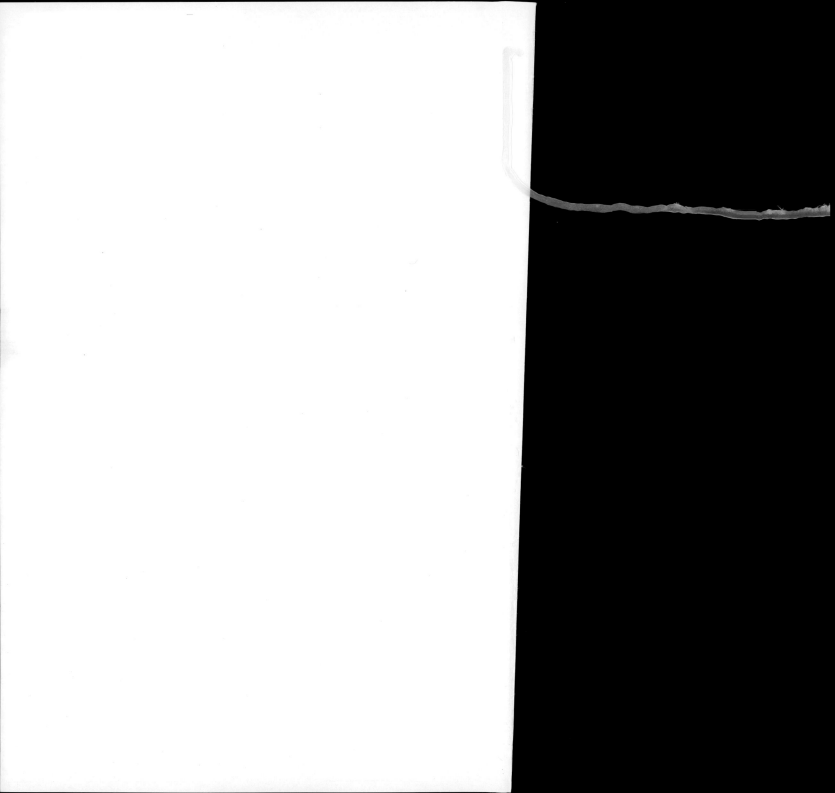

Contents

Part VIII Who's Who in Golf

Part IX The Government of the Game

Part X Golf History

Part XI Guide to Golfing Services and Places to Stay in the British Isles and Ireland

Part XII Clubs and Courses in the British Isles and Europe

CENTENARY CLUBS
2003

WE WOULD LIKE TO EXTEND OUR WARMEST WISHES TO THE FOLLOWING CLUBS IN THEIR CENTENARY YEAR.

ASHFORD (KENT) GOLF CLUB

Sandyhurst Lane,
Ashford, Kent TN25 4NT
Tel/Fax: (01233) 622655

Founded in 1903 the club moved to its current position in 1926. This beautiful parkland course is renowned as a good test of all round golfing ability. The course is 6,236 yards long with tree lined fairways and flowing streams. Visitors are always given a warm welcome all year round.

BALLYMENA GOLF CLUB

128 Raceview Road,
Ballymena,
Co Antrim,
Northern Ireland BT42 4HY
Tel/Fax: 028 2586 1487

Ballymena *(from the Irish middle town)* is situated 30 miles from Belfast and 20 miles from the port of Larne situated at the entrance to the famous Glens of Antrim. The parkland heath course is flat but drains exceptionally well and is playable all year round. The par 68 course is 5,299 metres.

DEESIDE GOLF CLUB

Golf Road,
Bieldside,
Aberdeen AB15 9DL
Tel/Fax: (01224) 869457

Set on the north bank of the river Dee only four miles from Aberdeen's City centre, the club enjoys the scenic splendour of Deeside. Founded in March 1903 a 9-hole course was in operation within six months. Recent developments have produced the current, testing 18- and 9-hole courses.

POWFOOT GOLF CLUB

(British Championship Golf Course)
Cummertrees, Annan,
Dumfriesshire DG12 5QE.
Tel/Fax: (01461) 700276

Founded in 1903 and designed by James Braid, this golf course is fast gaining a reputation as the finest links course in the South of Scotland. The fairways lined with the gorse and heather in full bloom make a stunning sight. Visitors will find a warm welcome at this gem of a course on the Scottish side of the Solway.

E-mail: bsutherland@powfootgolfclub.fsnet.co.uk Website: www.powfoot

THE WARRINGTON GOLF CLUB

Hill Warren, London Road,
Appleton Warrington,
Cheshire WA4 5HR

Tel: (01925) 261775 Fax: (01925) 265933
E-mail: secretary@warrington-golf-club.co.uk

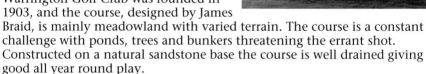

Warrington Golf Club was founded in 1903, and the course, designed by James Braid, is mainly meadowland with varied terrain. The course is a constant challenge with ponds, trees and bunkers threatening the errant shot. Constructed on a natural sandstone base the course is well drained giving good all year round play.

EAST BERKSHIRE GOLF CLUB

Ravenswood Avenue,
Crowthorne, Berkshire RG45 6BD
Tel: (01344) 772041 Fax: (01344) 777378

East Berkshire Golf Club has a beautiful heathland course that stands on the western end of what was known once as the Forest of Windsor. In 1903 a number of masters from Wellington College who played golf in the college grounds decided to formally recognise their association by setting up the East Berkshire Golf Club.

To satisfy their growing enthusiasm for the game in 1904 they purchased 100 acres of heathland located half a mile away and employed a well known golf professional Peter Paxton to design the course - a layout that has stood the test of time.

East Berkshire golf course at 6,344 is not a long course, but with dogleg boundaries, tree lined fairways and carrys across streams and heather. It will tax the skills of any golfer who decides to play a round of golf, but nevertheless he or she will have enjoyed every minute of it.

BARNEHURST GOLF COURSE

Mayplace Road East,
Barnehurst,
Kent DA7 6JU.
Tel: (01322) 523746 Fax: (01322) 523860

Opened in 1903, initially as an 18-hole ladies only course. It was converted to a 9-hole course - open to all - during the war. Now a well matured woodland course, providing a challenge to golfers of all abilities. Full clubhouse facilities are available, including a private function room. Golf societies and green fees are always made welcome. Tee time booking available seven days in advance.

MAGDALENE FIELDS GOLF CLUB

Berwick-upon-Tweed,
Northumberland TD15 1NE
Tel: (01289) 306130
Tel/Fax: (01289) 306384
Website: www.magdalene-fields.co.uk

Magdalene Fields Golf Course is the most northerly golf course in England. Opened on 4th June 1903 the course designer was Willie Park. Overlooked by the town's Elizabethan walls to the west with the North Sea to the east.
"The Fields" is a test of golf for all golfers.

BANGOR GOLF CLUB

Broadway,
Bangor, Co Down,
Northern Ireland BT20 4RH
Tel: 028 9127 0922 (Office)
028 9146 2164 (Pro Shop)
Fax: 028 9145 3394

Founded on 21st February 1903, Bangor Golf Club is located close to the town centre with splendid views over Bangor Bay and glimpses of Scotland on a clear day. The James Braid designed course quickly progressed from 9- to 18-holes and measures 6,410 yards from the medal tees offering a fair challenge to golfers of all abilities.
Visitors are welcome especially during the Bangor Open Tourism Golf Challenge in August. For reservations contact the office of the Professional.

PORTPATRICK (DUNSKEY) GOLF CLUB

Golf Course Road,
Portpatrick,
Stranraer DG9 8TB

Tel: (01776) 810273 Fax: (01776) 810811
E-mail: enquiries@portpatrickgolfclub.com

Portpatrick Golf Club, acclaimed the "Best Kept Secret in South West Scotland", is renowned for its friendly welcome. It boasts magnificent views across to Ireland and enjoys a temperate climate allowing play all the year round. Courses and yardage: Dunskey - 5,908 yards Par 70 SSS 69; Dinvin - 1,504 yards Par 27 (Par 3).

ST DAVIDS CITY GOLF CLUB

Whitesands,
St Davids,
Pembrokeshire SA62 6PT

Tel: (01437) 721751

Celebrating its Centenary, St Davids City Golf Club is Wales' most westerly golf course set in the Pembrokeshire coast National Park, with spectacular views across Ramsey Island, Whitesands Bay and St Davids Head. A 9-hole 18 tees links 6,117 yards par 70 SSS70 course which is dry and playable all year round and renowned for its quality greens.

OSWESTRY GOLF CLUB

Aston Park,
Oswestry,
Shropshire SY11 4JJ

Tel/Fax: (01691) 610535 (Secretary)
Tel: (01691) 610448 (Professional)
E-mail: secretary@oswestrygolfclub.co.uk

Founded in 1903 Oswestry spent its early years on nearby Llanymynech Hill before moving to Aston Park in 1931 when Sir Henry Cotton participated in an exhibition match to mark the opening of the new course.

James Braid designed a fine, gently undulating parkland layout set on free draining soils which ensures year-round play and called it "A Heaven Made Golf Course". It was at Oswestry that local member Ian Woosnam shot 57 only a few days before leaving to win the US Masters in 1981.

The club's history spans from the purchase of a harness, roller and slippers for the horse to computerisation in all departments.

Visitors will always find a warm welcome at our friendly club.

KENMARE GOLF CLUB

Kenmare, Co Kerry, Ireland

Tel: +353 64 41291
Fax: +353 64 42061
E-mail: info@kenmare.golfclub.com

Kenmare Golf Club boasts a breathtaking location set amongst the Kerry mountains and alongside the river Roughty Estuary. Designed by much praised Eddie Hackett the course features some very interesting holes. We pride ourselves on the high standard of the course all year round. Come and discover Ireland's best kept secret.

APPLEBY GOLF CLUB

Brackenber Moor,
Appleby in Westmorland,
Cumbria CA16 6LP

Tel: (017683) 51432 Fax: (017683) 52773

Appleby golf course is situated two miles east of the town just off the A66. The club enjoys a golfing history dating back to 1894 when the game was played on the Minsceugh just outside the town. In 1903 this club was reformed on its present location on Brackenber Moor. The former Open Champion Willie Fernie of Troon laid out the new course using the natural contours of the moor with short heathery rough and bracken to provide a challenging and delightful course described as "Gleneagles in the Raw". His creation is undeniably testing as the 5,901 yard par 68 course contains no par 5s but long challenging par 4s.

Off the course there is a warm welcome in the clubhouse and the course offers the best greens in the north of England at the best value for money in the country.

WALTON HEATH GOLF CLUB

**Deans Lane
Tadworth,
Surrey KT20 7TP**

**Tel: (01737) 812380 (Secretary)
Fax: (01737) 814225**

The Old Course features in the top 100 courses of the world. Both Old and New courses measure over 7,000 yards from the championship tees. Laid out by Herbert Fowler, they are recognised as one of the pioneers of modern golf course architecture. Home to James Braid, five times winner of the Open; host to numerous major amateur and professional tournaments including 20 PGA Matchplay tournaments; five European Opens and the 1981 Ryder Cup, the club was the venue for the 2002 English Amateur Championship and is the venue for the 2003 Varsity Match.

As Bernard Darwin once wrote "If there is anything that golfers want and do not get at Walton, I do not know what it can be".

KILLINEY GOLF CLUB

**Ballinclea Road,
Killiney,
Co Dublin,
Ireland.**

**Tel: +353 1 285 2823
Fax: +353 1 285 2823**

Killiney Golf Course was designed by James McKenna of Carrickmines and opened on Easter Monday 1903. In 1997 substantial alterations to the course came into play and now offers as fine a 9-hole layout as you will find.

The new clubhouse has been completed for the centenary year which has substantially increased the area but retained the old pavilion style. This facility will serve to enhance the clubs already significant reputation for hospitality to visitors.

Killiney Golf Club has counted many famous sports people among its members not least of whom was Dr Josh Pim who won both Singles and Doubles Wimbledon championships. In 1895 he was too busy to return to Wimbledon to defend his singles title.

LEATHERHEAD GOLF CLUB

Kingston Road,
Leatherhead,
Surrey KT22 0EE

Tel: (01372) 843966
Fax: (01372) 842241

E-mail: secretary@lgc-golf.co.uk
Website: www.lgc-golf.co.uk

Founded in 1903 as the Surrey Golf
Club but re-named shortly after in 1908 as
Leatherhead Golf Club. The course, which is situated in a delightful area of
the Surrey countryside in parkland and woodland, is maintained to a very
high standard and is undoubtedly an excellent challenge to all golfers.
As we look forward with great expectations to our Centenary Year we
extend our warmest wishes to all our members and visitors alike.

NORTH FORELAND GOLF CLUB

Convent Road,
Broadstairs,
Kent CT10 3PU

Tel (01843) 862140
Fax: (01843) 862663

Situated on the Kent
coast at the point where
the English Channel
becomes the North Sea,
is a cliff top downland
course that offers seaside
golf at its very best. Originally a 9-hole course it was extended when Lord
Northcliffe bought additional land in 1912 and employed Fowler &
Simpson to design the full 18-hole course. The 6,430 yards par 71 course
will be a final qualifying venue for the 2003 Open Championship.
With a view of the sea from every tee and every green, North Foreland
being a free running chalk-based course, is possibly Kent's premier all-year
round course which is confirmed by the number of returning societies and
visitors.
Special winter offers and society packages are available and visitors are
made welcome at the excellent, friendly clubhouse and fully stocked
professional shop.

E-mail: office@northforeland.co.uk

LALEHAM GOLF CLUB

Laleham Reach,
Chertsey,
Surrey KT16 8RP

Tel: (01932) 564211 (Secretary)
Fax: (01932) 564448

E-mail: sec@laleham-golf.co.uk
Website: www.laleham-golf.co.uk

Instituted as Chertsey Golf Club in October 1903, and designed by the 1904 Open Champion Jack White on land rented from the Earls of Lucan, Laleham Golf Club retains its unique character.

Standing on the Thames at a Roman ford and a medieval enclosure built by monks to graze their cattle on the lush pastures, the golfing challenge provided by bunkers, trees and water, suits all categories and abilities of club golfers.

Members bought the course in 1996 and celebrate its Centenary in the Victorian style clubhouse from October 2003 to September 2004. Why not visit us?

HENDON GOLF CLUB

Ashley Walk, Devonshire Road,
Mill Hill, London NW7 1DG

Tel: 020 8346 6023
Fax: 020 8343 1974

E-mail: hendongolf@talk21.com
Website: www.hendongolfclub.co.uk

Founded in 1903 the course, less than eight miles from the centre of London, was originally laid out under the direction of Harry Vardon and John H Taylor. With the acquisition of additional land in 1925, Harry Shapland Colt, the foremost golf architect of his day and designer of many notable courses, laid out the course as we know it today.

This delightful, undulating parkland course is renowned for the variety of its trees, its small, well-guarded greens and its bunkers, making it amongst the finest in London.

The clubhouse, built in 1964, with its air-conditioned lounge and dining room, commands a fine view of the course and provides a welcoming atmosphere to members and visitors alike.

Once visited you will want to come back again.

Foreword

Renton Laidlaw

Renton Laidlaw

Much work goes in each year to making the *Golfer's Handbook* as comprehensive as possible within the limits of the number of pages available. In this edition some past winners of top events have been put back in and the list of British and Irish international players has been split into nationalities for easier reference.

A new type and new design ideas have been adopted which hopefully makes the information more easily read. For this I am indebted to typographer Michael Card for all his valuable help and advice.

Collating and filing the mass of data required to keep the book as up-to-date as possible each year is a team effort. Results and addresses have been gathered with their usual professionalism by Alan and Heather Elliott. With Michael Card, Alan has streamlined the gathering of results and together they have produced a system that is second to none for efficiency and accuracy. Remember if you want to guarantee that your result is included please send it to him at the Royal and Ancient Golf Club of St Andrews.

David Davies of *The Guardian* has again written his stylishly comprehensive review of the 2002 majors, which produced two more wins for Tiger Woods, a dream victory for Ernie Els and a surprise triumph for Rich Beem at Hazeltine and Gordon Simpson, media director of the PGA European Tour, writes entertainingly when taking a closer look at Ernie Els the family man.

John Hopkins of *The Times* enjoyed recalling the drama, tension and passion of the delayed Ryder Cup match at The De Vere Belfry and in her review of the women's scene Lewine Mair of *The Daily Telegraph* highlights the continuing domination of the women's scene by Annika Sörenstam and the disappointment of defeats for home players in the Curtis Cup and Solheim Cup.

Mark Garrod of the Press Association, who also updates our records section each year, takes a comprehensive look back at the amateur year in men's golf while Ian Wooldridge of the *Daily Mail* is also in nostalgic mood. He reflects on the contribution the 'Big Three' – Arnold Palmer, Jack Nicklaus and Gary Player, winners collectively of 34 professional majors – made to golf. In addition St Andrews-based Keith Mackie, recalls past Championships at Royal St George's, this year's Open venue. To all contributors and to Shirley Card who did a splendid job as proofreader I am deeply indebted.

Finally my thanks to Morven Knowles who has acted as managing editor of the *Golfer's Handbook* for the last few years. Her disciplined yet friendly approach kept us all on our toes and the team wishes her well in her new more challenging role in national newspapers.

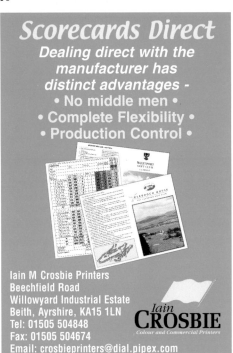
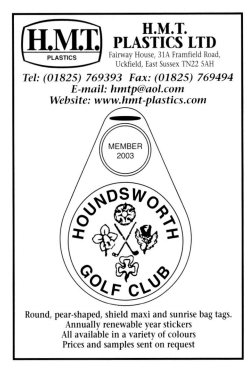

New R & A captain tees up a busy year

© GSR Photographic

John Whitmore, a former president, secretary and captain of the Oxford and Cambridge Golfing Society and a member at Royal Ashdown Forest and Rye is the new captain of the Royal and Ancient Golf Club of St Andrews. Last September he drove himself impressively into office watched by several hundred spectators including several past captains and the club's honorary professional John Panton.

Born in 1931 Mr Whitmore was educated at the Nautical College, Pangbourne, and Clare College, Cambridge, where he earned a Blue in 1953 and 1954. A member of the Royal and Ancient Golf Club of St Andrews since 1976 he has served on the club's championship committee and was for a time deputy chairman of the general committee. A former High Sheriff of East Sussex he has served as master of the Worshipful Company of Grocers and as chairman of the Board of Governers of Oundle School. Although he began and ended his career as a schoolmaster he spent over 30 years working in the family tanning business and in the fruit growing trade.

Mr Whitmore, who plays off 14 these days, includes cricket among his other interests and has been a member of the MCC for 40 years.

Random reflections on another interesting year

Renton Laidlaw looks back on 2002

The year 2002 will be remembered for many things but not least the wonderful three days of match-play competition at The De Vere Belfry when the Europeans captained by Sam Torrance beat the Americans to regain the Ryder Cup. After the over-exuberant scenes at the 1999 match at The Country Club in Brookline, both Torrance and the American captain Curtis Strange had been firm in their resolve to restore some dignity to the match without, of course, affecting the intense competition the match generates these days. They succeeded and with the crowds also behaving in the most sporting manner the reputation of the match has been fully restored.

Security was tighter than ever it has been for a golf event in Britain. Armed police patrolled the grounds throughout the week, an indication of the way of the world these days – a world which in golfing terms is a small one. Our top players travel around usually in their own planes to compete globally without giving it a thought. Although Justin Rose plays the South African and European Tours, he went to Japan and won early in the season. Sergio García who competes on both the US and European Tours slipped over for a week to win in Korea on the Davidoff Tour. As always most sponsors operating outside America – and assuming they still have the financial funds available – want a top US star in the field. Tiger Woods is as always the big draw card. He brought thousands to Heidelberg for the Deutsche Bank SAP Tournament Players Championship of Europe and then went head-to-head with Colin Montgomerie for the title. It was rivetting golf.

After winning The Masters for a third time and then his second US Open, the thought that he might just win all four in the same year – he has of course already held all four at the same time – gave an added edge to the Open at Muirfield but just like Jack Nicklaus, who had been on the same mission 30 years earlier, he stumbled, a victim of freakish Scottish weather, on the third day which saw him shoot 81, his highest score as a professional. Colin Montgomerie slumped to an 84 after a record equalling 64 the day before.

The winner that week was worldwide favourite – The Big Easy – Ernie Els, who had to survive a four-hole play-off and then sudden death against another cheery extrovert Frenchman Thomas Levet, taking on Jean Van de Velde's Carnoustie role this time, before getting his huge hands on the Claret Jug. If we all thought that was edge-of-seat exciting it was nothing compared to the Ryder Cup where Montgomerie headed an all-star cast of heroes to a triumph, which laid to rest all the talk that because the team had been chosen a year earlier many of the players were off form. True pre-Cup form in some cases did look distinctly ropey as far as handling Ryder Cup pressure was concerned but the pessimists were routed. Everyone raised their games to a new level on both sides with Montgomerie emerging for the second Cup running as the rock he had promised Sam Torrance he would

Bernhard Langer and Colin Montgomerie were a devastating partnership at the Ryder Cup.

© Phil Sheldon

Annika Sörenstam continues to rewrite the record book on the LPGA Tour.

Legendary Sam Snead's one regret – he never won the US Open.

Karrie Webb has now won all five LPGA Tour majors.

be. His masterly golf gave rise to thoughts that maybe that elusive major is not an impossibility after all. Few would begrudge him that.

In women's golf Karrie Webb coped best of all with the supreme test of Turnberry to win the Weetabix Women's Open Championship which owes so much to sponsor Richard George's enthusiasm and vision. Her win gave her her own Grand Slam. She has won all the women's majors, even the now defunct du Maurier which the British event replaced. The event is now officially on the US Women's Tour and it is hoped that sooner rather than later the Senior British Open for men will become an official US Senior Tour event in the same way as the Open is part of the main US Tour.

Dominating women's golf again throughout the year, however, was Annika Sörenstam who even before the end of October had amassed $2.5 million dollars in prize money, won nine times and finished in the top 10 in 16 out of 18 starts on the US Tour … and she revealed she does 250 sit-ups every night to keep herself fit.

There was talk throughout the year of maybe reducing the age of seniority from 50 to 45 in order to strengthen senior tour fields outside America but for the moment that is on hold but by no means forgotten. With more and more younger players making the grade quicker – there were more than 25 first time winners on both sides of the Atlantic – some players are finding their realistic top line competitive days are over not long after reaching 40. Of course there are exceptions – Eduardo Romero for one. He won the Barclays Scottish Open and only lost the Dunhill Links Championship in a play-off with Padraig Harrington, who continues to smile his way up the world rankings. In European Senior golf Neil Coles won again at the age of 67 and may well continue to win in his 70's, so smooth and repetitive is his swing, so sharp his competitive juices and so silky his putting stroke.

Gary Player is another old timer who remains evergreen and eager to add to an impressive list of victories stretching back to the mid 50's but he surprised not a few of us when he announced he was putting up for auction his golf trophies and memorabilia, including a Masters Green Jacket he technically should not have removed from the Augusta clubhouse. That is another story and so too is the drive by the equal rights lobby to have women as members of the National Golf Club founded by Bobby Jones and Clifford Roberts for their friends back in the 30's. With the world in such turmoil this campaign, even with its merits, seems strangely ill-timed. Augusta has always seemed to be an easy target.

For many years Sam Snead acted as an official starter at Augusta but the grand old man from Virginia died suddenly. I will always remember him kicking the upper lintel of a door in the Longniddry clubhouse in Scotland during a Seniors event some years back to prove his suppleness and athleticism. Legendary may be an overused expression but Slammin' Sam was a legend who stayed competitive by inventing a type of side-saddle action that did not break the rules preventing crocquet style putting.

In the 1947 US Open, he got into a play-off with Lew Worsham, a good player although not of Sam's class, and on the final hole left an approach putt exactly 30½ inches short. This is known because, when attempting to putt out, he was told it might be Worsham's turn. When measured Snead was found to be one inch further away than his opponent. The whole process took time and Snead's nerves suffered during the wait. He missed and when Worsham holed, the chance of winning the title had passed Sam by. It was a title he would never win yet probably the one he would have prized more than any other.

There is a fuller appreciation of his life a little later in this edition.

On this side of the Atlantic golf lost a well-respected benefactor in Lawrence Batley OBE,

who sponsored events for 20 years on first the main Tour and latterly on the European Seniors Tour. He was always a very visible sponsor and continued to compete in the Over 80's event he started. The international nature of the Senior Tour was highlighted when Seiji Ebihara from Japan finished top money earner, winning three titles during the season.

The year was notable in my mind for three emotional successes in Europe and one in America. When Justin Rose won his fourth title of the season at the Victor Chandler British Masters he was watched by his father Ken, who had done so much to help him in his career. Mr Rose Sen., battling leukaemia, died a few weeks later. Miles Tunnicliff's success at the Great North Open at Slaley Hall was something of a surprise to many but would not have been to his mother, who just before she died three weeks earlier had urged him to go out and win. She would have been immensely proud of the way he did so. And there was Malcolm Mackenzie's first ever Tour triumph in the French Open – on his 509th. appearance helped by a 200 yards second shot over water, under pressure, to 15 feet. He had waited for this win since 1981 and when it came he earned it with what was a strong candidate for shot of the year.

The other success which pleased fans around the world was the victory with Tiger Woods breathing down his neck of Craig 'Popeye' Parry in the NEC World Championship event at Sahalee in Washington. Parry, who earned his nickname because of his strong forearms, had waited 15 years for a first win in the US. When he did triumph in his 236th start he won a million.

John Jacobs OBE, a founder member of the Professional Golfers' Architects' Association and president of the PGA of Europe in 1999/2000, has been awarded life membership of the Professional Golfers Association – an elite award that numbers only seven others including Tony Jacklin CBE, Bernard Hunt MBE and John Panton MBE. The first executive director of the PGA European Tour, John is best known worldwide as 'Dr Golf'. His coaching expertise has earned him a place in the US Golf Hall of Fame and US Teaching Hall of Fame. During his remarkable career he has coached the English, Scottish, German, Spanish and Swedish national teams. He was awarded the Spanish Royal Golf Federation Medal of Merit for his 25 years service to the game in Spain. He coached the British and Irish Walker Cup team from 1963 to 1987 and worked, too, with several Curtis Cup sides. In 1965 he played in the Ryder Cup and captained the side in 1979 and 1981.

Max Faulkner, now 85 was honoured for his victory in the Open Championship over 50 years after he won the title at Royal Portrush in 1951. The

Australian Craig Parry had reason to thank Tiger Woods after winning his first title in America. Parry qualified for the NEC World Championship because he won the 2002 New Zealand Open – an event given enhanced status because Woods played in it as well.

© Phil Sheldon

recognition, which was long overdue, ends the controversy of why the oldest living Open champion had been ignored for so long. Still an active player at West Chiltington, the course he built with his son-in-law Brian Barnes, Faulkner played in his first Open at Princes in 1932 as a 15-year-old boy. Six shots clear with a round to go at Royal Portrush in 1951, the only year the event has ever been staged in Northern Ireland, it is alleged he was so confident of winning that he signed a ball 'Max Faulkner – 1951 Open champion' before he started the final round.

During the year the USGA and the Royal and Ancient Golf Club of St Andrews finally came together on the Rules of Golf regarding driving clubs. Not only was this significant in itself, but the lessons learnt have brought the two organisations closer together, making it much less likely in future that there will be any divisions over equipment rules.

The Council of National Golf Unions (CONGU) and the Ladies Golf Union (LGU) have been discussing ways of operating a unified handicapping system which could cater for men and women. The scheme is likely to be based on the CONGU scheme with amendments and additions that cater for situations unique to women's golf.

Déjà-vu as Tiger's Grand Slam dream is shattered

David Davies reviews the 2002 majors

So accustomed have we become to seeing Tiger Woods winning that the Championship year of 2002 was notable more for what he did not win rather than what he did. He took the first two majors of the season, the US Masters and the US Open and then, amidst a possible calendar year Grand Slam frenzy, he did not win the Open Championship. He did not collect another USPGA Championship either, but by then the excitement had abated. If Tiger is to do what no man has done before – add a Calendar Slam to his already unique achievement of four majors in succession – it must wait for another year.

There can be little doubt that after winning the first two majors of the season, Woods' goal was to land all four in the same season. This is not something he can ever be induced to admit, but then neither Bobby Jones nor Jack Nicklaus admitted that they had such grandiose projects in mind at the time. It was only long after his career had finished that Jones told the world that he set out in 1930 with the intention of giving his all towards winning the Open and Amateur Championships of Great Britain and America. He, of course, achieved that Impregnable Quadrilateral and in so doing became the only man who ever will.

Nicklaus, too, denied at the time that he was seeking a Calendar Slam, but after his major ambitions had evaporated he too agreed that in 1972 this was very much on his mind. He had looked at the venues for that year, Augusta for the Masters, Pebble Beach for the US Open, Muirfield for the Open and Oakland Hills for the US PGA and realised that not only did they all suit his game, he actually liked them as well.

Under the weather

Just as Woods was to do, however, he came to a shuddering halt at Muirfield. The parallel is not exact because Nicklaus failed only narrowly 30 years ago and it was, arguably, his own fault. Woods failed by a large margin and it was an act from on high that stopped him. In 1972 Nicklaus who had begun to believe that he could win any golf event by playing cautiously and letting the others make the mistakes, did just that ... but left himself with just too much to do in the last round. His closing 66 left him one behind Lee Trevino, no doubt he regretted leaving the driver out of his bag for the first three rounds.

Woods, on the other hand, ran into fearsome Muirfield weather. After two rounds he was handily placed and still the bookmakers favourite, but Saturday dawned grey, cold, wet and windy, and got worse. By the time Tiger got on the course it was blowing a gale and there was a curious sense of anticlimax as he hacked about in the hay, as one errant tee shot after another presented him with insoluble problems on this occasion.

We witnessed the implosion of a dream in almost Machiavellian surroundings as the winds howled, the rain first stung then soaked and the skies, bible-black as Dylan Thomas would have it, lent sepulchral surroundings to a demonic day.

At the end of it. Woods had taken 81, his highest professional score, understandable perhaps but he knew others had coped rather better with the bitter weather. In fact Woods has often said that he enjoys playing in wind and rain for the special challenges that kind of weather impose. Mhairi McKay, the former Curtis Cup and now Solheim Cup player, who was at Stamford University in California at the same time as Woods tells how, when the weather

Ernie Els' dream of winning the famous Claret Jug came true at Muirfield.

© Phil Sheldon

was foul, Tiger would be a solitary figure on the practice ground in an attempt to build a game for the kind of conditions he found at Muirfield. Maybe, but nothing can adequately prepare anyone for weather at its most loathsome and that Saturday was extreme! Des Smyth, the Irishman, who knows a bit about playing golf in bad weather, said it was 'more like January than July' and the eventual winner, Ernie Els, added: 'I kept dropping shots but they would not take me off the leaderboard! I knew nobody was having fun.' Perhaps the best indication of how bad it all was was shown in the Exhibition tent where all the umbrellas were sold out at £35 a time. At that price you can appreciate just how bad the weather was.

Sunshine sparkler

The Woods Calendar Slam dream died on Sunday at 1.07pm precisely, the moment that the US Tour journeyman Chris Riley holed a putt on the 72nd green that took him to one-under par, one better than the Woods total. There were, at that moment, 56 players still on the course, a measure of by how much Woods had failed.

There was still plenty of fascination and drama to come on the final day after the wind had died down. Gary Evans, ranked no.193 in the world, almost won the Open Championship. Although never a winner on the European tour, Evans has always been capable of stretches of brilliance, and he sparkled in the Sunday sunshine. He had eight birdies in his first 11 holes and had he birdied the long 17th, which most players did, Evans might well have become the lowliest ranked player to win a major since, well

Tiger Woods, seen here with the US Open trophy, had hopes of winning all four majors in the same year but ran into bad weather at Muirfield.

since 1999, when Paul Lawrie won the Open at Carnoustie when ranked 159th.

Evans, wholly unaccustomed to the kind of pressure he was experiencing, however, pulled his second at the long hole into some of the deepest rough and although some 150 people spent the regulation five minutes looking for it, all they found was a Titleist no.2, ironically the same make and number as Evans was playing, but not his!

He had to go back and proceeded to smash his fourth shot onto the green and hole the par putt from about 50-feet. It was almost unbearably exciting, but it was not quite enough and a dropped shot at the last cost him a place in what was to become a four-man, five hole play-off.

The participants were Els, Thomas Levet, Steve Elkington – who had prequalified – and Stuart Appleby, although Els really should have made sure of victory in regulation play. The South African, who had a 72 to Woods' 81 on Saturday, had the Championship won as he stood on the tee of the short 16th on Sunday with a two-stroke lead.

Els needed only a 7 iron for his tee shot but missed the green in the worst possible place, took a double bogey 5 and had to birdie the 17th and par the 18th to get into the four-hole aggregate play-off at the end of which the Australians Elkington and Appleby were eliminated and Els and Levet went back to the 18th to continue in sudden death.

Not the driver

Talk about déjà-vu. The only other Frenchman to get into a play-off for the Open had been Jean Van de Velde at Carnoustie in 1999. He could have prevented that by taking almost any club off the 18th tee in regular play other than the driver. Notoriously, he did take the driver, took 7 and eventually lost.

Now Levet stood on the 18th with a chance to win an Open, and proceeded to take the only club that could get him into severe trouble – the driver. And it did. He found a bunker, which meant an automatic bogey and although Els bunkered his second, he hit a magnificent shot to four feet for a winning par. Winner of the 1994 and 1997 US Opens, Ernie had at last won the title he had always desired. Three majors in nine years seems too few for a player of his enormous talent but, like everyone else, he has had to cope with Tiger. At Muirfield, however, it was his week.

Back in April, in Augusta, there was no suggestion that Woods' influence was waning. Quite the opposite as he strolled, almost casually, to his seventh major championship in his last 11 attempts. It was his third Green Jacket and, strange though it seems now, and stranger still as it seemed at the time, it was rather boring. The Augusta National car parks bore witness to that on Sunday afternoon as people streamed away from the course early. Yet this was emphatically not Tiger's fault. He did everything that he had to do to win a major and can

hardly be blamed if the rest of the cast, like little puppies, turned over to have their tummies tickled.

The lack of a challenge in the final round from some of the world's best players was pitiful. Retief Goosen, a winner of the US Open and paired with Woods, took 5 at the opening hole and disappeared from view. Els was almost but not quite out of it when he took 8 at the 13th, and Vijay Singh a Masters and US PGA champion, managed a 9 at the 15th.

Woods was never remotely pressurised; he was able, in his own words, to 'just plug along.' He did not try to do anything heroic. He never had the need to!

Lacking a challenger

Asked afterwards if he felt that this had been the easiest of his major championship wins, he said: 'You know, it was a tough day. The rain made it difficult, there were a lot of weird clubs to be hit because of the wet, and there were a lot of difficult pin positions.'

Not a word, you will notice, about anybody pressing him, because no one did. There is a school of thought that excellence, as displayed daily by Woods, can never be boring but while that extreme position can be occupied by the perfectionists, the fact is that for most of us great events demand great drama, and that only materialises when someone challenges the existing excellence. That simply did not happen on Sunday April 14 at Augusta.

Not surprisingly voices began to be heard from some of the game's previous greats, questioning the value of Woods' feats. Jack Nicklaus, Lee Trevino and Gary Player all wondered in print why it was that no one was standing up to Tiger, with Player asking a particularly pertinent question. 'The old timers,' he said 'can put up three great players from the same period who would back themselves to beat anybody, past or present. There was Ben Hogan, Sam Snead and Byron Nelson and later there was Jack, me and Lee, or Jack, Johnny Miller and me … but who would you pick now? Tiger, of course, but who else? Tiger, David Duval and Phil Mickelson? Or Tiger and Ernie and someone else? No, Tiger's on his own. The others don't measure up, or at least not yet.'

They continued not to measure up in the US Open played at Bethpage Black, a public course on Long Island, New York where, again, Woods won almost unopposed. This was partly because of his own talent, partly because he was still intimidating the opposition and partly because of the nature of the course. Although it was only 7214 yards long, the par fours were all extremely difficult. Seven of them were so long that the average club member would have struggled to get home in two, meaning that for him or her there were, in effect, 11 par 5s. For them it was a par 89! The course had been billed as 'Black Beauty' but, surrounded by knee-high rough it was 'Black Brutal' for all but the very best.

© Phil Sheldon

Rich Beem held off a late rally by Tiger Woods to win his first major at Hazeltine.

Sergio García led in the early stages of the first round, with an excellent 68, but even he, leading the driving statistics at the time, was cautious about the course. 'You have to hit the fairways here,' he said, 'because if you don't you will get pretty soon to a level where you just don't care.'

Be nice to Monty

That inveterate hitter of fairways, Colin Montgomerie, actually missed a few in his opening 75 and was despondent when he came off the course. That week had seen a campaign by *Golf Digest* to protect Monty from the viciously unfunny New York rednecks. The magazine had issued 25,000 buttons to spectators with the legend 'Be Nice To Monty.' Out early on Thursday, before the beer tents had done their worst, he escaped unheckled, but still unhappy. Ten-over made the cut and he missed it by one.

In the end there was only one person under par and it was, inevitably, Woods. He led by four after three rounds from García and by five from Mickelson and, as if by way of a change, issued an open invitation to the field to catch him by dropping shots at the first two holes of the final round. Yet not even such a generous gesture was accepted by his rivals. Woods played the remaining holes in level par and a final round of two-over par was good enough to win this major Championship by three shots.

Afterwards Woods, as he does, denied that there were no challenges. 'They're all difficult', he said, but what can he say? Imagine the furore if he said:

'Yeah, it was a doddle. No one's even giving me a game'.

He got a game, alright, at the Open, albeit from on high, and the predicted media interest in the US PGA, on the possibility of Woods going for a Grand Slam, suddenly slackened. He was a hot favourite to win, okay, but only three majors in a season? Small beer!

The story of Rich Beem and the US PGA is scarcely credible; a plot so over-the-top it would have been rejected as too improbable even in Hollywood. It features a talented golfer who gets bored with the game, goes off to sell hi-fi and stereo in a Seattle store, acquires a drinking problem, becomes an assistant pro and gets kicked out because he's hopeless at the etiquette then re-emerges on the US Tour because, quite simply, there's nothing else for him to do.

It emerges however that he is a late developer and what he developed into was not just a tournament winner – the Kemper Open and, two weeks before the PGA, the International – but a man who could withstand the pressures of Championship golf. In a final round full of drama he withstood one of the greatest charges ever seen at this level as Woods fought for what he regarded as rightfully his – another major title.

Beem was not the favourite at the start of the final round, and nor was Woods. Justin Leonard, former Open champion, led by three from Beem and by five from Woods and was playing so well he was widely expected to hold on.

That belief, however, was quickly shattered by a double-bogey at the eighth. On the back nine the championship developed into a duel between Beem, playing nicely, and Woods, as errant as he had been all week off the tee, but making up for that with a short game and putting to sell your soul for.

Beem led Woods by one at the turn but it was the playing of the long 11th that was to be crucial. Another awful drive from Woods meant he struggled to make par, while Beem, behind him, hit a drive 326 yards, a 5-wood 271 yards then holed from five feet for an absolutely brilliant eagle.

It gave him a three stroke lead and Woods, by now almost petulant, played the 13th and 14th as badly as it would be possible for him to play them dropping shots at both. That gave Beem a five-stroke lead after 14 holes, and he was to need nearly all of them. Up ahead Woods had said to himself: 'If I birdie the last four holes, I can still win this thing,' and, incredibly he hit a succession of fantastic shots – there was no luck involved – to birdie all four finishing holes! If Beem had not holed from 50 feet for a birdie on the 16th, Woods might well have won but, in the end, Beem did even with a three-putt on the last green. A day of the highest drama finished with the unlikeliest of winners. Not that he might not win again. He has a compact, quick-ish swing, hits the ball 'miles' and on this occasion, putted beautifully. He won deservedly and in so doing emphasised even more dramatically how difficult it is going to be for Woods to win all four majors in a calendar year.

There was not much of a threat of a European-born player winning a major. Sergio García was the only golfer to finish in the top 10 of all four and Padraig Harrington did so in the first three and missed out by one shot at the US PGA. Maybe in the near future they will take up, and beat, the Tiger Factor as effectively as Rich Beem did at Hazeltine.

Sergio García was the most consistent performer in the 2002 majors finishing in the top 10 in all four.

Padraig Harrington's continuing improvement augurs well for a major win in the near future.

© Phil Sheldon

Winning golf's Claret Jug was always Ernie's dream

Gordon Simpson on Els the family man

In the boisterous, euphoric aftermath of the 131st Open Golf Championship, Ernie Els paused to answer his mobile phone. The long-distance caller from South Africa turned out to be his 94-year-old grandfather, Ernie, after whom the newly-crowned Open Champion was named.

Els, quite naturally, expected fulsome praise from the aforementioned Ernie Vermaak following his epic triumph at the end of a memorable day of outrageous drama and high excitement at Muirfield.

'You know what?' said Els, a broad grin creasing his rugged features. 'He hadn't come on to congratulate me – he just wanted to give me some serious grief for not making a better job of my finish. Obviously I'm still not too old to get a ticking off from my grandad!'

That anecdote offers a perfect illustration as to the importance of family to the 33-year-old from Johannesburg and why, despite his wealth and vast accumulation of titles worldwide, Els can never be accused of becoming too big for his spiked golf shoes.

'We are a very close family, and always have been,' he explained. 'As well as my grandfather, I have my parents and a brother and sister to help me maintain a good grip of reality and normality. I think they are the reason I can keep my feet on the ground. Not that it's been particularly difficult, but I would never want to be accused of letting success go to my head, and everybody from my grandfather down wouldn't let that happen.'

That close family bond has been Ernie's driving force and source of inspiration since he first struck a golf ball, playing in the company of his grandfather and dad, Neels, who took up the game relatively late in life at the age of 28. Later, he would join forces with his elder brother, Dirk, and some of Dirk's friends, hitting golf balls from dawn to dusk in the relentless pursuit of perfection.

'I can't remember exactly the first time I held a golf club, but I must have been about four years old,' Els recalled. 'I was always around my dad, pulling the trolley or, when that became boring, just walking behind him or my grandfather with a club in my hand and trying to hit the ball.'

'For some reason I just loved the game. I had this inexplicable passion to play the game. I knew this

was the game for me. In South Africa, cricket was the summer game and rugby union in winter, but as I got older I would go to stay with my grandfather and Dirk and I would caddie for him and dad.'

'There was usually plenty of daylight left at the end of the day and I would play 18 holes before nightfall. Then all four of us would play on Sunday morning. It was a very tight family affair. We loved the game and it was perfect. I have very happy memories of those days.'

A supremely gifted all-rounder, Ernie excelled at a variety of sports. 'I played cricket and rugby all through school and at the age of 12 or 13 I was playing tennis to a very high standard. I was especially good at tennis. I believe you shouldn't get bogged down in one sport at an early age as you can lose the drive and passion if you concentrate on one thing.'

'However, the knocks were getting harder at rugby and I didn't want to leave South Africa to go

© Phil Sheldon

Open champion Ernie Els is very much the family man spending as much time with wife Liezl and his children Samantha and newest arrival Ben as his international schedule allows.

to America for tennis coaching. A lot of kids do that but I wanted to stay at home and do my own thing. I enjoyed my home life and a contented family environment. I still think I did the right thing.'

Blessed with a natural athleticism and imperturbable temperament – which in later years would lead to the apposite nickname of 'The Big Easy' – Ernie showed an aptitude for the game which was quickly recognised by Neels Els.

'Dad would often embarrass me,' he cringed. 'You can just imagine being a father with a son playing to a pretty good level. He kept saying: "Watch my son – he's going to win this or that one day". We can laugh about it now and although it wasn't much fun at the time I know he was just being a proud dad. He's great and I hope I've been able to repay him over the years.'

'The same with my grandfather. Sadly my gran passed away two years ago but I try to speak to grandad as often as I can on the phone. We hold a charity event at the end of every year now and the first prize is a statue of him. We call it the Ernie Vermaak Trophy and it's been going for seven years now. We have had to tell him not to make a speech any more because it takes him an hour to thank everybody!'

Victory at Muirfield after that astonishing sudden-death play-off with Thomas Levet of France, Stuart Appleby and Steve Elkington having been eliminated after the initial four hole play-off, provided Els with a deep sense of fulfillment.

Yet he knows he could have become, as he puts it, 'the talk of the town as the man who blew the Open.' He added: 'It has crossed my mind briefly since, but I don't want to dwell on it. I have blocked it out because it didn't happen.'.

The pent up emotion escaped in the moment he sank the winning putt, as Els hurled his baseball cap high into the air. Back in Greywalls Hotel, Els was sprayed with champagne by friends before returning to his home on Wentworth Estate for a victory celebration

'It took a long time to sink in,' he said. 'In fact, winning a major title doesn't really sink in properly until the week you have to hand back the trophy. That's the hardest part. You feel it's part of you. You spend the year being announced on the first tee as: "Open Champion" and it feels good. This is the one I waited most of my life for and now I've got it. To be honest, I have no intention of giving it up at Royal St George's!'

Ernie Els' major record

Year	Masters	US Open	Open	USPGA
1989	—	—	MC	—
1990	—	—	—	—
1991	—	—	—	—
1992	—	—	T5	MC
1993	—	T7	T6	MC
1994	T8	Won	T24	T25
1995	MC	MC	T11	T3
1996	T12	T5	T2	T61
1997	T17	Won	T10	T53
1998	T16	T49	T29	T21
1999	T27	MC	T24	MC
2000	2	T2	T2	T34
2001	T6	T66	T3	T13
2002	T5	T24	Won	T34

British Golf Museum
St Andrews

HEROIC

SURPRISING

STRIKING

HISTORIC

you can't miss this

Bruce Embankment, St Andrews, Fife KY16 9AB Telephone 01334 478880. Fax 01334 473306.
Opening Times Summer Hours: Easter to Mid October • 9.30am - 5.30pm Open 7 days
Winter Hours: 11am - 3pm Closed Tuesday & Wednesday.

Gamble pays off as Sam brings back the trophy

John Hopkins on the passion of the Ryder Cup

Late on Sunday 29 September, Sam Torrance sat in the corner of the Europe team room at The Belfry and reflected on the events of the previous few days. What he would later describe as the best week of his life had concluded a few hours earlier with remarkable scenes as Europe, the team he captained, had won one of the best ever Ryder Cups in the 75 years of the biennial competition against the US. The underdogs had triumphed. Form had been thrown out of the window. Individual brilliance was neutralised by team spirit. Few had predicted it but at the end of the three-day competition, which had set new standards for spectator behaviour and sporting skills, there was no doubt that Torrance's Europe team had deservedly achieved a famous victory, 15½–12 ½.

Who would have thought that in Sunday's singles, Phillip Price, the world's 119th player would crush Phil Mickelson, the world number two? Who would have thought Paul McGinley, ranked 71st in the world, would win two of the last six holes against Jim Furyk to eke out the half point that gave Europe victory. Who would have thought that Davis Love III, ranked 7th in the world, would halve with Pierre Fulke, ranked 88th or that Tiger Woods, unquestionably the most dominant golfer in the world with victories in seven of the past 13 major championships, would make no contribution to the singles, his half coming after the match was over? There had never been a day in the history of this biennial event when the US won only two of the 12 singles.

Astonishing feats

On this day of days there were echoes of the match at Brookline, outside Boston, three years earlier. Then one side had stormed to victory, one colour dominated the scoreboard, and noise reverberated in a throbbing din from all around the course. The difference was that then it was the US storming back to win by a point after trailing 10 - 6 at the end of the second day. Now it was Europe, moving away from a scoreline of 8-8 on Saturday night to record victory. The last day's astonishing feats included a holed bunker shot by Paul Azinger and remarkable displays by Europe's lesser players.

Colin Montgomerie was an inspiration, playing 82 holes without being behind in any of his five matches. This was a Ryder Cup for the spectators, who showed considerable restraint as a mark of respect for an event that was postponed and rescheduled after the tragedies of September 11, 2001. Their decorum helped establish the 34th Ryder Cup as a template for future Ryder Cups, one in which the respect the players felt for one another was channelled into astonishing golf and in which jingoism was kept to a minimum. It helped that though alcohol was sold on site, it had to be consumed in tents from which there was no view of the golf course.

So there was Torrance late at night, sitting sat back in his seat, a drink and a cigarette to hand and a smile playing around his lips as he surveyed the scene all around him. David Duval was singing lustily in one corner of the room. Nearby was Hal Sutton. Curtis Strange and Davis and Robin Love were also there. And so were Price and McGinley. Torrance looked across at the two Celts and remembered what he had said to Price before his match against Mickelson: 'You can have him Phillip,' Torrance said. Price nodded. 'You're right,' he replied.

'Tell 'em who I beat'

Torrance cast his mind back a few hours to a scene in the hotel bar where Lee Westwood had been acting as an impromptu master of ceremonies, introducing his teammates to the assembled raucous throng. As Westwood got to Price's name, Price leaned over and said: 'Tell 'em who I beat, tell 'em who I beat.'

Torrance smiled at the memory, as pleased for Price as he was proud at what Price had done. He thought there were signs of a return to form in the way the Welshman had played with Fulke in Saturday morning's foursomes, even though the men went down 2 & 1 to Mickelson and David Toms. Toms was Strange's secret weapon, winning more points for the US than any of his teammates. His most notable victory came over Sergio García in the singles. Toms is reminiscent in face, demeanour and golfing skills of Larry Nelson in the 1981 US team which triumphed handsomely over Europe. That team was captained by David Marr, and Nelson, who never lost a match, and was christened 'my baby-faced chicken killer.' Something similar could have been applied to the 2001 US PGA champion. He lost only one of his five matches.

Then Torrance moved his gaze to McGinley, the dark-haired Dubliner, who had been two down at the 12th against Furyk only to level the 17th and then hole the 10-foot putt on the 18th that gave Europe the Cup. 'These Irish,' Torrance must have thought to himself, shaking his head. 'These Irish!' He remembered Eamonn Darcy's putt on the 18th green at Muirfield Village in 1987 that set up victory in the US for the first time, Christy O'Connor Jnr's 2-iron second shot to the 18th at The Belfry in 1989, the year of the tied Ryder Cup and Philip Walton's defeat of Jay Haas in Europe's success in Rochester, New York, in 1995. And he thought of Padraig Harrington, who had lost both his matches on Friday, before coming under Montgomerie's wing for a victory on Saturday afternoon. Torrance thought how hard Harrington had practised with Torrance's father down the years and he was grateful to the Dubliner, especially since he had beaten Mark Calcavecchia so comfortably in the last day's singles. 'What is it about the Irish and the Ryder Cup?' Torrance wondered aloud.

If Torrance had thought back to the first two days he would surely have acknowledged how well Darren Clarke and Thomas Bjørn played in the first fourballs on Friday. Two men who had beaten Woods – Clarke at match play, Bjorn at stroke play – were drawn against Woods and Azinger in a match that he knew could set the tone for the Ryder Cup. Clarke's and Bjørn's was an important task – to help Europe get off to a good start. It was just as important for the two Americans that they did the same for their team and after going round in a better-ball score of 63, they might have felt they had achieved their aim – except that Clark and Bjørn went one better to win by one hole. It was just the quality of

golf we have come to expect in this fixture, players digging deep.

The first day was not one that Woods will want to remember. The world's leading golfer left a putt short to halve a hole, surely a cardinal sin. He missed two 3½ footers on successive greens. He lost both his matches. It was a reminder that Woods has never delivered as much as a player of his skill should in this event. After that Friday night's play his Ryder Cup record was: played 12, lost eight, halved one.

Vital half point

By Saturday evening when the score was 8–8 there had been three matches that were very significant, two of them involving Montgomerie. Montgomerie and Langer were three up after eight holes in Friday afternoon's foursomes against Mickelson and three up with four holes to play only for the Americans to snatch a half. That was just one of many passages of play that suggested that the US would triumph on Sunday evening. That unexpected half sent Strange in to dinner on Friday night with a smile on his face. Then Montgomerie and Harrington, stole one point from the same American pairing in Saturday afternoon's fourballs.

Finally, as dusk was gathering on Saturday, Clarke and McGinley got a half against Scott Hoch and Furyk when it looked as though the US would take a full point. The significance of that was that the two teams were dead level, 8-8, and as Mark James was later to remark, that meant that Strange was unable to guess how Torrance would send out his men the next morning. If Torrance had been one or two points behind then Strange would have realised that Torrance had to send out his best players to redress the situation.

The DeVere Belfry has been a happy hunting ground for Sam Torrance. He holed the winning putt there in the 1985 Ryder Cup then captained his team to success in 2002. The celebrations went on through the night.

© Phil Sheldon

Paul McGinley holes the winning putt and was hailed as a hero but he said he would have been one had he won out in the country!

As it happened Torrance went for the high risk, high return approach reasoning that if his top men got ahead then the sight of a predominantly blue scoreboard would inspire those following on. He sent out his best men one after the other expecting the first seven or eight to have secured the Cup before the match came down to the last few pairings. Strange did the opposite. He loaded three of his strongest men – Woods, Love and Mickelson, all of whom are among the top seven in the world – in his last three matches. 'If it was close and it was going to come down to the last match who would you want there other than Woods?' Strange asked.

High risk strategy

It was the first Ryder Cup in which Strange had captained the US team but not the first one in which he played a central role. Americans were a long time forgiving him for the way he was one up with two holes to play against Nick Faldo in 1995 and lost. Europe won that year, too.

Working out the order of play for Sunday's singles was a contest within a contest, one captain pitting his wits against the other, and again, as had happened so many times during the week, the cards fell Torrance's way. 'When we saw Sam's line-up we never said 'he should win, he should lose',' Langer, playing in his tenth Ryder Cup, said. 'With 24 of the best players in the world, anyone can beat anyone on a given day. But we felt confident nonetheless.'

Torrance' high risk strategy yielded the high reward he had gambled on. The US won only two of the first seven matches, Toms beating García and Verplank outplaying Westwood. Niclas Fasth halved with Azinger after the American holed from a bunker to win the 18th. Fulke and Parnevik, the Swedes, were playing better than some might have expected and would eventually halve with Love and Woods respectively.

But in the end it came down to Price, who holed a putt of 30 feet to beat Mickelson on the 16th, and then McGinley, who later revealed he had had a similar putt during the Benson and Hedges tournament. He appeared to play his putt quickly. 'I knew the line. There was no point in taking any longer. I wanted to get it over with.' When the ball went in McGinley thrust his arms up into the air and raced around the green looking, the *Washington Post* noted, like a penguin shuffling across the ice.

Many hours later, Torrance got up from his chair, did a little dance and took one more look around the room. He noted how some Americans had come to join his men. He spoke warmly to Curtis Strange. He gave Suzanne, his wife, a kiss as a thank you for her efforts. He thought to himself that nothing in sport could possibly better this. He even refused to allow the flattering comments made by his team to go to his head. Several of his men came up to him to urge him to stand as Ryder Cup captain in 2004 to attempt to do what only Tony Jacklin had ever done and captain a team to successive victories. 'But they were drunk,' Torrance would say later with a chuckle.

Then he looked at Price and McGinley once more. The words that David Purdie, the gynaecologist, had written for him to use during his official speeches came to his mind once again. 'They've got a Tiger but we've got 12 lions. Out of the shadows come heroes.' 'I didn't do anything,' Torrance said later. 'All I did was take them to the water. They drank copiously.'

> 'What came over to people on both sides of the Atlantic was the spirit of the game and the cameraderie between both sets of players, the wives, the caddies and the spectators. In the end I felt proud we got just about everything right' – *Sam Torrance*

Post-mortem time after women's cup defeats

Lewine Mair looks back on the year

The post-mortems stretched to the season's end after Great Britain and Ireland's amateurs lost the Curtis Cup in Pittsburgh and Europe's women professionals were defeated in the Solheim Cup at Interlachen.

Though the situation in the two events was very different going into the last day, with the amateurs behind and the professionals ahead, the last few hours had much in common. In both instances, the visiting teams had a chance of victory they could not quite seize.

In the Curtis Cup, the women were trailing 2–7 on the first day and were still 4–8 behind at the end of the second morning's foursomes. Then,they got off to an electrifying start in the singles, one which had the captain of the American team clutching at her head in horror and disbelief, as she glanced at the leaderboard. GB and Ireland were ahead in five matches and level in the other. If they could have

Redoubtable Carole Semple Thomson had the pleasure of holing the winning putt in the Curtis Cup.

© Phil Sheldon

kept things like that, they would have been celebrating one of the more famous victories of all time. As it was, the momentum changed again and, instead of a GB and Ireland triumph, the Americans prevailed 11–7.

Emma Duggleby and Rebecca Hudson went on to win, as did 19-year-old Sarah Jones, at once the youngest and the longest member of the British party. The matches which took a turn for the worse were those involving Alison Coffey, Vikki Laing and Heather Stirling. Coffey's match versus Meredith Duncan was always going to be a nail-biter of a contest but Laing and Stirling both seemed to have points in the bag when the Americans came back at them.

You had to hand it to the Americans, whose star of the show was none other than Carol Semple Thompson, 53 years of age and at least 31 years older than anyone else in her team. She had been three down after seven holes against Laing before winning four holes in a row.

Semple Thompson, who lived only 20 miles away and had a host of admirers in tow, went one up at the 17th as Laing caught the right-hand trap. Now she knew she could not lose but that was not enough for this grand dame of the American amateur scene. She wanted more.

Her chances looked more than a little remote when she barely caught the apron of the long 18th after Laing had hit splendidly to 12 feet from the flag. But, after sizing up the swirling putt with all the confidence of one who had known the course all her days, she holed to a rising roar which played its part in the American team's final surge.

'I cannot imagine a better script than this happening here in Fox Chapel in a Curtis Cup,' said the player who said, tentatively, that she could be making it a goal to play Curtis Cup golf in her 60s.

In the Solheim Cup, Europe won all four of the fourballs on the Saturday afternoon to go into the 12 singles with a 9–7 lead. In other words, five wins would have been enough for them to hang on to the trophy they had won two years before at a rain-lashed Loch Lomond.

The Americans were not going to let that happen. Led by their US Open champion, Juli Inkster, who defeated Raquel Carriedo by 4 and 3, they detonated alarm bells among the visitors by winning each of

the first three matches. Paula Marti was the victim in the second game, with Helen Alfredsson, one of Dale Reid's somewhat controversial wild-card choices, going down in the third.

It was Sam Torrance, the Ryder Cup captain, who talked of heroes emerging from shadows and, in the fourth of those Solheim Cup singles, it was the unsung Iben Tinning, who finally halted the European decline. She beat Kelly Keuhne by 3 and 2, while Sophie Gustafson won by the same margin against Cristie Kerr. Meanwhile, Suzann Pettersen notched a half which must have seemed like a win because she had been five down with five to play against Michel Redman.

The other halves belonged to Annika Sörenstam, who was shaping to break all records with her run of wins towards the end of the season, and Carin Koch. The Swede, incidentally, maintained her unbeaten Solheim Cup record from eight ties.

Both in the Curtis Cup and the Solheim Cup, there were arguments over the respective selection processes. Following GB and Ireland's Walker Cup win in 2000, there were those who felt that it would have made sense for the women to do as the men in giving the captain a say in who played in the team. Had Pam Benka, an excellent leader in every way, had that kind of input, she would surely have had a better chance of getting her head round who should play with whom in the foursomes.

In the Solheim Cup, it was more a matter of people not agreeing with Reid's wildcards. Why, they wanted to know, had she omitted Janice Moodie and Catriona Matthew, two Scots who have not only shone on the LPGA tour but whose match-play credentials are second to none?

Becky Brewerton of Wales had an answer at the ready for the amateur selectors. Upset at having been dumped from the side she made in 2000 after winning almost everything there was to win, Brewerton added the 2002 British women's stroke-play championship and European individual title to her list of successes. Then she had a good enough Home Internationals at the Berkshire to be chosen for the three-strong World Cup side who finished in the top 10 in Malaysia. She ended the season being named *Daily Telegraph* Golfer of the Year.

At the Ryder Cup, on the Sunday night Lee Westwood, took it upon himself to introduce each of his fellow players to those celebrating Europe's success in the bar of The Belfry.

Becky Brewerton had an outstanding year even if she missed out on the Curtis Cup.

© Phil Sheldon

When it was Phillip Price's turn to stand on the chair serving as a stage, the shy Welshman was by no means as reticent as you would have anticipated. 'Remember to tell them whom I beat,' he instructed Westwood, in a reference to his defeat of Phil Mickelson.

In their own way, Brewerton's scalps in the Home Internationals were also something to shout about.

Over the first two days, she was a cumulative ten under par in defeating two Curtis Cup players in Heather Stirling and Alison Coffey. If she could have had the better of Rebecca Hudson, on whom she was two up after ten, she would have had the set.

She was one up after a three at the 17th but, to her chagrin, took three putts from 30 feet on the home green.

New format but US are World Champions again

Mark Garrod on the Eisenhower Trophy

It was all change at the men's world amateur team championship in 2002, except for the name which ws inscribed on the Eisenhower Trophy, after the four days of competiion at the Saujana Club in Kuala Lumpur.

To accommodate the record number of 63 nations – including England, Scotland, Wales and Ireland entering separately for the first time rather than as a combined Grat Britain and Ireland side – each country was asked to send three not four golfers, with the best two scores each day counting rather than three out of four.

Whatever the format, the United States are always among the favourites and they fully justified that this time with a successful defence of the Cup and their 12th victory since the inaugural biennial event in 1958.

Seven years on from beating Tiger Woods in the Walker Cup, England's Gary Wolstenholme is still going strong. At the age of 41 he became the first overseas player to win the South African Amateur Strokeplay title. He has also been the British, Chinese, Finnish and Emirates champion in his career.

© Phil Sheldon

Not that it was a repeat of the previous runaway triumph. With a round to play France, seeking their maiden victory, had come from five behind to lead by three.

On a final day which saw heavy thunderstorms necessitate a cut to only the top 20 teams (Scotland and Ireland not among them), American college player of the year DJ Trahan, 10 over par after two rounds, produced a superb 66, the second lowest final round in the Championship's history. His score enabled himself, Hunter Mahan and Ricky Barnes to a three-stroke win on an eight-under aggregate of 568. There was double disappointment for leading French player Gregory Bourdy, who was pipped for the individual title by Australian Marcus Fraser's closing 70 for a seven-under 281.

England finished seventh, with Walker Cup pair Jamie Elson and Gary Wolstenholme eighth and 10th on their own ball respectively, and Wales 14th, David Price being their best performer in 16th position. With Great Britain and Ireland winners in 1998 and runners-up in 2000, the wisdom of splitting the home countries into four remains under scrutiny.

The Eisenhower Trophy brought the curtain down on an amateur season which began with a record-breaking achievement.

When Tiger Woods agreed to play in the New Zealand Open in January, the last thing he must have expected was to be competing against someone half his age, but 13-year-old Jae An not only won the qualifying tournament with a six-under-par 65, but also survived the halfway cut.

The Korean-born fourth former at Rotorua Boys High School is thought to be the youngest player ever to qualify for a national men's Open, a 10- and 12-year-old having competed in the US Women's Open.

Jae An's performance rather overshadowed the fact that another amateur, Australian Adam Groom, actually beat Woods in finishing fifth only four strokes behind winner Craig Parry.

The sport did not have to wait long for another notable feat by an amateur on the professional stage. Seventeen-year-old Rafael Cabrera, from the Canary Islands, came joint fourth in the Spanish Open, equalling the best-ever display by an amateur since the European Tour's launch in 1971.

And there was soon to be more cause for celebration in Spanish circles. Alejandro Larrazabal followed in very distinguished footsteps when he became Amateur champion at Royal Porthcawl.

In a history dating back to 1885 the only other two Spaniards to triumph have been José María Olazábal and Sergio García. Larrazabal, 22, did not arrive for the event with the same reputation, but golf is clearly in the blood. His mother Elena won the Spanish women's title three times and represented her country in the Espirito Trophy world team championship, while father Gustavo and younger brother Pablo have both played in the Eisenhower Trophy.

Four-up after 10 holes of the final against England's Martin Sell, Larrazabal was brought back to level with two to play, but then birdied the par five 17th and won on the last green after a superb seven-iron approach to six feet.

The week had started in astonishing fashion with a 10-under-par qualifying round of 61 by Richard Finch at Pyle and Kenfig. It broke the amateur course record by no fewer than seven strokes and if Finch was not that well-known at the time, he certainly was two months later, when he became English amateur champion at Walton Heath with a six and five win over Giles Legg.

Windyhill's Andrew McArthur, who turned his back on a possible career in football to concentrate on golf, became Scottish champion with a 2 and 1 victory over Scott Jamieson at Wetern Gailes, while John McGinn, of Greenore, lifted the Irish crown at Carlow with a three and one success against Ken Kearney.

Winner of the Welsh Amateur was David Price, from Vale of Glamorgan, who beat Lee Harpin at the 20th in a final cut to one round because of flooded fairways at Conwy, and down the coast at Royal St David's, Price then turned a great year into a never-to-be-forgotten one by helping Wales to their first-ever home international title. After waiting 70 years they became champions by beating defending champions and favourites England by one point, Ireland by two and then Scotland by three – even without Walker Cup man Nigel Edwards, who was laid low by stomach trouble.

Britain and Ireland retained the St Andrews Trophy against the Continent of Europe by a 14–10 margin in Lausanne – their 21st win in 24 matches – but the European amateur individual title went to France's Raphael Pellicioli, who finished five clear of England's James Heath at Troia in Portugal.

A familiar name was engraved on the Berkshire Trophy, 41-year-old Wolstenholme winning it for a third time with a tournament record 20 under par total of 267, four better than Elson, while Lee Corfield won the Lytham Trophy.

Graeme McDowell, another member of the triumphant 2001 Walker Cup side, will most remember the season for his maiden European tour victory at the Scandinavian Masters – only his fourth professional start. But an Amateur achievement of his is worthy of mention here as well.

The Ulsterman earned the number one ranking on the US collegiate scene during his time at the University of Alabama-Birmingham, finishing with a stroke average of 68.93 and winning nine tournaments.

Scotland's Simon Mackenzie beat a high-quality field to win the St Andrews Links Trophy, an event he has competed in every year since its inception in 1989, while 17-year-old South African Carl Schwartzel captured the English Open Amateur Strokeplay (Brabazon Trophy) at Royal Cinque Ports.

It was only the third time that the talented teenager, owner of a +5 handicap, had a links course, but having won the Indian amateur title, the amateur medal at the South African Open and been on the Sprinkbok side which won the world boy's team championship, notice had been served.

It was a further example of how quickly youngsters are now able to leave their mark – and here is another. At 15 Abbas-Ali Mawji hit the headlines by winning one of the regional qualifying competitions for the Open.

He did not go on to become the youngest player in the championship for over 100 years, but do not be surprised if somebody does soon.

Comrie's young sensations

Two teenagers with a combined age of 27 made history at the Comrie Club in Perthshire when they won the club's main Championship titles on the same day. Tiny 13-year-old Roseanne Niven, took the ladies' title with a 2 and 1 defeat over defending champion Mrs Jane Griffiths and 14-year-old Finlay White who plays off 3, beat Scottish youth cap Nicky Barr to land the men's title. Both are receiving coaching at the Scottish National Golf Centre at Drumoig near St Andrews. Later that same day the two youngsters danced together at the club's traditional evening celebration but, in the circumstances, neither provided the members with the usual whisky-filled trophies to mark the celebration.

How The Big Three turned a crisis into a triumph

Ian Wooldridge thanks three golfing pioneers

Such is now the pre-eminence of golf in the sporting firmament that it is astonishing to recall that 50 years ago the professional game was in a state of crisis. Watching an Open Championship then was rather like listening to The Archers – an everyday story of familiar folk reading from a repetitious script.

Between 1949 and 1958 Bobby Locke, of South Africa, and Peter Thomson, of Australia, each won the title four times. Both were wonderful to watch as they beat frequently lacklustre fields, but where were those damn Yankees who brought such a competitive cutting edge to everything they played in?

True, Ben Hogan paid a cursory visit in 1953 to reduce Carnoustie to scorched grass but even victory did not mollify him. He complained about his original accommodation until he was moved somewhere far grander, he refused a short trip around the bay even to glance at the treasures of St Andrews and was scornful about the prize money that left him well out of pocket for his visit to such barbary scores. He never came back and most of the glamourous figures of American golf heeded his disenchantment.

Thankfully three young men from starkly different backgrounds were emerging from their apprenticeships with far more adventurous ambitions. Two were Americans: Arnold Palmer, son of a greenkeeper, and Jack Nicklaus, collegiate hunk. The third, from the farmlands of South Africa, was Gary Player. Palmer was built like a highly-tuned middleweight boxer. Nicklaus, then, looked as though he lived on hamburgers and apple pie. Player, much the smallest of the three, oozed messianic determination.

It would be fatuous to suggest that they were to 'save' golf because golf will never need saving in that sense but is is not fatuous at all to suggest that these men, with their immense skills, their contrasting personalities and their impeccable manners both on and off the course, pulled golf in the expanding television era to heights undreamed of in the doldrums of the late 1950's. In the half century since then hundreds of professional golfers have risen to international celebrity and considerable, in some cases colossal, wealth in the tracks pioneered by men who broke the shackles of

© Phil Sheldon

The Big Three – Arnold Palmer, Gary Player and Jack Nicklaus – changed the face of golf forever.

provincialism and became known worldwide as The Big Three.

This, as they start to move from centre stage to their emeritus rocking chairs knowing that their chances of a 63 are receding, is a small tribute from a sportswriter of their own generation. Palmer is now 73 and has recovered from cancer. Player is 67, Nicklaus 63.

This is no statistical revue of their phenomenal achievements during the years that they almost dominated the major championships between them. These are recorded elsewhere in the *Golfer's Handbook*. This is more a close-up, at least of two of them, whom I am immensely privileged to call friends.

It was Arnold Palmer's successive victories at Royal Birkdale in 1961 and Royal Troon in 1962 that really blazed the trail for his American compatriots and made them realise the significance of what to them will always be known as the *British* Open Championship. Palmer, until the arrival years later of Severiano Ballesteros, was like Tarzan off the tees. He would hit it anywhere, confident that he could recover from the unfriendliest terrain Britain had to offer. Huge horseshoes of spectators would gather round him to watch what came next: clods of earth, clumps of grass, small flowers and field mice rising in the air as the ball flew free. His go-for-broke philosophy produced electrifying golf.

At the end of a round, trailed by the British satellite of Arnie's Army, he would slowly peel off his glove, walk to the edge of the green and hand it over to a young boy or a spectator sitting in a wheelchair. He would then proceed to the clubhouse, signing maybe three or four autographs on the way with a few words that the recipient would recall for ever. His secret was to *keep walking* in the process. Many a footballer and not a few cricketers should learn the trick.

Once in his youth, playing with his father, he hit an atrocious shot and in temper hurled his club into a tree. 'If you ever repeat that,' warned his father, 'you will never step on a golf course again.' He never did and, indeed, became one of the foremost guardians of golf's etiquette and traditions on the course and off it, in the many speeches he was required to deliver in that deep, growling voice. Politically, I suspect, he is to the right of Charlton Heston and John Wayne but that didn't stop American Presidents, Democrat as well as Republican, yearning to partner him in pro-ams or exhibition matches. The word is a cliché, but Arnold Palmer truly became an American icon.

Gary Player made his first real impact in world golf when, on a budget so restricted that he washed his own smalls in a bathroom handbasin, he won the Open Championship at Muirfield in 1959. Intense, garrulous, a dietary fanatic, he would spend his time on long haul flights to Britain or America squeezing squash balls in is hands to strengthen his arm muscles in order to compensate for his lack of height. He was to conquer both countries.

Coming from South Africa at the height of the republic's apartheid regime, he was to encounter the hostility that greeted many Springbok sportsmen at the time. The protesters were not to know that as his wealth proliferated he was setting up a school on his property back home for the education of deprived black children. When Gary appeared in golf gear vertically divided in black and white, many dismissed it as bizarre showmanship instead of understanding the humanitarian statement he was hoping to make.

As a showman he left Palmer and Nicklaus in the wings. Brylcreemed, burnished rather than merely shaven, immaculately dressed, with a handshake like a vice, he was always an interview waiting to happen on the front lawn of the August National Club or outside an Open Championship clubhouse. Some years ago a BBC radio news reporter covering his first Open asked me if I thought it would be possible to get a few words with the great man and, if so, would I help. I did. Half an hour later the exhausted reporter slumped down beside me and said: 'Jesus, how do I edit all that? I only wanted a minute.' That's Gary.

Jack Nicklaus I do not know, apart from attending many of his press conferences. Our paths never crossed at a personal level except when I once interviewed him for television and found him immensely polite and totally co-operative. When, however, I turned the conversation to his personal life, nothing intrusive but actually about his interest in antiques, he became suspicious that it was about to lead somewhere I had no intention of going. Nicklaus was the most private of the three and the most protective of his life off the course. Nicklaus was the greatest of The Big Three and arguably the greatest of all time, even allowing for Bobby Jones and Tiger Woods..

Thus the Big Three, brought together commercially by Mark McCormack at a critical time in the professional game's history. They were even greater for golf at the crossroads than the sum of their highly indivualistic parts.

Brilliant Norman created a championship record

Keith Mackie looks at Opens at Sandwich

Royal St George's, a distant outpost of links golf far removed from the game's roots on the east coast of Scotland, was the first course south of the border to stage the Open Championship. The year was 1894 and, in an effort to encourage Scottish professionals to undertake the long journey, a specially reduced fare was negotiated with the railway companies. Although the total entry set a new record at 94, a dozen more than the previous high at St Andrews, only 14 home-based Scots made the journey, but they were joined by another 21 who were already based at English clubs.

Yet it was Englishman J.H. Taylor who mastered the long and demanding course, winning by a margin of five shots despite never once breaking 80. His winning 72-hole total of 326 remains the highest in the history of the championship. Taylor, who was to win the title another four times in a lengthy career, had already acquired a reputation as one of the game's straightest hitters, a talent he enhanced with his ability to flight the ball high or low into the green. He needed all his skill to combat the fearsome St George's course.

From its inception seven years earlier the layout had attracted lavish praise and criticism in almost equal measure. Conceived by Scottish doctor Laidlaw Purves, an eminent consultant ophthalmologist at Guy's Hospital in London, the course took full advantage of the towering sandhills and narrow valleys. Purves, who had studied at the Universities of Edinburgh, Paris, Vienna and Berlin, was a powerful low handicap golfer and many critics accused him of designing a course to suit his own strengths. With hickory shafts and gutta percha golf balls, not many of his club companions could negotiate the numerous 150-yard carries. There were many blind shots and ferocious rough.

Freddie Tait, who won the Amateur Championship at St George's in 1896, summed up his opinions in a few words: 'A one-shot course, a paradise for the big hitter.' Bernard Darwin, pre-eminent golf correspondent of *The Times* and a member of the club, voiced similar concerns, stressing that 'the whole art of golf did not consist of hitting a ball over a sandhill and then running up to the top to see what had happened on the other side.'

Yet four Open Championships were played at St George's before any modifications were made to the course. Harry Vardon won the third of his six Opens, in 1899 and added his fourth after a play-off in 1911 when Arnaud Massy, trailing by six shots, conceded at the 35th hole. In 1904, the first Championship to feature rounds under 70 – J.H. Taylor had a 68, James Braid and winner Jack White

---

Walter Hagen a double winner at Sandwich

Only the American Walter Hagen has won twice at Royal St George's first used as a venue in 1894. En route to the titler in 1934 Henry Cotton shot a 65 – a score which was immortalised by being used as the name for a Dunlop golf ball. When the event was last played at the Sandwich course Australian Greg Norman set a new 72-hole record of 267 with rounds of 66, 68, 69 and 64.

Year	Winner	Score	Year	Winner	Score
1894	JH Taylor	326	1934	Henry Cotton	283
1899	Harry Vardon	310	1938	Reg Whitecombe	295
1904	Jack White	296	1949	Bobby Locke	283
1911	Harry Vardon	303	1981	Bill Rogers	276
1922	Walter Hagen	300	1985	Sandy Lyle	282
1928	Walter Hagen	292	1993	Greg Norman	267

scored 69s – the club received its royal title from Edward VII.

Flamboyant American Walter Hagen won twice at Royal St George's before Henry Cotton overcame his nerves to end a decade of US domination in 1934, setting a course record of 65 in the process, a score which gave the famous Dunlop golf ball its name. Reg Whitcombe claimed the title in 1938 with a final round of 78 that was a masterpiece of controlled scoring in gale force winds that ripped apart a large exhibition marquee and deposited torn canvas and golf merchandise across the links as far as the Prince's clubhouse almost a mile away. Downwind that day Alf Padgham, one of the game's most powerful players, drove the 384-yard 11th hole, but failed to reach the green into wind at the long 14th with four solid wooden shots.

Before Royal St George's vanished from the rota of championship courses for 32 years, it was to stage one more dramatic Open. In 1949 genial Irishman Harry Bradshaw had opened with a 68 and was in a relaxed state of mind in the second round when he discovered his ball lying in the bottom half of a broken beer bottle in the semi-rough to the right of the fifth fairway. Feeling that the rule covering an unplayable ball was not sufficiently clear, and fearing disqualification, he played the ball from its unusual spot. 'I picked my blaster, closed my eyes tightly and let fly,' he said.

The bottle disintegrated and the ball moved about 30 yards. Considerably shaken, he finished the hole with a 6. After four rounds he was tied with emerging South African golfer Bobby Locke and lost the 36-hole play-off by a dozen strokes. The free drop to which he was so clearly entitled could well have made him Open champion.

Lack of hotel accommodation in the immediate area and the network of small country lanes kept the Open away from the Kent coast until 1981 when a new road system was in place. The American entry was small, but a virtually unknown Texan, Bill Rogers won the title by four shots from Bernhard Langer. When the championship made a quick return in 1985 it was to mark the emergence of young Scot Sandy Lyle into the ranks of major winners, with a one shot margin over Payne Stewart. Three years later he was to claim the Masters title.

Yet perhaps the most dramatic of all St George's Opens was the 1993 triumph of Greg Norman. On the final day Nick Faldo scored a flawless 67 at the head of the field, but lost by two shots as Norman completed a masterly round of 64. Gene Sarazen, making a rare appearance in Britain at the age of 91, described the round as awesome. Norman said: 'I had never gone round a golf course before and not

© Phil Sheldon

Greg Norman set a new 72 hole record of 267 when he won the Open at Royal St George's in 1993.

miss-hit a single shot. I screwed up on only one little putt of 14 inches.' He later admitted: 'I didn't want that round to end.'

When Laidlaw Purves started his search for the perfect setting for a links course in the dying decades of the 19th century he tramped almost 200 miles of the southern England coastline before settling for the rugged dunes area south of Sandwich. Despite early criticism the course emerges in the 21st century with an enviable history of championship play. In addition to the Open it has staged 11 Amateur Championships and both the Walker and Curtis Cup matches as well as many high profile professional tournaments.

The two latest champions to claim the Open title at St George's sum up the challenge of the still rugged links this way. Sandy Lyle says: 'The premium is on driving and clever ball positioning.' Greg Norman says it is 'an all-round balanced golf course.'

The golfing hillbilly who became a world star

David Davies pays his tribute to a legend

American Samuel Snead – 'Slammin' Sam' as he was inevitably tagged – who died in 2002 aged 89, had a swing that was admired, coveted even, by more top-class players than perhaps any other golfer who ever lived. He appeared to be a complete natural, able to hit the ball vast distances, with a loose and easy action that looked as if it required no rehearsal. 'Sam,' said an envious rival, 'just walked up to the ball and poured honey all over it.'

Sam Snead was one of the game's great athletes whose fitness kept him competitive.

He was a complete contradiction, both in terms of his swing and character, to his two great contemporaries, Ben Hogan and Byron Nelson. Hogan worked all hours of the day and night to find a swing that worked, while Nelson was simply the most efficient scorer, and winner, of his day. But Snead, with his often casual air, his tall dominating manner, attracted the galleries – and the women – throughout his career, which ended with him winning the US Masters three times (1949, 1952, 1954), the US PGA three times (1942, 1949, 1951) and the Open Championship once (1946). Only six professionals in the history of the game have a better record that that.

Yet Snead never did win the US Open, a failure that prevented him from being listed among the four players with whom he naturally attracted comparison, the Grand Slam winners Gene Sarazen, Hogan, Jack Nicklaus and Gary Player. It was a failure that he always insisted did not bother him, but if it did not – and that is doubtful – it bothered a great many other people who felt that the exclusive Grand Slam club could only be enhanced by his presence.

Snead came from the backwoods of Virginia, from Hot Springs, where he maintained a home all his life – and where he died – although latterly he combined it with another winter house in Florida. When he first emerged on the fledgling US Tour, it was because he preferred that gypsy-style life to that of running a restaurant for his uncle, or working as a soda-jerk in a drugstore back home.

He had learned the game the hard way at White Sulphur Springs, the resort to which he was attached in the early days. It was the late 1930s, there was a depression on and everyone did what they could to earn a cent. This led to Snead telling a story against himself regarding the black art of gamesmanship. He was doing well in a tournament when a professional he knew approached him just before the final round and said: 'How do you expect to do well with that left elbow flying around like that?'

Snead said that he took notice of the remark, tried to do something about it, took eight at the second hole and finished with an 80, good only for third place. It was on a course, said Snead, 'that I could shoot 80 on with only two clubs,' and after that he resolved that if anyone tried to tamper with his mind he would say: 'Hey, beat me with your clubs.'

It was during that early period that his reputation for being slow on the uptake, for being the archetypal hillbilly, was created. He had just won a tournament in Oakland, California when he was approached by a photographer who took a victory picture. It was duly wired around the country and appeared in, among others, a New York newspaper. A few days later Sam happened to see a copy of the paper and said: 'Hey, how could they get my picture in New York. I ain't never been there.'

That remark was unprompted, but as it travelled around the world of golf, causing giggles wherever it went, the man in charge of the US Tour, a natural publicist called Fred Corcoran, seized upon it. He told Snead that the reporters of the time loved the idea of someone sneaking out from the sticks and playing great golf, and the man himself later admitted; 'I got the notion that playing the hillbilly wasn't a bad idea.'

But if he was notoriously slow on the uptake, that did not prevent him from asserting his opinion once it was formed. Snead was the captain of the 1969 US Ryder Cup team at Royal Birkdale when the match was halved because of a famous and quixotic gesture by Jack Nicklaus. The American conceded a short putt to Tony Jacklin that, had it been missed, would have meant yet another US victory. Most of the world applauded a wonderfully generous and sporting comment. Snead, for whom it meant that he was not now a winning captain, seethed. Furthermore, he let Nicklaus know how he seethed.

On another visit, to St Andrews for the 1946 Open Championship, which he won, he took no account of the fact that the nation had just been through a rather difficult time and decided, on the basis of the hotels of the period, that 'any time you leave the US you're just camping out.' He didn't like the Old Course either, a heresy then and now.

But Snead got away with almost everything during one of the most durable careers golf has seen. He was, most of the time, an amiable man, a man's man, and one with a fund of stories that were very definitely not for mixed company. He won around 140 tournaments during his career, the exact number depending on what constituted a proper tournament during his early years.   His swing is generally admitted to be the most graceful of them all, helping him to become the oldest man ever to win on the US Tour. He took the Greater Greensboro Open in 1965 at the age of 52 years; and, perhaps the most incredible feat of all, produced rounds of 67 and 66 in another Tour event, the Quad Cities Open. In his later years beating his age became an almost daily event.

He never admitted though, even to himself, that his failure to win the US Open troubled him. 'They say I couldn't win the big one', he would say. 'Well, what's big and what's small?'

His best chance of victory came in 1939 when the championship went to the Philadelphia Country Club. After 71 holes all Snead needed was a par five at the last hole, one he could reach in two shots, to win. But he had just bogied the 71st hole, he was upset and a little worried and not sure what he needed to win. Suspecting it was a birdie, he went for a big drive and hooked it into the rough. He topped a brassie second shot into the sand, tried to hit an eight iron out and hammered the ball into the face of the bunker. From there he went into another bunker, was on the green in five and took the inevitable three putts for an eight.

He was to play in the championship over a 40-year period: he finished second four times, third once and fifth twice but he never won the one title that would have meant the most to him.

Reproduced by permission of *The Guardian*

Sam's putting problems

Sam Snead always had problems with his putting but never more so than when on a tour of South Africa he lost 10 of the 12 matches he played against Bobby Locke who in contrast was one of the game's greatest putters.

He once described his attempts to putt as the equivalent of 'a monkey trying to wrestle with a football' but usually managed to find a way to get the ball into the hole using various methods. When he ended up straddling the line of the putt and using the putter croquet-style with his left hand on top of the shaft and his right hand half-way down it he thought he had found the permanent answer. The method worked but the ruling authorities decided this did not match up to the spirit of the game and was undignified. They banned that style of putting.

Sam Snead solved that problem very quickly. He used the same method but stood to putt with the ball to the right of his feet. It was called the sidewinder.

Venues and dates for the US majors and the Ryder Cup

	The Masters	US Open	US PGA Championship
2003	**April 10–13** Augusta National, Augusta, Georgia	**June 12–15** Olympia Fields, Illinois	**14–17 August** Oak Hill CC, New York
2004	**April 8–11** Augusta National, Augusta, Georgia	**June 17–20** Shinnecock Hills, Southampton, New York	**August** Whistling Straits, Kohler, Wisconsin
2005	**April 7–10** Augusta National, Augusta, Georgia	**June 16–19** Pinehurst No.2, Pinehurst, North Carolina	**August** The Country Club, Brookline, Massachusetts
2006	**April 6–9** Augusta National, Augusta, Georgia	**June 15–18** Winged Foot GC, Mamaroneck, New York	**August** Medinah CC, Medinah, Illinois
2007	**April 5–8** Augusta National, Augusta, Georgia	**June 14–17** Oakmont CC, Pennsylvania	**August** Southern Hills, Tulsa, Oklahoma
2008	**April 10–13** Augusta National, Augusta, Georgia		**August** Oakland Hills, Bloomfield Hills CC, Michigan
2009	**April 9–12** Augusta National, Augusta, Georgia		**August** Hazeltine National GC, Chaska, Minnesota
2010	**April 8–11** Augusta National, Augusta, Georgia		**August** Sahalee CC, Richmond, Washington
2011			**August** Atlanta AC, Deluth, Georgia

The US Masters normally begins on the Thursday following the first Sunday in April.
The US Open Championship normally begins on the Thursday following the second
  Sunday in June.
The US PGA Championship normally begins on the second Thursday in August.

Ryder Cup
The 2001 Ryder Cup was postponed to 2002 and the Cup will now be played in even years.

2002 at The Belfry, Sutton Coldfield, West Midlands on September 27–29
2004 at Oakland Hills Country Club, Birmingham, Michigan on September 26–28
2006 at The K Club, County Kildare, Ireland
2008 at Valhalla Golf Club, Louisville, Kentucky
2010 at Celtic Manor Resort, Newport, Wales
2012 at Medinah Country Club, Illinois
2014 at Gleneagles Hotel, Perthshire, Scotland
2016 at Hazeltine National GC, Chaska, Minnesota

Presidents Cup (USA *v* Rest of the World except Europe)
2003 at Fancourt Hotel and CC Estate (The Links Course), George, South Africa

R&A venues and dates for championships 2003–2005

	2003	2004	2005
The Amateur Championship	June 2–7 Royal Troon/ Irvine (Bogside)	May 31–June 5 St Andrews Old & Jubilee	May 30–June 4 Royal Birkdale Southport and Ainsdale
The Open Championship Regional Qualifying	July 7	July 5	July 4
The Open Championship Final Qualifying	July 13–14 Littlestone North Foreland Princes Royal Cinque Ports	July 11–12 TBA	July 10–11 TBA
The Junior Open Championship	Not played	July 13–15	Not played
The Open Championship	July 17–20 Royal St George's	July 15–18 Royal Troon	July 14–17 St Andrews
The Senior British Open	July 24–27 Turnberry	July TBA	TBA
The Seniors' Open Amateur Championship	August 6–8 Blairgowrie, Rosemount and Lansdowne	August 4–6 The Berkshire, Red and Blue Courses	August 3–5 Woburn Dukes and Duchess
The Boys' Home Internationals	August 5–7 Royal St David's	August 3–5 Royal Dublin	August 2–4 Woodhall Spa
The Boys' Amateur Championship	August 11–16 Royal Liverpool	August 9–14 Conwy (Caernarvonshire)	August 8–13 Huntstanton
British Mid-Amateur Championship	August 13–17 Jubilee Course, St Andrews	August 11–15 Royal Liverpool	August 10–14 Muirfield
The Jacques Léglise Trophy	August 29–30 Lahinch, Ireland	August 27–28 Nairn, Scotland	August 26–27 Royal Porthcawl
The St Andrews Trophy	Not played	August 27–28 Nairn, Scotland	Not played
The Walker Cup	September 6–7 Ganton	Not played	August 13–14 Chicago GC, Illinois
The Eisenhower Trophy	Not played	October 28–31 Puerto Rico	Not played

Schedules for the 2003 Season

European Team Championships

July 1–5	Amateur, Royal The Hague G&CC, Netherlands
July 8–12	Ladies, Wittelsbacher GC Rohrenfeld-Neuburg, Germany
July 8–12	Girls, Esjberg GC, Denmark
July 8–12	Boys, Astoria Cihelny (Karlovy Vary), Czech Republic

International European Championships

June 5–7	Mid-Amateur, Mosjö, Sweden
June 12–14	Seniors, Saint-Nom-La-Bretèche, France
July 24–26	European Young Masters, GC Augsburg, Germany
Aug 20–23	Amateur, Nairn GC, Scotland
Aug 27–30	Ladies, Shannon, Ireland
Oct 2–4	European Club Cup Trophy – Ladies, Racing Club de France, La Boulie, France
Oct 30–Nov 11	European Club Cup Trophy – Men, National GC of Antalya, Turkey

International Matches

| July 5–26 | Vagliano Trophy | Co. Louth GC, Ireland |
| Aug 29–30 | Jacques Léglise Trophy | La Hinch, Ireland |

Tournaments Recommended by the EGA

| April 2–5 | Sherry Cup, European Nations Championship | Sotogrande, Spain |

European International Calendar

Championships in bold type have not yet been confirmed

Feb 26–Mar 2	Spanish Ladies Amateur Championship, El Saler (Valencia)
Feb 26–Mar 2	Spanish Amateur Championship, Costa Ballena (Cádiz)
Mar 12–16	**Portuguese Ladies Amateur Championship**
Mar 12–16	**Portuguese Amateur Championship**
April 7–10	Israel Ladies Amateur Championship, Caesarea GC
April 7–10	Israel Amateur Championship, Caesarea GC
April 17–21	**French Lady Juniors Championship**
April 17–21	**French Boys Championship**
April 24–27	Spanish Lady Juniors Championship, Club Campo Villa de Madrid
April 25–27	German Ladies Amateur Championship, GC Am Alten, Fliess
April 25–27	German Amateur Championship, GC Am Alten, Fliess
April 26–27	**Scottish Ladies Open Stroke Play Championship**
May 2–4	Lytham Trophy, Royal Lytham & St Annes

European International Calendar continued

May 9–11	Irish Amateur Open Championship, Royal Dublin
May 16–18	English Open Stroke Play (Brabazon Trophy), Hunstanton
May 31– June 1	Welsh Open Youths Championship, Northop
June 2–7	The Amateur Championship, Royal Troon/Irvine
June 6–9	Austrian Ladies Amateur Championship, Colony Club, Gutenhof/Himberg
June 6–9	Austrian Amateur Championship, Colony Club, Gutenhof/Himberg
June 10–14	Ladies British Open Amateur Championship, Lindrick GC
June 13–15	Scottish Open Amateur Stroke Play Championship, Turnberry, Kintyre
June 20–22	Welsh Open Stroke Play Championship, Prestatyn
June 21–22	Scottish Youths Open Amateur Stroke Play Championship, Letham Grange
June 24–27	Russian Ladies Amateur Championship, Moscow G&CC
June 24–27	Russian Amateur Championship, Moscow G&CC
June 26–27	Irish Youths Amateur Open Championship, Douglas
June 27–29	**French Ladies Amateur Stroke Play Championship (Trophée Cécile Rothshild)**
June 27–29	**French Mens Amateur Stroke Play Championship (Coupe Murat)**
June 27–29	**Welsh Ladies Open Stroke Play Championship**
June 28–30	Polish Junior Open Championship, TBA
July 4–6	Ladies British Open Mid Amateur Championship, Royal Liverpool GC
July 16–18	**Slovak Amateur Championship**
July 16–20	Luxembourg Ladies Amateur Championship, GC Grand-Ducal
July 16–20	Luxembourg Amateur Championship, GC Grand-Ducal
July 17–19	Dutch Junior International, Toxandria
July 19–20	Irish Ladies' Open Amateur Strokeplay Championship, Rathsallagh
July 22–24	English Boys (under 18) Amateur Stroke Play Championship (Carris Trophy), Burnham & Berrow
July 29–31	Danish Girls Championship, Smorum GC
July 29–31	Danish Boys Championship, Smorum GC
July 29–30	**Scottish Lady Junior Stroke Play Championship**
Aug 1–3	Swiss Ladies Amateur Championship, Wylihof GC
Aug 1–3	Swiss Amateur Championship, Wylihof GC
Aug 5–9	Girls British Open Amateur Championship, Newport
Aug 6–8	British Senior Championship, Blairgowrie-Rosemount & Lansdowne
Aug 7–9	Finnish Ladies Amateur Championship, TBA
Aug 7–9	Finnish Amateur Championship, TBA
Aug 11–16	British Boys Championship, Royal Liverpool
Aug 12–15	**English Ladies Open Intermediate Championship**
Aug 13–16	Czech Ladies Amateur Championship, Praha Karlstejn GC
Aug 13–16	Czech Amateur Championship, Praha Karlstejn GC
Aug 13–17	British Mid-Amateur Championship, St Andrews, Jubilee
Aug 26–30	Belgian Lady Junior Championship, Royal GC de Belgique (Ravenstein)
Aug 26–30	Belgian Championship, Royal GC de Belgique (Ravenstein)
Aug 28–30	Porsche Hungarian Open Ladies Amateur Championship, Pannonia G&CC
Aug 28–30	Porsche Hungarian Open Amateur Championship, Pannonia G&CC
Sept 4–7	**Slovenian Ladies Amateur Championship**
Sept 4–7	**Slovenian Amateur Championship**
Sept 8–14	Spanish Junior Championship, Larrabea (Alava)
Sept 10–12	Ladies British Open Amateur Stroke Play Championship, Royal Portrush
Sept 10–13	Polish Open Amateur Championship, TBA
Sept 11–14	**Turkish Open Amateur Championship (Men)**
Sept 17–21	Italian International Ladies Amateur Championship, Gircolo Golf, Roma
Sept 17–21	Italian International Amateur Championship, Gircolo Golf, Roma
Sept 23–25	Senior Ladies British Open Amateur Championship, South Staffordshire GC
Sept 25–28	Hellenic Ladies Amateur Championship, Corfu
Sept 25–28	Hellenic Amateur Championship, Corfu
Oct 31–Nov 2	Cyprus Amateur Open, TBA

PGA European Tour

Nov 21–24	BMW Asian Open, Ta Shee Golf and Country Club, Taiwan
Nov 28–Dec 1	Omega Hong Kong Open, Hong Kong GC, Hong Kong
Jan 9–12	South African Airways Open, Erinvale GC, Cape Town, South Africa
Jan 16–19	Dunhill Championship, Houghton GC, Johannesburg, South Africa
Jan 23–26	Caltex Singapore Masters, Laguna National G&CC, Singapore
Jan 30–Feb 2	Heineken Classic, Royal Melbourne GC, Victoria, Australia
Feb 7–10	ANZ Championship, New South Wales GC, Sydney, Australia
Feb 13–16	Johnnie Walker Classic, Lake Karrinyup CC, Perth, Australia
Feb 19–23	Carlsberg Malaysian Open, The Mines Resort & GC, Kuala Lumpur, Malaysia
Feb 27–Mar 2	**WGC – Accenture Match Play,** La Costa Resort & Spa, Carlsbad, California, USA
Mar 6–9	Dubai Desert Classic, Emirates GC, Dubai
Mar 13–16	Qatar Masters, Doha GC, Qatar
Mar 20–23	Madeira Island Open, Santo da Serra, Madeira
Mar 27–30	TBA
Apr 3–6	TBA
Apr 10–13	**The Masters**, Augusta National, Georgia, USA
Apr 17–20	Algarve Open de Portugal, Vale de Lobo, Portugal
Apr 24–27	Canarias Open de España, TBC
May 1–4	Italian Open, TBC
May 8–11	Benson & Hedges International Open, The De Vere Belfry, Sutton Coldfield, England
May 15–18	Deutsche Bank – SAP Open TPC of Europe, Gut Kaden, Hamburg, Germany
May 22–25	**Volvo PGA Championship**, Wentworth Club, Surrey, England
May 29–Jun 1	The Celtic Manor Resort Wales Open, The Celtic Manor Resort, Newport, Wales
Jun 6–9	**British Masters**, Marriott Forest of Arden, Warwickshire, England
Jun 12–15	**US Open,** Olympia Fields CC, Matteson, Illinois, USA
Jun 19–22	Diageo Championship at Gleneagles, The Gleneagles Hotel, Perthshire, Scotland
Jun 26–29	Novotel Perrier Open de France, Le Golf National, Paris, France
Jul 3–6	Smurfit European Open, The K Club, Dublin, Ireland
Jul 10–13	The Barclays Scottish Open, Loch Lomond, Glasgow, Scotland
Jul 17–20	**132nd Open Golf Championship,** Royal St George's GC, Sandwich, Kent, England
Jul 24–27	TBA, Hilversumsche GC, Hilversum, Netherlands
July 31–Aug 3	Scandinavian Masters, Barsebäck G & CC, Malmo, Sweden
Aug 7–10	Nordic Open, Simons GC, Copenhagen, Denmark
Aug 14–17	**US PGA Championship,** Oak Hill CC, Rochester, New York, USA
Aug 14–17	TBA
Aug 21–24	**WGC – NEC Invitational,** Firestone CC, Akron, Ohio, USA
Aug 21–24	TBA
Aug 28–31	BMW International Open, Golfclub München Nord-Eichenried, Munich, Germany
Sep 4–7	Omega European Masters, Crans-sur-Sierre, Switzerland
Sep 11–14	Trophée Lancôme, Saint-Nom-La-Bretèche, Paris, France
Sep 18–22	Linde German Masters, Gut Lärchenhof, Cologne, Germany
Sep 25–28	Dunhill Links Championship, St Andrews Old, Kingsbarns and Carnoustie, Scotland
Oct 2–5	**WGC – American Express Championship,** Capitol City Club, Atlanta, USA
Oct 9–12	TBA
Oct 16–19	*Cisco World Match Play Championship, Wentworth Club, Surrey, England
Oct 23–26	Telefonica Open de Madrid, Club de Campo, Madrid, Spain
Oct 30–Nov 2	**Volvo Masters Andalucia,** Club de Golf, Valderrama, Spain
Nov 7–9	The Seve Trophy, San Roque Club, Spain
Nov 13–16	***WGC: – EMC^2 World Cup,** Kiwayah Island, USA

2004 Season

Nov 27–30	†BMW Asian Open, Westin Resort, Ta Shee, Taiwan
Dec 4–7	†Omega Hong Kong Open, Hong Kong GC, Hong Kong

Dates still to be confirmed: Irish Open, Dutch Open

---

*Bold type indicates a major   * denotes approved special events   † denotes 2004 Volvo Order of Merit*

US Men's Amateur Championship

Aug 18–24   Oakmost CC, Pittsburgh, PA

US Women's Amateur Championship

Aug 4–10   Philadelphia CC, PA

Mission Hills Golf Club to stage the first Dynasty Cup

China's Mission Hills Golf Club, the region's largest golf club with five 18-hole courses, will sponsor and stage the first clash between Asia and Japan for the inaugural Dynasty Cup.

The Ryder Cup-style tournament will pit Asia's leading players against the cream of Japanese golf from March 14–16 2003. The match will be staged biennially.

Mission Hills made a name for itself by hosting the 41st World Cup of Golf in November 1995 and last year invited world no.1 Tiger Woods to China for an exhibition match.

There are five championship courses at Mission Hills Golf Club in Shenzhen. Jack Nicklaus put his signature to the World Cup course, while the other courses were crafted by Nick Faldo, Ernie Els, Vijay Singh and Jumbo Ozaki. A decision has still to be taken on which course the Dynasty Cup will be staged.

Abbreviations

Alb	Albania	Ind	India	Pol	Poland
Arg	Argentina	Irl	Ireland	Por	Portugal
Aus	Australia	Isl	Iceland	Pur	Puerto Rico
Aut	Austria	Ita	Italy	Rus	Russia
Bel	Belgium	Jam	Jamaica	Sin	Singapore
Bra	Brazil	Jpn	Japan	RSA	South Africa
Can	Canada	Kor	Korea (South)	Sco	Scotland
Chi	China	Mal	Malaysia	Swe	Sweden
Chl	Chile	Mex	Mexico	Sui	Switzerland
Col	Colombia	Nam	Namibia	Tai	Taiwan
Den	Denmark	Ned	Netherlands	Tha	Thailand
Eng	England	NI	Northern Ireland	Tri	Trinidad and
Esp	Spain	Nor	Norway		Tobago
Fij	Fiji	NZ	New Zealand	USA	United States
Fin	Finland	Pan	Panama	Ven	Venezuela
Fra	France	Par	Paraguay	Wal	Wales
Ger	Germany	Per	Peru	Zim	Zimbabwe
Hun	Hungary	Phi	Philippines		

(am)	Amateur	(M)	Match play	jr	Junior
(D)	Defending champion	(S)	Stroke play	sr	Senior

Where available, total course yardage and the par for a course are displayed in square brackets, i.e.
[6686–70]

* indicates winner after play-off

Late Results

Tournament results that were obtained too late for inclusion in their
pertinent sections can be found on page 371

PART I

The Major Championships

The Open Championship

131st Open Championship at Muirfield (7034–71)

Prize Money £3.885 million. Entries: 2260. Regional qualifying courses: Alwoodley, Blackmoor, Co.Louth, Hadley Wood, Hindhead, Little Aston, Minchinhampton, Northamptonshire County, Notts, Ormskirk, Orsett, Renfrew, Silloth-on-Solway, Stockport, Trentham, Wildernesse. Final qualifying courses: Dunbar, Gullane No.1, Luffness New, North Berwick. Final Field: 156 (3 amateurs), of whom 83 (no amateurs) made the half-way cut on 144 or less.

1	Ernie Els (RSA)	70-66-72-70—278	£700000	€1095514
2	Stuart Appleby (Aus)	73-70-70-65—278	286667	448639
	Steve Elkington (Aus)	71-73-68-66—278	286667	448639
	Thomas Levet (Fra)	72-66-74-66—278	286667	448639

After a four-hole play-off, Appleby and Elkington were eliminated; Els won the sudden-death play-off with Levet at the first extra hole.

5	Gary Evans (Eng)	72-68-74-65—279	140000	219103
	Padraig Harrington (Irl)	69-67-76-67—279	140000	219103
	Shigeki Maruyama (Jpn)	68-68-75-68—279	140000	219103
8	Thomas Bjørn (Den)	68-70-73-69—280	77500	121289
	Sergio García (Esp)	71-69-71-69—280	77500	121289
	Retief Goosen (RSA)	71-68-74-67—280	77500	121289
	Søren Hansen (Den)	68-69-73-70—280	77500	121289
	Scott Hoch (USA)	74-69-71-66—280	77500	121289
	Peter O'Malley (Aus)	72-68-75-65—280	77500	121289
14	Justin Leonard (USA)	71-72-68-70—281	49750	77860
	Peter Lonard (Aus)	72-72-68-69—281	49750	77860
	Davis Love III (USA)	71-72-71-67—281	49750	77860
	Nick Price (Zim)	68-70-75-68—281	49750	77860
18	Bob Estes (USA)	71-70-73-68—282	41000	64166
	Scott McCarron (USA)	71-68-72-71—282	41000	64166
	Greg Norman (Aus)	71-72-71-68—282	41000	64166
	Duffy Waldorf (USA)	67-69-77-69—282	41000	64166
22	David Duval (USA)	72-71-70-70—283	32000	50081
	Toshimitsu Izawa (Jpn)	76-68-72-67—283	32000	50081
	Mark O'Meara (USA)	69-69-77-68—283	32000	50081
	Corey Pavin (USA)	69-70-75-69—283	32000	50081
	Chris Riley (USA)	70-71-76-66—283	32000	50081
	Justin Rose (Eng)	68-75-68-72—283	32000	50081
28	Bradley Dredge (Wal)	70-72-74-68—284	24000	37560
	Niclas Fasth (Swe)	70-73-71-70—284	24000	37560
	Pierre Fulke (Swe)	72-69-78-65—284	24000	37560
	Jerry Kelly (USA)	73-71-70-70—284	24000	37560
	Bernhard Langer (Ger)	72-72-71-69—284	24000	37560
	Jesper Parnevik (Swe)	72-72-70-70—284	24000	37560
	Loren Roberts (USA)	74-69-70-71—284	24000	37560
	Des Smyth (Irl)	68-69-74-73—284	24000	37560
	Tiger Woods (USA)	70-68-81-65—284	24000	37560
37	Darren Clarke (NI)	72-67-77-69—285	16917	26475
	Andrew Coltart (Sco)	71-69-74-71—285	16917	26475
	Neal Lancaster (USA)	71-71-76-67—285	16917	26475
	Stephen Leaney (Aus)	71-70-75-69—285	16917	26475
	Scott Verplank (USA)	72-68-74-71—285	16917	26475
	Ian Woosnam (Wal)	72-72-73-68—285	16917	26475
43	Trevor Immelman (RSA)	72-72-71-71—286	13750	21519

43T	Steve Jones (USA)	68-75-73-70—286	13750	21519
	Carl Pettersson (Swe)	67-70-76-73—286	13750	21519
	Esteban Toledo (Mex)	73-70-75-68—286	13750	21519
47	Paul Eales (Eng)	73-71-76-67—287	12000	18780
	Jeff Maggert (USA)	71-68-80-68—287	12000	18780
	Rocco Mediate (USA)	71-72-74-70—287	12000	18780
50	Fredrik Andersson (Swe)	74-70-74-70—288	10267	16068
	Warren Bennett (Eng)	71-68-82-67—288	10267	16068
	Ian Garbutt (Eng)	69-70-74-75—288	10267	16068
	Mikko Ilonen (Fin)	71-70-77-70—288	10267	16068
	Shingo Katayama (Jpn)	72-68-74-74—288	10267	16068
	Barry Lane (Eng)	74-68-72-74—288	10267	16068
	Ian Poulter (Eng)	69-69-78-72—288	10267	16068
	Bob Tway (USA)	70-66-78-74—288	10267	16068
59	Stewart Cink (USA)	71-69-80-69—289	9300	14555
	Joe Durant (USA)	72-71-73-73—289	9300	14555
	Nick Faldo (Eng)	73-69-76-71—289	9300	14555
	Richard Green (Aus)	72-72-75-70—289	9300	14555
	Kuboya Kenichi (Jpn)	70-73-73-73—289	9300	14555
	Paul Lawrie (Sco)	70-70-78-71—289	9300	14555
	Steve Stricker (USA)	69-70-81-69—289	9300	14555
66	Chris DiMarco (USA)	72-69-75-74—290	8800	13772
	Phil Mickelson (USA)	68-76-76-70—290	8800	13772
	Jarrod Moseley (Aus)	70-73-75-72—290	8800	13772
69	Stephen Ames (Tri)	68-70-81-72—291	8517	13329
	Jim Carter (USA)	74-70-73-74—291	8517	13329
	Matthew Cort (Eng)	73-71-78-69—291	8517	13329
	Len Mattiace (USA)	68-73-77-73—291	8517	13329
	Toru Taniguchi (Jpn)	71-73-76-71—291	8517	13329
	Mike Weir (Can)	73-69-74-75—291	8517	13329
75	Sandy Lyle (Sco)	68-76-73-75—292	8500	13303
	Chris Smith (USA)	74-69-71-78—292	8500	13303
77	Anders Hansen (Den)	71-72-79-71—293	8500	13303
	Roger Wessels (RSA)	72-71-73-77—293	8500	13303
79	David Park (Wal)	73-67-74-80—294	8500	13303
80	Mark Calcavecchia (USA)	74-66-81-74—295	8500	13303
	Lee Janzen (USA)	70-69-84-72—295	8500	13303
82	Colin Montgomerie (Sco)	74-64-84-75—297	8500	13303
83	David Toms (USA)	67-75-81-75—298	8500	13303

The following players missed the half-way cut:

84	Magnus Persson Atlevi (Swe)	72-73—145	95T	John Senden (Aus)	76-70—146
	John Bickerton (Eng)	73-72—145		Taichi Teshima (Jpn)	69-77—146
	Michael Campbell (NZ)	74-71—145		Tom Whitehouse (Eng)	75-71—146
	Marc Farry (Fra)	70-75—145	108	Robert Allenby (Aus)	73-74—147
	Brad Faxon (USA)	70-75—145		Luke Donald (Eng)	73-74—147
	Matt Kuchar (USA)	75-70—145		Jim Furyk (USA)	71-76—147
	José María Olazábal (Esp)	73-72—145		Mathias Grönberg (Swe)	75-72—147
	Jean-François Remesy (Fra)	68-77—145		David Howell (Eng)	73-74—147
	Eduardo Romero (Arg)	72-73—145		Raphaèl Jacquelin (Fra)	74-73—147
	Adam Scott (Aus)	77-68—145		Scott Laycock (Aus)	73-74—147
	Lee Westwood (Eng)	72-73—145		Tommy Nakajima (Jpn)	75-72—147
95	Alex Cejka (Ger)	73-73—146		Vijay Singh (Fij)	72-75—147
	Kyoung-Ju Choi (Kor)	73-73—146		Simon Young (Eng) (am)	76-71—147
	Tim Clark (RSA)	70-76—146	118	José Coceres (Arg)	70-78—148
	Scott Henderson (Sco)	78-68—146		Ricardo Gonzalez (Arg)	76-72—148
	Robert Karlsson (Swe)	72-74—146		Miguel Angel Jiménez (Esp)	73-75—148
	Tom Lehman (USA)	70-76—146		John Kemp (Eng) (am)	74-74—148
	Paul McGinley (Irl)	72-74—146		Andy Oldcorn (Sco)	79-69—148
	Billy Mayfair (USA)	71-75—146		Greg Owen (Eng)	76-72—148
	Craig Parry (Aus)	72-74—146		Ian Stanley (Aus)	76-72—148
	Tim Petrovic (USA)	73-73—146	125	Benn Barham (Eng)	76-73—149

130th Open Championship continued

125T	Adam Mednick (Swe)	75-74—149	136T	Kevin Sutherland (USA)	73-78—151
	Phillip Price (Wal)	75-74—149		Toru Suzuki (Jpn)	79-72—151
	Hal Sutton (USA)	74-75—149	144	Billy Andrade (USA)	77-75—152
129	Paul Casey (Eng)	72-78—150		Angel Cabrera (Arg)	73-79—152
	John Cook (USA)	74-76—150		Alejandro Larrazábal (Esp) (am)	77-75—152
	Mattias Eliasson (Swe)	78-72—150		Malcolm Mackenzie (Eng)	76-76—152
	Darren Fichardt (RSA)	80-70—150		John Riegger (USA)	78-74—152
	Frank Lickliter (USA)	74-76—150	149	Jamie Spence (Eng)	77-78—155
	Raymond Russell (Sco)	71-79—150		Tom Watson (USA)	77-78—155
	Dean Wilson (USA)	71-79—150	151	James Kingston (RSA)	76-81—157
136	Peter Baker (Eng)	75-76—151		Paul Mayoh (Eng)	84-73—157
	John Daly (USA)	74-77—151	153	Kiyoshi Miyazato (Jpn)	77-82—159
	Gary Emerson (Eng)	75-76—151	154	Roger Chapman (Eng)	74-DQ
	Dudley Hart (USA)	74-77—151		Thongchai Jaidee (Tha)	80-WD
	Fredrik Jacobson (Swe)	78-73—151		Jonathan Kaye (USA)	74-DQ
	Patrik Sjöland (Swe)	75-76—151			

2001 Open Championship at Royal Lytham & St Anne's   (7115–72)

Prize Money £3,229,748. Entries 2255. Regional qualifying courses: Alwoodley, Blackmoor, Burnham & Berrow, Carlisle, County Louth, Copt Heath, Coxmoor, Hadley Wood, Hindhead, Little Aston, Northamptonshire County, Orsett, Renfrew, Stockport, Wildernesse, Wilmslow. Final qualifying courses: Fairhaven, Hillside, St Anne's Old Links, Southport & Ainsdale. Final field comprised 156 players, of whom 70 (including one amateur) made the half-way cut on 144 or better.

1	Retief Goosen (RSA)	66-70-69-71—276	$900000	24	Steve Lowery	71-73-72-71—287	42523
2	Mark Brooks	72-64-70-70—276	530000		Joe Durant	71-74-70-72—287	42523
3	Stewart Cink	69-69-67-72—277	325310		Mark Calcavecchia	70-74-73-70—287	42523
4	Rocco Mediate	71-68-67-72—278	226777		Hal Sutton	70-75-71-71—287	42523
5	Tom Kite	73-72-72-64—281	172912		Tom Lehman	76-68-69-74—287	42523
	Paul Azinger	74-67-69-71—281	172912		Olin Browne	71-74-71-71—287	42523
7	Davis Love III	72-69-71-70—282	125172	30	Padraig Harrington		
	Vijay Singh (Fij)	74-70-74-64—282	125172		(Irl)	73-70-71-74—288	30055
	Angel Cabrera (Arg)	70-71-72-69—282	125172		Jesper Parnevik (Swe)	73-73-74-68—288	30055
	Phil Mickelson	70-69-68-75—282	125172		Dean Wilson	71-74-72-71—288	30055
	Kirk Triplett	72-69-71-70—282	125172		Bob Estes	70-72-75-71—288	30055
12	Tiger Woods	74-71-69-69—283	91734		Steve Jones	73-73-72-70—288	30055
	Sergio García (Esp)	70-68-68-77—283	91734		Gabriel Hjertstedt		
	Michael Allen	77-68-67-71—283	91734		(Swe)	72-74-70-72—288	30055
	Matt Gogel	70-69-74-70—283	91734		Darren Clarke (NI)	74-71-71-72—288	30055
16	David Duval	70-69-71-74—284	75337		Bob May	72-72-69-75—288	30055
	Scott Hoch	73-73-69-69—284	75337		Bryce Molder (am)	75-71-68-74—288	
	Chris DiMarco	69-73-70-72—284	75337		JL Lewis	68-68-77-75—288	30055
19	Corey Pavin	70-75-68-72—285	63426	40	Bernhard Langer		
	Chris Perry	72-71-73-69—285	63426		(Ger)	71-73-71-74—289	23933
	Mike Weir (Can)	67-76-68-74—285	63426		Tim Herron	71-74-73-71—289	23933
22	Scott Verplank	71-71-73-71—286	54813		Briny Baird	71-72-70-76—289	23933
	Thomas Bjørn (Den)	72-69-73-72—286	54813		Shaun Micheel	73-70-75-71—289	23933

Other Totals: Fred Funk, Toshimitsu Izawa (Jpn), Brandel Chamblee, Jeff Maggert, Duffy Waldorf, Kevin Sutherland, Tom Byrum 290; Eduardo Romero (Arg) 291; Loren Roberts, Colin Montgomerie (Sco), Mark Wiebe, Bob Tway, Hale Irwin, José Coceres (Arg), Scott Dunlap, Brandt Jobe, Frank Lickliter, Jimmy Walker 292; Jim Furyk, Dudley Hart, Richard Zokol (Can), Tim Petrovic 293; Ernie Els (RSA), Peter Lonard (Aus), Dan Forsman, David Toms, Harrison Frazar, David Peoples 294; Nick Faldo (Eng), Franklin Langham 295; Anthony Kang (Kor), Mathias Grönberg (Swe), Gary Orr (Sco), Thongchai Jaidee (Tha) 296; Jim McGovern 297; Stephen Gangluff 301

2000 Open Championship *at St Andrews* (7115–72)

Prize Money £2,722,150. Entries 2372. Regional qualifying courses: Alwoodley, Beau Desert, Blackmoor, Burnham & Berrow, Camberley Heath, Carlisle, Copt Heath, County Louth, Coxmoor, Hadley Wood, Hindhead, Northamptonshire County, Ormskirk, Renfrew, Romford, Stockport, Wildernesse. Final qualifying courses: Ladybank, Leven, Lundin, Scotscraig. Final field comprised 156 players, of whom 74 (none amateur) made the half-way cut on 144 or better.

1	Tiger Woods (USA)	67-66-67-69—269	£500000	11T	David Duval (USA)	70-70-66-75—281	37111
2	Ernie Els (RSA)	66-72-70-69—277	245000		Stuart Appleby (Aus)	73-70-68-70—281	37111
	Thomas Bjørn (Den)	69-69-68-71—277	245000		Davis Love III (USA)	74-66-74-67—281	37111
4	Tom Lehman (USA)	68-70-70-70—278	130000		Vijay Singh (Fij)	70-70-73-68—281	37111
	David Toms (USA)	69-67-71-71—278	130000		Phil Mickelson (USA)	72-66-71-72—281	37111
6	Fred Couples (USA)	70-68-72-69—279	100000		Bob May (USA)	72-72-66-71—281	37111
7	Loren Roberts (USA)	69-68-70-73—280	66250		Dennis Paulson (USA)	68-71-69-73—281	37111
	Paul Azinger (USA)	69-72-72-67—280	66250	20	Steve Flesch (USA)	67-70-71-74—282	25500
	Pierre Fulke (Swe)	69-72-70-69—280	66250		Padraig Harrington		
	Darren Clarke (NI)	70-69-68-73—280	66250		(Irl)	68-72-70-72—282	25500
11	Bernhard Langer (Ger)	74-70-66-71—281	37111		Steve Pate (USA)	73-70-71-68—282	25500
	Mark McNulty (Zim)	69-72-70-70—281	37111		Bob Estes (USA)	72-69-70-71—282	25500

Other Totals: Eduardo Romero (Arg), Sergio García (Esp), Jesper Parnevik (Swe), Craig Parry (Aus), José Coceres (Arg), Robert Allenby (Aus) 286; Nick Faldo (Eng), Justin Leonard (USA), Stewart Cink (USA), Jim Furyk (USA), Nick O'Hern (Aus), Jarrod Moseley (Aus), Gary Orr (Sco), Jeff Maggert (USA), Retief Goosen (RSA), Lucas Parsons (Aus), Tsuyoshi Yoneyama (Jpn) 287; Mike Weir (Can), Ian Garbutt (Eng), Rocco Mediate (USA), 288; David Frost (RSA), Tom Watson (USA), Shigeki Maruyama (Jpn), Greg Owen (Eng), Andrew Coltart (Sco) 289; Christy O'Connor jr (Irl), Jeff Sluman (USA), Steve Elkington (Aus), Kirk Triplett (USA) 290; Desvonde Botes (RSA), Ian Poulter (Eng), Per-Ulrik Johansson (Swe), Lee Westwood (Eng) 291; Gordon Brand jr (Sco), Ian Woosnam (Wal), 292; Tom Kite (USA), Kazuhiko Hosokawa (Jpn) 294; Peter Senior (Aus), Lionel Alexandre (Fra) 295; Dudley Hart (USA) Retd

1999 Open Championship *at Carnoustie* (7361–71)

Prize Money £2,009,550. Entries 2222. Regional qualifying courses: Beau Desert, Blackmoor, Burnham & Berrow, Carlisle, Copt Heath, County Louth, Coxmoor, Glenbervie, Hankley Common, Moortown, Northamptonshire County, Ormskirk, Romford, South Herts, Stockport, Wildernesse. Final qualifying courses: Downfield, Monifieth Links, Montrose Links, Panmure. Final field comprised 156 players, of whom 73 (none amateurs) made the half-way cut on 154 or better.

1	P Lawrie* (Sco)	73-74-76-67—290	£350000	18T	A Coltart (Sco)	74-74-72-77—297	20500
2	J Leonard (USA)	73-74-71-72—290	185000		F Nobilo (NZ)	76-76-70-75—297	20500
	J Van de Velde (Fra)	75-68-70-77—290	185000		P Sjöland (Swe)	74-72-77-74—297	20500
Lawrie won four-hole play-off					L Westwood (Eng)	76-75-74-72—297	20500
4	C Parry (Aus)	76-75-67-73—291	100000		C Rocca (Ita)	81-69-74-73—297	20500
	A Cabrera (Arg)	75-69-77-70—291	100000	24	P O'Malley (Aus)	76-75-74-73—298	15300
6	G Norman (Aus)	76-70-75-72—293	70000		E Els (RSA)	74-76-76-72—298	15300
7	D Frost (RSA)	80-69-71-74—294	50000		B Watts (USA)	74-73-77-74—298	15300
	D Love III (USA)	74-74-77-69—294	50000		I Woosnam (Wal)	76-74-74-74—298	15300
	T Woods (USA)	74-72-74-74—294	50000		MA Martin (Esp)	74-76-72-76—298	15300
10	J Parnevik (Swe)	74-71-78-72—295	34800	29	P Harrington (Irl)	77-74-74-74—299	13500
	S Dunlap (USA)	72-77-76-70—295	34800	30	J Maggert (USA)	75-77-75-73—300	11557
	R Goosen (RSA)	76-75-73-71—295	34800		D Clarke (NI)	76-75-76-73—300	11557
	H Sutton (USA)	73-78-72-72—295	34800		P Stewart (USA)	79-73-74-74—300	11557
	J Furyk (USA)	78-71-76-70—295	34800		P Fulke (Swe)	75-75-77-73—300	11557
15	T Yoneyama (Jpn)	77-74-73-72—296	26000		T Bjørn (Den)	79-73-75-73—300	11557
	C Montgomerie (Sco)	74-76-72-74—296	26000		T Herron (USA)	81-70-74-75—300	11557
	S Verplank (USA)	80-74-73-69—296	26000		L Mattiace (USA)	73-74-75-78—300	11557
18	B Langer (Ger)	72-77-73-75—297	20500				

Other Totals: M McNulty (Zim), D Hart (USA), P Baker (Eng), N Price (Zim), M Weir (Can), P Affleck (Wal) 301; D Waldorf (USA), M James (Eng) 302; S Pate (USA), N Ozaki (Jpn), J Sluman (USA), D Howell (Eng) 303; N Price (Eng), T Levet (Fra), K Tomori (Jpn), Kyoung-Ju Choi (Kor), B Hughes (Aus), D Robertson (Sco), B Estes (USA), S Allan (Aus), P Lonard (Aus) 304; D Paulson (USA), J Robinson (Eng), S Luna (Esp), P Price (Wal) 305; J Ryström (Swe), D Duval (USA), M Brooks (USA) 306; J Sandelin (Swe) 307; S Strüver (Ger) 308; L Thompson (Eng) 309; B Davis (Eng), J Huston (USA) 310; L Janzen (USA) 311; K Shingo (Jpn) 312; M Thompson (Eng), D Cooper (Eng) 313.

1998 Open Championship *at Royal Birkdale* (7018–70)

Prize money: £1,750,000. Entries: 2336. Regional qualifying courses: Beau Desert, Blackmoor, Burnham & Berrow, Carlisle, Copt Heath, County Louth, Coxmoor, Glenbervie, Hankley Common, Moortown, Northamptonshire County, Ormskirk, Romford, South Herts, Stockport and Wildernesse. Final qualifying courses: Hesketh, Hillside, Southport & Ainsdale and West Lancashire. Final field comprised 151 players, of whom 78 (including 3 amateurs) made the halfway cut on 146 or better.

1	M O'Meara (USA)*	72-68-72-68—280	£300000	19	C Strange (USA)	73-73-74-70—290	17220
2	B Watts (USA)	68-69-73-70—280	188000		V Singh (Fij)	67-74-78-71—290	17220
O'Meara won four-hole play-off					S Lyle (Sco)	71-72-75-72—290	17220
3	T Woods (USA)	65-73-77-66—281	135000		R Allenby (Aus)	67-76-78-69—290	17220
4	J Furyk (USA)	70-70-72-70—282	76666		M James (Eng)	71-74-74-71—290	17220
	J Parnevik (Swe)	68-72-72-70—282	76666	24	S Torrance (Sco)	69-77-75-70—291	12480
	R Russell (Sco)	68-73-75-66—282	76666		B Estes (USA)	72-70-76-73—291	12480
	J Rose (Eng) (am)	72-66-75-69—282			S Ames (Tri)	68-72-72-79—291	12480
8	D Love III (USA)	67-73-77-68—285	49500		P O'Malley (Aus)	71-71-78-71—291	12480
9	T Bjørn (Den)	68-71-76-71—286	40850		L Janzen (USA)	72-69-80-70—291	12480
	C Rocca (Ita)	72-74-70-70—286	40850	29	S Dunlap (USA)	72-69-80-71—292	10030
11	J Huston (USA)	65-77-73-72—287	33333		N Price (Zim)	66-72-82-72—292	10030
	B Faxon (USA)	67-74-74-72—287	33333		S Maruyama (Jpn)	70-73-75-74—292	10030
	D Duval (USA)	70-71-75-71—287	33333		L Roberts (USA)	66-76-76-74—292	10030
14	G Brand jr (Sco)	71-70-76-71—288	29000		E Els (RSA)	72-74-74-72—292	10030
15	P Baker (Eng)	69-72-77-71—289	23650		S García (am) (Esp)	69-75-76-72—292	
	G Turner (NZ)	68-75-75-71—289	23650	35	M Calcavecchia (USA)	69-77-73-74—293	8900
	JM Olazábal (Esp)	73-72-75-69—289	23650		S Luna (Esp)	70-72-80-71—293	8900
	D Smyth (Irl)	74-69-75-71—289	23650		S Strüver (Ger)	75-70-80-68—293	8900

Other Totals: P Sjöland (Swe), J Haeggman (Swe), P Walton (Irl), N Ozaki (Jpn), T Kite (USA), S Tinning (Den) 294; K Tomori (Jpn), D Howell (Eng), D Frost (RSA), R Davis (Aus), D Carter (Eng), N Faldo (Eng), P Stewart (USA), A Coltart (Sco) 295; S Stricker (USA), B Mayfair (USA), B Jobe (USA), L Mize (USA), F Minoza (Phi) 296; T Dodds (Nam), E Romero (Arg), S Jones (USA), J Leonard (USA), I Garrido (Esp), I Woosnam (Wal), L Westwood (Eng), C Daniel Franco (Par) 298; S Cink (USA), M Brooks (USA), M Campbell (NZ), F Couples (USA), M Long (NZ); D De Vooght (Bel) (am) 299; A Clapp (Eng) 300; G Evans (Eng) 301; B May (USA) 303; A McLardy (RSA) 304; F Jacobson (Swe) 305; K Hosokawa (Jpn) 306; R Giles (Irl) 307; P Mickelson (USA) 308; A Oldcorn (Sco) 309; D Hart (USA) 310.

1997 Open Championship *at Royal Troon* (7079–71)

Prize money: £1,586,300. Entries: 2133. Regional qualifying courses: Beau Desert, Burnham & Berrow, Carlisle, Copt Heath, Coxmoor, Glenbervie, Hankley Common, Moortown, North Hants, Romford, South Herts, Sundridge Park, Wilmslow. Final qualifying courses: Irvine Bogside, Glasgow Gailes, Kilmarnock Barassie, Western Gailes. 156 players took part, 70 (including 1 amateur) qualified for final 36 holes.

1	J Leonard (USA)	69-66-72-65—272	£250000	20	JM Olazábal (Esp)	75-68-73-67—283	14500
2	D Clarke (NI)	67-66-71-71—275	150000		M James (Eng)	76-67-70-70—283	14500
	J Parnevik (Swe)	70-66-66-73—275	150000		B Faxon (USA)	77-67-72-67—283	14500
4	J Furyk (USA)	67-72-70-70—279	90000		S Appleby (Aus)	72-72-68-71—283	14500
5	S Ames (Tri)	74-69-66-71—280	62500	24	P Lonard (Aus)	72-70-69-73—284	10362
	P Harrington (Irl)	75-69-69-67—280	62500		C Montgomerie (Sco)	76-69-69-70—284	10362
7	F Couples (USA)	69-68-70-74—281	40666		I Woosnam (Wal)	71-73-69-71—284	10362
	E Romero (Arg)	74-68-67-72—281	40666	24T	D A Russell (Eng)	75-72-68-69—284	10362
	P O'Malley (Aus)	73-70-70-68—281	40666		T Woods (USA)	72-74-64-74—284	10362
10	R Goosen (RSA)	75-69-70-68—282	24300		T Lehman (USA)	74-72-72-66—284	10362
	L Westwood (Eng)	73-70-67-72—282	24300		J Haas (USA)	71-70-73-70—284	10362
	T Watson (USA)	71-70-70-71—282	24300		P Mickelson (USA)	76-68-69-71—284	10362
	M Calcavecchia (USA)	74-67-72-69—282	24300	32	M McNulty (Zim)	78-67-72-68—285	8750
	R Allenby (Aus)	76-68-66-72—282	24300	33	J Lomas (Eng)	72-71-69-74—286	8283
	S Maruyama (Jpn)	74-69-70-69—282	24300		D Duval (USA)	73-69-73-71—286	8283
	T Kite (USA)	72-67-74-69—282	24300		R Davis (Aus)	73-73-70-70—286	8283
	D Love III (USA)	70-71-74-67—282	24300	36	A Magee (USA)	70-75-72-70—287	7950
	E Els (RSA)	75-69-69-69—282	24300		G Norman (Aus)	69-73-70-75—287	7950
	F Nobilo (NZ)	74-72-68-68—282	24300				

Other Totals: R Russell (Sco), M O'Meara (USA), J Kernohan (USA), M Bradley (USA), B Langer (Ger), V Singh (Fij) 288; J Coceres (Arg), D Tapping (Eng), C Strange (USA), J Kelly (USA) 289; S Jones (USA), J Payne (Eng), R Boxall (Eng) 290; A Cabrera (Arg), J Maggert (USA), W Riley (Aus), P Senior (Aus), C Pavin (USA), P Mitchell (Eng), N Faldo (Eng), G Turner (NZ) 291; P Stewart (USA) 292; J Nicklaus (USA), B Howard (Sco) (am) 293; T Purtzer (USA), J Spence (Eng), S Stricker (USA), P Teravainen (USA) 294; P McGinley (Irl), P-U Johansson (Swe), G Clark (Eng) 295; T Tolles (USA) 296; B Andrade (USA) 298.

1996 Open Championship at Royal Lytham & St Annes   (6892–71)

Prize money: £1,400,000. Entries: 1918. Regional qualifying courses: Beau Desert, Burnham & Berrow, Carlisle, Copt Heath, Coxmoor, Glenbervie, Hankley Common, Moortown, North Hants, Romford, South Herts, Sundridge Park, Wilmslow. Final qualifying courses: Fairhaven, Formby, St Anne's Old Links, Southport & Ainsdale. Qualified for final 36 holes: 77 (including 1 amateur).

1	T Lehman (USA)	67-67-64-73—271	£200000	18T	R Mediate (USA)	69-70-69-72—280	15500
2	M McCumber (USA)	67-69-71-66—273	125000	22	M James (Eng)	70-68-75-68—281	11875
	E Els (RSA)	68-67-71-67—273	125000		J Haas (USA)	70-72-71-68—281	11875
4	N Faldo (Eng)	68-68-68-70—274	75000		T Woods (USA) (am)	75-66-70-70—281	
5	J Maggert (USA)	69-70-72-65—276	50000		C Mason (Eng)	68-70-70-73—281	11875
	M Brooks (USA)	67-70-68-71—276	50000		S Stricker (USA)	71-70-66-74—281	11875
7	P Hedblom (Swe)	70-65-75-67—277	35000	27	B Crenshaw (USA)	73-68-71-70—282	9525
	G Norman (Aus)	71-68-71-67—277	35000		T Kite (USA)	77-66-69-70—282	9525
	G Turner (NZ)	72-69-68-68—277	35000		P Broadhurst (Eng)	65-72-74-71—282	9525
	F Couples (USA)	67-70-69-71—277	35000		C Pavin (USA)	70-66-74-72—282	9525
11	A Cejka (Ger)	73-67-71-67—278	27000		P Mitchell (Eng)	71-68-71-72—282	9525
	D Clarke (NI)	70-68-69-71—278	27000		F Nobilo (NZ)	70-72-68-72—282	9525
	V Singh (Fij)	69-67-69-73—278	27000	33	E Romero (Arg)	70-71-75-67—283	7843
14	M McNulty (Zim)	69-71-70-69—279	20250		T Tolles (USA)	73-70-71-69—283	7843
	D Duval (USA)	76-67-66-70—279	20250		S Simpson (USA)	71-69-73-70—283	7843
	P McGinley (Irl)	69-65-74-71—279	20250		E Darcy (Irl)	73-69-71-70—283	7843
	S Maruyama (Jpn)	68-70-69-72—279	20250		D Gilford (Eng)	71-67-71-74—283	7843
18	M Welch (Eng)	71-68-73-68—280	15500		M O'Meara (USA)	67-69-72-75—283	7843
	P Harrington (Irl)	68-68-73-71—280	15500		H Tanaka (Jpn)	67-71-70-75—283	7843
	L Roberts (USA)	67-69-72-72—280	15500		B Faxon (USA)	67-73-68-75—283	7843

Other Totals: M Calcavecchia (USA), P Mickelson (USA), K Eriksson (Swe), D Frost (RSA) 284; C Stadler (USA), B Mayfair (USA), P Jacobsen (USA), T Hamilton (Can), B Hughes (Aus), P Stewart (USA), R Boxall (Eng), J Nicklaus (USA), N Price (Zim), J Furyk (USA), J Parnevik (Swe) 285; J Payne (Eng), S Lyle (Sco), R Allenby (Aus), S Ames (Tri) 286; M Jonzon (Swe), DA Weibring (USA), J Sluman (USA), B Barnes (Sco) 287; C Suneson (Eng), C Rocca (Ita), G Law (Sco) 288; DA Russell (Eng), B Ogle (Aus), J Daly (USA) 289; H Clark (Eng) 290; B Charles (NZ) 291; D Hospital (Esp), R Todd (Can), C Strange (USA), R Chapman (Eng) 292; R Goosen (RSA) 293; A Langenaeken (Bel) 298.

1995 Open Championship at St Andrews   (6933–72)

Prize money: £1,250,000. Entries: 1836. Regional qualifying courses: Beau Desert, Blackwell, Glenbervie, Hankley Common, Lanark, Moortown, North Hants, Romford, Sherwood Forest, South Herts, Sundridge, Wilmslow. Final qualifying courses: Ladybank, Leven Links, Lundin, Scotscraig. Qualified for final 36 holes: 103 (including 4 amateurs).

1	J Daly (USA)*	67-71-73-71—282	£125000	20	P Mitchell (Eng)	73-74-71-70—288	13500
2	C Rocca (Ita)	69-70-70-73—282	100000		D Duval (USA)	71-75-70-72—288	13500
Daly won four-hole play-off					A Coltart (Sco)	70-74-71-73—288	13500
3	S Bottomley (Eng)	70-72-72-69—283	65666		B Lane (Eng)	72-73-68-75—288	13500
	M Brooks (USA)	70-69-73-71—283	65666	24	L Janzen (USA)	73-73-71-72—289	10316
	M Brooks (USA)	70-69-73-71—283	65666		S Webster (USA) (am)	70-72-74-73—289	
	M Campbell (NZ)	71-71-65-76—283	65666		B Langer (Ger)	72-71-73-73—289	10316
6	V Singh (Fij)	68-72-73-71—284	40500		J Parnevik (Swe)	75-71-70-73—289	10316
	S Elkington (Aus)	72-69-69-74—284	40500		M Calcavecchia (USA)	71-72-72-74—289	10316
8	M James (Eng)	72-75-68-70—285	33333		B Glasson (USA)	68-74-72-75—289	10316
	B Estes (USA)	72-70-71-72—285	33333		K Tomori (Jpn)	70-68-73-78—289	10316
	C Pavin (USA)	69-70-72-74—285	33333	31	R Drummond (Sco)	74-68-77-71—290	8122
11	P Stewart (USA)	72-68-75-71—286	26000		JM Olazábal (Esp)	72-72-74-72—290	8122
	B Ogle (Aus)	73-69-71-73—286	26000		D Frost (RSA)	72-72-74-72—290	8122
	S Torrance (Sco)	71-70-71-74—286	26000		H Sasaki (Jpn)	74-71-72-73—290	8122
	E Els (RSA)	71-68-72-75—286	26000		J Huston (USA)	71-74-72-73—290	8122
15	G Norman (Aus)	71-74-72-70—287	18200		P Jacobsen (USA)	71-76-70-73—290	8122
	R Allenby (Aus)	71-74-71-71—287	18200		D Clarke (NI)	69-77-70-74—290	8122
	B Crenshaw (USA)	67-72-76-72—287	18200		D Feherty (NI)	68-75-71-76—290	8122
	P-U Johansson (Swe)	69-78-68-72—287	18200		T Watson (USA)	67-76-70-77—290	8122
	B Faxon (USA)	71-67-75-74—287	18200				

Other Totals: S Ballesteros (Esp), W Bennett (Eng) (am), P Mickelson (USA), M McNulty (Zim), N Faldo (Eng), B Watts (USA), G Sherry (Sco) (am), J Cook (USA), N Price (Zim) 291; I Woosnam (Wal), A Forsbrand (Swe), M O'Meara (USA), T Nakajima (Jpn), B Claar (USA), K Green (USA) 292; J Gallagher (USA), P O'Malley (Aus), R Claydon (Eng) 293; P Senior (Aus), P Broadhurst (Eng), D Cooper (Eng), E Herrera (Col), T Kite (USA), P Lawrie (Sco), M Gates (Eng), R Floyd (USA), J Leonard (USA), D Gilford (Eng) 294; P Baker (Eng), J Maggert (USA), J Lomas (Eng), F Nobilo (NZ), G Player (RSA), O Karlsson (Swe), M Hallberg (Swe), S Hoch (USA), G Hallberg (USA), J Rivero (Esp), T Woods (Sco) (am) 295.

1994 Open Championship *at Turnberry* (6957–70)

Prize money: £1,100,000. Entries 1701. Regional qualifying courses: Blackwell, Glenbervie, Hankley Common, Lanark, Moortown, North Hants, Orsett, Sherwood Forest, South Herts, Sundridge Park, Wilmslow. Final qualifying courses: Glasgow Gailes, Irvine Bogside, Kilmarnock Barassie, Western Gailes. Qualified for final 36 holes: 81 (including 1 amateur). Non-qualifiers after 36 holes with scores of 143 or more: 75 (71 professionals, 4 amateurs)

1	N Price (Zim)	69-66-67-66—268	£110000	20	M Brooks (USA)	74-64-71-68—277	12500	
2	J Parnevik (Swe)	68-66-68-67—269	88000		V Singh (Fij)	70-68-69-70—277	12500	
3	F Zoeller (USA)	71-66-64-70—271	74000		G Turner (NZ)	65-71-70-71—277	12500	
4	A Forsbrand (Swe)	72-71-66-64—273	50666		P Senior (Aus)	68-71-67-71—277	12500	
	M James (Eng)	72-67-66-68—273	50666	24	B Estes (USA)	72-68-72-66—278	7972	
	D Feherty (NI)	68-69-66-70—273	50666		T Price (Aus)	74-65-71-68—278	7972	
7	B Faxon (USA)	69-65-67-73—274	36000		P Lawrie (Sco)	71-69-70-68—278	7972	
8	N Faldo (Eng)	75-66-70-64—275	30000		J Maggert (USA)	69-74-67-68—278	7972	
	T Kite (USA)	71-69-66-69—275	30000		T Lehman (USA)	70-69-70-69—278	7972	
	C Montgomerie (Sco)	72-69-65-69—275	30000		E Els (RSA)	69-69-69-71—278	7972	
11	R Claydon (Eng)	72-71-68-65—276	19333		M Springer (USA)	72-67-68-71—278	7972	
	M McNulty (Zim)	71-70-68-67—276	19333		L Roberts (USA)	68-69-69-72—278	7972	
	F Nobilo (NZ)	69-67-72-68—276	19333		P Jacobsen (USA)	69-70-67-72—278	7972	
	J Lomas (Eng)	66-70-72-68—276	19333		C Stadler (USA)	71-69-66-72—278	7972	
	M Calcavecchia (USA)	71-70-67-68—276	19333		A Coltart (Sco)	71-69-66-72—278	7972	
	G Norman (Aus)	71-67-69-69—276	19333	35	M Davis (Eng)	75-68-69-67—279	6700	
	L Mize (USA)	73-69-64-70—276	19333		L Janzen (USA)	74-69-69-67—279	6700	
	T Watson (USA)	68-65-69-74—276	19333		G Evans (Eng)	69-69-73-68—279	6700	
	R Rafferty (NI)	71-66-65-74—276	19333					

Other Totals: D Gilford (Eng), D Hospital (Esp), JM Olazábal (Esp), S Ballesteros (Esp), B Marchbank (Eng), D Clarke (NI) 280; J Van de Velde (Fra), D Love III (USA), M Ozaki (Jpn) 280; J Gallagher jr (USA), D Edwards (USA), G Kraft (USA), H Twitty (USA) 281; D Frost (RSA), M Lanner (Swe), K Tomori (Jpn), T Watanabe (Jpn) 282; P Baker (Eng), J Cook (USA), T Nakajima (Jpn), B Watts (USA), R McFarlane (Eng) 283; G Brand jr (Sco), H Meshiai (Jpn), B Langer (Ger), C O'Connor jr (Irl), P-U Johansson (Swe), R Allenby (Aus), W Grady (Aus) 284; S Elkington (Aus), M Roe (Eng), L Clements (USA), C Mason (Eng), R Alvarez (Arg) 285; W Bennett (Eng) (am), W Riley (Aus) 286; A Lyle (Sco) 287; C Ronald (Eng), C Gillies (Eng) 288; B Crenshaw (USA), C Parry (Aus), J Haeggman (Swe) 289; N Henning (RSA) 291; J Daly (USA) 292.

1993 Open Championship *at Royal St George's* (6860–70)

Prize money: £1,017,000. Entries 1827. Regional qualifying courses: Beau Desert, Blackwell, Coxmoor, Hankley Park, Lanark, Langley Park, North Hants, Orsett, Sherwood Forest, South Herts, Sundridge Park, Wilmslow. Final qualifying courses: Littlestone, North Foreland, Prince's and Royal Cinque Ports. Qualified for final 36 holes: 78 (77 professionals, 1 amateur). Non-qualifiers after 36 holes: 78 (73 professionals, 5 amateurs) with scores of 144 and above.

1	G Norman (Aus)	66-68-69-64—267	£100000	14T	T Kite (USA)	72-70-68-68—278	15214	
2	N Faldo (Eng)	69-63-70-67—269	80000	21	H Clark (Eng)	67-72-70-70—279	10000	
3	B Langer (Ger)	67-66-70-67—270	67000		J Parnevik (Swe)	68-74-68-69—279	10000	
4	C Pavin (USA)	68-66-68-70—272	50500		P Baker (Eng)	70-67-74-68—279	10000	
4	P Senior (Aus)	66-69-70-67—272	50500	24	R Davis (Aus)	68-71-71-70—280	8400	
6	N Price (Zim)	68-70-67-69—274	33166		D Frost (RSA)	69-73-70-68—280	8400	
	E Els (RSA)	68-69-69-68—274	33166		M Roe (Eng)	70-71-73-66—280	8400	
	P Lawrie (Sco)	72-68-69-65—274	33166	27	L Mize (USA)	67-69-74-71—281	7225	
9	W Grady (Aus)	74-68-64-69—275	25500		S Ballesteros (Esp)	68-73-69-71—281	7225	
	F Couples (USA)	68-66-72-69—275	25500		M James (Eng)	70-70-70-71—281	7225	
	S Simpson (USA)	68-70-71-66—275	25500		D Smyth (Irl)	67-74-70-70—281	7225	
12	P Stewart (USA)	71-72-70-63—276	21500		Y Mizumaki (Jpn)	69-69-73-70—281	7225	
13	B Lane (Eng)	70-68-71-68—277	20500		M Mackenzie (Eng)	72-71-71-67—281	7225	
14	J Daly (USA)	71-66-70-71—278	15214		I Pyman (Eng) (am)	68-72-70-71—281		
	F Zoeller (USA)	66-70-71-71—278	15214	34	H Twitty (USA)	71-71-67-73—282	6180	
	G Morgan (USA)	70-68-70-70—278	15214		R Floyd (USA)	70-72-67-73—282	6180	
	J Rivero (Esp)	68-73-67-70—278	15214		W Westner (RSA)	67-73-72-70—282	6180	
	M McNulty (Zim)	67-71-71-69—278	15214		P Broadhurst (Eng)	71-69-74-68—282	6180	
	M Calcavecchia (USA)	66-73-71-68—278	15214		J Van de Velde (Fra)	75-67-73-67—282	6180	

Other Totals: D Clarke (NI), C O'Connor jr (Irl), A Sorensen (Den), D Waldorf (USA), P Moloney (Aus), G Turner (NZ), C Mason (Eng), A Magee (USA), R Mediate (USA) 283; L Janzen (USA), S Elkington (Aus), J Huston (USA) 284; J Sewell (Eng), M Pinero (Esp), F Nobilo (NZ), S Torrance (Sco), MA Jiménez (Esp), I Woosnam (Wal), S Ames (Tri), I Garbutt (Eng) 285; C Parry (Aus), T Lehman (USA), V Singh (Fij), P Azinger (USA) 286; J Spence (Eng), O Karlsson (Swe), R Drummond (Eng) 287; T Pernice (USA), W Guy (Eng), J Cook (USA), M Sunesson (Swe) 288; I Baker-Finch (Aus), T Purtzer (USA), M Miller (Eng) 289; M Harwood (Aus), P Mitchell (Eng), P Fowler (Aus), D Forsman (USA) 290; M Krantz (Swe) 292; R Willison (Eng) 293.

Open Championship History

The Belt

Year	Winner	Score	Venue	Entrants
1860	W Park, Musselburgh	174	Prestwick	8
1861	T Morris sr, Prestwick	163	Prestwick	12
1862	T Morris sr, Prestwick	163	Prestwick	6
1863	W Park, Musselburgh	168	Prestwick	14
1864	T Morris Sr, Prestwick	167	Prestwick	6
1865	A Strath, St Andrews	162	Prestwick	10
1866	W Park, Musselburgh	169	Prestwick	12
1867	T Morris sr, St Andrews	170	Prestwick	10
1868	T Morris jr, St Andrews	154	Prestwick	12
1869	T Morris jr, St Andrews	157	Prestwick	14
1870	T Morris jr, St Andrews	149	Prestwick	17

Having won it three times in succession the Belt became the property of Young Tom Morris and the Championship was held in abeyance for a year. In 1872 the Claret Jug was, and still is, offered for annual competition.

The Claret Jug

Year	Winner	Score	Venue	Entrants
1872	T Morris jr, St Andrews	166	Prestwick	8
1873	T Kidd, St Andrews	179	St Andrews	26
1874	M Park, Musselburgh	159	Musselburgh	32
1875	W Park, Musselburgh	166	Prestwick	18
1876	B Martin, St Andrews	176	St Andrews	34
(D Strath tied but refused to play off)				
1877	J Anderson, St Andrews	160	Musselburgh	24
1878	J Anderson, St Andrews	157	Prestwick	26
1879	J Anderson, St Andrews	169	St Andrews	46
1880	B Ferguson, Musselburgh	162	Musselburgh	30
1881	B Ferguson, Musselburgh	170	Prestwick	22
1882	B Ferguson, Musselburgh	171	St Andrews	40
1883	W Fernie, Dumfries	158	Musselburgh	41
(After a tie with B Ferguson, Musselburgh)				
1884	J Simpson, Carnoustie	160	Prestwick	30
1885	B Martin, St Andrews	171	St Andrews	51
1886	D Brown, Musselburgh	157	Musselburgh	46
1887	W Park jr, Musselburgh	161	Prestwick	36
1888	J Burns, Warwick	171	St Andrews	53
1889	W Park Jr, Musselburgh	155	Musselburgh	42
(After a tie with A Kirkaldy)				
1890	J Ball, Royal Liverpool (am)	164	Prestwick	40
1891	H Kirkaldy, St Andrews	166	St Andrews	82

After 1891 the competition was extended to 72 holes and for the first time entry money was imposed

1892	H Hilton, Royal Liverpool (am)	305	Muirfield	66
1893	W Auchterlonie, St Andrews	322	Prestwick	72
1894	J Taylor, Winchester	326	Sandwich, R St George's	94
1895	J Taylor, Winchester	322	St Andrews	73
1896	H Vardon, Ganton	316	Muirfield	64
(Vardon won a 36 hole play-off after a tie with a score of 157 to Taylor's 161)				
1897	H Hilton, Royal Liverpool (am)	314	Hoylake, R Liverpool	86
1898	H Vardon, Ganton	307	Prestwick	78
1899	H Vardon, Ganton	310	Sandwich, R St George's	98
1900	J Taylor, Mid-Surrey	309	St Andrews	81
1901	J Braid, Romford	309	Muirfield	101
1902	A Herd, Huddersfield	307	Hoylake, R Liverpool	112
1903	H Vardon, Totteridge	300	Prestwick	127
1904	J White, Sunningdale	296	Sandwich, R St George's	144
1905	J Braid, Walton Heath	318	St Andrews	152
1906	J Braid, Walton Heath	300	Muirfield	183
1907	A Massy, La Boulie	312	Hoylake, R Liverpool	193
1908	J Braid, Walton Heath	291	Prestwick	180

Open Championship Claret Jug winners history *continued*

Year	Winner	Score	Venue	Entrants
1909	J Taylor, Mid-Surrey	295	Deal, R Cinque Ports	204
1910	J Braid, Walton Heath	299	St Andrews	210
1911	H Vardon, Totteridge	303	Sandwich, R St George's	226

(After a tie with A Massy. The tie was over 36 holes, but Massy picked up at the 35th hole before holing out. He had taken 148 for 34 holes, and when Vardon holed out at the 35th hole his score was 143)

Year	Winner	Score	Venue	Entrants
1912	E Ray, Oxhey	295	Muirfield	215
1913	J Taylor, Mid-Surrey	304	Hoylake, R Liverpool	269
1914	H Vardon, Totteridge	306	Prestwick	194
1915–19	*No Championship owing to Great War*			

Year	Winner	Score	Venue	Qualifiers	Entrants
1920	G Duncan, Hanger Hill	303	Deal, R Cinque Ports	81	190
1921	J Hutchison, Glenview, Chicago	296	St Andrews	85	158

(After a tie with R Wethered (am). Play-off scores: Hutchison 150; Wethered 159)

Year	Winner	Score	Venue	Qualifiers	Entrants
1922	W Hagen, Detroit, USA	300	Sandwich, R St George's	80	225
1923	A Havers, Coombe Hill	295	Troon	88	222
1924	W Hagen, Detroit, USA	301	Hoylake, R Liverpool	86	277
1925	J Barnes, USA	300	Prestwick	83	200
1926	R Jones, USA (am)	291	R Lytham and St Annes	117	293
1927	R Jones, USA (am)	285	St Andrews	108	207
1928	W Hagen, USA	292	Sandwich, R St George's	113	271
1929	W Hagen, USA	292	Muirfield	109	242
1930	R Jones, USA (am)	291	Hoylake, R Liverpool	112	296
1931	T Armour, USA	296	Carnoustie	109	215
1932	G Sarazen, USA	283	Sandwich, Prince's	110	224
1933	D Shute, USA	292	St Andrews	117	287

(After a tie with C Wood, USA. Play-off scores: Shute 149; Wood 154)

Year	Winner	Score	Venue	Qualifiers	Entrants
1934	T Cotton, Waterloo, Belgium	283	Sandwich, R St George's	101	312
1935	A Perry, Leatherhead	283	Muirfield	109	264
1936	A Padgham, Sundridge Park	287	Hoylake, R Liverpool	107	286
1937	T Cotton, Ashridge	290	Carnoustie	141	258
1938	R Whitcombe, Parkstone	295	Sandwich, R St George's	120	268
1939	R Burton, Sale	290	St Andrews	129	254
1940–45	*No Championship owing to Second World War*				
1946	S Snead, USA	290	St Andrews	100	225
1947	F Daly, Balmoral	293	Hoylake, R Liverpool	100	263
1948	T Cotton, Royal Mid-Surrey	284	Muirfield	97	272
1949	A Locke, RSA	283	Sandwich, R St George's	96	224

(After a tie with H Bradshaw, Kilcroney. Play-off scores: Locke 135; Bradshaw 147)

Year	Winner	Score	Venue	Qualifiers	Entrants
1950	A Locke, RSA	279	Troon	93	262
1951	M Faulkner, England	285	R Portrush	98	180
1952	A Locke, RSA	287	R Lytham and St Annes	96	275
1953	B Hogan, USA	282	Carnoustie	91	196
1954	P Thomson, Australia	283	Birkdale	97	349
1955	P Thomson, Australia	281	St Andrews	94	301
1956	P Thomson, Australia	286	Hoylake, R Liverpool	96	360
1957	A Locke, RSA	279	St Andrews	96	282
1958	P Thomson, Australia	278	R Lytham and St Annes	96	362

(After a tie with D Thomas, Sudbury. Play-off scores: Thomson 139; Thomas 143)

Year	Winner	Score	Venue	Qualifiers	Entrants
1959	G Player, RSA	284	Muirfield	90	285
1960	K Nagle, Australia	278	St Andrews	74	410
1961	A Palmer, USA	284	Birkdale	101	364
1962	A Palmer, USA	276	Troon	119	379
1963	R Charles, New Zealand	277	R Lytham and St Annes	119	261

(After a tie with P Rodgers, USA. Play-off scores: Charles 140; Rodgers 148)

Year	Winner	Score	Venue	Qualifiers	Entrants
1964	T Lema, USA	279	St Andrews	119	327
1965	P Thomson, Australia	285	R Birkdale	130	372
1966	J Nicklaus, USA	282	Muirfield	130	310
1967	R De Vicenzo, Argentina	278	Hoylake, R Liverpool	130	326
1968	G Player, RSA	289	Carnoustie	130	309
1969	A Jacklin, England	280	R Lytham and St Annes	129	424
1970	J Nicklaus, USA	283	St Andrews	134	468

(After a tie with Doug Sanders, USA. Play-off scores: Nicklaus 72; Sanders 73)

Year	Winner	Score	Venue	Qualifiers	Entrants
1971	L Trevino, USA	278	R Birkdale	150	528
1972	L Trevino, USA	278	Muirfield	150	570
1973	T Weiskopf, USA	276	Troon	150	569
1974	G Player, RSA	282	R Lytham and St Annes	150	679

Year	Winner	Score	Venue	Qualifiers	Entrants
1975	T Watson, USA	279	Carnoustie	150	629
(After a tie with J Newton, Australia. Play-off scores: Watson 71; Newton 72)					
1976	J Miller, USA	279	R Birkdale	150	719
1977	T Watson, USA	268	Turnberry	150	730
1978	J Nicklaus, USA	281	St Andrews	150	788
1979	S Ballesteros, Spain	283	R Lytham and St Annes	150	885
1980	T Watson, USA	271	Muirfield	151	994
1981	B Rogers, USA	276	Sandwich, R St George's	153	971
1982	T Watson, USA	284	R Troon	150	1121
1983	T Watson, USA	275	R Birkdale	151	1107
1984	S Ballesteros, Spain	276	St Andrews		1413
1985	A Lyle, Scotland	282	Sandwich, R St George's	149	1361
1986	G Norman, Australia	280	Turnberry	152	1347
1987	N Faldo, England	279	Muirfield	153	1407
1988	S Ballesteros, Spain	273	R Lytham and St Annes	153	1393
1989	M Calcavecchia, USA	275	R Troon	156	1481
(Calcavecchia won a four-hole play-off after a tie with W Grady, Australia, and G Norman, Australia)					
1990	N Faldo, England	270	St Andrews	152	1707
1991	I Baker-Finch, Australia	272	R Birkdale	156	1496
1992	N Faldo, England	272	Muirfield	156	1666
1993	G Norman, Australia	267	Sandwich, R St George's	156	1827
1994	N Price, Zimbabwe	268	Turnberry	156	1701
1995	J Daly, USA	282	St Andrews	159	1836
(Daly won a four-hole play-off after a tie with C Rocca, Italy)					
1996	T Lehman, USA	271	R Lytham and St Annes	156	1918
1997	J Leonard, USA	272	R Troon	156	2133
1998	M O'Meara, USA	280	R Birkdale	152	2336
(O'Meara won a four-hole play-off after a tie with B Watts, USA)					
1999	P Lawrie, Scotland	290	Carnoustie	156	2222
(Lawrie won a four-hole play-off after a tie with J Leonard, USA, and J Van de Velde, France)					
2000	T Woods, USA	269	St Andrews	156	2722
2001	David Duval, USA	274	R Lytham and St Annes	156	2255
2002	Ernie Els, RSA	278	Muirfield	156	2260

The US Open Championship

Players are of American nationality unless stated

102nd US Open *at Bethpage Black Course, Farmingdale, NY* (7214–70)

Prize Money \$5.5 million.   Entries: 8468.   Final Field: 156, of whom 72 (including 1 amateur) made the half-way cut on 150 or less.

1	Tiger Woods	67-68-70-72—277	\$1000000
2	Phil Mickelson	70-73-67-70—280	585000
3	Jeff Maggert	69-73-68-72—282	362356
4	Sergio García (Esp)	68-74-67-74—283	252546
5	Nick Faldo (Eng)	70-76-66-73—285	182882
	Scott Hoch	71-75-70-69—285	182882
	Billy Mayfair	69-74-68-74—285	182882
8	Tom Byrum	72-72-70-72—286	138669
	Padraig Harrington (Irl)	70-68-73-75—286	138669
	Nick Price (Zim)	72-75-69-70—286	138669
11	Peter Lonard (Aus)	73-74-73-67—287	119357
12	Robert Allenby (Aus)	74-70-67-77—288	102338
	Jay Haas	73-73-70-72—288	102338
	Dudley Hart	69-76-70-73—288	102338
	Justin Leonard	73-71-68-76—288	102338
16	Shigeki Maruyama (Jpn)	76-67-73-73—289	86372
	Steve Stricker	72-77-69-71—289	86372
18	Luke Donald (Eng)	76-72-70-72—290	68995
	Charles Howell III	71-74-70-75—290	68995
	Steve Flesch	72-72-75-71—290	68995
	Thomas Levet (Fra)	71-77-70-72—290	68995
	Mark O'Meara	76-70-69-75—290	68995
	Craig Stadler	74-72-70-74—290	68995
24	Jim Carter	77-73-70-71—291	47439
	Darren Clarke (NI)	74-74-72-71—291	47439
	Chris DiMarco	74-74-72-71—291	47439
	Ernie Els (RSA)	73-74-70-74—291	47439
	Davis Love III	71-71-72-77—291	47439
	Jeff Sluman	73-73-72-73—291	47439
30	Jason Caron	75-72-72-73—292	35639
	Kyoung-Ju Choi (Kor)	69-73-73-77—292	35639
	Paul Lawrie (Sco)	73-73-73-73—292	35639
	Scott McCarron	72-72-70-78—292	35639
	Vijay Singh (Fij)	75-75-67-75—292	35639
35	Shingo Katayama (Jpn)	74-72-74-73—293	31945
	Bernhard Langer (Ger)	72-76-70-75—293	31945
37	Stuart Appleby (Aus)	77-73-75-69—294	26783
	Thomas Bjørn (Den)	71-79-73-71—294	26783
	Niclas Fasth (Swe)	72-72-74-76—294	26783
	Donnie Hammond	73-77-71-73—294	26783
	Franklin Langham	70-76-74-74—294	26783
	Rocco Mediate	72-72-74-76—294	26783
	Kevin Sutherland	74-75-70-75—294	26783
	Hidemichi Tanaka (Jpn)	73-73-72-76—294	26783
45	Tom Lehman	71-76-72-76—295	20072
	Frank Lickliter	74-76-68-77—295	20072

45T	Kenny Perry	74-76-71-74—295	20072
	David Toms	74-74-70-77—295	20072
	Jean Van de Velde (Fra)	71-75-74-75—295	20072
50	Craig Bowden	71-77-74-74—296	16294
	Tim Herron	75-74-73-74—296	16294
	Robert Karlsson (Swe)	71-77-72-76—296	16294
	José María Olazábal (Esp)	71-77-75-73—296	16294
54	Harrison Frazar	74-73-75-75—297	14764
	Ian Leggatt (Can)	72-77-72-76—297	14764
	Jesper Parnevik (Swe)	72-76-69-80—297	14764
	Corey Pavin	74-75-70-78—297	14764
58	Brad Lardon	73-73-74-78—298	13988
59	John Maginnes	79-69-73-78—299	13493
	Greg Norman (Aus)	75-73-74-77—299	13493
	Bob Tway	72-78-73-76—299	13493
62	Andy Miller	76-74-75-75—300	12794
	Jeev Milkha Singh (Ind)	75-75-75-75—300	12794
	Paul Stankowski	72-77-77-74—300	12794
65	Spike McRoy	75-75-74-77—301	12340
66	Angel Cabrera (Arg)	73-73-79-77—302	12000
	Brad Faxon	75-74-73-80—302	12000
68	Kent Jones	76-74-74-79—303	11546
	Len Mattiace	72-73-78-80—303	11546
70	John Daly	74-76-81-73—304	11083
	Tom Gillis	71-76-78-79—304	11083
72	Kevin Warrick (am)	73-76-84-74—307	

The following players missed the half-way cut and received $1000 each:

73	Mark Calcavecchia	74-77—151
	John Cook	74-77—151
	Ben Crane	75-76—151
	David Duval	78-73—151
	J Brian Gay	75-76—151
	Lucas Glover	74-77—151
	Steve Haskins	74-77—151
	Matt Kuchar	76-75—151
	Colin Montgomerie (Sco)	75-76—151
	Peter O'Malley (Aus)	75-76—151
	Tom Pernice	75-76—151
	Todd Rose	71-80—151
	Kirk Triplett	73-78—151
86	Stewart Cink	70-82—152
	Jim Gallagher jr	75-77—152
	Per-Ulrik Johansson (Swe)	78-74—152
	Taichiro Kiyota (Jpn) (am)	73-79—152
	Steve Lowery	70-82—152
	Craig Perks (NZ)	76-76—152
	Philip Tataurangi (NZ)	74-78—152
	Mike Weir (Can)	78-74—152
94	Ricky Barnes (am)	78-75—153
	Mark Brooks	75-78—153
	Greg Chalmers (Aus)	72-81—153
	José Coceres (Arg)	77-76—153
	Ken Duke	76-77—153

94T	Scott Dunlap	75-78—153
	Jim Furyk	73-80—153
	Brent Geiberger	75-78—153
	John Huston	75-78—153
	Lee Janzen	76-77—153
	Tom Kite	80-73—153
	Scott Verplank	75-78—153
	Jimmy Walker	77-76—153
107	Stephen Ames (Tri)	77-77—154
	Billy Andrade	72-82—154
	Jay Don Blake	74-80—154
	Bob Estes	81-73—154
	Kelly Gibson	77-77—154
	Retief Goosen (RSA)	79-75—154
	Steve Jones	74-80—154
	Paul McGinley (Irl)	75-79—154
	Jim McGovern	75-79—154
	Ben Portie	77-77—154
	Andrew Sanders	77-77—154
	Hal Sutton	77-77—154
119	Woody Austin	79-76—155
	Michael Campbell (NZ)	72-83—155
	Pete Jordan	76-79—155
	Jerry Kelly	76-79—155
	Ryan Moore (am)	76-79—155
	Michael Muehr	77-78—155
	Joey Sindelar	76-79—155
126	Michael Allen	77-79—156
	David Frost (RSA)	75-81—156

126T	Blaine McCallister	77-79—156
	Mario Tiziani	76-80—156
130	Paul Azinger	75-82—157
	Olin Browne	76-81—157
	Trevor Dodds (Nam)	77-80—157
	Craig Parry (Aus)	79-78—157
	Steve Pate	82-75—157
	Pat Perez	76-81—157
	Adam Scott (Aus)	77-80—157
	Kaname Yokoo (Jpn)	78-79—157
138	Joe Durant	81-77—158
	Matt Gogel	78-80—158
	Paul Gow (Aus)	76-82—158
	Paul Goydos	80-78—158
	Jerry Haas	80-78—158
	George McNeill	79-79—158
144	David Howell (Eng)	78-81—159
	Charles Raulerson	78-81—159
146	Tony Soerries	84-76—160
147	Michael Clark II	83-80—163
	Hale Irwin	82-81—163
	Darrell Kestner	77-86—163
150	Scott Parel	82-83—165
	Heath Slocum	83-82—165
	Adam Speirs	80-85—165
153	Derek Tolan (am)	78-88—166
154	Wayne Grady (Aus)	84-83—167
155	Felix Casas (Phi)	82-92—174

2001 US Open at Southern Hills CC, Tulsa, Oklahoma (6874-71)

Prize money: $5,000,000. Entries: 8300

1	Tiger Woods	67-68-70-72—277	$1000000	24	Jim Carter	77-73-70-71—291		47439
2	Phil Mickelson	70-73-67-70—280	585000		Darren Clarke (NI)	74-74-72-71—291		47439
3	Jeff Maggert	69-73-68-72—282	362356		Chris DiMarco	74-74-72-71—291		47439
4	Sergio García (Esp)	68-74-67-74—283	252546		Ernie Els (RSA)	73-74-70-74—291		47439
5	Nick Faldo (Eng)	70-76-66-73—285	182882		Davis Love III	71-71-72-77—291		47439
	Scott Hoch	71-75-70-69—285	182882		Jeff Sluman	73-73-72-73—291		47439
	Billy Mayfair	69-74-68-74—285	182882	30	Jason Caron	75-72-72-73—292		35639
8	Tom Byrum	72-72-70-72—286	138669		Kyoung-Ju Choi			
	Padraig Harrington				(Kor)	69-73-73-77—292		35639
	(Irl)	70-68-73-75—286	138669		Paul Lawrie (Sco)	73-73-73-73—292		35639
	Nick Price (Zim)	72-75-69-70—286	138669		Scott McCarron	72-72-70-78—292		35639
11	Peter Lonard (Aus)	73-74-73-67—287	119357		Vijay Singh (Fij)	75-75-67-75—292		35639
12	Robert Allenby (Aus)	74-70-67-77—288	102338	35	Shingo Katayama			
	Jay Haas	73-73-70-72—288	102338		(Jpn)	74-72-74-73—293		31945
	Dudley Hart	69-76-70-73—288	102338		Bernhard Langer			
	Justin Leonard	73-71-68-76—288	102338		(Ger)	72-76-70-75—293		31945
16	Shigeki Maruyama			37	Stuart Appleby (Aus)	77-73-75-69—294		26783
	(Jpn)	76-67-73-73—289	86372		Thomas Bjørn (Den)	71-79-73-71—294		26783
	Steve Stricker	72-77-69-71—289	86372		Niclas Fasth (Swe)	72-72-74-76—294		26783
18	Luke Donald (Eng)	76-72-70-72—290	68995		Donnie Hammond	73-77-71-73—294		26783
	Charles Howell III	71-74-70-75—290	68995		Franklin Langham	70-76-74-74—294		26783
	Steve Flesch	72-72-75-71—290	68995		Rocco Mediate	72-72-74-76—294		26783
	Thomas Levet (Fra)	71-77-70-72—290	68995		Kevin Sutherland	74-75-70-75—294		26783
	Mark O'Meara	76-70-69-75—290	68995		Hidemichi Tanaka			
	Craig Stadler	74-72-70-74—290	68995		(Jpn)	73-73-72-76—294		26783

Other players who made the cut: Tom Lehman, Frank Lickliter, Kenny Perry, David Toms, Jean Van de Velde (Fra) 295; Craig Bowden, Tim Herron, Robert Karlsson (Swe), José María Olazábal (Esp) 296; Harrison Frazar, Ian Leggatt (Can), Jesper Parnevik (Swe), Corey Pavin 297; Brad Lardon 298; John Maginnes, Greg Norman (Aus), Bob Tway 299; Andy Miller, Jeev Milkha Singh (Ind), Paul Stankowski 300; Spike McRoy 301; Angel Cabrera (Arg), Brad Faxon 302; Kent Jones, Len Mattiace 303; John Daly. Tom Gillis 304; Kevin Warrick (am) 307

2000 US Open at Pebble Beach, CA (6874-71)

Prize money: $4,500,000. Entries: 8457 (record high)

1	Tiger Woods	65-69-71-67—272	$800000	22	Notah Begay III	74-75-72-73—294	53105
2	Miguel Angel Jiménez			23	Hal Sutton	69-73-83-70—295	45537
	(Esp)	66-74-76-71—287	391150		Bob May	72-76-75-72—295	45537
	Ernie Els (RSA)	74-73-68-72—287	391150		Tom Lehman	71-73-78-73—295	45537
4	John Huston	67-75-76-70—288	212779		Mike Brisky	71-73-79-72—295	45537
5	Padraig Harrington			27	Tom Watson	71-74-78-73—296	34066
	(Irl)	73-71-72-73—289	162526		Nick Price (Zim)	77-70-78-71—296	34066
	Lee Westwood (Eng)	71-71-76-71—289	162526		Steve Stricker	75-74-75-72—296	34066
7	Nick Faldo (Eng)	69-74-76-71—290	137203		Steve Jones	75-73-75-73—296	34066
8	Loren Roberts	68-78-73-72—291	112766		Hale Irwin	68-78-81-69—296	34066
	David Duval	75-71-74-71—291	112766	32	Tom Kite	72-77-77-71—297	28247
	Stewart Cink	77-72-72-70—291	112766		Chris Perry	75-72-78-72—297	28247
	Vijay Singh (Fij)	70-73-80-68—291	112766		Richard Zokol (Can)	74-74-80-69—297	28247
12	José María Olazábal				Rocco Mediate	69-76-75-77—297	28247
	(Esp)	70-71-76-75—292	86223		Lee Porter	74-70-83-70—297	28247
	Paul Azinger	71-73-79-69—292	86223	37	Woody Austin	77-70-78-73—298	22056
	Retief Goosen (RSA)	77-72-72-71—292	86223		Jerry Kelly	73-73-81-71—298	22056
	Michael Campbell				Larry Mize	73-72-76-77—298	22056
	(NZ)	71-77-71-73—292	86223		Craig Parry (Aus)	73-74-76-75—298	22056
16	Justin Leonard	73-73-75-72—293	65214		Bobby Clampett	68-77-76-77—298	22056
	Mike Weir (Can)	76-72-76-79—293	65214		Angel Cabrera (Arg)	69-76-79-74—298	22056
	Fred Couples	70-75-75-73—293	65214		Lee Janzen	71-73-79-75—298	22056
	Scott Hoch	73-76-75-69—293	65214		Ted Tryba	71-73-79-75—298	22056
	Phil Mickelson	71-73-73-76—293	65214		Charles Warren	75-74-75-74—298	22056
	David Toms	73-76-72-72—293	65214				

Other players who made the cut: Rick Hartmann, Sergio García (Esp), Colin Montgomerie (Sco), Scott Verplank, Thomas Bjørn (Den) 299; Warren Schutte (SA), Mark O'Meara 300; Darren Clarke (NI), Keith Clearwater, Jeff Coston 301; Kirk Triplett 302; Dave Eichelberger, Jimmy Green 303; Jeffrey Wilson (am) 304; Jim Furyk 305; Brandel Chamblee, Carlos Daniel Franco (Par) 306; Robert Damron 313

1999 US Open at Pinehurst No. 2, North Carolina   (7175–70)

Prize money: $3,500,000. Entries: 7889 (record high)

1	P Stewart	68-69-72-70—279	$625000	17T	S Verplank	72-73-72-74—291	46756
2	P Mickelson	67-70-73-70—280	370000	23	MA Jiménez (Esp)	73-70-72-77—292	33505
3	V Singh (Fij)	69-70-73-69—281	196791		N Price (Zim)	71-74-74-73—292	33505
	T Woods	68-71-72-70—281	196791		T Scherrer	72-72-74-74—292	33505
5	S Stricker	70-73-69-73—285	130655		B Watts	69-73-77-73—292	33505
6	T Herron	69-72-70-75—286	116935		DA Weibring	69-74-74-75—292	33505
7	D Duval	67-70-75-75—287	96260	28	D Berganio jr	68-77-76-72—293	26185
	J Maggert	71-69-74-73—287	96260		T Lehman	73-74-73-73—293	26185
	H Sutton	69-70-76-72—287	96260	30	B Estes	70-71-77-76—294	23804
10	D Clarke (NI)	73-70-74-71—288	78862		G Sisk	71-72-76-75—294	23804
	B Mayfair	67-72-74-75—288	78862	32	S Cink	72-74-78-71—295	22448
12	P Azinger	72-72-75-70—289	67347		S Strüver (Ger)	70-76-75-74—295	22448
	P Goydos	67-74-74-74—289	67347	34	B Fabel	69-75-78-74—296	19083
	D Love III	70-73-74-72—289	67347		C Franco (Par)	69-77-73-77—296	19083
15	J Leonard	69-75-73-73—290	58214		G Hjertstedt (Swe)	75-72-79-70—296	19083
	C Montgomerie (Sco)	72-72-74-72—290	58214		R Mediate	69-72-76-79—296	19083
17	J Furyk	69-73-77-72—291	46756		C Parry (Aus)	69-73-79-75—296	19083
	J Haas	74-72-73-72—291	46756		S Pate	70-75-75-76—296	19083
	D Hart	73-73-76-69—291	46756		C Pavin	74-71-78-73—296	19083
	J Huston	71-69-75-76—291	46756		E Toledo (Mex)	70-72-76-78—296	19083
	J Parnevik (Swe)	71-71-76-73—291	46756				

Other players who made the cut: S Allan (Aus), G Hallberg, L Mattiace, C Perry 297; R Allenby (Aus), B Chamblee, L Janzen, D Lebeck, 298; S Elkington (Aus), C Tidland 299; G Kraft, S McRoy, P Price (Wal), J Tyska 300; J Kelly, T Watson, K Yokoo (Jpn) 301; J Cook, T Kite 302; C Smith, B Tway 303; L Mize 304; H Kuehne (am) 306; B Burns, T Tryba 308; J Daly 309

1998 US Open at The Olympic Club, San Francisco   (6797–70)

Prize money: $3,000,000. Entries: 7117

1	L Janzen	73-66-73-68—280	$535000	18T	JM Olazábal (Esp)	68-77-71-74—290	41833
2	P Stewart	66-71-70-74—281	315000		T Woods	74-72-71-73—290	41833
3	B Tway	68-70-73-73—284	201730	23	C Martin	74-71-74-72—291	34043
4	N Price (Zim)	73-68-71-73—285	140597		G Day	73-72-71-75—291	34043
5	S Stricker	73-71-69-73—286	107392	25	DA Weibring	72-72-75-73—292	25640
	T Lehman	68-75-68-75—286	107392		P-U Johansson (Swe)	71-75-73-73—292	25640
7	D Duval	75-68-75-69—287	83794		E Romero (Arg)	72-70-76-74—292	25640
	L Westwood (Eng)	72-74-70-71—287	83794		C Perry	74-71-72-75—292	25640
	J Maggert	69-69-75-74—287	83794		V Singh (Fij)	73-72-73-74—292	25640
10	J Sluman	72-74-74-68—288	64490		T Bjørn (Den)	72-75-70-75—292	25640
	P Mickelson	71-73-74-70—288	64490		M Carnevale	67-73-74-78—292	25640
	S Appleby (Aus)	73-74-70-71—288	64490	32	M O'Meara	70-76-78-69—293	18372
	S Cink	73-68-73-74—288	64490		P Harrington (Irl)	73-72-76-72—293	18372
14	P Azinger	75-72-77-65—289	52214		B Zabriski	74-71-74-74—293	18372
	J Parnevik (Swe)	69-74-76-70—289	52214		S Pate	72-75-73-73—293	18372
	M Kuchar (am)	70-69-76-74—289			J Huston	73-72-72-76—293	18372
	J Furyk	74-73-68-74—289	52214		J Durant	68-73-76-76—293	18372
18	C Montgomerie (Sco)	70-74-77-69—290	41833		C DiMarco	71-71-74-77—293	18372
	L Roberts	71-76-71-72—290	41833		L Porter	72-67-76-78—293	18372
	F Lickliter II	73-71-72-74—290	41833				

Other players who made the cut: J Leonard, S McCarron, F Nobilo (NZ) 294; D Clarke (NI), J Sindelar, T Kite, J Acosta jr, O Browne, J Nicklaus 295; E Els (RSA), M Reid, B Faxon, S Verplank 296; F Couples, T Herron, J Johnston, J Daly 297; M Brooks 298; S Simpson 300; R Walcher 303; T Sipula 305.

1997 US Open at Congressional CC, Bethesda, Maryland (7213–70)

Prize money: $2,600,000. Entries: 7013

1	E Els (SA)	71-67-69-69—276	$465000	19T	P Stankowski	75-70-68-73—286	31915
2	C Montgomerie (Sco)	65-76-67-69—277	275000		H Sutton	66-73-73-74—286	31915
3	T Lehman	67-70-68-73—278	172828	24	L Mattiace	71-75-73-68—287	24173
4	J Maggert	73-66-68-74—281	120454		E Fryatt	72-73-73-69—287	24173
5	B Tway	71-71-70-70—282	79875		S Dunlap	75-66-75-71—287	24173
	O Browne	71-71-69-71—282	79875		S Elkington (Aus)	75-68-72-72—287	24173
	J Furyk	74-68-69-71—282	79875	28	P Goydos	73-72-74-69—288	17443
	J Haas	73-69-68-72—282	79875		P Azinger	72-72-74-70—288	17443
	T Tolles	74-67-69-72—282	79875		P Stewart	71-73-73-71—288	17443
10	S McCarron	73-71-69-70—283	56949		M McNulty (Zim)	67-73-75-73—288	17443
	S Hoch	71-68-72-72—283	56949		H Kase	68-73-73-74—288	17443
	D Ogrin	70-69-71-73—283	56949		F Zoeller	72-73-69-74—288	17443
13	L Roberts	72-69-72-71—284	47348		K Gibson	72-69-72-75—288	17443
	S Cink	71-67-74-72—284	47348	28	J Sluman	69-72-72-75—288	17443
	B Andrade	75-67-69-73—284	47348	36	J Leonard	69-72-78-70—289	13483
16	B Hughes (Aus)	75-70-71-69—285	40086		G Waite	72-74-72-71—289	13483
	JM Olazábal (Esp)	71-71-72-71—285	40086		S Stricker	66-76-75-72—289	13483
	D Love III	75-70-69-71—285	40086		M O'Meara	73-73-71-72—289	13483
19	N Price (Zim)	71-74-71-70—286	31915		S Appleby (Aus)	71-75-70-73—289	13483
	L Westwood (Eng)	71-71-73-71—286	31915		F Nobilo (NZ)	71-74-70-74—289	13483
	T Woods	74-67-73-72—286	31915		J Cook	72-71-71-75—289	13483

Other players who made the cut: D Clarke (NI), P Mickelson, F Funk, C Perry, C Parry (Aus) 290; J Parnevik (Swe), D Duval, N Faldo (Eng) 291; D White 292; L Janzen, J Nicklaus, H Irwin, F Couples, P Teravainen, P Broadhurst (Eng) 293; L Mize, C Rose 294; C Smith, D Waldorf, R Butcher, S Jones 295; T Watson 296; D Schreyer, B Crenshaw, B Faxon 297; T Kite, M Hulbert, G Kraft, J Morse, S Ames (Tri), T Björn (Den) 298; J Green 299; R Wylie, A Coltart (Sco) 300; D Mast, G Towne, V Singh (Fij), P Parker, D Hammond 301; J Ferenz 303; M Dawson 304; S Adams 306.

1996 US Open at Oakland Hills, Birmingham, Michigan (6990–70)

Prize money: $2,400,000. Entries: 5925

1	S Jones	74-66-69-69—278	$425000	16T	S Cink	69-73-70-73—285	33188
2	D Love III	71-69-70-69—279	204801		S Torrance (Sco)	71-69-71-74—285	33188
	T Lehman	71-72-65-71—279	204801	23	B Bryant	73-71-74-68—286	23806
4	J Morse	68-74-68-70—280	111235		P Jacobsen	71-74-70-71—286	23806
5	E Els (RSA)	72-67-72-70—281	84964		B Andrade	72-69-72-73—286	23806
	J Furyk	72-69-70-70—281	84964		W Austin	67-72-72-75—286	23806
7	S Hoch	73-71-71-67—282	66294	27	C Strange	74-73-71-69—287	17809
	V Singh (Fij)	71-72-70-69—282	66294		P Jordan	71-74-72-70—287	17809
	K Green	73-67-72-70—282	66294		J Nicklaus	72-74-69-72—287	17809
10	L Janzen	68-75-71-69—283	52591		P Stewart	67-71-76-73—287	17809
	G Norman (Aus)	73-66-74-70—283	52591		J Daly	72-69-73-73—287	17809
	C Montgomerie (Sco)	70-72-69-72—283	52591	32	M Swartz	72-72-74-70—288	14070
13	D Forsman	72-71-70-71—284	43725		T Purtzer	76-71-71-70—288	14070
	T Watson	70-71-71-72—284	43725		B Mayfair	72-71-74-71—288	14070
	F Nobilo (NZ)	69-71-70-74—284	43725		B Ogle (Aus)	70-75-72-71—288	14070
16	N Faldo (Eng)	72-71-72-70—285	33188		S Gotsche	72-70-74-72—288	14070
	D Begganio	69-72-72-72—285	33188		M Campbell (NZ)	70-73-73-72—288	14070
	M Brooks	76-68-69-72—285	33188		A Forsbrand (Swe)	74-71-71-72—288	14070
	M O'Meara	72-73-68-72—285	33188		S Murphy	71-75-68-74—288	14070
	J Cook	70-71-71-73—285	33188				

Other players who made the cut: L Parsons, JL Lucas, B Ford, S Simpson, W Riley (Aus), S Elkington (Aus), T Tolles, C Pavin, K Triplett, L Roberts 289; W Westner (RSA), B Gilder, K Perry, J Sluman, J Gullion, H Irwin, A Cejka (Ger), M Bradley, K Gibson, J Leonard 290; S Stricker, S Lowery, B Porter, W Murchison, M Leen (am), D Gilford (Eng), D Harrington 291; D Duval, A Morse, P Azinger, F Linkliter II, M Ozaki (Jpn), C Rocca (Ita), W Grady (Aus), D Ogrin, P O'Malley (Aus), C Byrum, J Gallagher jr, B Tway 292; T Kuehne (am), M Christie, I Woosnam (Wal) 293; T Woods (am), J Huston, K Jones, S Kendall, S McCarron, T Kite, B Faxon, N Lancaster 294; C Parry (Aus), J Sanchez, J O'Keefe, J Haas 295; A Rodriguez, T Pernice jr, P Mickelson 296; J Maggert, J Thorpe, B McCallister (Aus), P Walton (Irl) 297; O Uresti, O Browne 298; G Trevisonno 299; M Wiebe 300; S Scott (am), R Yokota (Jpn) 301; M Burke jr 302; S Kelly 309.

1995 US Open *at Shinnecock Hills, New York* (6944–70)

Prize money: $2,000,000. Entries: 6,001

1	C Pavin	72-69-71-68—280	$350000	21T	B Ogle (Aus)	71-75-72-69—287	20085
2	G Norman (Aus)	68-67-74-73—282	207000		P Jordan	74-71-71-71—287	20085
3	T Lehman	70-72-67-74—283	131974		B Andrade	72-69-74-72—287	20085
4	N Lancaster	70-72-77-65—284	66633		S Verplank	72-69-71-75—287	20085
	J Maggert	69-72-77-66—284	66633		I Woosnam (Wal)	72-71-69-75—287	20085
	B Glasson	69-70-76-69—284	66633	28	C Montgomerie (Sco)	71-74-75-68—288	13912
	J Haas	70-73-72-69—284	66633		MA Jiménez (Esp)	72-72-75-69—288	13912
	D Love III	72-68-73-71—284	66633		M Hulbert	74-72-72-70—288	13912
	P Mickelson	68-70-72-74—284	66633		M Ozaki (Jpn)	69-68-80-71—288	13912
10	F Nobilo (NZ)	72-72-70-71—285	44184		S Simpson	67-75-74-72—288	13912
	V Singh (Fij)	70-71-72-72—285	44184		D Duval	70-73-73-72—288	13912
	B Tway	69-69-72-75—285	44184		JM Olazábal (Esp)	73-70-72-73—288	13912
13	M McCumber	70-71-77-68—286	30934		G Hallberg	70-76-69-73—288	13912
	D Waldorf	72-70-75-69—286	30934	36	B Porter	73-70-79-67—289	9812
	Brad Bryant	71-75-70-70—286	30934		R Floyd	74-72-76-67—289	9812
	J Sluman	72-69-74-71—286	30934		H Sutton	71-74-76-68—289	9812
	M Roe (Eng)	71-69-74-72—286	30934		C Strange	70-72-76-71—289	9812
	L Janzen	70-72-72-72—286	30934		G Boros	73-71-74-71—289	9812
	N Price (Zim)	66-73-73-74—286	30934		S Elkington (Aus)	72-73-73-71—289	9812
	S Stricker	71-70-71-74—286	30934		C Byrum	70-70-76-73—289	9812
21	F Zoeller	69-74-76-68—287	20085		B Langer (Ger)	74-67-74-74—289	9812
	P Stewart	74-71-73-69—287	20085				

Other players who made the cut: B Lane (Eng) 290; J McGovern, C Pena, O Uresti, J Daly, N Faldo (Eng), B Hughes 291; B Burns, E Romero (Arg), T Tryba, P Jacobsen, M Gogel 292; B Faxon, T Watson, C Perry, S Lowery, S Hoch, G Bruckner 293; J Gallagher, J Cook, B Jobe, D Edwards, P Goydos 294; T Kite, M Brisky,T Armour III 295; J Connelly 296; B Crenshaw, J Maginnes 297; J Gullion 301

1994 US Open *at Oakmont, Pennsylvania* (6946–71)

Prize money: $1,700,000. Entries: 6010

1	E Els (RSA)*	69-71-66-73—279	$320000	18	S Verplank	70-72-75-70—287	22477
2	L Roberts	76-69-64-70—279	141828		S Ballesteros (Esp)	72-72-70-73—287	22477
	C Montgomerie (Sco)	71-65-73-70—279	141828		H Irwin	69-69-71-78—287	22477
*Els won at second sudden-death play-off hole against				21	S Torrance (Sco)	72-71-76-69—288	19464
Roberts after both shot 74 in 18-hole play-off. Montgomerie					S Pate	74-66-71-77—288	19464
shot 78.				23	B Langer (Ger)	72-72-73-72—289	17223
4	C Strange	70-70-70-70—280	75728		K Triplett	70-71-71-77—289	17223
5	J Cook	73-65-73-71—282	61318	25	M Springer	74-72-73-71—290	14705
6	C Dennis	71-71-70-71—283	49485		C Parry (Aus)	78-68-71-73—290	14705
	G Norman (Aus)	71-71-69-72—283	49485		C Beck	73-73-70-74—290	14705
	T Watson	68-73-68-74—283	49485	28	D Love III	74-72-74-72—292	11514
9	D Waldorf	74-68-73-69—284	37179		J Furyk	74-69-74-75—292	11514
	J Maggert	71-68-75-70—284	37179		L Clements	73-71-73-75—292	11514
	J Sluman	72-69-72-71—284	37179		J Nicklaus	69-70-77-76—292	11514
	F Nobilo (NZ)	69-71-68-76—284	37179		M Ozaki (Jpn)	70-73-69-80—292	11514
13	J McGovern	73-69-74-69—285	29767	33	M Carnevale	75-72-76-70—293	9578
	S Hoch	72-72-70-71—285	29767		T Lehman	77-68-73-75—293	9578
	D Edwards	73-65-75-72—285	29767		F Allen	73-70-74-76—293	9578
16	F Couples	72-71-69-74—286	25899		T Kite	73-71-72-77—293	9578
	S Lowery	71-74-68-76—286	25899		B Crenshaw	71-74-70-78—293	9578

Other players who made the cut: B Hughes, P Baker (Eng), G Brand Jr (Sco), B Jobe 294; F Quinn jr 295; P Goydos, F Funk, D Walsworth 296; T Dunlavey, O Browne, B Lane (Eng), M Emery, D Bergano, J Gallagher jr, W Levi, P Mickelson 297; T Armour III, H Royer III, S Simpson 298; S Richardson (Eng), F Zoeller 299; D Rummells, D Martin 301; E Humenik, M Smith, M Aubrey 302.

1993 US Open *at Baltusrol, Springfield, NJ* (7155–70)

Prize money: $1,600,000. Entries: 5905

1	L Janzen	67-67-69-69—272	$290000	16T	F Couples	68-71-71-71—281	21576
2	P Stewart	70-66-68-70—274	145000		M Standly	70-69-70-72—281	21576
3	C Parry (Aus)	66-74-69-68—277	78556	19	B McCallister	68-73-73-68—282	18071
	P Azinger	71-68-69-69—277	78556		D Forsman	73-71-70-68—282	18071
5	S Hoch	66-72-72-68—278	48730		C Pavin	68-69-75-70—282	18071
	T Watson	70-66-73-69—278	48730		T Lehman	71-70-71-70—282	18071
7	E Els (RSA)	71-73-68-67—279	35481		S Pate	70-71-71-70—282	18071
	R Floyd	68-73-70-68—279	35481		I Baker-Finch (Aus)	70-70-70-72—282	18071
	N Henke	72-71-67-69—279	35481	25	C Strange	73-68-75-67—283	14531
	F Funk	70-72-67-70—279	35481		J Ozaki (Jpn)	70-70-74-69—283	14531
11	L Roberts	70-70-71-69—280	26249		R Mediate	68-72-73-70—283	14531
	J Sluman	71-71-69-69—280	26249		C Beck	72-68-72-71—283	14531
	J Adams	70-70-69-71—280	26249		K Perry	74-70-68-71—283	14531
	D Edwards	70-72-66-72—280	26249		M Calcavecchia	70-70-71-72—283	14531
	N Price (Zim)	71-66-70-73—280	26249		J Cook	75-66-70-72—283	14531
16	B Lane (Eng)	74-68-70-69—281	21576		W Levi	71-69-69-74—283	14531

Other players who made the cut: S Lowery, C Montgomerie (Sco), B Gilder, J Ozaki (Jpn), G Twiggs, B Andrade, L Rinker, J Daly, C Stadler, R Allenby (Aus), D Love III, S Elkington (Aus), M Donald 284; S Simpson, M Brooks, M McCumber, B Claar, R Fehr, L Nelson 285; K Triplett, I Woosnam (Wal), F Allem (RSA), V Heafner, E Kirby, M Christie, K Clearwater, A Lyle (Sco), B Estes, J Maggert 286; M Hulbert, H Irwin, M Smith, A Knoll, J Edwards, JD Blake 287; F Zoeller, S Gotsche, J Leonard (am), B Faxon 288; J Nicklaus, N Faldo (Eng), G Waite, P Jordan, D Waldorf 289; M Wiebe, T Johnstone (Zim), J Haas, B Thompson 290; W Grady (Aus), T Schulz 291; S Stricker 292; S Flesch 294; D Weaver, J Flannery 295; R Wrenn 297; R Gamez 298.

US Open Championship History

Year	Winner	Runner-up	Venue	Score
1894	W Dunn	W Campbell	St Andrews, NY	2 holes

After 1894 decided by stroke play

Year	Winner	Venue	Score		Year	Winner	Venue	Score
1895	HJ Rawlins	Newport	173		1916	C Evans (am)	Minneapolis	286
1896	J Foulis	Southampton	152		1917-18	*No Championship*		
1897	J Lloyd	Wheaton, IL	162		1919	W Hagen	Braeburn	301
1898	F Herd	Shinnecock Hills	328		*(After a tie with M Brady Play-off: Hagen 77, Brady 78)*			
72 holes played from 1898					1920	E Ray (Eng)	Inverness	295
1899	W Smith	Baltimore	315		1921	J Barnes	Washington	289
1900	H Vardon (Eng)	Wheaton, IL	313		1922	G Sarazen	Glencoe	288
1901	W Anderson	Myopia, MA	315		1923	R Jones jr (am)	Inwood, LI	295
(After a tie with A Smith Play-off: Anderson 85, Smith 86)					*(After a tie with R Cruikshank. Play-off: Jones 76,*			
1902	L Auchterlonie	Garden City	305		*Cruikshank 78)*			
1903	W Anderson	Baltusrol	307		1924	C Walker	Oakland Hills	297
(After a tie with D Brown Play-off: Anderson 82, Brown 84)					1925	W MacFarlane	Worcester	291
1904	W Anderson	Glenview	304		*(After a tie with R Jones jr Play-off: MacFarlane 75-72,*			
1905	W Anderson	Myopia, MA	335		*Jones 75-73)*			
1906	A Smith	Onwentsia	291		1926	R Jones jr (am)	Scioto	293
1907	A Ross	Chestnut Hill, PA	302		1927	T Armour	Oakmont	301
1908	F McLeod	Myopia, MA	322		*(After a tie with H Cooper. Play-off: Armour 76, Cooper 79)*			
(After a tie with W Smith Play-off: McLeod 77, Smith 83)					1928	J Farrell	Olympia Fields	294
1909	G Sargent	Englewood, NJ	290		*(After a tie with R Jones Jr. Play-off: Farrell 143, Jones 144)*			
1910	A Smith	Philadelphia	289		1929	R Jones jr (Am)	Winged Foot, NY	294
(After a tie with J McDermott and M Smith)					*(After a tie with A Espinosa. Play-off: Jones 141,*			
1911	J McDermott	Wheaton, IL	307		*Espinosa 164)*			
(After a tie with M Brady and G Simpson					1930	R Jones jr (am)	Interlachen	287
Play-off: McDermott 80, Brady 82, Simpson 85)					1931	B Burke	Inverness	292
1912	J McDermott	Buffalo, NY	294		*(After a tie with G von Elm. Play-off: Burke 149-148,*			
1913	F Ouimet (am)	Brookline, MA	304		*von Elm 149-149)*			
(After a tie with H Vardon and E Ray)					1932	G Sarazen	Fresh Meadow	286
1914	W Hagen	Midlothian	297		1933	J Goodman (am)	North Shore	287
1915	J Travers (am)	Baltusrol	290		1934	O Dutra	Merion	293

Year	Winner	Venue	Score
1935	S Parks	Oakmont	299
1936	T Manero	Springfield	282
1937	R Guldahl	Oakland Hills	281
1938	R Guldahl	Cherry Hills	284
1939	B Nelson	Philadelphia	284
(After a tie with C Wood and D Shute)			
1940	W Lawson Little	Canterbury, OH	287
(After a tie with G Sarazen. Play-off: Little 70, Sarazen 73)			
1941	C Wood	Fort Worth, TX	284
1942–45	*No Championship*		
1946	L Mangrum	Canterbury	284
(After a tie with B Nelson and V Ghezzie)			
1947	L Worsham	St Louis	282
(After a tie with S Snead. Play-off: Worsham 69, Snead 70)			
1948	B Hogan	Los Angeles	276
1949	Dr C Middlecoff	Medinah, IL	286
1950	B Hogan	Merion, PA	287
(After a tie with L Mangrum and G Fazio. Play-off: Hogan 69, Mangrum 73, Fazio 75)			
1951	B Hogan	Oakland Hills, MI	287
1952	J Boros	Dallas, TX	281
1953	B Hogan	Oakmont	283
1954	E Furgol	Baltusrol	284
1955	J Fleck	San Francisco	287
(After a tie with B Hogan. Play-off: Fleck 69, Hogan 72)			
1956	Dr C Middlecoff	Rochester, NY	281
1957	D Mayer	Inverness	282
(After a tie with Dr C Middlecoff. Play-off: Mayer 72, Middlecoff 79)			
1958	T Bolt	Tulsa, OK	283
1959	W Casper	Winged Foot, NY	282
1960	A Palmer	Denver, CO	280
1961	G Littler	Birmingham, MI	281
1962	J Nicklaus	Oakmont	283
(After a tie with A Palmer. Play-off: Nicklaus 71, Palmer 74)			
1963	J Boros	Brookline, MA	293
(After a tie. Play-off: J Boros 70, J Cupit 73, A Palmer 76)			
1964	K Venturi	Washington	278
1965	G Player (RSA)	St Louis, MO	282
(After a tie with K Nagle. Play-off: Player 71, Nagle 74)			
1966	W Casper	San Francisco	278
(After a tie with A Palmer. Play-off: Casper 69, Palmer 73)			
1967	J Nicklaus	Baltusrol	275
1968	L Trevino	Rochester, NY	275
1969	O Moody	Houston, TX	281
1970	A Jacklin (Eng)	Hazeltine, MN	281
1971	L Trevino	Merion, PA	280
(After a tie with J Nicklaus. Play-off: Trevino 68, Nicklaus 71)			
1972	J Nicklaus	Pebble Beach	290
1973	J Miller	Oakmont, PA	279
1974	H Irwin	Winged Foot, NY	287
1975	L Graham	Medinah, IL	287
(After a tie with Mahaffey. Play-off: Graham 71, Mahaffey 73)			
1976	J Pate	Atlanta, GA	277
1977	H Green	Southern Hills, Tulsa	278
1978	A North	Cherry Hills	285
1979	H Irwin	Inverness, OH	284
1980	J Nicklaus	Baltusrol	272
1981	D Graham (Aus)	Merion, PA	273
1982	T Watson	Pebble Beach	282
1983	L Nelson	Oakmont, PA	280
1984	F Zoeller	Winged Foot	276
(After a tie with G Norman. Play-off: Zoeller 67, Norman 75)			
1985	A North	Oakland Hills, MI	279
1986	R Floyd	Shinnecock Hills, NY	279
1987	S Simpson	Olympic, San Francisco	277
1988	C Strange	Brookline, MA	278
(After a tie with N Faldo. Play-off: Strange 71, Faldo 75)			
1989	C Strange	Rochester, NY	278
1990	H Irwin	Medinah	280
(After a tie with M Donald won at 1st extra hole after 18-hole play-off tie)			
1991	P Stewart	Hazeltine, MN	282
(After a tie with S Simpson Play-off: Stewart 75, Simpson 77)			
1992	T Kite	Pebble Beach, FL	285
1993	L Janzen	Baltusrol	272
1994	E Els (RSA)	Oakmont, PA	279
(After a tie with L Roberts and C Montgomerie Play-off: Els 74, Roberts 74, Montgomerie 78. Els then defeated Roberts at the second hole of a sudden death play-off)			
1995	C Pavin	Shinnecock Hills, NY	280
1996	S Jones	Oakland Hills, MI	278
1997	E Els (RSA)	Congressional, Bethesda	276
1998	L Janzen	Olympic, San Francisco	280
1999	P Stewart	Pinehurst No. 2, NC	279
2000	T Woods	Pebble Beach, CA	272
2001	R Goosen (RSA)	Southern Hills CC, OK	276
2002	T Woods	Farmingdale, NY	277

The Masters

Players are of American nationality unless stated

66th Masters *at Augusta National GC, Georgia*   (7270–72)

Prize Money: $5 600 000.   Final field of 89, of whom two withdrew, and 45 (with no amateurs) survived the half-way cut on 147 or better.

1	Tiger Woods	70-69-66-71—276	$1008000
2	Retief Goosen (RSA)	69-67-69-74—279	604800
3	Phil Mickelson	69-72-68-71—280	380800
4	José María Olazábal (Esp)	70-69-71-71—281	268800
5	Ernie Els (RSA)	70-67-72-73—282	212800
	Padraig Harrington (Irl)	69-70-72-71—282	212800
7	Vijay Singh (Fij)	70-65-72-76—283	187600
8	Sergio García (Esp)	68-71-70-75—284	173600
9	Angel Cabrera (Arg)	68-71-73-73—285	151200
	Miguel Angel Jiménez (Esp)	70-71-74-70—285	151200
	Adam Scott (Aus)	71-72-72-70—285	151200
12	Chris DiMarco	70-71-72-73—286	123200
	Brad Faxon	71-75-69-71—286	123200
14	Nick Faldo (Eng)	75-67-73-72—287	98000
	Davis Love III	67-75-74-71—287	98000
	Shigeki Maruyama (Jpn)	75-72-73-67—287	98000
	Colin Montgomerie (Sco)	75-71-70-71—287	98000
18	Thomas Bjørn (Den)	74-67-70-77—288	81200
	Paul McGinley (Irl)	72-74-71-71—288	81200
20	Darren Clarke (NI)	70-74-73-72—289	65240
	Jerry Kelly	72-74-71-72—289	65240
	Justin Leonard	70-75-74-70—289	65240
	Nick Price (Zim)	70-76-70-73—289	65240
24	Mark Brooks	74-72-71-73—290	46480
	Stewart Cink	74-70-72-74—290	46480
	Tom Pernice	74-72-71-73—290	46480
	Jeff Sluman	73-72-71-74—290	46480
	Mike Weir (Can)	72-71-71-76—290	46480
29	Robert Allenby (Aus)	73-70-76-72—291	38080
	Charles Howell III	74-73-71-73—291	38080
	Jesper Parnevik (Swe)	70-72-77-72—291	38080
32	John Daly	74-73-70-75—292	32410
	Bernhard Langer (Ger)	73-72-73-74—292	32410
	Billy Mayfair	74-71-72-75—292	32410
	Craig Stadler	73-72-76-71—292	32410
36	Fred Couples	73-73-76-72—294	26950
	Rocco Mediate	75-68-77-74—294	26950
	Greg Norman (Aus)	71-76-72-75—294	26950
	David Toms	73-74-76-71—294	26950
40	Steve Lowery	75-71-76-73—295	22960
	Kirk Triplett	74-70-74-77—295	22960
	Tom Watson	71-76-76-72—295	22960
43	Scott Verplank	70-75-76-75—296	20720
44	Lee Westwood (Eng)	75-72-74-76—297	19600
45	Bob Estes	73-72-75-78—298	18480

The following players missed the half-way cut. Each professional player received $5000:

46	Paul Azinger	75-73—148	56T	Mark O'Meara	78-71—149	76	Robert Hamilton	
	Michael Campbell		61	Billy Andrade	75-75—150		(am)	77-77—154
	(NZ)	74-74—148		Bubba Dickerson			Tim Jackson (am)	76-78—154
	Joe Durant	74-74—148		(am)	79-71—150		Sandy Lyle (Sco)	73-81—154
	David Duval	74-74—148		Jim Furyk	73-77—150	79	Ian Woosnam (Wal)	77-78—155
	Michael Hoey (Irl)			Shingo Katayama		80	Seve Ballesteros	
	(am)	75-73—148		(Jpn)	78-72—150		(Esp)	75-81—156
	Tom Lehman	76-72—148		Tom Kite	77-73—150	81	Tommy Aaron	79-78—157
	Scott McCarron	75-73—148		Matt Kuchar	73-77—150	82	Ben Crenshaw	81-77—158
	Larry Mize	74-74—148		Kenny Perry	76-74—150		Gary Player (RSA)	80-78—158
	Rory Sabbatini			Toru Taniguchi (Jpn)	80-70—150	84	Stuart Appleby (Aus)	80-79—159
	(RSA)	73-75—148	69	Niclas Fasth (Swe)	76-75—151	85	Chez Reavie (am)	74-86—160
	Kevin Sutherland	78-70—148		Scott Hoch	76-75—151	86	Charles Coody	82-84—166
56	Mark Calcavecchia	79-70—149		Steve Stricker	75-76—151	87	Arnold Palmer	89-85—174
	Toshimitsu Izawa		72	Craig Perks (NZ)	81-71—152			
	(Jpn)	79-70—149		Fuzzy Zoeller	75-77—152		Frank Lickliter II and Hal Sutton	
	Lee Janzen	74-75—149	74	José Coceres (Arg)	74-79—153		withdrew.	
	Paul Lawrie (Sco)	75-74—149		Raymond Floyd	79-74—153			

2001 Masters

Prize money: $5,574,920. Entries: 93, of whom 47 made the half-way cut.

1	Tiger Woods	70-66-68-68—272	$1008000	24	Darren Clarke (NI)	72-67-72-73—284	53760
2	David Duval	71-66-70-67—274	604800	25	Tom Scherrer	71-71-70-73—285	49280
3	Phil Mickelson	67-69-69-70—275	380800	26	Fred Couples	74-71-73-68—286	44800
4	Toshimitsu Izawa			27	Padraig Harrington		
	(Jpn)	71-66-74-67—278	246400		(Irl)	75-69-72-71—287	40600
	Mark Calcavecchia	72-66-68-72—278	246400		Justin Leonard	73-71-72-71—287	40600
6	Bernhard Langer				Mike Weir (Can)	74-69-72-72—287	40600
	(Ger)	73-69-68-69—279	181300		Steve Jones	74-70-72-71—287	40600
	Jim Furyk	69-71-70-69—279	181300	31	Stuart Appleby		
	Ernie Els (RSA)	71-68-68-72—279	181300		(Aus)	72-70-70-76—288	33208
	Kirk Triplett	68-70-70-71—279	181300		Mark Brooks	70-71-77-70—288	33208
10	Brad Faxon	73-68-68-71—280	128800		Duffy Waldorf	72-70-71-75—288	33208
	Steve Stricker	66-71-72-71—280	128800		Lee Janzen	67-70-72-79—288	33208
	Miguel Angel				David Toms	72-72-71-73—288	33208
	Jiménez (Esp)	68-72-71-69—280	128800	36	Hal Sutton	74-69-71-75—289	28840
	Angel Cabrera			37	Loren Roberts	71-74-73-72—290	26320
	(Arg)	66-71-70-73—280	128800		Chris Perry	68-74-74-74—290	26320
	Chris DiMarco	65-69-72-74—280	128800		Scott Hoch	74-70-72-74—290	26320
15	José María			40	Steve Lowery	72-72-78-70—292	22960
	Olazábal (Esp)	70-68-71-72—281	95200		Shingo Katayama		
	Paul Azinger	70-71-71-69—281	95200		(Jpn)	75-70-73-74—292	22960
	Rocco Mediate	72-70-66-73—281	95200		Franklin Langham	72-73-75-72—292	22960
18	Vijay Singh (Fij)	69-71-73-69—282	81200	43	Dudley Hart	74-70-78-71—293	19600
	Tom Lehman	75-68-71-68—282	81200		Bob May	71-74-73-75—293	19600
20	Mark O'Meara	69-74-72-68—283	65240		Jonathan Kaye	74-71-74-74—293	19600
	Jesper Parnevik			46	Carlos Franco (Par)	71-71-77-75—294	17360
	(Swe)	71-71-72-69—283	65240	47	Robert Allenby		
	John Huston	67-75-72-69—283	65240		(Aus)	71-74-75-75—295	16240
	Jeff Maggert	72-70-70-71—283	65240				

2000 Masters

Prize money: $4,617,000. Entries: 95, of whom 57 made the half-way cut.

1	Vijay Singh (Fij)	72-67-70-69—278	$828000	28T	Justin Leonard	72-71-77-73—293	28673
2	Ernie Els (RSA)	72-67-74-68—281	496800		Stewart Cink	75-72-72-74—293	28673
3	Loren Roberts	73-69-71-69—282	266800		Mike Weir (Can)	75-70-70-78—293	28673
	David Duval	73-65-74-70—282	266800		Dudley Hart	75-71-72-75—293	28673
5	Tiger Woods	75-72-68-69—284	184000		Paul Azinger	72-72-77-72—293	28673
6	Tom Lehman	69-72-75-69—285	165600		Masashi Ozaki (Jpn)	72-72-74-75—293	28673
7	Davis Love III	75-72-68-71—286	143367		Thomas Bjørn (Den)	71-77-73-72—293	28673
	Carlos Franco (Par)	79-68-70-69—286	143367	37	Fred Funk	75-68-78-73—294	21620
	Phil Mickelson	71-68-76-71—286	143367		Jay Haas	75-71-75-73—294	21620
10	Hal Sutton	72-75-71-69—287	124200		Notah Begay III	74-74-73-73—294	21620
11	Greg Norman (Aus)	80-68-70-70—288	105800	40	Ian Woosnam (Wal)	74-70-76-75—295	17480
	Nick Price (Zim)	74-69-73-72—288	105800		Sergio García (Esp)	70-72-75-78—295	17480
	Fred Couples	76-72-70-70—288	105800		Jesper Parnevik (Swe)	77-71-70-77—295	17480
14	Chris Perry	73-75-72-69—289	80500		Darren Clarke (NI)	72-71-78-74—295	17480
	Jim Furyk	73-74-71-71—289	80500		Mark Brooks	72-76-73-74—295	17480
	John Huston	77-69-72-71—289	80500		Retief Goosen (RSA)	73-69-79-74—295	17480
	Dennis Paulson	68-76-73-72—289	80500	46	Shigeki Maruyama (Jpn)	76-71-74-75—296	13800
18	Jeff Sluman	73-69-77-71—290	69000		Scott Gump	75-70-78-73—296	13800
19	Padraig Harrington (Irl)	76-69-75-71—291	53820	48	Brandt Jobe	73-74-76-74—297	12604
	Steve Stricker	70-73-75-73—291	53820	49	Miguel Angel Jiménez		
	Jean Van de Velde (Fra)	76-70-75-70—291	53820		(Esp)	76-71-79-72—298	11623
	Colin Montgomerie				Steve Pate	78-69-77-74—298	11623
	(Sco)	76-69-77-69—291	53820		David Toms	74-72-73-79—298	11623
	Bob Estes	72-71-77-71—291	53820	52	Steve Elkington (Aus)	74-74-78-73—299	10948
	Glen Day	79-67-74-71—291	53820		Rocco Mediate	71-74-75-79—299	10948
25	Larry Mize	78-67-73-74—292	37567	54	Jack Nicklaus	74-70-81-78—303	10672
	Craig Parry (Aus)	75-71-72-74—292	37567		David Gossett (am)	75-71-79-78—303	10672
	Steve Jones	71-70-76-75—292	37567	56	Skip Kendall	76-72-77-83—308	10580
28	Nick Faldo (Eng)	72-72-74-75—293	28673	57	Tommy Aaron	72-74-86-81—313	10488
	Bernhard Langer (Ger)	71-71-75-76—293	28673				

1999 Masters

Prize money: $3,200,000. Entries: 96, of whom 56 made the half-way cut.

1	JM Olazábal (Esp)	70-66-73-71—280	$720000	27T	E Els (RSA)	71-72-69-80—292	29000
2	D Love III	69-72-70-71—282	432000		R Mediate	73-74-69-76—292	29000
3	G Norman (Aus)	71-68-71-73—283	272000	31	T Lehman	73-72-73-75—293	23720
4	B Estes	71-72-69-72—284	176000		S Maruyama (Jpn)	78-70-71-74—293	23720
	S Pate	71-75-65-73—284	176000		M O'Meara	70-76-69-78—293	23720
6	D Duval	71-74-70-70—285	125200		J Sluman	70-75-70-78—293	23720
	C Franco (Par)	72-72-68-73—285	125200		B Watts	73-73-70-77—293	23720
	P Mickelson	74-69-71-71—285	125200	36	J Huston	74-72-71-77—294	20100
	N Price (Zim)	69-72-72-72—285	125200		A Magee	70-77-72-75—294	20100
	L Westwood (Eng)	75-71-68-71—285	125200	38	B Andrade	76-72-72-75—295	18800
11	S Elkington (Aus)	72-70-71-74—287	92000		M Brooks	76-72-75-72—295	18800
	B Langer (Ger)	76-66-72-73—287	92000		R Floyd	74-73-72-76—295	18800
	C Montgomerie (Sco)	70-72-71-74—287	92000		C Stadler	72-76-70-77—295	18800
14	J Furyk	72-73-70-73—288	70000		S Stricker	75-72-69-79—295	18800
	L Janzen	70-69-73-76—288	70000		S García (Esp) (am)	72-75-75-73—295	
	B Jobe	72-71-74-71—288	70000	44	J Haas	74-69-79-75—297	14000
	I Woosnam (Wal)	71-74-71-72—288	70000		T Herron	75-69-74-79—297	14000
18	B Chamblee	69-73-75-72—289	52160		S Hoch	75-73-70-79—297	14000
	B Glasson	72-70-73-74—289	52160		T McKnight (am)	73-74-73-77—297	
	J Leonard	70-72-73-74—289	52160	48	S Lyle (Sco)	71-77-70-80—298	12000
	S McCarron	69-68-76-76—289	52160		C Parry (Aus)	75-73-73-77—298	12000
	T Woods	72-72-70-75—289	52160	50	C Perry	73-72-74-80—299	10960
23	L Mize	76-70-72-72—290	41600		M Kuchar (am)	77-71-73-78—299	
24	B Faxon	74-73-68-76—291	35200	52	O Browne	74-74-72-80—300	9980
	P-U Johansson (Swe)	75-72-71-73—291	35200		J Daly	72-76-71-81—300	9980
	V Singh (Fij)	72-76-71-72—291	35200		P Stewart	73-75-77-75—300	9980
27	S Cink	74-70-71-77—292	29000		B Tway	75-73-78-74—300	9980
	F Couples	74-71-76-71—292	29000	56	T Immelman (RSA) (am)	72-76-78-79—305	

1998 Masters

Prize money: $3,200,000. Entries: 88, of whom 46 made the half-way cut.

1	M O'Meara	74-70-68-67—279	$576000	23T	J Huston	77-71-70-71—289	33280
2	D Duval	71-68-74-67—280	281600		J Maggert	72-73-72-72—289	33280
	F Couples	69-70-71-70—280	281600	26	D Frost (RSA)	72-73-74-71—290	26133
4	J Furyk	76-70-67-68—281	153600		S Jones	75-70-75-70—290	26133
5	P Azinger	71-72-69-70—282	128000		B Faxon	73-74-71-72—290	26133
6	J Nicklaus	73-72-70-68—283	111200	29	M Bradley	73-74-72-72—291	23680
	D Toms	75-72-72-64—283	111200	30	S Elkington (Aus)	75-75-71-71—292	22720
8	D Clarke (NI)	76-73-67-69—285	89600	31	A Magee	74-72-74-73—293	21280
	J Leonard	74-73-69-69—285	89600		J Parnevik (Swe)	75-73-73-72—293	21280
	C Montgomerie (Sco)	71-75-69-70—285	89600	33	L Janzen	76-74-72-72—294	18112
	T Woods	71-72-72-70—285	89600		F Zoeller	71-74-75-74—294	18112
12	J Haas	72-71-71-72—286	64800		P Blackmar	71-78-75-70—294	18112
	P-U Johansson (Swe)	74-75-67-70—286	64800		J Daly	77-71-71-75—294	18112
	P Mickelson	74-69-69-74—286	64800		D Love III	74-75-67-78—294	18112
	JM Olazábal (Esp)	70-73-71-72—286	64800	38	T Kite	73-74-74-74—295	15680
16	M Calcavecchia	74-74-69-70—287	48000	39	B Langer (Ger)	75-73-74-74—296	14720
	E Els (RSA)	75-70-70-72—287	48000		P Stankowski	70-80-72-74—296	14720
	S Hoch	70-71-73-73—287	48000	41	C Pavin	73-77-72-75—297	13440
	I Woosnam (Wal)	74-71-72-70—287	48000		C Stadler	79-68-73-77—297	13440
	S McCarron	73-71-72-71—287	48000	43	J Cook	75-73-74-76—298	12480
21	W Wood	74-74-70-70—288	38400	44	L Westwood (Eng)	74-76-72-78—300	11840
	M Kuchar (am)	72-76-68-72—288			J Kribel (am)	74-76-76-75—301	
23	S Cink	74-76-69-70—289	33280	46	G Player (RSA)	77-72-78-75—302	11200

1997 Masters

Prize money: $2,500,000. Entries: 86, of whom 46 made the half-way cut.

1	T Woods	70-66-65-69—270	$486000	24	N Price (Zim)	71-71-75-74—291	24840
2	T Kite	77-69-66-70—282	291600		L Westwood (Eng)	77-71-73-70—291	24840
3	T Tolles	72-72-72-67—283	183600	26	L Janzen	72-73-74-73—292	21195
4	T Watson	75-68-69-72—284	129600		C Stadler	77-72-71-72—292	21195
5	C Rocca (Ita)	71-69-70-75—285	102600	28	P Azinger	69-73-77-74—293	19575
	P Stankowski	68-74-69-74—285	102600		J Furyk	74-75-72-72—293	19575
7	F Couples	72-69-73-72—286	78570	30	S McCarron	77-71-72-74—294	17145
	B Langer (Ger)	72-72-74-68—286	78570		L Mize	79-69-74-72—294	17145
	J Leonard	76-69-71-70—286	78570		C Montgomerie (Sco)	72-67-74-81—294	17145
	D Love III	72-71-72-71—286	78570		M O'Meara	75-74-70-75—294	17145
	J Sluman	74-67-72-73—286	78570	34	A Lyle (Sco)	73-73-74-75—295	14918
12	S Elkington (Aus)	76-72-72-67—287	52920		F Zoeller	75-73-69-78—295	14918
	P-U Johansson (Swe)	72-73-73-69—287	52920	36	D Waldorf	74-75-72-75—296	13905
	T Lehman	73-76-69-69—287	52920	37	D Frost (SA)	74-71-73-79—297	13230
	JM Olazábal (Esp)	71-70-74-72—287	52920	38	S Hoch	79-68-73-78—298	12690
	W Wood	72-76-71-68—287	52920	39	J Nicklaus	77-70-74-78—299	11610
17	M Calcavecchia	74-73-72-69—288	39150		S Torrance (Sco)	75-73-73-78—299	11610
	E Els (RSA)	73-70-71-74—288	39150		I Woosnam (Wal)	77-68-75-79—299	11610
	F Funk	73-74-69-72—288	39150	42	M Ozaki (Jpn)	74-74-74-78—300	10530
	V Singh (Fij)	75-74-69-70—288	39150	43	C Pavin	75-74-78-74—301	9720
21	S Appleby (Aus)	72-76-70-71—289	30240		C Rose	73-75-79-74—301	9720
	J Huston	67-77-75-70—289	30240	45	B Crenshaw	75-73-74-80—302	8910
	J Parnevik (Swe)	73-72-71-73—289	30240	46	F Nobilo (NZ)	76-72-74-81—303	8370

1996 Masters

Prize money: $2,500,000. Entries: 92, of whom 44 made the half-way cut.

1	N Faldo (Eng)	69-67-73-67—276	$450000	23	L Mize	75-71-77-68—291	25000
2	G Norman (Aus)	63-69-71-78—281	270000		L Roberts	71-73-72-75—291	25000
3	P Mickelson	65-73-72-72—282	170000	25	R Floyd	70-74-77-71—292	21000
4	F Nobilo (NZ)	71-71-72-69—283	120000		B Faxon	69-77-72-74—292	21000
5	S Hoch	67-73-73-71—284	95000	27	B Estes	71-71-79-72—293	18900
	D Waldorf	72-71-69-72—284	95000		J Leonard	72-74-75-72—293	18900
7	D Love III	72-71-74-68—285	77933	29	J Furyk	75-70-78-71—294	15571
	J Maggert	71-73-72-69—285	77933		J Gallagher jr	70-76-77-71—294	15571
	C Pavin	75-66-73-71—285	77933		H Irwin	74-71-77-72—294	15571
10	S McCarron	70-70-72-74—286	65000		S Simpson	69-76-76-73—294	15571
	D Frost (RSA)	70-68-74-74—286	65000		C Stadler	73-72-71-78—294	15571
12	B Tway	67-72-76-72—287	52500		J Daly	71-74-71-78—294	15571
	L Janzen	68-71-75-73—287	52500		I Woosnam (Wal)	72-69-73-80—294	15571
	E Els (RSA)	71-71-72-73—287	52500	36	F Funk	71-72-76-76—295	12333
15	F Couples	78-68-71-71—288	43750		J Haas	70-73-75-77—295	12333
	M Calcavecchia	71-73-71-73—288	43750		B Langer (Ger)	75-70-72-78—295	12333
17	J Huston	71-71-71-76—289	40000	39	C Montgomerie (Sco)	72-74-75-75—296	11050
18	P Azinger	70-74-76-70—290	32600		V Singh (Fij)	69-71-74-82—296	11050
	M O'Meara	72-71-75-72—290	32600	41	S Lowery (Sco)	71-74-75-77—297	10050
	T Lehman	75-70-72-73—290	32600		J Nicklaus	70-73-76-78—297	10050
	N Price (Zim)	71-75-70-74—290	32600	43	S Ballesteros (Esp)	73-73-77-76—299	9300
	D Duval	73-72-69-76—290	32600	44	A Cejka (Ger)	73-71-78-80—302	8800

1995 Masters

Prize money: $2,132,000. Entries: 86, of whom 47 made the half-way cut.

1	B Crenshaw	70-67-69-68—274	$396000	24T	D Edwards	69-73-73-71—286	18260
2	D Love III	69-69-71-66—275	237600		L Roberts	72-69-72-73—286	18260
3	J Haas	71-64-72-70—277	127600		N Faldo (Eng)	70-70-71-75—286	18260
	G Norman (Aus)	73-68-68-68—277	127600		D Waldorf	74-69-67-76—286	18260
5	S Elkington (Aus)	73-67-67-72—279	83600	29	B Estes	73-70-76-68—287	15300
	D Frost (RSA)	66-71-71-71—279	83600		M Ozaki (Jpn)	70-74-70-73—287	15300
7	S Hoch	69-67-71-73—280	70950	31	B Lietzke	72-71-71-74—288	13325
	P Mickelson	66-71-70-73—280	70950		P Jacobsen	72-73-69-74—288	13325
9	C Strange	72-71-65-73—281	63800		B Langer (Ger)	71-69-73-75—288	13325
10	F Couples	71-69-67-75—282	57200		M O'Meara	68-72-71-77—288	13325
	B Henninger	70-68-68-76—282	57200	35	D Forsman	71-74-74-71—290	10840
12	K Perry	73-70-71-69—283	48400		W Grady (Aus)	69-73-74-74—290	10840
	L Janzen	69-69-74-71—283	48400		J Nicklaus	67-78-70-75—290	10840
14	JM Olazábal (Esp)	66-74-72-72—284	39600		C Beck	68-76-69-77—290	10840
	T Watson	73-70-69-72—284	39600		M McCumber	73-69-69-79—290	10840
	H Irwin	69-72-71-72—284	39600	40	T Lehman	71-72-74-75—292	9500
17	C Montgomerie (Sco)	71-69-76-69—285	28786	41	M Calcavecchia	70-72-78-73—293	8567
	P Azinger	70-72-73-70—285	28786		T Woods (am)	72-72-77-72—293	
	B Faxon	76-69-69-71—285	28786		J Sluman	73-72-71-77—293	8567
	I Woosnam (Wal)	69-72-71-73—285	28786		P Stewart	71-72-72-78—293	8567
	R Floyd	71-70-70-74—285	28786	45	S Ballesteros (Esp)	75-68-78-75—296	7500
	C Pavin	67-71-72-75—285	28786		J Daly	75-69-71-81—296	7500
	J Huston	70-66-72-77—285	28786	47	R Fehr	76-69-69-83—297	6800
24	D Gilford (Eng)	67-73-75-71—286	18260				

1994 Masters

Prize money: $1,960,000. Entries: 86, of whom 51 made the half-way cut.

1	JM Olazábal (Esp)	74-67-69-69—279	$360000	27	S Simpson	74-74-73-73—294	14800
2	T Lehman	70-70-69-72—281	216000		V Singh (Fij)	70-75-74-75—294	14800
3	L Mize	68-71-72-71—282	136000		C Strange	74-70-75-75—294	14800
4	T Kite	69-72-71-71—283	96000	30	L Janzen	75-71-76-73—295	13300
5	J Haas	72-72-72-69—285	73000		C Parry (Aus)	75-74-73-73—295	13300
	J McGovern	72-70-71-72—285	73000	32	N Faldo (Eng)	76-73-73-74—296	12400
	L Roberts	75-68-72-70—285	73000	33	R Cochran	71-74-74-79—297	11500
8	E Els (RSA)	74-67-74-71—286	60000		S Torrance (Sco)	76-73-74-74—297	11500
	C Pavin	71-72-73-70—286	60000	35	D Frost (RSA)	74-71-75-78—298	10300
10	I Baker-Finch (Aus)	71-71-71-74—287	50000		N Price (Zim)	74-73-74-77—298	10300
	R Floyd	70-74-71-72—287	50000		F Zoeller	74-72-74-78—298	10300
	J Huston	72-72-74-69—287	50000	38	F Allem (RSA)	69-77-76-77—299	9000
13	T Watson	70-71-73-74—288	42000		F Funk	79-70-75-75—299	9000
14	D Forsman	74-66-76-73—289	38000		A Lyle (Sco)	75-73-78-73—299	9000
15	C Beck	71-71-75-74—291	34000	41	W Grady (Aus)	74-73-73-80—300	7400
	B Faxon	71-73-73-74—291	34000		A Magee	74-74-76-76—300	7400
	M O'Meara	75-70-76-70—291	34000		H Meshiai (Jpn)	71-71-80-78—300	7400
18	S Ballesteros (Esp)	70-76-75-71—292	24343		C Rocca (Ita)	79-70-78-73—300	7400
	B Crenshaw	74-73-73-72—292	24343		M Standly	77-69-79-75—300	7400
	D Edwards	73-72-73-74—292	24343	46	J Cook	77-72-77-75—301	6000
	B Glasson	72-73-75-72—292	24343		I Woosnam (Wal)	76-73-77-75—301	6000
	H Irwin	73-68-79-72—292	24343	48	J Daly	76-73-77-78—304	5250
	G Norman (Aus)	70-70-75-77—292	24343		H Twitty	73-76-74-81—304	5250
	L Wadkins	73-74-73-72—292	24343	50	J Maggert	75-73-82-75—305	5000
25	B Langer (Ger)	74-74-72-73—293	16800		J Harris (am)	72-76-80-77—305	
	J Sluman	74-75-71-73—293	16800				

1993 Masters

Prize money: $1,705,700. Entries: 90, of whom 61 made the half-way cut.

1	B Langer (Ger)	68-70-69-70—277	$306000	31T	A Magee	75-69-70-76—290	10533
2	C Beck	72-67-72-70—281	183600		G Norman (Aus)	74-68-71-77—290	10533
3	T Lehman	67-75-73-68—283	81600	34	G Sauers	74-71-75-71—291	8975
	J Daly	70-71-73-69—283	81600		B Gilder	69-76-75-71—291	8975
	S Elkington (Aus)	71-70-71-71—283	81600		P Mickelson	72-71-75-73—291	8975
	L Wadkins	69-72-71-71—283	81600		C Stadler	73-74-69-75—291	8975
7	JM Olazábal (Esp)	70-72-74-68—284	54850	38	J Haas	70-73-75-74—292	8000
	D Forsman	69-69-73-73—284	54850	39	N Faldo (Eng)	71-76-79-67—293	6817
9	P Stewart	74-70-72-69—285	47600		T Schulz	69-76-76-72—293	6817
	B Faxon	71-70-72-72—285	47600		D Waldorf	72-75-73-73—293	6817
11	A Forsbrand (Swe)	71-74-75-66—286	34850		K Clearwater	74-70-75-74—293	6817
	S Ballesteros (Esp)	74-70-71-71—286	34850		J Cook	76-67-75-75—293	6817
	C Pavin	67-75-73-71—286	34850		L Janzen	67-73-76-77—293	6817
	S Simpson	72-71-71-72—286	34850	45	M Ozaki (Jpn)	75-71-77-71—294	4940
	R Floyd	68-71-74-73—286	34850		N Ozaki (Jpn)	74-70-78-72—294	4940
	F Zoeller	76-67-71-73—286	34850		T Watson	71-75-73-75—294	4940
17	I Woosnam (Wal)	71-74-73-69—287	24650		JD Blake	71-74-73-76—294	4940
	M Calcavecchia	71-70-74-72—287	24650		C Parry (Aus)	69-72-75-78—294	4940
	H Twitty	70-71-73-73—287	24650	50	G Morgan	72-74-72-77—295	4250
	J Sluman	71-72-71-73—287	24650		B Ogle (Aus)	70-74-71-80—295	4250
21	M O'Meara	75-69-73-71—288	17000	52	D Peoples	71-73-78-74—296	4050
	F Couples	72-70-74-72—288	17000		C Montgomerie (Sco)	71-72-78-75—296	4050
	L Mize	67-74-74-73—288	17000	54	I Baker-Finch (Aus)	73-72-73-80—298	3900
	A Lyle (Sco)	73-71-71-73—288	17000		D Edwards	73-73-76-76—298	3900
	J Maggert	70-67-75-76—288	17000		D Love III	73-72-76-77—298	3900
	R Cochran	70-69-73-76—288	17000	57	C Coody	74-72-75-78—299	3800
27	J Nicklaus	67-75-76-71—289	12350		G Hallberg	72-74-78-75—299	3800
	H Irwin	74-69-74-72—289	12350	59	J Huston	68-74-84-75—301	3800
	J Sindelar	72-69-76-72—289	12350	60	G Player (RSA)	71-76-75-80—302	3700
	N Henke	76-69-71-73—289	12350	61	B Andrade	73-74-80-76—303	3700
31	B Lietzke	74-71-71-74—290	10533				

The Masters History

Year	Winner	Score	Year	Winner	Score
1934	H Smith	284	1970	W Casper*	279
1935	G Sarazen*	282	1971	C Coody	279
1936	H Smith	285	1972	J Nicklaus	286
1937	B Nelson	283	1973	T Aaron	283
1938	H Picard	285	1974	G Player (RSA)	278
1939	R Guldahl	279	1975	J Nicklaus	276
1940	J Demaret	280	1976	R Floyd	271
1941	C Wood	280	1977	T Watson	276
1942	B Nelson*	280	1978	G Player (RSA)	277
1946	H Keiser	282	1979	F Zoeller*	280
1947	J Demaret	281	1980	S Ballesteros (Esp)	275
1948	C Harmon	279	1981	T Watson	280
1949	S Snead	283	1982	C Stadler*	284
1950	J Demaret	282	1983	S Ballesteros (Esp)	280
1951	B Hogan	280	1984	B Crenshaw	277
1952	S Snead	286	1985	B Langer (Ger)	282
1953	B Hogan	274	1986	J Nicklaus	279
1954	S Snead*	289	1987	L Mize*	285
1955	C Middlecoff	279	1988	A Lyle (Sco)	281
1956	J Burke	289	1989	N Faldo (Eng)*	283
1957	D Ford	283	1990	N Faldo (Eng)*	278
1958	A Palmer	284	1991	I Woosnam (Wal)	277
1959	A Wall	284	1992	F Couples	275
1960	A Palmer	282	1993	B Langer (Ger)	277
1961	G Player (RSA)	280	1994	JM Olazábal (Esp)	279
1962	A Palmer*	280	1995	B Crenshaw	274
1963	J Nicklaus	286	1996	N Faldo (Eng)	276
1964	A Palmer	276	1997	T Woods	270
1965	J Nicklaus	271	1998	M O'Meara	279
1966	J Nicklaus*	288	1999	JM Olazábal (Esp)	280
1967	G Brewer	280	2000	V Singh (Fij)	278
1968	R Goalby	277	2001	T Woods	272
1969	G Archer	281	2002	T Woods	276

US PGA Championship

Players are of American nationality unless stated

84th US PGA Championship *Hazeltine National, Chaska, MN*   (7360–72)

Prize money: $5,500,000. Final field: 156 (one amateur), of whom 72 made the half-way cut on 148 or better.

1	Rich Beem	72-66-72-68—278	$990000
2	Tiger Woods	71-69-72-67—279	594000
3	Chris Riley	71-70-72-70—283	374000
4	Fred Funk	68-70-73-73—284	235000
	Justin Leonard	72-66-69-77—284	235000
6	Rocco Mediate	72-73-70-70—285	185000
7	Mark Calcavecchia	70-68-74-74—286	172000
8	Vijay Singh (Fij)	71-74-74-68—287	159000
9	Jim Furyk	68-73-76-71—288	149000
10	Robert Allenby (Aus)	76-66-77-70—289	110714
	Stewart Cink	74-74-72-69—289	110714
	José Coceres (Arg)	72-71-72-74—289	110714
	Pierre Fulke (Swe)	72-68-78-71—289	110714
	Sergio García (Esp)	75-73-73-68—289	110714
	Ricardo Gonzalez (Arg)	74-73-71-71—289	110714
	Steve Lowery	71-71-73-74—289	110714
17	Stuart Appleby (Aus)	73-74-74-69—290	72000
	Steve Flesch	72-74-73-71—290	72000
	Padraig Harrington (Irl)	71-73-74-72—290	72000
	Charles Howell III	72-69-80-69—290	72000
	Peter Lonard (Aus)	69-73-75-73—290	72000
22	Heath Slocum	73-74-75-69—291	57000
23	Michael Campbell (NZ)	73-70-77-72—292	44250
	Retief Goosen (RSA)	69-69-79-75—292	44250
	Bernhard Langer (Ger)	70-72-77-73—292	44250
	Justin Rose (Eng)	69-73-76-74—292	44250
	Adam Scott (Aus)	71-71-76-74—292	44250
	Jeff Sluman	70-75-74-73—292	44250
29	Brad Faxon	74-72-75-72—293	33500
	Tom Lehman	71-72-77-73—293	33500
	Craig Perks (NZ)	72-76-74-71—293	33500
	Kenny Perry	73-68-78-74—293	33500
	Kirk Triplett	75-69-79-70—293	33500
34	David Duval	71-77-76-70—294	26300
	Ernie Els (RSA)	72-71-75-76—294	26300
	Neal Lancaster	72-73-75-74—294	26300
	Phil Mickelson	76-72-78-68—294	26300
	Mike Weir (Can)	73-74-77-70—294	26300
39	Chris DiMarco	76-69-77-73—295	21500
	Joel Edwards	73-74-77-71—295	21500
	John Huston	74-74-75-72—295	21500
	Scott McCarron	73-71-79-72—295	21500
43	Briny Baird	79-69-73-75—296	17000
	Søren Hansen (Den)	73-69-78-76—296	17000
	Shigeki Maruyama (Jpn)	76-72-75-73—296	17000
	Loren Roberts	77-70-77-72—296	17000
	Kevin Sutherland	72-75-71-78—296	17000
48	Angel Cabrera (Arg)	71-73-77-76—297	13120

84th US PGA Championship *continued*

48T	Steve Elkington (Aus)	72-75-76-74—297	13120
	Davis Love III	70-75-76-76—297	13120
	Len Mattiace	74-73-76-74—297	13120
	Tom Watson	76-71-83-67—297	13120
53	Cameron Beckman	74-71-75-78—298	11742
	Tim Clark (RSA)	72-74-76-76—298	11742
	Brian Gay	73-74-78-73—298	11742
	Toshimitsu Izawa (Jpn)	72-73-75-78—298	11742
	Lee Janzen	70-76-77-75—298	11742
	Greg Norman (Aus)	71-74-73-80—298	11742
	Chris Smith	75-73-72-78—298	11742
60	Joe Durant	74-71-79-75—299	11200
	Nick Faldo (Eng)	71-76-74-78—299	11200
	Hal Sutton	73-73-75-78—299	11200
63	J J Henry	78-70-77-76—301	11000
64	Don Berry	76-71-80-75—302	10750
	Matt Gogel	74-73-83-72—302	10750
	J P Hayes	73-75-78-76—302	10750
	Joey Sindelar	77-71-78-76—302	10750
68	Dave Tentis	76-72-78-78—304	10500
69	José María Olazábal (Esp)	73-75-77-80—305	10400
70	Pat Perez	77-71-85-76—309	10300
71	Thomas Levet (Fra)	78-70-82-80—310	10200
72	Stephen Ames (Tri)	73-74—147	W/D

The following players missed the half-way cut. Each received $2000:

73	Thomas Bjørn (Den)	74-75—149	100	John Cooke	75-76—151	128	Scott Hoch	80-75—155
	Choi Kyoung-ju			Tim Herron	76-75—151		Jeff Maggert	78-77—155
	(Kor)	78-71—149		Mark O'Meara	75-76—151		Jesper Parnevik	
	Darren Clarke (NI)	79-70—149		David Toms	77-74—151		(Swe)	82-73—155
	David Gossett	72-77—149		Taichi Toshima (Jpn)	77-74—151		David Peoples	79-76—155
	Paul Lawrie (Sco)	75-74—149	105	Billy Andrade	75-77—152		Robert Thompson	78-77—155
	Ian Leggatt (Can)	75-74—149		James Blair III	74-78—152	133	Barry Evans	80-76—156
	J L Lewis	76-73—149		John Daly	76-76—152		Niclas Fasth (Swe)	79-77—156
	Larry Nelson	76-73—149		Robert Gamez	76-76—152		Joe Klinchock	79-77—156
	Nick Price (Zim)	72-77—149		Anders Hansen (Den)	79-73—152		Jeffrey Lankford	80-76—156
	Greg Owen (Eng)	76-73—149		Rick Hartmann	79-73—152		Scott Laycock (Aus)	80-76—156
	Rory Sabbatini			Shingo Katayama		138	Jim Carter	74-83—157
	(RSA)	74-75—149		(Jpn)	74-78—152		Bob Estes	81-76—157
	Scott Verplank	77-72—149		Matt Kuchar	78-74—152		Dudley Hart	82-75—157
	Fuzzy Zoeller	76-73—149		Colin Montgomerie			Craig Stevens (am)	82-75—157
86	Paul Azinger	76-74—150		(Sco)	74-78—152		Curtis Strange	81-76—157
	Chad Campbell	74-76—150		Craig Parry (Aus)	75-77—152	143	Tim Fleming	77-81—158
	Sean Farren	74-76—150		Carl Paulson	73-79—152		Lee Westwood (Eng)	75-83—158
	Jay Haas	77-73—150		Carl Petterson (Swe)	77-75—152	145	Paul Casey (Eng)	85-74—159
	Jonathan Kaye	77-73—150		Steve Stricker	74-78—152		Buddy Harston	76-83—159
	Jerry Kelly	77-73—150		Toru Taniguchi (Jpn)	75-77—152		Alan Morin	82-77—159
	Skip Kendall	74-76—150		Bruce Zabriski	75-77—152		Philip Price (Wal)	76-83—159
	Spike McRoy	74-76—150	120	Rob Labricz	78-75—153		Tim Weinhart	77-82—159
	John Rollins	77-73—150		Frank Lickliter II	77-76—153	150	Wayne DeFrancesco	78-82—160
	Eduardo Romero			Paul McGinley (Irl)	74-79—153	151	Steve Schneiter	86-76—162
	(Arg)	73-77—150		Billy Mayfair	77-76—153	152	Barry Mahlberg	80-86—166
	Bob Tway	74-76—150		Peter O'Malley (Aus)	79-74—153	153	Kent Stauffer	87-80—167
	Duffy Waldorf	77-73—150		Tim Thelen	75-78—153		Kim Thompson	87-80—167
	Dean Wilson	74-76—150	126	Mark Brooks	75-79—154	155	Tom Dolby	85-94—179
	Ian Woosnam (Wal)	77-73—150		Mike Gilmore	78-76—154	156	Bill Porter	W/D

2001 US PGA Championship *at Atlanta Athletic Club, Atlanta, Georgia*

Prize money: $5,205,049. Entries: 150, of whom 76 made the half-way cut. (7213–70)

1	David Toms	66-65-65-69—265	$936000	16T	Chris DiMarco	68-67-71-71—277	70666
2	Phil Mickelson	66-66-66-68—266	562000	22	Mark O'Meara	72-63-70-73—278	44285
3	Steve Lowery	67-67-66-68—268	354000		Shigeki Maruyama		
4	Mark Calcavecchia	71-68-66-65—270	222500		(Jpn)	68-72-71-67—278	44285
	Shingo Katayama (Jpn)	67-64-69-70—270	222500		Paul Azinger	68-67-69-74—278	44285
6	Billy Andrade	68-70-68-66—272	175000		Paul McGinley (Irl)	68-72-71-67—278	44285
7	Jim Furyk	70-64-71-69—274	152333		Briny Baird	70-69-72-67—278	44285
	Scott Verplank	69-68-70-67—274	152333		J Brian Gay	70-68-69-71—278	44285
	Scott Hoch	68-70-69-67—274	152333		Charles Howell III	71-67-69-71—278	44285
10	David Duval	66-68-67-74—275	122000	29	Greg Norman (Aus)	70-68-71-70—279	29437
	Justin Leonard	70-69-67-69—275	122000		Tiger Woods	73-67-69-70—279	29437
	Kirk Triplett	68-70-71-66—275	122000		Nick Price (Zim)	71-67-71-70—279	29437
13	Steve Flesch	73-67-70-66—276	94666		Kyoung-Ju Choi (Kor)	66-68-72-73—279	29437
	Jesper Parnevik (Swe)	70-68-70-68—276	94666		Bob Tway	69-69-71-70—279	29437
	Ernie Els (RSA)	67-67-70-72—276	94666		Carlos Franco (Par)	67-72-71-69—279	29437
16	Stuart Appleby (Aus)	66-70-68-73—277	70666		Niclas Fasth (Swe)	66-69-72-72—279	29437
	Mike Weir (Can)	69-72-66-70—277	70666		Christopher Smith	69-71-68-71—279	29437
	Dudley Hart	66-68-73-70—277	70666		José María Olazábal		
	José Coceres (Arg)	69-68-73-67—277	70666		(Esp)	70-70-68-71—279	29437
	Robert Allenby (Aus)	69-67-73-68—277	70666				

Other Totals: Fred Couples, Davis Love III, Bob Estes, Angel Cabrera (Arg), Andrew Coltart (Sco), Retief Goosen (RSA) 280; Andrew Oldcorn (Sco), Greg Chalmers (Aus), Jerry Kelly, Hal Sutton, Kenny Perry, Lee Westwood (Eng), Rick Schuller 281; Nick Faldo (Eng), Ian Woosnam (Wal), Joe Durant, Vijay Singh (Fij), Scott Dunlap, Tom Pernice, Chris Riley, Frank Lickliter 282; Brad Faxon, Stewart Cink, Phillip Price (Wal), Grant Waite (NZ) 283; Skip Kendall, Thomas Bjørn (Den), Jonathan Kaye, Rocco Mediate 284; Tom Watson, Steve Stricker, Robert Damron 285; Fred Funk, Scott McCarron 286; John Huston 287; Bob May 291; Paul Stankowski 293; Steve Pate 294; Colin Montgomerie (Sco) DQ

2000 US PGA Championship *at Valhalla GC, Louisville, Kentucky* (7167–72)

Prize money: $5,000,000. Entries: 150, of whom 80 made the half-way cut.

1	Tiger Woods	66-67-70-67—270	$900000	19T	JP Hayes	69-68-68-86—281	56200
2	Bob May	72-66-66-66—270	540000		Angel Cabrera (Arg)	72-71-71-67—281	56200
	Woods won after play-off				Robert Allenby (Aus)	73-71-68-69—281	56200
3	Thomas Bjørn (Den)	72-68-67-68—275	340000		Lee Janzen	76-70-70-65—281	56200
4	Greg Chalmers (Aus)	71-69-66-70—276	198667	24	Paul Azinger	72-71-66-73—282	41000
	José María Olazábal				Steve Jones	72-71-70-69—282	41000
	(Esp)	76-68-63-69—276	198667		Jarmo Sandelin (Swe)	74-72-68-68—282	41000
	Stuart Appleby (Aus)	72-69-68-69—276	198667	27	Brad Faxon	71-74-70-68—283	34167
7	Franklin Langham	72-71-65-69—277	157000		Skip Kendall	72-72-69-70—283	34167
8	Notah Begay III	72-66-70-70—278	145000		Tom Pernice	74-69-70-70—283	34167
9	Tom Watson	76-70-65-68—279	112500	30	Mike Weir (Can)	76-69-68-71—284	28875
	Fred Funk	69-68-74-68—279	112500		Jean Van de Velde		
	Davis Love III	68-69-72-70—279	112500		(Fra)	70-74-69-71—284	28875
	Darren Clarke (NI)	68-72-72-67—279	112500		Stephen Ames (Tri)	69-71-71-73—284	28875
	Scott Dunlap	66-68-70-75—279	112500		Kenny Perry	78-68-70-68—284	28875
	Phil Mickelson	70-70-69-70—279	112500	34	Sergio García (Esp)	74-69-73-69—285	24000
15	Stewart Cink	72-71-70-67—280	77500		Chris Perry	72-74-70-69—285	24000
	Lee Westwood (Eng)	72-72-69-67—280	77500		Mark Calcavecchia	73-74-71-67—285	24000
	Chris Dimarco	73-70-69-68—280	77500		Ernie Els (RSA)	74-68-72-71—285	24000
	Michael Clark II	73-70-67-70—280	77500		Blaine McCallister	73-71-70-71—285	24000
19	Tom Kite	70-72-69-70—281	56200				

Other Totals: Toshimitsu Izawa (Jpn), Colin Montgomerie (Sco) 286; Jeff Sluman, Justin Leonard, Paul Stankowski, Steve Pate, David Toms 287; Bernhard Langer (Ger), Mark O'Meara, Shigeki Maruyama (Jpn), Duffy Waldorf, Brian Henninger 288; Nick Faldo (Eng), Jesper Parnevik (Swe), Steve Lowery, Brian Watts, Glen Day, Andrew Coltart (Sco), Jonathan Kaye 289; Padraig Harrington (Irl), Loren Roberts, Curtis Strange, Carlos Franco (Par), Dennis Paulson, Joe Ogilvie 290; Wayne Grady (Aus), Craig Stadler, Bill Glasson, Miguel Angel Jiménez (Esp), Jay Haas 291; Greg Kraft, Kirk Triplett 292; John Huston 293; Jim Furyk, Paul Lawrie (Sco) 294; Robert Damron, Billy Mayfair, Scott Hoch 297; Masashi Ozaki (Jpn), Rory Sabbatini 299; Hidemichi Tanaka (Jpn) 301; Frank Dobbs 313

1999 US PGA Championship *at Medinah, Illinois* (7401–72)

Prize money: $3,000,000. Entries: 149, of whom 74 made the half-way cut.

1	T Woods	70-67-68-72—277	$630000	21	D Frost (RSA)	75-68-74-71—288	33200
2	S García (Esp)	66-73-68-71—278	378000		S Hoch	71-71-75-71—288	33200
3	S Cink	69-70-68-73—280	203000		S Kendall	74-65-71-78—288	33200
	J Haas	68-67-75-70—280	203000		JL Lewis	73-70-74-71—288	33200
5	N Price (Zim)	70-71-69-71—281	129000		K Wentworth	72-70-72-74—288	33200
6	B Estes	71-70-72-69—282	112000	26	F Couples	73-69-75-72—289	24000
	C Montgomerie (Sco)	72-70-70-70—282	112000		C Franco (Par)	72-71-71-75—289	24000
8	J Furyk	71-70-69-74—284	96500		J Kelly	69-74-71-75—289	24000
	S Pate	72-70-73-69—284	96500		H Sutton	72-73-73-71—289	24000
10	D Duval	70-71-72-72—285	72166		J Van de Velde (Fra)	74-70-75-70—289	24000
	MA Jiménez (Esp)	70-70-75-70—285	72166	31	P Goydos	73-70-71-76—290	20000
	J Parnevik (Swe)	72-70-73-70—285	72166		M James (Eng)	70-74-79-67—290	20000
	C Pavin	69-74-71-71—285	72166		T Tryba	70-72-76-72—290	20000
	C Perry	70-73-71-71—285	72166	34	S Flesch	73-71-72-75—291	15428
	M Weir (Can)	68-68-69-80—285	72166		P Lawrie (Sco)	73-72-72-74—291	15428
16	M Brooks	70-73-70-74—287	48600		T Lehman	70-74-76-71—291	15428
	G Hjertstedt (Swe)	72-70-73-72—287	48600		B Mayfair	75-69-75-72—291	15428
	B Jobe	69-74-69-75—287	48600		K Perry	74-69-72-76—291	15428
	G Turner (NZ)	73-69-70-75—287	48600		S Verplank	73-72-73-73—291	15428
	L Westwood (Eng)	70-68-74-75—287	48600		L Wadkins	72-69-74-76—291	15428

Other Totals: P Azinger, Angel Cabrera (Arg), C DiMarco, N Faldo (Eng), H Irwin, R Karlsson (Swe), D Waldorf, B Watts 292; O Browne, D Love III, R Mediate, V Singh (Fij), K Triplett 293; JP Hayes, A Magee, J Sluman 294; P Mickelson, M O'Meara, P Stewart, B Tway 295; M Calcavecchia, B Faxon, G Kraft, B Langer (Ger) 296; A Cejka (Ger), A Coltart (Sco), M Reid 297; S Dunlap, B Zabriski 298; R Beem, T Bjørn (Den), N Ozaki (Jpn) 299; F Funk 300

1998 US PGA Championship *at Sahalee, Seattle, Washington* (6906–70)

1	V Singh (Fij)	70-66-67-68—271	$540000	21	E Els (RSA)	72-72-71-66—281	32000
2	S Stricker	69-68-66-70—273	324000		A Magee	70-68-72-71—281	32000
3	S Elkington (Aus)	69-69-69-67—274	204000	23	P-U Johansson (Swe)	69-74-71-68—282	26000
4	F Lickliter	68-71-69-68—276	118000		F Funk	70-71-71-70—282	26000
	M O'Meara	69-70-69-68—276	118000		S Gump	68-69-72-73—282	26000
	N Price (Zim)	70-73-68-65—276	118000		G Kraft	71-73-65-73—282	26000
7	B Mayfair	73-67-67-70—277	89500	27	J Sluman	71-73-70-69—283	20500
	D Love III	70-68-69-70—277	89500		H Sutton	72-68-72-71—283	20500
9	J Cook	71-68-70-69—278	80000	29	G Day	68-71-75-70—284	17100
10	K Perry	69-72-70-68—279	69000		T Lehman	71-71-70-72—284	17100
	T Woods	66-72-70-71—279	69000		I Woosnam (Wal)	70-75-67-72—284	17100
	S Kendall	72-68-68-71—279	69000		L Rinker	70-70-71-73—284	17100
13	B Faxon	70-68-74-68—280	46000		S Hoch	72-69-70-73—284	17100
	F Couples	74-71-67-68—280	46000	34	P Mickelson	70-70-78-67—285	14250
	B Tway	69-76-67-68—280	46000		B Estes	68-76-69-72—285	14250
	P Azinger	68-73-70-69—280	46000		P Goydos	70-70-72-73—285	14250
	B Glasson	68-74-69-69—280	46000		R Cochran	69-71-70-75—285	14250
	S Flesch	75-69-67-69—280	46000	38	C Stadler	69-74-71-72—286	12750
	J Huston	70-71-68-71—280	46000		D Waldorf	74-70-70-72—286	12750
	R Allenby (Aus)	72-68-69-71—280	46000				

Other Totals: J Sindelar, J Haas, J Durant, C Franco (Par) 287; J Ozaki (Jpn), J Maggert, S Lowery, D Ogrin, K Sutherland, C Montgomerie (Sco), PH Horgan III, M Calcavecchia, D Hart, B Andrade 288; N Faldo (Eng), S Verplank 289; T Tryba, M Brooks, B Watts, J Carter, D Frost (RSA), JD Blake 290; T Dodds (Nam), T Byrum, O Browne 291; R Karlsson (Swe), S Maruyama (Jpn), L Roberts 292; S Leaney (Aus) 293; A Coltart (Sco) 294; D Sutherland 295; B Geiberger, C Parry (Aus), B Fabel 296; C Perry 297; T Herron 298

1997 US PGA Championship at Winged Foot CC, New York   (6987–70)

Prize money: $2,600,000. Entries: 150, of whom 77 made the half-way cut.

1	D Love III	66-71-66-66—269	470000	13T	B Tway	68-75-72-69—284	35100
2	J Leonard	68-70-65-71—274	280000		M O'Meara	69-73-75-67—284	35100
3	J Maggert	69-69-73-65—276	175000	23	M Calcavecchia	71-74-73-67—285	22500
4	L Janzen	69-67-74-69—279	125000		B Langer (Ger)	73-71-72-69—285	22500
5	T Kite	68-71-71-70—280	105000		D Martin	69-75-74-67—285	22500
6	P Blackmar	70-68-74-69—281	85000		S Maruyama (Jpn)	68-70-74-73—285	22500
	J Furyk	69-72-72-68—281	85000		K Perry	73-68-73-71—285	22500
	S Hoch	71-72-68-70—281	85000		J Cook	71-71-74-69—285	22500
9	T Byrum	69-73-70-70—282	70000	29	P Azinger	68-73-71-74—286	13625
10	T Lehman	69-72-72-70—283	60000		R Black	76-69-71-70—286	13625
	S McCarron	74-71-67-71—283	60000		F Couples	71-67-73-75—286	13625
	J Sindelar	72-71-71-69—283	60000		J Daly	66-73-77-70—286	13625
13	D Duval	70-70-71-73—284	35100		P Goydos	70-72-71-73—286	13625
	T Herron	72-73-68-71—284	35100		H Irwin	73-70-71-72—286	13625
	C Montgomerie (Sco)	74-71-67-72—284	35100		P Mickelson	69-69-73-75—286	13625
	G Norman (Aus)	68-71-74-71—284	35100		F Nobilo (NZ)	72-73-67-74—286	13625
	N Price (Zim)	72-70-72-70—284	35100		D Pooley	72-74-70-70—286	13625
	V Singh (Fij)	73-66-76-69—284	35100		P Stewart	70-70-72-74—286	13625
	T Tolles	75-70-73-66—284	35100		L Westwood (Eng)	74-68-71-73—286	13625
	K Triplett	73-70-71-70—284	35100		T Woods	70-70-71-75—286	13625

Other Totals: I Garrido (Esp), S Jones, D Ogrin, E Romero (Arg) 287; T Bjørn (Den), S Elkington (Aus), J Parnevik (Swe), S Torrance (Sco) 288; R Allenby (Aus), B Henninger, C Perry, L Roberts 289; O Browne, E Els (RSA), B Mayfair, T Smith, C Stadler 290; S Lowery, L Mize, L Wadkins 291; S Appleby (Aus), J Haas, R Cochran, F Funk, R Goosen (RSA), L Rinker 292; P Jacobsen, P-U Johansson (Swe), P Stankowski 293; C Franco (Par) 294; M Bradley, Y Kaneko (Jpn), L Nelson, C Rocca (Ita) 295; A Magee 296; P Jordan, K Sutherland 297.

1996 US PGA Championship at Valhalla, Louisville, Kentucky   (7144–72)

Prize money: $2,400,000. Entries: 150, of whom 87 made the half-way cut.

1	M Brooks*	68-70-69-70—277	$430000	17T	D Edwards	69-71-72-70—282	27285
2	K Perry	66-72-71-68—277	260000		J Furyk	70-70-73-69—282	27285
Brooks won play-off at extra hole					G Norman (Aus)	68-72-69-73—282	27285
3	S Elkington (Aus)	67-74-67-70—278	140000	24	E Aubrey	69-74-72-68—283	21500
	T Tolles	69-71-71-67—278	140000		MA Jiménez (Esp)	71-71-71-70—283	21500
5	J Leonard	71-66-72-70—279	86666	26	F Funk	73-69-73-69—284	18000
	J Parnevik (Swe)	73-67-69-70—279	86666		M O'Meara	71-70-74-69—284	18000
	V Singh (Fij)	69-69-69-72—279	86666		C Pavin	71-74-70-69—284	18000
8	L Janzen	68-71-71-70—280	57500		C Strange	73-70-68-73—284	18000
	P-U Johansson (Swe)	73-72-66-69—280	57500		S Stricker	73-72-72-67—284	18000
	P Mickelson	67-67-74-72—280	57500	31	P Azinger	70-75-71-69—285	13000
	L Mize	71-70-69-70—280	57500		M Bradley	73-72-70-70—285	13000
	F Nobilo (NZ)	69-72-71-68—280	57500		P Burke	71-72-69-73—285	13000
	N Price (Zim)	68-71-69-72—280	57500		J Haas	72-71-69-73—285	13000
14	M Brisky	71-69-69-72—281	39000		T Herron	71-73-68-73—285	13000
	T Lehman	71-71-69-70—281	39000	36	M Calcavecchia	70-74-70-72—286	9050
	J Sindelar	73-72-69-67—281	39000		R Mediate	71-72-67-76—286	9050
17	B Faxon	72-68-73-69—282	27285		D Ogrin	75-70-68-73—286	9050
	T Watson	69-71-73-69—282	27285		I Woosnam (Wal)	68-72-75-71—286	9050
	D A Weibring	71-73-71-67—282	27285		F Zoeller	76-67-72-71—286	9050
	R Cochran	68-72-65-77—282	27285				

Other Totals: G Day, D Duval, G Morgan, J Morse 287; J Sluman, F Couples 287; P Blackmar, J Cook, S McCarron, P Stankowski, B Watts 288; J Adams, B Boyd, A Cejka (Ger), J Gallagher Jr, L Rinker, C Rocca (Ita), N Lancaster, B Mayfair, T Nakajima (Jpn) 289; E Els (RSA), D Forsman, S Hoch, M Wiebe 290; N Faldo (Eng), W Grady (Aus), C Parry (Aus), W Wood 291; W Austin, B Crenshaw, N Henke, P Stewart 292; P Goydos, J Maggert 293; M Dawson 294; B Langer (Ger) 295; J Edwards 296; S Higashi (Jpn), S Ingraham 297; H Clark (Eng), J Reeves 298.

1995 US PGA Championship at Riviera, Los Angeles, California

(6956–71) Prize money: $2,000,000. Entries: 150, of whom 72 made the half-way cut.

1	S Elkington (Aus)*	68-67-68-64—267	$360000	20	G Norman (Aus)	66-69-70-72—277	21000
2	C Montgomerie (Sco)	68-67-67-65—267	216000		J Parnevik (Swe)	69-69-70-69—277	21000
Elkington won at first play-off hole					D Waldorf	69-69-67-72—277	21000
3	E Els (RSA)	66-65-66-72—269	116000	23	W Austin	70-70-70-68—278	15500
	J Maggert	66-69-65-69—269	116000		N Henke	68-73-67-70—278	15500
5	B Faxon	70-67-71-63—271	80000		P Jacobsen	69-67-71-71—278	15500
6	B Estes	69-68-68-68—273	68500		L Janzen	66-70-72-70—278	15500
	M O'Meara	64-67-69-73—273	68500		B Lietzke	73-68-67-70—278	15500
8	J Haas	69-71-64-70—274	50000		B Mayfair	68-68-72-70—278	15500
	J Leonard	68-66-70-70—274	50000		S Stricker	75-64-69-70—278	15500
	S Lowery	69-68-68-69—274	50000		S Torrance (Sco)	69-69-69-71—278	15500
	J Sluman	69-67-68-70—274	50000	31	P Azinger	70-70-72-67—279	8906
	C Stadler	71-66-66-71—274	50000		M Brooks	67-74-69-69—279	8906
13	J Furyk	68-70-69-68—275	33750		F Couples	70-69-74-66—279	8906
	MA Jiménez (Esp)	69-69-67-70—275	33750		N Faldo (Eng)	69-73-70-67—279	8906
	P Stewart	69-70-69-67—275	33750		G Morgan	66-73-74-66—279	8906
	K Triplett	71-69-68-67—275	33750		JM Olazábal (Esp)	72-66-70-71—279	8906
17	M Campbell (NZ)	71-65-71-69—276	26000		Joe Ozaki (Jpn)	71-70-65-73—279	8906
	C Rocca (Ita)	70-69-68-69—276	26000		DA Weibring	74-68-69-68—279	8906
	C Strange	72-68-68-68—276	26000				

Other Totals: L Clements, F Funk, A Lyle (Sco) 280; N Price (Zim), P Walton (Eng) 280; C Beck, B Crenshaw, J Gallagher jr, G Sauers, P Senior (Aus) 281; J Adams, B Claar, R Freeman, Jumbo Ozaki (Jpn), K Perry 282; M Bradley, H Irwin, T Kite, S Simpson 283; E Dougherty, P-U Johansson (Swe), S Pate, L Roberts, T Watson 284; B Lane (Eng), M Sullivan, L Wadkins 285; D Pruitt 286; D Frost (RSA); J Nicklaus 287; F Zoeller 288; B Kamm 289; C Byrum, W Defrancesco 291.

1994 US PGA Championship at Southern Hills, Tulsa, Oklahoma   (6834–70)

Prize money: $1,750,000. Entries: 151, of whom 76 made the half-way cut.

1	N Price (Zim)	67-65-70-67—269	$310000	19T	M McCumber	73-70-71-68—282	18666
2	C Pavin	70-67-69-69—275	160000		F Zoeller	69-71-72-70—282	18666
3	P Mickelson	68-71-67-70—276	110000		B Glasson	71-73-68-70—282	18666
4	N Faldo (Eng)	73-67-71-66—277	76666		C Strange	73-71-68-70—282	18666
	G Norman (Aus)	71-69-67-70—277	76666		C Parry (Aus)	70-69-70-73—282	18666
	J Cook	71-67-69-70—277	76666	25	B Lane (Eng)	70-73-68-72—283	13000
7	S Elkington (Aus)	73-70-66-69—278	57500		B Langer (Ger)	73-71-67-72—283	13000
	JM Olazábal (Esp)	72-66-70-70—278	57500		D Frost (RSA)	70-71-69-73—283	13000
9	I Woosnam (Wal)	68-72-73-66—279	41000		E Els (RSA)	68-71-69-75—283	13000
	T Kite	72-68-69-70—279	41000		J Sluman	70-72-66-75—283	13000
	T Watson	69-72-67-71—279	41000	30	B Faxon	72-73-73-66—284	8458
	L Roberts	69-72-67-71—279	41000		W Grady (Aus)	75-68-71-70—284	8458
	B Crenshaw	70-67-70-72—279	41000		B Boyd	72-71-70-71—284	8458
14	J Haas	71-66-68-75—280	32000		L Clements	74-70-69-71—284	8458
15	K Triplett	71-69-71-70—281	27000		S Torrance (Sco)	69-75-69-71—284	8458
	L Mize	72-72-67-70—281	27000		R Zokol (Can)	77-67-67-73—284	8458
	M McNulty (Zim)	72-68-70-71—281	27000	36	C Beck	72-70-72-71—285	7000
	G Day	70-69-70-72—281	27000		B McAllister	74-64-75-72—285	7000
19	C Stadler	70-70-74-68—282	18666		C Montgomerie (Sco)	67-76-70-72—285	7000

Other Totals: F Couples, B Mayfair, G Morgan, T Lehman, H Irwin 286; N Lancaster, D Edwards, D Gilford (Eng) 287; B Andrade, F Allem (RSA), B Estes, A Magee, F Nobilo (NZ), G Kraft, J Ozaki (Jpn), DA Weibring 288; D Hart, F Funk, H Sutton, T Dolby, K Perry, M Springer 289; R Floyd, T Nakajima (Jpn), R McDougal, L Wadkins, B Fleisher 290; L Janzen, JD Blake, P Stewart, J Inman, T Smith 291; D Hammond, P Senior (Aus) 292; A Lyle (Sco), D Pride 297; B Henninger, H Meshiai (Jpn) 298.

1993 US PGA Championship at Inverness, Toledo, Ohio   (6982–71)

Prize money: $1,700,000. Entries: 151, of whom 74 made the half-way cut.

1	P Azinger*	69-66-69-68—272	300000	22	G Sauers	68-74-70-69—281	14500
2	G Norman (Aus)	68-68-67-69—272	155000		F Nobilo (NZ)	69-66-74-72—281	14500
*Azinger won at second play-off hole					L Janzen	70-68-71-72—281	14500
3	N Faldo (Eng)	68-68-69-68—273	105000		I Woosnam (Wal)	70-71-68-72—281	14500
4	V Singh (Fij)	68-63-73-70—274	90000		G Twiggs	70-69-70-72—281	14500
5	T Watson	69-65-70-72—276	75000		J McGovern	71-67-69-74—281	14500
6	S Hoch	74-68-68-67—277	47812	28	P Jacobsen	71-67-76-72—282	10166
	N Henke	72-70-67-68—277	47812		B Mayfair	68-73-70-71—282	10166
	P Mickelson	67-71-69-70—277	47812		L Roberts	67-67-77-68—282	10166
	J Cook	72-66-68-71—277	47812	31	M Calcavecchia	68-70-77-68—283	7057
	S Simpson	64-70-71-72—277	47812		M McCumber	67-72-75-69—283	7057
	D Hart	66-68-71-72—277	47812		D Love III	70-72-72-69—283	7057
	B Estes	69-66-69-73—277	47812		S Ingraham	74-69-71-69—283	7057
	H Irwin	68-69-67-73—277	47812		F Zoeller	72-70-71-70—283	7057
14	B Fleisher	69-74-67-68—278	25000		N Price (Zim)	74-66-72-71—283	7057
	R Zokol (Can)	66-71-71-70—278	25000		T Wargo	71-70-71-71—283	7057
	S Elkington (Aus)	67-66-74-71—278	25000		F Allem (RSA)	70-71-70-72—283	7057
	G Hallberg	70-69-68-71—278	25000		M Hulbert	67-72-72-72—283	7057
	B Faxon	70-70-65-73—278	25000		H Sutton	69-72-70-72—283	7057
	L Wadkins	65-68-71-74—278	25000		C Parry (Aus)	70-73-68-72—283	7057
20	E Romero (Arg)	67-67-74-71—279	18500		F Couples	70-68-71-74—283	7057
	J Haas	69-68-70-72—279	18500		W Levi	69-73-66-75—283	7057

Other Totals: F Funk, DA Weibring, R Cochran, J Huston, D Forsman, P Stewart, J Ozaki (Jpn) 284; A Magee, J Daly, J Maggert, H Green, P Senior (Aus) 285; L Nelson, J M Olazábal (Esp), T Kite, R Fehr, A Lyle (Sco) 286; M Allen, J Sluman, B Crenshaw, D Hammond, M Standly 287; I Baker-Finch (Aus) 288; M Wiebe 289; B Ford, R Mediate 290; S Pate 292; K Burton, B Lane (Eng) 294; B Borowicz 295; J Adams 296.

US PGA Championship History

Year	Winner	Runner-up	Venue	By
1916	J Barnes	J Hutchison	Siwanoy	1 hole
1919	J Barnes	F McLeod	Engineers' Club	6 and 5
1920	J Hutchison	D Edgar	Flossmoor	1 hole
1921	W Hagen	J Barnes	Inwood Club	3 and 2
1922	G Sarazen	E French	Oakmont	4 and 3
1923	G Sarazen	W Hagen	Pelham	38th hole
1924	W Hagen	J Barnes	French Lick	2 holes
1925	W Hagen	W Mehlhorn	Olympic Fields	6 and 4
1926	W Hagen	L Diegel	Salisbury	4 and 3
1927	W Hagen	J Turnesa	Dallas, TX	1 hole
1928	L Diegel	A Espinosa	Five Farms	6 and 5
1929	L Diegel	J Farrell	Hill Crest	6 and 4
1930	T Armour	G Sarazen	Fresh Meadow	1 hole
1931	T Creavy	D Shute	Wannamoisett	2 and 1
1932	O Dutra	F Walsh	St Paul, MN	4 and 3
1933	G Sarazen	W Goggin	Milwaukee	5 and 4
1934	P Runyan	C Wood	Buffalo	38th hole
1935	J Revolta	T Armour	Oklahoma	5 and 4
1936	D Shute	J Thomson	Pinehurst	3 and 2
1937	D Shute	H McSpaden	Pittsburgh	37th hole
1938	P Runyan	S Snead	Shawnee	8 and 7
1939	H Picard	B Nelson	Pomonok	37th hole
1940	B Nelson	S Snead	Hershey, PA	1 hole
1941	V Ghezzie	B Nelson	Denver, CO	38th hole
1942	S Snead	J Turnesa	Atlantic City, NJ	2 and 1
1943	*No Championship*			
1944	B Hamilton	B Nelson	Spokane, WA	1 hole
1945	B Nelson	S Byrd	Dayton, OH	4 and 3
1946	B Hogan	E Oliver	Portland	6 and 4
1947	J Ferrier	C Harbert	Detroit	2 and 1
1948	B Hogan	M Turnesa	Norwood Hills	7 and 6
1949	S Snead	J Palmer	Richmond, VA	3 and 2

United States PGA Championship History *continued*

Year	Winner	Runner-up	Venue	By
1950	C Harper	H Williams	Scioto, OH	4 and 3
1951	S Snead	W Burkemo	Oakmont, PA	7 and 6
1953	W Burkemo	F Lorza	Birmingham, MI	2 and 1
1954	C Harbert	W Burkemo	St Paul, MN	4 and 3
1955	D Ford	C Middlecoff	Detroit	4 and 3
1956	J Burke	T Kroll	Boston	3 and 2
1957	L Hebert	D Finsterwald	Miami Valley, Dayton	3 and 1

Changed to stroke play

Year	Winner	Venue	Score	Year	Winner	Venue	Score
1958	D Finsterwald	Llanerch, PA	276	1981	L Nelson	Atlanta, GA	273
1959	B Rosburg	Minneapolis, MN	277	1982	R Floyd	Southern Hills, OK	272
1960	J Hebert	Firestone, Akron, OH	281	1983	H Sutton	Pacific Palisades, CA	274
1961	J Barber*	Olympia Fields, IL	277	1984	L Trevino	Shoal Creek, AL	273
1962	G Player (RSA)	Aronimink, PA	278	1985	H Green	Cherry Hills, Denver, CO	278
1963	J Nicklaus	Dallas, TX	279	1986	R Tway	Inverness, Toledo, OH	276
1964	B Nichols	Columbus, OH	271	1987	L Nelson*	PGA National, FL	287
1965	D Marr	Laurel Valley, PA	280	1988	J Sluman	Oaktree, OK	272
1966	A Geiberger	Firestone, Akron, OH	280	1989	P Stewart	Kemper Lakes, IL	276
1967	D January*	Columbine, CO	281	1990	W Grady (Aus)	Shoal Creek, AL	282
1968	J Boros	Pecan Valley, TX	281	1991	J Daly	Crooked Stick, IN	276
1969	R Floyd	Dayton, OH	276	1992	N Price (Zim)	Bellerive, MS	278
1970	D Stockton	Southern Hills, OK	279	1993	P Azinger*	Inverness, Toledo, OH	272
1971	J Nicklaus	PGA National, FL	281	1994	N Price (Zim)	Southern Hills, OK	269
1972	G Player (RSA)	Oakland Hills, MI	281	1995	S Elkington (Aus)*	Riviera, LA	267
1973	J Nicklaus	Canterbury, OH	277	1996	M Brooks*	Valhalla, Kentucky	277
1974	L Trevino	Tanglewood, NC	276	1997	D Love III	Winged Foot, NY	269
1975	J Nicklaus	Firestone, Akron, OH	276	1998	V Singh (Fij)	Sahalee, Seattle, WA	271
1976	D Stockton	Congressional, MD	281	1999	T Woods	Medinah, IL	277
1977	L Wadkins*	Pebble Beach, CA	287	2000	T Woods*	Valhalla, Louisville KY	270
1978	J Mahaffey*	Oakmont, PA	276	2001	D Toms	Atlanta Athletic Club, GA	265
1979	D Graham (Aus)*	Oakland Hills, MI	272	2002	R Beem	Hazeltine National, MN	278
1980	J Nicklaus	Oak Hill, NY	274				

First time winners a speciality at the US PGA Championship

Six of the last eight and 12 of the last 15 winners of the US PGA Championship, the fourth major of the season, have been first time winners.

They are: 1988 Jeff Sluman, 1989 Payne Stewart, 1990 Wayne Grady, 1991 John Daly, 1992 Nick Price, 1993 Paul Azinger 1995 Steve Elkington, 1996 Mark Brooks, 1997 Davis Love III, 1998 Vijay Singh, 2001 David Toms, 2002 Rich Beem.

Men's Major Title Table

Jack Nicklaus

Bobby Jones

Walter Hagen

All photographs © Phil Sheldon

	Open	US Open	Masters	US PGA	Amateur	US Amateur	Total Titles
Jack Nicklaus	3	4	6	5	0	2	20
Bobby Jones	3	4	0	0	1	5	13
Walter Hagen	4	2	0	5	0	0	11
Tiger Woods	1	2	3	2	0	3	11
John Ball	1	0	0	0	8	0	9
Ben Hogan	1	4	2	2	0	0	9
Gary Player	3	1	3	2	0	0	9
Arnold Palmer	2	1	4	0	0	1	8
Tom Watson	5	1	2	0	0	0	8
Harold Hilton	2	0	0	0	4	1	7
Gene Sarazen	1	2	1	3	0	0	7
Sam Snead	1	0	3	3	0	0	7
Harry Vardon	6	1	0	0	0	0	7
Lee Trevino	2	2	0	2	0	0	6
Nick Faldo	3	0	3	0	0	0	6

Weetabix Women's British Open Championship

2002 Weetabix Women's British Open Championship
at Ailsa Course, Turnberry, Ayrshire, Scotland   (6407–72)

Prize money: £1,000,000.   Final field of 144, of whom 66 (no amateurs) made the half-way cut.

1	Karrie Webb (Aus)	66-71-70-66—273	£154982	€249000
2	Michelle Ellis (Aus)	69-70-68-68—275	84990	136552
	Paula Marti (Esp)	69-68-69-69—275	84990	136552
4	Jeong Jang (Kor)	73-69-66-69—277	42308	67975
	Candie Kung (Tai)	65-71-71-70—277	42308	67975
	Catrin Nilsmark (Swe)	70-69-69-69—277	42308	67975
	Jennifer Rosales (Phi)	69-70-65-73—277	42308	67975
8	Beth Bauer (USA)	70-67-70-71—278	25164	40430
	Carin Koch (Swe)	68-68-68-74—278	25164	40430
	Meg Mallon (USA)	69-71-68-70—278	25164	40430
11	Sophie Gustafson (Swe)	69-73-69-68—279	19748	31728
	Se Ri Pak (Kor)	67-72-69-71—279	19748	31728
13	Natalie Gulbis (USA)	69-70-67-74—280	16581	26641
	Pat Hurst (USA)	69-70-69-72—280	16581	26641
	Angela Stanford (USA)	69-70-69-72—280	16581	26641
16	Tina Barrett (USA)	67-70-70-76—283	14348	23053
	Beth Daniel (USA)	73-68-68-74—283	14348	23053
18	Jean Bartholomew (USA)	71-72-72-69—284	12099	19439
	Wendy Doolan (Aus)	70-69-71-74—284	12099	19439
	Jane Geddes (USA)	71-69-70-74—284	12099	19439
	Marine Monnet (Fra)	71-70-70-73—284	12099	19439
	Fiona Pike (Aus)	72-73-67-72—284	12099	19439
	Rachel Teske (Aus)	67-74-68-75—284	12099	19439
24	Patricia Meunier Lebouc (Fra)	69-71-69-76—285	10249	16467
	Suzann Pettersen (Nor)	72-71-72-70—285	10249	16467
26	Dorothy Delasin (USA)	70-71-70-75—286	9366	15048
	Elisabeth Esterl (Ger)	67-71-72-76—286	9366	15048
	Emilee Klein (USA)	68-71-72-75—286	9366	15048
29	Brandie Burton (USA)	71-70-71-75—287	7949	12772
	Cristie Kerr (USA)	72-71-69-75—287	7949	12772
	Kelli Kuehne (USA)	75-67-71-74—287	7949	12772
	Yu Ping Lin (Tai)	73-69-74-71—287	7949	12772
	Iben Tinning (Den)	71-69-71-76—287	7949	12772
34	Toshimi Kimura (Jpn)	74-70-70-74—288	7249	11647
35	Kathryn Marshall (Sco)	70-71-76-72—289	6499	10442
	Catriona Matthew (Sco)	73-71-70-75—289	6499	10442
	Liselotte Neumann (Swe)	70-71-71-77—289	6499	10442
	Kelly Robbins (USA)	70-75-68-76—289	6499	10442
	Shani Waugh (Aus)	70-73-74-72—289	6499	10442
40	Helen Alfredsson (Swe)	70-75-71-74—290	5249	8434
	Lora Fairclough (Eng)	71-69-73-77—290	5249	8434
	Becky Iverson (USA)	69-76-72-73—290	5249	8434
	Karen Lunn (Aus)	73-71-72-74—290	5249	8434
	Sophie Sandolo (Ita)	71-74-68-77—290	5249	8434

45	Asa Gottmo (Swe)	72-72-72-75—291	£4399	€7069
	Mhairi McKay (Sco)	68-72-75-76—291	4399	7069
47	Heather Daly-Donofrio (USA)	70-71-77-74—292	3600	5783
	Federica Dassu (Ita)	68-72-75-77—292	3600	5783
	Tracy Hanson (USA)	70-73-75-74—292	3600	5783
	Johanna Head (Eng)	70-73-74-75—292	3600	5783
	Becky Morgan (Wal)	72-72-71-77—292	3600	5783
	Giulia Sergas (Ita)	73-67-73-79—292	3600	5783
53	Heather Bowie (USA)	78-65-73-77—293	2716	4364
	Grace Park (Kor)	73-69-71-80—293	2716	4364
	Suzanne Strudwick (Eng)	72-72-74-75—293	2716	4364
56	Raquel Carriedo (Esp)	70-72-71-81—294	2250	3615
	Karen Stupples (Eng)	73-72-72-77—294	2250	3615
	Wendy Ward (USA)	73-71-77-73—294	2250	3615
59	Betsy King (USA)	69-76-74-76—295	1950	3133
60	Vicki Goetze-Ackerman (USA)	73-72-75-76—296	1850	2972
61	Mi Hyun Kim (Kor)	68-76-75-78—297	1700	2731
	Charlotta Sörenstam (Swe)	72-72-77-76—297	1700	2731
63	Tonya Gill (USA)	72-72-74-80—298	1600	2570
64	Riikka Hakkarainen (Fin)	72-73-76-78—299	1550	2490
65	Marina Arruti (Esp)	71-72-74-84—301	1500	2410
66	Ana Larraneta (Esp)	72-72-75-83—302	1000	1607

The following 78 players missed the cut. Each professional player received £300:

67	Becky Brewerton (Wal) (am)	73-73—146		105T	Orie Fujino (Jpn)	77-73—150
	Silvia Cavalleri (Ita)	72-74—146			Trish Johnson (Eng)	78-72—150
	Cecilia Ekelundh (Swe)	73-73—146			Mikino Kubo (Jpn)	74-76—150
	Maria Hjörth (Swe)	76-70—146			Cecilie Lundgreen (Nor)	75-75—150
	Lorie Kane (Can)	74-72—146			Nancy Scranton (USA)	73-77—150
	Jung Yeon Lee (Kor)	75-71—146			Annika Sörenstam (Swe)	73-77—150
	Jill McGill (USA)	72-74—146			Kris Tschetter (USA)	77-73—150
	Janice Moodie (Sco)	72-74—146		113	Stephanie Keever (USA)	80-71—151
	Gloria Park (Kor)	74-72—146			Hiromi Kobayashi (Jpn)	75-76—151
	Nicole Stillig (Ger)	72-74—146			Michelle McGann (USA)	75-76—151
	Kimberley Williams (USA)	73-73—146			Joanne Morley (Eng)	76-75—151
78	Danielle Ammaccapane (USA)	73-74—147			Kirsty Taylor (Eng)	76-75—151
	Donna Andrews (USA)	71-76—147		118	Takayo Bando (Jpn)	77-75—152
	Stephanie Arricau (Fra)	75-72—147			Ana Belen Sanchez (Esp)	78-74—152
	Beth Bader (USA)	74-73—147			Maria Boden (Swe)	75-77—152
	Laura Diaz (USA)	69-78—147			Audra Burks (USA)	77-75—152
	Lynnette Brooky (NZ)	75-72—147			Corinne Dibnah (Aus)	74-78—152
	Wendy Dicks (Eng)	74-73—147			Kasumi Fujii (Jpn)	75-77—152
	Susan Ginter-Brooker USA)	74-73—147			Samantha Head (Eng)	78-74—152
	Kristal Parker-Manzo (USA)	73-74—147			Nina Karlsson (Swe)	74-78—152
	Cindy Schreyer (USA)	71-76—147		126	Juli Inkster (USA)	75-78—153
	Gina Scott (NZ)	75-72—147			Sandrine Mandiburu (Fra)	78-75—153
	Leslie Spalding (USA)	73-74—147			Nicola Moult (Eng)	76-77—153
	Vibeke Stensrud (Nor)	71-76—147		129	Virginie Auffret (Fra)	77-77—154
	Karen Weiss (USA)	73-74—147			Sara Eklund (Swe)	80-74—154
92	Catherine Cartwright (USA)	73-75—148			Nadina Taylor (Aus)	82-72—154
	Karine Icher (Fra)	72-76—148		132	Mia Lojdahl (Swe)	76-79—155
	Rosie Jones (USA)	75-73—148			Alison Nicholas (Eng)	78-77—155
	Laurette Maritz (RSA)	75-73—148			Emma Weeks (Eng)(am)	78-77—155
	Joanne Mills (Aus)	74-74—148		135	Denise Killeen (USA)	77-79—156
	Alison Munt (Aus)	76-72—148		136	Hilary Homeyer (USA)	76-81—157
	Sherri Steinhauer (USA)	73-75—148		137	Sarah Bennett (Eng)	77-81—158
	Mihoko Takahashi (Jpn)	76-72—148			Georgina Simpson (Eng)	78-80—158
100	Laura Davies (Eng)	74-75—149		139	Cherie Byrnes (Aus)	77-82—159
	Michelle Estill (USA)	76-73—149		140	Ashli Bunch (USA)	80-83—163
	Jackie Gallagher-Smith (USA)	75-74—149		141	Caroline Grady (Eng)	85-80—165
	Dale Reid (Sco)	71-78—149		142	Vanessa Vignali (Esp)	85-81—166
	Pearl Sinn (USA)	77-72—149		143	Permilla Sterner (Swe)	82-86—168
105	Jenna Daniels (USA)	71-79—150		144	Valerie Michaud (Fra)	77 Rtd

2001 Women's British Open Championship *at Sunningdale, Berkshire*

Prize money: £730,000   (6245–72)

1	Se Ri Pak (Kor)	71-70-70-66—277	£155000	21T Emilee Klein (USA)	71-70-71-73—285	11125
2	Mi Hyun Kim (Kor)	72-65-71-71—279	100000	Lora Fairclough (Eng)	71-70-67-77—285	11125
3	Laura Diaz (USA)	74-70-69-67—280	51813	25 Danielle Ammaccapane		
	Iben Tinning (Den)	71-69-72-68—280	51813	(USA)	75-68-74-69—286	9071
	Janice Moodie (Sco)	67-70-71-72—280	51813	Dina Ammaccapane		
	Catriona Matthew (Sco)	70-65-72-73—280	51813	(USA)	72-71-74-69—286	9071
7	Kristal Parker (USA)	72-71-71-67—281	25600	Silvia Cavalleri (Ita)	71-73-72-70—286	9071
	Marina Arruti (Esp)	71-73-70-67—281	25600	Maria Hjörth (Swe)	72-73-71-70—286	9071
	Kathryn Marshall (Sco)	75-71-68-67—281	25600	Gloria Park (Kor)	71-73-71-71—286	9071
	Kelli Kuehne (USA)	71-70-71-69—281	25600	Lee Ji Hee (Kor)	75-71-69-71—286	9071
	Kasumi Fujii (Jpn)	71-71-69-70—281	25600	Laura Davies (Eng)	68-73-69-76—286	9071
12	Raquel Carriedo (Esp)	73-70-70-69—282	17750	32 Annika Sörenstam (Swe)	70-74-74-69—287	6767
	Tracy Hanson (USA)	72-69-70-71—282	17750	Marisa Baena (Col)	72-74-72-69—287	6767
	Rosie Jones (USA)	70-69-71-72—282	17750	Suzann Pettersen (Nor)	78-64-74-71—287	6767
15	Brandie Burton (USA)	72-71-73-67—283	14400	Wendy Doolan (Aus)	72-68-75-72—287	6767
	Pearl Sinn (USA)	74-70-72-67—283	14400	Grace Park (USA)	70-71-74-72—287	6767
	Jill McGill (USA)	70-70-72-71—283	14400	Kelly Robbins (USA)	69-72-73-73—287	6767
	Karrie Webb (Aus)	74-67-68-74—283	14400	Mhairi McKay (Sco)	70-72-72-73—287	6767
19	Becky Morgan (Wal)	73-68-71-72—284	12575	Hee Won Han (Kor)	72-73-69-73—287	6767
	Trish Johnson (Eng)	70-67-72-75—284	12575	Hiromi Kobayashi (Jpn)	72-70-71-74—287	6767
21	Johanna Head (Eng)	68-70-75-72—285	11125	Rebecca Hudson (Eng)		
	Marlene Hedblom (Swe)	70-74-69-72—285	11125	(am)	71-70-70-76—287	

Other players who made the cut: Sophie Gustafson (Swe), Kellee Booth (USA), Joanne Morley (Eng), Vicki Goetze-Ackerman (USA) 288; Lorie Kane (Can), Suzanne Strudwick (Eng), Tina Barrett (USA), Cindy Schreyer (USA), Elisabeth Esterl (Ger), Riikka Hakkarainen (Fin) 289; Joanne Mills (Aus) 290; Becky Iverson (USA), Yu Ping Lin (Tai) 291; Liselotte Neumann (Swe) 292; Carin Koch (Swe), Jenny Lidback (Per), Marine Monnet (Fra), Diane Barnard (Eng) 293; Kaori Harada (Jpn), Laurette Maritz (RSA), Karin Icher (Fra), Lisa Hed (Swe) 294; Nicola Moult (Eng), Helen Alfredsson (Swe), Patricia Meunier-Lebouc (Fra) 295; Kirsty Taylor (Eng) 296; Judith Van Hagen (Ned), Claire Duffy (Eng) 297; Dorothy Delasin (USA) 298

2000 Women's British Open Championship *at Royal Birkdale*   (6285–73)

Prize money: £730,000

1	Sophie Gustafson (Swe)	70-66-71-75—282	£120000	20 Kelly Robbins (USA)	73-74-73-70—290	8475
2	Kirsty Taylor (Eng)	71-74-72-67—284	50713	Karen Weiss (USA)	73-70-75-72—290	8475
	Becky Iverson (USA)	70-70-75-69—284	50713	Rachel Hetherington		
	Liselotte Neumann (Swe)	71-73-71-69—284	50713	(Aus)	71-74-73-72—290	8475
	Meg Mallon (USA)	74-69-71-70—284	50713	Brandie Burton (USA)	72-74-71-73—290	8475
6	Laura Philo (USA)	72-73-72-68—285	27500	24 Michele Redman (USA)	74-73-73-71—291	7275
7	Karrie Webb (Aus)	68-75-72-71—286	23250	Alicia Dibos (Per)	72-73-74-72—291	7275
8	Janice Moody (Sco)	73-74-73-67—287	19500	Marine Monnet (Fra)	72-73-74-72—291	7275
	Vicki Goetze-Ackerman			Raquel Carriedo (Esp)	76-71-72-72—291	7275
	(USA)	77-69-73-68—287	19500	28 Riko Higashio (Jpn)	74-72-76-70—292	6313
10	Maggie Will (USA)	74-72-76-66—288	13250	Susan Redman (USA)	70-78-71-73—292	6313
	Michelle McGann (USA)	72-76-69-71—288	13250	Jill McGill (USA)	71-71-76-74—292	6313
	Juli Inkster (USA)	70-69-77-72—288	13250	Mhairi McKay (Sco)	74-71-71-76—292	6313
	Jenny Lidback (Per)	71-71-73-73—288	13250	32 Shani Waugh (Aus)	73-74-76-70—293	5400
	Trish Johnson (Eng)	71-72-72-73—288	13250	Michelle Estill (USA)	72-75-75-71—293	5400
	Kellee Booth (USA)	73-71-71-73—288	13250	Sofia Grönberg		
	Kathryn Marshall (Sco)	72-69-73-74—288	13250	Whitmore (Swe)	80-69-73-71—293	5400
17	Pat Bradley (USA)	74-71-74-70—289	9850	Gail Graham (Can)	79-71-71-72—293	5400
	Rosie Jones (USA)	72-72-73-72—289	9850	Betsey King (USA)	74-73-73-73—293	5400
	Annika Sörenstam (Swe)	70-76-71-72—289	9850			

Other players who made the cut: Giulia Sergas (Ita), Maria Hjörth (Swe), Tina Barrett (USA), Leigh Ann Mills (USA), Julie Forbes (Sco), Wendy Daden (Eng), Pernilla Sterner (Swe), Laura Davies (Eng) 294; Anna Berg (Swe), Yu Ping Lin (Tai), Aki Takamura (Jpn), Karen Pearce (Aus) 295; Silvia Cavalleri (Ita), Stephanie Arricau (Fra), Sara Eklund (Swe), Karen Stupples (Eng), Sandrine Mendiburu (Fra), Jenifer Feldott (USA), Helen Alfredsson (Swe), Anne-Marie Knight (Aus) 296; Federica Dassu (Ita) 297; Kristal Parker-Gregory (USA), Elizabeth Esterl (Ger) 298; Catrin Nilsmark (Swe), Smriti Mehra (Ind), Johanna Head (Eng) 299; Mardi Lunn (Aus), Mandy Adamson (RSA), Dale Reid (Sco) 300; Hiromi Kobayashi (Jpn), Lisa De Paulo (USA) 301; Hsui Feng Tseng (Chn), Nina Karlsson (Swe), Judith Van Hagen (Ned) 303; Emilee Klein (USA), Gina Marie Scott (NZ), Laurette Maritz (RSA) 304; Lora Fairclough (Eng) 306

1999 Women's British Open Championship at Woburn G&CC (6463–73)

Prize money: £575,000

1	S Steinhauer (USA)	71-71-68-73—283	£100000	17T	C Figg-Currier (USA)	69-76-72-73—290	6614
2	A Sörenstam (Swe)	69-71-72-72—284	60000		V Van		
3	H Dobson (Eng)	71-72-72-70—285	31666		Ryckeghem (Bel)	72-75-70-73—290	6614
	C Flom (USA)	71-74-69-71—285	31666		K Taylor (Eng)	73-71-72-74—290	6614
	F Pike (Aus)	70-70-71-74—285	31666	24	G Sergas (Ita) (am)	71-73-74-73—291	
6	E Klein (USA)	72-70-73-71—286	16000		J Morley (Eng)	70-75-73-73—291	5300
	S Gustafson (Swe)	73-69-72-72—286	16000		A Nicholas (Eng)	73-71-73-74—291	5300
	M Lunn (Aus)	71-72-70-73—286	16000		M Hjörth (Swe)	71-68-77-75—291	5300
	I Tinning (Den)	68-69-75-74—286	16000		S Lowe (Eng)	72-74-70-75—291	5300
	C McCurdy (USA)	73-70-68-75—286	16000		P Meunier-		
11	S Mehra (Ind)	70-70-76-71—287	11000		Lebouc (Fra)	73-70-72-76—291	5300
12	C Koch (Swe)	74-72-72-70—288	9625		M Yoneyama (Jpn)	73-70-72-76—291	5300
	S Strudwick (Eng)	71-70-76-71—288	9625	31	C Nilsmark (Swe)	72-71-76-73—292	4150
14	R Jones (USA)	73-71-73-72—289	8033		M Hirase (Jpn)	73-72-74-73—292	4150
	L Philo (USA)	69-71-75-74—289	8033		D Barnard (Eng)	73-72-74-73—292	4150
	L Neumann (Swe)	72-70-72-75—289	8033		K Marshall (Sco)	72-75-72-73—292	4150
17	D Richard (USA)	72-73-73-72—290	6614		S Cavalleri (Ita)	73-72-73-74—292	4150
	L Navarro (Esp)	70-70-77-73—290	6614		Yu Chen Huang (Tai)	71-75-72-74—292	4150
	M McNamara (Aus)	72-70-75-73—290	6614		R Hudson (Eng) (am)	72-69-75-76—292	
	T Kimura (Jpn)	69-74-74-73—290	6614				

Other players who made the cut: L Davies (Eng), T Barrett (USA), M McKay (Sco), C Dibnah (Aus), K Webb (Aus) J Head (Eng), R Higashio (Jpn) 293; C Sörenstam (Swe), J Moodie (Sco), L Hackney (Eng), J Forbes (Sco), J McGill (USA), K Orum (Den), F Dassu (Ita), A Belen Sanchez (Esp) 294; N Scranton (USA), M Baena (Col), H Kobayashi (Jpn), L Lambert (Aus), T Johnson (Eng), A Takamura (Jpn), E Poburski (Ger), M Dunn (USA), B Pestana (RSA) 297; J Mills (Aus), M Sutton (Eng), B Morgan (Wal) (am), C Schmitt (Fra) 299; P Wright (Sco), S Croce (Ita) 300; N Nijenhuis (Ned) (am), C Matthew (Sco) 301; M Hageman (Ned) 302; Le Kreutz (Fra), V Stensrud (Nor) 303

1998 Women's British Open Championship at Royal Lytham & St Annes

Prize money: £575,000   (6355–72)

1	S Steinhauer	81-72-70-69—292	£100000	20T	J Gallacher-Smith	76-74-74-79—303	6300
2	S Gustafson	78-71-74-70—293	50000		K Marshall	79-74-71-79—303	6300
	B Burton	71-74-77-71—293	50000	24	D Andrews	81-72-76-75—304	5600
4	J Moodie	75-72-72-75—294	30000		J Morley	79-74-74-77—304	5600
5	K Webb	76-76-71-73—296	25000		P Hurst	76-77-70-81—304	5600
6	L Spalding	76-70-75-76—297	17000	27	C Johnstone-Forbes	78-76-79-72—305	5100
	W Ward	76-71-74-76—297	17000		S Strudwick	75-72-75-83—305	5100
	S Mehra	73-77-71-76—297	17000	29	C Koch	79-74-76-77—306	4700
	B King	71-77-72-77—297	17000		K Saiki	80-76-73-77—306	4700
10	C Nilsmark	77-77-69-75—298	12000	31	C McCurdy	80-77-75-75—307	4216
11	T Johnson	72-77-77-73—299	9687		F Dassu	82-72-77-76—307	4216
	J Inkster	75-75-76-73—299	9687		A Nicholas	79-72-76-80—307	4216
	A Sörenstam	75-73-77-74—299	9687	34	L Fairclough	77-77-78-76—308	3300
	ML de Lorenzi	79-70-76-74—299	9687		SR Pak	78-74-79-77—308	3300
15	M McKay	75-74-75-76—300	8000		W Doolan	83-72-76-77—308	3300
16	M Murray	81-76-69-75—301	7300		L Baugh	77-80-74-77—308	3300
	D Reid	73-79-73-76—301	7300		C Dibnah	77-80-74-77—308	3300
	H Wadsworth	79-74-72-76—301	7300		H Dobson	80-71-79-78—308	3300
19	H Kobayashi	77-74-75-76—302	6800		C McMillan	76-78-76-78—308	3300
20	M Hjörth	82-73-72-76—303	6300		C Figg-Currier	78-78-74-78—308	3300
	K Tschetter	79-75-73-76—303	6300		V Odegard	82-73-74-79—308	3300

Other players who made the cut: E Klein, C Sörenstam, R Carriedo, S Lowe 309; S Dallongeville, L Philo 310; A Munt, C Hall, T Fischer 311; K Pearce, L Kane, B Whitehead, J Forbes, D Barnard 312; I Tinning, L Neumann 313; L Maritz, T Barrett, H Stacy 314; R Hakkerainen, A Berg 316; M Hirase 317; C Johnson 318; M Spencer-Devlin 319; E Knuth 321

1997 Women's British Open Championship *at Sunningdale*   (6255–72)

Prize money: £525,000

1	K Webb	65-70-63-71—269	£82500	19T	C Dibnah	72-71-70-73—286	5837
2	R Jones	70-70-66-71—277	52000		A Dibos	71-72-70-73—286	5837
3	A Sörenstam	72-70-69-67—278	36750	23	L Davies	74-73-69-71—287	5300
4	B Burton	73-69-71-67—280	27000		R Hetherington	75-70-71-71—287	5300
5	L Hackney	74-69-67-71—281	20000		K Tschetter	73-70-72-72—287	5300
	C Matthew	70-70-70-71—281	20000	26	E Klein	69-74-70-75—288	5000
7	W Doolan	74-70-68-70—282	14000	27	S Farron	72-75-75-67—289	4475
	T Barrett	70-72-70-70—282	14000		B Whitehead	71-74-77-67—289	4475
9	C Johnson	71-71-73-68—283	11500		J Morley	75-69-76-69—289	4475
10	C Sörenstam	71-70-72-71—284	10100		L Brooky	72-73-72-72—289	4475
	B King	71-72-68-73—284	10100		H Alfredsson	69-76-72-72—289	4475
12	J Lidback	71-74-70-70—285	7414		J Moodie	74-71-71-73—289	4475
	M Hirase	76-65-74-70—285	7414	33	K Lunn	74-71-75-70—290	3875
	L Neumann	68-75-71-71—285	7414		P Hurst	76-72-70-72—290	3875
	J Inkster	69-71-73-72—285	7414		S Cavalleri (am)	70-73-73-74—290	
	B Mucha	72-67-73-73—285	7414	36	S Maynor	72-74-74-71—291	3650
	H Dobson	73-69-69-74—285	7414	37	S Strudwick	72-74-74-72—292	3350
	K Marshall	70-68-73-74—285	7414		D Richard	71-72-75-74—292	3350
19	C Koch	76-71-71-68—286	5837		G Graham	73-73-71-75—292	3350
	L Lambert	70-73-73-70—286	5837				

Other players who made the cut: M Estill, S Steinhauer, K Parker-Gregory 293; P Meunier Lebouc, A Gottmo, S Prosser, A Fruhwirth, S Waugh 294; M Spencer-Devlin, H Kobayashi, F Dassu 295; T Green, A Yamaoka, T Johnson, E Esterl (Am) 296; S Croce, C Pierce, J Lee, W Dicks 297; M Koch, K Taylor, H Wadsworth, L Fairclough, L Kane, M Murray 298; C Figg-Currier 299; N Moult, D Barnard, S Gustafson 301; S Dallongeville 302.

1996 Women's British Open Championship *at Woburn G&CC* (6309–73)

Prize money: £500,000

1	E Klein	68-66-71-72—277	£80000	19T	D Reid	68-74-74-72—288	5675
2	P Hammel	71-70-72-71—284	42500		K Yamazaki	71-70-74-73—288	5675
	A Alcott	72-70-70-72—284	42500		H Alfredsson	69-76-69-74—288	5675
4	J Geddes	72-73-70-70—285	20416		J Lidback	68-73-73-74—288	5675
	L Hackney	71-69-73-72—285	20416	25	J Morley	72-71-74-72—289	4850
	A Nicholas	68-71-74-72—285	20416		K Marshall	71-72-73-73—289	4850
7	B Whitehead	76-70-71-69—286	9571		T Abitbol	70-75-70-74—289	4850
	D Richard	71-73-71-71—286	9571		T Barrett	71-74-69-75—289	4850
	ML de Lorenzi	74-72-68-72—286	9571		M Hjörth	70-70-71-78—289	4850
	P Bradley	70-75-69-72—286	9571	30	S Grönberg-Whitmore	75-73-71-71—290	4100
	C Johnson	72-69-73-72—286	9571		A Fukushima	74-74-69-73—290	4100
	R Jones	69-71-73-73—286	9571		C Sörenstam	76-70-71-73—290	4100
	T Kerdyk	70-70-72-74—286	9571		V Goetze	74-70-72-74—290	4100
14	B Mucha	73-71-74-69—287	6600		J Piers	68-73-72-77—290	4100
	D Eggeling	69-77-71-70—287	6600	35	B Daniel	77-71-71-72—291	3300
	C Nilsmark	72-76-68-71—287	6600		C Matthew	71-73-75-72—291	3300
	K Webb	69-70-74-74—287	6600		S Maynor	73-73-71-74—291	3300
	A Sörenstam	69-70-73-75—287	6600		T Fischer	72-71-74-74—291	3300
19	D Andrews	80-65-74-69—288	5675		D Pepper	71-72-72-76—291	3300
	L Davies	72-75-71-70—288	5675		W Doolan	72-74-67-78—291	3300

Other players who made the cut: H Kobayashi, T Hanson, M Hirase 292; E Knuth, K Parker-Gregory 293; M Mallon, S Strudwick, L Brooky, S Croce, E Orley, L Navarro 294; A-M Knight, P Sterner, S Redman, C Dibnah, P Rigby-Jinglov, M Figueras-Dotti, M Berteotti, C Figg-Currier 295; R Hetherington, J Crafter, B Hackett (Am) 296; R Carriedo, J Forbes, X Wunsch-Ruiz, M Estill 297; S Farwig, J Mcgill, C Hj Koch 298; N Harvey 300; K Weiss 302; M Sutton, K Harada 303.

1995 Women's British Open Championship at Woburn G&CC (6257–73)

Prize money: £360,000

1	K Webb	69-70-69-70—278	£60000	19T	A Gottmo	70-73-74-74—291	4032
2	J McGill	71-73-71-69—284	30000		B Burton	72-70-74-75—291	4032
	A Sörenstam	70-72-71-71—284	30000	23	R Hetherington	74-76-76-66—292	3710
4	M Berteotti	73-71-71-70—285	14333		J Morley	72-72-74-74—292	3710
	C Pierce	70-70-72-73—285	14333		E Orley	71-73-74-74—292	3710
	V Skinner	74-68-67-76—285	14333	26	V Michaud	76-73-75-69—293	3215
7	S Strudwick	73-68-71-74—286	9500		A Nicholas	73-72-76-72—293	3215
8	ML de Lorenzi	68-74-73-73—288	6937		S Dallongeville	76-72-72-73—293	3215
	W Doolan	73-71-70-74—288	6937		M McGuire	68-78-73-74—293	3215
	N Lopez	71-73-70-74—288	6937		T Fischer	76-66-77-74—293	3215
	L Neumann	67-74-71-76—288	6937		L Hackney	74-74-70-75—293	3215
12	K Tschetter	73-75-74-67—289	4957		L Fairclough	76-68-72-77—293	3215
	C Matthew	74-71-73-71—289	4957		M Lunn	73-67-73-80—293	3215
	V Goetze	73-72-71-73—289	4957	34	M McNamara	76-73-74-71—294	2585
	P Meunier	73-71-71-74—289	4957		T Johnson	75-74-74-71—294	2585
16	J Forbes	69-73-77-71—290	4430		Li Wen-Lin	74-71-75-74—294	2585
	S Prosser	70-74-74-72—290	4430		L West	73-75-71-75—294	2585
	H Kobayashi	72-70-74-74—290	4430		S Waugh	68-75-72-79—294	2585
19	L Brooky	69-74-76-72—291	4032		S Croce	71-71-73-79—294	2585
	K Pearce	74-71-72-74—291	4032				

Other players who made the cut: D Barnard, C Hall, T Hanson, C Hjalmarsson, P Hammel 296; L Davies, LA Mills, S Burnell, P Wright, W Dicks, E Klein, K Peterson-Parker 297; C Duffy, E Knuth 298; A Brighouse, K Orum, J Geddes 298; A Rogers, K Marshall, L Weima, C Eliasson-Wharton, S Gr-Whitmore 299; A Arruti, A Shapcott, T Barrett, K Davies 300; G Stewart, L Dermott (am) 301; S Moon, D Reid 302; J Soulsby, P Sterner 303; H Hopkins, C Evelyn Louw 304; K Stupples (am) 305; N Buxton 307.

1994 Women's British Open Championship at Woburn G&CC (6224–73)

Prize money: £335,000

1	L Neumann	71-67-70-72—280	£52500	17T	E Knuth	78-69-72-73—292	4100
2	D Mochrie	73-66-74-70—283	27250	21	P Wright	68-75-78-72—293	3740
	A Sörenstam	69-75-69-70—283	27250		K Pearce	70-74-75-74—293	3740
4	L Davies	74-66-73-71—284	14625		K Tschetter	68-76-75-74—293	3740
	C Dibnah	75-70-67-72—284	14625	24	K Cockerill	71-77-73-73—294	3425
6	C Figg-Currier	69-74-68-74—285	10750		A Alcott	74-74-75-71—294	3425
7	H Alfredsson	71-76-71-68—286	9250		B King	73-74-69-78—294	3425
8	T Hanson	74-73-66-74—287	8000		A Ritzman	69-76-75-74—294	3425
9	S Strudwick	71-71-71-75—288	6250	28	S Moon	72-78-74-71—295	2930
	V Skinner	77-71-66-74—288	6250		A Nicholas	72-73-70-80—295	2930
	C Pierce	70-75-71-72—288	6250		D Reid	76-72-75-72—295	2930
12	H Kobayashi	73-73-69-74—289	5100		M Lunn	73-75-75-72—295	2930
13	S Gautrey	69-74-72-75—290	4800		K Marshall	76-72-75-72—295	2930
14	T Abitbol	76-68-75-72—291	4526		L Fairclough	75-72-72-76—295	2930
	P Grice-Whittaker	77-72-72-70—291	4526		S Redman	74-71-76-74—295	2930
	M McGuire	71-73-78-69—291	4526	35	T Johnson	75-75-72-74—296	2480
17	S Grönberg-Whitmore	71-69-74-78—292	4100		E Orley	73-76-74-73—296	2480
	Li Wen-Lin	73-70-73-76—292	4100		K Albers	75-67-78-76—296	2480
	J Geddes	74-72-72-74—292	4100				

Other players who made the cut: LA Mills, H Person, C Hall, L Navarro, L West 297; T Barrett 298; M Figueras-Dotti, K Orum, W Doolan, T Fischer (am), J Forbes 299; ML de Lorenzi, C Hjalmarsson, I Maconi 300; X Wunsch-Ruiz, LR Sugg, K Noble 301; F Dassu, M De Boer, G Steward, F Descampe, C Nilsmark, S Prosser, M Spencer-Devlin, S Waugh, H Wadsworth, S Mendiburu, S Robinson 302; N Scranton 303; D Barnard, L Hackney, E Crosby 304; M Hageman 306; B New, M Burstrom, N Moult, M Lawrence Wengler 307; J Lawrence, S Gustafson 309.

1993 Women's British Open Championship at Woburn G&CC (6224–73)

Prize money: £300,000

1	K Lunn	71-69-68-67—275	£50000	21	J Soulsby	76-75-73-72—296	3685
2	B Burton	75-70-68-70—283	32000		C Figg-Currier	75-75-72-74—296	3685
3	K Marshall	73-71-69-73—286	21000	23	G Stewart	74-75-76-72—297	3505
4	Li Wen-Lin	70-71-74-72—287	14350		P Meunier (am)	73-76-77-71—297	
	J Geddes	76-75-72-64—287	14350		J Morley (am)	77-74-74-72—297	
6	P Sheehan	75-70-72-72—289	10500		V Michaud	79-73-70-75—297	3505
7	L Davies	69-76-75-70—290	7300	27	T Abitbol	77-74-74-73—298	3145
	ML de Lorenzi	73-77-72-68—290	7300		F Dassu	70-75-75-78—298	3145
	S Strudwick	72-71-73-74—290	7300		X Wunsch-Ruiz	73-79-71-75—298	3145
	C Nilsmark	76-71-74-69—290	7300		D Hanna	74-73-73-78—298	3145
11	A Nicholas	74-73-70-74—291	5400		K Cathrein	74-76-73-75—298	3145
12	T Johnson	72-75-77-69—293	4670		A Gottmo	77-70-74-77—298	3145
	D Reid	76-75-74-68—293	4670		N Buxton (am)	74-74-74-76—298	
	C Hjalmarsson	77-74-68-74—293	4670	34	L Neumann	74-72-80-73—299	2740
	H Alfredsson	77-71-74-71—293	4670		S Waugh	77-75-74-73—299	2740
16	S Grönberg-Whitmore	76-70-79-69—294	4180		C Hall	75-71-75-78—299	2740
	K Orum	75-72-73-74—294	4180	37	K Espinasse	77-74-74-75—300	2470
	S Gautrey	76-75-69-74—294	4180		F Descampe	75-77-74-74—300	2470
19	C Duffy	75-76-71-73—295	3880		A-C Jonasson (am)	72-74-78-76—300	
	R Hast	77-71-72-75—295	3880		L Cowan	74-77-75-74—300	2470

Other players who made the cut: C Dibnah, K Weiss, S Dallongeville (am) 301; S Moon, D Patterson, C Lambert (am) 302;
C Soules 303; L Brooky (am), V Palli 304; R Lautens, S Van Wyk, MG Estuesta, S Burnell (am), T Loveys, S Bennett 305;
M Sutton (am), H Wadsworth 306; K Leadbetter 307; D Barnard, C Sörenstam (am) 309; D Petrizzi 310; M Hageman 311

Women's British Open History

Year	Winner	Country	Venue	Score
1976	J Lee Smith	England	Fulford	299
1977	V Saunders	England	Lindrick	306
1978	J Melville	England	Foxhills	310
1979	A Sheard	South Africa	Southport and Ainsdale	301
1980	D Massey	USA	Wentworth (East)	294
1981	D Massey	USA	Northumberland	295
1982	M Figueras-Dotti	Spain	Royal Birkdale	296
1983	*Not played*			
1984	A Okamoto	Japan	Woburn	289
1985	B King	USA	Moor Park	300
1986	L Davies	England	Royal Birkdale	283
1987	A Nicholas	England	St Mellion	296
1988	C Dibnah*	Australia	Lindrick	296

* Won play-off after a tie with S Little

Year	Winner	Country	Venue	Score
1989	J Geddes	USA	Ferndown	274
1990	H Alfredsson*	Sweden	Woburn	288

* Won play-off at fourth extra hole after a tie with J Hill

Year	Winner	Country	Venue	Score
1991	P Grice-Whittaker	England	Woburn	284
1992	P Sheehan	USA	Woburn	207

Reduced to 54 holes by rain

Year	Winner	Country	Venue	Score
1993	K Lunn	Australia	Woburn	275
1994	L Neumann	Sweden	Woburn	280
1995	K Webb	Australia	Woburn	278
1996	E Klein	USA	Woburn	277
1997	K Webb	Australia	Sunningdale	269
1998	S Steinhauer	USA	Royal Lytham & St Annes	292
1999	S Steinhauer	USA	Woburn	283
2000	S Gustafson	Sweden	Royal Birkdale	282
2001	SR Pak	Korea	Sunningdale	277
2002	K Webb	Australia	Turnberry	273

US Women's Open Championship

Players are of American nationality unless stated

2002 US Women's Open Championship
at Prairie Dunes, Hutchinson, Kansas   (6293–70)

Prize Money $3,000,000. Prize Money $3 million. Entry 150, final field 69 (including 2 amateurs) on 149 or better made cut.

1	Juli Inkster	67-72-71-66—276	$535000
2	Annika Sörenstam (Swe)	70-69-69-70—278	315000
3	Shani Waugh (Aus)	67-73-71-72—283	202568
4	Raquel Carriedo (Esp)	75-71-72-66—284	141219
5	Se Ri Pak (Kor)	74-75-68-68—285	114370
6	Mhairi McKay (Sco)	70-75-71-70—286	101421
7	Beth Daniel	71-76-71-69—287	78016
	Laura Diaz	67-72-77-71—287	78016
	Kelli Kuehne	70-76-72-69—287	78016
	Janice Moodie (Sco)	71-72-71-73—287	78016
	Jennifer Rosales (Phi)	73-72-74-68—287	78016
12	Lynnette Brooky (NZ)	73-73-69-73—288	54201
	Stephanie Keever	72-71-73-72—288	54201
	Jill McGill	71-70-69-78—288	54201
	Joanne Morley (Eng)	78-68-73-69—288	54201
	Kelly Robbins	71-74-74-69—288	54201
	Rachel Teske (Aus)	75-71-72-70—288	54201
18	Donna Andrews	74-74-70-71—289	40738
	Beth Bauer	74-72-71-72—289	40738
	Lorie Kane (Can)	69-77-69-74—289	40738
	Grace Park (Kor)	71-77-71-70—289	40738
22	Danielle Ammaccapane	74-71-73-72—290	26894
	Michelle Ellis (Aus)	71-71-75-73—290	26894
	Susan Ginter-Brooker	74-72-70-74—290	26894
	Jeong Jang (Kor)	73-73-74-70—290	26894
	Rosie Jones	71-77-69-73—290	26894
	Mi Hyun Kim (Kor)	74-72-70-74—290	26894
	Meg Mallon	73-75-73-69—290	26894
	Catriona Matthew (Sco)	69-80-72-69—290	26894
	Stacy Prammanasudh	75-74-72-69—290	26894
	Michele Redman	71-69-73-77—290	26894
32	Brandie Burton	70-74-76-71—291	18730
	Laura Davies (Eng)	75-73-68-75—291	18730
	Hee-Won Han (Kor)	72-77-70-72—291	18730
	Cristie Kerr	74-71-72-74—291	18730
	Charlotta Sörenstam (Swe)	73-70-77-71—291	18730
37	Jenna Daniels	72-70-77-73—292	15209
	Wendy Doolan (Aus)	73-76-75-68—292	15209
	Jackie Gallagher-Smith	70-76-73-73—292	15209
	Carin Koch (Swe)	73-72-70-77—292	15209
	Liselotte Neumann (Swe)	72-74-70-76—292	15209
	Karen Stupples (Eng)	80-68-72-72—292	15209
	Kris Tschetter	72-77-72-71—292	15209
44	Jean Bartholomew	75-74-74-70—293	11122
	Audra Burke	70-76-77-70—293	11122

2002 US Women's Open Championship *continued*

44T	Mitzi Edge	74-75-75-69—293	11122
	Jung Yeon Lee (Kor)	71-75-75-72—293	11122
	Gloria Park (Kor)	73-74-72-74—293	11122
	Cindy Schreyer	70-74-73-76—293	11122
	Leslie Spalding	73-73-77-70—293	11122
51	Alicia Dibos (Per)	71-76-72-75—294	8673
	Vicki Goetze-Ackerman	78-70-71-75—294	8673
	Angela Jerman (am)	72-76-72-74—294	
	Ara Koh (Kor)	74-72-76-72—294	8673
	Sherri Steinhauer	70-79-71-74—294	8673
	Karen Weiss	75-73-72-74—294	8673
	Aree Song Wongluekiet (Tha) (am)	71-76-74-73—294	
58	Amy Fruhwirth	76-71-71-77—295	7884
	Kim Saiki	68-76-81-70—295	7884
	Sherri Turner	73-71-73-78—295	7884
61	Heather Bowie	75-72-74-75—296	7515
	Soo Young Moon (Kor)	75-74-77-70—296	7515
63	Patricia Meunier-Lebouc (Fra)	76-70-75-76—297	7330
64	Dawn Coe-Jones (Can)	72-72-81-73—298	7084
	Dorothy Delasin	76-73-78-71—298	7084
	Pearl Sin (Kor)	72-77-76-73—298	7084
67	Allison Finney	73-73-81-72—299	6838
68	Tracy Hanson	75-71-82-72—300	6715
69	Michele Vinieratos	72-76-76-77—301	6595

The following players missed the cut:

70	Patricia Baxter-Johnson	74-76—150	99	Anna Acker-Macosko	74-80—154	125T	Meredith Duncan (am)	78-79—157
	Moira Dunn	79-71—150		Allie Blomquist	79-75—154		Pat Hurst	79-78—157
	Karine Icher (Fra)	76-74—150		Angela Buzminski (Can)	78-76—154		Carol Semple Thompson (am)	81-76—157
	Becky Iverson	76-74—150		Maria Hjörth (Swe)	75-79—154	129	Elisaberth Esterl (Ger)	81-77—158
	Pamela Kerrigan	70-80—150		Jimin Kang	79-75—154		Tina Fischer (Ger)	78-80—158
	Betsy King	76-74—150		Kathryn Marshall (Sco)	75-79—154		Russamee Gulyanamitta (Tha)	82-76—158
	Leta Lindley	75-75—150		Michelle Murphy	74-80—154		Mayumi Nakajima (Jpn)	77-81—158
	Alison Nicholas (Eng)	72-78—150		Patty Sheehan	81-73—154		Kristin Tamulis (am)	83-75—158
	Namika Omata (Jpn)	76-74—150	107	Kristi Albers	75-80—155		Judith Vanhagen (Ned)	79-79—158
79	Annette Deluca	78-73—151		Marisa Baena (Col)	75-80—155	135	Beth Bader	77-82—159
	Yuri Fudoh (Jpn)	71-80—151		Michelle Estill	75-80—155		Mollie Fankhauser	77-82—159
	Natalie Gulbis	76-75—151		Michele Fuller	76-79—155	137	Jody Anschutz	79-81—160
	Emilee Klein	80-71—151		Tammie Green	78-77—155		Joellyn Erdmann	80-80—160
	Jenny Lidback	72-79—151		Sophie Gustafson (Swe)	79-76—155		Nancy Lopez	81-79—160
	Yu-Ping Lin (Tai)	77-74—151		Laurel Kean	73-82—155		Cindy Mueller	78-82—160
85	Kelly Cap	77-75—152		Smriti Mehra (Ind)	79-76—155		Nicole Perrot (Chi)	78-82—160
	Jeanne Cho (Kor) (am)	72-80—152		Angela Stanford	78-77—155		Tina Schneeburger (Aut)	79-81—160
	Jane Crafter (Aus)	75-77—152	116	Emily Bastel (am)	77-79—156	143	Dina Ammaccapane	81-80—161
	Eva Dahllof (Swe)	76-76—152		Heather Daly-Donofrio	79-77—156		Nancy Scranton	75-86—161
	Jennifer Feldott	74-78—152		Sue Daniels (Aus)	76-80—156	145	Tonya Gill	77-85—162
	Penny Hammel	78-74—152		Leigh Ann Hardin (am)	78-78—156	146	Catherine Cartwright	83-81—164
	Courtney Swaim (am)	73-79—152		Elizabeth Janangelo (am)	74-82—156	147	Nicole Hage (am)	82-86—168
	Karrie Webb (Aus)	79-73—152		Kristal Parker-Manzo	76-80—156	W/D	AJ Eathorne (Can)	82
93	Kate Golden	72-81—153		Julie Piers	78-78—156		Lorena Ochoa (Mex)	77
	Siew Ai Lim (Mal)	73-80—153		Wendy Ward	82-74—156		Deb Richard	82
	Leigh Ann Mills	74-79—153		Kimberley Williams	75-81—156			
	Laura Myerscough (am)	79-74—153	125	Colleen Cashman	75-82—157			
	Virada Nirapathpongporn (Tha) (am)	75-78—153						
	Fiona Pike (Aus)	77-76—153						

2001 US Women's Open Championship at Southern Pines, NC (6256–70)

Prize money: $2,700,000

1	Karrie Webb (Aus)	70-65-69-69—273	$520000	19T	Wendy Ward	70-71-74-73—288	37327
2	Se Ri Pak (Kor)	69-70-70-72—281	310000		Dorothy Delasin	75-70-70-73—288	37327
3	Dottie Pepper	74-69-70-69—282	202580	24	Beth Daniel	73-70-71-75—289	30091
4	Cristie Kerr	69-73-71-70—283	118697		Audra Burks	70-72-72-75—289	30091
	Sherri Turner	72-70-71-70—283	118697	26	Brandie Burton	73-70-77-70—290	24649
	Catriona Matthew (Sco)	72-68-70-73—283	118697		Helen Alfredsson (Swe)	71-73 74-72—290	24649
7	Lorie Kane (Can)	75-68-72-69—284	80726		Mi Hyun Kim (Kor)	68-76-72-74—290	24649
	Kristi Albers	71-69-74-70—284	80726		Janice Moodie (Sco)	71-70-73-76—290	24649
	Kelli Kuehne	70-71-72-71—284	80726	30	Kris Tschetter	72-74-77-68—291	20472
	Wendy Doolan	71-70-70-73—284	80726		Michelle Ellis	75-69-75-72—291	20472
11	Sophie Gustafson (Swe)	74-66-74-71—285	66581		Candy Hannemann (am)	73-73-72-73—291	
12	Kelly Robbins	72-68-76-70—286	57088		Meg Mallon	72-70-76-73—291	20472
	AJ Eathorne (Can)	67-71-75-73—286	57088	34	Pat Hurst	73-71-76-72—292	18408
	Juli Inkster	68-72-71-75—286	57088		Natalie Gulbis (am)	73-71-75-73—292	
	Yuri Fudoh (Jpn)	73-68-70-75—286	57088		Catrin Nilsmark (Swe)	70-76-72-74—292	18408
16	Emilee Klein	72-69-75-71—287	46885		Dina Ammaccapane	69-73-75-75—292	18408
	Michele Redman	70-72-73-72—287	46885		Karen Weiss	74-71-71-76—292	18408
	Annika Sörenstam (Swe)	70-72-73-72—287	46885	39	Marcy Newton	74-72-74-73—293	16061
19	Maria Hjörth (Swe)	70-71-77-70—288	37327		Liselotte Neumann (Swe)	70-73-76-74—293	16064
	Marisa Baena (Col)	71-72-75-70—288	37327		Rosie Jones	73-68-75-77—293	16061
	Jill McGill	68-76-72-72—288	37327		Grace Park (Kor)	76-70-69-78—293	16061

Other players who made the cut: Leta Lindley, Paula Marti (Esp), Amy Fruhwirth, Aki Nakano, Cindy Figg-Currier, Alison Nicholas (Eng) 294; Pearl Sinn (Kor) 295; Stephanie Keever (am), Christina Kim (am), Sherri Steinhauer 296; Smriti Mehra (Ind), Jean Bartholamew, Raquel Carriedo (Esp) 297; Terry-Jo Myers; Yu Ping Lin (Twn), Jamie Hullett 299, Lynnette Brooky, Lisa Strom 299

2000 US Women's Open Championship at Merit Club, Libertyville, IL

(6540–72)

Prize money: $2,700,000

1	Karrie Webb (Aus)	69-72-68-73—282	$500000	21T	Wendy Doolan (Aus)	77-69-74-75—295	34113
2	Cristie Kerr	72-71-74-70—287	240228	23	Donna Andrews	73-75-79-70—297	28404
	Meg Mallon	68-72-73-74—287	240228		Kristi Albers	71-77-73-76—297	28404
4	Rosie Jones	73-71-72-72—288	120119		Michele Redman	74-74-73-76—297	28404
	Mi Hyun Kim (Kor)	74-72-70-72—288	120119		Juli Inkster	70-74-73-80—297	28404
6	Grace Park (Kor)	74-72-73-70—289	90458	27	Charlotta Sörenstam (Swe)	75-74-76-73—298	21740
	Kelli Kuehne	71-74-73-71—289	90458		AJ Eathorne (Can)	73-77-73-75—298	21740
8	Beth Daniel	71-74-72-73—290	79345		Silvia Cavalleri (Ita)	72-73-75-78—298	21740
9	Annika Sörenstam (Swe)	73-75-73-70—291	67369		Joanne Morley (Eng)	73-72-74-79—298	21740
	Kelly Robbins	74-73-71-73—291	67369	31	Tina Barrett	72-78-75-74—299	17067
	Laura Davies (Eng)	73-71-72-75—291	67369		Danielle Ammaccapane	72-73-79-75—299	17067
12	Jennifer Rosales (Phi)	75-75-69-73—292	55355		Emilee Klein	77-72-75-75—299	17067
	Pat Hurst	73-72-72-75—292	55355		Fiona Pike (Aus)	72-74-77-76—299	17067
	Dorothy Delasin	76-68-72-76—292	55355		Kate Golden	75-72-76-76—299	17067
15	Se Ri Pak (Kor)	74-75-75-69—293	47846		Jenny Lidback (Per)	73-74-76-76—299	17067
	Kellee Booth	70-78-75-70—293	47846		Carin Koch (Swe)	75-73-73-78—299	17067
17	Janice Moodie (Sco)	73-77-75-69—294	40586		Sophie Gustafson (Swe)	72-78-71-78—299	17067
	Kathryn Marshall (Sco)	72-72-77-73—294	40586		Hiromi Kobayashi (Jpn)	77-72-70-80—299	17067
	Shani Waugh (Aus)	69-75-73-77—294	40586				
	Lorie Kane (Can)	71-74-72-77—294	40586				
21	Jackie Gallagher Smith	71-77-73-74—295	34113				

Other players who made the cut: Michelle Ellis (Aus), Valerie Skinner, Mary Beth Zimmerman, Naree Wongluekiet (am) 300; Catriona Matthew (Sco), Jill McGill 301; Leta Lindley, Nancy Scranton, Nancy Lopez, Jan Stephenson (Aus), Jae Jean Ro (am), Betsy King, Sara Sanders 302; Jean Zedlitz 304; Marisa Baena (Col), Anna Macosko 305; Hilary Homeyer (am) 306; Carri Wood 307; Barb Mucha 308; Pearl Sinn (Kor) 310; Michelle McGann 311

1999 US Women's Open Championship at Old Waverley, West Point, MS

Prize money: $1,750,000

(6421–72)

1	J Inkster	65-69-67-71—272	$315000	20T	L Lindley	72-72-73-70—287	21832
2	S Turner	69-69-68-71—277	185000		S Gustafson (Swe)	72-72-70-73—287	21832
3	K Kuehne	64-71-70-74—279	118227		D Andrews	69-71-72-75—287	21832
4	L Kane	70-64-71-75—280	82399		H Fukushima (Jpn)	69-70-71-77—287	21832
5	C Koch (Swe)	72-69-68-72—281	62938	25	K Saiki	70-71-73-74—288	16006
	M Mallon	70-70-69-72—281	62938		S Croce (Ita)	71-71-71-75—288	16006
7	K Webb (Aus)	70-70-68-74—282	53132		R Jones	71-70-72-75—288	16006
8	H Dobson (Eng)	71-70-73-69—283	45244		L Kiggens	71-67-73-77—288	16006
	M Hjörth (Swe)	73-69-70-71—283	45244		S Steinhauer	68-69-73-78—288	16006
	C Matthew (Sco)	69-68-74-72—283	45244	30	M Lunn (Aus)	72-71-74-72—289	11652
	G Park (Kor) (am)	70-67-73-73—283			J Zedlitz	75-67-75-72—289	11652
12	H Alfredsson (Swe)	72-68-70-74—284	37666		M McKay (Sco)	73-68-76-72—289	11652
	B Iverson	72-64-73-75—284	37666		N Scranton	69-72-75-73—289	11652
14	M Redman	72-71-75-67—285	32389		D Coe Jones	73-71-71-74—289	11652
	Se Ri Pak (Kor)	68-70-74-73—285	32389		A Acker Macosko	73-71-71-74—289	11652
	D Pepper	68-69-72-76—285	32389		K Robbins	70-70-74-75—289	11652
17	L Neumann (Swe)	73-71-69-73—286	27422	37	H Kobayashi (Jpn)	74-70-76-70—290	10078
	AJ Eathorne (Can)	69-71-71-75—286	27422		D Dormann	74-70-73-73—290	10078
	C Nilsmark (Swe)	69-71-70-76—286	27422		K Booth (am)	71-73-70-76—290	
20	C McCurdy	72-72-74-69—287	21832				

Other players who made the cut: M Estill, M Berteotti, K Tschetter, W Ward, M Dunn 291; P Kerrigan, S Strudwick (Eng) 292; B King, B Daniel, B Mucha, A Munt, W Doolan, V Odegard 293; M Will, R Hetherington (Aus) 294; J Lidback, L Hackney, C Figg-Currier, A Nicholas (Eng) 295; P Rizzo 296; J Feldott, P Hammel 297; K Millies 298; T Green 299

1998 US Women's Open Championship at Blackwolf Run, Wisconsin, WI

Prize money: $1,500,000

(6412–1)

1	Se Ri Pak* (Kor)	69-70-75-76—290	$267500	19T	J Lidback (Per)	71-73-79-75—298	18998
2	J Chuasiriporn (am)	72-71-75-72—290			A Fukushima (Jpn)	72-71-79-76—298	18998
	Se Ri Pak won at second extra hole after both were tied				R Jones	74-74-74-76—298	18998
	after 18 extra holes				W Ward	76-69-75-78—298	18998
3	L Neumann (Swe)	70-70-75-76—291	157500		D Andrews	70-75-75-78—298	18998
4	Dani Ammaccapane	76-71-74-71—292	77351		L Walters (Can)	76-70-74-78—298	18998
	P Hurst	69-75-75-73—292	77351	26	D Dormann	72-76-79-72—299	12972
	C Johnson	72-70-76-74—292	77351		N Scranton	76-72-78-73—299	12972
7	S Croce	74-71-76-72—293	46737		M Estill	75-74-76-74—299	12972
	T Green	73-71-76-73—293	46737		H Dobson (Eng)	71-75-77-76—299	12972
	M McKay (Sco)	72-70-73-78—293	46737		L Rinker Graham	75-71-77-76—299	12972
10	T Johnson (Eng)	73-71-77-73—294	39015	31	K Williams	68-81-79-72—300	10093
11	L Davies (Eng)	68-75-78-74—295	34929		P Hammel	71-79-77-73—300	10093
	D Pepper	71-71-78-75—295	34929		B Daniel	77-69-78-76—300	10093
13	C Koch (Swe)	72-74-77-73—296	30684		D Eggeling	71-72-79-78—300	10093
	H Alfredsson (Swe)	75-75-73-73—296	30684		K Webb (Aus)	76-73-73-78—300	10093
15	H Stacy	76-68-82-71—297	25871	36	D Coe Jones	71-74-83-73—301	8897
	A Acker Macosko	74-74-76-73—297	25871		I Blais (am)	74-73-78-76—301	
	Dina Ammaccapane	75-70-78-74—297	25871		K Tschetter	75-72-77-77—301	8897
	B Burton	74-72-77-74—297	25871		B Corrie Kuehn (am)	70-72-80-79—301	
19	L Kane (Can)	74-72-82-70—298	18998		L Spalding	69-74-78-80—301	8897

Other players who made the cut: H Wadsworth, E Klein, N Bowen, A Sörenstam, B Mucha 302; P Bradley, P Rizzo, P Sinn 304; K Albers, M Redman, M Lovander, K Booth (am), A De Luca 305; H Kobayashi 306; ML de Lorenz 307; S Lowe 308; J Stephenson, TJ Myers 309; JJ Robertson (am) 310; C Kerr 311; K Parker 314; K Baue 316

1997 US Women's Open Championship *at Pumpkin Ridge GC, Cornelius, OR*

Prize money: $1,300,000

(6365–71)

1	A Nicholas	70-66-67-71—274	$232500	21	K Kuehne	72-73-74-67—286	13800
2	N Lopez	69-68-69-69—275	137500		K Weiss	74-72-72-68—286	13800
3	K Robbins	68-69-74-66—277	86708		Se Ri Pak	68-74-75-69—286	13800
4	K Webb	73-72-65-68—278	60432		P Hurst	72-74-70-70—286	13800
5	S Croce	72-69-71-67—279	46159		L Bemvenuti	73-71-72-70—286	13800
	L Hackney	71-70-67-71—279	46159		C Pierce	71-71-73-71—286	13800
7	T Green	74-70-71-65—280	37542	27	C Matthew	76-69-70-72—287	10961
	M Redman	74-67-70-69—280	37542	28	S Smyers	71-71-75-71—288	9188
9	P Sheehan	72-71-71-68—282	28769		P Bradley	72-71-73-72—288	9188
	C Johnson	72-68-73-69—282	28769		K Marshall	72-71-73-72—288	9188
	D Coe-Jones	72-67-73-70—282	28769		B King	74-72-69-73—288	9188
	D Andrews	74-71-66-71—282	28769		J Pitcock	71-69-75-73—288	9188
	A Fukushima	71-71-69-71—282	28769	33	D Eggeling	71-74-76-70—291	7392
14	B Burton	73-72-69-70—284	21287		E Makings	72-73-75-71—291	7392
	D Pepper	72-70-72-70—284	21287		V Fergon	72-75-71-73—291	7392
	J Inkster	72-66-76-70—284	21287		M Morris	75-69-74-73—291	7392
	L Neumann	67-70-76-71—284	21287		R Jones	70-74-73-74—291	7392
	D Richard	68-70-73-73—284	21287		P Sinn	70-73-74-74—291	7392
19	T Johnson	69-74-71-71—285	17407		M McGann	73-70-73-75—291	7392
	K Williams	71-71-67-76—285	17407		C Nilsmark	76-70-69-76—291	7392

Other players who made the cut: A Dibos, J McGill 292; N Bowen, M McGeorge, M Mallon, J Lidback, E Wicoff 293; J Stephenson, H Alfredsson, L Kane 294; B Iverson, B Mucha 295; E Klein, J Gallagher-Smith, M Spencer-Devlin 296; T Hanson, S Redman, J Chuasiriporn (am) 297; D Dormann, N Harvey 298; M Edge, R Walton 299; B Corrie Kuehn (am) 302; P Dunlap 303.

1996 US Women's Open Championship

at Pine Needles Lodge & GC, Southern Pines, NC

(6207–70)

Prize money: $1,200,000

1	A Sörenstam	70-67-69-66—272	$212500	19T	B Daniel	69-78-68-72—287	14374
2	K Tschetter	70-74-68-66—278	125000		W Ward	76-68-71-72—287	14374
3	P Bradley	74-70-67-69—280	60372		M Hirase	74-69-69-75—287	14374
	J Geddes	71-69-70-70—280	60372	25	M Hattori	74-71-74-69—288	10482
	B Burton	70-70-69-71—280	60372		K Williams	69-78-69-72—288	10482
6	L Davies	74-68-70-69—281	40077		B Iverson	73-71-71-73—288	10482
7	C Nilsmark	72-73-68-69—282	35995		N Harvey	72-71-69-76—288	10482
8	C Rarick	73-70-72-68—283	29584	29	K Weiss	74-72-73-70—289	8134
	L Neumann	74-69-70-70—283	29584		S Redman	73-73-71-72—289	8134
	V Skinner	74-68-71-70—283	29584		R Jones	71-70-76-72—289	8134
	T Green	72-70-69-72—283	29584		T Kerdyk	73-72-69-75—289	8134
12	J Lidback	70-76-68-70—284	24654		E Klein	71-69-73-76—289	8134
13	A Nicholas	74-70-74-67—285	23243	34	C Pierce	72-75-73-70—290	7294
14	P Sheehan	74-71-72-69—286	19664		J Inkster	74-71-71-74—290	7294
	S Croce	72-70-74-70—286	19664	36	G Graham	72-70-76-73—291	6479
	C Schreyer	74-70-70-72—286	19664		H Kobayashi	77-71-69-74—291	6479
	M Will	71-72-70-73—286	19664		S Steinhauer	72-73-71-75—291	6479
	M Redman	70-73-69-74—286	19664		K Saiki	73-70-73-75—291	6479
19	C Johnston-Forbes	72-75-71-69—287	14374		B Mucha	74-71-70-76—291	6479
	M Mallon	77-68-72-70—287	14374		C Kerr (am)	73-73-76-69—291	
	K Webb	74-73-68-72—287	14374				

Other players who made the cut: K Albers, C Mockett, J Piers, M McGeorge, M McGann, I Shiotani, J Pitcock 292; J McGill, K Golden, T Johnson 293; Dani. Ammaccapane, C Matthew 294; S Farwig, J Stephenson, M Bell, M Baena (am) 295; K Robbins, S Turner, C Johnson 296; E Dahllof, N Foust 300.

1995 US Women's Open Championship

at The Broadmoor, Colorado Springs, CO (6398–70)

Prize money: $1,000,000

1	A Sörenstam	67-71-72-68—278	$175000	21	L Neumann	70-71-75-71—287	11154
2	M Malon	70-69-66-74—279	103500		A Okamoto	70-73-71-73—287	11154
3	B King	72-69-72-67—280	56238		A Ritzman	75-69-69-74—287	11154
	P Bradley	67-71-72-70—280	56238	24	C Hill	74-73-70-71—288	9287
5	L Lindley	70-68-74-69—281	35285		J Pitcock	72-73-72-71—288	9287
	R Jones	69-70-70-72—281	35285		L Davies	72-73-69-74—288	9287
7	T Green	68-70-75-69—282	28009		MB Zimmerman	72-72-68-76—288	9287
	D Coe-Jones	68-70-74-70—282	28009	28	A Fruhwirth	75-72-72-70—289	6841
	J Larsen	68-71-68-75—282	28009		B Burton	72-74-73-70—289	6841
10	M Morris	73-73-70-67—283	22190		N Lopez	72-73-74-70—289	6841
	P Sheehan	70-73-71-69—283	22190		M Hirase	70-74-73-72—289	6841
	V Skinner	68-72-72-71—283	22190		C Walker	69-73-75-72—289	6841
13	D Mochrie	73-70-69-72—284	18007		P Wright	72-73-71-73—289	6841
	K Tschetter	68-74-69-73—284	18007		D Miho Koyama	74-68-73-74—289	6841
	K Robbins	74-68-68-74—284	18007		J Bartholomew	67-71-77-74—289	6841
16	C Johnson	71-70-74-70—285	14454		G Graham	71-72-71-75—289	6841
	J Briles-Hinton	66-72-74-73—285	14454	37	S Strudwick	75-70-73-72—290	5218
	T Abitbol	67-72-72-74—285	14454		J Inkster	72-73-72-73—290	5218
	D Eggeling	70-68-73-74—285	14454		H Stacy	69-72-75-74—290	5218
20	M Redman	70-75-71-70—286	12449				

Other players who made the cut: H Alfredsson, J Dickinson, M McGann, A Dibos, C Hjalmarsson, J Geddes 291; K Peterson-Parker 292; L Kean, M McGeorge, P Hurst, A Nicholas 293; S Turner, J Stephenson, S Lebrun Ingram (am) 294; K Marshall, E Hayashida, V Goetze 295; K Albers, L Rinker-Graham, M Nause, K Noble, W Ward (am), K Booth (am) 296; A Alcott, E Crosby, A Benz, M Will, L Rittenhouse, M Estill, G Park (am) 297; S Rule, S Maynor, C Keggi 298; B Mucha, A Acker-Macosko 299; M Platt 303; A Munt 306.

1994 US Women's Open Championship

at Indianwood G&CC, Lake Orion, MI (6244–71)

Prize money: $850,000

1	P Sheehan	66-71-69-71—277	$155000	25	K Tschetter	71-73-72-73—289	8089
2	T Green	66-72-69-71—278	85000		D Richard	68-74-72-75—289	8089
3	L Neumann	69-72-71-69—281	47752		P Bradley	72-69-70-78—289	8089
4	T Abitbol	72-68-73-70—283	31132		P Wright	74-65-71-79—289	8089
	A Dibos	69-68-73-73—283	31132	29	K Lunn	72-72-77-69—290	7371
6	M Mallon	70-72-73-69—284	21486		V Goetze	71-73-73-73—290	7371
	H Alfredsson	63-69-76-77—285	16445	31	D Eggeling	67-73-79-72—291	6929
12	L Merten	74-68-75-69—286	12805		J Carner	69-74-75-73—291	6929
	D Mochrie	72-72-71-71—286	12805		A Read	68-72-76-75—291	6929
	L Grimes	72-73-69-72—286	12805		C Semple Thompson		
	J Dickinson	66-73-73-74—286	12805		(am)	66-75-76-74—291	
	M Estill	69-68-75-74—286	12805	35	C Walker	73-73-75-71—292	6048
	L Davies	68-68-75-75—286	12805		H Vaughn	74-70-76-72—292	6048
18	M McGann	71-70-77-69—287	10202		K Williams	72-74-72-74—292	6048
	J Inkster	75-72-69-71—287	10202		J Geddes	73-72-73-74—292	6048
	B Daniel	69-74-71-73—287	10202		D Coe-Jones	73-73-71-75—292	6048
	J Pitcock	74-72-67-74—287	10202		N Lopez	73-71-73-75—292	6048
22	S Maynor	73-70-76-69—288	9011		M McGeorge	69-73-75-75—292	6048
	L Walters	72-73-72-71—288	9011		K Monaghan	75-69-72-76—292	6048
	S Steinhauer	68-72-74-74—288	9011				

Other players who made the cut: V Fergon, M Berteotti, E Crosby, M Hirase, B Burton, S Little 293; N Bowen, A Okamoto 294; S Turner, D Dormann, E Klein (am) 295; J Stephenson, H Kobayashi, N Ramsbottom 296; C Pierce, T Fleming, A Ritzman, M Edge, S LeBrun Ingram (am) 297; T Kimura, L Kiggens 298; P Sinn, P Dunlap 300; J Sams 303; S McGuire 304

1993 US Women's Open Championship *at Crooked Stick GC, Carmel, IN*

Prize money: $800,000

(6311–72)

1	L Merten	71-71-70-68—280	$144000	17T	K Tschetter	73-71-69-75—288	9978
2	D Andrews	71-70-69-71—281	62431	21	M Mallon	73-72-69-75—289	9061
	H Alfredsson	68-70-69-74—281	62431	22	Dani Ammaccapane	73-74-73-70—290	8334
4	P Bradley	72-70-68-73—283	29249		A Finney	74-72-73-71—290	8334
	H Kobayashi	71-67-71-74—283	29249		M Redman	75-71-72-72—290	8334
6	P Sheehan	73-71-69-71—284	22379		D Coe-Jones	69-72-76-73—290	8334
7	B King	74-70-72-69—285	17525	26	L West	73-73-73-72—291	6894
	M McGann	70-66-78-71—285	17525		A Miller	73-68-78-72—291	6894
	N Lopez	70-71-70-74—285	17525		L Brower	73-73-72-73—291	6894
	A Okamoto	68-72-71-74—285	17525		J Larsen	76-71-70-74—291	6894
11	L Davies	73-71-69-73—286	13993		A Alcott	70-74-73-74—291	6894
	J Carner	71-69-73-73—286	13993		C Mah-Lyford	73-73-70-75—291	6894
13	T Barrett	73-73-70-71—287	11999		S Hamlin	74-68-73-76—291	6894
	C Johnson	71-75-69-72—287	11999		K Robbins	71-70-74-76—291	6894
	S Steinhauer	73-67-75-72—287	11999		Dina Ammaccapane	71-70-70-80—291	6894
	N Foust	71-71-71-74—287	11999		D Miho Koyama (am)	70-74-72-75—291	
17	D Mochrie	72-71-74-71—288	9978	36	J Dickinson	74-73-72-73—292	5907
	G Graham	72-73-70-73—288	9978		M Estill	74-70-75-73—292	5907
	B Mucha	75-69-71-73—288	9978		M Berteotti	72-75-70-75—292	5907

Other players who made the cut: Melissa McNamara, C Rarick, E Crosby, D Richard, J Inkster, B Burton 293; M McGeorge, P Wright, F Descampe, N Ramsbottom, L Rittenhouse 294; L Walters, J Geddes, V Goetze 295; A Read, B Daniel 296; B Bunkowsky 297; K Cathrein, J Anschutz 298; K Guadagnino, A Benz, S Ingram (am) 299; A Munt 301; L Neumann 303; J Myers 305.

US Women's Open History

Year	Winner	Runner-up	Venue	Score
1946	P Berg	B Jamieson	Spokane	5 and 4

Changed to strokeplay

Year	Winner	Venue	Score
1947	B Jamieson	Greensboro	300
1948	B Zaharias	Atlantic City	300
1949	L Suggs	Maryland	291
1950	B Zaharias	Wichita	291
1951	B Rawls	Atlanta	294
1952	L Suggs	Bala, PA	284
1953	B Rawls*	Rochester, NY	302

* Won play-off after a tie with J Pung 71-77

1954	B Zaharias	Peabody, MA	291
1955	F Crocker	Wichita	299
1956	K Cornelius*	Duluth	302

* Won play-off after a tie with B McIntire (am) 75-82

1957	B Rawls	Mamaroneck	299
1958	M Wright	Bloomfield Hills, MI	290
1959	M Wright	Pittsburgh, PA	287
1960	B Rawls	Worchester, MA	292
1961	M Wright	Springfield, NJ	293
1962	M Lindstrom	Myrtle Beach	301
1963	M Mills	Kenwood	289
1964	M Wright*	San Diego	290

* Won play-off after a tie with R Jessen, Seattle 70-72

1965	C Mann	Northfield, NJ	290
1966	S Spuzich	Hazeltine National, MN	297
1967	C Lacoste (Fra) (am)	Hot Springs, VA	294

US Women's Open Championship History *continued*

Year	Winner	Venue	Score
1968	S Berning	Moselem Springs, PA	289
1969	D Caponi	Scenic-Hills	294
1970	D Caponi	Muskogee, OK	287
1971	J Gunderson-Carner	Erie, PA	288
1972	S Berning	Mamaroneck, NY	299
1973	S Berning	Rochester, NY	290
1974	S Haynie	La Grange, IL	295
1975	S Palmer	Northfield, NJ	295
1976	J Carner*	Springfield, PA	292

* Won play-off after a tie with S Palmer 76-78

Year	Winner	Venue	Score
1977	H Stacy	Hazeltine, MN	292
1978	H Stacy	Indianapolis	299
1979	J Britz	Brooklawn, CN	284
1980	A Alcott	Richland, TN	280
1981	P Bradley	La Grange, IL	279
1982	J Alex	Del Paso, Sacramento, CA	283
1983	J Stephenson (Aus)	Broken Arrow, OK	290
1984	H Stacy	Salem, MA	290
1985	K Baker	Baltusrol, NJ	280
1986	J Geddes*	NCR	287

* Won play-off after a tie with S Little 71-73

Year	Winner	Venue	Score
1987	L Davies (Eng)*	Plainfield	285

* Won play-off after a tie with J Carner and A Okamoto – Davies 71, Okamoto 73, Carner 74

Year	Winner	Venue	Score
1988	L Neumann (Swe)	Baltimore	277
1989	B King	Indianwood, MI	278
1990	B King	Atlanta Athletic Club, GA	284
1991	M Mallon	Colonial, TX	283
1992	P Sheehan*	Oakmont, PA	280

* Won play-off after a tie with J Inkster 72-74

Year	Winner	Venue	Score
1993	L Merton	Crooked Stick	280
1994	P Sheehan	Indianwood, MI	277
1995	A Sörenstam (Swe)	The Broadmore, CO	278
1996	A Sörenstam (Swe)	Pine Needles Lodge, NC	272
1997	A Nicholas (Eng)	Pumpkin Ridge, OR	274
1998	SR Pak (Kor)*	Blackwolf Run, WI	290

* Won play-off after a tie with J Chausiriporn (am). Both shot 73 then Pak 5, 3 to 5, 4

Year	Winner	Venue	Score
1999	J Inkster	Old Waverley, West Point, MS	272
2000	K Webb (Aus)	Merit Club, Libertyville, IL	282
2001	K Webb (Aus)	Pine Needles Lodge & GC, NC	273
2002	J Inkster	Prairie Dunes, KS	276

McDonald's LPGA Championship

Players are of American nationality unless stated

2002 McDonald's LPGA Championship
at Du Pont CC, Wilmington, Delaware (6408–71)

Prize money: $1,500,000. Final field comprised 155, of whom 71 (all professionals) made the half-way cut on 150 or better.

1	Se Ri Pak (Kor)	71-70-68-70—279	225000
2	Beth Daniel	67-70-68-77—282	136987
3	Annika Sörenstam (Swe)	70-76-73-65—284	99375
4	Juli Inkster	69-75-70-71—285	69375
	Karrie Webb (Aus)	68-71-72-74—285	69375
6	Carin Koch (Swe)	68-73-73-72—286	46500
	Michele Redman	74-69-70-73—286	46500
8	Catriona Matthew (Sco)	70-73-75-70—288	37125
9	Kristi Albers	74-73-73-70—290	30625
	Michelle McGann	71-72-72-75—290	30625
	Karen Stupples (Eng)	75-70-70-75—290	30625
12	Meg Mallon	73-72-76-70—291	24650
	Kim Saiki	71-71-69-80—291	24650
	Karen Weiss	70-74-75-72—291	24650
15	Akiki Fukushima (Jpn)	71-71-76-74—292	19650
	Natalie Gulbis	72-72-75-73—292	19650
	Kelli Kuehne	71-75-74-72—292	19650
	Grace Park (Kor)	72-73-73-74—292	19650
	Rachel Teske (Aus)	72-71-77-72—292	19650
20	Laura Diaz	73-71-71-78—293	16950
	Barb Mucha	70-73-75-75—293	16950
22	Silvia Cavalleri (Ita)	72-73-73-76—294	15450
	Maria Hjörth (Swe)	78-70-75-71—294	15450
	Kelly Robbins	70-75-74-75—294	15450
25	Danielle Ammaccapane	73-76-73-73—295	12543
	Brandie Burton	74-76-74-71—295	12543
	Vicki Goetze-Ackerman	72-72-74-77—295	12543
	Tammie Green	70-78-73-74—295	12543
	Leta Lindley	72-77-71-75—295	12543
	Kathryn Marshall (Sco)	73-73-72-77—295	12543
	Gloria Park (Kor)	75-72-73-75—295	12543
	Kris Tschetter	74-75-75-71—295	12543
33	Eva Dahllof (Swe)	75-73-75-73—296	9056
	Dorothy Delasin	79-68-73-76—296	9056
	Moira Dunn	74-75-75-72—296	9056
	Michelle Ellis (Aus)	72-77-74-73—296	9056
	Lorie Kane (Can)	70-74-76-76—296	9056
	Mi Hyun Kim (Kor)	77-71-72-76—296	9056
	Charlotta Sörenstam (Swe)	75-73-74-74—296	9056
	Sherri Turner	74-73-76-73—296	9056
41	Jane Crafter (Aus)	74-75-74-74—297	6787
	Heather Daly-Donofrio	78-70-77-72—297	6787
	Tracy Hanson	76-74-72-75—297	6787
	Pat Hurst	71-75-75-76—297	6787
	Cristie Kerr	73-76-75-73—297	6787

2002 McDonald's LPGA Championship *continued*

41T	Mhairi McKay (Sco)	75-71-78-73—297	6787
47	Angela Buzminski	74-74-78-72—298	5490
	Jackie Gallagher-Smith	73-75-73-77—298	5490
	Betsy King	70-79-77-72—298	5490
	Joanne Morley (Eng)	73-74-74-77—298	5490
	Jennifer Rosales (Phi)	76-73-76-73—298	5490
52	Beth Bauer	72-74-79-74—299	4650
	Jenna Daniels	71-76-76-76—299	4650
	Michelle Estill	70-77-82-70—299	4650
	Liselotte Neumann (Swe)	75-74-78-72—299	4650
	Susie Parry	75-73-75-76—299	4650
57	Hee-Won Han (Kor)	75-70-76-79—300	4125
	Jeong Jang (Kor)	75-75-77-73—300	4125
59	Stephanie Keever	73-77-74-77—301	3825
	Angela Stanford	76-74-74-77—301	3825
61	Denise Killeen	76-74-75-77—302	3600
	Marnie McGuire (NZ)	74-75-77-76—302	3600
	Patricia Meunier-Lebouc (Fra)	76-73-75-78—302	3600
64	Emilee Klein	74-75-77-77—303	3450
65	Becky Iverson	74-74-82-74—304	3337
	Val Skinner	75-70-78-81—304	3337
67	Chris Johnson	76-73-76-80—305	3225
68	AJ Eathorne (Can)	75-74-81-77—307	3150
69	Karen Pearce (Aus)	77-73-80-78—308	3075
70	Alicia Dibos (Per)	78-72-80-79—309	2981
	Shiho Katano (Jpn)	78-72-81-78—309	2981

The following players missed the cut:

72	Dina Ammaccapane	76-75—151
	Patricia Baxter-Johnson	75-76—151
	Audra Burks	72-79—151
	Wendy Ward	76-75—151
	Kim Williams	74-77—151
77	Stefania Croce (Ita)	76-76—152
	Dawn Coe-Jones (Can)	75-77—152
	Candie Kung	75-77—152
	Jung Yeon Lee (Kor)	74-78—152
	Siew-Ai Lin (Mal)	79-73—152
	Mardi Lunn (Aus)	79-73—152
	Jill McGill	75-77—152
	Shani Waugh (Aus)	72-80—152
85	Jean Bartholomew	77-76—153
	Heather Bowie	76-77—153
	Diana D'Alessio	78-75—153
	Natascha Fink (Aut)	71-82—153
	Kate Golden	73-80—153
	Gail Graham (Can)	76-77—153
	Rosie Jones	76-77—153
	Laurel Kean	76-77—153
	Hironi Kobayashi (Jpn)	78-75—153
	Alison Nicholas (Eng)	76-77—153
	Deb Richard	73-80—153
	Laurie Rinker-Graham	78-75—153
	Leslie Spalding	75-78—153

85T	Sherri Steinhauer	77-76—153
99	Helen Alfredsson (Swe)	78-76—154
	Donna Andrews	77-77—154
	Marisa Baena (Col)	76-78—154
	Luciana Benvenuti (Bra)	77-77—154
	JoAnne Carner	82-72—154
	Amy Fruhwirth	82-72—154
	Jenny Lidback (Per)	78-76—154
	Yu Ping Lin (Tai)	75-79—154
	Cindy Schreyer	76-78—154
	Maggie Will	77-77—154
109	Beth Bader	80-75—155
	Jeanne-Marie Busuttil	76-79—155
	Tonya Gill	79-76—155
	Sophie Gustafson (Swe)	77-78—155
	Joanne Mills	79-76—155
	Namika Omata (Jpn)	76-79—155
115	Laura Davies (Eng)	76-80—156
	Penny Hammel	79-77—156
	Janice Moodie (Sco)	76-80—156
	Fiona Pike (Aus)	78-78—156
119	Ashli Bunch	80-77—157
	Cathy Johnston-Forbes	79-78—157
	Terry-Jo Myers	77-80—157

119T	Pearl Sinn (Kor)	76-81—157
	Jan Stephenson (Aus)	81-76—157
124	Tina Fischer (Ger)	82-76—158
	Pamela Kerrigan	80-78—158
126	Tina Barrett	78-81—159
	Kim Freeman	80-79—159
	Carmen Hajjar (Aus)	78-81—159
129	Dana Bates	79-81—160
	Jane Geddes	78-82—160
	Connie Masterson	78-82—160
	Patty Shehan	78-82—160
	Suzanne Strudwick (Eng)	78-82—160
134	Nancy Lopez	83-78—161
135	Sun Hee Lee (Kor)	82-80—162
	Kristal Parker-Manzo	83-79—162
137	Julie Hennessy	81-82—163
	Sally Little	80-83—163
139	DeDe Cusimano	83-81—164
140	Smriti Mehra (Ind)	84-81—165
141	Susan Kelley	85-89—174
WD	Nancy Scranton	
	Dale Eggeling	
DQ	Sally Dee	

2001 McDonald's LPGA Championship

Prize money: $1,400,000

1	Karrie Webb (Aus)	67-64-70-69—270	$225000	17T	Dottie Pepper	71-72-71-68—282	16819
2	Laura Diaz	67-71-66-68—272	139639		Kelly Robbins	69-74-71-68—282	16819
3	Maria Hjörth (Swe)	71-67-66-70—274	90577		Rachel Teske (Aus)	68-72-70-72—282	16819
	Wendy Ward	65-69-71-69—274	90577	26	Heather Daly-Donofrio	75-68-71-69—283	13162
5	Annika Sörenstam (Swe)	68-69-71-67—275	64157		Beth Daniel	71-71-70-71—283	13162
6	Laura Davies (Eng)	67-68-70-71—276	48684		Akiko Fukushima (Jpn)	66-72-73-72—283	13162
	Becky Iverson	66-73-67-70—276	48684		Nancy Scranton	73-68-70-72—283	13162
8	Mi Hyun Kim (Kor)	70-70-68-69—277	39250	30	Dawn Coe-Jones	72-69-71-72—284	11603
9	Helen Alfredsson (Swe)	68-66-74-70—278	35476		Catriona Matthew (Sco)	71-72-72-69—284	1 603
10	Michele Redman	69-66-73-71—279	30245		Grace Park (Kor)	71 72-71-70—284	11633
	Maggie Will	68-74-67-70—279	30245	33	Danielle Ammaccapane	69-71-71-74—285	10257
12	Rosie Jones	71-69-71-69—280	25013		Jane Crafter (Aus)	71-71-69-74—285	10257
	Lorie Kane (Can)	69-71-71-69—280	25013		Patricia Meunier-Lebouc		
	Liselotte Neumann (Swe)	69-72-68-71—280	25013		(Fra)	70-73-71-71—285	10257
15	Wendy Doolan (Aus)	70-71-72-68—281	21239		Sherri Turner	71-72-72-70—285	10257
	Juli Inkster	71-71-69-70—281	21239	37	Brandie Burton	69-74-68-75—286	9125
17	Pat Hurst	72-68-72-70—282	16819		Hee Won Han (Kor)	70-75-72-69—286	9125
	Carin Koch (Swe)	69-73-71-69—282	16819	39	Kathryn Marshall (Sco)	71-73-71-72—287	8011
	Leta Lindley	71-71-70-70—282	16819		Se Ri Pak (Kor)	71-73-69-74—287	8011
	Meg Mallon	71-74-67-70—282	16819		Deb Richard	72-71-73-71—287	8011
	Mhairi McKay (Sco)	68-72-70-72—282	16819		Kris Tschetter	71-74-69-73—287	8011
	Terry-Jo Myers	70-71-69-72—282	16819				

Other players who made the cut: Alicia Dibos, Vicki Goetze-Ackerman, Gloria Park (Kor), Kristal Parker 288; Suzy Green, Jenny Lidback (Per), Marnie McGuire 289; Mitzi Edge, Jackie Gallagher-Smith, Emilee Klein, Sara Sanders 290; Amy Alcott, Donna Andrews, Marisa Baena (Col), Susan Ginter, Betsy King, Charlotta Sörenstam (Swe), Leslie Spalding (Eng) 291; Dorothy Delasin, Alison Nicholas (Eng) 292; Jean Bartholomew, Gail Graham (Can), Joanne Morley (Eng) 293; Janice Moodie (Sco), Barb Mucha, Joan Pitcock 294; Annette DeLuca 296; Michelle McGann 299.

2000 McDonald's LPGA Championship

Prize money: $1,400,000

1	Juli Inkster*	72-69-65-75—281	$210000	23T	Betsy King	68-78-67-74—287	13304
	Winner after second play-off hole				Janice Moodie (Sco)	72-73-71-71—287	13304
2	Stefania Croce (Ita)	72-67-74-68—281	130330		Alison Nicholas (Eng)	72-72-71-72—287	13304
3	Se Ri Pak (Kor)	73-69-69-71—282	76319		Dottie Pepper	71-73-69-74—287	13304
	Nancy Scranton	72-70-67-73—282	76319	28	Rosie Jones	70-74-74-70—288	11191
	Wendy Ward	69-69-68-76—282	76319		Jenny Lidback (Per)	75-71-71-71—288	11191
6	Heather Bowie	74-70-70-69—283	42503		Gloria Park (Kor)	68-75-75-70—288	11191
	Jane Crafter (Aus)	72-69-69-73—283	42503		Karen Weiss	73-71-70-74—288	11191
	Laura Davies (Eng)	70-66-75-72—283	42503		Barb Whitehead	73-72-70-73—288	11191
9	Akiko Fukushima (Jpn)	71-72-71-70—284	29839	33	Beth Daniel	72-72-70-75—289	9698
	Jan Stephenson (Aus)	70-69-69-76—284	29839		Emilee Klein	74-71-71-73—289	9698
	Karrie Webb (Aus)	72-70-69-73—284	29839		Kim Saiki	77-69-71-72—289	9698
12	Amy Fruhwirth	74-71-70-70—285	21885	36	Jean Bartholomew	71-71-74-74—290	8464
	Mi Hyun Kim (Kor)	70-73-70-72—285	21885		Alicia Dibos (Per)	72-74-74-70—290	8464
	Leta Lindley	71-73-71-70—285	21885		Cindy McCurdy	73-74-71-72—290	8464
	Kelly Robbins	72-72-73-68—285	21885		Maggie Will	74-72-67-77—290	8464
	Annika Sörenstam (Swe)	70-73-70-72—285	21885	40	Sophie Gustafson		
17	Dawn Coe-Jones	71-73-72-70—286	16602		(Swe)	76-70-69-76—291	6820
	Wendy Doolan (Aus)	69-71-71-75—286	16602		Carin Koch (Swe)	74-70-73-74—291	6820
	Jane Geddes	66-74-73-73—286	16602		Barb Mucha	72-72-70-77—291	6820
	Pat Hurst	71-70-71-74—286	16602		Laura Philo	72-74-73-72—291	6820
	Meg Mallon	72-73-69-72—286	16602		Jennifer Rosales (Phi)	71-73-74-73—291	6820
	Michele Redman	70-70-70-76—286	16602		Sherri Steinhauer	70-75-68-78—291	6820
23	Pat Bradley	68-76-67-76—287	13304				

Other players who made the cut: Cindy Flom, Kathryn Marshall (Sco), Leigh Ann Mills, Patty Sheehan, Kris Tschetter, Mary Beth Zimmerman 292; Cindy Figg-Currier, Yu Ping Lin (Tre), 293; Jill McGill, Joanne Morley (Eng) 293; Marisa Baena (Col), AJ Eathorne (Can), Vicki Goetze-Ackerman, Kate Golden, Tracy Hanson, Catrin Nilsmark (Swe) 294; Ashli Bunch, Val Skinner, Leslie Spalding 295; Pamela Kerrigan, Nancy Lopez, Shani Waugh (Aus) 296; Danielle Ammaccapane, Debbi Koyama (Jpn) 298; Moira Dunn 299; Carmen Hajjar 300; Julie Piers 301; Dina Ammaccapane 305

1999 McDonald's LPGA Championship

Prize money: $1,400,000

1	J Inkster	68-66-69-65—268	$210000	22	L Kiggens	68-74-69-68—279	14063
2	L Neumann (Swe)	67-67-70-68—272	130330		A Fukushima (Jpn)	70-70-69-70—279	14063
3	M Lunn (Aus)	68-74-65-66—273	84538		V Odegard	69-70-70-70—279	14063
	N Scranton	69-68-66-70—273	84538		A Finney	67-69-71-72—279	14063
5	R Jones	64-72-68-70—274	54596	26	P Sinn	71-71-70-68—280	11087
	C Kerr	70-64-69-71—274	54596		Mi Hyun Kim (Kor)	70-70-71-69—280	11087
7	E Klein	72-68-67-68—275	35224		V Fergon	67-73-70-70—280	11087
	J McGill	70-69-68-68—275	35224		J Crafter	70-69-71-70—280	11087
	L Davies (Eng)	65-71-71-68—275	35224		L Lindley	70-72-67-71—280	11087
	Se Ri Pak (Kor)	68-69-67-71—275	35224		B Mucha	70-70-69-71—280	11087
11	M Hirase	70-73-68-65—276	23487		K Kuehne	68-67-72-73—280	11087
	S Sanders	70-68-68-70—276	23487		A Nicholas (Eng)	67-73-66-74—280	11087
	T Green	68-70-68-70—276	23487		T Johnson (Eng)	67-70-69-74—280	11087
	J Lidback	67-67-72-70—276	23487		L Kane	70-66-70-74—280	11087
	M Mallon	70-71-63-72—276	23487	36	T Tombs	71-71-69-70—281	8164
16	A Sörenstam (Swe)	73-68-68-68—277	18415		H Stacy	73-68-70-70—281	8164
	S Redman	70-68-70-69—277	18415		C Koch	68-73-70-70—281	8164
	J Stephenson	69-69-69-70—277	18415		N Bowen	70-72-68-71—281	8164
19	D Pepper	71-72-68-67—278	16301		S Waugh	70-69-71-71—281	8164
	S Steinhauer	74-69-65-70—278	16301		C Figg-Currier	71-70-67-73—281	8164
	H Kobayashi (Jpn)	70-67-71-70—278	16301				

Other players who made the cut: Dana Dormann, W Doolan, J Moodie (Sco), R Hetherington (Aus), M Spencer-Devlin 282;
C Flom, M Nause, B Iverson, M McGann, D Eggeling, S Croce (Ita), T Barrett 283; K Coats, K Tschetter, P Hammel,
C Nilsmark (Swe), K Saiki, D Richard, S Little, C Johnson, S Gustafson (Swe) 284; M Hjörth (Swe), M Will 285; P Bradley 286;
K Robbins 287; D Barnard 288; M McGeorge 289; B King, D Killeen 290; K Lunn (Aus) 299

1998 McDonald's LPGA Championship

Prize money: $1,300,000

1	Se Ri Pak	65-68-72-68—273	$195000	21T	H Dobson	76-70-70-68—284	13558
2	D Andrews	71-67-69-69—276	104666		P Hurst	71-73-68-72—284	13558
	L Hackney	70-66-69-71—276	104666		J Lidback	70-73-68-73—284	13558
4	K Webb	71-73-67-66—277	62145	25	D Dormann	71-74-74-66—285	11579
	W Ward	71-71-69-70—277	62145		M McGann	68-74-73-70—285	11579
6	M Mallon	71-69-68-70—278	39467		N Scranton	73-73-67-72—285	11579
	C Johnson	69-71-67-71—278	39467		S Redman	68-76-69-72—285	11579
	E Klein	72-67-68-71—278	39467		D Eggeling	68-69-74-74—285	11579
9	C Nilsmark	69-73-70-67—279	29110	30	W Doolan	73-72-71-70—286	9365
	K Robbins	69-71-68-71—279	29110		V Odegard	69-74-73-70—286	9365
11	J Pitcock	69-75-70-66—280	23180		A Sörenstam	73-71-71-71—286	9365
	A DeLuca	70-70-71-69—280	23180		R Hetherington	71-71-72-72—286	9365
	J Geddes	69-69-70-72—280	23180		L Kane	72-73-68-73—286	9365
14	T Green	72-68-70-71—281	19691		K Tschetter	71-71-71-73—286	9365
	L Walters	66-69-73-73—281	19691		J Morley	73-69-69-75—286	9365
16	M Hjörth	71-70-73-68—282	17402	37	S Steinhauer	73-73-71-70—287	7093
	J Inkster	70-71-69-72—282	17402		B King	71-73-72-71—287	7093
18	M Redman	70-71-74-68—283	15767		M Spencer-Devlin	74-71-70-72—287	7093
	C Koch	71-73-69-70—283	15767		L Neumann	73-69-73-72—287	7093
	C Johnston-Forbes	71-70-70-72—283	15767		M Halpin	73-73-68-73—287	7093
21	J Moodie	75-69-73-67—284	13558		M Estill	72-70-72-73—287	7093

Other players who made the cut: D Coe-Jones, S Little, N Lopez, L Davies, C McCurdy, M Figueras-Dotti, P Bradley 288;
C Figg-Currier, K Saiki, B Mucha, D Barnard, H Alfredsson 289; E Dahllof, C Sörenstam 290; C McMillan, K Albers,
K Monaghan, B Daniel, M Berteotti 291; H Stacy, M Dobek, P Hammel 292; G Graham, T Hanson 293; M McGeorge, B Burton
295; J Gallagher-Smith, M Morris 297; H Daly-Donofrio 298

1997 McDonald's LPGA Championship

Prize money: $1,200,000

1	C Johnson*	68-73-69-71—281	$180000	16T	K Saiki	68-75-69-77—289	15397
2	L Lindley	72-69-69-71—281	111711	20	A Fruhwirth	72-75-73-70—290	13586
Johnson won play-off at second extra hole					J Wyatt	73-75-71-71—290	13586
3	A Sörenstam	70-73-72-67—282	81519	22	M Lunn	72-77-75-67—291	12176
4	L Davies	67-75-74-68—284	57365		M Mallon	72-76-73-70—291	12176
	S Steinhauer	68-71-73-72—284	57365		T Barrett	69-77-75-70—291	12176
6	G Graham	69-79-71-66—285	38947	25	D Reid	74-75-73-70—292	10446
	D Coe-Jones	70-75-71-69—285	38947		W Ward	72-78-71-71—292	10446
8	T Johnson	70-73-72-71—286	31400		C Matthew	71-75-75-71—292	10446
9	K Webb	71-79-70-67—287	26871		M McGeorge	73-74-73-72—292	10446
	B Mucha	68-73-72-74—287	26871		A Dibos	71-76-73-72—292	10446
11	K Robbins	73-74-74-67—288	20047		C Figg-Currier	71-76-72-73—292	10446
	P Bradley	70-75-76-67—288	20047	31	S Strudwick	72-74-77-70—293	8423
	B Burton	71-73-76-68—288	20047		M McGann	74-76-71-72—293	8423
	D Dormann	70-73-75-70—288	20047		H Dobson	78-72-69-74—293	8423
	J Dickinson	75-72-68-73—288	20047		K Weiss	73-75-71-74—293	8423
16	W Doolan	74-72-74-69—289	15397		C Walker	72-74-73-74—293	8423
	L Kane	73-74-71-71—289	15397		N Bowen	73-72-73-75—293	8423
	D Andrews	73-71-73-72—289	15397				

Other players who made the cut: N Lopez, K Monaghan, D Richard, N Ramsbottom, D Pepper, M Edge, M Estill, K Parker-Gregory, B Whitehead 294; A Miller, K Albers, A Finney, K Marshall, J Lidback, M Morris, J Pitcock 295; B King, H Stacy, CH Koch, M Berteotti, S Redman, J Inkster 296; MB Zimmerman 297; J McGill, V Goetze-Ackerman, H Kobayashi, J Crafter, R Hetherington, K Peterson-Parker, N Scranton 298; C Mockett, H Alfredsson, Danielle Ammaccapane, J Geddes, D Killeen, A Alcott, J Gallagher-Smith, E Klein 299; M Hirase, M Spencer-Devlin, C Johnston-Forbes, A-M Palli, P Hurst 300; L Walters, V Skinner 301; Vickie Odegard 302.

1996 McDonald's LPGA Championship

Prize money: $1,200,000   Rain reduced event to 54 holes

1	L Davies	72-71-70—213	$180000	18T	S Steinhauer	74-71-74—219	13080
2	J Piers	72-72-70—214	111711		D Richard	74-70-75—219	13080
3	P Hammel	73-72-70—215	72461		A Benz	73-71-75—219	13080
	J Crafter	75-68-72—215	72461		N Lopez	70-73-76—219	13080
5	J Dickinson	71-74-71—216	37800		K Robbins	69-71-79—219	13080
	J Inkster	70-73-73—216	37800	26	J McGill	76-70-74—220	9744
	S Furlong	70-73-73—216	37800		S Redman	74-72-74—220	9744
	V Skinner	73-69-74—216	37800		D Pepper	70-76-74—220	9744
	H Kobayashi	71-70-75—216	37800		T-J Myers	74-71-75—220	9744
10	M Dobek	72-75-70—217	22342		J Geddes	71-74-75—220	9744
	P Sheehan	72-74-71—217	22342		C Pierce	75-69-76—220	9744
	M Mallon	69-75-73—217	22342		M McGeorge	74-70-76—220	9744
	K Albers	72-71-74—217	22342		B Daniel	72-72-76—220	9744
14	L Kiggens	75-70-73—218	17058	34	B Mucha	76-72-73—221	7366
	B King	72-72-74—218	17058		P Hurst	76-72-73—221	7366
	J Briles-Hinton	73-69-76—218	17058		T Johnson	75-73-73—221	7366
	A Sörenstam	69-73-76—218	17058		C Figg-Currier	73-74-74—221	7366
18	CH Koch	73-74-72—219	13080		L Grimes	74-70-77—221	7366
	K Tschetter	75-71-73—219	13080		E Dahllof	72-72-77—221	7366
	K Marshall	73-73-73—219	13080		R Hood	71-73-77—221	7366

Other players who made the cut: T Kerdyk, A Dibos, M Redman, K Monaghan, K Webb, M McGann, M Hirase, L Neumann, S Croce, T Hanson 222; D Dormann, P Bradley, G Graham, MB Zimmerman, B Whitehead, A Nicholas, M Nause 223; M Lunn, E Klein, S Maynor, S Strudwick, C Johnson 224; L West, D Andrews, B Iverson, B Burton, T Green, K Parker-Gregory 225; K Williams, R Jones, M Dunn 226; M Will, M Berteotti 227; M Morris, C Johnston-Forbes 228; A-M Palli, V Goetze 229; M Spencer-Devlin 231; M Estill 232.

1995 McDonald's LPGA Championship

Prize money: $1,200,000

1	K Robbins	66-68-72-68—274	$180000	18T	S Redman	73-71-71-71—286	13080
2	L Davies	68-68-69-70—275	111711		L Garbacz	71-71-72-72—286	13080
3	J Larsen	71-68-70-71—280	65416		K Tschetter	73-69-71-73—286	13080
	M Morris	67-71-70-72—280	65416		N Lopez	73-71-68-74—286	13080
	P Sheehan	67-68-72-73—280	65416		C Walker	70-70-72-74—286	13080
6	B Thomas	70-66-73-72—281	38947		A Finney	71-68-70-77—286	13080
	D Mochrie	67-70-71-73—281	38947	26	S Turner	73-74-70-70—287	10626
8	P Bradley	71-70-70-71—282	29890		K Guadagnino	72-73-68-74—287	10626
	T Green	69-72-70-71—282	29890		N Bowen	71-71-71-74—287	10626
10	A Sörenstam	71-71-72-69—283	25362	29	K Williams	72-71-75-70—288	9374
11	K Albers	71-71-72-70—284	20681		M Redman	75-68-72-73—288	9374
	D Eggeling	72-72-68-72—284	20681		J Geddes	71-71-71-75—288	9374
	J Pitcock	75-66-71-72—284	20681		M Estill	72-73-67-76—288	9374
	B King	69-71-72-72—284	20681	33	P Hurst	74-72-74-69—289	7970
15	L Kiggens	70-70-75-70—285	16504		K Peterson-Parker	74-73-71-71—289	7970
	M Mallon	70-72-71-72—285	16504		V Fergon	73-71-74-71—289	7970
	B Mucha	71-69-71-74—285	16504		E Gibson	73-69-74-73—289	7970
18	B Daniel	71-73-72-70—286	13080		R Jones	72-71-68-78—289	7970
	N Scranton	71-75-69-71—286	13080				

Other players who made the cut: J Carner, S Little, J Lidback, R Heiken, L Neumann, H Alfredsson, C Johnson, B Iverson, T Johnson 290; D Coe-Jones, A Nicholas, L Walters, T Kerdyk, J Inkster, M Edge, K Noble, V Skinner 291; A Ritzman, M Berteotti, J Dickinson, C Hill, J Crafter, M Figueras-Dotti 292; C Pierce, M McGeorge, C Johnston-Forbes, H Dobson, MB Zimmerman 293; D Massey, V Goetze, B Scherbak, C Mockett, A Benz 294; C Rarick 295; E Klein, T Hanson 296; J Briles-Hinton 297; E Dahllof 298; S Strudwick 299; L Tatum 300.

1994 McDonald's LPGA Championship

Prize money: $1,100,000

1	L Davies	70-72-69-68—279	$165000	17T	D Andrews	73-76-69-71—289	12257
2	A Ritzman	68-73-71-70—282	102402		B King	74-73-71-71—289	12257
3	E Crosby	76-71-69-67—283	54660		M McGeorge	75-71-70-73—289	12257
	P Bradley	73-73-70-67—283	54660		K Monaghan	72-72-72-73—289	12257
	H Kobayashi	72-73-71-67—283	54660		M Lunn	70-75-70-74—289	12257
	L Neumann	74-73-67-69—283	54660		R Walton	70-70-75-74—289	12257
7	S Steinhauer	75-70-72-68—285	27676	26	J Carner	73-75-74-68—290	9907
	A Alcott	71-75-70-69—285	27676		M McGann	70-76-75-69—290	9907
	B Daniel	72-74-68-71—285	27676	28	J Lidback	73-73-74-71—291	8460
	P Sheehan	72-68-72-73—285	27676		M Berteotti	75-70-75-71—291	8460
11	D Mochrie	68-78-70-70—286	20203		G Graham	73-71-76-71—291	8460
	M Mallon	71-71-69-75—286	20203		B Burton	76-70-73-72—291	8460
13	V Skinner	74-69-72-72—287	18266		A Okamoto	74-72-73-72—291	8460
14	J Inkster	69-76-74-69—288	16051		J Wyatt	72-74-73-72—291	8460
	D Dormann	71-76-71-70—288	16051		T Barrett	73-77-68-73—291	8460
	C Johnson	70-74-73-71—288	16051	35	D Eggeling	76-74-71-71—292	6891
17	B Mucha	73-74-75-67—289	12257		P Dunlap	71-74-75-72—292	6891
	N Bowen	73-75-73-68—289	12257		A Arruti	75-73-71-73—292	6891
	T Green	71-76-74-68—289	12257		H Alfredsson	73-74-71-74—292	6891

Other players who made the cut: J Dickinson, C Schreyer, M Spencer-Devlin, L Kiggens, K Guadagnino, L West 293; H Stacy 294; B Bunkowsky, L Merton, MB Zimmerman 295; M Morris, N Daghe, N Scranton, N Foust, K Tschetter 296; A Finney, L Walters, C Figg-Currier 297; P Sinn, K Noble, P Allen, M Estill, M Figueras-Dotti, J Anschutz 298; J Stephenson, A Benz, C Rarick 299; J Larsen, N Ramsbottom, C Johnston-Forbes, K Saiki, A Miller, C Keggi, M Edge 300; S Hamlin, N Harvey, V Goetze, M Will 301; D Coe-Jones 303; K Marshall 304; L Rinker-Graham, S Biago 305.

1993 McDonald's LPGA Championship

Prize money: $900,000

1	L Davies	66-69-73-69—277	$135000	20T	J Inkster	69-74-72-70—285	9747
2	S Steinhauer	69-72-70-67—278	83783		B Burton	74-74-66-71—285	9747
3	H Alfredsson	74-68-70-67—279	54346		J Carner	70-73-69-73—285	9747
	L Merten	68-69-72-70—279	54346	24	P Wright	75-73-70-68—286	8106
5	H Kobayashi	72-71-69-68—280	38494		R Hood	69-71-76-70—286	8106
6	P Bradley	73-70-71-67—281	25814		D Mochrie	70-71-74-71—286	8106
	MB Zimmerman	72-74-65-70—281	25814		D Lofland-Dormann	70-70-72-74—286	8106
	P Sheehan	68-73-70-70—281	25814		R Walton	74-65-72-75—286	8106
	G Graham	66-69-74-72—281	25814		A Dibos	70-71-69-76—286	8106
10	C Johnson	71-74-71-66—282	16756	30	P Sinn	72-75-70-70—287	6781
	N Lopez	73-69-70-70—282	16756		B Thomas	72-73-71-71—287	6781
	V Skinner	70-70-72-70—282	16756		L Kean	73-69-73-72—287	6781
	H Stacy	73-67-70-72—282	16756		M Berteotti	72-67-76-72—287	6781
14	B King	71-67-78-67—283	12793	34	D Coe-Jones	80-68-71-69—288	6090
	A Nicholas	73-74-67-69—283	12793		C Pierce	71-72-73-72—288	6090
	D Eggeling	70-76-68-69—283	12793	36	K Peterson-Parker	74-73-74-68—289	5411
	A Fukushima	72-69-68-74—283	12793		K Robbins	74-71-72-72—289	5411
18	J Dickinson	75-71-71-67—284	11095		L Neumann	71-75-69-74—289	5411
	T Barrett	73-72-71-68—284	11095		L Garbacz	73-69-72-75—289	5411
20	L Walters	69-73-76-67—285	9747				

Other players who made the cut: M Will, B Daniel, N Scranton, M Mallon, D Wilkins 290; N Ramsbottom, M Spencer-Devlin, J Larsen, A Alcott, M Murphy, E Crosby, E Gibson, J Crafter 291; K Albers, D Baldwin, J Briles-Hinton, M McGeorge, T Kerdyk, D Massey 292; T Green, P Rizzo, Dina Ammaccapane, J Pitcock, T-J Myers, C Figg-Currier, K Tschetter, P Dunlap, L Rinker-Graham 293; S Hamlin, Dani Ammaccapane, K Williams, S Turner 294; M Redman, J Wyatt, T Johnson 295; D Andrews, B Mucha, C Semple Thompson (am) 296; K Postlewait, L Baugh 297; T Tombs 298; N White, P Hammel 300; J Sams 303.

LPGA Championship History

The Championship was known simply as the LPGA Championship from its inauguration in 1955 until 1987. It was sponsored by Mazda from 1988 until 1993 when the sponsorship was taken over by McDonald's.

Year	Winner	Venue	Score
1955	B Hanson	Orchard Ridge	4 and 3
1956	M Hagg	Forest Lake	291
(After a tie with P Berg)			
1957	L Suggs	Churchill Valley	285
1958	M Wright	Churchill CC	288
1959	B Rawls	Churchill CC	288
1960	M Wright	French Lick	292
1961	M Wright	Stardust	287
1962	J Kimball	Stardust	282
1963	M Wright	Stardust	294
1964	M Mills	Stardust	278
1965	S Haynie	Stardust	279
1966	G Ehret	Stardust	282
1967	K Whitworth	Pleasant Valley	284
1968	S Post	Pleasant Valley	294
(After a tie with K Whitworth)			
1969	B Rawls	Concord	293
1970	S Englehorn	Pleasant Valley	285
(After a tie with K Whitworth)			
1971	K Whitworth	Pleasant Valley	288
1972	K Ahern	Pleasant Valley	293

LPGA Championship History *continued*

Year	Winner	Venue	Score
1973	M Mills	Pleasant Valley	288
1974	S Haynie	Pleasant Valley	288
1975	K Whitworth	Pine Ridge	288
1976	B Burfeindt	Pine Ridge	287
1977	C Higuchi (Jpn)	Bay Tree	279
1978	N Lopez	Kings Island	275
1979	D Caponi	Kings Island	279
1980	S Little (SA)	Kings Island	285
1981	D Caponi	Kings Island	280
1982	J Stephenson (Aus)	Kings Island	279
1983	P Sheehan	Kings Island	279
1984	P Sheehan	Kings Island	272
1985	N Lopez	Kings Island	273
1986	P Bradley	Kings Island	277
1987	J Geddes	Kings Island	275
1988	S Turner	Kings Island	281
1989	N Lopez	King's Island	274
1990	B Daniel	Bethesda	280
1991	M Mallon	Bethesda	274
1992	B King	Bethesda	267
1993	P Sheehan	Bethesda	275
1994	L Davies (Eng)	Wilmington, Delaware	275
1995	K Robbins	Wilmington, Delaware	274
1996	L Davies (Eng)	Wilmington, Delaware	213
(Reduced to 54 holes – bad weather)			
1997	C Johnson	Wilmington, Delaware	281
1998	Se Ri Pak (Kor)	Wilmington, Delaware	273
1999	J Inkster	Wilmington, Delaware	268
2000	J Inkster	Wilmington, Delaware	281
(After a tie with Stefania Croce (Ita))			
2001	K Webb (Aus)	Wilmington, Delaware	270
2002	Se Ri Pak (Kor)	Wilmington, Delaware	279

Lady golfer qualifies for US Tour event

Suzy Whaley, who hit the headlines when she became the first woman to play in the PGA Club Professionals Championship in June 2002, made history later in the year when she qualified for a place in the field for a Championship on the US Tour. She might have qualified for the Club Professionals Championship for the final major of 2002 – the US PGA Championship last June – but made herself ineligible by electing to play off tees sometimes 85–90 yards ahead of the men's tees.

Born in Cherry Hill, New Jersey she started playing golf at nine years of age at Syracuse. She played the LPGA Tour for four years in the early 90's before becoming club professional initially as an assistant in Bloomfield, Connecticut and now as head professional at Blue Fox Run in Avon, Connecticut. Her husband is general manager at the TPC at River Highlands, which hosts a US PGA Tour event – ironically the Canon Greater Hartford Open for which she qualified later in the year as a result of winning a qualifying competition.

Now she must decide whether to play against the men or not knowing that if she tees it up she will write her own chapter of golfing history.

Nabisco Dinah Shore

Players are of American nationality unless stated

2002 Nabisco Dinah Shore
at Mission Hills CC, Rancho Mirage, California (6460–72)

Prize Money $1,500,00 million. Final field comprised 103 players, of whom 74 (including three amateurs) made the half-way cut on 153 or less.

1	Annika Sörenstam (Swe)	70-71-71-68—280	$225000
2	Liselotte Neuman (Swe)	69-70-73-69—281	136987
3	Rosie Jones	72-69-72-69—282	88125
	Cristie Kerr	74-70-70-68—282	88125
5	Akiko Fukushima (Jpn)	73-76-68-66—283	56250
	Carin Koch (Swe)	73-73-71-66—283	56250
7	Karrie Webb (Aus)	75-70-67-72—284	42375
8	Lorena Ochoa (am)	75-69-71-70—285	
9	Becky Iverson	71-74-68-73—286	31050
	Lorie Kane (Can)	73-72-70-71—286	31050
	Leta Lindley	72-72-72-70—286	31050
	Se Ri Pak (Kor)	74-71-71-70—286	31050
	Grace Park (Kor)	75-73-70-68—286	31050
14	Vicki Goetze-Ackerman	74-73-68-72—287	21900
	Heather Bowie	75-71-72-69—287	21900
	Beth Daniel	71-70-75-71—287	21900
	Dorothy Delasin	72-73-69-73—287	21900
	Kris Tschetter	74-69-73-71—287	21900
19	Juli Inkster	73-76-71-68—288	18225
	Mhairi McKay (Sco)	73-72-73-70—288	18225
21	Laura Davies (Eng)	75-75-69-70—289	16350
	Wendy Doolan (Aus)	78-70-72-69—289	16350
	Mi Hyun Kim (Kor)	74-75-69-71—289	16350
	Janice Moodie (Sco)	73-73-73-70—289	16350
25	Sophie Gustafson (Swe)	77-69-71-73—290	13800
	Hee-Won Han (Kor)	74-74-73-69—290	13800
	Laurel Kean	79-71-74-66—290	13800
	Suzann Pettersen (Nor)	74-71-73-72—290	13800
	Michele Redman	75-70-72-73—290	13800
30	Laura Diaz	74-73-73-71—291	12225
	Aree Song Wongluekiet (am)	71-74-73-73—291	
32	Heather Daly-Donofrio	74-73-72-73—292	11100
	Kathryn Marshall (Sco)	75-72-73-72—292	11100
	Alison Nicholas (Eng)	76-71-70-75—292	11100
	Gloria Park (Kor)	70-76-75-71—292	11100
36	Marisa Baena (Col)	79-74-68-72—293	8524
	Maria Hjörth (Swe)	76-73-69-75—293	8524
	Pat Hurst	78-72-71-72—293	8524
	Chris Johnson	75-71-76-71—293	8524
	Betsy King	71-75-73-74—293	8524
	Kelli Kuehne	74-73-73-73—293	8524
	Meg Mallon	75-73-74-71—293	8524
	Sherri Steinhauer	73-78-70-72—293	8524
	Wendy Ward	77-74-73-69—293	8524
45	Helen Alfredsson (Swe)	74-73-72-75—294	6506
	Yuri Fudoh (Jpn)	78-75-71-70—294	6506
	Jeong Jang (Kor)	72-75-75-72—294	6506
	Yu Ping Lin (Tai)	74-74-74-72—294	6506

2001 Nabisco Dinah Shore *continued*

49	Donna Andrews	73-76-75-71—295	5812
	Barb Mucha	74-75-73-73—295	5812
51	Penny Hammel	78-70-73-75—296	5193
	Karin Icher (Fra)	77-69-78-72—296	5193
	Catriona Matthew (Sco)	74-77-71-74—296	5193
	Deb Richard	74-74-73-75—296	5193
55	Tina Barrett	76-74-75-73—298	4650
	Amy Fruhwirth	70-81-73-74—298	4650
	Jill McGill	76-73-73-76—298	4650
58	Moira Dunn	77-72-77-73—299	4200
	Kelly Robbins	77-76-71-75—299	4200
	Pearl Sinn (Kor)	75-73-74-77—299	4200
	Naree Song Wongluekiet (am)	76-73-74-76—299	
62	Brandie Burton	74-72-74-80—300	3775
	Charlotta Sörenstam (Swe)	81-70-74-75—300	3775
	Sherri Turner	76-75-77-72—300	3775
65	Dina Ammaccapane	77-75-74-75—301	3525
	Rachel Teske (Aus)	76-74-75-76—301	3525
	Karen Weiss	74-76-73-78—301	3525
68	Amy Alcott	72-75-77-78—302	3337
	Kate Golden	72-75-77-78—302	3337
70	Emilee Klein	76-77-77-73—303	3225
71	Patty Sheehan	73-76-75-81—305	3150
72	Tammie Green	78-75-76-77—306	3075
73	Meredith Duncan (am)	78-75-78-76—307	
74	Hiromi Kobayashi (Jpn)	77-76-79-80—312	3000

The following players missed the cut:

75	Danielle Ammaccapane	80-74—124	84	Michelle McGann	84-73—157
	Dale Eggeling	79-75—154	85	Nanci Bowen	76-82—158
	Jackie Gallagher-Smith	76-78—154	86	JoAnne Carner	84-75—159
	Tracy Hanson	78-76—154	87	Nancy Lopez	83-77—160
	Sally Little (RSA)	76-78—154	88	Chieko Amanuma (Jpn)	83-78—161
80	Catrin Nilsmark (Swe)	80-75—155		Mardi Lunn (Aus)	84-77—161
	Nancy Scranton	75-80—155	90	Tina Fischer (Ger)	81-81—162
82	Gail Graham	78-78—156	91	Terry-Jo Myers	84-82—166
	N Perrot (am)	76-80—156	DQ	Raquel Carriedo (Esp)	

2001 Nabisco Dinah Shore

Prize money: $1,250,000

1	Annika Sörenstam (Swe)	72-70-70-69—281	$225000		21T	Loreno Ochoa (Mex) (am)	72 71-74-73—290	
2	Karrie Webb (Aus)	73-72-70-69—284	87557		23	Becky Iverson	75-70-72-74—291	15955
	Janice Moodie (Sco)	72-72-70-70—284	87557		24	Maria Hjörth	73-72-75-72—292	14540
	Dottie Pepper	71-71-71-71—284	87557			Tammie Green	72-73-75-72—292	14540
	Akiko Fukushima (Jpn)	74-68-70-72—284	87557			Kelly Robbins	75-72-72-73—292	14540
	Rachel Teske (Aus)	72-73-66-73—284	87557			Penny Hammel	70-75-72-75—292	14540
7	Sophie Gustafson (Swe)	72-74-70-69—285	41891		28	Meg Mallon	74-71-78-70—293	12063
	Brandie Burton	74-69-72-70—285	41891			Grace Park (Kor)	75-75-72-71—293	12063
9	Laura Diaz	71-74-69-72—286	33589			Dina Ammaccapane	74-74-73-72—293	12063
	Pat Hurst	70-68-74-74—286	33589			Rosie Jones	73-73-75-72—293	12063
11	Laura Davies (Eng)	71-73-75-68—287	25957			Alison Nicholas (Eng)	71-75-75-72—293	12063
	Dorothy Delasin	73-70-74-70—287	25957			Stefania Croce (Ita)	74-72-73-74—293	12063
	Se Ri Pak (Kor)	73-69-73-72—287	25957			Emilee Klein	72-74-72-75—293	12063
	Tina Barrett	71-73-70-73—287	25957		35	Kelli Kuehne	75-70-75-74—294	10446
15	Mi Hyun Kim (Kor)	74-71-70-73—288	20736		36	Jan Crafter (Aus)	78-73-74-70—295	9124
	Carin Koch (Swe)	70-69-75-74—288	20736			Heather Bowie	77-73-74-71—295	9124
	Juli Inkster	70-75-68-75—288	20736			Charlotte Sörenstam (Swe)	78-71-75-71—295	9124
18	Liselotte Neumann (Swe)	70-74-74-71—289	18220			Nancy Scranton	72-75-75-73—295	9124
	Jeong Jang (Kor)	74-71-71-73—289	18220			Moira Dunn	78-73-70-74—295	9124
	Michele Redman	71-72-71-75—289	18220			Wendy Ward	76-73-70-76—295	9124
21	Jill McGill	75-71-70-74—290	16711					

Other players who made the cut: Amy Fruhwirth, Joanne Morley (Eng), Danielle Ammaccapane, Lorie Kane (Can) 296; Helen Alfredsson (Swe), Aree Wongluekiet (am) 297; Jenny Lidback (Per), Cindy Figg Currier, Nanci Bowen, Leta Lindley, Chris Johnson, Cathy Johnston Forbes, Donna Andrews 298; Beth Daniel, Laurie Kean, Pearl Sinn (Kor) 299; Jackie Gallagher Smith, Vickie Goetze Ackerman, Caroline McMillan, Vicki Fergon, Naree Wongluekiet (am) 300; Wendy Doolan (Aus), Nancy Lopez, Hiromi Kobayashi (Jpn) 301; Cristie Kerr, Susie Redman 302; Joan Pitcock, Catrin Nilsmark (Swe), Kellee Booth 303; Ok Hee Ku (Jpn) 305; Dawn Coe-Jones, Marine Monnet (Fra) 306; Betsy King 309

2000 Nabisco Dinah Shore

Prize money: $1,250,000

1	Karrie Webb (Aus)	67-70-67-70—274	$187500		17T	Kaori Higo (Jpn)	76-72-73-71—292	14321
2	Dottie Pepper	68-72-72-72—284	116366			Sherri Steinhauer	73-71-77-71—292	14321
3	Meg Mallon	75-70-73-67—285	84916			Charlotta Sörenstam (Swe)	75-75-70-72—292	14321
4	Cathy Johnston-Forbes	74-71-71-70—286	59755			Juli Inkster	76-71-73-72—292	14321
5	Michele Redman	73-73-69-71—286	59755			Nancy Bowen	75-72-73-72—292	14321
6	Helen Dobson (Eng)	73-74-72-68—287	40750			Carin Koch (Swe)	79-70-70-73—292	14321
	Chris Johnson	73-68-73-73—287	40750			Nancy Scranton	78-70-71-73—292	14321
8	Rosie Jones	74-71-74-69—288	31135			Barb Mucha	77-71-70-74—292	14321
	Kim Saiki	72-77-68-71—288	31135		27	Jane Geddes	74-72-78-69—293	10969
10	Jenny Lidback (Per)	75-72-74-68—289	24170			Leta Lindley	73-76-73-71—293	10969
	Wendy Doolan (Aus)	73-73-69-74—289	24170			Catriona Matthew (Sco)	72-77-73-71—293	10969
	Pat Hurst	72-72-70-75—289	24170			Alison Nicholas (Eng)	71-74-74-74—293	10969
	Aree Song Wongluekiet (am)	75-71-68-75—289			31	Susie Redman	73-75-74-72—294	9507
14	Kristi Albers	77-71-72-70—290	20845			Caroline McMillan (Eng)	73-74-74-73—294	9507
	Se Ri Pak (Kor)	73-71-77-70—291	18957			Gail Graham (Can)	71-75-75-73—294	9507
	Janice Moodie (Sco)	74-72-70-75—291	18957			Brandie Burton	74-75-71-74—294	9507
17	Kelly Robbins	79-69-73-71—292	14321					
	Annika Sörenstam (Swe)	76-72-73-71—292	14321					

Other players who made the cut: Akiko Fukushima (Jpn), Tina Barrett, Dawn Coe Jones, Laura Davies (Eng), Cristie Kerr, Fumiko Muraguchi (Jpn), Lorie Kane (Can), Beth Bauer (am) 295; Pearl Sinn (Kor), Nancy Lopez, Wendy Ward, Barb Whitehead 296; Cindy McCurdy, Becky Iverson, Mi Hyun Kim (Kor), Jill McGill, Patty Sheehan, Beth Daniel 297; Kris Tschetter, Donna Andrews, Mary Beth Zimmerman, Jan Stephenson (Aus) 298; Helen Alfredsson (Swe), Eva Dahlloff (Swe), Jackie Gallagher Smith, Catrin Nilsmark (Swe), Amy Fruhwirth 299; Mayumi Hirase (Jpn), Penny Hammel, Tammie Green, Sherri Turner, Rachel Hetherington (Aus) 300; Maggie Will, Ayako Okamoto (Jpn), Julie Piers, Kathryn Marshall (Sco) 301; Marnie McGuire (NZ) 302; Liselotte Neumann (Swe) 306; Dale Eggeling 309

1999 Nabisco Dinah Shore

Prize money: $1,000,000

1	D Pepper	70-66-67-66—269	$150000	13T	K Tschetter	68-70-73-75—286		13712
2	M Mallon	66-69-71-69—275	93093	21	M Spencer-Devlin	72-69-77-69—287		9692
3	K Webb (Aus)	73-71-70-66—280	67933		H Stacy	74-74-69-70—287		9692
4	K Robbins	69-73-67-72—281	52837		M Estill	70-76-71-70—287		9692
5	C Sörenstam (Swe)	72-68-76-66—282	42772		R Hetherington (Aus)	70-74-71-72—287		9692
6	J Inkster	72-66-71-74—283	35224		N Lopez	72-73-69-73—287		9692
7	C Matthew (Sco)	72-73-69-70—284	26502		D Eggeling	73-70-70-74—287		9692
	A Sörenstam (Swe)	70-73-71-70—284	26502		H Kobayashi (Jpn)	70-69-74-74—287		9692
	J Moodie (Sco)	69-68-75-72—284	26502		D Andrews	70-69-74-74—287		9692
10	S Steinhauer	70-72-72-71—285	19289	29	H Dobson (Eng)	74-72-74-68—288		7812
	M Hjörth (Swe)	77-68-68-72—285	19289		D Dormann	74-73-71-70—288		7812
	H Alfredsson (Swe)	69-71-73-72—285	19289		L Kane	73-74-71-70—288		7812
13	R Jones	73-70-73-70—286	13712		J Pitcock	77-68-73-70—288		7812
	M Will	72-71-73-70—286	13712	33	W Ward	74-73-72-70—289		6516
	M Redman	71-74-69-72—286	13712		A Alcott	74-71-71-73—289		6516
	P Bradley	73-69-72-72—286	13712		J Geddes	73-72-71-73—289		6516
	C McCurdy	70-74-69-73—286	13712		T Green	70-75-71-73—289		6516
	Se Ri Pak (Kor)	73-69-69-75—286	13712		B Mucha	73-75-67-74—289		6516
	M Hirase	70-72-69-75—286	13712		J Crafter	70-74-71-74—289		6516

Other players who made the cut: K Saiki, T Tombs, N Bowen, G Park (am) 290; K Marshall (Sco), E Klein, M Nause, P Hurst, B Daniel 291; G Graham, T Johnson, C Figg-Currier 292; T Barrett, C Johnson, M McGeorge, D Coe-Jones, K Albers, S Turner, A Nicholas (Eng) 293; L Neumann (Swe), M McGann, T Hanson, M Hattori 294; C Johnston-Forbes, P Sinn, L Kiggens 295; V Fergon, Dina Ammaccapane 296; D Richard, J Piers, J Chuasiriporn (am) 297; E Crosby, C Flom, L Davies (Eng) 298; P Sheehan, TJ Myers, Dani Ammaccapane, K Harada 299; B King 300; B Iverson 301; V Skinner, S Gustafson 302

1998 Nabisco Dinah Shore

Prize money: $1,000,000

1	P Hurst	68-72-70-71—281	$150000	18T	M Spencer-Devlin	72-70-76-73—291	12147
2	H Dobson	70-74-71-67—282	93093		L Hackney	71-71-73-76—291	12147
3	L Davies	75-70-70-68—283	60385	23	G Park (am)	77-73-71-71—292	
	H Alfredsson	70-73-70-70—283	60385	24	E Klein	76-74-73-70—293	9256
5	D Andrews	71-72-71-70—284	38998		J Inkster	74-75-74-70—293	9256
	L Neumann	69-71-71-73—284	38998		C Figg-Currier	74-72-77-70—293	9256
7	A Sörenstam	76-71-69-70—286	27928		B Iverson	74-72-77-70—293	9256
	K Webb	71-72-70-73—286	27928		B Mucha	72-75-74-72—293	9256
9	D Pepper	73-72-74-68—287	22393		T Green	72-72-76-73—293	9256
	S Steinhauer	69-76-71-71—287	22393		Dani Ammaccapane	75-73-71-74—293	9256
11	A Fruhwirth	73-71-73-71—288	18438		M McGann	74-71-72-76—293	9256
	D Coe-Jones	70-72-74-72—288	18438		M Hirase	73-69-73-78—293	9256
13	C Matthew	75-74-70-70—289	15670	33	H Kobayashi	77-71-77-69—294	6964
	P Hammel	73-72-71-73—289	15670		T Barrett	76-73-74-71—294	6964
	N Lopez	71-71-73-74—289	15670		M Halpin	72-77-74-71—294	6964
16	M Mallon	75-69-76-70—290	13658		G Graham	71-75-74-74—294	6964
	B Bauer (am)	76-70-72-72—290			A Nicholas	75-70-75-74—294	6964
18	L Kane	76-71-74-70—291	12147		J Geddes	73-75-71-75—294	6964
	R Jones	75-66-78-72—291	12147		D Dormann	73-74-72-75—294	6964
	J Carner	73-72-73-73—291	12147				

Other players who made the cut: A Alcott, J Stephenson 295; C McCurdy, K Saiki, J Crafter, P Sheehan, M Redman, J Pitcock, P Bradley, K Robbins 296; V Fergon, D Richard, D Eggeling, J Piers, B Burton 297; J Lidback, MB Zimmerman, K Marshall, L Walters 298; T Tombs, R Hetherington 299; C Rarick, B King, K Weiss 300; V Skinner 301; S Redman, P Rizzo, N Bowen 302; S Hamlin, T Johnson 303; M Morris 304; L Kiggens 305; B Daniel 306

1997 Nabisco Dinah Shore

Prize money: $900,000

1	B King	71-67-67-71—276	$135000	16T	L Davies	70-70-74-72—286	10898
2	K Tschetter	66-76-66-70—278	83783		K Marshall	66-73-73-74—286	10898
3	A Fruhwirth	69-70-68-72—279	54346	23	C Schreyer	72-74-73-68—287	8690
	K Robbins	70-67-68-74—279	54346		M Baena (am)	74-71-73-69—287	
5	N Bowen	70-74-70-68—282	35097		P Hammel	76-72-67-72—287	8690
	L Hackney	70-72-72-68—282	35097		T Johnson	70-72-73-72—287	8690
7	T Barrett	70-71-70-72—283	26720		N Lopez	70-74-69-74—287	8690
8	MB Zimmerman	75-74-72-63—284	21285	28	B Mucha	71-72-73-72—288	8000
	H Kobayashi	72-69-71-72—284	21285	29	K Webb	69-74-71-75—289	7728
	A Sörenstam	70-72-68-74—284	21285	30	M Hirase	70-77-72-71—290	6940
11	M Morris	71-75-72-67—285	15065		M Estill	72-73-73-72—290	6940
	D Andrews	73-71-72-69—285	15065		D Coe-Jones	73-72-72-73—290	6940
	J Geddes	68-75-72-70—285	15065		D Richard	68-75-74-73—290	6940
	J Crafter	70-71-72-72—285	15065		D Eggeling	68-72-75-75—290	6940
	D Pepper	69-70-71-75—285	15065	35	J Briles-Hinton	72-76-74-69—291	5668
16	T Green	72-73-71-70—286	10898		C Johnson	75-72-72-72—291	5668
	J Inkster	72-74-69-71—286	10898		E Klein	73-74-71-73—291	5668
	M McGann	74-70-71-71—286	10898		A-M Palli	73-74-70-74—291	5668
	L Neumann	74-71-69-72—286	10898		H Stacy	72-73-72-74—291	5668
	P Hurst	74-69-71-72—286	10898		P Bradley	69-72-73-77—291	5668

Other players who made the cut: A Nicholas, C Walker 292; V Skinner, J Lidback, C Rarick, B Iverson, L Walters 293; S Turner, B Burton, S Steinhauer, K Harada, J Pitcock, V Goetze-Ackerman 294; J Piers, R Hood, H Alfredsson 295; T Hanson, A Finney, A Alcott, K Monaghan 296; N Ramsbottom, R Walton 298; P Sheehan 299; A Okamoto 300; M Spencer-Devlin 301; A Ritzman, TJ Myers 302; B Bunkowsky-Scherbak, A Fukushima, L Kiggens 303; V Fergon, B Whitehead 304; T Kerdyk, A Benz 305.

1996 Nabisco Dinah Shore

Prize money: $900,000

1	P Sheehan	71-72-67-71—281	$135000	19T	T Kerdyk	67-72-77-72—288	10189
2	K Robbins	71-72-71-68—282	64158		J Inkster	70-70-74-74—288	10189
	M Mallon	71-70-71-70—282	64158	23	P Bradley	73-76-71-69—289	8111
	A Sörenstam	67-72-73-70—282	64158		J Geddes	74-72-74-69—289	8111
5	A Fruhwirth	71-73-68-71—283	32305		D Andrews	74-70-76-69—289	8111
	K Webb	72-70-70-71—283	32305		A Fukushima	74-68-78-69—289	8111
	B Burton	75-67-68-73—283	32305		A Alcott	68-78-71-72—289	8111
8	H Stacy	69-71-74-70—284	23550		P Hammel	75-69-73-72—289	8111
9	K Tschetter	71-74-70-70—285	21285		D Pepper	71-71-75-72—289	8111
10	D Richard	73-71-73-69—286	16212		N Bowen	76-70-70-73—289	8111
	L Neumann	73-69-75-69—286	16212	31	B Iverson	76-71-73-70—290	6544
	V Skinner	74-71-71-70—286	16212		S Redman	73-75-71-71—290	6544
	R Jones	72-67-75-72—286	16212		A Nicholas	75-72-72-71—290	6544
	T Hanson	69-69-74-74—286	16212		H Kobayashi	72-74-72-72—290	6544
15	N Lopez	73-72-73-69—287	12114	35	C Pierce	72-71-75-73—291	5411
	M McGeorge	74-70-74-69—287	12114		T Johnson	74-72-71-74—291	5411
	J Pitcock	71-74-71-71—287	12114		D Coe-Jones	72-73-72-74—291	5411
	L Davies	72-70-70-75—287	12114		P Sinn	73-73-70-75—291	5411
19	M Morris	76-71-71-70—288	10189		C Schreyer	72-71-73-75—291	5411
	S Farwig	71-73-73-71—288	10189		S Little	69-73-71-78—291	5411

Other players who made the cut: C Johnston-Forbes, K Parker-Gregory, N Ramsbottom, R Walton, B Mucha, G Graham, M Nause 292; J Piers, H Alfredsson, A Okamoto, T Barrett, J Wyatt, S Furlong 293; I Shiotani, L Lindley, V Fergon, M Redman 294; C Walker, K Marshall, M Estill, K Albers 295; J Dickinson, M McGann, MB Zimmerman, Dani Ammaccapane, A Ritzman 296; K Shipman, L Rinker-Graham 297; J Crafter 298; A Dibos, A Finney, S Strudwick, P Wright 299; A Benz, K Guadagnino, 301; S Palmer, E Klein 302; J Stephenson 303; J Carner, C Mackey 305.

1995 Nabisco Dinah Shore

Prize money: $850,000

1	N Bowen	69-75-71-70—285	$127500	16T	P Bradley	74-75-71-72—292	10056
2	S Redman	75-70-70-71—286	79129		J Inkster	76-70-73-73—292	10056
3	B Burton	76-71-71-69—287	42237		T-J Myers	77-68-73-74—292	10056
	S Turner	72-74-71-70—287	42237		M Estill	72-72-74-74—292	10056
	L Davies	75-69-70-73—287	42237		M Mallon	74-72-71-75—292	10056
	N Lopez	74-71-68-74—287	42237	24	A Sörenstam	76-74-74-69—293	8040
7	C Walker	74-73-69-72—288	23738		M Spencer-Devlin	69-79-74-71—293	8040
	T Green	71-70-70-77—288	23738		K Albers	76-72-72-73—293	8040
9	D Coe-Jones	71-75-71-72—289	20103	27	J Geddes	76-75-74-69—294	7014
10	C Pierce	77-71-73-69—290	17964		K Tschetter	75-74-73-72—294	7014
11	B King	77-75-71-68—291	14200		L West	74-75-71-74—294	7014
	D Mochrie	78-73-70-70—291	14200		K Robbins	76-67-76-75—294	7014
	B Mucha	74-74-72-71—291	14200		B Thomas	79-69-70-76—294	7014
	S Palmer	72-73-74-72—291	14200	32	D Eggeling	72-78-75-70—295	5859
	D Massey	71-75-72-73—291	14200		C Rarick	74-73-78-70—295	5859
16	A Dibos	77-74-75-66—292	10056		L Neumann	75-74-74-72—295	5859
	S Steinhauer	78-74-72-68—292	10056		J Larsen	74-76-72-73—295	5859
	A Nicholas	75-74-73-70—292	10056		K Noble	71-77-71-76—295	5859

Other players who made the cut: C Keggi, V Skinner, H Kobayashi, A Okamoto, N Ramsbottom, L Merten 296; P Sheehan, A Benz, L Walters, MB Zimmerman 297; Danielle Ammaccapane, C Schreyer, A Ritzman, B Daniel, P Jordan 298; R Jones, F Descampe, J Crafter, J Briles-Hinton, M McNamara 299; Jean Zedlitz, M McGann, I Shiotani, T Johnson, C Johnson, P Hammel 300; K Guadagnino, M Figueras-Dotti 301; L Kiggens, C Johnston-Forbes 302; P Sinn 303; A Finney, T Barrett, K Peterson-Parker, S Farwig, C Hill 304; J Stephenson, M Nause, D Andrews 305; M Berteotti 307; J Anschutz 311.

1994 Nabisco Dinah Shore

Prize money: $700,000

1	D Andrews	70-69-67-70—276	$105000	19T	C Keggi	72-73-72-71—288	7204
2	L Davies	70-68-69-70—277	65165		C Johnson	74-73-69-72—288	7204
3	T Green	70-72-69-68—279	47553		P Sheehan	73-71-72-72—288	7204
4	J Stephenson	70-69-70-71—280	36985		D Mochrie	74-73-68-73—288	7204
5	M McGann	70-68-70-73—281	29940		A Okamoto	69-74-72-73—288	7204
6	G Graham	73-71-71-68—283	21251		M McGeorge	72-71-70-75—288	7204
	K Robbins	73-70-69-71—283	21251	28	T Tombs	73-74-72-70—289	5670
	B Burton	73-73-65-72—283	21251		S Turner	72-74-71-72—289	5670
9	H Stacy	72-72-70-70—284	15674		V Skinner	72-72-72-73—289	5670
	N Lopez	68-72-73-71—284	15674		M Berteotti	71-73-72-73—289	5670
11	M Mallon	72-75-69-69—285	12064	32	T-J Myers	76-73-71-70—290	4913
	L Neumann	76-71-68-70—285	12064		H Kobayashi	72-77-71-70—290	4913
	D Dormann	73-71-70-71—285	12064		K Tschetter	73-69-76-72—290	4913
	D Eggeling	71-71-71-72—285	12064		S Steinhauer	76-68-72-74—290	4913
15	K Monaghan	70-76-70-70—286	9862	36	J Larsen	76-70-75-70—291	3949
	V Fergon	69-74-72-71—286	9862		K Albers	77-73-70-71—291	3949
17	L Merten	74-74-71-68—287	8982		C Rarick	72-74-74-71—291	3949
	N Scranton	75-70-69-73—287	8982		D Coe-Jones	74-70-75-72—291	3949
19	B Daniel	76-72-70-70—288	7204		Toshimi Kimura	71-74-73-73—291	3949
	J Geddes	70-77-71-70—288	7204		M Nause	74-71-72-74—291	3949
	P Bradley	71-75-71-71—288	7204		A Miller	68-71-77-75—291	3949

Other players who made the cut: M Spencer-Devlin, E Crosby, Danielle Ammaccapane, D Richard, T Johnson 292; J Crafter, J Carner, K Noble, S Strudwick, H Alfredsson, C Schreyer, J Dickinson, L Kean, B King, L Walters 293; C Figg-Currier, A Alcott 294; S Redman, M McNamara, T Kerdyk, L Garbacz 295; A Ritzman, M Will, R Hood, A Benz 296; M Estill 297; B Mucha, S Little, K Guadagnino 298; S Palmer, C Walker, P Wright 299; E Klein (am) 300; C Mackey 305; S Farwig 306; A-M Palli 307.

1993 Nabisco Dinah Shore

Prize money: $700,000

1	H Alfredsson	69-71-72-72—284	$105000		19T	N Scranton	73-72-71-75—291	8101
2	A Benz	72-73-71-70—286	49901		22	M McGann	78-70-75-69—292	7237
	T Barrett	70-73-72-71—286	49901			S Barrett	69-77-72-74—292	7237
	B King	71-74-67-74—286	49901		24	L Garbacz	75-75-72-71—293	6304
5	H Stacy	72-74-71-70—287	25126			C Keggi	74-74-73-72—293	6304
	M Berteotti	68-74-73-72—287	25126			Dani Ammaccapane	69-75-74-75—293	6304
	D Coe-Jones	72-68-72-75—287	25126			C Schreyer	75-70-72-76—293	6304
8	N Lopez	68-78-72-70—288	15762			A-M Palli	70-71-76-76—293	6304
	B Burton	73-73-68-74—288	15762			M Figueras-Dotti	68-72-75-78—293	6304
	T Johnson	74-68-72-74—288	15762		30	D Lofland-Dormann	76-75-75-68—294	4740
	J Crafter	71-72-70-75—288	15762			D Mochrie	77-73-74-70—294	4740
12	P Sheehan	73-70-76-70—289	10625			H Drew	79-70-74-71—294	4740
	D Massey	70-74-74-71—289	10625			V Skinner	73-75-74-72—294	4740
	T Green	72-73-72-72—289	10625			A Finney	70-73-79-72—294	4740
	L Davies	72-72-73-72—289	10625			C Rarick	76-75-70-73—294	4740
	P Wright	74-68-75-72—289	10625			S Turner	73-72-76-73—294	4740
	P Bradley	71-69-75-74—289	10625			T-J Myers	74-73-73-74—294	4740
18	K Monaghan	76-71-74-69—290	8806			J Pitcock	70-72-76-76—294	4740
19	D Andrews	73-74-72-72—291	8101			S Steinhauer	72-74-71-77—294	4740
	K Noble	74-72-70-75—291	8101					

Other players who made the cut: L Neumann, J Carner, P Rizzo, J Inkster, M Will, S Hamlin, K Postlewait, B Mucha, J Stephenson 295; F Descampe, J Dickinson, J Geddes, C Walker, M Mallon, S Little, L Walters 296; A Ritzman, A Alcott, C Figg-Currier, A Miller 297; K Tschetter, D Richard 298; R Jones, M Estill, V Fergon 299; S Redman, S Farwig, L Connelly, L Adams 300; E Crosby, B Daniel 301; N Foust, M Spencer-Devlin, P Jordan, L Merten 302; Marlene Hagge 304; C Johnson, S Palmer, B Pearson 305; A Okamoto 307; S Furlong, V Goetze (am) 308.

Nabisco Dinah Shore History

This event was inaugurated in 1972 as the Colgate Dinah Shore and continued to be sponsored by Colgate until 1981. Nabisco took over the sponsorship in 1982; and the Nabisco Dinah Shore was designated a Major Championship in 1983. Mission Hills CC, Rancho Mirage, California, is the event's permanent venue.

Year	Winner	Score		Year	Winner	Score
1972	J Blalock	213		1988	A Alcott	274
1973	M Wright	284		1989	J Inkster	279
1974	J Prentice	289		1990	B King	283
1975	S Palmer	283		1991	A Alcott	273
1976	J Rankin	285		1992	D Mochrie*	279
1977	K Whitworth	289		*Won play-off after a tie with J Inkster*		
1978	S Post	283		1993	H Alfredsson (Swe)	284
1979	S Post	276		1994	D Andrews	276
1980	D Caponi	275		1995	N Bowen	285
1981	N Lopez	277		1996	P Sheehan	281
1982	S Little	278		1997	B King	276
1983	A Alcott	282		1998	P Hurst	281
1984	J Inkster*	280		1999	D Pepper	269
Won play-off after a tie with P Bradley				2000	K Webb (Aus)	274
1985	A Miller	278		2001	A Sörenstam (Swe)	281
1986	P Bradley	280		2002	A Sörenstam (Swe)	280
1987	B King*	283				

Won play-off after a tie with P Sheehan

du Maurier Classic History

The du Maurier Classic was inaugurated in 1973 and designated a Major Championship in 1979. It was discontinued after 2000 and was replaced as a major on the US LPGA schedule by the Weetabix Women's British Open.

Players are of American nationality unless stated

Year	Winner	Venue	Score
1973	J Bourassa*	Montreal GC, Montreal	214

* Won play-off after a tie with S Haynie, J Rankin

1974	CJ Callison	Candiac GC, Montreal	208
1975	J Carner*	St George's CC, Toronto	214

* Won play-off after a tie with C Mann

1976	D Caponi*	Cedar Brae G&CC, Toronto	212

* Won play-off after a tie with J Rankin

1977	J Rankin	Lachute G&CC, Montreal	214
1978	J Carner	St George's CC, Toronto	278
1979	A Alcott	Richelieu Valley CC, Montreal	285
1980	P Bradley	St George's CC, Toronto	277
1981	J Stephenson (Aus)	Summerlea CC, Dorian, Quebec	278
1982	S Haynie	St George's CC, Toronto	280
1983	H Stacy	Beaconsfield CC, Montreal	277
1984	J Inkster	St George's CC, Toronto	279
1985	P Bradley	Beaconsfield CC, Montreal	278
1986	P Bradley*	Board of Trade CC, Toronto	276

* Won play-off after a tie with A Okamoto

1987	J Rosenthal	Islesmere GC, Laval, Quebec	272
1988	S Little (RSA)	Vancouver GC, Coquitlam, BC	279
1989	T Green	Beaconsfield GC, Montreal	279
1990	C Johnston	Westmount G&CC, Kitchener, Ontario	276
1991	N Scranton	Vancouver GC, Coquitlam, BC	279
1992	S Steinhauer	St Charles CC, Winnipeg, Manitoba	277
1993	B Burton*	London H&CC, Ontario	277

* Won play-off after a tie with B King

1994	M Nause	Ottawa Hunt Club, Ontario	279
1995	J Lidback	Beaconsfield CC, Montreal	280
1996	L Davies (Eng)	Edmonton CC, Edmonton, Alberta	277
1997	C Walker	Glen Abbey GC, Toronto	278
1998	B Burton	Essex G&CC, Ontario	270
1999	K Webb (Aus)	Priddis Greens G&CC, Calgary, Alberta	277
2000	M Mallon	Royal Ottawa GC, Aylmer, Quebec	282

Women's Major Title Table

Juli Inkster

Karrie Webb

Mickey Wright

All photographs © Phil Sheldon

	#British Open	US Open	LPGA	†Dinah Shore	*du Maurier	British Amateur	US Amateur	*Total Titles*
Juli Inkster	0	2	2	2	1	0	3	10
Karrie Webb (Aus)	3	2	1	1	1	0	0	8
Mickey Wright	0	4	4	0	0	0	0	8
Jo Anne Carner	0	2	0	0	0	0	5	7
Betsy King	1	2	1	3	0	0	0	7
Pat Bradley	0	1	1	1	3	0	0	6
Betsy Rawls	0	4	2	0	0	0	0	6
Glenna Collett Vare	0	0	0	0	0	0	6	6
Louise Suggs	0	2	1	0	0	1	1	5
Babe Zaharias	0	3	0	0	0	1	1	5
Amy Alcott	0	1	0	3	1	0	0	5
Laura Davies (Eng)	1	1	2	0	1	0	0	5

 # Designated a major on the US LPGA circuit from 2001   † Designated a major in 1983
* Designated a major in 1979, discontinued after 2000

PART II

Men's Professional Tournaments

Official World Rankings, Top 50 (at end US and European Tours 2002)

Ranking		Name	Country	Points Average	Total Points	No. of Events	2000/2001 Pts Lost	2002 Pts Gained
1	(1)	Tiger Woods	USA	18.03	757.30	42	−593.30	+676.96
2	(2)	Phil Mickelson	USA	8.80	431.09	49	−375.02	+375.52
3	(4)	Ernie Els	RSA	7.26	399.08	55	−355.13	+377.78
4	(10)	Retief Goosen	RSA	6.66	399.78	60	−248.45	+356.12
5	(7)	David Toms	USA	6.69	362.24	55	−248.42	+278.33
6	(6)	Sergio García	Esp	6.55	340.43	52	−229.74	+276.95
7	(8)	Vijay Singh	Fij	6.22	372.99	60	−272.15	+309.20
8	(11)	Padraig Harrington	Irl	5.84	280.38	48	−178.87	+217.74
9	(5)	Davis Love III	USA	5.20	239.13	46	−207.70	+175.72
10	(15)	Jim Furyk	USA	4.74	232.22	49	−167.32	+189.60
11	(14)	Colin Montgomerie	Sco	4.67	238.00	51	−168.99	+187.57
12	(29)	Nick Price	Zim	4.59	192.82	42	−138.21	+182.61
13	(20)	Chris DiMarco	USA	4.43	256.75	58	−198.13	+212.99
14	(34)	Angel Cabrera	Arg	4.13	185.85	45	−125.10	+164.54
15	(40)	Justin Leonard	USA	3.89	221.62	57	−142.30	+209.09
16	(27)	Michael Campbell	NZ	3.84	199.45	52	−164.99	+194.72
17	(13)	Bernhard Langer	Ger	3.83	195.11	51	−157.09	+112.87
18	(22)	Robert Allenby	Aus	3.82	232.80	61	−159.92	+160.83
19	(18)	Bob Estes	USA	3.81	197.92	52	−123.08	+129.43
20	(21)	Scott Hoch	USA	3.80	178.71	47	−150.00	+115.61
21	(30)	Rocco Mediate	USA	3.78	166.28	44	−129.81	+152.10
22	(3)	David Duval	USA	3.76	169.41	45	−232.42	+65.70
23	(80)	Eduardo Romero	Arg	3.67	146.98	40	−66.88	+151.82
24	(45)	Charles Howell III	USA	3.63	213.91	59	−75.36	+189.99
25	(279)	Rich Beem	USA	3.59	222.37	62	−37.36	+230.23
26	(9)	Darren Clarke	NI	3.53	190.69	54	−216.68	+125.81
27	(79)	Jerry Kelly	USA	3.47	211.86	61	−108.71	+222.56
28	(33)	Kenny Perry	USA	3.35	174.11	52	−121.67	+154.56
29	(63)	Shigeki Maruyama	Jpn	3.28	173.84	53	−107.09	+174.83
30	(51)	Scott McCarron	USA	3.27	173.45	53	−106.48	+160.25
31	(16)	Scott Verplank	USA	3.10	161.38	52	−168.11	+100.95
32	(91)	Fred Funk	USA	3.04	197.74	65	−85.12	+188.42
33	(24)	Thomas Björn	Den	3.00	153.20	51	−159.67	+109.24
34	(42)	Steve Lowery	USA	3.00	168.20	56	−113.84	+132.85
35	(46)	José Maria Olazábal	Esp	2.98	169.91	57	−138.20	+173.99
36	(43)	Stuart Appleby	Aus	2.95	177.12	60	−108.01	+136.73
37	(38)	Niclas Fasth	Swe	2.94	137.94	47	−85.34	+105.85
38	(12)	Mike Weir	Can	2.83	135.81	48	−188.19	+73.30
39	(44)	Brad Faxon	USA	2.80	143.75	52	−132.38	+143.60
40	(61)	Jeff Sluman	USA	2.78	173.61	63	−101.82	+149.45
41	(145)	Craig Parry	Aus	2.74	156.26	57	−57.09	+156.57
42	(162)	Justin Rose	Eng	2.68	152.82	57	−63.20	+161.90
43	(85)	Chris Riley	USA	2.67	160.39	60	−68.87	+140.69
44	(155)	Len Mattiace	USA	2.60	150.68	58	−73.29	+165.54
45	(48)	Toru Taniguchi	Jpn	2.60	150.54	58	−108.70	+132.14
46	(17)	Toshimitsu Izawa	Jpn	2.60	114.20	44	−115.65	+46.05
47	(49)	Adam Scott	Aus	2.56	153.88	60	−80.59	+126.38
48	(56)	Paul Lawrie	Sco	2.56	140.80	55	−76.93	+106.79
49	(188)	Choi Kyoung-Ju	Kor	2.47	140.51	57	−52.78	+146.74
50	(105)	John Cook	USA	2.45	122.48	50	−69.27	+120.08

Ranking in brackets indicates position at 31st December 2001

European Tour –
2002 and Past Results

2002 Volvo Order of Merit (at end of season)

1	Retief Goosen (RSA)	€2,360,127	59	Tobias Dier (Ger)	398,534
2	Padraig Harrington (Irl)	2,334,655	60	Simon Dyson (Eng)	397,290
3	Ernie Els (RSA)	2,251,708	61	Henrik Bjornstad (Nor)	388,581
4	Colin Montgomerie (Sco)	1,980,719	62	Joakim Haeggman (Swe)	386,388
5	Eduardo Romero (Arg)	1,811,329	63	Peter Fowler (Aus)	384,737
6	Sergio García (Esp)	1,488,728	64	Richard S Johnson (Swe)	383,505
7	Adam Scott (Aus)	1,361,775	65	Ignacio Garrido (Esp)	380,108
8	Michael Campbell (NZ)	1,325,403	66	Miguel Angel Jiménez (Esp)	362,452
9	Justin Rose (Eng)	1,323,528	67	Søren Kjeldsen (Den)	342,578
10	Paul Lowrie (Sco)	1,151,433	68	Steve Webster (Eng)	336,649
11	Angel Cabrera (Arg)	1,128,913	69	Santiago Luna (Esp)	325,336
12	Thomas Bjørn (Den)	1,110,213	70	Roger Chapman (Eng)	322,283
13	José Maria Olazábal (Esp)	1,066,082	71	Nick O'Hern (Aus)	321,618
14	Trevor Immelman (RSA)	1,064,085	72	Raphael Jacquelin (Fra)	319,580
15	Stephen Leaney (Aus)	1,055,029	73	Richard Bland (Eng)	318,773
16	Anders Hansen (Den)	1,047,920	74	David Howell (Eng)	315,409
17	Niclas Fasth (Swe)	982,849	75	Lee Westwood (Eng)	308,338
18	Bradley Dredge (Wal)	961,121	76	Raymond Russell (Sco)	303,749
19	Bernhard Langer (Ger)	947,232	77	Warren Bennett (Eng)	298,915
20	Søren Hansen (Den)	932,789	78	David Lynn (Eng)	295,737
21	Gary Evans (Eng)	862,656	79	Farren Fichardt (RSA)	290,509
22	Darren Clarke (NI)	848,023	80	Anthony Wall (Eng)	286,572
23	Alex Cejka (Ger)	846,734	81	Mark Pilkington (Wal)	283,758
24	Ian Poulter (Eng)	832,559	82	Ian Garbutt (Eng)	281,920
25	Thomas Levet (Fra)	821,430	83	Jonathan Lomas (Eng)	276,028
26	Carl Petersson (Swe)	806,892	84	Mathias Grönberg (Swe)	270,977
27	Nick Faldo (Eng)	771,471	85	Sam Torrance (Sco)	268,770
28	Ricardo Gonzalez (Arg)	748,354	86	Patrik Sjöland (Swe)	255,341
29	John Bickerton (Eng)	707,012	87	David Carter (Eng)	235,858
30	Frederik Jacobson (Swe)	703,400	88	Charlie Wi (Kor)	234,036
31	Barry Lane (Eng)	679,966	89	Arjun Atwal (Ind)	231,642
32	Peter O'Malley (Aus)	668,183	90	Jamie Donaldson (Wal)	229,892
33	Robert Karlsson (Swe)	625,087	91	Roger Wessels (RSA)	228,055
34	Ian Woosnam (Wal)	598,814	92	Miles Tunicliff (Eng)	223,170
35	Pierre Fulke (Swe)	563,825	93	Mark Foster (Eng)	220,239
36	Nick Dougherty (Eng)	562,508	94	Henrik Nystrom (Swe)	216,222
37	Greg Owen (Eng)	557,654	95	Mark Roe (Eng)	211,859
38	Jean-Francois Remesy (Fra)	549,440	96	Mikael Lundberg (Swe)	207,480
39	Brian Davis (Eng)	548,351	97	Stephen Gallacher (Sco)	205,607
40	Peter Lonard (Aus)	523,579	98	Marc Farry (Fra)	205,168
41	Steen Tinning (Den)	519,101	99	Märten Olander (Swe)	198,864
42	Alastair Forsyth (Sco)	504,442	100	Andrew Oldcorn (Sco)	198,481
43	Carlos Rodiles (Esp)	492,732	101	John Daly (USA)	194,486
44	Malcolm Mackenzie (Eng)	486,446	102	Diego Borrego (Esp)	194,022
45	Jarrod Moseley (Aus)	480,416	103	Mikko Ilonen (Fin)	192,142
46	Paul Casey (Eng)	475,848	104	Stephen Dodd (Wal)	189,482
47	Jarmo Sandelin (Swe)	474,041	105	Martin Maritz (RSA)	189,399
48	Phillip Price (Wal)	473,096	106	Sven Strüver (Ger)	188,996
49	Maarten Lafeber (Ned)	465,943	107	David Park (Wal)	183,671
50	David Gilford (Eng)	452,157	108	Greg Turner (NZ)	183,433
51	Richard Green (Aus)	449,524	109	Miguel Angel Martin (Esp)	183,167
52	Emanuele Canonica (Ita)	432,406	110	Gary Orr (Sco)	183,125
53	Rolf Muntz (Ned)	423,767	111	Klas Eriksson (Swe)	182,796
54	Andrew Coltart (Sco)	414,462	112	Kenneth Ferrie (Eng)	182,625
55	Jamie Spence (Eng)	414,075	113	Fredrik Andersson (Swe)	182,063
56	Graeme McDowell (NI)	412,203	114	David Drysdale (Sco)	178,379
57	Sandy Lyle (Sco)	407,599	115	Paul Eales (Eng)	176,218
58	Paul McGinley (Irl)	401,597	116	Gary Emerson (Eng)	175,491

Career Money List (at end of 2002 season)

1	Colin Montgomerie	(Sco)	€15,511,995	45	Tony Johnstone	(Zim)	2,756,539
2	Bernhard Langer	(Ger)	10,979,067	52	Peter Mitchell	(Eng)	2,743,692
3	Darren Clarke	(NI)	10,044,030	53	Miguel Angel Martin	(Esp)	2,730,370
4	Ernie Els	(RSA)	8,861,722	54	Jarmo Sandelin	(Swe)	2,675,169
5	Retief Goosen	(RSA)	8,792,476	55	Ignacio Garrido	(Esp)	2,631,039
6	Ian Woosnam	(Wal)	8,577,221	56	David Howell	(Eng)	2,617,124
7	José Maria Olazábal	(Esp)	8,213,195	57	Des Smyth	(Irl)	2,588,761
8	Lee Westwood	(Eng)	7,993,278	58	Greg Norman	(Aus)	2,587,241
9	Padraig Harrington	(Irl)	7,865,732	59	Joakim Haeggman	(Swe)	2,586,713
10	Nick Faldo	(Eng)	7,068,788	60	Mark Roe	(Eng)	2,576,531
11	Thomas Bjørn	(Den)	6,501,105	61	Rodger Davis	(Aus)	2,552,905
12	Vijay Singh	(Fij)	6,386,041	62	Stephen Leaney	(Aus)	2,550,860
13	Miguel Angel			63	Howard Clark	(Eng)	2,507,193
	Jiménez	(Esp)	6,260,752	64	Patrik Sjöland	(Swe)	2,505,814
14	Eduardo Romero	(Arg)	6,132,245	65	Adam Scott	(Aus)	2,406,521
15	Michael Campbell	(NZ)	5,445,877	66	Gary Evans	(Eng)	2,371,328
16	Sam Torrance	(Sco)	5,386,985	67	Eamonn Darcy	(Irl)	2,365,049
17	Seve Ballesteros	(Esp)	5,322,373	68	Sven Strüver	(Ger)	2,327,089
18	Paul Lawrie	(Sco)	5,021,752	69	Russell Claydon	(Eng)	2,324,403
19	Mark McNulty	(Zim)	4,822,028	70	Frank Nobilo	(NZ)	2,282,061
20	Paul McGinley	(Irl)	4,499,072	71	Santiago Luna	(Esp)	2,247,789
21	Mark James	(Eng)	4,481,604	72	Andrew Oldcorn	(Sco)	2,193,020
22	Angel Cabrera	(Arg)	4,436,877	73	Thomas Levet	(Fra)	2,087,157
23	Costantino Rocca	(Ita)	4,268,059	74	Fredrik Jacobson	(Swe)	2,086,101
24	Barry Lane	(Eng)	4,213,081	75	Peter Senior	(Aus)	2,085,950
25	Phillip Price	(Wal)	4,182,349	76	Justin Rose	(Eng)	2,053,344
26	Sergio García	(Esp)	4,120,950	77	Ricardo Gonzalez	(Arg)	2,045,401
27	Peter O'Malley	(Aus)	3,983,692	78	Malcolm Mackenzie	(Eng)	2,044,433
28	Robert Karlsson	(Swe)	3,970,237	79	Philip Walton	(Irl)	2,034,865
29	Andrew Coltart	(Sco)	3,885,486	80	Ian Poulter	(Eng)	2,016,527
30	Gordon Brand jr	(Sco)	3,778,706	81	Anders Hansen	(Den)	1,986,959
31	Pierre Fulke	(Swe)	3,496,352	82	Mark Mouland	(Wal)	1,977,277
32	Craig Parry	(Aus)	3,391,780	83	John Bickerton	(Eng)	1,923,666
33	David Gilford	(Eng)	3,374,628	84	Bob May	(USA)	1,921,213
34	Peter Baker	(Eng)	3,339,411	85	Steen Tinning	(Den)	1,892,251
35	Sandy Lyle	(Sco)	3,307,017	86	Steve Webster	(Eng)	1,884,732
36	Gary Orr	(Sco)	3,284,210	87	Steven Richardson	(Eng)	1,876,238
37	Jesper Parnevik	(Swe)	3,267,176	88	David Carter	(Eng)	1,865,235
38	Per-Ulrik Johansson	(Swe)	3,227,884	89	Raymond Russell	(Sco)	1,850,118
39	Ronan Rafferty	(NI)	3,110,339	90	Brian Davis	(Eng)	1,841,825
40	Anders Forsbrand	(Swe)	3,083,868	91	Greg Owen	(Eng)	1,833,133
41	Alex Cejka	(Ger)	3,022,240	92	Peter Fowler	(Aus)	1,816,426
42	Greg Turner	(NZ)	3,011,380	93	Wayne Riley	(Aus)	1,804,230
43	Jamie Spence	(Eng)	3,033,913	94	Søren Hansen	(Den)	1,772,727
44	Jean Van De Velde	(Fra)	2,963,606	95	Jonathan Lomas	(Eng)	1,749,801
45	Mathias Grönberg	(Swe)	2,955,190	96	Mats Lanner	(Swe)	1,719,398
46	Roger Chapman	(Eng)	2,953,727	97	Carl Mason	(Eng)	1,717,708
47	José Coceres	(Arg)	2,934,604	98	Richard Green	(Aus)	1,698,983
48	Niclas Fasth	(Swe)	2,852,072	99	Dean Robertson	(Sco)	1,593,889
49	Paul Broadhurst	(Eng)	2,811,345	100	Peter Lonard	(Aus)	1,583,323
50	José Rivero	(Esp)	2,759,861				

2002 Tour Statistics (Reuters Performance Data)

Stroke averages

Pos	Name	Avg
1	Padraig Harrington (Irl)	69.72
2	Ernue Els (RSA)	70.07
3	Retief Goosen (RSA)	70.15
4	Vijay Singh (Fij)	70.27
5T	Colin Montgomerie (Sco)	70.36
	Eduardo Romero (Arg)	70.36
7	Sergio García (Esp)	70.43
8	Adam Scott (Aus)	70.54
9	Michael Campbell (NZ)	70.56
10	Trevor Immelman (RSA)	70.67
11	Thomas Bjørn (Den)	70.77
12	Justin Rose (Eng)	70.80
13T	Bradley Dredge (Wal)	70.82
	Alex Cejka (Ger)	70.82
15	Ricardo Gonzalez (Arg)	70.88
16	Gary Evans (Eng)	70.91
17T	Joakim Haeggman (Swe)	70.93
	Angel Cabrera (Arg)	70.93
19	Des Terblanche (RSA)	70.94
20	Søren Hansen (Den)	70.95

Driving accuracy

Pos	Name	%
1	Peter O'Malley (Aus)	80.7
2	Richard Green (Aus)	76.9
3	Michele Reale (Ita)	76.0
4	Paul Eales (Eng)	72.2
5	David Gilford (Eng)	71.3
6T	John Bickerton (Eng)	70.6
	Stephen Dodd (Wal)	70.6
8	Ian Garbutt (Eng)	70.3
9	Jarrod Moseley (Aus)	70.1
10	Anders Hansen (Den)	69.4

Average putts per round

Pos	Name	Avg
1	Marcel Siem (Ger)	27.9
2T	Paul Casey (Eng)	28.2
	Sam Torrance (Sco)	28.2
4	Ricardo Gonzalez (Arg)	28.3
5T	Angel Cabrera (Arg)	28.4
	Olle Karlsson (Swe)	28.4
	Pierre Fulke (Swe)	28.4
	Sandy Lyle (Sco)	28.4
9T	Justin Rose (Eng)	28.5
	Jarmo Sandelin (Swe)	28.5

Driving distance

Pos	Name	Yds
1	Emanuele Canonica (Ita)	304.9
2	Des Terblanche (RSA)	301.7
3	Ricardo Gonzalez (Arg)	300.8
4	Angel Cabrera (Arg)	300.1
5	Ernie Els (RSA)	297.4
6	Santiago Luna (Esp)	296.0
7	Carl Suneson (Esp)	295.9
8	Stephen Dodd (Wal)	295.8
9	Paul Casey (Eng)	294.5
10	Michele Reale (Ita)	293.6

Sand saves

Pos	Name	%
1	Bernhard Langer (Ger)	81.3
2	Tony Johnstone (Zim)	72.4
3	Ignacio Garrido (Esp)	71.6
4	Miguel Angel Jiménez (Esp)	68.6
5	Justin Rose (Eng)	68.1
6	Scott Gardiner (Aus)	66.7
7	Jamie Donaldson (Wal)	66.4
8	Gary Evans (Eng)	65.8
9	Anders Hansen (Den)	65.6
10	Paul Eales (Eng)	65.4

Greens in regulation

Pos	Name	%
1	Thomas Levet (Fra)	75.8
2	Peter O'Malley (Aus)	74.3
3	Ian Garbutt (Eng)	72.7
4	Greg Owen (Eng)	72.6
5	Michele Reale (Ita)	72.4
6	Richard Green (Aus)	72.2
7	Eduardo Romero (Arg)	72.1
8	Ernie Els (RSA)	72.0
9	Bernhard Langer (Ger)	71.6
10	Alex Cejka (Ger)	71.4

Putts per green in regulation

Pos	Name	Avg
1	Michael Campbell (NZ)	1.704
2	Sam Torrance (Sco)	1.714
3	Colin Montgomerie (Sco)	1.716
4T	Paul Casey (Eng)	1.718
	Marcel Siem (Ger)	1.718
6	Retief Goosen (RSA)	1.720
7	Justin Rose (Eng)	1.727
8T	Darren Clarke (NI)	1.728
	Fredrik Jacobsen (Swe)	1.728
10	Ernie Els (RSA)	1.731

Tour Results (in chronological order)

BMW Asian Open at Westin Resort, Ta Shee, Taiwan   (7104–72)

1	Jarmo Sandelin (Swe)	72-66-72-68—278	£169632	€273702
2	Thongchai Jaidee (Tha)	74-70-68-67—279	90993	146818
	José María Olazábal (Esp)	70-70-72-67—279	90993	146818

Omega Hong Kong Open at Hong Kong GC   (6697–71)

1	José María Olazábal (Esp)	65-69-64-64—262	£80170	€128848
2	Henrik Bjornstad (Nor)	66-69-61-67—263	55247	88791
3	Adam Scott (Aus)	64-67-66-67—264	30763	49441

South African Open

2002 at Country Club, Durban, South Africa   (6733–72)

1903	LB Waters	1930	SF Brews	1958	AA Stewart (am)	1980	R Cole
1904	LB Waters	1931	SF Brews	1959	D Hutchinson (am)	1981	G Player
1905	AG Gray	1932	C McIlvenny	1960	G Player	1982	Not played
1906	AG Gray	1933	SF Brews	1961	R Waltman	1983	C Bolling
1907	LB Waters	1934	SF Brews	1962	HR Henning	1984	T Johnstone (Zim)
1908	G Fotheringham	1935	AD Locke (am)	1963	R Waltman	1985	G Levenson
1909	J Fotheringham	1936	CE Olander	1964	A Henning	1986	D Frost
1910	G Fotheringham	1937	AD Locke (am)	1965	G Player	1987	M McNulty
1911	G Fotheringham	1938	AD Locke	1966	G Player	1988	W Westner
1912	G Fotheringham	1939	AD Locke	1967	G Player	1989	S Wadsworth
1913	JAW Prentice (am)	1940	AD Locke	1968	G Player	1990	T Dodds
1914	G Fotheringham	1946	AD Locke	1969	G Player	1991	W Westner
1919	WH Horne	1947	RW Glennie (am)	1970	T Horton (Eng)	1992	E Els
1920	LB Waters	1948	JM Janks (am)*	1971	S Hobday	1993	C Whitelaw
1921	J Brews	1949	SF Brews	1972	G Player	1994	T Johnstone (Zim)
1922	F Jangle	1950	AD Locke	1973	RJ Charles (NZ)	1995	R Goosen
1923	J Brews	1951	AD Locke	1974	R Cole	1996	E Els
1924	BH Elkin	1952	SF Brews	1975	G Player	1997	V Singh (Fij)
1925	SF Brews	1953	JR Boyd (am)	1976	D Hayes	1998	E Els
1926	J Brews	1954	RC Taylor (am)	1976	G Player	1999	D Frost
1927	SF Brews	1955	AD Locke	1977	G Player	2000	M Grönberg (Swe)
1928	J Brews	1956	G Player	1978	H Baiocchi	2001	M McNulty (Zim)
1929	A Tosh	1957	HR Henning*	1979	G Player		

1	Tim Clark (RSA)	66-70-68-65—269	£79250	€128053
2	Steve Webster (Eng)	68-70-69-64—271	57500	92909
3	James Kingston (RSA)	66-67-74-68—275	29550	47747
	Jonathan Lomas (Eng)	68-67-71-69—275	29550	47747

Alfred Dunhill Championship

(1959–99 combined with South African PGA Championship)

1995	E Els	Wanderers Club	271		1999	E Els	Houghton GC	273
1996	S Strüver	Houghton GC	202 (54)		2000	A Wall	Houghton GC	204
1997	N Price	Houghton GC	269		2001	A Scott	Houghton GC	267
1998	T Johnstone	Houghton GC	271					

2002 at Houghton, Johannesburg, RSA   (7284–72)

1	Justin Rose (Eng)	71-66-66-65—268	£79000	€128174
2	Mark Foster (Eng)	69-67-65-69—270	38917	63140
	Retief Goosen (RSA)	68-67-70-65—270	38917	63140
	Martin Maritz (RSA)	72-64-63-71—270	38917	63140

Johnnie Walker Classic

1992	I Palmer	Bangkok	268	1997	E Els	Hope Island, Queensland	278
1993	N Faldo	Singapore Island	269	1999	Not played		
1994	G Norman	Blue Canyon, Phuket	277	2000	M Campbell	Ta Shee, Taiwan	276
1995	F Couples	Orchard GC, Manila	277	2001	T Woods	Bangkok	263
.1996	I Woosnam	Tanah Merah, Singapore	272				

2002 at Lake Karrinyup, Perth, Australia (6974–72)

1	Retief Goosen (RSA)	70-68-63-73—274	£150000	€243641
2	Pierre Fulke (Swe)	72-70-74-66—282	100000	162427
3	Sergio García (Esp)	69-73-72-69—283	56340	91511

Heineken Classic

1996	I Woosnam (Wal)	277	1999	Jarrod Moseley (Aus)	274
1997	MA Martin (Esp)	273	2000	M Campbell (NZ)	268
1998	T Bjørn (Den)	280	2001	M Campbell (NZ)	270

2002 at Royal Melbourne GC, Victoria, Australia (6981–72)

1	Ernie Els (RSA)	64-69-69-69—271	£135932	€221386
2	Peter Fowler (Aus)	69-70-70-67—276	54750	89169
	David Howell (Eng)	68-70-70-68—276	54750	89169
	Peter O'Malley (Aus)	68-68-70-70—276	54750	89169

The ANZ Championship at Lakes GC, Sydney, Australia (6904–73)

1	Richard Johnson (Swe)	3-16-16-11—46	£118676	€195080
2	Scott Laycock (Aus)	11-16-7-10—44	55877	91850
	Craig Parry (Aus)	10-18-9-7—44	55877	91850

WGC Accenture Match Play

2000 Darren Clarke (NI) beat Tiger Woods (USA) 4 and 3 at Carlsbad, CA, USA
2001 Steve Stricker (USA) beat Pierre Fulke (Swe) 2 and 1 at Melbourne, Australia

2002 at La Costa, Carlsbad, CA, USA

Final: Kevin Sutherland (USA) ($1000000) beat Scott McCarron (USA) ($500000) 1 hole

Consolation match: Brad Faxon (USA) ($400000) beat Paul Azinger (USA) at 19th

Fuller details of this event are to be found on p.171

Caltex Singapore Masters

2001 V Singh 263

2002 at Laguna National, Singapore (7112–72)

1	Arjun Atwal (Ind)	70-69-67-68—274	£104806	€171856
2	Richard Green (Aus)	69-72-68-70—279	69850	114536
3	Nick Faldo (Eng)	68-69-73-70—280	39357	64536

Carlsberg Malaysian Open

1992	V Singh	1996	S Fiesch	2000	Y Wei Tze
1993	G Norquist	1997	L Westwood	2001	V Singh
1994	J Haegmann	1998	E Fryatt		
1995	C Devers	1999	G Norquist		

Carlsberg Malaysian Open *continued*

2002 *at Royal Selangor, Kuala Lumpur, Malaysia* (6935–71)

1	Alastair Forsyth (Sco)*	63-65-69-70—267	£112894	€184366
2	Stephen Leaney (Aus)	67-67-66-67—267	77792	127041
3	Alex Cejka (Ger)	68-65-70-65—268	43319	70743

Dubai Desert Classic

1989	M James*	277	1996	C Montgomerie	270
1990	E Darcy	276	1997	R Green	272
1991	*Not played*		1998	JM Olazábal	269
1992	S Ballesteros*	272	1999	D Howell	275
1993	W Westner	274	2000	J Coceres	274
1994	E Els	268	2001	T Bjørn	266
1995	F Couples	268			

2002 *at Emirates GC, Dubai* (7185–72)

1	Ernie Els (RSA)	68-68-67-69—272	£166660	€273335
2	Niclas Fasth (Swe)	68-69-69-70—276	111110	182229
3	Carl Petterson (Swe)	70-73-65-69—277	62600	102669

Qatar Masters

1998	A Coltart	270	2000	R Muntz	280
1999	P. Lawrie	268	2001	T Johnstone	274

2002 *at Doha, Qatar* (7110–72)

1	Adam Scott (Aus)	67-66-69-67—269	£175722	€285651
2	Jean François Remesy (Fra)	68-69-68-70—275	91572	148858
	Nick Dougherty (Eng)	69-69-68-69—275	91572	148858

Madeira Island Open

1993	M James	Campo de Golf da Madeira	281	1998	M Lanner	Santo de Serra GC	277
1994	M Lanner	Campo de Golf da Madeira	206 (54)	1999	P Linhart	Santo da Serra GC	276
1995	S Luna	Campo de Golf da Madeira	272	2000	N Fasth	Santo de Serra GC	279
1996	J Sandelin	Campo de Golf da Madeira	279	2001	D Smyth	Santo de Serra GC	270
1997	P Mitchell	Santo de Serra GC	204 (54)				

2002 *at Santo da Serra, Madeira* (6664–72)

1	Diego Borrego (Esp)	72-68-72-69—281	£56800	€91660
2	Ivo Giner (Esp)	73-66-70-73—282	29602	47770
	Maarten Lafeber (Ned)	74-64-71-73—282	29602	47770

Algarve Open de Portugal

1953	EC Brown	Estoril	260		1967	A Gallardo	Estoril	214 (54)
1954	A Miguel	Estoril	263		1968	M Faulkner	Estoril	273
1955	F van Donck	Estoril	267		1969	R Sota	Estoril	270
1956	A Miguel	Estoril	268		1970	R Sota	Estoril	274
1958	P Alliss	Estoril	264		1971	L Platts	Estoril	277
1959	S Miguel	Estoril	265		1972	G Garrido	Estoril	196 (54)
1960	K Bousfield	Estoril	268		1973	J Benito*	Penina	294
1961	K Bousfield	Estoril	263		1974	BGC Huggett	Estoril	272
1962	A Angelini	Estoril	269		1975	H Underwood	Penina	292
1963	R Sota	Estoril	204 (54)		1976	S Balbuena	Quinta do Lago	283
1964	A Miguel	Estoril	279		1977	M Ramos	Penina	287
1966	A Angelini	Estoril	273		1978	H Clark	Penina	291

1979	B Barnes	Vilamoura	287		1992	R Rafferty	Vila Sol	273
1982	S Torrance	Penina	207 (54)		1993	D Gilford*	Vila Sol	275
1983	S Torrance	Troia	286		1994	P Price	Penha Longa	278
1984	A Johnstone	Quinta do Lago	274		1995	A Hunter*	Penha Longa	277
1985	W Humphreys	Quinta do Lago	279		1996	W Riley	Aroeira	271
1986	M McNulty	Quinta do Lago	270		1997	M Jonzon	Aroeira	269
1987	R Lee	Estoril	195 (54)		1998	P Mitchell	Algarve	274
1988	M Harwood	Quinta do Lago	280		1999	V Phillips*	Penina	276
1989	C Montgomerie	Quinta do Lago	264		2000	G Orr	Penina	275
1990	M McLean	Quinta do Lago	274		2001	P Price	Algarve	273
1991	S Richardson	Estela	283					

2002 at Vale do Lobo, Portugal   (7108–72)

1	Carl Pettersson (Swe)*	66-76—142	£76465	€125000
2	David Gilford (Eng)	70-72—142	50975	83330
3	Miguel Angel Martin (Esp)	73-70—143	23704	38750
	Henrik Nyström (Swe)	72-71—143	23704	38750
	Greg Owen (Eng)	72-71—143	23704	38750

The MASTERS at Augusta National, Georgia, USA   (7270–72)

1	Tiger Woods (USA)	70-69-66-71—276	£702439	€1144807
2	Retief Goosen (RSA)	69-67-69-74—279	421463	686884
3	Phil Mickelson (USA)	69-72-68-71—280	265366	432483

Fuller details of this event are included in Part I The Majors page 72

The Seve Trophy at Druids Glen, Wicklow, Ireland   (7076–71)

Great Britain and Ireland beat Continental Europe 14½–11½

Full details of this event are on page 191

Canarias Open de España

1912	A Massy (Fra)	Polo, Madrid		1955	H de Lamaze (Fra) (am)	Puerta de Hierro
1916	A de la Torre	Puerta de Hierro		1956	P Alliss (Eng)	El Prat
1917	A de la Torre	Puerta de Hierro		1957	M Faulkner (Eng)	Club de Campo
1919	A de la Torre	Puerta de Hierro		1958	P Alliss (Eng)	Puerta de Hierro
1921	E Lafitte	Puerta de Hierro		1959	PW Thomson (Aus)	El Prat
1923	A de la Torre	Puerta de Hierro		1960	S Miguel	Club de Campo
1925	A de la Torre	Puerta de Hierro		1961	A Miguel	Puerta de Hierro
1926	J Bernardino	Puerta de Hierro		1963	R Sota	El Prat
1927	A Massy (Fra)	Puerta de Hierro		1964	A Miguel	Tenerife
1928	A Massy (Fra)	Puerta de Hierro		1966	R de Vicenzo (Arg)	Sotogrande
1929	E Lafitte	Puerta de Hierro		1967	S Miguel	Sant Cugat
1930	J Bernardino	Puerta de Hierro		1968	R Shaw	La Galea
1932	G Gonzalez	Puerta de Hierro		1969	J Garaialde	RACE, Madrid
1933	G Gonzalez	Puerta de Hierro		1970	A Gallardo	Nueva Andalucia
1934	J Bernardino	Puerta de Hierro		1971	D Hayes (RSA)	El Prat
1935	A de la Torre	Puerta de Hierro		1972	A Garrido*	Pals
1941	M Provencio	Puerta de Hierro		1973	NC Coles (Eng)	La Manga
1942	G Gonzalez	Sant Cugat		1974	J Heard	La Manga
1943	M Provencio	Puerta de Hierro		1975	A Palmer (USA)	La Manga
1944	N Sagardia	Pedrena		1976	E Polland (NI)	La Manga
1945	C Celles	Puerta de Hierro		1977	B Gallacher (Sco)	La Manga
1946	M Morcillo	Pedrena		1978	B Barnes (Sco)	El Prat
1947	M Gonzalez (am)	Puerta de Hierro		1979	D Hayes (RSA)	Torrequebrada
1948	M Morcillo	Negun		1980	E Polland (NI)	Escorpion
1949	M Morcillo	Puerta de Hierro		1981	S Ballesteros	El Prat
1950	A Cerda	Cedana		1982	S Torrance (Sco)	Club de Campo
1951	M Provencio	Puerta de Hierro		1983	E Darcy (Irl)	Las Brisas
1952	M Faulkner (Eng)	Puerta de Hierro		1984	B Langer (Ger)	El Saler
1953	M Faulkner (Eng)	Puerta de Hierro		1985	S Ballesteros	Vallromanos
1954	S Miguel	Puerta de Hierro		1986	H Clark (Eng)	La Moraleja

Canarias Open de España continued

1987	N Faldo (Eng)	La Brisas		1995	S Ballesteros	Club de Campo
1988	M James (Eng)	Pedrena		1996	P Harrington (Irl)	Club de Campo
1989	B Langer (Ger)	El Saler		1997	M James* (Eng)	La Moraleja II
1990	R Davis (Aus)	Club de Campo		1998	T Bjørn (Swe)	El Prat
1991	E Romero* (Arg)	Club de Campo		1999	J Sandelin (Swe)	El Prat
1992	A Sherborne (Eng)	RACE, Madrid		2000	B Davis	PGA Golf de
1993	J Haeggman (Swe)	RACE, Madrid				Catalunya
1994	C Montgomerie (Sco)	Club de Campo		2001	R Karlsson (Swe)	El Saler

2002 at El Cortijo, Gran Canaria　　　　　　　　　　　　　　　(6899–72)

1	Sergio García (Esp)	67-68-67-73—275	£176360	€287000
2	Emanuele Canonica (Ita)	68-69-70-72—279	117572	191330
3	Greg Owen (Eng)	67-69-72-72—280	66241	107797

Novotel Perrier Open de France

1906	A Massy	La Boulie	292	1960	R De Vicenzo	St Cloud	275
1907	A Massy	La Boulie	294	1961	KDG Nagle	La Boulie	271
1908	JH Taylor	La Boulie	300	1962	A Murray	St Germain	274
1909	JH Taylor	La Boulie	290	1963	B Devlin	St Cloud	273
1910	J Braid	La Boulie	298	1964	R de Vicenzo	Chantilly	272
1911	A Massy	La Boulie	284	1965	R Sota	St Nom-la-Bretêche	268
1912	J Gassiat	La Boulie	284	1966	DJ Hutchinson	La Boulie	274
1913	G Duncan	Chantilly	304	1967	BJ Hunt	St Germain	271
1914	JD Edgar	Le Touquet	284	1968	PJ Butler	St Cloud	272
1920	W Hagen	La Boulie	298	1969	J Garaialde	St Nom-la-Bretêche	277
1921	A Boomer	Le Touquet	284	1970	D Graham	Chantaco	268
1922	A Boomer	La Boulie	284	1971	Lu Liang Huan	Biarritz	262
1923	J Ockenden	Dieppe	284	1972	B Jaeckel*	Biarritz & La Nivelle	265
1924	CJH Tolley (am)	La Boulie	290	1973	P Oosterhuis	La Boulie	280
1925	A Massy	Chantilly	291	1974	P Oosterhuis	Chantilly	284
1926	A Boomer	St Cloud	280	1975	B Barnes	La Boulie	281
1927	G Duncan	St Germain	290	1976	V Tshabalaia	Le Touquet	272
1928	CJH Tolley (am)	La Boulie	283	1977	S Ballesteros	Le Touquet	282
1929	A Boomer	Fourqueux	283	1978	D Hayes	La Baule	269
1930	ER Whitcombe	Dieppe	282	1979	B Gallacher	Lyons	284
1931	A Boomer	Deauville	291	1980	G Norman	St Cloud	268
1932	AJ Lacey	St Cloud	296	1981	A Lyle	St Germain	270
1933	B Gadd	Chantilly	283	1982	S Ballesteros	St Nom-la-Bretêche	278
1934	SF Brews	Dieppe	284	1983	N Faldo*	La Boulie	277
1935	SF Brews	Le Touquet	292	1984	B Langer	St Cloud	270
1936	M Dallemagne	St Germain	277	1985	S Ballesteros	St Germain	263
1937	M Dallemagne	St Cloud	278	1986	S Ballesteros	La Boulie	269
1938	M Dallemagne	Fourqueux	282	1987	J Rivero	St Cloud	269
1939	M Pose	Le Touquet	285	1988	N Faldo	Chantilly	274
1946	TH Cotton	St Cloud	269	1989	N Faldo	Chantilly	273
1947	TH Cotton	Chantilly	285	1990	P Walton*	Chantilly	275
1948	F Cavalo	St Cloud	287	1991	E Romero	National GC	281
1949	U Grappasonni	St Germain	275	1992	MA Martin	National GC	276
1950	R De Vicenzo	Chantilly	279	1993	C Rocca*	National GC	273
1951	H Hassanein	St Cloud	278	1994	M Roc	National GC	274
1952	AD Locke	St Germain	268	1995	P Broadhurst	National GC	274
1953	AD Locke	La Boulie	276	1996	R Allenby*	National GC	272
1954	F van Donck	St Cloud	275	1997	R Goosen	National GC	271
1955	B Nelson	La Boulie	271	1998	S Torrance	National GC	276
1956	A Miguel	Deauville	277	1999	R Goosen*	Golf du Médoc	272
1957	F van Donck	St Cloud	266	2000	C Montgomerie	Le Golf National	272
1958	F van Donck	St Germain	276	2001	JM Olazábal	Lyon GC	268
1959	DC Thomas	La Boulie	276				

2002 at Le Golf National, Paris, France　　　　　　　　　　　(7089–72)

1	Malcolm Mackenzie (Eng)	68-69-65-72—274	£205795	€333330
2	Trevor Immelman (RSA)	68-64-71-72—275	137197	222220
3	Kenneth Ferrie (Eng)	68-72-67-69—276	63797	103333
	Anders Hansen (Den)	69-70-65-72—276	63797	103333
	Ian Woosnam (Wal)	69-71-66-70—276	63797	103333

Benson and Hedges International Open

1971	A Jacklin*	Fulford	279	1987	N Ratcliffe	Fulford	275
1972	J Newton	Fulford	281	1988	P Baker*	Fulford	271
1973	V Baker	Fulford	276	1989	G Brand jr	Fulford	272
1974	P Toussaint*	Fulford	276	1990	JM Olazábal	St Mellion	279
1975	V Fernandez	Fulford	266	1991	B Langer	St Mellion	286
1976	G Marsh	Fulford	272	1992	P Senior*	St Mellion	287
1977	A Garrido	Fulford	280	1993	P Broadhurst	St Mellion	276
1978	L Trevino*	Fulford	274	1994	S Ballesteros	St Mellion	281
1979	M Bembridge	St Mellion	272	1995	P O'Malley	St Mellion	280
1980	G Marsh	Fulford	272	1996	S Ames	The Oxfordshire	283
1981	T Weiskopf	Fulford	272	1997	B Langer	The Oxfordshire	276
1982	G Norman	Fulford	283	1998	D Clarke	The Oxfordshire	273
1983	J Bland	Fulford	273	1999	C Montgomerie	The Oxfordshire	273
1984	S Torrance	Fulford	270	2000	JM Olazábal	The Belfry	275
1985	A Lyle	Fulford	274	2001	H Stenson	The Belfry	275
1986	M James*	Fulford	274				

2002 *at The Belfry, Sutton Coldfield, England*   (7118–72)

1	Angel Cabrera (Arg)	68-73-68-69—278	£183330	€294357
2	Barry Lane (Eng)	69-72-65-73—279	122220	196238
3	Michael Campbell (NZ)	70-69-71-70—280	56833	91252
	Padraig Harrington (Irl)	71-70-70-69—280	56833	91252
	Colin Montgomerie (Sco)	71-67-73-69—280	56833	91252

Deutsche Bank – SAP Open TPC of Europe

1977	N Coles	Foxhills	288	1990	M McLean	Quinta do Lago	274
1978	B Waites	Foxhills	286	1991	*not played*		
1979	M King	Moor Park	281	1992	*not played*		
1980	B Gallacher	Moortown	268	1993	*not played*		
1981	B Barnes*	Dalmahoy	276	1994	*not played*		
1982	N Faldo	Notts	270	1995	B Langer	Gut Kaden	270
1983	B Langer	St Mellion	269	1996	F Nobilo	Gut Kaden	270
1984	J Gonzalez*	St Mellion	265	1997	R McFarlane	Gut Kaden	282
1985	*Not played*			1998	L Westwood	Gut Kaden	265
1986	I Woosnam	The Belfry	277	1999	T Woods	St Leon-Rot	273
1987	*Not played*			2000	L Westwood	Gut Kaden, Hamburg	273
1988	*Not played*			2001	T Woods	St Leon-Rot	266
1989	C Montgomerie	Quinta do Lago	264				

2002 *at St Leon-Rot, Heidelberg, Germany*   (7255–72)

1	Tiger Woods* (USA)	69-67-64-68—268	£280859	€450000
2	Colin Montgomerie (Sco)	66-68-65-69—268	187239	300000
3	Justin Rose (Eng)	71-65-66-67—269	105490	169020

Volvo PGA Championship

1955	K Bousfield	Pannal	277	1969	B Gallacher	Ashburnham	293
1956	CH Ward	Maesdu	282	1972	A Jacklin	Wentworth Club	279
1957	P Alliss	Maesdu	286	1973	P Oosterhuis	Wentworth Club	280
1958	H Bradshaw	Llandudno	287	1974	M Bembridge	Wentworth Club	278
1959	DJ Rees	Ashburnham	283	1975	A Palmer	R St George's	285
1960	AF Stickley	Coventry	247 (63)	1976	NC Coles*	R St George's	280
1961	BJ Bamford	R Mid-Surrey	266	1977	M Piñero	R St George's	283
1962	P Alliss	Little Aston	287	1978	N Faldo	R Birkdale	278
1963	PJ Butler	R Birkdale	306	1979	V Fernandez	St Andrews	288
1964	AG Grubb	Western Gailes	287	1980	N Faldo	R St George's	283
1965	P Alliss	Prince's	286	1981	N Faldo	Ganton	274
1966	GB Wolstenholme	Saunton	278	1982	A Jacklin*	Hillside	284
1967	BGC Huggett	Thorndon Park	271	1983	S Ballesteros	R St George's	278
1967	ME Gregson	Hunstanton	275	1984	H Clark	Wentworth Club	204 (54)
1968	PM Townsend	R Mid-Surrey	275	1985	P Way*	Wentworth Club	282
1968	D Talbot	Dunbar	276	1986	R Davis*	Wentworth Club	281

Volvo PGA Championship *continued*

1987	B Langer	Wentworth Club	270	1995	B Langer	Wentworth Club	279
1988	I Woosnam	Wentworth Club	274	1996	C Rocca	Wentworth Club	274
1989	N Faldo	Wentworth Club	272	1997	I Woosnam	Wentworth Club	275
1990	M Harwood	Wentworth Club	271	1998	C Montgomerie	Wentworth Club	274
1991	S Ballesteros*	Wentworth Club	271	1999	C Montgomerie	Wentworth Club	270
1992	T Johnstone	Wentworth Club	272	2000	C Montgomerie	Wentworth Club	271
1993	B Langer	Wentworth Club	274	2001	A Oldcorn	Wentworth Club	272
1994	JM Olazábal	Wentworth Club	271				

2002 *at Wentworth Club, Virginia Water, Surrey* (7072–72)

1	Anders Hansen (Den)	68-65-66-70—269	£333330	€528708
2	Colin Montgomerie (Sco)	64-71-72-67—274	173710	275528
	Eduardo Romero (Arg)	67-68-71-68—274	173710	275528
4	Michael Campbell (NZ)	68-70-71-67—276	84933	134716
	Nick Faldo (Eng)	71-68-68-69—276	84933	134716
	Carlos Rodiles (Esp)	69-67-68-72—276	84933	134716
7	Darren Clarke (NI)	70-71-69-67—277	55000	87238
	Jarrod Moseley (Aus)	71-73-70-63—277	55000	87238
9	David Gilford (Eng)	68-71-70-70—279	42400	67252
	Peter O'Malley (Aus)	69-71-69-70—279	42400	67252
11	Peter Baker (Eng)	70-70-68-72—280	33500	53136
	Niclas Fasth (Swe)	71-71-71-67—280	33500	53136
	Maarten Lafeder (Ned)	71-70-67-72—280	33500	53136
	Stephen Leaney (Aus)	68-71-73-68—280	33500	53136
15	Gary Evans (Eng)	68-75-67-71—281	27600	43777
	Gregory Havret (Fra)	73-69-70-69—281	27600	43777
	Sam Torrance (Sco)	71-68-72-70—281	27600	43777
	Greg Turner (NZ)	68-71-69-73—281	27600	43777
19	John Bickerton (Eng)	71-68-73-70—282	22067	35001
	Thomas Bjørn (Den)	71-69-73-69—282	22067	35001
	Nick Dougherty (Eng)	72-70-71-69—282	22067	35001
	Ignacio Garrido (Esp)	69-71-69-73—282	22067	35001
	Ricardo Gonzales (Arg)	73-70-69-70—282	22067	35001
	Barry Lane (Eng)	71-71-69-71—282	22067	35001
	Mark McNulty (Zim)	67-69-71-75—282	22067	35001
	Phillip Price (Wal)	72-72-68-70—282	22067	35001
	Steen Tinning (Den)	67-76-70-69—282	22067	35001
28	Alastair Forsyth (Sco)	71-68-73-71—283	18400	29185
	Søren Hansen (Den)	75-69-71-68—283	18400	29185
	David J Russell (Eng)	68-76-73-66—283	18400	29185
31	Gary Clark (Eng)	69-72-73-70—284	16600	26330
	Robert Karlsson (Swe)	68-75-70-71—284	16600	26330
	Greg Owen (Eng)	71-72-75-66—284	16600	26330
34	Marc Farry (Fra)	71-72-73-69—285	14400	22840
	Tom Gillis (USA)	68-74-71-72—285	14400	22840
	Paul Lawrie (Sco)	73-70-68-74—285	14400	22840
	Andrew Marshall (Eng)	72-70-72-71—285	14400	22840
	Andrew Oldcorn (Sco)	68-75-72-70—285	14400	22840
	Patrik Sjöland (Swe)	71-71-71-72—285	14400	22840
40	Henrik Bjornstad (Nor)	72-71-72-71—286	11800	18716
	Angel Cabrera (Arg)	70-71-70-75—286	11800	18716
	David Carter (Eng)	71-72-72-71—286	11800	18716
	Sebastian Delagrange (Fra)	70-73-71-72—286	11800	18716
	Brett Rumford (Aus)	72-70-74-70—286	11800	18716
	Jean Van De Velde (Fra)	71-69-74-72—286	11800	18716
	Roger Wessels (RSA)	72-71-71-72—286	11800	18716
47	Jorge Berendt (Arg)	73-71-74-69—287	9800	15544
	Darren Fichardt (RSA)	72-72-69-74—287	9800	15544
	Stephen Gallacher (Sco)	71-71-72-73—287	9800	15544
50	Sion E Bebb (Wal)	71-71-75-71—288	8000	12689

50T	Mark Davis (Eng)	69-75-72-72—288	£8000	€12689
	Mikael Lundberg (Swe)	71-71-73-73—288	8000	12689
	Miguel Angel Martin (Esp)	70-73-75-70—288	8000	12689
	Lucas Parsons (Aus)	68-74-72-74—288	8000	12689
	José Rivero (Esp)	71-72-71-74—288	8000	12689
56	Diego Borrego (Esp)	68-74-76-71—289	6040	9580
	Gordon Brand jr (Sco)	70-73-77-69—289	6040	9580
	Andrew Coltart (Sco)	67-73-77-72—289	6040	9580
	Robert-Jan Derksen (Ned)	74-70-71-74—289	6040	9580
	Jarmo Sandelin (Swe)	69-71-73-76—289	6040	9580
61	Gary Emerson (Eng)	73-69-73-75—290	5100	8089
	Richard Green (Aus)	71-73-75-71—290	5100	8089
	Christopher Hanell (Swe)	72-72-72-74—290	5100	8089
	Jamie Spence (Eng)	72-72-76-70—290	5100	8089
65	Trevor Immelman (RSA)	69-74-73-75—291	4500	7138
	Wei-Tze Yeh (Tai)	73-71-73-74—291	4500	7138
67	Brian Davis (Eng)	72-70-76-74—292	4100	6503
	Mark Foster (Eng)	69-75-74-74—292	4100	6503
69	Desvonde Botes (RSA)	70-74-73-76—293	3725	5908
	Gary Marks (Eng)	71-70-77-75—293	3725	5908
71	Rolf Muntz (Ned)	69-75-77-73—294	2999	4757
	José María Olazábal (Esp)	68-73-75-78—294	2999	4757
73	Markus Brier (Aut)	71-72-78-74—295	2995	4751
	Ronan Rafferty (NI)	68-72-79-76—295	2995	4751
75	Paul Casey (Eng)	71-72-74-79—296	2992	4746
76	Muray Urquhart (Sco)	73-71-82-75—301	2990	4743

80 missed the cut on 144

Victor Chandler British Masters

1946T	AD Locke	Stoneham	286	1973	A Jacklin	St Pierre	272
	J Adams			1974	B Gallacher*	St Pierre	282
1947	A Lees	Little Aston	283	1975	B Gallacher	Ganton	289
1948	N Von Nida	Sunningdale	272	1976	B Dassu	St Pierre	271
1949	C Ward	St Andrews	290	1977	G Hunt*	Lindrick	291
1950	D Rees	Hoylake	281	1978	T Horton	St Pierre	279
1951	M Faulkner	Wentworth Club	281	1979	G Marsh	Woburn	283
1952	H Weetman	Mere	281	1980	B Langer	St Pierre	270
1953	H Bradshaw	Sunningdale	272	1981	G Norman	Woburn	273
1954	AD Locke	Prince's	291	1982	G Norman	St Pierre	267
1955	H Bradshaw	Little Aston	277	1983	L Woosnam	St Pierre	269
1956	C O'Connor	Prestwick	277	1985	L Trevino	Woburn	278
1957	E Brown	Hollinwell	275	1986	S Ballesteros	Woburn	275
1958	H Weetman	Little Aston	276	1987	M McNulty	Woburn	274
1959	C O'Connor	Portmarnock	276	1988	A Lyle	Woburn	273
1960	J Hitchcock	Sunningdale	275	1989	N Faldo	Woburn	267
1961	P Thomson	Porthcawl	284	1990	M James	Woburn	270
1962	D Rees	Wentworth Club	278	1991	S Ballesteros	Woburn	275
1963	B Hunt	Little Aston	282	1992	C O'Connor jr*	Woburn	270
1964	C Legrange	Royal Birkdale	288	1993	P Baker	Woburn	266
1965	B Hunt	Portmarnock	283	1994	I Woosnam	Woburn	271
1966	N Coles	Lindrick	278	1995	S Torrance	Collingtree Park	270
1967	A Jacklin	R St George's	274	1996	R Allenby*	Collingtree Park	284
1968	P Thomson	Sunningdale	274	1997	G Turner	Forest of Arden	275
1969	C Legrange	Little Aston	281	1998	C Montgomerie	Forest of Arden	281
1970	B Huggett	R Lytham & St Annes	293	1999	B May	Woburn	269
1971	M Bembridge	St Pierre	273	2000	G Orr	Woburn	267
1972	R J Charles	Northumberland	277	2001	T Levet*	Woburn	274

2002 *at Woburn, Milton Keynes, England*   (7214–72)

1	Justin Rose (Eng)	70-69-65-65—269	£208330	€329374
2	Ian Poulter (Eng)	68-67-67-68—270	78250	123715
3	Phillip Price (Wal)	68-65-68-72—273	62500	98814

The Compass Group English Open

1979	S Ballesteros	The Belfry	286	1993	I Woosnam	Forest of Arden	269
1980	M Piñero	The Belfry	286	1994	C Montgomerie	Forest of Arden	274
1981	R Davis	The Belfry	283	1995	P Walton*	Forest of Arden	274
1982	G Norman	The Belfry	279	1996	R Allenby	Forest of Arden	278
1983	H Baiocchi*	The Belfry	279	1997	P-U Johansson	Hanbury Manor	269
1988	H Clark	Royal Birkdale	279	1998	L Westwood	Hanbury Manor	271
1990	M James*	The Belfry	284	1999	D Clarke	Hanbury Manor	268
1991	D Gilford	The Belfry	278	2000	D Clarke	Forest of Arden	275
1992	V Fernandez	The Belfry	283	2001	P O'Malley	Forest of Arden	275

2002 at Forest of Arden, Warwickshire   (7213–72)

1	Darren Clarke (NI)	65-70-68-68—271	£133330	€208798
2	Søren Hansen (Den)	72-68-64-70—274	88880	139188
3	Raphaèl Jacquelin (Fra)	70-68-65-73—276	45040	70534
	Phillip Price (Wal)	68-68-70-70—276	45040	70534

US OPEN

2002 at Bethpage State Park, Farmingdale, NY, USA   (7214–70)

1	Tiger Woods (USA)	67-68-70-72—277	£684744	€1058313
2	Phil Mickelson (USA)	70-73-67-70—280	400575	618113
3	Jeff Maggert (USA)	69-73-68-72—282	248121	383486

Fuller details of this event are included in Part I The Majors page 64

The Great North Open   at Slaley Hall, Northumberland, England   (7088–72)

1996	R Goosen	277	1998	cancelled		2000	L Westwood	276
1997	C Montgomerie	270	1999	D Park	274	2001	A Coltart	277

2002

1	Miles Tunnicliff (Eng)	72-70-68-69—279	£100000	€155960
2	Sven Strüver (Ger)	71-65-74-73—283	66660	103963
3	Bradley Dredge (Wal)	68-71-75-70—284	33780	52683
	Malcolm Mackenzie (Eng)	72-72-69-71—284	33780	52683

Murphy's Irish Open

1927	G Duncan	Portmarnock	312	1979	M James	Portmarnock	282
1928	E Whitcombe	Newcastle	288	1980	M James	Portmarnock	284
1929	A Mitchell	Portmarnock	309	1981	S Torrance	Portmarnock	276
1930	C Whitcombe	Portrush	289	1982	J O'Leary	Portmarnock	287
1931	E Kenyon	Royal Dublin	291	1983	S Ballesteros	Royal Dublin	271
1932	A Padgham	Cork	283	1984	B Langer	Royal Dublin	267
1933	E Kenyon	Malone	286	1985	S Ballesteros*	Royal Dublin	278
1934	S Easterbrook	Portmarnock	284	1986	S Ballesteros	Portmarnock	285
.1935	E Whitcombe	Newcastle	292	1987	B Langer	Portmarnock	269
1936	R Whitcombe	Royal Dublin	281	1988	I Woosnam	Portmarnock	278
1937	B Gadd	Portrush	284	1989	I Woosnam*	Portmarnock	278
1938	A Locke	Portmarnock	292	1990	JM Olazábal	Portmarnock	282
1939	A Lees	Newcastle	287	1991	N Faldo	Killarney	283
1946	F Daly	Portmarnock	288	1992	N Faldo*	Killarney	274
1947	H Bradshaw	Portrush	290	1993	N Faldo*	Mount Juliet	276
1948	D Rees	Portmarnock	295	1994	B Langer	Mount Juliet	275
1949	H Bradshaw	Belvoir Park	286	1995	S Torrance*	Mount Juliet	277
1950	H Pickworth	Royal Dublin	287	1996	C Montgomerie	Druid's Glen	279
1953	E Brown	Belvoir Park	272	1997	C Montgomerie	Druid's Glen	269
1975	C O'Connor Jr	Woodbrook	275	1998	D Carter	Druid's Glen	278
1976	B Crenshaw	Portmarnock	284	1999	S García	Druid's Glen	268
1977	H Green	Portmarnock	283	2000	P Sjöland	Ballybunion	270
1978	K Brown	Portmarnock	281	2001	C Montgomerie	Fota Island	266

2002 at Fota Island, Cork, Ireland   (6927–71)

1	Søren Hansen (Den)*	69-69-64-68—270	£172678	€266660
2	Richard Bland (Eng)	69-71-63-67—270	77260	119310
	Niclas Fasth (Swe)	72-67-63-68—270	77260	119310
	Darren Fichardt (RSA)	71-68-64-67—270	77260	119310

Smurfit European Open

1978	B Wadkins*	Walton Heath	283	1990	P Senior	Sunningdale	267
1979	A Lyle	Turnberry	275	1991	M Harwood	Walton Heath	277
1980	T Kite	Walton Heath	284	1992	N Faldo	Sunningdale	262
1981	G Marsh	Royal Liverpool	275	1993	G Brand jr	E. Sussex National	275
1982	M Piñero	Sunningdale	266	1994	D Gilford	E. Sussex National	275
1983	L Aoki	Sunningdale	274	1995	B Langer*	The K Club	280
1984	G Brand jr	Sunningdale	270	1996	P-U Johansson	The K Club	277
1985	B Langer	Sunningdale	269	1997	P-U Johansson	The K Club	267
1986	G Norman*	Sunningdale	269	1998	M Grönberg	The K Club	275
1987	P Way	Walton Heath	279	1999	L Westwood	The K Club	271
1988	I Woosnam	Sunningdale	260	2000	L Westwood	The K Club	276
1989	A Murray	Walton Heath	277	2002	D Clarke	The K Club	273

2002 at The K Club, Dublin, Ireland   (7337–72)

1	Michael Campbell (NZ)	68-71-70-73—282	£333330	€515585
2	Bradley Dredge (Wal)	71-71-73-68—283	133055	205806
	Retief Goosen (RSA)	71-72-72-68—283	133055	205806
	Padraig Harrington (Irl)	72-69-69-73—283	133055	205806
	Paul Lawrie (Sco)	70-71-69-73—283	133055	205806

The Scottish Open

1986	D Feherty*	Haggs Castle	270	1995	W Riley	Carnoustie	276
1987	I Woosnam	Gleneagles	264	1996T	I Woosnam	Carnoustie	289
1988	B Lane	Gleneagles	271		T Bjørn	Loch Lomond	277
1989	M Allen	Gleneagles	272	1997	T Lehman	Loch Lomond	265
1990	I Woosnam	Gleneagles	269	1998	L Westwood	Loch Lomond	276
1991	C Parry	Gleneagles	268	1999	C Montgomerie	Loch Lomond	268
1992	P O'Malley	Gleneagles	262	2000	E Els	Loch Lomond	273
1993	J Parnevik	Gleneagles	271	2001	R Goosen	Loch Lomond	268
1994	C Mason	Gleneagles	265				

2002 at Loch Lomond, Glasgow, Scotland   (7083–71)

1	Eduardo Romero (Arg)*	72-66-65-70—273	£366660	€573016
2	Fredrik Jacobson (Swe)	66-65-71-71—273	244440	382011
3	Roger Chapman (Eng)	70-70-66-68—274	123860	193568
	Tim Clark (RSA)	71-68-67-68—274	123860	193568

OPEN CHAMPIONSHIP

2002 at Muirfield, Scotland   (7034–71)

1	Ernie Els (RSA)*	70-66-72-70—278	£700000	€1095514
2	Stuart Appleby (Aus)	73-70-70-65—278	286667	448639
	Steve Elkington (Aus)	71-73-68-66—278	286667	448639
	Thomas Levet (Fra)	72-66-74-66—278	286667	448639

Past results and fuller details in Part I The Majors page 54

TNT Open

Year	Player	Venue	Score		Year	Player	Venue	Score
1919	D Oosterveer	The Hague	158		1964	S Sewgolum	Eindhoven	275
1920	H Burrows	Kennemer	155		1965	A Miguel	Breda	278
1921	H Burrows	Domburg	151		1966	R Sota	Kennemer	276
1922	G Pannell	Noordwijk	160		1967	P Townsend	The Hague	282
1923	H Burrows	Hilversumsche	153		1968	J Cockin	Hilversumsche	292
1924	A Boomer	The Hague	138		1969	G Wolstenholme	Utrecht	277
1925	A Boomer	The Hague	144		1970	V Fernandez	Eindhoven	279
1926	A Boomer	The Hague	151		1971	R Sota	Kennemer	277
1927	P Boomer	The Hague	147		1972	J Newton	The Hague	277
1928	ER Whitcombe	The Hague	141		1973	D McClelland	The Hague	279
1929	JJ Taylor	Hilversumsche	153		1974	B Barnes	Hilversumsche	211 (54)
1930	J Oosterveer	The Hague	152		1975	H Baiocchi	Hilversumsche	279
1931	F Dyer	Kennemer	145		1976	S Ballesteros	Kennemer	275
1932	A Boyer	The Hague	137		1977	R Byman	Kennemer	278
1933	M Dallemagne	Kennemer	143		1978	R Byman	Noordwijkse	21 (54)
1934	SF Brews	Utrecht	286		1979	G Marsh	Noordwijkse	285
1935	SF Brews	Kennemer	275		1980	S Ballesteros	Hilversumsche	280
1936	F van Donck	Hilversumsche	285		1981	H Henning	The Hague	280
1937	F van Donck	Utrecht	286		1982	P Way	Utrecht	276
1938	AH Padgham	The Hague	281		1983	K Brown	Kennemer	274
1939	AD Locke	Kennemer	281		1984	B Langer	Rosendaelsche	275
1946	F van Donck	Hilversumsche	290		1985	G Marsh	Noordwijkse	282
1947	G Ruhl	Eindhoven	290		1986	S Ballesteros	Noordwijkse	271 (70)
-1948	C Denny	Hilversumsche	290		1987	G Brand jr	Hilversumsche	272
1949	J Adams	The Hague	294		1988	M Mouland	Hilversumsche	274
1950	R De Vicenzo	Breda	269		1989	JM Olazábal*	Kennemer	277
1951	F van Donck	Kennemer	281		1990	S McAllister	Kennemer	274
1952	C Denny	Hilversumsche	284		1991	P Stewart	Noordwijkse	267
1953	F van Donck	Eindhoven	286		1992	B Langer*	Noordwijkse	277
1954	U Grappasonni	The Hague	295		1993	C Montgomerie	Noordwijkse	281
1955	A Angelini	Kennemer	280		1994	MA Jiménez	Hilversumsche	270
1956	A Cerda	Eindhoven	277		1995	S Hoch	Hilversumsche	269
1957	J Jacobs	Hilversumsche	284		1996	M McNulty	Hilversumsche	266
1958	D Thomas	Kennemer	277		1997	S Strüver	Hilversumsche	266
1959	S Sewgolum	The Hague	283		1998	S Leaney	Hilversumsche	266
-1960	S Sewgolum	Eindhoven	280		1999	L Westwood	Hilversumsche	269
1961	BBS Wilkes	Kennemer	279		2000	S Leaney	Nordwijkse	269
1962	BGC Huggett	Hilversumsche	274		2001	B Langer*	Nordwijkse	269
1963	R Waltman	Wassenaar	279					

2002 at Hilversum, The Netherlands   (6617–70)

1	Tobias Dier (Ger)	60-67-67-69—263	£193019	€300000
2	Jamie Spence (Eng)	66-64-69-65—264	128679	200000
3	Padraig Harrington (Irl)	66-67-64-68—265	65202	101340
	Peter Lonard (Aus)	67-63-68-67—265	65202	101340

Volvo Scandinavian Masters

Year	Player	Venue	Score		Year	Player	Venue	Score
1991	C Montgomerie	Drottningholm	270		1997	J Haeggman	Barsebäck	270
1992	N Faldo	Barsebäck	277		1998	J Parnevik	Kungsängen	273
1993	P Baker*	Forsgårdens	278		1999	C Montgomerie	Barsebäck	268
1994	V Singh	Drottningholm	268		2000	L Westwood	Kungsängen	270
1995	J Parnevik	Barsebäck	270		2001	C Montgomerie	Kungsängen	274
1996	L Westwood	Forsgårdens	281					

2002 at Kungsängen, Stockholm, Sweden   (6761–71)

1	Graeme McDowell (NI)	64-73-66-67—270	£200143	€316660
2	Trevor Immelman (RSA)	70-67-67-67—271	133431	211110
3	Henrik Bjornstad (Nor)	70-69-66-67—272	67610	106970

The Wales Open at Celtic Manor Resort, Newport, Wales (7355–72)

2000	S Tinning	Newport	223	2001	P McGinley	Newport	138

2002

1	Paul Lawrie (Sco)	67-65-70-70—272	£183330	€291432
2	John Bickerton (Eng)	67-67-73-70—277	122220	194288
3	Mikko Ilonen (Fin)	70-68-70-70—278	68860	109464

US PGA CHAMPIONSHIP

2002 at Hazeltine National, Chaska, MN (7360–72)

1	Rich Beem (USA)	72-66-72-68—278	£649819	€1019144
2	Tiger Woods (USA)	71-69-72-67—279	389892	611487
3	Chris Riley (USA)	71-70-72-70—283	245487	385010

Past results and fuller details in Part I The Majors page 79

North West of Ireland Open

2001	T Dier (Ger)	Co. Cavan	271

2002 at Ballyliffin, Donegal, Ireland (7222–72)

1	Adam Mednick (Swe)	76-68-69-68—281	£37192	€58330
2	Andrew Coltart (Sco)	76-66-77-67—286	19380	30395
	Costantino Rocca (Ita)	71-69-74-72—286	19380	30395

WGC: NEC Invitational at Sahalee, Redmond, WA (6949–71)

1	Craig Parry (Aus)	72-65-66-65—268	£650533	€1016673
2	Robert Allenby (Aus)	69-63-71-69—272	266719	416836
	Fred Funk (USA)	68-68-68-68—272	266719	416836

Fuller details of this event are included in World Championship Events on page 171

Scottish PGA Championship

1999	W Bennett	2000	P Fulke	2001	P Casey

2002 at King's Course, Gleneagles, Scotland (7060–72)

1	Adam Scott (Aus)	67-65-67-63—262	£166660	€260461
2	Raymond Russell (Sco)	67-71-66-68—272	111110	173646
3	Sam Torrance (Sco)	69-68-69-67—273	62600	97833

BMW International Open

1989	D Feherty	Golfplatz, Munich	269	1996	M Farry	St Eurach L&GC	132
1990	P Azinger*	Golfplatz, Munich	277			(36 holes only)	
1991	A Lyle	Golfplatz, Munich	268	1997	R Karlsson	GC München	264
1992	P Azinger*	Golfplatz, Munich	266	1998	R Claydon	GC München	270
1993	P Fowler	Golfplatz, Munich	267	1999	C Montgomerie	GC München	268
1994	M McNulty	St Eurach L&GC	274	2000	T Bjørn	GC München	368
1995	F Nobilo	St Eurach L&GC	272	2001	J Daly	GC München	261

2002 at Golfclub München Nord-Eichenried, Munich (6963–72)

1	Thomas Bjørn (Den)	68-64-66-66—264	£191772	€300000
2	John Bickerton (Eng)	67-69-66-66—268	99939	156340
	Bernhard Langer (Ger)	64-69-67-68—268	99939	156340

Omega European Masters *at Crans-sur-Sierre, Switzerland* (since 1939)

Year	Player	Venue	Score		Year	Player	Score
1923	A Ross	Engen	149		1969	R Bernardini	277
1924	P Boomer	Engen	150		1970	G Marsh	274
1925	A Ross	Engen	148		1971	PM Townsend	270
1926	A Ross	Lucerne	145		1972	G Marsh	270
1929	A Wilson	Lucerne	142		1973	H Baiocchi	278
1930	A Boyer	Samedan	150		1974	RJ Charles	275
1931	M Dallemagne	Lucerne	145		1975	D Hayes	273
1934	A Boyer	Lausanne	133		1976	M Piñero	274
1935	A Boyer	Lausanne	137		1977	S Ballesteros	273
1936	F Francis (am)	Lausanne	134		1978	S Ballesteros	272
1937	M Dallemagne	Samedan	138		1979	H Baiocchi	275
1938	J Saubaber	Zumikon	139		1980	N Price	267
1939	F Cavalo	Crans-sur-Sierre	273		1981	M Piñero*	277
1948	U Grappasonni		285		1982	I Woosnam*	272
1949	M Dallemagne		270		1983	N Faldo*	268
1950	A Casera		276		1984	J Anderson	261
1951	EC Brown		267		1985	C Stadler	267
1952	U Grappasonni		267		1986	JM Olazábal	262
1953	F van Donck		267		1987	A Forsbrand	263
1954	AD Locke		276		1988	C Moody	268
1955	F van Donck		277		1989	S Ballesteros	266
1956	DJ Rees		278		1990	R Rafferty	267
1957	A Angelini		270		1991	J Hawkes	268
1958	K Bousfield		272		1992	J Spence*	271
1959	DJ Rees		274		1993	B Lane	270
1960	H Henning		270		1994	E Romero	266
1961	KDG Nagle		268		1995	M Grönberg	270
1962	RJ Charles*		272		1996	C Montgomerie	260
1963	DJ Rees*		278		1997	C Rocca	266
1964	HR Henning		276		1998	S Strüver	263
1965	HR Henning		208 (54)		1999	L Westwood	270
1966	A Angelini		271		2000	E Romero	261
1967	R Vines		272		2001	R Gonzalez	268
1968	R Bernardini		272				

2002

1	Robert Karlsson (Swe)	65-66-68-71—270	£158407	€250000
2	Trevor Immelman (RSA)	70-67-65-72—274	82549	130280
	Paul Lawrie (Sco)	66-70-66-72—274	82549	130280

Linde German Masters

Year	Player	Venue	Score		Year	Player	Venue	Score
1987	A Lyle*	Stuttgart	278		1995	A Forsbrand	Motzener See	264
1988	JM Olazábal	Stuttgart	279		1996	D Clarke	Motzener See	264
1989	B Langer	Stuttgart	276		1997	B Langer	Berliner G & CG	267
1990	S Torrance	Stuttgart	272		1998	C Montgomerie	Gut Lärchenhof	266
1991	B Langer*	Stuttgart	275		1999	S García	Gut Lärchenhof	277
1992	B Lane	Stuttgart	272		2000	M Campbell	Gut Lärchenhof	197
1993	S Richardson	Stuttgart	271		2001	B Langer	Gut Lärchenhof	266
1994	S Ballesteros*	Motzener See	270					

2002 *at Gut Lärchenhof, Cologne* (7289–72)

1	Stephen Leaney (Aus)	64-69-66-67—266	£315541	€500000
2	Alex Cejka (Ger)	68-68-63-68—267	210359	333330
3	Paul Casey (Eng)	68-67-62-71—268	97818	155000
	Nick Dougherty (Eng)	68-65-69-66—268	97818	155000
	Ian Woosnam (Wal)	68-64-68-68—268	97818	155000

WGC: American Express Stroke Play Championship

at Mount Juliet, Kilkenny, Ireland (7246–72)

1	Tiger Woods (USA)	65-65-67-66—263	£641643	€1026378
2	Retief Goosen (RSA)	67-67-68-62—264	346487	554244
3	Vijay Singh (Fij)	67-69-66-65—267	235804	377194

Fuller details of this event can be found in World Championship Events on page 171

Ryder Cup

at The Belfry, Sutton Coldfield

Result: Europe 15½, USA 12½

Fuller details of this event can be found in World Championship Events on page 171

Dunhill Links Championship

2001   P Lawrie

2002 *at St Andrews (Old Course), Carnoustie, Kingsbarns*

1	Padraig Harrington*(Irl)	66-66-68-69—269	£514535	€818661
2	Eduardo Romero (Arg)	65-68-67-69—269	342744	545771
3	Sandy Lyle (Sco)	69-67-67-68—271	159377	253785
	Colin Montgomerie (Sco)	70-69-69-63—271	159377	253785
	Vijay Singh (Fij)	70-67-64-70—271	159377	253785

Trophée Lancôme *at Saint-Nom-La-Bretèche, Paris* (6712–71)

1970	A Jacklin	206	(54)	1987	I Woosnam	264	
1971	A Palmer	202	(54)	1988	S Ballesteros	269	
1972	T Aaron	279		1989	E Romero	266	
1973	J Miller	277		1990	JM Olazábal	269	
1974	W Casper	283		1991	F Nobilo	267	
1975	G Player	278		1992	M Roe	267	
1976	S Ballesteros	283		1993	I Woosnam	267	
1977	G Marsh*	273		1994	V Singh	263	
1978	L Trevino	272		1995	C Montgomerie	269	
1979	J Miller	281		1996	J Parnevik	268	
1980	L Trevino	280		1997	M O'Meara	271	
1981	D Graham	280		1998	MA Jiménez	273	
1982	D Graham	276		1999	P Fulke	270	
1983	S Ballesteros	269		2000	R Goosen	271	
1984	A Lyle*	278		2001	S García	266	
1985	N Price*	275					
1986T	S Ballesteros*	274					
	B Langer*						

2002

1	Alex Cejka (Ger)	64-68-72-68—272	£150494	€239640
2	Carlos Rodiles (Esp)	67-69-72-66—274	100329	159760
3	Angel Cabrera (Arg)	69-68-71-67—275	50837	80950
	Jean-François Lucquin (Fra)	69-72-68-66—275	50837	80950

Cisco World Matchplay Championship

1964	A Palmer	N Coles	2 and 1	1969	R Charles	G Littler	37th hole
1965	G Player	P Thomson	3 and 2	1970	J Nicklaus	L Trevino	2 and 1
1966	G Player	J Nicklaus	6 and 4	1971	G Player	J Nicklaus	5 and 4
1967	A Palmer	P Thomson	1 hole	1972	T Weiskopf	L Trevino	4 and 3
1968	G Player	R Charles	1 hole	1973	G Player	G Marsh	40th hole

Cisco World Matchplay Championship *continued*

1974	H Irwin	G Player	3 and 1	1988	A Lyle	N Faldo	2 and 1
1975	H Irwin	A Geiberger	4 and 2	1989	N Faldo	I Woosnam	1 hole
1976	D Graham	H Irwin	38th hole	1990	I Woosnam	M McNulty	4 and 2
1977	G Marsh	R Floyd	5 and 3	1991	S Ballesteros	N Price	3 and 2
1978	I Aoki	S Owen	3 and 2	1992	N Faldo	J Sluman	8 and 7
1979	W Rogers	I Aoki	1 hole	1993	C Pavin	N Faldo	1 hole
1980	G Norman	A Lyle	1 hole	1994	E Els	C Montgomerie	4 and 2
1981	S Ballesteros	B Crenshaw	1 hole	1995	E Els	S Elkington	2 and 1
1982	S Ballesteros	A Lyle	37th hole	1996	E Els	V Singh	3 and 2
1983	G Norman	N Faldo	3 and 2	1997	V Singh	E Els	1 hole
1984	S Ballesteros	B Langer	2 and 1	1998	M O'Meara	T Woods	1 hole
1985	S Ballesteros	B Langer	6 and 5	1999	C Montgomerie	M O'Meara	3 and 2
1986	G Norman	A Lyle	2 and 1	2000	L Westwood	C Montgomerie	38th hole
1987	I Woosnam	A Lyle	1 hole	2001	I Woosnam	P Harrington	2 and 1

2002

First Round
Michael Campbell (NZ) beat Nick Faldo (Eng) at 43rd
Padraig Harrington (Irl) beat Mike Weir (Can) 4 and 3
Vijay Singh (Fij) beat Justin Rose (Eng) 1 hole
Colin Montgomerie (Sco) beat Fred Funk (USA) 3 and 2

Quarter Finals
Campbell beat Ian Woosnam (Wal) 3 and 2
Sergio García (Esp) beat Harrington 2 and 1
Singh beat Retief Goosen (RSA) 4 and 3
Ernie Els (RSA) beat Montgomerie 6 and 5

Semi-Finals
García beat Campbell 2 and 1
Els beat Singh 3 and 2

Final
Ernie Els beat Sergio García 2 and 1

Telefonica Open de Madrid
formerly BBVA Open Turespaña Masters de la Communidad de Madrid

1968	G Garrido	1977	A Garrido	1986	H Clark	1995	A Cejka
1969	R Soto	1978	H Clark	1987	I Woosnam	1996	D Borrego
1970	M Cabrera	1979	S Hobday	1988	D Cooper	1997	JM Olazábal
1971	V Barrios	1980	S Ballesteros	1989	S Ballesteros	1998	MA Jiménez
1972	J Kinsetta	1981	M Pineto	1990	B Langer	1999	MA Jiménez
1973	G Garrido	1982	S Ballesteros	1991	A Sherborne	2000	P Harrington
1974	M Pineto	1983	A Lyle	1992	D Feherty	2001	R Goosen
1975	K Shearer	1984	H Clark	1993	D Smyth		
1976	F Abreu	1985	M Pineto	1994	C Mason		

2002 *at Club de Campo, Madrid, Spain*   (6957–71)

1	Steen Tinning (Den)	68-68-62-67—265	£146507	€233330
2	Brian Davis (Eng)	65-72-66-63—266	65550	104396
	Andrew Coltart (Sco)	66-68-68-64—266	65550	104396
	Adam Scott (Aus)	67-65-66-68—266	65550	104396

Italian Open Telecom Italia

1925	F Pasquali	Stresa	154	1948	A Casera	San Remo	267
1926	A Boyer	Stresa	147	1949	H Hassanein	Villa d'Este	263
1927	P Alliss	Stresa	145	1950	U Grappasonni	Rome	281
1928	A Boyer	Villa d'Este	145	1951	J Adams	Milan	289
1929	R Golias	Villa d'Este	143	1952	E Brown	Milan	273
1930	A Boyer	Villa d'Este	140	1953	F van Donck	Villa d'Este	267
1931	A Boyer	Villa d'Este	141	1954	U Grappasonni	Villa d'Este	272
1932	A Boomer	Villa d'Este	143	1955	F van Donck	Venice	287
1934	N Nutley	San Remo	132	1956	A Cerda	Milan	284
1935	P Alliss	San Remo	262	1957	H Henning	Villa d'Este	273
1936	H Cotton	Sestriere	268	1958	P Alliss	Varese	282
1937	M Dallemagne	San Remo	276	1959	P Thomson	Villa d'Este	269
1938	F van Donck	Villa d'Este	276	1960	B Wilkes	Venice	285
1947	F van Donck	San Remo	263	1961	R Sota	Garlenda	282

1961–1971	*Not played*			1987	S Torrance*	Monticello	271
1972	N Wood	Villa d'Este	271	1988	G Norman	Monticello	270
1973	A Jacklin	Rome	284	1989	R Rafferty	Monticello	273
1974	P Oosterhuis	Venice	249 (63)	1990	R Boxall	Milan	267
1975	W Casper	Monticello	286	1991	C Parry	Castelconturbia	279
1976	B Dassu	Is Molas	280	1992	A Lyle	Monticello	270
1977	A Gallardo*	Monticello	286	1993	G Turner	Modena	267
1978	D Hayes	Pevero	293	1994	E Romero	Marco Simone	272
1979	B Barnes*	Monticello	281	1995	S Torrance	Le Rovedine	269
1980	M Mannelli	Rome	276	1996	J Payne	Bergamo GC	275
1981	J M Canizares*	Milan	280	1997	B Langer	Gardagolf	273
1982	M James	Is Molas	280	1998	JM Olazábal	Castelconturbia	195 (54)
1983	B Langer*	Ugolino	271	1999	D Robertson	Circolo GC, Torino	271
1984	A Lyle	Milan	277	2000	I Poulter	Is Molas	267
1985	M Piñero	Molinetto	267	2001	G Havret	Is Molas	268
1986	D Feherty*	Albarella, Venice	270				

2002 *at Olgiata GC Roma, Italy*

1	Ian Poulter (Eng)	61-67-69—197	£115276	€183330
2	Paul Lawrie (Sco)	66-63-70—199	76851	122220
3	Emanuele Canonica (Ita)	66-65-70—201	35736	56833
	Anders Hansen (Den)	64-71-66—201	35736	56833
	Anthony Wall (Eng)	69-67-65—201	35736	56833

Reduced to 56 holes because of rain

Volvo Masters Andalucia

1988	N Faldo	Valderrama	284	1995	A Cejka	Valderrama	282
1989	R Rafferty	Valderrama	282	1996	M McNulty	Valderrama	276
1990	M Harwood	Valderrama	286	1997	L Westwood	Montecastillo	200 (54)
1991	R Davis	Valderrama	280	1998	D Clarke	Montecastillo	271
1992	A Lyle	Valderrama	287	1999	MA Jiménez	Montecastillo	269
1993	C Montgomerie	Valderrama	274	2000	P Fulke	Montecastillo	272
1994	B Langer	Valderrama	276	2001	P Harrington	Montecastillo	204 (54)

2002 *at Valderrama, Spain* (6945–71)

1	Bernhard Langer* (Ger)	71-71-72-67—281	£277775	€435645
	Colin Montgomerie* (Sco)	70-69-72-70—281	277775	435645
3	Bradley Dredge (Wal)	68-71-71-73—283	125200	196357

* Declared a tie after 2 play-off holes because of darkness

European Challenge Tour 2002

Final Order of Merit (top 15 earn full Tour cards)

1	Lee S James (Eng)	€121,531	51	Richard Dinsdale (Wal)	18,972
2	Jean-François Lucquin (Fra)	101,544	52	Mattias Eliasson (Swe)	18,643
3	Matthew Blackey (Eng)	94,120	53	Sion E Bebb (Wal)	17,832
4	Peter Lawrie (Irl)	89,072	54	Allan Hogh (Den)	17,498
5	Iain Pyman (Eng)	75,674	55	Kariem Baraka (Ger)	17,304
6	Simon Hurd (Eng)	68,788	56	Alessandro Tadini (Ita)	17,134
7	Nicolas Vanhootegem (Bel)	63,823	57	James Hepworth (Eng)	16,755
8	John E Morgan (Eng)	62,047	58	Michael Jonzon (Swe)	16,225
9	Simon Wakefield (Eng)	58,922	59	Marc Cayeux (Zim)	16,120
10	Nicolas Colsaerts (Bel)	52,247	60	Stefano Reale (Ita)	15,999
11	Gary Birch jr (Eng)	51,219	61	Euan Little (Scot)	15,246
12	Gustavo Rojas (Arg)	50,873	62	David Ryles (Eng)	14,690
13	Benn Barham (Eng)	50,441	63	Martin Erlandsson (Swe)	13,802
14	Fredrik Widmark (Swe)	50,438	64	Gareth Paddison (NZ)	13,751
15	Julien Van Hauwe (Fr)	47,472	65	Roger Winchester (Eng)	13,750
16	Andrew Raitt (Eng)	47,254	66	Adam Crawford (Aus)	13,625
17	Titch Moore (RSA)	46,791	67	Kalle Brink (Swe)	13,491
18	Didier De Vooght (Bel)	46,266	68	Joakim Rask (Swe)	13,476
19	Mark Sanders (Eng)	44,671	69	Olivier David (Fra)	13,376
20	Massimo Florioli (It)	43,220	70	Dominique Nouailhac (Fra)	13,258
21	Ivo Giner (Esp)	38,788	71	Pehr Magnebrant (Swe)	13,212
22	Ed Stedman (Aus)	38,462	72	Garry Houston (Wal)	12,622
23	David J Geall (Eng)	38,384	73	Alberto Binaghi (Ita)	12,438
24	Ben Mason (Eng)	37,715	74	Kalle Vainola (Fin)	12,327
25	Damien McGrane (Irl)	37,358	75	Knud Storgaard (Den)	12,127
26	Jesus Maria Arruti (Esp)	36,870	76	Linus Petersson (Swe)	12,111
27	Wolfgang Huget (Ger)	36,055	77	Jean Pierre Cixous (Fra)	11,587
28	Gary Murphy (Irl)	34,747	78	Steven O'Hara (Scot)	11,362
29	Andrew Sherborne (Eng)	34,548	79	Per Nyman (Swe)	11,240
30	Richard Sterne (RSA)	34,537	80	Jean Louis Guepy (Fra)	11,114
31	Denny Lucas (Eng)	33,487	81	Marc Pendaries (Fra)	11,020
32	David Dixon (Eng)	33,361	82	Peter Malmgren (Swe)	10,819
33	Paul Dwyer (Eng)	32,755	83	Martin Maritz (RSA)	10,809
34	Ilya Goroneskoul (Fra)	31,477	84	Gianluca Baruffaldi (Ita)	10,764
35	Raimo Sjöberg (Swe)	31,110	85	Tuomas Tuovinen (Fin)	10,526
36	Guido Van der Valk (Ned)	30,909	86	Massimo Scarpa (Ita)	10,392
37	Hennie Otto (RSA)	29,956	87	Regis Gustave (St. Lucia)	10,247
38	Greig Hutcheon (Scot)	28,356	88	Marcel Siem (Ger)	10,049
39	Francois Delamontagne (Fra)	27,465	89	Carlos Quevedo (Esp)	10,038
40	Scott Kammann (USA)	27,348	90	Federico Bisazza (Ita)	9,937
41	Michael Archer (Eng)	25,761	91	Hampus Von Post (Swe)	9,816
42	Sam Little (Eng)	25,677	92	Bjorn Pettersson (Swe)	9,805
43	Hennie Walters (RSA)	24,714	93	Frédéric Cupillard (Fra)	9,535
44	Marcello Santi (Ita)	24,240	94	Steven Parry (Eng)	9,400
45	Thomas Norret (Den)	23,633	95	Van Phillips (Eng)	9,216
46	Thomas Besacenez (Fra)	21,862	96	Renaud Guillard (Fra)	9,192
47	Oskar Bergman (Swe)	21,149	97	Charles Challen (Eng)	8,862
48	Tim Milford (Eng)	20,030	98	Robin Byrd (USA)	8,855
49	Marco Bernardini (It)	19,784	99	Sebastien Branger (Fra)	8,832
50	Jamie Little (Eng)	19,047	100	Dennis Edlund (Swe)	8,804

Tour Results

Sameer Kenya Open	Muthaiga, Kenya	Lee S James (Eng)	265 (-19)
Stanbic Zambia Open	Lusaka, Zambia	Marc Cayeux (Zim)	270 (-22)
Madeira Island Open	Santo da Serra, Madeira	Diego Borrego (Esp)	281 (-7)
Panalpina BCM Moroccan Classic	Royal Dar Es Salam, Morocco	Jean-François Lucquin (Fra)	283 (-9)
Tessali Open del Sud	Riva dei Tessali, Italy	Simon Wakefield (Eng)	274 (-10)
Credit Suisse Private Banking Open	Patriziale, Ascona, Switzerland	abandoned	
Iski Challenge de España	Urturi, Vitoria, Spain	Fredrik Widmark (Swe)	276 (-16)
Austrian Open	Steiermärkischer Murhof, Austria	Markus Brier (Aut)	267 (-21)
Nykredit Danish Open	Horsens, Jutland, Denmark	Ed Stedman (Aus)	285 (-3)
Aa Open de Saint Omer	Aa Saint Omer, France	Nicolas Vanhootegem (Bel)	277 (-7)
Galeria Kaufhof Pokal Challenge	Rittergut Birkhof, Germany	Alex Cejka (Ger)	271 (-17)
Clearstream International Luxembourg Open	Kikuoka CC, Canach, Luxembourg	Lee James (Eng)	264 (-24)
Open des Volcans	Golf des Volcans, France	Scott Kammann (USA)	270 (-14)
PGA Triveneta Terme Euganee International Open	Montecchia, Italy	Wolfgang Huget (Ger)	268 (-20)
Volvo Finnish Open	Espoo, Finland	Thomas Norret (Den)	273 (-15)
Golf Challenge	Brunstorf, Hamburg, Germany	Iain Pyman (Eng)	204 (-12)
Charles Church Challenge Tour Championship	Bowood, Wiltshire, England	John E Morgan (Eng)	278 (-10)
Talma Finnish Challenge	Talma, Finland	Lee James (Eng)	239 (-19)
BMW Russian Open	Moscow, Russia	Iain Pyman (Eng)	269 (-19)
North West of Ireland Open	Ballyliffin, Donegal, Ireland	Adam Mednick (Swe)	281 (-7)
Skandia PGA Open	Halmstad, Sweden	Thomas Besancenez (Fra)	279 (-9)
Rolex Trophy	Genève, Switzerland	Simon Hurd (Eng)	268 (-20)
Formby Hall Challenge	Formby Hall, England	Matthew Blackey (Eng)	275 (-13)
Telia Grand Prix	Ljunghusens, Sweden	Matthew Blackey (Eng)	276 (-12)
PGA of Austria Masters	Kitzbühel Eichenheim, Austria		
Fortis Bank Challenge Open	Van Nymegen, Holland	Didier de Vooght (Bel)	270 (-18)
Challenge Tour Grand Final	Golf du Médoc, Bordeaux, France	Peter Lawrie (Irl)	272 (-12)

European Senior Tour 2002

Final Ranking

1	Seiji Ebihara (Jpn)	€330,210		51	Jeff Van Wagenen (USA)	35,570
2	Denis Durnian (Eng)	259,982		52	Bob Shearer (Aus)	31,819
3	Delroy Cambridge (Jam)	184,167		53	David Huish (Sco)	31,226
4	John Morgan (Eng)	157,216		54	Jay Horton (USA)	31,079
5	Christy O'Connor jr (Irl)	152,319		55	Bobby Verwey (RSA)	31,022
6	Steve Stull (USA)	137,468		56	Bill Hardwick (Can)	27,773
7	John Irwin (Can)	126,127		57	Martin Gray (Sco)	27,327
8	John Chillas (Sco)	125,829		58	Antonio Garrido (Esp)	25,135
9	Denis O'OSullivan (Irl)	125,361		59	Craig Defoy (Wal)	25,064
10	Nick Job (Eng)	122,319		60	Peter Dawson (Eng)	24,992
11	Neil Coles (Eng)	106,798		61	Liam Higgins (Irl)	23,222
12	Barry Vivian (NZ)	103,217		62	Mike Ferguson (Aus)	22,267
13	Keith MacDonald (Eng)	99,915		63	Manuel Piñero (Esp)	22,117
14	Tommy Horton (Eng)	96,574		64	Steve Wild (Eng)	21,378
15	David Good (Aus)	93,734		65	Paul Leonard (NI)	19,900
16	Jim Rhodes (Eng)	91,462		66	Hank Woodrome (USA)	19,680
17	Ian Mosey (Eng)	90,234		67	John Fourie (RSA)	19,189
18	Noel Ratcliffe (Aus)	89,380		68	Silvano Locatelli (Ita)	16,955
19	David Creamer (Eng)	88,768		69	David Ojala (USA)	16,117
20	Malcolm Gregson (Eng)	88,180		70	Renato Campagnoli (Ita)	12,956
21	Jerry Bruner (USA)	87,799		71	Lawrence Farmer (Wal)	12,679
22	Ray Carrasco (USA)	87,072		72	Norman Wood (Sco)	10,551
23	Ian Stanley (Aus)	80,197		73	Agim Bardha (Alb)	9,897
24	Mike Miller (Sco)	78,604		74	Ian Richardson (Eng)	8,995
25	Guillermo Encina (Chl)	76,937		75	David Vaughan (Wal)	8,862
26	David Oakley (USA)	76,692		76	John Benda (USA)	7,768
27	John Grace (USA)	76,330		77	Geoff Parslow (Aus)	7,325
28	Bernard Gallacher (Sco)	75,649		78	Tommy Price (USA)	7,077
29	Brian Jones (Aus)	66,075		79	Victor Garcia (Esp)	6,235
30	Alberto Croce (Ita)	65,592		80	Jan Sonnevi (Swe)	5,679
31	Gary Wintz (USA)	65,370		81	Brian Waites (Eng)	4,947
32	Dragon Taki (Jpn)	64,433		82	TR Jones (USA)	4,335
33	Ross Metherell (Aus)	63,567		83	David Snell (Eng)	3,801
34	Priscillo Diniz (Bra)	63,234		84	Jay Dolan III (USA)	3,667
35	Peter Townsend (Eng)	62,844		85	Kenny Stevenson (NI)	2,695
36	Terry Gale (Aus)	62,830		86	Barry Sandry (Eng)	1,557
37	Eamonn Darcy (Irl)	62,754		87	Graham Burroughs (Eng)	1,471
38	Eddie Polland (NI)	60,654		88	Michael Murphy (Irl)	1,040
39	Martin Foster (Eng)	58,813		89	Jan Dorrenstein (Ned)	981
40	Alan Tapie (USA)	58,229		90T	Manuel Sánchez (Esp)	777
41	John McTear (Sco)	57,852			Kurt Cox (USA)	777
42	Tony Jacklin (Eng)	55,506		92	Manuel Ballesteros (Esp)	621
43	Russell Weir (Sco)	51,114		93	John Turk (USA)	578
44	Bill Brask (USA)	50,119		94	Antero Baburin (Swe)	466
45	Simon Owen (NZ)	49,577		95	Hugh Dolan (Aus)	391
46	Joe McDermott (Irl)	46,475		96	Leonard Owens (Irl)	341
47	Maurice Bembridge (Eng)	38,363		97T	Roberto Bernardini (Ita)	255
48	Bob Lendzion (USA)	38,093			Gordon MacDonald (Sco)	255
49	David Jones (NI)	36,586		99	Roger Fidler (Eng)	225
50	John Mashego (RSA)	36,370		100	Deray Simon (USA)	213

Career Money List

1	Tommy Horton (Eng)	€1,329,478	51	Jay Horton (Eng)	212,750
2	Neil Coles (Eng)	817,588	52	Bill Brask (USA)	212,229
3	Noel Ratcliffe (Aus)	816,926	53	Peter Townsend (Eng)	200,476
4	John Morgan (Eng)	745,331	54	John Irwin (Can)	195,089
5	Malcolm Gregson (Eng)	647,773	55	John McTear (Sco)	188,414
6	Brian Huggett (Eng)	638,782	56	Norman Wood (Sco)	181,961
7	Seiji Ebihara (Jpn)	618,815	57	Joe McDermott (Irl)	174,699
8	Jim Rhodes (Eng)	580,072	58	Mike Miller (Sco)	168,319
9	David Oakley (USA)	572,600	59	Peter Butler (Eng)	155,984
10	Denis Durnian (Eng)	567,696	60	Hugh Inggs (RSA)	153,047
11	Ian Stanley (Aus)	558,784	61	John Chillas (Sco)	152,431
12	Denis O'Sullivan (Irl)	557,831	62	John Garner (Eng)	142,685
13	Maurice Bembridge (Eng)	530,872	63	Chick Evans (USA)	141,711
14	David Creamer (Eng)	529,210	64	David Butler (Eng)	141,202
15	Antonio Garrido (Esp)	520,799	65	Steve Stull (USA)	137,468
16	Jerry Bruner (USA)	501,265	66	Ian Richardson (Eng)	134,866
17	David Huish (Sco)	498,846	67	Noboru Sugai (Jpn)	129,863
18	Eddie Polland (NI)	495,780	68	David Snell (Eng)	125,509
19	Bobby Verwey (RSA)	488,430	69	Vincent Tshabalala (RSA)	122,481
20	Brian Waites (Eng)	482,279	70	Jay Dolan III (USA)	122,361
21	Bob Charles (NZ)	465,804	71	Steve Wild (Eng)	121,390
22	Alberto Croce (Ita)	428,937	72	Russell Weir (Sco)	120,663
23	Terry Gale (Aus)	418,260	73	Deray Simon (USA)	118,695
24	Christy O'Connor jr (Irl)	382,454	74	Agim Bardha (Alb)	118,051
25	Liam Higgins (Irl)	380,260	75	Michael Murphy (Irl)	113,602
26	David Good (Aus)	377,942	76	JR Delich (USA)	113,165
27	Bob Shearer (Aus)	377,885	77	Geoff Parslow (Aus)	112,714
28	Gary Player (RSA)	365,567	78	Doug Dalziel (USA)	112,220
29	Bernard Gallacher (Sco)	363,426	79	Tony Grubb (Eng)	111,240
30	Delroy Cambridge (Jam)	362,038	80	Barry Sandry (Eng)	109,740
31	John Fourie (RSA)	356,939	81	Tony Jacklin (Eng)	109,224
32	David Jones (NI)	355,956	82	Ian Mosey (Eng)	106,434
33	John Grace (USA)	352,899	83	Randall Vines (Aus)	104,772
34	Nick Job (Eng)	331,511	84	Roger Fidler (Eng)	103,628
35	Priscillo Diniz (Bra)	318,041	85	Joe Carr (USA)	102,745
36	Renato Campagnoli (Ita)	310,571	86	Snell Lancaster (USA)	101,667
37	Bill Hardwick (Can)	300,904	87	Tienie Britz (RSA)	94,886
38	Alan Tapie (USA)	286,973	88	Tommy Price (USA)	93,696
39	Craig Defoy (Wal)	284,441	89	Trevor Downing (Aus)	91,130
40	Paul Leonard (NI)	272,505	90	Roberto Bernardini (Ita)	89,034
41	Bob Lendzion (USA)	257,437	91	TR Jones (USA)	85,692
42	Simon Owen (NZ)	248,918	92	José Maria Roca (Esp)	85,082
43	Ross Metherell (Aus)	246,774	93	Harry Flatman (Eng)	83,946
44	Brian Barnes (Sco)	234,975	94	Hugh Boyle (Eng)	82,616
45	Ray Carrasco (USA)	233,901	95	Bernard Hunt (Eng)	82,382
46	John Bland (Eng)	228,535	96	George Burns (USA)	81,194
47	Barry Vivian (NZ)	225,426	97	Guillermo Encina (Chl)	76,937
48	Jeff Van Wagenen (USA)	221,340	98	Bryan Carter (Eng)	74,397
49	Peter Dawson (Eng)	215,689	99	Manuel Ballesteros (Esp)	72,966
50	Keith Macdonald (Eng)	214,158	100	Hedley Muscroft (Eng)	72,187

Tour Results

Royal Westmoreland Barbados Open	Royal Westmoreland, Barbados	Peter Townsend (Eng)	212 (-4)
Tobago Plantations Seniors Classic	Tobago	Steve Stull (USA)	205 (-11)
AIB Irish Seniors Open	Adare Manor, Ireland	Seiji Ebihara (Jpn)	208 (-8)
Legends in Golf	Flanders-Nippon, Belgium	Gary Wintz (USA)	205 (-11)
Microlease Jersey Seniors Masters	La Moye, Jersey	Delroy Cambridge (Jam)	205 (-11)
Lawrence Batley Seniors Open	Huddersfield, England	Neil Coles (Eng)	209 (-4)
Wales Seniors Open	Royal St David's, Wales	Seiji Ebihara (Jpn)	203 (-4)
The Mobile Cup	Stoke Park, England	Bernard Gallacher (Sco)	201 (-12)
SENIOR BRITISH OPEN	Royal Co Down, N Ireland	Noboru Sugai (Jpn)	281 (-3)
De Vere PGA Seniors Championship	Carden Park, England	Seiji Ebihara (Jpn)	267 (-21)
Bad Ragaz PGA Seniors Open	Bad Ragaz, Engadine, Switzerland	Dragon Taki (Jpn)	130 (-10)
Travis Perkins Senior Masters	Wentworth, Surrey, England	Ray Carrasco (USA)	206 (-10)
De Vere Hotels Seniors Classic	Slaley Hall, England	Brian Jones (Aus)	207 (-9)
Monte Carlo Invitational	Monte Carlo, France	Terry Gale (Aus)	197 (-10)
Bovis Lend-Lease European Senior Masters	Woburn, England	Delroy Cambridge (Jam)	207 (-9)
Scottish Seniors Open	The Roxburghe, Scotland	Denis Durnian (Eng)	206 (-10)
Daily Telegraph/Sodexho Senior Match Play Championship	Los Flamingos, Spain	Delroy Cambridge (Jam) beat Eddie Polland (NI) by 1 hole in final	
Tunisian Seniors Open	Port El Kantaoui, Tunisia	Denis O'Sullivan (Irl)	202 (-14)
Estoril Seniors Tour Championship	Campo de Golfe da Quinta da Marina, Portugal	Denis Durnian (Eng)*	208 (-5)

US PGA Tour 2002

Players are of US nationality unless stated

Final Ranking

The top 125 on the money list retained their cards for the 2003 season. The top 40 earned a spot at The Masters.

#	Player	Money
1	Tiger Woods	$6,912,625
2	Phil Mickelson	4,311,971
3	Vijay Singh (Fij)	3,756,563
4	David Toms	3,461,794
5	Ernie Els (RSA)	3,291,895
6	Jerry Kelly	2,946,889
7	Rich Beem	2,938,365
8	Justin Leonard	2,738,235
9	Charles Howell III	2,702,747
10	Retief Goosen (RSA)	2,617,004
11	Chris DiMarco	2,606,530
12	Sergio García (Esp)	2,401,993
13	Fred Funk	2,383,071
14	Jim Furyk	2,363,250
15	Jeff Sluman	2,250,187
16	Shigeki Maruyama (Jpn)	2,214,794
17	K.J. Choi (Kor)	2,204,907
18	Len Mattiace	2,194,327
19	Nick Price (Zim)	2,170,912
20	Robert Allenby (Aus)	2,115,771
21	Davis Love III	2,056,160
22	Rocco Mediate	2,040,676
23	Chris Riley	2,032,979
24	José Maria Olazábal (Esp)	1,987,027
25	John Rollins	1,956,565
26	Bob Estes	1,934,600
27	Kenny Perry	1,928,598
28	Loren Roberts	1,919,047
29	Scott McCarron	1,896,714
30	Steve Lowery	1,882,553
31	Brad Faxon	1,814,672
32	Stuart Appleby (Aus)	1,729,459
33	Phil Tataurangi (NZ)	1,643,686
34	Craig Perks (NZ)	1,632,042
35	John Cook	1,624,095
36	Kevin Sutherland	1,569,529
37	Craig Parry (Aus)	1,466,235
38	Scott Hoch	1,465,173
39	Jonathan Byrd	1,462,71
40	Pat Perez	1,451,726
41	Peter Lonard (Aus)	1,413,113
42	Billy Andrade	1,365,707
43	Chris Smith	1,361,963
44	Dan Forsman	1,305,790
45	John Huston	1,299,053
46	Stephen Ames (Tri)	1,278,301
47	Ian Leggatt (Can)	1,245,048
48	David Peoples	1,243,774
49	Matt Kuchar	1,237,725
50	Scott Verplank	1,217,022
51	Bob Burns	1,199,802
52	Steve Flesch	1,192,341
53	Mark Calcavecchia	1,164,169
54	Dudley Hart	1,161,080
55	Bob Tway	1,160,399
56	Lee Janzen	1,129,399
57	Matt Gogel	1,089,482
58	Luke Donald (Eng)	1,088,205
59	Steve Elkington (Aus)	1,084,535
60	Jonathan Kaye	1,082,803
61	Joel Edwards	1,077,651
62	Brandt Jobe	972,479
63	Jesper Parnevik (Swe)	964,304
64	Geoff Ogilvy (Aus)	957,184
65	JL Lewis	957,182
66	JP Hayes	955,271
67	Tim Herron	954,917
68	Rory Sabbatini (RSA)	936,664
69	Brian Gay	926,735
70	Ben Crane	921,076
71	Duffy Waldorf	909,003
72	Cameron Beckman	907,740
73	Stewart Cink	894,212
74	Tom Lehman	868,632
75	Billy Mayfair	864,745
76	Heath Slocum	864,615
77	Glen Day	859,930
78	Mike Weir (Can)	844,154
79	Kirk Triplett	843,273
80	David Duval	838,045
81	Chad Campbell	825,474
82	Briny Baird	817,514
83	Neal Lancaster	813,230
84	Jim Carter	812,610
85	Robert Gamez	807,892
86	Tim Petrovic	797,206
87	Joey Sindelar	790,750
88	Steve Stricker	789,713
89	Rod Pampling (Aus)	776,903
90	Paul Azinger	769,926
91	Esteban Toledo (Mex)	766,463
92	Hidemichi Tanaka (Jpn)	766,423
93	Frank Lickliter II	740,460
94	Jeff Maggert	733,198
95	Mark Brooks	731,671
96	Harrison Frazar	731,295
97	Mark O'Meara	730,132
98	Jay Haas	722,782
99	Gene Sauers	715,605
100	David Gossett	676,308
101	Skip Kendall	653,594
102	Carlos Franco (Col)	652,147
103	Fred Couples	646,703
104	Tom Pernice jr	645,110
105	Shaun Micheel	641,450
106	Greg Chalmers (Aus)	640,898
107	Tim Clark (RSA)	632,609
108	Notah Begay III	624,026
109	Tom Byrum	620,280
110	Spike McRoy	616,814
111	Olin Browne	615,828
112	John Daly	593,595
113	Brent Geiberger	582,592
114	John Senden (Aus)	578,613
115	David Berganio jr	573,151
116	JJ Henry	569,875
117	Carl Paulson	568,924
118	Paul Stankowski	565,294
119	Bernhard Langer (Ger)	559,395
120	Glen Hnatiuk	558,940
121	Per-Ulrik Johansson (Swe)	556,064
122	Andrew Magee	543,035
123	Pate Bates	537,284
124	Craig Barlow	528,569
125	Jay Williamson	515,445

Career Money List (at end of 2002 season)

1	Tiger Woods	$33,103,852	51	Duffy Waldorf	7,489,751
2	Phil Mickelson	22,149,969	52	Andrew Magee	7,380,467
3	Davis Love III	20,050,850	53	Steve Stricker	7,241,556
4	Vijay Singh (Fij)	18,281,015	54	Sergio García (Esp)	7,139,882
5	Nick Price (Zim)	16,648,337	55	Ben Crenshaw	7,091,166
6	David Duval	16,150,598	56	Robert Allenby (Aus)	7,077,119
7	Scott Hoch	16,018,375	57	Larry Mize	6,874,000
8	Ernie Els (RSA)	15,308,529	58	Chris Perry	6,866,671
9	Mark Calcavecchia	14,573,517	59	Dudley Hart	6,839,583
10	Hal Sutton	14,205,947	60	Joey Sindelar	6,760,441
11	Jim Furyk	13,856,843	61	Jerry Kelly	6,672,835
12	Justin Leonard	13,658,234	62	Dan Forsman	6,546,345
13	Fred Couples	13,327,971	63	Bruce Lietzke	6,474,794
14	Tom Lehman	12,957,027	64	Scott Simpson	6,473,578
15	Jeff Sluman	12,884,759	65	Scott McCarron	6,405,278
16	David Toms	12,874,480	66	Lanny Wadkins	6,355,681
17	Mark O'Meara	12,755,331	67	Chip Beck	6,199,550
18	Paul Azinger	12,457,891	68	Peter Jacobsen	6,177,393
19	Loren Roberts	11,785,532	69	Bill Glasson	6,136,653
20	Payne Stewart	11,737,008	70	José Maria Olazábal (Esp)	6,104,290
21	Brad Faxon	11,592,350	71	Steve Jones	5,983,270
22	John Cook	11,005,774	72	Hale Irwin	5,966,031
23	Tom Kite	10,920,309	73	Craig Parry (Aus)	5,916,109
24	Fred Funk	10,770,922	74	Jim Gallagher jr	5,838,475
25	John Huston	10,566,582	75	Fuzzy Zoeller	5,803,343
26	Bob Estes	10,415,855	76	Bernhard Langer (Ger)	5,797,534
27	Lee Janzen	10,131,975	77	Tim Herron	5,785,524
28	Jeff Maggert	10,006,019	78	Steve Flesch	5,755,205
29	Corey Pavin	9,898,182	79	Jack Nicklaus	5,722,901
30	Steve Elkington (Aus)	9,864,808	80	Glen Day	5,691,380
31	Tom Watson	9,773,761	81	Kevin Sutherland	5,532,775
32	Kenny Perry	9,557,012	82	Frank Lickliter II	5,404,690
33	Bob Tway	9,548,783	83	Ray Floyd	5,323,075
34	Jesper Parnevik (Swe)	9,276,274	84	Jay Don Blake	5,319,622
35	Rocco Mediate	9,271,474	85	Mark McCumber	5,309,688
36	Jay Haas	9,156,638	86	Gil Morgan	5,529,164
37	Billy Mayfair	9,138,307	87	Russ Cochran	5,240,987
38	Craig Stadler	9,008,663	88	Shigeki Maruyama (Jpn)	5,183,414
39	Scott Verplank	8,974,545	89	Len Mattiace	5,000,772
40	Steve Lowery	8,417,843	90	Blaine McCallister	4,890,955
41	Chris DiMarco	8,286,904	91	DA Weibring	4,753,416
42	Kirk Triplett	8,282,529	92	Wayne Levi	4,688,679
43	Billy Andrade	8,148,866	93	Mike Reid	4,686,774
44	David Frost (RSA)	8,001,237	94	Skip Kendall	4,659,139
45	Mike Weir (Can)	7,926,298	95	Carlos Franco (Col)	4,650,017
46	Mark Brooks	7,886,692	96	Joe Durant	4,505,639
47	Stewart Cink	7,872,432	97	Charles Howell III	4,486,912
48	Stuart Appleby (Aus)	7,621,734	98	David Edwards	4,441,324
49	Steve Pate	7,613,719	99	David Peoples	4,396,108
50	Curtis Strange	7,599,951	100	Brent Geiberger	4,368,683

Tour Statistics

Scoring averages

Pos	Name	Avg
1	Tiger Woods	68.56
2	Vijay Singh (Fij)	69.47
3	Ernie Els (RSA)	69.50
4	Phil Mickelson	69.58
5	Nick Price (Zim)	69.59
6	Retief Goosen (RSA)	69.69
7	David Toms	69.73
8	Justin Leonard	69.86
9	Fred Funk	69.99
10T	Peter Lonard (Aus)	70.00
	Sergio García (Esp)	70.00

Driving accuracy
(Percentage of fairways in regulation)

Pos	Name	%
1	Fred Funk	81.2
2	Scott Verplank	78.5
3T	Jim Furyk	77.6
	Heath Slocum	77.6
5	Glen Day	77.4
6	Fulton Allem (RSA)	77.3
7	Olin Browne	77.1
8	Glen Hnatiuk	76.9
9	Nick Price (Zim)	76.4
10	Joe Durant	75.6

Driving distance
(Average yards per drive)

Pos	Name	Yds
1	John Daly	306.8
2	Boo Weekley	297.3
3	Mathew Goggin (Aus)	296.1
4T	Dennis Paulson	293.7
	Charles Howell III	293.7
6	Tiger Woods	293.3
7	Tim Herron	292.7
8	Brett Wetterich	293.2
9	Chris Smith	292.2
10	Rich Beem	292.1

Sand saves

Pos	Name	%
1	José Maria Olazábal (Esp)	64.9
2	Brett Quigley	63.1
3	Bryce Molder	61.3
4	Brian Watts	60.7
5	Davis Love III	60.4
6	Miguel Angel Jimenez (Esp)	59.8
8	Len Mattiace	59.2
8T	Pat Perez	59.1
	Shigeki Maruyama (Jpn)	59.1
	Scott McCarron	59.1

Greens in regulation

Pos	Name	%
1	Tiger Woods	74.0
2	Jim Furyk	71.7
3	Chris Smith	71.6
4	Shaun Micheel	71.2
5	Fred Funk	71.1
6	Kenny Perry	70.8
7	Vijay Singh (Fij)	70.6
8T	Joe Durant	70.3
	Tom Lehman	70.3
9	David Toms	70.2

Putting averages
(Average per hole)

Pos	Name	Avg
1	Bob Heintz	1.682
2	David Toms	1.704
3	Chris Riley	1.713
4	Ben Crane	1.715
5	Phil Mickelson	1.717
6	Justin Leonard	1.722
7	Billy Andrade	1.729
8	Bryce Molder	1.730
9T	Chris DiMarco	1.730
	Scott Verplank	1.730

Tour Results (in chronological order)

Players are of American nationality unless stated

Mercedes Championships
Plantation Course, Kapalua, HI   (7263–73)

1	Sergio García (Esp)*	73-69-68-64—274	$720000
2	David Toms	69-66-72-67—274	432000
3	Kenny Perry	68-67-71-69—275	275000

Sony Open
Waialae CC, Honolulu, HI   (7060–70)

1	Jerry Kelly	66-65-65-70—266	$720000
2	John Cook	66-62-70-69—267	432000
3	Jay Don Blake	69-67-68-65—269	272000

Bob Hope Chrysler Classic
Bermuda Dunes (6927–72); Indian Wells (6478–72);
Tamarisk (6881–72); West Arnold Palmer (6950–72)

1	Phil Mickelson*	64-67-70-65-64—330	$720000
2	David Berganio jr	69-66-65-64-66—330	432000
3	Briny Baird	67-67-68-66-64—332	232000
	Cameron Beckman	67-67-64-65-69—332	232000

Phoenix Open
TPC Scottsdale, AZ   (7098–71)

1	Chris DiMarco	68-64-66-69—267	$720000
2	Kenny Perry	69-65-64-70—268	352000
	Kaname Yakoo (Jpn)	70-66-68-64—268	352000

AT&T Pebble Beach National Pro-Am
Pebble Beach, CA   (6816–72)

1	Matt Gogel	66-72-67-69—274	$720000
2	Pat Perez	66-65-70-76—277	432000
3	Lee Janzen	68-67-70-73—278	232000
	Andrew Magee	69-70-67-72—278	232000

Buick Invitational
Torrey Pines, CA   (S 7055–72; N 6874–72)

1	José María Olazábal (Esp)	71-72-67-65—275	$648000
2	JL Lewis	68-67-71-70—276	316800
	Mark O'Meara	67-69-70-70—276	316800

Nissan Open
Riviera CC, Pacific Palisades, CA (7078–71)

1	Len Mattiace	69-65-67-68—269	$666000
2	Brad Faxon	67-67-68-68—270	276266
	Scott McCarron	69-65-65-71—270	276266
	Rory Sabbatini (RSA)	69-68-65-68—270	276266

WGC Accenture Match Play
La Costa, Carlsbad, CA, USA

Final: Kevin Sutherland (USA) ($1000000) beat Scott McCarron (USA) ($500000) 1 hole

Consolation match: Brad Faxon (USA) ($400000) beat Paul Azinger (USA) ($300000) at 19th

Fuller details of this event are to be found on page 171

Touchstone Energy Tucson Open
Omni Tucson National, AZ (7109–72)

1	Ian Leggatt (Can)	68-71-65-64—268	$540000
2	David Peoples	67-68-68-67—270	264000
	Loren Roberts	65-70-69-66—270	264000

Genuity Championship
Doral (Blue), Miami, FL (7125–72)

1	Ernie Els (RSA)	66-67-66-72—271	$846000
2	Tiger Woods	67-70-70-66—273	507600
3	Peter Lonard	70-67-70-70—277	319600

Honda Classic
Heron Bay, Coral Springs, FL (7268–72)

1	Matt Kuchar	68-69-66-66—269	$630000
2	Brad Faxon	65-70-69-67—271	308000
	Joey Sindelar	68-67-66-70—271	308000

Bay Hill Invitational
Orlando, FL (7202–72)

1	Tiger Woods	67-65-74-69—275	$720000
2	Michael Campbell (NZ)	72-68-68-71—279	432000
3	John Huston	67-70-71-72—280	192000
	Len Mattiace	73-66-68-73—280	192000
	Rocco Mediate	69-70-71-70—280	192000
	Phil Mickelson	69-71-69-71—280	192000

The Players Championship
Sawgrass, Ponte Vedra Beach, FL (7093-72)

1	Craig Perks (NZ)	71-68-69-72—280	$1080000
2	Stephen Ames (Tri)	74-69-72-67—282	648000
3	Rocco Mediate	71-70-69-73—283	408000

Shell Houston Open
TPC, The Woodlands, TX   (7018–72)

1	Vijay Singh (Fij)	67-65-66-68—266	$720000
2	Darren Clarke (NI)	69-65-67-71—272	432000
3	José María Olazábal		
	(Esp)	71-68-64-70—273	272000

BellSouth Classic
TPC Sugarloaf, Duluth, GA   (7293–72)

1	Retief Goosen (RSA)	68-66-68-70—272	$684000
2	Jesper Parnevik (Swe)	66-69-76-65—276	410400
3	Phil Mickelson	65-68-71-73—277	258400

MASTERS
Augusta National, GA   (7270–72)

1	Tiger Woods (USA)	70-69-66-71—276	$1008000
2	Retief Goosen (RSA)	69-67-69-74—279	604800
3	Phil Mickelson (USA)	69-72-68-71—280	380800

Fuller details of this event are be found in Part I The Majors page 72

Worldcom Classic – The Heritage of Golf
Harbour Town, Hilton Head Island, SC   (6976–71)

1	Justin Leonard	67-64-66-73—270	$720000
2	Heath Slocum	67-68-66-70—271	432000
3	Phil Mickelson	65-64-72-71—272	272000

Greater Greensboro Chrysler Classic
Forest Oaks CC, NC   (7062–72)

1	Rocco Mediate	68-67-66-71—272	$684000
2	Mark Calcavecchia	65-69-69-72—275	410400
3	Jonathan Byrd	72-71-69-66—278	220400
	Chad Campbell	67-72-66-73—278	220400

Compaq Classic of New Orleans
English Turn, New Orleans, LA   (7116–72)

1	Kyung-ju Choi (Kor)	68-65-71-67—271	$810000
2	Dudley Hart	68-71-69-67—275	396000
	Geoff Ogilvy (Aus)	70-67-71-67—275	396000

Verizon Byron Nelson Classic
TPC Cottonwood Valley, Irving, TX   (7017–70)

1	Shigeki Maruyama (Jpn)	67-63-68-68—266	$864000
2	Ben Crane	68-67-68-65—268	518400
3	Tiger Woods	71-65-69-65—270	326400

MasterCard Colonial
Colonial CC, Fort Worth, TX   (7080–70)

1	Nick Price (Zim)	69-65-66-67—267	$774000
2	Kenny Perry	70-66-69-67—272	378400
	David Toms	71-71-64-66—272	378400

Memorial Tournament
Muirfield Village, Dublin, OH   (7224–72)

1	Jim Furyk	71-70-68-65—274	$810000
2	John Cook	73-69-65-69—276	396000
	David Peoples	69-74-65-68—276	396000

Kemper Insurance Open
TPC Avenal, Potomac, MD   (7005–71)

1	Bob Estes	65-69-69-70—273	$648000
2	Rich Beem	68-68-69-69—274	388800
3	Bob Burns	68-66-69-72—275	208800
	Steve Elkington (Aus)	70-67-69-69—275	208800

Buick Classic
Westchester CC, Harrison, NY   (6722–71)

1	Chris Smith	66-69-67-70—272	$630000
2	David Gossett	66-67-70-71—274	261333
	Pat Perez	67-70-67-70—274	261333
	Loren Roberts	64-68-71-71—274	261333

US OPEN
Bethpage, Farmingdale, NY   (7214–70)

1	Tiger Woods	67-68-70-72—277	$1000000
2	Phil Mickelson	70-73-67-70—280	585000
3	Jeff Maggert	69-73-68-72—282	362356

Fuller details of this event are to be found in Part I The Majors page 64

Canon Greater Hartford Open
TPC River Highlands, Cromwell, CT   (6820–70)

1	Phil Mickelson	69-67-66-64—266	$720000
2	Jonathan Kaye	65-67-65-70—267	352000
	Davis Love III	68-64-68-67—267	352000

FedEx St Jude Classic
TPC Southwind, Memphis, TN   (7030–71)

1	Len Mattiace	69-68-65-64—266	$684000
2	Tim Petrovic	65-68-66-68—267	410400
3	Notah Begay III	66-65-68-69—268	258400

Advil Western Open
Cog Hill, Lemont, IL   (7224–72)

1	Jerry Kelly	67-69-68-65—269	$720000
2	Davis Love III	67-70-68-66—271	432000
3	Brandt Jobe	69-69-69-66—273	272000

Greater Milwaukee Open
Brown Deer Park, Milwaukee, WI   (6759–71)

1	Jeff Sluman	64-66-63-68—261	$558000
2	Tim Herron	68-66-65-66—265	272800
	Steve Lowery	66-65-64-70—265	272800

OPEN CHAMPIONSHIP
Muirfield, Scotland   (7034–71)

1	Ernie Els (RSA)*	70-66-72-70—278	$1106140
2	Stuart Appleby (Aus)	73-70-70-65—278	452990
	Steve Elkington (Aus)	71-73-68-66—278	452990
	Thomas Levet (Fra)	72-66-74-66—278	452990

After a four-hole play-off, Appleby and Elkington were eliminated; Els won the sudden-death play-off with Levet at the first extra hole.

Fuller details of this event are to be found in Part I The Majors page 54

BC Open
En-Joie, Endicott, NY   (6974–72)

1	Spike McRoy	70-65-69-65—269	$378000
2	Fred Funk	71-66-66-67—270	226800
3	Glen Day	67-69-67-68—271	94710
	Robert Gamez	68-68-69-66—271	94710
	Brian Henninger	67-69-70-65—271	94710
	Cliff Kresge	72-67-70-62—271	94710
	Shaun Micheel	65-65-67-74—271	94710

John Deere Classic
TPC Deere Run, Silvas, IL   (7183–71)

1	JP Hayes	67-61-67-67—262	$540000
2	Robert Gamez	65-64-66-71—266	324000
3	Kirk Triplett	68-67-66-66—267	204000

The International
Castle Pines, Castle Rock, CO   (7559–72)

1	Rich Beem	10-0-15-19—44	$810000
2	Steve Lowery	8-13-6-16—43	486000
3	Mark Brooks	1-14-11-7—33	306000

Modified Stableford

Buick Open
Warwick Hills, Grand Blanc, MI (7105–72)

1	Tiger Woods	67-63-71-70—271	$594000
2	Fred Funk	71-66-67-71—275	217800
	Brian Gay	69-71-67-68—275	217800
	Mark O'Meara	68-69-70-68—275	217800
	Esteban Toledo (Mex)	68-67-67-73—275	217800

US PGA CHAMPIONSHIP
Hazeltine National, Chaska, MN (7360–72)

1	Rich Beem	72-66-72-68—278	$990000
2	Tiger Woods	71-69-72-67—279	594000
3	Chris Riley	71-70-72-70—283	374000

Fuller details of this event are included in Part I The Majors page 79

WGC – NEC Invitational
Sahalee, Redmond, WA (6949–71)

1	Craig Parry (Aus)	72-65-66-65—268	$1000000
2	Robert Allenby (Aus)	69-63-71-69—272	410000
	Fred Funk (USA)	68-68-68-68—272	410000

Fuller details of this event are to be found on page 172

Reno-Tahoe Open
Montreux GCC, Reno, NV (7472–72)

1	Chris Riley*	71-66-67-67—271	$540000
2	Jonathan Kaye	67-68-69-67—271	324000
3	J J Henry	68-69-70-68—275	174000
	Charles Howell III	65-73-73-64—275	174000

Air Canada Championship
Northview, Surrey, British Columbia, Canada (7072–71)

1	Gene Sauers	69-65-66-69—269	$630000
2	Steve Lowery	67-67-68-68—270	378000
3	Robert Allenby (Aus)	71-62-68-70—271	182000
	Craig Barlow	67-65-71-68—271	182000
	Vijay Singh (Fij)	70-69-67-65—271	182000

Bell Canadian Open
Angus Glen, Markham, Ontario, Canada (7112–72)

1	John Rollins*	70-71-66-65—272	$720000
2	Neal Lancaster	66-67-67-72—272	352000
	Justin Leonard	69-68-66-69—272	352000

SEI Pennsylvania Classic
Waynesborough, Paoli, PA (7244–71)

1	Dan Forsman	73-68-64-65—270	$594000
2	Robert Allenby (Aus)	71-68-67-65—271	290400
	Billy Andrade	66-68-68-69—271	290400

WGC Amex Championship
Mount Juliet, Kilkenny, Ireland   (7246–72)

1	Tiger Woods (USA)	65-65-67-66—263	$1000000
2	Retief Goosen (RSA)	67-67-68-62—264	540000
3	Vijay Singh (Fij)	67-69-66-65—267	367500

Tampa Bay Classic
Palm Harbor, FL   (7295–71)

1	Kyung-ju Choi (Kor)	63-68-68-68—267	$468000
2	Glen Day	68-67-70-69—274	280800
3	Mark Brooks	73-65-70-67—275	176800

RYDER CUP
at The Belfry, Sutton Coldfield

Result: Europe 15½, USA 12½

Fuller results of this event can be found on page 178

Valero Texas Open
La Cantera, San Antonio, TX   (6905–71)

1	Loren Roberts	67-63-67-64—261	$630000
2	Fred Couples	68-67-65-64—264	261333
	Fred Funk	68-68-64-64—264	261333
	Garrett Willis	71-61-66-66—264	261333

Michelob Championship at Kingsmill
Kingsmill, Williamsburg, VA   (6853–71)

1	Charles Howell III	70-65-68-67—270	$666000
2	Scott Hoch	66-70-67-69—272	325600
	Brandt Jobe	67-68-65-72—272	325600

Invensys Classic at Las Vegas
TPC Summerlin (7243–72)/The Canyons (7193–71)/Southern Highlands (7381–72)/Las Vegas, NV

1	Phil Tataurangi	67-66-67-68-62—330	$900000
2	Stuart Appleby (Aus)	66-68-64-67-66—331	440000
	Jeff Sluman	66-66-64-68-67—331	440000

Disney Golf Classic
Palm Lake Buena Vista, FL   (6967–72)

1	Bob Burns	63-68-67-65—263	$666000
2	Chris DiMarco	64-63-69-68—264	399600
3	Tiger Woods	66-69-67-63—265	251600

Buick Challenge
Callaway Gardens Mountain View Course, Pine Mountain, GA
                                                    (7057–72)
1	Jonathan Byrd	67-66-65-63—261	$666000
2	David Toms	66-68-63-65—262	399600
3	Phil Mickelson	65-67-70-63—268	251600

The Tour Championship
East Lake Country Club, GA   (6980–70)
1	Vijay Singh (Fij)	65-71-65-67—268	$900000
2	Charles Howell III	66-69-69-66—270	540000
3	David Toms	70-66-70-67—273	345000

Southern Farm Bureau Classic
Annandale GC, Madison, MA   (7199–72)
1	Luke Donald (Eng)	66-68-67—201	$468000
2	Deane Pappas (RSA)	66-68-68—202	280000
3	Brad Elder	65-67-71—203	176000

Reduced to 54 holes because of rain

Record number of first time winners

During 2002 thirty-one players scored breakthrough wins on the European and US PGA Tours

European Tour	US PGA Tour
Arjun Atwal	Bob Burns
Rich Beem	Jonathan Byrd
Tim Clark	K. J. Choi
Alastair Forsyth	Luke Donald
Anders Hansen	Matt Gogel
Søren Hansen	Charles Howell III
Richard S Johnson	Jerry Kelly
Graeme McDowell	Matt Kuchar
Malcolm Mackenzie	Ian Leggatt
Adam Mednick	Spike McRoy
Carl Pettersson	Len Mattiace
Justin Rose	Craig Parry
Kevin Sutherland	Craig Perks
Miles Tunnicliff	Chris Riley
	John Rollins
	Chris Smith
	Kevin Sutherland
	Phil Tataurangi

US Senior Tour 2002

Players are of American nationality unless stated

Final Ranking

1	Hale Irwin	$3,028,304	26	Walter Hall	785,327
2	Bob Gilder	2,367,637	27	Tom Purtzer	760,056
3	Bruce Fleisher	1,860,534	28	Wayne Levi	725,822
4	Tom Kite	1,631,930	29	Gary McCord	681,960
5	Doug Tewell	1,579,988	30	Rodger Davis (Aus)	673,895
6	Dana Quigley	1,569,972	31	Isao Aoki (Jpn)	653,836
7	Bruce Lietzke	1,527,676	32	Dave Eichelberger	642,487
8	Tom Watson	1,522,437	33	José Maria Canizares (Esp)	635,503
9	Jim Thorpe	1,511,591	34	Dave Stockton	594,943
10	Morris Hatalsky	1,391,044	35	Vicente Fernandez (Arg)	572,233
11	Gil Morgan	1,343,276	36	John Mahaffey	538,696
12	Allen Doyle	1,322,054	37	Bruce Summerhays	530,760
13	Bobby Wadkins	1,270,336	38	Tom Wargo	515,440
14	John Jacobs (Eng)	1,224,737	39	Jim Ahern	448,417
15	Tom Jenkins	1,220,872	40	James Mason	443,996
16	Hubert Green	1,218,392	41	Dick Mast	440,601
17	Don Pooley	1,155,456	42	JC Snead	439,713
18	Larry Nelson	1,143,224	43	Mike Smith	404,445
19	Stewart Ginn (Aus)	950,055	44	Jim Dent	383,601
20	Fuzzy Zoeller	945,211	45	John Schroeder	377,203
21	Mike McCullough	918,340	46	Graham Marsh (Aus)	356,100
22	Ed Dougherty	896,843	47	Mike Hill	351,284
23	Sammy Rachels	859,977	48	Andy North	350,048
24	Jay Sigel	843,526	49	Ted Goin	349,780
25	John Bland (RSA)	824,405	50	Walter Morgan	347,504

Career Money List

1	Hale Irwin	$22,916,208	20	Dana Quigley	7,861,578
2	Gil Morgan	16,351,756	21	Jim Thorpe	7,798,908
3	Tom Kite	15,150,699	22	Allen Doyle	7,714,206
4	Ray Floyd	13,758,298	23	Chi Chi Rodriguez (Pur)	7,663,317
5	Tom Watson	13,637,345	24	Gary Player (RSA)	7,568,073
6	Lee Trevino	13,094,733	25	Doug Tewell	7,493,275
7	Larry Nelson	13,057,022	26	Dale Douglass	7,335,675
8	Jim Colbert	12,393,509	27	Hubert Green	7,332,995
9	Dave Stockton	11,039,094	28	Ben Crenshaw	7,295,694
10	Bruce Fleisher	10,860,524	29	Jay Sigel	7,266,387
11	George Archer	10,159,437	30	Lanny Wadkins	7,227,687
12	Bob Charles (NZ)	9,310,404	31	Bob Gilder	7,188,383
13	Isao Aoki (Jpn)	9,172,355	32	Graham Marsh (Aus)	7,018,608
14	Bruce Lietzke	9,122,044	33	John Mahaffey	6,951,971
15	JC Snead	8,929,404	34	Fuzzy Zoeller	6,748,554
16	Jim Dent	8,780,452	35	Bruce Summerhays	6,553,047
17	Jack Nicklaus	8,765,906	36	Al Geiberger	6,548,182
18	Mike Hill	8,304,805	37	Tom Wargo	6,472,148
19	Bob Murphy	8,278,092	38	Dave Eichelberger	6,343,678

39	John Jacobs (Eng)	6,335,302
40	Bruce Crampton (Aus)	6,028,877
41	Leonard Thompson	5,992,213
42	Jim Albus	5,885,171
43	Mike McCullough	5,870,034
44	John Bland (RSA)	5,869,483
45	Ed Dougherty	5,868,555
46	David Graham (Aus)	5,867,966

47	Tom Jenkins	5,768,099
48	Miller Barber	5,605,420
49	Vicente Fernandez (Arg)	5,596,457
Others:		
53	José Maria Canizares (Esp)	5,298,152
63	Hugh Balocchi (RSA)	4,384,117
65	Simon Hobday (Zim)	4,182,988
67	Harold Henning (RSA)	4,124,514

Tour Statistics

Scoring average

Pos	Name	Rounds	Avg
1	Hale Irwin	82	68.93
2	Tom Watson	42	69.57
3	Tom Kite	72	69.64
4	Bruce Fleisher	93	69.73
5T	Morris Hatalsky	72	69.85
	Doug Tewell	81	69.85
7	Gil Morgan	69	69.88
8	Bruce Lietzke	69	69.96
9	Larry Nelson	77	70.09
10	Allen Doyle	98	70.21

Driving accuracy

Pos	Name	%
1	Doug Tewell	83.6
2	Allen Doyle	82.7
3	Lee Trevino	81.4
4	John Bland (RSA)	81.0
5	Hale Irwin	80.3
6	Bruce Fleisher	79.4
7T	John Mahaffey	77.0
	Graham Marsh (Aus)	77.0
9	Chi Chi Rodriquez (Pur)	76.9
10	Bob Murphy	76.7

Driving distance
(Average yards per drive)

Pos	Name	Yds
1	RW Eaks	295.1
2	Clyde Hughey	284.6
3	John Jacobs	284.5
4	Rodger David (Aus)	282.2
5	Jim Ahern	281.0
6	Tom Purtzer	280.6
7	Terry Dill	280.1
8	Sammy Rachels	280.0
9T	Tom Kite	279.4
	Bobby Wadkins	279.4

Putting leaders
(Average putts per hole)

Pos	Name	Avg
1	Hale Irwin	1.717
2	Morris Hatalsky	1.740
3	Ben Crenshaw	1.750
4	Don Pooley	1.756
5	Dana Quigley	1.759
6	Bob Gilder	1.760
7	Bruce Fleisher	1.761
8	Larry Nelson	1.762
9	Tom Wargo	1.763
10	Gil Morgan	1.765

Sand saves

Pos	Name	%
1	Jay Overton	65.1
2	Ed Dougherty	61.6
3	Morris Hatalsky	61.5
4	Vincente Fernandez (Arg)	60.5
5	Allen Doyle	59.2
6	Christy O'Connor jr (Ire)	57.4
7	Dana Quigley	56.7
8	Hale Irwin	55.8
9	Tom Purtzer	54.4
10	Dave Stockton	53.8

Greens in regulation

Pos	Name	Rounds	%
1	Tom Kite	72	75.9
2	Tom Watson	42	74.9
3	Doug Tewell	81	73.3
4	Tom Purtzer	70	73.0
5	Bruce Fleisher	93	72.9
6	Bobby Wadkins	89	72.8
7	David Eger	37	72.5
8	Sammy Rachels	81	72.4
9	Hale Irwin	82	72.2
10T	Tom Jenkins	101	71.8
	Wayne Levi	84	71.8

Tour Results

MasterCard Championship	Hualalai, Kaupulehu-Kona, HI	Tom Kite	199 (-17)
Senior Skins Game	Wailea, Maui, HI	Hale Irwin	11 skins
Royal Caribbean Classic	Crandon Park, Key Biscayne, FL	John Jacobs	133 (-11)
ACE Group Classic	Twin Eagles, Naples, FL	Hale Irwin	200 (-16)
Verizon Classic	TPC Tampa Bay, Lutz, FL	Doug Tewell	203 (-10)
Audi Senior Classic	Chapultepec, Mexico City	Bruce Lietske	208 (-8)
SBC Senior Classic	Valencia, Santa Clarita, CA	Tom Kite	212 (-4)
Toshiba Senior Classic	Newport Beach, CA	Hale Irwin	196 (-17)
Siebel Classic in Silicon Valley	Coyote Creek, San Jose, CA	Dana Quigley	212 (-4)
Emerald Coast Classic	The Moors, Milton, Pensacola, FL	Dave Eichelberger	130 (-10)
Liberty Mutual Legends of Golf	St Augustine, FL	Doug Tewell	205 (-11)
THE COUNTRYWIDE TRADITION	Superstition Mountain, AZ	Jim Thorpe	277 (-11)
Bruno's Memorial Classic	Greystone, Birmingham, AL	Sammy Rachels	201 (-15)
TD Waterhouse World Seniors Invitational	TPC Piper Glen, Charlotte, NC	Bruce Lietzke	133 (-11)
Instinet Classic	TPC Jasna Polana, Princeton, NJ	Isao Aoki (Jpn)	201 (-15)
Farmers Charity Classic	Egypt Valley, Ada, MI	Jay Siegel	203 (-13)
NFL Golf Classic	Upper Montclair, Clifton, NJ	James Mason	207 (-9)
SENIOR PGA CHAMPIONSHIP	Firestone CC, South Akron, OH	Fuzzy Zoeller	278 (-2)
BellSouth Senior Classic	Springhouse, Nashville, TN	Gil Morgan	202 (-14)
Greater Baltimore Classic	Hayfields, Hunt Valley, MD	JC Snead	203 (-13)
US SENIOR OPEN	Caves Valley, Baltimore, MD	Don Pooley	274 (-10)
AT&T Canada Senior Open	Essex CC, LaSalle, Ontario, Canada	Tom Jenkins	195 (-18)
FORD SENIOR PLAYERS CHAMPIONSHIP	TPC Michigan, Dearborn, MI	Stewart Ginn	274 (-14)
SBC Senior Open	Harborside, Chicago, IL	Bob Gilder	204 (-12)
FleetBoston Classic	Nashawtuc, Concord, MA	Bob Gilder	203 (-13)
Lightpath Long Island Classic	Meadow Brook, Jericho, NY	Hubert Green	199 (-14)
3M Championship	TPC Twin Cities, Blaine, MN	Hale Irwin	204 (-12)
Uniting Fore Care Classic	Park Meadows, Park City, UT	Morris Hatalsky	42 pts
Allianz Championship	Glen Oaks, West Des Moines, IA	Bob Gilder	200 (-13)
Kroger Senior Classic	TPC River's Bend, Maineville, OH	Bob Gilder	200 (-16)
RJR Championship	Tanglewood Park, Clemmons, NC	Bruce Fleisher	191 (-19)
SAS Championship	Prestonwood, Cary, NC	Bruce Lietzke	202 (-14)
Gold Rush Classic	Serrano, El Dorado Hills, CA	Tom Kite	194 (-22)
Turtle Bay Championship	Kahuku, HI	Hale Irwin	208 (-8)
The Trans America	Silverado, Napa, CA	Tom Kite	204 (-12)
SBC Championship	San Antonio, TX	Dana Quigley	201 (-12)
Senior Tour Championship	Gaillardia, Oklahoma City, OK	Tom Watson	274 (-14)

US Buy.com Tour 2002

Players are of American nationality unless stated

Final Ranking (Top 15 earned US Tour Card)

Pos	Name	Events	Prize $	Pos	Name	Events	Prize $
1	Patrick Moore	20	381,965	51	David Morland IV	7	91,924
2	Aaron Oberholser	20	319,883	52	Steve Haskins	25	91,444
3	Doug Barron	19	248,175	53	Charles Raulerson	22	91,408
4	Steven Alker (NZ)	24	247,008	54	Rob McKelvey	27	90,359
5	Cliff Kresge	22	245,265	55	Andy Sanders	13	84,177
6	Jason Gore	23	241,940	56	Brad Ott	23	80,683
7	Todd Fischer	26	234,777	57	Roger Tambellini	21	76,281
8	Marco Dawson	23	227,590	58	Tiaart van der Walt (RSA)	22	74,604
9	Darron Stiles	25	222,845	59	Chris Tidland	23	73,170
10	Aaron Baddeley (Aus)	17	216,536	60	Steve Ford	5	73,106
11	Jason Buha	25	204,938	61	Bryce Molder	4	72,064
12	Patrick Sheehan	27	201,231	62	Mark Wurtz	24	71,969
13	Gavin Coles	21	189,745	63	Ben Bates	26	71,804
14	Tag Ridings	25	187,494	64	Joe Daley	26	71,791
15	Todd Barranger	24	186,666	65	Wes Short	26	71,479
16	Charles Warren	24	177,294	66	DA Points	23	68,341
17	Omar Uresti	26	166,620	67	Lucas Glover	12	64,692
18	Jay Delsing	20	165,153	68	John Restino	18	64,287
19	Eric Meeks	27	165,027	69	Danny Briggs	21	62,986
20	Jason Caron	22	155,044	70	John Morse	13	61,621
21	Anthony Painter (Aus)	20	151,122	71	Chip Beck	16	61,525
22	Jeff Klauk	22	146,316	72	Stan Utley	9	59,811
23	Tyler Williamson	26	145,696	73	Vic Wilk	24	59,472
24	Barry Cheesman	25	144,948	74	Jimmy Walker	10	58,962
25	Keoke Cotner	27	144,816	75	Bob Friend	21	55,775
26	Mike Heinen	9	138,041	76	Jim McGovern	13	52,472
27	Brian Claar	16	131,623	77	Jason Dufner	25	51,832
28	Joel Kribel	26	129,146	78	Gene Sauers	11	51,467
29	Jace Bugg	20	128,687	79	Greg Gregory	22	50,087
30	Roland Thatcher	27	127,768	80	Kelly Gibson	13	49,725
31	Emlyn Aubrey	21	126,169	81	Billy Judah	25	48,748
32	Zoran Zorkic	28	124,386	82	Victor Schwamkrug	25	48,655
33	Mark Hensby	19	123,825	83	DJ Brigman	19	47,098
34	Peter O'Malley	3	121,125	84	James H McLean (RSA)	19	46,179
35	Andrew McLardy (RSA)	24	119,996	85	Chad Wright	21	45,782
36	Jeff Freeman	26	117,645	86	Trevor Dodds (Nam)	18	45,574
37	Tommy Blershenk	25	112,393	87	Kevin Johnson	21	43,370
38	Scott Sterling	16	112,357	88	Scott Petersen	16	42,597
39	David Branshaw	26	111,731	89	Jaxon Brigman	21	41,691
40	Dave Stockton jr	23	110,154	90	Daniel Chopra (Swe)	25	41,269
41	Ken Green	17	108,370	91	Todd Demsey	27	40,984
42	Gary Hallberg	21	106,317	92	Rob Bradley	22	40,634
43	Tom Carter	28	104,997	93	Pete Morgan	21	38,930
44	Hunter Haas	21	103,230	94	John Elliott	26	38,400
45	Andy Miller	6	103,157	95	Rocky Walcher	7	37,695
46	Brian Wilson	25	102,341	96	Shane Bertsch	20	37,354
47	Jeff Hart	22	97,595	97	Nolan Henke	19	37,251
48	John Maginnes	21	95,430	98	Tommy Tolles	8	36,766
49	Doug Garwood	27	94,438	99	Peter Fowler (Aus)	1	35,323
50	Rich Barcelo	25	92,547	100	Fran Quinn	1	34,703

Tour Results

Jacob's Creek Open Championship	Kooyonga, Adelaide, S Australia	Gavin Coles	279 (-9)
Holden Clearwater Classic	Christchurch, NZ	Peter O'Malley (Aus)	271 (-17)
Louisiana Open	Le Triomphe, Broussard, LA	Steve Alker	264 (-24)
Arkansas Classic	Diamante CC, Hot Springs Village, AR	Jace Bugg	271 (-17)
BMW Charity Pro-Am	Cliffs Valley, Travelers Rest, SC	Charles Warren	264 (-23)
Virginia Beach Open	Virginia Beach, VA	Cliff Kresge	277 (-11)
Richmond Open	Glen Allen, VA	Patrick Moore	268 (-20)
SAS Carolina Classic	Raleigh, NC	Zoran Zorkic	274 (-10)
NE Pennsylvania Classic	Moosic, PA	Gary Hallberg	275 (-9)
Samsung Canadian PGA Championship	Richmond Hill, Ontario	Arron Oberholser	268 (-16)
Lake Erie Charity Classic	Findley Lake, NY	Patrick Moore	275 (-13)
Knoxville Open	Fox Den, Knoxville, TN	Darron Stiles	204 (-12)
Hershey Open	Hershey, PA	Cliff Kresge	276 (-8)
Dayton Open	Centerville, OH	Jason Buha	265 (-23)
Fort Smith Classic	Hardscrabble, Fort Smith, AR	Todd Fischer	269 (-11)
Price Cutter Charity Championship	Highland Springs, Springfield, MO	Patrick Sheehan	269 (-19)
Omaha Classic	Champions Club, Omaha, NE	Jay Delsing	267 (-21)
LaSalle Bank Open	Kemper Lakes, Long Grove, IL	Marco Dawson	276 (-12)
Preferred Health Systems Wichita Open	Crestview, Wichita, KS	Tyler Williamson	272 (-8)
Permian Basin Open	Midland, TX	Tag Ridings	272 (-16)
Utah Classic	Sandy, UT	Arron Oberholser	202 (-14)
Oregon Classic	Junction City, OR	Jason Gore	270 (-18)
Boise Open	Hillcrest, Boise, ID	Jason Gore	273 (-11)
State Farm Open	Rancho Cucamonga, CA	Andy Miller*	272 (-12)
Monterey Peninsula Classic	Seaside, CA	Roland Thatcher	283 (-5)
Gila River Classic	Chandler, AZ	David Branshaw	262 (-22)
Shreveport Open	Southern Trace, Shreveport, LA	David Morland	197 (-19)
Buy.com Tour Championship	Capitol Hill, Prattville, AL	Patrick Moore	206 (-10)

Japan PGA Tour

Players are of Japanese nationality unless stated

Results 2001

Philip Morris Championship	ABC GC, Hyogo	Toshimitsu Izawa	272 (-16)
Casio World Open	Ibusuki GC, Kagoshima	Kiyoshi Murota	264 (-24)
Golf Nippon Series Cup	Yomiuri, Tokyo	Katsumasa Miyamoto	268 (-12)

Final Ranking 2001

1 Toshimitsu Izawa	¥217,934,583	6	Keng-Chi Lin (Tai)	96,713,000
2 Shingo Katayama	133,434,850	7	Hidemichi Tanaka	95,185,544
3 Dean Wilson (USA)	118,571,075	8	Katsumasa Miyamoto	87,455,177
4 Taichi Teshima	112,356,544	9	Tsuneyuki Nakajima	68,378,345
5 Toru Taniguchi	111,686,284	10	Keiichiro Fukabori	65,182,064

Results 2002

Token Corporation Cup	Kedoin GC, Kagoshima	Toru Taniguchi	272 (-18)
DyDo-Drinco Shizuoka Open	Hamaoka Course, Shizuoka	Kiyoshi Murota	276 (-12)
Tsuruya Open	Sports Shinko CC, Hyogo	Dean Wilson (USA)	271 (-11)
Chunichi Crowns	Nagoya GC, Aichi	Justin Rose (Eng)	266 (-14)
Fujisankei Classic	Kawana Hotel GC, Shizuoka	Nobuhito Sato	276 (-8)
JPGA Championship	Koma CC, Nara	Kenichi Kuboya	279 (-9)
Munsingwear Open KSB Cup	Ayutaki CC, Kagawa	Kenichi Kuboya	279 (-9)
Diamond Cup Tournament	Sayama GC, Saitama	Tsuneyuki Nakajima	269 (-19)
JCB Classic Sendai	Omotezaou Kokusai GC, Miyagi	Toru Suzuki	271 (-13)
Tamanoisu Yomiuri Open	Yomiuri CC, Hyogo	Toru Taniguchi	270 (-18)
Mizuno Open	Sentonaikai GC, Okayama	Dean Wilson (USA)	277 (-11)
Iiyama Cup JGT Championship	Horai CC, Tochigi	Nobuhito Sato	268 (-20)
Jukensangyo Open	Hiroshima CC	SK Ho (Tai)	274 (-14)
Sato Foods NST Niigata Open	Nakajo GC, Niigata	Yasuharu Imano	270 (-18)
Aiful Cup	Ajigasawa Kogen GC, Ishikawa	Yasuharu Imano	268 (-20)
Sun Chlorella Classic	Sapporo Bay GC, Hokkaido	Christian Pena (USA)	269 (-19)
Hisamitsu KBC Augusta	Keya GC, Fukuoka	Nobumitsu Yuhara	209 (-7)
Japan Matchplay Championship	Nidom Classic C, Hokkaido	Nobuhito Sato	
Suntory Open	Soubu CC, Chiba	Shingo Katayama	269 (-15)
ANA Open	Sapporo GC, Hokkaido	Masashi Ozaki	271 (-17)
Acom International	Ishioka GC, Ibaragi	Toru Taniguchi	197 (-16)
Georgia Tokai Classic	Miyoshi CC, Aichi	Toru Taniguchi	278 (-10)
Japan Open	Shimonoseki GC, Yamagichi	David Smail (NZ)	271 (-9)
Bridgestone Open	Sodegaura CC, Chiba	Scott Laycock (Aus)	272 (-16)
Philip Morris Championship	ABC GC, Hyogo	Brendan Jones (Aus)	269 (-19)
Mitsui Sumitomo VISA Taiheiyo Masters	Taiheiyo, Shizuoka	Toshimitsu Izawa	(D)
Dunlop Phoenix Tournament	Phoenix CC, Miyazaki	David Duval (USA)	(D)
Casio World Open	Ibusuki GC, Kagoshima	Kiyoshi Murota	(D)
Golf Nippon Series Cup	Tokyo Yomiuri CC, Tokyo	Katsumasa Miyamoto	(D)

Japan PGA Tour *continued*

Latest Ranking (after Philip Morris KK Championship)

1	Toru Taniguchi	¥136,642,600	11	Hiroyuki Fujita	53,544,085
2	Nobuhito Sato	124,889,344	12	David Smail (NZ)	51,973,576
3	Dean Wilson (USA)	89,396,100	13	SK Ho (Tai)	51,260,564
4	Shingo Katayama	78,056,750	14	Katsunori Kuwabara	48,466,317
5	Kenichi Kuboya	77,108,950	15	Naomichi Ozaki	47,485,571
6	Yasuharu Imano	66,799,705	16	Tomohiro Kondo	46,797,536
7	Brendan Jones (Aus)	64,699,735	17	Toshimitsu Izawa	46,626,951
8	Scott Laycock (Aus)	57,803,599	18	Hirofumi Miyase	45,625,905
9	Masashi Ozaki	56,811,342	19	Christian Pena (USA)	44,852,366
10	Tsuneyuki Nakajima	56,808,484	20	Toru Suzuki	42,804,302

Sutton named as next US Ryder Cup captain

The PGA of America wasted no time in naming Hal Sutton as captain of the 2004 American side for the match against Europe at Oakland Hills, Detroit.

The announcement came as no surprise. Forty-four-year-old Sutton, the 1983 US PGA champion and a team member four times between 1985 and 2001, had been widely tipped as successor to Curtis Strange.

Winner of 14 events on the US Tour, he is the 23rd US team captain and the 16th US PGA Championship winner to be given the opportunity to lead the side. 'I'm overwhelmed and honoured', said Sutton when the appointment was made. 'I'm looking forward to the challenge and will do my best to bring the Cup back to the United States. We are loaded with talent and just need to let that talent shine through'.

Three of the last five Ryder Cup matches have been decided by a single point. Europe has won five of the last nine and one match has been drawn.

At the time of going to press, Europe had not named a successor to Sam Torrance, who had indicated that he would not be seeking a second term as captain.

Davidoff Asian PGA Tour

Results 2001

BMW Asian Open	Westin Resort, Ta Shee, Taiwan	Jarmo Sandelin (Swe)	278 (-10)
Omega Hong Kong Open	Hong Kong GC	José María Olazábal (Esp)	262 (-22)

Final Ranking 2001

1	Thongchai Jaidee (Tha)	353060	11	Anthony Kang (Kor)	78636
2	Charlie Wi (Kor)	315857	12	Yang Yong-eun (Kor)	77526
3	Andrew Pitts (USA)	144393	13	Mamat (Sin)	76985
4	Thaworn Wiratchant (Tha)	120572	14	Choi Gwang-soo (Kor)	74709
5	Arjun Atwal (Ind)	111237	15	Park Do-kyu (Kor)	70381
6	Simon Yates (Sco)	100381	16	Zhang Lian-wei (Chi)	67616
7	James Kingston (RSA)	98807	17	Ted Oh (Kor)	67158
8	Kang Wook-soon (Kor)	87151	18	Thammanoon Sriroj (Tha)	66598
9	Vivek Bhandari (Ind)	86500	19	Yeh Wei-tze (Tai)	63524
10	Daniel Chopra (Swe)	83686	20	Clay Devers (USA)	61044

Results and Fixtures 2002–2003

Johnnie Walker Classic	Lake Karrinyup, Australia	Retief Goosen (RSA)	274 (-14)
London Myanmar Open	Yangon, Myanmar	Thongchai Jaidee (Tha)	277 (-11)
Hero Honda Masters		Harmeet Kahlon (Ind)	277 (-7)
Caltex Singapore Masters	Laguna	Arjun Atwal (Ind)	274 (-14)
Carlsberg Malaysian Open	Royal Selangor	Alastair Forsyth (Sco)	267 (-17)
Casino Filipino Philippine Open	Wack Wack	Rick Gibson (Can)	283 (-5)
Royal Challenge Indian Open	Delhi	Vijay Kumar (Ind)	275 (-13)
SK Telecom Open	Seoul, Korea	Charlie Wi (Kor)	272 (-16)
Maekyung LG Fashion Open	Nam Seoul	Eddie Lee Seung- Yong (Kor) (am)	268 (-20)
Mercuries Masters	Tamsui, Taiwan	Tsai Chi-Huang (Tai)	274 (-14)
Shinhan Donghae Open	Jae II CC, Seoul, Korea	Hur Suk-Ho (Kor)*	276 (-12)
Kolon Cup, Korean Open	Hanyang, Seoul, Korea	Sergio García (Esp)	265 (-23)
Volvo China Open	Silport, Shanghai	David Gleeson (Aus)	272 (-16)
Acer Taiwan Open	Sunrise GCC, Taiwan	Danny Chia (Mas)	291 (+3)
Davidoff Nations Cup	Palm Resort, Johor Bahru, Malaysia	Switzerland	
Macau Open	Macau	Zhang Lian-Wei (PRC)	277 (-7)
TCL Classic	Harbour Plaza, Dongguan, China		
BMW Asian Open	Ta Shee, Taiwan	Jarmo Sandelin (Swe)	
Omega Hong Kong Open	Hong Kong GC	JM Olazábal (Esp)	
Volvo Masters of Asia	Kota Permai, Malaysia		
Okinawa Open	Southern Links, Okinawa		

Latest Ranking (after Macau Open and with five events to play)

1	Arjun Atwal (Ind)	US$177675	11	Pablo del Olmo (Mex)	77370
2	Thammanoon Sriroj (Tha)	152924	12	James Kingston (RSA)	74970
3	David Gleeson (Aus)	118494	13	Harmeet Kahlon (Ind)	73494
4	Charlie Wi (Kor)	96320	14	Prayad Marksaeng (Tha)	73337
5	Brad Kennedy (Aus)	91468	15	Thongchai Jaidee (Tha)	71715
6	Tsai Chi-huang (Tai)	91431	16	Thaworn Wiratchant (Tha)	71306
7	Anthony Kang (Kor)	85966	17	Zhang Lian-Wei (PRC)	70273
8	Simon Yates (Sco)	82976	18	Kevin Na (Kor)	68354
9	Hur Suk-ho (Kor)	81566	19	Hsieh Yu-shu (Tai)	67109
10	Rick Gibson (Can)	79426	20	Chris Williams (RSA)	66764

Australasian Tour

Results 2001–2002

Players are of Australian nationality unless stated

Telstra New Zealand Open	ParaparaumauBeach	Craig Parry	273 (-11)
Johnnie Walker Classic*	Lake Karrinyup, Perth	Retief Goosen (RSA)	274 (-14)
Heineken Classic†	Royal Melbourne, Victoria	Ernie Els (RSA)	271 (-17)
ANZ Championship†	The Lakes, Sydney, NSA	Richard Johnson (Swe)	46 pts
New South Wales Masters	Longyard	Steve Collins	268 (-20)
Jacob's Creek Open Championship‡	Kooyonga	Gavin Coles	279 (-9)
Clearwater Classic‡	Clearwater Resort	Peter O'Malley	271 (-17)
Scenic Circle Hotels Dunedin Classic	Chisolm Links	Gareth Paddison	267 (-17)
South Australian PGA Championship	The Vines	Richard Ball	264 (-20)
Victorian PGA Championship	Kew Golf Club	Craig Carmichael*	278 (-10)
Victorian Open Championship	Sorrento & Portsea Golf	Andre Stolz†	274 (-8)
Queensland Open Championship	Ipswich Golf Club	Andrew Buckle	274 (-14)
New South Wales Open Championship	Horizons Golf Resort	Terry Price	279 (-9)
Holden Australian Open	Victoria GC, Melbourne	Stuart Appleby	(D)
Australian PGA	Coluum Resort, Queensland	Robert Allenby	(D)
Australian Ericsson Masters	Huntingdale GC, Melbourne	Colin Montgomerie (Sco)	(D)

* after a play-off with Craig Jones
†after play-off with David Bransdon

Latest Ranking 2001–2002 (after New South Wales Open)

1	Craig Parry	AUS$479851	11	Geoff Ogilvy	188000
2	Peter O'Malley	383142	12	Nick O'Hern	154259
3	Scott Laycock	374968	13	Terry Price	127005
4	Richard Johnson (Swe)	328700	14	Steve Alker (NZ)	119443
5	Stuart Appleby	270000	15	Peter Lonard	110481
6	Peter Fowler	265015	16	Greg Norman	100666
7	Gavin Coles	229131	17	Anthony Painter	98984
9	Robert Allenby	199520	18	Gareth Paddison	98925
9	Stephen Leaney	223410	19	Richard Lee (NZ)	95086
10	Andre Stolz	192920	20	Greg Turner (NZ)	94576

Fixtures 2003 (season ends December 14)

Jan 16–19	Holden New Zealand, Auckland Golf Club
Jan 30–Feb 2	†Heineken Classic, Royal Melbourne GC
Feb 6–9	†ANZ Championship, New South Wales Golf Club
Feb 13–16	*Johnnie Walker Classic, Lake Karrinyup Golf Club
Mar 6–9	‡Jacob's Creek Open, Kooyonga Golf Club
Mar 13–16	‡Clearwater Classic, Clearwater Resort
Nov 13–16	Perth International, venue to be confirmed
Nov 27–30	Holden Australian Open Championship, venue to be confirmed
Dec 4–7	MasterCard Masters, Huntingdale Golf Club
Dec 11–14	Australian PGA Championship

* Joint sanction with European Tour and Asian PGA Tour
† Joint sanction with European Tour
‡ Joint sanction with US PGA Tour

South African Sunshine Tour

Players are of South African nationality unless stated

Results 2001–2002

CABS/Old Mutual Zimbabwe Open	Chapman, Harare, Zimbabwe	Darren Fichardt	275 (-13)
PricewaterhouseCoopers Nelson Mandela Invitational	Pecanwood, Hartebeespoortdam	Simon Hobday/ Martin Maritz	123 (-21)
Nedbank Golf Challenge	Sun City	Sergio García* (Esp)	268 (-20)
Vodacom Players Championship	Royal Cape, Cape Town	Ernie Els	273 (-15)
South African Open	Mt Edgecombe/The Bluff, Durban	Tim Clark	269 (-19)
Dunhill Championship	Houghton, Johannesburg	Justin Rose (Eng)	268 (-20)
Telkom PGA Championship	Woodhill, Pretoria	Chris Williams	271 (-17)
Dimension Data Pro-Am	Sun City	Retief Goosen	268 (-20)
Nashua Masters	Centurion Lake/Zwartkop, Pretoria	Justin Rose (Eng)	265 (-15)
Tour Championship	Leopard Creek, Malelane	Nicholas Lawrence	274 (-14)

Final Ranking 2001–2002

1	Tim Clark	SAR1,069,900	11	Doug McGuigan (Sco)	367,890
2	Justin Rose (Eng)	1,476,006	12	Grant Muller	366,530
3	Retief Goosen	1,364,977	13	Alan McLean (Sco)	354,184
4	Martin Maritz	1,042,806	14	Marc Cayeux (Zim)	311,871
–	Mark Foster (Eng)	725,844	–	Paul McGinley (Irl)	311,466
5	James Kingston	706,234	15	Scott Drummond (Sco)	294,350
–	Ernie Els	621,311	16	Titch Moore	293,703
6	Roger Wessels	471,196	17	Chris Williams (Eng)	282,306
7	Nicholas Lawrence	416,055	18	Jaco Van Zyl	281,094
8	Darren Fichardt	397,023	19	Bruce Vaughan (USA)	276,734
9	Andre Cruse	386,619	20	Mark McNulty (Zim)	247,614
10	David Park (Wal)	376,412	21	Jamie Donaldson (Wal)	244,660

South African Sunshine Tour *continued*

Results and Fixtures 2002–2003

Royal Swazi Sun Open	Mbabane	Andrew McLardy	268 (20)
Stanbic Zambia Open	Lusaka, Zambia	Mark Cayeux	270 (-22)
FNB Botswana Open	Gabarone, Botswana	Hendrik Buhrmann	194 (-19)
Limpopo Industrelek Classic	Pietersburg	Hennie Otto	202 (-14)
Royal Swazi Sun Classic	Mbabane	James Kingston	204 (-12)
Vodacom Golf Classic	Royal Johannesburg/Kensington	Ashley Roestoff	205 (-11)
Bearing Man Highveld Classic	Witbank	Titch Moore	196 (-20)
Platinum Classic	Mooinooi, Rustenburg	Titch Moore	198 (-18)
Telcom PGA Championship	Woodhill, Pretoria		
Nashua Masters	Wild Coast Sun, Port Edward		
Vodacom Players Championship	Royal Cape, Cape Town		
Zimbabwe Open	Royal Harare, Zimbabwe		
South African Airways Open Championship	Erinvale, Somerset West		
Dunhill Championship	Houghton, Johannesburg		
Dimension Data Pro-Am	Sun City		
Tour Championship	Leopard Creek, Malelane		

Latest Ranking (after the Platinum Classic and with eight events to play)

1 Marc Cayeux (Zim)	SAR185547	
2 Titch Moore	149446	
3 Richard Sterne	124074	
4 Andre Cruse	109296	
5 Ashley Roestoff	93986	
6 Nic Henning	93613	
7 Andrew McLardy	79000	
8 Des Terblanche	70755	
9 Keith Horne	63653	
10 Brett Liddle	63658	
11 Doug McGuigan (Sco)	57500	
12 Hennie Otto	54710	
13 Simon Hurd (Eng)	53093	
14 Hendrik Buhrmann	52957	
15 Sean Farrell (Zim)	49292	
16 James Loughnane (Irl)	45760	
17 Bobby Lincoln	45000	
18 James Kingston	41157	
19 Bradford Vaughan	38086	
20 Grant Muller	35416	

Canadian Tour 2002

Players are of Canadian nationality unless stated

Panasonic Panama Open	Coronado Beach, Panama	Mario Tiziani* (USA)	273 (-15)
*after a play-off with David Kirkpatrick (Lakeland, FL) and Chad Wright (Ventura, CA)			
Texas Classic	KingWood, Houston, TX	Steve Scott (USA)	274 (-14)
Texas Challenge	Circle 'C' Ranch, Austin, TX	Hank Kuehne (USA)	270 (-18)
Scottsdale Swing, McCormick Ranch	Scottsdale, AZ	Jeff Quinney (USA)	265 (-23)
Scottsdale Swing, Eagle Mountain	Scottsdale, AZ	Jimmy Walker (USA)	261 (-19)
Michelin Ixtapa Classic	Palma Real, Ixtapa, Mexico	Pablo del Ohno (Mex)	267 (-21)
Barefoot Classic	Myrtle Beach, SC	Rob McMillan	277 (-11)
Myrtle Beach Barefoot Championship	Barefoot Resort Pete Dye course, Myrtle Beach, SC	Derek Gillespie (USA)	279 (-5)
Lewis Chitengwa Memorial Championship	Keswick, Charlottesville, VA	Chris Wisler (USA)	270 (-14)
Bay Mills Open	Wild Bluff, Brimley, MI	Jeff Quinney (USA)	282 (–6)
Ontario Open Heritage Classic	Grandview, Huntsville, ON	Mike Grob (USA)	274 (-14)
Vancouver Open	Swan-e-set Bay, Vancouver, BC	Iain Steel (Mal)	272 (-16)
Victoria Open	Uplands, Victoria, BC	Scott Hend (Aus)	263 (-17)
Telus Edmonton Open	Glendale, Edmonton, AB	Matt Daniel*	267 (-21)
*after a play-off with Stuart Anderson (Ft McMurray, AB)			
MTS Classic	Pine Ridge, Winnipeg, MB	Alex Quiroz (Mex)	272 (-12)
Telus Quebec Open	Le Versant, Terrebonne	Hank Kuehne* (USA)	273 (-15)
*after a play-off with Michael Harris (Troy, MI)			
Greater Toronto Open	Mandarin, Markham, ON	Chris Locker* (USA)	270 (-14)
*after a play-off with Derek Gillespie (Oshawa, ON)			
†Casino de Charlesvoix Cup	Le Manoir Richelieu, Pointe-au-Pic	Pete Bosquet and Jean Louis Lamarre	

† Unofficial event

Final Order of Merit 2002

1	Hank Kuehne (USA)	CAN$105959	21	Michael Kirk (RSA)	29917
2	Jeff Quinney (USA)	83011	22	Matt Daniel (USA)	29753
3	Derek Gillespie (USA)	73869	23	Jason Schultz (USA)	29148
4	Steve Scott (USA)	72855	24	Jason Enloc (USA)	26580
5	Mike Grob (USA)	59117	25	James Driscoll (USA)	24152
6	Aaron Barber (USA)	58470	26	Scott Ford (USA)	23681
7	Michael Harris (USA)	56721	27	David Mathis (USA)	23395
8	David Hearn (USA)	55426	28	Michael Henderson (USA)	22798
9	Iain Steel (Mal)	53490	29	Paul Scaletta (USA)	21228
10	Scott Hend (Aus)	49902	30	Chris Greenwood (USA)	20627
11	Alex Quiroz (Mex)	46539	31	Rich Massey (USA)	20148
12	David MacKenzie (Aus)	44800	32	Paul Devenport (NZ)	19763
13	Ken Duke (USA)	43414	33	Stuart Anderson	19140
14	Rob McMillan	43322	34	Darren Griff	18862
15	Mario Tiziani (USA)	39572	35	Bryn Parry	18698
16	Chris Locker (USA)	35410	36	Doug McGuigan	18247
17	Jason Bohn (USA)	32701	37	Stephen Woodard (USA)	17924
18	Dave Christensen (USA)	32634	38	Bryan DeCorso (USA)	17814
19	Alex Rocha (Bra)	31283	39	Mikkel Reese (USA)	17348
20	Andy Johnson (USA)	31006	40	Bobby Kalinowski (USA)	17243

Tour de las Americas

Results 2001–2002

Movinet Venezuela Open	Lagunita, Caracas, Venezuela	Rafael Alarcon (Mex)	268 (-12)
Abierto del Litoral	Rosario, Argentina	Marco Ruiz (Par)	278 (-6)
52nd Brazil Open Chevrolet	Sao Paulo, Brazil	Carlos Franco (Par)	273 (-11)
Torneo de Maestros Telefónica,	Olivos, Argentina	Angel Cabrera (Arg)	272 (-12)
Baviera Paraguay Open	Asunción, Paraguay	Raul Fretes (Par)	279 (-5)
Corona Caribbean Open	Our Lucaya, Freeport, Bahamas	Rafael Gomez (Arg)	278 (-10)
TLA-Los Encinos Open	Los Encinos, Mexico City	Roland Thatcher (USA)	278 (-10)
American Express Costa Rica Open	Cariari, San José, Costa Rica	Rafael Gomez (Arg)	289 (+5)
Gran Tikal Futura Guatemala Trophy	Mayan GC, Guatemala City	Sebastian Fernandez (Arg)	278 (-10)
LG Masters Panama	Summitt, Panama	Pedro Martinez (Par)	272 (-12)
TLA Players Championship Acapulco Fest	Fairmont Princess, Acapulco, Mexico	Roberto Coceres (Arg)	263 (-17)

Final Ranking 2001–2002

1	Rafael Gomez (Arg)	US$55639	11	Ramon Franco (Par)	16996
2	Marco Ruiz (Par)	35618	12	Pablo del Grosso (Arg)	16648
3	Gustavo Acosta (Arg)	30258	13	Rodolfo Gonzalez (Arg)	15602
4	Miguel Guzman (Arg)	29148	14	Alexandre Rocha (Bra)	15230
5	Rafael Alarcon (Mex)	27879	15	Angel Franco (Par)	15148
6	Roberto Coceres (Arg)	27438	16	Ruberlei Felizando (Bra)	13774
7	Carlos Franco (Par)	25935	17	Jon Levitt (USA)	11642
8	Sebastian Fernandez (Arg)	23633	18	Adam Armagost (USA)	10878
9	Pedro Martinez (Par)	22054	19	David Schuster (USA)	10030
10	Raul Fretes (Par)	17238	20	Alejandro Quiroz (Mex)	9640

World Championship Events

Accenture Match Play Championship
(formerly Anderson Consulting Match Play Championship

2000   Darren Clarke (NI) beat Tiger Woods (USA) 4 and 3 at La Costa Resort, Carlsberg, California
2001   Steve Stricker (USA) beat Pierre Fulke (Swe) 4 and 3 at Metropolitan GC, Melbourne, Australia

2002 *at La Costa, Carlsbad, CA, USA*   (7029–72)

First Round
Peter O'Malley (Aus) beat Tiger Woods (USA) 2 and 1
Nick Price (Zam) beat Angel Cabrera (Arg) 2 and 1
Scott Verplank (USA) beat Frank Lickliter (USA) at 20th
Bob Estes (USA) beat Stuart Appleby (Aus) 1 hole
Davis Love III (USA) beat Phillip Price (Wal) 2 and 1
Paul Azinger (USA) beat Jesper Parnevik (Swe) 1 hole
Vijay Singh (Fij) beat Toru Taniguchi (Jpn) 3 and 2
Niclas Fasth (Swe) beat Michael Campbell (NZ) 2 and 1

Sergio García (Esp) beat Lee Janzen (USA) 3 and 2
Charles Howell III (USA) beat Stewart Cink (USA) 4 and 3
Mike Weir (Can) beat Paul Lawrie (Sco) 3 and 2
Scott McCarron (USA) beat Colin Montgomerie (Sco) 2 and 1
Ernie Els (RSA) beat Jeff Sluman (USA) 4 and 3
Tom Lehman (USA) beat Hal Sutton (USA) 2 and 1
Matt Gogel (USA) beat Darren Clarke (NI) 2 and 1
Steve Lowery (USA) beat Scott Hoch (USA) 5 and 4

John Cook (USA) beat Phil Mickelson (USA) 3 and 2
Lee Westwood (Eng) beat Shingo Katayama (Jpn) 3 and 2
Adam Scott (Aus) beat Bernhard Langer (Ger) 2 and 1
Brad Faxon (USA) beat Kenny Perry (USA) 7 and 6
Retief Goosen (RSA) beat Bill Mayfair (USA) 4 and 3
José María Olazábal (Esp) beat Justin Leonard (USA) 1 hole
Chris DiMarco (USA) beat Steve Stricker (USA) 3 and 2
Mark Calcavecchia (USA) beat Jerry Kelly (USA) 3 and 2

Kevin Sutherland (USA) beat David Duval (USA) at 20th
Paul McGinley (Irl) beat Joe Durant (USA) 5 and 4
Jim Furyk (USA) beat Billy Andrade (USA) at 20th
Toshimitsu Izawa (Jpn) beat Pierre Fulke (Swe) 4 and 3
David Toms (USA) beat Rory Sabbatini (RSA) 1 hole
Rocco Mediate (USA) beat John Daly (USA) 5 and 4
Steve Flesch (USA) beat Padraig Harrington (Irl) 3 and 2
Kirk Triplett (USA) beat Robert Allenby (Aus) 3 and 2

Accenture Match Play Championship *continued*

Second Round
Price beat O'Malley 2 and 1
Estes beat Verplank at 20th
Azinger beat Love 1 hole
Fasth beat Singh 3 and 2
García beat Howell 1 hole
McCarron beat Weir 1 hole
Lehman beat Els at 19th
Gogel beat Lowery at 20th
Cook beat Westwood 1 hole
Faxon beat Scott 3 and 2
Olazábal beat Goosen 1 hole
Calcavecchia beat DiMarco 2 and 1
Sutherland beat McGinley 2 and 1
Furyk beat Izawa 3 and 1
Toms beat Mediate 1 hole
Flesch beat Triplett 3 and 2

Third Round
Estes beat Price 1 hole
Azinger beat Fasth at 20th
McCarron beat García 1 hole
Lehman beat Gogel 4 and 3
Faxon beat Cook 3 and 2
Olazábal beat Calcavecchia 2 holes

Sutherland beat Furyk 4 and 3
Toms beat Flesch 1 hole

Quarter-finals
Azinger beat Estes 2 and 1
McCarron beat Lehman 4 and 3
Faxon beat Olazábal at 20th
Sutherland beat Toms 3 and 2

Semi-finals
McCarron beat Azinger 1 hole
Sutherland beat Faxon 1 hole

Final (36 holes)
Kevin Sutherland beat Scott McCarron 1 hole

Consolation Match
Brad Faxon beat Paul Azinger at 19th

Winner:	$1,000,000	€1145476
Runner-up:	500,000	630012
3rd place:	400,000	515464
4th place:	300,000	412317
QF:	150,000	200458
3rd round:	75,000	97365
2nd round:	50,000	63001
1st round:	25,000	31500

NEC Invitational

(6949–71)

| 2000 | Tiger Woods (USA) | 64-61-67-67—259 | at Firestone CC, Aleron, Ohio |
| 2001 | T Woods (USA) | 66-67-66-69—268 | at Firestone CC, Aleron, Ohio |

2002 *at Sahalee, Redmond, WA*

1	Craig Parry (Aus)	72-65-66-65—268	$650533	€1016673
2	Robert Allenby (Aus)	69-63-71-69—272	266719	416836
	Fred Funk (USA)	68-68-68-68—272	266719	416836
4	Tiger Woods (USA)	68-70-67-68—273	139865	218585
5	Justin Rose (Eng)	67-67-72-68—274	121975	190626
6	Rich Beem (USA)	74-67-67-67—275	97580	152501
	Jim Furyk (USA)	70-67-68-70—275	97580	152501
8	Steve Lowery (USA)	67-65-73-71—276	78064	122001
9	Matt Gogel (USA)	68-69-68-72—277	68306	106751
	Phil Mickelson (USA)	66-69-71-71—277	68306	106751
11	Michael Campbell (NZ)	70-69-70-69—278	51230	80063
	Retief Goosen (RSA)	65-68-74-71—278	51230	80063
	Davis Love III (USA)	66-74-69-69—278	51230	80063
	Vijay Singh (Fij)	68-69-69-72—278	51230	80063
15	Thomas Bjørn (Den)	68-69-72-70—279	39601	61890
	Ernie Els (RSA)	71-67-67-74—279	39601	61890
	David Toms (USA)	69-68-71-71—279	39601	61890
	Lee Westwood (Eng)	68-69-72-70—279	39601	61890
19	Angel Cabrera (Arg)	72-70-70-68—280	32787	51240
	Kyoung-Ju Choi (Kor)	73-67-73-67—280	32787	51240
	Darren Clarke (NI)	66-74-68-72—280	32787	51240
	Bob Estes (USA)	71-71-69-69—280	32787	51240
	Peter Lonard (Aus)	70-71-72-67—280	32787	51240
24	Toshimitsu Izawa (Jpn)	65-73-73-71—282	29274	45750
	Rocco Mediate (USA)	68-69-73-72—282	29274	45750
	Kenny Perry (USA)	67-70-73-72 282	29274	45750
	Mike Weir (Can)	69-70-71-72—282	29274	45750

28	John Cook (USA)	70-74-69-70—283	$26835	€41938
	Chris DiMarco (USA)	68-70-74-71—283	26835	41938
	David Duval (USA)	72-75-71-65—283	26835	41938
	Ricardo Gonzalez (Arg)	71-72-68-72—283	26835	41938
	Justin Leonard (USA)	70-74-69-70—283	26835	41938
	Nick Price (Zim)	74-66-72-71—283	26835	41938
	Loren Roberts (USA)	70-66-76-71—283	26835	41938
	Kirk Triplett (USA)	71-69-70-73—283	26835	41938
36	Shigeki Maruyama (Jpn)	69-72-69-74—284	25208	39396
	Len Mattiace (USA)	69-72-72-71—284	25208	39396
38	Paul Azinger (USA)	68-72-73-72—285	24232	37871
	Matt Kuchar (USA)	71-68-71-75—285	24232	37871
	Bernhard Langer (Ger)	70-70-75-70—285	24232	37871
	Tom Lehman (USA)	72-70-69-74—285	24232	37871
42	Stuart Appleby (Aus)	70-72-74-70—286	22769	35584
	Carlos Daniel Franco (Par)	75-72-67-72—286	22769	35584
	Pierre Fulke (Swe)	69-73-73-71—286	22769	35584
	Craig Perks (NZ)	68-70-73-75—286	22769	35584
	Hal Sutton (USA)	73-71-70-72—286	22769	35584
47	Stewart Cink (USA)	73-71-73-70—287	21175	33093
	Joel Edwards (USA)	73-73-71-70—287	21175	33093
	Padraig Harrington (Irl)	72-70-73-72—287	21175	33093
	José María Olazábal (Esp)	71-68-75-73—287	21175	33093
	Eduardo Romero (Arg)	71-71-67-78—287	21175	33093
52	Notah Begay III (USA)	70-77-70-71—288	20329	31771
	Søren Hansen (Den)	76-69-69-74—288	20329	31771
	Graeme McDowell (NI)	72-69-73-74—288	20329	31771
55	Scott Hoch (USA)	72-77-69-71—289	19841	31009
	Greg Norman (Aus)	69-74-73-73—289	19841	31009
	Chris Smith (USA)	75-73-73-68—289	19841	31009
58	Niclas Fasth (Swe)	73-68-79-70—290	19191	29992
	Sergio García (Esp)	68-73-76-73—290	19191	29992
	Anders Hansen (Den)	71-76-74-69—290	19191	29992
	Kevin Sutherland (USA)	74-71-71-74—290	19191	29992
	Scott Verplank (USA)	71-75-76-68—290	19191	29992
63	Brad Faxon (USA)	71-72-71-77—291	18622	29102
	Charlie Wi (Kor)	73-73-73-72—291	18622	29102
65	Paul Lawrie (Sco)	73-69-81-70—293	18296	28594
	Nobuhito Sato (Jpn)	74-76-73-70—293	18296	28594
67	Paul McGinley (Irl)	79-69-73-74—295	18052	28213
68	Tobias Dier (Ger)	76-75-72-73—296	17727	27704
	Steve Elkington (Aus)	76-77-74-69—296	17727	27704
	Nicholas Lawrence (RSA)	76-72-78-70—296	17727	27704
71	Jesper Parnevik (Swe)	76-74-73-74—297	17320	27069
	Phillip Price (Wal)	73-73-73-78—297	17320	27069
73	John Daly (USA)	73-78-74-73—298	17077	26688
74	Mark Calcavecchia (USA)	74-81-75-69—299	16914	26434
75	José Coceres (Arg)	69-71-76-84—300	16670	26052
	Scott McCarron (USA)	74-74-77-75—300	16670	26052
77	Jerry Kelly (USA)	75-79-74-73—301	16426	25671
78	Colin Montgomerie (Sco)	71 Retired	16263	24417

American Express Challenge

2000 Mike Weir (Can) 68-75-65-69—277 at Sotogrande GC, Cadiz, Spain
2001 *Cancelled*

2002 *at Mount Juliet, Kilkenny, Ireland*

1	Tiger Woods (USA)	65-65-67-66—263	£641643	€1026378
2	Retief Goosen (RSA)	67-67-68-62—264	346487	554244
3	Vijay Singh (Fij)	67-69-66-65—267	235804	377194
4	Jerry Kelly (USA)	67-65-70-66—268	150786	241199

American Express Challenge *continued*

5	David Toms (USA)	66-67-69-66—268	£150786	€241199
6	Scott McCarron (USA)	71-67-64-67—269	115496	184748
7	Sergio García (Esp)	69-69-70-62—270	99455	159089
8	Davis Love III (USA)	69-67-68-67—271	83414	133429
9	Michael Campbell (NZ)	71-66-71-64—272	71222	113928
	Bob Estes (USA)	68-68-69-67—272	71222	113928
11	Stuart Appleby (Aus)	69-66-70-68—273	54058	86472
	Chris DiMarco (USA)	67-69-70-67—273	54058	86472
	Niclas Fasth (Swe)	68-69-72-64—273	54058	86472
	Justin Leonard (USA)	68-68-69-68—273	54058	86472
15	Gary Evans (Eng)	67-68-73-66—274	41707	66715
	Steve Lowery (USA)	66-67-69-72—274	41707	66715
	Rocco Mediate (USA)	69-67-67-71—274	41707	66715
	Nick Price (Zim)	68-71-69-66—274	41707	66715
	Scott Verplank (USA)	68-72-68-66—274	41707	66715
	Mike Weir (Can)	67-70-68-69—274	41707	66715
21	Padraig Harrington (Irl)	69-70-67-69—275	37215	59530
22	Kenny Perry (USA)	68-71-68-69—276	35932	57477
23	Ernie Els (RSA)	68-67-72-70—277	33686	53885
	Scott Hoch (USA)	71-68-67-71—277	33686	53885
	Stephen Leaney (Aus)	69-67-71-70—277	33686	53885
	Phil Mickelson (USA)	70-72-71-64—277	33686	53885
27	Thomas Bjørn (Den)	72-68-66-72—278	31120	49779
	Trevor Immelman (RSA)	71-71-67-69—278	31120	49779
	José María Olazábal (Esp)	68-72-69-69—278	31120	49779
	Kevin Sutherland (USA)	69-68-70-71—278	31120	49779
31	Robert Allenby (Aus)	72-70-67-70—279	29195	46700
	Colin Montgomerie (Sco)	72-70-69-68—279	29195	46700
33	Mark Calcavecchia (USA)	72-70-71-67—280	27591	44134
	Jim Furyk (USA)	69-69-69-73—280	27591	44134
	Bernhard Langer (Ger)	72-68-70-70—280	27591	44134
36	Angel Cabrera (Arg)	71-66-73-71—281	25666	41055
	José Coceres (Arg)	68-72-71-70—281	25666	41055
	Eduardo Romero (Arg)	70-71-70-70—281	25666	41055
39	Sören Hansen (Den)	75-68-65-74—282	23901	38233
	Tom Lehman (USA)	73-72-67-70—282	23901	38233
	Chris Riley (USA)	73-68-70-71—282	23901	38233
	Adam Scott (Aus)	70-70-69-73—282	23901	38233
43	Paul Azinger (USA)	73-73-71-66—283	22778	36436
	John Rollins (USA)	73-72-67-71—283	22778	36436
	Jeff Sluman (USA)	69-69-72-73—283	22778	36436
46	David Duval (USA)	71-65-72-76—284	21816	34897
	Len Mattiace (USA)	70-73-69-72—284	21816	34897
	Justin Rose (Eng)	73-70-72-69—284	21816	34897
49	Rich Beem (USA)	70-69-74-72—285	20533	32844
	John Cook (USA)	75-71-71-68—285	20533	32844
	Brad Faxon (USA)	70-77-67-71—285	20533	32844
	Fred Funk (USA)	69-70-72-74—285	20533	32844
	Craig Parry (Aus)	68-71-74-72—285	20533	32844
54	Paul Lawrie (Sco)	71-70-74-71—286	19249	30791
	Peter Lonard (Aus)	71-69-72-74—286	19249	30791
	Carl Pettersson (Swe)	72-72-68-74—286	19249	30791
57	Anders Hansen (Den)	71-72-72-74—289	18287	29252
	Thongchai Jaidee (Tha)	72-74-73-70—289	18287	29252
	Peter O'Malley (Aus)	75-73-71-70—289	18287	29252
60	Scott Laycock (Aus)	74-72-72-72—290	17645	28225
61	Craig Perks (NZ)	74-74-75-68—291	17324	27712
62	Tim Clark (RSA)	74-69-76-73—292	17004	27199
63	Darren Clarke (NI)	75-76-70-74—295	16683	26686
64	Kenichi Kuboya (Jpn)	77-72-73-76—298	16362	26173
65	Shigeki Maruyama (Jpn)	75 W/D	16041	25659

World Cup of Golf (Known as the Canada Cup until 1966)

Year	Winner	Runners-up	Venue	Score
1953	Argentina (A Cerda and R De Vincenzo) (Individual: A Cerda, Argentina, 140)	Canada (S Leonard and B Kerr)	Montreal	287
1954	Australia (P Thomson and K Nagle) (Individual: S Leonard, Canada, 275)	Argentina (A Cerda and R De Vincenzo)	Laval-Sur-Lac	556
1955	United States (C Harbert and E Furgol) (Individual: E Furgol, USA, after a play-off with P Thomson and F van Donck, 279)	Australia (P Thomson and K Nagle)	Washington	560
1956	United States (B Hogan and S Snead) (Individual: B Hogan, USA, 277)	South Africa (A Locke and G Player)	Wentworth	567
1957	Japan (T Nakamura and K Ono) (Individual: T Nakamura, Japan, 274)	United States (S Snead and J Demaret)	Tokyo	557
1958	Ireland (H Bradshaw and C O'Connor) (Individual: A Miguel, Spain, after a play-off with H Bradshaw, 286)	Spain (A Miguel and S Miguel)	Mexico City	579
1959	Australia (P Thomson and K Nagle) (Individual: S Leonard, Canada, 275, after a tie with P Thomson, Australia)	United States (S Snead and C Middlecoff)	Melbourne	563
1960	United States (S Snead and A Palmer) (Individual: F van Donck, Belgium, 279)	England (H Weetman and B Hunt)	Portmarnock	565
1961	United States (S Snead and J Demaret) (Individual: S Snead, USA, 272)	Australia (P Thomson and K Nagle)	Puerto Rico	560
1962	United States (S Snead and A Palmer) (Individual: R De Vicenzo, Argentina, 276)	Argentina (F de Luca and R De Vicenzo)	Buenos Aires	557
1963	United States (A Palmer and J Nicklaus) (Individual: J Nicklaus, USA, 237 [63 holes])	Spain (S Miguel and R Sota)	St Nom-La-Breteche	482
1964	United States (A Palmer and J Nicklaus) (Individual: J Nicklaus, USA, 276)	Argentina (R De Vicenzo and L Ruiz)	Maui, Hawaii	554
1965	South Africa (G Player and H Henning) (Individual: G Player, South Africa, 281)	Spain (A Miguel and R Sota)	Madrid	571
1966	United States (J Nicklaus and A Palmer) (Individual: G Knudson, Canada, and H Sugimoto, Japan, each 272; Knudson won play-off)	South Africa (G Player and H Henning)	Tokyo	548
1967	United States (J Nicklaus and A Palmer) (Individual: A Palmer, USA, 276)	New Zealand (R Charles and W Godfrey)	Mexico City	557
1968	Canada (A Balding and G Knudson) (Individual: A Balding, Canada, 274)	United States (J Boros and L Trevino)	Olgiata, Rome	569
1969	United States (O Moody and L Trevino) (Individual: L Trevino, USA, 275)	Japan (T Kono and H Yasuda)	Singapore	552
1970	Australia (B Devlin and D Graham) (Individual: R De Vicenzo, Argentina, 269)	Argentina (R De Vicenzo and V Fernandez)	Buenos Aires	545
1971	United States (J Nicklaus and L Trevino) (Individual: J Nicklaus, USA, 271)	South Africa (H Henning and G Player)	Palm Beach, Florida	555
1972	Taiwan (H Min-Nan and LL Huan) (Individual: H Min-Nan, Taiwan, 217 [3 rounds only])	Japan (T Kono and T Murakami)	Melbourne	438
1973	United States (J Nicklaus and J Miller) (Individual: J Miller, USA, 277)	South Africa (G Player and H Baiocchi)	Marbella, Spain	558
1974	South Africa (R Cole and D Hayes) (Individual: R Cole, South Africa, 271)	Japan (I Aoki and M Ozaki)	Caracas	554
1975	United States (J Miller and L Graham) (Individual: J Miller, USA, 275)	Taiwan (H Min-Nan and KC Hsiung)	Bangkok	554
1976	Spain (S Ballesteros and M Pinero) (Individual: EP Acosta, Mexico, 282)	United States (J Pate and D Stockton)	Palm Springs	574

Year	Winner	Runners-up	Venue	Score
1977	Spain	Philippines	Manilla, Philippines	591
	(S Ballesteros and A Garrido)	(R Lavares and B Arda)		
	(Individual: G Player, South Africa, 289)			
1978	United States	Australia	Hawaii	564
	(J Mahaffey and A North)	(G Norman and W Grady)		
	(Individual: J Mahaffey, USA, 281)			
1979	United States	Scotland	Glyfada, Greece	575
	(J Mahaffey and H Irwin)	(A Lyle and K Brown)		
	(Individual: H Irwin, USA, 285)			
1980	Canada	Scotland	Bogota	572
	(D Halldorson and J Nelford)	(A Lyle and S Martin)		
	(Individual: A Lyle, Scotland, 282)			
1981	*Not played*			
1982	Spain	United States	Acapulco	563
	(M Pinero and JM Canizares)	(B Gilder and B Clampett)		
	(Individual: M Pinero, Spain, 281)			
1983	United States	Canada	Pondok Inah, Jakarta	565
	(R Caldwell and J Cook)	(D Barr and J Anderson)		
	(Individual: D Barr, Canada, 276)			
1984	Spain	Scotland	Olgiata, Rome	414
	(JM Canizares and J Rivero)	(S Torrance and G Brand Jr)		
	(Individual: JM Canizares, Spain, 205. Played over 54 holes due to storm)			
1985	Canada	England	La Quinta, Calif.	559
	(D Halidorson and D Barr)	(H Clark and P Way)		
	(Individual: H Clark, England, 272)			
1986	*Not played*			
1987	Wales (won play-off)	Scotland	Kapalua, Hawaii	574
	(I Woosnam and D Llewelyn)	(S Torrance and A Lyle)		
	(Individual: I Woosnam, Wales, 274)			
1988	United States	Japan	Royal Melbourne,	560
	(B Crenshaw and M McCumber)	(T Ozaki and M Ozaki)	Australia	
	(Individual: B Crenshaw, USA, 275)			
1989	Australia	Spain	Las Brisas, Spain	278
	(P Fowler and W Grady)	(JM Olazábal and JM Canizares)		
	(Individual: P Fowler. Played over 36 holes due to storms.)			
1990	Germany	T England (M James andR Boxall)	Grand Cypress Resort,	
	(B Langer and T Giedeon)	Ireland (R Rafferty and D Feherty)	Orlando, Florida	556
	(Individual: P Stewart, USA, 271)			
1991	Sweden	Wales	La Querce, Rome	563
	(A Forsbrand and P-U Johansson)	(I Woosnam and P Price)		
	(Individual: I Woosnam, Wales, 273)			
1992	USA	Sweden	La Moraleja II,	548
	(F Couples and D Love III)	(A Forsbrand and P-U Johansson)	Madrid, Spain	
	(Individual: B Ogle, Australia, 270 after a tie with I Woosnam, Wales)			
1993	USA	Zimbabwe	Lake Nona, Orlando, FL	556
	(F Couples and D Love III)	(N Price and M McNulty)		
	(Individual: B Langer, Germany, 272)			
1994	USA	Zimbabwe	Dorado Beach,	536
	(F Couples and D Love III)	(M McNulty and T Johnstone)	Puerto Rico	
	(Individual: F Couples, USA, 265)			
1995	USA	Australia	Mission Hills, Shenzhen,	543
	(F Couples and D Love III)	(B Ogle and R Allenby)	China	
	(Individual: D Love III, USA, 267)			
1996	South Africa	USA	Erinvale, Cape Town	547
	(E Els and W Westner)	(T Lehman and S Jones)	South Africa	
	(Individual: E Els, S. Africa, 272)			
1997	Ireland	Scotland	Kiawah Island, SC	545
	(P Harrington and P McGinley)	(C Montgomerie and R Russell)		
	(Individual: C Montgomerie, Scotland, 266)			
1998	England	Italy	Gulf Harbour, Auckland	568
	(N Faldo and D Carter)	(C Rocca and M Florioli)	New Zealand	
	(Individual: Scott Verplank, USA, 279)			
1999	USA	Spain	The Mines Resort, KL	545
	(T Woods and M O'Meara)	(S Luna and MA Martin)	Malaysia	
	(Individual: Tiger Woods, USA, 263)			
2000	USA	Argentina	Buenos Aires GC	254
	(T Woods & D Duval)	(A Cabrera & E Romero)	Argentina	
2001	South Africa	New Zealand	The Taiheiyo Club,	254
	(E Els and R Goosen)	(Michael Campbell and David Smail)	Japan	
		USA		
		(David Duval and Tiger Woods)		
		Denmark		
		(Thomas Bjørn and Søren Hansen)		

The 48th EMC^2 World Cup of Golf is scheduled to played in Mexico between December 12 and 15 2002

Other International Events

Hassan II Trophy

1971	O Moody (USA)	1980	E Sneed (USA)	1993	P Stewart (USA)
1972	R Cerrudo (USA)	1981	B Eastwood (USA)	1994	M Gates (Eng)
1973	W Casper (USA)	1982	F Connor (USA)	1995	N Price (Zim)
1974	L Ziegler (USA)	1983	R Streck (USA)	1996	I Garrido (Esp)
1975	W Casper (USA)	1984	R Maltbie (USA)	1997	C Montgomerie (Sco)
1976	S Balbuena (USA)	1985	K Green (USA)	1998	S Luna (Esp)
1977	L Trevino (USA)	1986–90	Not played	1999	D Toms (USA)*
1978	P Townsend (Eng)	1991	V Singh (Fij)	2000	R Chapman (Eng)
1979	M Brannan (USA)	1992	P Stewart (USA)	2001	J Haegmann (Swe)

2002 event being played in December

Sun City Million Dollar Challenge

1982 (Jan)	J Miller (USA)	277	1990	D Frost (RSA)	284	1998	N Price* (Zim)	273
1982 (Dec)	R Floyd (USA)	280	1991	B Langer (Ger)	272	1999	E Els (RSA)	263
1983	S Ballesteros (Esp)	274	1992	D Frost (RSA)	276	2000	E Els (RSA)	268
1984	S Ballesteros (Esp)	279	1993	N Price (Zim)	264	2001	S García* (Esp)	268
1985	B Langer (Ger)	278	1994	N Faldo (Eng)	272			
1986	M McNulty (Zim)	282	1995	C Pavin (USA)	276			
1987	I Woosnam (Wal)	274	1996	C Montgomerie				
1988	F Allem (RSA)	278		(Sco)	274			
1989	D Frost (RSA)	276	1997	N Price (Zim)	275			

at Sun City, Bophutatswana, South Africa   (7597–72)

2002 event being played November 29–December 2

International Team Events

2002 Ryder Cup *at The Belfry, Sutton Coldfield*

Non-playing captains: Sam Torrance (Eur), Curtis Strange (USA)

Europe		USA	
***First Day, Morning* – Fourball**			
Bjørn & Clarke (1 hole)	1	Azinger & Woods	0
García & Westwood (4 and 3)	1	Duval & Love	0
Langer & Montgomerie (4 and 3)	1	Furyk & Hoch	0
Fasth & Harrington	0	Mickelson & Toms (1 hole)	1
	3		1
***Afternoon* – Foursomes**			
Bjørn & Clarke	0	Sutton & Verplank (2 and 1)	1
García & Westwood (2 and 1)	1	Calcavecchia & Woods	0
Langer & Montgomerie (halved)	½	Mickelson & Toms (halved)	½
Harrington & McGinley	0	Cink & Furyk (3 and 2)	1
	1½		2½

Match position: Europe 4½, USA 3½

Europe		USA	
***Second Day, Morning* – Foursomes**			
Fulke & Price	0	Mickelson & Toms (2 and 1)	1
García & Westwood (2 and 1)	1	Cink & Furyk	0
Langer & Montgomerie (1 hole)	1	Hoch & Verplank 1 hole	0
Bjørn & Clarke	0	Love & Woods (4 and 3)	1
	2		2
***Afternoon* – Fourball**			
Fasth & Parnevik	0	Calcavecchia & Duval (1 hole)	1
García & Westwood	0	Love & Woods (1 hole)	1
Harrington & Montgomerie (2 and 1)	1	Mickelson & Toms	0
Clarke & McGinley (halved)	½	Furyk & Hoch (halved)	½
	1½		2½

Match position: Europe 8, USA 8

Europe		USA	
***Third Day* – Singles**			
Colin Montgomerie (Sco) (5 and 4)	1	Scott Hoch	0
Sergio García (Esp)	0	David Toms (1 hole)	1
Darren Clarke (NI) (halved)	½	David Duval halved)	½
Bernhard Langer (Ger) (4 and 3)	1	Hal Sutton	0
Padraig Harrington (Irl) (5 and 4)	1	Mark Calcavecchia	0
Thomas Bjørn (Den) (2 and 1)	1	Stewart Cink	0
Lee Westwood (Eng)	0	Scott Verplank (2 and 1)	1
Niclas Fasth (Swe) (halved)	½	Paul Azinger (halved)	½
Paul McGinley (Irl) (halved)	½	Jim Furyk (halved)	½
Pierre Fulke (Swe) (halved)	½	Davis Love III (halved)	½
Phillip Price (Wal) (3 and 2)	1	Phil Mickelson	0
Jesper Parnevik (Swe) (halved)	½	Tiger Woods (halved)	½
	7½		4½

Result: Europe 15½, USA 12½

Great Britain v USA

1926 at Wentworth
Result: GB 13½, USA 1½

Singles
Abe Mitchell beat Jim Barnes 8 and 7
George Duncan beat Walter Hagen 6 and 5
Aubrey Boomer beat Tommy Armour 2 and 1
Archie Compston lost to Bill Mehlhorn 1 hole
George Gadd beat Joe Kirkwood 8 and 7
Ted Ray beat Al Watrous 6 and 5
Fred Robson beat Cyril Walker 5 and 4
Arthur Havers beat Fred McLeod 10 and 9
Ernest Whitcombe halved with Emmett French
Herbert Jolly beat Joe Stein 3 and 2

Foursomes
Mitchell & Duncan beat Barnes & Hagen 9 and 8
Boomer & Compston beat Armour & Kirkwood
3 and 2
Gadd & Havers beat Mehlhorn & Watrous 3 and 2
Ray & Robson beat Walker & McLeod 3 and 2
Whitcombe & Jolly beat French & Stein 3 and 2

RYDER CUP – Inaugurated 1927

1927 at Worcester, MA
Result: USA 9½, GBI 2½
Captains: W Hagen (USA), E Ray (GBI)

Foursomes
Hagen & Golden beat Ray & Robson 2 and 1
Farrell & Turnesa beat Duncan & Compston 8 and 6
Sarazen & Watrous beat Havers & Jolly 3 and 2
Diegel & Mehlhorn lost to Boomer & Whitcombe
7 and 5

Singles
Bill Mehlhorn beat Archie Compston 1 hole
Johnny Farrell beat Aubrey Boomer 5 and 4
Johnny Golden beat Herbert Jolly 8 and 7
Leo Diegel beat Ted Ray 7 and 5
Gene Sarazen halved with Charles Whitcombe
Walter Hagen beat Arthur Havers 2 and 1
Al Watrous beat Fred Robson 3 and 2
Joe Turnesa lost to George Duncan 1 hole

1929 at Moortown
Result: GBI 7, USA 5
*Captains: George Duncan (GBI),
Walter Hagen (USA)*

Foursomes
C Whitcombe & Compston halved with Farrell &
Turnesa
Boomer & Duncan lost to Diegel & Espinosa 7 and 5
Mitchell & Robson beat Sarazen & Dudley 2 and 1
E Whitcombe & Cotton lost to Golden & Hagen
2 holes

Singles
Charles Whitcombe beat Johnny Farrell 8 and 6
George Duncan beat Walter Hagen 10 and 8
Abe Mitchell lost to Leo Diegel 9 and 8
Archie Compston beat Gene Sarazen 6 and 4
Aubrey Boomer beat Joe Turnesa 4 and 3
Fred Robson lost to Horton Smith 4 and 2
Henry Cotton beat Al Watrous 4 and 3
Ernest Whitcombe halved with Al Espinosa

1931 at Scioto, Columbus, OH
Result: USA 9, GBI 3
*Captains: Walter Hagen (USA),
Charles Whitcombe (GBI)*

Foursomes
Sarazen & Farrell beat Compston & Davies 8 and 7
Hagen & Shute beat Duncan & Havers 10 and 9
Diegel & Espinosa lost to Mitchell & Robson 3 and 1
Burke & Cox beat Easterbrook & E Whitcombe 3 and 2

Singles
Billy Burke beat Archie Compston 7 and 6
Gene Sarazen beat Fred Robson 7 and 6
Johnny Farrell lost to William H Davies 4 and 3
Wilfred Cox beat Abe Mitchell 3 and 1
Walter Hagen beat Charles Whitcombe 4 and 3
Densmore Shute beat Bert Hodson 8 and 6
Al Espinosa beat Ernest Whitcombe 2 and 1
Craig Wood lost to Arthur Havers 4 and 3

1933 at Southport & Ainsdale
Result: GBI 6½, USA 5½
Captains: JH Taylor (GBI), Walter Hagen (USA)

Foursomes
Alliss & Whitcombe halved with Sarazen & Hagen
Mitchell & Havers beat Dutra & Shute 3 and 2
Davies & Easterbrook beat Wood & Runyan 1 hole
Padgham & Perry lost to Dudley & Burke 1 hole

Singles
Alf Padgham lost to Gene Sarazen 6 and 4
Abe Mitchell beat Olin Dutra 9 and 8
Arthur Lacey lost to Walter Hagen 2 and 1
William H Davies lost to Craig Wood 4 and 3
Percy Alliss beat Paul Runyan 2 and 1
Arthur Havers beat Leo Diegel 4 and 3
Syd Easterbrook beat Densmore Shute 1 hole
Charles Whitcombe lost to Horton Smith 2 and 1

1935 at Ridgewood, NJ
Result: USA 9, GBI 3
*Captains: Walter Hagen (USA),
Charles Whitcombe (GBI)*

Foursomes
Sarazen & Hagen beat Perry & Busson 7 and 6
Picard & Revolta beat Padgham & Alliss 6 and 5
Runyan & Smith beat Cox & Jarman 9 and 8
Dutra & Laffoon lost to C Whitcombe & E Whitcombe
1 hole

Singles
Gene Sarazen beat Jack Busson 3 and 2
Paul Runyon beat Dick Burton 5 and 3
Johnny Revolta beat Charles Whitcombe 2 and 1
Olin Dutra beat Alf Padgham 4 and 2
Craig Wood lost to Percy Alliss 1 hole
Horton Smith halved with Bill Cox
Henry Picard beat Ernest Whitcombe 3 and 2
Sam Parks halved with Alf Perry

1937 at Southport & Ainsdale
Result: USA 8, GBI 4
*Captains: Charles Whitcombe (GBI),
Walter Hagen (USA)*

Foursomes
Padgham & Cotton lost to Dudley & Nelson 4 and 2
Lacey & Bill Cox lost to Guldahl & Manero 2 and 1
Whitcombe & Rees halved with Sarazen & Shute
Alliss & Burton beat Picard & Johnny Revolta 2 and 1

1937 *continued*

Singles
Alf Padgham lost to Ralph Guldahl 8 and 7
Sam King halved with Densmore Shute
Dai Rees beat Byron Nelson 3 and 1
Henry Cotton beat Tony Manero 5 and 3
Percy Alliss lost to Gene Sarazen 1 hole
Dick Burton lost to Sam Snead 5 and 4
Alf Perry lost to Ed Dudley 2 and 1
Arthur Lacey lost to Henry Picard 2 and 1

1947 *at Portland, OR*

Result: USA 11, GBI 1
Captains: Ben Hogan (USA),
Henry Cotton (GBI)

Foursomes
Oliver & Worsham beat Cotton & Lees 10 and 9
Snead & Mangrum beat Daly & Ward 6 and 5
Hogan & Demaret beat Adams & Faulkner 2 holes
Nelson & Herman Barron beat Rees & King 2 and 1

Singles
Dutch Harrison beat Fred Daly 5 and 4
Lew Worsham beat Jimmy Adams 3 and 2
Lloyd Mangrum beat Max Faulkner 6 and 5
Ed Oliver beat Charlie Ward 4 and 3
Byron Nelson beat Arthur Lees 2 and 1
Sam Snead beat Henry Cotton 5 and 4
Jimmy Demaret beat Dai Rees 3 and 2
Herman Keiser lost to Sam King 4 and 3

1949 *at Ganton*

Result: USA 7, GBI 5
Captains: Charles Whitcombe (GBI),
Ben Hogan (USA)

Foursomes
Faulkner & Adams beat Harrison & Palmer 2 and 1
Daly & Ken Bousfield beat Hamilton & Alexander 4 and 2
Ward & King lost to Demaret & Heafner 4 and 3
Burton & Lees beat Snead & Mangrum 1 hole

Singles
Max Faulkner lost to Dutch Harrison 8 and 7
Jimmy Adams beat Johnny Palmer 2 and 1
Charlie Ward lost to Sam Snead 6 and 5
Dai Rees beat Bob Hamilton 6 and 4
Dick Burton lost to Clayton Heafner 3 and 2
Sam King lost to Chick Harbert 4 and 3
Arthur Lees lost to Jimmy Demaret 7 and 6
Fred Daly lost to Lloyd Mangrum 1 hole

1951 *at Pinehurst, NC*

Result: USA 9½, GBI 2½
Captains: Sam Snead (USA), Arthur Lacey (GBI)

Foursomes
Heafner & Burke beat Faulkner & Rees 5 and 3
Oliver & Henry Ransom lost to Ward & Lees 2 and 1
Mangrum & Snead beat Adams & Panton 5 and 4
Hogan & Demaret beat Daly & Bousfield 5 and 4

Singles
Jack Burke beat Jimmy Adams 4 and 3
Jimmy Demaret beat Dai Rees 2 holes
Clayton Heafner halved with Fred Daly
Lloyd Mangrum beat Harry Weetman 6 and 5
Ed Oliver lost to Arthur Lees 2 and 1
Ben Hogan beat Charlie Ward 3 and 2
Skip Alexander beat John Panton 8 and 7
Sam Snead beat Max Faulkner 4 and 3

1953 *at Wentworth*

Result: USA 6½, GBI 5½
Captains: Henry Cotton (GBI),
Lloyd Mangrum (USA)

Foursomes
Weetman & Alliss lost to Douglas & Oliver 2 and 1
Brown & Panton lost to Mangrum & Snead 8 and 7
Adams & Hunt lost to Kroll & Burke 7 and 5
Daly & Bradshaw beat Burkemo & Middlecoff 1 hole

Singles
Dai Rees lost to Jack Burke 2 and 1
Fred Daly beat Ted Kroll 9 and 7
Eric Brown beat Lloyd Mangrum 2 holes
Harry Weetman beat Sam Snead 1 hole
Max Faulkner lost to Cary Middlecoff 3 and 1
Peter Alliss lost to Jim Turnesa 1 hole
Bernard Hunt halved with Dave Douglas
Harry Bradshaw beat Fred Haas jr 3 and 2

1955 *at Palm Springs, CA*

Result: USA 8, GBI 4
Captains: Chick Harbert (USA),
Dai Rees (GBI)

Foursomes
Harper & Barber lost to Fallon & Jacobs 1 hole
Ford & Kroll beat Brown & Scott 5 and 4
Burke & Bolt beat Lees & Weetman 1 hole
Snead & Middlecoff beat Rees & Bradshaw 3 and 2

Singles
Tommy Bolt beat Christy O'Connor 4 and 2
Chick Harbert beat Syd Scott 3 and 2
Cary Middlecoff lost to John Jacobs 1 hole
Sam Snead beat Dai Rees 3 and 1
Marty Furgol lost to Arthur Lees 3 and 1
Jerry Barber lost to Eric Brown 3 and 2
Jack Burke beat Harry Bradshaw 3 and 2
Doug Ford beat Harry Weetman 3 and 2

1957 *at Lindrick*

Result: GBI 7½, USA 4½
Captains: Dai Rees (GBI), Jack Burke (USA)

Foursomes
Alliss & Hunt lost to Ford & Finsterwald 2 and 1
Bousfield & Rees beat Art Wall jr & Hawkins 3 and 2
Faulkner & Weetman lost to Kroll & Burke 4 and 3
O'Connor & Brown lost to Mayer & Bolt 7 and 5

Singles
Eric Brown beat Tommy Bolt 4 and 3
Peter Mills beat Jack Burke 5 and 3
Peter Alliss lost to Fred Hawkins 2 and 1
Ken Bousfield beat Lionel Hebert 4 and 3
Dai Rees beat Ed Furgol 7 and 6
Bernard Hunt beat Doug Ford 6 and 5
Christy O'Connor beat Dow Finsterwald 7 and 6
Harry Bradshaw halved with Dick Mayer

1959 *at Palm Desert, CA*

Result: USA 8½, GBI 3½
Captains: Sam Snead (USA),
Dai Rees (GBI)

Foursomes
Rosburg & Souchak beat Hunt & Brown 5 and 4
Ford & Wall lost to O'Connor & Alliss 3 and 2
Boros & Finsterwald beat Rees & Bousfield 2 holes
Snead & Middlecoff halved with Weetman & Thomas

Singles
Doug Ford halved with Norman Drew
Mike Souchak beat Ken Bousfield 3 and 2
Bob Rosburg beat Harry Weetman 6 and 5
Sam Snead beat Dave Thomas 6 and 5
Dow Finsterwald beat Dai Rees 1 hole
Jay Hebert halved with Peter Alliss
Art Wall jr beat Christy O'Connor 7 and 6
Cary Middlecoff lost to Eric Brown 4 and 3

1961 at Royal Lytham & St Anne's
Result: USA 14½, GBI 9½
Captains: Jerry Barber (USA), Dai Rees (GBI)
First Day: Foursomes – Morning
O'Connor & Alliss beat Littler & Ford 4 and 3
Panton & Hunt lost to Wall & Hebert 4 and 3
Rees & Bousfield lost to Casper & Palmer 2 and 1
Haliburton & Coles lost to Souchak & Collins 1 hole

Foursomes – Afternoon
O'Connor & Alliss lost to Wall & Hebert 1 hole
Panton & Hunt lost to Casper & Palmer 5 and 4
Rees & Bousfield beat Souchak & Collins 4 and 2
Haliburton& Coles lost to Barber & Finsterwald
1 hole
Second Day: Singles – Morning
Harry Weetman lost to Doug Ford 1 hole
Ralph Moffitt lost to Mike Souchak 5 and 4
Peter Alliss halved with Arnold Palmer
Ken Bousfield lost to Billy Casper 5 and 3
Dai Rees beat Jay Hebert 2 and 1
Neil Coles halved with Gene Littler
Bernard Hunt beat Jerry Barber 5 and 4
Christy O'Connor lost to Dow Finsterwald 2 and 1
Singles – Afternoon
Weetman lost to Wall 1 hole
Alliss beat Bill Collins 3 and 2
Hunt lost to Souchak 2 and 1
Tom Haliburton lost to Palmer 2 and 1
Rees beat Ford 4 and 3
Bousfield beat Barber 1 hole
Coles beat Finsterwald 1 hole
O'Connor halved with Littler

1963 at Atlanta, GA
Result: USA 23, GBI
Captains: Arnold Palmer (USA),
  John Fallon (GBI)
First Day: Foursomes – Morning
Palmer & Pott lost to Huggett & Will 3 and 2
Casper & Ragan beat Alliss & O'Connor 1 hole
Boros & Lema halved with Coles & B Hunt
Littler & Finsterwald halved with Thomas & Weetman
Foursomes – Afternoon
Maxwell & Goalby beat Thomas & Weetman 4 and 3
Palmer & Casper beat Huggett & Will 5 and 4
Littler & Finsterwald beat Coles & G Hunt 2 and 1
Boros & Lema beat Haliburton & B Hunt 1 hole
Second Day: Fourball – Morning
Palmer & Finsterwald beat Huggett & Thomas 5 and 4
Littler & Boros halved with Alliss & B Hunt
Casper & Maxwell beat Weetman & Will 3 and 2
Goalby & Ragan lost to Coles & O'Connor 1 hole
Fourball – Afternoon
Palmer & Finsterwald beat Coles & O'Connor 3 and 2
Lema & Pott beat Alliss & B Hunt 1 hole
Casper & Maxwell beat Haliburton & G Hunt 2 and 1
Goalby & Ragan halved with Huggett & Thomas

Third Day: Singles – Morning
Tony Lema beat Geoffrey Hunt 5 and 3
Johnny Pott lost to Brian Huggett 3 and 1
Arnold Palmer lost to Peter Alliss 1 hole
Billy Casper halved with Neil Coles
Bob Goalby beat Dave Thomas 3 and 2
Gene Littler lost to Tom Haliburton 6 and 5
Julius Boros lost to Harry Weetman 1 hole
Dow Finsterwald lost to Bernard Hunt 2 holes

Singles – Afternoon
Arnold Palmer beat George Will 3 and 2
Dave Ragan beat Neil Coles 2 and 1
Tony Lema halved with Peter Alliss
Gene Littler beat Tom Haliburton 6 and 5
Julius Boros beat Harry Weetman 2 and 1
Billy Maxwell beat Christy O'Connor 2 and 1
Dow Finsterwald beat Dave Thomas 4 and 3
Bob Goalby beat Bernard Hunt 2 and 1

1965 at Royal Birkdale
Result: GBI 12½, USA 19½
Captains: Harry Weetman (GBI),
  Byron Nelson (USA)
First Day: Foursomes – Morning
Thomas & Will beat Marr & Palmer 6 and 5
O'Connor & Alliss beat Venturi & January 5 and 4
Platts & Butler lost to Boros & Lema 1 hole
Hunt & Coles lost to Casper & Littler 2 and 1

Foursomes – Afternoon
Thomas & Will lost to Marr & Palmer 6 and 5
Martin & Hitchcock lost to Boros & Lema
5 and 4
O'Connor & Alliss beat Casper & Littler 2 and 1
Hunt & Coles beat Venturi & January 3 and 2

Second Day: Fourball – Morning
Thomas & Will lost to January & Jacobs 1 hole
Platts & Butler halved with Casper & Littler
Alliss & O'Connor lost to Marr & Palmer
5 and 4
Coles & Hunt beat Boros & Lema 1 hole

Fourball – Afternoon
Alliss & O'Connor beat Marr & Palmer 1 hole
Thomas & Will lost to January & Jacobs 1 hole
Platts & Butler halved with Casper & Littler
Coles & Hunt lost to Lema & Venturi 1 hole

Third Day: Singles – Morning
Jimmy Hitchcock lost to Arnold Palmer 3 and 2
Lionel Platts lost to Julius Boros 4 and 2
Peter Butler lost to Tony Lema 1 hole
Neil Coles lost to Dave Marr 2 holes
Bernard Hunt beat Gene Littler 2 holes
Peter Alliss beat Billy Casper 1 hole
Dave Thomas lost to Tommy Jacobs 2 and 1
George Will halved with Don January

Singles – Afternoon
Butler lost to Palmer 2 holes
Hitchcock lost to Boros 2 and 1
Christy O'Connor lost to Lema 6 and 4
Alliss beat Ken Venturi 3 and 1
Hunt lost to Marr 1 hole
Coles beat Casper 3 and 2
Will lost to Littler 2 and 1
Platts beat Jacobs 1 hole

1967 at Houston, TX
Result: USA 23½, GBI 8½
Captains: Ben Hogan (USA), Dai Rees (GBI)
First Day: Foursomes – Morning
Casper & Boros halved with Huggett & Will
Palmer & Dickinson beat Alliss & O'Connor 2 and 1
Sanders & Brewer lost to Jacklin & Thomas 4 and 3
Nichols & Pott beat Hunt & Coles 6 and 5

Foursomes – Afternoon
Boros & Casper beat Huggett & Will 1 hole
Dickinson & Palmer beat Gregson & Boyle 5 and 4
Littler & Geiberger lost to Jacklin & Thomas 3 and 2
Nichols & Pott beat Alliss & O'Connor 2 and 1

Second Day: Fourball – Morning
Casper & Brewer beat Alliss & O'Connor 3 and 2
Nichols & Pott beat Hunt & Coles 1 hole
Littler & Geiberger beat Jacklin & Thomas 1 hole
Dickinson & Sanders beat Huggett & Will 3 and 2

Fourball – Afternoon
Casper & Brewer beat Hunt & Coles 5 and 3
Dickinson & Sanders beat Alliss & Gregson 4 and 3
Palmer & Boros beat Will & Boyle 1 hole
Littler & Geiberger halved with Jacklin & Thomas

Third Day: Singles – Morning
Gay Brewer beat Hugh Boyle 4 and 3
Billy Casper beat Peter Alliss 2 and 1
Arnold Palmer beat Tony Jacklin 3 and 2
Julius Boros lost to Brian Huggett 1 hole
Doug Sanders lost to Neil Coles 2 and 1
Al Geiberger beat Malcolm Gregson 4 and 2
Gene Littler halved with Dave Thomas
Bobby Nichols halved with Bernard Hunt

Singles – Afternoon
Palmer beat Huggett 5 and 3
Brewer lost to Alliss 2 and 1
Gardner Dickinson beat Jacklin 3 and 2
Nichols beat Christy O'Connor 3 and 2
Johnny Pott beat George Will 3 and 1
Geiberger beat Gregson 2 and 1
Boros halved with Hunt
Sanders lost to Coles 2 and 1

1969 at Royal Birkdale
Result: USA 16, GBI 16
Captains: Eric Brown (GBI), Sam Snead (USA)
First Day: Foursomes – Morning
Coles & Huggett beat Barber & Floyd 3 and 2
Gallacher & Bembridge beat Trevino & Still 2 and 1
Jacklin & Townsend beat Hill & Aaron 3 and 1
O'Connor & Alliss halved with Casper & Beard

Foursomes – Afternoon
Coles & Huggett lost to Hill & Aaron 1 hole
Gallacher & Bembridge lost to Trevino & Littler 2 holes
Jacklin & Townsend beat Casper & Beard 1 hole
Hunt & Butler lost to Nicklaus & Sikes

Second Day: Fourball – Morning
O'Connor & Townsend beat Hill & Douglass 1 hole
Huggett & Alex Caygill halved with Floyd & Barber
Barnes & Alliss lost to Trevino & Littler 1 hole
Jacklin & Coles beat Nicklaus & Sikes 1 hole

Fourball – Afternoon
Townsend & Butler lost to Casper & Beard 2 holes
Huggett & Gallacher lost to Hill & Still 2 and 1
Bembridge & Hunt halved with Aaron & Floyd
Jacklin & Coles halved with Trevino & Barber

Third Day: Singles – Morning
Peter Alliss lost to Lee Trevino 2 and 1
Peter Townsend lost to Dave Hill 5 and 4
Neil Coles beat Tommy Aaron 1 hole
Brian Barnes lost to Billy Casper 1 hole
Christy O'Connor beat Frank Beard 5 and 4
Maurice Bembridge beat Ken Still 1 hole
Peter Butler beat Ray Floyd 1 hole
Tony Jacklin beat Jack Nicklaus 4 and 3

Singles – Afternoon
Barnes lost to Hill 4 and 2
Bernard Gallacher beat Trevino 4 and 3
Bembridge lost to Miller Barber 7 and 6
Butler beat Dale Douglass 3 and 2
O'Connor lost to Gene Littler 2 and 1
Brian Huggett halved with Casper
Coles lost to Dan Sikes 4 and 3
Jacklin halved with Nicklaus

1971 at St Louis, MO
Result: USA 18½, GBI 13½
Captains: Jay Hebert (USA), Eric Brown (GBI)
First Day: Foursomes – Morning
Casper & Barber lost to Coles & O'Connor 2 and 1
Palmer & Dickinson beat Townsend & Oosterhuis 2 holes
Nicklaus & Stockton lost to Huggett & Jacklin 3 and 2
Coody & Beard lost to Bembridge & Butler 1 hole

Foursomes – Afternoon
Casper & Barber lost to Bannerman & Gallacher 2 and 1
Palmer & Dickinson beat Townsend & Oosterhuis 1 hole
Trevino & Rudolph halved with Huggett and Jacklin
Nicklaus & Snead beat Bembridge & Butler 5 and 3

Second Day: Fourball – Morning
Trevino & Rudolph beat O'Connor & Barnes 2 and 1
Beard & Snead beat Coles & John Garner 2 and 1
Palmer & Dickinson beat Oosterhuis & Gallacher 5 and 4
Nicklaus & Littler beat Townsend & Bannerman 2 and 1

Fourball – Afternoon
Trevino & Casper lost to Oosterhuis & Gallacher 1 hole
Littler & Snead beat Huggett & Jacklin 2 and 1
Palmer & Nicklaus beat Townsend & Bannerman 1 hole
Coody & Beard halved with Coles & O'Connor

Third Day: Singles – Morning
Lee Trevino beat Tony Jacklin 1 hole
Dave Stockton halved with Bernard Gallacher
Mason Rudolph lost to Brian Barnes 1 hole
Gene Littler lost to Peter Oosterhuis 4 and 3
Jack Nicklaus beat Peter Townsend 3 and 2
Gardner Dickinson beat Christy O'Connor 5 and 4
Arnold Palmer halved with Harry Bannerman
Frank Beard halved with Neil Coles

Singles – Afternoon
Trevino beat Brian Huggett 7 and 6
JC Snead beat Jacklin 1 hole
Miller Barber lost to Barnes 2 and 1
Stockton beat Townsend 1 hole
Charles Coody lost to Gallacher 2 and 1
Nicklaus beat Coles 5 and 3
Palmer lost to Oosterhuis 3 and 2
Dickinson lost to Bannerman 2 and 1

1973 *at Muirfield*
Result: USA 19, GBI 13
Captains: Bernard Hunt (GBI), Jack Burke (USA)
First Day: **Foursomes – Morning**
Barnes & Gallacher beat Trevino & Casper 1 hole
O'Connor & Coles beat Weiskopf & Snead 3 and 2
Jacklin & Oosterhuis halved with Rodriguez & Graham
Bembridge & Polland lost to Nicklaus & Palmer 6 and 5
Fourball – Afternoon
Barnes & Gallacher beat Aaron & Brewer 5 and 4
Bembridge & Huggett beat Nicklaus & Palmer 3 and 1
Jacklin & Oosterhuis beat Weiskopf & Casper 3 and 1
O'Connor & Coles lost to Trevino & Blancas 2 and 1
Second Day: **Foursomes – Morning**
Barnes & Butler lost to Nicklaus & Weiskopf 1 hole
Jacklin & Oosterhuis beat Palmer & Hill 2 holes
Bembridge & Huggett beat Rodriguez & Graham
  5 and 4
O'Connor & Coles lost to Trevino & Casper 2 and 1
Fourball – Afternoon
Barnes & Butler lost to Snead & Palmer 2 holes
Jacklin & Oosterhuis lost to Brewer & Casper
  3 and 2
Clark & Polland lost to Nicklaus & Weiskopf 3 and 2
Bembridge & Huggett halved with Trevino &
  Blancas
Third Day: **Singles – Morning**
Brian Barnes lost to Billy Casper 2 and 1
Bernard Gallacher lost to Tom Weiskopf 3 and 1
Peter Butler lost to Homero Blancas 5 and 4
Tony Jacklin beat Tommy Aaron 3 and 1
Neil Coles halved with Gay Brewer
Christy O'Connor lost to JC Snead 1 hole
Maurice Bembridge halved with Jack Nicklaus
Peter Oosterhuis halved with Lee Trevino
Singles – Afternoon
Brian Huggett beat Blancas 4 and 2
Barnes lost to Snead 3 and 1
Gallacher lost to Brewer 6 and 5
Jacklin lost to Casper 2 and 1
Coles lost to Trevino 6 and 5
O'Connor halved with Weiskopf
Bembridge lost to Nicklaus 2 holes
Oosterhuis beat Arnold Palmer 4 and 2

1975 *at Laurel Valley, PA*
Result: USA 21, GBI 11
Captains: Arnold Palmer (USA),
  Bernard Hunt (GBI)
First Day: **Foursomes – Morning**
Nicklaus & Weiskopf beat Barnes & Gallacher
  5 and 4
Littler & Irwin beat Wood & Bembridge 4 and 3
Geiberger & Miller beat Jacklin & Oosterhuis 3 and 1
Trevino & Snead beat Horton & O'Leary 2 and 1
Fourball – Afternoon
Casper & Floyd lost to Jacklin & Oosterhuis 2 and 1
Weiskopf & Graham beat Darcy & Christy O'Connor jr
  3 and 2
Nicklaus & Murphy halved with Barnes & Gallacher
Trevino & Irwin beat Horton & O'Leary 2 and 1
Second Day: **Fourball – Morning**
Casper & Miller halved with Jacklin & Oosterhuis
Nicklaus & Snead beat Horton & Wood 4 and 2
Littler & Graham beat Barnes & Gallacher 5 and 3
Geiberger & Floyd halved with Darcy & Hunt

Foursomes – Afternoon
Trevino & Murphy lost to Jacklin & Barnes 3 and 2
Weiskopf & Miller beat O'Connor & O'Leary 5 and 3
Irwin & Casper beat Oosterhuis & Bembridge 3 and 2
Geiberger & Graham beat Darcy & Hunt 3 and 2
Third Day: **Singles – Morning**
Bob Murphy beat Tony Jacklin 2 and 1
Johnny Miller lost to Peter Oosterhuis 2 holes
Lee Trevino halved with Bernard Gallacher
Hale Irwin halved with Tommy Horton
Gene Littler beat Brian Huggett 4 and 2
Billy Casper beat Eamonn Darcy 3 and 2
Tom Weiskopf beat Guy Hunt 5 and 3
Jack Nicklaus lost to Brian Barnes 4 and 2
Singles – Afternoon
Ray Floyd beat Jacklin 1 hole
JC Snead lost to Oosterhuis 3 and 2
Al Geiberger halved with Gallacher
Lou Graham lost to Horton 2 and 1
Irwin beat John O'Leary 2 and 1
Murphy beat Maurice Bembridge 2 and 1
Trevino lost to Norman Wood 2 and 1
Nicklaus lost to Barnes 2 and 1

1977 *at Royal Lytham & St Anne's*
Result: USA 12½, GBI 7½
Captains: Brian Huggett (GBI),
  Dow Finsterwald (USA)
First Day: **Foursomes**
Gallacher & Barnes lost to Wadkins & Irwin 3 and 1
Coles & Dawson lost to Stockton & McGee 1 hole
Faldo & Oosterhuis beat Floyd & Graham 2 and 1
Darcy & Jacklin halved with Sneed & January
Horton & James lost to Nicklaus & Watson 5 and 4
Second Day: **Fourball**
Barnes & Horton lost to Watson & Green 5 and 4
Coles & Dawson lost to Sneed & Wadkins 5 and 3
Faldo & Oosterhuis beat Nicklaus & Floyd 3 and 1
Darcy & Jacklin lost to Hill & Stockton 5 and 3
James & Brown lost to Irwin & Graham 1 hole
Third Day: **Singles**
Howard Clark lost to Lanny Wadkins 4 and 3
Neil Coles lost to Lou Graham 5 and 3
Peter Dawson beat Don January 5 and 4
Brian Barnes beat Hale Irwin 1 hole
Tommy Horton lost to Dave Hill 5 and 4
Bernard Gallacher beat Jack Nicklaus 1 hole
Eamonn Darcy lost to Hubert Green 1 hole
Mark James lost to Ray Floyd 2 and 1
Nick Faldo beat Tom Watson 1 hole
Peter Oosterhuis beat Jerry McGee 2 holes

From 1979 GBI became a European team

1979 *at Greenbrier, WV*
Result: USA 17, Europe 11
Captains: Billy Casper (USA),
John Jacobs (Eur)
First Day: **Fourball – Morning**
Wadkins & Nelson beat Garrido & Ballesteros 2 and 1
Trevino & Zoeller beat Brown & James 3 and 2
Bean & Elder beat Oosterhuis & Faldo 2 and 1
Irwin & Mahaffey lost to Gallacher & Barnes 2 and 1

1979 *continued*

Foursomes – Afternoon
Irwin & Kite beat Brown & Smyth 7 and 6
Zoeller & Green lost to Garrido & Ballesteros 3 and 2
Trevino & Morgan halved with Lyle & Jacklin
Wadkins & Nelson beat Gallacher & Barnes 4 and 3

Second Day: Foursomes – Morning
Elder & Mahaffey lost to Lyle & Jacklin 5 and 4
Bean & Kite lost to Oosterhuis & Faldo 6 and 5
Zoeller & Hayes halved with Gallacher & Barnes
Wadkins & Nelson beat Garrido & Ballesteros 3 and 2

Fourball – Afternoon
Wadkins & Nelson beat Garrido & Ballesteros 5 and 4
Irwin & Kite beat Lyle & Jacklin 1 hole
Trevino & Zoeller lost to Gallacher & Barnes 3 and 2
Elder & Hayes lost to Oosterhuis & Faldo 1 hole

Third Day: Singles
Lanny Wadkins lost to Bernard Gallacher 3 and 2
Larry Nelson beat Seve Ballesteros 3 and 2
Tom Kite beat Tony Jacklin 1 hole
Mark Hayes beat Antonio Garrido 1 hole
Andy Bean beat Michael King 4 and 3
John Mahaffey beat Brian Barnes 1 hole
Lee Elder lost to Nick Faldo 3 and 2
Hale Irwin beat Des Smyth 5 and 3
Hubert Green beat Peter Oosterhuis 2 holes
Fuzzy Zoeller lost to Ken Brown 1 hole
Lee Trevino beat Sandy Lyle 2 and 1
Gil Morgan, Mark James: injury; match a half

1981 *at Walton Heath*

Result: USA 18½, Europe 9½
Captains: John Jacobs (Eur), Dave Marr (USA)

First Day: Foursomes – Morning
Langer & Pinero lost to Trevino & Nelson 1 hole
Lyle & James beat Rogers & Lietzke 2 and 1
Gallacher & Smyth beat Irwin & Floyd 3 and 2
Oosterhuis & Faldo lost to Watson & Nicklaus 4 and 3

Fourball – Afternoon
Torrance & Clark halved with Kite & Miller
Lyle & James beat Crenshaw & Pate 3 and 2
Smyth & Canizares beat Rogers & Lietzke 6 and 5
Gallacher & Darcy lost to Irwin & Floyd 2 and 1

Second Day: Fourball – Morning
Faldo & Torrance lost to Trevino & Pate 7 and 5
Lyle & James lost to Nelson & Kite 1 hole
Langer & Pinero beat Irwin & Floyd 2 and 1
Smyth & Canizares lost to Watson & Nicklaus 3 and 2

Foursomes – Afternoon
Oosterhuis & Torrance lost to Trevino & Pate 2 and 1
Langer & Pinero lost to Watson & Nicklaus 3 and 2
Lyle & James lost to Rogers & Floyd 3 and 2
Gallacher & Smyth lost to Nelson & Kite 3 and 2

Third Day: Singles
Sam Torrance lost to Lee Trevino 5 and 3
Sandy Lyle lost to Tom Kite 3 and 2
Bernard Gallacher halved with Bill Rogers
Mark James lost to Larry Nelson 2 holes
Des Smyth lost to Ben Crenshaw 6 and 4
Bernhard Langer halved with Bruce Lietzke
Manuel Pinero beat Jerry Pate 4 and 2
José Maria Canizares lost to Hale Irwin 1 hole
Nick Faldo beat Johnny Miller 2 and 1
Howard Clark beat Tom Watson 4 and 3
Peter Oosterhuis lost to Ray Floyd 2 holes
Eamonn Darcy lost to Jack Nicklaus 5 and 3

1983 *at PGA National, FL*

Result: USA 14½, Europe 13½
*Captains: Jack Nicklaus (USA),
    Tony Jacklin (Eur)*

First Day: Foursomes – Morning
Watson & Crenshaw beat Gallacher & Lyle 5 and 4
Wadkins & Stadler lost to Faldo & Langer 4 and 2
Floyd & Gilder lost to Canizares & Torrance 4 and 3
Kite & Peete beat Ballesteros & Way 2 and 1

Fourball – Afternoon
Morgan & Zoeller lost to Waites & Brown 2 and 1
Watson & Haas beat Faldo & Langer 2 and 1
Floyd & Strange lost to Ballesteros & Way 1 hole
Crenshaw & Peete halved with Torrance & Woosnam

Second Day: Foursomes – Morning
Floyd & Kite lost to Faldo & Langer 3 and 2
Wadkins & Morgan beat Canizares & Torrance 7 and 5
Gilder & Watson lost to Ballesteros & Way 2 and 1
Haas & Strange beat Waites & Brown 3 and 2

Fourball – Afternoon
Wadkins & Stadler beat Waites & Brown 1 hole
Crenshaw & Peete lost to Faldo & Langer 2 and 1
Haas & Morgan halved with Ballesteros & Way
Gilder & Watson beat Torrance & Woosnam 5 and 4

Third Day: Singles
Fuzzy Zoeller halved with Seve Ballesteros
Jay Haas lost to Nick Faldo 2 and 1
Gil Morgan lost to Bernhard Langer 2 holes
Bob Gilder beat Gordon J Brand 2 holes
Ben Crenshaw beat Sandy Lyle 3 and 1
Calvin Peete beat Brian Waites 1 hole
Curtis Strange lost to Paul Way 2 and 1
Tom Kite halved with Sam Torrance
Craig Stadler beat Ian Woosnam 3 and 2
Lanny Wadkins halved with José Maria Canizares
Ray Floyd lost to Ken Brown 4 and 3
Tom Watson beat Bernard Gallacher 2 and 1

1985 *at The Belfry*

Result: Europe 16½, USA 11½
Captains: Tony Jacklin (Eur), Lee Trevino (USA)

First Day: Foursomes – Morning
Ballesteros & Pinero beat Strange & O'Meara 2 and 1
Faldo & Langer lost to Kite & Peete 3 and 2
Brown & Lyle lost to Floyd & Wadkins 4 and 3
Clark & Torrance lost to Stadler & Sutton 3 and 2

Fourball – Afternoon
Way & Woosnam beat Green & Zoeller 1 hole
Ballesteros & Pinero beat Jacobsen & North 2 and 1
Canizares & Langer halved with Stadler & Sutton
Clark & Torrance lost to Floyd & Wadkins 1 hole

Second Day: Fourball – Morning
Clark & Torrance beat Kite & North 2 and 1
Way & Woosnam beat Green & Zoeller 4 and 3
Ballesteros & Pinero lost to O'Meara & Wadkins 3 and 2
Langer & Lyle halved with Stadler & Strange

Foursomes – Afternoon
Canizares & Rivero beat Kite & Peete 7 and 5
Ballesteros & Pinero beat Stadler & Sutton 5 and 4
Way & Woosnam lost to Jacobsen & Strange 4 and 3
Brown & Langer beat Floyd & Wadkins 3 and 2

Third Day: Singles
Manuel Pinero beat Lanny Wadkins 3 and 1
Ian Woosnam lost to Craig Stadler 2 and 1
Paul Way beat Ray Floyd 2 holes
Seve Ballesteros halved with Tom Kite
Sandy Lyle beat Peter Jacobsen 3 and 2

Bernhard Langer beat Hal Sutton 5 and 4
Sam Torrance beat Andy North 1 hole
Howard Clark beat Mark O'Meara 1 hole
Nick Faldo lost to Hubert Green 3 and 1
José Rivero lost to Calvin Peete 1 hole
José Maria Canizares beat Fuzzy Zoeller 2 holes
Ken Brown lost to Curtis Strange 4 and 2

1987 at Muirfield Village, OH
Result: Europe 15, USA 13
*Captains: Jack Nicklaus (USA),
Tony Jacklin (Eur)*
First Day: Foursomes – Morning
Kite & Strange beat Clark & Torrance 4 and 2
Pohl & Sutton beat Brown & Langer 2 and 1
Mize & Wadkins lost to Faldo & Woosnam 2 holes
Nelson & Stewart lost to Ballesteros & Olazábal 1 hole
Fourball – Afternoon
Crenshaw & Simpson lost to Brand & Rivero 3 and 2
Bean & Calcavecchia lost to Langer & Lyle 1 hole
Pohl & Sutton lost to Faldo & Woosnam 2 and 1
Kite & Strange lost to Ballesteros & Olazábal 2 and 1
Second Day: Foursomes – Morning
Kite & Strange beat Brand & Rivero 3 and 1
Mize & Sutton halved with Faldo & Woosnam
Nelson & Wadkins lost to Langer & Lyle 2 and 1
Crenshaw & Stewart lost to Ballesteros & Olazábal
1 hole
Fourball – Afternoon
Kite & Strange lost to Faldo & Woosnam 5 and 4
Bean & Stewart beat Brand & Darcy 3 and 2
Mize & Sutton beat Ballesteros & Olazábal 2 and 1
Nelson & Wadkins lost to Langer & Lyle 1 hole
Third Day: Singles
Andy Bean beat Ian Woosnam 1 hole
Dan Pohl lost to Howard Clark 1 hole
Larry Mize halved with Sam Torrance
Mark Calcavecchia beat Nick Faldo 1 hole
Payne Stewart beat José Maria Olazábal 2 holes
Scott Simpson beat José Rivero 2 and 1
Tom Kite beat Sandy Lyle 3 and 2
Ben Crenshaw lost to Eamonn Darcy 1 hole
Larry Nelson halved with Bernhard Langer
Curtis Strange lost to Seve Ballesteros 2 and 1
Lanny Wadkins beat Ken Brown 3 and 2
Hal Sutton halved with Gordon Brand jr

1989 at The Belfry
Result: Europe 14, USA 14
Captains: Tony Jacklin (Eur), Ray Floyd (USA)
First Day: Foursomes – Morning
Faldo & Woosnam halved with Kite & Strange
Clark & James lost to Stewart & Wadkins 1 hole
Ballesteros & Olazábal halved with Beck & Watson
Langer & Rafferty lost to Calcavecchia & Green
2 and 1
Fourball – Afternoon
Brand & Torrance beat Azinger & Strange 1 hole
Clark & James beat Couples & Wadkins 3 and 2
Faldo & Woosnam beat Calcavecchia & McCumber
1 hole
Ballesteros & Olazábal beat O'Meara & Watson 6 and 5
Second Day: Foursomes – Morning
Faldo & Woosnam beat Stewart & Wadkins 3 and 2
Brand & Torrance lost to Azinger & Beck 4 and 3

O'Connor & Rafferty lost to Calcavecchia & Green
3 and 2
Ballesteros & Olazábal beat Kite & Strange 1 hole
Fourball – Afternoon
Faldo & Woosnam lost to Azinger & Beck 2 and 1
Canizares & Langer lost to Kite & McCumber 2 and 1
Clark & James beat Stewart & Strange 1 hole
Ballesteros & Olazábal beat Calcavecchia & Green
4 and 2
Third Day: Singles
Seve Ballesteros lost to Paul Azinger 1 hole
Bernhard Langer lost to Chip Beck 3 and 1
José Maria Olazábal beat Payne Stewart 1 hole
Ronan Rafferty beat Mark Calvecchia 1 hole
Howard Clark lost to Tom Kite 8 and 7
Mark James beat Mark O'Meara 3 and 2
Christy O'Connor jr beat Fred Couples 1 hole
José Maria Canizares beat Ken Green 1 hole
Gordon Brand jr lost to Mark McCumber 1 hole
Sam Torrance lost to Tom Watson 3 and 1
Nick Faldo lost to Lanny Wadkins 1 hole
Ian Woosnam lost to Curtis Strange 1 hole

1991 at Kiawah Island, SC
Result: USA 14½, Europe 13½
*Captains: Dave Stockton (USA),
Bernard Gallacher (Eur)*
First Day: Morning – Foursomes
Ballesteros & Olazábal beat Azinger & Beck 2 and 1
Langer & James lost to Floyd & Couples 2 and 1
Gilford & Montgomerie lost to Wadkins & Irwin
4 and 2
Faldo & Woosnam lost to Stewart & Calcavecchia
1 hole
Afternoon – Fourball
Torrance & Feherty halved with Wadkins & O'Meara
Ballesteros & Olazábal beat Azinger & Beck 2 and 1
Richardson & James beat Pavin & Calcavecchia
5 and 4
Faldo & Woosnam lost to Floyd & Couples 5 and 3
Second Day: Morning – Foursomes
Torrance & Feherty lost to Irwin & Wadkins 4 and 2
James & Richardson lost to Calcavecchia & Stewart
1 hole
Faldo & Gilford lost to Azinger & O'Meara 7 and 6
Ballesteros & Olazábal beat Couples & Floyd
3 and 2
Afternoon – Fourball
Woosnam & Broadhurst beat Azinger & Irwin 2 and 1
Langer & Montgomerie beat Pate & Pavin 2 and 1
James & Richardson beat Wadkins & Levi 3 and 1
Ballesteros & Olazábal halved with Couples & Stewart
Third Day – Singles
Nick Faldo beat Ray Floyd 2 holes
David Feherty beat Payne Stewart 2 and 1
Colin Montgomerie halved with Mark Calcavecchia
José Maria Olazábal lost to Paul Azinger 2 holes
Steven Richardson lost to Corey Pavin 2 and 1
Seve Ballesteros beat Wayne Levi 3 and 2
Ian Woosnam lost to Chip Beck 3 and 1
Paul Broadhurst bat Mark O'Meara 3 and 1
Sam Torrance lost to Fred Couples 3 and 2
Mark James lost to Lanny Wadkins 3 and 2
Bernhard Langer halved with Hale Irwin
David Gilford (withdrawn) halved with Steve Pate
(withdrawn – injured)

1993 *at The Belfry*
Result: Europe 13, USA 15
Captains: Bernard Gallacher (Eur)
*   Tom Watson (USA)*

First Day: Morning – Foursomes
Torrance & James lost to Wadkins & Pavin 4 and 3
Woosnam & Langer beat Azinger & Stewart 7 and 5
Ballesteros & Olazábal lost to Kite & Love 2 and 1
Faldo & Montgomerie beat Floyd & Couples 4 and 3

Afternoon – Fourball
Woosnam & Baker beat Gallagher & Janzen 1 hole
Lane & Langer lost to Wadkins & Pavin 4 and 2
Faldo & Montgomerie halved with Azinger & Couples
Ballesteros & Olazábal beat Kite & Love 4 and 3

Second Day: Morning – Foursomes
Faldo & Montgomerie beat Wadkins & Pavin 3 and 2
Langer & Woosnam beat Couples & Azinger 2 and 1
Baker & Lane lost to Floyd & Stewart 3 and 2
Ballesteros & Olazábal beat Kite & Love 2 and 1

Afternoon – Fourball
Faldo & Montgomerie lost to Beck & Cook 2 holes
James & Rocca lost to Pavin & Gallagher 5 and 4
Woosnam & Baker beat Couples & Azinger 6 and 5
Olazábal & Haeggman lost to Floyd & Stewart 2 and 1

Third Day – Singles
Ian Woosnam halved with Fred Couples
Barry Lane lost to Chip Beck 1 hole
Colin Montgomerie beat Lee Janzen 1 hole
Peter Baker beat Corey Pavin 2 holes
Joakim Haeggman beat J Cook 1 hole
Sam Torrance (withdrawn at start of day) halved with
   Lanny Wadkins (withdrawn at start of day)
Mark James lost to Payne Stewart 3 and 2
Constantino Rocca lost to Davis Love III 1 hole
Seve Ballesteros lost to Jim Gallagher jr 3 and 2
José Maria Olazábal lost to Ray Floyd 2 holes
Bernhard Langer lost to Tom Kite 5 and 3
Nick Faldo halved with Paul Azinger

1995 *at Oak Hill, Rochester, NY*
Result: USA 13½, Europe 14½
Captains: Lanny Wadkins (USA),
*   Bernard Gallacher (Eur)*

First Day: Morning – Foursomes
Faldo & Montgomerie lost to Pavin & Lehman
   1 hole
Torrance & Rocca beat Haas & Couples 3 and 2
Clark & James lost to Love & Maggert 4 and 3
Langer & Johansson beat Crenshaw & Strange 1 hole

Afternoon – Fourball
Gilford & Ballesteros beat Faxon & Jacobsen 4 and 3
Torrance & Rocca lost to Maggert & Roberts 6 and 5
Faldo & Montgomerie lost to Couples & Love 3 and 2
Langer & Johansson lost to Pavin & Mickelson 6 and 4

Second Day: Morning – Foursomes
Faldo & Montgomerie beat Haas & Strange 4 and 2
Torrance & Rocca beat Love & Maggert 6 and 5
Woosnam & Walton lost to Roberts & Jacobsen 1 hole
Langer & Gilford beat Pavin & Lehman 4 and 3

Afternoon – Fourball
Torrance & Montgomerie lost to Faxon & Couples
   4 and 2
Woosnam & Rocca beat Love & Crenshaw 3 and 2
Ballesteros & Gilford lost to Haas & Mickelson 3 and 2
Faldo & Langer lost to Pavin & Roberts 1 hole

Third Day – Singles
Seve Ballesteros lost to Tom Lehman 4 and 3
Howard Clark beat Peter Jacobsen 1 hole
Mark James beat Jeff Maggert 4 and 3
Ian Woosnam halved with Fred Couples
Costantino Rocca lost to Davis Love III 3 and 2
David Gilford beat Brad Faxon 1 hole
Colin Montgomerie beat Ben Crenshaw 3 and 1
Nick Faldo beat Curtis Strange 1 hole
Sam Torrance beat Loren Roberts 2 and 1
Bernhard Langer lost to Corey Pavin 3 and 2
Philip Walton beat Jay Haas 1 hole
Per-Ulrik Johansson lost to Phil Mickelson 2 and 1

1997 Ryder Cup *at Valderrama, Spain*
Result: Europe 14½, USA 13½,
Captains: Seve Ballesteros (Eur),
*   Tom Kite (USA)*

First Day: Morning – Fourball
Olazábal & Rocca beat Love & Mickelson 1 hole
Faldo & Westwood lost to Couples & Faxon 1 hole
Parnevik & Johansson beat Lehman & Furyk 1 hole
Montgomerie & Langer lost to Woods & O'Meara 3 and 2

Afternoon – Foursomes
Rocca & Olazábal lost to Hoch & Janzen 1 hole
Langer & Montgomerie beat O'Meara & Woods 5 and 3
Faldo & Westwood beat Leonard & Maggert 3 and 2
Parnevik & Garrido halved with Lehman & Mickelson

Second Day: Morning – Fourball
Montgomerie & Clarke beat Couples & Love 1 hole
Woosnam & Bjørn beat Leonard & Faxon 2 and 1
Faldo & Westwood beat Woods & O'Meara 2 and 1
Olazábal & Garrido halved with Mickelson & Lehman

Afternoon – Foursomes
Montgomerie & Langer beat Janzen & Furyk 1 hole
Faldo & Westwood lost to Hoch & Maggert 2 and 1
Parnevik & Garrido halved with Leonard & Woods
Olazábal & Rocca beat Love & Couples 5 and 4

Third Day – Singles
Ian Woosnam lost to Fred Couples 8 and 7
Per-Ulrik Johansson beat Davis Love III 3 and 2
Costantino Rocca beat Tiger Woods 4 and 2
Thomas Bjørn halved with Justin Leonard
Darren Clarke lost to Phil Mickelson 2 and 1
Jesper Parnevik lost to Mark O'Meara 5 and 4
José Maria Olazábal lost to Lee Janzen 1 hole
Bernhard Langer beat Brad Faxon 2 and 1
Lee Westwood lost to Jeff Maggert 3 and 2
Colin Montgomerie halved with Scott Hoch
Nick Faldo lost to Jim Furyk 3 and 2
Ignacio Garrido lost to Tom Lehman 7 and 6

1999 Ryder Cup *at Brookline, MA*
Result: USA 14½, Europe 13½
Captains: Ben Crenshaw (USA),
*   Mark James (Eur)*

First Day: Morning – Foursomes
Montgomerie & Lawrie beat Duval & Mickelson 3 and 2
Parnevik & García beat Lehman & Woods 2 and 1
Jiménez & Harrington halved halved with Love &
   Stewart
Clarke & Westwood lost to Sutton & Maggert 3 and 2

Afternoon – Fourball
Montgomerie & Lawrie halved with Love & Leonard
Parnevik & García beat Mickelson & Furyk 1 hole
Jiménez & Olazábal beat Sutton & Maggert 2 and 1
Clarke & Westwood beat Duval & Woods 1 hole

Second Day: Morning – Foursomes
Montgomerie & Lawrie lost to Sutton & Maggert 1 hole
Clarke & Westwood beat Furyk & O'Meara 3 and 2
Jiménez & Harrington lost to Pate & Woods 1 hole
Parnevik & García beat Stewart & Leonard 3 and 2

Afternoon – Fourball
Clarke & Westwood lost to Mickelson & Lehman 2 and 1
Parnevik & García halved with Love & Duval
Jiménez & Olazábal halved with Leonard & Sutton
Montgomerie & Lawrie beat Pate & Woods 2 and 1

Third Day – Singles
Lee Westwood lost to Tom Lehman 3 and 2
Darren Clarke lost to Hal Sutton 4 and 2
Jarmo Sandelin lost to Phil Mickelson 4 and 3
Jean Van de Velde lost to Davis Love III 6 and 5
Andrew Coltart lost to Tiger Woods 3 and 2
Jesper Parnevik lost to David Duval 5 and 4
Padraig Harrington beat Mark O'Meara 1 hole
Miguel Angel Jiménez lost to Steve Pate 2 and 1
José Maria Olazábal halved with Justin Leonard
Colin Montgomerie beat Payne Stewart 1 hole
Sergio García lost to Jim Furyk 4 and 3
Paul Lawrie beat Jeff Maggert 4 and 3

As the match scheduled for 2001 was postponed the event will now continue in even-numbered years

INDIVIDUAL RECORDS

Matches were contested as Great Britain v USA from 1927–71; as Great Britain & Ireland v USA from 1973–77; and as Europe v USA from 1979. Bold type indicates captain; non-playing in brackets.

Europe

Name	Year	Played	Won	Lost	Halved
Jimmy Adams	*1939-47-49-51-53	7	2	5	0
Percy Alliss	1929-33-35-37	6	3	2	1
Peter Alliss	1953-57-59-61-63-65-67-69	30	10	15	5
Laurie Ayton	1949	0	0	0	0
Peter Baker	1993	4	3	1	0
Severiano Ballesteros (Esp)	1979-83-85-87-89-91-93-95-(97)	37	20	12	5
Harry Bannerman	1971	5	2	2	1
Brian Barnes	1969-71-73-75-77-79	25	10	14	1
Maurice Bembridge	1969-71-73-75	16	5	8	3
Thomas Bjørn (Den)	1997-2002	6	3	2	1
Aubrey Boomer	1927-29	4	2	2	0
Ken Bousfield	1949-51-55-57-59-61	10	5	5	0
Hugh Boyle	1967	3	0	3	0
Harry Bradshaw	1953-55-57	5	2	2	1
Gordon J Brand	1983	1	0	1	0
Gordon Brand jr	1987-89	7	2	4	1
Paul Broadhurst	1991	2	2	0	0
Eric Brown	1953-55-57-59-(69)-(71)	8	4	4	0
Ken Brown	1977-79-83-85-87	13	4	9	0
Stewart Burns	1929	0	0	0	0
Dick Burton	1935-37-*39-49	5	2	3	0
Jack Busson	1935	2	0	2	0
Peter Butler	1965-69-71-73	14	3	9	2
José Maria Canizares (Esp)	1981-83-85-89	11	5	4	2
Alex Caygill	1969	1	0	0	1
Clive Clark	1973	1	0	1	0
Howard Clark	1977-81-85-87-89-95	15	7	7	1
Darren Clarke	1997-99-2002	12	4	6	2
Neil Coles	1961-63-65-67-69-71-73-77	40	12	21	7
Andrew Coltart	1999	1	0	1	0
Archie Compston	1927-29-31	6	1	4	1
Henry Cotton	1929-*39-*39-47-(53)	6	2	4	0
Bill Cox	1935-37	3	0	2	1
Allan Dailey	1933	0	0	0	0
Fred Daly	1947-49-51-53	8	3	4	1
Eamonn Darcy	1975-77-81-87	11	1	8	2
William Davies	1931-33	4	2	2	0
Peter Dawson	1977	3	1	2	0
Norman Drew	1959	1	0	0	1
George Duncan	1927-**29**-31	5	2	3	0
Syd Easterbrook	1931-33	3	2	1	0
Nick Faldo	1977-79-81-83-85-87-89-91-93-95-97	46	23	19	4
John Fallon	1955-(63)	1	1	0	0
Niclas Fasth (Swe)	2002	3	0	2	1
Max Faulkner	1947-49-51-53-57	8	1	7	0

* In 1939 a GB&I team was named but the match was not played because of the Second World War

Ryder Cup European Individual Records *continued*

Name	Year	Played	Won	Lost	Halved
David Feherty	1991	3	1	1	1
Pierre Fulke (Swe)	2002	2	0	1	1
George Gadd	1927	0	0	0	0
Bernard Gallacher	1969-71-73-75-77-79-81-83-(91)-(93)-(95)	31	13	13	5
Sergio García (Esp)	1999-2002	10	6	3	1
John Garner	1971-73	1	0	1	0
Antonio Garrido (Esp)	1979	5	1	4	0
Ignacio Garrido (Esp)	1997	4	0	1	3
David Gilford	1991-95	6	3	3	0
Eric Green	1947	0	0	0	0
Malcolm Gregson	1967	4	0	4	0
Joakim Haeggman (Swe)	1993	2	1	1	0
Tom Haliburton	1961-63	6	0	6	0
Jack Hargreaves	1951	0	0	0	0
Padraig Harrington	1999-2002	7	3	3	1
Arthur Havers	1927-31-33	6	3	3	0
Jimmy Hitchcock	1965	3	0	3	0
Bert Hodson	1931	1	0	1	0
Reg Horne	1947	0	0	0	0
Tommy Horton	1975-77	8	1	6	1
Brian Huggett	1963-67-69-71-73-75-(77)	25	9	10	6
Bernard Hunt	1953-57-59-61-63-65-67-69-(73)-(75)	28	6	16	6
Geoffrey Hunt	1963	3	0	3	0
Guy Hunt	1975	3	0	2	1
Tony Jacklin	1967-69-71-73-75-77-79-(83)-(85)-(87)-(89)	35	13	14	8
John Jacobs	1955-(79)-(81)	2	2	0	0
Mark James	1977-79-81-89-91-93-95-(99)	24	8	15	1
Edward Jarman	1935	1	0	1	0
Miguel Angel Jiménez (Esp)	1999	5	1	2	2
Per-Ulrik Johansson (Swe)	1995-97	5	3	2	0
Herbert Jolly	1927	2	0	2	0
Michael King	1979	1	0	1	0
Sam King	1937-*39-47-49	5	1	3	1
Arthur Lacey	1933-37-(51)	3	0	3	0
Barry Lane	1993	3	0	3	0
Bernhard Langer (Ger)	1981-83-85-87-89-91-93-95-97-2002	42	21	15	6
Paul Lawrie	1999	5	3	1	1
Arthur Lees	1947-49-51-55	8	4	4	0
Sandy Lyle	1979-81-83-85-87	18	7	9	2
Paul McGinley (Irl)	2002	3	0	1	2
Jimmy Martin	1965	1	0	1	0
Peter Mills	1957-59	1	1	0	0
Abe Mitchell	1929-31-33	6	4	2	0
Ralph Moffitt	1961	1	0	1	0
Colin Montgomerie	1991-93-95-97-99-2002	28	16	7	5
Christy O'Connor jr	1975-89	4	1	3	0
Christy O'Connor sr	1955-57-59-61-63-65-67-69-71-73	36	11	21	4
José Maria Olazábal (Esp)	1987-89-91-93-97-99	28	15	8	5
John O'Leary	1975	4	0	4	0
Peter Oosterhuis	1971-73-75-77-79-81	28	14	11	3
Alf Padgham	1933-35-37-*39	6	0	6	0
John Panton	1951-53-61	5	0	5	0
Jesper Parnevik (Swe)	1997-99-2002	11	4	3	4
Alf Perry	1933-35-37	4	0	3	1
Manuel Pinero (Esp)	1981-85	9	6	3	0
Lionel Platts	1965	5	1	2	2
Eddie Polland	1973	2	0	2	0
Phillip Price	2002	2	1	1	0
Ronan Rafferty	1989	3	1	2	0
Ted Ray	1927	2	0	2	0
Dai Rees	1937-*39-47-49-51-53-55-57-59-61-(67)	18	7	10	1
Steven Richardson	1991	4	2	2	0
José Rivero (Esp)	1985-87	5	2	3	0
Fred Robson	1927-29-31	6	2	4	0
Costantino Rocca (Ita)	1993-95-97	11	6	5	0
Jarmo Sandelin (Swe)	1999	1	0	1	0
Syd Scott	1955	2	0	2	0
Des Smyth	1979-81	7	2	5	0
Dave Thomas	1959-63-65-67	18	3	10	5
Sam Torrance	1981-83-85-87-89-91-93-95-**2002**	27	7	15	5
Peter Townsend	1969-71	11	3	8	0

* In 1939 a GB&I team was named but the match was not played because of the Second World War

Name	Year	Played	Won	Lost	Halved
Jean Van de Velde (Fra)	1999	1	0	1	0
Brian Waites	1983	4	1	3	0
Philip Walton	1995	2	1	1	0
Charlie Ward	1947-49-51	6	1	5	0
Paul Way	1983-85	9	6	2	1
Harry Weetman	1951-53-55-57-59-61-63-(65)	15	2	11	2
Lee Westwood	1997-99-2002	10	5	5	0
Charles Whitcombe	1927-29-31-33-35-37-*39-(49)	9	3	2	4
Ernest Whitcombe	1929-31-35	6	1	4	1
Reg Whitcombe	1935-*39	1	0	1	0
George Will	1963-65-67	15	2	11	2
Norman Wood	1975	3	1	2	0
Ian Woosnam	1983-85-87-89-91-93-95-97	31	14	12	5

United States of America

Name	Year	Played	Won	Lost	Halved
Tommy Aaron	1969-73	6	1	4	1
Skip Alexander	1949-51	2	1	1	0
Paul Azinger	1989-91-93-2002	16	5	8	3
Jerry Barber	1955-61	5	1	4	0
Miller Barber	1969-71	7	1	4	2
Herman Barron	1947	1	1	0	0
Andy Bean	1979-87	6	4	2	0
Frank Beard	1969-71	8	2	3	3
Chip Beck	1989-91-93	9	6	2	1
Homero Blancas	1973	4	2	1	1
Tommy Bolt	1955-57	4	3	1	0
Julius Boros	1959-63-65-67	16	9	3	4
Gay Brewer	1967-73	9	5	3	1
Billy Burke	1931-33	3	3	0	0
Jack Burke	1951-53-55-57-59-(73)	8	7	1	0
Walter Burkemo	1953	1	0	1	0
Mark Calcavecchia	1987-89-91-2002	14	6	7	1
Billy Casper	1961-63-65-67-69-71-73-75-(79)	37	20	10	7
Stewart Cink	2002	3	1	2	0
Bill Collins	1961	3	1	2	0
Charles Coody	1971	3	0	2	1
John Cook	1993	2	1	1	0
Fred Couples	1989-91-93-95-97	20	7	9	4
Wilfred Cox	1931	2	2	0	0
Ben Crenshaw	1981-83-87-95-(99)	12	3	8	1
Jimmy Demaret	*1941-47-49-51	6	6	0	0
Gardner Dickinson	1967-71	10	9	1	0
Leo Diegel	1927-29-31-33	6	3	3	0
Dale Douglass	1969	2	0	2	0
Dave Douglas	1953	2	1	0	1
Ed Dudley	1929-33-37	4	3	1	0
Olin Dutra	1933-35	4	1	3	0
David Duval	1999-2002	7	2	3	2
Lee Elder	1979	4	1	3	0
Al Espinosa	1927-29-31	4	2	1	1
Johnny Farrell	1927-29-31	6	3	2	1
Brad Faxon	1995-97	6	2	4	0
Dow Finsterwald	1957-59-61-63-(77)	13	9	3	1
Ray Floyd	1969-75-77-81-83-85-(89)-91-93	31	12	16	3
Doug Ford	1955-57-59-61	9	4	4	1
Ed Furgol	1957	1	0	1	0
Marty Furgol	1955	1	0	1	0
Jim Furyk	1997-99-2002	11	3	6	2
Jim Gallagher jr	1993	3	2	1	0
Al Geiberger	1967-75	9	5	1	3
Vic Ghezzi	*1939-*41	0	0	0	0
Bob Gilder	1983	4	2	2	0
Bob Goalby	1963	5	3	1	1
Johnny Golden	1927-29	3	3	0	0
Lou Graham	1973-75-77	9	5	3	1
Hubert Green	1977-79-85	7	4	3	0
Ken Green	1989	4	2	2	0
Ralph Guldahl	1937-*39	2	2	0	0
Fred Haas jr	1953	1	0	1	0

* US teams were selected in 1939 and 1941, but did not play because of the Second World War

Ryder Cup American Individual Records *continued*

Name	Year	Played	Won	Lost	Halved
Jay Haas	1983-95	8	3	4	1
Walter Hagen	**1927-29-31-33-35-(37)**	9	7	1	1
Bob Hamilton	1949	2	0	2	0
Chick Harbert	1949-**55**	2	2	0	0
Chandler Harper	1955	1	0	1	0
EJ (Dutch) Harrison	1947-49-51	3	2	1	0
Fred Hawkins	1957	2	1	1	0
Mark Hayes	1979	3	1	2	0
Clayton Heafner	1949-51	4	3	0	1
Jay Hebert	1959-61-**(71)**	4	2	1	1
Lionel Hebert	1957	1	0	1	0
Dave Hill	1969-73-77	9	6	3	0
Jimmy Hines	*1939	0	0	0	0
Scott Hoch	1997-2002	7	2	3	2
Ben Hogan	*1941-**47**-**(49)**-51-**(67)**	3	3	0	0
Hale Irwin	1975-77-79-81-91	20	13	5	2
Tommy Jacobs	1965	4	3	1	0
Peter Jacobsen	1985-95	6	2	4	0
Don January	1965-77	7	2	3	2
Lee Janzen	1993-97	5	2	3	0
Herman Keiser	1947	1	0	1	0
Tom Kite	1979-81-83-85-87-89-93-**(97)**	28	15	9	4
Ted Kroll	1953-55-57	4	3	1	0
Ky Laffoon	1935	1	0	1	0
Tom Lehman	1995-97-99	10	5	3	2
Tony Lema	1963-65	11	8	1	2
Justin Leonard	1997-99	8	0	3	5
Wayne Levi	1991	2	0	2	0
Bruce Lietzke	1981	3	0	2	1
Gene Littler	1961-63-65-67-69-71-75	27	14	5	8
Davis Love III	1993-95-97-99-2002	21	8	9	4
Jeff Maggert	1995-97-99	11	6	5	0
John Mahaffey	1979	3	1	2	0
Mark McCumber	1989	3	2	1	0
Jerry McGee	1977	2	1	1	0
Harold McSpaden	*1939-*41	0	0	0	0
Tony Manero	1937	2	1	1	0
Lloyd Mangrum	*1941-47-49-51-**53**	8	6	2	0
Dave Marr	1965-**(81)**	6	4	2	0
Billy Maxwell	1963	4	4	0	0
Dick Mayer	1957	2	1	0	1
Bill Mehlhorn	1927	2	1	1	0
Dick Metz	*1939	0	0	0	0
Phil Mickelson	1995-97-99-2002	16	8	5	3
Cary Middlecoff	1953-55-59	6	2	3	1
Johnny Miller	1975-81	6	2	2	2
Larry Mize	1987	4	1	1	2
Gil Morgan	1979-83	6	1	2	3
Bob Murphy	1975	4	2	1	1
Byron Nelson	1937-*39-*41-47-**(65)**	4	3	1	0
Larry Nelson	1979-81-87	13	9	3	1
Bobby Nichols	1967	5	4	0	1
Jack Nicklaus	1969-71-73-75-77-81-**(83)**-**(87)**	28	17	8	3
Andy North	1985	3	0	3	0
Ed Oliver	1947-51-53	5	3	2	0
Mark O'Meara	1985-89-91-97-99	14	4	9	1
Arnold Palmer	1961-**63**-65-67-71-73-**(75)**	32	22	8	2
Johnny Palmer	1949	2	0	2	0
Sam Parks	1935	1	0	0	1
Jerry Pate	1981	4	2	2	0
Steve Pate	1991-99	4	2	2	0
Corey Pavin	1991-93-95	8	5	3	0
Calvin Peete	1983-85	7	4	2	1
Henry Picard	1935-37-*39	4	3	1	0
Dan Pohl	1987	3	1	2	0
Johnny Pott	1963-65-67	7	5	2	0
Dave Ragan	1963	4	2	1	1
Henry Ransom	1951	1	0	1	0
Johnny Revolta	1935-37	3	2	1	0
Loren Roberts	1995	4	3	1	0

* *US teams were selected in 1939 and 1941, but did not play because of the Second World War*

Name	Year	Played	Won	Lost	Halved
Chi Chi Rodriguez	1973	2	0	1	1
Bill Rogers	1981	4	1	2	1
Bob Rosburg	1959	2	2	0	0
Mason Rudolph	1971	3	1	1	1
Paul Runyan	1933-35-*39	4	2	2	0
Doug Sanders	1967	5	2	3	0
Gene Sarazen	1927-29-31-33-35-37-*41	12	7	2	3
Densmore Shute	1931-33-37	6	2	2	2
Dan Sikes	1969	3	2	1	0
Scott Simpson	1987	2	1	1	0
Horton Smith	1929-31-33-35-37-*39-*41	4	3	0	1
JC Snead	1971-73-75	11	9	2	0
Sam Snead	1937-*39-*41-47-49-**51**-53-55-**59**-**(69)**	13	10	2	1
Ed Sneed	1977	2	1	0	1
Mike Souchak	1959-61	6	5	1	0
Craig Stadler	1983-85	8	4	2	2
Payne Stewart	1987-89-91-93-99	19	7	10	2
Ken Still	1969	3	1	2	0
Dave Stockton	1971-77-**(91)**	5	3	1	1
Curtis Strange	1983-85-87-89-95-**2002**	20	6	12	2
Hal Sutton	1985-87-99-2002	16	7	5	4
David Toms	2002	5	3	1	1
Lee Trevino	1969-71-73-75-79-81-**(85)**	30	17	7	6
Jim Turnesa	1953	1	1	0	0
Joe Turnesa	1927-29	4	1	2	1
Ken Venturi	1965	4	1	3	0
Scott Verplank	2002	3	2	1	0
Lanny Wadkins	1977-79-83-85-87-89-91-93-**(95)**	33	20	11	2
Art Wall jr	1957-59-61	6	4	2	0
Al Watrous	1927-29	3	2	1	0
Tom Watson	1977-81-83-89-**(93)**	15	10	4	1
Tom Weiskopf	1973-75	10	7	2	1
Craig Wood	1931-33-35-*41	4	1	3	0
Tiger Woods	1997-99-2002	15	5	8	2
Lew Worsham	1947	2	2	0	0
Fuzzy Zoeller	1979-83-85	10	1	8	1

* US teams were selected in 1939 and 1941, but did not play because of the Second World War

The Seve Trophy (Instituted 2000)

2002 at Druids Glen, Co. Wicklow, Ireland

Captains: Seve Ballesteros (Europe); Colin Montgomerie (GB&I)

Continental Europe		GB&I	
First Day – **Greensomes**			
Bjørn & Karlsson (2 and 1)	1	Lawrie & Montgomerie	0
Jiménez & Olazábal	0	Woosnam & Webster (3 and 2)	1
Cejka & Grönberg	0	Harrington & McGinley (1 hole)	1
Jacquelin & Levet (2 and 1)	1	Clarke & Westwood	0
	2		2
Foursomes			
Fasth & Karlsson	0	Montgomerie & Oldcorn (2 and 1)	1
Jiménez & Olazábal (1 hole)	1	Casey & Webster	0
Jacquelin & Levet	0	Harrington & McGinley (1 hole)	1
Bjørn & Cejka	0	Clarke & Westwood (3 and 2)	1
	1		3

Match position: Continental Europe 3, GB&I 5

The Seve Trophy continued

Second Day – Fourball

Bjørn & Fasth	0	Casey & Lawrie (2 and 1)	1
Grönberg & Karlsson	0	Montgomerie & Woosnam (4 and 3)	1
Ballesteros & Olazábal (2 and 1)	1	Harrington & McGinley	0
Jacquelin & Jiménez	0	Clarke & Westwood (1 hole)	1
	1		**3**

Foursomes

Bjørn & Karlsson (halved)	½	Webster & Woosnam (halved)	½
Jacquelin & Levet (halved)	½	Lawrie & Oldcorn (halved)	½
Cejka & Fasth	0	Harrington & McGinley (1 hole)	1
Jiménez & Olazábal (1 hole)	1	Clarke & Montgomerie	0
	2		**2**

Match position: Continental Europe 6, GB&I 10

Third Day – Singles

Seve Ballesteros (Esp) (1 hole)	1	Colin Montgomerie (Sco)	0
Thomas Bjørn (Den)	0	Darren Clarke (NI) (4 and 3)	1
Miguel Angel Jiménez (Esp) (4 and 3)	1	Paul Casey (Eng)	0
Robert Karlsson (Swe) (1 hole)	1	Paul Lawrie (Sco)	0
Niclas Fasth (Swe) (halved)	½	Andrew Oldcorn (Sco) (halved)	½
Raphaèl Jacquelin (Fra)	0	Lee Westwood (Eng) (3 and 2)	1
José María Olazábal (Esp)	0	Padraig Harrington (Irl) (3 and 2)	1
Mathias Grönberg (Swe)	0	Paul McGinley (Irl) (4 and 3)	1
Thomas Levet (Fra) (2 and 1)	1	Steve Webster (Eng)	0
Alex Cejka (Ger) (5 and 4)	1	Ian Woosnam (Wal)	0
	5½		**4½**

Result: Continental Europe 11½; GB&I, 14½

2000 at Sunningdale, Berkshire, England

Captains: Colin Montgomerie (GB&I); Seve Ballesteros (Europe)

First Day – Foursomes
Montgomerie & Woosnam beat Jiménez & Olazábal 2 and 1
Clarke & Westwood beat Cejka & Langer 4 and 3
Harrington & Price beat Bjørn & Karlsson 1 hole
Lawrie & Orr lost to García & Van de Velde 3 and 2

Fourball
Howell & Westwood beat Ballesteros & Olazábal 2 and 1
Bickerton & Clarke lost to Bjørn & Jiménez 1 hole
Harrington & Woosnam lost to Cejka & Langer 2 and 1
Lawrie & Montgomerie lost to García & Sandelin 3 and 2

Second Day – Fourball
Montgomerie & Woosnam lost to Jiménez & Olazábal 6 and 5
Lawrie & Orr beat Karlsson & Sandelin 1 hole
Bickerton & Price lost to Bjørn & García 1 hole
Clarke & Westwood beat Cejka & Van de Velde 3 and 1

Greensomes
Lawrie & Orr halved with Jiménez & Olazábal
Howell & Montgomerie beat García & Van de Velde 2 and 1
Clarke & Westwood lost to Bjørn & Langer 4 and 3
Harrington & Price halved with Cejka & Karlsson

Third Day – **Singles**
Colin Montgomerie (Sco) lost to Seve Ballesteros (Esp) 2 and 1
Darren Clarke (NI) halved with Sergio García (Esp)
John Bickerton (Eng) lost to Jarmo Sandelin (Swe) 2 and 1
Lee Westwood (Eng) beat Thomas Bjørn (Den) 1 hole
Phillip Price (Wal) beat Alex Cejka (Ger) 2 and 1
Ian Woosnam (Wal) lost to Bernhard Langer (Ger) 4 and 3
David Howell (Eng) lost to Robert Karlsson (Swe) 2 and 1
Gary Orr (Sco) lost to José María Olazábal (Esp) 2 and 1
Paul Lawrie (Sco) beat Jean Van de Velde (Fra) 4 and 3
Padraig Harrington (Irl) beat Miguel Angel Jiménez (Esp) 1 hole

Result: GB&I, 12½; Continental Europe 13½

PGA Cup (Instituted 1973)

Great Britain and Ireland Club Professionals v United States Club Professionals

1973	USA	Pinehurst, NC	13–3				
1974	USA	Pinehurst, NC	11½–4½			*Played alternate years from 1984*	
1975	USA	Hillside, Southport, England	9½–6½	1986	USA	Knollwood, Lake Fore, IL	16–9
1976	USA	Moortown, Leeds, England	9½–6½	1988	USA	The Belfry, England	15½–10½
1977	Halved	Mission Hills, Palm Springs	8½–8½	1990	USA	Turtle Point, Kiawah Island, SC	19–7
1978	GB&I	St Mellion, Cornwall	10½–6½	1992	USA	K Club, Ireland	15–11
1979	GB&I	Castletown, Isle of Man	12½–4½	1994	USA	Palm Beach, Florida	15–11
1980	USA	Oak Tree, Edmond, OK	15–6	1996	Halved	Gleneagles, Scotland	13–13
1981	Halved	Turnberry Isle, Miami, FL	10½–10½	1998	USA	The Broadmoor, Colorado	
1982	USA	Holston Hills, Knoxville, TN	13–7			Springs, CO	11½–4½
1983	GB&I	Muirfield, Scotland	14½–6½	2000	USA	Celtic Manor, Newport, Wales	13½–12½
1984	GB&I	Turnberry, Scotland	12½–8½				

The match sheduled for 2002 was postponed and the event will now be played in 2003 and thereafter in odd-numbered years

Presidents Cup (Instituted 1994)

1994	USA	Lake Manassas, Virginia	20–12
1996	USA	Lake Manassas, Virginia	16½–15½
1998	International	Royal Melbourne, Australia	20½–11½
2000	USA	Robert Trent Jones GC, Gainsville	20½–11½

The match sheduled for 2002 was postponed and the event will now be played in 2003 at Fancourt, South Africa, and thereafter in odd-numbered years

Praia d'el Rey Rover European Cup

(European Seniors v Ladies' European PGA, instituted 1997)

at Praia d'el Rey, Obidos, Portugal

1997	European PGA Seniors beat ELPGA	13–7
1998	European PGA Seniors halved with ELPGA	10–10
1999	Ladies' European Tour beat European PGA Seniors	11–9
2000	*Not played*	
2001	*Not played*	
2002	*Not played*	

Alfred Dunhill Cup (Held at St Andrews from 1985 to 2000)

Year	Winner	Runner-up	Score
1985	Australia	USA	3–0
	(G Norman, G Marsh, D Graham)	(M O'Meara, R Floyd, C Strange)	
1986	Australia	Japan	3–0
	(R Davis, D Graham, G Norman)	(T Ozaki, N Ozaki, T Nakajima)	
1987	England	Scotland	2–1
	(N Faldo, G Brand, H Clark)	(S Lyle, S Torrance, G Brand Jr)	
1988	Ireland	Australia	2–1
	(D Smyth, R Rafferty, E Darcy)	(R Davis, D Graham, G Norman)	
1989	USA	Japan	3½–2½
	(M Calcavecchia, T Kite, C Strange)	(H Meshiai, N Ozaki, K Suzuki)	
1990	Ireland	England	3½–2½
	(P Walton, R Rafferty, D Feherty)	(M James, R Boxall, H Clark)	
1991	Sweden	South Africa	2–1
	(A Forsbrand, P-U Johansson, M Lanner)	(J Bland, D Frost, G Player)	
1992	England	Scotland	2–0
	(S Richardson, J Spence, D Gilford)	(G Brand Jr, C Montgomerie, S Lyle)	
1993	USA	England	2–1
	(P Stewart, F Couples, J Daly)	(M James, N Faldo, P Baker)	
1994	Canada	USA	2–1
	(D Barr, R Gibson, R Stewart)	(T Kite, C Strange, F Couples)	
1995	Scotland	Zimbabwe	2–1
	(A Coltart, C Montgomerie, S Torrance)	(T Johnstone, M McNulty, N Price)	
1996	USA	New Zealand	2–1
	(M O'Meara, P Mickelson, S Stricker)	(F Nobilo, G Turner, G Waite)	
1997	South Africa	Sweden	2–1
	(R Goosen, D Frost, E Els)	(J Parnevik, P-U Johansson, J Haeggman)	
1998	South Africa	Spain	2–1
	(R Goosen, D Frost, E Els)	(MA Jiménez, S Luna, JM Olazábal)	
1999	Spain	Australia	2–1
	(S García, JM Olazábal, MA Jiménez)	(C Parry, PO'Malley, S Leaney)	
2000	Spain	South Africa	2–1
	(MA Martin, MA Jiménez, JM Olazábal)	(D Frost, R Goosen, E Els)	

Tournament discontinued

Davidoff Nations Cup

2000   Korea   2001   China

2002 at Johor Bahru, Malaysia

1	Switzerland (André Bossart, Mark Chatelain)	64-66-66-68—264
2	Myanmar (Kyi Hla Han, Soe Kyaw Naing)	62-68-66-69—265
	Singapore (Mardan mamat, Lam Chih Bing)	64-69-63-69—265

Top three qualified for EMC^2 World Cup in Mexico from December 12–15

Other finishers: 4 Philippines; 5 Thailand; 6 Italy; 7 Netherlands; 8 Spain; 9 Finland; 10 Malaya; 11 India; 12 Pakistan; 13 Hong Kong; 14 China; 15 Taiwan; 16 Indonesia; 17 Greece; 18 Slovenia; 19 Czech Republic; 20 Mauritius

UBS Warburg Cup (Instituted 2001)

2001   USA

2002 at Sea Island, St Simons Island, GA

USA 14, Rest of World 9

Full results on page 371

National and Regional Championships

National Championships

Maxfli PGA Assistants' Championship

1984	G Weir	Coombe Hill	286	1993	C Everett	Oaklands	280
1985	G Coles	Coombe Hill	284	1994	M Plummer	Burnham & Berrow	278
1986	J Brennand	Sand Moor	280	1995	I Sparkes	The Warwickshire	285
1987	J Hawksworth	Coombe Hill	282	1996	S Purves	Moor Allerton	281
1988	J Oates	Coventry	284	1997	P Sefton	De Vere, Blackpool	273
1989	C Brooks	Hillside	291	1998	A Raitt	Bearwood Lakes	280
1990	A Ashton	Hillside	213 (54)	1999	I Harrison	Bearwood Lakes	274
1991	S Wood	Wentworth	288	2000	T Anderson	St Annes Old Links	273
1992	P Mayo	E Sussex National	285	2001	C Goodfellow	St Annes Old Links	207

2002 *at St Annes Old Links, Lytham*

1	David Orr (East Renfrewshire)	68-66-66-71—271
2	Craig Goodfellow (Eden)	65-75-69-63—272
3	Mark Nichols (unattached)	67-69-70-69—275

The De Vere PGA Seniors' Championship

1970	M Faulkner	Longniddry	288	1986	N Coles	Mere, Cheshire	276
1971	K Nagle	Elie	269	1987	N Coles	Turnberry	279
1972	K Bousfield	Longniddry	291	1988	P Thomson	North Berwick	287
1973	K Nagle	Elie	270	1989	N Coles	West Hill	277
1974	E Lester	Lundin	282	1990	B Waites	Brough	269
1975	K Nagle	Longniddry	268	1991	B Waites	Wollaton Park	277
1976	C O'Connor	Cambridgeshire Hotel	284	1992	T Horton	R Dublin	290
1977	C O'Connor	Cambridgeshire Hotel	288	1993	B Huggett	Sunningdale	204 (54)
1978	P Skerritt	Cambridgeshire Hotel	288	1994	J Morgan	Sunningdale	203
1979	C O'Connor	Cambridgeshire Hotel	280	1995	J Morgan	Sunningdale	204
1980	P Skerritt	Gleneagles Hotel	286	1996	T Gale	The Belfry	284
1981	C O'Connor	North Berwick	287	1997	W Hall	The Belfry	277
1982	C O'Connor	Longniddry	285	1998	T Horton	The Belfry	277
1983	C O'Connor	Burnham and Berrow	277	1999	R Metherall	The Belfry	276
1984	E Jones	Stratford-upon-Avon	280	2000	J Grace*	The Belfry	282
1985	N Coles	Pannal, Harrogate	284	2001	I Stanley	Carden Park	278

2002 *at Carden Park*

1	Seiji Ebihara (Jpn)	69-67-65-66—267
2	George Burns (USA)	72-66-66-73—277
	Steve Stull (USA)	71-39-71-66—277

Glenmuir Club Professionals' Championship

1973	DN Sewell	Calcot Park	276	1981	M Steadman	Woburn	289
1974	WB Murray	Calcot Park	275	1982	D Durnian	Hill Valley	285
1975	DN Sewell	Calcot Park	276	1983	J Farmer	Heaton Park	270
1976	WJ Ferguson	Moortown	283	1984	D Durnian	Bolton Old Links	278
1977	D Huish	Notts	284	1985	R Mann	The Belfry	291
1978	D Jones	Pannal	281	1986	D Huish	R Birkdale	278
1979	D Jones	Pannal	278	1987	R Weir	Sandiway	273
1980	D Jagger	Turnberry	286	1988	R Weir	Harlech	269

Glenmuir Club Professionals' Championship *continued*

1989	B Barnes	Sandwich, Prince's	280	1996	B Longmuir	Co Louth	280
1990	A Webster	Carnoustie	292	1997	B Rimmer	Northop	268
1991	W McGill	King's Lynn	285	1998	M Jones	Royal St David's	280
1992	J Hoskison	St Pierre	275	1999	S Bebb*	Kings Lynn	283
1993	C Hall	Coventry	274	2000	R Cameron*	St Andrews	295
1994	D Jones	North Berwick	278	2001	S Edwards	County Louth	275
1995	P Carman	West Hill	269				

2002 *at Saunton GC*

1	Bob Cameron (Sundridge Park)	66-72-67-75—280
2	John Dwyer (Ashbourne)	71-70-69-71—281
3	Graeme Bell (Eaglescliffe)	68-70-71-73—282
	Andrew Hare (Boston West)	71-71-68-72—282

Smurfit Irish PGA Championship

1960	C O'Connor	Warrenpoint	271	1981	D Jones	Woodbrook	283
1961	C O'Connor	Lahinch	280	1982	D Feherty	Woodbrook	287
1962	C O'Connor	Bangor	264	1983	L Higgins	Woodbrook	275
1963	C O'Connor	Little Island	271	1984	M Sludds	Skerries	277
1964	E Jones	Knock	279	1985	D Smyth	Co Louth	204 (54)
1965	C O'Connor	Mullingar	283	1986	D Smyth	Waterville	282
1966	C O'Connor	Warrenpoint	269	1987	P Walton	Co Louth	144 (36)
1967	H Boyle	Tullamore	214 (54)	1988	E Darcy	Castle, Dublin	269
1968	C Greene	Knock	282	1989	P Walton	Castle, Dublin	266
1969	J Martin	Dundalk	268	1990	D Smyth	Woodbrook	271
1970	H Jackson	Massareene	283	1991	P Walton	Woodbrook	277
1971	C O'Connor	Galway	278	1992	E Darcy	K Club	285
1972	J Kinsella	Bundoran	289	1993	M Sludds	K Club	285
1973	J Kinsella	Limerick	284	1994	D Clarke	Galway Bay	285
1974	E Polland	Portstewart	277	1995	P Walton	Belvoir Park	273
1975	C O'Connor	Carlow	275	1996	D Smyth	Slieve Russell GC	281
1976	P McGuirk	Waterville	291	1997	P McGinley	Fota Island	285
1977	P Skerritt	Woodbrook	281	1998	P Harrington*	Powerscourt	216 (54)
1978	C O'Connor	Dollymount	286	1999	N Manchip	The Island	271
1979	D Smyth	Dollymount	215 (54)	2000	P McGinley	Co Louth	270
1980	D Feherty	Dollymount	283	2001	D Smyth	Castle Rock	273

2002 *at Westport*

1	Paul McGinley (K Club)	76-72-65—213
2	John Dwyer (Ashbourne)	73-73-70—216
3	Philip Walton (Westpoint Fitness Centre)	70-79-68—217

Irish Club Professionals' Championship

1993	D Mooney	Royal Tara	208	1998	L Robinson	Nuremore	140
1994	K O'Donnell	Knockanally	216	1999	N Manchip	Nuremore	139
1995	D Jones	Fota Island	145	2000	L Walker	Nuremore	134
1996	B McGovern	Headfort	140	2001	M Allen*	Nuremore	142
1997	N Manchip	Mount Wolseley	141				

2002 *at Nuremore*

1	Neil Manchip (Royal Dublin)	70-65—135
2	Jimmy Bolger (Kilkenny)	66-71—137
	John Dwyer (Ashbourne)	68-69—137
	Brendan McGovern (Headfort)	70-67—137

Macallan Spey Bay Scottish Assistants' Championship

1980	F Mann	Dunbar	294	1991	G Hume	Kilmarnock Barassie	299
1981	M Brown	West Kilbride	290	1992	E McIntosh	Turnberry Hotel	266
1982	R Collinson	West Kilbride	294	1993	J Wither	Alloa	280
1983	A Webster	Stirling	285	1994	S Henderson	Newmacher	283
1984	C Elliott	Stirling	285	1995	A Tait	Newmacher	276
1985	C Elliott	Falkirk Tryst	284	1996	S Thompson	Newmacher	278
1986	P Helsby	Erskine	295	1997	M Hastie	Balbirnie Park	275
1987	C Innes	Hilton Park	284	1998	D Orr	Balbirnie Park	272
1988	G Collinson	Turnberry	289	1999	A Forsyth	Balbirnie Park	269
1989	C Brooks	Windyhill	282	2000	C Lee	Balbirnie Park	275
1990	P Lawrie	Cruden Bay	279	2001	C Kelly	Spey Bay	275

2002 *at Spey Bay*

1	Chris Kelly (Scotscraig)	67-71-69-70—277
2	Ross Cameron (McDonald)	71-65-68-77—281
3	Samuel Cairns (Carlisle)	70-71-75-68—284
	Chris Gilbert (Old Meldrum)	68-70-71-75—284

Scottish Match Play Championship

Sponsored by Aberdeen Asset Management at Meldrum House, Aberdeen

2002 *at Deeside* (Quarter- and Semi-Finals); *Balgownie* (Finals)

Quarter-Finals

Paul Lawrie (Meldrum House) beat Alan Reid (Brunston Castle) at 23rd

Ross Drummond (unattached) beat Craig Ronald (Carluke) 4 and 3

Paul Wardell (Whitekirk) beat Graham Rankin 1 hole

Craig Everett (Esporta Dougalston) beat Gary Collinson (Bearsden) 1 hole

Semi-Finals

Lawrie beat Drummond 1 hole

Wardell beat Everett 5 and 4

Final

Paul Lawrie beat Paul Wardell 3 and 2

Scottish Professionals' Championship

1965	EC Brown	Forfar	271	1983	B Gallacher	Dalmahoy	276
1966T	EC Brown	Cruden Bay	137 (36)	1984	I Young	Dalmahoy	276
	J Panton			1985	S Torrance	Dalmahoy	277
1967	H Bannerman	Montrose	279	1986	R Drummond	Glenbervie	270
1968	EC Brown	Monktonhall	286	1987	R Drummond	Glenbervie	268
1969	G Cunningham	Machrihanish	284	1988	S Stephen	Haggs Castle	283
1970	RDBM Shade	Montrose	276	1989	R Drummond	Monktonhall	274
1971	NJ Gallacher	Lundin Links	282	1990	R Drummond	Deer Park	278
1972	H Bannerman	Strathaven	268	1991	S Torrance	Erskine	274
1973	BJ Gallacher	Kings Links	276	1992	P Lawrie	Cardross	273
1974	BJ Gallacher	Drumpellier	276	1993	S Torrance	Dalmahoy	269
1975	D Huish	Duddingston	279	1994	A Coltart	Dalmahoy	281
1976	J Chillas	Haggs Castle	286	1995	C Gillies	Dalmahoy	278
1977	BJ Gallacher	Barnton	282	1996	B Marchbank	Dalmahoy	276
1978	S Torrance	Strathaven	269	1997	G Law	Downfield	284
1979	AWB Lyle	Glasgow Gailes	274	1998	C Gillies	Newmacher	273
1980	S Torrance	East Kilbride	273	1999	G Hutcheon	Gleneagles	288
1981	B Barnes	Dalmahoy	275	2000	A Forsyth	Gleneagles	255
1982	B Barnes	Dalmahoy	286	2001	J Chillas	Gleneagles	284

2002 *at Gleneagles*

1	Fraser Mann (Musselburgh)	73-72-69-66—280
2	David Orr (East Renfrewshire)	73-71-68-69—281
3	Scott Henderson (Kings Links)	69-71-66-76—282

Welsh National Championships

1960	RH Kemp jr	Llandudno	288	1981	C DeFoy	Cardiff	139
1961	S Mouland	Southerndown	286	1982	C DeFoy	Cardiff	137
1962	S Mouland	Porthcawl	302	1983	S Cox	Cardiff	136
1963	H Gould	Wrexham	291	1984	K Jones	Cardiff	135
1964	B Bielby	Tenby	297	1985	D Llewellyn	Whitchurch	132
1965	S Mouland	Penarth	281	1986	P Parkin	Whitchurch	142
1966	S Mouland	Conway	281	1987	A Dodman	Cardiff	132
1967	S Mouland	Pyle and Kenfig	219 (54)	1988	I Woosnam	Cardiff	137
1968	RJ Davies	Southerndown	292	1989	K Jones	Royal Porthcawl	140
1969	S Mouland	Llandudno	277	1990	P Mayo	Fairwood Park	136
1970	W Evans	Tredegar Park	289	1991	P Mayo	Fairwood Park	138
1971	J Buckley	St Pierre	291	1992	C Evans	Asburnham	142
1972	J Buckley	Porthcawl	298	1993	P Price	Caerphilly	138
1973	A Griffiths	Newport	289	1994	M Plummer	Northop	133
1974	M Hughes	Cardiff	284	1995	S Dodd	Northop	139
1975	C DeFoy	Whitchurch	285	1996	M Stanford	Northop	137
1976	S Cox	Radyr	284	1997	M Ellis	Vale of Glamorgan	139
1977	C DeFoy	Glamorganshire	135	1998	L Bond	Vale of Glamorgan	69 (18)
1978	BCC Huggett	Whitchurch	145	1999	R Dinsdale	Vale of Glamorgan	134
1979	*Cancelled*			2000	M Plummer	Newport	136
1980	A Griffiths	Cardiff	139	2001	S Dodd	Ashburnham	214

2002 *at Pyle & Kenfig*

1	Simon Edwards (Wrexham)*	72-67-71—210
2	Laurie Turner (Wepre Park)	67-69-74—210
3	Matthew Ellis (Vale of Llangollen)	71-69-71—211

PGA of Europe Championship

1983	Cees Renders (Ned)	1989	Russell Weir (Sco)	1997	Claude Grenier (Aut)
1984	Donald Armour (Ned)	1990	John Woof (Ned)	1998	Simon Brown (Eng)
1985	John Woof (Ned)	1991	Paul Carman (Eng)	1999	Richard Dinsdale (Wal)
1986	Stuart Brown (Eng)	1992	Tim Giles (Eng)	2000	Sion Bebb (Wal)
1987	Jim Rhodes (Eng)	1993	Russell Weir (Sco)	2001	A George (Eng)
1988	Russell Weir (Sco)	1994/1996	*– not played*		

2002 *at Pevero, Sardinia*   (6117m–72)

1	P Wesslingh (Eng)	71-68-67-74—280 (-8)
2	A George (Eng)	69-72-70-71—282 (-3)
3	B Rimmer (Eng)	70-69-68-78—285 (-3)

Regional Championships

Derbyshire Professionals

1993	K Cross	1998	J Mellor
1994	D Stafford	1999	D Russell
1995	A Carnall	2000	M Smith
1996	C Cross	2001	M Smith
1997	A Carnall	2002	M Poxon

Dorset PGA

2002	C Jessup

Devon Open

1993T	D Sheppard	1998	D Sheppard
	T McSherry	1999	J Langmead
1994	I Higgins	2000	B Austin
1995	B Austin	2001	B Austin
1996	J Langmead	2002	B Austin
1997	J Langmead		

East Anglian Open

1993	A George	1998	P Curry
1994	R Mann	1999	P Curry
1995	N Brown	2000	J Bevan
1996	N Brown	2001	D Parker
1997	I Poulter	2002	I Ellis

East Region PGA

1995	L Fickling	1999	S Khan
1996	T Charnley	2000	I Ellis
1997	R Mann	2001	P Barham
1998	T Charnley	2002	D Parker

Essex Open

1993	A Blackburn	1998	J Robson
1994	D Jones	1999	P Joiner
1995	J Robson	2000	S Khan
1996	S Khan	2001	R Coles
1997	V Cox	2002	D Parker

Essex Professionals

1993	T Wheals	1998	G Carter
1994	V Cox	1999	P Curry
1995	M Stokes	2000	W McColl
1996	P Joiner	2001	J Fryatt
1997	M Stokes	2002	P Barham

Hampshire PGA

1993	R Edwards	1998	G Hughes
1994	G Hughes	1999	J Barnes
1995	I Benson	2000	K Saunders
1996	R Bland	2001	S Cowie
1997	J Lovell	2002	K Saunders

Hampshire Match Play

1993	K Saunders	1998	D Harris
1994	M Wheeler	1999	J Lovell
1995	M Wheeler	2000	M Robbins
1996	J Le Roux	2001	P Bryden
1997	D Harris	2002	J Barnes

Hampshire, Isle of Wight and Channel Islands Open

1993	R Bland	1998	R Bland
1994	R Bland	1999	R Bland
1995	R Bland	2000	R Bland
1996	G Hughes	2001	S Cowie
1997	M Blackey	2002	R Tate

Herts Professionals

1993	L Jones	1998T	R Mitchell
1994T	N Brown		I Parker
	D Tapping	1999	L Jones
1995	N Brown	2000	R Mitchell
1996	R Hurd	2001	A Bailey
1997	P Winston	2002	D Field

Kent Open

1993	N Haynes	1998	D Parris
1994	T Berry	1999	R Cameron
1995	T Milford	2000	M McLean
1996	S Green	2001	J Marshall
1997	S Page	2002	M Day

Kent Professionals

1993	R Cameron	1998	T Milford
1994	M Lawrence	1999	R Cameron
1995	T Poole	2000	B Coomber
1996	A Butterfield	2001	S Wood
1997	P Lyons	2002	S Stevens

Lancashire Open

1993	L Edwards	1998	J Cheetham
1994	A Lancaster	1999	C Corrigan
1995	G Furey	2000	G Furey
1996	G Furey	2001	M Hollingsworth
1997	G Furey	2002	S Astin

Leicestershire and Rutland Open

1993	P Frith	1998	J Caylis (am)
1994	J Herbert	1999	I Ball
1995	I Lyner	2000	M Cort
1996	D Gibson	2001	I Ball
1997	N Bland	2002	G Shaw

Lincolnshire Open

1993	S Bennett	1998	M King (am)
1994	S Brewer	1999	M King (am)
1995	S Cox	2000	M King (am)
1996	S Bennett	2001	S Emery
1997	M King (am)	2002	

Midland Professionals

1993	C Clark (M)	1998	J Robinson (M)
	P Baker (S)		S Webster (S)
1994	N Turley (M)	1999	I Ball (M)
	P Baker (S)		C Hall (S)
1995	D Eddiford (M)	2000	R Rock (M)
	S Rose (S)		DJ Russell (S)
1996	S Bennett (M)	2001	J Robinson (M)
	DJ Russell (S)		T Rouse (S)
1997	J Higgins	2002	I Lyner (M)
	(M and S)		R Rock (S)

Midland Seniors

1993	J Humphries	1998	I Clark
1994	G Pope	1999	S Wild
1995	T Squires	2000	T Squires
1996	JC Thomas	2001	*Not played*
1997T	EW Hammond	2002	*Not played*
	C Moir		
	MA Smith		

Norfolk Open

1993	A Collison	1998	R Wilson
1994	J Hill	1999	P Little
1995	M Barrett	2000	M Jubb
1996	M Barrett	2001	D Henderson (am)
1997	N Lythgoe	2002	A Varney

Norfolk Professionals

1993	A Collison	1998	R Wilson
1994	A Collison	1999	I Ellis
1995	P Briggs	2000	M Jubb
1996	P Bower	2001	A Collison
1997	T Varney	2002	A Varney

Northern Region PGA

1993	C Smiley	1998	P Carman
1994	P Wesselingh	1999	R Wragg
1995	G Furey	2000	C Hislop
1996	S Townend	2001	B Sharrock
1997	G Furey	2002	P Archer

Northern Open

1993	K Stables	1998	L James
1994	K Stables	1999	A Forsyth
1995	J Higgins	2000	J Payne
1996	S Henderson	2001	G Rankin
1997	D Thomson	2002	F Mann

Northumberland and Durham Open

2002	B Rumney

South West PGA

1994	G Emerson	1999	G Ryall
1995	G Howell	2000	K Spurgeon
1996	M Stanford	2001	M Wiggett
1997	M Stanford	2002	B Austin
1998	S Little		

Southern Assistants

1993	R Edwards	1998	D Parris
1994	M Wheeler	1999	C Fromant
1995	P Lyons	2000	N Reilly
1996	D Parris	2001	C Roake
1997	A Lovelace	2002	P Schunter

Southern Assistants Match Play

1993	N Gorman	1998	B Hodkin
1994	M Groombridge	1999	M Nichols
1995	M Groombridge	2000	S Wells
1996	A Butterfield	2001	S Crooks
1997	B Hodkin	2002	G Lingard

Southern Professionals

1993	G Smith	1998	P Simpson
1994	R Edwards	1999	S Wood
1995	P Sefton	2000	P Robshaw
1996	P Hughes	2001	K Saunders
1997	P Sherman	2002	A Lovelace

Staffordshire Open

1993	M McGuire	1998	R Peace
1994	D Scott	1999	G Beddow
1995	I Proverbs	2000	J Cookson (am)
1996	B Rimmer	2001	R Maxfield (am)
1997	A Roger	2002	I Proverbs

Staffordshire and Shropshire

1993	J Rhodes	1999	P Wesselingh
1994	J Rhodes	2000	P Wesselingh
1995	B Stevens	2001	S Russell
1996	J Higgins	2002	G Gilligan (S)
1997	R Fisher		J Harrold (M)
1998	A Feriday		

Suffolk Open

1993	R Mann	1998	J Wright
1994	L Patterson	1999	S MacPherson
1995	R Mann	2000	J Keeley
1996	S MacPherson	2001	J Moul (am)
1997	P Wilby	2002	A Lucas

Suffolk Professionals

1993	K Golding	1998	K Golding (M)
1994	C Jenkins (M)		S MacPherson (S)
	L Patterson (S)	1999	R Mann (M)
1995	C Jenkins (M)		S MacPherson (S)
	R Mann (S)	2000	R Hitchcock (M)
1996	K Vince (M)		J Bevan (S)
	T Cooper (S)	2001	J Moul (am) (M)
1997T	A Cotton (M)		A Cotton (S)
	A Lucas (S)	2002	R Mann
	C Jenkins (S)		

Sunderland of Scotland Masters

1993	A Oldcorn	1998	M Miller*
1994	R Weir	1999	C Gillies
1995	M Jones	2000	S Martin
1996	C Ronald	2001	J Bevan
1997	L Vennet	2002	R Drummond

Surrey Open

1993	R Dickman	1998	P Sefton
1994	M Nichols	1999	H Stott
1995	A Wall	2000	C Gane
1996	P Hughes	2001	N Reilly
1997	M Nichols	2002	M Nichols

Sussex Open

1993	N Burke	1998	J Doherty (am)
1994	K Hinton	1999	P Lyons
1995	J Blamires	2000	P Lyons
1996	K Macdonald	2001	G Murray
1997	K Macdonald	2002	T Spence

Ulster Professionals

1993	D Jones	1998	D Mooney
1994	P Russell	1999	D Mooney
1995	R Burns	2000	P Collins
1996	J Heggarty	2001	J Dwyer
1997	D Mooney	2002	L Walker

Warwickshire Open

1993	A Bownes	1998	SJ Walker
1994	D White	1999	D Clayton
1995	C Dowling	2000	T Whitehouse (am)
1996	P Chalkley	2001	A Carey
1997	D Barton	2002	M Morris

Warwickshire Professionals

1993	A Bands (M)	1998	C Phillips (M)
	G Marston (S)		J Corns* (S)
1994	C Wicketts (M)	1999	D Clayton (M)
	S Webster (am)		A Bownes (S)
	(S)	2000	A Carey (M)
1995	J Cook		A Stokes (S)
	(M and S)	2001	A Stokes (M)
1996	C Phillips (M)		A Bownes (S)
	S Edwards (S)	2002	M Morris (M)
1997	L Bashford (M)		M Morris (S)
	C Phillips (S)		

West Region PGA

1993	P Mayo	1998	J Taylor
1994	S Little	1999	S Little
1995	M Thompson	2000	M Higley
1996	M McEwan	2001	I Ferrie
1997	M Thompson	2002	M Thompson

Hills Wiltshire Pro Champ

1993T	G Emerson	1998	R Blake
	D Ray	1999	S McDonald
1994	S Robertson	2000	A Beal
1995	G Laing	2001	S Robertson
1996	B Sandry	2002	D Hutton
1997	M Smith		

Worcestershire Open

1993	P Scarrett	1998	D Eddiford*
1994	S Edwards	1999	S Edwards
1995	C Clark	2000	N Turley
1996	D Clee	2001	N Turley
1997	P Scarrett	2002	R Wassell

Worcestershire Stroke Play

1993	F Clark	1998	D Eddiford
1994	C Clark	1999	F Clark
1995	I Clark	2000	J Jones
1996	F Clark	2001	N Turley
1997	I Clark	2002	M Toombes

Yorkshire Professionals

1993	A Nicholson	1998	G Brown
1994	L Turner	1999	G Brown
1995	R Golding	2000	G Walker
1996	N Ludwell	2001	A Ambler
1997	S Robinson	2002	A Ambler

Overseas National Championships

(Excluding European Tour or Affiliated Events)

Australian Open

1904 Hon Michael Scott (am)	1959 Kel Nagle
1905 Dan Soutar	1960 Bruce Devlin (am)
1906 Carnegie Clark (am)	1961 Frank Phillips
1907 Hon Michael Scott (am)	1962 Gary Player
1908 Clyde Pearce (am)	1963 Gary Player
1909 C Felstead (am)	1964 Jack Nicklaus
1910 Carnegie Clark (am)	1965 Gary Player
1911 Carnegie Clark (am)	1966 Arnold Palmer
1912 Ivo Whitton (am)	1967 Peter Thomson
1913 Ivo Whitton (am)	1968 Jack Nicklaus
1914-1919 *not played*	1969 Gary Player
1920 Joe Kirkwood	1970 Gary Player
1921 A Le Fevre	1971 Jack Nicklaus
1922 C Campbell	1972 Peter Thomson
1923 T Howard	1973 J C Snead
1924 A Russell (am)	1974 Gary Player
1925 Fred Popplewell	1975 Jack Nicklaus
1926 Ivo Whitton (am)	1976 Jack Nicklaus
1927 R Stewart	1977 David Graham
1928 Fred Popplewell	1978 Jack Nicklaus
1929 Ivo Whitton (am)	1979 Jack Newton
1930 F Eyre	1980 Greg Norman
1931 Ivo Whitton (am)	1981 Bill Rogers
1932 Mick Ryan (am)	1982 Bob Shearer
1933 M Kelly	1983 Peter Fowler
1934 Bill Bolger	1984 Tom Watson
1935 F McMahon	1985 Greg Norman
1936 Gene Sarazen	1986 Rodger Davis
1937 George Naismith	1987 Greg Norman
1938 Jim Ferrier (am)	1988 Mark Calcavecchia
1939 Jim Ferrier (am)	1989 Peter Senior
1940-1945 *not played*	1990 John Morse
1946 Ossie Pickworth	1991 Wayne Riley
1947 Ossie Pickworth	1992 Steve Elkington
1948 Ossie Pickworth	1993 Brad Faxon
1949 Eric Cremin	1994 Robert Allenby
1950 Norman Von Nida	1995 Greg Norman
1951 Peter Thomson	1996 Greg Norman
1952 Norman Von Nida	1997 Lee Westwood
1953 Norman Von Nida	1998 Greg Chalmers
1954 Ossie Pickworth	1999 Aaron Baddeley (am)
1955 Bobby Locke	2000 Aaron Baddeley
1956 Bruce Crampton	2001 Stuart Appleby
1957 Frank Phillips	2002 Stuart Appleby
1958 Gary Player	

Canadian Open

1904 J H Oke	1956 D Sanders (am)
1905 G Cumming	1957 G Bayer
1906 C Murray	1958 W Ellis jr
1907 P Barrett	1959 D Ford
1908 A Murray	1960 A Wall jr
1909 K Keffer	1961 J Cupit
1910 D Kenny	1962 T Kroll
1911 C Murray	1963 D Ford
1912 G Sargent	1964 KDG Nagle
1913 A Murray	1965 G Littler
1914 K Kesser	1966 D Massengale
1915-1918 *not played*	1967 W Casper
1919 J D Edgar	1968 RJ Charles
1920 J D Edgar	1969 T Aaron
1921 W H Trovinger	1970 D Zarley
1922 A Watrous	1971 L Trevino
1923 C W Hackney	1972 G Brewer jr
1924 L Diegel	1973 T Weiskopf
1925 L Diegel	1974 B Nichols
1926 M Smith	1975 T Weiskopf
1927 T Armour	1976 J Pate
1928 L Diegel	1977 L Trevino
1929 L Diegel	1978 B Lietzke
1930 T Armour	1979 L Trevino
1931 W Hagen	1980 B Gilder
1932 H Cooper	1981 P Oosterhuis
1933 J Kirkwood	1982 B Lietzke
1934 T Armour	1983 J Cook
1935 G Kunes	1984 G Norman
1936 L Little	1985 C Strange
1937 H Cooper	1986 B Murphy
1938 S Snead	1987 C Strange
1939 H McSpaden	1988 K Green
1940 S Snead	1989 S Jones
1941 S Snead	1990 W Levi
1942 C Wood	1991 N Price
1943-1944 *not played*	1992 G Norman
1945 B Nelson	1993 D Frost
1946 G Fazio	1994 N Price
1947 AD Locke	1995 M O'Meara
1948 CW Congdon	1996 D Hart
1949 E J Harrison	1997 S Jones
1950 J Ferrier	1998 B Andrade
1951 J Ferrier	1999 H Sutton
1952 J Palmer	2000 T Woods
1953 D Douglas	2001 S Verplank
1954 P Fletcher	2002 J Rollins
1955 A Palmer	

Austrian Open

1993	R Rafferty	1998	K Carissimi
1994	M Davis	1999	J Ciola
1995	A Cejka	2000	*Not played*
1996	P McGinley	2001	C Gane
1997	E Simsek	2002	M Brier

Hong Kong Open

1993	B Watts	1998	WS Kang
1994	D Frost	1999	P Sjöland
1995	G Webb	2000	S Dyson
1996	G Webb	2001	J M Olazábal
1997	F Nobilo	2002	*To be played*

Korean Open

1993	Y Kun Han	1998	DS Kim (am)
1994	M Cunning	1999	Choi Kyung Ju
1995	B Jobe	2000	T Jaidee
1996	Choi Kyung-Ju	2001	DS Kim (am)
1997	K Jong-Duck	2002	SGarcía

Indian Open

1993	A Sher	1998	A Firoz
1994	E Aubrey	1999	A Atwal
1995	J Rutledge	2000	J Randhawa
1996	H Shirakata	2001	T Jaidee
1997	E Fryatt	2002	V Kumar

New Zealand Open

1993	P Fowler	1998	G Turner
1994	C Jones	1999	M Lane
1995	L Parsons	2000	M Campbell
1996	M Long	2001	C Parry
1997	G Turner	2002	C Parry

Japanese Open

1993	S Okuda	1998	H Tanaka
1994	M Ozaki	1999	N Ozaki
1995	T Izwa	2000	N Ozaki
1996	P Teravainen	2001	T Teshima
1997	C Parry	2002	D Smail

Singapore Open

1993	P Maloney	1998	S Micheel
1994	KH Han	1999	J Milkha Singh
1995	S Conran	2000	J Randhawa
1996	J Kernohan	2001	T Warachant
1997	Z Moe	2002	*To be played*

Kenyan Open

1993	C Maltman	1998	R Gonzalez
1994	P Carman	1999	M Lafeber
1995	J Lee	2000	T Immelman
1996	M Miller	2001	A Roestoff
1997	J Berendt	2002	I James

Zambian Open

1993	P Harrison	1998	M Cayeux
1994	*Not played*	1999	*Not played*
1995	*Not played*	2000	J Loughnane
1996	D Botes	2001	M Foster
1997	*Not played*	2002	M Cayeux

Other 2002 Overseas National Championships

Caribbean Open	M Brier
Danish Open	E Stedman
Finnish Open	T Norret
Malaysian Open	A Forsyth

Russian Open	I Pyman
South African Open	T Clark
Taiwan Open	D Chia

PART III

Women's Professional Tournaments

Golf Weekly World Ranking for Women's Professional Golf

Latest ranking after Mizuno Classic

1	Annika Sörenstam (Swe)	756.83		51	Yu-Chen Huang (Chi)	69.48
2	Se Ri Pak (Kor)	500.93		52	Kirsty Taylor (Eng)	66.35
3	Karrie Webb (Aus)	410.63		53	Nicola Moult (Eng)	65.92
4	Mi Hyun Kim (Kor)	259.91		54	Beth Bauer (USA)	65.33
5	Laura Diaz (USA)	248.25		55	Pat Hurst (USA)	63.35
6	Juli Inkster (USA)	214.88		56	Shani Waugh (Aus)	59.57
7	Rosie Jones (USA)	203.63		57	Aki Takamura (Jpn)	59.10
8	Lorie Kane (Can)	199.13		58	Mihoko Takahashi (Jpn)	56.95
9	Carin Koch (Swe)	185.03		59	Johanna Head (Eng)	55.25
10	Laura Davies (Eng)	182.45		60	Kate Golden (USA)	55.00
11	Catriona Matthew (Sco)	179.94		61	Wendy Doolan (Aus)	54.56
12	Rachel Teske (Aus)	172.75		62	Kaori Harada (Jpn)	54.55
13	Grace Park (USA)	167.00		63	Silvia Cavalleri (Ita)	53.00
14	Sophie Gustafson (Swe)	162.38		64	Corinne Dibnah (Aus)	52.90
15	Michele Redman (USA)	160.25		65	Jennifer Rosales (Phi)	52.75
16	Kasumi Fujii (Jpn)	156.46		66	Hsiu-Feng Tseng (Jpn)	51.43
17	Cristie Kerr (USA)	153.01		67	Chieko Amanuma (Jpn)	50.42
18	Yuri Fudoh (Jpn)	140.89		68	Mikino Kubo (Jpn)	49.90
19	Maria Hjörth (Swe)	138.43		69	Nancy Scranton (USA)	49.55
20	Raquel Carriedo (Esp)	134.78		70	Michie Ohba (Jpn)	49.41
21	Mhairi McKay (Sco)	131.43		71	Becky Morgan (Wal)	49.12
22	Toshimi Kimura (Jpn)	128.77		72	Asa Gottmo (Swe)	48.96
23	Janice Moodie (Sco)	126.43		73	Mineko Nasu (Jpn)	48.88
24	Woo-Soon Ko (Kor)	122.34		74	Michiko Hattori (Jpn)	48.75
25	Meg Mallon (USA)	113.38		75	Ji-hee Lee (Kor)	47.88
26	Paula Marti (Esp)	109.57		76	Patricia Meunier Lebouc (Fra)	46.63
27	Beth Daniel (USA)	106.13		77	Marina Arruti (Esp)	45.83
28	Kelly Robbins (USA)	102.73		78	Donna Andrews (USA)	45.42
29	Karine Icher (Fra)	99.08		79	Candie Kung (Tai)	44.65
30	Akiko Fukushima (Jpn)	95.84		80	Betsy King (USA)	44.13
31	Michelle Ellis (Aus)	95.50		81	Midori Yonoyama (Jpn)	43.78
32	Dottie Pepper (USA)	92.26		82	Moira Dunn (USA)	43.75
33	Iben Tinning (Den)	92.26		83	Mikiyo Nishizuka (Jpn)	43.00
34	Suzann Pettersen (Nor)	91.25		84	Heather Bowie (USA)	42.82
35	Marine Monnet (Fra)	91.07		85	Vicki Goetze Ackerman (USA)	42.66
36	Hee-Won Han (Kor)	88.47		86	Chihiro Nakajima (Jpn)	42.60
37	Kaori Higo (Jpn)	86.81		87	Leta Lindley (USA)	41.98
38	Emilee Klein (USA)	86.51		88	Ana Belen Sanchez (Esp)	41.40
39	Gloria Park (Kor)	86.50		89	Kris Tschetter (USA)	39.55
40	Kelli Kuehne (USA)	84.46		90	Miyuki Shimabukuro (Jpn)	39.25
41	Wendy Ward (USA)	83.16		91	Kyoko Ono (Jpn)	38.15
42	Elisabeth Esterl (Ger)	82.70		92	Hiroko Yamaguchi (Jpn)	36.15
43	Danielle Ammaccapane (USA)	80.66		93	Gina Scott (NZ)	34.13
44	Liselotte Neumann (Swe)	79.51		94	Marnie McGuire (NZ)	34.10
45	Dorothy Delasin (USA)	76.50		95	Natalie Gulbis (USA)	34.00
46	Ikuyo Shiotani (Jpn)	75.87		96	Becky Iverson (USA)	33.53
47	Helen Alfredsson (Swe)	74.08		97	Jane Crafter (Aus)	33.13
48	Lynette Brooky (NZ)	73.68		98	Junko Yasui (Jpn)	32.79
49	Ok Hee Ku (Kor)	72.25		99	Karen Stupples (Eng)	32.53
50	Orie Fujino (Jpn)	70.25		100	Takayo Bandoh (Jpn)	32.50

Evian Ladies' European Tour, 2002

Final Order of Merit (The top 90 players retain a full card)

1	Paula Marti (Esp)	6589		52	Alison Nicholas (Eng)	796
2	Maria Hjörth (Swe)	6483		53	Jane Leary (Aus)	744
3	Sophie Gustafson (Swe)	5613		54	Sara Eklund (Swe)	743
4	Iben Tinning (Den)	5472		55	Nicole Stillig (Ger)	740
5	Asa Gottmo (Swe)	4851		56	Marlene Hedblom (Swe)	714
6	Karine Icher (Fra)	4642		57	Claire Duffy (Eng)	710
7	Marine Monnet (Fra)	4500		58	Natascha Fink (Aut)	706
8	Suzann Pettersen (Nor)	4403		59	Marieke Zelsman (Ned)	700
9	Laura Davies (Eng)	4359		60	Sandrine Mendiburu (Fra)	695
10	Raquel Carriedo (Esp)	4291		61	Pernilla Sterner (Swe)	694
11	Lynnette Brooky (NZ)	4138		62	Veronica Zorzi (Ita)	689
12	Elisabeth Esterl (Ger)	3599		63	Federica Dassu (Ita)	679
13	Johanna Head (Eng)	3456		64	Lisa Hed (Swe)	671
14	Kirsty Taylor (Eng)	3042		65	Rachel Kirkwood (Eng)	635
15	Mhairi McKay (Sco)	2928		66	Georgina Simpson (Eng)	601
16	Helen Alfredsson (Swe)	2852		67	Lara Tadiotto (Bel)	588
17	Ana Belen Sánchez (Esp)	2738		68	Loraine Lambert (Aus)	580
18	Nicola Moult (Eng)	2706		69	Ludivine Kreutz (Fra)	579
19	Catrin Nilsmark (Swe)	2682		70	Valerie Michaud (Fra)	579
20	Corinne Dibnah (Aus)	2225		71	Julie Forbes (Sco)	579
21	Silvia Cavalleri (Ita)	2054		72	Vibeke Stensrud (Nor)	574
22	Ana Larraneta (Esp)	2045		73	Suzanne O'Brien (Ire)	519
23	Samantha Head (Eng)	2009		74	Mia Lojdahl (Swe)	504
24	Kirsty S Taylor (Eng)	1812		75	Sara Jelander (Swe)	488
25	Becky Morgan (Wal)	1752		76	Valerie Van Ryckeghem (Bel)	423
26	Gina Scott (NZ)	1696		77	Alexandra Armas (Esp)	419
27	Trish Johnson (Eng)	1572		78	Nienke Nijenhuis (Ned)	407
28	Riikka Hakkainen (Fin)	1538		79	Anne-Marie Knight (Aus)	390
29	Karen Lunn (Aus)	1458		80	Jackie Kebbell (Eng)	388
30	Nadina Taylor (Aus)	1435		81	Judith Van Hagen (Ned)	387
31	Alison Munt (Aus)	1424		82	Marie-Laure de Lorenzi (Fra)	381
32	Marina Arruti (Esp)	1420		83	Wendy Dicks (Eng)	377
33	Cecilia Ekelundh (Swe)	1363		84	Regine Lautens (Swi)	353
34	Shani Waugh (Aus)	1356		85	Carina Vagner (Den)	349
35	Sara Beautell (Esp)	1353		86	Karen Margrethe Juul (Den)	331
36	Liselotte Neumann (Swe)	1345		87	Karolina Andersson (Swe)	328
37	Laurette Maritz (RSA)	1342		88	Anna Becker (Swe)	323
38	Kathryn Marshall (Sco)	1336		89	Malin Burstron (Swe)	297
39	Sophie Sandolo (Ita)	1295		90	Mandy Adamson (RSA)	284
40	Lora Fairclough (Eng)	1289				
41	Nina Karlsson (Swe)	1141		91	Kanna Takaneshi (Jpn)	263
42	Maria Boden (Swe)	1130		92	Elaine Ratcliffe (Eng)	255
43	Diana Luna (Ita)	1105		93	Sarah Bennett (Eng)	247
44	Stephanie Arricau (Fra)	1011		94	Jessica Lindbergh (Swe)	226
45	Caroline Hall (Eng)	975		95	Lesley Nicholson (Sco)	225
46	Cherie Byrnes (Aus)	958		96	Sara Forster (Eng)	213
47	Joanne Mills (Aus)	958		97	Johanna Westerberg (Swe)	208
48	Virginie Auffret (Fra)	926		98	Marie Hedberg (Swe)	207
49	Cecilie Lundgreen (Nor)	841		99	Isabella Maconi (Ita)	203
50	Diane Barnard (Eng)	829		100	Cecilia Sjoblom (Swe)	199
51	Dale Reid (Sco)	801				

Tour Results (in chronological order)

ANZ Ladies' Masters

Royal Pines, Gold Coast, Queensland   (5849–72)

1	Annika Sörenstam (Swe)*	74-64-71-69—278	€74093
2	Karrie Webb (Aus)	69-69-68-72—278	49395
3	Michelle Ellis (Aus)	68-70-70-72—280	34577

AAMI Women's Australian Open

Yarra Yarra, East Bentleigh, Victoria, Australia   (6051–72)

1	Karrie Webb (Aus)*	68-72-69-69—278	€49291
2	Suzann Pettersen (Nor)	70-70-69-69—278	32861
3	Michelle Ellis (Aus)	70-73-73-70—286	19716
	Becky Morgan (Wal)	73-70-72-71—286	19716

Ladies' Tenerife Open

Golf de Sur, San Miguel de Abona, Tenerife   (6123–72)

1	Raquel Carriedo (Esp)	73-71-77-71—292	€30000
2	Johanna Head (Eng)	72-74-79-68—293	20300
3	Elisabeth Esterl (Ger)	77-72-72-75—296	12400
	Marine Monnet (Fra)	76-72-77-71—296	12400

Ladies' Irish Open

Lackabane, Killarney, Co Kerry, Ireland   (6101–72)

1	Iben Tinning (Den)*	71-70-73—214	€24750
2	Suzann Pettersen (Nor)	71-71-72—214	16747
3	Maria Boden (Swe)	75-70-70—215	11550

La Perla Italian Open

Poggio dei Medici, Florence, Italy   (6252–73)

1	Iben Tinning (Den)	69-69-70-70—278	€28575
2	Silvia Cavalleri (Ita)	68-70-69-72—279	19336
3	Gina Scott (NZ)	67-74-73-69—283	13335

Ladies' Open of Costa Azul

Aroeira II, Lisbon, Portugal   (6113–72)

1	Kanna Takanashi (Jpn)	69-70—139	€10500
2	Julie Forbes (Sco)	72-68—140	8000
3	Lynnette Brooky (NZ)	71-70—141	5375
	Nicola Moult (Eng)	71-70—141	5375

Caja Duero Open de España Femenino

Campo de Golf, Salamanca, Spain (6201–72)

1	Karine Icher (Fra)	69-69-68-71—277	€37500
2	Raquel Carriedo (Esp)	70-68-70-70—278	25375
3	Lynnette Brooky (NZ)	66-73-69-72—280	15500
	Paula Marti (Esp)	70-72-71-67—280	15500

Evian Masters

Evian Les Bains, France (5975–72)

1	Annika Sörenstam (Swe)	68-67-65-69—269	€332243
2	Maria Hjörth (Swe)	71-68-70-64—273	187652
	Mu Hyun Kim (Kor)	66-70-68-69—273	187652

Arras Open de France Dames

Anzin St Aubin, France (5800–72)

1	Lynnette Brooky (NZ)	69-69-68-66—272	€41250
2	Paula Marti (Esp)	69-71-69-68—277	27912
3	Karine Icher (Fra)	70-68-71-70—279	15253
	Marine Monnet (Fra)	72-70-67-70—279	15253
	Iben Tinning (Den)	72-71-66-70—279	15253

P4 Norwegian Masters

Oslo, Norway (6129–72)

1	Laura Davies (Eng)*	73-69-68-73—283	€52800
2	Ana Larraneta (Esp)	68-69-78-68—283	35728
3	Karine Icher (Fra)	70-70-71-73—284	21824
	Marine Monnet (Fra)	71-72-71-70—284	21824

WEETABIX WOMEN'S BRITISH OPEN

Turnberry, Scotland (6407–72)

1	Karrie Webb (Aus)	66-71-70-66—273	€249007
2	Michelle Ellis (Aus)	69-70-68-68—275	136552
	Paula Marti (Esp)	69-68-69-69—275	136552

Fuller details of this event are included in Part I The Majors page 88

Compaq Open

Vasatorp, Helsingborg, Sweden (6170–72)

1	Annika Sörenstam (Swe)	67-66-68-70—271	€77123
2	Sophie Gustafson (Swe)	67-70-72-66—275	52186
3	Ana Belen Sánchez (Esp)	70-72-68-68—278	35991

The Wales WPGA Championship of Europe

Royal Porthcawl, Wales   (6183–73)

1	Asa Gottmo (Swe)	76-69-69-71—285	€94740
2	Maria Hjörth (Swe)	74-73-68-72—287	64107
3	Kirsty Taylor (Eng)	75-72-70-71—288	44212

The Solheim Cup *Interlachen CC, Madina, MN*   (6545–72)

USA beat Europe 15½–12½

Full details of this event can be found on page 219

Biarritz Ladies' Classic

Biarritz Le Phare, France   (5681-70)

1	Sophie Gustafson (Swe)*	69-67-64—200	€24750
2	Mhairi McKay (Sco)	67-67-66—200	16748
3	Helen Alfredsson (Swe)	65-65-71—201	10230
	Riikka Hakkarainen (Fin)	67-65-69—201	10230

US LPGA Tour 2002

Players are of American nationality unless stated

Money List Position with the Tyco/ADT Championship still to be played

Rank	Name	Events	Money Won
1	Annika Sörenstam (Swe)	22	$2,648,904
2	Se Ri Pak (Kor)	23	1,689,281
3	Juli Inkster	19	1,140,349
4	Mi Hyun Kim (Kor)	27	1,040,327
5	Karrie Webb (Aus)	20	923,700
6	Grace Park (Kor)	27	837,943
7	Laura Diaz	24	832.790
8	Carin Koch (Swe)	24	752,817
9	Rosie Jones	23	675,912
10	Cristie Kerr	25	668,643
11	Rachel Teske (Aus)	26	664,329
12	Lorie Cane (Can)	25	659,020
13	Michele Redman	24	654,599
14	Hee-Won Han (Kor)	27	612,747
15	Catriona Matthew (Sco)	27	553,394
16	Kelly Robbins	20	519,896
17	Mhairi McKay (Sco)	22	475,384
18	Beth Daniel	19	471.693
19	Beth Bauer	26	460,659
20	Gloria Park (Kor)	26	451,705
21	Meg Mallon	18	417,231
22	Janice Moody (Sco)	24	412,863
23	Kelli Kuehne	23	397,099
24	Danielle Ammaccapane	22	386,614
25	Michelle Ellis (Aus)	18	358,177
26	Shani Waugh	18	346,268
27	Maria Hjorth (Swe)	21	342,444
28	Laura Davies (Eng)	17	333,932
29	Jenny Rosales (Phi)	25	331,512
30	Patricia Meunier-Lebouc (Fra)	22	297,175
31	Dorothy Delasin	24	295,885
32	Liselotte Neumann (Swe)	19	295,225
33	Vicki Goetze-Ackerman	24	278,166
34	Jeong Jang (Kor)	26	276,820
35	Emilee Klein	27	272,036
36	Candi Kung	22	261,044
37	Heather Bowie	24	259,995
38	Kate Golden	24	259,143
39	Natalie Gulbis	26	257,310
40	Leta Lindley	23	252,061
41	Wendy Doolan	21	250,838
42	Akiko Fukushima (Jpn)	15	243,528
43	Pat Hurst	22	237,682
44	Donna Andrews	21	229,825
45	Agela Stanford	19	221,857
46	Karen Stupples (Eng)	22	214,760
47	Kris Tschetter	22	213,935
48	Joanne Morley	23	210,643
49	Jill McGill	26	202,375
50	Jackie Gallagher-Smith	25	187,180

Tour Results (in chronological order)

LPGA Takefuji Classic

Wailkoloa, HI   (6164–70)

1	Annika Sörenstam (Swe)*	64-66-66—196	$135000
2	Lorie Kane (Can)	63-66-67—196	82192
3	Heather Bowie	68-65-65—198	52875
	Gloria Park (Kor)	66-67-65—198	52875

PING Banner Health

Moon Valley, Phoenix, AZ   (6435–72)

1	Rachel Teske (Aus)*	70-69-71-71—281	$150000
2	Annika Sörenstam (Swe)*	67-70-68-76—281	91325
3	Akiko Fukushima (Jpn)	68-70-71-75—284	52916
	Cristie Kerr	70-69-70-75—284	52916
	Mi Hyun Kim (Kor)	75-70-67-72—284	52916

Welch's/Circle K Championship

Randolph Park, Tucson, AZ   (6222–72)

1	Laura Diaz	67-67-68-68—270	$120000
2	Juli Inkster	66-64-70-71—271	73060
3	Grace Park (Kor)	71-67-71-64—273	47000
	Kelly Robbins	71-67-68-67—273	47000

KRAFT NABISCO CHAMPIONSHIP

Mission Hills, Rancho Mirage, CA   (6460–72)

1	Annika Sörenstam (Swe)	70-71-71-68—280	$225000
2	Liselotte Neumann (Swe)	69-70-73-69—281	136987
3	Rosie Jones	72-69-72-69—282	88125
	Cristie Kerr	74-70-70-68—282	88125

Fuller details of this event are included in Part I The Majors page 111

The Office Depot Championship

El Caballero, Tarzana   (6394–72)

1	Se Ri Pak (Kor)	68-68-73—209	$150000
2	Annika Sörenstam (Swe)	71-68-71—210	91325
3	Laura Diaz	71-69-73—213	66250

Longs Drugs Challenge

Twelve Bridges GC, Lincoln, CA   (6388–72)

1	Cristie Kerr	66-72-67-75—280	$135000
2	Hee-Won Han (Kor)	74-70-67-70—281	82192
3	Heather Bowie	70-73-68-71—282	52875
	Jane Crafter (Aus)	69-71-70-72—282	52875

Chick-a-fil-A Charity Championship
Eagle's Landing, Stockbridge, GA   (6187–72)

1	Juli Inkster	66-66—132	$187500
2	Kelly Robbins	64-70—134	114156
3	Laura Diaz	66-69—135	82812

Aerus Electrolux USA Championship
The Legends Club, Franklin, TN   (6479–72)

1	Annika Sörenstam (Swe)	65-72-70-64—271	$120000
2	Pat Hurst	70-69-67-66—272	73060
3	Grace Park (Kor)	69-71-67-67—274	53000

Asahi Ryokuken International Championship
Mount Vintage, North Augusta, SC   (6455–72)

1	Janice Moodie (Sco)	70-66-67-70—273	$187500
2	Laura Davies (Eng)	67-71-69-73—280	114156
3	Rosie Jones	71-71-72-67—281	73437
	Annika Sörenstam (Swe)	72-70-67-72—281	73437

LPGA Corning Classic
Corning CC, NY   (6062–72)

1	Laura Diaz	66-69-69-70—274	$150000
2	Rosie Jones	69-69-67-71—276	91325
3	Silvia Cavalleri (Ita)	69-68-70-70—277	58750
	Marnie McGuire (NZ)	70-72-68-67—277	58750

Kellogg-Keebler Classic
Stonebridge, Aurora, IL   (6327–72)

1	Annika Sörenstam (Swe)	63-67-65—195	$180000
2	Danielle Ammaccapane	65-70-71—206	83529
	Mhairi McKay (Sco)	71-65-70—206	83529
	Michele Redman	64-74-68—206	83529

McDONALDS LPGA CHAMPIONSHIP
DuPont CC, Wilmington, DE   (6408–71)

1	Se Ri Pak (Kor)	71-70-68-70—279	$225000
2	Beth Daniel	67-70-68-77—282	136987
3	Annika Sörenstam (Swe)	70-76-73-65—284	99375

Fuller details of this event are included in Part I The Majors page 103

Evian Masters
Evian-les-Bains, France   (6091–72)

1	Annika Sörenstam (Swe)	68-67-65-69—269	$332243
2	Maria Hjörth (Swe)	71-68-70-64—273	187652
	Mi Hyun Kim (Kor)	66-70-68-69—273	187652

Wegmans Rochester International

Locust Hill, Pittsford, NY   (6200–72)

1	Karrie Webb (Aus)	64-72-72-68—276	$180000
2	Mi Hyun Kim (Kor)	69-67-67-74—277	109590
3	Se Ri Pak (Kor)	72-72-67-70—281	79500

ShopRite LPGA Classic

Bay Course, Marriott, Atlantic City, NJ   (6051–71)

1	Annika Sörenstam (Swe)	68-67-66—201	$180000
2	Kate Golden	64-69-71—204	83530
	Juli Inkster	65-67-72—204	83530
	Carin Koch (Swe)	71-66-67—204	83530

US WOMEN'S OPEN

Prairie Dunes, Hutchinson, KS   (6293–70)

1	Juli Inkster	67-72-71-66—276	$535000
2	Annika Sörenstam (Swe)	70-69-69-70—278	315000
3	Shani Waugh (Aus)	67-73-71-72—283	202568

Fuller details of this event are included in Part I The Majors page 95

Jamie Farr Kroger Classic

Highland Meadows, Sylvania, OH   (6365–71)

1	Rachel Teske (Aus)	67-73-64-66—270	$150000
2	Beth Bauer	69-67-67-69—272	91325
3	Laura Diaz	70-64-72-67—273	58750
	Karrie Webb (Aus)	72-65-66-70—273	58750

Giant Eagle LPGA Classic

Squaw's Creek, Vienna, OH   (6454–72)

1	Mi Hyun Kim (Kor)	65-68-69—202	$150000
2	Kelly Robbins	64-68-71—203	91325
3	Dorothy Delasin	69-69-67—205	58750
	Grace Park (Kor)	72-66-67—205	58750

Sybase Big Apple Classic

Wykagyl, New Rochelle, NY   (6161–71)

1	Gloria Park (Kor)*	71-67-63-69—270	$142500
2	Hee-Won Han (Kor)	70-67-66-67—270	86758
3	Annika Sörenstam (Swe)	71-66-64-70—271	62937

Wendy's Championship for Children

Tartan Fields, Dublin, OH   (6517–72)

1	Mi Hyun Kim (Kor)	68-67-73—208	$150000
2	Hee-Won Han (Kor)	73-66-70—209	91325
3	Danielle Ammaccapane	73-65-72—210	66250

WEETABIX WOMEN'S BRITISH OPEN

Ailsa Course, Turnberry, Scotland   (6407–72)

1	Karrie Webb (Aus)	66-71-70-66—273	$236383
2	Michelle Ellis (Aus)	69-70-68-68—275	129629
	Paula Marti (Esp)	69-68-69-69—275	126629

Fuller details of this event are included in Part I The Majors page 88

Bank of Montreal Canadian Women's Open

Summerlea, Vaudreuil-Dorian, Quebec   (6435–72)

1	Meg Mallon	71-71-69-73—284	$180000
2	Michelle Ellis (Aus)	69-71-73-74—287	83530
	Catriona Matthew (Sco)	70-70-70-77—287	83530
	Michele Redman	69-74-72-72—287	83530

First Union Betsy King Classic

Berkleigh, Kutztown, PA   (6197–72)

1	Se Ri Pak (Kor)	70-68-66-63—267	$180000
2	Angela Stanford	68-70-66-66—270	109590
3	Karrie Webb (Aus)	71-65-67-69—272	79500

State Farm Classic

Rail GC, Springfield, IL   (6403–72)

1	Patricia Meunier-Lebouc		
	(Fra)	64-67-72-67—270	$165000
2	Mi Hyun Kim (Kor)	67-68-68-69—272	86666
	Se Ri Pak (Kor)	70-69-68-65—272	86666

Williams Championship

Tulsa, OK   (6233–70)

1	Annika Sörenstam (Swe)	68-66-65—199	$150000
2	Lorie Kane (Can)	71-64-68—203	91325
3	Cristie Kerr	65-70-69—204	58750
	Joanne Mills (Aus)	69-68-67—204	58750

Safeway Classic

Columbia Edgewater, Portland, OR   (6318–72)

1	Annika Sörenstam (Swe)	69-62-68—199	$150000
2	Kate Golden	70-65-65—200	91325
3	Rosie Jones	67-69-68—204	58750
	Karen Stupples (Eng)	68-66-70—204	58750

The Solheim Cup *Interlachen CC, Madina, MN*

USA beat Europe 15½–12½

Full details of this event can be found on page 219

Samsung World Championship

Hiddenbrooke GC, Vallejo, CA

1	Annika Sörenstam (Swe)	66-67-68-65—266	$162000
2	Cristie Kerr	68-64-69-71—272	97000
3	Michele Redman	65-70-70-68—273	71000

Mobile LPGA Tournament of Champions

The Crossings, Semmes, AL

1	Se Ri Pak (Kor)	65-70-67-66—268	$122000
2	Carin Koch (Swe)	62-67-70-73—272	64875
	Catriona Matthew (Sco)	68-66-70-68—272	64875

Sports Today CJ Nine Bridges Classic

CJ Nine Bridges, Jeju Island, S Korea   (6306–72)

1	Se Ri Pak (Kor)	65-76-72—213	225000
2	Carin Koch (Swe)	70-76-73—219	139638
3	Lorie Kane (Can)	70-75-76—221	90576
	Mhairi McKay (Sco)	70-75-76—221	90576

Cisco World Ladies' Match Play Challenge

at Narita, Chiba, Japan

Semi-Finals
Grace Park (Kor) beat Carin Koch (Swe) 5 and 4
Midori Yoneyama (Jpn) beat Hee-Won Han (Kor) at 19th

Final
Grace Park beat Midori Yoneyama at 22nd

Winner: $153000; Runner-up: $96000

Mizuno Classic

Seta GC

1	Annika Sörenstam (Swe)	69-65-67—201	$169500
2	Grace Park (Kor)	66-69-68—203	105194
3	Se Ri Pak (Kor)	68-69-67—204	76763

Japan LPGA Tour

Players are of Japanese nationality unless stated

Results 2001

Daiohseishi Elleair Ladies Open	Elleair GC, Matsuyama	Ji-Hee Lee (Kor)	298 (-8)
JLPGA Tour Championship	Hibiscus GC, Miyazaki	Kaori Higo	275 (-13)

Final Ranking 2001

1	Yuri Fudoh	¥99,248,793	6	Aki Takamura	55,894,004
2	Kaori Higo	70,926,380	7	Miyuki Shimbakuro	55,069,918
3	Chieko Amanuma	69,867,902	8	Kaori Harada	51,692,852
4	Kasumi Fujii	58,661,828	9	Michie Ohba	51,346,162
5	Toshimi Kimura	56,922.288	10	Ji-Hee Lee (Kor)	48,308,650

Results 2002

Daikin Orchid Ladies	Ryukyu GC, Okinawa	Kasumi Fujii	208 (-8)
Promise Ladies	Tomisato GC	Mayumi Inoue	211 (-5)
Saishunkan Ladies	Kumamoto Airport CC	Ai-Yu Tu (Tai)	215 (-1)
Katokichi Queens	Yashima CC	Chieko Nishida	215 (-1)
Nichirei Cup World Ladies	Tokyo Yomiuri GC	Yuri Fudoh	271 (-17)
Vernal Ladies	Fukuoka Century CC	Mikino Kubo	213 (-3)
Chukyo TV/Bridgestone Open	Chukyo GC Ishino C	Shin Sora (Kor)	212 (-4)
Kosaido Ladies Golf Cup	Kosaido CC, Chiba	Orie Fujino	212 (-4)
Resort Trust Ladies	Grandy Naruto GC	Kozue Azuma	213 (-3)
We Love KOBE Suntory Ladies Open	Japan Memorial GC	Takayo Bandoh	280 (-8)
Apita Circle K Sunkus Ladies	U Gureen Nakatugawa GC	Mihoko Takahashi	209 (-7)
Belluna Ladies Cup	Obatagou GC	Orie Fujino	206 (-10)
Toyo Suisan Ladies Hokkaido	Sapporo Kitahiroshima Prince GC	Chihiro Nakajima	208 (-8)
Golf 5 Ladies	Mizunami CC, Gifu	Ikuyo Shiotani	206 (-10)
Vernal Open	Masters GC	Yuri Fudoh	210 (-6)
NEC Karuizawa 72	Karuizawa 72, Nagano	Akiko Fukushima	202 (-14)
New Caterpillar Mitsubishi Ladies	Dai Hakone CC	Kaori Higo	212 (-7)
Yonex Ladies	Yonex CC, Teradomari	Yuri Fudoh	201 (-15)
Fuji Sankei Ladies Classic	Fuji Sakura CC, Yamanash	Ok-Hee Ku (Kor)	206 (-7)
JLPGA Championship Konica Cup	Taiheiyo C Rokko C	Ok-Hee Ku (Kor)	283 (-5)
Munsingwear Tokai Classic	Ryosen GC, Mie	Kasumi Fujii	204 (-12)
Miyagi TV Cup Dunlop Open	Rainbow Hills GC, Tomiya	Mihoko Takahashi	211 (-5)
Japan Women's Open	Hakone CC	Woo-Soon Ko (Kor)	278 (-14)
Sankyo Ladies Open	Akagi CC	Toshimi Kimura	207 (-9)
Fujitsu Ladies	Tokyo 700 C, Chiba	Chihiro Nakajima	204 (-12)
Hisako Higuchi Classic	Taiheiyo C	Kasumi Fuji	209 (-7)

Japan LPGA Tour Results *continued*

Cisco World Ladies Matchplay	Narita GC	Grace Park (Kor)	
Mizuno Classic	Seta GC North C	Annika Sörenstam	
	Saitama	(Swe)	201 (-15)
Ito-En Ladies	Great Island C, Chiba	Laura Davies	(D)
Daio Paper Elleair Ladies Open	Ellair GC	Ji-Hee Lee (Kor)	(D)
Japan LPGA Championship	Hibiscus GC	Kaori Higo	(D)
(Ricoh Cup)			

Latest Ranking 2002 (after Mizuno Classic)

1	Yuri Fudoh	¥78,890,917	11	Kaori Higo	33,026,476
2	Kasumi Fujii	73,795,102	12	Ikuyo Shiotani	30,818,943
3	Toshimi Kumura	60,045,460	13	Kyoko Ono	29,782,602
4	Woo Soon Ko (Kor)	53,960,748	14	Chihiro Nakajima	29,074,802
5	Mikino Kubo	49,060,033	15	Hsiu-Feng Tseng	27,397,500
6	Orie Fujino	48,267,306	16	Tokayo Bandoh	26,818,121
7	Ok-Hee Ku (Kor)	44,315,344	17	Chieko Amanuma	24,422,844
8	Mihoko Takahashi	42,821,536	18	Mayumi Hirase	21,787,417
9	Yu Chen Huan (Chi)	38,403,236	19	Yun-Jue Wei	21,404,259
10	Midori Yonayama	37,864,917	20	Mikiyo Nishizuke	19,982,576

Three events had still to be played on the 2002 Japan LPGA circuit

---

Beverly Lewis to make PGA history in 2005

For the first time in 101 years, a lady professional is to be captain of the Professional Golfers' Association. Beverly Lewis from Essex will make history when she takes over the role from John Yeo in 2005 and 2006.

Beverly will be an ambassador for the Association and represent the membership at all the official functions and major golf events including The Open and The Masters. Her appointment is the latest in a series of achievements that have made her a role model for today's lady golfers.

She was a founder member of the Women's PGA in 1978, and later chaired that organisation between 1979 and 1981, and again in 1986. In 1982 she became one of the first lady professionals to acquire PGA membership.

During her eight-year tour career, Beverly scored two tournament wins before moving successfully into coaching and commentating with the BBC alongside Peter Alliss and with Channel Seven in Australia.

Beverly, a member at Thorndon Park for nearly 30 years, currently teaches at the Essex Golf Complex at Southend-on-Sea. She is one of the sport's most prolific authors with ten teaching books currently to her credit.

She has coached for the English Ladies' Golf Association and several county associations and lectured at European teaching conferences in Germany and Spain. She is also a qualified R&A referee.

'This is an unbelievable honour that brings enormous benefits to women's golf and I'm absolutely thrilled. There is no higher recognition in professional circles than being PGA Captain. It's an appointment I never ever considered would be within my grasp. I'm really looking forward to working alongside John Yeo for two years when he takes over from Dave Thomas in April and can't wait for 2005,' she said.

International Team Events

Solheim Cup

2002 *at Interlachen CC, Madina, MN*

Captains: Patty Sheehan (USA), Dale Reid (Sco) (Europe)

USA		Europe	
First Day – **Foursomes**			
Inkster & Diaz	0	Davies & Marti (2 holes)	1
Daniel & Ward (1 hole)	1	Carriedo & Tinning	0
Hurst & Robbins	0	Alfredsson & Pettersen (4 and 2)	1
Kuehne & Mallon	0	Koch & Sörenstam (3 and 2)	1
	1		3
Fourballs			
Jones & Kerr (1 hole)	1	Davies & Marti	0
Diaz & Klein (4 and 3)	1	Gustafson & Icher	0
Mallon & Redman (3 and 1)	1	Hjörth & Sörenstam	0
Inkster & Kuehne	0	Koch & McKay (3 and 2)	1
	3		1

Match Position: USA 4, Europe 4

Second Day – **Foursomes**			
Kerr & Redman	0	Koch & Sörenstam (4 and 3)	1
Klein & Ward (3 and 2)	1	McKay & Tinning	0
Inkster & Mallon (2 and 1)	1	Davies & Marti	0
Diaz & Robbins (3 and 1)	1	Alfredsson & Pettersen	0
	3		1
Fourballs			
Daniel & Ward	0	Koch & Sörenstam (4 and 3)	1
Hurst & Kuehne	0	Hjörth & Tinning (1 hole)	1
Jones & Kerr	0	Carriedo & Icher (1 hole)	1
Klein & Robbins	0	Davies & Gustafson (1 hole)	1
	0		4

Match Position: USA 7, Europe 9

Third Day – **Singles**			
Juli Inkster (4 and 3)	1	Raquel Carriedo (Esp)	0
Laura Diaz (5 and 3)	1	Paula Marti (Esp)	0
Emilee Klein (2 and 1)	1	Helen Alfredsson (Swe)	0
Kelli Kuehne	0	Iben Tinning (Den) (3 and 2)	1
Michele Redman (halved)	½	Suzann Pettersen (Nor) (halved)	½
Wendy Ward (halved)	½	Annika Sörenstam (Swe) (halved)	½
Kelly Robbins (5 and 3)	1	Maria Hjörth (Swe)	0
Cristie Kerr	0	Sophie Gustafson (Swe) (3 and 2)	1
Meg Mallon (3 and 2)	1	Laura Davies (Eng)	0
Pat Hurst (4 and 2)	1	Mhairi McKay (Sco)	0
Beth Daniel (halved)	½	Carin Koch (Swe) (halved)	½
Rosie Jones (3 and 2)	1	Karine Icher (Fra)	0
	8½		3½

Result: USA 15½, Europe 12½

Solheim Cup *continued*

1990 *at Lake Nona, FL*
Result: USA 11½, Europe 4½
Captains: Kathy Whitworth (USA),
 Mickey Walker (Europe)

First Day – Foursomes
Bradley & Lopez lost to Davies & Nicholas 2 and 1
Gerring & Mochrie beat Wright & Neumann 6 and 5
Sheehan & Jones beat Reid & Alfredsson 6 and 5
Daniel & King beat Johnson & de Lorenzi 5 and 4

Second Day – Fourball
Sheehan & Jones beat Johnson & de Lorenzi 2 and 1
Bradley & Lopez beat Reid & Alfredsson 2 and 1
King & Daniel beat Davies & Nicholas 4 and 3
Gerring & Mochrie lost to Neumann & Wright 4 and 2

Third Day – Singles
Cathy Gerring beat Helen Alfredsson 4 and 3
Rosie Jones lost to Laura Davies 3 and 2
Nancy Lopez beat Alison Nicholas 6 and 4
Betsy King halved with Pam Wright
Beth Daniel beat Liselotte Neumann 7 and 6
Patty Sheehan lost to Dale Reid 2 and 1
Dottie Mochrie beat Marie Laure de Lorenzi 4 and 2
Pat Bradley beat Trish Johnson 8 and 7

1992 *at Dalmahoy*
Result: Europe 11½, USA 6½
Captains: Mickey Walker (Europe),
 Kathy Whitworth (USA)

First Day – Foursomes
Davies & Nicholas beat King & Daniel 1 hole
Neumann & Alfredsson beat Bradley & Mochrie 2 and 1
Descampe & Johnson lost to Ammaccapane & Mallon
 1 hole
Reid & Wright halved with Sheehan & Inkster

Second Day – Fourball
Davies & Nicholas beat Sheehan & Inkster 1 hole
Johnson & Descampe halved with Burton & Richard
Wright & Reid lost to Mallon & King 1 hole
Alfredsson & Neumann halved with Bradley & Mochrie

Third Day – Singles
Laura Davies beat Brandie Burton 4 and 2
Helen Alfredsson beat Danielle Ammaccapane 4 and 3
Trish Johnson beat Patty Sheehan 2 and 1
Alison Nicholas lost to Juli Inkster 3 and 2
Florence Descampe lost to Beth Daniel 2 and 1
Pam Wright beat Pat Bradley 4 and 3
Catrin Nilsmark beat Meg Mallon 3 and 2
Kitrina Douglas lost to Deb Richard 7 and 6
Liselotte Neumann beat Betsy King 2 and 1
Dale Reid beat Dottie Pepper Mochrie 3 and 2

1994 *at the Greenbrier, WA*
Result: USA 13, Europe 7
Captains: JoAnne Carner (USA),
 Mickey Walker (Europe)

First Day – Foursomes
Burton & Mochrie beat 3 and 2
Daniel & Mallon lost to Nilsmark & Sörenstam 1 hole
Green & Robbins lost to Fairclough & Reid 2 and 1
Andrews & King lost to Davies & Nicholas 2 and 1
Sheehan & Steinhauer beat Johnson & Wright 2 holes

Second Day – Fourball
Burton & Mochrie beat Davies & Nicholas 2 and 1
Daniel & Mallon beat Nilsmark & Sörenstam 6 and 5

Green & Robbins lost to Fairclough & Reid 4 and 3
Andrews & King beat Johnson & Wright 3 and 2
Sheehan & Steinhauer lost to Alfredsson & Neumann
 1 hole

Third Day – Singles
Betsy King lost to Helen Alfredsson 2 and 1
Dottie Pepper Mochrie beat Catrin Nilsmark 6 and 5
Beth Daniel beat Trish Johnson 1 hole
Kelly Robbins beat Lora Fairclough 4 and 2
Meg Mallon beat Pam Wright 1 hole
Patty Sheehan lost to Alison Nicholas 3 and 2
Brandie Burton beat Laura Davies 1 hole
Tammie Green beat Annika Sörenstam 3 and 2
Sherri Steinhauer beat Dale Reid 2 holes
Donna Andrews beat Liselotte Neumann 3 and 2

1996 *at St Pierre, Chepstow*
Result: USA 17, Europe 11
Captains: (USA), Mickey Walker (Europe)

First Day – Foursomes
Sörenstam & Nilsmark halved with Robbins & McGann
Davies & Nicholas lost to Sheehan & Jones 1 hole
de Lorenzi & Reid lost to Daniell & Skinner 1 hole
Alfredsson & Neumann lost to Pepper & Burton 2 and 1

Fourball
Davies & Johnson beat Robbins & Bradley 6 and 5
Sörenstam & Marshall beat Skinner & Geddes 1 hole
Neumann & Nilsmark lost to Pepper & King 1 hole
Alfredsson & Nicholas halved with Mallon & Daniel

Second Day – Foursomes
Davies & Johnson beat Daniel & Skinner 4 and 3
Sörenstam & Nilsmark beat Pepper & Burton 1 hole
Neumann & Marshall halved with Mallon & Geddes
de Lorenzi & Alfredsson beat Robbins & McGann 4 and 3

Fourball
Davies & Hackney beat Daniel & Skinner 6 and 5
Sörenstam & Johnson halved with McGann & Mallon
de Lorenzi & Morley lost to Robbins & King 2 and 1
Nilsmark & Neumann beat Sheehan & Geddes 2 and 1

Third Day – Singles
Annika Sörenstam beat Pat Bradley 2 and 1
Kathryn Marshall lost to Val Skinner 2 and 1
Laura Davies lost to Michelle McGann 3 and 2
Liselotte Neumann halved with Beth Daniel
Lisa Hackney lost to Brandie Burton 1 hole
Trish Johnson lost to Dottie Pepper 3 and 2
Alison Nicholas halved with Kelly Robbins
Marie Laure de Lorenzi lost to Betsy King 6 and 4
Joanne Morley lost to Rosie Jones 5 and 4
Dale Reid lost to Jane Geddes 2 holes
Catrin Nilsmark lost to Patty Sheehan 2 and 1
Helen Alfredsson lost to Meg Mallon 4 and 2

1998 *at Muirfield Village, Dublin, OH*
Result: USA 16, Europe 12
Captains: Judy Rankin (USA),
 Pia Nilsson (Europe)

First Day – Foursomes
Pepper & Inkster beat Davies & Johnson 3 and 1
Mallon & Burton beat Alfredsson & Nicholas 3 and 1
Robbins & Hurst beat Hackney & Neumann 1 hole
A Sörenstam & Matthew beat Andrews & Green 3 and 2

Fourball
King & Johnson halved with Davies & C Sörenstam
Hurst & Jones beat Hackney & Gustafson 7 and 5
Robbins & Steinhauer lost to Alfredsson & de Lorenzi
   2 and 1
Pepper & Burton beat A Sörenstam & Nilsmark 2 holes

Second Day – Foursomes
Andrews & Steinhauer beat A Sörenstam & Matthew
   3 and 2
Mallon & Burton lost to Davies & C Sörenstam 3 and 2
Pepper & Inkster beat Alfredsson & de Lorenzi 1 hole
Robbins & Hurst beat Neumann & Nilsmark 1 hole

Fourball
King & Jones lost to A Sörenstam & Nilsmark 5 and 3
Johnson & Green lost to Davies & Hackney 2 holes
Andrews & Steinhauer beat Alfredsson & de Lorenzi
   4 and 3
Mallon & Inkster beat Neumann & C Sörenstam 2 and 1

Third Day – Singles
Pat Hurst lost to Laura Davies 1 hole
Juli Inkster lost to Helen Alfredsson 2 and 1
Donna Andrews lost to Annika Sörenstam 2 and 1
Brandie Burton lost to Liselotte Neumann 1 hole
Dottie Pepper beat Trish Johnson 3 and 2
Kelly Robbins beat Charlotta Sörenstam 2 and 1
Chris Johnson lost to Marie Laure de Lorenzi 1 hole
Rosie Jones beat Catrin Nilsmark 6 and 4
Tammie Green beat Alison Nicholas 1 hole
Sherri Steinhauer beat Catriona Matthew 3 and 2
Betsy King lost to Lisa Hackney 6 and 5
Meg Mallon halved with Sophie Gustafson

2000 *at Loch Lomond*
Result: Europe 14½, USA 11½
Captains: Dale Reid (Europe), Pat Bradley (USA)
First Day – Foursomes
Davies & Nicholas beat Pepper & Inkster 4 and 3
Johnson & Gustafson beat Robbins & Hurst 3 and 2
Nilsmark & Koch beat Burton & Iverson 2 and 1
Sörenstam & Moodie beat Mallon & Daniel 1 hole

Foursomes
Davies & Nicholas lost to Iverson & Jones 6 and 5
Johnson & Gustafson halved with Inkster & Steinhauer
Neumann & Alfredsson lost to Robbins & Hurst 2 holes
Moodie & Sörenstam beat Mallon & Daniel 1 hole

Second Day – **Fourball**
Nilsmark & Koch beat Scranton & Redman 2 and 1
Neumann & Meunier Labouc halved with Pepper & Burton
Davies & Carriedo halved with Mallon & Daniel
Sörenstam & Moodie lost to Hurst & Robbins 2 and 1
Johnson & Gustafson beat Jones & Iverson 3 and 2
Nicholas & Alfredsson beat Inkster & Steinhauer
   3 and 2

Third Day – Singles
Annika Sörenstam lost to Juli Inkster 5 and 4
Sophie Gustafson lost to Brandie Burton 4 and 3
Helen Alfredsson beat Beth Daniel 4 and 3
Trish Johnson lost to Dottie Pepper 2 and 1
Laura Davies lost to Kelly Robbins 3 and 2
Liselotte Neumann halved with Pat Hurst
Alison Nicholas halved with Sherri Steinhauer
Patricia Meunier Labouc lost to Meg Mallon 1 hole
Catrin Nilsmark beat Rosie Jones 1 hole
Raquel Carriedo lost to Becky Iverson 3 and 2
Carin Koch beat Michele Redman 2 and 1
Janice Moodie beat Nancy Scranton 1 hole

Solheim Cup – Individual Records

Brackets indicate non-playing captain

Europe

Name		Year	Played	Won	Lost	Halved
Helen Alfredsson	Swe	1990-92-94-96-98-2000-02	24	10	12	2
Raquel Carriedo	Esp	2000-02	5	1	3	1
Laura Davies	Eng	1990-92-94-96-98-2000-02	28	15	11	2
Florence Descampe	Bel	1992	3	0	2	1
Kitrina Douglas	Eng	1992	1	0	1	0
Lora Fairclough	Eng	1994	3	2	1	0
Sophie Gustafson	Swe	1998-2000-02	9	4	3	2
Lisa Hackney	Eng	1996-98	6	3	3	0
Maria Hjörth	Swe	2000	3	1	2	0
Karine Icher	Fra	2002	3	1	2	0
Trish Johnson	Eng	1990-92-94-96-98-2000	19	5	11	3
Carin Koch	Swe	2000-02	8	7	0	1
Marie Laure de Lorenzi	Fra	1990-96-98	11	3	8	0
Mhairi McKay	Sco	2002	3	1	2	0
Kathryn Marshall	Sco	1996	3	1	1	0
Paula Marti	Esp	2002	4	1	3	0
Catriona Matthew	Sco	1998	3	1	2	0
Patricia Meunier Lebouc	Fra	2000	2	0	1	1
Janice Moodie	Sco	2000	4	3	1	0
Joanne Morley	Eng	1996	2	0	2	0
Liselotte Neumann	Swe	1990-92-94-96-98-2000	21	6	10	5
Alison Nicholas	Eng	1990-92-94-96-98-2000	18	7	8	3
Catrin Nilsmark	Swe	1992-94-96-98-2000	16	8	7	1

Solheim Cup *continued*

Name		Year	Played	Won	Lost	Halved
Pia Nilsson	Swe	(1998)	0	0	0	0
Suzann Pettersen	Nor	2002	3	1	1	1
Dale Reid	Sco	1990-92-94-96-(**2000-02**)	11	4	6	1
Annika Sörenstam	Swe	1994-96-98-2000-02	22	12	7	3
Charlotta Sörenstam	Swe	1998	4	1	2	1
Iben Tinning	Den	2002	4	2	2	0
Mickey Walker	Eng	(1990)-(92)-(94)-(96)	0	0	0	0
Pam Wright	Sco	1990-92-94	6	1	4	1

United States

Name	Year	Played	Won	Lost	Halved
Danielle Ammaccapane	1992	2	1	1	0
Donna Andrews	1994-98	7	4	3	0
Pat Bradley	1990-92-96-(**2000**)	8	2	5	1
Brandie Burton	1992-94-96-98-2000	14	8	4	2
Jo Anne Carner	(1994)	0	0	0	0
Beth Daniel	1990-92-94-96-2000-02	19	8	7	4
Laura Diaz	2002	4	3	1	0
Jane Geddes	1996	4	1	2	1
Cathy Gerring	1990	3	2	1	0
Tammie Green	1994-98	6	2	4	0
Pat Hurst	1998-2000-02	11	6	4	1
Juli Inkster	1992-98-2000-02	15	7	6	2
Becky Iverson	2000	4	2	2	0
Chris Johnson	1998	3	0	2	1
Rosie Jones	1990-96-98-2000-02	15	9	6	0
Cristie Kerr	2002	4	1	3	0
Betsy King	1990-92-94-96-98	15	7	6	2
Emilee Klein	2002	4	3	1	0
Kelli Kuehne	2002	4	0	4	0
Nancy Lopez	1990	3	2	1	0
Michelle McGann	1996	4	1	1	2
Meg Mallon	1992-94-96-98-2000-02	22	11	6	5
Alice Miller	(1992)*	0	0	0	0
Dottie Pepper	1990-92-94-96-98-2000	20	13	5	2
Judy Rankin	(1996)-(98)	0	0	0	0
Michele Redman	2000-02	5	1	3	1
Deb Richard	1992	2	1	0	1
Kelly Robbins	1994-96-98-2000-02	20	10	8	2
Nancy Scranton	2000	2	0	2	0
Patty Sheehan	1990-92-94-96-(**2002**)	13	5	7	1
Val Skinner	1996	4	2	2	0
Sherri Steinhauer	1994-98-2000	10	5	1	2
Wendy Ward	2002	4	2	1	1
Kathy Whitworth	(1990)-(92)*	0	0	0	0

Professional Women's Overseas Championships

Australian Ladies Masters

1998	K Webb	2001	K Webb
1999	K Webb	2002	A Sörenstam
2000	K Webb		

AAMI Australian Women's Open

1995	L Neumann	1999	*Not played*
1996	C Matthew	2000	K Webb
1997	J Crafter	2001	S Gustafson
1998	M McGuire	2002	K Webb

French Ladies Open

1992	*Not played*	1998	*Not played*
1993	*Not played*	1999	T Johnson
1994	J Forbes	2000	P Meunier-Lebouc
1995	L Kreutz	2001	S Pettersen
1996	L Rolner	2002	L Brooky
1997	K Lunn		

Italian Ladies Open

1992	L Davies	1998	*Not played*
1993	A Arruti	1999	S Head
1994	C Dibnah	2000	S Gustafson
1995	D Booker	2001	P Marti
1996	L Davies	2002	I Tinning
1997	V Van Ryckegham		

Other 2002 Overseas Championships

Canadian Open	M Mallon
Japanese Open	M Murai
Norwegian Masters	L Davies
South African Ladies Masters	S Head
Spanish Open	K Icher

British Golf Museum
St Andrews

Willie and Laurie Auchterlonie in their workshop

Bruce Embankment, St. Andrews, Fife KY16 9AB
Phone 01334 460046 • Fax 01334 460064
Website www.britishgolfmuseum.co.uk

Opening Times:
Summer: Easter to Mid-October 9.30am–5.30pm • Open 7 days
Winter: 11am–3pm • Closed Tuesday and Wednesday

PART IV

Men's Amateur Tournaments

National and International Championships

Amateur Championship (inaugurated 1885)

Year	Winner	Runner-up	Venue	By	Ent
1885	A MacFie	H Hutchinson	Hoylake, Royal Liverpool	7 and 6	44
1886	H Hutchinson	H Lamb	St Andrews	7 and 6	42
1887	H Hutchinson	J Ball	Hoylake, Royal Liverpool	1 hole	33
1888	J Ball	J Laidlay	Prestwick	5 and 4	38
1889	J Laidlay	L Melville	St Andrews	2 and 1	40
1890	J Ball	J Laidlay	Hoylake, Royal Liverpool	4 and 3	44
1891	J Laidlay	H Hilton	St Andrews	20th hole	50
1892	J Ball	H Hilton	Sandwich, Royal St George's	3 and 1	45
1893	P Anderson	J Laidlay	Prestwick	1 hole	44
1894	J Ball	S Fergusson	Hoylake, Royal Liverpool	1 hole	64
1895	L Melville	J Ball	St Andrews	19th hole	68
From 1896 36 holes played					
1896	F Tait	H Hilton	Sandwich, Royal St George's	8 and 7	64
1897	A Allan	J Robb	Muirfield	4 and 2	74
1898	F Tait	S Fergusson	Hoylake, Royal Liverpool	7 and 5	77
1899	J Ball	F Tait	Prestwick	37th hole	101
1900	H Hilton	J Robb	Sandwich, Royal St George's	8 and 7	68
1901	H Hilton	J Low	St Andrews	1 hole	116
1902	C Hutchings	S Fry	Hoylake, Royal Liverpool	1 hole	114
1903	R Maxwell	H Hutchinson	Muirfield	7 and 5	142
1904	W Travis (USA)	E Blackwell	Sandwich, Royal St George's	4 and 3	104
1905	A Barry	Hon O Scott	Prestwick	3 and 2	148
1906	J Robb	C Lingen	Hoylake, Royal Liverpool	4 and 3	166
1907	J Ball	C Palmer	St Andrews	6 and 4	200
1908	E Lassen	H Taylor	Sandwich, Royal St George's	7 and 6	197
1909	R Maxwell	Capt C Hutchison	Muirfield	1 hole	170
1910	J Ball	C Aylmer	Hoylake, Royal Liverpool	10 and 9	160
1911	H Hilton	E Lassen	Prestwick	4 and 3	146
1912	J Ball	A Mitchell	Westward Ho!, Royal North Devon	38th hole	134
1913	H Hilton	R Harris	St Andrews	6 and 5	198
1914	J Jenkins	C Hezlet	Sandwich, Royal St George's	3 and 2	232
1915–19 No Championship owing to the Great War					
1920	C Tolley	R Gardner (USA)	Muirfield	37th hole	165
1921	W Hunter	A Graham	Hoylake, Royal Liverpool	12 and 11	223
1922	E Holderness	J Caven	Prestwick	1 hole	252
1923	R Wethered	R Harris	Deal, Royal Cinque Ports	7 and 6	209
1924	E Holderness	E Storey	St Andrews	3 and 2	201
1925	R Harris	K Fradgley	Westward Ho!, Royal North Devon	13 and 12	151
1926	J Sweetser (USA)	A Simpson	Muirfield	6 and 5	216
1927	Dr W Tweddell	D Landale	Hoylake, Royal Liverpool	7 and 6	197
1928	T Perkins	R Wethered	Prestwick	6 and 4	220
1929	C Tolley	J Smith	Sandwich, Royal St George's	4 and 3	253
1930	R Jones (USA)	R Wethered	St Andrews	7 and 6	271
1931	E Smith	J De Forest	Westward Ho!, Royal North Devon	1 hole	171
1932	J De Forest	E Fiddian	Muirfield	3 and 1	235
1933	Hon M Scott	T Bourn	Hoylake, Royal Liverpool	4 and 3	269
1934	W Lawson Little (USA)	J Wallace	Prestwick	14 and 13	225
1935	W Lawson Little (USA)	Dr W Tweddell	R Lytham and St Annes	1 hole	232
1936	H Thomson	J Ferrier (Aus)	St Andrews	2 holes	283
1937	R Sweeney jr (USA)	L Munn	Sandwich, Royal St George's	3 and 2	223
1938	C Yates (USA)	R Ewing	Troon	3 and 2	241
1939	A Kyle	A Duncan	Hoylake, Royal Liverpool	2 and 1	167
1940–45 Suspended during Second World War					
1946	J Bruen	R Sweeny (USA)	Birkdale	4 and 3	263
1947	W Turnesa (USA)	R Chapman (USA)	Carnoustie	3 and 2	200
1948	F Stranahan (USA)	C Stowe	Sandwich, Royal St George's	5 and 4	168
1949	S McCready	W Turnesa (USA)	Portmarnock	2 and 1	204

Year	Winner	Runner-up	Venue	By	Ent
1950	F Stranahan (USA)	R Chapman (USA)	St Andrews	8 and 6	324
1951	R Chapman (USA)	C Coe (USA)	Royal Porthcawl	5 and 4	192
1952	E Ward (USA)	F Stranahan (USA)	Prestwick	6 and 5	286
1953	J Carr	E Harvie Ward (USA)	Hoylake, Royal Liverpool	2 holes	279
1954	D Bachli (Aus)	W Campbell (USA)	Muirfield	2 and 1	286
1955	J Conrad (USA)	A Slater	Royal Lytham and St Annes	3 and 2	240
1956	J Beharrell	L Taylor	Troon	5 and 4	200
1957	R Reid Jack	H Ridgley (USA)	Formby	2 and 1	200
In 1956 and 1957 the Quarter Finals, Semi-Finals and Final were played over 36 holes					
1958	J Carr	A Thirlwell	St Andrews	3 and 2	488
In 1958, Semi-Finals and Final only were played over 36 holes					
1959	D Beman (USA)	W Hyndman (USA)	Sandwich, Royal St George's	3 and 2	362
1960	J Carr	R Cochran (USA)	Royal Portrush	8 and 7	183
1961	MF Bonallack	J Walker	Turnberry	6 and 4	250
1962	R Davies (USA)	J Povall	Hoylake, Royal Liverpool	1 hole	256
1963	M Lunt	J Blackwell	St Andrews	2 and 1	256
1964	G Clark	M Lunt	Ganton	39th hole	220
1965	MF Bonallack	C Clark	Royal Porthcawl	2 and 1	176
1966	R Cole (RSA)	R Shade	Carnoustie (18 holes)	3 and 2	206
1967	R Dickson (USA)	R Cerrudo (USA)	Formby	2 and 1	
1968	MF Bonallack	J Carr	Royal Troon	7 and 6	249
1969	MF Bonallack	W Hyndman (USA)	Hoylake, Royal Liverpool	3 and 2	245
1970	MF Bonallack	W Hyndman (USA)	Newcastle, Royal Co Down	8 and 7	256
1971	S Melnyk (USA)	J Simons (USA)	Carnoustie	3 and 2	256
1972	T Homer	A Thirlwell	Sandwich, Royal St George's	4 and 3	253
1973	R Siderowf (USA)	P Moody	Royal Porthcawl	5 and 3	222
1974	T Homer	J Gabrielsen (USA)	Muirfield	2 holes	330
1975	M Giles (USA)	M James	Hoylake, Royal Liverpool	8 and 7	206
1976	R Siderowf (USA)	J Davies	St Andrews	37th hole	289
1977	P McEvoy	H Campbell	Ganton	5 and 4	235
1978	P McEvoy	P McKellar	Royal Troon	4 and 3	353
1979	J Sigel (USA)	S Hoch (USA)	Hillside	3 and 2	285
1980	D Evans	D Suddards (RSA)	Royal Porthcawl	4 and 3	265
1981	P Ploujoux (Fra)	J Hirsch (USA)	St Andrews	4 and 2	256
1982	M Thompson	A Stubbs	Deal, Royal Cinque Ports	4 and 3	245
Qualifying round introduced					
1983	P Parkin	J Holtgrieve (USA)	Turnberry	5 and 4	288
1984	JM Olazábal (Esp)	C Montgomerie	Formby	5 and 4	291
1985	G McGimpsey	G Homewood	Royal Dornoch	8 and 7	457
1986	D Curry	G Birtwell	Royal Lytham and St Annes	11 and 9	427
1987	P Mayo	P McEvoy	Prestwick	3 and 1	373
1988	C Hardin (Swe)	B Fouchee (RSA)	Royal Porthcawl	1 hole	391
1989	S Dodd	C Cassells	Royal Birkdale	5 and 3	378
1990	R Muntz (Ned)	A Macara	Muirfield	7 and 6	510
1991	G Wolstenholme	B May (USA)	Ganton	8 and 6	345
1992	S Dundas	B Dredge	Carnoustie	7 and 6	364
1993	I Pyman	P Page	Royal Portrush	37th hole	279
1994	L James	G Sherry	Nairn	2 and 1	288
1995	G Sherry	M Reynard	Hoylake, Royal Liverpool	7 and 6	288
1996	W Bladon	R Beames	Turnberry	1 hole	288
1997	C Watson	T Immelman (RSA)	Royal St Georges, Royal Cinque Ports	3 and 2	369
1998	S García (Esp)	C Williams	Muirfield	7 and 6	537
1999	G Storm	A Wainwright	Royal County Down, Kilkeel	7 and 6	433
2000	M Ilonen	C Reimbold	Royal Liverpool and Wallasey	2 and 1	376
2001	M Hoey	I Campbell	Prestwick & Kilmarnock	1 hole	288

107th Amateur Championship *at Royal Porthcawl and Pyle & Kenfig*

286 entrants from 24 countries played in the 36-hole qualifying competition, 65 of whom qualified on 149 or better for the match play stage.

Leading Qualifier: Richard Finch (Hull) 76 + 61 [course record] = 137

First Round
Kevin McAlpine (Alyth) beat Ville Karhu (Fin) 2 and 1

Second Round
Mike Plate (USA) beat Richard Finch (Hull) 1 hole
Muhammad-Yasin Ali (Ealing) beat Mikko Korhonen (Fin) 3 and 1

Second Round *continued*
Andrew Buckle (Aus) beat Darren Henley (Stoneham) 5 and 4
Gareth Wright (West Linton) beat Kevin Freeman (Stoke Park) 1 hole
Graham Gordon (Newmachar) beat Joe Ferguson (Cleobury Mortimer) 4 and 3

Amateur Championship *continued*

Second Round *continued*

Christian Schunck beat Farren Keenan (Royal Mid-Surrey) 1 hole

Alex Smith (Pyle & Kenfig) beat Matthew Walkington (NZ) 5 and 3

Toni Karjalainen (Fin) beat Fraser Kelley (Ganton) 3 and 2

Nigel Edwards (Whitchurch) beat Craig Elliot (Ratho Park) at 19th

David Price (Vale of Glamorgan) beat Matthew Peel (Pyle & Kenfig) 2 holes

Erik Stenman (Fin) beat Paul Spargo (Aus) 3 and 2

Neil MacRae (Cawder) beat Darryl Berry (West Bradford) 3 and 2

Gregory Bourdy (Fra) beat David Skinns (Lincoln) 3 and 1

Albert Kruger (RSA) beat Christian Reimbold (Ger) 1 hole

Lee Corfield (Burnham & Berrow) beat Paul Bradshaw (Gainsborough) at 20th

Martin Sell (Wrag Barn) beat Jamie Moul (Stoke by Nayland) 1 hole

Thomas Sundstrom (Fin) beat Robert Funk (USA) 2 and 1

Roux Burger (RSA) beat Janne Mommo (Fin) 1 hole

Neil Mitchell (Murcar) beat Edoardo Molinari (Ita) 3 and 2

Stuart Wilson (Forfar) beat James Heath (Coombe Wood) 2 and 1

Richard Walker (Frodsham) beat Barry Hume (Haggs Castle) 1 hole

Jamie Elson (Kenilworth) beat Michael McGeady (City of Derry) 2 holes

Tim Rice (Limerick) beat Craig Watson (East Renfrewshire) 3 and 2

Graeme Clark (Doncaster) beat Pablo Martin (Esp) 2 holes

Kieran Staunton (Woodcote Park) beat Padraig Dooley (Cork) at 19th

Gary Wolstenholme (Kilworth Springs) beat Craig Shave (Cosby) 5 and 4

Charl Schwartzel (RSA) beat Sean Mason (Teignmouth) 4 and 2

Zane Scotland (Walton Heath) beat Marc Warren (East Kilbride) 4 and 3

Jack Doherty (Vale of Glamorgan) beat Steve Lewton (Woburn) 3 and 1

Second Round *continued*

Jamie Farnsworth (Coxmoor) beat Daniel Wardrop (Didsbury) 2 and 1

Richard Brookman (Creigiau) beat Inder Van Weerelt (Ned) 3 and 1

Alejandro Larrazábal (Esp) beat Kevin McAlpine (Alyth) 5 and 3

Third Round

Yasin Ali beat Plate 3 and 1

Buckle beat Wright at 19th

Gordon beat Schunk 3 and 1

Karjalainen beat Smith 2 holes

Price beat Edwards 3 and 2

MacRae beat Stenman 5 and 4

Bourdy beat Kruger 3 and 2

Sell beat Corfield 4 and 3

Sundstrom beat Burger 4 and 3

Wilson beat Mitchell 2 and 1

Elson beat Walker 2 and 1

Rice beat Clark 1 hole

Wolstenholme beat Staunton 3 and 2

Scotland beat Schwartzel 2 and 1

Doherty beat Farnsworth 3 and 2

Larrazábal beat Brookman 4 and 2

Fourth Round

Buckle beat Yasin Ali 4 and 3

Gordon beat Karjalainen 3 and 1

Price beat MacRae 3 and 2

Sell beat Bourdy 3 and 2

Sundstrom beat Wilson 4 and 3

Elson beat Rice 3 and 2

Scotland beat Wolstenholme 2 and 1

Larrazábal beat Doherty 4 and 3

Quarter Finals

Gordon beat Buckle 3 and 2

Sell beat Price 7 and 6

Elson beat Sundstrom 3 and 2

Larrazábal beat Scotland at 20th

Semi-Finals

Sell beat Gordon 1 hole

Larrazábal beat Elson at 19th

Final

Alejandro Larrazábal (Esp) beat Martin Sell (Wrag Barn) 1 hole

---

British Seniors' Open Amateur Championship (inaugurated 1969)

1969	R Pattinson	Formby	154	1977	Dr TE Donaldson	Panmure	228
1970	K Bamber	Prestwick	150	1978	RJ White	Formby	225
1971	GH Pickard	Royal Cinque Ports;		1979	RJ White	Harlech, R St David's	226
		Royal St George's	150	1980	JM Cannon	Prestwick St Nicholas	218
1972	TC Hartley	St Andrews	147	1981	T Branton	Hoylake, R Liverpool	227
1973	JT Jones	Longniddry	142	1982	RL Glading	Blairgowrie	218
1974	MA Ivor-Jones	Moortown	149	1983	AJ Swann (USA)	Walton Heath	222
1975	HJ Roberts	Turnberry	138	1984	JC Owens (USA)	Western Gailes	222
1976	WM Crichton	Berkshire	149	1985	D Morey (USA)	Hesketh	223

1986	AN Sturrock	Panmure	229		1995	G Steel	Hankley Common	218
1987	B Soyars (USA)	Royal Cinque Ports	226		1996	J Hirsch	Blairgowrie	210
1988	CW Green	Royal Burgess	221		1997	G Bradley (USA)	Sherwood Forest	216
1989	CW Green	Moortown, Alwoodley	226		1998	D Lane	Western Gailes/	
1990	CW Green	The Berkshire	207				Glasgow Gailes	221
1991	CW Green	Prestwick	219		1999	W Shean (USA)	Frilford Heath	219
1992	C Hartland	Purdis Heath	221		2000	J Hirsch (USA)	Gullane	218
1993	CW Green	Royal Aberdeen	150		2001	K Richardson		
1994	CW Green	Formby,				(USA)	Royal Portrush	217
		Southport & Ainsdale	223					

2002 *at Woodhall Spa*

1	John Baldwin (USA)	76-70-70—216
2	Earl Stewart (USA)	70-72-75—217
3	Roy Smethurst (Crewe)	70-74-74—218

British Mid-Amateur Championship (inaugurated 1995)

1995	GP Wolstenholme	S Vale	Sunningdale
1996	GP Wolstenholme	G Steel	Hillside, Lancs
1997	S Philipson	G Thomson	Prestwick
1998	GP Wolstenholme	S Twynholm	Ganton
1999	J Kemp	S East	Walton Heath
2000	A Farmer	J Kemp	Royal Troon
2001	S East	J McGroarty	Royal Troon

2002 *at Formby*

Quarter Finals

Jamie Donaldson (West Sussex) beat Richard Finch (Hull) 4 and 3

John Williams (Prestatyn) beat Andrew Inglis (Sunningdale Artisans) 1 hole

John Kemp (John O'Gaunt) beat Dennis Reiland (USA) at 20th

Barry Scott (Dumfries & Galloway) beat Gordon Forster (John O'Gaunt) 1 hole

Semi-Finals

Williams beat Donaldson 1 hole

Kemp beat Scott 5 and 4

Final

John Kemp beat John Williams 2 and 1

English Amateur Championship (inaugurated 1925)

1925	TF Ellison	S Robinson	Royal Liverpool	1 hole
1926	TF Ellison	Sq Ldr CH Hayward	Walton Heath	6 and 4
1927	TP Perkins	JB Beddard	Little Aston	2 and 1
1928	JA Stout	TP Perkins	R Lytham and St Annes	3 and 2
1929	W Sutton	EB Tipping	Northumberland	3 and 2
1930	TA Bourn	CE Hardman	Burnham & Berrow	3 and 2
1931	LG Crawley	W Sutton	Hunstanton	1 hole
1932	EW Fiddian	AS Bradshaw	Royal St George's	1 hole
1933	J Woollam	TA Bourn	Ganton	4 and 3
1934	S Lunt	LG Crawley	Formby	37th hole
1935	J Woollam	EW Fiddian	Hollinwell	2 and 1
1936	HG Bentley	JDA Langley	Royal Cinque Ports	5 and 4
1937	JJ Pennink	LG Crawley	Saunton	6 and 5
1938	JJ Pennink	SE Banks	Moortown	2 and 1
1939	AL Bentley	W Sutton	Royal Birkdale	5 and 4
1946	IR Patey	K Thom	Mid-Surrey	5 and 4
1947	GH Micklem	C Stow	Ganton	1 hole
1948	AGB Helm	HJR Roberts	Little Aston	2 and 1
1949	RJ White	C Stowe	Formby	5 and 4
1950	JDA Langley	IR Patey	Royal Cinque Ports	1 hole
1951	GP Roberts	H Bennett	Hunstanton	39th hole
1952	E Millward	TJ Shorrock	Burnham and Berrow	2 holes
1953	GH Micklem	RJ White	Royal Birkdale	2 and 1
1954	A Thirlwell	HG Bentley	Royal St George's	2 and 1
1955	A Thirlwell	M Burgess	Ganton	7 and 6
1956	GB Wolstenholme	H Bennett	R Lytham and St Annes	1 hole
1957	A Walker	G Whitehead	Royal Liverpool	4 and 3
1958	DN Sewell	DA Procter	Walton Heath	8 and 7

English Amateur Championship *continued*

1959	GB Wolstenholme	MF Bonallack	Formby	1 hole
1960	DN Sewell	MJ Christmas	Hunstanton	41st hole
1961	I Caldwell	GJ Clark	Wentworth	37th hole
1962	MF Bonallack	MSR Lunt	Moortown	2 and 1
1963	MF Bonallack	A Thirlwell	Burnham and Berrow	4 and 3
1964	Dr D Marsh	R Foster	Hollinwell	1 hole
1965	MF Bonallack	CA Clark	The Berkshire	3 and 2
1966	MSR Lunt	DJ Millensted	R Lytham and St Annes	3 and 2
1967	MF Bonallack	GE Hyde	Woodhall Spa	4 and 2
1968	MF Bonallack	PD Kelley	Ganton	12 and 11
1969	JH Cook	P Dawson	Royal St George's	6 and 4
1970	Dr D Marsh	SG Birtwell	R Birkdale	6 and 4
1971	W Humphreys	JC Davies	Burnham and Berrow	9 and 8
1972	H Ashby	R Revell	Northumberland	5 and 4
1973	H Ashby	SC Mason	Formby	5 and 4
1974	M James	JA Watts	Woodhall Spa	6 and 5
1975	N Faldo	D Eccleston	Royal Lytham and St Annes	6 and 4
1976	P Deeble	JC Davies	Ganton	3 and 1
1977	TR Shingler	J Mayell	Walton Heath	4 and 3
1978	P Downes	P Hoad	Royal Birkdale	1 hole
1979	R Chapman	A Carman	Royal St George's	6 and 5
1980	P Deeble	P McEvoy	Moortown	4 and 3
1981	D Blakeman	A Stubbs	Burnham & Berrow	3 and 1
1982	A Oldcorn	I Bradshaw	Royal Liverpool	4 and 3
1983	G Laurence	A Brewer	Wentworth	7 and 6
1984	D Gilford	M Gerrard	Woodhall Spa	4 and 3
1985	R Winchester	P Robinson	Little Aston	1 hole
1986	J Langmead	B White	Hillside	2 and 1
1987	K Weeks	R Eggo	Frilford Heath	37th hole
1988	R Claydon	D Curry	R Birkdale	38th hole
1989	S Richardson	R Eggo	Royal St George's	2 and 1
1990	I Garbutt	G Evans	Woodhall Spa	8 and 7
1991	R Willison	M Pullan	Formby	10 and 8
1992	S Cage	R Hutt	Royal Cinque Ports	3 and 2
1993	D Fisher	R Bland	Saunton	3 and 1
1994	M Foster	A Johnson	Moortown	8 and 7
1995	M Foster	S Jarman	Hunstanton	6 and 5
1996	S Webster	D Lucas	Hollinwell	6 and 4
1997	A Wainwright	P Rowe	Royal Liverpool	2 and 1
1998	M Sanders	S Gorry	Woodhall Spa	6 and 5
1999	P Casey	S Dyson	St Mellion	2 and 1
2000	P Casey	G Wolstenholme	Royal Lytham and St Annes	4 and 2
2001	S Godfrey	S Robinson	Saunton	4 and 3

2002 *at Walton Heath*

Quarter Finals

Giles Legg (Dudsbury) beat Richard Walker
   (Frodsham) 4 and 3
Robert Steele (Kenilworth) beat Geoff Harris
   (Reading) at 22nd
Richard Finch (Hull) beat Michael Hunt
   (Burnley) 6 and 5
Sam Osborne (Wentworth) beat George Cowan
   (Bellingham) 5 and 3

Semi-Finals

Legg beat Steele 2 and 1
Finch beat Osborne 1 hole

Final

Richard Finch beat Giles Legg 6 and 5

English Open Amateur Stroke Play Championship
(Brabazon Trophy) (inaugurated 1957)

1957	D Sewell	Moortown	287	1965T	CA Clark	Formby	289
1958	AH Perowne	Birkdale	289		DJ Millensted		
1959	D Sewell	Hollinwell	300		MJ Burgess		
1960	GB Wolstenholme	Ganton	286	1966	PM Townsend	Hunstanton	282
1961	RDBM Shade	Hoylake, R Liverpool	284	1967	RDBM Shade	Saunton	299
1962	A Slater	Woodhall Spa	209	1968	MF Bonallack	Walton Heath	210
1963	RDBM Shade	R Birkdale	306	1969T	R Foster	Moortown	290
1964	MF Bonallack	Deal, R Cinque Ports	290		MF Bonallack		

1970	R Foster	Little Aston	287	1987	JG Robinson	Ganton	287
1971	MF Bonallack	Hillside	294	1988	R Eggo	Saunton	289
1972	PH Moody	Hoylake, R Liverpool	296	1989T	C Rivett	Hoylake, R Liverpool	293
1973	R Revell	Hunstanton	294		RN Roderick		
1974	N Sundelson	Moortown	291	1990T	O Edmond	Burnham and Berrow	287
1975	A Lyle	Hollinwell	298		G Evans		
1976	P Hedges	Saunton	294	1991T	G Evans	Hunstanton	284
1977	A Lyle	Royal Liverpool	293		M Pullan		
1978	G Brand Jr	Woodhall Spa	289	1992	I Garrido	Notts	280
1979	D Long	Little Aston	291	1993	D Fisher	Stoneham	277
1980T	R Rafferty	Hunstanton	293	1994	G Harris	Little Aston	280
	P McEvoy			1995T	M Foster	Hillside	283
1981	P Way	Hillside	292		CS Edwards		
1982	P Downes	Woburn	299	1996	P Fenton	R St Georges	297
1983	C Banks	Hollinwell	294	1997	D Park	Saunton	271
1984	M Davis	Deal, R Cinque Ports	286	1998	P Hansson	Formby	287
1985T	R Roper	Seaton Carew	296	1999	M Side	Moortown	279
	P Baker			2000	J Lupprien (Ger)	Woodhall Spa	284
1986	R Kaplan	Sunningdale	286	2001	R Walker	Royal Birkdale	280

2002 Brabazon Trophy *at Royal Cinque Ports*

1	Charl Schwartzel (RSA)	69-73-70-70—282
2	Colm Moriarty (Athlone)	72-75-69-68—284
3	Nigel Edwards (Whitchurch)	71-74-70-72—287

English Seniors' Amateur Championship (inaugurated 1981)

1981	CR Spalding	Copt Heath	152	1993	G Edwards	John O'Gaunt	221
1982	JL Whitworth	Lindrick	152	1994T	G Steel	Parkstone,	
1983	B Cawthray	Ross-on-Wye	154		F Jones	Broadstone	72 (18)
1984	RL Glading	Thetford	150	1995	H Hopkinson	Copt Heath	226
1985	JR Marriott	Bristol and Clifton	153	1996T	G Edwards		
1986	R Hiatt	Northants County	153		B Berney	West Lancs	224
1987	I Caldwell	North Hants	72 (18)	1997	D Lane	West Hill	215
1988	G Edwards	Bromborough	222	1998	J Marks	Saunton	217
1989	G Clark	West Sussex	212	1999	D Lane	Shifnal	73 (18)
1990	N Paul	Enville, Bridgnorth	217	2000	R Smethurst	Moor Park	212
1991	W Williams	Gerrards Cross	217	2001	R Smethurst	Sherwood Forest	220
1992	B Cawthray	Fulford	223				

2002 *at Heswall & Bromborough*

1	Douglas Arnold (Copthorne)	73-77-74—224
2	Geoffrey Clay (Minchinhampton)	73-78-74—225
	Roy Smethurst (Crewe)	76-75-74—225

English Open Mid-Amateur Championship (Logan Trophy)

(inaugurated 1988)

1988	P McEvoy	Little Aston	284	1995	C Banks	Seacroft	222
1989	A Mew	Moortown	290	19 97	C Banks	Stockport	211
1990	A Mew	Wentworth	214	1998	S East	Broadstone	216
1991	I Richardson	West Lancashire	223	1999	S East	Little Aston	217
1992	A Mew	King's Lynn	222	2000	B Downing	Ponteland	208
1993	R Godley	Southport & Ainsdale	210	2001	S East	Lindrick	206
1994T	I Richardson	Trentham	217				
	A McLure						

2002 *at Prince's, Sandwich*

1	François Illouz (Fra)	72-72-73—217
	Stephen Crosby (Gorleston)	73-67-77—217 (Trophy shared)
3	Andrew Maw (Notts-Hollinwell)	75-69-74—218

English County Champions' Tournament (Formerly President's Bowl)
(inaugurated 1962)

1962T	G Edwards, Cheshire	1982	P Deeble, Northumberland
	A Thirwell, Northumberland	1983	N Chesses, Warwickshire
1963T	M Burgess, Sussex/R Foster, Yorks	1984T	N Briggs, Herts/P McEvoy, Warwickshire
1964	M Attenborough, Kent	1985	P Robinson, Herts
1965	M Lees, Lincs	1986	A Gelsthorpe, Yorks
1966	R Stephenson, Middx	1987T	F George, Berks, Bucks & Oxon
1967	P Benka, Surrey		D Fay, Surrey
1968	G Hyde, Sussex	1988	R Claydon, Cambridge
1969	A Holmes, Herts	1989	R Willison, Middlesex
1970	M King, Berks, Bucks and Oxon	1990T	P Streeter, Lincs/R Sloman, Kent
1971	M Lee, Yorks	1991	T Allen, Warwickshire
1972	P Berry, Glos	1992	L Westwood, Notts
1973	A Chandler, Lancs	1993	R Walker, Durham
1974T	G Hyde, Sussex/A Lyle, Shrops & Hereford	1994	GP Wolstenholme, Glos
1975	N Faldo, Herts	1995	S Webster, Warwickshire
1976	R Brown, Devon	1996T	J Herbert, Leics/G Wolstenholme, Glos
1977	M Walls, Cumbria	1997	J Herbert, Leicestershire & Rutland
1978	I Simpson, Notts	1998	GP Wolstenholme, Leics
1979	N Burch, Essex	1999	D Griffiths, Herts
1980	D Lane, Berks, Bucks and Oxon	2000	P Bradshaw, Lincolnshire
1981	M Kelly, Yorks	2001	G Wolstenholme

2002 *at Woodhall Spa*

Yorkshire beat Dorset 6½–2½
Yorkshire beat Hampshire, Isle of Wight & Channel Islands 7–2
Yorkshire beat Lincolnshire 6–3
Hampshire, Isle of Wight & Channel Islands beat Lincolnshire 5–4
Hampshire, Isle of Wight & Channel Islands beat Dorset 6½–2½
Dorset beat Lincolnshire 6–3

1 Yorkshire, 2 Hampshire, Isle of Wight & Channel Islands,
3 Dorset, 4 Lincolnshire

Winning team: David Appleyard, Darryl Berry, Graeme Clark, Richard Finch, Richard Jones, Fraser Kelley, Michael Skelton

Irish Amateur Open Championship (inaugurated 1892)

1892	A Stuart	JH Andrew	Royal Portrush	1 hole
1893	John Ball	LS Anderson	Newcastle	8 and 7
1894	John Ball	DL Low	Dollymount	9 and 7
1895	WB Taylor	JM Williamson	Royal Portrush	13 and 11
1896	WB Taylor	D Anderson	Newcastle	9 and 8
1897	HH Hilton	LS Anderson	Dollymount	5 and 4
1898	WB Taylor	ROJ Dallmyer	Royal Portrush	at 37th
1899	John Ball	JM Williamson	Portmarnock	13 and 11
1900	HH Hilton	SH Fry	Newcastle	11 and 9
1901	HH Hilton	P Dowie	Dollymount	6 and 5
1902	HH Hilton	WH Hamilton	Royal Portrush	5 and 4
1903	G Wilkie	HA Boyd	Portmarnock	1 hole
1904	JS Worthington	JF Mitchell	Newcastle	6 and 4
1905	HA Boyd	JF Mitchell	Dollymount	3 and 2
1906	HH Barker	JS Worthington	Royal Portrush	5 and 4
1907	JD Brown	SH Fry	Portmarnock	2 and 1
1908	JF Mitchell	HM Cairnes	Newcastle	3 and 2
1909	LO Munn	R Garson	Dollymount	2 holes
1910	LO Munn	G Lockhart	Royal Portrush	9 and 7
1911	LO Munn	Hon. Michael Scott	Portmarnock	7 and 6
1912	G Lockhart	P Jenkins	Newcastle	11 and 9
1913	CA Palmer	LA Phillips	Dollymount	4 and 3
1914–1918	*Not played due to First World War*			
1919	C Bretherton	TD Armour	Royal Portrush	5 and 3
1920	GNC Martin	CW Robertson	Portmarnock	6 and 5
1921	D Smyth	J Gorry	Newcastle	2 holes
1922	A Lowe	J Henderson	Royal Portrush	6 and 4
1923	GNC Martin	CO Hezlet	Newcastle	1 hole
1924	EF Spiller	JDA McCormack	Dollymount	3 and 1
1925	TA Torrance	CO Hezlet	Royal Portrush	4 and 3
1926	CO Hezlet	RM McConnell	Portmarnock	7 and 6

1927	RM McConnell	DEB Soulby	Newcastle	5 and 3
1928	GS Moon	EF Spiller	Dollymount	1 hole
1929	CO Hezlet	JA Lang	Royal Portrush	1 hole
1930	W Sutton	DA Fiddian	Portmarnock	4 and 2
1931	EA McRuvie	DEB Soulby	Newcastle	7 and 5
1932	J McLean	JC Brown	Dollymount	9 and 8
1933	J McLean	E Fiddian	Newcastle	3 and 2
1934	H Thomson	HG Bentley	Portmarnock	3 and 2
1935	H Thomson	J McLean	Royal Portrush	5 and 4
1936	JC Brown	WM O'Sullivan	Portmarnock	at 39th
1937	J Fitzsimmons	RA McKinna	Dollymount	4 and 3
1938	J Bruen jr	JR Mahon	Newcastle	9 and 8
1939–1945	*Not played due to Second World War*			
1946	JB Carr	AT Kyle	Royal Portrush	3 and 1
1947	J Burke	JB Carr	Dollymount	1 hole
1948	RC Ewing	JB Carr	Newcastle	1 hole
1949	WM O'Sullivan	BJ Scannell	Killarney	2 holes
1950	JB Carr	RC Ewing	Rosses Point	at 40th
1951	RC Ewing	JB Carr	Portmarnock	2 and 1
1952	NV Drew	CH Beamish	Royal Portrush	5 and 4
1953	NV Drew	WM O'Sullivan	Killarney	3 and 2
1954	JB Carr	RC Ewing	Dollymount	6 and 4
1955	JF Fitzgibbon	JW Hulme	Royal County Down	1 hole
1956	JB Carr	JR Mahon	Portmarnock	1 hole
1957	JL Bamford	W Meharg	Royal Portrush	at 37th

from 1958 decided by Stroke Play

1958	T Craddock	Dollymount	484
1959	J Duncan	Newcastle	313

not played 1960–1994

1995	P Harrington	Fota Island	283
1996	K Nolan	Fota Island	286
1997	K Nolan	Fota Island	279
1998	M Hoey	Royal Dublin	286
1999	G Cullen	Royal Dublin	282
2000	N Fox	Royal Dublin	284
2001	R McEvoy*	Royal Dublin	277

2002 *at Royal Dublin*

1	Louis Oosthuizen (RSA)	73-71-71-68—283
2	Paul Bradshaw (Gainsborough)	69-66-75-74—284
3	Justin Kehoe (Birr)	72-74-70-70—286

Irish Amateur Close Championship (inaugurated 1893)

1893	T Dickson	G Combe	Royal Portrush	2 holes
1894	R Magill jr	T Dickson	Newcastle	3 and 1
1895	WH Webb	J Stevenson	Dollymount	10 and 9
1896	J Stewart-Moore jr	HAS Upton	Royal Portrush	8 and 7
1897	HE Reade	WH Webb	Newcastle	2 and 1
1898	WH Webb	J Stewart-Moore jr	Dollymount	9 and 8
1899	HE Reade	JP Todd	Royal Portrush	3 and 2
1900	RGN Henry	J McAvoy	Portmarnock	4 and 3
1901	WH Boyd	HE Reade	Newcastle	7 and 5
1902	FB Newett	R Shaw	Dollymount	1 hole
1903	HE Reade	DRA Campbell	Royal Portrush	5 and 4
1904	HA Boyd	JP Todd	Portmarnock	4 and 2
1905	FB Newett	B O'Brien	Newcastle	6 and 5
1906	HA Boyd	HM Cairnes	Dollymount	at 38th
1907	HM Cairnes	HA Boyd	Royal Portrush	7 and 6
1908	LO Munn	A Babbington	Portmarnock	10 and 9
1909	AH Patterson	EF Spiller	Newcastle	at 37th
1910	JF Jameson	LO Munn	Dollymount	2 and 1
1911	LO Munn	HA Boyd	Royal Portrush	7 and 6
1912	AH Craig	P Halligan	Castlerock	13 and 11
1913	LO Munn	HA Boyd	Portmarnock	6 and 5
1914	LO Munn	Earl Annesley	Hermitage	10 and 8
1915–1918	*Not played due to First World War*			
1919	E Carter	WG McConnell	Portmarnock	9 and 7

Irish Amateur Close Championship *continued*

1920	CO Hezlet	CL Crawford	Castlerock	12 and 11
1921	E Carter	G Moore	Portmarnock	9 and 8
1922	EM Munn	WK Tillie	Royal Portrush	3 and 1
1923	JD McCormack	LE Werner	Milltown	2 and 1
1924	JD McCormack	DEB Soulby	Newcastle	4 and 2
1925	CW Robertson	HM Cairnes	Portmarnock	4 and 3
1926	AC Allison	OW Madden	Royal Portrush	7 and 6
1927	JD McCormack	HM Cairnes	Cork	at 37th
1928	DEB Soulby	JO Wisdom	Castlerock	7 and 5
1929	DEB Soulby	FP McConnell	Dollymount	4 and 3
1930	J Burke	FP McConnell	Lahinch	6 and 5
1931	J Burke	FP McConnell	Rosses Point	6 and 4
1932	J Burke	M Crowley	Royal Portrush	6 and 5
1933	J Burke	GT McMullan	Cork	3 and 2
1934	JC Brown	RM McConnell	Rosslare	6 and 5
1935	RM McConnell	J Burke	Galway	2 and 1
1936	J Burke	RM McConnell	Castlerock	7 and 6
1937	J Bruen jr	J Burke	Ballybunion	3 and 2
1938	J Bruen jr	R Simcox	Rathfarnham Castle	3 and 2
1939	GH Owens	RM McConnell	Rosses Point	6 and 5
1940	J Burke	WM O'Sullivan	Dollymount	4 and 3
1941–1945	*Not played due to Second World War*			
1946	J Burke	RC Ewing	Dollymount	2 and 1
1947	J Burke	J Fitzsimmons	Lahinch	2 holes
1948	RC Ewing	BJ Scannell	Royal Portrush	3 and 2
1949	J Carroll	P Murphy	Galway	4 and 3
1950	B Herlihy	BC McManus	Baltray	4 and 3
1951	M Power	JB Carr	Cork	3 and 2
1952	TW Egan	JC Brown	Royal Belfast	at 41st
1953	J Malone	M Power	Rosses Point	2 and 1
1954	JB Carr	I Forsythe	Carlow	4 and 3
1955	JR Mahon	G Crosbie	Lahinch	3 and 2
1956	AGH Love	G Crosbie	Malone	at 37th
1957	JB Carr	G Crosbie	Galway	2 holes
1958	RC Ewing	GA Young	Ballybunion	5 and 3
1959	T Craddock	JB Carr	Portmarnock	at 38th
1960	M Edwards	N Fogarty	Portstewart	6 and 5
1961	D Sheahan	J Brown	Rosses Point	5 and 4
1962	M Edwards	J Harrington	Baltray	42nd hole
1963	JB Carr	EC O'Brien	Killarney	2 and 1
1964	JB Carr	A McDade	Co Down	6 and 5
1965	JB Carr	T Craddock	Rosses Point	3 and 2
1966	D Sheahan	J Faith	Dollymount	3 and 2
1967	JB Carr	PD Flaherty	Lahinch	1 hole
1968	M O'Brien	F McCarroll	Royal Portrush	2 and 1
1969	V Nevin	J O'Leary	Co Sligo	1 hole
1970	D Sheahan	M Bloom	Grange	2 holes
1971	P Kane	M O'Brien	Ballybunion	3 and 2
1972	K Stevenson	B Hoey	Co Down	2 and 1
1973	RKM Pollin	RM Staunton	Rosses Point	1 hole
1974	R Kane	M Gannon	Portmarnock	5 and 4
1975	MD O'Brien	JA Bryan	Cork	5 and 4
1976	D Brannigan	D O'Sullivan	Royal Portrush	2 holes
1977	M Gannon	A Hayes	Westport	19th hole
1978	M Morris	T Cleary	Carlow	1 hole
1979	J Harrington	MA Gannon	Ballybunion	2 and 1
1980	R Rafferty	MJ Bannon	Co Down	8 and 7
1981	D Brannigan	E McMenamin	Co Sligo	19th hole
1982	P Walton	B Smyth	Woodbrook	7 and 6
1983	T Corridan	E Power	Killarney	2 holes
1984	CB Hoey	L McNamara	Malone	20th hole
1985	D O'Sullivan	D Branigan	Westport	1 hole
1986	J McHenry	P Rayfus	Dublin	4 and 3
1987	E Power	JP Fitzgerald	Tranmore	2 holes
1988	G McGimpsey	D Mulholland	Royal Portrush	2 and 1
1989	P McGinley	N Goulding	Rosses Point	3 and 2
1990	D Clarke	P Harrington	Baltray	3 and 2
1991	G McNeill	N Goulding	Ballybunion	3 and 1
1992	G Murphy	JP Fitzgerald	Portstewart	2 and 1
1993	E Power	D Higgins	Enniscrone	3 and 2
1994	D Higgins	P Harrington	Portmarnock	20th hole
1995	P Harrington	D Coughlan	Lahinch	3 and 2

1996	P Lawrie	G McGimpsey	Royal Co Down	3 and 2
1997	K Kearney	P Lawrie	Fota Island	5 and 4
1998	E Power	B Omelia	The Island	1 hole
1999	C McMonagle	M Sinclair	Killarney	2 and 1
2000	G McDowell	A McCormick	Royal Portrush	7 and 6
2001	G McNeill	S Browne	Co Sligo	20th hole

2002 at at Carlow

Leading Qualifier: Justin Kehoe (Birr) 137
Match Play: 64 qualified on 153 or better (4 out of 9 on 153)

Quarter Finals

Ken Kearney (Roscommon) beat Trevor Spence (Clandeboye) 6 and 5

Niall Goulding (Portmarnock) beat Mervyn Owens (Mallow) 4 and 2

Michael McGeady (City of Derry) beat Robert McCarthy (The Island) 3 and 2

John McGinn (Greenore) beat Adrian Morrow (Portmarnock)

Semi-Finals

Kearney beat Goulding 4 and 3

McGinn beat McGeady at 19th

Final

John McGinn beat Ken Kearney 3 and 1

Irish Seniors' Open Amateur Championship (inaugurated 1970)

1970	RC Ewing	Lahinch	153	1986	J Coey	Waterford	141
1971	J O'Sullivan	Rosslare	159	1987	J Murray	Castleroy	150
1972	BJ Scannell	Co. Sligo	152	1988	WB Buckley	Westport	154
1973	JW Hulme	Warrenpoint	147	1989	B McCrea	Royal Belfast	150
1974	P Walsh	Cork	155	1990	C Hartland	Cork	149
1975	SA O'Connor	Woodbrook	152	1991	C Hartland	Mullingar	147
1976	BJ Scannell	Athlone	150	1992	C Hartland	Athlone	145
1977	DB Somers	Warrenpoint	150	1993	P Breen	Bangor	147
1978	DP Herlihy	Limerick	150	1994	B Buckley	Tramore	151
1979	P Kelly	Royal Tara	153	1995	B Hoey	Dundalk	151
1980	GN Fogarty	Galway	144	1996	E Condren	Oughterard	148
1981	GN Fogarty	Bundoran	149	1997	B Wilson	The Knock	152
1982	J Murray	Douglas	141	1998	J Harrington	Thurles	149
1983	F Sharpe	Courtown	153	1999	A Lee	Thurles	150
1984	J Boston	Connemara	147	2000	D Jackson	Westport	151
1985	J Boston	Newcastle	155	2001	D Jackson	Clandeboye	153

2002 at Limerick

1	Tom Fox (Co. Louth)	70-76—146
2	Richie McDonnell (Seaport)	72-75—147
	Robert Wallace (Spa)	75-72—147

Scottish Amateur Championship (inaugurated 1922)

1922	J Wilson	E Blackwell	St Andrews	19th hole
1923	TM Burrell	Dr A McCallum	Troon	1 hole
1924	WW Mackenzie	W Tulloch	Aberdeen	3 and 2
1925	JT Dobson	W Mackenzie	Muirfield	3 and 2
1926	WJ Guild	SO Shepherd	Leven	2 and 1
1927	A Jamieson jr	Rev D Rutherford	Gailes	22nd hole
1928	WW Mackenzie	W Dodds	Muirfield	5 and 3
1929	JT Bookless	J Dawson	Aberdeen	5 and 4
1930	K Greig	T Wallace	Carnoustie	9 and 8
1931	J Wilson	A Jamieson Jr	Prestwick	2 and 1
1932	J McLean	K Greig	Dunbar	5 and 4
1933	J McLean	KC Forbes	Aberdeen	6 and 4
1934	J McLean	W Campbell	Western Gailes	3 and 1
1935	H Thomson	J McLean	St Andrews	2 and 1
1936	ED Hamilton	R Neill	Carnoustie	1 hole
1937	H McInally	K Patrick	Barassie	6 and 5
1938	ED Hamilton	R Rutherford	Muirfield	4 and 2
1939	H McInally	H Thomson	Prestwick	6 and 5
1946	EC Brown	R Rutherford	Carnoustie	3 and 2

Scottish Amateur Championship *continued*

1947	H McInally	J Pressley	Glasgow Gailes	10 and 8
1948	AS Flockhart	G Taylor	Royal Aberdeen	7 and 6
1949	R Wright	H McInally	Muirfield	1 hole
1950	WC Gibson	D Blair	Prestwick	2 and 1
1951	JM Dykes	J Wilson	St Andrews	4 and 2
1952	FG Dewar	J Wilson	Carnoustie	4 and 3
1953	DA Blair	J McKay	Western Gailes	3 and 1
1954	JW Draper	W Gray	Nairn	4 and 3
1955	RR Jack	AC Miller	Muirfield	2 and 1
1956	Dr FWG Deighton	A MacGregor	Troon	8 and 7
1957	JS Montgomerie	J Burnside	Balgownie	2 and 1
1958	WD Smith	I Harris	Prestwick	6 and 5
1959	Dr FWG Deighton	R Murray	St Andrews	6 and 5
1960	JR Young	S Saddler	Carnoustie	5 and 3
1961	J Walker	ST Murray	Western Gailes	4 and 3
1962	SWT Murray	R Shade	Muirfield	2 and 1
1963	RDBM Shade	N Henderson	Troon	4 and 3
1964	RDBM Shade	J McBeath	Nairn	8 and 7
1965	RDBM Shade	G Cosh	St Andrews	4 and 2
1966	RDBM Shade	C Strachan	Western Gailes	9 and 8
1967	RDBM Shade	A Murphy	Carnoustie	5 and 4
1968	GB Cosh	R Renfrew	Muirfield	4 and 3
1969	JM Cannon	A Hall	Troon	6 and 4
1970	CW Green	H Stuart	Royal Aberdeen	1 hole
1971	S Stephen	C Green	St Andrews	3 and 2
1972	HB Stuart	A Pirie	Prestwick	3 and 1
1973	IC Hutcheon	A Brodie	Carnoustie	3 and 2
1974	GH Murray	A Pirie	Western Gailes	2 and 1
1975	D Greig	G Murray	Montrose	7 and 6
1976	GH Murray	H Stuart	St Andrews	6 and 5
1977	A Brodie	P McKellar	Troon	1 hole
1978	IA Carslaw	J Cuddihy	Downfield	7 and 6
1979	K Macintosh	P McKellar	Prestwick	5 and 4
1980	D Jamieson	C Green	Royal Aberdeen	2 and 1 (18)
1981	C Dalgleish	A Thomson	Western Gailes	7 and 6
1982	CW Green	G Macgregor	Carnoustie	1 hole
1983	CW Green	J Huggan	Gullane	1 hole
1984	A Moir	K Buchan	Renfrew	3 and 3
1985	D Carrick	D James	Southerness	4 and 2
1986	C Brooks	A Thomson	Monifieth	3 and 2
1987	C Montgomerie	A Watt	Nairn	9 and 8
1988	J Milligan	A Coltart	Kilmarnock (Barassie)	1 hole
1989	A Thomson	A Tait	Moray	1 hole
1990	C Everett	M Thomson	Gullane	7 and 5
1991	G Lowson	L Salariya	Downfield	4 and 3
1992	S Gallacher	D Kirkpatrick	Glasgow Gailes	37th hole
1993	D Robertson	R Russell	Royal Dornoch	2 holes
1994	H McKibben	A Reid	Renfrew	39th hole
1995	S Mackenzie	H McKibben	Southerness	8 and 7
1996	M Brooks	A Turnbull	Dunbar	7 and 6
1997	C Hislop	S Cairns	Carnoustie	5 and 3
1998	G Rankin	M Donaldson	Prestwick	6 and 5
1999	C Heap	M Loftus	Cruden Bay	7 and 5
2000	S O'Hara	C Heap	Royal Dornoch	1 hole
2001	B Hume	C Watson	Downfield	4 and 3

2002 *at Western Gailes*

Quarter Finals

Christopher Campbell (Grantown-on-Spey) beat Craig Watson (East Renfrewshire) 1 hole

Scott Jamieson (Cathkin Braes) beat Russell Thornton (Cardross) 6 and 4

Terry Mathieson (Caledonian) beat Graeme Brown (Royal Montrose) 4 and 2

Andrew McArthur (Windyhill) beat Les McLaughlin (Cowglen) 6 and 4

Semi-Finals

Jamieson beat Campbell 2 and 1

McArthur beat Mathieson 1 hole

Final

Andrew McArthur beat Scott Jamieson 2 and 1

Scottish Open Amateur Stroke Play Championship

(inaugurated 1967)

1967	BJ Gallacher	Muirfield and Gullane	291
1968	RDBM Shade	Prestwick and Prestwick St Nicholas	282
1969	JS Macdonald	Carnoustie and Monifieth	288
1970	D Hayes	Glasgow Gailes and Barassie	275
1971	IC Hutcheon	Leven and Lundin	277
1972	BN Nicholas	Dalmahoy and Ratho Park	290
1973T	DM Robertson/GJ Clark	Dunbar and North Berwick	284
1974	IC Hutcheon	Blairgowrie and Alyth	283
1975	CW Green	Nairn and Nairn Dunbar	295
1976	S Martin	Monifieth and Carnoustie	299
1977	PJ McKellar	Muirfield and Gullane	299
1978	AR Taylor	Cawder	281
1979	IC Hutcheon	Blairgowrie	286
1980	G Brand jr	Musselburgh and R Musselburgh	207 (54 holes)
1981	F Walton	Erskine and Renfrew	287
1982	C Macgregor	Downfield and Camperdown	287
1983	C Murray	Irvine and Irvine Ravenspark	291
1984	CW Green	Blairgowrie	287
1985	C Montgomerie	Dunbar and North Berwick	274
1986	KH Walker	Carnoustie	289
1987	D Carrick	Lundin and Ladybank	282
1988	S Easingwood	Cathkin Braes and East Kilbride	277
1989	F Illouz	Blairgowrie	281
1990	G Hay	Royal Aberdeen and Murcar	133 (36 holes)
1991	A Coltart	Royal Troon and Troon Portland	291
1992	D Robertson	Mortonhall and Bruntsfield Links	281
1993	A Reid	St Andrews Jubilee and New	289
1994	D Downie	Letham Grange	288
1995	S Gallacher	Paisley and Renfrew	284
1996	A Forsyth	Cardross and Helensburgh	279
1997	DB Howard	Monifieth and Panmure	271
1998	L Kelly	Moray and Elgin	275
1999	G Rankin	St Andrews Old and Jubilee	286
2000	S McKenzie*	Letham Grange	278
2001	J Sutherland*	Nairn and Nairn Dunbar	279

2002 at Southerness

1	Barry Hume (Haggs Castle)	75-64-69-69—277
2	Simon Mackenzie (West Linton)	77-67-66-69—279
3	David Inglis (Glencorse)	73-69-67-70—279

Scottish Senior Championship (inaugurated 1978)

1978T	JM Cannon	Glasgow	149	1988	J Hayes	Royal Burgess	143
	GR Carmichael			1989	AS Mayer	Glasgow	139
1979	A Sinclair	Glasgow	143	1990	C Hartland	Royal Burgess	146
1980	JM Cannon	Royal Burgess	149	1991	CW Green	Glasgow	140
1981T	IR Harris	Glasgow	146	1992	G Clark	Royal Burgess	148
	Dr J Hastings			1993	J Maclean	Glasgow	141
	AN Sturrock			1994	DM Lawrie	Ladybank	149
1982T	JM Cannon	Royal Burgess	143	1995	CW Green	Glasgow	141
	J Niven			1996	CW Green	Western Gailes	146
1983	WD Smith	Glasgow	145	1997	CW Green	Glasgow	137
1984	A Sinclair	Royal Burgess	148	1998	CW Green	Ladybank	146
1985	AN Sturrock	Glasgow	143	1999	G Steel*	Glasgow	145
1986	RL Glading	Royal Burgess	153	2000	N Grant	Falkirk Tryst	142
1987	I Hornsby	Glasgow	145	2001	D Lane	Glasgow	140

2002 at Scotscraig

1	David Lane (Goring & Streatley)	72-70—142
2	David Smith (Stirling)	74-71—145
3	Gordon Broster (Padbrook Park)	71-74—145
	George Macgregor (Glencorse)	71-74—145

Scottish Champion of Champions (inaugurated 1970) *at Leven*

1970	A Horne	1981	I Hutcheon	1992	D Robertson
1971	D Black	1982	G Macgregor	1993	R Russell
1972	R Strachan	1983	D Carrick	1994	G Sherry
1973	*Not held*	1984	S Stephen	1995	S Gallacher
1974	M Niven	1985	I Brotherston	1996	M Brooks
1975	A Brodie	1986	I Hutcheon	1997	G Rankin
1976	A Brodie	1987	G Shaw	1998	G Rankin
1977	V Reid	1988	I Hutcheon	1999	D Patrick
1978	D Greig	1989	J Milligan	2000	G Fox
1979	B Marchbank	1990	J Milligan	2001	M Loftus
1980	I Hutcheon	1991	G Hay		

2002

1	Steven Carmichael (Cardross)*	69-68-66-73—276
2	Barry Hume (Haggs Castle)	75-64-65-72—276
	Marc Warren (East Kilbride)	73-68-70-65—276

Scottish Mid-Amateur Championship (inaugurated 1994)

1994	C Watson	1997	H McDonald	2000	J Cameron
1995	M Thomson	1998	G Campbell	2001	M Thompson
1996	B Smith	1999	G Crawford		

2002 *at Glenbervie*

Semi-Finals

Craig Elliot (Ratho Park) beat Les McLaughlin (Cowglen) 2 and 1
Mark Hislop (Glenbervie) beat Thomas Gilchrist (Falkirk Tryst) 1 hole

Final

Craig Elliot beat Mark Hislop 1 hole

Welsh Amateur Championship (inaugurated 1895)

Year	Winner	Runner-up	Venue	Score
1895	J Hunter	TM Barlow	Aberdovey	2 holes
1896	J Hunter	P Plunkett	Rhyl	1 hole
1897	FE Woodhead	J Hunter	Penarth	4 and 3
1898	FE Woodhead	Dr E Reid	Aberdovey	5 and 4
1899	FE Woodhead	TD Cummins	Conway	6 and 5
1900	TM Barlow	H Ludlow	Royal Porthcawl	2 and 1
1901	Major Green	P Plunkett	Aberdovey	8 and 7
1902	J Hunter	H Ludlow	Penarth	5 and 4
1903	J Hunter	TM Barlow	Rhos-on-Sea	2 holes
1904	H Ludlow	RM Brown	Ashburnham	13 and 11
1905	J Duncan jr	AP Cary Thomas	Conway	6 and 5
1906	G Renwick	WT Davies	Radyr	9 and 7
1907	LA Phillips	LH Gottwaltz	Royal Porthcawl	3 and 1
1908	G Renwick	LA Phillips	Southerndown	7 and 5
1909	J Duncan jr	EJ Byrne	Rhyl	9 and 8
1910	G Renwick	RM Brown	Swansea	2 holes
1911	HM Lloyd	TC Mellor	Conway	4 and 2
1912	LA Phillips	CH Turnbull	Royal Porthcawl	4 and 3
1913	HN Atkinson	CJ Hamilton	Chester	at 38th
1914–1919	*Not played due to First World War*			
1920	HR Howell	J Duncan jr	Southerndown	2 holes
1921	CEL Fairchild	E Rowe	Aberdovey	1 hole
1922	HR Howell	EDSN Carne	Tenby	12 and 11
1923	HR Howell	CEL Fairchild	Rhyl	3 and 1
1924	HR Howell	CH Turnbull	Radyr	2 and 1
1925	CEL Fairchild	GS Emery	Rhyl	10 and 8
1926	DR Lewis	K Stoker	Royal Porthcawl	1 hole
1927	DR Lewis	JL Jones	Tenby	4 and 3
1928	CC Marston	DR Lewis	Royal St David's	at 37th
1929	HR Howell	R Chapman	Southerndown	4 and 3

Year	Winner	Runner-up	Venue	Score
1930	HR Howell	DR Lewis	Tenby	2 and 1
1931	HR Howell	WG Morgan	Aberdovey	7 and 6
1932	HR Howell	HE Davies	Ashburnham	7 and 6
1933	JL Black	AA Duncan	Royal Porthcawl	2 and 1
1934	SB Roberts	GS Noon	Prestatyn	4 and 3
1935	R Chapman	GS Noon	Tenby	1 hole
1936	RM de Lloyd	G Wallis	Aberdovey	1 hole
1937	DH Lewis	R Glossop	Porthcawl	2 holes
1938	AA Duncan	SB Roberts	Rhyl	2 and 1
1939–1945 *Not played due to Second World War*				
1946	JV Moody	A Marshman	Porthcawl	9 and 8
1947	SB Roberts	G Breen Turner	Royal St David's	8 and 7
1948	AA Duncan	SB Roberts	Porthcawl	2 and 1
1949	AD Evans	MA Jones	Aberdovey	2 and 1
1950	JL Morgan	DJ Bonnell	Southerndown	9 and 7
1951	JL Morgan	WI Tucker	Royal St David's	3 and 2
1952	AA Duncan	JL Morgan	Ashburnham	4 and 3
1953	SB Roberts	D Pearson	Prestatyn	5 and 3
1954	AA Duncan	K Thomas	Tenby	6 and 5
1955	TJ Davies	P Dunn	Royal St David's	38th hole
1956	A Lockley	WI Tucker	Southerndown	2 and 1
1957	ES Mills	H Griffiths	Royal St David's	2 and 1
1958	HC Squirrell	AD Lake	Conway	4 and 3
1959	HC Squirrell	N Rees	Porthcawl	8 and 7
1960	HC Squirrell	P Richards	Aberdovey	2 and 1
1961	AD Evans	J Toye	Ashburnham	3 and 2
1962	J Povall	HC Squirrell	Royal St David's	3 and 2
1963	WI Tucker	J Povall	Southerndown	4 and 3
1964	HC Squirrell	WI Tucker	Royal St David's	1 hole
1965	HC Squirrell	G Clay	Porthcawl	6 and 4
1966	WI Tucker	EN Davies	Aberdovey	6 and 5
1967	JK Povall	WI Tucker	Asburnham	3 and 2
1968	J Buckley	J Povall	Conway	8 and 7
1969	JL Toye	EN Davies	Porthcawl	1 hole
1970	EN Davies	J Povall	Royal St David's	1 hole
1971	CT Brown	HC Squirrell	Southerndown	6 and 5
1972	EN Davies	JL Toye	Prestatyn	40th hole
1973	D McLean	T Holder	Ashburnham	6 and 4
1974	S Cox	EN Davies	Caernarvonshire	3 and 2
1975	JL Toye	WI Tucker	Porthcawl	5 and 4
1976	MPD Adams	WI Tucker	Royal St David's	6 and 5
1977	D Stevens	JKD Povall	Southerndown	3 and 2
1978	D McLean	A Ingram	Caernarvonshire	11 and 10
1979	TJ Melia	MS Roper	Ashburnham	5 and 4
1980	DL Stevens	G Clement	Prestatyn	10 and 9
1981	S Jones	C Davies	Porthcawl	5 and 3
1982	D Wood	C Davies	Royal St David's	8 and 7
1983	JR Jones	AP Parkin	Southerndown	2 holes
1984	JR Jones	A Llyr	Prestatyn	1 hole
1985	ED Jones	MA Macara	Ashburnham	2 and 1
1986	C Rees	B Knight	Conwy	1 hole
1987	PM Mayo	DK Wood	Porthcawl	2 holes
1988	K Jones	RN Roderick	Royal St David's	40th hole
1989	S Dodd	K Jones	Tenby	2 and 1
1990	A Barnett	A Jones	Prestatyn	1 hole
1991	S Pardoe	S Jones	Ashburnham	7 and 5
1992	H Roberts	R Johnson	Pyle & Kenfig	3 and 2
1993	B Dredge	M Ellis	Southerndown	3 and 1
1994	C Evans	M Smith	Royal Porthcawl	5 and 4
1995	G Houston	C Evans	Royal St David's	3 and 2
1996	Y Taylor	DH Park	Ashburnham	3 and 2
1997	JR Donaldson	M Pilkington	Pyle & Kenfig	5 and 4
1998	M Pilkington	K Sullivan	Prestatyn	2 and 1
1999	M Griffiths	R Brookman	Tenby	7 and 6
2000	JG Jermine	R Brookman	Royal St David's	1 hole
2001	C Williams	L Harpin	Royal Porthcawl	1 hole

Welsh Amateur Championship *continued*

2002 *at Conwy*

Quarter Finals
Nigel Edwards (Whitchurch) beat Roy Williams
  (Conwy) 2 holes
Lee Harpin (North Wales) beat Ryan Thomas
  (Aberdare) 2 and 1
David Price (Vale of Glamorgan) beat Arwel
  Roberts (Worthing) at 19th
Rhys Davies (Royal Porthcawl) beat Alwyn
  Thomas (Nefyn & District) 7 and 6

Semi-Finals
Harpin beat Edwards 4 and 2
Price beat Davies 3 and 2

Final
David Price beat Lee Harpin at 20th

Welsh Amateur Stroke Play Championship (inaugurated 1967)

1967	EN Davies	Harlech	295	1985	MA Macara	Harlech	291
1968	JA Buckley	Harlech	294	1986	M Calvert	Pyle & Kenfig	299
1969	DL Stevens	Tenby	288	1987	MA Macara	Llandudno (Maesdu)	290
1970	JK Povall	Newport	292	1988	RN Roderick	Tenby	283
1971T	EN Davies	Harlech	296	1989	SC Dodd	Conwy	304
	JL Toye						
1972	JR Jones	Pyle & Kenfig	299		*Open event since 1990*		
1973	JR Jones	Llandudno (Maesdu)	300	1990	G Houston	Pyle & Kenfig	288
1974	JL Toye	Tenby	307	1991	A Jones	Royal Porthcawl	290
1975	D McLean	Wrexham	288	1992	AJ Barnett	Royal St David's	278
1976	WI Tucker	Newport	282	1993	M Macara	Maesdu	280
1977	JA Buckley	Prestatyn	302	1994	N Van Hootegem	St Pierre	290
1978	HJ Evans	Pyle & Kenfig	300	1995	M Peet	Prestatyn	282
1979	D McLean	Holyhead	289	1996	M Blackey	Tenby	276
1980	TJ Melia	Tenby	291	1997	G Wolstenholme	Conwy	286
1981	D Evans	Wrexham	270	1998	DAJ Patrick	Southerndown	279
1982	JR Jones	Cradoc	287	1999	C Williams	Northop	288
1983	G Davies	Aberdovey	287	2000	J Donaldson	Ashburnham	283
1984	RN Roderick	Newport	292	2001	J Lupton	Maesdu	266

2002 *at Pyle & Kenfig*

1	Jack Doherty (Vale of Glamorgan)	74-68-70-70—282
2	Lee Corfield (Burnham & Berrow)	72-74-72-71—289
3	Graeme Clark (Doncaster)	71-70-73-76—290
	Richard Finch (Hull)	72-70-75-73—290
	Daniel Wardrop (Didsbury)	74-68-71-77—290

Welsh Seniors' Amateur Championship (inaugurated 1975) *at Aberdovey*

1975	A Marshman	77 (18)	1989	WI Tucker	160
1976	AD Evans	156	1990	I Hughes	159
1977	AE Lockley	154	1991	RO Ward	155
1978	AE Lockley	75 (18)	1992	I Hughes	150
1979	CR Morgan	158	1993	G Perks	149
1980	ES Mills	152	1994T	G Perks/I Hughes/	
1981	T Branton	153		A Prytherch	157
1982	WI Tucker	147	1995	I Hughes	147
1983	WS Gronow	153	1996	G Isaac	152
1984	WI Tucker	150	1997	I Hughes	148
1985	NA Lycett	149	1998	D Reidford	158
1986	E Mills	154	1999	G Isaac	150
1987	WS Gronow	146	2000	JR Jones*	145
1988	NA Lycett	150	2001	W Stowe	222

2002

1	B Cramb (Tenby)	70-74-77—221
2	WG Stowe (Aberdovey)	79-72-72—223
	J Whitcutt (Burnham & Berrow)	73-77-73—223
	D Williams (Newport, Gwent)	77-73-73—223

Welsh Tournament of Champions (inaugurated 1979) *at Cradoc*

1979	JL Toye	1987	JR Jones	1995	G Houston		
1980	JM Morrow	1988	SC Dodd	1996	MH Peat		
1981	AP Vicary	1989	P Sykes	1997	M Pilkington		
1982	PM Mayo	1990	G Gouston	1998	M Gwyther		
1983	PM Mayo	1991	G Houston	1999	R Williams		
1984	M Bearcroft	1992	B Dredge	2000	J Davidson		
1985	SC Dodd	1993	B Dredge	2001	N Oakley		
1986	SC Todd	1994	B Dredge				

2002

1	Tim Hayward (Pontnewydd)	138
2	I Clark (Pontnewydd)	142
3	R Butler (Borth & Ynyslas)	143

European Amateur Championship (inaugurated 1986)

1986	A Haglund (Swe)	Eindhoven, Netherlands	1996	D Olsson (Swe)	Karlstad, Sweden
1988	D Ecob (Aus)	Falkenstein, Germany	1997	D de Vooght (Bel)	Domaine Imperial,
1990	K Erikson (Swe)	Aalborg, Denmark			Switzerland
1991	J Payne (Eng)	Hillside, England	1998	P Gribben (Irl)	Golf du Medoc, France
1992	M Scarpa (Ita)	Le Querce, Italy	1999	G Havret (Fra)	Ascona, Switzerland
1993	M Backhausen (Den)	Dalmahoy, Scotland	2000	C Pettersson (Swe)	Murhof, Austria
1994	S Gallacher (Sco)	Aura, Finland	2001	S Browne (Irl)	Odense, Denmark
1995	S García (Esp)	El Prat, Spain			

2002 *at at Tróia, Portugal*

1	Raphaël Pellicioli (Fra)	70-71-70-73—284
2	James Heath (Eng)	71-77-70-71—289
3	Jeppe Huldahl (Den)	67-78-73-72—290

European Seniors' Championship (inaugurated 1999)

1999	H-J Ecklebe (Ger)	Switzerland	216	2001	G Steel (Eng)	Spain	216
2000	HH Giesen (Ger)	Spain	217				

2002 *at La Manga, Spain*

1	Andrew Morrison (Eng)	70-68-74—212
2	David J Smith (Sco)	75-72-74—221
3	Hans-Hubert Giesen (Ger)	74-72-77—223
	Jon Marks (Eng)	76-73-74—223
	Veit Pagel (Ger)	78-71-74—223

European Mid-Amateur Championship (inaugurated 1999)

1999	H-G Reiter (Ger)	Luxembourg	215	2001	B Downing (Eng)	Turkey	216
2000	F Illouz (Fra)	England	221				

2002 *at Kärntner, Dellach, Austria*

1	Hans-Günther Reiter (Ger)	72-71-67—210
2	Karl Bornemann (Irl)	73-73-69—215
3	Christian Sommer (Ger)	73-69-73—215

Lexus European Under 21 Championships (inaugurated 1988)

1998	Sergio García (Esp)	2000	Nicolas Colsaerts (Bel)	2002	*Not played*
1999	Nick Dougherty (Eng)	2001	B Hume (Sco)*		

National Orders of Merit

Ireland – Willie Gill Award 2002

1	Colm Moriarty (Athlone)	115	6T	Ken Kearney (Roscommon)	75
2	Noel Fox (Portmarnock)	110		Michael McDermott (Stackstown)	75
3	Stuart Paul (Tandragee)	95	8	Darren Crowe (Royal Dublin)	65
4	Justin Kehoe (Birr)	85	9	John McGinn (Greenore)	60
5	Gareth Maybin (Ballyclare)	80	10T	Robert McCarthy (The Island)	55
				Robert Forsythe (Hilton)	55

Scotland – Order of Merit 2002

1	Graham Gordon (Newmachar)	600	6	David Inglis (Glencorse)	292
2	Barry Hume (Haggs Castle)	472	7	Scott Jamieson (Cathkin Braes)	282
3	Jack Doherty (Vale of Glamorgan)	460	8	Stuart Wilson (Forfar)	233
4	Simon Mackenzie (West Linton)	362	9T	Andrew McArthur (Windyhill)	215
5	Bryan Innes (Murcar)	330		Graeme Brown (Royal Montrose)	215

Scottish Final Ranking 2002

1	Graham Gordon (Newmachar)	-2.143	6	Simon Mackenzie (West Linton)	-0.767
2	David Inglis (Glencorse)	-2.0	7	Stuart Wilson (Forfar)	-0.679
3	Bryan Innes (Murcar)	-1.842	8	Jonathan King (Cardross)	-0.514
4	Jamie McLeary (Glenrothes)	-1.688	9	Scott Jamieson (Cathkin Braes)	-0.5
5	Jack Doherty (Vale of Glamorgan)	-1.188	10	Steven Carmichael (Auchterarder)	-0.172

Wales – Konica Order of Merit 2002

1	Stuart Manley (Mountain Ash)	552	6	Gareth Wright (West Linton)	278
2	David Price (Vale of Glamorgan)	546	7	Neil Oakley (St Mellons)	272
3	Nigel Edwards (Whitchurch)	536	8	Richard Scott (Haverfordwest)	249
4	Lee Harpin (North Wales)	312	9	Craig Smith (St Mellons)	223
5	Alex Smith (Pyle & Kenfig)	279	10	Jonathon Holmes (Southerndown)	147

Daily Telegraph/*JJB* Order of Merit 2002

1	Gary Wolstenholme (Kilworth Springs)	11	Stuart Manley (Mountain Ash)
2	Nigel Edwards (Whitchurch)	12	Lee Corfield (Burnham & Berrow)
3	Graham Gordon (Newmachar)	13	David Price (Vale of Glamorgan)
4	Richard Walker (Frodsham)	14	Simon Mackenzie (West Linton)
5	Jonathan Lupton (Middlesbrough)	15	Lee Harpin (North Wales)
6	Jack Doherty (Vale of Glamorgan)	16	Colm Moriarty (Athlone)
7	Zane Scotland (Woodcote Park)	17	Stuart Wilson (Forfar)
8	Jamie Elson (Kenilworth)	18	David Inglis (Glencorse)
9	Graeme Clark (Doncaster)	19	Justin Kehoe (Birr)
10	Richard Finch (Hull)	20	Barry Hume (Haggs Castle)

Team Events

Walker Cup *(home team names first)*

21 May 1921 *at Hoylake*
Unofficial match — GBI v USA
Result: USA 9, GBI 3
Foursomes
Simpson & Jenkins lost to Evans & Jones 5 and 3
Tolley & Holderness lost to Ouimet & Guilford 3 and 2
de Montmorency & Wethered lost to Hunter & Platt
    1 hole
Aylmer & Armour lost to Wright & Fownes 4 and 2
Singles
CJH Tolley beat C Evans jr 4 and 3
JLC Jenkins lost to FD Ouimet 6 and 5
RH de Montmorency lost to RT Jones jr 4 and 3
JG Simpson lost to JP Guilford 2 and 1
CC Aylmer beat P Hunter 2 and 1
TD Armour beat JW Platt 2 and 1
EWE Holderness lost to F Wright 2 holes
RH Wethered lost to WC Fownes jr 3 and 1

1922 *at National Golf Links, New York*
Officially named the Walker Cup
Result: USA 8, GBI 4
Captains: WC Fownes (USA), R Harris (GBI)
Foursomes
Guilford & Ouimet beat Tolley & Darwin 8 and 7
Evans & Gardner lost to Wethered & Aylmer 5 and 4
Jones & Sweetser beat Torrance & Hooman 3 and 2
Marston & Fownes beat Caven & Mackenzie 2 and 1
Singles
JP Guilford beat CJH Tolley 2 and 1
RT Jones jr beat RH Wethered 3 and 2
C Evans jr beat J Caven 5 and 4
FD Ouimet beat CC Aylmer 8 and 7
RA Gardner beat WB Torrance 7 and 5
MR Marston lost to WW Mackenzie 6 and 5
WC Fownes jr lost to B Darwin 3 and 1
JW Sweetser lost to CVL Hooman at 37th

1923 *at St Andrews*
Result: USA 6½, GBI 5½
Captains: R Harris (GBI), RA Gardner (USA)
Foursomes
Tolley & Wethered beat Ouimet & Sweetser 6 and 5
Harris & Hooman lost to Gardner & Marston 7 and 6
Holderness & Hope beat Rotan & Herron 1 hole
Wilson & Murray beat Johnston & Neville
    4 and 3
Singles
RH Wethered halved with FD Ouimet
CJH Tolley beat JW Sweetser 4 and 3
R Harris lost to RA Gardner 1 hole
WW Mackenzie lost to GV Rotan 5 and 4
WL Hope lost to MR Marston 6 and 5
EWE Holderness lost to FJ Wright jr 1 hole
J Wilson beat SD Herron 1 hole
WA Murray lost to OF Willing 2 and 1

1924 *at Garden City, New York*
Result: USA 9, GBI 3
*Captains: RA Gardner (USA), CJH Tolley
    (GBI)*
Foursomes
Marston & Gardner beat Storey & Murray 3 and 1
Guilford & Ouimet beat Tolley & Hezlet 2 and 1
Jones & Fownes jr lost to Scott & Scott jr 1 hole
Sweetser & Johnston beat Torrance & Bristowe 4 and 3
Singles
MR Marston lost to CJH Tolley 1 hole
RT Jones jr beat CO Hezlet 4 and 3
C Evans jr beat WA Murray 2 and 1
FD Ouimet beat EF Storey 1 hole
JW Sweetser lost to Hon M Scott 7 and 6
RA Gardner beat WL Hope 3 and 2
JP Guilford beat TA Torrance 2 and 1
OF Willing beat DH Kyle 3 and 2

1926 *at St Andrews*
Result: USA 6½, GBI 5½
Captains: R Harris (GBI), RA Gardner (USA)
Foursomes
Wethered & Holderness beat Ouimet &
    Guilford 5 and 4
Tolley & Jamieson lost to Jones & Gunn 4 and 3
Harris & Hezlet lost to Von Elm & Sweetser 8 and 7
Storey & Brownlow lost to Gardner & MacKenzie
    1 hole
Singles
CJH Tolley lost to RT Jones jr 12 and 11
EWE Holderness lost to JW Sweetser 4 and 3
RH Wethered beat FD Ouimet 5 and 4
CO Hezlet halved with G Von Elm
R Harris beat JP Guilford 2 and 1
Hon WGE Brownlow lost to W Gunn 9 and 8
EF Storey beat RR MacKenzie 2 and 1
A Jamieson jr beat RA Gardner 5 and 4

1928 *at Wheaton, Chicago, IL*
Result: USA 11, GBI 1
*Captains: RT Jones jr (USA),
    W Tweddell (GBI)*
Foursomes
Sweetser & Von Elm beat Perkins & Tweddell 7 and 6
Jones & Evans beat Hezlet & Hope 5 and 3
Ouimet & Johnston beat Torrance & Storey 4 and 2
Gunn & MacKenzie beat Beck & Martin 7 and 5
Singles
RT Jones jr beat TP Perkins 13 and 12
G Von Elm beat W Tweddell 3 and 2
FD Ouimet beat CO Hezlet 8 and 7
JW Sweetser beat WL Hope 5 and 4
HR Johnston beat EF Storey 4 and 2
C Evans jr lost to TA Torrance 1 hole
W Gunn beat RH Hardman 11 and 10
RR MacKenzie beat GNC Martin 2 and 1

1930 *at St George's, Sandwich*
Result: USA 10, GBI 2
Captains: RH Wethered (GBI),
RT Jones jr (USA)

Foursomes
Tolley & Wethered beat Von Elm & Voigt 2 holes
Hartley & Torrance lost to Jones & Willing 8 and 7
Holderness & Stout lost to MacKenzie & Moe 2 and 1
Campbell & Smith lost to Johnston & Ouimet 2 and 1

Singles
CJH Tolley lost to HR Johnston 5 and 4
RH Wethered lost to RT Jones jr 9 and 8
RW Hartley lost to G Von Elm 3 and 2
EWE Holderness lost to GJ Voigt 10 and 8
JN Smith lost to OF Willing 2 and 1
TA Torrance beat FD Ouimet 7 and 6
JA Stout lost to DK Moe 1 hole
W Campbell lost to RR MacKenzie 6 and 5

1932 *at Brookline, MA*
Result: USA 9½, GBI 2½
Captains: FD Ouimet (USA), TA Torrance (GBI)

Foursomes
Sweetser & Voigt beat Hartley & Hartley 7 and 6
Seaver & Moreland beat Torrance & de Forest
    6 and 5
Ouimet & Dunlap beat Stout & Burke 7 and 6
Moe & Howell beat Fiddian & McRuvie 5 and 4

Singles
FD Ouimet halved with TA Torrance
JW Sweetser halved with JA Stout
GT Moreland beat RW Hartley 2 and 1
J Westland halved with J Burke
GJ Voigt lost to LG Crawley 1 hole
MJ McCarthy jr beat WL Hartley 3 and 2
CH Seaver beat EW Fiddian 7 and 6
GT Dunlap jr beat EA McRuvie 10 and 9

1934 *at St Andrews*
Result: USA 9½, GBI 2½
Captains: Hon M Scott (GBI),
FD Ouimet (USA)

Foursomes
Wethered & Tolley lost to Goodman & Little
    8 and 6
Bentley & Fiddian lost to Moreland & Westland
    6 and 5
Scott & McKinlay lost to Egan & Marston 3 and 2
McRuvie & McLean beat Ouimet & Dunlap 4 and 2

Singles
Hon M Scott lost to JG Goodman 7 and 6
CJH Tolley lost to WL Little jr 6 and 5
LG Crawley lost to FD Ouimet 5 and 4
J McLean lost to GT Dunlap jr 4 and 3
EW Fiddian lost to JW Fischer 5 and 4
SL McKinlay lost to GT Moreland 3 and 1
EA McRuvie halved with J Westland
TA Torrance beat MR Marston 4 and 3

1936 *at Pine Valley, NJ*
Result: USA 10½, GBI 1½
Captains: FD Ouimet (USA),
W Tweddell (GBI)

Foursomes
Goodman & Campbell beat Thomson & Bentley
    7 and 5
Smith & White beat McLean & Langley 8 and 7

Yates & Emery halved with Peters & Dykes
Givan & Voigt halved with Hill & Ewing

Singles
JG Goodman beat H Thomson 3 and 2
AE Campbell beat J McLean 5 and 4
JW Fischer beat RC Ewing 8 and 7
R Smith beat GA Hill 11 and 9
W Emery beat GB Peters 1 hole
CR Yates beat JM Dykes 8 and 7
GT Dunlap jr halved with HG Bentley
E White beat JDA Langley 6 and 5

1938 *at St Andrews*
Result: GBI 7½, USA 4½
Captains: JB Beck (GBI), FD Ouimet (USA)

Foursomes
Bentley & Bruen halved with Fischer & Kocsis
Peters & Thomson beat Goodman & Ward 4 and 2
Kyle & Stowe lost to Yates & Billows 3 and 2
Pennink & Crawley beat Smith & Haas 3 and 1

Singles
J Bruen jr lost to CR Yates 2 and 1
H Thomson beat JG Goodman 6 and 4
LG Crawley lost to JW Fischer 3 and 2
C Stowe beat CR Kocsis 2 and 1
JJF Pennink lost to MH Ward 12 and 11
RC Ewing beat RE Billows 1 hole
GB Peters beat R Smith 9 and 8
AT Kyle beat F Haas jr 5 and 4

1947 *at St Andrews*
Result: USA 8, GBI 4
Captains: JB Beck (GBI), FD Ouimet (USA)

Foursomes
Carr & Ewing lost to Bishop & Riegel 3 and 2
Crawley & Lucas beat Ward & Quick 5 and 4
Kyle & Wilson lost to Turnesa & Kammer 5 and 4
White & Stowe beat Stranahan & Chapman 4 and 3

Singles
LG Crawley lost to MH Ward 5 and 3
JB Carr beat SE Bishop 5 and 3
GH Micklem lost to RH Riegel 6 and 5
RC Ewing lost to WP Turnesa 6 and 5
C Stowe lost to FR Stranahan 2 and 1
RJ White beat AF Kammer jr 4 and 3
JC Wilson lost to SL Quick 8 and 6
PB Lucas lost to RD Chapman 4 and 3

1949 *at Winged Foot, New York*
Result: USA 10, GBI 2
Captains: FD Ouimet (USA), PB Lucas (GBI)

Foursomes
Billows & Turnesa lost to Carr & White 3 and 2
Kocsis & Stranahan beat Bruen & McCready 2 and 1
Bishop & Riegel beat Ewing & Micklem 9 and 7
Dawson & McCormick beat Thom & Perowne
    8 and 7

Singles
WP Turnesa lost to RJ White 4 and 3
FR Stranahan beat SM McCready 6 and 5
RH Riegel beat J Bruen jr 5 and 4
JW Dawson beat JB Carr 5 and 3
CR Coe beat RC Ewing 1 hole
RE Billows beat KG Thom 2 and 1
CR Kocsis beat AH Perowne 4 and 2
JB McHale jr beat GH Micklem 5 and 4

1951 *at Birkdale*
Result: USA 7½, GBI 4½
Captains: RH Oppenheimer (GBI),
*   WP Turnesa (USA)*

Foursomes
White & Carr halved with Stranahan & Campbell
Ewing & Langley halved with Coe & McHale
Kyle & Caldwell lost to Chapman & Knowles jr
   1 hole
Bruen jr & Morgan lost to Turnesa & Urzetta 5 and 4

Singles
SM McCready lost to S Urzetta 4 and 3
JB Carr beat FR Stranahan 2 and 1
RJ White beat CR Coe 2 and 1
JDA Langley lost to JB McHale jr 2 holes
RC Ewing lost to WC Campbell 5 and 4
AT Kyle beat WP Turnesa 2 holes
I Caldwell halved with HD Paddock jr
JL Morgan lost to RD Chapman 7 and 6

1953 *at Kittansett, MA*
Result: USA 9, GBI 3
Captains: CR Yates (USA), AA Duncan (GBI)

Foursomes
Urzetta & Venturi beat Carr & White 6 and 4
Ward & Westland beat Langley & AH Perowne 9 and 8
Jackson & Littler beat Wilson & MacGregor 3 and 2
Campbell & Coe lost to Micklem & Morgan
   4 and 3

Singles
EH Ward jr beat JB Carr 4 and 3
RD Chapman lost to RJ White 1 hole
GA Littler beat GH Micklem 5 and 3
J Westland beat RC MacGregor 7 and 5
DR Cherry beat NV Drew 9 and 7
K Venturi beat JC Wilson 9 and 8
CR Coe lost to JL Morgan 3 and 2
S Urzetta beat JDA Langley 3 and 2

1955 *at St Andrews*
Result: USA 10, GBI 2
Captains: GA Hill (GBI), WC Campbell (USA)

Foursomes
Carr & White lost to Ward & Cherry 1 hole
Micklem & Morgan lost to Patton & Yost 2 and 1
Caldwell & Millward lost to Conrad & Morey 3 and 2
Blair & Cater lost to Cudd & Jackson 5 and 4

Singles
RJ White lost to EH Ward jr 6 and 5
PF Scrutton lost to WJ Patton 2 and 1
I Caldwell beat D Morey 1 hole
JB Carr lost to DR Cherry 5 and 4
DA Blair beat JW Conrad 1 hole
EB Millward lost to BH Cudd 2 holes
RC Ewing lost to JG Jackson 6 and 4
JL Morgan lost to RL Yost 8 and 7

1957 *at Minikahda, MN*
Result: USA 8½, GBI 3½
Captains:CR Coe (USA), GH Micklem (GBI)

Foursomes
Baxter & Patton beat Carr & Deighton 2 and 1
Campbell & Taylor beat Bussell & Scrutton 4 and 3
Blum & Kocsis lost to Jack & Sewell 1 hole
Robbins & Rudolph halved with Shepperson &
   Wolstenholme

Singles
WJ Patton beat RR Jack 1 hole
WC Campbell beat JB Carr 3 and 2
R Baxter jr beat A Thirlwell 4 and 3
W Hyndman III beat FWG Deighton 7 and 6
JE Campbell lost to AF Bussell 2 and 1
FM Taylor jr beat D Sewell 1 hole
EM Rudolph beat PF Scrutton 3 and 2
H Robbins jr lost to GB Wolstenholme 2 and 1

1959 *at Muirfield*
Result: USA 9, GBI 3
Captains:GH Micklem (GBI), CR Coe (USA)

Foursomes
Jack & Sewell lost to Ward & Taylor 1 hole
Carr & Wolstenholme lost to Hyndman & Aaron 1 hole
Bonallack & Perowne lost to Patton & Coe 9 and 8
Lunt & Shepperson lost to Wettlander & Nicklaus
   2 and 1

Singles
JB Carr beat CR Coe 3 and 1
GB Wolstenholme lost to EH Ward jr 9 and 8
RR Jack beat WJ Patton 5 and 3
DN Sewell lost to W Hyndman III 4 and 3
AE Shepperson beat TD Aaron 2 and 1
MF Bonallack lost to DR Beman 2 holes
MSR Lunt lost to HW Wettlander 6 and 5
WD Smith lost to JW Nicklaus 5 and 4

1961 *at Seattle, WA*
Result: USA 11, GBI 1
Captains: J Westland (USA), CD Lawrie (GBI)

Foursomes
Beman & Nicklaus beat Walker & Chapman 6 and 5
Coe & Cherry beat Blair & Christmas 1 hole
Hyndman & Gardner beat Carr & G Huddy 4 and 3
Cochran & Andrews beat Bonallack & Shade
   4 and 3

Singles
DR Beman beat MF Bonallack 3 and 2
CR Coe beat MSR Lunt 5 and 4
FM Taylor jr beat J Walker 3 and 2
W Hyndman III beat DW Frame 7 and 6
JW Nicklaus beat JB Carr 6 and 4
CB Smith lost to MJ Christmas 3 and 2
RW Gardner beat RDBM Shade 1 hole
DR Cherry beat DA Blair 5 and 4

1963 *at Turnberry*
Result: USA 14, GBI 10
Captains: CD Lawrie (GBI), RS Tufts (USA)

First Day – Foursomes
Bonallack & Murray beat Patton & Sikes 4 and 3
Carr & Green lost to Gray & Harris 2 holes
Lunt & Sheahan lost to Beman & Coe 5 and 3
Madeley & Shade halved with Gardner &
   Updegraff

Singles
SWT Murray beat DR Beman 3 and 1
MJ Christmas lost to WJ Patton 3 and 2
JB Carr beat RH Sikes 7 and 5
DB Sheahan beat LE Harris 1 hole
MF Bonallack beat RD Davies 1 hole
AC Saddler halved with CR Coe
RDBM Shade beat AD Gray jr 4 and 3
MSR Lunt halved with CB Smith

Second Day – **Foursomes**
Bonallack & Murray lost to Patton & Sikes 1 hole
Lunt & Sheahan lost to Gray & Harris 3 and 2
Green & Saddler lost to Gardner & Updegraff 3 and 1
Madeley & Shade lost to Beman & Coe 3 and 2

Singles
Murray lost to Patton 3 and 2
Sheahan beat Davies 1 hole
Carr lost to Updegraff 4 and 3
Bonallack lost to Harris 3 and 2
Lunt lost to Gardner 3 and 2
Saddler halved with Beman
Shade beat Gray 2 and 1
Green lost to Coe 4 and 3

1965 at Five Farms, MD
Result: USA 12, GBI 12
Captains: JW Fischer (USA), JB Carr (GBI)

First Day – **Foursomes**
Campbell & Gray lost to Lunt & Cosh 1 hole
Beman & Allen halved with Bonallack & Clark
Patton & Tutwiler beat Foster & Clark 5 and 4
Hopkins & Eichelberger lost to Townsend & Shade
  2 and 1

Singles
WC Campbell beat MF Bonallack 6 and 5
DR Beman beat R Foster 2 holes
AD Gray jr lost to RDBM Shade 3 and 1
JM Hopkins lost to CA Clark 5 and 3
WJ Patton lost to P Townsend 3 and 2
D Morey lost to AC Saddler 2 and 1
DC Allen lost to GB Cosh 2 holes
ER Updegraff lost to MSR Lunt 2 and 1

Second Day – **Foursomes**
Campbell & Gray beat Saddler & Foster 4 and 3
Beman & Eichelberger lost to Townsend & Shade 2 and 1
Tutwiler & Patton beat Cosh & Lunt 2 and 1
Allen & Morey lost to CA Clark & Bonallack 2 and 1

Singles
Campbell beat Foster 3 and 2
Beman beat Saddler 1 hole
Tutwiler beat Shade 5 and 3
Allen lost to Cosh 4 and 3
Gray beat Townsend 1 hole
Hopkins halved with CA Clark
Eichelberger beat Bonallack 5 and 3
Patton beat Lunt 4 and 2

1967 at St George's, Sandwich
Result: USA 15, GBI 9
Captains: JB Carr (GBI), JW Sweetser (USA)

First Day – **Foursomes**
Shade & Oosterhuis halved with Murphy & Cerrudo
Foster & Saddler lost to Campbell & Lewis 1 hole
Bonallack & Attenborough lost to Gray & Tutwiler
  4 and 2
Carr & Craddock lost to Dickson & Grant 3 and 1

Singles
RDBM Shade lost to WC Campbell 2 and 1
R Foster lost to RJ Murphy jr 2 and 1
MF Bonallack halved with AD Gray jr
MF Attenborough lost to RJ Cerrudo 4 and 3
P Oosterhuis lost to RB Dickson 6 and 4
T Craddock lost to JW Lewis jr 2 and 1
AK Pirie halved with DC Allen
AC Saddler beat MA Fleckman 3 and 2

Second Day – **Foursomes**
Bonallack & Craddock beat Murphy & Cerrudo
  2 holes
Saddler & Pirie lost to Campbell & Lewis 1 hole
Shade & Oosterhuis beat Gray & Tutwiler 3 and 1
Foster & Millensted beat Allen & Fleckman
  2 and 1

Singles
Shade lost to Campbell 3 and 2
Bonallack beat Murphy 4 and 2
Saddler beat Gray 3 and 2
Foster halved with Cerrudo
Pirie lost to Dickson 4 and 3
Craddock beat Lewis 5 and 4
Oosterhuis lost to Grant 1 hole
Millensted lost to Tutwiler 3 and 1

1969 at Milwaukee, WI
Result: USA 13, GBI 11
*Captains: WJ Patton (USA),
  MF Bonallack (GBI)*

First Day – **Foursomes**
Giles & Melnyk beat Bonallack & Craddock
  3 and 2
Fleisher & Miller halved with Benka & Critchley
Wadkins & Siderowf lost to Green & A Brooks
W Hyndman III & Inman jr beat Foster & Marks
  2 and 1

Singles
B Fleisher halved with MF Bonallack
M Giles III beat CW Green 1 hole
AL Miller III beat B Critchley 1 hole
RL Siderowf beat LP Tupling 6 and 5
S Melnyk lost to PJ Benka 3 and 1
L Wadkins lost to GC Marks 1 hole
J Bohmann beat MG King 2 and 1
ER Updegraff beat R Foster 6 and 5

Second Day – **Foursomes**
Giles & Melnyk halved with Green & Brooks
Fleisher & Miller lost to Benka & Critchley 2 and 1
Siderowf & Wadkins beat Foster & King 6 and 5
Updegraff & Bohmann lost to Bonallack & Tupling
  4 and 3

Singles
Fleisher lost to Bonallack 5 and 4
Siderowf halved with Critchley
Miller beat King 1 hole
Giles halved with Craddock
Inman beat Benka 2 and 1
Bohmann lost to Brooks 4 and 3
Hyndman halved with Green
Updegraff lost to Marks 3 and 2

1971 at St Andrews
Result: GBI 13, USA 11
*Captains: MF Bonallack (GBI),
  JM Winters jr (USA)*

First Day – **Foursomes**
Bonallack & Humphreys beat Wadkins & Simons
  1 hole
Green & Carr beat Melnyk & Giles 1 hole
Marsh & Macgregor beat Miller & Farquhar
  2 and 1
Macdonald & Foster beat Campbell & Kite 2 and 1

1971 *continued*

Singles

CW Green lost to L Wadkins 1 hole
MF Bonallack lost to M Giles III 1 hole
GC Marks lost to AL Miller III 1 hole
JS Macdonald lost to S Melnyk 3 and 2
RJ Carr halved with W Hyndman III
W Humphreys lost to JR Gabrielsen 1 hole
HB Stuart beat J Farquhar 3 and 2
R Foster lost to T Kite 3 and 2

Second Day – **Foursomes**

Marks & Green lost to Melnyk & Giles 1 hole
Stuart & Carr beat Wadkins & Gabrielsen 1 hole
Marsh & Bonallack lost to Miller & Farquhar 5 and 4
Macdonald & Foster halved with Campbell & Kite

Singles

Bonallack lost to Wadkins 3 and 1
Stuart beat Giles 2 and 1
Humphreys beat Melnyk 2 and 1
Green beat Miller 1 hole
Carr beat Simons 2 holes
Macgregor beat Gabrielsen 1 hole
Marsh beat Hyndman 1 hole
Marks lost to Kite 3 and 2

1973 *at Brookline, MA*

Result: USA 14, GBI 10
Captains: JW Sweetser (USA), DM Marsh (GBI)

First Day – **Foursomes**

Giles & Koch halved with King & Hedges
Siderowf & Pfeil beat Stuart & Davies 5 and 4
Edwards & Ellis beat Green & Milne 2 and 1
West & Ballenger beat Foster & Homer 2 and 1

Singles

M Giles III beat HB Stuart 5 and 4
RL Siderowf beat MF Bonallack 4 and 2
G Koch lost to JC Davies 1 hole
M West lost to HK Clark 2 and 1
D Edwards beat R Foster 2 holes
M Killian lost to MG King 1 hole
W Rodgers lost to CW Green 1 hole
M Pfeil lost to WT Milne 4 and 3

Second Day – **Foursomes**

Giles & Koch & Homer & Foster 7 and 5
Siderowf & Pfeil halved with Clark & Davies
Edwards & Ellis beat Hedges & King 2 and 1
Rodgers & Killian beat Stuart & Milne 1 hole

Singles

Ellis lost to Stuart 5 and 4
Siderowf lost to Davies 3 and 2
Edwards beat Homer 2 and 1
Giles halved with Green
West beat King 1 hole
Killian lost to Milne 2 and 1
Koch halved with Hedges
Pfeil beat Clark 1 hole

1975 *at St Andrews*

Result: USA 15½, GBI 8½
Captains: DM Marsh (GBI),
ER Updegraff (USA)

First Day – **Foursomes**

James & Eyles beat Pate & Siderowf 1 hole
Davies & Poxon lost to Burns & Stadler
5 and 4
Green & Stuart lost to Haas & Strange 2 and 1
Macgregor & Hutcheon lost to Giles & Koch 5 and 4

Singles

M James beat J Pate 2 and 1
JC Davies halved with C Strange
P Mulcare beat RL Siderowf 1 hole
HB Stuart lost to G Koch 3 and 2
MA Poxon lost to J Grace 3 and 1
IC Hutcheon halved with WC Campbell
GRD Eyles lost to J Haas 2 and 1
G Macgregor lost to M Giles III 5 and 4

Second Day – **Foursomes**

Mulcare & Hutcheon beat Pate & Siderowf 1 hole
Green & Stuart lost to Burns & Stadler 1 hole
James & Eyles beat Campbell & Grace 5 and 3
Hedges & Davies lost to Haas & Strange 3 and 2

Singles

Hutcheon beat Pate 3 and 2
Mulcare lost to Strange 4 and 3
James lost to Koch 5 and 4
Davies beat Burns 2 and 1
Green lost to Grace 2 and 1
Macgregor lost to Stadler 3 and 2
Eyles lost to Campbell 2 and 1
Hedges halved with Giles

1977 *at Shinnecock Hills, NY*

Result: USA 16, GBI 8
Captains: LW Oehmig(USA),
AC Saddler (GBI)

First Day – **Foursomes**

Fought & Heafner beat Lyle & McEvoy 4 and 3
Simpson & Miller beat Davies & Kelley 5 and 4
Siderowf & Hallberg lost to Hutcheon & Deeble
1 hole
Sigel & Brannan beat Brodie & Martin 1 hole

Singles

L Miller beat P McEvoy 2 holes
J Fought beat IC Hutcheon 4 and 3
S Simpson beat GH Murray 7 and 6
V Heafner beat JC Davies 4 and 3
B Sander lost to A Brodie 4 and 3
G Hallberg lost to S Martin 3 and 2
F Ridley beat AWB Lyle 2 holes
J Sigel beat P McKellar 5 and 3

Second Day – **Foursomes**

Fought & Heafner beat Hutcheon & Deeble 4 and 3
Miller & Simpson beat McEvoy & Davies 2 holes
Siderowf & Sander lost to Brodie & Martin 6 and 4
Ridley & Brannan lost to Murray & Kelley 4 and 3

Singles

Miller beat Martin 1 hole
Fought beat Davies 2 and 1
Sander lost to Brodie 2 and 1
Hallberg beat McEvoy 4 and 3
Siderowf lost to Kelley 2 and 1
Brannan lost to Hutcheon 2 holes
Ridley beat Lyle 5 and 3
Sigel beat Deeble 1 hole

1979 *at Muirfield*

Result: USA 15½, GBI 8½
Captains: R Foster (GBI), RL Siderowf (USA)

First Day – **Foursomes**

McEvoy & Marchbank lost to Hoch & Sigel 1 hole
Godwin & Hutcheon beat West & Sutton
2 holes
Brand jr & Kelley lost to Fischesser & Holtgrieve
1 hole
Brodie & Carslaw beat Moody & Gove 2 and 1

Singles
P McEvoy halved with J Sigel
JC Davies lost to D Clarke 8 and 7
J Buckley lost to S Hoch 9 and 7
IC Hutcheon lost to J Holtgrieve 6 and 4
B Marchbank beat M Peck 1 hole
G Godwin beat G Moody 3 and 2
MJ Kelley beat D Fischesser 3 and 2
A Brodie lost to M Gove 3 and 2

Second Day – **Foursomes**
Godwin & Brand lost to Hoch & Sigel 4 and 3
McEvoy & Marchbank beat Fischesser & Holtgrieve
    2 and 1
Kelley & Hutcheon halved with West & Sutton
Carslaw & Brodie halved with Clarke & Peck

Singles
McEvoy lost to Hoch 3 and 1
Brand lost to Clarke 2 and 1
Godwin lost to Gove 3 and 2
Hutcheon lost to Peck 2 and 1
Brodie beat West 3 and 2
Kelley lost to Moody 3 and 2
Marchbank lost to Sutton 3 and 1
Carslaw lost to Sigel 2 and 1

1981 *at Cypress Point, CA*
Result: USA 15, GBI 9
Captains: J Gabrielsen (USA),
    R Foster (GBI)

First Day – **Foursomes**
Sutton & Sigel lost to Walton & Rafferty 4 and 2
Holtgrieve & Fuhrer beat Chapman & McEvoy
    1 hole
Lewis & von Tacky beat Deeble & Hutcheon 2 and 1
Commans & Pavin beat Evans & Way 5 and 4

Singles
H Sutton beat R Rafferty 3 and 1
J Rassett beat CR Dalgleish 1 hole
R Commans lost to P Walton 1 hole
B Lewis lost to R Chapman 2 and 1
J Mudd beat G Godwin 1 hole
C Pavin beat IC Hutcheon 4 and 3
D von Tacky lost to P Way 3 and 1
J Sigel beat P McEvoy 4 and 2

Second Day – **Foursomes**
Sutton & Sigel lost to Chapman & Way 1 hole
Holtgrieve & Fuhrer lost to Walton & Rafferty 6 and 4
Lewis & von Tacky lost to Evans & Dalgleish 3 and 2
Rassett & Mudd beat Hutcheon & Godwin 5 and 4

Singles
Sutton lost to Chapman 1 hole
Holtgrieve beat Rafferty 2 and 1
Fuhrer beat Walton 4 and 3
Sigel beat Way 6 and 5
Mudd beat Dalgleish 7 and 5
Commans halved with Godwin
Rassett beat Deeble 4 and 3
Pavin halved with Evans

1983 *at Hoylake*
Result: USA 13½, GBI 10½
Captains: CW Green (GBI), J Sigel (USA)

First Day – **Foursomes**
Macgregor & Walton beat Sigel & Fehr 3 and 2
Keppler & Pierse lost to Wood & Faxon 3 and 1
Lewis & Thompson lost to Lewis & Holtgrieve
    7 and 6
Mann & Oldcorn beat Hoffer & Tentis 5 and 4

Singles
P Walton beat J Sigel 1 hole
SD Keppler lost to R Fehr 1 hole
G Macgregor halved with W Wood
DG Carrick lost to B Faxon 3 and 1
A Oldcorn beat B Tuten 4 and 3
P Parkin beat N Crosby 5 and 4
AD Pierse lost to B Lewis jr 3 and 1
LS Mann lost to J Holtgrieve 6 and 5

Second Day – **Foursomes**
Macgregor & Walton lost to Crosby & Hoffer 2 holes
Parkin & Thompson beat Faxon & Wood 1 hole
Mann & Oldcorn beat Lewis & Holtgrieve 1 hole
Keppler & Pierse halved with Sigel & Fehr

Singles
Walton beat Wood 2 and 1
Parkin lost to Faxon 3 and 2
Macgregor lost to Fehr 2 and 1
Thompson lost to Tuten 3 and 2
Mann halved with Tentis
Keppler lost to Lewis 6 and 5
Oldcorn beat Holtgrieve 3 and 2
Carrick lost to Sigel 3 and 2

1985 *at Pine Valley, NJ*
Result: USA 13, GBI 11
Captains: J Sigel (USA), CW Green (GBI)

First Day – **Foursomes**
Verplank & Sigel beat Montgomerie & Macgregor
    1 hole
Waldorf & Randolph lost to Hawksworth & McGimpsey 4
    and 3
Sonnier & Haas lost to Baker & McEvoy 6 and 5
Podolak & Love halved with Bloice & Stephen

Singles
S Verplank beat G McGimpsey 2 and 1
S Randolph beat P Mayo 5 and 4
R Sonnier halved with J Hawksworth
J Sigel beat CS Montgomerie 5 and 4
B Lewis lost to P McEvoy 2 and 1
C Burroughs lost to G Macgregor 2 holes
D Waldorf beat D Gilford 4 and 2
J Haas lost to AR Stephen 2 and 1

Second Day – **Foursomes**
Verplank & Sigel halved with Mayo & Montgomerie
Randolph & Haas beat Hawksworth & McGimpsey
    3 and 2
Lewis & Burroughs beat Baker & McEvoy 2 and 1
Podolak & Love beat Bloice & Stephen 3 and 2

Singles
Randolph halved with McGimpsey
Verplank beat Montgomerie 1 hole
Sigel lost to Hawksworth 4 and 3
Love beat McEvoy 5 and 3
Sonnier lost to Baker 5 and 4
Burroughs lost to Macgregor 3 and 2
Lewis beat Bloice 4 and 3
Waldorf lost to Stephen 2 and 1

1987 *at Sunningdale*
Result: USA 16½, GBI 7½
Captains: GC Marks (GBI), F Ridley (USA)

First Day – **Foursomes**
Montgomerie & Shaw lost to Alexander & Mayfair
    5 and 4
Currey & Mayo lost to Kite & Mattice 2 and 1
Macgregor & Robinson lost to Lewis & Loeffler 2 and 1
McHenry & Girvan lost to Sigel & Andrade 3 and 2

1987 continued
Singles
D Currey beat B Alexander 2 holes
J Robinson lost to B Andrade 7 and 5
CS Montgomerie beat J Sorenson 3 and 2
R Eggo lost to J Sigel 3 and 2
J McHenry lost to B Montgomery 1 hole
P Girvan lost to B Lewis 3 and 2
DG Carrick lost to B Mayfair 2 holes
G Shaw beat C Kite 1 hole

Second Day – **Foursomes**
Currey & Carrick lost to Lewis & Loeffler 4 and 3
Montgomerie & Shaw lost to Kite & Mattice 5 and 3
Mayo & Macgregor lost to Sorenson & Montgomery 4 and 3
McHenry & Robinson beat Sigel & Andrade 4 and 2
Singles
Currey lost to Alexander 5 and 4
Montgomerie beat Andrade 4 and 2
McHenry beat Loeffler 3 and 2
Shaw halved with Sorenson
Robinson beat Mattice 1 hole
Carrick lost to Lewis 3 and 2
Eggo lost to Mayfair 1 hole
Girvan lost to Sigel 6 and 5

1989 at Peachtree, GA
Result: GBI 12½, USA 11½
Captains: F Ridley (USA), GC Marks (GBI)
First Day – **Foursomes**
Gamez & Martin beat Claydon & Prosser 3 and 2
Yates & Mickelson halved with Dodd & McGimpsey
Lesher & Sigel lost to McEvoy & O'Connell 6 and 5
Eger & Johnson lost to Milligan & Hare 2 and 1
Singles
R Gamez beat JW Milligan 7 and 6
D Martin lost to R Claydon 5 and 4
E Meeks halved with SC Dodd
R Howe lost to E O'Connell 5 and 4
D Yates lost to P McEvoy 2 and 1
P Mickelson beat G McGimpsey 4 and 2
G Lesher lost to C Cassells 1 hole
J Sigel halved with RN Roderick

Second Day – **Foursomes**
Gamez & Martin halved with McEvoy & O'Connell
Sigel & Lesher lost to Claydon & Cassells 3 and 2
Eger & Johnson lost to Milligan & Hare 2 and 1
Mickelson & Yates lost to McGimpsey & Dodd 2 and 1
Singles
Gamez beat Dodd 1 hole
Martin halved with Hare
Lesher beat Claydon 3 and 2
Yates beat McEvoy 4 and 3
Mickelson halved with O'Connell
Eger beat Roderick 4 and 2
Johnson beat Cassells 4 and 2
Sigel halved with Milligan

1991 at Portmarnock
Result: USA 14, GBI 10
Captains: G Macgregor (GBI), JR Gabrielsen (USA)
First Day – **Foursomes**
Milligan & Hay lost to Mickelson & May 5 and 3
Payne & Evans lost to Duval & Sposa 1 hole
McGimpsey & Willison lost to Voges & Eger 1 hole
McGinley & Harrington lost to Sigel & Doyle 2 and 1

Singles
A Coltart lost to P Mickelson 4 and 3
J Payne beat F Langham 2 and 1
G Evans beat D Duval 2 and 1
R Willison lost to B May 2 and 1
G McGimpsey beat M Sposa 1 hole
P McGinley lost to A Doyle 6 and 4
G Hay beat T Scherrer 1 hole
L White lost to J Sigel 4 and 3

Second Day – **Foursomes**
Milligan & McGimpsey beat Voges & Eger 2 and 1
Payne & Willison lost to Duval & Sposa 1 hole
Evans & Coltart beat Langham & Scherrer 4 and 3
White & McGinley beat Mickelson & May 1 hole
Singles
Milligan lost to Mickelson 1 hole
Payne beat Doyle 3 and 1
Evans lost to Langham 4 and 2
Coltart beat Sigel 1 hole
Willison beat Scherrer 3 and 2
Harrington lost to Eger 3 and 2
McGimpsey lost to May 4 and 3
Hay lost to Voges 3 and 1

1993 at Interlachen, Edina, MN
Result: USA 19, GBI 5
Captains: M Giles III (USA), G Macgregor (GBI)
First Day – **Foursomes**
Abandoned – rain & flooding
Singles
A Doyle beat I Pyman 1 hole
D Berganio lost to M Stanford 3 and 2
J Sigel lost to D Robertson 3 and 2
K Mitchum halved with S Cage
T Herron beat P Harrington 1 hole
D Yates beat P Page 2 and 1
T Demsey beat R Russell 2 and 1
J Leonard beat R Burns 4 and 3
B Gay lost to V Phillips 2 and 1
J Harris beat B Dredge 4 and 3

Second Day – **Foursomes**
Doyle & Leonard beat Pyman & Cage 4 and 3
Berganio & Demsey beat Stanford & Harrington 3 and 2
Sigel & Mitchum beat Dredge & Phillips 3 and 2
Harris & Herron beat Russell & Robertson 1 hole
Singles
Doyle beat Robertson 4 and 3
Harris beat Pyman 3 and 2
Yates beat Cage 2 and 1
Gay halved with Harrington
Sigel beat Page 5 and 4
Herron beat Phillips 3 and 2
Mitchum beat Russell 4 and 2
Berganio lost to Burns 1 hole
Demsey beat Dredge 3 and 2
Leonard beat Stanford 5 and 4

1995 at Royal Porthcawl
Result: GBI 14, USA 10
Captains: C Brown (GBI), AD Gray jr (USA)
First Day – **Foursomes**
Sherry & Gallacher lost to Harris & Woods 4 and 3
Foster & Howell halved with Bratton & Riley
Rankin & Howard lost to Begay & Jackson 4 and 3
Harrington & Fanagan beat Cox & Kuehne 5 and 3

Singles
G Sherry beat N Begay 3 and 2
L James lost to K Cox 1 hole
M Foster beat B Marucci 4 and 3
S Gallacher beat T Jackson 4 and 3
P Harrington beat J Courville jr 2 holes
B Howard halved with A Bratton
G Rankin lost to J Harris 1 hole
GP Wolstenholme beat T Woods 1 hole

Second Day – Foursomes
Sherry & Gallacher lost to Bratton & Riley 4 and 2
Howell & Foster beat Cox & Kuehne 3 and 2
Wolstenholme & James lost to Marucci & Courville
   6 and 5
Harrington & Fanagan beat Harris & Woods 2 and 1

Singles
Sherry beat Riley 2 holes
Howell beat Begay 2 and 1
Gallacher beat Kuehne 3 and 2
Fanagan beat Courville 3 and 2
Howard halved with Jackson
Foster halved with Marucci
Harrington lost to Harris 3 and 2
Wolstenholme lost to Woods 4 and 3

1997 *at Quaker Ridge, NY*
Result: USA 18, GBI 6
Captains: AD Gray jr (USA), C Brown (GBI)
First Day – Foursomes
Howard & Young lost to Elder & Kribel 4 and 3
Rose & Brooks lost to Courville & Marucci 5 and 4
Wolstenholme & Nolan lost to Gore & Harris
   6 and 4
Coughlan & Park lost to Leen & Wollman 1 hole
Singles
S Young beat D Delcher 5 and 4
C Watson beat S Scott 1 hole
B Howard lost to B Elder 5 and 4
J Rose beat J Kribel 1 hole
K Nolan lost to R Leen 3 and 2
G Rankin lost to J Gore 3 and 2
R Coughlan halved with C Wollman
GP Wolstenholme lost to J Harris 1 hole

Second Day – Foursomes
Young & Watson lost to Harris & Elder 3 and 2
Howard & Rankin lost to Courville & Marucci 5 and 4
Coughlan & Park lost to Delcher & Scott 1 hole
Wolstenholme & Rose beat Leen & Wollman 2 and 1
Singles
Young beat Kribel 2 and 1
Watson halved with Gore
Rose lost to Courville 3 and 2
Nolan lost to Elder 2 and 1
Brooks lost to Harris 6 and 5
Park lost to Marucci 4 and 3
Wolstenholme lost to Delcher 2 and 1
Coughlan lost to Scott 2 and 1

1999 *at Nairn*
Result: GBI 15, USA 9
Captains: P McEvoy (GBI), D Yates jr (USA)

First Day – Foursomes
Rankin & Storm lost to Haas & Miller 1 hole
Casey & Donald beat Byrd & Scott 5 and 3
Gribben & Kelly lost to Gossett & Jackson 3 and 1
Rowe & Wolstenholme beat Kuchar & Molder 1 hole

Singles
G Rankin lost to E Loar 4 and 3
L Donald beat T McKnight 4 and 3
G Storm lost to H Haas 5 and 3
P Casey beat S Scott 4 and 3
D Patrick lost to J Byrd 6 and 5
S Dyson halved with D Gossett
P Gribben halved with B Molder
L Kelly lost to T Jackson 3 and 1

Second Day – Foursomes
Rankin & Storm beat Loar & McKnight 4 and 3
Dyson & Gribben lost to Haas & Miller 1 hole
Casey & Donald beat Gossett & Jackson 1 hole
Rowe & Wolstenholme beat Kuchar & Molder 4 and 3
Singles
Rankin beat Scott 1 hole
Dyson lost to Loar 5 and 4
Casey beat Miller 3 and 2
Storm beat Byrd 1 hole
Donald beat Molder 3 and 2
Rowe beat Kuchar 1 hole
Gribben beat Haas 3 and 2
Wolstenholme beat Gossett 1 hole

2001 *at Ocean Forest, Sea Island, GA*
Result: GBI 15, USA 9
Captains: D Yates jr (USA), P McEvoy (GBI)
First Day – Foursomes
D Green & DJ Trahan lost to S O'Hara & GP Wolstenholme
   5 and 3
N Cassini & L Glover beat L Donald & N Dougherty
   4 and 3
D Eger & B Molder halved with J Elson & R McEvoy
J Driscoll & J Quinney lost to G McDowell & M Hoey
   3 and 1
Singles
E Compton beat G Wolstenholme 3 and 2
DJ Trahan beat S O'Hara 2 and 1
J Driscoll lost to N Dougherty 2 and 1
N Cassini beat N Edwards 5 and 4
J Harris lost to M Warren 5 and 4
J Quinney lost to L Donald 3 and 2
B Molder beat G McDowell 2 and 1
L Glover beat M Hoey 1 hole

Second Day – Foursomes
E Compton & J Harris lost to L Donald & N Dougherty
   3 and 2
N Cassini & L Glover lost to G McDowell & M Hoey
   2 and 1
D Eger & B Molder beat S O'Hara & M Warren 7 and 6
D Green & DJ Trahan lost to J Elson & R McEvoy 1 hole
Singles
L Glover lost to L Donald 3 and 2
J Harris lost to S O'Hara 4 and 3
DJ Trahan lost to N Dougherty 1 hole
J Driscoll lost to M Warren 2 and 1
B Molder beat G McDowell 1 hole
D Green lost to M Hoey 1 hole
E Compton halved with J Elson
N Cassini lost to GP Wolstenholme 4 and 3

Walker Cup – INDIVIDUAL RECORDS

Notes: Bold type indicates captain; in brackets, did not play
  † indicates players who have also played in the Ryder Cup

Great Britain and Ireland

Name		Year	Played	Won	Lost	Halved
MF Attenborough	Eng	1967	2	0	2	0
CC Aylmer	Eng	1922	2	1	1	0
†P Baker	Eng	1985	3	2	1	0
JB Beck	Eng	1928-(38)-(47)	1	0	1	0
PJ Benka	Eng	1969	4	2	1	1
HG Bentley	Eng	1934-36-38	4	0	2	2
DA Blair	Sco	1955-61	4	1	3	0
C Bloice	Sco	1985	3	0	2	1
MF Bonallack	Eng	1957-59-61-63-65-67-**69-71-73**	25	8	14	3
†G Brand jr	Sco	1979	3	0	3	0
OC Bristowe	Eng	(1923)-24	1	0	1	0
A Brodie	Sco	1977-79	8	5	2	1
A Brooks	Sco	1969	3	2	0	1
M Brooks	Sco	1997	2	0	2	0
C Brown	Wal	**1995**-(97)	0	0	0	0
Hon WGE Brownlow	Eng	1926	2	0	2	0
J Bruen	Irl	1938-49-51	5	0	4	1
JA Buckley	Wal	1979	1	0	1	0
J Burke	Irl	1932	2	0	1	1
R Burns	Irl	1993	2	1	1	0
AF Bussell	Sco	1957	2	1	1	0
S Cage	Eng	1993	3	0	2	1
I Caldwell	Eng	1951-55	4	1	2	1
W Campbell	Sco	1930	2	0	2	0
JB Carr	Irl	1947-49-51-53-55-57-59-61-63-(65)-**67**	20	5	14	1
RJ Carr	Irl	1971	4	3	0	1
DG Carrick	Sco	1983-87	5	0	5	0
IA Carslaw	Sco	1979	3	1	1	1
P Casey	Eng	1999	4	4	0	0
C Cassells	Eng	1989	3	2	1	0
JR Cater	Sco	1955	1	0	1	0
J Caven	Sco	1922	2	0	2	0
BHG Chapman	Eng	1961	1	0	1	0
R Chapman	Eng	1981	4	3	1	0
MJ Christmas	Eng	1961-63	3	1	2	0
†CA Clark	Eng	1965	4	2	0	2
GJ Clark	Eng	1965	1	0	1	0
†HK Clark	Eng	1973	3	1	1	1
R Claydon	Eng	1989	4	2	2	0
†A Coltart	Sco	1991	3	2	1	0
GB Cosh	Sco	1965	4	3	1	0
R Coughlan	Irl	1997	4	0	3	1
T Craddock	Irl	1967-69	6	2	3	1
LG Crawley	Eng	1932-34-38-47	6	3	3	0
B Critchley	Eng	1969	4	1	1	2
D Curry	Eng	1987	4	1	3	0
CR Dalgleish	Sco	1981	3	1	2	0
B Darwin	Eng	1922	2	1	1	0
JC Davies	Eng	1973-75-77-79	13	3	8	2
P Deeble	Eng	1977-81	5	1	4	0
FWG Deighton	Sco	(1951)-57	2	0	2	0
SC Dodd	Wal	1989	4	1	1	2
L Donald	Eng	1999-01	8	7	1	0
N Dougherty	Eng	2001	4	3	1	0
B Dredge	Wal	1993	3	0	3	0
†NV Drew	Irl	1953	1	0	1	0
AA Duncan	Wal	(1953)	0	0	0	0
JM Dykes	Sco	1936	2	0	1	1
S Dyson	Eng	1999	3	0	2	1
N Edwards	Wal	2001	1	0	1	0
R Eggo	Eng	1987	2	0	2	0

Walker Cup Individual Records *continued*

Name		Year	Played	Won	Lost	Halved
J Elson	Eng	2001	3	1	0	2
D Evans	Wal	1981	3	1	1	1
G Evans	Eng	1991	4	2	2	0
RC Ewing	Irl	1936-38-47-49-51-55	10	1	7	2
GRD Eyles	Eng	1975	4	2	2	0
J Fanagan	Irl	1995	3	3	0	0
EW Fiddian	Eng	1932-34	4	0	4	0
J de Forest	Eng	1932	1	0	1	0
M Foster	Eng	1995	4	2	0	2
R Foster	Eng	1965-67-69-71-73-(79)-(81)	17	2	13	2
DW Frame	Eng	1961	1	0	1	0
S Gallacher	Sco	1995	4	2	2	0
†D Gilford	Eng	1985	1	0	1	0
P Girvan	Sco	1987	3	0	3	0
G Godwin	Eng	1979-81	7	2	4	1
CW Green	Sco	1963-69-71-73-75-(83)-(85)	17	4	10	3
P Gribben	Irl	1999	4	1	2	1
RH Hardman	Eng	1928	1	0	1	0
A Hare	Eng	1989	3	2	2	0
†P Harrington	Irl	1991-93-95	9	3	5	1
R Harris	Sco	(1922)-23-26	4	1	3	0
RW Hartley	Eng	1930-32	4	0	4	0
WL Hartley	Eng	1932	2	0	2	0
J Hawksworth	Eng	1985	4	2	1	1
G Hay	Sco	1991	3	1	2	0
P Hedges	Eng	1973-75	5	0	2	3
CO Hezlet	Irl	1924-26-28	6	0	5	1
GA Hill	Eng	1936-(55)	2	0	1	1
M Hoey	Irl	2001	4	3	1	0
Sir EWE Holderness	Eng	1923-26-30	6	2	4	0
TWB Homer	Eng	1973	3	0	3	0
‡CVL Hooman	Eng	1922-23	3	†1	2	†0
WL Hope	Sco	1923-24-28	5	1	4	0
DB Howard	Sco	1995-97	6	0	4	2
D Howell	Eng	1995	3	2	0	1
G Huddy	Eng	1961	1	0	1	0
W Humphreys	Eng	1971	3	2	1	0
IC Hutcheon	Sco	1975-77-79-81	15	5	8	2
RR Jack	Sco	1957-59	4	2	2	0
L James	Eng	1995	2	0	2	0
†M James	Eng	1975	4	3	1	0
A Jamieson jr	Sco	1926	2	1	1	0
MJ Kelley	Eng	1977-79	7	3	3	1
L Kelly	Sco	1999	2	0	2	0
SD Keppler	Eng	1983	4	0	3	1
†MG King	Eng	1969-73	7	1	5	1
AT Kyle	Sco	1938-47-51	5	2	3	0
DH Kyle	Sco	1924	1	0	1	0
JA Lang	Sco	(1930)	0	0	0	0
JDA Langley	Eng	1936-51-53	6	0	5	1
CD Lawrie	Sco	(1961)-(63)	0	0	0	0
ME Lewis	Eng	1983	1	0	1	0
PB Lucas	Eng	(1936)-47-(49)	2	1	1	0
MSR Lunt	Eng	1959-61-63-65	11	2	8	1
†AWB Lyle	Sco	1977	3	0	3	0
AR McCallum	Sco	1928	1	0	1	0
SM McCready	Irl	1949-51	3	0	3	0
JS Macdonald	Sco	1971	3	1	1	1
G McDowell	Irl	2001	4	2	2	0
P McEvoy	Eng	1977-79-81-85-89-(99)-(01)	18	5	11	2
R McEvoy	Eng	2001	2	1	0	1
G McGimpsey	Irl	1985-89-91	11	4	5	2
P McGinley	Irl	1991	3	1	2	0
G Macgregor	Sco	1971-75-83-85-87-(91)-(93)	14	5	8	1
RC MacGregor	Sco	1953	2	0	2	0
J McHenry	Irl	1987	4	2	2	0
P McKellar	Sco	1977	1	0	1	0
WW Mackenzie	Sco	1922-23	3	1	2	0

‡*In 1922 Hooman beat Sweetser at the 37th – on all other occasions halved matches have counted as such.*

Name		Year	Played	Won	Lost	Halved
SL McKinlay	Sco	1934	2	0	2	0
J McLean	Sco	1934-36	4	1	3	0
EA McRuvie	Sco	1932-34	4	1	2	1
JFD Madeley	Irl	1963	2	0	1	1
LS Mann	Sco	1983	4	2	1	1
B Marchbank	Sco	1979	4	2	2	0
GC Marks	Eng	1969-71-(**87**)-(**89**)	6	2	4	0
DM Marsh	Eng	71-(**73**)-(**75**)	3	2	1	0
GNC Martin	Irl	1928	1	0	1	0
S Martin	Sco	1977	4	2	2	0
P Mayo	Wal	1985-87	4	0	3	1
GH Micklem	Eng	1947-49-53-55-(**57**)-(**59**)	6	1	5	0
DJ Millensted	Eng	1967	2	1	1	0
JW Milligan	Sco	1989-91	7	3	3	1
EB Millward	Eng	(**1949**)-55	2	0	2	0
WTG Milne	Sco	1973	4	2	2	0
†CS Montgomerie	Sco	1985-87	8	2	5	1
JL Morgan	Wal	1951-53-55	6	2	4	0
P Mulcare	Irl	1975	3	2	1	0
GH Murray	Sco	1977	2	1	1	0
SWT Murray	Sco	1963	4	2	2	0
WA Murray	Sco	1923-24-(26)	4	1	3	0
K Nolan	Irl	1997	3	0	3	0
E O'Connell	Irl	1989	4	2	0	2
S O'Hara	Sco	2001	4	2	2	0
A Oldcorn	Eng	1983	4	4	0	0
†PA Oosterhuis	Eng	1967	4	1	2	1
R Oppenheimer	Eng	(**1951**)	0	0	0	0
P Page	Eng	1993	2	0	2	0
D Park	Wal	1997	3	0	3	0
P Parkin	Wal	1983	3	2	1	0
D Patrick	Sco	1999	1	0	1	0
J Payne	Eng	1991	4	2	2	0
JJF Pennink	Eng	1938	2	1	1	0
TP Perkins	Eng	1928	2	0	2	0
GB Peters	Sco	1936-38	4	2	1	1
V Phillips	Eng	1993	3	1	2	0
AD Pierse	Irl	1983	3	0	2	1
AH Perowne	Eng	1949-53-59	4	0	4	0
AK Pirie	Sco	1967	3	0	2	1
MA Poxon	Eng	1975	2	0	2	0
D Prosser	Eng	1989	1	0	1	2
I Pyman	Eng	1993	3	0	3	0
†R Rafferty	Irl	1981	4	2	2	0
G Rankin	Sco	1995-97-99	8	2	6	0
D Robertson	Sco	1993	3	1	2	0
J Robinson	Eng	1987	4	2	2	0
RN Roderick	Wal	1989	2	0	1	1
J Rose	Eng	1997	4	2	2	0
P Rowe	Eng	1999	3	3	0	0
R Russell	Sco	1993	3	0	3	0
AC Saddler	Sco	1963-65-67-(**77**)	10	3	5	2
Hon M Scott	Eng	1924-**34**	4	2	2	0
R Scott, jr	Sco	1924	1	1	0	0
PF Scrutton	Eng	1955-57	3	0	3	0
DN Sewell	Eng	1957-59	4	1	3	0
RDBM Shade	Sco	1961-63-65-67	14	6	6	2
G Shaw	Sco	1987	4	1	2	1
DB Sheahan	Irl	1963	4	2	2	0
AE Shepperson	Eng	1957-59	3	1	1	1
G Sherry	Sco	1995	4	2	2	0
AF Simpson	Sco	(1926)	0	0	0	0
JN Smith	Sco	1930	2	0	2	0
WD Smith	Sco	1959	1	0	1	0
M Stanford	Eng	1993	3	1	2	0
AR Stephen	Sco	1985	4	2	1	1
EF Storey	Eng	1924-26-28	6	1	5	0
G Storm	Eng	1999	4	2	2	0
JA Stout	Eng	1930-32	4	0	3	1
C Stowe	Eng	1938-47	4	2	2	0

Walker Cup Individual Records *continued*

Name		Year	Played	Won	Lost	Halved
HB Stuart	Sco	1971-73-75	10	4	6	0
A Thirlwell	Eng	1957	1	0	1	0
KG Thom	Eng	1949	2	0	2	0
MS Thompson	Eng	1983	3	1	2	0
H Thomson	Sco	1936-38	4	2	2	0
CJH Tolley	Eng	1922-23-**24**-26-30-34	12	4	8	0
TA Torrance	Sco	1924-28-30-**32**-34	9	3	5	1
WB Torrance	Sco	1922	2	0	2	0
†PM Townsend	Eng	1965	4	3	1	0
LP Tupling	Eng	1969	2	1	1	0
W Tweddell	Eng	**1928**-(36)	2	0	2	0
J Walker	Sco	1961	2	0	2	0
†P Walton	Irl	1981-83	8	6	2	0
M Warren	Sco	2001	3	2	1	0
C Watson	Sco	1997	3	1	1	1
†P Way	Eng	1981	4	2	2	0
RH Wethered	Eng	1922-23-26-**30**-34	9	5	3	1
L White	Eng	1991	2	1	1	0
RJ White	Eng	1947-49-51-53-55	10	6	3	1
R Willison	Eng	1991	4	1	3	0
J Wilson	Sco	1923	2	2	0	0
JC Wilson	Sco	1947-53	4	0	4	0
GB Wolstenholme	Eng	1957-59	4	1	2	1
GP Wolstenholme	Eng	1995-97-99-01	13	7	6	0
S Young	Sco	1997	4	2	2	0

United States of America

Name	Year	Played	Won	Lost	Halved
†TD Aaron	1959	2	1	1	0
B Alexander	1987	3	2	1	0
DC Allen	1965-67	6	0	4	2
B Andrade	1987	4	2	2	0
ES Andrews	1961	1	1	0	0
D Ballenger	1973	1	1	0	0
R Baxter, jr	1957	2	2	0	0
N Begay III	1995	3	1	2	0
DR Beman	1959-61-63-65	11	7	2	2
D Berganio	1993	3	1	2	0
RE Billows	1938-49	4	2	2	0
SE Bishop	1947-49	3	2	1	0
AS Blum	1957	1	0	1	0
J Bohmann	1969	3	1	2	0
M Brannan	1977	3	1	2	0
A Bratton	1995	3	1	0	2
GF Burns	1975	3	2	1	0
C Burroughs	1985	3	1	2	0
J Byrd	1999	3	1	2	0
AE Campbell	1936	2	2	0	0
JE Campbell	1957	1	0	1	0
WC Campbell	1951-53-(**55**)-57-65-67-71-75	18	11	4	3
N Cassini	2001	4	2	2	0
RJ Cerrudo	1967	4	1	1	2
RD Chapman	1947-51-53	5	3	2	0
D Cherry	1953-55-61	5	5	0	0
D Clarke	1979	3	2	0	1
RE Cochran	1961	1	1	0	0
CR Coe	1949-51-53-(**57**)-**59**-61-63	13	7	4	2
R Commans	1981	3	1	1	1
E Compton	2001	3	1	1	1
JW Conrad	1955	2	1	1	0
J Courville jr	1995-97	6	4	2	0
K Cox	1995	3	1	2	0
N Crosby	1983	2	1	1	0
BH Cudd	1955	2	2	0	0

Name	Year	Played	Won	Lost	Halved
RD Davies	1963	2	0	2	0
JW Dawson	1949	2	2	0	0
D Delcher	1997	3	2	1	0
T Demsey	1993	3	3	0	0
RB Dickson	1967	3	3	0	0
A Doyle	1991-93	6	5	1	0
J Driscoll	2001	3	0	3	0
GT Dunlap jr	1932-34-36	5	3	1	1
†D Duval	1991	3	2	1	0
D Edwards	1973	4	4	0	0
HC Egan	1934	1	1	0	0
D Eger	1991-01	5	3	1	1
HC Eger	1989	3	1	2	0
D Eichelberger	1965	3	1	2	0
B Elder	1997	4	4	0	0
J Ellis	1973	3	2	1	0
W Emery	1936	2	1	0	1
C Evans jr	1922-24-28	5	3	2	0
J Farquhar	1971	3	1	2	0
†B Faxon	1983	4	3	1	0
R Fehr	1983	4	2	1	1
JW Fischer	1934-36-38-(65)	4	3	0	1
D Fischesser	1979	3	1	2	0
MA Fleckman	1967	2	0	2	0
B Fleisher	1969	4	0	2	2
J Fought	1977	4	4	0	0
WC Fownes jr	**1922-24**	3	1	2	0
F Fuhrer	1981	3	2	1	0
JR Gabrielsen	1977-(81)-(91)	3	1	2	0
R Gamez	1989	4	3	0	1
RA Gardner	1922-**23-24-26**	8	6	2	0
RW Gardner	1961-63	5	4	0	1
B Gay	1993	2	0	1	1
M Giles	1969-71-73-75	15	8	2	5
HL Givan	1936	1	0	0	1
L Glover	2001	4	2	2	0
JG Goodman	1934-36-38	6	4	2	0
J Gore	1997	3	2	0	1
D Gossett	1999	4	1	2	1
M Gove	1979	3	2	1	0
J Grace	1975	3	2	1	0
JA Grant	1967	2	2	0	0
AD Gray jr	1963-65-67-(95)-(97)	12	5	6	1
D Green	2001	3	0	3	0
JP Guilford	1922-24-26	6	4	2	0
W Gunn	1926-28	4	4	0	0
†F Haas jr	1938	2	0	2	0
H Haas	1999	4	3	1	0
†J Haas	1975	3	3	0	0
J Haas	1985	3	1	2	0
G Hallberg	1977	3	1	2	0
GS Hamer jr	(1947)	0	0	0	0
J Harris	1993-95-97-01	14	10	4	0
LE Harris jr	1963	4	3	1	0
V Heafner	1977	3	3	0	0
SD Herron	1923	2	0	2	0
T Herron	1993	3	3	0	0
†S Hoch	1979	4	4	0	0
W Hoffer	1983	2	1	1	0
J Holtgrieve	1979-81-83	10	6	4	0
JM Hopkins	1965	3	0	2	1
R Howe	1989	1	0	1	0
W Howell	1932	1	1	0	0
W Hyndman	1957-59-61-69-71	9	6	1	2
J Inman	1969	2	2	0	0
JG Jackson	1953-55	3	3	0	0
T Jackson	1995-99	6	3	2	1
K Johnson	1989	3	1	2	0
HR Johnston	1923-24-28-30	6	5	1	0
RT Jones jr	1922-24-26-**28-30**	10	9	1	0

Walker Cup Individual Records *continued*

Name	Year	Played	Won	Lost	Halved
AF Kammer	1947	2	1	1	0
M Killian	1973	3	1	2	0
C Kite	1987	3	2	1	0
†TO Kite	1971	4	2	1	1
RE Knepper	(1922)	0	0	0	0
RW Knowles	1951	1	1	0	0
G Koch	1973-75	7	4	1	2
CR Kocsis	1938-49-57	5	2	2	1
J Kribel	1997	3	1	2	0
M Kuchar	1999	3	0	3	0
T Kuehne	1995	3	0	3	0
F Langham	1991	3	1	2	0
R Leen	1997	3	2	1	0
†J Leonard	1993	3	3	0	0
G Lesher	1989	4	1	3	0
B Lewis jr	1981-83-85-87	14	10	4	0
JW Lewis	1967	4	3	1	0
WL Little jr	1934	2	2	0	0
†GA Littler	1953	2	2	0	0
E Loar	1999	3	2	1	0
B Loeffler	1987	3	2	1	0
†D Love III	1985	3	2	0	1
RR Mackenzie	1926-28-30	6	5	1	0
MJ McCarthy jr	(1928)-32	1	1	0	0
BN McCormick	1949	1	1	0	0
T McKnight	1999	2	0	2	0
JB McHale	1949-51	3	2	0	1
MR Marston	1922-23-24-34	8	5	3	0
D Martin	1989	4	1	1	2
B Marucci	1995-97	6	4	1	1
L Mattiace	1987	3	2	1	0
R May	1991	4	3	1	0
B Mayfair	1987	3	3	0	0
E Meeks	1989	1	0	0	1
SN Melnyk	1969-71	7	3	3	1
†P Mickelson	1989-91	8	4	2	2
AL Miller	1969-71	8	4	3	1
J Miller	1999	3	2	1	0
L Miller	1977	4	4	0	0
K Mitchum	1993	3	2	0	1
DK Moe	1930-32	3	3	0	0
B Molder	1999-01	8	3	3	2
B Montgomery	1987	2	2	0	0
G Moody	1979	3	1	2	0
GT Moreland	1932-34	4	4	0	0
D Morey	1955-65	4	1	3	0
J Mudd	1981	3	3	0	0
†RJ Murphy	1967	4	1	2	1
JF Neville	1923	1	0	1	0
†JW Nicklaus	1959-61	4	4	0	0
LW Oehmig	(1977)	0	0	0	0
FD Ouimet	1922-23-24-26-30-**32-34**-(**36**)-(**38**)-(**47**)-(**49**)	16	9	5	2
HD Paddock jr	1951	1	0	0	1
†J Pate	1975	4	0	4	0
WJ Patton	1955-57-59-63-65-(**69**)	14	11	3	0
†C Pavin	1981	3	2	0	1
M Peck	1979	3	1	1	1
M Pfeil	1973	4	2	1	1
M Podolak	1985	2	1	0	1
SL Quick	1947	2	1	1	0
J Quinney	2001	2	0	2	0
S Randolph	1985	4	2	1	1
J Rassett	1981	3	3	0	0
F Ridley	1977-(**87**)-(**89**)	3	2	1	0
RH Riegel	1947-49	4	4	0	0
C Riley	1995	3	1	1	1
H Robbins jr	1957	2	0	1	1
†W Rogers	1973	2	1	1	0

Name	Year	Played	Won	Lost	Halved
GV Rotan	1923	2	1	1	0
†EM Rudolph	1957	2	1	0	1
B Sander	1977	3	0	3	0
T Scherrer	1991	3	0	3	0
S Scott	1997-99	6	2	4	0
CH Seaver	1932	2	2	0	0
RL Siderowf	1969-73-75-77-(79)	14	4	8	2
J Sigel	1977-79-81-83-85-87-89-91-93	33	18	10	5
RH Sikes	1963	3	1	2	0
JB Simons	1971	2	0	2	0
†S Simpson	1977	3	3	0	0
CB Smith	1961-63	2	0	1	1
R Smith	1936-38	4	2	2	0
R Sonnier	1985	3	0	2	1
J Sorensen	1987	3	1	1	1
M Sposa	1991	3	2	1	0
†C Stadler	1975	3	3	0	0
FR Stranahan	1947-49-51	6	3	2	1
†C Strange	1975	4	3	0	1
†H Sutton	1979-81	7	2	4	1
‡JW Sweetser	1922-23-24-26-28-32-(67)-(73)	12	7	†4	†1
FM Taylor	1957-59-61	4	4	0	0
D Tentis	1983	2	0	1	1
DJ Trahan	2001	4	1	3	0
RS Tufts	(1963)	0	0	0	0
WP Turnesa	1947-49-51	6	3	3	0
B Tuten	1983	2	1	1	0
EM Tutweiler	1965-67	6	5	1	0
ER Updegraff	1963-65-69-(75)	7	3	3	1
S Urzetta	1951-53	4	4	0	0
K Venturi	1953	2	2	0	0
S Verplank	1985	4	3	0	1
M Voges	1991	3	2	1	0
GJ Voigt	1930-32-36	5	2	2	1
G Von Elm	1926-28-30	6	4	1	1
D von Tacky	1981	3	1	2	0
†JL Wadkins	1969-71	7	3	4	0
D Waldorf	1985	3	1	2	0
EH Ward	1953-55-59	6	6	0	0
MH Ward	1938-47	4	2	2	0
M West	1973-79	6	2	3	1
J Westland	1932-34-53-(61)	5	3	0	2
HW Wettlaufer	1959	2	2	0	0
E White	1936	2	2	0	0
OF Willing	1923-24-30	4	4	0	0
JM Winters jr	(1971)	0	0	0	0
C Wollman	1997	3	1	1	1
W Wood	1983	4	1	2	1
†T Woods	1995	4	2	2	0
FJ Wright	1923	1	1	0	0
CR Yates	1936-38-(53)	4	3	0	1
D Yates jr	1989-93-(99)-01	6	3	2	1
RL Yost	1955	2	2	0	0

World Amateur Team Championship (Eisenhower Trophy)

Year	Winners	Runners-up	Venue	Score
1958	Australia	United States	St Andrews	918
(After a tie, Australia won the play-off by two strokes: Australia 222, United States 224)				
1960	United States	Australia	Ardmore, USA	834
1962	United States	Canada	Kawana, Japan	854
1964	Great Britain & Ireland	Canada	Olgiata, Rome	895
1966	Australia	United States	Mexico City	877
1968	United States	Great Britain & Ireland	Melbourne	868
1970	United States	New Zealand	Madrid	857
1972	United States	Australia	Buenos Aires	865
1974	United States	Japan	Dominican Rep.	888
1976	Great Britain & Ireland	Japan	Penina, Portugal	892

‡ *In 1922 Hooman beat Sweetser at the 37th – on all other occasions halved matches have counted as such.*

World Amateur Team Championship *continued*

Year	Winners	Runners-up	Venue	Score
1978	United States	Canada	Fiji	873
1980	United States	South Africa	Pinehurst, USA	848
1982	United States	Sweden	Lausanne	859
1984	Japan	United States	Hong Kong	870
1986	Canada	United States	Caracas, Venezuela	860
1988	Great Britain & Ireland	United States	Ullva, Sweden	882
1990	Sweden	New Zealand	Christchurch, New Zealand	879
1992	New Zealand	United States	Capilano, Canada	823
1994	United States	Great Britain & Ireland	Paris, France	838
1996	Australia	Sweden	Manila, Philippines	838
1998	Great Britain and Ireland	Australia	Los Leones/La Dehesa, Chile	852
2000	United States	Great Britain & Ireland	Sporting Club, Berlin	841

2002 *at Saujana, Kuala Lumpur, Malaysia*

1   USA   568
   (Ricky Barnes, Hunter Mahan, DJ Trahan)

2   FRANCE   571
   (Eric Chaudouet, Raphael Pellicioli, Gregory Bourdy)

3T   AUSTRALIA   574
   (Marcus Fraser, Andrew Buckle, Adam Groom)

   PHILIPPINES   574
   (Angelo Que, Juvic Pagunsan, Jerome Delariarte)

5T   AUSTRIA   575
   (Martin Wiegele, Thomas Ortner, Thomas Kogler)

   NEW ZEALAND   575
   (Tim Wilkinson, Brad Shilton, Eddie Lee)

7   ENGLAND   578
   (Gary Wolstenholme, Richard Walker, Jamie Elson)

8   COLOMBIA   580
   (Camilo Villegas, Andres Mauricio Rodrigue, Manuel Jose Merizalde)

9   ITALY   581
   (Francesco Molinari, Edoardo Molinari, Andrea Romano)

10   SPAIN   582
   (Pablo Martin, Alfredo García, Gonzalo Fernandez-Castano)

Individual leader: Marcus Fraser (Aus)   281

Europe v Asia-Pacific (Bonallack Cup)

2002 *at Hirono GC, Japan*

First Day: **Morning – Fourball**

Chang and Meesawat halved with Warren and Wilson

Fujishima and Miyazato halved with Heredia and Molinari

Fraser and Hickmott lost to Reimbold and Wiegele 1 hole

Misra and Wilkinson beat N Edwards and de Sousa 3 and 2

Kwon and Jeong lost to C Edwards and Stanford 5 and 4

Afternoon – Foursome

Fujishima and Miyazato beat Warren and Wilson 4 and 3

Chang and Meesawat beat Heredia and Moloinari 2 and 1

Fraser and Hickmott halved with C Edwards and Stanford

Kapur and Misra lost to N Edwards and Hansen 2 and 1

Lee and Wilkinson lost to Reimbold and Wiegele 2 and 1

Second Day: **Morning – Fourball**

Lee and Wilkinson beat Warren and Wilson
5 and 4

Kwon and Jeong lost to Heredia and Molinari
5 and 3

Fujishima and Miyazato lost to Reimbold and
Wiegele 1 hole

Fraser and Hickmott beat Pilo and de Sousa
2 holes

Chang and Meesawat lost to C Edwards and
Stanford 2 and 1

Afternoon – Foursome

Kapur and Misra lost to Heredia and Molinari
4 and 3

Lee and Wilkinson beat Reimbold and Wiegele
3 and 2

Fraser and Hickmott beat N Edwards and Hansen
4 and 3

Chang and Meesawat halved with C Edwards and
Stanford

Fujishima and Miyazato beat Warren and Wilson
3 and 2

Match result: Asia-Pacific 18, Europe 14

Third Day: **Singles**

Prom Meesawat (Tha) beat Mark Warren (Sco)
6 and 5

Luke Hickmott (Aus) beat Christian Reimbold
(Ger) 1 hole

Eddie Lee (NZ) beat Edoardo Molinari (Ita)
5 and 4

Ki-Teak Kwon (Kor) lost to Martin Wiegele (Aut)
5 and 4

Keshav Misra (Ind) lost to Stuart Wilson (Sco)
4 and 3

Hong-Wei Chang (Tai) beat Alfredo Heredia (Esp)
1 hole

Yusaku Miyazato (Jpn) lost to Colin Edwards
(Eng) 1 hole

Ji-Ho Jeong (Kor) beat Mathew Stanford (Eng)
4 and 3

Shiv Kapur (Ind) lost to Nigel Edwards (Wal)
3 and 2

Tim Wilkinson (NZ) beat Mats Pilo (Swe)
3 and 2

Haruo Fujishima (Jpn) beat Anders Hansen (Den)
4 and 3

Marcus Fraser (Aus) beat Raphael de Sousa (Sui)
6 and 5

European Amateur Team Championship

Year	Winner	Runner-up	Venue
1959	Sweden	France	Barcelona, Spain
1961	Sweden	England	Brussels, Belgium
1963	England	Sweden	Falsterbo, Sweden
1965	Ireland	Scotland	St George's, England
1967	Ireland	France	Turin, Italy
1969	England	Germany	Hamburg, Germany
1971	England	Scotland	Lausanne, Switzerland
1973	England	Scotland	Penina, Portugal
1975	Scotland	Italy	Killarney, Ireland
1977	Scotland	Sweden	The Haagsche, Netherlands
1979	England	Wales	Esbjerg, Denmark
1981	England	Scotland	St Andrews, Scotland
1983	Ireland	Spain	Chantilly, France
1985	Scotland	Sweden	Halmstad, Sweden
1987	Ireland	England	Murhof, Austria
1989	England	Scotland	Royal Porthcawl, Wales
1991	England	Italy	Puerta de Hierro, Spain
1993	Wales	England	Marianske Lasne, Czech Republic
1995	Scotland	England	Royal Antwerp, Belgium
1997	Spain	Scotland	Portmarnock, Ireland
1999	Italy	Germany	Monticello, Italy
2001	Scotland	Ireland	Ljunghusens, Sweden

European Club Cup (Albacom Trophy)

1975	Club de Campo, Spain	Club de Campo		1985	El Prat, Spain	Aloha
1976	Växjö Golfklub, Sweden	El Prat		1986	Hamburger, Germany	Aloha
1977	Chantilly, France	RC Belgique		1987	Puerto de Hierro, Spain	Aloha
1978	Hamburger, Germany	Deauville		1988	Brokenhurst Manor, England	Aloha
1979	Hamburger, Germany	Santa Ponsa		1989	Ealing, England	Aloha
1980	Limerick, Ireland	Santa Ponsa		1990	Ealing, England	Aloha
1981	El Prat, Spain	Aloha		1991	Club de Golf Terramar, Spain	La Quinta
1982	El Prat, Spain	Aloha		1992	Hillerod, Denmark	La Quinta
1983	Rapallo, Italy	Aloha		1993	Lahden, Finland	La Quinta
1984	Hamburger, Germany	Aloha				

European Club Cup continued

1994	Kilmarnock (Barassie),			1998	Aalborg, Denmark	Parco de Medici
	Scotland	Vilamoura		1999	Aalborg, Denmark	Parco de Medici
1995	Racing C de France, France	Vilamoura		2000	Shandon Park,	
1996	Racing C de France, France	Vilamoura			Northern Ireland	Parco de Medici
1997	Racing C de France, France	Parco de Medici		2001	Shandon Park	La Boulie

2002 at Parco de Medici

1 Bordelais (France), 2 Vilamoura (Portugal, 3 Woodcote Park (England)

St Andrews Trophy (Great Britain & Ireland v Continent of Europe) Match instituted 1956, trophy presented 1962

1956	Great Britain & Ireland	Wentworth	12½–2½
1958	Great Britain & Ireland	St Cloud, France	10–5
1960	Great Britain & Ireland	Walton Heath	13–5
1962	Great Britain & Ireland	Halmstead, Sweden	18–12
1964	Great Britain & Ireland	Muirfield	23–7
1966	Great Britain & Ireland	Bilbao, Spain	19½–10½
1968	Great Britain & Ireland	Portmarnock	20–10
1970	Great Britain & Ireland	La Zoute, Belgium	17½–12½
1972	Great Britain & Ireland	Berkshire	19½–10½
1974	Continent of Europe	Punta Ala, Italy	16–14
1976	Great Britain & Ireland	St Andrews	18½–11½
1978	Great Britain & Ireland	Bremen, Germany	20½–9½
1980	Great Britain & Ireland	Sandwich, Royal St George's	19½–10½
1982	Continent of Europe	Rosendaelsche, Netherlands	14–10
1984	Great Britain & Ireland	Saunton, Devon	13–11
1986	Great Britain & Ireland	Halmstead, Sweden	14½–9½
1988	Great Britain & Ireland	St Andrews	15½–8½
1990	Great Britain & Ireland	El Saler, Spain	13–11
1992	Great Britain & Ireland	Royal Cinque Ports	14–10
1994	Great Britain & Ireland	Chantilly, France	14–10
1996	Great Britain & Ireland	Woodhall Spa	16–8
1998	Continent of Europe	Villa d'Este, Italy	14–10
2000	Great Britain & Ireland	The Ailsa Course, Turnberry	13–11

2002 at Lausanne, Switzerland

Continent of Europe		GB&I	
First Day – **Foursomes**			
Wiegele and Santos (4 and 3)	1	Walker and Clark	0
Lima and Clément (halved)	½	Wolstenholme and Edwards (halved)	½
Lemke and Sundström	0	Scotland and Elson (6 and 5)	1
García-Heredia and Larrazábal (1 hole)	1	Mackenzie and Gordon	0
	2½		**1½**
Singles			
Philippe Lima (Fra)	0	Gary Wolstenholme (Eng) (6 and 4)	1
Nicolas Sulzer (Sui) (5 and 4)	1	Richard Walker (Eng)	0
Martin Wiegele (Aut) (6 and 5)	1	Jonathan Lupton (Eng)	0
Alfredo García-Heredia	0	Zane Scotland (Eng) (1 hole)	1
Niklas Lemke (Swe) (2 holes)	1	Jamie Elson (Eng)	0
Hugo Santos (Por) (4 and 3)	1	Graeme Clark (Eng)	0
Julien Clément	0	Nigel Edwards (Wal) (1 hole)	1
Alejandro Larrazábal	0	Graham Gordon (Sco) (4 and 3)	1
	4		**4**

Match position: Continent of Europe 6½, GB&I 5½

Second Day – **Foursomes**			
Wiegele and Santos	0	Mackenzie and Gordon (1 hole)	1
Lemke and Sundström	0	Wolstenholme and Edwards (4 and 3)	1
Lima and Sulzer (7 and 6)	1	Scotland and Elson	0
García-Heredia and Larrazábal	0	Ilonen and Kylliainen (6 and 4)	1
	1		**3**

Singles

Lemke (halved)	½	Wolstenholme (halved)	½
Sulzer	0	Gordon (3 and 2)	1
Santos	0	Scotland (2 and 1)	1
Wiegele (2 and 1)	1	Elson	0
Sundström	0	Walker (2 and 1)	1
Clément (halved)	½	Simon Mackenzie (Sco)	½
Larrazábal	0	Clark (3 and 2)	1
García-Heredia (halved)	½	Edwards (halved)	½
	2½		5½

Captains: Wolfgang Wiegand (Ger), Garth McGimpsey (Irl)

Match Result: Continent of Europe 10, GB&I 14

Home Internationals

1932	Scotland	1959T	England/Ireland/Scotland	1979	No Internationals held
1933	Scotland	1960	England	1980	England
1934	Scotland	1961	Scotland	1981	Scotland
1935T	England/Ireland/Scotland	1962T	England/Ireland/Scotland	1982	Scotland
1936	Scotland	1963T	England/Ireland/Scotland	1983	Ireland
1937	Scotland	1964	England	1984	England
1938	England	1965	England	1985	England
1939–46	No Internationals held	1966	England	1986	Scotland
1947	England	1967	Scotland	1987	Ireland
1948	England	1968	England	1988	England
1949	England	1969	England	1989	England
1950	Ireland	1970	Scotland	1990	Ireland
1951T	Ireland and Scotland	1971	Scotland	1991	Ireland
1952	Scotland	1972T	Scotland/England	1992T	England and Ireland
1953	Scotland	1973	England	1993	England
1954	England	1974	England	1994	England
1955	Ireland	1975	Scotland	1995	England
1956	Scotland	1976	Scotland	1996	England
1957	England	1977	England		
1958	England	1978	England		

1997 at Burnham & Berrow

England beat Wales	10½ matches to 4½
Ireland beat Scotland	10½ matches to 4½
England beat Scotland	10½ matches to 4½
Ireland beat Wales	8½ matches to 6½
England halved with Ireland	7½ matches to 7½
Scotland beat Wales	9 matches to 6

Winners: England

1998 at Royal Porthcawl

Ireland beat Scotland	11 matches to 4
England beat Wales	11 matches to 4
Ireland halved with Wales	7½ matches each
England beat Scotland	9 matches to 6
England beat Ireland	8 matches to 7
Wales beat Scotland	11½ matches to 3½

Winners: England

1999 at Royal County Down

England beat Scotland	10 matches to 5
Ireland beat Wales	8 matches to 7
England beat Wales	11½ matches to 3½
Ireland beat Scotland	10½ matches to 4½
Scotland beat Wales	10½ matches to 4½
England beat Ireland	8½ matches to 6½

Winners: England

2000 at Carnoustie

England halved with Wales	7½ matches to 7½
Ireland halved with Scotland	7½ matches to 7½
England halved with Scotland	7½ matches to 7½
Wales beat Ireland	8 matches to 7
Scotland beat Wales	8½ matches to 6½
Ireland beat England	9½ matches to 5½

Winners: Scotland

2001 at Woodhall Spa

England beat Scotland	9 matches to 6
Ireland beat Wales	10½ matches to 4½
England halved with Wales	7½ matches to 7½
Scotland beat Ireland	8½ matches to 6½
Scotland beat Wales	10½ matches to 4½
England beat Ireland	11½ matches to 3½

Winners: England

2002 at Royal St David's

Wales beat England	8 matches to 7
Ireland halved with Scotland	7½ matches to 7½
Wales beat Ireland	8½ matches to 6½
Scotland beat England	10 matches to 5
England beat Ireland	10 matches to 5
Wales beat Scotland	9 matches to 6

Winners: Wales

Senior Home Internationals

2002 *Nairn Dunbar*

Result: 1 England 2½,   2 Scotland 2,   3 Ireland 1½,   4 Wales 0

English County Championship

1928	Warwickshire	1957	Surrey	1980	Surrey
1929	Lancashire	1958	Surrey	1981	Surrey
1930	Lancashire	1959	Northumberland	1982	Yorkshire
1931	Yorkshire	1961	Lancashire	1983	Berks, Bucks, Oxon
1932	Surrey	1962	Northumberland	1984	Yorkshire
1933	Yorkshire	1963	Yorkshire	1985T	Devon/Hertfordshire
1934	Worcestershire	1964	Northumberland	1986	Hertfordshire
1935	Worcestershire	1965	Northumberland	1987	Yorkshire
1936	Surrey	1966	Surrey	1988	Warwickshire
1937	Lancashire	1967	Lancashire	1989	Middlesex
1938	Staffordshire	1968	Surrey	1990	Warwickshire
1939	Worcestershire	1969	Berks, Bucks, Oxon	1991	Middlesex
1947	Staffordshire	1970	Gloucestershire	1992	Dorset
1948	Staffordshire	1971	Staffordshire	1993	Yorkshire
1949	Lancashire	1972	Berks, Bucks, Oxon	1994	Middlesex
1950	*Not played*	1973	Yorkshire	1995	Lancashire
1951	Lancashire	1974	Lincolnshire	1996	Hampshire
1952	Yorkshire	1975	Staffordshire	1997	Yorkshire
1953	Yorkshire	1976	Warwickshire	1998	Yorkshire
1954	Cheshire	1977	Warwickshire	1999	Yorkshire
1955	Yorkshire	1978	Kent	2000	Surrey
1956	Staffordshire	1979	Gloucestershire	2001	Yorkshire

2002 *at La Moye, Jersey*

Yorkshire beat Dorset 6½-2½
Yorkshire beat Hampshire, Isle of Wight & Channel Islands 7-2
Yorkshire beat Lincolnshire 6-3
Hampshire, Isle of Wight & Channel Islands beat Lincolnshire 5-4
Hampshire, Isle of Wight & Channel Islands beat Dorset 6½- 2½
Dorset beat Lincolnshire 6-3
Result: 1 Yorkshire, 2 Hampshire, Isle of Wight & Channel Islands, 3 Dorset, 4 Lincolnshire

English Club Championship

1989	Ealing	Southport and Ainsdale	1996	Hartlepool	Frilford Heath
1990	Ealing	Goring and Streatley	1997	Royal Mid-Surrey	Sandiway
1991	Trentham	Porters Park	1998	Moor Park	Northumberland
1992	Bristol & Clifton	South Staffs	1999	Royal Mid-Surrey	Moor Park
1993	Worksop	Rotherham	2000	Coxmoor	Berkhampstead
1994	Sandmoor	Coxmoor	2001	St Mellion	Minchinhampton
1995	Sandmoor	Ipswich			

2002 *at Northamptonshire County*

1	Woodcote Park* (Surrey)	285 (Stephen Russell, Kieran Staunton, Danny Lomas)
2	Southern Valley (Kent)	285
3	Kenilworth (Warwickshire)	287

Scottish Club Championship

2002 at Tulliallan

1	Tulliallan	279 (Mark Crichton, Alastair Ferguson, Neil Scaife)
2	Inverness	280
3	Blairgowrie	281

Scottish Area Team Championship

1990	North East	1994	Lothians	1998	Lanarkshire
1991	Glasgow	1995	North	1999	Lothians
1992	North East	1996	Renfrewshire	2000	North
1993	Lothians	1997	Lothians	2001	Perth and Kinross

2002 at East Renfrewshire

Semi-finals
Lanarkshire 7, Angus 2
Perth and Kinross 6½, Glasgow 2½

Final
Perth and Kinross 5, Lanarkshire 4

Scottish Foursomes Tournament – *Glasgow Evening Times* Trophy

1923 Gullane Comrades	1948 Melville College FP	1966 Bathgate	1983 Haggs Castle
1924 St Andrews New	1949 Troon Portland	1967 Prestonfield	1984 Royal Musselburgh
1925 St Andrews New	1950 '36 Club	1968 Troon St Meddans	1985 East Renfrewshire
1926 Pollok	1951 Troon Portland	1969 Irvine	1986 Hamilton
1927 Erskine	1952 Western Gailes	1970 Cardross	1987 Drumpellier
1928 Earlsferry Thistle	1953 Irvine	1971 Airdrie	1988 Irvine Ravenspark
1929 Pollok	1954 Glasgow University	1972 Scottish Building	1989 Cochrane Castle
1930 Mortonhall	1955 Haggs Castle	Contractors	1990 Pitreavie
1931 Royal Burgess	1956 Prestonfield	1973 Glasgow Insurance	1991 Irvine Ravenspark
1932 Hayston	1957 Falkirk Tryst	1974 Baberton	1992 Cochrane Castle
1933 Lothianburn	1958 Troon St Meddans	1975 Prestwick St Cuthbert	1993 Baberton
1934 Ayr Academy FP	1959 Cambuslang	1976 Wishaw	1994 Standard Life
1935 Ayr Academy FP	1960 Irvine	1977 Stirlingshire Jun.&	1995 Ratho Park
1936 Ayr Academy FP	1961 Falkirk Tryst	Youth Society	1996 Cardross
1937 Ayr Academy FP	1962 Irvine	1978 Helensburgh	1997 Cardross
1938 Western Gailes	1963 Clydebank & Dist	1979 Helensburgh	1998 Haggs Castle
1939–45 *Not played*	1964 Scottish Building	1980 Helensburgh	1999 Scottish Life
1946 St Andrews New	Contractors	1981 Duddingston	2000 Colville Park
1947 Western Gailes	1965 Falkirk Tryst	1982 Haggs Castle	2001 Hamilton

2002 at Glasgow Gailes

Final: Wishaw (Steven Taylor, Fraser McLaughlan) beat Falkirk Tryst (Tommy Gilchrist, Robert Smith)
      3-2

Welsh Inter-Counties Championship

2002 at Borth & Ynslas

1	Glamorgan	699
2	Caernarvonshire	704
3	Anglesey	720

Winning Team: Rhys Davies, Richard Evans, Jonathon Holmes, Llewellyn Matthews, Carl Rowe, James Williams

Individual winner: Roy Williams (Caernarvonshire) 68-67—135

Welsh Team Championship

2002 at Tenby

Semi-Finals: Monmouthshire beat Pontnewydd 3-2
      Tenby beat Pyle & Kenfig 3½-1½

Final: Monmouthshire beat Tenby 3-2

Principal 72 hole Tournaments

Including the National District Championships

Aberconwy Trophy (Inaugurated 1976) at Conwy/Llandudno (Maesdu), Gwynedd

1976	JR Jones	1985	MA Macara	1994	G Marsden
1977	EN Davies	1986	JR Berry	1995	S Andrew
1978	MG Mouland	1987	M Sheppard	1996	R Williams
1979	JM Morrow	1988	MG Hughes	1997	I Campbell
1980	JM Morrow	1989	JN Lee	1998	J Donaldson
1981	D Evans	1990	S Wilkinson	1999	J Donaldson
1982	G Tuttle	1991	S Wilkinson	2000	J Donaldson
1983	GH Brown	1992	MJ Ellis	2001	L Harpin*
1984	D McLean	1993	S Wilkinson		

2002

1	Richard Scott (Haverfordwest)	71-68-70-72—281
2	Lee Harpin (North Wales)	70-72-77-68—287
3	Craig Smith (St Mellons)	72-74-73-69—288

Berkshire Trophy (Inaugurated 1946) at The Berkshire

1946	R Sweeney	148	1964	R Foster	281	1983	S Hamer	288
1947	PB Lucas	298	1965	MF Bonallack	278	1984	JL Plaxton	276
1948	LG Crawley	301	1966	P Oosterhuis	287	1985	P McEvoy	279
1949	PB Lucas	300	1967	DJ Millensted	283	1986	R Muscroft	280
1950	PF Scrutton	296	1968	MF Bonallack	273	1987	J Robinson	275
1951	PF Scrutton	301	1969	JC Davies	278	1988	R Claydon	276
1952	PF Scrutton	286	1970	MF Bonallack	274	1989	J Metcalfe	272
1953	JL Morgan	289	1971T	MF Bonallack	277	1990	J O'Shea	271
1954T	Ft Lt K Hall	303		J Davies		1991	J Bickerton	280
	E Bromley-Davenport		1972	DP Davidson	280	1992	V Phillips	274
1955	GH Micklem	282	1973	PJ Hedges	278	1993	V Phillips	271
1956	GB Wolstenholme	285	1974	J Downie	280	1994T	J Knight	274
1957	MF Bonallack	291	1975	N Faldo	281		A Marshall	
1958T	GB Wolstenholme	284	1976	PJ Hedges	284	1995	G Harris	275
	AH Perowne		1977	A Lyle	279	1996	GP Wolstenholme	274
1959	JB Carr	279	1978	PJ Hedges	281	1997	GP Wolstenholme	275
1960	GB Wolstenholme	276	1979	D Williams	274	1998	M Hilton	284
1961	MF Bonallack	275	1980	P Downes	280	1999	D Henley	275
1962	SC Saddler	279	1981	D Blakeman	280	2000	C Edwards	281
1963	DW Frame	289	1982	SD Keppler	278	2001	G Evans	283

2002

1	Gary Wolstenholme (Kilworth Springs)	68-66-65-68—267
2	Jamie Elson (Kenilworth)	70-66-68-67—271
3	Kevin Freeman (Stoke Park)	66-71-69-66—272
	Jonathan Lupton (Middlesbrough)	66-70-68-68—272

Cameron Corbett Vase (Inaugurated 1897) at Haggs Castle, Glasgow

1897	AF Duncan	1933	W Tulloch	1970T	J McTear	
1898	AF Duncan	1934	JM Dykes		D Hayes	
1899	W Laidlaw	1935	H Thomson	1971	G Macgregor	
1900	GH Hutcheson	1936	J Gray	1972	HB Stuart	
1901	G Fox jr	1937	Tl Craig jr	1973	MJ Miller	
1902	AF Duncan	1938	JS Logan	1974	M Rae	
1903	G Fox jr	1939	A Steel	1975	D Barclay Howard	
1904	R Bone	1940–41	*No competition*	1976	GH Murray	
1905	R Bone	1942	AC Taylor	1977	MJ Miller	
1906	W Gemmill	1943–45	*No competition*	1978	GH Murray	
1907	G Wilkie	1946	JS Montgomerie	1979	KW Macintosh	
1908	AF Duncan	1947	W Maclaren	1980	IA Carslaw	
1909	EB Tipping	1948	J Pressley	1981	GH Murray	
1910	JH Irons	1949	GB Peters	1982	GH Murray	
1911	G Morris	1950	J Gray	1983	AS Oldcorn	
1912	R Scott jr	1951	GB Peters	1984	D Barclay Howard	
1913	R Scott jr	1952	J Stewart Thomson	1985	J McDonald	
1914	D Martin	1953	J Orr	1986	JW Milligan	
1915–18	*Not played due to First*	1954	JR Cater	1987	J Semple	
	World War	1955	RC Macgregor	1988	C Everett	
1919	HR Orr	1956	RC Macgregor	1989	AG Tait	
1920	DJ Murray Campbell	1957	I Rennie	1990	D Robertson	290
1921	HM Dickson	1958	DH Reid	1991	K Gallacher	281
1922	WS Macfarlane	1959	AS Kerr	1992	D Kirkpatrick	284
1923	JO Stevenson	1960	J Mackenzie	1993	R Russell	278
1924	JO Stevenson	1961	GB Cosh	1994	J Hodson	280
1925	A Jamieson jr	1962	JH Richmond	1995	D Barclay Howard	268
1926	G Chapple	1963	JA Davidson	1996	C Watson	282
1927	RS Rodger	1964	IA MacCaskill	1997	C Watson	268
1928	SL McKinlay	1965	H Frazer	1998	E Wilson	140 (36)
1929	D McBride	1966	D Black	1999	W Bryson	278
1930	HM Dickson	1967	JRW Walkinshaw	2000	P McKechnie	277
1931	HM Dickson	1968	CW Green	2001	P Gault	291
1932	W Stringer	1969	A Brooks			

2002

1	Barry Hume (Haggs Castle)*	66-72-70-67—275
2	Stuart Wilson (Forfar)	66-69-72-68—275
3	Graham Gordon (Newmachar)	73-67-73-70—283

Carad Trophy (Inaugurated 1971) at Radyr/Cardiff

1971	TA Rickard	292	1982	LR Absolem	292	1993	H Roberts	285	
1972	EN Davies	280	1983	P Mayo	283	1994	C Evans	267	
1973	RJ Jones	279	1984	AP Parkin	277	1995	A Harrhy	280	
1974	WI Tucker	283	1985	P Mayo	277	1996	NB Edwards	275	
1975	A Disley	284	1986	P Mayo	274	1997	NB Edwards	277	
1976	WI Tucker	277	1987	P Mayo	274	1998	NB Edwards	279	
1977	AB Morgan	287	1988	CS Dodd (54 holes)	204	1999	S Roberts	276	
1978	N Davies	293	1989	JL Peters	275	2000	N Edwards	275	
1979	R Broad	291	1990	R Johnson	278	2001	D Price	277	
1980	AP Parkin	284	1991	AV Jones					
1981	SR Davidson		1992	MJ Ellis	287				

2002

1	Jonathan Holmes (Southerndown)	70-72-68-73—283
2	Nigel Edwards (Whitchurch)	69-69-75-72—285
3	Stuart Manley (Mountain Ash)	71-77-69-69—286

Clwyd Open (Inaugurated 1991) at Prestatyn/Wrexham

1991	G Houston	1995	M Ellis	1999	L Harpin	
1992	C O'Carrol	1996	M Ellis	2000	K Sullivan	
1993	M Ellis	1997	D Park	2001	A Campbell	
1994	G Houston	1998	R Donovan			

Clwyd Open *continued*

2002

1	Gareth Wright (West Linton)	72-73-73-66—284
2	Craig Smith (St Mellons)	72-72-75-70—289
3	John Williams (Prestatyn)	69-78-74-71—292

Craigmillar Park Open *(Inaugurated 1961) at Craigmillar Park, Edinburgh*

1961	RDBM Shade	1975	IC Hutcheon	1989	RM Roper
1962	A Sinclair	1976	NA Faldo	1990	SJ Bannerman
1963	HM Campbell	1977	CW Green	1991	N Walton
1964	RDBM Shade	1978	DM McCart	1992	SJ Knowles
1965	GB Cosh	1979	IC Hutcheon	1993	R Russell
1966	RDBM Shade	1980	JB Dunlop	1994	BW Collier
1967	RDBM Shade	1981	GK MacDonald	1995	C Watson
1968	RDBM Shade	1982	AS Oldcorn	1996	GW Tough
1969	GB Cosh	1983	G Macgregor	1997	CD Hislop
1970	PJ Smith	1984	G Macgregor	1998	G Rankin
1971	CW Green	1985	C Bloice	1999	S Mackenzie
1972	CW Green	1986	SR Easingwood	2000	M Warren
1973	DF Campbell	1987	RM Roper	2001	S O'Hara
1974	GH Murray	1988	B Shields		

2002

1	Marc Warren (East Kilbride)	65-64-69-64—262
2	Craig Elliot (Ratho Park)	66-70-66-62—264
3	Keith Nicholson (Haddington)	65-66-67-68—266

Duncan Putter *(Inaugurated 1959) at Southerndown, Bridgend, Glamorgan*

1959	G Huddy	301	1974	S Cox	302	1988	S Dodd	290
1960	WI Tucker	289	1975	JG Jermine	295	1989	RN Roderick	280
1961T	G Huddy	295	1976T	WI Tucker	286	1990	R Willison	311
	WI Tucker			H Stott		1991	R Willison	267
1962	EN Davies	297	1977	H Stott	295	1992	R Dinsdale	213
1963	WI Tucker	296	1978	P McEvoy	295	1993	M Thomson	289
1964	JL Toye	293	1979	HJ Evans	292	1994	GP Wolstenholme	226
1965	P Townsend	305	1980	P McEvoy	296	1995	B Dredge	293
1966	MF Attenborough	291	1981T	R Chapman	294	1996	GP Wolstenholme	291
1967	D Millensted	297		PG Way		1997	M Pilkington	283
1968	JL Morgan	299	1982	D McLean	283	1998	M King	291
1969	WI Tucker	304	1983	JG Jermine	297	1999	GP Wolstenholme	216 (54)
1970	JL Toye	305	1984	JP Price	284	2000	J Donaldson	285
1971	W Humphreys	295	1985	P McEvoy	299	2001	N Edwards	140 (36)
1972	P Berry (3 rounds)	230	1986	D Wood	300			
1973	JKD Povall	299	1987	P McEvoy	278			

2002

1T	Stuart Manley (Mountain Ash)	71-70-70-75—286
	Neil Oakley (St Mellons)	71-68-75-72—286
3	Mark Laskey (Sprocket Hall)	73-73-72-71—289

Hampshire Salver *(Inaugurated 1979) at North Hants/Blackmoor*

1979	P McEvoy	280	1987	A Rogers	286	1995	M Treleaven	275
1980	J Morrow	282	1988	N E Holman	279	1996	J Knight	272
1981	A P Sherborne	211*	1989	P Dougan	286	1997	J P Rose	275
1982	I Gray	293	1990	J Metcalfe	272	1998	S J Dyson	275
1983	D G Lane	281	1991	G Evans	281	1999	B Mason	273
1984	D H Currie	283	1992	S R Cage	276	2000	M Young	207*
1985	A J Clapp	285	1993	D J Hamilton	281	2001	G Wolstenholme	271
1986	D Gilford	287	1994	W Bennett	279			

2002

1	Jamie Moul (Stoke-by-Nayland)	65-71-70-71—277
2	Gary Wolstenholme (Kilworth Springs)	66-66-73-73—278
3	Darryl Berry (West Bradford)	71-70-72-69—282

Lagonda Trophy (Inaugurated 1975) at Camberley Heath; from 1990 at Gog Magog

1975	WJ Reid	143	1984	MS Davis	289	1993	L James	279
1976	JC Davies	142	1985	J Robinson	283	1994	S Webster	276
1977	WS Gronow	145	1986	D Gilford	282	1995	P Nelson	274
1978	JC Davies	135	1987	DG Lane	290	1996	S Collingwood	283
1979	JG Bennett	142	1988	R Claydon	275	1997	L Donald	279
1980	P McEvoy	139	1989	T Spence	280	1998	K Ferrie	284
1981	N Mitchell	138	1990	L Parsons	273	1999	Z Scotland	284
1982	A Sherborne	290	1991	J Cook	277	2000	M Young	279
1983	I Sparkes	216 (54)	1992	L Westwood	279	2001	D Skinns	271

2002

1	Gary Wolstenholme (Kilworth Springs)	69-67-69-70—275
2	Mark Payne (Brickendon Grange)	67-73-65-71—276
3	William Bowe (Workington)	64-67-75-73—279

Standard Life Leven Gold Medal (Inaugurated 1870) at Leven Links, Fife

1870	J Elder	85	1910	W Whyte	76	1958	W McIntyre	71
1871	R Wallace	91	1911	G Wilkie	73	1959	W Moyes	71
1872	P Anderson	91	1912	G Wilkie	73	1960	T Taylor	69
1873	R Armit	95	1913	W Whyte	73	1963	W Moyes	68
1874	D Campbell	93	1914	GB Rattray	76	1961	A Cunningham	69
1875	AM Ross	90	1915–18 No competition			1962	W Moyes	71
1876	AM Ross	88	1919	G Wilkie	77	1964	A Cunningham	68
1877	J Wilkie	88	1920	JJ Smith	76	1965	PG Buchanan	71
1878	R Wallace	90	1921	GV Donaldson	77			
1879	C Anderson	89	1922	SO Shepperd	72	Two rounds played from 1966		
1880	C Anderson	89	1923	GV Donaldson	73	1966	GM Rutherford	144
1881	J Foggo	91	1924	JN Smith	76	1967	AO Maxwell	140
1882	J Wilkie	89	1925	A Robertson	73	1968	A Cunningham	140
1883	J Foggo	86	1926	T Ainslie	75			
1884	C Anderson	89	1927	EA McRuvie	72	Four rounds played from 1966		
1885	R Adam	84	1928	EA McRuvie	70	1969	P Smith	284
1886	R Adam	87	1929	EA McRuvie	72	1970	JC Farmer	277
1887	J Foggo	81	1930	EA McRuvie	68	1971	J Scott Macdonald	207
1888	DA Leitch	86	1931	A Dunsire	71	1972	J Rankine	282
1889	R Adam	81	1932	J Ballingall	72	1973	S Stephen	288
1890	W Marshall	80	1933	CA Danks	73	1974	P Smith	282
1891	DM Jackson	80	1934	EA McRuvie	67	1975	HB Stuart	286
1892	Col DW Mackinnon	85	1935	EG Stoddart	71	1976	IC Hutcheon	266
1893	HS Colt	79	1936	GA Buist	73	1977	IC Hutcheon	289
1894	J Bell jr	82	1937	JY Strachan	75	1978	R Wallace	287
1895	C Wllkie jr	80	1938	S Macdonald	71	1979	B Marchbank	274
1896	J Bell jr	78	1939	D Jamieson	72	1980	J Huggan	279
1897	J Bell jr	79	1940–45 No competition			1981	IC Hutcheon	282
1898	G Wilkie jr	82	1946	EA McRuvie	77	1982	IC Hutcheon	272
1899	G Wilkie jr	78	1947	JE Young	74	1983	J Huggan	274
1900	W Henderson	78	1948	J Imrie	77	1984	S Stephen	278
1901	R Simpson	76	1949	WM Ogg	76	1985	AD Turnbull	281
1902	J Bell	76	1950	E McRuvie	77	1986	P-U Johansson	275
1903	W Henderson	76	1951	J Imrie	72	1987	G Macgregor	271
1904	W Henderson	77	1952	HVS Thomson	69	1988	CE Everett	280
1905	G Wilkie	76	1953	O Rolland	70	1989	AJ Coltart	280
1906	G Wilkie	78	1954	JW Draper	73	1990	CE Everett	280
1907	M Goodwillie	73	1955	JW Draper	72	1991	GA Lowson	284
1908	W Henderson	77	1956	R Dishart	72	1992	D Robertson	279
1909	W Henderson	77	1957	I Pearson	72	1993	L Westwood	276

Standard Life Leven Gold Medal *continued*

1994	B Howard	265	1997	S Carmichael	278	2000	G Gordon	269
1995	S Mackenzie	273	1998	G Rankin	268	2001	P Whiteford*	271
1996	M Eliasson	267	1999	J Mathers	291			

2002

1	Jack Doherty (Vale of Glamorgan)	66-69-64-64—263
2	Graham Gordon (Newmachar)	66-68-65-68—267
	Jamie McLeary (Glenrothes)	67-70-65-65—267+

Lytham Trophy (Inaugurated 1965) *at Royal Lytham & St Annes and Fairhaven*

1965T	MF Bonallack	295	1974	CW Green	291	1988	P Broadhurst	296
	CA Clark		1975	G Macgregor	299	1989	N Williamson	286
1966	PM Townsend	290	1976	MJ Kelley	292	1990	G Evans	291
1967	R Foster	296	1977	P Deeble	296	1991	G Evans	284
1968	R Foster	286	1978	B Marchbank	288	1992	S Cage	294
1969T	T Craddock	290	1979	P McEvoy	279	1993	T McLure	292
	SG Birtwell		1980	IC Hutcheon	293	1994	W Bennett	285
1970T	JC Farmer	296	1981	R Chapman	221	1995	S Gallacher	281
	CW Green		1982	MF Sludds	306	1996	M Carver	284
	GC Marks		1983	S McAllister	299	1997	G Rankin	279
1971	W Humphreys	292	1984	J Hawksworth	289	1998	L Kelly	288
1972	MF Bonallack	281	1985	MPD Walls	291	1999	T Schuster	283
1973T	MG King	292	1986	S McKenna	297	2000	D Dixon	285
	SG Birtwell	292	1987	D Wood	293	2001	R McEvoy	276

2002

1	Les Corfield (Burnham & Berrow)	69-69-69-76—283
2	Richard Walker (Frodsham)	71-71-68-74—284
3	Graham Gordon (Newmachar)	72-68-73-73—286
	Jonathan Lupton (Middlesbrough)	71-73-67-75—286
	Gary Wolstenholme (Kilworth Springs)	67-70-76-73—286

St Andrews Links Trophy (Inaugurated 1989) *at St Andrews (Old and Jubilee)*

1989	R Claydon	284	1994	DB Howard	294	1999	D Patrick	152 (36)
1990	S Bouvier (Aus)	280	1995	G Rankin	276	2000	M King	140
1991	R Willison	289	1996	DB Howard	282	2001	S O'Hara	281
1992	C Watson	281	1997	J Rose	284			
1993	G Hay	280	1998	C Watson	276			

2002

1	Simon Mackenzie (West Linton)	76-71-72-70—289
2	Farren Keenan (Royal Mid-Surrey)	74-77-69-73—293
	Stuart Manley (Mountain Ash)	71-76-71-75—293

St David's Gold Cross (Inaugurated 1930) *at Royal St David's, Gwynedd*

1930	GC Stokoe	1950	DMG Sutherland	1965	MSR Lunt		
1931	EW Fiddian	1951	JL Morgan	1966	MSR Lunt		
1932	Dr W Tweddell	1952	SB Roberts	1967	MSR Lunt		
1933	IS Thomas	1953	S Lunt	1968	AW Holmes		
1934	SB Roberts	1954	GB Turner	1969	AJ Thomson		
1935	IS Thomas	1955	JL Morgan	1970	AJ Thomson		
1936	RMW Pritchard	1956	W Cdr CH Beamish	1971	A Smith		
1937	IS Thomas	1957	CD Lawrie	1972	EN Davies		
1938	SB Roberts	1958	GB Turner	1973	RD James		
1939	IS Thomas	1959	MSR Lunt	1974	GC Marks		
1940-45	*No competition*	1960	LJ Ranells	1975	CP Hodgkinson		
1946	SB Roberts	1961	MSR Lunt	1976	JR Jones		
1947	G Mills	1962	PD Kelley	1977	JA Fagan		
1948	CH Eaves	1963	JKD Povall	1978	S Wild		
1949	SB Roberts	1964	MSR Lunt	1979	MA Smith		

1980	CP Hodgkinson	1988	MW Calvert	1996	L Harpin
1981	G Broadbent	1989	AJ Barnett	1997	M Pilkington
1982	MW Calvert	1990	MA Macara	1998	L Harpin
1983	RD James	1991	RJ Dinsdale	1999	D Jones
1984	RJ Green	1992	B Dredge	2000	D Price
1985	KH Williams	1993	B Dredge	2001	C Williams
1986	RN Roderick	1994	C Evans		
1987	SR Andrew	1995	M Skinner		

2002

1	Alex Smith (Pyle & Kenfig)	73-69-68-73—283
2	Tim Dykes (Wrexham)	69-69-72-74—284
3	Lee Griffiths (Coed-y-Mwstwr)	75-69-71-70—285

Sherry Cup

1990	Alvaro Prat	1994	Francisco Cea	1998	Sergio García
1991	Padraig Harrington	1995	José Maria Zamora	1999	Marcel Siem
1992	Frederic Cupillard	1996	Alvaro Salto	2000	G Wolstenholme
1993	Francisco Valera	1997	Sergio García	2001	G Wolstenholme*

2002 *at Sotogrande, Spain*

1	Lee Harpin (Wales)	71-71-70—212
2	Gonzalo Fernandez-Castaño (Esp)	71-72-70—213
3	Michael McDermott (Irl)	71-72-72—215

Sutherland Chalice (Inaugurated 2000)

2000	G Gordon	275	2001	S Carmichael	274

2002 *at Dumfries & Galloway*

1	Graham Gordon (Newmachar)	65-62-68-69—264
2	Barry Scott (Dumfries & Galloway)	70-68-68-66—272
3	Wilson Bryson (Drumpellier)	68-68-69-69—274

Tennant Cup (Inaugurated 1880) *at Glasgow GC*

1880	AW Smith	1908	R Carson	1940–45	No competition
1881	AW Smith	1909	WS Colville	1946	JB Stevenson
1882	AM Ross	1910	R Andrew	1947	JC Wilson
1883	J Kirk	1911	WS Colville	1948	J Wallace
1884	W Doleman	1912	R Scott jr	1949	W Irvine
1885	TR Lamb	1913	SO Shepherd	1950	JW Mill
1886	D Bone	1914	John Caven	1951	WS McCleod
1887	JR Motion	1915–19	No competition	1952	GT Black
1888	D Bone	1920	G Lockhart	1953	AD Gray
1889	W Milne	1921	R Scott jr	1954	H McInally
1890	W Marshall	1922	WD Macleod	1955	LG Taylor
1891	D Bone	1923	FW Baldie	1956	JM Dykes
1892	D Bone	1924	J Barrie Cooper	1957	LG Taylor
1893	W Doleman	1925	R Scott jr	1958	Dr FWG Deighton
1894	W Doleman	1926	W Tulloch	1959	JF Milligan
1895	JA Shaw	1927	W Tulloch	1960	Dr FWG Deighton
1896	J Thomson	1928	A Jamieson jr	1961	R Reid Jack
1897	D Bone	1929	R Scott jr	1962	WS Jack
1898	R Bone	1930	JE Dawson	1963	SWT Murray
1899	W Hunter	1931	GNS Tweedale	1964	Dr FWG Deighton
1900	JG Macfarlane	1932	SL McInlay	1965	J Scott Cochran
1901	R Bone	1933	H Thomson	1966	AH Hall
1902	CB Macfarlane	1934	K Lindsay jr	1967	BJ Gallacher
1903	CB Macfarlane	1935	JM Dykes jr	1968	CW Green
1904	WS Colville	1936	JNW Dall	1969	J Scott Cochran
1905	TW Robb	1937	WS McCleod	1970	CW Green
1906	JG Macfarlane	1938	A Jamieson jr	1971	Andrew Brodie
1907	R Andrew	1939	GB Peters	1972	Allan Brodie

Tennant Cup *continued*

1973	PJ Smith	1984	E Wilson	1995	S Gallacher
1974	D McCart	1985	CJ Brooks	1996	G Rankin
1975	CW Green	1986	PG Girvan	1997	C Hislop
1976	IC Hutcheon	1987	J Rasmussen	1998	G Rankin
1977	S Martin	1988	C Dalgleish	1999	G Fox
1978	IA Carslaw	1989	DG Carrick	2000	G Fox
1979	G Hay	1990	C Everett	2001	C Watson
1980	Allan Brodie	1991	C Everett		
1981	G MacDonald	1992	D Robertson		
1982	LS Mann	1993	D Robertson		
1983	C Dalgleish	1994	G Rankin		

2002

1	Barry Hume (Haggs Castle)	65-63-71-65—264
2	Scott Jamieson (Cathkin Brae)	66-70-68-70—274
3	Jamie McLeary (Glenrothes)	68-70-68-69—275

Tillman Trophy (Inaugurated 1989)

1989	J Cook	1994	*Not played*	1999	J Conteh
1990	M Wiggett	1995	P Stuart	2000	B Welch
1991	A Tillman	1996	S Wakefield	2001	R Fisher
1992	D Probert	1997	M Searle		
1993	C Nowicki	1998	R Blaxhill		

2002 *at Woodhall Spa*

1	Adam Gee (Leatherhead)	69-70-70-73—282
2	David Skinns (Lincoln)	68-67-72-76—283
3	Matt Ford (Bearsted)	69-69-68-79—285

Trubshaw Cup (Inaugurated 1989) *at Ashburnham and Tenby*

1989	MA Macara	1996	M Ellis	1999	N Matthews
1990	TSM Wilkinson	1994	C Evans	2000	N Edwards
1991	S Pardoe	1995	B Dredge	2001	N Edwards
1992	B Dredge	1997	M Pilkington		
1993	B Dredge	1998	M Pilkington		

2002

1	Jack Doherty (Vale of Glamorgan)	69-69-72-71—281
2	Stuart Manley (Mountain Ash)	71-67-72-73—283
3	Nigel Edwards (Whitchurch)	70-71-72-74—287

Tucker Trophy

1999	J Donaldson	2000	I Campbell	2001	N Edwards

2002 *at Newport/Whitchurch*

1	Nigel Edwards (Whitchurch)	70-69-68-65—272
2	Stuart Manley (Mountain Ash)	69-73-70-66—278
	David Price (Vale of Glamorgan)	71-70-69-68—278

National District Championships

Midland Open (Inaugurated 1976)

1976	P Downes	1983	CA Banks	1990	J Bickerton	1997	P Streeter
1977	P Downes	1984	K Valentine	1991	P Sefton	1998	L Donald
1978	P McEvoy	1985	MC Hassall	1992	M McGuire	1999	G Davies
1979	M Tomlinson	1986	G Wolstenholme	1993	N Williamson	2000	D Dixon
1980	P Downes	1987	C Suneson	1994	D Howell	2001	M Lock
1981	P Baxter	1988	R Winchester	1995	G Harris		
1982	NJ Chesses	1989	J Cook	1996	M Carver		

2002 at Notts and Coxmoor

1	Gary Wolstenholme (Kilworth Springs)	72-72-74-70—288
2	Paul Dixon (Willesley Park)	69-71-78-72—290
3	John Kemp (John O'Gaunt)	69-70-76-76—291

West of England Open Match Play (Inaugurated 1912)

at Burnham & Berrow

1912	RA Riddell	1937	O Austreng	1964	DC Allen	1986	J Bennett
1913	Hon M Scott	1938	HJ Roberts	1965	DE Jones	1987	D Rosier
1914–18	No competition	1939–45	No competition	1966	A Forrester	1988	N Holman
1919	Hon M Scott	1946	JH Neal	1967	A Forrester	1989	N Holman
1920	Hon D Scott	1947	WF Wise	1968	SR Warrin	1990	I West
1921	CVL Hooman	1948	WF Wise	1969	SR Warrin	1991	S Amor
1922	Hon M Scott	1949	J Payne	1970	C Ball	1992	K Baker
1923	D Grant	1950	EB Millward	1971	G Irlam	1993	D Haines
1924	D Grant	1951	J Payne	1972	JA Bloxham	1994	A Emery
1925	D Grant	1952	EB Millward	1973	SC Mason	1995	A March
1926	K Whetstone	1953	F Griffin	1974	CS Mitchell	1996	M Carver
1927	GC Brooks	1954	EB Millward	1975	MR Lovett	1997	SJ Martin
1928	JA Pierson	1955	SJ Fox	1976	No competition	1998	D Dixon
1929	DE Landale	1956	SJ Fox	1977	AR Dunlop	1999	D Dixon
1930	RH de	1957	D Gardner	1978	R Broad	2000	J Morgan
	Montmorency	1958	AJN Young	1979	N Burch	2001	L Corfield
1931	DR Howard	1959	DM Woolmer	1980	JM Durbin		
1932	R Straker	1960	AW Holmes	1981	M Mouland		
1933	DM Anderson	1961	JM Leach	1982	M Higgins		
1934	Hon M Scott	1962	Sq Ldr WE	1983	C Peacock		
1935	JJF Pennink		McCrea	1984	GB Hickman		
1936	PH White	1963	KT Warren	1985	AC Nash		

2002

Quarter-Finals
Jamie Donaldson (West Sussex) beat Lewis Genney (Effingham) 4 and 3
Adam Ward (Whittington Heath) beat Rory Hunt (Teignmouth) 3 and 2
Ed Butler (Lansdown) beat Adam Meads (Burnham & Berrow) 4 and 3
John Whitcutt (Burnham & Berrow) beat Robert Narduzzo (Celtic Manor) 4 and 3

Semi-Finals
Donaldson beat Ward at 19th
Butler beat Whitcutt 1 hole

Final
J Donaldson beat E Butler at 19th

West of England Open Stroke Play (Inaugurated 1968)

1968	PJ Yeo	Saunton	297		1985	PE McEvoy	Saunton	307
1969	A Forrester	Saunton	304		1986	P Baker	R North Devon	282
1970	PJ Yeo	R North Devon	312		*Won at second extra hole after play-off with P McEvoy*			
1971	P Berry	Saunton	303		1987	G Wolstenholme	Saunton	296
1972	P Berry	R North Devon	310		1988	MC Evans	R North Devon	291
1973	SC Mason	Saunton	287		1989	AD Hare	Saunton	289
1974	R Abbott	R North Devon	301		1990	J Payne	Saunton	290
1975	BG Steer	Saunton	290		1991	D Lee	Saunton	286
1976	R Abbott	R North Devon	304		1992	M Stanford	R North Devon	291
1977	PE McEvoy	Saunton	298		1993	PR Trew	Saunton	279
1978	JG Bennett	R North Devon	291		1994	CP Nowicki	R North Devon	294
After play-off with PE McEvoy					1995	G Clark	Saunton	141 (36)
1979	R Kane	Saunton	296		1996	R Wiggins	Saunton	288
1980	PE McEvoy	R North Devon	288		1997	M Reynard	R North Devon	280
1981	N Taee	Saunton	245 (54)		1998	C Edwards	R North Devon	287
1982	MP Higgins	R North Devon	286		1999	D Griffiths	Saunton	286
1983	PE McEvoy	Saunton	298		2000	S Grewal	R North Devon	279
1984	A Sherborne	R North Devon	288		2001	R Finch	Saunton	279

2002 *at Royal North Devon*

1	Dean Barnes (Ferndown)	70-76-73—219
2	Chris McDonnell (Stocksfield)	76-74-71—221
3	Paul Bradshaw (Gainsborough)	71-76-76—223
	Lee Corfield (Burnham & Berrow)	71-73-79—223

East of Ireland Open

1989	D Clarke		1993	R Burns		1997	S Quinlivan	2001 K Kearney
1990	D O'Sullivan		1994	G McGimpsey		1998	G McGimpsey	
1991	P Hogan		1995	D Brannigan		1999	K Kearney	
1992	R Burns		1996	N Fox		2000	N Fox*	

2002 *at Co Louth*

1	Noel Fox (Portmarnock)	72-64-70-72—278
2	D Crowe (Royal Dublin)	72-70-68-73—283
3	Robert McCarthy (The Island)	76-70-70-71—287

North of Ireland Open

1989	N Anderson		1993	G McGimpsey		1997	M Sinclair	2001 S Paul
1990	D Clarke		1994	N Ludwell		1998	P Gribben	
1991	G McGimpsey		1995	F Nolan		1999	P Gribben	
1992	G McGimpsey		1996	M McGinley		2000	M Hoey	

2002 *at Royal Portrush*

Quarter-Finals

Chris Moriarty (Clandeboye) beat Michael McDermott (Stackstown) 2 and 1

N Crawford (Mourne) beat Tim Rice (Limerick) 6 and 4

Gareth Maybin (Ballyclare) beat Stuart Paul (Tandragee) 1 hole

Mark O'Sullivan (Galway) beat Colm Montgomery (Malone) 4 and 3

Semi-Finals

Moriarty beat Crawford 4 and 3; Maybin beat O'Sullivan at 19th

Final: Gareth Maybin beat Chris Moriarty 1 hole

Leading Qualifier: R Evans (Moyola Park) 75-64—139

South of Ireland Open

1989	S Keenan	1993	P Sheehan	1997	P Collier	2001	J Kehoe
1990	D Clarke	1994	D Higgins	1998	J Foster		
1991	P McGinley	1995	J Fanagan	1999	M Campbell		
1992	L MacNamara	1996	A Morrow	2000	G McDowell		

2002 *at Lahinch*

Quarter-Finals

Sean McTernan (Co. Sligo) beat Eddie Power (Kilkenny) at 20th
Barry Reddan (Co. Louth) beat Mark Campbell (Stackstown) 4 and 3
Mark Ryan (Grange) beat Michael McDermott (Stackstown) at 21st
Colm Moriarty (Athlone) beat Johnny Foster (Ballyclare) 2 and 1

Semi-Finals

McTernan beat Reddan 6 and 4;
Moriarty beat Ryan 4 and 2

Final: Colm Moriarty beat Sean McTernan at 19th

West of Ireland Open

1989	P McInerney	1993	G McGimpsey	1997	J Fanagan	2001	M McDermott
1990	N Goulding	1994	P Harrington	1998	N Fox		
1991	N Goulding	1995	E Brady	1999	M Ilonen (Fin)		
1992	K Kearney	1996	G McGimpsey	2000	E Brady		

2002 *at Co Sligo (Rosses Point)*

Semi-Finals

Stuart Paul (Tandragee) beat Colm Moriarty (Athlone) 2 and 1
Derek McNamara (Connemara) beat Ken Kearney (Roscommon) 6 and 5

Final: Stuart Paul beat Derek McNamara 1 hole

East of Scotland Open Stroke Play

1989	K Hird	1993	S Meiklejohn	1997	S Meiklejohn	2001	J King
1990	G Lawrie	1994	A Reid	1998	B Lamb (Aus)		
1991	R Clark	1995	G Davidson	1999	R Beames		
1992	ST Knowles	1996	C Hislop	2000	C Watson		

2002 *at Lundin GC*

1	David Inglis (Glencorse)	74-69-71-69—283
2	Graham Gordon (Newmachar)	71-74-68-71—284
3	Brian Heggie (St Andrews)	71-72-72-71—286
	Jamie McLeary (Glenrothes)	75-70-70-71—286

North of Scotland Open Stroke Play

1989	G Hickman	1993	D Downie	1997	G Crawford	2001	G Thomson
1990	S McIntosh	1994	E Forbes	1998	C Taylor		
1991	S Henderson	1995	R Beames	1999	N Steven*		
1992	K Buchan	1996	C Dunan	2000	C Watson		

2002 *at Elgin*

1	Wallace Booth (Crieff)	73-68-65-68—274
2	Craig Elliot (Ratho Park)	71-67-70-67—275
3	Bryan Innes (Murcar)	73-68-65-70—276

North-East Scotland District Championship

1999	BA Innes	2000	E Forbes	2001	G Gordon

2002 *at Murcar*

1	Bryan Innes (Murcar)	67-70-66—203
2	Graeme Brown (Royal Montrose)	73-66-67—206
3	Wallace Booth (Crieff)	69-72-68—209
	Barrie Edmond (Bon Accord)	73-68-68—209

South-East Scotland District Championship

1999	S Carmichael	2000	J King	2001	J Doherty

2002 *at Ratho Park*

1	Steven Armstrong (Ratho Park)	66-65-65-68—264
2	Lee Harper (Musselburgh)	73-66-67-67—273
3	Craig Neilson (Newbattle)	69-71-67-67—274

West of Scotland Open

1989	A Elliot	1993	B Howard	1997	C Hislop	2001	B Fitzsimmons
1990	S Knowles	1994	J Hodgson	1998	L Kelly		
1991	A Coltart	1995	G Rankin	1999	L Kelly		
1992	S Henderson	1996	C Hislop	2000	S O'Hara		

2002 *at Esporta Dougalston*

1	Graham Gordon (Newmachar)	69-73-66-73—281
2	Jack Doherty (Vale of Glamorgan)	70-71-71-71—283
3	David Sutton (Lockerbie)	71-69-74-74—288

Other Men's Amateur Tournaments

Berkhamsted Trophy (Inaugurated 1960)

Year	Winner	Score	Year	Winner	Score	Year	Winner	Score
1960	HC Squirrell	150	1974	P Fisher	144	1988	J Cowgill	146
1961	DW Frame	147	1975	PG Deeble	147	1989	J Payne	142
1962	DG Neech	149	1976	JC Davies	144	1990	J Barnes	144
1963	HC Squirrell	149	1977	AWB Lyle	144	1991	G Homewood	141
1964	PD Flaherty	149	1978	JC Davies	146	1992	P Page	141
1965	LF Millar	153	1979	JC Davies	147	1993	S Burnell	143
1966	P Townsend	150	1980	R Knott	143	1994	M Treleaven	140
1967	DJ Millensted	150	1981	P Dennett	146	1995	J Crampton	142
1968	PD Flaherty	144	1982	DG Lane	148	1996	L Donald	139
1969	MM Niven	149	1983	J Hawksworth	146	1997	P Streeter	143
1970	R Hunter	145	1984	R Willison	139	1998	G Storm	69 (18)
1971	A Millar	144	1985	F George	144	1999	GP Wolstenholme*	140
1972	C Cieslewicz	148	1986	P McEvoy	144	2000	J Wormald*	141
1973	SC Mason	141	1987	F George	141	2001	S Godfrey	140

2002

1	Gary Wolstenholme (Kilworth Springs)	69-71—140
2	Peter Appleyard (Chart Hills)	73-73—146
	James Cookson (Whittington Heath)	71-75—146

John Cross Bowl (Inaugurated 1957) *at Worplesdon, Surrey*

Year	Winner	Year	Winner	Year	Winner
1957	DW Frame	1972	AR Kerr	1987	B White
1958	G Evans	1973	DW Frame	1988	B White
1959	G Evans	1974	RPF Brown	1989	KG Jones
1960	DW Frame	1975	BJ Winteridge	1990	D Lee
1961	DW Frame	1976	DW Frame	1991	P Sefton
1962	DW Frame	1977	DW Frame	1992	R Watts
1963	PO Green	1978	RPF Brown	1993	J Collier
1964	RL Glading	1979	JG Bennett	1994	P Benka
1965	P Townsend	1980	JG Bennett	1995	M Galway
1966	P Townsend	1981	ME Johnson	1996	B Barham
1967	MJ Burgess	1982	R Boxall	1997	C Banks
1968	PJ Benka	1983	DG Lane	1998	J Wormald
1969	DW Frame	1984	I Gray	1999	M Galway
1970	P Dawson	1985	M Devetta	2000	R Mann*
1971	PBQ Drayson	1986	C Rotheroe	2001	J Bint

2002

1	D Holmes (Langley Park)	69-70—139
2	T Hunter (Ilford)	72-69—141
3	JM Bint (Chigwell)	73-69—142
4	K Staunton (Woodcote Park)	67-75—142

Frame Trophy (Inaugurated 1986 for players aged 50+) *at Worplesdon, Surrey*

1988	DW Frame	229	1993	DW Frame	216	1998	DG Lane	211
1989	JRW Walkinshaw	219	1994	DG Lane	222	1999	NH Barnes	220
1990	WJ Williams	224	1995	M Christmas	223	2000	DW Frame	213
1991	DB Sheahan	223	1996	DG Lane	217	2001	DW Frame	217
1992	DW Frame	223	1997	B Turner	226			

2002

1	BK Turner (Sunningdale Artisans)	73-65-71—209
2	DG Lane (Goring & Streatley)	71-72-68—211
3	HGA Steel (Moor Park)	70-74-72—216

Golf Illustrated Gold Vase (Inaugurated 1909)

1909	CK Hutchison	1949	RJ White	1975	MF Bonallack
1910	Abe Mitchell	1950	AW Whyte	1976	A Brodie
1911	R Harris	1951	JB Carr	1977	J Davies
1912	R Harris	1952	JDA Langley	1978	P Thomas
1913	Abe Mitchell	1953	JDA Langley	1979	KJ Miller
1914	H Hilton	1954	H Ridgeley	1980	G Brand jr
1919	D Darwin	1955	Major DA Blair	1981	P Garner
1920	DS Crowther	1956	Major DA Blair	1982	I Carslaw
1921	M Seymour	1957	GB Wolstenholme	1983	S Keppler
1922	WA Murray	1958	M Lunt	1984	JV Marks
1923	CJH Tolley	1959	A Bussell	1985	M Davis
1924	CC Aylmer	1960	D Sewell	1986	R Eggo
1925	JB Beck	1961T	DJ Harrison/MF Bonallack	1987	D Lane
1926T	CJH Tolley/TA Torrance	1962	BHG Chapman	1988	M Turner
1927	RH Wethered	1963	RH Mummery	1989	GP Wolstenholme
1928	CJH Tolley	1964	D Moffat	1990	A Rogers
1929	D Grant	1965	C Clark	1991	R Scott
1930	RT Jones (US)	1966	PM Townsend	1992	P Page
1931	WA Murray	1967T	MF Bonallack/	1993T	C Challen/V Phillips
1932	RW Hartley		RA Durrant	1994	S Burnell
1933	RW Hartley	1968	MF Bonallack	1995	A Wall
1934	WL Hartley	1969T	MF Bonallack/J Hayes	1996	*Not played*
1935	J Thomas	1970	D Harrison	1997	M James
1936	J Ferrier	1971	MF Bonallack	1998	R Rea*
1937	R Sweeney	1972T	H Ashby/DP Davidson/	1999	M Side
1938	CJ Anderson		R Hunter	2000	J Kemp
1939	SB Robert	1973	J Davies	2001	J Heath
1948	RD Chapman	1974	P Hedges		

2002 *at Walton Heath*

1	Andrew Inglis (Sunningdale)*	70-74—144 (at 2nd extra hole)
2	Terry Berry (Sundridge Park)	72-72—144
3	Crue Elliott (West Middlesex)	70-74—144

Hampshire Hog (Inaugurated 1957) *at Northants*

1957	MF Bonallack	1972	R Revell	1987	A Rogers
1958	PF Scrutton	1973	SC Mason	1988	S Richardson
1959	Col AA Duncan	1974	TJ Giles	1989	P McEvoy
1960	MF Attenborough	1975	HAN Stott	1990	J Metcalfe
1961	HC Squirrell	1976	MC Hughesdon	1991	M Welch
1962	FD Physick	1977	AWB Lyle	1992	S Graham
1963	Sqn Ldr WE McCrea	1978	GF Godwin	1993	D Hamilton
1964	DF Wilkie	1979	MF Bonallack	1994	B Ingleby
1965	T Koch de Gooreynd	1980	RA Durrant	1995	J Rose
1966	Major DA Blair	1981	G Brand jr	1996	R Tate
1967	Major DA Blair	1982	A Sherborne	1997	GP Wolstenholme
1968	MJ Burgess	1983	I Gray	1998	P Rowe
1969	B Critchley	1984	J Hawksworth	1999	C Rodgers
1970	Major DA Blair	1985	A Clapp	2000	M Booker
1971	DW Frame	1986	R Eggo	2001	J Lupton

2002

1	Gary Wolstenholme (Kilworth Springs)	66-66—132
2	Jamie Moul (Stoke-by-Nayland)	65-71—136
3	Ryan Henley (Stoneham)	70-68—138
	Farren Keenan (Royal Mid-Surrey)	67-71—138

King George V Coronation Cup *at Porters Park, Herts.*

1990	C Boal	141	1994	S Webster	146	1998	M King	65 (18)
1991	S Hoffman	142	1995	S Jarvis	140	1999	J Field*	141
1992	R Watts	141	1996	N Swaffield	134	2000	R Chattaway	142
1993	D Hamilton	134	1997	J Knight	136	2001	M Payne*	143

2002

1	Greg Evans (Ealing)	70-71—141
2	James Crampton (Spalding)	70-72—142
3	Paul Coburn (Sandy Lodge)	72-72—144

Prince of Wales Challenge Cup (Inaugurated 1928) *at Royal Cinque Ports*

1928	D Grant	142	1958T	BAF Belmore	158	1980T	B Nicholson	149
1929	NR Reeves	153	1959	D Johnstone	149	1981	JM Baldwin	146
1930	R Harris	156	1960	CG Moore	162	1982	SG Homewood	145
1931	RW Hartley	149	1961	RH Bazell	151	1983	M Davis	141
1932	EN Layton	151	1962	Dr J Pittar	154	1984T	F Wood	146
1933	JB Nash	148	1963	Sq Ldr WE McCrea	155		DH Niven	
1934	R Sweeney	304	1964	NA Paul	153.	1985	RJ Tickner	141
1935	HG Bentley	301	1965T	NA Paul	150	1986	JM Baldwin	149
1936	LOM Munn	301		VE Barton		1987	S Finch	148
1937	DHR Martin	291	1966	P Townsend	150	1988	MP Palmer	144
1938	EA Head	291	1967	MF Bonallack	141	1989T	T Lloyd	146
1939–46 *No competition*			1968T	NA Paul	144		NA Farrell	
1947	PB Lucas	154		GC Marks		1990T	G Homewood	
1948	Capt DA Blair	151	1969	MF Attenborough	152		BS Ingleby	145
1949	C Stowe	142	1970	J Butterworth	153	1991	S Pardoe	152
1950	I Caldwell	151	1971	VE Barton	147	1992	L Westwood	160
1951	I Caldwell	151	1972	PJ Hedges	162	1993	ML Welch	143
1952	I Caldwell	150	1973	PJ Hedges	138	1994	I Hardy	149
1953	JG Blackwell	159	1974	PJ Hedges	146	1995	L Ferris	152
1954	DLW Woon	143	1975	JC Davies	150	1996	J Maddock	142
1955T	C Taylor	153	1976	MJ Inglis	162	1997	J Carter	154
	GT Duncan		1977	PJ Hedges	154	1998	G Woodman	144
1956	PF Scrutton	151	1978	ER Dexter	145	1999	A Webster (Aus)	147
1957	*No competition*		1979	GF Godwin	148	2000	JM Bint	145
1958T	KR Mackenzie	158	1980T	GM Dunsire	149	2001	A Webster	140

2002

1	G Homewood (Ashford Manor)	73-78—151
2	R Kennedy (West Sussex)	78-75—153
3	T Hawkings (Royal St George's)	77-76—153
4	K Staunton (Woodcote Park)	76-77—153

Rosebery Challenge Cup (Inaugurated 1933) *at Ashridge*

1962	PR Johnston	1976	G Stradling	1990	C Tingey
1963	CA Murray	1977	J Ambridge	1991	M Thompson
1964	A Millar	1978	RJ Bevan	1992	R Harris
1965	EJ Wiggs	1979	JB Berney	1993	M Hooper
1966	A Holmes	1980	JA Watts	1994	P Wilkins
1967	A Holmes	1981	RY Mitchell	1995	P Wilkins
1968	A Holmes	1982	DG Lane	1996	J Kemp
1969	A Holmes	1983	N Briggs	1997	L Watcham
1970	PW Bent	1984	DG Lane	1998	S Vinnicombe
1971	AW Holmes	1985	P Wharton	1999	J Kemp
1972	AW Holmes	1986	JE Ambridge	2000	J Kemp
1973	AJ Mason	1987	HA Wilkerson	2001	J Ruebotham
1974	G Stradling	1988	N Leconte		
1975	JA Watts	1989	C Slattery		

2002

1	Robert Leonard (Harpenden Common)	68-69—137
2	Ewen Wilson (Porter's Park)	71-69—140
3	David Tanner (Hindley Hall)	71-70—141

St George's Grand Challenge Cup (Inaugurated 1888)

at Royal St George's, Sandwich, Kent

1888	J Ball	180	1927	WL Hartley	153	1968	MF Bonallack	142
1889	J Ball	169	1928	D Grant	146	1969	PJ Benka	150
1890	J Ball	175	1929	TA Torrance	148	1970	PJ Hedges	150
1891	J Ball	174	1930	RW Hartley	148	1971	EJS Garrett	143
1892	FA Fairlie	167	1931	WL Hartley	149	1972	JC Davies	149
1893	HH Hilton	165	1932	HG Bentley	151	1973	JC Davies	141
1894	HH Hilton	167	1933	JB Beck	151	1974	JC Davies	140
1895	E Blackwell	176	1934	AGS Penman	153	1975	JC Davies	147
1896	FG Tait	165	1935	Maj WHH Aitken	158	1976	JC Davies	158
1897	CE Hambro	162	1936	DHR Martin	150	1977	JC Davies	154
1898	FG Tait	163	1937	DHR Martin	144	1978	C Phillips	145
1899	FG Tait	155	1938	JJF Pennink	142	1979	CF Godwin	146
1900	R Maxwell	155	1939	AA McNair	153	1980	J Simmance	150
1901	SH Fry	165	1940–46	*No competition*		1981	MF Bonallack	151
1902	H Castle	162	1947	PB Lucas	147	1982	SJ Wood	145
1903	CK Hutchison	158	1948	M Gonzalez	144	1983	R Willison	155
1904	J Graham jr	154	1949	PF Scrutton	143	1984	SJ Wood	142
1905	R Harris	154	1950	E Bromley-Davenport	148	1985	SJ Wood	144
1906	S Mure Fergusson	155	1951	PF Scrutton	142	1986	RC Claydon	143
1907	CE Dick	161	1952	GH Micklem	148	1987	MR Coodwin	147
1908	AC Lincoln	157	1953	Major DA Blair	148	1988	T Ryan	143
1909	SH Fry	153	1954	H Berwick (Aus)	141	1989	S Green	149
1910	Capt CK Hutchison	157	1955	PF Scrutton	150	1990	P Sullivan	144
1911	E Martin Smith	148	1956	DAC Marr	148	1991	D Fisher	141
1912	Hon Michael Scott	146	1957	PF Scrutton	148	1992	L Westwood	146
1913	HD Gillies	153	1958	PF Scrutton	144	1993	P Sefton	137
1914	J Graham jr	146	1959	J Nicklaus (USA)	149	1994	M Welch	142
1915–19	*No competition*		1960	JG Blackwell	152	1995	J Harris	142
1920	R Harris	162	1961	Sq Ldr WE McCrea	143	1996	M Brooks	137
1921	WB Torrance	154	1962	Sq Ldr WE McCrea	145	1997	*Abandoned due to rain*	
1922	WI Hunter	156	1963	Sq Ldr WE McCrea	150	1998	C Gold*	145
1923	F Ouimet (USA)	153	1964	Major DA Blair	153	1999	M Williamson (Aus)	149
1924	RH Wethered	149	1965	MF Bonallack	144	2000	P Appleyard	151
1925	D Grant	149	1966	P Townsend	148	2001	A Gee	140
1926	Maj CO Hezlet	158	1967	Major DA Blair	154			

2002

1	B St John (Woodcote Park)	73-72—145
2	S Tiley (Royal Cinque Ports)	73-74—147
3	M Freidland (Guildford)	75-74—149

Selborne Salver (Inaugurated 1976) *at Blackmoor*

1976	A Miller	1985	SM Bottomley	1994	W Bennett
1977	CS Mitchell	1986	TE Clarke	1995	S Drummond
1978	GM Brand	1987	A Clapp	1996	J Knight
1979	P McEvoy	1988	NE Holman	1997	R Binney
1980	P McEvoy	1989	M Stamford	1998	M Side
1981	A Sherborne	1990	J Metcalfe	1999	B Mason
1982	IA Cray	1991	J Payne	2000	J Franks
1983	DG Lane	1992	M Treleaven	2001	G Wolstenholme
1984	D Curry	1993	M Welch		

2002

1	Graeme Clark (Doncaster)*	68-73—141
2	Jamie Moul (Stoke-by-Nayland)	70-71—141
3	Darryl Berry (West Bradford)	72-69—141

Foursomes Events

The Antlers (Inaugurated 1933) *at Royal Mid-Surrey*

1933	TFB Law and PWL Risdon	147	1970	JB Carr and R Carr	142
1934	GA Hill and HS Malik	153	1971	I Mosey and I Gradwell	144
1935	EF Storey and Sir WS Worthington Evans	152	1972	MJ Kelley and W Smith	144
1936	HG Bentley and F Francis	144	1973	DOJ Albutt and P Flaherty	148
1937	LG Crawley and C Stowe	145	1974	BF Critchley and MC Hughesdon	140
1938	RW Hartlev and PWL Risdon	149	1975	JC Davies and PJ Davies	140
1939	LG Crawley and H Thomson	148	1976	JK Tate and P Deeble	144
1940–47	*Not played due to Second World War*		1977	JC Davies and PJ Davies	141
1948	RC Quilter and E Bromley-Davenport	151	1978	R Chapman and R Fish	148
1949	LG Crawley and JC Wilson	143	1979	N Roche and D Williams	143
1950	L Gracey and I Caldwell	151	1980	G Coles and M Johnson	148
1951	LG Crawley and JC Wilson	147	1981	R Boxall and R Chapman	143
1952T	Major DA Blair and GH Micklem	145	1982	IA Carslaw and J Huggan	139
	LG Crawley and JC Wilson		1983	N Fox and G Lashford	147
1953	D Wilson and G Simmons	148	1984	M Palmer and M Belsham	147
1954	JR Thornhill and PF Scrutton	147	1985	S Blight and R Wilkins	143
1955	G Evans and D Sewell	147	1986	M Gerrard and B White	146
1956	GH Micklem and AF Bussell	141	1987	IA Carslaw and J Huggan	141
1957	Major DA Blair and CD Lawrie	138	1988	A Raitt and P Thornley	143
1958	D Sewell and G Evans	143	1989	A Howard and R Hunter	146
1959	HC Squirrell and P Dunn	146	1990	AC Livesey and RG Payne	143
1960	MSR Lunt and JC Behrrell	139	1991	WM Hopkinson and MR Cook	143
1961	HC Squirrell and P Dunn	145	1992	J C Davies and P J Davies	148
1962	AW Holmes and JM Leach	142	1993	M Benka and S Seman	138
1963	RC Pickering and MJ Cooper	146	1994	D Cowap and J Brant	142
1964	MF Bonallack and Dr DM Marsh	145	1995	R Neill and G Evans	141
1965	MSR Lunt and DE Rodway	146	1996	I Tottingham and R Harris	144
1966	PD Kelley and Dr DM Marsh	144	1997	S Kay and R Peacock	143
1967	Play abandoned		1998	G Willman and B Willman	142
1968	H Broadbent and G Birtwell	144	1999	D Lomas and K Staunton*	104
1969T	SR Warrin and JH Cook	146	2000	M Booker and R Rae	143
	J Povall and K Dabson		2001	M Booker and R Rae	142
1969T	JC Davies and W Humphreys	146			
	RD Watson-Jones and LOM Smith				

2002

1	Rupert Rea & Mark Booker (Royal Mid-Surrey)	71-67—138
2	Simon Cooper (Roehampton) & Tom Williams (Gog Magog)	75-68—143
3	A Walton & B Mann (Frilford Heath)	72-71—143

Burhill Family Foursomes (Inaugurated 1937) *at Burhill, Surrey*

1937	Captain JR Stroyan and Miss S Stroyan		1961	Mrs R Sutherland Pilch and J Sutherland Pilch
1938	W Price and Miss E Price		1962	JC Hubbard and Miss Trudi Hubbard
1939–1946	*No competition*		1963	GA Rowan-Robinson and
1947	Mrs GH Brooks and PJ Brooks			Miss 'Pooh' Rowan Robinson
1948	W Price and Miss E Price		1964	Mrs P Todhunter and T Todhunter
1949	Mrs EC Pepper and W Pepper		1965	Mrs WT Warrin and SR Warrin
1950	A Forbes Ilsley and Miss J Ilsley		1966	Mrs WT Warrin and SR Warrin
1951	Major E Loxley Land and Miss J Land		1967	Mrs WT Warrin and SR Warrin
1952	CHV Elliot and Miss S Elliott		1968	Mrs CHP Trollope and Nigel Trollope
1953	JC Hubbard and Miss A Hubbard		1969	Mrs EPP D'A Walton and JF Walton
1954	JC Hubbard and Miss A Hubbard		1970	JF Young and Miss EJ Young
1955	Mrs HP Thornhill and JR Thornhill		1971	PHA Brownrigg and Miss D Brownrigg
1956	Mrs HP Thornhill and JR Thornhill		1972	Mrs S Grant and NJ Grant
1957	CH Young and Mrs PBK Gracey		1973	MV Blake and Miss B Blake
1958	Mrs HM Winckley and JB Winckley		1974	Mrs NR Bailhache and WJ Bailhache
1959	Jack and Anna van Zwanenberg		1975	Mrs PR Williams and PM Williams
1960	Mrs M Kippax and JM Kippax		1976	Mrs D Gotla and C Gotla

1977	Mrs J Maudsley and C Maudsley	1990	Mrs M Maisey and S Maisey
1978	Mrs H Calderwood and WR Calderwood	1991	Mrs M Pollitt and R Pollitt
1979	Dr AG Wells and Miss E Wells	1992	R Stocks and Miss Joanna Stocks
1980	JL Hall and Miss Cynthia Hall	1993	Mrs M Bartlett and Jerome Bartlett
1981	Mrs J Fox and N Fox	1994	MJ Toole and Miss SJ Toole
1982	Mrs J Fox and N Fox	1995	Mrs G Warner and R Warner
1983	Mrs J Rowe and D Rowe	1996	Mrs AP Croft and MC Croft
1984	Mrs JS Gilbert and AS Gilbert	1997	Mrs J Clink and T Clink
1985	Mrs MM Pollitt and R Pollitt	1998	MJ Toole and Miss SJ Toole
1986	Mrs J Maudesley and C Maudesley	1999	MJ Toole and Miss SJ Toole
1987	Mrs A Croft and M Croft	2000	Mrs V Marchbanks and R Marchbanks
1988	Mrs V Hargreaves and R Hargreaves	2001	Mrs C Warren and R Warren
1989	Mrs J Lawson and P Lawson		

2002

Final

GR & TG Clark (Royal North Devon/Burhill) beat DFR & AM Lord (Northamptonshire County) 5 and 3

Fathers and Sons Foursomes *at West Hill, Surrey*

1991	DM and WK Laing	1995	J and D Niven	1999	R and K Boxall
1992	JA and R Piggott	1996	MJ and J Hickey	2000	G and M Steele
1993	B and R Groce	1997	DR and M Baxter	2001	J and D Niven
1994	RJ and P Hill	1998	SF and P Brown		

2002
Final

GR and TG Clark (Royal North Devon/Burhill) beat DFR and AM Lord (Northamptonshire County) 5 and 3

Sunningdale Foursomes (Inaugurated 1934) *at Sunningdale*

1934	Miss D Fishwick and EN Layton	1972	JC Davies and MG King
1935	Miss J Wethered and JSF Morrison	1973	J Putt and Miss M Everard
1936	Miss J Wethered and JSF Morrison	1974	PJ Butler and CA Clark
1937	AS Anderson and Dai Rees	1975	*Cancelled due to snow*
1938	Miss P Barton and Alf Padgham	1976	CA Clark and M Hughesdon
1939	C Rissik and EWH Kenyon	1977	GN Hunt and D Matthew
1940-47	*Not played due to Second World War*	1978	GA Caygill and Miss J Greenhalgh
1948	Miss Wanda Morgan and Sam King	1979	G Will and R Chapman
1949	RG French and SS Field	1980	NC Coles and D McClelland
1950	M Faulkner and J Knipe	1981	A Lyddon and G Brand jr
1951	Miss J Donald and TB Haliburton	1982	Miss MA McKenna and Miss M Madill
1952	PF Scrutton and Alan Waters	1983	J Davies and M Devetta
1953	Miss J Donald and TB Haliburton	1984	Miss M McKenna and Miss M Madill
1954	PF Scrutton and Alan Waters	1985	J O'Leary and S Torrance
1955	W Sharp and SS Scott	1986	R Rafferty and R Chapman
1956	G Knipe and DC Smalldon	1987	I Mosey and W Humphreys
1957	BGC Huggett and R Whitehead	1988	SC Mason and A Chandler
1958	Miss J Donald and Peter Alliss	1989	AD Hare and R Claydon
1959	MF Bonallack and D Sewell	1990	Miss D Reid and Miss C Dibnah
1960	Miss B McCorkindale and MJ Moir	1991	J Robinson and W Henry
1961	Mrs J Anderson and Peter Alliss	1992	R Boxall and D Cooper
1962	ER Whitehead and NC Coles	1993	A Beal and L James
1963	L Platts and D Snell	1994	S Webster and A Wall
1964	B Critchley and R Hunter	1995	D Cooper and R Boxall
1965	Mrs AD Spearman and T Fisher	1996	L Donald and M O'Connor
1966	RRW Davenport and A Walker	1997	Mrs J Hall and Miss H Wadsworth
1967	NC Coles and K Warren	1998	D Fisher and W Bennett
1968	JC Davies and W Humphreys	1999	L Walters and R McEvoy
1969	P Oosterhuis and PJ Benka	2000	S Head and J Head
1970	R Barrell and Miss A Willard	2001	C Lipscombe and S Little
1971	A Bird and H Flatman		

Sunningdale Foursomes *continued*

2002

Quarter Finals

Chloe Court (Goodwood) and Jamie Donaldson (Tall Pines) beat Barry Lane and Scott Evans (Bearwood Lakes) 4 and 2

John Kemp and Mark Wharton (John O'Gaunt) beat Carole and Richard Caldwell (Sunningdale) 3 and 2

Pereira Machado (Sunningdale) and Brito e Cunha (Estoril, Portugal) beat James York and Chris Drury (West Herts) 5 and 4

Glenn Ralph (Camberley Heath) & Tim Spence (Battle) beat Marcus Higley and Kevin Spurgeon (Yeovil) 4 and 3

Semi-Finals

Kemp and Wharton beat Court and Donaldson 1 hole

Ralph and Spence beat Pereira Machado and Brito e Cunha 3 and 2

Final

John Kemp and Mark Wharton beat Glenn Ralph and Tim Spence 1 hole

Worplesdon Mixed Foursomes (Inaugurated 1921) *at Worplesdon, Surrey*

1921	Miss Helme and TA Torrance	1965	Mrs G Valentine and JE Behrend
1922	Miss Joyce Wethered and R Wethered	1966	Mrs C Barclay and DJ Miller
1923	Miss Joyce Wethered and CJ Tolley	1967	JF Gancedo and Mlle C Lacoste
1924	Miss SR Fowler and EN Layton	1968	JD van Heel and Miss Dinah Oxley
1925	Miss Cecil Leitch and E Esmond	1969	Mrs R Ferguson and Alistair Wilson
1926	Mlle de la Chaume and R Wethered	1970	Miss R Roberts and RL Glading
1927	Miss Joyce Wethered and CJH Tolley	1971	Mrs D Frearson and A Smith
1928	Miss Joyce Wethered and JSF Morrison	1972	Miss B Le Garreres and CA Strang
1929	Miss M Gourlay and Maj CO Hezlet	1973	Miss T Perkins and RJ Evans
1930	Miss M Gourlay and Maj CO Hezlet	1974	Mrs S Birley and RL Glading
1931	Miss J Wethered and Hon M Scott	1975	Mr and Mrs JR Thornhill
1932	Miss J Wethered and RH Oppenheimer	1976	Mrs B Lewis and J Caplan
1933	Miss J Wethered and B Darwin beat	1977	Mrs D Henson and J Caplan
1934	Miss M Gourlay and TA Torrance	1978	Miss T Perkins and R Thomas
1935,	Miss G and J Craddock-Hartopp	1979	Miss J Melville and A Melville
1936	Miss J Wethered and Hon T Coke	1980	Mrs L Bayman and I Boyd
1937	Mrs Heppel and LG Crawley	1981	Mrs J Nicholsen and MN Stern
1938	Mrs MR Garon and EF Storey	1982	Miss B New and K Dobson
1939–45	*Not played due to Second World War*	1983	Miss B New and K Dobson
1946	Miss J Gordon and AA Duncan	1984	Mrs L Bayman and MC Hughesdon
1947	Miss J Gordon and AA Duncan	1985	Mrs H Kaye and D Longmuir
1948	Miss W Morgan and EF Storey	1986	Miss P Johnson and RN Roderick
1949	Miss F Stephens and LG Crawley	1987	Miss J Nicholson and B White
1950	Miss F Stephens and LG Crawley	1988	Mme A Larrezac and JJ Caplan
1951	Mrs AC Barclay and G Evans	1989	Miss S Kershaw and M Kershaw
1952	Mrs RT Peel and GW Mackie	1990	Miss S Keogh and A Rodgers
1953	Miss J Gordon and G Knipe	1991	J Rhodes and C Banks
1954	Miss F Stephens and WA Slark	1992	D Henson and B Turner
1955	Miss P Garvey and PF Scrutton	1993	A Macdonald and S Skeldon
1956	Mrs L Abrahams and Maj WD Henderson	1994	Mr and Mrs K Quinn
1957	Mrs B Singleton and WD Smith	1995	Mrs C Caldwell and P Carr
1958	Mr and Mrs M Bonallack	1996	Miss L Walters and M Naylor
1959	Miss J Robertson and I Wright	1997	Miss K Burton and G Wolstenholme
1960	Miss B Jackson and MJ Burgess	1998	Miss K Burton and J Smith
1961	Mrs R Smith and B Critchley	1999	Miss AM Boatman and RG Hodgkinson
1962	Viscomtesse de Saint Sauveur and DW Frame	2000	Mr and Mrs Galway
1963	Mrs G Valentine and JE Behrend	2001	Miss K Fisher and J Harper
1964	Mrs G Valentine and JE Behrend		

2002

Semi-Finals

Miss C Court (Goodwood) & J Donaldson (West Sussex) beat Mrs J Ballard & D Gatward (Calcot Park) 3 and 2

Miss M Allen (Moor Park) & J Maguire (Verulam) beat Mrs A Greenfield (Pycombe) & RM O'Connor (Ruby Hills) 3 and 2

Final

C Court & J Donaldson beat M Allen & J Maguire 1 hole

University and School Events

Halford-Hewitt Cup (Inaugurated 1924) at Deal

1924	Eton	1954	Rugby	1978	Harrow
1925	Eton	1955	Eton	1979	Stowe
1926	Eton	1956	Eton	1980	Shrewsbury
1927	Harrow	1957	George Watson's	1981	George Watson's
1928	Eton	1958	Harrow	1982	Charterhouse
1929	Harrow	1959	Wellington	1983	Charterhouse
1930	Charterhouse	1960	Rossall	1984	Charterhouse
1931	Harrow	1961	Rossall	1985	Harrow
1932	Charterhouse	1962	Oundle	1986	Repton
1933	Rugby	1963	Repton	1987	Merchiston
1934	Charterhouse	1964	Fettes	1988	Stowe
1935	Charterhouse	1965	Rugby	1989	Eton
1936	Charterhouse	1966	Charterhouse	1990	Tonbridge
1937	Charterhouse	1967	Eton	1991	Shrewsbury
1938	Marlborough	1968	Eton	1992	Tonbridge
1939	Charterhouse	1969	Eton	1993	Shrewsbury
1940–46 *No competition*		1970	Merchiston	1994	Tonbridge
1947	Harrow	1971	Charterhouse	1995	Harrow
1948	Winchester	1972	Marlborough	1996	Radley
1949	Charterhouse	1973	Rossall	1997	Oundle
1950	Rugby	1974	Charterhouse	1998	Charterhouse
1951	Rugby	1975	Harrow	1999	George Watson's
1952	Harrow	1976	Merchiston	2000	Epsom
1953	Harrow	1977	George Watson's	2001	Tonbridge

2002

Semi-Finals	Charterhouse beat Merchiston 3-2
	Whitgift beat Epsom 3-2
Final	Charterhouse beat Whitgift 3½-1½

Winning team: Mark Benka, Richard Caldwell, Michael Croft, Patric Foley-Brackley, Julian Hill, Robert Manning, Barnaby Mote, Tim Orgill, Simon Stilwell, Rupert Tate

Senior Halford-Hewitt Competitions (Inaugurated 2000)

Bernard Darwin Trophy (Original 16) at Woking GC

2000	Wellington College	2001	Malvern College	2002 Wellington College

Mellin Trophy (Second 16) at West Hill GC

2000	Lansing College	2001	Cheltenham College	2002 Shrewsbury School

Cyril Gray Trophy (Remaining 32) at Worplesdon

2000	Stoneyhurst School	2001	Canford School	2002 George Watson's College

Senior Halford-Hewitt Trophy (Play-off between winners of Darwin, Mellin and Gray Trophies)

2000	Wellington College beat Lansing College beat Stoneyhurst School at West Hill GC	2002	Wellington College beat George Watson's College beat Shrewsbury School at Worplesdon
2001	Canford School beat Malvern College beat Cheltenham College at Woking GC		

Grafton Morrish Trophy (Inaugurated 1963) *at Hunstanton and Brancaster*

1963	Tonbridge	1976	Charterhouse	1989	Tonbridge
1964	Tonbridge	1977	Haileybury	1990	Clifton
1965	Charterhouse	1978	Charterhouse	1991	Repton
1966	Charterhouse	1979	Harrow	1992	Charterhouse
1967	Charterhouse	1980	Charterhouse	1993	Malvern
1968	Wellington	1981	Charterhouse	1994	George Heriot's
1969	Sedbergh	1982	Marlborough	1995	Repton
1970	Sedbergh	1983	Wellington	1996	Coventry
1971	Dulwich	1984	Sedbergh	1997	George Heriot's
1972	Sedbergh	1985	Warwick	1998	Solihull
1973	Pangbourne	1986	Tonbridge	1999	George Heriot's
1974	Millfield	1987	Harrow	2000	Lancing
1975	Oundle	1988	Robert Gordon's	2001	King's College School

2002

Semi-Finals
Berkhamsted beat Solihull 2–1
George Heriot's beat Winchester 2–1

Winning team: John Archibald, Ron Bradly, David Campbell (captain), John Liddel, Bert Nicholson, Chris Paterson

Final
George Heriot's beat Berkhamsted 2–1

Oxford *v* Cambridge Varsity Match (Inaugurated 1878)

1878	Oxford	Wimbledon	1924	Cambridge	Hoylake
1879	Cambridge	Wimbledon	1925	Oxford	Hunstanton
1880	Oxford	Wimbledon	1926	Cambridge	Burnham and Berrow
1881	*Not played*		1927	Cambridge	Hoylake
1882	Cambridge	Wimbledon	1928	Cambridge	Prince's, Sandwich
1883	Oxford	Wimbledon	1929	Cambridge	Rye
1884	Oxford	Wimbledon	1930	Oxford	Hoylake
1885	Oxford	Wimbledon	1931	Oxford	Prince's, Sandwich
1886	Oxford	Wimbledon	1932	Oxford	Lytham St Annes
1887	Cambridge	Wimbledon	1933	Cambridge	Prince's, Sandwich
1888	Cambridge	Wimbledon	1934	Oxford	Formby
1889	Oxford	Wimbledon	1935	Cambridge	Burnham and Berrow
1890	Cambridge	Wimbledon	1936	Cambridge	Hoylake
1891	Cambridge	Wimbledon	1937	Cambridge	Prince's, Sandwich
1892	Cambridge	Wrlmbledon	1938	Cambridge	Westward Ho!
1893	Cambridge	Wimbledon	1939	Cambridge	Royal St George's
1894	Oxford	Sandwich	1940–45	*No competitions due to Second World War*	
1895	Cambridge	Sandwich	1946	Cambridge	Royal Lytham & St Annes
1896	Halved	Wimbledon	1947	Oxford	Rye
1897	Cambridge	Sandwich	1948	Oxford	Royal St George's
1898	Cambridge	Sandwich	1949	Cambridge	Hoylake
1899	Oxford	Sandwich	1950	Oxford	Royal Lytham & St Annes
1900	Oxford	Sandwich	1951	Cambridge	Rye
1901	Oxford	Sandwich	1952	Cambridge	Rye
1902	Oxford	Sandwich	1953	Cambridge	Rye
1903	Oxford	Sandwich	1954	Cambridge	Rye
1904	Oxford	Woking	1955	Cambridge	Rye
1905	Cambridge	Sunningdale	1956	Oxford	Formby
1906	Cambridge	Hoylake	1957	Oxford	Royal St George's
1907	Cambridge	Hoylake	1958	Cambridge	Rye

After 1907 the result was arrived at by matches won

			1959	Cambridge	Burnham & Berrow
			1960	Cambridge	Royal Lytham & St Annes
1908	Cambridge	Sunningdale	1961	Oxford	Royal St George's
1909	Oxford	Royal St George's	1962	Halved	Hunstanton
1910	Cambridge	Hoylake	1963	Cambridge	Royal Birkdale
1911	Oxford	Rye	1964	Oxford	Rye
1912	Halved	Prince's,	1965	Cambridge	Royal St George's
1913	Halved	Hoylake	1966	Cambridge	Hunstanton
1914	Oxford	Rye	1967	Cambridge	Rye
1915–19	*No competitions due to First World War*		1968	Cambridge	Porthcawl
1920	Cambridge	Sunningdale	1969	Cambridge	Formby
1921	Oxford	Hoylake	1970	Halved	Royal St George's
1922	Cambridge	Prince's, Sandwich	1971	Oxford	Rye
1923	Oxford	Rye	1972	Cambridge	Formby

1973	Oxford	Saunton		1988	Cambridge	Royal Porthcawl
1974	Cambridge	Ganton		1989	Cambridge	Rye
1975	Cambridge	Hoylake		1990	Cambridge	Muirfield
1976	Cambridge	Woodhall Spa		1991	Cambridge	Royal St George's
1977	Cambridge	Porthcawl		1992	Oxford	Royal Cinque Ports
1978	Oxford	Rye		1993	Oxford	Royal Liverpool
1979	Oxford	Harlech		1994	Oxford	Rye
1980	Oxford	Hoylake		1995	Oxford	Royal Lytham & St Annes
1981	Cambridge	Formby		1996	Oxford	Royal West Norfolk
1982	Cambridge	Hunstanton		1997	Oxford	Royal St Georges
1983	Cambridge	Royal St George's		1998	Cambridge	Rye
1984	Cambridge	Sunningdale		1999	Oxford	Royal Cinque Ports
1985	Oxford	Rye		2000	Cambridge	Porthcawl
1986	Oxford	Ganton		2001	Oxford	Formby
1987	Cambridge	Formby				

2002 *at Royal St George's*

Captains: DG Hayes (Oxford); AI Dodds (Cambridge)

Foursomes
Hayes & Locke beat Dodds & Weston 1 hole
Stacey & Edwards lost to Southworth & Macdonald 4 and 3
Greenhalgh & Simpson beat Robson & Colgan 1 hole
Sharples & Webster lost to Peacock & Bell 4 and 3
Mann & Meggs lost to Harvey & Dawson 4 and 3

Singles
DG Hayes (Corpus Christi) beat AI Dodds (Churchill) 5 and 4
JM Sharples (Corpus Christi) lost to DJ Robson (Emmanuel) 2 and 1
RC Mann (St Edmund Hall) beat JM Harvey (Caius) 5 and 4
TW Meggs (St Catherine's) beat AIRP Macdonald (St Catharine's) 5 and 4
MDS Webster (New College) halved with CJ Southworth (Trinity)
AR Edwards (Corpus Christi) lost to GC Colgan (Selwyn) 8 and 7
N Stacey (St Edmund Hall) lost to RC Bell (St John's) 5 and 4
RL Simpson (St Cross) lost to T Dawson (Emmanuel) 6 and 5
EAJ Greenhalgh (Brasenose) lost to BJ Peacock (Girton) 2 and 1
M Locke (Exeter) lost to PM Weston (Corpus Christi) 2 and 1

Result: Cambridge beat Oxford 9½–5½

Oxford and Cambridge Golfing Society
for the President's Putter (Inaugurated 1920) *at Rye*

1920	EWE Holderness	1948	Major AA Duncan	1971	GT Duncan
1921	EWE Holderness	1949	PB Lucas	1972	P Moody
1922	EWE Holderness	1950	DHR Martin	1973	AD Swanston
1923	EWE Holderness	1951	LG Crawley	1974	R Biggs
1924	B Darwin	1952	LG Crawley	1975	CJ Weight
1925	HD Gillies	1953	GH Micklem	1976	MJ Reece
1926T	EF Storey	1954	G Huddy	1977	AWJ Holmes
	RH Wethered	1955	G Huddy	1978	MJ Reece
1927	RH Wethered	1956	GT Duncan	1979	*Cancelled due to snow*
1928	RH Wethered	1957	AE Shepperson	1980	S Melville
1929	Sir EWE Holderness	1958	Lt-Col AA Duncan	1981	AWJ Holmes
1930	TA Bourn	1959	ID Wheater	1982	DMA Steel
1931	AG Pearson	1960	JME Anderson	1983	ER Dexter
1932	LG Crawley	1961	ID Wheater	1984	A Edmond
1933	AJ Peech	1962	MF Attenborough	1985	ER Dexter
1934	DHR Martin	1963	JG Blackwell	1986	J Caplan
1935	RH Wethered	1964	DMA Steel	1987	CD Meacher
1936	RH Wethered	1965	WJ Uzielli	1988	G Woollett
1937	JB Beck	1966	MF Attenborough	1989	M Froggatt
1938	CJH Tolley	1967	JR Midgley	1990	G Woollett
1939	JOH Greenly	1968	AWJ Holmes	1991	B Ingleby
1940–46 *No competition*		1969	P Moody	1992	M Cox
1947	LG Crawley	1970	DMA Steel	1993	C Weight

Oxford and Cambridge Golfing Society *continued*

1994	S Seman		1998	N Pabari
1995	A Woolnough		1999	C Dale
1996	C Rotheroe		2000	CJ Dale
1997	C Rotheroe		2001	B Streather

2002

Quarter-Finals

Andy Edmond beat Omar Malik 2 and 1
Dave McDowell beat Julius Stobbs 5 and 4
Tom Etridge beat John Turner 5 and 4
Steve Seman beat Dibran Zeqiri 3 and 2

Semi-Finals

McDowell beat Edmond 4 and 3
Etridge beat Seman 1 hole

Final

T Etridge beat D McDowell 2 and 1

Palmer Cup (USA university students *v* Great Britain & Ireland students)

1997	USA	19–5	Bay Hill, Orlando, Florida
1998	USA	12–12	St Andrews, Scotland
1999	USA	17½–6½	Honors, Tennessee
2000	GB&I	12½–11½	Royal Liverpool
2001	USA	14–2	Springfield, NJ

2002 *at Doonbeg, Co. Clare, Ireland*

First Day: **Fourball – Morning**

P Rowe & O Wilson beat B Mackenzie & N Watney
  1 hole
A Smith & J Walters beat R Hybl & L Williamson
  6 and 4
G Harris & S Manley lost to J Klauk & H Mahan 1 hole
J Kehoe & S Wilson lost to B Haas & DJ Trahan 1 hole

Foursomes – Afternoon

P Rowe & O Wilson halved with R Hybl &
  L Williamson
A Smith & J Walters lost to B Mackenzie &
  N Watney 6 and 4
G Harris & S Manley beat J Klauk & H Mahan
  5 and 4
J Kehoe & S Wilson lost to B Haas & DJ Trahan
  2 and 1

Second Day: **Singles – Morning**

Oliver Wilson lost to Bill Haas 2 holes
Philip Rowe lost to Nick Watney 1 hole
Geoff Harris lost to John Klauk 2 holes
Stuart Manley halved with Ryan Hybl
Stuart Wilson halved with Brock Mackenzie
Andy Smith lost to Lee Williamson 3 and 2
Justin Walters beat Hunter Mahan 2 and 1
Justin Kehoe lost to DJ Trahan 3 and 2

Singles – Afternoon

O Wilson lost to B Haas 2 holes
P Rowe lost to N Watney 1 hole
J Kehoe beat J Klauk 3 and 1
J Walters lost to R Hybl 7 and 6
S Wilson halved with B Mackenzie
S Manley halved with L Williamson
A Smith halved with H Mahan
G Harris halved with DJ Trahan

Result: Great Britain & Ireland 8½, United States 15½

Boyd Quaich (University Championship) *at St Andrews*

1946	AS Mayer	Glasgow	161		1964	AJ Low	St Andrews	299
1947T	H Brews	Johannesburg	148		1965	S MacDonald	Edinburgh	295
	FWG Deighton	Glasgow	148		1966	FE McCarroll	Queen's, Belfast	291
1948	JL Lindsay	St Andrews	203		1967	B Nicholson	Aberdeen	294
1949	FD Tatum	Oxford	217		1968	JW Johnston	Aberdeen	291
1950	GP Roberts	Liverpool	294		1969	PH Moody	Cambride	286
1951	H Dooley	Nottingham	299		1970	JT Moffat	Strathclyde	297
1952	G Parker	Glasgow	297		1971	JW Johnston	Aberdeen	289
1953	JL Bamford	Trinity, Dublin	290		1972	D Greig	Aberdeen	288
1954	I Caldwell	London	287		1973	J Rube	Sweden	285
1955	HC Squirrll	Birmingham	292		1974	G Cairns	Edinburgh	297
1956	JL Bamford	Trinity, Dublin	295		1975	S Dunlop	Trinity, Dublin	291
1957	DM Marsh	Liverpool	293		1976	R Watson	Dundee	297
1958	R Mummery	London	299		1977	R Watson	Dundee	297
1959-61	*Not played*				1978	R Watson	Dundee	298
1962	DB Sheahan	Univ. Coll., Dublin	217		1979	D McLeary	St Andrews	302
1963	S MacDonald	Edinburgh	295		1980	ME Lewis	Bath	290

1981	P Gallagher	Heriot-Watt	302	1992	L Walker	Trinity, Dublin	286
1982	ME Lewis	Bath	297	1993	G Sherry	Stirling	298
1983	R Risan	Lund, Sweden	296	1994	C Sanderson	Stellenbosch, SA	283
1984	J Huggan	Stirling	297	1995	C Sanderson	Stellenbosch, SA	290
1985	S Elgie	W. Ontario, Canada	299	1996	B Templeton	Heriot-Watt	294
1986	A Roberts	Hull	291	1997	G Maly	St Andrews	289
1987	M Pask	St Andrews	293	1998	D Simpson	Edinburgh	283
1988	A Mathers	Stirling	289	1999	O Lindsay	St Andrews	290
1989	A Mathers	Stirling	300	2000	G Greer	Glasgow	288
1990	A Mathers	Stirling	297	2001	P Botha*	Pretoria	292
1991	C Somner	Friberg, Switzerland	302				

2002

1	Gerrard Duncan (Heriot-Watt)	68-69-74-72—283
2	Andrew Lynch (Stirling)	74-71-69-73—287
3	Tim Dykes (Swansea)	74-73-72-72—291
	Daniel De Leon (SE Louisiana)	69-72-75-75—291

Queen Elizabeth Coronation Schools Trophy (inaugurated 1953)

at Royal Burgess, Barnton

1953	Watsonians	1978	Old Lorettonians
1954	Daniel Stewart's FP	1979	Gordonians
1955	Watsonians	1980	George Heriot's FP
1956	Watsonians	1981	Ayr Academicals
1957	Hillhead High School FP	1982	George Heriot's FP
1958	Watsonians	1983	Perth Academy FP
1959	Glasgow High School FP	1984	Glasgow High School FP
1960	Glasgow High School FP	1985	Glasgow High School FP
1961	Watsonians	1986	Watsonians
1962	Glasgow High School FP	1987	Daniel Stewart's/Melville FP
1963	Glasgow High School FP	1988	Watsonians
1964	Dollar Academicals	1989	Kelvinside Academicals
1965	Old Lorettonians	1990	Hutchesons' Grammar School FP
1966	Merchistonians	1991	Glasgow High School FP
1967	Merchistonians	1992	Daniel Stewart's/Melville FP
1968	Hillhead High School FP	1993	Merchistonians
1969	Kelvinside Academicals	1994	Perth Academy FP
1970	Dollar Academicals	1995	Glasgow High School FP
1971	Merchistonians	1996	Glasgow High School FP
1972	Merchistonians	1997	Old Uppinghamians
1973	Merchistonians	1998	Watsonians
1974	Old Carthusians	1999	Morrisonians
1975	Old Lorettonians	2000	Breadalbane Academicals
1976	Watsonians	2001	Old Carthusians
1977	Glasgow High School FP		

2002

Semi-Finals
Campbellians beat Carthusians 2-1
Breadalbane Academicals beat Lenzie Academicals 2-1

Final
Campbellians beat Breadalbane Academicals 2-1

Winning team: D Boyd, S Craig, K Lowry, R McAuley, R McDowell, J Pollin

County and Other Regional Championships

Anglesey

1993	M Perdue	1998	EO Jones
1994	J Campbell	1999	A Williams
1995	D McLean	2000	H Hughes
1996	A Williams	2001	H Hughes
1997	M Perdue	2002	M Perdue

Angus

1993	G Tough	1999	J Flynn
1994	E Wilson	2000	S Wilson
1995	J Rae	2001	M Lindsay (M)
1996	G Bell		A Johnston (S)
1997	P Cunningham	2002	GW Tough (M)
1998	E Ramsay		JA Watt (S)

Argyll and Bute

1993	G Tyre-Cole	1999	G Bolton
1994	G Bolton	2000	G McMillan
1995	G Tyre	2001	G Bolton (M)
1996	L Kelly		G Reynolds (S)
1997	S Campbell	2002	G Bolton (M)
1998	J Sharp		G Tyre (S)

Ayrshire

1993	H McKibben (M)	1998	I Robertson (M)
	G Sherry (S)		D Glass (S)
1994	J Cairney (M)	1999	G Holland
	G Lawrie (S)		(M and S)
1995	A Reid (M)	2000	L Bagnall (M)
	A Gourlay (S)		A Gourlay (S)
1996	J Cairney (M)	2001	A Gourlay (M)
	G Lawrie (S)		G Bryden (S)
1997	G Fox (M)	2002	A Gourlay (M)
	B Aitken (S)		R Duncan (S)

Bedfordshire

1993	C Beard	1998	M Wharton
1994	J Kemp	1999	J Kemp
1995	I Tottingham	2000	S Vinnecombe
1996	M Wharton	2001	J Kemp
1997	K Kemp	2002	M Wharton

Berks, Bucks and Oxon

1993	R Walton	1998	L Donald
1994	D Fisher	1999	L Rusher
1995	D Lane	2000	K Freeman
1996	J Carlsen	2001	C Bowler
1997	L Donald	2002	A Walton

Border Golfers' Association

1993	D Valentine	1998	D Ballantyne
1994	M Thomson	1999	J Paterson
1995	M Thomson	2000	M Thomson
1996	D Ballantyne	2001	M Thomson
1997	W Simpson	2002	RD Ballantyne

Caernarfon and District

1993	E Jones	1998	A Clishem
1994	D McLean	1999	R Williams
1995	S Pritchard	2000	H Hughes
1996	A Williams	2001	M Tottey
1997	*Not played*	2002	A Williams

Caernarfonshire Cup

1993	L Harpin	1998	M Pilkington
1994	J Dabecki	1999	E Angel
1995	J Dabecki	2000	M Wyn Jones
1996	M Pilkington	2001	A Thomas
1997	*Not played*	2002	A Thomas

Cambridgeshire

1993	LG Yearn	1998	L Yearn
1994	A Emery	1999	O Cousins
1995	S Jarvis	2000	LG Yearn
1996	P Rains	2001	LG Yearn
1997	O Cousins	2002	K Arthur

Cheshire

1993	J Hodgson	1998	J Donaldson
1994	J Hodgson	1999	SS Grewal
1995	C Smethurst	2000	FA Bibby
1996	D Vaughan	2001	GJ Bradley
1997	N Pabari	2002	D Wardrop

Clackmannanshire

1993	S Horne	1999	M Crichton
1994	P McLeod	2000	AC Fairbrother
1995	I Ross	2001	I Macaulay (M and S)
1996	R Stewart	2002	M Crichton (S)
1997	G Bowie		C Macaulay (M)
1998	B Stewart		

Cornwall

1993	C Phillips	1998	I Atkinson
1994	R Binney	1999	I Veale
1995	M Lock	2000	S Chapman
1996	I Veale	2001	C Llewellyn
1997	P Darlington	2002	IT Veale

Cumbria

1993	R Secular	1998	P Jack
1994	B Story	1999	J Longcake
1995	N Mitchell	2000	J Carr
1996	R Secular	2001	S Young
1997	G Watson	2002	N Bell

Derbyshire

1993	G Shaw	1998	L Walley
1994	J Feeney	1999	JP Feeney
1995	G Shaw	2000	N Vowles
1996	J Feeney	2001	P Gration
1997	AS Humpston	2002	P Gration

Devon

1993	R Goodey	1998	S Pike
1994	M Crossfield	1999	G Ruth
1995	A Capping	2000	S Davey
1996	D Eva	2001	G Ruth
1997	G Ruth	2002	K Harper

Dorset

1993	A Lawrence	1998	J Pounder
1994	M Davies	1999	C Jessup
1995	M Davies	2000	M Davies
1996	A Lawrence	2001	A Lawrence
1997	J Baldwin	2002	T Peacock

Dunbartonshire

1993	F Jardine (M and S)	1998	S Carmichael (M)
	F Jardine (S)		G Murphy (S)
1994	D Carrick (M)	1999	G Greer (M)
	F Hutchison (S)		J Hughes (S)
1995	T McKeown (M)	2000	J Devonney (M)
	F Jardine (S)		SR McIntosh (S)
1996	K MacNair (M)	2001	F Bone (M)
	A Leitch (S)		P Gault (S)
1997	S Carmichael (M)	2002	P Gault jr (M)
	S McLeitch (S)		K Smyth (S)

Durham

1993	R Walker	1998	C Hamilton
1994	J Kennedy	1999	A McLure
1995	A McLure	2000	AJ McLure
1996	S Ord	2001	M Ridley
1997	J Dryden	2002	J Harper

Essex

1993	R Coles	1998	B Taylor
1994	R Coles	1999	R Blaxhill
1995	D Salisbury	2000	S Middleton
1996	G Clark	2001	R Blaxill
1997	B Taylor	2002	P Ring

Fife

1993	DA Paton	1999	J McLeary
1994	C MacDougall	2000	R Bremner
1995	D Paton	2001	J McLeary (M)
1996	B Erskine		S Meiklejohn (S)
1997	S Meiklejohn	2002	R Dickson (M)
1998	J Bunch		JT Bunch (S)

Glamorgan

1993	M Stimson	1998	C Williams
1994	N Edwards	1999	S Roberts
1995	S Roberts	2000	N Edwards
1996	N Edwards	2001	N Edwards
1997	Y Taylor	2002	L James

Gloucestershire

1993	G Wolstenholme	1998	TP Smith
1994	G Wolstenholme	1999	D Young
1995	T Smith	2000	C Newman
1996	G Wolstenholme	2001	M Unwin
1997	M Unwin	2002	P Reed

Gwent
(Formerly Monmouthshire Amateur)

1993	A Harray	1998	N Povall
1994	B Dredge	1999	A Williams
1995	C Dinsdale	2000	CJ Dinsdale
1996	M Hayward	2001	S Westley
1997	R Price	2002	J Davidson

Hampshire, Isle of Wight and Channel Islands

1993	M Blackey	1998	C Hudson
1994	R Bland	1999	D Henley
1995	M Le Mesurier	2000	C McLaughlin
1996	M Blackey	2001	D Henley
1997	S Stanley	2002	R Elmes

Hertfordshire

1993	S Burnell	1998	R Conway-Lye
1994	G Maly	1999	D Griffiths
1995	H Steel	2000	I Farrant
1996	S Little	2001	M Payne
1997	C Duke	2002	B Connelly

Isle of Man

1993	G Wilson	1998	P McMullan
1994	R Sayle	1999	G Wilson
1995	G Wilson	2000	S Ellis
1996	G Wilson	2001	G Wilson
1997	P McMullan	2002	M Sutton

Kent

1993	G Brown	1998	D Ottaway
1994	B Barham	1999	J Carter
1995	T Milford	2000	D Curtis
1996	B Barham	2001	L Godwin
1997	D Ottoway	2002	L Campbell

Lanarkshire

1993	K Gallacher (M)	1999	W Bryson
	D Brown (S)		(M and S)
1994	M Moir (M)		W Bryson (S)
	W Bryson (S)	2000	I Duff (M)
1995	W Bryson (M)		C Heap (S)
	K Nisbet (S)	2001	C Gibson (M)
1996	J Ralston (M)		W Bryson (S)
	K Ralston (S)	2002	G Rodger (M)
1997	W Bryson (M)		S Douglas (S)
	E Moir (S)		
1998	R Hinshelwood (M)		
	M Warren (S)		

Lancashire

1993	G Helsby	1998	P Wiliams
1994	K Wallbank	1999	A Jackson
1995	G Boardman	2000	M Cox
1996	G Boardman	2001	R Bardsley
1997	D Johnson	2002	R Walker

Leicestershire and Rutland

1993	P Frith	1998	G Wolstenholme
1994	I Lyner	1999	D Gibson
1995	P Frith	2000	N Knighton
1996	J Herbert	2001	G Wolstenholme
1997	J Herbert	2002	C Shave

Lincolnshire

1993	J Crampton	1998	A White
1994	J Crampton	1999	D Skinns
1995	J Crampton	2000	P Bradshaw
1996	P Streeter	2001	LJ Toyne
1997	P Streeter	2002	P Bradshaw

Lothians

1993	S Smith	1999	C Swanston
1994	S Smith	2000	M Timmins
1995	S Smith	2001	K Nicholson (M)
1996	N Shillinglaw		D Thomson (S)
1997	K Nicholson	2002	B Smith (M)
1998	K Nicholson		G Corrigan (S)

Middlesex

1993	GA Homewood	1998	R Vaney
1994	WJ Bennett	1999	G Evans
1995	G Clark	2000	S Samphire
1996	S Kay	2001	S Samphire
1997	C Austin	2002	G Evans

Norfolk

1993	DA Edwards	1998	CJ Lamb
1994	J Durrant	1999	CJ Lamb
1995	I Ellis	2000	NJ Williamson
1996	P Little	2001	D Henderson
1997	G Price	2002	D Henderson

Northamptonshire

1993	S McIlwain	1998	G Keates
1994	A Print	1999	N Soto
1995	A Lord	2000	A Print
1996	I Dallas	2001	N Soto
1997	P Langrish-Smith	2002	M Peacock

Northumberland

1993	P Taylor	1998	J McCallum
1994	S Twynholm	1999	SE Philipson
1995	M Hall	2000	AR Paisley
1996	K Cademy-Taylor	2001	C McDonnell
1997	D Clark	2002	SE Phillipson

Nottinghamshire

1993	L Westwood	1998	AJ Liddle
1994	D Lucas	1999	AJ Liddle
1995	H Hopkinson	2000	M Allen
1996	D McJannet	2001	D McJannet
1997	O Wilson	2002	T Payne

Perth and Kinross

1993	T McLevy	1999	N Macdonald
1994	E Lindsay	2000	G Campbell
1995	S Herd	2001	G Campbell
1996	M Rose		(M and S)
1997	N Macdonald	2002	S Carruthers (M)
1998	K Grant		G Campbell (S)

Renfrewshire

1993	R Clark	1999	A McKay
1994	M Carmichael	2000	S Robertson
1995	R Adam	2001	A Craig (M)
1996	S Nicol		G Murphy (S)
1997	D Owens	2002	C Rossi (M)
1998	A McKay		GW Urquhart (S)

SE Scotland Championship

1993	D Wallis	1999	I Thomson
1994	I Reid	2000	BJ Scott
1995	B Scott	2001	I Brotherston (M)
1996	E Little		C Haddow (S)
1997	I Brotherston	2002	BJ Scott (S)
1998	D Sutton		J Power (M)

Shropshire and Herefordshire

1993	M Welch	1998	O Pughe
1994	M Welch	1999	K Baker
1995	D Park	2000	R Brown
1996	D Harris	2001	D McDonnell
1997	K Preece	2002	K Williams

Somerset

1993	C Edwards	1998	J Morgan
1994	C Edwards	1999	G Legg
1995	B Whittock	2000	D Dixon
1996	D Dixon	2001	C Edwards
1997	R Swords	2002	B Porter

Staffordshire

1993	C Poxon	1998	KD Hale
1994	R Mayfield	1999	R Chattaway
1995	T Ryder	2000	C Russell
1996	R Parkes	2001	MA Payne
1997	SD Wakefield	2002	A Cheese

Stirlingshire

1993	D Smith	1999	K McArthur
1994	K McArthur	2000	H Anderson
1995	K Brunton	2001	H Anderson (M)
1996	G McDonald		D Todd (S)
1997	A Ellison	2002	H Anderson (M)
1998	JR Johnson		D Buchanan (S)

Suffolk

1993	J Maddock	1998	J Wright
1994	J Maddock	1999	P Barnard
1995	D Quinney	2000	L Dodd
1996	J Keely	2001	L Dodd
1997	J Maddock	2002	J Wright

Surrey

1993	A Raitt	1998	C Rodgers
1994	M Ellis	1999	N Pimm
1995	A Wall	2000	J Franks
1996	M Palmer	2001	Z Scotland
1997	T Paterson	2002	D Lomas

Sussex

1993	M Galway	1998	M Harris
1994	P Clevely	1999	M Galway
1995	M Allen	2000	J Doherty
1996	M Harris	2001	S Nightingale
1997	M Harris	2002	C Newman

Warwickshire

1993	G Marston	1998	T Whitehouse
1994	N Connolly	1999	T Whitehouse
1995	S Webster	2000	T Whitehouse
1996	A Carey	2001	T Whitehouse
1997	T Whitehouse	2002	J Hemphill

Wiltshire

1993	RE Searle	1998	P Bicknell
1994	R Searle	1999	P Bicknell
1995	N Mumford	2000	S Surry
1996	A Mutch	2001	I Campbell
1997	P Bicknell	2002	J Huffam

Yorkshire

1993	J Healey (M)	1998	S Tarplett (M)
	J Roberts (S)		M Bugg /
1994	P Wood (M)		R Hodgkinson (S) (tied)
	N Ludwell (S)	1999	GA Clark (M)
1995	J Ellis (M)		SJ Dyson (S)
	N Gibson (S)	2000	JB Godbold (M)
	J Hepworth (S)		GA Clark (S)
1996	R Jones (M)		RM Hollins (S)
	N Emmerson (S)	2001	R Finch (M)
1997	R Jones (M)		R Finch (S)
	A Wright (S)	2002	DJ Berry (M)

Callaway handicapping

It frequently occurs in social competitions such as office or business association outings that many of the competitors do not have official handicaps. In such cases the best solution is to use the Callaway handicapping system, so called after the name of its inventor, as it is simple to use yet has proved equitable.

Competitors complete their round marking in their gross figures at every hole and their handicaps are awarded and deducted at the end of the 18 holes using the following table:

Competitor's Gross Score	Handicap Deduction
par or less	none
one over par – 75	½ worst hole
76–80	worst hole
81–85	worst hole plus ½ next worse
86–90	two worst holes
91–95	two worst holes plus 1½ next
96–100	three worst holes
101–105	three worst holes plus ½ next
106–110	four worst holes
111–115	four worst holes plus ½ next
116–120	five worst holes
121–125	five worst holes plus ½ next
126–130	six worst holes

Note 1: Worst hole equals highest score at any hole regardless of the par of the hole except that the maximum score allowed for any one hole is twice the par of the hole.

Note 2: The 17th and 18th holes are not allowed to be deducted.

Example: Competitor scores 104. From the table he should deduct as his handicap the total of his three worst (i.e. highest) individual hole scores plus half of his fourth worst hole. If he scored one 9, one 8 and several 7's he would therefore deduct a total of 27½ from his gross score of 104 to give a net score of 76½.

Overseas Amateur Championships

Australian (inaugurated 1894)

Year	Winner	Year	Winner	Year	Winner	Year	Winner
1894	LA Whyte	1924	H Sinclair	1954	P Toogood	1980	R Mackay
1895	RAA Balfour Melville	1925	H Sinclair	1955	J Rayner	1981	O Moore
		1926	Len Nettlefold	1956	H Berwick	1982	EM Couper
1896	HA Howden	1927	WS Nankivell	1957	BH Warren	1983	WJ Smith
1897	HA Howden	1928	Len Nettlefold	1958	K Hartley	1984	BP King
1898	HA Howden	1929	MJ Ryan	1959	BW Devlin	1985	B Ruangkit (Tha)
1899	CES Gillies	1930	HW Hattersley	1960	Ted Ball	1986	DJ Ecob
1900	LA Whyte	1931	HL William	1961	T Crow	1987	B Johns
1901	HA Howden	1932	Dr RH Bettington	1962	D Bachli	1988	S Bouvier
1902	H Macneil	1933	WL Hope	1963	J Hayes (RSA)	1989	SJ Conran
1903	DG Soutar	1934	TS McKay	1964	B Baker	1990	CD Gray
1904	JD Howden	1935	J Ferrier	1965	K Donohoe	1991	LKJ Parsons
1905	Hon. Michael Scott	1936	J Ferrier	1966	W Britten	1992	MS Campbell (NZ)
1906	EA Gill	1937	HL Williams	1967	J Muller	1993	GJ Chalmers
1907	Hon. Michael Scott	1938	J Ferrier	1968	R Stott	1994	W Bennett (Eng)
1908	Clyde Pearce	1939	J Ferrier	1969	RA Shearer	1995	MC Goggin
1909	Hon. Michael Scott	1940–45	Not played	1970	PA Bennett	1996	DC Gleeson
1910	Hon. Michael Scott	1946	AN Waterson	1971	GR Hicks	1997	K Felton
1911	JD Howden	1947	HW Hattersley	1972	CR Kaye	1998	B Rumford
1912	Hector Morrison	1948	D Bachli	1973	RJ Jenner	1999	BM Jones
1913	AR Lempriere	1949	WD Ackland-Horman	1974	TR Gale	2000	BP Lamb
1914–19	Not played			1975	C Bonython	2001	S Bowditch
1920	EL Apperley	1950	H Berwick	1976	P Sweeney	2002	K Barnes
1921	CL Winser	1951	Peter Heard	1977	AY Gresham		
1922	Ivo Witton	1952	R Stevens	1978	MA Clayton		
1923	Ivo Witton	1953	Peter Heard	1979	J Kelly		

Canadian (inaugurated 1895)

Year	Winner	Year	Winner	Year	Winner	Year	Winner
1895	TH Harley	1924	F Thompson	1954	E Harvie Ward	1979	R Alarcon (Mex)
1896	JS Gillespie	1925	DD Carrick	1955	M Norman	1980	G Olson
1897	WAH Kerr	1926	CR Somerville	1956	M Norman	1981	R Zokol
1898	GS Lyon	1927	DD Carrick	1957	N Weslock	1982	D Roxburgh
1899	Vere C Brown	1928	CR Somerville	1958	B Castator	1983	D Milovic
1900	GS Lyon	1929	E Held	1959	J Johnston	1984	W Swartz
1901	WAH Kerr	1930	CR Somerville	1960	RK Alexander	1985	B Franklin
1902	FR Martin	1931	CR Somerville	1961	G Cowan	1986	B Franklin
1903	GS Lyon	1932	GB Taylor	1962	R Taylor	1987	B Franklin
1904	J Percy Taylor	1933	A Campbell	1963	N Weslock	1988	D Roxburgh
1905	GS Lyon	1934	A Campbell	1964	N Weslock	1989	P Major
1906	GS Lyon	1935	CR Somerville	1965	N Weslock	1990	W Sye
1907	GS Lyon	1936	F Haas jr	1966	N Weslock	1991	J Kraemer
1908	Alex Wilson	1937	CR Somerville	1967	S Jones	1992	D Ritchie
1909	E Legge	1938	T Adams	1968	J Doyle	1993	G Simpson
1910	F Martin	1939	K Black	1969	Wayne McDonald	1994	W Sye
1911	GH Hutton	1940–44	Not played	1970	A Miller	1995	G Willis (USA)
1912	George S Lyon	1946	H Martell	1971	R Siderowf	1996	R McMillan
1913	GH Turpin	1947	FR Stranahan	1972	D Roxburgh	1997	D Goehring
1914	George S Lyon	1948	FR Stranahan	1973	G Burns	1998	C Matthew
1915–19	Not played	1949	RD Chapman	1974	D Roxburgh	1999	Han Lee (USA)
1920	CB Grier	1950	W Mawhinney	1975	J Nelford	2000	Han Lee (USA)
1921	F Thompson	1951	W McElroy	1976	J Nelford	2001	G Paddison
1922	CC Fraser	1952	L Bouchey	1977	R Spittle	2002	D Pruitt
1923	WJ Thompson	1953	D Cherry	1978	R Spittle		

New Zealand (inaugurated 1893)

1893	JA Somerville	1922	ADS Duncan	1953	DL Woon	1979	J Durry
1894	H Macneil	1923	J Goss jr	1954	DL Woon	1980	PE Hartstone
1895	G Gosset	1924	L Quin	1955	SG Jones	1981	T Cochrane
1896	MS Todd	1925	TH Horton	1956	PA Toogood	1982	J Peters
1897	D Pryde	1926	ADS Duncan	1957	EJ McDougall	1983	C Taylor
1898	W Pryde	1927	S Morpeth	1958	WJ Godfrey	1984	J Wagner
1899	ADS Duncan	1928	TH Horton	1959	SG Jones	1985	G Power
1900	ADS Duncan	1929	S Morpeth	1960	R Newdick	1986	P O'Malley
1901	ADS Duncan	1930	HA Black	1961	SG Jones	1987	O. Kendall
1902	SH Gollan	1931	R Wagg	1962	SG Jones	1988	B Hughes
1903	K Tareha	1932	R Wagg	1963	J Durry	1989	L Peterson
1904	AH Fisher	1933	BV Wright	1964	SG Jones	1990	M Long
1905	ADS Duncan	1934	BM Silk	1965	J Durry	1991	L Parsons
1906	SH Gollan	1935	JP Hornabrook	1966	SG Jones	1992	R Lee
1907	ADS Duncan	1936	JP Hornabrook	1967	J Durry	1993	P Tatamaugi
1908	HC Smith	1937	BM Silk	1968	BA Stevens	1994	P Fitzgibbon
1909	ADS Duncan	1938	PGF Smith	1969	G Stevenson	1995	S Bittle
1910	HB Lusk	1939	JP Hornabrook	1970	EJ McDougall	1996	D Somerville
1911	ADS Duncan	1940–45	*Not played*	1971	SG Jones	1997	C Johns
1912	BB Wood	1946	WG Horne	1972	RC Murray	1998	B MacDonald
1913	BB Wood	1947	BM Silk	1973	MN Nicholson	1999	A Duffin
1914	ADS Duncan	1948	A Gibbs	1974	RM Barltrop	2000	E Burgess
1915–18	*Not played*	1949	J Holden	1975	SF Reese	2001	B Gallie
1919	H Crosse	1950	DL Woon	1976	TR Pulman	2002	M Fraser
1920	S Morpeth	1951	DL Woon	1977	TR Pulman		
1921	AG Syme	1952	H Berwick	1978	F Nobilo		

South African (inaugurated 1892)

1892	D Walker	1922	WCE Stent	1952	M Janks	1978	EA Webber (Zim)
1893	DG Proudfoot	1923	WCE Stent	1953	R Brews	1979	L Norval
1894	DG Proudfoot	1924	AL Forster	1954	A Jackson	1980	E Grienewald
1895	DG Proudfoot	1925	TG McLelland	1955	B Keyter	1981	D Suddards
1896	DG Proudfoot	1926	WS Bryant	1956	RC Taylor	1982	N James
1897	DG Proudfoot	1927	GJ Chantler	1957	A Stewart	1983	C-C Yuan (Chi)
1898	DG Proudfoot	1928	B Wynne	1958	JR Boyd	1984	M Wiltshire
1899	DG Proudfoot	1929	C Hunter	1959	A Walker	1985	N Clarke
1900–01	*Not played*	1930	B Wynne	1960	WM Grinrod	1986	E Els
1902	DG Proudfoot	1931	C Coetzer	1961	JG Le Roux	1987	B Fouche
1903	R Law	1932	CE Olander	1962	J Hayes	1988	N Clarke
1904	JR Southey	1933	B Wynne	1963	D Symons	1989	C Rivett
1905	HCV Nicholson	1934	CE Olander	1964	JR Langridge	1990	R Goosen
1906	Lt. HM Ballinghall	1935	AD Locke	1965	P Vorster	1991	D Botes
1907	Lt. HM Ballinghall	1936	CE Olander	1966	Comrie du Toit	1992	B Davidson
1908	JAW Prentice	1937	AD Locke	1967	Derek Kemp	1993	L Chitengwa (Zim)
1909	JAW Prentice	1938	B Wynne	1968	R Williams	1994	B Vaughan
1910	Dr EL Steyn	1939	O Hayes	1969	D Thornton	1995	W Abery
1911	JAW Prentice	1940	HEP Watermeyer	1970	H Baiocchi	1996	T Moore
1912	HG Stewart	1941–45	*Not played*	1971	C Dreyer	1997	T Immelman
1913	JAW Prentice	1946	JR Boyd	1972	N Dundelson	1998	J Hugo
1914	SM McPherson	1947	C de G Watermeyer	1973	A. Oosthuizen	1999	R Sterne
1915–18	*Not played*	1948	RR Ryan	1974	T Lagerwey	2000	J Van Zyl
1919	HG Stewart	1949	RW Glennie	1975	P Vorster	2001	D Dixon (Eng)
1920	HG Stewart	1950	EADalton	1976	R Kotzen	2002	R Loubser
1921	AL Forster	1951	ES Irwin	1977	EA Webber (Zim)		

South African Stroke Play (inaugurated 1969)

1969	D Hayes	1978	D Suddards	1987	B Fouchee	1996	T Moore
1970	D Hayes	1979	D Suddards	1988	N Clarke	1997	U van den Berg
1971	K Suddards	1980	E Groenewald	1989	E Els	1998	T Immelman
1972	P Dunne	1981	C-C Yuan (Chi)	1990	P Pascoe	1999	J Hugo
1973	G Harvey (Zim)	1982	Li Wen-sheng	1991	N Henning	2000	C McMonagle (Ire)
1974	N Sundelson	1983	Peter van der Riet	1992	J Nelson	2001	R Sterne
1975	G Levenson	1984	D James	1993	D Kinnear	2002	G Wolstenholme
1976	G Harvey (Zim)	1985	D van Steden	1994	N Homann		(Eng)
1977	M McNulty	1986	C-S Hsieh	1995	M Murless		

United States

Year	Winner	Runner-up	Venue	By
1895	CB Macdonald	C Sands	Newport, RI	12 and 11
1896	HJ Whigham	JG Thorp	Shinnecock Hills, NY	8 and 7
1897	HJ Whigham	WR Betts	Wheaton, IL	8 and 6
1898	FS Douglas	WB Smith	Morris County, NJ	5 and 3
1899	HM Harriman	FS Douglas	Onwentsia, IL	3 and 2
1900	WJ Travis	FS Douglas	Garden City, NY	2 holes
1901	WJ Travis	WE Egan	Atlantic City, NJ	5 and 4
1902	LN James	EM Byers	Glenview, IL	4 and 3
1903	WJ Travis	EM Byers	Nassau, NY	5 and 4
1904	HC Egan	F Herreshof	Baltusrol, NJ	8 and 6
1905	HC Egan	DE Sawyer	Wheaton, IL	6 and 5
1906	EM Byers	GS Lyon	Englewood, NJ	2 holes
1907	JD Travers	A Graham	Cleveland, OH	6 and 5
1908	JD Travers	MH Behr	Garden City, NY	8 and 7
1909	RA Gardner	HC Egan	Wheaton, IL	4 and 3
1910	WC Fownes jr	WK Wood	Brookline, MA	4 and 3
1911	HH Hilton	F Herreshof	Apawamis, NY	37th
1912	JD Travers	C Evans jr	Wheaton, IL	7 and 6
1913	JD Travers	JG Anderson	Garden City, NY	5 and 4
1914	F Ouimet	JD Travers	Ekwanok, VT	6 and 5
1915	RA Gardner	JG Anderson	Detroit, MI	5 and 4
1916	C Evans jr	RA Gardner	Merion, PA	4 and 3
1917–18 *Not played due to First World War*				
1919	SD Herron	RT Jones jr	Oakmont, PA	5 and 4
1920	C Evans jr	F Ouimet	Roslyn, NY	7 and 6
1921	JP Guildford	RA Gardner	Clayton, MO	7 and 6
1922	JW Sweetser	C Evans jr	Brookline, MA	3 and 2
1923	MR Marston	JW Sweetser	Flossmoor, IL	38th
1924	RT Jones jr	G Von Elm	Merion, PA	9 and 8
1925	RT Jones jr	W Gunn	Oakmont, PA	8 and 7
1926	G Von Elm	RT Jones jr	Baltusrol, NJ	2 and 1
1927	RT Jones jr	C Evans jr	Minikahda, MN	8 and 7
1928	RT Jones jr	TP Perkins	Brae Burn, MA	10 and 9
1929	HR Johnston	OF Willing	Pebble Beach, CA	4 and 3
1930	RT Jones jr	EV Homans	Merion, PA	8 and 7
1931	F Ouimet	J Westland	Beverley, IL	6 and 5
1932	CR Somerville	J Goodman	Baltimore, MD	2 and 1
1933	GT Dunlap jr	MR Marston	Kenwood, OH	6 and 5
1934	W Lawson Little jr	D Goldman	Brookline, MA	8 and 7
1935	W Lawson Little jr	W Emery	Cleveland, OH	4 and 2
1936	JW Fischer	J McLean	Garden City, NY	37th
1937	J Goodman	RE Billows	Portland, OR	2 holes
1938	WP Turnesa	BP Abbott	Oakmont, PA	8 and 7
1939	MH Ward	RE Billows	Glenview, IL	7 and 5
1940	RD Chapman	WB McCullough	Winged Foot, NY	11 and 9
1941	MH Ward	BP Abbott	Omaha, NE	4 and 3
1946	SE Bishop	S Quick	Baltusrol, NJ	37th
1947	RH Riegel	JW Dawson	Pebble Beach, CA	2 and 1
1948	WP Turnesa	RE Billows	Memphis, TN	2 and 1
1949	CR Coe	R King	Rochester, NY	11 and 10
1950	S Urzetta	FR Stranahan	Minneapolis, MN	39th
1951	WJ Maxwell	J Gagliardi	Saucon Valley, PA	4 and 3
1952	J Westland	A Mengert	Seattle, WA	3 and 2

United States Amateur Championship *continued*

Year	Winner	Runner-up	Venue	By
1953	G Littler	D Morey	Oklahoma City, OK	1 hole
1954	A Palmer	R Sweeney	Detroit, MI	1 hole
1955	E Harvie Ward	W Hyndman	Richmond, VA	9 and 8
1956	E Harvie Ward	C Kocsis	Lake Forest, IL	5 and 4
1957	H Robbins	FM Taylor	Brookline, MA	5 and 4
1958	CR Coe	TD Aaron	San Francisco, CA	5 and 4
1959	JW Nicklaus	CR Coe	Broadmoor, CO	1 hole
1960	DR Beman	RW Gardner	St Louis, MO	6 and 4
1961	JW Nicklaus	HD Wysong	Pebble Beach, CA	8 and 6
1962	LE Harris jr	D Gray	Pinehurst, NC	1 hole
1963	DR Beman	RH Sikes	Des Moines, IA	2 and 1
1964	WC Campbell	EM Tutweiler	Canterbury, OH	1 hole

Changed to stroke play

Year	Winner	Venue	Score
1965	RJ Murphy	Tulsa, OK	291
1966	G Cowan	Merion, PA	285
1967	RB Dickson	Broadmoor, CO	285
1968	B Fleisher	Columbus, OH	284
1969	S Melnyk	Oakmont, PA	286
1970	L Wadkins	Portland, OR	280
1971	G Cowan	Wilmington, DE	280
1972	M Giles	Charlotte, NC	285

Reverted to match play

Year	Winner	Runner-up	Venue	By
1973	C Stadler	D Strawn	Inverness, OH	6 and 5
1974	J Pate	J Grace	Ridgewood, NJ	2 and 1
1975	F Ridley	K Fergus	Richmond, VA	2 holes
1976	B Sander	CP Moore	Bel-Air, CA	8 and 6
1977	J Fought	D Fischesser	Aronimink, PA	9 and 8
1978	J Cook	S Hoch	Plainfield, NJ	5 and 4
1979	M O'Meara	J Cook	Cleveland, OH	8 and 7
1980	H Sutton	B Lewis	Pinehurst, NC	9 and 8
1981	N Crosby	B Lindley	San Francisco, CA	37th
1982	J Sigel	D Tolley	Brookline, MA	8 and 7
1983	J Sigel	C Perry	Glenview, IL	8 and 7
1984	S Verplank	S Randolph	Oak Tree, OK	4 and 3
1985	S Randolph	P Persons	Montclair, NJ	1 hole
1986	S Alexander	C Kite	Shoal Creek, AL	5 and 3
1987	W Mayfair	E Rebmann	Jupiter Hills, FL	4 and 3
1988	E Meeks	D Yates	Hot Springs, VA	7 and 6
1989	C Patton	D Green	Merion, PA	3 and 1
1990	P Mickelson	M Zerman	Cherry Hills, CO	5 and 4
1991	M Voges	M Zerman	Chattanooga, TN	7 and 6
1992	J Leonard	T Scherrer	Muirfield Village, OH	8 and 7
1993	J Harris	D Ellis	Houston, TX	5 and 3
1994	T Woods	T Kuehne	Sawgrass, FL	2 holes
1995	T Woods	G Marucci	Newport, RI	2 holes
1996	T Woods	S Scott	Pumpkin Ridge, OR	38th
1997	M Kuchar	J Kribel	Cog Hill, Lemont, IL	2 and 1
1998	H Kuehne	T McKnight	Oak Hill, Rochester, NY	2 and 1
1999	D Gossett	Sung Yoon Kim	Pebble Beach, CA	9 and 8
2000	J Quinney	J Driscoll	Springfield, NJ	39th hole
2001	B Dickerson	R Hamilton	East Lake, Atlanta, GA	1 hole

2002 *at Oakland Hills, Bloomfield, MI*

Quarter Finals

Bill Haas (Greer, SC) beat John Klauk (Ponte Verde Beach, FL) 5 and 4
Ricky Barnes (Stockton, CA) beat Spencer Levin (Elk Grove, CA) 4 and 3
Hunter Mahon (McKinney, TX) beat Henry Liaw (Rowland Heights, CA) 3 and 2
Dustin Bray (Asheboro, NC) beat Ryan Moore (Puyallup, WA) 4 and 3

Semi-Finals

Barnes beat Haas 1 hole
Mahon beat Bray 1 hole

Final

Ricky Barnes beat Hunter Mahon 2 and 1

Other 2002 Overseas Amateur Championships

Austrian Open	Thomas Kogler (Aut)	**Kenyan Open**	Lee James (Eng)
Caribbean Open	Steven Bain (Bahamas)	**Korean Open**	Sergio García (Esp)
Czech Open	Svoboda Roman (Cze)	**Luxembourg Open**	Helge Schmeldt (Ger)
Danish Open	Ed Stedman (Aus)	**Malaysian Open**	Alastair Forsyth (Sco)
Finnish Open	Janne Mommo (Fin)	**Mexican Open**	Jamie Elson (Eng)
French Open	Eric Chaudouet (Fra)	**Portuguese Open**	Zane Scotland (Eng)
German Open	Richard Walker (Eng)	**Russian Open**	Iain Pyman (Eng)
Greek Open	James Heath (Eng)	**Singapore Open**	Matt Holden (NZ)
Hong Kong Open	José Mariía Olazábal (Esp)	**Spanish Open**	Zane Scotland (Eng)
Hungarian Open	Bernd Weisberger (Aut)	**Swiss Open**	Steve Rey (Sui)
Hungarian Close	Balázs Brúder	**Taiwan Open**	Danny Chia (Mal)
Indian Open	Vijay Kumar	**Turkish Open**	Eren Behcet (Eng)
Japanese Open	David Smail (NZ)	**Zambian Open**	Marc Cayeux (Zim)

PART V

Women's Amateur Tournaments

National and International Tournaments

Ladies British Amateur Championship (Inaugurated 1893)

1893	M Scott	I Pearson	St Annes	7 and 5
1894	M Scott	I Pearson	Littlestone	3 and 2
1895	M Scott	E Lythgoe	Portrush	5 and 4
1896	Miss Pascoe	L Thomson	Hoylake, Royal Liverpool	3 and 2
1897	EC Orr	Miss Orr	Gullane	4 and 2
1898	L Thomson	EC Neville	Yarmouth	7 and 5
1899	M Hezlet	Magill	Newcastle Co Down	2 and 1
1900	Adair	Neville	Westward Ho!, R North Devon	6 and 5
1901	Graham	Adair	Aberdovey	3 and 1
1902	M Hezlet	E Neville	Deal	19th hole
1903	Adair	F Walker-Leigh	Portrush	4 and 3
1904	L Dod	M Hezlet	Troon	1 hole
1905	B Thompson	ME Stuart	Cromer	3 and 2
1906	Kennon	B Thompson	Burnham	4 and 3
1907	M Hezlet	F Hezlet	Newcastle Co Down	2 and 1
1908	M Titterton	D Campbell	St Andrews	19th hole
1909	D Campbell	F Hezlet	Birkdale	4 and 3
1910	Miss Grant Suttie	L Moore	Westward Ho!, R North Devon	6 and 4
1911	D Campbell	V Hezlet	Portrush	3 and 2
1912	G Ravenscroft	S Temple	Turnberry	3 and 2

(Final played over 36 holes after 1912)

1913	M Dodd	Chubb	St Annes	8 and 6
1914	C Leitch	G Ravenscroft	Hunstanton	2 and 1
1915–18	*No Championship owing to the Great War*			
1919	*Should have been played at Burnham in October, but abandoned owing to railway strike*			
1920	C Leitch	M Griffiths	Newcastle Co Down	7 and 6
1921	C Leitch	J Wethered	Turnberry	4 and 3
1922	J Wethered	C Leitch	Prince's, Sandwich, Royal St George's	9 and 7
1923	D Chambers	A Macbeth	Burnham, Somerset	2 holes
1924	J Wethered	Mrs Cautley	Portrush	7 and 6
1925	J Wethered	C Leitch	Troon	37th hole
1926	C Leitch	Mrs Garon	Harlech	8 and 7
1927	T de la Chaume (Fra)	Miss Pearson	Newcastle Co Down	5 and 4
1928	N Le Blan (Fra)	S Marshall	Hunstanton	3 and 2
1929	J Wethered	G Collett (USA)	St Andrews	3 and 1
1930	D Fishwick	G Collett (USA)	Formby	4 and 3
1931	E Wilson	W Morgan	Portmarnock	7 and 6
1932	E Wilson	CPR Montgomery	Saunton	7 and 6
1933	E Wilson	D Plumpton	Gleneagles	5 and 4
1934	AM Holm	P Barton	Porthcawl	6 and 5
1935	W Morgan	P Barton	Newcastle Co Down	3 and 2
1936	P Barton	B Newell	Southport and Ainsdale	5 and 3
1937	J Anderson	D Park	Turnberry	6 and 4
1938	AM Holm	E Corlett	Burnham	4 and 3
1939	P Barton	T Marks	Portrush	2 and 1
1940–45	*No Championship owing to Second World War*			
1946	GW Hetherington	P Garvey	Hunstanton	1 hole
1947	B Zaharias (USA)	J Gordon	Gullane	5 and 4
1948	L Suggs (USA)	J Donald	Lytham St Annes	1 hole
1949	F Stephens	V Reddan	Harlech	5 and 4
1950	Vicomtesse de St Sauveur (Fra)	J Valentine	Newcastle Co Down	3 and 2
1951	PJ MacCann	F Stephens	Broadstone	4 and 3
1952	M Paterson	F Stephens	Troon	39th hole
1953	M Stewart (Can)	P Garvey	Porthcawl	7 and 6
1954	F Stephens	E Price	Ganton	4 and 3

1955	J Valentine	B Romack (USA)	Portrush	7 and 6
1956	M Smith (USA)	M Janssen (USA)	Sunningdale	8 and 7
1957	P Garvey	J Valentine	Gleneagles	4 and 3
1958	J Valentine	E Price	Hunstanton	1 hole
1959	E Price	B McCorkindale	Ascot	37th hole
1960	B McIntyre (USA)	P Garvey	Harlech	4 and 2
1961	M Spearman	DJ Robb	Carnoustie	7 and 6
1962	M Spearman	A Bonallack	Royal Birkdale	1 hole
1963	B Varangot (Fra)	P Garvey	Newcastle Co Down	3 and 1
1964	C Sorenson (USA)	BAB Jackson	Sandwich, Prince's, Royal St George's	37th hole
1965	B Varangot (Fra)	IC Robertson	St Andrews	4 and 3
1966	E Chadwick	V Saunders	Ganton	3 and 2
1967	E Chadwick	M Everard	Harlech	1 hole
1968	B Varangot (Fra)	C Rubin (Fra)	Walton Heath	20th hole
1969	C Lacoste (Fra)	A Irvin	Portrush	1 hole
1970	D Oxley	IC Robertson	Gullane	1 hole
1971	M Walker	B Huke	Alwoodley	3 and 1
1972	M Walker	C Rubin (Fra)	Hunstanton	2 holes
1973	A Irvin	M Walker	Carnoustie	3 and 2
1974	C Semple (USA)	A Bonallack	Porthcawl	2 and 1
1975	N Syms (USA)	S Cadden	St Andrews	3 and 2
1976	C Panton	A Sheard	Silloth	1 hole
1977	A Uzielli	V Marvin	Hillside	6 and 5
1978	E Kennedy (Aus)	J Greenhalgh	Notts	1 hole
1979	M Madill	J Lock (Aus)	Nairn	2 and 1
1980	A Quast (USA)	L Wollin (Swe)	Woodhall Spa	3 and 1
1981	IC Robertson	W Aitken	Conway	20th hole
1982	K Douglas	G Stewart	Walton Heath	4 and 2
1983	J Thornhill	R Lautens (Sui)	Silloth	4 and 2
1984	J Rosenthal (USA)	J Brown	Royal Troon	4 and 3
1985	L Beman (Irl)	C Waite	Ganton	1 hole
1986	McGuire (NZ)	L Briars (Aus)	West Sussex	2 and 1
1987	J Collingham	S Shapcott	Harlech	19th hole
1988	J Furby	J Wade	Deal	4 and 3
1989	H Dobson	E Farquharson	Royal Liverpool	6 and 5
1990	J Hall	H Wadsworth	Dunbar	3 and 2
1991	V Michaud (Fra)	W Doolan (Aus)	Pannal	3 and 2
1992	P Pedersen (Den)	J Morley	Saunton	1 hole
1993	C Lambert	K Speak	Royal Lytham	3 and 2
1994	E Duggleby	C Mourgue d'Algue	Newport	3 and 1
1995	J Hall	K Mourgue d'Algue	Royal Portrush	3 and 2
1996	K Kuehne (USA)	B Morgan	Royal Liverpool	5 and 3
1997	A Rose	M McKay	Cruden Bay	4 and 3
1998	K Rostron	C Nocera	Little Aston	3 and 2
1999	M Monnet (Fra)	R Hudson	Royal Birkdale	1 hole
2000	R Hudson	E Duggleby	Royal Birkdale	5 and 4
2001	M Prieto (Esp)	E Duggleby	Ladybank	4 and 3

2002 at Ashburnham

First Round

Alison Coffey (Ire) beat Karen Sjodin (Swe) 1 hole
Lisa Holm Sørensen (Den) beat Deana Rushworth (Woodsome Hall) 3 and 2
Vicky Uwland (Aus) beat Tiffany Woodyer (Saunton) 1 hole
Kathryn Evans (Conwy) beat Elaine Dowdell (Wexford) walkover
Sarah Jones (Pennard) beat Julie Ross (Whitley Bay) 4 and 2
Jo Pritchard (Tredegar Park) beat Emma Weeks (Hockley) 1 hole
Lucia Mar (Esp) beat Virginie Beauchet (Fra) 2 and 1
Ria Denise Oulazon (USA) beat Kerry Smith (Waterlooville) 5 and 4
Mireille Scalabre (Fra) beat Chloe Court (Goodwood) 5 and 4
Virginia Costa (Ita) beat Gwladys Nocera (Fra) 3 and 2
Lindsey Wright (Aus) beat Anja Monke (Ger) 3 and 2
Claire Coughlan (Cork) beat Anne Walker (Strathaven) 1 up
Sarah Heath (Shifnal) beat Camilla Guriby (Nor) 20th hole
Anna Knutsson (Swe) beat Karin Borjeskog (Swe) 2 holes
Fany Schaeffer (Fra) beat Susie Mathews (Aus) 1 hole
Linda Wessberg (Swe) beat Elizabeth McKinnon (NZ) 2 and 1
Denise Simon (Ger) beat Michaela Parmlid (Swe) 2 and 1

Ladies British Amateur Championship *continued*

First Round *continued*
Kerry Knowles (Worplesdon) beat Helena Svensson (Swe) 4 and 2
Macarena Campomanes (Esp) beat Marie Allen (Moor Park) 5 and 5
Marta Prieto (Esp) beat Tracey Boyes (Mean Valley) 19th hole
Eleanor Pilgrim (St Pierre) beat Tracy Atkin (Leamington and County GC) 3 and 2
Peggy Fraysse (Fra) beat Rachel Bell (Ganton) 19th hole
Rebecca Fry (Aus) beat Alex Keighley (Lightcliffe) 20th hole
Stephanie Doring (Aus) beat Lynn Kenny (University of Stirling) 2 and 1

Becky Brewerton (Abergele) beat Mette Buss (Den) 6 and 4
Miriam Hiller (Ger) beat Karen Haywood (Crompton) 8 and 7
Emma Duggleby (Malton & Norton) beat Clare Queen (Drumpellier) 21st hole
Rebecca Prout (Betchworth Park) beat Nathalie David (Fra) 19th hole
Martina Gillen (Beaverstown) beat Katie Dobson (Fulford) 3 and 2
Heather Stirling (Bridge of Allan) beat Anne Laing (Vale of Leven) 4 and 3
Anna Highgate (Cottrell Park) beat Jodie Dartford (Orsett) 5 and 4

Second Round
Coffey beat Sørensen 6 and 5
Uwland beat Evans 2 and 1
Pritchard beat Jones 3 and 2
Oulazon beat Mar 3 and 2
Costa beat Scalabra 1 hole
Wright beat Coughlan 3 and 2
Heath beat Knutsson 1 hole
Wessberg beat Schaeffer 5 and 3

Simon beat Knowles 2 and 1
Prieto beat Campomanes 21st hole
Fraysse beat Pilgrim 2 and 1
Fry beat Doring 3 and 2
Hudson beat Brewerton 4 and 3
Duggleby beat Hiller 2 holes
Gillen beat Prout 3 and 2
Highgate beat Stirling 6 and 5

Third Round
Coffey Beat Uwland 24th hole
Pritchard beat Oulazon 2 holes

Third Round *continued*
Wright beat Costa 2 and 1
Heath beat Wessberg 1 up
Simon beat Prieto 5 and 4
Fry beat Fraysse 2 holes
Hudson beat Duggleby 3 and 2
Gillen beat Highgate 1 hole

Quarter Finals
Coffey beat Pritchard 4 and 3
Wright beat Heath 3 and 2
Simon beat Fry 1 hole
Hudson beat Gillen 2 and 1

Semi-Finals
Wright beat Coffey 3 and 2
Hudson beat Simon 4 and 3

Final
Rebecca Hudson beat Lindsey Wright 5 and 4

Ladies British Open Amateur Stroke Play Championship

(Inaugurated 1969)

1969	A Irvin	Gosforth Park	295	1986	C Hourihane	Blairgowrie	291
1970	M Everard	Birkdale	313	1987	L Bayman	Ipswich	297
1971	IC Robertson	Ayr Belleisle	302	1988	K Mitchell	Porthcawl	317
1972	IC Robertson	Silloth	296	1989	H Dobson	Southerness	298
1973	A Stant	Purdis Heath	298	1990	V Thomas	Strathaven	287
1974	J Greenhalgh	Seaton Carew	302	1991	J Morley	Long Ashton	297
1975	J Greenhalgh	Gosforth Park	298	1992	J Hockley	Frilford Heath	287
1976	J Lee Smith	Fulford	299	1993	J Hall	Gullane	290
1977	M Everard	Lindrick	306	1994	K Speak	Woodhall Spa	297
1978	J Melville	Foxhills	310	1995	MJ Pons (Esp)	Princes	289
1979	M McKenna	Moseley	305	1996	C Kuld (Den)	Conwy (Caernarvonshire)	289
1980	M Mahill	Brancepeth Castle	304	1997	KM Juul (Den)	Silloth-on-Solway	293
1981	J Soulsby	Norwich	300	1998	N Nijenhuis	Stirling	297
1982	J Connachan	Downfield	294	1999	B Brewerton	Huddersfield	294
1983	A Nicholas	Moortown	292	2000	R Hudson	Newcastle, NI	294
1984	C Waite	Caernarvonshire	295	2001	R Hudson	Kilmarnock	300
1985	IC Robertson	Formby	300				

2002 *at Hunstanton*

1	Becky Brewerton (Abergele)	74-72-72-73—291
2	Clare Queen (Drumpellier)	72-74-77-71—294
3	Lynn Kenny (University of Stirling)	71-75-75-74—295

Ladies British Open Mid-Amateur Championship (inaugurated 2002)

2002 *at The Berkshire*

1	Anne Laing (Vale of Leven)	73-69-72—214
2	Kerry Smith (Waterlooville)	71-72-72—215
3	Emma Duggleby (Malton & Norton)	71-70-74—215

Senior Ladies British Open Amateur Stroke Play Championship

1981	BM King	Formby	159	1992	A Uzielli	Stratford-upon-Avon 148
1982	P Riddiford	Ilkley	161	1993	J Thornhill	Ashburnham 151
1983	M Birtwistle	Troon Portland	167	1994	D Williams	Nottingham 154
1984	O Semelaigne	Woodbridge	152	1995	A Uzielli	Blairgowrie 152
1985	Dr G Costello	Prestatyn	158	1996	V Hassett	Pyle & Kenfig 236
1986	P Riddiford	Longniddry	154	1997	T Wiesner (USA)	Frilford Heath 231
1987	O Semelaigne	Copt Heath	152	1998	A Uzielli	Powfoot 227
1988	C Bailey	Littlestone	156	1999	A Uzielli	Malone 229
1989	C Bailey	Wrexham	149	2000	B Mogensen (Den)	West Kilbride 242
1990	A Uzielli	Harrogate	153	2001	M McKenna	Aberdovy 230
1991	A Uzielli	Ladybank	154			

2002 *at Longniddry*

1	Ros Page (Henbury)	74-79-76—229
2	Christina Birke (Swe)	76-81-78—235
3	Diane Williams (Can)	74-87-75—236
	Sue Westall (Copt Heath)	83-78-75—236

English Ladies Close Amateur Championship (inaugurated 1912)

1912	M Gardner	Mrs Cautley	Sandwich	at 20th
1913	FW Brown	Mrs McNair	Hollinwell	1 hole
1914	Cecil Leitch	Miss Bastin	Walton Heath	2 and 1
1915–1918 *Not played due to First World War*				
1919	Cecil Leitch	Mrs Temple Dobell	St Annes Old	10 and 8
1920	Joyce Wethered	Cecil Leitch	Sheringham	2 and 1
1921	Joyce Wethered	Mrs Mudford	Lytham St Annes	12 and 11
1922	Joyce Wethered	J Stocker	Hunstanton	7 and 6
1923	Joyce Wethered	Mrs TA Lodge	Ganton	8 and 7
1924	Joyce Wethered	DR Fowler	Cooden Beach	8 and 7
1925	DR Fowler	J Winn	Westward Ho!	9 and 7
1926	Molly Gourlay	Elsie Corlett	Woodhall Spa	6 and 4
1927	Mrs H Guedalla	Enid Wilson	Pannal	1 hole
1928	Enid Wilson	Dorothy Pearson	Walton Heath	9 and 8
1929	Molly Gourlay	Diana Fishwick	Broadstone	6 and 5
1930	Enid Wilson	Mrs RO Porter	Aldeburgh	12 and 11
1931	Wanda Morgan	Molly Gourlay	Ganton	3 and 1
1932	Diana Fishwick	Miss B Brown	Royal Ashdown Forest	5 and 4
1933	Dorothy Pearson	M Johnson	Westward Ho!	5 and 3
1934	P Wade	M Johnson	Seacroft	4 and 3
1935	Mrs M Garon	Elsie Corlett	Birkdale	at 38th
1936	Wanda Morgan	P Wade	Hayling Island	2 and 1
1937	Wanda Morgan	M Fyshe	St Enodoc	4 and 2
1938	Elsie Corlett	J Winn	Aldeburgh	2 and 1
1939–1946 *Not played due to Second World War*				
1947	M Wallis	Elizabeth Price	Ganton	3 and 1
1948	Frances Stephens	Zara Bolton	Hayling Island	1 hole
1949	Diana Critchley	Lady Katharine Cairns	Burnham & Berrow	3 and 2
1950	Hon Mrs A Gee	Pamela Davies	Sheringham	8 and 6

English Ladies Close Amateur Championship *continued*

1951	Jeanne Bisgood	A Keiller	St Annes Old	2 and 1
1952	Pamela Davies	Jacqueline Gordon	Westwood Ho!	6 and 5
1953	Jeanne Bisgood	J McIntyre	Sandwich	6 and 5
1954	Frances Stephens	Elizabeth Price	Woodhall Spa	at 37th
1955	Frances Smith	Elizabeth Price	Moortown	4 and 3
1956	Bridget Jackson	Ruth Ferguson	Hunstanton	2 and 1
1957	Jeanne Bisgood	Margaret Nichol	Bournemouth	10 and 8
1958	Angela Bonallack	Bridget Jackson	Formby	3 and 2
1959	Ruth Porter	Frances Smith	Aldeburgh	5 and 4
1960	Margaret Nichol	Angela Bonallack	Burnham & Berrow	3 and 1
1961	Ruth Porter	Peggy Reece	Littlestone	2 holes
1962	Jean Roberts	Angela Bonallack	Woodhall Spa	3 and 1
1963	Angela Bonallack	Elizabeth Chadwick	Liphook	7 and 6
1964	Marley Spearman	Mary Everard	Lytham St Annes	6 and 5
1965	Ruth Porter	G Cheetham	Whittington Barracks	6 and 5
1966	Julia Greenhalgh	Jean Holmes	Hayling Island	3 and 1
1967	Ann Irvin	Margaret Pickard	Alwoodley	3 and 2
1968	Sally Barber	Dinah Oxley	Hunstanton	5 and 4
1969	Barbara Dixon	M Wenyon	Burnham & Berrow	6 and 4
1970	Dinah Oxley	Sally Barber	Rye	3 and 2
1971	Dinah Oxley	Sally Barber	Hoylake	5 and 4
1972	Mary Everard	Angela Bonallack	Woodhall Spa	2 and 1
1973	Mickey Walker	Carol Le Feuvre	Broadstone	6 and 5
1974	Ann Irvin	Jill Thornhill	Sunningdale	1 hole
1975	Beverly Huke	Lynne Harrold	Birkdale	2 and 1
1976	Lynne Harrold	Angela Uzielli	Hollinwell	3 and 2
1977	Vanessa Marvin	Mary Everard	Burnham & Berrow	1 hole
1978	Vanessa Marvin	Ruth Porter	West Sussex	2 and 1
1979	Julia Greenhalgh	Susan Hedges	Hoylake	2 and 1
1980	Beverley New	Julie Walker	Aldeburgh	3 and 2
1981	Diane Christison	S Cohen	Cotswold Hills	2 holes
1982	Julie Walker	C Nelson	Brancepeth Castle	4 and 3
1983	Linda Bayman	C Macintosh	Hayling Island	4 and 3
1984	Claire Waite	Linda Bayman	Hunstanton	3 and 2
1985	Patricia Johnson	Linda Bayman	Ferndown	1 hole
1986	Jill Thornhill	Susan Shapcott	Sandwich	3 and 1
1987	Joanne Furby	Maria King	Alwoodley	4 and 3
1988	Julie Wade	Susan Shapcott	Little Aston	at 19t
1989	Helen Dobson	Simone Morgan	Burnham & Berrow	4 and 3
1990	Angela Uzielli	Linzi Fletcher	Rye	2 and 1
1991	Nicola Buxton	Karen Stupples	Sheringham	2 holes
1992	Caroline Hall	Joanne Hockley	St Annes Old	1 hole
1993	Nicola Buxton	Sarah Burnell	St Enodoc	2 and 1
1994	Julie Wade	S Sharpe	The Berkshire	1 hole
1995	Julie Wade	Elaine Ratcliffe	Ipswich	2 and 1
1996	Joanne Hockley	Lisa Educate	Silloth-on-Solway	4 and 3
1997	Kim Rostron	K Burton	Saunton	4 and 2
1998	Elaine Ratcliffe	Lisa Walters	Walton Heath	at 19th
1999	Fiona Brown	Kerry Smith	Ganton	2 and 1
2000	Emma Duggleby	Rebecca Hudson	Hunstanton	4 and 3
2001	Rebecca Hudson	Emma Duggleby	West Sussex	at 20th

2002 *at Littlestone*

Quarter Finals
Alex Keighley (Lightcliffe) beat Rebecca Prout (Betchworth Park) 2 holes
Chloe Court (Goodwood) beat Lisa Ball (Parklands) 4 and 3
Nicola Timmins (Sene Valley) beat Emma Weeks (Hockley) 1 hole
Kerry Knowles (Worplesdon) beat Clare Lipscombe (Cirencester) 4 and 3

Semi-Finals
Court beat Keighley 3 and 1
Knowles beat Timmins 1 hole

Final
Kerry Knowles beat Chloe Court 6 and 5

English Ladies Close Amateur Stroke Play Championship
(Inaugurated 1984)

1984	P Grice	Moor Park	300	1993	J Hall	King's Norton	298
1985	P Johnson	Northants County	301	1994	F Brown	Ferndown	289
1986	S Shapcott	Broadstone	301	1995	L Walton	Hallamshire	289
1987	J Wade	Northumberland	296	1996	S Gallagher	Little Aston	290
1988	S Prosser	Wentworth	297	1997	L Tupholme	Hankley Common	293
1989	S Robinson	Notts	302	1998	E Duggleby	Broadstone	306
1990	K Tebbet	Saunton	299	1999	C Lipscombe	Gog Magog	300
1991	J Morley	Ganton	301	2000	R Hudson	Silloth-on-Solway	290
1992	J Morley	Littlestone	289	2001	C Marron*	Stoneham	291

2002 *at Whittington Heath*

1	Sara Garbutt (Ganton)	75-75-70-74—294
2	Danielle Masters (Rochester & Cobham Park)	73-77-75-71—296
3	Kerry Smith (Waterlooville)	75-74-74-74—297

English Ladies Under-23 Championship (Inaugurated 1978)

1978	S Bamford	Caldy	228	1990	K Tebbet	Saunton	299
1979	B Cooper	Coxmoor	223	1991	J Hockley	Saunton	303
1980	B Cooper	Porters Park	226	1992	N Buxton	Littlestone	292
1981	J Soulsby	Willesley Park	220	1993	R Millington	King's Norton	302
1982	M Gallagher	High Post	221	1994	F Brown	Ferndown	289
1983	P Grice	Hallamshire	219	1995	E Fields	Hallamshire	297
1984	P Johnson	Moor Park	300	1996	R Hudson	Little Aston	299
1985	P Johnson	Northants County	301	1997	R Bailey	Hankley Common	306
1986	S Shapcott	Broadstone	301	1998	L Meredith	Broadstone	307
1987	J Wade	Northumberland	296	1999	C Lipscombe	Gog Magog	300
1988	J Wade	Wentworth	299	2000	R Hudson	Silloth-on-Solway	290
1989	A Shapcott	Notts Ladies	302	2001	E Weeks	Stoneham	291

2002 *at Whittington Heath*

1	Sara Garbutt (Ganton)	75-75-70-74—294
2	Danielle Masters (Rochester & Cobham Park)	73-77-75-71—296
3	Kelly Hutcherson (Porter's Park)	71-81-76-72—300

English Senior Ladies Stroke Play Championship (Inaugurated 1986)

1988	A Thompson	Wentworth	158	1995	V Morgan	Tandridge	151
1989	C Bailey	Notts Ladies	163	1996	A Uzielli	Royal North Devon	153
1990	A Thompson	Fairhaven	162	1997	A Thompson	Formby Ladies	152
1991	C Bailey	Burnham and Berrow	155	1998	E Boatman	Royal Liverpool	154
1992	A Thompson	Pleasington	154	1999	S Westall	Northants County	151
1993	A Uzielli	Hunstanton	150	2000	E McCombe	Formby	162
1994	S Bassindale	Littlestone	163	2001	R Page	Woodhall Spa	159

2002 *at Saunton*

1	Carole Caldwell (Sunningdale)	82-76—158
2	Ros Page (Henbury)	77-82—159
3	Sue Timberlake (Edgbaston)	79-84—163

English Senior Ladies Match Play Championship (Inaugurated 1994)

1994	E Annison	S Bassindale	Whitting Heath
1995	A Thompson	G Palmer	R Ashdown Forest
1996	R Farrow	V Morgan	Lindrick
1997	G Palmer	C Means	S Winchester
1998	E McCombe	J Thornhill	West Sussex
1999	E McCombe	V Morgan	Lindrick
2000	E McCombe	M Griffiths	Burnham & Berrow
2001	A Vine	V Morgan	Beau Desert

English Senior Ladies Match Play Championship *continued*
2002 *at Ganton*

Semi-Finals
Chris Stirling (Meon Valley) beat Sue Timberlake (Edgbaston) 4 and 3
Carole Caldwell (Sunningdale) beat Ros Page (Henbury) 2 holes

Final
Chris Stirling beat Carole Caldwell 2 and 1

English Ladies Intermediate Championship (Inaugurated 1982)

1982	J Rhodes	Headingley	19th hole	1992	K Speak	South Staffs	3 and 1
1983	L Davies	Worksop	2 and 1	1993	K Speak	Seascale	2 and 1
1984	P Grice	Whittington Barracks	3 and 2	1994	J Oliver	Beaconsfield	2 up
1985	S Lowe	Caldy	2 and 1	1995	K Smith	Clitheroe	5 and 4
1986	S Moorcroft	Hexham	6 and 5	1996	R Bailey	Sandiway	3 and 2
1987	J Wade	Sheringham	2 and 1	1997	K Smith	Abbotsley	2 and 1
1988	S Morgan	Enville, Staffs	20th hole	1998	J Lamb	Hornsea	1 hole
1989	L Fairclough	Warrington	4 and 3	1999	K Fisher	Woodbury Park	1 hole
1990	L Fletcher	Whitley Bay	7 and 6	2000	K Keogh	Woodbury Park	1 hole
1991	J Morley	West Lancashire	6 and 5	2001	A Keighley	Pleasington	22nd hole

The event scheduled for 2002 was cancelled and replaced by the rescheduled English Ladies Close Amateur Championship

Irish Ladies Close Amateur Championship (Inaugurated 1894)

Year	Winner	Runner-up	Venue	Score
1894	Miss Mulligan	N Graham	Carnalea	3 and 2
1895	Miss Cox	Miss MacLaine	Portrush	3 and 2
1896	N Graham	N Brownrigg	Newcastle	4 and 3
1897	N Graham	Miss Magill	Dollymount	4 and 3
1898	Miss Magill	M Hezlet	Malone	1 hole
1899*	M Hezlet	Miss Adair	Newcastle	5 and 4
1900*	Miss Adair	V Hezlet	Portrush	9 and 7
1901	Miss Adair	F Walker-Leigh	Portmarnock	4 and 2
1902	Miss Adair	ME Stuart	Newcastle	9 and 7
1903	Miss Adair	V Hezlet	Portrush	7 and 5
1904	M Hezlet	F Walker-Leigh	Lahinch	3 and 2
1905	M Hezlet	F Hezlet	Portsalon	2 and 1
1906	M Hezlet	F Hezlet	Newcastle	2 and 1
1907	F Walker-Leigh	Mrs Fitzgibbon	Dollymount	4 and 3
1908	M Hezlet	F Hezlet	Portrush	5 and 4
1909	Miss Ormsby	V Hezlet	Lahinch	4 and 2
1910	M Harrison	Miss Magill	Newcastle	5 and 4
1911	M Harrison	F Walker-Leigh	Malahide	6 and 4
1912	M Harrison	Mrs Cramsie	Portsalon	5 and 3
1913	J Jackson	M Harrison	Lahinch	4 and 3
1914	J Jackson	Miss Meldon	Castlerock	3 and 2
1915–1918	*Not played due to First World War*			
1919	J Jackson	M Alexander	Portmarnock	5 and 4
1920	J Jackson	Mrs Cramsie	Portrush	5 and 4
1921	Miss Stuart French	M Fitzgibbon	Hermitage	4 and 3
1922	Mrs Claude Gotto	MR Hirsch	Newcastle	2 holes
1923	J Jackson	Mrs Babington	Portmarnock	5 and 4
1924	CG Thornton	Miss Hewitt	Castlerock	4 and 3
1925	J Jackson	JF Jameson	Lahinch	2 and 1
1926	P Jameson	CH Murland	Newcastle	5 and 3
1927	Miss McLoughlin	F Blake	Dollymount	2 holes
1928	Mrs Dwyer	H Clarke	Cork	3 and 2
1929	MA Hall	I Taylor	Rosapenna	1 hole
1930	JB Walker	JF Jameson	Portmarnock	2 and 1

* Final = 36 holes on these dates

Year	Winner	Runner-up	Venue	Score
1931	Miss Pentony	JH Todd	Rosses Point	2 and 1
1932	B. Latchford	D Ferguson	Ballybunion	7 and 5
1933	Miss Pentony	F Blacke	Newcastle	3 and 2
1934	P Sherlock Fletcher	JB Walker	Portmarnock	3 and 2
1935	D Ferguson	Miss Ellis	Rospenna	2 and 1
1936	C Tiernan	S Moore	Ballybunion	7 and 6
1937	HV Glendinning	EL Kidd	Portrush	37th hole
1938	J Beck	B Jackson	Portmarnock	5 and 4
1939	C MacGeagh	E Gikdea	Bundoran	1 hole
1940–1945	*Not played due to Second World War*			
1946	P Garvey	V Reddan	Lahinch	39th hole
1947	P Garvey	C Syme	Portrush	5 and 4
1948	P Garvey	V Reddan	Rosslare	9 and 7
1949	C Syme	J Beck	Baltray	9 and 7
1950	P Garvey	T Marks	Rosses Point	6 and 4
1951	P Garvey	D Forster	Ballybunion	12 and 10
1952	DM Forster	PG McCann	Newcastle	3 and 2
1953	P Garvey	Mrs Hegarty	Rosslare	8 and 7
1954	P Garvey	HV Glendinning	Portmarnock	13 and 12
1955	P Garvey	A O'Donohoe	Rosses Point	10 and 9
1956	P O'Sullivan	JF Hegarty	Killarney	14 and 12
1957	P Garvey	K McCann	Portrush	3 and 2
1958	P Garvey	Z Fallon	Carlow	7 and 6
1959	P Garvey	H Colhoun	Lahinch	12 and 10
1960	P Garvey	PG McCann	Cork	5 and 3
1961	K McCann	A Sweeney	Newcastle	5 and 3
1962	P Garvey	M Earner	Baltray	7 and 6
1963	P Garvey	E Barnett	Killarney	9 and 7
1964	Z Fallon	P O'Sullivan	Portrush	37th hole
1965	E Purcell	P O'Sullivan	Mullingar	3 and 2
1966	E Bradshaw	P O'Sullivan	Rosslare	3 and 2
1967	G Brandom	P O'Sullivan	Castlerock	3 and 2
1968	E Bradshaw	M McKenna	Lahinch	3 and 2
1969	M McKenna	C Hickey	Ballybunion	3 and 2
1970	P Garvey	M Earner	Portrush	2 and 1
1971	E Bradshaw	M Mooney	Baltray	3 and 1
1972	M McKenna	I Butler	Killarney	5 and 4
1973	M Mooney	M McKenna	Bundoran	2 and 1
1974	M McKenna	V Singleton	Lahinch	3 and 2
1975	M Gorry	E Bradshaw	Tramore	1 hole
1976	C Nesbitt	M McKenna	Rosses Point	20th hole
1977	M McKenna	R Hegarty	Ballybunion	2 holes
1978	M Gorry	I Butler	Grange	4 and 3
1979	M McKenna	C Nesbitt	Donegal	6 and 5
1980	C Nesbitt	C Hourihane	Lahinch	1 hole
1981	M McKenna	M Kenny	Laytown & Bettystown	1 hole
1982	M McKenna	M Madill	Portrush	2 and 1
1983	C Hourihane	V Hassett	Cork	6 and 4
1984	C Hourihane	M Madill	Rosses Point	19th hole
1985	C Hourihane	M McKenna	Waterville	4 and 3
1986	T O'Reilly	E Higgins	Castlerock	4 and 3
1987	C Hourihane	C Hickey	Lahinch	5 and 4
1988	L Bolton	E Higgins	Tramore	2 and 1
1989	M McKenna	C Wickham	West Port	19th hole
1990	ER McDaid	L Callan	The Island	2 and 1
1991	C Hourihane	E McDaid	Ballybunion	1 hole
1992	ER Power	C Hourihane	Co. Louth	1 hole
1993	E Higgins	A Rogers	R Belfast	2 and 1
1994	L Webb	H Kavanagh	Rosses Point	20th hole
1995	ER Power	S O'Brien-Kenney	Cork	1 hole
1996	B Hackett	L Behan	Tullamore	3 and 2
1997	S Fanagan	ER Power	Enniscrone	4 and 3
1998	L Behan	O Purfield	Clandeboye	19th hole
1999	C Coughlan	ER Power	Carlow	4 and 3
2000	A Coffey	C Coughlan	Co Louth	3 and 2
2001	A Coffey	C Coughlan	The European Club	4 and 3

2002 *at Cork*

Quarter Finals
Tricia Mangan (Ennis) beat Marian Riordan
   (Tipperary) 4 and 3
Alison Coffey (Warrenpoint) beat Maria Dunne
   (Skerries) 7 and 6
Martina Gillen (Beaverstown) beat Deirdre Smith
   (Co Louth) 4 and 3
Rebecca Coakley (Carlow) beat Pat Doran
   (Donabate) 4 and 3

Semi-Finals
Coffey beat Mangan 3 and 2
Coakley beat Gillen 1 hole

Final
Rebecca Coakley beat Alison Coffey 4 and 3

Irish Ladies Open Amateur Stroke Play Championship
(Inaugurated 1993)

1993	T Eakin	Milltown	293
1994	H Kavanagh	Milltown	286
1995	N Quigg	Grange	300
1996	ER Power	Grange	218
1997	Y Cassidy	Waterford Castle	217
1998	S O'Brien	Waterford Castle	141
1999	H Kavanagh	Waterford Castle	217
2000	R Cookley	Birr	205
2001	A Laing	Birr	214

2002 *at Dundalk*

1	Rebecca Coakley (Carlow)	74-65-75—214
2	Martina Gillen (Beaverstown)	73-69-72—214
3	A Larsson (Hillerød, Den)	76-70-70—216

Irish Senior Ladies Amateur Championship (Inaugurated 1988)

1988	M Magan		1993	G Costello	81	1998	M Moran	78
1989	Dr G Costello		1994	G Costello	80	1999	R Fanagan	80
1990	A Hesketh		1995	A Gaynor	81	2000	S Kearney	80
1991	C Hickey	77	1996	M Stuart	81	2001	M McKenna*	162
1992	C Hickey	79	1997	M O'Donnell	85			

2002 *at Co. Louth*

1	Pam Williamson (Baberton)	78-79—157
2	Diane Williams (USA)	78-83—161
3	Nancy Chaffee (USA)	85-79—164
	Anne Bigga (Tyneside)	85-79—164
	Mimmi Guglielmone (Ita)	79-85—164

Scottish Ladies Close Amateur Championship (Inaugurated 1903)

Year	Winner	Runner-up	Venue	Score
1903	AM Glover	MA Graham	St Andrews	1 hole
1904	MA Graham	M Bishop	Prestwick St Nicholas	6 and 5
1905	D Campbell	MA Graham	North Berwick	at 19th
1906	D Campbell	AM Glover	Cruden Bay	3 and 1
1907	FS Teacher	D Campbell	Troon	at 21st
1908	D Campbell	MA Cairns	Gullane	7 and 6
1909	EL Kyle	D Campbell	Machrihanish	3 and 1
1910	EL Kyle	AM Glover	Nairn	4 and 3
1911	E Grant-Suttie	EL Kyle	St Andrews	1 hole
1912	DM Jenkins	M Neil Fraser	Lossiemouth	4 and 2
1913	JW McCulloch	R Mackintosh	Machrihanish	4 and 3
1914	ER Anderson	FS Teacher	Muirfield	at 20th
1915–1919 *Not played due to First World War*				
1920	Mrs JB Watson	L Scroggie	Cruden Bay	5 and 3

Year	Winner	Runner-up	Venue	Score
1921	Mrs JB Watson	Mrs M Martin	Machrihanish	1 hole
1922	Mrs JB Watson	A Kyle	St Andrews	2 and 1
1923	Mrs WH Nicholson	Mrs JB Watson	Lossiemouth	2 and 1
1924	CPR Montgomery	H Cameron	Turnberry	5 and 4
1925	J Percy	E Grant-Suttie	Gullane	2 and 1
1926	MJ Wood	Mrs J Cochrane	Cruden Bay	2 and 1
1927	B Inglis	H Cameron	Machrihanish	1 hole
1928	JW McCulloch	P Ramsay	St Andrews	3 and 1
1929	Mrs JB Watson	Doris Park	Nairn	3 and 1
1930	Helen Holm	Doris Park	Turnberry	1 hole
1931	JW McCulloch	Doris Park	Gullane	at 19th
1932	Helen Holm	Mrs G Coates	Cruden Bay	at 23rd
1933	MJ Couper	Helen Holm	Turnberry	at 22nd
1934	Nan Baird	J Anderson	North Berwick	1 hole
1935	M Robertson-Durham	Nan Baird	Lossiemouth	at 20th
1936	Doris Park	CPR Montgomery	Turnberry	at 19th
1937	Helen Holm	Mrs I Bowhill	Gleneagles	3 and 2
1938	Jessie Anderson	Helen Holm	Nairn	2 holes
1939	Jessie Anderson	Catherine Park	Turnberry	at 19th
1939–1946	*Not played due to Second World War*			
1947	Jean Donald	J Kerr	Elie	5 and 3
1948	Helen Holm	Vivien Falconer	Gleneagles	5 and 4
1949	Jean Donald	Helen Holm	Troon	6 and 4
1950	Helen Holm	Charlotte Beddows (Mrs JB Watson)	St Andrews	6 and 5
1951	Mrs G Valentine	Moira Paterson	Nairn	3 and 2
1952	Jean Donald	Mrs RT Peel	Gullane	13 and 11
1953	Mrs G Valentine	Jean Donald	Carnoustie	8 and 7
1954	Mrs RT Peel	Mrs G Valentine	Turnberry	7 and 6
1955	Mrs G Valentine	Millicent Couper	North Berwick	8 and 6
1956	Mrs G Valentine	Helen Holm	Dornoch	8 and 7
1957	Marigold Speir	Helen Holm	Troon	7 and 5
1958	Dorothea Sommerville	Janette Robertson	Elie	1 hole
1959	Janette Robertson	Belle McCorkindale	Nairn	6 and 5
1960	Janette Robertson	Dorothea Sommerville	Turnberry	2 and 1
1961	JS Wright (*née* Robertson)	AM Lurie	St Andrews	1 hole
1962	JB Lawrence	C Draper	R Dornoch	5 and 4
1963	JB Lawrence	IC Robertson	Troon	2 and 1
1964	JB Lawrence	SM Reid	Gullane	5 and 3
1965	IC Robertson	JB Lawrence	Nairn	5 and 4
1966	IC Robertson	M Fowler	Machrihanish	2 and 1
1967	J Hastings	A Laing	North Berwick	5 and 3
1968	Joan Smith	J Rennie	Carnoustie	10 and 9
1969	JH Anderson	K Lackie	West Kilbride	5 and 4
1970	A Laing	IC Robertson	Dunbar	1 hole
1971	IC Robertson	A Ferguson	R Dornoch	3 and 2
1972	IC Robertson	CJ Lugton	Machrihanish	5 and 3
1973	I Wright	Dr AJ Wilson	St Andrews	2 holes
1974	Dr AJ Wilson	K Lackie	Nairn	22nd hole
1975	LA Hope	JW Smith	Elie	1 hole
1976	S Needham	T Walker	Machrihanish	3 and 2
1977	CJ Lugton	M Thomson	R Dornoch	1 hole
1978	IC Robertson	JW Smith	Prestwick	2 holes
1979	G Stewart	LA Hope	Gullane	2 and 1
1980	IC Robertson	F Anderson	Carnoustie	1 hole
1981	A Gemmill	W Aitken	Stranraer	2 and 1
1982	J Connachan	P Wright	R Troon	19th hole
1983	G Stewart	F Anderson	North Berwick	3 and 1
1984	G Stewart	A Gemmill	R Dornoch	3 and 2
1985	A Gemmill	D Thomson	Barassie	2 and 1
1986	IC Robertson	L Hope	St Andrews	3 and 2
1987	F Anderson	C Middleton	Nairn	4 and 3
1988	S Lawson	F Anderson	Southerness	3 and 1
1989	J Huggon	L Anderson	Lossiemouth	5 and 4
1990	E Farquharson	S Huggan	Machrihanish	3 and 2
1991	C Lambert	F Anderson	Carnoustie	3 and 2
1992	J Moody	E Farquharson	R Aberdeen	2 and 1
1993	C Lambert	M McKay	Prestwick St Nicholas	5 and 4
1994	C Matthew	V Melvin	Gullane	1 hole
1995	H Monaghan	S McMaster	Portpatrick	21st hole
1996	A Laing	A Rose	R Dornoch	1 hole

Scottish Ladies Close Amateur Championship *continued*

Year	Winner	Runner-up	Venue	Score
1997	A Rose	H Monaghan	W Kilbride	3 and 2
1998	E Moffat	C Agnew	North Berwick	4 and 3
1999	J Smith	A Laing	Nairn Dunbar	2 and 1
2000	L Kenny	H Stirling	Machrihanish	1 hole
2001	L Morton	L Mackay	Carnoustie	6 and 4

2002 *at Stranraer*

Quarter Finals

Heather Stirling (Bridge of Allan) beat Claire Hargan (Cardross) 2 and 1

Linzi Morton (Tulliallan) beat Fiona de Vries (St Rule) 5 and 4

Anne Laing (Vale of Leven) beat Sheena Wood (Aberdeen Ladies) 5 and 3

Lynn Kenny (University of Stirling) beat Jenna Wilson (Strathaven) 2 and 1

Semi-Finals

Stirling beat Morton 4 and 2

Laing beat Kenny 1 hole

Final

Heather Stirling beat Anne Laing 3 and 1

Scottish Ladies Open Strokeplay Championship (Helen Holm Trophy) (Inaugurated 1973)

1973	Belle Robertson	1981	Gillian Stewart	1989	Sara Robinson	1997	Kim Rostron
1974	Sandra Needham	1982	Wilma Aitken	1990	Catriona Lambert	1998	K-M Juul Esbjerg
1975	Muriel Thomson	1983	Jane Connachan	1991	Julie Wade	1999	L Nicholson
1976	Muriel Thomson	1984	Gillian Stewart	1992	Mhairi McKay	2000	Rebecca Hudson
1977	Beverly Huke	1985	Pamela Wright	1993	Julie Wade	2001	Fiona Brown
1978	Wilma Aitken	1986	Belle Robertson	1994	K Tebbet		
1979	Belle Robertson	1987	Elaine Farquharson	1995	Maria Hjörth		
1980	Wilma Aitken	1988	Elaine Farquharson	1996	J Hockley		

2002 *at Royal Troon and Troon Portland*

1	Heather Stirling (Bridge of Allan)	70-71-74—215
2	Becky Brewerton (Abergele)	72-71-76—219
3	Sarah Jones (Pennard)	70-70-80—220

Scottish Senior Ladies Amateur Championship (Inaugurated 1997)

1997	A Wilson	1999	P Williamson	2001	F Liddle
1998	I McIntosh	2000	P Hutton		

2002 *at Balcomie Links, Crail*

1	P Williamson (Baberton)	74-78—152
2	N Fenton (Merchants of Edinburgh)	80-77—157
3	J Clarke (Panmure)	80-80—160

Welsh Ladies Amateur Championship (Inaugurated 1905)

Year	Winner	Runner-up	Venue	Score
1905	E Young	B Duncan	Penarth	2 and 1
1906	B Duncan	Mrs Storry	Radyr	5 and 4
1907	B Duncan	Mrs Wenham	Royal Porthcawl	5 and 4
1908	B Duncan	Miss Lloyd Williams	Conwy	4 and 2
1909	B Duncan	Mrs Ellis Griffiths	Southerndown	4 and 3
1910	Miss Lloyd Roberts	Miss Leaver	Rhyl	4 and 3
1911	Miss Clay	Miss Allington-Hughes	Royal Porthcawl	2 and 1
1912	B Duncan	P Williams	Llandrindod Wells	4 and 2
1913	Miss Brooke	Miss Shaw	Rhos-on-Sea	at 19th
1914	Mrs Vivian Phillips	Miss Morgan	Tenby	4 and 3
1915–1919	*Not played due to First World War*			
1920	Mrs Rupert Phillips	M Marley	Royal Porthcawl	8 and 6

Year	Winner	Runner-up	Venue	Score
1921	M Marley	I Rieben	Aberdovey	7 and 5
1922	J Duncan	H Franklyn Thomas	Llandrindod Wells	9 and 8
1923	MR Cox	M Marley	Southerndown	at 39th
1924	MR Cox	B Pyman	Rhyl	11 and 10
1925	MR Cox	J Rhys	Tenby	9 and 7
1926	MC Justice	A Smalley	Aberdovey	4 and 3
1927	J Duncan	Mrs Blake	Porthcawl	1 hole
1928	J Duncan	I Rieben	Harlech	2 and 1
1929	I Rieben	B Pyman	Tenby	2 and 1
1930	MJ Jeffreys	I Rieben	Llandudno	2 holes
1931	MJ Jeffreys	B Pyman	Southerndown	4 and 3
1932	I Rieben	MJ Jeffreys	Aberdovey	2 and 1
1933	MJ Jeffreys	Mrs Bridge	Porthcawl	2 and 1
1934	I Rieben	MJ Jeffreys	Harlech	3 and 2
1935	*Abandoned – snow*			
1936	I Rieben	M Thompson	Prestatyn	2 and 1
1937	GS Emery	Dr P Whitaker	Porthcawl	10 and 9
1938	B Pyman	GS Emery	Llandudno	1 hole
1939	B Burrell	H Reynolds	Swansea	2 and 1
1940–1946	*Not played due to Second Word War*			
1947	M Barron	E Jones	Prestatyn	1 hole
1948	N Seely	M Barron	Prestatyn	12 and 11
1949	S Bryan Smith	E Brown	Newport	3 and 2
1950	Dr Garfield Evans	Nancy Cook	Porthcawl	2 and 1
1951	E Bromley-Davenport	Nancy Cook	Harlech	1 hole
1952	Elsie Lever	Pat Roberts	Southerndown	6 and 5
1953	Nancy Cook	Elsie Lever	Llandudno	3 and 2
1954	Nancy Cook	ED Brown	Tenby	1 hole
1955	Nancy Cook	Pat Roberts	Holyhead	2 holes
1956	Pat Roberts	M Barron	Royal Porthcawl	2 and 1
1957	M Barron	Pat Roberts	Royal St David's	6 and 4
1958	Nancy Cook Wright	Pat Roberts	Newport	1 hole
1959	Pat Roberts	A Gwyther	Conwy	6 and 4
1960	M Barron	E Brown	Tenby	8 and 6
1961	M Oliver	N Sneddon	Aberdovey	5 and 4
1962	M Oliver	P Roberts	Radyr	4 and 2
1963	P Roberts	N Sneddon	Royal St David's	7 and 5
1964	M Oliver	M Wright	Southerndown	1 hole
1965	M Wright	E Brown	Prestatyn	3 and 2
1966	A Hughes	P Roberts	Ashburnham	5 and 4
1967	M Wright	C Phipps	Royal St David's	21st hole
1968	S Hales	M Wright	Royal Porthcawl	3 and 2
1969	P Roberts	A Hughes	Caernarvonshire	3 and 2
1970	A Briggs	J Morris	Newport	19th hole
1971	A Briggs	EN Davies	Royal St David's	2 and 1
1972	A Hughes	J Rogers	Tenby	3 and 2
1973	A Briggs	J John	Holyhead	3 and 2
1974	A Briggs	Dr H Lyall	Ashburnham	3 and 2
1975	A Johnson (*née* Hughes)	K Rawlings	Prestatyn	1 hole
1976	T Perkins	A Johnson	Royal Porthcawl	4 and 2
1977	T Perkins	P Whitley	Aberdovey	5 and 4
1978	P Light	A Briggs	Newport	2 and 1
1979	V Rawlings	A Briggs	Caernarvonshire	2 holes
1980	M Rawlings	A Briggs	Tenby	2 and 1
1981	M Rawlings	A Briggs	Royal St David's	5 and 3
1982	V Thomas (*née* Rawlings)	M Rawlings	Ashburnham	7 and 6
1983	V Thomas	T Thomas (*née* Perkins)	Llandudno	1 hole
1984	S Roberts	K Davies	Newport	5 and 4
1985	V Thomas	S Jump	Prestatyn	1 hole
1986	V Thomas	L Isherwood	Royal Porthcawl	7 and 6
1987	V Thomas	S Roberts	Aberdovey	3 and 1
1988	S Roberts	F Connor	Tenby	4 and 2
1989	H Lawson	V Thomas	Conwy	2 and 1
1990	S Roberts	H Wadsworth	Ashburnham	3 and 2
1991	V Thomas	H Lawson	Royal St David's	4 and 3
1992	J Foster	S Boyes	Newport	4 and 3
1993	A Donne	V Thomas	Abergele & Pensarn	19th hole
1994	V Thomas	L Dermott	Royal Porthcawl	19th hole
1995	L Dermott	K Stark	Aberdovey	19th hole
1996	L Dermott	V Thomas	Tenby	4 and 3
1997	E Pilgrim	L Davis	Northop	4 and 2

Welsh Ladies Amateur Championship *continued*

Year	Winner	Runner-up	Venue	Score
1998	L Davis	R Morgan	Ashburnham	1 hole
1999	R Brewerton	R Morgan	Conwy	19th hole
2000	K Evans	K Phillips	Pyle & Kenfig	19th hole
2001	B Brewerton	S Jones	Royal St David's	2 and 1

2002 *at Newport*

Quarter Finals

El Pilgrim (St Pierre) beat Jo Pritchard
(Tredegar Park) 2 holes
Kathryn Evans (Conwy) beat Kate Philips
(Creigiau) 2 and 1
Stephanie Evans (Vale of Llangollen) beat Sara
Mountford (Wrexham) 3 and 2
Anna Highgate (Cottrell Park) beat Becky Brewerton
(Abergele) 2 and 1

Semi-Finals

Pilgrim beat K Evans 3 and 2
Highgate) beat S Evans 3 and 1

Final

El Pilgrim (St Pierre) beat Anna Highgate
(Cottrell Park) 1 hole

Welsh Ladies Open Amateur Strokeplay Championship

(Inaugurated 1976)

Year	Winner	Venue	Score	Year	Winner	Venue	Score
1976	P Light	Aberdovey	227	1989	V Thomas	Newport	220
1977	J Greenhalgh	Aberdovey	239	1990	L Hackney	Newport	218
1978	S Hedges	Aberdovey	49 holes	1991	M Sutton	R Porthcawl	224
1979	S Crowcroft	Aberdovey	228	1992	C Lambert	R Porthcawl	218
1980	T Thomas	Aberdovey	233	1993	J Hall	Newport	221
1981	V Thomas	Aberdovey	224	1994	A Rose	Newport	217
1982	V Thomas	Aberdovey	225	1995	F Brown	Newport	221
1983	J Thornhill	Aberdovey	239	1996	E Duggleby	Whitchurch	223
1984	L Davies	Aberdovey	230	1997	K Edwards	Whitchurch	216
1985	C Swallow	Aberdovey	219	1998	G Simpson	Rolls of Monmouth	154
1986	H Wadsworth	Aberdovey	223	1999	A Walker	Celtic Manor	230
1987	S Shapcott	Newport	225	2000	R Prout	Ashburnham	228
1988	S Shapcott	Newport	218	2001	V Laing	Royal Porthcawl	229

2002 *at Northop Country Park*

1	Vikki Laing (Musselburgh)	79-69-70—218
2	Heather Stirling (Bridge of Allan)	73-74-72—219
3	Becky Brewerton (Abergele)	75-74-73—222

Welsh Senior Ladies Championship (Inaugurated 1990)

Year	Winner	Venue	Score	Year	Winner	Venue	Score
1990	E Higgs	Vale of Llangollen	171	1996	C Thomas	Vale of Llangollen	157
1991	H Lyall	Pyle and Kenfig	160	1997	C Thomas	Fairwood Park	160
1992	P Morgan	Cardigan	83	1998	C Thomas	Padeswood	163
1993	P Morgan	Pwllheli	157	1999	V Mackenzie	St Mellons	153
1994	C Thomas	Llandudno	163	2000	F Shehan	Carmarthen	159
1995	C Thomas	Tredegar Park	157	2001	F Shehan	Porthmadog	159

2002 *at Creigiau*

1	Christine Thomas (Holyhead)	154
2	Verona MacKenzie (Whitchurch)	162
3	Angela Prichard (Royal Porthcawl)	172
4	Ruth James (Carmarthen)	172

Ladies European Open Amateur Championship (Inaugurated 1986)

1986	M Koch (Ger)	Morfontaine, France	286
1988	F Descampe (Bel)	Pedrena, Spain	289
1990	M Koch (Ger)	Zumicon, Switzerland	295
1991	D Bourson (Fra)	Schönborn, Austria	294
1992	J Morley (Eng)	Estoril, Portugal	284
1993	V Steinsrud (Nor)	Torino, Italy	277
1994	M Fischer (Ger)	Bastad, Sweden	288
1995	M Hjörth (Swe)	Berlin, Germany	284
1996	S Cavalleri (Ita)	Furesoe, Denmark	288
1997	S Cavalleri (Ita)	Formby, England	297
1998	G Sergas (Ita)	Noordwijk, Netherlands	295
1999	S Sandolo (Ita)	Karlovy Vary, Czech Republic	284
2000	E Duggleby (Eng)	Amber Baltic GC, Poland	283
2001	M Eberl (Ger)	Biella, Italy	217

2002 *at Kristianstad, Sweden*

1	Becky Brewerton (Wal)	73-70-70-75—288
2	Dewi-Claire Schreefel (Ned)	69-70-73-78—290
3	Pia Odefey (Ger)	69-73-74-79—295
	Nicola Timmins (Eng)	73-70-72-80—295

European Senior Ladies Championship (Inaugurated 2000)

2000	C Mourgue d'Algue (Fra)	La Manga	226
2001	C Mourgue d'Algue (Fra)	Torremirona	219

2002 *at La Manga*

1	Cecilia Mourgue D'Algue (Fra)	74-78-68—220
2	Clotilde Costa (Ita)	75-78-78—231
	Vicky Pertierra (Esp)	80-73-78—231

Lexus European Under 21 Championships (Inaugurated 1998)

1998	Kirsty Taylor (Eng)	2000	Rebecca Hudson (Eng)	2002	*Not played*
1999	Rebecca Hudson (Eng)	2001	Emma Cabrera (Esp)		

National Orders of Merit

English Order of Merit, 2002

1	Kerry Knowles (Worplesdon)	825
2	Nicola Timmins (Sene Valley)	810
3	Rebecca Hudson (Wheatley)	740

ILGU Irish Order of Merit, 2002

1	Alison Coffey (Warrenpoint)	1535
2	Rebecca Coakley (Carlow)	990
3	Martina Gillen (Beaverstown)	945

Dunfermline Building Society Scottish Order of Merit, 2002

1	Heather Stirling (Bridge of Allan)	3410
2	Lynn Kenny (University of Stirling)	1780
3	Anne Laing (Vale of Leven)	1705

Welsh Order of Merit, 2002

1	Becky Brewerton (Abergele)	1745
2	Eleanor Pilgrim (St Pierre)	965
3	Kathryn Evans (Conwy)	945

Team Events

Great Britain & Ireland v USA for the Curtis Cup
(home team names first)

2002 *at Fox Chapel, Pittsburgh, PA*

Captains: Mary Budke (USA), Pam Benka (GBI)

USA		Great Britain and Ireland	
First Day – Foursomes			
Duncan & Jerman (4 and 3)	1	Duggleby & Hudson	0
Fankhauser & Carol Semple Thompson (1 hole)	1	Laing & Stirling	0
Laura Myerscough & Swaim (3 and 2)	1	Alison Coffey & Kerry Smith	0
	3		0
Singles			
Emily Bastel	0	Rebecca Hudson (2 holes)	1
Leigh Anne Hardin (2 and 1)	1	Emma Duggleby	0
Meredith Duncan (5 and 4)	1	Fame More	0
Angela Jerman (6 and 5)	1	Sarah Jones	0
Courtney Swaim (4 and 2)	1	Heather Stirling	0
Mollie Fankhauser	0	Mollie Fankhauser (1 hole)	1
	4		2
Second Day – Foursomes			
Hardin & Bastel	0	Laing & Stirling (3 and 1)	1
Myerscough & Swaim (4 and 2)	1	Hudson & Smith	0
Duncan & Jerman	0	Coffey & Duggleby (4 and 2)	1
	1		2
Singles			
Fankhauser	0	Hudson (3 and 1)	1
Semple Thompson (1 hole)	1	Laing	0
Hardin	0	Duggleby (4 and 3)	1
Myerscough (2 holes)	1	Stirling	0
Duncan (3 and 1)	1	Coffey	0
Swaim	0	Jones (5 and 3)	1
	3		3

Result: USA 11, Great Britain and Ireland 7

1932 *at Wentworth*
Result: USA 5½, GBI 3½
Captains: J Wethered (GBI), M Hollins (USA)
Foursomes
Wethered & Morgan lost to Vare & Hill 1 hole
Wilson & JB Watson lost to Van Wie & Hicks 2 and 1
Gourlay & Doris Park lost to Orcutt & Cheney 1 hole
Singles
Joyce Wethered beat Glenna Collett Vare 6 and 4
Enid Wilson beat Helen Hicks 2 and 1
Wanda Morgan lost to Virginia Van Wie 2 and 1
Diana Fishwick beat Maureen Orcutt 4 and 3
Molly Gourlay halved with Opal Hill
Elsie Corlett lost to Leona Pressley Cheney 4 and 3

1934 *at Chevy Chase, MD*
Result: USA 6½, GBI 2½
*Captains: Glenna Collett Vare (USA),
    Doris Chambers (GBI)*
Foursomes
Van Wie & Glutting halved with Gourlay & Barton
Orcutt & Cheney beat Fishwick & Morgan 2 holes
Hill & Lucille Robinson lost to Plumpton & Walker
    2 and 1
Singles
Virginia Van Wie beat Diana Fishwick 2 and 1
Maureen Orcutt beat Molly Gourlay 4 and 2
Leona Pressley Cheney beat Pamela Barton 7 and 5
Charlotte Glutting beat Wanda Morgan
Opal Hill beat Diana Plumpton 3 and 2
Aniela Goldthwaite lost to Charlotte Walker 3 and 2

1936 *at Gleneagles*
Result: USA 4½, GBI 4½
Captains: Doris Chambers (GBI),
 Glenna Collett Vare (USA)

Foursomes
Morgan & Garon halved with Vare & Berg
Barton & Walker lost to Orcutt & Cheney 2 and 1
Anderson & Holm beat Hill & Glutting 3 and 2

Singles
Wanda Morgan lost to Glenna Collett Vare 3 and 2
Helen Holm beat Patty Berg 4 and 3
Pamela Barton lost to Charlotte Glutting 1 hole
Charlotte Walker lost to Maureen Orcutt 1 hole
Jessie Anderson beat Leona Pressley Cheney 1 hole
Marjorie Garon beat Opal Hill 7 and 5

1938 *at Essex, MA*
Result: USA 5½, GBI 3½
Captains: Frances Stebbins (USA),
 Mrs RH Wallace-Williamson (GBI)

Foursomes
Page & Orcutt lost to Holm & Tiernan 2 holes
Vare & Berg lost to Anderson & Corlett 1 hole
Miley & Kathryn Hemphill halved with Walker &
 Phyllis Wade

Singles
Estelle Lawson Page beat Helen Holm 6 and 5
Patty Berg beat Jessie Anderson 1 hole
Marion Miley beat Elsie Corlett 2 and 1
Glenna Collett Vare beat Charlotte Walker 2 and 1
Maureen Orcutt lost to Clarrie Tiernan 2 and 1
Charlotte Glutting beat Nan Baird 1 hole

1948 *at Birkdale*
Result: USA 6½, GBI 2½
Captains: Doris Chambers (GBI),
 Glenna Collett Vare (USA)

Foursomes
Donald & Gordon beat Suggs & Lenczyk 3 and 2
Garvey & Bolton lost to Kirby & Vare 4 and 3
Ruttle & Val Reddan lost to Page & Kielty 5 and 4

Singles
Philomena Garvey halved with Louise Suggs
Jean Donald beat Dorothy Kirby 2 holes
Jacqueline Gordon lost to Grace Lenczyk 5 and 3
Helen Holm lost to Estelle Lawson Page 3 and 2
Maureen Ruttle lost to Polly Riley 3 and 2
Zara Bolton lost to Dorothy Kielty 2 and 1

1950 *at Buffalo, NY*
Result: USA 7½, GBI 1½
Captains: Glenna Collett Vare (USA),
 Diana Fishwick Critchley (GBI)

Foursomes
Hanson & Porter beat Valentine & Donald 3 and 2
Helen Sigel & Kirk lost to Stephens & Price 1 hole
Dorothy Kirby & Kielty beat Garvey & Bisgood
 6 and 5

Singles
Dorothy Porter halved with Frances Stephens
Polly Riley beat Jessie Anderson Valentine 7 and 6
Beverly Hanson beat Jean Donald 6 and 5
Dorothy Kielty beat Philomena Garvey 2 and 1
Peggy Kirk beat Jeanne Bisgood 1 hole
Grace Lenczyk beat Elizabeth Price 5 and 4

1952 *at Muirfield*
Result: GBI 5, USA 4
Captains: Lady Katherine Cairns (GBI),
 Aniela Goldthwaite (USA)

Foursomes
Donald & Price beat Kirby & DeMoss 3 and 2
Stephens & JA Valentine lost to Doran & Lindsay
 6 and 4
Paterson & Garvey beat Riley & Patricia O'Sullivan
 2 and 1

Singles
Jean Donald lost to Dorothy Kirby 1 hole
Frances Stephens beat Marjorie Lindsay 2 and 1
Moira Paterson lost to Polly Riley 6 and 4
Jeanne Bisgood beat Mae Murray 6 and 5
Philomena Garvey lost to Claire Doran 3 and 2
Elizabeth Price beat Grace DeMoss 3 and 2

1954 *at Merion, PA*
Result: USA 6, GBI 3
Captains: Edith Flippin (USA),
 Mrs JB Beck (GBI)

Foursomes
Faulk & Riley beat Stephens & Price 6 and 4
Doran & Patricia Lesser beat Garvey & Valentine
 6 and 5
Kirby & Barbara Romack beat Marjorie Peel &
 Robertson 6 and 5

Singles
Mary Lena Faulk lost to Frances Stephens 1 hole
Claire Doran beat Jeanne Bisgood 4 and 3
Polly Riley beat Elizabeth Price 9 and 8
Dorothy Kirby lost to Philomena Garvey 3 and 1
Grace DeMoss Smith beat Jessie Anderson Valentine
 4 and 3
Joyce Ziske lost to Janette Robertson 3 and 1

1956 *at Prince's, Sandwich*
Result: GBI 5, USA 4
Captains: Zara Davis Bolton (GBI),
 Edith Flippin (USA)

Foursomes
Valentine & Garvey lost to Lesser & Smith 2 and 1
Smith & Price beat Riley & Romack 5 and 3
Robertson & Veronica Anstey lost to Downey & Carolyn
 Cudone 6 and 4

Singles
Jessie Anderson Valentine beat Patricia Lesser
 6 and 4
Philomena Garvey lost to Margaret Smith 9 and 8
Frances Stephens Smith beat Polly Riley 1 hole
Janette Robertson lost to Barbara Romack 6 and 4
Angela Ward beat Mary Ann Downey 6 and 4
Elizabeth Price beat Jane Nelson 7 and 6

1958 *at Brae Burn, MA*
Result: GBI 4½, USA 4½
Captains: Virginia Dennehy (USA),
 Daisy Ferguson (GBI)

Foursomes
Riley & Romack lost to Bonallack & Price 2 and 1
Gunderson & Quast lost to Robertson & Smith
 3 and 2
Johnstone & McIntire beat Jackson & Valentine
 6 and 5

1958 continued

Singles
JoAnne Gunderson beat Jessie Anderson Valentine
   2 holes
Barbara McIntire halved with Angela Ward Bonallack
Anne Quast beat Elizabeth Price 4 and 2
Anna Johnstone lost to Janette Robertson 3 and 2
Barbara Romack beat Bridget Jackson 3 and 2
Polly Riley lost to Frances Stephens Smith 2 holes

1960 at Lindrick

Result: USA 6½, GBI 2½
Captains: Maureen Garrett (GBI),
   Mildred Prunaret (USA)

Foursomes
Price & Bonallack beat Gunderson & McIntyre
   1 hole
Robertson & McCorkindale lost to Eller & Quast
   4 and 2
Frances Smith & Porter lost to Goodwin & Anna
   Johnstone 3 and 2

Singles
Elizabeth Price halved with Barbara McIntire
Angela Ward Bonallack lost to JoAnne Gunderson
   2 and 1
Janette Robertson lost to Anne Quast 2 holes
Philomena Garvey lost to Judy Eller 4 and 3
Belle McCorkindale lost to Judy Bell 8 and 7
Ruth Porter beat Joanne Goodwin 1 hole

1962 at Broadmoor, Colorado Springs, CO

Result: USA 8, GBI 1
Captains: Polly Riley (USA),
   Frances Stephens Smith (GBI)

Foursomes
Decker & McIntyre beat Spearman & Bonallack
   7 and 5
Jean Ashley & Anna Johnstone beat Ruth Porter &
   Frearson 8 and 7
Creed & Gunderson beat Vaughan & Ann Irvin
   4 and 3

Singles
Judy Bell lost to Diane Frearson 8 and 7
JoAnne Gunderson beat Angela Ward Bonallack
   2 and 1
Clifford Ann Creed beat Sally Bonallack 6 and 5
Anne Quast Decker beat Marley Spearman
   7 and 5
Phyllis Preuss beat Jean Roberts 1 hole
Barbara McIntyre beat Sheila Vaughan 5 and 4

1964 at Porthcawl

Result: USA 10½, GBI 1½
Captains: Elsie Corlett (GBI),
   Helen Hawes (USA)

First Day: Foursomes
Spearman & Bonallack beat McIntyre & Preuss
   2 and 1
Sheila Vaughan & Porter beat Gunderson & Roth
   3 and 2
Jackson & Susan Armitage lost to Sorenson & White
   8 and 6

Singles
Angela Ward Bonallack lost to JoAnne Gunderson
   6 and 5
Marley Spearman halved with Barbara McIntyre
Julia Greenhalgh lost to Barbara White 3 and 2
Bridget Jackson beat Carol Sorenson 4 and 3
Joan Lawrence lost to Peggy Conley 1 hole
Ruth Porter beat Nancy Roth 1 hole

Second Day: Foursomes
Spearman & Bonallack beat McIntyre & Preuss
   6 and 5
Armitage & Jackson lost to Gunderson & Roth
   2 holes
Porter & Vaughan halved with Sorenson & White

Singles
Spearman halved with Gunderson
Lawrence lost to McIntyre 4 and 2
Greenhalgh beat Phyllis Preuss 5 and 3
Bonallack lost to White 3 and 2
Porter lost to Sorenson 3 and 2
Jackson lost to Conley 1 hole

1966 at Hot Springs, VA

Result: USA 13, GBI 5
Captains: Dorothy Germain Porter (USA),
   Zara Bolton (GBI)

First Day: Foursomes
Ashley & Preuss beat Armitage & Bonallack 1 hole
Barbara McIntire & Welts halved with Joan Hastings &
   Robertson
Boddie & Flenniken beat Chadwick & Tredinnick
   1 hole

Singles
Jean Ashley beat Belle McCorkindale Robertson
   1 hole
Anne Quast Welts halved with Susan Armitage
Barbara White Boddie beat Angela Ward Bonallack
   3 and 2
Nancy Roth Syms beat Elizabeth Chadwick 2 holes
Helen Wilson lost to Ita Burke 3 and 1
Carol Sorenson Flenniken beat Marjory Fowler
   3 and 1

Second Day: Foursomes
Ashley & Preuss beat Armitage & Bonallack 2 and 1
McIntire & Welts lost to Burke & Chadwick 1 hole
Boddie & Flenniken beat Hastings & Robertson
   2 and 1

Singles
Ashley lost to Bonallack 2 and 1
Welts halved with Robertson
Boddie beat Armitage 3 and 2
Syms halved with Pam Tredinnick
Phyllis Preuss beat Chadwick 3 and 2
Flenniken beat Burke 2 and 1

1968 at Newcastle, Co Down

Result: USA 10½, GBI 7½
Captains: Zara Bolton (GBI),
   Evelyn Monsted (USA)

First Day: Foursomes
Irvin & Robertson beat Hamlin & Welts 6 and 5
Pickard & Saunders beat Conley & Dill 3 and 2
Howard & Pam Tredinnick lost to Ashley & Preuss
   1 hole

Singles
Ann Irvin beat Anne Quast Welts 3 and 2
Vivien Saunders lost to Shelley Hamlin 1 hole
Belle McCorkindale Robertson lost to Roberta Albers
  1 hole
Bridget Jackson halved with Peggy Conley
Dinah Oxley halved with Phyllis Preuss
Margaret Pickard beat Jean Ashley 2 holes

Second Day: Foursomes
Oxley & Tredinnick lost to Ashley & Preuss 5 and 4
Irvin & Robertson halved with Conley & Dill
Pickard & Saunders lost to Hamlin & Welts 2 and 1

Singles
Irvin beat Hamlin 3 and 2
Robertson halved with Welts
Saunders halved with Albers
Ann Howard lost to Mary Lou Dill 4 and 2
Pickard lost to Conley 1 hole
Jackson lost to Preuss 2 and 1

1970 at Brae Burn, MA
Result: USA 11½, GBI 6½
Captains: Carolyn Cudone (USA),
*   Jeanne Bisgood (GBI)*
First Day: Foursomes
Bastanchury & Hamlin lost to McKenna & Oxley 4 and 3
Preuss & Wilkinson beat Irvin & Robertson 4 and 3
Jane Fassinger & Hill lost to Everard & Greenhalgh
  5 and 3

Singles
Jane Bastanchury beat Dinah Oxley 5 and 3
Martha Wilkinson beat Ann Irvin 1 hole
Shelley Hamlin halved with Belle McCorkindale
  Robertson
Phyllis Preuss lost to Mary McKenna 4 and 2
Nancy Hager beat Margaret Pickard 5 and 4
Alice Dye beat Julia Greenhalgh 1 hole

Second Day: Foursomes
Preuss & Wilkinson beat McKenna & Oxley 6 and 4
Dye & Hill halved with Everard & Greenhalgh
Bastanchury & Hamlin beat Irvin & Robertson 1 hole

Singles
Bastanchury beat Irvin 4 and 3
Hamlin halved with Oxley
Preuss beat Robertson 1 hole
Wilkinson lost to Greenhalgh 6 and 4
Hager lost to Mary Everard 4 and 3
Cindy Hill beat McKenna 2 and 1

1972 at Western Gailes
Result: USA 10, GBI 8
Captains: Frances Stephens Smith (GBI),
*   Jean Ashley Crawford (USA)*
First Day: Foursomes
Everard & Beverly Huke lost to Baugh & Kirouac
  2 and 1
Frearson & Robertson beat Booth & McIntyre 2 and 1
McKenna & Walker beat Barry & Hollis Stacy 1 hole

Singles
Mickey Walker halved with Laura Baugh
Belle McCorkindale Robertson lost to Jane Bastanchury
  Booth 3 and 1
Mary Everard lost to Martha Wilkinson Kirouac
  4 and 3
Dinah Oxley lost to Barbara McIntire 4 and 3
Kathryn Phillips beat Lancy Smith 2 holes
Mary McKenna lost to Beth Barry 2 and 1

Second Day: Foursomes
McKenna & Walker beat Baugh & Kirouac 3 and 2
Everard & Huke lost to Booth & McIntyre 5 and 4
Frearson & Robertson halved with Barry & Stacy

Singles
Robertson lost to Baugh 6 and 5
Everard beat McIntyre 6 and 5
Walker beat Booth 1 hole
McKenna beat Kirouac 3 and 1
Diane Frearson lost to Smith 3 and 1
Phillips lost to Barry 3 and 1

1974 at San Francisco, CA
Result: USA 13, GBI 5
Captains: Sis Choate (USA),
*   Belle McCorkindale Robertson (GBI)*
First Day: Foursomes
Hill & Semple halved with Greenhalgh & McKenna
Booth & Sander beat Lee-Smith & LeFeuvre 6 and 5
Budke & Lauer lost to Everard & Walker 5 and 4

Singles
Carol Semple lost to Mickey Walker 2 and 1
Jane Bastanchury Booth beat Mary McKenna 5 and 3
Debbie Massey beat Mary Everard 1 hole
Bonnie Lauer beat Jennie Lee-Smith 6 and 5
Beth Barry beat Julia Greenhalgh 1 hole
Cindy Hill halved with Tegwen Perkins

Second Day: Foursomes
Booth & Sander beat McKenna & Walker 5 and 4
Budke & Lauer beat Everard & LeFeuvre 5 and 3
Hill & Semple lost to Greenhalgh & Perkins 3 and 2

Singles
Anne Quast Sander beat Everard 4 and 3
Booth beat Greenhalgh 7 and 5
Massey beat Carol LeFeuvre 6 and 5
Semple beat Walker 2 and 1
Mary Budke beat Perkins 5 and 4
Lauer lost to McKenna 2 and 1

1976 at Royal Lytham & St Annes
Result: USA 11½, GBI 6½
Captains: Belle McCorkindale Robertson (GBI),
*   Barbara McIntyre (USA)*
First Day: Foursomes
Greenhalgh & McKenna lost to Daniel & Hill 3 and 2
Cadden & Henson lost to Horton & Massey 6 and 5
Irvin & Perkins beat Semple & Syms 3 and 2

Singles
Ann Irvin lost to Beth Daniel 4 and 3
Dinah Oxley Henson beat Cindy Hill 1 hole
Suzanne Cadden lost to Nancy Lopez 3 and 1
Mary McKenna lost to Nancy Roth Syms 1 hole
Tegwen Perkins lost to Debbie Massey 1 hole
Julia Greenhalgh halved with Barbara Barrow

Second Day: Foursomes
Cadden & Irvin lost to Daniel & Hill 4 and 3
Henson & Perkins beat Semple & Syms 2 and 1
McKenna & Anne Stant lost to Barrow & Lopez 4 and 3

Singles
Henson lost to Daniel 3 and 2
Greenhalgh beat Syms 2 and 1
Cadden lost to Donna Horton 6 and 5
Jennie Lee-Smith lost to Massey 3 and 2
Perkins beat Hill 1 hole
McKenna beat Carol Semple 1 hole

1978 at Apawamis, NY

Result: USA 12, GBI 6

Captains: Helen Wilson (USA),
Carol Comboy (GBI)

First Day: Foursomes
Daniel & Brenda Goldsmith lost to Greenhalgh &
   Marvin 3 and 2
Cindy Hill & Smith lost to Everard & Thomson
   2 and 1
Cornett & Carolyn Hill halved with McKenna & Perkins

Singles
Beth Daniel beat Vanessa Marvin 5 and 4
Noreen Uihlein lost to Mary Everard 7 and 6
Lancy Smith beat Angela Uzielli 4 and 3
Cindy Hill beat Julia Greenhalgh 2 and 1
Carolyn Hill halved with Carole Caldwell
Judy Oliver beat Tegwen Perkins 2 and 1

Second Day: Foursomes
Cindy Hill & Smith beat Everard & Thomson 1 hole
Daniel & Goldsmith beat McKenna & Perkins 1 hole
Oliver & Uihlein beat Greenhalgh & Marvin 4 and 3

Singles
Daniel beat Mary McKenna 2 and 1
Patricia Cornett beat Caldwell 3 and 2
Cindy Hill lost to Muriel Thomson 2 and 1
Lancy Smith beat Perkins 2 holes
Oliver halved with Greenhalgh
Uihlein halved with Everard

1980 at St Pierre, Chepstow

Result: USA 13, GBI 5

Captains: Carol Comboy (GBI), Nancy Roth
Syms (USA)

First Day: Foursomes
McKenna & Nesbitt halved with Terri Moody &
   Smith
Stewart & Thomas lost to Castillo & Sheehan 5 and 3
Caldwell & Madill halved with Oliver & Semple

Singles
Mary McKenna lost to Patty Sheehan 3 and 2
Claire Nesbitt halved with Lancy Smith
Jane Connachan lost to Brenda Goldsmith 2 holes
Maureen Madill lost to Carol Semple 4 and 3
Linda Moore halved with Mary Hafeman
Carole Caldwell lost to Judy Oliver 1 hole

Second Day: Foursomes
Caldwell & Madill lost to Castillo & Sheehan 3 and 2
McKenna & Nesbitt lost to Moody & Smith 6 and 5
Moore & Thomas lost to Oliver & Semple 1 hole

Singles
Madill lost to Sheehan 5 and 4
McKenna beat Lori Castillo 5 and 4
Connachan lost to Hafeman 6 and 5
Gillian Stewart beat Smith 5 and 4
Moore beat Goldsmith 1 hole
Tegwen Perkins Thomas lost to Semple 4 and 3

1982 at Denver, CO

Result: USA 14½, GBI 3½

Captains: Betty Probasco (USA),
Maire O'Donnell (GBI)

First Day: Foursomes
Inkster & Semple beat McKenna & Robertson 5 and 4
Baker & Smith halved with Douglas & Soulsby
Benz & Hanlon beat Connachan & Stewart 2 and 1

Singles
Amy Benz beat Mary McKenna 2 and 1
Cathy Hanlon beat Jane Connachan 5 and 4
Mari McDougall beat Wilma Aitken 2 holes
Kathy Baker beat Belle McCorkindale Robertson 7 and 6
Judy Oliver lost to Janet Soulsby 2 holes
Juli Inkster beat Kitrina Douglas 7 and 6

Second Day: Foursomes
Inkster & Semple beat Aitken & Connachan 3 and 2
Baker & Smith beat Douglas & Soulsby 1 hole
Benz & Hanlon lost to McKenna & Robertson 1 hole

Singles
Inkster beat Douglas 7 and 6
Baker beat Gillian Stewart 4 and 3
Oliver beat Vicki Thomas 5 and 4
McDougall beat Soulsby 2 and 1
Carol Semple beat McKenna 1 hole
Lancy Smith lost to Robertson 5 and 4

1984 at Muirfield

Result: USA 9½, GBI 8½

Captains: Diane Robb Bailey (GBI),
Phyllis Preuss (USA)

First Day: Foursomes
New & Waite beat Pacillo & Sander 2 holes
Grice & Thornhill halved with Rosenthal & Smith
Davies & McKenna lost to Farr & Widman 1 hole

Singles
Jill Thornhill halved with Joanne Pacillo
Claire Waite lost to Penny Hammel 4 and 2
Claire Hourihane lost to Jody Rosenthal 3 and 1
Vicki Thomas beat Dana Howe 2 and 1
Penny Grice beat Anne Quast Sander 2 holes
Beverley New lost to Mary Anne Widman 4 and 3

Second Day: Foursomes
New & Waite lost to Rosenthal & Smith 3 and 1
Grice & Thornhill beat Farr & Widman 2 and 1
Hourihane & Thomas halved with Hammel & Howe

Singles
Thornhill lost to Pacillo 3 and 2
Laura Davies beat Sander 1 hole
Waite beat Lancy Smith 5 and 4
Grice lost to Howe 2 holes
New lost to Heather Farr 6 and 5
Hourihane beat Hammel 2 and 1

1986 at Prairie Dunes, KS

Result: GBI 13, USA 5

Captains: Judy Bell (USA),
Diane Robb Bailey (GBI)

First Day: Foursomes
Kessler & Schreyer lost to Behan & Thornhill 7 and 6
Ammaccapane & Mochrie lost to Davies & Johnson
   2 and 1
Gardner & Scrivner lost to McKenna & Robertson 1 hole

Singles
Leslie Shannon lost to Patricia (Trish) Johnson 1 hole
Kim Williams lost to Jill Thornhill 4 and 3
Danielle Ammaccapane lost to Lillian Behan 4 and 3
Kandi Kessler beat Vicki Thomas 3 and 2
Dottie Pepper Mochrie halved with Karen Davies
Cindy Schreyer beat Claire Hourihane 2 and 1

Second Day: Foursomes
Ammaccapane & Mochrie lost to Davies & Johnson 1 hole
Shannon & Williams lost to Behan & Thornhill 5 and 3
Gardner & Scrivner halved with McKenna & Belle
   McCorkindale Robertson

Singles
Shannon halved with Thornhill
Kathleen McCarthy Scrivner lost to Trish Johnson 5 and 3
Kim Gardner beat Behan 1 hole
Williams lost to Thomas 4 and 3
Kessler halved with Davies
Schreyer lost to Hourihane 5 and 4

1988 at Royal St George's
Result: GBI 11, USA 7
Captains: Diane Robb Bailey (GBI),
*   Judy Bell (USA)*
First Day: Foursomes
Bayman & Wade beat Kerdyk & Scrivner 2 and 1
Davies & Shapcott beat Scholefield & Thompson 5 and 4
Thomas & Thornhill halved with Keggi & Shannon

Singles
Linda Bayman halved with Tracy Kerdyk
Julie Wade beat Cindy Scholefield 2 holes
Susan Shapcott lost to Carol Semple Thompson 1 hole
Karen Davies lost to Pearl Sinn 4 and 3
Shirley Lawson beat Pat Cornett-Iker 1 hole
Jill Thornhill beat Leslie Shannon 3 and 2

Second Day: Foursomes
Bayman & Wade lost to Kerdyk & Scrivner 1 hole
Davies & Shapcott beat Keggi & Shannon 2 holes
Thomas & Thornhill beat Scholefield & Thompson
    6 and 5

Singles
Wade lost to Kerdyk 2 and 1
Shapcott beat Caroline Keggi 3 and 2
Lawson lost to Kathleen McCarthy Scrivner 4 and 3
Vicki Thomas beat Cornett-Iker 5 and 3
Bayman beat Sinn 1 hole
Thornhill lost to Thompson 3 and 2

1990 at Somerset Hills, NJ
Result: USA 14, GBI 4
Captains: Leslie Shannon (USA),
*   Jill Thornhill (GBI)*
First Day: Foursomes
Goetze & Anne Quast Sander beat Dobson & Lambert
    4 and 3
Noble & Margaret Platt lost to Wade & Imrie 2 and 1
Thompson & Weiss beat Farquharson & Helen
    Wadsworth 3 and 1

Singles
Vicki Goetze lost to Julie Wade 2 and 1
Katie Peterson beat Kathryn Imrie 3 and 2
Brandie Burton beat Linzi Fletcher 3 and 1
Robin Weiss beat Elaine Farquharson 4 and 3
Karen Noble beat Catriona Lambert 1 hole
Carol Semple Thompson lost to Vicki Thomas 1 hole

Second Day: Foursomes
Goetze & Sander beat Wade & Imrie 3 and 1
Noble & Platt lost to Dobson & Lambert 1 hole
Burton & Peterson beat Farquharson & Wadsworth
    5 and 4

Singles
Goetze beat Helen Dobson 4 and 3
Burton beat Lambert 4 and 3
Peterson beat Imrie 1 hole
Noble beat Wade 2 holes
Weiss beat Farquharson 2 and 1
Thompson beat Thomas 3 and 1

1992 at Hoylake
Result: GBI 10, USA 8
Captains: Elizabeth Boatman (GBI),
*   Judy Oliver (USA)*
First Day: Foursomes
Hall & Wade halved with Fruhwirth & Goetze
Lambert & Thomas beat Ingram & Shannon 2 and 1
Hourihane & Morley beat Hanson & Thompson 2 and 1

Singles
Joanne Morley halved with Amy Fruhwirth
Julie Wade lost to Vicki Goetze 3 and 2
Elaine Farquharson beat Robin Weiss 2 and 1
Nicola Buxton lost to Martha Lang 2 holes
Catriona Lambert beat Carol Semple Thompson 3 and 2
Caroline Hall beat Leslie Shannon 6 and 5

Second Day: Foursomes
Hall & Wade halved with Fruhwirth & Goetze
Hourihane & Morley halved with Lang & Weiss
Lambert & Thomas lost to Hanson & Thompson 3 and 2

Singles
Morley beat Fruhwirth 2 and 1
Lambert beat Tracy Hanson 6 and 5
Farquharson lost to Sarah LeBrun Ingram 2 and 1
Vicki Thomas lost to Shannon 2 and 1
Claire Hourihane lost to Lang 2 and 1
Hall beat Goetze 1 hole

1994 at Chattanooga, TN
Result: GBI 9, USA 9
Captains: Lancy Smith (USA),
*   Elizabeth Boatman (GBI)*
First Day: Foursomes
Sarah LeBrun Ingram & McGill halved with Matthew
    & Moodie
Klein & Thompson beat McKay & Kirsty Speak
    7 and 5
Kaupp & Port lost to Wade & Walton 6 and 5

Singles
Jill McGill halved with Julie Wade
Emilee Klein beat Janice Moodie 3 and 2
Wendy Ward lost to Lisa Walton 1 hole
Carol Semple Thompson beat Myra McKinlay 2 and 1
Ellen Port beat Mhairi McKay 2 and 1
Stephanie Sparks lost to Catriona Lambert Matthew
    1 hole

Second Day: Foursomes
Ingram & McGill lost to Wade & Walton 2 and 1
Klein & Thompson beat McKinlay & Eileen Rose
    Power 4 and 2
Sparks & Ward lost to Matthew & Moodie 3 and 2

Singles
McGill beat Wade 4 and 3
Klein lost to Matthew 2 and 1
Port beat McKay 7 and 5
Wendy Kaupp lost to McKinlay 3 and 2
Ward beat Walton 4 and 3
Thompson lost to Moodie 2 holes

1996 at Killarney
Result: GBI 11½, USA 6½
Captains: Ita Burke Butler (GBI),
*   Martha Lang (USA)*
First Day: Foursomes
Lisa Walton Educate & Wade lost to K Kuehne & Port
    2 and 1
Lisa Dermott & Rose beat B Corrie Kuehn & Jemsek 3 and 1
McKay & Moodie halved with Kerr & Thompson

1996 *continued*

Singles
Julie Wade lost to Sarah LeBrun Ingram 4 and 2
Karen Stupples beat Kellee Booth 3 and 2
Alison Rose beat Brenda Corrie Kuehn 5 and 4
Elaine Ratcliffe halved with Marla Jemsek
Mhairi McKay beat Cristie Kerr 1 hole
Janice Moodie beat Carol Semple Thompson 3 and 1

Second Day: Foursomes
McKay & Moodie beat Booth & Ingram 3 and 2
Dermott & Rose beat B Corrie Kuehn & Jemsek 2 and 1
Educate & Wade lost to K Kuehne & Port 1 hole
Singles
Wade lost to Kerr 1 hole
Ratcliffe beat Ingram 3 and 1
Stupples lost to Booth 3 and 2
Rose beat Ellen Port 6 and 5
McKay halved with Thompson
Moodie beat Kelli Kuehne 2 and 1

1998 *at Minikahda, Minneapolis, MN*
Result: USA 10, GBI 8
Captains: Barbara McIntire (USA),
  Ita Burke Butler (GBI)
First Day: Foursomes
Bauer & Chuasiriporn lost to Ratcliffe & Rostron
  1 hole
Booth & Corrie Kuehn beat Brown & Stupples
  2 and 1
Burke & Derby Grimes beat Morgan & Rose 3 and 2
Singles
Kellee Booth beat Kim Rostron 2 and 1
Brenda Corrie Kuehn beat Alison Rose 3 and 2
Jenny Chuasiriporn halved with Rebecca Hudson
Beth Bauer beat Hilary Monaghan 5 and 3
Jo Jo Robertson lost to Becky Morgan 2 and 1
Carol Semple Thompson lost to Elaine Ratcliffe
  3 and 2
Second Day: Foursomes
Booth & Corrie Kuehn beat Morgan & Rose 6 and 5
Bauer & Chuasiriporn lost to Brown & Hudson 2 holes
Burke & Derby Grimes beat Ratcliffe & Rostron 2 and 1

Singles
Booth beat Rostron 2 and 1
Corrie Kuehn beat Morgan 2 and 1
Thompson lost to Karen Stupples 1 hole
Robin Burke lost to Hudson 2 and 1
Robertson lost to Fiona Brown 1 hole
Virginia Derby Grimes halved with Ratcliffe

2000 *at Ganton*
Result: USA 10, GBI 8
Captains: Claire Hourihane Dowling (GBI),
  Jane Bastanchury Booth (USA)
First Day: Foursomes
Andrew & Morgan lost to Bauer & Carol Semple
  Thompson 1 hole
Brewerton & Hudson lost to Keever & Stanford
  1 hole
Duggleby & O'Brien halved with Derby Grimes &
  Homeyer
Singles
Kim Rostron Andrew lost to Beth Bauer 3 and 2
Fiona Brown lost to Robin Weiss 1 hole
Rebecca Hudson lost to Stephanie Keever 4 and 2
Lesley Nicholson halved with Angela Stanford
Singles *continued*
Suzanne O'Brien beat Leland Beckel 3 and 1
Emma Duggleby lost to Hilary Homeyer 1 hole
Second Day: Foursomes
Brewerton & Hudson beat Bauer & Thompson
  2 and 1
Duggleby & O'Brien beat Keever & Stanford
  7 and 6
Andrew & Morgan lost to Derby Grimes & Homeyer
  3 and 1
Singles
Hudson lost to Bauer 1 hole
O'Brien beat Weiss 3 and 2
Duggleby beat Keever 4 and 2
Becky Brewerton lost to Homeyer 3 and 2
Becky Morgan beat Stanford 5 and 4
Andrew beat Virginia Derby Grimes 6 and 5

Curtis Cup INDIVIDUAL RECORDS

Bold print: captain; bold print in brackets: non-playing captain
Maiden name in parentheses, former surname in square brackets

Great Britain and Ireland

Name		Year	Played	Won	Lost	Halved
Jean Anderson (Donald)	Sco	1948	6	3	3	0
Kim Andrew (Rostron)	Eng	1998-2000	8	2	6	0
Diane Bailey [Frearson] (Robb)	Eng	1962-72-**(84)**-**(86)**-**(88)**	5	2	2	1
Sally Barber (Bonallack)	Eng	1962	1	0	1	0
Pam Barton	Eng	1934-36	4	0	3	1
Linda Bayman	Eng	1988	4	2	1	1
Baba Beck (Pym)	Irl	**(1954)**	0	0	0	0
Charlotte Beddows [Watson] (Stevenson)	Sco	1932	1	0	1	0
Lilian Behan	Irl	1986	4	3	1	0
Veronica Beharrell (Anstey)	Eng	1956	1	0	1	0
Pam Benka (Tredinnick)	Eng	1966-68 **(2002)**	4	0	3	1
Jeanne Bisgood	Eng	1950-52-54-**(70)**	4	1	3	0
Elizabeth Boatman (Collis)	Eng	**(1992)**-**(94)**	0	0	0	0
Zara Bolton (Davis)	Eng	1948-**(56)**-**(66)**-**(68)**	2	0	2	0
Angela Bonallack (Ward)	Eng	1956-58-60-62-64-66	15	6	8	1

Name		Year	Played	Won	Lost	Halved
Becky Brewerton	Wal	2000	3	1	2	0
Fiona Brown	Eng	1998-2000	4	2	2	0
Ita Butler (Burke)	Irl	1966-(**96**)	3	2	1	0
Lady Katherine Cairns	Eng	(1952)	0	0	0	0
Carole Caldwell (Redford)	Eng	1978-80	5	0	3	2
Doris Chambers	Eng	(**1934**)-(**36**)-(**48**)	0	0	0	0
Alison Coffey	Irl	2002	3	1	2	0
Carol Comboy (Grott)	Eng	(**1978**)-(**80**)	0	0	0	0
Jane Connachan	Sco	1980-82	5	0	5	0
Elsie Corlett	Eng	1932-38-(**64**)	3	1	2	0
Diana Critchley (Fishwick)	Eng	1932-34-(**50**)	3	1	2	0
Alison Davidson (Rose)	Sco	1996-98	7	4	3	0
Karen Davies	Wal	1986-88	7	4	1	2
Laura Davies	Eng	1984	2	1	1	0
Lisa Dermott	Wal	1996	2	2	0	0
Helen Dobson	Eng	1990	3	1	2	0
Kitrina Douglas	Eng	1982	4	0	3	1
Claire Dowling (Hourihane)	Irl	1984-86-88-90-92-(**2000**)	8	3	3	2
Marjorie Draper [Peel] (Thomas)	Sco	1954	1	0	1	0
Emma Duggleby	Eng	2000	4	2	1	1
Lisa Educate (Walton)	Eng	1994-96	6	3	3	0
Mary Everard	Eng	1970-72-74-78	15	6	7	2
Elaine Farquharson	Sco	1990-92	6	1	5	0
Daisy Ferguson	Irl	(**1958**)	0	0	0	0
Marjory Ferguson (Fowler)	Sco	1966	1	0	1	0
Elizabeth Price Fisher (Price)	Eng	1950-52-54-56-58-60	12	7	4	1
Linzi Fletcher	Eng	1990	1	0	1	0
Maureen Garner (Madill)	Irl	1980	4	0	3	1
Marjorie Ross Garon	Eng	1936	2	1	0	1
Maureen Garrett (Ruttle)	Eng	1948-(**60**)	2	0	2	0
Philomena Garvey	Irl	1948-50-52-54-56-60	11	2	8	1
Carol Gibbs (Le Feuvre)	Eng	1974	3	0	3	0
Jacqueline Gordon	Eng	1948	2	1	1	0
Molly Gourlay	Eng	1932-34	4	0	2	2
Julia Greenhalgh	Eng	1964-70-74-76-78	17	6	7	4
Penny Grice-Whittaker (Grice)	Eng	1984	4	2	1	1
Caroline Hall	Eng	1992	4	2	0	2
Marley Harris [Spearman] (Baker)	Eng	1960-62-64	6	2	2	2
Dorothea Hastings (Sommerville)	Sco	1958	0	0	0	0
Lady Heathcoat-Amory (Joyce Wethered)	Eng	**1932**	2	1	1	0
Dinah Henson (Oxley)	Eng	1968-70-72-76	11	3	6	2
Helen Holm (Gray)	Sco	1936-38-48	5	3	2	0
Ann Howard (Phillips)	Eng	1956-68	2	0	2	0
Rebecca Hudson	Eng	1998-2000-02	11	5	5	1
Shirley Huggan (Lawson)	Sco	1988	2	1	1	0
Beverley Huke	Eng	1972	2	0	2	0
Ann Irvin	Eng	1962-68-70-76	12	4	7	1
Bridget Jackson	Eng	1958-64-68	8	1	6	1
Patricia Johnson	Eng	1986	4	4	0	0
Sarah Jones	Wal	2002	2	1	1	0
Vikki Laing	Sco	2002	4	2	2	0
Susan Langridge (Armitage)	Eng	1964-66	6	0	5	1
Joan Lawrence	Sco	1964	2	0	2	0
Wilma Leburn (Aitken)	Sco	1982	2	0	2	0
Jenny Lee Smith	Eng	1974-76	3	0	3	0
Kathryn Lumb (Phillips)	Eng	1970-72	2	1	1	0
Mhairi McKay	Sco	1994-96	7	2	3	2
Mary McKenna	Irl	1970-72-74-76-78-80-82-84-86	30	10	16	4
Myra McKinlay	Sco	1994	3	1	2	0
Suzanne McMahon (Cadden)	Sco	1976	4	0	4	0
Sheila Maher (Vaughan)	Eng	1962-64	4	1	2	1
Kathryn Marshall (Imrie)	Sco	1990	4	1	3	0
Vanessa Marvin	Eng	1978	3	1	2	0
Catriona Matthew (Lambert)	Sco	1990-92-94	12	7	4	1
Tegwen Matthews [Thomas] (Perkins)	Wal	1974-76-78-80	14	4	8	2
Moira Milton (Paterson)	Sco	1952	2	1	1	0
Hilary Monaghan	Sco	1998	1	0	1	0
Janice Moodie	Sco	1994-96	8	5	1	2

Curtis Cup Individual Records *continued*

Name		Year	Played	Won	Lost	Halved
Fame More	Eng	2002	1	0	1	0
Becky Morgan	Wal	1998-2000	7	2	5	0
Wanda Morgan	Eng	1932-34-36	6	0	5	1
Joanne Morley	Eng	1992	4	2	0	2
Nicola Murray (Buxton)	Eng	1992	1	0	1	0
Beverley New	Eng	1984	4	1	3	0
Lesley Nicholson	Sco	2000	1	0	0	1
Suzanne O'Brien	Irl	2000	4	3	0	1
Maire O'Donnell	Irl	(1982)	0	0	0	0
Margaret Pickard (Nichol)	Eng	1968-70	5	2	3	0
Diana Plumpton	Eng	1934	2	1	1	0
Elizabeth Pook (Chadwick)	Eng	1966	4	1	3	0
Doris Porter (Park)	Sco	1932	1	0	1	0
Eileen Rose Power (McDaid)	Irl	1994	1	0	1	0
Elaine Ratcliffe	Eng	1996-98	6	3	1	2
Clarrie Reddan (Tiernan)	Irl	1938-48	3	2	1	0
Joan Rennie (Hastings)	Sco	1966	2	0	1	1
Maureen Richmond (Walker)	Sco	1974	4	2	2	0
Jean Roberts	Eng	1962	1	0	1	0
Belle Robertson (McCorkindale)	Sco	1960-66-68-70-72-(74)-(76)-82-86	24	5	12	7
Claire Robinson (Nesbitt)	Irl	1980	3	0	1	2
Vivien Saunders	Eng	1968	4	1	2	1
Susan Shapcott	Eng	1988	4	3	1	0
Linda Simpson (Moore)	Eng	1980	3	1	1	1
Ruth Slark (Porter)	Eng	1960-62-64	7	3	3	1
Anne Smith [Stant] (Willard)	Eng	1976	1	0	1	0
Frances Smith (Stephens)	Eng	1950-52-54-56-58-60-(62)-(72)	11	7	3	1
Kerry Smith	Eng	2002	2	0	2	0
Janet Soulsby	Eng	1982	4	1	2	1
Kirsty Speak	Eng	1994	1	0	1	0
Gillian Stewart	Sco	1980-82	4	1	3	0
Heather Stirling	Sco	2002	4	1	3	0
Karen Stupples	Eng	1996-98	4	2	2	0
Vicki Thomas (Rawlings)	Wal	1982-84-86-88-90-92	13	6	5	2
Muriel Thomson	Sco	1978	3	2	1	0
Jill Thornhill	Eng	1984-86-88	12	6	2	4
Angela Uzielli (Carrick)	Eng	1978	1	0	1	0
Jessie Valentine (Anderson)	Sco	1936-38-50-52-54-56-58	13	4	9	0
Julie Wade	Eng	1988-90-92-94-96	19	6	10	3
Helen Wadsworth	Wal	1990	2	0	2	0
Claire Waite	Eng	1984	4	2	2	0
Mickey Walker	Eng	1972-74	4	3	0	1
Pat Walker	Irl	1934-36-38	6	2	3	1
Verona Wallace-Williamson	Sco	(1938)	0	0	0	0
Nan Wardlaw (Baird)	Sco	1938	1	0	1	0
Enid Wilson	Eng	1932	2	1	1	0
Janette Wright (Robertson)	Sco	1954-56-58-60	8	3	5	0
Phyllis Wylie (Wade)	Eng	1938	1	0	0	1

United States of America

Name	Year	Played	Won	Lost	Halved
Roberta Albers	1968	2	1	0	1
Danielle Ammaccapane	1986	3	0	3	0
Kathy Baker	1982	4	3	0	1
Barbara Barrow	1976	2	1	0	1
Beth Barry	1972-74	5	3	1	1
Emily Bastel	2002	2	0	2	0
Beth Bauer	1998-2000	7	4	3	0
Laura Baugh	1972	4	2	1	1
Leland Beckel	2000	1	0	1	0
Judy Bell	1960-62-(86)-(88)	2	1	1	0
Peggy Kirk Bell (Kirk)	1950	2	1	1	0
Amy Benz	1982	3	2	0	1
Patty Berg	1936-38	4	1	2	1
Barbara Fay Boddie (White)	1964-66	8	7	0	1
Jane Booth (Bastanchury)	1970-72-74-(2000)	12	9	3	0

Name	Year	Played	Won	Lost	Halved
Kellee Booth	1996-98	7	5	2	0
Mary Budke	1974-(**2002**)	3	2	1	0
Robin Burke	1998	3	2	1	0
Brandie Burton	1990	3	3	0	0
Jo Anne Carner (Gunderson)	1958-60-62-64	10	6	3	1
Lori Castillo	1980	3	2	1	0
Leona Cheney (Pressler)	1932-34-36	6	5	1	0
Sis Choate	(**1974**)	0	0	0	0
Jenny Chuasiriporn	1998	3	0	2	1
Peggy Conley	1964-68	6	3	1	2
Mary Ann Cook (Downey)	1956	2	1	1	0
Patricia Cornett	1978-88	4	1	2	1
Brenda Corrie Kuehn	1996-98	7	4	3	0
Jean Crawford (Ashley)	1962-66-68-(**72**)	8	6	2	0
Clifford Ann Creed	1962	2	2	0	0
Grace Cronin (Lenczyk)	1948-50	3	2	1	0
Carolyn Cudone	1956-(**70**)	1	1	0	0
Beth Daniel	1976-78	8	7	1	0
Virginia Dennehy	(**1958**)	0	0	0	0
Virginia Derby Grimes	1998-2000	6	3	1	2
Mary Lou Dill	1968	3	1	1	1
Meredith Duncan	2002	4	3	1	0
Alice Dye	1970	2	1	0	1
Mollie Fankhauser	2002	3	1	2	0
Heather Farr	1984	3	2	1	0
Jane Fassinger	1970	1	0	1	0
Mary Lena Faulk	1954	2	1	1	0
Carol Sorensen Flenniken (Sorensen)	1964-66	8	6	1	1
Edith Flippin (Quier)	(**1954**)-(**56**)	0	0	0	0
Amy Fruhwirth	1992	4	0	1	3
Kim Gardner	1986	3	1	1	1
Charlotte Glutting	1934-36-38	5	3	1	1
Vicki Goetze	1990-92	8	4	2	2
Brenda Goldsmith	1978-80	4	2	2	0
Aniela Goldthwaite	1934-(**52**)	1	0	1	0
Joanne Goodwin	1960	2	1	1	0
Mary Hafeman	1980	2	1	0	1
Shelley Hamkin	1968-70	8	3	3	2
Penny Hammel	1984	3	1	1	1
Nancy Hammer (Hager)	1970	2	1	1	0
Cathy Hanlon	1982	3	2	1	0
Beverley Hanson	1950	2	2	0	0
Tracy Hanson	1992	3	1	2	0
Patricia Harbottle (Lesser)	1954-56	3	2	1	0
Leigh Anne Hardin	2002	3	1	2	0
Helen Hawes	(**1964**)	0	0	0	0
Kathryn Hemphill	1938	1	0	0	1
Helen Hicks	1932	2	1	1	0
Carolyn Hill	1978	2	0	0	2
Cindy Hill	1970-74-76-78	14	5	6	3
Opel Hill	1932-34-36	6	2	3	1
Marion Hollins	(**1932**)	0	0	0	0
Hilary Homeyer	2000	4	3	0	1
Dana Howe	1984	3	1	1	1
Juli Inkster	1982	4	4	0	0
Maria Jemsek	1996	3	0	2	1
Angela Jerman	2002	3	2	1	0
Ann Casey Johnstone	1958-60-62	4	3	1	0
Mae Murray Jones (Murray)	1952	1	0	1	0
Wendy Kaupp	1994	2	0	2	0
Stephanie Keever	2000	4	2	2	0
Caroline Keggi	1988	3	0	2	1
Tracy Kerdyk	1988	4	2	1	1
Cristie Kerr	1996	3	1	1	1
Kandi Kessler	1986	3	1	1	1
Dorothy Kielty	1948-50	4	4	0	0
Dorothy Kirby	1948-50-52-54	7	4	3	0
Martha Kirouac (Wilkinson)	1970-72	8	5	3	0
Emilee Klein	1994	4	3	1	0
Nancy Knight (Lopez)	1976	2	2	0	0

Curtis Cup Individual Records *continued*

Name	Year	Played	Won	Lost	Halved
Kelli Kuehne	1996	3	2	1	0
Martha Lang	1992-(**96**)	3	2	0	1
Bonnie Lauer	1974	4	2	2	0
Sarah Le Brun Ingram	1992-94-96	7	2	4	1
Marjorie Lindsay	1952	2	1	1	0
Patricia Lucey (O'Sullivan)	1952	1	0	1	0
Mari McDougall	1982	2	2	0	0
Jill McGill	1994	4	1	1	2
Barbara McIntire	1958-60-62-64-66-72-(**76**)	16	6	6	4
Lucile Mann (Robinson)	1934	1	0	1	0
Debbie Massey	1974-76	5	5	0	0
Marion Miley	1938	2	1	0	1
Dottie Mochrie (Pepper)	1986	3	0	2	1
Evelyn Monsted	(**1968**)	0	0	0	0
Terri Moody	1980	2	1	0	1
Laura Myerscough	2002	3	3	0	0
Karen Noble	1990	4	2	2	0
Judith Oliver	1978-80-82-(**92**)	8	5	1	2
Maureen Orcutt	1932-34-36-38	8	5	3	0
Joanne Pacillo	1984	3	1	1	1
Estelle Page (Lawson)	1938-48	4	3	1	0
Katie Peterson	1990	3	3	0	0
Margaret Platt	1990	2	0	2	0
Frances Pond (Stebbins)	(**1938**)	0	0	0	0
Ellen Port	1994-96	6	4	2	0
Dorothy Germain Porter	1950-(**66**)	2	1	0	1
Phyllis Preuss	1962-64-66-68-70-(**84**)	15	10	4	1
Betty Probasco	(**1982**)	0	0	0	0
Mildred Prunaret	(**1960**)	0	0	0	0
Polly Riley	1948-50-52-54-56-58-(**62**)	10	5	5	0
Jo Jo Robertson	1998	2	0	2	0
Barbara Romack	1954-56-58	5	3	2	0
Jody Rosenthal	1984	3	2	0	1
Anne Sander [Welts] [Decker] (Quast)	1958-60-62-66-68-74-84-90	22	11	7	4
Cindy Scholefield	1988	3	0	3	0
Cindy Schreyer	1986	3	1	2	0
Kathleen McCarthy Scrivner (McCarthy)	1986-88	6	2	3	1
Carol Semple Thompson	1974-76-80-82-90-92-94-96-**98**-2000-02	33	16	13	4
Leslie Shannon	1986-88-90-92	9	1	6	2
Patty Sheehan	1980	4	4	0	0
Pearl Sinn	1988	2	1	1	0
Grace De Moss Smith (De Moss)	1952-54	3	1	2	0
Lancy Smith	1972-78-80-82-84-(**94**)	16	7	5	4
Margaret Smith	1956	2	2	0	0
Stephanie Sparks	1994	2	0	2	0
Hollis Stacy	1972	2	0	1	1
Claire Stancik (Doran)	1952-54	4	4	0	0
Angela Stanford	2000	4	1	2	1
Judy Street (Eller)	1960	2	2	0	0
Louise Suggs	1948	2	0	1	1
Courtney Swaim	2002	4	3	1	0
Nancy Roth Syms (Roth)	1964-66-76-(**80**)	9	3	5	1
Noreen Uihlein	1978	3	1	1	1
Virginia Van Wie	1932-34	4	3	0	1
Glenna Collett Vare (Collett)	1932-(**34**)-36-38-48-(**50**)	7	4	2	1
Wendy Ward	1994	3	1	2	0
Jane Weiss (Nelson)	1956	1	0	1	0
Robin Weiss	1990-92-2000	7	4	2	1
Donna White (Horton)	1976	2	2	0	0
Mary Anne Widman	1984	3	2	1	0
Kimberley Williams	1986	3	0	3	0
Helen Sigel Wilson (Sigel)	1950-66-(**78**)	2	0	2	0
Joyce Ziske	1954	1	0	1	0

Women's World Amateur Team Championship for the Espirito Santo Trophy

1964	France	United States	St Germain	588
1966	United States	Canada	Mexico	580
1968	United States	Australia	Melbourne	616
1970	United States	France	Madrid	598
1972	United States	France	Buenos Aires	583
1974	United States	GB&I, South Africa	Dominican Republic	620
1976	United States	France	Vilamoura, Portugal	605
1978	Australia	Canada	Fiji	596
1980	United States	Australia	Pinehurst, USA	588
1982	United States	New Zealand	Geneva, Switzerland	579
1984	United States	France	Hong Kong	585
1986	Spain	France	Caracas, Venezuela	580
1988	United States	Sweden	Drottningholm, Sweden	587
1990	United States	New Zealand	Christchurch, New Zealand	585
1992	Spain	GB&I	Vancouver, Canada	588
1994	United States	Korea	Paris, France	569
1996	Korea	Italy	Manila, Philippines	438
1998	United States	Italy	Santiago, Chile	558
2000	France	Korea	Sporting Club, Berlin	580

2002 *at Saujana, Kuala Lumpur* (Palm Course 6147–73; Bunga Raya Course 5994–73)
(Discarded scores in brackets)

1   AUSTRALIA*   578
(Katherine Hull, Vicky Uwland, Lindsey Wright; captain: Liz Cavill)
[won on third score of last round]

2   THAILAND   578
(Aree Song Wongluekiet, Naree Song Wongluekiet, Titiya Plucksataporn)

3   SPAIN   579
(N Clau, T Elosegui, M Prieto)

4   GERMANY   581
(M Eberl, P Odefey, D Simon)

5   USA   584
(E Bastel, B Lucidi, L Myerscough)

6   JAPAN   587
(K Furuya, A Mujasato, I Narita)

    KOREA   587
(Joo Mi Kim, Sung Ah Yim, Won Mi Park)

8T GREAT BRITAIN & IRELAND   588
(Becky Brewerton, Emma Duggleby, Heather Stirling)

    ITALY   588
(T Calzavara, C Grignolo, F Piovano)

    SWEDEN   588
(M Parmlid, K Sjodin, H Svensson)

11 Finland, 589; 12 Canada, Colombia, 593; 14 Taipei, 594; 15 Denmark, France, 597; 17 Mexico, 598; 18 Norway, 600; 19 Netherlands, 601; 20 New Zealand, 603; 21 Austria, 611; 22 Brazil, 615; 23 Argentina, Philippines, 616; 25 Switzerland, 620; 26 Chile; 27 Belgium; 28 Hong Kong, China; 29 Malaysia, South Africa; 31 Portugal; 32 Guatemala; 33 Russian Federation; 34 Slovakia; 35 Puerta Rico; 36 Bolivia; 37 Greece; 38 Croatia; 39 Islamic Republic of Iran.

Individual leader: Aree Song Wongluekiet (Tha), 288

Commonwealth Tournament (Instituted 1959, played every four years)

1959	Great Britain	St Andrews	1983	Australia	Glendale, Edmonton, Canada
1963	Great Britain	Royal Melbourne, Australia	1987	Canada	Christchurch, New Zealand
1967	Great Britain	Ancaster, Ontario, Canada	1991	Great Britain	Northumberland, England
1971	Great Britain	Hamilton, New Zealand	1995	Australia	Royal Sydney, Australia
1975	Great Britain	Ganton, England	1999	Australia	Marine Drive, Vancouver, Canada
1979	Canada	Lake Karrinup, Perth, Australia			

Women's European Amateur Team Championship

1967	England	France	Penina, Portugal	1985	England	Italy	Stavanger, Norway
1969	France	England	Tylosand, Sweden	1987	Sweden	Wales	Turnberry, Scotland
1971	England	France	Ganton, England	1989	France	England	Pals, Spain
1973	England	France	Brussels, Belgium	1991	England	Sweden	Wentworth, England
1975	France	Spain	Paris, France	1993	England	Spain	Royal Haagshe
1977	England	Spain	Sotogrande, Spain	1995	Spain	Scotland	Milan, Italy
1979	Ireland	Germany	Hermitage, Ireland	1997	Sweden	Scotland	Nordcenter, Finland
1981	Sweden	France	Troia, Portugal	1999	France	England	St Germain, France
1983	Ireland	England	Waterloo, Belgium	2001	Sweden	Spain	Pontevedra, Spain

Vagliano Trophy – Great Britain & Ireland v Continent of Europe

1959	GB & I	12–3	Wentworth	1981	Europe	14–10	P de Hierro
1961	GB & I	8–7	Villa d'Este	1983	GB & I	14–10	Woodhall Spa
1963	GB & I	20–10	Muirfield	1985	GB & I	14–10	Hamburg
1965	Europe	17–13	Cologne	1987	GB & I	15–9	The Berkshire
1967	Europe	15½–14½	Lytham	1989	GB & I	14½–9½	Venice
1969	Europe	16–14	Chantilly	1991	GB & I	13½–10½	Nairn
1971	GB & I	17½–12½	Worplesdon	1993	GB & I	13½–10½	Morfontaine
1973	GB & I	20–10	Eindhoven	1995	Europe	14–10	Ganton
1975	GB & I	13½–10½	Muirfield	1997	Europe	14–10	Halmstad
1977	GB & I	15½–8½	Malmo	1999	Europe	13–11	North Berwick
1979	Halved	12–12	R Porthcawl	2001	Europe	7–5	Venice

European Club Cup

2002

1	Germany (Bergisch-Land GC)	144-144-151—440
2	France (RCF La Boulle)	144-148-149—441
3	France (Saint Cloud)	143-153-154—450

Women's Home Internationals

2002 at The Berkshire

Ireland beat England	5 matches to 4	Wales beat England	5 matches to 4
Scotland beat Wales	5 matches to 4	England beat Wales	6½ matches to 2½
England beat Scotland	5½ matches to 3½	Scotland beat Ireland	6 matches to 3

Result: England 2; Scotland 2; Ireland 1; Wales 1

1948	England	R Lytham and St Annes
1949	Scotland	Harlech
1950	Scotland	Newcastle Co Down
1951	Scotland	Broadstone
1952	Scotland	Troon
1953	England	Porthcawl
1954T	England/Scotland	Ganton, Scotland
1955	England	Western Gailes
1956	Scotland	Sunningdale
1957	Scotland	Troon
1958	England	Hunstanton
1959	England	Hoylake
1960	England	Gullane
1961	Scotland	Portmarnock
1962	Scotland	Porthcawl
1963	England	Formby
1964	England	Troon
1965	England	Portrush
1966	England	Woodhall Spa
1967	England	Sunningdale
1968	England	Porthcawl
1969T	England/Scotland	Western Gailes
1970	England	Killarney
1971	England	Longniddry

1972	England	R Lytham and St Annes
1973	England	Harlech
1974T	England/Scotland/Ireland	Sandwich, Princes
1975	England	Newport
1976	England	Troon
1977	England	Cork
1978	England	Moortown
1979T	Scotland/Ireland	Harlech
1980	Ireland	Cruden Bay
1981	Scotland	Portmarnock
1982	England	Burnham and Barrow
1983	*Matches abandoned due to weather*	
1984	England	Gullane
1985	England	Waterville
1986	Ireland	Whittington Barracks
1987	England	Ashburnham
1988	Scotland	Kilmarnock (Barassie)
1989	England	Westport
1990	Scotland	Hunstanton
1991	Scotland	Aberdovey
1992	England	Hamilton
1993	England	Dublin

1994 at Huddersfield, Yorkshire

England beat Ireland	6½ matches to 2½
Scotland beat Wales	8½ matches to ½
England beat Wales	8 matches to 1
Scotland halved with Ireland	4½ matches to 4½
England beat Scotland	6 matches to 3
Ireland beat Wales	5½ matches to 3½

Result: England 3; Scotland 1½; Ireland 1½; Wales 0

1995 at Wrexham, Clwyd

England beat Scotland	6 matches to 3
Ireland halved with Wales	4½ matches to 4½
Ireland beat Scotland	5 matches to 4
Wales beat England	5 matches to 4
England beat Ireland	9 matches to 0
Scotland beat Wales	5 matches to 4

Result: England 2; Wales 1½; Ireland 1½; Scotland 1

1996 at Longniddry

Scotland beat Ireland	5½ matches to 3½
England beat Wales	6 matches to 3
Scotland beat Wales	5 matches to 4
England beat Ireland	6 matches to 3
England beat Scotland	5 matches to 4
Ireland beat Wales	5½ matches to 3½

Result: England 3; Scotland 2; Ireland 1; Wales 0

1997 at Lahinch, Ireland

Ireland beat Wales	6½ matches to 2½
England beat Scotland	6½ matches to 2½
England beat Ireland	6 matches to 3
Scotland beat Wales	5½ matches to 3½
England beat Wales	5 matches to 4
Ireland beat Scotland	7 matches to 2

Result: England 3; Ireland 2; Scotland 1; Wales 0

1998 at Burnham & Berrow

Ireland beat Wales	6 matches to 3
England beat Scotland	6 matches to 3
England beat Ireland	5 matches to 4
Ireland halved with Scotland	4½ matches to 4½
England beat Wales	6½ matches to 2½
Scotland halved with Wales	4½ matches to 4½

Result: England 3; Ireland 1½; Scotland 1; Wales ½

1999 at Royal Dornoch

Ireland beat Scotland	5 matches to 4
England halved with Wales	4½ matches to 4½
Wales beat Ireland	7½ matches to 1½
England beat Scotland	5 matches to 4
England beat Ireland	7 matches to 2
Wales beat Scotland	5½ matches to 3½

Result: Wales 2½; England 2½; Ireland 1; Scotland 0
(Wales won on individual games countback 17½–16½)

2000 at Royal St David's

Ireland halved with Wales	4½ matches to 4½
England beat Scotland	6 matches to 3
Wales beat Scotland	8 matches to 1
England beat Ireland	8 matches to 1
Ireland beat Scotland	5 matches to 4
England beat Wales	5 matches to 4

Result: England 3; Wales 1½; Ireland 1½; Scotland 0

2001 at Carlow

Ireland beat Wales	6 matches to 3
England beat Scotland	5½ matches to 3½
Wales halved with Scotland	4½ matches to 4½
England beat Ireland	5½ matches to 3½
England beat Wales	5 matches to 4
Ireland beat Scotland	5½ matches to 3½

Result: England 3; Ireland 2; Scotland & Wales ½

England and Wales Ladies County Championship

1908	Lancashire	1949	Surrey	1976	Staffordshire
1909	Surrey	1950	Yorkshire	1977	Essex
1910	Cheshire	1951	Lancashire	1978	Glamorgan
1911	Cheshire	1952	Lancashire	1979	Essex
1912	Cheshire	1953	Surrey	1980	Lancashire
1913	Surrey	1954	Warwickshire	1981	Glamorgan
1920	Middlesex	1955	Surrey	1982	Surrey
1921	Surrey	1956	Kent	1983	Surrey
1922	Surrey	1957	Middlesex	1984	Surrey/Yorkshire
1923	Surrey	1958	Lancashire	1985	Surrey
1924	Surrey	1959	Middlesex	1986	Glamorgan
1925	Surrey	1960	Lancashire	1987	Lancashire
1926	Surrey	1961	Middlesex	1988	Surrey
1927	Yorkshire	1962	Staffordshire	1989	Cheshire
1928	Cheshire	1963	Warwickshire	1990	Cheshire
1929	Yorkshire	1964	Lancashire	1991	Glamorgan
1930	Surrey	1965	Staffordshire	1992	Hampshire
1931	Middlesex	1966	Lancashire	1993	Lancashire
1932	Cheshire	1967	Lancashire	1994	Staffordshire
1933	Yorkshire	1968	Surrey	1995	Hampshire
1934	Surrey	1969	Lancashire	1996	Cheshire
1935	Essex	1970	Yorkshire	1997	Surrey
1936	Surrey	1971	Kent	1998	Yorkshire
1937	Surrey	1972	Kent	1999	Yorkshire
1938	Lancashire	1973	Northumberland	2000	Yorkshire
1947	Surrey	1974	Surrey	2001	Yorkshire
1948	Yorkshire	1975	Glamorgan		

2002 *at Moseley*

1 Lancashire; 2 Leicestershire & Rutland; 3 Kent; 4 Glamorgan

Scottish Ladies County Championship

1992	Dunbartonshire & Argyll	1996	East Lothian	2000	Northern Counties
1993	East Lothian	1997	Dunbartonshire & Argyll	2001	Stirlingshire &
1994	East Lothian	1998	East Lothian		Clackmannanshire
1995	Fife	1999	East Lothian		

2002 *at Portpatrick (Dunskey)*

1 Stirling & Clackmannan, 2 Aberdeen, 3 Dunbartonshire & Argyll, 4 Borders

Scottish Ladies Foursomes

1992	Haggs Castle	1996	Hilton Park	2000	Windyhill
1993	North Berwick	1997	Stirling	2001	Stirling
1994	Turnberry	1998	Prestonfield		
1995	Gullane	1999	Dunblane New		

2002 *at Alloa*

Ladies Panmure, Barry (Kathleen Sutherland, Susan Arbuckle)

Welsh Ladies Team Championship

1992	Whitchurch	1996	R. St Davids	2000	Pennard
1993	Pennard	1997	St Pierre	2001	Whitchurch
1994	St Pierre	1998	Wrexham		
1995	R. St Davids	1999	Pennard		

2002 *at Abergele*

Abergele

(Becky Brewerton, Glenys Jones, Pat Runcie, Karen Walford, Karen Weatherley)

Other Women's Amateur Tournaments

Lady Astor Salver (Inaugurated 1951) at *The Berkshire*

1951	Jeanne Bisgood	1964	Marley Spearman	1977	Angela Uzielli	1990T	Joanne Morley,
1952	Jeanne Bisgood	1965	Marley Spearman	1978	Mary Everard		Julie Wade
1953	Jeanne Bisgood	1966	Angela Bonallack	1979	Julia Greenhalgh	1991	EJ Smith
1954	Jean Donald	1967	Mary Everard	1980	Jane Lock	1992	Lisa Walton
1955	Elizabeth Price	1968	Mary Everard	1981	Angela Uzielli	1993	S Lambert
1956T	J Barton,	1969	Julia Greenhalgh	1982	*Abandoned*	1994	S Lambert
	Elizabeth Price	1970	B Whitehead	1983	Linda Denison-	1995	J Oliver
1957	Angela Ward	1971	Angela Uzielli		Pender Bayman	1996	S Gallagher
1958	Angela Ward	1972	Jill Thornhill	1984	Linda Bayman	1997	J Lamb
	Bonallack	1973T	Linda Denison-	1985	Helen Wadsworth	1998	R Morgan
1959	Elizabeth Price		Pender, Angela	1986	Caroline Pierce	1999	*Not played*
1960	Angela Bonallack		Uzielli	1987	Vicki Thomas	2000T	C Court,
1961	Angela Bonallack	1974	Cathy Barclay	1988	Jill Thornhill		K Taylor
1962	Ruth Porter	1975	Jill Thornhill	1989	Sarah Sutton	2001	E Pilgrim
1963	Ruth Porter	1976	Heather Clifford				

2002

No result: second round abandoned – rain and flood. After 18 holes, leaders were: Red Course: Kerry Smith (Waterlooville) 67; Blue Course: Lynn Kenny (Stirling University) 71

Bridget Jackson Bowl (Inaugurated 1982) at *Handsworth*

1982	Julie Brown (Leek)	1990	Susan Elliott (Henbury)	1996	Rebecca Hudson (Wheatley)
1983	Julie Brown (Leek)	1991	Fiona Edmund (Frinton-on-	1997	Kate MacIntosh (Aus)
1984	Trish Johnson (Pyle & Kenfig)		Sea)	1998	Claire Dowling (Copt Heath)
1985	Trish Johnson (Pyle & Kenfig)	1992	Fiona Brown (Heswall)	1999	Shelley McKevitt (Reading)
1986	Julia Hill (Hazel Grove)	1993	Simone Morgan (Hearsall)	2000	Rebecca Hudson (Wheatley)
1987	Vicki Thomas (Pennard)	1994	Kirsty Speak (Clitheroe)	2001	Laura Wright (Stanton-on-the-
1988	Vicki Thomas (Pennard)	1995	Karen Stupples (Royal Cinque		Wolds)
1989	Helen Dobson (Seacroft)		Ports)	2002	Claire Dowling (Copt Heath)

Hampshire Rose (Inaugurated 1973) at *North Hants*

1973	Carole Redford	1979	Carol Larkin	1987	Jill Thornhill	1995	J Oliver
1974	Pru Riddiford	1980	Beverley New	1988	Jill Thornhill	1996	K Stupples
1975	Vanessa Marvin	1981	Jillian Nicolson	1989	Alison MacDonald	1997	S Sanderson
1976T	Heather Clifford,	1982	Jill Thornhill	1990	S Keogh	1998	C Court
	Wendy Pithers	1983	J Pool	1991	K Egford	1999	C Court
1977	Julia Greenhalgh	1984	Carole Redford	1992	Angela Uzielli	2000	K Fisher
1978T	Heather Clifford		Caldwell	1993	C Hourihane	2001	K Smith
	Glyn-Jones,	1985	Angela Uzielli	1994T	K Shepherd,	2002	K Smith
	Vanessa Marvin	1986	Claire Hourihane		K Egford		

Liphook Scratch Cup (Inaugurated 1992) at *Liphook*

1992T	T Kernan,	1994	S Sharpe	1997	E Weeks	2000	K Smith
	K Shepherd	1995	K Shepherd	1998	K Knowles	2001	N Timmins
1993	K Egford	1996	K Shepherd	1999	R Prout	2002	F More

Roehampton Gold Cup (Inaugurated 1926) at Roehampton

1926	Mrs WM McNair	1953	Jeanne Bisgood	1973T	Ann Irvin,	1986T	Katherine
1927	Molly Gourlay	1954	Isabella Bromley		Carole Redford		Harridge,
1928	Cecil Leitch		Davenport	1974	Lyn Harrold		Patricia Johnson
1929	I Doxford	1955	Louisa Abrahams	1975T	Wendy Pithers,	1987	Diane Barnard
1930	Enid Wilson	1956	Shirley Allom		Carole Redford	1988	Alison Johns
1931	V Lamb	1957	Mary Roberts	1976T	Ann Irvin,	1989T	Catriona Lambert,
1932	Mrs A Gold	1958	Patricia Moore		Vanessa Marvin		Cathy Panton
1933	A Ramsden	1959	Mavis Glidewell	1977	Angela Uzielli	1990	Kathryn Imrie
1934	J Hamilton	1960	Elizabeth Price	1978T	Carole Redford	1991	K Hurley
1935	Pam Barton	1961	Louisa Abrahams		Caldwell,	1992	Mrs K Marshall
1936	B Newell	1962	Louisa Abrahams		Belle Robertson	1993	Beverley New
1937	Pam Barton	1963	Ruth Porter	1979	Belle Robertson	1994	C Hall
1938	Pam Barton	1964	RC Archer	1980	Angela Bonallack	1995	S Gallagher
1939	Pam Barton	1965	Marley Spearman	1981	Belle Robertson	1996T	Joanne Morley,
1940–42	Not played	1966	Gwen Brandon	1982	Belle Robertson		J Soulsby
1948	Maureen Ruttle	1967	Ann Irvin	1983T	Beverley New,	1997T	J Forbes, J Oliver
1949	Frances Stephens	1968	Ann Irvin		Vicki Thomas	1998T	K Lunn, J Head
1950	Maureen Ruttle	1969	Ann Irvin	1984	Beverley New	1999	K Taylor
	Garrett	1970	Mary Everard	1985	Vicki Thomas	2000	S Forster
1951	Jeanne Bisgood	1971	Beverly Huke			2001	T Loveys
1952	Jeanne Bisgood	1972	Ann Irvin			2002	F More

St Rule Trophy (Inaugurated 1984) at St Andrews

1984	P Hammel (USA)	149	1990	A Sörenstam	228	1996	A Laing	227
1985	K Imrie	151	1991	A Rose	237	1997	K Rostron	217
1986	T Hammond	153	1992	M Wright	222	1998	N Clau[1]	154 (36)
1987	J Morley	153	1993	C Lambert	215	1999	L Nicholson	227
1988	C Middleton	152	1994	C Matthew	217	2000	V Laing*	153 (36)
1989	C Middleton	232	1995	M Hjörth	220	2001	A Coffey	221

[1] At 16 years, the youngest ever winner

2002

1	Heather Stirling (Bridge of Allan)	71-71-76—218
2	Alison Coffey (Warrenpoint)	76-70-75—221
3	Lynn Kenny (Dunblane)	72-75-75—222

Sherry Cup at Soto Grande, Cadiz, Spain

1991	Caterina Quintarelli	1995	Maria Hjörth	1999	Martina Eberl
1992	Estafania Knuth	1996	Maria Hjörth	2000	Martina Eberl
1993	Ana F Johansson	1997	Marieke Zelsman	2001	Carmen Alonso Fuentes
1994	Ada O'Sullivan	1998	Nicole Stillia		

2002

1	Kathryn Evans (Wal)	74-72-72—218
2	Carmen Alonso (Esp)	75-75-74—224
3	Ursula Tuuti (Fin)	74-76-75—225

Women's Foursomes Events

London Ladies Foursomes

1992	Chelmsford	1996	The Berkshire	2000	Worplesdon
1993	Knebworth	1997	The Berkshire	2001	Porter's Park
1994	Knebworth	1998	The Berkshire	2002	Porter's Park
1995	The Berkshire	1999	The Berkshire		

Mothers and Daughters Foursomes *at Royal Mid-Surrey*

1992	Mrs P Carrick and Mrs A Uzielli
1993	Mrs P Carrick and Mrs A Uzielli
1994	Mrs P Carrick and Mrs A Uzielli
1995T	Mrs P Carrick and Mrs A Uzielli
	Mrs P Huntley and Miss J Huntley
1996T	Mrs A Uzielli and Miss C Uzielli
	Mrs E Boatman and Miss A Boatman
	Mrs S Lines and Miss K Lines

1997	Mrs S Lines and Miss K Lines
1998	Mrs H Joyce and Miss C Joyce
1999	Mrs E Boatman and Miss A Boatman
2000	Lady Bonallack and Mrs G Beasley
2001	Mrs and Miss Gay
2002	Mrs J Thornhill and Mrs C Weeks

Curtis Cup for St Andrews in 2008

For the first time the Curtis Cup match between Great Britain and Ireland and America is to be played at the home of golf. The Old course at St Andrews will be the venue for the match in 2008.

The Cup match has been played in Scotland on four previous occasions – 1936 at Gleneagles Hotel, 1952 at the Muirfield course of the Honourable Company of Edinburgh Golfers, in 1972 at Western Gailes and in 1984 again at Muirfield.

The Walker Cup, the men's amateur equivalent, has been played at St Andrews on eight occasions.

Women's Regional Amateur Championships

Aberdeenshire Ladies

1993	G Penny	1998	L Urquhart
1994	C Hunter	1999	L Urquhart
1995	J Matthews	2000	S Wood
1996	S Wood	2001	S Wood
1997	K Moggach	2002	S Wood

Angus Ladies

1993	M Summers	1998	L Fenton
1994	M Summers	1999	L Fenton
1995	K Sutherland	2000	A Ramsay
1996	S Simpson	2001	K Sutherland
1997	S Raitt	2002	D Dewar

Ayrshire Ladies

1993	M Wilson	1998	S Lambie
1994	A Gemmill	1999	S Lambie
1995	R Kennedy	2000	R Kennedy
1996	A Gemmill	2001	L Keohone
1997	A Gemmill	2002	S Lambie

Bedfordshire Ladies

1993	S Cormack	1998	S Cormack
1994	T Gale	1999	E Bruce
1995	A Bradley	2000	C Hoskin
1996	C Hoskin	2001	P Gale
1997	J Faris	2002	B Quinn

Berkshire Ladies

1993	A Uzielli	1998	S Sanderson
1994	J Guntrip	1999	L Webb
1995	A Uzielli	2000	L Webb
1996	S Sanderson	2001	E Cooper
1997	L Meredith	2002	L Webb

Border Counties Ladies

1993	D Turnbull	1998	A Hunter
1994	W Wells	1999	J Anderson
1995	A Fleming	2000	M Pow
1996	K Inkpen	2001	M Pow
1997	J Anderson	2002	J Anderson

Buckinghamshire Ladies

1993	C Watson	1998	C Watson
1994	P Williamson	1999	C Watson
1995	C Dowling	2000	C Watson
1996	C Watson	2001	S Mace
1997	C Watson	2002	C Watson

Caernarfonshire and Anglesey Ladies

1993	A Lewis	1998	F Vaughan-Thomas
1994	C Thomas	1999	K Evans
1995	L Davies	2000	L Davies
1996	L Davies	2001	L Davies
1997	F Vaughan-Thomas	2002	K Evans

Cambridgeshire and Huntingdonshire Ladies

1993	T Eakin	1998	J Walter
1994	T Eakin	1999	R Farrow
1995	P Parker	2000	J Walter
1996	J Walter	2001	P Parker
1997	J Walter	2002	J Walter

Cheshire Ladies

1993	J Morley	1998	E Ratcliffe
1994	F Brown	1999	R Adby
1995	E Ratcliffe	2000	O Briggs
1996	L Dermott	2001	R Adby
1997	E Ratcliffe	2002	S Beardsall

Cornwall Ladies

1993	J Ryder	1998	G Dowling
1994	E Fields	1999	G Dowling
1995	L Simpson	2000	G Dowling
1996	L Simpson	2001	S Sanderson
1997	L Simpson	2002	S Sanderson

Cumbria Ladies

1993	J Currie	1998	A Wood
1994	J Currie	1999	J Blaydes
1995	J Viles	2000	J Viles
1996	R Bruce	2001	J Blades
1997	J Blaydes	2002	E Woodhouse

Denbighshire and Flintshire Ladies

1993	S Lovatt	1998	B Jones
1994	A Donne	1999	R Brewerton
1995	S Lovatt	2000	S Mountford
1996	B Jones	2001	J Nicholson
1997	R Brewerton	2002	*Cancelled*

Derbyshire Ladies

1993	L Holmes	1998	L Shaw
1994	L Walters	1999	L Walters
1995	L Holmes	2000	R Wood
1996	L Shaw	2001	L Shaw
1997	L Walters	2002	R Wood

Devon Ladies

1993	K Tebbet	1998	C Copping
1994	K Tebbet	1999	K Clarke
1995	J Roberts	2000	K Clarke
1996	R Cirin	2001	K Clarke
1997	J Roberts	2002	E Frayn

Dorset Ladies

1993	S Sanderson	1998	A Monk
1994	W Russell	1999	S Phillips
1995	A Monk	2000	J Topp
1996	C Brown	2001	C Jones
1997	A Monk	2002	C Jones

Dumfriesshire Ladies

1993	G Adamson	1998	D MacDonald
1994	F Watson	1999	L Wells
1995	D Douglas	2000	L Wells
1996	C Adamson	2001	K Wells
1997	L Wells	2002	F Macgregor

Dunbartonshire and Argyll Ladies

1993	M McKinlay	1998	A Laing
1994	V Melvin	1999	V Melvin
1995	A Laing	2000	V Melvin
1996	V Melvin	2001	A Laing
1997	K Burns	2002	C McNeil

Durham Ladies

1993	L Keers	1998	P Dobson
1994	P Dobson	1999	L Keers
1995	K Lee	2000	P Simpson
1996	A Dobson	2001	A Dobson
1997	K Lee	2002	D Roseberry

East Lothian Ladies

1993	S McMester	1998	S McEwan
1994	C Matthew	1999	L Nicholson
1995	H Monaghan	2000	L Nicholson
1996	H Monaghan	2001	J Smith
1997	S McMaster	2002	S McMaster

Eastern Division Ladies (Scotland)

1993	A Rose	1998	F Lockhart
1994	J Ford	1999	L Kenny
1995	L Nicholson	2000	H Stirling
1996	H Monaghan	2001	H Stirling
1997	S Grant	2002	H Stirling

Essex Ladies

1993	T Poulton	1998	M Williams
1994	T Wilson	1999	E Gibson
1995	G Scase	2000	S Smith
1996	G Scase	2001	J Dartford
1997	S Barber	2002	J Dartford

Fife County Ladies

1993	K Milne	1998	K Milne
1994	L Bennett	1999	L Fury
1995	K Milne	2000	E Moffat
1996	E Moffat	2001	L Kenney
1997	J Hall	2002	S Millar

Galloway Ladies

1993	H Nesbit	1998	S McMurtrie
1994	C Meldrum	1999	S Booth
1995	T Dodds	2000	S McMurtrie
1996	A Cairns	2001	S McMurtrie
1997	S McMurtrie	2002	S McMurtrie

Glamorgan County Ladies

1993	V Thomas	1998	P Chugg
1994	V Thomas	1999	K Phillips
1995	J Thomas	2000	V Thomas
1996	V Thomas	2001	A Highgate
1997	V Thomas	2002	A Highgate

Gloucestershire Ladies

1993	C Hamilton	1998	C Lipscombe
1994	K Hamilton	1999	N Lumb
1995	N Sutton	2000	L Occleshaw
1996	J Clingan	2001	C Lipscombe
1997	C Lipscombe	2002	Z Lennox

Hampshire Ladies

1993	K Egford	1998	E Weekes
1994	K Egford	1999	K Taylor
1995	H Wheeler	2000	K Taylor
1996	C Stirling	2001	N Booth
1997	H Wheeler	2002	K Smith

Hertfordshire Ladies

1993	C Hawkes	1998	M Allen
1994	J Oliver	1999	H Skinner
1995	J Oliver	2000	K Evans
1996	K Evans	2001	S Matthews
1997	K Evans	2002	K Hutcherson

Kent Ladies

1993	M Sutton	1998	K Stupples
1994	M Sutton	1999	N Timmins
1995	C Caldwell	2000	D Masters
1996	K Stupples	2001	N Timmins
1997	S Butchers	2002	D Masters

Lanarkshire Ladies County

1993	M Hughes	1998	F Prior
1994	J Gardner	1999	F Prior
1995	R Rankin	2000	A Bell
1996	A Prentice	2001	C Queen
1997	L Lloyd	2002	C Queen

Lancashire Ladies

1993	K Rostron	1998	A Murray
1994	G Nutter	1999	K Fisher
1995	G Nutter	2000	C Blackshaw
1996	A Murray	2001	K Fisher
1997	G Nutter	2002	K Fisher

Leicestershire and Rutland Ladies

1993	M Page	1998	C Gay
1994	M Page	1999	J Morris
1995	C Gay	2000	H Lowe
1996	H Lowe	2001	C Gay
1997	J Morris	2002	R Rowlands

Lincolnshire Ladies

1993	R Broughton	1998	M Willerton
1994	S Brook	1999	S Hunter
1995	A Thompson	2000	S Walker
1996	M Willerton	2001	N Chantry
1997	A Thompson	2002	S Walker

Middlesex Ladies

1993	L Housman	1998	J Sadler
1994	M Henderson	1999	P Costello
1995	J Sadler	2000	D McCormack
1996	P Ramchand	2001	C Irons
1997	J Barnett	2002	P Ranchard

Midland Ladies

1993	R Bolas	1998	N Lawrenson
1994	J Morris	1999	S Pidgeon
1995	K Edwards	2000	S Walker
1996	S Gallagher	2001	K Hanwell
1997	R Bailey	2002	S Walker

Midlothian Ladies

1993	E Bruce	1998	V Laing
1994	E Bruce	1999	C Williamson
1995	P Silver	2000	B Murphy
1996	M Quigley	2001	F Hunter
1997	P Silver	2002	B Murphy

Mid-Wales Ladies

1993	A Owen	1998	A Hubbard
1994	G Gibb	1999	S Hughes
1995	J James	2000	J Dyer
1996	L Davies	2001	J Dyer
1997	K Humphries	2002	D Tuffnell

Monmouthshire Ladies

1993	S Musto	1998	S O'Sullivan
1994	E Pilgrim	1999	R Morgan
1995	E Pilgrim	2000	J Pritchard
1996	C Waite	2001	L Diggle
1997	S O'Sullivan	2002	E Pilgrim

Norfolk Ladies

1993	T Williamson	1998	T Williamson
1994	J Wilkerson	1999	R Shubrook
1995	J Wilkerson	2000	J Wilkerson
1996	C Grady	2001	J Wilkerson
1997	T Williamson	2002	J Wilkerson

Northamptonshire Ladies

1993	S Sharpe	1998	C Gibbs
1994	S Sharpe	1999	S Turbayne
1995	S Sharpe	2000	C Gibbs
1996	S Carter	2001	S Carter
1997	S Carter	2002	K Hanwell

Northern Counties (Scotland) Ladies

1993	S Alexander	1998	L Vass
1994	L Roxburgh	1999	L Mackay
1995	F McKay	2000	L Mackay
1996	F McLennan	2001	C Gruber
1997	E Vass	2002	L McKinnon

Northern Women's (ELGA)

1993	A Brighouse	1998	R Lomas
1994	G Nutter	1999	C Ritson
1995	K Rostron	2000	L Mackay
1996	K Rostron	2001	N Evans
1997	G Nutter	2002	N Edwards

Northern Women's Counties Championship

1993	Lancashire	1998	Yorkshire
1994	Lancashire	1999	Yorkshire
1995	Cheshire	2000	Yorkshire
1996	Lancashire	2001	Yorkshire
1997	Lancashire	2002	Cheshire

Northern Division Ladies (Scotland)

1993	S Alexander	1998	J Tough
1994	J Matthews	1999	L McLardy
1995	J Harrison	2000	J Yellowlees
1996	J Harrison	2001	S Wood
1997	C Hunter	2002	L Devenish

Northumberland Ladies

1993	H Wilson	1998	C Hall
1994	D Glenn	1999	J Ross
1995	H Wilson	2000	J Ross
1996	C Hall	2001	J Ross
1997	C Hall	2002	C Hall

Nottinghamshire Ladies

1993	L Rayner	1998	J Collingham
1994	G Palmer	1999	L Wright
1995	G Palmer	2000	L Wright
1996	L Wright	2001	*Event cancelled*
1997	J Collingham	2002	L Slack

Oxfordshire Ladies

1993	N Sparks	1998	N Woolford
1994	L King	1999	K Humphris
1995	L King	2000	N Woolford
1996	L King	2001	N Woolford
1997	L King	2002	J de Vere Hunt

Perth and Kinross Ladies

1993	E Wilson	1998	J Yellowlees
1994	C Dunbar	1999	A Murray
1995	F Farquharson	2000	C Meir
1996	E Wilson	2001	J Yellowlees
1997	N Harding	2002	D Butchart

Renfrewshire County Ladies

1993	K Fitzgerald	1998	K Fitzgerald
1994	C Agnew	1999	D Jackson
1995	D Jackson	2000	D Jackson
1996	D Jackson	2001	D Jackson
1997	L Robertson	2002	S Harman

Shropshire Ladies

1993	A Johnson	1998	L Archer
1994	A Johnson	1999	S Heath
1995	B Smith	2000	L Archer
1996	B Smith	2001	S Heath
1997	S Heath	2002	S Heath

Somerset Ladies

1993	R Murr	1998	G Pritchard
1994	S Burnell	1999	V McFarlane
1995	L Wixon	2000	A Pitt
1996	L Wixon	2001	B New
1997	L Wixon	2002	K Walls

South-Eastern Ladies

1993	K Smith	1998	A Waller
1994	K Egford	1999	K Knowles
1995	K Smith	2000	A Waller
1996	J Oliver	2001	K Smith
1997	L Evans	2002	R Prout

Southern Division Ladies (Scotland)

1993	C Meldrum	1998	D MacDonald
1994	D Douglas	1999	J Anderson
1995	J Anderson	2000	M Pow
1996	D Douglas	2001	A Shamash
1997	J Anderson	2002	L Fleming

South of Scotland Ladies

1993	D Douglas	1998	D Sutton
1994	F Rennie	1999	D MacDonald
1995	C Meldrum	2000	M Pow
1996	S McMurtrie	2001	M Pow
1997	J Anderson	2002	*Event cancelled*

South-Western Women's

1993	E Fields	1998	C Lipscombe
1994	R Morgan	1999	J Clingan
1995	E Fields	2000	E Pilgrim
1996	B Morgan	2001	C Lipsombe
1997	E Pilgrim	2002	K Walls

Staffordshire Ladies

1993	R Bolas	1998	K Edwards
1994	S Gallagher	1999	C Champion
1995	K Edwards	2000	J Peacock
1996	S Gallagher	2001	R Bolas
1997	K Edwards	2002	S Spenser

Stirling and Clackmannan County Ladies

1993	H Stirling	1998	L Kenny
1994	H Stirling	1999	H Stirling
1995	S Grant	2000	H Stirling
1996	H Hume	2001	L Kenny
1997	S Grant	2002	H Stirling

Suffolk Ladies

1993	J Hall	1998	J Hockley
1994	J Hockley	1999	A Boatman
1995	J Hall	2000	L Steadman
1996	J Hockley	2001	A Boatman
1997	L Wright	2002	A Boatman

Surrey Ladies

1993	S Lambert	1998	K Burton
1994	S Lambert	1999	R Prout
1995	J Thornhill	2000	K Knowles
1996	L McGowan	2001	L McGowan
1997	J Thornhill	2002	R Prout

Sussex Ladies

1993	C Titcomb	1998	J Galway
1994	J Head	1999	P Carver
1995	Z Steel	2000	C Court
1996	C Court	2001	C Court
1997	C Court	2002	A Greenfield

Warwickshire Ladies

1993	S Morgan	1998	C Dowling
1994	S Westhall	1999	C Dowling
1995	S Westhall	2000	T Atkin
1996	C Dowling	2001	C Dowling
1997	C Dowling	2002	F Johnson

Western Division Ladies (Scotland)

1993	J Moodie	1998	A Laing
1994	V Melvin	1999	A Laing
1995	A Hendry	2000	A Laing
1996	K Fitzgerald	2001	C Hargan
1997	C Malcolm	2002	A Laing

Wiltshire Ladies

1993	V Hanks	1998	W Martin
1994	S Sutton	1999	J Wheaton
1995	J Lamb	2000	J Wheaton
1996	J Lamb	2001	G Loughrey
1997	J Lamb	2002	G Loughrey

Worcestershire Ladies

1993	L Jones	1998	N Lawrenson
1994	N Lawrenson	1999	S Haslam
1995	S Tufnall	2000	S Nicklin
1996	N Lawrenson	2001	K Greenfield
1997	N Lawrenson	2002	L Day

Yorkshire Ladies

1993	N Buxton	1998	R Hudson
1994	N Buxton	1999	R Hudson
1995	R Hudson	2000	E Duggleby
1996	J Aldersley	2001	A Keighley
1997	R Hudson	2002	E Duggleby

Overseas Amateur Championships

Australian	Nikki Campbell (NSW)
Austrian	Denise Simon (Ger)
Canadian	Lisa Meldrum (Royal Montreal)
Czech Republic	Kvídová Petra
French	Virginie Beauchet (Fra)
Hungarian Open	Réka Kocsis (Hun)
Hungarian Close	Réka Kocsis
Luxembourg	Jessica Issler (Ger)
Netherlands	Dewi Claire Schreefel (Ned)
New Zealand Stroke Play	Brenda Ormsby (Rotarua)
Portuguese	Dewi Claire Schreefel
South African	Emma Duggleby (Eng)
Spanish Open	Martina Eberl (Ger)
Swiss Open	Regine Lautems (Sui)

United States Ladies Amateur Championship (Inaugurated 1895)

Year	Winner	Runner-up	Venue	By
1895	CS Brown	N Sargent	Meadowbrook, NY	132
Changed to match play				
1896	B Hoyt	A Tunure	Morristown, NJ	2 and 1
1897	B Hoyt	N Sargent	Essex County, MA	5 and 4
1898	B Hoyt	M Wetmore	Ardsley, NY	5 and 3
1899	R Underhill	M Fox	Philadelphia, PA	2 and 1
1900	FC Griscom	M Curtis	Shinnecock Hills, NY	6 and 5
1901	G Hecker	L Herron	Baltusrol, NJ	5 and 3
1902	G Hecker	LA Wells	Brookline, MA	4 and 3
1903	B Anthony	JA Carpenter	Wheaton, IL	7 and 6
1904	GM Bishop	EF Sanford	Merion, PA	5 and 3
1905	P Mackay	M Curtis	Morris County, NJ	1 hole
1906	HS Curtis	MB Adams	West Newton, MA	2 and 1
1907	M Curtis	HS Curtis	Blue Island, IL	7 and 6
1908	KC Harley	TH Polhemus	Chevy Chase, MD	6 and 5
1909	D Campbell	N Barlow	Merion, PA	3 and 2
1910	D Campbell	GM Martin	Homewood, IL	2 and 1
1911	M Curtis	LB Hyde	Baltusrol, NJ	5 and 4
1912	M Curtis	N Barlow	Essex County, MA	3 and 2
1913	G Ravenscroft	M Hollins	Wilmington, DE	2 holes
1914	KC Harley	EV Rosenthal	Nassau, NY	1 hole
1915	F Vanderbeck	M Gavin (Eng)	Onwentsia, IL	3 and 2
1916	A Stirling	M Caverly	Belmont Springs, MA	2 and 1
1917–1918 *Not played due to First World War*				
1919	A Stirling	M Gavin (Eng)	Shawnee, PA	6 and 5
1920	A Stirling	D Campbell Hurd	Cleveland, OH	5 and 4
1921	M Hollins	A Stirling	Deal, NJ	5 and 4
1922	G Collett	M Gavin (Eng)	Greenbrier, WV	5 and 4
1923	E Cummings	A Stirling	Westchester, NY	3 and 2
1924	D Campbell Hurd	MK Browne	Nyatt, RI	7 and 6
1925	G Collett	A Stirling Fraser	Clayton, MO	9 and 8
1926	H Stetson	E Goss	Merion, PA	2 and 1
1927	MB Horn	M Orcutt	Garden City, NY	5 and 4

United States Ladies' Amateur Championship *continued*

Year	Winner	Runner-up	Venue	By
1928	G Collett	V Van Wie	Hot Springs, VA	13 and 12
1929	G Collett	L Pressler	Oakland Hills, MI	4 and 3
1930	G Collett	V Van Wie	Beverly Hills, CA	6 and 5
1931	H Hicks	G Collett Vare	Williamsville, NY	2 and 1
1932	V Van Wie	G Collett Vare	Peabody, MA	10 and 8
1933	V Van Wie	H Hicks	Highland Park, IL	4 and 3
1934	V Van Wie	D Traung	Whitemarsh Valley, PA	2 and 1
1935	G Collett Vare	P Berg	Interlachen, MN	3 and 2
1936	P Barton (Eng)	M Orcutt	Canoe Brook, NJ	4 and 3
1937	EL Page	P Berg	Memphis, TN	7 and 6
1938	P Berg	EL Page	Westmoreland, IL	6 and 5
1939	B Jameson	D Kirby	Wee Burn, CT	3 and 2
1940	B Jameson	J Cochran	Pebble Beach, CA	6 and 5
1941	E Hicks Newell	H Sigel	Brookline, MA	5 and 3
1942–1945	*Not played due to Second World War*			
1946	B Zaharias	C Sherman	Tulsa, OK	11 and 9
1947	L Suggs	D Kirby	Franklin, MI	2 holes
1948	G Lenczyk	H Sigel	Pebble Beach, CA	4 and 3
1949	D Porter	D Kielty	Merion, PA	3 and 2
1950	B Hanson	M Murray	Atlanta, GA	6 and 4
1951	D Kirby	C Doran	St Paul, MN	2 and 1
1952	J Pung	S McFedters	Portland, OR	2 and 1
1953	ML Faulk	P Riley	West Barrington, RI	3 and 2
1954	B Romack	M Wright	Sewickley, PA	4 and 2
1955	P Lesser	J Nelson	Charlotte, NC	7 and 6
1956	M Stewart	J Gunderson	Indianapolis, IN	2 and 1
1957	J Gunderson	AC Johnstone	Del Paso, CA	8 and 6
1958	A Quast	B Romack	Wee Burn, CT	3 and 2
1959	B McIntyre	J Goodwin	Washington, DC	4 and 3
1960	J Gunderson	J Ashley	Tulsa, OK	6 and 5
1961	A Quast	P Preuss	Tacomac, WA	14 and 13
1962	J Gunderson	A Baker	Rochester, NY	9 and 8
1963	A Quast	P Conley	Williamstown, MA	2 and 1
1964	B McIntyre	J Gunderson	Prairie Dunes, KA	3 and 2
1965	J Ashley	A Quast	Denver, CO	5 and 4
1966	J Gunderson Carner	JD Stewart Streit	Sewickley, PA	41st hole
1967	ML Dill	J Ashley	Pasadena, CA	5 and 4
1968	J Gunderson Carner	A Quast	Birmingham, MI	5 and 4
1969	C Lacoste (Fra)	S Hamlin	Las Colinas, TX	3 and 2
1970	M Wilkinson	C Hill	Wee Burn, CT	3 and 2
1971	L Baugh	B Barry	Atlanta, GA	1 hole
1972	M Budke	C Hill	St Louis, MO	5 and 4
1973	C Semple	A Quast	Montclair, NJ	1 hole
1974	C Hill	C Semple	Seattle, WA	5 and 4
1975	B Daniel	D Horton	Brae Burn, MA	3 and 2
1976	D Horton	M Bretton	Del Paso, CA	2 and 1
1977	B Daniel	C Sherk	Cincinnati, OH	3 and 1
1978	C Sherk	J Oliver	Sunnybrook, PA	4 and 3
1979	C Hill	P Sheehan	Memphis, TN	7 and 6
1980	J Inkster	P Rizzo	Prairie Dunes, KA	2 holes
1981	J Inkster	L Goggin (Aus)	Portland, OR	1 hole
1982	J Inkster	C Hanlon	Colorado Springs, CO	4 and 3
1983	J Pacillo	S Quinlan	Canoe Brook, NJ	2 and 1
1984	D Richard	K Williams	Seattle, WA	37th hole
1985	M Hattori (Jpn)	C Stacy	Pittsburgh, PA	5 and 4
1986	K Cockerill	K McCarthy	Pasatiempo, CA	9 and 7
1987	K Cockerill	T Kerdyk	Barrington, RI	3 and 2
1988	P Sinn	K Noble	Minikahda, MN	6 and 5
1989	V Goetze	B Burton	Pinehurst, NC	4 and 3
1990	P Hurst	S Davis	Canoe Brook, NJ	37th hole
1991	A Fruhwirth	H Voorhees	Prairie Dunes, KA	5 and 4
1992	V Goetze	A Sörenstam (Swe)	Kemper Lakes, IL	1 hole
1993	J McGill	S Ingram	San Diego, CA	1 hole
1994	W Ward	J McGill	Hot Springs, VA	2 and 1
1995	K Kuehne	A-M Knight	Brookline, MA	4 and 2
1996	K Kuehne	M Baena	Lincoln, NE	2 and 1
1997	S Cavalleri (It)	R Burke	Brae Burn, MA	5 and 4
1998	G Park (Kor)	J Chuasiriporn	Blackwolf Run, WI	7 and 6
1999	D Delasin	J Kang	Biltmore Forest, NC	4 and 3

Year	Winner	Runner-up	Venue	By
2000	N Newton	L Myerscough	Biltmore Forest, NC	8 and 7
2001	M Duncan	N Perrot	Flint Hills, KS	at 37th

2002 *at Sleepy Hollow, Scarborough, NY*

Quarter Finals
Becky Lucidi (Poway, CA) beat Emily Bastel (Upper Sandusky, OH) 3 and 1
Lindsey Wright (Aus) beat Walailak Satarak (Tha) 4 and 3
Brandi Jackson (Belton, SC) beat Mollie Fankhauser (Columbus, OH) at 20th
Maru Martinez (Ven) beat Virada Nirapthpongporn (Tha) 2 holes

Semi-Finals
Lucidi b Wright 3 and 2
Jackson beat Martinez at 19th

Final
Becky Lucidi beat Brandi Jackson 3 and 2

PART VI

Junior Tournaments and Events

Boys' and Youths' Tournaments

Boys Amateur Championship

Year	Winner	Runner-up	Venue	By
1921	ADD Mathieson	GH Lintott	Ascot	37th hole
1922	HS Mitchell	W Greenfield	Ascot	4 and 2
1923	ADD Mathieson	HS Mitchell	Dunbar	3 and 2
1924	RW Peattie	P Manuevrier (Fra)	Coombe Hill	2 holes
1925	RW Peattie	A McNair	Barnton	4 and 3
1926	EA McRuvie	CW Timmis	Coombe Hill	1 hole
1927	EW Fiddian	K Forbes	Royal Burgess	4 and 2
1928	S Scheftel	A Dobbie	Formby	6 and 5
1929	J Lindsay	J Scott-Riddell	Royal Burgess	6 and 4
1930	J Lindsay	J Todd	Fulwell	9 and 8
1931	H Thomson	F McGloin	Glasgow (Killermont)	5 and 4
1932	IS MacDonald	LA Hardie	Royal Lytham and St Annes	2 and 1
1933	PB Lucas	W McLachlan	Carnoustie	3 and 2
1934	RS Burles	FB Allpass	Moortown	12 and 10
1935	JDA Langley	R Norris	Royal Aberdeen	6 and 5
1936	J Bruen	W Innes	Birkdale	11 and 9
1937	IM Roberts	J Stewart	Bruntsfield	8 and 7
1938	W Smeaton	T Snowball	Moor Park	3 and 2
1939	SB Williamson	KG Thom	Carnoustie	4 and 2
1940-45	*Suspended during War*			
1946	AFD MacGregor	DF Dunstan	Bruntsfield	7 and 5
1947	J Armour	I Caldwell	Hoylake	5 and 4
1948	JD Pritchett	DH Reid	Kilmarnock (Barassie)	37th hole
1949	H MacAnespie	NV Drew	St Andrews	3 and 2
1950	J Glover	I Young	Royal Lytham and St Annes	2 and 1
1951	N Dunn	MSR Lunt	Prestwick	6 and 5
1952	M Bonallack	AE Shepperson	Formby	37th hole
1953	AE Shepperson	AT Booth	Dunbar	6 and 4
1954	AF Bussell	K Warren	Hoylake	38th hole
1955	SC Wilson	BJK Aitken	Kilmarnock (Barassie)	39th hole
1956	JF Ferguson	CW Cole	Sunningdale	2 and 1
1957	D Ball	J Wilson	Carnoustie	2 and 1
1958	R Braddon	IM Stungo	Moortown	4 and 3
1959	AR Murphy	EM Shamash	Pollok	3 and 1
1960	P Cros (Fra)	PO Green	Olton	5 and 3
1961	FS Morris	C Clark	Dalmahoy	3 and 2
1962	PM Townsend	DC Penman	Royal Mid-Surrey	1 hole
1963	AHC Soutar	DI Rigby	Prestwick	2 and 1
1964	PM Townsend	RD Gray	Formby	9 and 8
1965	GR Milne	DK Midgley	Gullane	4 and 2
1966	A Phillips	A Muller	Moortown	12 and 11
1967	LP Tupling	SC Evans	Western Gailes	4 and 2
1968	SC Evans	K Dabson	St Annes Old Links	3 and 2
1969	M Foster	M Gray	Dunbar	37th hole
1970	ID Gradwell	JE Murray	Hillside	1 hole
1971	H Clark	G Harvey	Kilmarnock (Barassie)	6 and 5
1972	G Harvey	R Newsome	Moortown	7 and 5
1973	DM Robertson	S Betti (Ita)	Blairgowrie	5 and 3
1974	TR Shannon	A Lyle	Hoylake	10 and 9
1975	B Marchbank	A Lyle	Bruntsfield	1 hole
1976	M Mouland	G Hargreaves	Sunningdale	6 and 5
1977	I Ford	CR Dalgleish	Downfield	1 hole
1978	S Keppler	M Stokes	Seaton Carew	3 and 2
1979	R Rafferty	D Ray	Kilmarnock (Barassie)	6 and 5
1980	D Muscroft	A Llyr	Formby	7 and 6

Year	Winner	Runner-up	Venue	By
1981	J Lopez (Esp)	R Weedon	Gullane	4 and 3
1982	M Grieve	G Hickman	Burnham and Barrow	37th hole
1983	JM Olazábal (Esp)	M Pendaries	Glenbervie	6 and 5
1984	L Vannett	A Mednick (Swe)	Royal Porthcawl	2 and 1
1985	J Cook	W Henry	Royal Burgess	5 and 4
1986	L Walker	G King	Seaton Carew	5 and 4
1987	C O'Carrol	P Olsson (Swe)	Barassie	3 and 1
1988	S Pardoe	D Haines	Formby	3 and 2
1989	C Watts	C Fraser	Nairn	5 and 3
1990	M Welch	M Ellis	Hunstanton	3 and 1
1991	F Valera (Esp)	R Walton	Montrose	4 and 3
1992	L Westerberg (Swe)	F Jacobson (Swe)	Royal Mid-Surrey	3 and 2
1993	D Howell	V Gustavsson (Swe)	Glenbervie	3 and 1
1994	C Smith	C Rodgers	Little Aston	2 and 1
1995	S Young	S Walker	Dunbar	7 and 6
1996	K Ferrie	M Pilkington	Littlestone	2 and 1
1997	S García (Esp)	R Jones	Saunton	6 and 5
1998	S O'Hara	S Reale (Ita)	Ladybank	1 hole
1999	A Gutierrez (Esp)	M Skelton	Royal St David's	1 hole
2000	D Inglis	D Skinns	Hillside	1 hole
2001	P Martin	R Cabrera	Ganton	3 and 2

2002 *at Carnoustie*

Quarter Finals

Fernando García (Esp) beat Pablo Martin (Esp) at 19th

Mark Pilling (Astbury) beat Robert Leonard (Harpenden Common) at 20th

Rhys Davies (Royal Porthcawl) beat Stefan Wiedergrun (Ger) 3 and 2

Matthew Richardson (Pinner Hill) beat Xavier Poncelet (Fra) 4 and 3

Semi-Finals

Pilling beat García 3 and 1

Davies beat Richardson 3 and 2

Final

Mark Pilling beat Rhys Davies at 37th

British Youths Open Amateur Championship

This championship bridged the gap between the Boys and the Men's tournaments from 1954 until 1995, when it was discontinued because it was no longer needed. The date on the schedule was used to introduce the Mid-Amateur (over 25s).

Year	Winner	Club	Venue	Score
1954	JS More	Swanston	Erskine	287
1955	B Stockdale	Royal Lytham & St Annes	Pannal	287
1956	AF Bussell	Coxmoor	Royal Burgess	287
1957	G Will	St Andrews	Pannal	290
1958	RH Kemp	Glamorganshire	Dumfries & County	281
1959	RA Jowle	Moseley	Pannal	286
1960	GA Caygill	Sunningdale	Pannal	279
1961	JS Martin	Kilbirnie Place	Bruntsfield	284
1962	GA Caygill	Sunningdale	Pannal	287
1963	AJ Low	St Andrews U	Pollok	283
1964	BW Barnes	Burnham & Berrow	Pannal	290
1965	PM Townsend	Porters Park	Gosforth Park	281
1966	PA Easterhouse	Dulwich & Sydenham Hill	Dalmahoy	219 (54 holes)
1967	PJ Benka	Addington	Copt Heath	278
1968	PJ Benka	Addington	Ayr Belleisle	281
1969	JH Cook	Calcot Park	Lindrick	289
1970	B Dassu	Italy	Royal Burgess	276
1971	P Elson	Coventry	Northamptonshire County	277
1972	AH Chandler	Regent Park (Bolton)	Glasgow Gailes	281
1973	SC Mason	Goring & Streatley	Southport & Ainsdale	284
1974	DM Robertson	Dunbar	Downfield	284
1975	N Faldo	Welwyn Garden City	Pannal	278
1976	ME Lewis	Henbury	Gullane	277
1977	AWB Lyle	Hawkstone Park	Moor Park	285
1978	B Marchbank	Auchterarder	East Renfrewshire	278
1979	G Brand jr	Knowle	Woodhall Spa	291
1980	G Hay	Hilton Park	Royal Troon	303

British Youths Open Amateur Championship *continued*

Year	Winner	Club	Venue	Score
1981	T Antevik	Sweden	West Lancashire	290
1982	AP Parkin	Newtown	St Andrews New	280
1983	P Mayo	Newport	Sunningdale	290
1984	R Morris	Padeswick & Buckley	Blairgowrie	281
1985	JM Olazábal	Spain	Ganton	281
1986	D Gilford	Trentham Park	Carnoustie	283
1987	J Cook*	Leamington & County	Hollinwell	283
1988	C Cevaer*	France	Royal Aberdeen	275
1989	M Smith*	Brokenhurst Manor	Ashburnham	285
1990	M Gronberg	Sweden	Southerness	275
1991	J Payne	Sandilands	Woodhall Spa	287
1992	W Bennett	Ruislip	Northumberland	283
1993	L Westwood	Worksop	Glasgow Gailes	278
1994	F Jacobson	Sweden	Royal St Davids	277

English Boys Stroke Play Championship (formerly Carris Trophy)

Year	Winner	Score	Year	Winner	Score	Year	Winner	Score
1935	R Upex	75 (18)	1962	FS Morris	145	1983	P Baker	288
1936	JDA Langley	152	1963	EJ Threlfall	147	1984	J Coe	283
1937	RJ White	149	1964	PM Townsend	148	1985	P Baker	286
1938	IP Garrow	147	1965	G McKay	145	1986	G Evans	292
1939	CW Warren	149	1966	A Black	151	1987	D Bathgate	289
1946	AH Perowne	158	1967	RF Brown	147	1988	P Page	284
1947	I Caldwell	159	1968	P Dawson	149	1989	I Garbutt	285
1948	I Caldwell	152	1969	ID Gradwell	150	1990	M Welch	276
1949	PB Hine	148	1970	MF Foster	146	1991	I Pyman	284
1950	J Glover	144	1971	RJ Evans	146	1992	M Foster	286
1951	I Young	154	1972	L Donovan	143	1993	J Harris	285
1952	N Thygesen	150	1973	S Hadfield	148	1994	R Duck	280
1953	N Johnson	148	1974	KJ Brown	304	1995	J Rose	266
1954	K Warren	149	1975	A Lyle	270	1996	G Storm	281
1955	ID Wheater	151	1976	H Stott	285	1997	D Griffiths	283
1956	G Maisey	141	1977	R Mugglestone	293	1998	S Godfrey	286
1957	G Maisey	145	1978	J Plaxton	144	1999	D Porter	275
1958	J Hamilton	149	1979	P Hammond	288	2000	G Lockerbie	279
1959	RT Walker	152	1980	MP McLean	290	2001	M Richardson*	138
1960	PM Baxter	150	1981	D Gilford	290			
1961	DJ Miller	143	1982	M Jarvis	298			

2002 *at Beau Desert*

1	Carlos Del Moral (Esp)	74-70-68-70—282
2	Jamie Moul (Stoke-by-Nayland)	70-70-71-74—285
3	Julian Munns (John o' Gaunt)	76-74-69-70—289

English Boys Under-16 Championship (McGregor Trophy)

Year	Winner	Score	Year	Winner	Score	Year	Winner	Score
1994	G Storm	291	1997	R Paolillo	285	2000	M Skelton	289
1995	J Rose	287	1998	MY Ali	280	2001	P Waring	212
1996	E Molinari	291	1999	J Heath	280			

2002 *at Sheringham*

1	Matthew Baldwin (Hesketh)	72-74-68-75—289
2	Chris Drabble (Workington)	73-72-76-73—294
3	Paul Oakley (Billingham)	73-75-74-73—295

IMSL Irish Boys Championship (inaugurated 1983)

1983	J Carvill	J Farrell	Curragh	144
1984	E O'Connell	J Farrell	Mullingar	142
1985	K Kearney	D Clarke	Athlone	145
1986	D Errity	G McNeill	Royal Tara	147
1987	G McNeill	P McCartan	Warrenpoint	143
1988	D McGrane	P Harrington	Birr	219
1989	D Higgins	JWH Clark	Mullingar	221
1990	R Burns	G Murphy	Kilkenny	213
1991	R Coughlan	R Burns	Thurles	207
1992	J O'Sullivan	D Dunne	Athlone	210
1993	H Armstrong	C McMonagle/P Byrne	Warrenpoint	222
1994	P Byrne	R Leonard/A Thomas	Nenagh	209
1995	L Dalton	M McGreedy	Mullingar	222
1996	M Campbell	L Dalton	Galway	213
1997	M Hoey	D Jones	Galway	217
1998	D Jones	D O'Connor	Youghal	214
1999	M McTernan	M O'Sullivan	Kilkenny	210
2000	D McNamara	C Doran	Strandhill	268
2001	M McHugh*	K Fahey	Donaghadee	280

2002 *at Thurles*

1	C McNamara (Limerick)	71-69-70-69—279
2	G Shaw (Lurgan)	70-70-69-72—281
3	A O'Callaghan (Douglas)	71-72-73-70—286

Irish Youths Open Amateur Championship (inaugurated 1969)

1969	D Branigan	Delgany	142	1986	JC Morris	Carlow	280
1970	LA Owens	Tullamore	286	1987	C Everett	Killarney	300
1971	MA Gannon	Athlone	277	1988	P McGinley	Malone	283
1972	MA Gannon	Mullingar	291	1989	A Mathers	Athlone	280
1973	J Purcell	Tullamore	289	1990	D Errity	Dundalk	293
1974	S Dunlop	Athlone	293	1991	R Coughlan	Lahinch	288
1975	P McNally	Mullingar	287	1992	K Nolan	Clandeboye	275
1976	R McCormack	Tullamore	294	1993	CD Hislop	Co Sligo	279
1977	B McDaid	Athlone	290	1994	B O'Melia	Tullamore	272
1978	T Corridan	Thurles	279	1995	S Young	Ballybunion	286
1979	R Rafferty	Tullamore	293	1996	S Young	Royal Portrush	291
1980	J McHenry	Clandeboye	296	1997	N Howley	Galway	284
1981	J McHenry	Westport	303	1998	A Murray	Headfort	281
1982	K O'Donnell	Mullingar	286	1999	G McDowall	Cork	284
1983	P Murphy	Cork	287	2000	G McDowall	Malone	276
1984	JC Morris	Bangor	292	2001	M Ryan	Enniscrone	298
1985	J McHenry	Co Sligo	287				

2002 *at Seapoint*

1	Gareth Wright (West Linton)	72-71-73-72—288
2	D Price (Vale of Glamorgan)	72-71-73-77—293
3	Philip McLaughlin (Ballyliffin)	78-73-67-77—295

Scottish Boys Championship

1960	L Carver	S Wilson	North Berwick	6 and 5
1961	K Thomson	G Wilson	North Berwick	10 and 8
1962	HF Urquhart	S MacDonald	North Berwick	3 and 2
1963	FS Morris	I Clark	North Berwick	9 and 8
1964	WR Lockie	MD Cleghorn	North Berwick	1 hole
1965	RL Penman	J Wood	North Berwick	9 and 8
1966	J McTear	DG Greig	North Berwick	4 and 3
1967	DG Greig	I Cannon	North Berwick	2 and 1
1968	RD Weir	M Grubb	North Berwick	6 and 4
1969	RP Fyfe	IP Doig	North Berwick	4 and 2
1970	S Stephen	M Henry	North Berwick	38th hole
1971	JE Murray	AA Mackay	North Berwick	4 and 3
1972	DM Robertson	G Cairns	North Berwick	9 and 8

Scottish Boys Championship *continued*

1973	R Watson	H Alexander	North Berwick	8 and 7
1974	DM Robertson	J Cuddihy	North Berwick	6 and 5
1975	A Brown	J Cuddihy	North Berwick	6 and 4
1976	B Marchbank	J Cuddihy	Dunbar	2 and 1
1977	JS Taylor	GJ Webster	Dunbar	3 and 2
1978	J Huggan	KW Stables	Dunbar	2 and 1
1979	DR Weir	S Morrison	West Kilbride	5 and 3
1980	R Gregan	AJ Currie	Dunbar	2 and 1
1981	C Stewart	G Mellon	Dunbar	3 and 2
1982	A Smith	J White	Dunbar	39th hole
1983	C Gillies	C Innes	Dunbar	38th hole
1984	K Buchan	L Vannet	Dunbar	2 and 1
1985	AD McQueen	FJ McCulloch	Dunbar	1 hole
1986	AG Tait	EA McIntosh	Dunbar	6 and 5
1987	AJ Coltart	SJ Bannerman	Dunbar	37th hole
1988	CA Fraser	F Clark	Dunbar	9 and 8
1989	M King	D Brolls	Dunbar	8 and 7
1990	B Collier	D Keeney	West Kilbride	2 and 1
1991	C Hislop	R Thorton	West Kilbride	11 and 9
1992	A Reid	A Forsyth	West Kilbride	2 and 1
1993	S Young	A Campbell	West Kilbride	4 and 2
1994	S Young	E Little	Dunbar	2 and 1
1995	S Young	M Donaldson	Royal Aberdeen	7 and 6
1996	S Whiteford	I McLaughlin	West Kilbride	3 and 2
1997	M Donaldson	L Rhind	Dunbar	1 hole
1998	S O'Hara	D Sutton	Murcar	2 holes
1999	L Harper	M Syme	West Kilbride	6 and 5
2000	S Buckley	M Risbridger	Dunbar	7 and 6
2001	S Brown	R Gill	Royal Aberdeen	6 and 4

2002 *at West Kilbride*

Quarter Finals
Ross Benvie (Braehead) beat Ben Renfrew (Middlesbrough) at 20th
John Hempstock (Dumfries & Galloway) beat Paul Betty (Hayston) 2 and 1
Mark Wilkie (Royal Aberdeen) beat David Aitchison (Royal Dornoch) 2 and 1
Robert Taylor (Cardross) beat Steven Ferguson (Falkirk Tryst) 1 hole

Semi-Finals
Hempstock beat Benvie 5 and 4
Taylor beat Wilkie 4 and 2

Final
John Hempstock beat Robert Taylor 2 and 1

Scottish Boys Stroke Play Championship

1970	D Chillas	Carnoustie	298	1986	G Cassells	Edzell	294
1971	JE Murray	Lanark	274	1987	C Ronald	Lanark	287
1972	S Martin	Montrose	280	1988	M Urquhart	Dumfries and County	280
1973	S Martin	Royal Burgess	284	1989	C Fraser	Stirling	282
1974	PW Gallacher	Lundin Links	290	1990	N Archibald	Monifieth	292
1975	A Webster	Kilmarnock (Barassie)	286	1991	S Gallacher	Crieff	280
1976	A Webster	Forfar	292	1992	S Gallacher	Monifieth	288
1977T	J Huggan	Renfrew	303	1993	J Bunch	Powfoot	292
	L Mann			1994	S Young	Drumpellier	288
1978	R Fraser	Arbroath	283	1995	C Lee	Arbroath	284
1979	L Mann	Stirling	289	1996	M Brown	Dullatur	286
1980	ASK Glen	Forfar	288	1997	L Rhind	Downfield	287
1981	J Gullen	Bellshill	296	1998	G Holland	Burntisland	281
1982	D Purdie	Monifieth	296	1999	B Hume	Nairn Dunbar	281
1983	L Vannet	Kilmarnock (Barassie)	286	2000	C Ries (RSA)	Cawder	275
1984	K Walker	Carnoustie	280	2001	S Jamieson	Lanark	275
1985	G Matthew	Baberton	297				

2002 *at Peterhead*

1	Mark Lamb (Haddington)	67-72-66-70—275
2	Chris Johnston (Dunbar)	71-70-66-69—276
3	Paul Doherty (Vale of Glamorgan)	70-69-72-67—278
	Duncan Stewart (Grantown-on-Spey)	67-73-68-70—278

Scottish Boys Under-16 Stroke Play Championship

1990	G Davidson	W Linton	148	1996	P Whiteford	Bothwell	143
1991	D Patrick	R Musselburgh	152	1997	D Inglis	Glenbervie	139
1992	*Not played*			1998	D Inglis	Braehead	139
1993	S Lamond	Old Ranfurly	150	1999	G Murray	Lundin	141
1994	S Fraser	Crieff	142	2000	W Booth	The Hirsel	138
1995	C Campbell	Shotts	73 (18)	2001	C Johnston	Edzell	143

2002 *at Ratho Park*

1	Scott Borrowman (Dollar)	72-70—142
2	Paul O'Hara (Colville Park)	70-73—143
3	Simon Hislop (Selkirk)	72-72—144
	James Wilkinson (Brampton)	72-72—144

Scottish Youths Stroke Play Championship

1979	A Oldcorn	Dalmahoy	217	1991	D Robertson	Hilton Park	273
1980	G Brand jr	Monifieth & Ashludie	281	1992	R Russell	Nairn	296
1981	S Campbell	Cawder and Keir	279	1993	CD Hislop	West Kilbride	284
1982	LS Mann	Leven and Scoonie	270	1994	S Gallacher	Crieff	275
1983	A Moir	Mortonhall	284	1995	E Little	Irvine, Ayr	280
1984	B Shields	Eastwood, Renfrew	280	1996	E Little	Stranraer & Portpatrick	280
1985	H Kemp	East Kilbride	282	1997	S Young	Cawder	269
1986	A Mednick	Cawder	282	1998	T Rice*	Bruntsfield/R. Burgess	287
1987	K Walker	Bogside	291	1999	J Hendry*	Crieff & Aucterarder	142
1988	P McGinley	Ladybank & Glenrothes	281	2000	J Hendry	Newmachar	285
1989	J Mackenzie	Longniddry	281	2001	J McLeary	Crail	287
1990	S Bannerman	Portpatrick & Stranraer	213				

2002 *at Murrayshall*

1	Gregory Bourdy (Fra)	74-64-68-70—276
2	David Inglis (Glencorse)	67-67-70-74—278
	Jamie McLeary (Glenrothes)	71-67-72-68—278

Welsh Boys' Championship (inaugurated 1954)

1954	JWH Mitchell	DA Rees	Llandrindod Wells	8 and 6
1955	EW Griffith	DA Rees	Llandrindod Wells	3 and 2
1956	DA Rees	JP Hales	Llandrindod Wells	2 and 1
1957	P Waddilove	JG Jones	Llandrindod Wells	2 and 1
1958	P Waddilove	J Williams	Llandrindod Wells	1 hole
1959	C Gilford	JG Jones	Llandrindod Wells	6 and 4
1960	C Gilford	JL Toye	Llandrindod Wells	5 and 4
1961	AR Porter	JL Toye	Llandrindod Wells	3 and 2
1962	RC Waddilove	W Wadrup	Harlech	20th hole
1963	G Matthews	R Witchell	Penarth	6 and 5
1964	D Lloyd	M Walters	Conway	2 and 1
1965	G Matthews	DG Lloyd	Wenvoe Castle	7 and 6
1966	J Buckley	DP Owen	Holyhead	4 and 2
1967	J Buckley	DL Stevens	Glamorganshire	2 and 1
1968	J Buckley	C Brown	Maesdu	1 hole
1969	K Dabson	P Light	Glamorganshire	5 and 3
1970	P Tadman	A Morgan	Conway	2 and 1
1971	R Jenkins	TJ Melia	Ashburnham	3 and 2
1972	MG Chugg	RM Jones	Wrexham	3 and 2
1973	R Tate	N Duncan	Penarth	2 and 1
1974	D Williams	S Lewis	Llandudno	5 and 4
1975	G Davies	PG Garrett	Glamorganshire	20th hole
1976	JM Morrow	MG Mouland	Caernarvonshire	1 hole
1977	JM Morrow	MG Mouland	Glamorganshire	2 and 1
1978	JM Morrow	A Laking	Harlech	2 and 1
1979	P Mayo	M Hayward	Penarth	24th hole
1980	A Llyr	DK Wood	Llandudno (Maesdu)	2 and 1
1981	M Evans	P Webborn	Pontypool	5 and 4
1982	CM Rees	KH Williams	Prestatyn	2 holes

Welsh Boys Championship *continued*

1983	MA Macara	RN Roderick	Radyr	1 hole
1984	GA Macara	D Bagg	Llandudno	1 hole
1985	B Macfarlane	R Herbert	Cardiff	1 hole
1986	C O'Carroll	A Salmon	Rhuddlan	1 hole
1987	SJ Edwards	A Herbert	Abergavenny	19th hole
1988	C Platt	P Murphy	Holyhead	2 and 1
1989	R Johnson	RL Evans	Southerndown	2 holes
1990	M Ellis	C Sheppard	Llandudno (Maesdu)	3 and 2
1991	B Dredge	A Cooper	Tenby	2 and 1
1992	Y Taylor	J Pugh	Wrexham	1 hole
1993	R Davies	S Raybould	Pyle and Kenfig	3 and 2
1994	R Peet	K Sullivan	Abergele & Pensarn	7 and 6
1995	M Palmer	O Pughe	Newport	4 and 3
1996	A Smith	M Griffiths	Borth & Ynyslas	at 19th hole
1997	A Lee	I Campbell	Glamorganshire	4 and 3
1998	M Setterfield	D Price	Llandudno	3 and 2
1999	C Mills	D Price	Neath	3 and 2
2000	R Narduzzo	G Dobson-Jones	Pwllheli	1 hole
2001	J Morgan	B Briscoe	St Mellons	3 and 2

2002 *at Radyr*

Quarter Finals

Chris Cole (Monmouthshire) beat Llew Matthews (Southerndown) 6 and 5

Greg Williams (Pontypridd) beat Luke Thomas (Pontypridd) 1 hole

James Morgan (Alice Springs) beat Rhys Davies (Royal Porthcawl) at 19th

Mark Laskey (Brockett Hall) beat Carl Wakeley (Whitchurch) 2 and 1

Semi-Finals

Cole beat Williams 3 and 2

Morgan beat Laskey 2 and 1

Final

Chris Cole beat James Morgan 4 and 3

Welsh Boys Stroke Play Championship (inaugurated 1995)

at Borth & Ynyslas

2002 *at Radyr*

1	Chris Cole (Monmouthshire)	66-67—133
2	Carl Wakeley (Whitchurch)	68-71—139
3	Rhys Davies (Royal Porthcawl)	73-67—140

Welsh Boys Under-15 Championship (inaugurated 1985)

2002 *at Radyr*

1	Z Gould (Vale of Glamorgan)	72-70—142
2	A Runcie (Abergele)	76-69—145
3	E Hodgson (Mold)	75-75—150
	D Horseman (Pontypool)	76-74—150
	L Jones (Conwy)	78-72—150

Welsh Open Youths Championship (inaugurated 1993)

1993	A McKenna	Langland Bay	310	1998	M Hearne	Carmarthen	294
1994	D Quinney	Vale of Llangollen	290	1999	D Price	Rhuddlan	281
1995	R Warner	Glamorganshire	289	2000	B Welch	Cottrell Park	276
1996	D Harris	Porthmadog	295	2001	T Dykes	Wrexham	281
1997	N Matthews	Cradoc	294				

2002 *at Cardiff*

1	J Ruth (Tavistock)	72-70-74-67—283
2	S Tiley (Royal Cinque Ports)	69-74-77-66—286
3	L James (Brynhill)	71-75-73-69—288
	R Narduzzo (Celtic Manor)	74-65-76-73—288

Peter McEvoy Trophy *at Copt Heath*

1988	P Sefton	1993	S Webster	1998	J Rose
1989	D Bathgate	1994	J Harris	1999	D Porter
1990	P Sherman	1995	C Duke	2000	Z Scotland
1991	L Westwood	1996	M Pilkington	2001	B Harvey
1992	B Davis	1997	P Rowe		

2002 *at Copt Heath*

1	Matthew Richardson (Pinner Hill)	69-73-73-66—281
2	Adam Stott (Reddish Vale)	72-70-72-69—283
3	James Ruth (Tavistock)	78-71-72-68—289
	Paul Waring (Bromborough)	70-71-77-71—289

R&A Junior Open Championhips (Boys and Girls)

1994	Orn Aevar Hjartanson (Isl)	2000	Steven Jeppeson (Swe) (Gold)
1996	Antti Hiltunen (Fin)		Luis Cargiulo (Pan) (Silver)
1998	David Inglis (Sco)	2001	*Not played*

2002 *at Royal Musselburgh*

1	Cian McNamara (Irl)	71-65-71—207
2	Da-Sol Chung (Kor)	71-69-70—210
3	Laurence Allen (Eng)	72-75-64—211

Nick Faldo Junior Series

1997	N Dougherty		
1998	G Hyde	Loch Lomond	138
1999	N Dougherty	The Belfry	109 (27 holes)
2000	N Dougherty	Royal Liverpool	140
2001	G Bondarenko*	Saunton	152

2002 *at Burhill*

1	James Heath (Walton Heath)	138
2	Danny Wardrop (Worsley Park)	141

Under 18 winner: Alex Murrell (Eden)   138

Under 17 winner: Paul Doherty (Vale of Glamorgan)   138

Under 16 winner: Seve Benson (Guildford)   143

Under 15 winner: Matthew Evans (Rotherham)   147

Nick Faldo Junior Series (International Trophy)

1999	Etienne Bond (Fra)	The Belfry	111 (27 holes)
2000	A Kruger (RSA)	Royal Liverpool	150
2001	P Erofejeff (Fin)	Saunton	153

2001 *at Burhill*

1	Caroline Westrup (Swe)	68-74—142
2	Andreas Danewid (Swe)	70-78—148
3	Stenna Westerlund (Fin)	73-76—149

Midland Boys Amateur Championship

1989	M Wilson	1994	R Duck	1998	E Vernon
1990	ML Welch	1995	C Richardson	1999	C Stevenson
1991	S Drummond	1996T	S Walker	2000	J Prince
1992	S Drummond		K Cliffe	2001	O West
1993	S Webster	1997	K Hale		

2002 *at Hinckley*

Ben Stafford (Maxstoke Park)   71-71—142

Team Events

World Junior Team Championship

1995	USA	643	1998	England	874	2001	RSA	856
1996	Japan	625	1999	England	863	2002	*Not played*	
1997	USA	864	2000	USA	859			

European Boys Team Championship

1980	Spain	El Prat, Barcelona	1991	Sweden	Oslo, Norway
1981	England	Olgiata, Rome	1992	Scotland	Conwy, Wales
1982	Italy	Frankfurt, Germany	1993	Sweden	Ascona, Switzerland
1983	Sweden	Helsinki, Finland	1994	England	Vilamoura, Portugal
1984	Scotland	Royal St George's, England	1995	England	Woodhall Spa
1985	England	Troia, Portugal	1996	Spain	Gut Murstatten, Austria
1986	England	Turin, Italy	1997	Spain	Bled, Slovenia
1987	Scotland	Chantilly, France	1998	Ireland	Gullane, Scotland
1988	France	Renfrew, Scotland	1999	England	Uppsala, Sweden
1989	England	Lyckoma, Sweden	2000	Scotland	Noord Nederlandse
1990	Spain	Reykjavik, Iceland	2001	Sweden	Amber Baltic, Poland

2002 *at Reykjavik, Iceland*

Final Ranking:
1 Spain, 2 Sweden, 3 France, 4 Wales, 5 England, 6 Scotland
19 teams played

European Youths Team Championship

1990	Italy	Sweden	Turin, Italy
1992	Sweden	England	Helsinki, Finland
1994	Ireland	Sweden	Esbjerg, Denmark
1996	Scotland	Spain	Madeira
1998	Wales	Sweden	Royal Waterloo, Belgium
2000	England	Scotland	Kilmarnock (Barassie), Scotland

2002 *at Gdansk, Poland*

Final Ranking:
1 Sweden, 2 England, 3 Spain, 4 Scotland, 5 Austria, 6 Finland
20 teams played

Great Britain & Ireland v Continent of Europe
(Jacques Léglise Trophy)

1958	GB&I	11½–½	Moortown	1985	GB&I	7½–4½	Royal Burgess
1959	GB&I	7–2	Pollok	1986	Europe	8½–3½	Seaton Carew
1960	GB&I	8–7	Olton	1987	GB&I	7½–4½	Kilmarnock (Barassie)
1961	GB&I	11–4	Dalmahoy	1988	GB&I	5½–2½	Formby
1962	GB&I	11–4	Royal Mid-Surrey	1989	GB&I	7½–4½	Nairn
1963	GB&I	12–3	Prestwick	1990	GB&I	10–2	Hunstanton
1964	GB&I	12–1	Formby	1991	GB&I	6½–5½	Montrose
1965	GB&I	12–1	Gullane	1992	GB&I	8–7	Royal Mid–Surrey
1966	GB&I	10–2	Moortown	1993	GB&I	8–7	Glenbervie
1967–76 Not played				1994	GB&I	12½–2½	Little Aston
1977	Europe	7–6	Downfield	1995	GB&I	9–6	Dunbar
1978	Europe	7–6	Seaton Carew	1996	Europe	13–11	Woodhall Spa
1979	GB&I	9½–2½	Kilmarnock (Barassie)	1997	Europe	12½–11½	Aberdeen
1980	GB&I	7–5	Formby	1998	GB&I	14–10	Villa d'Este, Italy
1981	GB&I	8–4	Gullane	1999	GB&I	15–9	Burnham & Berrow
1982	GB&I	11–1	Burnham & Berrow	2000	GB&I	16–8	Turnberry
1983	GB&I	6½–5½	Glenbervie	2001	Europe	16–8	Chantilly
1984	GB&I	6½–5½	Royal Porthcawl				

2002 *at Lausanne, Switzerland* (European names first):

Captains: Gonzalo Fernandez-Castaño (Esp); Rhys Davies (Wal)

First Day, Morning – Foursomes
Del Moral & Romano lost to Bowe & Shaw
   3 and 1
Ahokas & Lorenzo beat Waring & Pilling 1 hole
Adell & Floren lost to Davies & Richardson
   2 holes
Cabrera & Benavides lost to Skelton & Keenan
   2 and 1

Afternoon – Singles
Gustav Adell (Swe) lost to Clancey Bowe (Irl)
   4 and 2
Antti Ahokas (Fin) lost to Jamie Moul (Eng)
   3 and 2
Peter Baunsee (Den) lost to Matt Richardson (Eng)
   5 and 4
Andrea Romano (Ita) beat Farren Keenan (Eng)
   2 holes
Rafael Cabrera (Esp) beat Paul Waring (Eng)
   2 holes
Carlos Del Moral (Esp) halved with Rhys Davies
   (Wal)
Pablo Martin Benavides (Esp) beat Gareth Shaw
   (Irl) 4 and 2
Oscar Floren (Swe) lost to Michael Skelton (Eng)
   4 and 3

Second Day, Morning – Foursomes
Adell & Floren beat Davies & Richardson
   3 and 2
Ahokas & Lorenzo lost to Waring & Moul
   2 and 1
Benavides & Romano halved with Skelton &
   Keenan
Cabrera & Del Moral lost to Bowe & Shaw
   5 and 4

Afternoon – Singles
Ahokas lost to Richardson 5 and 4
Romano lost to Moul 2 holes
Baunsee beat Keenan 5 and 3
Adell beat Waring 1 hole
Michael Lorenzo (Fra) lost to Davies 5 and 3
Floren beat Bowe 2 and 1
Cabrera beat Mark Pilling 1 hole
Benavides lost to Skelton 5 and 4

Result: C of E 10; GB&I 14

Boys Home Internationals (R&A Trophy) (Instituted 1985)

1985T	England/Ireland	Royal Burgess	1994	England	Little Aston
1986	Ireland	Seaton Carew	1995	Scotland	Dunbar
1987	Scotland	Barassie	1996	England	Littlestone
1988	England	Formby	1997	Ireland	Royal North Devon
1989	England	Nairn	1998	England	St Andrews
1990	Scotland	Hunstanton	1999	England	Conwy
1991	England	Montrose	2000	England	Portmanock
1992T	Wales/Scotland	Royal Mid-Surrey	2001	England	Moortown
1993	England	Glenbervie			

2002 *at Lansdowne, Blairgowrie*

Scotland beat Ireland	10½–4½
England beat Wales	9–6
England beat Scotland	13–2
Wales beat Ireland	8½–6½
Wales beat Scotland	9½–4½
England beat Ireland	10–5

Result: 1 England; 2 Wales; 3 Scotland; 4 Ireland

English Boys County Finals

2000 Surrey   2001 Lancashire

2002 *at St Annes Old Links*
1 Yorkshire,
2 Kent
3 Cornwall
4 Nottinghamshire

Scottish Boys Team Championship

2000 Lothians   355   2001 Dunbartonshire   347

2002 *at East Kilbride*

1	Lothians	370
2	North	377
3	North-East	378

The Junior Ryder Cup

1995	Rochester, USA	Exhibition Match won by Europe
1997	San Roque & Alcaidesa, Spain	United States won 7–5
1999	Cape Cod, USA	Europe won 10½–1½

2002 at The K Club, Dublin, Ireland

Captains: Macarena Campomanes, Charlie Westrup (Eur); Susan Addis, Tom Addis (USA)

Teams

Under 16

Emma Cabrera (Esp)	Tiffany Chudy (CA)	
Claire Grignolo (Ita)	Stephanie Connelly (MD)	
Peter-Max Hamm (Ger)	Jennifer Davis (TN)	
Matteo del Podio (Ita)	Travis Esway (CA)	
Rony Raillard (Fra)	Shaun Felchner (HI)	
Benjamin Regent (Fra)	Lauren Mielbrecht (FL)	
Dewi-Claire Schreefel (Ned)	Adam Porzak (CA)	
Katharina Werdinig (Aut)	Colin Wilcox (CA)	

Under-18

Carmen Alonso (Esp)	Mallory Code (FL)
Farren Keenan (Eng)	Taylor Hall (GA)
Denise Simon (Ger)	Jenny Suh (VA)
Raphael De Sousa (Sui)	Casey Wittenberg (TN)

First Day – Girls and Boys Fourball

Grignolo & Schreefel halved with Connelly & Suh
De Sousa & Hamm beat Hall & Wittenburg 4 and 3
Cabrera & Werdinig beat Davis & Mielbrecht 5 and 4
del Podio & Keenan beat Esway & Porzak 4 and 3
Alonso & Simon beat Chudy & Code 4 and 3
Raillard & Regent lost to Felchner & Wilcox 5 and 3

Result: Europe 4½, USA 1½

Second Day – Mixed Fourball

Werdinig & Keenan lost to Code & Wittenburg 5 and 4
Alonso & Raillard beat Suh & Hall 1 hole
Schreefel & del Podio beat Connelly & Porzak 1 hole
Cabrera & Regent beat Mielbrecht & Esway 6 and 5
Grignolo & de Sousa beat Davis & Felchner 2 holes
Simon & Hamm beat Chudy & Wilcox 2 and 1

Final result: Europe 9½, USA 2½

Girls' and Junior Ladies' Tournaments

Girls British Open Championship

Year	Winner	Runner-up	Venue	By
1960	S Clarke	AL Irvin	Kilmarnock (Barassie)	2 and 1
1961	D Robb	J Roberts	Beaconsfield	3 and 2
1962	S McLaren-Smith	A Murphy	Foxton Hall	2 and 1
1963	D Oxley	B Whitehead	Gullane	2 and 1
1964	P Tredinnick	K Cumming	Camberley Heath	2 and 1
1965	A Willard	A Ward	Formby	3 and 2
1966	J Hutton	D Oxley	Troon Portland	20th hole
1967	P Burrows	J Hutton	Liphook	2 and 1
1968	C Wallace	C Reybroeck	Leven	4 and 3
1969	J de Witt Puyt	C Reybroeck	Ilkley	2 and 1
1970	C Le Feuvre	Michelle Walker	North Wales	2 and 1
1971	J Mark	Maureen Walker	North Berwick	4 and 3
1972	Maureen Walker	S Cadden	Norwich	2 and 1
1973	AM Palli	N Jeanson	Northamptonshire	2 and 1
1974	R Barry	T Perkins	Dunbar	1 hole
1975	S Cadden	L Isherwood	Henbury	4 and 3
1976	G Stewart	S Rowlands	Pyle and Kenfig	5 and 4
1977	W Aitken	S Bamford	Formby Ladies	2 and 1
1978	M L de Lorenzi	D Glenn	Largs	2 and 1
1979	S Lapaire	P Smilie	Edgbaston	19th hole
1980	J Connachan	L Bolton	Wrexham	2 holes
1981	J Connachan	P Grice	Woodbridge	20th hole
1982	C Waite	M Mackie	Edzell	6 and 5
1983	E Orley	A Walters	Leeds	7 and 6
1984	C Swallow	E Farquharson	Maesdu	1 hole
1985	S Shapcott	E Farquharson	Hesketh	3 and 1
1986	S Croce	S Bennett	West Kilbride	5 and 4
1987	H Dobson	S Croce	Barnham Broom	19th hole
1988	A Macdonald	J Posener	Pyle and Kenfig	3 and 2
1989	M McKinlay	S Eriksson	Carlisle	19th hole
1990	S Cavalleri	E Valera	Penrith	5 and 4
1991	M Hjorth	J Moodie	Whitchurch	3 and 2
1992	M McKay	L Navarro	Northamptonshire	2 holes
1993	M McKay	A Vincent	Helensburgh	4 and 3
1994	A Vincent	R Hudson	Gog Magog	1 up
1995	A Lemoine	J Krantz	Northop Park	3 and 2
1996	M Monnet	C Laurens	Formby	4 and 3
1997	C Laurens	M Nagl	West Kilbride	2 and 1
1998	M Beautell	M Nagl	Holyhead	4 and 3
1999	S Pettersen	M Nagl	High Post	3 and 1
2000	T Calzavara	R Bell	Blairgowrie	1 hole
2001	C Queen	C Alonso	Brough	1 hole

2002 *at Sandiway*

Rain washed out this tournament in its later stages. Awards were made to the top qualifiers, and to the Quarter Finalists.

Qualifiers

1	Emma Cabrera (Esp)	69-69—138
2	Louise Stable (Swe)	72-67—139
3	Maria Hernandez (Esp)	68-71—139

Girls British Open Championship *continued*

Quarter finalists in knock-out: Madeleine Augustsson (Swe), Elisa Serramia (Esp), Giusy Paolillo (Ita), Claire Grignolo (Ita), Maria Hernandez (Esp), Anparo Gala (Esp), Melodie Bourdy (Fra), Louise Stable (Swe).

The team event was won by Spain (Emma Cabrera, Elisa Serramia, Maria Recasens).

English Girls Close Championship

Year	Winner	Runner–up	Venue	By
1964	S Ward	P Tredinnick	Wollaton Park	2 and 1
1965	D Oxley	A Payne	Edgbaston	2 holes
1966	B Whitehead	D Oxley	Woodbridge	1 hole
1967	A Willard	G Holloway	Burhill	1 hole
1968	K Phillips	C le Feuvre	Harrogate	6 and 5
1969	C le Feuvre	K Phillips	Hawkstone Park	2 and 1
1970	C le Feuvre	M Walker	High Post	2 and 1
1971	C Eckersley	J Stevens	Liphook	4 and 3
1972	C Barker	R Kelly	Trentham	4 and 3
1973	S Parker	S Thurston	Lincoln	19th hole
1974	C Langford	L Harrold	Knowle	2 and 1
1975	M Burton	R Barry	Formby	6 and 5
1976	H Latham	D Park	Moseley	3 and 2
1977	S Bamford	S Jolly	Chelmsford	21st hole
1978	P Smillie	J Smith	Willesley Park	3 and 2
1979	L Moore	P Barry	Cirencester	1 hole
1980	P Smillie	J Soulsby	Kedleston Park	3 and 2
1981	J Soulsby	C Waite	Worksop	7 and 5
1982	C Waite	P Grice	Wilmslow	3 and 2
1983	P Grice	K Mitchell	West Surrey	2 and 1
1984	C Swallow	S Duhig	Bath	3 and 1
1985	L Fairclough	K Mitchell	Coventry	6 and 5
1986	S Shapcott	N Way	Huddersfield	7 and 6
1987	S Shapcott	S Morgan	Sandy Lodge	1 hole
1988	H Dobson	S Shapcott	Long Ashton	1 hole
1989	H Dobson	A MacDonald	Edgbaston	3 and 1
1990	C Hall	J Hockley	Bolton Old Links	20th hole
1991	N Buxton	C Hall	Knole Park	2 and 1
1992	F Brown	L Nicholson	Finham Park	2 and 1
1993	G Simpson	L Wixon	Cotswold Hills	7 and 5
1994	K Hamilton	S Forster	Whitley Bay	3 and 2
1995	R Hudson	G Nutter	Porters Park	2 and 1
1996	R Hudson	D Rushworth	Bedford	8 and 6
1997	S McKevitt	C Ritson	Kingsdown	3 and 2
1998	L Walters	K Lawton	Harrogate	5 and 4
1999	S Heath	A Cook	Chigwell	6 and 4
2000	S Walker	R Wood	Sheringham	1 hole
2001	A Marshall	S Walker	Long Ashton	3 and 2

2002 *at Fairhaven*

Quarter Finals

Faye Sanderson (Heworth) beat Emma McBride (Upton-by-Chester) 6 and 4

Natalie Haywood (Rotherham) beat Annabel Silk (Corhampton) at 19th

Alex Marshall (North Foreland) beat Sian Reddick (Sene Valley) 2 and 1

Laura Eastwood (Yelverton) beat Corisande Lee (Pleasington) 2 holes

Semi-Finals

Haywood beat Sanderson

Eastwood beat Marshall

Final

Laura Eastwood beat Natalie Haywood 1 hole

Irish Girls Championship (inaugurated 1951)

Year	Winner	Runner–up	Venue	By
1951	J Davies	I Hurst	Milltown	3 and 2
1952	J Redgate	A Phillips	Grange	at 22nd
1953	J Redgate	I Hurst	Grange	4 and 3
1954–60	*Suspended*			
1961	M Coburn	C McAuley	Portrush	6 and 5
1962	P Boyd	P Atkinson	Elm Park	4 and 3
1963	P Atkinson	C Scarlett	Donaghadee	8 and 7
1964	C Scarlett	A Maher	Milltown	6 and 5
1965	V Singleton	P McKenzie	Ballycastle	7 and 6
1966	M McConnell	D Hulme	Dun Laoghaire	3 and 2
1967	M McConnell	C Wallace	Portrush	6 and 5
1968	C Wallace	A McCoy	Louth	3 and 1
1969	EA McGregor	M Sheenan	Knock	6 and 5
1970	EA McGregor	J Mark	Greystones	3 and 2
1971	J Mark	C Nesbitt	Belfast	3 and 2
1972	P Smyth	M Governey	Elm Park	1 hole
1973	M Governey	R Hegarty	Mullingar	3 and 1
1974	R Hegarty	M Irvine	Castletroy	2 holes
1975	M Irvine	P Wickham	Carlow	2 and 1
1976	P Wickham	R Hegarty	Castle	5 and 3
1977	A Ferguson	R Walsh	Birr	3 and 2
1978	C Wickham	B Gleeson	Killarney	1 hole
1979	L Bolton	B Gleeson	Milltown	3 and 2
1980	B Gleeson	L Bolton	Kilkenny	5 and 3
1981	B Gleeson	E Lynn	Donegal	1 hole
1982	D Langan	S Lynn	Headfort	5 and 4
1983	E McDaid	S Lynn	Ennis	20th hole
1984	S Sheehan	L Tormey	Thurles	6 and 4
1985	S Sheehan	D Hanna	Laytown/Bettystown	5 and 4
1986	D Mahon	T Eakin	Mallow	4 and 3
1987	V Greevy	B Ryan	Galway	8 and 7
1988	L McCool	P Gorman	Courtown	3 and 2
1989	A Rogers	R MacGuigan	Athlone	2 and 1
1990	G Doran	L McCool	Royal Portrush	3 and 1
1991	A Rogers	D Powell	Mallow	2 and 1
1992	M McGreevy	N Gorman	Kilkenny	2 and 1
1993	M McGreevy	E Dowdall	Strandhill	2 and 1
1994	A O'Leary	D Doyle	Mullingar	23rd hole
1995	P Murphy	G Hegarty	Douglas	5 and 4
1996	P Murphy	C Smyth	Warren Point	2 holes
1997	J Gannon	C Coughlan	Lay/Bettystown	3 and 2
1998	P Murphy	C Coughlan	Galway	5 and 4
1999	P Murphy	M Gillen	Tullamore	20th hole
2000	M Gillen	N Mullooly	Limerick	6 and 5
2001	DM Conaty	H Nolan	Belvoir Park	3 and 2

2002 at Athenry

Quarter Finals

Heather Nolan (Shannon) beat Alison Kingston (Bandon)
3 and 2

Dawn Marie Conaty (Ashbourne) beat Danielle McVeigh
(RCDL) 4 and 2

Karen Delaney (Carlow) beat Tara Delany (Carlow)
2 and 1

Sinead O'Sullivan (Galway) beat Joanne Cronin
(Killarney) 1 hole

Semi-Finals

Nolan beat Conaty 2 and 1

Delany beat O'Sullivan 1 hole

Final

Karen Delany beat Heather Nolan 4 and 3

Scottish Ladies Junior Open Stroke Play Championship
(inaugurated 1955)

1955	M Fowler	Erskine		1979	A Gemmill	Royal Troon, Portland
1956	B McCorkindale	Erskine		1980	J Connachan	Kirkcaldy
1957	M Fowler	Kilmacolm		1981	K Douglas	Downfield
1958	R Porter	Ranfurly Castle		1982	J Rhodes	Dumfries & Galloway
1959	D Robb	Helensburgh		1983	S Lawson	Largs
1960	J Greenhalgh	Ranfurly Castle		1984	S Lawson	Dunbar
1961	D Robb	Whitecraigs		1985	K Imrie	Ballater
1962	S Armitage	Dalmahoy		1986	K Imrie	Dumfries and County
1963	A Irvin	Dumfries		1987	K Imrie	Douglas Park
1964	M Nuttall	Dalmahoy		1988	C Lambert	Baberton
1965	I Wylie	Carnoustie		1989	C Lambert	Dunblane New
1966	J Smith	Douglas Park		1990	J Moodie	Royal Troon
1967	J Bourassa	Dunbar		1991	C Macdonald	Alyth
1968	K Phillips	Dumfries		1992	L McCool	North Berwick
1969	K Phillips	Prestonfield		1993	J Moodie	Dumfries and County
1970	B Huke	Leven		1994	C Agnew	Dumfries and County
1971	B Huke	Dalmahoy		1995	R Hakkarainen (Fin)	Lanark
1972	L Hope	Troon, Portland		1996	L Moffat	Auchterarder
1973	G Cadden	Edzell		1997	L Nicholson	Stranraer
1974	S Lambie	Stranraer		1998	V Laing	Duff House Royal
1975	S Cadden	Lanark		1999	L Kenny	Alyth
1976	S Cadden	Prestonfield		2000	L Morton	Cardross
1977	S Cadden	Edzell		2001	L Kenny	Southerness
1978	J Connachan	Peebles				

2002 at Baberton

1	Kelly Brotherton (Tuliallan)	69-69—138
2	Clare Queen (Drumpellier)	70-69—139
3	Heather MacRae (Dunblane New)	68-73—141

Scottish Girls Close Championship (inagurated 1960)

Year	Winner	Runner-up	Venue	By
1960	J Hastings	A Lurie	Kilmacolm	6 and 4
1961	I Wylie	W Clark	Murrayfield	3 and 1
1962	I Wylie	U Burnet	West Kilbride	3 and 1
1963	M Norval	S MacDonald	Carnoustie	6 and 4
1964	JW Smith	C Workman	West Kilbride	2 and 1
1965	JW Smith	I Walker	Leven	7 and 5
1966	J Hutton	F Jamieson	Arbroath	2 holes
1967	J Hutton	K Lackie	West Kilbride	4 and 2
1968	M Dewar	J Crawford	Dalmahoy	2 holes
1969	C Panton	A Coutts	Edzell	23rd hole
1970	M Walker	L Bennett	Largs	3 and 2
1971	M Walker	S Kennedy	Edzell	1 hole
1972	G Cadden	C Panton	Stirling	3 and 2
1973	M Walker	M Thomson	Cowal, Dunoon	1 hole
1974	S Cadden	D Reid	Arbroath	3 and 1
1975	W Aitken	S Cadden	Leven	1 hole
1976	S Cadden	D Mitchell	Dumfries and County	4 and 2
1977	W Aitken	G Wilson	West Kilbride	2 holes
1978	J Connachan	D Mitchell	Stirling	7 and 5
1979	J Connachan	G Wilson	Dunbar	3 and 1
1980	J Connachan	P Wright	Dumfries and County	21st hole
1981	D Thomson	P Wright	Kilmarnock (Barassie)	2 and 1
1982	S Lawson	D Thomson	Montrose	1 hole
1983	K Imrie	D Martin	Leven	2 and 1
1984	T Craik	D Jackson	Peebles	3 and 2
1985	E Farquharson	E Moffat	West Kilbride	2 holes
1986	C Lambert	F McKay	Nairn	4 and 3
1987	S Little	L Moretti	Stirling	3 and 2
1988	J Jenkins	F McKay	Dumfries and County	4 and 3
1989	J Moodie	V Melvin	Kilmacolm	19th hole
1990	M McKay	J Moodie	Duff House Royal	3 and 2
1991	J Moodie	M McKay	Leven Links	5 and 4
1992	M McKay	L Nicholson	Powfoot	2 and 1

Year	Winner	Runner–up	Venue	By
1993	C Agnew	H Stirling	Baberton	19th hole
1994	C Nicholson	L Moffat	Deeside	3 and 1
1995	L Moffat	F Lockhart	Paisley	2 and 1
1996	V Laing	C Hunter	Peebles	5 and 4
1997	V Laing	A Walker	Dunfermline	5 and 4
1998	V Laing	L Moffat	Kilmarnock Barassie	at 21st hole
1999	V Laing	L Wells	Edzell	3 and 2
2000	L Kenney	F Gilbert	Dunblane New	3 and 2
2001	H MacRea	L Kenney	Glenbervie	1 hole

2002 at Powfoot

Quarter Finals
Gemma Webster (Hilton Park) beat Kerri Harper (Inverness) 3 and 2

Clare-Marie Carlton (Fereneze) beat Rowena Hay (Nairn Dunbar) at 19th

Laura Walker (Nairn Dunbar) beat Kate O'Sullivan (Cochrane Castle) 2 and 1

Dawn Dewar (Monifieth) beat Lesley Hendry (Routenburn) at 19th

Semi-Finals
Webster beat Carlton 2 and 1

Walker beat Dewar 2 and 1

Final
Laura Walker beat Gemma Webster 2 and 1

Welsh Girls Championship (inaugurated 1957)

Year	Winner	Runner–up	Venue	By
1957	A Coulman	S Wynne-Jones	Newport	1 hole
1958	S Wynne-Jones	A Coulman	Conwy	3 and 1
1959	C Mason	T Williams	Glamorgan	3 and 2
1960	A Hughes	D Wilson	Llandrindod Wells	6 and 4
1961	J Morris	S Kelly	North Wales	3 and 2
1962	J Morris	P Morgan	Southerndown	4 and 3
1963	A Hughes	A Brown	Conway	8 and 7
1964	A Hughes	M Leigh	Holyhead	5 and 3
1965	A Hughes	A Reardon-Hughes	Swansea Bay	19th hole
1966	S Hales	J Rogers	Prestatyn	1 hole
1967	E Wilkie	L Humphreys	Pyle and Kenfig	1 hole
1968	L Morris	J Rogers	Portmadoc	1 hole
1969	L Morris	L Humphreys	Wenvoe Castle	5 and 3
1970	T Perkins	P Light	Rhuddlan	2 and 1
1971	P Light	P Whitley	Glamorganshire	4 and 3
1972	P Whitley	P Light	Llandudno (Maesdu)	2 and 1
1973	V Rawlings	T Perkins	Whitchurch	19th hole
1974	L Isherwood	S Rowlands	Wrexham	4 and 3
1975	L Isherwood	S Rowlands	Swansea Bay	1 hole
1976	K Rawlings	C Parry	Rhuddlan	5 and 4
1977	S Rowlands	D Taylor	Clyne	7 and 5
1978	S Rowlands	G Rees	Abergele	3 and 2
1979	M Rawlings	J Richards	St Mellons	19th hole
1980	K Davies	M Rawlings	Vale of Llangollen	19th hole
1981	M Rawlings	F Connor	Radyr	4 and 3
1982	K Davies	K Beckett	Wrexham	6 and 5
1983	N Wesley	J Foster	Whitchurch	4 and 2
1984	J Foster	J Evans	Pwllheli	6 and 5
1985	J Foster	S Caley	Langland Bay	6 and 5
1986	J Foster	L Dermott	Holyhead	3 and 2
1987	J Lloyd	S Bibbs	Cardiff	2 and 1
1988	L Dermott	A Perriam	Builth Wells	2 holes
1989	L Dermott	N Stroud	Carmarthen	4 and 2
1990	L Dermott	N Stroud	Padeswood and Buckley	6 and 4
1991	S Boyes	R Morgan	Clyne	3 and 1
1992	B Jones	S Musto	Rhuddlan	2 and 1
1993	K Stark	S Tudor-Jones	Radyr	3 and 2
1994	K Stark	J Evans	Wrexham	4 and 3
1995	E Pilgrim	L Davis	Borth and Ynyslas	2 holes
1996	K Stark	S Bourne	Monmouth	4 and 3
1997	R Brewerton	K Stark	Perhos	19th hole
1998	B Brewerton	L Archer	Old Padeswood	3 and 1
1999	K Phillips	R Last	Pontardawe	6 and 5

Welsh Girls Championship *continued*

2000	K Phillips	J Pritchard	Northop Country Park	1 hole
2001	S Jones	J Dyer	Carmarthen	3 and 2

2002 *at North Wales GC*

Quarter Finals

Rebecca Adlam (Monmouthshire) beat Stephanie Evans (Vale of Llangollen) 3 and 2

Rosie Vaughan-Jones (Cardigan) beat Melanie Peake (Rhuddlan) 1 hole

Donna Jones (Caernarfon) beat Laura Weatherill (The Gower) 5 and 4

Lucy Gould (Bargoed) beat Brianne Loucks (Wrexham) at 20th

Semi-Finals

Vaughan-Jones beat Adlam 1 hole

Gould beat Jones 1 hole

Final

Lucy Gould beat Rosie Vaughan-Jones 4 and 3

Nick Faldo Junior Series

1998	K Philips	Loch Lomond	154
1999	A Highgate	The Belfry	114 (27 holes)
2000	A Highgate	Royal Liverpool	146
2001	O Rotmistrova	Saunton	155

2002 *at Burhill*

1	Florentyna Parker (Gut Waldhof, Germany)	77-75—152
2	Natalie Haywood (Rotherham)	77-76—153
3	Ouliana Rotmistrova (Moscow City)	80-74—154

Now there is a golfing Tigress!

Cheyenne Woods, the niece of World No. 1 Tiger Woods, may be set to follow her uncle into the golfing record books. She is just four feet tall but already can hit a ball 220 yards, has won over 50 events including the Under 10 World Championship and had two holes-in-one on adult courses.

She is the daughter of Earl Woods Jr., Tiger's half-brother from Earl Woods' first marriage. Kent Chase, her golfing coach in San Diego, has been teaching her for five years after asking for a volunteer to hit bunker shots at a junior clinic he was holding.

Team Events

European Girls Team Championship

Year	Winner	Venue
1995	Sweden	Luxembourg
1997	Spain	Germany
1999	Germany	Finland
2001	Spain	Portugal

European Lady Juniors Team Championship

Year	Winner	Second	Venue
1990	Sweden	England	Shannon, Ireland
1992	Spain	Sweden	St Nom–la–Breteche, France
1994	Sweden	France	Gutenhof, Vienna, Austria
1996	France	Spain	Nairn, Scotland
1998	Spain	Italy	Oslo, Norway
2000	Italy	England	Castelconturbia GC, Italy

Girls Home Internationals (Stroyan Cup)

Year	Winner	Venue	Year	Winner	Venue
1966	Scotland	Troon (Portland)	1984	Scotland	Llandudno (Maesdu)
1967	England	Liphook	1985	England	Hesketh GC
1968	England	Leven	1986	England	West Kilbride
1969	England	Ilkley	1987	England	Barnham Broom
1970	England	North Wales	1988	England	Pyle and Kenfig
1971	England	North Berwick	1989	England	Carlisle
1972	Scotland	Royal Norwich	1990	England	Penrith
1973	Scotland	Northamptonshire County	1991	England	Whitchurch
1974	England	Dunbar	1992	Scotland	Moseley
1975	England	Henbury	1993	Scotland	Helensburgh
1976	Scotland	Pyle and Kenfig	1994	Scotland	Gog Magog
1977	England	Formby Ladies	1995	England	Northop
1978	England	Largs	1996	England	Formby
1979	England	Edgbaston	1997	England	Forfar
1980	England	Wrexham	1998	England	Mullingar
1981	England	Woodbridge	1999	Wales	High Post
1982	England	Edzell	2000	England	Downfield
1983	England	Alwoodley	2001	England	Brough

2002 *at The Hermitage*

England beat Ireland	5½–3½
Wales beat Scotland	5½–3½
England beat Scotland	7–2
Ireland beat Wales	6–3
Ireland beat Scotland	7½–1½
England beat Wales	7–2

Result: 1 England, 2 Ireland, 3 Wales, 4 Scotland

The Junior Ryder Cup *at The K Club, Dublin, Ireland*

For full results and team members see page 353

Golf Foundation Events

Weetabix Age Group Championships

Boys

Year	Under 16	Under 15	Under 14
1990	C Lane (Kingsthorpe)	G Harris (Broome Manor)	P Collier (Limerick)
1991	G Harris (Broome Manor)	C Richardson (Burghley Park)	J Bajcer (Church Stretton)
1992	C Leach (Gillingham)	S Walker (Walmley)	D Kirton (Worksop)
1993	K Godfrey (St Enodoc)	S Young (Seascale)	J Rose (North Hants)
1994	A Smith (Rhondda)	T Hilton (Lewes)	A Smith (Enville)
1995	G Legg (Enmore Park)	S Robinson (Seaton Carew)	D Inglis (Glencorse)
1996	S Fromant (Orsett)	D Skinns (Canwick Park)	C Smith (Cotgrave Place)
1997	M Stam (Royal Liverpool)	G Lockerbie (Keswick)	S Robinson (Thames Ditton)
1998	D Rix (Malton and Norton)	M Skelton (Hunley Hall)	L Shepherd (Cleckheaton & District)
1999	W Schucksmith (Sand Moor)	J Moul (Stoke by Nayland)	T Robinson (Middlesbrough)
2000	M Jones (Upton-by-Chester)	S Taylor (Blundells Hill)	S Hufton (Copt Heath)
2001	J Cundy (Kings Lynn)	M Baldwin (Hesketh)	T Chambers (Coxmoor)

Year	Under 13
1990	S Walker (Boldmere)
1991	N Rossin (John O'Gaunt)
1992	D Main (Moray)
1993	S Godfrey (St Enodoc)
1994	D Tarbotton (Hull)
1995	D Porter (Wellow)
1996	J Maxwell (Muckhart)
1997	J Turner (Newmarket Links)
1998	C Paisley (Stocksfield)
1999	J Haugh (Salisbury and S Wilts)
2000	J Stevenson (Torrington)
2001	Z Gould (Vale of Glamorgan)

2002 at Forest of Arden, Meriden

Under 16
John Parry (Harrogate)	70-67	137
Matthew Baldwin (Hesketh)	70-68	138
Matthew Jones (Pontypridd)	67-74	141
Daniel Taylor (Woburn)	72-70	142
Edward Meredith (Shropshire)	69-73	142
Richard Graham (Hayston)	75-68	143

Under 15
Lee Lewis (Fairwood Park)	71-71	142
Laurence Eltham (Goring & Streatley)	73-70	143
Matthew Lord (Fulford, York)	68-76	144
Andrew Sullivan (Purley Chase)	70-74	144
Adam Hinkins (Chiltern Forest)	74-71	145
Simon Ward (Nuremore)	72-73	145

Under 14
Matthew Swales (Bowood)	74-73	147
Oliver Fisher (West Essex)	74-73	147
Christian Stone (Chevin)	76-75	151
Lewis Edmunds (West Cornwall)	71-81	152
Jack Walker (Lancaster)	77-76	153
Tom Hardy (Llanymynech)	73-82	155

Under 13
Nicholas Eardley (Burslem)	74-76	150
Henry Smart (Banstead Downs)	76-76	152
Peter Stevenson (Torrington)	74-79	153
Mathew Law (Bowood)	73-81	154
Mikhail Ishaq (Bondhay)	79-77	156

Girls

Year	Under 17	Under 16	Under 15
1990		T Poulton (Boyce Hill)	V Hanks (Broome Manor)
1991		G Simpson (Cleckheaton & District)	D Doyle (Lahinch)
1992		H Stirling (Bridge of Allan)	G Nutter (Prestwich)
1993		K Wrigglesworth (Hornsea)	R Hudson (Wheatley)
1994		L Meredith (Wentworth)	L Moffat (W. Kilbride)
1995	R Hudson (Wheatley)	L Moffat (W. Kilbride)	V Laing (Musselburgh)
1996	K Fisher (Leyland)	F More (Lindrick)	L Archer (Lilleshall Hall)
1997	V Laing (Musselburgh)	R Bell (Northcliff)	L Kenney (Pitreavie)
1998	J Pritchard (Tredegar Park)	L Archer (Lilleshall Hall)	A Marshall (Burghley Park)
1999	P Willett (Enfield)	H MacRae (Callander)	A Marshall (Burghley Park)
2000	C Queen (Drumpelier)	L Eastwood (Yelverton)	N Haywood (Rotherham)
2001	L Eastwood (Yelverton)	N Haywood (Rotherham)	F Johnson (Harborne)

2002 at Forest of Arden, Meriden

Under 17

Janet Phipps (Gog Magog)	79-72	151
Roseann Youngman (Oundle)	73-81	154
Rosie Vaughan-Jones (Cardigan)	84-80	134
Jodi Campbell (Hull)	85-82	167

Under 16

Anna Scott (Consett & District)	68-79	147
Katrina Holford (Ingestre Park)	75-76	151
Jessica Pearcey (Ferndown)	75-77	152
Portia Abbott (Kingsdown)	75-78	153
Natasha Morgan (Alice Springs)	75-80	155

Under 15

Melissa Reid (Chevin)	70-73	143
Joanne Hodge (Knowle)	76-75	151
Breanne Loucks (Wrexham)	77-75	152
Laura Harvey (Richmond, Yorks)	78-77	155
Rachael Jennings (Izaak Walton)	76-80	156

Duke of York Trophy Winners (For best 36-hole aggregate)

Year	Boys	Girls
1991	Gary Harris (Broome Manor)	Georgina Simpson (Cleckheaton)
1992	Christopher Leach (Gillingham)	Heather Stirling (Bridge of Allan)
1993	Kristian Godfrey (St Enodoc)	Katy Wrigglesworth (Hornsea)
1994	Alex Smith (Rhondda)	Lisa Meredith (Wentworth)
1995	Gavin Legg (Enmore Park)	Rebecca Hudson (Wheatley)
1996	Stuart Fromant (Orsett)	Fame More (Lindrick)
1997	Marcus Stam (Royal Liverpool)	Louise Kenney (Pitreavie)
1998	Darren Rix (Malton & Norton)	Laura Archer (Lilleshall Hall)
1999	William Shucksmith (Sand Moor)	Alexandra Marshall (Burghley Park) and Polly Willett (Enfield)
2000	Sam Hufton (Copt Heath)	Natalie Haywood (Rotherham)
2001	James Cundy (King's Lynn)	Natalie Haywood (Rotherham)
2002	John Parry (Harrogate)	Melissa Reid (Chevin)

Golf Foundation Schools Team Championship (for the R&A Trophy)

Year	Winner	Country	Venue
1990	Lycée Bellevue	France	St Andrews
1991	Lycée Bellevue	France	Sunningdale
1992	Lycée Bellevue	France	St Andrews
1993	Lycée Bellevue	France	Gleneagles
1994	Lycée Bellevue	France	St Andrews
1995	Kelvin Grove High School	Australia	Sunningdale
1996	Welkom Gymnasium	South Africa	Blairgowrie
1997	Lycée Bellevue	France	Loch Lomond
1998	Damelin College, Randburg	South Africa	Sunningdale
1999	Kooralbyn International School	Australia	St Andrews
2000	Rotorua Boys' High School	New Zealand	Royal County Down
2001	Rotorua Boys' High School	New Zealand	The Berkshire

PGA European Tour Trophy

Sam Hunt (NZ)   72-68—140

Golf Foundation Award Winners

Year	Winner	Club
1982	Lindsey Anderson	Tain
1983	Nigel Osborne Clarke	Shirehampton
1984	Wayne Henry	Redbourn
1985	David Grantham	Hull
1986	Matthew Stanford	Saltford
1987	Jane Marchant	Whittington Barracks
1988	*Boys:* Ian Garbutt	Wheatley
	Girls: Lisa Dermott	St Melyd
1989	*Boys:* Lee Westwood	Worksop
	Girls: Lynn McCool	Strabane
1990	*Boys:* Keith Law	Forfar
	Girls: Mhairi McKay	Turnberry
1991	*Boys:* Gary Harris	Broome Manor
	Girls: Nicola Buxton	Woodsome Hall
1992	*Boys:* Shaun Devenney	Strabane
	Girls: Mhairi McKay	Turnberry
1993	*Boys:* Craig Williams	Greigiau
	Girls: Georgina Simpson	Cleckheaton & Dist
1994	*Boys:* Denny Lucas	Worksop
	Girls: Rebecca Hudson	Wheatley
1995	*Boys:* Justin Rose	North Hants
	Girls: Rebecca Hudson	Wheatley
1996	*Boys:* Mark Pilkington	Nefyn & District GC and Pwllheli
	Girls: Fame More	Chesterfield GC and Lindrick GC
1997	*Boys:* Nicholas Dougherty	Shaw Hill, Lancs
	Girls: Rebecca Brewerton	Abergele & Pensarn
1998	*Boys:* Steven O'Hara	Colville Park
	Girls: Vikki Laing	Musselburgh
1999	*Boys:* Barry Hume	Haggs Castle
	Girls: Rebecca Brewerton	Abergele
2000	*Boys:* David Inglis	Glencorse
	Girls: Sophie Walker	Kenwick Park

Discontinued

PART VII

Awards

Awards

Association of Golf Writers' Trophy (Awarded to the man or woman who, in the opinion of golf writers, has done most for European golf during the year)

1951	Max Faulkner	1976	Great Britain & Ireland Eisenhower Trophy Team
1952	Miss Elizabeth Price	1977	Christy O'Connor
1953	Joe Carr	1978	Peter McEvoy
1954	Mrs Roy Smith (Miss Frances Stephens)	1979	Severiano Ballesteros
1955	Ladies' Golf Union's Touring Team	1980	Sandy Lyle
1956	John Beharrell	1981	Bernhard Langer
1957	Dai Rees	1982	Gordon Brand Jr
1958	Harry Bradshaw	1983	Nick Faldo
1959	Eric Brown	1984	Severiano Ballesteros
1960	Sir Stuart Goodwin (sponsor of international golf)	1985	European Ryder Cup Team
1961	Commdr Charles Roe (ex-hon secretary, PGA)	1986	GB&I Curtis Cup Team
1962	Mrs Marley Spearman, British Ladies' Champion 1961–1962	1987	European Ryder Cup Team
		1988	Sandy Lyle
1963	Michael Lunt, Amateur Champion, 1963	1989	Great Britain & Ireland Walker Cup Team
1964	GB&I Eisenhower Trophy Team	1990	Nick Faldo
1965	Gerald Micklem, golf administrator, President, English Golf Union	1991	Severiano Ballesteros
		1992	European Solheim Cup Team
1966	Ronnie Shade	1993	Bernhard Langer
1967	John Panton	1994	Laura Davies
1968	Michael Bonallack	1995	European Ryder Cup Team
1969	Tony Jacklin	1996	Colin Montgomerie
1970	Tony Jacklin	1997	Alison Nicholas
1971	Great Britain & Ireland Walker Cup Team	1998	Lee Westwood
1972	Miss Michelle Walker	1999	Sergio García
1973	Peter Oosterhuis	2000	Lee Westwood
1974	Peter Oosterhuis	2001	Great Britain & Ireland Walker Cup Team
1975	Golf Foundation	2002	*Not yet decided*

Harry Vardon Trophy (Awarded to the PGA member heading the Order of Merit at the end of the season)

1937	Charles Whitcombe	1963	Neil Coles	1984	Bernhard Langer
1938	Henry Cotton	1964	Peter Alliss	1985	Sandy Lyle
1939	Roger Whitcombe	1965	Bernard Hunt	1986	Severiano Ballesteros
1940–45	*In abeyance*	1966	Peter Alliss	1987	Ian Woosnam
1946	Bobby Locke	1967	Malcolm Gregson	1988	Severiano Ballesteros
1947	Norman Von Nida	1968	Brian Huggett	1989	Ronan Rafferty
1948	Charlie Ward	1969	Bernard Gallacher	1990	Ian Woosnam
1949	Charlie Ward	1970	Neil Coles	1991	Severiano Ballesteros
1950	Bobby Locke	1971	Peter Oosterhuis	1992	Nick Faldo
1951	John Panton	1972	Peter Oosterhuis	1993	Colin Montgomerie
1952	Harry Weetman	1973	Peter Oosterhuis	1994	Colin Montgomerie
1953	Flory van Donck	1974	Peter Oosterhuis	1995	Colin Montgomerie
1954	Bobby Locke	1975	Dale Hayes	1996	Colin Montgomerie
1955	Dai Rees	1976	Severiano Ballesteros	1997	Colin Montgomerie
1956	Harry Weetman	1977	Severiano Ballesteros	1998	Colin Montgomerie
1957	Eric Brown	1978	Severiano Ballesteros	1999	Colin Montgomerie
1958	Bernard Hunt	1979	Sandy Lyle	2000	Lee Westwood
1959	Dai Rees	1980	Sandy Lyle	2001	Retief Goosen
1960	Bernard Hunt	1981	Bernhard Langer	2002	Retief Goosen
1961	Christy O'Connor	1982	Greg Norman		
1962	Christy O'Connor	1983	Nick Faldo		

Sir Henry Cotton European Rookie of the Year

1960	Tommy Goodwin	1982	Gordon Brand Jr
1961	Alex Caygill	1983	Grant Turner
1962	No Award	1984	Philip Parkin
1963	Tony Jacklin	1985	Paul Thomas
1964	No Award	1986	José Maria Olazàbal
1966	Robin Liddle	1987	Peter Baker
1967	No Award	1988	Colin Montgomerie
1968	Bernard Gallacher	1989	Paul Broadhurst
1969	Peter Oosterhuis	1990	Russell Claydon
1970	Stuart Brown	1991	Per-Ulrik Johansson
1971	David Llewellyn	1992	Jim Payne
1972	Sam Torrance	1993	Gary Orr
1973	Philip Elson	1994	Jonathan Lomas
1974	Carl Mason	1995	Jarmo Sandelin
1975	No Award	1996	Thomas Bjorn
1976	Mark James	1997	Scott Henderson
1977	Nick Faldo	1998	Olivier Edmond
1978	Sandy Lyle	1999	Sergio García
1979	Mike Miller	2000	Ian Poulter
1980	Paul Hoad	2001	Paul Casey
1981	Jeremy Bennett	2002	Nick Dougherty

Daily Telegraph Woman Golfer of the Year

1982	Jane Connachan
1983	Jill Thornhill
1984	Gillian Stewart and Claire Waite
1985	Belle Robertson
1986	GB&I Curtis Cup Team
1987	Linda Bayman
1988	GB&I Curtis Cup Team
1989	Helen Dobson
1990	Angela Uzielli
1991	Joanne Morley
1992	GB&I Curtis Cup Team, Captain Liz Boatman
1993	Catriona Lambert and Julie Hall
1994	GB&I Curtis Cup Team, Captain Liz Boatman
1995	Julie Hall
1996	GB&I Curtis Cup Team
1997	Alison Rose
1998	Kim Andrew
1999	Welsh International Team
2000	Rebecca Hudson
2001	Rebecca Hudson
2002	Becky Brewerton

Bobby Jones Award

(Awarded by USGA for distinguished sportsmanship in golf)

1955	Francis Ouimet	1979	Tom Kite
1956	Bill Campbell	1980	Charles Yates
1957	Babe Zaharias	1981	JoAnne Carner
1958	Margaret Curtis	1982	Billy Joe Patton
1959	Findlay Douglas	1983	Maureen Garrett
1960	Charles Evans Jr	1984	Jay Sigel
1961	Joe Carr	1985	Fuzzy Zoeller
1962	Horton-Smith	1986	Jess W Sweetser
1963	Patty Berg	1987	Tom Watson
1964	Charles Coe	1988	Isaac B Grainger
1965	Mrs Edwin Vare	1989	Chi-Chi Rodriquez
1966	Gary Player	1990	Peggy Kirk Bell
1967	Richard Tufts	1991	Ben Grenshaw
1968	Robert Dickson	1992	Gene Sarazen
1969	Gerald Micklem	1993	PJ Boatwright Jr
1970	Roberto De Vicenzo	1994	Lewis Oehmig
1971	Arnold Palmer	1995	Herbert Warren
1972	Michael Bonallack		Wind
1973	Gene Littler	1996	Betsy Rawls
1974	Byron Nelson	1997	Fred Brand
1975	Jack Nicklaus	1998	Nancy Lopez
1976	Ben Hogan	1999	Ed Updegraff
1977	Joseph C Dey	2000	Barbara McIntyre
1978	Bob Hope and	2001	Thomas Cousins
	Bing Crosby	2002	Judy Rankin

Arnold Palmer Award

(Awarded to the US PGA Tour leading money-winner)

1981	Tom Kite	1991	Corey Pavin
1982	Craig Stadler	1992	Fred Couples
1983	Hal Sutton	1993	Nick Price
1984	Tom Watson	1994	Nick Price
1985	Curtis Strange	1995	Greg Norman
1986	Greg Norman	1996	Tom Lehman
1987	Paul Azinger	1997	Tiger Woods
1988	Curtis Strange	1998	David Duval
1989	Tom Kite	1999	Tiger Woods
1990	Greg Norman	2000	Tiger Woods

The US Vardon Trophy

(The award is made by the PGA of America to the member of the US Tour who completes 60 rounds or more, with the lowest scoring average over the calendar year)

1937	Harry Cooper		1952	Jack Burke	70.54	1963	Billy Casper	70.58
1938	Sam Snead		1953	Lloyd Mangrum	70.22	1964	Arnold Palmer	70.01
1939	Byron Nelson		1954	Ed Harrison	70.41	1965	Billy Casper	70.85
1940	Ben Hogan		1955	Sam Snead	69.86	1966	Billy Casper	70.27
1941	Ben Hogan		1956	Cary Middlecoff	70.35	1967	Arnold Palmer	70.18
1942–46	No Awards – World War II		1957	Dow Finsterwald	70.30	1968	Billy Casper	69.82
1947	Jimmy Demarel	69.90	1958	Bob Rosburg	70.11	1969	Dave Hill	70.34
1948	Ben Hogan	69.30	1959	Art Wall	70.35	1970	Lee Trevino	70.64
1949	Sam Snead	69.37	1960	Billy Casper	69.95	1971	Lee Trevino	70.27
1950	Sam Snead	69.23	1961	Arnold Palmer	69.85	1972	Lee Trevino	70.89
1951	Lloyd Mangrum	70.05	1962	Arnold Palmer	70.27	1973	Bruce Crampton	70.57

The US Vardon Trophy *continued*

1974	Lee Trevino	70.53	1984	Calvin Peete	70.56	1994	Greg Norman	69.81
1975	Bruce Crampton	70.51	1985	Don Pooley	70.36	1995	Steve Elkington	69.82
1976	Don January	70.56	1986	Scott Hoch	70.08	1996	Tom Lehman	69.32
1977	Tom Watson	70.32	1987	Dan Pohl	70.25	1997	Nick Price	68.98
1978	Tom Watson	70.16	1988	Chip Beck	69.46	1998	David Duval	69.13
1979	Tom Watson	70.27	1989	Greg Norman	69.49	1999	Tiger Woods	68.43
1980	Lee Trevino	69.73	1990	Greg Norman	69.10	2000	Tiger Woods	67.79
1981	Tom Kite	69.80	1991	Fred Couples	69.59	2001	Tiger Woods	68.81
1982	Tom Kite	70.21	1992	Fred Couples	69.38	2002	Tiger Woods	68.56
1983	Ray Floyd	70.61	1993	Nick Price	69.11			

Jack Nicklaus Award

(Decided by US PGA Tour members ballot)

1990	Wayne Levi	1997	Tiger Woods
1991	Fred Couples	1998	Mark O'Meara
1992	Fred Couples	1999	Tiger Woods
1993	Nick Price	2000	Tiger Woods
1994	Nick Price	2001	Tiger Woods
1995	Greg Norman	2002	*Not yet decided*
1996	Tom Lehman		

US PGA Rookie of the Year

(Decided by PGA Tour members ballot)

1990	Robert Gamez	1997	Stewart Cink
1991	John Daly	1998	Steve Flesch
1992	Mark Carnevale	1999	Carlos Franco
1993	Vijay Singh	2000	Michael Clark II
1994	Ernie Els	2001	Charles Howell III
1995	Woody Austin	2002	*Not yet decided*
1996	Tiger Woods		

US PGA Player of the Year

1948	Ben Hogan	1976	Jack Nicklaus
1949	Sam Snead	1977	Tom Watson
1950	Ben Hogan	1978	Tom Watson
1951	Ben Hogan	1979	Tom Watson
1952	Julius Boros	1980	Tom Watson
1953	Ben Hogan	1981	Bill Rogers
1954	Ed Furgol	1982	Tom Watson
1955	Doug Ford	1983	Hal Sutton
1956	Jack Burke	1984	Tom Watson
1957	Dick Mayer	1985	Lanny Wadkins
1958	Dow Finsterwald	1986	Bob Tway
1959	Art Wall	1987	Paul Azinger
1960	Arnold Palmer	1988	Curtis Strange
1961	Jerry Barner	1989	Tom Kite
1962	Arnold Palmer	1990	Nick Faldo
1963	Julius Boros	1991	Corey Pavin
1964	Ken Venturi	1992	Fred Couples
1965	Dave Marr	1993	Nick Price
1966	Billy Casper	1994	Nick Price
1967	Jack Nicklaus	1995	Greg Norman
1968	*not awarded*	1996	Tom Lehman
1969	Orville Moody	1997	Tiger Woods
1970	Billy Casper	1998	Mark O'Meara
1971	Lee Trevino	1999	Tiger Woods
1972	Jack Nicklaus	2000	Tiger Woods
1973	Jack Nicklaus	2001	Tiger Woods
1974	Johnny Miller	2002	Tiger Woods
1975	Jack Nicklaus		

US LPGA Louise Suggs Rookie of the Year

1962	Mary Mills	1985	Penny Hammel
1963	Clifford Ann Creed	1986	Jody Rosenthal
1964	Susie Berning	1987	Tammi Green
1965	Margie Masters	1988	Liselotte Neumann
1966	Jan Ferraris		(Swi)
1967	Sharron Moran	1989	Pamela Wright (Sco)
1968	Sandra Post	1990	Hiromi Kobayashi
1969	Jane Blalock		(Jpn)
1970	JoAnne Carner	1991	Brandie Burton
1971	Sally Little	1992	Helen Alfredsson
1972	Jocelyne Bourassa		(Swe)
1973	Laura Baugh	1993	Suzanne Strudwick
1974	Jan Stephenson		(Eng)
1975	Amy Alcott	1994	Annika Sörenstam
1976	Bonnie Lauer		(Swe)
1977	Debbie Massey	1995	Pat Hurst
1978	Nancy Lopez	1996	Karrie Webb (Aus)
1979	Beth Daniel	1997	Lisa Hackney (Eng)
1980	Myra Van Hoose	1998	Se Ri Pak (Kor)
1981	Patty Sheehan	1999	Mi Hyun Kim (Kor)
1982	Patti Rizzo	2000	Dorothy Delason
1983	Stephanie Farwig	2001	Hee Won Han (Kor)
1984	Juli Inkster	2002	Beth Bauer

US LPGA Rolex Player of the Year

1966	Kathy Whitworth	1985	Nancy Lopez
1967	Kathy Whitworth	1986	Pat Bradley
1968	Kathy Whitworth	1987	Ayako Okamoto
1969	Kathy Whitworth	1988	Nancy Lopez
1970	Sandra Haynie	1989	Betsy King
1971	Kathy Whitworth	1990	Beth Daniel
1972	Kathy Whitworth	1991	Pat Bradley
1973	Kathy Whitworth	1992	Dottie Mochrie
1974	JoAnne Carner	1993	Betsy King
1975	Sandra Palmer	1994	Beth Daniel
1976	Judy Rankin	1995	Annika Sörenstam
1977	Judy Rankin	1996	Laura Davies
1978	Nancy Lopez	1997	Annika Sörenstam
1979	Nancy Lopez	1998	Annika Sörenstam
1980	Beth Daniel	1999	Karrie Webb
1981	Jo Anne Carner	2000	Karrie Webb
1982	Jo Anne Carner	2001	Annika Sörenstam
1983	Patty Sheehan	2002	Beth Bauer
1984	Betsy King		

Players' Player of the Year

1995	Annika Sörenstam (Swe)
1996	Laura Davies (Eng)
1997	Alison Nicholas (Eng)
1998	Sophie Gustafson (Swe)
1999	Laura Davies (Eng)
2000	Sophie Gustafson (Swe)
2001	Raquel Carriedo (Esp)
2002	Annika Sörenstam (Swe)

Joyce Wethered Trophy

(Awarded to the outstanding amateur under 25)

1994	Janice Moodie	1999	Becky Brewerton
1995	Rebecca Hudson	2000	Sophie Walker
1996	Mhairi McKay	2001	Clare Queen
1997	Rebecca Hudson	2002	Sarah Jones
1998	Liza Walters		

Bill Johnson Trophy

Awarded to the Rookie of the Year on the Evian Tour

1984	Katrina Douglas (Eng)
1085	Laura Davies (Eng)
1986	Patricia Gonzales
1987	Trish Johnson (Eng)
1988	Laurette Maritz (USA)
1989	Helen Alfredsson (Swe)
1990	Pearl Sinn (Kor)
1991	Helen Wdsworth (Wal)
1992	Sandrine Mendiburu (Fra)
1993	Annika Sörenstam (Swe)
1994	Tracy Hansen (USA)
1995	Karrie Webb (Aus)
1996	Anne-Marie Knight (Aus)
1997	Anna Berg (Swe)
1998	Laura Philo (USA)
1999	Elaine Ratcliffe (Eng)
2000	Guila Sergas (Ita)
2001	Suzann Pettersen (Nor)
2002	Kirsty S Taylor (Eng)

Evian Tour Stroke Average Winners

		Scoring average
1991	Alison Nicholas	71.71
1992	Laura Davies	70.35
1993	Laura Davies	71.63
1994	Liselotte Neumann	69.56
1995	Annika Sörenstam	69.75
1996	Marie Laure de Lorenzi	71.39
1997	Marie Laure de Lorenzi	72.20
1998	Laura Davies	71.96
1999	Elaine Ratcliffe	73.76
2000	Laura Davies	70.50
2001	Catriona Mathew	70.08
2002	Sophie Gustafson	70.59

Evian Tour Order or Merit

1979	Catherine Panton-Lewis (Sco)	1991	Corinne Dibnah (Aus)
1980	Muriel Thomson (Sco)	1992	Laura Davies (Eng)
1981	Jenny Lee-Smith (Eng)	1993	Karen Lunn (Aus)
1982	Jenny Lee-Smith (Eng)	1994	Liselotte Neumann (Swe)
1983	Muriel Thomson (Sco)	1995	Annika Sörenstam (Swe)
1984	Dale Reid (Sco)	1996	Laura Davies (Eng)
1985	Laura Davies (Eng)	1997	Alison Nicholas (Eng)
1986	Laura Davies (Eng)	1998	Helen Alfredsson (Swe)
1987	Dale Reid (Sco)	1999	Laura Davies (Eng)
1988	Marie-Laure Taud (Fra)	2000	Sophie Gustafson (Swe)
1989	Marie-Laure de Laurenzi (Fra)	2001	Raquel Carriedo (Esp)
1990	Trish Johnson (Eng)	2002	Paula Marti (Esp)

US LPGA Vare Trophy

		Scoring average			Scoring average
1953	Patty Berg	75.00	1978	Nancy Lopez	71.76
1954	Babe Zaharias	75.48	1979	Nancy Lopez	71.20
1955	Patty Berg	74.47	1980	Amy Alcott	71.51
1956	Patty Berg	74.57	1981	Jo Anne Carner	71.75
1957	Louise Suggs	74.64	1982	Jo Anne Carner	71.49
1958	Beverly Hanson	74.92	1983	Jo Anne Carner	71.41
1959	Betsy Rawls	74.03	1984	Patty Sheehan	71.40
1960	Mickey Wright	73.25	1985	Nancy Lopez	70.73
1961	Mickey Wright	73.55	1986	Pat Bradley	71.10
1962	Mickey Wright	73.67	1987	Betsy King	71.14
1963	Mickey Wright	72.81	1988	Colleen Walker	71.26
1964	Mickey Wright	72.46	1989	Beth Daniel	70.38
1965	Kathy Whitworth	72.61	1990	Beth Daniel	70.54
1966	Kathy Whitworth	72.60	1991	Pat Bradley	70.66
1967	Kathy Whitworth	72.74	1992	Dottie Mochrie	70.80
1968	Carol Mann	72.04	1993	Nancy Lopez	70.83
1969	Kathy Whitworth	72.38	1994	Beth Daniel	70.90
1970	Kathy Whitworth	72.26	1995	Annika Sörenstam	71.00
1971	Kathy Whitworth	72.88	1996	Annika Sörenstam	70.47
1972	Kathy Whitworth	72.38	1997	Karrie Webb	70.01
1973	Judy Rankin	73.08	1998	Annika Sörenstam	69.99
1974	JoAnne Carner	72.87	1999	Karrie Webb	69.43
1975	JoAnne Carner	72.40	2000	Karrie Webb	70.05
1976	Judy Rankin	72.25	2001	Annika Sörenstam	69.42
1977	Judy Rankin	72.16	2002	*Not yet decided*	

Tiger Woods becomes first to capture four straight PGA Player of the Year honours

Tiger Woods has won his fourth consecutive Vardon Trophy – the showcase award for a season's scoring consistency – and his fourth straight PGA Player of the Year award. He clinched his fourth straight and fifth overall PGA Player of the Year award in August. The PGA of America presents both awards.

Woods concluded the regular season at the 2002 Tour Championship by finishing with a 68.56 adjusted scoring average based on 68 rounds. Vijay Singh, winner of the Tour Championship, was runner-up with a 69.47 average through 96 rounds. Ernie Els was third at 69.50 based on 62 rounds.

Since joining the PGA Tour in 1996, Woods has won PGA Player of the Year honours in 1997, 1999, 2000, 2001 and 2002. He has won the Vardon Trophy every year since 1999.

He established the lowest adjusted scoring average record of 67.79 in 2000 and his actual scoring average of 68.17 broke Byron Nelson's scoring mark of 68.33 set in 1945. This year Woods' actual scoring average was 69.00, while Fred Funk and David Toms shared second at 69.64.

Since 1937 the Vardon Trophy, named in honour of famed British golfer Harry Vardon, has been awarded annually to the touring professional with the lowest adjusted scoring average. It is based on a minimum of 60 rounds, with no incomplete rounds, in events co-sponsored or designated by the PGA Tour.

The PGA Player of the Year award was first presented in 1948 and is decided on a points system taking in tournament victories, official money and scoring averages.

Late Results

Men's Amateur County and Regional Championships

Channel Islands	R Ramskill
Flintshire	N Tomlinson
South-Western Counties	B Welch
Worcestershire	S Braithwaite
Yorkshire Stroke Play	N Sweet

Overseas Amateur Championships

Italian Ladies'	Arnaud Gabellon (Fra)
Italian Men's	Marta Prieto (Esp)
New Zealand Ladies'	Melanie Holmes-Smith (Aus)

International Team Events

UBS Warburg Cup (Instituted 2001)

USA v Rest of World   *Captains:* Arnold Palmer (USA); Gary Player (Rest of World)

2002 at Sea Island, St Simons Island, GA

First Day – **Foursomes**
Palmer & Strange lost to Player & Faldo 1 hole
Azinger & Hoch halved with Langer & Romero
Floyd & Lehman beat Torrance & Woosnam 1 hole
Funk & Gilder lost to Aoki & Ebihara 3 and 1
Irwin & Kite beat Davis & Ginn 3 and 2
Watson & O'Meara beat Durnian & Lane 2 and 1

First day result: USA 3½, Rest of World 2½

Second Day – **Fourballs**
Palmer & Watson beat Player & Langer 3 and 2
Floyd & Lehman beat Torrance & Woosnam 2 and 1
Funk & Gilder beat Aoki & Ebihara 1 hole
Strange & Irwin lost to Faldo & Romero 1 hole
Kite & Hoch lost to Durnian & Lane 4 and 3
Azinger & O'Meara lost to Davis & Ginn 4 and 2

Second day result: USA 3, World 3
Overall result after two days: USA 6½, World 5½

Third Day – **Singles**
Arnold Palmer lost to Gary Player (RSA)
  6 and 5
Curtis Strange beat Sam Torrance (Sco) 4 and 3
Paul Azinger beat Bernhard Langer (Ger)
  4 and 3
Tom Lehman beat Eduardo Romero (Arg)
  2 and 1
Scott Hoch lost to Barry Lane (Eng) 1 hole
Mark O'Meara beat Nick Faldo (Eng) 3 and 2
Tom Kite lost to Ian Woosnam (Wal) 3 and 2
Hale Irwin beat Rodger Davis (Aus) 2 and 1
Fred Funk halved with Isao Aoki (Jpn)
Bob Gilder beat Stewart Ginn (Aus) 1 hole
Raymond Floyd beat Seiji Ebihara (Jpn)
  2 and 1
Tom Watson halved with Denis Durnian (Eng)

Third day result: USA 8, World 4

Overall result: USA 14, World 9

PART VIII

Who's Who
in Golf

British, Irish and Continental Players

Alfredsson, Helen (Swe)
Born Gothenburg, 9 April 1965
Turned professional 1989
After earning Rookie of the Year on the 1989 European Tour she won the 1992 Ladies' British Open. Two years later she was Gatorade Rookie of the Year on the American LPGA Tour. She has competed in the seven Solheim Cup matches played to date and has won titles in Europe, America. Japan and Australia.

Alliss, Peter (GB)
Born Berlin, 28 February 1931
Turned professional 1946
Following a distinguished career as a tournament golfer in which he won 18 titles between 1954 and 1966 and played eight times in the Ryder Cup between 1953 and 1969, he turned to golf commentating. In Britain he works for the BBC and in America for the ABC network. Twice captain of the PGA in 1962 and 1987 he won the Spanish, Italian and Portuguese Opens in 1958. Author or co-author of several golf books and a novel with a golfing background, he has also designed several courses including the Brabazon course at The Belfry in association with Dave Thomas.

Andrew, Kim (née Rostron) (GB)
Born 12 February 1974
After taking the English and Scottish Ladies stroke play titles in 1997 she won the Ladies British Open Amateur a year later. She played in the 1998 and 2000 Curtis Cup matches.

Bailey MBE, Mrs Diane (Frearson née Robb) (GB)
Born Wolverhampton, 31 August 1943
After playing in the 1962 and 1972 Curtis Cup matches she captained the side in 1984, 1986 and 1988. In 1984 at Muirfield the Great Britain and Ireland side lost narrowly to the Americans but she led the side to a first ever victory on American soil at Prairie Dunes in Kansas two years later. The result was a convincing 13-5. She was in charge again when the GB & I side held on to the Cup two years later this time by 11-7 at Royal St George's.

Baker, Peter (GB)
Born Shifnal, Shropshire, 7 October 1967
Rookie of the year in 1987, Peter was hailed as the best young newcomer by Nick Faldo when he beat Faldo in a play-off for the Benson and Hedges International in 1988. Several times a winner since then he played in the 1993 Ryder Cup scoring three points out of four. In the singles he beat Corey Pavin.

Ballesteros, Severiano (Esp)
Born Pedrena, 9 April 1957
Turned professional 1974
Charismatic Spaniard who won 52 titles between 1976 and 1999 including three Opens (1979, 1984 at St Andrews and 1988) and The Masters at Augusta in 1980 and again in 1983. One of four brothers all of whom play golf. He was introduced to the game by big brother Manuel and first hit the headlines when he and Jack Nicklaus finished second to Johnny Miller at Royal Birkdale in 1976. He played in eight Ryder Cups and captained the side to victory at Valderrama in 2000. Never one of golf's straightest hitters his powers of recovery from seemingly impossible positions have been legendary throughout his career. He was the driving force in getting a match started between the British and Irish golfers and the Continentals in 2000. Sadly has lost his game but not his hope that one day it will return.

Barnes, Brian (GB)
Born Addington, Surrey, 3 June 1945
Turned professional 1964
Extrovert Scottish professional whose father-in-law is former Open champion Max Faulkner. He was a ten times winner on the European Tour between 1972 and 1981 and was twice British Seniors champion successfully defending the title in 1996. He played in six Ryder Cup matches most notably at Laurel Valley in 1975 when, having beaten Jack Nicklaus in the morning, he beat him again in the afternoon. Now prevented from continuing to play on the US Senior Tour because of rheumatoid arthritis he is expanding his career as a commentator on both sides of the Atlantic.

Beharrell, John Charles (GB)
Born Birmingham, 14 January 1935
Youngest winner of the Amateur Championship when he took the title at Troon (now Royal Troon) in 1956. Held the post of captain of the Royal and Ancient Golf Club of St Andrews in 1998/99. Married Veronica Anstey, former Curtis Cup player, Australian and New Zealand Ladies champion.

Benka, Peter (GB)
Born London, 18 September 1946
Former Walker Cup player who won the British Youths Championship in 1967 and 1968. Now chairman of the R&A Selection Committee.

Bennett, Warren (GB)
Born Ruislip, 20 August 1971
Turned professional 1994
Leading amateur in the 1994 Open Championship and winner of the Australian Centennial Amateur Championship the same year. Now a professional, he won the 1999 Scottish PGA Championship.

Bisgood CBE, Jeanne (GB)
Born Richmond, Surrey, 11 August 1923
Three times English Ladies champion in 1951, 1953 and 1957. Having played in three Curtis Cups she captained the side in 1970. Between 1952 and 1955 she won the Swedish, Italian, German, Portuguese and Norwegian Ladies titles.

Bjørn, Thomas (Den)
Born Silkeborg, 18 February 1971
Turned professional 1993
A former Danish Amateur champion in 1990 and 1991, he became the first Dane to play in the Ryder Cup when he made the team in 1997. Four down after four holes against Justin Leonard in the last day singles at Valderrama he fought back to halve the match and gain a valuable half-point in the European victory. He missed out on the 1999 match because of injury but was in the 2001 side and beat Stewart Cink in the singles. Won four times in the Challenge Tour before gaining his full European card. He came joint second to Tiger Woods in the 2000 Open at St Andrews just a few weeks after finishing third behind Woods in the US Open at Pebble Beach. In Japan in 1999 he beat Sergio García at the fourth hole of a play-off for the Dunlop Phoenix title. In 2001 he beat Tiger Woods in the Dubai Desert Classic.

Bonallack Kt OBE, Sir Michael (GB)
Born Chigwell, Essex, 31 December 1934
One of only three golfing knights (the others are the late Sir Henry Cotton and Sir Bob Charles) he won the Amateur Championship five times between 1961 and 1970 and was five times English champion between 1962 and 1968. He also won the English stroke play title four times and was twice leading amateur in the Open in 1968 and 1971. In his hugely impressive career he played in nine Walker Cup matches captaining the side on two occasions. He participated in five Eisenhower Trophy matches and five Commonwealth team competitions. He scored his first national title win in the 1952 British Boys' Championship and took his Essex County title 11 times between 1954 and 1972. After serving as secretary of the R&A from 1983 to 1999 he was captain in 1999/2000. Twice winner of the Association of Golf Writers' award in 1968 and 1999, he also received the Bobby Jones award in 1972, the Donald Ross and Gerald Micklem awards in 1991 and the Ambassador of Golf award in 1995. In 2000 he was inducted into the World Hall Golf of Fame. A former chairman of the R&A selection committee, he served as chairman of the PGA from 1976 to 1981 and is now a non-executive director of the PGA European Tour. He was chairman of the Golf Foundation in 1977 and president of the English Golf Union in 1982.

His wife Lady Angela is the former English champion Angela Ward. Sir Michael is currently captain of the Duke's Club of St Andrews. His wife is lady captain.

Bonallack, Lady Angela (née Ward) (GB)
Born Birchington, Kent, 7 April 1937
Wife of Sir Michael Bonallack OBE she played in six Curtis Cup matches. She was leading amateur in the 1975 and 1976 Colgate European Opens, won two English Ladies titles and had victories, too, in the Swedish, German, Scandinavian and Portuguese Championships.

Brown, Ken (GB)
Born Harpenden, Hertfordshire, 9 January 1957
Turned professional 1974
Renowned as a great short game exponent, especially with his hickory-shafted putter, he won four times in Europe between 1978 and 85, and took the Southern Open on the US tour in 1987. He played in two winning Ryder Cup sides in 1985 and 1987 having previously played in the 1977, 1979 and 1983 matches. Latterly he has carved out a new career for himself as a television commentator initially, for Sky TV, now with Peter Alliss on the BBC.

Butler, Ita (née Burke) (Ire)
Born Nenagh, County Tipperary
Having played in the Curtis Cup in 1966, she captained the side that beat the Americans by 5 points at Killarney thirty years later.

Canizares, José Maria (Esp)
Born Madrid, 18 February 1947
Turned professional 1967
A seven-time winner on the European Tour between 1972 and 1992 the popular Spaniard now plays full time on the US Senior Tour where his consistency has enabled him to earn $3.47 million from his first 104 events. A former caddie, he played in four Ryder Cup matches in the 80s winning five and halving two of his 11 games.

Carr, Joe (Ire)
Born Dublin, 18 February 1922
Winner of the Amateur Championship in 1953, 1958 and 1960, he is Ireland's most successful post-war amateur golfer. Between 1954 and 1967 he won six Irish championships, and was Irish Open Amateur champion four times between 1946 and 1956. He won the south of Ireland Open Amateur Championship three times, but took the East of Ireland title and West of Ireland title twelve times each. He played in ten Walker cups and captained the side twice. He was leading amateur in the Open in 1956 and 1958, was awarded the Association of Golf Writers' Trophy in 1953 and was presented with the Bobby Jones Award in 1961 and the Walter Hagen Award in 1967. He captained the R&A in 1991/92.

Casey, Paul (GB)
Born Cheltenham, 21 July 1977
Turned professional 2001
Winner of the English Amateur Championship in 1999 and 2000, he attended Arizona State University where

he was a three time All American in NCAA Golf. While at college he broke records set by Phil Mickelson and Tiger Woods. In the 1999 Walker Cup match, which the Great Britain and Ireland side won at Nairn, he won all of his four games. After turning professional he earned his European Tour card after just five events helped by a second-equal finish in the Great North Open 2001 and twelfth place finishes in the Compass English Open and Benson and Hedges International. He became a winner in his 11th event when taking the Gleneagles Scottish PGA title over the PGA Centenary course. His coach is Peter Kostis. In 2002 he shot a course record 62 at Gut Lärchenhof in the Linde German Masters won by Stephen Leaney.

Cavalleri, Silvia (Ita)
Born Milan, 10 October 1972
Turned professional 1997
Became the first Italian to win the US Amateur when she beat Robin Burke 5 and 4 at Brae Burn in the final. She was five times Italian National Junior champion and won the British Girls title in 1990 with a 5 and 4 success over E Valera at Penrith. As a professional her best finish to date is tied second in the 2000 Ladies' Italian Open.

Chapman, Roger (GB)
Born Nakuru, Kenya, 1 May 1959
Turned professional 1981
After playing on the European Tour for eighteen years without success, he lost his card and had to return to the qualifying school in 1999. Regaining his playing privileges with a twelfth place finish in the six round competition, he made his break-through win by beating Padraig Harrington at the second hole of a play-off in the Brazil Rio de Janeiro Five Hundred Years Open. Later that year he won the Hassan II Trophy at Dar-Es-Salaam in Morocco. A former English Amateur Champion in 1981 he played in the Walker Cup the same year beating Hal Sutton twice in a day at Cypress Point.

Clark, Clive (GB)
Born Winchester, 27 June 1945
Turned professional 1965
In the 1965 Walker Cup at Five Farms East in Maryland, he holed a 35-foot putt to earn a half point against Mark Hopkins and ensure a drawn match against the Americans. After turning professional he played in the 1973 Ryder Cup and was a four time winner of titles between 1966 and 1974. Following a career as commentator with the BBC he continued his golf course architecture work in America, and has received awards for his innovative designs.

Clark, Howard (GB)
Born Leeds, 26 August 1954
Turned professional 1973
A scratch player by the age of 16 he turned professional after playing in the 1973 Walker Cup. An eleven-time winner on the European tour he played in six Ryder Cups and was in the winning team three times – in 1985 at The Belfry, 1987 at Muirfield Village, when the Europeans won for the first time on American soil, and in 1995 when

he gained a vital point helped by a hole in one in the last day singles against Peter Jacobsen. In the 1985 World Cup played at La Quinta in Palm Springs he was the individual champion. He played 494 tournaments before giving up full-time competition to concentrate on his job as a golf analyst on the Sky TV commentary team.

Clarke, Darren (GB)
Born Dungannon, Northern Ireland, 14 August 1968
Turned professional 1990
He became the first European Tour player to shoot 60 twice when he returned that record low score at the European Open at the K Club in 1999. Seven years earlier he had shot a nine under par 60 at Mont Agel in the European Monte Carlo Open, but his 60 in Dublin was 12 under par. With his second 60 he also equalled two other records. With twelve birdies on the card he matched the best birdie total in a round and he also scored a record-equalling eight birdies in a row. Tied second in the 1997 Open behind Justin Leonard, he was third equal in 2001 at Lytham, Clarke played particularly well in the 2000 Andersen Consulting Match Play Championship at La Costa in California beating Paul Azinger, Mark O'Meara, Thomas Bjørn, Hal Sutton and David Duval to reach the final against Tiger Woods. He became the first European to win a World Golf Championship event when he beat Woods 4 and 3 and picked up the million dollar first prize. He played in the 1997, 1999 and 2001 Ryder Cup matches making a vital half point on the final day with David Duval in the 2001 match.

Coles MBE, Neil (GB)
Born 26 September 1934
Turned professional 1950
Remarkably he has won golf tournaments in six decades. In 1956 he won the Gor-Ray tournament and made golfing history when he took the Microlease Jersey Seniors Open at La Moye in 2000. From 1973 to 1979 he played in 68 events on the main European Tour without missing a half-way cut and became the then oldest winner when he won the Sanyo Open in Barcelona in 1982 at the age of 48 years and 14 days. (Des Smyth has since become an even older winner.) Coles remains, however, the oldest winner on the European Senior tour scoring his Jersey win when aged 65 years and 10 months and the following year won the Lawrence Batley Seniors Open at Huddersfield. A member of eight Ryder Cup teams, he has represented his country nineteen times since turning professional at the age of sixteen with a handicap of 14. He has been chairman of the PGA European Tour's Board of Directors since its inception in 1971 and in 2000 was inducted into the World Golf Hall of Fame. Internationally respected he might well have won more in America but for an aversion to flying caused by a bad experience on an internal flight from Edinburgh to London.

Coltart, Andrew (GB)
Born Dumfries, 12 May 1970
Turned professional 1991
Twice Australian PGA champion in 1994 and 1997 he was the Australasian circuit's top money earner for the

1997/98 season. He made his Ryder Cup debut at Brookline in 1999 as a captain's pick and on the final day found himself up against Tiger Woods. He played well but still lost. A former Walker Cup and Eisenhower Trophy player he was a member of the only Scottish team to win the Alfred Dunhill Cup at St Andrews in 1995. His European Tour successes include the 1998 Qatar Masters and 2001 Great North Open. His sister Laurae is married to fellow professional Lee Westwood.

Darcy, Eamonn (Ire)
Born Dalgeny, 7 August 1952
Turned professional 1969
One of Ireland's best known players who has played more than 600 tournament appearances on the European Tour despite suffering for many years with back trouble. First played when he was 10 years old and is renowned for his very distinctive swing incorporating a flying right elbow. He played in four Ryder Cups including the memorable one at Muirfield Village in 1987 when Europe won for the first time in America. He scored a vital point in the last day singles holing a tricky left to right downhill seven footer for a valuable point against Ben Crenshaw. In 2002 he joined the European Senior Tour.

Davidson, Alison (née Rose) (GB)
Born Stirling, Scotland, 18 June 1968
Twice a Curtis Cup player in 1996 and 1998. She won the Ladies British Open Amateur in 1997.

Davies CBE, Laura (GB)
Born 10 October 1963
Turned professional 1985
Record-breaking performer who has won over 60 events worldwide including the US and British Women's Opens. For six days in 1987 she held both titles having won the American event before joining the US Tour. Was a founder member of the Women's Tour in Europe where she has won a record 33 times. Still holds the record for the number of birdies in a round – 11 which she scored in the 1987 Open de France Feminin. Her 16-shot victory, by a margin of five shots, in the 1995 Guardian Irish Holidays Open at St Margaret's remains the biggest in European Tour history. Her 267 totals in the 1988 Biarritz Ladies Open and the 1995 Guardian Irish Holidays Open are the lowest on Tour. Other major victories include the LPGA Championship twice and the du Maurier Championship. A big-hitting 5ft 10 ins blonde she has won every year in America since 1988 except in 1990, 1992 and 1999 when her best finish was second. Between 1985 and 1999 she had won in Europe at least once a season. In 1999 became the first European Tour player to pass through the £1 million in prize-money earnings and finished European No. 1 that year for a record fifth time. The 1996 Rolex Player of the Year in America she has won almost $5.5 million in US prize-money. Originally honoured with an MBE by Her Majesty the Queen in 1988, she became a CBE in 2000. Enjoys all sports including soccer (she supports Liverpool FC). Among other awards she has received

during her career have been the Association of Golf Writers' Trophy for her contribution to European golf in 1994 and the American version in 1994 and 1996 for her performances on the US Tour. In 1994 she became the first golfer to score victories on five different Tours – European, American, Australasian, Japanese and Asian in one calendar year. As an amateur she played for Surrey and was a Curtis Cup player in 1984. She has competed in all seven Solheim Cup matches. In 2000 was recognised by the LPGA in their top 50 players and teachers.

Donald, Luke (GB)
Born Hemel Hempstead, Hertfordshire, 7 December 1977
Member of the winning Great Britain and Ireland team against the Americans in the 1999 Walker Cup at Nairn and again in 2001 before turning professional. In 1999 won the NCAA Championship and was named NCAA Player of the Year. Has played most of his golf in 2002 in America and he scored his first win on the US Tour when he took the rain-shortened Southern Farms Bureau title, becoming the 18th first-time winner of the season.

Dowling, Clare (née Hourihane) (Ire)
Born 18 February 1958
Won three Irish Ladies Championships in a row – 1983, 1984 and 1985 and won the title again in 1987 and 1991. She won the 1986 British Ladies Stroke play amateur title. Two years earlier she had made the first of five playing appearances in the Curtis Cup before acting as non-playing captain in 2000.

Drew, Norman (GB)
Born Belfast, 25 May 1932
Turned professional 1958
Twice Irish Open Amateur champion in 1952 and 1953 he played in the 1953 Walker Cup and six years later represented Great Britain and Ireland in the Ryder Cup.

Duggelby, Emma (GB)
Born Fulford, York, 5 October 1971
Talented English golfer who won the British Ladies Open Amateur Championship in 1994 and the English Ladies in 2000 when she also made her Curtis Cup début.

Faldo MBE, Nick (GB)
Born Welwyn Garden City, 18 July 1957
Turned professional 1976
Decided to turn professional after watching the US Masters on television and being impressed by Jack Nicklaus's performance. Europe's most successful major title winner having won three Open Championships in 1987, 1990 at St Andrews and 1992 and three Masters titles in 1989, 1990 and 1996. Of current day players only Tom Watson with eight wins has won more majors. When he successfully defended the Masters in 1990 he became only the second man (after Nicklaus) to win in successive years. Staged a dramatic last day revival to win the 1996 Masters having started the last round six behind Greg Norman. When he realised his swing was not good enough to win

majors he completely revamped it with the help of coach David Leadbetter. His 31 European Tour victories include a record three Irish Open victories in a row. In 1992 became the first player to win over £1 million in prize-money during a season. He played with distinction in 11 Ryder Cup matches including the winning teams in 1985, 1987, 1995 and 1997. He holds the record for most games played in the Cup – 46 – and most points won – 25. In 1995 at Oak Hill came from behind to score a vital last day point against Curtis Strange, the American who had beaten him in a play-off for the US Open title in 1988 at The Country Club in Boston. He became the first international player to be named USPGA Player of the Year in 1990 and led the official World Golf Rankings for 81 weeks in 1993-1994. After having teamed up with Swedish caddie Fanny Sunesson for ten years they split only to be reunited as one of golf's best-known partnerships in 2001.

Fasth, Niclas (Swe)
Born Gothenburg, Sweden, 29 April 1972
Turned professional 1989
Tried to play both US and European tours in 1998 but found it too difficult. Made the headlines in 2001 when finishing second to David Duval in the Open. Played in the 2001 Ryder Cup side and made a half point against Paul Azinger on the final day.

Faulkner OBE, Max (GB)
Born Bexhill, Sussex, 29 July 1916
Turned professional 1933
One of the game's most extrovert and colourful characters who played in five Ryder Cups but whose career highlight was winning the Open at Royal in 1951. After having been ignored for an honour for 50 years he was deservedly recognised in 2001 when awarded an OBE. He is father-in-law of Brian Barnes.

Feherty, David (GB)
Born Bangor, Northern Ireland, 13 August 1958
Turned professional 1976
Quick-witted Ulsterman who gave up his competitive golfing career to become a hugely successful commentator for CBS in America where his one-liners are legendary. Had five European title wins and three victories on the South African circuit before switching his golf clubs for a more lucrative career with a microphone.

Fiddian, Eric Westwood (GB)
Born Stourbridge, Worcestershire, 28 March 1910
Best remembered for having had two holes in one during the final of the 1933 Irish Open Amateur Championship but still lost by 3 and 2 to J. McLean.

Foster, Rodney (GB)
Born Shipley, Yorkshire, 13 October 1941
Played in the Walker Cup five times between 1965 and 1973 and captained the side in 1979. He also captained the Eisenhower Trophy team in 1980.

Fulke, Pierre (Swe)
Born Nyköping, Sweden, 21 February 1971
Turned professional 1993
Son of a Swedish swimming champion he finished runner-up to Steve Stricker in the 2001 Accenture Matchplay Championship a few weeks after winning the Volvo Masters. Played on the 2001 winning Ryder Cup side.

Gallacher CBE, Bernard (GB)
Born Bathgate, Scotland, 9 February 1949
Turned professional 1967
For many years combined tournament golf with the club professional's post at Wentworth where he was honoured in 2000 by being appointed captain. He took up golf at the age of 11 and nine years later was European No.1. He has scored 30 victories worldwide. Gallacher was the youngest Ryder Cup player when he made his début in the 1969 match in which he beat Lee Trevino in the singles. He played in eight Cup matches and captained the side three times losing narrowly in 1991 at Kiawah Island and 1993 at The Belfry before leading the team to success at Oak Hill in 1995. He is a member of the European Tour's Board of Directors. Now plays on the European Senior Tour and made his break-through win in 2002 when he took first prize in the Mobile Cup at Stoke Park.

García, Sergio (Esp)
Born Castellon, 9 January 1980
Turned professional 1999
The extrovert Spaniard having won the French and Amateur Championships in 1997 took the British title in 1998 and in both years was European Amateur Masters champion. Son of a greenkeeper/professional who now plays on the European Senior Tour, Sergio's future was always going to be in professional golf but he waited until after the 1999 Masters in which he was leading amateur before joining the paid ranks at the Spanish Open. Although only just starting to collect Ryder Cup points he easily made the 1999 team and formed an invaluable partnership with Jesper Parnevik at Brookline scoring three and a half points out of four on the first two days. Victories in the Murphy's Irish Open and Linde German Masters helped him to the 1999 Rookie of the Year title in Europe but arguably an even better performance was finishing runner-up to Tiger Woods in the US PGA Championship at Medinah outside Chicago. Although he did not win in 2000 he won the Mastercard Colonial and Buick Classic on the US Tour in 2001 and the Mercedes Championship, the Canaries Open de España and the Kolon Cup in Korea. He was in the 2001 Ryder Cup team and formed a useful partnership with Lee Westwood winning 3 out of 4 points in the first two days.

Garrett, Maureen (*née* Ruttle) (GB)
Born 22 August 1922
President of the Ladies' Golf Union from 1982 to 1985, she captained the Curtis Cup (1960) and Vagliano Trophy (1961) teams. In 1983 won the Bobby Jones

award presented annually by the United States Golf Association to a person who emulates Jones' spirit, personal qualities and attitude to the game and its players.

Garrido, Ignacio (Esp)
Born Madrid, 27 March 1972
Turned professional 1993
Eldest son of Antonio Garrido who played in the 1979 Ryder Cup, Ignacio emulated his father when he made the team at the 1997 match at Valderrama having earlier that year won the Volvo German Open. Before turning professional with a handicap of 4 he won the English Amateur Stroke Play title (the Brabazon Trophy) in 1992. In the 80s used to caddie for his father who has since caddied for him on occasion.

Garvey, Philomena (Ire)
Born Drogheda, Co Louth, 27 April 1927
Turned professional 1964 but later reinstated
Winner of the Irish Ladies title 15 times between 1946 and 1970 and six times a Curtis Cup player between 1948 and 1960 she remains one of Ireland's most successful players. In 1957 she won the British Ladies Open Amateur title.

Glover, John (GB)
Born Belfast, 3 March 1933
He was secretary of the R&A Rules of Golf committee from 1980 until his retirement in 1995. He played eight times for Ireland between 1951 and 1970.

Goldschmid Isa (*née* Bevione) (Ita)
Born Italy, 15 October 1925
One of Italy's greatest amateurs she won her national title 21 times between 1947 and 1974 and was ten times Italian Open champion between 1952 and 1969. Among her other triumphs were victories in the 1952 Spanish Ladies and the 1973 French Ladies.

Green OBE, Charlie (GB)
Born Dumbarton, 2 August 1932
One of Scotland's most successful amateur golfers who was leading amateur in the 1962 Open Championship. A prolific winner he took the Scottish Amateur title three times in 1970, 1982 and 1983. He played in five and was non-playing captain in two more Walker Cups and was awarded the Frank Moran Trophy for his services to Scottish sport in 1974.

Gustafson, Sophie (Swe)
Born Saro, 27 December 1973
Turned professional 1992
Winner of the 2000 Weetabix Women's British Open she had studied marketing, economics and law before turning to professional golf. Credits Seve Ballesteros and Laura Davies as the two players most influencing her career. Her first European victory was the 1996 Swiss Open and her first on the US LPGA Tour was the Chick-fil-A Charity Cup in 2000. Played in the 1998, 2000 and 2002 Solheim Cups.

Haeggman, Joakim (Swe)
Born Kalmar, 28 August 1969
Turned professional 1989
Became the first Swedish player to play in the Ryder Cup when he made the side which lost to the Americans at The Belfry in 1993. He received one of team captain Bernard Gallacher's 'wild cards' and beat John Cook in his last day singles. Gave up ice hockey after dislocating his shoulder and breaking ribs in 1994. Realised then that ice hockey and golf do not mix but has become an enthusiastic angler when not on the links. Equalled the world record of 27 for the first nine holes in the Alfred Dunhill Cup over the Old course at St Andrews in 1997. Occasionally acts as commentator for Swedish TV and was a member of Sam Torrance's Ryder Cup back-room team at The Belfry last year.

Hall, Julie (GB)
Born Ipswich, Suffolk, 10 March 1967
Secretary of the Ladies Golf Union from 1996 to 2000 she was one of the most successful competitors in both individual and team golf. Among the many titles she won were the English Stroke Play in 1987 and 1993, the British Ladies Stroke Play in 1993 and the Scottish Stroke Play in 1991 and 1993. She shared Britain's Golfer of the Year award in 1993 and won it again in 1995 on her own. She played in five Curtis Cups matches including the victories at Royal Liverpool 1992 and Killarney in 1996 and the drawn match in 1994 at Chattanooga. Now works with the R&A.

Harrington, Padraig (Ire)
Born Dublin, Ireland, 31 August 1971
Turned professional 1995
A qualified accountant, he was Irish Open and Close Amateur champion (1995) and played three times in the Walker Cup player before turning professional. Played in the 1999 Ryder Cup at Brookline and beat Mark O'Meara in the singles. He was a member of the victorious European team for the postponed 2001 match beating Mark Calcavecchia in the final day singles. Remembered in 2000 for being disqualified on the final day of the Benson and Hedges International at The Belfry after having moved into a five shot lead at the 54-hole stage. It was only then discovered that one of his playing partners had signed Harrington's card on the first day and not Harrington himself. The manner in which he accepted this disappointment greatly impressed observers. In the autumn of 2002 he won the US$800,000 first pize in the Dunhill Links Championship beating Eduardo Romero at the 2nd play-off hole at St Andrews.

Harris, Marley (*née* Spearman) (GB)
Born January 11 1982
Superb ambassadress for golf in the 1950s and 1960s whose exuberance and joie de vivre is legendary. Three times a Curtis Cup player she won the British Ladies in 1961 and again in 1962. She was English champion in 1964. In 1962 was awarded the Association of Golf Writers' Trophy for her services to golf.

Hjörth, Maria (Swe)
Born Falun, 10 October 1973
Turned professional 1996
After an excellent amateur career when she won titles in Finland, Norway and Spain (where she won the prestigious Sherry Cup), she attended Stirling University in Scotland on a golf bursary and graduated with a BA honours degree in English before turning professional. In 2002 she played in the Solheim Cup.

Horton MBE, Tommy (GB)
Born St Helens, Lancashire, 16 June 1961
Turned professional 1957
A former Ryder Cup player who was no.1 earner on the European Seniors Tour in 1993 and for four successive seasons between 1996 and 1999. Awarded an MBE by Her Majesty the Queen for his services to golf, Tommy is a member of the European Tour Board and is chairman of the European Seniors Tour committee. A distinguished coach, broadcaster, author and golf course architect, Tommy retired as club professional at Royal Jersey in 1999 after 25 years in the post.

Howard, Barclay (GB)
Born Johnstone, Scotland, 27 January 1953
Leading amateur in the Open Championship at Royal Troon in 1997, he has successfully battled cancer which affected his golfing career after he had played in both the 1995 and 1997 Walker Cup matches. When Dean Robertson won the Italian Open at Turin in 1999 he dedicated his victory to him as a tribute to his courage in adversity.

Hudson, Rebecca (GB)
Born Doncaster, Yorkshire, 13 June 1979
Turned professional 2002
A member of the 1998 and 2000 and 2002 Curtis Cup teams Rebecca is one of the most gifted of younger players. In 2000 she won both the British Match Play and Stroke Play titles, the Scottish and English Stroke play Championships and the Spanish Women's Open. In addition she made the birdie that ensured Great Britain and Ireland won a medal in the World Team Championship for the Espirito Santo Trophy in Berlin in 2000.

Huggett MBE, Brian (GB)
Born Porthcawl, Wales, 18 November 1936
Turned professional 1951
Brian won the first of his 16 European Tour titles in Holland in 1962 and was still winning in 2000 when he landed the Beko Seniors Classic in Turkey after a play-off. A dogged competitor he played in six Ryder Cup matches before being given the honour of captaining the side in 1977 – the last year the Americans took on players from only Great Britain and Ireland. A respected golf course designer, Huggett was awarded the MBE for his services to golf and in particular Welsh golf.

Hunt MBE, Bernard (GB)
Born Atherstone, Warwickshire, 2 February 1930
Turned professional 1946
One of Britain's most accomplished professionals he won 22 times between 1953 and 1973. He was third in the 1960 Open at the Old Course behind Kel Nagle and fourth in 1964 when Tony Lema took the title at St Andrews. Among his other victories were successes in Egypt and Brazil. Having made eight appearances in the Ryder Cup he captained the side in 1973 and again in 1975. He was PGA captain in 1966 and won the Harry Vardon Trophy as leading player in the Order of Merit on three occasions.

Ilonen, Mikko (Fin)
Born Lahti, 18 December 1979
Turned professional 2001
Became the first Finnish golfer to win the Amateur Championship when he beat Christian Reimbold from Germany 2 and 1 in the final at Royal Liverpool. He has won both the Finnish match play and stroke play titles.

Irvin, Ann (GB)
Born 11 April 1943
Winner of the British Ladies' title in 1973, she played in four Curtis Cup matches between 1962 and 1976. She was Daks Woman Golfer of the Year in 1968 and 1969 and has been active in administration at junior and county level.

Jacklin CBE, Tony (GB)
Born Scunthorpe, 7 July 1944
Turned professional 1962
Played an important and often under-rated role in the growth of the PGA European Tour after it became a self-supporting organisation in 1971. Although playing most of his golf in America he was encouraged by John Jacobs, the then executive director of the European Tour, to return to Europe to help build up the circuit. In 1969 he won the Open Championship at Royal Lytham and St Annes – the first British winner of the title since Max Faulkner in 1951. A year later he led from start to finish to win the US Open at Hazeltine – the first British player to win that event since Ted Ray had been successful in 1920 and the only one to have done so to date. He was the first player since Harry Vardon to hold the British and American Open titles simultaneously. He might well have won further Opens but a thunderstorm halted his bid for the title at St Andrews in 1970, he came third in 1971 and in 1972 Lee Trevino chipped in at the 17th at Muirfield and went on to win a title the British player had seemed set to win.

Jackson, Bridget (GB)
Born Birmingham, 10 July 1936
A former President of the Ladies Golf Union she played in three Curtis Cup matches and captained the Vagliano Trophy side twice after having played four times. Although the best she managed in the British Championship was runner-up in 1964 she did win the English, German and Canadian titles.

Jacobs OBE, John (GB)
Born Lindrick, Yorkshire, 14 March 1925
The first Executive Director of the independently run PGA European Tour, John Jacobs was awarded the OBE in 2000 for his services to golf as a player,

administrator and coach. Known as 'Dr Golf' Jacobs has built up an awesome reputation as a teacher around the world and is held in high esteem by the golfing world. Top American coach Butch Harmon summed up Jacobs' contribution in this field of golf when he said: 'There is not one teacher who does not owe something to John. He wrote the book on coaching.' With 75 per cent of the votes he was inducted into the World Golf Teachers Hall of Fame and was described at that ceremony as 'the English genius'. Last year he was also, quite correctly, welcomed into the World Golf Hall of Fame in America. Having played in the 1955 Ryder Cup match he captained the side in 1979 when Continental players were included for the first time and again in 1981. Ken Schofield who succeeded him as European Tour supremo believes that Jacobs changed the face of golf sponsorship allowing, as he points out, more than 10 players a season to earn a living.

James, Mark (GB)
Born Manchester, 28 October 1953
Turned professional 1976
Veteran of over 500 European tournaments who is now chairman of the European Tour's Tournament committee. A seven-time Ryder Cup player including the 1995 match at Oak Hill when he scored a vital early last day point against Jeff Maggert, he captained the side at Brookline in 1999. Four times a top five finisher in the Open Championship Mark has been involved in his fair share of controversy especially in the early days. He has won 18 European Tour events and four elsewhere but these days having successfully battled cancer, he is just as happy working in his Yorkshire garden. Caused some raised eyebrows with some of his comments in his book reviewing the 1999 Ryder Cup entitled 'Into the Bear Pit'. Affectionately known as Jesse to his friends.

Jarman, Ted (GB)
Born Margate 2 July 1907
Oldest living GB&I Ryder Cup player who competed in the 1935 match at Ridgewood, New Jersey.

Jiménez, Miguel Angel (Esp)
Born Malaga, 4 January 1954
Turned professional 1982
Talented Spaniard who was runner-up to Tiger Woods in the 2000 US Open. This was a year after making his successful début in the Ryder Cup. One of seven brothers he did not take up golf until his mid-teens. He loves cars, drives a Ferrari and has been nicknamed 'The Mechanic' by his friends. His best-remembered shot was the 3-wood he hit into the hole for an albatross 2 at the infamous 17th hole at Valderrama in the Volvo Masters but he was credited with having played the Canon Shot of the Year when he chipped in at the last to win 1998 Trophée Lancôme. In 2000 lost in a play-off at Valderrama in a World Championship to Tiger Woods. He played on both sides of the Atlantic in 2002.

Johansson, Per-Ulrik (Swe)
Born Uppsala, 6 December 1966
Turned professional 1990
A former amateur international at both junior and senior level he became the first Swede to play in two Ryder Cups when he made the 1995 and 1997 teams. In 1997 he played Phil Mickelson with whom he had studied at Arizona State University. In 1991 he was winner of the Sir Henry Cotton Rookie of the Year award in Europe.

Johnson, Trish (GB)
Born Bristol, 17 January 1966
Turned professional 1987
Another stalwart of the Women's Tour in Europe who learned the game at windy Westward Ho. Regular winner on Tour both in Europe and America, she scored two and a half points out of four in Europe's dramatic Solheim Cup win over the Americans at Loch Lomond in 2000. She has played in six Solheim Cup matches. She was European no.1 earner in 1990. A loyal supporter of Arsenal FC she regularly attends games at Highbury.

King, Sam (GB)
Born Sevenoaks, Kent, 27 March 1911
Turned professional 1933
He played Ryder Cup golf immediately before and after World War II and came third in the 1939 Open Championship. In the 1947 Ryder Cup he prevented an American whitewash in the singles by beating Herman Kaiser.

Koch, Karin (Swe)
Born Kungalv, Sweden, 2 February 1971
She has been playing golf since she was nine and in two Solheim Cups remains unbeaten. In 2000 she won 3 points out of 3 and in 2002 2½ points out of 3.

Lane, Barry (GB)
Born Hayes, Middlesex, 21 June 1960
Turned professional 1976
After winning his way into the 1993 Ryder Cup he hit the headlines when he won the first prize of $1 million in the Andersen Consulting World Championship in beating David Frost in the final at Greyhawk in Arizona. He has played over 400 European events.

Langer, Bernhard (Ger)
Born Anhausen, 27 August 1957
Turned professional 1972
One of the game's most respected figures and consistent performers he is best known for having conquered the putting yips on more than one occasion. Twice winner of the US Masters in 1985 and 1993 he has never managed to win the Open despite coming second twice and third on three occasions. Deeply religious he was for many years Germany's only top player. He has been an inspiration to many taking his own National title on 12 occasions and winning 37 titles in Europe between 1980 and 2000. In 1979 he won the Cacherel Under 25s Championship by 17 shots. He played nine times in the Ryder Cup between 1981 and

1997 proving a mainstay in foursomes and fourballs with 11 different partners. He regained his place for the 2001 match after having been overlooked for a captain's pick in 1999 and made 3½ points – 2½ of them partnering Colin Montgomerie. Now plays both the US and European Tours. Has won 11 times in Germany including five German Opens.

Lawrence, Joan (GB)
Born Kinghorn, Fife, 20 April 1930
After a competitive career in which she three times won the Scottish championship and played in the 1964 Curtis Cup, she has played her part in golf administration. She had two four-year spells as an LGU selector, is treasurer of the Scottish Ladies Golf Association and has also served on the LGU executive.

Lawrie MBE, Paul (GB)
Born Aberdeen, 1 January 1969
Turned professional 1986
Made golfing history when he came from 10 shots back on the final day to win the 1999 Open Championship at Carnoustie after a play-off against former winner Justin Leonard and Frenchman Jean Van de Velde. With his win he became the first home-based Scot since Willie Auchterlonie in 1893 to take the title. Still based in Aberdeen he hit the opening tee shot in the 1999 Ryder Cup and played well in partnership with Colin Montgomerie in foursomes and four balls and in the singles earned a point against Jeff Maggert. Originally an assistant at Banchory Golf Club on Royal Deeside Lawrie has had a hole named after him at the club. Coached by former Tour player Adam Hunter and Scottish Rugby Union psychologist Dr Richard Cox, Lawrie has been awarded an MBE for his achievements in golf.

Lee-Smith, Jennifer (GB)
Born Newcastle-upon-Tyne, 2 December 1948
Turned professional 1977
After winning the Ladies British Open as an amateur in 1976 was named Daks Woman Golfer of the Year. She played twice in the Curtis Cup before turning professional and winning nine times in a six year run from 1979. For a time she ran her own driving range in southern England but now lives in Florida.

De Lorenzi, Marie-Laure (Fra)
Born Biarritz, 21 January 1961
Turned professional 1986
The stylish French golfer won 20 titles in Europe between 1987 and 1997 setting a record in 1988 when she won eight times but for family reasons never spent time on the US Tour. Jointly holds the record for 54 holes on the European Tour with her 201 total in the 1995 Dutch Open.

Lunt, Michael (GB)
Born Birmingham, 20 May 1935
Won the Amateur Championship in 1963 beating John Blackwell in the final then reached the final again the following year. He was English Amateur champion in 1966 and played four times in the Walker Cup.

Lyle MBE, Sandy (GB)
Born Shrewsbury, 9 February 1958
Turned professional in 1977
With his win in the 1985 Open Championship at Royal St. George's became the first British player to take the title since Tony Jacklin in 1969. He was also the first British player to win a Green Jacket in the Masters at Augusta in 1988 helped by a majestic 7-iron second shot out of sand at the last for a rare winning birdie 3. Although he represented England as an amateur at boys', youths' and senior level he became Scottish when he turned professional, something he was entitled to do at the time because his late father, the professional at Hawkstone Park, was a Scot. This is no longer allowed. He made his international début at age 14 and, two years later, qualified for and played 54 holes in the 1974 Open at Royal Lytham and St Annes. A tremendously talented natural golfer he fell a victim later in his career to becoming over-technical. Now lives in Perthshire in Scotland but still competes when possible on the US Tour and on the European Tour.

McDowell, Graeme (GB)
Born Ballymoney, Northern Ireland, 30 July 1979
Turned professional 2002
A member of the winning Great Britain and Ireland Walker Cup team in 2001, he earned his European Tour card in just his fourth event as a professional. McDowell, who had been signed up to represent the Kungsangen Golf Club in Sweden just two weeks earlier, received a last minute sponsor's invitation to play there in the Volvo Scandinavian Masters ... and not only won the event but also broke the course record with an opening round of 64. He beat Trevor Immelman into second place with former US PGA champion Jeff Sluman third. McDowell's winning score of 270 – 14-under-par – earned him a first prize of over £200,000 and a place in the World Golf Championship NEC event at Sahalee in Washington. He was the European Tour's 12th first time winner of the season and at 23 the youngest winner of the title.

McEvoy, Peter (GB)
Born London, 22 March 1953
The most capped player for England who has had further success as a captain of Great Britain and Ireland's Eisenhower Trophy and Walker Cup sides. The Eisenhower win came in 1998 and the Walker Cup ttriumphs at Nairn in 1999 and at Ocean Forest, Sea Island, Georgia in 2001. On both occasions his team won 15-9. A regular winner of amateur events McEvoy was amateur champion in 1977 and 1978 and won the English stroke play title in 1980. He reached the final of the English Amateur the same year. In 1978 he played all four rounds in the Masters at Augusta and that year received the Association of Golf Writers' Trophy for his contribution to European golf. He was leading amateur in two Open Championships – 1978 and 1979.

McGimpsey, Garth (Ire)
Born 17 July 1955
A long hitter who was Irish long-driving champion in 1977 and UK long-driving title holder two years later. He was amateur champion in 1985 and Irish champion the same year and again in 1988. He played in three Walker Cup matches and competed in the home internationals for Ireland in 1978 and from 1980 to 1998. He will captain the Walker Cup side in 2003.

McGinley, Paul (Ire)
Born Dublin, 16 December 1966
Turned Professional 1991
Popular Irish golfer who turned to the game after breaking his left kneecap playing Gaelic football. With Padraig Harrington won the 1977 World Cup at Kiawah and made his Ryder Cup début when the postponed 2001 match was played in 2002. In a tense finish to his match with Jim Furyk he holed from 9 feet to get the half point the Europeans needed for victory.

Macgregor, George (GB)
Born Edinburgh, 19 August 1944
After playing in five Walker Cup matches he captained the side in 1991 and later served as chairman of the R&A Selection committee. He won the Scottish Stroke Play title in 1982 after having been runner up three times.

McKenna, Mary (Ire)
Born Dublin, 29 April 1949
Winner of the British Ladies Amateur Stroke play title in 1979 and eight times Irish champion between 1969 and 1989. One of Ireland's most successful golfers she played in nine Curtis Cup matches and nine Vagliano Trophy matches between 1969 and 1987. She captained the Vagliano team in 1995. Three times a member of the Great Britain and Ireland Espirito Santo Trophy side she went on to captain the team in 1986. She was Daks Woman Golfer of the Year in 1979.

Marks, Geoffrey (GB)
Born Hanley, Stoke-on-Trent, November 1938
President of the English Golf Union in 1995 he captained the Walker Cup side in 1987 after having played on two previous occasions. He made eight appearances for England in the home internationals before captaining the team in a non-playing capacity at the start of the 1980s. He is a former England selector and was chairman of the R&A selection committee for four years from 1989.

Marsh, Dr David (GB)
Born Southport, Lancashire, 29 April 1934
Twice winner of the English Amateur Championship in 1964 and 1970, he was captain of the R&A in 1990/1991. He played in the 1971 Walker Cup match at St Andrews and helped the home side win by scoring a vital one hole victory in the singles against Bill Hyndman. He captained the team in 1973 and 1975 and had a distinguished career as a player and then captain for England between 1956 and 1972. He was chairman of the R&A selection committee from 1979 to 1983 and in 1987 was president of the English Golf Union.

Milligan, Jim (GB)
Born Irvine, Ayrshire, 15 June 1963
The 1988 Scottish Amateur champion had his moment of international glory in the 1989 Walker Cup which was won by the Great Britain and Ireland side for only the third time in the history of the event and for the first time on American soil. With GB&I leading by a point at Peachtree in Atlanta only Milligan and his experienced opponent Jay Sigel were left on the course. The American looked favourite to gain the final point and force a draw. The American was two up with three to play but Milligan hit his approach from 100 yards to a few inches to win the 16th with a birdie then chipped in after both had fluffed chips to square at the 17th. The last was halved leaving the Great Britain and Ireland side historic winners by a point.

Montgomerie MBE, Colin (GB)
Born Glasgow, 23 June 1963
Turned professional 1987
Europe's most consistent golfer who topped the Volvo Order of Merit an unprecedented seven years in a row between 1993 and 1999. Although he has yet to win a major he has come close losing a play-off for the US Open to Ernie Els in 1994 and again being pipped by Els in the 1997 Championship. He was third behind Tom Kite in the 1992 US Open. In 1995 he was beaten in a play-off for the US PGA Championship by Australian Steve Elkington. He has had over 30 victories around the world and has played with distinction in six Ryder Cups. At Brookline in 1999 and at The Belfry in 2002 he was a pillar of strength for the team in difficult on-course conditions. In the 2002 match he was never down and was top points scorer making 4½ out of 5 points. He has twice won the Association of Golf Writers' Golfer of the Year award and has been three times Johnnie Walker Golfer of the Year in Europe. His low round in Europe is 61 achieved at Crans-sur-Sierre in the Canon European Masters in 1996. He has been honoured by Her Majesty the Queen for his record-breaking golfing exploits but is troubled these days by a persistent back injury.

Moodie, Janice (GB)
Born Glasgow, 31 May 1973
Turned professional 1997
The 1992 Scottish Women's Stroke play champion played in two winning Curtis Cup teams and earned All American honours at San Jose State University where she graduated with a degree in psychology. She plays both the European and American Tours and in 2000 finished 17th in America and ninth in Europe. Started playing at age 11 and has been helped considerably by Cawder professional Ken Stevely. In the 2000 Solheim Cup she won three out of four points but was controversially left out of the 2002 team despite having won the Asahi Ryokuken International on the LPGA tour.

Neumann, Liselotte (Swe)
Born Finspang, 20 May 1966
Turned professional 1985
Having won the US Women's Open in 1988 she won the Weetabix British Women's title in 1990 to become

one of six players to complete the Transatlantic double. The others are Laura Davies, Alison Nicholas, Jane Geddes, Betsy King and Patty Sheehan. The 1988 Rookie of the Year on the LPGA Tour she has played in all six Solheim Cup matches.

Nicholas MBE, Alison (GB)
Born Gibraltar, 6 February 1978
In Solheim Cup golf had a successful partnership with Laura Davies. In addition they have both won the British and US Open Championship. Alison's first win on the European Tour came in the 1987 Weetabix British Open and she added the US Open ten years later after battling with Nancy Lopez who was trying to win her national title for the first time. Alison is a former winner of the Association of Golf Writers' Golfer of the Year award and has been honoured with an MBE.

Nilsmark, Catrin (Swe)
Born Gothenburg, Sweden, 28 Aug 1967
Holed the winning putt in Europe's Solheim Cup victory in 1992. Her early career affected by whiplash injury after a car crash. Used to hold a private pilot's licence but now rides Harley Davidson motorcycles. She will captain the 2003 European Solheim Cup side for the match being played in Sweden.

O'Connor Sr, Christy (Ire)
Born Galway, 21 December 1924
Turned professional 1946
Never managed to win the Open but came close on three occasions finishing runner-up to Peter Thomson in 1965 and being third on two other occasions. Played in ten Ryder Cup matches between 1955 and 1973 and scored 24 wins in tournament play between 1955 and 1972. Known affectionately as 'Himself' by Irish golfing fans who have long admired his talent with his clubs. He is a brilliant shot maker.

O'Connor Jr, Christy (Ire)
Born Galway, 19 August 1948
Turned professional 1965
Nephew of Christy Sr, he finished third in the 1985 Open Championship. A winner on the European and Safari circuits he won the 1999 and 2000 Senior British Open – only the second man to successfully defend. Played in two Ryder Cup matches hitting a career best 2-iron to the last green at The Belfry in 1989 to beat Fred Couples and ensure a drawn match enabling Europe to keep the trophy. Now plays on the US Senior Tour but his career was interrupted when he broke a leg in a motorcycle accident.

Olazábal, José Maria (Esp)
Born Fuenterrabia, 5 February 1966
Turned professional 1985
Twice a winner of the Masters, his second triumph was particularly emotional. He had won in 1994 but had to withdraw from the 1995 Ryder Cup with a foot problem eventually diagnosed as rheumatoid polyarthritis in three joints of the right foot and two of the left. He was out of golf for eighteen months but treatment from

Munich doctor Hans-Wilhelm Muller-Wohlfahrt helped him back to full fitness after a period when he was house bound and unable to walk. At that point it seemed as if his career was over, but he came back in 1999 to beat Davis Love III by two shots at Augusta. With over twenty victories in Europe and a further seven abroad, the son of a Real Sebastian greenkeeper who took up the game at the age of four has been one of the most popular players in the game. He competed in six Ryder Cups between 1987 and 1999 frequently partnering Severiano Ballesteros. He is a former British Boys Youths and Amateur champion. His best performance in the Open was third in 1992 when Nick Faldo won at Muirfield.

O'Leary, John (Ire)
Born Dublin, 19 August 1949
Turned professional 1979
After a successful career as a player including victory in the Carrolls Irish Open in 1982 he retired because of injury and now is director of golf at the Buckinghamshire Club. He is a member of the PGA European Tour Board of Directors.

Oosterhuis, Peter (GB)
Born London, 3 May 1948
Turned professional 1968
Twice runner up in the Open Championship in 1974 and 1982, he was also the leading British player in 1975 and 1978. He finished third in the US Masters in 1973, had multiple wins on the European tour and in Africa and won the Canadian Open on the US tour in 1981. He played in six Ryder Cups partnering Nick Faldo at Royal Lytham and St Annes in 1977 when Faldo made his début. He was top earner in Europe four years in a row from 1971. Following his retirement from top-line golf he moved to America and after a spell working for the Golf Channel he is now a respected member of the CBS commentary team.

Panton-Lewis, Cathy (GB)
Born Bridge of Allan, Stirlingshire, 14 June 1955
Turned professional 1978
A former Ladies British Open Amateur Champion in 1976 when she was named Scottish Sportswoman of the year. She notched up thirteen victories as a professional on the European tour between 1979 and 1988. Daughter of John Panton, MBE.

Panton MBE, John (GB)
Born Pitlochry, Perthshire, 9 October 1916
Turned professional 1935
Honorary professional since 1988 to the Royal & Ancient Golf Club of St Andrews, he is one of Scotland's best known and admired professionals. He was leading British player in the 1956 Open and beat Sam Snead for the World Senior's title in 1967. He played in three Ryder Cup matches and was twelve times a contestant in the World Cup with the late Eric Brown as his regular partner. He won the Association of Golf Writer's Trophy for his contribution to the game in 1967 and has been honoured with an MBE.

Parnevik, Jesper (Swe)
Born Danderyd, Stockholm, 7 March 1965
Turned professional 1986
Son of a well-known Swedish entertainer he is one of the most extrovert of golfers best known for his habit of wearing a baseball cap with the brim turned up and brightly coloured drain-pipe style trousers. Winner of events on both sides of the Atlantic he plays most of his golf these days in America where he has won five times since 1998 but made history in 1995 when he became the first Swede to win in Sweden when he took the Scandinavian Masters at Barseback in Malmo. Has twice finished runner-up in the Open at Turnberry in 1994 when he was two ahead but made a bogey at the last and was passed by Nick Price who finished with an eagle and a birdie in the last three holes. He led by two with a round to go in 1998 but shot 73 and finished tied second with Darren Clarke behind Justin Leonard. Played in the 1997 and 1999 Ryder Cup teaming up successfully with Sergio García to win three and a half points in 1999. Was also in the 2001 team and halved with Tiger Woods in the singles. Has had health problems suffering injuries and illness and has resorted at times to unusual remedies including eating volcanic dust to cleanse the system.

Prado, Catherine (*née* Lacoste) (Fra)
Born Paris 27 June 1945
The only amateur golfer ever to win the US Women's Open she won the title at Hot Springs, Virginia in 1967. She was also the first non-American to take the title and the youngest. Two years later she won both the US and British Amateur titles. She was a four times winner of her own French Championship in 1967, 1969, 1970 and 1972 and won the Spanish title in 1969, 1972 and 1976. She comes from a well-known French sporting family.

Price Fisher, Elizabeth (GB)
Born London, 17 January 1923
Turned professional 1968 but reinstated as an amateur
three years later
Between 1950 and 1960 she played in six Curtis Cup matches and, in addition to her 1959 victory in the British Ladies Championship, also won national titles in Denmark and Portugal. For many years worked for the Daily Telegraph.

Price, Phillip (GB)
Born Pontypridd, 21 October 1966
Turned professional 1989
Winner of the 1994 Portuguese Open he abandoned plans to play the US Tour in 2002. He made his Ryder Cup début in 2002 and produced a sterling last day performance when he beat the world no.2 Phil Mickelson 3 and 2 for a vital point.

Rafferty, Ronan (GB)
Born Newry, Northern Ireland, 13 January 1964
Turned professional 1981
Won the Irish Amateur Championship as a 16 year old in 1980 when he also won the English Amateur Open Stroke Play title, competed in the Eisenhower Trophy and played against Europe in the home internationals. Winner of the British Boys, Irish Youths' and Ulster Youths' titles in 1979, he also played in the senior Irish side against Wales that year. A regular winner on the European tour between 1988 and 1993 he was also victorious in tournaments played in South America, Australia and New Zealand. A wrist injury has curtailed his career but he is active on the corporate golf front and often commentates for Sky TV. He has an impressive wine collection.

Reid MBE, Dale (GB)
Born Ladybank, Fife, 20 March 1959
Turned professional 1979
Scored twenty-one wins in her professional career between 1980 and 1991 and was so successful in leading Europe's Solheim Cup side to victory against the Americans at Loch Lomond in 2000 that she was again captain in 2002 when the Americans won. Following the team's success in the 2000 Solheim Cup she received an MBE.

Rivero, José (Esp)
Born Madrid, 20 September 1955
Turned professional 1973
One of only eight Spaniards who have played in the Ryder Cup he competed in the winning 1985 and 1987 sides. Worked as a caddie but received a grant from the Spanish Federation to pursue his golf career. With José Maria Canizares won the World Cup in 1984 at Olgiata in Italy.

Robertson MBE, Belle (GB)
Born Southend, Argyll, 11 April 1936
One of Scotland's most talented amateur golfers who was Scottish Sportswoman of the Year in 1968, 1971, 1978 and 1981. She was Woman Golfer of the Year in 1971, 1981 and 1985. A former Ladies British Open Amateur Champion and six times Scottish Ladies Champion, she competed in nine Curtis Cups acting as non-playing captain in 1974 and 1976.

Rocca, Costantino (Ita)
Born Bergamo, 4 December 1956
Turned professional 1981
The first and to date only Italian to play in the Ryder Cup. In the 1999 match at Valderrama he beat Tiger Woods 4 and 2 in a vital singles. Left his job in a polystyrene box making factory to become a club professional and graduated to the tournament scene through Europe's Challenge Tour. In 1995 he fluffed a chip at the final hole in the Open at St Andrews only to hole from 60 feet out of the Valley of Sin to force a play-off against John Daly which he then lost.

Rose, Justin (GB)
Born Johannesburg, South Africa, 30 July 1980
Turned professional 1998
Walker Cup player who shot to attention in the 1998 Open Championship when he finished top amateur and third behind winner Mark O'Meara after holing his third shot at the last on the final day for a closing birdie.

Immediately after that Open he turned professional and missed his first 21 half-way cuts before finding his feet. In 2002 was a multiple winner in Europe and also won in Japan and South Africa. Delighted his father who watched him win the Victor Chandler British Masters just a few weeks before he died of leukemia.

Sandelin, Jarmo (Swe)
Born Imatra, Finland, 10 May 1967
Turned professional 1987
Extrovert Swede who made his début in the Ryder Cup at Brookline in 1999 although he did not play until the singles. Has always been a snazzy dresser on course where he is one of the game's longest hitters often in the early days with a 54-inch shafted driver. Five time winner on Tour he met his partner Linda when she asked to caddie for him at a Stockholm pro-am.

Saunders, Vivien (GB)
Born Sutton, Surrey, 24 November 1946
Turned professional 1969
Founder of the Women's Professional Golfers' Association (European Tour) in 1978 and chairman for the first two years. In 1969 she was the first European golfer to qualify for the LPGA Tour in America.

Segard, Mme Patrick (de St Saveur, *née* Lally Vagliano) (Fra)
Former chairperson of the Women's Committee of the World Amateur Golf Council holding the post from 1964 to 1972. A four times French champion (1948, 50, 51 and 52) she also won the British (1950), Swiss (1949 and 1965), Luxembourg (1949), Italian (1949 and 1951) and Spanish (1951) amateur titles. She represented France from 1937 to 1939, from 1947 to 1965 and again in 1970.

Smyth, Des (Ire)
Born Drogheda, Ireland, 12 February
Turned professional 1973
Became the oldest winner on the PGA European Tour when he won the Madeira Island Open in 2001. Smyth was several months older than Neil Coles had been when he won the Sanyo Open in Barcelona. One of the Tour's most consistent performers he is fast approaching his 600th appearance at European Tour events since 1974. Five times Irish National Champion he was a member of the winning Irish side in the 1988 Alfred Dunhill Cup.

Sörenstam, Annika (Swe)
Born Stockholm, 9 October 1970
Turned professional 1992
Winner of the US Open in 1995 and 1996 she and Karrie Webb of Australia have battled for the headlines on the US LPGA Tour over the past few years. A prolific winner of titles in America (24 wins to the end July 2001) she won four in a row in early summer 2000 as she and Webb battled again for the No. 1 spot in 2001. Sörenstam was the No. 1 earner in 1995, 1997 and 1998, Webb in 1996, 1999 and 2000. At the Standard Register Ping event she became the first golfer to shoot 59 on the LPGA Tour. Her second round score 59 included 13 birdies, 11 of them in her first 12 holes. Her 36-hole total of 124 beat the previous record set by Webb the previous season by three. Her 54-hole score of 193 matched the record set by Karrie Webb and her 72-hole total of 261 which gave her victory by three shots from Se Ri Pak matched the low total on Tour set by Se Ri Pak in 1998. Sörenstam's 27-under-par winning score was a new record for the Tour beating the 26-under-par score Webb returned in the Australian Ladies' Masters in 1999. Her sister Charlotta also plays on the LPGA and Evian Tours. Before turning professional she finished runner-up in the 1992 US Women's Championship. Sörenstam continued on her winning way in 2002 when her victories included another major – the Kraft Nabisco Championship. By the end of August she had won six times in the US and once more in Europe. By the beginning of October she had won nine times on the 2002 LPGA Tour and collected her 40th LPGA title. Only four players have won more than 9 events in one LPGA season. By October she had won $2.5 million worldwide. When Annika won the Mizuno Classic in Japan she became the first player for 34 years to win 10 titles in a season.

Thomas, David (GB)
Born Newcastle-upon-Tyne, 16 August 1934
Twice runner-up in the Open Championship Welshman Thomas lost a play-off to Peter Thomson in 1958. He played 11 times in the World Cup for Wales and four times in the Ryder Cup. In all he won 10 tournaments between 1961 and 1969 before retiring to concentrate on golf course design. Along with Peter Alliss he designed the Ryder Cup course at The Belfry. Was appointed captain of the Professional Golfers' Association for 2001 – their Centenary year – and for 2002.

Thomas, Vicki (*née* Rawlings) (GB)
Born Northampton, 27 October 1954
One of Wales' most accomplished players who took part in six Curtis Cup matches between 1982 and 1992. She won the Welsh Championship eight times between 1979 and 1994 as well as the British Ladies Stroke Play in 1990.

Torrance MBE, Sam (GB)
Born Largs, Ayrshire, 24 August 1953
Turned professional 1970
Between 1976 and 1998 he won 21 times on the European Tour in which he has played over 650 events. Captain of the 2001 European Ryder Cup side having previously played in eight matches notably holing the winning putt in 1985 to end a 28-year run of American domination. He was an inspired captain when the 2001 match was played in September 2002. Tied 8 points each, Torrance's men won the singles for only the third time since 1979 to win 15½–12½. His father Bob, who has been his only coach, looks after the swings these days of several others on the European Tour including Paul McGinley who holed the nine foot putt that brought the Ryder Cup back to Europe. He was awarded the MBE in 1996. European Tour officials worked out that in his first 28 years Torrance walked an

estimated 14,000 miles and played 15,000 shots earning at the rate of £22 per stroke.

Valentine MBE, Jessie (née Anderson) (GB)

Born Perth, Scotland, 18 March 1915
Turned professional 1960
A winner of titles before and after World War II, she was an impressive competitor and was one of the first ladies to make a career out of professional golf. She won the British Ladies as an amateur in 1937 and again in 1955 and 1958 and was Scottish champion in 1938 and 1939 and four times between 1951 and 1956. But for the war years it is certain she would have had more titles and victories. She played in seven Curtis Cups between 1936 and 1958 and represented Scotland in the Home Internationals on 17 occasions between 1934 and 1958.

Van de Velde, Jean (Fra)

Born Mont de Marsan, 29 May 1966
Turned professional 1987
Who ever remembers who came second? Everybody will remember Jean Van de Velde, however, for finishing runner-up after a play-off with eventual winner Paul Lawrie and American Justin Leonard when the Open returned to a somewhat tricked-up Carnoustie in 1999. Playing the last hole he led by three but refused to play safe and paid a severe penalty. He ran up a triple bogey 7 after seeing his approach ricochet off a stand into the rough and his next into the Barry Burn. He appeared to contemplate playing the half-submerged ball when taking off his shoes and socks and wading in but that was never a possibility. Took up the game as a youngster when holidaying with his parents in Biarritz. Has scored only one win in Europe (the Roma Masters in 1993) and has returned to the European Tour after a spell in America. Made his Ryder Cup début at Brookline in 1999.

Varangot, Brigitte (Fra)

Born Biarritz, 1 May 1940
Winner of the French Amateur title five times in six years from 1961 and again in 1973. Her run in the French Championship was impressive from 1960 when her finishes were 2, 1, 1, 2, 1, 1, 1, 2. She was also a triple winner of the British Championship in 1963, 1965 and 1968. One of France's most successful players she also won the Italian title in 1970.

Walker OBE, Mickey (GB)

Born Alwoodley, Yorkshire, 17 December 1952
Turned professional 1973
Always a popular and modest competitor she followed up an excellent amateur career by doing well as a professional. Twice a Curtis Cup player she won the Ladies British Open Amateur in 1971 and 1972, the English Ladies in 1973 and had victories, too, in Portugal, Spain and America where she won the 1972 Trans-Mississippi title. She won six times as a professional but is perhaps best known for her stirring captaincy of the first four European Solheim Cup sides

leading them to a five point success at Dalmahoy. In 1992 she galvanised her side by playing them tapes of the men's Ryder Cup triumphs. Now a club professional she also works regularly as a television commentator.

Walton, Philip (Ire)

Born Dublin, 28 March 1962
Turned professional 1983
Twice a Walker Cup player he is best remembered for two-putting the last to beat Jay Haas by one hole and clinch victory in the 1995 Ryder Cup at Oak Hill. He played in five Alfred Dunhill Cup competitions at St Andrews and was in the winning side in 1990.

Westwood, Lee (GB)

Born Worksop, Nottinghamshire, 24 April 1973
Turned professional 1993
A former British Youths champion who missed out on Walker Cup honours, he quickly made the grade in the professional ranks. In 2000 he ended the seven-year reign of Colin Montgomerie by taking the top spot in the Volvo Order of Merit. He was six-time winner that year in Europe taking five order of merit titles and beating Montgomerie at the second extra hole of the Cisco World Match Play final at Wentworth. Among his overseas victories are three successful Taiheiyo Masters titles in Japan, the Australian Open in 1997 when he beat Greg Norman in a play-off and the Freeport McDermott Classic at New Orleans on the US Tour. He has already won titles on every major circuit. He is married to Laurae Coltart, sister of fellow professional Andrew Coltart. He has been a member of the last three Ryder Cup teams and in the 2001 match won 3 points out of 4.

White, Ronnie (GB)

Born Wallasey, Cheshire, 9 April 1921
A five times Walker Cup team member between 1947 and 1953 he was one of the most impressive players in post-war amateur golf. He won six and halved one of the 10 Walker Cup matches he played and won the English Amateur in 1949 and the English Open stroke play title the following two years.

Wolstenholme, Gary (GB)

Born Egham, Surrey, 21 August 1960
The 1991 Amateur champion he has been one of the most regular title winners in the past 11 years. Son of former professional the late Guy Wolstenholme he won the 1995 and 1996 British Mid-Amateur Championship, the Chinese Amateur title in 1993, the Emirates Amateur in 1995 and the Finnish Amateur in 1996. He also won the 2002 Australian Amateur Championship title and the 2002 South African stroke-play title. He was England County champion of champions in 1994 and 1996 and he highlighted his appearances in Walker Cup golf by beating Tiger Woods by one hole in the first day singles of the 1995 match at Royal Porthcawl. Great Britain and Ireland won that year but Woods gained his revenge on Wolstenholme by beating him on the second day.

Woosnam MBE, Ian (GB)

Born Oswestry, Shropshire, 2 March 1958
Turned professional 1976

Highlight of his career was winning the Green Jacket at the Masters in 1991 after a last day battle with Spaniard José Maria Olazábal who went on to win in 1994 and again in 1999. Teamed up very successfully with Nick Faldo in Ryder Cup golf and was in four winning teams in 1985, 1987, 1995 and 1997. Was vice-captain in 2001 to Sam Torrance. He has scored 28 European Tour victories and twice won the World Match Play Championship in 1987 when he beat Sandy Lyle, with whom he used to play boys' golf in Shropshire, in 1990 when his opponent was Zimbabwean Mark McNulty and in 2001 when he beat Retief Goosen, then US Open Champion, Colin Montgomerie, Lee Westwood and then Padraig Harrington in the final. In 1989 he lost a low-scoring final to Nick Faldo on the last green. His lowest round was a 60 he returned in the 1990 Monte Carlo Open at Mont Agel. Partnered by David Llewellyn he won the World Cup of Golf in 1987 beating Scotland's Sam Torrance and Sandy Lyle in a play-off. Honoured with an MBE from Her Majesty the Queen he now lives with his family in Jersey. Finished joint third in the 2001 Open at Lytham after having been penalised two shots for discovering on the second tee he had 15 clubs (one over the limit) in his bag.

Wright, Janette (*née* Robertson) (GB)

Born Glasgow, 7 January 1935

Another of Scotland's most accomplished amateur players she competed four times in the Curtis Cup and was four times Scottish champion between 1959 and 1973. Formerly married to the late golf professional Innes Wright her daughter Pamela plays professionally on the LPGA Tour in America.

Wright, Pamela (GB)

Born Aboyne, Scotland, 26 June 1964
Turned professional 1988

Daughter of former Scottish champion and Curtis Cup golfer Janette Wright and the late Aboyne professional Innes Wright. She played in the first three Solheim Cup matches being a member of the winning team at Dalmahoy in 1992 and was vice-captain in 2000. She was an All-American in 1987 and again in 1988 when she also won Collegiate Golfer of the Year honours. She was LPGA Tour rookie of the year in 1989.

Overseas Players

Aaron, Tommy (USA)
Born Gainesville, Georgia, 22 February 1937
Turned professional 1961
After finishing runner-up in the 1972 US PGA Championship he won the 1973 Masters. He was a member of the 1969 and 1973 Ryder Cup teams. Inadvertently marked down a 4 on Roberto de Vicenzo's card for the 17th hole in the 1968 Masters when the Argentinian took 3. De Vicenzo signed for the 4 and lost out by one shot on a play-off for the Green Jacket.

Allenby, Robert (Aus)
Born Melbourne, 12 July 1971
Turned professional 1992
Pipped by a shot from winning the Australian Open as an amateur in 1991 by Wayne Riley's birdie, birdie, birdie finish at Royal Melbourne he won the title three years later as a professional. After competing on the European Tour and winning four times, he now plays on the US Tour. He has played in two Presidents Cup matches in 1996 and 2000.

Isao, Aoki (Jpn)
Born Abiko, Chiba, 31 August 1942
Turned professional 1964
Successful international performer whose only victory on the main US Tour came dramatically in Hawaii in 1983 when he holed a 128 yards pitch for an eagle 3 at the last at Waialae to beat Jack Renner. Only Japanese golfer to win on the main European Tour taking the European Open in 1983. He also won the World Match Play in 1978 beating Simon Owen and was runner up the following year. He holed in one at Wentworth in that event to win a condominium at Gleneagles. He was top earner five times in his own country and is the Japanese golfer who has come closest to winning a major title finishing runner-up two shots behind Jack Nicklaus in the 1980 US Open at Baltusrol.

Azinger, Paul (USA)
Born Holyoke, Massachusetts, 6 January 1960
Turned professional 1981
Helped by a second hole play-off victory against Greg Norman in the 1993 US PGA Championship at Inverness he made almost $1.5 million to finish second on the US money list to Nick Price. The following year he played only four events after having been diagnosed with lymphoma in his right shoulder blade. Happily he made a good recovery and scored his 12th US Tour victory in 2000 and his first since his 1993 US PGA win when he opened with a 63 and led from start to finish in the Sony Open in Hawaii. He played in three Ryder Cup matches in 1989, 1991 and 1993 and was on the 2001 team making headlines by holing a bunker shot at the last to halve with Niclas Fasth. In 1987 he was joint runner-up with Rodger Davis in the Open at Muirfield won by Nick Faldo.

Baddeley, Aaron (Aus)
Born New Hampshire, USA, 17 March 1981
Turned professional 2000
Became the first amateur to win the Australian Open since Bruce Devlin in 1969 and the youngest when he took the title at Royal Sydney in 2000. Then, having turned professional he successfully defended it at Kingston Heath. He had shown considerable promise when at age 15, he qualified for the Victorian Open. Represented Australia in the Eisenhower Trophy and holds both Australian and American passports. Played a limited schedule in 2002 despite having a European Tour card.

Baiocchi, Hugh (RSA)
Born Johannesburg, 17 August 1946
Turned professional 1971
A scratch golfer when he was 15, Hugh Baiocchi joined the Senior PGA Tour after playing with distinction for 23 years on the European Tour. He has played in 31 different countries around the world winning in many of them. He gained an extra special delight at winning the 1978 South African Open emulating his long-time golfing hero Gary Player who is a multiple winner of that title.

Baker-Finch, Ian (Aus)
Born Namour, Queensland, 24 October 1960
Turned professional 1979
Impressive winner of the Open Championship in 1991 he emerged as a tremendous ambassador for golf. Sadly in attempting to hit the ball further off the tee he lost his game completely when teeing up in Tour events and was forced, after an agonising spell, to retire prematurely. After having been given the chance to commentate in Australia, he took up the opportunity to do a similar job for the American ABC network.

Beem, Rich (USA)
Born Phoenix Arizona 24 August 1974
Turned professional 1994.
Playing in only his fourth major championship he hit the headlines in 2002 when he held off the spirited challenge of Tiger Woods to win the US PGA

Championship at Hazeltine. The 31-year-old from Phoenix who now lives in Texas admitted he was 'flabbergasted to have won' having arrived with no expectations, although a winner of two US Tour titles – the 1999 Kemper Open and the 2002 International event at Castle Pines just a few weeks before the US PGA title. Just a year after turning professional Beem had given up the game to sell car stereos and mobile phones before becoming an assistant club professional before returning once again to tournament play in 1999. On the final day at Hazeltine, Beem hit two great shots – a fairway wood to to seven feet for an eagle at the at the 587 yards 11th. and a 40 foot putt for a birdie at the 16th. which helped him hold off Woods who finished with four birdies in a row. Beem prevented Woods from winning three majors in a year for the second time. From 73rd in the World Rankings Beem jumped to 26th.

Berg, Patty (USA)

Born Minneapolis, 13 February 1918
Turned professional 1940
A founder member of the LPGA Tour in America, she won 57 times in her career including the 1946 US Women's Open. She was leading US money winner in 1954, 1955 and 1957. The first president of the LPGA she was honoured several times winning, among others, the Bobby Jones award in 1963 and the Ben Hogan award and Hall of Fame in 1976.

Bradley, Pat (USA)

Born Westford, Massachusetts, 24 March 1951
Turned professional 1974
Winner of four US LPGA majors – the Nabisco Championship, the US Women's Open, the LPGA Championship and the du Maurier Classic, she won 31 times on the American circuit. An outstanding skier and ski instructor as well she started playing golf when she was 11. Every time she won her mother would ring a bell on the porch of the family home whatever the time of day. The bell is now in the World Golf Hall of Fame. She played in four Solheim Cup sides and captained the team in 2000 at Loch Lomond. Inducted into the LPGA Hall of Fame in 1991 she was Rolex Player of the Year in 1986 and 1991.

Brooks, Mark (USA)

Born Fort Worth, Texas, 25 March 1961
Turned professional 1983
A seven-time winner on the US Tour between 1988 and 1996 he took the US PGA Championship title in 1996 after a play-off with Kenny Perry at Valhalla. On that occasion he birdied the 72nd hole and the first extra hole to win but he was beaten by South African Retief Goosen in the 18-hole play-off for the 2000 US Open at Southern Hills in Tulsa. Goosen shot 70, Brooks 72.

Calcavecchia, Mark (USA)

Born Laurel, Nebraska, 12 June 1960
Turned professional 1981
Winner of the 1989 Open Championship at Royal Troon after the first ever four-hole play-off against

Australians Greg Norman and Wayne Grady. He was runner-up in the 1987 Masters at Augusta to Sandy Lyle and came second to Jodie Mudd in the 1990 Players' Championship. He played in the 1987, 1989, 1991 and 2001 Ryder Cup sides.

Campbell, William Cammack (USA)

Born West Virginia, 5 May 1923
One of America's most distinguished players and administrators. He won the US Amateur Championship in 1964 and was runner-up in the Amateur Championship in Britain to Australian Doug Bachli at Muirfield. One of a select group who have been both President of the United States Golf Association (in 1983) and captain of the Royal and Ancient Golf Club of St Andrews (in 1987/1988). He played in eight Ryder Cup matches between 1951 and 1975 captaining the side in 1955.

Caponi, Donna (USA)

Born Detroit, Michigan, 29 January 1945
Turned professional 1965
Twice winner of the US Women's Open in 1969 and 1970 she collected 24 titles between 1969 and 1981 on the LPGA Tour. Winner of the 1975 Colgate European Open at Sunningdale, she is now a respected commentator/analyst.

Carner, Jo Anne (*née* Gunderson) (USA)

Born Kirkland, Washington, 4 April 1939
Turned professional 1970
Had five victories in the US Ladies' Amateur Championship (1957, 1960, 1962, 1966 and 1968) before turning professional and winning the 1971 and 1976 US Women's Open. She remains the last amateur to win on the LPGA Tour after having taken the 1969 Burdine's Invitational. Between 1970 and 1985 scored 42 victories on the LPGA Tour and was Rolex Player of the Year in 1974, 1981 and 1982. She was inducted into the LPGA Hall of Fame in 1982 and the World Golf Hall of Fame in 1985. She won the Bobby Jones award in 1981 and the Mickey Wright award in 1974 and 1982.

Casper, Billy (USA)

Born San Diego, California, 24 June 1931
Turned professional 1954
A three-time major title winner he took the US Open in 1959 and 1966 and the US Masters in 1970. In 1966 he came back from seven strokes behind Arnold Palmer with nine to play to force a play-off which he then won. Between 1956 and 1975 he picked up 51 first prize cheques on the US Tour. His European victories were the 1974 Trophée Lancôme and Lancia D'Oro and the 1975 Italian Open. As a senior golf he won nine times between 1982 and 1989 including the US Senior Open in 1983. Played in eight Ryder Cups and captained the American side in 1979 at Greenbrier. He and wife Shirley have 11 children several of them adopted. He was named Father of the Year in 1966. Started playing golf aged 5 and rates Ben Hogan, Byron Nelson and Sam Snead as his

heroes. Five times Vardon Trophy winner (for low season stroke-average) and twice top money earner he was US PGA Player of the Year in 1966 and 1970. He was inducted into the World Golf Hall of Fame in 1978 and the US PGA Hall of Fame in 1982.

Charles, Sir Bob (NZ)
Born Auckland, 14 March 1936
Turned professional 1960

Three years after turning professional he became the first and still the only New Zealander and left-hander to win the Open Championship. He defeated Phil Rodgers in the last 36-hole play-off for the title at Royal Lytham and St Annes then was runner-up in 1968 to Gary Player at Carnoustie and in 1969 to Tony Jacklin again at Lytham. Earlier in 1954 he had won the first of his four New Zealand Opens as an amateur. Between 1954 and 1960 worked in a bank before embarking on a golf career which has seen him win extensively around the world on golf's main Tours and the US Senior Tour. He won seven times on the US Tour, nine times in Europe, 24 times in New Zealand and has also won in Canada, Japan and South Africa. He does everything right-handed except games requiring two hands. In 1972 received the OBE from Her Majesty the Queen, the CBE in 1992 and was knighted in 1999 for his services to golf.

Cink, Stewart (USA)
Born Huntsville, Alabama, 21 May 1973
Turned professional 1995

The Rookie of the Year on the US Tour in 1997 when he won the Canon Greater Hartford Classic. The year before he had been top rookie on the Buy.com tour. Although he made the 2001 Ryder Cup side he missed a two foot putt on the last and, as a result, a play-off for the US Open with Mark Brooks and winner Retief Goosen.

Coe, Charles (USA)
Born Oklahoma City, 26 October 1923

Another fine American amateur golfer who finished runner-up with Arnold Palmer to Gary Player in the 1961 Masters at Augusta. Twice US Amateur champion in 1949 and 1958, he played in six Walker Cup matches and was non-playing captain in 1959. He won seven and halved two of the 13 games he played. Winner of the Bobby Jones award in 1964.

Cole, Bobby (RSA)
Born Springs, 11 May 1948
Turned professional 1966

Winner of the Amateur Championship in 1966 when he beat R.D.B.M. Shade in the final which because of haar (fog) was reduced to 18 holes. Among his victories when he turned professional were two South African Opens in 1974 and 1980.

Cook, John (USA)
Born Toledo, Ohio, 2 October 1957
Turned professional 1979

A regular winner on the US Tour he gave Nick Faldo a fright in the 1992 Open at Muirfield. Three strokes behind with eight to play Cook had moved out in front

after 16 holes on the final day but finished 5,5 to Faldo's 4,4. He was also tied second that year in the US PGA Championship. Given much help in his early years by Jack Nicklaus and Tom Weiskopf.

Couples, Fred (USA)
Born Seattle, Washington, 3 October 1959
Turned professional 1980

Troubled continually with a back problem he has managed to win only one major – the 1992 US Masters but is one of the most popular of all American players. Although he has been known to say he enjoys watching television lying on the sofa, he is no stay-at-home in a golfing sense. He has always been willing to travel and his overseas victories include two Johnnie Walker World Championships, the Johnnie Walker Classic, the Dubai Desert Classic and the Tournoi Perrier de Paris. On the US Tour he won 14 times between 1983 and 1998. He played five Ryder Cup matches and three times teed up for the US in the Presidents Cup.

Crenshaw, Ben (USA)
Born Austin, Texas, 11 January 1952

One of golf's great putters who followed up his victory in the 1984 US Masters with an emotional repeat success in 1995 just a short time after the death of his long-time coach and mentor Harvey Pennick. He played in four Ryder Cup matches between 1981 and 1995 before captaining the side in 1999 when the Americans came from four points back to win with a scintillating last day performance. Winner of the Byron Nelson award in 1976 he was also named Bobby Jones award winner in 1991. Now combines playing with an equally successful career as a golf course designer and is an acknowledged authority on every aspect of the history of the game.

Daly, John (USA)
Born Sacramento, California, 28 April 1966
Turned professional 1987

Winner of two majors – the 1991 US PGA Championship and the 1995 Open Championship at St Andrews after a play-off with Costantino Rocca, his career has not been without its ups and downs. He admits he has battled alcoholism and, on occasions, has been his own worst enemy when having run-ins with officialdom but he remains one of the most popular and likeable if sometimes unorthodox players on Tour because of his long hitting. His average drive is over 300 yards. When he won the US PGA Championship at Crooked Stick he got in as ninth alternate, drove through the night to tee it up without a practice round and shot 69, 67, 69, 71 to beat Bruce Lietzke by three. Given invaluable help at times by Fuzzy Zoeller he writes his own songs and is a mean performer on the guitar. In 2001 took the BMW International Open title at Munich. In 2002 was a member of both the US and European Tours.

Daniel, Beth (USA)
Born Charleston, South Carolina, 14 October 1956
Turned professional 1978

A member of the LPGA Hall of Fame she won 32 times between 1979 and 1995 including the 1990 US LPGA

Championship. She was Rolex Player of the Year in 1980, 1990 and 1994. Before turning professional she won the US Women's Amateur title in 1975 and 1977 and played in the 1976 and 1978 Curtis Cup teams. She has played in five Solheim Cup competitions since it began in 1990, missing only the 1998 match.

Davis, Rodger (Aus)
Born Sydney, 18 May 1951
Turned professional 1974
Experienced Australian competitor who came joint second in the 1987 Open Championship behind Nick Faldo at Muirfield. A regular on the European Tour he hopes to extend his playing career on the US Senior circuit. Winner of 27 titles, 19 of them on the Australasian circuit where, in 1988, he picked up an Aus$1 million first prize in the Bicentennial event at Royal Melbourne. Gave up golf for a while but lost all his money in a hotel venture that went wrong and took up tournament play again. For many years played in trade mark 'plus twos'.

Dibnah, Corinne (Aus)
Born Brisbane, 29 July 1962
Turned professional 1984
A former Australian and New Zealand amateur champion, she joined the European Tour after turning professional and won 13 times between 1986 and 1994. A pupil of Greg Norman's first coach Charlie Earp, she was Europe's top earner in 1991.

Dickson, Robert B (USA)
Born McAlester, Oklahoma, 25 January 1944
Turned professional 1968
Best remembered for being one of only four players to complete a Transatlantic amateur double. In 1967 he won the US Amateur Championship at Broadmoor with a total of 285 (the Championship was played over 72 holes from 1965 to 1972) and the British Amateur title with a 2 and 1 win over fellow American Ron Cerrudo at Formby. After turning professional scored two wins on the US Tour.

Duval, David (USA)
Born Jacksonville, Florida, 19 November 1971
Turned professional 1993
A regular winner on the US Tour who wears dark glasses because of an eye stigmatism which is sensitive to light, he won his first major at Royal Lytham and St Annes last year when he became only the second American professional to win the Open over that course. He was the first player in US Tour history to win titles by play-off in consecutive weeks. Played 86 events and had seven second-place finishes and four thirds before making his break-through win in the Michelob Championship then won the following week as well. His father Bob plays the US Senior Tour. He was a winner of the US Tour Championship in 1997 and the Players' Championship in 1999. In the 1998 and 2001 Masters he came second and was third in that event in 2000. He played in 1991 Walker Cup and was a member of the winning Ryder Cup side on his début

in 1999 and was also a member of the 2002 Cup side halving his match with Darren Clarke in the singles.

Elkington, Steve (Aus)
Born Inverell, 8 December 1962
Turned professional 1985
A former Australian (1990 and 1991) and New Zealand (1990) champion he is a regular winner these days on the US Tour despite an allergy to grass. At Riviera CC in Los Angeles in 1995 he beat Colin Montgomerie in a play-off for the US PGA Championship, the only major he has won to date. Winner of the 1992 Australian Open he has one of the finest swings in golf. He is also an accomplished artist in his spare time. He has played four times since 1994 in the Presidents Cup. In 2002 after prequalifying for the event at Dunbar he played off for the Open title at Muirfield with Thomas Levet, Stuart Appleby and eventual winner Ernie Els.

Els, Ernie (RSA)
Born Johannesburg, 17 October 1969
Turned professional 1989
Teenage winner of the South African Amateur Championship in 1996 he is renowned as one of the game's big hitters. His short game can be deadly too and when on song he is one of the most impressive international performers. He has won two US Opens – in 1994 at Oakmont after a play-off against Loren Roberts and Colin Montgomerie and at Congressional where he beat Montgomerie into second place. Although proficient at Rugby Union and cricket he decided to concentrate on golf when he played off scratch at age 14. He has matched Gary Player's record of winning three successive South African Opens and has collected the South African PGA and Masters titles as well. In 1994 he equalled the European Tour record of 12 birdies in the 61 he fired en route to victory in the Dubai Desert Classic. He was made an honorary member of the PGA European Tour in recognition of his two US Open wins and his three successive World Match Play title successes round the famous West Course. Going for a fourth successive win in 1997 he lost on the last green to Vijay Singh. In 2002 Els won the Heineken Classic at Royal Melbourne, the Dubai Desert Classic and the Genuity Championship on the US Tour before realising his life-long dream by winning the Open Championship at Muirfield 43 years after Gary Player had won at the same venue. He beat Frenchman Thomas Levet in a sudden-death play-off at the first extra hole after tieing with him in a four hole play-off which also involved Australians Stuart Appleby and Steve Elkington. All had finished on six-under-par 268. Els played a brilliant recovery from an awkward lie in a greenside trap at the 18th to make the par that earned him his third major title victory. By winning he ended Tiger Woods' hopes of winning all four majors in the same year. Woods had won the Masters and US Open earlier.

Faxon, Brad (USA)
Born Oceanport, New Jersey, 1 August 1961
Turned professional 1983
A former Walker Cup player who competed in the 1983 match he has played twice in the Ryder Cup (1995 and

1997). A seven-time winner on the US Tour he also putted superbly to win the Australian Open at Metropolitan in 1993.

Fernandez, Vicente (Arg)

Born Corrientes, 5 May 1946
Turned professional 1964

After playing on the European Tour where he won five times between 1975 and 1992 he joined the US Senior Tour competing with considerable success. In this respect he was following in the footsteps of fellow Argentinian Roberto de Vicenzo. Born with one leg shorter than the other which is why he limps, he is remembered in Europe for the 87 foot putt he holed up three tiers on the final green at The Belfry in 1992 to win the Murphy's English Open. His nickname is 'Chino'.

Finsterwald, Dow (USA)

Born Athens, Ohio, 6 September 1929
Turned professional 1951

Winner of the 1958 US PGA Championship he won 11 other competitions between 1955 and 1963. He played in four Ryder Cup matches in a row from 1957 and captained the side in 1977. He was US PGA Player of the Year in 1958.

Floyd, Raymond (USA)

Born Fort Bragg, North Carolina, 4 September 1942
Turned professional 1961

A four time major winner whose failure to win an Open Championship title prevented his completing a Slam of Majors. He won the US Open in 1986, the Masters in 1976 when he matched the then 72-hole record set by Jack Nicklaus to win by eight strokes and took the US PGA title in 1969 and 1982. In addition to coming second and third in the Open he was also runner-up three times in the Masters and in the US PGA once. After scoring 22 victories on the main US Tour he has continued to win as a senior. Inducted into the World Golf Hall of Fame in 1989 he is an avid Chicago Cubs baseball fan. Played in eight Ryder Cup matches between 1969 and 1993 making history with his last appearance by being the oldest player to take part in the match. He was 49. He was non-playing captain in 1989 when the match was drawn at The Belfry.

Ford, Doug (USA)

Born West Haven, Connecticut, 6 August 1922
Turned professional 1949

His 25 wins on the US Tour between 1955 and 1963 included the 1975 US Masters. US PGA Player of the Year in 1955, he competed in four Ryder Cup matches in succession from 1955.

Franco, Carlos (Par)

Born Asunción, 24 May 1965
Turned professional 1986

Emerged on to the international stage from humble beginnings. He was one of a family of nine who shared a one-room home at the course where his father was greens superintendent and caddie. All five of his brothers play golf and he was appointed Paraguayan Minister of Sport in 1999. Won twice in his rookie year on the US Tour and became the first player to make more than $1 million in his first two seasons. Has scored three wins on the US circuit, five times in Japan where he had 11 top 10 finishes in 1997, once in the Philippines and 19 times in South America. First made headlines at St Andrews when he beat Sam Torrance in the Alfred Dunhill Cup.

Frost, David (RSA)

Born Cape Town, 11 September 1959
Turned professional 1981

Although now based permanently in the United States has won as many titles overseas as on the US Tour. The 1993 season was his best in America when he made over $1 million in prize money and finished fifth on the money list. He has established a vineyard in South Africa growing 100 acres of vines on the 300-acre estate. He has very quickly earned a reputation for producing quality wines.

Furyk, Jim (USA)

Born West Chester, Pennsylvania, 12 May 1970
Turned professional 1992

Clearly enjoys playing in Las Vegas where he has won three Invitational events in 1995, 1999 and 1998. Has teed it up in two Presidents Cups and two Ryder Cups beating Nick Faldo in the singles at Valderrama in 1997. He was also in the 2001 side. Has one of the most easily recognisable if idiosyncratic swings in top line golf. His father Mike has been his only coach.

Geddes, Jane (USA)

Born Huntingdon, New York, 5 February 1960
Turned professional 1983

In 1986 she was the 13th player on the LPGA Tour to score her first victory at the US Women's Open. A year later she won the US LPGA title and took the British Women's title in 1989. She won 11 times on the US Tour between 1986 and 1994.

Goosen, Retief (RSA)

Born Pietersburg, 3 February 1969
Turned professional 1990

Introduced to golf at the age of 11 he scored his first major success when leading from start to finish at the 2001 US Open at Tulsa and then beating Mark Brooks in the 18-hole play-off by two shots. Although he suffered health problems after being hit by lightning as a teenager he has enjoyed a friendly rivalry with South Africa's other talented young player Ernie Els. Winner of the 1990 South African Amateur title, he scored his first professional victory in the Iscor Newcastle Classic a year later. In Europe where he has been helped by Belgian psychologist Jos Vanstiphout, golf's quiet achiever enjoys playing in France where he has won two French Championships (1997 and 1999) and the Trophée Lancôme in 2000. Just weeks after his US Open win in 2001 he led again from start to finish to win the Scottish Open at Loch Lomond. In 2002 he was

a runaway eight shot winner in the Johnnie Walker Classic at Lake Karynup in Perth, Australia.

Grady, Wayne (Aus)
Born Brisbane, 26 July 1957
Turned professional 1973 and again in 1978
One of Australia's most popular players he won the US PGA Championship at Shoal Creek by three shots over Fred Couples. A year earlier he had tied with Greg Norman and eventual winner Mark Calcavecchia for the Open Championship losing out in the first ever four-hole play-off for the title. Took over in 2001 as chairman of the Australasian Tour from Jack Newton.

Graham, David (Aus)
Born Windsor, Tasmania, 23 May 1946
Turned professional 1962
Played superbly for a closing 67 round Merion to win the 1981 US Open Championship from George Burns and Bill Rogers. That day he hit every green in regulation. Two years earlier he had beaten Ben Crenshaw at the third extra hole at Oakland Hills to win the US PGA Championship. When he took up the game at age 14 he played with left-handed clubs before making the switch to a right-handed set. Awarded the Order of Australia for his services to golf he is a member of the Cup and Tee committee that sets up Augusta each year for the Masters. A regular winner around the world in the 70s and 80s he won eight times on the US Tour between 1972 and 1983. Now plays on the US Senior Tour but also has gained a considerable reputation as a course designer.

Graham, Lou (USA)
Born Nashville, Tennessee, 7 January 1938
Turned professional 1962
Won the US Open at Medinah in 1975 after a play-off against John Mahaffey.

Green, Hubert (USA)
Born Birmingham, Alabama, 18 December 1946
Turned professional 1970
Beat Lou Graham for the 1977 US Open at Southern Hills despite being told with four holes to play that he had received a death threat. Three times a Ryder Cup player he also won the 1985 US PGA Championship. His only European Tour victory was the 1977 Irish Open. Best known for his unorthodox swing and distinctive crouching putting style.

Harper, Chandler (USA)
Born Portsmouth, Virginia, 10 March 1914
Turned professional 1934
Winner of the 1950 US PGA Championship he won over ten tournaments and was elected to the US PGA Hall of Fame in 1969. Once shot 58 (29-29) round a 6100 yards course in Portsmouth.

Hayes, Dale (RSA)
Born Pretoria, 1 July 1952   Turned professional 1970
Former South African amateur stroke play champion who was a regular winner in South Africa and Europe

after turning professional. He was Europe's top money earner in 1975 but retired from competitive golf to move into business. He is now a successful television commentator in South Africa with a weekly programme of his own.

Haynie, Sandra (USA)
Born Fort Worth, Texas, 4 June 1943
Turned professional 1961
Twice a winner of the US Open (1965 and 1974) she won 42 times between 1962 and 1982 on the US LPGA Tour. She was elected to the LPGA Hall of Fame in 1977.

Henning, Harold (RSA)
Born Johannesburg, 3 October 1934
Turned professional 1953
One of three brothers from a well-known South African golf family he was a regular winner of golf events in his home country and Europe and had two wins on the US Tour. Played ten times for South Africa in the World Cup winning the event with Gary Player in Madrid in 1965.

Hoch, Scott (USA)
Born Raleigh, North Carolina, 24 November 1955
Turned professional 1979
Ryder Cup, Presidents Cup, Walker Cup and Eisenhower Trophy player who is a regular winner on the US Tour. Has scored 10 wins on the US Tour between 1980 and 2001 and has had six more victories worldwide. In 1989 he donated $100,000 of his Las Vegas Invitational winnings to the Arnold Palmer Children's Hospital in Orlando where his son Cameron had been successfully treated for a rare bone infection in his right knee.

Inkster, Juli (USA)
Born Santa Cruz, California, 24 June 1960
Turned professional 1983
Winner of two majors in 1984 (the Nabisco Championship and the du Maurier) she also had a double Major year in 1999 when she won the US Women's Open and the LPGA Championship which she won for a second time in 2000. In 2002 she won the US Women's Open for a second time. In all she has won 10 major titles. In her amateur career she became the first player since 1934 to win the US Women's amateur title three years in a row (1980, 81, 82). Only four other women and one man (Tiger Woods) have successfully defended the national titles twice in a row. Coached for a time by the late London-based Leslie King at Harrods Store.

Irwin, Hale (USA)
Born Joplin, Montana, 3 June 1945
Turned professional 1968
A three time winner of the US Open (1974, 1979 and 1990) he has been a prolific winner on the main US Tour and, since turning 50, on the US Senior Tour. He had 20 wins on the main Tour including the 1990 US Open triumph where he holed a 45-foot putt on the final

green at Medinah to force a play-off with Mike Donald then after both were still tied following a further 18 holes became the oldest winner of the Championship at 45 when he sank a 10-foot birdie putt at the first extra hole of sudden death. Joint runner-up to Tom Watson in the 1983 Open at Royal Birkdale where he stubbed the ground and missed a tap-in putt on the final day – a slip that cost him the chance of a play-off. Three times top earner on the Senior Tour where, prior to the start of the 2001 season, he had averaged $90,573 per start in 130 events coming in the top three in 63 of those events and finishing over par in only nine of them.

January, Don (USA)
Born Plainview, Texas, 20 November 1929
Turned professional 1955
Winner of the US Open in 1967 he followed up his successful main Tour career in which he had 11 wins between 1956 and 1976 with double that success as a Senior winning 22 times. Much admired for his easy rhythmical style.

Janzen, Lee (USA)
Born Austin, Minnesota, 28 August 1964
Turned professional 1986
Twice a winner of the US Open in 1993 and again in 1998 when he staged the best final round comeback since Johnny Miller rallied from six back to win the title 25 years earlier. Five strokes behind the late Payne Stewart after 54 holes at Baltusrol he closed with a 67 to beat Stewart with whom he had also battled for the title in 1993.

Jones, Steve (USA)
Born Artesia, New Mexico, 27 December 1958
Turned professional 1981
First player since Jerry Pate in 1976 to win the US Open after having had to qualify. His 1996 victory was the result of inspiration he received from reading a Ben Hogan book given to him the week before the Championship at Oakland Hills. Uses a reverse overlapping grip as a result of injury. Indeed his career was put on hold for three years after injury to his left index finger following a dirt-bike accident. He dominated the 1997 Phoenix Open shooting 62, 64, 65 and 67 for an 11 shot victory over Jesper Parnevik That week his 258 winning total was just one outside the low US Tour record set by Mike Souchak in 1955.

King, Betsy (USA)
Born Reading, Pennsylvania, 13 August 1955
Turned professional 1977
Another stalwart of the LPGA Tour in America she has won 34 times between 1984 and 2001. Winner of the British Open in 1985 she has also won the US Open in 1989 and 1990, the Nabisco Championship three times in 1987, 1990 and 1997 and the LPGA Championship in 1990. She never managed to win the du Maurier event although finishing in the top six on nine occasions. Three times Rolex Player of the Year in 1984, 1989 and 1993 she was elected to the LPGA Hall of Fame in 1995.

Kite, Tom (USA)
Born Austin, Texas, 9 December 1949
Turned professional 1972
He won the US Open at Pebble Beach in 1992 in difficult conditions when aged 42 to lose the 'best player around never to have won a Major' tag. With 19 wins on the main Tour he was the first to top $6million, $7 million, $8 million and $9 million dollars in prize money. Has been playing since he was 11 and after a lifetime wearing glasses had laser surgery to correct acute near-sightedness. The Ryder Cup captain in 1997 he now plays the US Senior Tour.

Klein, Emilee (USA)
Born Santa Monica, California, 11 June 1974
Turned professional 1994
The former Curtis Cup player who played in the 1994 match scored her biggest triumph as a professional when winning the Weetabix British Women's Open at Woburn in 1996.

Kuchar, Matt (USA)
Born Lake Mary, Florida, 21 June 1978
Turned professional 2002
Winner of the US Amateur in 1997 he was leading amateur in the 1998 Masters and US Open Championship. Scored his first win as a professional when he landed the 2002 Honda Classic.

Kuehne, Kelli (USA)
Born Dallas, Texas, 11 May 1977
Turned professional 1998
Having won the US Women's Amateur Championship in 1995 she successfully defended the title the following year when she also won the British Women's title – the first player to win both in the same year. She was also the first player to follow up her win in the US Junior Girls Championship in 1994 with victory in the US Women's event the following year. Her brother Hank is also a professional.

Lehman, Tom (USA)
Born Austin, Minnesota, 7 March 1959
Turned professional 1982
Winner of the Open Championship at Royal Lytham and St Annes in 1996 he was runner-up in the US Open in 1996 and third in 1997. He was runner-up in the 1994 US Masters having come third the previous year. Has played in four Ryder Cup matches.

Leonard, Justin (USA)
Born Dallas, Texas, 15 June 1972
Turned professional 1994
Winner of the 1997 Open at Royal Troon when he beat Jesper Parnevik and Darren Clarke into second place with a closing 65 and nearly won the title again in 1999 when he lost a four-hole play-off with Jean Van de Velde and Paul Lawrie to the Scotsman at Carnoustie. In 1998 came from five back to beat Lee Janzen in the Players Championship and is

remembered for his fight back against José Maria Olazábal on the final day of the 1999 Ryder Cup at Brookline. Four down after 11 holes he managed to share a half-point with the Spaniard to help America win the Cup.

Littler, Gene (USA)
Born San Diego, California, 21 July 1930
Turned professional 1954
Winner of the 1953 US Amateur Championship he had a distinguished professional career scoring 26 victories on the US Tour between 1955 and 1977. He scored his only major triumph at Pebble Beach in 1971 when he beat Bob Goalby and Doug Sanders at Oakland Hills. He had been runner-up in the US Open in 1954 and was runner-up in the 1977 US PGA Championship and the 1970 US Masters. A seven-time Ryder Cup player between 1961 and 1977 he is a former winner of the Ben Hogan, Bobby Jones and Byron Nelson awards. He won the Hogan award after successfully beating cancer.

Lopez, Nancy (née Knight) (USA)
Born Torrance, California, 6 January 1957
Turned professional 1977
One of the game's bubbliest personalities and impressive performers who took her first title – the New Mexico Women's Amateur title at age 12. Between 1978 and 1995 she won 48 times on the LPGA Tour and was Rolex Player of the Year on four occasions (1978, 79, 85 and 88). In 1978, her rookie year, she won nine titles including a record five in a row. That year she also lost two play-offs and remains the only player to have won the Rookie of the Year, Player of the Year and Vare Trophy (scoring average) in the same season. A year later she won eight tournaments. Three times a winner of the LPGA Championship in 1978, 1985 and 1989 she has never managed to win the US Open although she was runner-up in 1975 as an amateur, in 1977, 1989 and most recently 1997 when she lost out to Britain's Alison Nicholas. She has now retired from competitive golf.

Love III, Davis (USA)
Born Charlotte, North Carolina, 13 April 1964
Turned professional 1985
Son of one of America's most highly rated teachers who died in a plane crash in 1988, Love has won only one major – the 1997 US PGA Championship at Winged Foot where he beat Justin Leonard by five shots. He has been runner-up in the US Open (1996) and the US Masters (1999). In the World Cup of Golf won the title in partnership with Fred Couples four years in a row (1992–1995). He has played in five Ryder Cups.

Lunn, Karen (Aus)
Born Sydney, 21 March 1966
Turned professional 1985
A former top amateur she won the British Women's Open in 1993 at Woburn following the success in the

European Ladies Open earlier in the year by her younger sister Mardi.

McIntire, Barbara (USA)
Born Toledo, Ohio, 1935
One of America's best amateurs who finished runner-up in the 1956 US Women's Open to Kathy Cornelius at Northland Duluth. Winner of the US Women's Amateur title in 1959 and 1964 she also won the British Amateur title in 1960. She played in six Curtis Cups between 1958 and 1962.

McNulty, Mark (Zim)
Born Zimbabwe, 25 October 1953
Turned professional 1977
Recognised as one of the best putters in golf he was runner-up to Nick Faldo in the 1990 Open at St Andrews. Although hampered throughout his career by a series of injuries and illness he has scored 16 wins on the European Tour and 33 around the world including 23 on the South African Sunshine circuit. He won the South African Open in 1987 and again in 2001 holing an 18-foot putt on the last at East London to beat Justin Rose.

Maggert, Jeff (USA)
Born Columbia, Missouri, 20 February 1964
Turned professional 1986
A three times Ryder Cup player who competed in the 1995, 1997 and 1999 matches he won the World Golf Championship Match Play event in 1999 to land a million. A quiet achiever he has come third in the US PGA twice in 1995 and 1997.

Mallon, Meg (USA)
Born Natwick, Maryland, 14 April 1963
Turned professional 1986
Winner of the 1991 US Women's Open, 1991 Mazda LPGA Championship, the 2000 du Maurier Classic and 11 other events between 1991 and 2002.

Mann, Carole (USA)
Born Buffalo, New York, 3 February 1940
Turned professional 1960
Winner of 38 events on the LPGA Tour in her 22 years on Tour. A former president of the LPGA she was a key figure in the founding of the Tour and received the prestigious Babe Zaharias award. In 1964 she won the Western Open, then a Major, and in 1965 the US Women's Open but in 1968 she had a then record 23 rounds in the 60s, won 11 times and won the scoring averages prize with a score of 72.04.

Marsh, Graham (Aus)
Born Kalgoorlie, Western Australia, 14 January 1944
Turned professional 1968
A notable Australian who followed up his international playing career by gaining a reputation for designing fine courses. Although he played in Europe, America and Australasia he spent most of his time on the

Japanese circuit where he had 17 wins between 1971 and 1982 but won 11 times in Europe and scored victories also in the United States, India, Thailand and Malaysia. He now plays on the US Senior Tour.

Massey, Debbie (USA)
Born Grosse Pointe, Michigan, 5 November 1950
Turned professional 1977
Best known for winning the British Women's Open in 1980 and 1981.

Melnyk, Steve (USA)
Born Brunswick, Georgia, 26 February 1947
Turned professional 1971
US Amateur champion in 1969 and British champion in 1971. His professional career was cut short because of an ankle injury. Today he commentates for CBS, one of the US networks.

Mickelson, Phil (USA)
Born San Diego, California, 16 June 1970
Turned professional 1992
Plays all sports right-handed except golf and claims to have started hitting golf balls at 18 months. Although he won the 2000 Tour Championship is still without a major victory. His best finishes in Majors are second in the 2001 US PGA Championship and the 1999 US Open and third in the 1994 US PGA Championship. His 19 victories on the US Tour include a win as an amateur in the 1995 Tucson Open. His 65 at the Masters in 1996 is lowest score by a left-hander at that event. One of only three players to win the NCAA Championship and US Amateur in the same year. The others – Jack Nicklaus and Tiger Woods. He has played in two Walker Cups, four times in Presidents Cup and in four Ryder Cup matches.

Miller, Johnny (USA)
Born San Francisco, California, 29 April 1947
Turned professional 1969
Dreamed of winning the Open after Tony Lema, another member of the Olympic Club in San Francisco, did so in 1964. Realised his dream when he beat Jack Nicklaus and Seve Ballesteros into second place in the 1976 Open at Royal Birkdale. His US Open win in 1973 came with the help of a brilliant last round 63 which set the record since equalled for the lowest round in the Championship. Was involved with Tom Weiskopf and Jack Nicklaus in one of the greatest finishes to a US Masters in 1975 which Nicklaus won. He scored 24 wins between 1971 and 1984 and in 1975 shot 49 under par when winning the Phoenix and Tucson Opens in successive weeks. Now commentates for NBC.

Mize, Larry (USA)
Born Augusta, Georgia, 23 September 1958
Turned professional 1980
Only local player ever to win the Masters and he did it in dramatic style holing a 140-foot pitch and run at the second extra hole to edge out Greg Norman and Seve Ballesteros. He had made the play-off by holing a 10-

foot birdie on the final green. In 1993 he beat an international field to take the Johnnie Walker World Championship title at Tryall in Jamaica. His middle name is Hogan.

Nagle, Kel (Aus)
Born North Sydney, 21 December 1920
Turned professional 1946
In the dramatic Centenary Open at St Andrews in 1960 he edged out Arnold Palmer, winner already that year of the Masters and US Open, to become champion. It was the finest moment in the illustrious career of a golfer who has been a wonderful ambassador for his country. Along with Peter Thomson he competed nine times in the World Cup winning the event in 1954. He is an honorary member of the Royal and Ancient Golf Club of St Andrews.

Nelson, Byron (USA)
Born Fort Worth, Texas, 4 February 1912
Turned professional 1932
In the 1945 US season he won 18 times including 11 events in a row between March and August – a record unlikely ever to be broken. Between 1935 and 1946 he won 54 times but although he won the US Open in 1939, the US PGA Championship in 1940 and 1945 and the US Masters in 1937 and 1942 he never managed to complete the set of four majors. His only win in Europe was the 1955 French Open. He remains a father figure in US golf and until he retired in 2001 was one of the Masters honorary starters along with the late Gene Sarazen and the late Sam Snead.

Nelson, Larry (USA)
Born Fort Payne, Alabama, 10 September 1947
Turned professional 1971
Often underrated he learned to play by reading Ben Hogan's The Five Fundamentals of Golf and broke 100 first time out and 70 after just nine months. Active as well these days on course design he has won the Jack Nicklaus award. He has been successful in the US Open (1983 at Oakmont) and two US PGA Championships (in 1981 at the Atlanta Athletic Club and in 1987 after a play-off with Lanny Wadkins at PGA National). Three times a Ryder Cup player he has competed equally successfully as a Senior having won 15 titles (at end of July 2001). He did not play as a youngster but visited a driving range after completing his military service and was hooked. He was named Senior PGA Tour Player of the Year for finishing top earner and winning six times in 2000. At the end of his third full season on the Senior Tour and after 87 events he had won just short of $10 million.

Newton, Jack (Aus)
Born Sydney, 30 January 1950
Turned professional 1969
Runner-up to Tom Watson after a play-off in the 1975 Open at Carnoustie and runner-up to Seve Ballesteros in the 1980 Masters at Augusta, he was a popular personality on both sides of the Atlantic and in his native Australia only to have his playing career ended

prematurely when he walked into the whirling propeller of a plane at Sydney airport. He lost an eye, an arm and had considerable internal injuries but the quick action of a surgeon who happened to be around probably saved his life. Learned to play one-handed and still competes in pro-ams successfully. Until his retirement in 2000 he was chairman of the Australasian Tour and remains Australia's most successful golf commentator working exclusively for Channel Seven.

Nicklaus, Jack (USA)

Born Columbus, Ohio, 21 January 1940
Turned professional 1961
The greatest golfer of the 20th century and possibly of all time depending on what Tiger Woods manages to achieve. After winning two US Amateurs he went on to win 18 professional major titles. His record is phenomenal. He won the Open in 1966, 1970 and 1978, the last two at St Andrews and was runner-up seven times and third on two further occasions. He won the US Open in 1962, 1967, 1972 and 1980 and came second four times. He won five US PGA titles in 1963, 1971, 1973, 1975 and 1980 and was runner-up four times and third on two further occasions and he won six Masters in 1963, 1965, 1966, 1972, 1975 and 1986 when at the age of 46 he became the oldest winner of a Green Jacket. In addition he was runner-up four times and third twice. In 1966 he became the first player to successfully defend the Masters (a feat later matched by Nick Faldo in 1990). He won six Australian Opens (1964, 1968, 1971, 1975, 1976 and 1978) and played in six Ryder Cups, captaining two more in 1983 at Palm Beach Gardens when America won and in 1987 at Muirfield Village where his side were losers for the first time on home soil. Credited with saving the Cup match after suggesting that Continental golfers should be included in the side from 1979. Ten years earlier he conceded the 18-inch putt that Jacklin had for a half at the last when the result of the match depended on the result of that game. The match was drawn. After winning 71 times between 1962 and 1984 on the main Tour he won a further ten times on the Senior US Tour. He has won almost every honour you can win in golf including the Byron Nelson, Ben Hogan and Walter Hagen awards. He was the US top money earner in seasons 1964, 1965, 1967, 1971, 1972, 1973, 1975 and 1976 and is a honorary member of the Royal and Ancient Golf Club of St Andrews. Bobby Jones once said of Nicklaus that 'he played a game with which I am not familiar'. With the constant support of his wife Barbara, Nicklaus has been the personification of all that is good about the game. He has designed over 200 courses worldwide.

Nobilo, Frank (NZ)

Born Auckland, 14 May 1960
Turned professional 1979
Injury has affected his career in recent years but he remains one of his country's most popular players with an excellent swing. After winning regularly in Europe he moved to America where in 1997 he won the Greater Greensboro Classic. He has represented New Zealand in nine World Cup matches between 1982 and 1999,

played in 11 Alfred Dunhill Cups and three Presidents Cup sides.

Norman, Greg (Aus)

Born Mount Isa, Queensland, 10 February 1955
Turned professional 1976
Australia's most prolific winner in recent years credited with 77 victories worldwide (as of July 2001) but has slowed down because of injury and trimmed his schedule in recent times. He won the Open in tough conditions at Turnberry in 1986 and again in glorious weather at Royal St George's in 1993 when he fired the lowest winning aggregate of 267 (66, 68, 69, 64). Decided to take up golf after caddying for his mother and abandoned plans to join the Australian Air Force. One of the few golfers to have topped the official money lists on both sides of the Atlantic he received his first winner's cheque in the Westlake Classic on the Australian Tour in 1976. Has the unhappy reputation of having lost Majors in three different types of play-off – the 1987 Masters to Larry Mize and the 1993 US PGA to Paul Azinger in sudden death, the Open to Mark Calcavecchia at Royal Troon n a four-hole play-off in 1989 and the US Open over 18 holes to Fuzzy Zoeller at Winged Foot in 1984. In 1986 he led going into the final round of all four Majors that year and won only the Open. During his career he has set all kinds of money records on the US Tour but is jinxed at the US Masters where he has finished second three times. He has also been runner-up on five other occasions in Majors. Today spends as much time in the boardroom looking after his business interests as he does playing.

North, Andy (USA)

Born Thorp, Wisconsin, 9 March 1950
Turned professional 1972
Although this tall American found it difficult to win Tour events he did pick up two US Open titles. His first Championship success came at Cherry Hills in Denver in 1986 when he edged out Dave Stockton and J C Snead and the second at Oakland Hills in 1985 when he finished just a shot ahead of Dave Barr, T C Chen and Denis Watson who had been penalised a shot during the Championship for waiting longer than the regulation 10 seconds at one hole to see if his ball would drop into the cup. North is now a very successful golf commentator whose analytical comments are much admired.

Okamoto, Ayako (Jpn)

Born Hiroshima, 12 April 1951
Turned professional 1976
Although she won the British Women's Open in 1984 she managed only a runner-up spot in the US Women's Open and US LPGA Championships despite finishing in the top 20 28 times and missing the cut only four times. In the LPGA Championships she finished second or third five times in six years from 1986. She scored 17 victories in the USA between 1982 and 1992, won the 1990 German Open and was Japanese Women's champion in 1993 and 1997.

O'Meara, Mark (USA)

Born Goldsboro, North Carolina, 13 January 1957
Turned professional 1980

A former US Amateur Champion in 1979 Mark was 41 when he won his first Major – the US Masters at Augusta. That week in 1998 he did not three putt once on Augusta's glassy greens. Three months later he won the Open at Royal Birkdale battling with, among others, Tiger Woods with whom he has had a particular friendship. They both live at Isleworth in Florida. He is the oldest player to win two Majors in the same year and was chosen as PGA Player of the Year that season. When he closed birdie, birdie to win the Masters he joined Arnold Palmer and Art Wall as the only players to do that and became only the fifth player in Masters history to win without leading in the first three rounds. He won his Open championship title in a four hole play-off against Brian Watts. O'Meara played in five Ryder Cups between 1985 and 1999.

Ozaki, 'Jumbo' (Jpn)

Born Kaiman Town, Tokushima, 24 January 1947
Turned professional 1980

Along with Isao Aoki is Japan's best known player, but unlike Aoki has maintained his base in Japan where he has scored over 80 victories. His only overseas win was the New Zealand Open early in his career. He is a golfing icon in his native country. His two brothers Joe (Naomichi) and Jet also play professionally.

Pak, Se Ri (Kor)

Born Daejeon, 28 September 1977
Turned professional 1996

In 1998 she was awarded the Order of Merit by the South Korean government – the highest honour given to an athlete – for having won two Majors in her rookie year on the US Tour. She won the McDonald LPGA Championship matching Liselotte Neumann in making a major her first tour success. When she won the US Women's Open later that year after an 18-hole play-off followed by two extra holes of sudden death against amateur Jenny Chuasiriporn, she became the youngest golfer to take that title. By the middle of 2001 she had won 12 events on the US tour including the Weetabix Women's British Open at Sunningdale – an event included on the US Tour as well as the European Circuit for the first time. In 2002 she was again a multiple winner on the US Tour adding to her majors by winning the McDonald's LPGA Championship. As an amateur in Korea she won 30 titles.

Palmer, Arnold (USA)

Born Latrobe, Pennsylvania, 10 September 1929
Turned professional 1954

Winner of 61 titles on the US Tour between 1956 and 1980, he is one of the most charismatic players in golf who has been credited with starting the golfing boom in the latter part of the 20th century. A former US Amateur champion in 1954, his performances were always exciting to watch and for years he was followed around by his own ever-loyal army of fans... indeed still is when he tees up on the US Senior Tour. He won eight Major titles – the 1960 US Open and the 1961 and 1962 Opens at Royal Birkdale in very stormy weather and at Royal Troon where he beat Kel Nagle by six shots and the rest of the field by 13. He won the US Masters in 1958, 1960, 1962 and 1964 but never managed to win the US PGA although he finished second three times. The first player to pass the $1 million mark in earnings he helped Keith Mackenzie the then secretary of the Royal and Ancient Golf Club of St Andrews revive the Open and is now a distinguished honorary member of the club. In 1960 having won the US Masters and US Open he came to St Andrews for the Centenary Open hoping to match three majors in a season – a record held at the time by Ben Hogan but he was beaten by Australian Kel Nagle. Son of the greenkeeper at Ligonier in the Pennsylvanian mountains – he later bought the club – he has remained a respected golfing idol noted for his remarkable strength and his attacking golf. With Jack Nicklaus and Gary Player he became a member of the modern Big Three – a concept developed by his manager Mark McCormack whose first client he was.

Parry Craig (Aus)

Born Sunshine, Victoria, Australia 12 January 1966.
Turned professional 1985.

Australian Parry, winner of 18 titles internationally but never a winner on the US Tour, put that right in 2002 when he landed the World Golf Championship NEC Invitational at Sahalee in Washington to pick up his largest career cheque – $1 million. After 15 years of trying to win in America the chances of him being successful at Salahee seemed slim having missed the four previous cuts. However, the 300-1 long-shot played and putted beautifully covering the last 48 holes without making a bogey to win by four from another Australian Robert Allenby and American Fred Funk. Tiger Woods, trying to win the event for a record fourth-successive year was fourth. Only Gene Sarazen and Walter Hagen have ever won the same four titles in successive years. It was Parry's 236th tournament in the United States and moved him from 118th in the world to 45th.

Pate, Jerry (USA)

Born Macon, Georgia, 16 September 1953
Turned professional 1975

Winner of the 1976 US Open when he hit a 5-iron across water to three feet at the 72nd hole at the Atlanta Athletic Club. He was a member of what is regarded as the strongest ever Ryder Cup side that beat the Europeans at Walton Heath in 1981. Has now retired from golf and commentates for one of the American networks.

Pavin, Corey (USA)

Born Oxnard, California, 26 May 1961
Turned professional 1983

Although not one of golf's longer hitters he battled with powerful Greg Norman to take the 1995 US Open title

at Shinnecock Hills. A runner-up in the 1994 US PGA Championship and third in the 1992 US Masters he won 13 times between 1984 and 1996. His only victory in Europe came when he took the German Open title in 1983 while on honeymoon.

Pepper (Mochrie, Scarinzi), Dottie (USA)

Born Saratoga Springs, Florida, 17 August 1965
Turned professional 1987
Winner of 17 events (through to July 2001) on the US LPGA Tour including two majors. A fierce competitor she took the Nabisco Dinah Shore title in 1992 and again in 1999. She played in all Solheim Cup matches to 2000.

Player, Gary (RSA)

Born Johannesburg, 1 November 1935
Turned professional 1953
One of the modern Big Three with Arnold Palmer and Jack Nicklaus, he has won 167 titles worldwide including nine Majors between 1959 and 1978 and nine senior Majors between 1986 and 1997. His Major wins include three Open Championships in 1959 at Muirfield, 1968 at Carnoustie and 1974 at Royal Lytham and St Annes, three US Masters in 1961, 1974 and 1978, the US Open in 1965 when he completed a Grand Slam of major titles and the US PGA Championship in 1962 and 1972. A life-long fitness fanatic who has won titles in five decades he is one of only five players to have won all four Major titles. Gene Sarazen, Ben Hogan, Jack Nicklaus and Tiger Woods are the others. He considers the greatest thrill of his life was becoming the third man in history to do so. Having never based himself full-time in the US he has travelled more miles than any other golfer during his career – an estimated 12 million by the end of 2000. He entered his first Open in 1955 and failed to qualify but finished fourth in 1956 and played for the last time at Royal Lytham and St Annes in 2001 when 66. One of his most dramatic major performances came when he went into the last round seven shots behind Hubert Green at the 1974 US Masters, came home in 30 and equalled the then record 64 to win. He scored a record seven wins in the Australian Open, took the South African Open a record 13 times and won the World Match Play title a record-equalling five times coming from seven down after 19 holes in one tie in 1965 to beat Tony Lema at the 37th. Credited as being one of the game's greatest bunker players he remains as enthusiastic about competing today as he did when he first took up the game.

Price, Nick (Zim)

Born Durban, South Africa, 28 January 1957
Turned professional 1977
One of the game's most popular players his greatest season was 1990 when he took six titles including the Open at Turnberry when he beat Jesper Parnevik and the US PGA at Southern Hills when Corey Pavin was second. He had scored his first Major triumph two years earlier when he edged out John Cook, Nick Faldo, Jim Gallagher Jr and Gene Sauers at the US PGA at Bellerive, St Louis. Along with Tiger Woods his record of 15 wins in the 90s

was the most by any player. One of only seven players to win consecutive Majors, the others being Ben Hogan, Jack Nicklaus, Arnold Palmer, Lee Trevino, Tom Watson and Tiger Woods. Four times a Presidents Cup player he jointly holds the Augusta National record of 63 with Greg Norman. One of only two players in the 90s to win two Majors in a year, the others being Nick Faldo in 1990 and Mark O'Meara in 1998. Born of English parents but brought up in Zimbabwe he played his early golf with Mark McNulty and Tony Johnstone. Winner of 40 titles by end of August 2002.

Rawls, Betsy (USA)

Born Spartanburg, South Carolina, 4 May 1928
Turned professional 1951
Winner of the 1951, 1953, 1957 and 1960 US Women's Open and the US LPGA Championship in 1959 and 1969 as well as two Western Opens when the Western Open was a Major, she scored 55 victories on the LPGA Tour between 1951 and 1972. One of the best shot makers in women's golf who was noted for her game around and on the greens.

Rogers, Bill (USA)

Born Waco, Texas, 10 September 1951
Turned professional 1974
US PGA Player of the Year in 1981 when he won the Open at Royal St George's and was runner-up in the US Open. That year he also won the Australian Open but retired from top line competitive golf not long after because he did not enjoy all the travelling. A former Walker Cup player in 1973 he only entered the Open in 1981 at the insistence of Ben Crenshaw. Now a successful club professional and sometime television commentator.

Romero, Eduardo (Arg)

Born Cordoba, Argentina, 12 July 1954
Turned professional 1982
Son of the Cordoba club professional he learned much from former Open champion Roberto de Vicenzo and has inherited his grace and elegance as a competitor. A wonderful ambassador for Argentina he briefly held a US Tour card in 1994 but prefers to play his golf these days on the European Tour where he has won seven times including impressively at the 1999 Canon European Masters where he improved his concentration after studying Indian yoga techniques. Used his own money to sponsor Angel Cabrera with whom he finished second in the 2000 World Cup in Buenos Aries behind Tiger Woods and David Duval. Beat Frederick Andersson in a play-off in 2002 to win the Barclays Scottish Open at Loch Lomond but lost to Padraig Harrington in a play-off for the US$800,000 first prize in the Dunhill Links Championship at St Andrews.

Sander, Anne (Welts, Decker, *née* Quast) (USA)

Born Marysville, 1938
A three time winner of the US Ladies title in 1958, 1961 and 1963, she also won the British Ladies title in 1980.

She made eight appearances in the Curtis Cup stretching from 1958 to 1990. Only Carole Semple Thompson has played more often having played ten times.

Scott, Adam (Aus)
Born Adelaide, 16 July 1980
Turned professional 2000
Highly regarded young Australian who was ranked World No 2 amateur when he turned professional in 2000. Coached in the early days by his father Phil, himself a golf professional Scott now uses Butch Harmon whom he met while attending the University of Las Vegas. Swings very much like another Harmon client Tiger Woods. He made headlines as an amateur when he fired a 10-under-par 63 at the Lakes in the Greg Norman Holden International in 2000 but has shot 62 in the US Junior Championship at Los Coyotes CC. Made his European Tour card in just eight starts and secured his first Tour win when beating Justin Rose in the 2001 Alfred Dunhill Championship at Houghton in Johannesburg. In 2002 he won at Qatar and at Gleneagles Hotel when he won the Diageo Scottish PGA Championship by ten shots with a 26 under par total. He was 22 under par that week for the par 5 holes.

Semple Thompson, Carol (USA)
Born 1950
Winner of six USGA titles including the US Ladies title in 1973 and the British Ladies in 1974. She has played in 12 Curtis Cups between 1974 and 2002 and holed the 27-foot winning putt in the 2002 match. At 53 she is the oldest US Curtis Cup Player.

Senior, Peter (Aus)
Born Singapore, 31 July 1959
Turned professional 1978
One of Australia's most likeable and underrated performers who has been a regular winner over the years on the Australian, Japanese and European circuits. Converted to the broomstick putter by Sam Torrance – a move that saved his playing career. A former winner of the Australian Open, Australian PGA and Australian Masters titles he had considerable success off the course when he bought a share in a pawn-broking business.

Sheehan, Patty (USA)
Born Middlebury, Vermont, 27 October 1956
Turned professional 1980
Scored 35 victories between 1981 and 1996 including six Majors – the LPGA Championship in 1983, 1984 and 1994, the US Women's Open in 1993 and 1994 and the Nabisco Championship in 1996. As an amateur she won all her four games in the 1980 Curtis Cup. She is a member of the LPGA Hall of Fame.

Siderowf, Dick (USA)
Twice a winner of the British Amateur title in 1973 when he beat Peter Moody at Royal Porthcawl and again in 1976 when he had to go to the 37th hole to beat John Davies. He was leading amateur in the 1968 US Open and played in four Walker Cups (1969, 1973, 1975 and 1977) before captaining the winning side in 1979.

Sigel, Jay (USA)
Born Narbeth, Pennsylvania, 13 November 1943
Turned professional 1993
Winner of the Amateur Championship in 1979 when he beat Scott Hoch 3 and 2 at Hillside, he also won the US Amateur in successive years 1982 and 1983. He was leading amateur in the US Open in 1984 and leading amateur in the US Masters in 1981, 1982 and 1988. He played in nine Walker Cup matches between 1977 and 1993 and has a record 18 points to his credit. Turned professional in order to join the US Senior Tour where he has had several successes.

Simpson, Scott (USA)
Born San Diego, California, 17 September 1955
Turned professional 1977
Winner of the US Open in 1987 at San Francisco's Olympic Club, he was beaten in a play-off for the title four years later at Hazeltine when the late Payne Stewart won the 18-hole play-off.

Singh, Vijay (Fij)
Born Lautoka, 22 February 1963
Turned professional 1982
An international player who began his career in Australasia he became the first Fijian to win a major when he won the 1998 US PGA Championship at Sahalee but may well be remembered more for his victory in the 2000 US Masters which effectively prevented Tiger Woods winning all four Majors in a year. Tiger went on to win the US Open, Open and US PGA Championship that year and won the Masters the following year to hold all four Major titles at the one time. Introduced to golf by his father, an aeroplane technician, Vijay modelled his swing on that of Tom Weiskopf. Before making the grade on the European Tour where he won the 1992 Volvo German Open by 11 shots he was a club professional in Borneo. He has won tournaments in South Africa, Malaysia, the Ivory Coast, Nigeria, France, Zimbabwe, Morocco, Spain, England, Germany, Sweden, Taiwan and the United States. He ended Ernie Els' run of victories in the World Match Play Championship when he beat him in the final by one hole in 1997 when the South African was going for a fourth successive title. One of the game's most dedicated practisers.

Stadler, Craig (USA)
Born San Diego, California, 2 June 1953
Turned professional 1975
Nicknamed 'The Walrus' because of his moustache and stocky build, he was the winner of the 1982 Masters at Augusta. Winner of 12 titles on the US Tour between 1980 and 1996 he played in two Ryder Cups (1983 and 1985). As an amateur he played in the 1975 Walker Cup two years after winning the US Amateur.

Steinhauer, Sherri (USA)
Born Madison, Wisconsin, 27 December 1962
Turned professional 1985
Winner of the Women's British Open in 1998 at Royal Lytham and St Annes and the following year at Woburn. She has played in the last three Solheim Cup matches.

Stephenson, Jan (Aus)
Born Sydney, 22 December 1951
Turned professional 1973
She won three majors on the LPGA Tour – the 1981 du Maurier Classic, the 1982 UPGA Championship and the 1983 US Women's Open. She was twice Australian Ladies champion in 1973 and 1977.

Stockton, Dave (USA)
Born San Bernardino, California, 2 November 1941
Turned professional 1964
Winner of two US PGA Championships in 1970 and 1976, he has won more Senior Tour titles (14 as of end July 2001) than he did on the main Tour (11). Captained the American Ryder Cup team in the infamous 'War on the Shore' match at Kiawah Island in 1991.

Stranahan, Frank R (USA)
Born Toledo, Ohio, 5 August 1922
Turned professional 1954
One of America's most successful amateurs he won the Amateur championship at Royal St George's in 1948 and 1950. He also won the US Amateur in 1950, the Mexican Amateur in 1946, 1948 and 1951 and the Canadian title in 1947 and 1948. He was also leading amateur in the Open in 1947, 1949, 1950, 1951 and 1953 behind Ben Hogan. He played in three Walker Cups in 1947, 1949 and 1951.

Strange, Curtis (USA)
Born Norfolk, Virginia, 20 January 1955
Turned professional 1976
Winner of successive US Opens in 1988 and again in 1989 when he beat Nick Faldo in an 18-hole play-off at The Country Club Brookline after getting up and down from a bunker at the last to tie on 278. Winner of 17 US Tour titles he won at least one event for seven successive years from 1983. Having played in five Ryder Cup matches he captained the US side when the 2001 match was played at The Belfry in 2002. Now commentates for the ABC Network.

Streit, Marlene Stewart (Can)
Born Cereal, Alberta, 9 March 1934
One of Canada's most successful amateurs she won her national title ten times between 1951 and 1973. She won the 1953 British Amateur, the US Amateur in 1956 and the Australian Ladies in 1963. She was Canadian Woman Athlete of the Year in 1951, 1953, 1956, 1960 and 1963.

Stricker, Steve (USA)
Born Egerton, Wisconsin, 23 February 1967
Turned professional 1990
Started 2001 by winning the $1 million first prize in the Accenture Match Play Championship, one of the World Golf Championship series. In the final he beat Pierre Fulke. Was a member of the winning American Alfred Dunhill Cup side in 1996.

Suggs, Louise (USA)
Born Atlanta, Georgia, 7 September 1923
Turned professional 1948
Winner of 58 titles on the LPGA Tour after a brilliant amateur career which included victories in the 1947 US Amateur and the 1948 British Amateur Championships. She won 11 Majors including the US Open in 1949 and 1952 and the LPGA Championship in 1957. A founder member of the US Tour she was an inaugural honoree when the LPGA Hall of Fame was instituted in 1967.

Sutton, Hal (USA)
Born Shreveport, Louisiana, 28 April 1958
Turned professional 1981
Winner of the 1983 US PGA Championship at the Riviera CC in Los Angeles beating Jack Nicklaus into second place. Played in the 1985 and 1987 Ryder Cup matches and returned to the side in 1999 at Brookline when he beat Darren Clarke 4 and 2 in the singles. He made the 2001 side as well.

Thomson CBE, Peter (Aus)
Born Melbourne, 23 August 1929
Turned professional 1949
He is one of only four players who have won five Open Championships. At the start of the 20th century J.H. Taylor and James Braid won five, and Tom Watson won five in eight years from 1975 while Thomson completed his five victories between 1954 and 1965. In one seven-year spell from 1952 Thomson never finished worse than second in the Championship. His run of finishes from 1952 was 2, 2, 1, 1, 1, 2, 1. His fifth victory, arguably his most impressive, came at Royal Birkdale in 1965 when more Americans were in the field. He played only three times in the US Open finishing fourth in 1956. He played in five US Masters with fifth his best finish in 1957. He won three Australian Opens and in Europe had 24 victories between 1954 and 1972. With one of the most fluent and reliable swings he made golf look easy. Instrumental in developing the game throughout Asia, Africa and the Middle East he was ready to retire from golf and pursue a career in Australian politics but he was not elected and turned instead to the US Senior Tour with great success. In 1985 he won nine Senior Tour titles. Has captained three Rest of the World Presidents Cup sides, was elected to the World Golf Hall of Fame in 1988 and is an honorary member of the Royal and Ancient Golf Club of St Andrews. After his retirement from top-line golf he concentrated on his hugely successful golf course designing business based in Melbourne completing projects in many countries around the world.

Toms, David (USA)
Born Monroe, LA, 4 January 1967
Turned professional 1989
Most important of his six wins on the US Tour was his first Major success by beating Phil Mickelson into second place in the 2001 USPGA Championship. Toms shot 66, 65, 65 and 69 for a 265 record winning aggregate at the Atlanta Athletic Club. This is the lowest aggregate in any Major. The previous year he had come joint fourth to Tiger Woods in the Open. Made his Ryder Cup début in 2001 and was the American side's top points scorer with 3½ points.

Trevino, Lee (USA)
Born Dallas, Texas, 1 December 1939
Turned professional 1961
Twenty times a winner on the US Tour between 1968 and 1981 'Supermex', as he was nicknamed by his peers, hit the headlines in 1971 when he won the US Open beating Jack Nicklaus in a play-off at Merion, the Canadian Open at Montreal and the Open at Royal Birkdale in succession. One of the most extrovert of golfers who followed up his 27 victories on the main Tour with 29 on the US Senior Tour was entirely self-taught. He won six Majors – the Open in 1971 and 1972 when he chipped in at the 71st hole to end Tony Jacklin's hopes of winning, the US Open in 1968 and 1971 and the US PGA Championship in 1974 and 1984 but he never finished better than tenth twice in the Masters at Augusta – a course with so many right to left dog-legs that he felt it did not suit his game. In 1975 he was hit by lightning while playing in the Western Open in Chicago and had to undergo back surgery in order to keep competing. He was involved in one of the low scoring matches in the World Match Play Championship with Tony Jacklin in 1972 when he again came out on top.

Verplank, Scott (USA)
Born Dallas, Texas, 9 July 1964
When he won the Western Open as an amateur in 1985 he was the first to do so since Doug Sanders took the 1956 Canadian Open. Missed most of the 1991 and 1992 seasons because of an elbow injury and the injury also affected his 1996 season. He has diabetes and wears an insulin pump while playing to regulate his medication. Curtis Strange chose him as one of his two 'picks' for the 2001 US Ryder Cup side. In the singles on the final day he beat Lee Westwood 2 and 1.

De Vicenzo, Roberto (Arg)
Born Buenos Aires, 14 April 1923
Turned professional 1938
Although he won the Open in 1967 at Royal Liverpool this impressive South American is perhaps best known for the Major title he might have won. In 1968 he finished tied with Bob Goalby at Augusta or he thought he had. He had finished birdie, bogey to do so but sadly signed for the par 4 that had been inadvertently and carelessly put down for the 17th by Tommy Aaron who was marking his card. Although everyone watching on television and at the course saw the Argentinian make 3 the fact that he signed for 4 was indisputable and he had to accept that there would be no play-off. It remains one of the saddest incidents in golf with the emotion heightened by the fact that that Sunday was de Vicenzo's 45th birthday. The gracious manner in which he accepted the disappointments was remarkable. What a contrast to the scenes at Hoylake nine months earlier when, after years of trying, he finally won the Open beating Jack Nicklaus and Clive Clark in the process thanks to a pressure-packed brilliant last round 70. In fact he was runner-up in the event in 1950 and came third six times. The father of South American golf he was a magnificent driver and is credited with having won over 200 titles in his extraordinary career including nine Argentinian Opens between 1944 and 1974 plus the 1957 Jamaican, 1950 Belgian, 1950 Dutch, 1950, 1960 and 1964 French, 1964 German Open and 1966 Spanish Open titles. He played 15 times for Argentina in the World Cup and four times for Mexico. Inducted into the World Golf Hall of Fame in 1989 he is an honorary member of the Royal and Ancient Golf Club of St Andrews.

Wadkins, Lanny (USA)
Born Richmond, Virginia, 5 December 1949
Turned professional 1971
His 21 victories on the US Tour between 1972 and 1992 include the 1977 US PGA Championship, his only Major. He won that after a play-off with Gene Littler at Pebble Beach but lost a play-off for the same title in 1987 to Larry Nelson at Palm Beach Gardens. He was second on two other occasions to Ray Floyd in 1982 and to Lee Trevino in 1984. In other Majors his best finish was third three times in the US Masters (1990, 1991 and 1993), tied second in the US Open (1986) and tied fourth in the 1984 Open at St Andrews. One of the fiercest of competitors he played eight Ryder Cups between 1977 and 1993 winning 20 of his 33 games, but was a losing captain at Oak Hill in 1995.

Ward, Harvie (USA)
Born Tarboro, North Carolina 1926
Turned professional 1973
Winner of the Amateur Championship in 1952 when he beat Frank Stranahan 6 and 5 at Prestwick, he went on to win the US title in 1955 and 1956 and the Canadian Amateur in 1964. He played in the 1953, 1955 and 1959 Walker Cup matches and won all of his six games.

Watson, Tom (USA)
Born Kansas City, Missouri, 4 September 1949
Turned professional 1971
Winner of 34 career titles, he won at least three a year on the main US Tour in a six-year spell between 1977 and 1982. He is best known for having won five Open championships in eight years between 1975 and 1983 to match the feat of J.H. Taylor, James Braid and Peter Thomson. When he had a chance to win a sixth Open and tie Harry Vardon's record at St Andrews in 1984 he hit his second close to the wall through the green at the

17th and lost out to Seve Ballesteros. Watson's wins came at Carnoustie in 1975 after a play-off with Jack Newton; a memorable 1977 triumph in which he edged out Jack Nicklaus at Turnberry shooting 65, 65 over the weekend to Nicklaus' 65, 66; 1980 at Muirfield where he beat Lee Trevino; 1982 at Royal Troon where Peter Oosterhuis and Nick Price came second and 1983 when Andy Bean and Hale Irwin were runners-up. Watson also won the 1982 US Open chipping in from the rough at the 17th on the final day to go on and beat Nicklaus and two US Masters in 1977 and 1981 but he never did better than tied second in the 1977 US PGA Championship to miss out joining Gene Sarazen, Ben Hogan, Gary Player, Jack Nicklaus and Tiger Woods as a winner of all four Majors. Became the oldest winner on the US Tour when he won the Mastercard Colonial in 1998 nearly 24 years after scoring his first win in the Western Open. He was 48, two years older than the previous oldest Ben Hogan, when he won the same event for the fifth time in 1959. Six times Player of the Year he played in four Ryder Cups and captained the side to victory in 1993 at The Belfry. Now plays on the US Senior Tour Inducted into the World Golf Hall of Fame in 1988, he is an honorary member of the Royal and Ancient Golf Club of St Andrews.

Webb, Karrie (Aus)

Born Ayr, Queensland, 21 December 1974
Turned professional 1994

Blonde Australian who is rewriting the record books with her performances on the LPGA Tour. Peter Thomson, the five times Open champion considers she is the best golfer male or female there is and Greg Norman, who was her inspiration as a teenager, believes she can play at times better than Tiger Woods although Webb herself hates comparisons. She scored her first Major win in 1995 when she took the Weetabix Women's British Open – a title she won again in 1997. When she joined the LPGA Tour she won the 1999 du Maurier Classic, the 2000 Nabisco Championship and the 2000 and 2001 US Women's Open – five Majors out of eight (by the end of July 2001) – the most impressive run since Mickey Wright won five out of six in the early 1960s. In 2002 she became the first player to complete a career Grand Slam when she won her third Weetabix British Open which had become an official major on the US LPGA Tour. It was her sixth major title in four years. Her winning total at Turnberry was 15 under par 273. Enjoys a close rivalry with Annika Sörenstam.

Weir, Mike (Can)

Born Sarnia, Ontario, 12 May 1970
Turned professional 1992

A left-hander, he was the first Canadian to play in the Presidents Cup when he made the side in 2000 and the first from his country to win a World Golf Championship event when he took the American Express Championship at Valderrama in 2000. Wrote to Jack Nicklaus as a 13-year-old to enquire whether or not he should switch from playing golf left-handed to right-handed and was told not to switch. In 1997 he led the scoring averages on the Canadian Tour with a score of 69.29.

Weiskopf, Tom (USA)

Born Massillon, Ohio, 9 November 1942
Turned professional 1946

Winner of only one Major – the 1973 Open Championship at Royal Troon, he lived in the shadow of Jack Nicklaus throughout his competitive career. He was runner-up in the 1976 US Open to Jerry Pate and was twice third in 1973 and 1977. His best finish in the US PGA Championship was third in 1975 – the year he had to be content for the fourth time with second place at the US Masters. He had been runner-up for a Green Jacket in 1969, 1972 and 1974 previously but played perhaps his best golf ever in 1975 only to be pipped at the post by Nicklaus. With 22 wins to his name he now plays the US Senior Tour with a curtailed schedule because of his course design work for which he and his original partner Jay Morrish have received much praise. One of their designs is Loch Lomond, venue of the revived Scottish Open. Played in just two Ryder Cup matches giving up a place in the team one year in order to go Bighorn sheep hunting in Alaska.

Whitworth, Kathy (USA)

Born Monahans, Texas, 27 September 1939
Turned professional 1958

Won 88 titles on the LPGA Tour between 1959 and 1991 – more than any one else male or female. Her golden period was in the 1960s when she won eight events in 1965, nine in 1966, eight in 1967 and 10 in 1968. When she finished third in the 1981 US Women's Open she became the first player to top $1 million in prize money on the LPGA Tour. She was the seventh member of the LPGA Tour Hall of Fame when inducted in 1975. Began playing golf at the age of 15 and made golfing history when she teamed up with Mickey Wright to play in the previously all male Legends of Golf event. Winner of six Majors – including three LPGA Championship wins in 1967, 1971 and 1975. In addition she won two Titleholders Championships (1966 and 1967) and the 1967 Western Open when they were Majors. Enjoyed a winning streak of 17 successive years on the LPGA Tour.

Woods, Eldrick 'Tiger' (USA)

Born Cypress, California, 30 December 1975
Turned professional 1996

First golfer in history to hold all four Majors simultaneously. He won the 2000 US Open, the Open at St Andrews and the US PGA Championship after a play-off with Bob May then scored his second victory at Augusta when he won the 2001 US Masters. He is rewriting the record books. As an amateur he successfully made two defences of the US Championship to win the event a record three years in a row but the meteoric start to his professional career gives rise to the view that he might beat Jack Nicklaus' 18 major title wins record. In 2000 he was 53-under-par for the four Majors with Ernie Els next best at 17-under.

His nine Tour victories in a season was the most by anyone since Ben Hogan won 11 in 1950. When he won the AT and T at Pebble Beach in 2000 he became the first player since Ben Hogan in 1948 to win on six successive starts on the US Tour. At Pebble Beach in the US Open he shot 65, 69, 71, 67 to tie the US Open record of 272 but his 12-under-par score was a new sub-par record. Having won the US Masters for the first time with a record 270 total which gave him a 12 shot victory in 1997 and taken the US PGA title in 1999 he needed only to win the Open in Britain to become the youngest and only the fifth player in history (the others were Gene Sarazen, Ben Hogan, Gary Player and Jack Nicklaus) to have won all four Majors. At the Old Course at St Andrews he romped home by eight shots with a new British Open and major Championship record total of 269 – 19-under-par. He needed extra holes to beat Bob May at Valhalla to successfully defend the US PGA title a few weeks later. With that victory he joined Ben Hogan (1953) as a winner of three Majors in a season but beat that record when he took the US Masters Green Jacket for a second time in 2001. His current Majors tally is six. His chance of winning all four Majors in one season was lost when he did not successfully defend his US Open title later in the year. During the 2000 season he set or tied 27 records and his average score on the US Tour of 68.1 beat Sam Snead's record of 69.23 set in 1945. Named Tiger after a Vietnamese soldier who was a friend of his father's he was born to play golf, hitting shots on the Bob Hope Show when aged two and shooting 48 for nine holes at age three. He is the youngest player to have won 20 events on the US Tour. He is so far ahead in the World rankings that he is unlikely to be deposed for some considerable time. He played in the 1997 and 1999 Ryder Cup matches and is a member of the 2001 side. Woods won the Masters title again in 2002 beating Retief Goosen into second place at Augusta on a final day when both Ernie Els and Vijay Singh challenged strongly before the South African ran up a 7 and the Fijian a 9 on the back nine. When he also won the US Open again at Bethpage Park in New York State he was in line to win all four majors in the same year but just like Jack Nicklaus 30 years earlier he lost out at Muirfield where Ernie Els was the winner of the Open. Caught in severe weather on the third day Woods fired a career high professional score of 81 but hit back with

a closing 65 to finish joint 28th. In the US PGA Championship at Hazeltine he closed with four birdies but lost his chance of a ninth major in six years to Rich Beem. He has played in three Ryder Cups and with David Duvall won the World Cup of Golf in 2001.

Wright, Mickey (USA)

Born San Diego, California, 14 February 1935
Turned professional 1954

Her 82 victories on the LPGA Tour between 1956 and 1973 was bettered only by Kathy Whitworth who has 88 official victories. One of the greatest golfers in the history of the Tour she had a winning streak of 14 successive seasons. Winner of 13 Major titles she is the only player to date to have won three in one season. In 1961 she took the US Women's Open, the LPGA Championship and the Titleholders Championship. That year she became only the second player to win both the US Women's Open and LPGA Championship in the same year having done so previously in 1958. Scored 79 of her victories between 1956 and 1969 when averaging almost eight wins a season. During this time she enjoyed a tremendous rivalry with Miss Whitworth. Truly a golfing legend.

Yates, Charles Richard (Charlie) (USA)

Born Atlanta, Georgia, 9 September 1913

Great friend of the late Bobby Jones he was top amateur in the US Masters in 1934, 1939 and 1940. In 1938 came to Royal Troon and won the British Amateur title beating R. Ewing 3 and 2. For many years acted as chairman of the press committee at the US Masters and annually stages an overseas golf writers party in the Augusta Clubhouse.

Zoeller, Fuzzy (USA)

Born New Albany, Indiana, 11 November 1951
Turned professional 1973

Winner of the US Masters in 1979 after a play-off with Ed Sneed (who had dropped shots at the last three holes in regulation play) and Tom Watson and the US Open in 1984 at Winged Foot after an 18-hole play-off with Greg Norman. A regular winner on the US Tour between 1979 and 1986, he played in three Ryder Cups (1979, 1983 and 1985).

British Isles International Players, Professional Men

Key

RC	Ryder Cup GBI till 1977; Europe thereafter.	DC	Dunhill Cup – by home country
		CC	Canada Cup
USA	1921, 1926: pre-Ryder Cup	WbC	Warburg Cup
RoW	Rest of World	(S)Eur	European Seniors v Ladies European Tour
FT	Four Tours World Championship, Players represented European Tour; also in Nissan Cup and Kirin Cup	*	indicates winning team
		'to' indicates inclusive dates: e.g.'1908 to 1911' means '1908-09-10-11'; otherwise individual years are shown.	
Eur	GBI v Continent of Europe		
WC	World Cup – by home country; was Canada (Cup) till 1966	Captaincy is indicated by the year printed in bold type; non-playing captaincy in brackets	

ENGLAND

Alliss, Percy
RC 1929-31-33-35-37; Sco 1932 to 1937; Irl 1932-38; Wal 1938; (GBI) Fra 1939

Alliss, Peter
RC 1953-57-59-61-63-65-67-69; CC 1954-55-57-58-59-61-62-64-66; WC 1967

Baker, Peter
RC 1993; DC 1993 (r/u)-98; WC 1999

Bamford, BJ
CC 1961

Barber, T
Irl 1932-33

Batley, JB
Sco 1912

Beck, AG
Wal, Irl 1938

Bembridge, Maurice
RC 1969-71-73-75; SA 1976; WC 1974-75; (S) Eur 1997

Bickerton, J
Eur 2000

Boomer, Aubrey
USA 1926; RC 1927-29

Bousfield, Ken
RC 1949-51-55-57-59-61; CC 1956-57

Boxall, R
WC 1990; DC 1990

Branch, WJ
Sco 1936

Brand, Gordon J
RC 1983; Nissan 1986; WC 1983; DC 1986-87*

Broadhurst, Paul
RC 1991; FT 1991-95; WC 1997; DC 1991

Burton, J
Irl 1933

Burton, R (Dick)
RC 1935-37-49; Sco 1935-36-37; Sco, Wal, Irl 1938

Busson, JH
Sco 1938

Busson, Jack J
RC 1935; Sco 1934-35-36-37

Butler, Peter J
RC 1965-69-71-73; Eur 1976; WC 1969-70-73

Carter, D
DC 1998; WC 1998*

Cawsey, GH
Sco 1906-07

Caygill, G Alex
RC 1969

Chapman, R
DC 2000

Clark, Clive
RC 1973

Clark, Howard K
RC 1977-81-85-87-89-95; Aus 1988; Eur 1978-84; Nissan 1985; WC 1978-84-85-87; DC 1985-86-87*-89-90-94-95

Claydon, R
DC 1997

Coles, Neil C
RC 1961-63-65-67-69-71-73-77; Eur 1974-76-78-80; (S) Eur 1998-99; Can 1963; WC 1968

Collinge, T
Sco 1937

Collins, JF
Sco 1903-04

Compston, Archie
USA 1926; RC 1927-29-31; Fra 1929; Sco, Irl 1932; Sco 1935

Cotton, T Henry
RC 1929-37-47; Fra 1929

Cox, WJ (Bill)
RC 1935-37; Sco 1935-36-37

Curtis, D
Sco 1934; Sco, Wal, Irl 1938

Davis, B
DC 2000

Davies, William H
RC 1931-33; Sco, Irl 1932-33

Dawson, Peter
RC 1977; WC 1977

Denny, Charles S
Sco 1936

Durnian, Denis
WC 1989; DC 1989; WbC 2001-02

Easterbrook, Syd
RC 1931-33; Sco 1932 to 35; 38; Irl 1933

Faldo, Nick A
RC 1977-79-81-83-85-87-89-91-93-95-97; Eur 1978-80-82-84; RoW 1982; Nissan 1986; Kirin 1987; FT 1990; WC 1977-91-98*; DC 1985-86-87*-88-91-93; WbC 2001-02

Faulkner, Max
RC 1947-49-51-53-57

Foster, M
Eur 1976; WC 1976

Gadd, B
Sco, Irl 1933; Sco 1935; Sco, Irl, Wal 1938

Gadd, George
USA 1926; RC 1927

Garner, John R
RC 1971-71

Gaudin, PJ
Sco 1905-06-07-09-12-13

Gilford, David
RC 1991-95; WC 1992-93; DC 1992*

Gray, E
Sco 1904-05-07

Green, Eric
RC 1947

Green, T
Sco 1935; also Wal v Sco, Irl 1937 and Sco, Eng 1938

Gregson, Malcolm
RC 1967; WC 1967; (S) Eur 1997

Hargreaves, Jack
RC 1951

Havers, AG
USA 1921-26; RC 1927-31-33; Fra 1929; Sco, Irl 1932-33; Sco 1934

Hitchcock, Jimmy
RC 1965

Horne, Reg
RC 1947

Horton, Tommy
RC 1975-77; Eur 1974-76; WC 1976; (S) Eur 1997-(98)-(99)

Howell, D
Eur 2000; DC 1999

Hunt, Bernard J
RC 1953-57-59-61-63-65-67-69; Can 1958-59-60-62-63-64; WC 1968

Hunt, Guy L
RC 1975; Eur 1974; WC 1972-75

Hunt, Geoffrey M
RC 1963

Jacklin, A (Tony)
RC 1967-69-71-73-75-77-79-(83)-(85)-(87)-(89); Eur 1976-82; RoW 1982; Can 1966; WC 1970-71-72

Jacobs, John RM
RC 1955

Jagger, D
Eur 1976

James, Mark H
RC 1977-79-81-89-91-93-95-(99); Eur 1978-80-82; RoW 1982; Aus 1988; Kirin 1988; FT 1989-90; WC 1978-79-82-84-87-88-93-97-99; DC 1988-89-90-93-95-97-99

Jarman, Edward W
RC 1935; Sco 1935

Job, Nick
Eur 1980

Jolly, Herbert C
USA 1926; RC 1927; Fra 1929

Jones, D
(S)Eur 1998-99

Jones, R
Sco 1903 to 07; 09-10-12-13

Kenyon, EWH
Sco, Irl 1932

King, Michael
RC 1979; WC 1979

King, Sam L
RC 1937-47-49; Sco 1934-36-37; Sco, Wal, Irl 1938

Lacey, Arthur J
RC 1933-37; Sco, Irl 1932-33; Sco 1934-36-37; Sco, Irl, Wal 1938

Lane, Barry
RC 1993; WC 1988-94; DC 1988-94-95-96; WbC 2002

Lees, Arthur
RC 1947-49-51-55; Sco, Wal, Irl 1938

Mason, SC
Eur 1980; WC 1980

Mayo, CH
Sco 1907-09-10-12-13

Mills, R Peter
RC

Mitchell, Abe
USA 1921-26; RC 1929-31-33; Sco 1932-33-34

Mitchell, P
WC 1996

Moffitt, Ralph
RC 1961

Morgan, J
(S)Eur 1997-99

Ockenden, J
USA 1921

Oke, WG
Sco 1932

Oosterhuis, Peter A
RC 1971-73-75-77-79-81; Eur 1974; WC 1971

O'Sullivan, DF
(S)Eur 1998

Padgham, Alf H
RC 1933-35-37; Sco, Irl 1932-33; Sco 1934 to 37; Sco, Irl, Wal 1938

Payne, J
WC 1996

Perry, Alf
RC 1933-35-37; Irl 1932; Sco 1933-36-38

Platts, Lionel
RC 1965

Rainford, P
Sco 1903-07

Ray, E (Ted)
USA 1921-26; RC 1927; Sco 1903 to 07; 09-10-12-13

Reid, W
Sco 1906-07

Renouf, TG
Sco 1903-04-05-10-13

Rhodes, J
(S)Eur 1998

Richardson, Steven
RC 1991; FT 1991; WC 1992; DC 1991-92*

Robson, F
USA1926; RC 1927-29-31; Sco 1909-10

Roe, Mark
WC 1989-94-95; DC 1994

Rowe, AJ
Sco 1903-06-07

Scott, Syd S
RC 1955

Seymour, M
(SCO) Irl 1932; (ENG): Sco, Irl 1932-33

Sherlock, JG
USA 1921; Sco 1903 to 07; 09-10-12-13

Snell, D
Canada 1965

Spence, J
DC 1992*-2000

Sutton, M
Can 1955

Taylor, JH
USA 1921; Sco 1903 to 07; 09-10-12-13

Taylor, JJ
Sco 1937

Taylor, Josh
USA 1921; Sco 1913

Tingey, A
Sco 1903-05

Townsend, Peter
RC 1969-71; Eur 1974; WC 1969-74

Twine, WT
Irl 1932

Vardon, Harry
USA 1921

Waites, Brian J
RC 1983; Eur 1980-82-84; RoW 1982; WC 1980-82-83; (S)Eur 1997-98

Ward, Charlie H
RC 1947-49-51; Irl 1932

Way, Paul
RC 1983-85; WC 1985; DC 1985-99

Weetman, Harry
RC 1951-53-55-57*-59-61-63;
Can 1954-56-60

Westwood, Lee
RC 1997-99-2002; Eur 2000; DC
1996-97-98-99

Whitcombe, Charles A
RC 1927-29-31-33-35-37; Fra
1929; Sco 1932 to 38; Irl 1933

Whitcombe, EE
Sco, Wal, Irl 1938

Whitcombe, Ernest R
USA 1926; RC 1929-31-35; Fra
1929; Sco 1932; Irl 1933

Whitcombe, Reg A
RC 1935; Sco 1933 to 38

Wilcock, P
WC 1973

Williamson, T
Sco 1904 to 07; 09-10-12-13

Wilson, RG
Sco 1913

Wolstenholme, Guy B
Can 1965

IRELAND

Boyle, Hugh F
RC 1967; WC 1967

Bradshaw, Harry
RC 1953-55-57; Can 1954 to1959;
Sco 1937-38; Wal 1937; Eng 1938

Carrol, LJ
Sco, Wal 1937; Sco, Eng 1938

Cassidy, D
Sco 1936; Sco, Wal 1937

Cassidy, J
Eng 1933; Sco 1934-35

Clarke, Darren
RC 1997-99-2002; Eur 2000; DC
1994 to 99; WC 1994-95-96

Daly, Fred
RC 1947-49-51-53; Sco 1936; Sco,
Wal 1937; Sco, Eng 1938; Can
1954-55

Darcy, Eamonn
RC 1975-77-81-87; Eur 1976-84;
SA 1976; WC 1976-77-83-84-85-
87; DC 1987-88*-91

Drew, Norman V
RC 1959; Can 1960-61

Edgar, J
Sco 1938

Fairweather, S
Eng 1932; Sco 1933; [SCO] Eng
1933-35-36; Irl, Wal 1938

Feherty, David
RC 1991; FT 1990-91; DC 1985-
86-90*-91-93; WC 1990

Greene, C
Can 1965

Hamill, J
Eng 1932; Eng, Sco 33; Sco 34-35

Harrington, Padraig
RC 1999-2002; Eur 2000; DC
1996 to 99; WC 1996-97*-98-99-
2000

Holley, W
Sco 1933-34-35-36-38; Eng 1932-
33-38

Jackson, H
WC 1970-71

Jones, E
Can 1965

Kinsella, J
WC 1968-69-72-73

Kinsella, W
Sco 1937; Sco, Eng 1938

McCartney, J
Sco 1932 to 38; Eng 1932-33-38;
Wal 1937

McDermott, M
Sco, Eng 1932

McGinley, Paul
RC 2002; WC 1993-94-97*-98-99-
2000; DC 1993-94-96-97-98-99

McGinn, John
HI 2002

McKenna, J
Sco 1936; Sco, Wal 1937; Sco,
Wal, Eng 1938

McKenna, R
Sco, Eng 1933; Sco 1935

McNeill, H
Eng 1932

Mahon, PJ
Sco 1932 to 38; Eng 1932-33-38;
Wal 1937-38

Martin, Jimmy
RC 1965; Can 1962-63-64-66; WC
1970

O'Brien, W
Sco 1934-36; Sco, Wal 1937

O'Connor, Christy
RC 1955-57-59-61-63-65-67-69-
71-73; Can 1956 to 64; 66; WC
1967-68-69-71-73

O'Connor, Christy jr
RC 1975-89; Eur 1974-84; SA
1976; (S)Eur 1998; WC 1974-75-
78-85-89-92; DC 1985-89-92

O'Connor, CJ
(S)Eur 1998

O'Connor, P
Sco, Eng 1932-33; Sco 1934-35-36

O'Leary, John E
RC 1975; Eur 1976-78-82; RoW
1982; WC 1972-80-82

O'Neill, J
Eng 1933

O'Neill, M
Sco, Eng 1933; Sco 1934

Patterson, E
Sco 1933 to 36; Eng 1933; Wal
1937

Polland, Eddie
RC 1973; Eur 1974-76-78-80;
(S)Eur 1998-99; WC 1973-74-76-
77-78-79

Pope, CW
Sco, Eng 1932

Rafferty, Ronan
RC 1989; Eur 1984; Kirin 1988;
FT 1989-90-91; Aus 1988; WC
1983-84-87-88; 90 to 93; DC
1986-87-88*-89-90*-91-92-93-95

Smyth, Des
RC 1979-81; Eur 1980-82-84;
RoW 1982; WC 1979-80-82-83-
88-89; DC 1985-86-87-88*-2000;
WbC 2001

Stevenson, P
Sco 1933 to 36; 38; Eng 1933-38

Wallace, L
Sco, Eng 1932

Walton, Philip
RC 1995; WC 1995; DC 1989-
90*-92-94-95

SCOTLAND

Adams, J
RC 1947-49-51-53; Eng 1932 to
1938; Wal 1937-38; Irl 1937-38

Ainslie, T
Irl 1936

Anderson, Joe
Irl 1932

Anderson, W
Irl 1936; Eng, Wal 1937

Ayton, LB
Eng 1910-12-13-33-34

Ayton, Laurie B jr
RC 1949; Eng 1937

Ballantine, J
Eng 1932-36

Ballingall, J
Eng, Irl, Wal 1938

Bannerman, Harry
RC 1993; WC 1967-72

Barnes, Brian
RC 1969-71-73-75-77-79; Eur
1974-76-78-80; SA 1976; WC
1974-75-76-77

Braid, James
USA 1921; Eng 1903 to 07; 10-12

Brand, Gordon jr
RC 1987-89; Aus 1988; Nissan
1985; Kirin 1988; FT 1989; WC

1984-85-88-89-90-92-94; DC 1985
to 89; 91 to 94; 97

Brown, Eric C
RC 1953-55-57-59; Can 1954 to
62; 65-66; WC 1967-68

Brown, Ken
RC 1977-79-83-85-87; Eur 1978;
Kirin 1987; WC 1977-78-79-83

Burns, Stewart
RC 1929; Eng 1932

Callum, WS
Irl 1935

Campbell, J
Irl 1936

Coltart, Andrew
RC 1999; DC 1994-95*-96-98-
2000; WC 1994-95-96-98

Coltart, F
Eng 1909

Dailey, Allan
RC 1933; Eng 1932 to 36; Eng, Irl,
Wal 1938

Davis, W
Irl 1933 to 36; Irl, Eng, Wal 1937-
38

Dobson, T
Eng, Irl 1932 to 1936; Eng, Irl,
Wal 1937; Irl, Wal 1938

Don, W
Irl 1935-36

Donaldson, J
Eng 1932-35-38; Irl, Wal 1937

Dorman, R
Irl 1932

Duncan, George
USA 1921-26; RC 1927-29-31;
Eng 1906-07-09-10-12-13-32-34 to
37

Durward, JG
Irl 1934; Eng 1937

Fairweather, S
[IRL] Eng 1932; Sco 1933; [SCO]
Eng 1933-35-36; Irl, Wal 1938

Fallon, John
RC 1955; Eng 1936; Eng, Irl, Wal
1937-38

Fenton, WB
Eng, Irl 1932; Irl 1933

Fernie, TR
Eng 1910-12-13-33

Gallacher, Bernard
RC 1969-71-73-75-77-79-81-83-
(91)-(93)-(95); Eur 1974-78-82-84;
SA 1976; RoW 1982; WC 1969-
71-74-82-83

Good, G
Eng 1934-36

Gow, A
Eng 1912

Grant, T
Eng 1913

Haliburton, Tom B
RC 1961-63; Can 1954; Irl 1935-
36; Irl, Wal, Eng 1938

Hastings, W
Eng, Wal, Irl 1937-38

Hepburn, J
Eng 1903-05-06-07-09-10-12-13

Herd, A (Sandy)
Eng 1903-04-05-06-09-10-12-13-32

Houston, D
Irl 1934

Huish, D
WC 1973

Hunter, W
Eng 1906-07-09-10

Hutton, GC
Irl 1936; Irl, Eng, Wal 1937; Eng
1938

Ingram, D
WC 1973

Knight, G
Eng 1937

Laidlaw, W
Eng 1935-36-38; Irl, Wal 1937

Lawrie, Paul
RC 1999; WC 1996; DC 1999

Lockhart, G
Irl 1934-35

Lyle, AWB (Sandy)
RC 1979-81-83-85-87; Eur 1980-
82-84; RoW 1982; Aus 1988;
Nissan 1985-86; Kirin 1987; WC
1979-80-87; DC 1985 to 90; 92

McCulloch, D
Eng, Irl 1932 to 35; Eng 1936-37

McDowall, J
Eng 1932; Eng, Irl 1933 to 36

McEwan, P
Eng 1907

McIntosh, G
Eng, Irl, Wal 1938

McMillan, J
Eng, Irl 1933-34; Eng 1935

McMinn, W
Eng 1932-33-34

Martin, S
WC 1980

Montgomerie, Colin
RC 1991-93-95-97-99-2002; Eur
2000; FT 1991; WC 1988-91-92-
93-97 (individual winner)-98-99;
DC 1988; 91 to 98 (winners 95);
2000

Orr, Gary
Eur 2000; DC 1998-99-2000

Panton, John
RC 1951-53-61; Can 1955 to 66;
WC 1968

Park, J
Eng 1909

Ritchie, WL
Eng 1913

Robertson, F
Irl 1933; Eng 1938

Robertson, P
Eng, Irl 1932; Irl 1934

Russell, Raymond
WC 1997; DC 1996-97

Sayers, Ben jr
Eng 1906-07-09

Seymour, M
Irl 1932; (ENG): Sco, Irl 1932-33

Shade, Ronnie DBM
WC 1970-71-72

Simpson, A
Eng 1904

Smith, CR
Eng 1903-04-07-09-13

Smith, GE
Irl 1932

Spark, W
Irl 1933; Irl, Eng 1935; Irl, Wal
1937

Thompson, R
Eng 1903 to 07; 09-10-12

Torrance, Sam
RC 1981-83-85-87-89-91-93-95-
(2002); Eur 1976-78-80-82-84;
RoW 1982; Nissan 1985; FT 1991;
WC 1976-78-82-84-85-87-89-90-
93-95; DC 1985-86-87-89-90-91-
93-95*; WbC 2001-02

Walker, RT
Can 1964

Watt, T
Eng 1907

Watt, W
Eng 1912-13

White, J
Eng 1903 to 07; 09; 12-13

Will, George
RC 1963-65-67; Can 1963; WC
1969-70

Wilson, T
Irl 1932; Irl, Eng 1933-34

Wood, Norman
RC 1975; WC 1975

WALES

Affleck, P
DC 1995-96

Cox, S
WC 1975

Davies, R
WC 1968

De Foy, Craig B
WC 1971; 73 to 78

Dobson, K
WC 1972

Gould, H
Can 1954-55

Grabham, C
Eng, Sco 1938

Healing, SF
Sco 1938

Hill, EF
Sco, Irl 1937; Sco, Eng 1938

Hodson, Bert
RC 1931; Sco, Irl 1937; Sco, Eng 1938; also Eng v Irl 1933

Huggett, Brian GC
RC 1963-67-69-71-73-75; Eur 1974-78; Can 1963-64-65; WC 1968-69-70-71-76-79; (S) Eur 1998

James, G
Sco, Irl 1937

Jones, DC
Sco, Irl 1937; Sco, Eng 1938

Jones, T
Sco 1936; Irl 1937; Eng 1938

Llewellyn, D
Eur 1984; WC 1974-85-87*-88; DC 1985-88

Lloyd, F
Sco, Irl 1937; Sco, Eng 1938

Mayo, Paul
DC 1993

Mouland, Mark
Kirin 1988; WC 1988-89-90-92-93-95-96; DC 1986-87-88-89-93-95-96

Mouland, S
Can 1965-66; WC 1967

Park, D
DC 2000

Parkin, P
Eur 1984; WC 1984-89; DC 1985-86-87-89-90-91

Pickett, C
Sco, Irl 1937; Sco, Eng 1938

Price, Phillip
RC 2002; Eur 2000; WC 1994-95-97-98-2000; DC 1991-96

Rees, Dai J
RC 1937-47-49-51-53-(55)-(57)*-(59)-(61)-**(67)**

Smalldon, D
Can 1955-56

Thomas, Dave C
RC 1959-63-65-67; Can 1957 to 63; 66; WC 1967-69-70

Vaughan, DI
WC 1972-73-77-78-79-80

Williams, K
Sco, Irl 1937; Sco, Eng 1938

Woosnam, Ian
RC 1983-85-87-89-91-93-95-97; Eur 1982-84-2000; RoW 1982; Aus 1988; Nissan 1985-86; Kirin 1987; FT 1989-90; WC 1980; 82 to 85; 87*; 90 to 94; 96-97-98; DC 1985 to 91; 93-95-2000; WbC 2001-02

British Isles International Players, Professional Women

Non-playing captaincy in brackets

ENGLAND

Davies, Laura
SOLHEIM CUP 1990-92-94-96-98-2000-2002

Douglas, Kitrina
SOLHEIM CUP 1992

Fairclough, Lora
SOLHEIM CUP 1994

Hackney, Lisa
SOLHEIM CUP 1996-98

Johnson, Trish
SOLHEIM CUP 1990-92-94-96-98-2000

Morley, Joanne
SOLHEIM CUP 1996

Nicholas, Alison
SOLHEIM CUP 1990-92-94-96-98-2000

Walker, Mickey
SOLHEIM CUP (1990)-(92)-(94)-(96)

SCOTLAND

McKay, Mhairi
SOLHEIM CUP 2002

Marshall, Kathryn
SOLHEIM CUP 1996

Matthew, Catriona
SOLHEIM CUP 1998

Moodie, Janice
SOLHEIM CUP 2000

Reid, Dale
SOLHEIM CUP 1990-92-94-96-(2000)-(2002)

Wright, Pam
SOLHEIM CUP 1990-92-94

British Isles International Players, Amateur Men

Key

WC	Walker Cup
CT	Commonweath Tournament
ET	Eisenhower Trophy
ETC	played in European Team Championship for home country
HI	played in Home International matches
NNC	Nixdorf Nations Cup

Scan   Scandinavia
*   indicates winning team
'to' indicates inclusive dates: e.g. '1908 to 1911' means '1908-09-10-11'; otherwise individual years are shown.
Captaincy is indicated by the year printed in bold type; non-playing captaincy in brackets

ENGLAND

Ashby, H
Dominican Int 1973; Eur 1974; HI 1972-73-74

Attenborough, MF
WC 1967; Eur 1966-68; HI 1964-66-67-68; ETC 1967

Aylmer, CC
USA 1921; WC 1922; Sco 1911-22-23-24

Baker, P
WC 1985; Eur 1986; HI 1985

Ball, J
Sco 1902 to 12

Banks, C
HI 1983

Banks, SE
HI 1934-38

Bardsley, R
HI 1987; Fra 1988

Barker, HH
Sco 1907

Barry, AG
Sco 1906-07

Bathgate, D
HI 1990

Bayliss, RP
Irl 1929; HI 1933-34

Beck, JB
WC 1928-(38)*-(47); Sco 1926-30; HI 1933

Beddard, JB
Wal/Irl 1925; Sco 1927-28; Sco, Irl 1929

Beharrell, JC
HI 1956

Bell, RK
HI 1947

Benka, PJ
WC 1969; Eur 1970; HI 1967-68-69-70; ETC 1969

Bennett, H
HI 1948-49-51

Bennett, S
Sco 1979

Bennett, W
ET 1994; Eur 1994; HI 1992-93-94; Fra 1994

Bentley, AL
HI 1936-37; Fra 1937-39

Bentley, HG
WC 1934-36-38; Sco, Irl 1931; HI 1932 to 38; 47; Fra 1934 to 37; 39; 54

Berry, P
Eur 1972; HI 1972

Birtwell, SG
HI 1968-70-73

Blackey, M
HI 1995-96-97; ETC 1997; Fra 1994-96; Esp 1995

Bladon,W
Eur 1996; HI 1996

Blakeman, D
HI 1981; Fra 1982

Bland, R
HI 1994-95; Esp 1995

Bloxham, JA
HI 1966

Bonallack, Sir Michael F
WC 1957 to 73; [69-71*]; ET 1960 to 72; CT 1959-63-67-71; Eur 1958; 62 to 72; HI 1957 to 74; ETC 1969-71

Bottomley, S
HI 1986

Bourn, TA
Aus 1934; Irl 1928; Sco 1930; HI 1933-34; Fra 1934

Bowman, TH
HI 1932

Boxall, R
HI 1980-81-82; Fra 1982

Bradshaw, AS
HI 1932

Bradshaw, EI
Sco 1979; ETC 1979

Bramston, JAT
Sco 1902

Brand, GJ
Eur 1976; HI 1976

Bretherton, CF
Sco 1922 to 25; Wal/Irl 1925

Bristowe, OC
WC 1923-24

Broadhurst. P
Eur 1988; HI 1986-87; Fra 1988

Bromley-Davenport, E
HI 1938-51

Brough, S
Eur 1960; HI 1952-55-59-60; Fra 1952-60

Brownlow, Hon WGE
WC 1926

Burch, N
HI 1974

Burgess, MJ
HI 1963-64-67; ETC 1967

Butterworth, JR
Fra 1954

Cage, S
WC 1993; HI 1992

Caldwell, I
WC 1951-55; HI 1950 to 59; 61; Fra 1950

Cannon, JHS
Irl/Wal 1925

Carman, A
Sco 1979; HI 1980

Carr, FC
Sco 1911

Carrigill, PM
HI 1978

Carver, M
HI 1996; ETC 1997

Casey, P
WC 1999; ET 2000; Eur 2000; HI 1999

Cassells, C
HI 1989

Castle, H
Sco 1903-04

Chapman, BHG
WC 1961; Eur 1962; HI 1961-62

Chapman, R
WC 1981; Eur 1980; Sco 1979; HI 1980-81; ETC 1981

Christmas, MJ
WC 1961-63; Eur 1962-64; ET 1962; HI 1960 to 64

Clark, CA
WC 1965; Eur 1964; HI 1964

Clark, Graeme
HI 1995-2002; ETC 2001; Esp 2001; Fra 2002

Clark, GJ
WC 1965; Eur 1964-66

Clark, HK
WC 1973; HI 1973

Claydon, Russell
WC 1989; HI 1988; ETC 1989

Colt, HS
Sco 1908

Cook, J
HI 1989-90

Cook, JH
HI 1969

Corfield, Lee
HI 2002

Crawley, Leonard G
WC 1932-34-38-47; Sco, Irl 1931; HI 1932-33-34-36-37-38-47-48-49-54-55; Fra 1936-37-38-49

Critchley, Bruce
WC 1969; Eur 1970; HI 1962-69-70; ETC 1969

Curry, DH
WC 1987; ET 1986; Eur 1986-88; HI 1984-86-87; Fra 1988

Darwin, Bernard
WC 1922; Sco 1902-04-05-08-09-10-23-24

Davies, JC
WC 1973-75-77-79; ET 1974-76*; Eur 1972-74-76-78; HI 1969-71-72-73-74-78; ETC 1973-75-77

Davies, M
HI 1984-85

Davison, C
HI 1989

Dawson, P
HI 1969

De Bendern, Count J (John de Forest)
WC **1932**; Sco, Irl **1931**

Deeble, P
WC 1977-81; Eur 1978; Colombian Int 1978; HI 1975-76-77-78-80-81-83-84; Sco 1979; ETC 1979-81; Fra 1982

Dixon, D
HI 2000; RSA Esp 2001

Donald, Luke
WC 1999-2001; ET 1998*-2000; Eur 2000; HI 1996-97-98;ETC 1999-2001; Fra 1996

Dougherty, Nick
WC2001; Eur 2000; HI 2000; ETC 2001; Fra 2000; Esp, RSA 2001

Downes, P
Eur 1980; HI 1976-77-78-80-81-82; ETC 1977-79-81

Downie, JJ
HI 1974

Drummond, S
HI 1995

Duck, R
HI 1997

Dunn, NW
Irl 1928

Durrant, RA
HI 1967; ETC 1967

Dyson, S
WC 1999; HI 1998-99; ETC 1999; Esp 1999

Edwards, CS
HI 1991 to 95; 97-98; ETC 1995-99; Fra 1992-94-96-2000; Esp 1993-95-99-2001

Eggo, R
WC 1987; Eur 1988; HI 1986 to 90; Fra 1988

Ellis, HC
Sco 1902-12

Ellison, TF
Sco 1922-25-26-27

Elson, Jamie
WC2001; HI 2000-01-02; Fra 2000-02; Esp 2001

Evans, G
HI 1961

Evans, G
WC 1991; ET 1990; HI 1990; ETC 1991

Eyles, GR
WC 1975; ET 1974; Eur 1974; HI 1974-75; ETC 1975

Fairbairn, KA
HI 1988

Faldo, N
CT 1975; HI 1975

Fenton, P
HI 1996

Ferrie, K
HI 1998

Fiddian, EW
WC 1932-34; Sco, Irl 1929-30-31; HI 1932 to 35; Fra 1934

Finch, Richard
HI 2000-02; Fra 2000-02

Fisher, D
Eur 1994; HI 1993-94; Fra 1994

Fogg, HN
HI 1933

Foster, M
WC 1995; HI 1994-95; ETC 1995; Esp 1995

Foster, MF
HI 1973

Foster, R
WC 1965-67-69-71-73-**(79)-(81)**; ET 1964-70-**80**; Eur 1964-66-68-70; CT 1967-71; HI 1963-64; 66 to 72; ETC 1967-69-71-73

Fowler, WH
Sco 1903-04-05

Fox, SJ
HI 1956-57-58

Frame, DW
WC 1961; HI 1958 to 63

Francis, F
HI 1936; Fra 1935-36

Frazier, K
HI 1938

Fry, SH
Sco 1902 to 09

Garbutt, I
Eur 1992; HI 1990-91-92; ETC 1991; Fra 1992

Garner, PF
HI 1977-78-80; Sco 1979

Garnet, LG
Aus 1934; Fra 1934

Gent, J
Irl 1930; HI 1938

Gilford, David
WC 1985; ET 1984; Eur 1986; HI 1983-84-85

Gillies, HD
Sco 1908-25-26-27

Godfrey, S
HI 2001

Godwin, G
WC 1979-81; HI 1976-77-78-80-81; Sco 1979; ETC 1979-81; Fra 1982

Gray, CD
HI 1932

Green, HB
Sco 1979

Green, PO
CT 1963; HI 1961-62-63

Griffiths, D
HI 1999-2000-01; Fra 2000; RSA, Esp 2001

Hambro, AV
Sco 1905-08-09-10-22

Hamer, S
HI 1983-84

Hardman, RH
WC 1928; Sco 1927-28

Hare, A
WC 1989; HI 1988; ETC 1989

Harris, G
HI 1994; ETC 1995; Esp 1995

Harris, M
Eur 2000; HI 1998-99

Hartley, RW
WC 1930-32; Sco 1926 to 31; Irl 1928 to 31; HI 1933-34-35

Hartley, WL
WC 1932; Irl/Wal 1925; Sco 1927-31; Irl 1928-31; HI 1932-33; Fra 1935

Hassall, JE
Sco 1923; Irl/Wal 1925

Hawksworth, J
WC 1985; HI 1984-85

Hayward, CH
Sco 1925; Irl 1928

Hedges, PJ
WC 1973-75; ET 1976; Eur 1974-76; HI 1970; 73 to 78;82-83; ETC 1973-75-77

Helm, AGB
HI 1948

Henriques, GLQ
Irl 1930

Henry, W
HI 1987; Fra 1988

Hill, GA
WC 1936-(1955); HI 1936-37

Hilton, HH
Sco 1902 to 07; 09 to 12

Hilton, M
Esp 1999

Hoad, PGJ
HI 1978; Sco 1979

Hodgson, C
Sco 1924

Hodgson, J
HI 1994

Holderness, Sir EWE
USA 1921; WC 1923-26-30; Sco 1922 to 26; 28

Holmes, AW
HI 1962

Homer, TWB
WC 1973; ET 1972; Eur 1972; HI 1972-73; ETC 1973

Homewood, G
HI 1985-91; ETC 1991

Hooman, CVL
WC 1922-23; Sco 1910-22

Howell, D
WC 1995; HI 1994-95; ETC 1995; Esp 1995

Huddy, G
WC 1961; HI 1960-61-62

Humphreys, W
WC 1971; Eur 1970; HI 1970-71; ETC 1971

Hutchings, C
Sco 1902

Hutchinson, HG
Sco 1902-03-04-06-07-09

Hutt, R
HI 1991-92-93

Hyde, GE
HI 1967-68

Illingworth, G
Sco 1929; Fra 1937

Inglis, MJ
HI 1977

James, L
WC 1995; ET 1994; Eu 1994; HI 1993-94-95; ETC 1995; Fra 1994; Esp 1995

James, M
WC 1975; HI 1974-75; ETC 1975

James, RD
HI 1974-75

Jobson, RH
Irl 1928

Jones, JW
HI 1948 to 52; 54-55

Kelley, MJ
WC 1977-79; ET 1976*; Eur 1976-78; Colombian Int 1978; HI 1974 to 78; 80-81-82-(88); ETC 1977-79; Fra 1982

Kelley, PD
HI 1965-66-68

Keppler, SD
WC 1983; HI 1982-83; Fra 1982

King, M
WC 1969-73; Eur 1970-72; CT 1971; HI 1969 to 73; ETC 1971-73

Kitchin, JE
Fra 1949

Knight, J
Fra 1996

Langley, JDA
WC 1936-51-53; HI 1950 to 53; Fra 1950

Langmead, J
HI 1986

Lassen, EA
Sco 1909 to 12

Laurence, C
HI 1983-84-85

Layton, EN
Sco 1922-23-26; Irl/Wal 1925

Lee, M
HI 1950

Lee, MG
HI 1965

Lewis, ME
WC 1983; HI 1980-81-82-(99)-(2001); Fra 1982

Lincoln, AC
Sco 1907

Logan, GW
HI 1973

Lucas, D
HI 1996

Lucas, PB
WC 1936-47-(49); HI 1936-48-49; Fra 1936

Ludwell, N
HI 1991; Fra 1992

Lunt, MSR
WC 1959-61-63-65; ET 1964; Eur 1964; CT 1963; HI 1956 to 60; 62-63-64-66

Lunt, S
HI 1932 to 35; Fra 1934-35-39

Lupton, Jonathan
HI 2001-02; Fra 2002

Lyle, AWB (Sandy)
WC 1977; Eur 1976; CT 1975; HI 1975-76-77; ETC 1977

Lynn, D
HI 1995

Lyon, JS
HI 1937-38

McCarthy, S
HI 1998

McEvoy, Peter
WC 1977-79-81-85-89-(1999)*-(2001)*; ET 1978-80-84-86-88*; Eur 1978-80-86-88; HI 1976-77-78; 80-81; 83 to 89; 91; (94) to (97); Sco 1979; ETC 1977-79-81-89; Fra 1982-88-92-(02)

McEvoy, R
WC2001; HI 2000-01; ETC 2001; Fra 2000; Esp 2001

McGuire, M
HI 1992

Marks, GC
WC 1969-71-(87)-(89)*; ET 1970; Eur 1968-70; CT 1975; Colombian Int 1975; HI 1963; 67 to 71; 74-75-82; ETC 1967-69-71-75; Fra (1982)

Marsh, David M
WC 1959-71-(73)-(75); Eur 1958; HI 1956 to 60; 64-66; 68 to 72; ETC 1971

Martin, DHR
HI 1938; Fra 1934-49

Mason, B
HI 1998-99; Esp 1999

Mason, SC
HI 1973

Mellin, GL
Sco 1922

Metcalfe, J
Eur 1990; HI 1989

Micklem, Gerald H
WC 1947-49-53-55-(57)-(59); ET 1958; HI 1947 to 55

Millensted, Dudley J
WC 1967; CT 1967; HI 1966; ETC 1967

Millward, EB
WC 1949-55; HI 1950; 52 to 55

Mitchell, Abe
Sco 1910-11-12

Mitchell, CS
HI 1975-76-78

Mitchell, FH
Sco 1906-07-08

Moffat, DM
HI 1961-63-67; Fra 1959-60

Montmorency, RH de
USA 1921; Sco 1908; Wal/Irl
1925; SA 1927

Moody, PH
Eur 1972; HI 1971-72

Morgan, J
Fra 2000

Morrison, JSF
Irl 1930

Mosey, IJ
HI 1971

Muscroft, R
HI 1986

Nash, A
HI 1988-89

Neech, DG
HI 1961

Nelson, P
Fra 1996

Newey, AS
HI 1932

Oldcorn, Andrew
WC 1983; ET 1982; HI 1982-83

Oosterhuis, Peter A
WC 1967; ET 1968; Eur 1968; HI
1966-67-68

Oppenheimer, RH
WC (1951); Irl 1928-29; Irl, Sco
1930

Page, P
WC 1993; HI 1993

Palmer, DJ
HI 1962-63

Patey, IR
HI 1925; Fra 1948-49-50

Pattinson, R
HI 1949

Payne, J
HI 1950-51

Payne, J
WC 1991; Eur 1990; HI 1989-90;
ETC 1991

Pearson, AG
SA 1927

Pearson, MJ
HI 1951-52

Pease, JWB (Lord Wardington)
Sco 1903 to 06

Pennink, JJF
WC 1938; HI 1937-38-47; Fra
1937-38-39

Perkins, TP
WC 1928; Sco 1927-28-29

Perowne, AH
WC 1949-53-59; ET 1958; HI
1947 to 51; 53-54-55-57

Philipson, S
HI 1997

Phillips, V
WC 1993

Plaxton, J
HI 1983-84

Pollock, VA
Sco 1908

Powell, WA
Sco 1923-24; Wal/Irl 1925

Poxon, Martin A
WC 1975; HI 1975-76; ETC 1975

Prosser, D
ETC 1989

Pullan, M
HI 1991-92

Pyman, I
WC 1993; HI 1993

Rawlinson, D
HI 1949-50-52-53

Ray, D
HI 1982; Fra 1982

Revell, RP
HI 1972-73; ETC 1973

Reynard, M
HI 1996-97; Fra 1996

Richardson, S
HI 1986-87-88

Risdon, PWL
HI 1935-36

Roberts, GP
HI 1951-53; Fra 1949

Roberts, HJ
HI 1947-48-53

Robertson, A
HI 1986-87; Fra 1988

Robinson, J
Irl 1928

Robinson, J
WC 1987; HI 1986

Robinson, S
Sco 1925; Irl 1928-29-30

Rodgers, C
HI 1999; Esp 1999

Rogers, A
HI 1991; Fra 1992

Roper, HS
Sco, Irl 1931

Roper, R
HI 1984 to 87

Rose, Justin
WC 1997; HI 1997; ETC 1997

Rothwell, J
HI 1947-48

Rowe, Philip
WC 1999; Asia Pacific 2000; HI
1997-98-2000; ETC 1999; Esp 1999

Ryles, D
HI 2000

Sanders, M
HI 1998-99; Esp 1999

Sandywell, A
HI 1990; ETC 1991

Scotland, Zane
HI 2000-01-02; Fra 2000-02

Scott, KB
HI 1937-38; Fra 1938

Scott, Hon Michael
WC 1924-(34); Aus 1934; Sco
1911-12; 23 to 26

Scott, Hon O
Sco 1902-05-06

Scrutton, EWHB
Sco 1912

Scrutton, PF
WC 1955-57; HI 1950-55

Sewell, D
WC 1957-59; ET 1960; CT 1959;
HI 1956 to 60

Shepperson, AE
WC 1957-59; HI 1956 to 60; 62

Sherborne, A
HI 1982-83-84

Shingler, TR
HI 1977

Shorrock, TJ
Fra 1952

Side, M
HI 1999

Skinns, David
HI 2001-02; Fra 2002

Slark, WA
HI 1957

Slater, A
HI 1955-62

Smith, Eric M
Sco, Irl 1931

Smith, Everard
Sco 1908-09-10-12

Smith, GF
Sco 1902-03

Smith, JR
HI 1932

Smith, LOM
HI 1963

Smith, W
Eur 1972; HI 1972

Snowdon, J
HI 1934

Stanford, M
WC 1993; ET 1992; Eur 1992; HI
1991-92-93; Fra 1992

Steel, Donald MA
HI 1970

Stevens, LB
Sco 1912

Storey, EF
WC 1924-26-28; Sco 1924 to 28;
30; HI 1936; Fra 1936

Storm, G
WC 1999; HI 1999; ETC 1999

Stott, HAN
HI 1976-77

Stout, JA
WC 1930-32; Sco 1928 to 31; Irl 1929-31

Stowe, C
WC 1938-47; HI 1935 to 38; 47-49-54; Fra 1938-39-49

Straker, R
HI 1932

Streeter, P
HI 1992; Fra 1994-96

Stubbs, AK
HI 1982

Suneson, C
HI 1988; ETC 1989

Sutherland, DMG
HI 1947

Sutton, W
Sco 1929-31; Irl 1929-30-31

Tate, JK
HI 1954-55-56

Taylor, HE
Sco 1911

Thirlwell, A
WC 1957; Eur 1956-58-64; CT 1953-64; HI 1951-52; 54 to 58; 63-64

Thirsk, TJ
Irl 1929; HI 1933 to 38; Fra 1935 to 39

Thom, KG
WC 1949; HI 1947-48-49-53

Thomas, I
HI 1933

Thompson, ASG
HI 1935-37

Thompson, MS
WC 1983; HI 1982

Timmis, CT
Irl 1930; HI 1936-37

Tipping, EB
Irl 1930

Tipple, ER
Irl 1928-29; HI 1932

Tolley, Cyril JH
USA 1921; WC 1922-23-**24**-26-30-34; SA 1927; Sco 1922 to 30; Irl/Wal 1925; HI 1936-37-38; Fra 1938

Townsend, Peter M
WC 1965; ET 1966; Eur 1966; HI 1965-66

Tredinnick, SV
HI 1950

Tupling, LP
WC 1969; HI 1969; ETC 1969

Turner A
HI 1952

Tweddell, W
WC **1928-(36)**; Sco 1928-29-30; HI 1935

Wainwright, A
HI 1997-99

Walker, MS
Irl/Wal 1925

Walker, Richard
HI 2001-02; Fra 2002

Wallbank, K
HI 1996-97; Fra 1996

Walls, MPD
HI 1980-81-85

Walton, AR
HI 1934-35

Warren, KT
HI 1962

Watts, C
HI 1991-92; Fra 1992

Way, Paul
WC 1981; HI 1981; ETC 1981

Webster, S
HI 1995-96; ETC 1997

Weeks, K
HI 1987-88; Fra 1988

Welch, M
HI 1993-94; Fra 1994

Wells, J
HI 1999

Westwood, Lee
HI 1993

Wethered, Roger H
USA 1921; WC 1922-23-26-**30**-34; Sco 1922 to 30

White, L
WC 1991; HI 1990; ETC 1991

White, RJ
WC 1947-49-51-53-55; HI 1947-48-49-53-54

Whitehouse, Tom
HI 2000

Wiggett, M
HI 1990

Wiggins, R
Eur 1996; HI 1996; ETC 1997

Williams, DF
Sco 1979

Willison, R
WC 1991; ET 1990; Eur 1990; HI 1988-89-90; ETC 1989-91

Wilson, Oliver
HI 2002; Fra 2002

Winchester, R
HI 1985-87-89

Winter, G
HI 1991

Wise, WS
HI 1947

Wolstenholme, Guy G
WC 1957-59; ET 1958-60; CT 1959; HI 1953; 55 to 60

Wolstenholme, Gary P
WC 1995-97-99*-2001*; ET 1996-98*; Eur 1992-94; Asia Pacific 2000; HI 1988 to 2001-02;

ETC 1995-97-99-2001; Fra 1988-92-94-2000-02; Esp 1989-91-95-99-2001; RSA 2001

Woollam, J
HI 1933-34-35; Fra 1935

Woolley, FA
Sco 1910-11-12

Worthington, JS
Sco 1905

Yasin Ali
HI 2002

Yeo, J
HI 1971

Zacharias, JP
HI 1935

Zoete, HW de
Sco 1903-04-06-07

IRELAND

Allison, A
Eng 1928; Sco 1929

Anderson, N
Eur 1988; HI 1985 to 90; 93; ETC 1989

Babington, A
Wal 1913

Baker, RN
HI 1975

Bamford, JL
HI 1954-56

Beamish, CH
HI 1950-51-53-56

Bell, HE
Wal 1930; HI 1932

Bowen, J
HI 1961

Boyd, HA
Wal 1913-23

Brady, E
HI 1995-98; ETC 1999

Branigan, D
HI 1975-76-77-80-81-82-86; ETC 1977-81; WGer, Fra, Swe 1976

Briscoe, A
Eng 1928 to 31; Sco, Wal 1929-30-31; HI 1932-33-38

Brown, JC
HI 1933 to 38; 48-52-53

Browne, S
HI 2001; ETC 2001

Bruen, J
WC 1938-49-51; HI 1937-38-49-50

Burke, J
WC 1932; Eng, Wal 1929; Eng, Wal, Sco 1930-31; HI 1932 to 38; 47-48-49

Burns, M
HI 1973-75-83

Burns, R
WC 1993; ET 1992; Eur 1992; HI 1991-92

Cairnes, HM
Sco, Eng 1904; Wal 1913-25; Sco 1927

Campbell, MK
HI 1999

Carr, Joe B
WC 1947 to 63; (65)-**(67)**; ET 1958-60; Eur 1954-56-64-66-68; HI 1947 to 69; ETC 1965-67-69

Carr, JJ
HI 1981-82-83

Carr, JR
Wal 1930; Wal, Eng 1931; HI 1933

Carr, R
WC 1971; HI 1970-71; ETC 1971

Carroll, CA
Wal 1924

Carroll, JP
HI 1948-49-50-51-62

Carroll, W
Wal 1913-23-24-25; Eng 1925; Sco 1929; HI 1932

Carvill, J
Eur 1990; HI 1989; ETC 1989

Cashell, BG
HI 1978; Fra, WGer, Swe 1978

Caul, P
HI 1968-69; 1971 to 75

Clarke, D
Eur 1990; HI 1987-89

Cleary, T
HI 1976-77-78; 82 to 86; Wal 1979; Fra, WGer, Swe 1976

Corcoran, DK
HI 1972-73; ETC 1973

Corridan, T
HI 1983-84-91-92

Coughlan, R
WC 1997; HI 1991-94; ETC 1997

Crabbe, JL
Wal 1925; Sco 1927-28

Craddock, T
WC 1967-69; HI 1955 to 60; 67 to 70

Craigan, RM
HI 1963-64

Crosbie, GF
HI 1953-55-56-57-**(88)**

Crowe, Darren
HI 2002

Crowley, M
Eng 1928 to 31; Wal 1929-31; Sco 1929-30-31; HI 1932

Cullen, G
Asia Pacific 2000; HI 1999; ETC 1999

Davies, FE
Wal 1923

Dickson, JR
HI 1980; ETC 1977

Donellan, B
HI 1952

Dooley, Padraig
HI 2002

Drew, Norman V
WC 1953; HI 1952-53

Duncan, J
HI 1959-60-61

Dunne, D
HI 1997

Dunne, E
HI 1973-74-76-77-**(2001)**; Wal 1979; ETC 1975

Edwards, B
HI 1961-62; 64 to 69; 73

Edwards, M
HI 1956-57-58-60-61-62

Egan, TW
HI 1952-53-59-60-62-67-68; ETC 1967-69

Elliot, IA
HI 1975-77-78; ETC 1975; Fra, WGer, Swe 1978

Errity, D
HI 1990

Ewing, RC
WC 1936-38-47-49-51-55; HI 1934 to 38; 47 to 51; 53 to 58

Fanagan, J
WC 1995; Eur 1992-96; HI 1989 to 97; ETC 1995-97

Ferguson, M
HI 1952

Ferguson, WJ
HI 1952-54-55-58-59-61

French, WF
Sco 1929; HI 1932

Fitzgibbon, JF
HI 1955-56-57

Fitzsimmons, J
HI 1938-47-48

Flaherty, JA
HI 1934 to 37

Flaherty, PD
HI 1967; ETC 1967-69

Fleury, RA
HI 1974

Fogarty, GN
HI 1956-58-63-64-67

Foster, J
HI 1998-2000-01

Fox, Noel
Eur 2000; HI 1996 to 99; 2001-02; ETC 1997-2001

Froggatt, P
HI 1957

Gannon, MA
Eur 1974-78; HI 1973-74-77-78-80-81-83-84; 87 to 90; ETC 1979-81-89; Fra, WGer, Swe 1978-80

Gill, WJ
Wal 1931; HI 1932 to 37

Glover, J
HI 1951-52-53-55-59-60-70

Goulding, N
HI 1988 to 92; ETC 1991

Graham, JSS
HI 1938-50-51

Greene, R
HI 1933

Gribben, P
WC 1999; ET 1998*; HI 1997-98-99

Guerin, M
HI 1961-62-63

Hanway, M
HI 1971-74

Harrington, J
HI 1960-61-74-75-76; Wal 1979; ETC 1975

Harrington, Padraig
WC 1991-93-95; Eur 1992-94; HI 1990 to 95; ETC 1991-95

Hayes, JA
HI 1977

Healy, TM
Sco, Eng 1931

Heather, D
HI 1976; Fra, WGer, Swe 1976

Hegarty, J
HI 1975

Hegarty, TD
HI 1957

Henderson, J
Wal 1923

Herlihy, B
HI 1950

Heverin, AJ
HI 1978; Fra, WGer, Swe 1978

Hezlet, CO
WC 1924-26-28; SA 1927; Wal 1923-25-27-29-31; Sco 1927 to 31; Eng 1929-30-31

Higgins, D
HI 1993-94

Higgins, L
HI 1968-70-71

Hoey, M
WC2001; HI 1999-2000-01; ETC 1999-2001

Hoey, TBC
HI 1970 to 73; 77-84; ETC 1971-77

Hogan, P
HI 1985 to 88; ETC 1991

Hulme, WJ
HI 1955-56-57

Humphreys, AR
Eng 1957

Hutton, R
HI 1991

Jameson, JF
Wal 1913-24

Johnson, TWG
Eng 1929

Jones, D
HI 1998

Kane, RM
Eur 1974; HI 1967-68-71-72-74-78; Wal 1979; ETC 1971-79

Kearney, Ken
HI 1988-89-90-92-94-95-97-98-2002; ETC 1999

Keenan, S
HI 1989

Kehoe, Justin
HI 2000-01-02

Kelleher, WA
HI 1962

Kelly, NS
HI 1966

Kilduff, AJ
Sco 1928

Kissock, B
HI 1961-62-74-76; Fra, WGer, Swe 1978

Lawrie, P
HI 1996; ETC 1997

Lehane, N
HI 1976; Fra, WGer, Swe 1976

Leyden, PJ
HI 1953-55-56-57-59

Long, D
HI 1973-74; 80 to 84; Wal 1979; ETC 1979

Lowe, A
Wal 1924; Eng 1925-28; Sco 1927-28

Lyons, P
HI 1986

McCarroll, F
HI 1968-69

McCarthy, L
HI 1953 to 56

McConnell, FP
Wal, Eng 1929; Wal, Eng, Sco 1930-31; HI 1934

McConnell, RM
Wal 1924-25-29-30-31; Eng 1925; 28 to 31; Sco 1927-28-29-31; HI 1934 to 37

McConnell, WG
Eng 1925

McCormack, JD
Wal 1913-24; Eng 1928; HI 1932 to 37

McCormick, Andrew
HI 1997 to 2002

McCrea, WE
HI 1965-66-67; ETC 1965

McCready, SM
WC 1949-51; HI 1947-49-50-52-54

McDaid, B
Wal 1979

McDermott, M
HI 2000-01; ETC 2001

McDowell, G
WC 2001; HI 2000; ETC 2001

McGimpsey, G
WC 1985-89-91; ET 1984-86-88*; Eur 1986-88-90-92; HI 1978; 80 to 99; Wal 1979; ETC 1981-89-91-95-97-99

McGinley, M
HI 1996

McGinley, P
WC 1991; HI 1989-90; ETC 1991

McGinn, John
HI 2002

McHenry, J
WC 1987; HI 1985-86

McInally, RH
HI 1949-51

Mackeown, HN
HI 1973; ETC 1973

McMenamin, E
HI 1981

McMonagle, C
HI 1999-2000; ETC 1999

McMullan, C
HI 1933-34-35

MacNamara, L
HI 1977; 83 to 92; ETC 1977-91

McNeill, G
HI 1991-93-2001

McTernan, Sean
HI 2002

Madeley, JFD
WC 1963; Eur 1962; HI 1959 to 64

Mahon, RJ
HI 1938-52-54-55

Malone, B
HI 1959-64-69-71-75; ETC 1971-75

Manley, N
Wal 1924; Sco 1927-28; Eng 1928

Marren, JM
Wal 1925

Martin, GNC
WC 1928; Wal 1923-29; Sco 1928-29-30; Eng 1929-30

Meharg, W
HI 1957

Moore, GJ
Eng 1928; Wal 1929

Moriarty, Colm
HI 2001-02

Morris, JC
HI 1993 to 98; ETC 1995

Morris, MF
HI 1978-80-82-83-84; Wal 1979; ETC 1979; Fra, WGer, Swe 1980

Morrow, AJC
HI 1975-83-92-93-96-97-99-2000

Mulcare, P
WC 1975; Eur 1972; HI 1968 to 72; 74-78-80; ETC 1975-79; Fra, WGer, Swe 1978-80

Mulholland, D
HI 1988

Munn, E
Wal 1913-23-24; Sco 1927

Munn, L
Wal 1913-23-24; HI 1936-37

Murphy, G
HI 1992 to 95; ETC 1995

Murphy, M
HI 2000

Murphy, P
HI 1985-86

Murray, P
HI 1995-96

Neill, JH
HI 1938-47-48-49

Nestor, JM
HI 1962-63-64

Nevin, V
HI 1960-63-65-67-69-72; ETC 1967-69-73

Nicholson, J
HI 1932

Nolan, K
WC 1997; ET 1996; Eur 1996; HI 1992 to 96; ETC 1995-97

O'Boyle, P
ETC 1977

O'Brien, MD
HI 1968 to 72; 75-76-77; ETC 1971; Fra, WGer, Swe 1976

O'Connell, A
HI 1967-70-71

O'Connell, E
WC 1989; ET 1988*; Eur 1988; HI 1985; ETC 1989

O'Leary, JE
HI 1969-70; ETC 1969

O'Neill, JJ
HI 1968

O'Rourke, P
HI 1980-81-82-84-85

O'Sullivan, DF
HI 1976-85-86-87-91; ETC 1977

O'Sullivan, WM
HI 1934 to 38; 47 to 51; 53-54

Omelia, B
HI 1994 to 97

Ownes, GH
HI 1935-37-38-47

Patterson, AH
Wal 1913

Paul, Stuart
HI 2001-02

Pierse, AD
WC 1983; ET 1982; Eur 1980; HI 1976-77-78; 80 to 85; 87-88; Wal 1979; ETC 1981; Fra, WGer, Swe 1980

Pollin, RKM
HI 1971; ETC 1973

Power, E
HI 1987-88-93-94-95-97-98-99

Power, M
HI 1947 to 52; 54

Purcell, M
HI 1973

Rafferty, Ronan
WC 1981; ET 1980; Eur 1980;
Wal 1979; HI 1980-81; ETC 1981;
Fra, WGer, Swe 1980

Rainey, WHE
HI 1962

Rayfus, P
HI 1986-87-88

Reade, HE
Wal 1913

Reddan, B
HI 1987

Rice, JH
HI 1947-52

Rice, T
HI 2000-01; ETC 2001

Robertson, CT
Wal, Sco 1930

Scannel, BJ
HI 1947 to 51; 53-54

Sheals, HS
Wal 1929; Eng 1929-30-31; Sco
1930; HI 1932-33

Sheahan, D
WC 1963; Eur 1962-64-67; HI
1961 to 67; 70

Simcox, R
Wal, Sco 1930; Wal, Sco, Eng
1931; HI 1932 to 36; 38

Sinclair, M
HI 1999

Slattery, B
HI 1947-48

Sludds, MF
HI 1982

Smyth, D
HI 1972-73; ETC 1973

Smyth, DW
Wal 1923-30; Eng 1930; Sco 1931;
HI 1933

Smyth, V
HI 1981-82

Soulby, DEB
Sco, Wal, Eng 1929-30

Spiller, EF
Wal 1924; Eng 1928; Sco 1928-29

Spring, G
HI 1996

Staunton, R
HI 1964-65-72; ETC 1973

Stevenson, JF
Wal 1923-24; Eng 1925

Stevenson, K
HI 1972

Taggart, J
HI 1953

Timbey, JC
Sco 1928-31; Wal 1931

Waddell, G
Wal 1925

Walton, P
WC 1981-83; ET 1982; Wal 1979;
HI 1980-81; ETC 1981; Fra,
WGer, Swe 1980

Webster, F
HI 1949

Welch, L
HI 1936

Werner, LE
Wal 1925

West, CH
Eng 1928; HI 1932

Young, D
HI 1969-70-77

SCOTLAND

Aitken, AR
Eng 1906-07-08

Alexander, DW
HI 1958; Scan 1958

Anderson, RB
HI 1962-63; Scan 1960-62

Andrew, R
Eng 1905 to 10

Armour, A
Eng 1922

Armour, TD
USA 1921

Bannerman, SJ
HI 1988; Swe 1990

Barrie, GC
HI 1981-83; Swe 1983

Beames, Roger
Eur 1996; HI 1995-96-99; Esp
1996; Fra, Swe 1997

Beveridge, HW
Eng 1908

Birnie, J
Irl 1927

Black, D
HI 1966-67

Black, FC
Eur 1966; HI 1962-64-65-66-68;
ETC 1965-67; Scan 1962

Black, GT
HI 1952-53; SA 1954

Black, WC
HI 1964-65

Blackwell, EBH
Eng 1902, 1904 to 1907, 1909-10-
12, 1923-24-25

Blair, DA
WC 1955-61; CT 1954; HI 1948-
49-51-52-53-55-56-57; Scan 1956-
58-62

Bloice, C
WC 1985; HI 1985-86; ETC 1985;
Fra 1985; Ita, Swe 1986

Blyth, AD
Eng 1904

Bookless, JT
Eng, Irl 1930; Eng, Wal 1931

Braid, HM
Eng 1922-23

Brand, Gordon jr
WC 1979; ET 1978-80; Eur 1978-
80; HI 1978-80

Brock, J
Irl 1929; HI 1932

Brodie, Allan
WC 1977-79; ET 1978; Eur 1974-
76-78-80; HI 1970, 1972 to 1978,
1980; Eng 1979; ETC 1973-77;
Bel, Esp 1977; Fra 1978; Ita 1979

Brodie, Andrew
HI 1968-69; Esp 1974

Brooks, A
WC 1969; HI 1968-69; ETC 1969

Brooks, CJ
Eur 1986; HI 1984-85; Swe 1984;
Swe, Ita 1986

Brooks, M
WC 1997; ET 1996; Eur 1996; HI
1995-96; ETC 1997; Aut 1994;
Esp 1996; Fra, Swe 1997

Brotherston, IR
HI 1984-85; ETC 1985; Fra 1985

Bryson, WS
HI 1991-92-93; Swe, Ita 1992; Fra
1993; Esp 1994

Bucher, AMM
HI 1954-55-56; Scan 1956

Burnside, J
HI 1956-57

Burrell, TM
Eng 1924

Bussell, AF
WC 1957; Eur 1956-62; HI 1956-
57-58-61; Scan 1956-60

Cairns, S
HI 1997

Cameron, D
HI 1938-51

Campbell, C
HI 1999

Campbell, Sir Guy, Bt
Eng 1909-10-11

Campbell, HM
Eur 1964; HI 1962-64-68; ETC
1965-(79); Scan 1962; Aus 1964

Campbell, JGS
HI 1947-48

Campbell, W
WC 1930; Irl 1927; Irl, Eng 1928-
29-30; Irl, Eng, Wal 1931; HI 1933
to 36

Cannon, JM
HI 1969; Esp 1974

Carmichael, Steven
HI 1998-99-2001-02; Swe 1999;
Esp, Ita 2002

Carrick, DG
WC 1983-87; Eur 1986; HI 1981
to 89; ETC 1987-(89)-(91); WGer
1987; Ita 1984-86-88; Fra 1987-89;
Swe 1983-84-86

Carslaw, IA
WC 1979; Eur 1978; HI 1976-77-
78-80-81; ETC 1977-79; Eng
1979; Esp 1977; Fra 1978-83; Bel
1978; Ita 1979

Cater, JR
WC 1955; HI 1952 to 56; SA
1954; Scan 1956

Caven, J
WC 1922; Eng 1926

Chillas, D
HI 1971

Cochran, JS
HI 1966

Collier, B
HI 1994; Aut 1994

Coltart, Andrew
WC 1991; ET 1990; Eur 1990; HI
1988-89-90; ETC 1989-91; NNC
1990; Ita, Swe 1990; Fra 1991

Cosh, GB
WC 1965; ET 1966-68; Eur 1966-
68; CT 1967; HI 1964 to 69; ETC
1965-(69)

Coutts, FJ
HI 1980-81-82; ETC 1981-83; Fra
1981-82-83

Crawford, DR
HI 1990-91; ETC 1991; Fra 1991

Crawford, G
Esp 2002

Cuddihy, J
HI 1977-78

Dalgleish, CR
WC 1981; Eur 1982; HI 81-82-83-
89-(95); ETC 1981-83-(93)-(95);
Fra 1982; NNC 1989

Dawson, JE
Irl 1927-29; Irl, Eng 1930; Irl, Eng,
Wal 1931; HI 1932-33-34-37

Dawson, M
HI 1963-65-66

Deboys, A
HI 1956-59-60; Scan 1960

Deighton, Frank WG
WC 1951-57; CT 1954-59; HI
1950-52-53-56-58-59-60; SA
1954; NZ 1954; Scan 1956

Denholm, RB
Irl 1927-29; Irl, Wal, Eng 1931; HI
1932-33-34

Dewar, FG
HI 1952-53-55; SA 1954; ETC
(1971)-(73)

Dick, CE
Eng 1902-03-04-05-09-12

Dickson, HM
Irl 1929-31

Doherty, Jack
HI 2001-02; Swe 2001; Esp, Ita
2002

Dowie, Andrew
HI 1949

Downie, D
HI 1993-94; Esp, Ita 1994; Fra,
Swe 1995

Draper, JW
HI 1954

Dundas, S
HI 1992-93

Dykes, J Morton
WC 1936; HI 1934-35-36-48-49-
51

Easingwood, SR
HI 1986-87-88-90; ETC 1989; Fra
1987-89; Ita 1988-90

Elliot, A
HI 1989; ETC 1989; Fra 1989

Elliot, C
HI 1982; Fra 1983

Everett, C
HI 1988-89-90; ETC 1989-91;
NNC 1989-90; Ita 1988-90; Fra
1988-89-91; Swe 1990

Fairlie, WE
Eng 1912

Farmer, A
HI 1997; Swe 1999

Farmer, JC
HI 1970

Ferguson, S Mure
Eng 1902-03-04

Fleming, J
HI 1987

Flockhart, AS
HI 1948-49

Forbes, E
HI 1996-98-2000-01; Ita 1996-
2000; Fra 1997; Swe 1997-99; Esp
2002

Forsyth, A
HI 1996; ETC 1997; Ita 1996; Fra,
Swe 1997

Fox, G
HI 1997-98-99; ETC 1999; Swe
1999

Gairdner, JR
Eng 1902

Gallacher, Bernard J
HI 1967

Gallacher, S
WC 1995; ET 1994; HI 1992 to
95; ETC 1993-95; Ita, Esp 1994;
Fra, Swe 1995

Galloway, RF
HI 1957-58-59; Scan 1958

Garson, R
Irl 1927-28-29

Gibb, C
Eng 1927; Irl 1928

Gibson, WC
HI 1950-51

Girvan, P
WC 1987; HI 1986; ETC 1987;
WGer 1987

Gordon, Graham
HI 2000-02

Graham, AJ
Eng 1925

Graham, J
Eng 1902 to 11

Green, CT
WC 1963-69-71-73-75-(83)-(85);
ET 1970-72-(84)-(86);Eur 1962-
66-68-70-72-74-76; CT 1971; HI
1961 to 78; Eng 1979; ETC 1965
to 83; Scan 1962; Aus 1964; Bel
1973-75-77-78; Esp 1977; Ita
1979

Greig, DG
CT 1975; HI 1972-73-75

Greig, K
HI 1933

Guild, WJ
Eng 1925; Eng, Irl 1927-28

Hall, AH
HI 1962-66-69

Hamilton, ED
HI 1936-37-38

Hare, WCD
HI 1953; NZ 1954

Harris, IR
HI 1955-56-58-59

Harris, R
WC 1922-23-26; Eng 1905-08-10-
11-12; 22 to 28

Hastings, JL
HI 1957-58; Scan 1958

Hay, G
WC 1991; Eur 1980; Eng 1979; HI
1980-88-90-91-92; ETC 1991-93;
Bel 1980; Fra 1980-82-89-91-93;
Ita 1988-92-94; Swe 1992; Esp
1994

Hay, J
HI 1972

Heap, Craig
HI 1999-2001; ETC 2001

Henderson, N
HI 1963-64

Hird, K
HI 1987-88-89; NNC 1989; Ita
1990

Hislop, Craig
HI 1994-96; Aut 1994; Ita 1996

Hope, WL
WC 1923-24-28; Eng 1923; 25 to
29

Horne, A
HI 1971

Horne, S
HI 1997-98

Hosie, JR
HI 1936

Howard, D Barclay
WC 1995-97; ET 1996; Eur 1980-94-96; Eng 1979; HI 1980 to 83; 93 to 96; ETC 1981-95-97; Bel 1980; Fra 1980-81-83-95-97; Ita 1984-94; Esp 1994-96; Swe 1995-97

Huggan, J
HI 1981 to 84; ETC 1981; Fra 1982-83; Swe 1983; Ita 1984

Hume, B
HI 1999-2000-01; ETC 2001; Ita 2000; Swe 2001

Hunter, NM
1903-12

Hunter, R
HI 1966

Hunter, WI
Eng 1922

Hutcheon, I
WC 1975-77-79-81; ET 1974-76*-80; Eur 1974-76; CT 1975; Dominican Int 1973; Colombian Int 1975; HI 1971 to 78; 80; ETC 1973-75-77-79-81; Bel 1973-75-77-78-80; Esp 1977; Fra 1978-80-81; Ita 1979; Swe 1983

Hutchison, CK
Eng 1904 to 12

Inglis, David
HI 2001-02

Jack, R Reid
WC 1957-59; ET 1958; Eur 1956; CT 1959; HI 1950-51; 54 to 59; 61; NZ 1954; Scan 1956-58

Jack, WS (Billy)
HI 1955

James, D
HI 1985

Jamieson, A jr
WC 1926; Eng 1927; Eng, Irl 1928; Eng, Irl, Wal 1931; HI 1932-33-36-37

Jamieson, D
HI 1980

Jamieson, Scott
HI 2002

Jenkins, JLC
USA 1921; Eng 1908-12-22-24-26-28; Irl 1928

Johnston, JW
HI 1970-71

Kelly, L
WC 1999; ET 1998*; HI 1997-98; ETC 1999; Swe 1999

Killey, GC
Irl 1928

King, Jonathan
HI 2001-02; Swe 2001; Esp 2002

Kirkpatrick, D
HI 1992; ETC 1993; Fra 1993

Knowles, ST
HI 1990-91-92; Fra 1991

Kyle, AT
WC 1938-47-51; SA 1952; HI 1938-47; 49 to 53

Kyle, DH
WC 1924; Eng 1924-30

Kyle, EP
Eng 1925

Laidlay, JE
Eng 1902 to 11

Lang, JA
WC 1930; Irl, Eng 1929; Irl 1930; Irl, Eng, Wal 1931

Lawrie, CD
WC (1961)-(1963); ET (1960)-(1962); Eur (1960)-(1962); HI 1949-50; 55 to 58; Swe 1950; Scan 1956-58

Lee, IGF
HI 1958 to 62; Scan 1960

Lindsay, J
HI 1933 to 36

Little, E
Ita 1996

Lockhart, G
Eng 1911-12

Loftus, M
Eur 2000; HI 1999-2000; Ita 2000

Low, AJ
HI 1963-64; ETC 1965; Aus 1964

Low, JL
Eng 1904

Lowdon, CJ
Irl 1927

Lowson, AG
HI 1989-90-91-97; Swe 1990; Swe, Ita 1992

Lygate, M
HI 1970-75-(88); ETC 1971-85-87

McAllister, SD
HI 1983; ETC 1983; Swe 1983

McArthur, Andrew
HI 2002

McArthur, W
HI 1952-54; SA 1954

McBeath, J
HI 1964

McBride, D
HI 1932

McCallum, AR
WC 1928; Eng 1929

McCart, DM
HI 1977-78; Bel, Fra 1978

MacDonald, GK
HI 1978-81-82; Eng 1979; Fra 1981-82-83

McDonald, H
HI 1970

Macdonald, J Scott
WC 1971; Eur 1970; HI 1969 to 72; ETC 1971; Bel 1973

Macfarlane, CB
Eng 1912

Macgregor, A
Scan 1956

Macgregor, G
WC 1971-75-83-85-87-(91)-(93); ET 1982; Eur 1970-74-84; CT 1971-75; HI 1969 to 76; 80 to 87; (99); Eng 1979; ETC 1971-73-75-81-83-85-87; Bel 1973-75-80; Fra 1981-82-85-87; Swe 1983-84-86; Ita 1984-86

MacGregor, RC
WC 1953; HI 1951 to 54; NZ 1954

McInally, H
HI 1937-47-48

McIntosh, EA
HI 1989

Macintosh, KW
Eur 1980; Eng 1979; HI 1980; Bel, Fra 1980

McKay, G
HI 1969

McKay, JR
HI 1950-51-52-54; NZ 1954

McKechnie, P
HI 1998

McKellar, PJ
WC 1977; Eur 1978; HI 1976-77-78; Eng 1979; Bel, Fra 1978

Mackenzie, F
Eng 1902-03

Mackenzie, S
HI 1990; 93 to 2001; ETC 1999-2001; Esp 1994-96-02; Ita 1994-2000; Fra 1997; Swe 1997-99

Mackenzie, WW
WC 1922-23; Eng 1923-26-27-29; Irl 1930

McKibbin, H
HI 1994-95; ETC 1995; Fra, Swe 1995; Esp 1996

Mackie, GW
HI 1948-50

McKinlay, SL
WC 1934; Eng 1929-30-31; Irl 1930; Wal 1931; HI 1932-33-35-37- 47

McKinna, RA
HI 1938

McKinnon, A
HI 1947-52

McLean, J
WC 1934-36; Aus 1934; HI 1932 to 36

McLeary, Jamie
HI 2002

McLeod, AE
HI 1937-38

McLeod, WS
HI 1935-37-38; 47 to 51; Swe 1950

McNair, AA
Irl 1929

MacRae, Neil
Ita 2002

McRuvie, Eric A
WC 1932-34; Eng 1929; Eng, Irl 1930; Eng, Irl, Wal 1931; HI 1932 to 36

McTear, J
HI 1971

Manford, GC
Eng 1922-23

Mann, LS
WC 1983; HI 1982-83; ETC 1983; Swe 1983

Marchbank, Brian
WC 1979; ET 1978; Eur 1976-78; HI 1978; ETC 1979; Ita 1979

Martin, S
WC 1977; ET 1976; Eur 1976; HI 1975-76-77; ETC 1977; Bel, Esp 1977

Maxwell, R
Eng 1902 to 07; 09-10

Melville, LM Balfour
Eng 1902-03

Melville, TE
HI 1974

Menzies, A
Eng 1925

Mill, JW
HI 1953-54

Miller, AC
HI 1954-55

Miller, MJ
HI 1974-75-77-78; Bel, Fra 1978

Milligan, JW
WC 1989-91; ET 1988*-90; Eur 1988-92; HI 1986 to 92; ETC 1987-89-91; NNC 1989; Swe 1986-90-92; WGer 1987; Fra 1987-89-91; Ita 1988-90-92

Milne, WTG
WC 1973; HI 1972-73; ETC 1973; Bel 1973

Moir, A
Eur 1984; HI 1983-84; ETC 1985; Swe, Ita 1984; Fra 1985

Montgomerie, Colin S
WC 1985-87; ET 1984-86; Eur 1986; HI 1984-85-86; ETC 1985-87; Ita 1984; Swe 1984-86; Fra 1985; WGer 1987

Montgomerie, JS
HI 1957; ETC 1965; Scan 1958

Morris, FS
HI 1963

Morrison, JH
Scan 1960

Munro, RAG
HI 1960

Murdoch, D
HI 1964

Murphy, AR
HI 1961-67

Murray, GH
WC 1977; Eur 1978; HI 1973 to 78; 83; ETC 1975-77; Esp 1974-77; Bel 1975-77

Murray, SWT
WC 1963; Eur 1958-62; HI 1959 to 63; Scan 1960

Murray, WA
WC 1923-24; Eng 1923 to 27

Murray, WB
HI 1967-68-69; ETC 1969

Neill, R
HI 1936

Noon, J
HI 1987

O'Hara, Steven
WC 2001; ET 2000; Eur 2000; HI 1999-2000; ETC 2001; Ita 2000; Swe 2001

Osgood, TH
Eng 1925

Paton, DA
HI 1991

Patrick, D
WC 1999; Asia Pacific 2000; HI 1997-98-99; ETC 1999; Swe 1999

Patrick, KG
HI 1937

Peters, GB
WC 1936-38; HI 1934 to 38

Pirie, AK
WC 1967; Eur 1970; HI 1966 to 75; ETC 1967-69; Bel 1973-75; Esp 1974

Pressley, J
HI 1947-48-49

Raeside, A
Irl 1929

Ramsay, Eric
HI 2002; Ita 2002

Rankin, G
WC 1995-97-99; HI 1994-95-97-98; ETC 1995-97-99; Swe 1995-97-99; Fra 1995-97; Esp 1996

Reid, A
HI 1993-94-95; ETC 1993-95; Esp, Ita 1994; Fra 1995

Renfrew, RL
HI 1964

Robb, J jr
Eng 1902-03-05-06-07

Robb, WM
HI 1935

Roberts, AT
Irl 1931

Roberts, GW
HI 1937-38

Robertson, Dean
WC 1993; ET 1992; Eur 1992; HI 1991-92-93; ETC 1993; Swe, Ita 1992; Fra 1993

Robertson, DM
HI 1973-74; Esp 1974

Robertson-Durham, JA
Eng 1911

Russell, R
WC 1993; HI 1992-93; ETC 1993; Fra 1993

Rutherford, DS
Irl 1929

Rutherford, R
HI 1938-47

Saddler, AC
WC 1963-65-67-(77); ET 1962-(76)*; Eur 1960-62-64-66; CT 1959-63-67; HI 1959 to 64; 66; ETC 1965-67-(75)-(77); Scan 1962

Scott, R jr
WC 1924; Eng 1924-28

Scott, WGF
Irl 1927

Scroggie, FH
Eng 1910

Shade, Ronnie DBM
WC 1961-63-65-67; ET 1962-64-66-68; Eur 1960-62-64-66; CT 1963-67; Aus 1964; HI 1957; 60 to 68; ETC 1965-67; Scan 1960-62

Shaw, G
WC 1987; HI 1984-86-87-88-90; ETC 1987; Swe 1984; Fra, WGer 1987

Sherry, Gordon
WC 1995; ET 1994; Eur 1994; HI 1993-94-95; ETC 1995; Fra 1993-95; Esp 1994; Swe 1995

Shields, B
HI 1986

Simpson, AF
Eng 1927; Irl 1928

Simpson, JG
USA 1921; Eng 1907-08-09-11-12-22-24-26

Sinclair, A
HI 1950; ETC (1967)

Smith, JN
WC 1930; Irl 1928; Irl, Eng 1930; Irl, Eng, Wal 1931; HI 1932-33-34

Smith, S
Aut 1994

Smith, WD
WC 1959; Eur 1958; HI 1957 to 60; 63; Scan 1958-60

Stephen, AR (Sandy)
WC 1985; Eur 1972; HI 1971 to 77; 84-85; ETC 1975-85; Esp 1974; Bel 1975-77-78; Fra 1985

Stevenson, A
HI 1949

Stevenson, JB
Irl 1931; HI 1932-38-47-49-50-51

Strachan, CJL
HI 1965-66-67; ETC 1967

Stuart, HB
WC 1971-73-75; ET 1972; Eur 1968-72-74; CT 1971; HI 1967 to 74; 76; ETC 1969-71-73-75; Bel 1973-75

Stuart, JE
HI 1959

Tait, AG
HI 1987-88-89; NNC 1989

Taylor, GN
HI 1948

Taylor, JS
Eng 1979; HI 1980; Bel, Fra 1980

Taylor, LG
HI 1955-56

Thomson, AP
HI 1970; ETC 1971

Thomson, G
HI 1996

Thomson, Hector
WC 1936-38; HI 1934 to 38

Thomson, JA
HI 1981 to 89; 91-92; ETC 1983; WGer 1987; Ita 1984-86-88-90; Swe 1990

Thomson, Mike
HI 1998

Thorburn, K
Irl 1927; Eng 1928

Torrance, TA
WC 1924-28-30-**32**-34; Eng 1922-23-25-26-28-29-30; HI 1933

Torrance, WB
WC 1922; Eng 1922-23-24-26-27-28-30; Irl 1928-29-30

Tulloch, W
Eng 1927-29; Eng, Irl 1930; Eng, Irl, Wal 1931; HI 1932

Turnbull, A
HI 1995-96-97; Fra 1995; Esp 1996

Twynholm, S
HI 1990; NNC 1990

Urquhart, M
HI 1993; Ita 1996

Vannet, Lee
HI 1984

Walker, J
WC 1961; Eur 1958-60; HI 1954-55-57-58; 60 to 63; Scan 1958-62

Walker, KH
HI 1985-86

Walker, RS
HI 1935-36

Warren, Marc
WC 2001; HI 2000-01; ETC 2001; Ita 2000; Swe 2001

Watson, Craig R
WC 1997; HI 1991-92; 94 to 2000; **2001**; ETC 1997-99-2001; Swe 1992-97-2001; Ita 1992; Aut 1994; Esp 1996-2002; Fra 1997

Watt, AW
HI 1987

Webster, AJ
HI 1978

Wemyss, DS
HI 1937

Whyte, AW
HI 1934

Wight, R
Swe 1950

Wilkie, DF
HI 1962-63-65-67-68

Wilkie, G
Eng 1911

Williamson, SB
HI 1947-48-49-51-52

Wilson, E
HI 1985

Wilson, J
WC 1923; Eng 1922-23-24-26; Irl 1932

Wilson, JC
WC 1947-53; CT 1954; SA 1954; HI 1947-48-49-51-52-53; Swe 1950; NZ 1954

Wilson, P
HI 1976; Bel 1977

Wilson, Stuart
HI 2000-02; Esp, Ita 2002

Wright, I
HI 1958 to 61; Scan 1960-62

Young, ID
Eur 1982; HI 1981-82; Fra 1982

Young, JR
Eur 1960; HI 1960-61-65; Scan 1960

Young, S
WC 1997; HI 1996; ETC 1997; Ita 1996

WALES

Adams, MPD
HI 1969 to 72; 75-76-77

Atkinson, HN
Irl 1913

Barnett, A
HI 1989-90-91; ETC 1991

Bayne, PWGA
HI 1949

Bevan, RJ
HI 1964-65-66-67-73-74

Black, JL
HI 1932 to 1936

Bonnell, DJ
HI 1949-50-51

Broad, RD
Irl 1979; HI 1980-81-82-84; ETC 1981

Brookman, R
HI 1999-2000

Brown, CT
WC (1995)*-(97); Eur [1996]; HI 1970 to 75; 77-78-80-[88]; ETC 1973; Den 1977; Irl 1979; Den, Esp, Sui 1980

Brown, D
Irl 1923-30-31; Eng 1925; Sco 1931

Buckley, JA
WC 1979; HI 1967-68-69-76-77-78; ETC 1967-69; Den 1976-77

Calvert, M
HI 1983-84-86-87-89-91

Campbell, A
HI 1996-97-2000-01

Campbell, I
HI 1998-99-2001; ETC 1999-2001

Carr, JP
Irl 1913

Chapman, JA
Irl 1923-29-30-31; Eng 1925; Sco 1931

Chapman, R
Irl 1929; HI 1932-34-35-36

Charles, WB
Irl 1924

Clark, MD
Irl 1947

Clay, G
HI 1962

Clement, G
Irl 1979

Coulter, JG
HI 1951-52

Cox, S
HI 1970 to 74; ETC 1971-73

Davies, EN
HI 1959 to 74; ETC 1969-71-73

Davies, G
HI 1981-82-83; Den 1977

Davies, HE
HI 1933-34-36

Davies, Rhys
HI 2002

Davies, TJ
HI 1954 to 60

Dinsdale, R
HI 1991-92-93

Disley, A
HI 1976-77-78-**(99)**; Irl 1979; Den 1977

Dodd, SC
WC 1989; HI 1985-87-88-89

Donaldson, J
ET 2000; Eur 2000; HI 1996 to 2000; ETC 1997-99

Dredge, Bradley
WC 1993; ET 1992; Eur 1994; HI 1992 to 95; ETC 1995

Duffy, I
HI 1975

Duncan, AA
WC (1953); HI 1933-34-36-38; 47 to 59

Duncan, GT
HI 1952 to 58

Duncan, J jr
Irl 1913

Dykes, Tim
HI 2001-02

Eaves, CH
HI 1935-36-38-47-48-49

Edwards, Nigel
WC 2001; HI 1995 to 2002; ETC 1997-99-2001

Edwards, S
HI 1992

Edwards, TH
HI 1947

Ellis, M
Eur 1996; HI 1992 to 96

Emerson, T
HI 1932

Emery, G
Irl 1925; HI 1933-36-38

Evans, AD
Sco, Irl 1931; Sco 1935; HI 1932 to 35; 38; 47 to 56; 61

Evans, C
1990 to 95; ETC 1995

Evans, Duncan
WC 1981; Eur 1980; HI 1978-80-81; Irl 1979; ETC 1981

Evans, HJ
HI 1976-77-78-80-81-84-85-87-88; Irl 1979; ETC 1979-81; Fra 1976; Den 1977-80; Esp, Sui 1980

Evans, M Gear
Irl 1930; Sco, Irl 1931

Fairchild, CEL
Irl 1923; Eng 1925

Fairchild, IJ
Irl 1924

Gilford, CF
HI 1963 to 67

Glossop, R
HI 1935-37-38-47

Griffiths, HGB
Irl 1923-24-25

Griffiths, HS
Eng 1958

Griffiths, JA
HI 1933

Griffiths, M
HI 1999-2000-01; ETC 2001

Hales, JP
Sco 1963

Hall, A
HI 1994

Hall, D
HI 1932-37

Hall, K
HI 1955-59

Hamilton, CJ
Irl 1913

Harpin, Lee
HI 1996; 1998 to 2002; ETC 1999-2001

Harrhy, A
HI 1988-89-95

Harris, D
HI 1997

Harrison, JW
HI 1937-50

Herne, KTC
Irl 1913

Houston, G
HI 1990 to 95; ETC 1991-95

Howell, HR
Irl 1923-24-25-29-30-31; Eng 1925; Sco 1931; HI 1932; 34 to 38; 47

Howell H Logan
Irl 1925

Hughes, I
HI 1954-55-56

Humphrey, JG
Irl 1925

Humphreys, DI
HI 1972

Isitt, GH
Irl 1923

Jacob, NE
HI 1932 to 36

Jermine, JG
HI 1972 to 76; 82; 2000; ETC 1975-77; Fra 1975

Johnson, R
Eur 1994; HI 1990-92-93-94; ETC 1991

Jones, A
HI 1989-90; ETC 1991

Jones, DK
HI 1973

Jones, EO
HI 1983-85-86

Jones, JG Parry
HI 1959-60

Jones, JL
HI 1933-34-36

Jones, JR
HI 1970-72-73-77-78; 80 to 85; Irl 1979; ETC 1973-79-81; Den 1976; Den, Sui, Esp 1980

Jones, KG
HI 1988

Jones, MA
HI 1947 to 51; 53-54-57

Jones, Malcolm F
HI 1933

Jones, SP
HI 1981 to 86; 88-89-91-93

Knight, B
HI 1986

Knipe, RG
HI 1953 to 56

Knowles, WR
Eng 1948

Lake, AD
HI 1958

Last, CN
HI 1975

Lee, JN
HI 1988-89; ETC 1991

Lewis, DH
HI 1935 to 38

Lewis, DR
Irl 1925-29-30-31; Sco 1931; HI 1932-34

Lewis, R Cofe
Irl 1925

Lloyd, HM
Irl 1913

Lloyd, RM de
Sco, Irl 1931; HI 1932 to 38; 47-48

Llyr, A
HI 1984-85

Lockley, AE
HI1956-57-58-62

Macara, MA
HI 1983-84-85; 87; 89 to 93

McLean, D
HI 1968 to 78; 80 to 83; 85-86-88-90; Irl 1979; ETC 1975-77-79-81; Fra 1975; Fra, Den 1976; Den, Sui, Esp 1980

Maliphant, FR
HI 1932

Manley, Stuart
HI 2001-02

Marsden, G
HI 1994

Marshman, A
HI 1952

Marston, CC
Irl 1929-30; Irl, Sco 1931

Mathias-Thomas, FEL
Irl 1924-25

Matthews, N
HI 1999; ETC 1999

Matthews, RL
HI 1935-37

Mayo, PM
WC 1985-87; HI 1982-88

Melia, TJ
HI 1976-77-78-80-81-82; Irl 1979; ETC 1977-79; Den 1976; Den, Sui, Esp 1980

Mills, ES
HI 1957

Mitchell, JWH
HI 1964-65-66-67

Moody, JV
HI 1947-48-49-51-56; 58 to 61

Morgan, JL
WC 1951-53-55; HI 1948 to 62;
64-68

Morris, R
HI 1983-86-87

Morris, TS
Irl 1924-29-30

Morrow, JM
Irl 1979; HI 1980-81; ETC 1979-81; Den, Sui, Esp 1980

Moss, AV
HI 1965-66-68

Mouland, MG
HI 1978-81; Irl 1979; ETC 1979

Moxon, GA
Irl 1929-30

Newman, JE
HI 1932

Newton, H
Irl 1929

Noon, GS
HI 1935-36-37

Oakley, Neil
HI 2002

O'Carroll, C
HI 1989 to 93; ETC 1991

Owen, JB
HI 1971

Owens, GF
HI 1960-61

Palferman, H
HI 1950-53

Palmer, M
HI 1998

Pardoe, S
HI 1991

Parfitt, RWM
Irl 1924

Park, D
WC 1997; HI 1994 to 97; ETC 1995-97

Parkin, AP
WC 1983; HI 1980-81-82

Parry, JR
HI 1966-75-76-77; Fra 1976

Peet, M
HI 1995-96

Peters, JL
HI 1987-88-89

Phillips, LA
Irl 1913

Pilkington, M
HI 1997-98; ETC 1997

Pinch, AG
HI 1969

Povall, J
Eur 1962; HI 1960 to 63; 65 to 77; ETC 1967-69-71-73-75-77; Fra 1975; Fra, Den 1976

Pressdee, RNG
HI 1958 to 62

Price, David
HI 1999-2000-01-02

Price, JP
HI 1986-87-88

Price, Rhodri
HI 1994-96-97

Pugh, RS
Irl 1923-24-29

Pughe, O
HI 1997-98

Rees, CN
HI 1986-88-89-91-92; 94 to 97

Rees, DA
HI 1961 to 64

Renwick, G jr
Irl 1923

Ricardo, W
Irl 1930; Irl, Sco 1931

Rice-Jones, L
Irl 1924

Richards, PM
HI 1960 to 63; 71

Roberts, H
HI 1992-93

Roberts, J
HI 1937

Roberts, S
HI 1998-99

Roberts, SB
HI 1932 to 35; 37-38; 47 to 54

Roberts, WJ
HI 1948 to 54

Roderick, RN
WC 1989; Eur 1988; HI 1983 to 88

Rolfe, B
HI 1963-65

Roobottom, EL
HI 1967

Roper, MS
Irl 1979

Sheppard, M
HI 1990

Smith, Alex
HI 1998-2000-02

Smith, Craig
HI 2002

Smith, M
HI 1993 to 97; ETC 1995-97

Smith, VH
Irl 1924-25

Squirrel, HC
HI 1955 to 71; 73-74-75; ETC 1967-69-71-75; Fra 1975

Stevens, DI
HI 1968-69-70; 74 to 78; 80-82; ETC 1969-77; Fra 1976; Den 1977

Stoker, K
Irl 1923-24

Stokoe, GC
Eng 1925; Irl 1929-30

Sullivan, Kyron
HI 1998 to 2001; ETC 2001

Symonds, A
Irl 1925

Taylor, TPD
HI 1963

Taylor, Y
HI 1995-96-97; ETC 1995-97

Thomas, KR
HI 1951-52

Tooth, EA
Irl 1913

Toye, JL
HI 1963 to 67; 69 to 74; 76-78; ETC 1971-73-75-77; Fra 1975

Tucker, WI
HI 1949 to 72; 74-75; ETC 1967-69-75; Fra 1975

Turnbull, CH
Irl 1913-25

Turner, GB
HI 1947 to 52; 55-56

Wallis, G
HI 1934-36-37-38

Walters, EM
HI 1967-68-69; ETC 1969

Wilkie, GT
HI 1938

Wilkinson, S
HI 1990-91

Willcox, FS
Sco, Irl 1931

Williams, Craig
Asia Pacific 2000; HI 1998 to 2001; ETC 1999-2001

Williams, James
HI 2001-02

Williams, KH
HI 1983 to 87

Williams, PG
Irl 1925

Wills, M
HI 1990

Winfield, HB
Irl 1913

Wood, DK
HI 1982 to 87

Woosnam, Ian
Fra 1976

Wright, Garwth
HI 2002

British Isles International Players, Amateur Women

Key

Entries for the Curtis Cup, Commonwealth Tournament, World Amateur Team Championship and Vagliano Trophy, indicate that the player is representing Great Britain and Ireland. Other entries are for the home country.

CC	Curtis Cup
CT	Commonwealth Tournament
ES	World Amateur Team Championship (Espirito Santo)
VT	Vagliano Trophy
ELTC	played in European Ladies Team Championship for home country
HI	played in Home International matches
*	indicates winning team

'to' indicates inclusive dates: e.g. '1908 to 1911' means '1908-09-10-11'; otherwise individual years are shown.

Captaincy is indicated by the year printed in bold type; non-playing captaincy in brackets

[1998] indicates Espirito Santo Team selection which was subsequently advised not to travel to Chile

Maiden names are shown in brackets; other surnames and titles in square brackets

ENGLAND

Allen, F
HI 1952

Andrew, Kim (Rostron)
CC 1998-2000; HI 1996-97-99-2001; ELTC 1997-2001; (GBI) VT 1997-99-2001; ES [1998]; CT 1999

Archer, A (Rampton)
HI (1968)

Bailey [Frearson](Robb)
CC 1962-72-(84)-(86)*-(88)*; VT 1961-(83)-(85); CT 1983; HI 1961-62-71; ELTC 1968-(93)

Barber (Bonallack)
CC 1962; ES (1996); VT 1961-63-69; CT (1995); HI 1960-61-62-68-70-72-77-(78); ELTC 1969-71

Bargh Etherington, B (Whitehead)
HI 1974

Barry, L
HI 1911 to 14

Barry, P
HI 1982

Barton, Pam
CC 1934-36; HI 1935 to 39

Bastin, G
HI 1920 to 25

Bayman, Linda (Denison Pender)
CC 1988; ES 1988; VT 1971-85-87; HI 1971-72-73-83-84-85-87-88-(95)-(96); ELTC 1985-87-89-(97)-(2001)

Beharrell, Veronica (Anstey)
CC 1956; HI 1955-56-57-(61)

Benka, Pam (Tredinnick)
CC 1966-68-(2002); VT 1967; HI 1967

Biggs, A (Whittaker)
VT 1959

Bisgood, Jeanne
CC 1950-52-54-(70); HI 1949 to 54; 56-58

Blaymire, J
HI 1971-88-(89)

Boatman, Elizabeth A (Collis)
CC (1992)*-(94); CT (1987)-(91); HI 1974-80-(84)-(85)-(90)-(91); ELTC (1985)-(87)

Bolas, R
HI 1992

Bolton, Zara (Bonner Davis)
CC 1948-(56)-(66)-(68); CT 1967; HI 1939; 48 to 51; (55)-(56)

Bonallack, Angela (Ward) [Lady Bonallack]
CC 1956-58-60-62-64-66; VT 1959-61-63; HI 1956 to 66; 72

Bostock, M
HI (1954)

Bourn, Mrs
HI 1909-12

Brown, Fiona
CC 1998-2000; VT 1999-2001; CT 1999; HI 1994; 96 to 2001; ELTC 1997-99-2001

Brown, J
HI 1984

Burnell, S
HI 1993; ELTC 1993

Burton, M
ELTC 1997

Cairns, Lady Katherine
CC (1952)*; HI 1947-48; 50 to 54

Caldwell, Carole (Redford)
CC 1978-80; VT 1973; HI 1973-78-79-80

Cann, M (Nuttall)
HI 1966

Carrick, P (Bullard)
HI 1939-47

Cautley, B (Hawtrey)
HI 1912-13-14; 22 to 25; 27

Chambers, Doris
(1934)-(36)-(38); 1906-07; 09 to 12; 20-24-25

Christison, D
HI 1981

Clark, G (Atkinson)
HI 1955

Clarke, Mrs ML
HI 1933-35

Clarke, Nickie
HI (2002)

Clarke, P
HI 1981

Clement, V
HI 1932-34-35

Close, M (Wenyon)
VT 1969; HI 1968-69; ELTC 1969

Collett, P
HI 1910

Collingham, J (Melville)
VT 1979-87; CT 1987; HI 1978-79-81-84-86-87-92; ELTC 1989

Comboy, Carol (Grott)
CC **(1978)-(80)**; ES **(1978)**; VT (1977)-(79); CT **(1979)**; HI **(1975)-(76)**

Corlett, Elsie
CC 1932-38-(64); HI 1927; 29 to 33; 35 to 39

Cotton, S (German)
VT 1967; HI 1967-68; ELTC 1967

Court, C
HI 2000

Critchley, Diana (Fishwick)
CC 1932-34-(50); HI 1930 to 33; 35-36-(47)

Croft, A
HI 1927

Crummack, Miss
HI 1909

Davies, Laura
CC 1984; HI 1983-84

Dobson, Helen
CC 1990; VT 1989; HI 1987-88-89; ELTC 1989

Dod, L
HI 1905

Douglas, K
CC 1982; VT 1983; HI 1981-82-83

Dowling, D
HI 1979

Duggleby, Emma
CC 2000-02; VT 1995-2001; HI 1994-95-96-99-2000-01-02; ELTC 1995-99-2001

Durrant, B [Green] (Lowe)
HI 1954

Edmond, F (Macdonald)
VT 1991; HI 1991; ELTC 1991

Educate, Lisa (Walton)
CC 1994-96; VT 1993-95; CT 1995; HI 1991-94-95; ELTC 1993-95

Egford, K
HI 1992-94

Evans, H
HI 1908

Everard, Mary
CC 1970-72-74-78; ES 1968-72-78; VT 1967-69-71-73; CT 1971; HI 1964-67-69-70-72-73-77-78; ELTC 1967-71-77

Fairclough, L
VT 1989; HI 1988-89-90; ELTC 1989

Ferguson, R (Ogden)
HI 1957

Fields, E
HI 1995-96

Fisher, Kirsty
VT 2001; HI 1998 to 2002; ELTC 1999-2001

Fletcher, Linzi
CC 1990; CT 1991; HI 1989-90; ELTC 1991

Foster, C
HI 1905-06-09

Fowler, J
HI 1928

Furby, J
HI 1987-88; ELTC 1987

Fyshe, M
HI 1938

Garbutt, Sara
HI 2002

Garon, Marjorie Ross
CC 1936; HI 1927-28-32-33-34-36-37-38

Garrett, Maureen (Ruttle)
CC 1948-(60); VT 1959; HI 1947-48-50-53-(59)-(60)-(63)

Gee, Hon. J (Hives)
HI 1950-51-52

Gibb, M (Titterton)
HI 1906-07-08-10-12

Gibbs, Carol (Le Feuvre)
CC 1974; VT 1973; HI 1971 to 74

Gold, N
HI 1929-31-32

Gordon, Jacqueline
CC 1948; HI 1947-48-49-52-53

Gourlay, Molly
CC 1932-34; HI 1923-24; 27 to 30; 32-33-34-38-(57)

Green, B (Pockett)
HI 1939

Grice-Whitaker, Penny (Grice)
CC 1984; ES 1984; HI 1983-84

Griffiths, M
HI 1920-21

Guadella, E (Leitch)
HI 1908-10-20-21-22; 27 to 30; 33

Hackney, L
HI 1990

Hall, Caroline
CC 1992; VT 1991; HI 1991-92; ELTC 1991

Hall, CM
HI 1985

Hambro, W (Martin Smith)
HI 1914

Hamilton, J
HI 1937-38-39

Hammond, T
HI 1985

Hampson, M
HI 1954

Harris, Marley [Spearman] (Baker)
CC 1960-62-64; ES 1964; VT 1959-61-65; HI 1955 to 65; ELTC 1965-71

Harrold, L
HI 1974-75-76

Hartill, D
HI 1923

Hartley, E
HI **(1964)**

Hayter, J (Yuille)
HI 1956

Heath, Sarah (Gleeson)
HI 2001-02; ELTC 2001

Heathcoat-Amory, Lady (Joyce Wethered)
CC **1932**; HI 1921 to 25; 29

Hedges, S (Whitlock)
VT 1979; CT 1979; HI 1979

Helme, E
HI 1911-12-13-20

Heming Johnson, G
HI 1909-11-13

Henson, Dinah (Oxley)
CC 1968-70-72-76; ES 1970; VT 1967-69-71; CT 1967-71; HI 1967 to 70; 75 to 78; ELTC 1971-77

Hetherington, Mrs (Gittens)
HI 1909

Hill, J
HI 1986

Hockley, J
ES 1992; VT 1993; HI 1991-92-93-96

Hodge, Susan (Shapcott)
CC 1988; ES 1988; VT 1987; CT 1987; HI 1986-88; ELTC 1987

Hodgson, M
HI 1939

Holmes, A
HI 1931

Holmes [Hetherington] (McClure)
HI 1956-66-(67)

Hooman, EM (Gavin)
HI 1910-11

Howard, Ann (Phillips)
CC 1956-58; HI 1953 to 58; **(79)-(80)**

Hudson, Rebecca
CC 1998-2000-02; ES [1998]-2000; VT 1997-2001; CT 1999; HI 1996-2001-02; ELTC 1997-99-2001

Huke, Beverley
CC 1972; VT 1975; HI 1971-72-75-76-77

Hunter, D (Tucker)
HI 1905

Irvin, Ann
CC 1962-68-70-76; ES **(1982)**; VT 1961 to 75; CT 1967-75; HI 1962-63-65; 67 to 73; 75; ELTC 1965-67-69-71

Jackson, Bridget
CC 1958-64-68; ES 1964; VT 1959-63-65-67-**(73)**-**(75)**; CT 1959-67; HI 1955 to 59; 63 to 66; **(73)**-**(74)**

Johns, A
HI 1987-88-89

Johnson, M
HI 1934-35

Johnson, Patricia M
CC 1986; ES 1986; VT 1985; HI 1984-85-86; ELTC 1985

Kaye, H (Williamson)
HI **(1986)**-**(87)**

Keighley, Alex
HI 2002

Keiller, G (Style)
HI 1948-49-52

Kennedy, D (Fowler)
HI 1923-24-25-27-28-29

Kennion, Mrs (Kenyon Stow)
HI 1910

Kyle, B [Rhodes] (Norris)
HI 1937-38-39-48-49

Lamb, J
HI 1998-99

Lambert, S (Cohen)
VT 1979-95; HI 1979-80-93-94-95; ELTC 1995

Langridge, Susan (Armitage)
CC 1964-66; VT 1963-65; HI 1963 to 66; ELTC 1965

Large, P (Davies)
HI 1951-52-**(81)**-**(82)**

Latham Hall, E (Chubb)
HI 1928

Lee Smith, Jenny
CC 1974-76; ES 1976; CT 1975; HI 1973 to 76

Leitch, C
HI 1910 to 14; 20-21-22-24-25-27-28

Lipscombe, Clare
HI 1999

Lobbett, P
HI 1922-24-27-29-30

Luckin, B (Cooper)
HI 1980

Lumb, Kathryn (Phillips)
CC 1972; VT 1969-71; HI 1968 to 71; ELTC 1969

Lyons, T (Ross Steen)
VT 1959; HI 1959

Macbeth, M (Dodd)
HI 1913-14; 20 to 25

Macdonald, F
HI 1990

McIntosh, B (Dixon)
VT 1969; HI 1969-70; ELTC 1969

McIntyre, J
HI 1949-54

McNair, W
HI 1921

Maher, Sheila (Vaughan)
CC 1962-64; VT 1961; CT 1963; HI 1960 to 64

Marvin, Vanessa
CC 1978; VT 1977; HI 1977-78; ELTC 1977

Merrill, Julia (Greenhalgh)
CC 1964-70-74-76-78; ES 1970-**74**-78; VT 1961-65-75-77; CT 1963; HI 1960-61-63-66-69-70-71; 75 to 78; ELTC 1971-77

Moorcroft, S
HI 1985-86; ELTC 1985-87

Morant, E
HI 1906-10

More, Fame
CC 2002; VT 2001; HI 2000-01-02; ELTC 2001

Morgan, S
HI 1989; ELTC 1989

Morgan, Wanda
CC 1932-34-36; HI 1931 to 37

Morley, Joanne
CC 1992; ES 1992; VT 1991-93; HI 1990 to 93; ELTC 1991-93

Morris, L (Moore)
HI 1912-13

Morrison, G (Cheetham)
VT 1965; HI 1965-**(69)**

Morrison, G (Cradock-Hartopp)
HI 1936

Murray, Nicola (Buxton)
CC 1992; VT 1991-93; HI 1991-92-93; ELTC 1991-93

Murray, S (Jolly)
HI 1976

Nes, K (Garnham)
HI 1931-32-33; 36 to 39

Neville, E
HI 1905-06-08-10

New, Beverley
CC 1984; VT 1983; HI 1980 to 83

Newell, B
HI 1936

Newton, B (Brown)
HI 1930; 33 to 37

Oliver, J
HI 1995

Parker, S
HI 1973

Pearson, D
HI 1928 to 32; 34

Phillips, ME
HI 1905

Pickard, Margaret (Nichol)
CC 1968-70; VT 1959-61-67; HI 1958 to 61; 67-69; **(83)**

Pook, Elizabeth (Chadwick)
CC 1966; VT 1963-67; CT 1967; HI 1963-65-66-67

Porter, M (Lazenby)
HI 1931-32

Price, M (Greaves)
HI **(1956)**

Price Fisher, Elizabeth (Price)
CC 1950-52-54-56-58-60; VT 1959; CT 1959; HI 1948; 51 to 60

Prout, Rebecca
HI 2000

Rabbidge, R
HI 1931

Ratcliffe, Elaine
CC 1998; ES 1996; VT 1997; HI 1995-96-97; ELTC 1995-97

Read, P
HI 1922

Reece, P (Millington)
HI 1966

Remer, H
HI 1909

Richardson, Mrs
HI 1907-09

Robinson, S
HI 1989

Roskrow, M
HI 1948-50

Rudgard, G
HI 1931-32-50-51-52

Sabine, Diana (Plumpton)
CC 1934; HI 1934-35

Saunders, Vivien
CC 1968; VT 1967; CT 1967; HI 1967-68; ELTC 1967

Sheppard, E (Pears)
HI 1947

Simpson, Linda (Moore)
CC 1980; HI 1979-80

Slark, Ruth (Porter)
CC 1960-62-64; ES 1964-66; VT 1959-61-65; CT 1963; HI 1959 to 62; 64-65-66-68-78; ELTC 1965

Smillie, P
HI 1985-86

Smith, Anne [Stant] (Willard)
CC 1976; VT 1975; CT **1959-63**; HI 1974-75-76

Smith, E
HI 1991

Smith, Frances (Stephens)
CC 1950-52-54-56-58-60; **(62)**-**(72)**; VT 1959-71; CT 1959-63; HI 1947 to 55; 59; **(62)**-**(71)**-**(72)**

Smith, Kerry
CC 2002; VT 2001; HI 1997 to 2002; ELTC 1999

Soulsby, Janet
CC **1982**

Speak, Kirsty
CC 1994; ES 1994; VT 1993; HI 1993-94; ELTC 1993

Steel, E
HI 1905 to 08; 11

Stocker, J
HI 1922-23

Stupples, Karen
CC 1996-98; VT 1997; HI 1995 to 98; ELTC 1995-97

Sugden, J (Machin)
HI 1953-54-55

Sumpter, Mrs
HI 1907-08-12-14-24

Sutherland Pilch, R (Barton)
HI 1947-49-50-(58)

Swallow, C
HI 1985; ELTC 1985

Tamworth, Mrs
HI 1908

Tebbet, K
HI 1990-94

Temple, S
HI 1913-14

Temple Dobell, G (Ravenscroft)
HI 1911 to 14; 20-21-25-30

Thompson, M (Wallis)
HI 1948-49

Thornhill, J (Woodside)
CC 1984-86-88; VT 1965-83-85-87-(89); CT 1983-87; HI 1965-74; 82 to 88; ELTC 1965-85-87

Thomlinson, J [Evans] (Roberts)
CC 1962; VT 1963; HI 1962-64

Turner, B
HI 1908

Uzielli, Angela (Carrick)
CC 1978; VT 1977; HI 1976-77-78-90; (92)-(93); ELTC 1977

Wade, Julie
CC 1988-90-92-94-96; ES 1988-90-94; VT 1989-91-93-95; CT 1991-95; HI 1987 to 95; ELTC 1987 to 95

Waite, Claire
CC 1984; ES 1984; VT 1983; CT 1983; HI 1981 to 84; ELTC 1985

Walker, B (Thompson)
HI 1905 to 09; 11

Walker, Mickey
CC 1972-74; VT 1971; CT 1971; HI 1970-72; ELTC 1971

Walker-Leigh, F
HI 1907-08-09; 11 to 14

Walter, J
HI 1974-79-80-82-86

Walters, L
HI 1998

Watson, C (Nelson)
HI 1982

Westall, S (Maudsley)
HI 1973

Williamson, C (Barker)
HI 1979-80-81

Willock-Pollen, G
HI 1907

Wilson, Enid
CC 1932; HI 1928-29-30

Winn, J
HI 1920-21-23-25

Wragg, M
HI 1929

Wylie, Phyllis (Wade)
CC 1938; HI 1934 to 38; 47

IRELAND

Alexander, M
HI 1920-21-22-30

Arbuthnot, M
HI 1921

Armstrong, M
HI 1906

Barlow, Mrs
HI 1921

Beck, Baba (Pim)
HI 1930 to 34; 36-37; 47 to 56; 58-59-61

Beckett, J
HI 1962-66-67-68

Behan, L
CC 1986; VT 1985; HI 1984-85-86-96-98

Birmingham, M
HI (1967)

Blake, Miss
HI 1931 to 36

Boyd, J
HI 1912-13-14

Bradshaw, E
VT 1969-71; HI 1964; 66 to 71; 74-75-(80)-(81); ELTC 1969-71-75

Brandom, G
VT 1967; HI 1965 to 68; ELTC 1967

Brennan, R (Hegarty)
HI 1974 to 79; 81

Brice, Mrs
HI 1948

Brinton, Mrs
HI 1922

Brooks, E
HI 1953-54-56

Brown, B
HI 1960

Brownlow, Miss
HI 1923

Butler, I (Burke)
CC 1966-(96)*; ES 1964-66; VT 1965; 1962 to 66; 68; 70 to 73; 76 to 79; (86)-(87); ELTC 1967

Byrne, A (Sweeney)
HI 1959 to 63; (90)-(91)

Callen, L
HI 1990

Casement, M (Harrison)
HI 1909 to 14

Cassidy, Yvonne
HI 1994-95-2000-01

Clarke, Mrs
HI 1922

Coffey, Alison
CC 2002; ES 2000; VT 1999-2001; HI 1995 to 2002; ELTC 1997-99-2001

Colquhoun, H
HI 1959-60-61-63

Coote, Miss
HI 1925-28-29

Costello, G
HI 1973-(84)-(85)

Coughlan, Claire
HI 1999-2000-01; ELTC 1999-2001

Cramsie, F (Hezlet)
HI 1905 to 10; 13-20-24

Cuming, Mrs
HI 1910

Cuthell, R (Adair)
HI 1908

Dering, Mrs
HI 1923

Dickson, E
HI 1999-2000; ELTC 1999

Dickson, M
HI 1909

Dowdall, Elaine
HI 1997 to 2001

Dowling, Claire (Hourihane)
CC 1984-86-88-90-92-(2000); ES 1986-90-[98]; VT 1981-83-85-87-89-91-(99); HI 1979 to 92; ELTC 1981-83-85-87-89-(97)

Durlacher, Mrs
HI 1905 to 10; 14

Dwyer, Mrs
HI 1928

Eakin, P (James)
HI 1967

Eakin, T
HI 1990 to 94; ELTC 1993

Earner, M
HI 1960 to 63; 70

Ellis, E
HI 1932-35-37-38

Ferguson, A
HI 1989

Ferguson, Daisy
CC (1958); HI 1927 to 32; 34 to 38; (61)

Fitzgibbon, M
HI 1920-21; 29 to 33

Fitzpatrick, O (Heskin)
HI 1967

Fletcher, P (Sherlock)
HI 1932-34-35-36-38-39-54-55-(66)

Gardiner, A
HI 1927-29

Garvey, Philomena
CC 1948-50-52-54-56-60; VT 1959-63; HI 1947 to 53; **54-56-57-58-59-60**-61-62-63-68-69

Gaynor, Z (Fallon)
ES 1964; HI 1952 to 65; 68-69-70; **(72)**

Gildea, Miss
HI 1936 to 39

Gillen, Martina
HI 1999-2001-02; ELTC 2001

Glendinning, D
HI 1937-54

Gorman, S
HI 1976; 79 to 82; **(92)-(93)**; ELTC **(1993)**

Gorry, Mary
VT 1977; HI 1971 to 80; 88-**(89)**; ELTC 1971-75

Gotto, Mrs C
HI 1923

Gotto, Mrs L
HI 1920

Graham, N
HI 1908-09-10-12

Gubbins, Miss
HI 1905

Hackett, B
HI 1993-94-96

Hall, Mrs
HI 1927-30

Hanna, D
HI 1987-88

Harrington, D
HI 1923

Hazlett, VP
HI **(1956)**

Healy, B
HI 1980-82

Hegarty, G
HI 1955-56-**(64)**

Heskin, A
HI 1968-69-70-72-75-77-**(82)-(83)**

Hewett, G
HI 1923-24

Hezlet, Mrs
HI 1910

Hickey, C
HI 1969-**(75)-(76)**

Higgins, E
HI 1981 to 88; 91 to 96; ELTC 1987-93-**(2001)**

Holland, I (Hurst)
HI 1958

Hulton, V (Hezlet)
HI 1905-07; 09 to 12; 20-21

Humphreys, D (Forster)
HI 1951-52-53-55-57

Hyland, B
HI 1964-65-66;

Jackson, B
HI 1937-38-39-50

Jackson, Mrs H
HI 1921

Jackson, J
HI 1912-13-14; 20 to 25; 27 to 30

Jackson, Mrs L
HI 1910-12-14-20-22-25

Jameson, S (Tobin)
HI 1913-14-20-24-25-27

Kavanagh, H
VT 1995; HI 1993-94-95-97-98-2001; ELTC 1997-2001

Keane, Sinead
HI 2000-02; ELTC 2001

Keenan, D
HI 1989

Kidd, Mrs
HI 1934-37

King, Mrs
HI 1923-25-27-29

Kirkwood, Mrs
HI 1955

Larkin, C (McAuley)
HI 1966 to 72; ELTC 1971

Latchford, B
HI 1931-33

Lauder, G
HI 1911

Lauder, R
HI 1911

Lowry, Mrs
HI 1947

MacCann, K
HI 1984-85-86

MacCann, K (Smye)
HI 1947 to 54; 56-57-58-60-61-62-64-**(65)**

McCarthy, A
HI 1951-52

McCarthy, D
HI 1988-90-91-95; ELTC 1993

McCool, L
HI 1993

McDaid, E (O'Grady)
HI 1959

MacGeach, C
HI 1938-39-48-49-50

McGowan, Darragh
HI 2002

McGreevy, V
HI 1987-90-92

McKenna, Mary
CC 1970 to 86; ES 1970-74-76-**(86)-(90)**; VT 1969 to 81; 85-87; **(95)**; HI 1968 to 91; 93; **(2002)**; ELTC 1969-71-75-87

McNeile, CL
HI 1906

McQuillan, Y
HI 1985-86

Madeley, M (Coburn)
HI 1964-69; ELTC 1969

Madill, Maureen
CC 1980; ES 1980; VT 1979-81-85; CT 1979; HI 1978 to 85

Madill, Mrs
HI 1920-24-25-27-28-29-33

Magill, J
HI 1907-11-13

Mahon, D
HI 1989-90

Mallam, Mrs S
HI 1922-23

Mangan, Tricia
HI 1998-2000-02

Marks, Mrs T
HI 1950

Marks, Mrs
HI 1930-31-33-35

Menton, D
HI 1949

Millar, D
HI 1928

Milligan, J (Mark)
HI 1971-72-73

Mitchell, J
HI 1930

Mooney, M
VT 1973; HI 1972-73; ELTC 1971

Moore, S
HI 1937-38-39-47-48-49-**(68)**

Moran, V (Singleton)
HI 1970-71-73-74-75; ELTC 1971-75

Moriarty, M (Irvine)
HI 1979

Morris, Mrs de B
HI 1933

Murray, Rachel
HI 1952

Nolan, Heather
HI 2002

Nutting, P (Jameson)
HI 1927-28

O'Brien, A
HI 1969

O'Brien, Suzanne (Fanagan)
CC 2000; ES 2000; VT 1999; HI 1995 to 2000; ELTC 1997-99

O'Brien Kenney, S
HI 1977-78; 83 to 86

O'Donnell, Maire
CC **(1982)**; VT **(1981)**; HI 1974-77-**(78)**-**(79)**; ELTC **(1980)**

O'Donohue, A
HI 1948 to 51; 53; **(73)**-**(74)**

O'Hare, S
HI 1921-22

O'Reilly, T (Moran)
HI 1977-78-86-88; **(95)**; ELTC 1987

O'Sullivan, A
HI 1982-83-84-92-94-95-96; ELTC 1993-97

O'Sullivan, P
HI 1950 to 60; 63 to 67; **(69)**-**(70)**-**(71)**; ELTC **(1971)**

Ormsby, Miss
HI 1909-10-11

Orr, P (Boyd)
HI 1971

Pim, Mrs
HI 1908

Power, Eileen Rose (McDaid)
CC 1994; VT 1995-97; HI 1987 to 97; 2001-02; ELTC 1987-93-97-99

Purcell, E
HI 1965-66-67-72-73

Purfield, O
HI 1998-99

Reddan, Clarrie (Tiernan)
CC 1938-48; HI 1935-36-38-39-47-48-49

Reddan, MV
HI 1955

Rice, J
HI 1924-27-29

Riordan, Marian
HI 2002

Roberts, E (Pentony)
HI 1932 to 36; 39

Roberts, E (Barnett)
HI 1961 to 65; ELTC 1964

Robinson, C (Nesbitt)
CC 1980; VT 1979; HI 1974 to 81

Robinson, R (Bayly)
HI 1947-56-57

Roche, Mrs
HI 1922

Rogers, A
HI 1992-93; ELTC 1993

Ross, M (Hezlet)
HI 1905 to 08; 11-12

Slade, Lady
HI 1906

Smith, Deirdre
HI 1999; ELTC 2001

Smith, Mrs L
HI 1913-14-21-22-23-25

Smythe, M
HI 1947 to 56; 58-59; **(62)**

Starrett, L (Malone)
HI 1975 to 78; 80

Stuart, M
HI 1905-07-08

Stuart-French, Miss
HI 1922

Sweeney, L
HI 1991

Taylor, I
HI 1930

Thornhill, Miss
HI 1924-25

Thornton, Mrs
HI 1924

Todd, Mrs
HI 1931 to 36

Tynte, V
HI 1905-06-08-09; 11 to 14

Walker, Pat
CC 1934-36-38; HI 1928 to 39; 48

Walsh, R
HI 1987

Webb, L (Bolton)
HI 1981-82-88-89-91-92-94

Wickham, C
HI 1983-89

Wickham, P
HI 1976-83-87; ELTC 1987

Wilson, Mrs
HI 1931

SCOTLAND

Agnew, C
HI 1995

Aitken, E (Young)
HI 1954

Anderson, E
HI 1910-11-12-21-25

Anderson, F
VT 1987; HI 1977-79-80-81-83-84-87 to 92; ELTC 1979-83-87-91

Anderson, H
VT 1969; HI 1964-65-68-69-70-71; ELTC 1969

Anderson, Jean (Donald)
CC 1948-50-52; HI 1947 to 52

Anderson, L
HI 1986 to 89; ELTC 1987-89

Anderson, VH
HI 1907

Bald, J
HI 1968-69-71; ELTC 1969

Barclay, C (Brisbane)
HI 1953-61-68

Baynes, Mrs CE
HI 1921-22

Beddows, C [Watson] (Stevenson)
CC 1932; HI 1913-14-21-22-23-27; 29 to 37; 39; 47 to 51

Bennett, Lorna
HI 1977-80-81

Benton, MH
HI 1914

Blair, N (Menzies)
HI 1955

Bowhill, M (Robertson-Durham)
HI 1936-37-38

Broun, JG
HI 1905-06-07-21

Brown, Mrs FW (Gilroy)
HI 1905 to 11; 13-21

Brown, TWL
HI 1924-25

Burns, K
HI 1999

Burton, H (Mitchell)
VT 1961; HI 1931-55-56-**(59)**

Cadden, G
VT **(1997)**; HI 1974-75-(95)-(96); ELTC **(1997)**

Campbell, J (Burnett)
HI 1960

Coats, Mrs G
HI 1931 to 34

Cochrane, K
HI 1924-25-28-29-30

Connachan, J
CC 1980-82; ES 1980-82; VT 1981-83; CT 1983; HI 1979 to 83

Copley, K (Lackie)
HI 1974-75

Couper, M
HI 1929; 34 to 37; 39-56

Craik, T
HI 1988

Crawford, I (Wylie)
HI 1970-71-72

Cresswell, K (Stuart)
HI 1909 to 12; 14

Cruickshank, DM (Jenkins)
HI 1910-11-12

Davidson, Alison (Rose)
CC 1996-98; VT 1995-97; CT 1995; HI 1990 to 98; 2000; ELTC 1991-93-95-97-99

Davidson, B (Inglis)
HI 1928

Draper, Marjorie [Peel] (Thomas)
CC 1954; VT **(1963)**; HI 1929-34-38; 49 to 53; **(54)**-**(55)**; 56-57-58; **(61)**; 62

Duncan, MJ (Wood)
HI 1925-27-28-39

Falconer, V (Lamb)
HI 1932-36-37; 47 to 56

Farie-Anderson, J
HI 1924

Farquharson-Black, Elaine (Farquharson)
CC 1990-92; VT 1989-91; CT 1991; HI 1987 to 91; 97-98; **(2002)**; ELTC 1989-91

Feggans, Pamela
HI 2002

Ferguson, Marjory (Fowler)
CC 1966; VT 1965; HI 1959; 62 to 67; 69-70-85; ELTC 1965-67-71

Forbes, J
HI 1985 to 89; ELTC 1987-89

Ford, J
HI 1993-94-95

Gallagher, S
HI 1983-84

Gemmill, A
HI 1981-82; 84 to 89; 91-**(97)**

Glennie, H
HI 1959

Glover, A
HI 1905-06-08-09-12

Gow, J
HI 1923-24-27-28

Graham, MA
HI 1905-06

Granger Harrison, Mrs
HI 1922

Grant-Suttie, E
HI 1908-10-11-14-22-23

Grant-Suttie, R
HI 1914

Greenlees, E
HI 1924

Greenlees, Y
HI 1928-30-31-33-34-35-38

Hamilton, S (McKinven)
HI 1965

Hargan, Claire
HI 1999-2000-01; ELTC 2001

Hastings, Dorothea (Sommerville)
CC 1958; VT 1963; HI 1955 to 63

Hay, J (Pelham Burn)
HI 1959

Holm, Helen (Gray)
CC 1936-38-48; HI 1932 to 38; 47-48-50-51-55-57

Hope, LA
HI 1975-76-80; 84 to 87; **(88)-(89)-(90)**

Huggan, Shirley (Lawson)
CC 1988; VT 1989; HI 1985 to 89; ELTC 1985-87-89

Hurd [Howe] (Campbell)
HI 1905-06-08-09-11-28-30

Jack, E (Philip)
HI 1962-63-64-**(81)-(82)**

Jackson, D
HI 1990

Kelway Bamber, Mrs
HI 1923-27-33

Kenny, Lynn
HI 2000-01-02

Kerr, J
HI 1947-48-49-54

Kinloch, Miss
HI 1913-14

Knight, Mrs
HI 1922

Kyle, E
HI 1909-10

Laing, A
VT 1967; HI 1966-67-70-71-**(73)-(74)**

Laing, Anne
VT 1999; CT 1999; HI 1995 to 99; 2001-02; ELTC 1997-99-2001

Laing, Susannah
HI 2002

Laing, Vicki
CC 2002; HI 1997-98; ELTC 2001

Lambie, S
HI 1976

Lawrence, Joan B
CC 1964; ES 1964; VT 1963-65; CT 1971; HI 1959 to 70; **(77)**; ELTC 1965-67-69-71

Leburn, Wilma (Aitken)
CC 1982; VT 1981-83; HI 1978 to 83; 85

Leete, Mrs IG
HI 1933

Little, S
HI 1993

Lugton, C
HI 1968-72-73-**75-76**-77-78-80

MacAndrew, F
HI 1913-14

McCulloch, J
HI 1921 to 24; 27; 29 to 33; 35; **(60)**

Macdonald, K
HI 1928-29

MacIntosh, I
HI **(1991)-(92)-(93)**; ELTC **(1993)**

McKay, F
HI 1992-93-94; ELTC 1993

Mackay, Lesley
HI 1999-2000-01-02; ELTC 2001

McKay, Mhairi
CC 1994-96; ES 1996; VT 1993-95-97; CT 1995; HI 1991-93-94-96; ELTC 1993-95

Mackenzie, A
HI 1921

McKinlay, Myra
CC 1994; HI 1990-92-93; ELTC 1993

McLarty, E
HI **(1966)-(67)-(68)**

McMahon, Suzanne (Cadden)
CC 1976; VT 1975; HI 1974 to 77; 79

McMaster, S
HI 1994 to 97; ELTC 1995-97

McNeil, K
HI **(1969)-(70)**

Main, M (Farquhar)
HI 1950-51

Maitland, M
HI 1905-06-08-12-13

Marr, H (Cameron)
HI 1927 to 31

Marshall, Kathryn (Imrie)
CC 1990; VT 1989; HI 1984-85-89; ELTC 1987-89

Mather, H
HI 1905-09-12-13-14

Matthew, Catriona (Lambert)
CC 1990-92-94; ES 1992; VT 1989-91-93; CT 1991; HI 1989 to 93; ELTC 1989-91-93

Mellis, Mrs
HI 1924-27

Melvin, V
HI 1994-96

Menzies, M
HI **(1962)**

Milton, Moira (Paterson)
CC 1952; HI 1948 to 52

Moffat, L
VT 1999; HI 1996-98-2001

Monaghan, Hilary
CC 1998; VT 1999; HI 1995 to 98; 2000; ELTC 1997-99

Moodie, Janice
CC 1994-96; ES 1996; VT 1993-95-97; CT 1995; HI 1990-91-92; ELTC 1991-93-95-97

Morton, Linzi
HI 2000-01-02; ELTC 2001

Myles, M
HI 1955-57-59-60-67

Neill-Fraser, M
HI 1905 to 14

Nicholson, J (Hutton)
CT 1971; HI 1969-70; ELTC 1971

Nicholson, Lesley
CC 2000; VT 1999; HI 1994 to 99; ELTC 1995-97-99

Nicholson, Mrs WH
HI 1910-13

Nimmo, H
HI 1936-38-39

Norris, J (Smith)
VT 1977; HI 1966 to 72; 75 to 79; **(83)-(84)**; ELTC 1971

Norwell, I (Watt)
HI 1954

Panton-Lewis, C (Panton)
ES 1976; VT 1977; HI 1972-73-76-77-78

Park, Mrs
HI 1952

Patey, Mrs
HI 1922-23

Percy, G (Mitchell)
HI 1927-28-30-31

Porter, Doris (Park)
CC 1932; HI 1922-25-27; 29 to 35; 37-38; 47-48

Provis, I (Kyle)
HI 1910-11

Purvis-Russell-Montgomery, C
HI 1921-22-23-25; 28 to 39; 47 to 50; 52

Queen, Clare
HI 2002

Rawlinson, T (Walker)
VT 1973; HI 1970-71-73-76

Reid, A (Lurie)
VT 1961; HI 1960 to 64; 66

Reid, A (Kyle)
HI 1923-24-25

Reid, D
HI 1978-79

Rennie, J (Hastings)
CC 1966; VT 1961-67; 1961-65-66-67-71-72; ELTC 1967

Richmond, M (Walker)
CC 1974; VT 1975; HI 1972 to 75; 77-78

Rigby, F (Macbeth)
HI 1912-13

Ritchie, C (Park)
HI 1939-47-48-51-52-53-(64)

Roberts, M (Brown)
ES 1964; HI (1965)

Robertson, B (McCorkindale)
CC 1960-66-68-70-72-(74)-(76)-82-86; ES 1964-66-(68)-72-80-82; VT 1959-63-69-71-81-85; CT 1971-(75); HI 1958 to 66; 69-72-73-78-80-81-82-84-85-86; ELTC 1965-67-69-71

Robertson, D
HI 1907

Robertson, E
HI 1924

Robertson, G
HI 1907-08-09

Roxburgh, L
HI 1993-94-95

Roy, S (Needham)
VT 1973-75; HI 1969; 71 to 76; 83

Rusack, J
HI 1908

Singleton, B (Henderson)
HI 1939; 52 to 58; 60 to 65

Smith, J
HI 1999; ELTC 1999

Speir, Marigold
HI 1957-64-68-(71)-(72)

Stavert, M
HI 1979

Steel, Mrs DC
HI 1925

Stewart, Gillian
CC 1980-82; VT 1979-81-83; CT 1979-83; HI 1979 to 84; ELTC 1982-4

Stewart, L (Scraggie)
HI 1921-22-23

Stirling, Heather
CC 2002; HI 1999-2000-01-02

Summers, M (Mackie)
HI 1986

Teacher, F
HI 1908-09-11-12-13

Thompson, M
HI 1949

Thomson, D
HI 1982-83-85-87

Thomson, M
HI 1907

Thomson, Muriel
CC 1978; VT 1977; HI 1974 to 78; ELTC 1978

Valentine, Jessie (Anderson)
CC 1938-48-50-52-54-56-58; CT 1959; HI 1934 to 39; 47; 49 to 55; 56; 57-58

Veitch, F
HI 1912

Wallace-Williamson, Verona
CC 1938; HI 1932

Wardlaw, Nan (Baird)
CC 1938; HI 1932; 35 to 39; 47-48

Wilson, A
HI 1973-74-(85)

Wood, S
HI 1999-2000

Wooldridge, W (Shaw)
HI 1982

Wright, Janette (Robertson)
CC 1954-56-58-60; VT 1959-61-63; CT 1959; HI 1952 to 61; 63-65-67-73; (78)-(79)-(80)-(86); ELTC 1965

Wright, M
HI 1990-91-92; ELTC 1991

Wright, P
VT 1981; HI 1981 to 84; ELTC 1987

WALES

Allington-Hughes, Miss
HI 1908-09-10-12-14-22-25

Archer, L
HI 1999

Ashcombe, Lady
HI 1950 to 54

Aubertin, Mrs
HI 1908-09-10

Baker, J
HI 1990

Barron, M
HI 1929-30-31; 34 to 39; 47 to 58; 60 to 63

Bayliss, Mrs
HI 1921

Bloodworth, D (Lewis)
HI 1954 to 57; 60

Boyes, S
HI 1992

Bradley, K (Rawlings)
HI 1975 to 79; 82-83

Brearley, M
HI 1937-38

Brewerton, R [Becky]
CC 2000; VT 2001; HI 1997 to 2002; ELTC 1999-2001

Bridges, Mrs
HI 1933-38-39

Briggs, A (Brown)
VT 1971-75; HI 1969 to 80; 81-82-83; 84; 93; ELTC 1971-75

Bromley-Davenport, I (Rieben)
HI 1932 to 36; 48; 50 to 56

Brook, D
HI 1913

Brown, E (Jones)
HI 1947 to 50; 52-53; 57 to 66; 68-69-70

Brown, J
HI 1960-61-62-64-65; ELTC 1965-69

Brown, Mrs
HI 1924-25-27

Bryan-Smith, S
HI 1947 to 52; 56

Burrell, Mrs
HI 1939

Caryl, M
HI 1929

Chugg, Pam (Light)
HI 1973 to 78; 86-87-88; 96; (2002); ELTC 1975-87-(2001)

Clarkson, H (Reynolds)
HI 1935-38-39

Clay, E
HI 1912

Cole, C
HI 1998

Cowley, Lady
HI 1907-09

Cox, Margaret
HI 1924-25

Cox, Nell
HI 1954

Cross, M
HI 1922

Cunninghame, S
HI 1922-25-29-31

Dampney, S
HI 1924-25; 27 to 30

David, Mrs
HI 1908

Davies, Karen
CC 1986-88; VT 1987; CT 1987;
HI 1981-82-83; ELTC 1987

Davies, P (Griffiths)
HI 1965 to 68; 70-71-73; ELTC
1971

Davis, Louise
HI 1997-98-2000-01-02; ELTC
1997-99

Deacon, Mrs
HI 1912-14

Dermott, Lisa
CC 1996; HI 1987-88-89; 91 to
96; ELTC 1991-93

Donne, A
HI 1993-94; ELTC 1993

Duncan, B
HI 1907 to 10; 12

Duncan, M
HI 1922-23-28-34

Edwards, E
HI 1949-50

Edwards, J
HI 1932-33-34-36-37

Edwards, J (Morris)
HI 1962-63; 66 to 70; **(77)-(78)-(79)**; ELTC 1967-69-(93)

Ellis Griffiths, Mrs
HI 1907-08-09-12-13

Emery, MJ
HI 1928 to 38; 47

Evans, Kathryn
HI 1999-2000-01-02

Evans, N
HI 1908-09-10-13

Evans, Natalee
HI 1996 to 99; ELTC 1997-99

Evans, Stephanie
HI 2002

Franklin Thomas, E
HI 1909

Freeguard, C
HI 1927

Garfield Evans, PR (Whittaker)
HI 1948 to 54; **(55)-(56)-(57)-(58)**

Gear Evans, A
HI 1932-33-34

Gethin Griffith, S
HI 1914-22-23-24; 28 to 31; 35

Gibbs, S
HI 1933-34-39

Griffith, W
HI 1981

Haig, J (Mathias Thomas)
HI 1938-39

Hartley, R
HI 1958-59-62

Hedley Hill, Miss
HI 1922

Highgate, Anna
HI 1999-2001-02; ELTC 2001

Hill, Mrs
HI 1924

Hort, K
HI 1929

Hughes, J
HI 1967-71-88-**(89)**; ELTC 1971

Hughes, Miss
HI 1907

Humphreys, A (Coulman)
HI 1969-70-71

Hurst, Mrs
HI 1921-22-23-25-27-28

Inghram, E (Lever)
HI 1947 to 58; 64-65

Irvine, Miss
HI 1930

Isaac, Mrs
HI 1924

Isherwood, L
HI 1972-76-77-78-80-86; 88 to 91

Jenkin, B
HI 1959

Jenkins, J (Owen)
HI 1953-56

John, J
HI 1974

Johnson, A (Hughes)
HI 1964; 66 to 76; 78-79-85; **(95)**;
ELTC 1965-67-69-71

Johnson, J (Roberts)
HI 1955

Johnson, R
HI 1955

Jones, A (Gwyther)
HI 1959

Jones, B
HI 1994-95-96-98; ELTC 1993

Jones, K
HI **(1959)-(60)-(61)**

Jones, M (De Lloyd)
HI 1951

Jones, Sarah
CC 2002; HI 2000-01-02; ELTC
2001

Jones, Mrs
HI 1932-35

Justice, M
HI 1931-32

Laming Evans, Mrs
HI 1922-23

Langford, Mrs
HI 1937

Lawson, H
HI 1989 to 92; 97-98; ELTC 1991-93-97

Leaver, B
HI 1912-14-21

Llewellyn, Miss
HI 1912-13-14-21-22-23

Lloyd, J
HI 1988

Lloyd, P
HI 1935-36

Lloyd Davies, VH
HI 1913

Lloyd Roberts, V
HI 1907-08-10

Lloyd Williams, Miss
HI 1909-10-12-14

Lovatt, S
HI 1994-95

MacKean, Mrs
HI 1938-39-47

MacTier, Mrs
HI 1927

Magee, A-M
HI 1991 to 94

Marley, MV
HI 1921-22-23-30-37

Martin, P [Whitworth Jones] (Low)
HI 1948-50-56-59-60-61

Mason, Mrs
HI 1923

Matthews, Tegwen [Thomas] (Perkins)
CC 1974-76-78-80; ES 1974; VT
1973-75-77-79; CT 1975-79; HI
1972 to 84

Mills, I
HI 1935-36-37-39-47-48

Morgan, R [Becky]
CC 1998-2000; ES [1998]; VT
1997-99; CT 1999; HI 1996 to 99;
ELTC 2001

Morgan, Miss
HI 1912-13-14

Mountford, Sara
HI 1989 to 92; ELTC 1991-2001

Musgrove, Mrs
HI 1923-24

Newman, L
HI 1927-31

Nicholls, M
HI **(1962)**

Oliver, M (Jones)
ES 1964; HI 1955; 60 to 66

Orr, Mrs
HI 1924

Owen, E
HI 1947

Perriam, A
HI 1988-90-91-92

Phelips, M
HI 1913-14-21

Phillips, Kate
HI 1999-2000-01-02; ELTC 2001

Phillips, Mrs
HI 1921

Pilgrim, Eleanor
HI 1995-97-2000-01; ELTC 1997-99-2001

Powell, M
HI 1908-09-10-12

Pritchard, Jo
HI 2002

Proctor, Mrs
HI 1907

Pyman, B
HI 1921-22-23-25; 28 to 39; 47 to 50; 52

Rawlings, M
VT 1981; HI 1979-80-81; 83 to 87

Rees, G
HI 1981

Rees, MB
HI 1927-31

Rhys, J
HI 1979

Richards, D
HI 1994-95-96

Richards, J
HI 1980-82-83-85

Richards, S
HI 1967

Rieben, Mrs
HI 1927 to 33

Roberts, B
HI **(1984)-(85)-(86)**

Roberts, G
HI 1949-52-53-54

Roberts, P
ES 1964; HI 1950-51-53; 55 to 63; **(64)-(65)-(66)-(67)**; 68-69-70; ELTC 1965-67-69

Roberts, S
HI 1983 to 90; ELTC 1983-87

Rogers, J
HI 1972

Scott Chard, Mrs
HI 1928-30

Seddon, N
HI 1962-63; **(74)-(75)-(76)**

Selkirk, H
HI 1925-28

Shaw, P
HI 1913

Sheldon, A
HI 1981

Slocombe, E (Davies)
HI 1974-75

Smalley, Mrs A
HI 1924-25; 31 to 34

Sowter, Mrs
HI 1923

Stark, K
HI 1995-96

Stockton, Mrs
HI 1949

Storry, Mrs
HI 1910-14

Stroud, N
HI 1989

Thomas, C (Phipps)
HI 1959; 63 to 73; 76-77-80

Thomas, I
HI 1910

Thomas, J (Foster)
HI 1984 to 87; 92-93-95; ELTC 1987-89-91-93

Thomas, O
HI 1921

Thomas, S (Rowlands)
HI 1977-82-84-85

Thomas, Vicki (Rawlings)
CC 1982-84-86-88-90; ES 1990; VT 1979-83-85-87-89-91; CT 1979-83-87-91; HI 1971 to 98; ELTC 1973 to 83; 87-91-97-99

Thompson, M
HI 1937-38-39

Treharne, A (Mills)
HI 1952-61

Turner, S (Jump)
HI 1982-84-85-86-91-93

Valentine, P (Whitley)
HI 1973-74-75; 77 to 80; **(90)**

Wadsworth, Helen
CC 1984; HI 1987 to 90; ELTC 1987-**90**

Wakelin, H
HI 1955

Webster, S (Hales)
HI 1968-69-72; (91)

Wesley, N
HI 1986

Weston, R
HI 1927

Whieldon, Miss
HI 1908

Williams, M
HI 1936

Wilson Jones, D
HI 1952

Wright, N (Cook)
ES 1964; HI 1938-47-48-49; 51 to 54; 57 to 60; 62-63-64-66-67-68; **(71)-(72)-(73)**; ELTC 1965; **(71)**

PART IX

Government of the Game

The Royal and Ancient and the modern game

The Royal and Ancient Golf Club of St Andrews holds a unique position within the game. Formed in 1754 as a private members' club, it has evolved through two and a half centuries as golf's senior authority. There are now three distinct areas of responsibility within the framework of administration undertaken by the R&A.

At international level, outside North America, the club has been the governing authority for the Rules of Golf since 1897, with more than 120 countries, unions and associations affiliated to it.

The running of the Open and Amateur Championships has also been part of the R&A remit since 1920, a national commitment now enlarged with the running of the Boys, Mid-Amateur and Seniors Championships and, more recently, the Junior Open. The R&A selects teams to represent Great Britain & Ireland in events such as the Walker Cup (GB&I v USA) and the St Andrews Trophy (GB&I v Europe), and organises these events when they are played in Britain and Ireland.

As a private club the R&A has 2500 members throughout the world, many of whom are leading administrators within their own country's golf authority. With representatives on the World Amateur Golf Council, the R&A also is involved in the running of the Eisenhower Trophy (the world amateur men's team championship) and the Espirito Santo Trophy (the world amateur women's team championship). Both these tournaments are held every two years. This wealth of expertise makes a wide range of experience available to all R&A committees.

In 2002, the new Golf Course Committee replaced the Golf Course Advisory Panel and is concerned with all aspects of the golf course, paying particular attention to environmental and ecological issues; the use of water and chemicals; climate change; planning of new courses and levels of play. It also offers best-practice professional advice and information to architects, golf associations and federations, planners, government agencies, golf clubs, greenkeepers and other relevant groups.

Promoting the game

Another major aspect of the R&A's leadership is the allocation of funds from Open Championship revenues to help finance projects large and small which promote and expand the game worldwide. Many millions have been ploughed back into grassroots golf in this way.

The Royal and Ancient Golf Club staged the first international golf conference in 1970 bringing together representatives from Britain and Europe. This developed ten years later into a truly international gathering at which 33 affiliated countries were represented. At the sixth conference in 2001, more than 150 delegates from 69 organisations around the world were involved in discussing topics vital to the growth and development of the game.

Judgements made by the R&A on all aspects of the game are made against a background of history and tradition established over six centuries, but always with an understanding of modern demands.

Refining the laws of the ancient game

During a 10-year period towards the end of the 19th century, when the number of golf clubs in Britain rose from fewer than 200 to almost 1000, the need for a governing body to bring conformity to the rules became a matter of serious debate. Until that time each club could set and administer its own regulations for playing the game.

The R&A was already recognised as something of a father figure and eventually agreed to pressure from the leading clubs to take responsibility for the laws of the game. On September 28, 1897, the Rules of Golf Committee was formed and the R&A moved from its position as a highly regarded advisor to a firmly established governing authority with well-defined powers.

With the exception of the United State and Mexico, whose allegiance lies with the United States Golf Association, and Canada, which is self-governing but affiliated to the R&A, every country where the game is played has affiliated to the Royal and Ancient and accepts the club's authority over the laws of the game and the regulation on amateur status. Following a four-day meeting in the House of Lords between the R&A and the USGA, a uniform code of rules has been applied world-wide since 1952. Yet, even today, the R&A does not impose the Rules of Golf, but rather governs by consent.

The main thrust of the work of the Rules of Golf Committee is in the area of interpretation and constant review, revision and simplification of the laws. To this end the R&A and USGA meet twice a year to discuss possible changes, which will then be examined at great length in consultation with amateur and professional golfing bodies worldwide. Any agreed changes to the rules are made every four years.

The Rules Committee is composed of 12 members of the R&A with up to a further 12 representatives from golfing bodies at home and abroad. In addition to the USGA, there are advisory members from Britain's Council of National Golf Unions and the Ladies Golf Union, plus delegates from Europe, Australia, New Zealand, Canada, South Africa, South America, Asia and the Pacific, and Japan.

Since the creation of the first Rules Committee in 1897, the R&A has spawned two further offspring to meet the ever-increasing pressures of administration. The Implements and Ball Committee investigates and rules on the admissibility or otherwise of newly developed clubs and golf balls, and the Amateur Status Committee defines the laws which govern acceptable levels of prizes, tournament rules, grants and scholarships and applications for reinstatement to the amateur ranks.

The Open Championship

The R&A first became involved with the Open Championship after Young Tom Morris won the original championship belt outright in 1870 and Prestwick Golf Club, which had inaugurated the event 10 years earlier, asked the Royal and Ancient and the Honourable Company of Edinburgh Golfers to join them in providing a new trophy and staging the championship.

By 1919 a total of 26 golf clubs had become involved in the organisation of the Open and Amateur Championships. It was a cumbersome and at times chaotic situation, which was resolved when the clubs invited the R&A to take full responsibility for both events from 1920.

Significant changes had taken place over the first 60 years since the first Championship in 1860. Entries had increased from eight to more than 250, qualifying rounds were introduced and play changed from three rounds of Prestwick's 12-hole course in one day to four rounds of 18 holes over two days.

Those changes pale into insignificance when set beside the modern championship. Well over 2000 entries are received each year. Prize money has reached almost £4 million and spectators number more than 200,000. The tented village is virtually a small township, with more than 7000 people involved as volunteers or paid employees.

It is not just the Open, however, which occupies the talents of Championship Committee members. They are also responsible for the Amateur, Boys, Mid-Amateur and Seniors Championships and the Junior Open. International events also come under their umbrella. These include organisation of the Walker Cup, St Andrews and Jacques Léglise Trophies when they are played in Great Britain and Ireland.

The Selection Committee, which reports directly to the General Committee, has the responsibility for teams representing Great Britain & Ireland and involves members from each of the four home countries.

Profits from the Open Championship are channelled back into the game through the External Funds Supervisory Committee which recommends grants and loans for projects throughout the world, particularly those concerned with the training and development of junior golf and encourages golf in countries where the game is in its infancy.

The R&A as a private club

Although the worldwide membership of the R&A is 2500, those resident in St Andrews barely number three figures. Many who wear the R&A tie are also members of leading clubs in other golfing nations and bring a wealth of experience to committee discussions.

Yet despite its pre-eminent position, the club has no golf course. For many years the upkeep of the Old Course was paid for by the R&A and the New Course was built and maintained at the members' expense. This arrangement ws modified in 1953 by the creation of the Joint Links Committee which consisted of an equal number of R&A and Town Council members and took responsibility for the then four courses at St Andrews. Since 1974 the St Andrews courses, now numbering seven, have been administered by the Links Trust.

Now the St Andrews courses are administered by a Links Trust and Links Management Committee on which the R&A has the right to appoint representation and the club still makes significant contributions to the maintenance and improvement of the courses with grants and loans.

Members gather from around the world for the club's spring and autumn meetings and in September each year the new captain follows tradition by driving into office to the resounding boom of an ancient cannon.

Duke of York to be next R & A captain

When His Royal Highness The Duke of York takes over as captain of the Royal and Ancient Golf Club of St Andrews in the autumn of 2003 he will be the sixth member of the Royal Family to have captained the Club. The others have been:

1863 – HRH The Prince of Wales (later King Edward VII)
1876 – HRH Prince Leopold
1922 – HRH The Prince of Wales (later King Edward VIII)
1930 – HRH The Duke of York (later King George VI)
1937 – HRH The Duke of Kent.

Golf's Complicated Rules Ensure Game's Integrity

Keith Mackie on recent rules decisions

Two balls on the putting green are moved by the wind. One player must play the ball from its new position without penalty. The other must replace the ball and take a one stroke penalty. Why? The dilemma was perfectly illustrated at the final two holes of the 2002 United States Open Championship over the Black Course at Bethpage Park, New York.

On the 17th green Steve Stricker had just placed a marker behind his ball when a gust of wind moved the ball. On the final green his playing partner, Frank Lickliter, was about to putt when the wind shifted his ball.

In the first case Stricker had done nothing to cause the ball to move. He checked with rules officials who assured him that the ball had to be played from its new position without penalty as neither wind nor water is an outside agency. Had the ball been moved by another ball or a spectator it would have been replaced, but again without penalty. The fact that Stricker had placed a marker behind the ball made no difference to the ruling as the ball remains in play until it has been lifted.

In Lickliter's case the important difference was that he had addressed the ball. Once a player has taken his stance and grounded his club any movement of the ball is considered to have been caused by the player. In these circumstances the ball must be replaced in its original position and a one stroke penalty is applied.

On fast, sloping greens in windy conditions players can avoid the possibility of incurring a penalty by keeping the head of the putter off the ground as they prepare to putt. Players are permitted to take their stance, but they have not addressed the ball until the club is grounded.

The rules official with the Lickliter match was not aware of any infringement until the player called the penalty on himself.

The integrity of professional golfers was also clearly illustrated by Stuart Appleby in the first round of the 2002 Masters at Augusta. The Australian, who was to feature in the four-man play-off for the Open Championship at Muirfield later in the year, was attempting to play a recovery from a water hazard. After the stroke he told a rules official that he thought he had felt something on his backswing and that his club may have touched the water, but he could not be sure.

There is a two-shot penalty for touching the water at address or in the backswing in a water hazard, just as there is for touching the sand in a bunker. A video replay of Appleby's stroke showed that he had, in fact, brushed the surface of the water with the clubhead on his backswing.

If that penalty seems harsh for an action that gained no advantage, there are good reasons. One of the basic principles behind the rules of the game is that the ball should be played as it lies. Grounding the club behind the ball in a bunker could have the effect of teeing the ball up. Allowing the club to touch the sand in the backswing could create a furrow which would make the shot easier. In a water hazard a player is prohibited from touching the water to prevent testing the depth before attempting to play a ball which is lying in or submerged by water.

The rules must necessarily provide that certain actions result in penalties whether they are accidental or deliberate and whether or not they lead to an advantage.

If Appleby's error was known to no-one but himself, the drama which surrounded Gary Evans' final round in the Open Championship was witnessed by millions. On his way to a 65, to finish just one shot short of the play-off for the title, he hit his second shot at the 17th into heavy rough short and left of the green. Despite a frantic search, assisted by a large number of spectators, the ball was never found.

Several balls were unearthed, including a Titleist 2, the same make and number as Evans was playing, but it did not bear his own identification mark. Players use a variety of methods to ensure they do not play a wrong ball. Some cover the ball with large letters, others with dots. Some prefer the minimalist approach. Arnold Palmer used to puncture the ball with two small pin pricks beside the maker's name.

Where tournament players have an advantage over club golfers is that spectators start the search for a ball as soon as it disappears from sight, but the official five minute search period does not begin until the player or his caddie reaches the spot where he believes the ball was lost. Players cannot, however, hang back in order to prolong the time.

A more unusual lost ball incident occurred at the Scottish PGA Championship at Gleneagles where

defending title-holder Paul Casey laid up safely in the fairway at the second hole, but could find no sign of his ball. Spectators reported hearing a noise that could have been the ball striking a sprinkler head and the area of search was widened, but still without success. Casey was forced to retrace his steps and play another ball before it was discovered that his original ball had lodged beneath the broken sprinkler head cover. Had spectators clearly seen the ball lodge in the sprinkler he could have dropped at the nearest point of relief without penalty, even if the ball could not be seen in the obstruction ... but, sadly for him, none had.

Rules Booklet

The Rules of Golf are available in booklet form free from the Royal and Ancient Golf Club of St Andrews, which also has for sale a book detailing decisions taken regarding the rules.

R&A Contacts

The history of the Royal and Ancient Golf Club of St Andrews and up-to-date news of its activities worldwide can be found at the website
www.randa.org

Full details of the Open Championship can be found at
www.opengolf.com

R&A officials can be contacted on: Tel 01334 460000 Fax 01334 460001

Secretary: Peter Dawson

Assistant Secretary: Michael Tate

Championship Secretary: David Hill

Commercial Secretary: Angus Farquhar

Financial Secretary: Mark Dobell

Golf Development Secretary: Duncan Weir

Golf Heritage Secretary: Peter Lewis

Members' Secretary: Aubyn Stewart-Wilson

Projects Secretary: Lachlan McIntosh

Rules Secretary: David Rickman

RULES
OF GOLF

As Approved by
The Royal and Ancient Golf Club
of St. Andrews, Scotland
and the
United States Golf Association

29th EDITION
EFFECTIVE 1st JANUARY 2000

HOW TO USE THE RULE BOOK

Understand the words
The Rules book is written in a very precise and deliberate fashion. You should be aware of and understand the following differences in word use.

may	=	optional
should	=	recommendation
shall/must	=	instruction (and penalty if not carried out)
a ball	=	you may substitute another ball (e.g. Rules 26, 27 or 28)
the ball	=	you may not substitute another ball (e.g. Rules 24-2 or 25-1)

Know the definitions
There are over forty defined terms and these form the foundation around which the Rules of play are written. A good knowledge of the defined terms (which are italicised throughout the book) is very important to the correct application of the Rules.

Which rule applies?
The Contents pages may help you find the relevant Rule, alternatively there is an Index at the back of the book.

What is the ruling
To answer any question on the Rules you must first establish the facts of the case. To do so, you should identify:

1. The form of play (e.g. match play or stroke play, single, foursome or four-ball?)
2. Who is involved (e.g. the player, his partner or caddie, an outside agency?)
3. Where the incident occurred (e.g. on the teeing ground, in a bunker or water hazard, on the putting green or elsewhere on the course).

In some cases it might also be necessary to establish:

4. The player's intentions (e.g. what was he doing and what does he want to do?)
5. Any subsequent events (e.g. the player has returned his score card or the competition has closed).

Refer to the book
It is recommended that you carry a Rule book in your golf bag and use it whenever a question arises. If in doubt, play the course as you find it and play the ball as it lies. Once back in the Clubhouse, reference to Decisions on the Rules of Golf should help resolve any outstanding queries.

CONTENTS

SECTION I — ETIQUETTE

COURTESY ON THE COURSE

Safety
Prior to playing a stroke or making a practice swing, the player should ensure that no one is standing close by or in a position to be hit by the club, the ball or any stones, pebbles, twigs or the like which may be moved by the stroke or swing.

Consideration for Other Players
The player who has the honour should be allowed to play before his opponent or fellow-competitor tees his ball.

No one should move, talk or stand close to or directly behind the ball or the hole when a player is addressing the ball or making a stroke.

No player should play until the players in front are out of range.

Pace of Play
In the interest of all, players should play without delay.

If a player believes his ball may be lost outside a water hazard or out of bounds, to save time, he should play a provisional ball.

Players searching for a ball should signal the players behind them to pass as soon as it becomes apparent that the ball will not easily be found. They should not search for five minutes before doing so. They should not continue play until the players following them have passed and are out of range.

When the play of a hole has been completed, players should immediately leave the putting green.

If a match fails to keep its place on the course and loses more than one clear hole on the players in front, it should invite the match following to pass.

PRIORITY ON THE COURSE

In the absence of special rules, two-ball matches should have precedence over and be entitled to pass any three- or four-ball match, which should invite them through.

A single player has no standing and should give way to a match of any kind.

Any match playing a whole round is entitled to pass a match playing a shorter round.

CARE OF THE COURSE

Holes in Bunkers
Before leaving a bunker, a player should carefully fill up and smooth over all holes and footprints made by him.

Repair Divots, Ball-Marks and Damage by Spikes
A player should ensure that any divot hole made by him and any damage to the putting green made by a ball is carefully repaired. On completion of the hole by all players in the group, damage to the putting green caused by golf shoe spikes should be repaired.

Damage to Greens — Flagsticks, Bags, etc.
Players should ensure that, when putting down bags or the flagstick, no damage is done to the putting green and that neither they nor their caddies damage the hole by standing close to it, in handling the flagstick or in removing the ball from the hole. The flagstick should be properly replaced in the hole before the players leave the putting green. Players should not damage the putting green by leaning on their putters, particularly when removing the ball from the hole.

Golf Carts
Local notices regulating the movement of golf carts should be strictly observed.

Damage Through Practice Swings
In taking practice swings, players should avoid causing damage to the course, particularly the tees, by removing divots.

SECTION II — DEFINITIONS

The Definitions are placed in alphabetical order and some are also repeated at the beginning of their relevant Rule.

In the Rules themselves, defined terms which may be important to the application of a Rule are italicised the first time they appear.

Abnormal Ground Conditions

An 'abnormal ground condition' is any casual water, ground under repair or hole, cast or runway on the course made by a burrowing animal, a reptile or a bird.

Addressing the Ball

A player has 'addressed the ball' when he has taken his stance and has also grounded his club, except that in a hazard a player has addressed the ball when he has taken his stance.

Advice

'Advice' is any counsel or suggestion which could influence a player in determining his play, the choice of a club or the method of making a stroke.

Information on the Rules or on matters of public information, such as the position of hazards or the flagstick on the putting green, is not advice.

Ball Deemed to Move

See 'Move or Moved'.

Ball Holed

See 'Holed'.

Ball Lost

See 'Lost Ball'.

Ball in Play

A ball is 'in play' as soon as the player has made a stroke on the teeing ground. It remains in play until holed out, except when it is lost, out of bounds or lifted, or another ball has been substituted whether or not such substitution is permitted; a ball so substituted becomes the ball in play.

Bunker

A 'bunker' is a hazard consisting of a prepared area of ground, often a hollow, from which turf or soil has been removed and replaced with sand or the like. Grass-covered ground bordering or within a bunker is not part of the bunker. The margin of a bunker extends vertically downwards, but not upwards. A ball is in a bunker when it lies in or any part of it touches the bunker.

Burrowing Animal

A 'burrowing animal' is an animal that makes a hole for habitation or shelter, such as a rabbit, mole, ground hog, gopher or salamander.

Note: A hole made by a non-burrowing animal, such as a dog, is not an abnormal ground condition unless marked or declared as ground under repair.

Caddie

A 'caddie' is one who carries or handles a player's clubs during play and otherwise assists him in accordance with the Rules.

When one caddie is employed by more than one player, he is always deemed to be the caddie of the player whose ball is involved, and equipment carried by him is deemed to be that player's equipment, except when the caddie acts upon specific directions of another player, in which case he is considered to be that other player's caddie.

Casual Water

'Casual water' is any temporary accumulation of water on the course which is visible before or after the player takes his stance and is not in a water hazard. Snow and natural ice, other than frost, are either casual water or loose impediments, at the option of the player. Manufactured ice is an obstruction. Dew and frost are not casual water. A ball is in casual water when it lies in or any part of it touches the casual water.

Committee

The 'Committee' is the committee in charge of the competition or, if the matter does not arise in a competition, the committee in charge of the course.

Competitor

A 'competitor' is a player in a stroke competition. A 'fellow-competitor' is any person with whom the competitor plays. Neither is partner of the other.

In stroke play foursome and four-ball competitions, where the context so admits, the word 'competitor' or 'fellow-competitor' includes his partner.

Course

The 'course' is the whole area within which play is permitted (see Rule 33-2).

Equipment

'Equipment' is anything used, worn or carried by or for the player except any ball he has played at the hole being played and any small object, such as a coin or a tee, when used to mark the position of a ball or the extent of an area in which a ball is to be dropped. Equipment includes a golf cart, whether or not motorised. If such a cart is shared by two or more players, the cart and everything in it are deemed to be the equipment of the player whose ball is involved except that, when the cart is being moved by one of the players sharing it, the cart and everything in it are deemed to be that player's equipment.

Note: A ball played at the hole being played is equipment when it has been lifted and not put back into play.

Fellow-Competitor
See 'Competitor".

Flagstick
The 'flagstick' is a movable straight indicator, with or without bunting or other material attached, centred in the hole to show its position. It shall be circular in cross-section.

Forecaddie
A 'forecaddie' is one who is employed by the Committee to indicate to players the position of balls during play. He is an outside agency.

Ground Under Repair
'Ground under repair' is any part of the course so marked by order of the Committee or so declared by its authorised representative. It includes material piled for removal and a hole made by a greenkeeper, even if not so marked.

All ground and any grass, bush, tree or other growing thing within the ground under repair is part of the ground under repair. The margin of ground under repair extends vertically downwards, but not upwards. Stakes and lines defining ground under repair are in such ground. Such stakes are obstructions. A ball is in ground under repair when it lies in or any part of it touches the ground under repair.

Note 1: Grass cuttings and other material left on the course which have been abandoned and are not intended to be removed are not ground under repair unless so marked.

Note 2: The Committee may make a Local Rule prohibiting play from ground under repair or an environmentally sensitive area which has been defined as ground under repair.

Hazards
A 'hazard' is any bunker or water hazard.

Hole
The 'hole' shall be 4¼ inches (108 mm) in diameter and at least 4 inches (100 mm) deep. If a lining is used, it shall be sunk at least 1 inch (25 mm) below the putting green surface unless the nature of the soil makes it impracticable to do so; its outer diameter shall not exceed 4¼ inches (108 mm).

Holed
A ball is 'holed' when it is at rest within the circumference of the hole and all of it is below the level of the lip of the hole.

Honour
The player who is to play first from the teeing ground is said to have the 'honour'.

Lateral Water Hazard
A 'lateral water hazard' is a water hazard or that part of a water hazard so situated that it is not possible or is deemed by the Committee to be impracticable to drop a ball behind the water hazard in accordance with Rule 26-1b.

That part of a water hazard to be played as a lateral water hazard should be distinctively marked. A ball is in a lateral water hazard when it lies in or any part of it touches the lateral water hazard.

Note 1: Lateral water hazards should be defined by red stakes or lines.

Note 2: The Committee may make a Local Rule prohibiting play from an environmentally-sensitive area which has been defined as a lateral water hazard.

Note 3: The Committee may define a lateral water hazard as a water hazard.

Line of Play
The 'line of play' is the direction which the player wishes his ball to take after a stroke, plus a reasonable distance on either side of the intended direction. The line of play extends vertically upwards from the ground, but does not extend beyond the hole.

Line of Putt
The 'line of putt' is the line which the player wishes his ball to take after a stroke on the putting green. Except with respect to Rule 16-1e, the line of putt includes a reasonable distance on either side of the intended line. The line of putt does not extend beyond the hole.

Loose Impediments
'Loose impediments' are natural objects such as stones, leaves, twigs, branches and the like, dung, worms and insects and casts or heaps made by them, provided they are not fixed or growing, are not solidly embedded and do not adhere to the ball.

Sand and loose soil are loose impediments on the putting green, but not elsewhere.

Snow and natural ice, other than frost, are either casual water or loose impediments, at the option of the player. Manufactured ice is an obstruction.

Dew and frost are not loose impediments.

Lost Ball
A ball is 'lost' if:

a. It is not found or identified as his by the player within five minutes after the player's side or his or their caddies have begun to search for it; or

b. The player has put another ball into play under the Rules, even though he may not have searched for the original ball; or

c. The player has played any stroke with a provisional ball from the place where the original ball is likely to be or from a point nearer the hole than that place, whereupon the provisional ball becomes the ball in play.

Time spent in playing a wrong ball is not counted in the five-minute period allowed for search.

Marker
A 'marker' is one who is appointed by the Committee to record a competitor's score in stroke play. He may be a fellow-competitor. He is not a referee.

Matches
See 'Sides and Matches'.

Move or Moved
A ball is deemed to have 'moved' if it leaves its position and comes to rest in any other place.

Nearest Point of Relief
The 'nearest point of relief' is the reference point for taking relief without penalty from interference by an immovable obstruction (Rule 24-2), an abnormal ground condition (Rule 25-1) or a wrong putting green (Rule 25-3).

It is the point on the course, nearest to where the ball lies, which is not nearer the hole and at which, if the ball were so positioned, no interference (as defined) would exist.

Note: The player should determine his nearest point of relief by using the club with which he expects to play his next stroke to simulate the address position and swing for such stroke.

Observer
An 'observer' is one who is appointed by the Committee to assist a referee to decide questions of fact and to report to him any breach of a Rule. An observer should not attend the flagstick, stand at or mark the position of the hole, or lift the ball or mark its position.

Obstructions
An 'obstruction' is anything artificial, including the artificial surfaces and sides of roads and paths and manufactured ice, except:

a. Objects defining out of bounds, such as walls, fences, stakes and railings;
b. Any part of an immovable artificial object which is out of bounds; and
c. Any construction declared by the Committee to be an integral part of the course.

An obstruction is a movable obstruction if it may be moved without unreasonable effort, without unduly delaying play and without causing damage. Otherwise, it is an immovable obstruction.

Note: The Committee may make a Local Rule declaring a movable obstruction to be an immovable obstruction.

Out of Bounds
'Out of bounds' is beyond the boundaries of the course or any part of the course so marked by the Committee.

When out of bounds is defined by reference to stakes or a fence, or as being beyond stakes or a fence, the out of bounds line is determined by the nearest inside points of the stakes or fence posts at ground level excluding angled supports.

Objects defining out of bounds such as walls, fences, stakes and railings, are not obstructions and are deemed to be fixed.

When out of bounds is defined by a line on the ground, the line itself is out of bounds.

The out of bounds line extends vertically upwards and downwards.

A ball is out of bounds when all of it lies out of bounds.

A player may stand out of bounds to play a ball lying within bounds.

Outside Agency
An 'outside agency' is any agency not part of the match or, in stroke play, not part of the competitor's side, and includes a referee, a marker, an observer and a forecaddie. Neither wind nor water is an outside agency.

Partner
A 'partner' is a player associated with another player on the same side.

In a threesome, foursome, best-ball or four-ball match, where the context so admits, the word 'player' includes his partner or partners.

Penalty Stroke
A 'penalty stroke' is one added to the score of a player or side under certain Rules. In a threesome or foursome, penalty strokes do not affect the order of play.

Provisional Ball
A 'provisional ball' is a ball played under Rule 27-2 for a ball which may be lost outside a water hazard or may be out of bounds.

Putting Green
The 'putting green' is all ground of the hole being played which is specially prepared for putting or otherwise defined as such by the Committee. A ball is on the putting green when any part of it touches the putting green.

Referee
A 'referee' is one who is appointed by the Committee to accompany players to decide questions of fact and apply the Rules. He shall act on any breach of a Rule which he observes or is reported to him.

A referee should not attend the flagstick, stand at or mark the position of the hole, or lift the ball or mark its position.

Rub of the Green
A 'rub of the green' occurs when a ball in motion is accidentally deflected or stopped by any outside agency (see Rule 19-1).

Rule or Rules
The term 'Rule' includes:

a. The Rules of Golf;
b. Any Local Rules made by the Committee under Rule 33-8a and Appendix I; and
c. The specifications on clubs and the ball in Appendices II and III.

Sides and Matches
Side: A player, or two or more players who are partners.

Single: A match in which one plays against another.

Threesome: A match in which one plays against two, and each side plays one ball.

Foursome: A match in which two play against two, and each side plays one ball.

Three-ball: A match play competition in which three play against one another, each playing his own ball. Each player is playing two distinct matches.

Best-ball: A match in which one plays against the better ball of two or the best ball of three players.

Four-ball: A match in which two play their better ball against the better ball of the two other players.

Stance
Taking the 'stance' consists in a player placing his feet in position for and preparatory to making a stroke.

Stipulated Round
The 'stipulated round' consists of playing the holes of the course in their correct sequence unless otherwise authorised by the Committee. The number of holes in a stipulated round is 18 unless a smaller number is authorised by the Committee. As to extension of stipulated round in match play, see Rule 2-3.

Stroke
A 'stroke' is the forward movement of the club made with the intention of fairly striking at and moving the ball, but if a player checks his downswing voluntarily before the clubhead reaches the ball he is deemed not to have made a stroke.

Teeing Ground
The 'teeing ground' is the starting place for the hole to be played. It is a rectangular area two club-lengths in depth, the front and the sides of which are defined by the outside limits of two tee-markers. A ball is outside the teeing ground when all of it lies outside the teeing ground.

Through the Green
'Through the green' is the whole area of the course except:

a. The teeing ground and putting green of the hole being played; and
b. All hazards on the course.

Water Hazard
A 'water hazard' is any sea, lake, pond, river, ditch, surface drainage ditch or other open water course (whether or not containing water) and anything of a similar nature.

All ground or water within the margin of a water hazard is part of the water hazard. The margin of a water hazard extends vertically upwards and downwards. Stakes and lines defining the margins of water hazards are in the hazards. Such stakes are obstructions. A ball is in a water hazard when it lies in or any part of it touches the water hazard.

Note 1: Water hazards (other than lateral water hazards) should be defined by yellow stakes or lines.

Note 2: The Committee may make a Local Rule prohibiting play from an environmentally-sensitive area which has been defined as a water hazard.

Wrong Ball
A 'wrong ball' is any ball other than the player's:

a. Ball in play,
b. Provisional ball, or
c. Second ball played under Rule 3-3 or Rule 20-7b in stroke play.

Note: Ball in play includes a ball substituted for the ball in play whether or not such substitution is permitted.

Wrong Putting Green
A 'wrong putting green' is any putting green other than that of the hole being played. Unless otherwise prescribed by the Committee, this term includes a practice putting green or pitching green on the course.

SECTION III — THE RULES OF PLAY

THE GAME

Rule 1. The Game

1-1. General
The Game of Golf consists in playing a ball from the *teeing ground* into the *hole* by a *stroke* or successive strokes in accordance with the *Rules*.

1-2. Exerting Influence on Ball
No player or caddie shall take any action to influence the position or the movement of a ball except in accordance with the *Rules*.
(Removal of movable obstructions – see Rule 24-1.)
PENALTY FOR BREACH OF RULE 1-2:
Match play – Loss of hole;
Stroke play – Two strokes.
Note: In the case of a serious breach of Rule 1-2, the *Committee* may impose a penalty of disqualification.

1-3. Agreement to Waive Rules
Players shall not agree to exclude the operation of any *Rule* or to waive any penalty incurred.
PENALTY FOR BREACH OF RULE 1-3:
Match play – Disqualification of both sides;
Stroke play – Disqualification of competitors concerned.
(Agreeing to play out of turn in stroke play – see Rule 10-2c.)

1-4. Points Not Covered by Rules
If any point in dispute is not covered by the *Rules*, the decision shall be made in accordance with equity.

Rule 2. Match play

2-1. Winner of Hole; Reckoning of Holes
In match play the game is played by holes.
Except as otherwise provided in the *Rules*, a hole is won by the side which holes its ball in the fewer strokes. In a handicap match the lower net score wins the hole.
The reckoning of holes is kept by the terms: so many 'holes up' or 'all square', and so many 'to play'.
A side is 'dormie' when it is as many holes up as there are holes remaining to be played.

2-2. Halved Hole
A hole is halved if each side holes out in the same number of strokes.
When a player has holed out and his opponent has been left with a stroke for the half, if the player

thereafter incurs a penalty, the hole is halved.

2-3. Winner of Match
A match (which consists of a *stipulated round*, unless otherwise decreed by the *Committee*) is won by the side which is leading by a number of holes greater than the number of holes remaining to be played.
The Committee may, for the purpose of settling a tie, extend the stipulated round to as many holes as are required for a match to be won.

2-4. Concession of Next Stroke, Hole or Match
When the opponent's ball is at rest or is deemed to be at rest under Rule 16-2, the player may concede the opponent to have holed out with his next *stroke* and the ball may be removed by either side with a club or otherwise.
A player may concede a hole or a match at any time prior to the conclusion of the hole or the match.
Concession of a stroke, hole or match may not be declined or withdrawn.

2-5. Claims
In match play, if a doubt or dispute arises between the players and no duly authorised representative of the *Committee* is available within a reasonable time, the players shall continue the match without delay. Any claim, if it is to be considered by the Committee, must be made before any player in the match plays from the next *teeing ground* or, in the case of the last hole of the match, before all players in the match leave the *putting green*.
No later claim shall be considered unless it is based on facts previously unknown to the player making the claim and the player making the claim had been given wrong information (Rules 6-2a and 9) by an opponent. In any case, no later claim shall be considered after the result of the match has been officially announced, unless the Committee is satisfied that the opponent knew he was giving wrong information.

2-6. General Penalty
The penalty for a breach of a *Rule* in match play is loss of hole except when otherwise provided.

Rule 3. Stroke Play

3-1. Winner
The competitor who plays the *stipulated round* or rounds in the fewest strokes is the winner.

3-2. Failure to Hole Out
If a competitor fails to hole out at any hole and does not correct his mistake before he plays a *stroke* from

the next *teeing ground* or, in the case of the last hole of the round, before he leaves the *putting green*, he shall be disqualified.

3-3. Doubt as to Procedure
a. Procedure
In stroke play only, when during play of a hole a competitor is doubtful of his rights or procedure, he may, without penalty, play a second ball. After the situation which caused the doubt has arisen, the competitor should, before taking further action, announce to his *marker* or a *fellow-competitor* his decision to invoke this Rule and the ball with which he will score if the *Rules* permit.

The competitor shall report the facts to the *Committee* before returning his score card unless he scores the same with both balls; if he fails to do so, he shall be disqualified.

b. Determination of Score for Hole
If the *Rules* allow the procedure selected in advance by the competitor, the score with the ball selected shall be his score for the hole.

If the competitor fails to announce in advance his decision to invoke this Rule or his selection, the score with the original ball or, if the original ball is not one of the balls being played, the first ball put into play shall count if the Rules allow the procedure adopted for such ball.

Note 1: If a competitor plays a second ball, *penalty strokes* incurred solely by playing the ball ruled not to count and *strokes* subsequently taken with that ball shall be disregarded.

Note 2: A second ball played under Rule 3-3 is not a *provisional ball* under Rule 27-2.

3-4. Refusal to Comply with a Rule
If a competitor refuses to comply with a *Rule* affecting the rights of another competitor, he shall be disqualified.

3-5. General Penalty
The penalty for a breach of a *Rule* in stroke play is two strokes except when otherwise provided.

Rule 4. Clubs
A player in doubt as to the conformity of a club should consult the Royal and Ancient Golf Club of St. Andrews.

A manufacturer should submit to the Royal and Ancient Golf Club of St. Andrews a sample of a club which is to be manufactured for a ruling as to whether the club conforms with the *Rules*. If a man-

ufacturer fails to submit a sample before manufacturing and/or marketing the club, the manufacturer assumes the risk of a ruling that the club does not conform to the Rules. Any sample submitted to the Royal and Ancient Golf Club of St. Andrews will become its property for reference purposes.

4-1. Form and Make of Clubs
a. General
The player's clubs shall conform with this Rule and the provisions, specifications and interpretations set forth in Appendix II.

b. Wear and Alteration
A club which conforms with the *Rules* when new is deemed to conform after wear through normal use. Any part of a club which has been purposely altered is regarded as new and must, in its altered state, conform with the Rules.

4-2. Playing Characteristics Changed and Foreign Material
a. Playing Characteristics Changed
During a *stipulated round*, the playing characteristics of a club shall not be purposely changed by adjustment or by any other means.

b. Foreign Material
Foreign material must not be applied to the club face for the purpose of influencing the movement of the ball.

PENALTY FOR BREACH
OF RULE 4-1 or -2: Disqualification.

4-3. Damaged Clubs:
Repair and Replacement
a. Damage in Normal Course of Play
If, during a *stipulated round*, a player's club is damaged in the normal course of play, he may:
(i) use the club in its damaged state for the remainder of the *stipulated round*; or
(ii) without unduly delaying play, repair it or have it repaired; or
(iii) as an additional option available only if the club is unfit for play, replace the damaged club with any club. The replacement of a club must not unduly delay play and must not be made by borrowing any club selected for play by any other person playing on the *course*.

PENALTY FOR BREACH OF RULE 4-3a:
See Penalty Statement for Rule 4-4a or b.
Note: A club is unfit for play if it is substantially damaged, e.g. the shaft breaks into pieces or the clubhead becomes loose, detached or significantly deformed. A

club is not unfit for play solely because the shaft is bent, the club's lie or loft has been altered or the club-head is scratched.

b. Damage Other Than in Normal Course of Play
If, during a *stipulated round*, a player's club is damaged other than in the normal course of play rendering it non-conforming or changing its playing characteristics, the club shall not subsequently be used or replaced during the round.

c. Damage Prior to Round
A player may use a club damaged prior to a round provided the club, in its damaged state, conforms with the *Rules*.

Damage to a club which occurred prior to a round may be repaired during the round, provided the playing characteristics are not changed and play is not unduly delayed.

PENALTY FOR BREACH OF
RULE 4-3b or c: Disqualification.
(Undue delay – see Rule 6-7.)

4-4. Maximum of Fourteen Clubs
a. Selection and Addition of Clubs
The player shall start a *stipulated round* with not more than fourteen clubs. He is limited to the clubs thus selected for that round except that, if he started with fewer than fourteen clubs, he may add any number provided his total number does not exceed fourteen.

The addition of a club or clubs must not unduly delay play (Rule 6-7) and must not be made by borrowing any club selected for play by any other person playing on the course.

b. Partners May Share Clubs
Partners may share clubs, provided that the total number of clubs carried by the partners so sharing does not exceed fourteen.

PENALTY FOR BREACH OF
RULE 4-4a or b, *regardless of number of excess clubs carried*: Match play – At the conclusion of the hole at which the breach is discovered, the state of the match shall be adjusted by deducting one hole for each hole at which a breach occurred. Maximum deduction per round: two holes.
Stroke play – Two strokes for each hole at which any breach occurred; maximum penalty per round: four strokes.
Bogey and par competitions – Penalties as in match play.
Stableford competitions – see Note 1 to Rule 32-1b.

c. Excess Club Declared Out of Play
Any club carried or used in breach of this Rule shall be declared out of play by the player immediately upon discovery that a breach has occurred and thereafter shall not be used by the player during the round.

PENALTY FOR BREACH OF RULE 4-4c:
Disqualification.

Rule 5. The Ball

5-1. General
The ball the player uses shall conform to requirements specified in Appendix III.

Note: The *Committee* may require, in the conditions of a competition (Rule 33-1), that the ball the player uses must be named on the current List of Conforming Golf Balls issued by the Royal and Ancient Golf Club of St. Andrews.

5-2. Foreign Material
Foreign material must not be applied to a ball for the purpose of changing its playing characteristics.

PENALTY FOR BREACH OF
RULE 5-1 or 5-2: Disqualification.

5-3. Ball Unfit for Play
A ball is unfit for play if it is visibly cut, cracked or out of shape. A ball is not unfit for play solely because mud or other materials adhere to it, its surface is scratched or scraped or its paint is damaged or discoloured.

If a player has reason to believe his ball has become unfit for play during the play of the hole being played, he may during the play of such hole lift his ball without penalty to determine whether it is unfit.

Before lifting the ball, the player must announce his intention to his opponent in match play or his *marker* or a *fellow-competitor* in stroke play and mark the position of the ball. He may then lift and examine the ball without cleaning it and must give his opponent, marker or fellow-competitor an opportunity to examine the ball.

If he fails to comply with this procedure, he shall incur a penalty of one stroke.

If it is determined that the ball has become unfit for play during play of the hole being played, the player may substitute another ball, placing it on the spot where the original ball lay. Otherwise, the original ball shall be replaced.

If a ball breaks into pieces as a result of a *stroke*, the stroke shall be cancelled and the player shall play a ball without penalty as nearly as possible at the spot from which the original ball was played (see Rule 20-5).

*PENALTY FOR BREACH OF RULE 5-3:
Match play – Loss of hole;
Stroke play – Two strokes.
*If a player incurs the general penalty for breach of Rule5-3, no additional penalty under the Rule shall be applied.

Note: If the opponent, marker or fellow-competitor wishes to dispute a claim of unfitness, he must do so before the player plays another ball.
(Cleaning ball lifted from putting green or under any other Rule – see Rule 21.)

PLAYER'S RESPONSIBILITIES

Rule 6. The Player

Definition
A **marker** is one who is appointed by the *Committee* to record a *competitor's* score in stroke play. He may be a *fellow-competitor*. He is not a *referee*.

6-1. Rules; Conditions of Competition
The player is responsible for knowing the *Rules* and the conditions under which the competition is to be played (Rule 33-1).

6-2. Handicap
a. Match Play
Before starting a match in a handicap competition, the players should determine from one another their respective handicaps. If a player begins the match having declared a higher handicap which would affect the number of strokes given or received, he shall be disqualified; otherwise, the player shall play off the declared handicap.

b. Stroke Play
In any round of a handicap competition, the competitor shall ensure that his handicap is recorded on his score card before it is returned to the *Committee*. If no handicap is recorded on his score card before it is returned, or if the recorded handicap is higher than that to which he is entitled and this affects the number of strokes received, he shall be disqualified from the handicap competition; otherwise, the score shall stand.
   Note: It is the player's responsibility to know the holes at which handicap strokes are to be given or received.

6-3. Time of Starting and Groups
a. Time of Starting
The player shall start at the time laid down by the *Committee*.

b. Groups
In stroke play, the competitor shall remain throughout the round in the group arranged by the *Committee* unless the Committee authorises or ratifies a change.
   PENALTY FOR BREACH OF RULE 6-3:
   Disqualification.
   (Best-ball and four-ball play – see Rules 30-3a and 31-2.)

Note: The *Committee* may provide in the conditions of a competition (Rule 33-1) that, if the player arrives at his starting point, ready to play, within five minutes after his starting time, in the absence of circumstances which warrant waiving the penalty of disqualification as provided in Rule 33-7, the penalty for failure to start on time is loss of the first hole in match play or two strokes at the first hole in stroke play instead of disqualification.

6-4. Caddie
The player may have only one *caddie* at any one time, under penalty of disqualification.
   For any breach of a *Rule* by his caddie, the player incurs the applicable penalty.

6-5. Ball
The responsibility for playing the proper ball rests with the player. Each player should put an identification mark on his ball.

6-6. Scoring in Stroke Play
a. Recording Scores
After each hole the *marker* should check the score with the competitor and record it. On completion of the round the marker shall sign the card and hand it to the competitor. If more than one marker records the scores, each shall sign for the part for which he is responsible.

b. Signing and Returning Card
After completion of the round, the competitor should check his score for each hole and settle any doubtful points with the *Committee*. He shall ensure that the *marker* has signed the card, countersign the card himself and return it to the Committee as soon as possible.
   PENALTY FOR BREACH OF RULE 6-6b:
   Disqualification.

c. Alteration of Card
No alteration may be made on a card after the competitor has returned it to the *Committee*.

d. Wrong Score for Hole
The competitor is responsible for the correctness of the score recorded for each hole on his card. If he returns a score for any hole lower than actually taken, he shall be disqualified. If he returns a score for any hole higher than actually taken, the score as returned shall stand.
   Note 1: The *Committee* is responsible for the addition of scores and application of the handicap recorded on the card – see Rule 33-5.
   Note 2: In four-ball stroke play, see also Rule 31-4 and -7a.

6-7. Undue Delay; Slow Play
The player shall play without undue delay and in accordance with any pace of play guidelines which may be laid down by the *Committee*. Between completion of a hole and playing from the next *teeing ground*, the player shall not unduly delay play.
   PENALTY FOR BREACH OF RULE 6-7:
   Match play – Loss of hole;
   Stroke play – Two strokes.
   Bogey and par competitions – See Note 2
   to Rule 32-1a.
   Stableford competitions – See Note 2
   to Rule 32-1b.
   For subsequent offence – Disqualification.

Note 1: If the player unduly delays play between holes, he is delaying the play of the next hole and, except for bogey, par and Stableford competitions (see Rule 32), the penalty applies to that hole.

Note 2: For the purpose of preventing slow play, the *Committee* may, in the conditions of a competition (Rule 33-1), lay down pace of play guidelines including maximum periods of time allowed to complete a stipulated round, a hole or a stroke.

In stroke play only, the Committee may, in such a condition, modify the penalty for a breach of this Rule as follows:

First offence – One stroke;
Second offence – Two strokes.
For subsequent offence – Disqualification.

6-8. Discontinuance of Play; Resumption of Play
a. When Permitted
The player shall not discontinue play unless:

 (i) the *Committee* has suspended play;
 (ii) he believes there is danger from lightning;
 (iii) he is seeking a decision from the *Committee* on a doubtful or disputed point (see Rules 2-5 and 34-3); or
 (iv) there is some other good reason such as sudden illness.

Bad weather is not of itself a good reason for discontinuing play.

If the player discontinues play without specific permission from the *Committee*, he shall report to the Committee as soon as practicable. If he does so and the Committee considers his reason satisfactory, the player incurs no penalty. Otherwise, the player shall be disqualified.

Exception in match play: Players discontinuing match play by agreement are not subject to disqualification unless by so doing the competition is delayed.

Note: Leaving the course does not of itself constitute discontinuance of play.

b. Procedure When Play Suspended by Committee
When play is suspended by the *Committee*, if the players in a match or group are between the play of two holes, they shall not resume play until the Committee has ordered a resumption of play. If they are in the process of playing a hole, they may continue provided they do so without delay. If they choose to continue, they shall discontinue either before or immediately after completing the hole.

The players shall resume play when the Committee has ordered a resumption of play.

PENALTY FOR BREACH OF RULE 6-8b:
Disqualification.

Note: The *Committee* may provide in the conditions of a competition (Rule 33-1) that, in potentially dangerous situations, play shall be discontinued immediately following a suspension of play by the

Committee. If a player fails to discontinue play immediately, he shall be disqualified unless circumstances warrant waiving such penalty as provided in Rule 33-7.

c. Lifting Ball When Play Discontinued
When a player discontinues play of a hole under Rule 6-8a, he may lift his ball without penalty only if the *Committee* has suspended play or there is a good reason to lift it. Before lifting the ball the player must mark its position. If the player discontinues play and lifts his ball without specific permission from the Committee, when reporting to the Committee (Rule 6-8a), he shall, at that time, report the lifting of the ball.

If the player lifts the ball without a good reason to do so, fails to mark the position of the ball before lifting it or fails to report the lifting of the ball, he shall incur a penalty of one stroke.

d. Procedure When Play Resumed
Play shall be resumed from where it was discontinued, even if resumption occurs on a subsequent day. The player shall, either before or when play is resumed, proceed as follows:

 (i) if the player has lifted the ball, he shall, provided he was entitled to lift it under Rule 6-8c, place a ball on the spot from which the original ball was lifted. Otherwise, the original ball must be replaced;
 (ii) if the player entitled to lift his ball under Rule 6-8c has not done so, he may lift, clean and replace the ball, or substitute a ball on the spot from which the original ball was lifted. Before lifting the ball he must mark its position; or
 (iii) if the player's ball or ball-marker is moved (including by wind or water) while play is discontinued, a ball or ball-marker shall be placed on the spot from which the original ball or ball-marker was moved.

(Spot not determinable – see Rule 20-3c.)

*PENALTY FOR BREACH OF RULE 6-8d:
Match play – Loss of hole;
Stroke play – Two strokes.
*If a player incurs the general penalty for a breach of Rule 6-8d, no additional penalty under Rule 6-8c shall be applied.

Rule 7. Practice

Definition
The **course** is the whole area within which play is permitted (see Rule 33-2).

7-1. Before or Between Rounds
a. Match Play
On any day of a match play competition, a player may practise on the competition *course* before a round.

b. Stroke Play
On any day of a stroke competition or play-off, a competitor shall not practise on the competition *course* or test the surface of any *putting green* on the course before a round or play-off. When two or more rounds of a stroke competition are to be played over consecutive days, a competitor shall not practise between those rounds on any competition course remaining to be played, or test the surface of any putting green on such course.

Exception: Practice putting or chipping on or near the first *teeing ground* before starting a round or play-off is permitted.

PENALTY FOR BREACH OF RULE 7-1b:
Disqualification.

Note: The *Committee* may in the conditions of a competition (Rule 33-1) prohibit practice on the competition course on any day of a match play competition or permit practice on the competition course or part of the course (Rule 33-2c) on any day of or between rounds of a stroke competition.

7-2. During Round
A player shall not play a practice *stroke* either during the play of a hole or between the play of two holes except that, between the play of two holes, the player may practise putting or chipping on or near the *putting green* of the hole last played, any practice putting green or the *teeing ground* of the next hole to be played in the round, provided such practice stroke is not played from a hazard and does not unduly delay play (Rule 6-7).

Strokes played in continuing the play of a hole, the result of which has been decided, are not practice strokes.

Exception: When play has been suspended by the *Committee*, a player may, prior to resumption of play, practise (a) as provided in this Rule, (b) anywhere other than on the competition *course* and (c) as otherwise permitted by the Committee.

PENALTY FOR BREACH OF RULE 7-2:
Match play – Loss of hole;
Stroke play – Two strokes.

In the event of a breach between the play of two holes, the penalty applies to the next hole.

Note 1: A practice swing is not a practice *stroke* and may be taken at any place, provided the player does not breach the *Rules*.

Note 2: The *Committee* may prohibit practice on or near the *putting green* of the hole last played.

Rule 8. Advice;
Indicating Line of Play

Definitions
Advice is any counsel or suggestion which could influence a player in determining his play, the choice of a club or the method of making a *stroke*.

Information on the *Rules* or on matters of public information, such as the position of *hazards* or the *flagstick* on the *putting green*, is not advice.

The **line of play** is the direction which the player wishes his ball to take after a *stroke*, plus a reasonable distance on either side of the intended direction. The line of play extends vertically upwards from the ground, but does not extend beyond the *hole*.

8-1. Advice
During a *stipulated round*, a player shall not give *advice* to anyone in the competition except his partner and may ask for advice only from his partner or either of their caddies.

8-2. Indicating Line of Play
a. Other Than on Putting Green
Except on the *putting green*, a player may have the *line of play* indicated to him by anyone, but no one shall be positioned by the player on or close to the line or an extension of the line beyond the hole while the *stroke* is being played. Any mark placed during the play of a hole by the player or with his knowledge to indicate the line shall be removed before the stroke is played.

Exception: Flagstick attended or held up – see Rule 17-1.

b. On the Putting Green
When the player's ball is on the *putting green*, the player, his partner or either of their caddies may, before but not during the *stroke*, point out a line for putting, but in so doing the putting green shall not be touched. No mark shall be placed anywhere to indicate a line for putting.

PENALTY FOR BREACH OF RULE:
Match play – Loss of hole;
Stroke play – Two strokes.

Note: The *Committee* may, in the conditions of a team competition (Rule 33-1), permit each team to appoint one person who may give *advice* (including pointing out a line for putting) to members of that team. The Committee may lay down conditions relating to the appointment and permitted conduct of such person, who must be identified to the Committee before giving advice.

Rule 9. Information as to
Strokes Taken

9-1. General
The number of *strokes* a player has taken shall include any penalty strokes incurred.

9-2. Match Play
A player who has incurred a penalty shall inform his opponent as soon as practicable, unless he is obviously proceeding under a *Rule* involving a penalty and this has been observed by his opponent. If he fails so

to inform his opponent, he shall be deemed to have given wrong information, even if he was not aware that he had incurred a penalty.

An opponent is entitled to ascertain from the player, during the play of a hole, the number of strokes he has taken and, after play of a hole, the number of strokes taken on the hole just completed.

If during the play of a hole the player gives or is deemed to give wrong information as to the number of strokes taken, he shall incur no penalty if he corrects the mistake before his opponent has played his next stroke. If the player fails so to correct the wrong information, he shall lose the hole.

If after play of a hole the player gives or is deemed to give wrong information as to the number of strokes taken on the hole just completed and this affects the opponent's understanding of the result of the hole, he shall incur no penalty if he corrects his mistake before any player plays from the next *teeing ground* or, in the case of the last hole of the match, before all players leave the *putting green*. If the player fails so to correct the wrong information, he shall lose the hole.

9-3. Stroke Play

A competitor who has incurred a penalty should inform his *marker* as soon as practicable.

ORDER OF PLAY

Rule 10. Order of Play

Definition

The player who is to play first from the *teeing ground* is said to have the **honour**.

10-1. Match Play
a. Teeing Ground

The side which shall have the *honour* at the first *teeing ground* shall be determined by the order of the draw. In the absence of a draw, the honour should be decided by lot.

The side which wins a hole shall take the honour at the next teeing ground. If a hole has been halved, the side which had the honour at the previous teeing ground shall retain it.

b. Other Than on Teeing Ground

When the balls are *in play*, the ball farther from the hole shall be played first. If the balls are equidistant from the hole, the ball to be played first should be decided by lot.

Exception: Rule 30-3c (best-ball and four-ball match play).

c. Playing Out of Turn

If a player plays when his opponent should have played, the opponent may immediately require the player to cancel the stroke so played and, in correct order, play a ball without penalty as nearly as possible at the spot from which the original ball was last played (see Rule 20-5).

10-2. Stroke Play
a. Teeing Ground

The competitor who shall have the *honour* at the first *teeing ground* shall be determined by the order of the draw. In the absence of a draw, the honour should be decided by lot.

The competitor with the lowest score at a hole shall take the honour at the next teeing ground. The competitor with the second lowest score shall play next and so on. If two or more competitors have the same score at a hole, they shall play from the next teeing ground in the same order as at the previous teeing ground.

b. Other Than on Teeing Ground

When the balls are *in play*, the ball farthest from the hole shall be played first. If two or more balls are equidistant from the hole, the ball to be played first should be decided by lot.

Exceptions: Rules 22 (ball interfering with or assisting play) and 31-5 (four-ball stroke play).

c. Playing Out of Turn

If a competitor plays out of turn, no penalty is incurred and the ball shall be played as it lies. If, however, the *Committee* determines that competitors have agreed to play in an order other than that set forth in Clauses 2a, 2b and 3 of this Rule to give one of them an advantage, they shall be disqualified.

(Playing stroke while another ball in motion after stroke from putting green – see Rule 16-1f.)

(Incorrect order of play in threesomes and foursomes stroke play – see Rule 29-3.)

10-3. Provisional Ball or
Second Ball from Teeing Ground

If a player plays a *provisional ball* or a second ball from a *teeing ground*, he shall do so after his opponent or *fellow-competitor* has played his first *stroke*. If a player plays a provisional ball or a second ball out of turn, Clauses 1c and 2c of this Rule shall apply.

10-4. Ball Moved in Measuring

If a ball is moved in measuring to determine which ball is farther from the hole, no penalty is incurred and the ball shall be replaced.

TEEING GROUND

Rule 11. Teeing Ground

Definition

The **teeing ground** is the starting place for the hole to be played. It is a rectangular area two club-lengths in depth, the front and the sides of which are defined by the outside limits of two tee-markers. A ball is outside the teeing ground when all of it lies outside the teeing ground.

11-1. Teeing
In teeing, the ball may be placed on the ground, on an irregularity of surface created by the player on the ground or on a tee, sand or other substance in order to raise it off the ground.

A player may stand outside the *teeing ground* to play a ball within it.

11-2. Tee-Markers
Before a player plays his first *stroke* with any ball from the *teeing ground* of the hole being played, the tee-markers are deemed to be fixed. In such circumstances, if the player moves or allows to be moved a tee-marker for the purpose of avoiding interference with his stance, the area of his intended swing or his line of play, he shall incur the penalty for a breach of Rule 13-2.

11-3. Ball Falling Off Tee
If a ball, when not *in play*, falls off a tee or is knocked off a tee by the player in addressing it, it may be re-teed without penalty, but if a *stroke* is made at the ball in these circumstances, whether the ball is moving or not, the stroke counts but no penalty is incurred.

11-4. Playing from Outside Teeing Ground
a. Match Play
If a player, when starting a hole, plays a ball from outside the *teeing ground*, the opponent may immediately require the player to cancel the *stroke* so played and play a ball from within the teeing ground, without penalty.

b. Stroke Play
If a competitor, when starting a hole, plays a ball from outside the *teeing ground*, he shall incur a penalty of two strokes and shall then play a ball from within the teeing ground.

If the competitor plays a stroke from the next teeing ground without first correcting his mistake or, in the case of the last hole of the round, leaves the *putting green* without first declaring his intention to correct his mistake, he shall be disqualified.

The stroke from outside the teeing ground and any subsequent strokes by the competitor on the hole prior to his correction of the mistake do not count in his score.

11-5. Playing from Wrong Teeing Ground
The provisions of Rule 11-4 apply.

PLAYING THE BALL

Rule 12. Searching for and Identifying the Ball

Definitions
A **hazard** is any bunker or water hazard.
A **bunker** is a *hazard* consisting of a prepared area of ground, often a hollow, from which turf or soil has been removed and replaced with sand or the like. Grass-covered ground bordering or within a bunker is not part of the bunker. The margin of a bunker extends vertically downwards, but not upwards. A ball is in a bunker when it lies in or any part of it touches the bunker.

A **water hazard** is any sea, lake, pond, river, ditch, surface drainage ditch or other open water course (whether or not containing water) and anything of a similar nature.

All ground or water within the margin of a water hazard is part of the water hazard. The margin of a water hazard extends vertically upwards and downwards. Stakes and lines defining the margins of water hazards are in the hazards. Such stakes are *obstructions*. A ball is in a water hazard when it lies in or any part of it touches the water hazard.

Note 1: Water hazards (other than *lateral water hazards*) should be defined by yellow stakes or lines.

Note 2: The *Committee* may make a Local Rule prohibiting play from an environmentally-sensitive area which has been defined as a water hazard.

12-1. Searching for Ball; Seeing Ball
In searching for his ball anywhere on the *course*, the player may touch or bend long grass, rushes, bushes, whins, heather or the like, but only to the extent necessary to find and identify it, provided that this does not improve the lie of the ball, the area of his intended swing or his *line of play*.

A player is not necessarily entitled to see his ball when playing a *stroke*.

In a *hazard*, if a ball is believed to be covered by *loose impediments* or sand, the player may remove by probing, raking or other means as much thereof as will enable him to see a part of a ball. If an excess is removed, no penalty is incurred and the ball shall be re-covered so that only a part of the ball is visible. If the ball is moved in such removal, no penalty is incurred; the ball shall be replaced and, if necessary, re-covered. As to removal of loose impediments outside a hazard, see Rule 23.

If a ball lying in an *abnormal ground condition* is accidentally moved during search, no penalty is incurred; the ball shall be replaced, unless the player elects to proceed under Rule 25-1b. If the player replaces the ball, he may still proceed under Rule 25-1b if applicable.

If a ball is believed to be lying in water in a *water hazard*, the player may probe for it with a club or otherwise. If the ball is moved in so doing, no penalty is incurred; the ball shall be replaced, unless the player elects to proceed under Rule 26-1.

PENALTY FOR BREACH OF RULE 12-1:
      Match play – Loss of hole;
      Stroke play – Two strokes.

12-2. Identifying Ball
The responsibility for playing the proper ball rests with the player. Each player should put an identification mark on his ball.

Except in a *hazard*, the player may, without penalty, lift a ball he believes to be his own for the purpose of identification and clean it to the extent necessary for identification. If the ball is the player's ball, he shall replace it. Before lifting the ball, the player must announce his intention to his opponent in match play or his *marker* or a *fellow-competitor* in stroke play and mark the position of the ball. He must then give his opponent, marker or fellow-competitor an opportunity to observe the lifting and replacement. If he lifts his ball without announcing his intention in advance, marking the position of the ball or giving his opponent, marker or fellow-competitor an opportunity to observe, or if he lifts his ball for identification in a hazard, or cleans it more than necessary for identification, he shall incur a penalty of one stroke and the ball shall be replaced.

If a player who is required to replace a ball fails to do so, he shall incur the penalty for a breach of Rule 20-3a, but no additional penalty under Rule 12-2 shall be applied.

Rule 13. Ball Played as It Lies

Definitions
A **hazard** is any *bunker* or *water hazard*.

A **bunker** is a *hazard* consisting of a prepared area of ground, often a hollow, from which turf or soil has been removed and replaced with sand or the like. Grass-covered ground bordering or within a bunker is not part of the bunker. The margin of a bunker extends vertically downwards, but not upwards. A ball is in a bunker when it lies in or any part of it touches the bunker.

A **water hazard** is any sea, lake, pond, river, ditch, surface drainage ditch or other open water course (whether or not containing water) and anything of a similar nature.

All ground or water within the margin of a water hazard is part of the water hazard. The margin of a water hazard extends vertically upwards and downwards. Stakes and lines defining the margins of water hazards are in the hazards. Such stakes are *obstructions*. A ball is in a water hazard when it lies in or any part of it touches the water hazard.

Note 1: Water hazards (other than *lateral water hazards*) should be defined by yellow stakes or lines.

Note 2: The *Committee* may make a Local Rule prohibiting play from an environmentally-sensitive area which has been defined as a water hazard.

The **line of play** is the direction which the player wishes his ball to take after a *stroke*, plus a reasonable distance on either side of the intended direction. The line of play extends vertically upwards from the ground, but does not extend beyond the *hole*.

Taking the **stance** consists in a player placing his feet in position for and preparatory to making a *stroke*.

13-1. General
The ball shall be played as it lies, except as otherwise provided in the Rules. (Ball at rest moved – see Rule 18.)

13-2. Improving Lie, Area of Intended Stance or Swing, or Line of Play
Except as provided in the *Rules*, a player shall not improve or allow to be improved:

    the position or lie of his ball,

    the area of his intended stance or swing,

    his *line of play* or a reasonable extension of that line beyond the *hole,* or

    the area in which he is to drop or place a ball

by any of the following actions:

    moving, bending or breaking anything growing or fixed (including immovable *obstructions* and objects defining *out of bounds*),

    creating or eliminating irregularities of surface,

    removing or pressing down sand, loose soil, replaced divots or other cut turf placed in position, or

    removing dew, frost or water

except as follows:

    as may occur in fairly taking his *stance*,

    in making a *stroke* or the backward movement of his club for a stroke,

    on the *teeing ground* in creating or eliminating irregularities of surface, or

    on the *putting green* in removing sand and loose soil as provided in Rule 16-1a or in repairing damage as provided in Rule 16-1c.

The club may be grounded only lightly and shall not be pressed on the ground.

Exception: Ball in hazard – see Rule 13-4.

13-3. Building Stance
A player is entitled to place his feet firmly in taking his *stance*, but he shall not build a stance.

13-4. Ball in Hazard
Except as provided in the *Rules*, before making a *stroke* at a ball which is in a *hazard* (whether a *bunker* or a *water hazard*) or which, having been lifted from a hazard, may be dropped or placed in the hazard, the player shall not:

a. Test the condition of the hazard or any similar hazard,

b. Touch the ground in the hazard or water in the water hazard with a club or otherwise, or

c. Touch or move a *loose impediment* lying in or touching the hazard.

Exceptions:
1. Provided nothing is done which constitutes testing the condition of the hazard or improves the lie of the ball, there is no penalty if the player (a)

touches the ground in any hazard or water in a water hazard as a result of or to prevent falling, in removing an *obstruction,* in measuring or in retrieving, lifting, placing or replacing a ball under any Rule or (b) places his clubs in a hazard.

2. The player after playing the *stroke,* or his *caddie* at any time without the authority of the player, may smooth sand or soil in the hazard, provided that, if the ball is still in the hazard, nothing is done which improves the lie of the ball or assists the player in his subsequent play of the hole.

Note: At any time, including at address or in the backward movement for the *stroke,* the player may touch with a club or otherwise any *obstruction,* any construction declared by the *Committee* to be an integral part of the course or any grass, bush, tree or other growing thing.

PENALTY FOR BREACH OF RULE:
Match play – Loss of hole;
Stroke play – Two strokes.
(Searching for ball – see Rule 12-1.)

Rule 14. Striking the Ball

Definition
A **stroke** is the forward movement of the club made with the intention of fairly striking at and moving the ball, but if a player checks his downswing voluntarily before the clubhead reaches the ball he is deemed not to have made a stroke.

14-1. Ball to be Fairly Struck At
The ball shall be fairly struck at with the head of the club and must not be pushed, scraped or spooned.

14-2. Assistance
In making a *stroke,* a player shall not:

a. accept physical assistance or protection from the elements, or
b. allow his *caddie,* his partner or his partner's caddie to position himself on or close to an extension of the *line of play* or the *line of putt* behind the ball.

PENALTY FOR BREACH OF
RULE 14-1 or -2: Match play – Loss of hole;
Stroke play – Two strokes.

14-3. Artificial Devices and Unusual Equipment
A player in doubt as to whether use of an item would constitute a breach of Rule 14-3 should consult the Royal and Ancient Golf Club of St. Andrews.

A manufacturer may submit to the Royal and Ancient Golf Club of St. Andrews a sample of an item which is to be manufactured for a ruling as to whether its use during a *stipulated round* would cause a player to be in breach of Rule 14-3. Such sample will become the property of the Royal and Ancient Golf Club of St. Andrews for reference pur-

poses. If a manufacturer fails to submit a sample before manufacturing and/or marketing the item, he assumes the risk of a ruling that use of the item would be contrary to the *Rules.*

Except as provided in the Rules, during a stipulated round the player shall not use any artificial device or unusual equipment:

a. Which might assist him in making a *stroke* or in his play; or
b. For the purpose of gauging or measuring distance or conditions which might affect his play; or
c. Which might assist him in gripping the club, except that:
   (i) plain gloves may be worn;
   (ii) resin, powder and drying or moisturising agents may be used; and
   (iii) a towel or handkerchief may be wrapped around the grip.

PENALTY FOR BREACH OF RULE 14-3:
Disqualification.

14-4. Striking the Ball More Than Once
If a player's club strikes the ball more than once in the course of a *stroke,* the player shall count the stroke and add a penalty stroke, making two strokes in all.

14-5. Playing Moving Ball
A player shall not play while his ball is moving.

Exceptions:
Ball falling off tee – Rule 11-3.
Striking the ball more than once – Rule 14-4.
Ball moving in water – Rule 14-6.

When the ball begins to move only after the player has begun the *stroke* or the backward movement of his club for the stroke, he shall incur no penalty under this Rule for playing a moving ball, but he is not exempt from any penalty incurred under the following Rules:

Ball at rest moved by player – Rule 18-2a.
Ball at rest moving after address – Rule 18-2b.
Ball at rest moving after loose impediment touched – Rule 18-2c.

(Ball purposely deflected or stopped by player, partner or caddie – see Rule 1-2.)

14-6. Ball Moving in Water
When a ball is moving in water in a *water hazard,* the player may, without penalty, make a *stroke,* but he must not delay making his stroke in order to allow the wind or current to improve the position of the ball. A ball moving in water in a water hazard may be lifted if the player elects to invoke Rule 26.

PENALTY FOR BREACH OF
RULE 14-5 or -6: Match play – Loss of hole;
Stroke play – Two strokes.

Rule 15. Wrong Ball; Substituted Ball

Definition
A **wrong ball** is any ball other than the player's:

a. *Ball in play*,
b. *Provisional ball*, or
c. Second ball played under Rule 3-3 or Rule 20-7b in stroke play.

Note: Ball in play includes a ball substituted for the ball in play whether or not such substitution is permitted.

15-1. General

A player must hole out with the ball played from the *teeing ground* unless a *Rule* permits him to substitute another ball. If a player substitutes another ball when not so permitted, that ball is not a *wrong ball*; it becomes the *ball in play* and, if the error is not corrected as provided in Rule 20-6, the player shall incur a penalty of loss of hole in match play or two strokes in stroke play.
(Playing from wrong place – see Rule 20-7.)

15-2. Match Play

If a player plays a *stroke* with a *wrong ball* except in a *hazard*, he shall lose the hole.

If a player plays any strokes in a hazard with a wrong ball, there is no penalty. Strokes played in a hazard with a wrong ball do not count in the player's score. If the wrong ball belongs to another player, its owner shall place a ball on the spot from which the wrong ball was first played.

If the player and opponent exchange balls during the play of a hole, the first to play the wrong ball other than from a hazard shall lose the hole; when this cannot be determined, the hole shall be played out with the balls exchanged.

15-3. Stroke Play

If a competitor plays a *stroke* or strokes with a *wrong ball*, he shall incur a penalty of two strokes, unless the only stroke or strokes played with such ball were played when it was in a *hazard*, in which case no penalty is incurred.

The competitor must correct his mistake by playing the correct ball. If he fails to correct his mistake before he plays a stroke from the next *teeing ground* or, in the case of the last hole of the round, fails to declare his intention to correct his mistake before leaving the *putting green*, he shall be disqualified.

Strokes played by a competitor with a wrong ball do not count in his score.

If the wrong ball belongs to another competitor, its owner shall place a ball on the spot from which the wrong ball was first played.
(Lie of ball to be placed or replaced altered – see Rule 20-3b.)

THE PUTTING GREEN

Rule 16. The Putting Green

Definitions
The **putting green** is all ground of the hole being played which is specially prepared for putting or otherwise defined as such by the *Committee*. A ball is on the putting green when any part of it touches the putting green.

The **line of putt** is the line which the player wishes his ball to take after a *stroke* on the *putting green*. Except with respect to Rule 16-1e, the line of putt includes a reasonable distance on either side of the intended line. The line of putt does not extend beyond the *hole*.

A ball is **holed** when it is at rest within the circumference of the *hole* and all of it is below the level of the lip of the hole.

16-1. General
a. Touching Line of Putt
The *line of putt* must not be touched except:

(i)   the player may move sand and loose soil on the *putting green* and other *loose impediments* by picking them up or by brushing them aside with his hand or a club without pressing anything down;
(ii) in *addressing the ball*, the player may place the club in front of the ball without pressing anything down;
(iii) in measuring – Rule 10-4;
(iv) in lifting the ball – Rule 16-1b;
(v)   in pressing down a ball-marker;
(vi) in repairing old hole plugs or ball marks on the putting green – Rule 16-1c; and
(vii) in removing movable *obstructions* – Rule 24-1.

(Indicating line for putting on putting green – see Rule 8–2b.)

b. Lifting Ball
A ball on the *putting green* may be lifted and, if desired, cleaned. A ball so lifted shall be replaced on the spot from which it was lifted.

c. Repair of Hole Plugs, Ball Marks and Other Damage
The player may repair an old hole plug or damage to the *putting green* caused by the impact of a ball, whether or not the player's ball lies on the putting green. If a ball or ball-marker is accidentally moved in the process of such repair, the ball or ball-marker shall be replaced, without penalty. Any other damage to the putting green shall not be repaired if it might assist the player in his subsequent play of the hole.

d. Testing Surface
During the play of a hole, a player shall not test the surface of the *putting green* by rolling a ball or roughening or scraping the surface.

e. Standing Astride or on Line of Putt

The player shall not make a *stroke* on the *putting green* from a *stance* astride, or with either foot touching, the *line of putt* or an extension of that line behind the ball.

f. Playing Stroke While Another Ball in Motion

The player shall not play a *stroke* while another ball is in motion after a stroke from the *putting green*, except that, if a player does so, he incurs no penalty if it was his turn to play.

(Lifting ball interfering with or assisting play while another ball in motion – see Rule 22.)

PENALTY FOR BREACH OF RULE 16-1:
Match play – Loss of hole;
Stroke play – Two strokes.
(Position of caddie or partner – see Rule 14-2.)
(Wrong putting green – see Rule 25-3.)

16-2. Ball Overhanging Hole

When any part of the ball overhangs the lip of the *hole*, the player is allowed enough time to reach the hole without unreasonable delay and an additional ten seconds to determine whether the ball is at rest. If by then the ball has not fallen into the hole, it is deemed to be at rest. If the ball subsequently falls into the hole, the player is deemed to have holed out with his last stroke, and he shall add a penalty stroke to his score for the hole; otherwise there is no penalty under this Rule.

(Undue delay – see Rule 6-7.)

Rule 17. The Flagstick

Definition

The **flagstick** is a movable straight indicator, with or without bunting or other material attached, centred in the hole to show its position. It shall be circular in cross-section.

17-1. Flagstick Attended, Removed or Held Up

Before and during the *stroke*, the player may have the *flagstick* attended, removed or held up to indicate the position of the *hole*. This may be done only on the authority of the player before he plays his stroke.

If, prior to the stroke, the flagstick is attended, removed or held up by anyone with the player's knowledge and no objection is made, the player shall be deemed to have authorised it. If anyone attends or holds up the flagstick or stands near the hole while a stroke is being played, he shall be deemed to be attending the flagstick until the ball comes to rest.

17-2. Unauthorised Attendance

a. Match Play

In match play, an opponent or his *caddie* shall not, without the authority or prior knowledge of the play-

er, attend, remove or hold up the *flagstick* while the player is making a *stroke* or his ball is in motion.

b. Stroke Play

In stroke play, if a *fellow-competitor* or his *caddie* attends, removes or holds up the *flagstick* without the competitor's authority or prior knowledge while the competitor is making a *stroke* or his ball is in motion, the fellow-competitor shall incur the penalty for breach of this Rule. In such circumstances, if the competitor's ball strikes the flagstick, the person attending it or anything carried by him, the competitor incurs no penalty and the ball shall be played as it lies, except that, if the stroke was played from the *putting green*, the stroke shall be cancelled, the ball replaced and the stroke replayed.

PENALTY FOR BREACH OF
RULE 17-1 or -2: Match play – Loss of hole;
Stroke play – Two strokes.

17-3. Ball Striking Flagstick or Attendant

The player's ball shall not strike:

a. The *flagstick* when attended, removed or held up by the player, his *partner* or either of their *caddies*, or by another person with the player's authority or prior knowledge; or

b. The player's *caddie*, his partner or his partner's caddie when attending the *flagstick*, or another person attending the flagstick with the player's authority or prior knowledge or anything carried by any such person; or

c. The *flagstick* in the hole, unattended, when the ball has been played from the *putting green*.

PENALTY FOR BREACH OF RULE 17-3:
Match play – Loss of hole;
Stroke play – Two strokes,
and the ball shall be played as it lies.

17-4. Ball Resting Against Flagstick

If the ball rests against the *flagstick* when it is in the *hole*, the player or another person authorised by him may move or remove the flagstick and if the ball falls into the hole, the player shall be deemed to have holed out with his last stroke; otherwise the ball, if *moved*, shall be placed on the lip of the hole, without penalty.

BALL MOVED, DEFLECTED OR STOPPED

Rule 18. Ball at Rest Moved

Definitions

A ball is deemed to have **moved** if it leaves its position and comes to rest in any other place.

An **outside agency** is any agency not part of the match or, in stroke play, not part of the competitor's *side*, and includes a *referee*, a *marker*, an *observer* and a *forecaddie*. Neither wind nor water is an outside agency.

Equipment is anything used, worn or carried by or for the player except any ball he has played at the hole being played and any small object, such as a coin or a tee, when used to mark the position of a ball or the extent of an area in which a ball is to be dropped. Equipment includes a golf cart, whether or not motorised. If such a cart is shared by two or more players, the cart and everything in it are deemed to be the equipment of the player whose ball is involved except that, when the cart is being moved by one of the players sharing it, the cart and everything in it are deemed to be that player's equipment.

Note: A ball played at the hole being played is equipment when it has been lifted and not put back into play.

A player has **addressed the ball** when he has taken his *stance* and has also grounded his club, except that in a *hazard* a player has addressed the ball when he has taken his stance.

Taking the **stance** consists in a player placing his feet in position for and preparatory to making a *stroke*.

18-1. By Outside Agency
If a ball at rest is moved by an *outside agency*, the player shall incur no penalty and the ball shall be replaced before the player plays another *stroke*.

(Player's ball at rest moved by another ball – see Rule 18–5.)

18-2. By Player, Partner, Caddie or Equipment
a. General
When a player's ball is *in play*, if:

(i) the player, his *partner* or either of their *caddies* lifts or *moves* it, touches it purposely (except with a club in the act of addressing it) or causes it to *move* except as permitted by a *Rule*, or

(ii) *equipment* of the player or his *partner* causes the ball to *move*,

the player shall incur a penalty stroke. The ball shall be replaced unless the movement of the ball occurs after the player has begun his swing and he does not discontinue his swing.

Under the *Rules* no penalty is incurred if a player accidentally causes his ball to move in the following circumstances:

In measuring to determine which ball farther from hole – Rule 10-4
In searching for covered ball in *hazard* or for ball in an *abnormal ground condition* – Rule 12-1
In the process of repairing hole plug or ball mark – Rule 16-1c
In the process of removing *loose impediment* on *putting green* – Rule 18-2c
In the process of lifting ball under a Rule – Rule 20-1
In the process of placing or replacing ball under a Rule – Rule 20-3a
In removal of movable *obstruction* – Rule 24-1.

b. Ball Moving After Address
If a player's *ball in play moves* after he has *addressed* it (other than as a result of a *stroke*), the player shall be deemed to have moved the ball and shall incur a penalty stroke. The player shall replace the ball unless the movement of the ball occurs after he has begun his swing and he does not discontinue his swing.

c. Ball Moving After Loose Impediment Touched
Through the green, if the ball *moves* after any *loose impediment*, lying within a club-length of it has been touched by the player, his *partner* or either of their *caddies* and before the player has *addressed* it, the player shall be deemed to have moved the ball and shall incur a penalty stroke. The player shall replace the ball unless the movement of the ball occurs after he has begun his swing and he does not discontinue his swing.

On the *putting green*, if the ball or the ball-marker moves in the process of removing any loose impediment, the ball or the ball-marker shall be replaced. There is no penalty provided the movement of the ball or the ball-marker is directly attributable to the removal of the loose impediment. Otherwise, the player shall incur a penalty stroke under Rule 18-2a or 20-1.

18-3. By Opponent, Caddie or Equipment in Match Play
a. During Search
If, during search for a player's ball, the ball is *moved* by an opponent, his *caddie* or his *equipment*, no penalty is incurred and the player shall replace the ball.

b. Other Than During Search
If, other than during search for a ball, the ball is touched or *moved* by an opponent, his *caddie* or his *equipment*, except as otherwise provided in the *Rules*, the opponent shall incur a penalty stroke. The player shall replace the ball.

(Ball moved in measuring to determine which ball farther from the hole – see Rule 10-4.)
(Playing a wrong ball – see Rule 15-2.)

18-4. By Fellow-Competitor, Caddie or Equipment in Stroke Play
If a competitor's ball is *moved* by a *fellow-competitor*, his *caddie* or his *equipment*, no penalty is incurred. The competitor shall replace his ball.
(Playing a wrong ball – see Rule 15-3.)

18-5. By Another Ball
If a *ball in play* and at rest is *moved* by another ball in motion after a *stroke*, the moved ball shall be replaced.

*PENALTY FOR BREACH OF RULE:
Match play – Loss of hole;
Stroke play – Two strokes.

*If a player who is required to replace a ball fails to do so, he shall incur the general penalty for breach of Rule 18 but no additional penalty under Rule 18 shall be applied.

Note 1: If a ball to be replaced under this Rule is not immediately recoverable, another ball may be substituted.

Note 2: If it is impossible to determine the spot on which a ball is to be placed, see Rule 20-3c.

Rule 19. Ball in Motion Deflected or Stopped

Definitions

An **outside agency** is any agency not part of the match or, in stroke play, not part of the competitor's side, and includes a *referee*, a *marker*, an *observer* and a *forecaddie*. Neither wind nor water is an outside agency.

Equipment is anything used, worn or carried by or for the player except any ball he has played at the hole being played and any small object, such as a coin or a tee, when used to mark the position of a ball or the extent of an area in which a ball is to be dropped. Equipment includes a golf cart, whether or not motorised. If such a cart is shared by two or more players, the cart and everything in it are deemed to be the equipment of the player whose ball is involved except that, when the cart is being moved by one of the players sharing it, the cart and everything in it are deemed to be that player's equipment.

Note: A ball played at the hole being played is equipment when it has been lifted and not put back into play.

19-1. By Outside Agency

If a ball in motion is accidentally deflected or stopped by any *outside agency*, it is a *rub of the green*, no penalty is incurred and the ball shall be played as it lies except:

a. If a ball in motion after a *stroke* other than on the *putting green* comes to rest in or on any moving or animate *outside agency*, the player shall, *through the green* or in a *hazard,* drop the ball, or on the putting green place the ball, as near as possible to the spot where the outside agency was when the ball came to rest in or on it, and

b. If a ball in motion after a *stroke* on the *putting green* is deflected or stopped by, or comes to rest in or on, any moving or animate *outside agency* except a worm or an insect, the stroke shall be cancelled, the ball replaced and the stroke replayed.

If the ball is not immediately recoverable, another ball may be substituted.

(Player's ball deflected or stopped by another ball – see Rule 19-5.)

Note: If the *referee* or the *Committee* determines that a player's ball has been purposely deflected or

stopped by an *outside agency*, Rule 1-4 applies to the player. If the outside agency is a *fellow-competitor* or his *caddie*, Rule 1-2 applies to the fellow-competitor.

19-2. By Player, Partner, Caddie or Equipment
a. Match Play

If a player's ball is accidentally deflected or stopped by himself, his *partner* or either of their *caddies* or *equipment,* he shall lose the hole.

b. Stroke Play

If a competitor's ball is accidentally deflected or stopped by himself, his *partner* or either of their *caddies* or *equipment,* the competitor shall incur a penalty of two strokes. The ball shall be played as it lies, except when it comes to rest in or on the competitor's, his partner's or either of their caddies' clothes or equipment, in which case the competitor shall *through the green* or in a *hazard* drop the ball, or on the *putting green* place the ball, as near as possible to where the article was when the ball came to rest in or on it.

Exception: Dropped ball – see Rule 20-2a.

(Ball purposely deflected or stopped by player, partner or caddie – see Rule 1-2.)

19-3. By Opponent, Caddie or Equipment in Match Play

If a player's ball is accidentally deflected or stopped by an opponent, his *caddie* or his *equipment,* no penalty is incurred. The player may play the ball as it lies or, before another *stroke* is played by either side, cancel the stroke and play a ball without penalty as nearly as possible at the spot from which the original ball was last played (see Rule 20-5).

If the ball has come to rest in or on the opponent's or his caddie's clothes or equipment, the player may *through the green* or in a *hazard* drop the ball, or on the *putting green* place the ball, as near as possible to where the article was when the ball came to rest in or on it.

Exception: Ball striking person attending flagstick – see Rule 17-3b.

(Ball purposely deflected or stopped by opponent or caddie – see Rule 1-2.)

19-4. By Fellow-Competitor, Caddie or Equipment in Stroke Play

See Rule 19-1 regarding ball deflected by *outside agency.*

19-5. By Another Ball
a. At Rest

If a player's ball in motion after a *stroke* is deflected or stopped by a *ball in play* and at rest, the player shall play his ball as it lies.

In match play, no penalty is incurred. In stroke play, there is no penalty unless both balls lay on the *putting green* prior to the stroke, in which case the player incurs a penalty of two strokes.

b. In Motion
If a player's ball in motion after a *stroke* is deflected or stopped by another ball in motion after a stroke, the player shall play his ball as it lies. There is no penalty unless the player was in breach of Rule 16-1f, in which case he shall incur the penalty for breach of that Rule.

Exception: If the player's ball is in motion after a *stroke* on the *putting green* and the other ball in motion is an *outside agency* – see Rule 19-1b.

PENALTY FOR BREACH OF RULE:
Match play – Loss of hole;
Stroke play – Two strokes.

RELIEF SITUATIONS AND PROCEDURE

Rule 20. Lifting, Dropping and Placing; Playing from Wrong Place

20-1. Lifting and Marking
A ball to be lifted under the *Rules* may be lifted by the player, his partner or another person authorised by the player. In any such case, the player shall be responsible for any breach of the Rules.

The position of the ball shall be marked before it is lifted under a Rule which requires it to be replaced. If it is not marked, the player shall incur a penalty of one stroke and the ball shall be replaced. If it is not replaced, the player shall incur the general penalty for breach of this Rule but no additional penalty under Rule 20-1 shall be applied.

If a ball or ball-marker is accidentally moved in the process of lifting the ball under a Rule or marking its position, the ball or the ball-marker shall be replaced. There is no penalty provided the movement of the ball or the ball-marker is directly attributable to the specific act of marking the position of or lifting the ball. Otherwise, the player shall incur a penalty stroke under this Rule or Rule 18-2a.

Exception: If a player incurs a penalty for failing to act in accordance with Rule 5-3 or 12-2, no additional penalty under Rule 20-1 shall be applied.

Note: The position of a ball to be lifted should be marked by placing a ball-marker, a small coin or other similar object immediately behind the ball. If the ball-marker interferes with the play, *stance* or *stroke* of another player, it should be placed one or more clubhead-lengths to one side.

20-2. Dropping and Re-Dropping
a. By Whom and How
A ball to be dropped under the *Rules* shall be dropped by the player himself. He shall stand erect, hold the ball at shoulder height and arm's length and drop it. If a ball is dropped by any other person or in any other manner and the error is not corrected as provided in Rule 20-6, the player shall incur a penalty stroke.

If the ball touches the player, his partner, either of their *caddies* or their *equipment* before or after it strikes a part of the *course*, the ball shall be re-dropped, without penalty. There is no limit to the number of times a ball shall be re-dropped in such circumstances.
(Taking action to influence position or movement of ball – see Rule 1-2.)

b. Where to Drop
When a ball is to be dropped as near as possible to a specific spot, it shall be dropped not nearer the hole than the specific spot which, if it is not precisely known to the player, shall be estimated.

A ball when dropped must first strike a part of the *course* where the applicable *Rule* requires it to be dropped. If it is not so dropped, Rules 20-6 and -7 apply.

c. When to Re-Drop
A dropped ball shall be re-dropped without penalty if it:

(i) rolls into and comes to rest in a *hazard*;
(ii) rolls out of and comes to rest outside a *hazard*;
(iii) rolls onto and comes to rest on a *putting green*;
(iv) rolls and comes to rest *out of bounds*;
(v) rolls to and comes to rest in a position where there is interference by the condition from which relief was taken under Rule 24-2b (immovable obstruction), Rule 25-1 (abnormal ground conditions), Rule 25-3 (wrong putting green) or a Local Rule (Rule 33-8a) or rolls back into the pitch-mark from which it was lifted under Rule 25-2 (embedded ball);
(vi) rolls and comes to rest more than two club-lengths from where it first struck a part of the course; or
(vii) rolls and comes to rest nearer the hole than:
    (a) its original position or estimated position (see Rule 20-2b) unless otherwise permitted by the *Rules*; or
    (b) the nearest point of relief or maximum available relief (Rule 24-2, 25-1 or 25-3); or
    (c) the point where the original ball last crossed the margin of the *water hazard* or *lateral water hazard* (Rule 26-1).

If the ball when re-dropped rolls into any position listed above, it shall be placed as near as possible to the spot where it first struck a part of the course when re-dropped.

If a ball to be re-dropped or placed under this Rule is not immediately recoverable, another ball may be substituted.

Note: If a ball when dropped or re-dropped comes to rest and subsequently *moves*, the ball shall be played as it lies, unless the provisions of any other *Rule* apply.

20-3. Placing and Replacing

a. By Whom and Where

A ball to be placed under the *Rules* shall be placed by the player or his partner. If a ball is to be replaced, the player, his partner or the person who lifted or moved it shall place it on the spot from which it was lifted or moved. In any such case, the player shall be responsible for any breach of the Rules.

If a ball or ball-marker is accidentally *moved* in the process of placing or replacing the ball, the ball or the ball-marker shall be replaced. There is no penalty provided the movement of the ball or the ball-marker is directly attributable to the specific act of placing or replacing the ball or removing the ball-marker. Otherwise, the player shall incur a penalty stroke under Rule 18-2a or 20-1.

b. Lie of Ball to be Placed or Replaced Altered

If the original lie of a ball to be placed or replaced has been altered:

(i) except in a *hazard*, the ball shall be placed in the nearest lie most similar to the original lie which is not more than one club-length from the original lie, not nearer the hole and not in a hazard;

(ii) in a *water hazard*, the ball shall be placed in accordance with Clause (i) above, except that the ball must be placed in the water hazard;

(iii) in a *bunker,* the original lie shall be recreated as nearly as possible and the ball shall be placed in that lie.

c. Spot Not Determinable

If it is impossible to determine the spot where the ball is to be placed or replaced:

(i) *through the green*, the ball shall be dropped as near as possible to the place where it lay but not in a *hazard* or on a *putting green*;

(ii) in a *hazard*, the ball shall be dropped in the hazard as near as possible to the place where it lay;

(iii) on the *putting green*, the ball shall be placed as near as possible to the place where it lay but not in a *hazard*.

d. Ball Fails to Come to Rest on Spot

If a ball when placed fails to come to rest on the spot on which it was placed, it shall be replaced without penalty. If it still fails to come to rest on that spot:

(i) except in a *hazard,* it shall be placed at the nearest spot where it can be placed at rest which is not nearer the hole and not in a hazard;

(ii) in a hazard, it shall be placed in the hazard at the nearest spot where it can be placed at rest which is not nearer the hole.

If a ball when placed comes to rest on the spot on which it is placed, and it subsequently *moves*, there is no penalty and the ball shall be played as it lies, unless the provisions of any other *Rule* apply.

PENALTY FOR BREACH OF RULE 20-1,
-2 or -3: Match play – Loss of hole;
    Stroke play – Two strokes.

20-4. When Ball Dropped or Placed Is in Play

If the player's *ball in play* has been lifted, it is again in play when dropped or placed.

A substituted ball becomes the ball in play when it has been dropped or placed.

(Ball incorrectly substituted – see Rule 15-1.)

(Lifting ball incorrectly substituted, dropped or placed – see Rule 20-6.)

20-5.   Playing Next Stroke from Where Previous Stroke Played

When, under the *Rules*, a player elects or is required to play his next *stroke* from where a previous stroke was played, he shall proceed as follows: if the stroke is to be played from the *teeing ground*, the ball to be played shall be played from anywhere within the teeing ground and may be teed; if the stroke is to be played from *through the green* or a *hazard,* it shall be dropped; if the stroke is to be played on the *putting green*, it shall be placed.

PENALTY FOR BREACH OF RULE 20-5: Match
    play – Loss of hole;
    Stroke play – Two strokes.

20-6. Lifting Ball Incorrectly Substituted, Dropped or Placed

A ball incorrectly substituted, dropped or placed in a wrong place or otherwise not in accordance with the *Rules* but not played may be lifted, without penalty, and the player shall then proceed correctly.

20-7. Playing from Wrong Place

For a ball played from outside the *teeing ground* or from a wrong teeing ground – see Rule 11-4 and -5.

a. Match Play

If a player plays a *stroke* with a ball which has been dropped or placed in a wrong place, he shall lose the hole.

b. Stroke Play

If a competitor plays a *stroke* with his *ball in play* (i) which has been dropped or placed in a wrong place or (ii) which has been *moved* and not replaced in a case where the *Rules* require replacement, he shall, provided a serious breach has not occurred, incur the penalty prescribed by the applicable Rule and play out the hole with the ball.

If, after playing from a wrong place, a competitor becomes aware of that fact and believes that a serious breach may be involved, he may, provided he has not played a stroke from the next *teeing ground* or, in the case of the last hole of the round, left the *putting green*, declare that he will play out the hole with a second ball dropped or placed in accordance with the Rules. The competitor shall report the facts to the *Committee* before returning his score card; if he fails

to do so, he shall be disqualified. The Committee shall determine whether a serious breach of the Rule occurred. If so, the score with the second ball shall count and the competitor shall add two penalty strokes to his score with that ball.

If a serious breach has occurred and the competitor has failed to correct it as prescribed above, he shall be disqualified.

Note: If a competitor plays a second ball, *penalty strokes* incurred solely by playing the ball ruled not to count and *strokes* subsequently taken with that ball shall be disregarded.

Rule 21. Cleaning Ball

A ball on the *putting green* may be cleaned when lifted under Rule 16-1b. Elsewhere, a ball may be cleaned when lifted except when it has been lifted:

a. To determine if it is unfit for play (Rule 5-3);
b. For identification (Rule 12-2), in which case it may be cleaned only to the extent necessary for identification; or
c. Because it is interfering with or assisting play (Rule 22).

If a player cleans his ball during play of a hole except as provided in this Rule, he shall incur a penalty of one stroke and the ball, if lifted, shall be replaced.

If a player who is required to replace a ball fails to do so, he shall incur the penalty for breach of Rule 20-3a, but no additional penalty under Rule 21 shall be applied.

Exception: If a player incurs a penalty for failing to act in accordance with Rule 5-3, 12-2 or 22, no additional penalty under Rule 21 shall be applied.

Rule 22. Ball Interfering With or Assisting Play

Any player may:
a. Lift his ball if he considers that the ball might assist any other player or
b. Have any other ball lifted if he considers that the ball might interfere with his play or assist the play of any other player,

but this may not be done while another ball is in motion. In stroke play, a player required to lift his ball may play first rather than lift. A ball lifted under this Rule shall be replaced.

PENALTY FOR BREACH OF RULE:
Match play – Loss of hole;
Stroke play – Two strokes.

Note: Except on the *putting green*, the ball may not be cleaned when lifted under this Rule – see Rule 21.

Rule 23. Loose Impediments

Definition
Loose impediments are natural objects such as stones, leaves, twigs, branches and the like, dung, worms and insects and casts or heaps made by them, provided they are not fixed or growing, are not solidly embedded and do not adhere to the ball.

Sand and loose soil are loose impediments on the *putting green* but not elsewhere.

Snow and natural ice, other than frost, are either *casual water* or loose impediments, at the option of the player. Manufactured ice is an *obstruction*.

Dew and frost are not loose impediments.

23-1. Relief
Except when both the *loose impediment* and the ball lie in or touch the same *hazard,* any loose impediment may be removed without penalty. If the ball *moves*, see Rule 18-2c.

When a ball is in motion, a loose impediment which might influence the movement of the ball shall not be removed.

PENALTY FOR BREACH OF RULE:
Match play – Loss of hole;
Stroke play – Two strokes.

(Searching for ball in hazard – see Rule 12-1.)
(Touching line of putt – see Rule 16-1a.)

Rule 24. Obstructions

Definitions
The **nearest point of relief** is the reference point for taking relief without penalty from interference by an immovable *obstruction* (Rule 24-2), an *abnormal ground condition* (Rule 25-1) or a *wrong putting green* (Rule 25-3).

It is the point on the *course,* nearest to where the ball lies, which is not nearer the hole and at which, if the ball were so positioned, no interference (as defined) would exist.

Note: The player should determine his nearest point of relief by using the club with which he expects to play his next stroke to simulate the address position and swing for such stroke.

An **obstruction** is anything artificial, including the artificial surfaces and sides of roads and paths and manufactured ice, except:

a. Objects defining *out of bounds*, such as walls, fences, stakes and railings;
b. Any part of an immovable artificial object which is *out of bounds*; and
c. Any construction declared by the *Committee* to be an integral part of the course.

An obstruction is a movable obstruction if it may be moved without unreasonable effort, without unduly delaying play and without causing damage. Otherwise, it is an immovable obstruction.

Note: The *Committee* may make a Local Rule declaring a movable obstruction to be an immovable obstruction.

24-1. Movable Obstruction

A player may obtain relief from a movable *obstruction* as follows:

a. If the ball does not lie in or on the *obstruction*, the obstruction may be removed. If the ball *moves*, it shall be replaced, and there is no penalty provided that the movement of the ball is directly attributable to the removal of the obstruction. Otherwise, Rule 18-2a applies.

b. If the ball lies in or on the *obstruction*, the ball may be lifted, without penalty, and the obstruction removed. The ball shall *through the green* or in a *hazard* be dropped, or on the *putting green* be placed, as near as possible to the spot directly under the place where the ball lay in or on the obstruction, but not nearer the hole.

The ball may be cleaned when lifted under Rule 24-1.

When a ball is in motion, an obstruction which might influence the movement of the ball, other than an attended *flagstick* or *equipment* of the players, shall not be removed.

(Exerting influence on the ball – see Rule 1-2.)

Note: If a ball to be dropped or placed under this Rule is not immediately recoverable, another ball may be substituted.

24-2. Immovable Obstruction
a. Interference

Interference by an immovable *obstruction* occurs when a ball lies in or on the *obstruction*, or so close to the obstruction that the obstruction interferes with the player's *stance* or the area of his intended swing. If the player's ball lies on the *putting green*, interference also occurs if an immovable obstruction on the putting green intervenes on his *line of putt*. Otherwise, intervention on the *line of play* is not, of itself, interference under this Rule.

b. Relief

Except when the ball is in a *water hazard* or a *lateral water hazard*, a player may obtain relief from interference by an immovable *obstruction*, without penalty, as follows:

(i) **Through the Green:** If the ball lies *through the green*, the *nearest point of relief* shall be determined which is not in a *hazard* or on a *putting green*. The player shall lift the ball and drop it within one club-length of and not nearer the hole than the nearest point of relief, on a part of the *course* which avoids interference (as defined) by the immovable *obstruction* and is not in a hazard or on a putting green.

(ii) **In a Bunker:** If the ball is in a *bunker,* the player shall lift and drop the ball in accordance with Clause (i) above, except that the *nearest point of relief* must be in the bunker and the ball must be dropped in the bunker.

(iii) **On the Putting Green:** If the ball lies on the *putting green,* the player shall lift the ball and place it at the nearest *point of relief* which is not in a *hazard*. The nearest point of relief may be off the putting green.

The ball may be cleaned when lifted under Rule 24-2b.

(Ball rolling to a position where there is interference by the condition from which relief was taken – see Rule 20-2c(v).)

Exception: A player may not obtain relief under Rule 24–2b if (a) it is clearly unreasonable for him to play a stroke because of interference by anything other than an immovable *obstruction* or (b) interference by an immovable obstruction would occur only through use of an unnecessarily abnormal *stance*, swing or direction of play.

Note 1: If a ball is in a *water hazard* (including a *lateral water hazard*), the player is not entitled to relief without penalty from interference by an immovable *obstruction*. The player shall play the ball as it lies or proceed under Rule 26-1.

Note 2: If a ball to be dropped or placed under this Rule is not immediately recoverable, another ball may be substituted.

Note 3: The *Committee* may make a Local Rule stating that the player must determine the *nearest point of relief* without crossing over, through or under the *obstruction*.

c. Ball Lost

It is a question of fact whether a ball lost after having been struck toward an immovable *obstruction* is lost in the obstruction. In order to treat the ball as lost in the obstruction, there must be reasonable evidence to that effect. In the absence of such evidence, the ball must be treated as a *lost ball* and Rule 27 applies.

If a ball is lost in an immovable obstruction, the spot where the ball last entered the obstruction shall be determined and, for the purpose of applying this Rule, the ball shall be deemed to lie at this spot.

(i) **Through the Green:** If the ball last entered the immovable *obstruction* at a spot *through the green*, the player may substitute another ball without penalty and take relief as prescribed in Rule 24-2b(i).

(ii) **In a Bunker:** If the ball last entered the immovable *obstruction* at a spot in a *bunker*, the player may substitute another ball without penalty and take relief as prescribed in Rule 24-2b(ii).

(iii) **In a Water Hazard (including a Lateral Water Hazard):** If the ball last entered the immovable *obstruction* at a spot in a *water hazard*, the player is not entitled to relief without penalty. The player shall proceed under Rule 26-1.

(iv) **On the Putting Green:** If the ball last entered the immovable *obstruction* at a spot on the

putting green, the player may substitute another ball without penalty and take relief as prescribed in Rule 24-2b(iii).

PENALTY FOR BREACH OF RULE:
Match play – Loss of hole;
Stroke play – Two strokes.

Rule 25. Abnormal Ground Conditions, Embedded Ball and Wrong Putting Green

Definitions

An **abnormal ground condition** is any *casual water*, *ground under repair* or hole, cast or runway on the *course* made by a *burrowing animal*, a reptile or a bird.

A **burrowing animal** is an animal that makes a hole for habitation or shelter, such as a rabbit, mole, ground hog, gopher or salamander.

Note: A hole made by a non-burrowing animal, such as a dog, is not an *abnormal ground condition* unless marked or declared as *ground under repair*.

Casual water is any temporary accumulation of water on the *course* which is visible before or after the player takes his *stance* and is not in a *water hazard*. Snow and natural ice, other than frost, are either casual water or *loose impediments*, at the option of the player. Manufactured ice is an *obstruction*. Dew and frost are not casual water. A ball is in casual water when it lies in or any part of it touches the casual water.

Ground under repair is any part of the *course* so marked by order of the *Committee* or so declared by its authorised representative. It includes material piled for removal and a hole made by a greenkeeper, even if not so marked.

All ground and any grass, bush, tree or other growing thing within the ground under repair is part of the ground under repair. The margin of ground under repair extends vertically downwards, but not upwards. Stakes and lines defining ground under repair are in such ground. Such stakes are *obstructions*. A ball is in ground under repair when it lies in or any part of it touches the ground under repair.

Note 1: Grass cuttings and other material left on the *course* which have been abandoned and are not intended to be removed are not ground under repair unless so marked.

Note 2: The *Committee* may make a Local Rule prohibiting play from ground under repair or an environmentally-sensitive area which has been defined as ground under repair.

The **nearest point of relief** is the reference point for taking relief without penalty from interference by an immovable *obstruction* (Rule 24-2), an *abnormal ground condition* (Rule 25-1) or a *wrong putting green* (Rule 25-3).

It is the point on the *course*, nearest to where the ball lies, which is not nearer the hole and at which,

if the ball were so positioned, no interference (as defined) would exist.

Note: The player should determine his nearest point of relief by using the club with which he expects to play his next stroke to simulate the address position and swing for such stroke.

A **wrong putting green** is any *putting green* other than that of the hole being played. Unless otherwise prescribed by the *Committee*, this term includes a practice putting green or pitching green on the *course*.

25-1. Abnormal Ground Conditions
a. Interference

Interference by an *abnormal ground condition* occurs when a ball lies in or touches the condition or when such a condition interferes with the player's *stance* or the area of his intended swing. If the player's ball lies on the *putting green*, interference also occurs if such condition on the putting green intervenes on his *line of putt*. Otherwise, intervention on the *line of play* is not, of itself, interference under this Rule.

Note: The *Committee* may make a Local Rule denying the player relief from interference with his *stance* by an *abnormal ground condition*.

b. Relief

Except when the ball is in a *water hazard* or a *lateral water hazard*, a player may obtain relief from interference by an *abnormal ground condition* as follows:

(i) **Through the Green:** If the ball lies *through the green*, the *nearest point of relief* shall be determined which is not in a *hazard* or on a *putting green*. The player shall lift the ball and drop it without penalty within one club-length of and not nearer the hole than the nearest point of relief, on a part of the *course* which avoids interference (as defined) by the condition and is not in a hazard or on a putting green.

(ii) **In a Bunker:** If the ball is in a *bunker,* the player shall lift and drop the ball either:

  (a) Without penalty, in accordance with Clause (i) above, except that the *nearest point of relief* must be in the bunker and the ball must be dropped in the bunker, or if complete relief is impossible, in the bunker as near as possible to the spot where the ball lay, but not nearer the hole, on a part of the *course* which affords maximum available relief from the condition; or

  (b) Under penalty of one stroke, outside the bunker keeping the point where the ball lay directly between the hole and the spot on which the ball is dropped, with no limit to how far behind the bunker the ball may be dropped.

(iii) **On the Putting Green:** If the ball lies on the *putting green,* the player shall lift the ball and place it without penalty at the *nearest point of relief* which is not in a *hazard*, or if complete

relief is impossible, at the nearest position to where it lay which affords maximum available relief from the condition, but not nearer the hole nor in a hazard. The nearest point of relief or maximum available relief may be off the putting green.

The ball may be cleaned when lifted under Rule 25-1b.

(Ball rolling to a position where there is interference by the condition from which relief was taken – see Rule 20-2c(v).)

Exception: A player may not obtain relief under Rule 25-1b if (a) it is clearly unreasonable for him to play a stroke because of interference by anything other than an *abnormal ground condition* or (b) interference by such a condition would occur only through use of an unnecessarily abnormal *stance*, swing or direction of play.

Note 1: If a ball is in a *water hazard* (including a *lateral water hazard*), the player is not entitled to relief without penalty from interference by an *abnormal ground condition*. The player shall play the ball as it lies (unless prohibited by Local Rule) or proceed under Rule 26-1.

Note 2: If a ball to be dropped or placed under this Rule is not immediately recoverable, another ball may be substituted.

c. Ball Lost
It is a question of fact whether a ball lost after having been struck toward an *abnormal ground condition* is lost in such condition. In order to treat the ball as lost in the abnormal ground condition, there must be reasonable evidence to that effect. In the absence of such evidence, the ball must be treated as a *lost ball* and Rule 27 applies.

If a ball is lost in an abnormal ground condition, the spot where the ball last entered the condition shall be determined and, for the purposes of applying this Rule, the ball shall be deemed to lie at this spot.

(i) **Through the Green:** If the ball last entered the *abnormal ground condition* at a spot *through the green*, the player may substitute another ball without penalty and take relief as prescribed in Rule 25-1b(i).

(ii) **In a Bunker:** If the ball last entered the *abnormal ground condition* at a spot in a *bunker*, the player may substitute another ball without penalty and take relief as prescribed in Rule 25-1b(ii).

(iii) **In a Water Hazard (including a Lateral Water Hazard):** If the ball last entered the *abnormal ground condition* at a spot in a *water hazard*, the player is not entitled to relief without penalty. The player shall proceed under Rule 26-1.

(iv) **On the Putting Green:** If the ball last entered the *abnormal ground condition* at a spot on the *putting green*, the player may substitute another ball without penalty and take relief as prescribed in Rule 25-1b(iii).

25-2. Embedded Ball
A ball embedded in its own pitch-mark in the ground in any closely-mown area *through the green* may be lifted, cleaned and dropped, without penalty, as near as possible to the spot where it lay but not nearer the hole. The ball when dropped must first strike a part of the *course* through the green. 'Closely-mown area' means any area of the course, including paths through the rough, cut to fairway height or less.

25-3. Wrong Putting Green
a. Interference
Interference by a *wrong putting green* occurs when a ball is on the wrong putting green.

Interference to a player's *stance* or the area of his intended swing is not, of itself, interference under this Rule.

b. Relief
If a player has interference by a *wrong putting green*, the player must take relief, without penalty, as follows:

The *nearest point of relief* shall be determined which is not in a *hazard* or on a *putting green*. The player shall lift the ball and drop it within one club-length of and not nearer the hole than the nearest point of relief, on a part of the *course* which avoids interference (as defined) by the wrong putting green and is not in a *hazard* or on a putting green. The ball may be cleaned when so lifted.

PENALTY FOR BREACH OF RULE:
Match play – Loss of hole;
Stroke play – Two strokes.

Rule 26. Water Hazards (including Lateral Water Hazards)

Definitions
A **water hazard** is any sea, lake, pond, river, ditch, surface drainage ditch or other open water course (whether or not containing water) and anything of a similar nature.

All ground or water within the margin of a water hazard is part of the water hazard. The margin of a water hazard extends vertically upwards and downwards. Stakes and lines defining the margins of water hazards are in the hazards. Such stakes are *obstructions*. A ball is in a water hazard when it lies in or any part of it touches the water hazard.

Note 1: Water hazards (other than *lateral water hazards*) should be defined by yellow stakes or lines.

Note 2: The *Committee* may make a Local Rule prohibiting play from an environmentally-sensitive area which has been defined as a water hazard.

A **lateral water hazard** is a *water hazard* or that part of a water hazard so situated that it is not possible or is deemed by the *Committee* to be

impracticable to drop a ball behind the water hazard in accordance with Rule 26-1b.

That part of a water hazard to be played as a lateral water hazard should be distinctively marked. A ball is in a lateral water hazard when it lies in or any part of it touches the lateral water hazard.

Note 1: Lateral water hazards should be defined by red stakes or lines.

Note 2: The *Committee* may make a Local Rule prohibiting play from an environmentally-sensitive area which has been defined as a lateral water hazard.

Note 3: The Committee may define a lateral water hazard as a water hazard.

26-1. Ball in Water Hazard

It is a question of fact whether a ball lost after having been struck toward a *water hazard* is lost inside or outside the hazard. In order to treat the ball as lost in the hazard, there must be reasonable evidence that the ball lodged in it. In the absence of such evidence, the ball must be treated as a *lost ball* and Rule 27 applies.

If a ball is in or is lost in a water hazard (whether the ball lies in water or not), the player may under penalty of one stroke:

a. Play a ball as nearly as possible at the spot from which the original ball was last played (see Rule 20-5); or

b. Drop a ball behind the water hazard, keeping the point at which the original ball last crossed the margin of the water hazard directly between the hole and the spot on which the ball is dropped, with no limit to how far behind the water hazard the ball may be dropped; or

c. As additional options available only if the ball last crossed the margin of a lateral water hazard, drop a ball outside the water hazard within two club-lengths of and not nearer the hole than (i) the point where the original ball last crossed the margin of the water hazard or (ii) a point on the opposite margin of the water hazard equidistant from the hole.

The ball may be cleaned when lifted under this Rule.

(Ball moving in water in a water hazard – see Rule 14-6.)

26-2. Ball Played Within Water Hazard
a. Ball Comes to Rest in the Hazard

If a ball played from within a *water hazard* comes to rest in the same hazard after the *stroke*, the player may:

(i) proceed under Rule 26-1; or

(ii) under penalty of one stroke, play a ball as nearly as possible at the spot from which the last stroke from outside the hazard was played (see Rule 20-5).

If the player proceeds under Rule 26-1a, he may elect not to play the dropped ball. If he so elects, he may:

a. proceed under Rule 26-1b, adding the additional penalty of one stroke prescribed by that Rule; or

b. proceed under Rule 26-1c, if applicable, adding the additional penalty of one stroke prescribed by that Rule; or

c. add an additional penalty of one stroke and play a ball as nearly as possible at the spot from which the last stroke from outside the hazard was played (see Rule 20-5).

b. Ball Lost or Unplayable Outside Hazard or Out of Bounds

If a ball played from within a *water hazard* is *lost* or declared unplayable outside the hazard or is *out of bounds*, the player, after taking a penalty of one stroke under Rule 27-1 or 28a, may:

(i) play a ball as nearly as possible at the spot in the hazard from which the original ball was last played (see Rule 20-5); or

(ii) proceed under Rule 26-1b, or if applicable Rule 26-1c, adding the additional penalty of one stroke prescribed by the Rule and using as the reference point the point where the original ball last crossed the margin of the hazard before it came to rest in the hazard; or

(iii) add an additional penalty of one stroke and play a ball as nearly as possible at the spot from which the last stroke from outside the hazard was played (see Rule 20-5).

Note 1: When proceeding under Rule 26-2b, the player is not required to drop a ball under Rule 27-1 or 28a. If he does drop a ball, he is not required to play it. He may alternatively proceed under Clause (ii) or (iii).

Note 2: If a ball played from within a water hazard is declared unplayable outside the hazard, nothing in Rule 26-2b precludes the player from proceeding under Rule 28b or c.

PENALTY FOR BREACH OF RULE:
Match play – Loss of hole;
Stroke play – Two strokes.

Rule 27. Ball Lost or Out of Bounds; Provisional Ball

Definitions

A ball is *lost* if:

a. It is not found or identified as his by the player within five minutes after the player's *side* or his or their *caddies* have begun to search for it; or

b. The player has put another ball into play under the *Rules*, even though he may not have searched for the original ball; or

c. The player has played any stroke with a *provisional ball* from the place where the original ball is likely to be or from a point nearer the hole than that place, whereupon the provisional ball becomes the *ball in play*.

Time spent in playing a *wrong ball* is not counted in the five-minute period allowed for search.

Out of bounds is beyond the boundaries of the *course* or any part of the course so marked by the *Committee.*

When out of bounds is defined by reference to stakes or a fence, or as being beyond stakes or a fence, the out of bounds line is determined by the nearest inside points of the stakes or fence posts at ground level excluding angled supports.

Objects defining out of bounds such as walls, fences, stakes and railings, are not *obstructions* and are deemed to be fixed.

When out of bounds is defined by a line on the ground, the line itself is out of bounds.

The out of bounds line extends vertically upwards and downwards.

A ball is out of bounds when all of it lies out of bounds.

A player may stand out of bounds to play a ball lying within bounds.

A **provisional ball** is a ball played under Rule 27-2 for a ball which may be *lost* outside a *water hazard* or may be *out of bounds.*

27-1. Ball Lost or Out of Bounds

If a ball is *lost* or is *out of bounds*, the player shall play a ball, under penalty of one stroke, as nearly as possible at the spot from which the original ball was last played (see Rule 20-5).

Exceptions:

1. If there is reasonable evidence that the original ball is lost in a *water hazard*, the player shall proceed in accordance with Rule 26-1.
2. If there is reasonable evidence that the original ball is lost in an immovable *obstruction* (Rule 24-2c) or an *abnormal ground condition* (Rule 25-1c) the player may proceed under the applicable Rule.

PENALTY FOR BREACH OF RULE 27-1: Match
play – Loss of hole;
Stroke play – Two strokes.

27-2. Provisional Ball
a. Procedure

If a ball may be *lost* outside a *water hazard* or may be *out of bounds*, to save time the player may play another ball provisionally in accordance with Rule 27-1. The player shall inform his opponent in match play or his *marker* or a *fellow-competitor* in stroke play that he intends to play a *provisional ball*, and he shall play it before he or his partner goes forward to search for the original ball.

If he fails to do so and plays another ball, such ball is not a provisional ball and becomes the *ball in play* under penalty of stroke and distance (Rule 27-1); the original ball is deemed to be lost.

(Order of play from teeing ground – see Rule 10-3.)

b. When Provisional Ball Becomes Ball in Play

The player may play a *provisional ball* until he reaches the place where the original ball is likely to be. If he plays a *stroke* with the provisional ball from the place where the original ball is likely to be or from a point nearer the hole than that place, the original ball is deemed to be *lost* and the provisional ball becomes the *ball in play* under penalty of stroke and distance (Rule 27-1).

If the original ball is lost outside a *water hazard* or is *out of bounds*, the provisional ball becomes the ball in play, under penalty of stroke and distance (Rule 27-1).

If there is reasonable evidence that the original ball is lost in a water hazard, the player shall proceed in accordance with Rule 26-1.

Exception: If there is reasonable evidence that the original ball is lost in an immovable *obstruction* (Rule 24-2c) or an *abnormal ground condition* (Rule 25-1c), the player may proceed under the applicable Rule.

c. When Provisional Ball to be Abandoned

If the original ball is neither *lost* nor *out of bounds*, the player shall abandon the *provisional ball* and continue play with the original ball. If he fails to do so, any further *strokes* played with the provisional ball shall constitute playing a *wrong ball* and the provisions of Rule 15 shall apply.

Note: Strokes taken and *penalty strokes* incurred solely in playing a *provisional ball* subsequently abandoned under Rule 27-2c shall be disregarded.

Rule 28. Ball Unplayable

The player may declare his ball unplayable at any place on the *course* except when the ball is in a *water hazard*. The player is the sole judge as to whether his ball is unplayable.

If the player deems his ball to be unplayable, he shall, under penalty of one stroke:

a. Play a ball as nearly as possible at the spot from which the original ball was last played (see Rule 20-5); or
b. Drop a ball within two club-lengths of the spot where the ball lay, but not nearer the hole; or
c. Drop a ball behind the point where the ball lay, keeping that point directly between the hole and the spot on which the ball is dropped, with no limit to how far behind that point the ball may be dropped.

If the unplayable ball is in a *bunker*, the player may proceed under Clause a, b or c. If he elects to proceed under Clause b or c, a ball must be dropped in the bunker.

The ball may be cleaned when lifted under this Rule.

PENALTY FOR BREACH OF RULE:
Match play – Loss of hole;
Stroke play – Two strokes.

OTHER FORMS OF PLAY

Rule 29. Threesomes and Foursomes

Definitions
Threesome: A match in which one plays against two, and each side plays one ball.
Foursome: A match in which two play against two, and each side plays one ball.

29-1. General
In a *threesome* or a *foursome*, during any *stipulated round* the *partners* shall play alternately from the *teeing grounds* and alternately during the play of each hole. *Penalty strokes* do not affect the order of play.

29-2. Match Play
If a player plays when his *partner* should have played, his side shall lose the hole.

29-3. Stroke Play
If the *partners* play a *stroke* or *strokes* in incorrect order, such stroke or strokes shall be cancelled and the side shall incur a penalty of two strokes. The side shall correct the error by playing a ball in correct order as nearly as possible at the spot from which it first played in incorrect order (see Rule 20-5). If the side plays a stroke from the next *teeing ground* without first correcting the error or, in the case of the last hole of the round, leaves the *putting green* without declaring its intention to correct the error, the side shall be disqualified.

Rule 30. Three-Ball, Best-Ball and Four-Ball Match Play

Definitions
Three-Ball: A match play competition in which three play against one another, each playing his own ball. Each player is playing two distinct matches.
Best-Ball: A match in which one plays against the better ball of two or the best ball of three players.
Four-Ball: A match in which two play their better ball against the better ball of two other players.

30-1. Rules of Golf Apply
The Rules of Golf, so far as they are not at variance with the following special Rules, shall apply to three-ball, best-ball and four-ball matches.

30-2. Three-Ball Match Play
a. Ball at Rest Moved by an Opponent
Except as otherwise provided in the *Rules*, if the player's ball is touched or *moved* by an opponent, his *caddie* or *equipment* other than during search, Rule 18-3b applies. That opponent shall incur a penalty stroke in his match with the player, but not in his match with the other opponent.

b. Ball Deflected or Stopped by an Opponent Accidentally
If a player's ball is accidentally deflected or stopped by an opponent, his *caddie* or *equipment,* no penalty shall be incurred. In his match with that opponent the player may play the ball as it lies or, before another stroke is played by either side, he may cancel the stroke and play a ball without penalty as nearly as possible at the spot from which the original ball was last played (see Rule 20-5). In his match with the other opponent, the ball shall be played as it lies.
Exception: Ball striking person attending flagstick – see Rule 17-3b.
(Ball purposely deflected or stopped by opponent – see Rule 1-2.)

30-3. Best-Ball and Four-Ball Match Play
a. Representation of Side
A side may be represented by one *partner* for all or any part of a match; all partners need not be present. An absent partner may join a match between holes, but not during play of a hole.

b. Maximum of Fourteen Clubs
The side shall be penalised for a breach of Rule 4-4 by any partner.

c. Order of Play
Balls belonging to the same side may be played in the order the side considers best.

d. Wrong Ball
If a player plays a *stroke* with a *wrong ball* except in a *hazard,* he shall be disqualified for that hole, but his *partner* incurs no penalty even if the wrong ball belongs to him. If the wrong ball belongs to another player, its owner shall place a ball on the spot from which the wrong ball was first played.

e. Disqualification of Side
(i) A side shall be disqualified for a breach of any of the following by any *partner*:
Rule 1-3 – Agreement to Waive Rules.
Rule 4-1 or -2 – Clubs.
Rule 5-1 or -2 – The Ball.
Rule 6-2a – Handicap (playing off higher handicap).
Rule 6-4 – Caddie.
Rule 6-7 – Undue Delay; Slow Play (repeated offence).
Rule 14-3 – Artificial Devices and Unusual Equipment.

(ii) A side shall be disqualified for a breach of any of the following by all *partners*:
Rule 6-3 – Time of Starting and Groups.
Rule 6-8 – Discontinuance of Play.

f. Effect of Other Penalties
If a player's breach of a *Rule* assists his *partner's* play or adversely affects an opponent's play, the

partner incurs the applicable penalty in addition to any penalty incurred by the player.

In all other cases where a player incurs a penalty for breach of a Rule, the penalty shall not apply to his partner. Where the penalty is stated to be loss of hole, the effect shall be to disqualify the player for that hole.

g. Another Form of Match Played Concurrently

In a best-ball or four-ball match when another form of match is played concurrently, the above special Rules shall apply.

Rule 31. Four-Ball Stroke Play

In four-ball stroke play two competitors play as *partners*, each playing his own ball. The lower score of the partners is the score for the hole. If one partner fails to complete the play of a hole, there is no penalty.

31-1. Rules of Golf Apply

The Rules of Golf, so far as they are not at variance with the following special Rules, shall apply to four-ball stroke play.

31-2. Representation of Side

A *side* may be represented by either *partner* for all or any part of a *stipulated round*; both partners need not be present. An absent competitor may join his partner between holes, but not during play of a hole.

31-3. Maximum of Fourteen Clubs

The *side* shall be penalised for a breach of Rule 4-4 by either *partner*.

31-4. Scoring

The *marker* is required to record for each hole only the gross score of whichever *partner's* score is to count. The gross scores to count must be individually identifiable; otherwise the *side* shall be disqualified. Only one of the partners need be responsible for complying with Rule 6-6b. (Wrong score – see Rule 31-7a.)

31-5. Order of Play

Balls belonging to the same *side* may be played in the order the side considers best.

31-6. Wrong Ball

If a competitor plays a *stroke* or strokes with a *wrong ball* except in a *hazard*, he shall add two penalty strokes to his score for the hole and shall then play the correct ball. His *partner* incurs no penalty even if the wrong ball belongs to him.

If the wrong ball belongs to another competitor, its owner shall place a ball on the spot from which the wrong ball was first played.

31-7. Disqualification Penalties
a. Breach by One Partner

A *side* shall be disqualified from the competition for a breach of any of the following by either *partner*:

Rule 1-3 –	Agreement to Waive Rules.
Rule 3-4 –	Refusal to Comply with Rule.
Rule 4-1 or -2 –	Clubs.
Rule 5-1 or -2 –	The Ball.
Rule 6-2b –	Handicap (playing off higher handicap; failure to record handicap).
Rule 6-4 –	Caddie.
Rule 6-6b –	Signing and Returning Card.
Rule 6-6d –	Wrong Score for Hole, i.e. when the recorded score of the partner whose score is to count is lower than actually taken. If the recorded score of the partner whose score is to count is higher than actually taken, it must stand as returned.
Rule 6-7 –	Undue Delay; Slow Play (repeated offence).
Rule 7-1 –	Practice Before or Between Rounds.
Rule 14-3 –	Artificial Devices and Unusual Equipment.
Rule 31-4 –	Gross Scores to Count Not Individually Identifiable.

b. Breach by Both Partners

A *side* shall be disqualified:

(i) for a breach by both *partners* of Rule 6-3 (Time of Starting and Groups) or Rule 6-8 (Discontinuance of Play), or

(ii) if, at the same hole, each *partner* is in breach of a *Rule* the penalty for which is disqualification from the competition or for a hole.

c. For the Hole Only

In all other cases where a breach of a *Rule* would entail disqualification, the competitor shall be disqualified only for the hole at which the breach occurred.

31-8. Effect of Other Penalties

If a competitor's breach of a *Rule* assists his *partner's* play, the partner incurs the applicable penalty in addition to any penalty incurred by the competitor.

In all other cases where a competitor incurs a penalty for breach of a Rule, the penalty shall not apply to his partner.

Rule 32. Bogey, Par and Stableford Competitions

32-1. Conditions

Bogey, par and Stableford competitions are forms of stroke competition in which play is against a fixed score at each hole. The Rules for stroke play, so far

as they are not at variance with the following special Rules, apply.

a. Bogey and Par Competitions

The reckoning for bogey and par competitions is made as in match play. Any hole for which a competitor makes no return shall be regarded as a loss. The winner is the competitor who is most successful in the aggregate of holes.

The *marker* is responsible for marking only the gross number of strokes for each hole where the competitor makes a net score equal to or less than the fixed score.

Note 1: Maximum of 14 Clubs – Penalties as in match play – see Rule 4-4.

Note 2: Undue Delay; Slow Play (Rule 6-7) – The competitor's score shall be adjusted by deducting one hole from the overall result.

b. Stableford Competitions

The reckoning in Stableford competitions is made by points awarded in relation to a fixed score at each hole as follows:

Hole Played in	Points
More than one over fixed score or no score returned	0
One over fixed score	1
Fixed score	2
One under fixed score	3
Two under fixed score	4
Three under fixed score	5
Four under fixed score	6

The winner is the competitor who scores the highest number of points.

The *marker* shall be responsible for marking only the gross number of strokes at each hole where the competitor's net score earns one or more points.

Note 1: Maximum of 14 Clubs (Rule 4-4) – Penalties applied as follows: From total points scored for the round, deduction of two points for each hole at which any breach occurred; maximum deduction per round: four points.

Note 2: Undue Delay; Slow Play (Rule 6-7) – The competitor's score shall be adjusted by deducting two points from the points total scored for the round.

32-2. Disqualification Penalties

a. From the Competition

A competitor shall be disqualified from the competition for a breach of any of the following:

Rule 1-3 –	Agreement to Waive Rules.
Rule 3-4 –	Refusal to Comply with Rule.
Rule 4-1 or -2 –	Clubs.
Rule 5-1 or -2 –	The Ball.
Rule 6-2b –	Handicap (playing off higher handicap; failure to record handicap).
Rule 6-3 –	Time of Starting and Groups.
Rule 6-4 –	Caddie.
Rule 6-6b –	Signing and Returning Card.
Rule 6-6d –	Wrong Score for Hole, except that no penalty shall be incurred when a breach of this Rule does not affect the result of the hole.
Rule 6-7 –	Undue Delay; Slow Play (repeated offence).
Rule 6-8 –	Discontinuance of Play.
Rule 7-1 –	Practice Before or Between Rounds.
Rule 14-3 –	Artificial Devices and Unusual Equipment.

b. For a Hole

In all other cases where a breach of a *Rule* would entail disqualification, the competitor shall be disqualified only for the hole at which the breach occurred.

ADMINISTRATION

Rule 33. The Committee

33-1.   Conditions; Waiving Rule

The *Committee* shall lay down the conditions under which a competition is to be played.

The Committee has no power to waive a Rule of Golf.

Certain special rules governing stroke play are so substantially different from those governing match play that combining the two forms of play is not practicable and is not permitted. The results of matches played and the scores returned in these circumstances shall not be accepted.

In stroke play the Committee may limit a *referee's* duties.

33-2. The Course

a. Defining Bounds and Margins

The *Committee* shall define accurately:

(i) the *course* and *out of bounds*,
(ii) the margins of *water hazards* and *lateral water hazards*,
(iii) *ground under repair*, and
(iv) *obstructions* and integral parts of the course.

b. New Holes

New *holes* should be made on the day on which a stroke competition begins and at such other times as the *Committee* considers necessary, provided all competitors in a single round play with each hole cut in the same position.

Exception: When it is impossible for a damaged *hole* to be repaired so that it conforms with the Definition, the *Committee* may make a new hole in a nearby similar position.

Note: Where a single round is to be played on more than one day, the *Committee* may provide in the conditions of a competition that the *holes* and *teeing grounds* may be differently situated on each

day of the competition, provided that, on any one day, all competitors play with each hole and each teeing ground in the same position.

c. Practice Ground
Where there is no practice ground available outside the area of a competition *course,* the *Committee* should lay down the area on which players may practise on any day of a competition, if it is practicable to do so. On any day of a stroke competition, the Committee should not normally permit practice on or to a *putting green* or from a *hazard* of the competition course.

d. Course Unplayable
If the *Committee* or its authorised representative considers that for any reason the *course* is not in a playable condition or that there are circumstances which render the proper playing of the game impossible, it may, in match play or stroke play, order a temporary suspension of play or, in stroke play, declare play null and void and cancel all scores for the round in question. When a round is cancelled, all penalties incurred in that round are cancelled.

(Procedure in discontinuing and resuming play – see Rule 6-8.)

33-3. Times of Starting and Groups
The *Committee* shall lay down the times of starting and, in stroke play, arrange the groups in which competitors shall play.

When a match play competition is played over an extended period, the Committee shall lay down the limit of time within which each round shall be completed. When players are allowed to arrange the date of their match within these limits, the Committee should announce that the match must be played at a stated time on the last day of the period unless the players agree to a prior date.

33-4. Handicap Stroke Table
The *Committee* shall publish a table indicating the order of holes at which handicap strokes are to be given or received.

33-5. Score Card
In stroke play, the Committee shall issue for each competitor a score card containing the date and the competitor's name or, in foursome or four-ball stroke play, the competitors' names.

In stroke play, the Committee is responsible for the addition of scores and application of the handicap recorded on the card.

In four-ball stroke play, the Committee is responsible for recording the better-ball score for each hole and in the process applying the handicaps recorded on the card, and adding the better-ball scores.

In bogey, par and Stableford competitions, the Committee is responsible for applying the handicap recorded on the card and determining the result of each hole and the overall result or points total.

33-6. Decision of Ties
The *Committee* shall announce the manner, day and time for the decision of a halved match or of a tie, whether played on level terms or under handicap.

A halved match shall not be decided by stroke play. A tie in stroke play shall not be decided by a match.

33-7. Disqualification Penalty; Committee Discretion
A penalty of disqualification may in exceptional individual cases be waived, modified or imposed if the *Committee* considers such action warranted.

Any penalty less than disqualification shall not be waived or modified.

33-8. Local Rules
a. Policy
The *Committee* may make and publish Local Rules for local abnormal conditions if they are consistent with the policy set forth in Appendix I.

b. Waiving or Modifying a Rule
A Rule of Golf shall not be waived by a Local Rule. However, if a *Committee* considers that local abnormal conditions interfere with the proper playing of the game to the extent that it is necessary to make a Local Rule which modifies the *Rules*, the Local Rule must be authorised by the Royal and Ancient Golf Club of St. Andrews.

Rule 34. Disputes and Decisions

34-1. Claims and Penalties
a. Match Play
In match play if a claim is lodged with the *Committee* under Rule 2-5, a decision should be given as soon as possible so that the state of the match may, if necessary, be adjusted.

If a claim is not made within the time limit provided by Rule 2-5, it shall not be considered unless it is based on facts previously unknown to the player making the claim and the player making the claim had been given wrong information (Rules 6-2a and 9) by an opponent. In any case, no later claim shall be considered after the result of the match has been officially announced, unless the Committee is satisfied that the opponent knew he was giving wrong information.

There is no time limit on applying the disqualification penalty for a breach of Rule 1-3.

b. Stroke Play
Except as provided below, in stroke play, no penalty shall be rescinded, modified or imposed after the competition has closed. A competition is deemed to have closed when the result has been officially announced or, in stroke play qualifying followed by match play, when the player has teed off in his first match.

Exceptions: A penalty of disqualification shall be imposed after the competition has closed if a competitor:

(i) was in breach of Rule 1-3 (Agreement to Waive Rules); or

(ii) returned a score card on which he had recorded a handicap which, before the competition closed, he knew was higher than that to which he was entitled, and this affected the number of strokes received (Rule 6-2b); or

(iii) returned a score for any hole lower than actually taken (Rule 6-6d) for any reason other than failure to include a penalty which, before the competition closed, he did not know he had incurred; or

(iv) knew, before the competition closed, that he had been in breach of any other *Rule* for which the prescribed penalty is disqualification.

34-2. Referee's Decision
If a *referee* has been appointed by the *Committee*, his decision shall be final.

34-3. Committee's Decision
In the absence of a *referee*, any dispute or doubtful point on the *Rules* shall be referred to the *Committee*, whose decision shall be final.

If the Committee cannot come to a decision, it shall refer the dispute or doubtful point to the Rules of Golf Committee of the Royal and Ancient Golf Club of St. Andrews, whose decision shall be final.

If the dispute or doubtful point has not been referred to the Rules of Golf Committee, the player or players have the right to refer an agreed statement through the Secretary of the Club to the Rules of Golf Committee for an opinion as to the correctness of the decision given. The reply will be sent to the Secretary of the Club or Clubs concerned.

If play is conducted other than in accordance with the Rules of Golf, the Rules of Golf Committee will not give a decision on any question.

APPENDIX I
LOCAL RULES; CONDITIONS OF THE COMPETITION

Part A: Local Rules

As provided in Rule 33-8a, the Committee may make and publish Local Rules for local abnormal conditions if they are consistent with the policy set forth in this Appendix.

In addition, detailed information regarding acceptable and prohibited Local Rules is provided in 'Decisions on the Rules of Golf' under Rule 33-8.

If local abnormal conditions interfere with the proper playing of the game and the Committee considers it necessary to modify a Rule of Golf, authorisation from the Royal and Ancient Golf Club of St. Andrews must be obtained.

1. Defining Bounds and Margins
Specifying means used to define out of bounds, water hazards, lateral water hazards, ground under repair, obstructions and integral parts of the course (Rule 33-2a).

2. Water Hazards
a. Lateral Water Hazards
Clarifying the status of water hazards which may be lateral water hazards (Rule 26).

b. Provisional Ball
Permitting play of a provisional ball for a ball which may be in a water hazard of such character that if the original ball is not found, there is reasonable evidence that it is lost in the water hazard and it would be impracticable to determine whether the ball is in the hazard or to do so would unduly delay play. The ball shall be played provisionally under any of the available options under Rule 26-1 or any applicable Local Rule. In such a case, if a provisional ball is played and the original ball is in a water hazard, the player may play the original ball as it lies or continue with the provisional ball in play, but he may not proceed under Rule 26-1 with regard to the original ball.

3. Areas of the Course Requiring Preservation; Environmentally-Sensitive Areas
Assisting preservation of the course by defining areas, including turf nurseries, young plantations and other parts of the course under cultivation, as 'ground under repair' from which play is prohibited.

When the Committee is required to prohibit play from environmentally-sensitive areas which are on or adjoin the course, it should make a Local Rule clarifying the relief procedure.

4. Temporary Conditions – Mud, Extreme Wetness, Poor Conditions and Protection of Course
a. Lifting an Embedded Ball, Cleaning
Temporary conditions which might interfere with the proper playing of the game, including mud and extreme wetness, warranting relief for an embedded ball anywhere through the green or permitting lifting, cleaning and replacing a ball anywhere through the green or on a closely-mown area through the green.

b. 'Preferred Lies' and 'Winter Rules'
Adverse conditions, including the poor condition of the course or the existence of mud, are sometimes so general, particularly during winter months, that the Committee may decide to grant relief by temporary Local Rule either to protect the course or to promote fair and pleasant play. Such Local Rule shall be withdrawn as soon as the conditions warrant.

5. Obstructions
a. General
Clarifying the status of objects which may be obstructions (Rule 24).

Declaring any construction to be an integral part of the course and, accordingly, not an obstruction, e.g. built-up sides of teeing grounds, putting greens and bunkers (Rules 24 and 33-2a).

b. Stones in Bunkers

Allowing the removal of stones in bunkers by declaring them to be 'movable obstructions' (Rule 24-1).

c. Roads and Paths

(i) Declaring artificial surfaces and sides of roads and paths to be integral parts of the course, or

(ii) Providing relief of the type afforded under Rule 24-2b from roads and paths not having artificial surfaces and sides if they could unfairly affect play.

d. Fixed Sprinkler Heads

Providing relief from intervention by fixed sprinkler heads on or within two club-lengths of the putting green when the ball lies within two club-lengths of the sprinkler head.

e. Protection of Young Trees

Providing relief for the protection of young trees.

f. Temporary Obstructions

Providing relief from interference by temporary obstructions (e.g. grandstands, television cables and equipment, etc.).

6. Dropping Zones (Ball Drops)

Establishing special areas on which balls may or shall be dropped when it is not feasible or practicable to proceed exactly in conformity with Rule 24-2b or 24-2c (Immovable Obstruction), Rule 25-1b or 25-1c (Abnormal Ground Conditions), Rule 25-3 (Wrong Putting Green), Rule 26-1 (Water Hazards and Lateral Water Hazards) or Rule 28 (Ball Unplayable).

Part B: Specimen Local Rules

Within the policy set out in Part A of this Appendix, the Committee may adopt a Specimen Local Rule by referring, on a score card or notice board, to the examples given below. However, Specimen Local Rules 3a, 3b, 3c, 6a and 6b should not be printed or referred to on a score card as they are all of limited duration.

1. Areas of the Course Requiring Preservation; Environmentally-Sensitive Areas
a. Ground Under Repair; Play Prohibited

If the Committee wishes to protect any area of the course, it should declare it to be ground under repair and prohibit play from within that area. The following Local Rule is recommended:

'The _____ (defined by ____) is ground under repair from which play is prohibited. If a player's ball lies in the area, or if it interferes with the player's stance or the area of his intended swing, the player must take relief under Rule 25-1.

PENALTY FOR BREACH OF LOCAL RULE:
  Match play – Loss of hole;
  Stroke play – Two strokes.'

b. Environmentally-Sensitive Areas

If an appropriate authority (i.e. a Government Agency or the like) prohibits entry into and/or play from an area on or adjoining the course for environmental reasons, the Committee should make a Local Rule clarifying the relief procedure.

The Committee has some discretion in terms of whether the area is defined as ground under repair, a water hazard or out of bounds. However, it may not simply define such an area to be a water hazard if it does not meet the Definition of a 'Water Hazard' and it should attempt to preserve the character of the hole. The following Local Rule is recommended:

'**1. Definition**

An environmentally-sensitive area is an area so declared by an appropriate authority, entry into and/or play from which is prohibited for environmental reasons. Such an area may be defined as ground under repair, a water hazard, a lateral water hazard or out of bounds at the discretion of the Committee provided that, in the case of an environmentally-sensitive area which has been defined as a water hazard or a lateral water hazard, the area is, by Definition, a water hazard.

Note: The Committee may not declare an area to be environmentally-sensitive.

2. Ball in Environmentally-Sensitive Area
a. Ground Under Repair

If a ball is in an environmentally-sensitive area which is defined as ground under repair, a ball must be dropped in accordance with Rule 25-1b.

If there is reasonable evidence that a ball is lost within an environmentally-sensitive area which is defined as ground under repair, the player may take relief without penalty as prescribed in Rule 25-1c.

b. Water Hazards and Lateral Water Hazards

If a ball is in or there is reasonable evidence that it is lost in an environmentally-sensitive area which is defined as a water hazard or lateral water hazard, the player must, under penalty of one stroke, proceed under Rule 26-1.

Note: If a ball dropped in accordance with Rule 26 rolls into a position where the environmentally-sensitive area interferes with the player's stance or the area of his intended swing, the player must take relief as provided in Clause 3 of this Local Rule.

c. Out of Bounds

If a ball is in an environmentally-sensitive area which is defined as out of bounds, the player

shall play a ball, under penalty of one stroke, as nearly as possible at the spot from which the original ball was last played (see Rule 20-5).

3. Interference with Stance or Area of Intended Swing

Interference by an environmentally-sensitive area occurs when such a condition interferes with the player's stance or the area of his intended swing. If interference exists, the player must take relief as follows:

(i) Through the Green: If the ball lies through the green, the point on the course nearest to where the ball lies shall be determined which (a) is not nearer the hole, (b) avoids interference by the condition and (c) is not in a hazard or on a putting green. The player shall lift the ball and drop it without penalty within one club-length of the point thus determined on a part of the course that fulfils (a), (b) and (c) above.

(ii) In a Hazard: If the ball is in a hazard, the player shall lift the ball and drop it either:
  (a) Without penalty, in the hazard, as near as possible to the spot where the ball lay, but not nearer the hole, on a part of the course which provides complete relief from the condition; or
  (b) Under penalty of one stroke, outside the hazard, keeping the point where the ball lay directly between the hole and the spot on which the ball is dropped, with no limit to how far behind the hazard the ball may be dropped.
Additionally, the player may proceed under Rule 26 or 28 if applicable.

(iii) On the Putting Green: If the ball lies on the putting green, the player shall lift the ball and place it without penalty in the nearest position to where it lay which affords complete relief from the condition, but not nearer the hole or in a hazard.

The ball may be cleaned when so lifted under Clause 3 of this Local Rule.

Exception: A player may not obtain relief under Clause 3 of this Local Rule if (a) it is clearly unreasonable for him to play a stroke because of interference by anything other than a condition covered by this Local Rule or (b) interference by such a condition would occur only through use of an unnecessarily abnormal stance, swing or direction of play.

PENALTY FOR BREACH OF LOCAL RULE: Match play – Loss of hole; Stroke play – Two strokes.

Note: In case of a serious breach of this Local Rule, the Committee may impose a penalty of disqualification.'

2. Protection of Young Trees

When it is desired to prevent damage to young trees, the following Local Rule is recommended:
'Protection of young trees identified by _____ . If such a tree interferes with a player's stance or the area of his intended swing, the ball must be lifted, without penalty, and dropped in accordance with the procedure prescribed in Rule 24-2b (Immovable Obstruction). If the ball lies in a water hazard, the player shall lift and drop the ball in accordance with Rule 24-2b(i) except that the nearest point of relief must be in the water hazard and the ball must be dropped in the water hazard or the player may proceed under Rule 26. The ball may be cleaned when so lifted.

Exception: A player may not obtain relief under this Local Rule if (a) it is clearly unreasonable for him to play a stroke because of interference by anything other than such tree or (b) interference by such tree would occur only through use of an unnecessarily abnormal stance, swing or direction of play.

PENALTY FOR BREACH OF LOCAL RULE: Match play – Loss of hole; Stroke play – Two strokes.'

3. Temporary Conditions – Mud, Extreme Wetness, Poor Conditions and Protection of the Course
a. Relief for Embedded Ball; Cleaning Ball
Rule 25-2 provides relief without penalty for a ball embedded in its own pitch-mark in any closely-mown area through the green. On the putting green, a ball may be lifted and damage caused by the impact of a ball may be repaired (Rules 16-1b and c). When permission to take relief for an embedded ball anywhere through the green would be warranted, the following Local Rule is recommended:

'Through the green, a ball which is embedded in its own pitch-mark in the ground, other than sand, may be lifted without penalty, cleaned and dropped as near as possible to where it lay but not nearer the hole. The ball when dropped must first strike a part of the course through the green.

Exception: A player may not obtain relief under this Local Rule if it is clearly unreasonable for him to play a stroke because of interference by anything other than the condition covered by this Local Rule.

PENALTY FOR BREACH OF LOCAL RULE: Match play – Loss of hole; Stroke play – Two strokes.'

Alternatively, conditions may be such that permission to lift, clean and replace the ball will suffice. In

such circumstances, the following Local Rule is recommended:

'(Specify area) a ball may be lifted, cleaned and replaced without penalty.
Note: The position of the ball shall be marked before it is lifted under this Local Rule – see Rule 20-1.
PENALTY FOR BREACH OF LOCAL RULE: Match play – Loss of hole; Stroke play – Two strokes.'

b. 'Preferred Lies' and 'Winter Rules'

The R&A does not endorse 'preferred lies' or 'winter rules' and recommends that the Rules of Golf be observed uniformly. Ground under repair is provided for in Rule 25 and occasional local abnormal conditions which might interfere with fair play and are not widespread should be defined as ground under repair.

However, adverse conditions are sometimes so general throughout a course that the Committee believes 'preferred lies' or 'winter rules' would promote fair play or help protect the course. Heavy snows, spring thaws, prolonged rains or extreme heat can make fairways unsatisfactory and sometimes prevent use of heavy mowing equipment.

When a Committee adopts a Local Rule for 'preferred lies' or 'winter rules' it should be set out in detail and should be interpreted by the Committee, as there is no established code for 'winter rules'. Without a detailed Local Rule, it is meaningless for a Committee to post a notice merely saying 'Winter Rules today.'

The following Local Rule would seem appropriate for the conditions in question, but the R&A will not interpret it:

'A ball lying on a closely-mown area through the green may, without penalty, be moved or may be lifted, cleaned and placed within (specify area, e.g., six inches, one club-length, etc.) of where it originally lay, but not nearer the hole and not in a hazard or on a putting green. A player may move or place his ball once and after the ball has been so moved or placed, it is in play.
PENALTY FOR BREACH OF LOCAL RULE: Match play – Loss of hole; Stroke play – Two strokes.'

Before a Committee adopts a Local Rule permitting 'preferred lies' or 'winter rules', the following facts should be considered:
1. Such a Local Rule conflicts with the Rules of Golf and the fundamental principle of playing the ball as it lies.
2. 'Winter rules' are sometimes adopted under the guise of protecting the course when, in fact, the practical effect is just the opposite – they permit moving the ball to the best turf, from which divots are then taken to injure the course further.

3. 'Preferred lies' or 'winter rules' tend generally to lower scores and handicaps, thus penalising the players in competition with players whose scores for handicaps are made under the Rules of Golf.
4. Extended use or indiscriminate use of 'preferred lies' or 'winter rules' will place players at a disadvantage when competing at a course where the ball must be played as it lies.

c. Aeration Holes

When a course has been aerated, a Local Rule permitting relief, without penalty, from an aeration hole may be warranted. The following Local Rule is recommended:

'Through the green, a ball which comes to rest in or on an aeration hole may be lifted without penalty, cleaned and dropped, as near as possible to the spot where it lay but not nearer the hole. The ball when dropped must first strike a part of the course through the green.

On the putting green, the player shall place the ball at the nearest spot not nearer the hole which avoids such situation.
PENALTY FOR BREACH OF LOCAL RULE: Match play – Loss of hole; Stroke play – Two strokes.'

4. Stones in bunkers

Stones are, by definition, loose impediments and, when a player's ball is in a hazard, a stone lying in or touching the hazard may not be touched or moved (Rule 13-4). However, stones in bunkers may represent a danger to players (a player could be injured by a stone struck by the player's club in an attempt to play the ball) and they may interfere with the proper playing of the game.

When permission to lift a stone in a bunker would be warranted, the following Local Rule is recommended:

'Stones in bunkers are movable obstructions (Rule 24-1 applies).'

5. Fixed Sprinkler Heads

Rule 24-2 provides relief without penalty from interference by an immovable obstruction, but it also provides that, except on the putting green, intervention on the line of play is not, of itself, interference under this Rule.

However, on some courses, the aprons of the putting greens are so closely mown that players may wish to putt from just off the green. In such conditions, fixed sprinkler heads on the apron may interfere with the proper playing of the game and the introduction of the following Local Rule providing additional relief without penalty from intervention by a fixed sprinkler head would be warranted:

'All fixed sprinkler heads are immovable obstructions and relief from interference by

them may be obtained under Rule 24-2. In addition, if a ball lies off the putting green but not in a hazard and such an obstruction on or within two club-lengths of the putting green and within two club-lengths of the ball intervenes on the line of play between the ball and the hole, the player may take relief as follows:

The ball shall be lifted and dropped at the nearest point to where the ball lay which (a) is not nearer the hole, (b) avoids such intervention and (c) is not in a hazard or on a putting green. The ball may be cleaned when so lifted.

PENALTY FOR BREACH OF LOCAL RULE:Match play – Loss of hole; Stroke play – Two strokes.'

6. Temporary Obstructions

When temporary obstructions are installed on or adjoining the course, the Committee should define the status of such obstructions as movable, immovable or temporary immovable obstructions.

a. Temporary Immovable Obstructions

If the Committee defines such obstructions as temporary immovable obstructions, the following Local Rule is recommended:

'1. Definition

A temporary immovable obstruction is a non-permanent artificial object which is often erected in conjunction with a competition and which is fixed or not readily movable.

Examples of temporary immovable obstructions include, but are not limited to, tents, scoreboards, grandstands, television towers and lavatories.

Supporting guy wires are part of the temporary immovable obstruction unless the Committee declares that they are to be treated as elevated power lines or cables.

2. Interference

Interference by a temporary immovable obstruction occurs when (a) the ball lies in front of and so close to the obstruction that the obstruction interferes with the player's stance or the area of his intended swing, or (b) the ball lies in, on, under or behind the obstruction so that any part of the obstruction intervenes directly between the player's ball and the hole; interference also exists if the ball lies within one club-length of a spot where such intervention would exist.

Note: A ball is under a temporary immovable obstruction when it is below the outer most edges of the obstruction, even if these edges do not extend downwards to the ground.

3. Relief

A player may obtain relief from interference by a temporary immovable obstruction, including

a temporary immovable obstruction which is out of bounds, as follows:

a. Through the Green – If the ball lies through the green, the point on the course nearest to where the ball lies shall be determined which (a) is not nearer the hole, (b) avoids interference as defined in Clause 2 and (c) is not in a hazard or on a putting green. The player shall lift the ball and drop it without penalty within one club-length of the point thus determined on a part of the course which fulfils (a), (b) and (c) above.

b. In a Hazard: If the ball is in a hazard, the player shall lift and drop the ball either:

(i) Without penalty, in the hazard, on the nearest part of the course affording complete relief within the limits specified in Clause 3a above or, if complete relief is impossible, on a part of the course within the hazard which affords maximum available relief; or

(ii) Under penalty of one stroke, outside the hazard as follows: the point on the course nearest to where the ball lies shall be determined which (a) is not nearer the hole, (b) avoids interference as defined in Clause 2 and (c) is not in a hazard. The player shall drop the ball within one club-length of the point thus determined on a part of the course which fulfils (a), (b) and (c) above.

The ball may be cleaned when lifted under Clause 3.

Note 1: If the ball lies in a hazard, nothing in this Local Rule precludes the player from proceeding under Rule 26 or Rule 28, if applicable.

Note 2: If the ball to be dropped under this Local Rule is not immediately recoverable, another ball may be substituted.

Note 3: A Committee may make a Local Rule (a) permitting or requiring a player to use a dropping zone or ball drop when taking relief from a temporary immovable obstruction or (b) permitting a player, as an additional relief option, to drop the ball on the opposite side of the obstruction from the point established under Clause 3, but otherwise in accordance with Clause 3.

Exceptions:

If a player's ball lies in front of or behind the temporary immovable obstruction (not in, on or under the obstruction) he may not obtain relief under Clause 3 if:

1. It is clearly unreasonable for him to play a stroke or, in the case of intervention, to play a stroke such that the ball could finish on a direct line to the hole, because of interference

by anything other than the temporary immovable obstruction;

2. Interference by the temporary immovable obstruction would occur only through use of an unnecessarily abnormal stance, swing or direction of play; or

3. In the case of intervention, it would be clearly unreasonable to expect the player to be able to strike the ball far enough towards the hole to reach the temporary immovable obstruction.

Note: A player not entitled to relief due to these exceptions may proceed under Rule 24-2, if applicable.

4. Ball Lost

If there is reasonable evidence that the ball is lost in, on or under a temporary immovable obstruction, a ball may be dropped under the provisions of Clause 3 or Clause 5, if applicable. For the purpose of applying Clauses 3 and 5, the ball shall be deemed to lie at the spot where it last entered the obstruction (Rule 24-2c).

5. Dropping Zones (Ball Drops)

If the player has interference from a temporary immovable obstruction, the Committee may permit or require the use of a dropping zone or ball drop. If the player uses a dropping zone in taking relief, he must drop the ball in the dropping zone nearest to where his ball originally lay or is deemed to lie under Clause 4 (even though the nearest dropping zone may be nearer the hole).

Note 1: A Committee may make a Local Rule prohibiting the use of a dropping zone or ball drop which is nearer the hole.

Note 2: If the ball is dropped in a dropping zone, the ball shall not be re-dropped if it comes to rest within two club-lengths of the spot where it first struck a part of the course even though it may come to rest nearer the hole or outside the boundaries of the dropping zone.

PENALTY FOR BREACH OF LOCAL RULE:
Match play – Loss of hole;
Stroke play – Two strokes.'

b. Temporary Power Lines and Cables

When temporary power lines, cables, or telephone lines are installed on the course, the following Local Rule is recommended:

'Temporary power lines, cables, telephone lines and mats covering or stanchions supporting them are obstructions:

1. If they are readily movable, Rule 24-1 applies.

2. If they are fixed or not readily movable, the player may, if the ball lies through the green or in a bunker, obtain relief as provided in Rule 24-2b. If the ball lies in a water hazard, the player may obtain relief under Rule 24-2b(i) except that the nearest point of relief must be in

the water hazard and the ball must be dropped in the water hazard or the player may proceed under Rule 26.

3. If a ball strikes an elevated power line or cable, the stroke shall be cancelled and replayed, without penalty (see Rule 20-5). If the ball is not immediately recoverable another ball may be substituted.

Note: Guy wires supporting a temporary immovable obstruction are part of the temporary immovable obstruction unless the Committee, by Local Rule, declares that they are to be treated as elevated power lines or cables.

Exception: Ball striking elevated junction section of cable rising from the ground shall not be replayed.

4. Grass-covered cable trenches are ground under repair even if not so marked and Rule 25-1b applies.'

Part C: Conditions of the Competition

Rule 33-1 provides, 'The Committee shall lay down the conditions under which a competition is to be played.' Such conditions should include many matters such as method of entry, eligibility, number of rounds to be played, etc. which it is not appropriate to deal with in the Rules of Golf or this Appendix. Detailed information regarding such conditions is provided in 'Decisions on the Rules of Golf' under Rule 33-1.

However, there are seven matters which might be covered in the Conditions of the Competition to which the Committee's attention is specifically drawn by way of a Note to the appropriate Rule. These are:

1. Specification of the Ball (Note to Rule 5-1)

The following two conditions are recommended only for competitions involving expert players:

a. List of Conforming Golf Balls

The R&A periodically issues a List of Conforming Golf Balls which lists balls that have been tested and found to conform. If the Committee wishes to require use of a brand of golf ball on the List, the List should be posted and the following condition of competition used:

'The ball the player uses shall be named on the current List of Conforming Golf Balls issued by the Royal and Ancient Golf Club of St Andrews.

PENALTY FOR BREACH OF CONDITION: Disqualification.'

b. One Ball Condition

If it is desired to prohibit changing brands and types of golf balls during a stipulated round, the following condition is recommended:

'Limitation on Balls Used During Round: (Note to Rule 5-1)

(i) 'One Ball' Condition
During a stipulated round, the balls a player uses must be of the same brand and type as detailed by a single entry on the current List of Conforming Golf Balls.

PENALTY FOR BREACH OF CONDITION: Match play – At the conclusion of the hole at which the breach is discovered, the state of the match shall be adjusted by deducting one hole for each hole at which a breach occurred; maximum deduction per round: Two holes.
Stroke play – Two strokes for each hole at which any breach occurred; maximum penalty per round: Four strokes.

(ii) Procedure When Breach Discovered
When a player discovers that he has used a ball in breach of this condition, he shall abandon that ball before playing from the next teeing ground and complete the round using a proper ball; otherwise, the player shall be disqualified. If discovery is made during play of a hole and the player elects to substitute a proper ball before completing that hole, the player shall place a proper ball on the spot where the ball used in breach of the condition lay.'

2. Time of Starting (Note to Rule 6-3a)
If the Committee wishes to act in accordance with the Note, the following wording is recommended:

'If the player arrives at his starting point, ready to play, within five minutes after his starting time in the absence of circumstances which warrant waiving the penalty of disqualification as provided in Rule 33-7, the penalty for failure to start on time is loss of the first hole to be played in match play or two strokes in stroke play. Penalty for lateness beyond five minutes is disqualification.'

3. Pace of Play
The Committee may lay down pace of play guidelines to help prevent slow play, in accordance with Note 2 to Rule 6-7.

4. Suspension of Play Due to a Dangerous Situation (Note to Rule 6-8b)
As there have been many deaths and injuries from lightning on golf courses, all clubs and sponsors of golf competitions are urged to take precautions for the protection of persons against lightning. Attention is called to Rules 6-8 and 33-2d. If the Committee desires to adopt the condition in the Note under Rule 6-8b, the following wording is recommended:

'When play is suspended by the Committee for a dangerous situation, if the players in a match or group are between the play of two holes,

they shall not resume play until the Committee has ordered a resumption of play. If they are in the process of playing a hole, they shall discontinue play immediately and shall not thereafter resume play until the Committee has ordered a resumption of play. If a player fails to discontinue play immediately, he shall be disqualified unless circumstances warrant waiving such penalty as provided in Rule 33-7.
The signal for suspending play due to a dangerous situation will be a prolonged note of the siren.'

The following signals are generally used and it is recommended that all Committees do similarly:
Discontinue Play Immediately: One prolonged note of siren.
Discontinue Play: Three consecutive notes of siren, repeated.
Resume Play: Two short notes of siren, repeated.

5. Practice
a. General
The Committee may make regulations governing practice in accordance with the Note to Rule 7-1, Exception (c) to Rule 7-2, and Rule 33-2c.

b. Practice Between Holes (Note 2 to Rule 7)
It is recommended that a condition of competition prohibiting practice putting or chipping on or near the putting green of the hole last played is only introduced in stroke play competitions. The following wording is recommended:

'A player shall not play any practice stroke on or near the putting green of the hole last played. If a practice stroke is played on or near the putting green of the hole last played, the player shall incur a penalty of two strokes at the next hole, except that in the case of the last hole of the round, he incurs the penalty at that hole.'

6. Advice in Team Competitions
If the Committee wishes to act in accordance with the Note under Rule 8, the following wording is recommended:

'In accordance with the Note to Rule 8 of the Rules of Golf, each team may appoint one person (in addition to the persons from whom advice may be asked under the Rule) who may give advice to members of that team. Such person (if it is desired to insert any restriction on who may be nominated insert such restriction here) shall be identified to the Committee before giving advice.'

7. New Holes
The Committee may provide, in accordance with the Note to Rule 33-2b, that the holes and teeing grounds for a single round competition, being held on more than one day, may be differently situated on each day.

Other conditions of the competition might include:

Transportation

If it is desired to require players to walk in a competition, the following condition is recommended:

'Players shall walk at all times during a stipulated round.

PENALTY FOR BREACH OF CONDITION:

Match play – At the conclusion of the hole at which the breach is discovered, the state of the match shall be adjusted by deducting one hole for each hole at which a breach occurred. Maximum deduction per round: Two holes.

Stroke play – Two strokes for each hole at which any breach occurred; maximum penalty per round: Four strokes. In the event of a breach between the play of two holes, the penalty applies to the next hole.

Match or stroke play – Use of any unauthorised form of transportation shall be discontinued immediately upon discovery that a breach has occurred. Otherwise, the player shall be disqualified.'

How to Decide Ties

Rule 33-6 empowers the Committee to determine how and when a halved match or a stroke play tie shall be decided. The decision should be published in advance.

The R&A recommends:

Match Play

A match which ends all square should be played off hole by hole until one side wins a hole. The play-off should start on the hole where the match began. In a handicap match, handicap strokes should be allowed as in the prescribed round.

Stroke Play

(a) In the event of a tie in a scratch stroke play competition, a play-off is recommended. Such a play-off may be over 18 holes or a smaller number of holes as specified by the Committee. If that is not feasible or there is still a tie, a hole-by-hole play-off is recommended.

(b) In the event of a tie in a handicap stroke play competition, a play-off with handicaps is recommended. Such a play-off may be over 18 holes or a smaller number of holes as specified by the Committee. If the play-off is less than 18 holes, the percentage of 18 holes to be played should be applied to the players' handicaps to determine their play-off handicaps. Handicap stroke fractions of one-half stroke or more should count as a full stroke and any lesser fraction should be disregarded.

(c) In either a scratch or handicap stroke play competition, if a play-off of any type is not feasible, matching score cards is recommended. The method of matching cards should be announced in advance. An acceptable method of matching cards is to determine the winner on the basis of the best score for the last nine holes. If the tying players have the same score for the last nine, determine the winner on the basis of the last six holes, last three holes and finally the 18th hole. If such a method is used in a handicap stroke play competition, one-half, one-third, one-sixth, etc. of the handicaps should be deducted. Fractions should not be disregarded. If such a method is used in a competition with a multiple tee start, it is recommended that the 'last nine holes, last six holes, etc.' is considered to be holes 10-18, 13-18, etc.

(d) If the conditions of the competition provide that ties shall be decided over the last nine, last six, last three and last hole, they should also provide what will happen if this procedure does not produce a winner.

Draw for Match Play

Although the draw for match play may be completely blind or certain players may be distributed through different quarters or eighths, the General Numerical Draw is recommended if matches are determined by a qualifying round.

General Numerical Draw

For purposes of determining places in the draw, ties in qualifying rounds other than those for the last qualifying place shall be decided by the order in which scores are returned, with the first score to be returned receiving the lowest available number, etc. If it is impossible to determine the order in which scores are returned, ties shall be determined by a blind draw.

Upper half	Lower Half	Upper Half	Lower Half
64 Qualifiers		*32 Qualifiers*	
1 vs 64	2 vs 63	1 vs 32	2 vs 31
32 vs 33	31 vs 34	16 vs 17	15 vs 18
16 vs 49	15 vs 50	8 vs 25	7 vs 26
17 vs 48	18 vs 47	9 vs 24	10 vs 23
8 vs 57	7 vs 58	4 vs 29	3 vs 30
25 vs 40	26 vs 39	13 vs 20	14 vs 19
9 vs 56	10 vs 55	5 vs 28	6 vs 27
24 vs 41	23 vs 42	12 vs 21	11 vs 22
4 vs 61	3 vs 62	*16 Qualifiers*	
29 vs 36	30 vs 35	1 vs 16	2 vs 15
13 vs 52	14 vs 51	8 vs 9	7 vs 10
20 vs 45	19 vs 46	4 vs 13	3 vs 14
5 vs 60	6 vs 59	5 vs 12	6 vs 11
28 vs 37	27 vs 38	*8 Qualifiers*	
12 vs 53	11 vs 54	1 vs 8	2 vs 7
21 vs 44	22 vs 43	4 vs 5	3 vs 6

APPENDICES II AND III

Any design in a club or ball which is not covered by Rules 4 and 5 and Appendices II and III, or which might significantly change the nature of the game, will be ruled on by the Royal and Ancient Golf Club of St. Andrews.

The dimensions contained in Appendices II and III are referenced in imperial measurements. A metric conversion is also referenced for information, calculated using a conversion rate of 1 inch = 25.4 mm. In the event of any dispute over the conformity of a club or ball, the imperial measurement shall take precedence.

APPENDIX II
Design of Clubs

A player in doubt as to the conformity of a club should consult the Royal and Ancient Golf Club of St. Andrews.

A manufacturer should submit to the Royal and Ancient Golf Club of St. Andrews a sample of a club which is to be manufactured for a ruling as to whether the club conforms with the *Rules*. If a manufacturer fails to submit a sample before manufacturing and/or marketing the club, the manufacturer assumes the risk of a ruling that the club does not conform with the Rules. Any sample submitted to the Royal and Ancient Golf Club of St. Andrews will become its property for reference purposes.

The following paragraphs prescribe general regulations for the design of clubs, together with specifications and interpretations.

Where a club, or part of a club, is required to have some specific property, this means that it must be designed and manufactured with the intention of having that property. The finished club or part must have that property within manufacturing tolerances appropriate to the material used.

1. Clubs
a. General
A club is an implement designed to be used for striking the ball and generally comes in three forms: woods, irons and putters distinguished by shape and intended use. A putter is a club with a loft not exceeding ten degrees designed primarily for use on the putting green.

The club shall not be substantially different from the traditional and customary form and make. The club shall be composed of a shaft and a head. All parts of the club shall be fixed so that the club is one unit, and it shall have no external attachments except as otherwise permitted by the *Rules*.

b. Adjustability
Woods and irons shall not be designed to be adjustable except for weight. Putters may be designed to be adjustable for weight and some other forms of adjustability are also permitted. All methods of adjustment permitted by the *Rules* require that:

(i) the adjustment cannot be readily made;

(ii) all adjustable parts are firmly fixed and there is no reasonable likelihood of them working loose during a round; and

(iii) all configurations of adjustment conform with the Rules.

The disqualification penalty for purposely changing the playing characteristics of a club during a *stipulated round* (Rule 4-2a) applies to all clubs including a putter.

c. Length
The overall length of the club shall be at least 18 inches (457.2 mm) measu grip along the axis of the shaft or a straight line extension of it to the sole of the club.

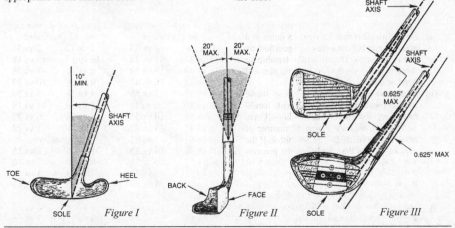

Figure I   *Figure II*   *Figure III*

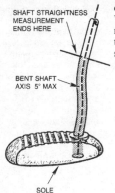

SHAFT STRAIGHTNESS
MEASUREMENT
ENDS HERE

BENT SHAFT
AXIS 5° MAX

SOLE

Figure IV

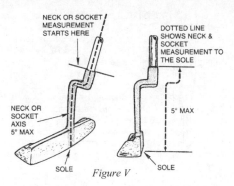

NECK OR SOCKET
MEASUREMENT
STARTS HERE

DOTTED LINE
SHOWS NECK &
SOCKET
MEASUREMENT TO
THE SOLE

NECK OR
SOCKET
AXIS
5° MAX

5° MAX

SOLE   SOLE

Figure V

d. Alignment
When the club is in its normal address position the shaft shall be so aligned that:

(i) the projection of the straight part of the shaft on to the vertical plane through the toe and heel shall diverge from the vertical by at least 10 degrees (see Fig. I).

(ii) the projection of the straight part of the shaft on to the vertical plane along the intended line of play shall not diverge from the vertical by more than 20 degrees (see Fig. II).

Except for putters, all of the heel portion of the club shall lie within 0.625 inches (15.88 mm) of the plane containing the axis of the straight part of the shaft and the intended (horizontal) line of play (see Fig. III).

2. Shaft
a. Straightness
The shaft shall be straight from the top of the grip to a point not more than 5 inches (127mm) above the sole, measured from the point where the shaft ceases to be straight along the axis of the bent part of the shaft and the neck and/or socket (see Fig. IV).

b. Bending and Twisting Properties
At any point along its length, the shaft shall:

(i) bend in such a way that the deflection is the same regardless of how the shaft is rotated about its longitudinal axis; and
(ii) twist the same amount in both directions.

c. Attachment to Clubhead
The shaft shall be attached to the clubhead at the heel either directly or through a single plain neck and/or socket. The length from the top of the neck and/or socket to the sole of the club shall not exceed 5 inches (127mm), measured along the axis of, and following any bend in, the neck and/or socket (see Fig. V).

  Exception for Putters: The shaft or neck or socket of a putter may be fixed at any point in the head.

3. Grip (See Fig. VI)
The grip consists of material added to the shaft to enable the player to obtain a firm hold. The grip shall be straight and plain in form, shall extend to the end of the shaft and shall not be moulded for any part of the hands. If no material is added, that portion of the shaft designed to be held by the player shall be considered the grip.

(i) For clubs other than putters the grip must be circular in cross-section, except that a continuous, straight, slightly raised rib may be incorporated along the full length of the grip, and a slightly indented spiral is permitted on a wrapped grip or a replica of one.

(ii) A putter grip may have a non-circular cross-section, provided the cross-section has no concavity, is symmetrical and remains generally similar throughout the length of the grip. (See Clause (v) below.)

(iii) The grip may be tapered but must not have any bulge or waist. Its cross-sectional dimensions measured in any direction must not exceed 1.75 inches (44.45 mm).

(iv) For clubs other than putters the axis of the grip must coincide with the axis of the shaft.

(v) A putter may have two grips provided each is circular in cross-section, the axis of each coincides with the axis of the shaft, and they are separated by at least 1.5 inches (38.1 mm).

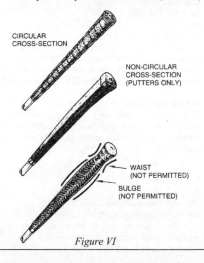

CIRCULAR
CROSS-SECTION

NON-CIRCULAR
CROSS-SECTION
(PUTTERS ONLY)

WAIST
(NOT PERMITTED)

BULGE
(NOT PERMITTED)

Figure VI

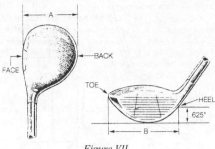

Figure VII

4. Clubhead
a. Plain in Shape
The clubhead shall be generally plain in shape. All parts shall be rigid, structural in nature and functional. It is not practicable to define plain in shape precisely and comprehensively but features which are deemed to be in breach of this requirement and are therefore not permitted include:

(i) holes through the head,
(ii) transparent material added for other than decorative or structural purposes,
(iii) appendages to the main body of the head such as knobs, plates, rods or fins,

for the purpose of meeting dimensional specifications, for aiming or for any other purpose. Exceptions may be made for putters.

Any furrows in or runners on the sole shall not extend into the face.

b. Dimensions
The distance from the heel to the toe of the clubhead shall be greater than the distance from the face to the back. These dimensions are measured, with the clubhead in its normal address position, on horizontal lines between vertical projections of the outermost points of (i) the heel and the toe and (ii) the face and the back (see Fig. VII, dimension A). If the outermost point of the heel is not clearly defined, it is deemed to be 0.625 inches (15.88 mm) above the horizontal plane on which the club is resting in its normal address position (see Fig. VII, dimension B).

c. Striking Faces
The clubhead shall only have one striking face, except that a putter may have two such faces if their characteristics are the same, and they are opposite each other.

5. Club Face
a. General
The material and construction of, or any treatment to, the face or clubhead shall not have the effect at impact of a spring (test on file), or impart significantly more spin to the ball than a standard steel face, or have any

other effect which would unduly influence the movement of the ball.

The face of the club shall be hard and rigid (some exceptions may be made for putters) and, except for such markings listed below, shall be smooth and shall not have any degree of concavity.

b. Impact Area Roughness and Material
Except for markings specified in the following paragraphs, the surface roughness within the area where impact is intended (the 'impact area') must not exceed that of decorative sandblasting, or of fine milling (see Fig. VIII).

The whole of the impact area must be of the same material. Exceptions may be made for wooden clubs.

c. Impact Area Markings
Markings in the impact area must not have sharp edges or raised lips as determined by a finger test. Grooves or punch marks in the impact area must meet the following specifications:

(i) **Grooves.** A series of straight grooves with diverging sides and a symmetrical cross-section may be used (see Fig. IX). The width and cross-section must be consistent across the face of the club and along the length of the grooves. Any rounding of groove edges shall be in the form of a radius which does not exceed 0.020 inches (0.508 mm). The width of the grooves shall not exceed 0.035 inches (0.9mm), using the 30 degree method of measurement on file with the Royal and Ancient Golf Club of St. Andrews. The distance between edges of adjacent grooves must not be less than three times the width of a groove, and not less than 0.075 inches (1.905 mm). The depth of a groove must not exceed 0.020 inches (0.508 mm).

(ii) **Punch Marks.** Punch marks may be used. The area of any such mark must not exceed 0.0044 square inches (2.84 sq.mm). A mark must not be closer to an adjacent mark than 0.168 inches (4.27 mm) measured from centre to centre. The depth of a punch mark must not exceed 0.040 inches (1.02 mm). If punch marks are used in combination with grooves, a punch mark must not be closer to a groove than 0.168 inches (4.27 mm), measured from centre to centre.

d. Decorative Markings
The centre of the impact area may be indicated by a design within the boundary of a square whose sides are 0.375 inches (9.53 mm) in length. Such a design must not unduly influ-

Figure VIII

ence the movement of the ball. Decorative markings are permitted outside the impact area.

e. Non-metallic Club Face Markings
The above specifications apply to clubs on which the impact area of the face is of metal or a material of similar hardness. They do not apply to clubs with faces made of other materials and whose loft angle is 24 degrees or less, but markings which could unduly influence the movement of the ball are prohibited. Clubs with this type of face and a loft angle exceeding 24 degrees may have grooves of maximum width 0.040 inches (1.02 mm) and maximum depth 1½ times the groove width, but must otherwise conform to the markings specifications above.

f. Putter Face
The specifications above with regard to roughness, material and markings in the impact area do not apply to putters.

APPENDIX III
The Ball

1. Weight
The weight of the ball shall not be greater than 1.620 ounces avoirdupois (45.93 gm).

2. Size
The diameter of the ball shall be not less than 1.680 inches (42.67mm). This specification will be satisfied if, under its own weight, a ball falls through a 1.680 inches diameter ring gauge in fewer than 25 out of 100 randomly selected positions, the test being carried out at a temperature of $23 \pm 1°C$.

3. Spherical Symmetry
The ball must not be designed, manufactured or intentionally modified to have properties which differ from those of a spherically symmetrical ball.

4. Initial Velocity
The initial velocity of the ball shall not exceed the limit specified (test on file) when measured on apparatus approved by the Royal and Ancient Golf Club of St. Andrews.

5. Overall Distance Standard
The combined carry and roll of the ball, when tested on apparatus approved by the Royal and Ancient Golf Club of St. Andrews, shall not exceed the distance specified under the conditions set forth in the Overall Distance Standard for golf balls on file with the Royal and Ancient Golf Club of St. Andrews.

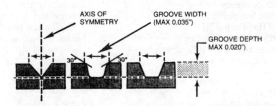

EXAMPLES OF PERMISSIBLE GROOVE CROSS-SECTIONS

Figure IX

INDEX

The Rules of Golf are here indexed according to the
pertinent rule number, definition or appendix that has gone before.

HANDICAPS

The Rules of Golf do not legislate for the allocation and adjustment of handicaps. Such matters are within the jurisdiction of the National Union concerned and queries should be directed accordingly.

RULES OF AMATEUR STATUS
As approved by the Royal and Ancient Golf Club of St Andrews
Effective from 1st January 2000

Preamble
The Royal and Ancient Golf Club of St. Andrews reserves the right to change the Rules and to make and change the interpretations relating to Amateur Status at any time.

Definitions

The Definitions are placed in alphabetical order and some are also repeated at the beginning of their relevant Rule.

In the Rules themselves, defined terms are italicised.

Amateur Golfer
An 'Amateur Golfer' is one who plays the game as a non-remunerative and non-profit-making sport and who does not receive remuneration for teaching golf or for other activities because of *golf skill or reputation*, except as provided in the *Rules*.

Committee
The 'Committee' is the appropriate Committee of the *Governing Body*.

Golf Skill or Reputation
Generally, an *Amateur golfer* is only considered to have golf skill if he has gained representative honours at county or national level. Golf reputation can only be gained through golf skill and does not include prominence for service to the game of golf as an administrator. It is a matter for a *Governing Body* to decide whether a particular *Amateur golfer* has 'golf skill or reputation'.

Governing Body
The 'Governing Body' for the Rules of Amateur Status in any country is the national union of that country.

Note: In Great Britain and Ireland, the Royal and Ancient Golf Club of St. Andrews is the *Governing Body*.

Instruction
'Instruction' covers teaching the physical aspects of playing golf i.e. the actual mechanics of swinging a golf club and hitting a golf ball.

Junior Golfer
A 'junior golfer' is an *Amateur golfer* who has not reached his 18th birthday in the year prior to the event, unless a different age is decided by the *Governing Body*.

Prize Voucher
A 'prize voucher' is a voucher issued by the Committee in charge of a competition for the purchase of goods from a Professional's shop or other retail source.

Retail Value
The 'retail value' of a prize is the normal recommended selling price at which merchandise is available to anyone at a retail source.

Rule or Rules
The term 'Rule' or 'Rules' refers to the Rules of Amateur Status as determined by the *Governing Body*.

Symbolic Prize
A 'symbolic prize' is a trophy made of gold, silver, ceramic, glass or the like which is permanently and distinctively engraved.

Testimonial Award
A 'testimonial award' relates to notable performances or contributions to golf as distinguished from competition prizes. A testimonial award may not be a monetary award.

Rule 1. Amateurism

Definitions

An **Amateur golfer** is one who plays the game as a non-remunerative and non-profit-making sport and who does not receive remuneration for teaching golf or for other activities because of *golf skill or reputation*, except as provided in the *Rules*.

The term **Rule** or **Rules** refers to the Rules of Amateur Status as determined by the *Governing Body*.

1-1. General

An *Amateur golfer* must play the game and conduct himself in accordance with the *Rules*.

1-2. Amateur Status

Amateur Status is a universal condition of eligibility for playing in golf competitions as an *Amateur golfer*. A person who acts contrary to the *Rules* may forfeit his status as an *Amateur golfer* and as a result will be ineligible to play in Amateur competitions.

1-3. Purpose and Spirit of the Rules

The purpose and spirit of the *Rules* is to maintain the distinction between Amateur golf and Professional golf and keep the Amateur game as free as possible from the abuses which may follow from uncontrolled sponsorship and financial incentive. It is considered necessary to safeguard Amateur golf, which is largely self-regulating with regard to the Rules of play and handicapping, so that it may be fully enjoyed by all *Amateur golfers*.

1-4. Doubt as to Rules

Any person who wishes to be an *Amateur golfer* and who is in doubt as to whether taking a proposed course of action is permitted under the *Rules* should consult the *Governing Body*.

Any organiser or sponsor of an Amateur golf competition or a competition involving *Amateur golfers*, who is in doubt as to whether a proposal is in accordance with the *Rules* should consult the *Governing Body*.

Rule 2. Professionalism

2-1. General

An *Amateur golfer* must not take any action for the purpose of becoming a Professional golfer, including entering into an agreement, written or oral, with a sponsor or Professional agent.

Exception: Applying unsuccessfully for the position of an Assistant Professional.

Note: An *Amateur golfer* may enquire as to his likely prospects as a Professional and he may work in a Professional's shop and receive a salary, provided he does not infringe the *Rules* in any other way.

2-2. Professional Golfers' Associations

An *Amateur golfer* must not hold or retain membership of any Professional Golfers' Association.

2-3. Professional Tournament Players

An *Amateur golfer* must not file an application to a final or sole qualifying competition for a Professional Tour.

Note: If an *Amateur golfer* must pre-qualify for a final qualifying competition, he may enter such a pre-qualifying competition without forfeiting his Amateur Status.

Rule 3. Prizes

Definitions

The **Governing Body** for the Rules of Amateur Status in any country is the national union of that country.

Note: In Great Britain and Ireland, the Royal and Ancient Golf Club of St. Andrews is the *Governing Body*.

A **prize voucher** is a voucher issued by the Committee in charge of a competition for the purchase of goods from a Professional's shop or other retail source.

The **retail value** of a prize is the normal recommended selling price at which merchandise is available to anyone at a retail source.

A **symbolic prize** is a trophy made of gold, silver, ceramic, glass or the like which is permanently and distinctively engraved.

A **testimonial award** relates to notable performances or contributions to golf as distinguished from competition prizes. A testimonial award may not be a monetary award.

3-1. Playing for Prize Money

An *Amateur golfer* must not play golf for prize money.

3-2. Prize Limits
a. General

An *Amateur golfer* must not accept a prize (other than a *symbolic prize*) or *prize voucher* of *retail value* in excess of the prescribed limits. These limits apply to the total prizes or *prize vouchers* received by an *Amateur golfer* in any one competition or series of competitions, excluding any hole-in-one prize.

In Europe	£300	or the equivalent
Elsewhere	$US500	or the equivalent

or such lesser figure as may be decided by the *Governing Body*.

b. Hole-in-One Prizes

The limits prescribed in Rule 3-2a apply to a prize for a hole-in-one. However, such a prize may be accepted in addition to any other prize won in the same competition.

c. Exchanging Prizes

An *Amateur golfer* must not exchange a prize or *prize voucher* for cash.

Exception: An *Amateur golfer* may submit a *prize voucher* to a national or county union and thereafter be reimbursed from the value of that voucher for expenses incurred in participating in a golf competition, provided the reimbursement of such expenses is permitted under Rule 4-2.

Note 1: The onus of proving the *retail value* of a particular prize rests with the Committee in charge of the competition.

Note 2: It is recommended that the total value of scratch prizes, or each division of handicap prizes, should not exceed twice the prescribed limit in an 18-hole competition, three times in a 36-hole competition, four times in a 54-hole competition and five times in a 72-hole competition.

3-3. Testimonial Awards
a. General

An *Amateur golfer* must not accept a *testimonial award* of *retail value* in excess of the limits prescribed in Rule 3-2a.

b. Multiple Awards

An *Amateur golfer* may accept more than one *testimonial award* from different donors, even though their total *retail value* exceeds the prescribed limit, provided they are not presented so as to evade the limit for a single award.

Rule 4. Expenses

Definitions

The **Governing Body** for the Rules of Amateur Status in any country is the national union of that country.

Note: In Great Britain and Ireland, the Royal and Ancient Golf Club of St. Andrews is the *Governing Body*.

A **junior golfer** is an *Amateur golfer* who has not reached his 18th birthday in the year prior to the event, unless a different age is decided by the *Governing Body*.

4-1. General

Except as provided in the *Rules*, an *Amateur golfer* must not accept expenses, in money or otherwise, from any source to play in a golf competition or exhibition.

4-2. Receipt of Expenses

An *Amateur golfer* may receive expenses, not exceeding the actual expenses incurred, to play in a golf competition or exhibition as follows:-

a. Family support

An *Amateur golfer* may receive expenses from a member of his family or a legal guardian.

b. Junior Golfers

A *junior golfer* may receive expenses when competing in a competition limited exclusively to *junior golfers*.

c. Team Events

(i) An *Amateur golfer*, who is representing his country, county or club (or similar body) in a team competition or at a training camp may receive expenses; and

(ii) An *Amateur golfer*, who is representing his country by taking part in a national championship abroad immediately before or after an international team competition may receive expenses.

The expenses must be paid by the body he represents or the body controlling golf in the country he is visiting.

d. Individual Events

An *Amateur golfer* may receive expenses when competing in individual events provided he complies with the following provisions:

(i) The player must be nominated to play in the competition by either his club, county or national union.

(ii) Where the competition is to take place in the player's own country and the nomination has been made by a club or county union, the approval of the national union, or the county union in the area in which the competition is to be staged, must first be obtained.

(iii) Where the competition is to take place in another country, the approval of the national union of the country in which the competition is to be staged and, if the nominating body is not the national union of the country from which the nomination is made, the approval of the national union must first be obtained by the nominating body.

(iv) The expenses must be paid only by the national union or county union responsible in the area from which the nomination is made or, subject to the approval of the nominating body, by the body controlling golf in the territory he is visiting.

(v) The expenses must be limited to a specific number of competitive days in any one calendar year as may be determined by the *Governing Body* in the country from which the nomination is made. The expenses are deemed to include reasonable travelling time and practice days in connection with the competitive days.

e. Celebrities, Business Associates, etc.

An *Amateur golfer* who is invited to take part in a competition for reasons unrelated to *golf skill* may receive expenses.

f. Exhibitions

An *Amateur golfer* who is participating in an exhibition in aid of a recognised charity may receive

expenses, provided that the exhibition is not run in connection with another golfing event.

g. Sponsored Handicap Competitions
An *Amateur golfer* may receive expenses when competing in a sponsored handicap competition, provided the competition has been approved as follows:

(i) Where the competition is to take place in the player's own country, the annual approval of the *Governing Body* must first be obtained in advance by the sponsor; and

(ii) Where the competition is to take place in more than one country or involves golfers from another country, the approval of the two or more *Governing Bodies* must first be obtained in advance by the sponsor. The application for this approval should be sent to the *Governing Body* in the country where the competition commences.

Rule 5. Instruction

Definitions
Instruction covers teaching the physical aspects of playing golf, i.e. the actual mechanics of swinging a golf club and hitting a golf ball.

A **junior golfer** is an *Amateur golfer* who has not reached his 18th birthday in the year prior to the event, unless a different age is decided by the *Governing Body*.

5-1. General
Except as provided in the *Rules*, an *Amateur golfer* must not receive payment or compensation for giving *instruction* in playing golf.

5-2. Where Payment Permitted
a. Schools, Colleges, etc.
An *Amateur golfer*, who is an employee of an educational institution or system, may receive payment or compensation for golf *instruction* to students of the institution or system, provided that during a year the total time devoted to golf *instruction* comprises less than 50 percent of the time spent in the performance of all duties as such an employee.

b. Junior Golfers
An *Amateur golfer* may receive expenses, not exceeding the actual expenses incurred, for giving golf *instruction* to *junior golfers* as part of a programme which has been approved in advance by the *Governing Body*.

5-3. Instruction in Writing
An *Amateur golfer* may receive payment or compensation for *instruction* in writing, provided his ability or reputation as a golfer was not a major factor in his employment or in the commission or sale of his work.

Note: *Instruction* does not cover the many psychological aspects of the game or the Rules or Etiquette of Golf.

Rule 6. Use of Golf Skill or Reputation

Definitions
Generally, an *Amateur golfer* is only considered to have golf skill if he has gained representative honours at county or national level. Golf reputation can only be gained through golf skill and does not include prominence for service to the game of golf as an administrator. It is a matter for a *Governing Body* to decide whether a particular *Amateur golfer* has **golf skill or reputation**.

The **Governing Body** for the Rules of Amateur Status in any country is the national union of that country.

Note: In Great Britain and Ireland, the Royal and Ancient Golf Club of St. Andrews is the *Governing Body*.

Instruction covers teaching the physical aspects of playing golf, i.e. the actual mechanics of swinging a golf club and hitting a golf ball.

6-1. General
Except as provided in the *Rules*, an *Amateur golfer* of *golf skill or reputation* must not use that skill or reputation to promote, advertise or sell anything or for any financial gain.

6-2. Lending Name or Likeness
An *Amateur golfer* of *golf skill or reputation* must not use that skill or reputation to obtain payment, compensation, personal benefit or any financial gain for allowing his name or likeness to be used for the advertisement or sale of anything.

Note: An *Amateur golfer* may accept equipment from anyone dealing in such equipment provided no advertising is involved.

6-3. Personal Appearance
An *Amateur golfer* of *golf skill or reputation* must not use that skill or reputation to obtain payment, compensation, personal benefit or any financial gain for a personal appearance.

Exception: An *Amateur golfer* may receive actual expenses in connection with a personal appearance provided no golf competition or exhibition is involved.

6-4. Broadcasting and Writing
An *Amateur golfer* of *golf skill or reputation* must not use that skill or reputation to obtain payment, compensation, personal benefit or any financial gain for broadcasting concerning golf or writing golf articles or books.

Exception: An *Amateur golfer* may receive payment, compensation, personal benefit or any financial gain from broadcasting or writing provided:

(a) the player is actually the author of the commentary, article or books; and

(b) *instruction* in playing golf is not included.

6-5. Grants, Scholarships and Bursaries

An *Amateur golfer* of *golf skill or reputation* must not accept the benefits of a grant, scholarship or bursary, except one whose terms and conditions have been approved by the *Governing Body*.

6-6. Membership

An *Amateur golfer* of *golf skill or reputation* must not accept an offer of membership in a Golf Club without full payment for the class of membership if such an offer is made as an inducement to play for that Club.

Rule 7. Other Conduct Incompatible with Amateurism

Definitions

An **Amateur golfer** is one who plays the game as a non-remunerative and non-profit-making sport and who does not receive remuneration for teaching golf or for other activities because of *golf skill or reputation*, except as provided in the *Rules*.

The term **Rule** or **Rules** refers to the Rules of Amateur Status as determined by the *Governing Body*.

7-1. Conduct Detrimental to Golf

An *Amateur golfer* must not act in a manner which is considered detrimental to the best interests of the game.

7-2. Conduct Contrary to the Purpose and Spirit of the Rules

An *Amateur golfer* must not take any action, including actions relating to golf gambling, which is contrary to the purpose and spirit of the *Rules*.

Rule 8. Procedure for Enforcement of the Rules

Definitions

The **Committee** is the appropriate Committee of the *Governing Body*.

The **Governing Body** for the Rules of Amateur Status in any country is the national union of that country.

Note: In Great Britain and Ireland, the Royal and Ancient Golf Club of St. Andrews is the *Governing Body*.

8-1. Decision on a Breach

If a possible breach of the *Rules* by a person claiming to be an *Amateur golfer* comes to the attention of the *Committee*, it is a matter for the *Committee* to decide whether a breach has occurred. Each case will be investigated to the extent deemed appropriate by the *Committee* and considered on its merits. The decision of the *Committee* shall be final, subject to an Appeal as provided in these *Rules*.

8-2. Enforcement

Upon a decision that a person has breached the *Rules*, the *Committee* may declare the Amateur Status of the person forfeited or require the person to refrain or desist from specified actions as a condition of retaining his Amateur Status.

The *Committee* must use its best endeavours to ensure that the person is notified and may notify any interested golf union of any action taken under Rule 8-2.

8-3. Appeals Procedure

A person affected by a decision made by the Amateur Status Committee of the Royal and Ancient Golf Club of St. Andrews in respect of the enforcement of these *Rules*, may raise an appeal of that decision with the Amateur Status Appeals Committee.

Note: Each *Governing Body* should put in place a procedure whereby any decision in respect of forfeiture of Amateur Status may be appealed by the person affected by such decision.

Rule 9. Reinstatement of Amateur Status

Definitions

The **Committee** is the appropriate Committee of the *Governing Body*.

The **Governing Body** for the Rules of Amateur Status in any country is the national union of that country.

Note: In Great Britain and Ireland, the Royal and Ancient Golf Club of St. Andrews is the *Governing Body*.

9-1. General

The *Committee* has sole power to reinstate a person to Amateur Status or to deny reinstatement, subject to an Appeal as provided in these *Rules*. Each application for reinstatement shall be considered on its merits.

9-2. Applications for Reinstatement

In considering an application for reinstatement, the *Committee* shall normally be guided by the following principles:

a. Awaiting Reinstatement

The Professional is considered to hold an advantage over the *Amateur golfer* by reason of having devoted himself to the game as his profession; other persons infringing the *Rules* also obtain advantages not available to the *Amateur golfer*. They do not necessarily lose such advantages merely by deciding to cease infringing the *Rules*. Therefore, an applicant for reinstatement to Amateur Status must undergo a period awaiting reinstatement as prescribed by the *Committee*.

The period awaiting reinstatement starts from the date of the person's last breach of the *Rules* unless the *Committee* decides that it starts from the date when the person's last breach became known to the *Committee*.

b. Period Awaiting Reinstatement
(i) Professionalism

The period awaiting reinstatement is normally related to the period the person was in breach. However, no applicant is normally eligible for reinstatement until he has conducted himself in accordance with the *Rules* for a period of at least one year.

It is recommended that the following guidelines on periods awaiting reinstatement are applied by the *Committee:*

Period of Breach:	Period Awaiting Reinstatement:
under 2 years	1 year
2-10 years	2 years
over 10 years	3 years

The *Committee* reserves the right to extend or to shorten such a period. Players of national prominence who have been in breach for more than five years are not normally eligible for reinstatement.

(ii) Other Breaches of the Rules

The period awaiting reinstatement is normally related to the seriousness of the breach, i.e. the value of the excessive prize, the amount of unauthorised expenses received, etc. However, no applicant is normally eligible for reinstatement until he has conducted himself in accordance with the *Rules* for a period of at least two years.

The *Committee* reserves the right to extend or shorten such a period.

(iii) Second Reinstatement

The period awaiting reinstatement is normally three years irrespective of the period of breach.

The *Committee* reserves the right to extend or shorten such a period.

c. Number of Reinstatements

A person is not normally reinstated more than twice.

d. Status While Awaiting Reinstatement

During the period awaiting reinstatement an applicant for reinstatement must comply with these *Rules* as they apply to an *Amateur golfer*.

He is not eligible to enter competitions as an *Amateur golfer*. However, he may enter competitions and win a prize solely among members of a Club of which he is a member, subject to the approval of the Club; but he may not represent such Club against other Clubs.

9-3. Procedure for Applications

Each application for reinstatement must be submitted to the *Committee*, in accordance with such procedures as may be laid down and it must include such information as the *Committee* may require.

9-4. Appeals Procedure

A person affected by a decision made by the Amateur Status Committee of the Royal and Ancient Golf Club of St. Andrews in respect of reinstatement of Amateur Status, may raise an appeal of that decision with the Amateur Status Appeals Committee.

Note: Each *Governing Body* should put in place a procedure whereby any decision in respect of reinstatement of Amateur Status may be appealed by the person affected by such a decision.

Rule 10. Committee Decision

Definition

The **Committee** is the appropriate Committee of the *Governing Body*.

10-1. Committee's Decision

The *Committee's* decision is final, subject to an Appeal as provided in Rules 8-3 and 9-4.

10-2. Doubt as to Rules

If the *Committee* considers the case to be doubtful or not covered by the *Rules*, it may, prior to making its decision, consult with the Amateur Status Committee of the Royal and Ancient Golf Club of St. Andrews.

Today's Highly-qualified PGA Professional

With the first hundred years of providing a service to golf now behind it, The Professional Golfers' Association is looking forward to the future with confidence. The development of the game and the quality of service is being continually enhanced especially within the Training Programme, now available to all aspiring professionals.

Initially placed on the agenda by Eddie Whitcombe in a letter to the Association's Executive Committee in 1936, the formal structure of the Association's Training Programme only crystalised after a chance meeting with James Braid at Walton Heath in 1950. With Braid's blessing the Executive Committee instructed Whitcombe to design a training programme for all potential club professional golfers. The first courses were held at Maesdu Golf Club in North Wales in 1952 with instruction and discussion centred on teaching the golf swing, running a golf shop and repairing golf clubs.

In those early days Whitcombe relied upon the assistance of Tom Jones, Professional at Maesdu, and friends Reg Cox, Sid Collins, and Eddie Musty to run the courses. For the aspiring professional simple attendance was sufficient in those early days to grant full membership of the Association.

The commitment to the game and its development is stronger than ever today. There is a stronger belief that the responsible development of the game must be in qualified hands. Since the days of Eddie Whitcombe and his Maesdu courses, the Association's Training programme has continued to improve. There is greater involvement of existing members, all using their experience to pass on their knowledge to the new breed of recruits eager to pursue a career in the professional game.

Academic courses now include Rules of Golf and Tournament Administration coupled with Commercial Studies – a new name for the old Running a Business course. Trainees are required to maintain a playing stan-

dard throughout their early professional days that reflects their ability as golfers. Indeed entrance onto the programme can only be achieved from the amateur ranks if the applicant has a handicap of 4 or better.

The handicap requirement was lowered as the growth of the sport gained a higher profile in the wake of Tony Jacklin's famous successes in The Open Championship in 1969 and the US Open in 1970. With more trainee professionals applying during the 1970s and 1980s the existing training facilities offered by Inverclyde, Lilleshall and Bisham Abbey proved inadequate and in June 1996 Eddie Whitcombe and Reg Cox attended a special occasion at the PGA's National Headquarters at The De Vere Belfry.

On 4 June, 1996, HRH The Duke of York presided over the opening of the Association's state of the art, purpose built training academy – a far cry from the thoughts offered by Whitcombe in his letter sixty years earlier. Adjacent to six new accommodation buildings for use by the trainees during their course attendance, the newly revamped Training Diploma Programme offers a degree-style course to the prospective golf professional providing exposure to the new disciplines of Sports Science (including nutrition and fitness), Teaching and Theory of the

PGA professionals must take a highly sophisticated three-year course before they become fully qualified club professionals and teachers.

Golf Swing, Club Technology, Business Management, Rules of Golf and Tournament administration.

The courses are designed on distance learning modules with the primary focus at grass roots club level. There the trainee is required to work closely with their employing professional while having access at all times to a specialized team of training

with the rigorous assessment procedures reflect the degree of professionalism now expected of PGA Members. Nor does education end on graduation. The PGA now provides a Continuous Professional Development Programme, and an Advanced Education Programme, for qualified PGA members to ensure that the PGA Golf Professional is equipped

© PGA

executives at the Training Academy plus the support of other senior qualified teaching PGA members as their mentors. Successful graduation at the end of their intensive training ensures that all new PGA registered professionals are fully equipped to meet the challenges that the game now presents as more and more people discover golf and want to learn not just how to play it but also the etiquette which is so much a part of the game's integrity.

The study period is concentrated over three years, and the strictly enforced entry requirements coupled

to meet the continually changing circumstances in the modern game.

The high profile success of individual players such as 1999 Open Champion, Paul Lawrie, Ryder Cup players Ken Brown, Gordon Brand and Barry Lane and 2000 Rookie of the Year Ian Poulter, who have all met the relevant qualification criteria, proves that the carefully planned PGA qualification courses are designed to embrace both the tour player and the club professional alike, ensuring the future of the game is in safe hands at both ends of the spectrum.

Professional Governing Bodies

The Professional Golfers' Association

The Professional Golfers' Association was founded in 1901 to promote interest in the game of golf; to protect and advance the mutual and trade interests of its members; to arrange and hold meetings and tournaments periodically for the members; to institute and operate funds for the benefit of the members; to assist the members to obtain employment; and effect any other objects of a like nature as may be determined from time to time by the Association.

Classes of Membership

There shall be nine classes of membership:

(i) **Class A** Members engaged as the nominated professional on a full-time basis at a PGA Club, PGA Course or PGA Driving Range in one of the seven Regions; and members engaged as the nominated professional on a full-time basis, at an establishment in one of the seven Regions at which the public can play and/or practise which, in the opinion of the Executive Committee does not qualify as a PGA Club, Course or Driving Range but does warrant Class A status. *Note:* Class A(T) – Class A members currently engaged at an establishment which has been inspected and approved as a PGA Training Establishment and currently holds that status will be identified where appropriate by the suffix (T) after their classification.

(ii) **Class B** Members engaged by a Class A or D member to assist the nominated professional at any PGA Establishment in one of the seven Regions on a full-time basis.

(iii) **Class C** Tournament playing members (men and women).

(iv) **Class D** Members engaged as the nominated professional on a full-time basis at a PGA Establishment within the seven Regions which does not qualify as a 'Class A' establishment, or engaged on a full-time basis within the seven Regions by any other Company or any other individual designated by the Executive Committee for this purpose. (Former Class G.)

(v) **Class E** Honorary Associate Members (HAM). Those who in the opinion of the Executive Committee through their past or continuing membership justify retaining the full privileges of membership as Honorary Associate Members (HAM).

(vi) **Class F** Associate Members (AM).

(a) Those who have ceased to be eligible for other categories of membership who in the opinion of the Executive Committee through their past membership justify retaining limited privileges of membership as Associate Members; and (b) Members of the PGA European Tour or WPGET who do not qualify for Class C membership but who in the opinion of the Executive Committee justify limited privileges of membership as Associate Members.

(vii) **Class G** Honorary Life Members (HLM). Those recommended by the Board to a Special General Meeting of the Association for election as Honorary Life Members. No form of application is needed nor need reference be made to the Regional Committee concerned.

(viii) **Class H** Members who are qualified members of the Association, and ineligible for any other class of membership, engaged on a full-time basis at an establishment acceptable to the Association outside the jurisdiction of the seven Regions. (Overseas)

(ix) **Class O** Members who have not qualified at the official training centre of the Association, who are ineligible for any other class of membership, and who are current members of another PGA approved by the Association and have held such member- ship for not less than two years.

The Management of the Association is under the overall direction and control of a Board. The Association is divided into seven Regions each of which employs a full-time secretary and runs tournaments for the benefit of members within its Region.

The Association is responsible for arranging and obtaining sponsorship of the Ryder Cup, Club Professionals' Championship, PGA Cup matches, Seniors' Championship, PGA Assistants' Championship, Assistants' Matchplay Championship and other National Championships.

Anyone who intends to become a club professional must serve a minimum of three years in registration and qualify at the PGA Training School before election as a full Member.

The Professional Golfers' Associations of Europe

The PGA of Europe was created in 1989 as an Association of national European PGAs to ensure uniformity of professional standards and objectives.

In its first ten years the PGAE grew to a body comprising 33 member PGAs, five of them Associate Members from outside the continent of Europe. These 33 PGAs are made up of a total of 12,000 professionals comprising Directors of Golf, Club Professionals, Teaching Professionals, all of whom provide a comprehensive service to the entire golfing community.

The purpose of the PGA or Europe is to:

(1) Unify and improve standards of education and qualification;
(2) Advise and assist golf professionals to achieve properly rewarded employment;
(3) Provide relevant playing opportunities;
(4) Be the central point of advice, information and support;
(5) Be a respected link with other golfing bodies throughout Europe and the rest of the world – all for the benefit of its members and the enhancement of the sport.

PGA European Tour

To be eligible to become a member of the PGA European Tour a player must possess certain minimum standards which shall be determined by the Tournament Committee. In 1976 a Qualifying School for potential new members was introduced to be held annually. The leading players are awarded cards allowing them to compete in PGA European Tour tournaments.

In 1985 the PGA European Tour became ALL EXEMPT with no more Monday pre-qualifying. Full details can be obtained from the Wentworth Headquarters.

The Evian Tour (Ladies' European Tour)

The Evian Tour was founded in 1988 to further the development of women's professional golf throughout Europe and its membership is open to all nationalities. A qualifying school is held annually and an amateur wishing to participate must be 18 years of age and have a handicap of 1 or less. Full details can be obtained from the Tour Headquarters at Tytherington.

Amateur Governing Bodies

Home Unions

The English Golf Union

The English Golf Union was founded in 1924 and embraces 34 County Unions with 1895 affiliated clubs, 24 clubs overseas, and 500 Golfing Societies and Associations. Its objects are:

(1) To further the interests of Amateur Golf in England.
(2) To assist in maintaining a uniform system of handicapping.
(3) To arrange an English Championship; an English Strokeplay Championship; an English County Championship, International and other Matches and Competitions.
(4) To cooperate with the Royal & Ancient Golf Club of St Andrews and the Council of National Golf Unions.
(5) To cooperate with other National Golf Unions and Associations in such manner as may be decided.

The Scottish Golf Union

The Scottish Golf Union was founded in 1920 and embraces 695 clubs. Subject to the stipulation and declaration that the Union recognises the Royal & Ancient Golf Club of St Andrews as the Ruling Authority in the game of golf, the objects of the Union are:

(a) To foster and maintain a high standard of amateur golf in Scotland and to administer and organise and generally act as the governing body of amateur golf in Scotland.
(b) To institute and thereafter carry through annually a Scottish Amateur Championship, a Scottish Open Amateur Strokeplay Championship and other such competitions and matches as they consider appropriate.
(c) To administer and apply the rules of the Standard Scratch Score and Handicapping Scheme as approved by the Council of National Golf Unions from time to time.
(d) To deal with other matters of general or local interest to amateur golfers in Scotland.

The Union's organisation consists of Area Committees covering the whole of Scotland. There are 16 Areas, each having its own Association or Committee elected by the Clubs in that particular area and each Area Association or Committee elects one delegate to serve on the Executive of the Union.

Golfing Union of Ireland

The Golfing Union of Ireland, founded in 1891, embraces 398 Clubs. Its objects are:

(1) Securing the federation of the various Clubs.
(2) Arranging Amateur Championships, Inter-Provincial and Inter-Club Competitions, and International Matches.
(3) Securing a uniform standard of handicapping.
(4) Providing for advice and assistance, other than financial, to affiliated Clubs in all matters appertaining to Golf, and generally to promote the game in every way, in which this can be better done by the Union than by individual Clubs.

Its functions include the holding of the Close Championship for Amateur Golfers and Tournaments for Team Matches.

Its organisation consists of Provincial Councils in each of the four Provinces elected by the Clubs in the Province – each province electing a limited number of delegates to the Central Council which meets annually.

Welsh Golfing Union

The Welsh Golfing Union was founded in 1895 and is the second oldest of the four National Unions. Unlike the other Unions it is an association of Golf Clubs and Golfing Organisations. The present membership is 159. For the purpose of electing the Executive Council, Wales is divided into ten districts which between them return 22 members. The objects of the Union are:

(a) To take any steps which may be deemed necessary to further the interests of the amateur game in Wales.
(b) To hold a Championship Meeting or Meetings each year.
(c) To encourage, financially and/or otherwise, Inter-Club, Inter-County, and International Matches, and such other events as may be authorised by the Council.
(d) To assist in setting up and maintaining a uniform system of Handicapping.
(e) To assist in the establishment and maintenance of high standards of greenkeeping.

Note: The union recognises the Royal & Ancient Golf Club of St Andrews as the ruling authority.

The Council of National Golf Unions

At a meeting of Representatives of Golf Unions and Associations in Great Britain and Ireland, called at the

special request of the Scottish Golf Union, and held in York, on 14th February, 1924, resolutions were adopted from which the Council of National Golf Unions was constituted.

The Council holds an Annual Meeting in March, and such other meetings as may be necessary. Two representatives are elected from each national Home Union – England, Scotland, Ireland and Wales and one from the Royal and Ancient Golf Club of St Andrews – and hold office until the next Annual meeting when they are eligible for re-election.

The principal function of the Council, as laid down by the York Conference, was to formulate a system of Standard Scratch Scores and Handicapping, and to co-operate with the Royal & Ancient Championship Committee in matters coming under their jurisdiction. The responsibilities undertaken by the Council at the instance of the Royal & Ancient Golf Club or the National Unions are as follows:

1   The Standard Scratch Score and Handicapping Scheme, formulated in March, 1926, approved by the Royal & Ancient, and last revised in 2001.
2   The nomination of one member on the Board of Management of The Sports Turf Research Institute, with an experimental station at St Ives, Bingley, Yorkshire.
3   The management of the Annual Amateur International Matches between the four countries – England, Scotland, Ireland and Wales.

United States Golf Association

The USGA is the national governing body of golf in the United States, dedicated to promoting and conserving the best interests and true spirit of the game.

Founded on 22 December 1894 by representatives of five American golf clubs, the USGA was originally charged with conducting national championships, implementing a uniform code of rules, and maintaining a national system of handicapping.

Today, the principal functions of the association remain lagely unchanged. Each year, the USGA conducts thirteen national championships for amateur and professional golfers; biennial competitions include State Team Championships for men and women, the Walker Cup, Curtis Cup, and World Amateur Team Championships. In cooperation with the Royal & Ancient Golf Club of St. Andrews, Scotland, the USGA continues to write and interpret the Rules of Golf, and oversees the standards regulating the equipment used to play the game. The association also maintains a national handicapping system, providing handicap computation services to state and regional golf associations through the Golf Handicap and Information Network.

Additional responsibilities assumed by the association encompass turfgrass and environmental research conducted by the USGA Green Section; preservation and promotion of the game's rich history in the Museum and Archives; oversight of the Rules of Amateur Status; publication of *Golf Journal*, the USGA's official magazine; and direction of the USGA Members Program, with over 900,000 members globally. Since 1965, the USGA Foundation has functioned as the association's broad-based philanthropic arm, dedicated to maintaining and improving the opportunities for all individuals to participate fully in the game.

Tel: +1 908 234 2300\ Fax: +1 908 234 9687

Government of the Amateur and Open Golf Championship

In December 1919, on the invitation of the clubs who had hitherto controlled the Amateur and Open Golf Championships, the Royal & Ancient took over the government of those events. These two championships are now controlled by a committee appointed by the Royal & Ancient Golf Club of St Andrews. The Committee is called the Royal and Ancient Golf Club Championship Committee and consists of eight members of the Club elected by the Club.

Ladies' Golf Union (LGU)

The Ladies' Golf Union was founded in 1893 with the following objectives:

(1)   To promote the interests of the game of Golf.
(2)   To obtain a uniformity of the rules of the game by establishing a representative legislative authority.
(3)   To establish a uniform system of handicapping.
(4)   To act as a tribunal and court of reference on points of uncertainty.
(5)   To arrange the Annual Championship Competition and obtain the funds necessary for that purpose.

After 100 years, only the language has changed, the present Constitution defines the objectives as:

(1)   To uphold the rules of the game, to advance and safeguard the interests of women's golf and to decide all doubtful and disputed points in connection therewith.
(2)   To maintain, regulate and enforce the LGU Handicapping System.
(3)   To employ the funds of The Union in such a manner as shall be deemed best for the interests of women's golf, with power to borrow or raise money to use for the same purpose.
(4)   To maintain and regulate International events, Championships and Competitions held under the LGU regulations and to promote the interests of Great Britain and Ireland in Ladies International Golf.

(5) To make, maintain and publish such regulations as may be considered necessary for the above purposes.

The constituents of the LGU are:

Home Countries. The English Ladies' Golf Association (founded 1952), the Irish Ladies' Golf Union (founded 1893), the Scottish Ladies' Golfing Association (founded 1904), the Welsh Ladies' Golf Union (founded 1904), plus ladies' societies, girls' schools and ladies' clubs affiliated to these organisations.

Overseas. Affiliated ladies' golf unions and golf clubs in the Commonwealth and any other overseas ladies' golfing organisation affiliated to the LGU.

Individual lady members of clubs within the above categories are regarded as members of the LGU.

The Rules of the Game and of Amateur Status, which the LGU is bound to uphold, are those published by the Royal & Ancient Golf Club of St Andrews.

In endeavouring to fulfil its responsibilities towards advancing and safeguarding women's golf, the LGU maintains contact with other golfing organisations – the Royal & Ancient Golf Club of St Andrews, the Council of National Golf Unions, the Golf Foundation, the Central Council of Physical Recreation, the Sports Council, the Women Professional Golfers' European Tour and the Women's Committee of the United States Golf Association. This contact ensures that the LGU is informed of developments and projected developments and has an opportunity to comment upon and to influence the future of the game for women.

Either directly or through its constituent national organisations the LGU advises and is the ultimate authority on doubts or disputes which may arise in connection with the handicapping system and regulations governing competitions played under LGU conditions.

The handicapping system, together with the system for assessment of Scratch Scores, is formulated and published by the LGU. Handicap Certificates are provided by the LGU and distributed through the National Organisations and appointed club officials to every member of every affiliated club which has fulfilled the requisite conditions for obtaining an LGU handicap.

The funds of the LGU are administered by the Hon. Treasurer on the authority of the Executive Council, and the accounts are submitted annually for adoption in General Meeting.

The Women's British Open Championship, Ladies' British Open Amateur Championship, Ladies' British Open Amateur Stroke Play Championship, Girls' British Open Amateur Championship, Senior Ladies' British Open Amateur Championship, Ladies British Open Mid-Amateur Championship and the Home International matches are organised annually by the LGU. International events involving a British or a combined British and Irish team are organised and controlled by the LGU

when held in this country and the LGU acts as the coordinating body for the Commonwealth Tournament in whichever of the five participating countries it is held, four-yearly, by rotation. The LGU selects and trains the teams, provides the uniforms and pays all the expenses of participation, whether held in this country or overseas. The LGU also maintains and regulates certain competitions played under handicap, such as Medal Competitions, Coronation Foursomes, Challenge Bowls, Australian Spoons and the LGU Pendant Competition.

The day-to-day administration of certain of the LGU responsibilities in the home countries is undertaken by the National Organisations, such as that concerned with handicapping regulations, Scratch Scores, and the organisation of Challenge Bowls and Australian Spoons Competitions.

Membership subscriptions to the LGU are assessed on a per capita basis of the club membership. To save unnecessary expense and duplication of administrative work in the home countries LGU subscriptions are collected by the National Organisations along with their own, and transmitted in bulk to the LGU.

Policy is determined and control over all the LGU's activities is exercised by an Executive Council of eight members – two each elected by the English, Irish, Scottish and Welsh national organisations. The Chairman is elected annually by the Councillors. During her chairmanship her place on the Council is taken by her Deputy and she has no vote other than a casting vote. The President and the Hon. Treasurer of the Union also attend and take part in Council meetings but with no vote. The Council meets five times a year.

The Annual General Meeting is held in January. The formal business includes presentation of the Report of the Executive Council for the previous year and of the Accounts for the last completed financial year, the election or re-election of President, Vice-Presidents, Hon. Treasurer and Auditors, and a report of the election of Councillors and their Deputies for the ensuing year and of the European Championship Committee representative. Voting is on the following basis: Executive Council, one each (8); members in the four home countries, one per national organisation (4) and in addition one per 100 affiliated clubs or part thereof; one per overseas Commonwealth Union with a membership of 50 or more clubs, and one per 100 individually affiliated clubs.

The Lady Golfer's Handbook is published annually by the LGU and is distributed free to all affiliated clubs and organisations and to appointed Handicap Advisers. It is also available for sale to anyone interested. It contains the regulations for British Championships and international matches (with results for the past twenty years) and for LGU competitions, and sets out the Rules of the Union. It also lists every affiliated organisation, with names and addresses of officials, and every affiliated club, with Scratch Score, county of affiliation, number of members, and other useful information.

Championship and International Match Conditions

Championship Conditions

Men

The Amateur Championship

The Championship, until 1982, was decided entirely by match play over 18 holes except for the final which was over 36 holes. Since 1983 the Championship has comprised two stroke play rounds of 18 holes each from which the leading 64 players and ties over the 36 holes qualify for the match play stages. Matches are over 18 holes except for the final which is over 36 holes. Full particulars can be obtained from the Championship Entries Department, Royal and Ancient Golf Club, St Andrews, Fife KY16 9JD. Tel: 01334 460000   Fax: 01334 460001

The Seniors Open Amateur Championship

The Championship consists of 18 holes on each of two days, the leading 50 players and ties over the 36 holes then playing a further 18 holes the following day. Entrants must have attained the age of 55 years prior to the first day of the Championship. Full particulars can be obtained from the Championship Entries Department, Royal and Ancient Golf Club, St Andrews, Fife KY16 9JD. Tel: 01334 460000   Fax: 01334 460001

National Championships

The English, Scottish, Irish and Welsh Amateur Championships are played by holes, each match consisting of one round of 18 holes except the final which is contested over 36 holes. Full particulars of conditions of entry and method of play can be obtained from the secretaries of the respective national Unions.

English Open Amateur Stroke Play Championship

The Championship consists of one round of 18 holes on each of two days after which the leading 40 and those tying for 40th place play a further two rounds. The remainder are eliminated.

Conditions for entry include: entrants must have a handicap not exceeding three; where the entries exceed 130, an 18-hole qualifying round is held the day before the Championship. Certain players are exempt from qualifying.

Full particulars of conditions of entry and method of play can be obtained from the Secretary, English Golf Union, National Golf Centre, The Broadway, Woodhall Spa, Lincs LN10 6PU. Tel: 01526 354500   Fax: 01526 354020

Scottish Open Amateur Stroke Play Championship

The Championship consists of one round of 18 holes on each of two days after which the leading 40 and those tying for 40th place play a further two rounds. The remainder are eliminated. Full particulars of conditions of entry and method of play can be obtained from the Scottish Golf Union, Scottish National Golf Centre, Drumoig, Leuchars, St Andrews, Fife KY 16 0DW. Tel: 01382 549500   Fax: 01382 549510

British Mid-Amateur Championship

The Championship comprises two stroke play rounds of 18 holes from which the leading 64 players over the 36 holes qualify for the match play stages. All matches including the final are over 18 holes. Entrants must have attained the age of 25 years prior to the first day of the Championship. Full particulars can be obtained from the Championship Entries Department, Royal and Ancient Golf Club, St Andrews, Fife KY16 9JD. Tel: 01334 460000   Fax: 01334 460001

Boys

Boys Amateur Championship

The Championship is played by match play, each match including the final consisting of one round of 18 holes. Entrants must be under 18 years of age at 00.00 hours on 1st January in the year of the Championship. Full particulars can be obtained from the Championship Entries Department, Royal and Ancient Golf Club, St Andrews, Fife KY16 9JD. Tel: 01334 460000   Fax: 01334 460001

Ladies

Ladies' British Open Amateur Championship

The Championship consists of one 18-hole qualifying round on each of two days. The players returning the 64 lowest scores over 36 holes shall qualify for match play. Ties for 64th place shall be decided by hole-by-hole play-off.

Ladies' British Open Amateur Stroke Play Championship

The Championship consists of 72 holes stroke play; 18 holes are played on each of two days after which the first 40 and all ties for 40th place qualify for a further 36 holes on the third day. Handicap limit is 6.4.

Ladies' British Open Championship

The Championship consists of 72 holes stroke play. 18 holes are played on each of four days, the field being reduced after the first 36 holes.

Entries accepted from lady amateurs with a handicap not exceeding scratch and from lady professionals. Full particulars for all three Championships can be obtained from the LGU, The Scores, St Andrews, Fife KY16 9AT. Tel: 01334 475811   Fax: 01334 472818

National Championships

Conditions of entry and method of play for the English, Scottish, Welsh and Irish Ladies' Close Championships can be obtained from the Secretaries of the respective associations.

Other championships organised by the respective national associations, from whom full particulars can be obtained, include English Ladies', Intermediate, English Ladies' Stroke Play, Scottish Girls' Open Amateur Stroke Play (under 21) and Welsh Ladies' Open Amateur Stroke Play.

Girls

Girls' British Open Amateur Championship

The Championship consists of two 18-hole qualifying rounds, followed by match play in two flights, the first of 32 and the second of 16 players.
Conditions of entry include:
Entrants must be under 18 years of age on the 1st January in the year of the Championship.

Competitors are required to hold a certified LGU international handicap not exceeding 12.4.

Full particulars can be obtained from the Administrator, LGU, The Scores, St Andrews, Fife KY16 9AT. Tel: 01334 475811   Fax: 01334 472818

National Championships

The English, Scottish, Irish and Welsh Girls' Close Championships are open to all girls of relevant nationality and appropriate age which may vary from country to country. A handicap limit may be set by some countries. Full particulars can be obtained via the secretaries of the respective associations.

International European Amateur Championships

Founded in 1986 by the European Golf Association, the International Amateur and Ladies Amateur Championships are held on an annual basis since 1990. These Championships consist of one round of 18 holes on each of three days after which the leading 70 and those tying for 70th place play one further round.

Full particulars of conditions of entry and method of play can be obtained from the European Golf Association.

Since 1991, the European Golf Association also holds an International Mid-Amateur Championship on an annual basis. The Championship consist of one round of 18 holes on each of two days after which the leading 90 and those tying for 90th place play one further round.

Full particulars of conditions of entry and method of play can be obtained from the European Golf Association.

Since 1996, the European Golf Association holds an International Seniors Championship for ladies and men on an annual basis.

The Championship consists of one round of 18 holes on each of two days after which there is a cut in both ladies and men categories. The competitors who pass the cut play one further round.

Additionally, a nation's cup is played within the tournament on the first two days. Teams are composed of three players. The two best gross scores out of three will count each day. The total aggregate of the four scores over two days will constitute the team's score.

Full particulars of conditions of entry and method of play can be obtained from the European Golf Association, Place de la Croix-Blanche 19, PO Box CH-1066 Epilanges, Switzerland. Tel: +41 21 784 32 32 Fax: +412 1 784 35 91

International Match Conditions

Men's Amateur Matches

Walker Cup – Great Britain and Ireland v United States of America

Mr GH Walker of the United States presented a Cup for international competition to be known as *The United States Golf Association International Challenge Trophy*, popularly described as *The Walker Cup*.

The Cup shall be played for by teams of amateur golfers selected from Clubs under the jurisdiction of the United States Golf Association on the one side and from England, Ireland, Scotland and Wales on the other.

The Walker Cup shall be held every two years in the United States of America and Great Britain and Ireland alternately.

The teams shall consist of not more than ten players and a captain.

The contest consists of four foursomes and eight singles matches over 18 holes on each of two days.

St Andrews Trophy – Great Britain and Ireland *v* Continent of Europe

First staged in 1956, the St Andrews Trophy is a biennial international match played between two selected teams of amateur golfers representing Great Britain and Ireland and the Continent of Europe. Each team consists of nine players and the match is played over two consecutive days with four morning foursomes followed each afternoon by eight singles. Selection of the Great Britain and Ireland team is carried out by the Selection Committee of The Royal and Ancient Golf Club. The European Golf Association select the Continent of Europe team.

Eisenhower Trophy – Men's World Team Championship

Founded in recognition of the need for an official world amateur team championship, the first event was played at St Andrews in 1958 and the Trophy has been played for every second year in different countries around the world.

Each country enters a team of four players who play strokeplay over 72 holes, the total of the three best individual scores to be counted for each round.

European Team Championship

Founded in 1959 by the European Golf Association for competition among member countries of the Association. The Championship is held biennially and played in rotation round the countries, which are grouped in four geographical zones.

Each team consists of six players who play two qualifying rounds of 18 holes, the five best scores of each round constituting the team aggregate. Flights for match play are then arranged according to qualifying rankings. The match play consists of two foursomes and five singles on each of three days.

A similar championship is held in alternate years for Youths teams, under 21 years of age and every year for Boys teams, under 18 years of age.

Raymond Trophy – Home Internationals

The first official International Match recorded was in 1902 at Hoylake between England and Scotland who won 32 to 25 on a holes up basis.

In 1932 International Week was inaugurated under the auspices of the British Golf Unions' Joint Advisory Council with the full approval of the four National Golf Unions. The Council of National Golf Unions is now responsible for running the matches. Teams of 11 players from England, Scotland, Ireland and Wales engage in matches consisting of five foursomes and ten singles over 18 holes, the foursomes being in the morning and the singles in the afternoon. Each team plays every other team.

The eligibility of players to play for their country shall be their eligibility to play in the Amateur Championship of their country.

Sir Michael Bonallack Trophy – Europe v Asia /Pacific

First staged in 1998, the Sir Michael Bonallack Trophy is a biennial international match played between two selected teams of amateur golfers representing Europe and Asia/Pacific. Each team consists of 12 players and the match is played over three days with five four balls in the morning and five foursomes in the afternoon of the first two days, followed by 12 singles on the last day. Selection of the European team is carried out by the European Golf Association. The Asia/Pacific Golf Confederation selects the Asia/Pacific team.

Men's Professional Matches

Ryder Cup – Europe v United States of America

This Cup was presented by Mr Samuel Ryder, St Albans, England (who died 2nd January, 1936), for competition between a team of British professionals and a team of American professionals. The trophy was first competed for in 1927. In 1929 the original conditions were varied to confine the British team to British-born professionals resident in Great Britain, and the American team to American-born professionals resident in the United States, in the year of the match. In 1979 the British team was extended to include European players. The matches are played

biennially, in alternate continents, in accordance with the conditions as agreed between the respective PGAs.

World Cup (formerly Canada Cup)

Founded in America by John Jay Hopkins in 1955 as a team event for professional golfers with the object of spreading international goodwill. Each country is represented by two players with the best team score over 72 holes producing the winners of the World Cup and the best individual score the winner of the International Trophy. Played for annually (but not in 1986) the event was run until 1999 by the International Gold Association but it is now organised as part of the new World Championship series of events by representatives of the leading professional golf tours.

Seve Ballesteros Trophy – Great Britain and Ireland v Continent of Europe

A match instituted in 2000 at Sunningdale and played along Ryder Cup lines in alternate years.

Llandudno Trophy (PGA Cup) – Great Britain and Ireland v United States of America

The Llandudno International Trophy was first awarded to England in 1939 after winning the first Home Tournament Series against Ireland, Scotland and Wales. With the outbreak of war the series was abolished and the Trophy formed part of Percy Alliss's personal collection. After Percy's death his son Peter donated the Llandudno Trophy to be awarded to the winner of the then annual PGA Cup Match. Now it is a biennial match played since 1973 in Ryder Cup format between Great Britain and Ireland and the United States of America involving top club professionals. No prize money is awarded to the competitors who compete solely for their country. Selection of the Great Britain and Ireland team is determined following completion of the Glenmuir PGA Club Professionals Championship.

Ladies Amateur Matches

Curtis Cup – Great Britain and Ireland v United States

For a trophy presented by the late Misses Margaret and Harriot Curtis of Boston, USA, for biennial competition between amateur teams from the United States of America and Great Britain and Ireland. The match is sponsored jointly by the United States Golf Association and the Ladies' Golf Union who may select teams of not more than eight players.

The match consists of three foursomes and six singles of 18 holes on each of two days, the foursomes being played each morning.

Vagliano Trophy – Great Britain and Ireland v Continent of Europe

For a trophy presented to the Comité des Dames de la Fédération Française de Golf and the Ladies' Golf Union by Monsieur AA Vagliano, originally for annual competition between teams of women amateur golfers from France and Great Britain and Ireland but, since 1959, by mutual agreement, for competition between teams from the Continent of Europe and Great Britain and Ireland.

The match is played biennially, alternately in Great Britain and Ireland and on the Continent of Europe, with teams of not more than nine players plus a non-playing captain. The match consists of four foursomes and eight singles, of 18 holes on each of two days. The foursomes are played each morning.

Espirito Santo Trophy – Women's World Team Championship

Presented by Mrs Ricardo Santo of Portugal for biennial competition between teams of not more than three women amateur golfers who represent a national association affiliated to the World Amateur Golf Council. First competed for in 1964. The Championship consists of 72 holes strokeplay, 18 holes on each of four days, the two best scores in each round constituting the team aggregate.

Lady Astor Trophy – Commonwealth Tournament

For a trophy presented by the late Viscountess Astor CH, and the Ladies' Golf Union for competition once in every four years between teams of women amateur golfers from Commonwealth countries.

The inaugural Commonwealth Tournament was played at St Andrews in 1959 between teams from Australia, Canada, New Zealand, South Africa and Great Britain and was won by the British team. The tournament is played in rotation in the competing countries, for the present Great Britain, Australia, Canada, and New Zealand, each country being entitled to nominate six players including a playing or non-playing captain.

Each team plays every other team and each team match consists of two foursomes and four singles over 18 holes. The foursomes are played in the morning and the singles in the afternoon.

European Team Championships

Founded in 1959 by the European Golf Association for competition among member countries of the Association. The Championship is held biennially and played in rotation round the countries, which are grouped in four geographical zones.

Each team consists of six players who play two qualifying rounds of 18 holes, the five best scores of each round constituting the team aggregate. Flights for matchplay are then arranged according to qualifying rankings. The matchplay consists of two foursomes and five singles on each of three days.

A similar championship is held in alternate years for Lady Juniors teams, under 21 years of age and every year for Girls teams, under 18 years of age.

Home Internationals

Teams from England, Scotland, Ireland and Wales compete annually for a trophy presented to the LGU by the late Mr TH Miller. The qualifications for a player being eligible to play for her country are the same as those laid down by each country for its Close Championship.

Each team plays each other team. The matches consist of six singles and three foursomes, each of 18 holes. Each country may nominate teams of not more than eight players.

Ladies Professional Matches

Solheim Cup – Europe v United States

The Solheim Cup, named after Karsten Solheim who founded the sponsoring Ping company, is the women's equivalent of the Ryder Cup. In 1990 the inaugural competition between the top women professional golfers from Europe and America took place in Florida.

The matches are played biennially in alternate continents. The format is foursomes and fourball matches on the first two days, followed by singles on the third in accordance with the conditions as agreed between the Evian Tour and the United States LPGA Tour.

World Cup

Started in 2000 by the LPGA and the International management Group, the event is held along similar lines to the men's World Cup with each country represented by two players. There is also an individual competiton incorporated in the regulations. It had been planned as an annual fixture but the 2001 Championship scheduled for Adelaide was cancelled.

Boys Matches

R & A Trophy – Home Internationals

Teams comprising 11 players from England, Scotland, Ireland and Wales compete against one another over three days in a single round robin format. Each fixture comprises five morning foursomes followed by ten afternoon singles.

To be eligible for selection, players must be under the age of 18 at 00.00 hours on 1st January in the year of the matches and have eligibility to play in their national championships

Jacques Léglise Trophy – Great Britain and Ireland v Continent of Europe

The Jacques Léglise Trophy is an annual international match played between two selected teams of amateur boy golfers representing Great Britain and Ireland and the Continent of Europe. Each team consists of nine players and the match is played over two consecutive days with four morning foursomes followed each afternoon by eight singles. Selection of the Great Britain and Ireland team is carried out by the Selection Committee of The Royal and Ancient Golf Club. The European Golf Association selects the Continent of Europe team

To be eligible for selection, players must be under the age of 18 at 00.00 hours on 1st January in the year of the matches.

Junior Ryder Cup

First staged in 1995, the Junior Ryder Cup is a biennial international match played between two selected teams of amateur golfers representing Europe and the USA, prior to the Ryder Cup. Each team consists of four girls and four boys under 16 as well as two girls and two boys under 18. The match is played over two consecutive days with six four balls on the first day and six mixed four balls on the second day.

Selection of the European team is carried out by the European Golf Association. Players and captains are then invited to watch the Ryder Cup.

Girls

Home Internationals

Teams from England, Scotland, Ireland and Wales compete annually for the Stroyan Cup. The qualifications for a player for the Girls' International Matches shall be the same as those laid down by each country for its Girls' Close Championship except that a player shall be under 18 years on the 1st January in the year of the Championship.

Each team, consisting of not more than eight players, plays each other team, a draw taking place to decide the order of play between the teams. The matches consist of three foursomes and six singles, each of 18 holes.

Golf Associations

The National Association of Public Golf Courses (Affiliated to English Golf Union)

The Association was founded in 1927 by golf course architect FG Hawtree and five-times Open Champion JH Taylor who saw the need for cohesion of private golf, public golf and the local councils. Until 1939 the Association was sustained by a small amount of financial support from the *News of the World*, which enabled the the Public Courses Championship of England, the so-called Unofficial Championship to be staged. After the War the Association was revitalised and the Championship was recognised by the National Union. Some 3500 public course golfers now try to qualify for the Unofficial Championship.

The success and importance of this prompted the inauguration of the Ladies' Championship and, subsequently, the Junior Championship. Various club team events came soon after, and these have now progressed to national level with a vast following from club members. Thus the Association now organises some 14 national events annually.

Many of the local councils' course management authorities (CMAs) are now full subscribing members, and many others permit the courtesy of the course for all the Association's national and zonal tournaments. Advice is offered to CMAs, when requested, on such matters as course construction, club formation and integration, establishment of Standard Scratch Score and par values, and many other topics concerned with the management of the game of golf. Overseas organisations and councils can seek advice and help in forming their own courses, clubs and associations.

The constitutional aims have not changed over the years, and the Association is proud to have maintained them. The aims are:

1. To unite the clubs formed on public courses in England and Wales, and their course managements in the furtherance of the interests of amateur golf.
2. To promote annual public course championships and such other matches, competitions and tournaments as shall be authorised by the executive of the Association.
3. To afford direct representation of public course interests in the National Union.

The organisation of the Association is wholly voluntary and honorary. Contact details p.514.

Association of Golf Club Secretaries

Membership is over 2,300, consisting of secretaries/managers and retired secretaries of clubs and golfing associations situated in the UK and Europe. The Association offers advice on all aspects of managing a golf club, including the use of an extensive information library, mainly available direct to members through its website. A national conference is held every three years. Potential and newly appointed secretaries can attend a residential training course while regular seminars are available to all members. The Association's journal, *Golf Club Management*, is published monthly and circulated to all members. The regular business of the Association is conducted from the 17 regions of the UK, along with a number of golf meetings. After five years members can apply for membership of the Institute of Golf Club Management, which is part of the Association. Contact details p.513.

The Association of Golf Writers

A group of 30 newspapermen attending the Walker Cup Match at St Andrews on 2 June 1938 decided there was a need for an organisation to 'protect the interests of golf writers'. Their main objective was to establish close liaison with the governing bodies and promoters of golf. Thus was born The Association of Golf Writers, now solidly established and rightly respected as the official negotiating body of the golfing press. The Association owes much to a membership which has included many internationally recognised names who have contributed to elevating the Association to a unique level among British sports writers' associations. Contact details p.513.

The Sports Turf Research Institute (STRI) (Bingley, West Yorkshire)

The STRI is officially recognised as the national centre for sports and amenity turf and is the official agronomist to the Championship Committee of the R&A. It is a non-profit distributing company limited by guarantee, its affairs managed by a small Executive Committee drawn from its Members Body comprising most sports controlling bodies. Golf is represented by the nominees of the R&A, the four home Golf Unions and the Council of National Golf Unions. The British Institute of Golf Course Architects, the British & International Greenkeepers Association and the PGA European Tour are also represented on its Members Body and Golf Committee.

STRI's mission is to carry out research and promote innovation; to provide advisory and consultancy services; and to provide education and publications for subscribing clubs, sports controlling bodies and the turfgrass industry at large. Contact details on p.514.

The European Institute of Golf Course Architects (EIGCA)

The European Institute of Golf Course Architects reprsents the vast majority of qualified and experienced golf course architects throughout Europe. EIGCA's goals include enhancing the professional status of the profession, developing the role of eduation and increasing the opportunities for its members to practise in countries throughout the world. EIGCA also provides educational courses to train future golf course architects and is the authoritative voice on all related matters, being recognised by the Royal and Ancient Golf Club of St Andrews. Contact details p.514.

The British Association of Golf Course Constructors

The BAGCC has always maintained its small though highly prestigious membership by 'invitation only', those selected proven by example to have performed work to the highest standard in every aspect of golf course construction: from initial consultation, survey, through design and construction to regular course maintenance. New members are admitted only if they satisfy the criteria of experience, professionalism and quality of workmanship set by the association. Membership remains an identity of considerable pride, worn in the same way, as, say, that of a qualified architect or surveyor. In simple terms it indicates that 'This organisation is skilled at its job, it is highly profesional and is recognised by its peers.' Contact details p.514.

British and International Golf Greenkeepers' Association (BIGGA)

Formed in 1987 from an amalgamation of the British, English and Scottish Associations. Objectives are to promote and advance all aspects of greenkeeping; to assist and encourage the proficiency of members; to arrange an international annual conference, educational seminars, functions and competitions; to collaborate with any body or organisation which may benefit the Association or its members or with which there may be a common interest; to carry out and perform any other duties which shall be in the general interests of the Association or its members. The Association has an official magazine, *Greenkeeping International*, which is issued free to all members. The Association also organised the annual BIGGA Turf Management Exhibition (BTME) which is Europe's largest indoor turf show. Currently the Association has over 7,300 members in the United Kingdom and world wide. Contact details p.514.

National Golf Clubs' Advisory Association

Founded in 1922, the Association's objectives are to protect the interests of golf clubs in general and to give legal advice and direction, under the opinion of Counsel, on the administrative and legal responsibilities of golf clubs. Financial assistance may sometimes be given in cases taken to the courts for decisions on points which, in the opinion of the Executive Committee, involve principles affecting the general interests of affiliated clubs. Contact details p.514.

European Golf Association
Association Européenne de Golf

Formed at a meeting held 20 November 1937 in Luxembourg, membership is restricted to European national amateur golf associations or unions. The Association concerns itself solely with matters of an international character. The association is presently composed of 30 member countries and is governed by the following committees:

- Executive Committee
- Championship Committee
- Professional Technical Committee
- EGA Handicapping & Course Rating Committee

Prime objectives are:

(a) To encourage international development of golf, to strengthen bonds of friendship existing between it members.
(b) To encourage the formation of new golf organisations representing the golf activities of European countries.
(c) To co-ordinate the dates of the Open and Amateur championships of its members and to arrange, in conjuction with host Federations, European champion-ships and specific matches of international character.
(d) To ratify and publish the calendar dates of the major Amateur and Professional championships and international matches in Europe.
(e) To create and maintain international relationships in the field of golf and undertake any action useful to the cause of golf on an international level.

The headquarters are situated in Epalinges, Switzerland. Contact details p.522.

Golf Club Stewards' Association

The Golf Club Stewards' Association was founded as early as 1912. Its members are Stewards in golf clubs throughout the UK and Ireland. It has a National Committee and Regional Branches in the South, North-West, Midlands, East Anglia, Yorkshire, Wales and the West, North-East Scotland and Ireland. The objectives of the Association are to promote the interests of members; to administer a Benevolent Fund for members in need; and to arrange golf competitions and matches. It also serves as an agency for the employment of Stewards in golf clubs. Contact details p.514.

Directory of Golfing Organisations Worldwide

National Associations

Great Britain and Ireland

Royal and Ancient Golf Club
Sec, Peter Dawson, St Andrews, Fife KY16 9JD
Tel (01334) 460000   *Fax* (01334) 460001
E-mail thesecretary@randagc.org
Website www.randa.org

Council of National Golf Unions
Sec, Kevin McIntyre, Dromin, Dunleer, Co.Louth,
Ireland
Tel +353 41 686 1476
E-mail golfinmcinere@hotmail.com

The Evian Tour (Ladies European Tour)
Ch Execs, I Randall and R Gibson, The
Tytherington Club, The Old Hall, Macclesfield,
Cheshire SK10 2LQ
Tel (01625) 611444   *Fax* (01625) 610406
E-mail mail@ladieseuropeantour.com
Website www.eviantour.com

Ladies' Golf Union
Sec, Andy Salmon, The Scores, St Andrews, Fife
KY16 9AT
Tel (01334) 475811   *Fax* (01334) 472818
E-mail info@lgu.org
Website www.lgu.org

The Professional Golfers' Association
Ch Exec, Sandy Jones, Centenary House, The De
Vere Belfry, Sutton Coldfield, B76 9PT
Tel (01675) 470333   *Fax* (01675) 477888
Website www.pga.org.uk

East Region: *Sec*, J Smith, John O'Gaunt GC,
Sutton Park, Sandy, Beds SG19 2LY
Tel (01767) 261888   *Fax* (01767) 261381
E-mail john.smith@pga.org.uk
Midland Region: *Sec*, J Sewell, King's Norton GC,
Brockhill Lane, Weatheroak, Nr Alvechurch, Worcs
B48 7ED
Tel (01564) 824909
Fax (01564) 822805
E-mail jon.sewell@pga.org.uk
North Region: *Sec*, J Croxton, No 2 Cottage, Bolton
GC, Lostock Park, Chorley New Road, Bolton,
Lancs BL6 4AJ
Tel (01204) 496137
Fax (01204) 847959
E-mail jim.croxton@pga.org.uk

South Region: *Sec*, P Ward, Clandon Regis GC,
Epsom Road, West Clandon, Guildford, Surrey
GU4 7TT
Tel (01483) 224200   *Fax* (01483) 223224
E-mail peter.ward@pga.org.uk
West Region: *Sec*, R Ellis, Exeter G&CC, Topsham
Road, Countess Wear, Exeter, EX2 7AE
Tel (01392) 877657   *Fax* (01392) 876382
E-mail ray.ellis@pga.org.uk
Irish Region: *Sec*, M McCumiskey, Dundalk GC,
Blackrock, Dundalk, Co Louth, Eire
Tel (00 353) 42 932 1193
Fax (00 353) 42 932 1899
E-mail michael.mccumiskey@pga.org.uk
Scottish Region: *Sec*, P Lloyd, King's Lodge,
Gleneagles, Auchterarder, PH3 1NE
Tel (01764) 661840   *Fax* (01764) 661841
E-mail peter.lloyd@pga.org.uk

PGA European Tour
Exec Dir, KD Schofield CBE, PGA European Tour,
Wentworth Drive, Virginia Water, Surrey
GU25 4LX
Tel (01344) 840400   *Fax* (01344) 840451
E-mail kschofield@europeantour.com
Website www.europeantour.com

PGA of Europe
Sec, LE Thornton, Centenary House, The De Vere
Belfry, Sutton Coldfield, B76 9PT
Tel (01675) 477899   *Fax* (01675) 477890
E-mail info@pgae.com   *Website* www.pgae.com

Artisan Golfers' Association
Hon Sec, K Stevens, 85 The Avenue,
Lightwater, Surrey GU18 5RG
Tel 01276 475103

Association of Golf Club Secretaries
Sec, R Burniston, 7a Beaconsfield Road,
Weston-super-Mare, BS23 1YE
Tel (01934) 641166   *Fax* (01934) 644254
E-mail hq@agcs.org.uk
Website www.agcs.org.uk

Association of Golf Writers
Sec, M Garrod, 106 Byng Drive, Potters Bar,
EN6 1UJ
Tel/Fax (01707) 654112
E-mail pasport@markgarrod.fsbusiness.co.uk

British Association of Golf Course Constructors
Sec, D White, Fore! The Dormy House, Cooden
Beach GC, Bexhill-on-Sea, TN39 4TR
Tel (01424) 842380   *Fax* (01424) 843375
E-mail mightyspyder@aol.com
Website www.bagcc.org.uk

British Golf Collectors' Society
Sec, CH Ibbetson, PO Box 13704, North Berwick,
EH39 4ZB
Tel/Fax (01620) 895561
E-mail bgcs@globalnet.co.uk
Website www.britgolfcollectors.wyenet.co.uk

The British Golf Museum
Dir, PN Lewis; *Curator*, Kathryn Baker, Bruce
Embankment, St Andrews, Fife KY16 9AB
Tel (01334) 460046   *Fax* (01334) 460064
E-mail kathrynbaker@randagc.org
Website www.britishgolfmuseum.co.uk

**British & International Golf Greenkeepers'
Association**
Exec Dir, N Thomas, Bigga House, Aldwark, Alne,
York YO61 1UF
Tel (01347) 833800   *Fax* (01347) 833801
E-mail reception@bigga.co.uk
Website www.bigga.org.uk

British Turf & Landscape Irrigation Association
PO Box 709, Garstang, PR3 1GT
Tel/Fax (07041) 363 130
Website www.btlia.org.uk

**The European Institute of Golf Course Architects
(EIGCA)**
Pres, D Williams, Merrist Wood House,
Worplesdon, Surrey GU3 3PE
Tel (01483) 884036   *Fax* (01483) 884037
E-mail info@eigca.org
Website www.eigca.org

Golf Club Stewards' Association
Sec, Peter Payne, 3 St George's Drive,
Ickenham, Middx UB10 4HW
Tel (01895) 674325

Golf Foundation
Foundation House, The Spinney, Hoddesdon Rd,
Stanstead Abbots, SG12 8GF
Tel (01920) 876200   *Fax* (01920) 876211
E-mail info@golf-foundation.org
Website www.golf-foundation.org

Golf Society of Great Britain
Sec, Mrs J Hesketh, Inglewood Farm, Minshull
Vernon, Middlewich, Cheshire CW10 0LS
Tel/Fax (01270) 522533
E-mail jackie@hesketh2000.freeserve.co.uk

Hole in One Golf Society
Sec, B Dickinson, PO Box 109, New Line,
Greengates, Bradford, BD10 9UY
Tel (01274) 598878   *Fax* (01274) 590878

National Association of Public Golf Courses
Hon Sec, E Mitchell, 12 Newton Close,
Redditch, B98 7YR
Tel (01527) 542106   *Fax* (01527) 455320

National Golf Clubs' Advisory Association
Sec, Michael Shaw LLM, Suite 2 Angel House,
Portland Square, Bakewell, Derbyshire DE45 1HB
Tel (01629) 813844   *Fax* (01629) 812614
Website www.ngcaa.org.uk

Public Schools Old Boys Golf Association
Hon Sec, P de Pinna, Bruins, Wythwood,
Haywards Heath, West Sussex RH16 4RD
Tel (01444) 454883   *Fax* (01444) 415117

Public Schools' Golfing Society
Hon Sec, JNS Lowe, Basement, Magdalen House,
148 Tooley St, London SE1 2TU
Tel (020) 7234 0007   *Fax* (020) 7234 0008
E-mail jlowe@solo-di.demon.co.uk

The Sports Turf Research Institute (STRI)
Ch Exec, Dr IG McKillop; *Head Ext Affairs*,
Anne Wilson, St Ives Estate, Bingley, West Yorks
BD16 1AU.
Tel (01274) 565131   *Fax* (01274) 561891
E-mail info@stri.co.uk
Website www.stri.co.uk

Regional Associations

England

English Golf Union
Sec, PM Baxter, National Golf Centre, The Broadway,
Woodhall Spa, Lincs LN10 6PU
Tel (01526) 354500   *Fax* (01526) 354020
E-mail info@englishgolfunion.org
Website www.englishgolfunion.org

Midland Group: *Sec*, RJW Baldwin, Chantry
Cottage, Friar Street, Droitwich, Worcs WR9 8EQ
Tel (01905) 778560   *Fax* (01905) 795848
E-mail secretary@midlandgolfunion.co.uk
Website www.midlandgolfunion.co.uk

Northern Group: *Sec*, JE Allen, West Pines, 16
Macclesfield Rd, Prestbury, Cheshire SK10 4BN
Tel/Fax (01625) 828130

South Eastern Group: *Sec*, JW Gilding,
10 Mansion Lane, Iver, Bucks SL0 9RH
Tel (01753) 819686
Fax (01753) 771809
E-mail secretary@southeastgolfunion.co.uk

South Western Group: *Sec*, DR King, 41 West
Town Lane, Brislington, Bristol, BS4 5DD
Tel (01179) 773330

English Men's County Golf Unions

Bedfordshire CGU
Hon Sec, C Allen, 102 Tyne Crescent, Bedford,
MK41 7UW
Tel/Fax (01234) 216835
E-mail bedsgusec@aol.com
Website www.bedsgolfunion.org

Berks, Bucks & Oxon UGC
Sec, PMJ York, Bridge House, Station Approach,
Great Missenden, HP16 9AZ
Tel (01494) 867341   *Fax* (01494) 867342
E-mail secretary@bbogolf.com
Website www.bbogolf.com

Cambridgeshire Area GU
Sec, RAC Blows, 73 Pheasant Rise, Bar Hill,
Cambridge, CB3 8SB
Tel (01954) 780887

Cheshire UGC
Hon Sec, BH Nattrass, 'Whitecliff', 6 Bryn Seiriol,
Llandudno, LL30 1PD
Tel/Fax (01492) 580518
E-mail secretary@cheshiregolf.org.uk
Website www.cheshiregolf.org.uk

Cornwall GU
Hon Sec, JG Rowe, 11 St Winnolls Park, Looe,
PL13 1DG
Tel/Fax (01503) 265814

Cumbria UGC
Hon Sec, W Ward, Moss View, Low Asby,
Lamplugh, Workington, CA14 4RT
Tel/Fax (01946) 861600

Derbyshire UGC
Hon Sec, CRJ Ibbotson, 4 The Spinney, Luke Lane,
Brailsford, nr Ashbourne, DE6 3BS
Tel (01335) 360889   *Fax* (01335) 361198
E-mail cliveibbotson@lineone.net
Website www.dugc.co.uk

Devon CGU
Sec, John Hirst, 20 Plymouth Rd, Tavistock, PL19 8AY
Tel (01822) 610640   *Fax* (01822) 610540
E-mail info@devongolfunion.org.uk
Website www.devon.golfunion.org.uk

Dorset CGU
Hon Sec, Douglas Pratt, 5 Farm Close, Southill,
Weymouth, DT4 0EG
Tel (01305) 786184
E-mail douglas.pratt@virgin.net
Website www.dorsct.golfunion.com

Durham CGU
Hon Sec, GP Hope, 7 Merrion Close, Moorside,
Sunderland, SR3 2QP
Tel/Fax (0191) 522 8605

Essex County Amateur GU
Sec, AT Lockwood, 2d Maldon Road, Witham,
Essex CM8 2AB
Tel (01376) 500 998   *Fax* (01376) 500 842
E-mail info@essexgolfunion.org
Website www.essexgolfunion.org

Gloucestershire GU
Sec, I Watkins, The Vyse, Olde Lane, Toddington,
Glos GL54 5DQ
Tel/Fax (01242) 612476
E-mail secretary@gloucestershiregolfunion.com.uk
Website www.gloucestershire.golfunion.com.uk

Hampshire, Isle of Wight & Channel Islands GU
Sec, K Maplesden, c/o Liphook GC, Wheatsheaf
Enclosure, Liphook, Hants GU30 7EH
Tel (01428) 725580
Fax (01428) 729232
E-mail hgu@hampshiregolf.co.uk
Website www.hampshiregolf.org.uk

Hertfordshire GU
Hon Sec, JC Harkett, 5 Willow Way, Harpenden,
AL5 5JF
Tel (01582) 760841
Fax (01582) 462608
E-mail hertsgolfunionsec@lineone.net

Isle of Man GU
Hon Sec, Joe Boyd, Cheu-Ny-Hawiney,
Phildraw Rd, Ballasilla, Isle of Man IM9 3EG
Tel/Fax (01624) 823098

Kent CGU
Sec, SS Fullager, St Andrew's Road, Littlestone,
New Romney, Kent TN28 8RB
Tel (01797) 367725   *Fax* (01797) 367726
E-mail kcgu@kentgolf.co.uk
Website www.kentgolf.org.uk

Lancashire UGC
Sec, AV Moss, 5 Dicconson Terrace, Lytham
St Annes, FY8 5JY
Tel (01253) 733323   *Fax* (01253) 795721
E-mail secretary@lancashiregolf.fsnet.co.uk

Leicestershire & Rutland GU
Hon Sec, C Chamberlain, 10 Shipton Close, The
Meadows, Wigston Magna, Leicester LE18 3WL
Tel/Fax (0116) 288 9862
E-mail secretary@lrgu.co.uk
Website www.lrgu.co.uk

Lincolnshire UGC
Hon Sec, GH Moore OBE, Authorpe House,
36 Horncastle Road, Woodhall Spa,
LN10 6UZ
Tel/Fax (01526) 352792

Middlesex CGU
Sec, JAL Williams, Television House, Office no.6,
269 Field End Rd, Eastcote, Ruislip, HA4 9LS
Tel (0208) 429 9206   *Fax* (0208) 429 9156
E-mail mcgu@dial.pipex.com

Norfolk CGU
Hon Sec, RJ Trower, 12a Stanley Avenue, Thorpe,
Norwich, Norfolk NR7 0BE
Tel/Fax (01603) 431026

Northamptonshire GU
Hon Sec, G Brooks, 17 Water Lane, Chelveston,
Wellingborough, NN9 6AP
Tel/Fax (01933) 625032
E-mail secretary@ngu.org.uk

Northumberland UGC
Hon Sec, WE Procter, 5 Oakhurst Drive, Kenton
Park, Gosforth, Newcastle-upon-Tyne, NE3 4JS
Tel/Fax (0191) 285 4981
E-mail elliott.procter@ukonline.co.uk

Nottinghamshire UGC
Hon Sec, E Peters, 48 Weaverthorpe Road,
Woodthorpe, NG5 4NB
Tel/Fax (0115) 926 6560
E-mail peters@btinternet.com
Website www.nottsgolfunion.com

Shropshire & Herefordshire UGC
Hon Sec, JR Davies, 23 Poplar Crescent, Bayston
Hill, Shrewsbury, SY3 0QB
Tel/Fax (01743) 872655
E-mail bdavies@blueyonder.co.uk

Somerset GU
Hon Sec, GA Yates, Little Manor, Greinton,
Nr Bridgwater, TA7 9BW
Tel/Fax (01458) 210179
E-mail grahamyates@greinton.freeserve.co.uk
Website www.somerset.golfunion.com

Staffordshire UGC
Sec, BA Cox, 34 Lordswood Square, Harborne,
Birmingham B17 9BS
Tel (0121) 427 4962   *Fax* {0121) 426 6366
E-mail staffs.golf@virgin.net
Website www.staffsgolf.com

Suffolk CGU
Hon Sec, RA Kent, 77 Bennett Avenue,
Bury St Edmunds, IP33 3JJ
Tel/Fax (01284) 705765
E-mail golfsgu@aol.com

Surrey CGU
Sec, MW Ashton, Sutton Green GC, New Lane,
Sutton Green, GU4 7QF
Tel (01483) 755788
Fax (01483) 751771
E-mail cgu@surreygolf.org
Website www.surreygolf.org

Sussex CGU
Sec, DJ Harmer, Suite 1, 216 South Coast Road,
Peacehaven, East Sussex BN10 8JR
Tel (01273) 589791
Fax (01273) 585705
E-mail sussexgolf@tinyworld.co.uk
Website www.sussexgolf.org

Warwickshire UGC
Sec, J Stubbings, Quaker Cottage, Wiggins Hill
Road, Wishaw, Sutton Coldfield, B76 9QE
Tel/Fax (01675) 470809
E-mail stubbings@wugc.fsnet.co.uk
Website www.warksgolf.co.uk

Wiltshire CGU
Sec, EK Hodges, 13 Elm Close, Boweshill,
Melksham, Wilts SN12 6SD
Tel/Fax (01225) 703255
E-mail keithhodges@tinyworld.co.uk

Worcestershire UGC
Hon Sec, A Boyd, The Bears Den, Upper Street,
Defford, Worcester, WR8 9BG
Tel (01386) 750657   *Fax* (01386) 750472
E-mail aboydgolf@aol.com
Website www.wugc.co.uk

Yorkshire UGC
Hon Sec, KH Dowswell, 33 George Street,
Wakefield, WF1 1LX.
Tel (01924) 383869   *Fax* (01924) 383634
E-mail yorkshiregolf@lineone.net
Website www.yorkshireunionofgolf.co.uk

English Ladies' Golf Association
Sec, Mrs S Dennis, Edgbaston GC, Church Road,
Birmingham B15 3TB
Tel (0121) 456 2088   *Fax* (0121) 454 5542
E-mail office@englishladiesgolf.org
Website www.englishladiesgolf.org

English Senior Ladies Golf Association
Hon.Sec. Mrs J Buchanan, Bell House, Meonstoke,
Southampton SO32 3NJ
Tel (01489) 878 228
Email jobuchanan@bellhouse71.fsnet.co.uk
Website www.eslga.org.uk

Northern Division: *Hon Sec*, Mrs R Horsfall, Rock
Bottom, Daisy Lea Lane, Edgerton, Huddersfield,
HD3 3LL
Tel (01484)533444
E-mail horsfall@rockbottom.fsnet.co.uk

Midlands Division: *Hon Sec*, Mrs J Latch, 3 The
Barns, Soulbury Rd, Burcott, Leighton Buzzard,
LU7 0JU
Tel (01296) 681214
E-mail jill.latch@talk21.com

South-Eastern Division: *Hon Sec*, Mrs R Wallis,
The Bungalow, The Green, Pirbright, Woking,
GU24 0JE
Tel (01483) 476528
E-mail rhwallis@ukgateway.net

South-Western Division: *Hon Sec*, Mrs A Bates,
25 Brinsea Rd, Congresbury, nr Bristol, BS49 5JF
Tel (01934) 833470
E-mail audrey@batesinvestigations.fsnet.co.uk

English Ladies' County Golf Associations

Bedfordshire LCGA
Hon Sec, Mrs N Cole, 6 Church Lane, Eaton Bray,
Beds LU6 2DJ
Tel (01525) 220479
E-mail 8noreen.cole@ic24.net

Berkshire LCGA
Hon Sec, Mrs M Shepherd, 40 Florence Road,
College Town, Sandhurst, GU47 0QD
Tel/Fax (01276) 35937

Buckinghamshire LCGA
Hon Sec, Mrs C Hawksworth, 22 Copthall Lane,
Chalfont St Peter, SL9 0DB
Tel (01753) 883088

Cambs & Hunts LCGA
Hon Sec, Mrs S Ramsay, 11 Marriotts Yard,
Ramsey, Huntingdon PE26 1HN
Tel (01487) 710824

Cheshire County LGA
Hon Sec, Mrs B Walker, 12 Higher Downs,
Knutsford, Cheshire WA16 8AW
Tel (01565) 634124

Cornwall LCGA
Hon Sec, Mrs C Penhale, 2 Scolars Close, St Ive,
Liskeard, PL14 3UX
Tel (01579) 384595

Cumbria LCGA
Hon Sec, Mrs L Mayne, Jasmine Cottage, Stainton,
Nr Penrith, CA11 0ES
Tel/Fax (01768) 865495

Derbyshire LCGA
Hon Sec, Mrs J Morgan, Upper Burrows Farm,
Brailsford, Derby DE6 3BN
Tel (01335) 360250

Devon County Ladies' Golf Association
Hon Sec, Mrs J Shayler, 2 Bystock Mews, Exmouth
EX8 5EP
Tel (01395) 272801

Dorset LCGA
Hon Sec, Mrs J Dando, 130 Radipole Lane,
Weymouth DT4 0TG
Tel (01305) 774560

Durham County LGA
Sec, Mrs E Whittle, 23 Kitswell Road, Lanchester,
Co Durham DH7 0JJ
Tel (01207) 520581

Essex LCGA
Hon Sec, Mrs M Low, 15 Rushdene Road,
Brentwood, CM15 9ES
Tel (01277) 230849

Gloucestershire LCGA
Hon Sec, Mrs G Merry, Myles House, Ashmead,
Dursley, GL11 3EN
Tel (01453) 542569

Hampshire LCGA
Sec, Mrs A Grosvenor, 16A Salterns Lane, Hayling
Island, PO11 9PJ
Tel (023) 9246 5710

Hertfordshire County LGA
Hon Sec, Mrs M Broadbent, 6 Earlsmead,
Letchworth, SG6 3UE
Tel (01462) 682767

Kent County LGA
Hon Sec, Mrs S Daniel, 6 Wyvern Close, Dartford,
DA1 2NA
Tel (01322) 271583

Lancashire LCGA
Hon Sec, Mrs J Rogers, 19 Lonsdale Rd, Formby,
Liverpool L37 3HD
Tel (01704) 831009

Leicestershire & Rutland LCGA
Hon Sec, Mrs AL Adams, 23 Fisher Close,
Cossington, Leicester, LE7 4US
Tel (01509) 812869

Lincolnshire LCA
Hon Sec, Mrs K Craigs, 11 Sylvan Avenue,
Woodhall Spa, LN10 6SL
Tel (01526) 352293

Middlesex LCGA
Hon Sec, Mrs E Thomas, 62 Highview Avenue,
Edgware, HA8 9UA
Tel (020)8905 3631

Norfolk LCA
Hon Sec, Miss MA Fisher, 33 Brettingham Avenue,
Norwich NR4 6XQ
Tel (01603) 501181
E-mail fisher.m@btinternet.com

Northamptonshire LCGA
Hon Sec, Mrs SE Clark, The Leys, 32 West St, Earls
Barton, Northampton NN6 0EW
Tel (01604) 810257

Northumberland LCGA
Hon Sec, Mrs PA Smith, Clonreher, Armstrong
Cottages, Bamburgh, Northumberland NE69 7BA
Tel (01668) 214216

Nottinghamshire County LGA
Hon Sec, Mrs BA Patrick, 18 Delville Avenue,
Keyworth, Nottingham NG12 5JA
Tel (0115) 937 3237

Oxfordshire LCGA
Hon Sec, Mrs EA Sadler, 84 Mably Grove,
Wantage, Oxon OX12 9XN
Tel (01235) 760997

Shropshire LCGA
Hon Sec, Mrs HF Davies, Brooklands, Old Woods,
Bomere Heath, Shrewsbury, SY4 3AX
Tel (01939) 290427

Somerset LCGA
Hon Sec, Mrs A Meek, The Old Barn, Woolverton,
Bath BA2 7QT
Tel (01373) 832828

Staffordshire LCGA
Hon Sec, Mrs PM Barrow, Heron's Pool, Roman Rd,
Little Aston, Sutton Coldfield, B74 3AA
Tel/Fax (0121) 353 5753

Suffolk LCGA
Hon Sec, Mrs W Wootton, Mill Cottage, Mill Lane,
Great Blakenham, Ipswich, IP6 0NJ
Tel (01473) 831843

Surrey LCGA
Hon Sec, Mrs W Elliott, SLCGA c/o Sutton Green
GC, New Lane, Sutton Green, GU4 7OF
Tel (01483) 751622
Fax (01483) 751771

Sussex County LGA
Hon Sec, Mrs JM Scott, Preferred Lie, Rufwood,
Crawley Down, West Sussex RH10 4HD
Tel (01342) 712213

Warwickshire LCGA
Hon Sec, Mrs I Howell, 7 Coppice Walk, Cheswick
Green, Solihull B90 4HY
Tel (01564) 200091

Wiltshire LCGA
Sec, Mrs F Pinder, Pippins, Mill Orchard, Fovant,
Salisbury, SP3 5JS
Tel (01722) 714767

Worcestershire County LGA
Hon Sec, Mrs J Purnell, 14 Bank Farm Close,
Pedmore, Stourbridge DY9 0TT
Tel (01562) 885043

Yorkshire LCGA
Hon Sec, Mrs A McMullen, 88 Ash Hill Drive,
Shadwell, Leeds LS17 8JR
Tel (01132) 737257

English County PGAs

Bedfordshire & Cambridgeshire PGA
Sec, B Wake, 6 Gazelle Close, Eaton Socon,
St Neots, PE19 3QF
Tel (01480) 219760

Berks, Bucks & Oxon PGA
Hon Sec, Mrs M Green, Wayside, Aylesbury Road,
Monks Risborough, Aylesbury, HP27 0JS
Tel (01844) 343012

Cheshire and North Wales PGA
Sec, J Croxton, No 2 Cottage, Bolton GC, Lostock
Park, Chorley New Road, Bolton, BL6 4AJ
Tel (01204) 496137   *Fax* (01204) 847959

Cornwall PGA
Sec, B Gripe, 3 Redannick Crescent, Truro, TR1 2DG
Tel (01872) 276989

Derbyshire PGA
Sec, F McCabe, Hillside, Lower Hall Close,
Holbrook, Derby DE56 0TN
Tel (01332) 880411

Devon PGA
Sec, I Marshall, Staddon Heights GC, Plymstock,
Plymouth, PL9 9SP
Tel (01752) 492630

Dorset PGA
Sec/Treas, JM Nicholls, 230 St Michaels Avenue,
Yeovil, Somerset BA21 4LZ
Tel (01935) 472839
E-mail nicholls.john@lineone.net

Essex PGA
Sec, J Stott, 1 The Paddocks, Great Totham,
Maldon, CM9 8PF
Tel (01621) 890113
E-mail jstott@essexpga.co.uk
Website www.essexpga.co.uk

Gloucestershire & Somerset PGA
Sec, E Goodwin, Cotswold Hills GC, Ullenwood,
Cheltenham, GL53 9QT
Tel (01242) 515263

Hampshire PGA
Sec, DL Wheeler, South Winchester GC, Pitt,
Winchester, SO22 5QW
Tel/Fax (01962) 860928
E-mail hampshirepga@yahoo.co.uk
Website www.hampshirepga.com

Hertfordshire PGA
Sec, Malcolm Plumbley, Stavonga Dell, Pasture Rd,
Letchworth SG6 3LP
Tel/Fax (01462) 485268
E-mail meplumbley@stavonga.co.uk

Kent PGA
Sec, Miss K Page, Kent PGA Office, West Malling
GC, London Road, Addington,
Maidstone, ME19 5AR
Tel/Fax (01732) 843420
E-mail karen@kpga.fsnet.co.uk
Website www.kentpga.co.uk

Lancashire PGA
Sec, J Croxton, No 2 Cottage, Bolton GC, Lostock
Park, Chorley New Road, Bolton, BL6 4AJ
Tel (01204) 496137
Fax (01204) 847959

Leicestershire PGA
Sec, J Ashton, 2 Rose Tree Avenue, Birstall,
Leicester, LE4 4CR
Tel (0116) 267 1316

Lincolnshire PGA
Sec, D Drake, Gainsborough GC, Thonock,
Gainsborough, DN21 1PZ
Tel (01522) 703331

Middlesex PGA
Sec, B Eady, 8 Woodbank Drive, Chalfont St Giles,
HP8 4RP
Tel (01494) 874487
E-mail brianeady@ukonline.co.uk

Norfolk PGA
Sec, R Evans, 4 Malton Drive, Thorpe Marriott,
Norwich, NR8 6TT
Tel (01603) 868404
E-mail ronevans@supanet.com

North East & North West PGA
Hon Sec, R Sentance, 7 Larchlea, Ponteland,
Newcastle upon Tyne, NE20 9LG
Tel/Fax (01661) 821336
E-mail ray@pgane.f9.co.uk

Northamptonshire PGA
Sec, Kash Naidu, Langholm, Kettering Rd,
Walgrave, NN6 9PH
Tel (01604) 781353
Fax (01604) 781313
E-mail kashnaidu@hotmail.com

Nottinghamshire PGA
Sec, Mrs D Ashley, 31 Orchid Drive, Newark,
NG24 3TX
Tel (01636) 686391
E-mail dianeashley@supanet.com

Shropshire & Hereford PGA
Sec, P Hinton, 1 Stanley Lane Cottages, Bridgnorth,
Shropshire
Tel (01746) 762045

Staffordshire PGA
Sec, DJ Lewis, 59 Chester Crescent, The
Westlands, Newcastle-under-Lyme, ST5 3RR
Tel/Fax (01782) 613415

Suffolk PGA
Sec, A Sleath, 21 Hasketon Rd, Woodbridge, IP12 4LD
Tel (01394) 380011

Surrey PGA
Sec, K Parry, Clandon Regis GC, Epsom Road, West
Clandon, Guildford, GU4 7TT
Tel (01483) 223031   *Fax* (01483) 223224
E-mail celia.shipp@pga.org.uk

Sussex PGU
Sec, C Pluck, 96 Cranston Avenue, Bexhill, East
Sussex TN39 3NL
Tel/Fax (01424) 221298
E-mail cliff@spgu.freeserve.co.uk
Website www.spgu.freeserve.co.uk

Warwickshire PGA
Sec, J Tunnicliff, 80 Wychwood Ave, Knowle,
Solihull, B93 9DQ
Tel (01564) 773168

Wiltshire PGA
Sec, R Blake, Upavon GC, Douglas Avenue,
Upavon, Pewsey, SN9 6BQ
Tel (01980) 630281   *Fax* (01980) 635103
E-mail richard@richardblake.co.uk

Worcestershire PGA
Sec, K Ball, 136 Alvechurch Road, West Heath,
Birmingham B31 3PW
Tel (0121) 475 7400

Yorkshire PGA
Sec, J Pape, 1 Summerhill Gardens, Leeds, Yorks
LS8 2EL
Tel (0113) 266 4746

English Blind Golf Association
Sec, R Tomlinson, 93 St Barnabas Road, Woodford
Green, Essex IG8 7BT
Tel/Fax (020) 8505 2085
E-mail ron@blindgolf.demon.co.uk
Website www.englishblindgolf.com

Ireland

Golfing Union of Ireland
Gen Sec, S Smith, Glencar House, 81 Eglinton Road,
Donnybrook, Dublin 4
Tel +353 1 269 4111   *Fax* +353 1 269 5368
E-mail gui@iol.ie   *Website* www.gui.ie

Irish Men's Branches

Connacht Branch: *Gen Sec*, E Lonergan,
2 Springfield Terrace, Castlebar, Mayo
Tel +353 94 28141   *Fax* +353 94 28143
E-mail guicb@eircom.net

Leinster Branch: *Exec.Off*, P Smyth,
1 Clonskeagh Square, Clonskeagh Road, Dublin 14
Tel +353 1 269 6977   *Fax* +353 1 269 3602
E-mail guilb@indigo.ie

Munster Branch: *Hon Sec*, S MacMahon,
6 Town View, Mallow, Co Cork
Tel +353 22 21026   *Fax* +353 22 42373
E-mail guimb@iol.ie

Ulster Branch: *Sec*, BG Edwards, MBE,
58a High Street, Holywood, Co Down BT18 9AE
Tel (028) 9042 3708   *Fax* (028) 9042 6766
E-mail ulster.gui@virgin.net

Irish Ladies' Golf Union
Sec, Mrs T Thompson, 1 Clonskeagh Square,
Clonskeagh Road, Dublin 14
Tel +353 1 269 6244   *Fax* +353 1 283 8670
E-mail info@ilgu.ie   *Website* www.ilgu.ie

Irish Ladies' Districts

Eastern District: *Hon Sec*, Mrs T Morgan, Orchard
House, Station Road, Dunleer, Co.Louth
Tel +353 686 2857

Midland District: *Hon Sec*, Mrs B McTague,
Athlone Rd, Ferbane, Co Offaly
Tel +353 902 54961

Northern District: *Hon Sec*, Ms A Dickson, 12 The
Meadows, Strangford Road, Downpatrick, Co Down
BT20 6LN
Tel (028) 446 12286

Southern District: *Hon Sec*, Mrs M McMahon,
Ballysallach, Newmarket-on-Fergus, Co.Clare
Tel +353 61 368 288

Western District: *Hon Sec*, Mrs K Reilly, Old
Church Street, Athenry, Co Galway
Tel +353 91 845417

Scotland

Scottish Golf Union
Sec, H Grey, Scottish National Golf Centre,
Drumoig, Leuchars, St Andrews, KY16 0DW
Tel (01382) 549500   *Fax* (01382) 549510
E-mail sgu@scottishgolf.com
Website www.scottishgolf.com

Scottish Men's Area Golf Associations

Angus: *Sec*, D Speed, 7 Eastgate, Friockheim,
Arbroath, DD11 4TG
Tel (01241) 828544   *Fax* (01241) 828455
E-mail david@speedd.fsnet.co.uk

Argyll & Bute: *Sec*, G Duncanson, 4 Shore Rd, Port Bannatyne, Isle of Bute, PA20 0LQ
Tel (01700) 502468

Ayrshire: *Sec*, RL Crawford, 81 Connel Crescent, Mauchline, Ayrshire KA5 5AU
Tel (01290) 551434   *Fax* (01290) 551078
E-mail secretaryaga@btinternet.com

Borders: *Sec*, RG Scott, 3 Whytbank Row, Clovenfords, Galashiels, TD1 3NE
Tel/Fax (01896) 850570
E-mail ronscott@bordergolf.freeserve.co.uk

Clackmannanshire: *Sec*, T Johnson, 75 Dewar Avenue, Kincardine on Forth, FK10 4RR
Tel/Fax (01259) 731168
E-mail thjohn01@aol.com

Dunbartonshire: *Sec*, AW Jones, 107 Larkfield Road, Lenzie, Glasgow G66 3AS
Tel /Fax (0141) 776 7430
E-mail alanjones@larky14.fsnet.co.uk

Fife: *Sec*, J Scott, Lauriston, East Links, Leven, KY8 4JL
Tel (01333) 423798   *Fax* (01333) 439910
E-mail jscott@care4free.net

Glasgow: *Sec*, RJG Jamieson, 32 Eglinton Street, Beith, KA15 1AH
Tel/Fax (01505) 503000

Lanarkshire: *Sec*, T Logan, 41 Woodlands Drive, Coatbridge, ML5 1LB.
Tel (01236) 428799   *Fax* (01236) 429358
E-mail tlogan@btinternet.com

Lothians: *Sec*, A Shaw, 34 Caroline Terrace, Edinburgh EH12 8QX
Tel 0131 334 7291   *Fax* 0131 334 9269
E-mail AllanGShaw@hotmail.com

North: *Sec*, J Macpherson, Pinetops, 11 Granary Park, Rafford, Forres IV36 2JZ
Tel/Fax (01309) 671576
E-mail js.macpherson@virgin.net

North-East: *Sec*, G McIntosh, 35 School Road, Peterculter, AB14 0TB
Tel (01224) 733836
E-mail kayashish@msn.com

Perth & Kinross: *Sec*, DY Rae, 18 Carlownie Place, Auchterarder, PH3 1BT
Tel (01764) 662837   *Fax* (01764) 662886

Renfrewshire: *Sec*, JI McCosh, 'Muirfield', 20 Williamson Place, Johnstone, PA5 9DW
Tel (01505) 344613

South: *Sec*, J Burns, Glanavan, 14 Millfield Avenue, Stranraer, DG9 0EG
Tel/Fax (01776) 704778
E-mail glanavan@tesco.net

Stirlingshire: *Sec*, J Elliot, 65 Rosebank Avenue, Falkirk, FK1 5JR
Tel (01324) 634118

Scottish Blind Golf Society
Co.Sec. Jim Gales, 38 Crawley Crescent, Springfield, Cupar, KY15 5SF
Tel/Fax (01334) 653 767

Scottish Golfers' Alliance
Sec/Treas, Mrs MA Caldwell, 5 Deveron Avenue, Giffnock, Glasgow G46 6NH
Tel (0141) 638 2066

Scottish Ladies' Golfing Association
Sec, Peter Smith, Scottish National Golf Centre, Drumoig, Leuchars, Fife KY16 0DW
Tel (01382) 549 502
Fax (01382) 549 512
E-mail slga@scottishgolf.com
Website www.scottishgolf.com

Scottish Veteran Ladies' Golfing Association
Hon Sec, Mrs I McDonald, 3A York Road, North Berwick, East Lothian EH39 4LS
Tel 01620 895 347

Scottish Ladies County Golf Associations

Aberdeen LCGA
Hon Sec, Mrs M Robinson, 7 Carnegie Gardens, Aberdeen AB15 4AW
Tel (01224) 313 582

Angus LCGA
Hon Sec, Mrs D Gordon, 11 Golf Avenue, Monifieth, DD5 4AS
Tel (01382) 532 799

Ayrshire LCGA
Hon Sec, Miss AD Cree, 19 Woodfield Road, Ayr KA8 8LZ
Tel (01292) 260 702

Border Counties' LGA
Hon Treas, Miss M Blair, 6 Chapel Street, Innerleithen EH44 6HN
Tel (01896) 830365

Dumfriesshire LCGA
Hon Sec, Miss MJ Greig, 10 Nelson Street, Dumfries DG2 9AY
Tel (01387) 254429

Dunbartonshire & Argyll LCGA
Hon Sec, Mrs M Johnston, Ardleish, 43 Hillside Road, Cardross, Dumbarton G82 5LU
Tel (01389) 841 528

East Lothian LCGA
Hon Sec, Mrs C Bowe, Birkhill, Newbyth, East Linton, EH40 3DU
Tel (01620) 860 321

Fife County LGA
Hon Sec, Mrs A Robertson, 24 Abbey Court, St Andrews, KY16 9TL
Tel (01334) 473 863

Galloway LCGA
Hon Sec, Mrs P Magill, Church St, Kirkcolm, Stranraer, DG9 0NN
Tel (01776) 853 254

Lanarkshire LCGA
Hon Sec, Mrs M Heggie, 80 Weirwood Avenue, Garrowhill, Glasgow G69 6LN
Tel (0141) 771 3802

Midlothian County LGA
Hon Sec, Mrs A Leslie, 18 Swanston Grove,
Edinburgh EH10 7BW
Tel (0131) 445 2411

Northern Counties' LGA
Hon Sec, Mrs J Corbett, Sandle Wood, 18 Edward
Avenue, Banff
Tel (01261) 812 848

Perth & Kinross LCGA
Hon Sec, Mrs D Butchart, 16 Airlie Street, Alyth,
Blairgowrie PH11 8AJ
Tel (01828) 633000

Renfrewshire LCGA
Hon Sec, Mrs C Finlayson, Hazel Lodge, Hazeldon
Rd, Mearnskirk, Glasgow G77 6RR
Tel (0141) 639 5418

Stirling & Clackmannan LGA
Hon Sec, Mrs A Hunter, 22 Muirhead Road,
Stenhousemuir, FK5 4JA
Tel (01324) 554 515

Wales

Welsh Golfing Union
Sec, R Dixon, Catsash, Newport, Gwent NP18 1JQ
Tel (01633) 430 830   *Fax* (01633) 430 843
E-mail wgu@welshgolf.org
Website www.welshgolf.org

Welsh Men's Golf Unions

Anglesey GU
Hon Sec, GP Jones, 20 Gwelfor Estate, Cemaes Bay,
Anglesey LL67 0NL
Tel (01407) 710755

Brecon & Radnor GU
Hon Sec, DJ Davies, Garden House, Howey,
Llandrindod Wells, Powys LD1 5PU
Tel (01597) 824316

Caernarfonshire & District GU
Hon Sec, RE Jones, 23 Bryn Rhos, Rhosbodrual,
Caernarfon, Gwynedd LL55 2BT
Tel (01286) 673486

Denbighshire GU
Hon Sec, EG Howells, 10 Lon Howell, Myddleton
Park, Dinbych, LL16 4AN North Wales
Tel/Fax (01745) 813849

Dyfed GU
Hon Sec, AE Scott, 40 Clover Park, Haverfordwest,
Dyfed SA61 1UE
Tel (01437) 767578
E-mail ascott4347@aol.com

Union of Flintshire Golf Clubs
Hon Sec, JF Snead, 1 Cornist Cottages, Cornist Park,
Flint, Clwyd CH6 5RH, North Wales
Tel (01352) 733461

Glamorgan County GU
Hon Sec, DC Thomas, 168 North Road, Ferndale,
Rhondda CF43 4RA
Tel (01443) 730722

Gwent GU
Sec, CM Buckley, 20 St Peters Drive, Libanus
Fields, Blackwood, NP12 2ER, Gwent
Tel (01495) 223 520

North Wales PGA see **Cheshire & North Wales PGA**

South Wales PGA
Sec, RC Thomas, 17 South Place, Porthcawl, Mid
Glamorgan CF36 3DB
Tel (01656) 783 377

Welsh Ladies' Golf Union
Sec, Mrs Liz Edwards, Catsash, Newport NP18 1JQ
Tel (01633) 422 911
Fax (01633) 431106
E-mail wlgu@quinweb.net

Welsh Ladies' County Golf Associations

Caernarvonshire & Anglesey LCGA
Hon Sec, Mrs J Ellwood, Ty Ni, Morfa Nefyn,
Pwllheli LL53 6DG
Tel (01758) 720193

Denbighshire & Flintshire LCGA
Sec, Mrs HP Williams, 4 Green Meadows,
Hawarden, Flintshire CH5 3SL
Tel (01244) 534 549

Glamorgan LCGA
Sec, Miss J Brown, Trefelin, 2 Windmill Lane,
Cowbridge, Vale of Glamorgan CF71 7HX
Tel (01446) 773292

Mid Wales LCGA
Sec, Miss A James, Flat 4, Penbryn Court,
Lampeter, Dyfed SA48 7EU
Tel (01570) 422 463

Monmouthshire LCGA
Hon Sec, Mrs E Davidson, Jon-Len, Goldcliff,
Newport NP18 2AU
Tel (01633) 274 477

Overseas Associations

Europe

European Golf Association
Gen Sec, JC Storjohann, Place de la Croix Blanche 19, Case Postale CH-1066 Epalinges, Switzerland
Tel +41 21 784 35 32   *Fax* +41 21 784 35 91
E-mail info@ega-golf.ch
Website www.ega-golf.ch

Austrian Golf Association
Gen Sec, Mrs Waltraud Neuwirth, Haus des Sports, Prinz-Eugen-Strasse 12, A-1040 Wien
Tel +43 1 505 3245   *Fax* +43 1 505 4962
E-mail oegv@golf.at
Website www.golf.at

Royal Belgian Golf Federation
Gen Sec, E Steghers, Chausée de la Hulpe 110, B-1000 Brussels
Tel +32 2 672 2389   *Fax* +32 2 672 0897
E-mail info@golfbelgium.be
Website www.golfbelgium.be

Bulgarian Golf Association
Gen Sec, Stoil Stoilov, 66 Charni Vrah Blvd, 1407 Sofia
Tel +359 268 1820   *Fax* +359 262 4226
E-mail golfbg@hotmail.com

Croatian Golf Federation
Sec, D Kasapovic, Hotel Esplanade, Mihanoviceva 1, HR-10 000 Zagreb
Tel +385 1 456 6631   *Fax* +385 1 457 7907

Cyprus Golf Federation
Gen Sec, T Murray, PO Box 62085, 8062 Pafos
Tel +357 26 642 774   *Fax* +357 26 642 776
E-mail golfers2@cytanet.com.cy

Czech Golf Federation
Gen Sec, Z Kodejs, Erpet Golf Centre, Strakonickà 2860, CZ-150 00 Prague 5-Smichov
Tel +420 2 5731 7865   *Fax* +420 2 5731 8618
E-mail cgf@cgf.cz
Website www.cgf.cz

Danish Golf Union
Gen Sec, K Thuen, Idraettens Hus, Brøndby Stadion 20, DK-2605 Brøndby
Tel +45 43 262 700   *Fax* +45 43 262 701
E-mail info@dgu-golf.dk
Website www.dgu-golf.dk

Estonian Golf Association
Sec Gen, M Schmidt, Narva mnt. 24, EE-10120 Tallinn
Tel +372 640 0450   *Fax* +372 631 2229
E-mail mait@eestiehitus.ee

Finnish Golf Union
Gen Sec, K Hagfors, Radiokatu 20, FIN-00093 Slu
Tel +358 9 3481 2520   *Fax* +358 9 147 145
E-mail office@golf.slu.fi
Website www.golf.fi

French Golf Federation
Dir Gen, H Chesneau, 68 Rue Anatole France, F-92309 Levallois-Perret Cedex
Tel +33 1 41 497 700   *Fax* +33 1 41 497 701
E-mail ffg@ffgolf.org
Website www.ffgolf.org

German Golf Association
Gen Sec, Ullrich Libor, Postfach 2106, D-65011 Wiesbaden
Tel +49 611 990 200   *Fax* +49 611 990 2040
E-mail info@dgv.golf.de
Website www.golf.de

Hellenic Golf Federation
Hon Sec, P Papalavrentis, PO Box 70003, GR-166 10 Glyfada Athens
Tel +30 10 894 1933   *Fax* +30 10 894 5162
E-mail hgfederation@attglobal.net

Hungarian Golf Federation
Gen Sec, T Szlávy, Dózsa György út 1-3, H-1143 Budapest
Tel/Fax +36 1 221 5923
E-mail hungolf@hungolf.hu

Iceland Golf Union
Gen Sec, H Thorsteinsson, Sport Center, Laugardal, IS-104 Reykjavik
Tel +354 514 4050   *Fax* +354 514 4051
E-mail gsi@isisport.is
Website www.golf.is

Italian Golf Federation
Sec Gen, S Manca, Viale Tiziano 74, I-00196 Roma
Tel +39 06 323 1825   *Fax* +39 06 322 0250
E-mail fig@federgolf.it
Website www.federgolf.it

Latvia Golf Federation
Gen Sec, N Mazjanis, Elizabetes Str.49 LV-1050 Riga
Tel +371 925 6220   *Fax* +371 782 8078
E-mail noris@navigators.lv

Luxembourg Golf Federation
Sec, Jules Heisbourg, 1 Route de Trèves, L-2633 Senningerberg
Tel +352 34 0090   *Fax* +352 34 8391
E-mail flgsecretariat@flgolf.lu
Website www.flgolf.lu

Malta Golf Federation
Hon Sec, Alexander Mangion, c/o Royal Malta GC, Marsa LQA 06, Malta
Tel +356 23 9302   *Fax* +356 22 7020
E-mail info@maltagolf.org
Website www.maltagolf.org

Netherlands Golf Federation
Gen Sec, HL Heyster, PO Box 221, NL-3454 ZL De Meern
Tel +31 30 242 6370   *Fax* +31 30 242 6380
E-mail golf@ngf.nl
Website www.golfsite.nl

Norwegian Golf Federation
Gen Sec, G Ove Berg, PO Box 163, Lilleaker,
N-0216 Oslo
Tel +47 22 73 6620   *Fax* +47 22 73 6621
E-mail golfforbundet@ngf.golf.no

Polish Golf Union
Pres, Andrzej Person, Centralny Osrodek Sportu, Ul.
Lazienkowska 6A, PL-00-449 Warszawa
Tel +48 22 5298 716   *Fax* +48 22 5298 916
Website www.golf.pl

Portuguese Golf Federation
Sec, J A Moreira, Av das Tulipas, Edifico
Miraflores 17°, Miraflores, P-1495-161 Algés
Tel +351 214 123 780   *Fax* +351 214 107 972
E-mail fpg@fpg.pt
Website www.fpg.pt

Russian Golf Association
Pres, A Kovalev, Office 331, 8 Luzhnetskaya nab,
RU-119992 Moskow
Tel /Fax +7 095 725 4719

San Marino Golf Federation
Gen Sec, F Sandro, Via XXV, Marzo 11, 47031
Domagnano
Tel +39 549 907 159   *Fax* +39 549 992 746

Slovak Golf Union
Gen Sec, P Spacek, Mliekarenska 10, SK-824
92 Bratislava
Tel/Fax +421 2 5341 2623
E-mail sgu@golfs.sk
Website www.sgu.sk

Slovenian Golf Association
Sec, M Azman, Dunajska 51, SLO-1000
Ljubljana
Tel +386 1 236 1190   *Fax* +386 1 236 1190
E-mail golfzveza@golfzveza-slovenije.si
Website www.golfzveza-slovenije.si

Royal Spanish Golf Federation
Sec, L Alvarez, Capitán Haya 9, E-28020 Madrid
Tel +34 91 555 2682   *Fax* +34 91 556 3290
E-mail rfeg@golfspain.com
Website www.golfspainfederacion.com

Swedish Golf Federation
Gen Sec, Mats Enquist, PO Box 84, Kevingstrand,
S-182 11 Danderyd
Tel +46 8 622 1500   *Fax* +46 8 755 8439
E-mail info@sgf.golf.se
Website www.golf.se

Swiss Golf Association
Sec, JC Storjohann, Place de la Croix Blanche 19,
Case Postale, CH-1066 Epalinges
Tel +41 21 784 3531   *Fax* +41 21 784 3536
E-mail info@asg.ch
Website www.asg.ch

Turkish Golf Federation
Co-ord, I Aktekin, GSGM Ulus Is Hani, A Blok 2
Kat, 205 Ulus 06050, Ankara
Tel +90 312 309 3945
Fax +90 312 309 1840

European Professional Associations

Austria PGA
Sec, R Hagan, A-8724 Spielberg,
Frauenbachstrasse 51
Tel +43 664 304 5078   *Fax* +43 351 282 171
E-mail pga-austria@aon.at

Belgian PGA
Sec, B De Bruyckere, Norkerseweg 126b, B-8790
Waregem
Tel +32 2672 2389   *Fax* +32 5644 0546
E-mail info@pga.be
Website www.pga.be

Denmark PGA
Sec, J Sunds, Centervej 1, Gatten 9640, Farso
Tel +45 98 662 235   *Fax* +45 98 662 238
E-mail pga@golfonline.dk
Website www.golfonline.dk.pga

Finland PGA
Sec, M Rantanen, Radiokatu 20, FIN-00093 SLU
Tel +358 9 3481 2377   *Fax* +358 9 3481 2378
E-mail pgafinland@pga.fi
Website www.pga.fi

French PGA
Dir, Alain Serra, National Golf Club, 2 Avenue du
Golf, 78 280 Guyancourt, France
Tel +33 1 34 52 0846
Fax +33 1 34 52 0548
E-mail pgafra@club-internet.fr
Website www.pgafrance.com

PGA of Germany
Sec, Rainer Goldrian, Werner Haas Str 6, D-86153
Augsburg
Tel +49 821 568 710
Fax +49 821 568 7129
E-mail info@pga.de
Website www.pga.de

Italy PGA
Sec, L Rendina, Palazzo Galileo, Via Maragoni 3,
I-20124 Milano
Tel +39 02 670 5670
Fax +39 02 669 3600
E-mail pgaitaly@tin.it
Website www.pga.it

Netherlands PGA
Sec, Mrs R Vonk Mundt, Burg van der Borchlaan 1,
3722 GZ Bilthoven
Tel +31 30 228 7018
Fax +31 30 225 0261
E-mail npga@wxs.nl
Website www.PGAholland.com

Portugal PGA
Sec, R Pinto, Av das Tulipas, Edifico Miraflores 17°,
Miraflores, P-1495-161 Algés
Tel +351 21 412 3788
Fax +351 21 410 7972
E-mail pga.portugal@neto.pt
Website www.fpg.pt

Spain PGA
Sec, M Santamaría, c/Capitán Haya 22-5C,
E-28020 Madrid
Tel +34 91 555 1393
Fax +34 91 597 0170
E-mail apge@wanadoo.es
Website www.golfexcel.com/apg

Swedish PGA
Sec, M Sorling, Tylösand, S-302 73 Halmstad
Tel +46 35 320 30
Fax +46 35 320 25
E-mail pga@golf.se
Website www.pga.golf.se

Swiss PGA
Gen Sec, C Blattmann, Hauserstrasse 14, PO Box
CH-8030 Zürich
Tel +41 1 267 3401
Fax +41 1 267 3411
E-mail info@swisspga.ch
Website www.swisspga.ch

North America: Canada and USA

Royal Canadian Golf Association
Exec Dir, SD Ross, Golf House, Glen Abbey, 1333
Dorval Drive, Oakville, Ontario L6J 4Z3
Tel +1 905 849 9700   *Fax* +1 905 845 7040
E-mail golfhouse@rcga.org
Website www.rcga.org

Canadian Ladies' Golf Association
Exec Dir, LJ Murphy, Golf House, Glen Abbey,
1333 Dorval Drive, Oakville, Ontario L6J 4Z3
Tel +1 905 849 2542   *Fax* +1 905 849 0188
E-mail clga@clga.org   *Website* www.clga.org

Canadian PGA
Pres, Ch Exec, David J Colling, 13450 Dublin Line
RR#1, Acton, Ontario L7J 2W7
Tel +1 519 853 5450   *Fax* +1 519 853 5449
E-mail cpga@canadianpga.org
Website www.cpga.com

Canadian Tour
Comm, Ian Mansfield, 212 King Street West, Suite
203, Toronto, Ontario Canada M58 1K5
Tel +1 416 204 1564   *Fax* +1 416 204 1368
Website cantour.com

Ladies' Professional Golf Association
Pres, 100 International Golf Drive, Daytona Beach,
Florida 32124-1092
Tel +1 386 274 6200   *Fax* +1 386 274 1099
Website www.lpga.com

National Golf Foundation
Pres, 1150 South US Highway One, Jupiter,
Florida 33477
Tel +1 561 744 6006   *Website* www.ngf.org

PGA of America
Pres, Box 109601, 100 Avenue of the Champions,
Palm Beach Gardens, Florida 33418.
Tel +1 561 624 8400   *Fax* +1 561 624 8448
Website www.pgaonline.com

PGA Tour
Pres, The Commissioner, PGA Tour, 112 PGA Tour
Boulevard, Ponte Vedra Beach, Florida 32082
Tel +1 904 285 3700   *Fax* +1 904 285 7913
Website www.pgatour.com

United States Golf Association
Pres, Golf House, PO Box 708, Far Hills,
NJ 07931-0708
Tel +1 908 234 2300   *Fax* +1 908 234 9687
E-mail usga@usga.org   *Website* www.usga.org

The Caribbean and Central America

Caribbean Golf Association
Sec, David G Bird, PO Box 31329 SMB, Grand
Cayman, Cayman Islands
Tel +345 947 1903   *Fax* +345 947 3439
E-mail bird@candw.ky

Bahamas Golf Federation
Pres, Ambrose Gouthro, PO Box F-41790, Freeport,
Grand Bahama
Tel +242 373 7295   *Fax* +242 373 7926
E-mail agouthro@blvdnet.com
Website www.bgfnet.com

Barbados Golf Association
Sec, Trenton Weekes, PO Box 585, Bridgetown,
Barbados
Tel +246 430 0808   *Fax* +246 437 7792
E-mail carib@caribsurf.com
Website www.bajangolf.4mg.com

Bermuda Golf Association
Sec, Tom Smith, PO Box HM 433, Hamilton,
Bermuda HM-BX
Tel +1 441 238 1367   *Fax* +1 441 238 0983
E-mail bdagolf@ibl.bm

Cayman Islands Golf Association
Sec, David G Bird, PO Box 31329 SMB, Grand
Cayman
Tel +345 947 1903   *Fax* +345 947 3439
E-mail bird@candw.ky

National Golf Association of Costa Rica
Pres, F Solano, PO Box 10969, 1000 San Jose
Tel +506 221 8129   *Fax* +506 257 0439
E-mail fsolano@sol.racsa.co.cr
Website www.edenia.com/amagolf

Fedogolf (Dominican Republic)
Exec Dir, Rudys Soler, Campo Nacional de Golf,
Las Lagunas S.A., Autopito Duarte Km 20, Santo
Domingo, Dominican Republic
Tel +809 231 4719
Fax +809 372 7406
E-mail fedogolf@hotmail.com
Website www.fedogolf.org

El Salvador Golf Federation
Sec, G Aceto Marini, Apartado Postal 631, San
Salvador C.A.
Tel +503 285 8503
Fax +503 289 1378
E-mail fesagolf@yahoo.com

Guatemalan Golf Federation
Exec Sec, Adolfo Rios, Diagonal 6 10-76, Zona 10,
Guatemala
Tel +502 360 9435
Fax +502 360 9475

Hondurena Golf Association
Sec, LF Gutiérrez, Apartado Postal 3175,
Tegucigalpa, Honduras
Tel +504 37 2084
Fax +504 38 0456

Jamaica Golf Association
Hon Sec, Herman McDonald, PO Box 743, Kingston
8
Tel +1 876 925 2325
Fax +1 876 924 6330
E-mail jamgolf@n5.com.jm
Website www.jamaicagolfassociation.com

Mexican Golf Federation
Sec, IA Herroz, Av.Lomas de Sotelo No.1112 int.2,
Col.Lomas de Sotelo C.P.11200 Mexico
Tel +525 580 6121
Fax +525 580 2263
E-mail fedmexgolf@compuserve.com.mx
Website www.mexgolf.org

Nicaraguan Golf Association
Pres, Alfonso Llanes, Nicabox 538, PO Box 25640,
Miami, FL 33102, USA
Tel +350 441 7596
Fax +350 385 1464

OECS Golf Association
Sec, Joan Paul, PO Box 189, Castries, St Lucia
Tel +758 452 3079   *Fax* +758 452 3885
E-mail joanpaul@candw.lc

Panama Golf Association
Pres, Anibal Galindo, PO Box 8613, Panama 5
Tel +507 266 7436   *Fax* +507 220 3994
E-mail master@pty.com

Puerto Rico Golf Association
Pres, Sidney Wolf, 58 Caribe St, San Juan, Puerto
Rico 00907-1909
Tel +787 721 7742   *Fax* +787 723 5760
E-mail golfpuertorico@prga.org
Website www.prga.org

Trinidad & Tobago Golf Association
Pres, Clarence Wilcox, c/o 36 Methuen St,
Woodbrook, Port of Spain, Trinidad
Tel +868 625 2115   *Fax* +868 625 4764
E-mail wilent@wow.net

Turks & Caicos Golf Association
Pres, John Phillips, PO Box 64, Suite C12,
Providenciales, Turks & Caicos Islands
Tel +649 946 4109   *Fax* +649 946 4939
E-mail claymore@tciway.tc

Virgin Islands Golfers' Federation
Pres, Bruce Streibich, PO Box 3457,
Christiansted, St Croix, US Virgin Islands 00822
Tel +340 773 3119   *Fax* +340 773 4032
E-mail bstreibich@vipower.net

South America

South American Golf Federation
Exec Sec, Juan Pablo Gutiérrez, Carrera 49A
No 99-30, Bogotá, Colombia
Tel +57 1 226 3489   *Fax* +57 1 226 7788
E-mail fedesud@latino.net.co

Argentine Golf Association
Exec Dir, Jorge V Garasino, Corrientes 538-Pisos
11y12, 1043 Buenos Aires
Tel +54 11 4325 1113   *Fax* +54 11 4325 8660
E-mail golf@aag.com.ar
Website www.aag.com.ar

Bolivian Golf Federation
Sec, Juan E Maclean, Edif.Camara de Comercio Piso
6-Oficina 604, C.P. 10217, La Paz
Tel/Fax +591 2 315853
E-mail fbgolf@ceibo.entelnet.bo
Website www.bolivia-golf.com

Brazilian Golf Confederation
Sec, MA Aguiar Giusti, Rua Paes de Araujo,
29cjs.42 e 43, CEP 04531-090-São
Paulo-SP.
Tel/Fax +55 11 3846
E-mail golfe@cbg.com.br
Website www.cbg.com.br

Chilean Golf Federation
Sec, Carlos Amenabar, Av el Golf 266, Las
Condes, Santiago
Tel +56 2 362 0777   *Fax* +56 2 362 0929
E-mail secretaria@chilegolf.cl
Website www.chilegolf.cl

Colombian Golf Federation
Sec, Dr V Rodríguez Posada, Carrera 7A, No 72-64
Int 26, Apartado aéreo 88768, Bogotá
Tel +57 1 310 7664
Fax +57 1 235 5091
E-mail fedegolf@cable.net.co
Website www.federacioncolombianadegolf.com

Ecuador Golf Federation
Sec, Patricia Pazmiño, C.P. 17012411, Quito
Tel + 593 22 491 512
Fax + 593 22 491 254
E-mail fedecuat@feg.org.ec
Website www.feg.org.ec

Paraguay Golf Association
Pres, Victor M Ricciardi, Casilla de Correo No 76,
Asunción
Tel +595 21 447 923
Fax +595 21 495 796
E-mail apg@mmail.com.py
Website www.apg.com.py

Peru Golf Federation
Sec, Juan Neira, Estadio Nacional Puerta 4 Piso 3,
Lima 1
Tel +51 1 433 6515
Fax +51 1 433 8018
E-mail mail@fpg.org.pe
Website www.fpg.org.pe

Uruguay Golf Association
Sec, P Pereira Micoud, Casilla de Correo 1484, Montevideo
Tel +598 2 701 721
E-mail augolf@adinet.com.uy

Venezuela Golf Federation
Exec Dir, Julio L Torres, Av. Juan B Arismendi, Unidad Comercial La Florida, Mezzanina, local 8.Urb.La Florida, Caracas 1050
Tel +582 731 7662
Fax +582 730 2731
E-mail fvg@fvg.org
Website www.fvg.org

Africa

Algerian Golf Federation
Sec, Benmiloud Noureddine, rue Ahmed Ouaked, Dely-Ibrahim
Tel +213 236 3059   *Fax* +213 261 4133

Botswana Golf Union
Sec, SE Palframan, PO Box 1033, Gaborone

Botswana Ladies Golf Union
Hon Sec, Mrs D Beesley, PO Box 1362, Gaborone

The Egyptian Golf Federation
Chair, Khaled Abou Taleb, 29 Abdel Moneim Hafaz Street, Heliopolis, Cairo
Tel +202 291 9101   *Fax* +202 291 9102
E-mail attar@internetalex.com

Ghana Golf Association
Hon Sec, Col JA Kabore, PO Box 8, Achimota, Accra
Tel/Fax 233-21-400221
E-mail vaghq@ghana.com

Ghana Ladies Golf Union
Hon Sec, Miss E Adzakpo, PO Box 8, Achimota, Accra

Côte d'Ivoire National Golf Federation
Sec, I Keita, O8 BP 1297, Abidjan 08
Tel +225 213 874   *Fax* +225 227 112

Kenya Golf Union
Chair, Vishy Talwas, PO Box 49609, Nairobi
Tel +254 2 763 898   *Fax* +254 2 765 118
E-mail kgu@connect.co.ke
Website www.kgu.org.ke

Kenya Ladies' Golf Union
Hon Sec, Mrs S Royle, PO Box 16751, Nairobi

KwaZulu-Natal Golf Union
Sec, RT Runge, PO Box 1939, Durban 4000
Tel +27 (0)31 202 7636 *Fax* +27 (0)31 202 1022
E-mail kzngu@kzngolf.co.za

Libyan Golf Federation
Pres, Mohamed El-Kheituni, PO Box 3674, Tripoli

Malawi Golf Union
Sec, J Hinde, PO Box 1198, Blantyre
Tel +265 643988   *Fax* +265 640135
E-mail jhinde@illovo.co.za

Malawi Ladies' Golf Union
Hon Sec, Mrs J Mullock, PO Box 5319, Limbe

Mauritius Golf Federation
Pres, Raj Ramlackhan, 42 Sir William Newton Street, Port Louis
Tel +230 208 2440
Fax +230 208 2438
E-mail ramn@intnet.mu

The Royal Moroccan Golf Federation
Sec, Sad Benkirane, Royal Golf Rabat Dar-es-Salam, Route des Zaers, Rabat
Tel +212 775 5636
Fax +212 775 1026

Namibian Golf Union
Treas, Hugh Mortimer, PO Box 2122, Windhoek, Namibia
E-mail wcc@iafrica.com.na

Nigeria Golf Union
Sec, IBB International G&CC, PO Box 6935, Wuse, Abuja
Tel +234 9 523 2015
Fax +234 9 523 2014
E-mail scovir@skannet.com

Nigerian Ladies Golf Union
Sec, Mrs P Ojebuoboh, c/o Ikoyi GC, PO Box 239, Ikoyi, Lagos

Sierra Leone Golf Federation
Pres, Freetown GC, PO Box 237, Lumley Beach, Freetown

South Africa Sunshine Tour
Exec Dir, Louis Martin, 15 Postnet Suite #185, Private Bag X15, Somerset West 7129
Tel +27 21 850 6500   *Fax* +27 21 852 8271

South African Golf Association
Exec Dir, BA Younge, PO Box 391994, Bramley, South Africa 2018
Tel +27 11 442 3723   *Fax* +27 11 442 3753
E-mail sagolf@global.co.za

South African Ladies' Golf Union
Hon Sec, Mrs V Horak, PO Box 209, Randfontein 1760, RSA
Tel/Fax +27 11 416 1263
E-mail salgu@golfing-sa.co.za
Website www.safgu.co.za

South African PGA
Sec, PO Box 66201, Woodhill, 0076 RSA
Tel +27 12 998 1356   *Fax* +27 12 993 0597
E-mail pgasa@worldonline.co.za
Website www.pgasa.com

South African Women's PGA
Sec, Mrs V Harrington, PO Box 781547, Sandton 2146
Tel/Fax +27 11 477 8606

Swaziland Golf Union
Sec, J Resting, PO Box 1739, Mbabane
Tel/Fax +268 404 2227
E-mail johnrest@realnet.co.sz

Tanzania Golf Union
Sec, Rafik Meghji, PO Box 6018, Dar-es-Salaam
Tel +255 22 215 1706   *Fax* +255 22 215 0626
E-mail tgu@tzgolfun.com
Website www.tzgolfun.com

Tanzania Ladies' Golf Union
Hon Sec, Mrs S Torr, PO Box 286, Dar-es-Salaam

Tunisian Golf Federation
Pres, Anror Atallah, Choutrana II, 2036 Soukra
Tel +216 1 865 745
Fax +216 1 865 700

Uganda Golf Union
Pres, GW Eggadu, Kitante Road, PO Box 2574,
Kampala

Uganda Ladies Golf Union
Hon Sec, Mrs R Tumusiime, PO Box 624, Kampala

Zambia Golf Union
Hon Sec, M Doogan, PO Box 71784, Ndola.
Tel +260 2 650697/621438   *Fax* +260 2 621834
E-mail collalum@coppernet.com

Zambia Ladies' Golf Union
Hon Sec, Mrs P Barker, PO Box 31051, Lusaka

Zimbabwe Golf Association
Sec, JL Nixon, PO Box 3327, Harare
Tel +263 4 746 141   *Fax* +263 4 746 228

Zimbabwe Ladies' Golf Union
Hon Sec, Mrs F Benzon, 15 Brompton Rd,
Highlands, Harare
E-mail benzon@africaonline.com.zw

Middle East

Bahrain Golf Committee
Gen Sec, Daij Khalifa, PO Box 38938, Riffa
Tel +973 778 620   *Fax* +973 778 595
E-mail bgcom@batelco.com.bh

**The Golf Federation of the Islamic Republic of
Iran**
Sec Gen, Sayad Nasrolla Sadjadi, PO Box
15815-1881, Tehran
Tel +98 21 829 671   *Fax* +98 21 834 333

Israel Golf Federation
Gen Sec, I Gvirtzman, PO Box 4858, Caesarea
38900
Tel +972 4 636 1172   *Fax* +972 4 636 1173
E-mail andis@caesarea.il
Website www.caesarea.fm

Lebanese Golf Federation
Pres, Faysal Alamldine, c/o GC of Lebanon,
PO Box 11-3099, Beirut
Tel +961 1 822 470   *Fax* +961 1 822 474
Email info@golfclub.org.lb

Qatar Golf Association
Pres, Sheikh Abdullah Bin Ahmed Al Thani, PO
Box 6177, Doha
Tel +974 454 284   *Fax* +974 430 132

Saudi Golf Committee
Sec Gen, Ali M.Al-Suhaim, PO Box 102201, Riyadh
11675, Saudi Arabia
Tel/Fax +966 1 402 1079

United Arab Emirates Golf Association
Sec Gen, Khalid Al Halyan, PO Box 31410, Dubai,
UAE
Tel +971 4 295 6440
Fax +971 4 295 6026
E-mail uaegolf@emirates.net.ae
Website www.uaegolf.com

Asia

Asia-Pacific Golf Confederation
Sec, Bertie To Jr, c/o HKR International Ltd, Room
203, Discovery Bay Office Centre, No.2 Plaza Lane,
Discovery Bay, Lantau Island, Hong Kong
Tel +852 2238 3330
Fax +852 2987 6432
E-mail bertieto@dbgc.com.hk

Asian PGA
Sec, Ramlan Dato'harun, 415-417 Block A Kelana
Business Centre, 97 Jalan SS 7/2 Kelana Jaya,
Selangor, Malaysia
Tel +603 7492 0099
Fax +603 7492 0098
Website www.asianpgatour.com

Asia PGA Tour
Chief Exec Off, Justin Strachan, 15/F, One
Harbourfront, 18 Tak Fung Street, Hunghom,
Kowloon, Hong Kong
Tel +852 2330 8227
Fax +852 2801 5743
E-mail apgatour@asiaonline.net
Website www.asianpgatour.com

China Golf Association
Sec, Cui Zhi Qiang (David Cui), 5 Tiyuguan Rd,
Beijing, China 100763
Tel +8610 858 18873   *Fax* +8610 858 25994
E-mail cga-cra@263.net

Golf Association of the Republic of China
Sec Gen, Lung-Kuo Chien, 12 F-1, 125 Nan-King
East Road, Section 2, Taipei, Taiwan 104 R.O.C.
Tel +886 2 516 5611   *Fax* +886 2 516 3208

PGA Republic of China
2nd Floor 196 Cheng-Teh Road, Taipei, Taiwan
Tel +886 2 8220318   *Fax* +886 2 8229684

Hong Kong Golf Association Ltd
Ch Exec, David Roberts, Room 2003, Sports House,
1 Stadium Path, So Kon Po, Causeway Bay, Hong
Kong
Tel +852 2522 8804
Fax +852 2845 1553
E-mail hkga@netvigator.com
Website www.hkga.com

Hong Kong PGA
Sec, Mr M Lai Wai Sing, Room 702 Landmark
North, Sheung Shui, NT Hong Kong
Tel +852 523 3171

Indian Golf Union
Sec, Mr PK Bhattacharyya, 'Sukh Sagar' 2nd Floor,
2/5 Sarat Bose Road, Calcutta 700 020
Tel +91 33 4745 795   *Fax* +91 33 4748 914
E-mail ingolf.union@gems.vsnl.net.in

Indonesian Golf Association
Sec Gen, Kusman Ismukanto, Rawamangun Muka
Raya, Jakarta 13220
Tel/Fax +62 21 470 1019
E-mail pgi@pgionline.org
Website www.pgionline.org

Japan Golf Association
Sec, Naomi Yokoyama, 606-6th Floor, Palace
Building, Marunouchi, Chiyoda-ku, Tokyo
100-0005
Tel +81 3 3215 0003   *Fax* +81 3 3214 2831
Email info@jpa.org.jp

Japan Ladies PGA
7-16-3 Ginza, Nitetsu Kobiki Bldg 8F, Chuo-ku,
Tokyo 104-0061
Tel +81 3 3546 7801   *Fax* +81 3 3546 7805

Japan PGA
Int Com, Seien Kobayakawa, Top Hamamatsucho
Bldg, 1-5-12 Shiba.Minato-Ku, 8FL, Tokyo
105-0014
Tel +81 3 5419 2614   *Fax* +81 3 5419 2622
E-mail bp@pga.or.jp

Korean Golf Association
Sec Gen, Dong Wook Kim, 1318 Rm Manhattan
Bldg, 36-2 Yeo Eui Du-Dong, Yeong Deung Po Ku,
Seoul
Tel +82 2 783 4748   *Fax* +82 2 783 4747
E-mail kogolf@chollian.net

Malaysian Golf Association
Sec, Tay Chong-Min, 12A Persiaran Ampang, 55000
Kuala Lumpur
Tel +60 3 4577931   *Fax* +60 3 4565596
E-mail mga@tm.net.my

PGA of Malaysia
Sec, Brig-Gen Mahendran, 1B Jalan Mamanda 7,
Ampang Point, 6800 Selangor Darul Ehsan,
Malaysia

Myanmar Golf Federation
Sec, U Aung Kyi, c/o Aung San Stadium,
Rangoon
Tel +95 01 663 930   *Fax* +95 01 289 563

Pakistan Golf Federation
Hon Sec, W/Cdr Iftikhar Ahmed Khan, Hamayun
Rashid, Jhelum Road, PO Box
No 1295, Rawalpindi
Tel +92 51 256 995   *Fax* +92 51 584 566

Philippines Golf Association
Sec Gen, Alfredo M Masigan, 209 Administration
Building, Rizal Memorial Sports Complex, Vito
Cruz, Manila-1000
Tel +63 2 588845
Fax +63 2 521 1587
Email rpgolf@pworld.net.ph

Singapore Golf Association
Hon Sec, Yik Nam Yeong, Tanglin Road Post
Office, PO Box 457, Singapore 912416
Tel +65 256 1318   *Fax* +65 256 1917
E-mail sga@pacific.net.sg

Sri Lanka Golf Union
Hon Sec, AGG Punchihewa, PO Box 309, 223
Model Farm Road, Colombo 8, Sri Lanka

Thailand Golf Association
Sec Gen, Pongnat Vatanasak, Room 212/213
Rajmangala National Stadium, 2088 Ramkamhaeng
Rd, Hua Mark, Bangkapi, Bangkok 10240
Tel +66 2 369 3777 *Fax* +66 2 369 3776
E-mail pongnat_v@yahoo.com
Website www.tga.or.th

Australasia and the Pacific

Australian Golf Union
Sec, Colin Phillips, Golf Australia House, 153–155
Cecil Street, South Melbourne, Victoria 3205
Tel +61 3 9699 7944   *Fax* +61 3 9690 8510
E-mail agu@agu.org.au   *Website* www.agu.org.au

Women's Golf Australia
Exec Dir, Maisie Mooney, 355 Moray Street, South
Melbourne, Victoria 3205
Tel +61 3 9690 9344   *Fax* +61 3 9696 2060
E-mail info@womensgolfaus.org.au
Website www.womensgolfaus.org.au

Australian PGA
Ch Exec, Max Garske, PO Box 1314, Crows Nest,
New South Wales
Tel +61 2 9439 8111   *Fax* +61 2 9439 7888
E-mail maxgpga@oze-mail.com.au
Website www.pga.org.au

PGA Tour Australasia
Exec Dir, Andrew Georgiou, Suite 302, 77 Berry St,
North Sydney, NSW 2060
Tel +61 2 9956 0000   *Fax* +61 2 9956 0099
Website pgatour.com.au

Cook Islands Golf Association
Pres, Hugh M N Henry, Rarotonga GC, PO Box
151, Rarotonga, Cook Islands
Tel +682 27 360   *Fax* +682 25 420

National Golf Association of Fiji
Hon Sec, CM Lenz, GPO Box 13843, Suva, Fiji
Tel +679 301 897   *Fax* +679 301 647
E-mail fasanoc@is.com.fj

New Zealand Golf Association
Ch Exec, N Woodbury, PO Box 11842 Wellington
Tel +64 4 385 4330   *Fax* +64 4 385 4331
E-mail nzga@nzga.co.nz
Website www.nzga.co.nz

Womens' Golf New Zealand Inc
Exec Dir, Mrs J Mackay, PO Box 11187,
65 Victoria Street, Wellington
Tel +64 4 4726 733   *Fax* +64 4 4726 732
E-mail golf@womensgolf.org.nz

New Zealand PGA
Exec Dir, PG Wyllie, PO Box 11-934,
Wellington
Tel +64 4 4722 687   *Fax* +64 4 4712 152
E-mail postmaster@pga.org.nz
Website www.pga.org.nz

Papua New Guinea Golf Association
Hon Sec, c/o Lae G.C., PO Box 164, Lae MP, Papua
New Guinea
Tel +675 323 1120   *Fax* +675 323 1300

Papua New Guinea Ladies Golf Association
Hon Sec, Mrs L Illidge, PO Box 348,
Lae MP 411

Vanuatu Golf Association
Chairman, Bernie Cain, PO Box 358, Port Vila,
Vanuatu, Pacific Ocean
Tel +678 22178   *Fax* +678 25037
E-mail vilaref@vanuatu.com.vu

Websites

Royal and Ancient Golf Club	www.randa.org
Ladies Golf Union	www.lgu.org
United States Golf Association	www.usga.org
European Golf Association	www.ega-golf.ch
English Golf Union	www.englishgolfunion.org
English Ladies (ELGA)	www.englishladiesgolf.org
Golf Union of Ireland	www.gui.ie
Irish Ladies (ILGU)	www.ilgu.ie
Scottish Golf Union & Scottish Ladies (SLGA)	www.scottishgolf.com
Welsh Golfing Union	www.welshgolf.org
Professional Golfers Association	www.pga.org.uk
PGA of Europe	www.pgae.com
PGA of America	www.pga.com
PGA European Tour	www.europeantour.com
Evian Tour (Women's European)	www.eviantour.com
US PGA Tour	www.pgatour.com
US LPGA Tour	www.lpga.com
Davidoff Tour (Asia)	www.asianpgatour.com
Australasian Tour	www.pgatour.com.au
South African Sunshine Tour	www.sunshinetour.com
Other tours via Golf Web	www.golfweb.com
BBC Online – Golf	www.bbc.co.uk/sport
The Golf Channel	www.thegolfchannel.com
Golf Illustrated	www.golfillustrated.com
Nick Faldo (Junior Series)	www.nickfaldo.org
Jack Nicklaus	www.nicklaus.com
Tiger Woods	www.tigerwoods.com

PART X

Golf History

History of Championships and Team Events run by the R&A

The following entries highlight the history of championship and team events that are organised by the Royal and Ancient Golf Club of St Andrews, or by the R&A in conjunction with other bodies.

Championships that come solely under the administration of the R&A are:
The Open Championship
The Amateur Championship
The Seniors Open Amateur Championship
The British Mid-Amateur Championship
The Boys Amateur Championship
The Junior Open Championships

Team events organised by the R&A and other bodies are:
The Walker Cup (R&A/USGA)
The Eisenhower Trophy (R&A/World Amateur Golf Council)
The St Andrews Trophy (R&A/EGA)
The Jacques Léglise Trophy (R&A/EGA)

Team events organised by the R&A are:
The Boys Home Internationals

The aim has been to focus on the origins and structural growth of each event, noting key changes in format and conditions. Current championship and international match conditions are defined elsewhere in the volume.

The Open Championship

The Open Championship began in 1860 at the Prestwick Golf Club and the original trophy was an ornate Challenge Belt, presented by the Earl of Eglinton. What is now recognised as the first Open Championship was played on October 17, 1860 at the end of the club's autumn meeting. A total of eight players competed in three rounds of the 12 hole course. No prize money for the Open was awarded until 1863, the winner simply received the Belt for a year. In 1863 it was decided to give money prizes to those finishing second, third and fourth but the winner still only received the Belt. It was not until 1864 that the winner received £6. The average field in the 1860s was only 12 players.

The original rules of the competition stated that the Belt 'becomes the property of the winner by being won

three years in succession.' In 1870 Tom Morris Junior won for the third year in a row and took possession of the Belt. He won £6 for his efforts out of a total prize fund of £12. No championship was held in 1871 whilst the Prestwick Club entered into discussions with the Royal and Ancient Golf Club and the Honourable Company of Edinburgh Golfers over the future of the event.

One of the key turning points in the history of the Open took place at the spring meeting of the Prestwick Club in April 1871. At that meeting it was proposed that 'in contemplation of St Andrews, Musselburgh and other clubs joining in the purchase of a Belt to be played for over four or more greens, it is not expedient for the Club to provide a Belt to be played solely for at Prestwick.' From that date onwards, the Open ceased to be under the sole control of the Prestwick Golf Club.

The Championship was played again under this new agreement in 1872 and the new trophy was the now famous Claret Jug. Until 1891, the host club remained responsible for all arrangements regarding the Championship, which continued to be played over 36 holes in one day.

In 1892, the Honourable Company of Edinburgh Golfers took four radical steps to transform the Open Championship. It expanded the Championship to 72 holes over two days, imposed an entrance charge for all competitors, moved the Championship to a new course at Muirfield and increased the total prize fund from £28 10s to £100. These actions were all taken unilaterally by the club, with the increased purse to counter a rival tournament held at Musselburgh.

A meeting was held between the three host clubs on June 9, 1893, for the purpose of 'placing the competition for the Open Championship on a basis more commensurate with its importance than had hitherto existed.' Three resolutions were agreed. Two English clubs, St George's, Sandwich and Royal Liverpool, would be invited to stage the Championship and join the rota, now of five clubs. Four rounds of 18 holes would be played over two days. Each of the five clubs would contribute £15 annually to the cost and the balance would come from an entry fee for all competitors. The prize money would total £100, with £30 for the winner. The date of each year's championship would be set by the host club, which would also bear

any additional necessary expenses. The representatives of the five clubs became known as the Delegates of the Associated Clubs.

The increasing number of entrants caused a cut to be introduced after two rounds in 1898 and between 1904 and 1906 the Championship was played over three days. It then reverted to two days in 1907 with the introduction of qualifying rounds. The entire field had to qualify and there were no exemptions.

On January 24, 1920, the Delegates of the Associated Clubs asked the R&A to take over 'the management of the Championship and the custody of the Challenge Cup.' The new Championship Committee was responsible for running both the Open and Amateur Championships and in 1922 it was decided that the Open should only be played over links courses. The venues included in today's circuit are: Carnoustie, Muirfield, Royal Birkdale, Royal Liverpool, Royal Lytham & St Annes, Royal St George's, Royal Troon, the Old Course, St Andrews and Turnberry.

Prestwick, birth place of the Open, played host to the Championship 24 times, the last in 1925. Other courses that have been used in the past are: Musselburgh (1874, 1877, 1880, 1883, 1886, 1889); Royal Cinque Ports, Deal (1909, 1920); Princes, Sandwich (1932); Royal Portrush (1951).

The Open was played regularly over three days starting in 1926, with a round on each of the first two days and two rounds on the final day, which from 1927 onwards was a Friday. The total prize money had reached £500 by 1939. The prize money was increased to £1000 in 1946 and reached £5000 in 1959.

As the Open went into its second century in the 1960s, it grew tremendously both as a championship and a spectator event. In 1963, exemptions from pre-qualifying were introduced for the leading players. Play was extended to four days in 1966, with the Championship finishing with a single round on the Saturday. In 1968, a second cut after 54 holes was introduced to further reduce the field on the final day and this remained in effect until 1985. To cope with the increasing spectator numbers, facilities were much improved. Grandstands were first introduced at the 1960 Open and they became a standard feature from 1963 onwards.

Regional qualifying had been tried as an experiment for one year in 1926, but did not become a regular feature until 1977. Some players were exempt but had to take part in final qualifying, while others were exempt from both regional and final qualifying.

Since 1980, the Championship has been scheduled to end on a Sunday instead of a Saturday. In the event of a tie for first place, play-offs took place over 36 holes up until 1963, when they were reduced to 18 holes. In 1985 a four-hole play-off, followed by sudden death, was introduced to guarantee a finish in four days.

The Open Championship was first televised by the BBC in 1955. The first live broadcast to America was in 1966 and was shown on ABC. In 1958, the television coverage lasted for a total of three hours, one and a half hours on each of the final two days. In 2001, the Open was broadcast for 1038 hours worldwide.

Admission charges to watch the Open were introduced in 1926. Paid admissions went over 50,000 for the first time in 1968 at Carnoustie and over 100,000 for the first time at St Andrews in 1978. The 200,000 attendance figure was reached for the first time at St Andrews in 1990. A new record was set at the Home of Golf in 2000 when 238,787 watched the Millennium Open.

Growth of prize money by decade

Year	Total Prize Money	First Prize
1862	£0	£0
1872	£20	£8
1882	£45	£12
1892	£100	£35
1902	£125	£50
1912	£135	£50
1922	£225	£75
1932	£500	£100
1946	£1000	£150
1952	£1700	£300
1962	£8500	£1400
1972	£50,000	£5500
1982	£250,000	£32,000
1992	£950,000	£95,000
2002	£3,800,000	£700,000

Harry Vardon has scored most victories in the Open Championship. He won it six times between 1896 and 1914. J.H. Taylor, James Braid, Peter Thomson and Tom Watson have all won the Open five times each. Between 1860 and 1889, all the Open winners were Scottish. John Ball jr became the first Englishman and the first amateur to claim the title in 1890. Arnaud Massy from France was the first Continental winner in 1907.

Four players have completed a hat trick of Open wins: Tom Morris jr 1868–1870; Jamie Anderson 1877–1879; Bob Ferguson 1880–1882; Peter Thomson 1954–1956.

The Open has been won by an amateur six times – John Ball in 1890, Harold Hilton in 1892 and 1897 and Bobby Jones in 1926, 1927 and 1930. Walter Hagen was the first native born American to win the Open when he triumphed in 1922. Jock Hutchison, who had won the previous year, was resident in America at the time of his victory but was born in St Andrews.

The Amateur Championship

What became recognised at the first Amateur Championship was held at Hoylake in 1885, although earlier national amateur competitions had been played at St Andrews in 1857, 1858 and 1859. The R&A had considered holding a national amateur tournament in 1876 but decided not to proceed with the idea.

In December 1884, Thomas Owen Potter, the Secretary of Royal Liverpool Golf Club, proposed holding a championship for amateur players. The event was to be open to members of recognised clubs and it was hoped that it would make the game more popular and lead to improved standards of play.

A total of 44 players from 12 clubs entered the first championship. The format was matchplay, with the ruling that if two players tied they would both advance to the following round and play one another again. There were three semi-finalists: John Ball, Horace Hutchinson and Allan Macfie. After a bye to the final, Macfie beat Hutchinson 7 and 6.

Following the success of the first tournament, it was agreed that a championship open to all amateurs should be played at St Andrews, Hoylake and Prestwick in rotation.

A total of 24 golf clubs subscribed for the trophy, which was acquired in 1886. They were:

Alnmouth	Royal Aberdeen
Bruntsfield	Royal Albert (Montrose)
Dalhousie	Royal & Ancient
Formby	Royal Blackheath
Gullane	Royal Burgess
Honourable Company	Royal Liverpool
Innerleven	Royal North Devon
Kilspindie	Royal St George's
King James VI	Royal Wimbledon
New North Berwick	Tantallon
Panmure	Troon
Prestwick	West Lancashire

Representatives, known as Delegates of the Associated Clubs, were elected from these clubs to run the Championship and in 1919 they approached the R&A to accept future management. The Club agreed and in 1920 formed the Championship Committee. This committee became responsible for organising the Amateur and Open and for making decisions on the conditions of play. It was not until 1922, however, that the 1885 tournament was officially recognised as the first Amateur Championship and Allan Macfie the first winner.

The venue circuit gradually increased. Sandwich was added in 1892, Muirfield in 1897 and Westward Ho! in 1912. In its entire history the event has been to 22 locations throughout Britain. It first went to Ireland in 1949 (Portmarnock) and Wales in 1951 (Porthcawl).

Prior to 1930, only two non-British players won the Amateur Championship title, Walter Travis, who won in 1904, and Jesse Sweetser, who won in 1926. Both hailed from the United States, the former via Australia.

The Americans began to make their presence felt more strongly in the 1930s, with four Americans winning five Amateur Championships. Bobby Jones took the title at St Andrews 1930, the year in which he achieved the Grand Slam. Lawson Little won in 1934 and 1935, Robert Sweeney in 1937 and Charles Yates in 1938.

Following a break during World War II, the Amateur Championship resumed in 1946 at Birkdale when the handicap limit was raised from one to two as an encouragement to those amateurs who had been on war service.

Attempts were made during the 1950s and 1960s to control large numbers of entries. In 1956 the field was limited to 200 so that the quarter-final and semi-final matches and the final could be played over 36 holes.

This experiment lasted two years, when it was decided that only the semi-finals and final should be played over two rounds.

Regional qualifying over 36 holes was introduced in 1958 when 14 courses throughout the UK were selected. Using this method, the original entry of 500 was reduced to 200. Any player with a handicap of 5 or better could enter.

In 1961 regional qualifying was scrapped and the quarter-finals and semi-finals were played over 18 holes. Then in 1983 at Turnberry, 36 holes of strokeplay qualifying were introduced during the first two days. This format continues, with the leading 64 players and ties qualifying for the matchplay stages.

The Seniors Open Amateur Championship

The Seniors Open Amateur Championship was the first tournament to be initiated by the R&A. Prestwick Golf Club was responsible for starting the Open Championship, while Royal Liverpool Golf Club introduced the Amateur Championship. Other events, such as the Boys Amateur Championship and Boys Home Internationals were started by private individuals and then handed over, by agreement, to the R&A.

The Seniors Open Amateur Championship made its debut at Formby in 1969. It started as a means to help choose a Great Britain and Ireland team for the World Senior Amateur Team Championship which had begun in 1967 at Pinehurst, North Carolina, under the auspices of the World Amateur Golf Council.

Initially, the World Senior team event was to be played every two years, alternating with the competition for the Eisenhower Trophy, but it did not survive beyond 1969. The success of the Seniors Open Amateur Championship, however, was evident from the start and it became a popular event in its own right.

It began as a 36-hole strokeplay event, held over two days for players over the age of 55. The handicap limit was 5 and the field was restricted to 100. The winner was Reg Pattinson, who duly played his way onto the World Amateur Senior team. He was partnered by Alan Cave, A.L. Bentley and A.T. Kyle. The short-lived World Senior event was played in 1969 over the Old Course at St Andrews and was won for the second time by the United States. Great Britain and Ireland finished third out of an entry of only 13 teams.

Before the present format was introduced, various alternatives were tried, in order to satisfy increasing entry demands. Two courses were used in 1971, allowing an entry of 250 when the handicap limit was increased to 9. In 1974, a limit of 130 was imposed. Subsidiary competitions were introduced according to age group: 55–59, 60–64 and 65 and over. A fourth age group was added in 1975 for the over 70s and the entry limit was increased to 140. The special categories changed in 1999, to one only for the 65 and over age group.

Today, the Seniors Open Amateur Championship attracts a wide international field, the initial entry of

252 playing two rounds and the leading 50 and ties completing a further 18 holes. Scotland's Charlie Green is a multiple winner, having claimed the title six times between 1988 and 1994.

The British Mid-Amateur Championship

Introduced as recently as 1995, the British Mid-Amateur Championship does, in fact, have a longer history. In 1954, Sam Bunton founded the British Youths Open Championship for amateurs and assistant professionals under the age of 22. The aim was to provide a category for those players who were too old to compete in the Boys Championship, which catered for players under the age of 18, and who were too young to compete in major tournaments.

By the end of the 1950s, the British Youths had become a well established, popular event, with entries exceeding 200, but its future came under discussion in 1962 when the R&A Championship Committee was notified that the sponsor was anxious to hand over the event to another authority.

The R&A began its administration of the event in 1963. While it continued as an event for youths aged between 18 and 22, it was decided that professional entries should be excluded. The R&A also changed the title, renaming it the British Youths Open Amateur Championship.

The handicap limit, which was originally 6, was lowered in 1968 to 4. At the same time, the minimum age requirement was abolished and this format continued until 1994 when the Championship Committee decided to replace it with a new fixture. The British Mid-Amateur Championship made its debut at Sunningdale in 1995. Entries are accepted from competitors who have reached the age of 25 prior to the first day of the Championship. Gary Wolstenholme holds the record of most wins, claiming victory in 1995, 1996 and 1998.

The Boys Amateur Championship

The Boys Amateur Championship was introduced in 1921 for the under-16 age group. For the first two years it was played at Royal Ascot under the guidance of D.M. Mathieson and Colonel Thomas South. In 1948, Colonel South announced his intention to retire from his duties in connection with the event, declaring that 'nothing would give him greater pleasure than that the Royal and Ancient Golf Club should take over the conduct of the Championship.'

The venue for the first Boys Amateur Championship to be played under the administration of the R&A was the Old Course, St Andrews. A sub-committee ran the event until 1952 when it was finally handed over to the Championship Committee.

Since that year a prize has been presented to the best performing 16-year-old. This, the Peter Garner Bowl, commemorates the death of a competitor who was killed in a road accident while returning from the 1951 Championship.

Sir Michael Bonallack enjoyed early success in the Boys Amateur Championship. He won in 1952, and went on to win the Amateur Championship in 1961, 1965, 1968, 1969 and 1970.

Professionals who won the title earlier in their careers include Ronan Rafferty (1979), José María Olazábal (1983) and more recently Sergio García (1997).

The Junior Open Championships

Inaugurated in 1994, the Junior Open Championships came under the R&A's administrative control in 2000. All national golf unions and federations are invited to send their leading boy and girl under the age of 16 to compete in the three-day event. In previous years, only one player from each union or federation could enter. The biennial event is run on a course close to the Open Championship and in the same week so that all participants can spend time watching the world's finest players in action.

To encourage entries worldwide, there are three categories of competition defined by varying handicap limits. Gold is for those with a handicap of 3 and under, silver 4–9 and bronze 10–21.

The Walker Cup

The United States Golf Association International Challenge Trophy was originally intended to be presented to the winners of a contest to which all golf playing nations would be invited. However, as the R&A tactfully pointed out to their counterparts in the USGA in 1921, the only two countries capable of entering a team were Britain and America.

By this simple process of elimination the trophy presented by USGA President George Herbert Walker became the focal point of a biennial series between the finest amateur players of the two countries. The first unofficial match was played in 1921 on the eve of the Amateur Championship at Hoylake when 19-year-old Bobby Jones helped the American team to a 9–3 victory. For the next three years the event was played annually, but settled into its biennial pattern after 1924.

It was not until 1938 at St Andrews that Great Britain and Ireland recorded a first victory. In 1965 there was a 12–12 tie on American soil and St Andrews was again the venue for the next GB&I triumph in 1971.

Only after the first success in America, with a 12½–11½ victory at Peachtree in Georgia in 1989, did the GB&I team finally end American domination of the matches. In the years that followed there were home wins at Porthcawl in 1995 and Nairn in 1999. GB&I successfully defended the trophy two years later at Sea Island in Georgia by a convincing 15–9 margin.

The man after whom the trophy and the matches are named has another claim to a place in world his-tory. His grandson, George Herbert Walker Bush and his great-grandson have both held office as President of the United States of America.

The Eisenhower Trophy

The United States Golf Association approached the R&A in 1958 with the proposal that the two bodies should sponsor a world-wide amateur golf event. The new competition was to take place biennially in non-Walker Cup years, and the first to be played at St Andrews in October 1958. All golfing bodies which observed the Rules of Golf and Amateur Status as approved by the R&A and the USGA were invited to send one representative to a meeting in Washington at which President Dwight D. Eisenhower presented a trophy to be awarded to the winning country. The controlling committee of the event was to be known as the World Amateur Golf Council.

The key objective of the new council was 'to foster friendship and sportsmanship among the peoples of the world through the conduct of an Amateur Team Championship for The Eisenhower Trophy.' In a meeting with the President in the Rose Garden of the White House, Eisenhower offered his advice to the delegates: 'I suggest, aside from the four hotshot golfers you bring, that you take along some high-handicap fellows and let them play at their full handicaps … This way golf doesn't become so important.' This observation led to the creation of a 'Delegates and Duffers Cup' for officials and non-playing captains.

The format decided for the Eisenhower Trophy was strokeplay. Each team consisted of four players who would play four rounds. The team score for each round was the three best individual scores. The first competition was held in St Andrews and attracted 29 teams. After 72 holes of golf, the American and Australian teams were both tied on an aggregate score of 918. A play-off was held and the Australian team won by two strokes. So far this has been the only play-off in the history of the event.

Australia went on to win the trophy twice more, in 1966 and 1996. However, the USA have dominated the event, winning it 11 times in total. The Great Britain and Ireland team won four times, in 1964, 1976, 1988 and 1998. In 2002 teams were reduced from four to three players with the best two scores counting in each round and for the first time England, Ireland, Scotland and Wales entered separate teams. In 2002 in Malaysia there was a field of 56 teams.

The St Andrews Trophy

In November 1955 the Championship Committee of The Royal and Ancient Golf Club put forward a recommendation that 'the European Golf Association should be approached with a view to arranging an international match between a Great Britain and Ireland and European side.'

The GB&I team, captained by Gerald Micklem, duly triumphed by a score of 12½ to 2½ in the first match played over the West Course at Wentworth in 1956. The event was so successful that it was immediately established as a biennial event in non-Walker Cup years and in 1964 the R&A donated the St Andrews Trophy to be presented to the winning team.

Although Great Britain and Ireland have dominated the match, winning 21 of the 24 encounters, the Continent of Europe had a convincing victory at Villa d'Este in Italy in 1998 and suffered only a narrow 13–11 defeat at Turnberry in 2000. GB&I won the event 14–10 in 2002.

The Jacques Léglise Trophy

The annual boys international match involving GB&I against a team from the Continent of Europe was introduced in 1958. This event was dominated originally by the British side, which won every match through 1966 prompting the match to be discontinued because it was a one-sided affair.

The match was revived in 1977 when the Continental team won by 7 points to 6. A new trophy, donated by Jean-Louis Dupont on behalf of Golf de Chantilly in memory of Jacques Léglise. a leading French golf administrator, was presented for the first time in 1978 when the Continental team again won. Since then the Continental players have triumphed in 1986 and again in 1996, 1997 and 2001. The match was played in conjunction with the Boys Amateur Championship and Home International events until 1996, since when it has been staged independently.

The Boys Home Internationals

Introduced at Dunbar in 1923, the Boys Home Internationals started off as a match played between England and Scotland. It was traditionally associated with the Boys Amateur Championship, being played the day before and acting as a prelude to the main event.

The R&A accepted responsibility for the Boys Amateur Championship in 1949 and with it the running of the England v Scotland match. The Championship Committee originally carried out team selection. Today, representatives from the four Home Unions select the teams.

In 1972, a team match between Ireland and Wales was added to the fixture and the current format was established in 1996. The four home countries compete against one another over three consecutive days in a round robin series. Each fixture comprises five morning foursomes, followed by the afternoon singles.

In 1997, there was a significant break with the past when, for the first time, the venue chosen for the Boys Home Internationals differed to that for the Boys Amateur Championship. This practice has remained, helping to shape the individual identity of the international matches. Since 1985, the R&A Trophy has been awarded to the winning team.

Famous Players of the Past

In making the difficult choice of the names to be included, effort has been made to acknowledge the outstanding players and personalities of each successive era from the early pioneers to the stars of recent times.

Alliss, Percy   (1897–1975)

Finished in the top six in the Open Championship seven times, including joint third at Carnoustie in 1931, two strokes behind Tommy Armour. Twice winner of the Match Play Championship, five times German Open champion and twice winner of the Italian Open. Ryder Cup player in 1933–35–37, an international honour also gained by his son Peter. Spent much of his career as professional at the Wansee Club in Berlin.

Anderson, Jamie   (1842–1912)

Winner of three consecutive Open Championships – 1877–78–79. A native St Andrean, he once claimed to have played 90 consecutive holes on the Old Course without a bad or unintended shot. He was noted for his straight hitting and accurate putting.

Anderson, Willie   (1878–1910)

Took his typically Scottish flat swing to America where he won the US Open four times in a five year period from 1901. Only Bobby Jones, Ben Hogan and Jack Nicklaus have also won the US Open four times.

Armour, Thomas D.   (1896–1968)

Born in Edinburgh, he played for Britain against America as an amateur and, after emigrating, for America against Britain as a professional in the forerunners of the Walker and Ryder Cup matches. Won the US Open in 1927, the USPGA in 1930 and the 1931 Open at Carnoustie. Became an outstanding coach and wrote several bestselling instruction books.

Auchterlonie, William   (1872–1963)

Won the Open at Prestwick in 1893 at the age of 21 with a set of seven clubs he had made himself. Founded the famous family club-making business in St Andrews. He believed that golfers should master half, three-quarter and full shots with each club. Appointed Honorary Professional to the R&A in 1935.

Ball, John   (1861–1940)

Finished fourth in the Open of 1878 at the age of 16 and became the first amateur to win the title in 1890. He won the Amateur Championship eight times and shares with Bobby Jones the distinction of being the winner of the Open and Amateur in the same year. He grew up on the edge of the links area which became the Royal Liverpool Golf Club and the birthplace of the Amateur. He was a master at keeping the ball low in the wind, but with the same straight-faced club could cut the ball up for accurate approach shots. His run of success could have been greater but for military service in the South African campaign and the First World War.

Barton, Pamela   (1917–1943)

At the age of 19 she held both the British and American Ladies Championships in 1936. She was French champion at 17, runner-up in the British in both 1934 and '35 and won the title again in 1939. A Curtis Cup team member in 1934 and '36 she was a Flight Officer in the WAAF when she was killed in a plane crash at an RAF airfield in Kent.

Boros, Julius   (1920–1994)

Became the oldest winner of a major championship when he won the USPGA in 1968 at the age of 48. He twice won the US Open, in 1952 and again 11 years later at Brookline when he was 43. In a play-off he

Pam Barton   Popperfoto

beat Jackie Cupit by three shots and Arnold Palmer by six. He played in four Ryder Cup matches between 1959–67, winning nine of his 16 matches and losing only three.

Bousfield, Kenneth (1919–2000)

Although a short hitter even by the standards of his era, he won five out of 10 matches in six Ryder Cup appearances from 1949–61. He captured the PGA Match Play Championship in 1955, one of eight tournament victories in Britain, and also won six European Opens. He represented England in the World Cup at Wentworth in 1956 and Tokyo in 1957

Braid, James (1870–1950)

Together with Harry Vardon and JH Taylor he formed the Great Triumvirate and dominated the game for 20 years before the 1914–18 war. In a 10-year period from 1901 he became the first player in the history of the event to win the Open five times – and also finished second on three occasions. In that same period he won the Match Play Championship four times and the French Open. He was a tall, powerful player who hit the ball hard but always retained an appearance of outward calm. He was one of the founder members of the Professional Golfers' Association and did much to elevate the status of the professional golfer. He was responsible for the design of many golf courses and served as professional at Walton Heath for 45 years. He was an honorary member of that club for 25 years and became one of its directors. He was also an honorary member of the R&A.

Bruen, Jimmy (1920–1972)

Won the Irish Amateur at the age of 17 and defended his title the following year. At 18 he became the youngest ever Walker Cup player and in practice for the match at St Andrews in 1938 equalled the amateur course record of 68 set by Bobby Jones.

Campbell, Dorothy Iona (1883–1946)

One of only two golfers to win the British, American and Canadian Ladies titles. In total she won these three major championships seven times.

Compston, Archie (1893–1962)

Beat Walter Hagen 18 and 17 in a 72-hole challenge match at Moor Park in 1928 and tied for second place in the 1925 Open. Played in the Ryder Cup in 1927–29–31.

Cotton, Sir Henry (1907–1987)

The first player to be knighted for services to golf, he died a few days before the announcement of the award was made. He won the Open Championship three times, which included a round of 65 at Royal St George's in 1934 after which the famous Dunlop golf ball was named. His final 71 at Carnoustie to win the 1937 championship in torrential

rain gave him great satisfaction and he set another record with a 66 at Muirfield on the way to his third triumph in 1948. He won the Match Play Championship three times and was runner-up on three occasions. He also won 11 Open titles in Europe, played three times in the Ryder Cup and was non-playing captain in 1953. Sir Henry worked hard to promote the status of professional golf and also championed the cause of young golfers, becoming a founder member of the Golf Foundation. He was a highly successful teacher, author and architect, spending much time at Penina, a course he created in southern Portugal. He was an honorary member of the R&A.

Crawley, Leonard (1903–1981)

Played four times in the Walker Cup in 1932–34–38–47 and won the English Amateur in 1931. He also played first-class cricket for Worcestershire and Essex and toured the West Indies with the MCC in 1936. After the Second World War he was golf correspondent for the *Daily Telegraph* for 30 years.

The Curtis sisters, Harriet (1878–1944)
Margaret (1880–1965)

Donors of the Curtis Cup still contested biennially between the USA and GB&I. Harriet won the US Women's Amateur in 1906 and lost in the following year's final to her sister Margaret, who went on to win the championship three times.

Daly, Fred (1911–1990)

Daly won the Open at Royal Liverpool in 1947 and in four of the next five years was never out of the top four in the Championship. At Portrush, where he was born, he finished fourth to Max Faulkner in 1951, the only time the Open has been played in Northern Ireland. He was Ulster champion 11 times and three times captured the prestigious PGA Match Play Championship. He was a member of the Ryder Cup team four times, finishing on a high note at Wentworth in 1953 when he won his foursomes match in partnership with Harry Bradshaw and then beat Ted Kroll 9 and 7 in the singles.

Darwin, Bernard (1876–1961)

One of the most gifted and authoritative writers on golf, he was also an accomplished England international player for more than 20 years. While in America to report the 1922 Walker Cup match for The Times, he was called in to play and captain the side when Robert Harris became ill. A grandson of Charles Darwin, he was captain of the R&A in 1934–35. In 1937 he was awarded the CBE for services to literature.

Demaret, Jimmy (1910–1983)

Three times Masters champion, coming from five strokes behind over the final six holes to beat Jim Ferrier by two in 1950, he also won six consecutive tournaments in 1940 while still performing as a night club

singer. He won all six Ryder Cup matches he played in the encounters of 1947–49–51.

Duncan, George (1884–1964)

Won the Open in 1920 by making up 13 shots on the leader over the last two rounds and came close to catching Walter Hagen for the title two years later. Renowned as one of the fastest players, his book was entitled *Golf at the Gallop*.

Ferguson, Bob (1848–1915)

The Open Championship winner three times in succession between 1880–82. He then lost a 36-hole play-off for the title by one stroke to Willie Fernie in 1883. At 18 he had won the Leith Tournament against the game's leading professionals.

Fernie, Willie (1851–1924)

In 1882 he was second to Bob Ferguson in the Open over his home course at St Andrews. The following year he beat the same player in a 36-hole play-off for the championship over Ferguson's home links at Musselburgh.

Hagen, Walter (1892–1969)

A flamboyant character who used a hired Rolls Royce as a changing room because professionals were not allowed in many clubhouses, he once gave his £50 cheque for winning the Open to his caddie. He won four consecutive USPGA Championships from 1924 when it was still decided by matchplay. He was four times a winner of the Open, in 1922–24–28–29 and captured the US Open title in 1914 and 1919. He captained and played in five Ryder Cup encounters between 1927–35, winning seven of his nine matches and losing only once. He was non-playing captain in 1937.

Herd, Alexander 'Sandy' (1868–1944)

When he first played in the Open at the age of 17 he possessed only four clubs. His only championship success came in the 1902 Open at Hoylake, the first player to capture the title using the new rubber-cored ball. He won the Match Play Championship at the age of 58 and took part in his last Open at St Andrews in 1939 at the age of 71.

Hilton, Harold (1869–1942)

Winner of the Amateur Championship four times between 1900 and 1913, he also became the first player and the only Briton to hold both the British and US Amateur titles in the same year 1911. He won the Open in 1892 at Muirfield, the first time the championship was extended to 72 holes. A small but powerful player he was the first editor of *Golf Monthly*.

Hogan, Ben (1912–1997)

One of only five players to have won all four major championships, his record of capturing three in the same season has been matched by Tiger Woods. He dominated the golfing scene in America after the Second World War and in 1953 won the Masters, US Open and the Open Championship. A clash of dates between the Open and USPGA prevented an attempt on the Grand Slam, but his poor state of health after a near fatal car crash four years earlier would have made the matchplay format of 10 rounds in six days in the USPGA an impossibility. After his car collided with a Greyhound bus in fog, it was feared that Hogan might never walk again. He had won three majors before the accident and he returned to capture six more. His only appearance in the Open was in his tremendous season of 1953 and he recorded rounds of 73-71-70-68 to win by four strokes at Carnoustie. His dramatic life story was made into a Hollywood film entitled *Follow the Sun*.

Hutchinson, Horace (1859–1932)

Runner-up in the first Amateur Championship in 1885, he won the title in the next two years and reached the final again in 1903. Represented England from 1902–07. He was a prolific writer on golf and country life and became the first English captain of the R&A in 1908.

Jones, Bobby (1902–1971)

Always remembered for his incredible and unrepeatable achievement in 1930 of winning the Open and Amateur Championships of Britain and America in one outstanding season – the original and unchallenged Grand Slam. At the end of that year he retired from competitive golf at the age of 28. His victories included four US Opens, five US Amateur titles, three Opens in Britain and one Amateur Championship. Although his swing was stylish and fluent, he suffered badly from nerves and was often sick and unable to eat during championships.

He was also an accomplished scholar, gaining first-class honours degrees in law, English literature and mechanical engineering at three different universities. He subsequently opened a law practice in Atlanta and developed the idea of creating the Augusta National course and staging an annual invitation event which was to become known as the Masters.

He was made an honorary member of the Royal and Ancient Golf Club in 1956 and two years later was given the freedom of the Burgh of St Andrews at an emotional ceremony. He died after many years of suffering from a crippling spinal disease and a hole on the Old Course bears his name.

Kirkaldy, Andrew (1860–1934)

First honorary professional appointed by the R&A, he lost a play-off for the Open Championship of 1889 to Willie Park at Musselburgh. He was second in the championship three times, a further three times finished third and twice fourth. A powerful player, he was renowned for speaking his mind.

Bobby Jones   Popperfoto

Laidlay, John Ernest   (1860–1940)

The man who first employed the overlapping grip which was later credited to Harry Vardon and universally known as the Vardon grip, Laidlay was a finalist in the Amateur Championship six times in seven years from 1888, winning the title twice at a time when John Ball, Horace Hutchinson and Harold Hilton were at their peak. He was runner-up in the Open to Willie Auchterlonie at Prestwick in 1893. Among the 130 medals he won, were the Gold Medal and Silver Cross in R&A competitions.

Leitch, 'Cecil'   (1891–1977)

Christened Charlotte Cecilia, but universally known as Cecil, her list of international victories would undoubtedly have been greater but for the blank golfing years of the first world war. She first won the British Ladies Championship in 1908 at the age of 17. In 1914 she took the English, French and British titles and successfully defended all three when competition was resumed after the war. In all she won the French Championship five times, the British four times, the English twice, the Canadian once. Her total of four victories in the British has never been beaten and has

been equalled only by her great rival Joyce Wethered. The victory in Canada was by a margin of 17 and 15 in the 36-hole final.

Lema, Tony   (1934–1966)

His first visit to Britain, leaving time for only 27 holes of practice around the Old Course at St Andrews, culminated in Open Championship victory in 1964 by five shots over Jack Nicklaus. He had won three tournaments in four starts in America before arriving in Scotland and gave great credit for his Open success to local caddie Tip Anderson. He played in the Ryder Cup in 1963 and 1965 with an outstanding record. He lost only once in 11 matches, halved twice and won eight. Lema and his wife were killed when a private plane in which they were travelling to a tournament crashed in Illinois.

Little, Lawson   (1910–1968)

Won the Amateur Championships of Britain and America in 1934 and successfully defended both titles the following year. He then turned his amateur form into a successful professional career, starting in 1936 with victory in the Canadian Open. He won the US Open in 1940 after a play-off against Gene Sarazen.

Locke, Bobby   (1917–1987)

The son of Northern Irish emigrants to South Africa, Arthur D'Arcy Locke was playing off plus four by the age of 18 and won the South African Boys, Amateur and Open Championships. On his first visit to Britain in 1936 he was leading amateur in the Open Championship. Realising that his normal fade was leaving him well short of the leading players, he deliberately developed the hook shot to get more run on the ball. It was to become his trade-mark throughout a long career.

He was encouraged to try the American tour in 1947 and won five tournaments, one by the record margin of 16 shots. More successes followed and the USPGA framed a rule which banned him from playing in their events, an action described by Gene Sarazen as 'the most disgraceful action by any golf organisation'.

Disillusioned by the American attitude, Locke played most of his golf in Europe, winning the Open four times. He shared a period of domination with Peter Thomson between 1949–1958 when they won the championship four times each, only Max Faulkner and Ben Hogan breaking the sequence. In his final Open victory at St Andrews in 1957 he failed to replace his ball in the correct spot on the 18th green after moving it from fellow competitor Bruce Crampton's line. The mistake, which could have led to disqualification, was only spotted on television replays. The R&A Championship Committee rightly decided that Locke, who had won by three strokes, had gained no advantage, and allowed the result to stand.

Following a career in which he won over 80 events around the world he was made an honorary member of the R&A in 1976.

Bobby Locke   Popperfoto

Longhurst, Henry (1909–1978)

Captain of Cambridge University golf team, runner-up in the French and Swiss Amateur Championships and winner of the German title in 1936, he became the most perceptive and readable golf correspondent of his time and a television commentator who never wasted a single word. His relaxed, chatty style was based on the premise that he was explaining the scene to a friend in his favourite golf club bar. For 25 years his Sunday Times column ran without a break and became compulsory reading for golfers and non-golfers alike. He had a brief spell as a member of parliament and was awarded the CBE for services to golf.

Mackenzie, Alister (1870–1934)

A family doctor and surgeon, he became involved with Harry S. Colt in the design of the Alwoodley course in Leeds, where he was a founder member and honorary secretary and eventually abandoned his medical career and worked full time at golf course architecture. There are many outstanding examples of his work in Britain, Australia, New Zealand and America. His most famous creation, in partnership with Bobby Jones, is the Augusta National course in Georgia, home of the US Masters.

Massy, Arnaud (1877–1958)

The first non-British player to win the Open Championship. Born in Biarritz, France, he defeated J.H. Taylor by two strokes at Hoylake in 1907. Four years later

he tied for the title with Harry Vardon at Royal St George's, but conceded at the 35th hole when he was five strokes behind. He won the French Open four times, the Spanish on three occasions and the Belgian title once.

Micklem, Gerald (1911–1988)

A pre-war Oxford Blue, he won the English Amateur Championship in 1947 and 1953 and played in the Walker Cup team four times between 1947 and 1955. He was non-playing captain in 1957 and 1959. In 1976 he set a record of 36 consecutive appearances in the President's Putter, an event that he won in 1953. In addition to his playing success he was a tireless administrator, serving as chairman of the R&A Rules, Selection and Championship Committees. He was president of the English Golf Union and the European Golf Association and captain of the R&A. In 1969 he received the Bobby Jones award for services to golf.

Middlecoff, Cary (1921–1998)

Dentist turned golf professional, he became one of the most prolific winners on the US tour, with 37 victories that included two US Opens and a Masters victory. In the US Open of 1949 he beat Sam Snead and Clayton Heafner at Medinah, and seven years later recaptured the title by one shot ahead of Ben Hogan and Julius Boros at Oak Hill. His Masters success came in 1955 when he established a record seven-shot winning margin over Hogan.

Mitchell, Abe (1897–1947)

Said by J.H. Taylor to be the finest player never to win an Open, he finished in the top six five times. He was more successful in the Match Play Championship, with victories in 1919, 1920 and 1929. He taught the game to St Albans seed merchant Samuel Ryder and is the figure depicted on top of the famous trophy.

Morgan, Wanda (1910–1995)

Three-time English Amateur champion, in 1931–36–37, she also captured the British title in 1935 and played three times in the Curtis Cup from 1932–36.

Morris, Old Tom (1821–1908)

Apprenticed as a feathery ball maker to Allan Robertson in St Andrews at the age of 18 he was one of the finest golfers of his day when he took up the position of Keeper of the Green at Prestwick, where he laid out the original 12-hole course. He was 39 when he finished second in the first Open in 1860, but subsequently won the title four times, and played in every Open until 1896 when he was 75. His success rate might have been much greater if he had been a better putter. His son once said: 'He would be a much better player if the hole was a yard closer.'

A man of fierce conviction, he returned to St Andrews to take up the duties of looking after the Old

Course at a salary of £50 per year, paid by the R&A. He came to regard the course as his own property and was once publicly reprimanded for closing it without authority because he considered it needed a rest. A testimonial in 1896 raised £1,240 pounds towards his old age from golfers around the world and when he retired in 1903 the R&A continued to pay his salary. He died after a fall on the stairs of the New Club in 1908, having outlived his wife, his daughter and his three sons.

Morris, Young Tom   (1851–1875)

Born in St Andrews, but brought up in Prestwick, where his father had moved to become Keeper of the Green, he won a tournament against leading professionals at the age of 13. He was only 17 when he succeeded his father as Open champion in 1868 and then defended the title successfully in the following two years to claim the winner's belt outright. There was no championship in 1971, but when the present silver trophy became the prize in 1872, Young Tom's was the first name engraved on its base.

His prodigious talent was best demonstrated in his third successive Open victory in 1870 when he played 36 holes at Prestwick in 149 strokes, 12 shots ahead of his nearest rival, superb scoring given the equipment and the condition of the courses at that time.

He married in November 1874 and was playing with his father in a money match at North Berwick the following year when a telegram from St Andrews sent them hurrying back across the Firth of Forth in a private yacht. Young Tom's wife and baby had both died in childbirth. He played golf only twice after that, in matches that had been arranged long in advance, and fell into moods of deep depression. He died on Christmas morning of that same year from a burst artery in the lung. He was 24 years old. A public subscription paid for a memorial which still stands above his grave in the cathedral cemetery.

Ouimet, Francis   (1893–1967)

Regarded as the player who started the American golf boom after beating Harry Vardon and Ted Ray in a play-off for the 1913 US Open as a young amateur. Twice a winner of the US Amateur, he was a member of every Walker Cup team from 1922 to 1934 and non-playing captain from then until 1949. In 1951 he became the first non-British national to be elected captain of the R&A and was a committee member of the USGA for many years.

Park, William   (1834–1903)

Winner of the first Open Championship in 1860. He won the title three more times, in 1863, 1866 and 1875, and was runner-up on four occasions. For 20 years he issued a standing challenge to play any man in the world for £100 a side. His reputation was built largely around a successful putting stroke and he always stressed the importance of never leaving putts short.

Park, Mungo   (1839–1904)

Younger brother to Willie Park, he spent much of his early life at sea, but won the Open Championship in 1874 at the age of 35, beating Young Tom Morris into second place by two shots on his home course at Musselburgh.

Park, William jr   (1864–1925)

Son of the man who won the first Open Championship, Willie Park jr captured the title twice – in 1887 and 1889 – and finished second to Harry Vardon in 1898. He was also an accomplished clubmaker who did much to popularise the bulger driver with its convex face and he patented the wry-neck putter in 1891. One of the first and most successful professionals to design golf courses, he was responsible for many layouts in Britain, Europe and America and also wrote two highly successful books on the game.

Philp, Hugh   (1782–1856)

One of the master craftsmen in St Andrews in the early days of the 19th century, he was renowned for his skill in creating long-nosed putters. After his death his business was continued by Robert Forgan. Philp's clubs are much prized collector's items.

Picard, Henry   (1907–1997)

Winner of the 1938 US Masters and the 1939 USPGA Championship, where he birdied the final hole to tie with Byron Nelson and birdied the first extra hole for the title. Ill health cut short a career in which he won 27 tournaments.

Ray, Ted   (1877–1943)

Born in Jersey, his early years in golf were in competition with Channel Islands compatriot Harry Vardon and his fellow members of the Great Triumvirate, J.H. Taylor and James Braid. His only victory in the Open came in 1912, but he was runner-up to Taylor the following year and second again, to Jim Barnes of America, in 1925 when he was 48 years of age He claimed the US Open title in 1920 and remains one of only three British players to win the Open on both sides of the Atlantic. The others are Vardon and Tony Jacklin.

Rees, Dai   (1913–1983)

One of Britain's outstanding golfers for three decades, he played in nine Ryder Cup matches between 1937 and 1961 and was playing captain of the 1957 team which won the trophy for the first time since 1933. He was non-playing captain in 1967. He was runner-up in the Open three times and won the PGA Match Play title four times. He was made an honorary member of the Royal and Ancient Golf Club in 1976.

Robertson, Allan   (1815–1858)

So fearsome was Robertson's reputation as a player that when the R&A staged an annual competition for

Dai Rees   Popperfoto

local professionals, he was not allowed to take part so as to give the others a chance. A famous maker of feather golf balls, he strongly resisted the advance of the more robust gutta percha. Tom Morris senior was his apprentice and they were reputed never to have lost a foursomes match in which they were partners.

Ryder, Samuel (1858–1936)

The prosperous seed merchant was so impressed with the friendly rivalry between British and American professionals at an unofficial match at Wentworth in 1926 that he donated the famous gold trophy for the first Ryder Cup match the following year. The trophy is still presented today for the contest between America and Europe.

Sarazen, Gene (1902–1999)

Advised to find an outdoor job to improve his health, Sarazen became a caddie and then an assistant professional. At the age of 20 he became the first player to win the US Open and PGA titles in the same year. In claiming seven major titles he added the Open at Prince's in 1932 and when he won the second Masters tournament in 1935 he became the first of only five players to date who have won all four Grand Slam trophies during their careers. He played 'the shot heard around the world' on his way to Masters victory, holing a four-wood across the lake at the 15th for an albatross two. At the age of 71 he played in the Open at Troon and holed-in-one at the

Postage Stamp eighth. The next day be holed from a bunker for a two at the same hole. He acted as an honorary starter at the Masters, hitting his final shot only a month before his death at the age of 97.

Sayers, Ben (1857–1924)

A twinkling, elphin figure, the diminutive Sayers played a leading part in the game for more than four decades. He represented Scotland against England from 1903 to 1913 and played in every Open from 1880 to 1923.

Smith, Frances – *née* Bunty Stephens (1925–1978)

Dominated post-war women's golf, winning the British Ladies Championship in 1949 and 1954, was three times a winner of the English and once the victor in the French Championship. She represented Great Britain & Ireland in six consecutive encounters from 1950, losing only three of her 11 matches, and was non-playing captain of the team in 1962 and 1972. She was awarded the OBE for her services to golf.

Smith, Horton (1908–1963)

In his first winter on the professional circuit as a 20-year-old in 1928–29 he won eight out of nine tournaments. He was promoted to that year's Ryder Cup team and played again in 1933 and 1935 and remained unbeaten He won the first Masters in 1934 and repeated that success two year's later. He received the Ben Hogan Award for overcoming illness or injury and the Bobby Jones Award for distinguished sportsmanship in golf.

Smith, Macdonald (1890–1949)

Born into a talented Carnoustie golfing family, he was destined to become one of the finest golfers never to win the Open. He was second in 1930 and 1932, was twice third and twice fourth. His best chance came at Prestwick in 1925 when he led the field by five strokes with one round to play, but the enthusiastic hordes of Scottish supporters destroyed his concentration and he finished with an 82 for fourth place.

Snead, Samuel Jackson (1912–2002)

Few would argue that 'Slammin' Sam Snead' possessed the sweetest swing in the history of the game. 'He just walked up to the ball and poured honey all over it', it was said. Raised during the Depression in Hot Springs, Virginia, he also died there on May 23 2002, four days short of his 90th birthday. His seven major titles comprised three Masters, three US PGA Championships and the 1946 Open at St Andrews, while he was runner-up four times in the US Open. But for the Second World War he would surely have added several more. He achieved a record 82 PGA Tour victories in America, the last of them at age 52, and was just as prolific round the world across six

decades. He played in seven Ryder Cup matches, captained the 1969 United States team which tied at Royal Birkdale and after his retirement acted as honorary starter at the Masters until his death. Perhaps his greatest achievement came in the 1979 Quad Cities Open when he scored 67 and 66. He was 67 years of age at the time.

Stewart, Payne   (1957–1999)

Four months after winning his second US Open title Payne Stewart was killed in a plane crash. Only a month earlier he had been on the winning United States Ryder Cup team. His first major victory was in the 1989 USPGA Championship and he claimed his first US Open title two years later after a play-off against Scott Simpson. In 1999 he holed an 18-foot winning putt to beat Phil Mickleson for the US title he was never able to defend. In 1985 he finished a stroke behind Sandy Lyle in the Open at Royal St George's and five years later he shared second place as Nick Faldo won the Championship at St Andrews.

Tait, Freddie   (1870–1900)

In 1890 Tait set a new record of 77 for the Old Course, lowering that to 72 only four years later. He was three times the leading amateur in the Open Championship and twice won the Amateur Championship, in 1896 and 1898. The following year he lost at the 37th hole of an historic final to John Ball at Prestwick. He was killed while leading a charge of the Black Watch at Koodoosberg Drift in the Boer War.

Taylor, John Henry   (1871–1963)

Winner of the Open Championship five times between 1894 and 1913, Taylor was part of the Great Triumvirate with James Braid and Harry Vardon. He tied for the title with Vardon in 1896, but lost in the play-off and was runner-up another five times. He also won the French and German Opens and finished second in the US Open. A self-educated man, he was a thoughtful and compelling speaker and became the founding father of the Professional Golfers' Association. He was made an honorary member of the R&A in 1949.

Tolley, Cyril   (1896–1978)

Won the first of his two Amateur Championships in 1920 while still a student at Oxford and played in the unofficial match which preceded the Walker Cup a year later. He played in six Walker Cup encounters and was team captain in 1924. Tolley is the only amateur to have won the French Open, a title he captured in 1924 and 1928. After winning the Amateur for the second time in 1929 he was favourite to retain the title at St Andrews the following summer but was beaten by a stymie at the 19th hole in the fourth round by Bobby Jones in his Grand Slam year.

Travis, Walter   (1862–1925)

Born in Australia, he won the US Amateur Championship in 1900 at the age of 38, having taken up the game only four years earlier. He won again the following year and in 1903. He became the first overseas player to win the Amateur title in Britain in 1904, using a centre-shafted Schenectady putter he had just acquired. The club was banned a short time later. He was 52 years old when he last reached the semi-finals of the US Amateur in 1914.

Vardon, Harry   (1870–1937)

Still the only player to have won the Open Championship six times, Vardon, who was born in Jersey, won his first title in 1896, in a 36-hole play-off against J.H. Taylor and his last in 1914, this time beating Taylor by three shots. He won the US Open in 1900 and was beaten in a play-off by Francis Ouimet in 1913. He popularised the overlapping grip which still bears his name, although it was first used by Johnny Laidlay. He was also the originator of the modern upright swing, moving away from the flat sweeping action of previous eras. After his Open victory of 1903, during which he was so ill he thought he would not be able to finish, he was diagnosed with tuberculosis. His legendary accuracy and low scoring are commemorated with the award of the Vardon Trophy each year to the player on the European Tour with the lowest stroke average.

Vare, Glenna – née Collett   (1903–1989)

Won the first of her six US Ladies Amateur titles at the age of 19 in 1922 and the last in 1935. A natural athlete, she attacked the ball with more power than was normal in the women's game. The British title eluded her, although at St Andrews in 1929 she was three-under par and five up on Joyce Wethered after 11 holes, but lost to a blistering counter-attack. She played in the first Curtis Cup match in 1932 and was a member of the team in 1936, 1938 and 1948 and captain in 1934 and 1950.

Walker, George   (1874–1953)

The President of the United States Golf Association who donated the trophy for the first match in 1922, at Long Island, New York, and which is still presented to the winning team in the biennial matches beteeen the USA and Great Britain & Ireland. His grandson and great grandson, George Walker Bush and George Bush jr have both become Presidents of the United States.

Ward, Charles Harold   (1911–2001)

Charlie Ward played in three Ryder Cup matches from 1947–1951 and was twice third in the Open, behind Henry Cotton at Muirfield in 1948 and Max Faulkner at Royal Portrush in 1951.

Wethered, Joyce – Lady Heathcoat-Amory (1901–1997)

Entered her first English Ladies Championship in 1920 at the age of 18 and beat holder Cecil Leitch in

the final. She remained unbeaten for four years, winning 33 successive matches. After they had played together at St Andrews, Bobby Jones remarked: 'I had never played golf with anyone, man or woman, amateur or professional, who made me feel so utterly outclassed.'

Wethered, Roger (1899–1983)

Amateur champion in 1923 and runner-up in 1928 and 1930, he played five times in the Walker Cup, acting as playing captain at Royal St George's in 1930, and represented England against Scotland every year from 1922 to 1930. In the Open Championship at St Andrews in 1921 he tied with Jock Hutchison despite incurring a penalty for treading on his own ball. Due to play in a cricket match in England the following day, he was persuaded to stay in St Andrews for the play-off, but lost by 150-159 over 36 holes.

Whitcombe, Ernest (1890–1971)
Charles (1895–1978)
Reginald (1898–1957)

The remarkable golfing brothers from Burnham, Somerset, were all selected for the Ryder Cup team of 1935. Charlie and Eddie were paired togther and won the only point in the foursomes in a heavy 9-3 defeat by the American team. Reg won the gale-lashed Open at Royal St George's in 1938, with a final round of 78 as the exhibition tent was blown into the sea. Ernest finished second to Walter Hagen in 1924 and Charlie was third at Muirfield in 1935.

Wilson, Enid (1910–1996)

Completed a hat-trick of victories in the Ladies British Amateur Championship from 1931–33. She was twice a semi-finalist in the American Championship, won the British Girls and English Ladies titles and played in the inaugural Curtis Cup match, beating Helen Hicks 2 and 1 in the singles. Retiring early from competitive golf, she was never afraid to express strongly held views on the game in her role as wormen's golf correspondent of the *Daily Telegraph*.

Wood, Craig (1901–1968)

Both Masters and US Open champion in 1941, Wood finally made up for a career of near misses, having lost play-offs for all four major championships between 1933 and 1939. He was three times a member of the American Ryder Cup team.

Zaharias, Mildred – *née* Didrickson (1915–1956)

As a 17-year-old, Babe, as she was universally known, broke three records in the 1932 Los Angeles Olympics – the javelin, 80 metres hurdles and high jump, but her high jump medal was denied her when judges decided her technique was illegal. Turning her attention to golf, she rapidly established herself as the most powerful woman golfer of the time. She won the final of the US Amateur by 11 and 9 in 1946, became the first American to win the British title the following year, then helped launch the women's professional tour. She won the US Women's Open in 1948, 1950 and 1954 and in 1950 won six of the nine events on the tour. In 1952 she had a major operation for cancer, but when she won her third and final Open two years later it was by the margin of 12 shots. She was voted Woman Athlete of the Year five times between 1932 and 1950 and Greatest Female Athlete of the Half-Century in 1949.

Interesting Facts and Unusual Incidents

Royal Golf Clubs

● The right to the designation *Royal* is bestowed by the favour of the Sovereign or a member of the Royal House. In most cases the title is granted along with the bestowal of royal patronage on the club. The Perth Golfing Society was the first to receive the designation *Royal*. That was accorded in June 1833. King William IV bestowed the honour on the Royal & Ancient Club in 1834. The most recent Club to be so designated is the Royal Troon in 1978.

Royal and Presidential Golfers

● In the long history of the Royal and Ancient game no reigning British monarch has played in an open competition. In 1922 the Duke of Windsor, when Prince of Wales, competed in the Royal & Ancient Autumn Medal at St Andrews. He also took part in competitions at Mid-Surrey, Sunningdale, Royal St George's and in the Parliamentary Handicap. He occasionally competed in American events, sometimes partnered by a professional. On a private visit to London in 1952, he competed in the Autumn competition of Royal St George's at Sandwich, scoring 97. As Prince of Wales he played on courses all over the world and, after his abdication, as Duke of Windsor he continued to enjoy the game for many years.

● King George VI, when still Duke of York, in 1930, and the Duke of Kent, in 1937, also competed in the Autumn Meeting of the Royal & Ancient, when they had formally played themselves into the Captaincy of the Club and each returned his card in the medal round.

● King Leopold of Belgium played in the Belgian Amateur Championship at Le Zoute, the only reigning monarch ever to have played in a national championship. The Belgian King played in many competitions subsequent to his abdication. In 1949 he reached the quarter-finals of the French Amateur Championship at St Cloud, playing as Count de Rethy.

● King Baudouin of Belgium in 1958 played in the triangular match Belgium-France-Holland and won his match against a Dutch player. He also took part in the Gleneagles Hotel tournament (playing as Mr B. de Rethy), partnered by Dai Rees in 1959.

● United States President George Bush accepted an invitation in 1990 to become an Honorary Member of the Royal & Ancient Golf Club of St Andrews. The honour recognised his long connection and that of his family with golf and the R&A. Both President Bush's father, Prescott Bush Sr, and his grandfather, George Herbert Walker – who donated the Walker Cup – were presidents of the United States Golf Association. Other Honorary Members of the R&A include Kel Nagle, Jack Nicklaus, Arnold Palmer, Gene Sarazen, Peter Thomson, Roberto de Vicenzo, Gary Player and five-times Open Championship winner Tom Watson, who was made an honorary member in 1999 on his 50th birthday.

● In September 1992, the Royal & Ancient Golf Club of St Andrews announced that His Royal Highness The Duke of York had accepted the Club's invitation of Honorary Membership. The Duke of York is the third member of the Royal Family to accept membership along with Their Royal Highnesses The Duke of Edinburgh and The Duke of Kent. He has since become a single handicapper, and has appeared in a number of pro-ams, partnering Open and Masters champion Mark O'Meara to victory in the Alfred Dunhill Cup pro-am at St Andrews in 1998. His Royal Highness has been named captain-elect for 2004–5, when the club will celebrate its 250th anniversary.

First Lady Golfer

● Mary Queen of Scots, who was beheaded on 8th February, 1587, was probably the first lady golfer so mentioned by name. As evidence of her indifference to the fate of Darnley, her husband who was murdered at Kirk o' Field, Edinburgh, she was charged at her trial with having played at golf in the fields beside Seton a few days after his death.

Record Championship Victories

● In the Amateur Championship at Muirfield, 1920, Captain Carter, an Irish golfer, defeated an American entrant by 10 and 8. This is the only known instance where a player has won every hole in an Amateur Championship tie.

● In the final of the Canadian Ladies' Championship at Rivermead, Ottawa, in 1921, Cecil Leitch defeated Mollie McBride by 17 and 15. Miss Leitch lost only 1 hole in the match, the ninth. She was 14 up at the end of the first round, making only 3 holes necessary in the second. She won 18 holes out of 21 played, lost 1, and halved 2.

● In the final of the French Ladies' Open Championship at Le Touquet in 1927, Mlle de la Chaume (St Cloud) defeated Mrs Alex Johnston (Moor Park)

by 15 and 14, the largest victory in a European golf championship.

● At Prestwick in 1934, W. Lawson Little of Presidio, San Francisco, defeated James Wallace, Troon Portland, by 14 and 13 in the final of the Amateur Championship, the record victory in the Championship. Wallace failed to win a single hole.

Players who have won Two or More Majors in the Same Year

(The first Masters Tournament was played in 1934.)

1922 Gene Sarazen – USPGA, US Open
1924 Walter Hagen – USPGA, Open
1926 Bobby Jones – US Open, Open
1930 Bobby Jones – US Open, Open (Bobby Jones also won the US Amateur and British Amateur in this year.)
1932 Gene Sarazen – US Open, Open
1941 Craig Wood – Masters, US Open
1948 Ben Hogan – USPGA, US Open
1949 Sam Snead – USPGA, Masters
1951 Ben Hogan – Masters, US Open
1953 Ben Hogan – Masters, US Open, Open
1956 Jack Burke – USPGA, Masters
1960 Arnold Palmer – Masters, US Open
1962 Arnold Palmer – Masters, Open
1963 Jack Nicklaus – USPGA, Masters
1966 Jack Nicklaus – Masters, Open
1971 Lee Trevino – US Open, Open
1972 Jack Nicklaus – Masters, Open
1974 Gary Player – Masters, Open
1975 Jack Nicklaus – USPGA, Masters
1977 Tom Watson – Masters, Open
1980 Jack Nicklaus – USPGA, US Open
1982 Tom Watson – US Open, Open
1990 Nick Faldo – Masters, Open
1994 Nick Price – Open, US PGA
1998 Mark O'Meara – Masters, Open
2000 *Tiger Woods – US Open, Open, USPGA

*Woods also won the 2001 Masters to become the first player to hold all four Majors at the same time. He was 65-under-par for the four events.

Outstanding Records in Championships, International Matches and on the Professional Circuit

● The record number of victories in the Open Championship is six, held by Harry Vardon who won in 1896-98-99-1903-11-14.

● Five-time winners of the Championship are J.H. Taylor in 1894-95-1900-09-13; James Braid in 1901-05-06-08-10; Peter Thomson in 1954-55-56-58-65 and Tom Watson in 1975-77-80-82-83. Thomson's 1965 win was achieved when the Championship had become a truly international event. In 1957 he finished second behind Bobby Locke. By winning again in 1958 Thomson was prevented only by Bobby Locke from winning five consecutive Open Championships.

● Four successive victories in the Open by *Young* Tom Morris is a record so far never equalled. He won in 1868-69-70-72. (The Championship was not played in 1871.) Other four-time winners are Bobby Locke in 1949-50-52-57, Walter Hagen in 1922-24-28-29, Willie Park 1860-63-66-75, and *Old* Tom Morris 1861-62-64-67.

● Since the Championship began in 1860, players who have won three times in succession are Jamie Anderson, Bob Ferguson, and Peter Thomson.

● Robert Tyre Jones won the Open three times in 1926-27-30; the Amateur in 1930; the American Open in 1923-26-29-30; and the American Amateur in 1924-25-27-28-30. In winning the four major golf titles of the world in one year (1930) he achieved a feat unlikely ever to be equalled. Jones retired from competitive golf after winning the 1930 American Open, the last of these Championships, at the age of 28.

● Jack Nicklaus has had the most wins (six) in the US Masters Tournament, followed by Arnold Palmer with four.

● In modern times there are four championships generally regarded as standing above all others – the Open, US Open, US Masters, and USPGA. Five players have held all these titles, Gene Sarazen, Ben Hogan, Gary Player, Jack Nicklaus and Tiger Woods. In 1978 Nicklaus became the first player to have held each of them at least three times. His record in these events is: Open 1966-70-78; US Open 1962-67-72-80; US Masters 1963-65-66-72-75-86; USPGA 1963-71-73-75-80. His total of major championships is now 18. In 1998 at the age of 58, Nicklaus finished joint sixth in the Masters. By not playing in the Open Championship that year, he ended a run of 154 successive major championships for which he was eligible (stretching back to 1957).

In 1953 Ben Hogan won the Masters, US Open and Open, but did not compete in the USPGA because the date clashed with the Open.

In 2000 Tiger Woods won the US Open by 15 strokes (a major championship record), the Open by eight strokes, and the USPGA in the play-off. In 2001 he then added the Masters winning by two shots to become the first player to hold all four major titles at the same time. He was 65-under-par for the four events.

● In the 1996 English Amateur Championship at Hollinwell, Ian Richardson (50) and his son, Carl, of Burghley Park, Lincolnshire, both reached the semi-finals. Both lost.

● The record number of victories in the US Open is four, held by W. Anderson, Bobby Jones, Ben Hogan and Jack Nicklaus.

● Bobby Jones (amateur), Gene Sarazen, Ben Hogan, Lee Trevino, Tom Watson and Tiger Woods are the only players to have won the Open and US Open Championships in the same year. Tony Jacklin won the Open in 1969 and the US Open in 1970 and for a few weeks was the holder of both.

● In winning the Amateur Championship in 1970 Michael Bonallack became the first player to win in three consecutive years.

● The English Amateur record number of victories is held by Michael Bonallack, who won the title five times.

● John Ball holds the record number of victories in the Amateur Championship, which he won eight times. Next comes Michael Bonallack (who was internationally known as *The Duke*) with five wins.

● Cecil Leitch and Joyce Wethered each won the British Ladies' title four times.

● The Scottish Amateur record was held by Ronnie Shade, who won five titles in successive years, 1963 to 1967. His long reign as Champion ended when he was beaten in the fourth round of the 1968 Championship after winning 44 consecutive matches.

● Joyce Wethered established an unbeaten record by winning the English Ladies' in five successive years from 1920 to 1924 inclusive.

● In winning the Amateur Championships of Britain and America in 1934 and 1935 Lawson Little won 31 consecutive matches. Other dual winners of these championships in the same year are R.T. Jones (1930) and Bob Dickson (1967).

● Peter Thomson's victory in the 1971 New Zealand Open Championship was his ninth in that championship.

● In a four-week spell in 1971, Lee Trevino won in succession the US Open, the Canadian Open and the Open Championships.

● Michael Bonallack and Bill Hyndman were the Amateur Championship finalists in both 1969 and 1970. This was the first time the same two players reached the final in successive years.

● On the US professional circuit the greatest number of consecutive victories is 11, achieved by Byron Nelson in 1945. Nelson also holds the record for most victories in one calendar year, again in 1945 when he won a total of 18 tournaments.

● Raymond Floyd, by winning the Doral Classic in March 1992, joined Sam Snead as the only winners of US Tour events in four different decades.

● Sam Snead won tournaments in six decades. His first win was the 1936 West Virginia PGA. In 1980 he won the *Golf Digest* Commemorative and in 1982 the Legends of Golf with Don January.

● Neil Coles became the second golfer to win a professional event in six different decades when he won the Microlease Jersey Seniors Open at La Moye in June 2000. He was 65 at the time and had won his maiden title in 1958.

● Jack Nicklaus and the late Walter Hagen have had five wins each in the USPGA Championship. All Hagen's wins were at match play; all Nicklaus's at stroke play.

● In 1953 Flori van Donck of Belgium had seven major victories in Europe, including the Open Championships of Switzerland, Italy, Holland, Germany and Belgium.

● Mrs Anne Sander won four major amateur titles each under a different name. She won the US Ladies' in 1958 as Miss Quast, in 1961 as Mrs Decker, in 1963 as Mrs Welts and the British Ladies' in 1980 as Mrs Sander.

● The highest number of appearances in the Ryder Cup matches is held by Nick Faldo who made his eleventh appearance in 1997.

● The greatest number of appearances in the Walker Cup matches is held by Irishman Joe Carr who made his tenth appearance in 1967.

● In the Curtis Cup Mary McKenna made her ninth consecutive appearance in 1986.

● Players who have represented their country in both Walker and Ryder Cup matches are: for the United States, Fred Haas, Ken Venturi, Gene Littler, Jack Nicklaus, Tommy Aaron, Mason Rudolph, Bob Murphy, Lanny Wadkins, Scott Simpson, Tom Kite, Jerry Pate, Craig Stadler, Jay Haas, Bill Rodgers, Hal Sutton, Curtis Strange, Davis Love III, Brad Faxon, Scott Hoch, Phil Mickelson, Corey Pavin, Justin Leonard, Tiger Woods and David Duval; and for Great Britain & Ireland, Norman Drew, Peter Townsend, Clive Clark, Peter Oosterhuis, Howard Clark, Mark James, Michael King, Gordon Brand Jr, Paul Way, Ronan Rafferty, Sandy Lyle, Philip Walton, David Gilford, Colin Montgomerie, Peter Baker, Padraig Harrington and Andrew Coltart.

Remarkable Recoveries in Matchplay

● There have been two remarkable recoveries in the Walker Cup Matches. In 1930 at Sandwich, J.A. Stout, Great Britain, round in 68, was 4 up at the end of the first round against Donald Moe. Stout started in the second round, 3, 3, 3, and was 7 up. He was still 7 up with 13 to play. Moe, who went round in 67, won back the 7 holes to draw level at the 17th green. At the 18th or 36th of the match, Moe, after a long drive placed his iron shot within three feet of the hole and won the match by 1 hole.

● In 1936 at Pine Valley, George Voigt and Harry Girvan for America were 7 up with 11 to play against Alec Hill and Cecil Ewing. The British pair drew level at the 17th hole, or the 35th of the match, and the last hole was halved.

● In the 1965 Piccadilly Match Play Championship Gary Player beat Tony Lema after being 7 down with 17 to play.

● Bobby Cruickshank, the old Edinburgh player, had an extraordinary recovery in a 36-hole match in a USPGA Championship for he defeated Al Watrous after being 11 down with 12 to play.

● In a match at the Army GC, Aldershot, on 5th July, 1974, for the Gradoville Bowl, M.C. Smart was 8 down with 8 to play against Mike Cook. Smart succeeded in winning all the remaining holes and the 19th for victory.

● In the 1982 Suntory World Match Play Championship Sandy Lyle beat Nick Faldo after being 6 down with 18 to play.

Oldest Champions

Open Championship: Belt Tom Morris in 1867 – 46 years 99 days. *Cup* Roberto de Vicenzo, 44 years 93 days, in 1967; Harry Vardon, 44 years 42 days, in 1914; J.H. Taylor, 42 years 97 days, in 1913.

Amateur Championship Hon. Michael Scot, 54, at Hoylake in 1933.

British Ladies Amateur Mrs Jessie Valentine, 43, at Hunstanton in 1958.

Scottish Amateur J.M. Cannon, 53, at Troon in 1969.

English Amateur Terry Shingler, 41 years 11 months at Walton Heath 1977; Gerald Micklem, 41 years 8 months, at Royal Birkdale 1947.

Welsh Amateur John Jermine, 56, at St David's, in 2000

US Open Hale Irwin, 45, at Medinah, Illinois, in 1990.

US Amateur Jack Westland, 47, at Seattle in 1952 (He had been defeated in the 1931 final, 21 years previously, by Francis Ouimet).

US Masters Jack Nicklaus, 46, in 1986.

European Tour Neil Coles, 48, in 1983.

European Senior Tour Neil Coles, 65, in 2000

USPGA Julius Boros, 48, in 1968. Lee Trevino, 44, in 1984.

USPGA Tour Sam Snead, 52, at Greensborough Open in 1965. Sam Snead, 61, equal second in Glen Campbell Open 1974.

Youngest Champions

Open Championship: Belt Tom Morris, Jr, 17 years 5 months, in 1868. *Cup* Willie Auchterlonie, 21 years 24 days, in 1893; Tom Morris, Jr, 21 years 5 months, in 1872; Severiano Ballesteros, 22 years 103 days, in 1979.

Amateur Championship J.C. Beharrell, 18 years 1 month, at Troon in 1956; R. Cole (SA) 18 years 1 month, at Carnoustie in 1966.

British Ladies Amateur May Hezlett, 17, at Newcastle, Co Down, in 1899; Michelle Walker, 18, at Alwoodley in 1971.

English Amateur Nick Faldo, 18, at Lytham St Annes in 1975; Paul Downes, 18, at Birkdale in 1978; David Gilford, 18, at Woodhall Spa in 1984; Ian Garbutt, 18, at Woodhall Spa in 1990; Mark Foster, 18, at Moortown in 1994.

English Amateur Strokeplay Ronan Rafferty, 16, at Hunstanton in 1980.

British Ladies Open Strokeplay Helen Dobson, 18, at Southerness in 1989.

British Boys Championship Mark Mouland (Wales) 15 years 120 days at Sunningdale in 1976; Pablo Martin (Spain) 15 years 120 days at Ganton 2001.

Disqualifications

Disqualifications are now numerous, usually for some irregularity over signing a scorecard or for late arrival at the first tee. We therefore show here only incidents in major events involving famous players or players who were in a winning position or incidents which were in themselves unusual.

● J.J. McDermott, the American Open Champion 1911–12, arrived for the Open Championship at Prestwick in 1914 to discover that he had made a mistake of a week in the date the championship began. The American could not play, as the qualifying rounds were completed on the day he arrived.

● In the Amateur Championship at Sandwich in 1937, Brigadier-General Critchley, arriving at Southampton from New York on the *Queen Mary*, which had been delayed by fog, flew by specially chartered aeroplane to Sandwich. He circled over the clubhouse, so the officials knew he was nearly there, but he arrived six minutes late, and his name had been struck out. At the same championship a player, entered from Burma, who had travelled across the Pacific and the American Continent, and was also on the *Queen Mary*, travelled from Southampton by motor car and arrived four hours after his starting time to find after journeying more than halfway round the world he was *struck out*.

● An unprecedented disqualification was that of A. Murray in the New Zealand Open Championship, 1937. Murray, who was New Zealand Champion in 1935, was playing with J.P. Hornabrook, New Zealand Amateur Champion, and at the 8th hole in the last round, while waiting for his partner to putt, Murray dropped a ball on the edge of the green and made a practice putt along the edge. Murray returned the lowest score in the championship, but he was disqualified for taking the practice putt.

● At the Open Championship at St Andrews in 1946, John Panton, Glenbervie, in the evening practised putting on a green on the New Course, which was one of the qualifying courses. He himself reported his inadvertence to the Royal & Ancient and he was disqualified.

● At the Open Championship, Sandwich, 1949, C. Rotar, an American, qualified by four strokes to compete in the championship but he was disqualified because he had used a putter which did not conform to the accepted form and make of a golf club, the socket being bent over the centre of the club head. This is the only case where a player has been disqualified in the Open Championship for using an illegal club.

● In the 1957 American Women's Open Championship, Mrs Jackie Pung had the lowest score, 298 over four rounds, but lost the championship. The card she signed for the final round read *five* at the 4th hole instead of the correct *six*. Her total of 72 was correct but the error, under rigid rules, resulted in her disqualification. Betty Jameson, who partnered Mrs Pung and also returned a wrong score, was also disqualified.

Longest Match

● W.R. Chamberlain, a retired farmer, and George New, a postmaster at Chilton Foliat, on 1st August, 1922, met at Littlecote, the 9-hole course of Sir Ernest Wills, and agreed to play every Thursday afternoon over the course. This continued until New's sudden death on 13th January, 1938. An accurate record of the match was kept, giving details of each round including wind direction and playing conditions. In the elaborate system nearly two million facts were

recorded. They played 814 rounds, and aggregated 86,397 strokes, of which Chamberlain took 44,008 and New 42,371. New, therefore, was 1,637 strokes up. The last round of all was halved, a suitable end to such an unusual contest.

Longest Ties

● The longest known ties in 18-hole match play rounds in major events were in an early round of the News of the World Match Play Championship at Turnberry in 1960, when W.S. Collins beat W.J. Branch at the 31st hole and in the third round of the same tournament at Walton Heath in 1961 when Harold Henning beat Peter Alliss also at the 31st hole.
● In the 1970 Scottish Amateur Championship at Balgownie, Aberdeen, E. Hammond beat J. McIvor at the 29th hole in their second round tie.
● C.A. Palmer beat Lionel Munn at the 28th hole at Sandwich in 1908. This is the record tie of the British Amateur Championship. Munn has also been engaged in two other extended ties in the Amateur Championship. At Muirfield, in 1932, in the semi-final, he was defeated by John de Forest, the ultimate winner, at the 26th hole, and at St Andrews, in 1936, in the second round he was defeated by J.L. Mitchell, again at the 26th hole.

The following examples of long ties are in a different category for they occurred in competitions, either stroke play or match play, where the conditions stipulated that in the event of a tie, a further stated number of holes had to be played – in some cases 36 holes, but mostly 18. With this method a vast number of extra holes was sometimes necessary to settle ties.

● The longest known was between two American women in a tournament at Peterson (New Jersey) when 88 extra holes were required before Mrs Edwin Labaugh emerged as winner.
● In a match on the Queensland course, Australia, in October, 1933, H.B. Bonney and Col H.C.H. Robertson versus B.J. Canniffe and Dr Wallis Hoare required to play a further four 18-hole matches after being level at the end of the original 18 holes. In the fourth replay Hoare and Caniffe won by 3 and 2 which meant that 70 extra holes had been necessary to decide the tie.
● After finishing all square in the final of the Dudley GC's foursomes competition in 1950, F.W. Mannell and A.G. Walker played a further three 18-hole replays against T. Poole and E. Jones, each time finishing all square. A further 9 holes were arranged and Mannell and Walker won by 3 and 2 making a total of 61 extra holes to decide the tie.
● R.A. Whitcombe and Mark Seymour tied for first prize in the Penfold £750 Tournament at St Annes-on-Sea, in 1934. They had to play off over 36 holes and tied again. They were then required to play another 9 holes when Whitcombe won with 34 against 36. The tournament was over 72 holes. The first tie added 36 holes and the extra 9 holes made an aggregate of 117 holes to decide the winner. This is a record in first-

class British golf but in no way compares with other long ties as it involved only two replays – one of 36 holes and one of 9.
● In the American Open Championship at Toledo, Ohio, in 1931, G. Von Elm and Billy Burke tied for the title. Each returned aggregates of 292. On the first replay both finished in 149 for 36 holes but on the second replay Burke won with a score of 148 against 149. This is a record tie in a national open championship.
● Cary Middlecoff and Lloyd Mangrum were declared co-winners of the 1949 Motor City Open on the USPGA Tour after halving 11 sudden death holes.
● Australian David Graham beat American Dave Stockton at the tenth extra hole in the 1998 Royal Caribbean Classic, a record on the US Senior Tour.
● Paul Downes was beaten by Robin Davenport at the 9th extra hole in the 4th round of the 1981 English Amateur Championship, a record marathon match for the Championship.
● Severiano Ballesteros was beaten by Johnny Miller at the 9th extra hole of a sudden-death play-off at the 1982 Million Dollar Sun City Challenge.
● José Maria Olazábal beat Ronan Rafferty at the 9th extra hole to win the 1989 Dutch Open on the Kennemer Golf and Country Club course.

Long Drives

It is impossible to state with any certainty what is the longest ever drive. Many long drives have never been measured and many others have most likely never been brought to our attention. Then there are several outside factors which can produce freakishly long drives, such as a strong following wind, downhill terrain or bonehard ground. Where all three of these favourable conditions prevail outstandingly long drives can be achieved. Another consideration is that a long drive made during a tournament is a different proposition from one made for length alone, either on the practice ground, a long driving competition or in a game of no consequence. All this should be borne in mind when considering the long drives shown here.

● When professional Carl Hooper hit a wayward drive on the 3rd hole (456 yards) at the Oak Hills Country Club, San Antonio, during the 1992 Texas Open, he wrote himself into the record books but out of the tournament. The ball kept bouncing and rolling on a tarmac cart path until it was stopped by a fence – 787 yards away. It took Hooper two recovery shots with a 4-iron and then an 8-iron to return to the fairway. He eventually holed out for a double bogey six and failed to survive the half-way qualifying cut.
● Tommie Campbell of Portmarnock hit a drive of 392 yards at Dun Laoghaire GC in July 1964.
● Playing in Australia, American George Bayer is reported to have driven to within chipping distance of a 589 yards hole. *It was certainly a drive of over 500 yards,* said Bayer acknowledging the strong following wind, sharp downslope where his ball landed and the bone-hard ground.

● In September, 1934, over the East Devon course, T.H.V. Haydon, Wimbledon, drove to the edge of the 9th green which was a hole of 465 yards, giving a drive of not less than 450 yards.
● E.C. Bliss drove 445 yards at Herne Bay in August, 1913. The drive was measured by a government surveyor who also measured the drop in height from tee to resting place of the ball at 57 feet.

Long Carries

● At Sitwell Park, Rotherham, in 1935 the home professional, W. Smithson, drove a ball which carried a dyke at 380 yards from the 2nd tee.
● George Bell, of Penrith GC, New South Wales, Australia, using a number 2 wood drove across the Nepean River, a certified carry of 309 yards in a driving contest in 1964.
● After the 1986 Irish Professional Championship at Waterville, Co. Kerry, four long-hitting professionals tried for the longest-carry record over water, across a lake in the Waterville Hotel grounds. Liam Higgins, the local professional, carried 310 yards and Paul Leonard 311, beating the previous record by 2 yards.
● In the 1972 Algarve Open at Penina, Henry Cotton vouched for a carry of 305 yards over a ditch at the 18th hole by long-hitting Spanish professional Francisco Abreu. There was virtually no wind assistance.
● At the Home International matches at Portmarnock in 1949 a driving competition was held in which all the players in all four teams competed. The actual carry was measured and the longest was 280 yards by Jimmy Bruen.
● On 6th April, 1976, Tony Jacklin hit a number of balls into Vancouver harbour, Canada, from the 495-foot high roof of a new building complex. The longest carry was measured at 389 yards.

Long Hitting

There have been numerous long hits, not on golf courses, where an outside agency has assisted the length of the shot. Such an example was a 'drive' by Liam Higgins in 1986, on the Airport runway at Baldonal, near Dublin, of 632 yards.

Longest Albatrosses

● The longest-known albatrosses (three under par) recorded at par 5 holes are:
● 647 yards-2nd hole at Guam Navy Club by Chief Petty Officer Kevin Murray of Chicago on 3rd January, 1982.
● 609 yards-15th hole at Mahaka Inn West Course, Hawaii, by John Eakin of California on 12th November, 1972.
● 602 yards-16th hole at Whiting Field Golf Course, Milton, Florida, by 27-year-old Bill Graham with a drive and a 3-wood, aided by a 25 mph tail wind.
● The longest-known albatrosses in open championships are: 580 yards 14th hole at Crans-sur-Sierre, by American Billy Casper in the 1971 Swiss

Open; 558 yards 5th hole at Muirfield by American Johnny Miller in the 1972 Open Championship.
● In the 1994 German Amateur Championship at Wittelsbacher GC, Rohrenfield, Graham Rankin, a member of the visiting Scottish national team, had a two at the 592 yard 18th.

Eagles (Multiple and Consecutive)

● Wilf Jones scored three consecutive eagles at the first three holes at Moor Hall GC when playing in a competition there on August Bank Holiday Monday 1968. He scored 3, 1, 2 at holes measuring 529 yards, 176 yards and 302 yards.
● In a round of the 1980 Jubilee Cup, a mixed foursomes match play event of Colchester GC, Mrs Nora Booth and her son Brendan scored three consecutive gross eagles of 1, 3, 2 at the eighth, ninth and tenth holes.
● Three players in a four-ball match at Kington GC, Herefordshire, on 22nd July, 1948, all had eagle 2s at the 18th hole (272 yards). They were R.N. Bird, R. Morgan and V. Timson.
● Four Americans from Wisconsin on holiday at Gleneagles in 1977 scored three eagles and a birdie at the 300-yard par-4 14th hole on the King's course. The birdie was by Dr Kim Lulloff and the eagles by Dr Gordon Meiklejohn, Richard Johnson and Jack Kubitz.
● In an open competition at Glen Innes GC, Australia on 13th November, 1977, three players in a four-ball scored eagle 3s at the 9th hole (442 metres). They were Terry Marshall, Roy McHarg and Jack Rohleder.
● David McCarthy, a member of Moortown Golf Club, Leeds, had three consecutive eagles (3, 3, 2) on the 4th, 5th and 6th holes during a Pro-Am competition at Lucerne, Switzerland, on 7th August, 1992.

Speed of Golf Ball and Club Head and Effect of Wind and Temperature

● In *The Search for the Perfect Swing*, a scientific study of the golf swing, a first class golfer is said to have the club head travelling at 100 mph at impact. This will cause the ball to leave the club at 135 mph. An outstandingly long hitter might manage to have the club head travelling at 130 mph which would produce a ball send-off speed of 175 mph. The resultant shot would carry 280 yards.
● According to Thomas Hardman, Wilson's director of research and development, wind will reduce or increase the flight of a golf ball by approximately 1½ yards for every mile per hour of wind. Every two degrees of temperature will make a yard difference in a ball's flight.

Most Northerly Course

● Although the most northerly course used to be in Iceland, Björkliden Arctic Golf Club, Sweden, 250 km north of the Arctic Circle, has taken over that role. This may soon change, however, when a course opens

in Narvic, Norway, which could be a few metres further north than Björkliden.

Most Southerly Course

● Golf's most southerly course is Scott Base Country Club, 13° north of the South Pole. The course is run by the New Zealand Antarctic Programme and players must be kitted in full survival gear. The most difficult aspect is finding the orange golf balls which tend to get buried in the snow. Other obstacles include penguins, seals and skuas. If the ball is stolen by a skua then a penalty of one shot is incurred; but if the ball hits a skua it counts as a birdie.

Highest Golf Courses

● The highest golf course in the world is thought to be the Tuctu GC in Peru which is 14,335 feet above sea-level. High courses are also found in Bolivia with the La Paz GC being about 13,500 feet. In the Himalayas, near the border with Tibet, a 9-hole course at 12,800 feet has been laid out by keen golfers in the Indian Army.
● The highest course in Europe is at Sestriere in the Italian Alps, 6,500 feet above sea-level.
● The highest courses in Great Britain are West Monmouthshire in Wales at 1,513 feet, Leadhills in Scotland at 1,500 feet and Church Stratton in England at 1,250 feet.

Longest Courses

● The longest course in the world is Dub's Dread GC, Piper, Kansas, USA measuring 8,101 yards (par 78).
● The longest course for the Open Championship was 7,252 yards at Carnoustie in 1968.

Longest Holes

● The longest hole in the world, as far as is known, is the 6th hole measuring 782 metres (860 yards) at Koolan Island GC, Western Australia. The par of the hole is 7. There are several holes over 700 yards throughout the world.
● The longest hole for the Open Championship is the 577 yards 6th hole at Royal Troon.

Longest Tournaments

● The longest tournament held was over 144 holes in the World Open at Pinehurst, N Carolina, USA, first held in 1973. Play was over two weeks with a cut imposed at the halfway mark.
● An annual tournament, played in Germany on the longest day of the year, comprises 100 holes' medal play. Best return, in 1995, was 399 strokes.

Largest Entries

● The Open – 2460, St Andrews, 2000.
● The Amateur – 537, Muirfield, 1998.
● US Open – 8457, Pebble Beach, 2000.
● The largest entry for a PGA European Tour event was 398 for the 1978 Colgate PGA Championship.

Since 1985, when the all-exempt ruling was introduced, all PGA tournaments have had 144 competitors, slightly more or less.
● In 1952, Bobby Locke, the Open Champion, played a round at Wentworth against any golfer in Britain. Cards costing 2s. 6d. each (12½p), were taken out by 24,000 golfers. The challenge was to beat the local par by more than Locke could beat the par at Wentworth. 1,641 competitors, including women, succeeded in *beating* the Champion and each received a certificate signed by him. As a result of this challenge the British Golf Foundation benefited to the extent of £3,026, the proceeds from the sale of cards. A similar tournament was held in the US and Canada when 87,094 golfers participated; 14,667 players bettered Ben Hogan's score under handicap. The fund benefited by $80,024.

Largest Prize Money

● The Machrie Tournament of 1901 was the first tournament with a first prize of £100. It was won by J.H. Taylor, then Open Champion, who beat James Braid in the final.
● The richest event in the world is currently the Players' Championship in Florida. It has a total purse of $6 million and a first prize of $1.08 million.

Holing-in-One – Odds Against

● At the Wanderers Club, Johannesburg in January, 1951, forty-nine amateurs and professionals each played three balls at a hole 146 yards long. Of the 147 balls hit, the nearest was by Koos de Beer, professional at Reading Country Club, which finished 10½ inches from the hole. Harry Bradshaw, the Irish professional who was touring with the British team in South Africa, touched the pin with his second shot, but the ball rolled on and stopped 3 feet 2 inches from the cup.
● A competition on similar lines was held in 1951 in New York when 1,409 players who had done a hole-in-one held a competition over several days at short holes on three New York courses. Each player was allowed a total of five shots, giving an aggregate of 7,045 shots. No player holed-in-one, and the nearest ball finished 3½ inches from the hole.
● A further illustration of the element of luck in holing-in-one is derived from an effort by Harry Gonder, an American professional, who in 1940 stood for 16 hours 25 minutes and hit 1,817 balls trying to do a 160 yard hole-in-one. He had two official witnesses and caddies to tee and retrieve the balls and count the strokes. His 1,756th shot struck the hole but stopped an inch from the hole. This was his nearest effort.
● From this and other similar information an estimate of the odds against holing-in-one at any particular hole within the range of one shot was made at somewhere between 1,500 and 2,000 to 1 by a proficient player. Subsequently, however, statistical analysis in America has come up with the following odds: a male professional or top amateur 3,708 to 1; a female professional or top amateur 4,648 to 1; an average golfer 42,952 to 1.

Hole-in-One First Recorded

● Earliest recorded hole-in-one was in 1868 at the Open Championship when Tom Morris (Young Tom) did the 145-yard 8th hole Prestwick in one stroke. This was the first of four Open Championships won successively by Young Tom.

● The first hole-in-one recorded with the 1.66 in ball was in 1972 by John G. Salvesen, a member of the R&A Championship Committee. At the time this size of ball was only experimental. Salvesen used a 7-iron for his historical feat at the 11th hole on the Old Course, St Andrews.

Holing-in-One in Important Events

Since the day of the first known hole-in-one by Tom Morris Jr, at the 8th hole (145 yards) at Prestwick in the 1868 Open Championship, holes-in-one, even in championships, have become too numerous for each to be recorded. Only where other unusual or interesting circumstances prevailed are the instances shown here.

● All hole-in-one achievements are remarkable. Many are extraordinary. Among the more amazing was that of 2-handicap Leicestershire golfer Bob Taylor, a member of the Scraptoft Club. During the final practice day for the 1974 Eastern Counties Foursomes Championship on the Hunstanton Links, he holed his tee shot with a one-iron at the 188-yard 16th. The next day, in the first round of the competition, he repeated the feat, the only difference being that because of a change of wind he used a six-iron. When he stepped on to the 16th tee the following day his partner jokingly offered him odds of 1,000,000 to one against holing-in-one for a third successive time. Taylor again used his six-iron – and holed in one!

● 1878 – Jamie Anderson, competing in the Open Championship at Prestwick, holed the 17th hole in one. Anderson was playing the next to last hole, and though it seemed then that he was winning easily, it turned out afterwards that if he had not taken this hole in one stroke he would very likely have lost. Anderson was just about to make his tee shot when Andy Stuart (winner of the first Irish Open Championship in 1892), who was acting as marker to Anderson, remarked he was standing outside the teeing ground, and that if he played the stroke from there he would be disqualified. Anderson picked up his ball and teed it in a proper place. Then he holed-in-one. He won the Championship by one stroke.

● On a Friday the 13th in 1990, Richard Allen holed-in-one at the 13th at the Barwon Heads Golf Club, Victoria, Australia, and then lost the hole. He was giving a handicap stroke to his opponent, brother-in-law Jason Ennels, who also holed-in-one.

● 1906 – R. Johnston, North Berwick, competing in the Open Championship, did the 14th hole at Muirfield in one. Johnston played with only one club throughout – an adjustable head club.

● 1959 – The first hole-in-one in the US Women's Open Championship was recorded. It was by Patty Berg on the 7th hole (170 yards) at Churchill Valley CC, Pittsburgh.

● 1962 – On 6th April, playing in the second round of the Schweppes Close Championship at Little Aston, H. Middleton of Shandon Park, Belfast, holed his tee shot at the 159-yard 5th hole, winning a prize of £1,000. Ten minutes later, playing two matches ahead of Middleton, R.A. Jowle, son of the professional, Frank Jowle, holed his tee shot at the 179-yard 9th hole. As an amateur he was rewarded by the sponsors with a £30 voucher.

● 1963 – By holing out in one stroke at the 18th hole (156 yards) at Moor Park on the first day of the Esso Golden round-robin tournament, H.R. Henning, South Africa, won the £10,000 prize offered for this feat.

● 1967 – Tony Jacklin in winning the Masters tournament at St George's, Sandwich, did the 16th hole in one. His ace has an exceptional place in the records for it was seen by millions on TV, the ball was in view in its flight till it went into the hole in his final round of 64.

● 1971 – John Hudson, 25-year-old professional at Hendon, achieved a near miracle when he holed two consecutive holes-in-one in the Martini Tournament at Norwich. They were at the 11th and 12th holes (195 yards and 311 yards respectively) in the second round.

● 1971 – In the Open Championship at Birkdale, Lionel Platts holed-in-one at the 212-yard 4th hole in the second round. This was the first instance of an Open Championship hole-in-one being recorded by television. It was incidentally Platts' seventh ace of his career.

● There have been four holes-in-one in the Ryder Cup: by Peter Butler at Muirfield in 1973, Nick Faldo at the Belfry in 1993, and by Costantino Rocca and Howard Clark at Oak Hill in 1995.

● 1973 – In the 1973 Open Championship at Troon, two holes-in-one were recorded, both at the 8th hole, known as the Postage Stamp, in the first round. They were achieved by Gene Sarazen and amateur David Russell, who were by coincidence respectively the oldest and youngest competitors.

● Mrs Argea Tissies, whose husband Hermann took 15 at Royal Troon's Postage Stamp 8th hole in the 1950 Open, scored a hole-in-one at the 2nd hole at Punta Ala in the second round of the Italian Ladies' Senior Open of 1978. Exactly five years later on the same date, at the same time of day, in the same round of the same tournament at the same hole, she did it again with the same club.

● In less than two hours play in the second round of the 1989 US Open at Oak Hill Country Club, Rochester, New York, four competitors – Doug Weaver, Mark Wiebe, Jerry Pate and Nick Price – each holed the 167-yard 6th hole in one. The odds against four professionals achieving such a record in a field of 156 are reckoned at 332,000 to 1.

● On 20th May, 1998, British golf journalist Derek Lawrenson, an eight-handicapper, won a Lamborghini Diablo car, valued at over £180,000, by holing his three-iron tee shot to the 175-yard 15th hole at Mill Ride, Berkshire. He was taking part in a charity day and was partnering England football stars Paul Ince and Steve McManaman.

● David Toms took the lead in the 2001 USPGA Championship at Atlanta Athletic Club with a hole-in-one at the 15th hole in the third round and went on to win. Nick Faldo (4th hole) and Scott Hoch (17th hole) also had holes-in-one during the event.

Holing-in-One – Longest Holes

● Bob Mitera, as a 21-year-old American student, standing 5 feet 6 inches and weighing under 12 stones, claimed the world record for the longest hole-in-one. Playing over the appropriately named Miracle Hill course at Omaha, on 7th October, 1965, Bob holed his drive at the 10th hole, 447 yards long. The ground sloped sharply downhill.

● Two longer holes-in-one have been achieved, but because they were at dog-leg holes they are not generally accepted as being the longest holes-in-one. They were 496 yards (17th hole, Teign Valley) by Shaun Lynch in July 1995 and 480 yards (5th hole, Hope CC, Arkansas) by L. Bruce on 15th November, 1962.

● In March, 1961, Lou Kretlow holed his tee shot at the 427-yard 16th hole at Lake Hefner course, Oklahoma City, USA.

● The longest known hole-in-one in Great Britain was the 393-yard 7th hole at West Lancashire GC, where in 1972 the assistant professional Peter Parkinson holed his tee shot.

● Other long holes-in-one recorded in Great Britain have been 380 yards (5th hole at Tankersley Park) by David Hulley in 1961; 380 yards (12th hole at White Webbs) by Danny Dunne on 30th July, 1976; 370 yards (17th hole at Chilwell Manor, distance from the forward tee) by Ray Newton in 1977; 365 yards (10th hole at Harewood Downs) by K. Saunders in 1965; 365 yards (7th hole at Catterick Garrison GC) by Leslie Bruckner on 18th July, 1980.

● The longest-recorded hole-in-one by a woman was that accomplished in September, 1949 by Marie Robie – the 393-yard hole at Furnace Brook course, Wollaston, Mass, USA.

Holing-in-One – Greatest Number by One Person

59–Amateur Norman Manley of Long Beach, California.

50–Mancil Davis, professional at the Trophy Club, Forth Worth, Texas.

31–British professional C.T. le Chevalier who died in 1973.

22–British amateur, Jim Hay of Kirkintilloch GC.

At One Hole

13–Joe Lucius at 15th hole of Mohawk, Ohio.

5–Left-hander, the late Fred Francis at 7th (now 16th) hole of Cardigan GC.

Holing-in-One – Greatest Frequency

● The greatest number of holes-in-one in a calendar year is 11, by J.O. Boydstone of California in 1962.

● John Putt of Frilford Heath GC had six holes-in-one in 1970, followed by three in 1971.

● Douglas Porteous, of Ruchill GC, Glasgow, achieved seven holes-in-one in the space of eight months. Four of them were scored in a five-day period from 26th to 30th September, 1974, in three consecutive rounds of golf. The first two were achieved at Ruchill GC in one round, the third there two days later, and the fourth at Clydebank and District GC after another two days. The following May, Porteous had three holes-in-one, the first at Linn Park GC incredibly followed by two more in the one round at Clober GC.

● Mrs Kathleen Hetherington of West Essex has holed-in-one five times, four being at the 15th hole at West Essex. Four of her five aces were within seven months in 1966.

● Mrs Dorothy Hill of Dumfries and Galloway GC holed-in-one three times in 11 days in 1977.

● James C. Reid of Brodick, aged 59 and 8 handicap in 1987, achieved 14 holes-in-one, all but one on Isle of Arran courses. His success was in spite of severe physical handicaps of a stiff left knee, a damaged right ankle, two discs removed from his back and a hip replacement.

● Jean Nield, a member at Chorlton-cum-Hardy and Bramall Park, has had eleven holes-in-one and her husband Brian, who plays at Bramall Park, has had five – a husband and wife total of 16.

Holing Successive Holes-in-One

● Successive holes-in-one are rare; successive par 4 holes-in-one may be classed as near miracles. N.L. Manley performed the most incredible feat in September, 1964, at Del Valle Country Club, Saugus, California, USA. The par 4 7th (330 yards) and 8th (290 yards) are both slightly downhill, dog-leg holes. Manley had *aces* at both, en route to a course record of 61 (par 71).

● The first recorded example in Britain of a player holing-in-one stroke at each of two successive holes was achieved on 6th February, 1964, at the Walmer and Kingsdown course, Kent. The young assistant professional at that club, Roger Game (aged 17) holed out with a 4-wood at the 244-yard 7th hole, and repeated the feat at the 256-yard 8th hole, using a 5-iron.

● The first occasion of holing-in-one at consecutive holes in a major professional event occurred when John Hudson, 25-year-old professional at Hendon, holed-in-one at the 11th and 12th holes at Norwich during the second round of the 1971 Martini tournament. Hudson used a 4-iron at the 195-yard 11th and a driver at the 311-yard downhill 12th hole.

● Assistant professional Tom Doty (23 years), playing in a friendly match on a course near Chicago in October, 1971, had a remarkable four-hole score which included two consecutive holes-in-one, sandwiched either side by an albatross and an eagle: 4th hole (500 yards)-2; 5th hole (360 yards dog-leg)-1; 6th hole (175 yards)-1; 7th hole (375 yards)-2. Thus he was 10 under par for four consecutive holes.

● At the Standard Life Loch Lomond tournament on the European Tour in July 2000 Jarmo Sandelin holed-in-one at the 17th with the final shot there in the third round and fellow Swede Mathias Gronberg holed-in-one with the first shot there in the last round. A prize of $100,000 was only on offer in the last round.

Holing-in-One Twice (or More) in the Same Round by the Same Person

What might be thought to be a very rare feat indeed – that of holing-in-one twice in the same round – has in fact happened on many occasions as the following instances show. It is, nevertheless, compared to the number of golfers in the world, still something of an outstanding achievement. The first known occasion was in 1907 when J. Ireland playing in a three-ball match at Worlington holed the 5th and 18th holes in one stroke and two years later in 1909 H.C. Josecelyne holed the 3rd (175 yards) and the 14th (115 yards) at Acton on 24th November.

● The first mention of two holes-in-one in a round by a woman was followed later by a similar feat by another lady at the same club. On 19th May, 1942, Mrs W. Driver, of Balgowlah Golf Club, New South Wales, holed out in one at the 3rd and 8th holes in the same round, while on 29th July, 1948, Mrs F. Burke at the same club holed out in one at the second and eighth holes.

● The Rev Harold Snider, aged 75, scored his first hole-in-one on 9th June, 1976 at the 8th hole of the Ironwood course, near Phoenix. By the end of his round he had scored three holes-in-one, the other two being at the 13th (110 yards) and 14th (135 yards). Ironwood is a par-3 course, giving more opportunity of scoring holes-in-one, but, nevertheless, three holes-in-one in one round on any type of course is an outstanding achievement.

● When the Hawarden course in North Wales comprised only nine holes, Frank Mills in 1994 had two holes-in-one at the same hole in the same round. Each time, he hit a seven iron to the 134-yard 3rd and 12th.

● The youngest player to achieve two holes-in-one in the same round is thought to be Christopher Anthony Jones on 14 September, 1994. At the age of 14 years and 11 months he holed-in-one at the Sand Moor, Leeds, 137-yard 10th hole and then at the 156-yard 17th.

● The youngest woman to have performed the feat was a 17-year-old, Marjorie Merchant, playing at the Lomas Athletic GC, Argentina, at the 4th (170 yards) and 8th (130 yards) holes.

● Tony Hannam, left-handed, handicap 16 and age 71, followed a hole-in-one at the 142 yards 4th of the Bude and North Cornwall Golf Club course with another at the 143-yard 10th hole on Friday, 18th September, 1992.

● Brothers Eric and John Wilkinson were playing together at the Ravensworth Golf Club on Tyneside in 2001 and both holed-in-one at the 148 yards eighth.

Eric (46) played first and then John to the hidden green but there is no doubting this unusual double ace. The club's vice-captain Dave Johnstone saw both balls go in! Postman Eric plays off 9. John, a county planner, has a handicap of 20. Next time they played the hole both missed the green.

Holes-in-One on the Same Day

● In July 1987, at the Skerries Club, Co Dublin, Rank Xerox sponsored two tournaments, a men's 18-hole four-ball with 134 pairs competing and a 9-hole mixed foursomes with 33 pairs. During the day each of the four par-3 holes on the course were holed-in-one: the 2nd by Noel Bollard, the 5th by Bart Reynolds, the 12th by Jackie Carr and the 15th by Gerry Ellis.

● Wendy Russell holed-in-one at the consecutive par threes in the first round of the British Senior Ladies' at Wrexham in 1989.

● Clifford Briggs, aged 65, holed-in-one at the 14th at Parkstone GC on the same day as his wife Gwen, 60, aced the 16th.

● In the final round of the 2000 Victor Chandler British Masters at Woburn Alastair Forsyth holed-in-one at the second. Playing partner Roger Chapman then holed-in-one at the eighth.

Two Holes-in-One at the Same Hole in the Same Game

● *First in World:* George Stewart and Fred Spellmeyer at the 18th hole, Forest Hills, New Jersey, USA in October 1919.

● *First in Great Britain:* Miss G. Clutterbuck and Mrs H.M. Robinson at the 15th hole (120 yards), St Augustine GC, Ramsgate, on 8th May, 1925.

● *First in Denmark:* In a Club match in August 1987 at Himmerland, Steffan Jacobsen of Himmerland and Peter Forsberg of Himmerland halved the 15th hole in one shot, the first known occasion in Denmark.

● *First in Australia:* Dr & Mrs B. Rankine, playing in a mixed 'Canadian foursome' event at the Osmond Club near Adelaide, South Australia in April 1987, holed-in-one in consecutive shots at the 2nd hole (162 metres), he from the men's tee with a 3-iron and his wife from the ladies' tee with a 1½ wood.

● Jack Ashton, aged 76, holed-in-one at the 8th hole of the West Kent Golf Club at Downe but only got a half. Opponent Ted Eagle, in receipt of shot, made a 2, net 1.

● Dr Martin Pucci and Trevor Ironside will never forget one round at the Macdonald Club in Ellon last year. Playing in an open competition the two golfers with Jamie Cowthorne making up the three-ball reached the tee at the 169yards short 11th. Dr Pucci, with the honour, hit a 5-iron, Mr Ironside a 6-iron at the hole where only the top of the flag is visible. Both hit good shots but when they reached the green they could spot only one ball and that was Mr Cowthorne's. Then they realised that something amazing might have happened. When they reached the putting

surface they discovered that both Dr Pucci's and Mr Ironside's balls were wedged into the hole. Both had made aces. It was Dr Pucci's sixth and Mr Ironside's second.

● Eric and John Wilkinson went out for their usual weekly game at the Ravensworth Golf Club in Wrekenton on Tyneside in 2001 and both holed in one at the 148 yards eighth. Neither Eric, a 46-year-old 9-handicapper who has been playing golf since he was 14, nor John, who has been playing golf for ten years and has a handicap of 20, saw the balls go in because the green is over a hill but club vice-captain Dave Johnston did and described the incident as 'amazing' Next time the brothers played the hole both missed the green!

Holing-in-One – Youngest and Oldest players

● In January 1985 Otto Bucher of Switzerland holed-in-one at the age of 99 on La Manga's 130-yard 12th hole.

● Bob Hope had a hole-in-one at Palm Springs, California, at the age of 90.

● The youngest player ever to achieve a hole in one is now believed to be Matthew Draper, who was only five when he aced the 122-yard fourth hole at Cherwell Edge, Oxfordshire, in June 1997. He used a wood.

● Six-year-old Tommy Moore aced the 145-yard fourth hole at Woodbrier, West Virginia, in 1968. He had another at the same hole before his seventh birthday.

● Alex Evans, aged eight, holed-in-one with a 4-wood at the 136-yard 4th hole at Bromborough, Merseyside, in 1994.

Holing-in-One – Miscellaneous Incidents

● Chemistry student Jason Bohn, aged 19, of State College, Pennsylvania, supported a charity golf event at Tuscaloosa, Alabama, in 1992 when twelve competitors were invited to try to hole-in-one at the 135-yard second hole for a special prize covered by insurance. One attempt only was allowed. Bohn succeeded and was offered US$1m (paid at the rate of $5,000 a month for the next 20 years) at the cost of losing his amateur status. He took the money.

● The late Harry Vardon, who scored the greatest number of victories in the Open Championship, only once did a hole-in-one. That was in 1903 at Mundesley, Norfolk, where Vardon was convalescing from a long illness.

● In a guest day at Rochford Hundred, Essex, in 1994, there were holes-in-one at all the par threes. First Paul Cairns, of Langdon Hills, holed a 4-iron at the 205-yard 15th, next Paul Francis, a member of the home club, sank a 7-iron at the 156-yard seventh and finally Jim Crabb, of Three Rivers, holed a 9-iron at the 136-yard 11th.

● In April 1988, Mary Anderson, a bio-chemistry student at Trinity College, Dublin, holed-in-one at the 290-yard 6th hole at Island GC, Co Dublin.

● In April 1984 Joseph McCaffrey and his son, Gordon, each holed-in-one in the Spring Medal at the 164-yard 12th hole at Vale of Leven Club, Dunbartonshire.

● In 1977, 14-year-old Gillian Field after a series of lessons holed-in-one at the 10th hole at Moor Place GC in her first round of golf.

● When he holed-in-one at the second hole in a match against D. Graham in the 1979 Suntory World Match Play at Wentworth, Japanese professional Isao Aoki won himself a Bovis home at Gleneagles worth, inclusive of furnishings, £55,000.

● On the morning after being elected captain for 1973 of the Norwich GC, J.S. Murray hit his first shot as captain straight into the hole at the 169-yard 1st hole.

● At Nuneaton GC in 1999 the men's captain and the ladies' captain both holed-in-one during their captaincies.

● Using the same club and ball, 11-handicap left-hander Christopher Smyth holed-in-one at the 2nd hole (170 yards) in two consecutive medal competitions at Headfort GC, Co Meath, in January, 1976.

● Playing over Rickmansworth course at Easter, 1960, Mrs A.E. (Paddy) Martin achieved a remarkable sequence of aces. On Good Friday she sank her tee shot at the 3rd hole (125 yards). The next day, using the same ball and the same 8-iron, at the same hole, she scored another one. And on the Monday (same ball, same club, same hole) she again holed out from the tee.

● At Barton-on-Sea in February 1989 Mrs Dorothy Huntley-Flindt, aged 91, holed-in-one at the par-3 13th. The following day Mr John Chape, a fellow member in his 80s, holed the par- 3 5th in one.

● In 1995 Roy Marsland of Ratho Park, Edinburgh, had three holes in one in nine days: at Prestonfield's 5th, at Ratho Park's 3rd and at Sandilands' 2nd.

● Michael Monk, age 82, a member of Tandridge Golf Club, Surrey, waited until 1992 to record his first hole-in-one. It continued a run of rare successes for his family. In the previous 12 months, Mr Monk's daughter, Elizabeth, 52, daughter-in-law, Celia, 48, and grandson, Jeremy, 16, had all holed in one on the same course.

● Lou Holloway, a left-hander, recorded his second hole-in-one at the Mount Derby course in New Zealand 13 years after acing the same hole while playing right-handed.

● Ryan Procop, an American schoolboy, holed-in-one at a 168-yard par 3 at Glen Eagles GC, Ohio, with a putter. He confessed that he was so disgusted with himself after a 12 on the previous hole that he just grabbed his putter and hit from the tee.

● Ernie and Shirley Marsden, of Warwick Golf Club, are believed in 1993 to have equalled the record for holes-in-one by a married couple. Each has had three, as have another English couple, Mr and Mrs B.E. Simmonds.

● Russell Pugh, a 12-handicapper from Nottinghamshire, holed-in-one twice in three days at the 274-yard par-4 18th hole at Sidmouth in Devon in 1998. The hole has a blind tee shot.

Challenge Matches

One of the first recorded professional challenge matches was in 1843 when Allan Robertson beat Willie Dunn in a 20-round match at St Andrews over 360 holes by 2 rounds and 1 to play. Thereafter until about 1905 many matches are recorded, some for up to £200 a side – a considerable sum for the time. The Morrises, the Dunns and the Parks were the main protagonists until Vardon, Braid and Taylor took over in the 1890s. Often matches were on a home-and-away basis over 72 holes or more, with many spectators; Vardon and Willie Park Jr attracted over 10,000 at North Berwick in 1899.

Between the wars Walter Hagen, Archie Compston, Henry Cotton and Bobby Locke all played several such matches. Compston surprisingly beat Hagen by 18 up and 17 to play at Moor Park in 1928; yet typically Hagen went on to win the Open the following week at Sandwich. Cotton played classic golf at Walton Heath in 1937 when he beat Densmore Shute for £500-a-side at Walton Heath by 6 and 5 over 72 holes.

Curious and Large Wagers

(See also bets recorded under Cross-Country Matches *and in* Challenge Matches*)*

● In the Royal and Ancient Club minutes an entry on 3rd November, 1870 was made in the following terms:

Sir David Moncrieffe, Bart, of Moncrieffe, backs his life against the life of John Whyte-Melville, Esq, of Strathkinnes, for a new silver club as a present to the St Andrews Golf Club, the price of the club to be paid by the survivor and the arms of the parties to be engraved on the club, and the present bet inscribed on it. No balls to be attached to it. In testimony of which this bet is subscribed by the parties thereto.

Thirteen years later, Mr Whyte-Melville, in a feeling and appropriate speech, expressed his deep regret at the lamented death of Sir Robert Moncrieffe, one of the most distinguished and zealous supporters of the club. Whyte-Melville, while lamenting the cause that led to it, had pleasure in fulfilling the duty imposed upon him by the bet, and accordingly delivered to the captain the silver putter. Whyte-Melville in 1883 was elected captain of the club a second time; he died in his eighty-sixth year in July, 1883, before he could take office and the captaincy remained vacant for a year. His portrait hangs in the Royal & Ancient clubhouse and is one of the finest and most distinguished pictures in the smoking room.

● In 1914 Francis Ouimet, who in the previous autumn had won the American Open Championship after a triangular tie with Harry Vardon and Ted Ray, came to Great Britain with Jerome D. Travers, the holder of the American amateur title, to compete in the British Amateur Championship at Sandwich. An American syndicate took a bet of £30,000 to £10,000 that one or other of the two United States champions would be the winner. It only took two rounds to decide the bet against the Americans. Ouimet was beaten by a then quite unknown player, H.S. Tubbs, while Travers was defeated by Charles Palmer, who was 56 years of age at the time.

● 1907 John Ball for a wager undertook to go round Hoylake during a dense fog in under 90, in not more than two and a quarter hours and without losing a ball. Ball played with a black ball, went round in 81, and also beat the time.

● The late Ben Sayers, for a wager, played the 18 holes of the Burgess Society course scoring a four at every hole. Sayers was about to start against an American, when his opponent asked him what he could do the course in. *Fours* replied Sayers, meaning 72, or an average of 4s for the round. A bet was made, then the American added, *Remember a three or a five is not a four.* There were eight bogey 5s and two 3s on the Burgess course at the time Old Ben achieved his feat.

Feats of Endurance

Although golf is not a game where endurance, in the ordinary sense in which the term is employed in sport, is required, there are several instances of feats on the links which demanded great physical exertion.

● Four British golfers, Simon Gard, Nick Harley, Patrick Maxwell and his brother Alastair Maxwell, completed 14 rounds in one day at Iceland's Akureyri Golf Club, the most northern 18-hole course in the world, during June 1991 when there was 24-hour daylight. It was claimed a record and £10,000 was raised for charity.

● In 1971 during a 24-hour period from 6 pm on 27th November until 5.15 pm on 28th November, Ian Colston completed 401 holes over the 6,061 yards Bendigo course, Victoria, Australia. Colston was a top marathon athlete but was not a golfer. However prior to his golfing marathon he took some lessons and became adept with a 6-iron, the only club he used throughout the 401 holes. The only assistance Colston had was a team of harriers to carry his 6-iron and look for his ball, and a band of motor-cyclists who provided light during the night. This is, as far as is known, the greatest number of holes played in 24 hours on foot on a full-size course.

● In 1934 Col Bill Farnham played 376 holes in 24 hours 10 minutes at the Guildford Lake Course, Guildford, Connecticut, using only a mashie and a putter.

● To raise funds for extending the Skipton GC course from 12 to 18 holes, the club professional, 24-year-old Graham Webster, played 277 holes in the hours of daylight on Monday 20th June, 1977. Playing with nothing longer than a 5-iron he averaged 81 per 18-hole round. Included in his marathon was a hole-in-one.

● Michael Moore, a 7 handicap 26-year-old member of Okehampton GC, completed on foot 15 rounds 6 holes (276 holes) there on Sunday, 25th June, 1972, in the hours of daylight. He started at 4.15 am and stopped at 9.15 pm. The distance covered was estimated at 56 miles.

● On 21st June, 1976, 5-handicapper Sandy Small played 15 rounds (270 holes) over his home course Cosby GC, length 6,128 yards, to raise money for the Society of Physically Handicapped Children. Using only a 5-iron, 9-iron and putter, Small started at 4.10 am and completed his 270th hole at 10.39 pm with the aid of car headlights. His fastest round was his first (40 minutes) and slowest his last (82 minutes). His best round of 76 was achieved in the second round.
● During the weekend of 20th–21st June, 1970, Peter Chambers of Yorkshire completed over 14 rounds of golf over the Scarborough South Cliff course. In a non-stop marathon lasting just under 24 hours, Chambers played 257 holes in 1,168 strokes, an average of 84.4 strokes per round.
● Bruce Sutherland, on the Craiglockhart Links, Edinburgh, started at 8.15 pm on 21st June, 1927, and played almost continuously until 7.30 pm on 22nd June, 1927. During the night four caddies with acetylene lamps lit the way, and lost balls were reduced to a minimum. He completed fourteen rounds. Mr Sutherland, who was a physical culture teacher, never recovered from the physical strain and died a few years later.
● Sidney Gleave, motorcycle racer, and Ernest Smith, golf professional at Davyhulme Club, Manchester, on 12th June, 1939, played five rounds of golf in five different countries – Scotland, Ireland, Isle of Man, England and Wales. Smith had to play the five rounds under 80 in one day to win the £100 wager. They travelled by plane, and the following was their programme:

    Start 3.40a.m. at Prestwick St Nicholas (Scotland), finished 1 hour 35 minutes later on 70.
    2nd Course – Bangor, Ireland. Started at 7.15 a.m. and took 1 hour 30 minutes to finish on 76.
    3rd Course – Castletown, Isle of Man. Started 10.15 am, scored 76 in 1 hour 40 minutes.
    4th Course – Blackpool, Stanley Park, England. Started at 1.30 pm and scored 72 in 1 hour 55 minutes.
    5th Course – Hawarden, Wales, started at 6 pm and finished 2 hours 15 minutes later with a score of 72.

● On 19th June, 1995, Ian Botham, the former England cricketer, played four rounds of golf in Ireland, Wales, Scotland and England. His playing companions were Gary Price, the professional at Branston, and Tony Wright, owner of Craythorne, Burton-on-Trent, where the last 18 holes were completed. The other courses were St Margaret's, Anglesey and Dumfries & Galloway. The first round began at 4.30 am and the last was completed at 8.30 pm.
● On Wednesday, 3rd July, 1974, E.S. Wilson, Whitehead, Co Antrim and Dr G.W. Donaldson, Newry, Co. Down, played a nine-hole match in each of seven countries in the one day. The first 9 holes was at La Moye (Channel Islands) followed by Hawarden (Wales), Chester (England), Turnberry (Scotland), Castletown (Isle of Man), Dundalk (Eire)

and Warrenpoint (N Ireland). They started their first round at 4.25 am and their last round at 9.25 pm. Wilson piloted his own plane throughout.
● In June 1986 to raise money for the upkeep of his medieval church, the Rector of Mark with Allerton, Somerset, the Rev Michael Pavey, played a sponsored 18 holes on 18 different courses in the Bath & Wells Diocese. With his partner, the well-known broadcaster and music, Antony Hopkins, they played the 1st at Minehead at 5.55 am and finished playing the 18th at Burnham and Berrow at 6.05 pm. They covered 240 miles in the 'round' including the distances to reach the correct tee for the 'next' hole on each course. Par for the 'round' was 70. Together the pair raised £10,500 for the church.
● To raise funds for the Marlborough Club's centenary year (1988), Laurence Ross, the Club professional, in June 1987, played eight rounds in 12 hours. Against a par of 72, he completed the 576 holes in 3 under par, playing from back tees and walking all the way.
● As part of the 1992 Centenary Celebrations of the Royal Cinque Ports Golf Club at Deal, Kent, and to support charity, a six-handicap member, John Brazell, played all 37 royal courses in Britain and Ireland in 17 days. He won 22 matches, halved three, lost 12; hit 2,834 shots for an average score of 76.6; lost 11 balls and made 62 birdies. The aim was to raise £30,000 for Leukaemia Research and the Spastics Society.
● To raise more than £500 for the Guide Dogs for the Blind charity in the summer of 1992, Mrs Cheryle Power, a member of the Langley Park Golf Club, Beckenham, Kent, played 100 holes in a day – starting at 5 am and finishing at 8.45 pm.
● David Steele, a former European Tour player, completed 17½ rounds, 315 holes, between 6 am and 9.45 pm in 1993 at the San Roque club near Gibraltar in a total of 1,291 shots. Steele was assisted by a caddie cart and raised £15,000 for charity.

Fastest Rounds

● Dick Kimbrough, 41, completed a round on foot on 8th August, 1972, at North Platte CC, Nebraska (6,068 yards) in 30 minutes 10 seconds. He carried only a 3-iron.
● At Mowbray Course, Cape Town, November 1931, Len Richardson, who had represented South Africa in the Olympic Games, played a round which measured 6,248 yards in 31 minutes 22 seconds.
● The women's all-time record for the fastest round played on a course of at least 5,600 yards is held by Sue Ledger, 20, who completed the East Berks course in 38 minutes 8 seconds, beating the previous record by 17 minutes.
● In April, 1934, after attending a wedding in Bournemouth, Hants, Captain Gerald Moxom hurried to his club, West Hill in Surrey, to play in the captain's prize competition. With daylight fading and still dressed in his morning suit, he went round in 65 minutes and won the competition with a net 71 into the bargain.

● On 14th June, 1922, Jock Hutchison and Joe Kirkwood (Australia) played round the Old Course at St Andrews in 1 hour 20 minutes. Hutchison, out in 37, led by three holes at the ninth and won by 4 and 3.

● Fastest rounds can also take another form – the time taken for a ball to be propelled round 18 holes. The fastest known round of this type is 8 minutes 53.8 seconds on 25th August, 1979 by 42 members at Ridgemount CC Rochester, New York, a course measuring 6,161 yards. The Rules of Golf were observed but a ball was available on each tee; to be driven off the instant the ball had been holed at the preceding hole.

● The fastest round with the same ball took place in January 1992 at the Paradise Golf Club, Arizona. It took only 11 minutes 24 seconds; 91 golfers being positioned around the course ready to hit the ball as soon as it came to rest and then throwing the ball from green to tee.

● In 1992 John Daly and Mark Calcavecchia were both fined by the USPGA Tour for playing the final round of the Players' Championship in Florida in 123 minutes. Daly scored 80, Calcavecchia 81.

Curious Scoring

● C.W. Allen of Leek Golf Club chipped-in four times in a round in which he was partnered by K. Brint against G. Davies and R. Hollins. The shortest chip was a yard, the longest 20 yards.

● Tony Blackwell, playing off a handicap of four, broke the course record at Bull Bay, Anglesey, by four strokes when he had a gross 60 (net 56) in winning the club's town trophy in 1996. The course measured 6,217 yards.

● In the third round of the 1994 Volvo PGA Championship at Wentworth, Des Smyth, of Ireland, made birdie twos at each of the four short holes, the 2nd, 5th, 10th and 14th. He also had a two at the second hole in the fourth round.

● Also at Wentworth, in the 1994 World Match Play Championship, Seve Ballesteros had seven successive twos at the short holes – and still lost his quarter-final against Ernie Els.

● R.H. Corbett, playing in the semi-final of the Tangye Cup at Mullion in 1916, did a score of 27. The remarkable part of Corbett's score was that it was made up of nine successive 3s, bogey being 5, 3, 4, 4, 5, 3, 4, 4, 3.

● At Little Chalfont in June 1985 Adrian Donkersley played six successive holes in 6, 5, 4, 3, 2, 1 from the 9th to the 14th holes against a par of 4, 4, 3, 4, 3, 3.

● On 2nd September, 1920, playing over Torphin, near Edinburgh, William Ingle did the first five holes in 1, 2, 3, 4, 5.

● In the summer of 1970, Keith McMillan, on holiday at Cullen, had a remarkable series of 1, 2, 3, 4, 5 at the 11th to 15th holes.

● Marc Osborne was only 14 years of age when he equalled the Betchworth Park amateur course record

with a 66 in July, 1993. He was playing in the Mortimer Cup, a 36-hole medal competition, and had at the time a handicap of 6.8.

● Playing at Addington Palace, July, 1934, Ronald Jones, a member of Hendon Club, holed five consecutive holes in 5, 4, 3, 2, 1.

● Harry Dunderdale of Lincoln GC scored 5, 4, 3, 2, 1 in five consecutive holes during the first round of his club championship in 1978. The hole-in-one was the 7th, measuring 294 yards.

● At the Open Amateur Tournament of the Royal Ashdown Forest in 1936 Bobby Locke in his morning round had a score of 72, accomplishing every hole in 4.

● George Stewart of Cupar had a four at every hole over the Queen's course at Gleneagles despite forgetting to change into his golf shoes and therefore still wearing his street shoes.

● Henry Cotton told of one of the most extraordinary scoring feats ever. With some other professionals he was at Sestrieres in the 30s for the Italian Open Championship and Joe Ezar, a colourful character in those days on both sides of the Atlantic, accepted a wager from a club official – 1,000 lira for a 66 to break the course record; 2,000 for a 65; and 4,000 for a 64. *I'll do 64*, said Ezar, and proceeded to jot down the hole-by-hole score figures he would do next day for that total. With the exception of the ninth and tenth holes where his predicted score was 3, 4 and the actual score was 4, 3, he accomplished this amazing feat exactly as nominated.

● Nick Faldo scored par figures at all 18 holes in the final round of the 1987 Open Championship at Muirfield to win the title.

● During the Colts Championship at Knowle Golf Club, Bristol, Chris Newman (Cotswold Hills) scored eight consecutive 3s with birdies at four of the holes.

● At the Toft Hotel Golf Club captain's day event L. Heffernan had an ace, D. Patrick a 2, R. Barnett a 3 and D. Heffernan a 4 at the 240 yard par-4 ninth.

● In the European Club Championship played at the Parco de Medici Club in Rome in 1998, Belgian Dimitri van Hauwaert from Royal Antwerp had an albatross 2, Norwegian Marius Bjornstad from Oslo an eagle 3 and Scotsman Andrew Hogg from Turriff a birdie 4 at the 486 metre par-5 eighth hole.

High Scores

● In the qualifying competition at Formby for the 1976 Open Championship, Maurice Flitcroft, a 46-year-old crane driver from Barrow-in-Furness, took 121 strokes for the first round and then withdrew saying, *I have no chance of qualifying*. Flitcroft entered as a professional but had never before played 18 holes. He had taken the game up 18 months previously but, as he was not a member of a club, had been limited to practising on a local beach. His round was made up thus: 7, 5, 6, 6, 6, 6, 12, 6, 7-61; 11, 5, 6, 8, 4, 9, 5, 7, 5-60, total 121. After his round Flitcroft said, 'I've made a lot of progress in the last few months and I'm sorry I did not do better. I was trying too hard at

the beginning but began to put things together at the end of the round.' R&A officials, who were not amused by the bogus professional's efforts, refunded the £30 entry money to Flitcroft's two fellow-competitors. Flitcroft has since tried to qualify for the Open under assumed names: Gerard Hoppy from Switzerland and Beau Jolley (as in the wine)!

● Playing in the qualifying rounds of the 1965 Open Championship at Southport, an American self-styled professional entrant from Milwaukee, Walter Danecki, achieved the inglorious feat of scoring a total of 221 strokes for 36 holes, 81 over par. His first round over the Hillside course was 108, followed by a second round of 113. Walter, who afterwards admitted he felt *a little discouraged and sad*, declared that he entered because he was *after the money*.

● The highest individual scoring ever known in the rounds connected with the Open Championship occurred at Muirfield, 1935, when a Scottish professional started 7, 10, 5, 10, and took 65 to reach the 9th hole. Another 10 came at the 11th and the player decided to retire at the 12th hole. There he was in a bunker, and after playing four shots he had not regained the fairway.

● In 1883 in the Open Championship at Musselburgh, Willie Fernie, the winner, had a 10, the only time double figures appeared on the card of the Open Champion of the year. Fernie won after a tie with Bob Ferguson, and his score for the last hole in the tie was 2. He holed from just off the green to win by one stroke.

● In the first Open Championship at Prestwick in 1860 a competitor took 21, the highest score for one hole ever recorded in this event. The record is preserved in the archives of the Prestwick Golf Club, where the championship was founded.

● In the first round of the 1980 US Masters, Tom Weiskopf hit his ball into the water hazard in front of the par-3 12th hole five times and scored 13 for the hole.

● In the French Open at St Cloud, in 1968, Brian Barnes took 15 for the short 8th hole in the second round. After missing putts at which he hurriedly snatched while the ball was moving he penalised himself further by standing astride the line of a putt. The amazing result was that he actually took 12 strokes from about three feet from the hole. The highest scores on the European Tour were also recorded in the French Open. Philippe Porquier had a 20 at La Baule in 1978 and Ian Woosnam a 16 at La Boulie in 1986.

● US professional Dave Hill 6-putted the fifth green at Oakmont in the 1962 US Open Championship.

● Many high scores have been made at the Road Hole at St Andrews. Davie Ayton, on one occasion, was coming in a certain winner of the Open Championship when he got on the road and took 11. In 1921, at the Open Championship, one professional took 13. In 1923, competing for the Autumn Medal of the Royal & Ancient, J.B. Anderson required a five and a four to win the second award, but he took 13 at

the Road Hole. Anderson was close to the green in two, was twice in the bunkers in the face of the green, and once on the road. In 1935, R.H. Oppenheimer tied for the Royal Medal (the first award) in the Autumn Meeting of the Royal & Ancient. On the play-off he was one stroke behind Captain Aitken when they stood on the 17th tee. Oppenheimer drove three balls out of bounds and eventually took 11 to the Road Hole.

● British professional Mark James scored 111 in the second round of the 1978 Italian Open. He played the closing holes with only his right hand due to an injury to his left hand.

● In the 1927 Shawnee Open, Tommy Armour took 23 strokes to the 17th hole. Armour had won the American Open Championship a week earlier. In an effort to play the hole in a particular way, Armour hooked ball after ball out of bounds and finished with a 21 on the card. There was some doubt about the accuracy of this figure and on reaching the clubhouse Armour stated that it should be 23. This is the highest score by a professional in a tournament.

Freak Matches

● In 1912, the late Harry Dearth, an eminent vocalist, attired in a complete suit of heavy armour, played a match at Bushey Hall. He was beaten 2 and 1.

● In 1914, at the start of the First World War, J.N. Farrar, a native of Hoylake, was stationed at Royston, Herts. A bet was made of 10-1 that he would not go round Royston under 100 strokes, equipped in full infantry marching order, water bottle, full field kit and haversack. Farrar went round in 94. At the camp were several golfers, including professionals, who tried the same feat but failed.

● Captain Pennington took part in a match *from the air* against A.J. Young, the professional at Sonning. Captain Pennington, with 80 golf balls in the locker of his machine, set out to find the Sonning greens by dropping the balls as he circled over the course. The balls were covered in white cloth to ensure that they did not bounce once they struck the ground. The airman completed the course in 40 minutes, taking 29 *strokes*, while Young occupied two hours for his round of 68. Captain Pennington was eventually killed in an air crash in 1933.

● In April 1924, at Littlehampton, Harry Rowntree, an amateur golfer, played the better ball of Edward Ray and George Duncan, receiving an allowance of 150 yards to use as he required during the round. Rowntree won by 6 and 5 and had used only 50 yards 2 feet of his handicap. At one hole Duncan had a two – Rowntree, who was 25 yards from the hole, took this distance from his handicap and won the hole in one. Ray (died 1945) afterwards declared that, conceding a handicap of one yard per round, he could win every championship in the world. And he might, when reckoning is taken of the number of times a putt just stops an inch or two or how much difference to a shot three inches will make for the lie of the ball, either in a bunker or on the fairway. Many single

matches on the same system have been played. An 18 handicap player opposed to a scratch player should make a close match with an allowance of 50 yards.

● The first known instance of a golf match by telephone occurred in 1957, when the Cotswold Hills Golf Club, Cheltenham, England, won a golf tournament against the Cheltenham Golf Club, Melbourne, Australia, by six strokes. A large crowd assembled at the English club to wait for the 12,000 miles telephone call from Australia. The match had been played at the suggestion of a former member of the Cotswold Hills Club, Harry Davies, and was open to every member of the two clubs. The result of the match was decided on the aggregate of the eight best scores on each side and the English club won by 564 strokes to 570.

Golf Matches Against Other Sports

● H.H. Hilton and Percy Ashworth, many times racket champion, contested a driving match, the former driving a golf ball with a driver, and the latter a racket ball with a racket. Best distances: Against breeze – Golfer 182 yards; Racket player 125 yards. Down wind – Golfer 230 yards; Racket player 140 yards. Afterwards Ashworth hit a golf ball with the racket and got a greater distance than with the racket ball, but was still a long way behind the ball driven by Hilton.

● In 1913, at Wellington, Shropshire, a match between a golfer and a fisherman casting a $2\frac{1}{2}$ oz weight was played. The golfer, Rupert May, took 87; the fisherman J.J.D. Mackinlay, in difficulty because of his short casts, 102. His longest cast, 105 yards, was within 12 yards of the world record at the time, held by French angler, Decautelle. When within a rod's length of a hole he ran the weight to the rod end and dropped into the hole. Five times he broke his line, and was allowed another shot without penalty.

● In December, 1913, F.M.A. Webster, of the London Athletic Club, and Dora Roberts, with javelins, played a match with the late Harry Vardon and Mrs Gordon Robertson, who used the regulation clubs and golf balls. The golfers conceded two-thirds in the matter of distance, and they won by 5 up and 4 to play in a contest of 18 holes. The javelin throwers had a mark of two feet square in which to *hole out* while the golfers had to get their ball into the ordinary golf hole. Mr Webster's best throw was one of 160 feet.

● Several matches have taken place between a golfer on the one side and an archer on the other. The wielder of the bow and arrow has nearly always proved the victor. In 1953 at Kirkhill Golf Course, Lanarkshire, five archers beat six golfers by two games to one. There were two special rules for the match; when an archer's arrow landed six feet from the hole or the golfer's ball three feet from the hole, they were counted as holed. When the arrows landed in bunkers or in the rough, archers lifted their arrow and added a stroke. The sixth archer in this match called off and one archer shot two arrows from each of the 18 tees.

● In 1954, at the Southbroom Club, South Africa, a match over 9 holes was played between an archer and a fisherman against two golfers. The participants were all champions of their own sphere and consisted of Vernon Adams (archer), Dennis Burd (fisherman), Jeanette Wahl (champion of Southbroom and Port Shepstone), and Ron Burd (professional at Southbroom). The conditions were that the archer had holed out when his arrows struck a small leather bag placed on the green beside the hole and in the event of his placing his approach shot within a bow's length of the pin he was deemed to have 1-putted. The fisherman, to achieve a 1-putt, had to land his sinker within a rod's length of the pin. The two golfers were ahead for brief spells, but it was the opposition who led at the deciding 9th hole where *Robin Hood* played a perfect approach for a birdie.

● An *Across England* combined match was begun on 11th October, 1965, by four golfers and two archers from Crowborough Beacon Golf Club, Sussex, accompanied by *Penny*, a white Alsatian dog, whose duty it was to find lost balls. They teed off from Carlisle Castle via Hadrian's Wall, the Pennine Way, finally holing out in the 18th hole at Newcastle United GC in 612 teed shots. Casualties included 110 lost golf balls and 19 lost or broken arrows. The match took 5½ days, and the distance travelled was about 60 miles. The golfers were Miss P. Ward, K. Meaney, K. Ashdown and C.A. Macey; the archers were W.H. Hulme and T. Scott. The first arrow was fired from the battlements of Carlisle Castle, a distance of nearly 300 yards, by Cumberland Champion R. Willis, who also fired the second arrow right across the River Eden. R. Clough, president of Newcastle United GC, holed the last two putts. The match was in aid of *Guide Dogs for the Blind* and *Friends of Crowborough Hospital.*

Cross-country Matches

● Taking 1 year, 114 days, Floyd Rood golfed his way from coast to coast across the United States. He took 114,737 shots including 3,511 penalty shots for the 3,397 mile course.

● Two Californian teenagers, Bob Aube (17) and Phil Marrone (18) went on a golfing safari in 1974 from San Francisco to Los Angeles, a trip of over 500 miles lasting 16 days. The first six days they played alongside motorways. Over 1,000 balls were used.

● In 1830, the Gold Medal winner of the Royal & Ancient backed himself for 10 sovereigns to drive from the 1st hole at St Andrews to the toll bar at Cupar, distance nine miles, in 200 teed shots. He won easily.

● In 1848, two Edinburgh golfers played a match from Bruntsfield Links to the top of Arthur's Seat – an eminence overlooking the Scottish capital, 822 feet above sea level.

● On a winter's day in 1898, Freddie Tait backed himself to play a gutta ball in 40 teed shots from Royal St George's Clubhouse, Sandwich, to the Cinque Ports Club, Deal. He was to hole out by hitting any part of the Deal Clubhouse. The distance as the

crow flies was three miles. The redoubtable Tait holed out with his 32nd shot, so effectively that the ball went through a window.

● In 1900 three members of the Hackensack (NJ) Club played a game of four-and-a-half hours over an extemporised course six miles long, which stretched from Hackensack to Paterson. Despite rain, corn-fields, and wide streams, the three golfers – J.W. Hauleebeek, Dr E.R. Pfaare, and Eugene Crassons – completed the round, the first and the last named taking 305 strokes each, and Dr Pfaare 327 strokes. The players used only two clubs, the mashie and the cleek.

● On 3rd December, 1920, P. Rupert Phillips and W. Raymond Thomas teed up on the first tee of the Radyr Golf Club and played to the last hole at Southern-down. The distance as the crow flies was 15½ miles, but circumventing swamps, woods, and plough, they covered, approximately, 20 miles. The wager was that they would not do the hole in 1,000 strokes, but they holed out at their 608th stroke two days later. They carried large ordnance maps.

● On 12th March, 1921, A. Stanley Turner, Macclesfield, played from his house to the Cat and Fiddle Inn, five miles distance, in 64 strokes. The route was broken and hilly with a rise of nearly 1,000 feet. Turner was allowed to tee up within two club lengths after each shot and the wagering was 6-4 against his doing the distance in 170 strokes.

● In 1919, a golfer drove a ball from Piccadilly Circus and, proceeding via the Strand, Fleet Street and Ludgate Hill, *holed out* at the Royal Exchange, London. The player drove off at 8 am on a Sunday, a time when the usually thronged thoroughfares were deserted.

● On 23rd April, 1939, Richard Sutton, a London stockbroker, played from Tower Bridge, London, to White's Club, St James's Street, in 142 strokes. The bet was he would not do *the course* in under 200 shots. Sutton used a putter, crossed the Thames at Southwark Bridge, and hit the ball short distances to keep out of trouble.

● Golfers produced the most original event in Ireland's three-week national festival of An Tostal, in 1953 – a cross-country competition with an advertised £1,000,000 for the man who could hole out in one. The 150 golfers drove off from the first tee at Kildare Club to hole out eventually on the 18th green, five miles away, on the nearby Curragh course, a distance of 8,800 yards. The unusual hazards to be negotiated included the main Dublin-Cork railway line and high-way, the Curragh Racecourse, hoofprints left by Irish thoroughbred racehorses out exercising on the plains from nearby stables, army tank tracks and about 150 telephone lines. The Golden Ball Trophy, which is played for annually – a standard size golf ball in gold, mounted on a black marble pillar beside the silver fig-ure of a golfer on a green marble base, designed by Captain Maurice Cogan, Army GHQ, Dublin – was for the best gross. And it went to one of the longest hitters in international golf – Amateur Champion,

Irish internationalist and British Walker Cup player Joe Carr, with the remarkable score of 52.

● In 1961, as a University Charities Week stunt, four Aberdeen University students set out to golf their way up Ben Nevis (4,406 feet). About half-way up, after losing 63 balls and expending 659 strokes, the quartet conceded victory to Britain's highest mountain.

● Among several cross-country golfing exploits, one of the most arduous was faced by Iain Williamson and Tony Kent, who teed off from Cained Point on the summit of Fairfield in the Lake District. With the hole cut in the lawn of the Bishop of Carlisle's home at Rydal Park, it measured 7,200 yards and passed through the summits of Great Rigg Mann, Heron Pike and Nab Scar, descending altogether 1,900 feet. Eight balls were lost and the two golfers holed out in a com-bined total of 303 strokes.

Long-lived Golfers

● James Priddy, aged 80, played in the Seniors' Open at his home club, Weston-super-Mare, Avon, on 27th June, 1990, and scored a gross 70 to beat his age by ten shots.

● The oldest golfer who ever lived is believed to have been Arthur Thompson of British Columbia, Canada. He equalled his age when 103 at Uplands GC, a course of over 6,000 yards. He died two years later.

● Nathaniel Vickers celebrated his 103rd birthday on Sunday, 9th October, 1949, and died the following day. He was the oldest member of the United States Senior Golf Association and until 1942 he competed regularly in their events and won many trophies in the various age divisions. When 100 years old, he apolo-gised for being able to play only nine holes a day. Vickers predicted he would live until 103 and he died a few hours after he had celebrated his birthday.

● American George Miller, who died in 1979 aged 102, played regularly when 100 years old.

● In 1999 94-year-old Mr W. Seneviratne, a retired schoolmaster who lived and worked in Malaysia, was still practising every day and regularly competing in medal competitions at the Royal Colombo Golf Club which was founded in 1879.

● Phyllis Tidmarsh, aged 90, won a Stableford com-petition at Saltford Golf Club, near Bath, when she returned 42 points. Her handicap was cut from 28 to 27.

● George Swanwick, a member of Wallasey, celebrated his 90th birthday with a lunch at the club on 1st April, 1971. He played golf several times a week, carrying his own clubs, and had holed-in-one at the ages of 75 and 85. His ambition was to com-plete the sequence aged 95 ... but he died in 1973 aged 92.

● The 10th Earl of Wemyss played a round on his 92nd birthday, in 1910, at Craigielaw. At the age of 87 the Earl was partnered by Harry Vardon in a match at Kilspindie, the golf course on his East Lothian estate at Gosford. After playing his ball the venerable

earl mounted a pony and rode to the next shot. He died on 30th June, 1914.

● F.L. Callender, aged 78, in September 1932, played nine consecutive rounds in the Jubilee Vase, St Andrews. He was defeated in the ninth, the final round, by 4 and 2. Callender's handicap was 12. This is the best known achievement of a septuagenarian in golf.

● George Evans shot a remarkable one over par 71 at Brockenhurst Manor – remarkable because Mr Evans was 87 at the time. Playing with him that day was Hampshire, Isle of Wight and Channel Islands President John Nettell and former Ferndown pro Doug Sewell. 'It's good to shoot a score under your age, but when its 16 shots better that must be a record', said Mr Nettell. Mr Evans qualified for four opens while professional at West Hill, Surrey.

● Bernard Matthews, aged 82, of Banstead Downs Club, handicap 6, holed the course in 72 gross in August 1988. A week later he holed it in 70, twelve shots below his age. He came back in 31, finishing 4, 3, 3, 2, 3, against a par of 5, 4, 3, 3, 4. Mr Matthews's eclectic score at his Club is 37, or one over 2's.

Playing in the Dark

On numerous occasions it has been necessary to hold lamps, lighted candles, or torches at holes in order that players might finish a competition. Large entries, slow play, early darkness and an eclipse of the sun have all been causes of playing in darkness.

● Since 1972, the Whitburn Golf Club at South Shields, Tyne and Wear, has held an annual Summer Solstice Competition. All competitors, who draw lots for starting tees, must begin before 4.24 and 13 seconds am, the time the sun rises over the first hole on the longest day of the year.

● At the Open Championship in Musselburgh in November 1889 many players finished when the light had so far gone that the adjacent street lamps were lit. The cards were checked by candlelight. Several players who had no chance of the championship were paid small sums to withdraw in order to permit others who had a chance to finish in daylight. This was the last championship at Musselburgh.

● At the Southern Section of the PGA tournament on 25th September, 1907, at Burnham Beeches, several players concluded the round by the aid of torch lights placed near the holes.

● In the Irish Open Championship at Portmarnock in September, 1907, a tie in the third round between W.C. Pickeman and A. Jeffcott was postponed owing to darkness, at the 22nd hole. The next morning Pickeman won at the 24th.

● The qualifying round of the American Amateur Championship in 1910 could not be finished in one day, and several competitors had to stop their round on account of darkness, and complete it early in the morning of the following day.

● On 10th January, 1926, in the final of the President's Putter, at Rye, E.F. Storey and R.H. Wethered

were all square at the 24th hole. It was 5 pm and so dark that, although a fair crowd was present, the balls could not be followed. The tie was abandoned and the Putter held jointly for the year. Each winner of the Putter affixes the ball he played; for 1926 there are two balls, respectively engraved with the names of the finalists.

● In the 1932 Walker Cup contest at Brooklyn, a total eclipse of the sun occurred.

● At Perth, on 14th September, 1932, a competition was in progress under good clear evening light, and a full bright moon. The moon rose at 7.10 and an hour later came under eclipse to the earth's surface. The light then became so bad that on the last three greens competitors holed out by the aid of the light from matches.

● At Carnoustie, 1932, in the competition for the *Craw's Nest* the large entry necessitated competitors being sent off in 3-ball matches. The late players had to be assisted by electric torches flashed on the greens.

● In February, 1950, Max Faulkner and his partner, R. Dolman, in a Guildford Alliance event finished their round in complete darkness. A photographer's flash bulbs were used at the last hole to direct Faulkner's approach. Several of the other competitors also finished in darkness. At the last hole they had only the light from the clubhouse to aim at and one played his approach so boldly that he put his ball through the hall doorway and almost into the dressing room.

● On the second day of the 1969 Ryder Cup contest, the last 4-ball match ended in near total darkness on the 18th green at Royal Birkdale. With the help of the clubhouse lights the two American players, Lee Trevino and Miller Barber, along with Tony Jacklin for Britain each faced putts of around five feet to win their match. All missed and their game was halved.

The occasions mentioned above all occurred in competitions where it was not intended to play in the dark. There are, however, numerous instances where players set out to play in the dark either for bets or for novelty.

● On 29th November, 1878, R.W. Brown backed himself to go round the Hoylake links in 150 strokes, starting at 11 pm. The conditions of the match were that Mr Brown was only to be penalised *loss of distance* for a lost ball, and that no one was to help him to find it. He went round in 147 strokes, and won his bet by the narrow margin of three strokes.

● In 1876 David Strath backed himself to go round St Andrews under 100, in moonlight. He took 95, and did not lose a ball.

● In September 1928, at St Andrews, the first and last holes were illuminated by lanterns, and at 11 pm four members of the Royal and Ancient set out to play a foursome over the 2 holes. Electric lights, lanterns, and rockets were used to brighten the fairway, and the headlights of motor cars parked on Links Place formed a helpful battery. The 1st hole was won in four, and each side got a five at the 18th. About 1,000

spectators followed the freak match, which was played to celebrate the appointment of Angus Hambro to the captaincy of the club.

● In 1931, Rufus Stewart, professional, Kooyonga Club, South Australia, and former Australian Open Champion, played 18 holes of exhibition golf at night without losing a single ball over the Kooyonga course, and completed the round in 77.

● At Ashley Wood Golf Club, Blandford, Dorset, a night-time golf tournament was arranged annually with up to 180 golfers taking part over four nights. Over £6000 has been raised in four years for the Muscular Dystrophy Charity.

● At Pannal, 3rd July, 1937, R.H. Locke, playing in bright moonlight, holed his tee shot at the 15th hole, distance 220 yards, the only known case of holing-in-one under such conditions.

Fatal and Other Accidents on the Links

The history of golf is, unfortunately, marred by a great number of fatal accidents on or near the course. In the vast majority of such cases they have been caused either by careless swinging of the club or by an uncontrolled shot when the ball has struck a spectator or bystander. In addition to the fatal accidents there is an even larger number on record which have resulted in serious injury or blindness. We do not propose to list these accidents except where they have some unusual feature. We would remind all golfers of the tragic consequences which have so often been caused by momentary carelessness. The fatal accidents which follow have an unusual cause and other accidents given may have their humorous aspect.

● English tournament professional Richard Boxall was three shots off the lead in the third round of the 1991 Open Championship when he fractured his left leg driving from the 9th tee at Royal Birkdale. He was taken from the course to hospital by ambulance and was listed in the official results as 'retired' which entitled him to a consolation prize of £3000.

A month later, Russell Weir of Scotland, was competing in the European Teaching Professionals' Championship near Rotterdam when he also fractured his left leg driving from the 7th tee in the first round.

● In July, 1971, Rudolph Roy, aged 43, was killed at a Montreal course; in playing out of woods, the shaft of his club snapped, rebounded off a tree and the jagged edge plunged into his body.

● Harold Wallace, aged 75, playing at Lundin Links with two friends in 1950, was crossing the railway line which separates the fifth green and sixth tee, when a light engine knocked him down and he was killed instantly.

● In the summer of 1963, Harold Kalles, of Toronto, Canada, died six days after his throat had been cut by a golf club shaft, which broke against a tree as he was trying to play out of a bunker.

● At Jacksonville, Florida, on 18th March, 1952, two women golfers were instantly killed when hit simultaneously by the whirling propeller of a navy fighter plane. They were playing together when the plane with a dead engine coming in out of control, hit them from behind.

● In May, 1993, at Ponoka Community GC, Alberta, Canada, Richard McCulough hit a poor tee shot on the 13th hole and promptly smashed his driver angrily against a golf cart. The head of the driver and six inches of shaft flew through the air, piercing McCulough's throat and severing his carotid artery. He died in hospital.

● Britain's first national open event for competitors aged over 80, at Moortown, Leeds in September, 1992, was marred when 81-year-old Frank Hart collapsed on the fourth tee and died. Play continued and Charles Mitchell, aged 80, won the Stableford competition with a gross score of 81 for 39 points.

● Playing in the 1993 Carlesburg-Tetley Cornish Festival at Tehidy Park, Ian Cornwell was struck on the leg by a wayward shot from a player two groups behind. Later, as he was leaving the 16th green, he was hit again, this time below the ear, by the same player, knocking him unconscious. This may be the first time that a player has been hit twice in the same round by the same player.

Lightning on the Links

There have been a considerable number of fatal and serious accidents through players and caddies having been struck by lightning on the course. The Royal & Ancient and the USGA have, since 1952, provided for discontinuance of play during lightning storms under the Rules of Golf (Rule 37, 6) and the United States Golf Association has given the following guide for personal safety during thunderstorms:

(a) Do not go out of doors or remain out during thunderstorms unless it is necessary. Stay inside of a building where it is dry, preferably away from fireplaces, stoves, and other metal objects.

(b) If there is any choice of shelter, choose in the following order:
   1. Large metal or metal-frame buildings.
   2. Dwellings or other buildings which are protected against lightning.
   3. Large unprotected buildings.
   4. Small unprotected buildings.

(c) If remaining out of doors is unavoidable, keep away from:
   1. Small sheds and shelters if in an exposed location.
   2. Isolated trees.
   3. Wire fences.
   4. Hilltops and wide open spaces.

(d) Seek shelter in:
   1. A cave.
   2. A depression in the ground.
   3. A deep valley or canyon.
   4. The foot of a steep or overhanging cliff.
   5. Dense woods.
   6. A grove of trees.

Note – Raising golf clubs or umbrellas above the head is dangerous.

● A serious incident with lightning involving well-known golfers was at the 1975 Western Open in Chicago when Lee Trevino, Jerry Heard and Bobby Nichols were all struck and had to be taken to hospital. At the same time Tony Jacklin had a club thrown 15 feet out of his hands.

● Two well-known competitors were struck by lightning in European events in 1977. They were Mark James of Britain in the Swiss Open and Severiano Ballesteros of Spain in the Scandinavian Open. Fortunately neither appeared to be badly injured.

● Two spectators were killed by lightning in 1991: one at the US Open and the other at US PGA Championship.

Spectators Interfering with Balls

● Deliberate interference by spectators with balls in play during important money matches was not unknown in the old days when there was intense rivalry between the *schools* of Musselburgh, St Andrews, and North Berwick, and disputes arose in stake matches caused by the action of spectators in kicking the ball into either a favourable or an unfavourable position.

● Tom Morris, in his last match with Willie Park at Musselburgh, refused to go on because of interference by the spectators, and in the match on the same course about 40 years later, in 1895, between Willie Park Jr and J.H. Taylor, the barracking of the crowd and interference with play was so bad that when the Park-Vardon match came to be arranged in 1899, Vardon refused to accept Musselburgh as a venue.

● Even in modern times spectators have been known to interfere deliberately with players' balls, though it is usually by children. In the 1972 Penfold Tournament at Queen's Park, Bournemouth, Christy O'Connor Jr had his ball stolen by a young boy, but not being told of this at the time had to take the penalty for a lost ball. O'Connor finished in a tie for first place, but lost the play-off.

● In 1912 in the last round of the final of the Amateur Championship at Westward Ho! between Abe Mitchell and John Ball, the drive of the former to the short 14th hit an open umbrella held by a lady protecting herself from the heavy rain, and instead of landing on the green the ball was diverted into a bunker. Mitchell, who was leading at the time by 2 holes, lost the hole and Ball won the Championship at the 38th hole.

● In the match between the professionals of Great Britain and America at Southport in 1937 a dense crowd collected round the 15th green waiting for the Sarazen-Alliss match. The American's ball landed in the lap of a woman, who picked it up and threw it so close to the hole that Sarazen got a two against Alliss' three.

● In a memorable tie between Bobby Jones and Cyril Tolley in the 1930 Amateur Championship at St Andrews, Jones' approach to the 17th green struck spectators massed at the left end of the green and led to controversy as to whether it would otherwise have gone on to the famous road. Jones himself had deliberately played for that part of the green and had requested stewards to get the crowd back. Had the ball gone on to the road, the historic Jones Quadrilateral of the year – the Open and Amateur Championships of Britain and the United States – might not have gone into the records.

● In the 1983 Suntory World Match Play Championship at Wentworth Nick Faldo hit his second shot over the green at the 16th hole into a group of spectators. To everyone's astonishment and discomfiture the ball reappeared on the green about 30ft from the hole, propelled there by a thoroughly misguided and anonymous spectator. The referee ruled that Faldo should play the ball where it lay on the green. Faldo's opponent, Graham Marsh, understandably upset by the incident, took three putts against Faldo's two, thus losing a hole he might well otherwise have won. Faldo won the match 2 and 1, but lost in the final to Marsh's fellow Australian Greg Norman by 3 and 2.

Golf Balls Killing Animals and Fish, and Incidents with Animals

● An astounding fatality to an animal through being hit by a golf ball occurred at St Margaret's-at-Cliffe Golf Club, Kent on 13th June, 1934, when W.J. Robinson, the professional, killed a cow with his tee shot to the 18th hole. The cow was standing in the fairway about 100 yards from the tee, and the ball struck her on the back of the head. She fell like a log, but staggered to her feet and walked about 50 yards before dropping again. When the players reached her she was dead.

● J.W. Perret, of Ystrad Mynach, playing with Chas R. Halliday, of Ralston, in the qualifying rounds of the Society of One Armed Golfers' Championship over the Darley course, Troon, on 27th August, 1935, killed two gulls at successive holes with his second shots. The *deadly* shots were at the 1st and 2nd holes.

● On the first day of grouse shooting of the 1975 season (12th August), 11-year-old schoolboy Willie Fraser, of Kingussie, beat all the guns when he killed a grouse with his tee shot on the local course.

● On 10th June, 1904, while playing in the Edinburgh High Constables' Competition at Kilspindie, Captain Ferguson sent a long ball into the rough at the Target hole, and on searching for it found that it had struck and killed a young hare.

● Playing in a mixed open tournament at the Waimairi Beach Golf Club in Christchurch, New Zealand, in the summer of 1961, Mrs R.T. Challis found her ball in fairly long spongy grass where a placing rule applied. She picked up, placed the ball and played her stroke. A young hare leaped into the air and fell dead at her feet. She had placed the ball on the leveret without seeing it and without disturbing it.

● In 1906 in the Border Championship at Hawick, a gull and a weasel were killed by balls during the afternoon's play.

● A golfer at Newark, in May, 1907, drove his ball into the river. The ball struck a trout 2lb in weight and killed it.

● On 24th April, 1975, at Scunthorpe GC, Jim Tollan's drive at the 14th hole, called *The Mallard*, struck and killed a female mallard duck in flight. The duck was stuffed and is displayed in the Scunthorpe Clubhouse.

● A. Samuel, Melbourne Club, at Sandringham, was driving with an iron club from the 17th tee, when a kitten, which had been playing in the long grass, sprang suddenly at the ball. Kitten and club arrived at the objective simultaneously, with the result that the kitten took an unexpected flight through the air, landing some 20 yards away.

● As Susan Rowlands was lining up a vital putt in the closing stages of the final of the 1978 Welsh Girls' Championship at Abergele, a tiny mouse scampered up her trouser leg. After holing the putt, the mouse ran down again. Susan, who won the final, admitted that she fortunately had not known it was there.

Interference by Birds and Animals

● Crows, ravens, hawks and seagulls frequently carry off golf balls, sometimes dropping the ball actually on the green, and it is a common incident for a cow to swallow a golf ball. A plague of crows on the Liverpool course at Hoylake are addicted to golf balls – they stole 26 in one day – selecting only new balls. It was suggested that members should carry shotguns as a 15th club!

● A match was approaching a hole in a rather low-lying course, when one of the players made a crisp chip from about 30 yards from the hole. The ball trickled slowly across the green and eventually disappeared into the hole. After a momentary pause, the ball was suddenly ejected on to the green, and out jumped a large frog.

● A large black crow named Jasper which frequented the Lithgow GC in New South Wales, Australia, stole 30 golf balls in the club's 1972 Easter Tournament.

● As Mrs Molly Whitaker was playing from a bunker at Beachwood course, Natal, South Africa, a large monkey leaped from a bush and clutched her round the neck. A caddie drove it off by clipping it with an iron club.

● In Massachusetts a goose, having been hit rather hard by a golf ball which then came to rest by the side of a water hazard, took revenge by waddling over to the ball and kicking it into the water.

● In the summer of 1963, S.C. King had a good drive to the 10th hole at the Guernsey Club. His partner, R.W. Clark, was in the rough, and King helped him to search. Returning to his ball, he found a cow eating it. Next day, at the same hole, the positions were reversed, and King was in the rough. Clark placed his woollen hat over his ball, remarking, *I'll make sure the cow doesn't eat mine.* On his return he found the cow thoroughly enjoying his hat; nothing was left but the pom-pom.

● On 5 August 2000 in the first round of the Royal Westmoreland Club Championship in Barbados, Kevin Edwards, a five-handicapper, hit a tee shot at the short 15th to a few feet of the hole. A monkey then ran onto the green, picked up the ball, threw it into the air a few times, then placed it in the hole before running off. Mr Edwards had to replace his ball, but was obliged afterwards to buy everyone a drink at the bar by virtue of a newly written rule.

Armless, One-armed, Legless and Ambidextrous Players

● In September, 1933, at Burgess Golfing Society of Edinburgh, the first championship for one-armed golfers was held. There were 43 entries and 37 of the competitors had lost an arm in the 1914-18 war. Play was over two rounds and the championship was won by W.E. Thomson, Eastwood, Glasgow, with a score of 169 (82 and 87) for two rounds. The Burgess course was 6,300 yards long. Thomson drove the last green, 260 yards. The championship and an international match are played annually.

● In the Boys' Amateur Championship 1923, at Dunbar and 1949 at St Andrews, there were competitors each with one arm. The competitor in 1949, R.P. Reid, Cupar, Fife, who lost his arm working a machine in a butcher's shop, got through to the third round.

● There have been cases of persons with no arms playing golf. One, Thomas McAuliffe, who held the club between his right shoulder and cheek, once went round Buffalo CC, USA, in 108.

● Group Captain Bader, who lost both legs in a flying accident prior to the World War 1939-45, took part in golf competitions and reached a single-figure handicap in spite of his disability.

● In 1909, Scott of Silloth, and John Haskins of Hoylake, both one-armed golfers, played a home and away match for £20-a-side. Scott finished five up at Silloth. He was seven up and 14 to play at Hoylake but Haskins played so well that Scott eventually only won by 3 and 1. This was the first match between one-armed golfers. Haskins in 1919 was challenged by Mr Mycock, of Buxton, another one-armed golfer. The match was 36 holes, home and away. The first half was played over the Buxton and High Peak Links, and the latter half over the Liverpool Links, and resulted in a win for Haskins by 11 and 10. Later in the same year Haskins received another challenge to play against Alexander Smart of Aberdeen. The match was 18 holes over the Balgownie Course, and ended in favour of Haskins.

● In a match, November, 1926, between the Geduld and Sub Nigel Clubs – two golf clubs connected with the South African gold mines of the same names – each club had two players minus an arm. The natural consequence was that the quartet were matched. The

players were – A.W.P. Charteris and E. Mitchell, Sub Nigel; and E.P. Coles and J. Kirby, Geduld. This is the first record of four one-armed players in a foursome.

● At Joliet Country Club, USA, a one-armed golfer named D.R. Anderson drove a ball 300 yards.

● Left-handedness, but playing golf right-handed, is prevalent and for a man to throw with his left hand and play golf right-handed is considered an advantage, for Bobby Jones, Jesse Sweetser, Walter Hagen, Jim Barnes, Joe Kirkwood and more recently Johnny Miller were eminent golfers who were left-handed and ambidextrous.

● In a practice round for the Open Championship in July, 1927, at St Andrews, Len Nettlefold and Joe Kirkwood changed sets of clubs at the 9th hole. Nettlefold was a left-handed golfer and Kirkwood right-handed. They played the last nine, Kirkwood with the left-handed clubs and Nettlefold with the right-handed clubs.

● The late Harry Vardon, when he was at Ganton, got tired of giving impossible odds to his members and beating them, so he collected a set of left-handed clubs, and rating himself at scratch, conceded the handicap odds to them. He won with the same monotonous regularity.

● Ernest Jones, who was professional at the Chislehurst Club, was badly wounded in the war in France in 1916 and his right leg had to be amputated below the knee. He persevered with the game, and before the end of the year he went round the Clacton course balanced on his one leg in 72. Jones later settled in the United States where he built fame and fortune as a golf teacher.

● Major Alexander McDonald Fraser of Edinburgh had the distinction of holding two handicaps simultaneously in the same club – one when he played left-handed and the other for his right-handed play. In medal competitions he had to state before teeing up which method he would use.

● Former England test cricketer Brian Close once held a handicap of 2 playing right-handed, but after retiring from cricket in 1977 decided to apply himself as a left-handed player. His left-handed handicap at the time of his retirement was 7. Close had the distinction of once beating Ted Dexter, another distinguished test cricketer and noted golfer twice in the one day, playing right-handed in the morning and left-handed in the afternoon.

Blind and Blindfolded Golf

● Major Towse, VC, whose eyes were shot out during the South African War, 1899, was probably the first blind man to play golf. His only stipulations when playing the game were that he should be allowed to touch the ball with his hands to ascertain its position, and that his caddie could ring a small bell to indicate the position of the hole. Major Towse, who played with considerable skill, was also an expert oarsman and bridge player. He died in 1945, aged 81.

● The United States Blind Golfers' Association in 1946 promoted an Invitational Golf Tournament for the blind at Inglewood, California, to be held annually. In 1953 there were 24 competitors, of which 11 completed the two rounds of 36 holes. The winner was Charley Boswell who lost his eyesight leading a tank unit in Germany in 1944.

● In July, 1954, at Lambton Golf and Country Club, Toronto, the first international championship for the blind was held. It resulted in a win for Joe Lazaro, of Waltham, Mass., with a score of 220 for the two rounds. He drove the 215-yard 16th hole and just missed an ace, his ball stopping 18 inches from the hole. Charley Boswell, who won the United States Blind Golfers' Association Tournament in 1953, was second. The same Charles Boswell, of Birmingham, Alabama, holed the 141-yard 14th hole at the Vestavia CC in one in October, 1970.

● Another blind person to have holed-in-one was American Ben Thomas while on holiday in South Carolina in 1978.

● Rick Sorenson undertook a bet in which, playing 18 holes blindfolded at Meadowbrook Course, Minneapolis, on 25th May, 1973, he was to pay $10 for every hole over par and receive $100 for every hole in par or better. He went round in 86 losing $70 on the deal.

● Alfred Toogood played blindfolded in a match against Tindal Atkinson at Sunningdale in 1912. Toogood was beaten 8 and 7. Previously, in 1908, I. Millar, Newcastle-upon-Tyne, played a match blindfolded against A.T. Broughton, Birkdale, at Newcastle, County Down.

● Wing-Commander *Laddie* Lucas, DSO, DFC, MP, played over Sandy Lodge golf course in Hertfordshire on 7th August, 1954, completely blindfolded and had a score of 87.

Trick Shots

● Joe Kirkwood, Australia, specialised in public exhibitions of trick and fancy shots. He played all kinds of strokes after nominating them, and among his ordinary strokes nothing was more impressive than those hit for low flight. He played a full drive from the face of a wrist watch, and the toe of a spectator's shoe, full strokes at a suspended ball, and played for slice and pull at will, and exhibited his ambidexterity by playing left-handed strokes with right-handed clubs. Holing six balls, stymieing, a full shot at a ball catching it as it descended, and hitting 12 full shots in rapid succession, with his face turned away from the ball, were shots among his repertoire. In playing the last named Kirkwood placed the balls in a row, about six inches apart, and moved quickly along the line. Kirkwood, who was born in Australia lived for many years in America. He died in November, 1970 aged 73.

● On 2nd April, 1894, a 3-ball match was played over Musselburgh course between Messrs Grant, Bowden, and Waggot, the clubmaker, the latter teeing on the face of a watch at each tee. He finished the round in 41 the watch being undamaged in any way.

● In a match at Esher on 23rd November, 1931, George Ashdown, the professional, played his tee shot for each of the 18 holes from a rubber tee strapped to the forehead of Miss Ena Shaw.

● E.A. Forrest, a South African professional in a music hall turn of trick golf shots, played blindfolded shots, one being from the ball teed on the chin of his recumbent partner.

● The late Paul Hahn, an American trick specialist could hit four balls with two clubs. Holding a club in each hand he hit two balls, hooking one and slicing the other with the same swing. Hahn had a repertoire of 30 trick shots. In 1955 he flew round the world, exhibiting in 14 countries and on all five continents.

Balls Colliding and Touching

● Competing in the 1980 Corfu International Championship, Sharon Peachey drove from one tee and her ball collided in mid-air with one from a competitor playing another hole. Her ball ended in a pond.

● Playing in the Cornish team championship in 1973 at West Cornwall GC Tom Scott-Brown, of West Cornwall GC, and Paddy Bradley, of Tehidy GC, saw their drives from the fourth and eighth tees collide in mid-air.

● During a fourball match at Guernsey Club in June, 1966, near the 13th green from the tee, two of the players, D.G. Hare and S. Machin, chipped up simultaneously; the balls collided in mid-air and Machin's ball hit the green, then the flagstick, and dropped into the hole for a birdie 2.

● In May, 1926, during the meeting of the Army Golfing Society at St Andrews, Colonel Howard and Lieutenant-Colonel Buchanan Dunlop, while playing in the foursomes against J. Rodger and J. Mackie, hit full iron shots for the seconds to the 16th green. Each thought he had to play his ball first, and hidden by a bunker the players struck their balls simultaneously. The balls, going towards the hole about 20 yards from the pin and five feet in the air, met with great force and dropped either side of the hole five yards apart.

● In 1972, before a luncheon celebrating the centenary year of the Ladies' Section of Royal Wimbledon GC, a 12-hole competition was held during which two competitors, Mrs L. Champion and Mrs A. McKendrick, driving from the eighth and ninth tees respectively, saw their balls collide in mid-air.

● In 1928, at Wentworth Falls, Australia, Dr Alcorn and E.A. Avery, of Leura Club, were playing with professional E. Barnes. The tee shots of Avery and Barnes at the 9th hole finished on opposite sides of the fairway. Both players unknowingly hit their seconds (chip shots) at the same time. Dr Alcorn, standing at the pin, suddenly saw two balls approaching the hole from different angles. They met in the air and dropped into the hole.

● At Rugby, 1931, playing in a 4-ball match, H. Fraser pulled his drive from the 10th tee in the direction of the ninth tee. Simultaneously a club member, driving from the ninth tee, pulled his drive. The tees were about 350 yards apart. The two balls collided in mid-air.

● Two golf balls, being played in opposite directions, collided in flight over Longniddry Golf Course on 27th June, 1953. Immediately after Stewart Elder, of Longniddry, had driven from the third tee, another ball, which had been pulled off line from the second fairway, which runs alongside the third, struck his ball about 20 feet above the ground. S.J. Fleming, of Tranent, who was playing with Elder, heard a loud crack and thought Elder's ball had exploded. The balls were found undamaged about 70 yards apart.

Three and Two Balls Dislodged by One Shot

● In 1934 on the short 3rd hole (now the 13th) of Olton Course, Warwickshire, J.R. Horden, a scratch golfer of the club, sent his tee shot into long wet grass a few feet over the back of the green. When he played an *explosion* shot three balls dropped on to the putting green, his own and two others.

● A.M. Chevalier, playing at Hale, Cheshire, March, 1935, drove his ball into a grass bunker, and when he reached it there was only part of it showing. He played the shot with a niblick and to his amazement not one but three balls shot into the air. They all dropped back into the bunker and came to rest within a foot of each other. Then came another surprise. One of the *finds* was of the same manufacture and bore the same number as the ball he was playing with.

● Playing to the 9th hole, at Osborne House Club, Isle of Wight, George A. Sherman lost his ball which had sunk out of sight on the sodden fairway. A few weeks later, playing from the same tee, his ball again was plugged, only the top showing. Under a local rule he lifted his ball to place it, and exactly under it lay the ball he had lost previously.

Balls in Strange Places

● Playing at the John O' Gaunt Club, Sutton, near Biggleswade (Beds), a member drove a ball which did not touch the ground until it reached London – over 40 miles away. The ball landed in a vegetable lorry which was passing the golf course and later fell out of a package of cabbages when they were unloaded at Covent Garden, London.

● In the English Open Amateur Stroke Play at Moortown in 1974, Nigel Denham, a Yorkshire County player, in the first round saw his overhit second shot to the 18th green bounce up some steps into the clubhouse. His ball went through an open door, ricocheted off a wall and came to rest in the men's bar, 20 feet from the windows. As the clubhouse was not out of bounds Denham decided to play the shot back to the green and opened a window 4 feet by 2 feet through which he pitched his ball to 12 feet from the flag. (Several weeks later the R&A declared that Denham should have been penalised two shots for opening the window. The clubhouse was an immovable obstruction and no part of it should have been moved.)

● In the Open Championship at Sandwich, 1949, Harry Bradshaw, Kilcroney, Dublin, at the 5th hole in his second round, drove into the rough and found his ball inside a beer bottle with the neck and shoulder broken off and four sharp points sticking up. Bradshaw, if he had treated the ball as in an unplayable lie might have been involved in a disqualification, so he decided to play it where it lay. With his blaster he smashed the bottle and sent the ball about 30 yards. The hole, a par 4, cost him 6.

● Kevin Sharman of Woodbridge GC hit a low, very straight drive at the club's 8th hole in 1979. After some minutes' searching, his ball was found embedded in a plastic sphere on top of the direction post.

● On the Dublin Course, 16th July, 1936, in the Irish Open Championship, A.D. Locke, the South African, played his tee shot at the 100-yard 12th hole, but the ball could not be found on arrival on the green. The marker removed the pin and it was discovered that the ball had been entangled in the flag. It dropped near the edge of the hole and Locke holed the short putt for a birdie two.

● While playing a round on the Geelong Golf Club Course, Australia, Easter, 1923, Captain Charteris topped his tee shot to the short 2nd hole, which lies over a creek with deep and steep clay banks. His ball came to rest on the near slope of the creek bank. He elected to play the ball as it lay, and took his niblick. After the shot, the ball was nowhere to be seen. It was found later embedded in a mass of gluey clay stuck fast to the face of the niblick. It could not be shaken off. Charteris did what was afterwards approved by the R&A, cleaned the ball and dropped it behind without penalty.

● In October, 1929, at Blackmoor Golf Club, Bordon, Hants, a player driving from the first tee holed out his ball in the chimney of a house some 120 yards distant and some 40 yards out of bounds on the right. The owner and his wife were sitting in front of the fire when they heard a rattle in the chimney and were astonished to see a golf ball drop into the fire.

● A similar incident occurred in an inter-club match between Musselburgh and Lothianburn at Prestongrange in 1938 when a member of the former team hooked his ball at the 2nd hole and gave it up for lost. To his amazement a woman emerged from one of the houses adjacent to this part of the course and handed back the ball which she said had come down the chimney and landed on a pot which was on the fire.

● In July, 1955, J. Lowrie, starter at the Eden Course, St Andrews, witnessed a freak shot. A visitor drove from the first tee just as a north-bound train was passing. He sliced the shot and the ball disappeared through an open window of a passenger compartment. Almost immediately the ball emerged again, having been thrown back on to the fairway by a man in the compartment, who waved a greeting which presumably indicated that no one was hurt.

● At Coombe Wood Golf Club a player hit a ball towards the 16th green where it landed in the vertical exhaust of a tractor which was mowing the fairway.

The greenkeeper was somewhat surprised to find a temporary loss of power in the tractor. When sufficient compression had built up in the exhaust system, the ball was forced out with tremendous velocity, hit the roof of a house nearby, bounced off and landed some three feet from the pin on the green.

● When carrying out an inspection of the air conditioning system at St John's Hospital, Chelmsford, in 1993, a golf ball was found in the ventilator immediately above the operating theatre. It was probably the result of a hooked drive from the first tee at Chelmsford Golf Club, which is close by, but the ball can only have entered the duct on a rebound through a three-inch gap under a ventilator hood and then descended through a series of sharp bends to its final resting place.

● There have been many occasions when misdirected shots have finished in strange places after an unusual line of flight and bounce. At Ashford, Middlesex, John Miller, aged 69, hit his tee shot out of bounds at the 12th hole (237 yards). It struck a parked car, passed through a copse, hit more cars, jumped a canopy, flew through the clubhouse kitchen window, finishing in a cooking stock-pot, without once touching the ground. Mr Miller had previously done the hole in one on four occasions.

Balls Hit To and From Great Heights

● In 1798 two Edinburgh golfers undertook to drive a ball over the spire of St Giles' Cathedral, Edinburgh, for a wager. Mr Sceales, of Leith, and Mr Smellie, a printer, were each allowed six shots and succeeded in sending the balls well over the weathercock, a height of more than 160 feet from the ground.

● Some years later Donald McLean, an Edinburgh lawyer, won a substantial bet by driving a ball over the Melville Monument in St Andrew Square, Edinburgh – height, 154 feet.

● Tom Morris in 1860, at the famous bridge of Ballochmyle, stood in the quarry beneath and, from a stick elevated horizontally, attempted to send golf balls over the bridge. He could raise them only to the pathway, 400 feet high, which was in itself a great feat with the gutta ball.

● Captain Ernest Carter, on 28th September, 1922, drove a ball from the roadway at the 1st tee on Harlech Links against the wall of Harlech Castle. The embattlements are 200 feet over the level of the roadway, and the point where the ball struck the embattlements was 180 yards from the point where the ball was teed. Captain Carter, who was laid odds of £100 to £1, used a baffy.

● In 1896 Freddie Tait, then a subaltern in the Black Watch, drove a ball from the Rookery, the highest building on Edinburgh Castle, in a match against a brother officer to hole out in the fountain in Princes Street Gardens 350 feet below and about 300 yards distant.

● Prior to the 1977 Lancôme Tournament in Paris, Arnold Palmer hit three balls from the second stage of

the Eiffel Tower, over 300 feet above ground. The longest was measured at 403 yards. One ball was hooked and hit a bus but no serious damage was done as all traffic had been stopped for safety reasons.

● Long drives have been made from mountain peaks, across the gorge at Victoria Falls, from the Pyramids, high buildings in New York, and from many other similar places. As an illustration of such freakish *drives* a member of the New York Rangers' Hockey Team from the top of Mount Edith Cavell, 11,033 feet high, drove a ball which struck the Ghost Glacier 5000 feet below and bounced off the rocky ledge another 1000 feet – a total drop of 2000 yards. Later, in June, 1968, from Pikes Peak, Colorado (14,110 feet), Arthur Lynskey hit a ball which travelled 200 yards horizontally but 2 miles vertically.

Remarkable Shots

● Remarkable shots are as numerous as the grains of sand; around every 19th hole, legends are recalled of astounding shots. One shot is commemorated by a memorial tablet at the 17th hole at the Lytham and St Annes Club. It was made by Bobby Jones in the final round of the Open Championship in 1926. He was partnered by Al Watrous, another American player. They had been running neck and neck and at the end of the third round, Watrous was just leading Jones with 215 against 217. At the 16th Jones drew level then on the 17th he drove into a sandy lie in broken ground. Watrous reached the green with his second. Jones took a mashie-iron (the equivalent to a 4-iron today) and hit a magnificent shot to the green to get his 4. This remarkable recovery unnerved Watrous, who 3-putted, and Jones, getting another 4 at the last hole against 5, won his first Open Championship with 291 against Watrous' 293. The tablet is near the spot where Jones played his second shot.

● Arnold Palmer (USA), playing in the second round of the Australian Wills Masters tournament at Melbourne, in October, 1964, hooked his second shot at the 9th hole high into the fork of a gum tree. Climbing 20 feet up the tree, Palmer, with the head of his 1-iron reversed, played a hammer stroke and knocked the ball some 30 yards forward, followed by a brilliant chip to the green and a putt.

● In the foursome during the Ryder Cup at Moortown in 1929, Joe Turnesa hooked the American side's second shot at the last hole behind the marquee adjoining the clubhouse, Johnny Farrel then pitched the ball over the marquee on to the green only feet away from the pin and Turnesa holed out for a 4.

Miscellaneous Incidents and Strange Golfing Facts

● Gary Player of South Africa was honoured by his country by having his portrait on new postage stamps which were issued on 12th December, 1976. It was the first time a specific golfer had ever been depicted on any country's postage stamps. In 1981 the US Postal Service introduced stamps featuring Bobby

Jones and Babe Zaharias. They are the first golfers to be thus honoured by the United States.

● Gary Harris, aged 18, became the first player to make five consecutive appearances for England in the European Boys Team Championship at Vilamoura, Portugal, in 1994.

● In February, 1971, the first ever golf shots on the moon's surface were played by Captain Alan Shepard, commander of the Apollo 14 spacecraft. Captain Shepard hit two balls with an iron head attached to a makeshift shaft. With a one-handed swing he claimed he hit the first ball 200 yards aided by the reduced force of gravity on the moon. Subsequent findings put this distance in doubt. The second was a shank. Acknowledging the occasion the R&A sent Captain Shepard the following telegram: *Warmest congratulations to all of you on your great achievement and safe return. Please refer to Rules of Golf section on etiquette, paragraph 6, quote – before leaving a bunker a player should carefully fill up all holes made by him therein, unquote.* Shepard presented the club to the USGA Museum in 1974.

● Charles (Chick) Evans competed in every US Amateur Championship held between 1907 and 1962 by which time he was 72 years old. This amounted to 50 consecutive occasions discounting the six years of the two World Wars when the championship was not held.

● In winning the 1977 US Open at Southern Hills CC, Tulsa, Oklahoma, Hubert Green had to contend with a death threat. Coming off the 14th green in the final round, he was advised by USGA officials that a phone call had been received saying that he would be killed. Green decided that play should continue and happily he went on to win, unharmed.

● It was discovered at the 1977 USPGA Championship that the clubs with which Tom Watson had won the Open Championship and the US Masters earlier in the year were illegal, having grooves which exceeded the permitted specifications. The set he used in winning the 1975 Open Championship were then flown out to him and they too were found to be illegal. No retrospective action was taken.

● Mrs Fred Daly, wife of the former Open champion, saved the clubhouse of Balmoral GC, Belfast, from destruction when three men entered the professional's shop on 5th August, 1976, and left a bag containing a bomb outside the shop beside the clubhouse when refused money. Mrs Daly carried the bag over to a hedge some distance away where the bomb exploded 15 minutes later. The only damage was broken windows. On the same day several hours afterwards, Dungannon GC in Co. Tyrone suffered extensive damage to the clubhouse from terrorist bombs. Co. Down GC, proposed venue of the 1979 home international matches suffered bomb damage in May that year and through fear for the safety of team members the 1979 matches were cancelled.

● The Army Golfing Society and St Andrews on 21st April, 1934, played a match 200-a-side, the largest golf match ever played. Play was by foursomes. The Army won 58, St Andrews 31 and 11 were halved.

● Jamie Ortiz-Patino, owner of the Valderrama Golf Club at Sotogrande, Spain, paid a record £84,000 (increased to £92,400 with ten per cent buyers premium) for a late seventeenth- or early eighteenth-century rake iron offered at auction in Musselburgh in July, 1992. The iron, which had been kept in a garden shed, was bought to be exhibited in a museum being created in Valderrama.

● A Christie's golf auction during the week of the 1991 Open Championship created two world records. An American dealer bought a blacksmith-made iron club head dating from the seventeenth century for £44,000. It had been found 10 years before in a hedge near the North Berwick Golf Club in Scotland. Also, £165,000 was paid by a Japanese collector for an oil painting by Sir Francis Grant (1810–1878) of the 1823 Royal & Ancient captain, John Whyte-Melville, standing beside the Swilcan Burn at St Andrews. The same Japanese buyer successfully bid £35,200 for a rare gutty golf ball marking device from the workshops of Old Tom Morris in St Andrews, while an unused feathery golf ball by Allan Robertson fetched £11,000.

● In 1986 Alistair Risk and three colleagues on the 17th green at Brora, Sutherland, watched a cow giving birth to twin calves between the markers on the 18th tee, causing them to play their next tee shots from in front of the tee. Their application for a ruling from the R&A brought a Rules Committee reply that while technically a rule had been broken, their action was considered within the spirit of the game and there should be no penalty. The Secretary added that the Rules Committee hoped that mother and twins were doing well.

● In view of the increasing number of people crossing the road (known as Granny Clark's Wynd) which runs across the first and 18th fairways of the Old Course, St Andrews, as a right of way, the St Andrews Links committee decided in 1969 to control the flow by erecting traffic lights, with appropriate green for go, yellow for caution and red for stop. The lights are controlled from the starter's box on the first tee. Golfers on the first tee must wait until the lights turn to green before driving off and a notice has been erected at the Wynd warning pedestrians not to cross at yellow or stop.

● A traffic light for golfers was also installed in 1971 on one of Japan's most congested courses. After putting on the uphill 9th hole of the Fukuoka course in Southern Japan, players have to switch on a go-ahead signal for following golfers waiting to play their shots to the green.

● A 22-year-old professional at Brett Essex GC, Brentwood, David Moore, who was playing in the Mufulira Open in Zambia in 1976, was shot dead it is alleged by the man with whom he was staying for the duration of the tournament. It appeared his host then shot himself.

● Peggy Carrick and her daughter, Angela Uzielli, won the Mothers and Daughters Tournament at Royal Mid-Surrey in 1994 for the 21st time.

● Patricia Shepherd has won the ladies' club championship at Turriff GC Aberdeenshire 30 consecutive times from 1959 to 1988.

● Mrs Jackie Mercer won the South African Ladies' Championship in 1979, 31 years after her first victory in the event as Miss Jacqueline Smith.

● During the Royal & Ancient Golf Club of St Andrews' medal meeting on 25th September, 1907, a member of the Royal & Ancient drove a ball which struck the sharp point of a hatpin in the hat of a lady who was crossing the course. The ball was so firmly impaled that it remained in position. The lady was not hurt.

● John Cook, former English Amateur Champion, narrowly escaped death during an attempted coup against King Hassan of Morocco in July 1971. Cook had been playing in a tournament arranged by King Hassan, a keen golfer, and was at the King's birthday party in Rabat when rebels broke into the party demanding that the King give up his throne. Cook and many others present were taken hostage.

● When playing from the 9th tee at Lossiemouth golf course in June, 1971, Martin Robertson struck a Royal Navy jet aircraft which was coming in to land at the nearby airfield. The plane was not damaged.

● At a court in Inglewood, California, in 1978, Jim Brown was convicted of beating and choking an opponent during a dispute over where a ball should have been placed on the green.

● During the Northern Ireland troubles a home-made hand grenade was found in a bunker at Dungannon GC, Co. Tyrone, on Sunday, 12th September, 1976.

● Tiger Woods, 18, became both the youngest and the first black golfer to win the United States Amateur Championship at Sawgrass in 1994. He went on to win the title three years in a row and then won the first major championship he played as a professional, the 1997 Masters, by a record 12 strokes and with a record low aggregate of 270, 18 under par.

● To mark the centenary of the Jersey Golf Club in 1978, the Jersey Post Office issued a set of four special stamps featuring Jersey's most famous golfer, Harry Vardon. The background of the 13p stamp was a brief biography of Vardon's career reproduced from the *Golfer's Handbook*.

● Forty-one-year-old John Mosley went for a round of golf at Delaware Park GC, Buffalo, New York, in July, 1972. He stepped on to the first tee and was challenged over a green fee by an official guard. A scuffle developed, a shot was fired and Mosley, a bullet in his chest, died on the way to hospital. His wife was awarded $131,250 in an action against the City of Buffalo and the guard. The guard was sentenced to $7\frac{1}{2}$ years for second-degree manslaughter.

● When three competitors in a 1968 Pennsylvania pro-am event were about to drive from the 16th tee, two bandits (one with pistol) suddenly emerged from the bushes, struck one of the players and robbed them of wristwatches and $300.

● In the 1932 Walker Cup match at Brooklyn, Leonard Crawley succeeded in denting the cup. An

errant iron shot to the 18th green hit the cup, which was on display outside the clubhouse.

● In Johannesburg, South Africa, three golf officials appeared in court accused of violating a 75-year-old Sunday Observance Law by staging the final round of the South African PGA championship on Sunday, 28th February, 1971. The Championship should have been completed on the Saturday but heavy rain prevented any play.

● In the Open Championship of 1876, at St Andrews, Bob Martin and David Strath tied at 176. A protest was lodged against Strath alleging he played his approach to the 17th green and struck a spectator. The Royal & Ancient ordered the replay, but Strath refused to play off the tie until a decision had been given on the protest. No decision was given and Bob Martin was declared the Champion.

● At Rose Bay, New South Wales, on 11th July, 1931, D.J. Bayly MacArthur, on stepping into a bunker, began to sink. MacArthur, who weighed 14 stone, shouted for help. He was rescued when up to the armpits. He had stepped on a patch of quicksand, aggravated by excess of moisture.

● The late Bobby Cruickshank was the victim of his own jubilation in the 1934 US Open at Merion. In the 4th round while in with a chance of winning he half-topped his second shot at the 11th hole. The ball was heading for a pond in front of the green but instead of ending up in the water it hit a rock and bounced on to the green. In his delight Cruickshank threw his club into the air only to receive a resounding blow on the head as it returned to earth.

● A dog with an infallible nose for finding lost golf balls was, in 1971, given honorary membership of the Waihi GC, Hamilton, New Zealand. The dog, called Chico, was trained to search for lost balls, to be sold back to the members, the money being put into the club funds.

● By 1980 Waddy, an 11-year-old beagle belonging to Bob Inglis, the secretary of Brokenhurst Manor GC, had found over 35,000 golf balls.

● Herbert M. Hepworth, Headingley, Leeds, Lord Mayor of Leeds in 1906, scored one thousand holes in 2, a feat which took him 30 years to accomplish. It was celebrated by a dinner in 1931 at the Leeds club. The first 2 of all was scored on 12th June, 1901, at Cobble Hall Course, Leeds, and the 1,000th in 1931 at Alwoodley, Leeds. Hepworth died in November, 1942.

● Fiona MacDonald was the first female to play in the Oxford and Cambridge University match at Ganton in 1986.

● Mrs Sara Gibbon won the Farnham (Surrey) Club's Grandmother's competition 48 hours after her first grand-child was born.

● At Carnoustie in the first qualifying round for the 1952 Scottish Amateur Championship a competitor drove three balls in succession out of bounds at the 1st hole and thereupon withdrew.

● In 1993, the Clark family from Hagley GC, Worcs, set a record for the county's three major professional events. The Worcestershire Stroke Play Championship was won by Finlay Clark, the eldest son, who beat his father Iain and younger brother Cameron, who tied second. In the Match Play Iain beat his son Finlay by 2 and 1 in the final; Cameron won the play-off for third place. Then in the Worcestershire Annual Pro-Am it was Cameron's turn to win, with his brother Finlay coming second and father Iain third. To add to the achievements of the family, Cameron also won the Midland Professional Match Play Championship.

● During a Captain–Pro foursomes challenge match at Chelmsford in 1993, Club Professional Dennis Bailey, put the ball into a hole only once in all 18 holes – when he holed-in-one at the fourth.

Strange Local Rules

● The Duke of Windsor, who played on an extraordinary variety of the world's courses, once took advantage of a local rule at Jinja in Uganda and lifted his ball from a hippo's footprint without penalty.

● At the Glen Canyon course in Arizona a local rule provides that *If your ball lands within a club length of a rattlesnake you are allowed to move the ball.*

● Another local rule in Uganda read: *If a ball comes to rest in dangerous proximity to a crocodile, another ball may be dropped.*

● The 6th hole at Koolan Island GC, Western Australia, also serves as a local air strip and a local rule reads: *Aircraft and vehicular traffic have right of way at all times.*

● A local rule at the RAF Waddington GC reads: *When teeing off from the 2nd, right of way must be given to taxiing aircraft.*

Record Scoring

In the Major Championships nobody has shot lower than 63. There have been seven 63s in the Open, three 63s in the US Open, two 63s in The Masters and eight 63s in the USPGA Championship. The lowest first 36 holes is 130 by Nick Faldo in the 1992 Open at Muirfield and the lowest 72 hole total is 265 by David Toms in the 2001 USPGA Championship at the Atlanta Athletic Club.

The Open Championship

Most times champions

6 Harry Vardon, 1896–98–99–1903–11–14
5 James Braid, 1901–05–06–08–10; J.H. Taylor, 1894–95–1900–09–13; Peter Thomson, 1954–55–56–58–65; Tom Watson, 1975–77–80–82–83

Most times runner-up

7 Jack Nicklaus, 1964–67–68–72–76–77–79
6 J.H. Taylor, 1896–1904–05–06–07–14

Oldest winner

Old Tom Morris, 46 years 99 days, 1867
Roberto De Vicenzo, 44 years 93 days, 1967

Youngest winner

Young Tom Morris, 17 years 5 months 8 days, 1868
Willie Auchterlonie, 21 years 24 days, 1893
Severiano Ballesteros, 22 years 3 months 12 days, 1979

Youngest and oldest competitor

Young Tom Morris, 15 years, 4 months, 29 days, 1866
Gene Sarazen, 71 years 4 months 13 days, 1973

Widest margin of victory

13 strokes Old Tom Morris, 1862
12 strokes Young Tom Morris, 1870
8 strokes J.H. Taylor, 1900 and 1913; James Braid, 1908; Tiger Woods, 2000
6 strokes Harry Vardon, 1903; J.H. Taylor, 1909; Bobby Jones, 1927; Walter Hagen, 1929; Arnold Palmer, 1962; Johnny Miller, 1976

Lowest winning aggregates

267 Greg Norman, 66-68-69-64, Sandwich, 1993
268 Tom Watson, 68-70-65-65, Turnberry, 1977; Nick Price, 69-66-67-66, Turnberry, 1994
269 Tiger Woods, 67-66-67-69, St Andrews, 2000
270 Nick Faldo, 67-65-67-71, St Andrews, 1990

Lowest in relation to par

19 under Tiger Woods, St Andrews, 2000
18 under Nick Faldo, St Andrews, 1990

Lowest aggregate by runner-up

269 (68-70-65-66), Jack Nicklaus, Turnberry, 1977;
(69-63-70-67) Nick Faldo, Sandwich, 1993;
(68-66-68-67) Jesper Parnevik, Turnberry, 1994

Lowest aggregate by an amateur

281 (68-72-70-71), Iain Pyman, Sandwich, 1993;
(75-66-70-70), Tiger Woods, Royal Lytham, 1996

Lowest round

63 Mark Hayes, second round, Turnberry, 1977;
Isao Aoki, third round, Muirfield, 1980; Greg orman, second round, Turnberry, 1986; Paul Broadhurst, third round, St Andrews, 1990; Jodie Mudd, fourth round, Royal Birkdale, 1991; Nick Faldo, second round, Payne Stewart, fourth round, Sandwich, 1993

Lowest round by an amateur

66 Frank Stranahan, fourth round, Troon, 1950;
Tiger Woods, second round, Royal Lytham, 1996;
Justin Rose, second round, Royal Birkdale, 1998

Lowest first round

64 Craig Stadler, Royal Birkdale, 1983; Christy O'Connor Jr, Royal St George's, 1985; Rodger Davis, Muirfield, 1987; Steve Pate, Ray Floyd, Muirfield, 1992

Lowest second round

63 Mark Hayes, Turnberry, 1977; Greg Norman, Turnberry, 1986; Nick Faldo, Sandwich, 1993

Lowest third round

63 Isao Aoki, Muirfield, 1980; Paul Broadhurst, St Andrews, 1990

Lowest fourth round

63 Jodie Mudd, Royal Birkdale, 1991; Payne Stewart, Sandwich, 1993

Lowest first 36 holes

130 (66-64), Nick Faldo, Muirfield, 1992
132 (67-65), Henry Cotton, Sandwich, 1934; Nick Faldo (67-65) and Greg Norman (66-66), St Andrews, 1990; Nick Faldo (69-63), Sandwich, 1993

Lowest second 36 holes

130 (65-65), Tom Watson, Turnberry, 1977;
(64-66) Ian Baker-Finch, Royal Birkdale, 1991;
(66-64) Anders Forsbrand, Turnberry, 1994

Lowest first 54 holes

198 (67-67-64) Tom Lehman, Royal Lytham, 1996
199 (67-65-67), Nick Faldo, St Andrews, 1990;
(66-64-69) Nick Faldo, Muirfield, 1992

Lowest final 54 holes

199 (66-67-66) Nick Price, Turnberry, 1994
200 (70-65-65), Tom Watson, Turnberry, 1977
(63-70-67), Nick Faldo, Sandwich, 1993
(66-64-70), Fuzzy Zoeller, Turnberry, 1994
(66-70-64), Nick Faldo, Turnberry 1994

Lowest 9 holes

28 Denis Durnian, first 9, Royal Birkdale, 1983

Champions in three decades

Harry Vardon, 1986, 1903, 1911
J.H. Taylor, 1894, 1900, 1913
Gary Player, 1959, 1968, 1974

Biggest span between first and last victories

19 years, J.H. Taylor, 1894–1913
18 years, Harry Vardon, 1896–1914
15 years, Willie Park, 1860–75
15 years, Gary Player, 1959–74
14 years, Henry Cotton, 1934–48

Successive victories

4 Young Tom Morris, 1868–72 (no championship in 1871)
3 Jamie Anderson, 1877–79; Bob Ferguson, 1880–82, Peter Thomson, 1954–56
2 Old Tom Morris, 1861–62; J.H. Taylor, 1894–95; Harry Vardon, 1898–99; James Braid, 1905–06; Bobby Jones, 1926–27; Walter Hagen, 1928–29; Bobby Locke, 1949–50; Arnold Palmer, 1961–62; Lee Trevino, 1971–72; Tom Watson, 1982–83

Victories by amateurs

3 Bobby Jones, 1926–27–30
2 Harold Hilton, 1892–97
1 John Ball, 1890
Roger Wethered lost a play-off in 1921

Highest number of top five finishes

16 J.H. Taylor and Jack Nicklaus
15 Harry Vardon and James Braid

Players with four rounds under 70

Greg Norman (66-68-69-64), Sandwich, 1993; Ernie Els (68-69-69-68), Sandwich, 1993; Nick Price (69-66-67-66), Turnberry, 1994; Jesper Parnevik (68-66-68-67), Turnberry, 1994; Tiger Woods (67-66-67-69), St Andrews, 2000

Highest number of rounds under 70

34   Nick Faldo
33   Jack Nicklaus
27   Tom Watson
23   Greg Norman
21   Lee Trevino
20   Severiano Ballesteros and Nick Price

Outright leader after every round (since Championship became 72 holes in 1892)

James Braid, 1908; Ted Ray, 1912; Bobby Jones, 1927; Gene Sarazen, 1932; Henry Cotton, 1934; Tom Weiskopf, 1973

Record leads (since 1892)

After 18 holes: 4 strokes, Bobby Jones, 1927; Henry Cotton, 1934; Christy O'Connor Jr, 1985
After 36 holes: 9 strokes, Henry Cotton, 1934
After 54 holes: 10 strokes, Henry Cotton, 1934; 7 strokes, Tony Lema, 1964; 6 strokes, James Braid, 1908; Tom Lehman, 1996; Tiger Woods, 2000

Champions with each round lower than previous one

Jack White, 1904, Sandwich, 80-75-72-69
James Braid, 1906, Muirfield, 77-76-74-73
Ben Hogan, 1953, Carnoustie, 73-71-70-68
Gary Player, 1959, Muirfield, 75-71-70-68

Champion with four rounds the same

Densmore Shute, 1933, St Andrews, 73-73-73-73 (excluding the play-off)

Biggest variation between rounds of a champion

14 strokes, Henry Cotton, 1934, second round 65, fourth round 79
11 strokes, Jack White, 1904, first round 80, fourth round 69; Greg Norman, 1986, first round 74, second round 63, third round 74

Biggest variation between two rounds

20 strokes: R.G. French, 1938, second round 71, third round 91; Colin Montgomerie, 2002, second round 64, third round 84
18 strokes: A. Tingey Jr, 1923, first round 94, second 76
17 strokes, Jack Nicklaus, 1981, first round 83, second round 66; Ian Baker-Finch, 1986, first round 86, second round 69

Best comeback by champions

After 18 holes: Harry Vardon, 1896, 11 strokes behind the leader
After 36 holes: George Duncan, 1920, 13 strokes behind leader
After 54 holes: Paul Lawrie, 1999, 10 strokes behind the leader (won four-hole play-off)

Best comeback by non-champions

Of non-champions, Greg Norman, 1989, seven strokes behind the leader and lost in a play-off

Best finishing round by a champion

64 Greg Norman, Sandwich, 1993
65 Tom Watson, Turnberry, 1977; Severiano Ballesteros, Royal Lytham, 1988; Justin Leonard, Royal Troon, 1997

Worst finishing round by a champion since 1920

79 Henry Cotton, Sandwich, 1934
78 Reg Whitcombe, Sandwich, 1938
77 Walter Hagen, Hoylake, 1924

Best opening round by a champion

66 Peter Thomson, Royal Lytham, 1958; NickFaldo, Muirfield, 1992; Greg Norman, Sandwich, 1993
67 Henry Cotton, Sandwich, 1934; Tom Watson, Royal Birkdale, 1983; Severiano Ballesteros, Royal Lytham, 1988; Nick Faldo, St Andrews, 1990; John Daly, St Andrews, 1995, Tom Lehman, Royal Lytham, 1996, Tiger Woods, St Andrews, 2000

Worst opening round by a champion since 1919

80 George Duncan, Deal, 1920 (he also had a second round of 80)
77 Walter Hagen, Hoylake, 1924

Biggest recovery in 18 holes by a champion

George Duncan, Deal, 1920, was 13 strokes behind the leader, Abe Mitchell, after 36 holes and level after 54

Most consecutive appearances

47 Gary Player, 1955–2001

Championship since 1946 with the fewest rounds under 70

St Andrews, 1946; Hoylake, 1947; Portrush, 1951; Hoylake, 1956; Carnoustie, 1968. All had only two rounds under 70

Longest course

Carnoustie, 1999, 7361 yds

Largest entries

2460 in 2000, St Andrews

Courses most often used

St Andrews, 26; Prestwick, 24 (but not since 1925); Muirfield, 15; Sandwich, 12; Hoylake, 10; Royal Lytham and St Annes, 10; Royal Birkdale, 8; Royal Troon 7; Musselburgh, 6; Carnoustie, 6; Turnberry, 3; Deal, 2; Royal Portrush and Prince's, 1

Albatrosses (Double-Eagles)

Both Jeff Maggert (6th hole, 2nd round) and Greg Owen (11th hole, 3rd round) made albatrosses during the 2001 Open Championship at Royal Lytham and St Annes. No complete record of albatrosses in the history of the event is available but since 1980 there had been only three others – by Johnny Miller (Muirfield 5th hole) in 1980, Bill Rogers (Royal Birkdale 17th hole) 1983 and Manny Zerman (St Andrews) 2000.

US Open

Most times champion

4 Willie Anderson, 1901–03–04–05; Bobby Jones, 1923–26–29–30; Ben Hogan, 1948–50–51–53; Jack Nicklaus, 1962–67–72–80

Most times runner-up

4 Bobby Jones, 1922–24–25–28; Sam Snead, 1937–47–49–53; Arnold Palmer, 1962–63–66–67; Jack Nicklaus, 1960 (am)–68–71–82

Oldest winner

Hale Irwin, 45 years, 15 days, Medinah, 1990

Youngest winner

Johnny McDermott, 19 years, 10 months, 12 days, Chicago, 1911

Biggest winning margin

15 strokes Tiger Woods, Pebble Beach, 2000

Prize Money

Year	Total	First Prize £	Year	Total	First Prize £	Year	Total	First Prize £
1860	nil	nil	1959	5000	1,000	1985	530,000	65,000
1863	10	nil	1960	7000	1,250	1986	600,000	70,000
1864	16	6	1961	8500	1,400	1987	650,000	75,000
1876	20	20	1963	8500	1,500	1988	700,000	80,000
1889	22	8	1965	10,000	1,750	1989	750,000	80,000
1891	28.50	10	1966	15,000	2,100	1990	815,000	85,000
1892	110	(am)	1968	20,000	3,000	1991	900,000	90,000
1893	100	30	1969	30,000	4,250	1992	950,000	95,000
1910	125	50	1970	40,000	5,250	1993	1,000,000	100,000
1920	225	75	1971	45,000	5,500	1994	1,100,000	110,000
1927	275	100	1972	50,000	5,500	1995	1,250,000	125,000
1930	400	100	1975	75,000	7,500	1996	1,400,000	200,000
1931	500	100	1977	100,000	10,000	1997	1,586,300	250,000
1946	1000	150	1978	125,000	12,500	1998	1,774,150	300,000
1949	1700	300	1979	155,000	15,500	1999	2,029,950	350,000
1953	2450	500	1980	200,000	25,000	2000	2,722,150	500,000
1954	3500	750	1982	250,000	32,000	2001	3,229,748	600,000
1955	3750	1,000	1983	300,000	40,000	2002	3,880,998	700,000
1958	4850	1,000	1984	451,000	55,000			

Attendances

Year	Attendance	Year	Attendance	Year	Attendance	Year	Attendance
1962	37,098	1973	78,810	1984	193,126	1995	180,000
1963	24,585	1974	92,796	1985	141,619	1996	170,000
1964	35,954	1975	85,258	1986	134,261	1997	176,797
1965	32,927	1976	92,021	1987	139,189	1998	180,000
1966	40,182	1977	87,615	1988	191,334	1999	158,000
1967	29,880	1978	125,271	1989	160,639	2000	230,000
1968	51,819	1979	134,501	1990	207,000	2001	178,000
1969	46,001	1980	131,610	1991	192,154	2002	161,000
1970	82,593	1981	111,987	1992	150,100		
1971	70,076	1982	133,299	1993	140,100		
1972	84,746	1983	142,892	1994	128,000		

Lowest winning aggregate
272 Jack Nicklaus, Baltusrol, 1980; Lee Janzen, Baltusrol, 1993; Tiger Woods, Pebble Beach, 2000

Lowest in relation to par
12 under Tiger Woods, Pebble Beach, 2000

Lowest round
63 Johnny Miller, fourth round, Oakmont, 1973; Jack Nicklaus, first round, Baltusrol, 1980; Tom Weiskopf, first round, Baltusrol, 1980

Lowest 9 holes
29 Neal Lancaster, Shinnecock Hills, 1995, and Oakland Hills, 1996

Lowest first 36 holes
134 Jack Nicklaus, Baltusrol, 1980; Tze-chung Chen, Oakland Hills, 1985; Tiger Woods, Pebble Beach, 2000

Lowest final 36 holes
132 Larry Nelson, Oakmont, 1983

Most consecutive appearances
44 Jack Nicklaus 1957 to 2000

Successive victories
3 Willie Anderson, 1903–04–05

Players with four rounds under 70
Lee Trevino, 69-68-69-69, Oak Hill, 1968; Lee Janzen, 67-67-69-69, Baltusrol, 1993

Outright leader after every round
Walter Hagen, Midlothian, 1914; Jim Barnes, Col-umbia, 1921; Ben Hogan, Oakmont, 1953; Tony Jacklin, Hazeltine, 1970; Tiger Woods, Pebble Beach, 2000; Tiger Woods, Bethpage, 2002

Best opening round by a champion
63 Jack Nicklaus, Baltusrol, 1980

Worst opening round by a champion
91 Horace Rawlins, Newport, RI, 1895
Since World War II: 76 Ben Hogan, Oakland Hills, 1951; Jack Fleck, Olympic, 1955

US Masters

Most times champion
6 Jack Nicklaus, 1963–65–66–72–75–86
4 Arnold Palmer, 1958–60–62–64

Most times runner-up
4 Ben Hogan, 1942–46–54–55; Jack Nicklaus, 1964–71–77–81

Oldest winner
Jack Nicklaus, 46 years, 2 months, 23 days, 1986

Youngest winner
Tiger Woods, 21 years, 3 months, 15 days, 1997

Biggest winning margin
12 strokes Tiger Woods, 1997

Lowest winning aggregate
270 Tiger Woods, 1997

Lowest in relation to par
18 under Tiger Woods, Augusta, 1997

Lowest aggregate by an amateur
281 Charles Coe, 1961 (joint second)

Lowest round
63 Nick Price, 1986; Greg Norman, 1996

Lowest 9 holes
29 Mark Calcavecchia, 1992; David Toms, 1998

Lowest first 36 holes
131 Raymond Floyd, 1976

Lowest final 36 holes
131 Johnny Miller, 1975

Most appearances
49 Doug Ford 1952 to 2001

Successive victories
2 Jack Nicklaus, 1965–66; Nick Faldo, 1989–90; Tiger Woods, 2001–02

Players with four rounds under 70
None

Outright leader after every round
Craig Wood, 1941; Arnold Palmer, 1960; Jack Nicklaus, 1972; Raymond Floyd, 1976

Best opening round by a champion
65 Raymond Floyd, 1976

Worst opening round by a champion
75 Craig Stadler, 1982

Albatrosses
There have been three albatross twos in the Masters at Augusta National: by Gene Sarazen at the 15th, 1935; by Bruce Devlin at the eighth, 1967; and by Jeff Maggert at the 13th, 1994.

USPGA Championship

Most times champion
5 Walter Hagen, 1921–24–25–26–27; Jack Nicklaus 1963–71–73–75–80

Most times runner-up
4 Jack Nicklaus, 1964–65–74–83

Oldest winner
Julius Boros, 48 years 4 months 18 days, Pecan Valley, 1968

Youngest winner
Gene Sarazen, 20 years 5 months 22 days, Oakmont, 1922

Biggest winning margin
7 strokes Jack Nicklaus, Oak Hill, 1980

Lowest winning aggregate
265 (-15) David Toms, Atlanta Athletic Club, 2001
267 Steve Elkington and Colin Montgomerie, Riviera, 1995 – Montgomerie lost sudden death play-off

Lowest aggregate by runner-up
266 (-14) Phil Michelson, Atlanta Athletic Club, 2001

Lowest in relation to par
18 under Tiger Woods and Bob May, Valhalla, 2000 (May lost three-hole play-off)

Lowest round
63 Bruce Crampton, Firestone, 1975; Raymond Floyd, Southern Hills, 1982; Gary Player, Shoal Creek, 1984; Vijay Singh, Inverness, 1993; Michael Bradley and Brad Faxon, Riviera, 1995; José Maria Olazábal, Valhalla, 2000; Mark O'Meara, Atlanta Athletic Club, 2001

Most successive victories
4 Walter Hagen, 1924–25–26–27

Lowest 9 holes
28 Brad Faxon, Riviera, 1995

Lowest first 36 holes
131 Hal Sutton, Riviera, 1983; Vijay Singh, Inverness, 1993; Ernie Els and Mark O'Meara, Riviera, 1995; Shingo Katayama and David Toms, Atlanta Athletic Club, 2001

Lowest final 36 holes
131 Mark Calcavecchia, Atlanta Athletic Club, 2001
132 Miller Barber, Dayton, 1969; Steve Elkington and Colin Montgomerie, Riviera, 1995

Most appearances
37 Arnold Palmer; Jack Nicklaus

Outright leader after every round
Bobby Nichols, Columbus, 1964; Jack Nicklaus, PGA National, 1971; Raymond Floyd, Southern Hills, 1982; Hal Sutton, Riviera, 1983

Best opening round by a champion
63 Raymond Floyd, Southern Hills, 1982

Worst opening round by a champion
75 John Mahaffey, Oakmont, 1978

European PGA Tour

Lowest 72-hole aggregate
258 (14 under par) David Llewellyn (Wal), AGF Biarritz Open, 1988; (18 under) Ian Woosnam (Wal), Monte Carlo Open, 1990.
259 (25 under par) Mark McNulty (Zim), German Open at Frankfurt, 1987; (21 under par) Tiger Woods (USA), NEC Invitational, 2000
Note: In relation to par, the 27-under 261 of Jerry Anderson (Can) to win the 1984 Ebel European Masters–Swiss Open at Crans-sur-Sierre is the record. John Daly equalled this at the 2001 BMW International Open at Munchen Nord-Richenreid, but preferred lies were in operation in the third round.

Lowest 9 holes
27 (9 under par) José María Canizares (Esp), Swiss Open at Crans-sur-Sierre, 1978; (7 under) Robert Lee (Eng), Johnnie Walker Monte Carlo Open at Mont Agel, 1985; (6 under) Robert Lee, Portuguese Open at Estoril, 1987; (9 under) Joakim Haeggman (Swe), Alfred Dunhill Cup at St Andrews, 1997

Lowest 18 holes
60 (-11) Baldovino Dassu (Ita), Swiss Open at Crans-sur-Sierre, 1971; David Llewellyn (Wal), AGF Biarritz Open, 1988; (-9) Ian Woosnam (Wal), Torras Monte Carlo Open at Mont Agel, 1990; (-12) Jamie Spence, Canon European Masters at Crans-sur-Sierre, 1992; (-10) Paul Curry, Bell's Scottish Open at Gleneagles, 1992; (-9) both Darren Clarke and Johan Rystrom, Monte Carlo Open at Mont Agel, 1992; (-12) Bernhard Langer (Ger), Linde German Masters at Motzener See, 1997; (-12) Darren Clarke, Smurfit European Open at K Club, 1999; (-10) Tobias Dier TNT Open, Hilversum, 2002

Lowest 36 holes
124 (18 under par) Colin Montgomerie (Sco), Canon European Masters at Crans-sur-Sierre, 1996 (3rd and 4th rounds)

Lowest first 36 holes
125 Tiger Woods, NEC Invitational World
Championship, Firestone, Akron, Ohio, 2000

Lowest 54 holes
192 (24 under) Anders Forbrand (Swe), Ebel
European Masters Swiss Open at Crans-sur-Sierre,
1987; (18 under) Tiger Woods, NEC Invitational,
Firestone, Akron, Ohio, 2000

Largest winning margin
17 strokes Bernhard Langer, Cacharel Under-25s'
Championship in Nîmes, 1979.

Highest winning score
306 Peter Butler (Eng), Schweppes PGA Close
Championship at Royal Birkdale, 1963.

Youngest winner
Dale Hayes, 18 years 290 days, Spanish Open, 1971

Oldest winner
Des Smyth (Ire), 48 years 34 days, Madeira Island
Open, 2001

Most wins in one season
7 Norman von Nida (Aus), 1947

US Tour

Lowest 72-hole aggregate
256 (28 under par) Mark Calcavecchia (USA),
65-60-64-67, Phoenix Open, TPC of Scottsdale, 2001
Note: John Huston's 260 at the 1998 Hawaiian
Open was also 28 under

Lowest 18 holes
59 Sam Snead, 3rd round, Greenbrier Open (Sam
Snead Festival), White Sulphur Springs, West
Virginia, 1959; Al Geiberger, 2nd round, Danny
Thomas Memphis Classic, Colonial CC, 1977 (when
preferred lies were in operation); (-13) Chip Beck on
the 6,914-yards Sunrise GC course, Las Vegas, 3rd
round, Las Vegas Invitational, 1991 (finished third
but won a bonus prize of $500,000 and another
$500,000 for charities; (-13) David Duval on
6,940-yd PGA West Arnold Palmer course, CA,
final round, Bob Hope Chrysler Classic, 1999 (won
tournament with last hole eagle)

Lowest 9 holes
27 Mike Souchak, Texas Open, 1955; Andy North,
BC Open, 1975

Lowest 36 holes
124 (18 under) Mark Calcavecchia (USA), Phoenix
Open, 2001 (2nd and 3rd rounds)

Lowest first 36 holes
125 (17 under) Mark Calcavecchia (USA), Phoenix
Open, 2001; (15 under) Tiger Woods (USA), NEC
Invitational World Championship,
Firestone, Akron, Ohio, 2000

Lowest 54 holes
189 Chandler Harper, Texas Open (last three
rounds), 1954; Mark Calcavecchia (USA), Phoenix
Open (first three rounds), 2001

Largest winning margin
16 strokes J. Douglas Edgar, Canadian Open
Championship, 1919; Bobby Locke, Chicago Victory
National Championship, 1948

Youngest winner
Johnny McDermott, 19 years 10 months, US Open,
1911

Oldest winner
Sam Snead, 52 years 10 months, Greater Greensboro
Open, 1965

Most wins in one season
18 Byron Nelson, 1945

National opens – excluding Europe and USA

Lowest 72-hole aggregate
255 Peter Tupling, Nigerian Open, Lagos, 1981.

Lowest 36-hole aggregate
124 (18 under par) Sandy Lyle, Nigerian Open,
Ikoyi GC, Lagos, 1978 (his first year as a
professional)

Lowest 18 holes
59 Gary Player, second round, Brazilian Open,
Gavea GC (6,185 yards), Rio de Janeiro, 1974.

Professional events – excluding Europe and USA

Lowest 72-hole aggregate
260 Bob Charles, Spalding Masters at Tauranga,
New Zealand, 1969; Jason Bohn (USA), Bayer
Classic, Huron Oaks, Canada, 2001.

Lowest 18-hole aggregate
58 (13 under) Jason Bohn (USA), Bayer Classic,
Huron Oaks, Canada, 2001.

Lowest 9-hole aggregate
27 Bill Brask (USA) at Tauranga in the New
Zealand PGA in 1976.

Miscellaneous British

72-hole aggregate
Andrew Brooks recorded a 72-hole aggregate of 259
in winning the Skol (Scotland) tournament at
Williamwood in 1974.

Lowest rounds

Playing on the ladies' course (4,020 yards) at Sunningdale on 26th September, 1961, Arthur Lees, the professional there, went round in 52, 10 under par. He went out in 26 (2, 3, 3, 4, 3, 3, 3, 3, 2) and came back in 26 (2, 3, 3, 3, 2, 3, 4, 3, 3).

On 1st January, 1936, A.E. Smith, Woolacombe Bay professional, recorded a score of 55 in a game there with a club member. The course measured 4,248 yards. Smith went out in 29 and came back in 26 finishing with a hole-in-one at the 18th.

Other low scores recorded in Britain are by C.C. Aylmer, an English International who went round Ranelagh in 56; George Duncan, Axenfels in 56; Harry Bannerman, Banchory in 56 in 1971; Ian Connelly, Welwyn Garden City in 56 in 1972; James Braid, Hedderwick near Dunbar in 57; H. Hardman, Wirral in 58; Norman Quigley, Windermere in 58 in 1937; Robert Webster, Eaglescliffe in 58, in 1970. Harry Weetman scored 58 in a round at the 6171 yards Croham Hurst on 30th January, 1956.

D. Sewell had a round of 60 in an Alliance Meeting at Ferndown, Bournemouth, a full-size course. He scored 30 for each half and had a total of 26 putts. In September 1986, Jeffrey Burn, handicap 1, of Shrewsbury GC, scored 60 in a club competition, made up of 8 birdies, an eagle and 9 pars. He was 30 out and 30 home and no. 5 on his card. Andrew Sherborne, as a 20-year-old amateur, went round Cirencester in 60 strokes. Dennis Gray completed a round at Broome Manor, Swindon (6906 yards, SSS 73) in the summer of 1976 in 60 (28 out, 32 in).

Playing over Aberdour on 13th June, 1936, Hector Thomson, British Amateur champion, 1936, and Jack McLean, former Scottish Amateur champion, each did 61 in the second round of an exhibition. McLean in his first round had a 63, which gave him an aggregate 124 for 36 holes.

Steve Tredinnick in a friendly match against business tycoon Joe Hyman scored a 61 over West Sussex (6211 yards) in 1970. It included a hole-in-one at the 12th (198 yards) and a 2 at the 17th (445 yards).

Another round of 61 on a full-size course was achieved by 18-year-old Michael Jones on his home course, Worthing GC (6274 yards), in the first round of the President's Cup in May, 1974.

In the Second City Pro-Am tournament in 1970, at Handsworth, Simon Fogarty did the second 9 holes in 27 against the par of 36.

Miscellaneous USA

Lowest rounds

The lowest known scores recorded for 18 holes in America are 55 by E.F. Staugaard in 1935 over the 6419 yards Montebello Park, California, and 55 by Homero Blancas in 1962 over the 5002 yards Premier course in Longview, Texas. Staugaard in his round had 2 eagles, 13 birdies and 3 pars.

Equally outstanding is a round of 58 (13 under par) achieved by a 13-year-old boy, Douglas Beecher, on 6th July, 1976, at Pitman CC, New Jersey. The course measured 6180 yards from the back tees, and the middle tees, off which Douglas played, were estimated by the club professional to reduce the yardage by under 180 yards.

In 1941 at a 6100 yards course in Portsmouth, Virginia, Chandler Harper scored 58.

Jack Nicklaus in an exhibition match at Breakers Club, Palm Beach, California, in 1973 scored 59 over the 6200-yard course.

The lowest 9-hole score in America is 25, held jointly by Bill Burke over the second half of the 6384 yards Normandie CC, St Louis in May, 1970 at the age of 29; by Daniel Cavin, who had seven 3s and two 2s on the par 36 Bill Brewer Course, Texas, in September, 1959; and by Douglas Beecher over the second half of Pitman CC, New Jersey, on 6th July, 1976, at the amazingly young age of 13. The back 9 holes of the Pitman course measured 3150 yards (par 35) from the back tees, but even though Douglas played off the middle tees, the yardage was still over 3000 yards for the 9 holes. He scored 8 birdies and 1 eagle.

Horton Smith scored 119 for two consecutive rounds in winning the Catalina Open in California in December, 1928. The course, however, measured only 4700 yards.

Miscellaneous – excluding GB and USA

Tony Jacklin won the 1973 Los Lagartos Open with an aggregate of 261, 27 under par.

Henry Cotton in 1950 had a round of 56 at Monte Carlo (29 out, 27 in).

In a Pro-Am tournament prior to the 1973 Nigerian Open, British professional David Jagger went round in 59.

Max Banbury recorded a 9-hole score of 26 at Woodstock, Ontario, playing in a competition in 1952.

Women

The lowest score recorded on a full-size course by a woman is 59 by Sweden's Annika Sörenstam on the 6459 yards, par 72 Moon Valley course in Phoenix, Arizona. It broke by two the previous record of 61 by South Korean Se Ri Pak. Sörenstam had begun the tournament with a 65 and by adding rounds of 69 and 68 she equalled the LPGA record of 261 set by Pak (71-61-63-66) at Highland Meadows in Ohio in 1998. Sörenstam's score represents 27 under par, Pak's 23 under.

The lowest 9-hole score on the US Ladies' PGA circuit is 28, first achieved by Mary Beth Zimmerman in the 1984 Rail Charity Classic and since equalled by Pat Bradley, Muffin Spencer-Devlin,

Peggy Kirsch, Renee Heiken, Anika Sörenstam and Danielle Ammaccapane.

The Lowest 36-hole score is the 124 (20 under par) by Sörenstam at Moon Valley and the lowest 54-hole score 193 (23 under) by Karrie Webb at Walnut Hills, Michigan, in the 2000 Oldsmobile Classic and equalled by Sörenstam at Moon Valley.

Patty Berg holds the record for the most number of women's majors with 15; Kathy Whitworth achieved a record number of tournament wins with 88; Mickey Wright's 13 wins in 1963 was the most in one season and the youngest and oldest winners of LPGA events were Marlene Hagge, 18 years and 14 days when she won the 1952 Sarasota Open and JoAnne Carner, 46 years 5 months 11 days when she won the 1985 Safeco Classic.

The lowest round on the European LPGA is 62 (11 under par) by Trish Johnson in the 1996 French Open. A 62 was also achieved by New Zealand's Janice Arnold at Coventry in 1990 during a Women's Professional Golfers' Association tournament.

The lowest 9-hole score on the European LPGA circuit is 29 by Kitrina Douglas, Regine Lautens, Laura Davies, Anne Jones and Trish Johnson.

In the Women's World Team Championship in Mexico in 1966, Mrs Belle Robertson, playing for the British team, was the only player to break 70. She scored 69 in the third round.

At Westgate-on-Sea GC (measuring 5002 yards), Wanda Morgan scored 60 in an open tournament in 1929.

Since scores cannot properly be taken in matchplay no stroke records can be made in matchplay events. Nevertheless we record here two outstanding examples of low scoring in the finals of national championships. Mrs Catherine Lacoste de Prado is credited with a score of 62 in the first round of the 36-hole final of the 1972 French Ladies' Open Championship at Morfontaine. She went out in 29 and came back in 33 on a course measuring 5933 yards. In the final of the English Ladies' Championship at Woodhall Spa in 1954, Frances Stephens (later Mrs Smith) did the first nine holes against Elizabeth Price (later Mrs Fisher) in 30. It included a hole-in-one at the 5th. The nine holes measured 3280 yards.

Amateurs

National championships

The following examples of low scoring cannot be regarded as genuine stroke play records since they took place in match play. Nevertheless they are recorded here as being worthy of note.

Michael Bonallack in beating David Kelley in the final of the English championship in 1968 at Ganton did the first 18 holes in 61 with only one putt under two feet conceded. He was out in 32 and home in 29. The par of the course was 71.

Charles McFarlane, playing in the fourth round of the Amateur Championship at Sandwich in 1914 against Charles Evans did the first nine holes in 31, winning by 6 and 5.

This score of 31 at Sandwich was equalled on several occasions in later years there. Then, in 1948, Richard Chapman of America went out in 29 in the fourth round eventually beating Hamilton McInally, Scottish Champion in 1937, 1939 and 1947, by 9 and 7.

In the fourth round of the Amateur Championship at Hoylake in 1953, Harvie Ward, the holder, did the first nine holes against Frank Stranahan in 32. The total yardage for the holes was 3474 yards and included one hole of 527 yards and five holes over 400 yards. Ward won by one hole.

Francis Ouimet in the first round of the American Amateur Championship in 1932 against George Voigt did the first nine holes in 30. Ouimet won by 6 and 5.

Open competitions

The 1970 South African Dunlop Masters Tournament was won by an amateur, John Fourie, with a score of 266, 14 under par. He led from start to finish with rounds of 65, 68, 65, 68, finally winning by six shots from Gary Player.

Jim Ferrier, Manly, won the New South Wales championship at Sydney in 1935 with 266. His rounds were: 67, 65, 70, 64, giving an aggregate 16 strokes better than that of the runner-up. At the time he did this amazing score Ferrier was 20 years old and an amateur. Aaron Baddeley became the first amateur to win the Australian Open since Bruce Devlin in 1960 when he took the title at Royal Sydney in 1999. After turning pro he successfully defended the title the following year at Kingston Heath.

Holes below par

Most holes below par

E.F. Staugaard in a round of 55 over the 6419 yards Montbello Park, California, in 1935, had two eagles, 13 birdies and three pars.

American Jim Clouette scored 14 birdies in a round at Longhills GC, Arkansas, in 1974. The course measured 6257 yards.

Jimmy Martin in his round of 63 in the Swallow-Penfold at Stoneham in 1961 had one eagle and 11 birdies.

In the Ricarton Rose Bowl at Hamilton, Scotland, in August, 1981, Wilma Aitken, a women's amateur internationalist, had 11 birdies in a round of 64, including nine consecutive birdies from the 3rd to the 11th.

Mrs Donna Young scored nine birdies and one eagle in one round in the 1975 Colgate European Women's Open.

Jason Bohn had two eagles and 10 birdies in his closing 58 at the 2001 Bayer Classic on the Canadian Tour at the par 71 Huron Oaks.

Consecutive holes below par

Lionel Platts had ten consecutive birdies from the 8th to 17th holes at Blairgowrie GC during a practice round for the 1973 Sumrie Better-Ball tournament.

Roberto De Vicenzo in the Argentine Centre of the Republic Championship in April, 1974 at the Cordoba GC, Villa Allende, broke par at each of the first nine holes. (By starting his round at the 10th hole they were in fact the second nine holes played by Vicenzo.) He had one eagle (at the 7th hole) and eight birdies. The par for the 3,602 yards half was 37, completed by Vicenzo in 27.

Nine consecutive holes under par have been recorded by Claude Harmon in a friendly match over Winged Foot GC, Mamaroneck, NY, in 1931; by Les Hardie at Eastern GC, Melbourne, in April, 1934; by Jimmy Smith at McCabe GC, Nashville, Tenn, in 1969; by 13-year-old Douglas Beecher in 1976, at Pitman CC, New Jersey; by Rick Sigda at Greenfield CC, Mass, in 1979; and by Ian Jelley at Brookman Park in 1994.

T.W. Egan in winning the East of Ireland Championship in 1962 at Baltray had eight consecutive birdies (2nd to 9th) in the third round.

On the United States PGA tour, eight consecutive holes below par have been achieved by three players – Bob Goalby in the 1961 St Petersburg Open, Fuzzy Zoeller in the 1976 Quad Cities Open and Dewey Arnette in the 1987 Buick Open.

Fred Couples set a PGA European Tour record with 12 birdies in a round of 61 during the 1991 Scandinavian Masters on the 72-par Drottningholm course. This has since been equalled by Ernie Els (1994 Dubai Desert Classic) and by Russell Claydon and Fredrik Lindgren (1995 German Masters). Ian Woosnam, Tony Johnstone, Severiano Ballesteros, John Bickerton, Mark O'Meara and Raymond Russell share another record with eight successive birdies.

The United States Ladies' PGA record is seven consecutive holes below par achieved by Carol Mann in the Borden Classic at Columbus, Ohio in 1975.

Miss Wilma Aitken recorded nine successive birdies (from the 3rd to the 11th) in the 1981 Ricarton Rose Bowl.

This has since been equalled by Ernie Els (1994 Dubai Desert Classic), Russell Claydon and Fredrik Lindgren (1995 German Masters) and Darreb Clarke (1999 Smurfit European Open). Ian Woosnam, Tony Johnstone, Severiano Ballesteros, John Bickerton, Mark O'Meara, Raymond Russell, Darren Clarke and Marcello Santi and Marten Olander share another record with eight successive birdies.

Low scoring rarities

At Standerton GC, South Africa, in May 1937, F.F. Bennett, playing for Standerton against Witwatersrand University, did the 2nd hole, 110 yards, in three

2s and a 1. Standerton is a 9-hole course, and in the match Bennett had to play four rounds.

In 1957 a fourball comprising H.J. Marr, E. Stevenson, C. Bennett and W.S. May completed the 2nd hole (160 yards) in the grand total of six strokes. Marr and Stevenson both holed in one while Bennett and May both made 2.

The old Meadow Brook Club of Long Island, USA, had five par 3 holes and George Low in a round there in the 1950s scored two at each of them.

In a friendly match on a course near Chicago in 1971, assistant professional Tom Doty (23 years) had a remarkable low run over four consecutive holes: 4th (500 yards) 2; 5th (360 yards, dogleg) 1; 6th (175 yards) 1; 7th (375 yards) 2.

R.W. Bishop, playing in the Oxley Park, July medal competition in 1966, scored three consecutive 2s. They occurred at the 12th, 13th and 14th holes which measured 151, 500 and 136 yards respectively.

In the 1959 PGA Close Championship at Ashburnham, Bob Boobyer scored five 2s in one of the rounds.

American Art Wall scored three consecutive 2s in the first round of the US Masters in 1974. They were at the 4th, 5th and 6th holes, the par of which was 3, 4 and 3.

Nine consecutive 3s have been recorded by R.H. Corbett in 1916 in the semi-final of the Tangye Cup; by Dr James Stothers of Ralston GC over the 2056 yards 9-hole course at Carradale, Argyll, during the summer of 1971; by Irish internationalist Brian Kissock in the Homebright Open at Carnalea GC, Bangor, in June, 1975; and by American club professional Ben Toski.

The most consecutive 3s in a British PGA event is seven by Eric Brown in the Dunlop at Gleneagles (Queen's Course) in 1960.

Hubert Green scored eight consecutive 3s in a round in the 1980 US Open.

The greatest number of 3s in one round in a British PGA event is 11 by Brian Barnes in the 1977 Skol Lager tournament at Gleneagles.

Fewest putts

The lowest known number of putts in one round is 14, achieved by Colin Collen-Smith in a round at Betchworth Park, Dorking, in June, 1947. He single-putted 14 greens and chipped into the hole on four occasions.

Professional Richard Stanwood in a round at Riverside GC, Pocatello, Idaho on 17th May, 1976 took 15 putts, chipping into the hole on five occasions.

Several instances of 16 putts in one round have been recorded in friendly games.

For 9 holes, the fewest putts is five by Ron Stutesman for the first 9 holes at Orchard Hills G&CC, Washington, USA in 1978.

Walter Hagen in nine consecutive holes on one occasion took only seven putts. He holed long putts on seven greens and chips at the other two holes.

In competitive stroke rounds in Britain and Ireland, the lowest known number of putts in one round is 18,

in a medal round at Portpatrick Dunskey GC, Wilmslow GC professional Fred Taggart is reported to have taken 20 putts in one round of the 1934 Open Championship. Padraigh Hogan (Elm Park), when competing in the Junior Scratch Cup at Carlow in 1976, took only 20 putts in a round of 67.

The fewest putts in a British PGA event is believed to be 22 by Bill Large in a qualifying round over Moor Park High Course for the 1972 Benson and Hedges Match Play.

Overseas, outside the United States of America, the fewest putts is 19 achieved by Robert Wynn (GB) in a round in the 1973 Nigerian Open and by Mary Bohen (US) in the final round of the 1977 South Australian Open at Adelaide.

The USPGA record for fewest putts in one round is 18, achieved by Andy North (1990); Kenny Knox (1989); Mike McGee (1987) and Sam Trehan (1979). For 9 holes the record is eight putts by Kenny Knox (1989), Jim Colbert (1987) and Sam Trehan (1979).

The fewest putts recorded for a 72-hole US PGA Tour event is 93 by Kenny Knox in the 1989 Heritage Classic at Harbour Town Golf Links.

The fewest putts recorded by a woman is 17, by Joan Joyce in the Lady Michelob tournament, Georgia, in May, 1982.

Amazing Golfing Double

Dr Martin Pucci and Trevor Ironside will never forget one round at the Macdonald Club in Ellon last year. Playing in an open competition the two golfers, with Jamie Cowthorne making up the three-ball, reached the tee at the 169 yards short 11th. Dr Pucci, with the honour, hit a 5-iron, Mr Ironside a 6-iron at the hole where only the top of the flag is visible. Both hit good shots but when they reached the green they could spot only one ball and that was Mr Cowthorne's. Then they realised that something amazing might have happened.

When they reached the putting surface they discovered that both Dr Pucci's and Mr Ironside's balls were wedged into the hole. Both had made aces. It was Dr Pucci's sixth and Mr Ironside's second.

They were not the first golfers to achieve this. In 1919 at Forest Hills, New Jersey, George Stewart and Fred Spellmeyer achieved the feat and in 1925 Miss G. Clutterbuck and Mrs H. M. Robinson did the same at the 15th hole at the St Augustine club in Ramsgate.

Last year brothers Eric and John Wilkinson also both aced the 148 yards eighth at the Ravensworth Golf Club in Wrekenton while playing their usual weekly game. Similar incidents have occurred – in Denmark when Steffan Jacobsen and Peter Forsbeg holed in one at the 15th hole in a club match at Himmerland, and in Australia where Dr B. Rankine holed in one from the men's tee at the short second at the Osmond club in South Australia only to be followed into the hole by his partner, his wife, playing from the ladies' tee.

PART XI

Guide to Golfing Services and Places to Stay in the British Isles and Ireland

Buyer's Guide to Good Golfing and Golf Course Maintenance

This compact but informative guide to manufacturers and organisations offering services to golf clubs and individual golfers includes a wide number of categories, from services to personal accessories and golfing equipment to golf course maintenance.

ACADEMIC QUALIFICATIONS
AGRONOMY
ARCHITECTS & CONSULTANTS
AWARDS, PRIZES & TROPHIES
BAG/MEMBERSHIP TAGS
BAGS/GOLF ACCESSORIES
BALL COLLECTORS
BOOKSELLERS & PUBLISHERS
CARTS, TROLLEYS & BUGGIES
CLOTHING/GOLFWEAR
COMPUTER SOFTWARE/SYSTEMS
CORPORATE GIFTS & EVENTS
COURSE CONSTRUCTION & UPGADING
COURSE MEASUREMENT
DISTRIBUTORS & WHOLESALERS
DRIVING RANGE & PRACTICE EQUIPMENT
EDUCATION
ELECTRIC GOLF CARS
ELECTRONIC POINT OF SALE
FINANCE
FIXTURE BOOKS
FLOODLIGHTING & FENCING
GIFTS & NOVELTIES
GOLF BALL MANUFACTURERS/SUPPLIERS
GOLF CLUB MANUFACTURERS/SUPPLIERS
GOLF COURSE DESIGN CONSULTANTS
GOLF COURSE DISTANCE GUIDES
GOLF COURSE MAINTENANCE & UPGRADING
GOLF DEVELOPMENT/MANAGEMENT
GOLF HOLIDAYS
GOLF RANGE DESIGN
GOLFING AIDS/PRACTICE EQUIPMENT
GREENKEEPING & DRIVING RANGE VEHICLES
GREENKEEPING INFORMATION SERVICE

GRIPS & SHAFTS
GROUP PURCHASING
INSURANCE
INTERNET TEE-TIME BOOKING
IRRIGATION CONSULTANTS/DESIGN & INSTALLATION
JEWELLERY
MAIL ORDER
PATHWAYS
PERSONAL EQUIPMENT & ACCESSORIES
PERSONALISED PRODUCTS
PICTURES & PRINTS
PLAY AND STAY
PORTUGAL
PRACTICE NETTING/CAGES
PRINTING
PROFESSIONAL ASSOCIATIONS (see pages 633-635)
PUTTER & CHIPPERS MANUFACTURERS/SUPPLIERS
RANGE BALL MANUFACTURERS/SUPPLIERS
RECRUITMENT CONSULTANTS
REMOTE CONTROLLED TROLLEYS
RIDE-ON BUGGIES
SCORECARDS & PLANNERS
SIMULATORS/ANALYSERS
SYNTHETIC SURFACES
TEE SIGNS
THERMAL WEAR
TRAINING & TEACHING AIDS
TROPHIES
TUITION
WATER RESOURCES/RESERVOIR DESIGN
WATER STORAGE/TANKS
WEATHERWEAR
WINTER ALL-WEATHER TEE MATS

ACADEMIC QUALIFICATIONS

Bournemouth University

School of Service Industries,
Fern Barrow,
Poole,
Dorset BH12 5BB.
Tel (01202) 595146 Fax (01202) 515707
E-mail: mcustard@bournemouth.ac.uk
*Website: www.bournemouth.ac.uk/
service_industries*

The university has developed a unique degree for those interested in a career in golf and/or sports management. With the support of local golf clubs, the BSc(Hons) in Sports Management (golf) is a 4-year sandwich degree which provides graduates with the technical expertise as well as the managerial skills necessary to succeed in this dynamic industry. Contact: Programme Administrator, School of Service Industries.

AGRONOMY

British Rootzone & Topdressing Manufacturers Association

Federation House,
NAC,
Stoneleigh Park,
Warwickshire CV8 2RF.
Tel 024 7641 4999 Fax 024 7641 4990
E-mail: brtma@sportslife.org.uk
Website: www.brtma.com

The Association is a collaboration of experience and expertise in the manufacture of rootzone materials to offer architects, constructors and agronomists a recognised focal point for the industry.

PSD Agronomy Ltd

42 Garstang
Road,
Preston,
Lancashire PR1 1NA.
Tel (01772) 884450 Fax (01772) 884445
E-mail: psdgb@aol.com
Website: www.psdagronomy.com

A specialist team of golf course agronomists working throughout the UK and Europe. Whether building a new course, extending an existing one or just making the best of what you have - we have the technical expertise to help.

STRI - The Sports Turf Research Institute

St Ives Estate, Bingley,
West Yorkshire BD16 1AU.
Tel (01274) 565131 Fax (01274) 561891
E-mail: info@stri.co.uk
Website: www.stri.co.uk

Independent specialists offering you help and advice for the design, construction, management and maintenance, irrigation or renovation of your golf course. Comprehensive in-house support services for ecology, testing, turf pathology and research.

ARCHITECTS & CONSULTANTS

David Griffith

20 Clwyd Avenue, Dyserth,
Denbighshire LL18 6HN.
Tel (01745) 570659 Fax (01745) 571382
Mobile: 07778 494123
E-mail: david@griffithgolf.co.uk

Golf course architect. Years of experience in a variety of golf projects ensures that no stone is left unturned in fulfilling the potential of a site. A satisfaction guarantee is given to all projects.

David Williams Golf Design

187 Llanelian Road, Old Colwyn,
Colwyn Bay, North Wales LL29 8UW.
Tel (01492) 512070 Fax (01492) 512077
E-mail: david@williamsgolf.co.uk

Golf course architects and project managers. Fully integrated service *from conception through construction to completion*. Over 20 new courses built in Britain within last ten years. Alterations, improvements and upgrades undertaken through the country. Member of the European Institute of Golf Course Architects (EIGCA).

European Institute of Golf Course Architects - EIGCA

Chiddingfold Golf Club, Petworth Road,
Chiddingfold, Surrey GU8 4SL.
Tel/Fax +44 (0) 1428 681528
E-mail: info@eigca.org
Website: www.eigca.org

The EIGCA represents the vast majority of qualified and experienced golf course architects throughout Europe. Our goals include enhancing the professional status of the profession, developing the role of education and increasing the opportunities for its members to practice in countries throughout

the world. EIGCA also provides educational courses to train future golf course architects and is authoritative voice on all related matters, being recognised by the R&A Golf Club of St Andrews. Contact: Julia Green, Executive Officer.

Gaunt & Marnoch
- Golf Course Architects
Head Office: Hilltop, Lakeside,
Bakewell, Derbyshire DE45 1GN.
Tel+44 (0) 1629 815453
Fax+44 (0) 1629 815170
E-mail: info@gauntandmarnoch.com
Website: www.gauntandmarnoch.com

Gaunt & Marnoch provides a comprehensive, cost-conscious and environmentally sympathetic golf course design service. An international and award-winning company who are flexible and offer a top quality service from feasibility through planning to construction supervision and opening the course for play. We are committed to better golf through good design. Ring for brochure. *(See advertisement page 18 for further details.)*

Grassform Ltd
- Golf Courses, Sports Grounds and Land Drainage Contractors
Dunsteads Farm, Trueloves Lane,
Ingatestone, Essex CM4 0NJ.
Tel (01277) 355500 Fax (01277) 355504
E-mail: sales@grassform.co.uk
Website: www.grassform.co.uk

Grassform Limited undertakes all types of golf course projects. From new build to re-construction of tees, greens and bunkers. We also install land drainage systems, sand banding, lakes, water features, footpaths, buggy paths and driving ranges. For further information please contact Mark Dunning.

Hawtree Ltd - Golf Course Architects & Consultants
5 Oxford Street, Woodstock,
Oxon OX20 1TQ.
Tel (01993) 811976 Fax (01993) 812448
E-mail: mail@hawtree.co.uk
Website: www.hawtree.co.uk

Founded in 1912, Hawtree Limited is the longest continuous golf course practice, having designed and renovated over 800 golf courses worldwide. Just some of these include the renowned Birkdale, Portmarnock, Lahinch and Vilamoura golf courses.

J D Edgar
- Golf Course Architect
Wheathampstead Pay & Play Golf Course,
Harpenden Road,
St Albans, Hertfordshire AL4 8EZ.
Tel/Fax (01582) 833941

Doug Edgar the golf professional and golf course architect is a member of the PGA and PGAA. He designs and builds courses and can offer you a complete design consultancy service.

Philip Sparks
Professional Golf Designs
Peak House,
Hawksdown,
Walmer, Deal, Kent CT12 5BE.
Tel (01304) 374119 Fax (01843) 853090

'Creating future links with the Past'. Specialising in golf course remodelling and renovation. Toro student architect of the year 2000. First golf professional in the world to gain an EIGCA diploma in golf course architecture.

Ritson Golf Design
2nd Floor Office,
29 William Street,
Rugby,
Warwickshire CV21 3HA.
Tel/Fax (01788) 573866
E-mail: steve.ritson@telinco.co.uk
Website: www.golf-course-architect.com

Golf course and landscape architects, undertaking a wide range of golf design projects both in the UK and abroad, from championship to par 3 courses, remodelling existing courses and the creation of exciting driving ranges.

Robin Hiseman
Golf Course Design
Berrymeadow Cottage,
4 West Cairnbeg Cottages,
Laurencekirk,
Aberdeenshire AB30 1SR.
Tel/Fax (01561) 320827
E-mail:
robin@hisemangolf.freeserve.co.uk

Scotland's EIGCA qualified golf architect provides a personal, professional and superior design service for existing clubs and new developers. A specialist in the alteration and extension of existing courses. Major projects completed for Royal Dornoch, Boat of Garten, Deeside and Nairn Dunbar.

STRI - The Sports Turf Research Institute

St Ives Estate, Bingley,
West Yorkshire BD16 1AU.
Tel (01274) 565131 Fax (01274) 561891
E-mail: info@stri.co.uk
Website: www.stri.co.uk

Independent specialists offering you help and advice for the design, construction, management and maintenance, irrigation or renovation of your golf course. Comprehensive in-house support services for ecology, testing, turf pathology and research.

Simon Gidman International Golf Course Architects

Wychwood House, 43 Shipton Road,
Ascott Under Wychwood, Oxon OX7 6AG.
Tel (01993) 830441 Fax (01993) 831860
Mobile: 07768 600102
E-mail: srg@gidmangolf.co.uk
Website: www.gidmangolf.co.uk

A full member of the European Institute of Golf Course Architects (EIGCA), Simon Gidman has been involved with some 50 projects in Europe and throughout the world. The company alsospecialises in preparing reports and studies for the restoration and upgrading of existing golf courses.

Swan Golf Designs Ltd

Telfords Barn, Willingale,
Ongar, Essex CM5 0QF.
Tel (01277) 896229 Fax (01277) 896300
E-mail: swangolfdesigns@btinternet.com
Website: www.swangolfdesigns.com

Professional golf course architects with traditional values, offering initial appraisals, conceptual designs, detailed design work and construction management. Specialising in improvements of existing golf courses, extensions, re-design of greens and tees etc, including restorations of classic old courses.

York & Martin

39 Salisbury Street,
Fordingbridge, Hampshire SP6 1AB.
Tel (01425) 652087 Fax (01425) 652476
E-mail: msm@yorkandmartin.com
Website: www.yorkandmartin.com

Independent irrigation consultants providing objective advice on all irrigation related matters including water sourcing, existing system evaluation, system designs and specifications, project supervision etc. Operating throughout the UK and mainland Europe.

AWARDS, PRIZES & TROPHIES

Bryants of Leeds

Speedwell Street,
Meanwood Road, Leeds LS6 2TD.
Tel 0113-242 8330 Fax 0113-242 6330
Website: www.dimplygolf.com

The leading supplier of personalised golf merchandise. Golf club membership tags and labels, green fee stationery. Captain's Day, Society events and Corporate Golf Day merchandise. Call for a free colour brochure or visit us on our website.

Derek Burridge (Wholesale) Ltd

Awards House, Unit 15,
The Metro Centre, Springfield Road,
Hayes, Middlesex UB4 0LE.
Tel 020 8569 0123 Fax 020 8569 0111

The country's leading suppliers of golf prizes, celebrating their 43rd year. We offer a vast range of silverplate, crystal, china, clocks, leather goods and sporting trophies, all at trade prices. Glass and silverplate in-house engraving service. Next day delivery throughout the UK. Call for brochure. (See advertisement page 18 for further details.)

Fine Art Golf

Rodono House, St Mary's Loch,
Yarrow Valley, Scottish Borders TD7 5LH.
Tel (01750) 42215
E-mail: info@FineGolfArt.com
Website: www.finegolfart.com

Specialist supplier of beautiful, hand-framed-in-Scotland golfing pictures, providing golf prints, cartoons and rare hand-coloured caricatures for corporate gifts, retirement presents, special birthday gifts and top quality trophies for corporate golf days.

Galloway Crystal & Glass Ltd

Beeswing, by Dumfries DG2 8ED.
Tel (01387) 760643 Fax (01387) 760537
E-mail: mccallum@gallowayglass.com
Websites: www.gallowayglass.com
www.crystalforgolfers.com

Specialist plain and cut crystal suppliers and engravers. Many innovative golfing gift ideas through our special collections. Personalisation our speciality. Ask for our catalogue along with club and reseller price lists.

Grandison Golf Gallery
'Gowanbank',
5 Sorley's Brae,
Dollar FK14 7AS.
Tel (01259) 740318
E-mail: info@grandisongolfgallery.com
Website: www.grandisongolfgallery.com

Finest quality limited edition prints of the
world's premier golfing venues by one of the
world's leading golf artists, William Grandison.
Each print is individually signed and
numbered. Gifts and prizes of distinction for
the discerning golfer. Private commissions.

Hymax Products (UK) Ltd
Unit 19
Team Valley Business Centre,
Earlsway Team Valley,
Gateshead NE11 0RG.
Tel 0191-491 1138 Fax 0191-491 1911
E-mail: info@hymax.co.uk
Website: www.hymax.co.uk

Manufacturers of golf accessories and
corporate gift packs. Unique and innovative
British made goods. *Gifts that the golfer uses.*

Richard Chorley Golf Art
159 Lonsdale Road,
Stevenage,
Hertfordshire SG1 5DG.
Tel/Fax (01438) 727901

Richard Chorley, England's premier golf artist.
Private commissions, original oil paintings,
drawings and limited edition prints. Prints
signed by the artist, numbered and embossed.
Collection of classic courses and golfing greats.
Ideal corporate and captain's prizes gifts.

Solent Souvenirs Ltd
Hamble Bank,
40 Newtown Road,
Warsash,
Southampton,
Hampshire SO31 9FZ.
Tel (01489) 577985 Fax (01489) 577886
E-mail: solentsouvenirs@aol.com

Britain's premier supplier of specialised golf
jewellery and quality gifts. Many items
designed and manufactured exclusively for us
and unobtainable elsewhere. Replace that
traditional trophy with an elegant prize which
will be both useful and cherished. Most items
delivered overnight.

BAG/MEMBERSHIP TAGS

H M T Plastics Ltd
Fairway House,
31A Framfield Road,
Uckfield, East Sussex TN22 5AH.
Tel (01825) 769393 Fax (01825) 769494
E-mail: hmt@aol.com
Website: www.hmt-plastics.com

Bag tags supplied in nine colours either round,
pear shaped, shield maxi or sunrise to
accommodate club logo, from a choice of print
colours. Adhesive Year Stickers available in
choice of nine colours and sold separately. *(See
advertisement page 16 for further details.)*

BAGS/GOLF ACCESSORIES

Prosimmon Golf (UK) Ltd
21 Monkspath Business Park,
Highlands Road,
Shirley,
Solihull, West Midlands B90 4NZ.
Tel 0121-744 9551 Fax 0121-744 9541

Manufacturers of premium golf clubs, bags and
accessories. Designers of unique *Matchplay*
computerised custom club fitting system.

Teltale
6 Skye Road,
Shawfarm Industrial Estate,
Prestwick KA9 2TA.
Tel/Fax (01292) 475125
E-mail: john@teltale.uk.com
Website: www.teltale.uk.com

Waterproof nylon raincovers made from
durable nylon with pocket for scorecard. Fits
all bag sizes and packs into a neat zipped
wallet. Available in six colours. Cost £11.50.

BALL COLLECTORS

European Golf Machinery
Street Garage, Bucklesham,
Ipswich, Suffolk IP10 0DN.
Tel (01473) 659815 Fax (01473) 659045
E-mail: sales@europeangolf.prestel.co.uk
*Website: www.web-marketing.co.uk/
europeangolfmachinery*

Manufacturers of driving range equipment
including golf ball collectors, dispensers, ball
washers and elevators. Kawasaki ATV and
Mule distributors. *(See advertisement page 18 for
further details.)*

BOOKSELLERS & PUBLISHERS

Pitchcare.com Limited - A Single Solution for the Perfect Surface.

The Technology Centre,
Wolverhampton Science Park,
Wolverhampton,
West Midlands WV10 9RU.
Tel (01902) 824392 Fax (01902) 824393
E-mail: enquiries@pitchcare.com
Website: www.pitchcare.com

Unique interactive website magazine produced by professional groundsmen for everyone who has an interest in sports turf and lawns. Latest news on products and opportunities to find out how professionals achieve the finest sporting surfaces in the world - buy top quality products at group purchasing prices from leading manufacturers. Take advantage of our weather news and many other specialist services. Membership is FREE. Golf England approved supplier.

STRI - The Sports Turf Research Institute

St Ives Estate,
Bingley,
West Yorkshire BD16 1AU.
Tel (01274) 565131 Fax (01274) 561891
E-mail: info@stri.co.uk
Website: www.stri.co.uk

A specialist provider and supplier of books and training courses. Over 200 titles available from our on-line bookshop (www.stri.co.uk). Catalogue and training course details on request.

Steve Schofield Golf Books

29 Nichols Way,
Wetherby,
West Yorkshire LS22 6AD.
Tel/Fax (01937) 581276
E-mail: golfbooks@steveschofield.com

Classic golf books for sale, new, old and antiquarian. Books on golf history, architecture, biography, club and ball collecting and instruction. Free catalogue on request.

Mention The Royal & Ancient Golfer's Handbook when making your enquiries

CARTS, TROLLEYS & BUGGIES

A La Carts

Beechwood, Bakeham Lane,
Englefield Green TW20 9TU.
Tel/Fax (01784) 472982
E-mail: jt@alacarts.co.uk
Website: www.alacarts.tsx.org

Manufacturers and distributors of single and two-seater golf buggies. Also powered trolleys.

Middlemore Ltd

Sharrocks Street, Wolverhampton,
West Midlands WV1 3RP.
Tel (01902) 870077 Fax (01902) 455200
E-mail: electra-caddie@thama.co.uk
Website: www.thama.co.uk

European distributors of the world's foremost remote controlled powered golf trolley - the *LECTRONIC KADDY 'Dyna Steer 2000'.* Your hand held transmitter helps you to turn this amazing machine left to right and right to left with great ease. The Original all-alluminium lightweight machine that helps you break par, not your back. Free colour brochure on request. *(See advertisement page 18 for further details.)*

Patterson Products

Unit 6, Fordwater Trading Estate,
Ford Road, Chertsey, Surrey KT16 8HG.
Tel (01932) 570016 Fax (01932) 570084
E-mail: info@patterson.co.uk
Website: www.patterson.co.uk

Manufacturers and retailers of the *Trio* single-seat, transportable golf cart. Major suppliers and consultants to Handigolf, a charity for the severely disabled golfer. The *Trio* is now in its 16th year with over 4,500 happy users.

Teltale

6 Skye Road, Shawfarm Industrial Estate,
Prestwick KA9 2TA.
Tel/Fax (01292) 475125
E-mail: john@teltale.uk.com
Website: www.teltale.uk.com

The TopCart is sturdy, light (8kg) and powerful. Folded size an incredible 33"x 14.7" x 10" and available in three colours. Our new Teltale ride-on buggy, is an innovative and user-friendly design, quickly folded down in seconds to fit small hatchback cars. High power motors and extra wide tyres. Ideally suitable for hire.

Yamaha Motor (UK) Ltd
Sopwith Drive, Brooklands,
Weybridge, Surrey KT13 0UZ.
Tel (01932) 358096 Fax (01932) 358090

Suppliers of petrol and electric golf cars for clubs and individuals. Fleet contracts with optional purchase and lease schemes, full maintenance and service support. On and off-course utility vehicles, multi-passenger cars and beverage units.

CLOTHING/GOLFWEAR

Sunderland of Scotland Ltd
PO Box 14, Glasgow G2 1ER.
Tel 0141-572 5220 Fax 0141-572 5221
Website: www.sunderlandgolf.com

Sunderland of Scotland manufacture high quality golf rainwear in Scotland. All rainsuits are tour-tested and guaranteed waterproof and breathable, a variety of fabrics including Goretex being used. Sunderlands also manufacture the famous Sunderland Original Weatherbeater, Classic windproof Pullovers and Fleece. Official supplier to PGA, PGAE, LPGA, LET and St Andrews Links Trust.

COMPUTER SOFTWARE/SYSTEMS

Euro Systems Projects (ESP)
Europa House, 1 Kimpton Link Business Park, Kimpton Road, Sutton, Surrey SM3 9QP.
Tel 020 8251 5100 Fax 020 8251 5101
E-mail: enquiries@e-s-p.com
Website: www.e-s-p.com

ESP is universally recognised as the UK's market leader for the supply of integrated point of sale and management systems. Designed specifically for the golf industry their system incorporates modules to efficiently manage: membership; bookings; retail; food and beverage and access control and many others and is used by over 200 clubs and courses throughout the UK and Europe.

Links Software
6 Ascot Avenue,
Westerlands Park, Glasgow G12 0AX.
Tel/Fax 0141-581 6759
E-mail: ac.provan@ntlworld.com
Website: www.linksgolf.co.uk

The complete software solution for golf clubs. Membership and subscriptions, handicaps, bookings, point of sale and stock control.

Compatible with most swipecards. Fully networkable. Modules start from £450.

Sports Coach Systems Ltd
Curtis Road, Dorking, Surrey RH4 1XD.
Tel +44 (0) 1306 741888
Fax +44 (0) 1306 877888
E-mail: sportscoachsys@aol.com
Website: www.sports-coach.com

Manufacturers of the world's finest range of golf electronics and software. Projected systoms from under £6,000, club, ball and swing analysis, Links LS Simulators, Photographic Simulators and Driving Ranges. As well as digital firewire with the world famous Sports Coach 2003. Europe's largest manufacturer of golf mats, Portarange nets and cage nets.

CORPORATE GIFTS & EVENTS

Bryants of Leeds
Speedwell Street,
Meanwood Road, Leeds LS6 2TD.
Tel 0113-242 8330 Fax 0113-242 6330
Website: www.dimplygolf.com

The leading supplier of personalised golf merchandise. Golf club membership tags and labels, green fee stationery. Captain's Day, Society events and Corporate Golf Day merchandise. Call for a free colour brochure or visit us on our website.

Derek Burridge (Wholesale) Ltd
Awards House, Unit 15,
The Metro Centre, Springfield Road,
Hayes, Middlesex UB4 0LE.
Tel 020 8569 0123 Fax 020 8569 0111

The country's leading suppliers of golf prizes, celebrating their 43rd year, offer a vast range of silverplate, crystal, china, clocks, leather goods and sporting trophies, all at trade prices. Glass and silverplate in-house engraving service. Next day delivery throughout the UK. Call for our brochure. *(See advertisement page 18 for further details.)*

Fine Art Golf
Rodono House, St Mary's Loch,
Yarrow Valley, Scottish Borders TD7 5LH.
Tel (01750) 42215
E-mail: info@FineGolfArt.com
Website: www.finegolfart.com

Specialist supplier of beautiful, hand-framed-in-Scotland golfing pictures, providing golf

prints, cartoons and rare hand-coloured caricatures for corporate gifts, retirement presents, special birthday gifts and top quality trophies for corporate golf days.

Hymax Products (UK) Ltd
Unit 19 Team Valley Business Centre,
Earlsway Team Valley,
Gateshead NE11 0RG.
Tel 0191-491 1138 Fax 0191-491 1911
E-mail: info@hymax.co.uk
Website: www.hymax.co.uk

Manufacturers of golf accessories and corporate gift packs. Unique and innovative British made goods. *Gifts that the golfer uses.*

COURSE CONSTRUCTION & UPGADING

M J Abbott Ltd
Bratch Lane, Dinton,
Salisbury, Wiltshire SP3 5EB.
Tel (01722) 716361 Fax (01722) 716828
E-mail: enquiries@mjabbott.co.uk
Website: www.mjabbott.co.uk

M J Abbott Limited offer a range of specialist services to the golf and leisure industry. Recognised as one of Britain's leading companies offering Rain Bird irrigation systems. Land drainage, golf course construction and maintenance are all undertaken by experienced employees utilising the company's own specially adapted machinery.

Brian D Pierson
32 New Road,
Ringwood,
Hampshire BH24 3AU.
Tel (01202) 822372 Fax (01202) 826447

The Golf Course Builder - 35 years' experience on over 200 golf courses. New construction - alterations - project management. Contracts completed in USA, Canada, mainland Europe and British Isles. Work completed on seven Open Championship courses.

British Association of Golf Course Constructors - BAGCC
The Dormy House, Cooden Beach Golf Club, Bexhill-on-Sea TN39 4TR.
Tel (01424) 842380 Fax (01424) 843375
E-mail: mightyspyder@aol.com
Website: www.bagcc.org.uk

Secretary: David White. Constructors who appear on the BAGCC membership roster qualify only by passing a critical vetting process undertaken by their peers, who look for excellence in construction and a clear demonstration of skills pertinent only to the golf course industry. Utilising the services of a BAGCC member therefore ensures absolute professionalism.

David Williams Golf Design
187 Llanelian Road,
Old Colwyn,
Colwyn Bay,
North Wales LL29 8UW.
Tel (01492) 512070 Fax (01492) 512077
E-mail: david@williamsgolf.co.uk

Golf course architects and project managers. Fully integrated service *from conception through construction to completion.* Over 20 new courses built in Britain within last ten years. Alterations, improvements and upgrades undertaken through the country. Member of the European Institute of Golf Course Architects (EIGCA).

Grassform Ltd
- Golf Courses, Sports Grounds and Land Drainage Contractors
Dunsteads Farm,
Trueloves Lane,
Ingatestone, Essex CM4 0NJ.
Tel (01277) 355500 Fax (01277) 355504
E-mail: sales@grassform.co.uk
Website: www.grassform.co.uk

Grassform Limited undertakes all types of golf course projects. From new build to re-construction of tees, greens and bunkers. We also install land drainage systems, sand banding, lakes, water features, footpaths, buggy paths and driving ranges. For further information please contact Mark Dunning.

John Greasley Ltd
Ashfield House,
1154 Melton Road,
Syston,
Leicester LE7 2HB.
Tel 0116-269 6766 Fax 0116-269 6866

John Greasley established his company in 1984 and has specialised in the construction of new courses, along with alterations, improvements and refurbishment on existing ones. Works have been completed on some of the countries oldest and most prestigious courses.

Land Unit Construction Ltd
Hanslope,
Milton Keynes,
Buckinghamshire MK19 7BX.
Tel (01908) 510414 Fax (01908) 511056
E-mail: sales@landunitconstruction.co.uk
Website: www.landunitconstruction.co.uk

We have the knowledge and experience gained over 25 years in golf course construction and constantly work with many of the country's leading golf course architects to provide clients with unparalleled quality of service.

PSD Agronomy Ltd
42 Garstang Road,
Preston,
Lancashire PR1 1NA.
Tel (01772) 884450 Fax (01772) 884445
E-mail: psdgb@aol.com
Website: www.psdagronomy.com

A specialist team of golf course agronomists working throughout the UK and Europe. Whether building a new course, extending an existing one or just making the best of what you have - we have the technical expertise to help.

STRI - The Sports Turf Research Institute
St Ives Estate,
Bingley,
West Yorkshire BD16 1AU.
Tel (01274) 565131 Fax (01274) 561891
E-mail: info@stri.co.uk
Website: www.stri.co.uk

Independent specialists offering you help and advice for the design, construction, management and maintenance, irrigation or renovation of your golf course. Comprehensive in-house support services for ecology, testing, turf pathology and research.

Simon Gidman International Golf Course Architects
Wychwood House, 43 Shipton Road,
Ascott Under Wychwood, Oxon OX7 6AG.
Tel (01993) 830441 Fax (01993) 831860
Mobile: 07768 600102
E-mail: srg@gidmangolf.co.uk
Website: www.gidmangolf.co.uk

A full member of the European Institute of Golf Course Architects (EIGCA), Simon Gidman has been involved with some 50 projects in Europe and throughout the world. The company alsospecialises in preparing reports and studies for the restoration and upgrading of existing golf courses.

Swan Golf Designs Ltd
Telfords Barn,
Willingale,
Ongar, Essex CM5 0QF.
Tel (01277) 896229 Fax (01277) 896300
E-mail: swangolfdesigns@btinternet.com
Website: www.swangolfdesigns.com

Professional golf course architects with traditional values, offering initial appraisals, conceptual designs, detailed design work and construction management. Specialising in improvements of existing golf courses, extensions, re-design of greens and tees etc, including restorations of classic old courses.

COURSE MEASUREMENT

Eagle Promotions Ltd
Eagle House,
1 Clearway Court,
139-141 Croydon Road,
Caterham, Surrey CR3 6PF.
Tel (01883) 344244 Fax (01883) 341777
E-mail: info@eaglepromotions.co.uk
Website: www.eaglepromotions.co.uk

Eagle Promotions offer a comprehensive range of products from certified course measurement and tee signs through to scorecards, yardage books, green fee tickets, members' tags, event and leader boards, honours boards, clubhouse and general course signage. For further information please contact Philip McInley on 01883 344244.

DISTRIBUTORS & WHOLESALERS

Aldila UK
12 Heather Road,
Binley Woods,
Coventry CV3 2DE.
Tel/Fax 024 7654 5651
E-mail: heath.chapman@1way.co.uk

Aldila Golf equipment distributors: Diamond Golf Ltd, 4/5 Rudford Industrial Estate, Ford Road, Arundel BN18 0BS Tel (01903) 726999 Fax (01903) 726998; Golfsmith (Europe) Ltd, Ormond House, Nuffield Road, St Ives, Cambridgeshire PE27 3LX Tel (01480) 308800 Fax (01480) 308801.

British Golf Industry Association

Federation House,
Stoneleigh Park, Warwickshire CV8 2RF.
Tel 024 7641 7141 Fax 024 7641 4990
E-mail: bgia@sportslife.org.uk

Trade association for manufacturers and distributors of golf equipment.

Eaton Ltd - Golf Pride Grips

Units 1 & 2 The Stirling Centre,
Northfields Industrial Estate,
Market Deeping,
Nr Peterborough PE6 8EQ.
Tel (01778) 341555 Fax (01778) 344025

Manufacturers of golf grips for over 50 years, Eaton have been the leader in golf grip technology and the leader in rubber and cord grip sales for both professional and amateur players alike.

Yonex UK Ltd

Yonex House, 74 Wood Lane,
White City, London W12 7RH.
Tel 020 8742 9777 Fax 020 8742 9612
E-mail: cservice@yonexuk.com
Website: www.yonexuk.com

Manufacturer and distributor of Yonex premium golf equipment. All models are designed and manufactured using the latest in high technology materials and world class quality standards.

DRIVING RANGE & PRACTICE EQUIPMENT

European Golf Machinery

Street Garage, Bucklesham,
Ipswich, Suffolk IP10 0DN.
Tel (01473) 659815 Fax (01473) 659045
E-mail: sales@europeangolf.prestel.co.uk
Website: www.web-marketing.co.uk/
europeangolfmachinery

Manufacturers of driving range equipment including golf ball collectors, dispensers, ball washers and elevators. Kawasaki ATV and Mule distributors. *(See advertisement page 18 for further details.)*

Tildenet Ltd

Hartcliffe Way, Bristol BS3 5RJ.
Tel 0117-966 9684 Fax 0117-923 1251
E-mail: enquiries@tildenet.co.uk
Website: www.tildenet.co.uk

Tildenet supply and install a comprehensive range of quality products to the Golfing World. These include perimeter ball stop netting, practice nets and mats for the professional enthusiast. Anti-ball plug nets, target nets, target greens and anti-dazzle netting for clubs, and grass germination and bunker membranes for the greenkeeper.

EDUCATION

Bournemouth University

School of Service Industries,
Fern Barrow,
Poole, Dorset BH12 5BB.
Tel (01202) 595146 Fax (01202) 515707
E-mail: mcustard@bournemouth.ac.uk
Website: www.bournemouth.ac.uk/
service_industries

The university has developed a unique degree for those interested in a career in golf and/or sports management. With the support of local golf clubs, the BSc(Hons) in Sports Management (golf) is a 4-year sandwich degree which provides graduates with the technical expertise as well as the managerial skills necessary to succeed in this dynamic industry. Contact: Programme Administrator, School of Service Industries.

ELECTRIC GOLF CARS

Yamaha Motor (UK) Ltd

Sopwith Drive,
Brooklands,
Weybridge, Surrey KT13 0UZ.
Tel (01932) 358096 Fax (01932) 358090

Suppliers of petrol and electric golf cars for clubs and individuals. Fleet contracts with optional purchase and lease schemes, full maintenance and service support. On and off-course utility vehicles, multi-passenger cars and beverage units.

ELECTRONIC POINT OF SALE

Euro Systems Projects (ESP)

Europa House, 1 Kimpton Link Business Park, Kimpton Road,
Sutton, Surrey SM3 9QP.
Tel 020 8251 5100 Fax 020 8251 5101
E-mail: enquiries@e-s-p.com
Website: www.e-s-p.com

ESP is universally recognised as the UK's market leader for the supply of integrated point of sale and management systems. Designed specifically for the golf industry their system incorporates modules to efficiently manage:

membership; bookings; retail; food and beverage and access control and many others and is used by over 200 clubs and courses throughout the UK and Europe.

FINANCE

Humberclyde Groundscare Finance
Northern Cross,
Basing View,
Basingstoke, Hampshire RG21 4HL
Tel (01256) 377429 Fax (01256) 377222
E-mail: enquiries@humberclyde.co.uk
Website: www.humberclyde.co.uk

Providing finance solutions to proprietary and membership golf clubs for over 30 years, we have a team of specialists available to help you find the finance package most suited to your needs. *(See advertisement page 31 for further details.)*

FIXTURE BOOKS

Iain Crosbie Printers
Beechfield Road,
Willowyard Industrial Estate,
Beith,
Ayrshire KA15 1LN.
Tel (01505) 504848 Fax: (01505) 504674
E-mail: crosbieprinters@dial.pipex.com

At Crosbie Printers we have over 20 years' experience in printing associated with golf and commerce. We manufacture scorecards (standard and bespoke), fixture books/diaries, green fee tickets, marketing brochures/leaflets and all associated printed stationery. *(See advertisement page 16 for further details.)*

FLOODLIGHTING & FENCING

Mike Copson Associates Golf Driving Range Design & Construction Specialists
42 Bewdley Hill,
Kidderminster,
Worcestershire DY11 6JA.
Tel/Fax (01562) 863937
Mobile: 0836 371180
E-mail: mike@mikecopson.co.uk
Website: www.mikecopson.co.uk

Mike Copson has been designing and building driving ranges since 1988. During this time he has completed 26 major golfing projects.

Clients include: British Coal, Whitbread's, Bovis (La Manga) abroad and many private golf clubs and local authorities. Our experience also extends to the design of high perimeter fencing and floodlighting designs. We can offer a full turnkey package or individually designed packages to suit each client or act as a consultant.

GIFTS & NOVELTIES

Derek Burridge (Wholesale) Ltd
Awards House,
Unit 15,
The Metro Centre,
Springfield Road, Hayes,
Middlesex UB4 0LE.
Tel 020 8569 0123 Fax 020 8569 0111

The country's leading suppliers of golf prizes, celebrating their 43rd year. We offer a vast range of silverplate, crystal, china, clocks, leather goods and sporting trophies, all at trade prices. Glass and silverplate in-house engraving service. Next day delivery throughout the UK. Call for brochure. *(See advertisement page 18 for further details.)*

Hymax Products (UK) Ltd
Unit 19
Team Valley Business Centre,
Earlsway Team Valley,
Gateshead NE11 0RG.
Tel 0191-491 1138 Fax 0191-491 1911
E-mail: info@hymax.co.uk
Website: www.hymax.co.uk

Manufacturers of golf accessories and corporate gift packs. Unique and innovative British made goods. *Gifts that the golfer uses.*

Solent Souvenirs Ltd
Hamble Bank,
40 Newtown Road,
Warsash,
Southampton,
Hampshire SO31 9FZ.
Tel (01489) 577985 Fax (01489) 577886
E-mail: solentsouvenirs@aol.com

Britain's premier supplier of specialised golf jewellery and quality gifts. Many items designed and manufactured exclusively for us and unobtainable elsewhere. Replace that traditional trophy with an elegant prize which will be both useful and cherished. Most items delivered overnight.

GOLF BALL MANUFACTURERS/SUPPLIERS

Wilson Sporting Goods Co Ltd
Ayr Road, Irvine, Ayrshire KA12 8HG.
Tel (01294) 316270 Fax (01294) 316300
Website: www.wilsonsports.com

Manufactures and supplies a full range of game improvement products specifically designed to enhance performance for golfers of all standards. Superstar products for 2003 include the new Deep Red family of drivers, fairway woods, irons and putters. Also new for 2003 is the Staff True family of premium balls available in three models, to cater for all performance requirements. Call us or visit our website for details of your nearest stockist.

GOLF CLUB MANUFACTURERS/SUPPLIERS

Adams Golf UK Ltd
Unit 6 Corium House,
Douglas Drive, Catteshall Lane,
Godalming, Surrey GU7 1JX.
Tel (01483) 239333 Fax (01483) 239334
E-mail: sales@adamsgolf.co.uk
Website: www.adamsgolf.co.uk

Adams Golf supply a complete range of Tight Lie products with a choice of either their patented multi material or graphite shafts. GT drivers and fairway woods are complemented by irons, putters, wedges and accessories. The products are endorsed by, amongst others - Tom Watson, Larry Nelson and Bruce Lietzke.

Aldila UK
12 Heather Road,
Binley Woods, Coventry CV3 2DE.
Tel/Fax 024 7654 5651
E-mail: heath.chapman@1way.co.uk

World's leading manufacturer of graphite golf shafts, including the Aldila One, HM 2000, HM 40, Excelerator Series. Speciality Series and Value Series.

Bronty Golf
3 Musgrave Mount, Eccleshill,
Bradford, West Yorkshire BD2 3LA.
Tel/Fax +44 (0) 1274 773585
Mobile:+44 (0) 7950 397603
E-mail: brontygolf1@activemail.co.uk
Website: www.brontygolf.co.uk

Manufacturers of high quality British made custom golf clubs, putters and specialist clubs. Authentic replicas and hickory shafted putters etc.

Callaway Golf Europe Ltd
Unit 27 Barwell Business Park,
Leatherhead Road,
Chessington, Surrey KT9 2NY.
Tel +44 (0) 20 8391 0111

Manufacturer of golf clubs, golf balls and accessories. Callaway Golf is now the distributor for Odyssey Golf.

Prosimmon Golf (UK) Ltd
21 Monkspath Business Park,
Highlands Road, Shirley, Solihull,
West Midlands B90 4NZ.
Tel 0121-744 9551 Fax 0121-744 9541

Manufacturers of premium golf clubs, bags and accessories. Designers of unique *Matchplay* computerised custom club fitting system.

True Temper UK/Europe
c/o Tucker Fasteners
Walsall Road, Birmingham B42 1BP.
Tel 0121-331 2276 Fax 0121-331 2286

Golf shaft manufacturer both steel and graphite. In 2002 achieved over 120 Tournament wins on PGA Tours. Dynamic Gold used by leading players. Sensicore continues to grow in usage by both Tournament players and amateurs.

Wilson Sporting Goods Co Ltd
Ayr Road, Irvine, Ayrshire KA12 8HG.
Tel (01294) 316270 Fax (01294) 316300
Website: www.wilsonsports.com

Manufactures and supplies a full range of game improvement products specifically designed to enhance performance for golfers of all standards. Superstar products for 2003 include the new Deep Red family of drivers, fairway woods, irons and putters. Also new for 2003 is the Staff True family of premium balls available in three models, to cater for all performance requirements. Call us or visit our website for details of your nearest stockist.

Yonex UK Ltd
Yonex House, 74 Wood Lane,
White City, London W12 7RH.
Tel 020 8742 9777 Fax 020 8742 9612
E-mail: cservice@yonexuk.com
Website: www.yonexuk.com

Manufacturer and distributor of Yonex premium golf equipment. All models are designed and manufactured using the latest in high technology materials and world class quality standards.

GOLF COURSE DESIGN CONSULTANTS

David Griffith
20 Clwyd Avenue,
Dyserth,
Denbighshire LL18 6HN.
Tel (01745) 570659 Fax (01745) 571382
Mobile: 07778 494123
E-mail: david@griffithgolf.co.uk

Golf course architect. Years of experience in a variety of golf projects ensures that no stone is left unturned in fulfilling the potential of a site. A satisfaction guarantee is given to all projects.

David Williams Golf Design
187 Llanelian Road,
Old Colwyn,
Colwyn Bay, North Wales LL29 8UW.
Tel (01492) 512070 Fax (01492) 512077
E-mail: david@williamsgolf.co.uk

Golf Course architects and project managers. Fully integrated service *from conception through construction to completion.* Over 20 new courses built in Britain within last ten years. Alterations, improvements and upgrades undertaken through the country. Member of the European Institute of Golf Course Architects (EIGCA).

European Institute of Golf Course Architects - EIGCA
Chiddingfold Golf Club,
Petworth Road,
Chiddingfold,
Surrey GU8 4SL.
Tel/Fax +44 (0) 1428 681528
E-mail: info@eigca.org
Website: www.eigca.org

The EIGCA represents the vast majority of qualified and experienced golf course architects throughout Europe. Our goals include enhancing the professional status of the profession, developing the role of education and increasing the opportunities for its members to practice in countries throughout the world. EIGCA also provides educational courses to train future golf course architects and is the authoritative voice on all related matters, being recognised by the R&A Golf Club of St Andrews. Contact: Julia Green, Executive Officer.

Gaunt & Marnoch - Golf Course Architects
Head Office: Hilltop, Lakeside,
Bakewell, Derbyshire DE45 1GN.
Tel+44 (0) 1629 815453
Fax+44 (0) 1629 815170
E-mail: info@gauntandmarnoch.com
Website: www.gauntandmarnoch.com

Gaunt & Marnoch provides a comprehensive, cost-conscious and environmentally sympathetic golf course design service. An international and award-winning company who are flexible and offer a top quality service from feasibility through planning to construction supervision and opening the course for play. We are committed to better golf through good design. Ring for brochure. *(See advertisement page 18 for further details.)*

Hawtree Ltd - Golf Course Architects & Consultants
5 Oxford Street,
Woodstock,
Oxon OX20 1TQ.
Tel (01993) 811976 Fax (01993) 812448
E-mail: mail@hawtree.co.uk
Website: www.hawtree.co.uk

Founded in 1912, Hawtree Limited is the longest continuous golf course practice, having designed and renovated over 800 golf courses worldwide. Just some of these include the renowned Birkdale, Portmarnock, Lahinch and Vilamoura golf courses.

Peter Alliss - Golf Ltd
25 St Johns Road,
Farnham,
Surrey GU9 8NV.
Tel (01252) 717711 Fax (01252) 717722
E-mail: roy@allissgolf.demon.co.uk

Designers of golf courses and re-design of existing courses. Contact Peter Alliss or Roy Cooper.

Philip Sparks Professional Golf Designs
Peak House,
Hawksdown,
Walmer, Deal, Kent CT12 5BE.
Tel (01304) 374119 Fax (01843) 853090

'Creating future links with the Past'. Specialising in golf course remodelling and renovation. Toro student architect of the year 2000. First golf professional in the world to gain an EIGCA diploma in golf course architecture.

Ritson Golf Design

2nd Floor Office,
29 William Street,
Rugby,
Warwickshire CV21 3HA.
Tel/Fax (01788) 573866
E-mail: steve.ritson@telinco.co.uk
Website: www.golf-course-architect.com

Golf course and landscape architects, undertaking a wide range of golf design projects both in the UK and abroad, from championship to par 3 courses, remodelling existing courses and the creation of exciting driving ranges.

Robin Hiseman Golf Course Design

Berrymeadow Cottage,
4 West Cairnbeg Cottages,
Laurencekirk,
Aberdeenshire AB30 1SR.
Tel/Fax (01561) 320827
E-mail:
robin@hisemangolf.freeserve.co.uk

Scotland's EIGCA qualified golf architect provides a personal, professional and superior design service for existing clubs and new developers. A specialist in the alteration and extension of existing courses. Major projects completed for Royal Dornoch, Boat of Garten, Deeside and Nairn Dunbar.

GOLF COURSE DISTANCE GUIDES

Strokesport

Abbey Mill Business Centre,
Paisley PA1 1TJ.
Tel 0141-848 1199 Fax 0141-887 1642

We are publishers of *Strokesaver Distance Guides* which are recognised as the most accurate and useful golf course management aids worldwide. *Strokesaver* provides professionals and clubs with a constant profit centre. Course Measurement - Measurement and survey to professional standard. Certification accepted by National Golf unions. Leading specialists in course measurement. *(See advertisement page 16 for further details.)*

GOLF COURSE MAINTENANCE & UPGRADING

Arden Lea Irrigation Ltd

160 Moss Lane, Hesketh Bank,
Preston, Lancashire PR4 6AE.
Tel (01772) 812433 Fax (01772) 815371
E-mail: alirrig@aol.com

Arden Lea Irrigation established nearly 30 years ago specialises in irrigation on golf courses and other leisure facilities. With our experienced staff we have completed work on many well known golf courses throughout the UK and Southern Ireland. We are an independent company and can supply any type of irrigation equipment. Full member of the British Turf and Landscape Irrigation Association.

Brian D Pierson

32 New Road, Ringwood,
Hampshire BH24 3AU.
Tel (01202) 822372 Fax (01202) 826447

The Golf Course Builder - 35 years' experience on over 200 golf courses. New construction - alterations - project management. Contracts completed in USA, Canada, mainland Europe and British Isles. Work completed on seven Open Championship courses.

Glen Farrow (UK) Ltd

Spalding Road, Pinchbeck,
Spalding, Lincolnshire PE11 3UE.
Tel (01775) 722327 Fax (01775) 725444
E-mail: info@glenfarrow.co.uk
Website: www.glenfarrow.co.uk

With over 30 years' experience and an excellent reputation for workmanship, Glen Farrow offer a full design, supply and installation service using competitive and cost-effective solutions, contract maintenance and emergency repairs also undertaken.

Grassform Ltd - Golf Courses, Sports Grounds and Land Drainage Contractors

Dunsteads Farm, Trueloves Lane,
Ingatestone, Essex CM4 0NJ.
Tel (01277) 355500 Fax (01277) 355504
E-mail: sales@grassform.co.uk
Website: www.grassform.co.uk

Grassform Limited undertakes all types of golf course projects. From new build to re-construction of tees, greens and bunkers. We also install land drainage systems, sand

banding, lakes, water features, footpaths, buggy paths and driving ranges. For further information please contact Mark Dunning.

Land Unit Construction Ltd
Hanslope, Milton Keynes,
Buckinghamshire MK19 7BX.
Tel (01908) 510414 Fax (01908) 511056
E-mail: sales@landunitconstruction.co.uk
Website: www.landunitconstruction.co.uk

We have the knowledge and experience gained over 25 years in golf course construction and constantly work with many of the country's leading golf course architects to provide clients with unparalleled quality of service.

Peter Alliss - Golf Ltd
25 St Johns Road, Farnham,
Surrey GU9 8NV.
Tel (01252) 717711 Fax (01252) 717722
E-mail: roy@allissgolf.demon.co.uk

Designers of golf courses and re-design of existing courses. Contact Peter Alliss or Roy Cooper.

Toro Commercial Products - Lely (UK) Ltd
Station Road, St Neots, Huntingdon,
Cambridgeshire PE19 1QH.
Tel (01480) 226800 Fax (01480) 226801
E-mail: toro.info@lely.co.uk
Website: www.toro.com

Toro offer an extensive range of professional turf maintenance equipment which includes: greens mowers, fairway mowers, triplex mowers, rotary mowers, aeration and utility vehicles. *Toro* manufacture to an exceptionally high quality and give unrivalled quality of cut.

GOLF DEVELOPMENT/MANAGEMENT

Association of Golf Club Secretaries
7A Beaconsfield Road,
Weston-Super-Mare, Somerset BS23 1YE.
Tel (01934) 641166 Fax (01934) 644254
E-mail: hq@agcs.org.uk
Website: www.agcs.org.uk

Membership is available to golf secretaries and managers, course owners and others involved in golf club administration. The following services are available: monthly journal, information library, training courses. seminars, conferences, regional meetings and employment support.

Barrelfield Golf Ltd
302 Ewell Road,
Surbiton,
Surrey KT6 7AQ.
Tel 020 8390 6566 Fax 020 8390 8830
Website: www.barrelfieldgolf.co.uk

Barrelfield Golf Limited has an unrivalled track record in the development, marketing, management and maintenance of profitable golf clubs in Britain. Other services include feasibility studies and arranging finance. For further information contact Melvin Thomas 020 8390 6566.

Bournemouth University
School of Service Industries,
Fern Barrow,
Poole,
Dorset BH12 5BB.
Tel (01202) 595146 Fax (01202) 515707
E-mail: mcustard@bournemouth.ac.uk
*Website: www.bournemouth.ac.uk/
service_industries*

The university has developed a unique degree for those interested in a career in golf and/or sports management. With the support of local golf clubs, the BSc(Hons) in Sports Management (golf) is a 4-year sandwich degree which provides graduates with the technical expertise as well as the managerial skills necessary to succeed in this dynamic industry. Contact: Programme Administrator, School of Service Industries.

The Council of National Golf Unions
Dromin,
Dunleer,
Co Louth,
Ireland.
Tel/Fax +353 41 6861476
E-mail: golfinmcinere@hotmail.com

The handicapping authority for Great Britain and Ireland. The Standard Scratch Score and Handicapping scheme has been in operation since March 1926. The Consultative Committee consists of representatives from the English, Ireland, Scottish and Welsh golf unions. They receive and consider schemes for fixing scratch scores and adjustments to handicaps throughout Great Britain and Ireland and submit their proposals to the Royal & Ancient of St Andrews for approval.

English Golf Union - EGU

The National Golf Centre,
The Broadway,
Woodhall Spa,
Lincolnshire LN10 6PU.
Tel (01526) 354500 Fax (01526) 354020
E-mail: info@englishgolfunion.org
Website: www.englishgolfunion.org

As the governing body for men's amateur golf in England the EGU organises championships and coaching for players and representative teams at all levels and offers an advisory service on all aspects of golf administration and management.

Golf Consultants Association - GCA

Federation House,
Stoneleigh Park,
Warwickshire CV8 2RF.
Tel (02476) 414999 Fax (02476) 414990
E-mail: gca@sportslife.org.uk

The GCA provides a point of reference for those requiring independent, professional, golf consultancy services throughout the world.

The Golf Foundation - Developing Junior Golf

Foundation House,
The Spinney,
Hoddesdon Road,
Stanstead Abbotts,
Hertfordshire SG12 8GF.
Tel (01920) 876200 Fax (01920) 876211
Website: www.golf-foundation.org

An organisation dedicated to the promotion and development of grass roots junior golf across the British Isles. *The Golf Foundation is a registered charity.*

Golf Search - The Golfing Recruitment Specialists

Kildare House,
102-104 Sheen Road,
Richmond-on-Thames, Surrey TW9 1UF.
Tel 020 8334 1125 Fax 020 8334 1177

Golf Search has years of recruitment experience and the largest database of golf management personnel in Europe. We carry out comprehensive interviews and reference checks on all candidates. The professional service provided offers exceptional value for money, our fees are 10% of salary. Please phone for further information.

National Association of Public Golf Courses - NAPGC

12 Newton Close, Redditch B98 7YR.
Tel (01527) 542106 Fax (01527) 455320
E-mail: eddiemitchell@blueyonder.co.uk
Website: www.napgc.org.uk

The Association provides competition golf for men and lady players of all handicaps and age. It also offers help and advice to its member clubs - those playing over courses that they do not own.

National Golf Clubs' Advisory Association - NGCAA

First Floor Chambers,
18-20 Stamford Street,
Stalybridge, Cheshire SK15 2JZ.
Tel 0161-338 8680 Fax 0161-338 8408
E-mail: ngcaa@idealnet.co.uk
Website: www.ngcaa.org.uk

A non-profit making organisation providing legal advice and support to golf clubs throughout the UK. The Association is the only independent body supporting golf clubs in areas of activity other than those arising from playing the game.

Portfolio International

5 Bream's Buildings, London EC4A 1DY.
Tel +44 (0) 207 520 5000
Fax +44 (0) 207 520 5002
E-mail: suzie.boyd@portfoliointl.com
Website: www.portfoliointernational.com

Seventeen years' experience providing specialist recruitment services to the hospitality industry using executive search, database search techniques. Our golf division can save you valuable time and expense providing key management to golf clubs and resorts. Please phone or e-mail Suzie Boyd for further information.

GOLF HOLIDAYS

Portugal Fairways - Go-Golf-Pay-Less

Estrada de Pera, Sesmarias, 8200 Albufeira, Portugal.
Tel +44 (0) 1908 311768
E-mail: info@go-golf-pay-less.com
Website: www.go-golf-pay-less.com

Algarve, Estoril and Costa Azul golfing breaks - let Go-Golf-Pay-Less book your courses, preferred dates and tee times at discounted

prices at no charge to you! Accommodation in a choice of hotels, villas, motels and apartments. Car rental and airport transfers.

famous Sports Coach 2003. Europe's largest manufacturer of golf mats, Portarange nets and cage nets.

GOLF RANGE DESIGN

Mike Copson Associates
Golf Driving Range Design
& Construction Specialists
42 Bewdley Hill, Kidderminster,
Worcestershire DY11 6JA.
Tel/Fax (01562) 863937
Mobile: 0836 371180
E-mail: mike@mikecopson.co.uk
Website: www.mikecopson.co.uk

Mike Copson has been designing and building driving ranges since 1988. During this time he has completed 26 major golfing projects. Clients include: British Coal, Whitbread's, Bovis (La Manga) abroad and many private golf clubs and local authorities. Our experience also extends to the design of high perimeter fencing and floodlighting designs. We can offer a full turnkey package or individually designed packages to suit each client or act as a consultant.

GOLFING AIDS/PRACTICE EQUIPMENT

Pan European (Golf) 1973 (PEP)
Old Mill Works, High Street,
Maldon, Essex CM9 5EH.
Tel (01621) 851700 Fax (01621) 850417
E-mail: info@golfpep.co.uk
Website: www.golfpep.co.uk

Products include a wide range of practice nets and mats for beginners through to professionals. We also make a commercial range of nets and mats for clubs, stores and leisure centres. Worldwide export sales our speciality.

Sports Coach Systems Ltd
Curtis Road, Dorking, Surrey RH4 1XD.
Tel +44 (0) 1306 741888
Fax +44 (0) 1306 877888
E-mail: sportscoachsys@aol.com
Website: www.sports-coach.com

Manufacturers of the world's finest range of golf electronics and software. Projected systoms from under £6,000, club, ball and swing analysis, Links LS Simulators, Photographic Simulators and Driving Ranges. As well as digital firewire with the world

GREENKEEPING & DRIVING RANGE VEHICLES

European Golf Machinery
Street Garage,
Bucklesham,
Ipswich,
Suffolk IP10 0DN.
Tel (01473) 659815 Fax (01473) 659045
E-mail: sales@europeangolf.prestel.co.uk
Website: www.web-marketing.co.uk/europeangolfmachinery

Manufacturers of driving range equipment including golf ball collectors, dispensers, ball washers and elevators. Kawasaki ATV and Mule distributors. *(See advertisement page 18 for further details.)*

Humberclyde Groundscare Finance
Northern Cross,
Basing View,
Basingstoke,
Hampshire RG21 4HL
Tel (01256) 377429 Fax (01256) 377222
E-mail: enquiries@humberclyde.co.uk
Website: www.humberclyde.co.uk

Providing finance solutions to proprietary and membership golf clubs for over 30 years, we have a team of specialists available to help you find the finance package most suited to your needs. *(See advertisement page 31 for further details.)*

Toro Commercial Products - Lely (UK) Ltd
Station Road,
St Neots,
Huntingdon,
Cambridgeshire PE19 1QH.
Tel (01480) 226800 Fax (01480) 226801
E-mail: toro.info@lely.co.uk
Website: www.toro.com

Toro offer an extensive range of professional turf maintenance equipment which includes: greens mowers, fairway mowers, triplex mowers, rotary mowers, aeration and utility vehicles. *Toro* manufacture to an exceptionally high quality and give unrivalled quality of cut.

GREENKEEPING INFORMATION SERVICE

British & International Golf Greenkeepers Association - BIGGA

**BIGGA House, Aldwark,
Alne, North Yorkshire YO61 1UF.**
*Tel (01347) 833800 Fax (01347) 833801
E-mail: reception@bigga.co.uk
Website: www.bigga.org.uk*

BIGGA has over 7,000 members and is the professional body that represents greenkeepers throughout the UK and has members in 32 countries worldwide. As well as providing extensive education and training programmes for its members BIGGA produces a monthly magazine 'Greenkeeper International' and each January in Harrogate organises the BIGGA Turf Management Exhibition and the Clubhouse Exhibition. Contact Neil Thomas, Executive Director.

Pitchcare.com Limited - A Single Solution for the Perfect Surface.

**The Technology Centre,
Wolverhampton Science Park,
Wolverhampton,
West Midlands WV10 9RU.**
*Tel (01902) 824392 Fax (01902) 824393
E-mail: enquiries@pitchcare.com
Website: www.pitchcare.com*

Unique interactive website magazine produced by professional groundsmen for everyone who has an interest in sports turf and lawns. Latest news on products and opportunities to find out how professionals achieve the finest sporting surfaces in the world - buy top quality products at group purchasing prices from leading manufacturers. Take advantage of our weather news and many other specialist services. Membership is FREE. Golf England approved supplier.

GRIPS & SHAFTS

Eaton Ltd - Golf Pride Grips

**Units 1 & 2 The Stirling Centre,
Northfields Industrial Estate,
Market Deeping,
Nr Peterborough PE6 8EQ.**
Tel (01778) 341555 Fax (01778) 344025

Manufacturers of golf grips for over 50 years, Eaton have been the leader in golf grip technology and the leader in rubber and cord grip sales for both professional and amateur players alike.

True Temper UK/Europe c/o Tucker Fasteners

Walsall Road, Birmingham B42 1BP.
Tel 0121-331 2276 Fax 0121-331 2286

Golf shaft manufacturer both steel and graphite. In 2002 achieved over 120 Tournament wins on PGA Tours. Dynamic Gold used by leading players. Sensicore continues to grow in usage by both Tournament players and amateurs.

GROUP PURCHASING

Pitchcare.com Limited - A Single Solution for the Perfect Surface.

**The Technology Centre,
Wolverhampton Science Park,
Wolverhampton,
West Midlands WV10 9RU.**
*Tel (01902) 824392 Fax (01902) 824393
E-mail: enquiries@pitchcare.com
Website: www.pitchcare.com*

Unique interactive website magazine produced by professional groundsmen for everyone who has an interest in sports turf and lawns. Latest news on products and opportunities to find out how professionals achieve the finest sporting surfaces in the world - buy top quality products at group purchasing prices from leading manufacturers. Take advantage of our weather news and many other specialist services. Membership is FREE. Golf England approved supplier.

INSURANCE

Golfplan - International Golf & Travel Insurance

**Redcliffe House, Whitehouse Street,
Bristol BS3 4AY.**
*Tel 0117-963 6198 Fax 0117-923 1058
E-mail: info@golfplan.co.uk
Website: www.golfplan.co.uk*

Golfplan, endorsed by the PGA, is Europe's largest specialist golf insurance provider. A Golfplan policy covers individual golfers against personal liability; accidental damage to third party property; golf equipment; personal effects; equipment hire charges; tournament

entry fees; membership fees; personal accident; Hole-in-One. Contact your professional or call Golfplan quoting Ref: GHB7.

INTERNET TEE-TIME BOOKING

Links Software
6 Ascot Avenue,
Westerlands Park,
Glasgow G12 0AX.
Tel/Fax 0141-581 6759
E-mail: ac.provan@ntlworld.com
Website: www.linksgolf.co.uk

The complete software solution for golf clubs. Membership and subscriptions, handicaps, bookings, point of sale and stock control. Compatible with most swipecards. Fully networkable. Modules start from £450.

IRRIGATION CONSULTANTS/DESIGN & INSTALLATION

2iC - International Irrigation Consultants
Offices in Surrey: Cranbourne, Avenue Road, Cranleigh, Surrey GU6 7LL.
Tel/Fax (01483) 278416
Lincolnshire: 10 Peregrine Close, Sleaford, Lincolnshire NG34 7UY.
Tel/Fax (01529) 300224
E-mail: bill@2ic.co.uk Marcus@2ic.co.uk

Independent consulting irrigation engineers - for all your irrigation and water issues. Cost-effective trouble shooting of golf course irrigation systems. Detailed new designs, installation supervision and contract management. GPS surveys and AutoCAD draughting.

M J Abbott Ltd
Bratch Lane,
Dinton,
Salisbury, Wiltshire SP3 5EB.
Tel (01722) 716361 Fax (01722) 716828
E-mail: enquiries@mjabbott.co.uk
Website: www.mjabbott.co.uk

M J Abbott Limited offer a range of specialist services to the golf and leisure industry. Recognised as one of Britain's leading companies offering Rain Bird irrigation systems. Land drainage, golf course construction and maintenance are all undertaken by experienced employees utilising the company's own specially adapted machinery.

Arden Lea Irrigation Ltd
160 Moss Lane, Hesketh Bank,
Preston, Lancashire PR4 6AE.
Tel (01772) 812433 Fax (01772) 815371
E-mail: alirrig@aol.com

Arden Lea Irrigation established nearly 30 years ago specialises in irrigation on golf courses and other leisure facilities. With our experienced staff we have completed work on many well known golf courses throughout the UK and Southern Ireland. We are an independent company and can supply any type of irrigation equipment. Full member of the British Turf and Landscape Irrigation Association.

Glen Farrow (UK) Ltd
Spalding Road, Pinchbeck,
Spalding, Lincolnshire PE11 3UE.
Tel (01775) 722327 Fax (01775) 725444
E-mail: info@glenfarrow.co.uk
Website: www.glenfarrow.co.uk

With over 30 years' experience and an excellent reputation for workmanship, Glen Farrow offer a full design, supply and installation service using competitive and cost-effective solutions, contract maintenance and emergency repairs also undertaken.

Grassform Ltd - Golf Courses, Sports Grounds and Land Drainage Contractors
Dunsteads Farm, Trueloves Lane,
Ingatestone, Essex CM4 0NJ.
Tel (01277) 355500 Fax (01277) 355504
E-mail: sales@grassform.co.uk
Website: www.grassform.co.uk

Grassform Limited undertakes all types of golf course projects. From new build to re-construction of tees, greens and bunkers. We also install land drainage systems, sand banding, lakes, water features, footpaths, buggy paths and driving ranges. For further information please contact Mark Dunning.

ISS Aquaturf Systems Ltd
Unit 18, Downton Industrial Estate,
Batten Road, Downton, Salisbury,
Wiltshire SP5 3HU.
Tel (01725) 513880 Fax (01725) 513003

ISS Aquaturf Systems Limited are master dealers for *Toro & Hunter* operating throughout southern England in the design, supply and installation of automatic pop-up irrigation systems for golf courses. The company has

been in business for 20 years and specialises in providing quality systems at competitive prices.

L S Systems Ltd
188 Blackgate Lane, Tarleton,
Preston, Lancashire PR4 6UU.
Tel (01772) 815080 Fax (01772) 815417
E-mail: sales@lssystems.co.uk
Website: www.lssystems.co.uk

L S Systems are TORO Elite contractors. We provide a comprehensive design and installation service for complete irrigation solutions for all golf clubs. We are the largest stockist of TORO equipment in the north of England. Please call for a no obligation estimate.

Landline Ltd
1 Bluebridge Industrial Estate,
Halstead, Essex CO9 2EX.
Tel (01784) 476699 Fax (01784) 472507
E-mail: info@landline.co.uk
Website: www.landline.co.uk

Landline are specialist suppliers, installers of lake pond and irrigation reservoir linings. Free technical advisory service is available for all aspects of liner installation. We offer a complete service to customers backed by over 20 years' practical experience.

Oakdale T & G Irrigation
175 Westgate Road, Belton,
Doncaster DN9 1QA.
Tel (01427) 874200 Fax (01427) 875333
E-mail: david@oakdale.uk.com
Website: www.oakdale.uk.com

We design and install all types of turf irrigation systems and water storage solutions. Our engineers respond rapidly to service/maintenance enquiries. We supply all makes of irrigation equipment and undertake all sizes of contracts.

Ocmis Irrigation (UK) Ltd
Head Office: Higher Burrow,
Kingsbury, Martock, Somerset TA12 6BU.
Scotland: Broadmeadow, Harburn,
West Calder, West Lothian EH55 8RT.
Ireland: 1 Glenageary Avenue,
Dun Laoghaire, Co Dublin.
Main telephone and fax numbers
for all offices:
Tel 0870 600 5131 Fax 0870 600 5132

Ocmis Irrigation offer the complete irrigation service including the design, supply and installation of Rain Bird, Buckner and Hunter irrigation systems. Complete after-sales service, full maintenance and service contracts for all types and makes of irrigation systems.

Robin Hume Associates Ltd
Unit 13 Hardwicke Stables,
Hadnall, Shrewsbury,
Shropshire SY4 4AS.
Tel (01939) 210417 Fax (01939) 210890
E-mail: info@irrigationconsultants.co.uk
Website: www.irrigationconsultants.co.uk

Independent consultants offering advice on all aspects of golf course irrigation - water resourcing - contract management - design and operation.

STRI - The Sports Turf Research Institute
St Ives Estate,
Bingley,
West Yorkshire BD16 1AU.
Tel (01274) 565131 Fax (01274) 561891
E-mail: info@stri.co.uk
Website: www.stri.co.uk

Independent specialists offering you help and advice for the design, construction, management and maintenance, irrigation or renovation of your golf course. Comprehensive in-house support services for ecology, testing, turf pathology and research.

Toro Irrigation Products - Lely (UK) Ltd
Station Road,
St Neots, Huntingdon,
Cambridgeshire PE19 1QH.
Tel (01480) 226800 Fax (01480) 226801
E-mail: toro.info@lely.co.uk
Website: www.toro.com

Toro provides customers with a complete range of innovative, high quality irrigation products and systems, including upgrade controllers, to help grow and maintain the best turf - the only brand to offer both commercial and irrigation equipment.

York & Martin
39 Salisbury Street,
Fordingbridge, Hampshire SP6 1AB.
Tel (01425) 652087 Fax (01425) 652476
E-mail: msm@yorkandmartin.com
Website: www.yorkandmartin.com

Independent irrigation consultants providing objective advice on all irrigation related matters

including water sourcing, existing system evaluation, system designs and specifications, project supervision etc. Operating throughout the UK and mainland Europe.

JEWELLERY

Solent Souvenirs Ltd
Hamble Bank,
40 Newtown Road,
Warsash,
Southampton, Hampshire SO31 9FZ.
Tel (01489) 577985 Fax (01489) 577886
E-mail: solentsouvenirs@aol.com

Britain's premier supplier of specialised golf jewellery and quality gifts. Many items designed and manufactured exclusively for us and unobtainable elsewhere. Replace that traditional trophy with an elegant prize which will be both useful and cherished. Most items delivered overnight.

MAIL ORDER

Steve Schofield Golf Books
29 Nichols Way,
Wetherby, West Yorkshire LS22 6AD.
Tel/Fax (01937) 581276
E-mail: golfbooks@steveschofield.com

Classic golf books for sale, new, old and antiquarian. Books on golf history, architecture, biography, club and ball collecting and instruction. Free catalogue on request.

PATHWAYS

Dura-Sport Ltd
- Synthetic Surfaces for Golf
Road Barn Farm,
Croft Road,
Cosby, Leicestershire LE9 1SG.
Tel 0116-286 3800 Fax 0116-286 3888
E-mail: sales@dura-sport.co.uk

The leading supplier of proven synthetic surface solutions for pathways, waiting areas, winter tees and putting/pitching areas including the revolutionary and patented Sure-Step surfacing.

Mention The Royal & Ancient Golfer's Handbook when making your enquiries

PERSONAL EQUIPMENT & ACCESSORIES

Mycoal Warm Packs Ltd
Unit 1, Imperial Park,
Empress Road,
Southampton, Hampshire SO14 0JW.
Tel 023 8021 1068 Fax 023 8023 1398
Website: www.mycoal.co.uk

Suppliers and manufacturers of the ever popular handwarmers and thermo-mittens. All enquiries welcome - small or large.

PERSONALISED PRODUCTS

Bryants of Leeds
Speedwell Street,
Meanwood Road,
Leeds LS6 2TD.
Tel 0113-242 8330 Fax 0113-242 6330
Website: www.dimplygolf.com

The leading supplier of personalised golf merchandise. Golf club membership tags and labels, green fee stationery. Captain's Day, Society events and Corporate Golf Day merchandise. Call for a free colour brochure or visit us on our website.

Derek Burridge (Wholesale) Ltd
Awards House,
Unit 15,
The Metro Centre,
Springfield Road, Hayes,
Middlesex UB4 0LE.
Tel 020 8569 0123 Fax 020 8569 0111

The country's leading suppliers of golf prizes, celebrating their 43rd year, offer a vast range of silverplate, crystal, china, clocks, leather goods and sporting trophies, all at trade prices. Glass and silverplate in-house engraving service. Next day delivery throughout the UK. Call for our brochure. (See advertisement page 18 for further details.)

Galloway Crystal & Glass Ltd
Beeswing,
by Dumfries DG2 8ED.
Tel (01387) 760643 Fax (01387) 760537
E-mail: mccallum@gallowayglass.com
Websites: www.gallowayglass.com
www.crystalforgolfers.com

Specialist plain and cut crystal suppliers and engravers. Many innovative golfing gift ideas through our special collections. Personalisation our speciality. Ask for our catalogue along with club and reseller price lists.

H M T Plastics Ltd

Fairway House,
31A Framfield Road,
Uckfield, East Sussex TN22 5AH.
Tel (01825) 769393 Fax (01825) 769494
E-mail: hmt@aol.com
Website: www.hmt-plastics.com

Bag tags supplied in nine colours either round, pear shaped, shield maxi or sunrise to accommodate club logo, from a choice of print colours. Adhesive Year Stickers available in choice of nine colours and sold separately. *(See advertisement page 16 for further details.)*

PICTURES & PRINTS

Grandison Golf Gallery

'Gowanbank',
5 Sorley's Brae,
Dollar FK14 7AS.
Tel (01259) 740318
E-mail: info@grandisongolfgallery.com
Website: www.grandisongolfgallery.com

Finest quality limited edition prints of the world's premier golfing venues by one of the world's leading golf artists, William Grandison. Each print is individually signed and numbered. Gifts and prizes of distinction for the discerning golfer. Private commissions.

Richard Chorley Golf Art

159 Lonsdale Road,
Stevenage,
Hertfordshire SG1 5DG.
Tel/Fax (01438) 727901

Richard Chorley, England's premier golf artist. Private commissions, original oil paintings, drawings and limited edition prints. Prints signed by the artist, numbered and embossed. Collection of classic courses and golfing greats. Ideal corporate and captain's prizes gifts.

PLAY AND STAY

Portugal Fairways - Go-Golf-Pay-Less

Estrada de Pera,
Sesmarias,
8200 Albufeira, Portugal.
Tel +44 (0) 1908 311768
E-mail: info@go-golf-pay-less.com
Website: www.go-golf-pay-less.com

Algarve, Estoril and Costa Azul golfing breaks - let Go-Golf-Pay-Less book your courses, preferred dates and tee times at discounted prices at no charge to you! Accommodation in a choice of hotels, villas, motels and apartments. Car rental and airport transfers.

PORTUGAL

Portugal Fairways - Go-Golf-Pay-Less

Estrada de Pera,
Sesmarias,
8200 Albufeira,
Portugal.
Tel +44 (0) 1908 311768
E-mail: info@go-golf-pay-less.com
Website: www.go-golf-pay-less.com

Algarve, Estoril and Costa Azul golfing breaks - let Go-Golf-Pay-Less book your courses, preferred dates and tee times at discounted prices at no charge to you! Accommodation in a choice of hotels, villas, motels and apartments. Car rental and airport transfers.

PRACTICE NETTING/CAGES

Pan European (Golf) 1973 (PEP)

Old Mill Works,
High Street,
Maldon, Essex CM9 5EH.
Tel (01621) 851700 Fax (01621) 850417
E-mail: info@golfpep.co.uk
Website: www.golfpep.co.uk

Products include a wide range of practice nets and mats for beginners through to professionals. We also make a commercial range of nets and mats for clubs, stores and leisure centres. Worldwide export sales our speciality.

Tildenet Ltd

Hartcliffe Way,
Bristol BS3 5RJ.
Tel 0117-966 9684 Fax 0117-923 1251
E-mail: enquiries@tildenet.co.uk
Website: www.tildenet.co.uk

Tildenet supply and install a comprehensive range of quality products to the Golfing World. These include perimeter ball stop netting, practice nets and mats for the professional enthusiast. Anti-ball plug nets, target nets, target greens and anti-dazzle netting for clubs, and grass germination and bunker membranes for the greenkeeper.

PRINTING

Iain Crosbie Printers
Beechfield Road,
Willowyard Industrial Estate,
Beith, Ayrshire KA15 1LN.
Tel (01505) 504848 Fax: (01505) 504674
E-mail: crosbieprinters@dial.pipex.com

At Crosbie Printers we have over 20 years' experience in printing associated with golf and commerce. We manufacture scorecards (standard and bespoke), fixture books/diaries, green fee tickets, marketing brochures/leaflets and all associated printed stationery. *(See advertisement page 16 for further details.)*

PUTTER & CHIPPERS MANUFACTURERS/ SUPPLIERS

Bronty Golf
3 Musgrave Mount, Eccleshill,
Bradford, West Yorkshire BD2 3LA.
Tel/Fax +44 (0) 1274 773585
Mobile: +44 (0) 7950 397603
E-mail: brontygolf1@activemail.co.uk
Website: www.brontygolf.co.uk

Manufacturers of high quality British made custom golf clubs, putters and specialist clubs. Authentic replicas and hickory shafted putters etc.

Callaway Golf Europe Ltd
Unit 27 Barwell Business Park,
Leatherhead Road,
Chessington, Surrey KT9 2NY.
Tel +44 (0) 20 8391 0111

Manufacturer of golf clubs, golf balls and accessories. Callaway Golf is now the distributor for Odyssey Golf.

RANGE BALL MANUFACTURERS/ SUPPLIERS

European Golf Machinery
Street Garage,
Bucklesham,
Ipswich, Suffolk IP10 0DN.
Tel (01473) 659815 Fax (01473) 659045
E-mail: sales@europeangolf.prestel.co.uk
Website: www.web-marketing.co.uk/ europeangolfmachinery

Manufacturers of driving range equipment including golf ball collectors, dispensers, ball washers and elevators. Kawasaki ATV and Mule distributors. *(See advertisement page 18 for further details.)*

RECRUITMENT CONSULTANTS

Golf Search - The Golfing Recruitment Specialists
Kildare House,
1012-104 Sheen Road,
Richmond-on-Thames,
Surrey TW9 1UF.
Tel 020 8334 1125 Fax 020 8334 1177

Golf Search has years of recruitment experience and the largest database of golf management personnel in Europe. We carry out comprehensive interviews and reference checks on all candidates. The professional service provided offers exceptional value for money, our fees are 10% of salary. Please phone for further information.

Portfolio International
5 Breams Buildings,
London EC4A 1DY.
Tel +44 (0) 207 520 5000
Fax +44 (0) 207 520 5007
E-mail: suzie.boyd@portfoliointl.com
Website: www.portfoliointernational.com

Fifteen years' experience providing specialist recruitment services to the hospitality industry. Executive search, database search (over 36,000 contacts) or advertised search. Our golf division can save you valuable time and expense providing key management to golf clubs and resorts. Please phone for further information.

REMOTE CONTROLLED TROLLEYS

Middlemore Ltd
Sharrocks Street,
Wolverhampton,
West Midlands WV1 3RP.
Tel (01902) 870077 Fax (01902) 455200
E-mail: electra-caddie@thama.co.uk
Website: www.thama.co.uk

Manufacturers of *ELECTRA CADDIE* 'Premier' and 'Compact' one-piece foldaway powered trolleys and the 4-wheel single seater *RYDEON '2000'* buggy - simply load it into the boot of your car! Break par, not your back! Free colour brochure on request. *(See advertisement page 18 for further details.)*

RIDE-ON BUGGIES

A La Carts
Beechwood,
Bakeham Lane,
Englefield Green TW20 9TU.
Tel/Fax (01784) 472982
E-mail: jt@alacarts.co.uk
Website: www.alacarts.tsx.org
Manufacturers and distributors of single and two-seater golf buggies. Also powered trolleys.

Patterson Products
Unit 6, Fordwater Trading Estate,
Ford Road,
Chertsey, Surrey KT16 8HG.
Tel (01932) 570016 Fax (01932) 570084
E-mail: info@patterson.co.uk
Website: www.patterson.co.uk
Manufacturers and retailers of the *Trio* single-seat, transportable golf cart. Major suppliers and consultants to Handigolf, a charity for the severely disabled golfer. The *Trio* is now in its 16th year with over 4,500 happy users.

Teltale
6 Skye Road,
Shawfarm Industrial Estate,
Prestwick KA9 2TA.
Tel/Fax (01292) 475125
E-mail: john@teltale.uk.com
Website: www.teltale.uk.com
Teltale ride-on buggy. New design and innovative user-friendly buggy. Can be quickly folded down in a few seconds to fit into small hatchback car. High power motors and extra wide tyres. Ideally suitable for hire.

SCORECARDS & PLANNERS

Eagle Promotions Ltd
Eagle House, 1 Clearway Court,
139-141 Croydon Road,
Caterham, Surrey CR3 6PF.
Tel (01883) 344244 Fax (01883) 341777
E-mail: info@eaglepromotions.co.uk
Website: www.eaglepromotions.co.uk
Eagle Promotions offer a comprehensive range of products from certified course measurement and tee signs through to scorecards, yardage books, green fee tickets, members' tags, event and leader boards, honours boards, clubhouse and general course signage. For further information please contact Philip McInley on 01883 344244.

Iain Crosbie Printers
Beechfield Road,
Willowyard Industrial Estate,
Beith,
Ayrshire KA15 1LN.
Tel (01505) 504848 Fax: (01505) 504674
E-mail: crosbieprinters@dial.pipex.com
At Crosbie Printers we have over 20 years' experience in printing associated with golf and commerce. We manufacture scorecards (standard and bespoke), fixture books/diaries, green fee tickets, marketing brochures/leaflets and all associated printed stationery. *(See advertisement page 16 for further details.)*

SIMULATORS/ANALYSERS

Sports Coach Systems Ltd
Curtis Road,
Dorking,
Surrey RH4 1XD.
Tel +44 (0) 1306 741888
Fax +44 (0) 1306 877888
E-mail: sportscoachsys@aol.com
Website: www.sports-coach.com
Manufacturers of the world's finest range of golf electronics and software. Projected systoms from under £6,000, club, ball and swing analysis, Links LS Simulators, Photographic Simulators and Driving Ranges. As well as digital firewire with the world famous Sports Coach 2003. Europe's largest manufacturer of golf mats, Portarange nets and cage nets.

SYNTHETIC SURFACES

Dura-Sport Ltd
- Synthetic Surfaces for Golf
Road Barn Farm,
Croft Road,
Cosby, Leicestershire LE9 1SG.
Tel 0116-286 3800 Fax 0116-286 3888
E-mail: sales@dura-sport.co.uk
The leading supplier of proven synthetic surface solutions for pathways, waiting areas, winter tees and putting/pitching areas including the revolutionary and patented Sure-Step surfacing.

TEE SIGNS

Eagle Promotions Ltd

Eagle House, 1 Clearway Court,
139-141 Croydon Road,
Caterham, Surrey CR3 6PF.
Tel (01883) 344244 Fax (01883) 341777
E-mail: info@eaglepromotions.co.uk
Website: www.eaglepromotions.co.uk

Eagle Promotions offer a comprehensive range
of products from certified course measurement
and tee signs through to scorecards, yardage
books, green fee tickets, members' tags, event
and leader boards, honours boards, clubhouse
and general course signage. For further
information please contact Philip McInley on
01883 344244.

THERMAL WEAR

Mycoal Warm Packs Ltd

Unit 1, Imperial Park, Empress Road,
Southampton, Hampshire SO14 0JW.
Tel 023 8021 1068 Fax 023 8023 1398
Website: www.mycoal.co.uk

Suppliers and manufacturers of the ever
popular handwarmers and thermo-mittens. All
enquiries welcome - small or large.

TRAINING & TEACHING AIDS

STRI - The Sports Turf Research Institute

St Ives Estate,
Bingley,
West Yorkshire BD16 1AU.
Tel (01274) 565131 Fax (01274) 561891
E-mail: info@stri.co.uk
Website: www.stri.co.uk

A specialist provider and supplier of books and
training courses. Over 200 titles available from
our on-line bookshop (www.stri.co.uk).
Catalogue and training course details on
request.

Sports Coach Systems Ltd

Curtis Road,
Dorking, Surrey RH4 1XD.
Tel +44 (0) 1306 741888
Fax +44 (0) 1306 877888
E-mail: sportscoachsys@aol.com
Website: www.sports-coach.com

Manufacturers of the world's finest range of
golf electronics and software. Projected

systoms from under £6,000, club, ball and
swing analysis, Links LS Simulators,
Photographic Simulators and Driving Ranges.
As well as digital firewire with the world
famous Sports Coach 2003. Europe's largest
manufacturer of golf mats, Portarange nets and
cage nets.

TROPHIES

Derek Burridge (Wholesale) Ltd

Awards House,
Unit 15,
The Metro Centre,
Springfield Road,
Hayes, Middlesex UB4 0LE.
Tel 020 8569 0123 Fax 020 8569 0111

The country's leading suppliers of golf prizes,
celebrating their 43rd year, offer a vast range of
silverplate, crystal, china, clocks, leather goods
and sporting trophies, all at trade prices. Glass
and silverplate in-house engraving service.
Next day delivery throughout the UK. Call for
our brochure. *(See advertisement page 18 for
further details.)*

Fine Art Golf

Rodono House,
St Mary's Loch,
Yarrow Valley,
Scottish Borders TD7 5LH.
Tel (01750) 42215
E-mail: info@FineGolfArt.com
Website: www.finegolfart.com

Specialist supplier of beautiful, hand-framed-
in-Scotland golfing pictures, providing golf
prints, cartoons and rare hand-coloured
caricatures for corporate gifts, retirement
presents, special birthday gifts and top quality
trophies for corporate golf days.

Galloway Crystal & Glass Ltd

Beeswing,
by Dumfries DG2 8ED.
Tel (01387) 760643 Fax (01387) 760537
E-mail: mccallum@gallowayglass.com
Websites: www.gallowayglass.com
www.crystalforgolfers.com

Specialist plain and cut crystal suppliers and
engravers. Many innovative golfing gift ideas
through our special collections. Personalisation
our speciality. Ask for our catalogue along with
club and reseller price lists.

TUITION

Beaufort Golf Course
Churchtown, Beaufort,
Killarney, Co Kerry, Ireland.
Tel +353 64 44440 Fax +353 64 44752

A traditional Kerry welcome awaits you at *the Friendliest Course in Kerry*. Challenging 18-hole par 71 championship course, buggies and caddies for hire, excellent golf shop, bar food and snacks. Tuition can be arranged with our golf professional. Societies and groups welcome. *(See advertisement page 27 for further details.)*

Cannington Golf Course
Cannington College,
Cannington, Bridgwater,
Somerset TA5 2LS.
Tel/Fax (01278) 655050

Designed by Martin Hawtree of Oxford and built to highest international specifications in 1992 by Brian Pierson Limited under the consultancy of top agronomists Jim Arthur and Gordon Child. Together they have produced arguably the best 9-hole golf course with its 18 tees in the west of England. With its 'Links-Like' appearance in high summer the subtle contours make for a testing round of golf for the scratch golfer, yet it is receptive to the beginner with its wide spaces at 2,929 yards par 34. Beating par will take skill and courage.

European Golf Teachers Federation - EGTF
5 Hastings Road, Bromley, Kent BR2 8NZ.
Tel 020 8462 4120 Fax 020 8462 3983
E-mail: egtf@dial.pipex.com
Website: www.egtf.co.uk

We offer intensive teaching courses for professionals and amateurs who would like to know how to teach the game simply. The EGTF is the leader in the field of golf instruction.

Rodway Hill Golf Course
Newent Road, Highnam,
Gloucestershire GL2 8DN.
Tel (01452) 384222

An 18-hole, par 70 course, open to the public, two miles south west of Gloucester, with panoramic views of the Cotswolds. It has a well stocked shop, practice and teaching facilities. Hire kit available. Bar and restaurant facilities. Societies welcome.

WATER RESOURCES/RESERVOIR DESIGN

2iC - International Irrigation Consultants
Offices in Surrey: Cranbourne, Avenue Road, Cranleigh, Surrey GU6 7LL.
Tel/Fax (01483) 278416
Lincolnshire: 10 Peregrine Close, Sleaford, Lincolnshire NG34 7UY.
Tel/Fax (01529) 300224
E-mails: bill@2ic.co.uk Marcus@2ic.co.uk

Independent consulting engineers specialising in the sourcing of water and the design and construction management of irrigation reservoirs. Hydrological monitoring projects and abstraction licence applications. 2iC - for more water and somewhere to store it!

L S Systems Ltd
188 Blackgate Lane,
Tarleton, Preston,
Lancashire PR4 6UU.
Tel (01772) 815080 Fax (01772) 815417
E-mail: sales@lssystems.co.uk
Website: www.lssystems.co.uk

L S Systems are TORO Elite contractors. We provide a comprehensive design and installation service for complete irrigation solutions for all golf clubs. We are the largest stockist of TORO equipment in the north of England. Please call for a no obligation estimate.

Landline Ltd
1 Bluebridge Industrial Estate,
Halstead, Essex CO9 2EX.
Tel (01784) 476699 Fax (01784) 472507
E-mail: info@landline.co.uk
Website: www.landline.co.uk

Landline are specialist suppliers, installers of lake pond and irrigation reservoir linings. Free technical advisory service is available for all aspects of liner installation. We offer a complete service to customers backed by over 20 years' practical experience.

Robin Hume Associates Ltd
Unit 13 Hardwicke Stables, Hadnall,
Shrewsbury, Shropshire SY4 4AS.
Tel (01939) 210417 Fax (01939) 210890
E-mail: info@irrigationconsultants.co.uk
Website: www.irrigationconsultants.co.uk

Independent consultants offering advice on all aspects of golf course irrigation - water resourcing - contract management - design and operation.

WATER STORAGE/TANKS

ISS Aquaturf Systems Ltd
Unit 18, Downton Industrial Estate,
Batten Road, Downton, Salisbury,
Wiltshire SP5 3HU.
Tel (01725) 513880 Fax (01725) 513003

ISS Aquaturf Systems Limited are master
dealers for *Toro & Hunter* operating throughout
southern England in the design, supply and
installation of automatic pop-up irrigation
systems for golf courses. The company has
been in business for 20 years and specialises in
providing quality systems at competitive prices.

Landline Ltd
1 Bluebridge Industrial Estate,
Halstead, Essex CO9 2EX.
Tel (01784) 476699 Fax (01784) 472507
E-mail: info@landline.co.uk
Website: www.landline.co.uk

Landline are specialist suppliers, installers of
lake pond and irrigation reservoir linings. Free
technical advisory service is available for all
aspects of liner installation. We offer a
complete service to customers backed by over
20 years' practical experience.

Oakdale T & G Irrigation
175 Westgate Road, Belton,
Doncaster DN9 1QA.
Tel (01427) 874200 Fax (01427) 875333
E-mail: david@oakdale.uk.com
Website: www.oakdale.uk.com

We design and install all types of turf irrigation
systems and water storage solutions. Our
engineers respond rapidly to service/
maintenance enquiries. We supply all makes of
irrigation equipment and undertake all sizes of
contracts.

Ocmis Irrigation (UK) Ltd
Head Office: Higher Burrow, Kingsbury,
Martock, Somerset TA12 6BU.
Scotland: Broadmeadow, Harburn,
West Calder, West Lothian EH55 8RT.
Ireland: 1 Glenageary Avenue,
Dun Laoghaire, Co Dublin.
*Main telephone and fax numbers
for all offices:*
Tel 0870 600 5131 Fax 0870 600 5132

Ocmis Irrigation offer the complete irrigation
service including the design, supply and
installation of Rain Bird, Buckner and Hunter
irrigation systems. Complete after-sales service,
full maintenance and service contracts for all
types and makes of irrigation systems.

WEATHERWEAR

Mycoal Warm Packs Ltd
Unit 1, Imperial Park, Empress Road,
Southampton, Hampshire SO14 0JW.
Tel 023 8021 1068 Fax 023 8023 1398
Website: www.mycoal.co.uk

Suppliers and manufacturers of the ever
popular handwarmers and thermo-mittens. All
enquiries welcome - small or large.

Sunderland of Scotland Ltd
PO Box 14, Glasgow G2 1ER.
Tel 0141-572 5220 Fax 0141-572 5221
Website: www.sunderlandgolf.com

Sunderland of Scotland manufacture high
quality golf rainwear in Scotland. All rainsuits
are tour-tested and guaranteed waterproof and
breathable, a variety of fabrics including
Goretex being used. Sunderlands also
manufacture the famous Sunderland Original
Weatherbeater, Classic windproof Pullovers
and Fleece. Official supplier to PGA, PGAE,
LPGA, LET and St Andrews Links Trust.

WINTER ALL-WEATHER TEE MATS

Dura-Sport Ltd
- Synthetic Surfaces for Golf
Road Barn Farm, Croft Road,
Cosby, Leicestershire LE9 1SG.
Tel 0116-286 3800 Fax 0116-286 3888
E-mail: sales@dura-sport.co.uk

The leading supplier of proven synthetic
surface solutions for pathways, waiting areas,
winter tees and putting/pitching areas including
the revolutionary and patented Sure-Step
surfacing.

Choose from among
the best hotels in
the British Isles and Ireland

Golfing Hotel Compendium

The Golfing Hotel Compendium is a comprehensive source of information for golfers wishing to find the most comfortable place to stay at or close to some of the finest courses in the country. This section has been compiled from the premier hotels, guest houses and self-catering facilities in the British Isles which include golf among their many attractions.

If readers wish especially to recommend an establishment which is not listed in this section of the Royal & Ancient Golfer's Handbook the editors will be happy to be advised.

ENGLAND

South West

Burnham & Berrow - The Dormy
Burnham and Berrow Golf Club,
St Christopher's Way,
Burnham-on-Sea, Somerset TA8 2PE.
Tel (01278) 785760
E-mail: Secretary@BurnhamandBerrow.
freeserve.co.uk

18-hole championship links golf course and 9-hole course. Dormy accommodation available. *(See advertisement page 613 for further details.)*

China Fleet Country Club
Saltash, Cornwall PL12 6LJ.
Tel (01752) 848668 Fax (01752) 848456
E-mail: sales@china-fleet.co.uk
Website: www.china-fleet.co.uk

Situated in 180 acres of Cornish countryside, 40 self-catering 4- and 6-berth apartments, 18-hole par 72 golf, 28-bay driving range, pool, health suite, gymnasium, raquet sports, bars, restaurant and coffee shop. *(See advertisement page 615 for further details.)*

The Dorset Golf & Country Club Golf Hotel
Bere Regis,
Nr Poole,
Dorset BH20 7NT.
Tel (01929) 472244 Fax (01929) 471294
E-mail: admin@dorsetgolfresort.com
Website: www.dorsetgolfresort.com

3-Crown Commended golf hotel in beautiful Hardy country overlooking Purbeck Hills. Excellent English cuisine with 16 twin bedded rooms. Reputation for personal service. Lakeland 18-hole and woodland 9-hole courses. Floodlit covered driving range. Golf packages available. Conference facilities available.

Fircroft Hotel
Owls Road,
Bournemouth, Dorset BH5 1AE.
Tel (01202) 309771 Fax (01202) 395644

The hotel is situated close to sea and shops with many superb golf courses in the area. Fine restaurant with choice of menus. Large car park. Late bar. Free use of leisure club 9am to 6pm, with indoor pool, jacuzzi, sauna steam room and gym.

Golf View Hotel
Headland Road,
Newquay,
Cornwall TR7 1HN.
Tel/Fax (01637) 875082

An outstanding hotel overlooking Newquay
Golf Course and Newquay's world famous
Fistral beach (150 yards from the hotel). Most
rooms en suite. Own car park. Reduced green
fees on most courses. Special party rates.

Pines Hotel
Burlington Road,
Swanage,
Dorset BH19 1LT.
Tel (01929) 425211 Fax (01929) 422075
E-mail: reservations@pineshotel.co.uk
Website: www.pineshotel.co.uk

50-bedroom family run 3-Star hotel. All
bedrooms have private bathroom, telephone
and colour TV. One and a half miles from Isle
of Purbeck Golf Club. Within easy reach of all
Dorset courses. Award-winning restaurant.
Cliff top position with stunning sea views.

Tewkesbury Park Hotel, Golf & Country Club
Lincoln Green Lane,
Tewkesbury, Gloucestershire GL20 7DN.
Tel (01684) 295405 Fax (01684) 292386
Website: www.corushotels.co.uk

An elegant extended 18th-century manor house
with stunning views across to the Malvern
Hills. The hotel has extensive leisure facilities
including an 18-hole par 3 parkland golf course
including wooded areas and water hazards.
(See advertisement page 4 for further details.)

Trevose Golf & Country Club
Constantine Bay,
Padstow, North Cornwall PL28 8JB.
Tel (01841) 520208 Fax (01841) 521057
E-mail: reception@trevose-gc.co.uk
Website: www.trevose-gc.co.uk/

Trevose offers not only great golf
(championship 18-hole course, a 9-hole full
length (3,100 yards) par 35 plus a 9-hole short
course) but also a first class clubhouse and
restaurant, three hard all-weather tennis courts,
a heated outdoor swimming pool in the
summer, a games room for the kids and a
boutique. Accommodation is available in
bungalows, chalets, trehuel flats, dormy flats
and cabins. Send for our detailed colour
brochure. Open all year. Societies welcome.

Woodbury Park Golf & Country Club
Woodbury Castle,
Woodbury, Exeter, Devon EX5 1JJ.
Tel (01395) 233382 Fax (01395) 233384

Luxury 55-bedroom hotel with five superb
lodges. The Nigel Mansell owned resort
encompasses 27 holes, including the Oaks
championship course, in addition to extensive
leisure facilities. The ideal venue for your
golfing break.

South East

The Bell Hotel
The Quay, Sandwich, Kent CT13 9EF.
Tel (01304) 613388 Fax (01304) 615308
E-mail: hotel@princes-leisure.co.uk
Website: www.princes-leisure.co.uk

The perfect base when playing Royal St
Georges, Prince's and Royal Cinque Ports - all
within ten minutes' drive. Relax in traditional
comfort in historic surroundings. Individually
designed rooms with en suite throughout.
Special inclusive golf breaks with the *Prince's
Golf Club. (See advertisement page 615 for further
details.)*

Botley Park Hotel Golf & Country Club
Winchester Road, Boorley Green,
Botley, Southampton SO32 2UA.
Tel (01489) 780888 Fax (01489) 789242
*E-mail: info@botleypark.macdonald-
hotels.co.uk*
Website: www.macdonaldhotels.co.uk

Set in 176 acres of rolling Hampshire
countryside, this 4-Star hotel has 100 en suite
bedrooms, superb restaurant, extensive leisure
facilities and its own picturesque and
challenging 18-hole par 70 golf course and
driving range. *(See advertisement page 613 for
further details.)*

Briggens House Hotel
Briggens Park, Stanstead Road (A414),
Stanstead Abbotts,
Nr Harlow, Hertfordshire SG12 8LD.
Tel (01279) 829955 Fax (01279) 793685
Website: www.corushotels.co.uk

A 17th-century house set in 80 acres of
parkland with a 9-hole professional golf course,
outdoor swimming pool and tennis courts. An
ideal base to visit Cambridge, London and the

Bluewater Shopping Centre, all within a 45 minutes' drive. *(See advertisement page 4 for further details.)*

Corus and Regal Hotels
**Blakelands House, Yeomans Drive,
Blakelands, Milton Keynes MK14 5HG.**
Reservations 0845 3000 2000
Websites: www.regalhotels.co.uk
www.corushotels.co.uk

Corus and Regal hotels have over 90 hotels throughout the country, ideally located for touring the best of Britain's golf courses. *(See advertisement page 4 for further details.)*

Coulsdon Manor
- Coulsdon Golf Centre
**Coulsdon Court Road,
Coulsdon, Surrey CR5 2LL.**
Tel 020 8660 6083 Fax 020 8668 3118
E-mail:
coulsdonmanor@marstonhotels.com
Website: www.marstonhotels.com

A relaxing yet challenging par 70 golf course set in 140 acres of Surrey parkland. Golf societies made very welcome. Excellent restaurant and bar facilities at the Manor. *(See advertisement page 615 for further details.)*

Flackley Ash Hotel
**Peasmarsh,
Nr Rye, East Sussex TN31 6YH.**
Tel (01797) 230651 Fax (01797) 230510
E-mail: enquiries@flackleyashhotel.co.uk
Website: www.flackleyashhotel.co.uk

3-Star Georgian country house hotel set in beautiful grounds with putting green. Indoor swimming pool, whirlpool spa, saunas, steam room, gym, massage and beauty treatments. Extensive wine list, good food and a friendly welcome.

Gatton Manor Hotel
Golf & Country Club Ltd
Ockley, Nr Dorking, Surrey RH5 5PQ.
Tel (01306) 627555
E-mail: gattonmanor@enterprise.net
Website: www.gattonmanor.co.uk

Set amidst its own 18-hole golf course in 200 acres of parklands and lakes, situated between London and the south coast, in the heart of the Surrey countryside. Superb all en suite accommodation overlooking the golf course and grounds. À la carte restaurants, large lounge bar, conference suites, gym and health club.

Lansdowne Hotel
**King Edward's Parade,
Eastbourne,
East Sussex BN21 4EE.**
Tel (01323) 725174 Fax (01323) 739721
E-mail: reception@lansdowne-hotel.co.uk
Website: www.lansdowne-hotel.co.uk

RAC/AA 3-Star. Play 36 holes a day on choice of seven courses; we book your tee-off time. Two nights with green fees, light lunch at club and use of our drying room. 17 January to 28 February £150; 1 to 31 March £160; 1 April to 31 May £169; 1 June to 30 September £179; 1 October to 31 December £162. Extra days pro rata. *(See advertisement page 613 for further details.)*

Parasampia Golf & Country Club
**Grove Road,
Donnington,
Newbury, Berkshire RG14 2LA.**
Tel (01635) 581000 Fax (01635) 552259
Website: www.parasampia.com

18-hole parkland/moorland championship course designed by Dave Thomas. The clubhouse and hotel are located within a beautifully renovated 18th-century gothic mansion. This will provide an ideal setting for your society, company golf day or conference stay.

Seaford - The Dormy House
**Seaford Golf Club,
East Blatchington,
Seaford, East Sussex BN25 2JD.**
Tel (01323) 892442

The Dormy House provides comfortable accommodation for 20 guests in 10 twin-bedded en suit bedrooms on the first floor of the clubhouse, and 2 single rooms in our bungalow annexe. For latest brochure ring 01323 892442.

Wokefield Park Golf Club
**Mortimer,
Reading,
Berkshire RG7 3AE.**
Tel 0118-933 4013 Fax 0118-933 4031

Set amid the Berkshire countryside this challenging 7,000 yards golf course has mature trees, winding streams, nine lakes and large bunkers. Wokefield also features 320 bedrooms, teaching academy and leisure facilities. Call the golf sales team on 0118-933 4018 and 4017.

East Anglia

Abbotsley Golf Hotel & Country Club
Eynesbury Hardwicke,
St Neots,
Cambridgeshire PE19 4XN.
Tel (01480) 474000 Fax (01480) 471018

Set in 250 acres of idyllic countryside, offering two 18-hole courses, a par 3, driving range, squash courts, fitness centre and a 42-bedroom hotel. Golf breaks and residential packages available. Operated by American Golf (UK) Limited.

Beaumaris Hotel
15 South Street,
Sheringham, Norfolk NR26 8LL.
Tel (01263) 822370 Fax (01263) 821421
E-mail: beauhotel@aol.com
Website: www.thebeaumarishotel.co.uk

Established and run by the same family for 55 years with a reputation for personal service and excellent English cuisine. 21 en suite bedrooms. AA 2-Star Ashley Courtenay Recommended; ETC 2-Star; Good Hotel Guide. Three minutes' walk Sheringham's exhilerating cliff top golf course.

Cambridgeshire Moat House Hotel
Bar Hill,
Cambridge CB3 8EU.
Tel (01954) 249988 (Hotel)
(01954) 780098 (Club) Fax (01954) 780010
Website: www.moathousehotels.com

Superb 18-hole 6,734 yard championship golf course set within 134 acres of parkland. Host to the East Anglian Open 2001, 2002 and 2003. This 134-bedroomed hotel has full leisure facilities, two excellent restaurants and three bars. Golf packages available.

Stoke By-Nayland Club Hotel
Leavenheath, Colchester, Essex CO6 4PZ.
Tel (01206) 262836 Fax (01205) 263356
E-mail: in@golf-club.co.uk
Website: www.stokebynaylandclub.co.uk

Recognised as one of the finest golf and leisure facilities in East Anglia. Two 18-hole championsip golf courses, covered driving range, all year round buggy availability. En suite accommodation in our luxury hotel. Renowned excellent cuisine. Superb indoor pool and gymnasium.

Wentworth Hotel
Wentworth Road,
Aldeburgh,
Suffolk IP15 5BD.
Tel (01728) 452312 Fax (01728) 454343
E-mail: stay@wentworth-aldeburgh.co.uk
Website: www.wentworth-aldeburgh.com

Country house hotel with sea views. Thirty-seven bedrooms, two comfortable, spacious lounges and Terrace Bar. AA Rosette restaurant serving local seafood. We know how to look after golfers. Visit our website.

White Horse Hotel - Leiston
Station Road,
Leiston, Suffolk IP16 4HD.
Tel (01728) 830694 Fax (01728) 833105

Close to three excellent courses in the heart of Suffolk Heritage Coast. Friendly bars, excellent food, 12 rooms, 11 en suite, all with TV and telephone. Bargain weekend breaks all year.

Northamptonshire

Farthingstone Hotel & Golf Course
Farthingstone,
Towcester, Northamptonshire NN12 8HA.
Tel (01327) 361291 Fax (01327) 361645

Set in glorious wooded countryside, just 90 minutes outside London. Farthingstone Hotel offers 16 superb en suite rooms, a challenging 18-hole golf course, squash court, full size snooker tables, and a carvery restaurant. Highly competitive tariffs.

Hellidon Lakes Hotel Golf & Country Club
Hellidon, Daventry,
Northamptonshire NN11 6GG.
Tel (01327) 262550 Fax (01327) 262559
E-mail: hellidon@marstonhotels.com
Website: www.marstonhotels.com

27 holes of golf through woodland and over lakes. Buggies for hire. Corporate, Society and residential packages available. 71 well appointed bedrooms and suites, country club with extensive health and fitness facilities including pool, gym and treatment rooms. Indoor golf simulator and 10-pin bowling. Only 20 minutes from junction 11 of the M40 and junction 16 of the M1, one and a half hours from M25. *(See advertisement page 617 for further details.)*

East Midlands

Dower House Hotel
Manor Estate,
Woodhall Spa,
Lincolnshire LN10 6PY.
Tel/Fax (01526) 352588

Situated within the Manor Estate the Dower House overlooks the new Woodhall 18-hole golf course. The hotel is renowned for food and wine. 3 Diamond. Golfing parties' tariff available.

The Grange & Links Hotel
Sea Lane,
Sandilands,
Sutton-on-Sea,
Lincolnshire LN12 2RA.
Tel (01507) 441334 Fax (01507) 443033
E-mail: grangelinks@ic24.net
Website: www.grangeandlinkshotel.com

3-Star 30-bedroom hotel with own 18-hole links course. Two tennis courts, snooker and ballroom. Award-winning hotel renowned for superb cuisine, friendliness, comfort and service.

North Shore Hotel
Golf Club & Course
North Shore Road,
Skegness PE25 1DN.
Tel (01754) 763298 Fax (01754) 761902
E-mail: golf@north-shore.co.uk
Website: www.north-shore.co.uk

A mature and challenging 18-hole part parkland and part links course with sea views on the edge of Skegness. Good all year round climate. Rarely closed in winter with no winter greens. Rarely closed bars, superb bar food and à la carte restaurant. 36 bedrooms available.

Petwood Hotel
Woodhall Spa,
Lincolnshire LN10 6QF.
Tel (01526) 352411 Fax (01526) 353473
Website: www.petwood.co.uk

Built in the early 1900s, this luxurious hotel is set in a 30-acre estate, close to Woodhall Spa's championship golf course. 50 en suite bedrooms and a popular restaurant specialising in local produce. Special golf packages available - ask for our golf brochure for further details.

West Midlands

Telford Golf & Country Club
Great Hay Drive,
Sutton Heights,
Telford, Shropshire TF7 4DT.
Tel (01952) 429977 Fax (01952) 586602
Website: www.corushotels.co.uk

The perfect place for a weekend away, this lovely hotel has its own 18-hole championship golf course together with well equipped leisure facilities. Visit the Ironbridge Gorge Museums and the nearby Tudor market town of Shrewsbury. *(See advertisement page 620 for further details.)*

Whitefields Hotel
Golf & Country Club
Coventry Road,
Thurlaston,
Nr Rugby,
Warwickshire CV23 9JR.
Tel (01788) 521800 Fax (01788) 521695
Website: www.whitefields/hotel.co.uk

18-hole course 6,223 yards. Driving range, putting green 18. Four conference rooms. 50 en suite rooms. Bars and à la carte restaurant. Societies welcome seven days. Call the secretary on 01788 815555. Reservations 01788 521800.

Yorkshire & Humberside

Aldwark Manor Hotel
Golf & Country Club
Aldwark,
Alne,
York, North Yorkshire YO61 1UF.
Tel (01347) 838146 (Hotel)
(01347) 838353 (Golf)
Fax (01347) 838867
E-mail: aldwark@marstonhotels.com
Website: www.marstonhotels.com

Victorian 60-bedroomed manor house set within beautiful parkland with the river Ure meandering through the 18-hole golf course. Within easy reach of York, Harrogate and Knaresborough. Ideal for visiting the Yorkshire Dales and moors. Health spa with highly trained therapists, swimming pool and sauna. Award-winning creative menus available in both restaurant and brasserie with friendly, efficient service. *(See advertisement page 617 for further details.)*

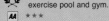

Cave Castle Hotel & Country Club
South Cave, East Yorkshire HU15 2EU.
Tel (01430) 422245 Fax (01430) 421118

Superb country manor house with 53 en suite bedrooms in tranquil 160-acre parkland setting with easy access to M62 motorway. Excellent, traditional cuisine is served in our character restaurant. Choice of two 18-hole golf courses (Cave Castle and Boothferry Park), plus use of leisure facilities, including 19m indoor pool, gym, sauna, steam and spa. This is a Unique Leisure Experience not to be missed! Golf and leisure breaks, visiting parties and non-golfers welcome.

Hotel Majestic - Scarborough
57 Northstead Manor Drive,
Scarborough, North Yorkshire YO12 6AG.
Tel/Fax (01723) 363806

ETB 2-Star. Privately owned hotel overlooking Peasholm Park. Minutes from Northcliffe Golf Course. All 19 bedrooms have en suite, double glazed, fully centrally heated. Cocktail bar. Draught beers. Golf parties welcomed. Flexible evening dinner times can be arranged.

The Royal Hotel - Scarborough
St Nicholas Street,
Scarborough, North Yorkshire YO11 2HE.
Tel (01723) 364333 Fax (01723) 500618
E-mail: royalhotel@englishrosehotels.com
Website: www.englishrosehotels.com

The historic and famous Royal Hotel is a quality 3-Star hotel in the central position overlooking Scarborough's South Bay and close to both North and South Cliff golf clubs. The championship course at Ganton is a short distance away. The hotel has been selected by the US, Great Britain and Ireland teams together with the R&A officials as their base for the 2003 Walker Cup competition. *(See advertisement page 617 for further details.)*

Rudding Park Hotel & Golf
Follifoot, Harrogate,
North Yorkshire HG3 1JH.
Tel (01423) 871350 Fax (01243) 872286
E-mail: sales@ruddingpark.com
Website: www.ruddingpark.com

The Rudding Park Estate, just two miles south of Harrogate, is an ideal venue for the discerning golfer. The contemporary award-winning 4-Star AA hotel and AA 2-Rosette Clocktower Restaurant, coupled with the magnificent 18-hole, par 72, parkland golf course, ensures a relaxing break. Golfing packages and special seasonal offers are available.

Wrangham House Hotel
10 Stonegate, Hunmanby,
Nr Filey, North Yorkshire YO14 0NS.
Tel (01723) 891333 Fax (01723) 892973
E-mail: mervynpoulter@lineone.net
Website: www.wranghamhouse.co.uk

Secluded Georgian country house hotel with 12 en suite rooms, dining room and bar. Ideally situated for golfers visiting Ganton, Riley, Scarborough and Bridlington courses.

North West

The Allerdale Court Hotel
Market Place,
Cockermouth, Cumbria CA13 9NQ.
Tel (01900) 823654 Fax (01900) 823033
Website: www.allerdalecourthotel.co.uk

2-Star Commended. Excellent restaurant, 24 en suite rooms, well stocked 19th hole. Two miles from Cockermouth Golf Club and near to Keswick and Silloth courses. Good value package deals for groups, societies and individuals.

The Fishermans Arms Hotel
The Coast Road,
Baycliff, Ulverston, Cumbria LA12 9RJ.
Tel (01229) 869387

Family run hotel built and styled in 1930's decor. Overlooking Morecombe Bay the ever changing real ales and good food add to the warm and welcoming atmosphere of the establishment. Nearest hotel to the Ulverston course.

Lancaster Golf Club
Ashton Hall,
Ashton with Stodday, Lancaster LA2 0AJ.
Tel (01524) 751247 Fax (01524) 752742
E-mail: sec@lancastergc.freeserve.co.uk
Website: www.lancastergc.co.uk

Facilities to accommodate 18 guests, all en suite bedrooms mainly twin rooms with a limited number of singles. First class catering, well stocked bar with a wide selection of fine wines and malt whiskies. Resident club professional. *(See advertisement page 22 for further details.)*

Metropole Hotel
3 Portland Street,
Southport, Merseyside PR8 1LL.
Tel (01704) 536836 Fax (01704) 549041
E-mail:
metropole.southport@btinternet.com
Website: www.btinternet.com/-
metropole.southport

RAC/AA 2-Star hotel. Centrally situated and close to Royal Birkdale and other championship courses. Fully licensed - late bar facilities for residents. Full size snooker table. Reduced rates for golfers. Golfing proprietors will assist with tee reservations.

Northcote Manor
Northcote Road,
Langho, Blackburn, Lancashire BB6 8BE.
Tel (01254) 240555 Fax (01254) 246568
E-mail: sales@northcotemanor.com
Website: www.northcotemanor.com

Premier country house hotel famous for its award-winning restaurant. Fabulous range of wines from the cellar. Fourteen excellent individual bedrooms. Within easy reach of five championship golf courses. Fully inclusive Golf Gourmet packages available - transport to all courses available. Fabulous venue for special occasions, weddings and corporate events. *(See advertisement page 619 for further details.)*

The Prince of Wales Hotel
Lord Street,
Southport, Merseyside PR8 1JS.
Tel (01704) 536688 Fax (01704) 543932

Since 1876 the Prince of Wales Hotel has been the premier golfers hotel in Southport. Used as the base for the Ryder Cup and British Open over the years, the hotel provides quality 4-Star accommodation. 103 rooms, two restaurants and bar. We are able to arrange tee-times at any of the twelve courses with prior arrangement in the area. The hotel is located centrally in Southport and offer on-site car parking. *(See advertisement page 617 for further details.)*

Royal Lytham St Anne's - The Dormy House
Royal Lytham & St Anne's Golf Club
Links Gate,
Lytham St Anne's,
Lancashire FY8 3LQ.
Tel (01253) 724206 Fax (01253) 780946

Ideal for small parties wishing to play the championship course. Accommodation for men only. Apply to the assistant secretary. *(See advertisement page 4 for further details.)*

Shaw Hill Golf & Country Club
Preston Road,
Whittle-Le-Woods,
Chorley, Lancashire PR6 7PP.
Tel (01257) 269221 Fax (01257) 261223

Shaw Hill comprises a 72 par 18-hole golf course, a fully equipped leisure centre and an AA award-winning restaurant and we can offer wedding and conference facilities. *(See advertisement page 619 for further details.)*

Isle of Man

Castletown Golf Links Hotel
Fort Island,
Derbyhaven,
Isle of Man IM9 1UA.
Tel (01624) 822201 Fax (01624) 824633
E-mail: golflinks@manx.net
Website: www.golfiom.com

An 18-hole links championship course voted number 73 in the UK by *Golf World* magazine. Measuring 6,711 yards SSS 72 established since 1892 is set on the peninsula of Langness surrounded by sea on three sides and overlooking the Manx rolling hills. Accommodation is available twelve months of the year, three bars, excellent local cuisine served in both the table d'hôte and à la carte restaurants. Visiting parties and non-members welcome.

North East

George Washington Golf & Country Club
Stone Cellar Road,
High Usworth,
District 12,
Washington, Tyne & Wear NE37 1PH.
Tel 0191-402 9988 Fax 0191-415 1166
Website: www.corushotels.co.uk

A hotel with something for everyone with its own 18-hole championship golf course and leisure centre including an indoor pool and beauty treatments. Ideal for shopping or touring Northumbria's historical sites and beautiful coastlines. *(See advertisement page 4 for further details.)*

HOTEL, RESTAURANT & COUNTRY CLUB
TENBURY WELLS, WORCESTERSHIRE

Idyllic lakeside setting in a private estate, perfect venue for weddings, conferences and private functions. Our own 9-hole golf course Par 68 5132 yards SSS65 on the Estate.

Indoor 16 metre pool and leisure facilities. Two excellent fishing lakes - fly and coarse fishing and bowls.

Warm welcoming ambiance and log fires in winter. 14 en-suite bedrooms. Excellent cuisine prepared with imagination and flair using only fresh local produce.

SPECIAL 2-DAY GOLF AND FISHING BREAKS CAN BE ARRANGED.

CALL US, WE ARE WELL WORTH A VISIT!
01584 810044

De Vere
St David's Park Hotel
Golf Club

RAC
★ ★ ★ ★
AA

ST. DAVID'S PARK HOTEL and Northop Country Park Golf Club offer luxury accommodation and superb facilities second to none, including our *championship 18 hole golf course, Health Club, swimming pool, fully equipped gymnasium, beautician, tennis courts, professional golf shop, Club Cafe and renowned restaurants.*

OUR GOLF CLUB AT NORTHOP COUNTRY PARK is set amongst mature trees and wonderful parkland. *The first class pavilion style Clubhouse offers a superb selection of facilities to complete the all round leisure experience.*

for further information call
01244 520800
or visit us at
E-mail: reservations.stdavidspark@devere-hotels.com
Website: www.devereonline.co.uk
fax: 01244 520930

at the Heart of everything

Gormanstown Manor
"Farm Guest House"
A Golfer's Paradise in Wicklow The Garden of Ireland

Near Wicklow Town and Brittas Bay
Co Wicklow, Ireland.
(Just outside Dublin City off N11)

OPEN ALL YEAR

Spectacular par 3 golf course 18-hole pitch and putt, and golf driving range with a qualified golf professional in attendance daily. Ideally located for the golfer who wishes to play on the top 25 courses in the area.

A warm welcome awaits at this charming family manor. Peaceful, relaxed atmosphere, spectacular surroundings. Extensive landscaped gardens with breathtaking scenery. En-suite bedrooms, sitting/lounge, dining rooms, TVs and telephones and open log fires.

EARLY BOOKING IS ESSENTIAL

Please phone or fax Margaret for details
Tel: +353 404 69432 Fax: +353 404 61832

E-mail: gormanstownmanor@tinet.ie
Website: www.homepage.eircom.net/~gormanstownmanor

Renvyle House Hotel awaits being discovered by you.......

A romantic, historic coastal hotel set in the wild splendour of Connemara amidst the beauty of the sea and mountains, where warmth and comfort is assured. Turf fires, cosy lounges and award-winning cuisine complete your relaxation.

Wonderful walks, tennis, horse riding, swimming pool, snooker, boating, fishing and cycling all available. For the discerning golfer there is the added bonus of our own 9-hole par 36 golf course and golf clinics.

Renvyle House Hotel
Connemara, Co Galway, Ireland.
Tel: +353 95 43511 Fax: +353 95 43515
E-mail: renvyle@iol.ie
Website: www.renvyle.com

Hall Garth
Golf & Country Club Hotel
Coatham Mundeville,
Darlington,
Co Durham DL1 3LU.
Tel (01325) 300400 Fax (01325) 310083
Website: www.corushotels.co.uk

A 16th-century country house adjoining 67
acres of parkland with its own 9 par 72-hole
golf course and extensive leisure club facilities.
(See advertisement page 4 for further details.)

Linden Hall
Longhorsley,
Morpeth,
Northumberland NE65 8XF.
Tel (01670) 500011 Fax (01670) 500001
Website: www.lindenhall.co.uk

Linden Hall golf course is located in the serene
grounds of Linden Hall Hotel, a 3-Star, 52-
bedroom luxury country house hotel with
swimming pool, health spa, gymnasium and
conference facilities. An added facility is the
14-bedroom, Linden Dormy House ideal for
golfing parties. The 18-hole, 6,846 yard SSS
73 golf course completely surrounds the hotel
and is set within mature woodland, rolling
parkland with established burns and lakes
amidst the stunning backdrop of the Cheviot
hills and Northumbrian coastline.

Ramside Hall Hotel & Golf Club
Carrville,
Durham DH1 1TD.
Tel 0191-386 5282 Fax 0191-386 0399

Set in 220 acres on the outskirts of the
cathedral city of Durham and surrounded by a
stimulating 27-hole golf course. 3-Star; 4-
Crown Highly Commended. 80 luxury
bedrooms, restaurant, grill room and carvery.
Conference and banqueting facilities. Superb
floodlit driving range and practice areas. *(See
advertisement page 619 for further details.)*

White Swan Hotel
Bondgate Within,
Alnwick,
Northumberland NE66 1TD.
Tel (01665) 602109 Fax (01665) 510400

AA 3-Star 17th-century coaching inn. Over ten
courses within 25 miles. Packages arranged,
tee-times booked. Spectacular coastline. Also
racing breaks. Visit our magnificent Olympic
suite from the Titanic's sister ship.

SCOTLAND
Scottish Borders
The Marine Hotel
Cromwell Road,
North Berwick,
East Lothian EH39 4LZ.
Tel 0870 400 8129 Fax (01620) 894480
Website: www.macdonaldhotels.co.uk

Superb 83-bedroom sporting hotel overlooking
the North Berwick West Links with fabulous
sea and golfing views. Home-from-home for
many of the world's top golfers and famed for
friendly service and traditional value for money
holidays. For non-golfers there is swimming,
tennis and snooker. Families, individuals and
golfing parties enjoy the relaxed atmosphere of
this all-year-round holiday hotel. Special
seasonal leisure breaks and holiday rates. *(See
advertisement page 621 for further details.)*

The Roxburghe Hotel
& Golf Course
Heiton, By Kelso,
Roxburghshire TD5 8JZ.
Tel (01573) 450331 Fax (01573) 450611
E-mail: golf@roxburghe.net
Website: www.roxburghe.net

The Roxburghe Golf Course is the only
championship course in the Scottish Borders,
home to the Scottish Seniors Open. Designed
by Dave Thomas to follow the natural contours
and features of the Roxburghe Estate, the
7,111 yard course suits and challenges all levels
of player. The 22-bedroom country house hotel
owned by the Duke and Duchess of Roxburghe
offers luxury accommodation, superb cuisine
and excellent bar in the library.

Central & East
Ballathie House Hotel
Kinclaven, Stanley, Perthshire PH1 4QN.
Tel (01250) 883268 Fax (01250) 883396
E-mail: email@ballathiehousehotel.com
Website: www.ballathiehousehotel.com

STB 4-Star, AA 2-Rosettes, Taste of Scotland
and Thistle Award winner. Standing in its own
grounds overlooking the river Tay near Perth,
Ballathie House offers Scottish hospitality in a
house of character and distinction. Fifteen
minutes from Rosemount Golf Club and many
other courses.

Carnoustie Hotel Golf Resort & Spa
The Links, Carnoustie, Angus DD7 7JE.
Tel (01241) 411999 Fax (01241) 411998
E-mail: enquiries@carnoustie-hotel.com
Website: www.carnoustie-hotel.com

Deluxe 4-Star hotel situated on the world class links, home to 128th Open Championship. Residents can take advantage of the first class facilities and reserve guaranteed starting times on the par 72 championship course, or the Burnside and Buddon 18-hole courses. *(See advertisement page 621 for further details.)*

Crusoe Hotel
2 Main Street, Lower Largo, Fife KY8 6BT.
Tel (01333) 320759 Fax (01333) 320865

Family run hotel on seafront of historic Lower Largo. Good food in bars and restaurant. Great golfing centre, St Andrews only fifteen minutes. Groups welcome - late bar.

Dalmunzie House Hotel
Spittal O'Glenshee,
Blairgowrie, Perthshire PH10 7QG.
Tel (01250) 885224 Fax (01250) 885225

Set in the Highlands with our own 9-hole course. This friendly country house offers an ideal base for a golfing holiday with excellent local courses at Blairgowrie, Pitlochry, Alyth and many more. *(See advertisement page 619 for further details.)*

Goldenstones Hotel
Queens Road,
Dunbar, East Lothian EH42 1LG.
Tel (01368) 862356 Fax (01368) 865644
E-mail: info@goldenstones.co.uk
Website: www.goldenstones.co.uk

STB 2-Star. We can arrange tee-times for you at some of the finest Scottish golf courses, including Muirfield, Dunbar and North Berwick. There are nineteen superb courses all within half an hour of the hotel. £30.00 B&B.

Golf Hotel
34 Dirleton Avenue,
North Berwick, East Lothian EH39 4BH.
Tel (01620) 892202 Fax (01620) 892290
Website: www.thegolfhotel.net

Family run hotel ideal for golfers wishing to play any of East Lothian's eighteen courses. Starting times arranged. Lounge bar, TV lounge, all rooms with private bathroom and colour TV.

Kenmore Hotel
The Square, Kenmore,
Nr Aberfeldy,
Perthshire PH15 2NU.
Tel (01887) 830205 Fax (01887) 830262
E-mail: reception@kenmorehotel.co.uk
Website: www.kenmorehotel.com

Scotland's Oldest Inn (1572). Forty en suite bedrooms refurbished 2000. Scotland's finest scenery by the river and Loch Tay. Adjacent to Taymouth Castle Golf Course (James Braid design) and Kenmore Golf Course. Ideal for touring, walking, fishing, cycling and water sports. *(See advertisement page 621 for further details.)*

Kinloch House Hotel
by Blairgowrie,
Perthshire PH10 6SG.
Tel (01250) 884237 Fax: (01250) 884333

Kinloch House offers an almost unique proposition for golfers. 35 courses within an hour's drive, planning of rounds and booking of tee-times, sportsman's room with every facility and the best of Scottish hospitality. In-house health and fitness centre. AA 3-Red Star; 3-Rosette; STB 5-Star. *(See advertisement page 621 for further details.)*

Loch Monzievaird Chalets
Ochtertyre,
Crieff,
Perthshire PH7 4JR.
Tel (01764) 652586 Fax (01764) 652555

The beautiful grounds at Loch Monzievaird, are hidden away one mile from Crieff. Our Norwegian and Danish chalets are laid out amongst ancient oak, beech and scots pine. 20 golf courses within half an hour's drive!

Old Course Hotel - Golf Resort & Spa
St Andrews,
Fife KY16 9SP.
Tel (01334) 474371 Fax (01334) 477668

This luxury 134-bedroom hotel overlooks the 17th Road Hole of the Old Course and is a five minute walk to the beach and town. Facilities include health spa with swimming pool, whirlpool, fitness room and full range of massage and beauty treatments. The hotel has its own championship golf course, the Duke's Course. Open to non-residents, with residents enjoying guaranteed tee-times and reduced green fees.

The Sandford Country House Hotel

Newton Hill,
Wormit,
(Nr St Andrews) Fife DD6 8RG.
Tel (01382) 541802 Fax (01382) 542136

Cuisine at the Sandford is exceptional. The award-winning kitchen uses only the finest local produce to create varied and imaginative seasonal menus. Neighbouring Newton Hill Sports offer clay pigeon, fly fishing and off-roading.

The Scores Hotel

St Andrews,
Fife, KY16 9BB.
Tel (01334) 472451 Fax (01334) 473947

Overlooking the R&A clubhouse and first tee of the Old course, this famous golfers 3-Star hotel enjoys a commanding position with panoramic views over one of Scotland's most beautiful bays. The Scorecard bar offers a fascinating collection of golf memorabilia, including a comprehensive collection of the actual players' scorecards from *The Open* and *Dunhill Cups*. A stay at the Scores Hotel is part of the St Andrews Experience.

St Andrews Golf Hotel

St Andrews,
Fife KY16 9AS.
Tel (01334) 472611 Fax (01334) 472188
E-mail: reception@standrews-golf.co.uk
Website: www.standrews-golf.co.uk

AA 3-Star; 2-Rosettes; STB 4-Star.Victorian town house hotel offering great comfort and traditional Scottish hospitality. Award-winning restaurant and cellar. Two hundred yards from the first tee of the Old Course. Let us take the hassle out of arranging your golfing trip.

St Andrews Hazelbank Hotel

28 The Scores,
St Andrews,
Fife KY16 9AS.
Tel/Fax (01334) 472466
Website: www.hazelbank.com

Situated 200 yards from the R&A Clubhouse overlooking St Andrews Bay, this family run hotel offers quality accommodation (STB 3-Star) at affordable prices. All rooms en suite. Rates for 2003 £35 - £55 per person B&B, double/twin. Single supplement applies.

Highlands & Islands

Aurora Hotel - Italian Restaurant

2 Academy Street,
Nairn,
Inverness-shire IV12 4RJ.
Tel (01667) 453551 Fax (01667) 456577
E-mail: aurorahotelnairn@aol.com

A family run 10-bedroomed hotel with traditional Italian restaurant offers a warm welcome and comfortable accommodation. Close to both of Nairn's championship courses, many more within 30 miles. Beautiful beaches, whisky and castle trails.

Machrie Hotel & Golf Links

Port Ellen,
Isle of Islay, Argyll PA42 7AN.
Tel (01496) 302310 Fax (01496) 302404
E-mail: machrie@machrie.com
Website: www.machrie.com

Play a hidden gem of a course. Traditional 18-hole championship links course situated on the doorstep of the Machrie Hotel. Excellent accommodation, fine food and friendly service. Self-catering and golf packages also available.

West

Dunduff House

Dunduff Farm,
Dunure, Ayr KA7 4LH.
Tel (01292) 500225 Fax (01292) 500222

Situated on the edge of Dunure overlooking Arran and Firth of Clyde. Golf courses include Royal Troon, Turnberry and many more interesting courses. All rooms have TV, radio, tea-making facilities, wash hand basin. Two double rooms have en suite facilities. STB 4-Star; AA/RAC 5-Diamonds. Self-catering cottage available - sleeps four.

Fairfield House Hotel

12 Fairfield Road,
Ayr KA7 2AR.
Tel (01292) 267461 Fax (01292) 261456
Website: www.fairfieldhotel.co.uk

The 4-Star Fairfield House is simply the most luxurious hotel of its type in the area, with a well deserved reputation for comfort and fine dining. Local courses include Turnberry and Royal Troon.

Langley Bank Guest House
39 Carrick Road,
Ayr KA7 2RD.
Tel (01292) 264246 Fax (01292) 282628
Website: www.accommodation-ayr.co.uk

Langley Bank is an elegantly refurbished
Victorian house offering quality
accommodation at affordable prices. Centrally
situated and in close proximity to all local golf
courses. En suite facilities, direct dial
telephone. Private car park.

Parkstone Hotel
Central Esplanade,
Prestwick,
Ayrshire KA9 1QN.
Tel (01292) 477286 Fax (01292) 477671
E-mail: info@parkstonehotel.co.uk
Website: www.parkstonehotel.co.uk

Seafront location adjacent to Prestwick Golf
Club and close to town centre. 22 bedrooms all
en suite. AA 3-Star; AA Rosette. Special breaks
available and all golfing arrangements can be
made.

The Westin Turnberry Resort, Scotland
Turnberry,
Ayrshire KA26 9LT.
Tel +44 (0) 1655 331000
Fax +44 (0) 1655 331706
E-mail: turnberry@westin.com
Website: www.westin.com/turnberry

World renowned hotel located in spectacular
coastal surroundings with unrivalled facilities.
Savour the finest international cuisine, stay in
luxuriously appointed hotel and lodge
bedrooms, relax in the award-winning spa or
enjoy a range of exciting outdoor pursuits.

WALES

Welsh Borders

Belmont Lodge & Golf
Belmont, Hereford HR2 9SA.
Tel (01432) 352666 Fax (01432) 358090

18-hole golf course running along the beautiful
Wye Valley with a 30-bedroomed hotel on-site.
Other facilities include bar, restaurant, fishing,
bowling and tennis. Only a mile and a half
from Hereford City centre.

Cadmore Lodge Hotel
St Michaels,
Tenbury Wells,
Worcestershire WR15 8TQ.
Tel/Fax (01584) 810044

A warm welcome awaits at Cadmore Lodge
Hotel. Excellent cuisine from chefs with
imagination and flair. Our own 9-hole golf
course par 68 SSS 65 (18 holes). Two fishing
lakes for trout and course fishing. Indoor
swimming pool, with spa, steam room and
cardio-vascular equipment. *(See advertisement
page 624 for further details.)*

North

De Vere St David's Park Hotel
St David's Park,
Ewloe,
Nr Chester, Flintshire CH5 3YB.
Tel (01244) 520800 Fax (01244) 520930
E-mail:
reservations.stdavidspark@devere-
hotels.com
Website: www.devereonline.co.uk

AA 4-Star hotel with extensive leisure facilities,
including gym and swimming pool. 145
bedrooms and suites, excellent restaurant.
Northop Country Park Golf Club only five
minutes away. Special golf packages available.
(See advertisement page 624 for further details.)

Imperial Hotel - Llandudno
The Promenade,
Llandudno, Gwynedd LL30 1AP.
Tel (01492) 877466 Fax (01492) 878043
Website: www.theimperial.co.uk

100-bedroomed hotel with extensive leisure
facilities including 45' indoor swimming pool.
Ideally situated for all North Wales' golf
courses. Award-winning restaurant and private
dining room for up to 30 available.

Central

Penrhos Golf & Country Club
Llanrhystud, Ceredigion SY23 5AY.
Tel (01974) 202999 Fax (01974) 202100
Website: www.penrhosgolf.co.uk

Fifteen American-style suites. 18-hole
championship length course, driving range,
indoor swimming pool, sauna, steam room,
gymnasium, tennis courts, spa, solarium and
bowling green.

South & South West

The Best Western Lamphey Court Hotel
Lamphey,
Pembroke, Pembrokeshire SA71 5NT.
Tel (01646) 672273 Fax (01646) 672480
E-mail: info@lampheycourt.co.uk
Website: www.lampheycourt.co.uk

One of Wales' leading country hotels. Deluxe bedrooms, superb leisure centre, swimming pool, jacuzzi, gym, sauna and floodlit tennis. Special arrangements with Tenby, South Pembrokeshire, Trefloyne and Haverfordwest golf clubs. Excellent food and wine.

Royal Porthcawl - The Dormy
Royal Porthcawl Golf Club,
Rest Bay,
Porthcawl,
Mid Glamorgan CF36 3UW.
Tel (01656) 782251 Fax (01656) 771687
E-mail: royalporthcawl@aol.com
Website: www.royalporthcawl.com

Luxury dormy accommodation for parties of up to twelve persons. Apply to the secretary. (See advertisement page 28 for further details.)

St Mary's Hotel Golf & Country Club
St Mary's Hill,
Pencoed, Vale of Glamorgan CF35 5EA.
Tel (01656) 861100 Fax (01656) 863400

24-bedroom hotel, 18-hole membership and pay course. 9-hole pay as you play, 15-bay floodlit driving range, clubhouse and restaurant conservatory and three bars. Fully stocked golf shop. Floodlit chipping and putting area and resident golf professional Mr John Peters.

CHANNEL ISLANDS

La Grande Mare Hotel Golf Club
La Grande Mare,
Vazon, Castel, Guernsey.
Tel (01481) 256576 & 253544
Fax (01481) 255194
Website: www.lgm.guernsey.net

Beautifully appointed luxury hotel with 18-hole golf course. Professional shop and tuition on-site. First class, well priced restaurant. 2-AA Rosettes. Beachside location. Golfing breaks catered for.

The Moorings Hotel & Restaurant
Gorey Pier, Gorey, Jersey JE3 6EW.
Tel (01534) 853633 Fax (01534) 857618

3-Star intimate and luxurious 15-bedroom hotel overlooking the quaint Gorey harbour and the sandy bay of Grouville. Half a mile from the Royal Jersey Golf Club. Renowned for its superb food, seafood a speciality. Open all year. Special rates for golfers at any time.

St Pierre Park Hotel
Rohais, St Peter Port, Guernsey GYI 1FD.
Tel (01481) 728282 Fax (01481) 712041

This 4-Star hotel offers extensive leisure facilities including a 9-hole par 3 golf course, designed by Tony Jacklin. Three tennis courts and a health suite with heated indoor swimming pool, spa bath, saunas, steam rooms, solaria and exercise room.

NORTHERN IRELAND

Bushmills Inn Hotel & Restaurant
9 Dunluce Road,
Bushmills, Co Antrim BT57 8QG.
Tel +44 (0) 28 207 32339
Fax +44 (0) 28 207 32048
E-mail: rna@bushmillsinn.com
Website: www.bushmillsinn.com

Just four scenic miles from Royal Portrush this multi award-winning hotel and restaurant has been outstandingly successful in recreating its origins as an old coaching inn. Turf fires, gas lights and stripped pine set the scene at this 'living museum of Ulster hospitality'. A Perry Golf 'Partner'; Member of Ireland's Blue Book and Best-Loved Hotels of the World.

REPUBLIC OF IRELAND

Arnolds Hotel
Dunfanaghy, Co Donegal, Ireland.
Tel +353 74 36208 Fax +353 74 36352
Website: www.arnoldshol.ie

Family hotel established since 1922 situated at the entrance to the village overlooking Horn Head and Sheephaven Bay. Ideal base to play the many scenic links of north west Donegal.

Bloomfield House Hotel & Leisure Club

Belvedere,
Mullingar,
Co Westmeath, Ireland.
Tel +353 44 40894 Fax +353 44 43767
E-mail: sales@bloomfieldhouse.com
Website: www.bloomfieldhouse.com

This beautifully appointed hotel boasts 65 en suite bedrooms. Leisure club and healing rooms offering a range of treatments. Adjacent to Mullingar's Championship Golf Course. Glasson, Esker Hills and Tullamore golf courses are also nearby.

Byrne's Mal Dua House

Clifden,
Connemara,
Co Galway, Ireland.
Tel: +353 95 21171 Fax +353 95 21739
UK Freefone 0800 9047532
USA Toll Free 1866 8919420
E-mail: info@maldua.com
Website: www.maldua.com

AA/RAC-5-Star; Bord Failte 4-Star. In the heart of Connemara, award-winning guesthouse, close to Connemara Golf Club, Byrne's Mal Dua House offers luxury in a relaxed atmosphere. Courtesy mini-bus. Bicycles for hire. Visit our website.

Casey's of Baltimore Hotel

Baltimore,
Co Cork,
Ireland.
Tel +353 28 20197 Fax +353 28 20509
E-mail: caseys@eircom.net
Website: www.caseysofbaltimore.com

3-Star family run 14 en suite bedroom hotel. Seafood restaurant and traditional pub. Golf available at Skibbereen 18-hole golf course. Special rates for residents.

Castletroy Park Hotel

Dublin Road,
Limerick, Ireland.
Tel +353 61 335566 Fax +353 61 331117
E-mail: sales@castletroy-park.ie
Website: www.castletroy-park.ie

The newly refurbished Castletroy Park Hotel lies at the heart of the south west of Ireland. The region boasts over 23 golf courses, including the renowned Ballybunion course, all within an hour's drive of the hotel.

Charleville Lodge

268-272 North Circular Road,
Phibsborough, Dublin 7, Ireland.
Tel +353 838 6633 Fax +353 838 5854
E-mail: charleville@indigo.ie
Website: www.charlevillelodge.ie

We are located in the heart of Dublin, surrounded by championship courses and beside all entertainment and restaurants. A warm welcome awaits you. Let us make your golf arrangements for you.

Coffey's Loch Lein House Hotel

Golf Course Road, Fossa,
Killarney, Co Kerry, Ireland.
Tel +353 64 31260 Fax +353 64 36151
E-mail: ecoffey@indigo.ie
Website: www.lochlein.com

On the shores of Killarney's lower lake with magnificent views, a warm welcome awaits you at this family run hotel. Recently extended the relaxed atmosphere and service remain unchanged. Four excellent 18-hole championship golf courses nearby.

Druids Glen Marriott Hotel & Country Club

Newtownmountkennedy,
Co Wicklow, Ireland.
Tel +353 1 2870800 Fax +353 1 2870801
E-mail:
events.druids@marriotthotels.com
Website: www.marriotthotels.com/dubgs

Situated within Druids Glen Golf Resort and only 20 miles south of Dublin, lies the new Druids Glen Marriott Hotel & Country Club - the perfect venue in which to relax and enjoy championship golf, holistic spa treatment, excellent cuisine and abosolute comfort. A second championship course, Druid's Heath, is due to open in Autumn 2003.

Gormanstown Manor - Farm Guest House

Gormanstown,
Near Wicklow Town and Brittas Bay,
Co Wicklow, Ireland.
Tel +353 404 69432 Fax +353 404 61832
E-mail: gormanstownmanor@tinet.ie
*Website: www.homepage.eircom.net/-
gormanstownmanor*

We have a spectactular par 3 golf course 18-hole pitch and putt and a golf driving range with a qualified golf professional in attendance daily. Gormanstown Manor is ideally located

for the golfer who wishes to play golf on the top 25 golf courses in the area. We are just outside Dublin City off the N11. *(See advertisement page 624 for further details.)*

Gregans Castle Hotel
Ballyvaughan,
Co Clare, Ireland.
Tel +353 65 7077 005 Fax +353 65 7077 111
E-mail: res@gregans.ie
Website: www.gregans.ie

To play Lahinch, Doonbeg, Galway Bay and Gort. Luxury country house hotel with 22 very comfortable rooms and suites. Quiet, rural location with magnificent views of mountains and Galway Bay. Suitable for the up-market golfer, who enjoys high standards of hotel keeping. Only one hour from user-friendly Shannon International Airport. Early check-in possible. AA Red Star and Rosettes for good food.

Hunter's Hotel
Rathnew,
Co Wicklow, Ireland.
Tel +353 404 40106 Fax +353 404 40338
E-mail: reception@hunters.ie
Website: www.hunters.ie

270 year old coaching inn run by the same family for the past 170 years. Ideal centre for golf holidays. Twenty 18-hole courses within half an hour, nearest three minutes' drive away.

Inishowen Gateway Hotel
Gateway Health & Fitness Club
Railway Road, Buncrana,
Inishowen, Co Donegal, Ireland.
Tel +353 77 61144 Fax +353 77 62278
E-mail: info@inishowengateway.com
Website: www.inishowengateway.com

Stylish hotel, 63 en suite bedrooms, with adjoining luxurious health and fitness club. Enjoying a delightful location on the white sandy shores of Lough Swilly. Ideal for golf at the 'Faldo famous' Ballyliffin courses and North West Golf Club.

Jurys Hotel Waterford
Ferrybank, Waterford, Ireland.
Tel +353 51 832111 Fax +353 51 832863

Situated on 38 acres of parkland and overlooking Waterford City, this hotel has 98 bedrooms. Facilities include an extensive leisure centre, bar and restaurant. There are six 18-hole courses within a ten mile radius.

The Killarney Park Hotel
Kenmare Place,
Killarney, Co Kerry, Ireland.
Tel +353 64 35555 Fax +353 64 35266
E-mail: info@killarneyparkhotel.ie
Website: www.killarneyparkhotel.ie

Voted Irish Golf Hotel of the Year for 2001 by the IGTOA. Superbly located in the heart of Killarney town, this 5-Star hotel is the perfect location to access the finest golf courses in the south west of Ireland. Spacious deluxe, air conditioned rooms or magnificent suites. Relax and unwind in the friendly Garden Bar, billiards room and library. Leisure facilities include 20m pool, outdoor hot tub, sauna and health spa. Drying room for golf club storage.

King Sitric Fish Restaurant & Accommodation
East Pier, Howth,
Co Dublin, Ireland.
Tel +353 1 8325235 Fax +353 1 8392442

Beautifully located in picturesque Howth harbour, with panoramic sea views. Famous seafood restaurant, established 1971, now with quality accommodation. Many golf courses of Dublin and Fingal within half an hour. Dart into Dublin 25 minutes; Dublin airport only 20 minutes.

Lake of Shadows Hotel
Grianan Park, Buncrana,
Inishowen, Co Donegal, Ireland.
Tel +353 77 61005 Fax +353 77 62131
Website: www.lakeofshadows.com

Family run hotel with 23 en suite bedrooms, cosy, warm and just oozing with charm. Close to beautiful sandy beaches and is an ideal location for golfing at world famous Ballyliffin (two courses) and North West Golf Club.

Mount Juliet
Thomastown, Co Kilkenny, Ireland.
Tel +353 56 73000 Fax +353 56 73019
E-mail: info@mountjuliet.ie
Website: www.mountjuliet.ie

Deluxe accommodation in the elegant Mount Juliet House or the informal club rooms. Ireland's premier sporting estate offers guests on-site fishing, horse riding, tennis, leisure centre and fully dedicated spa. Golf Academy with PGA professionals. 18-hole putting course. Irish Open venue 1993-95. Host to WGC American Express Championship in September 2002.

Renvyle House Hotel
Connemara,
Go Galway, Ireland.
Tel +353 95 43511 Fax +353 95 43515
E-mail: renvyle@iol.ie
Website: www.renvyle.com

Set in the wild splendour of Connemara in truly magical surroundings. Originally the home of Oliver St John Gogarty, Renvyle House has played host to many famous people - Augustus John, Yeats and Churchill to name but a few. Warmth, comfort and award-winning fare awaits. Excellent golf and golf clinics are available on-site. *(See advertisement page 624 for further details.)*

Rosapenna Hotel & Golf Links
Rosapenna,
Downings, Donegal, Ireland.
Tel +353 74 55301 Fax +353 74 55128

Rosapenna Hotel is set in the middle of its own 36-hole golf links course. Half a mile from the fishing village of Downings.

The Slieve Russell Hotel Golf & Country Club
Ballyconnell,
Co Cavan, Ireland.
Tel +353 49 9526444 Fax +353 49 9526474
Website: www.quinnhotels.com

Located only two hours' drive from both Dublin and Belfast, the Slieve Russell is a complete resort with its 5-Star leisure facilities, championship 18-hole golf course, 159 superbly appointed bedrooms and a selection

of restaurants and bars, conference and banqueting suites - 'The *Perfect* location for business or pleasure.'

The Smugglers Inn
Cliff Road,
Waterville,
Co Kerry, Ireland.
Tel +353 66 9474330 Fax +353 66 9474422
E-mail: thesmugglersinn@eircom.net
*Website: www.welcome.to/
thesmugglersinn*

Situated in a quiet location, 2km sandy beach, adjacent to Waterville golf links. Gourmet restaurant, chef proprietors Harry and Henry Hunt. 17 rooms all en suite. Wonderful views to the Atlantic and golf course.

St Helen's Bay Golf & Country Club
St Helens,
Kilrane,
Rosslare Harbour,
Co Wexford, Ireland.
Tel +353 53 33234 Fax +353 53 33803
E-mail: sthelens@iol.ie
Website: sthelensbay.com

Luxury on-site accommodation together with tennis courts, leisure room and sauna. Full bar/catering facilities available in the clubhouse. Superbly located championship 18-hole golf course, which has blended the best of parkland characteristics with a finish that is true links and plenty of difficulty. Situated only five minutes from Rosslare ferryport. Green fee and society friendly, playable all year round.

Professional Associations

Association of Golf Club Secretaries

7A Beaconsfield Road,
Weston-Super-Mare, Somerset BS23 1YE.
Tel (01934) 641166 Fax (01934) 644254
E-mail: hq@agcs.org.uk
Website: www.agcs.org.uk

Membership is available to golf secretaries and managers, course owners and others involved in golf club administration. The following services are available: monthly journal, information library, training courses. seminars, conferences, regional meetings and employment support.

British & International Golf Greenkeepers Association

BIGGA House,
Aldwark,
Alne, North Yorkshire YO61 1UF.
Tel (01347) 833800 Fax (01347) 833801
E-mail: reception@bigga.co.uk
Website: www.bigga.org.uk

BIGGA has over 7,000 members and is the professional body that represents greenkeepers throughout the UK and has members in 32 countries worldwide. As well as providing extensive education and training programmes for its members BIGGA produces a monthly magazine 'Greenkeeper International' and each January in Harrogate organises the BIGGA Turf Management Exhibition and the Clubhouse Exhibition. Contact Neil Thomas, Executive Director.

British Association of Golf Course Constructors

The Dormy House,
Cooden Beach
Golf Club,
Bexhill-on-Sea TN39 4TR.
Tel:(01424) 842380 Fax: (01424) 843375
E-mail: mightyspyder@aol.com
Website: www.bagcc.org.uk

Secretary: David White. Constructors who appear on the BAGCC membership roster qualify only by passing a critical vetting process undertaken by their peers, who look for excellence in construction and a clear demonstration of skills pertinent only to the golf course industry. Utilising the services of a BAGCC member therefore ensures absolute professionalism.

British Golf Industry Association - BGIA

Federation House,
Stoneleigh Park,
Warwickshire CV8 2RF.
Tel 024 7641 7141 Fax 024 7641 4990
E-mail: bgia@sportslife.org.uk

Trade association for manufacturers and distributors of golf equipment.

British Rootzone & Topdressing Manufacturers Association

Federation House, NAC,
Stoneleigh Park,
Warwickshire CV8 2RF.
Tel 024 7641 4999 Fax 024 7641 4990
E-mail: brtma@sportslife.org.uk
Website: www.brtma.com

The Association is a collaboration of experience and expertise in the manufacture of rootzone materials to offer architects, constructors and agronomists a recognised focal point for the industry.

The Council of National Golf Unions

Dromin,
Dunleer,
Co Louth, Ireland.
Tel/Fax +353 41 6861476
E-mail: golfinmcinere@hotmail.com

The handicapping authority for Great Britain and Ireland. The Standard Scratch Score and Handicapping scheme has been in operation since March 1926. The Consultative Committee consists of representatives from the English, Ireland, Scottish and Welsh golf unions. They receive and consider schemes for fixing scratch scores and adjustments to handicaps throughout Great Britain and Ireland and submit their proposals to the Royal & Ancient of St Andrews for approval.

English Golf Union - EGU

The National Golf Centre, The Broadway,
Woodhall Spa, Lincolnshire LN10 6PU.
Tel (01526) 354500 Fax (01526) 354020
E-mail: info@englishgolfunion.org
Website: www.englishgolfunion.org

As the governing body for men's amateur golf in England the EGU organises championships and coaching for players and representative teams at all levels and offers an advisory service on all aspects of golf administration and management.

European Golf Teachers Federation

5 Hastings Road,
Bromley, Kent BR2 8NZ.
Tel 020 8462 4120 Fax 020 8462 3983
E-mail: egtf@dial.pipex.com
Website: www.egtf.co.uk

EUROPEAN GOLF TEACHERS FEDERATION LTD
Leaders in the Field of Golf Instruction

We offer intensive teaching courses for professionals and amateurs who would like to know how to teach the game simply. The EGTF is the leader in the field of golf instruction.

European Institute of Golf Course Architects

Chiddingfold Golf Club, Petworth Road,
Chiddingfold, Surrey GU8 4SL.
Tel/Fax +44 (0) 1428 681528
E-mail: info@eigca.org
Website: www.eigca.org

EIGCA

The EIGCA represents the vast majority of qualified and experienced golf course architects throughout Europe. EIGCA's goals include enhancing the professional status of the profession, developing the role of education and increasing the opportunities for its members to practice in countries throughout the world. EIGCA also provids educational courses to train future golf course architects and is the authoritive voice on all related matters, being recognised by the R&A Golf Club of St Andrews. Contact: Julia Green, Executive Officer.

Golf Consultants Association

Federation House,
Stoneleigh
Park, Warwickshire CV8 2RF.
Tel (02476) 414999 Fax (02476) 414990
E-mail: gca@sportslife.org.uk

The GCA provides a point of reference for those requiring independent, professional, golf consultancy services throughout the world.

The Golf Foundation - Developing Junior Golf

Foundation House,
The Spinney,
Hoddesdon Road,
Stanstead Abbotts,
Hertfordshire SG12 8GF.
Tel (01920) 876200 Fax (01920) 876211
Website: www.golf-foundation.org

An organisation dedicated to the promotion and development of grass roots junior golf across the British Isles. *The Golf Foundation is a registered charity.*

National Association of Public Golf Courses - NAPGC

12 Newton Close,
Redditch B98 7YR.
Tel (01527) 542106 Fax (01527) 455320
E-mail: eddiemitchell@blueyonder.co.uk
Website: www.napgc.org.uk

The Association provides competition golf for men and lady players of all handicaps and age. It also offers help and advice to its member clubs - those playing over courses that they do not own.

National Golf Clubs' Advisory Association

First Floor Chambers,
18-20 Stamford Street,
Stalybridge,
Cheshire SK15 2JZ.
Tel 0161-338 8680 Fax 0161-338 8408
E-mail: ngcaa@idealnet.co.uk
Website: www.ngcaa.org.uk

A non-profit making organisation providing legal advice and support to golf clubs throughout the UK. The Association is the only independent body supporting golf clubs in areas of activity other than those arising from playing the game.

STRI - The Sports Turf Research Institute

St Ives Estate,
Bingley,
West Yorkshire BD16 1AU.
Tel (01274) 565131 Fax (01274) 561891
E-mail: info@stri.co.uk
Website: www.stri.co.uk

Independent specialists offering you help and advice for the design, construction, management and maintenance, irrigation or renovation of your golf course. Comprehensive in-house support services for ecology, testing, turf pathology and research.

Golf Club Facilities

This section lists clubs which can offer hotel accommodation, and hotels which have their own golf facilties. They are able to provide for society or corporate days, and in some instances offer an extensive range of other sports and leisure activities.

Abbotsley Golf Hotel & Country Club
Eynesbury Hardwicke, St Neots, Cambridgeshire PE19 4XN.
Tel (01480) 474000 Fax (01480) 471018

Set in 250 acres of idyllic countryside, offering two 18-hole courses, a par 3, driving range, squash courts, fitness centre and a 42-bedroom hotel. Golf breaks and residential packages available. Operated by American Golf (UK) Limited.

Aldwark Manor Hotel Golf & Country Club
Aldwark, Alne, York, North Yorkshire YO61 1UF.
Tel: (01347) 838146 (Hotel)
(01347) 838353 (Golf)
Fax (01347) 838867
E-mail: aldwark@marstonhotels.com
Website: www.marstonhotels.com

Aldwark Manor extends a warm welcome to everyone. Situated in the Vale of York is a 6,154 yards par 71 golf course, laid out in easy walking parkland with the river Ure meandering beside a number of fairways. The ideal venue for your Society or company golf day. *(See advertisement page 617 for further details.)*

Beaufort Golf Course
Churchtown, Beaufort, Killarney, Co Kerry, Ireland.
Tel +353 64 44440 Fax +353 64 44752

A traditional Kerry welcome awaits you at *the Friendliest Course in Kerry.* Challenging 18-hole par 71 championship course, buggies and caddies for hire, excellent golf shop, bar food and snacks. Tuition can be arranged with our golf professional. Societies and groups welcome. *(See advertisement page 27 for further details.)*

Belmont Lodge & Golf
Belmont, Hereford HR2 9SA.
Tel (01432) 352666 Fax (01432) 358090

18-hole golf course running along the beautiful Wye Valley with a 30-bedroomed hotel on-site. Other facilities include bar, restaurant, fishing, bowling and tennis. Only a mile and a half from Hereford City centre.

Borth & Ynyslas Golf Club
Borth, Ceredigion SY24 5JS.
Tel (01970) 871202
E-mail: secretary@borthgolf.co.uk

18-hole links course adjoining Borth beach. Humps and hollows provide great variation, although the topography and springy turf make for easy walking. Professional's shop, practice area, modern clubhouse with bar and catering. Tuition available.

Botley Park Hotel Golf & Country Club
Winchester Road, Boorley Green, Botley, Southampton SO32 2UA.
Tel (01489) 780888 Fax (01489) 789242
E-mail:
info@botleypark.macdonald-hotels.co.uk
Website: www.macdonaldhotels.co.uk

Set in 176 acres of rolling Hampshire countryside, this 4-Star hotel has 100 en suite bedrooms, superb restaurant, extensive leisure facilities and its own picturesque and

challenging 18-hole par 70 golf course and driving range. *(See advertisement page 613 for further details.)*

Burnham & Berrow Golf Club
St Christopher's Way,
Burnham-on-Sea,
Somerset TA8 2PE.
Tel (01278) 785760
E-mail:
Secretary@BurnhamandBerrow.freeserve.co.uk

18-hole championship links golf course and 9-hole course. Dormy accommodation available. *(See advertisement page 613 for further details.)*

Bushey Hall Golf Club
Bushey Hall Drive, Bushey,
Hertfordshire WD23 2EP.
Tel (01923) 222253
(01923) 225802 (proshop)
Website: www.golfclubuk.co.uk

Established in 1890 Bushey Hall Golf Club has one of the oldest and best established courses in Hertfordshire. Facilities include a fully equipped pro shop, practice net, clubhouse restaurant and bar. Open for membership. Pay as you play operated. *(See advertisement page 22 for further details.)*

Cadmore Lodge Hotel
St Michaels, Tenbury Wells,
Worcestershire WR15 8TQ.
Tel/Fax (01584) 810044

A warm welcome awaits at Cadmore Lodge Hotel. Excellent cuisine from chefs with imagination and flair. Our own 9-hole golf course par 68 SSS 65 (18 holes). Two fishing lakes for trout and course fishing. Indoor swimming pool, with spa, steam room and cardio-vascular equipment. *(See advertisement page 624 for further details.)*

Cambridgeshire Moat House Hotel
Bar Hill, Cambridge CB3 8EU.
Tel (01954) 249988 (Hotel)
(01954) 780098 (Club)
Fax (01954) 780010
Website: www.moathousehotels.com

Superb 18-hole 6,7334 yards championship golf course set within 134 acres of parkland. Host to the East Anglian Open 2001, 2002 and 2003. This 134-bedroomed hotel has full leisure facilities, two excellent restaurants and three bars. Golf packages available.

Cannington Golf Course
Cannington College, Cannington,
Bridgwater, Somerset TA5 2LS.
Tel/Fax (01278) 655050

Designed by Martin Hawtree of Oxford and built to highest international specifications in 1992 by Brian Pierson Limited under the consultancy of top agronomists Jim Arthur and Gordon Child. Together they have produced arguably the best 9-hole golf course with its 18 tees in the west of England. With its 'Links-Like' appearance in high summer the subtle contours make for a testing round of golf for the scratch golfer yet it is receptive to the beginner with its wide spaces at 2,929 yards par 34. Beating par will take skill and courage.

Carnoustie Hotel Golf Resort & Spa
The Links, Carnoustie, Angus DD7 7JE.
Tel (01241) 411999 Fax (01241) 411998
E-mail: enquiries@carnoustie-hotel.com
Website: www.carnoustie-hotel.com

Deluxe 4-Star hotel situated on the world class links, home to 128th Open Championship. Residents can take advantage of the first class facilities and reserve guaranteed starting times on the par 72 championship course, or the Burnside and Buddon 18-hole courses. *(See advertisement page 621 for further details.)*

Castletown Golf Links Hotel
Fort Island,
Derbyhaven, Isle of Man IM9 1UA.
Tel (01624) 822201 Fax (01624) 824633
E-mail: golflinks@manx.net
Website: www.golfiom.com

An 18-hole links championship course voted number 73 in the UK by *Golf World* magazine. Measuring 6,711 yards SSS 72 established since 1892 is set on the peninsula of Langness surrounded by sea on three sides and overlooking the Manx rolling hills. Accommodation is available twelve months of the year, three bars, excellent local cuisine, table d'hôte and à la carte in both restaurants. Visiting parties and non-members welcome.

Cave Castle Hotel & Country Club
South Cave, East Yorkshire HU15 2EU.
Tel (01430) 422245 Fax (01430) 421118

Superb country manor house with 53 en suite bedrooms in tranquil 160-acre parkland setting with easy access to M62 motorway. Excellent,

traditional cuisine is served in our character restaurant. Choice of two 18-hole golf courses (Cave Castle and Boothferry Park), plus use of leisure facilities, including 19m indoor pool, gym, sauna, steam and spa. This is a Unique Leisure Experience not to be missed! Golf and leisure breaks, visiting parties and non-golfers welcome.

Charleville Golf Club
Charleville,
Co Cork, Ireland.
Tel +353 63 81257 Fax +353 63 81274
E-mail: charlevillegolf@eircom.net

Located in the foothills of Ballyhoura mountains enjoy uncrowded golf at our 27-hole championship parkland course renowned for its lush fairways and excellent greens. Driving range, full bar and catering facilities in our friendly clubhouse. Open from 7.30am to sunset.

China Fleet Country Club
Saltash,
Cornwall PL12 6LJ.
Tel (01752) 848668 Fax (01752) 848456
E-mail: sales@china-fleet.co.uk
Website: www.china-fleet.co.uk

Situated in 180 acres of Cornish countryside, 40 self-catering 4 and 6-berth apartments, 18-hole par 72 golf, 28-bay driving range, pool, health suite, gymnasium, racquet sports, bars, restaurant and coffee shop. *(See advertisement page 615 for further details.)*

Coulsdon Golf Centre - Coulsdon Manor
Coulsdon Court Road,
Coulsdon,
Surrey CR5 2LL.
Tel 020 8660 6083 Fax 020 8668 3118
E-mail:
coulsdonmanor@marstonhotels.com
Website: www.marstonhotels.com

A relaxing yet challenging par 70 golf course set in 140 acres of Surrey parkland. Golf societies made very welcome. Excellent restaurant and bar facilities at the Manor. *(See advertisement page 615 for further details.)*

> ## Use this listing for arranging your society day

Courtown Golf Club
Kiltennel, Gorey, Co Wexford, Ireland.
Tel +353 55 25166 Fax +353 55 25553
E-mail: courtown@iol.ie
Website: www.courtowngolfclub.com

This 18-hole heavily wooded parkland course features four challenging par 3's and three long par 5's. The variety (no two holes are alike) and excellence of this course is matched by its luxurious clubhouse and bar and catering facilities.

Dalmunzie House Hotel
Spittal O'Glenshee,
Blairgowrie,
Perthshire PH10 7QG.
Tel (01250) 885224 Fax (01250) 885225

Set in the Highlands with our own 9-hole course. This friendly country house offers an ideal base for a golfing holiday with excellent local courses at Blairgowrie, Pitlochry, Alyth and many more. *(See advertisement page 619 for further details.)*

De Vere Northop Country Park Golf Club
Northop, Flintshire CH7 6WA.
Tel (01352) 840440 Fax (01352) 840445
Website: www.devereonline.co.uk

John Jacob's designed par 72, 18-hole championship course in 247 acres of mature parkland. Driving range, pratice greens and pro shop plus two all-weather tennis courts, gym and sauna. Award-winning restaurant. Overnight accommodation available at nearby De Vere St David's Park Hotel five minutes away. *(See advertisement page 624 for further details.)*

The Dorset Golf & Country Club
Bere Regis,
Nr Pool, Dorset BH20 7NT.
Tel (01929) 472244 Fax (01929) 471294
E-mail: admin@dorsetgolfresort.com
Website: www.dorsetgolfresort.com

Hawtree design course - 7,027 yards SSS 74 with the record of 65. Other tees available! The lakeland course features all-the-year-round greens protected by large bunkers with water coming into play on several holes. Floodlit 22-bay driving range and golf buggies available for hire. Beautiful Hardy country overlooking Purbeck Hills. Superb accommodation in our Dorset Golf Hotel - see Golfing Hotel Compendium.

Druids Glen Golf Club

Newtownmountkennedy,
Co Wicklow,
Ireland.
Tel +353 1 287 3600 Fax +353 1 287 3699
E-mail: druids@indigo.ie
Website: www.druidsglen.ie

Venue for the 2001 Seve Trophy. European Golf Course of the Year 2000. Home of Murphy's Irish Open 1996 to 1999. Facilities include an 18-hole championship golf course, 3-hole teaching academy, practice ground and sumptuously converted 18th-century clubhouse with full bar and dining facilities. Visitors always welcome.

Edmondstown Golf Club

Rathfarnham,
Dublin 16, Ireland.
Tel +353 1 493 1082 Fax +353 1 493 3152
E-mail: info@edmondstowngolfclub.ie
Website: www.edmondstowngolfclub.ie

Edmondstown Golf Club is situated amongst the most delightful surroundings on the foothills of the Dublin mountains, and only seven miles from Dublin City centre. A testing parkland course - it lends itself to the golfer who desires a socially enjoyable round of golf - on a well maintained and manicured golf course. *(See advertisement page 28 for further details.)*

Farthingstone Hotel & Golf Course

Farthingstone,
Towcester, Northamptonshire NN12 8HA.
Tel (01327) 361291 Fax (01327) 361645

Set in glorious wooded countryside, just 90 minutes outside London. Farthingstone Hotel offers 16 superb en suite rooms, a challenging 18-hole golf course, squash court, full size snooker tables, and a carvery restaurant. Highly competitive tariffs.

Gatton Manor Hotel Golf & Country Club Ltd

Ockley,
Nr Dorking, Surrey RH5 5PQ.
Tel (01306) 627555

Set amidst its own 18-hole golf course in 200 acres of parklands and lakes, situated between London and the south coast, in the heart of the Surrey countryside. Superb all en suite accommodation overlooking the golf course and grounds. À la carte restaurants, large lounge bar, conference suites, gym and health club.

Gormanstown Manor - Farm Guest House

Gormanstown,
Near Wicklow Town and Brittas Bay,
Co Wicklow, Ireland.
Tel +353 404 69432 Fax +353 404 61832
E-mail: gormanstownmanor@tinet.ie
Website: www.homepage.eircom.net/-gormanstownmanor

We have a spectacular par 3 golf course 18-hole pitch and putt and a golf driving range with a qualified golf professional in attendance daily. Gormanstown Manor is ideally located for the golfer who wishes to play golf on the top 25 golf courses in the area. We are just outside Dublin City off the N11. *(See advertisement page 624 for further details.)*

The Grange & Links Hotel

Sea Lane,
Sandilands,
Sutton-on-Sea,
Lincolnshire LN12 2RA.
Tel (01507) 441334 Fax (01507) 443033
E-mail: grangelinks@ic24.net
Website: www.grangeandlinkshotel.com

3-Star 30-bedroom hotel with own 18-hole links course. Two tennis courts, snooker and ballroom. Award-winning hotel renowned for superb cuisine, friendliness, comfort and service.

Harrogate Golf Club

Forest Lane Head,
Harrogate,
North Yorkshire HG2 7TF.
Tel (01423) 862999

A long established 18-hole golf course set amongst mature trees formerly part of the Forest of Knaresborough. Visitors are assured of a warm reception in the extensively refurbished clubhouse and restaurant. *(See advertisement page 28 for further details.)*

Hellidon Lakes Hotel Golf & Country Club

Hellidon,
Daventry,
Northamptonshire NN11 6GG.
Tel (01327) 262550 Fax (01327) 262559
E-mail: hellidon@marstonhotels.com
Website: www.marstonhotels.com

27 holes of golf through woodland and over lakes. Buggies for hire. Corporate, Society and residential packages available. 71 well

appointed bedrooms and suites, country club with extensive health and fitness facilities including pool, gym and treatment rooms. Indoor golf simulator and 10-pin bowling. Only 20 minutes from junction 11 of the M40 and junction 16 of the M1, one and a half hours from M25. *(See advertisement page 617 for further details.)*

Hollywood Lakes Golf Club
Ballyboughal,
Co Dublin, Ireland.
Tel +353 1 843 3406/7 Fax +353 1 843 3002

Parkland course featuring water hazards and lakes at 6 holes and also the longest par 5 in Ireland at 639 yards (14th hole). Green fees weekday E30.00; weekend E35.00. *(See advertisement page 27 for further details.)*

Howth Golf Club
St Fintan's,
Carrickbrack Road,
Sutton, Dublin 13, Ireland.
Tel +353 1 832 3055 Fax +353 1 832 1793
E-mail: secretary@howthgolfclub.ie
Website: www.howthgolfclub.ie

Howth Golf Club is a long established heathland course located within ten miles of Dublin City centre and Dublin airport. The club boasts a fine clubhouse and enjoys panoramic views of land and sea scapes.

The Island Golf Club
Corballis,
Donabate, Co Dublin, Ireland.
Tel +353 1 843 6462 Fax +353 1 843 6860
E-mail: islandgc@iol.ie
Website: www.theislandgolfclub.com

Continuing a tradition of links golf since its inception in 1890. The magnificent splendour and solitude associated with the Island, is highlighted by undulating fairways rolling through majestic sand dunes.

La Grande Mare Hotel Golf Club
La Grande Mare,
Vazon, Castel, Guernsey.
Tel (01481) 256576 & 253544 Fax (01481) 255194
Website: www.lgm.guernsey.net

Beautifully appointed luxury hotel with 18-hole golf course. Professional shop and tuition on-site. First class, well priced restaurant. 2-AA Rosettes. Beachside location. Golfing breaks catered for.

Lancaster Golf Club
Ashton Hall,
Ashton with Stodday, Lancaster LA2 0AJ.
Tel (01524) 751247 Fax (01524) 752742
E-mail: sec@lancastergc.freeserve.co.uk
Website: www.lancastergc.co.uk

The parkland course laid out by James Braid is 6,500 yards par 71. Accommodation at the Dormy House at Ashton Hall is available. Inclusive packages (minimum two night stay) at very competitive rates. First class catering well stocked bar with a wide selection of fine wines and malt whiskies. Resident club professional. *(See advertisement page 22.)*

Linden Hall
Longhorsley, Morpeth,
Northumberland NE65 8XF.
Tel (01670) 500011 Fax (01670) 500001
Website: www.lindenhall.co.uk

Linden Hall golf course is located within the grounds of Linden Hall Hotel, a 3-Star, 52-bedroom luxury country house hotel, with swimming pool, health spa, gymnasium and conferece facilities. An added facility is the 14-bedroom Linden Dormy House ideal for golfing parties. The 18-hole, 6,846 yard SSS 73 golf course completely surrounds the hotel and is set within mature woodland, rolling parkland with established burns and lakes amidst the stunning backdrop of the Cheviot hills and Northumbrian coastline.

Machrie Hotel & Golf Links
Port Ellen, Isle of Islay, Argyll PA42 7AN.
Tel (01496) 302310 Fax (01496) 302404
E-mail: machrie@machrie.com
Website: www.machrie.com

Play a hidden gem of a course. Traditional 18-hole championship links course situated on the doorstep of the Machrie Hotel. Excellent accommodation, fine food and friendly service. Self-catering and golf packages also available.

Malone Golf Club
240 Upper Malone Road,
Dunmurry, Belfast BT17 9LB.
Tel 028 9061 2758 Fax 028 9043 1394
E-mail: manager@malonegolfclub.co.uk
Website: www.malonegolfclub.co.uk

Superb 27-hole championship course set in 330 acres of rolling parkland. Five miles from Belfast City centre. Societies, groups and visitors welcome by arrangement. Full bar and catering facilities. *(See advertisement page 22.)*

Mentmore Golf & Country Club

Mentmore,
Nr Leighton Buzzard,
Bedfordshire LU7 0UA.
Tel (01296) 662020 Fax (01296) 662592
E-mail: mentmore.events@clubhaus.com

Two 180-hole championship golf courses.
Rothschild Course par 72, 6,763 yards,
Rosebery Course par 72, 6,777 yards. Practice
range. Restaurant, swimming pool, sauna,
jacuzzi and steam room. Leisure club and
tennis courts.

Mersey Valley Golf Club (1995)

Warrington Road,
Bold Heath,
Widnes, Cheshire WA8 3XL.
Tel 0151-424 6060 Fax 0151-257 9097

Conference facilities, corporate golf days and
memberships, societies and visitors welcome.
Buggy hire. We specialise in corporate golf days
- easy walking course. 20 minutes from
Liverpool and Manchester, two miles junction
7 on the M62. Superb bar and catering
facilities.

Mount Juliet

Thomastown,
Co Kilkenny, Ireland.
Tel +353 56 73000 Fax +353 56 73019
E-mail: info@mountjuliet.ie
Website: www.mountjuliet.ie

Deluxe accommodation in the elegant Mount
Juliet House or the informal club rooms.
Ireland's premier sporting estate offers guests
on-site fishing, horse riding, tennis, leisure
centre and fully dedicated spa. Golf Academy
with PGA professionals. 18-hole putting
course. Irish Open venue 1993-95. Host to
WGC American Express Championship in
September 2002.

North Shore Hotel Golf Club & Course

North Shore Road,
Skegness PE25 1DN.
Tel (01754) 763298 Fax (01754) 761902
E-mail: golf@north-shore.co.uk
Website: www.north-shore.co.uk

A mature and challenging 18-hole part
parkland and part links course with sea views
on the edge of Skegness. Good all year round
climate. Rarely closed in winter with no winter
greens. Rarely closed bars, superb bar food and
à la carte restaurant. 36 bedrooms available.

Old Course Hotel - Golf Resort & Spa

St Andrews,
Fife KY16 9SP.
Tel (01334) 474371 Fax (01334) 477668

This luxury 134-bedroom hotel overlooks the
17th Road Hole of the Old Course and is a five
minute walk to the beach and town. Facilities
include health spa with swimming pool,
whirlpool, fitness room and full range of
massage and beauty treatments. The hotel has
its own championship golf course, the Duke's
Course. Open to non-residents, with residents
enjoying guaranteed tee-times and reduced
green fees.

Parasampia Golf & Country Club

Grove Road,
Donnington,
Newbury,
Berkshire RG14 2LA.
Tel (01635) 581000 Fax (01635) 552259
Website: www.parasampia.com

18-hole parkland/moorland championship
course designed by Dave Thomas. The
clubhouse and hotel are located within a
beautifully renovated 18th-century gothic
mansion. This will provide an ideal setting for
your society, company golf day or conference
stay.

Penrhos Golf & Country Club

Llanrhystud,
Ceredigion SY23 5AY.
Tel (01974) 202999 Fax (01974) 202100
Website: www.penrhosgolf.co.uk

Fifteen American-style suites. 18-hole
championship length course, driving range,
indoor swimming pool, sauna, steam room,
gymnasium, tennis courts, spa, solarium and
bowling green.

Penrith Golf Club

Salkeld Road,
Penrith,
Cumbria CA11 8SG.
Tel (01768) 891919

The club, which is 112 years old, is easily
accessible from junction 41 on the M6
motorway and lies half a mile east of Penrith,
enjoying panoramic views to the Lakeland hills.
Visitors are very welcome to play this excellent
course.

Powerscourt Golf Club
Enniskerry,
Co Wicklow, Ireland.
Tel +353 1 204 6033 Fax +353 1 276 1303
E-mail: golfclub@powerscourt.ie
Website: www.powerscourt.ie

An Inspiring Course in a Spectacular Location. Powerscourt is a free draining course with links characteristics. Built to championship standard, with top quality tees and exceptional tiered greens, it is set in some of Ireland's most beautiful parkland. *(See advertisement page 27 for further details.)*

Prince's Golf Club
Sandwich Bay,
Sandwich, Kent CT13 9QB.
Tel (01304) 611118 Fax (01304) 612000
E-mail: hotel@princes-leisure.co.uk
Website: www.princes-leisure.co.uk

This previous Open Championship venue offers a challenging 27-hole course 6,690 yards par 71-72 and excellent driving range with friendly clubhouse making visitors welcome. For overnight accommodation the Bell Hotel in Sandwich is within a ten minutes' drive where you can relax after a days golfing and enjoy imaginative cuisine and friendly service. *(See advertisement page 615 for further details.)*

Ramside Hall Hotel & Golf Club
Carrville,
Durham DH1 1TD.
Tel 0191-386 5282 Fax 0191-386 0399

Set in 220 acres on the outsksirts of the cathedral city of Durham and surrounded by a stimulating 27-hole golf course. 3-Star; 4-Crown Highly Commended. 80 luxury bedrooms, restaurant, grill room and carvery. Conference and banqueting facilities. Superb floodlit driving range and practice areas. *(See advertisement page 619 for further details.)*

Renvyle House Hotel
Connemara,
Go Galway, Ireland.
Tel +353 95 43511 Fax +353 95 43515
E-mail: renvyle@iol.ie
Website: www.renvyle.com

Set in the wild splendour of Connemara in truly magical surroundings. Originally the home of Oliver St John Gogarty, Renvyle House has played host to many famous people - Augustus John, Yeats and Churchill to name but a few. Warmth, comfort and award-

winning fare awaits. Excellent golf and golf clinics are available on-site. *(See advertisement page 624 for further details.)*

Rodway Hill Golf Course
Newent Road,
Highnam,
Gloucestershire GL2 8DN.
Tel (01452) 384222

An 18-hole, par 70 course, open to the public, two miles south west of Gloucester, with panoramic views of the Cotswolds. It has a well stocked shop, practice and teaching facilities. Hire kit available. Bar and restaurant facilities. Societies welcome.

Rosapenna Hotel & Golf Links
Rosapenna,
Downings, Donegal, Ireland.
Tel +353 74 55301 Fax +353 74 55128

Rosapenna Hotel is set in the middle of its own 36-hole golf links course. Half a mile from the fishing village of Downings.

The Roxburghe Hotel & Golf Course
Heiton, By Kelso,
Roxburghshire TD5 8JZ.
Tel (01573) 450331 Fax (01573) 450611
E-mail: golf@roxburghe.net
Website: www.roxburghe.net

The Roxburghe Golf Course is the only championship course in the Scottish Borders, home to the Scottish Seniors Open. Designed by Dave Thomas to follow the natural contours and features of the Roxburghe Estate, the 7,111 yard course suits and challenges all levels of player. The 22-bedroom country house hotel owned by the Duke and Duchess of Roxburghe offers luxury accommodation, superb cuisine and excellent bar in the library.

The Royal Dublin Golf Club
North Bull Island,
Dollymount,
Dublin 3, Ireland.
Tel +353 1 833 6346 Fax +353 1 833 6504

The Royal Dublin Golf Club is Ireland's second oldest golf club and one of the country's premier sporting theatres. Royal Dublin provides visiting players with a combination of a superb championship links and a degree of hospitality that mirrors its historic development. *(See advertisement page 28 for further details.)*

Royal Lytham & St Anne's Golf Club

Links Gate,
Lytham St Anne's,
Lancashire FY8 3LQ.
Tel (01253) 724206 Fax (01253) 780946

Ideal for small parties wishing to play the championship course. Accommodation for men only. Apply to the assistant secretary. *(See advertisement page 22 for further details.)*

Royal Porthcawl Golf Club

Rest Bay,
Porthcawl,
Mid Glamorgan CF36 3UW.
Tel (01656) 782251 Fax (01656) 771687
E-mail: royalporthcawl@aol.com
Website: www.royalporthcawl.com

Luxury dormy accommodation for parties of up to twelve persons. Apply to the secretary. *(See advertisement page 28 for further details.)*

Rudding Park

Follifoot,
Harrogate,
North Yorkshire HG3 1DJ.
Tel (01423) 872100 Fax (01423) 873011
E-mail: sales@ruddingpark.com
Website: www.ruddingpark.com

Rudding Park, just two miles south of Harrogate provides the complete golfing experience. The 18-hole, par 72 Martin Hawtree designed parkland golf course together with the award-winning hotel, make for an enjoyable visit. The golf academy not only boasts an 18-bay floodlit covered driving range but also four PGA professionals. Corporate and Society events welcome.

Seaford Golf Club

East Blatchington,
Seaford,
East Sussex BN25 2JD.
Tel (01323) 892442

The Dormy House provides comfortable accommodation for 20 guests in 10 twin-bedded en suite bedrooms on the first floor of the clubhouse, and 2 single rooms in our bungalow annexe. For latest brochure ring 01323 892442.

Shaw Hill Golf & Country Club

Preston Road,
Whittle-Le-Woods,
Chorley, Lancashire PR6 7PP.
Tel (01257) 269221 Fax (01257) 261223

Shaw Hill comprises a 72 par 18-hole golf course, a fully equipped leisure centre and an AA award-winning restaurant and we can offer wedding and conference facilities. *(See advertisement page 619 for further details.)*

The Slieve Russell Hotel Golf & Country Club

Ballyconnell,
Co Cavan, Ireland.
Tel +353 49 9526444 Fax +353 49 9526474
Website: www.quinnhotels.com

Located only two hours' drive from both Dublin and Belfast, the Slieve Russell is a complete resort with its 5-Star leisure facilities, championship 18-hole golf course, 159 superbly appointed bedrooms and a selection of restaurants and bars, conference and banqueting suites - 'The *Perfect* location for business or pleasure.

Sparkwell Golf Course

Blacklands,
Sparkwell,
Plymouth, Devon PL7 5DF.
Tel/Fax (01752) 837219

A testing 9-hole, pay as you play course and a par 3 course, set in 60 acres of parkland. Facilities include a well equipped golf shop, excellent restaurant and friendly bar. Open to the public. Golf societies welcome.

St Helen's Bay Golf & Country Club

St Helens,
Kilrane,
Rosslare Harbour,
Co Wexford, Ireland.
Tel +353 53 33234 Fax +353 53 33803
E-mail: sthelens@iol.ie
Website: www.sthelensbay.com

Superbly located championship 18-hole golf course, which has blended the best of parkland characteristics with a finish that is true links and plenty of difficulty. Luxury on-site
continued over page

accommodation together with tennis courts. Full bar and catering facilities available in the clubhouse. Situated only five minutes from Rosslare ferryport. Green fee and society-friendly, playable all year.

St Mary's Hotel Golf & Country Club
St Mary's Hill,
Pencoed, Vale of Glamorgan CF35 5EA.
Tel (01656) 861100 Fax (01656) 863400

24-bedroom hotel, 18-hole membership and pay course. 9-hole pay as you play, 15-bay floodlit driving range, clubhouse and restaurant conservatory and three bars. Fully stocked golf shop. Floodlit chipping and putting area and resident golf professional Mr John Peters.

St Pierre Park Hotel
Rohais,
St Peter Port,
Guernsey GYI 1FD.
Tel (01481) 728282 Fax (01481) 712041

This 4-Star hotel offers extensive leisure facilities including a 9-hole par 3 golf course, designed by Tony Jacklin. Three tennis courts and a health suite with heated indoor swimming pool, spa bath, saunas, steam rooms, solaria and exercise room.

The Stoke By Nayland Club Hotel
Leavenheath,
Colchester, Essex CO6 4PZ.
Tel (01206) 262836 Fax (01206) 263356
E-mail: info@golf-club.co.uk
Website: www.stokebynaylandclub.co.uk

Recognised as one of the finest golf and leisure facilities in East Anglia. Two 18-hole championship golf courses and covered driving range, all year round buggy availability. En suite accommodation in our luxury hotel. Renowned excellent cuisine, superb indoor pool and gymnasium.

Telford Golf & Country Club
Great Hay,
Sutton Heights,
Telford, Shropshire TF7 4DT.
Tel (01952) 429977 Fax (01952) 586602
Website: www.corushotels.co.uk

Overlooking the Ironbridge Gorge, the 96-bedroom hotel offers its own 18-hole championship course. Floodlit driving range and practice areas. The extensive leisure facilities include squash courts, snooker, swimming pool, gymnasium, whirlpool, sauna and steam rooms. Resident masseur. Corporate, Society and residential packages.

Trevose Golf & Country Club
Constantine Bay,
Padstow, North Cornwall PL28 8JB.
Tel (01841) 520208 Fax (01841) 521057
E-mail: reception@trevose-gc.co.uk
Website: www.trevose-gc.co.uk/

Trevose offers not only great golf (championship 18-hole course, a 9-hole full length (3,100 yards) par 35 plus a 9-hole short course) but also a first class clubhouse and restaurant, three hard all-weather tennis courts, a heated outdoor swimming pool in the summer, a games room for the kids and a boutique. Accommodation is available in bungalows, chalets, trehuel flats, dormy flats and cabins. Send for our detailed colour brochure. Open all year. Societies welcome.

The Westin Turnberry Resort, Scotland
Turnberry,
Ayrshire KA26 9LT.
Tel +44 (0) 1655 331000
Fax +44 (0) 1655 331706
E-mail: turnberry@westin.com
Website: www.westin.com/turnberry

One of the finest golfing destinations in the world. Turnberry has two championship links courses, the legendary Ailsa (host to three Open's) and the highly acclaimed Kintyre. Whilst Colin Montgomerie Links Golf Academy offers world class teaching and practice facilities.

Wheathampstead Pay & Play Golf Course
Harpenden Road,
St Albans, Hertfordshire AL4 8EZ.
Tel/Fax (01582) 833941

A 9-hole par 33 golf course and large practice area. Everyone is welcome. Doug Edgar, who built and designed the course, will help you with all your golfing needs. Telephone 01582 833941.

Whitefields Hotel Golf & Country Club
Coventry Road, Thurlaston,
Nr Rugby, Warwickshire CV23 9JR.
Tel (01788) 521800 Fax (01788) 521695
Website: www.whitefields/hotel.co.uk

18-hole course 6,223 yards. Driving range,
putting green 18. Four conference rooms. 50
en suite rooms. Bars and à la carte restaurant.
Societies welcome seven days. Call the
secretary on 01788 815555. Reservations
01788 521800.

Wicklow Golf Club
Dunbur Road, Wicklow, Ireland.
Tel +353 404 67379 Tel/Fax +353 404 66122

A challenging and spectacular test of golf is
promised here at Wicklow Golf Club. Par 71
SSS 70 5,720 metres featuring the natural
contours of the terrain. Open from sunrise to
sunset. Enjoy uncrowded golf and excellent
clubhouse facilities. Visitors made very
welcome.

Wokefield Park Golf Club
Mortimer, Reading, Berkshire RG7 3AE.
Tel 0118-933 4013 Fax 0118-933 4031

Set amid the Berkshire countryside this
challenging 7,000 yards golf course has mature
trees, winding streams, nine lakes and large
bunkers. Wokefield also features 320
bedrooms, teaching academy and leisure
facilities. Call the golf sales team on 0118-933
4018 and 4017.

Woodbury Park Golf & Country Club
Woodbury Castle,
Woodbury,
Exeter, Devon EX5 1JJ.
Tel (01395) 233382 Fax (01395) 233384

Luxury 55-bedroom hotel with five superb
lodges. The Nigel Mansell owned resort
encompasses 27 holes, including the Oaks
championship course, in addition to extensive
leisure facilities. The ideal venue for your
golfing break.

Index of Advertisers

PART XII

Clubs and Courses in the British Isles and Europe

Compiled by Jan Bennett

Club Centenaries

1903

Appleby
Arbroath Artisan
Ashford
Ballymena
Bangor
Barnehurst
Bishopshire
Bromborough
Caldwell
Castlefields
Deeside
Diss
East Berkshire
Hale
Hendon
Laleham
Leatherhead
Magdalene Fields
Newport
Normanton
North Foreland
Oswestry
Pontypool
Portpatrick
Powfoot
Ralston
Ross-on-Wye
Rossendale
Rotherham
Shooter's Hill
Silecroft
St Davids City
St Fillans
St Michaels
Walton Heath
Warrington

1904

Alness
Auchterderran
Bamburgh Castle
Blackpool North Shore
Blankney
Bonar Bridge/Ardgay
Coombe Wood
Erskine
Fereneze

1904 *continued*

Fintona
Flackwell Heath
Fulwell
Gifford
Haverfordwest
Highgate
Hindhead
Holywood
Hull
Isles of Scilly
Keighley
Kibworth
Kirkcaldy
Langland Bay
Lutterworth
Machynlleth
North Hants
Osborne
Piltdown
Pontefract & District
Saddleworth
Saltford
Shirehampton Park
Spey Bay
Staddon Heights
Stand
Wath
Whitehead
Whiteleaf
Wolstanton
Wrexham
Yelverton

1905

Banchory
Bellshill
Blyth
Bramhall
Bridlington
Broomieknowe
Burley
Burnley
Caerphilly
Castle Douglas
Chapel-en-le-Frith
Clydebank & District
Colvend

1905 *continued*

Criccieth
Dunmurry
Ellesborough
Erewash Valley
Hindley Hall
Huyton & Prescot
Knighton
Knowle
Lee-on-the-Solent
Letchworth
Llandrindod Wells
Llanishen
Mannings Heath
Maryport
Morecambe
Mount Ellen
North Middlesex
Nuneaton
Old Ranfurly
Pontypridd
Porthmadog
Prenton
Prestatyn
Queens Park (Bournemouth)
Redditch
Sandyhills
Sleaford
Southerndown
St Medan
Stockport
Stranraer
Tenterden
The Dunnerholme
Verulam
Whitecraigs
Woodhall Hills
Worthing
Wrekin

1906

Allendale
Alston Moor
Bradford Moor
Brandhall
Carholme
Carradale
Chilwell Manor

1906 *continued*

Chipstead
Clayton
Cowglen
Deane
Dinsdale Spa
Dunstable Downs
Elgin
Enmore Park
Fulford
Glen (North Berwick)
Gorleston
Gosforth
Halesowen
Halifax West End
Hartlepool
Harwich & Dovercourt
Holywell
Knighton
Kyles of Bute
Leigh
Longcliffe
Matlock
Morpeth
Ormonde Fields
Otley
Outlane
Pannal
Prince's
Ravensworth
Serlby Park
Silverdale
South Bradford
South Leeds
Southport & Ainsdale
St Deiniol
Stafford Castle
Stanton-on-the-Wolds
The Dyke
Turnberry Hotel
Walmersley
West Byfleet
West Monmouthshire
Whitsand Bay Hotel
Whittaker
Williamwood
Wrotham

Golf Clubs and Courses in the British Isles and Europe

How to use this section

Clubs in England, Ireland and Wales are listed in alphabetical order by country and county. Note that some clubs and courses are affiliated to a county different to that in which they are physically located. Clubs in Scotland are grouped under recognised administrative regions. The Great Britain and Ireland county index can be found on page 650.

European clubs are listed alphabetically by country and grouped under regional headings. The index for this can be found on page 846. In most European countries, only 18 hole courses are included.

All clubs and courses are listed in the the general index at back of the book.

Club details (see Key to Symbols below)

The date after the name of the club indicates the year it was founded. Courses are private unless otherwise stated. Many public courses play host to members' clubs. Information on these can be obtained from the course concerned.

The address is the postal address.

Telephone: club telephone number for general use.

Membership: total number of playing members. The number of lady members (L) and juniors (J) is sometimes shown separately.

Secretary/Professional: telephone numbers for secretaries and professionals are shown separately.

Holes: the length of the course refers in most cases to the yardage from the medal tees.

Visitors: indicates the playing opportunities and restrictions for unaccompanied visitors.

Fees: green fees, the most up-to-date supplied, are quoted for visitors playing without a member. The basic cost per round or per day (D) is shown first, with the weekend rate in brackets. The cost of a weekly (W) ticket is sometimes shown.

Location: general location of club/course.

Miscellaneous: other golf facilities.

Architect: course architect/designer.

Abbreviations

WD	Weekdays.
WE	Weekends.
BH	Bank Holidays.
H	Handicap certificate required.
M	With a member, i.e. casual visitors are not allowed: only visitors playing with a member are permitted on the days stated.
NA	No visitors allowed.
SOC	Recognised Golfing Societies welcome if previous arrangements made with secretary.
U	Unrestricted.
CR	Course Rating (Europe)
SR	Slope Rating (Europe)

We are indebted to club secretaries in the British Isles and continental Europe for the information supplied.

Key to Symbols

☎ Telephone	✓ Professional	⊕ Miscellaneous
🖳 Fax	⊳ Holes	⌂ Architect
✉ E-mail	👫 Visitors	■ Website
📖 Membership	£€ Fees	
✍ Secretary	⚒ Location	

Great Britain and Ireland County Index

England

Bedfordshire

Aspley Guise & Woburn Sands (1914)
West Hill, Aspley Guise, Milton Keynes, MK17 8DX
- ☎ (01908) 583596
- ⌨ (01908) 583596
- ▥ 590
- ✍ (01908) 583596
- ✎ C Clingan (01908) 582974
- �︎ 18 L 6079 yds Par 71 SSS 70
- ⛹ WD–H WE/BH–MH SOC–Wed & Fri
- £€ £27 D–£38
- ⛳ 2 miles W of M1 Junction 13
- ⛨ Herd/Sandow

Aylesbury Vale (1991)
Wing, Leighton Buzzard, LU7 0UJ
- ☎ (01525) 240196
- ⌨ (01525) 240848
- ▥ 500
- ✍ C Wright (Sec/Mgr)
- ✎ G Goble (01525) 240197
- �︎ 18 L 6612 yds Par 72 SSS 72
- ⛹ WD–U WE–U–phone first SOC–WD
- £€ £15 (£25)
- ⛳ 3 miles W of Leighton Buzzard on Wing-Stewkley road
- ⊕ Driving range
- ⛨ Sq Ldr Don Wright

Beadlow Manor Hotel G&CC (1973)
Beadlow, Shefford, SG17 5PH
- ☎ (01525) 860800
- ⌨ (01525) 861345
- ▥ 700
- ✍ R Tommey (01525) 843398
- ✎ P Hetherington (01525) 861292
- �︎ 18 L 6238 yds SSS 71
  18 L 6042 yds SSS 70
- ⛹ U H SOC
- £€ On application
- ⛳ 2 miles W of Shefford on A507
- ⊕ Driving range

Bedford (1999)
Carnoustie Drive, Great Denham, Biddenham, MK40 4BF
- ☎ (01234) 320022
- ⌨ (01234) 320023
- ✍ M Rizzi (01234) 330559
- ✎ J Bodicoat
- �︎ 18 L 6560 yds Par 72
- ⛹ WD–U WE–M SOC–WD
- £€ £25 (£40)
- ⛳ 2 miles W of Bedford (A428)
- ⊕ Driving range
- ⛨ David Pottage

Bedford & County (1912)
Green Lane, Clapham, Bedford, MK41 6ET
- ☎ (01234) 352617
- ⌨ (01234) 357195
- ✉ olga@bedcounty.fsnet.co.uk
- ▥ 600
- ✍ RP Walker (Mgr), O Ebsworth (Asst Mgr)
- ✎ R Tattersall (01234) 359189
- ⏞ 18 L 6399 yds SSS 70
- ⛹ WD–U H WE–M SOC
- £€ D–£30
- ⛳ 2 miles NW of Bedford on A6
- ⬛ www.bedfordandcountygolfclub.co.uk

Bedfordshire (1891)
Spring Lane, Stagsden, Bedford, MK43 8SR
- ☎ (01234) 822555
- ⌨ (01234) 825052
- ▥ 600
- ✍ DE Romans (Gen Mgr)
- ✎ D Armor (01234) 826100
- ⏞ 18 L 6565 yds SSS 72
- ⛹ WD–U (phone first) WE–M before noon SOC–WD
- £€ On application
- ⛳ 3 miles W of Bedford (A422). M1 Junction 14, 5 miles

Chalgrave Manor
Dunstable Road, Chalgrave, Toddington, LU5 6JN
- ☎ (01525) 876556
- ⌨ (01525) 876556
- ▥ 450
- ✍ S Rumball
- ✎ T Bunyan
- ⏞ 18 L 6382 yds Par 72 SSS 70
- ⛹ U SOC–WD
- £€ £15 (£20)
- ⛳ 2 miles W of M1 Junction 12 on A5120
- ⊕ Practice range
- ⛨ Mike Palmer

Colmworth (1992)
Proprietary
New Road, Colmworth, MK44 2NV
- ☎ (01234) 378181
- ⌨ (01234) 376235
- ▥ 200
- ✍ A Willis (01234) 402674
- ✎ M Fields
- ⏞ 18 L 6435 yds Par 72 SSS 71
  9 hole Par 3 course
- ⛹ U SOC
- £€ £12 (£18)
- ⛳ 6 miles N of Bedford, off B660. 4 miles W of A1
- ⊕ Driving range
- ⛨ John Glasgow
- ⬛ www.colmworthgolfclub.co.uk

Colworth (1985)
Unilever Research, Sharnbrook, Bedford, MK44 1LQ
- ☎ (01933) 353269 (Sec)
- ▥ 405
- ✍ E Thompson
- ⏞ 9 L 2626 yds Par 68 SSS 66
- ⛹ M
- £€ D–£8
- ⛳ Sharnbrook, 10 miles N of Bedford, off A6

Dunstable Downs (1906)
Whipsnade Road, Dunstable, LU6 2NB
- ☎ (01582) 604472
- ⌨ (01582) 478700
- ▥ 640
- ✍ GB Woodcock
- ✎ M Weldon (01582) 662806
- ⏞ 18 L 5903 yds SSS 69
- ⛹ WD–H WE–M SOC–WD exc Wed
- £€ £25 D–£40
- ⛳ 2 miles SW of Dunstable on B4541. M1 Junction 11
- ⛨ James Braid

Griffin (1985)
Chaul End Road, Caddington, LU1 4AX
- ☎ (01582) 415573
- ⌨ (01582) 415314
- ▥ 500
- ✍ D Sweetnam
- ✎ D Marsden
- ⏞ 18 L 6240 yds Par 71 SSS 70
- ⛹ WD–U WE/BH–phone first SOC
- £€ £14 Fri–£17 (£20)
- ⛳ 3 miles W of Luton on A505 between Dunstable and Caddington. M1 Junction 10/11

Henlow (1985)
RAF Henlow, Henlow, SG16 6DN
- ☎ (01462) 851515 Ext 7083
- ⌨ (01462) 816780
- ▥ 250
- ✍ A Smythe (01462) 851515 (Ext 7473)
- ⏞ 9 L 5618 yds SSS 67
- ⛹ M
- £€ D–£10
- ⛳ 3 miles SE of Shefford on A600
- ⊕ Driving range
- ⬛ www.henlowgolfclub.co.uk

John O'Gaunt (1948)
Sutton Park, Sandy, Biggleswade, SG19 2LY
- ☎ (01767) 260360
- ⌨ (01767) 262834
- ✉ admin@johnogauntgolfclub.co.uk
- ▥ 1450
- ✍ SD Anthony
- ✎ L Scarbrow (01767) 260094
- ⏞ John O'Gaunt 18 L 6513 yds SSS 71
  Carthagena 18 L 5869 yds SSS 69

‡ H–phone first SOC–WD
££ £45 (£50)
⊶ 3 miles NE of Biggleswade on
    B1040
⌂ Hawtree

Leighton Buzzard   (1925)
Plantation Road, Leighton Buzzard,
LU7 7JF
☎ **(01525) 373811/373812**
⌨ 650
✍ D Mutton (01525) 373811
✓ M Campbell (01525) 372143
▷ 18 L 6101 yds SSS 70
‡ WD exc Tues–U H WE/BH–MH
££ £32 D–£35
⊶ Heath and Reach, 1 mile N of
    Leighton Buzzard. M1 Junction 12

Millbrook   (1980)
Ampthill, MK45 2JB
☎ **(01525) 840252**
⌨ (01525) 406249
✉ info@themillbrook.com
⌨ 385
✍ DC Cooke
✓ G Dixon (01525) 402269
▷ 18 L 7021 yds SSS 73
‡ WD–U after 12.30pm SOC
££ £22 (£28)
⊶ 4 miles from M1 Junctions 12 or 13
    on A507
⊕ Practice range
⌂ W Sutherland
■ www.themillbrook.com

Mount Pleasant   (1992)
Proprietary
Station Road, Lower Stondon, Henlow,
SG16 6JL
☎ **(01462) 850999**
⌨ (01462) 850257
✉ davidsimsmpgolf@aol.com
⌨ 300
✍ D Simkins (Prop) (01462) 850999
✓ M Roberts (01462) 850999
▷ 9 L 6003 yds Par 70 SSS 69
‡ U SOC–WD
££ 9 holes–£8 (£10.50) 18 holes–£14
    (£18)
⊶ 4 miles N of Hitchin, off A600
⌂ Derek Young
■ www.mountpleasantgolfclub.co.uk

Mowsbury   (1975)
Public
Kimbolton Road, Bedford, MK41 8DQ
☎ **(01234) 216374/771041**
⌨ 460
✍ LW Allan
✓ M Summers
▷ 18 L 6514 yds SSS 71
‡ U
££ £13.30 (£14)
⊶ 2 miles N of Bedford on B660
⊕ Driving range
⌂ Hawtree

Pavenham Park   (1994)
Pavenham, Bedford, MK43 7PE
☎ **(01234) 822202**
⌨ (01234) 826602

✉ kolvengolf@ukonline.co.uk
⌨ 850
✍ E Thompson
✓ ZL Thompson
▷ 18 L 6353 yds SSS 71
‡ WD–U WE–M SOC–WD
££ £25 (£40)
⊶ 4 miles NW of Bedford on A6
⌂ Zac Thompson
■ www.kolvengolf.com

South Beds   (1892)
Warden Hill Road, Luton, LU2 7AE
☎ **(01582) 575201**
⌨ (01582) 495381
⌨ 850
✍ RJ Wright (01582) 591500
✓ E Cogle (01582) 591209
▷ Galley 18 L 6467 yds SSS 71
    Warden 9 L 4914 yds SSS 64
‡ Galley WD–H (Ladies Day–Tues)
    WE/BH–H exc comp days–NA
    SOC Warden–U
££ Galley £22 D–£32 (£34 D–£43)
    Warden £10 (£13)
⊶ 3 miles N of Luton, E of A6

Stockwood Park   (1973)
Public
Stockwood Park, London Rd, Luton,
LU1 4LX
☎ **(01582) 413704**
⌨ (01582) 481001
✉ secretary@stockwoodparkgc
    .freeserve.co.uk
⌨ 900
✍ Mrs B McMillan (01582) 431788
✓ G McCarthy
▷ 18 L 6049 yds SSS 69
‡ U
££ £9.50 (£12.70)
⊶ 1 mile S of Luton on A6. M1
    Junction 10
⊕ Driving range

Tilsworth   (1972)
Pay and play
Dunstable Rd, Tilsworth, Dunstable,
LU7 9PU
☎ **(01525) 210721/210722**
⌨ (01525) 210465
⌨ 370
✍ G Brandon-White
✓ N Webb (Mgr)
▷ 18 L 5303 yds Par 69 SSS 67
‡ U SOC
££ £14 (£16)
⊶ 2 miles N of Dunstable (A5)
⊕ Driving range
■ www.tilsworthgolf.co.uk

Wyboston Lakes   (1978)
Public
Wyboston Lakes, Wyboston, MK44 3AL
☎ **(01480) 223004**
⌨ (01480) 407330
⌨ 300
✍ DJ Little (Mgr)
✓ P Ashwell (01480) 223004
▷ 18 L 5995 yds Par 70 SSS 69
‡ WD–U WE–booking SOC

££ £15 (£20)
⊶ S of St Neots, off A1 and St Neots
    by-pass
⊕ Driving range
⌂ Neil Ockden
■ www.wybostonlakes.co.uk

Berkshire

Bearwood   (1986)
Mole Road, Sindlesham, Wokingham,
RG41 5DB
☎ **(0118) 976 0060**
⌨ (0118) 977 2687
⌨ 500
✍ BFC Tustin (Mgr) (0118) 976 0060
✓ BJ Tustin (0118) 976 0156
▷ 9 L 5614 yds SSS 68
‡ WD–H before 4pm –M after 4pm
££ 18 holes–£18 (£22) 9 holes–£10
    (£12)
⊶ 1 mile SW of Winnersh, on B3030.
    M4 Junction 10
⊕ Driving range

Bearwood Lakes   (1996)
Bearwood Road, Sindlesham, RG41 4SJ
☎ **(0118) 979 7900**
⌨ (0118) 979 2911
✉ info@bearwoodlakes.co.uk
⌨ 800
✍ S Evans (Gen Mgr)
✓ T Waldron (0118) 978 3030
▷ 18 L 6800 yds Par 72 SSS 72
‡ M H
⊶ 1 mile S of M4 Junction 10,
    between Wokingham and
    Sindlesham
⌂ Martin Hawtree
■ www.bearwoodlakes.co.uk

The Berkshire   (1928)
Swinley Road, Ascot, SL5 8AY
☎ **(01344) 621495**
⌨ (01344) 623328
⌨ 935
✍ Lt Col JCF Hunt (01344) 621496
✓ P Anderson (01344) 622351
▷ Red 18 L 6379 yds SSS 71
    Blue 18 L 6260 yds SSS 71
‡ WD–I WE/BH–M
££ On application
⊶ 3 miles from Ascot on A332. M3
    Junction 3
⌂ Herbert Fowler

Billingbear Park
Pay and play
The Straight Mile, Wokingham,
RG40 5SJ
☎ **(01344) 869259**
⌨ (01344) 869259
⌨ 50
✍ Mrs JR Blainey
✓ MW Blainey
▷ 9 L 5700 yds Par 68
    9 hole Par 3 course
‡ U
££ £8 (£10)

2 miles E of Wokingham via B3034. M4 Junction 10

Bird Hills (1985)
Public
Drift Road, Hawthorn Hill, Maidenhead, SL6 3ST
- ☎ **(01628) 771030**
- ☐ (01628) 631023
- ✉ info@birdhills.co.uk
- ☐ 400
- ♟ S Farrin (Gen Mgr)
- ✓ N Slimming
- ⏸ 18 L 6212 yds SSS 69
- ⚭ U SOC–WD
- ££ On application
- 🚗 4 miles S of Maidenhead on A330
- ⊕ Floodlit driving range
- ■ www.birdhills.co.uk

Blue Mountain Golf Centre (1993)
Pay and play
Wood Lane, Binfield, RG42 4EX
- ☎ **(01344) 300220**
- ☐ (01344) 360960
- ☐ 500
- ✓ I Looms (01344) 488858
- ⏸ 18 L 6097 yds SSS 70
- ⚭ U SOC
- ££ £18 Fri–£20 (£24)
- 🚗 1 mile W of Bracknell on B3408. M4 Junction 10
- ⊕ Driving range. Golf Academy

Calcot Park (1930)
Bath Road, Calcot, Reading, RG31 7RN
- ☎ **(0118) 942 7124**
- ☐ (0118) 945 3373
- ✉ info@calcotpark.com
- ☐ 550
- ♟ JR Cox
- ✓ IJ Campbell (0118) 942 7797
- ⏸ 18 L 6216 yds SSS 70
- ⚭ WD–H WE/BH–M SOC–WD
- ££ £40 After 2pm–£25
- 🚗 3 miles W of Reading on A4. 1¹⁄₂ miles E of M4 Junction 12
- ⏠ HS Colt

Castle Royle (1994)
Knowl Hill, Reading, RG10 9XA
- ☎ **(01628) 825442**
- ♟ M Harris (Gen Mgr)
- ✓ R Watts
- ⏸ 18 L 6828 yds Par 72 SSS 73
- ⚭ N/A
- ££ N/A
- 🚗 2 miles W of Maidenhead (A4). M4 Junction 8/9
- ⏠ Neil Coles

Datchet (1890)
Buccleuch Road, Datchet, SL3 9BP
- ☎ **(01753) 543887 (Clubhouse)**
- ☐ (01753) 541872
- ✉ secretary@datchetgolfclub.co.uk
- ☐ 210 50(L) 30(J)
- ♟ KR Smith (01753) 541872
- ✓ I Godleman (01753) 545222

- ⏸ 9 L 6087 yds SSS 69
- ⚭ WD–U M after 3pm WE–M SOC
- ££ £18.50 D–£25.50
- 🚗 Slough, Windsor 2 miles
- ⏠ JH Taylor
- ■ www.datchetgolfclub.co.uk

Deanwood Park (1995)
Pay and play
Stockcross, Newbury, RG20 8JS
- ☎ **(01635) 48772**
- ☐ (01635) 48772
- ☐ 300
- ♟ J Bowness
- ✓ J Purton
- ⏸ 9 L 4230 yds Par 64 SSS 60
- ⚭ U
- ££ £14.50 (£17.50)
- 🚗 2 miles W of Newbury (B4000). M4 Junction 13, 2 miles
- ⊕ Driving range

Donnington Valley (1985)
Snelsmore House, Snelsmore Common, Newbury, RG14 3BG
- ☎ **(01635) 568140**
- ☐ (01635) 568141
- ☐ 550
- ♟ LC Storey (01635) 568145
- ✓ M Balfour
- ⏸ 18 L 6335 yds SSS 71
- ⚭ U
- ££ £22 (£28)
- 🚗 N of Newbury, off Old Oxford road
- ■ www.donningtonvalley.co.uk

Downshire (1973)
Public
Easthampstead Park, Wokingham, RG11 3DH
- ☎ **(01344) 302030**
- ☐ (01344) 301020
- ♟ P Stanwick (Golf Mgr)
- ✓ W Owers
- ⏸ 18 L 6416 yds SSS 69
- ⚭ U SOC
- ££ £13.50 (£17)
- 🚗 Off Nine Mile Ride
- ⊕ Driving range. Pitch & putt

East Berkshire (1903)
Ravenswood Ave, Crowthorne, RG45 6BD
- ☎ **(01344) 772041**
- ☐ (01344) 777378
- ☐ 700
- ♟ DP Kelly
- ✓ J Brant (01344) 774112
- ⏸ 18 L 6345 yds SSS 70
- ⚭ WD–H WE/BH–M SOC
- ££ £40
- 🚗 Nr Crowthorne Station
- ⏠ P Paxton

Goring & Streatley (1895)
Rectory Road, Streatley-on-Thames, RG8 9QA
- ☎ **(01491) 873229**
- ☐ (01491) 875224
- ☐ 740 115(L) 50(J)
- ♟ I McColl (Sec/Mgr)

- ✓ J Hadland (01491) 873715
- ⏸ 18 L 6355 yds SSS 70
- ⚭ WD–U WE/BH–M SOC–WD
- ££ £28 D–£35 (£35)
- 🚗 10 miles NW of Reading on A417
- ⏠ Tom Dunne
- ■ www.goringgc.org

Hennerton (1992)
Crazies Hill Road, Wargrave, RG10 8LT
- ☎ **(0118) 940 1000/4778**
- ☐ (0118) 940 1042
- ☐ 450
- ♟ PJ Hearn
- ✓ W Farrow (0118) 940 4778
- ⏸ 9 L 2730 yds SSS 34
- ⚭ WD–U WE–pm only SOC
- ££ 18 holes–£17 (£20) 9 holes–£12 (£17)
- 🚗 Between Maidenhead and Reading (A4/A321)
- ⊕ Driving range
- ⏠ Dion Beard
- ■ www.hennertongolfclub.co.uk

Hurst (1979)
Public
Sandford Lane, Hurst, Wokingham, RG10 0SQ
- ☎ **(01734) 344355**
- ♟ AG Poncia (Hon)
- ✓ P Watson
- ⏸ 9 L 3015 yds SSS 70
- ££ On application
- 🚗 Reading 5 miles. Wokingham 3 miles

Maidenhead (1896)
Shoppenhangers Road, Maidenhead, SL6 2PZ
- ☎ **(01628) 624693**
- ☐ 600
- ♟ TP Jackson
- ✓ S Geary (01628) 624067
- ⏸ 18 L 6360 yds SSS 70
- ⚭ WD–H Fri–M after noon WE–M
- ££ D–£35
- 🚗 Off A308, nr Maidenhead Station

Mapledurham (1992)
Mapledurham, Reading, RG4 7UD
- ☎ **(0118) 946 3353**
- ☐ (0118) 946 3363
- ☐ 400
- ♟ D Burton
- ✓ S O'Keefe
- ⏸ 18 L 5625 yds SSS 69
- ⚭ U
- ££ £19 (£24)
- 🚗 4 miles NW of Reading, off A4074
- ⏠ MRM Sandow

Mill Ride (1990)
Mill Ride, Ascot, SL5 8LT
- ☎ **(01344) 886777**
- ☐ (01344) 886820
- ☐ 300
- ♟ G Irvine (Gen Mgr)
- ✓ M Palmer
- ⏸ 18 L 6752 yds SSS 72
- ⚭ H SOC

£€ On application
🚗 2 miles W of Ascot
⊕ www.mill-ride.com
🏠 Donald Steel

Newbury & Crookham
(1873)
Bury's Bank Road, Greenham Common, Newbury, RG19 8BZ
☎ **(01635) 40035**
🖳 (01635) 40045
📧 steve.myers@newburygolf.co.uk
📖 626
🏌 S Myers
⚲ DW Harris (01635) 31201
🏳 18 L 5918 yds SSS 69
👥 WD–U H WE–M (recognised club members)
£€ £30
🚗 2 miles SE of Newbury. M4 Junction 13

Newbury Racecourse   (1994)
The Racecourse, Newbury, RG14 7NZ
☎ **(01635) 551464**
🖳 (01635) 528354
📖 300
🏌 R Osgood (01635) 400015
⚲ N Mitchell (01635) 551464
🏳 18 L 6311 yds Par 70 SSS 70
👥 U SOC
£€ £13 (£17)
🚗 4 miles S of M4 Junction 13 on A34/A39
⊕ Driving range
■ www.nrgc.co.uk

Parasampia G&CC
Donnington Grove, Grove Road, Donnington, RG14 2LA
☎ **(01635) 581000**
🖳 (01635) 552259
📧 enquiries@parasampia.com
📖 350
🏌 S Greenacre (Mgr)
⚲ G Williams
🏳 18 L 7108 yds Par 72 SSS 74
👥 U SOC–WD/BH
£€ £35 D–£45 (£40 D–£55)
🚗 NW of Newbury, off old Oxford road (B4494). M4 Junction 13, 3¹/₂ miles
🏠 Dave Thomas
■ www.parasampia.com

Reading   (1910)
17 Kidmore End Road, Emmer Green, Reading, RG4 8SG
☎ **(0118) 947 2909**
🖳 (0118) 946 4468
📖 585
🏌 R Brown (0118) 947 2909
⚲ S Fotheringham (0118) 947 6115
🏳 18 L 6251 yds SSS 70
👥 Mon–Thurs–UH Fri/WE/BH–M SOC–Tues–Thurs
£€ £27.50 D–£40
🚗 2 miles N of Reading, off Peppard Road (B481)
🏠 James Braid

Royal Ascot   (1887)
Winkfield Road, Ascot, SL5 7LJ
☎ **(01344) 625175**
🖳 (01344) 872330
📖 600
🏌 Mrs S Thompson
⚲ A White (01344) 624656
🏳 18 L 5716 yds SSS 68
👥 M SOC
£€ On application
🚗 On Ascot Heath, inside Ascot racecourse. Windsor 4 miles
🏠 JH Taylor

The Royal Household   (1901)
Crown Estates Office, Windsor Castle, Windsor
☎ **(020) 7930 4832**
🖳 (020) 7839 5950
📖 200
🏌 G Begley
🏳 9 L 4560 yds SSS 62
👥 Strictly by invitation
🚗 Home Park, Windsor Castle
🏠 Muir Ferguson

Sand Martins   (1993)
Finchampstead Road, Wokingham, RG40 3RQ
☎ **(0118) 979 2711**
🖳 (0118) 977 0282
📖 750
🏌 Ms E Roginski
⚲ AJ Hall (0118) 977 0265
🏳 18 L 6204 yds Par 70 SSS 70
👥 WD–U WE–NA SOC
£€ £30
🚗 1 mile S of Wokingham. M4 Junction 10
⊕ Driving range
🏠 ET Fox
■ www.sandmartins.com

Sonning   (1911)
Duffield Road, Sonning, Reading, RG4 6GJ
☎ **(0118) 969 3332**
🖳 (0118) 944 8409
📧 secretary@sonning-golf-club.co.uk
📖 750
🏌 AJ Tanner
⚲ RT McDougall (0118) 969 2910
🏳 18 L 6366 yds SSS 70
👥 WD–H WE–M
£€ On application
🚗 1¹/₂ miles E of A329(M). S of A4, nr Sonning

Sulham Valley   (1992)
Pincents Lane, Calcot, Reading, RG3 5UQ
☎ **(01734) 305959**
🖳 (01734) 305002
📖 700
🏌 To be appointed
⚲ Tina Tetley
🏳 18 L 6121 yds Par 71
👥 U SOC
£€ £20 (£25)
🚗 M4 Junction 12, 1 mile

Swinley Forest   (1909)
Coronation Road, Ascot, SL9 5LE
☎ **(01344) 620197**
🖳 (01344) 874733
📧 swinleyfgc@aol.com
📖 350
🏌 IL Pearce (01344) 874979
⚲ S Hill (01344) 874811
🏳 18 L 6045 yds Par 69 SSS 70
👥 M
£€ £75
🚗 S of Ascot
🏠 HS Colt

Temple   (1909)
Henley Road, Hurley, Maidenhead, SL6 5LH
☎ **(01628) 824795**
🖳 (01628) 828119
📖 566
🏌 KGM Adderley (01628) 824795
⚲ J Whiteley (01628) 824254
🏳 18 L 6248 yds SSS 70
👥 H SOC
£€ £36 (£44)
🚗 Between Maidenhead and Henley on A4130. M4 Junction 8/9. M40 Junction 4
🏠 Willie Park Jr

Theale
North Street, Theale, Reading, RG6 5EX
☎ **(01189) 305331**
🖳 (01189) 305331
🏌 M Lowe
⚲ L Newman
🏳 18 L 6392 yds Par 72 SSS 71
👥 U SOC
£€ £16 (£20)
🚗 1 mile from M4 Junction 12
⊕ Driving range
🏠 M Lowe

West Berkshire   (1975)
Chaddleworth, Newbury, RG20 7DU
☎ **(01488) 638574**
📖 700
🏌 Mrs CM Clayton
⚲ P Simpson (01488) 638851
🏳 18 L 7001 yds SSS 74
👥 WD–U WE–M SOC–WD
£€ £25 D–£35 (£35)
🚗 Off A338 to Wantage. M4 Junction 14

Winter Hill   (1976)
Grange Lane, Cookham, SL6 9RP
☎ **(01628) 527613**
📖 800
🏌 M Goodenough
⚲ R Frost (01628) 527610
🏳 18 L 6408 yds SSS 71
👥 WD–U WE–M SOC
£€ D–£30 After 2pm–£21
🚗 Maidenhead 3 miles
🏠 Charles Lawrie

Wokefield Park   (1998)
Mortimer, Reading, RG7 3AE
☎ **(0118) 933 4013/4018/4017**
🖳 (0118) 933 4031

wokefieldgolf@initialstyle.co.uk
J Morgan (Hon), M Clark
G Smith (0118) 933 4078
18 L 6961 yds Par 72 SSS 73
WD–U WE–NA before 9.30am SOC
£€ £30 (£45)
8 miles SW of Reading, off A33. M4 Junction 11
Driving range
Jonathan Gaunt
www.golf-isc.co.uk

Buckinghamshire

Abbey Hill (1975)
Monks Way, Two Mile Ash, Milton Keynes, MK8 8AA
☎ (01908) 563845
300
J Falconer
G Woodham
18 L 6193 yds SSS 69
Par 3 course
U
£€ On application
2 miles S of Stony Stratford
Driving range

Aylesbury Golf Centre (1992)
Public
Hulcott Lane, Bierton, HP22 5GA
☎ (01296) 393644
K Partington (Mgr)
A Saary
18 L 5965 yds SSS 69
U
£€ £10 (£15)
1 mile N of Aylesbury on A418
Driving range
TS Benwell

Aylesbury Park (1996)
Oxford Road, Aylesbury, HP17 8QQ
☎ (01296) 399166/395381
(01296) 336830
340
Carole Barnes (01296) 399196
D Boot (01296) 399196
18 L 6150 yds SSS 69
U
£€ £12.50 (£18)
SW of Aylesbury (A418). M40 Junction 8, 12 miles
Driving range
Martin Hawtree

Beaconsfield (1902)
Seer Green, Beaconsfield, HP9 2UR
☎ (01494) 676545
(01494) 681148
secretary@beaconsfieldgolfclub .co.uk
850
KR Wilcox
M Brothers (01494) 676616
18 L 6493 yds Par 72 SSS 71
WD–H WE–M SOC

£€ £35 D–£50
2 miles E of Beaconsfield. M40 Junction 2
Driving range
HS Colt

Buckingham (1914)
Tingewick Road, Buckingham, MK18 4AE
☎ (01280) 813282 (Clubhouse)
(01280) 821812
680
T Gates (Gen Mgr) (01280) 815566
G Hannah (01280) 815210
18 L 6082 yds SSS 69
WD–U WE–M SOC–Tues & Thurs
£€ £28
2 miles SW of Buckingham on A421

Buckinghamshire (1992)
Denham Court Mansion, Denham Court Drive, Denham, UB9 5PG
☎ (01895) 835777
(01895) 835210
golf@bucks.dircon.co.uk
650
E Roca (01895) 836804
J O'Leary (01895) 836814
18 L 6880 yds Par 72 SSS 73
I or M SOC–WD exc Fri
£€ £70 (£80)
Off A40(M). M25 Junction 16b/M40 Junction 1
Driving range (Members)
John Jacobs
www.buckinghamshire-golfclub .co.uk

Burnham Beeches (1891)
Green Lane, Burnham, Slough, SL1 8EG
☎ (01628) 661448
(01628) 668968
enquiries@bbgc.co.uk
670
AJ Buckner (Mgr) (01628) 661448
R Bolton (01628) 661661
18 L 6449 yds SSS 71
WD–I WE/BH–M H
£€ £38 D–£56
4 miles W of Slough
www.bbgc.co.uk

Chartridge Park (1989)
Chartridge, Chesham, HP5 2TF
☎ (01494) 791772
700
Mr & Mrs P Gibbins
P Gibbins
18 L 5580 yds SSS 66
U SOC
£€ £25 (£30)
2 miles NW of Chesham. 9 miles W of M25 Junction 18
John Jacobs
www.cpgc.co.uk

Chesham & Ley Hill (1900)
Ley Hill, Chesham, HP5 1UZ
☎ (01494) 784541
(01494) 785506

the.secretary@clhgolfclub.co.uk
322
B Durand
9 L 5240 yds SSS 65
WD–U exc Tues–NA before 3pm WE/BH–M SOC–Thurs & Fri
£€ £13
Chesham 2 miles
Course closed Sun after 2pm from 1st Apr–30th Sept

Chiltern Forest
Aston Hill, Halton, Aylesbury, HP22 5NQ
☎ (01296) 631267
(01296) 631267
650
S Thornton (01296) 631267
A Lavers (01296) 631817
18 L 5765 yds SSS 70
WD–U WE–M SOC
£€ £20 D–£25
5 miles SE of Aylesbury, off A4011
www.chilternforest.co.uk

Denham (1910)
Tilehouse Lane, Denham, UB9 5DE
☎ (01895) 832022
(01895) 835340
775
MJ Miller
S Campbell (01895) 832801
18 L 6462 yds SSS 71
Mon–Thurs–I H Fri–Sun/BH–M
£€ £50–£68
2 miles NW of Uxbridge
HS Colt

Ellesborough (1905)
Butlers Cross, Aylesbury, HP17 0TZ
☎ (01296) 622114
(01296) 622114
admin@ellesboroughgolf.co.uk
700
B Weeds (Gen Mgr)
M Squire (01296) 623126
18 L 6283 yds SSS 71
WE/BH–M WD–I or H SOC–Wed & Thurs only
£€ On application
1 mile W of Wendover
www.ellesboroughgolf.co.uk

Farnham Park (1974)
Public
Park Road, Stoke Poges, Slough, SL2 4PJ
☎ (01753) 643332
450
Mrs M Brooker (01753) 647065
P Warner
18 L 6172 yds SSS 71
U
£€ £14.50
2 miles N of Slough
Hawtree

Flackwell Heath (1904)
Treadaway Road, Flackwell Heath, High Wycombe, HP10 9PE
☎ (01628) 520929
(01628) 530040

☐ 700
🏌 SJ Chandler
✓ P Watson (01628) 523017
▷ 18 L 6211 yds SSS 70
🏠 WD–H WE–M SOC–Wed & Thurs
££ £24
🏌 Between High Wycombe and
   Beaconsfield, off A40. M40
   Junction 3/4
🏠 J Turner

Gerrards Cross   (1921)

Chalfont Park, Gerrards Cross, SL9 0QA
☎ **(01753) 883263**
🖳 (01753) 883593
☐ 725
🏌 Inger Perkins
✓ M Barr (01753) 885300
▷ 18 L 6212 yds SSS 70
🏠 WD–H WE/BH–M SOC
££ £38 D–£52
🏌 1 mile from Station, off A413
🏠 B Pedlar

Harewood Downs   (1907)

Cokes Lane, Chalfont St Giles, HP8 4TA
☎ **(01494) 762308**
🖳 (01494) 766869
✉ secretyary@hdgc.co.uk
☐ 700
🏌 SJ Thornton (01494) 762184
✓ GC Morris (01494) 764102
▷ 18 L 5958 yds SSS 69
🏠 H
££ £33 (£38)
🏌 2 miles E of Amersham, off A413

Harleyford   (1996)

*Harleyford Estate, Henley Road,
Marlow, SL7 2SP*
☎ **(01628) 402149**
🖳 (01628) 478434
☐ 750
🏌 M Newey
✓ L Jackson
▷ 18 L 6587 yds Par 72 SSS 72
🏠 U SOC–WD after 10am SOC–WE
   after 1pm
££ £40 (£60)
🏌 1 mile W of Marlow on A4155
⊕ Driving range
🏠 Donald Steel

Hazlemere   (1982)

*Penn Road, Hazlemere, High Wycombe,
HP15 7LR*
☎ **(01494) 719300**
🖳 (01494) 713914
☐ 500
🏌 BF Cable
✓ P Harrison (01494) 719306
▷ 18 L 5807 yds SSS 69
🏠 WD–U WE–booking req SOC–WD
££ £20 (£30)
🏌 3 miles NE of High Wycombe on
   B474
🏠 Terry Murray

Iver   (1983)

Hollow Hill Lane, Iver, SL0 0JJ
☎ **(01753) 655615**
🖳 (01753) 654225

☐ 500
🏌 J Lynch (Golf Dir)
✓ J Lynch
▷ 9 L 6300 yds SSS 72
🏠 U SOC
££ 18 holes–£13 (£16) 9 holes–£7.50
   (£9)
🏌 ¹/₂ mile from Langley station, off
   Langley Park Road. M4 Junction 5,
   2 miles

Ivinghoe   (1967)

*Wellcroft, Ivinghoe, Leighton Buzzard,
LU7 9EF*
☎ **(01296) 668696**
🖳 (01296) 662755
☐ 250
🏌 Mrs SE Garrad (01296) 662478
✓ PW Garrad (01296) 668696
▷ 9 L 4508 yds SSS 62
🏠 WD–U WE–U after 8am SOC
££ 18 holes–£9. 9 holes–£6
🏌 3 miles N of Tring. M1 Junction 11,
   5 miles
🏠 R Garrad

The Lambourne Club
(1992)

Dropmore Road, Burnham, SL1 8NF
☎ **(01628) 666755**
🖳 (01628) 663301
☐ 550
🏌 B Sparks (Gen Mgr)
✓ D Hart (Golf Dir) (01628) 662936
▷ 18 L 6771 yds SSS 73
🏠 H
££ £50 (£75)
🏌 1 mile N of Burnham. M40
   Junction 2. M4 Junction 7
⊕ Driving range
🏠 Donald Steel

Little Chalfont   (1981)

*Lodge Lane, Little Chalfont, Amersham,
HP8 4AJ*
☎ **(01494) 764877**
🖳 (01494) 762860
☐ 400
🏌 JM Dunne
✓ B Woodhouse (01494) 762942
▷ 9 L 5752 yds SSS 68
🏠 U SOC
££ £11.50 (£13.50)
🏌 Chalfont & Latimer Station ¹/₂ mile.
   M25 Junction 18, 1 mile
🏠 JM Dunne

Magnolia Park

Arncott Road, Boarstall, HP18 9XX
☎ **(01844) 239700**
🖳 (01844 238991
☐ 300
🏌 A Rutter (Gen Mgr)
✓ A Taylor (Golf Dir)
▷ 18 holes Par 73 SSS 73
   9 hole course
🏠 U SOC–WD
££ D–£40
🏌 10 miles NW of Thame (B4011)
⊕ Golf Academy
🏠 Johnathan Gaunt

Mentmore G&CC   (1992)

Mentmore, Leighton Buzzard, LU7 0UA
☎ **(01296) 662020**
🖳 (01296) 662592
✉ m.barley@clubhaus.com
☐ 1100
🏌 M Barley
✓ R Davies
▷ Rothschild 18 L 6777 yds SSS 72;
   Rosebery 18 L 6850 yds SSS 73
🏠 WD–U WE/BH–U after 11am
   SOC
££ £30 (£40)
🏌 4 miles S of Leighton Buzzard
⊕ Driving range
🏠 Bob Sandow
■ www.clubhaus.com

Oakland Park   (1994)

*Three Households, Chalfont St Giles,
HP8 4LW*
☎ **(01494) 871277**
🖳 (01494) 874692
☐ 750
🏌 SF Balmforth (Sec/Dir),
   A King (Gen Mgr)
✓ A Thatcher
▷ 18 L 5246 yds Par 67 SSS 66
🏠 U SOC–WD
££ £25
🏌 3 miles N of M40 Junction 2
⊕ Driving range
🏠 Jonathan Gaunt

Princes Risborough   (1990)

*Lee Road, Saunderton Lee, Princes
Risborough, HP27 9NX*
☎ **(01844) 346989 (Clubhouse)**
🖳 (01844) 274938
☐ 400
🏌 JF Tubb (Man Dir)
✓ S Lowry (01844) 274567
▷ 9 L 5440 yds Par 68 SSS 67
🏠 U SOC
££ 18 holes–£15 (£20) 9 holes–£12
   (£14)
🏌 7 miles NW of High Wycombe on
   A4010
🏠 Guy Hunt
■ www.prgc.co.uk

Richings Park G&CC
(1996)

North Park, Iver, SL0 9DL
☎ **(01753) 655352**
🖳 (01753) 655409
☐ 650
🏌 A Garland (01753) 655370
✓ S Kelly (01753) 655352
▷ 18 L 6094 yds Par 70 SSS 69
   Par 3 Academy course
🏠 WD–U WE–M
££ £17
🏌 Nr M4 Junction 5
⊕ Driving range
🏠 Alan Higgins
■ www.richingspark.co.uk

Silverstone   (1992)

Proprietary
*Silverstone Road, Stowe, Buckingham,
MK18 5LH*
☎ **(01280) 850005**

☎ (01280) 850156
✉ sgc@zonal.co.uk
📖 500
✍ B Major
✓ R Holt
☞ 18 L 6558 yds Par 72 SSS 71
👤 U–booking advisable SOC
££ £15 (£21)
🚗 Opposite Silverstone Race Circuit, N of Buckingham
⊕ Driving range
🏛 David Snell

Stoke Poges (1908)
Park Road, Stoke Poges, SL2 4PG
☎ **(01753) 717171**
🖥 (01753) 717181
✉ info@stokeparkclub.com
📖 850
✓ S Collier
☞ 18 L 6721 yds SSS 72
9 L 3074 yds
👤 U
££ £125 (£200)
🚗 5 miles N of Windsor
🏛 HS Colt

Stowe (1974)
Stowe, Buckingham, MK18 5EH
📖 300
✍ Mrs CM Shaw (01280) 818282
☞ 9 L 4472 yds SSS 62
👤 WD/WE 8am–1pm & after 7pm–M; School holidays–M SOC
££ On application
🚗 M1 Junction 16. 4 miles NW of Buckingham

Thorney Park (1992)
Thorney Mill Lane, Iver, SL0 9AL
☎ **(01895) 422095**
🖥 (01895) 431307
📖 300
✍ A Killing
✓ A Killing
☞ 18 L 5731 yds Par 69 SSS 68
👤 U SOC
££ £18 (£20)
🚗 3 miles N of M4 Junction 5 (B470)

Three Locks (1992)
Great Brickhill, Milton Keynes, MK17 9BH
☎ **(01525) 270470**
🖥 (01525) 270470
📖 300
✍ P Critchley
☞ 18 L 6025 yds Par 70 SSS 68
👤 U SOC exc Sun
££ £16.50 (£20)
🚗 N of Leighton Buzzard on A4146. M1 Junction 14
🏛 MRM Sandow

Wavendon Golf Centre (1990)
Lower End Road, Wavendon, Milton Keynes, MK17 8DA
☎ **(01908) 281811**

☎ (01908) 281257
📖 250
✍ J Drake
✓ G Iron
☞ 18 L 5460 yds Par 67 SSS 66
9 hole pitch & putt course
👤 U SOC
££ £12.50 (£18)
🚗 2 miles W of M1 Junction 13
⊕ Floodlit driving range

Weston Turville (1973)
New Road, Weston Turville, Aylesbury, HP22 5QT
☎ **(01296) 424084**
🖥 (01296) 395376
📖 600
✍ D Allen
✓ G George (01296) 425949
☞ 18 L 6008 yds SSS 69
👤 U
££ £20 (£25)
🚗 1½ miles SE of Aylesbury

Wexham Park (1979)
Pay and play
Wexham Street, Wexham, Slough, SL3 6ND
☎ **(01753) 663271**
🖥 (01753) 663318
📖 850
✍ J Dunne
✓ J Kennedy (01753) 663425
☞ 18 L 5251 yds SSS 66
Green 9 L 2219 yds SSS 32
Red 9 L 2727 yds SSS 34
👤 U SOC–WD/Sat & Sun pm
££ 18 hole:£12.50 (£16.50) 9 hole:£7 (£7.50)
🚗 2 miles N of Slough. M4 Junction 4
⊕ Driving range
🏛 David Morgan
■ www.wexhamparkgolfcourse.co.uk

Whiteleaf (1904)
Whiteleaf, Princes Risborough, HP27 0LY
☎ **(01844) 343097/274058**
🖥 (01844) 275551
✉ whiteleafgc@tiscali.co.uk
📖 300
✍ D Hill (01844) 274058
✓ KS Ward (01844) 345472
☞ 9 L 5391 yds SSS 66
👤 WD–U WE–M SOC
££ £20
🚗 Princes Risborough 2 miles

Windmill Hill (1972)
Pay and play
Tattenhoe Lane, Bletchley, MK3 7RB
☎ **(01908) 631113 (Bookings)**
🖥 (01908) 630034
📖 130
✍ B Smith
✓ C Clingan (01908) 378623
☞ 18 L 6720 yds Par 73 SSS 72
👤 U SOC after 11am
££ £11 (£15)
🚗 W of Milton Keynes on A421. M1 Junctions 13 & 14

⊕ Driving range
🏛 Sir Henry Cotton

Woburn (1976)
Little Brickhill, Milton Keynes, MK17 9LJ
☎ **(01908) 370756**
🖥 (01908) 378436
✉ enquiries@woburngolf.com
📖 1300
✍ E Bullock (Man Dir), Glenna Beasley (Sec)
✓ L Blacklock (01908) 626600
☞ Duke's 18 L 6976 yds SSS 74
Duchess 18 L 6651 yds SSS 72
Marquess 18 L 7214 yds SSS 74
👤 WD–H (by arrangement) WE–M
££ By arrangement
🚗 ½ mile E of A5. 4 miles W of M1 Junction 13
🏛 Charles Lawrie (Duke's/Duchess)
■ www.woburngolf.com

Wycombe Heights (1991)
Public
Rayners Avenue, Loudwater, High Wycombe, HP10 9SZ
☎ **(01494) 816686**
🖥 (01494) 816728
✉ info@wycombeheightsgc.co.uk
📖 600
✍ P Talbot (01494) 816686
✓ (01494) 812862
☞ 18 L 6300 yds Par 70 SSS 72
18 hole Par 3 course
👤 U SOC
££ £13 (£18.50)
🚗 ½ mile from M40 Junction 3, on A40 to Wycombe
⊕ Driving range
🏛 John Jacobs

Cambridgeshire

Abbotsley (1986)
Proprietary
Eynesbury Hardwicke, St Neots, PE19 6XN
☎ **(01480) 474000**
🖥 (01480) 403280
✉ abbotsley@americangolf.uk.com
📖 440
✍ J Tubb (01480) 474000
✓ S Connolly
☞ 18 L 6311 yds SSS 72
👤 WD/BH–U WE–M before 1pm –U after 1pm SOC
££ £19 (£30)
🚗 2 miles SE of St Neots on B1046. M11 Junction 13 (A428)
🏛 Vivien Saunders

Bourn (1991)
Toft Road, Bourn, Cambridge, CB3 7TT
☎ **(01954) 718057**
🖥 (01954) 718908
📖 600
✍ C Watson (01954) 718958

⚐ 18 L 6417 yds SSS 71
👥 WD–U WE–U after 1pm SOC–WD
£€ On application
🚗 8 miles W of Cambridge, off B1046. M11 Junction 12

Brampton Park   (1991)
Buckden Road, Brampton, Huntingdon, PE28 4NF
☎ **(01480) 434700**
📠 (01480) 411145
📧 admin@bramptonparkgc.co.uk
📖 650
🏌 RK Oakes (Gen Mgr)
🏌 A Currie (01480) 434705
⚐ 18 L 6300 yds SSS 72
👥 U SOC
£€ £25 (D–£35)
🚗 3 miles W of Huntingdon, off A1/A604
⊕ Driving range
🏠 Simon Gidman
■ www.bramptonparkgc.co.uk

Cambridge
Station Road, Longstanton, Cambridge, CB4 5DR
☎ **(01954) 789388**
📖 300
🏌 K Green
🏌 G Huggett, A Engleman
⚐ 18 L 6736 yds Par 72 SSS 74
👥 U SOC
£€ £10 (£13)
🚗 5 miles NW of Cambridge, off A14 (B1050)
⊕ Floodlit driving range

Cambridge National
Proprietary
Comberton Road, Toft, Cambridge, CB3 7RY
☎ **(01223) 264700**
📠 (01223) 264701
📧 meridian@golfsocieties.com
📖 500
🏌 Ingrid van Rooyen, Vivien Saunders
🏌 M Clemons (01223) 264702
⚐ 18 L 6732 yds Par 73 SSS 72
👥 U SOC
£€ £15 (£20)
🚗 3 miles SW of Cambridge on B1046. M11 Junction 12
🏠 Alliss/Clark
■ www.golfsocieties.com

Cambridgeshire Moat House   (1974)
Bar Hill, Cambridge, CB3 8EU
☎ **(01954) 249988 (Hotel)**
📠 (01954) 780010
📖 650
🏌 (01954) 249971
🏌 P Simpson (01954) 780098
⚐ 18 L 6734 yds Par 72 SSS 73
👥 U SOC–WD
£€ £20 (£30)
🚗 5 miles NW of Cambridge on A14
■ www.cambridgeshiregolf.co.uk

Cromwell
Proprietary
Eynesbury Hardwicke, St Neots, PE19 6XN
☎ **(01480) 215153**
📠 (01480) 406463
📖 250
🏌 J Tubb (01480) 474000
🏌 S Connolly
⚐ 18 L 6087 yds SSS 69
9 hole Par 3 course
👥 U SOC
£€ £10 (£17)
🚗 2 miles SE of St Neots on B1046. M11 Junction 13 (A428)
⊕ Floodlit driving range
🏠 Vivien Saunders

Elton Furze   (1993)
Bullock Road, Haddon, Peterborough, PE7 3TT
☎ **(01832) 280189**
📠 (01832) 280299
📖 540
🏌 Barbara Knights
🏌 F Kiddie (01832) 280614
⚐ 18 L 6289 yds SSS 70
👥 WD–phone in advance SOC
£€ £22 (£32)
🚗 4 miles W of Peterborough on old A605
⊕ Driving range
🏠 Roger Fitton
■ www.eltonfurzegolfclub.co.uk

Ely City   (1961)
107 Cambridge Road, Ely, CB7 4HX
☎ **(01353) 662751**
📠 (01353) 668636
📖 840
🏌 MS Hoare (Mgr) (01353) 662751
🏌 A George (01353) 663317
⚐ 18 L 6627 yds SSS 72
👥 WD–H WE–H SOC–Tues–Fri
£€ £30 (£36)
🚗 12 miles N of Cambridge
🏠 Henry Cotton
■ www.elygolf.co.uk

Girton   (1936)
Dodford Lane, Girton, CB3 0QE
☎ **(01223) 276169**
📠 (01223) 277150
📧 secretary@girtongolfclub.co.uk
📖 800
🏌 Miss VM Webb
🏌 S Thomson (01223) 276991
⚐ 18 L 6012 yds SSS 69
👥 WD–U WE/BH–M SOC–WD
£€ £20
🚗 3 miles N of Cambridge (A14)
■ www.girtongolfclub.co.uk

The Gog Magog   (1901)
Shelford Bottom, Cambridge, CB2 4AB
☎ **(01223) 247626**
📠 (01223) 414990
📧 secretary@gogmagog.co.uk
📖 1300
🏌 IM Simpson

🏌 I Bamborough (01223) 246058
⚐ Old 18 L 6398 yds SSS 70
Wandlebury 18 L 6735 yds SSS 72
👥 WD–I or H WE/BH–M SOC–Tues & Thurs
£€ On application
🚗 2 miles S of Cambridge on A1307 (A604)
🏠 Hawtree
■ www.gogmagog.co.uk

Hemingford Abbots   (1991)
Proprietary
New Farm Lodge, Cambridge Road, Hemingford Abbots, PE28 9HQ
☎ **(01480) 495000**
📠 (01480) 496000
📖 220
🏌 RD Paton
⚐ 9 L 5468 yds SSS 68
👥 U
£€ On application
🚗 2 miles S of Huntingdon on A14
⊕ Floodlit driving range
■ www.astroman.co.uk

Heydon Grange G&CC   (1994)
Heydon, Royston, SG8 7NS
☎ **(01763) 208988**
📠 (01763) 208926
📖 200
🏌 S Akhtar
⚐ 18 L 6512 yds SSS 72
9 L 3249 yds SSS 36
👥 U SOC
£€ £15 (£20)
🚗 4 miles E of Royston on A505. M11 Junction 10
⊕ Driving range
🏠 Cameron Sinclair
■ www.heydongrange.co.uk

Lakeside Lodge   (1992)
Fen Road, Pidley, Huntingdon, PE17 3DD
☎ **(01487) 740540**
📠 (01487) 740852
📖 550
🏌 Mrs J Hopkins
🏌 S Waterman (01487) 741541
⚐ 18 L 6865 yds SSS 73
9 L 2601 yds SSS 33
👥 U SOC
£€ £10 (£16)
🚗 4 miles N of St Ives on B1040
⊕ Driving range
🏠 A Headley

Malton   (1993)
Pay and play
Malton Lane, Meldreth, Royston, SG8 6PE
☎ **(01763) 262200**
📠 (01763) 262209
📧 info@maltongolf.co.uk
📖 300
🏌 A Boyce (01638) 751222
🏌 B Lyon
⚐ 18 L 6708 yds Par 72 SSS 72
👥 U SOC–exc WE–NA before 11am

£€ £10 (£16)
⊕ 8 miles SW of Cambridge, off A10.
5 miles SW of M11 Junction 11
⊕ Driving range
🛈 Bruce Critchley
■ www.maltongolf.co.uk

March (1922)
*Frogs Abbey, Grange Rd, March,
PE15 0YH*
☎ (01354) 652364
▥ 400
✍ Lt Cdr LE Taylor RN
✓ J Hadland
▷ 9 L 6210 yds SSS 70
👥 H SOC–WD
£€ £17
⊕ 18 miles E of Peterborough on
A141

Old Nene G&CC (1992)
*Muchwood Lane, Bodsey, Ramsey,
PE26 2XQ*
☎ (01487) 813519/815622
▥ 200
✍ PB Cade
✓ I Galloway (01487) 710122
▷ 9 L 5605 yds SSS 68
👥 U SOC
£€ 18 holes–£11 (£16) 9 holes–£7 (£9)
⊕ 1 mile N of Ramsey, towards
Ramsey Mereside
⊕ Floodlit driving range
🛈 Richard Edrich

Orton Meadows (1987)
Public
Ham Lane, Peterborough, PE2 5UU
☎ (01733) 237478
▥ 450
✍ WL Stocks (01733) 234769
✓ A Howard
▷ 18 L 5664 yds SSS 68
👥 U–phone Pro
£€ £11.50 (£15.20)
⊕ 2 miles SW of Peterborough on old
A605
⊕ 12 hole pitch & putt
🛈 D & R Fitton
■ www.ortonmeadowsgolfcourse
.co.uk

Peterborough Milton (1937)
Milton Ferry, Peterborough, PE6 7AG
☎ (01733) 380489
▯ (01733) 380489
✉ miltongolfclub@aol.com
▥ 850
✍ AB Izod (01733) 380489
✓ M Gallagher (01733) 380793
▷ 18 L 6505 yds SSS 72
👥 U SOC H
£€ £30 (£40)
⊕ 4 miles W of Peterborough on A47
🛈 James Braid
■ www.Peterboroughmiltongolfclub
.co.uk

Ramsey (1964)
*4 Abbey Terrace, Ramsey, Huntingdon,
PE26 1DD*
☎ (01487) 812600

▯ (01487) 815746
▥ 750
✍ M Kjenstad
✓ S Scott (01487) 813022
▷ 18 L 6163 yds Par 71 SSS 70
👥 WD–H WE/BH–M SOC
£€ £25
⊕ 12 miles SE of Peterborough
🛈 J Hamilton Stutt

St Ives (1923)
St Ives, Huntingdon, PE27 6DH
☎ (01480) 464459
▯ (01480) 468392
▥ 385
✍ BE Dunn (01480) 468392
✓ D Glasby (01480) 466067
▷ 9 L 6180 yds SSS 70
👥 WD–U H WE–M
£€ D–£20
⊕ 5 miles E of Huntingdon

St Neots (1890)
Crosshall Road, St Neots, PE19 7GE
☎ (01480) 472363
▯ (01480) 472363
✉ office@stneots-golfclub.co.uk
▥ 600
✍ F Thorpe (Mgr) (01480) 472363
✓ J Boast (01480) 476513
▷ 18 L 6074 yds SSS 69
👥 WD–H WE–M
£€ On application
⊕ By A1/B1048 Junction
🛈 Harry Vardon

Stilton Oaks (1997)
Proprietary
*High Street, Stilton, Peterborough,
PE7 3RA*
☎ (01733) 245233
▥ 200
✍ Mrs M Smith
✓ None
▷ 18 hole course
👥 U
£€ £10 (£12)
⊕ 5 miles S of Peterborough. A1(M)
Junction 16

Thorney Golf Centre (1991)
Public
*English Drove, Thorney, Peterborough,
PE6 0TJ*
☎ (01733) 270570
▯ (01733) 270842
▥ 400
✍ Jane Hind
✓ M Templeman
▷ Fen 18 L 6104 yds SSS 69
Lakes 18 L 6402 yds SSS 71
9 hole Par 3 course
👥 Lakes WD–U SOC WE–M
£€ Fen £7 (£9) Lakes £11.50 (£18.50)
⊕ 8 miles E of Peterborough, off
A47
⊕ Floodlit driving range
🛈 A Dow

Thorpe Wood (1975)
Pay and play
Nene Parkway, Peterborough, PE3 6SE
☎ (01733) 267701
▯ (01733) 332774
✉ enquiries@thorpewoodgolfcourse
.co.uk
✍ R Palmer
✓ R Fitton
▷ 18 L 7086 yds SSS 74
👥 U–booking required SOC–WD
£€ £11.50 (£15.20)
⊕ 3 miles W of Peterborough on A47
(Junction 15)
🛈 Alliss/Thomas
■ www.thorpewoodgolfcourse.co.uk

Waterbeach (1968)
*Waterbeach Barracks, Waterbeach,
Cambridge, CB5 9PA*
☎ (01223) 575260 (Sec)
▯ (01223) 511525
✍ ES Rowlands (Hon)
▷ 9 L 6236 yds Par 70 SSS 70
👥 M SOC–WD
£€ £10
⊕ 6 miles NE of Cambridge, off A10

Channel Islands

Alderney
Route des Carrieres, Alderney, GY9 3YD
☎ (01481) 822835
▯ (01481) 823609
▥ 420
✍ Barbara Dale (01481) 823563
▷ 9 L 5006 yds Par 64 SSS 65
👥 U SOC H
£€ D–£20 (D–£25)
⊕ 1 mile E of St Anne

La Grande Mare (1994)
Vazon Bay, Castel, Guernsey, GY5 7LL
☎ (01481) 255313
▯ (01481) 255194
✉ golflgm@gtonline.net
▥ 750
✍ J Vermeulen (01481) 253544
✓ M Groves (01481) 253432
▷ 18 L 5112 yds SSS 66
👥 U–booking necessary SOC
£€ D–£27 (£29)
⊕ Vazon Bay, W coast of Guernsey
🛈 Hawtree
■ www.LGM.Guernsey.net

Les Mielles G&CC (1994)
St Ouens Bay, Jersey, JE3 7FQ
☎ (01534) 482787
▯ (01534) 485414
▥ 1500
✍ J Le Brun (Golf
Dir) (01534) 482787 Ext 4
✓ L Elstone (01534) 483699 W
Osmand (01534) 483252
▷ 18 L 5770 yds Par 70 SSS 69
👥 H or Green Card SOC
£€ £22 (£25)
⊕ Five Mile Road, St Ouens Bay

⊕ Driving range
🏠 Le Brun/Whitehead
⌨ www.lesmielles.com

La Moye (1902)
La Moye, St Brelade, Jersey, JE3 8GQ
☎ (01534) 743401,
   (01534) 747166 (Bookings)
💻 (01534) 747289
🕮 1350
✍ CHM Greetham
✎ M Deeley (01534) 743130
🏌 18 L 6664 yds SSS 73
👤 I H SOC–9.30–11am and 2.30–4pm
   WE–after 2.30pm
£ £45 D–£75 (£50)
⚲ 2 miles from Jersey Airport
⊕ Driving range
🏠 James Braid

Les Ormes (1996)
Pay and play
Mont à la Brune, St Brelade, Jersey, JE3 8FL
☎ (01534) 497000
💻 (01534) 499122
🕮 1200
✍ M Graham (01534) 497002
✎ A Chamberlain (01534) 497000
🏌 9 L 5018 yds Par 66 SSS 65
👤 U SOC
£ 9 holes–£13 (£16) 18 holes–£19.50 (£24)
⚲ Mont à la Brune, nr Airport
⊕ Driving range

Royal Guernsey (1890)
L'Ancresse, Guernsey, GY3 5BY
☎ (01481) 247022
💻 (01481) 243960
✉ bobby@rggc.fsnet.co.uk
🕮 1520
✍ M de Laune (01481) 246523
   R Eggo (Golf Mgr)
✎ N Wood (01481) 245070
🏌 18 L 6215 yds SSS 70
👤 WD–H WE–M
£ £38
⚲ 3 miles N of St Peter Port
⊕ Driving range

Royal Jersey (1878)
Grouville, Jersey, JE3 9BD
☎ (01534) 854416
💻 (01534) 854684
🕮 1300
✍ DJ Attwood
✎ D Morgan (01534) 852234
🏌 18 L 6100 yds SSS 70
👤 WD–H after 10am WE/BH–H after 2.30pm
£ £45 (£45)
⚲ 4 miles E of St Helier

St Clements (1925)
Public
St Clements, Jersey, JE2 6QN
☎ (01534) 821938
✎ R Marks
🏌 9 L 3972 yds SSS 61

👤 U exc Sun am–NA
£ On application
⚲ 1 mile E of St Helier

St Pierre Park
Rohais, St Peter Port, Guernsey, GY1 1FD
☎ (01481) 727039
🕮 290
✎ R Corbet (Mgr)
🏌 9 hole Par 3 course
👤 U SOC
£ 18 holes–£15 (£17)
⚲ 1 mile W of St Peter Port
⊕ Driving range
🏠 Tony Jacklin

Cheshire

Alder Root (1993)
Alder Root Lane, Winwick, Warrington, WA2 8RZ
☎ (01925) 291919
💻 (01925) 291961
🕮 450
✍ E Lander
✎ C McKevitt (01925) 291932
🏌 10 L 5820 yds Par 69 SSS 68
👤 WD–U SOC
£ £12 (£20)
⚲ 4 miles N of Warrington (A49). M6 Junction 22. M62 Junction 9
🏠 Millington/Lander

Alderley Edge (1907)
Brook Lane, Alderley Edge, SK9 7RU
☎ (01625) 585583
🕮 212 90(L) 40(J) 40(5)
✍ RC Harrison
✎ P Bowring (01625) 584493
🏌 9 L 5823 yds SSS 68
👤 M or H SOC
£ £22 (£27.50)
⚲ 12 miles S of Manchester
■ www.aegc.co.uk

Aldersey Green
Aldersey, Chester, CH3 9EH
☎ (01829) 782157
✍ S Bradbury
✎ S Bradbury (01829) 782157
🏌 18 L 6150 yds Par 70
👤 U SOC
£ £12 (£15)
⚲ 8 miles S of Chester, off A41

Altrincham Municipal (1893)
Public
Stockport Road, Timperley, Altrincham, WA15 7LP
☎ (0161) 928 0761
🕮 276
✍ B Simpson
✎ S Partington
🏌 18 L 6385 yds Par 71 SSS 70

👤 U SOC
£ £8.30 (£11.50)
⚲ 1 mile W of Altrincham (A560)
⊕ Driving range

Alvaston Hall (1992)
Proprietary
Middlewich Road, Nantwich, CW5 6PD
☎ (01270) 628473
💻 (01270) 623395
🕮 340
✍ N Perkins (01270) 760206
✎ K Valentine
🏌 9 L 3708 yds Par 64 SSS 59
👤 U
£ £10 (£10)
⚲ 11 miles W of M6 Junction 16 on A530
⊕ Driving range
🏠 K Valentine

Antrobus
Foggs Lane, Antrobus, Northwich, CW9 6JQ
☎ (01925) 730890
💻 (01925) 730100
🕮 550
✍ Miss C Axford
✎ P Farrance (01925) 730900
🏌 18 L 6220 yds Par 71 SSS 72
👤 H SOC
£ £22 (£25)
⚲ Nr M56 Junction 10, on A559 to Northwich
⊕ Driving range
🏠 Michael Slater
■ www.antrobusgolfclub.co.uk

Ashton-on-Mersey (1897)
Church Lane, Sale, M33 5QQ
☎ (0161) 973 3220 (Clubhouse)
💻 (0161) 976 4390
✉ golf@aomgc.fsnet.co.uk
🕮 190 65(L) 40(J)
✍ CW Hill (0161) 976 4390
✎ MJ Williams (0161) 962 3727
🏌 9 L 3073 yds SSS 69
👤 WD–U H exc Tues–NA before 3pm WE–M
£ £20.50
⚲ 5 miles W of Manchester. M60 Junction 7, 1½ miles

Astbury (1922)
Peel Lane, Astbury, Congleton, CW12 4RE
☎ (01260) 272772
🕮 700
✍ FM Reed (01260) 272772
✎ A Salt (01260) 272772
🏌 18 L 6296 yds SSS 70
👤 WD–H or M WE–M SOC–Thurs only
£ £30 SOC–£25
⚲ 1 mile S of Congleton, off A34
■ www.astburygolfclub.com

Birchwood (1979)
Kelvin Close, Birchwood, Warrington, WA3 7PB
☎ (01925) 818819

⛟ (01925) 822403
📖 745
🏌 F Craig
✓ P McEwan (01925) 816574
▷ 18 L 6727 yds Par 71 SSS 73
👥 U SOC–Mon/Wed/Thurs
££ £18 D–£26 (£34)
🚗 M62 Junction 11, 2 miles. Signs to 'Science Park North'
🏠 TJA Macauley

Bramall Park (1894)

20 Manor Road, Bramhall, Stockport, SK7 3LY
☎ **(0161) 485 3119 (Clubhouse)**
🖳 (0161) 485 7101
📖 715
🏌 IR McNeill (0161) 485 7101
✓ M Proffit (0161) 485 2205
▷ 18 L 6214 yds SSS 70
👥 I
££ £30 (£40)
🚗 8 miles S of Manchester (A5102)

Bramhall (1905)

Ladythorn Road, Bramhall, Stockport, SK7 2EY
☎ **(0161) 439 6092**
🖳 (0161) 439 0264
✉ office@bramhallgolfclub.com
📖 325 155(L) 85(J)
🏌 B Hill (Hon) (0161) 439 6092
✓ R Green (0161) 439 1171
▷ 18 L 6300 yds SSS 70
👥 U H exc Thurs SOC–Wed
££ £30 D–£35 (£37 D–£46)
🚗 S of Stockport, off A5102
■ www.bramhallgolfclub.com

Carden Park

Chester, CH3 9DQ
☎ **(01829) 731600**
🖳 (01829) 731629
📖 234
🏌 D Llewellyn
✓ S Edwards (01829) 731500
▷ Cheshire 18 L 6824 yds SSS 72; Nicklaus 18 L 7045 yds Par 72 9 hole Par 3 course
👥 H SOC
££ Cheshire–£40 Nicklaus–£60
🚗 10 miles S of Chester on A534
⊕ Golf Academy. Driving range

Cheadle (1885)

Shiers Drive, Cheadle Road, Cheadle, SK8 1HW
☎ **(0161) 491 4452**
📖 350
🏌 BR Woodhouse
✓ S Booth (0161) 428 9878
▷ 9 L 5006 yds SSS 65
👥 H or I exc Tues & Sat–NA SOC
££ £20 (£25)
🚗 1 mile S of Cheadle. M63 Junction 11, 2 miles

Chester (1901)

Curzon Park, Chester, CH4 8AR
☎ **(01244) 675130**
🖳 (01244) 676667

📖 840
🏌 VFC Wood (01244) 677760
✓ G Parton (01244) 671185
▷ 18 L 6461 yds SSS 71
👥 U H SOC
££ £30 (£35)
🚗 Chester 1 mile

Congleton (1898)

Biddulph Road, Congleton, CW12 3LZ
☎ **(01260) 273540**
🖳 (01260) 290902
✉ congletongolfclub@hotmail.com
📖 440
🏌 R Brindley
✓ JA Colclough
▷ 12 L 5119 yds Par 68 SSS 65
👥 U H SOC
££ £21 (£31)
🚗 1½ miles E of Congleton on A527

Crewe (1911)

Fields Road, Haslington, Crewe, CW1 5TB
☎ **(01270) 584227 (Steward)**
🖳 (01270) 256482
✉ secretary@crewegolfclub.co.uk
📖 628
🏌 A Whittingham (01270) 584099
✓ D Wheeler (01270) 585032
▷ 18 L 6404 yds SSS 71
👥 WD–U WE/BH–M SOC
££ £27 After 1pm–£22
🚗 Haslington, 2 miles NE of Crewe Station, off A534. 5 miles W of M6 Jun
■ www.crewegolfclub.co.uk

Davenport (1913)

Worth Hall, Middlewood Road, Poynton, SK12 1TS
☎ **(01625) 876951**
🖳 (01625) 877489
📖 650
✓ G Norcott (01625) 877319
▷ 18 L 6027 yds SSS 69
👥 U exc Wed & Sat–NA SOC–Tues & Thurs
££ £30 (£40)
🚗 5 miles S of Stockport. 7 miles N of Macclesfield

Delamere Forest (1910)

Station Road, Delamere, Northwich, CW8 2JE
☎ **(01606) 883264**
🖳 (01606) 889444
📖 400
🏌 TG Owen (01606) 883800
🏌 EB Jones (01606) 883307
▷ 18 L 6328 yds SSS 71
👥 WD–U WE–2 ball only SOC
££ £30 D–£45 (£45)
🚗 10 miles E of Chester, off B5152
🏠 Herbert Fowler

Disley (1889)

Stanley Hall Lane, Disley, Stockport, SK12 2JX
☎ **(01663) 762071**
🖳 (01663) 762678

📖 500
🏌 Dianne Bradley (01663) 764001
✓ AG Esplin (01663) 762884
▷ 18 L 5942 yds Par 70
👥 WD–U exc Thurs WE/BH–M
££ £25 (£30)
🚗 6 miles S of Stockport on A6

Dukinfield (1913)

Yew Tree Lane, Dukinfield, SK16 5DB
☎ **(0161) 338 2340**
🖳 (0161) 303 0205
✉ dgc@telinco.co.uk
📖 300 80(L) 65(J)
🏌 K Marsh (0161) 368 6457
✓ A Jowett (0161) 338 2340
▷ 18 L 5338 yds SSS 66
👥 WD–U exc Wed pm WE–M SOC
££ £16.50
🚗 6 miles E of Manchester. M67 Junction 3
■ www.dukinfieldgolfclub.co.uk

Dunham Forest G&CC (1961)

Oldfield Lane, Altrincham, WA14 4TY
☎ **(0161) 928 2605**
🖳 (0161) 929 8975
✉ email@dunhamforestgolfclub.com
📖 600
🏌 Mrs S Klaus
✓ I Wrigley (0161) 928 2727
▷ 18 L 6636 yds SSS 72
👥 WD–U WE/BH–M SOC exc 12–1pm
££ £40 (£45)
🚗 1 mile SW of Altrincham. M56 Junction 7

Eaton (1965)

Guy Lane, Waverton, Chester, CH3 7PH
☎ **(01244) 335885**
🖳 (01244) 335782
✉ kerrybrown@eatongolfclub.co.uk
📖 550
🏌 K Brown
✓ W Tye (01244) 335826
▷ 18 L 6562 yds SSS 71
👥 H SOC
££ On application
🚗 3 miles SE of Chester, off A41
⊕ Driving range
🏠 Donald Steel

Ellesmere Port (1971)

Public
Chester Road, Childer Thornton, South Wirral, CH66 1QF
☎ **(0151) 339 7689**
📖 350
🏌 C Craggs
✓ T Roberts
▷ 18 L 6432 yds SSS 71
👥 WD–U WE–arrange with Pro SOC–WD
££ £6.70 (£7.40)
🚗 9 miles N of Chester on A41. M53 Junction 5

For list of abbreviations and key to symbols see page 649

Frodsham   (1990)

Simons Lane, Frodsham, WA6 6HE
- ☎ **(01928) 732159**
- ☐ (01928) 734070
- ✉ office@frodshamgolfclub.co.uk
- ☐ 600
- ♬ EI Roylance
- ⌇ G Tonge (01928) 739442
- ⟡ 18 L 6298 yds SSS 70
- ♛ WD–U WE/BH–M SOC–WD
- ££ £36
- ⬣ 9 miles NE of Chester (A56). M56 Junction 12, 3 miles
- ⌂ John Day
- ■ www.frodshamgolfclub.co.uk

Gatley   (1911)

Waterfall Farm, Styal Road, Heald Green, Cheadle SK8 3TW
- ☎ **(0161) 437 2091**
- ☐ 450
- ♬ RWR Salt
- ⌇ J Matterson (0161) 436 2830
- ⟡ 9 L 5934 yds SSS 68
- ♛ WD exc Tues–arrange with Pro WE/Tues–NA
- ££ £21
- ⬣ 7 miles S of Manchester. Manchester Airport 2 miles

Hale   (1903)

Rappax Road, Hale, WA15 0NU
- ☎ **(0161) 980 4225**
- ☐ 350
- ♬ JT Goodman
- ⌇ A Bickerdike (0161) 904 0835
- ⟡ 9 L 5780 yds SSS 68
- ♛ WD–U exc Thurs–NA before 5pm WE/BH–M SOC
- ££ D–£25
- ⬣ 2 miles SE of Altrincham

Hazel Grove   (1913)

Buxton Road, Hazel Grove, Stockport, SK7 6LU
- ☎ **(0161) 483 3217 (Clubhouse)**
- ☐ 550
- ♬ FA Williams (0161) 483 3978
- ⌇ J Hopley (0161) 483 7272
- ⟡ 18 L 6263 yds SSS 70
- ♛ U SOC–Thurs & Fri
- ££ £25.50 D–£30.50 (£30.50, D–£35.50)
- ⬣ 3 miles S of Stockport (A6)

Heaton Moor   (1892)

Mauldeth Road, Heaton Mersey, Stockport, SK4 3NX
- ☎ **(0161) 432 2134**
- ☐ (0161) 432 2134
- ✉ hmgc@ukgateway.net
- ☐ 550
- ♬ JR Smith
- ⌇ SJ Marsh (0161) 432 0846
- ⟡ 18 L 5968 yds SSS 69
- ♛ U SOC
- ££ £23 (£31)
- ⬣ 2 miles from M63 Junction 12, off A5145

Helsby   (1901)

Tower's Lane, Helsby, Frodsham, WA6 0JB
- ☎ **(01928) 722021**
- ☐ (01928) 725384
- ✉ secathgc@aol.com
- ☐ 620
- ♬ LJ Norbury
- ⌇ M Jones (01928) 725457
- ⟡ 18 L 6265 yds SSS 70
- ♛ H WE–NA SOC–Tues & Thurs
- ££ £25 (£37)
- ⬣ 1 mile SE of M56 Junction 14, off Primrose Lane
- ⊕ Driving range
- ⌂ James Braid
- ■ www.ukgolfer.org/clubs/helsby

Heyrose   (1989)

Budworth Road, Tabley, Knutsford, WA16 0HZ
- ☎ **(01565) 733664**
- ☐ (01565) 734578
- ☐ 600
- ♬ Mrs H March (01565) 733664
- ⌇ C Iddon (01565) 734267
- ⟡ 18 L 6513 yds SSS 71
- ♛ U SOC
- ££ £20 (£25)
- ⬣ 3 miles W of Knutsford, off Pickmere Lane. M6 Junction 19, 1 mile
- ⌂ CN Bridge

Houldsworth   (1910)

Houldsworth Park, Houldsworth Street, Reddish, Stockport SK5 6BN
- ☎ **(0161) 442 1712**
- ☐ (0161) 947 9678
- ☐ 625
- ♬ D Robertson (0161) 442 1712
- ⌇ D Naylor (0161) 442 1714
- ⟡ 18 L 6209 yds Par 70 SSS 70
- ♛ U SOC
- ££ £20 (£25)
- ⬣ 4 miles S of Manchester

Knights Grange   (1983)

Public
Grange Lane, Winsford, CW7 2PT
- ☎ **(01606) 552780**
- ♬ Mrs P Littler (Mgr)
- ⌇ G Moore (01606) 853564
- ⟡ 18 L 6253 yds SSS 70
- ♛ U SOC
- ££ £8 (10)
- ⬣ Knights Grange Sports Complex. M6 Junctions 18 & 19

Knutsford   (1891)

Mereheath Lane, Knutsford, WA16 6HS
- ☎ **(01565) 633355**
- ☐ 250
- ♬ DM Burgess
- ⌇ G Ogden
- ⟡ 9 L 6203 yds SSS 70
- ♛ H exc Wed–NA SOC
- ££ £25 (£30)
- ⬣ Knutsford ½ mile

Leigh   (1906)

Kenyon Hall, Culcheth, Warrington, WA3 4BG
- ☎ **(01925) 763130**
- ☐ (01925) 765097
- ☐ 850
- ♬ DA Taylor (01925) 762943
- ⌇ A Baguley (01925) 762013
- ⟡ 18 L 5892 yds SSS 68
- ♛ U H SOC
- ££ £30 (£40)
- ⬣ 5 miles NE of Warrington
- ⌂ James Braid

Lymm   (1907)

Whitbarrow Road, Lymm, WA13 9AN
- ☎ **(01925) 755020**
- ☐ (01925) 755020
- ☐ 400 100(L) 75(J) 50(5)
- ♬ S Nash
- ⌇ S McCarthy (01925) 755054
- ⟡ 18 L 6341 yds SSS 70
- ♛ WD–H WE–M SOC–Wed
- ££ £24 (£32)
- ⬣ 5 miles SE of Warrington. M6 Junction 20
- ■ www.lymm-golf-club.co.uk

Macclesfield   (1889)

The Hollins, Macclesfield, SK11 7EA
- ☎ **(01625) 423227**
- ☐ (01625) 260061
- ✉ secretary@maccgolfclub.co.uk
- ☐ 600
- ♬ DJ English (01625) 615845
- ⌇ T Taylor (01625) 616952
- ⟡ 18 L 5714 yds SSS 68
- ♛ WD/BH–H WE–M SOC–WD
- ££ £25 (£30)
- ⬣ SE edge of Macclesfield, off A523
- ⌂ Hawtree
- ■ www.maccgolfclub.co.uk

Malkins Bank   (1980)

Public
Betchton Road, Malkins Bank, Sandbach, CW11 4XN
- ☎ **(01270) 765931**
- ☐ (01270) 764730
- ⌇ D Hackney
- ⟡ 18 L 6071 yds SSS 69
- ♛ U SOC
- ££ £8.80 (£10.30)
- ⬣ 2 miles S of Sandbach via A534/A533. M6 Junction 17

Marple   (1892)

Barnsfold Road, Hawk Green, Marple, Stockport SK6 7EL
- ☎ **(0161) 427 2311**
- ☐ (0161) 427 1125
- ☐ 435 100(L) 60(J)
- ♬ MR Baguley (0161) 427 1125
- ⌇ D Myers (0161) 427 1195
- ⟡ 18 L 5552 yds SSS 67
- ♛ WD–U exc Thurs–NA WE/BH–M SOC
- ££ £20 (£30)
- ⬣ 2 miles from High Lane North, off A6

Mellor & Townscliffe (1894)

Tarden, Gibb Lane, Mellor, Stockport SK6 5NA

- ☎ (0161) 427 9700 (Clubhouse)
- 🖳 (0161) 427 0103
- 📖 700
- 🏌 G Lee (0161) 427 2208
- ✏ G Broadley (0161) 427 5759
- ⟾ 18 L 5925 yds SSS 69
- 👥 WD–U WE–M SOC
- ££ £22 (£31)
- 🚗 7 miles SE of Stockport, off A626
- ■ www.mellorgolf.co.uk

Mere G&CC (1934)

Chester Road, Mere, Knutsford, WA16 6LJ

- ☎ (01565) 830155
- 🖳 (01565) 830713
- 📖 375 200(L) 40(J)
- ✏ P Eyre (01565) 830219
- ⟾ 18 L 6817 yds SSS 73
- 👥 WE/BH–M Wed & Fri–M Mon/Tues/Thurs–H SOC
- ££ D–£70
- 🚗 1 mile E of M6 Junction 19. 2 miles W of M56 Junction 7
- ⊕ Driving range-members and green fees only
- 🏠 James Braid

Mersey Valley (1995)

Warrington Road, Bold Heath, Widnes, WA8 3XL

- ☎ (0151) 424 6060
- 🖳 (0151) 257 9097
- 📖 550
- 🏌 A Stevenson
- ✏ A Stevenson
- ⟾ 18 L 6300 yds SSS 70
- 👥 U
- ££ £18 (£20)
- 🚗 M62 Junction 7, 2 miles
- 🏠 RMR Bush

Mobberley

Burleyhurst Lane, Mobberley, Knutsford, WA16 7JZ

- ☎ (01505) 880188
- 🖳 (01505) 880178
- 🏌 N Donaghy
- ✏ J Cheetham
- ⟾ 9 L 5542 yds Par 67
- 👥 U SOC
- ££ £14.50 (£18)
- 🚗 Mobberley. M56 Junction 6

Mollington Grange (1999)

Townfield Lane, Mollington, Chester, CH1 6NJ

- ☎ (01244) 851185
- 🖳 (01244) 851349
- 📖 500
- 🏌 MJ Olney-Smith
- ✏ L Corcoran
- ⟾ 18 L 6696 yds Par 72 SSS 72
- 👥 WD–U WE–NA before noon SOC–WD
- ££ £25 (£30)
- 🚗 2 miles N of Chester on A540. End of M56, 2 miles

- ⊕ Driving range
- ■ www.mollingtongolfclub.co.uk

Mottram Hall Hotel (1991)

Wilmslow Road, Mottram St Andrew, Prestbury, SK10 4QT

- ☎ (01625) 828135
- 🖳 (01625) 829284
- 📖 500
- 🏌 M Turnock
- ✏ T Rastall
- ⟾ 18 L 7006 yds SSS 74
- 👥 U H
- ££ £45 (£50)
- 🚗 4 miles SE of Wilmslow
- ⊕ Driving range
- 🏠 Dave Thomas

Peover

Plumley Moor Road, Lower Peover, WA16 9SE

- ☎ (01565) 723337
- 🖳 (01565) 723311
- 📖 350
- 🏌 PA Naylor
- ⟾ 18 L 6702 yds Par 72
- 👥 U SOC–WD
- ££ £18 (£23)
- 🚗 3 miles SW of Knutsford, off A556. M6 Junction 19
- 🏠 Peter Naylor

Portal G&CC (1992)

Cobblers Cross Lane, Tarporley, CW6 0DJ

- ☎ (01829) 733933
- 🖳 (01829) 733928
- ✉ portalgolf@aol.com
- 📖 250
- 🏌 D Wills (Golf Dir)
- ✏ A Hill
- ⟾ 18 L 7037 yds SSS 74
- 👥 U H SOC
- ££ £50
- 🚗 11 miles SE of Chester on A51. M6 Junctions 16 or 19
- ⊕ Driving range
- 🏠 Donald Steel
- ■ www.portalgolf.co.uk

Portal Premier (1990)

Forest Road, Tarporley, CW6 0JA

- ☎ (01829) 733884
- 🖳 (01829) 733666
- 📖 550
- 🏌 D Wills (Golf Dir)
- ✏ Miss J Statham (01829) 733703
- ⟾ 18 L 6508 yds SSS 71
- 👥 U SOC–WD
- ££ £30 (£35)
- 🚗 1 mile N of Tarporley on A49 Warrington road
- ⊕ Driving range
- 🏠 Tim Rouse

Poulton Park (1980)

Dig Lane, Cinnamon Brow, WA2 0SH

- ☎ (01925) 812034/822802
- 🖳 (01925) 822802
- 📖 360

- 🏌 E Caise
- ✏ A Matthews (01925) 825220
- ⟾ 9 L 4978 metres SSS 66
- 👥 WD–NA 5–6pm WE–NA
- ££ £15 (£17)
- 🚗 Off Crab Lane, Fearnhead

Prestbury (1920)

Macclesfield Road, Prestbury, Macclesfield, SK10 4BJ

- ☎ (01625) 828241
- 🖳 (01625) 828241
- ✉ office@prestburygolfclub.com
- 📖 700
- 🏌 DM Bebbington
- ✏ N Summerfield (01625) 828242
- ⟾ 18 L 6359 yds SSS 71
- 👥 WD–I WE–M SOC–Thurs
- ££ £45
- 🚗 2 miles NW of Macclesfield
- 🏠 HS Colt

Pryors Hayes (1993)

Willington Road, Oscroft, Tarvin, CH3 8NL

- ☎ (01829) 741250
- 🖳 (01829) 749077
- 📖 600
- 🏌 JM Quinn
- ✏ M Redrup (01829) 740140
- ⟾ 18 L 6054 yds Par 69 SSS 69
- 👥 U SOC
- ££ £20 (£30)
- 🚗 Tarvin, 5 miles E of Chester
- 🏠 John Day
- ■ www.pryors-hayes.co.uk

Queens Park (1985)

Public

Queens Park Drive, Crewe, CW2 7SB

- ☎ (01270) 662378
- 📖 250
- 🏌 RJ Sparks (01270) 580424
- ✏ J Lowe
- ⟾ 9 L 4920 yds SSS 64
- 👥 WD–U WE–U after 12 noon SOC
- ££ £6.50 (£8.50)
- 🚗 2 miles from Crewe, off Victoria Avenue

Reaseheath (1987)

Reaseheath College, Reaseheath, Nantwich, CW5 6DF

- ☎ (01270) 625131
- 🖳 (01270) 625665
- ✉ chrisb@reaseheath.ac.uk
- 📖 600
- 🏌 CK Bishop (Hon)
- ⟾ 9 L 3726 yds SSS 58
- 👥 M SOC–WD
- ££ £7
- 🚗 2 miles NW of Nantwich on College campus
- 🏠 D Mortram

Reddish Vale (1912)

Southcliffe Road, Reddish, Stockport, SK5 7EE

- ☎ (0161) 480 2359
- 🖳 (0161) 477 8242
- ✉ admin@reddishvalegolfclub.co.uk

- 550
- BJD Rendell JP
- RE Freeman (0161) 480 3824
- 18 L 6086 yds SSS 69
- WD–U exc 12.30–1.30pm–M WE–M SOC–WD
- £€ £25
- 1 mile NNE of Stockport
- Dr A MacKenzie
- www.reddishvalegolfclub.co.uk

Ringway (1909)
Hale Mount, Hale Barns, Altrincham, WA15 8SW
- ☎ (0161) 904 9609
- enquiries@ringwaygolfclub.co.uk
- 345 165(L) 41(J)
- A Scully (0161) 980 2630
- N Ryan (0161) 980 8432
- 18 L 6494 yds SSS 71
- Tues–NA before 3pm Fri–M Sun–NA before 11am SOC–Thurs
- £€ £35 (£45)
- 8 miles S of Manchester, off M56 Junction 6 (A538)

Romiley (1897)
Goosehouse Green, Romiley, Stockport, SK6 4LJ
- ☎ (0161) 430 2392
- (0161) 430 7258
- office@romileygolfclub.org
- 625
- PR Trafford
- RN Giles (0161) 430 7122
- 18 L 6412 yds Par 70 SSS 71
- U SOC
- £€ £30 (£40)
- Station 3/4 mile (B6104)

Runcorn (1909)
Clifton Road, Runcorn, WA7 4SU
- ☎ (01928) 572093 (Members)
- (01928) 574214
- 375 80(L) 80(J)
- BR Griffiths (01928) 574214
- D Ingman (01928) 564791
- 18 L 6035 yds SSS 69
- WD–U H exc comp days WE–M SOC–Mon & Fri only
- £€ £24
- Runcorn (A557). M56 Junction 12

St Michaels Jubilee (1977)
Public
Dundalk Road, Widnes, WA8 8BS
- ☎ (0151) 424 6230
- 200
- KB Stevenson
- R Bilton (01295) 65241
- 18 L 5612 yds SSS 67
- U
- £€ On application
- Widnes

Sale (1913)
Sale Lodge, Golf Road, Sale, M33 2XU
- ☎ (0161) 973 3404
- (0161) 962 4217
- 750
- KG Fraser (Hon) (0161) 973 1638

- M Stewart (0161) 973 1730
- 18 L 6126 yds SSS 70
- U SOC–WD
- £€ £28 (£33)
- N of Sale. M60 Junction 6

Sandbach (1895)
Middlewich Road, Sandbach, CW11 1FH
- ☎ (01270) 762117
- 240 115(L) 50(J)
- GF Wood
- 9 L 5598 yds SSS 67
- WD–U WE/BH–M
- £€ D–£20
- 1 mile W of Sandbach (A533). M6 Junction 17

Sandiway (1921)
Chester Road, Sandiway, CW8 2DJ
- ☎ (01606) 883247
- (01606) 888548
- info@sandiwaygolf.fsnet.co.uk
- 730
- RH Owens
- W Laird (01606) 883180
- 18 L 6435 yds SSS 72
- H SOC
- £€ £40 (£50)
- 15 miles E of Chester on A556
- Ted Ray
- www.sandiwaygolf.co.uk

Shrigley Hall Hotel & CC (1989)
Shrigley Park, Pott Shrigley, Macclesfield, SK10 5SB
- ☎ (01625) 575757
- (01625) 575437
- 500
- Louisa Lawton
- T Stevens (01625) 575626
- 18 L 6281 yds SSS 71
- U SOC
- £€ £36 (£41)
- 15 miles from centre of Manchester. Airport 10 miles
- Donald Steel

Stamford (1901)
Oakfield House, Huddersfield Road, Stalybridge, SK15 3PY
- ☎ (01457) 832126
- 700
- BD Matthews
- B Badger (01457) 834829
- 18 L 5701 yds SSS 68
- WD–U WE comp days–after 2.30pm SOC–WD
- £€ £20 (£25)
- NE boundary of Stalybridge on B6175

Stockport (1905)
Offerton Road, Offerton, Stockport, SK2 5HL
- ☎ (0161) 427 2001 (Members)
- (0161) 449 8293
- stockportgolf@oz.co.uk
- 510
- JE Flanagan (0161) 427 8369
- M Peel (0161) 427 2421
- 18 L 6326 yds SSS 71

- SOC–WD
- £€ £40 (£50)
- 4 miles SE of Stockport on A627
- Herd/Hawtree

Styal (1994)
Station Road, Styal, SK9 4JN
- ☎ (01625) 531359 (Bookings)
- (01625) 530063
- 850
- W Higham (01625) 530063
- S Forrest (01625) 528910
- 18 L 6504 yds Par 70 SSS 70 9 hole Par 3 course
- U SOC
- £€ £12
- 2 miles from M56 Junction 5. Manchester Airport 5 mins
- Floodlit driving range
- T Holmes
- www.styalgolf.co.uk

Sutton Hall
Aston Lane, Sutton Weaver, Runcorn, WA7 3ED
- ☎ (01928) 790747
- (01928) 759174
- 600 30(J)
- M Faulkner
- I Smith (01928) 714872
- 18 L 6608 yds Par 72
- U SOC–WD
- £€ £20 (£24)
- 3 miles S of M56 Junction 12

The Tytherington Club (1986)
Macclesfield, SK10 2JP
- ☎ (01625) 506000
- (01625) 506040
- 800
- To be appointed
- G McLeod
- 18 L 6737 yds SSS 73
- U H SOC–WD
- £€ £28 D–£35 (£34 D–£45)
- N of Macclesfield (A523)
- Driving range
- Thomas/Dawson

Upton-by-Chester (1934)
Upton Lane, Chester, CH2 1EE
- ☎ (01244) 381183
- (01244) 376955
- 750
- F Hopley (01244) 381183
- S Dewhurst (01244) 381183
- 18 L 5850 yds SSS 68
- U SOC–WD
- £€ £20 D–£30 (£20 D–£30)
- Off Liverpool road, near 'Frog' PH

Vale Royal Abbey (1998)
Whitegate, Northwich, CW8 2BA
- ☎ (01606) 301291
- (01606) 301414
- 650
- R Stockdale (01606) 301702
- 18 holes Par 71 SSS 71

👤 U SOC
££ £35
⛳ 2 miles W of Hartford, off A556
🏠 Simon Gidman
⬛ www.crownsportsplc.com

Vicars Cross   (1939)
Tarvin Road, Great Barrow, Chester,
CH3 7HN
☎ **(01244) 335174**
🖥 (01244) 335686
📖 800
🐦 Mrs K Hunt
✒ JA Forsythe (01244) 335595
🏴 18 L 6428 yds SSS 71
👤 U SOC–Tues & Thurs
££ £25 (£25)
⛳ 3 miles E of Chester on A51
⊕ Driving range
🏠 E Parr

Walton Hall   (1972)
Public
Warrington Road, Higher Walton,
Warrington, WA4 5LU
☎ **(01925) 266775**
📖 350
🐦 I England
✒ J Jackson (01925) 263061
🏴 18 L 6843 yds Par 72 SSS 73
👤 U SOC
££ £9 (£11)
⛳ 2 miles S of Warrington. M56
Junctions 10/11
🏠 Thomas/Alliss

Warrington   (1903)
Hill Warren, Appleton, WA4 5HR
☎ **(01925) 261620**
🖥 (01925) 265933
📖 875
🐦 NF Morrall (01925) 261775
✒ R Mackay (01925) 265431
🏴 18 L 6210 yds SSS 70
👤 U SOC–Wed
££ On application
⛳ 3 miles S of Warrington on A49.
M56 Junction 10
⬛ www.warrington-golf-club.co.uk

Werneth Low   (1912)
Werneth Low Road, Gee Cross, Hyde,
SK14 3AF
☎ **(0161) 368 2503**
🖥 (0161) 320 0053
📖 315 60(L) 40(J)
🐦 M Gregg (0161) 336 9496
✒ T Bacchus (0161) 367 9376
🏴 11 L 6113 yds Par 70 SSS 69
👤 U exc Sun–NA Sat/BH–M SOC
££ £18
⛳ 2 miles SE of Hyde, nr Gee Cross.
M67 Junction 4
🏠 Peter Campbell

Widnes   (1924)
Highfield Road, Widnes, WA8 7DT
☎ **(0151) 424 2440**
🖥 (0151) 495 2849
✉ arudder.wgc@uhu.co.uk
📖 600

🐦 VA Rudder (0151) 424 2995
✒ J O'Brien (0151) 420 7467
🏴 18 L 5729 yds SSS 68
👤 WD–U WE–H NA on comp days
SOC–Wed & Thurs
££ £18 (£24)
⛳ Station ½ mile. M62 Junction 7

Wilmslow   (1889)
Great Warford, Mobberley, Knutsford,
WA16 7AY
☎ **(01565) 872148**
🖥 (01565) 872172
📖 785
🐦 Mrs MI Padfield
✒ LJ Nowicki (01565) 873620
🏴 18 L 6607 yds SSS 72
👤 U H exc Wed–NA before 3pm
££ £40 (£50)
⛳ 3 miles W of Alderley Edge
⬛ www.wilmslowgolfclub.ukf.net

Cornwall

Bowood Park   (1992)
Valley Truckle, Lanteglos, Camelford,
PL32 9RF
☎ **(01840) 213017**
🖥 (01840) 212622
✉ golf@bowoodpark.com
📖 300
✒ J Phillips
🏴 18 L 6692 yds SSS 72
👤 H (phone first) SOC
££ £40
⛳ 2 miles SW of Camelford, off A39,
on to B3266
⊕ Driving range

Bude & North Cornwall
(1891)
Burn View, Bude, EX23 8DA
☎ **(01288) 352006**
🖥 (01288) 356855
📖 682 106(L) 38(J)
🐦 Mrs PM Ralph
✒ J Yeo (01288) 353635
🏴 18 L 6057 yds Par 71 SSS 70
👤 WD–U 9.30–12.30pm, 2–5pm and
after 6.30pm WE–restricted
££ D–£27 (£32)
⛳ Bude town centre
⬛ www.budegolf.co.uk

Budock Vean Hotel   (1922)
Mawnan Smith, Falmouth,
TR11 5LG
☎ **(01326) 252102**
🖥 (01326) 250892
✉ relax@budockvean.co.uk
📖 150
🐦 RM Whitwam
✒ A Ramsden (Golf Mgr)
🏴 9 L 5153 yds SSS 65
👤 H
££ D–£18 (D–£20)
⛳ Falmouth 5 miles
🏠 James Braid

Cape Cornwall G&CC
(1990)
St Just, Penzance, TR19 7NL
☎ **(01736) 788611**
🖥 (01736) 788611
📖 450
🐦 M Waters
✒ M Atherton (01736) 788867
🏴 18 L 5650 yds SSS 68
👤 WD/Sat–U Sun–NA before noon
SOC
££ £20 (£20)
⛳ 1 mile W of St Just. 8 miles W of
Penzance, off A3071
🏠 R Hamilton

Carlyon Bay   (1926)
Carlyon Bay, St Austell, PL25 3RD
☎ **(01726) 814250**
📖 500
🐦 Y Lister, P Clemo
✒ M Rowe (01726) 814228
🏴 18 L 6560 yds SSS 71
👤 U–book with Pro
££ £37
⛳ 2 miles E of St Austell
🏠 J Hamilton Stutt

China Fleet CC   (1991)
Saltash, PL12 6LJ
☎ **(01752) 848668**
🖥 (01752) 848456
✉ sales@china-fleet.co.uk
📖 600
🐦 DW O'Sullivan
✒ N Cook
🏴 18 L 6551 yds SSS 72
👤 H–by arrangement SOC
££ On application
⛳ 1 mile from Tamar Bridge, off A38
⊕ Floodlit driving range
🏠 Martin Hawtree

Culdrose
Royal Naval Air Station, Culdrose
☎ **(01326) 574121 Ext 2413**
📖 173
🐦 VC Williams (01326) 572540
🏴 18 L 6432 yds Par 72 SSS 71
👤 M–play restricted to WE and
evenings
££ D–£5 (D–£5)
⛳ Culdrose, 1 mile S of Helston on
A3083

Falmouth   (1894)
Swanpool Road, Falmouth, TR11 5BQ
☎ **(01326) 311262/314296**
🖥 (01326) 317783
✉ falmouthgolfclub@freezone.co.uk
📖 500
🐦 R Wooldridge (01326) 314296
✒ B Patterson (Golf Dir)
🏴 18 L 6037 yds Par 71 SSS 70
👤 U H SOC
££ On application
⛳ ¼ mile W of Swanpool Beach
⊕ Driving range
⬛ www.falmouthgolfclub.co.uk

Isles of Scilly (1904)

St Mary's, Isles of Scilly, TR21 0NF
☎ **(01720) 422692**
🖥 (01720) 422049
📖 130
🏌 S Watt
🏞 9 L 6001 yds SSS 69
👥 U
£€ £19
🚗 Hughtown 1¹/₂ miles
🏛 Horace Hutchinson

Killiow (1987)

Killiow, Kea, Truro, TR3 6AG
☎ **(01872) 270246**
🖥 (01872) 240915
📖 500
🏌 J Crowson (01872) 240915
🏞 18 L 5274 yds Par 70 SSS 68
👥 U
£€ £15.50
🚗 2¹/₂ miles S of Truro, off A39
⊕ Driving range

Lanhydrock (1991)

Lostwithiel Road, Bodmin, PL30 5AQ
☎ **(01208) 73600**
🖥 (01208) 77325
📖 300
🏌 G Bond (Gen Mgr)
✓ J Broadway
🏞 18 L 6100 yds Par 70 SSS 70
👥 U SOC
£€ On application
🚗 1 mile S of Bodmin, off B3268
⊕ Driving range
🏛 J Hamilton Stutt
■ www.lanhydrock-golf.co.uk

Launceston (1927)

St Stephen, Launceston, PL15 8HF
☎ **(01566) 773442**
🖥 (01566) 777506
📖 900
🏌 C Hicks
✓ J Tozer
🏞 18 L 6415 yds SSS 71
👥 WD–U H WE–NA
£€ D–£25
🚗 1 mile N of Launceston, off Bude road
🏛 J Hamilton Stutt
■ www.launcestongolfclub.com

Looe (1933)

Bin Down, Looe, PL13 1PX
☎ **(01503) 240239**
🖥 (01503) 240864
📖 600
🏌 T Day (Hon)
✓ A MacDonald
🏞 18 L 5940 yds Par 70 SSS 69
👥 U SOC
£€ On application
🚗 3 miles E of Looe
🏛 Harry Vardon

Lostwithiel G&CC (1990)

Lower Polscoe, Lostwithiel, PL22 0HQ
☎ **(01208) 873550**
🖥 (01208) 873479

✉ reception@golf-hotel.co.uk
📖 350
🏌 D Higman
✓ T Nash (01208) 873822
🏞 18 L 5984 yds Par 72
👥 U SOC
£€ £25 (£29)
🚗 ¹/₂ mile E of Lostwithiel, off A390
⊕ Driving range
🏛 Stuart Wood
■ www.golf-hotel.co.uk

Merlin (1991)

Proprietary
Mawgan Porth, Newquay, TR8 4DN
☎ **(01841) 540222**
🖥 (01841) 541031
🏌 Mrs M Oliver
🏞 18 L 6210 yds Par 71 SSS 71
👥 U SOC
£€ 18 holes–£15. 9 holes–£11
🚗 4 miles N of Newquay
⊕ Driving range
🏛 Ross Oliver

Mullion (1895)

Cury, Helston, TR12 7BP
☎ **(01326) 240685**
🖥 (01326) 240685
📖 700
🏌 G Fitter
✓ P Blundell (01326) 241176
🏞 18 L 6037 yds SSS 70
👥 H (restricted comp days and open days) SOC–WD
£€ D–£23 (£28)
🚗 6 miles S of Helston
⊕ Golf academy
🏛 W Sich

Newquay (1890)

Tower Road, Newquay, TR7 1LT
☎ **(01637) 872091**
🖥 (01637) 874066
✉ newquaygolfclub@smartone.co.uk
📖 600
🏌 G Binney (01637) 874354
✓ M Bevan (01637) 874830
🏞 18 L 6151 yds SSS 69
👥 WD/Sat–H Sun–H SOC
£€ £30 (£30) W–£90
🚗 Newquay town centre
🏛 HS Colt
■ www.newquaygolfclub.com

Perranporth (1927)

Budnic Hill, Perranporth, TR6 0AB
☎ **(01872) 572454**
🖥 (01872) 573701
📖 600
🏌 DC Mugford (01872) 573701
✓ DC Michell (01872) 572317
🏞 18 L 6286 yds SSS 72
👥 WD–U WE–H SOC
£€ £25 (£30)
🚗 ¹/₂ mile NW of Perranporth
🏛 James Braid

Porthpean (1992)

Porthpean, St Austell, PL26 6AY
☎ **(01726) 64613**

🏞 18 L 5210 yds Par 67 SSS 66
👥 U SOC
£€ £14
🚗 2 miles SE of St Austell on coast
⊕ Driving range

Praa Sands (1971)

Praa Sands, Penzance, TR20 9TQ
☎ **(01736) 763445**
🖥 (01736) 763399
📖 225
🏌 D & K Phillips (Props)
🏞 9 L 4122 yds Par 62 SSS 60
👥 U exc Sun am
£€ £15 D–£20
🚗 7 miles E of Penzance on A394 Penzance-Helston road
🏛 RA Hamilton

St Austell (1911)

Tregongeeves, St Austell, PL26 7DS
☎ **(01726) 74756**
📖 780
🏌 K Trahair
✓ T Pitts (01726) 68621
🏞 18 L 5981 yds SSS 69
👥 SOC exc comp days
£€ On application
🚗 1¹/₂ miles W of St Austell

St Enodoc (1890)

Rock, Wadebridge, PL27 6LD
☎ **(01208) 863216**
🖥 (01208) 862976
✉ stenodocgolfclub@aol.com
📖 1360
🏌 TD Clagett
✓ NJ Williams (01208) 862402
🏞 Church 18 L 6243 yds SSS 70 Holywell 18 L 4103 yds SSS 61
👥 Church H–max 24 SOC Holywell–U
£€ Church £38 (£45) Holywell £15 (£15)
🚗 6 miles NW of Wadebridge
🏛 James Braid

St Kew (1993)

Proprietary
St Kew Highway, Wadebridge, Bodmin, PL30 3EF
☎ **(01208) 841500**
🖥 (01208) 841500
✉ st-kew-golf-club@ic24.net
📖 270
🏌 J Brown (Prop)
✓ N Rogers
🏞 9 L 4543 yds SSS 62
👥 U SOC
£€ 9 holes–£10. 18 holes–£15
🚗 2¹/₂ miles N of Wadebridge on A39
⊕ Covered driving range
🏛 David Derry

St Mellion Hotel G&CC (1976)

St Mellion, Saltash, PL12 6SD
☎ **(01579) 351351**
🖥 (01579) 350537
📖 850

✓ D Moon
🏳 Old 18 L 5782 yds SSS 68
Nicklaus 18 L 6651 yds SSS 72
👥 U SOC
££ From £15
🚗 Tamar Bridge, 5 miles NW of Saltash
⊕ Driving range
🏠 Hamilton Stutt/Nicklaus
■ www.stmellion.co.uk

Tehidy Park (1922)
Camborne, TR14 0HH
☎ **(01209) 842208**
🖳 (01209) 843680
🖂 secretary-manager @tehidyparkgolfclub.co.uk
📖 1000
🏠 R Parker (Sec/Mgr)
✓ J Dumbreck (01209) 842914
🏳 18 L 6241 yds SSS 71
👥 H
££ £25 (£30)
🚗 3 miles N of Camborne
■ www.tehidyparkgolfclub.co.uk

Tregenna Castle Hotel (1982)
St Ives, TR26 2DE
☎ **(01736) 795254 Ext 121**
📖 297
🏠 J Goodman
🏳 18 L 3549 yds SSS 57
👥 U SOC
££ On application
🚗 St Ives 1 mile, off A3074

Treloy (1991)
Treloy, Newquay, TR7 4JN
☎ **(01637) 878554**
📖 145
🏠 J Paull
🏳 9 L 2143 yds SSS 31
👥 U SOC
££ 18 holes–£12.50 9 holes–£8
🚗 2 miles E of Newquay on A3059
🏠 MRM Sandow

Trethorne
Kennards House, Launceston, PL15 8QE
☎ **(01566) 86903**
🖳 (01566) 86981
📖 450
🏠 C Willis
✓ M Boundy
🏳 18 L 6188 yds Par 71 SSS 71
👥 U
££ £24
🚗 2 miles SW of Launceston (A30)
⊕ Driving range
🏠 Frank Frayne

Trevose (1924)
Constantine Bay, Padstow, PL28 8JB
☎ **(01841) 520208**
🖳 (01841) 521057
📖 1500
🏠 P Gammon (Prop), N Gammon (Sec/Mgr)
✓ G Alliss (01841) 520261

🏳 18 L 6608 yds SSS 72
9 L 3031 yds SSS 35
9 L 1360 yds SSS 29
👥 H SOC
££ On application
🚗 4 miles W of Padstow
⊕ 3 & 4 ball times restricted (phone first)
🏠 HS Colt
■ www.trevose-gc.co.uk

Truro (1937)
Treliske, Truro, TR1 3LG
☎ **(01872) 272640**
🖳 (01872) 278684
📖 900
🏠 HWD Leicester (Sec/Mgr) (01872) 278684
✓ NK Bicknell (01872) 276595
🏳 18 L 5347 yds SSS 66
👥 U H SOC
££ £20 (£25)
🚗 1 mile W of Truro on A390
🏠 Colt/Alison/Morrison
■ www.trurogolf.com

West Cornwall (1889)
Lelant, St Ives, TR26 3DZ
☎ **(01736) 753401**
🖳 (01736) 753401
📖 825
🏠 IJ Veale
✓ P Atherton (01736) 753177
🏳 18 L 5884 yds SSS 69
👥 H SOC
££ £25 (£30)
🚗 2 miles E of St Ives
■ www.westcornwallgolfclub.co.uk

Whitsand Bay Hotel (1906)
Portwrinkle, Torpoint, PL11 3BU
☎ **(01503) 230470 (Clubhouse)**
🖳 (01503) 230329
📖 320
🏠 GG Dyer (01503) 230164
✓ S Poole (01503) 230778
🏳 18 L 5953 yds SSS 69
👥 U SOC
££ £20 (£22.50)
🚗 6 miles W of Plymouth
🏠 Willie Fernie

Cumbria

Alston Moor (1906)
The Hermitage, Alston, CA9 3DB
☎ **(01434) 381675**
🖳 (01434) 381675
📖 180
🏠 H Robinson (01434) 381354
🏳 10 L 5380 yds SSS 66
👥 U SOC
££ D–£10 (D–£12)
🚗 2 miles S of Alston on B6277
■ www.cybermoor.org.guest.golf

Appleby (1903)
Brackenber Moor, Appleby, CA16 6LP
☎ **(017683) 51432**

🖳 (017683) 52773
🖂 www.applebygolfclub.org.uk
📖 736
🏠 JMF Doig (Hon)
✓ J Taylor (017683) 52922
🏳 18 L 5901 yds SSS 68
👥 U H
££ £19 (£23)
🚗 2 miles SE of Appleby. ½ mile N of A66
🏠 Willie Fernie

Barrow (1921)
Rakesmoor Lane, Hawcoat, Barrow-in-Furness, LA14 4QB
☎ **(01229) 825444**
📖 505 91(L) 67(J)
🏠 J Slater (Hon)
🏳 18 L 6184 yds Par 71 SSS 70
👥 U H Ladies Day–Fri SOC
££ £20 W–£85
🚗 2 miles E of Barrow, off A590

Brampton (Talkin Tarn) (1907)
Tarn Road, Brampton, CA8 1HN
☎ **(016977) 2255**
🖳 (016977) 41487
🖂 secretary@bramptongolfclub.com
📖 750
🏠 IJ Meldrum (01900) 827985
✓ S Wilkinson (016977) 2000
🏳 18 L 6407 yds Par 72 SSS 71
👥 U
££ D–£22 (D–£30)
🚗 B6413, 1 mile SE of Brampton
⊕ Driving range
🏠 James Braid

Brayton Park (1986)
Pay and play
Lakeside Inn, Brayton Park, Aspatria, CA5 3TD
☎ **(016973) 20840**
📖 60
🏠 D Warwick
🏳 9 L 2521 yds SSS 65
👥 U
££ 9 holes–£5 (£6) 18 holes–£7 (£8)
🚗 1 mile N of Aspatria. 10 miles N of Cockermouth

Carlisle (1908)
Aglionby, Carlisle, CA4 8AG
☎ **(01228) 513029**
🖳 (01228) 513303
📖 735
🏠 Mrs HM Rowell
✓ M Heggie (01228) 513241
🏳 18 L 6278 yds SSS 70
👥 WD–U exc Tues–NA Sat–M Sun–restricted SOC–Mon/Wed/Fri
££ £25 D–£40 (£30 D–£40)
🚗 ½ mile E of M6 Junction 43, on A69
🏠 Mackenzie Ross

Carus Green (1996)
Pay and play
Burneside Road, Kendal, LA9 6EB
☎ **(01539) 721097/737277**

☎ (01539) 721097
📖 400
🏌 B Lumsden
🏌 D Turner
🏴 18 L 5642 yds Par 70 SSS 68
🏌 U SOC
££ £14 (£16)
🏁 1 mile N of Kendal on Burneside
　　Road
⬛ www.carusgreen.co.uk

Casterton

Sedbergh Road, Casterton, Carnforth,
LA6 2LA
☎ (015242) 71592
📠 (015242) 74387
📧 castertongc@hotmail.com
📖 300
🏌 J & E Makinson (Props)
🏌 R Williamson
🏴 9 L 3015 yds Par 35
🏌 U SOC
££ £10 (£14)
🏁 1 mile NE of Kirkby Lonsdale on
　　A683. M6 Junction 36, 6 miles
🏁 Will Adamson
⬛ www.castertongc.co.uk

Cockermouth　(1896)

Embleton, Cockermouth, CA13 9SG
☎ (017687) 76223/76941
📠 (017687) 76941
📖 539
🏌 RD Pollard (01900) 822650
🏌 None
🏴 18 L 5496 yds SSS 67
🏌 WD–U before 3.30pm exc Wed
　　WE–restricted SOC
££ £18 (£22)
🏁 4 miles E of Cockermouth
🏁 James Braid

Dalston Hall　(1990)

Dalston Hall, Dalston, Carlisle,
CA5 7JX
☎ (01228) 710165
📖 270
🏌 Jane Simpson
🏴 9 L 2700 yds SSS 67
🏌 U
££ 9 holes–£6.50 (£7.50) 18 holes–£10
　　(£13)
🏁 5 miles SW of Carlisle on B5299. 6
　　miles W of M6 Junction 42

The Dunnerholme　(1905)

Duddon Road, Askam-in-Furness,
LA16 7AW
☎ (01229) 462675
📖 400
🏌 LA Haines (01229) 826198
🏴 10 L 6075 yds SSS 70
🏌 U
££ £10 (£12)
🏁 6 miles N of Barrow on A595

Eden　(1992)

Crosby-on-Eden, Carlisle, CA6 4RA
☎ (01228) 573003
📠 (01228) 818435
📖 700

🏌 S Harrison (01228) 573003
🏴 18 L 6368 yds SSS 72
🏌 U SOC
££ £28 (£32)
🏁 5 miles NE of Carlisle, off A689.
　　M6 Junction 44
⊕ Driving range. Golf academy

Furness　(1872)

Walney Island, Barrow-in-Furness,
LA14 3LN
☎ (01229) 471232
📖 625
🏌 JW Anderson
🏌 None
🏴 18 L 6363 yds SSS 71
🏌 H SOC
££ £20 (£25)
🏁 Walney Island. M6 Junction 36

Grange Fell　(1952)

Fell Road, Grange-over-Sands,
LA11 6HB
☎ (015395) 32536
📖 300
🏌 M Higginson (015395) 34098
🏴 9 L 4840 metres SSS 66
🏌 U
££ £15 (£20)
🏁 W of Grange-over-Sands, towards
　　Cartmel

Grange-over-Sands　(1919)

Meathop Road, Grange-over-Sands,
LA11 6QX
☎ (015395) 33180
📠 (015395) 33754
📖 430 170(L) 40(J)
🏌 SD Wright (015395) 33754
🏌 A Pickering (015395) 35937
🏴 18 L 5938 yds SSS 69
🏌 H SOC
££ £20 D–£25 (£25 D–£30)
🏁 E of Grange, off B5277
🏁 A Mackenzie

Haltwhistle　(1967)

Wallend Farm, Greenhead, Carlisle,
CA6 7HN
☎ (01697) 747367
📠 (01434) 344311
📖 300
🏌 JD Gilbertson (Hon)
🏌 None
🏴 18 L 5522 yds Par 69 SSS 69
🏌 U SOC
££ D–£12 (£15)
🏁 3 miles W of Haltwhistle on A69
🏁 Andrew Mair

Kendal　(1891)

The Heights, Kendal, LA9 4PQ
☎ (01539) 736466 (Clubhouse),
　　(01539) 723499 (Bookings)
📠 (01539) 733708
📖 731
🏌 A Dunn (01539) 733708
🏌 P Scott (01539) 723499
🏴 18 L 5785 yds Par 70 SSS 68
🏌 U H SOC
££ £22 (£27.50)
🏁 1 mile NW of Kendal

Keswick　(1978)

Threlkeld Hall, Keswick, CA12 4SX
☎ (017687) 79010 (Bookings)
📠 (017687) 79861
📖 900
🏌 RC Jackson (017687) 79324
🏌 P Rawlinson (017687) 79010
🏴 18 L 6225 yds SSS 72
🏌 U H–book with Pro SOC
££ D–£20 (£25)
🏁 4 miles E of Keswick (A66)
🏁 E Brown

Kirkby Lonsdale

Scaleber Lane, Barbon, Kirkby Lonsdale,
LA6 2LJ
☎ (015242) 76365
📠 (015242) 76503
📧 KLGolf@Dial/Pipex.com
📖 550 50(J)
🏌 G Hall (015242) 76365
🏌 C Barrett (015242) 76366
🏴 18 L 6481 yds SSS 71
🏌 U SOC
££ £25 (£30)
🏁 3 miles N of Kirkby Lonsdale, off
　　A683
🏁 W Squires
⬛ www.klgolf.dial.pipex.com

Maryport　(1905)

Bankend, Maryport, CA15 6PA
☎ (01900) 812605
📠 (01900) 815626
📖 430
🏌 HL Hayston (Chairman)
🏴 18 L 6088 yds SSS 70
🏌 U SOC
££ D–£17 (£22)
🏁 1 mile N of Maryport, off B5300

Penrith　(1890)

Salkeld Road, Penrith, CA11 8SG
☎ (01768) 891919/865429
📖 750
🏌 D Noble (01768) 891919
🏌 G Key (01768) 891919
🏴 18 L 6026 yds SSS 69
🏌 WD–H WE/BH–H 10.06–11.30am
　　& after 3pm
££ £20 D–£25 (£25 D–£30)
🏁 ¹/₂ mile E of Penrith

St Bees　(1929)

Peckmill, Beach Road, St Bees,
CA27 0EJ
☎ (01946) 822515,
　　(01946) 824300 (Clubhouse)
📖 400
🏌 BG Ritson
🏴 9 L 5122 yds SSS 65
🏌 WD–U exc Wed–NA after 4pm
　　WE–NA before 3pm
££ £12 (£12)
🏁 4 miles S of Whitehaven

Seascale　(1893)

Seascale, CA20 1QL
☎ (019467) 28202/28800
📠 (019467) 28202

📖 570
🏌 JDH Stobart (019467) 28202
✒ S Rudd (019467) 21779
🏁 18 L 6416 yds Par 71 SSS 71
👥 U SOC
££ £24 D–£29 (£27 D–£32)
🚗 15 miles S of Whitehaven
🏠 Campbell/Lowe

Sedbergh (1896)
Dent Road, Sedbergh, LA10 5SS
☎ (015396) 21551
📠 (015396) 20993
📧 sedberghgc@btinternet.com
📖 350
🏌 AD Lord (015396) 20993
✒ J Garner
🏁 9 L 5588 yds Par 70 SSS 68
👥 U–phone in advance SOC H
££ £18 D–£23 (£20 D–£25)
🚗 1 mile S of Sedbergh on Dent road. M6 Junction 37, 5 miles
🏠 WG Squires

Silecroft (1903)
Silecroft, Millom, LA18 4NX
☎ (01229) 774250
📠 (01229) 774342
📖 300
🏌 DLA MacLardie (01229) 774342
✒ None
🏁 9 L 5877 yds Par 68 SSS 68
👥 WD–U WE/BH–restricted
££ D–£15 (£20)
🚗 3 miles W of Millom

Silloth-on-Solway (1892)
Silloth, Wigton, CA7 4BL
☎ (016973) 31304
📠 (016973) 31782
📖 700
✒ (016973) 32404
🏁 18 L 6614 yds SSS 73
👥 U H–booking advisable SOC
££ D–£30 (£40)
🚗 22 miles W of Carlisle (B5302). M6 Junction 43
🏠 David Grant

Silverdale (1906)
Red Bridge Lane, Silverdale, Carnforth, LA5 0SP
☎ (01524) 701300
📠 (01524) 702074
📧 silverdalegolfclub@ecosse.net
📖 500
🏌 KD Smith (01524) 702074
🏁 18 L 5535 yds Par 70 SSS 68
👥 U exc Sun (Summer)–M
££ £20 (£25)
🚗 3 miles NW of Carnforth, by Silverdale Station

Stony Holme (1974)
Public
St Aidan's Road, Carlisle, CA1 1LS
☎ (01228) 625511
📖 375
🏌 WJ Hodgson (01228) 527112
✒ S Ling (01228) 625511
🏁 18 L 5775 yds Par 69 SSS 68

👥 U SOC
££ £8.30 (£10.30)
🚗 1 mile E of Carlisle, off A69. M6 Junction 43
🏠 Frank Pennink

Ulverston (1895)
Bardsea Park, Ulverston, LA12 9QJ
☎ (01229) 582824
📧 ulverstongolf@bardseapark.freeserve.co.uk
📖 745
🏌 K Oliver
✒ MR Smith (01229) 582806
🏁 18 L 6201 yds SSS 70
👥 H or I SOC
££ £25 D–£30 (£30 D–£35) Summer £14 D–£18 (£18 D–£22) Winter
🚗 1¹/₂ miles SW of Ulverston on A5087
🏠 Herd/Colt

Windermere (1891)
Cleabarrow, Windermere, LA23 3NB
☎ (015394) 43123
📠 (015394) 43123
📖 700
🏌 KR Moffat
✒ WSM Rooke (015394) 43550
🏁 18 L 5132 yds SSS 65
👥 H SOC
££ £24 (£28)
🚗 1¹/₂ miles E of Bowness
🏠 George Lowe

Workington (1893)
Branthwaite Road, Workington, CA14 4SS
☎ (01900) 603460/67818
📠 (01900) 607122
📖 600 110(L) 85(J)
🏌 TF Stout
✒ A Drabble
🏁 18 L 6252 yds SSS 70
👥 H SOC
££ £20 (£25)
🚗 2 miles SE of Workington
🏠 James Braid

Derbyshire

Alfreton (1892)
Oakerthorpe, Alfreton, DE55 7LH
☎ (01773) 832070
📖 300
🏌 E Brown
✒ J Mellor (01773) 831901
🏁 11 L 5393 yds SSS 66
👥 WD–U H before 4.30pm –M after 4.30pm WE–M SOC H
££ £16
🚗 W of Alfreton (A38). M1 Junction 28

Allestree Park (1949)
Public
Allestree Hall, Allestree, Derby, DE22 2EU
☎ (01332) 550616

📖 200
🏌 A Maguire
✒ L Woodward
🏁 18 L 5714 yds SSS 68
👥 WD–U WE–booking req SOC
££ £11
🚗 2 miles N of Derby on A6

Ashbourne (1886)
Wyaston Road, Ashbourne, DE6 1NB
☎ (01335) 342078
📠 (01335) 347937
📧 sec@ashbournegc.fsnet.co.uk
📖 600
🏌 P Cook (01335) 342078
✒ A Smith (01335) 347960
🏁 18 L 6365 yds SSS 71
👥 WD–U SOC
££ £20 (£30)
🚗 1¹/₂ miles SW of Ashbourne, off A52
🏠 David Hemstock
■ www.ashbournegolfclub.co.uk

Bakewell (1899)
Station Road, Bakewell, DE4 1GB
☎ (01629) 812307
📖 305 67(L) 25(J)
🏌 F Parker
✒ None
🏁 9 L 5240 yds SSS 66
👥 WD–U WE/BH–by arrangement SOC
££ £15 (£20)
🚗 ¹/₂ mile NE of Bakewell and A6

Birch Hall
Sheffield Road, Unstone, S18 5DH
☎ (01246) 291979
📖 300
🏌 G Jackson
✒ None
🏁 18 L 6509 yds Par 73 SSS 71
👥 U
££ On application
🚗 2 miles N of Chesterfield (B60557)
🏠 David Tucker

Blue Circle (1985)
Cement Works, Hope, S33 2RP
☎ (01433) 622315
📖 230
🏌 DS Smith
🏁 9 L 5350 yds SSS 66
👥 M
🚗 Hope Valley

Bondhay (1991)
Bondhay Lane, Whitwell, Worksop, S80 3EH
☎ (01909) 723608
📠 (01909) 720226
📧 bondhay@aol.com
📖 520
🏌 H Hardisty
✒ M Ramsden
🏁 18 L 6785 yds Par 72 9 hole course
👥 U SOC
££ £17 (£22)
🚗 2 miles E of M1 Junction 30, off A619

⊕ Driving range
⌂ Donald Steel

Brailsford   (1994)
Proprietary
Pools Head Lane, Brailsford,
Ashbourne, DE6 3BU
☎ **(01335) 360096**
⌸ 131
⚹ K Wilson
╱ D McCarthy
▷ 9 L 3148 yds Par 36 SSS 35
⚇ U SOC
£€ 9 holes–£9 (£11.50) 18
   holes–£13.50 (£16.50)
⚱ On A52 between Derby and
   Ashbourne
⊕ Driving range

Breadsall Priory Hotel
G&CC   (1976)
Moor Road, Morley, Derby, DE7 6DL
☎ **(01332) 832235**
⌨ (01332) 833509
⌸ 900
⚹ P Le Roi (Gen Mgr)
╱ D Steels (01332) 834425
▷ 18 L 6201 yds SSS 70
   18 L 6028 yds SSS 69
⚇ WD–U SOC–WD only
£€ £25–£42
⚱ Morley, 5 miles N of Derby (A61).
   M1 Junction 25, 9 miles
⊕ Driving range

Broughton Heath
Bent Lane, Church Broughton,
DE65 5BA
☎ **(01283) 521235**
⌨ (01283) 521235
⌸ 435
⚹ J Bentley
╱ A Hyland
▷ 18 L 3087 yds Par 54 SSS 53
⚇ WD–U WE–booking necessary
   SOC
£€ £8.50 (£11)
⚱ Church Broughton, 1 mile N of
   A516 at Hatton
⌂ K Tunnicliffe

Burton-on-Trent   (1894)
43 Ashby Road East, Burton-on-Trent,
DE15 0PS
☎ **(01283) 568708 (Clubhouse)**
⌨ (01283) 544551
⌑ burtongolfclub@btinternet.com
⌸ 600
⚹ D Hartley (01283) 544551
╱ G Stafford (01283) 562240
▷ 18 L 6579 yds SSS 71
⚇ I H WD–NA before 9am or 1–2pm
   SOC
£€ £28 (£32)
⚱ 3 miles E of Burton on A511
⌂ HS Colt

Buxton & High Peak   (1887)
Townend, Buxton, SK17 7EN
☎ **(01298) 26263**

⌨ (01298) 26333
⌑ secretary@bhpgc.fsnet.co.uk
⌸ 450
⚹ H Smith
╱ G Brown (01298) 23112
▷ 18 L 5954 yds SSS 69
⚇ U
£€ £23 (£29)
⚱ NE boundary of Buxton (A6)
■ www.buxtonandhighpeakgolfclub
   .co.uk

Carsington Water   (1994)
Pay and play
Carsington, Wirksworth
☎ **(01629) 85650**
⌸ 300
⚹ GWR Coleman (Mgr)
   (01403) 784864
╱ To be appointed
▷ 9 L 6000yds SSS
⚇ U SOC
£€ On application
⚱ 8 miles NE of Ashbourne, off
   B5035
⌂ John Ludlow

Cavendish   (1925)
Gadley Lane, Buxton, SK17 6XD
☎ **(01298) 23494**
⌨ (01298) 79708
⌸ 600
⚹ JD Rushton (01298) 79708
╱ P Hunstone (01298) 25052
▷ 18 L 5833 yds SSS 68
⚇ U H SOC–by prior arrangement
   with Pro
£€ £26 (£35)
⚱ ³/₄ mile W of Buxton Station. St
   John's Road (A53)
⊕ Driving range
⌂ Dr A Mackenzie

Chapel-en-le-Frith   (1905)
The Cockyard, Manchester Road,
Chapel-en-le-Frith, SK23 9UH
☎ **(01298) 812118**
⌨ (01298) 814990
⌑ info@chapelgolf.co.uk
⌸ 640
⚹ J Hilton (01298) 813943
╱ DJ Cullen (01298) 812118
▷ 18 L 6434 yds SSS 71
⚇ U
£€ £24 (£35)
⚱ 13 miles SE of Stockport, off A6
   (B5470)
■ www.chapelgolf.co.uk

Chesterfield   (1897)
Walton, Chesterfield, S42 7LA
☎ **(01246) 279256**
⌨ (01246) 276622
⌸ 600
⚹ BG Broughton
╱ M McLean (01246) 276297
▷ 18 L 6281 yds Par 71 SSS 70
⚇ WD–U H WE–M SOC–WD
£€ £26–£35
⚱ 2 miles SW of Chesterfield on
   A623

Chesterfield Municipal
   (1934)
Public
Murray House, Crow Lane,
Chesterfield, S41 0EQ
☎ **(01246) 273887,**
   (01246) 239500 (Bookings)
⌨ (01246) 558024
⌸ 350
⚹ J Hearnshaw
╱ A Carnall (01246) 239500
▷ 18 L 6013 yds SSS 69
   9 hole course
⚇ U
£€ On application
⚱ ¹/₄ mile past Chesterfield station
⊕ Pitch & putt

Chevin   (1894)
Duffield, Derby, DE56 4EE
☎ **(01332) 841864**
⌨ (01332) 844028
⌑ secretary@chevingolf.fsnet.co.uk
⌸ 500 100(L) 80(J) 70(5D)
⚹ JA Milner
╱ W Bird (01332) 841112
▷ 18 L 6057 yds SSS 69
⚇ WD–U WE–M SOC–WD H
£€ £25 D–£30
⚱ 5 miles N of Derby on A6

Derby Sinfin   (1923)
Public
Wilmore Road, Sinfin, Derby,
DE24 9HD
☎ **(01332) 766323**
⚹ P Davidson
╱ J Siddons (01332) 766462
▷ 18 L 6163 yds SSS 69
⚇ U SOC
£€ On application
⚱ 1 mile S of Derby, off A52

Erewash Valley   (1905)
Stanton-by-Dale, DE7 4QR
☎ **(0115) 932 3258**
⌨ (0115) 932 2984
⌸ 675
⚹ JA Beckett (0115) 932 2984
╱ MJ Ronan (0115) 932 4667
▷ 18 L 6547 yds SSS 71
⚇ WE/BH–NA before noon
   SOC–WD
£€ £24 D–£29 (D–£29)
⚱ 10 miles E of Derby, off A52. M1
   Junction 25, 3 miles

Glossop & District   (1894)
Sheffield Road, Glossop, SK13 7PU
☎ **(01457) 865247 (Clubhouse)**
⌸ 300
⚹ DS Booth
╱ D Marsh (01457) 853117
▷ 11 L 5800 yds SSS 68
⚇ U SOC
£€ £20 (£25)
⚱ 1 mile E of Glossop, off A57

Grassmoor Golf Centre
Pay and play
North Wingfield Road, Grassmoor, Chesterfield, S42 5EA
- ☎ **(01246) 856044**
- 🖴 (01246) 853486
- ✉ helen.chester@ruffordpark.co.uk
- 📖 390
- ♟ H Hagues
- ✔ G Hagues
- ► 18 L 5721 yds Par 69
- 👥 U–advance booking required SOC
- ££ £10 (£14)
- ⚐ 2 miles S of Chesterfield on B6038. M1 Junction 29, 3 miles
- ⊕ Floodlit driving range
- ♠ Hawtree
- www.grassmoorgolf.co.uk

Horsley Lodge (1992)
Smalley Mill Road, Horsley, DE21 5BL
- ☎ **(01332) 780838**
- 🖴 (01332) 781118
- 📖 600
- ♟ G Johnson
- ✔ G Lyall (01332) 780838
- ► 18 L 6336 yds SSS 70
- 👥 WD–U H
- ££ On application
- ⚐ 4 miles NE of Derby. M1 Junction 28
- ⊕ Driving range
- ♠ GM White

Ilkeston (1929)
Public
Peewit West End Drive, Ilkeston, DE7 5GH
- ☎ **(0115) 930 4550**
- 📖 100
- ♟ M Ogden (0115) 944 2304
- ✔ None
- ► 9 L 4116 yds Par 62 SSS 60
- 👥 U SOC–WD
- ££ On application
- ⚐ ½ mile E of Ilkeston

Kedleston Park (1947)
Kedleston, Quarndon, Derby, DE22 5JD
- ☎ **(01332) 840035**
- 🖴 (01332) 840035
- 📖 784
- ♟ GR Duckmanton
- ✔ P Wesselingh (01332) 841685
- ► 18 L 6675 yds SSS 72
- 👥 WD–H–soft spikes only
- ££ £35 (£45)
- ⚐ 4 miles N of Derby. National Trust signs to Kedleston Hall
- ♠ James Braid

Matlock (1906)
Chesterfield Road, Matlock Moor, Matlock, DE4 5LZ
- ☎ **(01629) 582191**
- 🖴 (01629) 582135
- 📖 496 78(L) 55(J)
- ♟ J Odell (01629) 582191
- ✔ M Whithorn (01629) 584934
- ► 18 L 5804 yds SSS 68

- 👥 WD–U exc 12.30–1.30pm–NA WE/BH–M SOC–WD
- ££ D–£25
- ⚐ 1½ miles NE of Matlock (A632)

Maywood (1990)
Rushy Lane, Risley, Derby, DE7 3ST
- ☎ **(0115) 939 2306**
- 📖 500
- ♟ WJ Cockeram
- ✔ S Sherratt (0115) 949 0043
- ► 18 L 6424 yds Par 72 SSS 71
- 👥 WD–U before 4pm WE–restricted SOC
- ££ £15 (£20)
- ⚐ Between Nottingham and Derby. M1 Junction 25
- ♠ P Moon

Mickleover (1923)
Uttoxeter Road, Mickleover, DE3 9AD
- ☎ **(01332) 513339 (Clubhouse)**
- 🖴 (01332) 512092
- 📖 800
- ♟ D Rodgers (01332) 512092
- ✔ T Coxon (01332) 518662
- ► 18 L 5708 yds SSS 68
- 👥 U SOC–Tues & Thurs
- ££ £25 (£30)
- ⚐ 3 miles W of Derby on A516/B5020

New Mills (1907)
Shaw Marsh, New Mills, High Peak, SK22 4QE
- ☎ **(01663) 743485**
- 📖 420
- ♟ P Jenkinson (01663) 744305
- ✔ C Cross (01663) 746161
- ► 18 L 5604 yds SSS 67
- 👥 WD–U WE–M SOC
- ££ £15 (£20)
- ⚐ 8 miles SE of Stockport
- ♠ David Williams

Ormonde Fields (1906)
Nottingham Road, Codnor, Ripley, DE5 9RG
- ☎ **(01773) 742987**
- 🖴 (01773) 744848
- 📖 660
- ♟ K Constable
- ► 18 L 6504 yds SSS 72
- 👥 U SOC
- ££ On application
- ⚐ A610 Ripley to Nottingham road. M1 Junction 26, 5 miles
- ♠ John Fearn

Pastures (1969)
Pastures Hospital, Mickleover, DE3 5DQ
- ☎ **(01332) 521074**
- 📖 320
- ♟ S McWilliams
- ► 9 L 5095 yds SSS 65
- 👥 M SOC–WD
- ⚐ 4 miles W of Derby
- ♠ JF Pennink

Shirland (1977)
Lower Delves, Shirland, DE55 6AU
- ☎ **(01773) 834935**
- 📖 450
- ♟ G Towle (01246) 874224
- ✔ NB Hallam (01773) 834935
- ► 18 L 6072 yds SSS 70
- 👥 WD–U WE–U after 2pm SOC
- ££ £17 (£20)
- ⚐ 1 mile N of Alfreton, off A61 by Shirland Church

Sickleholme (1898)
Bamford, Sheffield, S33 0BH
- ☎ **(01433) 651306**
- 📖 250 100(L) 72(J)
- ♟ PH Taylor (Mgr)
- ✔ PH Taylor
- ► 18 L 6064 yds SSS 69
- 👥 U exc Wed am
- ££ £26 (£32)
- ⚐ W of Sheffield, between Hathersage and Hope (A625)

Stanedge (1934)
Walton Hay Farm, Chesterfield, S45 0LW
- ☎ **(01246) 566156**
- 📖 325
- ♟ W Tyzack (01246) 276568
- ► 9 L 5786 yds SSS 68
- 👥 WD–U before 2pm –M after 2pm WE–M SOC
- ££ £15
- ⚐ 5 miles SW of Chesterfield, off B5057

Devon

Ashbury (1991)
Fowley Cross, Okehampton, EX20 4NL
- ☎ **(01837) 55453**
- 🖴 (01837) 55468
- 📖 100
- ♟ N Agnew
- ✔ R Cade
- ► 18 L 5244 yds SSS 66
  18 L 5881 yds SSS 68
  18 hole Par 3 course
- 👥 WD–U after 12 noon
- ££ £15 (£20)
- ⚐ 4 miles W of Okehampton, off A3079
- ♠ DJ Fensom
- ■ www.ashburyhotel.co.uk

Axe Cliff (1894)
Squires Lane, Axmouth, Seaton, EX12 4AB
- ☎ **(01297) 24371**
- 📖 400
- ♟ Mrs H Kenworthy
- ✔ M Dack (01297) 21754
- ► 18 L 5969 yds SSS 70
- 👥 U H SOC
- ££ £20 (£22)
- ⚐ Nr Yacht Club at Axmouth Bridge

Bigbury (1923)

Bigbury-on-Sea, TQ7 4BB
☎ **(01548) 810055 (Clubhouse)**
🖥 (01548) 810207
📖 800
🏌 MJ Lowry (01548) 810557
✍ S Lloyd (01548) 810412
⛳ 18 L 6061 yds Par 70 SSS 69
👥 H SOC
££ £27 (£30)
⛳ 15 miles SE of Plymouth on B3392
🏠 JH Taylor
■ www.bigburygolfclub.com

Chulmleigh (1976)

Pay and play
Leigh Road, Chulmleigh, EX18 7BL
☎ **(01769) 580519**
🖥 (01769) 580519
✉ chulmleighgolf@aol.com
📖 100
🏌 RW Dow
⛳ Summer 18 L 1450 yds SSS 54
Winter 9 L 2309 yds SSS 54
👥 U
££ £6.50 D–£12
⛳ 1 mile N of A377 at Chulmleigh
🏠 John Goodban
■ www.chulmleighgolf.co.uk

Churston (1890)

Churston, Brixham, TQ5 0LA
☎ **(01803) 842751**
🖥 (01803) 845738
✉ manager@churstongc.freeserve
.co.uk
📖 983
🏌 SR Bawden (01803) 842751
✍ N Holman (01803) 843442
⛳ 18 L 6208 yds SSS 70
👥 H exc Tues am–NA
SOC–Mon/Thurs/Fri
££ £30 (£35)
⛳ 5 miles S of Torquay
🏠 HS Colt
■ www.churstongolfclubunited.co.uk

Dainton Park (1993)

*Totnes Road, Ipplepen, Newton Abbot,
TQ12 5TN*
☎ **(01803) 815000**
📖 600
🏌 M Penlington
✍ M Tyson
⛳ 18 L 6210 yds SSS 70
👥 U SOC
££ £18 (£20)
⛳ 2 miles S of Newton Abbot on
A381
⊕ Driving range
🏠 Adrian Stiff

Dartmouth G&CC (1992)

Blackawton, Totnes, TQ9 7DE
☎ **(01803) 712686**
🖥 (01803) 712628
✉ info@dgcc.co.uk
📖 800
🏌 J Waugh
✍ S Dougan (01803) 712650
⛳ Ch'ship 18 L 7191 yds SSS 74
Dartmouth 18 L 4791 yds SSS 64

👥 WD–U phone first WE–H SOC
££ Ch'ship £29 (£36). Dartmouth £16
(£17)
⛳ 4 miles NE of Dartmouth on A3122
⊕ Driving range
🏠 Jeremy Pern
■ www.dgcc.co.uk

Dinnaton (1989)

Ivybridge, PL21 9HU
☎ **(01752) 892512/892452**
🖥 (01752) 698334
📖 300
🏌 B Rimes
✍ D Ridyard (01752) 691288
⛳ 9 L 4100 yds SSS 59
9 hole course Par 64
👥 U SOC
££ D–£10 (D–£12.50)
⛳ 12 miles SE of Plymouth, off
A38/B3213
🏠 Pink/Cotton

Downes Crediton (1976)

Hookway, Crediton, EX17 3PT
☎ **(01363) 773991**
🖥 (01363) 775060
📖 700
🏌 PT Lee (01363) 773025
✍ S Macaskill (01363) 774464
⛳ 18 L 5954 yds Par 70 SSS 69
👥 H SOC
££ £24 (£27)
⛳ 2 miles S of Crediton, off A377

East Devon (1902)

Links Road, Budleigh Salterton, EX9 6DG
☎ **(01395) 442018**
🖥 (01395) 445547
✉ secretary@edgc.co.uk
📖 850
🏌 R Burley (01395) 443370
✍ T Underwood (01395) 445195
⛳ 18 L 6231 yds SSS 70
👥 WD–H NA before 10am
SOC–Thurs only
££ £30 (£40)
⛳ 12 miles SE of Exeter

Elfordleigh Hotel G&CC (1932)

*Colebrook, Plympton, Plymouth,
PL7 5EB*
☎ **(01752) 348425**
🖥 (01752) 344581
✉ elfordleigh@btinternet.com
📖 500
🏌 IC Roberts (01752) 348446
✍ J Nolan (01752) 348425
⛳ 18 L 5527 yds SSS 67
👥 U H–phone first SOC
££ £25 (£30)
⛳ 4 miles E of Plymouth, off
Plympton road
🏠 JH Taylor

Exeter G&CC (1895)

Countess Wear, Exeter, EX2 7AE
☎ **(01392) 874139**
🖥 (01392) 874139

✉ info@Exetergcc.co.uk
📖 850
🏌 KJ Ham (Golf
Mgr) (01392) 874639
✍ M Rowett (01392) 875028
⛳ 18 L 6008 yds SSS 69
👥 WD–U H WE–I H SOC–Thurs
££ On application
⛳ 4 miles SE of Exeter
🏠 James Braid

Fingle Glen (1992)

Tedburn St Mary, Exeter, EX6 6AF
☎ **(01647) 61817**
🖥 (01647) 61135
📖 450
🏌 P Miliffe
✍ S Gould
⛳ 9 L 2466 yds SSS 63
👥 U SOC
££ 18 holes–£11.50 (£15) 9 holes–£8
(£9)
⛳ 5 miles W of Exeter on A30
⊕ Driving range

Hartland Forest (1980)

*Hartland Forest Golf Parc, Woolsery,
EX39 5RA*
☎ **(01237) 431442**
🖥 (01237) 431734
📖 90
⛳ 18 L 4923 yds Par 70 SSS 68
👥 U SOC
££ £15
⛳ 6 miles S of Clovelly, off A39
🏠 Alan Cartwright

Hele Park Golf Centre (1993)

Pay and play
*Ashburton Road, Newton Abbot,
TQ12 6JN*
☎ **(01626) 336060**
🖥 (01626) 332661
✉ info@heleparkgolf.co.uk
📖 300
🏌 AJ Taylor (01626) 336060
✍ J Langmead
⛳ 9 L 2584 yds SSS 65
👥 U SOC
££ £16 (£18)
⛳ W of Newton Abbot on A383
⊕ Driving range
🏠 M Craig
■ www.heleparkgolf.co.uk

Holsworthy (1937)

Kilatree, Holsworthy, EX22 6LP
☎ **(01409) 253177**
🖥 (01409) 253177
✉ hgcsecretary@aol.com
📖 450
🏌 B Megson
✍ G Webb (01409) 254771
⛳ 18 L 6100 yds SSS 69
👥 WD–U Sun–U after 2.30pm
££ £25
⛳ 1 mile W of Holsworthy. 7 miles E
of Bude (A3072)

For list of abbreviations and key to symbols see page 649

Honiton (1896)

Middlehills, Honiton, EX14 9TR
- ☎ **(01404) 44422**
- 🖶 (01404) 46383
- 📖 800
- 🏌 BM Young
- ✎ A Cave (01404) 42943
- ⛳ 18 L 5902 yds Par 69 SSS 68
- 👥 U (recognised club member) SOC
- ££ £23 (£28)
- 🚗 2 miles S of Honiton

Hurdwick (1990)

Tavistock Hamlets, Tavistock, PL19 8PZ
- ☎ **(01822) 612746**
- 📖 175
- 🏌 Maj RW Cullen (Mgr)
- ⛳ 18 L 5335 yds Par 67
- 👥 U SOC
- ££ £15 (£15)
- 🚗 1 mile N of Tavistock, on Brentor Church road
- 🏠 Hawtree/Bartlett

Ilfracombe (1892)

Hele Bay, Ilfracombe, EX34 9RT
- ☎ **(01271) 862176**
- 🖶 (01271) 867731
- 📧 ilfracombe.golfclub@virgin.net
- 📖 500
- 🏌 B Wright
- ✎ M Davies (01271) 863328
- ⛳ 18 L 5795 yds Par 69 SSS 68
- 👥 WD–H SOC WE/BH–U after 10am –NA 12–1pm
- ££ £20 (£25)
- 🚗 2 miles E of Ilfracombe, towards Combe Martin
- ⊕ Driving range
- 🏠 TK Weir
- ■ www.ilfracombegolfclub.com

Libbaton (1990)

High Bickington, Umberleigh, EX37 9BS
- ☎ **(01769) 560269**
- 📖 475
- 🏌 JH Brough
- ✎ Sarah Burnell
- ⛳ 18 L 6494 yds SSS 72
- 👥 U SOC
- ££ £18 (£22)
- 🚗 1 mile S of High Bickington on B3217. M5 Junction 27
- ⊕ Floodlit driving range

Manor House Hotel (1929)

Moretonhampstead, TQ13 8RE
- ☎ **(01647) 440998**
- 🖶 (01647) 440961
- 📧 manortee@aol.com
- 📖 250
- 🏌 R Lewis
- ✎ R Lewis
- ⛳ 18 L 6016 yds SSS 69 Par 3 course
- 👥 U H SOC
- ££ £30 (£35)
- 🚗 15 miles SW of Exeter on B3212. M5 Junction 31
- 🏠 JF Abercromby

Mortehoe & Woolacombe (1992)

Easewell, Mortehoe, Ilfracombe, EX34 7EH
- ☎ **(01271) 870225**
- 📖 225
- 🏌 M Wilkinson (01271) 870745
- ⛳ 9 L 4852 yds SSS 63
- 👥 U
- ££ 9 holes–£7 18 holes–£12
- 🚗 E of Mortehoe village
- 🏠 David Hoare

Newton Abbot (Stover) (1930)

Newton Abbot, TQ12 6QQ
- ☎ **(01626) 352460**
- 🖶 (01626) 330210
- 📖 750
- 🏌 GW Rees
- ✎ M Craig (01626) 362078
- ⛳ 18 L 5764 yds SSS 68
- 👥 U H SOC
- ££ D–£30 (£28)
- 🚗 3 miles N of Newton Abbot on A382. A38 Drumbridges Junction
- 🏠 James Braid
- ■ www.stovergolfclub.com

Okehampton (1913)

Okehampton, EX20 1EF
- ☎ **(01837) 52113**
- 🖶 (01837) 52734
- 📧 okehamptongc@btconnect.com
- 📖 500
- 🏌 C Yeo (Admin)
- ✎ A Moon (01837) 53541
- ⛳ 18 L 5268 yds SSS 65
- 👥 H SOC
- ££ On application
- 🚗 S boundary of Okehampton
- 🏠 JH Taylor
- ■ www.okehamptongc.co.uk

Padbrook Park (1992)

Pay and play
Cullompton, EX15 1RU
- ☎ **(01884) 38286**
- 🖶 (01884) 34359
- 📖 450
- 🏌 R Chard (Mgr)
- ✎ S Adwick (01884) 820805
- ⛳ 9 L 6108 yds SSS 70
- 👥 U SOC–WD
- ££ 18 holes–£12 (£18). 9 holes–£10 (£15)
- 🚗 10 miles E of Exeter. M5 Junction 28, 1 mile
- 🏠 Bob Sandow

Portmore Golf Park (1993)

Pay and play
Landkey Road, Barnstaple, EX32 9LB
- ☎ **(01271) 378378**
- 🖶 (01271) 378378
- 📖 400
- 🏌 C Webber
- ✎ S Gould, D Everett
- ⛳ 9 L 3048 yds Par 70 9 hole Par 3 course

- 👥 U
- ££ 9 holes–£10. 18 holes–£12 Par 3 course–£7–£10
- 🚗 1 mile E of Barnstaple, off A361
- ⊕ Floodlit driving range
- 🏠 Hawtree/Cox

Royal North Devon (1864)

Golf Links Road, Westward Ho!, EX39 1HD
- ☎ **(01237) 473824 (Clubhouse)**
- 🖶 (01237) 423456
- 📧 info@royalnorthdevongolfclub.co.uk
- 📖 1100
- 🏌 R Fowler (01237) 473817
- ✎ R Herring (01237) 477598
- ⛳ 18 L 6665 yds SSS 72
- 👥 U H
- ££ £32 D–£38 (£38 D–£42)
- 🚗 2 miles N of Bideford (A39)
- ⊕ Golf Museum
- 🏠 Old Tom Morris
- ■ www.royalnorthdevongolfclub.co.uk

Saunton (1897)

Saunton, Braunton, EX33 1LG
- ☎ **(01271) 812436**
- 🖶 (01271) 814241
- 📖 1450
- 🏌 TC Reynolds
- ✎ AT Mackenzie (01271) 812013
- ⛳ East 18 L 6729 yds SSS 72 West 18 L 6403 yds SSS 71
- 👥 U H SOC
- ££ £45 D–£65 inc lunch
- 🚗 6 miles W of Barnstaple
- 🏠 Fowler/Pennink
- ■ www.sauntongolf.co.uk

Sidmouth (1889)

Cotmaton Road, Sidmouth, EX10 8SX
- ☎ **(01395) 513023**
- 🖶 (01395) 514661
- 📖 850
- 🏌 IM Smith (01395) 513451
- ✎ G Tapper (01395) 516407
- ⛳ 18 L 5068 yds SSS 65
- 👥 U SOC
- ££ £20 (£20)
- 🚗 1/2 mile W of Sidmouth. 12 miles SE of M5 Junction 30
- 🏠 JH Taylor

Sparkwell (1993)

Pay and play
Sparkwell, Plymouth, PL7 5DF
- ☎ **(01752) 837219**
- 🖶 (01752) 837219
- 📖 108
- 🏌 G Adamson
- ✎ None
- ⛳ 9 L 5772 yds SSS 68
- 👥 U SOC
- ££ 18 holes–£10 (£12) 9 holes–£6 (£7)
- 🚗 8 miles NE of Plymouth. A38 Plympton Junction
- ⊕ 9 hole pitch & putt
- 🏠 J Gabb

Staddon Heights　(1904)
Plymstock, Plymouth, PL9 9SP
- ☎ **(01752) 402475**
- 🖷 (01752) 401998
- 📖 740
- ⚐ RW Brown
- ✓ I Marshall (01752) 492630
- ⮞ 18 L 5845 yds SSS 70
- 👤 WE–H SOC–WD
- ££ D–£18 (D–£22)
- ⛐ SE Plymouth, via Plymstock

Tavistock　(1890)
Down Road, Tavistock, PL19 9AQ
- ☎ **(01822) 612344**
- 🖷 (01822) 612344
- 📖 700
- ⚐ MJ O'Dowd
- ✓ D Rehaag (01822) 612316
- ⮞ 18 L 6250 yds SSS 70
- 👤 SOC–WD
- ££ £24 (£30)
- ⛐ Whitchurch Down

Teign Valley　(1995)
Christow, Exeter, EX6 7PA
- ☎ **(01647) 253026**
- 🖷 (01647) 253026
- ✉ welcome@teignvalleygolf.co.uk
- 📖 300
- ⚐ M Daniels
- ✓ S Amiet (01647) 253127
- ⮞ 18 L 5913 yds Par 70 SSS 68
- 👤 U SOC
- ££ £17 (£20)
- ⛐ SW of Exeter, via A38 (B3193)
- 🛈 Peter Nicholson

Teignmouth　(1924)
Exeter Road, Teignmouth, TQ14 9NY
- ☎ **(01626) 777070**
- 🖷 (01626) 777070
- 📖 900
- ⚐ W Hendry (01626) 777070
- ✓ P Ward (01626) 772894
- ⮞ 18 L 6227 yds SSS 69
- 👤 WD–H (recognised club member)
  WE–by appointment SOC–WD
- ££ £25 (£27.50)
- ⛐ 2 miles N of Teignmouth on B3192
- 🛈 Dr A Mackenzie

Thurlestone　(1897)
Thurlestone, Kingsbridge, TQ7 3NZ
- ☎ **(01548) 560405**
- 🖷 (01548) 562149
- 📖 770
- ⚐ JR Scott (01548) 560405
- ✓ P Laugher (01548) 560715
- ⮞ 18 L 6340 yds Par 71 SSS 70
- 👤 I or H
- ££ £32 W–£115
- ⛐ 5 miles W of Kingsbridge, off A379
- 🛈 HS Colt
- ■ www.thurlestonegc.co.uk

Tiverton　(1932)
Post Hill, Tiverton, EX16 4NE
- ☎ **(01884) 252114 (Clubhouse)**

- 🖷 (01884) 251607
- ✉ tivertongolfclub@lineone.net
- 📖 600 130(L) 45(J)
- ⚐ R Jessop (Sec/Mgr)
  (01884) 252187
- ✓ M Hawton (01884) 254836
- ⮞ 18 L 6236 yds SSS 70
- 👤 H
- ££ On application
- ⛐ 5 miles W of M5 Junction 27. 1¹/₂ miles E of Tiverton on B3391
- 🛈 Braid/Cotton

Torquay　(1909)
Petitor Road, St Marychurch, Torquay, TQ1 4QF
- ☎ **(01803) 327471**
- 🖷 (01803) 316116
- ✉ torquaygolfclub@skynow.net
- 📖 800
- ⚐ BG Long (01803) 314591
- ✓ M Ruth (01803) 329113
- ⮞ 18 L 6198 yds Par 69 SSS 69
- 👤 H SOC
- ££ £25 (£30)
- ⛐ 2 miles N of Torquay
- ■ www.torquaygolfclub.org.uk

Torrington　(1895)
Weare Trees, Torrington, EX38 7EZ
- ☎ **(01805) 622229**
- 🖷 (01805) 623878
- 📖 400
- ⚐ Mrs JM Cudmore
- ✓ None
- ⮞ 9 L 4423 yds Par 64 SSS 63
- 👤 U exc Sun am–NA SOC–Tues/Wed am
- ££ D–£12
- ⛐ 1 mile W of Torrington on Weare Giffard road

Warren　(1892)
Dawlish Warren, EX7 0NF
- ☎ **(01626) 862255**
- 🖷 (01626) 888005
- ✉ secretary@dwgc.co.uk
- 📖 600
- ⚐ T Aggett
- ✓ D Prowse (01626) 864002
- ⮞ 18 L 5912 yds Par 69 SSS 68
- 👤 H SOC–Mon/Wed/Fri
- ££ £22 (£25)
- ⛐ 1¹/₂ miles E of Dawlish. M5 Junction 30
- 🛈 James Braid

Waterbridge　(1992)
Pay and play
Down St Mary, Crediton, EX17 5LG
- ☎ **(01363) 85111**
- ⚐ G & A Wren (Props)
- ✓ D Ridyard (01837) 83406
- ⮞ 9 L 1955 yds Par 32
- 👤 U
- ££ 18 holes–£10 (£12) 9 holes–£6 (£7)
- ⛐ 1 mile N of Copplestone on A337
- 🛈 David Taylor
- ■ www.waterbridge.business.co.uk

Woodbury Park　(1992)
Woodbury Castle, Woodbury, EX5 1JJ
- ☎ **(01395) 233500**
- 🖷 (01395) 233384
- 📖 720
- ⚐ A Richards (Mgr)
- ✓ A Richards
- ⮞ 18 L 6870 yds SSS 73
  9 L 4582 yds SSS 62
- 👤 U H
- ££ 18 hole:£30 (£40). 9 hole:£11 (£12)
- ⛐ 10 miles E of Exeter on A3052. M5 Junction 30, 6 miles
- ⊕ Driving range
- 🛈 J Hamilton Stutt

Wrangaton　(1895)
Golf Links Road, Wrangaton, South Brent, TQ10 9HJ
- ☎ **(01364) 73229**
- 🖷 (01364) 73229
- 📖 600
- ⚐ G Williams (01364) 73229
- ✓ G Richards (01364) 72161
- ⮞ 18 L 6083 yds SSS 69
- 👤 U SOC
- ££ £20
- ⛐ Dartmoor, 3 miles E of Ivybridge
- 🛈 Donald Steel

Yelverton　(1904)
Golf Links Road, Yelverton, PL20 6BN
- ☎ **(01822) 852824**
- 🖷 (01822) 854869
- ✉ secretary@yelvertongc.co.uk
- 📖 600
- ⚐ SM Barnes (01822) 852824
- ✓ T McSherry (01822) 853593
- ⮞ 18 L 6353 yds Par 71 SSS 71
- 👤 H SOC
- ££ D–£30 (£40)
- ⛐ 6 miles N of Plymouth on A386
- 🛈 Herbert Fowler

Dorset

The Ashley Wood　(1896)
Wimborne Road, Blandford Forum, DT11 9HN
- ☎ **(01258) 452253**
- 🖷 (01258) 450590
- 📖 670
- ⚐ P Bodle
- ✓ J Shimmons
- ⮞ 18 L 6270 yds Par 70 SSS 70
- 👤 WD–U WE–H after 1pm
- ££ Phone in advance
- ⛐ 1¹/₂ miles SE of Blandford on B3082
- 🛈 Patrick Tallack

Bridport & West Dorset (1891)
Burton Road, Bridport, DT6 4PS
- ☎ **(01308) 421095/422597**
- 📖 550
- ⚐ PJ Ridler (01308) 421095
- ✓ D Parsons (01308) 421491

---

18 L 5860 yds Par 71 SSS 68
WD/Sat–U after 9.30am Sun–U after 1pm SOC
££ £22. After noon–£16
1 mile E of A35 Bridport by-pass on B3157
Driving range
9 hole pitch & putt course (Summer).
F Hawtree

Broadstone (1898)

Wentworth Drive, Broadstone, BH18 8DQ
☎ (01202) 692595
(01202) 642520
admin@broadstonegolfclub.com
650
C Robinson (01202) 642521
N Tokely (01202) 692835
18 L 6315 yds SSS 70
WD–H from 9.30–11.30am and 2–4pm WE/BH–restricted SOC–WD
££ £35 (£55)
4 miles N of Poole, off A349
Dunn(1898)/Colt(1920)
www.broadstonegolfclub.com

Bulbury Woods (1989)

Bulbury Lane, Lytchett Minster, Poole, BH16 6EP
☎ (01929) 459574
(01929) 459000
enquiries@bulbury-woods.co.uk
400
D Adams
18 L 6002 yds Par 71 SSS 69
U SOC–WD
££ £15 (£20)
3 miles NW of Poole, off A35
www.bulbury-woods.co.uk

Came Down (1896)

Came Down, Dorchester, DT2 8NR
☎ (01305) 813494
(01305) 813494
700
R Kelly (Mgr) (01305) 813494
N Rodgers (01305) 812670
18 L 6244 yds SSS 71
H Sun am–NA SOC
££ £24 (£28)
2 miles S of Dorchester on A354
Taylor/Colt

Canford Magna

Knighton Lane, Wimborne, BH21 3AS
☎ (01202) 592552
(01202) 592550
1000
T Smith (Mgr) (01202) 592505
M Cummins (01202) 591212
Parkland 18 L 6495 yds Par 71 SSS 71
Riverside 18 L 6214 yds Par 70 SSS 70
Knighton 9 L 1377 yds Par 27
££ £7–£25
2 miles E of Wimborne on A341

Driving range. Golf Academy. 6 holes pitch & putt course
Swan/Smith
www.canfordmagnagc.co.uk

Canford School

Canford School, Wimborne, BH21 3AD
☎ (01202) 841254
(01202) 881009
360
M Burley (Mgr)
9 L 5918 yds SSS 68
M SOC
££ £12
1 mile SE of Wimborne, off A341
P Boult

Charminster (1998)

Proprietary
Wolfedale Golf Course, Charminster, Dorchester, DT2 7SG
☎ (01305) 260186
(01305) 261376
140
D Cox (Prop/Mgr) (01305) 260186
T Lovegrove (01305) 260186
18 L 5467 yds Par 69 SSS 67
U
££ £11 (£11)
2 miles N of Dorchester

Chedington Court (1991)

South Perrott, Beaminster, DT8 3HU
☎ (01935) 891413
(01935) 891217
450
D Astill (Man Dir)
S Cronin
18 L 5950 yds SSS 70
U SOC
££ £16 (£20)
4 miles SE of Crewkerne on A356
Chapman/Hemstock/Astill

Christchurch (1977)

Pay and play
Riverside Avenue, Bournemouth, BH7 7ES
☎ (01202) 436436 (Bookings)
320
ME Harvey (01202) 436412
L Moxon
18 L 6277 yds course
9 hole short course
U SOC
££ 18 hole:£14.50 (£17.50) 9 hole:£10 (£12)
Bournemouth/Christchurch boundary
Driving range

Crane Valley (1992)

The Clubhouse, Verwood, BH31 7LE
☎ (01202) 814088
(01202) 813407
600
A Blackwell (Gen Mgr)
J Ranson
18 L 6421 yds Par 72 SSS 71
9 L 2030 yds Par 33 SSS 60
H SOC 9 hole–U
££ 18 hole:£25 (£35) 9 hole:£5.50 (£6.50)

Nr Ringwood, on B3081 Verwood–Cranborne road
Floodlit driving range
Donald Steel

The Dorset G&CC (1978)

Bere Regis, Wareham, BH20 7NT
☎ (01929) 472244
(01929) 471294
850
G Packer (Gen Mgr)
D Honan (Golf Dir)
Lakeland 18 L 7027 yds SSS 72; Woodland 18 L 4887 yds SSS 64
U SOC
££ Lakeland–£30 (£35) Woodland–£21 (£23)
5 miles S of Bere Regis, off Wool road
Driving range
Martin Hawtree
www.dorsetgolfresort.com

Dudsbury (1992)

Proprietary
64 Christchurch Road, Ferndown, BH22 8ST
☎ (01202) 593499
(01202) 594555
golf@dudsbury.demon.co.uk
GH Legg
K Spurgeon (01202) 594488
18 L 6903 yds Par 71 SSS 73
U
££ £35 (£40)
3 miles N of Bournemouth (B3073)
Driving range. Academy course
Donald Steel
www.thedudsbury.co.uk

Ferndown (1923)

119 Golf Links Road, Ferndown, BH22 8BU
☎ (01202) 874602
(01202) 873926
700
MC Davies (Mgr) (01202) 874602
IAB Parker (01202) 873825
18 L 6452 yds SSS 71
9 L 5604 yds SSS 68
WD–I H after 9.30am SOC–Tues & Fri
££ Old £45 (£60) President's £18 (£20)
6 miles N of Bournemouth
Harold Hilton

Ferndown Forest (1993)

Forest Links Road, Ferndown, BH22 9QE
☎ (01202) 876096
(01202) 894095
400
M Dodd
M Dodd (01202) 894990
18 L 5200 yds Par 68 SSS 65
U SOC
££ £11 (£13)
5 miles N of Bournemouth. N of Ferndown Bypass
Floodlit driving range
Hunt/Grafham

● www.ferndown_forest_leisure
.co.uk

Halstock (1988)
Pay and play
Common Lane, Halstock, BA22 9SF
☎ (01935) 891689
📠 (01935) 891839
📖 200
🏌 LR Church (Mgr)
🏳 18 L 4481 yds Par 66 SSS 63
👥 U SOC
£€ £11 (£13)
⛳ 6 miles S of Yeovil, off A37
⊕ Driving range

Highcliffe Castle (1913)
107 Lymington Road, Highcliffe-on-Sea,
Christchurch, BH23 4LA
☎ (01425) 272210/272953
📠 (01425) 272210
📖 350 100(L) 50(J)
🏌 G Fisher (01425) 272210
🏳 18 L 4776 yds Par 64 SSS 63
👥 H SOC
£€ £25.50 (£35.50)
⛳ 8 miles E of Bournemouth

Isle of Purbeck (1892)
Studland, BH19 3AB
☎ (01929) 450361
📠 (01929) 450501
📖 400
🏌 Mrs J Robinson (Man Dir)
✓ I Brake (01929) 450354
🏳 18 L 6295 yds SSS 70
   9 L 2007 yds SSS 30
👥 U SOC
£€ £35 D–£45 (£40 D–£47.50)
⛳ 3 miles N of Swanage on B3351.
   Ferry from Sandbanks to Studland
🏛 HS Colt
● www.purbeckgolf.co.uk

Knighton Heath (1976)
Francis Avenue, West Howe,
Bournemouth, BH11 8NX
☎ (01202) 572633
📠 (01202) 590774
📧 khgc@btinternet.com
📖 700
🏌 R Bestwick
✓ P Brown (01202) 578275
🏳 18 L 6065 yds SSS 69
👥 WD–H after 9.30am WE–M
£€ On application
⛳ 3 miles N of Poole, at junction of
   A348/A3049

Lyme Regis (1893)
Timber Hill, Lyme Regis, DT7 3HQ
☎ (01297) 442043 (Clubhouse)
📖 750
🏌 B Wheeler (01297) 442963
✓ D Driver (01297) 443822
🏳 18 L 6283 yds SSS 70
👥 H WD–U after 9.30am (2.30pm
   Thurs) Sun–U after noon SOC
£€ £25 After 2pm–£20
⛳ Between Lyme Regis and
   Charmouth, off A3502/A35

Lyons Gate (1991)
Proprietary
Lyons Gate Farm, Lyons Gate,
Dorchester, DT2 7AZ
☎ (01300) 345239
📖 80
🏌 NW Pires (01300) 345239
🏳 9 L 3834 yds Par 60 SSS 60
👥 U SOC
£€ 18 holes–£10 (£11) 9 holes–£6 (£7)
⛳ Middle Marsh, 12 miles N of
   Dorchester (A352)
🏛 Ken Abel
● www.lyonsgategolfclub.co.uk

Meyrick Park (1890)
Pay and play
Central Drive, Meyrick Park,
Bournemouth, BH2 6LH
☎ (01202) 786000,
   (01202) 786040 (Bookings)
📧 meyrickpark.lodge@clubhaus.com
📖 400
✓ D Miles
🏳 18 L 5637 yds Par 69
👥 U
£€ £17 (£20)
⛳ ½mile behind Town Hall,
   Bournemouth
🏛 Dunn(1894)/Colt(1925)
● www.clubhaus.com

Moors Valley (1988)
Public
Horton Road, Ringwood, BH24 2ET
☎ (01425) 480448
📠 (01425) 480799
📖 310
🏌 M Dean
✓ M Torrens (01425) 479776
🏳 18 L 6270 yds SSS 70
   4-hole short course
👥 U
£€ On application
⛳ 4 miles SW of Ringwood, off A31
🏛 Martin Hawtree

Parkstone (1910)
Links Road, Parkstone, Poole,
BH14 9QS
☎ (01202) 707138
📠 (01202) 706027
📖 500 160(L) 75(J)
🏌 Christine Radford (Gen Mgr)
✓ M Thompson (01202) 708092
🏳 18 L 6250 yds SSS 70
👥 H WD–NA before 9.38am and
   12.30–2.10pm WE–NA before
   9.45am and 12.30–2.30pm
£€ £35 D–£50 (£45 D–£60)
⛳ 3 miles W of Bournemouth, off
   A35
⊕ Practice range
🏛 W Park Jr/Braid

Parley Court
Proprietary
Parley Green Lane, Hurn, Christchurch,
BH23 6BB
☎ (01202) 591600
📧 info@parleygolf.co.uk

📖 200
🏌 Mrs SD Mitchell
🏳 9 L 2469 yds SSS 64
👥 U SOC
£€ 18 holes–£8.50 (£9.50). 9 holes–£6
   (£7)
⛳ Nr Bournemouth Airport (B3073)
● www.parleygolf.co.uk

Queens Park (Bournemouth) (1905)
Public
Queens Park West Drive, Queens Park,
Bournemouth, BH8 9BY
☎ (01202) 302611,
   (01202) 396198 (Bookings)
📠 (01202) 302611
📧 dgibb@qbbgc.fsnet.co.uk
📖 350
🏌 Mrs DJ Gibb (01202) 302611
✓ R Hill (01202) 396817
🏳 18 L 6090 yds SSS 69
👥 U SOC
£€ £15 (£18)
⛳ 2 miles NE of Bournemouth

Riversmeet Par Three
Stony Lane South, Christchurch,
BH23 1HW
☎ (01202) 477987
📠 (01202) 470853
📖 250
🏌 N Williams
🏳 18 L 1650 yds Par 54
👥 U
£€ On application
⛳ 2 miles W of Bournemouth

Sherborne (1894)
Higher Clatcombe, Sherborne, DT9 4RN
☎ (01935) 812274
📠 (01935) 814218
📖 700
🏌 P Gamble (01935) 814431
✓ A Tresidder (01935) 812274
🏳 18 L 5882 yds Par 70 SSS 68
👥 H
£€ £22 (£36)
⛳ 1 mile N of Sherborne, off B3145
🏛 James Braid

Solent Meads Par Three
Public
Rolls Drive, Hengistbury
Head, Bournemouth
☎ (01202) 420795
🏳 18 L 2325 yds Par 54
👥 U
£€ On application
⛳ Hengistbury Head, S of
   Christchurch
⊕ Driving range

Sturminster Marshall (1992)
Moor Lane, Sturminster Marshall,
BH21 4AH
☎ (01258) 858444
📠 (01258) 858262
📖 490
🏌 DR Holdsworth

√ G Howell
ℙ 9 L 5026 yds SSS 65
👭 U SOC
££ 18 holes–£11. 9 holes–£8
🚗 8 miles N of Poole on A350
🏠 John Sharkey

Wareham (1908)

Sandford Road, Wareham, BH20 4DH
☎ **(01929) 554147/557995**
🖳 (01929) 557993
📖 550
🏌 G Prince
ℙ 18 L 5753 yds SSS 68
👭 WD–after 9.30am WE–after 1pm SOC–WD
££ £22 D–£28 (£25)
🚗 N of Wareham on A351
🏠 C Whitcombe
■ www.warehamgolfclub.com

Weymouth (1909)

Links Road, Weymouth, DT4 0PF
☎ **(01305) 773981**
🖳 (01305) 788029
✉ weymouthgolfclub@aol.com
📖 750
🏌 BR Chatham
√ D Lochrie (01305) 773997
ℙ 18 L 5981 yds Par 70 SSS 69
👭 H SOC–WD
££ £24 (£30)
🚗 1 mile from town centre (A354), off Manor roundabout
🏠 Braid/Hamilton Stutt
■ www.weymouthgolfclub.co.uk

Durham

Barnard Castle (1898)

Harmire Road, Barnard Castle, DL12 8QN
☎ **(01833) 638355**
🖳 (01833) 695551
📖 700
🏌 WC Raine
√ D Pearce (01833) 631980
ℙ 18 L 6406 yds SSS 71
👭 U SOC
££ £20 D–£26 (£27 D–£32)
🚗 N boundary of Barnard Castle on B6278
■ www.barnardcastlegolfclub.org.uk

Beamish Park (1950)

Beamish, Stanley, DH9 0RH
☎ **(0191) 370 1382**
🖳 (0191) 370 2937
📖 560
🏌 G Cushlow (0191) 370 1382
√ C Cole (0191) 370 1984
ℙ 18 L 6205 yds SSS 70
👭 WD/Sat–U before 4pm Sun–NA SOC
££ £16 (£24)
🚗 Beamish, nr Stanley
🏠 Henry Cotton

Billingham (1967)

Sandy Lane, Billingham, TS22 5NA
☎ **(01642) 554494/533816**
🖳 (01642) 533816
📖 850
✉ (01642) 533816
√ M Ure (01642) 557060
ℙ 18 L 6391 yds SSS 70
👭 WD–H after 9am WE/BH–H after 10am SOC
££ D–£25 (£40)
🚗 W boundary of Billingham by A19, E of bypass
🏠 Frank Pennink

Bishop Auckland (1894)

High Plains, Durham Road, Bishop Auckland, DL14 8DL
☎ **(01388) 602198**
🖳 (01388) 607005
✉ enquiries@bagc.co.uk
📖 860
🏌 A Milne (01388) 663648
√ D Skiffington (01388) 661618
ℙ 18 L 6420 yds SSS 70
👭 H (closed Good Friday and Christmas Day)
££ £22 D–£26 (£28)
🚗 ½ mile NE of Bishop Auckland
🏠 James Kay
■ www.bagc.co.uk

Blackwell Grange (1930)

Briar Close, Blackwell, Darlington, DL3 8QX
☎ **(01325) 464464**
🖳 (01325) 464458
✉ secretary@blackwell-grange.demon.co.uk
📖 700
🏌 PB Burkill (Hon) (01325) 464458
√ J Furby (01325) 462088
ℙ 18 L 5621 yds Par 68 SSS 67
👭 U exc Wed 11am–2.30pm–NA Sat–booking req Sun–restricted SOC
££ £20 D–£25 (£30)
🚗 1 mile S of Darlington on A66
🏠 Frank Pennink

Brancepeth Castle (1924)

Brancepeth Village, Durham, DH7 8EA
☎ **(0191) 378 0075**
🖳 (0191) 378 3835
📖 768 118(L) 74(J)
🏌 B Cullen
√ D Howdon (0191) 378 0183
ℙ 18 L 6400 yds SSS 70
👭 SOC–WD WE–NA
££ £30 (£35)
🚗 4 miles W of Durham on A690
🏠 HS Colt
■ www.brancepeth-castle-golf.co.uk

Castle Eden & Peterlee (1927)

Castle Eden, Hartlepool, TS27 4SS
☎ **(01429) 836220**
📖 650
🏌 D Livingston (01429) 836510

√ P Jackson (01429) 836689
ℙ 18 L 6262 yds SSS 70
👭 U
££ £24 (£34)
🚗 2 miles S of Peterlee
🏠 Henry Cotton
■ www.ceden-golf.co.uk

Chester-Le-Street (1908)

Lumley Park, Chester-Le-Street, DH3 4NS
☎ **(0191) 388 3218**
🖳 (0191) 388 1220
📖 435 130(L) 90(J)
🏌 B Forster
√ D Fletcher (0191) 389 0157
ℙ 18 L 6437 yds SSS 71
👭 WD–H after 9.30am –NA 12–1pm WE–NA before 10.30am or 12–2pm
££ £22 (£27.50)
🚗 E of Chester-Le-Street
🏠 JH Taylor

Consett & District (1911)

Elmfield Road, Consett, DH8 5NN
☎ **(01207) 502186**
🖳 (01207) 505060
📖 650
🏌 IB Murray (01207) 529324
√ J Ord (01207) 580210
ℙ 18 L 6020 yds SSS 69
👭 WD–U SOC–exc Sat
££ £18 (£26)
🚗 14 miles N of Durham on A691
🏠 Harry Vardon

Crook (1919)

Low Job's Hill, Crook, DL15 9AA
☎ **(01388) 762429/767926**
📖 450
🏌 JW Laing
√ C Dilley (01388) 768145
ℙ 18 L 6102 yds SSS 69
👭 U SOC
££ From £12
🚗 ½ mile E of Crook (A689)

Darlington (1908)

Haughton Grange, Darlington, DL1 3JD
☎ **(01325) 355324**
🖳 (01325) 488126
✉ darlington.golfclub@virgin.net
📖 825
🏌 GW Storey (Fax 01325 480668)
√ C Dilley (01325) 484198
ℙ 18 L 6181 yds Par 70 SSS 69
👭 WD–U from 10am–12 & 2–4pm WE–M
££ £22 D–£31
🚗 Off Salters Lane, NE of Darlington
🏠 Dr Alistair Mackenzie

Dinsdale Spa (1906)

Middleton St George, Darlington, DL2 1DW
☎ **(01325) 332222**
🖳 (01325) 332222
📖 875
🏌 EP Davison (01325) 332297
√ N Metcalfe (01325) 332515

🏴 18 L 6090 yds Par 71 SSS 69
🏌 WD–U exc Tues–NA WE–M
££ D–£25
🚗 5 miles SE of Darlington

Durham City (1887)
Littleburn, Langley Moor, Durham, DH7 8HL
☎ **(0191) 378 0069**
📠 (0191) 378 4265
📖 750
🖊 LTI Wilson (0191) 386 4434
✔ S Corbally (0191) 378 0029
🏴 18 L 6326 yds SSS 70
🏌 WD–U SOC
££ £24 (£30)
🚗 1¹/₂ miles W of Durham, off A690
🏠 CC Stanton

Eaglescliffe (1914)
Yarm Road, Eaglescliffe, Stockton-on-Tees, TS16 0DQ
☎ **(01642) 780098 (Clubhouse)**
✉ egcsec@lineone.net
📖 835
🖊 MR Sample (01642) 780238
✔ G Bell (01642) 790122
🏴 18 L 6275 yds SSS 70
🏌 U SOC
££ £26 D–£35 (£36 D–£50)
🚗 3 miles S of Stockton-on-Tees on A135
🏠 Braid/Cotton
■ www.eaglescliffegolfclub.co.uk

Hartlepool (1906)
Hart Warren, Hartlepool, TS24 9QF
☎ **(01429) 274398**
📠 (01429) 274129
📖 700
🖊 LG Gordon (01429) 261723
✔ G Laidlaw (01429) 267473
🏴 18 L 6255 yds SSS 70
🏌 WD–U SOC
££ £26 (£38)
🚗 N boundary of Hartlepool
■ www.hartlepoolgolfclub.co.uk

High Throston (1997)
Hart Lane, Hartlepool, TS26 0UG
☎ **(01429) 275325**
📖 240
🖊 Mrs J Sturrock (01429) 268071
✔ None
🏴 18 L 6247 yds Par 71 SSS 70
🏌 U SOC
££ £16 (£19)
🚗 2 miles NW of Hartlepool (A179)
🏠 Jonathan Gaunt

Hobson Municipal (1978)
Public
Hobson, Burnopfield, Newcastle-upon-Tyne, NE16 6BZ
☎ **(01207) 271605**
🖊 RJ Handrick
✔ J Ord
🏴 18 L 6403 yds SSS 71
🏌 U SOC
££ £15 (£18)
🚗 Between Gateshead and Consett on A692

Knotty Hill Golf Centre (1992)
Pay and play
Sedgefield, Stockton-on-Tees, TS21 2BB
☎ **(01740) 620320**
📠 (01740) 622227
✉ khgc21@btinternet.com
🖊 D Craggs (Mgr)
🏴 Princes 18 L 6577 yds Par 72 SSS 71
   Bishops 18 L 5886 yds Par 70
🏌 U SOC
££ £12 (£14)
🚗 1 mile N of Sedgefield on A177. A1(M) Junction 60, 2 miles
⊕ Floodlit driving range
🏠 Chris Stanton

Mount Oswald (1924)
South Road, Durham City, DH1 3TQ
☎ **(0191) 386 7527**
📠 (0191) 386 0975
✉ info@mountoswald.co.uk
📖 120
🖊 N Galvin
🏴 18 L 5984 yds SSS 69
🏌 U SOC
££ £13.50 D–£22 (£16 D–£26)
🚗 SW of Durham on A177
■ www.mountoswald.co.uk

Norton (1989)
Pay and play
Junction Road, Norton, Stockton-on-Tees, TS20 1SU
☎ **(01642) 676385**
📠 (01642) 608467
🏴 18 L 5870 yds SSS 71
🏌 U SOC
££ £10 (£12)
🚗 1 mile E of A177 on B1274
🏠 Tim Harper

Oakleaf Golf Complex (1993)
Pay and play
School Aycliffe Lane, Newton Aycliffe, DL5 6QZ
☎ **(01325) 310820**
📠 (01325) 300873
🖊 A Bailey (Mgr) (01325) 300700
✔ A Waites
🏴 18 L 5821 yds SSS 68
🏌 WD–U WE–booking necessary
££ £7.80 (£8.85)
🚗 1 mile W of Aycliffe on A6072, from A68
⊕ Floodlit driving range

Ramside (1995)
Ramside Hall Hotel, Carrville, Durham, DH1 1TD
☎ **(0191) 386 9514**
📠 (0191) 386 9519
📖 300
🖊 TI Flowers
✔ R Lister (0191) 386 9514
🏴 27 holes:
   6217-6851 yds SSS 70-73
🏌 U SOC Soft spikes only

££ £28 (£35)
🚗 2 miles NE of Durham on A690. A1(M) Junction 62
⊕ Driving range. Golf Academy
🏠 J Gaunt

Roseberry Grange (1986)
Public
Grange Villa, Chester-Le-Street, DH2 3NF
☎ **(0191) 370 0670**
📠 (0191) 370 2047
📖 500
🖊 R McDermott (Hon)
✔ A Hartley (0191) 370 0660
🏴 18 L 5892 yds SSS 68
🏌 U SOC
££ £12 (£15)
🚗 3 miles W of Chester-Le-Street on A693
⊕ Driving range

Ryhope (1992)
Public
Leechmere Way, Hollycarrside, Ryhope, Sunderland SR2 0DH
☎ **(0191) 523 7333**
📠 (0191) 521 3811
📖 300
🖊 A Brown
✔ None
🏴 18 L 4601 yds SSS 65
🏌 U
££ £6 (£6)
🚗 2 miles SW of Sunderland, off A1018
🏠 Jonathan Gaunt

Seaham (1911)
Shrewsbury Street, Dawdon, Seaham, SR7 7RD
☎ **(0191) 581 2354**
📖 550
🖊 V Smith (0191) 581 1268
✔ G Jones (0191) 513 0837
🏴 18 L 5972 yds SSS 69
🏌 U SOC
££ On application
🚗 Dawdon, 2 miles NE of A19

Seaton Carew (1874)
Tees Road, Hartlepool, TS25 1DE
☎ **(01429) 266249/261040**
📖 650
🖊 PR Wilson (01429) 261473
✔ M Rogers (01429) 890660
🏴 Old 18 L 6613 yds SSS 72
   Brabazon 18 L 6855 yds SSS 73
🏌 U SOC
££ £34 (£44)
🚗 Hartlepool 2 miles
🏠 Dr A Mackenzie

South Moor (1923)
The Middles, Craghead, Stanley, DH9 6AG
☎ **(01207) 232848/283525**
📠 (01207) 284616
📖 650
🖊 B Davison (0191) 388 4523

✓ S Cowell (01207) 283525
🏃 18 L 6271 yds Par 72 SSS 70
👥 WD–H WE/BH–M SOC–WD/Sat
£€ £15 (£26)
🚗 6 miles W of Chester-le-Street
🏠 Dr A Mackenzie
■ www.south-moorgolfclub.co.uk

Stressholme (1976)
Public
Snipe Lane, Darlington, DL2 2SA
☎ (01325) 461002
🖥 (01325) 351826
✍ R Givens
✓ R Givens
🏃 18 L 6511 yds SSS 71
👥 U
£€ On application
🚗 2 miles S of Darlington on A66
⊕ Floodlit driving range

Woodham G&CC (1983)
Proprietary
Burnhill Way, Newton Aycliffe, DL5 4PN
☎ (01325) 320574
🖥 (01325) 315254
📖 610
✍ JD Jenkinson
✓ E Wilson (01325) 315257
🏃 18 L 6688 yds Par 73 SSS 72
👥 WD–U WE/BH–booking SOC
£€ £16.50 D–£22 (£26.50)
🚗 1 mile N of Newton Aycliffe. 6 miles from A1 (A689)
🏠 J Hamilton Stutt

The Wynyard Club
Wellington Drive, Wynyard Park, Billingham, TS22 5QJ
☎ (01740) 644399
🖥 (01740) 644599
✍ C Mounter (Golf Dir)
✓ C Mounter
🏃 18 holes Par 72 SSS 73
👥 M SOC–H
£€ On application
🚗 5 miles E of Sedgefield, between A1 and A19
⊕ Floodlit driving range. Golf Academy
🏠 Hawtree

Essex

Abridge G&CC (1964)
Epping Lane, Stapleford Tawney, RM4 1ST
☎ (01708) 688396
🖥 (01708) 688550
✉ lynne@abridgegolf.freeserve.co.uk
📖 650
✍ Miss L Payne (01708) 688396
✓ S Layton (01708) 688333
🏃 18 L 6703 yds SSS 72
👥 WD–H WE/BH–NA
£€ £30
🚗 Theydon Bois/Epping Stations 3 miles
🏠 Henry Cotton

Ballards Gore G&CC (1980)
Gore Road, Canewdon, Rochford, SS4 2DA
☎ (01702) 258917
🖥 (01702) 258571
📖 600
✍ A Hall
✓ R Emery
🏃 18 L 6874 yds SSS 73
👥 WD–U WE–M after 12.30pm (summer) 11.30am (winter) SOC
£€ £20 D–£25
🚗 1½ miles NE of Rochford

Basildon (1967)
Public
Clayhill Lane, Sparrow's Hearne, Basildon, SS16 5JP
☎ (01268) 533297
🖥 (01268) 533849
📖 300
✍ AM Burch
✓ M Oliver (01268) 533532
🏃 18 L 6236 yds Par 72 SSS 70
👥 U SOC
£€ £9.50 (£16)
🚗 1 mile S of Basildon, off A176 at Kingswood roundabout
■ www.basgolfclub.fsnet.co.uk

Belfairs (1926)
Public
Eastwood Road North, Leigh-on-Sea, SS9 4LR
☎ (01702) 525345 (Starter)
🏃 18 L 5802 yds SSS 68
👥 WD–U exc Thurs am. Booking necessary
£€ £11 (£16)
🚗 Between A127 and A13

Belhus Park G&CC (1972)
Pay and play
Belhus Park, South Ockendon, RM15 4QR
☎ (01708) 854260
📖 280
✍ J Cleary
✓ G Lunn
🏃 18 L 5188 yds SSS 68
👥 U
£€ £9.50 (£14)
🚗 1 mile N of A13/M25 Dartford Tunnel
⊕ Floodlit driving range

Bentley G&CC (1972)
Ongar Road, Brentwood, CM15 9SS
☎ (01277) 373179
🖥 (01277) 375097
📖 550
✍ JA Vivers
✓ N Garrett (01277) 372933
🏃 18 L 6709 yds SSS 72
👥 WD–UH WE–M after noon BH–after 11am SOC–WD
£€ £22 D–£30
🚗 18 miles E of London. M25 Junction 28, 3 miles

Benton Hall (1993)
Wickham Hill, Witham, CM8 3LH
☎ (01376) 502454
🖥 (01376) 521050
✉ g.barre@clubhaus.com
✍ D Reeves
✓ C Fairweather
🏃 18 L 6570 yds SSS 72
9 hole Par 3 course
👥 U SOC–WD
£€ £20–£30
🚗 Witham, 8 miles NE of Chelmsford, off A12
⊕ Driving range
🏠 Walker/Cox
■ www.clubhaus.com

Birch Grove (1970)
Layer Road, Colchester, CO2 0HS
☎ (01206) 734276
🖥 (01206) 734276
📖 280
✍ Mrs M Marston
🏃 9 L 4532 yds SSS 63
👥 U exc Sun–U after 1pm SOC
£€ D–£12
🚗 3 miles S of Colchester on B1026

Boyce Hill (1921)
Vicarage Hill, Benfleet, SS7 1PD
☎ (01268) 793625
🖥 (01268) 750497
✉ boycehill@hotmail.com
📖 700
✍ PD Keeble
✓ G Burroughs (01268) 752565
🏃 18 L 6003 yds SSS 69
👥 WD–UH WE/BH–MH SOC–Thurs only
£€ D–£25
🚗 4 miles W of Southend
🏠 James Braid

Braintree (1891)
Kings Lane, Stisted, Braintree, CM77 8DD
☎ (01376) 346079
🖥 (01376) 348677
📖 700
✍ N Wells
✓ T Parcell (01376) 343465
🏃 18 L 6228 yds SSS 70
👥 WD–U H SOC
£€ £25 (£42)
🚗 1 mile E of Braintree, off A120 towards Stisted
🏠 Hawtree

Braxted Park (1953)
Braxted Park, Witham, CM8 3EN
☎ (01376) 572372
🖥 (01621) 892840
📖 100
✍ Mrs V Keeble
✓ J Hudson
🏃 9 L 5704 yds Par 70 SSS 68
👥 WD–U SOC–WD
£€ 18 holes–£12.50 9 holes–£9.50
🚗 1½ miles off A12, nr Kelvedon
🏠 Sir Allen Clark

Bunsay Downs (1982)
Public
Little Baddow Road, Woodham Walter,
Maldon, CM9 6RW
- ☎ **(01245) 412648/412369**
- 🖉 MFL Durham
- 🏌 H Roblin (01245) 222648
- ⛳ 9 L 2913 yds SSS 68
  9 hole Par 3 course
- 👥 WD–U WE/BH–book in advance
  SOC–WD
- ££ On application
- 🚗 7 miles E of Chelmsford, off A414
- ⊕ Indoor driving range

Burnham-on-Crouch (1923)
Ferry Road, Creeksea, Burnham-on-Crouch, CM0 8PQ
- ☎ **(01621) 782282/785508**
- 🖥 (01621) 784489
- 📖 600
- 🖉 Mrs D Evers
- 🏌 S Cardy (01621) 782282
- ⛳ 18 L 6056 yds SSS 69
- 👥 WD–H
- ££ £26
- 🚗 1½ miles W of Burnham
- 🏠 D Swan

The Burstead (1995)
Tye Common Road, Little Burstead,
Billericay, CM12 9SS
- ☎ **(01277) 631171**
- 🖥 (01277) 632766
- 📖 800
- 🖉 L Mence
- 🏌 K Bridges
- ⛳ 18 L 6275 yds SSS 70
- 👥 WD–U H WE–NA pm SOC
- ££ £20
- 🚗 2 miles S of Billericay, off A176
- 🏠 Patrick Tallack

Canons Brook (1962)
Elizabeth Way, Harlow, CM19 5BE
- ☎ **(01279) 421482**
- 🖥 (01279) 626393
- 📖 700
- 🖉 Mrs SJ Langton
- 🏌 A McGinn (01279) 418357
- ⛳ 18 L 6763 yds SSS 73
- 👥 WD–U WE/BH–M
- ££ £25 D–30
- 🚗 25 miles N of London
- 🏠 Henry Cotton
- ■ www.canonsbrook.com

Castle Point (1988)
Public
Waterside Farm, Somnes Avenue,
Canvey Island, SS8 9FG
- ☎ **(01268) 510830**
- 📖 240
- 🖉 Mrs D Archer (01268) 696298
- 🏌 M Utteridge (01268) 510830
- ⛳ 18 L 6153 yds SSS 69
- 👥 U SOC
- ££ £9 (£13)
- 🚗 On A130 to Canvey Island, off A13
  Eastbound

- ⊕ Driving range
- 🏠 Golf Landscapes

Channels (1974)
Belsteads Farm Lane, Little Waltham,
Chelmsford, CM3 3PT
- ☎ **(01245) 440005**
- 🖥 (01245) 442032
- ✉ info@channelsgolf.co.uk
- 📖 650
- 🖉 AM Squire
- 🏌 IB Sinclair (01245) 441056
- ⛳ 18 L 6402 yds Par 71 SSS 71
  18 L 4779 yds Par 67 SSS 63
- 👥 WD–U WE–M SOC
- ££ £30 D–£45
- 🚗 3 miles NE of Chelmsford on A130
- ⊕ Pitch & putt course. Driving range
- ■ www.channelsgolf.co.uk

Chelmsford (1893)
Widford, Chelmsford, CM2 9AP
- ☎ **(01245) 256483**
- 🖥 (01245) 256483
- ✉ office@chelmsfordgc.sagehost
  .co.uk
- 📖 650
- 🖉 G Winckless (01245) 256483
- 🏌 M Welch (01245) 257079
- ⛳ 18 L 5981 yds SSS 69
- 👥 WD–H WE/BH–M SOC
- ££ £36 D–£46
- 🚗 Off A1016 at Widford roundabout
- 🏠 HS Colt
- ■ www.chelmsfordgc.co.uk

Chigwell (1925)
High Road, Chigwell, IG7 5BH
- ☎ **(020) 8500 2059**
- 🖥 (020) 8501 3410
- 📖 780
- 🖉 RH Danzey
- 🏌 R Beard (020) 8500 2384
- ⛳ 18 L 6279 yds SSS 70
- 👥 WD–H WE/BH–M
- ££ £35 D–£45
- 🚗 13 miles NE of London (A113)
- 🏠 Hawtree/Taylor

Chingford
158 Station Road, Chingford, London E4
- ☎ **(0208) 524 0788**
- 🖉 B Sinden
- 🏌 A Trainor
- ⛳ 18 L 6342 yds Par 71 SSS 70
- 👥 U
- ££ £11.70 (£15.30)

Clacton-on-Sea (1892)
West Road, Clacton-on-Sea, CO15 1AJ
- ☎ **(01255) 421919**
- 🖥 (01255) 424602
- ✉ clactongolfclub@btclick.com
- 📖 650
- 🖉 JH Wiggam (01255) 421919
- 🏌 SJ Levermore (01255) 426304
- ⛳ 18 L 6532 yds SSS 71
- 👥 H WE/BH–H after 11am SOC–WD
- ££ £20 (£30)
- 🚗 On Clacton sea front. 13 miles E of
  Colchester (A120)

Colchester (1907)
21 Braiswick, Colchester, CO4 5AU
- ☎ **(01206) 853396**
- 🖥 (01206) 852698
- ✉ colchester.golf@btinternet.com
- 📖 756
- 🖉 WM Beckett
- 🏌 M Angel (01206) 853920
- ⛳ 18 L 6347 yds SSS 70
- 👥 WD/WE–H BH–NA SOC
- ££ £30 D–£40 (£40)
- 🚗 ¾ mile NW of Colchester North
  Station, towards West Berholt on
  B1508
- 🏠 James Braid

Colne Valley (1991)
Station Road, Earls Colne, CO6 2LT
- ☎ **(01787) 224343**
- 🖥 (01787) 224126
- 📖 500
- 🖉 T Smith (01787) 224343
- 🏌 R Taylor (01787) 224233
- ⛳ 18 L 6301 yds SSS 70
- 👥 WD–U WE/BH–after 11am SOC
- ££ £25 (£30)
- 🚗 12 miles W of Colchester (A1124)
- 🏠 Howard Swann

Crondon Park (1994)
Proprietary
Stock Road, Stock, CM4 9DP
- ☎ **(01277) 841115**
- 🖥 (01277) 841356
- 📖 875
- 🖉 P Cranwell
- 🏌 P Barham (01277) 841887
- ⛳ 18 L 6585 yds SSS 71
  9 hole course
- 👥 WD–U WE–M SOC–WD
- ££ £20 (£30)
- 🚗 5 miles S of Chelmsford on B1007.
  M25 Junction 28
- ⊕ Driving range
- 🏠 Martin Gillett
- ■ www.crondon.com

Elsenham Golf Centre (1997)
Hall Road, Elsenham, Bishop's
Stortford, CM22 6DH
- ☎ **(01279) 812865**
- 🖥 (01279) 816970
- ✉ golfacad@compuserve.com
- 🖉 O McKenna (Prop)
- 🏌 O McKenna
- ⛳ 9 L 5854 yds Par 70
- 👥 U
- ££ 9 holes–£10 (£12) 18 holes–£14
  (£16)
- 🚗 Off M11, by Stansted Airport
- ⊕ Driving range
- ■ www.agcltd.co.uk

Essex G&CC (1990)
Earls Colne, Colchester, CO6 2NS
- ☎ **(01787) 224466**
- 🖥 (01787) 224410
- 📖 600
- 🖉 DJ Clark

✓ L Cocker
⚑ 18 L 6958 yds Par 73
9 L 2190 yds Par 34
👥 WD–U WE–U after 11am SOC
£€ £25 (£30)
🚗 2 miles N of A120 at Coggeshall on B1024
⊕ Floodlit driving range.
🏠 Reg Plumbridge
■ www.the-essex.co.uk

The Essex Golf Complex (1993)

Pay and play
Garon Park, Eastern Avenue, Southend-on-Sea, SS9 4PT
☎ (01702) 601701
🖥 (01702) 601033
📖 700
🖊 Mrs J Jacom
✓ G Jacom
⚑ 18 L 6237 yds SSS 70
9 hole Par 3 course
👥 U SOC
£€ £17 (£23)
🚗 E side of Southend-on-Sea. M25 Junction 29
⊕ Floodlit driving range
🏠 Walker/Cox

Fairlop Waters (1987)

Public
Forest Road, Barkingside, Ilford, IG6 3JA
☎ (020) 8500 9911
📖 135
🖊 L Quinn
✓ B Preston (0181) 501 1881
⚑ 18 L 6288 yds SSS 72
9 hole Par 3 course
👥 U
£€ £7.50 (£11)
🚗 2 miles from S end of M11, by Fairlop underground station
⊕ Driving range

Five Lakes Hotel G&CC (1974)

Colchester Road, Tolleshunt Knights, Maldon, CM9 8HX
☎ (01621) 868888 (Hotel),
(01621) 862307 (Bookings)
🖥 (01621) 869696
📖 600
🖊 N Popper
✓ G Carter (01621) 862326
⚑ Links 18 L 6250 yds SSS 70
Lakes 18 L 6765 yds SSS 72
👥 U BH–U after 1pm SOC
£€ Links £22 (£28). Lakes £29 (£38)
🚗 8 miles S of Colchester, off B1026
⊕ Driving range
🏠 Neil Coles

Forrester Park (1975)

Beckingham Road, Great Totham, Maldon, CM9 8EA
☎ (01621) 891406
🖥 (01621) 891406
📖 900

🖊 T Forrester-Muir
✓ G Pike (01621) 893456
⚑ 18 L 6073 yds SSS 69
👥 WD–U WE–NA before noon SOC–WD
£€ £19 (£21)
🚗 3 miles NE of Maldon on B1022
🏠 Everett/Forrester-Muir

Frinton (1895)

1 The Esplanade, Frinton-on-Sea, CO13 9EP
☎ (01255) 674618
🖥 (01255) 682450
✉ frintongolf@lineone.net
📖 850
🖊 Lt Col RW Attrill
✓ P Taggart (01255) 671618
⚑ 18 L 6259 yds SSS 70
9 L 2508 yds SSS 33
👥 18 hole: H WE/BH–NA before 11.30am SOC
£€ 18 hole: D–£30. 9 hole:£10
🚗 18 miles E of Colchester
🏠 W Park Jr/HS Colt
■ www.frintongolfclub.com

Gosfield Lake (1986)

The Manor House, Gosfield, Halstead, CO9 1SE
☎ (01787) 474747
🖥 (01787) 476044
✉ gosfieldlakegc@btconnect.com
📖 800
🖊 JA O'Shea (Sec/Mgr)
✓ R Wheeler (01787) 474488
⚑ Lakes 18 L 6756 yds Par 72 SSS 72
Meadows 9 L 4180 yds Par 66
👥 Lakes WD–H WE(pm)–H by arrangement SOC. Meadows–U
£€ Lakes £30 D–£35. Meadows £15 D–£18
🚗 7 miles N of Braintree (A1017)
🏠 Sir H Cotton/Swann
■ www.gosfield-lake-golf-club.co.uk

Hainault Forest (1912)

Public
Romford Road, Chigwell Row, IG7 4QW
☎ (020) 8500 2131 (Caddy Master),
(020) 8500 2097 (Clubhouse)
📖 630
🖊 Mrs V Krinks (0181) 500 0385
✓ CS Hope (0181) 500 2131
⚑ No 1 18 L 5754 yds SSS 67
No 2 18 L 6600 yds SSS 71
👥 U
£€ On application
🚗 Hog Hill, Redbridge

Hanover G&CC (1991)

Owned privately
Hullbridge Road, Rayleigh, SS6 9QS
☎ (01702) 232377
🖥 (01702) 231811
📖 700
🖊 T Harrold
✓ A Blackburn
⚑ Georgian 18 L 6669 yds SSS 73
Regency 18 L 3700 yds SSS 58
👥 Georgian:WD–H WE–M SOC
Regency:U SOC

£€ Georgian £25 D–£35.
Regency £12.50 (£15)
🚗 3 miles NW of Southend
🏠 Reg Plumbridge

Hartswood (1967)

Pay and play
King George's Playing Fields, Brentwood, CM14 5AE
☎ (01277) 214830 (Bookings)
📖 270
🖊 D Mancey (01227) 218850
✓ S Cole (01277) 218714
⚑ 18 L 6192 yds SSS 70
👥 WD–U after 10am SOC
£€ £11 (£16)
🚗 E of Brentwood on A128

Harwich & Dovercourt (1906)

Station Road, Parkeston, Harwich, CO12 4NZ
☎ (01255) 503616
🖥 (01255) 503323
📖 400
🖊 AR Boddy
✓ None
⚑ 9 L 2950 yds SSS 69
👥 WD–H WE–M SOC
£€ £20
🚗 A120 to roundabout to Harwich Port, course entrance 20 yds on LHS

Ilford (1907)

291 Wanstead Park Road, Ilford, IG1 3TR
☎ (020) 8554 2930
🖥 (020) 8554 0822
📖 500
🖊 GH Smith
✓ S Dowsett (020) 8554 0094
⚑ 18 L 5299 yds SSS 66
👥 WD–U WE–phone Pro SOC
£€ £16 (£20)
🚗 S end of M11, off A406

Langdon Hills (1991)

Lower Dunton Road, Bulphan, RM14 3TY
☎ (01268) 548444/544300
🖥 (01268) 490084
📖 500
🖊 B Hardie
✓ T Moncur (01268) 544300
⚑ 27 holes:
Langdon 9 L 3132 yds Par 35
Bulphan 9 L 3372 yds Par 37
Horndon 9 L 3054 yds Par 36
👥 U SOC
£€ £14.85 (£19.75)
🚗 SW of Basildon between A127 and A13. M25 Junction 29, 8 miles
⊕ Floodlit driving range
🏠 MRM Sandow

Lexden Wood (1993)

Pay and play
Bakers Lane, Colchester, CO3 4AU
☎ (01206) 843333
🖥 (01206) 854775

📖 850
🏌 L Cole
◦ P Grice
▷ 18 L 5160 yds Par 67 SSS 65
👥 U SOC
££ £18 (£20)
⊶ NW of Colchester, off A12
⊕ Driving range. Pitch & putt course
🏠 Jon Johnson

Loughton (1981)
Public
Clays Lane, Debden Green, Loughton, IG10 2RZ
☎ **(020) 8502 2923**
📖 100
🏌 A Day
◦ R Layton
▷ 9 L 4735 yds SSS 63
👥 U–booking required SOC
££ 18 holes–£11.50 (£13.50)
    9 holes–£7 (£8)
⊶ M25 Junction 26

Maldon (1891)
Beeleigh Langford, Maldon, CM9 6LL
☎ **(01621) 853212**
📠 (01621) 855232
✉ maldon.golf@virgin.net
📖 380
🏌 GR Bezant
▷ 9 L 6253 yds Par 71 SSS 70
👥 WD–U H WE–M SOC
££ £15 D–£20
⊶ 3 miles NW of Maldon on B1019

Maylands (1936)
Harold Park, Romford, RM3 0AZ
☎ **(017083) 42055**
📠 (017083) 73080
📖 600
🏌 (017083) 73080
◦ JS Hopkin (017083) 46466
▷ 18 L 6351 yds SSS 70
👥 WD–H WE/BH–M SOC H
££ £25 (£40)
⊶ 2 miles E of Romford on A12. M25 Junction 28, 1 mile
🏠 HS Colt

Nazeing (1992)
Middle Street, Nazeing, EN9 2LW
☎ **(01992) 893798/893915**
📠 (01992) 893882
📖 350
🏌 J Speller (01992) 893915
◦ R Green (01992) 893798
▷ 18 L 6598 yds SSS 71
👥 WD–H WE/BH–H after 11am SOC
££ £20 (£28)
⊶ 3 miles SW of Harlow. M11 Junction 7
⊕ Open air driving range
🏠 Martin Gillett

North Weald (1996)
Rayley Lane, North Weald, Epping, CM16 6AR
☎ **(01992) 522118**
📠 (01992) 522881

📖 500
🏌 PH Newson
◦ D Rawlings (01992) 524725
▷ 18 L 6311 yds Par 71 SSS 70
👥 U SOC–WD
££ £20 (£27.50)
⊶ 1½ miles E of M11 Junction 7 on A414
⊕ Driving range
🏠 David Williams

The Notleys (1995)
The Green, Black Notley, Witham, CM8 1RG
☎ **(01376) 329328**
📖 300
🏌 R Mortier
◦ D Bugg
▷ 18 L 6022 yds Par 71
    9 hole Par 3 course
👥 U SOC
££ £11 (£15)
⊶ Black Notley, S of Braintree, off A120
⊕ Practice range
🏠 John Day

Orsett (1899)
Brentwood Road, Orsett, RM16 3DS
☎ **(01375) 891352**
📠 (01375) 892471
📖 700
🏌 DT Howe (01375) 893409
◦ P Joiner (01375) 891797
▷ 18 L 6614 yds SSS 72
👥 WD–H WE–M SOC–WD exc Thurs & Fri
££ £35–£50
⊶ 4 miles NE of Grays on A128. M25 Junction 30/31
🏠 James Braid

The Priors (1992)
Horseman's Side, Tysea Hill, Stapleford Abbotts, RM4 1JU
☎ **(01708) 381108,
    (01708) 373344 (Bookings)**
📠 (01708) 386345
🏌 D Eagle (Gen Mgr)
◦ J Stanion
▷ 18 L 5720 yds SSS 68
👥 U SOC
££ £11–£15
⊶ 3 miles N of Romford. M25 Junction 28
🏠 Howard Swann

Regiment Way Golf Centre (1995)
Pay and play
Back Lane, Little Waltham, Chelmsford, CM3 3PR
☎ **(01245) 361100**
🏌 R Pamphilon
◦ D Marsh
▷ 9 L 4887 yds Par 65 SSS 64
👥 U
££ 9 holes–£8 (£9) 18 holes–£11 (£12)
⊶ 3 miles NE of Chelmsford (A130)
⊕ Floodlit driving range

Risebridge (1972)
Pay and play
Risebridge Chase, Lower Bedfords Road, Romford, RM1 4DG
☎ **(01708) 741429**
📖 175
🏌 L Bushell
◦ P Jennings (01708) 741429
▷ 18 L 6394 yds SSS 71
    9 hole Par 3 course
👥 U
££ £13.50 (£15.50)
⊶ 2 miles from M25 Junction 28, off A12
⊕ Driving range
🏠 F Hawtree

Rivenhall Oaks (1994)
Pay and play
Forest Road, Witham, Essex, CM8 2PS
☎ **(01376) 510222**
📖 135
🏌 S Brice
◦ J Hudson
▷ 9 L 3128 yds Par 36
    9 hole Par 3 course
👥 U
££ £8 (£11)
⊶ 4 miles E of Witham, off A12
⊕ Floodlit driving range
🏠 Alan Walker

Rochford Hundred (1893)
Rochford Hall, Hall Road, Rochford, SS4 1NW
☎ **(01702) 544302**
📠 (01702) 541343
📖 375 90(L) 60(J)
🏌 AH Bondfield
◦ GS Hill
▷ 18 L 6256 yds SSS 70
👥 WD–U H WE–M
££ On application
⊶ 4 miles N of Southend-on-Sea
🏠 James Braid

Romford (1894)
Heath Drive, Gidea Park, Romford, RM2 5QB
☎ **(01708) 740007 (Members)**
📠 (01708) 752157
📖 680
🏌 Mrs H Robinson (01708) 740986
◦ H Flatman (01708) 749393
▷ 18 L 6395 yds SSS 70
👥 WD–I WE–NA SOC
££ £25 D–£35
⊶ 1 mile E of Romford. 3 miles W of M25 Junction 29
🏠 HS Colt

Royal Epping Forest (1888)
Forest Approach, Station Road, Chingford, London E4 7AZ
☎ **(020) 8529 6407**
📠 (020) 8559 4664
✉ office@refgc.co.uk
📖 300 50(L) 25(J)
🏌 R Bright-Thomas (0181) 529 2195
◦ A Traynor (0181) 529 5708
▷ 18 L 6342 yds Par 71 SSS 70

For list of abbreviations and key to symbols see page 649

鬥 U–booking necessary SOC
££ £11.30 (£15.70)
🚗 Nr Chingford station. M25 Junction 26
⊕ Red coats or trousers compulsory

Saffron Walden (1919)

Windmill Hill, Saffron Walden, CB10 1BX
☎ (01799) 522786
🖳 (01799) 522786
✉ office@swgc.com
📖 950
🏌 GL Pearce (01799) 522786
⌿ P Davis (01799) 527728
🏴 18 L 6606 yds SSS 72
鬥 WD–U H WE/BH–M SOC
££ £35
🚗 Saffron Walden, on B184

St Cleres

St Cleres Hall, Stanford-le-Hope, SS17 0LX
☎ (01375) 361565
📖 500
🏌 D Wood (01375) 361565
⌿ D Wood (01375) 361565
🏴 18 holes Par 72 SSS 71
鬥 U H SOC
££ £15 (£20)
🚗 5 miles E of M25 Junction 30/31 (A13)
⊕ Driving range
🏠 Adrian Stiff

South Essex G&CC

Herongate, Brentwood, CM13 3LW
☎ (01277) 811289
🖳 (01277) 811304
✉ southessex@americangolf.uk.com
📖 600
🏌 R Brewer (Gen Mgr)
⌿ G Stewart
🏴 18 L 6851 yds Par 72 SSS 73
9 L 3102 yds Par 35
鬥 U SOC
££ £16 (£22)
🚗 4 miles E of M25 Junction 29 (A127/A128)
⊕ Driving range. Golf Academy
🏠 Reg Plumbridge
■ www.americangolf.com

Stapleford Abbotts (1989)

Horseman's Side, Tysea Hill, Stapleford Abbotts, RM4 1JU
☎ (01708) 381108
🖳 (01708) 386345
📖 750
🏌 G Ivory
⌿ J Cornish (01708) 381108
🏴 18 L 6501 yds SSS 71
9 hole Par 3 course
鬥 WD–U WE–H SOC
££ £25–£45
🚗 3 miles N of Romford. M25 Junction 28
🏠 Howard Swann

Stock Brook Manor (1992)

Queen's Park Avenue, Stock, Billericay, CM12 0SP
☎ (01277) 653616
🖳 (01277) 633063
📖 850
🏌 C Laurence (Golf Dir)
⌿ C Laurence
🏴 18 L 6905 yds SSS 73
9 L 2952 yds SSS 69
鬥 H–booking necessary
££ £25 (£30)
🚗 5 miles S of Chelmsford on B1007
⊕ Driving range. Par 3 course
🏠 Martin Gillett

Theydon Bois (1897)

Theydon Bois, Epping, CM16 4EH
☎ (01992) 813054
🖳 (01992) 815602
✉ theydonboisgolf@btconnect.com
📖 600
🏌 MC Slatter (01992) 813054
⌿ RJ Hall (01992) 812460
🏴 18 L 5480 yds SSS 68
鬥 U exc Thurs am–restricted SOC
££ £26 After 2pm–£22
🚗 1 mile S of Epping. M25 Junction 26
🏠 James Braid

Thorndon Park (1920)

Ingrave, Brentwood, CM13 3RH
☎ (01277) 810345
🖳 (01277) 810645
✉ tpgc@btclick.com
📖 450 140(L) 60(J)
🏌 Lt Col RM Estcourt
⌿ BV White (01277) 810736
🏴 18 L 6492 yds SSS 71
鬥 WD–I WE/BH–M
££ £40 D–£55
🚗 2 miles SE of Brentwood on A128
🏠 HS Colt

Thorpe Hall (1907)

Thorpe Hall Avenue, Thorpe Bay, SS1 3AT
☎ (01702) 582205
🖳 (01702) 584498
📖 750
🏌 RM O'Hara
⌿ WJ McColl (01702) 588195
🏴 18 L 6319 yds SSS 71
鬥 WD–H SOC–Fri only
££ On application
🚗 E of Southend-on-Sea

Three Rivers (1973)

Stow Road, Purleigh, Chelmsford, CM3 6RR
☎ (01621) 828631
🖳 (01621) 828060
📖 800
🏌 J Martin (Gen Mgr)
⌿ S Clark
🏴 Kings 18 L 6449 yds Par 72 SSS 71
Jubilee 18 L 4501 yds Par 64
SSS 62

鬥 WD–U exc Mon & Wed–NA before 11.30am WE–U after 1.30pm SOC
££ Kings £20 (£25) Jubilee £10 (£12.50)
🚗 Cold Norton, 5 miles S of Maldon
🏠 Hawtree
■ www.clubhaus.com

Toot Hill (1991)

School Road, Toot Hill, Ongar, CM5 9PU
☎ (01277) 365747
🖳 (01277) 364509
📖 400
🏌 Mrs Cameron
⌿ M Bishop
🏴 18 L 6053 yds Par 70 SSS 69
鬥 H WE–NA before 1pm SOC–WD
££ £25 (£30)
🚗 2 miles W of Ongar
⊕ Practice range
🏠 Martin Gillett

Top Meadow (1986)

Fen Lane, North Ockendon, RM14 3PR
☎ (01708) 852239 (Clubhouse)
✉ info@topmeadow.co.uk
🏌 D Stock
⌿ R Porter (01708) 859545
🏴 18 L 6227 yds Par 72
鬥 WD–U WE–M SOC
££ £12
🚗 N Ockendon, off B186
⊕ Driving range
■ www.topmeadow.co.uk

Towerlands (1985)

Panfield Road, Braintree, CM7 5BJ
☎ (01376) 326802
🖳 (01376) 552487
📖 300
🏌 R Crane
⌿ (01376) 347951
🏴 9 L 5559 yds Par 68
鬥 WD–U exc Wed & Fri–NA after 4.30pm WE–NA before 1pm SOC
££ 18 holes–£10 (£12) 9 holes–£8
🚗 1 mile NW of Braintree (B1053)

Upminster (1928)

114 Hall Lane, Upminster, RM14 1AU
☎ (01708) 222788
🖳 (01708) 222484
📖 1070
🏌 J Collantine
⌿ S Cipa (01708) 220000
🏴 18 L 6031 yds SSS 69
鬥 WD–U H exc Tues am Ladies Day WE/BH–NA SOC
££ £25 D–£30
🚗 Station 3/4 mile

Wanstead (1893)

Wanstead, London, E11 2LW
☎ (020) 8989 0604
🖳 (020) 8532 9138
📖 650
🏌 K Jones (020) 8989 3938
⌿ D Hawkins (020) 8989 9876
🏴 18 L 6262 yds SSS 69

WD–H WE/BH–M
££ D–£28
⊶ Off A12, nr Wanstead station
🏠 James Braid
■ www.wanstead.golf.org.uk

Warley Park (1975)
Magpie Lane, Little Warley, Brentwood, CM13 3DX
☎ (01277) 224891
🖷 (01277) 200679
📖 800
🏌 K Regan
⌖ J Groat (01277) 200441
🏳 27 hole course
🏌 WD–H
££ £30
⊶ 2 miles S of Brentwood. M25 Junction 29
🏠 Reg Plumbridge

Warren (1932)
Woodham Walter, Maldon, CM9 6RW
☎ (01245) 223258/223198
🖷 (01245) 223989
📖 800
🏌 MFL Durham (01245) 223258
⌖ D Brooks (01245) 224662
🏳 18 L 6211 yds SSS 69
🏌 WD–H WE–M SOC
££ £30 D–£35
⊶ 7 miles E of Chelmsford, off A414
⊕ Golf Academy (01245) 223198
■ www.warrengolfclub.co.uk

Weald Park (1994)
Coxtie Green Road, South Weald, Brentwood, CM14 5RJ
☎ (01277) 375101
🖷 (01277) 374888
📖 600
🏌 M Orwin (Gen Mgr)
⌖ K Clark
🏳 18 L 6612 yds SSS 72
🏌 U–booking necessary WE–U after 11am SOC
££ £18 (£24)
⊶ 3 miles from M25 Junction 28 (A1023)
⊕ Driving range
🏠 Reg Plumbridge
■ www.americangolf.com

West Essex (1900)
Bury Road, Sewardstonebury, Chingford, London E4 7QL
☎ (020) 8529 7558
🖷 (020) 8524 7870
📖 690
🏌 D Wilson
⌖ R Joyce (020) 8529 4367
🏳 18 L 6289 yds SSS 70
🏌 WD–U H WE/BH–M H SOC–Mon/Wed/Fri
££ £32 D–£37
⊶ 2 miles N of Chingford BR station. M25 Junction 26
⊕ Driving range
🏠 James Braid

Woodford (1890)
2, Sunset Avenue, Woodford Green, IG8 0ST
☎ (020) 8504 0553 (Clubhouse)
🖷 (020) 8559 0504
📖 430
🏌 RS Crofts (020) 8504 3330
⌖ R Layton (020) 8504 4254
🏳 9 L 5867 yds SSS 68
🏌 WD–U exc Tues am–NA Sat–M Sun–NA before noon SOC
££ £10–£15
⊶ 11 miles NE of London
⊕ Major item of red clothing to be worn on course
🏠 Tom Dunn

Woolston Manor (1994)
Woolston Manor, Abridge Road, Chigwell, IG7 6BX
☎ (020) 8500 2549
🖷 (020) 8501 5452
📖 650
🏌 P Spargo
⌖ P Eady (0181) 559 8272
🏳 18 L 6408 yds SSS 71
🏌 H SOC–WD
££ £35 (£45)
⊶ 1 mile from M11 Junction 5
⊕ Floodlit driving range
🏠 Neil Coles

Gloucestershire

Brickhampton Court
Cheltenham Road, Churchdown, GL2 9QF
☎ (01452) 859444
🖷 (01452) 859333
✉ info@brickhampton.co.uk
🏌 R East
⌖ B Wilson
🏳 Spa 18 L 6449 yds Par 71 SSS 71 Glevum 9 L 1859 yds Par 31
🏌 U SOC–WD
££ Spa £20 D–£35 (£26 D–£45) Glevum £9 (£14)
⊶ Between Cheltenham and Gloucester on B4063. M5 Junction 11, 3 miles
⊕ Floodlit driving range
🏠 Simon Gidman
■ www.brickhampton.co.uk

Bristol & Clifton (1891)
Beggar Bush Lane, Failand, Clifton, Bristol BS8 3TH
☎ (01275) 393474/393117
🖷 (01275) 394611
📖 650
🏌 CR Vane Percy (01275) 393474
⌖ P Mitchell (01275) 393031
🏳 18 L 6316 yds SSS 70
🏌 WD–UH WE/BH–UH after 11am SOC
££ On request
⊶ 2 miles W of suspension bridge. 4 miles S of M5 Junction 19
⊕ Driving range
■ www.bristolgolf.co.uk

Broadway (1895)
Willersey Hill, Broadway, Worcs, WR12 7LG
☎ (01386) 858997
🖷 (01386) 858643
📖 515 165(L) 75(J)
🏌 B Carnie (Sec/Mgr) (01386) 853683
⌖ M Freeman (01386) 853275
🏳 18 L 6228 yds Par 72 SSS 70
🏌 H exc Sat–M SOC
££ £30 (£37)
⊶ 1½ miles E of Broadway (A44)
🏠 James Braid

Canons Court (1982)
Bradley Green, Wotton-under-Edge, GL12 7PN
☎ (01453) 843128
📖 200
⌖ I Watts
🏳 9 L 5724 yds SSS 65
🏌 U
££ £10
⊶ 3 miles E of M5 Junction 14, off B4058

Chipping Sodbury
Chipping Sodbury, Bristol, BS37 6PU
☎ (01454) 312024 (Members)
🖷 (01454) 320052
📖 750
🏌 R Wilmott (01454) 319042
⌖ M Watts (01454) 314087
🏳 18 L 6786 yds SSS 73
🏌 WD–U WE–pm only Sat/Sun am–XL SOC
££ £22 (£27)
⊶ 12 miles NE of Bristol. M4 Junction 18, 5 miles. M5 Junction 14, 9 miles.
⊕ Driving range
🏠 Fred Hawtree
■ www.chippingsodburygolfclub .co.uk

Cirencester (1893)
Cheltenham Road, Bagendon, Cirencester, GL7 7BH
☎ (01285) 653939
🖷 (01285) 650665
✉ info@cirencestergolfclub.co.uk
📖 800
🏌 IA Gray (01285) 652465
⌖ P Garratt (01285) 656124
🏳 18 L 6055 yds Par 70 SSS 69
🏌 H SOC–WD
££ £25 (£30)
⊶ 1½ miles N of Cirencester on A435
🏠 James Braid
■ www.cirencestergolfclub.co.uk

Cleeve Hill (1892)
Pay and play
Cleeve Hill, Cheltenham, GL52 3PW
☎ (01242) 672025
✉ golf@cleevehill.com
🏌 S Gilman (Mgr)
⌖ D Finch (01242) 672592
🏳 18 L 6496 yds Par 72 SSS 71

U exc Sat 11–3pm/Sun am–NA
SOC
£€ £12 (£15)
🚗 3 miles N of Cheltenham on A46 to
Winchcombe
⊕ Tee booking 7 days in advance
■ www.clevehill.com

Cotswold Edge (1980)
*Upper Rushmire, Wotton-under-Edge,
GL12 7PT*
☎ (01453) 844167
🖷 (01453) 845120
📖 800
🏌 NJ Newman
✓ DJ Gosling (01453) 844398
🏳 18 L 5816 yds SSS 69
👥 WD–U WE–M SOC
£€ £15
🚗 2 miles NE of Wotton-under-Edge
on B4058 Tetbury road. M5
Junction 14

Cotswold Hills (1902)
Ullenwood, Cheltenham, GL53 9QT
☎ (01242) 515264
🖷 (01242) 515317
📧 golf@chgc.freeserve.co.uk
📖 750
🏌 P Burroughes (Gen Mgr)
✓ N Allen (01242) 515263
🏳 18 L 6801 yds SSS 72
👥 U–recognised club members SOC
£€ £27 D–£34 (£34 D–£40)
🚗 3 miles S of Cheltenham. M5
Junction 11A
🏠 MD Little

Dymock Grange (1995)
*The Old Grange, Leominster Road,
Dymock, GL18 2AN*
☎ (01531) 890840
🖷 (01531) 890852
📖 180
🏌 BA Crossman (Gen Mgr)
✓ None
🏳 9 L 2696 yds Par 36
9 L 1695 yds Par 30
👥 U
£€ £12 (£15)
🚗 14 miles NW of Gloucester
(B4215)

Filton (1909)
Golf Course Lane, Bristol, BS34 7QS
☎ (0117) 969 2021
🖷 (0117) 931 4359
📧 thesecretary@filtongolfclub.co.uk
📖 700
🏌 Mrs E Mannering (0117) 969 4169
✓ D Robinson (0117) 969 6968
🏳 18 L 6208 yds SSS 70
👥 WD–U WE/BH–M SOC–WD
£€ £22 D–£27
🚗 4 miles N of Bristol
🏠 Hawtree

Forest Hills (1992)
Proprietary
Mile End Road, Coleford, GL16 7BY
☎ (01594) 810620

🖷 (01594) 810823
📖 550
🏌 N Antice (01594) 810620
✓ R Ballard (01594) 810620
🏳 18 L 6300 yds SSS 72
👥 U SOC
£€ £17 (£22)
🚗 1 mile E of Coleford (B4028)
⊕ Driving range
🏠 Adrian Stiff
■ www.fweb.org.uk/forestgolf

Forest of Dean (1973)
Lords Hill, Coleford, GL16 8BE
☎ (01594) 832583
🖷 (01594) 832584
📧 enquiries@bellshotel.co.uk
📖 500
🏌 R Sanzen-Baker
✓ A Gray (01594) 833689
🏳 18 L 5682 yds SSS 69
👥 U SOC
£€ £18 (£25)
🚗 ¹/₂ mile SE of Coleford on Parkend
road. M50, 10 miles
🏠 John Day

The Gloucestershire (1976)
*Tracy Park Estate, Bath Road, Wick,
Bristol BS30 5RN*
☎ (0117) 937 2251,
(0117) 303 9123 (Bookings)
🖷 (0117) 937 4288
📧 golf@thegloucestershire.com
📖 700
🏌 D Knipe (Dir)
✓ D Morgan
🏳 Crown 18 L 6252 yds SSS 70
Cromwell 18 L 6246 yds SSS 70
👥 U–phone first SOC
£€ £30 (£38)
🚗 3 miles NW of Bath, off A420. M4
Junction 18
⊕ Driving range
■ www.thegloucestershire.com

Gloucester Hotel (1976)
Matson Lane, Gloucester, GL4 9EA
☎ (01452) 525653
📖 750
🏌 P Darnell
✓ P Darnell (01452) 411311
🏳 18 L 6127 yds SSS 69
9 L 1980 yds SSS 27
👥 U
£€ £19 (£25)
🚗 2 miles S of Gloucester, off
Painswick road. M5 Junction 11
⊕ Driving range

Henbury (1891)
Westbury-on-Trym, Bristol, BS10 7QB
☎ (0117) 950 0660
🖷 (0117) 959 1928
📖 760
🏌 (0117) 950 0044
✓ N Riley (0117) 950 2121
🏳 18 L 6007 yds SSS 70
👥 WD–H WE–M SOC–Tues & Fri
£€ £25
🚗 3 miles N of Bristol, off A4018. M5
Junction 17
■ www.henburygolfclub.co.uk

Hilton Puckrup Hall Hotel (1992)
Puckrup, Tewkesbury, GL20 6EL
☎ (01684) 296200/271591
🖷 (01684) 850788
📖 500
🏌 G Spring
✓ K Pickett
🏳 18 L 6189 yds SSS 70
👥 WD–H SOC WE–residents
£€ £25 (£30)
🚗 2 miles N of Tewkesbury on A38.
M50 Junction 1. M5 Junction 8
🏠 Simon Gidman

Kendleshire
*Henfield Road, Coalpit Heath, Bristol,
BS36 2TG*
☎ (0117) 956 7007
🖷 (0117) 957 3433
📧 info@kendleshire.co.uk
📖 750
🏌 P Murphy
✓ M Bessell (0117) 956 7000
🏳 27 L 6249-6544 yds Par 70-71
👥 U SOC
£€ £27 (£35)
🚗 1 mile NE of Bristol. M32 Junction 1
⊕ Driving range. Golf Academy
🏠 Adrian Stiff

Knowle (1905)
*Fairway, West Town Lane, Brislington,
Bristol BS4 5DF*
☎ (0117) 977 6341
🖷 (0117) 972 0615
📖 700
🏌 MJ Harrington (0117) 977 0660
✓ R Hayward (0117) 977 9193
🏳 18 L 6006 yds SSS 69
👥 WD exc Thurs–H WE/BH–H
SOC–Thurs
£€ £22 D–£27 (£27 D–£32)
🚗 Brislington Hill, 3 miles S of
Bristol, off A4
🏠 JH Taylor

Lilley Brook (1922)
*Cirencester Road, Charlton Kings,
Cheltenham, GL53 8EG*
☎ (01242) 526785
🖷 (01242) 256880
📖 900
🏌 MF Jordan (Gen Mgr)
✓ F Hadden (01242) 525201
🏳 18 L 6226 yds SSS 70
👥 WD–H or I (recognised club
members) WE–M SOC–WD
£€ £25 D–£30 (£30 D–£35)
🚗 3 miles SE of Cheltenham on A435.
M5 Junction 11 or 11A

Long Ashton (1893)
*Clarken Coombe, Long Ashton, Bristol,
BS41 9DW*
☎ (01275) 392229
🖷 (01275) 394395
📧 info@longashtongolfclub.co.uk
📖 750
🏌 R Williams (01275) 392229
✓ M Hart (01275) 392229

18 L 6077 yds SSS 70
WD–U H WE/BH–I H SOC–Wed & Fri
££ £30 (£35)
3 miles S of Bristol on B3128
JH Taylor
www.longashtongolfclub.co.uk

Lydney (1909)

Lakeside Avenue, Lydney, GL15 5QA
☎ (01594) 842614
dennis@barnard.fsnet.co.uk
300
DA Barnard (01594) 843940
9 L 5430 yds SSS 66
WD–U WE/BH–M SOC
££ £10
20 miles SW of Gloucester
www.members.tripod.co.uk/kenfar/lgc

Mangotsfield (1975)

Carsons Road, Mangotsfield, Bristol, BS17 3LW
☎ (0117) 956 5501
600
C Main
C Trewin
18 L 5337 yds SSS 66
U
££ On application
6 miles NE of Bristol

Minchinhampton (1889)

Minchinhampton, Stroud, GL6 9BE
☎ (01453) 832642 (Old), (01453) 833840 (New)
(01453) 837360
1860
DT Calvert (01453) 833866
C Steele (01453) 837351
Old 18 L 6019 yds SSS 69;
Avening 18 L 6263 yds SSS 70;
Cherington 18 L 6387 yds SSS 70
H SOC
££ Old–£10 (£13). New–£20 (£32)
Old-3 miles E of Stroud. New-5 miles E of Stroud
Old: R Wilson. Avening: F Hawtree.
Cherington: M Hawtree

Naunton Downs (1993)

Naunton, Cheltenham, GL54 3AE
☎ (01451) 850090
(01451) 850091
750
Charlotte Thomas
N Ellis (01451) 850092
18 L 6135 yds Par 71 SSS 69
WD–U–by arrangement WE–NA before 11am
££ £19 (£27.50)
5 miles SW of Stow-on-the-Wold, on B4068
Jacob Pott
www.nauntondowns.fsnet.co.uk

Newent (1994)

Pay and play
Coldharbour Lane, Newent, GL18 1DJ
☎ (01531) 820478

(01531) 820478
50
W Russell
T Brown
9 L 2100 yds Par 33 SSS 59
U SOC
££ 9 holes–£6 (£7) 18 holes–£10 (£12)
10 miles NW of Gloucester on B4215. M50 Junction 3, 4 miles

Painswick (1891)

Painswick, Stroud, GL6 6TL
☎ (01452) 812180
(01452) 814423
430
AB Layton-Smith (01452) 612622
None
18 L 4780 yds SSS 63
WD/Sat–U Sun–M SOC
££ £17.50 Sat–£22.50
½ mile N of Painswick on A46
David Brown

Rodway Hill (1991)

Pay and play
Newent Road, Highnam, GL2 8DN
☎ (01452) 384222
(01452) 313814
350
R Howe
T Grubb
18 L 6040 yds Par 70 SSS 69
U SOC
££ 18 holes–£12 (£14). 9 holes–£8 (£9)
2 miles W of Gloucester (B4215)
J Gabb

Sherdons Golf Centre (1993)

Pay and play
Tredington, Tewkesbury, GL20 7BP
☎ (01684) 274782
(01684) 275358
300
R Chatham
P Clark, J Parker
9 L 2654 yds Par 34 SSS 66
U
££ 18 holes–£11 (£14) 9 holes–£6.50 (£7.50)
2 miles S of Tewkesbury, off A38
Driving range

Shirehampton Park (1904)

Park Hill, Shirehampton, Bristol, BS11 0UL
☎ (0117) 982 3059
(0117) 982 5280
info@shirehamptonparkgolfclub.co.uk
600
A Hobbs (0117) 982 2083
B Ellis (0117) 982 2488
18 L 5430 yds Par 67 SSS 66
WD–H WE–M SOC
££ £20 (£17)
2 miles E of M5 Junction 18, on B4054

Stinchcombe Hill (1889)

Stinchcombe Hill, Dursley, GL11 6AQ
☎ (01453) 542015

(01453) 549545
stinchcombehill@golfers.net
550
PH Jones
P Bushell (01453) 543878
18 L 5734 yds SSS 68
U–phone Pro SOC
££ £24 (£30)
1 mile W of Dursley. M5 Junction 14
A Hoare

Tewkesbury Park Hotel (1976)

Lincoln Green Lane, Tewkesbury, GL20 7DN
☎ (01684) 295405 (Hotel)
(01684) 292386
600
RS Nichol (01684) 272322
C Boast (01684) 272320
18 L 6533 yds Par 73 SSS 71
6 hole Par 3 course
WD–U H WE–restricted SOC–WD
££ £25 (£30)
½ mile S of Tewkesbury on A38. M5 Junction 9, 2 miles
Driving range
www.corushotels.com/tewkesburypark

Thornbury Golf Centre (1992)

Bristol Road, Thornbury
☎ (01454) 281144
(01454) 281177
500
I Gibson
S Hubbard
18 L 6207 yds SSS 69 Par 71
18 L 2195 yds Par 54
U SOC–WD
££ £17 (£21.50)
10 miles N of Bristol, off A38
Driving range
Hawtree

Westonbirt (1971)

Westonbirt, Tetbury, GL8 8QG
☎ (01666) 880242
200
Bursar, Westonbirt School
9 L 4504 yds SSS 61
U SOC–WD
££ On application
3 miles S of Tetbury, off A433

Woodlands G&CC (1989)

Pay and play
Woodlands Lane, Almondsbury, Bristol, BS32 4JZ
☎ (01454) 619319
(01454) 619397
golf@woodlands-golf.com
I Knipe
N Warburton
18 L 6100 yds SSS 70
U SOC
££ £12 (£14)
Nr M5 Junction 16
www.woodlands-golf.com

Woodspring G&CC (1994)
Yanley Lane, Long Ashton, Bristol,
BS41 9LR
- ☎ (01275) 394378
- 📠 (01275) 394473
- 🖎 M Pierce (Gen Mgr)
- / N Beer
- ⊱ 27 holes:
  6209-6587 yds Par 71 SSS 70-71
- 👥 W–H SOC
- ££ £25 (£28.50)
- ⌘ 2 miles S of Bristol on A38.
- ⊕ Floodlit driving range
- ⌂ Allis/Clark

Hampshire

Alresford (1890)
Cheriton Road, Alresford, SO24 0PN
- ☎ (01962) 733746
- 📠 (01962) 736040
- 🖎 secretary@alresford-golf.demon
  .co.uk
- 📖 625
- 🖎 T Adams
- / M Scott (01962) 733998
- ⊱ 18 L 5905 yds Par 69 SSS 68
- 👥 U H SOC–WD
- ££ £25 D–£35 (£40)
- ⌘ 1 mile S of Alresford on B3046
- ⌂ Scott Webb Young
- ■ www.alresfordgolf.com

Alton (1908)
Old Odiham Road, Alton, GU34 4BU
- ☎ (01420) 82042
- 📖 370
- 🖎 R Keeling
- / R Keeling (01420) 86518
- ⊱ 9 L 5744 yds SSS 68
- 👥 WD–U WE–H or M SOC–WD
- ££ 18 holes–£15 D–£20 9 holes–£10
- ⌘ 2 miles N of Alton. 6 miles S of
  Odiham, off B3349
- ⌂ James Braid

Ampfield Par Three (1963)
Winchester Road, Ampfield, Romsey,
SO51 9BQ
- ☎ (01794) 368480
- 📖 500
- 🖎 Ms L Hilman
- / R Benfield (01794) 368750
- ⊱ 18 L 2478 yds SSS 53
- 👥 WD–U WE/BH–H (phone first)
  SOC
- ££ £9 (£15.50)
- ⌘ 5 miles E of Romsey on A31
- ⌂ Henry Cotton

Andover (1907)
51 Winchester Road, Andover, SP10 2EF
- ☎ (01264) 323980
- 📠 (01264) 358040
- 🖎 play@andovergolfclub.fsnet.co.uk
- 📖 460 30(L) 45(J)
- 🖎 M Bennet (01264) 358040
- / D Lawrence (01264) 324151
- ⊱ 9 L 6096 yds SSS 69

- 👥 U H SOC
- ££ £15 (£20)
- ⌘ ¹/₂ mile S of Andover on A3057
- ⌂ JH Taylor

Army (1883)
Laffan's Road, Aldershot, GU11 2HF
- ☎ (01252) 336776
- 📠 (01252) 337562
- 🖎 agc@ic24.net
- 📖 750
- 🖎 Maj (Retd) JWG Douglass
  (01252) 337272
- / G Cowley (01252) 336722
- ⊱ 18 L 6579 yds SSS 71
- 👥 WD–H–contact Sec/Mgr SOC
- ££ Special rates for Forces
- ⌘ Between Aldershot and
  Farnborough
- ■ www.whichgolfclub.com/army

Barton-on-Sea (1897)
Milford Road, New Milton, BH25 5PP
- ☎ (01425) 615308
- 📠 (01425) 621457
- 📖 1000
- 🖎 N Hallam-Jones
- / P Rodgers (01425) 611210
- ⊱ 27 holes:
  L 6289-6505 yds Par 72
- 👥 H NA before 9am SOC–WD exc
  Tues
- ££ D–£35 (D–£40)
- ⌘ 1 mile from New Milton, off
  B3058. M27 Junction 1
- ⌂ J Hamilton Stutt
- ■ www.barton-on-sea-golf.co.uk

Basingstoke (1928)
Kempshott Park, Basingstoke, RG23 7LL
- ☎ (01256) 465990
- 📠 (01256) 331793
- 🖎 basingstokegolfclub@ukonline
  .co.uk
- 📖 700
- 🖎 WA Jefford
- / G Shoesmith (01256) 351332
- ⊱ 18 L 6350 yds SSS 70
- 👥 WD–H WE–M SOC–Wed & Thurs
- ££ £28 D–£38
- ⌘ 3 miles W of Basingstoke on A30.
  M3 Junction 7
- ⌂ James Braid
- ■ www.basingstokegolfclub.co.uk

Bishopswood (1978)
Proprietary
Bishopswood Lane, Tadley, Basingstoke,
RG26 4AT
- ☎ (0118) 981 2200/5213
- 📠 (0118) 940 8606
- 📖 400
- 🖎 M Collins (0118) 982 0312
- / S Ward
- ⊱ 9 L 6474 yds Par 72 SSS 71
- 👥 WD–U WE–M SOC
- ££ 9 holes–£11. 18 holes–£16.50
- ⌘ 6 miles N of Basingstoke, off A340
- ⊕ Floodlit driving range
- ⌂ Blake/Phillips
- ■ www.bishopswoodgolfcourse.co.uk

Blackmoor (1913)
Whitehill, Bordon, GU35 9EH
- ☎ (01420) 472775
- 📠 (01420) 487666
- 🖎 admin@blackmoorgolf.co.uk
- 📖 680 100(L) 70(J)
- 🖎 AN Harris
- / S Clay (01420) 472345
- ⊱ 18 L 6213 yds SSS 70
- 👥 WD–H SOC–WD
- ££ £35 D–£47
- ⌘ ¹/₂ mile W of Whitehill on A325
- ⌂ HS Colt
- ■ www.blackmoorgolf.co.uk

Blacknest (1993)
Blacknest, GU34 4QL
- ☎ (01420) 22888
- 📠 (01420) 22001
- 🖎 info@huntswoodgolf.com
- 📖 397
- / T Cook
- ⊱ 18 L 5938 yds SSS 69
  9 hole Par 3 course
- 👥 U SOC
- ££ £17 (£22)
- ⌘ 7 miles SW of Farnham, off A325
- ⊕ Driving range
- ■ www.huntswoodgolf.com

Blackwater Valley
Chandlers Lane, Yateley, Surrey,
GU46 7SZ
- ☎ (01252) 874725
- 📠 (01252) 874725
- 📖 50
- / J Rodger
- ⊱ 9 L 2365 yds Par 66
- 👥 U SOC
- ££ £7 (£9)
- ⌘ 5 miles W of Camberley (B3272)
- ⊕ Floodlit driving range
- ⌂ HJ Allenby

Botley Park Hotel G&CC
(1989)
Winchester Road, Boorley Green, Botley,
SO3 2UA
- ☎ (01489) 780888 Ext 451
- 📠 (01489) 789242
- 📖 700
- 🖎 Miss M Johnstone
- / T Barter (01489) 789771
- ⊱ 18 L 6341 yds SSS 70
- 👥 H SOC
- ££ £30
- ⌘ 6 miles E of Southampton on
  B3354. M27 Junction 7. 8 miles SE
  of M3 Junction 11
- ⊕ Driving range
- ⌂ Potterton/Murray

Bramshaw (1880)
Brook, Lyndhurst, SO43 7HE
- ☎ (023) 8081 3433
- 📠 (023) 8081 3460
- 📖 1200
- 🖎 RD Tingey
- / C Bonner (023) 8081 3434
- ⊱ Forest 18 L 5774 yds SSS 68
  Manor 18 L 6517 yds SSS 71

U H
£€ Forest–£28. Manor–£33
🚗 10 miles SW of Southampton. M27
Junction 1, 1 mile
■ www.bramshaw.co.uk

Brokenhurst Manor   (1919)

Sway Road, Brockenhurst, SO42 7SG
☎ (01590) 623332
📠 (01590) 624140
✉ pclifford@bmgcltd.freeserve.co.uk
📖 800
🏌 PE Clifford
⚲ B Parker (01590) 623092
⮞ 18 L 6222 yds SSS 70
🚹 WD–H after 9.30am exc
Tues–Ladies' Day SOC–Thurs only
£€ £45 D–£55 (£55 D–£70)
🚗 1 mile SW of Brockenhurst on
B3055
🏠 HS Colt

Burley   (1905)

Cott Lane, Burley, Ringwood, BH24 4BB
☎ (01425) 403737 (Clubhouse)
📠 (01425) 404168
✉ secretary@burleygolfclub.fsnet
.co.uk
📖 520
🏌 GJ Stride (01425) 402431
⮞ 9 L 6149 yds Par 71 SSS 69
🚹 U H–preferred
£€ £16 (£20) W–£75
🚗 4 miles SE of Ringwood

Cams Hall Estate

Cams Hall Estate, Fareham, PO16 8UP
☎ (01329) 827222
📠 (01329) 827111
📖 950
🏌 S Wright (Sec/Mgr)
⚲ J Neve (01329) 837732
⮞ 27 L 6244-6477 yds SSS 70-71
🚹 U SOC
£€ £22 (£29)
🚗 8 miles W of Portsmouth. M27
Junction 11
🏠 Alliss/Clarke

Chilworth   (1989)

*Main Road, Chilworth, Southampton,
SO16 7JP*
☎ (023) 8074 0544
📠 (023) 8073 3166
📖 650
🏌 Mrs E Garner
⮞ 18 L 5740 yds SSS 69
🚹 U
£€ £12 (£15)
🚗 Between Romsey and Southampton
on A27
⊕ Floodlit driving range

Corhampton   (1891)

Corhampton, Southampton, SO32 3LP
☎ (01489) 877279
📠 (01489) 877680
✉ secretary@corhamptongc.co.uk
📖 800
🏌 Mrs L Collins
⚲ I Roper (01489) 877638

⮞ 18 L 6444 yds SSS 71
🚹 WD–U H WE/BH–M SOC–Mons
& Thurs
£€ £24 D–£34
🚗 9 miles S of Winchester
■ www.corhamptongc.co.uk

Dibden Golf Centre   (1974)

Public
*Main Road, Dibden, Southampton,
SO45 5TB*
☎ (023) 8020 7508 (Bookings)
📖 700
⚲ P Smith (023) 8084 5596
⮞ 18 L 5986 yds SSS 69
9 hole course
🚹 U
£€ £12.50 (£14.60)
🚗 10 miles W of Southampton, off
A326 at Dibden roundabout
⊕ Floodlit driving range
■ www.nfdc.gov.uk/golf

Dummer   (1993)

Dummer, Basingstoke, RG25 2AR
☎ (01256) 397888
📠 (01256) 397889
✉ golf@dummergc.co.uk
📖 700
🏌 R Corkhill
⚲ A Fannon (01256) 397950
⮞ 18 L 6403 yds SSS 71
🚹 U SOC
£€ £30 (£40)
🚗 4 miles SW of Basingstoke, by M3
Junction 7
⊕ Driving range
🏠 Alliss/Clark
■ www.dummergc.co.uk

Dunwood Manor   (1969)

*Danes Road, Awbridge, Romsey,
SO51 0GF*
☎ (01794) 340549
📠 (01794) 341215
✉ admin@dunwood-golf.co.uk
📖 600
🏌 JR Basford
⚲ H Teschner (01794) 340663
⮞ 18 L 5767 yds SSS 69
🚹 WE/BH–restricted SOC–WD
£€ £25 (£37)
🚗 Romsey 4 miles, off A27
■ www.dunwood-golf.co.uk

Fareham Woods   (1997)

*Skylark Meadows, Whiteley, Fareham,
PO15 6RS*
☎ (01329) 844441
📠 (01329) 844442
📖 600
🏌 M Woodman
⚲ S Edwards
⮞ 18 L 5622 yds Par 70 SSS 67
🚹 WD–U WE–M SOC–WD
£€ £15
🚗 6 miles W of Fareham. M27
Junction 9

Fleetlands   (1961)

Fareham Road, Gosport, PO13 0AW
☎ (023) 9254 4492
📖 140
⚲ M Barnes (023) 9254 4592
⮞ 9 L 4852 yds SSS 64
🚹 M at all times
🚗 2 miles S of Fareham on A32
Gosport road. M27 Junction 12

Fleming Park   (1973)

Public
*Fleming Park, Magpie Lane, Eastleigh,
SO50 9LH*
☎ (023) 8061 2797
🏌 A Wheavil
⚲ C Strickett
⮞ 18 L 4436 yds SSS 62
🚹 U SOC–WD
£€ On application
🚗 6 miles N of Southampton

Four Marks   (1994)

*Headmore Lane, Four Marks, Alton,
GU34 3ES*
☎ (01420) 587214
📠 (01420) 587313
✉ fourmarksgolf@btopenworld.com
📖 238
🏌 W Falloon
⚲ P Chapman (01420) 587214
⮞ 9 L 2077 yds Par 62 SSS 61
🚹 U SOC
£€ 9 holes–£8 (£9) 18 holes–£10.90
(£11.90)
🚗 6 miles SW of Alton (A31)
🏠 Wright/Falloon/Wrigglesworth

Furzeley   (1993)

Pay and play
Furzeley Road, Denmead, PO7 6TX
☎ (023) 9223 1180
📠 (023) 9223 0921
🏌 T Brown
⚲ D Brown
⮞ 18 L 4363 yds Par 62 SSS 61
🚹 U SOC
£€ £11 (£12.50)
🚗 2 miles NW of Waterlooville

Gosport & Stokes Bay
(1885)

Fort Road, Haslar, Gosport, PO12 2AT
☎ (023) 9258 1625
📠 (023) 9252 7941
📖 450
🏌 P Lucas (023) 9252 7941
⮞ 9 L 5995 yds SSS 69
🚹 U exc Sun–NA SOC–Mon/Wed/Fri
£€ £15 (£20)
🚗 S boundary of Gosport

The Hampshire

*Winchester Road, Goodworth Clatford,
Andover, SP11 7TB*
☎ (01264) 357555
📠 (01264) 356606
📖 735
🏌 T Fiducia
⚲ S Cronin
⮞ 18 L 6376 yds Par
9 hole Par 3 course

🦅 U SOC
£€ £15 (£25)
🚗 1 mile SW of Andover (A3057)
⊕ Covered driving range
🏠 T Fiducia

Hartley Wintney (1891)
London Road, Hartley Wintney, Hook, RG27 8PT
☎ **(01252) 842214**
📠 (01252) 844211
📖 750
🏌 MG Bryant (01252) 844211
🏌 M Smith (01252) 843779
🏳 18 L 6240 yds SSS 71
🦅 Wed–Ladies Day
   WE/BH–restricted SOC
£€ £25 (£35)
🚗 A30 between Camberley and Basingstoke

Hayling (1883)
Links Lane, Hayling Island, PO11 0BX
☎ **(023) 9246 3712**
📠 (023) 9246 1119
📧 hgcltd@aol.com
📖 900
🏌 CJ Cavill (023) 9246 4446
🏌 R Gadd (023) 9246 4491
🏳 18 L 6531 yds SSS 71
🦅 H WE/BH–after 10am SOC–Tues & Wed
£€ £36 (£44)
🚗 5 miles S of Havant on A3023
🏠 Taylor (1905)/Simpson (1933)

Hockley (1915)
Twyford, Winchester, SO21 1PL
☎ **(01962) 713165**
📠 (01962) 713612
📧 hockleygolfclub@aol.com
📖 750
🏌 Mrs L Dyer
🏳 18 L 6336 yds SSS 70
🦅 U H SOC
£€ On application
🚗 2 miles S of Winchester on B3335
🏠 James Braid
■ www.hockleygolfclub.org.uk

Leckford (1929)
Leckford, Stockbridge, SO20 6JS
☎ **(01264) 810320**
📠 (01264) 810439
📖 400
🏌 J Wood
🏌 T Ashton (01264) 338175
🏳 Old 9 L 3251 yds SSS 71
   New 9 L 2281 yds SSS 62
🦅 M
£€ £10 (£14)
🚗 5 miles W of Andover

Lee-on-the-Solent (1905)
Brune Lane, Lee-on-the-Solent, PO13 9PB
☎ **(023) 9255 0207**
📠 (023) 9255 4233
📧 enquiries@leeonthesolentgolfclub.co.uk
📖 715
🏌 M Topper (Mgr) (023) 92551170

🏌 R Edwards (01705) 551181
🏳 18 L 5943 yds SSS 69
🦅 WD–U H WE–M H SOC–Thurs
£€ D–£30 (£35)
🚗 3 miles S of Fareham. M27 Junction 11
■ www.leeonthesolentgolfclub.co.uk

Liphook (1922)
Liphook, GU30 7EH
☎ **(01428) 723271/723785**
📠 (01428) 724853
📧 liphookgolfclub@btconnect.com
📖 700
🏌 Maj JB Morgan MBE (01428) 723785/723271
🏌 G Lee
🏳 18 L 6167 yds SSS 69
🦅 I H (max 24) Sun–NA before 1pm SOC
£€ £39 D–£46 (D–£55)
🚗 1 mile S of Liphook on B2070 (old A3)
🏠 ACG Groome

Marriott Meon Valley Hotel (1977)
Sandy Lane, Shedfield, Southampton, SO32 2HQ
☎ **(01329) 833455**
📠 (01329) 834411
📖 730
🏌 GF McMenemy (Golf Dir)
🏌 R Cameron
🏳 18 L 6520 yds SSS 71
   9 L 2885 yds SSS 68
🦅 H SOC
£€ 18 hole:£36 (£45) 9 hole:£12
🚗 2 miles NW of Wickham. N off A334
⊕ Driving range
🏠 J Hamilton Stutt

New Forest (1888)
Southampton Road, Lyndhurst, SO43 7BU
☎ **(023) 8028 2752**
📧 barbara@nfgc.sagehost.co.uk
📖 650
🏌 Mrs B Shaw, R Macdonald (Prop) (023) 8028 2484
🏌 W Butcher
🏳 18 L 5742 yds SSS 68
🦅 U exc Sun am SOC–WD
£€ £12 (£15)
🚗 8 miles W of Southampton on A35

North Hants (1904)
Minley Road, Fleet, GU51 1RF
☎ **(01252) 616443**
📠 (01252) 811627
📖 550
🏌 G Hogg
🏌 S Porter (01252) 616655
🏳 18 L 6519 yds Par 71 SSS 72
🦅 WD–H by prior arrangement
   WE/BH–MH SOC–Tues & Wed
£€ On application
🚗 3 miles W of Farnborough on B3013. M3 Junction 4A
🏠 James Braid

Old Thorns (1982)
Pay and play
Longmoor Road, Griggs Green, Liphook, GU30 7PE
☎ **(01428) 724555**
📠 (01428) 725036
🏌 GM Jones (Gen Mgr)
🏌 K Stevenson
🏳 18 L 6533 yds SSS 71
🦅 U SOC
£€ £35 (£45)
🚗 Griggs Green exit off A3
⊕ Driving range
🏠 Cdr John Harris

Otterbourne Golf Centre (1995)
Poles Lane, Otterbourne, Winchester, SO21 2EL
☎ **(01962) 775225**
🏌 JM Garner (Mgr)
🏳 9 L 1939 yds Par
🦅 U
£€ £4 (£5)
🚗 On A31 between Otterbourne and Hursley
⊕ Driving range

Park (1995)
Pay and play
Avington, Winchester, SO21 1DA
☎ **(01962) 779945 (Clubhouse)**
📠 (01962) 779530
📖 350
🏌 R Stent (Prop) (01962) 779955
🏌 None
🏳 9 L 1907 yds Par 61 SSS 58
🦅 U SOC
£€ 9 holes–£8 (£11). 18 holes–£12 (£16.50)
🚗 4 miles E of Winchester. M3 Junction 9

Paultons Golf Centre
Pay and play
Old Salisbury Road, Ower, Romsey, SO51 6AN
☎ **(023) 8081 3992**
📠 (023) 8081 3993
🏌 R Pilbury
🏌 (023) 8081 4626
🏳 18 L 6238 yds SSS 71
   9 hole Academy course
🦅 U SOC
£€ 18 holes–£16 (£20) 9 holes–£6 (£6)
🚗 Nr M27 Junction 2, at Ower
⊕ Driving range

Petersfield (1892)
Tankerdale Lane, Liss, GU33 7QY
☎ **(01730) 895165**
📠 (01730) 894713
📖 730
🏌 RR Hine
🏌 G Hughes (01730) 895216
🏳 18 L 6450 yds Par 72 SSS 71
🦅 WD–U WE/BH–NA before noon
   SOC–Mon/Wed/Fri
£€ £25 (£30)
🚗 Off A3, at Liss exit (B3006)
🏠 Hawtree

Petersfield Sussex Road

Pay and play
Sussex Road, Petersfield
- ☎ **(01730) 267732**
- ⚐ RR Hine
- ✓ G Hughes
- ⊢ 9 L 3005 yds
- 👤 U
- ££ 9 holes–£7 (£9) 18 holes–£11 (£13)
- ⊷ Petersfield

Portsmouth   (1926)

Public
Crookhorn Lane, Widley, Waterlooville, PO7 5QL
- ☎ **(023) 9237 2210**
- ⚐ (023) 9220 0766
- 📖 650
- ⚐ D Houlihan (023) 9220 1827
- ✓ J Banting (023) 9237 2210
- ⊢ 18 L 6139 yds SSS 70
- 👤 U SOC–arrange with Pro
- ££ £6.50–£13.50
- ⊷ 1 mile N of Portsmouth, on B2177
- ■ www.portsmouthgc.com

Romsey   (1900)

Nursling, Southampton, SO16 0XW
- ☎ **(023) 8073 2218**
- ⚐ (023) 8074 1036
- 📖 825
- ⚐ MTF Rees (023) 8073 4637
- ✓ M Desmond (023) 8073 6673
- ⊢ 18 L 5856 yds SSS 68
- 👤 WD–H WE/BH–M H
- ££ £23 D–£29
- ⊷ 2 miles SE of Romsey on A3057. M27/M271 Junction 3

Rowlands Castle   (1902)

Links Lane, Rowlands Castle, PO9 6AE
- ☎ **(023) 9241 2216**
- ⚐ (023) 9241 3649
- ✉ manager@rowlandscastlegolfclub .co.uk
- 📖 800 150(L) 50(J)
- ⚐ KD Fisher (023) 9241 2784
- ✓ P Klepacz (023) 9241 2785
- ⊢ 18 L 6618 yds Par 72 SSS 72
- 👤 WD–U H exc Wed am–restricted WE–phone first Sat–M SOC–Tues & Thurs
- ££ £30 (£35)
- ⊷ 9 miles S of Petersfield, off A3(M). 3 miles N of Havant
- 🏠 HS Colt

Royal Winchester   (1888)

Sarum Road, Winchester, SO22 5QE
- ☎ **(01962) 852462**
- ⚐ (01962) 865048
- 📖 750
- ⚐ D Thomson (Mgr)
- ✓ S Hunter (01962) 862473
- ⊢ 18 L 6204 yds SSS 70
- 👤 WD–U H WE/BH–M SOC–Mon/Tues/Wed
- ££ On application
- ⊷ W of Winchester. M3 Junction 11
- 🏠 JH Taylor

Sandford Springs   (1988)

Wolverton, Tadley, RG26 5RT
- ☎ **(01635) 296800**
- ⚐ (01635) 296801
- ✉ garye@leaderboardgolf.co.uk
- 📖 700
- ⚐ G Edmunds
- ✓ G Edmunds (01635) 296808
- ⊢ 27 L 6100 yds SSS 70
- 👤 WD–prior booking WE–M SOC–WD
- ££ £28 D–£37
- ⊷ 8 miles N of Basingstoke on A339
- 🏠 Hawtree

Somerley Park   (1995)

Somerley, Ringwood, BH24 3PL
- ☎ **(01425) 461496**
- 📖 169
- ⚐ J Staley, R Curtis (Props)
- ✓ J Waring (01202) 821703
- ⊢ 9 L 2155 yds Par 33 SSS 62
- 👤 M SOC
- ££ £10
- ⊷ 5 miles W of Ringwood
- 🏠 John Jacobs OBE

South Winchester

Romsey Road, Winchester, SO22 5QW
- ☎ **(01962) 877800**
- ⚐ (01962) 877900
- 📖 750
- ⚐ S Wright (Gen Mgr)
- ✓ R Adams (01962) 840469
- ⊢ 18 L 7086 yds SSS 74
- 👤 H SOC
- ££ £25 (£35)
- ⊷ S side of Winchester
- ⊕ Driving range
- 🏠 Thomas/Alliss
- ■ www.southwinchester.com

Southampton Municipal
(1935)

Public
Golf Course Road, Bassett, Southampton, SO16 7AY
- ☎ **(023) 8076 8407**
- ✓ J Cave
- ⊢ 18 L 6218 yds SSS 70
  9 L 2391 yds SSS 33
- 👤 U
- ££ On application
- ⊷ 2 miles N of Southampton

Southsea   (1914)

Public
The Clubhouse, Burrfields Road, Portsmouth, PO3 5JJ
- ☎ **(023) 9266 4549**
- ⚐ (023) 9265 0525
- 📖 350
- ⚐ K Parker (023) 9266 8667
- ✓ T Healy
- ⊢ 18 L 5970 yds SSS 68
- 👤 U SOC
- ££ £11 (£13)
- ⊷ 1 mile off M27 on A2030
- ⊕ Driving range

Southwick Park   (1977)

Pinsley Drive, Southwick, PO17 6EL
- ☎ **(023) 9238 0131**
- ⚐ (023) 9221 0289
- 📖 650 80(L)
- ⚐ NW Price
- ✓ J Green (023) 9238 0442
- ⊢ 18 L 5884 yds SSS 69
- 👤 WD–U booking necessary WE–NA before 2pm SOC
- ££ On application. Service Personnel reduced rate
- ⊷ 5 miles N of Portsmouth, off B2177

Southwood   (1977)

Public
Ively Road, Farnborough, GU14 0LJ
- ☎ **(01252) 548700**
- ⚐ (01252) 549091
- 📖 480
- ⚐ MJ Pettifor
- ✓ J Willmott
- ⊢ 18 L 5738 yds Par 69 SSS 68
- 👤 U
- ££ £15.50 (£18)
- ⊷ 1 mile W of Farnborough, off A325
- 🏠 M Hawtree

Stoneham   (1908)

Monks Wood Close, Bassett, Southampton, SO16 3TT
- ☎ **(023) 8076 9272**
- ⚐ (023) 8076 6320
- ✉ richard.penley-martin @stonehamgolfclub.org.uk
- 📖 600
- ⚐ R Penley-Martin (Mgr) (023) 8076 9272
- ✓ I Young (023) 8076 8397
- ⊢ 18 L 6387 yds SSS 70
- 👤 H SOC–Mon/Thurs/Fri
- ££ £32 D–£36 (£44 D–£55)
- ⊷ 2 miles N of Southampton on A27
- 🏠 Willie Park

Test Valley   (1992)

Micheldever Road, Overton, Basingstoke, RG25 3DS
- ☎ **(08707) 459020**
- ⚐ (08707) 459023
- 📖 550
- ⚐ A Briggs (Mgr) (08707) 459021
- ✓ A Briggs
- ⊢ 18 L 6897 yds SSS 73
- 👤 U SOC
- ££ £18 (£24)
- ⊷ 2 miles S of Overton on Micheldever road. M3 Junction 8 (A303)
- 🏠 Wright/Darcy

Tournerbury Golf Centre
(1993)

Pay and play
Tournerbury Road, Hayling Island, PO11 9DL
- ☎ **(023) 9246 2266**
- ✓ R Brown
- ⊢ 9 L 2956 yds SSS 35
- 👤 U SOC

£€   9 holes–£7 (£8.30)
⬧   E coast of Hayling Island. 3 miles S
     of Havant
⊕   Driving range

Tylney Park   (1973)

Rotherwick, Basingstoke, RG27 9AY
☎   **(01256) 762079**
🖥   (01256) 763079
📖   700
🏌   MR Alcock
🏑   C de Bruin (Mgr)
🏳   18 L 6108 yds SSS 69
🚹   WD–U WE–M or H SOC
£€   On application
⬧   2 miles NW of Hook. M3 Junction
     5

Waterlooville   (1907)

*Cherry Tree Ave, Cowplain,
Waterlooville, PO8 8AP*
☎   **(023) 9226 3388**
🖥   (023) 9234 7513
📖   800
🏌   D Nairne
🏑   J Hay (023) 9225 6911
🏳   18 L 6602 yds SSS 72
🚹   WD/WE–M H (Sun am–XL) SOC
£€   £30 D–£35
⬧   10 miles N of Portsmouth on A3
🏠   Henry Cotton
🖳   www.waterloovillegolfclub.co.uk

Wellow   (1991)

*Ryedown Lane, East Wellow, Romsey,
SO51 6BD*
☎   **(01794) 322872**
🖥   (01794) 323832
📖   600
🏌   Mrs C Gurd
🏑   N Bratley (01794) 323833
🏳   27 L 6000 yds SSS 69
🚹   U SOC–WD
£€   £17 (£21)
⬧   2 miles W of Romsey. M27
     Junction 2, via A36
🏠   W Wiltshire

Weybrook Park   (1971)

*Rooksdown Lane, Basingstoke,
RG24 9NT*
☎   **(01256) 320347**
🖥   (01256) 812973
🖂   office_weybrookpark@barbox.net
📖   600
🏌   A Dillon (Mgr)
🏑   A Dillon (01256) 333232
🏳   18 L 6468 yds SSS 71
🚹   WD–U WE–contact Mgr SOC
£€   £21.50 (£28)
⬧   1½ miles N of Basingstoke

Wickham Park

*Titchfield Lane, Wickham, Fareham,
PO17 5PJ*
☎   **(01329) 833342**
🖥   (01329) 834798
🖂   wpgc@crownsportsplc.com
🏌   I Yates (Mgr)
🏑   S Edwards

🏳   18 L 5898 yds Par 69 SSS 68
🚹   U SOC–WD
£€   £13 (£16)
⬧   2 miles N of Fareham. M27
     Junction 10
🏠   Jon Payn
🖳   www.wickhampark.co.uk

Worldham Park   (1993)

Pay and play
*Cakers Lane, Worldham, Alton,
GU34 3AG*
☎   **(01420) 543151/544606**
📖   500
🏌   NV Harvey (01420) 544606
🏑   J Le Roux (01420) 543151
🏳   18 L 6500 yds SSS 71
🚹   WD–U WE–U after 11am
     SOC–WD
£€   £11 (£14)
⬧   ½ mile E of Alton on B3004 to
     Bordon
⊕   Driving range
🏠   Troth/Whidborne

Herefordshire

Belmont Lodge   (1983)

Belmont, Hereford, HR2 9SA
☎   **(01432) 352666**
🖥   (01432) 358090
🖂   info@belmont-hereford.co.uk
📖   500
🏌   B Macaskill (Mgr)
🏑   M Welsh (01432) 352717
🏳   18 L 6511 yds SSS 71
🚹   U SOC
£€   On application
⬧   1½ miles S of Hereford on A465
🏠   B Sandow
🖳   www.belmont-hereford.co.uk

Burghill Valley   (1991)

*Tillington Road, Burghill, Hereford,
HR4 7RW*
☎   **(01432) 760456**
🖥   (01432) 761654
🖂   golf@bvgc.co.uk
🏌   K Smith (Mgr)
🏑   N Clarke (01432) 760808
🏳   18 L 6239 yds SSS 70
🚹   U SOC
£€   £20 (£25)
⬧   3 miles N of Hereford, off A4110
🖳   www.bvgc.co.uk

Cadmore Lodge   (1990)

Pay and play
*Berrington Green, Tenbury Wells,
Worcester, WR15 8TQ*
☎   **(01584) 810044**
🖥   (01584) 810044
📖   150
🏌   RV Farr
🏑   None
🏳   9 L 5129 yds Par 68 SSS 65
🚹   U
£€   D–£10 (D–£14)
⬧   2 miles S of Tenbury Wells on
     A4112
🖳   www.cadmorelodge.demon.co.uk

Hereford Municipal   (1983)

Public
Holmer Road, Hereford, HR4 9UD
☎   **(01432) 344376**
🖥   (01432) 266281
📖   200
🏌   G Evans
🏑   G Morgan (01432) 344376
🏳   9 L 3060 yds Par 70 SSS 69
🚹   U SOC
£€   18 holes–£6.90 (£8.50) 9
     holes–£4.60 (£5.60)
⬧   Hereford Leisure Centre, A49
     Leominster road

Herefordshire   (1896)

*Raven's Causeway, Wormsley, Hereford,
HR4 8LY*
☎   **(01432) 830219**
🖥   (01432) 830095
📖   770 150(L) 55(J)
🏌   TG Horobin (Hon)
🏑   D Hemming (01432) 830465
🏳   18 L 6031 yds SSS 69
🚹   U–phone first SOC
£€   £20 D–£25 (£25 D–£32)
⬧   6 miles NW of Hereford

Kington   (1926)

Bradnor Hill, Kington, HR5 3RE
☎   **(01544) 230340**
🖥   (01544) 340270
📖   500
🏌   GR Wictome (01544) 340270
🏑   A Gealy (01544) 231320
🏳   18 L 5840 yds SSS 68
🚹   WE–NA before 10.15am –restricted
     1.30–2.45pm SOC
£€   £16 D–£21 (£22 D–£27)
⬧   1 mile N of Kington
🏠   CK Hutchinson

Leominster   (1967)

Ford Bridge, Leominster, HR6 0LE
☎   **(01568) 612863 (Clubhouse)**
🖥   (01568) 610055
📖   450
🏌   L Green (01568) 610055
🏑   A Ferriday (01568) 611402
🏳   18 L 6026 yds SSS 69
🚹   U SOC
£€   £15.50 D–£19 (£22 D–£25)
⬧   3 miles S of Leominster on A49
     (Leominster By-pass)
🏠   R Sandow

Ross-on-Wye   (1903)

*Two Park, Gorsley, Ross-on-Wye,
HR9 7UT*
☎   **(01989) 720267**
🖥   (01989) 720212
🖂   secretary@therossonwyegolfclub
     .co.uk
📖   760
🏌   P Plumb
🏑   N Catchpole (01989) 720439
🏳   18 L 6500 yds Par 72 SSS 71
🚹   U SOC–Wed–Fri (min 16 players)
£€   £36–£46 SOC–£28–£40
⬧   5 miles N of Ross-on-Wye, by M50
     Junction 3

⊕ Parkland driving range
⌂ CK Cotton
■ www.rossonwyegolfclub.co.uk

Sapey   (1991)
Proprietary
Upper Sapey, Worcester, WR6 6XT
☎ **(01886) 853288**
⌨ (01886) 853485
✉ anybody@sapeygolf.co.uk
▥ 450
♙ Miss L Stevenson
✓ C Knowles
▷ 18 L 5895 yds SSS 68
   9 hole Par 3 course
♙ WD–U WE–NA before 10am SOC
£€ £20 (£25)
♠ 6 miles N of Bromyard on B4203.
   M5 Junction 5
■ www.sapeygolf.co.uk

South Herefordshire   (1992)
Twin Lakes, Upton Bishop, Ross-on-Wye, HR9 7UA
☎ **(01989) 780535**
⌨ (01989) 780535
▥ 300
♙ RLA Lee (Mgr)
✓ E Litchfield
▷ 18 L 6672 yds Par 71 SSS 72
   9 hole Par 3 course
♙ U SOC
£€ £15 (£20)
♠ 3 miles NE of Ross-on-Wye. M50
   Junction 4
⊕ Floodlit driving range
⌂ John Day

Hertfordshire

Aldenham G&CC   (1975)
Church Lane, Aldenham, Watford, WD25 8NN
☎ **(01923) 853929**
⌨ (01923) 858472
✉ aldenhamgolf@ukonline.co.uk
▥ 500
♙ Mrs J Phillips
✓ T Dunstan (01923) 857889
▷ 18 L 6456 yds SSS 71
   9 L 2350 yds
♙ WD–U WE–U after 12.30pm
£€ 18 hole: £26 (£35). 9 hole: £10
   (£12)
♠ 3 miles E of Watford, off B462. M1
   Junction 5

Aldwickbury Park   (1995)
Piggottshill Lane, Wheathampstead Road, Harpenden, AL5 1AB
☎ **(01582) 765112**
⌨ (01582) 760113
✉ enquiries
   @aldwickburyparkgolfclub.com
▥ 700
♙ A Knott
✓ P Toyer (01582) 760112
▷ 18 L 6032 yds Par 71 SSS 69
   9 hole Par 3 course

♙ WD–U booking necessary WE–U
   after 1pm SOC–WD
£€ £25 (£30)
♠ E of Harpenden on
   Wheathampstead road. M1 Junction
   9. A1(M) Junction 4
⌂ Gillett/Brown
■ www.aldwickburyparkgolfclub.com

Arkley   (1909)
Rowley Green Road, Barnet, EN5 3HL
☎ **(020) 8449 0394**
⌨ (020) 8440 5214
▥ 350
♙ D Reed
✓ M Porter (020) 8440 8473
▷ 9 L 6106 yds SSS 69
♙ WD–U WE–M SOC–Wed–Fri
£€ £24
♠ NW of Barnet, off A1(M)
⌂ James Braid

Ashridge   (1932)
Little Gaddesden, Berkhamsted, HP4 1LY
☎ **(01442) 842244**
⌨ (01442) 843770
✉ info@ashridgegolfclub.ltd.uk
▥ 700
♙ MS Silver
✓ A Ainsworth (01442) 842307
▷ 18 L 6505 yds SSS 71
♙ WD only–phone Sec
£€ On application
♠ 5 miles N of Berkhamsted on
   B4506
⌂ Campbell/Hutchison/Hotchkin
■ www.ashridgegolfclub.ltd.uk

Barkway Park   (1992)
Nuthampstead Road, Barkway, Royston, SG8 8EN
☎ **(01763) 849070**
▥ 285
♙ GS Cannon
✓ J Bates (01763) 848215
▷ 18 L 6997 yds SSS 74
♙ U
£€ £10 (£15)
♠ 5 miles SE of Royston, on B1368
⌂ Vivien Saunders

Batchwood Hall   (1935)
Pay and play
Batchwood Drive, St Albans, AL3 5XA
☎ **(01727) 833349**
⌨ (01582) 833530
▥ 425
♙ B Hudson
▷ 18 L 6487 yds SSS 71
♙ WD–U WE–NA before 10am
£€ £10.80 (£13.90)
♠ NW of St Albans on A5081. 5
   miles S of M1 Junction 9
⌂ JH Taylor

Batchworth Park   (1996)
London Road, Rickmansworth, WD3 1JS
☎ **(01923) 711400**
⌨ (01923) 710200

▥ 750
✓ S Proudfoot (01923) 714922
▷ 18 L 6723 yds Par 72 SSS 72
♙ M
£€ N/A
♠ 1 mile SE of Rickmansworth on
   A404. M25 Junction 18
⊕ Indoor Academy. Practice range
⌂ Dave Thomas

Berkhamsted   (1890)
The Common, Berkhamsted, HP4 2QB
☎ **(01442) 865832**
⌨ (01442) 863730
✉ barryh@berkhamstedgc.co.uk
▥ 450 120(L) 50(J)
♙ BJ Hill
✓ J Clarke (01442) 865851
▷ 18 L 6605 yds Par 71 SSS 72
♙ U H WE–M before 11.30am
   SOC–Wed & Fri
£€ On application
♠ 1 mile N of Berkhamsted. M25
   Junction 21 (A41). M1 Junction 8
⌂ HS Colt/James Braid

Bishop's Stortford   (1910)
Dunmow Road, Bishop's Stortford, CM23 5HP
☎ **(01279) 654715**
⌨ (01279) 655215
✉ bishopstortfordgc@hotmail.com
▥ 900
♙ B Collins
✓ SM Bryan (01279) 651324
▷ 18 L 6404 yds SSS 71
♙ WD–U H WE–M SOC–WD exc
   Tues
£€ £28 D–£35
♠ E of Bishop's Stortford on A1250.
   M11 Junction 8,¹/₂mile
⌂ James Braid
■ www.bsgc.co.uk

Boxmoor   (1890)
18 Box Lane, Hemel Hempstead, HP3 0DJ
☎ **(01442) 242434 (Clubhouse)**
▥ 290
♙ CJ Horsted (07976) 747567
✓ None
▷ 9 L 4854 yds SSS 64
♙ U exc Sun–NA
£€ £12 Sat–£14
♠ 1 mile W of Hemel Hempstead on
   B4505 to Chesham
■ www.boxmoorgolfclub.co.uk

Brickendon Grange (1964)
Pembridge Lane, Brickendon, Hertford, SG13 8PD
☎ **(01992) 511258**
⌨ (01992) 511411
✉ genman@brickendongrangegc
   .co.uk
▥ 700
♙ C Day
✓ G Tippett (01992) 511218
▷ 18 L 6325 yds SSS 70
♙ WD–U H WE/BH–M SOC

££ £28 D–£38
⊛ Bayford, 3 miles S of Hertford
⌂ CK Cotton
■ www.brickendongrangegc.co.uk

Bridgedown (1994)

St Albans Road, Barnet, EN5 4RE
☎ (020) 8440 4120
🖳 (020) 8441 7649
▦ 400
✍ Mrs A Menai-Davis (020) 8441 7649
✓ L Jones
▷ 18 L 6626 yds Par 72 SSS 72
👥 U
££ £15 (£17)
⊛ 1 mile S of South Mimms on A1081. M25 Junction 23
⊕ Practice range
⌂ Howard Swann

Briggens House Hotel (1988)

Briggens Park, Stanstead Road, Stanstead Abbotts, SG12 8LD
☎ (01279) 793742
🖳 (01279) 793685
▦ 280
✍ A Battle (Mgr)
▷ 9 L 5825 yds SSS 69
👥 U SOC
££ 9 holes–£11 (£15)
⊛ 4 miles E of Hertford, off A414

Brocket Hall (1992)

Welwyn, AL8 7XG
☎ (01707) 335241
✉ paulden@brocket-hall.co.uk
▦ 790
✍ P Densham (01707) 335241
✓ K Wood (01707) 390063
▷ Melbourne 18 L 6616 yds SSS 72; Palmerston 18 L 6925 yds SSS 73
👥 M H
⊛ On B653 to Wheathampstead. A1(M) Junction 4
⊕ Driving range. Nick Faldo Golf Institute
⌂ Melbourne-Alliss/Clark. Palmerston-Steel

Brookmans Park (1930)

Brookmans Park, Hatfield, AL9 7AT
☎ (01707) 652487
🖳 (01707) 661851
▦ 800
✍ PA Gill
✓ I Jelley (01707) 652468
▷ 18 L 6473 yds SSS 71
👥 WD–UH WE/BH–M SOC
££ £32
⊛ 3 miles S of Hatfield, off A1000
⌂ Hawtree/Taylor

Bushey G&CC (1980)

High Street, Bushey, WD2 1BJ
☎ (020) 8950 2283
🖳 (020) 8386 1181
▦ 446
✍ B Worthington

✓ G Atkinson (020) 8950 2215
▷ 9 L 3030 yds SSS 70
👥 WD–U before 6pm WE/BH–U after 3.30pm Wed–closed SOC–WD exc Wed
££ 18 holes–£18 (£21). 9 holes–£12 (£14)
⊛ 2 miles S of Watford on A4008
⊕ Driving range

Bushey Hall (1890)

Bushey Hall Drive, Bushey, WD23 2EP
☎ (01923) 222253
🖳 (01923) 229759
✉ roy@golfclubuk.co.uk
▦ 460
✍ R Penman
✓ K Wickham (01923) 225802
▷ 18 L 6055 yds SSS 70
👥 U SOC–WD
££ £25 (£32)
⊛ 1 mile SE of Watford. M1 Junction 5
⌂ James Braid
■ www.golfclubuk.co.uk

Chadwell Springs (1974)

Hertford Road, Ware, SG12 9LE
☎ (01920) 463647
▦ 350
✍ M Scott (01920) 461447
✓ M Wall (01920) 462075
▷ 9 L 3021 yds SSS 69
👥 WD–U WE–M
££ £20
⊛ Between Ware and Hertford on A119

Chesfield Downs (1991)

Pay and play
Jack's Hill, Graveley, Stevenage, SG4 7EQ
☎ (08707) 460020
🖳 (08707) 460021
▦ 550
✍ P Barnfather
✓ K Bond
▷ 18 L 6646 yds SSS 71
9 holes Par 3 course
👥 U SOC
££ 18 hole:£18 (£26). 9 hole:£5 (£6)
⊛ B197, N of Stevenage. A1(M) Junctions 8 or 9
⊕ Driving range
⌂ Jonathan Gaunt

Cheshunt (1976)

Public
Park Lane, Cheshunt, EN7 6QD
☎ (01992) 29777
▦ 280
✍ B Furne
✓ D Banks (01992) 24009
▷ 18 L 6608 yds SSS 71
👥 U–booking required
££ £12 (£16.50)
⊛ Off A10 at Church Lane, Cheshunt. M25 Junction 25, 3 miles
⌂ Hawtree

Chorleywood (1890)

Common Road, Chorleywood, WD3 5LN
☎ (01923) 282009
🖳 (01923) 286739
✉ chorleywood.gc@btclick.com
▦ 320
✍ RA Botham
✓ None
▷ 9 L 2856 yds SSS 67
👥 WD–U exc Tues am WE–U after 11.30am SOC
££ £20 (£25)
⊛ 3 miles N of Rickmansworth, off A404. M25 Junction 18

Danesbury Park (1992)

Codicote Road, Welwyn, AL6 9SD
☎ (01438) 840100
🖳 (01727) 846109
▦ 300
✍ D Snowdon
✓ G Harvey
▷ 9 L 4150 yds SSS 60
👥 U SOC–WD
⊛ ³/₄ mile from A1(M) Junction 6 on B656 Hitchin road
⌂ Derek Snowdon

Dyrham Park CC (1963)

Galley Lane, Barnet, EN5 4RA
☎ (020) 8440 3361
🖳 (020) 8441 9836
▦ 600
✍ K Sutton
✓ W Large (020) 8440 3904
▷ 18 L 6422 yds SSS 71
👥 M SOC–Wed
⊛ 10 miles N of London. M25 Junction 23
⌂ CK Cotton

East Herts (1899)

Hamels Park, Buntingford, SG9 9NA
☎ (01920) 821923
🖳 (01920) 823700
▦ 700
✍ C Day (01920) 821978
✓ G Culmer (01920) 821922
▷ 18 L 6456 yds SSS 71
👥 WD–H exc Wed–NA before 1pm WE–M
££ On application
⊛ ¹/₄ mile N of Puckeridge on A10

Elstree (1984)

Watling Street, Elstree, WD6 3AA
☎ (020) 8238 6947 (Clubhouse)
🖳 (020) 8207 6390
✉ admin@elstree-golf.co.uk
▦ 400
✍ K Roberts (020) 8238 6942
✓ M Warwick (020) 8238 6941
▷ 18 L 6556 yds Par 73 SSS 72
👥 U SOC
££ On application
⊛ A5183, 1 mile N of Elstree. M1 Junction 4
⊕ Floodlit driving range
⌂ Donald Steel
■ www.elstree-golfclub.co.uk

Forest Hills (1994)

Newgate Street, SG13 8EW
- ☎ **(01707) 876825**
- 🖥 (01707) 876825
- 📖 170
- 🏌 G Spearpoint
- 🏑 C Easton
- ⛳ 9 L 3220 yds Par 72 SSS 71
- 👥 WD–U WE/BH–by arrangement
- ££ £15 (£20)
- ⛳ 3 miles W of Cheshunt. M25 Junction 25
- 🏛 Mel Flannagan

Great Hadham (1993)

Great Hadham Road, Bishop's Stortford, SG10 6JE
- ☎ **(01279) 843558**
- 🖥 (01279) 842122
- 📖 700
- 🏌 I Bailey
- 🏑 K Lunt (01279) 843888
- ⛳ 18 L 6854 yds Par 72 SSS 73
- 👥 WD–U WE/BH–NA before 12 noon SOC
- ££ £20 (£27)
- ⛳ 3 miles SW of Bishops Stortford (B1004). M11 Junction 8
- ⊕ Driving range

Hadley Wood (1922)

Beech Hill, Hadley Wood, Barnet, EN4 0JJ
- ☎ **(020) 8449 4328**
- 🖥 (020) 8364 8633
- 📧 gen.mgr@hadleywoodgc.com
- 📖 635
- 🏌 CS Silcox (Gen Mgr)
- 🏑 P Jones (020) 8449 3285
- ⛳ 18 L 6514 yds SSS 71
- 👥 WD–H WE/BH–M SOC
- ££ On application
- ⛳ 10 miles N of London, off A111 between Potters Bar and Cockfosters. 2 miles S of M25 Junction 24
- ⊕ Practice range
- 🏛 Dr A Mackenzie
- ■ www.hadleywoodgc.com

Hanbury Manor G&CC (1990)

Ware, SG12 0SD
- ☎ **(01920) 487722**
- 🖥 (01920) 487692
- 📧 brian.alderson@marriotthotels .co.uk
- 📖 500
- 🏌 S Emms
- 🏑 D Ingram
- ⛳ 18 L 7016 yds SSS 74
- 👥 M H + Hotel guests
- ££ £85
- ⛳ 8 miles N of M25 Junction 25 on A10 at Thundridge
- 🏛 Jack Nicklaus II

Harpenden (1894)

Hammonds End, Harpenden, AL5 2AX
- ☎ **(01582) 712580**
- 🖥 (01582) 712725

- 📧 office@harpendengolfclub.co.uk
- 📖 800
- 🏌 FLK Clapp (Gen Mgr)
- 🏑 P Cherry (01582) 767124
- ⛳ 18 L 6381 yds SSS 70
- 👥 WD–U exc Thurs WE/BH–M SOC–WD exc Thurs
- ££ £26 D–£36
- ⛳ 6 miles N of St Albans on B487
- 🏛 Hawtree/Taylor

Harpenden Common (1931)

East Common, Harpenden, AL5 1BL
- ☎ **(01582) 712856**
- 🖥 (01582) 715959
- 📖 740
- 🏌 GD Eastwood (01582) 715959
- 🏑 D Fitzsimmons (01582) 460655
- ⛳ 18 L 6214 yds SSS 70
- 👥 WD–U H WE–M SOC
- ££ £25 (£30)
- ⛳ 4 miles N of St Albans, on A1081
- 🏛 K Brown (1995)

Hartsbourne G&CC (1946)

Hartsbourne Avenue, Bushey Heath, WD2 1JW
- ☎ **(020) 8950 1133**
- 🖥 (020) 8950 5357
- 📖 750
- 🏌 S Whyte
- 🏑 A Cardwell (020) 8950 2836
- ⛳ 18 L 6385 yds SSS 70
-    9 L 5773 yds SSS 68
- 👥 NA SOC
- ⛳ 5 miles SE of Watford, off A4008
- 🏛 Hawtree/Taylor

Hatfield London CC (1976)

Pay and play
Bedwell Park, Essendon, Hatfield, AL9 6HN
- ☎ **(01707) 663131**
- 🖥 (01707) 278475
- 📖 260
- 🏌 H Takeda
- 🏑 N Greer (01707) 650431
- ⛳ 18 L 6808 yds SSS 72
-    18 hole course
- 👥 U SOC
- ££ £19 (£27)
- ⛳ 4 miles E of Hatfield on B158. M25 Junction 24. A1(M) Junction 4
- ⊕ 9 hole pitch & putt course
- 🏛 Fred Hawtree

The Hertfordshire (1995)

Proprietary
Broxbournebury Mansion, White Stubbs Lane, Broxbourne, EN10 7PY
- ☎ **(01992) 466666**
- 🖥 (01992) 470326
- 📧 hertfordshire@americangolf .co.uk
- 📖 690
- 🏌 J Hetherington
- 🏑 D Smith
- ⛳ 18 L 6400 yds Par 70 SSS 70
- 👥 U H SOC
- ££ £30
- ⛳ 8 miles N of M25 Junction 25, off A10

- ⊕ Floodlit driving range
- 🏛 Jack Nicklaus II

Kingsway Golf Centre (1991)

Cambridge Road, Melbourn, Royston, SG8 6EY
- ☎ **(01763) 262727**
- 🖥 (01763) 263298
- 📖 200
- 🏌 B Smith
- 🏑 S Brown
- ⛳ 9 L 2500 yds Par 33
-    9 hole Par 3 course
- 👥 U SOC
- ££ 9 holes–£5.50 (£7.50). 18 holes–£9 (£12)
- ⛳ N of Royston on A10
- ⊕ Driving range

Knebworth (1908)

Deards End Lane, Knebworth, SG3 6NL
- ☎ **(01438) 812752 (Clubhouse)**
- 🖥 (01438) 815216
- 📖 1000
- 🏌 M Parsons MBE (01438) 812752
- 🏑 G Parker (01438) 812757
- ⛳ 18 L 6492 yds SSS 71
- 👥 WD–U H WE–M SOC–Mon/Tues/Thurs
- ££ £30
- ⛳ 1 mile S of Stevenage on B197. A1(M) Junction 7
- 🏛 Willie Park

Lamerwood (1996)

Codicote Road, Wheathampstead, AL4 8GB
- ☎ **(01582) 833013**
- 🖥 (01582) 832604
- 📧 lamerwood.cc@virgin.net
- 🏌 S Takabatake (Golf Dir)
- 🏑 M Masters (01582) 833013
- ⛳ 18 L 6953 yds Par 72
-    9 hole Par 3 course
- 👥 U
- ££ £24 (£35)
- ⛳ 5 miles W of A1(M) Junction 4 on B653
- ⊕ Driving range
- 🏛 Cameron Sinclair

Letchworth (1905)

Letchworth Lane, Letchworth, SG6 3NQ
- ☎ **(01462) 683203**
- 🖥 (01462) 484567
- 📧 letchworthgolfclub@uk2.net
- 📖 900
- 🏌 AR Bailey
- 🏑 (01462) 682713
- ⛳ 18 L 6181 yds SSS 69
- 👥 WD–H WE–M SOC–Wed–Fri
- ££ £28
- ⛳ S of Letchworth, off A505. A1(M) Junction 9
- ⊕ Driving range
- 🏛 Harry Vardon

For list of abbreviations and key to symbols see page 649

Little Hay Golf Complex

(1977)

Pay and play

Box Lane, Bovingdon, Hemel
Hempstead, HP3 0DQ

- ☎ **(01442) 833798**
- 🖳 (01442) 831399
- ✍ C Gordon (Golf Mgr)
- ⌁ N Allen
- ⊳ 18 L 6592 yds SSS 71
- ⋀ U SOC
- £€ £12 (£16.50)
- ⊷ 2 miles W of Hemel Hempstead, on B4505 to Chesham
- ⊕ Driving range. Pitch & putt
- ⌂ Hawtree

Manor of Groves G&CC

(1991)

High Wych, Sawbridgeworth, CM21 0LA

- ☎ **(01279) 721486/603543**
- 🖳 (01279) 726972
- ⌨ 595
- ✍ R Walker (01279) 722247
- ⌁ R Hurd
- ⊳ 18 L 6280 yds SSS 70
- ⋀ WD–U WE–NA before noon SOC
- £€ On application
- ⊷ 1 mile N of Harlow
- ⌂ S Sharer

Mid Herts   (1892)

Gustard Wood, Wheathampstead,
AL4 8RS

- ☎ **(01582) 832242**
- 🖳 (01582) 834834
- ✉ secretary@mid-hertsgolfclub.co.uk
- ⌨ 500(M) 125(L)
- ✍ RJH Jourdan
- ⌁ B Puttick (01582) 832788
- ⊳ 18 L 6060 yds SSS 69
- ⋀ WD–UH exc Tues & Wed pm WE/BH–M SOC
- £€ On application
- ⊷ 6 miles N of St Albans on B651
- ■ www.mid-hertsgolfclub.co.uk

Mill Green   (1994)

Gypsy Lane, Mill Green, Welwyn Garden
City, AL7 4TY

- ☎ **(01707) 276900**
- 🖳 (01707) 276898
- ✍ D Naughton (Gen Mgr)
- ⌁ I Parker (01707) 270542
- ⊳ 18 L 6615 yds Par 72 SSS 72 Par 3 course
- ⋀ U SOC–WD
- £€ £25 (£30)
- ⊷ S of Welwyn Garden City, off A414. A1 Junction 4
- ⌂ Clark/Alliss

Moor Park   (1923)

Rickmansworth, WD3 1QN

- ☎ **(01923) 773146**
- 🖳 (01923) 777109
- ⌨ 1700
- ✍ JM Moore (01923) 773146
- ⌁ L Farmer (01923) 774113
- ⊳ High 18 L 6713 yds SSS 72 West 18 L 5823 yds SSS 68

- ⋀ WD–H WE/BH–M SOC
- £€ High £65. West £40
- ⊷ 1 mile SE of Rickmansworth, off Batchworth roundabout (A4145). M25 Junction 18, 2 miles
- ⌂ HS Colt
- ■ www.moorparkgc.co.uk

Old Fold Manor   (1910)

Old Fold Lane, Hadley Green, Barnet,
EN5 4QN

- ☎ **(020) 8440 9185**
- 🖳 (020) 8441 4863
- ✉ manager@oldfoldmanor.co.uk
- ⌨ 526
- ✍ AW Dickens (Mgr)
- ⌁ P McEvoy (020) 8440 7488
- ⊳ 18 L 6466 yds SSS 71
- ⋀ WD–H WE–M SOC–Thurs & Fri
- £€ £25 D–£35
- ⊷ 1 mile N of Barnet on A1000
- ■ www.oldfoldmanor.co.uk

Oxhey Park

Prestwick Road, South Oxhey, Watford,
WD19 7EX

- ☎ **(01923) 248213/210118**
- ⌨ 110
- ✍ AT Duggan (Prop)
- ⌁ J Wright
- ⊳ 9 L 1637 yds Par 58
- ⋀ U
- £€ 9 holes–£6 (£8). 18 holes–£8 (£10)
- ⊷ 2 miles SW of Watford. M1 Junction 5
- ⊕ Driving range

Panshanger Golf Complex

(1976)

Old Herns Lane, Welwyn Garden City,
AL7 2ED

- ☎ **(01707) 333312/333350 (Bookings)**
- ⊳ 18 L 6167 yds SSS 70 9 hole Par 3 course
- ⋀ U
- £€ On application
- ⊷ 2 miles off A1, via B1000 to Hertford

Porters Park   (1899)

Shenley Hill, Radlett, WD7 7AZ

- ☎ **(01923) 854127**
- 🖳 (01923) 855475
- ⌨ 850
- ✍ P Marshall
- ⌁ D Gleeson (01923) 854366
- ⊳ 18 L 6313 yds SSS 70
- ⋀ WD–H (phone first) WE/BH–M SOC–Wed & Thurs
- £€ £30–£45
- ⊷ E of Radlett on Shenley road. M25 Junction 22

Potters Bar   (1923)

Darkes Lane, Potters Bar, EN6 1DE

- ☎ **(01707) 652020**
- 🖳 (01707) 655051
- ⌨ 600
- ✍ PK Watson (Mgr)
- ⌁ G A'ris, J Harding (01707) 652987

- ⊳ 18 L 6279 yds SSS 70
- ⋀ WD–H WE/BH–M SOC–WD exc Wed
- £€ £25 D–£35
- ⊷ 1 mile N of M25 Junction 24, off A1000
- ⌂ James Braid
- ■ www.pottersbargolfclub.com

Redbourn   (1970)

Kinsbourne Green Lane, Redbourn, St
Albans, AL3 7QA

- ☎ **(01582) 793493**
- 🖳 (01582) 794362
- ✉ enquiries@redbourngolfclub.com
- ✍ R Fay
- ⌁ S Hunter
- ⊳ 18 L 6506 yds SSS 71 9 hole Par 3 course
- ⋀ WD–U booking necessary WE/BH–H SOC–WD
- £€ 18 hole: £25 (£30) 9 hole: £7 (£10)
- ⊷ 4 miles N of St Albans, off A5. 1 mile S of M1 Junction 9
- ⊕ Target golf range
- ■ www.redbourngolfclub.com

Rickmansworth   (1937)

Public

Moor Lane, Rickmansworth, WD3 1QL

- ☎ **(01923) 775278**
- 🖳 (01923) 775278
- ⌨ 250
- ⌁ A Dobbins (01923) 775278
- ⊳ 18 L 4493 yds SSS 62 9 hole Par 3 course
- ⋀ U
- £€ £11 (£15.50)
- ⊷ ½ mile SE of Rickmansworth, off Batchworth roundabout (A4145). M25 Junction 18, 2 miles
- ⌂ HS Colt

Royston   (1892)

Baldock Road, Royston, SG8 5BG

- ☎ **(01763) 242696**
- 🖳 (01763) 246910
- ✉ roystongolf@btconnect.com
- ⌨ 750
- ✍ J Beech (01763) 242696
- ⌁ S Clark (01763) 243476
- ⊳ 18 L 6086 yds SSS 70
- ⋀ WD–H WE–M SOC–WD
- £€ £25 D–£30
- ⊷ SW of Royston on A505
- ⌂ H Vardon

Sandy Lodge   (1910)

Sandy Lodge Lane, Northwood, Middx,
HA6 2JD

- ☎ **(01923) 825429**
- 🖳 (01923) 824319
- ⌨ 700
- ✍ JC Coombes
- ⌁ J Pinsent (01923) 825321
- ⊳ 18 L 6328 yds SSS 71
- ⋀ H or M SOC
- £€ On application
- ⊷ Adjacent Moor Park Station
- ⌂ Harry Vardon

Shendish Manor　(1988)
Pay and play
Shendish Manor, London Road, Apsley, HP3 0AA
☎ **(01442) 251806**
🖥 (01442) 230683
📧 golf@shendish-manor.com
🏌 T Concannon
⛳ 18 L 5660 yds Par 70 SSS 68
👥 U SOC
£€ £15 (£25)
🚗 S of Hemel Hempstead, off A41. M25 Junction 20
🏠 Cotton/Steel
■ www.shendish-manor.com

South Herts　(1899)
Links Drive, Totteridge, London, N20 8QU
☎ **(020) 8445 0117**
🖥 (020) 8445 7569
📖 850
🏌 KA Bravant (020) 8445 2035
✓ RY Mitchell (020) 8445 4633
⛳ 18 L 6470 yds SSS 71
　 9 L 1581 yds
👥 WD–IH WE/BH–M
£€ On application
🚗 Totteridge Lane
🏠 Harry Vardon

Stevenage　(1980)
Public
Aston Lane, Stevenage, SG2 7EL
☎ **(01438) 880424**
📖 450
🏌 Mrs S Elwin (01438) 880322
✓ S Barker (01438) 880424
⛳ 18 L 6451 yds SSS 71
　 9 hole Par 3 course
👥 U
£€ £12 (£16)
🚗 Off A602 to Hertford. A1(M) Junction 7
⊕ Driving range
🏠 John Jacobs

Stocks Hotel G&CC　(1994)
Stocks Road, Aldbury, Tring, HP23 5RX
☎ **(01442) 851341**
🖥 (01442) 851253
📖 440
🏌 R Darling (Golf Mgr)
✓ PR Lane (Ext 311)
⛳ 18 L 7016 yds SSS 74
👥 H SOC
£€ £30 (£40)
🚗 Aldbury, 2 miles E of Tring. A41(T), 2 miles
⊕ Practice range
🏠 M Billcliffe

Verulam　(1905)
226 London Road, St Albans, AL1 1JG
☎ **(01727) 853327**
🖥 (01727) 812201
📖 712
🏌 JR Maguire (Gen Mgr)
✓ N Burch (01727) 861401
⛳ 18 L 6448 yds Par 72 SSS 71
👥 WD–H exc Mon–U WE/BH–M

SOC–Tues & Thurs
£€ £25 Mon–£20
🚗 1 mile SE of St Albans on A1081. M25 Junction 21A or 22. M1 Junction 6
⊕ Practice range
🏠 Braid/Steel
■ www.verulamgolf.co.uk

Welwyn Garden City　(1922)
Mannicotts, High Oaks Road, Welwyn Garden City, AL8 7BP
☎ **(01707) 325243**
🖥 (01707) 393213
📖 900
🏌 R Blower (Gen Mgr) (01707) 325243
✓ R May (01707) 325525
⛳ 18 L 6100 yds SSS 69
👥 WD–H WE/BH–NA
£€ On application
🚗 1 mile N of Hatfield. A1(M) Junction 4 - B197 to Valley Road
🏠 Hawtree

West Herts　(1890)
Cassiobury Park, Watford, WD3 3GG
☎ **(01923) 236484**
🖥 (01923) 222300
📖 700
🏌 CC Dodman
✓ CS Gough (01923) 220352
⛳ 18 L 6488 yds SSS 71
👥 WD–U WE/BH–M SOC–Wed & Fri
£€ £30 (£38)
🚗 Off A412, between Watford and Rickmansworth
🏠 Morris/Mackenzie

Wheathampstead　(2001)
Pay and play
Harpenden Road, Wheathampstead, St Albans, AL4 8EZ
☎ **(01582) 833941**
🖥 (01582) 833941
🏌 JD Edgar
✓ JD Edgar
⛳ 9 L 2100 yds Par 31 SSS 31
👥 U SOC
£€ £13 (£14). 9 holes–£8.50
🚗 1 mile W of Wheathampstead (B653)
⊕ Driving range
🏠 JD Edgar

Whipsnade Park　(1974)
Studham Lane, Dagnall, HP4 1RH
☎ **(01442) 842330**
🖥 (01442) 842090
📧 whipsnadeparkgc@talk21.com
📖 600
🏌 Andrea King
✓ D Turner
⛳ 18 L 6812 yds SSS 72
👥 WD–U WE–M SOC–WD
£€ £27 D–£37
🚗 8 miles N of Hemel Hempstead, off A4147
■ www.whipsnadeparkgc.com

Whitehill　(1990)
Dane End, Ware, SG12 0JS
☎ **(01920) 438495**
🖥 (01920) 438891
📧 whitehillgolfcentre@btinternet.com
📖 550
🏌 Mr & Mrs A Smith (Props)
✓ J Belsham
⛳ 18 L 6802 yds SSS 72
👥 U
£€ £21 (£25.50)
🚗 4 miles N of Ware (A10)
⊕ Floodlit driving range

Isle of Man

Castletown Golf Links　(1892)
Fort Island, Derbyhaven, IM9 1UA
☎ **(01624) 822201**
🖥 (01624) 824633
📧 golflinks@manx.net
📖 500
🏌 B Watts (Hon)
✓ M Crowe (01624) 822211
⛳ 18 L 6711 yds SSS 72
👥 U SOC
£€ £35 (£40)
🚗 1 mile E of Castletown. 3 miles from Airport
🏠 Old Tom Morris
■ www.golfiom.com

Douglas Municipal　(1927)
Public
Pulrose Park, Douglas, IM2 1AE
☎ **(01624) 675952 (Clubhouse)**
📖 300
🏌 M Murray
✓ K Parry (01624) 661558
⛳ 18 L 5922 yds Par 69 SSS 69
👥 U
£€ £8.50 (£10.50)
🚗 Douglas Pier 2 miles
🏠 Dr A Mackenzie

King Edward Bay　(1893)
Groudle Road, Onchan, IM3 2JR
☎ **(01624) 620430/673821**
🖥 (01624) 676794
📖 400
🏌 B Holt (01624) 670977
✓ D Jones (01624) 672709
⛳ 18 L 5457 yds SSS 65
👥 U SOC
£€ £10 (£12)
🚗 1 mile N of Douglas
🏠 Tom Morris (1893 course)

Mount Murray G&CC (1994)
Santon, IM4 2HT
☎ **(01624) 661111**
🖥 (01624) 611116
📖 360
🏌 AD Dyson (Ext 3023)
✓ AD Dyson (Ext 3023)
⛳ 18 L 6664 yds SSS 72

U H SOC
££ £18 (£24)
⊕ 3 miles SW of Douglas
⊕ Driving range

Peel (1895)
Rheast Lane, Peel, IM5 1BG
☎ **(01624) 842227**
▱ (01624) 843456
▥ 600
✍ MND Robinson (01624) 843456
✔ M Crowe
ᛙ 18 L 5874 yds SSS 69
ᛟ WD–U WE/BH–NA before
    10.30am SOC
££ £20 (£28)
⊕ 10 miles W of Douglas via A1
⛨ James Braid
▪ www.geocities.com/peelgc

Port St Mary (1936)
Public
Kallow Road, Port St Mary, IM9 5EJ
☎ **(01624) 834932**
✍ T Boyle (Hon)
✔ M Crowe (01624) 822221
ᛙ 9 L 2711 yds SSS 66
ᛟ WD–U WE–NA before 10.30am
    SOC
££ On application
⊕ 6 miles S of Castletown via A5
⛨ George Duncan

Ramsey (1891)
Brookfield, Ramsey, IM8 2AH
☎ **(01624) 813365/812244**
▱ (01624) 815833
▥ 700
✍ Mrs J Hignett (01624) 812244
✔ C Wilson (01624) 814736
ᛙ 18 L 6019 yds SSS 69
ᛟ WD–U after 10am WE–M SOC
££ £23 (£26)
⊕ N of Douglas via A18. W boundary
    of Ramsey
⛨ James Braid

Rowany (1895)
Rowany Drive, Port Erin, IM9 6LN
☎ **(01624) 834108**
▱ (01624) 834072
✉ rowany@iommail.net
▥ 500
✍ DG Street (Mgr) (01624) 834072
ᛙ 18 L 5774 yds SSS 69
ᛟ U SOC
££ £15 (£20)
⊕ 6 miles W of Castletown via A5

Isle of Wight

Cowes (1909)
Crossfield Avenue, Cowes, PO31 8HN
☎ **(01983) 280135**
▥ 300
✍ D Weaver (01983) 292303
ᛙ 18 L 5878 yds SSS 68
ᛟ H Thurs–NA before 3pm (Ladies
    Day) Fri–NA after 5pm Sun
    am–NA

££ £15 (£18)
⊕ Nr Cowes High School
⛨ J Hamilton Stutt

Freshwater Bay (1894)
Afton Down, Freshwater, PO40 9TZ
☎ **(01983) 752955**
▱ (01983) 756704
▥ 500
✍ T Riddett (01983) 752955
ᛙ 18 L 5725 yds SSS 68
ᛟ H–NA before 9.30am SOC
££ £20 (£24)
⊕ 400 yds off Military Road (A3055)
▪ www.isle-of-wight.uk.com/golf

Newport (1896)
*St George's Down, Shide, Newport,
PO30 3BA*
☎ **(01983) 525076**
▥ 350
✍ C Bradshaw (01983) 525076
ᛙ 9 L 5674 yds SSS 68
ᛟ WD–U exc Wed–NA 12–2.30pm
    Sat–NA before 3.30pm Sun–NA
    before noon SOC
££ £15 (£17.50)
⊕ 1 mile SE of Newport
⛨ Guy Hunt

Osborne (1904)
*Osborne House Estate, East Cowes,
PO32 6JX*
☎ **(01983) 295421**
▥ 260 90(L)
✍ RS Jones
ᛙ 9 L 6372 yds SSS 70
ᛟ WD–U exc Ladies Day (Tues)
    9am–1pm–NA WE–NA before
    noon SOC
££ £20 (£22) 5D–£65
⊕ S of East Cowes in grounds of
    Osborne House

Ryde (1895)
Binstead Road, Ryde, PO33 3NF
☎ **(01983) 614809**
▱ (01983) 567418
▥ 450
✍ ARJ Goodall
✔ None
ᛙ 9 L 5287 yds SSS 66
ᛟ WD–U exc Wed pm Sun–NA
    before noon
££ £15 (£20)
⊕ On main Ryde/Newport road
⛨ J Hamilton Stutt

Shanklin & Sandown (1900)
The Fairway, Lake, Sandown, PO36 9PR
☎ **(01983) 403217**
▱ (01983) 403007
▥ 650
✍ AC Creed
✔ P Hammond (01983) 404424
ᛙ 18 L 6063 yds SSS 69
ᛟ WD–U WE–NA before 12 noon
££ £27.50 (£33) 3WD–£66
⊕ 1 mile off A3055 in Lake
⛨ James Braid

Ventnor (1892)
*Steephill Down Road, Ventnor,
PO38 1BP*
☎ **(01983) 853326**
✉ ventnorgolf@lineone.net
▥ 250
✍ S Blackmore
ᛙ 12 L 5767 yds Par 70 SSS 68
ᛟ WD–U exc Mon Sun–NA before
    1pm SOC
££ On application
⊕ NW boundary of Ventnor
▪ www.ventnorgolfclub.co.uk

Westridge
Brading Road, Ryde, PO33 1QS
☎ **(01983) 613131**
ᛙ 9 L 3225 yds Par
ᛟ U
££ £10 (£11)
⊕ 2 miles S of Ryde (A3054)
⊕ Driving range

Kent

Aquarius (1913)
*Marmora Rd, Honor Oak, London,
SE22 0RY*
☎ **(020) 8693 1626**
▥ 400
✍ J Halliby
✔ F Private
ᛙ 9 L 5246 yds SSS 66
ᛟ M
££ On application

Ashford (1903)
Sandyhurst Lane, Ashford, TN25 4NT
☎ **(01233) 620180**
▱ (01233) 622655
▥ 650
✍ AH Story (01233) 622655
✔ H Sherman (01233) 629644
ᛙ 18 L 6284 yds SSS 70
ᛟ WD–H WE/BH–H SOC
££ £28 D–£38 (£35)
⊕ Ashford 1½ miles (A20)
⛨ Cotton

Austin Lodge (1991)
Eynsford, Swanley, DA4 0HU
☎ **(01322) 863000**
▱ (01322) 862406
▥ 600
✍ S Bevan
✔ P Edwards
ᛙ 18 L 6600 yds Par 73 SSS 71
ᛟ WD–U WE–NA before noon SOC
££ £16 (£25)
⊕ Off A225, nr Eynsford Station.
    M25 Junction 3, 3 miles
⊕ Driving range for members and
    guests
⛨ Peter Bevan

Barnehurst (1903)
Public
*Mayplace Road East, Bexley Heath,
DA7 6JU*
☎ **(01322) 523746**

☎ (01322) 554612
📖 300
⛳ 9 L 5448 yds SSS 69
👥 U SOC
£€ £9.25 (£12.60)
🚗 Between Crayford and
　　Bexleyheath
🏌 James Braid

Bearsted (1895)

Ware Street, Bearsted, Maidstone,
ME14 4PQ
☎ (01622) 738389
🖷 (01622) 738198
📖 780
🖉 Mrs LM Siems (01622) 738198
⛳ T Simpson (01622) 738024
⛳ 18 L 6253 yds SSS 70
👥 WD–I H WE–H M (recognised GC
　　members) SOC
£€ £27 D–£36
🚗 2¹/₂ miles E of Maidstone

Beckenham Place Park
(1907)

Public
Beckenham Hill Road, Beckenham,
BR3 2BP
☎ (020) 8650 2292
🖷 (020) 8663 1201
⛳ H Davies-Thomas
⛳ 18 L 5722 yds SSS 68
👥 U
£€ £7.60 (£12.40) WE–booking fee
🚗 Off A21 on A222

Bexleyheath (1907)

Mount Road, Bexleyheath, BR8 7RJ
☎ (020) 8303 6951
📖 350
🖉 D Clark
⛳ 9 L 5239 yds SSS 66
👥 WD–H before 4pm
£€ £20
🚗 Station 1 mile

Birchwood Park (1990)

Birchwood Road, Wilmington, Dartford,
DA2 7HJ
☎ (01322) 660554
🖷 (01322) 667283
📖 450
🖉 Mrs J Smith (Mgr) (01322) 662038
⛳ S Cranfield (01322) 615209
⛳ 18 L 6364 yds Par 71 SSS 70
　　9 hole course
👥 U SOC
£€ £17 (£22)
🚗 2 miles S of A2/A2018 Junction
⊕ Driving range
🏌 Howard Swann
■ www.birchwoodparkgc.co.uk

Boughton (1993)

Pay and play
Brickfield Lane, Boughton, Faversham,
ME13 9AJ
☎ (01227) 752277
🖷 (01227) 752361
📖 300
🖉 S Hall

⛳ T Poole
⛳ 18 L 6452 yds SSS 71
👥 U SOC–WD
£€ £16 (£22)
🚗 NE of Boughton, nr M2/A2
　　interchange. 6 miles W of
　　Canterbury
⊕ Driving range
🏌 Philip Sparks

Broke Hill (1993)

Sevenoaks Road, Halstead, TN14 7HR
☎ (01959) 533225
🖷 (01959) 532680
🖉 C Winning (Gen Mgr)
⛳ C McKillop (01959) 533810
⛳ 18 L 6374 yds Par 72 SSS 71
👥 WD–U before 5pm WE–NA
　　SOC–WD
£€ £35
🚗 4 miles S of Bromley on A21. M25
　　Junction 4
🏌 David Williams
■ www.brokehillgolf.co.uk

Bromley (1948)

Public
Magpie Hall Lane, Bromley, BR2 8JF
☎ (020) 8462 7014
🖷 (020) 8462 6916
📖 100
🖉 A Hodgson
⛳ 9 L 5538 yds SSS 66
👥 U
£€ £6 (£7.85)
🚗 Off Bromley Common (A21)

Broome Park (1981)

Broome Park Estate, Barham,
Canterbury, CT4 6QX
☎ (01227) 830728
🖷 (01227) 832591
📖 600
🖉 G Robins
⛳ T Britz (01227) 831126
⛳ 18 L 6580 yds SSS 71
👥 H WE–NA before noon SOC–WD
£€ £30 (£35)
🚗 M2/A2-A260 Folkestone road, 1¹/₂
　　miles on RH side
⊕ Driving range
🏌 Donald Steel
■ www.broomepark.co.uk

Canterbury (1927)

Scotland Hills, Littlebourne Road,
Canterbury, CT1 1TW
☎ (01227) 453532
🖷 (01227) 784277
📧 cgc@freeola.com
📖 680
⛳ P Everard (01227) 462865
⛳ 18 L 6272 yds SSS 70
👥 WD–U H WE–NA before 11.30am
　　SOC–Tues/Thurs/Fri
£€ £36 D–£36 (£40)
🚗 1 mile E of Canterbury on A257
🏌 HS Colt
■ www.canterburygolfclub.org.uk

Chart Hills (1993)

Weeks Lane, Biddenden, Ashford,
TN27 8JX
☎ (01580) 292222
🖷 (01580) 292233
📖 495
⛳ D French (Golf Mgr)
　　(01580) 292148
⛳ 18 L 7135 yds SSS 74
👥 U exc Mon/Wed/Sat–NA SOC
£€ On application
🚗 12 miles W of Ashford (A262)
⊕ Golf Academy
🏌 Nick Faldo

Chelsfield Lakes Golf
Centre (1992)

Pay and play
Court Road, Orpington, BR6 9BX
☎ (01689) 896266
🖷 (01689) 824577
📖 650
🖉 P Smith (Mgr)
⛳ N Lee, B Hodkin
⛳ 18 L 6077 yds Par 71 SSS 69
　　9 hole Par 3 course
👥 U–booking required
🚗 1 mile from M25 Junction 4 (A224)
⊕ Target golf range
🏌 MRM Sandow
■ www.clubhaus.com

Cherry Lodge (1969)

Jail Lane, Biggin Hill, Westerham,
TN16 3AX
☎ (01959) 572250
🖷 (01959) 540672
📧 info@cherrylodgegc.co.uk
📖 650
🖉 W Tombling
⛳ N Child (01959) 572989
⛳ 18 L 6652 yds SSS 73
👥 WD–U WE–M SOC–WD before
　　3pm
£€ £30 D–£40
🚗 3 miles N of Westerham, off A233
⊕ Driving range
🏌 John Day
■ www.cherrylodgegc.co.uk

Chestfield (1925)

103 Chestfield Road, Whitstable, CT5 3LU
☎ (01227) 794411
🖷 (01227) 794454
📧 secretary@chestfield-golfclub
　　.co.uk
📖 600
🖉 C Maxted (01227) 794411
⛳ J Brotherton (01227) 793563
⛳ 18 L 6208 yds SSS 70
👥 WD–U WE–NA before noon SOC
£€ £22 (£25)
🚗 ¹/₂ mile S of A2990 and Chestfield
　　Station
🏌 Donald Steel
■ www.chestfield-golfclub.co.uk

Chislehurst (1894)

Camden Place, Camden Park Road,
Chislehurst, BR7 5HJ
☎ (020) 8467 3055
🖷 (020) 8295 0874

☐ 740
✍ D Bowles (020) 8467 2782
✓ J Bird (020) 8467 6798
► 18 L 5128 yds SSS 65
♔ WD–H WE–M SOC
£€ £25
⊕ M25 Junction 3/A20/A222

Cobtree Manor Park (1984)
Public
Chatham Road, Boxley, Maidstone,
ME14 3AZ
☎ **(01622) 753276**
✍ A Ferras
► 18 L 5716 yds SSS 68
♔ WD–U WE/BH–(book 1 wk in
advance) SOC–WD
£€ £10 (£18)
⊕ 3 miles N of Maidstone on A229
⌂ F Hawtree

Cray Valley (1972)
Pay and play
Sandy Lane, St Paul's Cray, Orpington,
BR5 3HY
☎ **(01689) 837909**
🖳 (01689) 891428
☐ 600
✍ J Scappatura (01689) 839677
✓ G Sheriff (01689) 837909
► 18 L 5624 yds SSS 67
9 L 2100 yds SSS 60
♔ U
£€ £13 (£19)
⊕ Off A20 Ruxley roundabout at
Sidcup

Darenth Valley (1973)
Pay and play
Station Road, Shoreham, Sevenoaks,
TN14 7SA
☎ **(01959) 522944 (Clubhouse),**
(01959) 522922 (Bookings)
🖳 (01959) 525089
📧 darenthvalleygolfcourse
@shoreham2000.fsbusiness.co.uk
✍ JR Cooper (Mgr)
✓ D Copsey (01959) 522922
► 18 L 6258 yds Par 72 SSS 71
♔ U–booking required SOC
£€ £17.50 (£23)
⊕ 3 miles N of Sevenoaks, off A225.
M25 Junctions 3 or 5

Dartford (1897)
Heath Lane, Dartford, DA1 2TN
☎ **(01322) 223616**
📧 dartfordgolf@hotmail.com
☐ 750
✍ KJ Rawlins (01322) 226455
✓ J Gregory (01322) 226409
► 18 L 5909 yds Par 69 SSS 69
♔ WD–I WE–M H
£€ £22.50
⊕ Dartford 2 miles. Dartford Heath
turn off A2
⌂ James Braid

Deangate Ridge (1972)
Public
Duxcourt Road, Hoo, Rochester,
ME3 8RZ
☎ **(01634) 251950**

☐ 560
✍ Mrs CJ Williams (01634) 251950
✓ R Fox (01634) 251180
► 18 L 6300 yds SSS 70
♔ U SOC
£€ On application
⊕ 7 miles NE of Rochester on A228.
M2, 5 miles
⊕ Driving range. Pitch & putt

Edenbridge G&CC (1973)
Crouch House Road, Edenbridge,
TN8 5LQ
☎ **(01732) 867381**
🖳 (01732) 867029
☐ 800
✍ Mrs C Lloyd (Gen Mgr)
✓ K Burkin (01732) 865202
► 18 L 6577 yds SSS 72
18 L 5605 yds SSS 67
9 hole course
♔ WD/WE–booking necessary
£€ £20 (£27.50)
⊕ 2 miles W of Edenbridge. M25
Junction 6
⊕ Floodlit driving range
⌂ David Williams

Eltham Warren (1890)
Bexley Road, Eltham, London, SE9 2PE
☎ **(020) 8850 1166**
📧 secretary@elthamwarren.tdps.co.uk
☐ 430
✍ DJ Clare (020) 8850 4477
✓ G Brett (020) 8859 7909
► 9 L 5850 yds SSS 68
♔ WD–I WE/BH–M SOC–Thurs only
£€ D–£28 (£14)
⊕ ¹/₂ mile from Eltham station on
A210
⌂ James Braid
■ www.elthamwarrengolfclub.co.uk

Etchinghill (1995)
Pay and play
Canterbury Road, Etchinghill,
Folkestone, CT18 8FA
☎ **(01303) 863863**
🖳 (01303) 863210
☐ 550
✍ S Garside (Mgr)
✓ C Hodgson (01303) 863966
► 18 L 6013-6116 yds Par 70 SSS 69
9 hole Par 3 course
♔ WD–U WE–NA 7am–11am
£€ £18 (£24)
⊕ 1 mile N of M20 Junction 12 on
B2065
⊕ Driving range
⌂ John Sturdy

Faversham (1902)
Belmont Park, Faversham, ME13 0HB
☎ **(01795) 890561**
🖳 (01795) 890760
☐ 850
✍ J Edgington
✓ S Rokes (01795) 890275
► 18 L 6030 yds Par 70 SSS 69
♔ WD–I or H WE–M
£€ £30
⊕ Faversham and M2, 2 miles

Fawkham Valley (1987)
Gay Dawn Farm, Fawkham, Dartford,
DA3 8LZ
☎ **(01474) 707144**
🖳 (01474) 707911
☐ 350
✍ A Dart
✓ C McKillop
► 9 L 6547 yds Par 72 SSS 72
♔ WD–U H WE/BH–NA before 1pm
SOC
£€ £20 (£27.50)
⊕ 4 miles S of Dartford Tunnel. E of
Brands Hatch along Fawkham
Valley road
■ www.fawkhamvalley.co.uk

Gillingham (1908)
Woodlands Road, Gillingham, ME7 2AP
☎ **(01634) 850999**
🖳 (01634) 574749
☐ 450 100(L) 50(J)
✍ Mrs M Scott (01634) 853017
✓ S Green (01634) 855862
► 18 L 5509 yds SSS 67
♔ WD–I H WE/BH–M
£€ £20 D–£28
⊕ A2/M2, 2 miles
⌂ Braid/Steel

Hawkhurst (1968)
High Street, Hawkhurst, TN18 4JS
☎ **(01580) 754074/752396**
🖳 (01580) 754074
📧 hawkhead@tesco.net
☐ 450
✍ B Morrison (Gen Mgr)
✓ T Collins (01580) 753600
► 9 L 5751 yds Par 70 SSS 68
♔ WD–U WE–M SOC
£€ 18 holes–£18 (£20) 9 holes–£12
⊕ 14 miles S of Tunbridge Wells on
A268
■ HawkhurstGolfClub.org.uk

Hemsted Forest (1969)
Golford Road, Cranbrook, TN17 4AL
☎ **(01580) 712833**
🖳 (01580) 714274
✍ K Stevenson
► 18 L 6305 yds SSS 70
♔ WD–U WE/BH–restricted SOC
£€ £28 (£36)
⊕ 15 miles S of Maidstone. M25
Junction 5-A21/A262
⌂ Cdr J Harris

Herne Bay (1895)
Eddington, Herne Bay, CT6 7PG
☎ **(01227) 374097**
☐ 500
✍ B Warren (01227) 373964
✓ S Dordoy (01227) 374727
► 18 L 5567 yds SSS 68
♔ WD–U WE/BH–H after noon
SOC–WD
£€ £18 D–£25 (£25)
⊕ A2299 Thanet road

Hever (1993)

Hever Road, Hever, TN8 7NP
- ☎ **(01732) 700771**
- 🖥 (01732) 700775
- 🕮 700
- ⌨ R Tinworth
- ⮞ 18 L 7002 yds SSS 75
  9 L 2784 yds
- 👥 H SOC
- ££ £35 (£55)
- ⛳ 2 miles E of Edenbridge
- ⊕ Driving range
- 🏠 Peter Nicholson
- ■ www.hever.com

High Elms (1969)

Public
High Elms Road, Downe, Orpington, BR6 7SZ
- ☎ **(01689) 858175**
- 🖥 (01689) 856326
- ⌨ Mrs P O'Keeffe (Hon)
- ⌨ P Remy
- ⮞ 18 L 6221 yds Par 71 SSS 70
- 👥 U
- ££ On application
- ⛳ Off A21 via Shire Lane

Hythe Imperial (1950)

Prince's Parade, Hythe, CT21 6AE
- ☎ **(01303) 233745**
- 🖥 (01303) 267554
- 🕮 445
- ⌨ B Duncan (01303) 267554
- ⌨ G Ritchie (01303) 233745
- ⮞ 9 L 5560 yds SSS 67
- 👥 H SOC
- ££ £15 (£20)
- ⛳ On coast, 4 miles W of Folkestone

Kings Hill (1996)

Kings Hill, West Malling, ME19 4AF
- ☎ **(01732) 875040/842121
  (Bookings)**
- 🖥 (01732) 875019
- 🕮 530
- ⌨ Margaret Gilbert (Mgr)
- ⌨ D Hudspith (01732) 842121
- ⮞ 18 L 6622 yds Par 72 SSS 72
- 👥 WD–U SOC–WD
- ££ £30
- ⛳ 3 miles from M20 Junction 4, off A228
- 🏠 David Williams

Knole Park (1924)

Seal Hollow Road, Sevenoaks, TN15 0HJ
- ☎ **(01732) 452709**
- 🖥 (01732) 463159
- 🕮 700
- ⌨ AP Mitchell (01732) 452150
- ⌨ P Sykes (01732) 451740
- ⮞ 18 L 6266 yds SSS 70
- 👥 WD–restricted WE/BH–M H SOC
- ££ £40 D–£50
- ⛳ ¹/₂ mile from Sevenoaks centre
- 🏠 JF Abercromby
- ■ www.kentgolf.co.uk/knolepark

Lamberhurst (1890)

Church Road, Lamberhurst, TN3 8DT
- ☎ **(01892) 890241**
- 🖥 (01892) 891140
- ✉ secretary@lamberhurstgolfclub.com
- 🕮 700
- ⌨ RJ Walden (01892) 890591
- ⌨ BM Impett (01892) 890552
- ⮞ 18 L 6364 yds SSS 70
- 👥 WD–U H WE–NA before noon
- ££ £26 D–£36 (£41)
- ⛳ 5 miles SE of Tunbridge Wells, off A21
- ■ www.lamberhurstgolfclub.com

Langley Park (1910)

Barnfield Wood Road, Beckenham, BR3 6SZ
- ☎ **(020) 8650 2090**
- 🖥 (020) 8658 6310
- ✉ manager@langleyparkgolfclub.co.uk
- 🕮 750
- ⌨ R Pollard (Gen Mgr) (020) 8658 6849
- ⌨ C Staff (020) 8650 1663
- ⮞ 18 L 6488 yds SSS 71
- 👥 WD–H WE–M SOC–WD
- ££ £25 D–£35
- ⛳ Bromley South Station 1 mile. M25 Junction 4
- 🏠 JH Taylor
- ■ www.langleyparkgolfclub.co.uk

Leeds Castle (1928)

Pay and play
Leeds Castle, Hollingbourne, Maidstone, ME17 1PL
- ☎ **(01622) 880467/767828**
- 🖥 (01622) 735616
- ⌨ S Purves
- ⮞ 9 L 2451 yds Par 33
- 👥 U SOC–WD
- ££ 9 holes–£11 (£13)
- ⛳ 4 miles E of Maidstone (A20). M20 Junction 8, 1 mile
- ⊕ 6-day advance booking
- 🏠 Neil Coles

Littlestone (1888)

St Andrews Road, Littlestone, New Romney, TN28 8RB
- ☎ **(01797) 362310**
- 🖥 (01797) 362740
- ✉ secretary@littlestonegolfclub.org.uk
- 🕮 550
- ⌨ Col C Moorhouse (01797) 363355
- ⌨ A Jones (01797) 362231
- ⮞ 18 L 6676 yds Par 71 SSS 73
- 👥 WD–H WE–by arrangement SOC
- ££ £36 (£50)
- ⛳ 2 miles E of New Romney. 15 miles SE of Ashford. M20 Junction 10
- 🏠 W Laidlaw Purves/Dr A Mackenzie
- ■ www.littlestonegolfclub.org.uk

London Beach (1998)

Pay and play
Ashford Road, St michaels, Ashford, TN30 6SP
- ☎ **(01580) 766279**
- 🖥 (01580) 766681
- ✉ enquiries@londonbeach
- ⌨ P Edmonds
- ⌨ M Chilcott (01580) 764135
- ⮞ 9 L 5860 yds
- 👥 U SOC
- ££ 9 holes–£15 (£20). 18 holes–£20 (£25)
- ⛳ M20 Junction 8
- ⊕ Driving range. Pitch & putt
- ■ enwww.londonbeach.com

The London Golf Club (1993)

South Ash Manor Estate, Stansted Lane, Ash, TN15 7EN
- ☎ **(01474) 879899**
- 🖥 (01474) 879912
- 🕮 550
- ⌨ D Loh
- ⌨ B Longmuir
- ⮞ Heritage 18 L 7208 yds Par 72 SSS 74;
  International 18 L 7005 yds Par 72 SSS 74
- 👥 M I SOC–WD
- ££ On application
- ⛳ Off A20, nr Brands Hatch
- ⊕ Driving range. Academy
- 🏠 Nicklaus/Kirby
- ■ www.londongolf.co.uk

Lullingstone Park (1967)

Public
Parkgate Road, Chelsfield, Orpington, BR6 7PX
- ☎ **(01959) 533793**
- ⌨ BMS Vallance
- ⌨ M Watt
- ⮞ 18 L 6779 yds SSS 72
  9 L 2445 yds Par 33
- 👥 U
- ££ On application
- ⛳ Off Orpington by-pass (A224) towards Well Hill. M25 Junction 4
- ⊕ Driving range. 9 hole pitch & putt course

Lydd

Pay and play
Romney Road, Lydd, Romney Marsh, TN29 9LS
- ☎ **(01797) 320808**
- 🖥 (01797) 321482
- ✉ info@lyddgolfclub.co.uk
- 🕮 576
- ⌨ BM Evans, S Balcomb (Gen Mgr)
- ⌨ S Smith (01797) 321201
- ⮞ 18 L 6517 yds Par 71 SSS 71
  Driving range
- 👥 U SOC
- ££ £17 (£25)
- ⛳ 15 miles SE of Ashford, by Lydd Airport (B2075). M20 Junction 10
- ⊕ Driving range
- 🏠 M Smith
- ■ www.lyddgolfclub.co.uk

Mid Kent (1908)
Singlewell Road, Gravesend, DA11 7RB
- ☎ **(01474) 568035**
- 🖳 (01474) 564218
- 📖 870
- ✎ M Foreman (01474) 332810
- ⊳ 18 L 6104 yds SSS 69
- 👥 WD–H WE–M
- ££ On application
- 🚗 SE of Gravesend, nr A2
- ⌂ Frank Pennink

Moatlands (1993)
Watermans Lane, Brenchley, Tonbridge, TN12 6ND
- ☎ **(01892) 724400**
- 🖳 (01892) 723300
- ✉ moatlandsgolf@btconnect.com
- 📖 600
- ✎ K Wiley
- ✎ J Eldridge (01892) 724252
- ⊳ 18 L 7060 yds Par 72 SSS 74
- 👥 WD–U H WE–H NA before noon SOC–WD exc Wed
- ££ £29 (£39)
- 🚗 Between Matfield and Paddock Wood, off B2160
- ⊕ Driving range
- ⌂ T Saito
- ■ www.moatlands.com

Nizels (1992)
Nizels Lane, Hildenborough, Tonbridge, TN11 8NU
- ☎ **(01732) 833833**
- 🖳 (01732) 835492
- ✉ nizels@clubhaus.com
- 📖 700
- ✎ J Martin (Gen Mgr)
- ✎ A Mellor (01732) 838926
- ⊳ 18 L 6297 yds SSS 71
- 👥 WD–U SOC
- ££ £30 (£40)
- 🚗 4 miles from M25 on B245. A21 Tonbridge North Junction
- ⌂ Lennan/Purnell
- ■ www.clubhaus.com

North Foreland (1903)
Convent Road, Broadstairs, Thanet, CT10 3PU
- ☎ **(01843) 862140**
- 🖳 (01843) 862663
- ✉ office@northforeland.co.uk
- 📖 1100
- ✎ BJ Preston
- ✎ D Parris (01843) 604471
- ⊳ 18 L 6430 yds SSS 71 18 hole Par 3 course
- 👥 WD–H WE–NA am –H pm
- ££ £30 (£40)
- 🚗 B2052, 1½ miles N of Broadstairs
- ⌂ Fowler/Simpson

Oastpark (1992)
Malling Road, Snodland, ME6 5LG
- ☎ **(01634) 242661**
- 🖳 (01634) 240744
- 📖 300
- ✎ Lesley Murrock (01634) 242818
- ✎ D Porthouse (01634) 242661

- ⊳ 9 L 2850 yds Par 34 SSS 34
- 👥 U SOC
- ££ 9 holes–£7 (£8) 18 holes–£12 (£14)
- 🚗 1 mile E of M20 Junction 4
- ⊕ Driving range

Park Wood (1994)
Proprietary
Chestnut Avenue, Tatsfield, Westerham, TN16 2EG
- ☎ **(01959) 577744**
- 🖳 (01959) 572702
- ✉ mail@parkwoodgolf.co.uk
- 📖 450
- ✎ Miss RLR Gold Smith (Man Dir)
- ✎ N Terry (01959) 577177
- ⊳ 18 L 6573 yds Par 72 SSS 72
- 👥 U SOC
- ££ £32–£36 (£42–£50)
- 🚗 Tatsfield, nr Westerham. M25 Junction 4
- ■ www.parkwoodgolf.co.uk

Poult Wood (1974)
Public
Higham Lane, Tonbridge, TN11 9QR
- ☎ **(01732) 364039 (Bookings), (01732) 366180 (Clubhouse)**
- 📖 481
- ✎ S Taylor
- ✎ C Miller
- ⊳ 18 L 5524 yds Par 68 SSS 66 9 L 2562 yds par 28
- 👥 U–booking required SOC–WD
- ££ £12.50 (£18)
- 🚗 1 mile N of Tonbridge, off A227
- ⌂ Hawtree

Prince's (1906)
Proprietary
Sandwich Bay, Sandwich, CT13 9QB
- ☎ **(01304) 611118**
- 🖳 (01304) 612000
- ✉ golf@princes-leisure.co.uk
- 📖 250
- ✎ WM Howie (Dir)
- ✎ D Barbour (01304) 613797
- ⊳ 27 hole course (3 x 9 holes): Dunes/Himalayas/Shore Length 6813-7063 yds Par 71-72 SSS 72-73
- 👥 U SOC
- ££ On application
- 🚗 Sandwich Bay (A256)
- ⊕ Driving range
- ⌂ Morrison/Campbell
- ■ www.princes-leisure.co.uk

Redlibbets
West Yoke, Ash, Nr Sevenoaks, TN15 7HT
- ☎ **(01474) 879190**
- 🖳 (01474) 879290
- 📖 500
- ✎ J Potter
- ✎ R Taylor (01474) 872278
- ⊳ 18 L 6651 yds Par 72
- 👥 U SOC
- ££ £40
- 🚗 Off A20 between Fawkham and Ash. M20 Junction 2. M25 Junct. 3
- ⌂ Jonathan Gaunt

The Ridge (1993)
Chartway Street, East Sutton, Maidstone, ME17 3JB
- ☎ **(01622) 844382**
- 🖳 (01622) 844168
- ✎ J Callister (Gen Mgr)
- ✎ T Dungate (01622) 844243
- ⊳ 18 L 6254 yds SSS 72
- 👥 U SOC
- ££ £20 (£25)
- 🚗 3 miles E of Maidstone, off A274. M20 Junction 8
- ⊕ Driving range
- ⌂ Patrick Dawson

Riverside (1991)
Pay and play
Summerton Way, Thamesmead, London, SE28 8PP
- ☎ **(020) 8310 7975**
- ⊳ 9 L 5485 yds Par 66
- 👥 U SOC–WD
- ££ £7 (£9)
- 🚗 Woolwich

Riverside Golf Centre (1991)
Pay and play
Fairway Drive, Summerton Way, Thamesmead, London SE28 8PP
- ☎ **(020) 8310 7975**
- 🖳 (020) 8312 3441
- ✎ BD Jarrett
- ✎ Sarah Jarrett
- ⊳ 9 L 5462 yds Par 70 SSS 66
- 👥 U SOC
- ££ 18 holes–£10.50 (£12) 9 holes–£6.50 (£8.50)
- ⊕ Floodlit driving range
- ■ www.riversidegolf.co.uk

Rochester & Cobham Park (1891)
Park Pale, by Rochester, ME2 3UL
- ☎ **(01474) 823411**
- 🖳 (01474) 824446
- 📖 720
- ✎ DW Smith (Mgr)
- ✎ I Higgins (01474) 823658
- ⊳ 18 L 6596 yds SSS 71
- 👥 WD–U H WE–M before 5pm SOC–Tues & Thurs. Soft spikes only
- ££ £30
- 🚗 3 miles E of Gravesend exit (A2)
- ⊕ Driving range
- ⌂ D Steel
- ■ www.rochesterandcobhamgc.co.uk

Romney Warren (1993)
Pay and play
St Andrews Road, Littlestone, New Romney, TN28 8RB
- ☎ **(01797) 362231**
- 🖳 (01797) 362740
- 📖 250
- ✎ E Purkiss (Hon)
- ✎ S Watkins
- ⊳ 18 L 5126 yds SSS 65
- 👥 U SOC
- ££ £13 (£18)

- 2 miles E of New Romney. 15 miles SE of Ashford
- Evans/Lewis
- www.romneywarrengolfclub.co.uk

Royal Blackheath   (1608)
Court Road, Eltham, London, SE9 5AF
- ☎ (020) 8850 1795
- 🖥 (020) 8859 0150
- ✉ secretary@rbgc.com
- 📖 700
- ✍ AG Dunlop
- ↗ R Harrison (020) 8850 1763
- ▷ 18 L 6219 yds SSS 70
- ⚭ WD–I or H WE/BH–M SOC
- ££ £40 D–£60
- ⚬ 5 miles W of M25 Junction 3
- ⊕ Golf Museum
- ⛳ James Braid
- www.rbgc.com

Royal Cinque Ports   (1892)
Golf Road, Deal, CT14 6RF
- ☎ (01304) 374007 (Office), (01304) 374328 (Clubhouse)
- 🖥 (01304) 379530
- 📖 1000+
- ✍ CC Hammond (01304) 367856
- ↗ A Reynolds (01304) 374170
- ▷ 18 L 6467 yds SSS 71
- ⚭ WD–H after 9.30am SOC
- ££ On application
- ⚬ A258, N of Deal
- ⊕ Driving range
- www.royalcinqueports.com

Royal St George's   (1887)
Sandwich, CT13 9PB
- ☎ (01304) 613090
- 🖥 (01304) 611245
- ✉ secretary@royalstgeorges.com
- 📖 725
- ✍ HCG Gabbey
- ↗ A Brooks (01304) 615236
- ▷ 18 L 7102 yds Par 70 SSS 74
- ⚭ WD–I H WE–M SOC–WD
- ££ £75 D–£110
- ⚬ 1 mile E of Sandwich
- ⛳ Dr Laidlaw Purves
- www.royalstgeorges.com

Ruxley Park   (1975)
Pay and play
Sandy Lane, St Paul's Cray, Orpington, BR5 3HY
- ☎ (01689) 871490
- 🖥 (01689) 891428
- 📖 500
- ✍ J Scappatura
- ↗ A Langoon
- ▷ 18 L 6027 yds SSS 69 9 hole Par 3 course
- ⚭ U
- ££ £11 (£18)
- ⚬ Off A20 Ruxley roundabout at Sidcup
- ⊕ Floodlit driving range

St Augustines   (1907)
Cottington Road, Cliffsend, Ramsgate, CT12 5JN
- ☎ (01843) 590333

- 🖥 (01843) 590444
- ✉ sagc@ic24.net
- 📖 650 55(J)
- ✍ LP Dyke
- ↗ DB Scott (01843) 590222
- ▷ 18 L 5254 yds SS 66
- ⚭ H SOC–WD
- ££ £15 (£16.50)
- ⚬ 2 miles SW of Ramsgate from A253 or A256. Signs to St Augustines Cross
- ⛳ Tom Vardon

Sene Valley   (1888)
Sene, Folkestone, CT18 8BL
- ☎ (01303) 268513
- 🖥 (01303) 237513
- ✉ svgc@freeserve.co.uk
- 📖 650
- ✍ G Sykes (Mgr)
- ↗ N Watson (01303) 268514
- ▷ 18 L 6215 yds SSS 70
- ⚭ H SOC
- ££ £20 (£30)
- ⚬ 2 miles N of Hythe on B2065
- ⛳ Henry Cotton
- ■ www.sceneatsene.co.uk

Sheerness   (1906)
Power Station Road, Sheerness, ME12 3AE
- ☎ (01795) 662585
- 🖥 (01795) 668100
- ✉ thesecretary@sheernessgc.freeserve.co.uk
- 📖 600
- ✍ AF Jones
- ↗ L Stanford (01795) 583060
- ▷ 18 L 6460 yds SSS 71
- ⚭ WD–U SOC
- ££ £20
- ⚬ 9 miles N of Sittingbourne. M20, M2 or A2 to A249

Shooter's Hill   (1903)
Lowood, Eaglesfield Road, London, SE18 3DA
- ☎ (020) 8854 1216
- 🖥 (020) 8854 0469
- 📖 596 69(L) 46(J)
- ✍ Sandy Watt (020) 8854 6368
- ↗ D Brotherton (020) 8854 0073
- ▷ 18 L 5721 yds SSS 68
- ⚭ WD–I WE/BH–M SOC–Tues & Thurs only
- ££ £22 D–£27
- ⚬ Off A207 nr Blackheath
- ⛳ Willie Park

Shortlands   (1894)
Meadow Road, Shortlands, Bromley, BR2 0DX
- ☎ (020) 8460 2471
- 🖥 (020) 8460 8828
- 📖 525
- ✍ PS May (020) 8460 8828
- ↗ M Taylor (020) 8464 6182
- ▷ 9 L 5261 yds SSS 66
- ⚭ M
- ££ 18 holes–£15. 9 holes–£10
- ⚬ Ravensbourne Ave, Shortlands

Sidcup   (1891)
7 Hurst Road, Sidcup, DA15 9AE
- ☎ (020) 8300 2864
- 🖥 (020) 8300 2150
- 📖 400
- ✍ J Auchterlony (020) 8300 2150
- ↗ N Willis (020) 8309 0679
- ▷ 9 L 5571 yds Par 68 SSS 68
- ⚭ WD–H WE/BH–M SOC–WD
- ££ £18
- ⚬ On A222. A2/A20, 2 miles

Sittingbourne & Milton Regis   (1929)
Wormdale, Newington, Sittingbourne, ME9 7PX
- ☎ (01795) 842261
- 🖥 (01795) 844117
- ✉ sittingbourne@golfclub.totalserve.co.uk
- 📖 575 100(L) 50(J)
- ✍ HDG Wylie
- ↗ JR Hearn (01795) 842775
- ▷ 18 L 6291 yds SSS 70
- ⚭ WD–H Sat–NA Sun–M SOC–Tues & Thurs
- ££ £25
- ⚬ N of M2 Junction 5, towards Danaway

Southern Valley   (1999)
Pay and play
Thong Lane, Shorne, Gravesend DA12 4LF
- ☎ (01474) 740026, (01474) 568568 (Bookings)
- 🖥 (01474) 360366
- ✉ info@southernvalley.co.uk
- 📖 380
- ✍ Anne Green
- ↗ L Batchelor
- ▷ 18 L 6100 yds Par 69 SSS 69
- ⚭ U SOC
- ££ 9 holes–£10 (£12.50). 18 holes–£16 (£19)
- ⚬ S of Gravesend, off A2
- ⛳ Weller/Richardson

Staplehurst Golf Centre
Cradducks Lane, Staplehurst, TN12 0DR
- ☎ (01580) 893362
- ✍ C Jenkins
- ↗ C Jenkins
- ▷ 9 L 6114 yds Par 72 SSS 70
- ⚭ U
- ££ £12 (£13)
- ⚬ 8 miles S of Maidstone on A229
- ⊕ Driving range
- ⛳ Sayner/Jenkins

Sundridge Park   (1901)
Garden Road, Bromley, BR1 3NE
- ☎ (020) 8460 0278
- 🖥 (020) 8289 3050
- ✉ secretary@spgc.co.uk
- 📖 1200
- ✍ R Burden (020) 8460 0278
- ↗ B Cameron (020) 8460 5540
- ▷ East 18 L 6538 yds SSS 71 West 18 L 6019 yds SSS 69
- ⚭ H SOC–WD
- ££ D–£55

🚗 1 mile N of Bromley, by Sundridge Park Station. M25 Junctions 3/4

Sweetwoods Park (1994)
Cowden, Edenbridge, TN8 7JN
☎ **(01342) 850729**
🖬 (01342) 850866
📧 danhowe@sweetwoodspark.com
📖 750
🏌 D Howe (01342) 850942
🏌 P Lyons (01342) 850729
🏳 18 L 5299-6610 yds Par 72 SSS 69-73
🏌 U SOC
££ £24 (£32)
🚗 5 miles E of E Grinstead on A264
⊕ Driving range
🏠 P Strand
■ www.sweetwoodspark.com

Tenterden (1905)
Woodchurch Road, Tenterden, TN30 7DR
☎ **(01580) 763987**
🖬 (01580) 763987
📖 650
🏌 N Taylor (Sec/Mgr)
🏌 K Kelsall (01580) 762409
🏳 18 L 6050 yds Par 70 SSS 69
🏌 WD–U WE/BH–M Sun–NA before noon SOC–WD
££ On application
🚗 1 mile E of Tenterden on B2067
■ www.tenterdengolfclub.co.uk

Tudor Park (1988)
Proprietary
Ashford Road, Bearsted, Maidstone, ME14 4NQ
☎ **(01622) 734334**
🖬 (01622) 735360
📖 750
🏌 J Ladbrook (01622) 777119
🏌 N McNally (01622) 739412
🏳 18 L 6041yds SSS 69
🏌 H SOC
££ £35 (£40)
🚗 3 miles E of Maidstone on A20. M20 Junction 8
⊕ Driving range
🏠 Donald Steel

Tunbridge Wells (1889)
Langton Road, Tunbridge Wells, TN4 8XH
☎ **(01892) 523034**
🖬 (01892) 536918
📖 212 44(L) 61(J)
🏌 RF Mealing (01892) 536918
🏌 M Barton (01892) 541386
🏳 9 L 4725 yds SSS 62
🏌 U H SOC
££ £14 (£20)
🚗 Tunbridge Wells, next to Spa Hotel

Upchurch River Valley (1991)
Pay and play
Oak Lane, Upchurch, Sittingbourne, ME9 7AY
☎ **(01634) 360626**

🖬 (01634) 387784
📖 640
🏌 D Candy (01634) 260594
🏌 R Cornwell (01634) 379592
🏳 18 L 6237 yds SSS 70
9 hole course
🏌 U SOC–WD
££ 18 hole:£11.45 (£14.45) 9 hole:£6.75 (£7.75)
🚗 3 miles NE of Rainham, off A2. M2 Junction 4
⊕ Floodlit driving range
🏠 David Smart

Walmer & Kingsdown (1909)
The Leas, Kingsdown, Deal, CT14 8EP
☎ **(01304) 373256**
🖬 (01304) 382336
📖 627
🏌 J Morgan
🏌 M Paget (01304) 363017
🏳 18 L 6444 yds Par 72 SSS 71
🏌 WD–H WE–after noon SOC
££ D–£25 (£30)
🚗 2½ miles S of Deal on clifftop
🏠 James Braid

Weald of Kent (1992)
Pay and play
Maidstone Road, Headcorn, TN27 9PT
☎ **(01622) 890866**
🖬 (01622) 890070
📖 500
🏌 K Brown (Golf Dir)
🏳 18 L 6169 yds SSS 69
🏌 U–booking 5 days in advance SOC
££ £16 (£20)
🚗 5 miles S of Maidstone on A274. M20 Junction 8
🏠 John Millen

West Kent (1916)
West Hill, Downe, Orpington, BR6 7JJ
☎ **(01689) 851323**
🖬 (01689) 858693
📧 golf@wkgc.co.uk
📖 750
🏌 AP Barclay
🏌 RS Fidler (01689) 856863
🏳 18 L 6399 yds Par 70 SSS 70
🏌 WD–H or I–phone to arrange WE/BH–M
££ On application
🚗 5 miles S of Orpington
■ www.wkgc.co.uk

West Malling (1974)
Addington, Maidstone, ME19 5AR
☎ **(01732) 844785**
🖬 (01732) 844795
📖 900
🏌 MR Ellis
🏌 D Lambert
🏳 Spitfire 18 L 6142 yds Par 70 Hurricane 18 L 6240 yds Par 70
🏌 WD–U WE–U H after noon
££ £25 (£35)
🚗 12 miles W of Maidstone (A20)
⊕ Driving range
🏠 Max Faulkner
■ www.westmallinggolf.com

Westerham
Valence Park, Brasted Road, Westerham, TN16 1LJ
☎ **(01959) 567100**
🖬 (01959) 567101
📖 700
🏌 S Hodsdon (Gen Mgr)
🏌 R Sturgeon
🏳 18 L 6272 yds Par 72
🏌 WD–U WE–after 12.30pm
££ £27 (£35)
🚗 E of Westerham (A25), off M25 Junction 5
⊕ Driving range
🏠 David Williams
■ www.westerhamgc.co.uk

Westgate & Birchington (1893)
176 Canterbury Road, Westgate-on-Sea, CT8 8LT
☎ **(01843) 831115/833905**
📖 325
🏌 TJ Sharp
🏌 R Game
🏳 18 L 4889 yds SSS 64
🏌 WD–NA before 10am WE–NA before 11am SOC
££ £15 (£18)
🚗 1 mile W of Westgate (A28)

Whitstable & Seasalter (1911)
Collingwood Road, Whitstable, CT5 1EB
☎ **(01227) 272020**
🖬 (01227) 280822
📖 350
🏌 C Chapman
🏳 9 L 5357 yds Par 63 SSS 63
🏌 U
££ 18 holes–£15
🚗 1 mile W of Whitstable

Wildernesse (1890)
Seal, Sevenoaks, TN15 0JE
☎ **(01732) 761526**
📖 700
🏌 RA Foster (01732) 761199
🏌 CA Walker (01732) 761527
🏳 18 L 6440 yds Par 72 SSS 71
🏌 WD–I H SOC–Mon/Thurs/Fri
££ £40 D–£60
🚗 2 miles E of Sevenoaks (A25). M25 Junction 5

Woodlands Manor (1928)
Woodlands, Tinkerpot Lane, Sevenoaks, TN15 6AB
☎ **(01959) 523806**
🖬 (01959) 524398
📖 650
🏌 CG Robins (01959) 523806
🏌 P Womack (01959) 524161
🏳 18 L 6000 yds SSS 69
🏌 WD–U WE–H NA before noon SOC–WD
££ On application
🚗 4 miles S of M25 Junction 3. Off A20 between West Kingsdown and Otford

⊕ Driving range
⌂ Coles/Lyons

Wrotham Heath (1906)
Seven Mile Lane Comp, Sevenoaks, TN15 8QZ
☎ **(01732) 884800**
▭ 424 75(L) 50(J)
⌸ LJ Byrne
⟋ H Dearden (01732) 883854
⟣ 18 L 5954 yds SSS 69
⚇ WD–H WE/BH–M SOC–Thurs & Fri
£€ £25 D–£35
⚘ 8 miles W of Maidstone on B2016. M26/A20 Junction, 1 mile
⌂ Donald Steel

Lancashire

Accrington & District
(1893)
West End, Oswaldtwistle, Accrington, BB5 4LS
☎ **(01254) 381614**
▭ (01254) 233273
✉ info@accrington-golf-club.fsnet .co.uk
⌸ 350
⚐ GA Dixon (01254) 265620
⟋ W Harling (01254) 231091
⟣ 18 L 6044 yds SSS 69
⚇ WD/WE–U H SOC–H
£€ On application
⚘ 3 miles SW of Accrington. M65 Junctions 6/7
■ www.accrington-golf-club.fsnet.co.uk

Ashton & Lea (1913)
Tudor Ave, Off Blackpool Rd, Lea, Preston PR4 0XA
☎ **(01772) 726480**
▭ (01772) 735762
✉ ashtonleagolf@supanet.com
⌸ 750
⚐ I Hulley (01772) 735282
⟋ M Greenough (01772) 720374
⟣ 18 L 6334 yds SSS 71
⚇ U SOC
£€ £24 (£27)
⚘ 3 miles W of Preston, off A5085. Nr M6, M55 and M65
⌂ J Steer

Ashton-in-Makerfield
(1902)
Garswood Park, Liverpool Road, Ashton-in-Makerfield, WN4 0YT
☎ **(01942) 727267**
▭ (01942) 719330
⌸ 675
⚐ JW Ball (01942) 719330
⟋ P Allan (01942) 724229
⟣ 18 L 6212 yds SSS 70
⚇ WD–U exc Wed WE/BH–M SOC
£€ £28
⚘ 1 mile W of Ashton-in-Makerfield on A58. M6 Junction 23/24

Ashton-under-Lyne (1912)
Gorsey Way, Hurst, Ashton-under-Lyne, OL6 9HT
☎ **(0161) 330 1537**
▭ (0161) 330 6673
⌸ 600
⚐ A Jackson (0161) 330 1537
⟋ C Boyle (0161) 308 2095
⟣ 18 L 6209 yds SSS 70
⚇ WD–U WE/BH–M SOC
£€ On application
⚘ 8 miles E of Manchester. M60 Junction 23

Bacup (1910)
Maden Road, Bankside Lane, Bacup, OL13 8HN
☎ **(01706) 873170**
▭ (01706) 867726
⌸ 396
⚐ T Leyland (01706) 879644
⟣ 9 L 6008 yds SSS 69
⚇ U
£€ On application
⚘ Bankside Lane

Baxenden & District (1913)
Top o' th' Meadow, Baxenden, Accrington, BB5 2EA
☎ **(01254) 234555**
⌸ 400
⚐ N Turner (01706) 225423
⟣ 9 L 5702 yds SSS 68
⚇ WD–U WE/BH–M
£€ £15
⚘ 2 miles SE of Accrington
■ www.baxendengolf.co.uk

Beacon Park (1982)
Public
Beacon Lane, Dalton, Up Holland, WN8 7RU
☎ **(01695) 627500**
⌸ 250
⚐ T Harris
⟋ G Nelson (01695) 622700
⟣ 18 L 5927 yds SSS 69
⚇ U–book 6 days in advance SOC
£€ On application
⚘ Nr Ashurst Beacon and M58/M6 Junction 26
⊕ Driving range

Blackburn (1894)
Beardwood Brow, Blackburn, BB2 7AX
☎ **(01254) 51122**
▭ (01254) 665578
⌸ 476 65(L) 104(J)
⚐ K Taylor (01254) 51122
⟋ A Rodwell (01254) 55942
⟣ 18 L 6144 yds SSS 70
⚇ U SOC–WD WE/BH–restricted
£€ £25 (£30)
⚘ 1 mile NW of Blackburn (A677). M6 Junction 31

Blackpool North Shore
(1904)
Devonshire Road, Blackpool, FY2 0RD
☎ **(01253) 351017**

▭ (01253) 591240
✉ office@bnsgc.com
⌸ 750
⚐ JW Morris (01253) 352054
⟋ B Ward (01253) 354640
⟣ 18 L 6443 yds SSS 71
⚇ WD–U WE–restricted SOC
£€ £30 (£35)
⚘ ½ mile E of Queens Promenade (B5124)
⌂ HS Colt

Blackpool Park (1925)
Public
North Park Drive, Blackpool, FY3 8LS
☎ **(01253) 397916**
▭ (01253) 397916
⌸ 600
⚐ D Stones (01253) 397916
⟋ B Purdie (01253) 391004
⟣ 18 L 6192 yds SSS 69
⚇ U–no telephone booking
£€ £12.50 (£14.50)
⚘ 2 miles E of Blackpool, signposted off M55
⌂ Dr A Mackenzie

Bolton (1891)
Lostock Park, Bolton, BL6 4AJ
☎ **(01204) 843278**
▭ (01204) 843067
✉ boltongolf@lostockpark.fsbusiness .co.uk
⌸ 600
⚐ Mrs HM Stuart (01204) 843067
⟋ R Longworth (01204) 843073
⟣ 18 L 6237 yds Par 70 SSS 70
⚇ U SOC
£€ £30 D–£36 (£33 D–£40)
⚘ 3 miles W of Bolton. M61 Junction 6, 2 miles

Bolton Old Links (1891)
Chorley Old Road, Montserrat, Bolton, BL1 5SU
☎ **(01204) 840050**
▭ (01204) 842307
✉ mail@boltonoldlinks.co.uk
⌸ 600
⚐ Mrs J Boardman (01204) 842307
⟋ P Horridge (01204) 843089
⟣ 18 L 6469 yds SSS 71
⚇ U H exc comp Sats SOC
£€ £30 (£40)
⚘ 3 miles NW of Bolton on B6226
⌂ Dr A Mackenzie
■ www.boltonoldlinks.co.uk

Bolton Open Golf Course
Pay and play
Longsight Park, Longsight Lane, Harwood, BL2 4JX
☎ **(01204) 597659/309778**
⌸ 250
⚐ D Fletcher (Sec/Mgr) (01204) 597659
⟋ A Duncan (Golf Dir) (01204) 309778
⟣ 18 holes Par 70 SSS 68
⚇ WD–U WE–booking necessary SOC
£€ £8 (£12)

🚗 2 miles NE of Bolton (A666)
⊕ Driving range

Brackley Municipal (1977)
Public
Bullows Road, Little Hulton, Worsley, M38 9TR
☎ **(0161) 790 6076**
✓ S Lomax (Mgr)
🏌 9 L 3003 yds SSS 69
👤 U
££ On application
🚗 2 miles NW of Walkden, off A6

Breightmet (1911)
Red Bridge, Ainsworth, Bolton, BL2 5PA
☎ **(01204) 527381**
📖 240
✍ SP Griffiths
🏌 9 L 6416 yds SSS 71
👤 WD–H WE–NA SOC–WD
££ £15 (£18)
🚗 3 miles E of Bolton

Brookdale (1896)
Medlock Road, Woodhouses, Failsworth, M35 9WQ
☎ **(0161) 681 4534**
📠 (0161) 688 6872
📖 725
✍ MJ Chadwick
✓ T Cuppello (0161) 681 2655
🏌 18 L 5841 yds SSS 68
👤 WD–U SOC–WD
££ £22
🚗 5 miles NE of Manchester
🖥 www.brookdalegolfclub.co.uk

Burnley (1905)
Glen View, Burnley, BB11 3RW
☎ **(01282) 421045**
📠 (01282) 451281
📖 520
✍ RDM Wills (01282) 451281
✓ P McEvoy (01282) 455266
🏌 18 L 5939 yds SSS 69
👤 H SOC
££ £20 (£25)
🚗 Via Manchester Road to Glen View Road
🖥 www.burnleygolfclub@on the green.co.uk

Bury (1890)
Unsworth Hall, Blackford Bridge, Bury, BL9 9TJ
☎ **(0161) 766 4897**
📠 (0161) 796 3480
📖 750
✍ R Adams
✓ D Procter (0161) 766 2213
🏌 18 L 5927 yds SSS 69
👤 H SOC
££ £26 (£30)
🚗 A56, 5 miles N of Manchester. 3 miles N of M62 Junction 17

Castle Hawk (1975)
Chadwick Lane, Castleton, Rochdale, OL11 3BY
☎ **(01706) 640841**

📠 (01706) 860587
📧 teeoff@castlehawk.co.uk
📖 200
✍ L Entwistle
✓ A Duncan
🏌 18 L 5398 yds SSS 68
   9 L 3158 yds SSS 55
👤 U SOC
££ WD/Sat D–£9 Sun D–£11
🚗 Castleton Station 1 mile. M62 Junction 20
⊕ Driving range

Chorley (1897)
Hall o' th' Hill, Heath Charnock, Chorley, PR6 9HX
☎ **(01257) 480263**
📠 (01257) 480722
📧 secretary@chorleygolfclub.freeserve.co.uk
📖 550
✍ Mrs A Allen (01257) 480263
✓ M Bradley (01257) 481245
🏌 18 L 6240 yds SSS 70
👤 WD–I or H WE–NA SOC
££ On application
🚗 1 mile S of Chorley at junction A6/A673
🏠 JA Steer
🖥 www.chorleygolfclub.co.uk

Clitheroe (1891)
Whalley Road, Clitheroe, BB7 1PP
☎ **(01200) 422618 (Clubhouse)**
📠 (01200) 422292
📧 secretary@clitheroegolfclub.com
📖 700
✍ T Ashton (01200) 422292
✓ J Twissell (01200) 424242
🏌 18 L 6326 yds SSS 71
👤 WD–U H SOC
££ £28 D–£33 (£39)
🚗 2 miles S of Clitheroe
⊕ Range
🏠 James Braid
🖥 www.clitheroegolfclub.com

Colne (1901)
Law Farm, Skipton Old Road, Colne, BB8 7EB
☎ **(01282) 863391**
📖 354
✍ JT Duerden (Hon)
✓ None
🏌 9 L 5961 yds SSS 69
👤 U exc comp days SOC–WD
££ £16 (£20)
🚗 1½ miles N of Colne. From end of M65, signs to Keighley and then Lothersdale

Crompton & Royton (1913)
High Barn, Royton, Oldham, OL2 6RW
☎ **(0161) 624 2154**
📠 (0161) 652 4711
📖 620
✍ JB Lord (0161) 624 0986
✓ DA Melling (0161) 624 2154
🏌 18 L 6186 yds SSS 70
👤 U SOC–WD
££ £25 (£35)
🚗 3 miles NW of Oldham

Darwen (1893)
Winter Hill, Duddon Avenue, Darwen, BB3 0LB
☎ **(01254) 701287**
📠 (01254) 773833
📖 375 70(L) 60(J)
✍ JR Lawson (01254) 704367
✓ W Lennon (01254) 776370
🏌 18 L 5863 yds Par 69 SSS 68
👤 U exc Tues & Sat–NA
££ £25 (£30)
🚗 Darwen 1½ miles. M65 Junction 4

Dean Wood (1922)
Lafford Lane, Up Holland, Skelmersdale, WN8 0QZ
☎ **(01695) 622219**
📠 (01695) 622245
📧 office@dwgc.fsnet.co.uk
📖 750
✍ A McGregor
✓ S Danchin
🏌 18 L 6148 yds SSS 70
👤 WD–U WE/BH–M SOC
££ £30 (£33)
🚗 4 miles W of Wigan (A577)
🏠 James Braid

Deane (1906)
Off Junction Road, Deane, Bolton, BL3 4NS
☎ **(01204) 61944**
📖 490
✍ DA Thompson (01204) 651808
✓ D Martindale
🏌 18 L 5652 yds SSS 67
👤 WD–U WE–restricted SOC–Tues/Thurs/Fri
££ £24 (£28)
🚗 2 miles W of Bolton. M61 Junction 5, 1 mile

Dunscar (1908)
Longworth Lane, Bromley Cross, Bolton, BL7 9QY
☎ **(01204) 598228**
📠 (01204) 303321
📧 secretary@dunscargolfclub.fsnet.co.uk
📖 600
✍ JW Jennings (01204) 303321
✓ G Treadgold (01204) 592992
🏌 18 L 6085 yds Par 71 SSS 69
👤 WD–U WE–restricted SOC
££ £20 (£30)
🚗 3 miles N of Bolton, off A666

Duxbury Park (1975)
Public
Duxbury Hall Road, Duxbury Park, Chorley, PR7 4AS
☎ **(01257) 265380**
📠 (01257) 241378
✍ PA Smith
✓ D Clarke
🏌 18 L 6270 yds SSS 70
👤 U
££ £8 (£10.50)
🚗 1½ miles S of Chorley, off Wigan Lane

Fairhaven (1895)

Lytham Hall Park, Ansdell, Lytham St Annes, FY8 4JU
- ☎ **(01253) 736741**
- 🖷 (01253) 731461
- 📖 900
- 🏌 H Fielding
- ✎ (01253) 736976
- ⏴ 18 L 6883 yds SSS 73
- 👥 WD–U WE–NA before 9am SOC–WD
- £€ £33 (£40)
- 🚗 Lytham 2 miles. St Annes 2 miles. M55 Junction 4

Fishwick Hall (1912)

Glenluce Drive, Farringdon Park, Preston, PR1 5TD
- ☎ **(01772) 798300**
- 🖷 (01772) 704600
- 📖 750
- 🏌 JP Davis
- ✎ M Watson (01772) 795870
- ⏴ 18 L 5857 yds SSS 69
- Apply to Sec SOC
- £€ £26 (£31)
- 🚗 1 mile E of Preston, nr junction of A59 and M6 Junction 31

Fleetwood (1932)

Golf House, Princes Way, Fleetwood, FY7 8AF
- ☎ **(01253) 873114 (Clubhouse)**
- 🖷 (01253) 773573
- ✉ fleetwoodgc@aol.com
- 📖 548
- 🏌 N Robinson (01253) 773573
- ✎ S McLaughlin (01253) 873661
- ⏴ L 18 L 6308 yds SSS 70
- 👥 U H exc Tues SOC
- £€ £30 (£40)
- 🚗 1 mile W of Fleetwood centre
- 🏠 A Steer
- ■ www.fleetwoodgolfclub.org.uk

Gathurst (1913)

Miles Lane, Shevington, Wigan, WN6 8EW
- ☎ **(01257) 252861 (Clubhouse)**
- 🖷 (01257) 255953
- ✉ gathurst.golfclub@02.co.uk
- 📖 675
- 🏌 Mrs I Fyffe (01257) 255235
- ✎ D Clarke (01257) 255882
- ⏴ 18 L 6089 yds Par 70 SSS 69
- 👥 WD–U before 5pm WE/BH/Wed–M SOC–WD
- £€ £26
- 🚗 4 miles W of Wigan. 1 mile S of M6 Junction 27
- 🏠 N Pearson-ADAS

Ghyll (1907)

Ghyll Brow, Barnoldswick, Colne, BB18 6JH
- ☎ **(01282) 842466**
- ✉ secretary@ghyllgc.freeserve.com
- 📖 310
- 🏌 JL Gill (01524) 412958
- ⏴ 9 L 5708 yds SSS 68
- 👥 U exc Sun–NA

- £€ D–£15 (D–£18)
- 🚗 7 miles N of Colne, off A56 (B6252)
- ■ www.ghyllgc.co.uk

Great Harwood (1896)

Harwood Bar, Great Harwood, BB6 7TE
- ☎ **(01254) 884391**
- 🖷 (01254) 879495
- 📖 195 65(L) 45(J)
- 🏌 J Spibey (01254) 879494
- ⏴ 9 L 6404 yds SSS 71
- 👥 U SOC
- £€ £16 (£22)
- 🚗 5 miles NE of Blackburn. M65 Junction 7

Green Haworth (1914)

Green Haworth, Accrington, BB5 3SL
- ☎ **(01254) 237580**
- 🖷 (01254) 396176
- 📖 250
- 🏌 W Halstead
- ⏴ 9 L 5556 yds SSS 67
- 👥 WD–U exc Wed–Ladies only after 5pm WE/BH–M SOC
- £€ On application
- 🚗 Willows Lane

Greenmount (1920)

Greenmount, Bury, BL8 4LH
- ☎ **(01204) 883712**
- 📖 220
- 🏌 MD Barron (Hon)
- ✎ J Seed
- ⏴ 9 L 6044 yds SSS 70
- 👥 WD–U exc Tues WE–M
- £€ £15
- 🚗 3 miles N of Bury

Haigh Hall (1972)

Public
Haigh Hall Country Park, Haigh, Wigan, WN2 1PE
- ☎ **(01942) 833337 (Clubhouse)**
- 🖷 (01942) 831417
- 📖 300
- 🏌 W Fleetwood
- ✎ I Lee (01942) 831107
- ⏴ 9 L 1446 yds
- 18 L 6350 yds (open June 2002)
- 👥 U
- £€ £3.60 (£4.60)
- 🚗 2 miles NW of Wigan. M6 Junction 27. M61 Junction 6
- 🏠 Gaunt/Marnoch

Harwood (1926)

Roading Brook Road, Bolton, BL2 4JD
- ☎ **(01204) 522878**
- 🖷 (01204) 524233
- ✉ secretary@harwoodgolfclub.co.uk
- 📖 604
- 🏌 IW Lund (01204) 524233
- ✎ P Slater (01204) 362834
- ⏴ 18 L 5786 yds SSS 68
- 👥 WD–H WE–M SOC
- £€ £20
- 🚗 4 miles NE of Bolton (B6391)
- 🏠 J Shuttleworth
- ■ www.harwoodgolfclub.co.uk

Heysham (1910)

Trumacar Park, Middleton Road, Heysham, Morecambe LA3 3JH
- ☎ **(01524) 851011**
- 🖷 (01524) 853030
- 📖 685
- 🏌 FA Bland (Sec/Mgr)
- ✎ R Dône (01524) 852000
- ⏴ 18 L 6258 yds SSS 70
- 👥 U H SOC
- £€ £25 D–£30 (£40)
- 🚗 2 miles S of Morecambe. M6 Junction 34, 5 miles
- 🏠 A Herd

Hindley Hall (1905)

Hall Lane, Hindley, Wigan, WN2 2SQ
- ☎ **(01942) 255131**
- 🖷 (01942) 253871
- 📖 430
- 🏌 Louise Marrow (01942) 255131
- ✎ D Clarke (01942) 255991
- ⏴ 18 L 5913 yds SSS 68
- 👥 U SOC
- £€ £20 (£27)
- 🚗 2 miles S of Wigan. M61 Junction 6

Horwich (1895)

Victoria Road, Horwich, BL6 5PH
- ☎ **(01204) 696980**
- 🖷 (01942) 205316
- 📖 300
- 🏌 C Sherborne
- ✎ B Sharrock
- ⏴ 9 L 5404 yds SSS 66
- 👥 U SOC–WD
- £€ £16
- 🚗 5 miles W of Bolton
- 🏠 George Lowe

Hurlston Hall (1994)

Hurlston Lane, Southport Road, Scarisbrick, L40 8HB
- ☎ **(01704) 840400**
- 🖷 (01704) 841404
- ✉ hurlston_hall@btinternet.com
- 📖 650
- 🏌 M Atherton
- ✎ J Esclapez (01704) 841120
- ⏴ 18 L 6746 yds SSS 72
- 👥 H SOC
- £€ £35 (£40)
- 🚗 2 miles NW of Ormskirk (A570). M58 Junction 3
- ⊕ Floodlit driving range
- 🏠 Donald Steel
- ■ www.hurlstonhall.co.uk

Ingol (1981)

Tanterton Hall Road, Ingol, Preston, PR2 7BY
- ☎ **(01772) 734556**
- 📖 700
- 🏌 H Parker
- ✎ S Laycock
- ⏴ 18 L 5868 yds SSS 68
- 👥 U SOC–WD
- £€ £15 (£25)
- 🚗 1½ miles NW of Preston (A6). M6 Junction 32

Knott End (1910)

Wyreside, Knott End-on-Sea, Poulton-le-Fylde, FY6 0AA
- ☎ **(01253) 810254 (Clubhouse)**
- ☎ (01253) 813446
- ✉ knottendgolfclub@btinternet.com
- 🏛 660
- ✍ A Crossley (01253) 810576
- ⚲ P Walker (01253) 811365
- ⮑ 18 L 5849 yds SSS 68
- ⚭ WD–U WE/BH–by arrangement SOC–WD
- ££ D–£25 (£30)
- ⌘ Over Wyre, 12 miles NE of Blackpool (A588)
- 🏠 James Braid

Lancaster (1932)

Ashton Hall, Ashton-with-Stodday, Lancaster, LA2 0AJ
- ☎ **(01524) 752090 (Clubhouse)**
- ☎ (01524) 752742
- 🏛 530 170(L) 62(J)
- ✍ PJ Irvine (01524) 751247
- ⚲ DE Sutcliffe (01524) 751802
- ⮑ 18 L 6500 yds SSS 71
- ⚭ WD–H SOC–WD
- ££ £32
- ⌘ 2 miles S of Lancaster (A588)
- ⊕ Dormy House
- 🏠 James Braid

Lansil (1947)

Caton Road, Lancaster, LA4 3PE
- ☎ **(01524) 39269**
- 🏛 450
- ✍ J Ollerton (01995) 601451
- ⮑ 9 L 5608 yds Par 70 SSS 67
- ⚭ WD–U Sun–U after 1pm
- ££ £12 (£12)
- ⌘ A683, 2 miles E of Lancaster

Leyland (1924)

Wigan Road, Leyland, PR25 5UD
- ☎ **(01772) 436457**
- ☎ (01772) 436457
- ✉ manager@leylandgolfclub.com
- 🏛 750
- ✍ J Ross
- ⚲ C Burgess (01772) 423425
- ⮑ 18 L 6298 yds SSS 70
- ⚭ WD–U WE–M SOC–WD
- ££ £25
- ⌘ M6 Junction 28, ¹/₂mile
- 🖥 www.leylandgolfclub.com

Lobden (1888)

Whitworth, Rochdale, OL12 8XJ
- ☎ **(01706) 343228**
- ☎ (01706) 343228
- ✉ lobdengc@hotmail.com
- 🏛 220
- ✍ J Keate (01706) 345598
- ⮑ 9 L 5697 yds Par 70 SSS 68
- ⚭ U
- ££ £12 (£15)
- ⌘ 4 miles N of Rochdale

Longridge (1877)

Fell Barn, Jeffrey Hill, Longridge, Preston PR3 2TU
- ☎ **(01772) 783291**

- ☐ (01772) 783022
- 🏛 700
- ✍ DC Wensley
- ⚲ S Taylor (01772) 783291
- ⮑ 18 L 5969 yds SSS 69
- ⚭ U
- ££ £15 (£20)
- ⌘ 8 miles NE of Preston, off B6243

Lowes Park (1915)

Hilltop, Lowes Road, Bury, BL9 6SU
- ☎ **(0161) 764 1231**
- ☐ (0161) 763 9503
- 🏛 350
- ✍ J Entwistle
- ⮑ 9 L 6006 yds Par 70 SSS 69
- ⚭ WD–U exc Wed–NA WE/BH–by arrangement
- ££ Summer £10 (£15) Winter £5 (£10)
- ⌘ 1 mile NE of Bury, off A56

Lytham Green Drive (1922)

Ballam Road, Lytham, FY8 4LE
- ☎ **(01253) 734782**
- ☐ (01253) 731350
- ✉ sec@greendrive.fsnet.co.uk
- 🏛 700
- ✍ S Higham (01253) 737390
- ⚲ A Lancaster (01253) 737379
- ⮑ 18 L 6163 yds SSS 69
- ⚭ WD–U H WE–NA SOC–WD
- ££ £30 (£38)
- ⌘ Lytham St Annes. M55 Junction 4
- 🏠 JA Steer

Marland (1928)

Public
Springfield Park, Bolton Road, Rochdale, OL11 4RE
- ☎ **(01706) 649801**
- ☐ (01706) 523082
- 🏛 300
- ✍ J Wallis
- ⚲ D Wills
- ⮑ 18 L 5237 yds SSS 66
- ⚭ WD–U WE–booking necessary
- ££ £7.50 (£9.50)
- ⌘ W of Rochdale (A58). M62 Junctions 19/20, 2 miles

Marsden Park (1969)

Public
Townhouse Road, Nelson, BB9 8DG
- ☎ **(01282) 661912**
- ✍ N Standage (01282) 865133
- ⚲ M Ross (01282) 661912
- ⮑ 18 L 5813 yds Par 70 SSS 68
- ⚭ U SOC
- ££ On application
- ⌘ M65 Junction 13, signposted Walton Lane

Morecambe (1905)

Bare, Morecambe, LA4 6AJ
- ☎ **(01524) 418050**
- ☐ (01524) 400088
- ✉ morecambegolf@btconnect.com
- 🏛 850
- ✍ Mrs J Atkinson (01524) 412841
- ⚲ S Fletcher (01524) 415596

- ⮑ 18 L 5750 yds SSS 69
- ⚭ U H SOC
- ££ On application
- ⌘ On coast road towards Carnforth (A5105)

Mossock Hall (1996)

Liverpool Road, Bickerstaffe, L39 0EE
- ☎ **(01695) 421717**
- ☐ (01695) 424961
- 🏛 600
- ✍ K Brain
- ⚲ P Atkis (01695) 424969
- ⮑ 18 L 6375 yds Par 71 SSS 71
- ⚭ U exc comp days SOC
- ££ £30 (£35)
- ⌘ 4 miles S of Ormskirk
- 🏠 Steve Marnoch

Mytton Fold Hotel (1994)

Proprietary
Whalley Road, Langho, BB6 8AB
- ☎ **(01254) 240662 (Hotel)**
- ☐ (01254) 248119
- ✉ gary@myttonfold.co.uk
- 🏛 350
- ✍ G Lucas
- ⚲ G Coope (01254) 245392
- ⮑ 18 L 6155 yds SSS 69
- ⚭ U SOC
- ££ £16 (£16)
- ⌘ 6 miles N of Blackburn, off A59. M6 Junction 31
- 🏠 F Hargreaves
- 🖥 www.smoothhound.co.uk/hotels/mytton

Nelson (1902)

Kings Causeway, Brierfield, Nelson, BB9 0EU
- ☎ **(01282) 614583**
- ☐ (01282) 606226
- 🏛 550
- ✍ BR Thomason (01282) 611834
- ⚲ N Reeves (01282) 617000
- ⮑ 18 L 6006 yds Par 70 SSS 69
- ⚭ WD–U H exc Thurs–NA WE–U exc Sat before 4pm SOC
- ££ £25 (£30)
- ⌘ 2 miles N of Burnley. M65 Junction 12
- 🏠 Dr A MacKenzie

Oldham (1892)

Lees New Road, Oldham, OL4 5PN
- ☎ **(0161) 624 4986**
- 🏛 300 45(L) 35(J)
- ✍ J Brooks
- ⚲ D Green (0161) 626 8346
- ⮑ 18 L 5045 yds SSS 65
- ⚭ U SOC
- ££ On application
- ⌘ Off Oldham-Stalybridge road

Ormskirk (1899)

Cranes Lane, Lathom, Ormskirk, L40 5UJ
- ☎ **(01695) 572112**
- 🏛 300
- ✍ RDJ Lawrence (01695) 572227

J Hammond (01695) 572074
18 L 6358 yds SSS 71
I exc Sat–NA SOC
££ £35 Wed–£40 Sun–£40 D–£50
2 miles E of Ormskirk

Pennington
Pennington Country Park, Leigh, WN7 3PA
☎ (01942) 682852
122
BW Lythgoe
T Kershaw (01942) 682852
9 L 5521 yds Par 70 SSS 67
U SOC
££ £3.60 (£4.60)
¹/₂ mile off A580, on Leigh By-Pass

Penwortham (1908)
Blundell Lane, Penwortham, Preston, PR1 0AX
☎ (01772) 744630
(01772) 740172
820
N Annandale
S Holden (01772) 742345
18 L 6056 yds SSS 69
WD–U WE–no parties
££ £25 (£33)
1¹/₂ miles W of Preston (A59)

Pleasington (1891)
Pleasington, Blackburn, BB2 5JF
☎ (01254) 202177
(01254) 201028
jean@pleasington-golf.co.uk
545
M Trickett
GJ Furey (01254) 201630
18 L 6445 yds SSS 71
H
££ £38 (£42)
3 miles SW of Blackburn

Poulton-le-Fylde (1982)
Public
Myrtle Farm, Breck Road, Poulton-le-Fylde, FY6 7HJ
☎ (01253) 892444
250
P Drew
J Greenwood
9 L 2979 yds SSS 69
U
££ On application
3 miles NE of Blackpool
⊕ Indoor driving range

Preston (1892)
Fulwood Hall Lane, Fulwood, Preston, PR2 8DD
☎ (01772) 700011
(01772) 794234
prestongolfclub@btinternet.com
800
J Chadwick
A Greenbank (01772) 700022
18 L 6312 yds SSS 71
WD–U H WE–M SOC–WD
££ D–£35
1¹/₂ miles W of M6 Junction 32

⊕ Driving range. Golf academy
James Braid

Regent Park (Bolton) (1931)
Public
Links Road, Chorley New Road, Bolton, BL6 4AF
☎ (01204) 844170
260
J Rogers
B Longworth (01204) 842336
18 L 6221yds Par 70 SSS 69
U SOC–WD
££ £8 (£10)
A673, 3 miles W of Bolton. M61 Junction 6

Rishton (1927)
Eachill Links, Hawthorn Drive, Rishton, BB1 4HG
☎ (01254) 884442
(01254) 887701
msm@cwcom.net
302
T Charnock
9 L 6097 yds SSS 69
WD–U WE–M
££ £15
3 miles E of Blackburn
Thomas/Alliss

Rochdale (1888)
Edenfield Road, Bagslate, Rochdale, OL11 5YR
☎ (01706) 646024 (Clubhouse)
(01706) 861113
750
P Chappell (01706) 643818
A Laverty (01706) 522104
18 L 6031 yds SSS 69
U
££ £20 (£25)
3 miles from M62 Junction 20 on A680
George Lowe

Rossendale (1903)
Ewood Lane Head, Haslingden, Rossendale, BB4 6LH
☎ (01706) 831339
(01706) 228669
713
NC Readett
SJ Nicholls (01706) 213616
18 L 6293 yds SSS 71
WD/Sun–U Sat–M
££ £25 (£30) (1999)
7 miles N of Bury, nr end of M66

Royal Lytham & St Annes (1886)
Links Gate, Lytham St Annes, FY8 3LQ
☎ (01253) 724206
(01253) 780946
bookings@royallytham.org
600
RJG Cochrane
E Birchenough (01253) 720094
18 L 6685 yds SSS 73
WD–I H
££ £100

St Annes 1 mile (A584)
⊕ Dormy House

Saddleworth (1904)
Mountain Ash, Uppermill, Oldham, OL3 6LT
☎ (01457) 873653
(01457) 820647
secretary@saddleworthgolfclub.org.uk
700
AE Gleave
RI Johnson
18 L 5976 yds SSS 69
U
££ £23 (£30)
Uppermill, 5 miles E of Oldham
Mackenzie/Leaver

St Annes Old Links (1901)
Highbury Road East, Lytham St Annes, FY8 2LD
☎ (01253) 723597
(01253) 781506
secretary@coastalgolf.co.uk
945
RV Beach
D Webster (01253) 722432
18 L 6684 yds SSS 72
WD–NA before 9.30am and 12–1.30pm WE/BH–arrange with Sec SOC
££ £38 (£50)
Between St Annes and Blackpool, off A584
Herd
www.coastalgolf.co.uk

Shaw Hill Hotel G&CC (1925)
Preston Road, Whittle-le-Woods, Chorley, PR6 7PP
☎ (01257) 269221
(01257) 261223
info@shaw-hill.co.uk
500
DFW Dimsdale
D Clarke (01257) 279222
18 L 6246 yds Par 73 SSS 70
WD–U H SOC
££ £30 (£40)
A6, 1¹/₂ miles N of Chorley. M61 Junction 8. M6 Junction 28

Standish Court (1995)
Rectory Lane, Standish, Wigan, WN6 0XD
☎ (01257) 425777
(01257) 425888
300
G O'Neill
B Toone
18 L 5266 yds Par 68 SSS 66
U SOC
££ £10 (£15)
M6 Junction 27, 2 miles
Patrick Dawson
www.standishgolf.co.uk

Stonyhurst Park (1980)
Stonyhurst, Hurst Green, Clitheroe, BB7 9QB
☎ (01254) 826478

  380
JM Aitken (01254) 823666
9 L 5572 yds SSS 67
WD–U WE–NA
£15
5 miles SW of Clitheroe (B6243)
Green fees payable at Bayley Arms, Hurst Green

Towneley (1932)
Public
Towneley Park, Todmorden Road, Burnley, BB11 3ED
☎ (01282) 451636
280
N Clark (01282) 414555
(01282) 438473
18 L 5811 yds Par 70 SSS 68
9 hole course
U
£9.55 (£10.60)
1¹/₂ miles E of Burnley

Tunshill (1901)
Kiln Lane, Milnrow, Rochdale, OL16 3TS
☎ (01706) 342095
300
G Hurst (01706) 650566
9 L 5745 yds SSS 68
WD–U WE–M SOC
£16
2 miles E of Rochdale. M62 Junction 21

Turton (1908)
Wood End Farm, Chapeltown Road, Bromley Cross, Bolton BL7 9QH
☎ (01204) 852235
300 56(L) 51(J)
D Fairclough (01204) 592024
None
18 L 6159 yds Par 70 SSS 70
WD–U exc Wed–NA 11.30–3.30pm WE/BH–M SOC
£20 (£25)
3¹/₂ miles N of Bolton, nr Last Drop Village

De Vere Herons Reach
(1993)
Pay and play
East Park Drive, Blackpool, FY3 8LL
☎ (01253) 838866/766156
(01253) 798800
550
P Heaton
R Bowman (01253) 766156
18 L 6461 yds SSS 72
U H SOC
£40 (£45)
M55 Junction 4. Follow signs to Blackpool Zoo
Floodlit driving range
Alliss/Clark

Walmersley (1906)
Garrett's Close, Walmersley, Bury, BL9 6TE
☎ (0161) 764 1429

(0161) 764 7770
450
RO Goldstein (0161) 764 7770
P Thorpe (0161) 763 9050
18 L 5341 yds SSS 67
WD–U exc Tues–NA Sat–NA Sun–M SOC–Wed–Fri
D–£20
2 miles N of Bury (A56). S of M66 Junction 1
SG Marnoch

Werneth (1908)
Green Lane, Garden Suburb, Oldham, OL8 3AZ
☎ (0161) 624 1190
400
JH Barlow
R Penny
18 L 5363 yds SSS 66
WD–U WE–M SOC
D–£16.50
2 miles S of Oldham
Sandy Herd

Westhoughton (1929)
Long Island, Westhoughton, Bolton, BL5 2BR
☎ (01942) 811085/608958
230
F Donohue
J Seed
9 L 5834 yds SSS 68
WD–U WE/BH–M
D–£16
4 miles SW of Bolton on A58

Whalley (1912)
Long Leese Barn, Clerkhill Road, Whalley, BB7 9DR
☎ (01254) 822236
(01254) 824760
350
P Lord (01282) 779167
J Hunt (01254) 822236
9 L 6258 yds Par 72 SSS 71
U exc Sat (Apr–Oct) SOC–WD
£16 (£20)
7 miles NE of Blackburn
■ www.whalleygolfclub.co.uk

Whittaker (1906)
Littleborough, OL5 0LH
☎ (01706) 378310
S Noblett (01706) 842541
9 L 5666 yds SSS 67
WD/Sat–U Sun–NA
£14 (£18)
1¹/₂ miles N of Littleborough, off A58. M62 Junction 21
NP Stott

Wigan (1898)
Arley Hall, Haigh, Wigan, WN1 2UH
☎ (01257) 421360
300
E Walmsley
18 L 6008 yds SSS 70
U exc Tues & Sat
£25 (£30)

4 miles N of Wigan, off A5106/B5239. M6 Junction 27
Gaunt/Marnoch

Wilpshire (1890)
72 Whalley Road, Wilpshire, Blackburn, BB1 9LF
☎ (01254) 248260
(01254) 248260
650
HE Aspden
W Slaven (01254) 249558
18 L 5911 yds SSS 69
WD–U WE/BH–on request
£25 (£30)
3 miles NE of Blackburn, off A666

Leicestershire

Beedles Lake (1993)
170 Broome Lane, East Goscote, LE7 3WQ
☎ (0116) 260 6759/7086
336
L Emery (Gen Mgr) (0116) 260 4414
S Byrne
18 L 6732 yds Par 72 SSS 71
U SOC
£11 (£14)
4 miles N of Leicester on B5328, off A46. M1, 8 miles
Driving range
D Tucker

Birstall (1900)
Station Road, Birstall, Leicester, LE4 3BB
☎ (0116) 267 4450
(0116) 267 4322
400 80(L) 50(J)
Mrs SE Chilton (0116) 267 4322
D Clark (0116) 267 5245
18 L 6213 yds SSS 70
WD–I WE–M SOC
£25 D–£30
3 miles N of Leicester (A6)

Blaby (1991)
Pay and play
Lutterworth Road, Blaby, LE8 3DB
☎ (0116) 278 4804
B Morris
9 L 2600 yds SSS 68
U
18 holes–£6 (£8)
S of Blaby village
Driving range

Breedon Priory (1990)
Green Lane, Wilson, Derby, DE73 1LG
☎ (01332) 863081
(01332) 865319
✉ bpgc@barbox.net
500
M Mayfield
L Sheldon
18 L 5777 yds Par 69 SSS 68
WD–U WE–NA before 2pm (phone first) SOC–WD

££   £20 (£25)
⊶   3¹/₂ miles W of M1 Junction 23A
on A453
🛉   Snell/Ashton

Charnwood Forest (1890)

Breakback Road, Woodhouse Eaves,
Loughborough, LE12 8TA
☎   (01509) 890259
🖥   (01509) 890925
✉   secretary@charnwoodforestgc
.co.uk
📖   330
🏌   Mrs J Bowler
⚐   9 L 5960 yds SSS 69
👥   WD–H WE/BH–NA
SOC–Wed–Fri
££   £20 (£25)
⊶   M1 Junction 22/23, 3 miles

Cosby (1895)

Chapel Lane, Broughton Road, Cosby,
Leicester LE9 1RG
☎   (0116) 286 4759
🖥   (0116) 286 4484
✉   secretary@cosby-golf-club.co.uk
📖   690
🏌   GT Kirkpatrick (0116) 286 4759
⚐   M Wing (0116) 284 8275
⚐   18 L 6410 yds Par 71 SSS 71
👥   WD–U H before 4pm WE/BH–M
H SOC–WD–H
££   £22 D–£29
⊶   ¹/₂ mile S of Cosby. 7 miles S of
Leicester
■   www.cosby-golf-club.co.uk

Enderby (1986)

Public
Mill Lane, Enderby, Leicester, LE19 4LX
☎   (0116) 284 9388
⚐   C D'Araujo
⚐   9 L 5712 yds SSS 71
👥   U
££   18 holes–£6.75 (£9)
⊶   Enderby 2 miles. M1 Junction 21

Glen Gorse (1933)

Glen Road, Oadby, Leicester, LE2 4RF
☎   (0116) 271 4159
🖥   (0116) 271 4159
✉   secretary@gggc.co.uk
📖   440 115(L) 60(J)
🏌   Mrs J James (0116) 271 4159
⚐   D Fitzpatrick (0116) 271 3748
⚐   18 L 6648 yds SSS 72
👥   WD–U WE/BH–M SOC–WD
££   £25 D–£30
⊶   3 miles S of Leicester on A6

Hinckley (1894)

Leicester Road, Hinckley, LE10 3DR
☎   (01455) 615124
🖥   (01455) 890841
📖   650
🏌   R Coley, L Jackson (Admin)
⚐   R Jones (01455) 615014
⚐   18 L 6527 yds SSS 71
👥   WD–U exc Tues Sat–NA before
4pm Sun–M after 11am SOC
££   £25 D–£35

⊶   NE of Hinckley on B4668, nr M69
■   www.hinckleygolfclub.com

Humberstone Heights

(1978)
Public
Gipsy Lane, Leicester, LE5 0TB
☎   (0116) 299 5570/1
🖥   (0116) 299 5569
📖   350
🏌   Mrs H Cotter
⚐   P Highfield (0116) 299 5570
⚐   18 L 6343 yds SSS 70
👥   U SOC
££   On application
⊶   3 miles E of Leicester, off A47
⊕   Driving range. Pitch & putt course
🛉   Hawtree

Kibworth (1904)

Weir Road, Kibworth Beauchamp,
Leicester, LE8 0LP
☎   (0116) 279 2301
🖥   (0116) 279 6434
📖   700
🏌   J Noble (Mgr)
⚐   R Larratt (0116) 279 2283
⚐   18 L 6354 yds SSS 71
👥   WD–U WE–M SOC–WD
££   £23
⊶   9 miles SE of Leicester, off A6
⊕   Driving range

Kilworth Springs (1993)

South Kilworth Road, North Kilworth,
Lutterworth, LE17 6HJ
☎   (01858) 575082
🖥   (01858) 575078
📖   514
🏌   Ann Vicary
⚐   A Markert
⚐   18 L 6718 yds SSS 72
👥   U SOC
££   £18 (£21)
⊶   4 miles E of M1 Junction 20
⊕   Driving range

Kirby Muxloe (1893)

Station Road, Kirby Muxloe, Leicester,
LE9 2EP
☎   (0116) 239 3457
🖥   (0116) 239 3457
📖   630
🏌   GB Woodcock (0116) 239 3457
⚐   B Whipham (0116) 239 2813
⚐   18 L 6307 yds Par 71 SSS 70
👥   WD–U before 3.45pm exc
Tues–NA WE–Captain's
permission only SOC–H
££   £25 D–£30
⊶   3 miles W of Leicester. M1
Junctions 21 or 21A
⊕   Driving range for members and
green fees only

Langton Park G&CC

(1994)
Langton Hall, Leicester, LE16 7TY
☎   (01858) 545374
🖥   (01858) 545358

📖   200
🏌   J Window
⚐   18 L 6724 yds SSS 72
👥   H or I SOC
££   On application
⊶   12 miles SE of Leicester, off A6. 2
miles N of Market Harborough
🛉   Hawtree

Leicestershire (1890)

Evington Lane, Leicester, LE5 6DJ
☎   (0116) 273 8825
🖥   (0116) 273 1900
✉   enquiries@thelgc.co.uk
📖   750
🏌   CR Chapman
⚐   DT Jones (0116) 273 6730
⚐   18 L 6329 yds SSS 71
👥   U H SOC–arrange with Sec or Pro
££   £24 (£29)
⊶   2 miles E of Leicester
■   www.thelgc.co.uk

Leicestershire Forest

(1991)
Markfield Lane, Botcheston, LE9 9FJ
☎   (01455) 824800
📖   460
🏌   M Fixter
⚐   M Wing
⚐   18 L 6111 yds SSS 69
👥   U–phone first
££   On application
⊶   6 miles W of Leicester. M1
Junction 22, 4 miles
⊕   Driving range
🛉   York/Fixter

Lingdale (1967)

Joe Moore's Lane, Woodhouse Eaves,
Loughborough, LE12 8TF
☎   (01509) 890703
🖥   (01509) 890703
📖   659
🏌   M Green
⚐   P Sellears (01509) 890684
⚐   18 L 6545 yds SSS 71
👥   U SOC
££   D–£30 (£40)
⊶   6 miles S of Loughborough. M1
Junction 23, 4 miles

Longcliffe (1906)

Snells Nook Lane, Nanpantan,
Loughborough, LE11 3YA
☎   (01509) 216321
✉   longcliffegolf@btconnect.com
📖   650
🏌   P Keeling (01509) 239129
⚐   DC Mee (01509) 231450
⚐   18 L 6695 yds SSS 72
👥   WD–H WE–M
££   £30
⊶   3 miles SW of Loughborough. M1
Junction 23

Lutterworth (1904)

Rugby Road, Lutterworth, LE17 4HN
☎   (01455) 552532
🖥   (01455) 553586

780
🐦 J Faulks (01455) 552532
✓ R Tisdall (01455) 557199
⛳ 18 L 6226 yds SSS 70
👥 WD–U WE–M SOC–WD
£€ £22 D–£30
🚗 By M1 Junction 20 and M6 Junction 1

Market Harborough   (1898)

Great Oxendon Road, Market Harborough, LE16 8NF
☎ **(01858) 463684**
📠 (01858) 432906
📖 650
🐦 AP Price-Jones
✓ FJ Baxter (01858) 463684
⛳ 18 L 6022 yds Par 70 SSS 69
👥 WD–U WE–M SOC–WD
£€ £25 D–£30
🚗 1 mile S of Mkt Harborough on A508
🏠 Howard Swan

Melton Mowbray   (1925)

Waltham Rd, Thorpe Arnold, Melton Mowbray, LE14 4SD
☎ **(01664) 562118**
📠 (01664) 562118
📧 mmgc@LE144SD.fsbusiness.co.uk
📖 575
✓ N Curtis (01664) 569629
⛳ 18 L 6222 yds SSS 70
👥 U H before 3pm –M after 3pm SOC
£€ £20 (£23)
🚗 2 miles NE of Melton Mowbray on A607

Oadby   (1974)

Public
Leicester Road, Oadby, Leicester, LE2 4AJ
☎ **(0116) 270 9052/270 0215**
📖 350
🐦 P Goodall (0116) 270 3828
✓ A Wells (0116) 270 9052
⛳ 18 L 6311 yds Par 72 SSS 70
👥 WD–U WE/BH–book with Pro SOC–WD
£€ £10 (£13)
🚗 Leicester Racecourse, 2 miles SE of Leicester (A6)

Park Hill   (1994)

Park Hill, Seagrave, LE12 7NG
☎ **(01509) 815454**
📠 (01509) 816062
📧 mail@parkhillgolf.co.uk
📖 500
🐦 JP Hutson
✓ M Ulyett (01509) 815775
⛳ 18 L 7219 yds Par 73 SSS 74
👥 U SOC
£€ £22 D–£30 (£26 D–£38)
🚗 6 miles N of Leicester on A46. M1 Junction 21A
⊕ Driving range
🌐 www.parkhillgolf.co.uk

Rothley Park   (1911)

Westfield Lane, Rothley, Leicester, LE7 7LH
☎ **(0116) 230 2019**

550
📠 (0116) 230 2809
📧 secretary@rothleypark.co.uk
🐦 SG Winterton (0116) 230 2809
✓ D Spillane (0116) 230 3023
⛳ 18 L 6487 yds SSS 71
👥 WD–H exc Tues–NA WE/BH–NA SOC
£€ £25 D–£30
🚗 6 miles N of Leicester, W of A6
🌐 www.rothleypark.com

Scraptoft   (1928)

Beeby Road, Scraptoft, Leicester, LE7 9SJ
☎ **(0116) 241 9000**
📠 (0116) 241 9000
📖 600
🐦 H Taylor (0116) 241 9000
✓ S Wood (0116) 241 9138
⛳ 18 L 6151 yds Par 70 SSS 70
👥 WD–U WE–M SOC–WD
£€ £24 D–£29
🚗 3 miles E of Leicester

Six Hills

Pay and play
Six Hills, Melton Mowbray, LE14 3PR
☎ **(01509) 881225**
📠 (01509) 889090
📖 100
🐦 Mrs J Showler
✓ T Westwood
⛳ 18 L 5758 yds Par 71 SSS 69
👥 U
£€ £10 (£13)
🚗 10 miles N of leicester, off A46

Ullesthorpe Court Hotel   (1976)

Frolesworth Road, Ullesthorpe, Lutterworth, LE17 5BZ
☎ **(01455) 209023**
📠 (01455) 202537
📖 600
🐦 PE Woolley
✓ D Bowring (01455) 209150
⛳ 18 L 6650 yds SSS 72
👥 U SOC–WD
£€ £20 D–£35
🚗 3 miles NW of Lutterworth, off B577. M1 Junction 20, 5 miles
🌐 www.ullesthorpecourt.co.uk

Western Park   (1920)

Public
Scudamore Road, Leicester, LE3 1UQ
☎ **(0116) 287 2339/287 6158**
📖 300
🐦 IA Nicholson
✓ BN Whipham (0116) 287 2339
⛳ 18 L 6532 yds SSS 71
👥 U
£€ On application
🚗 4 miles W of Leicester. M1 Junction 21, 3 miles

Whetstone   (1965)

Cambridge Road, Cosby, Leicester, LE9 5SH
☎ **(0116) 286 1424**
📠 (0116) 286 1424

550
🐦 D Dalby
✓ N Leatherland, D Raitt
⛳ 18 L 5795 yds Par 68 SSS 68
👥 U SOC
£€ £15
🚗 S boundary of Leicester
⊕ Driving range
🏠 E Callaway

Willesley Park   (1921)

Measham Road, Ashby-de-la-Zouch, LE65 2PF
☎ **(01530) 411532**
📠 (01530) 414596
📖 600 99(L) 38(J)
🐦 RE Brown (01530) 414596
✓ BJ Hill (01530) 414820
⛳ 18 L 6304 yds SSS 70
👥 WD–H WE/BH–H after 9.30am SOC
£€ £30 (£35)
🚗 2 miles S of Ashby on B5006. M1 Junctions 22/23/24. A42(M) Junction 12
🏠 James Braid

Lincolnshire

Ashby Decoy   (1936)

Ashby Decoy, Burringham Road, Scunthorpe, DN17 2AB
☎ **(01724) 842913**
📠 (01724) 271708
📧 ashby.decoy@btclick.com
📖 520 130(L) 65(J)
🐦 Mrs J Harrison (01724) 866561
✓ A Miller (01724) 868972
⛳ 18 L 6281 yds SSS 71
👥 WD–H Sat–M SOC–WD exc Tues
£€ £18 (£23)
🚗 2 miles SW of Scunthorpe
🌐 www.ashbydecoy.co.uk

Belton Park   (1890)

Belton Lane, Londonthorpe Road, Grantham, NG31 9SH
☎ **(01476) 567399**
📠 (01476) 592078
📖 900
🐦 T Ireland
✓ B McKee (01476) 563911
⛳ 27 holes:
Brownlow L 6452 yds SSS 71
Ancaster L 6305 yds SSS 70
Belmont L 6075 yds SSS 69
👥 U H SOC–WD exc Tues
£€ £30 (£36)
🚗 2 miles N of Grantham
🏠 T Williamson
🌐 www.greatgolfatbeltonpark.co.uk

Belton Woods Hotel (1991)

Belton, Grantham, NG32 2LN
☎ **(01476) 593200**
📠 (01476) 574547
📖 350
🐦 A Ozolins (01636) 672305

✎ S Sayers
✐ Lakes 18 L 6831 yds SSS 73
  Woodside 18 L 6623 yds SSS 72
  9 hole Par 3 course
👥 U SOC
££ £27 D–£45 (£30 D–£50)
🚗 2 miles N of Grantham on A607
  towards Lincoln
⊕ Driving range
🏠 Cayford

Blankney (1904)

Blankney, Lincoln, LN4 3AZ
☎ **(01526) 320263**
🖶 (01526) 322521
🏛 664 138(L) 50(J)
✐ DA Priest
✎ G Bradley (01526) 320202
✐ 18 L 6638 yds SSS 73
👥 U H SOC
££ £24 (£30)
🚗 10 miles SE of Lincoln on B1188
🏠 Cameron Sinclair
■ www.blankneygolf.co.uk

Boston (1900)

*Cowbridge, Horncastle Road, Boston,
PE22 7EL*
☎ **(01205) 362306**
🖶 (01205) 350589
🏛 650 115L) 60(J)
✐ SP Shaw (01205) 350589
✎ N Hiom (01205) 362306
✐ 18 L 6483 yds Par 72 SSS 71
👥 WD–U WE/BH–U H
££ £20 (£25)
🚗 2 miles N of Boston on B1183

Boston West (1995)

Hubbert's Bridge, Boston, PE20 3QX
☎ **(01205) 290670**
🖶 (01205) 290725
✉ info@bostonwestgolfclub.co.uk
🏛 650
✐ MJ Couture (01205) 290670
✎ A Hare (01529) 303970
✐ 18 L 6333 yds Par 72 SSS 70
  6 hole Par 3 course
👥 U
££ £14 (£16)
🚗 2 miles W of Boston on B1192
⊕ Floodlit driving range
🏠 Michael Zara
■ www.bostonwestgolfclub.co.uk

Burghley Park (1890)

St Martin's, Stamford, PE9 3JX
☎ **(01780) 753789**
🖶 (01780) 753789
✉ burghley.golf@lineone.net
🏛 750 140(L) 100(J)
✐ PH Mulligan (01780) 753789
✎ G Davies (01780) 762100
✐ 18 L 6236 yds SSS 70
👥 WD–I or H WE/BH–M SOC–WD
££ £25
🚗 1 mile S of Stamford, off A1 to
  B1081
🏠 Rev JD Day

Canwick Park (1893)

*Canwick Park, Washingborough Road,
Lincoln, LN4 1EF*
☎ **(01522) 542912/522166**
🖶 (01522) 526997
✉ manager@canwickpark.co.uk
🏛 650
✐ P Roberts (01522) 542912
✎ S Williamson (01522) 536870
✐ 18 L 6150 yds SSS 69
👥 WD–U WE–M before 2.30pm
  SOC–WD
££ £17 (£21)
🚗 1 mile SE of Lincoln
🏠 Hawtree
■ www.canwickpark.co.uk

Carholme (1906)

Carholme Road, Lincoln, LN1 1SE
☎ **(01522) 523725**
🖶 (01522) 533733
✉ info@carholme-golf-club.co.uk
🏛 600
✐ J Lammin
✎ R Hunter (01522) 536811
✐ 18 L 6215 yds Par 71 SSS 70
👥 WD–U WE–U after 2pm BH–SOC
££ £18 (£22)
🚗 Lincoln 1 mile (A57)
■ www.carholme-golf-club.co.uk

Cleethorpes (1894)

Kings Road, Cleethorpes, DN35 0PN
☎ **(01472) 814060 (Pro)**
🏛 750
✐ JG Ashton (01472) 816110
✎ P Davies (01472) 814060
✐ 18 L 6349 yds SSS 70
👥 WD–U exc Wed pm SOC–exc
  Tues/Wed/Sat
££ D–£20 (D–£25)
🚗 1 mile S of Cleethorpes

Elsham (1900)

Barton Road, Elsham, Brigg, DN20 0LS
☎ **(01652) 680291**
🖶 (01652) 680308
🏛 650
✐ T Hartley (Mgr) (01652) 680291
✎ S Brewer (01652) 680432
✐ 18 L 6402 yds SSS 71
👥 H SOC–WD
££ £24 D–£30
🚗 3 miles N of Brigg. M180 Junction
  5

Forest Pines (1996)

Ermine Street, Brigg, DN20 0AQ
☎ **(01652) 650756**
🖶 (01652) 650495
🏛 350
✐ D Edwards (Golf Dir)
✎ D Edwards
✐ 27 holes:6393-6859 yds
  Par 71-73 SSS 70-73
👥 U SOC
££ £30 D–£40
🚗 M180 Junction 4, on A15 to
  Scunthorpe
🏠 John Morgan
■ www.forestpines.co.uk

Gainsborough (1894)

Thonock, Gainsborough, DN21 1PZ
☎ **(01427) 613088**
🖶 (01427) 810172
🏛 600
✐ D Bowers
✎ S Cooper
✐ 18 L 6266 yds Par 70 SSS 70
  18 L 6724 yds Par 72 SSS 72
👥 U
££ £25 D–£35
🚗 N of Gainsborough
⊕ Floodlit driving range
🏠 Neil Coles

Gedney Hill (1991)

Public
*West Drove, Gedney End Hill,
PE12 0NT*
☎ **(01406) 330922**
🏛 400
✐ M Page
✎ D Hutton
✐ 18 L 5450 yds SSS 66
👥 U SOC–WD
££ £6.50 (£11)
🚗 4 miles from A47 on B1166
⊕ Driving range
🏠 C Britton

Grange Park (1992)

Pay and play
*Butterwick Road, Messingham,
Scunthorpe, DN17 3PP*
☎ **(01724) 762945**
🖶 (01724) 762851
✐ I Cannon (Mgr)
✎ J Drury
✐ 13 L 4122 yds SSS 48
  9 hole Par 3 course
👥 U
££ £6.50 (£8.50)
🚗 5 miles from Scunthorpe. M180
  Junction 3
⊕ Floodlit driving range
🏠 RW Price

Grimsby (1922)

Littlecoates Road, Grimsby, DN34 4LU
☎ **(01472) 342823 (Clubhouse)**
🖶 (01472) 342630
🏛 720 150(L) 70(J)
✐ V McAfee (01472) 342630
✎ R Smith (01472) 356981
✐ 18 L 6057 yds Par 70 SSS 69
👥 WD–U Sat pm/Sun am–XL
  SOC–WD
££ £22 D–£28
🚗 1 mile W of Grimsby, off A46. 1
  mile from A180
🏠 HS Colt

Hirst Priory Park

Crowle, Scunthorpe, DN17 4BU
☎ **(07715) 420519**
🏛 400
✐ M Thompson
✎ (01724) 711619
✐ 18 L 6199 yds Par 71 SSS 69
👥 U SOC
££ £13.75 (£17.50)

⚐ ³/₄ mile N of M180 Junction 2, on A161 to Crowle
🏠 David Baxter

Holme Hall (1908)

Holme Lane, Bottesford, Scunthorpe, DN16 3RF
☎ **(01724) 862078**
📠 (01724) 862078
📧 tracey.curtis@btconnect.com
📖 470 90(L) 30(J)
🏌 Miss TL Curtis
🏌 R McKiernan (01724) 851816
🏁 18 L 6404 yds SSS 70
👥 WD–U WE–M H SOC–WD
££ £22 D–£30
⚐ 4 miles SE of Scunthorpe. M180 Junction 4

Horncastle (1990)

West Ashby, Horncastle, LN9 5PP
☎ **(01507) 526800**
📖 300
🏌 D Hardy
🏌 EC Wright
🏁 18 L 5717 yds SSS 70
👥 U SOC
££ £15 D–£20
⚐ 1 mile N of Horncastle, off A158
🏠 EC Wright

Humberston Park

Humberston Avenue, Humberston, DN36 4SJ
☎ **(01472) 210404**
📖 230
🏌 R Bean (01472) 690361
🏁 9 L 3670 yds Par 60 SSS 57
👥 U exc Wed pm/Thurs am/Sun am SOC
££ £8 (£10)
⚐ Humberston, 3 miles S of Grimsby (A1031)
🏠 T Barraclough

Immingham (1975)

St Andrews Lane, Off Church Lane, Immingham, DN40 2EU
☎ **(01469) 575298**
📠 (01469) 577636
📖 650
🏌 N Harding (01469) 575493
🏁 18 L 6215 yds SSS 70
👥 WD–U Sun–NA before noon SOC–WD
££ £16 D–£23
⚐ N of St Andrew's Church, Immingham
🏠 Hawtree/Pennink
■ www.immgc.com

Kenwick Park (1992)

Kenwick Hall, Louth, LN11 8NY
☎ **(01507) 605134**
📠 (01507) 606556
🏌 PG Shillington
🏌 E Sharp (01507) 607161
🏁 18 L 6815 yds Par 72 SSS 73
👥 U SOC
££ D–£25 (£35)
⚐ 1 mile SE of Louth

⊕ Teaching Academy. Driving range
🏠 Patrick Tallack

Kingsway (1971)

Public
Kingsway, Scunthorpe, DN15 7ER
☎ **(01724) 840945**
🏌 C Mann
🏌 C Mann
🏁 9 L 1915 yds SSS 59
👥 U
££ On application
⚐ ³/₄ mile W of Scunthorpe, off A18

Kirton Holme (1992)

Pay and play
Holme Road, Kirton Holme, Boston, PE20 1SY
☎ **(01205) 290669**
📖 350
🏌 Mrs T Welberry (01205) 290560
🏁 9 L 2884 yds SSS 68
👥 U SOC–WD
££ D–£9 (£10)
⚐ 3 miles W of Boston, off A52
🏠 DW Welberry

Lincoln (1891)

Torksey, Lincoln, LN1 2EG
☎ **(01427) 718721**
📠 (01427) 718721
📧 info@lincolngc.co.uk
📖 700
🏌 DB Linton
🏌 A Carter (01427) 718273
🏁 18 L 6438 yds SSS 71
👥 WD–H SOC
££ £26 D–£32
⚐ 12 miles NW of Lincoln, off A156
■ www.lincolngc.co.uk

Louth (1965)

Crowtree Lane, Louth, LN11 9LJ
☎ **(01507) 603681**
📠 (01507) 608501
📧 louthgolfclub1992@btinternet.com
📖 700
🏌 M Covey (Mgr) (01507) 603681
🏌 AJ Blundell (01507) 604648
🏁 18 L 6430 yds SSS 71
👥 U SOC
££ £20 D–£26 (£30 D–£35)
⚐ W side of Louth
■ www.louthgolfclub.com

Manor (Laceby) (1992)

Laceby Manor, Laceby, Grimsby, DN37 7EA
☎ **(01472) 873468**
📠 (01472) 276706
📖 550
🏌 Mrs J Mackay, G Mackay (Mgr)
🏁 18 L 6354 yds SSS 70
👥 U SOC
££ D–£18 (£22)
⚐ 5 miles W of Grimsby at Barton Street (A18)
🏠 Nicholson/Rushton

Market Rasen & District (1912)

Legsby Road, Market Rasen, LN8 3DZ
☎ **(01673) 842319**
📖 600
🏌 JA Brown
🏌 AM Chester (01673) 842416
🏁 18 L 6209 yds SSS 70
👥 WD–I WE/BH–M SOC
££ £20 D–£29
⚐ 1 mile E of Market Rasen

Market Rasen Racecourse

Legsby Road, Market Rasen, LN8 3EA
☎ **(01673) 843434**
📠 (01673) 844532
🏁 9 L 2350 yds Par
👥 U
££ On application
⚐ Market Rasen Racecourse

Martin Moor

Martin Road, Blankney, LN4 3BE
☎ **(01526) 378243**
📠 (01526) 378243
📖 170
🏌 B Wallis
🏁 9 L 6325 yds Par 72 SSS 70
👥 U
££ £8.50 (£10)
⚐ 3 miles E of Metheringham (B1189)
🏠 Harrison/Lovett

Millfield (1985)

Laughterton, Lincoln, LN1 2LB
☎ **(01427) 718473**
📠 (01427) 718473
📖 500
🏌 P Grey-Guthrie
🏁 18 L 6004 yds SSS 69
   18 L 4585 yds
   9 hole Par 3 course
👥 U
££ £5 – £8
⚐ 9 miles W of Lincoln, nr Torksey (B1133)
⊕ Driving range
🏠 C Watson

Normanby Hall (1978)

Public
Normanby Park, Scunthorpe, DN15 9HU
☎ **(01724) 280444 Ext 852 (Bookings)**
📖 850
🏌 P McNicholas (01724) 853212
🏌 C Mann (01724) 720226
🏁 18 L 6548 yds SSS 71
👥 U SOC–WD
££ £11.50 D–£16 (£13.50)
⚐ 5 miles N of Scunthorpe
🏠 Hawtree

North Shore (1910)

North Shore Road, Skegness, PE25 1DN
☎ **(01754) 763298**
📠 (01754) 761902

450
- B Howard (01754) 763298
- J Cornelius (01754) 764822
- 18 L 6254 yds SSS 71
- H–soft spikes only Apr–Oct SOC–WD
- ££ £22 D–£33 (£31 D–£45)
- 1 mile N of Skegness
- James Braid
- www.north-shore.co.uk

Pottergate
Moor Lane, Branston, Lincoln
- ☎ (01522) 794867
- 300
- G McFee
- L Tasker
- 9 L 5164 yds Par 68 SSS 65
- U
- ££ £8 (£9.50)
- 3 miles SE of Lincoln (B1188)
- WT Bailey

RAF Coningsby   (1972)
RAF Coningsby, Lincoln, LN4 4SY
- ☎ (01526) 342581 Ext 6828
- 220
- S Ellis (01526) 347640
- 9 L 5354 yds Par 68 SSS 66
- WD–U before 5pm SOC–WD
- ££ £8
- Between Woodhall Spa and Coningsby on B1192

RAF Waddington
Waddington, Lincoln, LN5 9NB
- ☎ (01522) 720271 Ext 7958
- 90
- D Bennett
- 9 L 5519 yds SSS 69
- By prior arrangement
- ££ On application
- 4 miles S of Lincoln (A607)

Sandilands   (1901)
Sandilands, Sutton-on-Sea, LN12 2RJ
- ☎ (01507) 441432
- (01507) 441617
- 300
- C Carpenter (01507) 441432
- 18 L 6068 yds SSS 69
- U SOC
- ££ £18 (£20)
- 1 mile S of Sutton-on-Sea, off A52

Seacroft   (1895)
Drummond Road, Seacroft, Skegness, PE25 3AU
- ☎ (01754) 763020
- (01754) 763020
- enquiries@seacroft-golfclub.co.uk
- 328 107(L) 87(J)
- R England (Sec/Mgr)
- J R Lawie (01754) 769624
- 18 L 6479 yds SSS 71
- U H SOC
- ££ £30 (£35)
- S boundary of Skegness, nr Nature Reserve
- Willie Fernie
- www.seacroft-golfclub.co.uk

Sleaford   (1905)
Willoughby Road, South Rauceby, Sleaford, NG34 8PL
- ☎ (01529) 488273
- (01529) 488326
- sleafordgolfclub@btinternet.com
- 630
- TE Gibbons
- J Wilson (01529) 488644
- 18 L 6503 yds SSS 71
- U H exc Sun–NA (Winter) SOC–WD
- ££ £22 (£36)
- 1 mile W of Sleaford on A153
- Tom Williamson

South Kyme   (1990)
Skinners Lane, South Kyme, Lincoln, LN4 4AT
- ☎ (01526) 861113
- (01526) 861080
- southkymegc@hotmail.com
- P Chamberlain (Golf Dir)
- J P Chamberlain
- 18 L 6597 yds SSS 71
- U SOC
- ££ £15 (£18)
- 2 miles from A17 on B1395
- ⊕ 6 hole practice course
- Graham Bradley
- www.skgc.co.uk

Spalding   (1907)
Surfleet, Spalding, PE11 4EA
- ☎ (01775) 680386
- (01775) 680988
- 750
- BW Walker (01775) 680386
- J Spencer (01775) 680474
- 18 L 6483 yds SSS 71
- U H SOC–Tues after 2pm & Thurs
- ££ £20 (£30)
- 4 miles N of Spalding, off A16
- Spencer/Ward/Price

Stoke Rochford   (1924)
Great North Rd, Grantham, NG33 5EW
- ☎ (01476) 530275
- 570
- J Martindale (01572) 756305
- J A Dow (01476) 530218
- 18 L 6252 yds SSS 70
- WD–U WE/BH–U after 10.30am
- ££ On application
- 6 miles S of Grantham (A1)
- Maj Hotchkin (1935)

Sudbrook Moor   (1991)
Public
Charity Street, Carlton Scroop, Grantham, NG32 3AT
- ☎ (01400) 250796
- Judith Hutton
- J T Hutton (01400) 250796
- 9 L 4827 yds Par 66 SSS 64
- U–phone first
- ££ D–£7 (D–£9)
- Carlton Scroop, 6 miles NE of Grantham (A607)
- Tim Hutton
- www.sudbrookmoor.co.uk

Sutton Bridge   (1914)
New Road, Sutton Bridge, Spalding, PE12 9RQ
- ☎ (01406) 350323 (Clubhouse)
- 320
- NE Davis (01945) 582447
- J Alison Johns (01406) 351422
- 9 L 5820 yds SSS 68
- WD–H WE–M SOC
- ££ £18
- 8 miles N of Wisbech (A17)
- ⊕ Driving range

Tetney
Station Road, Tetney, Grimsby, DN36 5HY
- ☎ (01472) 211644
- (01472) 211644
- 425
- J Abrams
- J J Abrams
- 18 L 6100 yds Par 71 SSS 69
- U SOC
- ££ £10 (£11)
- 5 miles S of Grimsby, off A16
- ⊕ Driving range

Toft Hotel   (1988)
Proprietary
Toft, Bourne, PE10 0JT
- ☎ (01778) 590616
- (01778) 590264
- 500
- R Morris (01778) 590654
- J M Jackson
- 18 L 6486 yds Par 72 SSS 71
- U
- ££ £25 (£35)
- 8 miles from Stamford on A6121
- D & R Fitton

Waltham Windmill   (1997)
Proprietary
Cheapside, Waltham, Grimsby, DN37 0HT
- ☎ (01472) 824109
- (01472) 828391
- 600
- GW Fielding (01472) 824109
- J N Burkitt (01472) 823963
- 18 L 6400 yds Par 71 SSS 71
- WD–U SOC
- ££ £20 (£27)
- 2 miles S of Grimsby, off A16
- Fox/Payne

Welton Manor   (1995)
Proprietary
Hackthorn Road, Welton, LN2 3PD
- ☎ (01673) 862827
- (01673) 860917
- golf@weltonmanorgolfcentre.co.uk
- 650
- J Barlow
- J G Leslie (01673) 862827
- 18 L 5703 yds SSS 67
- U SOC
- ££ £12 (£15)
- Off A46 Lincoln to Grimsby road
- ⊕ Driving range
- www.weltonmanorgolfcentre.co.uk

Woodhall Spa (1891)

Woodhall Spa, LN10 6PU
☎ **(01526) 351835,**
   (01526) 352511 (Bookings)
🖳 (01526) 352778
📖 525
🏌 M Underwood
✎ S Williams (01526) 351831
🏴 Hotchkin 18 L 7047 yds SSS 75;
   Bracken 18 L 6735 yds SSS 74
👥 Booking essential SOC
££ Hotchkin–£60 D–£100
   Bracken–£40 D–£65
⛳ 19 miles SE of Lincoln (B1191)
⊕ Driving range. Teaching Academy
🏠 Hotchkin/Steel

Woodthorpe Hall (1986)

Woodthorpe, Alford, LN13 0DD
☎ **(01507) 450000**
🖳 (01507) 450000
📧 secretary@woodthorpehallgolfclub
   .fsnet.co.uk
📖 200
✎ Joan Smith (01507) 450000
🏴 18 L 5140 yds Par 67 SSS 65
👥 U SOC
££ £10 D–£15
⛳ 3 miles N of Alford, off B1373. 8
   miles SE of Louth
⬛ www.woodthorpehall.co.uk

London Clubs

Aquarius *Kent*
Beckenham Place Park *Kent*
Central London Golf Centre *Surrey*
Dulwich & Sydenham Hill *Surrey*
Eltham Warren *Kent*
Finchley *Middlesex*
Hampstead *Middlesex*
Hendon *Middlesex*
Highgate *Middlesex*
Lee Valley *Middlesex*
London Scottish *Surrey*
Mill Hill *Middlesex*
Muswell Hill *Middlesex*
North Middlesex *Middlesex*
Richmond Park *Surrey*
Roehampton *Surrey*
Royal Blackheath *Kent*
Royal Epping Forest *Essex*
Royal Wimbledon *Surrey*
Shooter's Hill *Kent*
South Herts *Hertfordshire*
Trent Park *Middlesex*
Wanstead *Essex*
West Essex *Essex*
Wimbledon Common *Surrey*
Wimbledon Park *Surrey*

Manchester

Blackley (1907)

*Victoria Avenue East, Manchester,
M9 7HW*
☎ **(0161) 643 2980**

📖 800
✎ CB Leggott (0161) 654 7770
✎ C Gould (0161) 643 3912
🏴 18 L 6235 yds SSS 70
👥 WD–U WE–M SOC–WD exc
   Thurs
££ £24
⛳ North Manchester

Boysnope Park (1998)

Proprietary
*Liverpool Road, Barton Moss, Eccles,
M30 7RF*
☎ **(0161) 707 6125**
🖳 (0161) 707 3622
✎ Jean Stringer (0161) 707 6125
✎ S Currie (0161) 787 8687
🏴 18 L 3506 yds Par 72 SSS 71
👥 U SOC
££ £11 (£12)
⛳ SW of Manchester on A57. M60
   Junction 11, 1 mile
⊕ Driving range
⬛ www.boysnopegolfclub.co.uk

Chorlton-cum-Hardy
(1902)

*Barlow Hall, Barlow Hall Road,
Manchester, M21 7JJ*
☎ **(0161) 881 3139**
🖳 (0161) 881 4532
📖 800
✎ IR Booth (0161) 881 5830
✎ DR Valentine (0161) 881 9911
🏴 18 L 5980 yds SSS 69
👥 U H SOC–Thurs & Fri
££ £25 (£30)
⛳ 4 miles S of Manchester
   (A5103/A5145)
⬛ www.chorltoncumhardygolfclub
   .sagenet.co.uk

Davyhulme Park (1911)

*Gleneagles Road, Davyhulme,
Manchester, M41 8SA*
☎ **(0161) 748 2260**
🖳 (0161) 747 4067
📖 700
✎ LB Wright
✎ D Butler (0161) 748 3931
🏴 18 L 6237 yds SSS 70
👥 WD–H exc Wed & Fri–NA
   Sat–NA Sun–M
   SOC–Mon/Tues/Thurs
££ £24. 27 holes–£30
⛳ 7 miles SW of Manchester

Denton (1909)

*Manchester Road, Denton, Manchester,
M34 2GG*
☎ **(0161) 336 3218**
🖳 (0161) 336 4751
📖 686
✎ EW Tewson
✎ M Hollingworth (0161) 336 2070
🏴 18 L 6496 yds SSS 71
👥 WD–U WE/BH–NA before 3pm
   SOC
££ £25 (£30)
⛳ M60 Junction 24, A57 to
   Manchester

Didsbury (1891)

*Ford Lane, Northenden, Manchester,
M22 4NQ*
☎ **(0161) 998 9278**
🖳 (0161) 902 3060
📧 golf@didsburygolfclub.com
📖 760
✎ AL Watson (Mgr)
✎ P Barber (0161) 998 2811
🏴 18 L 6210 yds SSS 70
👥 WD–U H exc 9–10am &
   12–1.30pm–NA WE–U H
   10.30–11.30am & after 4pm
££ £28 (£32)
⛳ 6 miles S of Manchester. M60
   Junction 5
⬛ www.didsburygolfclub.com

Ellesmere (1913)

*Old Clough Lane, Worsley, Manchester,
M28 7HZ*
☎ **(0161) 790 2122**
📧 honsec@ellesmeregolf.fsnet.co.uk
📖 380 80(L) 75(J)
✎ A Chapman (0161) 799 0554
✎ T Morley (0161) 790 8591
🏴 18 L 6248 yds SSS 70
👥 U exc comp days (check with Pro)
   SOC–WD
££ £22 (£28)
⛳ 6 miles W of Manchester, nr
   junction of M60/A580
⬛ www.ellesmeregolf.co.uk

Fairfield Golf & Sailing
Club (1892)

*Booth Road, Audenshaw, Manchester,
M34 5GA*
☎ **(0161) 301 4528**
📧 secretary@fairfieldgolf.co.uk
📖 550
✎ IS James (Sec/Mgr)
   (0161) 370 2808
✎ SA Pownell (0161) 370 2292
🏴 18 L 5664 yds SSS 68
👥 WD–U WE–NA before noon
   SOC–WD
££ £20 (£25)
⛳ 5 miles E of Manchester on A635

Flixton (1893)

*Church Road, Flixton, Urmston,
Manchester M41 6EP*
☎ **(0161) 748 2116**
🖳 (0161) 748 2116
📖 400
✎ EG Gill (0161) 748 2116
✎ D Wade (0161) 746 7160
🏴 9 L 6410 yds SSS 71
👥 WD–U exc Wed SOC
££ £16
⛳ 6 miles SW of Manchester on
   B5213. M60 Junction 10

Great Lever & Farnworth
(1901)

*Plodder Lane, Farnworth, Bolton,
BL4 0LQ*
☎ **(01204) 656493**
🖳 (01204) 656137

- 600
- ✍ MJ Ivill (01204) 656137
- ✓ T Howarth (01204) 656650
- ⏞ 18 L 6064 yds SSS 69
- ⚇ H SOC–WD
- £€ £20 (£27)
- ⛳ 2 miles S of Bolton. M61 Junction 4

Heaton Park Golf Centre (1912)

Public
Heaton Park, Middleton Road, Prestwich, M25 2SW
- ☎ **(0161) 654 9899**
- ✍ JK Mort (Mgr)
- ⏞ 18 L 5755 yds SSS 68 18 hole Par 3 course
- ⚇ U SOC
- £€ £10 (£12.50)
- ⛳ North Manchester, via M60 Junction 19 to Middleton Road
- ⊕ Driving range
- ⛨ JH Taylor

Manchester (1882)

Hopwood Cottage, Rochdale Road, Middleton, Manchester M24 6QP
- ☎ **(0161) 643 2718,**
  (0161) 643 0023 (Bookings)
- 🖴 (0161) 643 9174
- 📖 700
- ✍ KG Flett (0161) 643 3202
- ✓ B Connor (0161) 643 2638
- ⏞ 18 L 6450 yds SSS 72
- ⚇ WD–H WE–NA SOC
- £€ D–£30 (£45)
- ⛳ 7 miles N of Manchester. M62 Junction 20
- ⊕ Driving range-members and green fees only
- ⛨ HS Colt
- ■ www.manchestergc.co.uk

New North Manchester (1894)

Rhodes House, Manchester Old Road, Middleton, M24 4PE
- ☎ **(0161) 643 9033**
- 🖴 (0161) 643 7775
- ✉ secretary@nmgc.co.uk
- 📖 700
- ✍ D Parkinson
- ✓ J Peel (0161) 643 7094
- ⏞ 18 L 6598 yds SSS 72
- ⚇ H
- £€ £25 (£28)
- ⛳ 5 miles N of Manchester. M60 Junction 19
- ⛨ A Compston
- ■ www.nmgc.co.uk

Northenden (1913)

Palatine Road, Manchester, M22 4FR
- ☎ **(0161) 998 47079**
- 🖴 (0161) 945 5592
- ✉ northenden.golfclub@btopenworld.com
- 📖 700
- ✍ Francesca Woodworth (Sec/Mgr) (0161) 998 4738
- ✓ J Curtis (0161) 945 3386

- ⏞ 18 L 6503 yds SSS 71
- ⚇ U SOC
- £€ £28 (£32)
- ⛳ 5 miles S of Manchester. M60 Junction 5

Old Manchester (1818)

Club
c/o 9 Ashbourne Grove, Whitefield, M45 7NJ
- ☎ **(0161) 766 4157**
- ✍ PT Goodall
- ⏞ Club without a course

Pike Fold (1909)

Hills Lane, Pole Lane, Unsworth, Bury BL9 8QP
- ☎ **(0161) 766 3561**
- 🖴 (0161) 796 3569
- 📖 250
- ✍ J O'Donnell
- ✓ A Cory
- ⏞ 9 L 6312 yds Par 72 SSS 71
- ⚇ WD–U WE/BH–M
- £€ On application
- ⛳ 8 miles N of Manchester, by M66

Prestwich (1908)

Hilton Lane, Prestwich, M25 9XB
- ☎ **(0161) 772 0700**
- 🖴 (0161) 772 0700
- ✉ 1908@prestwichgc.fsnet.co.uk
- 📖 500
- ✍ P Moore
- ✓ S Wakefield (0161) 773 1404
- ⏞ 18 L 5103 yds SSS 64
- ⚇ WD–H WE–NA before 3pm SOC
- £€ £20 (£20)
- ⛳ 2¹/₂ miles N of Manchester, off A56. M63 Junction 17

Stand (1904)

The Dales, Ashbourne Grove, Whitefield, Manchester M45 7NL
- ☎ **(0161) 766 2388**
- 🖴 (0161) 796 3234
- 📖 600
- ✍ TE Thacker (0161) 766 3197
- ✓ M Dance (0161) 766 2214
- ⏞ 18 L 6411 yds SSS 71
- ⚇ U SOC–WD
- £€ £25 (£30)
- ⛳ 5 miles N of Manchester. M60 Junction 17
- ⛨ Alex Herd

Swinton Park (1926)

East Lancashire Road, Swinton, Manchester, M27 5LX
- ☎ **(0161) 794 1785**
- 🖴 (0161) 281 0698
- 📖 450 120(L) 50(J)
- ✍ TH Glover (0161) 794 0861
- ✓ J Wilson (0161) 793 8077
- ⏞ 18 L 6726 yds SSS 72
- ⚇ WD–U WE–M SOC–Tues
- £€ On application
- ⛳ On A580, 5 miles NW of Manchester

Whitefield (1932)

Higher Lane, Whitefield, Manchester, M45 7EZ
- ☎ **(0161) 351 2700**
- 🖴 (0161) 351 2712
- 📖 538
- ✍ Mrs A Schofield
- ✓ P Reeves (0161) 351 2709
- ⏞ 18 L 6045 yds SSS 69
  18 L 5755 yds SSS 68
- ⚇ U SOC–WD
- £€ £25 (£35)
- ⛳ 4 miles N of Manchester. M60 Junction 17

William Wroe (1973)

Public
Pennybridge Lane, Flixton, Manchester, M31 3DL
- ☎ **(0161) 748 8680**
- ✓ B Parkinson
- ⏞ 18 L 4395 yds SSS 61
- ⚇ U–booking necessary
- £€ On application
- ⛳ 6 miles SW of Manchester, by M63 Junction 4

Withington (1892)

243 Palatine Road, West Didsbury, Manchester, M20 2UE
- ☎ **(0161) 445 3912**
- 🖴 (0161) 445 5210
- 📖 340 97(L) 38(J)
- ✍ B Grundy (0161) 445 9544
- ✓ RJ Ling (0161) 445 4861
- ⏞ 18 L 6410 yds SSS 70
- ⚇ WD–H exc Thurs SOC
- £€ On application
- ⛳ 6 miles S of Manchester on B5166

Worsley (1894)

Stableford Avenue, Monton Green, Eccles, Manchester M30 8AP
- ☎ **(0161) 789 4202**
- 🖴 (0161) 789 3200
- 📖 625
- ✍ R Hamlett (Hon)
- ✓ C Cousins
- ⏞ 18 L 6217 yds SSS 70
- ⚇ H SOC
- £€ £30 (£35)
- ⛳ 5 miles W of Manchester

Merseyside

Allerton Municipal (1934)

Public
Allerton Road, Liverpool, L18 3JT
- ☎ **(0151) 428 1046**
- ✓ B Large
- ⏞ 18 L 5494 yds SSS 65
  9 hole course
- ⚇ U SOC
- £€ On application
- ⛳ 5 miles S of Liverpool

Arrowe Park (1931)

Public

Arrowe Park, Woodchurch, Birkenhead, CH49 5LW

☎ **(0151) 677 1527**
♘ C Jones
✓ C Disbury
⊳ 18 L 6396 yds SSS 70
♚ U
££ £7.70 (£7.70)
⛳ 3 miles S of Birkenhead on A552. M53 Junction 3, 1 mile

Bidston (1913)

Bidston Link Road, Wallasey, Wirral, CH44 2HR

☎ **(0151) 638 3412**
▥ 500
♘ JR Whitton (Hon)
✓ (0151) 638 3412
⊳ 18 L 6207 yds SSS 70
♚ WD–U WE–U after 3pm SOC
££ £18 (£25)
⛳ Off Bidston Link Road. M53 Junction 1

Blundells Hill

Blundells Lane, Rainhill, L35 6NA

☎ **(0151) 430 0100**
▭ (0151) 426 5256
▥ 600
♘ A Roberts
✓ R Burbidge
⊳ 18 L 6347 yds Par 71
♚ U SOC
££ £25 (£30)
⛳ 2 miles SW of St Helens. M62 Junction 7
⊕ Driving range
♙ Steve Marnoch
▮ www.blundellshill.co.uk

Bootle (1934)

Dunnings Bridge Road, Litherland, L30 2PP

☎ **(0151) 928 6196**
▥ 400
♘ J Morgan
✓ A Bradshaw (0151) 928 1371
⊳ 18 L 6362 yds SSS 70
♚ U–book by phone SOC
££ £7.50 (£9.50)
⛳ 5 miles N of Liverpool (A565)
♙ Fred Stevens

Bowring (1913)

Public

Bowring Park, Roby Road, Huyton, L36 4HD

☎ **(0151) 489 1901**
✓ D Weston
⊳ 9 L 5592 yds SSS 66
♚ U
££ On application
⛳ 6 miles N of Liverpool. M62 Junction 5

Brackenwood (1933)

Public

Brackenwood Lane, Bebington, Wirral, L63 2LY

☎ **(0151) 608 3093**
✓ K Lamb
⊳ 18 L 6232 yds SSS 70
♚ U SOC
££ On application
⛳ Nr M53 Junction 4

Bromborough (1903)

Raby Hall Road, Bromborough, CH63 0NW

☎ **(0151) 334 2155**
▭ (0151) 334 7300
▥ 800
♘ JT Barraclough (0151) 334 2155
✓ G Berry (0151) 334 4499
⊳ 18 L 6547 yds SSS 72
♚ U–contact Pro in advance
££ £35 (£35)
⛳ Mid Wirral, M53 Junction 4
▮ www.bromborough-golf-club.freeserve.co.uk

Caldy (1907)

Links Hey Road, Caldy, Wirral, CH48 1NB

☎ **(0151) 625 5660**
▭ (0151) 625 7394
✉ gail@caldygolfclub.fsnet.co.uk
▥ 900
♘ Gail Copple
✓ K Jones (0151) 625 1818
⊳ 18 L 6601 yds SSS 72
♚ WD–U exc before 9.30am and from 1–2pm (booking necessary) SOC
££ On application
⛳ 1 1/2 miles S of West Kirby

Childwall (1913)

Naylor's Road, Gateacre, Liverpool, L27 2YB

☎ **(0151) 487 0654**
▭ (0151) 487 0882
▥ 650
♘ J Tully (Mgr)
✓ N Parr (0151) 487 9871
⊳ 18 L 6425 yds SSS 71
♚ WD–Tues–restricted. WE/BH–restricted SOC
££ £30 (£40)
⛳ 7 miles E of Liverpool. M62 Junction 6, 2 miles
♙ James Braid

Eastham Lodge (1973)

117 Ferry Road, Eastham, Wirral, CH62 0AP

☎ **(0151) 327 1483 (Clubhouse)**
▭ (0151) 327 7574
▥ 750
♘ CS Camden (0151) 327 3003
✓ N Sargent (0151) 327 3008
⊳ 18 L 5706 yds SSS 68
♚ WD–U WE/BH–M SOC–Tues
££ £22
⛳ 6 miles S of Birkenhead, off A41. M53 Junction 5. Signs to Eastham Country Park
♙ Hawtree/Hemstock

Formby (1884)

Golf Road, Formby, Liverpool, L37 1LQ

☎ **(01704) 872164**

▭ (01704) 833028
✉ info@formbygolfclub.co.uk
▥ 400
♘ CCH Barker (01704) 872164
✓ GH Butler (01704) 873090
⊳ 18 L 6993 yds SSS 74
♚ WD–I H SOC
££ £78 (£88)
⛳ By Freshfield Station, Formby
♙ Willie Park
▮ www.formbygolfclub.co.uk

Formby Hall

Southport Old Road, Formby, L37 0AB

☎ **(01704) 875699**
✓ D Lloyd
⊳ 18 L 6875 yds Par 73
♚ WD–U SOC
££ On application
⛳ Off Formby by-pass
⊕ Floodlit driving range

Formby Ladies' (1896)

Golf Road, Formby, Liverpool, L37 1YH

☎ **(01704) 873493**
▭ (01704) 873493
✉ secretary@formbyladiesgolfclub.co.uk
♘ Mrs J Houghton (01704) 873493
✓ G Butler (01704) 873090
⊳ 18 L 5374 yds SSS 71
♚ U–phone first SOC
££ £35 (£40)
⛳ Formby, off A565
▮ www.formbyladiesgolfclub.co.uk

Grange Park (1891)

Prescot Road, St Helens, WA10 3AD

☎ **(01744) 22980 (Members)**
▭ (01744) 26318
▥ 730
♘ CV Hadley (01744) 26318
✓ P Roberts (01744) 28785
⊳ 18 L 6446 yds SSS 71
♚ I SOC–WD exc Tues
££ £26 (£33)
⛳ 1 1/2 miles W of St Helens on A58
▮ www.ukgolfer.org

Haydock Park (1877)

Golborne Park, Newton Lane, Newton-le-Willows, WA12 0HX

☎ **(01925) 224389**
▭ (01925) 228525
▥ 400 120(L)
♘ Mrs V Wiseman (01925) 228525
✓ PE Kenwright (01925) 226944
⊳ 18 L 6058 yds SSS 69
♚ H or I SOC–WD exc Tues
££ £28
⛳ 1 mile E of M6 Junction 23

Hesketh (1885)

Cockle Dick's Lane, Cambridge Road, Southport, PR9 9QQ

☎ **(01704) 530226**
▭ (01704) 539250
✉ hesketh@ukgolfer.org
▥ 650
♘ MG Senior (01704) 536897
✓ J Donoghue (01704) 530050

18 L 6649 yds SSS 72
WD–U WE/BH–restricted SOC
£€ £40 D–£50 (£50)
1 mile N of Southport (A565)
JOF Morris
www.ukgolfer.org

Heswall (1902)

Cottage Lane, Gayton, Heswall,
CH60 8PB
☎ **(0151) 342 1237**
🖳 (0151) 342 6140
📖 902
✍ A Brooker
🏌 AE Thompson (0151) 342 7431
18 L 6492 yds SSS 72
U H BH–NA SOC–Wed & Fri
£€ £35 (£40)
8 miles NW of Chester off A540.
M53 Junction 4

Hillside (1911)

Hastings Road, Hillside, Southport,
PR8 2LU
☎ **(01704) 569902**
🖳 (01704) 563192
📧 hillside@ukgolfer.org
📖 800
✍ JG Graham (01704) 567169
🏌 B Seddon (01704) 568360
18 L 6850 yds SSS 74
By arrangement with Sec
£€ £55 D–£70
Southport
Hawtree

Houghwood (1996)

Billinge Hill, Crank Road, Crank, St
Helens WA11 8RL
☎ **(01744) 894754**
🖳 (01744) 894754
📖 630
✍ B Haigh
🏌 P Dickenson (01744) 894444
18 L 6268 yds SSS 70
WD–U SOC–WD
£€ £17.50 (£25)
3 miles N of St Helens, off A580
(B5201). M6 Junctions 23 or 26
N Pearson

Hoylake Municipal (1933)

Public
Carr Lane, Hoylake, Wirral, L47 4BG
☎ **(0151) 632 2956/4883 (Bookings)**
✍ ME Down (0151) 632 6823
🏌 S Hooton
18 L 6330 yds SSS 70
WD–U WE–phone booking 1 week
in advance SOC
£€ £8
4 miles W of Birkenhead
James Braid

Huyton & Prescot (1905)

Hurst Park, Huyton Lane, Huyton,
L36 1UA
☎ **(0151) 489 1138**
🖳 (0151) 489 0797
📖 700
✍ D Ponsonby (0151) 489 3948

🏌 J Fisher (0151) 489 2022
18 L 5839 yds SSS 68
WD–U WE–H SOC–WD
£€ On application
7 miles E of Liverpool. 1 mile S of
Prescot on B5199. M57 Junction 2

Leasowe (1891)

Leasowe Road, Moreton, Wirral,
CH46 3RD
☎ **(0151) 677 5852**
🖳 (0151) 604 1448
📖 610
✍ L Jukes
🏌 AJ Ayre (0151) 678 5460
18 L 6263 yds SSS 70
U SOC–H
£€ D–£25.50 (D–£30.50)
1 mile N of Queensway Tunnel.
M53 Junction 1
John Ball Jr

Lee Park (1954)

Childwall Valley Road, Gateacre,
Liverpool, L27 3YA
☎ **(0151) 487 9861 (Clubhouse)**
📖 580
✍ A Fagan (0151) 487 3882
18 L 6108 yds Par 72 SSS 70
U SOC
£€ On application
7 miles SE of Liverpool (B5171)

Liverpool Municipal (1967)

Public
Ingoe Lane, Kirkby, Liverpool, L32 4SS
☎ **(0151) 546 5435**
🏌 D Weston
18 L 6571 yds SSS 71
U WE–booking required SOC
£€ On application
M57 Junction 6 to B5192

Prenton (1905)

Golf Links Road, Prenton, Birkenhead,
CH42 8LW
☎ **(0151) 608 1461**
🖳 (0151) 608 4659
📖 470 100(L) 80(J)
✍ N Brown (0151) 608 1053
🏌 R Thompson (0151) 608 1636
18 L 6429 yds SSS 71
U SOC–Mon/Wed/Fri
£€ £30 (£35)
Outskirts of Birkenhead. M53
Junction 3
www.prentongolfclub.co.uk

RLGC Village Play (1895)

Club
c/o 18 Waverley Road, Hoylake, Wirral,
CH47 3DD
📖 40
✍ PD Williams (0151) 632 5156
Play over Royal Liverpool,
Hoylake

Royal Birkdale (1889)

Waterloo Road, Birkdale, Southport,
PR8 2LX
☎ **(01704) 567920**

(01704) 562327
📧 royalbirkdalegc@dial.pipex.com
✍ MC Gilyeat
🏌 B Hodgkinson (01704) 568857
18 L 6703 yds SSS 73
I H SOC
£€ £120 D–£145 (£135)
1½ miles S of Southport (A565)
George Lowe
www.royalbirkdale.com

Royal Liverpool (1869)

Meols Drive, Hoylake, CH47 4AL
☎ **(0151) 632 3101/3102**
🖳 (0151) 632 6737
📧 sec@royal-liverpool-golf.com
📖 810
✍ Gp Capt CT Moore CBE
🏌 J Heggarty (0151) 632 5868
18 L 7165 yds SSS 74
H SOC
£€ On application
On A553 from M53 Junction 2
www.royal-liverpool-golf.com

Sherdley Park Municipal

Public
Sherdley Park, St Helens
☎ **(01744) 813149**
🖳 (01744) 817967
✍ B Collins (Mgr)
18 L 5974 yds SSS 69
U SOC
£€ £7.20 (£8.50)
2 miles E of St Helens (A570). M62
Junction 7, 2 miles
⊕ Driving range

Southport & Ainsdale (1906)

Bradshaws Lane, Ainsdale, Southport,
PR8 3LG
☎ **(01704) 578000**
🖳 (01704) 570896
📧 secretary@sandagolfclub.co.uk
📖 452 94(L) 51(J)
✍ CA Birrell
🏌 J Payne (01704) 577316
18 L 6687 yds Par 72 SSS 73
WD–H WE–NA before noon
£€ £55 D–£75 (£75)
3 miles S of Southport on A565
James Braid
www.sandagolfclub.co.uk

Southport Municipal (1914)

Public
Park Road West, Southport, PR9 0JS
☎ **(01704) 535286**
🏌 W Fletcher
18 L 6253 yds SSS 69
U SOC
£€ On application
N end of Southport promenade

Southport Old Links (1926)

Moss Lane, Southport, PR9 7QS
☎ **(01704) 228207**
🖳 (01704) 505353
📖 450

🏌 BE Kenyon
🏴 9 L 6349 yds SSS 71
👥 U exc WE comp days/BH–NA
SOC–WD
££ £22 (£30)
🏌 Churchtown, 3 miles NE of
Southport

Wallasey (1891)

Bayswater Road, Wallasey, CH45 8LA
☎ **(0151) 691 1024**
🖥 (0151) 638 8988
✉ wallaseygc@aol.com
📖 450 90(L) 50(J)
🏌 CF Smith (0151) 691 1024
🏌 M Adams (0151) 638 3888
🏴 18 L 6503 yds SSS 72
👥 H SOC
££ £45 (£60)
🏌 M53–signs to New Brighton
🏠 Tom Morris
■ www.wallaseygolf.com

Warren (1911)

Public
*Grove Road, Wallasey, Wirral,
CH45 0JA*
☎ **(0151) 639 8323 (Clubhouse)**
🏌 DA Farrington
🏌 S Konrad (0151) 639 5730
🏴 9 L 5914 yds SSS 68
👥 U
££ On application
🏌 Wallasey
■ www.warrengc.freeserve.co.uk

West Derby (1896)

Yew Tree Lane, Liverpool, L12 9HQ
☎ **(0151) 228 1540**
🖥 (0151) 259 0505
📖 550
🏌 AP Milne (0151) 254 1034
🏌 A Witherup (0151) 220 5478
🏴 18 L 6277 yds SSS 70
👥 SOC–WD after 9.30am
££ £27 (£36)
🏌 2 miles E of Liverpool, off A580-
West Derby Junction

West Lancashire (1873)

*Hall Road West, Blundellsands,
Liverpool, L23 8SZ*
☎ **(0151) 924 4115**
🖥 (0151) 931 4448
📖 700
🏌 S King (0151) 924 1076
🏌 G Edge (0151) 924 5662
🏴 18 L 6767 yds SSS 73
👥 H SOC–WD exc Tues
££ £50 D–£65 (£70)
🏌 Between Liverpool and Southport,
off A565
🏠 CK Cotton
■ www.westlancashiregolf.co.uk

Wirral Ladies (1894)

*93 Bidston Road, Birkenhead, Wirral,
CH43 6TS*
☎ **(0151) 652 1255**
🖥 (0151) 653 4323
📖 450

🏌 Mrs SA Headford
🏌 A Law (0151) 652 2468
🏴 18 L 4948 yds SSS 69 (Ladies)
18 L 5185 yds SSS 65 (Men)
👥 U H SOC–WD
££ £25 (£25)
🏌 Birkenhead ¹/₂ mile. M53, 2 miles

Woolton (1900)

*Doe Park, Speke Road, Woolton,
Liverpool L25 7TZ*
☎ **(0151) 486 1601**
🖥 (0151) 486 1664
📖 750
🏌 K Hamilton (0151) 486 2298
🏌 D Thompson (0151) 486 1298
🏴 18 L 5706 yds SSS 68
👥 U exc comp days
££ £24 (£35)
🏌 SE Liverpool. End of M62/M57

Middlesex

Airlinks (1984)

Public
Southall Lane, Hounslow, TW5 9PE
☎ **(020) 8561 1418**
🖥 (020) 8813 6284
🏌 S Brewster
🏌 T Martin
🏴 18 L 6001 yds SSS 69
👥 U
££ £10 (£16)
🏌 Just off M4 Junction 3
⊕ Floodlit driving range
🏠 Alliss/Taylor

Ashford Manor (1898)

Fordbridge Road, Ashford, TW15 3RT
☎ **(01784) 424644**
🖥 (01784) 424649
✉ ashfordmanorgolfclub@fsnet.co.uk
📖 700
🏌 I Buchan (Mgr) (01784) 424644
🏌 I Partington (01784) 255940
🏴 18 L 6352 yds SSS 70
👥 WD–U WE–H
££ £30 D–£35
🏌 A308 Ashford. M25 Junction 13
🏠 T Hogg

Brent Valley (1938)

Public
Church Road, Hanwell, London, W7 3BE
☎ **(020) 8567 4230 (Clubhouse),
(020) 8567 1287 (Bookings)**
📖 195
🏌 Ms M Griffin
🏌 P Bryant (020) 8567 1287
🏴 18 L 5426 yds SSS 66
👥 U SOC
££ On application

Bush Hill Park (1895)

*Bush Hill, Winchmore Hill, London,
N21 2BU*
☎ **(020) 8360 5738**
🖥 (020) 8360 5583
📖 630

🏌 Miss R Meade
🏌 A Andrews (020) 8360 4103
🏴 18 L 5825 yds SSS 68
👥 WD–H WE–NA SOC
££ £27.50
🏌 S of Enfield
■ www.bushhillparkgolfclub.co.uk

C & L Country Club (1991)

West End Road, Northolt UB5 6RD
☎ **(020) 8845 5662**
🏴 9 L 4440 yds SSS 62
👥 U SOC
££ £10
🏌 A40, opp Northolt Airport
🏠 Patrick Tallack

Crews Hill (1920)

*Cattlegate Road, Crews Hill, Enfield,
EN2 8AZ*
☎ **(020) 8363 0787**
🖥 (020) 8363 2343
📖 600
🏌 AD Stewart (020) 8363 6674
🏌 N Wichelow (020) 8366 7422
🏴 18 L 6273 yds SSS 70
👥 WD–I H WE/BH–M SOC
££ On application
🏌 2¹/₂ miles N of Enfield. M25
Junction 24
🏠 HS Colt

Ealing (1898)

Perivale Lane, Greenford, UB6 8SS
☎ **(020) 8997 0937**
🖥 (020) 8998 0756
📖 600
🏌 June Mackison (Gen Mgr)
🏌 D Barton (020) 8997 3959
🏴 18 L 6216 yds SSS 70
👥 WD–U H WE/BH–M
££ On application
🏌 Marble Arch 6 miles on A40-
Perivale junction
🏠 HS Colt

Enfield (1893)

Old Park Road South, Enfield, EN2 7DA
☎ **(020) 8363 3970**
🖥 (020) 8342 0381
📖 625
🏌 NA Challis
🏌 L Fickling (020) 8366 4492
🏴 18 L 6154 yds SSS 70
👥 WD–H WE/BH–M SOC–WD
££ £25 D–£30
🏌 1 mile NE of Enfield. M25 Junction
24-A1005
🏠 James Braid
■ www.enfieldgolfclub.co.uk

Finchley (1929)

*Nether Court, Frith Lane, London,
NW7 1PU*
☎ **(020) 8346 2436**
🖥 (020) 8343 4205
✉ secretary@finchleygolfclub.co.uk
📖 550
🏌 WD Keene
🏌 DM Brown (020) 8346 5086
🏴 18 L 6356 yds SSS 71

WD–U WE–pm only SOC
£€ On application
⊕ M1 Junction 2
⌂ James Braid
■ www.finchleygolfclub.co.uk

Fulwell   (1904)
Wellington Road, Hampton Hill,
TW12 1JY
☎ **(020) 8977 2733**
🖀 (020) 8977 7732
✉ secretary@fulwellgolfclub.co.uk
⌘ 750
🏌 PF Butcher
✔ N Turner (020) 8977 3844
► 18 L 6544 yds SSS 71
WD–I WE–M SOC
£€ £30 (£35)
⊕ Opposite Fulwell Station

Grim's Dyke   (1910)
Oxhey Lane, Hatch End, Pinner,
HA5 4AL
☎ **(020) 8428 4539**
🖀 (020) 8421 5494
⌘ 600
🏌 KR Skingle (020) 8428 4539
✔ N Stephens (020) 8428 7484
► 18 L 5600 yds SSS 67
WD–U H WE–M SOC exc BH–NA
£€ £26 D–£31
⊕ 2 miles NW of Harrow (A4008).
M1 Junctions 4/5
⌂ James Braid

Hampstead   (1893)
Winnington Road, London, N2 0TU
☎ **(020) 8455 0203**
🖀 (020) 8731 6194
⌘ 450
🏌 ACM Harris
✔ PJ Brown (020) 8455 7089
► 9 L 5812 yds SSS 68
H–phone Pro first
£€ £30 (£35)
⊕ 1 mile from Hampstead, nr
Spaniards Inn
⌂ Tom Dunn

Harrow School   (1978)
High Street, Harrow-on-the-Hill,
HA1 3HW
⌘ 440 100(L) 10(J)
🏌 CV Davies (020) 8872 8232
► 9 L 3690 yds SSS 57
M H
⊕ Harrow School, NW London
⌂ Donald Steel

Haste Hill   (1933)
Public
The Drive, Northwood, HA6 1HN
☎ **(01923) 825224**
🖀 (01923) 826485
⌘ 250
🏌 M Groves
✔ C Smillie
► 18 L 5736 yds SSS 68
U SOC
£€ £12.50 (£17.50)
⊕ Northwood–Hillingdon

Heath Park   (1975)
Stockley Road, West Drayton
☎ **(01895) 444232**
🖀 (01895) 444232
✉ heathparkgolf@yahoo.co.uk
⌘ 180
🏌 B Sharma (Prop)
► 9 L 3236 yds SSS 56
WD–U Sun–NA before 11am SOC
£€ £8 (£9)
⊕ Crowne Plaza Hotel, Heathrow
⌂ Neil Coles
■ www.hpgc.co.uk

Hendon   (1903)
Ashley Walk, Devonshire Road, London,
NW7 1DG
☎ **(020) 8346 6023**
🖀 (020) 8343 1974
⌘ 560
🏌 DE Cooper
✔ M Deal (020) 8346 8990
► 18 L 6289 yds Par 70 SSS 70
WD–U WE/BH–bookings SOC
£€ £30 D–£35 (£35)
⊕ M1 Junction 2, on to Holders Hill
Road
⌂ HS Colt

Highgate   (1904)
Denewood Road, Highgate, London,
N6 4AH
☎ **(020) 8340 1906 (Clubhouse)**
🖀 (020) 8348 9152
⌘ 700
🏌 JG Wilson (020) 8340 3745
✔ R Turner (020) 8340 5467
► 18 L 5964 yds SSS 69
WD–U exc Wed–NA before noon
WE/BH–M SOC
£€ £30
⊕ Off Sheldon Avenue/Hampstead
Lane
⌂ Cuthbert Butchart
■ www.highgategolfclub.freeserve
.co.uk

Hillingdon   (1892)
18 Dorset Way, Hillingdon, Uxbridge,
UB10 0JR
☎ **(01895) 239810**
🖀 (01895) 233956
⌘ 375
🏌 KJ Newton (01895) 233956
✔ PCR Smith (01895) 460035
► 9 L 5459 yds SSS 67
WD–U exc Thurs 12–4pm WE
pm–M H SOC–WD
£€ £15 D–£27
⊕ Off Uxbridge Road, opposite St
John's Church

Horsenden Hill   (1935)
Public
Woodland Rise, Greenford, UB6 0RD
☎ **(020) 8902 4555**
⌘ 84
🏌 AK Witte
✔ J Quarshie
► 9 L 3264 yds SSS 56
U

£€ 9 holes–£4.40 (£6.40)
⊕ Greenford

Hounslow Heath   (1979)
Public
Staines Road, Hounslow, TW4 5DS
☎ **(020) 8570 5271**
⌘ 130
🏌 R Mulford
► 18 L 5901 yds Par 69 SSS 68
WD–U WE–booking essential
£€ £9 (£13)
⊕ Opposite Green Lane, Staines Road
(A315)
⌂ Fraser

Lee Valley   (1973)
Pay and play
Lee Valley Leisure, Picketts Lock Lane,
Edmonton, London N9 0AS
☎ **(020) 8803 3611**
✔ RG Gerken
► 18 L 4974 yds SSS 64
WD–U WE–booking advisable
£€ £12 (£15)
⊕ 1 mile N of north Circular Road,
Edmonton on Meridian Way
⊕ Floodlit driving range

London Golf Centre   (1984)
Public
Ruislip Road, Northolt, UB5 6QZ
☎ **(020) 8841 6162/845 2332**
🖀 (020) 8842 2097
🏌 JP Clifford (Gen Mgr)
✔ G Newall (020) 8845 3180
► 9 L 5838 yds SSS 69
U SOC
£€ 9 holes–£5. 18 holes–£9
⊕ Off A40, nr Polish war memorial
⊕ Driving range

Mill Hill   (1925)
100 Barnet Way, Mill Hill, London,
NW7 3AL
☎ **(020) 8959 2282**
🖀 (020) 8906 0731
✉ haslehurstd@aol.com
⌘ 570
🏌 RE Haslehurst (020) 8959 2339
✔ D Beal (020) 8959 7261
► 18 L 6309 yds SSS 70
WD–U H WE/BH–U H after
11.30am SOC–WD
£€ £25 (£30)
⊕ ½ mile N of Apex Corner, nr
A1/A41 junction
⌂ Abercromby/Colt

Muswell Hill   (1893)
Rhodes Avenue, Wood Green, London,
N22 7UT
☎ **(020) 8888 2044**
🖀 (020) 8889 9380
⌘ 600
🏌 J Underhill (020) 8888 1764
✔ D Wilton (020) 8888 8046
► 18 L 6474 yds SSS 71
WD–U WE–book with Pro SOC
£€ £30 D–£40 (£35)

🚭 1 mile from Bounds Green Station.
Central London 7 miles
🏠 Braid/Wilson

North Middlesex (1905)

*The Manor House, Friern Barnet Lane,
Whetstone, London N20 0NL*
☎ (020) 8445 1732
🖳 (020) 8445 5023
✉ office@northmiddlesexgc.co.uk
📖 500
🏌 Ms A McDonald (Mgr)
(020) 8445 1604
✓ (020) 8445 3060
🏳 18 L 5594 yds SSS 67
👥 WE/BH–restricted SOC–WD
£€ £25 (£30)
🚭 5 miles S of M25 Junction 23,
between Barnet and Finchley
🏠 Willie Park Jr
◼ www.northmiddlesexgc.co.uk

Northolt (1991)

Pay and play
Huxley Close, Northolt, UB5 5UL
☎ (020) 8841 5550
📖 250
🏌 L Gribben
✓ I Godleman
🏳 9 hole course Par 56 SSS 55
👥 U SOC
£€ £5
🚭 Nr M40 Target roundabout
⊕ Driving range

Northwood (1891)

*Rickmansworth Road, Northwood,
HA6 2QW*
☎ (01923) 825329
🖳 (01923) 840150
✉ secretary@northwoodgc
📖 560
🏌 Maj (Retd) KP Loosemore
(01923) 821384
✓ CJ Holdsworth (01923) 820112
🏳 18 L 6553 yds Par 71 SSS 71
👥 WD–H WE/BH–NA SOC
£€ £30 (£40)
🚭 3 miles SE of Rickmansworth
(A404)
🏠 James Braid

Perivale Park (1932)

Public
*Stockdove Way, Argyle Road, Greenford,
UB6 8EN*
☎ (020) 8575 7116
📖 140
🏌 P Smith
✓ P Bryant (020) 8575 7116
🏳 9 L 5296 yds SSS 67
👥 U
£€ 9 holes–£4.40 (£6.50) 18
holes–£11.50
🚭 1 mile E of Greenford, off A40

Pinner Hill (1927)

Southview Road, Pinner Hill, HA5 3YA
☎ (020) 8866 0963
🖳 (020) 8868 4817
✉ pinnerhillgc.@uk2.net

📖 770
🏌 IN Prentice (020) 8866 0963
✓ M Grieve (020) 8866 2109
🏳 18 L 6388 yds SSS 71
👥 WD–H exc Wed & Thurs–U
Sun/BH–M SOC
£€ £30 (£35) exc Wed & Thurs–£15
🚭 1 mile W from Pinner Green
🏠 JH Taylor
◼ www.pinnerhillgc.co.uk

Ruislip (1936)

Public
Ickenham Road, Ruislip, HA4 7DQ
☎ (01895) 638835
🖳 (01895) 622172
📖 325
🏌 G Bannister (01895) 637659
✓ P Glozier
🏳 18 L 5571 yds Par 69 SSS 67
👥 U SOC
£€ £12.50 (£18.50)
🚭 W Ruislip BR/LTE Station
⊕ Driving range
🏠 A Herd

Stanmore (1893)

29 Gordon Avenue, Stanmore, HA7 2RL
☎ (020) 8954 2599
🖳 (020) 8954 6418
✉ office@stanmoregolfclub.fsnet
.co.uk
📖 590
🏌 Maria Bateman
✓ VR Law (020) 8954 2646
🏳 18 L 5860 yds SSS 68
👥 WD–H WE/BH–M SOC
£€ £15 – £22 (£30)
🚭 Between Stanmore and Belmont,
off Old Church Lane

Stockley Park (1993)

Pay and play
*The Clubhouse, Stockley Park, Uxbridge,
UB11 1AQ*
☎ (020) 8813 5700/561 6339
(Bookings)
🖳 (020) 8813 5655
🏌 C Kennedy
✓ A Knox
🏳 18 L 6548 yds SSS 71
👥 U SOC
£€ £25 (£35)
🚭 Heathrow Airport, 1 mile. M4
Junction 4, 1 mile
🏠 Robert Trent Jones Sr

Strawberry Hill (1900)

*Wellesley Road, Strawberry Hill,
Twickenham, TW2 5SD*
☎ (020) 8894 0165
🖳 (020) 8898 0786
📖 350
🏌 (020) 8894 0165
✓ P Buchan (020) 8898 2082
🏳 9 L 2381 yds Par 64 SSS 62
👥 WD–U WE–M
£€ £20
🏠 Strawberry Hill Station
🏠 JH Taylor

Sudbury (1920)

Bridgewater Road, Wembley, HA0 1AL
☎ (020) 8902 3713
🖳 (020) 8903 2966
✉ alecpoole@sudburygolfclub
.sagehost.co.uk
📖 640
🏌 AJ Poole (Gen Mgr)
✓ N Jordan (020) 8902 7910
🏳 18 L 6282 yds SSS 70
👥 WD–H WE–M SOC–Tues–Fri
£€ On application
🚭 Junction of A4005/A4090
◼ www.sudburygolfclubltd.co.uk

Sunbury (1993)

Proprietary
Charlton Lane, Shepperton, TW17 8QA
☎ (01932) 770298
🖳 (01932) 789300
📖 350
🏌 J Wright (Gen Mgr)
(01932) 770298
✓ A Hardaway (01932) 772898
🏳 18 L 5103 yds Par 68 SSS 65
9 L 2444 yds Par 33
👥 U–phone Pro SOC
£€ £15 (£22)
🚭 SE of Queen Mary Reservoir, nr
Charlton. M3 Junction 1, 2 miles
⊕ Floodlit driving range

Trent Park (1973)

Public
*Bramley Road, Southgate, London,
N14 4UW*
☎ (020) 8367 4653
🖳 (020) 8366 4581
✓ R Stocker
🏳 18 L 6008 yds SSS 69
👥 WD–U SOC WE–NA before 11am
£€ £13.50 (£17)
🚭 Nr Oakwood Tube station
⊕ Driving range

Twickenham (1977)

Pay and play
Staines Road, Twickenham, TW2 5JD
☎ (020) 8783 1698
🖳 (020) 8941 9134
✓ Suzy Watt (020) 8783 1698
🏳 9 L 6014 yds SSS 69
👥 U
£€ £6.50 (£7)
🚭 2 miles NW of Hampton Court, nr
end of M3
⊕ Floodlit driving range

Uxbridge (1947)

Public
*The Drive, Harefield Place, Uxbridge,
UB10 8AQ*
☎ (01895) 231169
🖳 (01895) 810262
✓ T Atkins (01895) 272457
(01895) 237287
🏳 18 L 5711 yds SSS 68
👥 U SOC
£€ £12.50 (£18.50)
🚭 2 miles N of Uxbridge. B467 off
A40 towards Ruislip. M25 Junction
16, 3 miles

For list of abbreviations and key to symbols see page 649

West Middlesex (1891)
Greenford Road, Southall, UB1 3EE
- ☎ **(020) 8574 3450**
- 📠 (020) 8574 2383
- ✉ westmid.gc@virgin.net
- 🕮 650
- ⚷ E Marper
- ✓ IP Harris (020) 8574 1800
- ⮞ 18 L 6119 yds SSS 69
- 👥 WD–U WE–NA before 3pm (phone Pro) SOC–Tues/Thurs/Fri
- ££ Mon–£13 Tues/Thurs/Fri–£20 Wed–£15 W/E–£30
- 🚗 Junction of Uxbridge Road and Greenford Road
- 🏠 James Braid
- ▪ www.westmiddxgolfclub.co.uk

Whitewebbs (1932)
Public
Beggars Hollow, Clay Hill, Enfield, EN2 9JN
- ☎ **(020) 8363 2951**
- 🕮 200
- ⚷ IF Forsyth
- ✓ P Garlick (020) 8363 4454
- ⮞ 18 L 5863 yds SSS 68
- 👥 U
- ££ £10 (£12)
- 🚗 1 mile N of Enfield

Wyke Green (1928)
Syon Lane, Isleworth, Osterley, TW7 5PT
- ☎ **(020) 8560 8777**
- 📠 (020) 8569 8392
- ✉ office@wykegreengolfclub.co.uk
- 🕮 700
- ⚷ D Pearson
- ✓ N Smith (020) 8847 0685
- ⮞ 18 L 6211 yds SSS 70
- 👥 WD–U exc Fri–NA WE/BH–H after 4pm SOC
- ££ £28 D–£40 After 5pm–£20
- 🚗 ¹/₂ mile from Gillette Corner (A4)
- ⊕ Practice range
- 🏠 Hawtree/Taylor

Norfolk

Barnham Broom Hotel
(1977)
Honingham Road, Barnham Broom, Norwich, NR9 4DD
- ☎ **(01603) 759393 (Hotel), (01603) 759552 (Golf Shop)**
- 📠 (01603) 758224
- 🕮 500
- ⚷ P Ballingall (Golf Dir) (01603) 759393 Ext 278
- ✓ A Rudge
- ⮞ Valley 18 L 6483 yds Par 72 SSS 71
  Hill 18 L 6495 yds Par 71 SSS 71
- 👥 U SOC
- ££ £30 (£40)
- 🚗 10 miles SW of Norwich, off A47. 5 miles NW of Wymondham, off A11
- ⊕ 3 Academy holes
- 🏠 Pennink/Steel
- ▪ www.barnham-broom.co.uk

Bawburgh (1978)
Glen Lodge, Marlingford Road, Bawburgh, Norwich NR9 3LU
- ☎ **(01603) 740404**
- 📠 (01603) 740403
- ✉ info@bawburgh.com
- 🕮 650
- ⚷ I Ladbrooke (Golf Dir), J Barnard
- ✓ C Potter (01603) 742323
- ⮞ 18 L 6209 yds SSS 70
- 👥 U–phone first SOC
- ££ £25 (£30)
- 🚗 2 miles W of Norwich, off A47 Norwich Southern Bypass
- ⊕ Floodlit driving range. Golf Academy
- 🏠 Shaun Manser

Caldecott Hall
Caldecott Hall, Beccles Road, Fritton, NR31 9EY
- ☎ **(01493) 488488**
- 📠 (01493) 488561
- 🕮 600
- ⚷ R Beales
- ✓ S Shulver
- ⮞ 18 L 6536 yds Par 72 SSS 71
  9 hole Par 3 course
- 👥 H SOC
- ££ £20 (£26)
- 🚗 5 miles SW of Gt Yarmouth on A413
- ⊕ Floodlit driving range. 9 holes pitch & putt course

Costessey Park (1983)
Costessey Park, Costessey, Norwich, NR8 5AL
- ☎ **(01603) 746333**
- 📠 (01603) 746185
- 🕮 600
- ⚷ GC Stangoe
- ✓ A Young (01603) 747085
- ⮞ 18 L 5900 yds Par 71 SSS 69
- 👥 U SOC–WD
- ££ On application
- 🚗 3 miles W of Norwich, off A47 at Round Well PH

Dereham (1934)
Quebec Road, Dereham, NR19 2DS
- ☎ **(01362) 695900**
- 📠 (01362) 695904
- ✉ derehamgolfclub@dgolfclub .freeserve.co.uk
- 🕮 400
- ⚷ S Kaye
- ✓ R Curtis (01362) 695631
- ⮞ 9 L 6225 yds SSS 70
- 👥 H
- ££ £17.50 D–£22.50
- 🚗 Dereham ¹/₂ mile

Dunham (1979)
Proprietary
Little Dunham, Swaffham, PE32 2DF
- ☎ **(01328) 701718**
- 📠 (01328) 701906
- ✉ garympotter@hotmail.com
- 🕮 200
- ⚷ G & S Potter (Props) (01328) 701906

- ✓ G Potter (01328) 701906
- ⮞ 9 L 2560 yds Par 66 SSS 64
- 👥 U SOC
- ££ £12 (£15)
- 🚗 4 miles NE of Swaffham, off A47. Signs from Necton
- 🏠 Cecil Denny
- ▪ www.dunhamgolfclub.com

Eagles (1990)
39 School Road, Tilney All Saints, Kings Lynn, PE34 4RS
- ☎ **(01553) 827147**
- 📠 (01553) 829777
- 🕮 200
- ⚷ D Horn (Prop)
- ✓ N Pickerell
- ⮞ 9 L 2142 yds SSS 61
  9 hole Par 3 course
- 👥 U
- ££ 9 holes–£ 7.50 (£8.50)
- 🚗 5 miles W of Kings Lynn on A47
- ⊕ Driving range
- 🏠 David Horn
- ▪ www.eagles-golf-tennis.co.uk

Eaton (1910)
Newmarket Road, Norwich, NR4 6SF
- ☎ **(01603) 451686**
- 📠 (01603) 451686
- ✉ administrator@eatongc.co.uk
- 🕮 640 135(L) 70(J)
- ⚷ Mrs LA Bovill
- ✓ M Allen (01603) 452478
- ⮞ 18 L 6114 yds SSS 70
- 👥 H WE–NA before noon SOC–WD
- ££ £30 (£40)
- 🚗 S Norwich, off A11
- ▪ www.eatongc.co.uk

Fakenham (1973)
The Race Course, Fakenham, NR21 7NY
- ☎ **(01328) 862867**
- 🕮 510
- ⚷ G Cocker (01328) 855665
- ✓ C Williams (01328) 863534
- ⮞ 9 L 6174 yds SSS 69
- 👥 WD–U WE–NA before 12 noon SOC
- ££ £14 (£18)
- 🚗 Fakenham racecourse

Feltwell (1976)
Thor Ave, Wilton Road, Feltwell, IP26 4AY
- ☎ **(01842) 827644**
- 📠 (01842) 827644
- ✉ secretary@feltwellgolfclub.force9 .co.uk
- 🕮 400
- ⚷ SJ Waller
- ✓ C Puttock (01842) 829089
- ⮞ 9 L 6488 yds SSS 71
- 👥 U SOC–WD pm
- ££ £15 (£24)
- 🚗 1 mile S of Feltwell on B1112
- ⊕ Former Feltwell aerodrome
- ▪ www.clubnoticeboard.co.uk

Gorleston (1906)
Warren Road, Gorleston, Gt Yarmouth, NR31 6JT
- ☎ **(01493) 661911**

□ (01493) 661911
🕮 900
🏌 NP Longbottom (01493) 661911
🏌 N Brown (01493) 662103
🏳 18 L 6400 yds SSS 71
👤 U H SOC
£€ £25 (£30) W–£85
🚗 S of Gorleston, off A12
🏠 JH Taylor

Great Yarmouth & Caister (1882)

Beach House, Caister-on-Sea, Gt Yarmouth, NR30 5TD
☎ (01493) 728699
□ (01493) 728831
🕮 700
🏌 HJ Harvey
🏌 M Clarke (01493) 720421
🏳 18 L 6330 yds SSS 70
👤 WE–NA before noon SOC
£€ £30 (£35)
🚗 Caister-on-Sea
■ www.caistergolf.com

Hunstanton (1891)

Golf Course Road, Old Hunstanton, PE36 6JQ
☎ (01485) 532811
□ (01485) 532319
✉ hunstanton.golf.@eidosnet.co.uk
🕮 650 250(L) 60(J)
🏌 DP Thomson
🏌 J Dodds (01485) 532751
🏳 18 L 6759 yds SSS 73
👤 WD–H after 9.30am WE–H after 10.30am SOC
£€ D–£55 (£65)
🚗 1¹/₂ miles NE of Hunstanton
⊕ 2-ball play only
🏠 George Fernie

King's Lynn (1923)

Castle Rising, King's Lynn, PE31 6BD
☎ (01553) 631654
□ (01553) 631036
🕮 910
🏌 MP Sackrée (01553) 633000
🏌 J Reynolds (01553) 631655
🏳 18 L 6609 yds SSS 73
👤 U H SOC
£€ £40 (£50)
🚗 4 miles NE of King's Lynn, off A149
🏠 Alliss/Thomas

Links Country Park Hotel

West Runton, Cromer, NR27 9QH
☎ (01263) 838383
□ (01263) 838264
✉ sales@links-hotel.co.uk
🕮 300
🏌 CB Abbott
🏌 A Collison (01263) 838215
🏳 9 L 4814 yds Par 66 SSS 64
👤 U
£€ £25 (£30)
🚗 3 miles W of Cromer (A149)
🏠 JH Taylor
■ www.links-hotel.co.uk

Marriott Sprowston Manor Hotel (1980)

Wroxham Road, Sprowston, Norwich, NR7 8RP
☎ (01603) 410657
□ (01603) 788884
🕮 500
🏌 J O'Malley (Golf Dir) (01603) 254294
🏌 G Ireson (01603) 417264
🏳 18 L 5982 yds SSS 70
👤 U SOC
£€ £19 (£25)
🚗 2 miles NE of Norwich on A1151
⊕ Floodlit driving range

Mattishall (1990)

South Green, Mattishall, Dereham
☎ (01362) 850464
🕮 180
🏌 B Hall
🏳 9 L 6170 yds Par 70 SSS 69
👤 WD–U WE–U before noon SOC
£€ £8 (£10)
🚗 6 miles E of Dereham (B1063)
⊕ 9 hole pitch & putt
🏠 BC Todd

Middleton Hall (1989)

Proprietary
Middleton, King's Lynn, PE32 1RH
☎ (01553) 841800
□ (01553) 841800
✉ middleton-hall@btclick.com
🕮 600
🏌 J Holland
🏌 S White (01553) 841801
🏳 18 L 6004 yds Par 71 SSS 69
👤 U SOC
£€ £25 (£30)
🚗 2 miles SE of King's Lynn on A47
⊕ Driving range
🏠 D Scott
■ www.middletonhall.co.uk

Mundesley (1901)

Links Road, Mundesley, NR11 8ES
☎ (01263) 720279
□ (01263) 720279
🕮 500
🏌 J Woodhouse (Sec/Mgr) (01263) 720095
🏌 TG Symmons (01263) 720279
🏳 9 L 5377 yds SSS 66
👤 WD–U H exc Wed 10.30–3.30pm WE–NA before 3.30pm
£€ £18 (£25)
🚗 5 miles SE of Cromer

The Norfolk G&CC (1993)

Hingham Road, Reymerston, Norwich, NR9 4QQ
☎ (01362) 850297
□ (01362) 850614
🕮 530
🏌 M de Boltz
🏌 T Varney (01362) 850297
🏳 18 L 6609 yds SSS 72
👤 WD–U before 4pm –M after 4pm WE/BH–NA before noon SOC
£€ £22 (£27)

🚗 14 miles W of Norwich, off B1135 Dereham to Wymondham road
⊕ Driving range. 9 hole pitch & putt course
■ www.thenorfolk.co.uk

RAF Marham (1974)

RAF Marham, Kings Lynn, PE33 9NP
🕮 290
🏌 WR Benton (01760) 337261 (Ext 6507)
🏳 9 L 5244 yds SSS 66
👤 By prior arrangement–U exc Sun am
🚗 11 miles SE of King's Lynn, nr Narborough
⊕ Course situated on MOD land, and may be closed without prior notice

Richmond Park (1990)

Saham Road, Watton, IP25 6EA
☎ (01953) 881803
□ (01953) 881817
🕮 600
🏌 A Hemsley
🏌 A Hemsley
🏳 18 L 6300 yds SSS 70
👤 WD–U WE–H before noon SOC
£€ £22 (£30)
🚗 ¹/₂ mile NW of Watton
⊕ Driving range
🏠 Scott/Jessup

Royal Cromer (1888)

Overstrand Road, Cromer, NR27 0JH
☎ (01263) 512884
□ (01263) 512430
✉ general.manager@royal-cromer .co.uk
🕮 700
🏌 Mrs DC Hopkins
🏌 L Patterson (01263) 512267
🏳 18 L 6508 yds SSS 72
👤 H SOC–WD
£€ D–£35 (D–£40)
🚗 1 mile E of Cromer on B1159
🏠 Morris/Taylor/Braid/Pennink
■ www.royal-cromer.com

Royal Norwich (1893)

Drayton High Road, Hellesdon, Norwich, NR6 5AH
☎ (01603) 425712
□ (01603) 417945
✉ mail@royalnorwichgolf.co.uk
🕮 700
🏌 J Meggy (Mgr) (01603) 429928
🏌 D Futter (01603) 408459
🏳 18 L 6506 yds Par 72 SSS 72
👤 WE/BH–restricted SOC
£€ D–£38 (£46)
🚗 ¹/₂ mile W of Norwich ring road, on Fakenham road
🏠 James Braid
■ www.royalnorwichgolf.co.uk

Royal West Norfolk (1892)

Brancaster, King's Lynn, PE31 8AX
☎ (01485) 210223
□ (01485) 210087
🕮 760
🏌 Maj NA Carrington Smith (01485) 210087

✓ S Rayner (01485) 210616
☞ 18 L 6427 yds SSS 71
♔ M No four balls allowed Mid July–mid Sept WE–NA before 10am SOC
£€ £65 (£75)
⊷ 7 miles E of Hunstanton on A419
⌂ Holcombe Ingleby

Ryston Park (1932)
Ely Road, Denver, Downham Market, PE38 0HH
☎ **(01366) 382133**
☐ (01366) 383834
▱ 320
✍ WJ Flogdell
✓ None
☞ 9 L 6310 yds SSS 70
♔ WD–H WE/BH–M SOC
£€ £15 D–£20
⊷ 1 mile S of Downham Market on A10
⌂ James Braid

Sheringham (1891)
Sheringham, NR26 8HG
☎ **(01263) 822038 (Clubhouse)**
☐ (01263) 825189
📧 sgc.sec@care4free.net
▱ 700
✍ MC Davies (01263) 823488
✓ MW Jubb (01263) 822980
☞ 18 L 6456 yds SSS 71
♔ WD–U H after 9.30am SOC
£€ £40 (£50)
⊷ ¹/₂ mile W of Sheringham (A149)
⌂ Tom Dunn
◼ www.sheringhamgolfclub.co.uk

Swaffham (1922)
Cley Road, Swaffham, PE37 8AE
☎ **(01760) 721621**
☐ (01760) 721621
▱ 500
✍ MA Rust
✓ P Field (01760) 721611
☞ 18 L 6539 yds SSS 71
♔ WD–U WE–M exc Sun am–NA
£€ £25
⊷ 1¹/₂ miles SW of Swaffham
◼ www.swaffhamgc.supanet.com

Thetford (1912)
Brandon Road, Thetford, IP24 3NE
☎ **(01842) 752258 (Clubhouse)**
☐ (01842) 766212
📧 sally@thetfordgolfclub.co.uk
▱ 700
✍ Mrs SA Redpath (01842) 752169
✓ G Kitley (01842) 752662
☞ 18 L 6879 yds SSS 73
♔ H SOC–Wed–Fri
£€ £35
⊷ 2 miles W of Thetford (B1107), off A11 By-pass
⌂ CH Mayo

De Vere Dunston Hall (1994)
Pay and play
Ipswich Road, Dunston, Norwich, NR14 8PQ
☎ **(01508) 470178**

☐ (01508) 471499
▱ 400
✍ P Briggs
✓ P Briggs
☞ 18 L 6200 yds Par 71 SSS 70
♔ U
£€ £25 (£30)
⊷ 5 miles S of Norwich on A140
⊕ Floodlit driving range
⌂ John Glasgow

Wensum Valley (1990)
Beech Avenue, Taverham, Norwich, NR8 6HP
☎ **(01603) 261012**
☐ (01603) 261664
▱ 850
✍ Mrs B Hall
✓ P Whittle
☞ 18 L 6223 yds SSS 70
   9 L 2906 yds SSS 68
♔ U SOC
£€ £20
⊷ 4 miles NW of Norwich on A1067
⊕ Floodlit driving range
⌂ BC Todd
◼ www.wensumvalleyhotel.co.uk

Weston Park (1993)
Weston Longville, Norwich, NR9 5JW
☎ **(01603) 872363**
☐ (01603) 873040
📧 golf@weston-park.co.uk
▱ 450
✍ RR Wright
✓ MR Few (01603) 872998
☞ 18 L 6603 yds SSS 72
♔ WD–U H
£€ £30 (£38)
⊷ 7 miles NW of Norwich, off A1067
⌂ John Glasgow
◼ www.weston-park.co.uk

Northamptonshire

Brampton Heath
Sandy Lane, Church Brampton, NN6 8AX
☎ **(01604) 843939**
☐ (01604) 843885
📧 slawrence@bhgc.co.uk
▱ 500
✍ S Lawrence (01604) 843939
✓ R Hudson (01604) 843939
☞ 18 L 6450 yds Par 72 SSS 71
   9 hole short course
♔ U SOC
£€ £15 (£19)
⊷ 4 miles N of Northampton between A5008 and A428
⊕ Driving range
◼ www.bhgc.co.uk

Cold Ashby (1974)
Stanford Road, Cold Ashby, Northampton, NN6 6EP
☎ **(01604) 740548**
☐ (01604) 740548
📧 coldashby.golfclub@virgin.net

▱ 600 40(L) 40(J)
✍ DA Croxton (Prop) (01604) 740548
✓ S Rose (01604) 740099
☞ 27 L 6308 yds Par 72 SSS 70
♔ WD–U WE–U after 12 noon (if booked) SOC
£€ £15 (£18)
⊷ 11 miles N of Northampton, nr A5199/A14 Junction 1. 7 miles E of M1 Junction 18
⌂ David Croxton
◼ www.coldashbygolfclub.com

Collingtree Park (1990)
Windingbrook Lane, Northampton, NN4 0XN
☎ **(01604) 700000**
☐ (01604) 702600
▱ 900
✍ J Hammond (Gen Mgr)
✓ G Pook
☞ 18 L 6776 yds SSS 72
♔ H SOC
£€ £25 (£30)
⊷ ¹/₂ mile E of M1 Junction 15
⊕ Floodlit driving range
⌂ Johnny Miller
◼ www.collingtreeparkgolf.com

Daventry & District (1911)
Norton Road, Daventry, NN11 5LS
☎ **(01327) 702829**
▱ 350
✍ E Smith
✓ None
☞ 9 L 5812 yds Par 69 SSS 68
♔ WD–U Sun–NA before 11am SOC–phone Sec
£€ £10 (£15)
⊷ ¹/₂ mile E of Daventry

Delapre (1976)
Public
Eagle Drive, Nene Valley Way, Northampton, NN4 7DU
☎ **(01604) 764036/763957**
☐ (01604) 706378
📧 ruth@delapre.northampton.gov.uk
▱ 750
✍ JS Corby (01604) 763957
✓ J Corby, J Cuddihy (01604) 764036
☞ Oaks 18 L 6293 yds SSS 70
   Hardingstone 9 L 2146 yds SSS 32
   2 x 9 holes Par 3 courses
♔ U SOC
£€ £12 (£16)
⊷ 3 miles from M1 Junction 15, on A508/A45
⊕ Pitch & putt. Driving range
⌂ Jacobs/Corby
◼ www.delapregolf.co.uk

Embankment (1975)
The Embankment, Wellingborough, NN8 1LD
☎ **(01933) 228465**
▱ 175
✍ JB Andrew, E Walden (Mgr)
☞ 9 L 3400 yds SSS 56
♔ WD–M
£€ £4

∞ 1 mile SE of Wellingborough
🏠 TH Neal

Farthingstone Hotel (1974)

Farthingstone, Towcester, NN12 8HA
☎ **(01327) 361291**
📠 (01327) 361645
📧 interest@farthingstone.co.uk
📖 400
🏌 DC Donaldson (Prop/Mgr)
✓ G Lunn (01327) 361533
🏴 18 L 6299 yds SSS 70
🙎 U SOC
££ £17 D–£22 (£25 D–£30) SOC–£19
∞ 4 miles W of A5 on Farthingstone-Everdon road. M1 Junction 16, 6 miles
■ www.farthingstone.co.uk

Hellidon Lakes Hotel G&CC (1991)

Hellidon, Daventry, NN11 6GG
☎ **(01327) 262550**
📠 (01327) 262559
📖 500
🏌 MA Thomas
✓ G Wills (01327) 262551
🏴 18 L 6700 yds SSS 72
9 L 5582 yds SSS 67
🙎 U H SOC
££ £20 (£30)
∞ 7 miles SW of Daventry, via A361. M40 Junction 11 and M1 Junction 16,
🏠 David Snell
■ www.hellidon.co.uk

Kettering (1891)

Headlands, Kettering, NN15 6XA
☎ **(01536) 511104**
📠 (01536) 511104
📧 kgc@ukgateway.net
📖 700 100(L) 50(J)
🏌 DG Buckby (01536) 511104
✓ K Theobald (01536) 81014
🏴 18 L 6087 yds SSS 69
🙎 WD–U WE/BH–M SOC
££ D–£30
∞ S boundary of Kettering
🏠 Tom Morris
■ www.kettering-golf.co.uk

Kingfisher Hotel

Proprietary
Buckingham Road, Deanshanger, Milton Keynes, MK19 6JY
☎ **(01908) 560354/562332**
📠 (01908) 260857
📖 98
🏌 D Barraclough
✓ B Mudge
🏴 9 L 5690 yds Par 70 SSS 67
🙎 U exc Sun–restricted SOC
££ 9 holes–£7.50 (£10). 18 holes–£11 (£14)
∞ NW of Milton Keynes on A422 to Buckingham. M1 Junction 15
⊕ Driving range
🏠 Donald Steel
■ www.kingfisher-hotelandgolf.co.uk

Kingsthorpe (1908)

Kingsley Road, Northampton, NN2 7BU
☎ **(01604) 711173**
📠 (01604) 710610
📧 secretary@kingsthorpe-golf.co.uk
📖 600
🏌 JE Harris (01604) 710610
✓ P Armstrong (01604) 719602
🏴 18 L 5918 yds SSS 69
🙎 WD–U WE/BH–M H SOC–WD
££ D–£25
∞ 2 miles N of Northampton centre, off A508
🏠 Alison /Colt
■ www.kingsthorpe-golf.co.uk

Northampton (1893)

Harlestone, Northampton, NN7 4EF
☎ **(01604) 845102 (Clubhouse)**
📠 (01604) 820262
📧 golf@northamptongolfclub.co.uk
📖 635 148(L) 72(J)
🏌 S Malherbe (01604) 845155
✓ K Dickens (01604) 845167
🏴 18 L 6615 yds Par 72 SSS 72
🙎 H WD–U WE–M SOC–WD
££ £35
∞ 4 miles NW of Northampton, on A428 beyond Harlestone
🏠 Donald Steel
■ www.northamptongolfclub.co.uk

Northamptonshire County (1909)

Church Brampton, Northampton, NN6 8AZ
☎ **(01604) 842170**
📠 (01604) 843463
📖 650
🏌 (01604) 843025
✓ T Rouse (01604) 842226
🏴 18 L 6505 yds SSS 72
🙎 H SOC
££ Summer–£45 (£45) Winter–£30 (£30)
∞ 5 miles NW of Northampton, between A428 and A50
🏠 HS Colt

Oundle (1893)

Benefield Road, Oundle, PE8 4EZ
☎ **(01832) 273267**
📠 (01832) 273267
📖 650
🏌 D Foley
✓ R Keys (01832) 272273
🏴 18 L 6265 yds Par 72 SSS 70
🙎 WD–U H WE–M before 10.30am –U H after 10.30am SOC
££ £18.50 D–£25.50 (£35.50)
∞ 1¹/2 miles W of Oundle on A427

Overstone Park (1994)

Watermark Leisure, Billing Lane, Northampton, NN6 0AP
☎ **(01604) 647666**
📠 (01604) 642635
📧 enquiries@overstonepark.co.uk
📖 450
🏌 J Stewart

✓ B Mudge (01604) 643555
🏴 18 L 6602 yds SSS 72
🙎 WD–U SOC
££ £25 (£32)
∞ 4 miles E of Northampton, off A45. M1 Junction 15
⊕ Driving range
🏠 Donald Steel
■ www.overstonepark.co.uk

Priors Hall (1965)

Public
Stamford Road, Weldon, Corby, NN17 3JH
☎ **(01536) 260756**
📠 (01536) 260756
📖 400
🏌 T Arnold
✓ G Bradbrook
🏴 18 L 6631 yds SSS 72
🙎 U SOC–WD
££ On application
∞ 4 miles E of Corby (A43)
🏠 Hawtree

Rushden (1919)

Kimbolton Road, Chelveston, Wellingborough, NN9 6AN
☎ **(01933) 418511**
📖 350
🏌 SP Trayhorn
🏴 10 L 6335 yds Par 71 SSS 70
🙎 WD–U exc Wed pm WE/BH–M SOC
££ £18
∞ On B645, 2 miles E of Higham Ferrers

Staverton Park (1977)

Staverton Park, Staverton, Daventry, NN11 6JT
☎ **(01327) 302000/302118**
📠 (01327) 311428
🏌 D Entwhistle (Gen Mgr), Mrs A Radford (Sec)
✓ R Mudge (01327) 705506
🏴 18 L 6602 yds SSS 72
🙎 U SOC
££ On application
∞ 1 mile SW of Daventry, off A425. M1 Junctions 16/18. M40 Junct. 11
⊕ Driving range

Stoke Albany (1997)

Ashley Road, Stoke Albany, Market Harborough, LE16 8PL
☎ **(01858) 535208**
📠 (01858) 535505
📖 450
🏌 R Want
✓ A Clifford
🏴 18 L 6132 yds Par 71 SSS 69
🙎 U SOC
££ £13 (£18)
∞ Between Market Harborough and Corby (A427)
🏠 Hawtree

Wellingborough (1893)

Harrowden Hall, Great Harrowden, Wellingborough, NN9 5AD
☎ **(01933) 677234/673022**

☎ (01933) 679379
✉ info@wellingboroughgolfclub.org
🏢 850
♣ R Tomlin (01933) 677234
✓ D Clifford (01933) 678752
▷ 18 L 6620 yds SSS 72
♙ WD–U H exc Tues WE–M
  SOC–WD exc Tues
££ D–£40
♣ 2 miles N of Wellingborough on
  A509
🏠 Hawtree

Whittlebury Park G&CC
(1992)
Whittlebury, Towcester, NN12 8XW
☎ **(01327) 858092**
📠 (01327) 858009
🏢 400
♣ PJ Tomlin
▷ 36 holes:
  5000-7000 yds SSS 66-72
♙ U H SOC
££ £18 D–£30 (£25 D–£35)
♣ 4 miles S of Towcester on A413
⊕ Driving range
🏠 Cameron Sinclair

Northumberland

Allendale   (1906)
*High Studdon, Allenheads Road,
Allendale, Hexham NE47 9DH*
☎ **(01434) 683926**
📠 (01434) 683926
🏢 145 26(L) 35(J)
♣ TS Norton (Hon)
▷ 9 L 4501 yds Par 66 SSS 64
♙ U
££ D–£10 (D–£10)
♣ 1¹/₂ miles S of Allendale on B6295
■ www.allendale-golf.org

Alnmouth   (1869)
Foxton Hall, Alnmouth, NE66 3BE
☎ **(01665) 830231**
📠 (01665) 830922
✉ secretary@alnmouthgolfclub.com
🏢 750
♣ P Simpson
✓ Shop (01665) 830043
▷ 18 L 6484 yds SSS 71
♙ Mon/Tues/Thurs–H (restricted)
  SOC
££ £27 D–£32
♣ 5 miles SE of Alnwick
⊕ Dormy House
🏠 HS Colt

Alnmouth Village   (1869)
Marine Road, Alnmouth, NE66 2RZ
☎ **(01665) 830370**
📠 (01665) 602096
🏢 340
♣ W Maclean (01665) 602096
▷ 9 L 6020 yds SSS 70
♙ H
££ £15 (£20)
♣ Alnmouth

Alnwick   (1907)
Swansfield Park, Alnwick, NE66 1AB
☎ **(01665) 602632**
✉ mail@alnwickgolfclub.co.uk
🏢 450
♣ LE Stewart (01665) 602499
▷ 18 L 6250 yds SSS 70
♙ U
££ D–£20 (D–£25)
♣ Alnwick, off A1
🏠 Rochester/Rae
■ www.alnwickgolfclub.co.uk

Arcot Hall   (1909)
Dudley, Cramlington, NE23 7QP
☎ **(0191) 236 2794**
📠 (0191) 217 0370
🏢 700
♣ F Elliott (0191) 236 2794
✓ J Metcalfe (0191) 236 2794
▷ 18 L 6389 yds SSS 70
♙ WD–H WE/BH–M SOC
££ D–£26 (£30) After 3pm–£21
♣ 7 miles N of Newcastle, off A1
🏠 James Braid
■ www.arcothallgolfclub.com

Bamburgh Castle   (1904)
*The Club House, 40 The Wynding,
Bamburgh, NE69 7DE*
☎ **(01668) 214378**
📠 (01668) 214607
🏢 730
♣ RA Patterson (01668) 214321
▷ 18 L 5621 yds Par 68 SSS 67
♙ WD–U H WE/BH–M SOC
££ D–£30 (£30 D–£35)
♣ 5 miles E of A1, via B1341 or
  B1342
🏠 George Rochester

Bedlingtonshire   (1972)
*Acorn Bank, Hartford Road, Bedlington,
NE22 6AA*
☎ **(01670) 822457**
📠 (01670) 823048
🏢 750
♣ FM Hanson (01670) 822457
✓ M Webb (01670) 822457
▷ 18 L 6224 metres SSS 73
♙ U SOC
££ £17 (£24)
♣ 12 miles N of Newcastle (A1068)
🏠 Frank Pennink

Belford   (1993)
South Road, Belford, NE70 7HY
☎ **(01668) 213433**
📠 (01668) 213919
🏢 200
♣ AM Gilhome
✓ None
▷ 9 L 6304 yds SSS 70
♙ U SOC
££ On application
♣ 15 miles N of Alnwick, off A1
⊕ Driving range
🏠 Nigel Williams

Bellingham   (1893)
Boggle Hole, Bellingham, NE48 2DT
☎ **(01434) 220530/220152**
📠 (01434) 220160
✉ admin@bellinghamgolfclub.com
🏢 420
♣ P Cordiner (01434) 220182
▷ 18 L 6093 yds Par 70 SSS 70
♙ U SOC
££ £20 (£25)
♣ 15 miles N of Hexham, off B6320
⊕ Driving range
🏠 I Wilson

Berwick-upon-Tweed   (1890)
*Goswick, Berwick-upon-Tweed,
TD15 2RW*
☎ **(01289) 387256**
📠 (01289) 387334
✉ goswickgc@btconnect.com
🏢 600
♣ D Wilkinson
✓ P Terras (01289) 387380
▷ 18 L 6686 yds SSS 72
♙ WD–U 9.30–11.30am & after 2pm
  WE–U 10–11.30am & after 2.30pm
  SOC
££ £27 (£32)
♣ 5 miles S of Berwick, off A1
🏠 James Braid
■ www.goswicklinksgc.co.uk

Blyth   (1905)
New Delaval, Blyth, NE24 4DB
☎ **(01670) 540110**
📠 (01670) 540134
✉ blythgc@lineone.net
🏢 800
♣ J Wright (01670) 540110
✓ A Brown (01670) 356514
▷ 18 L 6456 yds SSS 71
♙ WD–U before 4pm WE/BH–U after
  2pm SOC
££ £21 D–£25
♣ 3 miles SW of Blyth, off A1061
  (B1532)
🏠 J Hamilton Stutt

Burgham Park   (1994)
Felton, Morpeth, NE65 8QP
☎ **(01670) 787898**
📠 (01670) 787164
🏢 570
♣ J Carr
✓ A Hartley (01670) 787898
▷ 18 L 6751 yds SSS 72
♙ U SOC
££ £15 (£18)
♣ 5 miles N of Morpeth on A1
⊕ Pitch & putt course
🏠 Andrew Mair

Close House   (1968)
*Close House, Heddon-on-the-Wall,
Newcastle-upon-Tyne, NE15 0HT*
☎ **(01661) 852953**
🏢 900
♣ ME Pearse
▷ 18 L 5606 yds SSS 67
♙ M SOC–WD
££ SOC D–£18

🐾 9 miles W of Newcastle on A69
🏠 Hawtree

Dunstanburgh Castle (1900)
Embleton, NE66 3XQ
☎ (01665) 576562
🖫 396
🏌 PFC Gilbert (Mgr)
🅿 18 L 6298 yds SSS 70
🏵 U
£€ £16 (£20)
🐾 7 miles NE of Alnwick on B1339
🏠 James Braid

Hexham (1892)
Spital Park, Hexham, NE46 3RZ
☎ (01434) 603072
🖳 (01434) 601865
🖫 750
🏌 Dawn Wylie (01434) 603072
✓ MW Forster (01434) 604904
🅿 18 L 6272 yds SSS 70
🏵 U
£€ £30 (£40)
🐾 21 miles W of Newcastle (A69)
🏠 Vardon/Caird
■ www.hexhamgolfclub.ntb.org.uk

Linden Hall (1997)
Longhorsley, Morpeth, NE65 8XF
☎ (01670) 500011
🖳 (01670) 500001
🖫 350
🏌 D Curry (Sec/Mgr)
✓ D Curry (01670) 500011
🅿 18 L 6846 yds Par 72 SSS 73
🏵 U H SOC
£€ £25 (£28)
🐾 8 miles NW of Morpeth, off A697
⊕ Driving range
🏠 Jonathan Gaunt

Longhirst Hall (1997)
Longhirst Hall, Longhirst, NE61 3LL
☎ (01670) 791509 (Clubhouse),
   (01670) 858519 (Admin)
🖳 (01670) 818309
📧 enquiries@longhirstgolf.co.uk
🖫 2250
🏌 J Boulton (01670) 812442
✓ G Cant
🅿 18 L 6570 yds Par 72
   9 hole course
🏵 U SOC
£€ £20 (£20)
🐾 4 miles NE of Morpeth, via A197/B1337
⊕ Driving range
🏠 B Poole
■ www.longhirstgolf.co.uk

Magdalene Fields (1903)
Pay and play
Magdalene Fields, Berwick-upon-Tweed, TD15 1NE
☎ (01289) 306384
🖫 330
🏌 MJ Lynch
🅿 18 L 6407 yds SSS 71
🏵 U SOC
£€ £17 (£19)

🐾 Berwick-upon-Tweed 1 mile
🏠 Park/Jefferson/Thompson
■ www.magdalene-fields.co.uk

Matfen Hall Hotel (1994)
Matfen, Hexham, NE20 0RH
☎ (01661) 886500 (Hotel),
   (01661) 886400 (Bookings)
🖳 (01661) 886055
📧 golf@matfenhall.fsnet.co.uk
🖫 500
🏌 D Burton
✓ J Harrison
🅿 18 L 6516 yds Par 72
   9 hole Par 3 course
🏵 WD–U WE–U after 10am
£€ £27.50 (£30)
🐾 12 miles W of Newcastle, off B6318
⊕ Driving range
🏠 Mair/James/Gaunt
■ www.matfenhall.com

Morpeth (1906)
The Clubhouse, Morpeth, NE61 2BT
☎ (01670) 504942
🖳 (01670) 504918
🖫 700
🏌 KD Cazaly (01670) 504942
✓ MR Jackson (01670) 515675
🅿 18 L 5671 metres SSS 69
🏵 H SOC
£€ £22 (£27)
🐾 1 mile S of Morpeth on A197

Newbiggin (1884)
Newbiggin-by-the-Sea, NE64 6DW
☎ (01670) 817344 (Clubhouse)
🖳 (01670) 520236
🖫 500
🏌 GW Beattie (01670) 852959
🅿 18 L 6516 yds SSS 71
🏵 U after 10am exc comp days–NA SOC
£€ D–£20 (D–£25)
🐾 Newbiggin, nr Church Point
🏠 Willie Park

Ponteland (1927)
53 Bell Villas, Ponteland, Newcastle-upon-Tyne, NE20 9BD
☎ (01661) 822689
🖳 (01661) 860077
📧 secretary@thepontelandgolfclub.co.uk
🖫 480 170(L) 115(J)
🏌 JN Dobson
✓ A Robson-Crosby
🅿 18 L 6524 yds SSS 71
🏵 WD–U SOC–Tues & Thurs
£€ £25
🐾 6 miles NW of Newcastle on A696, nr Airport

Prudhoe (1930)
Eastwood Park, Prudhoe-on-Tyne, NE42 5DX
☎ (01661) 832466
🖳 (01661) 830710
🖫 450
🏌 ID Pauw

✓ J Crawford (01661) 836188
🅿 18 L 5839 yds SSS 69
🏵 WD–U WE–NA before 3pm SOC
£€ £20 (£25)
🐾 12 miles W of Newcastle (A1/A695 junction)

Rothbury (1891)
Old Race Course, Rothbury, Morpeth, NE65 7TR
☎ (01669) 621271
🖫 298
🏌 WT Bathgate (01669) 620718
✓ None
🅿 9 L 5779 yds Par 68 SSS 67
🏵 WD–U exc Tues after 4pm & Wed am WE–by arrangement
£€ D–£11 (D–£16)
🐾 15 miles N of Morpeth on A697. W side of Rothbury
🏠 JB Radcliffe

Seahouses (1913)
Beadnell Road, Seahouses, NE68 7XT
☎ (01665) 720794
🖳 (01665) 721994
📧 seahousesgolfclub@breathemail.net
🖫 600
🏌 JA Gray
🅿 18 L 5542 yds SSS 67
🏵 U SOC
£€ £18 (£25)
🐾 14 miles N of Alnwick. 9 miles E of A1 on B1340

Stocksfield (1913)
New Ridley, Stocksfield, NE43 7RE
☎ (01661) 843041
🖳 (01661) 843046
🖫 426 100(L) 75(J)
🏌 B Slade
✓ D Mather
🅿 18 L 5998 yds SSS 70
🏵 U SOC–exc Wed & Sat
£€ £25 (£30)
🐾 2 miles S of Stocksfield. 3 miles E of A68
🏠 F Pennink
■ www.sgcgolf.co.uk

Swarland Hall (1993)
Coast View, Swarland, Morpeth, NE65 9JG
☎ (01670) 787940 (Clubhouse)
🏌 K Rutter (01670) 787010
✓ Shop (01670) 787010
🅿 18 L 6628 yds SSS 72
🏵 U
£€ £15 (£20)
🐾 8 miles S of Alnwick, 1 mile W of A1

Tynedale (1908)
Public
Tyne Green, Hexham, NE46 3HQ
☎ (01434) 608154
🏌 J McDiarmid
✓ Mrs C Brown
🅿 9 L 5706 yds SSS 68
🏵 U exc Sun–booking necessary
£€ £10 (£12) (1993)
🐾 S side of Hexham

For list of abbreviations and key to symbols see page 649

De Vere Slaley Hall　(1988)

Slaley, Hexham, NE47 0BY
- ☎ **(01434) 673350**
- 📠 (01434) 673152
- 📖 350
- ✍ M Stancer (Golf Mgr)
- ✓ M Stancer (01434) 673154
- ⚐ Hunting 18 L 7073 yds Par 72 SSS 71-74;
  Priestman 18 L 7010 Par 72 SSS 71-74
- 👥 U SOC
- ££ Hunting–£70. Priestman–£42.50
- ⛳ 20 miles W of Newcastle. 7 miles S of Corbridge, off A68
- ⊕ Driving range. Golf Academy
- ⌂ Hunting-Dave Thomas. Priestman-Neil Coles
- ■ www.deverehotels.com

Warkworth　(1891)

The Links, Warkworth, Morpeth, NE65 0SW
- ☎ **(01665) 711596**
- 📖 400
- ✍ M Rowe
- ⚐ 9 L 5986 yds SSS 69
- 👥 U exc Tues & Sat SOC
- ££ D–£12 (D–£20)
- ⛳ 9 miles SE of Alnwick (A1068)
- ⌂ Old Tom Morris

Wooler　(1975)

Dod Law, Doddington, Wooler, NE71 6EA
- ☎ **(01668) 282135**
- 📖 250
- ✍ S Lowrey (01668) 281631
- ✓ None
- ⚐ 9 L 6372 yds SSS 70
- 👥 U SOC
- ££ D–£10 (D–£15)
- ⛳ 3 miles N of Wooler on B6525

Nottinghamshire

Beeston Fields　(1923)

Beeston, Nottingham, NG9 3DD
- ☎ **(0115) 925 7062**
- 📠 (0115) 925 4280
- 📖 510 148(L) 58(J)
- ✍ J Lewis
- ✓ A Wardle (0115) 922 0872
- ⚐ 18 L 6404 yds SSS 71
- 👥 U H SOC
- ££ £26 (£31)
- ⛳ 4 miles W of Nottingham. M1 Junction 25
- ⌂ Tom Williamson
- ■ www.beestonfields.co.uk

Brierley Forest　(1993)

Main Street, Huthwaite, Sutton-in-Ashfield, NG17 2LG
- ☎ **(01623) 550761**
- 📠 (01623) 550761
- 📖 130
- ✍ D Crafts
- ✓ None

⚐ 18 L 6008 yds Par 72 SSS 69
👥 WD–U bookings only WE–NA before noon
££ £11.50
⛳ W of Sutton-in-Ashfield. M1 Junction 28, 2 miles

Bulwell Forest　(1902)

Public
Hucknall Road, Bulwell, Nottingham, NG6 9LQ
- ☎ **(0115) 977 0576 (Clubhouse)**
- ☎ (0115) 976 3172 (Pro)
- 📖 350
- ✍ D Waddilove (Hon) (0115) 960 8435
- ✓ L Rawlings (0115) 976 3172
- ⚐ 18 L 5746 yds Par 68 SSS 67
- 👥 U SOC
- ££ £12 (£15). 4ball–£44 (£48)
- ⛳ 4 miles N of Nottingham. M1 Junction 26, 3 miles

Chilwell Manor　(1906)

Meadow Lane, Chilwell, Nottingham, NG9 5AE
- ☎ **(0115) 925 8958**
- 📠 (0115) 922 0575
- ✉ chilwellmanorgolfclub@barbox.net
- 📖 700
- ✍ RA Westcott
- ✓ P Wilson (0115) 925 8993
- ⚐ 18 L 6255 yds Par 70 SSS 71
- 👥 U SOC
- ££ £20 (£20)
- ⛳ 4 miles W of Nottingham on A6005
- ⌂ Tom Williamson

College Pines　(1994)

Worksop College Drive, Sparken Hill, Worksop, S80 3AP
- ☎ **(01909) 501431**
- 📠 (01909) 481227
- 📖 550
- ✍ C Snell (Golf Dir)
- ✓ C Snell (01909) 501431
- ⚐ 18 L 6801 yds SSS 73
- 👥 U–phone first SOC
- ££ £12 (£18)
- ⛳ 1 mile SE of Worksop on B6034, off Worksop Bypass
- ⊕ Driving range
- ⌂ David Snell

Cotgrave Place G&CC　(1991)

Owned privately
Stragglethorpe, Cotgrave, NG12 3HB
- ☎ **(0115) 933 3344**
- 📠 (0115) 933 4567
- ✉ cotgrave@americangolf.com
- 📖 780
- ✍ M Evans
- ✓ R Smith
- ⚐ Open 18 L 6303 yds SSS 70 Masters 18 L 5887 yds SSS 68
- 👥 U SOC
- ££ Open £20 (£25) Masters £19 (£25)
- ⛳ 4 miles SE of Nottingham, off A52
- ⊕ Driving range
- ⌂ Small/Glasgow/Alliss

Coxmoor　(1913)

Coxmoor Road, Sutton-in-Ashfield, NG17 5LF
- ☎ **(01623) 557359**
- 📠 (01623) 557359
- ✉ coxmoor@freeuk.com
- 📖 650
- ✍ JB Noble
- ✓ D Ridley (01623) 559906
- ⚐ 18 L 6501 yds SSS 72
- 👥 H exc Ladies Day–Tues WE–NA SOC
- ££ £37 D–£48
- ⛳ 1¹/₂ miles S of Mansfield. 4 miles NE of M1 Junction 27 on A611
- ■ www.coxmoor-golf.co.uk

Edwalton　(1982)

Public
Edwalton, Nottingham, NG12 4AS
- ☎ **(0115) 923 4775**
- 📖 700
- ✍ Mrs DJ Parkes (Hon)
- ✓ J Staples
- ⚐ 9 L 3336 yds SSS 36 9 hole Par 3 course
- 👥 U
- ££ On application
- ⛳ 2 miles S of Nottingham (A606)

Kilton Forest　(1978)

Public
Blyth Road, Worksop, S81 0TL
- ☎ **(01909) 486563**
- 📖 340
- ✍ A Mansbridge (Hon) (01909) 486269
- ✓ S Betteridge (01909) 486563
- ⚐ 18 L 6424 yds Par 72 SSS 71
- 👥 WD–U WE–booking necessary SOC
- ££ £12 (£15)
- ⛳ 1 mile NE of Worksop on B6045

Leen Valley Golf Centre　(1994)

Pay and play
Wigwam Lane, Hucknall, NG15 7TA
- ☎ **(0115) 964 2037**
- 📠 (0115) 964 2724
- 📖 670
- ✍ BR Goodman (Gen Mgr)
- ✓ J Lines (01623) 422764
- ⚐ 18 L 6233 yds Par 72 SSS 70 9 hole Par 3 course
- 👥 U SOC
- ££ £10 (£14.50)
- ⛳ ¹/₂ mile from Hucknall town centre
- ⌂ Tom Hodgetts

Mansfield Woodhouse　(1973)

Public
Mansfield Woodhouse, NG19 9EU
- ☎ **(01623) 23521**
- ✍ M Stuart
- ✓ L Highfield Jr
- ⚐ 9 L 2411 yds SSS 65
- 👥 U
- ££ £3
- ⛳ 2 miles N of Mansfield (A60)

Mapperley (1907)

Central Avenue, Plains Road, Mapperley, Nottingham NG3 5RH
- ☎ **(0115) 955 6672**
- 🖳 (0115) 955 6670
- 📖 650
- 🏌 A Newton
- 🏌 J Barker (0115) 955 6673
- ⛳ 18 L 6307 yds SSS 70
- 👥 U SOC
- £€ £17 D–£20
- 🚗 3 miles NE of Nottingham, off B684
- 🏠 J Mason

Newark (1901)

Coddington, Newark, NG24 2QX
- ☎ **(01636) 626282**
- 🖳 (01636) 626497
- 📖 650
- 🏌 P Snow (01636) 626282
- 🏌 PA Lockley (01636) 626492
- ⛳ 18 L 6458 yds SSS 71
- 👥 H SOC
- £€ £23 (£28)
- 🚗 4 miles E of Newark on A17

Norwood Park (1999)

Norwood Park, Southwell, NG25 0PF
- ☎ **(01636) 816626**
- 🖳 (01636) 815756
- 📧 norwoodgolf@mail.com
- 📖 470
- 🏌 R Beckett (01636) 813226
- 🏌 P Thornton (01636) 816626
- ⛳ 18 L 6805 yds Par 72 SSS 72
- 👥 U SOC
- £€ £16 D–£28 (£22 D–£36)
- 🚗 ¹/₂ mile W of Southwell, off Kirklington road
- ⊕ Driving range
- 🏠 Clyde Johnston
- ■ www.norwoodpark.org.uk

Nottingham City (1910)

Public
Lawton Drive, Bulwell, Nottingham, NG6 8BL
- ☎ **(0115) 927 8021**
- 🖳 (0115) 927 6916
- 📖 460
- 🏌 (0115) 927 6916
- 🏌 CR Jepson (0115) 927 2767
- ⛳ 18 L 6218 yds SSS 70
- 👥 WD–U WE–NA before noon SOC
- £€ £11 (£11)
- 🚗 5 miles N of Nottingham. M1 Junction 26

Notts (1887)

Hollinwell, Kirkby-in-Ashfield, NG17 7QR
- ☎ **(01623) 753225**
- 🖳 (01623) 753655
- 📖 500
- 🏌 NI Symington
- 🏌 A Thomas (01623) 753087
- ⛳ 18 L 7103 yds Par 72 SSS 75
- 👥 WD–H WE/BH–M
- £€ On application
- 🚗 4 miles S of Mansfield on A611.

- M1 Junction 27
- ⊕ Driving range-green fees only
- 🏠 Willie Park Jr

Oakmere Park (1974)

Oaks Lane, Oxton, NG25 0RH
- ☎ **(0115) 965 3545**
- 🖳 (0115) 965 5628
- 📖 450
- 🏌 D St-John Jones
- 🏌 D St-John Jones (0115) 965 3545
- ⛳ 18 L 6617 yds SSS 72
  9 L 3495 yds SSS 37
- 👥 WD–U WE/BH–arrange times with Mgr SOC
- £€ 18 hole:£18 (£25) 9 hole:£6 (£8)
- 🚗 8 miles NE of Nottingham on A614
- ⊕ Floodlit driving range
- 🏠 F Pennink
- ■ www.oakmerepark.co.uk

Radcliffe-on-Trent (1909)

Dewberry Lane, Cropwell Road, Radcliffe-on-Trent, NG12 2JH
- ☎ **(0115) 933 3000**
- 🖳 (0115) 911 6991
- 📧 les.rotgc@talk21.com
- 📖 670
- 🏌 L Wake
- 🏌 C George (0115) 933 2396
- ⛳ 18 L 6381 yds Par 70 SSS 71
- 👥 H SOC–Wed only
- £€ £23 (£28)
- 🚗 6 miles E of Nottingham, off A52
- 🏠 Tom Williamson
- ■ www.radcliffeontrentgc.co.uk

Ramsdale Park Golf Centre (1992)

Pay and play
Oxton Road, Calverton, NG14 6NU
- ☎ **(0115) 965 5600**
- 🖳 (0115) 965 4105
- 📧 info@ramsdaleparkgc.co.uk
- 🏌 N Birch (Mgr)
- 🏌 R Macey
- ⛳ 18 L 6546 yds SSS 71
  18 hole Par 3 course
- 👥 U SOC–WD
- £€ £16 (£20)
- 🚗 5 miles NE of Nottingham on B6386. M1 Junction 27
- ⊕ Floodlit driving range
- 🏠 Hawtree
- ■ www.ramsdaleparkgc.co.uk

Retford (1921)

Brecks Road, Ordsall, Retford, DN22 7UA
- ☎ **(01777) 703733**
- 🖳 (01777) 710412
- 📖 700
- 🏌 Linda Colclough (01777) 860682
- 🏌 C Morris
- ⛳ 18 L 6370 yds SSS 70
- 👥 WD–U WE–after 2pm SOC–WD
- £€ £15 D–£20 (£18)
- 🚗 2 miles SW of Retford, off A638 or A620. M1 Junction 30

Ruddington Grange (1988)

Wilford Road, Ruddington, Nottingham, NG11 6NB
- ☎ **(0115) 984 6141**
- 🖳 (0115) 940 5165
- 📧 info@ruddingtongrange.com
- 📖 600
- 🏌 A Johnson
- 🏌 R Simpson (0115) 921 1951
- ⛳ 18 L 6490 yds SSS 72
- 👥 WD–U SOC
- £€ D–£17.50 (£25)
- 🚗 3 miles S of Nottingham
- 🏠 J Small

Rufford Park Golf Centre

Rufford Lane, Rufford, Newark, NG22 9DG
- ☎ **(01623) 825253**
- 🖳 (01623) 825254
- 📖 450
- 🏌 Mrs K Whitehead
- 🏌 J Vaughan, J Thompson
- ⛳ 18 L 6286 yds Par 70 SSS 70
- 👥 U–booking necessary SOC–WD/WEpm
- £€ £15 D–£20 (£20)
- 🚗 Nr Rufford Abbey on A614. 8 miles S of A1/A614 junction
- ⊕ Floodlit driving range

Rushcliffe (1909)

Stocking Lane, East Leake, Loughborough, LE12 5RL
- ☎ **(01509) 852959**
- 🖳 (01509) 852688
- 📧 secretary.rushcliffegc @btopenworld.com
- 📖 704
- 🏌 KW Hodkinson
- 🏌 C Hall (01509) 852701
- ⛳ 18 L 6090 yds SSS 69
- 👥 SOC–WD
- £€ £25 (£30)
- 🚗 9 miles S of Nottingham. M1 Junction 24

Serlby Park (1906)

Serlby, Doncaster, DN10 6BA
- ☎ **(01777) 818268**
- 📖 250
- 🏌 KJ Crook (01302) 742280
- ⛳ 9 L 5370 yds SSS 66
- 👥 M SOC–WD
- £€ £20
- 🚗 12 miles S of Doncaster, between A614 and A638

Sherwood Forest (1895)

Eakring Road, Mansfield, NG18 3EW
- ☎ **(01623) 626689**
- 🖳 (01623) 420412
- 📖 648
- 🏌 Ms A Miles
- 🏌 K Hall (01623) 627403
- ⛳ 18 L 6843 yds SSS 74
- 👥 H SOC–WD
- £€ On application to Sec
- 🚗 2 miles E of Mansfield (A617)
- 🏠 HS Colt/James Braid

Southwell (1993)

Proprietary
*Southwell Racecourse, Rolleston,
Newark, NG25 0TS*
☎ **(01636) 816501**
🖥 (01636) 812271
📖 400
🏌 M Harness (01636) 821651
⛳ S Meade (01636) 813706
🏁 18 L 5770 yds Par 70 SSS 68
👥 U SOC
££ £15 (£18)
🚗 6 miles W of Newark on A617.
Course adjacent to racetrack
🏠 RA Muddle

Springwater (1991)

Pay and play
*Moor Lane, Calverton, Nottingham,
NG14 6FZ*
☎ **(0115) 965 2129**
📖 400
🏌 W Turner (0115) 965 2565
⛳ P Drew (0115) 965 2129
🏁 18 L 6244 yds Par 71
👥 U SOC
££ £15 (£20)
🚗 Off A6097 between Lowdham and
Oxton
🏠 ADAS/McEvoy

Stanton-on-the-Wolds

(1906)
*Golf Road, Stanton-on-the-Wolds,
Nottingham, NG12 5BH*
☎ **(0115) 937 2044**
🖥 (0115) 937 4885
📖 500 167(L) 100(J)
🏌 AR Evans (0115) 937 4885
⛳ N Hernon ((0115) 937 2390
🏁 18 L 6421 yds SSS 71
👥 WD–U exc comp days WE–M SOC
££ £23 D–£31 SOC–£25–£30
🚗 9 miles S of Nottingham

Trent Lock Golf Centre

(1991)
*Lock Lane, Sawley, Long Eaton,
NG10 3DD*
☎ **(0115) 946 4398**
🖥 (0115) 946 1183
📖 550
🏌 R Gregory
⛳ M Taylor
🏁 18 L 5730 yds Par 69 SSS 68
9 L 2908 yds Par 36
👥 U SOC
££ £12.50 (£15) 9 hole:£5
🚗 S of Long Eaton. M1 Junction 25
⊕ Driving range
🏠 E McCausland

Wollaton Park (1927)

Wollaton Park, Nottingham, NG8 1BT
☎ **(0115) 978 7574**
🖥 (0115) 970 0736
🖂 wollatonparkgc@aol.com
📖 700
🏌 MT Harvey
⛳ J Lower (0115) 978 4834

🏁 18 L 6445 yds SSS 71
👥 U SOC
££ On application
🚗 2 miles SW of Nottingham. M1
Junction 25, 5 miles
🏠 T Williamson

Worksop (1911)

Windmill Lane, Worksop, S80 2SQ
☎ **(01909) 472696**
🖥 (01909) 477731
📖 500
🏌 DA Dufall (01909) 477731
⛳ C Weatherhead (01909) 477732
🏁 18 L 6660 yds Par 72 SSS 73
👥 WD–H (phone first) WE/BH–M
SOC
££ On application
🚗 1 mile SE of Worksop, off A6034
via by-pass (A57). M1 Junction 30,
9 miles

Oxfordshire

Aspect Park (1988)

*Remenham Hill, Henley-on-Thames,
RG9 3EH*
☎ **(01491) 578306**
🖥 (01491) 578306
📖 600
🏌 T Winsland
⛳ T Notley (01491) 577562
🏁 18 L 6559 yds Par 72 SSS 71
👥 WD–U WE–restricted before noon
SOC
££ £20 (£25)
🚗 1 mile E of Henley. M40 Junction
4, 8 miles
⊕ Driving range. Pitch & putt
🏠 T Winsland

Badgemore Park (1972)

Proprietary
Henley-on-Thames, RG9 4NR
☎ **(01491) 572206**
🖥 (01491) 576899
🖂 info@badgemorepark.com
📖 600
🏌 J Connell (Mgr) (01491) 572206
⛳ J Dunn (01491) 574175
🏁 18 L 6129 yds SSS 69
👥 WD–U exc Tues am–NA WE–U
after 11am SOC–Wed & Fri
££ £24 (£36)
🚗 1 mile NW of Henley on
Rotherfield Greys road
🏠 B Sandow
■ www.badgemorepark.com

Banbury Golf Centre (1993)

*Aynho Road, Adderbury, Banbury,
OX17 3NT*
☎ **(01295) 810419**
🖥 (01295) 810056
🖂 office@banburygolfcentre.co.uk
📖 300
🏌 MA Reed (Prop)
⛳ S Kier (01295) 812880
🏁 27 holes :
L 5766-6706 yds Par 72 SSS 72

👥 U SOC
££ £16 (£23)
🚗 6 miles S of Banbury on B4100.
M40 Junction 10/11
🏠 Reed/Payn
■ www.banburygolfcentre.co.uk

Bicester G&CC (1973)

Chesterton, Bicester, OX26 1TE
☎ **(01869) 241204**
🖂 bicestergolf@ukonline.co.uk
📖 650
🏌 P Fox (01869 241204
⛳ J Goodman (01869) 242023
🏁 18 L 6013 yds SSS 70
👥 U SOC–WD
££ £25 (£35)
🚗 2 miles SW of Bicester. M40
Junction 9

Brailes (1992)

*Sutton Lane, Lower Brailes, Banbury,
OX15 5BB*
☎ **(01608) 685336**
🖥 (01608) 685205
🖂 office@brailes-golf-club.co.uk
📖 580
🏌 RAS Malir
⛳ A Brown (01608) 685633
🏁 18 L 6310 yds Par 71 SSS 70
👥 U SOC–WD
££ £20 (£30)
🚗 3 miles E of Shipston-on-Stour on
B4035. M40 Junction 11, 10 miles
⊕ Driving range
🏠 BA Hull
■ www.brailes-golf-club.co.uk

Burford (1936)

Burford, OX18 4JG
☎ **(01993) 822583**
🖥 (01993) 822801
📖 710
🏌 RP Thompson
⛳ M Ridge (01993) 822344
🏁 18 L 6432 yds SSS 71
👥 WD–H SOC
££ On application
🚗 19 miles W of Oxford on A40

Carswell CC (1993)

Carswell, Faringdon, SN7 8PU
☎ **(01367) 870422**
🖥 (01367) 870592
🖂 info@carswellcountryclub.co.uk
📖 500
🏌 G Lisi (Prop)
⛳ S Parker
🏁 18 L 6133 yds Par 72
👥 U SOC–WD
££ £18 (£25)
🚗 12 miles W of Oxford on A420
⊕ Floodlit driving range

Cherwell Edge (1980)

Chacombe, Banbury, OX17 2EN
☎ **(01295) 711591**
🖥 (01295) 712404
📖 462
🏌 RA Beare
⛳ J Kingston

18 L 5947 yds SSS 68
U SOC–WD
££ £12 (£16)
3 miles E of Banbury on B4525
Driving range

Chipping Norton (1890)

*Southcombe, Chipping Norton,
OX7 5QH*
☎ (01608) 642383
(01608) 645422
900
S Chislett
N Rowlands (01608) 643356
18 L 6280 yds SSS 70
WD–U WE–M
££ £28
1 mile E of Chipping Norton on
A44

Drayton Park (1992)

Pay and play
*Steventon Road, Drayton, Abingdon,
OX14 2RR*
☎ (01235) 550607/528989
(01235) 525731
draytonpark@btclick.com
400
(01235) 528989
M Morbey (01235) 550607
18 L 5535 yds SSS 67
9 hole Par 3 course
U SOC
££ £17.75 (£19.75)
5 miles S of Oxford on A34. M4
Junction 13
Floodlit driving range
Hawtree

Frilford Heath (1908)

Frilford Heath, Abingdon, OX13 5NW
☎ (01865) 390864
(01865) 390823
1250 210(L)
S Styles
DC Craik (01865) 390887
Red 18 L 6884 yds SSS 73
Green 18 L 6006 yds SSS 69
Blue 18 L 6728 yds SSS 72
H SOC
££ £50 (£65)
3 miles W of Abingdon on A338
Blue-Simon Gidman

Hadden Hill (1990)

Wallingford Road, Didcot, OX11 9BJ
☎ (01235) 510410
(01235) 510410
420 62(L)
MV Morley
A Waters
18 L 6563 yds SSS 71
WD–U SOC–WD
££ £15 (£20)
E of Didcot on A4130
Floodlit driving range
MV Morley
www.haddenhillgolf.co.uk

Henley (1907)

*Harpsden, Henley-on-Thames,
RG9 4HG*
☎ (01491) 575781
(01491) 412179
henleygolfclub@btinternet.com
750
AM Chaundy (01491) 575742
M Howell (01491) 575710
18 L 6329 yds SSS 70
WD–H WE–M SOC
££ D–£30
1 mile S of Henley (A4155)
James Braid
www.henleygc.com

Hinksey Heights (1995)

South Hinksey, Oxford, OX1 5AB
☎ (01865) 327775
(01865) 736930
play@oxford-golf.co.uk
360
K Martin (Gen Mgr)
D Bolton (01865) 327775
18 L 6936 yds Par 74 SSS 73
9 hole Par 3 course
U SOC
££ £17.50 (£25)
W of Oxford, off A34 at South
Hinksey, between Oxford and
Abingdon
Practice range. Golf academy
D Heads
www.oxford-golf.co.uk

Huntercombe (1901)

Nuffield, Henley-on-Thames, RG9 5SL
☎ (01491) 641207
(01491) 642060
800
KS McCrea
D Reffin (01491) 641241
18 L 6173 yds SSS 70
H–by appointment only SOC–WD
££ D–£40
6 miles W of Henley on A4130
Foursomes and singles only
Willie Park Jr

Kirtlington (1995)

Kirtlington, OX5 3JY
☎ (01869) 351133
(01869) 331143
info@kirtlingtongolfclub.co.uk
350
P Smith (Sec/Mgr)
18 holes Par 70 SSS 69
U SOC
££ £20 (£25)
1 mile from Kirtlington on A4095.
M40 Junction 9
Driving range
G Webster

North Oxford (1907)

Banbury Road, Oxford, OX2 8EZ
☎ (01865) 554415
(01865) 515921
secretary@nogc.com
701
GW Pullin (01865) 554924

R Harris (01865) 553977
18 L 5805 yds SSS 67
WD–U SOC–WD exc Thurs
££ £18 D–£25 After 5pm–£14
4 miles N of Oxford, off A4260 to
Kidlington
www.nogc.co.uk

The Oxfordshire (1993)

*Rycote Lane, Milton Common, Thame,
OX9 2PU*
☎ (01844) 278300
(01844) 278003
600
R Moan
N Pike
18 L 7187 yds Par 72 SSS 75
I H WE–NA before noon
££ On application
1½ miles W of Thame on A329.
M40 Junction 7, 1½ miles. M40
Junction 8, 4 miles
Driving range
Rees Jones

RAF Benson (1975)

*Royal Air Force, Benson, Wallingford,
OX10 6AA*
☎ (01491) 837766 Ext 7322
200
B Sowerby (01235) 848472
9 L 4412 yds Par 63 SSS 61
M
££ £7
3½ miles NE of Wallingford

Rye Hill

Milcombe, Banbury, OX15 4RU
☎ (01295) 721818
(01295) 720089
T Pennock
18 L 6919 yds Par 72
U–booking necessary SOC
££ £17 (£22)
5 miles SW of Banbury, off A361.
M40 Junction 11
3 x Par 3 holes

Southfield (1875)

Hill Top Road, Oxford, OX4 1PF
☎ (01865) 242158
(01865) 242158
700
N Stone (Gen Mgr)
A Rees (01865) 244258
18 L 6230 yds SSS 70
WD–U WE/BH–M H SOC
££ £25
2 miles E of Oxford
HS Colt

The Springs Hotel (1998)

*Wallingford Road, North Stoke,
Wallingford, OX10 6BE*
☎ (01491) 827310
(01491) 827312
550
D Allen (01491) 827307
L Atkins (01491) 827310
18 L 6470 yds Par 72 SSS 71
By arrangement SOC

££ £27.50 (£34)
⊗ 2 miles SW of Wallingford on B4009. M40 Junction 6
⌂ Brian Huggett
■ www.thespringshotel.com

Studley Wood (1996)

The Straight Mile, Horton-cum-Studley, Oxford, OX33 1BF
☎ (01865) 351144
⌨ (01865) 351166
✉ admin@swgc.co.uk
⌕ 770
⚴ R Booth (01865) 351144
✓ T Williams (01865) 351122
⊳ 18 L 6722 yds Par 73 SSS 72
⚇ WD–U WE–NA before noon SOC
££ £32 (£40)
⊗ 4 miles NE of Oxford. M40 Junction 8
⊕ Driving range. Golf academy
⌂ Simon Gidman
■ www.studleywoodgolf.co.uk

Tadmarton Heath (1922)

Wigginton, Banbury, OX15 5HL
☎ (01608) 737278
⌨ (01608) 730548
✉ thgc@btinternet.com
⌕ 650
⚴ IM Kirkwood
✓ T Jones (01608) 730047
⊳ 18 L 5917 yds SSS 69
⚇ WD–H by appointment WE–M SOC–WD
££ £38 (£40). After 2pm–£28
⊗ 5 miles SW of Banbury, off B4035
⌂ Maj CJ Hutchison
■ www.thgc.btinternet.co.uk

Waterstock (1994)

Pay and play
Thame Road, Waterstock, Oxford, OX33 1HT
☎ (01844) 338093
⌨ (01844) 338036
⌕ 500
⚴ AJ Wyatt
✓ P Bryant
⊳ 18 L 6535 yds Par 73
⚇ U SOC
££ £17 (£20)
⊗ E of Oxford on A418. M40 Junction 8
⊕ Floodlit driving range
⌂ Donald Steel

Witney Lakes (1994)

Downs Road, Witney, OX8 5SY
☎ (01993) 893010
⌨ (01993) 778866
⌕ 450
⚴ M Percival
✓ A South, A Campbell
⊳ 18 L 6460 yds SSS 71
⚇ U
££ £16 (£22)
⊗ 2 miles W of Witney on B4047
⊕ Floodlit driving range
⌂ Simon Gidman
■ www.witney-lakes.co.uk

Wychwood (1992)

Proprietary
Lyneham, Chipping Norton, OX7 6QQ
☎ (01993) 831841
⌨ (01993) 831775
✉ golf@wychwoodgc.freeserve.co.uk
⌕ 780
⚴ CJT Howkins
✓ J Fincher
⊳ 18 L 6669 yds SSS 72
⚇ WD–U WE–U after 11am SOC
££ £22 (£26)
⊗ 4 miles W of Chipping Norton, off A361
⊕ Driving range
⌂ D Carpenter
■ www.golf@lynehamgc.freeserve.co.uk

Rutland

Greetham Valley (1992)

Greetham, Oakham, LE15 7NP
☎ (01780) 460004
⌨ (01780) 460623
✉ gvgc@webleicester.co.uk
⌕ 1000
⚴ FE Hinch
✓ J Pengelly (01780) 460666
⊳ 18 holes SSS 71
 18 holes SSS 68
 9 hole Par 3 course
⚇ U SOC–WD
££ £28 (£32)
⊗ 5 miles NE of Oakham (B668), nr A1
⊕ Floodlit driving range

Luffenham Heath (1911)

Ketton, Stamford, PE9 3UU
☎ (01780) 720205
⌨ (01780) 722146
✉ jringleby@theluffenhamheathgc.co.uk
⌕ 555
⚴ JR Ingleby
✓ I Burnett (01780) 720298
⊳ 18 L 6315 yds SSS 70
⚇ U H SOC–WD
££ £40 D–£50 (£40 D–£50)
⊗ 5 miles W of Stamford on A6121
⌂ James Braid
■ www.luffenhamheath.co.uk

RAF Cottesmore (1982)

Oakham, Leicester, LE15 7BL
☎ (01572) 812241 Ext 6706
⌕ 150
⚴ GA Lawrence
⊳ 9 L 5767 yds SSS 67
⚇ By arrangement
££ £10
⊗ RAF Cottesmore

RAF North Luffenham (1975)

RAF North Luffenham, Oakham, LE15 8RL
☎ (01780) 720041 Ext 7523

⌕ 350 62(L) 25(J)
⚴ S Nicholson
⊳ 9 L 6048 yds Par 70 SSS 69
⚇ U SOC
££ D–£8
⊗ ¹/₂ mile from S shore of Rutland Water

Rutland County (1991)

Great Casterton, Stamford, PE9 4AQ
☎ (01780) 460239/460330
⌨ (01780) 460437
⚴ S Lowe (Golf Dir)
⊳ 18 L 6401 yds SSS 71
 9 hole Par 3 course
⚇ U H SOC
££ £25 (£30)
⊗ 3 miles N of Stamford on A1
⊕ Driving range
⌂ Cameron Sinclair

Shropshire

Aqualate

Proprietary
Stafford Road, Newport, TF10 9JT
☎ (01952) 811699
⌨ (01952) 825343
⌕ 160
⚴ HB Dawes (Mgr) (01952) 825343
✓ K Short (01952) 811699
⊳ 18 L 5659 yds Par 69 SSS 67
⚇ U
££ £10 (£13)
⊗ 1 mile E of Newport (A518/A41 junction)
⊕ Floodlit driving range
■ www.aqualategolf.f2s.com

Arscott (1992)

Arscott, Pontesbury, Shrewsbury, SY5 0XP
☎ (01743) 860114
⌨ (01743) 860114
⌕ 550
⚴ BK Harper
✓ (01743) 860881
⊳ 18 L 6112 yds SSS 69
⚇ WD–U WE/BH–M before 2pm SOC
££ £16 (£20)
⊗ 5 miles SW of Shrewsbury, off A488
⌂ Martin Hamer

Bridgnorth (1889)

Stanley Lane, Bridgnorth, WV16 4SF
☎ (01746) 763315
⌨ (01746) 761381
✉ bridgnorth-golf@supanet.com
⌕ 690
⚴ GC Kelsall
✓ P Hinton (01746) 762045
⊳ 18 L 6582 yds SSS 72
⚇ H SOC
££ £26 (£32)
⊗ 1 mile N of Bridgnorth

Chesterton Valley
Chesterton, Worfield, Bridgnorth, WV15 5NX
- ☎ **(01746) 783682**
- ⌂ 350
- ✍ P Hinton
- ✒ P Hinton
- ⏴ 18 L 5860 yds Par 69 SSS 67
- ♟ U–phone first SOC
- ££ £14.50 (£15.50)
- ⛳ 10 miles W of Wolverhampton on B4176

Church Stretton   (1898)
Trevor Hill, Church Stretton, SY6 6JH
- ☎ **(01694) 722281**
- ⌂ 410
- ✒ J Townsend (01694) 722281
- ⏴ 18 L 5020 yds SSS 65
- ♟ H WE–NA before 10.30am SOC
- ££ £18 (£26)
- ⛳ ¹/₂ mile W of Church Stretton, off A49
- ⛩ James Braid

Cleobury Mortimer   (1993)
Wyre Common, Cleobury Mortimer, DY14 8HQ
- ☎ **(01299) 271112 (Clubhouse)**
- ⌨ (01299) 271468
- ⌂ 704
- ✍ G Pain (Gen Mgr)
- ✒ J Jones, M Payne
- ⏴ 27 holes:
  L 6147-6438 yds SSS 69-71
- ♟ WD–U H WE–M H SOC
- ££ £20 (£30)
- ⛳ 10 miles SW of Kidderminster on A4117
- ■ www.cleoburygolfclub.com

Hawkstone Park   (1920)
Weston-under-Redcastle, Shrewsbury, SY4 5UY
- ☎ **(01939) 200611**
- ⌨ (01939) 200311
- ✉ info@hawkstone.co.uk
- ⌂ 700
- ✍ T Harrop
- ✒ T Roberts
- ⏴ Hawkstone 18 L 6491 yds SSS 72;
  Windmill 18 L 6764 yds SSS 72
  Academy 6 holes Par 3 course
- ♟ U
- ££ £28 D–£42 (£36 D–£50)
- ⛳ 10 miles S of Whitchurch. 14 miles N of Shrewsbury on A49
- ⊕ Driving range
- ⛩ Braid/Huggett
- ■ www.hawkstone.co.uk

Hill Valley G&CC   (1975)
Terrick Road, Whitchurch, SY13 4JZ
- ☎ **(01948) 663584**
- ⌨ (01948) 665927
- ⌂ 600
- ✍ JS Pickering
- ✒ AR Minshall, CT Burgess
- ⏴ Emerald 18 L 6628 yds Par 73
  Sapphire 18 L 4801 yds Par 66
- ♟ U

- ££ Emerald £20 (£25) Sapphire £11 (£15)
- ⛳ 1 mile N of Whitchurch, off A41/A49 Bypass
- ⊕ 6-bay practice range
- ⛩ Alliss/Thomas

Horsehay Village   (1999)
Pay and play
Wellington Road, Horsehay, Telford, TF4 3BT
- ☎ **(01952) 632070**
- ⌨ (01952) 632074
- ✉ horsehayvillagegolfcentre@wrekin
  .gov.uk
- ⌂ 350
- ✍ M Morgan
- ✒ D Thorp (01952) 632070
- ⏴ 18 L 5929 yds Par 70 SSS 69
- ♟ U SOC
- ££ £12 (£14)
- ⛳ Nr M54 Junction 6
- ⊕ Driving range. Pitch & putt course
- ⛩ Howard Swan

Lilleshall Hall   (1937)
Abbey Road, Lilleshall, Newport, TF10 9AS
- ☎ **(01952) 603840/604776**
- ⌨ (01952) 604776
- ⌂ 600
- ✍ BC Stephens (01952) 604776
- ✒ S McKane (01952) 604104
- ⏴ 18 L 5813 yds SSS 68
- ♟ WD–U WE–M SOC
- ££ £22
- ⛳ 3 miles S of Newport between Lilleshall and Sheriffhales. M54 Junction 4
- ⛩ HS Colt

Llanymynech   (1933)
Pant, Oswestry, SY10 8LB
- ☎ **(01691) 830542**
- ⌂ 760
- ✍ DR Thomas (01691) 830983
- ✒ A Griffiths (01691) 830879
- ⏴ 18 L 6114 yds Par 70 SSS 69
- ♟ U before 4.30pm –M after 4.30pm SOC–WD
- ££ £20 (£25)
- ⛳ 5 miles S of Oswestry on A483

Ludlow   (1889)
Bromfield, Ludlow, SY8 2BT
- ☎ **(01584) 856285**
- ⌨ (01584) 856366
- ✉ ludlowgc@barbox.net
- ⌂ 550
- ✍ RJ Heath (01584) 856285 (am)
- ✒ R Price (01584) 856366
- ⏴ 18 L 6277 yds SSS 70
- ♟ H SOC–WD
- ££ £20 (£25)
- ⛳ 2 miles N of Ludlow (A49)

Market Drayton   (1926)
Sutton, Market Drayton, TF9 1LX
- ☎ **(01630) 652266**
- ⌂ 550
- ✍ DB Palmer

- ✒ R Clewes (01630) 656237
- ⏴ 18 L 6290 yds SSS 71
- ♟ WD–U WE–NA
- ££ £24
- ⛳ 1 mile S of Market Drayton

Meole Brace   (1976)
Public
Meole Brace, Shrewsbury SY2 6QQ
- ☎ **(01743) 364050**
- ⌨ (01743) 364050
- ✒ N Bramall
- ⏴ 9 L 2915 yds SSS 68
- ♟ WD–U WE–book in advance
- ££ On application
- ⛳ 1 mile S of Shrewsbury, off A49

Mile End   (1992)
Proprietary
Mile End, Oswestry, SY11 4JE
- ☎ **(01691) 671246**
- ⌨ (01691) 670580
- ✉ mileendgc@aol.com
- ✍ R Thompson
- ✒ S Carpenter (01691) 671246
- ⏴ 18 L 6194 yds SSS 69
- ♟ U SOC
- ££ £16 D–£24 (£22 D–£30)
- ⛳ 1 mile SE of Oswestry, off A5
- ⊕ Driving range
- ⛩ Price/Gough
- ■ www.mileendgolfclub.co.uk

Oswestry   (1903)
Aston Park, Oswestry, SY11 4JJ
- ☎ **(01691) 610221**
- ⌨ (01691) 610535
- ⌂ 880
- ✍ PB Turner (01691) 610535
- ✒ D Skelton (01691) 610448
- ⏴ 18 L 6038 yds SSS 69
- ♟ M or H SOC–WD
- ££ £23 (£31)
- ⛳ 3 miles SE of Oswestry on A5
- ⛩ James Braid

Patshull Park Hotel G&CC   (1980)
Pattingham, WV6 7HR, WV6 7HR
- ☎ **(01902) 700100**
- ⌨ (01902) 700874
- ⌂ 395
- ✍ M Ellam
- ✒ R Bissell (01902) 700342
- ⏴ 18 L 6412 yds SSS 71
- ♟ U H SOC
- ££ £30 (£40)
- ⛳ 7 miles W of Wolverhampton, off A41. M54 Junction 3, 5 miles
- ⛩ John Jacobs
- ■ www.patshull-park.co.uk

Severn Meadows   (1990)
Pay and play
Highley, Bridgnorth, WV16 6HZ
- ☎ **(01746) 862212**
- ⌂ 190
- ✍ C Harrison
- ✒ None

▷ 18 L 6357 yds Par 72 SSS 70
⋈ WD–U WE–booking required
££ £12 (£14)
⊷ 8 miles S of Bridgnorth on B4555

Shifnal (1929)
Decker Hill, Shifnal, TF11 8QL
☎ **(01952) 460467/460330**
⌨ (01952) 461127
✉ secretary@shifnalgolfclub.co.uk
📖 700
⅍ M Vanner (01952) 460330
✓ J Flanaghan (01952) 460457
▷ 18 L 6422 yds SSS 71
⋈ WD–phone first WE/BH–M
££ £25
⊷ 1 mile NE of Shifnal. M54 Junction 4, 2 miles
⌂ Pennink
■ www.shifnalgolfclub.co.uk

Shrewsbury (1891)
Condover, Shrewsbury, SY5 7BL
☎ **(01743) 872976**
⌨ (01743) 874647
✉ info@shrewsbury-golf-club.co.uk
📖 525 184(L) 70(J)
⅍ Mrs SM Kenny (01743) 872977
✓ P Seal (01743) 874581
▷ 18 L 6178 yds Par 70 SSS 69
⋈ H SOC
££ £22 (£25)
⊷ 4 miles S of Shrewsbury
■ www.shrewsbury-golf-club.co.uk

The Shropshire (1992)
Pay and play
Muxton, Telford, TF2 8PQ
☎ **(01952) 677866**
⌨ (01952) 677622
📖 500
⅍ S Glass
✓ A Holmes
▷ 27 L 6589-6637 yds SSS 70-72
⋈ U SOC
££ £18 (£23)
⊷ 4 miles NW of Telford (B5060). M54 Junction 4
⊕ Floodlit driving range. Pitch & putt course
⌂ Martin Hawtree
■ www.theshropshire.co.uk

Telford (1976)
Great Hay Drive, Sutton Heights, Telford, TF7 4DT
☎ **(01952) 429977**
⌨ (01952) 586602
✉ ibarklem@aol.com
📖 400
⅍ I Lucas (01952) 422960
✓ D Bateman (01952) 586052
▷ 18 L 6741 yds SSS 72
⋈ H SOC
££ On application
⊷ 4 miles SE of Telford, off A442
⊕ Driving range
⌂ John Harris
■ www.telford-golfclub.co.uk

Worfield (1991)
Worfield, Bridgnorth, WV15 5HE
☎ **(01746) 716541**
⌨ (01746) 716302
📖 500
⅍ W Weaver (Gen Mgr) (01746) 716372
✓ S Russell (01746) 716541
▷ 18 L 6660 yds SSS 72
⋈ U SOC
££ £20 (£25)
⊷ 7 miles W of Wolverhampton on A454
⌂ Gough/Williams

Wrekin (1905)
Wellington, Telford, TF6 5BX
☎ **(01952) 244032**
⌨ (01952) 252906
✉ wrekingolfclub@lineone.net
📖 400 100(L) 90(J)
⅍ D Briscoe
✓ K Housden (01952) 223101
▷ 18 L 5657 yds SSS 67
⋈ WD–U before 5pm –M after 5pm SOC
££ £22 (£30)
⊷ Wellington, off B5061

Somerset

Bath (1880)
Sham Castle, North Road, Bath, BA2 6JG
☎ **(01225) 425182**
⌨ (01225) 331027
✉ enquiries@bathgolfclub.org.uk
📖 730
⅍ PE Ware (01225) 463834
✓ P Hancox (01225) 466953
▷ 18 L 6442 yds SSS 71
⋈ H SOC
££ £28 (£34)
⊷ 1¹/₂ miles SE of Bath, off A36
⌂ HS Colt
■ www.bathgolfclub.org.uk

Brean (1973)
Coast Road, Brean, Burnham-on-Sea, TA8 2QY
☎ **(01278) 752111**
⌨ (01278) 752111
✉ golf@brean.com
📖 400
⅍ I Ross (Hon)
✓ D Haines (01278) 752111
▷ 18 L 5565 yds SSS 67
⋈ WD–U WE–pm only SOC
££ £18 (£20)
⊷ 4 miles N of Burnham-on-Sea. M5 Junction 22, 6 miles

Burnham & Berrow (1890)
St Christopher's Way, Burnham-on-Sea, TA8 2PE
☎ **(01278) 783137**
⌨ (01278) 795440
✉ secretary@burnhamandberrow .freeserve.co.uk

📖 800
⅍ JM Harper (01278) 785760
✓ M Crowther-Smith (01278) 784545
▷ 18 L 6606 yds SSS 73
9 L 6332 yds SSS 72
⋈ I H SOC
££ 18 hole:£40 (£60) 9 hole:£12
⊷ 1 mile N of Burnham-on-Sea on B3140. M5 Junction 22
⊕ Dormy House

Cannington (1993)
Pay and play
Cannington College, Bridgwater, TA5 2LS
☎ **(01278) 655050**
⌨ (01278) 652479
📖 200
⅍ R Macrow (Mgr)
✓ R Macrow
▷ 9 L 6072 yds Par 68 SSS 70
⋈ U exc Wed eve–restricted
££ 18 holes–£13 (£16.50) 9 holes–£9 (£11)
⊷ 4 miles NW of Bridgwater on A39. M5 Junction 24
⊕ Driving range
⌂ Hawtree

Clevedon (1891)
Castle Road, Clevedon, BS21 7AA
☎ **(01275) 874057**
⌨ (01275) 341228
📖 800
⅍ J Cunning (01275) 874057
✓ R Scanlan (01275) 874704
▷ 18 L 6557 yds Par 72 SSS 72
⋈ WD–U H exc WE/BH–U H (phone first) SOC–WD
££ £25 (£40)
⊷ Off Holly Lane, Walton, Clevedon. M5 Junction 20
⌂ JH Taylor

Enmore Park (1906)
Enmore, Bridgwater, TA5 2AN
☎ **(01278) 671244 (Members)**
⌨ (01278) 671740
✉ golfclub@enmore.fsnet.co.uk
📖 780
⅍ D Weston (01278) 671481
✓ N Wixon (01278) 671519
▷ 18 L 6411 yds SSS 71
⋈ U SOC–WD
££ £25 (£35)
⊷ 3 miles W of Bridgwater, off Durleigh road. M5 Junctions 23/24
⌂ Hawtree
■ www.golfdirector.com/enmore

Entry Hill (1985)
Public
Entry Hill, Bath, BA2 5NA
☎ **(01225) 834248**
⅍ J Sercombe
✓ T Tapley
▷ 9 L 4206 yds SSS 61
⋈ WD/WE–booking only
££ 18 holes–£10.50. 9 holes–£6.85
⊷ 1 mile S of Bath, off A367

Farrington (1992)
Marsh Lane, Farrington Gurney, Bristol,
BS39 6TS
- ☎ **(01761) 451596**
- 📠 (01761) 451021
- ✉ info@farringtongolfclub.net
- 📖 620
- 🏌 SG Cook (01761) 451596
- ⚐ J Cowgill (01761) 451046
- ⛳ 18 L 6716 yds Par 72 SSS 72
  9 L 3002 yds Par 54 SSS 53
- 👥 WD–U H SOC–WD
- £€ 18 hole:£20 (£30). 9 hole:£6 (£8)
- ⚘ 12 miles S of Bristol (A37). 10
  miles S of Bath (A39)
- ⊕ Floodlit driving range
- 🏠 Peter Thompson

Fosseway CC (1970)
Charlton Lane, Midsomer Norton,
Radstock, BA3 4BD
- ☎ **(01761) 412214**
- 📠 (01761) 418357
- 📖 270
- 🏌 PJ Jordan (Mgr)
- ⛳ 9 L 4565 yds SSS 63
- 👥 WD–U exc Wed–M after 5pm
  WE–NA before 1.30pm
- £€ £15
- ⚘ 10 miles SW of Bath on A367

Frome (1994)
Proprietary
Critchill Manor, Frome, BA11 4LJ
- ☎ **(01373) 453410**
- 📠 (01373) 453410
- ✉ fromegolfclub@yahoo.co.uk
- 📖 400
- 🏌 Mrs S Austin
- ⚐ T Issacs
- ⛳ 18 hole course Par 69 SSS 67
- 👥 U
- £€ £14 D–£19 (£16 D–£20)
- ⚘ 12 miles S of Bath
- ⊕ Driving range
- 🖥 www.fromegolfclub.fsnet.co.uk

Isle of Wedmore (1992)
Lineage, Lascots Hill, Wedmore,
BS28 4QT
- ☎ **(01934) 712452**
- 📠 (01934) 713696
- 📖 600
- 🏌 AC Edwards (01934) 712222
- ⚐ G Coombe (01934) 712452
- ⛳ 18 L 6006 yds Par 70 SSS 69
- 👥 U SOC–WD
- £€ £18 (£22)
- ⚘ ¾ mile N of Wedmore. M5
  Junction 22
- 🏠 Terry Murray

Kingweston (1983)
(Sec) Mead Run, Compton Street,
Compton Dundon, Somerton TA11 6PP
- ☎ **(01458) 43921**
- 📖 200
- 🏌 JG Willetts
- ⛳ 9 L 4516 yds SSS 62
- 👥 M exc Wed & Sat 2–5pm–NA
- £€ NA

⚘ 1 mile SE of Butleigh. 2 miles SE
of Glastonbury

Lansdown (1894)
Lansdown, Bath, BA1 9BT
- ☎ **(01225) 422138**
- 📠 (01225) 339252
- ✉ admin@lansdowngolfclub.co.uk
- 📖 750
- 🏌 Mrs E Bacon
- ⚐ T Mercer (01225) 420242
- ⛳ 18 L 6316 yds SSS 70
- 👥 H SOC
- £€ £22
- ⚘ 2 miles NW of Bath, by racecourse.
  M4 Junction 18, 6 miles
- 🏠 HS Colt
- 🖥 www.lansdowngolfclub.co.uk

Long Sutton (1991)
Pay and play
Long Load, Langport, TA10 9JU
- ☎ **(01458) 241017**
- 📠 (01458) 241022
- 📖 600
- 🏌 GC Bennett
- ⚐ A Hayes
- ⛳ 18 L 6367 yds SSS 71
- 👥 WD–U WE–booking required SOC
- £€ £16 (£20)
- ⚘ 3 miles E of Langport
- ⊕ Floodlit driving range
- 🏠 Patrick Dawson

The Mendip (1908)
Gurney Slade, Radstock, BA3 4UT
- ☎ **(01749) 840570**
- 📠 (01749) 841439
- ✉ secretary@mendipgolfclub.co.uk
- 📖 800
- 🏌 J Scott
- ⚐ A Marsh (01749) 840793
- ⛳ 18 L 6383 yds SSS 71
- 👥 WD–U WE–H SOC–WD
- £€ £24 (£35)
- ⚘ 3 miles N of Shepton Mallet (A37)
- 🏠 CK Cotton
- 🖥 www.mendipgolfclub.co.uk

Mendip Spring (1992)
Honeyhall Lane, Congresbury, BS49 5JT
- ☎ **(01934) 853337/852322**
- 📠 (01934) 853021
- 📖 400
- 🏌 A Melhuish
- ⚐ J Blackburn
- ⛳ 18 L 6334 yds SSS 70
  9 L 4784 yds SSS 66
- 👥 U
- £€ 18 hole:£24 (£35). 9 hole:£8.50 (£9)
- ⚘ Congresbury. M5 Junction 21
- ⊕ Driving range
- 🏠 Langholt

Minehead & West Somerset (1882)
The Warren, Minehead, TA24 5SJ
- ☎ **(01643) 702057**
- 📠 (01643) 705095
- ✉ secretary@mineheadgolf.co.uk

- 📖 604
- 🏌 RAJ Rayner
- ⚐ I Read (01643) 704378
- ⛳ 18 L 6228 yds SSS 70
- 👥 U after 9.30am SOC
- £€ £26 (£30) W–£100
- ⚘ E end of sea front
- 🖥 www.mineheadgolf.co.uk

Oake Manor (1993)
Oake, Taunton, TA4 1BA
- ☎ **(01823) 461993**
- 📠 (01823) 461995
- 📖 600
- 🏌 R Gardner (Golf Mgr)
- ⚐ R Gardner
- ⛳ 18 L 6109 yds Par 70 SSS 69
- 👥 U–phone first SOC
- £€ £19 (£25)
- ⚘ 4 miles W of Taunton, off B3227.
  M5 Junctions 25/26 onto A38
- ⊕ Driving range. Academy course
- 🏠 Adrian Stiff
- 🖥 www.oakemanor.com

Orchardleigh (1996)
Frome, BA11 2PH
- ☎ **(01373) 454200/454206**
  (Bookings)
- 📠 (01373) 454202
- 📖 500
- 🏌 T Atkinson (Mgr)
- ⚐ I Ridsdale
- ⛳ 18 L 6810 yds Par 72 SSS 73
- 👥 WD/BH–U WE–U after 11am SOC
- £€ £25 D–£37.50 (£35)
- ⚘ 2 miles NW of Frome on A362. 12
  miles S of Bath
- ⊕ Practice range
- 🏠 Brian Huggett

Puxton Park (1992)
Pay and play
Puxton, Weston-super-Mare, BS24 6TA
- ☎ **(01934) 876942**
- ⚐ C Ancsell
- ⛳ 18 L 6600 yds Par 72
- 👥 U SOC
- £€ £8 (£10)
- ⚘ A370, 2 miles E of M5 Junction 21

Saltford (1904)
Golf Club Lane, Saltford, Bristol,
BS18 3AA
- ☎ **(01225) 873220**
- 📠 (01225) 873525
- 📖 650
- 🏌 V Radnedge (01225) 873513
- ⚐ D Millensted (01225) 872043
- ⛳ 18 L 6225 yds SSS 70
- 👥 WD–U SOC–Mon & Thurs
- £€ £24
- ⚘ 7 miles SE of Bristol

Stockwood Vale (1991)
Public
Stockwood Lane, Keynsham, Bristol,
BS31 2ER
- ☎ **(0117) 986 6505**
- 📠 (0117) 986 8974
- 📖 500

For list of abbreviations and key to symbols see page 649

M Edenborough
J Richards
18 L 6031 yds SSS 71
U SOC–WD
££ £15 (£17.50)
1 mile SE of Bristol, off A4174
Driving range
Ramsay
www.stockwoodvale.com

Tall Pines (1991)

*Cooks Bridle Path, Downside, Backwell,
Bristol BS48 3DJ*
☎ (01275) 472076
(01275) 474869
500
T Murray
A Murray
18 L 6100yds Par 70 SSS 69
U SOC
££ £18 (£18)
8 miles SW of Bristol (A470/A38)
Terry Murray

Taunton & Pickeridge (1892)

Corfe, Taunton, TA3 7BY
☎ (01823) 421876
(01823) 421742
sec@taunt-pickgolfclub.sagehost
.co.uk
660
MPD Walls (01823) 421537
G Milne (01823) 421790
18 L 5927 yds SSS 68
H SOC
££ £22 (£30)
5 miles S of Taunton on B3170
Hawtree

Taunton Vale (1991)

Creech Heathfield, Taunton, TA3 5EY
☎ (01823) 412220
(01823) 413583
tvgc@easynet.co.uk
750
M Keitch (01823) 412880
18 L 6167 yds Par 70 SSS 69
9 L 2004 yds Par 64 SSS 60
U SOC
££ 18 hole:£20 (£24). 9 hole:£10 (£12)
3 miles N of Taunton, off A361.
M5 Junctions 24/25
Floodlit driving range
John Pyne
www.tauntonvalegolf.co.uk

Tickenham (1991)

*Clevedon Road, Tickenham, Bristol,
BS21 6RY*
☎ (01275) 856626
1250
A Sutcliffe
9 L 2000 yds
U–phone first SOC
££ 18 holes–£10 (£12)
2 miles E of M5 Junction 20 on
B3130, nr Nailsea
Floodlit driving range
Andrew Sutcliffe
www.tickenhamgolf.co.uk

Vivary (1928)

Public
Vivary Park, Taunton, TA1 3JW
☎ (01823) 289274 (Clubhouse)
300
D Pike
D Hawker (01823) 333875
18 L 4620 yds SSS 63
U SOC–WD
££ £8.40
Centre of Taunton
Herbert Fowler

Wells (1893)

East Horrington Road, Wells, BA5 3DS
☎ (01749) 675005
(01749) 675005
750
A Bishop (01749) 679059
18 L 6015 yds SSS 69
WD–U WE–H SOC–WD
££ £20 (£25)
1½ miles E of Wells, off Bath road
(B3139)
Floodlit driving range

Weston-super-Mare (1892)

*Uphill Road North, Weston-super-Mare,
BS23 4NQ*
☎ (01934) 626968
(01934) 621360
752
Mrs K Drake (01934) 626968
M La Band (01934) 633360
18 L 6251 yds SSS 70
H SOC
££ £24 (£35) W–£75
Weston-super-Mare
T Dunn

Wheathill (1993)

Wheathill, Somerton, TA11 7HG
☎ (01963) 240667
(01963) 240230
400
A Lyddon (Sec/Mgr)
A England
18 L 5362 yds SSS 66
4 holes Par 3 course
U SOC
££ £15 (£20)
3 miles W of Castle Cary on B3153

Windwhistle (1932)

Cricket St Thomas, Chard TA20 4DG
☎ (01460) 30231
(01460) 30055
info@windwhistlegolf.co.uk
550
IN Dodd
P Deeprose
18 L 6510 yds SSS 71
U–phone first SOC
££ On application
Windwhistle, 3 miles E of Chard on
A30. M5 Junction 25, 12 miles
Driving range
JH Taylor/L Fisher
www.windwhistlegolf.co.uk

Worlebury (1908)

*Monks Hill, Worlebury, Weston-super-
Mare, BS22 9SX*
☎ (01934) 625789
(01934) 621935
secretary@worleburyg.c.co.uk
640
MW Wake
G Marks (01934) 418473
18 L 5963 yds SSS 69
H SOC–WD
££ £23 (£30)
2 miles NE of Weston, off A370
H Vardon
www.worlebury.g.c.co.uk

Yeovil (1919)

Sherborne Road, Yeovil, BA21 5BW
☎ (01935) 475949 (Clubhouse)
(01935) 411283
720 123(L) 85(J)
GR Dodd (01935) 422965
G Kite (01935) 473763
18 L 6144 yds SSS 70
9 L 4876 yds SSS 65
WD–U H WE/BH–H
(WD/WE–phone Pro) SOC
££ 18 hole:£25 (£30). 9 hole:£18 (£20)
1 mile from Yeovil on A30 to
Sherborne
Fowler/Alison

Staffordshire

Alsager G&CC (1992)

*Audley Road, Alsager, Stoke-on-Trent,
ST7 2UR*
☎ (01270) 875700
(01270) 882207
660
M Davenport
R Brown
18 L 6225 yds SSS 70
WD–U before 5pm –M after 5pm
SOC
££ £25
5 miles W of Crewe. M6 Junction
16
www.alsagergolfclub.com

Aston Wood (1994)

Blake Street, Sutton Coldfield, B74 4EU
☎ (0121) 580 7803
(0121) 353 0354
enquiries@astonwoodgolfclub
.co.uk
850
K Heathcote (0121) 580 7803
S Smith (0121) 580 7801
18 holes Par 71 SSS 71
WD–M before 5pm WE–M SOC
££ £22 (£33)
3 miles NE of Sutton Coldfield on
A4026. M6 Junction 7. M42
Junction 9
Driving range
Alliss/Clarke
www.astonwoodgolfclub.co.uk

For list of abbreviations and key to symbols see page 649

Barlaston (1987)

Meaford Road, Stone, ST15 8UX
- ☎ **(01782) 372867**
- 🖳 (01782) 372867
- 📖 650
- ✎ I Rogers (01782) 372795
- ↱ 18 L 5800 yds SSS 68
- ♙ WD–U WE–NA before 10am
- ££ On application
- ⊶ ½ mile S of Barlaston. M6 Junction 14/15

Beau Desert (1921)

Hazel Slade, Cannock, WS12 5PJ
- ☎ **(01543) 422626/422773**
- 🖳 (01543) 451137
- ✉ bdgc@btconnect.com
- 📖 650
- ✎ JN Bradbury (01543) 422626
- ✎ B Stevens (01543) 422492
- ↱ 18 L 6310 yds Par 70 SSS 71
- ♙ WD–U WE–phone in advance BH–NA SOC
- ££ £40 (£50)
- ⊶ 4 miles NE of Cannock, off A460
- ⊕ Driving range
- ⌂ WH Fowler
- ■ www.bdgc.co.uk

Bloxwich (1924)

136 Stafford Road, Bloxwich, WS3 3PQ
- ☎ **(01922) 476593**
- 🖳 (01922) 493449
- ✉ bloxwich.golf-club@virgin.net
- 📖 700
- ✎ DA Frost (01922) 476593
- ✎ RJ Dance (01922) 476889
- ↱ 18 L 6257 yds SSS 71
- ♙ WD–U WE–M SOC
- ££ £30 (£35)
- ⊶ N of Walsall on A34

Branston G&CC (1975)

Burton Road, Branston, Burton-on-Trent, DE14 3DP
- ☎ **(01283) 543207**
- 🖳 (01283) 566984
- ✉ sales@branston-golf-club.co.uk
- 📖 800
- ✎ G Pyle (Golf Mgr)
- ✎ J Sture
- ↱ 18 L 6697 yds Par 72 SSS 72
- 9 L 1856 yds Par 30
- ♙ WD–U WE–M before noon SOC
- ££ £28 (£40)
- ⊶ ½ mile S of Burton (A38)
- ⊕ Driving range
- ⌂ G Hamshall

Brocton Hall (1894)

Brocton, Stafford, ST17 0TH
- ☎ **(01785) 662627**
- 🖳 (01785) 661591
- 📖 500
- ✎ G Ashley (01785) 661901
- ✎ N Bland (01785) 661485
- ↱ 18 L 6095 yds SSS 69
- ♙ I H SOC
- ££ £33 (£40)
- ⊶ 4 miles SE of Stafford, off A34
- ⌂ Harry Vardon

Burslem (1907)

Wood Farm, High Lane, Stoke-on-Trent, ST6 7JT
- ☎ **(01782) 837006**
- 📖 300
- ✎ Mrs J Mountford (01782) 258028
- ↱ 9 L 5274 yds SSS 66
- ♙ WD–U WE–NA
- ££ £16
- ⊶ Burslem 2 miles

Calderfields (1983)

Aldridge Road, Walsall, WS4 2JS
- ☎ **(01922) 646888 (Clubhouse),**
  (01922) 632243 (Bookings)
- 🖳 (01922) 638787
- 📖 750
- ✎ Mrs K Williams
- ✎ I Roberts (01922) 613675
- ↱ 18 L 6636 yds SSS 72
- ♙ U SOC
- ££ £18
- ⊶ 1 mile N of Walsall (A454). M6 Junction 10
- ⊕ Floodlit driving range
- ■ www.calderfieldsgolf.com

Cannock Park (1993)

Public
Stafford Road, Cannock, WS11 2AL
- ☎ **(01543) 578850**
- 🖳 (01543) 578850
- 📖 230
- ✎ CB Milne (01543) 571091
- ✎ D Dunk
- ↱ 18 L 5149 yds SSS 65
- ♙ U SOC–WD
- ££ £9 (£11)
- ⊶ ½ mile N of Cannock on A34. M6 Junction 11, 2 miles
- ⌂ John Mainland

The Chase (1999)

Pottal Pool Road, Penkridge, ST19 5RN
- ☎ **(01785) 712191**
- 🖳 (01785) 712692
- ✉ tcgc@crownsportsplc.com
- 📖 600
- ✎ M Clarke (01785) 712888
- ✎ A Preston (01785) 712191
- ↱ 18 L 6354 yds Par 72 SSS 72
- ♙ U H
- ££ £16 (£21)
- ⊶ 10 miles S of Stafford, off A449. M6 Junctions 12 & 13
- ⊕ Driving range

The Craythorne (1972)

Craythorne Road, Stretton, Burton-on-Trent, DE13 0AZ
- ☎ **(01283) 564329**
- 🖳 (01283) 511908
- ✉ admin@craythorne.co.uk
- 📖 450
- ✎ AA Wright (Man Dir)
- ✎ S Hadfield (01283) 533745
- ↱ 18 L 5556 yds Par 68 SSS 68
- Pitch & putt course
- ♙ WD–U SOC
- ££ £24 (£30)
- ⊶ Stretton, 1½ miles N of Burton. A38/A5121 Junction

- ⊕ Floodlit driving range
- ■ www.craythorne.co.uk

Dartmouth (1910)

Vale Street, West Bromwich, B71 4DW
- ☎ **(0121) 588 2131**
- 📖 350
- ✎ C Wade
- ✎ S Joyce
- ↱ 9 L 6036 yds SSS 71
- ♙ WD–U WE–M SOC–Tues & Thurs
- ££ D–£20
- ⊶ 1 mile from W Bromwich, behind Churchfields High School. Junction M5/M6

Denstone College

Denstone, Uttoxeter, ST14 5HN
- ☎ **(01889) 590484**
- ✎ M Raisbeck (Mgr)
- ✎ None
- ↱ 9 L 4404 yds Par 64 SSS 62
- ♙ M SOC
- ££ £6
- ⊶ Grounds of Denstone College. 6 miles N of Uttoxeter
- ⌂ MP Raisbeck

Drayton Park (1897)

Drayton Park, Tamworth, B78 3TN
- ☎ **(01827) 251139**
- 🖳 (01827) 284035
- 📖 650
- ✎ DO Winter
- ✎ MW Passmore (01827) 251478
- ↱ 18 L 6473 yds SSS 73
- ♙ WD–H WE/BH–NA SOC–Tues & Thurs
- ££ D–£34
- ⊶ 2 miles S of Tamworth (A4091)
- ⌂ James Braid

Druids Heath (1974)

Stonnall Road, Aldridge, WS9 8JZ
- ☎ **(01922) 455595**
- 🖳 (01922) 452887
- 📖 539 80(L) 50(J)
- ✎ KI Taylor
- ✎ G Williams (01922) 459523
- ↱ 18 L 6661 yds Par 72 SSS 73
- ♙ WD–U WE–NA before 2pm SOC–WD
- ££ £30 (£38)
- ⊶ 6 miles NW of Sutton Coldfield, off A452

Enville (1935)

Highgate Common, Enville, Stourbridge, DY7 5BN
- ☎ **(01384) 872074**
- 🖳 (01384) 873396
- 📖 900
- ✎ RJ Bannister (Sec/Mgr) (01384) 872074
- ✎ S Power (01384) 872585
- ↱ Highgate 18 L 6531 yds SSS 72; Lodge 18 L 6290 yds SSS 70
- ♙ WD–U WE/BH–M H SOC
- ££ £30–£40
- ⊶ 6 miles W of Stourbridge

For list of abbreviations and key to symbols see page 649

Goldenhill (1983)

Public
Mobberley Road, Goldenhill, Stoke-on-Trent, ST6 5SS
☎ **(01782) 784715**
🖷 (01782) 775940
📖 600
🏌 P Jones
⚲ A Clingan
🏴 18 L 5957 yds SSS 68
👤 U SOC–book with Pro
💷 £6 (£7)
🚗 Between Tunstall and Kidsgrove, off A50

Great Barr (1961)

Chapel Lane, Birmingham, B43 7BA
☎ **(0121) 357 1232**
📖 600
🏌 Mrs HK Devey (0121) 358 4376
⚲ R Spragg (0121) 357 5270
🏴 18 L 6459 yds SSS 72
👤 WD–U WE–I (h'cap max 18) SOC
💷 £32
🚗 6 miles NW of Birmingham. M6 Junction 7

Greenway Hall (1908)

Stockton Brook, Stoke-on-Trent, ST9 9LJ
☎ **(01782) 503158**
🖂 jackbarker_greenwayhallgolfclub @hotmail.com
📖 300
🏌 M Armitage
⚲ M Armitage
🏴 18 L 5676 yds SSS 67
👤 U SOC
💷 £10 (£13.50)
🚗 5 miles N of Stoke, off A53
■ www.jackbarker.com

Handsworth (1895)

11 Sunningdale Close, Handsworth Wood, Birmingham, B20 1NP
☎ **(0121) 554 3387**
🖷 (0121) 554 6144
🖂 info@handsworthgolfclub.net
📖 850
🏌 PS Hodnett (Hon)
⚲ L Bashford (0121) 523 3594
🏴 18 L 6267 yds SSS 70
👤 WD–U WE/BH–M SOC
💷 £35
🚗 3 miles NW of Birmingham. M5 Junction 1. M6 Junction 7

Himley Hall (1980)

Public
Himley Hall Park, Dudley, DY3 4DF
☎ **(01902) 895207**
📖 300
🏌 M Harris
⚲ J Nicholls
🏴 9 L 3145 yds SSS 36
   9 hole short course
👤 WD–U WE/BH–restricted
💷 18 holes–£9.50. 9 holes–£6.50
🚗 Grounds of Himley Hall Park. B4176, off A449
🏛 A & K Baker

Ingestre Park (1977)

Ingestre, Stafford, ST18 0RE
☎ **(01889) 270061**
🖂 ipgc@lineone.net
🖷 (01889) 271434
📖 740
🏌 CJ Radmore (Mgr) (01889) 270845
⚲ D Scullion (01889) 270304
🏴 18 L 6268 yds SSS 70
👤 WD–H before 3.30pm WE/BH–M SOC–WD exc Wed
💷 £25 D–£30
🚗 6 miles E of Stafford, off Tixall Road. M6 Junctions 13/14
🏛 Hawtree

Izaak Walton

Cold Norton, Stone, ST15 0NS
☎ **(01785) 760900**
📖 425
🏌 TT Tyler
⚲ J Brown
🏴 18 L 6281 yds SSS 72
👤 U SOC
💷 £15 (£20)
🚗 7 miles NW of Stafford on B5026. M6 Junction 14
⊕ Driving range

Keele Golf Centre (1973)

Public
Keele Road, Newcastle-under-Lyme, ST5 5AB
☎ **(01782) 717417**
🖷 (01782) 712972
🏌 GA Bytheway
⚲ C Smith
🏴 18 L 5822 metres SSS 70
👤 U
💷 £6.50 (£8.40)
🚗 2 miles W of Newcastle on A525, opposite University. M6 Junction 15
⊕ Floodlit driving range
🏛 Hawtree

Lakeside (1969)

Rugeley Power Station, Rugeley, WS15 1PR
☎ **(01889) 575667**
📖 550
🏌 T Moore
🏴 18 L 5765 yds Par 71 SSS 69
👤 M
🚗 2 miles SE of Rugeley on A513

Leek (1892)

Big Birchall, Leek, ST13 5RE
☎ **(01538) 385889**
🖷 (01538) 384535
📖 520 135(L) 65(J)
🏌 JB Cooper (01538) 384779
⚲ I Benson (01538) 384767
🏴 18 L 6218 yds SSS 70
👤 U H before 3pm –M after 3pm SOC–Wed only
💷 £26 (£32)
🚗 1 mile S of Leek on A520

Little Aston (1908)

Streetly, Sutton Coldfield, B74 3AN
☎ **(0121) 353 2066**
🖷 (0121) 580 8387
📖 250
🏌 AE Dibble (Mgr) (0121) 353 2942
⚲ (0121) 353 0330
🏴 18 L 6670 yds SSS 73
👤 H WE–by prior arrangement SOC–WD
💷 £50 D–£60
🚗 4 miles NW of Sutton Coldfield, off A454
🏛 Harry Vardon
■ www.littleastongolf.co.uk

Manor (Kingstone) (1991)

Leese Hill, Kingstone, Uttoxeter, ST14 8QT
☎ **(01889) 563234**
🖷 (01889) 563234
📖 300
🏌 A Campbell
🏴 18 hole course
👤 U
💷 £12 (£20)
🚗 4 miles W of Uttoxeter on A518
🏛 E Anderson

Newcastle-under-Lyme (1908)

Whitmore Road, Newcastle-under-Lyme, ST5 2QB
☎ **(01782) 616583**
🖷 (01782) 617531
📖 575
🏌 KP Geddes (Sec/Mgr) (01782) 617006
⚲ P Symonds (01782) 618526
🏴 18 L 6317 yds SSS 71
👤 WD–U H WE/BH–M SOC
💷 On application
🚗 2 miles SW of Newcastle-under-Lyme on A53

Onneley (1968)

Onneley, Crewe, Cheshire, CW3 5QF
☎ **(01782) 750577**
📖 410
🏌 P Ball (01782) 846759
⚲ None
🏴 13 L 5781 yds SSS 68
👤 WD–U Sat/BH–M Sun–NA SOC–Thurs
💷 D–£20
🚗 8 miles W of Newcastle, off A525
🏛 A Benson

Oxley Park (1913)

Stafford Road, Bushbury, Wolverhampton, WV10 6DE
☎ **(01902) 425892**
🖷 (01902) 712241
🖂 secretary@oxleyparkgolfclub.fsnet .co.uk
📖 550
🏌 RJ Wormstone (01902) 425892
⚲ LA Burlison (01902) 425445
🏴 18 L 6226 yds SSS 71
👤 U SOC

For list of abbreviations and key to symbols see page 649

££ £25 (£25)
🚗 2 miles S of M54 Junction 2, off A449
🏠 HS Colt

Parkhall (1989)
Public
Hulme Road, Weston Coyney, Stoke-on-Trent, ST3 5BH
☎ **(01782) 599584**
🏌 N Worrall (Mgr) (01831) 456409
⛳ A Clingan
🏳 18 L 2335 yds Par 54
👫 WE–booking necessary SOC
££ On application
🚗 3 miles E of Stoke. Longton 1 mile

Penn (1908)
Penn Common, Wolverhampton, WV4 5JN
☎ **(01902) 341142**
🖥 (01902) 620504
📧 secretary@penn-golf.freeserve.co.uk
🏨 650
🏌 MH Jones
⛳ B Burlison (01902) 330472
🏳 18 L 6487 yds SSS 72
👫 WD–U WE–M SOC
££ £20. Nov–Feb £15
🚗 2 miles SW of Wolverhampton, off A449

Perton Park (1990)
Wrottesley Park Road, Perton, Wolverhampton, WV6 7HL
☎ **(01902) 380103/380073**
🖥 (01902) 326219
🏨 300
🏌 E Greenway (Mgr)
⛳ J Harrold (01902) 380073
🏳 18 L 6520 yds SSS 72
👫 U SOC
££ £12 (£18)
🚗 6 miles W of Wolverhampton, off A454
⊕ Driving range

St Thomas's Priory (1995)
Armitage Lane, Armitage, Rugeley, WS15 1ED
☎ **(01543) 491116**
🖥 (01543) 492244
🏨 500
🏌 J Bissell
⛳ RMR O'Hanlon (01543) 492096
🏳 18 L 5969 yds SSS 70
👫 H SOC–WD
££ £20 (£25)
🚗 1 mile SE of Rugeley on A513, opp Ash Tree Inn
🏠 Paul Mulholland
■ www.st-thomass-golfclub.com

Sandwell Park (1895)
Birmingham Road, West Bromwich, B71 4JJ
☎ **(0121) 553 4637**
🖥 (0121) 525 1651
📧 secretary@sandwellparkgolfclub.co.uk

🏨 600
🏌 DA Paterson
⛳ N Wylie (0121) 553 4384
🏳 18 L 6468 yds SSS 73
👫 WD–U WE–MH SOC–WD
££ £30–£40
🚗 West Bromwich/Birmingham boundary. By M5 Junction 1
🏠 HS Colt
■ www.sandwellparkgolfclub.co.uk

Sedgley (1992)
Pay and play
Sandyfields Road, Sedgley, Dudley, DY3 3DL
☎ **(01902) 880503**
📧 info@sedgleygolf.co.uk
🏨 150
🏌 JA Cox
⛳ G Mercer
🏳 9 L 3150 yds SSS 71
👫 U
££ 9 holes–£6. 18 holes–£8
🚗 ¹/₂ mile from Sedgley, off A463 between Dudley and Wolverhampton
⊕ Driving range
🏠 WG Cox
■ www.sedgleygolf.co.uk

Seedy Mill (1991)
Pay and play
Elmhurst, Lichfield, WS13 8HE
☎ **(01543) 417333**
🖥 (01543) 418098
📧 k.denver@clubhaus.com
🏨 1100
🏌 R Gee
⛳ C Stanley
🏳 18 L 6305 yds SSS 70
9 hole Par 3 course
👫 WD–U WE–U after 12 noon SOC
££ £23 (£28)
🚗 2 miles N of Lichfield on A515
⊕ Floodlit driving range
🏠 Hawtree
■ www.clubhaus.com

South Staffordshire (1892)
Danescourt Road, Tettenhall, Wolverhampton, WV6 9BQ
☎ **(01902) 754406**
🖥 (01902) 741753
📧 manager@ssgc.fsnet.co.uk
🏨 550
🏌 WR Benton (Mgr) (01902) 751065
⛳ M Sparrow (01902) 754816
🏳 18 L 6500 yds SSS 71
👫 WD–U WE/BH–M or by arrangement SOC
££ £36 D–£42 (£50)
🚗 3 miles W of Wolverhampton, off A41
🏠 Harry Vardon

Stafford Castle (1906)
Newport Road, Stafford, ST16 1BP
☎ **(01785) 223821**
🏨 440
🏌 Mrs S Calvert
🏳 9 L 6382 yds Par 71 SSS 70

👫 WD–U WE–after 1pm
££ £16 (£20)
🚗 ¹/₂ mile W of Stafford

Stone (1896)
The Fillybrooks, Stone, ST15 0NB
☎ **(01785) 813103**
🏨 314
🏌 PR Farley (01785) 284875
🏳 9 L 6299 yds Par 71 SSS 70
👫 WD–U WE/BH–M SOC–WD
££ £20
🚗 ¹/₂ mile W of Stone on A34

Swindon (1976)
Bridgnorth Road, Swindon, Dudley, DY3 4PU
☎ **(01902) 897031**
🖥 (01902) 326219
🏨 500
🏌 E Greenway (Mgr)
⛳ P Lester (01902) 896191
🏳 18 L 6121 yds SSS 70
9 hole Par 3 course
👫 U SOC–WD
££ £20 (£30)
🚗 5 miles SW of Wolverhampton on B4176
⊕ Driving range

Tamworth (1976)
Public
Eagle Drive, Amington, Tamworth, B77 4EG
☎ **(01827) 709303**
🖥 (01827) 709304
🏨 500
⛳ W Allcock
🏳 18 L 6695 yds SSS 72
👫 U SOC–WD
££ £13
🚗 2¹/₂ miles E of Tamworth on B5000. M42, 3 miles
⊕ Driving range

Trentham (1894)
14 Barlaston Old Road, Trentham, Stoke-on-Trent, ST4 8HB
☎ **(01782) 642347**
🖥 (01782) 644024
📧 secretary@trenthamgolf.org
🏨 420
🏌 RN Portas (01782) 658109
⛳ S Wilson (01782) 657309
🏳 18 L 6644 yds SSS 72
👫 WD–U H WE/BH–M (or enquire Sec) SOC–WD
££ £40 (£50)
🚗 3 miles S of Newcastle-under-Lyme on A5305, off A34. M6 Junction 15
■ www.trenthamgolf.org

Trentham Park (1936)
Trentham Park, Stoke-on-Trent, ST4 8AE
☎ **(01782) 642245**
🖥 (01782) 658800
📧 trevor.berrisford@barbox.net
🏨 500 100(L) 50(J)
🏌 T Berrisford (01782) 658800
⛳ B Rimmer (01782) 642125
🏳 18 L 6425 yds SSS 71

H SOC–Wed & Fri
££ £25 (£32)
4 miles S of Newcastle on A34. M6 Junction 15, 1 mile

Uttoxeter (1970)

Wood Lane, Uttoxeter, ST14 8JR
(01889) 566552
(01889) 567501
700
A Griffiths
AD McCandless (01889) 564884
18 L 5801 yds Par 70 SSS 69
WD–U WE–by arrangement SOC
££ D–£20 (£30)
Close to A50, by Uttoxeter racecourse

Walsall (1907)

Broadway, Walsall, WS1 3EY
(01922) 613512
(01922) 616460
600
JK Harding (01922) 613512
R Lambert (01922) 626766
18 L 6259 yds SSS 71
WD–U WE–M SOC
££ £33
1 mile S of Walsall, off A34. M6 Junction 7
McKenzie

Wergs (1990)

Pay and play
Keepers Lane, Tettenhall, WV6 8UA
(01902) 742225
(01902) 744748
150
Mrs G Parsons
S Weir (07973) 899607
18 L 6949 yds Par 72 SSS 73
U
££ D–£15 (£20)
3 miles W of Wolverhampton on A41
CW Moseley

Westwood (1923)

Newcastle Road, Wallbridge, Leek, ST13 7AA
(01538) 398385
(01538) 382485
800
C Plant
D Squire
18 L 6207 yds SSS 70
U SOC–WD
££ WD–£18
W boundary of Leek on A53

Whiston Hall (1971)

Whiston, Cheadle, ST10 2HZ
(01538) 266260
500
LC & RM Cliff (Mgr)
18 L 5742 yds SSS 69
U SOC
££ £10
8 miles NE of Stoke-on-Trent on A52, nr Alton Towers

Whittington Heath (1886)

Tamworth Road, Lichfield, WS14 9PW
(01543) 432317 (Admin),
(01543) 432212 (Steward)
(01543) 433962
670
Mrs JA Burton
AR Sadler (01543) 432261
18 L 6490 yds SSS 71
WD–H or I WE/BH–M SOC–Wed & Thurs
££ £35 D–£50
2¹/₂ miles E of Lichfield on Tamworth road (A51)

Wolstanton (1904)

Dimsdale Old Hall, Hassam Parade, Wolstanton, Newcastle ST5 9DR
(01782) 616995
625
Mrs VJ Keenan (01782) 622413
S Arnold (01782) 622718
18 L 5807 yds SSS 68
WD–H WE–M SOC–WD
££ £25
1¹/₂ miles NW of Newcastle (A34)

Suffolk

Aldeburgh (1884)

Aldeburgh, IP15 5PE
(01728) 452890
(01728) 452937
879
GM Gadney
K Preston (01728) 453309
18 L 6323 yds Par 68 SSS 71
9 L 2114 yds SSS 64
H–2 ball play only SOC
££ On application
6 miles E of A12 (A1094)
W Fernie/J Thompson
www.aldeburghgolfclub.co.uk

Beccles (1899)

The Common, Beccles, NR34 9BX
(01502) 712244
150
DW Trunks (01502) 714616
9 L 2696 yds SSS 67
WD–U Sun–M SOC
££ £5 (£10)
10 miles W of Lowestoft (A146)

Brett Vale (1992)

Noakes Road, Raydon, Ipswich, IP7 5LR
(01473) 310718
(01473) 312270
620
JS Reid
P Bate
18 L 5797 yds Par 70 SSS 67
U–booking advisable. Soft spikes only. SOC–WD
££ £20 (£25)
5 miles N of Colchester, off A12 (B1070), towards Hadleigh
Driving range. 3 x 3 Par 3 holes
Howard Swan
www.brettvale.com

Bungay & Waveney Valley (1889)

Outney Common, Bungay, NR35 1DS
(01986) 892337
(01986) 892222
bury.golf@talk21.com
673
JF Taylor
N Whyte
18 L 6044 yds Par 69 SSS 69
WD–U WE–M SOC–WD
££ £24 D–£30
¹/₂ mile W of Bungay, on N side of A143
James Braid

Bury St Edmunds (1922)

Tut Hill, Bury St Edmunds, IP28 6LG
(01284) 755979
(01284) 763288
750 180(L)
JC Sayer
M Jillings (01284) 755978
18 L 6669 yds Par 72 SSS 72
9 L 2217 yds Par 31 SSS 31
WD/BH–U WE–M SOC–WD
££ 18 hole:£25 9 hole:£12 (£15)
2 miles W of Bury St Edmunds on B1106, off A14
Ted Ray
www.club-noticeboard.co.uk /burystedmunds

Cretingham (1984)

Grove Farm, Cretingham, Woodbridge, IP13 7BA
(01728) 685275
(01728) 685037
300
Mrs K Jackson
N Jackson
9 L 4969 yds Par 33
9 hole short course
U SOC
££ 18 holes–£14 (£16)
2 miles SE of Earl Soham. 11 miles N of Ipswich
Practice range
J Austin

Diss (1903)

Stuston Common, Diss, IP21 4AA
(01379) 641025
(01379) 644586
sec.dissgolf@virgin.net
750
C Wellstead (01379) 641025
N Taylor (01379) 644399
18 L 6206 yds Par 70 SSS 69
WD–UH WE–phone first SOC
££ £25
1 mile SE of Diss, off A140

Felixstowe Ferry (1880)

Ferry Road, Felixstowe, IP4 9RY
(01394) 283060
(01394) 273679
secretary@felixstowegolf.co.uk
1000
R Tibbs (01394) 286834
I Macpherson (01394) 283975

⛳ 18 L 6308 yds SSS 70
9 L 2986 yds Par 35
👥 WD–H after 9am WE–H after 2.30pm SOC. 9 hole course–U
££ 18 hole: £18 (£30). 9 hole: £9 (£10)
🚗 2 miles NE of Felixstowe, towards Ferry
🏠 Henry Cotton (1947)
■ www.felixstowegolf.co.uk

Flempton (1895)
Bury St Edmunds, IP28 6HQ
☎ (01284) 728291
📖 250
✍ JF Taylor
✓ M Jillings
⛳ 9 L 6240 yds SSS 70
👥 WD–H WE/BH–M
££ D–£35 (£35)
🚗 4 miles NW of Bury St Edmunds on A1101
🏠 JH Taylor

Fynn Valley (1991)
Proprietary
Witnesham, Ipswich, IP6 9JA
☎ (01473) 785267
🖳 (01473) 785632
📧 enquiries@fynn-valley.co.uk
📖 650
✍ AR Tyrrell (01473) 785267
✓ K Vince (01473) 785463
⛳ 18 L 6361 yds Par 70 SSS 71
9 hole Par 3 course
👥 U exc Sun am SOC
££ £22 (£25)
🚗 2 miles N of Ipswich on B1077
⊕ Driving range
🏠 AR Tyrrell
■ www.fynn-valley.co.uk

Halesworth (1990)
Bramfield Road, Halesworth, IP19 9XA
☎ (01986) 875567
🖳 (01986) 874565
📖 400
✓ R Whyte
⛳ 18 L 6383 yds SSS 72
9 hole course SSS 33
👥 H SOC
££ 18 hole:£15 D–£19 (£21) 9 hole:£7.50
🚗 1 mile S of Halesworth, off A144
⊕ Floodlit driving range
🏠 JW Johnson

Haverhill (1974)
Coupals Road, Haverhill, CB9 7UW
☎ (01440) 761951
🖳 (01440) 761951
📧 haverhillgolf@coupalsroad.fsnet.co.uk
📖 700
✍ Mrs J Edwards, D Renyard (Mgr)
✓ N Duc (01440) 712628
⛳ 18 L 5929 yds SSS 70
👥 U–phone Pro SOC–WD
££ £25 (£30)
🚗 1 mile E of Haverhill, off A1107
🏠 Lawrie/Pilgrem
■ www.club-noticeboard.co.uk

Hintlesham Hall (1991)
Hintlesham, Ipswich, IP8 3NS
☎ (01473) 652761
🖳 (01473) 652750
📧 office@hintleshamhallgolfclub.com
📖 475
✍ I Procter (Mgr)
✓ A Spink
⛳ 18 L 6638 yds SSS 72
👥 WD–U after 10.30am WE–NA SOC
££ £34 – £42
🚗 4 miles W of Ipswich on A1071
🏠 Hawtree

Ipswich (Purdis Heath) (1895)
Purdis Heath, Bucklesham Road, Ipswich, IP3 8UQ
☎ (01473) 727474 (Steward)
🖳 (01473) 715236
📖 740
✍ NM Ellice (01473) 728941
✓ SJ Whymark (01473) 724017
⛳ 18 L 6435 yds Par 71 SSS 71
9 L 1930 yds Par 31
👥 18 hole:H SOC 9 hole:U
££ 18 hole:£40 (£43) 9 hole:£12.50
🚗 3 miles E of Ipswich
🏠 James Braid
■ www.ipswichgolfclub.com

Links (Newmarket) (1902)
Cambridge Road, Newmarket, CB8 0TG
☎ (01638) 663000
🖳 (01638) 661476
📧 secretary@linksgc.fsbusiness.co.uk
📖 750
✍ ML Hartley
✓ J Sharkey (01638) 662395
⛳ 18 L 6424 yds SSS 72
👥 H exc Sun–M before 11.30am SOC
££ £24 D–£32 (£28 D–£36)
🚗 1 mile SW of Newmarket

Newton Green (1907)
Newton Green, Sudbury, CO10 0QN
☎ (01787) 77501
📖 650
✍ K Mazdon (01787) 377217
✓ T Cooper (01787) 313215
⛳ 18 L 5893 yds SSS 69
👥 WD–U WE–M SOC
££ £15.50
🚗 4 miles S of Sudbury on A134

Rookery Park (1891)
Carlton Colville, Lowestoft, NR33 8HJ
☎ (01502) 560380
🖳 (01502) 560380
📖 1000
✍ T Atkinson
✓ M Elsworthy (01502) 515103
⛳ 18 L 6714 yds SSS 72
9 hole Par 3 course
👥 WD–U Sat/BH–after 11am Sun–NA SOC
££ £25 (£30)
🚗 3 miles W of Lowestoft (A146)

Royal Worlington & Newmarket (1893)
Golf Links Road, Worlington, Bury St Edmunds, IP28 8SD
☎ (01638) 712216 (Clubhouse)
🖳 (01638) 717787
📖 325
✍ KJ Weston (01638) 717787
✓ M Hawkins (01638) 715224
⛳ 9 L 6210 yds SSS 70
👥 I or H–phone first (2 ball or foursomes only) WE–NA
££ D–£50. After 2pm–£37
🚗 6 miles NE of Newmarket, off A11
🏠 Tom Dunn

Rushmere (1927)
Rushmere Heath, Ipswich, IP4 5QQ
☎ (01473) 725648
🖳 (01473) 273852
📖 770
✍ AN Harris (01473) 725648
✓ NTJ McNeill (01473) 728076
⛳ 18 L 6262 yds SSS 70
👥 WD–H WE/BH–H after 2.30pm
££ £25
🚗 3 miles E of Ipswich, off Woodbridge road (A1214)
🏠 David Williams (1999)

Seckford (1991)
Seckford Hall Road, Great Bealings, Woodbridge, IP13 6NT
☎ (01394) 388000
🖳 (01394) 382818
📧 info@seckfordgolf.co.uk
📖 400
✍ N Gruntvig (Sec/Mgr)
✓ S Jay
⛳ 18 L 5392 yds Par 68 SSS 66
👥 U–booking necessary SOC
££ £19 (£25)
🚗 SW of Woodbridge, off A12
■ www.seckfordgolf.co.uk

Southwold (1884)
The Common, Southwold, IP18 6TB
☎ (01502) 723234
📖 450
✍ PJ Obern (01502) 723248
✓ B Allen (01502) 723790
⛳ 9 L 6050 yds SSS 69
👥 U (subject to fixtures)
££ £26 (£28)
🚗 35 miles NE of Ipswich

Stoke-by-Nayland (1972)
Keepers Lane, Leavenheath, Colchester, CO6 4PZ
☎ (01206) 262836
🖳 (01206) 263356
📧 info@golf-club.co.uk
📖 1400
✍ PG Barfield (01206) 265815
✓ K Lovelock (01206) 262769
⛳ Gainsborough 18 L 6498 yds SSS 71;
Constable 18 L 6544 yds SSS 71
👥 WD–U WE/BH–H after 10am SOC
££ £25 (£35)
🚗 Off A134 Colchester-Sudbury road on B1068

⊕ Driving range
■ www.stokebynaylandclub.co.uk

Stowmarket (1962)
Lower Road, Onehouse, Stowmarket, IP14 3DA
☎ (01449) 736392
🖷 (01449) 736826
▦ 600
🏌 GR West (01449) 736473
✓ D Burl
⊳ 18 L 6119 yds SSS 69
👤 H SOC–Thurs & Fri
£€ £28 (£34)
🚗 2¹/₂ miles SW of Stowmarket
⊕ Driving range
■ www.club-noticeboard.co.uk/stowmarket

The Suffolk G&CC (1974)
Fornham St Genevieve, Bury St Edmunds, IP28 6JQ
☎ (01284) 706777
🖷 (01284) 706721
✉ the-lodge@the-suffolk.co.uk
▦ 600
🏌 M Aho
✓ S Hall
⊳ 18 L 6376 yds SSS 71
👤 U SOC
£€ £25 (£30)
🚗 2 miles NW of Bury St Edmunds, off B1106
■ www.the-suffolk.co.uk

Thorpeness Hotel (1923)
Thorpeness, Leiston, IP16 4NH
☎ (01728) 452176
🖷 (01728) 453868
▦ 300
🏌 J Montague
✓ (01728) 454926
⊳ 18 L 6281 yds SSS 71
👤 U
£€ £32 (£37)
🚗 2 miles N of Aldeburgh
🏠 James Braid
■ www.thorpeness.co.uk

Ufford Park Hotel (1992)
Yarmouth Road, Ufford, Woodbridge, IP12 1QW
☎ (01394) 382836
🖷 (01394) 383582
▦ 350
🏌 B Tidy
✓ S Robertson
⊳ 18 L 6485 yds SSS 71
👤 U H SOC
£€ £25 (£30)
🚗 2 miles N of Woodbridge, off A12
⊕ Golf Academy
🏠 P Pilgrim
■ www.uffordpark.co.uk

Waldringfield Heath (1983)
Newbourne Road, Waldringfield, Woodbridge, IP12 4PT
☎ (01473) 736768
🖷 (01473) 736436
▦ 640

🏌 LJ McWade
✓ R Mann, A Lucas (01473) 736417
⊳ 18 L 6141 yds SSS 69
👤 WD–U WE/BH–M before noon SOC–WD
£€ On application
🚗 3 miles E of Ipswich, off A12
🏠 P Pilgrem

Woodbridge (1893)
Bromeswell Heath, Woodbridge, IP12 2PF
☎ (01394) 382038
🖷 (01394) 382392
✉ woodbridgegc@anglianet.co.uk
▦ 925
🏌 A Theunissen
✓ C Elliott (01394) 383213
⊳ 18 L 6299 yds SSS 70
9 L 6382 yds SSS 70
👤 WD–H WE/BH–M SOC
£€ 18 hole:£40. 9 hole:£18
🚗 2 miles E of Woodbridge on A1152 towards Orford
🏠 F Hawtree

Surrey

Abbey Moor (1991)
Pay and play
Green Lane, Addlestone, KT15 2XU
☎ (01932) 570741/570765
▦ 300
🏌 T Stannard (01932) 561313
✓ P Trigwell (01932) 570741
⊳ 9 L 5277 yds Par 68
👤 U
£€ £9.50 (£11)
🚗 Nr M25 Junction 11, off A318
🏠 D Walker

The Addington (1913)
205 Shirley Church Road, Croydon, CR0 5AB
☎ (020) 8777 1055
🖷 (020) 8777 1701
✉ theaddgc@dialstart.net
🏌 RAR Hill
⊳ 18 L 6338 yds SSS 71
👤 H SOC–WD
£€ On application
🚗 E Croydon 2¹/₂ miles
🏠 JF Abercromby

Addington Court (1931)
Pay and play
Featherbed Lane, Addington, Croydon, CR0 9AA
☎ (020) 8657 0281 (Bookings)
🖷 (020) 8651 0282
✉ addington@americangolf.uk.com
▦ 600
🏌 T O'Keefe (020) 8651 5270
✓ T O'Keefe (020) 8657 0281
⊳ Championship 18 L 5577 yds SSS 67
Falconwood 18 L 5472 yds SSS 67
9 L 1804 yds SSS 62
18 hole pitch & putt course
👤 U SOC

£€ Championship £16.35 (£19.60)
Falconwood £14.35 (£17.60)
9 hole:£9 (£10)
🚗 3 miles SE of Croydon
⊕ Driving range
🏠 F Hawtree Sr

Addington Palace (1923)
Addington Park, Gravel Hill, Addington, CR0 5BB
☎ (020) 8654 3061
🖷 (020) 8655 3632
▦ 700
🏌 DMG Monk
✓ R Williams (020) 8654 1786
⊳ 18 L 6410 yds SSS 71
👤 WD–H WE/BH–M
£€ £35 D–£40
🚗 2 miles E of Croydon Station

Banstead Downs (1890)
Burdon Lane, Belmont, Sutton, SM2 7DD
☎ (020) 8642 2284
🖷 (020) 8642 5252
▦ 700
🏌 RHA Steele
✓ I Golding (020) 8642 6884
⊳ 18 L 6194 yds SSS 69
👤 WD–H WE/BH–M SOC–Thurs
£€ £35 After 12 noon–£25
🚗 1 mile S of Sutton

Barrow Hills (1970)
Longcross, Chertsey, KT16 0DS
☎ (01344) 635770
▦ 230
🏌 R Hammond (01483) 234807
⊳ 18 L 3090 yds SSS 53
👤 M
£€ On application
🚗 4 miles W of Chertsey

Betchworth Park (1911)
Reigate Road, Dorking, RH4 1NZ
☎ (01306) 882052
🖷 (01306) 877462
✉ manager@betchworthparkgc.co.uk
▦ 725
🏌 J Holton (Mgr)
✓ A Tocher (01306) 884334
⊳ 18 L 6266 yds SSS 70
👤 WD–by arrangement exc Tues & Wed am WE–NA exc Sun pm SOC–Mon & Thurs
£€ £34 (£45)
🚗 1 mile E of Dorking on A25
🏠 HS Colt

Bletchingley (1993)
Church Lane, Bletchingley, RH1 4LP
☎ (01883) 744666
🖷 (01883) 744284
▦ 550
🏌 Mrs N Robinson (Mgr)
✓ A Dyer (01883) 744848
⊳ 18 L 6504 yds Par 72 SSS 71
👤 WD–U WE–M before 2.15pm SOC
£€ £25 (£30)
🚗 1 mile S of M25 Junction 6 on A25
🏠 Paul Wright
■ www.bletchingleygolfclub.co.uk

Bowenhurst Golf Centre

Mill Lane, Crondall, Farnham,
GU10 5RP
☎ **(01252) 851695**
🖳 (01252) 852039
📖 202
🏌 GL Corbey (01252) 851695
⛳ A Carter (01252) 851344
🏴 9 L 2007 yds Par 62 SSS 60
👥 U SOC
££ 18 holes–£11 (£14). 9 holes–£8
   (£9.50)
🚗 2 miles SW of Farnham on A287.
   M3 Junction 5
⊕ Driving range
🏠 G Finn, N Finn

Bramley (1913)

Bramley, Guildford, GU5 0AL
☎ **(01483) 892696**
🖳 (01483) 894673
📧 secretary@bramleygolfclub.co.uk
📖 800
🏌 Ms M Lambert (01483) 892696
⛳ G Peddie (01483) 893685
🏴 18 L 5990 yds SSS 69
👥 WD–U WE–M SOC–WD
££ £30 D–£35
🚗 3 miles S of Guildford on A281
⊕ Driving range – members and green
   fees only
🏠 Mayo/Braid

Broadwater Park

Guildford Road, Farncombe,
Godalming, GU7 3BU
☎ **(01483) 429955**
📖 126
🏌 RJ Ashby
⛳ KD Milton
🏴 9 L 1301 yds Par 27
👥 U
££ £5.25 (£6)
🚗 1 mile SE of Godalming (A3100)
🏠 KD Milton

Burhill (1907)

Burwood Road, Walton-on-Thames,
KT12 4BL
☎ **(01932) 227345**
🖳 (01932) 267159
📖 1100
🏌 D Cook (Gen Mgr)
⛳ L Johnson (01932) 221729
🏴 Old 18 L 6479 yds SSS 71
   New 18 L 6597 yds SSS 71
👥 WD–H WE/BH–M
££ On application
🚗 Between Walton-on-Thames and
   Cobham, off Burwood Road
⊕ Game Improvement Centre
🏠 Willie Park/Gidman

Camberley Heath (1912)

Golf Drive, Camberley, GU15 1JG
☎ **(01276) 23258**
🖳 (01276) 692505
📖 725
🏌 J Greenwood
⛳ G Ralph (01276) 27905
🏴 18 L 6326 yds SSS 71

👥 WD–H WE–M SOC H
££ On application
🚗 1½ miles S of Camberley on A325
🏠 HS Colt

Central London Golf Centre (1992)

Public
Burntwood Lane, Wandsworth, London,
SW17 0AT
☎ **(020) 8871 2468**
🖳 (020) 8874 7447
📖 200
🏌 J Robson
⛳ J Robson
🏴 9 L 4658 yds SSS 62
👥 U SOC
££ £9 (£11)
🚗 Off Burntwood Lane SW17
⊕ Driving range
🏠 Patrick Tallack
■ www.clgc.co.uk

Chessington Golf Centre (1983)

Pay and play
Garrison Lane, Chessington KT9 2LW
☎ **(020) 8391 0948**
🖳 (020) 8397 2068
📧 info@chessingtongolf.co.uk
📖 85
🏌 M Bedford
⛳ M Janes
🏴 9 L 1679 yds Par 60 SSS 55
👥 U
££ £7.50 (£9)
🚗 Off A243, opp Chessington South
   Station. M25 Junction 9
⊕ Driving range

Chiddingfold (1994)

Petworth Road, Chiddingfold, GU8 4SL
☎ **(01428) 685888**
🖳 (01428) 685939
📖 400
🏌 Miss C Mentz (Gen Mgr)
⛳ G Wallis
🏴 18 L 5482 yds Par 70 SSS 67
👥 U SOC
££ £16 (£22)
🚗 On A283 between Petworth and
   Guildford
🏠 Johnathan Gaunt

Chipstead (1906)

How Lane, Chipstead, Coulsdon,
CR5 3LN
☎ **(01737) 555781**
🖳 (01737) 555404
📧 office@chipsteadgolf.co.uk
📖 600
🏌 Mrs SA Wallace
   (Admin) (01737) 555781
⛳ G Torbett
   (Golf Dir) (01737) 554939
🏴 18 L 5450 yds SSS 67
👥 WD–U WE/BH–M
££ £30. After 4pm–£20
🚗 M25 Junction 8 (A217)
■ www.chipsteadgolf.co.uk

Chobham (1994)

Chobham Road, Knaphill, Woking,
GU21 2TZ
☎ **(01276) 855584**
🖳 (01276) 855663
📖 750
🏌 C Kennedy
⛳ T Coombes (01276) 855748
🏴 18 L 5959 yds Par 69 SSS 69
👥 M H–restricted SOC
££ £36
🚗 3 miles E of M3 Junction 3 between
   Chobham and Knaphill (A3046)
🏠 Alliss/Clark
■ www.chobhamgolfclub.co.uk

Clandon Regis (1994)

Epsom Road, West Clandon, GU4 7TT
☎ **(01483) 224888**
🖳 (01483) 211781
📧 office@clandonregis-golfclub.co.uk
📖 650
🏌 Mrs WR Savage
⛳ S Lloyd (01483) 223922
🏴 18 L 6419 yds Par 72 SSS 71
👥 WD–U WE–NA before 10.30am
   SOC–WD
££ £25 (£35)
🚗 3 miles E of Guildford on A246
🏠 David Williams
■ www.clandonregis-golfclub.co.uk

Coombe Hill (1911)

Golf Club Drive, Coombe Lane West,
Kingston, KT2 7DF
☎ **(020) 8336 7600**
🖳 (020) 8336 7601
📖 553
🏌 Mrs C De Foy
⛳ C De Foy (020) 8949 3713
🏴 18 L 6293 yds SSS 71
👥 WD–I or H WE–NA SOC
££ £60 D–£80
🚗 1 mile W of New Malden on A238
🏠 JF Abercromby
■ www.coombehillgolfclub.com

Coombe Wood (1904)

George Road, Kingston Hill, Kingston-
upon-Thames, KT2 7NS
☎ **(020) 8942 3828 (Clubhouse)**
🖳 (020) 8942 0388
📧 cwoodgc@ukonline.co.uk
📖 580
🏌 PM Urwin (020) 8942 0388
⛳ D Butler (020) 8942 6764
🏴 18 L 5299 yds SSS 66
👥 WD–U WE–NA before 1pm
   SOC–WD
££ £25 (£35)
🚗 1 mile E of Kingston-upon-Thames,
   off A3 at Robin Hood roundabout
   or Coombe junction
🏠 Williamson

Coulsdon Manor (1937)

Pay and play
Coulsdon Court Road, Old Coulsdon,
Croydon, CR5 2LL
☎ **(020) 8660 6083**
🖳 (020) 8668 3118

☎ D Copsey (020) 8660 6083
🖥 18 L 6037 yds SSS 70
👤 U
💶 £13.50 (£16.75)
🚗 5 miles S of Croydon on B2030.
M25 Junction 7
🏠 HS Colt

The Cranleigh (1985)

Barhatch Lane, Cranleigh, GU6 7NG
☎ **(01483) 268855**
🖥 (01483) 267251
📖 650
🏌 MG Kateley
⚐ T Longmuir (01483) 277188
🏳 18 L 5648 yds SSS 67
👤 WD–U WE/BH–pm only
SOC–WD
💶 £24 (£26)
🚗 1 mile from Cranleigh, off A281
⊕ Driving range

Croham Hurst (1911)

Croham Road, South Croydon, CR2 7HJ
☎ **(020) 8657 5581**
🖥 (020) 8657 3229
📧 secretary@chgc.co.uk
📖 515 110(L) 50(J)
🏌 DS Free
⚐ E Stillwell (020) 8657 7705
🏳 18 L 6290 yds SSS 70
👤 WD–I WE/BH–M
💶 £40 (£50)
🚗 1 mile from S Croydon. M25
Junction 6-A22-B270-B269
🏠 Braid/Hawtree
■ www.chgc.co.uk

Cuddington (1929)

Banstead Road, Banstead, SM7 1RD
☎ **(020) 8393 0951**
🖥 (020) 8786 7025
📖 760
🏌 DM Scott (020) 8393 0952
⚐ M Warner (020) 8393 5850
🏳 18 L 6614 yds SSS 71
👤 WD–I WE–M
💶 £40 (£50)
🚗 Nr Banstead Station
🏠 HS Colt

Dorking (1897)

*Deepdene Avenue, Chart Park, Dorking,
RH5 4BX*
☎ **(01306) 886917**
🖥 (01306) 886917
📖 360
🏌 P Napier (Mgr)
⚐ P Napier
🏳 9 L 5163 yds SSS 65
👤 WD–U WE/BH–M SOC–WD
💶 £14
🚗 1 mile S of Dorking on A24
🏠 James Braid

Drift (1976)

The Drift, East Horsley, KT24 5HD
☎ **(01483) 284641**
🖥 (01483) 284642
📖 700
🏌 G Backett (Sec/Mgr)

⚐ L Greasley (01483) 284772
🏳 18 L 6425 yds SSS 72
👤 WD–U WE–U after 3pm SOC
💶 £30 (£45)
🚗 2 miles off A3 (B2039). M25
Junction 10
⊕ Driving range
🏠 Robert Sandow

Dulwich & Sydenham Hill (1894)

*Grange Lane, College Road, London,
SE21 7LH*
☎ **(020) 8693 3961**
🖥 (020) 8693 2481
📧 secretary@dulwichgolf.co.uk
📖 850
🏌 BW O'Farrell
⚐ D Baillie (020) 8693 8491
🏳 18 L 6051 yds SSS 69
👤 WD–H WE/BH–M SOC
💶 £30

Dunsfold Aerodrome (1965)

*Dunsfold Aerodrome, Godalming,
GU8 4BS*
☎ **(01483) 265403**
🖥 (01483) 265670
📖 270
🏌 F Tuck
⚐ None
🏳 9 L 6236 yds Par 72 SSS 70
👤 M
💶 £6 (£6)
🚗 10 miles S of Guildford, off A281
🏠 Sharkey/Hayward

Effingham (1927)

Guildford Road, Effingham, KT24 5PZ
☎ **(01372) 452203**
🖥 (01372) 459959
📧 secretary@effinghamgolfclub.com
📖 980
🏌 S Sheppard
⚐ S Hoatson (01372) 452606
🏳 18 L 6524 yds SSS 71
👤 WD–H WE/BH–M
💶 £35 – £45
🚗 8 miles E of Guildford on A246.
M25 Junctions 9 or 10
🏠 HS Colt

Epsom (1889)

*Longdown Lane South, Epsom Downs,
Epsom, KT17 4JR*
☎ **(01372) 721666**
🖥 (01372) 817183
📖 800
🏌 LR Anderson
⚐ R Goudie (01372) 741867
🏳 18 L 5658 yds SSS 68
👤 WD–U exc Tues am WE/BH–NA
before noon SOC
💶 £29 (£32)
🚗 ³/₄ mile NE of Epsom Racecourse

Farleigh Court (1997)

Proprietary
Old Farleigh Road, Farleigh, CR6 9PX
☎ **(01883) 627733 (Bookings)**

🖥 (01883) 627722
🏌 C Dryden (Mgr) (01883) 627711
⚐ S Graham (01883) 627733
🏳 18 hole course Par 72 SSS 71
9 hole course par 36
👤 WD–U after 10am WE–U after 12
noon
💶 18 hole:£30 (£40) 9 hole:£14 (£17)
🚗 5 miles SE of Croydon. M25
Junction 6
⊕ Driving range
🏠 John Jacobs

Farnham (1896)

The Sands, Farnham, GU10 1PX
☎ **(01252) 783163**
🖥 (01252) 781185
📧 info@farnhamgolfclub.com
📖 750
🏌 Judy Elliott (01252) 782109
⚐ G Cowlishaw (01252) 782198
🏳 18 L 6313 yds SSS 71
👤 WD–H WE–M
SOC–Wed/Thurs/Fri
💶 £40 D–£45
🚗 1 mile E of Farnham, off A31

Farnham Park Par Three (1966)

Pay and play
Farnham Park, Farnham, GU9 0AU
☎ **(01252) 715216**
🖥 (01252) 718246
📖 75
🏌 A Curtis
⚐ A Curtis
🏳 9 L 1163 yds Par 54
👤 U
💶 £4.50 (£5)
🚗 By Farnham Castle
🏠 Henry Cotton

Foxhills (1975)

Stonehill Road, Ottershaw, KT16 0EL
☎ **(01932) 872050**
🖥 (01932) 874762
📖 975
🏌 A Laking (Mgr)
⚐ A Good (01932) 873961
🏳 18 L 6680 yds SSS 73
18 L 6547 yds SSS 72
9 hole course
👤 WD–U WE–NA before noon
SOC–WD am
💶 £60 D–£80 (£70)
🚗 2 miles SW of Chertsey on B386
⊕ Driving range
🏠 FW Hawtree
■ www.foxhills.co.uk

Gatton Manor Hotel G&CC (1969)

*Standon Lane, Ockley, Dorking,
RH5 5PQ*
☎ **(01306) 627555**
🖥 (01306) 627713
📧 gattonmanor@enterprise.net
📖 250
🏌 LC Heath
⚐ R Sargent (01306) 627557
🏳 18 L 6653 yds SSS 72

For list of abbreviations and key to symbols see page 649

🐦 U exc Sun before 1 pm–NA
SOC–WD
£€ £23 (£30)
🚗 1¹/₂ miles SW of Ockley, off A29.
M25 Junction 9, S on A24
⊕ Driving range
🏠 Henry Cotton
■ www.gattonmanor.co.uk

Goal Farm Par Three
Proprietary
Gole Road, Pirbright, GU24 OP2
☎ (01483) 473183/473205
🔑 R & J Church (Props)
▷ 9 hole Par 3 course
🐦 Sat/Thurs am–restricted SOC–WD
£€ £4.50 (£4.75)
🚗 7 miles NW of Guildford

Guildford (1886)
High Path Road, Merrow, Guildford, GU1 2HL
☎ (01483) 563941
🖥 (01483) 453228
📖 600
🔑 BJ Green
✓ PG Hollington (01483) 566765
▷ 18 L 6090 yds SSS 70
🐦 WD–U WE–M SOC–WD
£€ £35
🚗 2 miles E of Guildford on A246
🏠 Taylor/Hawtree

Hampton Court Palace
(1895)
Hampton Wick, Kingston-upon-Thames, KT1 4AD
☎ (020) 8977 2423
🖥 (020) 8977 5938
📖 650
✓ A Weller (Gen Mgr)
(020) 8977 2658
▷ 18 L 6584 yds SSS 71
🐦 WD–U WE–U after 1.30pm
£€ £30 (£40)
🚗 1 mile W of Kingston

Hankley Common (1896)
Tilford, Farnham, GU10 2DD
☎ (01252) 792493
🖥 (01252) 795699
📖 700
🔑 JSW Scott
✓ P Stow (01252) 793761
▷ 18 L 6438 yds SSS 71
🐦 WD–U WE–H at discretion of Sec
SOC
£€ £50 (£65)
🚗 3 miles SE of Farnham on Tilford road

Happy Valley (1999)
Rook Lane, Chaldon, Caterham, CR3 5AA
☎ (01883) 344555
🖥 (01883) 344422
📖 550
🔑 S Hodsdon (Gen Mgr)
✓ D Kent
▷ 18 L 6858 yds Par 72 SSS 73
🐦 WD–U WE–NA before 11.30am
SOC

£€ £20 (£27)
🚗 5 miles S of Croydon. M25 Junction 7
⊕ Driving range
🏠 David Williams
■ www.happyvalley.co.uk

Hazelwood Golf Centre
Pay and play
Croysdale Avenue, Green Street, Sunbury-on-Thames, TW16 6QU
☎ (01932) 770932
🖥 (01932) 770933
📖 292
🔑 J Reed
✓ F Sheridan (01932) 770932
▷ 9 L 5660 yds Par 35 SSS 67
🐦 U SOC
£€ £7 (£8.50)
🚗 M3 Junction 1, 1 mile
⊕ Driving range. Golf academy
🏠 Jonathan Gaunt

Hersham Village
Assher Road, Hersham, Walton-on-Thames, KT12 4RA
☎ (01932) 267666
🖥 (01932) 240975
🔑 R Hutton (Golf Dir)
✓ R Hutton
▷ 9 L 3097 yds Par 36
🐦 U
£€ 18 holes–£15
🚗 5 miles N of M25 Junction 10 (B365)
⊕ Floodlit driving range

Hindhead (1904)
Churt Road, Hindhead, GU26 6HX
☎ (01428) 604614
🖥 (01428) 608508
✉ secretary@hindhead-golfclub.co.uk
📖 500 76(L) 107(J)
🔑 JA Davies
✓ N Ogilvy (01428) 604458
▷ 18 L 6356 yds SSS 70
🐦 WD–U WE–by arrangement H SOC–Wed & Thurs
£€ £36 (£46)
🚗 1¹/₂ miles N of A3 on A287. M25 Junction 10, 25 miles

Hoebridge Golf Centre
(1982)
Public
Old Woking Road, Old Woking, GU22 8JH
☎ (01483) 722611
🖥 (01483) 740369
📖 480
🔑 P Dawson (Mgr)
✓ TD Powell
▷ 18 L 6587 yds SSS 71
Inter 9 L 2294 yds Par 33
18 hole Par 3 course
🐦 U SOC–WD
£€ 18 hole: £17.50 (£21) Inter:£9.
Par 3: £7.20
🚗 Between Old Woking and West Byfleet on B382
⊕ Floodlit driving range

🏠 Jacobs/Hawtree
■ www.hoebridge.co.uk

Horne Park
Croydon Barn Lane, Horne, South Godstone, RH9 8JP
☎ (01342) 844715
🖥 (01342) 844443
✉ hornepark@pncl.co.uk
📖 360
🔑 N Bedward (Mgr)
✓ N Bedward (01342) 844715
▷ 9 L 2718 yds Par 34
🐦 U
£€ 9 holes–£9.50 (£10.50)
🚗 Off A22. M25 Junction 6
⊕ Driving range
🏠 Howard Swann
■ www.horneparkgolf.co.uk

Horton Park G&CC (1987)
Pay and play
Hook Road, Epsom, KT19 8QG
☎ (020) 8393 8400 (Enquiries),
(020) 8394 2626 (Bookings)
🖥 (020) 8394 1369
✉ hortonparkgc@aol.com
📖 450
✓ M Hirst (020) 8394 2626
▷ 18 L 5728 yds SSS 70
9 L 3274 yds Par 60
🐦 U SOC
£€ £16 (£18)
🚗 1 mile from A3, W of Epsom. M25 Junction 9
⊕ Driving range
🏠 P Nicholson

Hurtmore (1992)
Pay and play
Hurtmore Road, Hurtmore, Godalming, GU7 2RN
☎ (01483) 426492
🖥 (01483) 426121
📖 200
🔑 Maxine Burton (01483) 426492
✓ Maxine Burton (01483) 424440
▷ 18 L 5530 yds Par 70 SSS 67
🐦 U SOC
£€ £12 (£17)
🚗 6 miles S of Guildford on A3. M25 Junction 10
🏠 Alliss/Clark

Kingswood (1928)
Sandy Lane, Kingswood, Tadworth, KT20 6NE
☎ (01737) 833316
🖥 (01737) 833920
📖 770
🔑 L Andrews (Admin)
(01737) 832188
✓ T Sims (01737) 832334
▷ 18 L 6904 yds SSS 73
🐦 U SOC
£€ £36 (£50)
🚗 5 miles S of Sutton on A217. M25 Junction 8, 2 miles
⊕ Driving range
🏠 James Braid

Laleham (1903)

Laleham Reach, Chertsey KT16 8RP
- ☎ **(01932) 564211**
- 🖳 (01932) 564448
- ✉ sec@laleham-golf.co.uk
- 📖 600
- ⚑ Mrs PA Kennett
- ✓ H Stott (01932) 562877
- ⊳ 18 L 6203 yds SSS 70
- ⚇ WD–U 9.30–4.30pm WE–M
  SOC–Mon–Wed
- ££ £25 – £30
- ⚘ 2 miles S of Staines, opp Thorpe
  Park
- ■ www.laleham-golf.co.uk

Leatherhead (1903)

Proprietary
Kingston Road, Leatherhead, KT22 0EE
- ☎ **(01372) 843966**
- 🖳 (01372) 842241
- ✉ secretary@lgc-golf.co.uk
- 📖 600
- ⚑ A Norman (01372) 843966
- ✓ S Norman (01372) 843956
- ⊳ 18 L 6203 yds Par 71 SSS 70
- ⚇ WD–U WE–NA before 2pm SOC
- ££ £37.50 (£47.50)
- ⚘ On A243 to Chessington. M25
  Junction 9
- ■ www.lgc-golf.co.uk

Limpsfield Chart (1889)

Westerham Road, Limpsfield, RH8 0SL
- ☎ **(01883) 723405/722106**
- 📖 300
- ⚑ MA Baker
- ✓ None
- ⊳ 9 L 5718 yds SSS 68
- ⚇ WD–U exc Thurs (Ladies Day)
  WE–M or by appointment SOC
- ££ £18 (£20)
- ⚘ 1 mile E of Oxted on A25

Lingfield Park (1987)

Racecourse Road, Lingfield, RH7 6PQ
- ☎ **(01342) 834602**
- 🖳 (01342) 836077
- ✉ cmorley@lingfieldpark.co.uk
- 📖 700
- ⚑ C Morley
- ✓ C Morley (01342) 832659
- ⊳ 18 L 6500 yds SSS 72
- ⚇ WD–U WE/BH–M SOC–WD
- ££ £40 (£50)
- ⚘ Next to Lingfield racecourse. M25
  Junction 6
- ⊕ Driving range

London Scottish (1865)

*Windmill Enclosure, Wimbledon
Common, London, SW19 5NQ*
- ☎ **(020) 8788 0135**
- 🖳 (020) 8789 7517
- ✉ secretary.lsgc@virgin.net
- 📖 250
- ⚑ S Barr (020) 8789 7517
- ✓ S Barr (020) 8789 1207
- ⊳ 18 L 5458 yds Par 68 SSS 66
- ⚇ WD–U WE/BH–NA SOC
- ££ £15 Mon–£10

- ⚘ Wimbledon Common
- ⊕ Red upper garment must be worn
- 🏠 Willie Dunn/Tom Dunn

Malden (1893)

Traps Lane, New Malden, KT3 4RS
- ☎ **(020) 8942 0654**
- 🖳 (020) 8336 2219
- ✉ maldengolfclub@lwcdial.net
- 📖 800
- ⚑ Mrs A Besant (Mgr)
- ✓ R Hunter (Golf Mgr)
  (020) 8942 6009
- ⊳ 18 L 6295 yds SSS 70
- ⚇ WD–U WE–restricted
  SOC–Wed–Fri
- ££ On application
- ⚘ Off A3, between Wimbledon and
  Kingston
- ■ www.maldengolfclub.com

Merrist Wood (1997)

*Coombe Lane, Worplesdon, Guildford,
GU3 3PE*
- ☎ **(01483) 238890**
- 🖳 (01483) 238896
- 📖 700
- ⚑ P Flavin
- ✓ C Connell (01483) 238894
- ⊳ 18 L 6575 yds Par 72 SSS 71
- ⚇ H–soft spikes only SOC
- ££ £30 D–£45
- ⚘ 2 miles W of Guildford, off A323
- ⊕ Driving range
- 🏠 David Williams
- ■ www.merristwood-golfclub.co.uk

Milford

Proprietary
Station Lane, Milford, GU8 5HS
- ☎ **(01483) 419200**
- 🖳 (01483) 419199
- ✉ milford@americangolf.uk.com
- 📖 750
- ⚑ R Griffiths (Mgr)
- ✓ P Creamer (01483) 416291
- ⊳ 18 L 5960 yds Par 69 SSS 68
- ⚇ WD–U WE–after 12 noon SOC
- ££ £25 (£30)
- ⚘ 3 miles SW of Guildford, off A3
- 🏠 Alliss/Clark

Mitcham (1924)

*Carshalton Road, Mitcham Junction,
CR4 4HN*
- ☎ **(020) 8648 1508,**
  (020) 8640 4280 (Bookings)
- 🖳 (020) 8648 4197
- 📖 500
- ⚑ WJ Dutch (020) 8648 4197
- ✓ JA Godfrey (020) 8640 4280
- ⊳ 18 L 5931 yds SSS 68
- ⚇ WD–U WE–NA before 1.30pm
  SOC
- ££ £16 (£18)
- ⚘ Mitcham Junction Station

Moore Place (1926)

Public
Portsmouth Road, Esher, KT10 9LN
- ☎ **(01372) 463533**

- 🖳 (01372) 460274
- 📖 80
- ⚑ P Hirsch
- ✓ D Allen
- ⊳ 9 L 4216 yds SSS 58
- ⚇ U
- ££ £5.80 (£7.70)
- ⚘ Centre of Esher
- 🏠 D Allen

New Zealand (1895)

Woodham Lane, Addlestone, KT15 3QD
- ☎ **(01932) 345049**
- 🖳 (01932) 342891
- ✉ roger.marrett@nzgc.org
- 📖 300
- ⚑ RA Marrett (01932) 342891
- ✓ VR Elvidge (01932) 349619
- ⊳ 18 L 6075 yds SSS 69
- ⚇ By request
- ££ On application
- ⚘ Woking 3 miles. West Byfleet 1
  mile. Weybridge 5 miles
- 🏠 Simpson/Fergusson

North Downs (1899)

*Northdown Road, Woldingham,
Caterham, CR3 7AA*
- ☎ **(01883) 652057**
- 🖳 (01883) 652832
- ✉ info@northdownsgolfclub.co.uk
- 📖 550
- ⚑ DM Sinden (Mgr) (01883) 652057
- ✓ MJ Homewood (01883) 653004
- ⊳ 18 L 5857 yds Par 69 SSS 68
- ⚇ WD–U WE–M SOC–WD
- ££ £25
- ⚘ 3 miles E of Caterham. M25
  Junction 6
- 🏠 JF Pennink
- ■ www.northdownsgolfclub.co.uk

Oak Park (1984)

*Heath Lane, Crondall, Farnham,
GU10 5PB*
- ☎ **(01252) 850850**
- 🖳 (01252) 850851
- 📖 500
- ⚑ N Dainton
- ✓ G Murton (01252) 850066
- ⊳ Woodland 18 L 6352 yds Par 70
  SSS 70;
  Village 9 L 3279 yds Par 36
- ⚇ U SOC
- ££ Woodland £20 (£30) Village £10
  (£12)
- ⚘ Off A287 Farnham-Odiham road.
  M3 Junction 5, 4 miles
- ⊕ Driving range
- 🏠 Patrick Dawson

Oaks Sports Centre (1973)

Public
*Woodmansterne Road, Carshalton,
SM5 4AN*
- ☎ **(020) 8643 8363**
- 🖳 (020) 8770 7303
- 📖 1000
- ✓ G Horley
- ⊳ 18 L 6033 yds SSS 69
  9 hole course
- ⚇ U

££ 18 hole:£16.25 (£19.75)
    9 hole:£8.15 (£9.90)
⟳ 2 miles from Sutton on B278
⊕ Floodlit driving range

Pachesham Park Golf Centre (1990)
Pay and play
Oaklawn Road, Leatherhead, KT22 0BT
☎ (01372) 843453
🖰 (01372) 844076
✉ phil.taylor@pacheshamgolf.co.uk
📖 250
⚐ P Taylor
✓ P Taylor
🏳 9 L 2804 yds Par 35
👥 U SOC
££ 9 holes–£9 (£10.50)
⟳ NW of Leatherhead, off A244. M25 Junction 9
⊕ Driving range
🏠 P Taylor
■ www.pacheshamgolf.co.uk

Pine Ridge (1992)
Pay and play
Old Bisley Road, Frimley, Camberley, GU16 9NX
☎ (01276) 20770
🖰 (01276) 678837
✉ enquiry@pineridgegolf.co.uk
⚐ CD Smith (Sec/Mgr) (01276) 675444
✓ P Sefton
🏳 18 L 6458 yds SSS 71
👥 U SOC
££ £22.50 (£29)
⟳ Off Maultway, between Lightwater and Frimley. M3 Junction 3, 2 miles
⊕ Floodlit driving range
🏠 Clive D Smith
■ www.pineridgegolf.co.uk

Purley Downs (1894)
106 Purley Downs Road, South Croydon, CR2 0RB
☎ (020) 8657 8347
🖰 (020) 8651 5044
✉ info@purleydowns.co.uk
📖 660
⚐ PC Gallienne
✓ G Wilson (020) 8651 0819
🏳 18 L 6275 yds SSS 70
👥 WD–I WE–M SOC–WD exc Tues am
££ On application
⟳ 3 miles S of Croydon (A235)
■ www.purleydowns.co.uk

Puttenham (1894)
Puttenham, Guildford, GU3 1AL
☎ (01483) 810498
🖰 (01483) 810988
📖 500
⚐ G Simmons
✓ D Lintott (01483) 810277
🏳 18 L 6212 yds SSS 74
👥 WD–by prior appointment WE/BH–M SOC–Wed & Thurs
££ On application

⟳ Between Guildford and Farnham, on Hog's Back

Pyrford (1993)
Warren Lane, Pyrford, GU22 8XR
☎ (01483) 723555
🖰 (01483) 729777
✉ pyrford@americangolf.uk.com
📖 650
⚐ I Bartlett
✓ D Brewer (01483) 751070
🏳 18 L 6256 yds SSS 70
👥 WD–U WE–M before noon SOC–WD
££ £40 (£45)
⟳ 2 miles from A3 at Ripley
🏠 Alliss/Clark

Redhill (1993)
Pay and play
Canada Avenue, Redhill, RH1 5BF
☎ (01737) 770204
🖰 (01737) 760046
📖 90
⚐ S Furlonger
✓ J Edgar
🏳 9 L 1903 yds Par 31 SSS 59
👥 U SOC
££ 9 holes–£4.95 (£5.95)
⟳ 1¹/₂ miles S of Redhill on A23, off Three Arch Road
⊕ Floodlit driving range

Redhill & Reigate (1887)
Clarence Lodge, Pendleton Road, Redhill, RH1 6LB
☎ (01737) 244626/244433
🖰 (01737) 242117
📖 500
✓ W Pike (01737) 240777
✓ W Pike (01737) 244433
🏳 18 L 5272 yds SSS 68
👥 WD–U WE–phone first SOC
££ £20 (£30)
⟳ 1 mile S of Redhill on A23

Reigate Heath (1895)
The Club House, Reigate Heath, RH2 8QR
☎ (01737) 242610
🖰 (01737) 249226
📖 330 80(L) 60(J)
⚐ RJ Perkins (01737) 226793
✓ B Davies
🏳 9 L 5658 yds SSS 67
👥 WD–U Sun/BH–M SOC–Wed & Thurs
££ On application
⟳ W boundary of Reigate Heath

Reigate Hill
Gatton Bottom, Reigate, RH2 0TU
☎ (01737) 645577
🖰 (01737) 642650
📖 550
⚐ I Donnelly
✓ C Forsyth (01737) 646070
🏳 18 L 6175 yds Par 72 SSS 70
👥 WD–U WE–M SOC
££ £25
⟳ 1 mile from M25 Junction 8, off A217
🏠 David Williams

Richmond (1891)
Sudbrook Park, Richmond, TW10 7AS
☎ (020) 8940 1463
🖰 (020) 8332 7914
✉ generalmanager.rgc@tiscali.co.uk
📖 700
⚐ D Cromie (020) 8940 4351
✓ N Job (020) 8940 7792
🏳 18 L 6007 yds SSS 69
👥 WD–H
££ £37
⟳ Between Richmond and Kingston-upon-Thames

Richmond Park (1923)
Public
Roehampton Gate, Richmond Park, London, SW15 5JR
☎ (020) 8876 3205/1795
🖰 (020) 8878 1354
✉ gcmgolf@hotmail.com
⚐ AJ Gourvish
✓ D Bown
🏳 Dukes 18 L 6036 yds SSS 68
    Princes 18 L 5868 yds SSS 67
👥 WD–U WE–booking necessary SOC–WD
££ On application
⟳ In Richmond Park
⊕ Driving range
🏠 Hawtree

Roehampton Club (1901)
Roehampton Lane, London, SW15 5LR
☎ (020) 8480 4200
🖰 (020) 8480 4265
✉ admin@roehamptonclub.co.uk
📖 1400
⚐ M Wilson (Chief Exec) (020) 8480 4200
✓ AL Scott (020) 8876 3858
🏳 18 L 6065 yds Par 71
👥 WD/WE–Introduced by member
££ On application
⟳ 1 mile W of Putney, off South Circular
■ www.roehamptonclub.co.uk

Roker Park (1993)
Pay and play
Holly Lane, Aldershot Road, Guildford, GU3 3PB
☎ (01483) 236677
📖 200
⚐ C Tegg
✓ K Warn (01483) 236677
🏳 9 L 3037 yds SSS 72
👥 U SOC
££ £8.50 (£10)
⟳ 2 miles W of Guildford on A323
⊕ Driving range
🏠 Alan Helling

Royal Automobile Club (1913)
Woodcote Park, Epsom, KT18 7EW
☎ (01372) 276311
🖰 (01372) 276117
⚐ D Adams (01372) 273091
✓ I Howieson (01372) 279514
🏳 Old 18 L 6709 yds SSS 72
    Coronation 18 L 6223 yds SSS 70

For list of abbreviations and key to symbols see page 649

M SOC
Epsom Station 2 miles
Fowler/Myddleton

Royal Mid-Surrey (1892)
Old Deer Park, Richmond, TW9 2SB
☎ (020) 8940 1894
▢ (020) 8332 2957
✉ secretary@rmsgc.co.uk
▥ 1420
✎ P Talbot (020) 8940 0459
▷ Outer 18 L 6385 yds SSS 70
Inner 18 L 5446 yds SSS 67
WD–H or M WE/BH–M SOC
€€ D–£68
Nr Richmond roundabout, off A316
JH Taylor
■ www.rmsgc.co.uk

Royal Wimbledon (1865)
29 Camp Road, Wimbledon Common, London, SW19 4UW
☎ (020) 8946 2125
▢ (020) 8944 8652
✉ secretary@rwgc.co.uk
▥ 800
✎ NI Smith
✎ DR Jones (020) 8946 4606
▷ 18 L 6348 yds SSS 70
WD–H by arrangement
Wimbledon Common, 2 miles S of A23 Tibbets Corner
HS Colt
■ www.rwgc.co.uk

Rusper (1992)
Rusper Road, Newdigate, RH5 5BX
☎ (01293) 871456,
(01293) 871871 (Bookings)
▢ (01293) 871456
✉ jill@ruspergolfclub.co.uk
▥ 235
✎ Mrs J Thornhill
✎ Janice Arnold (01293) 871871
▷ 18 L 6621 yds SSS 72
U SOC
€€ 18 holes–£15 (£18.50). 9 holes–£10 (£13.50).
5 miles S of Dorking, off A24
⊕ Driving range

AW Blunden

St George's Hill (1912)
Golf Club Road, St George's Hill, Weybridge, KT13 0NL
☎ (01932) 847758
▢ (01932) 821564
✉ admin@stgeorgeshillgolfclub.co.uk
▥ 600
✎ J Robinson
✎ AC Rattue (01932) 843523
▷ 27 L 6097-6496 yds SSS 69-71
WD–I H WE/BH–M SOC–Wed–Fri
€€ £80 – £105
2 miles N of M25/A3 Junction, on B374
HS Colt
■ www.stgeorgeshillgolfclub.co.uk

Sandown Park Golf Centre (1970)
Public
More Lane, Esher, KT10 8AN
☎ (01372) 461234
▢ (01372) 461203
▥ 500
✎ D Parr (Mgr)
✎ J Skinner (01372) 461282
▷ 9 L 5658 yds SSS 67
9 hole Par 3 course
U–closed on race days
€€ £6.75 (£8.50)
Sandown Park Racecourse
⊕ Floodlit driving range
John Jacobs
■ www.sandown.co.uk

Selsdon Park Hotel (1929)
Addington Road, Sanderstead, South Croydon, CR2 8YA
☎ (020) 8657 8811
▢ (020) 8657 3401
✎ Mrs C Screene
✎ M Churchill (020) 8657 4129
▷ 18 L 6473 yds SSS 71
U SOC (min 12 golfers)
€€ £20 (£30)
3 miles S of Croydon on A2022 Purley-Addington road
⊕ Driving range
JH Taylor

Shirley Park (1914)
194 Addiscombe Road, Croydon, CR0 7LB
☎ (020) 8654 1143
▢ (020) 8654 6733
▥ 600
✎ D Roy
✎ (020) 8654 8767
▷ 18 L 6210 yds SSS 70
WD–U WE/BH–M SOC
€€ £35
On A232, 1 mile E of East Croydon Station
Simpson/Fowler
■ www.shirleyparkgolfclub.co.uk

Silvermere (1976)
Pay and play
Redhill Road, Cobham, KT11 1EF
☎ (01932) 867275
▢ (01932) 868259
✉ sales@silvermere.freeserve.co.uk
▥ 750
✎ Mrs P Devereux
✎ D McClelland
▷ 18 L 6027 yds SSS 71
WD–U WE–NA before 11am SOC
€€ £22.50 (£32.50)
½ mile from M25 Junction 10 on B366 to Byfleet
⊕ Floodlit driving range
■ www.crowngolf.co.uk

Sunningdale (1900)
Ridgemount Road, Sunningdale, Berks, SL5 9RR
☎ (01344) 621681

▢ (01344) 624154
▥ 900
✎ S Zuill
✎ K Maxwell (01344) 620128
▷ Old 18 L 6581 yds SSS 72
New 18 L 6617 yds SSS 73
Mon–Thurs–I Fri/WE–M
€€ Old–£120 New–£85
Sunningdale Station ¼ mile, off A30
Willie Park/HS Colt

Sunningdale Ladies (1902)
Cross Road, Sunningdale, SL5 9RX
☎ (01344) 620507
✉ ladiesgolf@lineone.net
▥ 400
✎ JF Darroch
▷ 18 L 3622 yds SSS 60
WD/WE–by appointment. No 3 or 4 balls before 10.30am
€€ £22 (£25)
Sunningdale Station ¼ mile
HS Colt

Surbiton (1895)
Woodstock Lane, Chessington, KT9 1UG
☎ (020) 8398 3101
▢ (020) 8339 0992
▥ 800
✎ DR Crockford
✎ P Milton (020) 8398 6619
▷ 18 L 6055 yds SSS 69
WD–H WE/BH–M
€€ £30 D–£45
2 miles E of Esher

Surrey Downs (2001)
Pay and play
Outwood Lane, Kingswood, KT20 6JS
☎ (01737) 839090
▢ (01737) 839080
✎ Miss L Hafele (Admin)
✎ S Blacklee (01737) 832726
▷ 18 L 6356 yds Par 71 SSS 70
U SOC
€€ £25 (£35)
N of Kingswood, off A217/B2032. M25 Junction 8
⊕ Golf academy
Peter Alliss

Sutton Green (1994)
New Lane, Sutton Green, Guildford, GU4 7QF
☎ (01483) 747898
▢ (01483) 750289
✉ admin@suttongreengc.co.uk
▥ 600
✎ J Buchanan
✎ P Tedder (01483) 766849
▷ 18 L 6300 yds Par 71 SSS 70
WD–U WE–U after 2pm
€€ £40 (£50)
2 miles S of Woking
Walker/Davies

Tandridge (1925)
Oxted, RH8 9NQ
☎ (01883) 712273 (Clubhouse)
▢ (01883) 730537
▥ 750

🖉 Lt Cdr SE Kennard RN
(01883) 712274
✒ C Evans (01883) 713701
↦ 18 L 6250 yds SSS 70
👥 Mon/Wed/Thurs only–H
SOC–Mon/Wed/Thurs
££ On application
🚗 5 miles E of Redhill, off A25. M25
Junction 6
🏠 HS Colt
■ www.tandridgegolfclub.com

Thames Ditton & Esher
(1892)
Portsmouth Road, Esher, KT10 9AL
☎ (020) 8398 1551
🖵 150
🖉 A Barry
✒ R Jones
↦ 9 L 5419 yds SSS 65
👥 WD–U WE–by arrangement
££ £10 (£12)
🚗 Esher

Tyrrells Wood (1924)
*Tyrrells Wood, Leatherhead,
KT22 8QP*
☎ (01372) 376025 (2 lines)
🖵 (01372) 360836
🖵 744
🖉 CGR Kydd
✒ S DeFoy (01372) 375200
↦ 18 L 6282 yds SSS 70
👥 WD–I BH/Sat–NA Sun–NA before
noon SOC
££ £34 (£44)
🚗 2 miles SE of Leatherhead, off A24
nr Headley. M25 Junction 9, 1 mile
■ www.tyrrellswood-golfclub.co.uk

Walton Heath (1903)
*Deans Lane, Walton-on-the-Hill,
Tadworth, KT20 7TP*
☎ (01737) 812060
🖵 (01737) 814225
🖵 900
🖉 MW Bawden (01737) 812380
✒ K Macpherson (01737) 812152
↦ Old 18 L 6801 yds SSS 73
New 18 L 6609 yds SSS 72
👥 WD–H booking necessary
WE/BH–M SOC–WD
££ On application
🚗 18 miles S of London on
A217/B2032. 2 miles N of M25
Junction 8
🏠 WH Fowler
■ www.whgc.co.uk

Wentworth Club (1924)
*Wentworth Drive, Virginia Water,
GU25 4LS*
☎ (01344) 842201
🖵 (01344) 842804
🖵 3622
🖉 S Christie (Admin)
✒ D Rennie (01344) 846306
↦ West 18 L 7047 yds SSS 74
East 18 L 6201 yds SSS 70
Edinburgh 18 L 7004 yds SSS 74
Executive 9 L 1902 yds Par 27

👥 WD–H by prior arrangement
WE–M SOC–WD
££ On application
🚗 21 miles SW of London at
A30/A329 junction. M25 Junction
13, 3 miles
⊕ Driving range
🏠 HS Colt (East/West). Jacobs/Player
(Edinburgh)
■ www.wentworthclub.com

West Byfleet (1906)
*Sheerwater Road, West Byfleet,
KT14 6AA*
☎ (01932) 345230
🖵 (01932) 340667
🖵 550
🖉 DG Lee (Gen Mgr)
(01932) 343433
✒ D Regan (01932) 346584
↦ 18 L 6211 yds SSS 70
👥 WD–U WE/BH–NA SOC
££ £40 D–£50
🚗 West Byfleet ¹/₂ mile on A245.
M25 Junction 10 or 11
🏠 CS Butchart

West Hill (1907)
Bagshot Road, Brookwood, GU24 0BH
☎ (01483) 474365/472110
🖵 (01483) 474252
🖵 550
🖉 MC Swatton
✒ JA Clements (01483) 473172
↦ 18 L 6322 yds Par 69 SSS 71
👥 WD–H WE–M SOC
££ £47 D–£65
🚗 5 miles W of Woking on A322
🏠 CS Butchart
■ www.westhill-golfclub.co.uk

West Surrey (1910)
Enton Green, Godalming, GU8 5AF
☎ (01483) 421275
🖵 (01483) 415419
🖵 750
🖉 RT Crabb
✒ A Tawse (01483) 417278
↦ 18 L 6300 yds SSS 70
👥 H SOC–Wed/Thurs/Fri
££ £27 (£48)
🚗 ¹/₂ mile SE of Milford Station
🏠 Herbert Fowler

Wildwood CC (1992)
Horsham Road, Alfold, GU6 8JE
☎ (01403) 753255
🖵 (01403) 752005
✉ wayne@wildwoodgolf.co.uk
🖵 640
🖉 W Berry (Gen Mgr)
✒ S Andrews
↦ 18 L 6655 yds SSS 73
Par 3 course
👥 WE–NA before noon SOC
££ £30 (£45)
🚗 10 miles S of Guildford on A281
⊕ Driving range
🏠 Hawtree
■ www.wildwoodgolf.co.uk

Wimbledon Common
(1908)
*19 Camp Road, Wimbledon Common,
London, SW19 4UW*
☎ (020) 8946 0294
🖵 (020) 8947 8697
🖵 275
🖉 RJW Pierce (020) 8946 7571
✒ JS Jukes
↦ 18 L 5438 yds SSS 66
👥 WD–U WE–M SOC
££ WD–£15 exc Mon–£10
🚗 Wimbledon Common
⊕ Pillarbox red outer garment must be
worn. London Scottish play here
🏠 Willie Dunn/Tom Dunn

Wimbledon Park (1898)
Home Park Road, London, SW19 7HR
☎ (020) 8946 1002
🖵 (020) 8944 8688
🖵 650
🖉 Mrs E Inwood (020) 8946 1250
✒ D Wingrove (020) 8946 4053
↦ 18 L 5492 yds SSS 66
👥 WD–H I WE/BH–after 3pm SOC
££ D–£40 (£40)
🚗 2 miles from A3 at Tibbets Corner
■ www.wpgc.co.uk

Windlemere (1978)
Pay and play
*Windlesham Road, West End, Woking,
GU24 9QL*
☎ (01276) 858727
🖵 (01276) 678837
🖉 CD Smith
✒ D Thomas
↦ 9 L 5346 yds SSS 66
👥 U
££ 9 holes–£9 (£10.50)
🚗 A319 at Lightwater/West End
⊕ Floodlit driving range
🏠 Clive D Smith

Windlesham (1994)
Grove End, Bagshot, GU19 5HY
☎ (01276) 452220
🖵 (01276) 452290
✉ admin@windleshamgolf.com
🖵 800
🖉 R Park
✒ L Mucklow (01276) 472323
↦ 18 L 6650 yds SSS 72
👥 H–phone first WE–pm only
SOC–WD
££ £25 (£35)
🚗 ¹/₂ mile N of M3 Junction 3, off
A30/A322
⊕ Driving range
🏠 Tommy Horton
■ www.windleshamgolf.com

The Wisley (1991)
Ripley, Woking, GU23 6QU
☎ (01483) 211022
🖵 (01483) 211662
🖵 700
🖉 AD Lawrence (Gen Mgr)
✒ D Pugh (01483) 211213

27 holes SSS 73:
Church 9 L 3356 yds; Garden 9 L
3385 yds;
Mill 9 L 3473 yds
👤 M
🚗 1 mile S of M25 Junction 10
🏠 Robert Trent Jones Jr

Woking   (1893)
*Pond Road, Hook Heath, Woking,
GU22 0JZ*
☎ **(01483) 760053**
📠 (01483) 772441
📖 500
✍ G Ritchie
⌕ C Bianco (01483) 769582
📐 18 L 6340 yds SSS 70
👤 WD–H WE/BH–M SOC–WD
£€ £55
🚗 W of Woking in St John's / Hook
Heath area
🏠 Tom Dunn

The Woldingham   (1996)
*Halliloo Valley Road, Woldingham,
CR3 7HA*
☎ **(01883) 653501**
📠 (01883) 653502
📖 650
✍ P Harrison
⌕ N Carter (01883) 653541
📐 18 L 6322 yds Par 71 SSS 70
👤 WD–U WE–NA before noon SOC
£€ £25 (£40)
🚗 2¹/₂ miles N of M25 Junction 6, off
A22
⊕ Practice range
🏠 Bradford Benz

Woodcote Park   (1912)
*Meadow Hill, Bridle Way, Coulsdon,
CR5 2QQ*
☎ **(020) 8668 2788**
📠 (020) 8660 0918
✉ info@woodcotepgc.com
📖 630
✍ K Brabbins
⌕ W Grant (020) 8668 1843
📐 18 L 6680 yds Par 71 SSS 72
👤 WD–U WE–M
£€ £35 D–£45
🚗 Purley 2 miles. M25 Junction 7
🏠 HS Colt

Worplesdon   (1908)
*Heath House Road, Woking,
GU22 0RA*
☎ **(01483) 472277**
📠 (01483) 473303
📖 600
✍ JT Christine
⌕ JT Christine (01483) 473287
📐 18 L 6440 yds SSS 71
👤 WD–H WE–M
£€ On application
🚗 E of Woking, off A322. 6 miles N
of Guildford (A3). 6 miles S of M3
Junction 3

Sussex (East)

Brighton & Hove   (1887)
Devils Dyke Road, Brighton, BN1 8YJ
☎ **(01273) 556482**
📠 (01273) 554247
📖 320
✍ P Bonsall (Golf Dir)
⌕ P Bonsall (01273) 556686
📐 9 L 5704 yds SSS 68
👤 U SOC Sun–NA before noon
£€ £18 (£25)
🚗 4 miles N of Brighton
🏠 James Braid

Cooden Beach   (1912)
*Cooden Beach, Bexhill-on-Sea,
TN39 4TR*
☎ **(01424) 842040**
📠 (01424) 842040
📖 700
✍ TE Hawes
⌕ J Sim (01424) 843938
📐 18 L 6500 yds SSS 71
👤 H SOC
£€ £32 (£35)
🚗 W boundary of Bexhill
🏠 Herbert Fowler

Crowborough Beacon
(1895)
Beacon Road, Crowborough, TN6 1UJ
☎ **(01892) 661511**
📠 (01892) 611988
✉ cbgc@eastsx.fsnet.co.uk
📖 700
✍ Mrs V Harwood (01892) 661511
⌕ D Newnham (01892) 653877
📐 18 L 6273 yds SSS 70
👤 WD–H WE/BH–H after 2pm SOC
£€ £27.50 – £40
🚗 9 miles S of Tunbridge Wells on
A26
■ www.crowboroughbeacongolfclub
.co.uk

Dale Hill Hotel   (1973)
Ticehurst, Wadhurst, TN5 7DQ
☎ **(01580) 200112**
📠 (01580) 201249
📖 1000
✍ Ms M Harris (Sec/Mgr)
⌕ M Woods (01580) 201090
📐 18 L 5856 yds SSS 69
Woosnam 18 L 6512 yds SSS 71
👤 U SOC
£€ £25 (£35) Woosnam–£50 (£60)
🚗 B2087, off A21 at Flimwell
⊕ Driving range
■ www.dalehill.co.uk

Dewlands Manor   (1992)
Cottage Hill, Rotherfield, TN6 3JN
☎ **(01892) 852266**
📠 (01892) 853015
✍ T Robins
⌕ N Godin
📐 9 L 3186 yds Par 36
👤 U–phone first
£€ 9 holes–£15 (£17). 18 holes–£25
(£30)

🚗 ¹/₂ mile S of Rotherfield, off
A267/B2101. 10 miles S of
Tunbridge Wells. M25 Junction 5
🏠 Reg Godin

The Dyke   (1906)
*Devil's Dyke, Devil's Dyke Road,
Brighton, BN1 8YJ*
☎ **(01273) 857296**
📠 (01273) 857078
✉ secretary@dykegolfclub.org.uk
📖 750
✍ MD Harrity (Sec/Mgr)
⌕ R Arnold (01273) 857260
📐 18 L 6611 yds SSS 72
👤 WD–U H WE–U H after noon
SOC–WD
£€ £28 D–£38 (£35)
🚗 4 miles N of Brighton
🏠 Fred Hawtree
■ www.dykegolfclub.co.uk

East Brighton   (1893)
Roedean Road, Brighton, BN2 5RA
☎ **(01273) 604838**
📠 (01273) 680277
✉ msw@ebgc.co.uk
📖 650
✍ ME Page
⌕ M Stuart-William (Golf Mgr)
(01273) 603989
📐 18 L 6346 yds SSS 70
👤 WD–U H after 9am WE–NA before
11am SOC
£€ £27.50 D–£37.50 (£32.50)
🚗 1¹/₂ miles E of Town Centre,
overlooking Marina
🏠 James Braid

East Sussex National
(1989)
Little Horsted, Uckfield, TN22 5ES
☎ **(01825) 880088**
📠 (01825) 880066
📖 770
✍ B Street (Gen Mgr)
⌕ S MacLennan (01825) 880088
📐 East 18 L 7138 yds SSS 74
West 18 L 7154 yds SSS 74
👤 U on one course
£€ Summer–£40 (£45). Winter–£35
(£40)
🚗 2 miles S of Uckfield, on A22
⊕ Driving range. Golf academy
🏠 Bob Cupp
■ www.eastsussexnational.co.uk

Eastbourne Downs   (1908)
*East Dean Road, Eastbourne,
BN20 8ES*
☎ **(01323) 720827**
📠 (01323) 412506
📖 550
✍ AJ Reeves
⌕ T Marshall (01323) 732264
📐 18 L 6601 yds SSS 72
👤 WD–U WE–NA before 11am
£€ D–£23
🚗 ¹/₂ mile W of Eastbourne on A259
🏠 JH Taylor

For list of abbreviations and key to symbols see page 649

Eastbourne Golfing Park (1992)

Pay and play
Lottbridge Drove, Eastbourne, BN23 6QJ
☎ **(01323) 520400**
🖳 (01323) 520400
📖 250
🏌 J Plumley
✓ B Finch
⛳ 9 L 5046 yds SSS 65
🏌 U
££ £9 (£14)
🚗 ¹/₂ mile S of Hampden Park
⊕ Floodlit driving range
🏛 David Ashton

Hastings G&CC (1973)

Beauport Park, Battle Road, St Leonards-on-Sea, TN37 7BP
☎ **(01424) 854243**
🖳 (01424) 854244
📖 300
🏌 M Strevett
✓ C Giddins (01424) 852981
⛳ 18 L 6180 yds SSS 71
🏌 U–booking necessary SOC
££ £14 (£17.50)
🚗 3 miles N of Hastings, off A2100 Battle road
⊕ Driving range
▪ www.hastingsgolfclub.com

Highwoods (1925)

Ellerslie Lane, Bexhill-on-Sea, TN39 4LJ
☎ **(01424) 212625**
🖳 (01424) 216866
📧 secretary@highwoodsgolfclub .co.uk
📖 800
🏌 LM Dennis-Smither
✓ MJ Andrews (01424) 212770
⛳ 18 L 6218 yds SSS 70
🏌 WD/Sat–H Sun am–M Sun pm–H
££ £30 (£35)
🚗 2 miles N of Bexhill
🏛 JH Taylor

Hollingbury Park (1908)

Public
Ditchling Road, Brighton, BN1 7HS
☎ **(01273) 552010**
🖳 (01273) 552010
📖 300
🏌 Mrs M Bailey
✓ G Crompton (01273) 500086
⛳ 18 L 6415 yds SSS 71
🏌 U SOC
££ £12 (£17)
🚗 1 mile NE of Brighton
▪ www.hollingburygolfclub.co.uk

Holtye (1893)

Holtye, Cowden, Edenbridge, TN8 7ED
☎ **(01342) 850635**
🖳 (01342) 850576
📖 430
🏌 JP Holmes (01342) 850576
✓ K Hinton (01342) 850957
⛳ 9 L 5325 yds SSS 66

🏌 WD–U exc Wed/Thurs am–NA WE–NA before noon SOC–Tues & Fri
££ D–£16 (£18)
🚗 4 miles E of E Grinstead on A264

Horam Park (1985)

Pay and play
Chiddingly Road, Horam, TN21 0JJ
☎ **(01435) 813477**
🖳 (01435) 813677
📧 angie@horamgolf.freeserve.co.uk
📖 400
🏌 Mrs A Briggs
✓ G Velvick
⛳ 9 L 6128 yds SSS 70
🏌 U SOC
££ 18 holes–£16.50 (£18) 9 holes–£10.50 (£11)
🚗 ¹/₂ mile S of Horam towards Chiddingley. 12 miles N of Eastbourne on A267
⊕ Floodlit driving range. Pitch & putt course
🏛 Glen Johnson
▪ www.horamparkgolf.co.uk

Lewes (1896)

Chapel Hill, Lewes, BN7 2BB
☎ **(01273) 473245**
🖳 (01273) 483474
📖 650
🏌 Miss J Raffety (01273) 483474
✓ P Dobson (01273) 483823
⛳ 18 L 6190 yds Par 71 SSS 70
🏌 WD–U WE–NA before 2pm SOC
££ £25 (£36)
🚗 ¹/₂ mile from Lewes at E end of Cliffe High Street

Mid Sussex (1995)

Proprietary
Spatham Lane, Ditchling, BN6 8XJ
☎ **(01273) 846567**
🖳 (01273) 845767
📧 admin@midsussexgolfclub.co.uk
📖 600
🏌 A McNiven (Golf Dir)
✓ N Plimmer
⛳ 18 L 6450 yds Par 71 SSS 71
🏌 WD–U WE–pm only SOC–WD
££ £25 (£25)
🚗 1 mile E of Ditchling
⊕ Driving range
🏛 David Williams
▪ www.midsussexgolfclub.co.uk

Nevill (1912)

Benhall Mill Road, Tunbridge Wells, TN2 5JW
☎ **(01892) 525818**
🖳 (01892) 517861
📧 manager@nevillgolfclub.co.uk
📖 800
🏌 TJ Fensom
✓ P Huggett (01892) 532941
⛳ 18 L 6349 yds SSS 70
🏌 WD–H WE/BH–M
££ £25 D–£40
🚗 Tunbridge Wells 1 mile

Peacehaven (1895)

Brighton Road, Newhaven, BN9 9UH
☎ **(01273) 514049**
🖳 (01273) 512571
📧 golf@peacehavengc.freeserve.co.uk
📖 290
🏌 Mrs D Corke (01273) 512571
✓ I Pearson (01273) 512602
⛳ 9 L 5488 yds SSS 67
🏌 WD–U WE/BH–after 11am SOC
££ £15 (£20)
🚗 8 miles E of Brighton on A259
🏛 James Braid

Piltdown (1904)

Piltdown, Uckfield, TN22 3XB
☎ **(01825) 722033**
🖳 (01825) 724192
📖 400
🏌 CM Lewis (Hon)
✓ J Partridge (01825) 722389
⛳ 18 L 6070 yds SSS 69
🏌 I or H exc BH/Tues am/Thurs am/Sun am SOC
££ £30 D–£40
🚗 1 mile W of Maresfield, off A272 towards Isfield

Royal Ashdown Forest (1888)

Chapel Lane, Forest Row, East Grinstead, RH18 5LR
☎ **(01342) 822018/823014 (Old), (01342) 824866 (West)**
🖳 (01342) 825211/824869
📖 450
🏌 DED Neave
✓ MA Landsborough (01342) 822247
⛳ Old 18 L 6477 yds SSS 71 West 18 L 5606 yds SSS 67
🏌 On application–phone first
££ Old–£45 D–£55 (£60 R/D) West £18 (£23)
🚗 4 miles S of E Grinstead on B2110 Hartfield road. M25 Junction 6
▪ www.royalashdown.co.uk

Royal Eastbourne (1887)

Paradise Drive, Eastbourne, BN20 8BP
☎ **(01323) 729738**
🖳 (01323) 729738
📖 850
🏌 P Jeynes
✓ A Harrison (01323) 736986
⛳ Devonshire 18 L 6131 yds SSS 69 Hartington 9 L 2147 yds SSS 61
🏌 U H SOC–WD
££ Devonshire–£25 (£40) Hartington–£15
🚗 ¹/₂ mile from Town Hall

Rye (1894)

Camber, Rye, TN31 7QS
☎ **(01797) 225241**
🖳 (01797) 225460
📖 1000 125(L) 100(J)
🏌 JAL Smith
✓ MP Lee (01797) 225218
⛳ 18 L 6308 yds SSS 71 9 L 6141 yds SSS 70

M
3 miles E of Rye on B2075
HS Colt

Seaford (1887)

East Blatchington, Seaford, BN25 2JD
☎ (01323) 892442
🖩 (01323) 894113
📖 420 110(L) 37(J)
🏌 PAA Court (Gen Mgr)
/ (01323) 894160
🏳 18 L 6233 yds SSS 70
🏌 WD–U after 10am exc Tues WE–M
SOC
£€ D–£30 (£35)
🚗 1 mile N of Seaford (A259)
⊕ Driving range
🏠 JH Taylor
■ www.seafordgolfclub.co.uk

Seaford Head (1907)

Public
Southdown Road, Seaford, BN25 4JS
☎ (01323) 890139
🏌 I Perkins (01323) 894843
/ AJ Lowles (01323) 890139
🏳 18 L 5812 yds SSS 68
🏌 U
£€ £15 (£18)
🚗 8 miles W of Eastbourne. 3/4 mile S
of A259

Sedlescombe (1990)

Kent Street, Sedlescombe, TN33 0SD
☎ (01424) 871700
🖩 (01424) 871712
✉ golf@golfschool.co.uk
📖 380
🏌 T Underhill
/ J Andrews
🏳 18 L 6269 yds Par 72 SSS 70
🏌 U SOC
£€ On application
🚗 5 miles N of Hastings
⊕ Floodlit driving range
🏠 Glen Johnson

Waterhall (1923)

Public
Waterhall Road, Brighton, BN1 8YR
☎ (01273) 508658
📖 300
🏌 LB Allen
/ P Charman
🏳 18 L 5775 yds SSS 68
🏌 WD–U WE–U after 8am
£€ £11.50 (£11.50)
🚗 3 miles N of Brighton between A23
and A27. 1 mile N of A2308

Wellshurst G&CC (1992)

North Street, Hellingly, BN27 4EE
☎ (01435) 813636
🖩 (01435) 812444
✉ info@wellshurst.com
📖 400
🏌 M Adams (Man Dir)
/ M Jarvis (01435) 813456
🏳 18 L 5992 yds SSS 69
🏌 U SOC
£€ £18 (£22)

🚗 2 miles N of Hailsham on A267
⊕ Driving range

West Hove (1910)

Church Farm, Hangleton, Hove, BN3 8AN
☎ (01273) 413411 (Clubhouse)
🖩 (01273) 439988
📖 600
🏌 Megan Bibby (Mgr)
(01273) 419738
/ D Cook (01273) 413494
🏳 18 L 6201 yds SSS 70 Par 70
🏌 U–phone first SOC
£€ On application
🚗 N of Brighton By-pass. 2nd
junction W from A23 flyover
⊕ Practice driving range
🏠 Hawtree
■ www.westhovegolfclub.co.uk

Willingdon (1898)

*Southdown Road, Eastbourne,
BN20 9AA*
☎ (01323) 410981
🖩 (01323) 411510
📖 550
🏌 Mrs J Packham (01323) 410981
/ T Moore (01323) 410984
🏳 18 L 6049 yds SSS 69
🏌 WD–U H WE–MH exc Sun
am–NA SOC–H
£€ D–£25 (£28)
🚗 1/2 mile N of Eastbourne, off A22
🏠 JH Taylor/Dr A Mackenzie

Sussex (West)

Avisford Park (1990)

Pay and play
*Yapton Lane, Walberton, Arundel,
BN18 0LS*
☎ (01243) 554611
📖 200
🏌 N Upjohn
/ R Beach
🏳 18 L 5390 yds Par 67 SSS 66
🏌 U SOC
£€ £12 (£15)
🚗 4 miles W of Arundel on A27

Bognor Regis (1892)

*Downview Road, Felpham, Bognor
Regis, PO22 8JD*
☎ (01243) 865867
🖩 (01243) 860719
✉ sec@bognorgolfclub.co.uk
📖 750
🏌 PD Badger (01243) 821929
/ S Bassil (01243) 865209
🏳 18 L 6238 yds Par 70 SSS 70
🏌 WD–I or H after 9.30am
WE/BH–M (Apr–Sept) –I H
(Oct–Mar) SOC–WD
£€ £25 (£35)
🚗 2 miles E of Bognor Regis, off
A259
🏠 James Braid
■ www.bognorgolfclub.co.uk

Brinsbury College (1991)

North Heath, Pulborough, RH20 1DZ
☎ (01798) 872218
🖩 (01798) 875222
📖 200
🏌 S Hall (01798) 877421
/ S Hall (01798) 877421
🏳 9 holes Par 62 SSS 57
🏌 WD–U WE–U exc Sun am–NA
SOC–WD
£€ £8 (£12)
🚗 2 miles N of Pulborough on A29
⊕ Driving range

Burgess Hill Golf Centre

Pay and play
Cuckfield Road, Burgess Hill
☎ (01444) 258585
🖩 (01444) 247318
🏌 CJ Collins (Mgr)
/ M Groombridge
🏳 9 hole Par 3 course
🏌 U
£€ On application
🚗 N of Burgess Hill
⊕ Floodlit driving range
🏠 Steel/Collins
■ www.golfsussex.co.uk

Chartham Park (1993)

Proprietary
Felcourt, East Grinstead, RH19 2JT
☎ (01342) 870340
🖩 (01342) 870719
🏌 PJ Smith (Gen Mgr)
/ D Hobbs (01342) 870008
🏳 18 L 6688 yds Par 72 SSS 72
🏌 WD–U WE–U after 12 noon
£€ £30 (£35)
🚗 2 miles N of East Grinstead, off
A22. M25 Junction 6
⊕ Driving range
🏠 Neil Coles

Chichester (1990)

Hunston Village, Chichester, PO20 6AX
☎ (01243) 533833
🖩 (01243) 539922
✉ enquiries@chichestergolf.com
📖 575
/ J Slinger
🏳 18 L 6442 yds SSS 71
18 L 6109 yds SSS 69
9 hole Par 3 course
🏌 U SOC
£€ £16–£21 (£18–£29)
🚗 2 miles S of A27 on B2145 to
Selsey
⊕ Driving range
🏠 Phillip Sanders
■ www.chichestergolf.com

Copthorne (1892)

Borers Arm Road, Copthorne, RH10 3LL
☎ (01342) 712508
🖩 (01342) 717682
✉ info@copthornegolfclub.co.uk
📖 565
🏌 JP Pyne (01342) 712033
/ J Burrell (01342) 712405
🏳 18 L 6435 yds SSS 71

WD–U WE/BH–after 1pm SOC
££ £32 (£40)
1 mile E of M23 Junction 10, on A264
James Braid
www.copthornegolfclub.co.uk

Cottesmore (1975)

Proprietary
Buchan Hill, Pease Pottage, Crawley, RH11 9AT
☎ (01293) 528256
(01293) 522819
cottesmore@americangolf.uk.com
800
B Pearmaine
C Callan (01293) 535399
Griffin 18 L 6248 yds Par 71 SSS 70
Phoenix 18 L 5514 yds Par 69 SSS 67
U SOC
££ Griffin–£22.50 (£30)
Phoenix–£12 (£16)
4 miles S of Crawley, off M23 Junction 11
MD Rogerson

Cowdray Park (1920)

Petworth Road, Midhurst, GU29 0BB
☎ (01730) 813599
(01730) 815900
700
P Fairminer
R Gough (01730) 813599
18 L 6212 yds SSS 70
WD–H WE/BH–H NA before 11.30am SOC
££ £38
1 mile E of Midhurst on A272
T Simpson

Effingham Park (1980)

West Park Road, Copthorne, RH10 3EU
☎ (01342) 716528
(01342) 716039
300
IWB McRobbie (Hon)
M Root
9 L 1815 yds Par 30 SSS 57
WD–U exc Wed & Thurs before 12 noon WE–U after 11.30am
££ £10 D–£15 (£12 D–£17)
B2028/B2039. M23 Junction 10
Golf academy
Francisco Escario

Foxbridge (1993)

Foxbridge Lane, Plaistow, RH14 0LB
☎ (01403) 753303 (Bookings)
(01403) 753433
300
PA Clark
S Hall
9 L 3118 yds SSS 70
U SOC
££ £18 (£25)
15 miles S of Guildford, off B2133
Paul Clark

Goodwood (1892)

Kennel Hill, Goodwood, Chichester, PO18 0PN
☎ (01243) 774968
(01243) 781741
900
Carole Davison (01243) 774968
K MacDonald (01243) 774994
18 L 6401 yds SSS 71
WD–H after 9am WE–H after 10am SOC–Wed & Thurs
££ £32 (£42)
3 miles NE of Chichester, on road to racecourse
James Braid

Goodwood Park G&CC (1989)

Goodwood, Chichester, PO18 0QB
☎ (01243) 520117
700
M Pierce
A Wratting
18 L 6530 yds SSS 72
WD–H WE/BH–NA before noon H SOC
££ £28 (£35)
4 miles N of Chichester
Driving range
Donald Steel

Ham Manor (1936)

West Drive, Angmering, Littlehampton, BN16 4JE
☎ (01903) 783288
(01903) 850886
860
VJ Chaszczewski
S Buckley (01903) 783732
18 L 6216 yds SSS 70
WD/WE–H
££ On application
Between Worthing and Littlehampton
HS Colt
www.hammanor.co.uk

Hassocks (1995)

Pay and play
London Road, Hassocks, BN6 9NA
☎ (01273) 846990
(01273) 846070
350
Mrs J Brown (Gen Mgr) (01273) 846630
C Ledger (01273) 846990
18 L 5754 yds Par 70 SSS 68
U
££ £15 (£19.50)
1 mile S of Burgess Hill on A273. 7 miles N of Brighton
Paul Wright
www.hassocksgolfclub.co.uk

Haywards Heath (1922)

High Beech Lane, Haywards Heath, RH16 1SL
☎ (01444) 414457
(01444) 458319
771

GB Kullner
M Henning (01444) 414866
18 L 6248 yds SSS 70
WD/WE–H–restricted SOC–Wed & Thurs
££ £26 (£36)
2 miles N of Haywards Heath, off B2112

Hill Barn (1935)

Public
Hill Barn Lane, Worthing, BN14 9QE
☎ (01903) 237301
AP Higgins
18 L 6224 yds SSS 70
U
££ £12.50 (£13.50)
NE of A27 at Warren Road roundabout
Hawtree

Horsham (1993)

Pay and play
Worthing Road, Horsham, RH13 7AX
☎ (01403) 271525
(01403) 274528
300
E Purton (01403) 271525
L Morris
9 L 2061 yds Par 33 SSS 30
U SOC
££ 9 holes–£7 (£8)
1 mile S of Horsham, off A24

Ifield (1927)

Rusper Road, Ifield, Crawley, RH11 0LN
☎ (01293) 520222
(01293) 612973
875
DJ Knight
J Earl (01293) 523088
18 L 6330 yds SSS 70
WD–H WE–M SOC
££ £26 D–£36
W of Crawley. M23 Junction 11
Hawtree/Taylor

Littlehampton (1889)

170 Rope Walk, Littlehampton, BN17 5DL
☎ (01903) 717170
(01903) 726629
lgc@talk21.com
650
S Graham (01903) 717170
G McQuitty (01903) 716369
18 L 6244 yds SSS 70
WD–U after 9.30am WE/BH–NA before noon SOC
££ £28 (£35)
W bank of River Arun, Littlehampton
Hawtree

Mannings Heath (1905)

Fullers, Hammerpond Road, Mannings Heath, Horsham RH13 6PG
☎ (01403) 210228
(01403) 270974
730
S Kershaw

✓ C Tucker (01403) 210228
▶ Waterfall 18 L 6378 yds SSS 70;
  Kingfisher 18 L 6217 yds SSS 70
👥 U H SOC
££ £34 (£42)
🚗 3 miles SE of Horsham (A281).
  M23 Junction 11
⊕ Driving range
🏠 Kingfisher-David Williams
■ www.exclusivehotels.co.uk

Paxhill Park   (1990)

East Mascalls Lane, Lindfield, RH16 2QN
☎ (01444) 484467
📠 (01444) 482709
✉ johnbowen@paxhillpark.fsnet
  .co.uk
📖 540
✍ JD Bowen
✓ M Green
▶ 18 L 6196 yds SSS 68
👥 WD–U WE–pm only
££ £15 (£20)
🚗 1 mile N of Lindfield, off B2028. 4
  miles NE of Haywards Heath
⊕ Driving range
🏠 Patrick Tallack

Pease Pottage   (1986)

Horsham Road, Pease Pottage, Crawley,
RH11 9AP
☎ (01293) 521706
📖 56
✍ A Venn
✓ D Blair
▶ 9 L 3511 yds SSS 57
👥 U
££ £8.50 (£11)
🚗 S of Crawley, off A23. M23
  Junction 11
⊕ Driving range

Petworth   (1989)

Pay and play
London Road, Petworth, GU28 9LX
☎ (01798) 344097
📠 (01798) 342528
📖 105
✍ A Long (Mgr) (01798) 344097
✓ J Little (01428) 605093
▶ 18 L 6191 yds Par 71 SSS 69
👥 U SOC
££ £10 D–£13.50
🚗 2¹/₂ miles N of Petworth on A283
⊕ Driving range
🏠 C & T Duncton

Pyecombe   (1894)

Clayton Hill, Pyecombe, Brighton,
BN45 7FF
☎ (01273) 845372
📠 (01273) 843338
✉ pycombegc@btopenworld.com
📖 650
✍ IR Bradbery
✓ CR White (01273) 845398
▶ 18 L 6278 yds SSS 70
👥 WD–U exc Tues after 9.15am
  WE–U after 2pm
  SOC–Mon/Wed/Thurs
££ £25 (£30)
🚗 6 miles N of Brighton on A273

Rustington   (1992)

Public
Golfers Lane, Angmering, BN16 4NB
☎ (01903) 850790
📠 (01903) 850982
✍ SP Langmead
✓ (01903) 850790
▶ 18 L 5735 yds Par 70 SSS 68
  9 hole Par 3 course
👥 U SOC
££ On application
🚗 On A259 between Worthing and
  Littlehampton
⊕ Floodlit driving range
🏠 David Williams
■ www.rgcgolf.com

Selsey   (1908)

Golf Links Lane, Selsey, PO20 9DR
☎ (01243) 605176 (Members)
📠 (01243) 602203
📖 400
✍ P Carter (01243) 602203
✓ P Grindley
▶ 9 L 5834 yds SSS 68
👥 U
££ 18 holes–£11 (£18). 9 holes–£10
  (£14)
🚗 7 miles S of Chichester

Shillinglee Park   (1980)

Pay and play
Chiddingfold, Godalming, GU8 4TA
☎ (01428) 653237
📠 (01428) 644391
📖 400
✍ G Baxter (Prop)
✓ M Dowdell
▶ 9 L 2516 yds Par 32
👥 U SOC exc Sat am
££ 18 holes–£13 (£15) 9 holes–£8.50
  (£9.50)
🚗 2¹/₂ miles SE of Chiddingfold
⊕ Pitch & putt course
🏠 Roger Mace

Singing Hills   (1992)

Proprietary
Albourne, Brighton, BN6 9EB
☎ (01273) 835353
📠 (01273) 835444
📖 400
✍ DO Weston
✓ W Street
▶ 27 holes SSS 69-72:
  River 9 L 2826 yds
  Valley 9 L 3348 yds
  Lakes 9 L 3253 yds
👥 U SOC
££ £23 (£31)
🚗 6 miles N of Brighton, off B2117
⊕ Driving range
🏠 MRM Sandow

Slinfold Park   (1993)

Stane Street, Slinfold, Horsham,
RH13 7RE
☎ (01403) 791154 (Clubhouse)
📠 (01403) 791465
📖 600
✍ S Blake (Gen Mgr)

✓ T Clingan (01403) 791555
▶ 18 L 6450 yds SSS 71
  9 hole course
👥 U SOC
££ £25 (£30)
🚗 3 miles W of Horsham (A29)
⊕ Driving range. Academy course
🏠 John Fortune
■ www.slinfoldpark.co.uk

Tilgate Forest   (1982)

Public
Titmus Drive, Tilgate, Crawley,
RH10 5EU
☎ (01293) 530103
📠 (01293) 523478
📖 320
✍ T Reagan
✓ S Trussell, D McClelland
▶ 18 L 6359 yds SSS 70
  9 hole Par 3 course
👥 U SOC–Mon–Thurs
££ 18 hole:£12 (£16) 9 hole:£4 (£5.30)
🚗 1¹/₂ miles SE of Crawley. M23
  Junction 11
⊕ Driving range

West Chiltington   (1988)

Proprietary
Broadford Bridge Road, West
Chiltington, RH20 2YA
☎ (01798) 813574
📠 (01798) 812631
✉ cottongolf@westchiltington
  .fsbusiness.co.uk
📖 500
✍ G McKay
✓ Lorraine Cousins
  (01798) 812115
▶ 18 L 5969 yds Par 70 SSS 69
  9 hole Par 3 course
👥 U SOC
££ £18 (£22.50)
🚗 2 miles E of Pulborough
⊕ Driving range
🏠 Faulkner/Barnes

West Sussex   (1930)

Golf Club Lane, Wiggonholt,
Pulborough, RH20 2EN
☎ (01798) 872563
📠 (01798) 872033
✉ secretary@westsussexgolf.co.uk
📖 800
✍ CP Simpson
✓ T Packham (01798) 872426
▶ 18 L 6223 yds SSS 70
👥 WD–I H after 9.30am exc Fri–M
  SOC–Wed & Thurs
££ On application
🚗 1¹/₂ miles E of Pulborough on A283
⊕ Driving range
🏠 Campbell/Hutcheson
■ www.westsussexgolf.co.uk

Worthing   (1905)

Links Road, Worthing, BN14 9QZ
☎ (01903) 260801
📠 (01903) 694664
📖 1000
✍ IJ Evans (01903) 260801
✓ S Rolley (01903) 260718

☞ Lower 18 L 6530 yds Par 71
SSS 72
Upper 18 L 5243 yds Par 66 SSS 66
☺ WD–U H WE–confirm in advance
with Pro
£€ On application
⛳ Central Station 1½ miles (A27), nr
A24 Junction
⛳ HS Colt
■ www.worthinggolf.co.uk

Tyne & Wear

Backworth (1937)
*The Hall, Backworth, Shiremoor,
Newcastle-upon-Tyne NE27 0AH*
☎ (0191) 268 1048
🖵 400
✍ GM Sales
✓ None
☞ 9 L 5930 yds SSS 69
☺ Mon & Fri–U Tues–Thurs–M after
5pm WE–after 12.30pm exc comp
Sats–after 6pm
£€ On application
⛳ Off Tyne Tunnel link road,
Holystone roundabout

Birtley (1922)
Birtley Lane, Birtley, DH3 2LR
☎ (0191) 410 2207
🖵 230
✍ RC Landells
☞ 9 L 5660 yds SSS 67
☺ WD–U exc Fri pm–M WE/BH–M
SOC
£€ £14.50
⛳ 3 miles from Birtley service area on
A1(M)

Boldon (1912)
Dipe Lane, East Boldon, NE36 0PQ
☎ (0191) 536 4182 (Clubhouse)
🖵 (0191) 537 2270
✉ info@boldongolfclub.co.uk
🖵 700
✍ RW Benton (0191) 536 5360
✓ Phipps Golf (0191) 536 5835
☞ 18 L 6348 yds SSS 70
☺ WD–U WE/BH–NA before 3.30pm
£€ £20 (£24)
⛳ 8 miles SE of Newcastle
⊕ Driving range
⛳ H Vardon
■ www.boldongolfclub.co.uk

City of Newcastle (1891)
*Three Mile Bridge, Gosforth, Newcastle-
upon-Tyne, NE3 2DR*
☎ (0191) 285 1775
🖵 (0191) 284 0700
🖵 400 110(L) 60(J)
✍ AJ Matthew (Mgr)
✓ S McKenna (0191) 285 5481
☞ 18 L 6528 yds SSS 71
☺ U SOC
£€ £25 D–£30 (£30)
⛳ B1318, 3 miles N of Newcastle
⛳ Harry Vardon

Garesfield (1922)
Chopwell, NE17 7AP
☎ (01207) 561309
🖵 (01207) 561309
🖵 700
✍ WG Dunn
✓ D Race (01207) 563082
☞ 18 L 6458 yds SSS 71
☺ WD–U WE/BH–NA before 4.30pm
SOC
£€ On application
⛳ 7 miles SW of Newcastle, between
High Spen and Chopwell

Gosforth (1906)
*Broadway East, Gosforth, Newcastle
upon Tyne, NE3 5ER*
☎ (0191) 285 6710
🖵 (0191) 284 6274
🖵 380 100(L) 60(J)
✍ B Pluse (0191) 285 3495
✓ G Garland (0191) 285 0553
☞ 18 L 6024 yds SSS 69
☺ U SOC
£€ £25 (£25)
⛳ 3 miles N of Newcastle, off A6125

Hetton-le-Hole
Pay and play
*Elemore Golf Course, Elemore Lane,
DH5 0QB*
☎ (0191) 517 3057
🖵 (0191) 517 3054
✍ E Booth
☞ 18 L 5950 yds Par 69
☺ U SOC
£€ £9.50 (£12.50)
⛳ 4 miles E of A1(M)/A690 junction

Heworth (1912)
*Gingling Gate, Heworth, Gateshead,
NE10 8XY*
☎ (0191) 469 4424
✉ theheworthgolfclub@supanet.com
🖵 800
✍ G Holbrow
✓ A Marshall
☞ 18 L 6404 yds SSS 71
☺ WD–U WE–NA before noon
£€ £18
⛳ SE boundary of Gateshead

Houghton-le-Spring (1908)
Copt Hill, Houghton-le-Spring, DH5 8LU
☎ (0191) 584 1198
🖵 600
✍ N Wales (0191) 584 0048
✓ (0191) 584 7421
☞ 18 L 6416 yds Par 72 SSS 71
☺ U SOC
£€ £20 (£27)
⛳ 3 miles SW of Sunderland

Newcastle United (1892)
*Ponteland Road, Cowgate, Newcastle-
upon-Tyne, NE5 3JW*
☎ (0191) 286 4693 (Clubhouse)
🖵 700
✍ J Simpson (Hon)
✓ (0191) 286 9998

☞ 18 L 6617 yds SSS 72
☺ WD–U WE/BH–M
£€ On application
⛳ Nuns Moor, 2 miles W of city
centre

Northumberland (1898)
*High Gosforth Park, Newcastle-upon-
Tyne, NE3 5HT*
☎ (0191) 236 2498
🖵 (0191) 236 2498
🖵 500
✍ JM Forteath QGM
✓ None
☞ 18 L 6629 yds SSS 72
☺ WD–I BH–M
£€ £35–£45
⛳ 5 miles N of Newcastle
⛳ HS Colt/James Braid

Parklands (1971)
*High Gosforth Park, Newcastle-upon-
Tyne, NE3 5HQ*
☎ (0191) 236 4480/4867
🖵 500
✍ B Woof
✓ B Rumney
☞ 18 L 6013 yds Par 71 SSS 69
☺ U
£€ £15 (£18)
⛳ 5 miles N of Newcastle
⊕ 9 hole pitch & putt course. Driving
range

Ravensworth (1906)
*Moss Heaps, Wrekenton, Gateshead,
NE9 7UU*
☎ (0191) 487 6014/2843
🖵 550
✍ RW Hill (091) 442 1042
✓ S Cowell (0191) 491 3475
☞ 18 L 5872 yds SSS 68
☺ U H SOC
£€ £19 (£28)
⛳ 3 miles S of Newcastle on B1296

Ryton (1891)
*Doctor Stanners, Clara Vale, Ryton,
NE40 3TD*
☎ (0191) 413 3253
🖵 (0191) 413 1642
✉ secretary@rytongolfclub.co.uk
🖵 600
✍ S Dix
☞ 18 L 5499 metres SSS 69
☺ WD–U WE–M SOC
£€ £16 (£21)
⛳ 7 miles W of Newcastle, off A695

South Shields (1893)
Cleadon Hills, South Shields, NE34 8EG
☎ (0191) 456 0475
✉ thesecretary@south-shields-
golf.freeserve.co.uk
🖵 700
✍ R Stanness (0191) 456 8942
✓ G Parsons (0191) 456 0110
☞ 18 L 5984 yds SSS 69
☺ U SOC
£€ On application
⛳ Cleadon Hills

Tynemouth (1913)

Spital Dene, Tynemouth, North Shields,
NE30 2ER
- ☎ **(0191) 257 4578**
- 📠 (0191) 259 5193
- 📖 855
- 🏌 W Storey (0191) 257 3381
- ⛳ J McKenna (0191) 258 0728
- ▷ 18 L 6359 yds SSS 70
- 👥 WD–U 9.30am–5pm –NA before
  9.30am and after 5pm WE/BH–M
- ££ £20 D–£25
- 🚗 8 miles E of Newcastle
- 🏠 Willie Park

Tyneside (1879)

Westfield Lane, Ryton, NE40 3QE
- ☎ **(0191) 413 2177**
- 📠 (0191) 413 2742
- 📖 660
- 🏌 E Stephenson (0191) 413 2742
- ⛳ M Gunn (0191) 413 1600
- ▷ 18 L 6033 yds SSS 69
- 👥 WD–U exc 11.30–1.30pm Sat–NA
  Sun–NA before 3pm SOC
- ££ £20 (£20)
- 🚗 7 miles W of Newcastle. S of river,
  off A695
- 🏠 HS Colt

Wallsend (1973)

Public
Rheydt Avenue, Bigges Main, Wallsend,
NE28 8SU
- ☎ **(0191) 262 1973**
- ⛳ D Souter
- ⛳ K Phillips (0191) 262 4231
- ▷ 18 L 6608 yds SSS 72
- 👥 U
- ££ £15.50 (£17.50)
- 🚗 Between Newcastle and Wallsend
  on coast road
- ⊕ Driving range
- 🏠 G Showball

Washington (1979)

Stone Cellar Road, High Usworth,
District 12, Washington NE37 1PH
- ☎ **(0191) 417 8346**
- 📠 (0191) 415 1166
- 📖 600
- 🏌 G Robinson
- ⛳ D Patterson
- ▷ 18 L 6604 yds SSS 72
  9 hole Par 3 course
- 👥 WD–U WE–after 10.30am SOC
- ££ £20 (£25)
- 🚗 Off A1(M), on A195
- ⊕ Driving range
- 🖥 www.corushotels.com/hotels
  /wasgeo

Wearside (1892)

Coxgreen, Sunderland, SR4 9JT
- ☎ **(0191) 534 2518**
- 📠 (0191) 534 6186
- 📖 800
- 🏌 M Gowland
- ⛳ D Brolls (0191) 534 4269
- ▷ 18 L 6315 yds SSS 70
  Par 3 course

- 👥 H SOC
- ££ £20 (£26)
- 🚗 2 miles W of Sunderland, off A183,
  by A19

Westerhope (1941)

Whorlton Grange, Westerhope,
Newcastle-upon-Tyne, NE5 1PP
- ☎ **(0191) 286 9125**
- 📖 778
- 🏌 R Pears (0191) 286 7636
- ⛳ N Brown (0191) 286 0594
- ▷ 18 L 6407 yds SSS 71
- 👥 WD–U
- ££ £16
- 🚗 5 miles W of Newcastle

Whickham (1911)

Hollinside Park, Fellside Road,
Whickham, Newcastle-upon-Tyne
NE16 5BA
- ☎ **(0191) 488 7309 (Clubhouse)**
- 📠 (0191) 488 1577
- 📖 650
- 🏌 Mrs J Miller (0191) 488 1576
- ⛳ G Lisle (0191) 488 8591
- ▷ 18 L 5878 yds Par 68 SSS 68
- 👥 U SOC–WD
- ££ £20 (£25)
- 🚗 5 miles SW of Newcastle

Whitburn (1931)

Lizard Lane, South Shields, NE34 7AF
- ☎ **(0191) 529 2144**
- 📠 (0191) 529 4944
- 📖 580 73(L) 85(J)
- 🏌 Mrs V Atkinson (0191) 529 4944
- ⛳ D Stephenson (0191) 529 4210
- ▷ 18 L 5899 yds Par 70 SSS 68
- 👥 U SOC–WD exc Tues
- ££ £20 (£26)
- 🚗 2 miles N of Sunderland on coast
- 🏠 Colt/Alison/Morrison

Whitley Bay (1890)

Claremont Road, Whitley Bay,
NE26 3UF
- ☎ **(0191) 252 0180**
- 📠 (0191) 297 0030
- 📧 secretary@whitleybaygolfclub
  .co.uk
- 📖 700
- 🏌 H Hanover
- ⛳ G Shipley (0191) 252 5688
- ▷ 18 L 6579 yds SSS 71
- 👥 WD–U WE–M
- ££ £22 D–£30
- 🚗 10 miles E of Newcastle
- 🖥 www.wbgolf.free-online.co.uk

Warwickshire

Ansty (1992)

Brinklow Road, Ansty, Coventry,
CV7 9JH
- ☎ **(024) 7662 1341/7660 2568**
- 📠 (024) 7660 2568
- 📖 375
- 🏌 S Firkins
- ⛳ S Firkins

- ▷ 18 L 6079 yds Par 71 SSS 69
  Par 3 course
- 👥 U SOC
- ££ £10 (£14)
- 🚗 Between Ansty and Brinklow
  (B4029). M6 Junction 2, 1 mile.
- ⊕ Driving range
- 🏠 D Morgan

Atherstone (1894)

The Outwoods, Coleshill Road,
Atherstone, CV9 2RL
- ☎ **(01827) 713110**
- 📠 (01827) 715686
- 📖 400 40(L) 40(J)
- 🏌 VA Walton (01827) 892568
- ▷ 18 L 6012 yds Par 72 SSS 70
- 👥 WD–U BH/Sat–M Sun–M after
  5pm SOC–WD
- ££ D–£25 Mon–£15
- 🚗 ¼ mile from Atherstone on
  Coleshill road

The Belfry (1977)

Public
Wishaw, B76 9PR
- ☎ **(01675) 470301**
- 📠 (01675) 470174
- 🏌 R Maxfield
- ⛳ P McGovern
- ▷ Brabazon 18 L 7118 yds SSS 74
  Derby 18 L 6009 yds SSS 69
  PGA National 18 L 6737 yds
  SSS 72
- 👥 H SOC
- ££ Brabazon £70–£130. PGA National
  £40–£65. Derby £20–£35
- 🚗 2 miles N of M42 Junction 9, off
  A446
- ⊕ Driving range
- 🏠 Brabazon & Derby-Alliss/Thomas;
  PGA National-Thomas

Bidford Grange (1992)

Stratford Road, Bidford-on-Avon,
B50 4LY
- ☎ **(01789) 490319**
- 📠 (01789) 778184
- 📖 310
- 🏌 M Smith (Mgr)
- ⛳ D Webber
- ▷ 18 L 7233 yds Par 72 SSS 74
- 👥 U SOC
- ££ £12 (£15)
- 🚗 5 miles W of Stratford-on-Avon on
  B439
- 🏠 Swann/Tillman/Granger

Boldmere (1936)

Public
Monmouth Drive, Sutton Coldfield,
Birmingham, BJ3 6JR
- ☎ **(0121) 354 3379**
- 📧 boldmeregolfclub@hotmail.com
- 📖 300
- 🏌 R Leeson
- ⛳ T Short
- ▷ 18 L 4463 yds SSS 62
- 👥 U
- ££ £9 (£11)
- 🚗 By Sutton Park, 1 mile W of Sutton
  Coldfield

Bramcote Waters

Pay and play
Bazzard Road, Bramcote, Nuneaton, CV11 6QJ
☎ **(01455) 220807**
🖷 (01203) 388775
✒ N Gilks
⊳ 9 L 4995 yds Par 66 SSS 64
♟ U
£€ £12 (£13)
⛳ 4 miles SE of Nuneaton, off B4114
🏠 David Snell

City of Coventry (Brandon Wood) (1977)

Public
Brandon Lane, Coventry, CV8 3GQ
☎ **(024) 7654 3141**
🖷 (024) 7654 5108
📖 400
✒ C Gledhill
✒ C Gledhill
⊳ 18 L 6521 yds SSS 71
♟ U SOC
£€ On application
⛳ 6 miles SE of Coventry, off A45(S)
⊕ Floodlit driving range

Copt Heath (1907)

1220 Warwick Road, Knowle, Solihull, B93 9LN
☎ **(01564) 772650**
🖷 (01564) 771022
🖳 golf@copt-heath.co.uk
📖 700
✒ CV Hadley
✒ BJ Barton (01564) 776155
⊳ 18 L 6508 yds SSS 71
♟ WD–H WE/BH–M SOC
£€ £40 – £50
⛳ 2 miles S of Solihull on A4141. M42 Junction 5

Coventry (1887)

St Martins Road, Finham Park, Coventry, CV3 6RJ
☎ **(024) 7641 1123**
🖷 (024) 7669 0131
🖳 coventrygolfclub@hotmail.com
📖 750
✒ GL Pearce (024) 7641 4152
✒ P Weaver (024) 7641 1298
⊳ 18 L 6601 yds SSS 73
♟ WD–H
£€ £35
⛳ 2 miles S of Coventry on A444/B4113
🏠 Vardon/Hawtree
■ www.coventrygolfcourse.co.uk

Coventry Hearsall (1894)

Beechwood Avenue, Coventry, CV5 6DF
☎ **(024) 7671 3470**
🖷 (024) 7669 1534
📖 600
✒ Mrs ME Hudson
✒ M Tarn (024) 7671 3156
⊳ 18 L 6005 yds SSS 69
♟ WD–U WE–M
£€ D–£30
⛳ 1¹/₂ miles S of Coventry, off A45

Edgbaston (1896)

Church Road, Edgbaston, Birmingham, B15 3TB
☎ **(0121) 454 1736**
🖷 (0121) 454 2395
🖳 secretary@edgbastongc.co.uk
📖 950
✒ P Heath
✒ J Cundy (0121) 454 3226
⊳ 18 L 6106 yds SSS 69
♟ H SOC
£€ £40 (£50)
⛳ 1¹/₂ miles S of Birmingham, off A38
🏠 HS Colt
■ www.edgbastongc.co.uk

Harborne (1893)

40 Tennal Road, Harborne, Birmingham, B32 2JE
☎ **(0121) 427 1728**
🖷 (0121) 427 4039
📖 600
✒ GA Tozer (0121) 427 3058
✒ A Quarterman (0121) 427 3512
⊳ 18 L 6210 yds SSS 70
♟ WD–U WE/BH–M SOC
£€ £30 D–£35
⛳ 3 miles SW of Birmingham. M5 Junction 3
🏠 HS Colt

Harborne Church Farm (1926)

Public
Vicarage Road, Harborne, Birmingham, B17 0SN
☎ **(0121) 427 1204**
🖷 (0121) 428 3126
📖 180
✒ B Flanagan
✒ P Johnson
⊳ 9 L 4882 yds Par 66 SSS 64
♟ U
£€ 18 holes–£8.50 (£10) 9 holes–£6 (£7)
⛳ 3 miles SW of Birmingham
■ www.learnaboutgolf.co.uk

Hatchford Brook (1969)

Public
Coventry Road, Sheldon, Birmingham, B26 3PY
☎ **(0121) 743 9821**
🖷 (0121) 743 3420
🖳 idt@hbgc.freeserve.co.uk
📖 400
✒ ID Thomson (0121) 742 6643
✒ M Hampton
⊳ 18 L 6137 yds Par 70 SSS 69
♟ U SOC
£€ £9 (£10)
⛳ City boundary close to airport. A45/M42 Junction
■ www.golfpro-direct.co.uk/hbgc

Henley G&CC (1994)

Birmingham Road, Henley-in-Arden, B95 5QA
☎ **(01564) 793715**
🖷 (01564) 795754
🖳 enquiries@henleygcc.co.uk
📖 600
✒ TN Collingwood (Gen Mgr)
✒ N Hyde
⊳ 18 L 6933 yds SSS 73
9 hole Par 3 course
♟ U–booking required SOC
£€ £25 (£30)
⛳ N of Stratford-on-Avon on A3400. M40 Junction 16, 3 miles
⊕ Driving range
🏠 N Selwyn-Smith

Hilltop (1979)

Public
Park Lane, Handsworth, Birmingham, B21 8LJ
☎ **(0121) 554 4463**
✒ K Highfield (Mgr)
✒ K Highfield
⊳ 18 L 6114 yds SSS 69
♟ U
£€ £9.50 (£11)
⛳ Sandwell Valley. M5 Junction 1

Ingon Manor (1993)

Ingon Lane, Snitterfield, Stratford-on-Avon, CV37 0QE
☎ **(01789) 731857**
🖳 info@ingonmanor.co.uk
📖 350
✒ P Taylor (01789) 731938
⊳ 18 L 6575 yds Par 73 SSS 71
♟ U H SOC
£€ £25 (£30)
⛳ 3 miles N of Stratford-on-Avon, off A461. M40 Junction 15
⊕ Driving range
🏠 David Hemstock
■ www.ingonmanor.co.uk

Kenilworth (1889)

Crewe Lane, Kenilworth, CV8 2EA
☎ **(01926) 854296**
🖷 (01926) 864453
🖳 info@kenilworthgolfclub.fsnet.co.uk
📖 750
✒ J McTavish (01926) 858517
✒ S Yates (01926) 512732
⊳ 18 L 6400 yds SSS 71
♟ U H BH–M SOC–WD
£€ £32 (£40)
⛳ 1¹/₂ miles E of Kenilworth. 5 miles S of Coventry
🏠 Hawtree
■ www.kenilworthgolfclub.org.uk

Ladbrook Park (1908)

Poolhead Lane, Tanworth-in-Arden, Solihull, B94 5ED
☎ **(01564) 742264**
🖷 (01564) 742909
📖 700
✒ Mrs SE Burrows (Admin)
✒ R Mountford (01564) 742581
⊳ 18 L 6427 yds SSS 71
♟ WD–U H WE/BH–M H
£€ On application
⛳ 12 miles S of Birmingham. M42 Junction 3
🏠 HS Colt

Leamington & County
(1908)

Golf Lane, Whitnash, Leamington Spa, CV31 2QA

- ☎ **(01926) 425961**
- 📠 (01926) 425961
- ✉ secretary@leamingtongolf.co.uk
- 📖 650
- ✍ SM Cooknell
- ⛳ J Mellor (01926) 428014
- ⛳ 18 L 6439 yds SSS 71
- 👤 U SOC
- ££ £27 (£40)
- ⛳ 1½ miles S of Leamington Spa
- ⛳ HS Colt

Marconi (Grange GC)
Copsewood, Coventry, CV3 1HS

- ☎ **(024) 7656 3339**
- 📖 350
- ✍ REC Jones (Hon)
- ⛳ 9 L 6048 yds SSS 71
- 👤 WD–U before 2.30pm exc Wed–NA Sat–NA Sun–NA before noon
- ££ £12 Sun–£15
- ⛳ 2½ miles E of Coventry on A428
- ⛳ TJ McAuley

Marriott Forest of Arden Hotel (1970)
Maxstoke Lane, Meriden, Coventry, CV7 7HR

- ☎ **(01676) 522335**
- 📠 (01676) 523711
- 📖 650
- ✍ M Newey (Golf Dir)
- ⛳ P Hoye
- ⛳ Arden 18 L 6719 yds Par 72 SSS 73
      Aylesford 18 L 5801 yds Par 69 SSS 68
- 👤 WD–U SOC–WD
- ££ Arden–£70 (£80)
      Aylesford–£35 (£45)
- ⛳ 9 miles W of Coventry, off A45. M6 Junction 4
- ⊕ Driving range
- ⛳ Donald Steel

Maxstoke Park (1898)
Castle Lane, Coleshill, Birmingham, B46 2RD

- ☎ **(01675) 466743**
- 📠 (01675) 466185
- ✉ @maxstokepark.fsnet.co.uk
- 📖 780
- ✍ GE Crawford
- ⛳ N McEwan (01675) 464915
- ⛳ 18 L 6442 yds SSS 71
- 👤 WD–U H WE–M
- ££ £27.50
- ⛳ 3 miles SE of Coleshill. M6 Junction 6

Moor Hall (1932)
Moor Hall Drive, Four Oaks, Sutton Coldfield, B75 6LN

- ☎ **(0121) 308 6130**
- 📠 (0121) 308 6130
- ✉ manager@moorhallgolfclub.fsnet .co.uk
- 📖 668
- ✍ DJ Etheridge
- ⛳ A Partridge (0121) 308 5106
- ⛳ 18 L 6249 yds SSS 70
- 👤 WD–U H exc Thurs–U after 1pm WE/BH–M
- ££ £33 D–£44
- ⛳ 1 mile E of Sutton Coldfield

Newbold Comyn (1973)
Public

Newbold Terrace East, Leamington Spa, CV32 4EW

- ☎ **(01926) 421157**
- 📖 191
- ✍ CV Baker (01926) 887220
- ⛳ R Carvell
- ⛳ 18 L 6315 yds SSS 70
- 👤 WD–U WE–booking 1 week in advance SOC
- ££ £8 (£12.30)
- ⛳ Off Willes Road (B4099)

North Warwickshire (1894)
Hampton Lane, Meriden, Coventry, CV7 7LL

- ☎ **(01676) 522464 (Clubhouse)**
- 📠 (01676) 523004
- 📖 450
- ✍ AJ Finn (Hon) (01676) 522915
- ⛳ A Bownes (01676) 522259
- ⛳ 9 L 6374 yds SSS 71
- 👤 WD–U WE/BH–M SOC
- ££ £20
- ⛳ 6 miles W of Coventry, off A45

Nuneaton (1905)
Golf Drive, Whitestone, Nuneaton, CV11 6QF

- ☎ **(024) 7634 7810**
- 📠 (024) 7632 7563
- 📖 650
- ✍ P Smith
- ⛳ J Salter (024) 7634 0201
- ⛳ 18 L 6412 yds SSS 71
- 👤 WD–U H WE–M SOC
- ££ £28 D–£33
- ⛳ 2 miles S of Nuneaton, off Lutterworth road

Oakridge
Arley Lane, Ansley Village, Nuneaton, CV10 9PH

- ☎ **(01676) 541389**
- 📠 (01676) 542709
- 📖 500
- ✍ Mrs S Lovric (Admin)
- ⛳ 18 L 6242 yds Par 72 SSS 70
- 👤 U SOC–WD
- ££ £16
- ⛳ B4112 from Nuneaton. M6 Junction 3
- ⛳ Algie Jayes

Olton (1893)
Mirfield Road, Solihull, B91 1JH

- ☎ **(0121) 705 1083**
- 📠 (0121) 711 2010
- ✉ mailbox@oltongolfclub.fsnet.co.uk

- 📖 600
- ✍ BG Smith (0121) 704 1936
- ⛳ C Haynes (0121) 705 7296
- ⛳ 18 L 6232 yds SSS 71
- 👤 WD–U exc Wed am WE–M
- ££ £25–£35
- ⛳ 7 miles SE of Birmingham (A41)
- 🌐 www.oltongolf.co.uk

Purley Chase (1980)
Pipers Lane, Ridge Lane, Nuneaton, CV10 0RB

- ☎ **(024) 7639 3118**
- ✉ enquiries@purley-chase.co.uk
- 📖 600
- ✍ Linda Jackson
- ⛳ 18 L 6772 yds SSS 72
- 👤 WD/BH–U WE–U after 2.30pm SOC
- ££ On application
- ⛳ 4 miles WNW of Nuneaton on B114 (A47). A5 Mancetter Island

Pype Hayes (1932)
Public

Eachelhurst Road, Walmley, Sutton Coldfield, B76 8EP

- ☎ **(0121) 351 1014**
- 📠 (0121) 313 0206
- 📖 320
- ✍ L Brogan
- ⛳ J Kelly
- ⛳ 18 L 5996 yds SSS 69
- 👤 U
- ££ On application
- ⛳ 5 miles NE of Birmingham

Robin Hood (1893)
St Bernards Road, Solihull, B92 7DJ

- ☎ **(0121) 706 0061**
- 📠 (0121) 706 0061
- 📖 650
- ⛳ A Harvey (0121) 706 0806
- ⛳ 18 L 6635 yds SSS 72
- 👤 WD–U WE/BH–M SOC–WD H
- ££ £30 D–£35
- ⛳ 7 miles S of Birmingham
- ⛳ HS Colt

Rugby (1891)
Clifton Road, Rugby, CV21 3RD

- ☎ **(01788) 544637 (Clubhouse)**
- 📠 (01788) 542306
- ✉ golf@rugbygc.fsnet.co.uk
- 📖 750
- ✍ N Towler (01788) 542306
- ⛳ N Summers (01788) 575134
- ⛳ 18 L 5614 yds SSS 67
- 👤 WD–U WE/BH–M SOC
- ££ On application
- ⛳ 1 mile N of Rugby on B5414

Shirley (1956)
Stratford Road, Monkspath, Shirley, Solihull B90 4EW

- ☎ **(0121) 744 6001**
- 📠 (0121) 745 8220
- 📖 650
- ✍ Mrs VA Duggan
- ⛳ S Bottrill (0121) 745 4979
- ⛳ 18 L 6510 yds SSS 71

WD–U WE–M SOC
£€ £25 D–£35
⊶ 8 miles S of Birmingham, nr M42 Junction 4
⌂ John Morrison

Sphinx (1948)
Sphinx Drive, Coventry, CV3 1WA
☎ (024) 7645 1361
⌨ 300
✍ GE Brownbridge (024) 7659 7731
⮞ 9 L 4262 yds SSS 60
Fri/WE–M after 4.30pm SOC
£€ £8 (£10)
⊶ Nr Binley Road, Coventry

Stonebridge Golf Centre
Somers Road, Meriden, CV7 7PL
☎ (01676) 522442
⌨ (01676) 522447
⌨ 400
✍ R Grier
⚲ R Grier
⮞ 18 L 6250 yds Par 70
U
£€ £15.50 (£18.50)
⊶ 2 miles E of M42 Junction 6
⊕ Driving range

Stoneleigh Deer Park (1992)
The Old Deer Park, Coventry Road, Stoneleigh, CV8 3DR
☎ (024) 7663 9991
⌨ (024) 7651 1533
⌨ 800
✍ C Reay
⚲ M McGuire
⮞ 18 L 6023 yds SSS 71
9 hole Par 3 course
WD–U WE–NA before 2pm SOC
£€ On application
⊶ ¹/₂ mile E of Stoneleigh

Stratford Oaks (1991)
Bearley Road, Snitterfield, Stratford-on-Avon, CV37 0EZ
☎ (01789) 731980
⌨ (01789) 731981
✉ admin@stratfordoaks.co.uk
⌨ 700
✍ ND Powell (Golf Dir)
⚲ A Dunbar
⮞ 18 L 6100 yds SSS 71
WD–U WE–U booking necessary
£€ £21 (£26)
⊶ 4 miles NE of Stratford-on-Avon
⊕ Driving range
⌂ Howard Swann

Stratford-on-Avon (1894)
Tiddington Road, Stratford-on-Avon, CV37 7BA
☎ (01789) 205749
⌨ (01789) 414909
⌨ 770
✍ NS Dodd (01789) 205749
⚲ D Sutherland (01789) 205677
⮞ 18 L 6374 yds SSS 70
U H SOC
£€ £35 (£40)
⊶ ¹/₂ mile E of Stratford-on-Avon on B4086

⌂ JH Taylor
◼ www.stratfordgolf.co.uk

Sutton Coldfield (1889)
110 Thornhill Road, Sutton Coldfield, B74 3ER
☎ (0121) 580 7878
⌨ (0121) 353 5503
⌨ 600
✍ RG MItchell, KM Tempest (0121) 353 9633
⚲ JK Hayes (0121) 580 7878
⮞ 18 L 6541 yds SSS 71
U H SOC
£€ £30 D–£40 (£40)
⊶ 9 miles N of Birmingham, off B4138

Tidbury Green (1994)
Pay and play
Tilehouse Lane, Shirley, Solihull, B90 1HP
☎ (01564) 824460
⌨ 300
✍ Lucy Broadhurst
⚲ R Thompson
⮞ 9 L 2473 yds Par 34
U SOC
£€ 18 holes–£9 (£9) 9 holes–£6 (£6)
⊶ 2 miles from M42 Junction 4, nr Earlswood Lakes
⊕ Driving range
⌂ Derek Stevenson

Walmley (1902)
Brooks Road, Wylde Green, Sutton Coldfield, B72 1HR
☎ (0121) 377 7272
⌨ (0121) 377 7272
⌨ 700
✍ MJ Roberts
⚲ CJ Wicketts (0121) 373 7103
⮞ 18 L 6585 yds SSS 72
WD–U WE–M SOC
£€ £30 D–£35
⊶ N boundary of Birmingham

Warwick (1971)
Public
Warwick Racecourse, Warwick, CV34 6HW
☎ (01926) 494316
✍ Mrs R Dunkley
⚲ P Sharp (01926) 491284
⮞ 9 L 2682 yds SSS 66
U exc while racing in progress & Sun am
£€ £10 (£11)
⊶ Centre of Warwick Racecourse
⊕ Driving range
⌂ DG Dunkley

The Warwickshire (1993)
Proprietary
Leek Wootton, Warwick, CV35 7QT
☎ (01926) 409409
⌨ (01926) 408409
⌨ 1100
✍ B Fotheringham (Golf Mgr)
⚲ M Dulson
⮞ 18 L 7178 yds SSS 74

18 L 7154 yds SSS 74
9 hole Par 3 course
H SOC
£€ £39 (£49)
⊶ 1 mile N of Warwick, off A46. M40 Junction 15
⊕ Driving range
⌂ Karl Litton

Welcombe Hotel
Warwick Road, Stratford-on-Avon, CV37 0NR
☎ (01789) 413800
⌨ (01789) 414666
⌨ 200
✍ N Price (01789) 295252
⚲ K Hayler (01789) 413800
⮞ 18 L 6294 yds SSS 70
U H
£€ D–£40 (D–£50)
⊶ 1¹/₂ miles NE of Stratford-on-Avon on A439 towards Warwick. M40 Junction 15
⊕ Driving range
⌂ T McAuley

Whitefields Hotel (1992)
Coventry Road, Thurlaston, Rugby, CV23 9JR
☎ (01788) 815555
⌨ (01788) 521695
✉ mail@whitefields-hotel.co.uk
⌨ 400
✍ B Coleman (01788) 815555
⚲ D Price
⮞ 18 L 6289 yds Par 71 SSS 70
U SOC
£€ £16 (£22)
⊶ 3 miles SW of Rugby at A45/M45 Junction
⊕ Driving range

◼ www.whitefields-hotel.co.uk

Widney Manor (1993)
Pay and play
Saintbury Drive, Widney Manor, Solihull, B91 3SZ
☎ (0121) 704 0704
⌨ (0121) 704 7999
⌨ 503
✍ M Harrhy (Sec/Mgr)
⚲ T Atkinson
⮞ 18 L 5284 yds Par 69
U–booking 5 days in advance SOC
£€ £9.95 (£14.95)
⊶ 3 miles from M42 Junction 4, off A34
⊕ Driving range

Windmill Village (1990)
Birmingham Road, Allesley, Coventry, CV5 9AL
☎ (024) 7640 4041
⌨ (024) 7640 4042
✉ leisure@windmillvillagehotel.co.uk
⌨ 450
✍ M Hartland (Mgr)
⚲ R Hunter (024) 7640 4041
⮞ 18 L 5213 yds Par 70
U SOC
£€ £14.50 (£17.95)

☎ 3 miles W of Coventry on A45
🏠 Hunter/Harrhy

Wishaw (1995)

Bulls Lane, Wishaw, Sutton Coldfield, B76 9AA
☎ **(0121) 313 2110**
▥ 250
✎ PM Lewington
🏴 18 L 5397 yds Par 71 SSS 66
👤 U SOC
££ £12 (£18)
☎ 3 miles NW of M42 Junction 9

Wiltshire

Bowood G&CC (1992)

Proprietary
Derry Hill, Calne, SN11 9PQ
☎ **(01249) 822228**
🖥 (01249) 822218
✉ golfclub@bowood.org
▥ 450
✎ Karen Elson (Mgr)
🏴 M Taylor
🏴 18 L 7317 yds Par 72 SSS 73
👤 U–booking required WE–M before noon SOC
££ £36 (£39)
☎ 3 miles SE of Chippenham on A342. M4 Junction 14 (A4)
⊕ Driving range. 3 Academy holes
🏠 David Thomas
■ www.bowood.org

Bradford-on-Avon (1991)

Trowbridge Road, Bradford-on-Avon
☎ **(01225) 868268**
🏴 G Sawyer
🏴 9 L 2100 metres SSS 61
👤 WD–U WE–pm only
££ 9 holes–£6.50. 18 holes–£10
☎ SE of Bradford, nr River Avon

Brinkworth (1984)

Longmans Farm, Brinkworth, Chippenham, SN15 5DG
☎ **(01666) 510277**
▥ 250
✎ J Sheppard
🏴 18 L 5900 yds SSS 69
👤 U SOC
££ On application
☎ 2 miles from Brinkworth (B4042). 12 miles NE of Chippenham

Broome Manor (1976)

Public
Pipers Way, Swindon, SN3 1RG
☎ **(01793) 532403**
🖥 (01793) 433255
✉ bmgc.sec@eclipse.co.uk
▥ 800
✎ JE Poolman (01793) 823462
🏴 B Sandry (01793) 532403
🏴 18 L 6283 yds SSS 70
  9 L 2690 yds SSS 67
👤 U
££ 18 hole:£14. 9 hole:£9

☎ Swindon 2 miles. M4 Junction 15
⊕ Floodlit driving range
🏠 F Hawtree
■ www.bmgc.co.uk

Chippenham (1896)

Malmesbury Road, Chippenham, SN15 5LT
☎ **(01249) 652040**
🖥 (01249) 446681
▥ 650
✎ D Maddison
🏴 W Creamer (01249) 655519
🏴 18 L 5540 yds SSS 67
👤 U WE–M SOC
££ £22 (£27)
☎ 1 mile N of Chippenham, off A350. M4 Junction 17

Cricklade Hotel (1992)

Common Hill, Cricklade SN6 6HA
☎ **(01793) 750751**
🖥 (01793) 751767
▥ 70
✎ C Withers
🏴 I Bolt
🏴 9 L 1830 yds Par 62 SSS 58
👤 WD–U SOC–WD
££ £16 D–£25
☎ ½ mile W of Cricklade on B4040. M4 Junctions 15/16
🏠 Bolt/Smith

Cumberwell Park (1994)

Bradford-on-Avon, BA15 2PQ
☎ **(01225) 863322**
🖥 (01225) 868160
✉ enquiries@cumberwellpark.co.uk
▥ 1250
🏴 J Jacobs (Golf Dir)
🏴 27 hole course
👤 U SOC
££ £25 (£30)
☎ Between Bradford-on-Avon and Bath on A363. M4 Junction 18
⊕ Driving range
🏠 Adrian Stiff
■ www.cumberwellpark.co.uk

Defence Academy (1953)

Shrivenham, Swindon, SN6 8LA
☎ **(01793) 785725**
▥ 500
✎ R Humphrey (Mgr)
🏴 18 L 5684 yds SSS 69
👤 M SOC
££ £10 (£10)
☎ Grounds of Defence Academy. Entry must be arranged with Mgr

Erlestoke Sands (1992)

Erlestoke, Devizes, SN10 5UB
☎ **(01380) 831069**
🖥 (01380) 831284
✉ info@erlestokesands.co.uk
▥ 620
✎ M Pugsley
🏴 M Walters (01380) 831027
🏴 18 L 6406 yds Par 73 SSS 71
👤 U–book with Pro SOC
££ £20 (£25)

☎ 6 miles E of Westbury on B3098
⊕ Driving area. 3 Academy holes
🏠 Adrian Stiff

Hamptworth G&CC (1994)

Elmtree Farmhouse, Hamptworth Road, Landford, SP5 2DU
☎ **(01794) 390155**
🖥 (01794) 390022
✎ P Stevens
🏴 M White
🏴 18 L 6516 yds SSS 71
👤 H
££ £25 D–£30
☎ 10 miles SE of Salisbury, off A36/B3079. M27 Junction 2, 6 miles
⊕ Driving range
■ www.hamptworthgolf.co.uk

High Post (1922)

Great Durnford, Salisbury, SP4 6AT
☎ **(01722) 782356**
🖥 (01722) 782674
▥ 600
✎ P Grimes (01722) 782356
🏴 I Welding (01722) 782219
🏴 18 L 6305 yds Par 70 SSS 70
👤 WD–U WE/BH–H SOC
££ £28 D–£37 (£35 D–£45) SOC–£30
☎ 4 miles N of Salisbury on A345
🏠 Hawtree

Highworth (1990)

Swindon Road, Highworth, SN6 7SJ
☎ **(01793) 766014**
✎ KW Loveday
🏴 9 L 3220 yds SSS 70
👤 U
££ £7.90
☎ 5 miles N of Swindon (A361). M4 Junction 15
⊕ 9 hole pitch & putt course

Kingsdown (1880)

Kingsdown, Corsham, SN13 8BS
☎ **(01225) 742530**
▥ 640 105(L) 45(J)
✎ JE Elliott (01225) 743472
🏴 A Butler (01225) 742634
🏴 18 L 6445 yds SSS 71
👤 WD–H WE–M
££ £26
☎ 5 miles E of Bath

Manor House (1992)

Proprietary
Castle Combe, SN14 7JW
☎ **(01249) 782982**
🖥 (01249) 782992
✉ enquiries@manorhousegolfclub.com
▥ 400
✎ Susan Auld (Gen Mgr)
🏴 P Green
🏴 18 L 6286 yds SSS 71
👤 U H–booking necessary SOC
££ £50 Fri/WE–£60
☎ N of Castle Combe, off B4039. M4 Junction 17, 4 miles
⊕ Driving range

🏠 Alliss/Clarke
■ www.manorhousegolfclub.com

Marlborough (1888)
The Common, Marlborough, SN8 1DU
☎ (01672) 512147
🖥 (01672) 513164
📧 contactus@marlboroughgolfclub
.co.uk
📖 750
🏌 JAD Sullivan
✓ S Amor (01672) 512493
🏳 18 L 6514 yds SSS 71
👫 WD/WE–H SOC
££ £26 D–£34 (£31.50 D–£42)
🚗 ¹/₂ mile N of Marlborough (A346). 7
miles S of M4 Junction 15
■ www.marlboroughgolfclub.co.uk

Monkton Park Par Three
(1965)
Pay and play
Chippenham, SN15 3PP
☎ (01249) 653928
🖥 (01249) 653928
📖 100
🏌 MR & BJ Dawson (Props)
🏳 9 hole Par 3 course
👫 U
££ 18 holes–£6 9 holes–£4
🚗 Centre of Chippenham. M4 Junction
17
🏠 M Dawson
■ www.pitchandputtgolf.com

North Wilts (1890)
Bishops' Cannings, Devizes, SN10 2LP
☎ (01380) 860257
🖥 (01380) 860877
📧 secretary@northwiltsgolf.com
📖 625 105(L) 90(J)
🏌 Mrs P Stephenson (01380) 860627
✓ GJ Laing (Golf
Mgr) (01380) 860330
🏳 18 L 6414 yds SSS 71
👫 U exc Xmas Day–Jan 31–M SOC
££ £21 (£24)
🚗 1 mile from A4, E of Calne
■ www.northwiltsgolf.com

Oaksey Park (1991)
Pay and play
Oaksey, Malmesbury, SN16 9SB
☎ (01666) 577995
🖥 (01666) 577174
🏳 9 L 2900 yds SSS 68
👫 U SOC
££ £10 (£15)
🚗 8 miles NE of Malmesbury, off
A429
⊕ Driving range
🏠 Chapman/Warren

Ogbourne Downs (1907)
*Ogbourne St George, Marlborough,
SN8 1TB*
☎ (01672) 841327
🖥 (01672) 841101
📖 700
🏌 Miss M Green (01672) 841327

✓ A Kirk (01672) 841287
🏳 18 L 6363 yds Par 71 SSS 70
👫 WD–H WE–M SOC–WD
££ £30 (£35)
🚗 5 miles S of M4 Junction 15, on
A346
🏠 JH Taylor

Rushmore Park
Tollard Royal, Salisbury, SP5 5QB
☎ (01725) 516326
🖥 (01725) 516466
📖 370
🏌 S McDonagh
✓ S McDonagh
🏳 18 hole course
👫 U SOC
££ £14 (£17)
🚗 8 miles SE of Shaftesbury
(B3081)
⊕ Driving range
🏠 T Crouch

Salisbury & South Wilts
(1888)
Netherhampton, Salisbury, SP2 8PR
☎ (01722) 742645
🖥 (01722) 742645
📧 mail@salisburygolf.co.uk
📖 1100
🏌 Pat Clash (Gen Mgr)
✓ J Cave (01722) 742929
🏳 18 L 6485 yds SSS 71
9 hole course Par 34
👫 WD–U SOC–WD
££ £25 (£40)
🚗 Wilton, 3 miles SW of Salisbury on
A3094
🏠 Taylor/Gidman
■ www.salisburygolf.co.uk

Shrivenham Park (1967)
Pay and play
*Penny Hooks Lane, Shrivenham,
Swindon, SN6 8EX*
☎ (01793) 783853
🖥 (01793) 782999
📖 20
🏌 S Ash (01793) 783853
✓ T Pocock (01793) 783853
🏳 18 L 5769 yds SSS 69
👫 U SOC
££ £12 (£15)
🚗 4 miles E of Swindon, off A420. M4
Junction 15

Thoulstone Park (1992)
Chapmanslade, Westbury, BA13 4AQ
☎ (01373) 832825
🖥 (01373) 832821
🏌 Mrs J Pearce
✓ T Isaacs (01373) 832808
🏳 18 L 6300 yds Par 71 SSS 70
👫 U SOC–WD
££ £18 (£24)
🚗 12 miles S of Bath, off A36
⊕ Driving range
🏠 MRM Sandow

Tidworth Garrison (1908)
Bulford Road, Tidworth, SP9 7AF
☎ (01980) 842321 (Clubhouse)
🖥 (01980) 842301
📧 tidworth@garrison-
golfclub.fsnet.co.uk
📖 800
🏌 T Harris (01980) 842301
✓ T Gosden (01980) 842393
🏳 18 L 6320 yds Par 70 SSS 70
👫 WD–U H SOC–Tues & Thurs
££ £29
🚗 1 mile SW of Tidworth on Bulford
road (A338)
🏠 Donald Steel
■ www.tidworthgolfclub.co.uk

Upavon (1918)
Douglas Avenue, Upavon, SN9 6BQ
☎ (01980) 630787
🖥 (01980) 630787
📖 550
🏌 L Mitchell
✓ R Blake (01980) 630281
🏳 18 L 6415 yds SSS 71
👫 WD–U WE–M before noon –U after
noon SOC–WD
££ £18 D–£24 (£20)
🚗 2 miles SE of Upavon on A342
🏠 R Blake

West Wilts (1891)
Elm Hill, Warminster, BA12 0AU
☎ (01985) 213133
🖥 (01985) 219809
📖 570 70(L) 50(J)
🏌 GN Morgan
✓ S Swales (01985) 212110
🏳 18 L 5754 yds SSS 68
👫 WD–U H WE–U H after noon –NA
before noon
££ £22 D–£30 (£27 D–£38)
🚗 1 mile off A350, on Westbury to
Warminster road
🏠 JH Taylor
■ www.westwiltsgolfclub.co.uk

Whitley (1993)
Pay and play
*Corsham Road, Whitley, Melksham,
SN12 7QE*
☎ (01225) 790099
📖 250
🏌 C Tomkins (01225) 790099
✓ None
🏳 9 L 2200 yds Par 33 SSS 61
👫 U
££ 18 holes–£9. 9 holes–£7
🚗 1 mile N of Melksham on B3553
⊕ Driving range
🏠 Laurence Ross

The Wiltshire
*Vastern, Wootton Bassett, Swindon,
SN4 7PB*
☎ (01793) 849999
🖥 (01793) 849988
📖 600
🏌 RG Lipscombe (Gen Mgr)
✓ A Gray
🏳 18 L 6666 yds SSS 72

U SOC
££ £30 (£30)
🚗 1 mile S of Wootton Bassett on A3102. M4 Junction 16
🏠 Alliss/Clark

Wrag Barn G&CC (1990)
Shrivenham Road, Highworth, Swindon, SN6 7QQ
☎ **(01793) 861327**
🖳 (01793) 861325
📖 600
🎣 M Betteridge
⌇ B Loughrey (01793) 766027
🏌 18 L 6600 yds SSS 71
🏌 WD–U WE–NA before noon SOC–WD
££ £27 (£32)
🚗 6 miles NE of Swindon on B4000. M4 Junction 15, 8 miles
⊕ Driving range. 6-hole Academy course
🏠 Hawtree
■ www.wragbarn.com

Worcestershire

Abbey Hotel G&CC (1985)
Dagnell End Road, Redditch, B98 7BE
☎ **(01527) 406600**
🖳 (01527) 406514
📧 info@theabbeyhotel.co.uk
📖 400
⌇ R Davies (01527) 406500
🏌 18 L 6499 yds SSS 72
🏌 WD–U SOC
££ £17 (£23)
🚗 B4101, off A441 Birmingham road. M42 Junction 2
⊕ Driving range
🏠 Donald Steel

Bank House Hotel G&CC (1992)
Bransford, Worcester, WR6 5JD
☎ **(01886) 833551**
🖳 (01886) 832461
📖 350
🎣 PAD Holmes
⌇ C George
🏌 18 L 6204 yds SSS 71
🏌 U SOC
££ £18 (£25)
🚗 3 miles SW of Worcester on A4103 Hereford road. M5 Junction 7
⊕ Driving range
🏠 Bob Sandow
■ www.bankhousehotel.com

Blackwell (1893)
Blackwell, Bromsgrove, Worcestershire, B60 1PY
☎ **(0121) 445 1994**
🖳 (0121) 445 4911
📖 304 67(L) 6(J)
🎣 JT Mead
⌇ N Blake (0121) 445 3113
🏌 18 L 6260 yds SSS 71
🏌 WD–U H WE/BH–M

££ £50 D–£60
🚗 3 miles E of Bromsgrove. M42 Junction 1 (South)

Brandhall (1906)
Public
Heron Road, Oldbury, Warley, B68 8AQ
☎ **(0121) 552 7475**
📖 300
⌇ C Yates (0121) 552 2195
🏌 18 L 5813 yds Par 71 SSS 68
🏌 U exc first 1¹⁄₂ hrs Sat/Sun
££ £11
🚗 6 miles NW of Birmingham. M5 Junction 2, 1¹⁄₂ miles

Bromsgrove Golf Centre (1992)
Proprietary
Stratford Road, Bromsgrove, B60 1LD
☎ **(01527) 575886**
🖳 (01527) 570964
📧 enquiries@bromsgrovegolf.f9.co.uk
📖 900
🎣 D Went
⌇ G Long (01527) 575886
🏌 18 L 5969 yds SSS 69
🏌 U SOC
££ £15.50 (£20.50)
🚗 Junction of A38/A448. M42 Junction 1. M5 Junction 4/5
⊕ Driving range
🏠 Hawtree
■ www.bromsgrovegolfcentre.co.uk

Churchill & Blakedown (1926)
Churchill Lane, Blakedown, Kidderminster, DY10 3NB
☎ **(01562) 700018**
📖 300
🎣 MJ Taylor
🏌 9 L 6472 yds Par 72 SSS 71
🏌 WD–U WE–M
££ £20
🚗 3 miles N of Kidderminster on A456

Cocks Moor Woods (1926)
Public
Alcester Road, South King's Heath, Birmingham, B14 4ER
☎ **(0121) 464 3584**
⌇ S Ellis
🏌 18 L 5769 yds SSS 67
🏌 U
££ On application
🚗 6 miles S of Birmingham (A435)

Droitwich G&CC (1897)
Ford Lane, Droitwich, WR9 0BQ
☎ **(01905) 774344**
🖳 (01905) 797290
📖 782
🎣 M Ashton (01905) 774344
⌇ CS Thompson (01905) 770207
🏌 18 L 6058 yds Par 69 SSS 68
🏌 WD–U WE/BH–M SOC–Wed & Fri
££ £18 – £26

🚗 1 mile N of Droitwich, off A38. M5 Junction 5

Dudley (1893)
Turners Hill, Rowley Regis, B65 9DP
☎ **(01384) 253719**
🖳 (01384) 233177
📧 info@dudleygc.fsnet.co.uk
📖 320
🎣 RP Fortune (01384) 233877
⌇ G Dean (01384) 254020
🏌 18 L 5730 yds SSS 68
🏌 WD–U WE–M
££ On application
🚗 2 miles S of Dudley

Evesham (1894)
Craycombe Links, Fladbury, Pershore, WR10 2QS
☎ **(01386) 860395**
🖳 (01386) 861356
📧 eveshamgolfclub@talk21.com
📖 360
🎣 Mrs L Tattersall (01386) 860395
⌇ D Cummins (01386) 861144
🏌 9 L 6415 yds SSS 71
🏌 WD–H WE–M NA on comp/match days SOC
££ D–£20
🚗 Fladbury, 4 miles W of Evesham (A4538)

Fulford Heath (1933)
Tanners Green Lane, Wythall, Birmingham, B47 6BH
☎ **(01564) 822806 (Clubhouse)**
🖳 (01564) 822629
📧 secretary@fulfordheath.co.uk
📖 750
🎣 Mrs MA Tuckett (01564) 824758
⌇ R Dunbar (01564) 822930
🏌 18 L 6179 yds SSS 70
🏌 WD–H WE/BH–M SOC–Tues & Thurs
££ On application
🚗 8 miles S of Birmingham. M42 Junction 3
🏠 Braid/Hawtree

Gay Hill (1913)
Hollywood Lane, Birmingham, B47 5PP
☎ **(0121) 430 6523/7077**
🖳 (0121) 436 7796
📖 700
🎣 Mrs J Morris (0121) 430 8544
⌇ A Potter (0121) 474 6001
🏌 18 L 6532 yds SSS 72
🏌 WD–U H WE–M SOC
££ £28.50
🚗 7 miles S of Birmingham on A435. M42 Junction 3, 3 miles

Habberley (1924)
Low Habberley, Kidderminster, DY11 5RG
☎ **(01562) 745756**
🖳 (01562) 745756
📖 250
🎣 B Blakeway
🏌 9 L 5440 yds SSS 67
🏌 WD–U WE–M SOC

££ £12 (£15)
⊶ 3 miles NW of Kidderminster

Hagley (1980)
Proprietary
Wassell Grove, Hagley, Stourbridge,
DY9 9JW
☎ (01562) 883701
🖥 (01562) 887518
📖 750
🏌 GF Yardley (01562) 883701
⌇ I Clark (01562) 883852
🏳 18 L 6376 yds SSS 72
👥 WD–U WE–M after 10am
   SOC–WD
££ £23 D–£28
⊶ 5 miles SW of Birmingham on
   A456. M5 Junction 3
▦ www.hagleygolfandcountryclub
   .co.uk

Halesowen (1906)
The Leasowes, Halesowen, B62 8QF
☎ (0121) 501 3606
🖥 (0121) 501 3606
📖 680
🏌 P Crumpton
⌇ J Nicholas (0121) 503 0593
🏳 18 L 5754 yds SSS 69
👥 WD–U WE–M SOC–WD exc Wed
££ £25 D–£30
⊶ M5 Junction 3, 2 miles

Kidderminster (1909)
Russell Road, Kidderminster,
DY10 3HT
☎ (01562) 822303
🖥 (01562) 827866
📖 900
🏌 M Burnand
⌇ NP Underwood (01562) 740090
🏳 18 L 6405 yds SSS 71
👥 WD–H WE–M SOC–Thurs
££ £30 D–£40
⊶ Signposted off A449
   Wolverhampton-Worcester road

Kings Norton (1892)
Brockhill Lane, Weatheroak, Alvechurch,
Birmingham B48 7ED
☎ (01564) 826789
🖥 (01564) 826955
📖 1050
🏌 T Webb (Mgr)
⌇ K Hayward (01564) 822822
🏳 9 L 3382 yds SSS 36
   9 L 3372 yds SSS 36
   9 L 3290 yds SSS 36
👥 WD–U WE–NA SOC
££ £32 D–£40
⊶ 7 miles S of Birmingham. 1 mile N
   of M42 Junction 3
⊕ 12 hole short course
🏛 Fred Hawtree
▦ www.kingsnortongolfclub.co.uk

Lickey Hills (1927)
Public
Lickey Hills, Rednal, Birmingham,
B45 8RR
☎ (0121) 453 3159

🏌 AG Cushing
⌇ J Kelly
🏳 18 L 6010 yds SSS 69
👥 U
££ On application
⊶ 10 miles SW of Birmingham. M5
   Junction 4

Little Lakes (1975)
Lye Head, Bewdley, Worcester,
DY12 2UZ
☎ (01299) 266385
🖥 (01299) 266398
📖 400 50(L)
🏌 J Dean (01562) 741704
⌇ M Laing
🏳 18 L 5644 yds SSS 68
👥 U SOC
££ £15 (£20)
⊶ 3 miles W of Bewdley, off
   A456

Moseley (1892)
Springfield Road, Kings Heath,
Birmingham, B14 7DX
☎ (0121) 444 2115
🖥 (0121) 441 4662
📖 600
🏌 AM Sanders (0121) 444 4957
⌇ M Griffin (0121) 444 2063
🏳 18 L 6315 yds SSS 71
👥 WD–H or M
££ £37
⊶ South Birmingham
🏛 HS Colt

North Worcestershire
(1907)
Frankley Beeches Road, Northfield,
Birmingham, B31 5LP
☎ (0121) 475 1047
🖥 (0121) 476 8681
📖 550
🏌 D Wilson
⌇ IF Clark (0121) 475 5721
🏳 18 L 5907 yds SSS 69
👥 WD–U WE/BH–M
££ £25 D–£35
⊶ 7 miles SW of Birmingham, off
   A38
🏛 James Braid

Ombersley (1991)
Bishopswood Road, Ombersley,
Droitwich, WR9 0LE
☎ (01905) 620747
🖥 (01905) 620047
📧 enquiries@ombersleygolfclub
   .co.uk
📖 750
🏌 G Glenister (Gen Mgr)
⌇ G Glenister
🏳 18 L 6139 yds SSS 69
👥 U
££ £16.20 (£22.50)
⊶ 6 miles N of Worcester, off
   A449
⊕ Driving range
🏛 David Morgan
▦ www.ombersleygolfclub.co.uk

Perdiswell Park
Pay and play
Bilford Road, Worcester, WR3 8DX
☎ (01905) 754668
🖥 (01905) 756608
📖 286
🏌 R Gardner
⌇ M Woodward (01905) 754668
🏳 18 L 5297 yds SSS 68
👥 U
££ 9 holes–£5.50 (£7.15) 18
   holes–£8.70 (£11.20)
⊶ Worcester. M5 Junction 6

Pitcheroak (1973)
Public
Plymouth Road, Redditch, B97 4PB
☎ (01527) 541054
📖 148
🏌 R Barnett
⌇ D Stewart
🏳 9 L 4561 yds Par 65 SSS 62
👥 U
££ 18 holes–£8.90 (£10.30) 9
   holes–£6.85 (£7.60)
⊶ Redditch

Ravenmeadow
Hindlip Lane, Clanes, Worcester,
WR3 8SA
☎ (01905) 757525
🖥 (01905) 759184
📖 250
🏌 T Senter (Mgr) (01905) 458876
⌇ P Brookes (01905) 756665
🏳 9 L 5440 yds Par 67
👥 U
££ £8–£12 (£10–£15)
⊶ 3 miles N of Worcester, off A38.
   M50 Junction 6
⊕ Driving range
🏛 R Baldwyn

Redditch (1913)
Lower Grinsty, Green Lane, Callow Hill,
Redditch B97 5PJ
☎ (01527) 543079
🖥 (01527) 547413
📖 883
🏌 SF Hickin
⌇ D Down (01527) 546372
🏳 18 L 6494 yds SSS 72
👥 WD–U SOC
££ £28
⊶ 3 miles SW of Redditch, off A441
🏛 F Pennink

Stourbridge (1892)
Worcester Lane, Pedmore, Stourbridge,
DY8 2RB
☎ (01384) 393062
🖥 (01384) 444660
📖 850
🏌 Mrs MA Betts (01384) 395566
⌇ M Male (01384) 393129
🏳 18 L 6231 yds SSS 70
👥 WD–U exc Wed before 4pm–M
   WE/BH–M
££ £30
⊶ 1 mile S of Stourbridge on
   Worcester road. M5 Junctions 3/4
▦ www.stourbridge-golf-club.co.uk

Tolladine   (1898)

The Fairway, Tolladine Road,
Worcester, WR4 9BA
☎ **(01905) 21074 (Clubhouse)**
⌨ 270
✍ D Turner
✓ M Slater
🏴 9 L 5174 yds SSS 67
👥 WD–U before 4pm –M after 4pm
   WE/BH–M SOC
£€ On application
🚗 M5 Junction 6, 1 mile

The Vale   (1991)

Bishampton, Pershore, WR10 2LZ
☎ **(01386) 462781**
⌨ (01386) 462597
📖 800
✍ D Gutteridge (Gen Mgr)
✓ Caroline Griffiths (01386) 462520
🏴 18 L 6644 yds SSS 72
   9 L 2628 yds SSS 65
👥 WD–U WE–U after 1pm SOC–WD
£€ On application
🚗 6 miles NW of Evesham, off
   A4538. M5 Junction 6, 12 miles
⊕ Driving range
🏠 M Sandow
🌐 www.crownsportsplc.com

Warley   (1921)

Public
Lightwoods Hill, Warley, B67 5EQ
☎ **(0121) 429 2440**
✍ A Woolridge
✓ D Ashington
🏴 9 L 2606 yds SSS 64
👥 U SOC
£€ On application
🚗 5 miles W of Birmingham, off
   A456

Wharton Park   (1992)

Longbank, Bewdley, DY12 2QW
☎ **(01299) 405222**
⌨ (01299) 405121
📧 enquiries@wharton park.co.uk
📖 550
✓ A Hoare (01299) 405163
🏴 18 L 6435 yds Par 72 SSS 71
👥 U SOC–WD
£€ £20 (£25)
🚗 Bewdley By-pass on A456
⊕ Practice ground
🏠 Howard Swann

Worcester G&CC   (1898)

Boughton Park, Worcester, WR2 4EZ
☎ **(01905) 421132 (Clubhouse)**
⌨ (01905) 749090
📖 1005
✍ DG Bettsworth (01905) 422555
✓ C Colenso (01905) 422044
🏴 18 L 6251 yds SSS 70
👥 WD–H WE–M SOC
£€ £30
🚗 1 mile W of Worcester on A4103
🏠 Dr A Mackenzie (1926)/
   C Colenso (1991)

Worcestershire   (1879)

Wood Farm, Malvern Wells, WR14 4PP
☎ **(01684) 575992**
⌨ (01684) 893334
📧 secretary
   @theworcestershiregolfclub.co.uk
📖 770
✍ Mrs JP Howe (Sec/Mgr)
   (01684) 575992
✓ RAF Lewis (01684) 564428
🏴 18 L 6449 yds SSS 71
👥 WD–H WE–H after 10am
£€ £25 (£34)
🚗 2 miles S of Gt Malvern, off
   A449/B4209
🌐 www.theworcestershiregolfclub
   .co.uk

Wyre Forest Golf Centre

Pay and play
Zortech Avenue, Kidderminster,
DY11 7EX
☎ **(01299) 822682**
⌨ (01299) 879433
📧 simonprice@wyreforestgolf.com
📖 363
✍ S Price (Mgr)
✓ S Price
🏴 18 L 5790 yds Par 70 SSS 68
👥 U SOC
£€ £12 (£16)
🚗 18 miles S of Birmingham on
   A451, between Kidderminster and
   Stourport
⊕ Floodlit driving range

Yorkshire (East)

Allerthorpe Park

Allerthorpe, York, YO42 4RL
☎ **(01759) 306686**
⌨ (01759) 304308
📖 475
✍ JD Atkinson (Sec/Mgr)
✓ (01759) 306686
🏴 18 L 5506 yds Par 67 SSS 66
👥 U SOC
£€ £18 (£18)
🚗 2 miles W of Pocklington, off
   A1079
🏠 JG Hatcliffe & Partners

Beverley & East Riding   (1889)

The Westwood, Beverley, HU17 8RG
☎ **(01482) 867190**
⌨ (01482) 868757
📖 530
✍ M Drew (01482) 868757
✓ A Ashby (01482) 869519
🏴 18 L 5972 yds SSS 69
👥 U SOC
£€ £15 (£20)
🚗 Beverley-Walkington road (B1230)

Boothferry Park   (1982)

Spaldington Lane, Spaldington, Goole,
DN14 7NG
☎ **(01430) 430364**

⌨ (01430) 430567
✍ Christine Welton (Golf Admin)
   (01430) 430364
✓ N Bundy (01430) 430364
🏴 18 L 6593 yds SSS 72
👥 U SOC
£€ £10 (£15)
🚗 3 miles N of Howden on B1288.
   M62 Junction 37, 2 miles
🏠 Donald Steel

Bridlington   (1905)

Belvedere Road, Bridlington, YO15 3NA
☎ **(01262) 672092/606367**
⌨ (01262) 606367
📖 623
✍ C Greenwood (01262) 606367
✓ ARA Howarth (01262) 674721
🏴 18 L 6638 yds Par 72 SSS 72
👥 U exc Sun–NA
£€ £19 (£29)
🚗 1¹/₂ miles S of Bridlington, off
   A165
🏠 James Braid

The Bridlington Links   (1993)

Pay and play
Flamborough Road, Marton,
Bridlington, YO15 1DW
☎ **(01262) 401584**
⌨ (01262) 401702
📖 300
✍ PM Hancock (Gen Mgr)
✓ S Raybould
🏴 18 L 6720 yds SSS 72
   9 hole course
👥 U
£€ £12 (£15)
🚗 2 miles N of Bridlington on B1255
⊕ Floodlit driving range. 3 Academy
   holes
🏠 Howard Swann

Brough   (1893)

Cave Road, Brough, HU15 1HB
☎ **(01482) 667374**
⌨ (01482) 669873
📖 700
✍ GW Townhill (Golf Dir)
   (01482) 667291
✓ GW Townhill (01482) 667483
🏴 18 L 6075 yds SSS 69
👥 WD–U exc Wed–NA
£€ £32
🚗 10 miles W of Hull on A63
🌐 www.brough-golfclub.co.uk

Cave Castle   (1989)

South Cave, Nr Brough, HU15 2EU
☎ **(01430) 421286**
⌨ (01430) 421118
✍ C Welton (Admin)
✓ S MacKinder (01430) 421286
🏴 18 L 6409 yds SSS 71
👥 U SOC
£€ £12.50 (£18)
🚗 10 miles W of Hull. Junction of
   A63/M62

Cherry Burton (1993)

Pay and play

Leconfield Road, Cherry Burton,
Beverley, HU17 7RB

☎ **(01964) 550924**
📖 220
🏌 A Ashby (Mgr)
/ A Ashby
🏴 9 L 2278 yds Par 33 SSS 62
👥 U SOC
££ £7 (£10)
⛳ 2 miles N of Beverley, off Malton road
⊕ Driving range

Cottingham (1984)

Woodhill Way, Cottingham, Hull,
HU16 5RZ

☎ **(01482) 842394**
📠 (01482) 845932
📖 600
🏌 RJ Wiles (01482) 846030
/ CW Gray (01482) 842394
🏴 18 L 6459 yds Par 72 SSS 71
👥 WD–U WE/BH–restricted SOC after 2pm
££ £16 D–£24 (£24 D–£36)
⛳ 3 miles N of Hull, off A164
⊕ Driving range
🏠 Wiles/Litten
■ www.golf-in-england.co.uk/cottingham

Driffield (1923)

Sunderlandwick, Driffield, YO25 9AD

☎ **(01377) 240448 (Clubhouse),**
   (01377) 253116 (Office)
📠 (01377) 240599
📖 670
🏌 PJ Mounfield
/ K Wright (01377) 241224
🏴 18 L 6212 yds SSS 70
👥 H I SOC
££ £20 D–£25 (£30 D–£40)
⛳ S of Driffield on A164

Flamborough Head (1932)

Lighthouse Road, Flamborough,
Bridlington, YO15 1AR

☎ **(01262) 850333/850417**
📠 (01262) 850279
📧 secretary
   @flamboroughheadgolfclub.co.uk
📖 400
🏌 GS Thornton
/ P Harrison (01262) 850333
🏴 18 L 6189 yds Par 71 SSS 69
👥 U
££ £18 (£20) 5D–£68
⛳ 5 miles NE of Bridlington
■ www.flamboroughheadgolfclub .co.uk

Ganstead Park (1976)

Longdales Lane, Coniston, Hull,
HU11 4LB

☎ **(01482) 811280 (Steward)**
📠 (01482) 817754
📧 secretary@gansteadpark.co.uk
📖 700
🏌 G Drewery (01482) 817754
/ M Smee (01482) 811121
🏴 18 L 6801 yds SSS 73
👥 U H WE–NA before noon SOC
££ On application
⛳ 5 miles E of Hull on A165
🏠 Peter Green
■ www.gansteadpark.co.uk

Hainsworth Park (1983)

Brandesburton, Driffield, YO25 8RT

☎ **(01964) 542362**
📠 (01964) 542362
📖 550
🏌 P Hounsfield, BW Atkin (Prop)
/ PR Binnington (01964) 542362
🏴 18 L 6362 yds SSS 71
👥 SOC
££ £16 (£20)
⛳ 6 miles NW of Beverley, off A165 at Brandesburton roundabout

Hessle (1898)

Westfield Road, Raywell, Cottingham,
HU16 5YL

☎ **(01482) 650171**
📠 (01482) 652679
📖 680
🏌 D Pettit
/ G Fieldsend (01482) 650190
🏴 18 L 6604 yds SSS 72
👥 WD–U exc Tues 9am–1pm WE–NA before 11.30am
££ £25 (£32)
⛳ 3 miles SW of Cottingham
🏠 Thomas/Alliss

Hornsea (1898)

Rolston Road, Hornsea, HU18 1XG

☎ **(01964) 532020**
📠 (01964) 532020
📖 600
🏌 Angela Howard (01964) 532020
/ S Wright (01964) 534989
🏴 18 L 6661 yds SSS 72
👥 WD–U WE–restricted SOC
££ £22 D–£30
⛳ 300 yds past Hornsea Free Port
🏠 Mackenzie/Braid

Hull (1921)

The Hall, 27 Packman Lane, Kirk Ella,
Hull HU10 7TJ

☎ **(01482) 653026**
📠 (01482) 658919
📖 821
🏌 R Toothill (Gen Mgr) (01482) 658919
/ D Jagger (01482) 653074
🏴 18 L 6246 yds SSS 70
👥 WD–U WE–NA
££ £26.50 D–£32
⛳ 5 miles W of Hull
🏠 James Braid

Kilnwick Percy (1995)

Pocklington, York, YO42 1UF

☎ **(01759) 303090**
📖 350
🏌 Mrs A Clayton (Sec/Mgr)
/ J Townhill
🏴 18 L 6214 yds Par 70 SSS 70
👥 U SOC
££ £15 (£18)
⛳ 1 mile E of Pocklington, off B1246
🏠 John Day

Springhead Park (1930)

Public

Willerby Road, Hull, HU5 5JE

☎ **(01482) 656309**
🏌 Mrs J Garforth (01482) 656958
🏴 18 L 6402 yds SSS 71
👥 U SOC–WD
££ £7.50 (£9)
⛳ 4 miles W of Hull

Sutton Park (1935)

Public

Salthouse Road, Hull, HU8 9HF

☎ **(01482) 374242**
📠 (01482) 701428
📖 300
🏌 CR Alsop
/ (01482) 711450
🏴 18 L 6251 yds SSS 70
👥 U SOC–exc Sun
££ £7.50 (£9.50)
⛳ 3 miles E of Hull on A165

Withernsea (1909)

Chestnut Avenue, Withernsea,
HU19 2PG

☎ **(01964) 612258 (Clubhouse)**
📖 329 30(L) 36(J)
🏌 K Purdue (Admin) (01694) 612078
🏴 9 L 6207 yds Par 72 SSS 70
👥 WD–U WE/BH–M before 1pm SOC
££ £10
⛳ 17 miles E of Hull on A1033. S side of Withernsea

Yorkshire (North)

Aldwark Manor (1978)

Aldwark, Alne, York, YO61 1UF

☎ **(01347) 838353**
📠 (01347) 830007
📖 400
🏌 GF Platt (Mgr) (01347) 838353
🏴 18 L 6187 yds Par 72 SSS 70
👥 U SOC
££ £25 D–£35 (£30 D–£40)
⛳ 5 miles SE of Boroughbridge, off A1. 13 miles NW of York, off A19

Ampleforth College (1972)

Castle Drive, Gilling East, York,
YO62 4HP

☎ **(01439) 788212**
📖 200
🏌 Dr M Wilson (01904) 768861
🏴 9 L 5567 yds Par 69 SSS 69
👥 U exc 2–4pm during term time
££ £12 (£12)
⛳ Gilling East, 18 miles N of York (B1363)
⊕ Green fees payable at Fairfax Arms, Gilling East
🏠 Rev Jerome Lambert OSB
■ www.ampleforthgolf.co.uk

Bedale (1894)

Leyburn Road, Bedale, DL8 1EZ
- ☎ (01677) 422568
- ✉ bedalegolfclub@aol.com
- 📖 600 60(J)
- ✍ G Brown (01677) 422451
- ⌁ AD Johnson (01677) 422443
- ⛳ 18 L 6610 yds SSS 72
- ⛹ U SOC
- ££ £22 (£33)
- ⮐ N boundary of Bedale

Bentham (1922)

Robin Lane, Bentham, Lancaster, LA2 7AG
- ☎ (015242) 62455
- ✉ (015242) 62470
- ✉ secretary@benthamgolfclub.co.uk
- 📖 450
- ✍ T Tudor (015242) 62455
- ⛳ 9 L 5820 yds SSS 69
- ⛹ U SOC
- ££ D–£20
- ⮐ NE of Lancaster on B6480 towards Settle. 13 miles E of M6 Junction 34
- ⊕ Extension to 18 holes in 2003
- ■ www.benthamgolfclub.co.uk

Catterick (1930)

Leyburn Road, Catterick Garrison, DL9 3QE
- ☎ (01748) 833268
- ✉ (01748) 833268
- 📖 700
- ✍ G McDonnell (Sec/Mgr)
- ⌁ A Marshall (01748) 833671
- ⛳ 18 L 6329 yds SSS 71
- ⛹ H WE–NA before 10am SOC
- ££ £25 (£30)
- ⮐ 6 miles SW of Scotch Corner, via A1
- ⟰ Arthur Day
- ■ www.catterickgolfclub.co.uk

Cleveland (1887)

Majuba Road, Redcar, TS10 5BJ
- ☎ (01642) 471798
- ✉ (01642) 471798
- 📖 800
- ✍ P Bacon (01642) 471798
- ⌁ (01642) 483462
- ⛳ 18 L 6696 yds SSS 72
- ⛹ WD–U WE/BH–by arrangement SOC
- ££ £25 (£28)
- ⮐ S bank of River Tees
- ■ www.clevelandgolfclub.co.uk

Cocksford (1992)

Stutton, Tadcaster, LS24 9NG
- ☎ (01937) 834253
- ✉ (01937) 834253
- ✍ F Judson
- ⌁ G Thompson
- ⛳ 18 L 5570 yds Par 71 SSS 69
- ⛹ WD–U WE–by arrangement SOC
- ££ £19 D–£25 (£25 D–28)
- ⮐ 1¹/₂ miles S of Tadcaster
- ■ www.cocksfordgolfclub.freeserve.co.uk

Crimple Valley (1976)

Pay and play
Hookstone Wood Road, Harrogate, HG2 8PN
- ☎ (01423) 883485
- ✉ (01423) 881018
- 📖 200
- ✍ P Lumb
- ⌁ P Lumb
- ⛳ 9 L 2500 yds SSS 33
- ⛹ U
- ££ 9 holes–£5 (£6) 18 holes–£8 D–£11
- ⮐ 1 mile S of Harrogate, off A61, by Yorkshire Showground
- ⟰ R Lumb

Drax (1989)

Drax, Selby, YO8 8PQ
- ☎ (01757) 618041
- 📖 450
- ✍ K Onions (01405) 860872
- ⛳ 9 L 5434 yds Par 68 SSS 66
- ⛹ M SOC
- ££ £8 (£8)
- ⮐ 5 miles S of Selby, off A1041
- ⟰ JM Scott

Easingwold (1930)

Stillington Road, Easingwold, York, YO61 3ET
- ☎ (01347) 821486
- ✉ (01347) 822474
- ✉ brian@easingwold-golf-club.fsnet.co.uk
- 📖 690
- ✍ DB Stockley (01347) 822474
- ⌁ J Hughes (01347) 821964
- ⛳ 18 L 6627 yds Par 72 SSS 72
- ⛹ U
- ££ D–£25 D–£30 (£30)
- ⮐ 12 miles N of York on A19. S end of Easingwold
- ⊕ Target golf
- ⟰ Hawtree/OCM
- ■ www.easingwold-golf-club.co.uk

Filey (1897)

West Ave, Filey, YO14 9BQ
- ☎ (01723) 513293
- ✉ (01723) 514952
- ✉ info@fileygolfclub.freeserve.co.uk
- 📖 768
- ✍ JR Nicholson
- ⌁ GM Hutchinson (01723) 513134
- ⛳ 18 L 6112 yds SSS 69
- 9 L 1513 yds Par 30
- ⛹ U H SOC
- ££ £23 (£30) Summer
- £18 (£25) Winter
- ⮐ 1 mile S of Filey centre
- ⟰ James Braid

Forest of Galtres (1993)

Moorlands Road, Skelton, York, YO32 2RF
- ☎ (01904) 766198
- ✉ (01904) 769400
- 📖 450
- ✍ Mrs SJ Procter
- ⌁ P Bradley
- ⛳ 18 L 6412 yds Par 72 SSS 70

- ⛹ U SOC–WD/Sun
- ££ £20 (£27)
- ⮐ Skelton, 4 miles N of York. 1¹/₂ miles off A19
- ⊕ Driving range
- ⟰ Simon Gidman
- ■ www.forestofgaltres.co.uk

Forest Park (1991)

Stockton-on Forest, York, YO32 9UW
- ☎ (01904) 400425
- ✉ secretary@forestparkgolfclub.co.uk
- 📖 650
- ✍ N Crossley (01904) 400688
- ⌁ None
- ⛳ 18 L 6660 yds Par 71 SSS 72
- 9 L 3186 yds Par 70 SSS 70
- ⛹ U SOC
- ££ £18 D–£24 (£23 D–£32) 9 hole:£8 (£10)
- ⮐ 1¹/₂ miles from E end of A64 York By-pass
- ⊕ Driving range
- ■ www.forestparkgolfclub.co.uk

Fulford (1906)

Heslington Lane, York, YO10 5DY
- ☎ (01904) 413579
- ✉ (01904) 416918
- 📖 750
- ✍ I Mackland
- ⌁ M Brown (01904) 412882
- ⛳ 18 L 6775 yds SSS 72
- ⛹ By arrangement with Mgr
- ££ £37 D–£48 (£48)
- ⮐ 2 miles S of York (A64)
- ⟰ Major C McKenzie

Ganton (1891)

Station Road, Ganton, Scarborough, YO12 4PA
- ☎ (01944) 710329
- ✉ (01944) 710922
- ✉ secretary@gantongolfclub.com
- 📖 550
- ✍ Maj RG Woolsey
- ⌁ G Brown (01944) 710260
- ⛳ 18 L 6734 yds SSS 73
- ⛹ By prior arrangement
- ££ On application
- ⮐ 11 miles SW of Scarborough on A64
- ⟰ Dunn/Vardon/Braid/Colt
- ■ www.gantongolfclub.com

Harrogate (1892)

Forest Lane Head, Harrogate, HG2 7TF
- ☎ (01423) 863158 (Clubhouse)
- ✉ (01423) 860073
- 📖 700
- ✍ (01423) 862999
- ⌁ P Johnson (01423) 862547
- ⛳ 18 L 6241 yds SSS 70
- ⛹ WD–U WE/BH–enquire first SOC–WD exc Tues
- ££ £30 D–£35 (£40)
- ⮐ 2 miles E of Harrogate on Knaresborough road (A59)
- ⟰ Sandy Herd
- ■ www.harrogate-gc.co.uk

Heworth (1911)

Muncaster House, Muncastergate, York,
YO31 9JY

- ☎ **(01904) 424618**
- 📠 (01904) 426156
- ✉ golf@heworth-gc.fsnet.co.uk
- 📖 345 80(L) 50(J)
- ✍ RJ Hunt (01904) 426156
- ✓ S Burdett (01904) 422389
- ⛳ 12 L 6141 yds Par 70 SSS 69
- 👥 U
- £€ £18 (£20)
- 🚗 NE boundary of York (A1036)

Hunley Hall (1993)

Brotton, Saltburn, TS12 2QQ

- ☎ **(01287) 676216**
- 📠 (01287) 678250
- ✉ enquiries@hunleyhall.co.uk
- 📖 500
- ✍ E Lillie (01287) 676216
- ✓ A Brook (01287) 677444
- ⛳ 27 holes:
  5948-6918 yds Par/SSS 68-73
- 👥 U SOC–exc Sun
- £€ £20 (£30)
- 🚗 15 miles SE of Middlesbrough on A174
- ⊕ Floodlit driving range
- 🏠 John Morgan
- ■ www.hunleyhall.co.uk

Kirkbymoorside (1951)

Manor Vale, Kirkbymoorside, York,
YO62 6EG

- ☎ **(01751) 431525**
- 📠 (01751) 433190
- ✉ enqs@kmsgolf.fsnet.co.uk
- 📖 630
- ✍ RJ Butter
- ✓ J Hinchliffe (01751) 430402
- ⛳ 18 L 6047 yds SSS 69
- 👥 U after 9am
- £€ £20 (£27)
- 🚗 A170 between Helmsley and Pickering
- ■ www.kirkbymoorsidegolf.co.uk

Knaresborough (1920)

Boroughbridge Road, Knaresborough,
HG5 0QQ

- ☎ **(01423) 864865**
- 📠 (01423) 869345
- 📖 795
- ✍ JL Hall (Mgr) (01423) 862690
- ✓ GJ Vickers (01423) 864865
- ⛳ 18 L 6413 yds Par 70 SSS 71
- 👥 U SOC
- £€ £28.50 (£35.50)
- 🚗 1¹/₂ miles N of Knaresborough on A6055
- 🏠 Hawtree

Malton & Norton (1910)

Welham Park, Welham Road, Norton,
Malton YO17 9QE

- ☎ **(01653) 692959**
- 📠 (01653) 697912
- 📖 820
- ✍ E Harrison (01653) 697912
- ✓ SI Robinson (01653) 693882

- ⛳ 27 holes:
  Welham L 6456 yds SSS 71
  Park L 6242 yds SSS 70
  Derwent L 6286 yds SSS 70
- 👥 WD–U WE–restricted on match days H SOC
- £€ £25 (£30)
- 🚗 18 miles NE of York (A64)
- ⊕ Driving range

Masham (1895)

Burnholme, Swinton Road, Masham,
Ripon HG4 4HT

- ☎ **(01765) 689379**
- 📠 (01765) 688054
- 📖 327
- ✍ Mrs J McGee (01765) 688054
- ⛳ 9 L 6120 yds SSS 69
- 👥 WD–U before 5pm WE–M BH–NA
- £€ £20
- 🚗 10 miles N of Ripon, off A6108

Middlesbrough (1908)

Brass Castle Lane, Marton,
Middlesbrough, TS8 9EE

- ☎ **(01642) 311515**
- 📠 (01642) 319607
- 📖 975
- ✍ PM Jackson
- ✓ DJ Jones (01642) 311766
- ⛳ 18 L 6278 yds SSS 70
- 👥 WD–U H exc Tues–NA before 1.30pm Sat–NA SOC
- £€ D–£32 (£37)
- 🚗 3 miles S of Middlesbrough
- 🏠 James Braid
- ■ www.middlesbroughgolfclub.co.uk

Middlesbrough Municipal (1977)

Public
Ladgate Lane, Middlesbrough, TS5 7YZ

- ☎ **(01642) 315533**
- 📠 (01642) 300726
- 📖 625
- ✍ JC Taylor (Hon)
- ✓ A Hope (01642) 300720
- ⛳ 18 L 6333 yds SSS 70
- 👥 U
- £€ £11 (£14)
- 🚗 2 miles S of Middlesbrough on A174
- ⊕ Floodlit driving range

Oakdale (1914)

Oakdale, Harrogate, HG1 2LN

- ☎ **(01423) 567162**
- 📠 (01423) 536030
- 📖 775
- ✍ MJ Cross
- ✓ C Dell (01423) 560510
- ⛳ 18 L 6456 yds SSS 71
- 👥 WD–U 9.30–12.30 and after 2pm SOC–WD
- £€ £30 D–£45
- 🚗 ¹/₂ mile NE of Royal Hall, Harrogate
- 🏠 Dr A Mackenzie

The Oaks (1996)

Aughton Common, Aughton, York,
YO42 4PW

- ☎ **(01757) 288001 (Clubhouse),**
  (01757) 288007 (Bookings)
- 📠 (01757) 289029
- 📖 675
- ✍ Mrs S Nutt (01757) 288577
- ✓ J Townhill
- ⛳ 18 L 6743 yds Par 72 SSS 72
- 👥 WD–U WE–M SOC–WD
- £€ £22 D–£35
- 🚗 1 mile N of Bubwith on B1228. 14 miles SE of York. M62 Junction 37
- ⊕ Driving range
- 🏠 Julian Covey
- ■ www.theoaksgolfclub.co.uk

Pannal (1906)

Follifoot Road, Pannal, Harrogate,
HG3 1ES

- ☎ **(01423) 871641**
- 📠 (01423) 870043
- ✉ secretary@pannelgc.co.uk
- 📖 780
- ✍ R Braddon (01423) 872628
- ✓ D Padgett (01423) 872620
- ⛳ 18 L 6622 yds SSS 72
- 👥 WD–H 9.30–12 and after 1.30pm WE–H 11–12 and after 2.30pm SOC
- £€ £41 D–£51 (£51)
- 🚗 2¹/₂ miles S of Harrogate, on A61
- 🏠 Herd/Mackenzie

Pike Hills (1920)

Tadcaster Road, Askham Bryan, York,
YO23 3UW

- ☎ **(01904) 700797**
- 📠 (01904) 700797
- 📖 750
- ✍ L Hargrave
- ✓ I Gradwell (01904) 708756
- ⛳ 18 L 6146 yds SSS 70
- 👥 WD–U H before 4.30pm –M after 4.30pm SOC–WD
- £€ £20 D–£26
- 🚗 3 miles SW of York on A64

Richmond (1892)

Bend Hagg, Richmond, DL10 5EX

- ☎ **(01748) 825319**
- 📖 600
- ✍ BD Aston (01748) 823231
- ✓ P Jackson (01748) 822457
- ⛳ 18 L 5886 yds SSS 68
- 👥 U
- £€ £20 D–£22 (£25 D–£30)
- 🚗 3 miles SW of Scotch Corner
- 🏠 Frank Pennink

Ripon City (1907)

Palace Road, Ripon, HG4 3HH

- ☎ **(01765) 603640**
- 📠 (01765) 692880
- ✉ office@ripongolf.com
- 📖 650 100(L) 45(J)
- ✍ CJ Webb
- ✓ T Davis (01765) 600411
- ⛳ 18 L 6084 yds SSS 69
- 👥 U SOC

£€ £23 (£30)
⇔ 1 mile N of Ripon on A6108
⊕ Driving range
🏠 ADAS
■ www.ripongolf.com

Romanby (1993)
Pay and play
Yafforth Road, Northallerton,
DL7 0PE
☎ (01609) 779988
📠 (01609) 779084
📖 550
🏌 G McDonnell (01609) 778855
🏌 T Jenkins
🏴 18 L 6663 yds SSS 72
🏌 U SOC
£€ £25 (£30)
⇔ 1 mile W of Northallerton on B6271
⊕ Floodlit driving range
🏠 Will Adamson

Rudding Park (1995)
Pay and play
Rudding Park, Harrogate, HG3 1DJ
☎ (01423) 872100
📠 (01423) 873011
📖 500
🏌 J Watson
🏌 M Moore (01423) 873400
🏴 18 L 6871 yds SSS 72
🏌 U H SOC
£€ £22.50. Fri/WE–£27.50
⇔ 2 miles S of Harrogate (A658)
⊕ Driving range. Golf Academy
🏠 Hawtree
■ www.ruddingpark.com

Saltburn (1894)
Hob Hill, Saltburn-by-the-Sea,
TS12 1NJ
☎ (01287) 622812
📠 (01287) 625988
📖 900
🏌 J Walton
🏌 M Nutter (01287) 624653
🏴 18 L 5846 yds SSS 68
🏌 H SOC
£€ £23 (£29)
⇔ 1 mile S of Saltburn

Scarborough North Cliff
(1909)
North Cliff Avenue, Burniston Road,
Scarborough, YO12 6PP
☎ (01723) 360786
📠 (01723) 362134
📖 860
🏌 JR Freeman
🏌 SN Deller (01723) 365920
🏴 18 L 6425 yds Par 71 SSS 71
🏌 U H exc Sat am, Sun before 10am and comp days SOC
£€ £22 D–£28 (£25 D–£30)
⇔ 2 miles N of Scarborough on coast road
🏠 James Braid
■ www.ncgc.co.uk

Scarborough South Cliff
(1902)
Deepdale Avenue, Scarborough,
YO11 2UE
☎ (01723) 374737
📠 (01723) 374737
✉ secretary@scarboroughgolfclub.co.uk
📖 700
🏌 D Roberts
🏌 T Skingle (01723) 365150
🏴 18 L 6039 yds SSS 69
🏌 U H
£€ £22 (£27)
⇔ 1 mile S of Scarborough, off A165
🏠 Dr A Mackenzie

Scarthingwell (1993)
Scarthingwell, Tadcaster, LS24 9DG
☎ (01937) 557878
📠 (01937) 557909
📖 400
🏌 S Footman (01937) 557864
🏴 18 L 6642 yds Par 71 SSS 72
🏌 U SOC
£€ £16 (£20)
⇔ 4 miles S of Tadcaster on A162

Selby (1907)
Mill Lane, Brayton, Selby, YO8 9LD
☎ (01757) 228622
📠 (01757) 228785
📖 749
🏌 JN Proctor
🏌 A Smith (01757) 228785
🏴 18 L 6374 yds SSS 71
🏌 WD–H WE–NA SOC–WD
£€ £30 D–£35
⇔ 3 miles SW of Selby, off A19 at Brayton. 5 miles N of M62 Junction 34
🏠 JH Taylor/Hawtree
■ www.selbygolfclub.co.uk

Settle (1895)
Giggleswick, Settle, BD24 0DH
☎ (01729) 825288
📖 250
🏌 J Ketchell (01729) 823727
🏴 9 L 5414 yds SSS 66
🏌 U exc Sun–restricted SOC
£€ D–£15
⇔ 1 mile N of Settle on A65
🏠 Tom Vardon

Skipton (1893)
Short Lee Lane, Skipton, BD23 3LF
☎ (01756) 793922
📠 (01756) 796665
📖 720
🏌 TH Newman (01756) 795657
🏌 P Robinson (01756) 793257
🏴 18 L 6076 yds SSS 70
🏌 U SOC
£€ £24 (£26)
⇔ 1 mile N of Skipton on A59

Teesside (1901)
Acklam Road, Thornaby, TS17 7JS
☎ (01642) 676249

📠 (01642) 676252
✉ teessidegolfclub@btconnect.com
📖 690
🏌 PB Hodgson (01642) 616516
🏌 K Hall (01642) 673822
🏴 18 L 6535 yds Par 72 SSS 71
🏌 WD–U before 4.30pm WE–U after 11am BH–M before 11am SOC
£€ D–£26 (£30)
⇔ 2 miles S of Stockton on A1130. ¹/₂ mile from A19 on A1130
🏠 Makepeace/Summerville
■ www.teessidegolfclub.com

Thirsk & Northallerton
(1914)
Thornton-le-Street, Thirsk, YO7 4AB
☎ (01845) 522170
📠 (01845) 525115
📖 500
🏌 GS Batterbee (01845) 525115
🏌 R Garner (01845) 526216
🏴 18 L 6495 yds SSS 71
🏌 WD/Sat–U H Sun–M SOC
£€ £22 D–£28 Sat/BH–£28 D–£33
⇔ 2 miles N of Thirsk, nr A19 and A168 roundabout
🏠 ADAS

Whitby (1892)
Sandsend Road, Low Straggleton,
Whitby, YO21 3SR
☎ (01947) 602768
📠 (01947) 600660
📖 900
🏌 T Graham (01947) 600660
🏌 T Mason (01947) 602719
🏴 18 L 6134 yds SSS 69
🏌 U H SOC
£€ £22 (£28)
⇔ 2 miles N of Whitby on A174

Wilton (1952)
Wilton, Redcar, Cleveland, TS10 4QY
☎ (01642) 465265/465886
📠 (01642) 465463
✉ secretary@wiltongolfclub.co.uk
📖 863
🏌 R Douglas (01642) 465265
🏌 Pat Smillie (01642) 452730
🏴 18 L 6145 yds Par 70 SSS 69
🏌 WD–U after 10am Sat–NA Sun/BH–U after 10am SOC–WD exc Tues & Thurs
£€ D–£22 (D–£26)
⇔ 3 miles W of Redcar on A174–signs to Wilton Castle
■ www.wiltongolfclub.co.uk

York (1890)
Lords Moor Lane, Strensall, York,
YO32 5XF
☎ (01904) 491840
📠 (01904) 491852
📖 400 129(L) 78(J)
🏌 SG Watson
🏌 AP Hoyles (01904) 490304
🏴 18 L 6301 yds SSS 70
🏌 U–phone Sec SOC
£€ £30–£40 (£40–£45)

🐾 4 miles N of York ring road (A1237)
🏠 JH Taylor

Yorkshire (South)

Abbeydale (1895)
Twentywell Lane, Dore, Sheffield, S17 4QA
☎ **(0114) 236 0763**
🖳 (0114) 236 0762
📖 650
🏌 GL Lord
⌁ N Perry (0114) 236 5633
🏴 18 L 6323 yds SSS 70
👥 U SOC–H by arrangement
££ £30 (£45)
🐾 5 miles S of Sheffield, off A621
🏠 Herbert Fowler
■ www.abbeydalegolf.co.uk

Barnsley (1925)
Public
Wakefield Road, Staincross, Barnsley, S75 6JZ
☎ **(01226) 382856**
📖 500
🏌 M Gillott
⌁ S Wyke (01226) 380358
🏴 18 L 5951 yds Par 69 SSS 69
👥 U
££ £10 (£12)
🐾 4 miles N of Barnsley on A61

Bawtry G&CC (1974)
Cross Lane, Austerfield, Doncaster, DN10 6RF
☎ **(01302) 710841**
📖 490 25(L) 20(J)
🏌 PD Ludbrook
⌁ H Selby-Green
🏴 18 L 6900 yds Par 73 SSS 73
👥 U SOC
££ £14 (£18)
🐾 2 miles NE of Bawtry, on A614
⊕ Driving range
🏠 E & M Baker

Beauchief (1925)
Public
Abbey Lane, Beauchief, Sheffield, S18 0DB
☎ **(0114) 236 7274**
📖 450
🏴 18 L 5452 yds SSS 66
👥 U
££ £8.50 – £10
🐾 A621 Sheffield

Birley Wood (1974)
Public
Birley Lane, Sheffield, S12 3BP
☎ **(0114) 264 7262**
📧 birleysec@hotmail.com
📖 218
🏌 P Renshaw (0114) 265 3784
⌁ P Ball
🏴 18 L 5647 yds Par 68 SSS 67
👥 U

££ £8.50 (£10)
🐾 4 miles S of Sheffield on A616. M1 Junction 30
■ www.birleywood.free-online.co.uk

Concord Park (1952)
Pay and play
Shiregreen Lane, Sheffield, S5 6AE
☎ **(0114) 257 7378**
🏌 GR Gunnee
⌁ W Allcroft
🏴 18 L 4872 yds Par 67 SSS 64
👥 U
££ £8 (£10)
🐾 M1 Junction 34, 1 mile
⊕ Driving range

Crookhill Park (1974)
Public
Conisborough, Doncaster, DN12 2AH
☎ **(01709) 862979**
📖 50
🏌 TA Cusack
🏴 18 L 5860 yds SSS 68
👥 U
££ £9.95 (£11.30)
🐾 3 miles W of A1(M)/A630 junction

Doncaster (1894)
Bawtry Road, Bessacarr, Doncaster, DN4 7PD
☎ **(01302) 865632**
🖳 (01302) 865994
📧 doncastergolf@aol.com
📖 375
🏌 DR Barton
⌁ G Bailey (01302) 868404
🏴 18 L 6220 yds SSS 70
👥 WD–U H WE/BH–NA before 11.30am SOC–WD
££ £30 D–£36 (£15)
🐾 4½ miles S of Doncaster on A638
🏠 Mackenzie/Hawtree

Doncaster Town Moor (1895)
Bawtry Road, Belle Vue, Doncaster, DN4 5HU
☎ **(01302) 533778**
📖 540
🏌 J Stoddart
⌁ S Shaw (01302) 535286
🏴 18 L 6001 yds SSS 69
👥 U exc Sun–NA before 3.30pm SOC
££ £16 (£17)
🐾 Inside racecourse. Clubhouse on A638

Dore & Totley (1913)
Bradway Road, Bradway, Sheffield, S17 4QR
☎ **(0114) 236 0492**
🖳 (0114) 235 3436
📖 580
🏌 JR Johnson (0114) 236 9872
⌁ G Roberts (0114) 236 6844
🏴 18 L 6265 yds Par 70 SSS 70
👥 WD–restricted Sat–NA Sun–restricted before 1pm SOC–Tues & Thurs
££ £26 (£30) Sun–£15 after 2pm
🐾 5 miles SW of Sheffield, off A61

Grange Park (1972)
Pay and play
Upper Wortley Road, Kimberworth, Rotherham, S61 2SJ
☎ **(01709) 558884**
📖 150
🏌 RP Townley (01709) 558884
⌁ E Clark (01709) 559497
🏴 18 L 6461 yds SSS 71
👥 U SOC–phone Pro
££ £10.20 (£12.75)
🐾 2 miles W of Rotherham on A629
⊕ Driving range

Hallamshire (1897)
Sandygate, Sheffield, S10 4LA
☎ **(0114) 230 1007**
🖳 (0114) 230 2153
📖 600
🏌 Mrs KE Renshaw (0114) 230 2153
⌁ G Tickell (0114) 230 5222
🏴 18 L 6333 yds SSS 71
👥 H SOC–WD
££ £39 (£43)
🐾 W boundary of Sheffield

Hallowes (1892)
Dronfield, Sheffield, S18 1UR
☎ **(01246) 413734**
🖳 (01246) 413734
📖 550
🏌 T Marshall
⌁ P Dunn (01246) 411196
🏴 18 L 6342 yds SSS 71
👥 WD–U WE–M
££ £30 D–£35
🐾 6 miles S of Sheffield on B6057

Hickleton (1909)
Hickleton, Doncaster, DN5 7BE
☎ **(01709) 896081**
🖳 (01709) 896083
📖 525
🏌 JA Mills
⌁ PJ Audsley (01709) 888436
🏴 18 L 6208 yds SSS 71
👥 WD–U WE–NA before noon SOC
££ £20 (£27)
🐾 6 miles W of Doncaster on A635
🏠 Huggett/Coles

Hillsborough (1920)
Worrall Road, Sheffield, S6 4BE
☎ **(0114) 234 3608 (Clubhouse)**
🖳 (0114) 234 9151
📧 admin@hillsboroughgolfclub.co.uk
📖 534
🏌 TC Pigott (0114) 234 9151
⌁ L Horsman (0114) 233 2666
🏴 18 L 6035 yds SSS 70
👥 H SOC
££ £30 (£35)
🐾 Wadsley, Sheffield

Lees Hall (1907)
Hemsworth Road, Norton, Sheffield, S8 8LL
☎ **(0114) 255 4402**
🖳 (0114) 255 2900
📖 550

🏌 JW Poulson (0114) 255 2900
⛳ S Berry
🏳 18 L 6171 yds SSS 70
👥 U SOC
💷 £20 (£30)
🏌 3 miles S of Sheffield. E of A61

Lindrick (1891)

Lindrick Common, Worksop, Notts,
S81 8BH
☎ (01909) 485802
🖥 (01909) 488685
📖 500
🏌 J Armitage (01909) 475282
⛳ JR King (01909) 475820
🏳 18 L 6486 yds Par 71 SSS 71
👥 U H–by prior arrangement exc Tues
   SOC–WD
💷 £48 (£48)
🏌 4 miles W of Worksop on A57. M1
   Junction 31
■ www.lindrickgolf.com

Owston Park (1988)

Public
Owston Lane, Owston Carcroft
DN6 8EP
☎ (01302) 330821
🏌 MT Parker
🏳 9 L 6148 yds SSS 71
👥 U
💷 On application
🏌 5 miles N of Doncaster on A19
🏠 Michael Parker

Phoenix (1932)

Pavilion Lane, Brinsworth, Rotherham,
S60 5PA
☎ (01709) 363788
🖥 (01709) 363788
📖 700
🏌 A Webb (01709) 365905
⛳ M Roberts (01709) 382624
🏳 18 L 6181 yds SSS 70
👥 U
💷 £18 D–£24 (£24 D–£32)
🏌 2 miles S of Rotherham. M1
   Junction 34
⊕ Driving range
🏠 H Cotton

Renishaw Park (1911)

Golf House, Mill Lane, Renishaw,
Sheffield S21 3UZ
☎ (01246) 432044
📖 450
🏌 TJ Childs
⛳ J Oates (01246) 435484
🏳 18 L 6262 yds SSS 70
👥 H SOC
💷 £26 D–£35.50 (£40)
🏌 7 miles SE of Sheffield. 2 miles W
   of M1 Junction 30

Robin Hood (1996)

Owston Hall, Owston, Doncaster,
DN6 9JF
☎ (01302) 722800
🖥 (01302) 728885
📖 200
🏌 C Tanswell

⛳ J Laszkowicz (01302) 722231
🏳 18 L 6937 yds Par 72 SSS 73
👥 U SOC
💷 £16 (£22)
🏌 5 miles N of Doncaster on A19
   (B1220)
🏠 Will Adamson

Rother Valley Golf Centre (1997)

Mansfield Road, Wales Bar, Sheffield,
S26 5PQ
☎ (0114) 247 3000
🖥 (0114) 247 6000
✉ rother-jackbarker@btinternet.com
📖 300
🏌 Mrs M Goodman
⛳ JK Ripley
🏳 18 L 6602 yds Par 72 SSS 72
   9 hole Par 3 course
👥 U SOC
💷 £12 (£16)
🏌 Rother Valley Country Park, 2
   miles S of M1 Junction 31
⊕ Floodlit driving range
🏠 Shattock/Roe

Rotherham (1903)

Thrybergh Park, Rotherham, S65 4NU
☎ (01709) 850466
🖥 (01709) 859517
📖 400
🏌 G Smalley (01709) 850466
⛳ S Thornhill (01709) 850480
🏳 18 L 6324 yds SSS 70
👥 WD–U SOC
💷 £30 (£35)
🏌 4 miles E of Rotherham on A630

Roundwood (1976)

Green Lane, Rawmarsh, Rotherham,
S62 6LA
☎ (01709) 523471
📖 700
🏌 M Pantry (01709) 527583
🏳 18 L 5620 yds Par 67 SSS 67
👥 WE–NA before 5pm on comp days
   SOC–WD
💷 £15 (£18)
🏌 2 miles N of Rotherham on A633

Sandhill (1993)

Pay and play
Little Houghton, Barnsley, S72 0HW
☎ (01226) 753444
🖥 (01226) 753444
📖 420
🏌 BD Murray
🏳 18 L 6250 yds SSS 70
👥 U SOC
💷 £11 (£15)
🏌 6 miles E of Barnsley, off A635
⊕ Driving range
🏠 John Royston

Sheffield Transport (1923)

Meadow Head, Sheffield, S8 7RE
☎ (0114) 237 3216
📖 125
🏌 AE Mason

🏳 18 L 3966 yds SSS 62
👥 M
🏌 S of Sheffield on A61

Silkstone (1893)

Field Head, Elmhirst Lane, Silkstone,
Barnsley S75 4LD
☎ (01226) 790328
🖥 (01226) 792653
📖 600
🏌 J Goulding
⛳ K Guy (01226) 790128
🏳 18 L 6069 yds SSS 70
👥 WD–U SOC–WD
💷 £22 D–£28 SOC(12+)–£40
🏌 1 mile W of M1 Junction 37 on
   A628

Sitwell Park (1913)

Shrogs Wood Road, Rotherham, S60 4BY
☎ (01709) 541046
🖥 (01709) 703637
📖 500
🏌 G Simmonite
⛳ N Taylor (01709) 540961
🏳 18 L 6250 yds SSS 70
👥 WD–U Sat–M Sun–NA before
   11.30am SOC
💷 £25 D–£30 (£30)
🏌 2¹/₂ miles E of Rotherham on A631.
   M18 Junction 1
🏠 Dr A Mackenzie

Stocksbridge & District (1924)

Royd Lane, Deepcar, Sheffield, S36 2RZ
☎ (0114) 288 7479
🖥 (0114) 288 2003
📖 300
🏌 J Willers (0114) 288 2003
⛳ T Brookes (0114) 288 2779
🏳 18 L 5200 yds Par 65 SSS 65
👥 U SOC
💷 £20 (£30)
🏌 9 miles W of Sheffield (A616)

Tankersley Park (1907)

Park Lane, High Green, Sheffield,
S35 4LG
☎ (0114) 246 8247
🖥 (0114) 245 7818
📖 574
🏌 A Brownhill (0114) 246 8247
⛳ I Kirk (0114) 245 5583
🏳 18 L 6212 yds Par 69 SSS 70
👥 WD–U WE–M SOC–WD
💷 £27 D–£36 (£36)
🏌 Chapeltown, 7 miles N of Sheffield.
   M1 Junctions 35A/36
🏠 Hawtree

Thorne (1980)

Pay and play
Kirton Lane, Thorne, Doncaster,
DN8 5RJ
☎ (01405) 812084
🖥 (01405) 741899
📖 120
🏌 R Highfield
⛳ ED Highfield (01405) 812084

18 L 5294 yds SSS 66
U
£€ £9 (£10)
10 miles NE of Doncaster. M18 Junction 5/6
RD Highfield

Tinsley Park (1920)
Public
High Hazels Park, Darnall, Sheffield, S9 4PE
☎ (0114) 203 7435
500
ML Shillito
AP Highfield (0114) 203 7435
18 L 6084 yds SSS 69
WD–U WE–by arrangement SOC
£€ £10
M1 Junction 33, 3 miles (A6102)

Wath (1904)
Abdy Rawmarsh, Rotherham, S62 7SJ
☎ (01709) 878609
(01709) 877097
wathgolf@aol.com
680
M Godfrey (01709) 583174
C Bassett (01709) 878609
18 L 6123 yds SSS 69
WD–U WE/BH–M SOC
£€ £22 D–£27
Abdy Farm, 1½ miles S of Wath-upon-Dearne

Wheatley (1913)
Armthorpe Road, Doncaster, DN2 5QB
☎ (01302) 831655
(01302) 812736
wheatleygolfclub@route56.co.uk
385 100(L) 50(J)
RTJ Bruno
S Fox (01302) 834085
18 L 6405 yds SSS 71
U SOC
£€ £27 (£33)
3 miles NE of Doncaster

Wombwell Hillies (1989)
Public
Wentworth View, Wombwell, Barnsley, S73 0LA
☎ (01226) 754433
(01226) 758635
J Hayes (01226) 756761
9 L 2095 yds SSS 60
U
£€ On application
4 miles SE of Barnsley

Wortley (1894)
Hermit Hill Lane, Wortley, Sheffield, S35 7DF
☎ (0114) 288 8469
(0114) 288 8488
wortleygolfclub@virgin.net
500
Dr FA Wilson
I Kirk (0114) 288 6490
18 L 6035 yds SSS 69
WD–U WE–NA before 10am SOC
£€ £28 (£35)

2 miles W of M1 Junction 36, off A629

Yorkshire (West)

Alwoodley (1907)
Wigton Lane, Alwoodley, Leeds, LS17 8SA
☎ (0113) 268 1680
(0113) 293 9458
via website
450
CD Wilcher
JR Green (0113) 268 9603
18 L 6785 yds SSS 73
U SOC–WD
£€ £60 (£75)
5 miles N of Leeds on A61
Dr A Mackenzie
www.alwoodley.co.uk

Bagden Hall Hotel (1993)
Wakefield Road, Scissett, HD8 9LE
☎ (01484) 865330
(01484) 861001
175
J Rinder
N Hirst (Golf Dir)
9 L 3022 yds Par 56 SSS 55
U
£€ £10 (£13)
On A636 between Derby Dale and Scissett. M1 Junction 39
F O'Donnell

Baildon (1896)
Moorgate, Baildon, Shipley, BD17 5PP
☎ (01274) 584266
(01274) 530551
750
JA Cooley
R Masters (01274) 595162
18 L 6231 yds SSS 70
WD–U before 5pm (restricted Tues) WE/BH–restricted
£€ £16 (£20)
5 miles N of Bradford, off A6038
Tom Morris/James Braid

Ben Rhydding (1947)
High Wood, Ben Rhydding, Ilkley, LS9 8SB
☎ (01943) 608759
195 60(L) 45(J)
A Leverton
9 L 4611 yds SSS 63
WD–U exc Wed pm & Thurs am WE–M
£€ £12 (£17)
2 miles SE of Ilkley

Bingley St Ives (1931)
St Ives Estate, Bingley, BD16 1AT
☎ (01274) 562436
(01274) 511788
Mrs M Welch
R Firth (01274) 562506
18 L 6480 yds SSS 71
WD–U before 4pm

£€ £25 D–£30
6 miles NW of Bradford, off A650

Bracken Ghyll (1993)
Skipton Road, Addingham, Ilkley, LS29 0SL
☎ (01943) 831207
400
JW Williams
None
18 L 5310 yds Par 69 SSS 66
WD/BH–U WE–NA before noon on comp days SOC
£€ £18 (£20)
3 miles W of Ilkley on old A65 to Addingham
Indoor practice area

Bradford (1891)
Hawksworth Lane, Guiseley, Leeds, LS20 8NP
☎ (01943) 875570
(01943) 875570
650
T Eagle
S Weldon (01943) 873719
18 L 6259 yds SSS 71
WD–U WE–NA before noon SOC–WD
£€ On application
8 miles N of Bradford, off A6038. 10 miles N of Leeds on A650

Bradford Moor (1906)
Scarr Hall, Pollard Lane, Bradford, BD2 4RW
☎ (01274) 771716
350
CP Bedford (01274) 771693
9 L 5854 yds SSS 68
WD–U
£€ £10
2 miles N of Bradford

Bradley Park (1978)
Public
Bradley Road, Huddersfield, HD2 1PZ
☎ (01484) 223772
(01484) 451613
300
K Blackwell
PE Reilly
18 L 6202 yds SSS 70
9 hole Par 3 course
U SOC
£€ £12.50 (£15.20)
2 miles N of Huddersfield, off A6107, M62 Junction 25
Floodlit driving range

Branshaw (1912)
Branshaw Moor, Oakworth, Keighley, BD22 7ES
☎ (01535) 643235
(01535) 648011
branshaw@golfclub.fslife.co.uk
525
T O'Hara
M Tyler (01535) 647441
18 L 5858 yds SSS 68
WD–U SOC–WD

£€ D–£20 (D–£30)
⟷ 2 miles SW of Keighley on B6143
⌂ James Braid/Dr A Mackenzie

Calverley   (1984)

Woodhall Lane, Pudsey, LS28 5QY
☎ **(0113) 256 9244**
⌨ (0113) 256 4362
📖 600
🗝 N Wendel-Jones (Mgr)
✓ N Wendel-Jones
🏴 18 L 5527 yds SSS 67
    9 L 2137 yds Par 33
👤 WD–U WE–pm only
£€ £12 (£15)
⟷ 4 miles NE of Bradford
⊕ Driving range

Castlefields   (1903)

Rastrick Common, Brighouse, HD6 3HL
☎ **(01484) 713276**
📖 180
🗝 FC Tolley
🏴 6 L 2406 yds Par 54 SSS 50
👤 M
£€ £6 (£8)
⟷ 1 mile S of Brighouse

City of Wakefield   (1936)

Public
Lupset Park, Horbury Road, Wakefield, WF2 8QS
☎ **(01924) 367442**
✓ R Holland (01924) 360282
🏴 18 L 6319 yds SSS 70
👤 U SOC–WD
£€ On application
⟷ A642, 2 miles W of Wakefield. 2 miles E of M1 Junction 39/40
⌂ JSF Morrison

Clayton   (1906)

Thornton View Road, Clayton, Bradford, BD14 6JX
☎ **(01274) 880047**
📖 170 26(L) 54(J)
🗝 DA Smith (01274) 572311
🏴 9 L 5515 yds SSS 67
👤 WD–U Sat–U Sun–after 4pm
£€ £12 D–£14 (£14)
⟷ 3 miles W of Bradford, off A647

Cleckheaton & District
(1900)

483 Bradford Road, Cleckheaton, BD19 6BU
☎ **(01274) 874118 (Clubhouse)**
⌨ (01274) 871382
✉ info@cleckheatongolf.fsnet.co.uk
📖 572
🗝 Mrs R Newsholme (Asst Sec) (01274) 851266
✓ M Ingham (01274) 851267
🏴 18 L 5860 yds SSS 69
👤 U SOC
£€ £25 D–£30 (£30)
⟷ Nr M62 Junction 26-A638
🖥 www.cleckheatongolfclub.fsnet .co.uk

Cookridge Hall

Cookridge Lane, Cookridge, Leeds, LS16 7NL
☎ **(0113) 230 0641**
⌨ (0113) 203 0198
✉ cookridgehall@americangolf.uk .com
📖 650
🗝 W Carr (Gen Mgr) (0113) 230 0641
✓ M Pearson
🏴 18 L 6788 yds Par 72 SSS 72
👤 WD–U Sat–U after 2pm Sun–U after 12 noon SOC
£€ £18 (£20)
⟷ 5 miles NW of Leeds, via A660
⊕ Driving range. Golf Academy
⌂ Karl Litten

Crosland Heath   (1914)

Felk Stile Road, Crosland Heath, Huddersfield, HD4 7AF
☎ **(01484) 653216**
⌨ (01484) 461079
📖 600
🗝 D Walker (Sec/Mgr) (01484) 653216
✓ J Eyre (01484) 653877
🏴 18 L 6004 yds SSS 70
👤 U SOC
£€ On application
⟷ 3 miles W of Huddersfield, off A62

Crow Nest Park   (1994)

Coach Road, Hove Edge, Brighouse, HD6 2LN
☎ **(01484) 401121**
⌨ (01484) 720975
📖 300
🗝 A Naylor
✓ P Everitt (01484) 401121
🏴 9 L 6020 yds Par 70 SSS 69
👤 WD–U WE–U before noon
£€ 18 holes–£22. 9 holes–£11
⟷ 5 miles E of Halifax. M62 Junction 25
⊕ Driving range
⌂ Will Adamson

Dewsbury District   (1891)

The Pinnacle, Sands Lane, Mirfield, WF14 8HJ
☎ **(01924) 492399**
📖 650
🗝 DM Ellis
✓ N Hirst (01924) 496030
🏴 18 L 6360 yds SSS 71
👤 WD–U WE–M –U after 3pm SOC
£€ £18 (£15)
⟷ 2 miles W of Dewsbury, off A644
⌂ Tom Morris/Alliss/Thomas

East Bierley   (1928)

South View Road, Bierley, Bradford, BD4 6PP
☎ **(01274) 681023**
📖 156 47(L) 30(J)
🗝 RJ Welch (01274) 683666
🏴 9 L 4692 yds SSS 63
👤 U exc Mon–NA after 4pm Sun–NA
£€ £14 (£16)
⟷ 4 miles SE of Bradford

Elland   (1910)

Hammerstones Leach Lane, Hullen Edge, Elland, HX5 0TA
☎ **(01422) 372505**
📖 280
🗝 AD Blackburn (01422) 372014
✓ N Krzywicki (01422) 374886
🏴 9 L 5498 yds Par 66 SSS 67
👤 U
£€ £15 (£25)
⟷ Elland 1 mile. M62 Junction 24, signpost Blackley

Fardew   (1993)

Pay and play
Nursery Farm, Carr Lane, East Morton, Keighley BD20 5RY
☎ **(01274) 561229**
⌨ (01274) 561229
✉ fardew@dial.pipex.com
📖 100
🗝 GA Richardson
✓ I Bottomley
🏴 9 L 3104 yds Par 72 SSS 70
👤 U SOC
£€ 9 holes–£8 (£9) 18 holes–£12 (£14)
⟷ 2 miles W of Bingley on A650
⌂ Will Adamson

Ferrybridge 'C'   (1976)

PO Box 39, Stranglands Lane, Knottingley, WF11 8SQ
☎ **(01977) 884165**
📖 305
🗝 TD Ellis
🏴 9 L 5137 yds SSS 65
👤 M
£€ D–£6 (D–£7)
⟷ ¹/₂ mile off A1, on B6136
⌂ NE Pugh

Fulneck   (1892)

Fulneck, Pudsey, LS28 8NT
☎ **(0113) 256 5191**
📖 290
🗝 Mrs P Warburton (0113) 256 2606
🏴 9 L 5456 yds SSS 67
👤 WD–U WE/BH–M SOC
£€ £15
⟷ 5 miles W of Leeds

Garforth   (1913)

Long Lane, Garforth, Leeds, LS25 2DS
☎ **(0113) 286 2021**
⌨ (0113) 286 3308
📖 550
🗝 NG Douglas (0113) 286 3308
✓ K Findlater (0113) 286 2063
🏴 18 L 6304 yds SSS 70
👤 WD–U H WE/BH–M SOC
£€ £30 D–£35
⟷ 9 miles E of Leeds, between Garforth and Barwick-in-Elmet
⊕ Driving range
🖥 www.garforthgolfclub.co.uk

Gotts Park   (1933)

Public
Armley Ridge Road, Armley, Leeds, LS12 2QX
☎ **(0113) 234 2019**

🖩 300
🏌 M Gill (0113) 256 2994
✓ J Marlor
🏳 18 L 4960 yds SSS 64
👤 U
££ On application
🚗 2 miles W of Leeds

Halifax (1895)
Union Lane, Ogden, Halifax, HX2 8XR
☎ (01422) 244171
🖥 (01422) 241459
🖩 450
✓ M Allison (01422) 240047
🏳 18 L 6037 yds SSS 69
👤 U WD–parties welcome SOC
££ £20 (£25)
🚗 4 miles N of Halifax on A629
🏠 Alex Herd/James Braid

Halifax Bradley Hall (1907)
Holywell Green, Halifax, HX4 9AN
☎ (01422) 374108
🖩 608
🏌 M Dredge (01484) 374108
✓ P Wood (01422) 370231
🏳 18 L 6138 yds SSS 70
👤 U SOC
££ £20 (£28)
🚗 S of Halifax on A6112

Halifax West End (1904)
Paddock Lane, Highroad Well, Halifax, HX2 0NT
☎ (01422) 341878
🖥 (01442) 341878
🖩 340 100(L) 60(J)
🏌 G Gower (01422) 341878
✓ D Rishworth (01422) 363293
🏳 18 L 5951 yds SSS 69
👤 U SOC
££ £25 (£30)
🚗 2 miles NW of Halifax

Hanging Heaton (1922)
Whitecross Road, Bennett Lane, Dewsbury, WF12 7DT
☎ (01924) 461606
🖥 (01924) 430100
✉ ken.wood@hhgc.org
🖩 400
🏌 K Wood (01924) 430100
✓ (01924) 467077
🏳 9 L 2923 yds SSS 68
👤 WD–U WE–M
££ £16
🚗 Dewsbury ¾ mile (A653)

Headingley (1892)
Back Church Lane, Adel, Leeds, LS16 8DW
☎ (0113) 267 3052 (Clubhouse)
🖥 (0113) 281 7334
🖩 675
🏌 JR Burns JP (Mgr) (0113) 267 9573
✓ NM Harvey (0113) 267 5100
🏳 18 L 6298 yds SSS 70
👤 WD–U before 3.30pm SOC
££ £30 D–£35 (£40)
🚗 5 miles NW of Leeds, off A660
🏠 Dr A MacKenzie

Headley (1907)
Headley Lane, Thornton, Bradford, BD13 3LX
☎ (01274) 833481
🖥 (01274) 833481
🖩 270 35(L) 35(J)
🏌 A Goodman
🏳 9 L 4914 yds SSS 64
👤 WD–U WE–M SOC
££ On application
🚗 5 miles W of Bradford (B6145)

Hebden Bridge (1930)
Great Mount, Wadsworth, Hebden Bridge, HX7 8PH
☎ (01422) 842896
🖩 300
🏌 R Priestley (01422) 842896
🏳 9 L 5242 yds Par 68 SSS 67
👤 WD–U
££ £10–£12 (£15)
🚗 1 mile N of Hebden Bridge

Horsforth (1907)
Layton Rise, Layton Road, Horsforth, Leeds LS18 5EX
☎ (0113) 258 6819
✉ horsforthgolf@btconnect.com
🖩 365 90(L) 85(J)
🏌 Mrs J Kenny
✓ (0113) 258 5200
🏳 18 L 6293 yds SSS 70
👤 U SOC
££ D–£26 (£38)
🚗 6 miles NW of Leeds

Howley Hall (1900)
Scotchman Lane, Morley, Leeds, LS27 0NX
☎ (01924) 350100
🖥 (01924) 350104
✉ office@howleyhall.co.uk
🖩 492
🏌 D Jones (01924) 350100
✓ G Watkinson (01924) 350102
🏳 18 L 6058 yds Par 71 SSS 69
👤 U SOC–WD/Sun before 5pm
££ £29 D–£35 (£39)
🚗 4 miles SW of Leeds on B6123

Huddersfield (1891)
Fixby Hall, Lightridge Road, Huddersfield, HD2 2EP
☎ (01484) 420110
🖥 (01484) 424623
🖩 682
🏌 JM Seatter (Gen Mgr), Mrs D Lockett (01484) 426203
✓ P Carman (01484) 426463
🏳 18 L 6432 yds SSS 71
👤 U SOC–WD
££ £37 D–£47 (£47 D–£57)
🚗 2 miles N of Huddersfield, off A6107. M62 Junction 24
⊕ Driving range
🌐 www.huddersfield-golf.co.uk

Ilkley (1890)
Myddleton, Ilkley, LS29 0BE
☎ (01943) 607277

🖥 (01943) 816130
🖩 530
🏌 PG Richardson (01943) 600214
✓ JL Hammond (01943) 607463
🏳 18 L 6260 yds SSS 70
👤 U
££ £37 (£42)
🚗 NW of Ilkley, off A65

Keighley (1904)
Howden Park, Utley, Keighley, BD20 6DH
☎ (01535) 604778
🖥 (01535) 610572
✉ manager@keighleygolfclub.com
🖩 600
🏌 G Cameron Dawson
✓ M Bradley (01535) 665370
🏳 18 L 6141 yds SSS 70
👤 WD–NA before 9.30am & 12–1.30pm Sat–NA Sun/BH–NA before 2pm
££ £28 D–£32 (£32 D–£38)
🚗 1 mile W of Keighley on A629

Leeds (1896)
Elmete Road, Roundhay, Leeds, LS8 2LJ
☎ (0113) 265 8775
🖥 (0113) 232 3369
🖩 545
🏌 SJ Clarkson (0113) 265 9203
✓ S Longster (0113) 265 8786
🏳 18 L 6092 yds SSS 69
👤 WD–U WE–M SOC
££ £25 D–£32
🚗 4 miles NE of Leeds, off A58
⬛ www.leedsgolfclub.com

Leeds Golf Centre (1994)
Pay and play
Wike Ridge Lane, Shadwell, Leeds, LS17 9JW
☎ (0113) 288 6000
🖥 (0113) 288 6185
🖩 500
🏌 D Dourambeis
✓ M Pinkett
🏳 18 L 6800 yds SSS 72
12 hole Par 3 course
👤 U SOC
££ £14.50 (£18)
🚗 NE of Leeds, between A58 and A61
⊕ Driving range. Golf Academy
🏠 Donald Steel
🌐 www.leedsgolfcentre.com

Lightcliffe (1907)
Knowle Top Road, Lightcliffe, HX3 8SW
☎ (01422) 202459
🖩 180 95(L) 84(J)
🏌 CCD Balaam (01422) 201650
✓ R Kershaw
🏳 9 L 5368 metres SSS 68
👤 U H–exc Wed Sun am–M SOC
££ £16 (£20)
🚗 3 miles E of Halifax (A58)

Lofthouse Hill
Leeds Road, Lofthouse Hill, Wakefield, WF3 3LR
☎ (01924) 823703

☎ (01924) 823703
🖉 N Todd
✒ B Janes (01924) 820048
ᴾ 9 L 3167 yds Par 35
👥 M SOC
££ 18 holes–£17.50 9 holes–£10
🚗 Between Leeds and Wakefield
⊕ Driving range

Longley Park (1910)
Maple Street, Huddersfield, HD5 9AX
☎ (01484) 426932
📖 400
✒ N Leeming (01484) 422304
ᴾ 9 L 5212 yds Par 66 SSS 66
👥 WD–U exc Thurs WE–restricted
££ £13.50 (£16)
🚗 Huddersfield ¹/₂ mile

Low Laithes (1925)
*Park Mill Lane, Flushdyke, Ossett,
WF5 9AP*
☎ (01924) 273275
🖥 (01924) 266067
📧 info@low-laithes-golf-club.co.uk
📖 610
🖉 P Browning (Sec/Mgr)
(01924) 266067
✒ P Browning (01924) 274667
ᴾ 18 L 6468 yds SSS 71
👥 U WE–no parties SOC–WD
££ £22 D–£25 (£36)
🚗 2 miles W of Wakefield. M1
Junction 40
🏠 Dr A Mackenzie

The Manor
*Bradford Road, Drighlington, Bradford,
BD11 1AB*
☎ (0113) 285 2644
📖 300
🖉 J Crompton (Sec/Mgr)
✒ J Crompton
ᴾ 18 L 6508 yds Par 72 SSS 71
👥 U SOC–exc Sat
££ £15 (£15)
🚗 1 mile from M62 Junction 27, off
A650
⊕ Floodlit driving range. 6 holes pitch
& putt course
🏠 David Hemstock

Marriott Hollins Hall
Hotel (1999)
*Hollins Hill, Baildon, Shipley,
BD17 7QW*
☎ (01274) 534212
🖥 (01274) 534220
📖 300
🖉 Janice Dornom (01274) 534250
ᴾ 18 L 6700 yds Par 71 SSS 72
👥 H
££ £40
🚗 6 miles N of Bradford on A6038
🏠 Ross McMurray

Marsden (1921)
*Hemplow, Marsden, Huddersfield,
HD7 6NN*
☎ (01484) 844253

📖 200 50(L) 50(J)
🖉 GM Sykes (01484) 686665
✒ N Krzywicki
ᴾ 9 L 5702 yds SSS 68
👥 WD–U Sat–NA before 4pm Sun–M
SOC
££ £10 (£15)
🚗 8 miles W of Huddersfield, off
A62
🏠 Dr A Mackenzie

Meltham (1908)
*Thick Hollins Hall, Meltham,
Huddersfield, HD9 4DQ*
☎ (01484) 850227
🖥 (01484) 859051
📧 meltham@thegolfcourse.co.uk
📖 650
🖉 CJ Naylor (Hon)
✒ PF Davies (01484) 851521
ᴾ 18 L 6396 yds SSS 70
👥 H
££ £22 (£27)
🚗 5 miles SW of Huddersfield
(B6107)
🖥 www.meltham-golf.co.uk

Mid Yorkshire (1993)
*Havercroft Lane, Darrington,
Pontefract, WF8 3BP*
☎ (01977) 704522
🖥 (01977) 600823
📖 600
🖉 Linda Darwood
✒ A Corbett (01977) 600844
ᴾ 18 L 6340 yds SSS 71
👥 U H SOC
££ £15 (£25)
🚗 Nr A1/M62 junction
⊕ Floodlit driving range
🏠 Steve Marnoch

Middleton Park (1933)
Public
*Ring Road, Beeston Park, Middleton,
LS10 3TN*
☎ (0113) 270 0449
📧 lynn@ratcliffel.fsnet.co.uk
📖 250
🖉 Mrs L Ratcliffe
✒ None
ᴾ 18 L 5233 yds SSS 66
👥 U
££ On application
🚗 3 miles S of Leeds

Moor Allerton (1923)
Coal Road, Wike, Leeds, LS17 9NH
☎ (0113) 266 1154
🖥 (0113) 237 1124
📖 800
🖉 N Lomas
✒ R Lane (0113) 266 5209
ᴾ 27 L 6470-6843 yds SSS 73-74
👥 WD/Sat–U Sun–NA SOC
££ £45 D–£50 (£60 D–£65)
🚗 5¹/₂ miles N of Leeds, off A61
⊕ Driving range
🏠 Robert Trent Jones Sr

Moortown (1909)
Harrogate Road, Leeds, LS17 7DB
☎ (0113) 268 6521
🖥 (0113) 268 0986
📖 600
🖉 KC Bradley
✒ B Hutchinson (0113) 268 3636
ᴾ 18 L 6995 yds SSS 74
👥 H
££ £55 (£65)
🚗 5¹/₂ miles N of Leeds on A61
🏠 Dr A Mackenzie

Normanton (1903)
*Hatfield Hall, Aberford Road, Stanley,
Wakefield WF3 4JP*
☎ (01924) 200900
🖥 (01924) 200777
📖 600
🖉 RJ Metcalfe
✒ F Houlgate
ᴾ 18 L 6191 yds Par 72 SSS 69
👥 U SOC
££ £22
🚗 3 miles N of Wakefield (A642).
M62 Junction 30
🖥 www.normantongolf.co.uk

Northcliffe (1921)
*High Bank Lane, Shipley, Bradford,
BD18 4LJ*
☎ (01274) 584085
🖥 (01274) 596731
📧 northcliffe@bigfoot.com
📖 867
🖉 I Collins (01274) 596731
✒ M Hillas (01274) 587193
ᴾ 18 L 6113 yds SSS 70
👥 U SOC
££ £25 (£30)
🚗 3 miles NW of Bradford, off A650
Keighley road
🏠 James Braid
🖥 www.northcliffegolfclubshipley
.co.uk

Otley (1906)
West Busk Lane, Otley, LS21 3NG
☎ (01943) 465329
🖥 (01943) 850387
📧 office@otley-golfclub.co.uk
📖 700
🖉 PJ Clarke Ext 202
✒ S Tomkinson Ext 203
ᴾ 18 L 6245 yds SSS 70
👥 U exc Sat–NA SOC
££ £29 (£36)
🚗 1 mile W of Otley, off A6038
🖥 www.otley-golfclub.co.uk

Oulton Park (1990)
Public
Oulton, Rothwell, Leeds, LS26 8EX
☎ (0113) 282 3152
🖥 (0113) 282 6290
📖 390
🖉 A Cooper (Mgr)
✒ S Gromett
ᴾ 18 L 6479 yds SSS 71
9 L 3287 yds SSS 35
👥 U SOC–WD

££   18 hole: £10.15 (£13.15) 9 hole:
£5.95 (£6.95)
⊕   5 miles SE of Leeds, off A642. N of
M62 Junction 30
⊕   Driving range
↟   Alliss/Thomas

Outlane   (1906)

Slack Lane, New Hey Road, Outlane,
HD3 3YL
☎   (01422) 374762
⊟   (01422) 311789
⊞   500
♨   P Jackson
✓   D Chapman
⊬   18 L 6010 yds SSS 69
⋔   U SOC
££   £19 (£29)
⊕   4 miles W of Huddersfield, off
A640. M62 Junction 23

Painthorpe House   (1961)

Painthorpe Lane, Crigglestone,
Wakefield, WF4 3HE
☎   (01924) 255083
⊟   (01924) 252022
⊞   180
♨   H Kershaw (01924) 274527
⊬   9 L 4520 yds SSS 62
⋔   U
££   £5 (£6)
⊕   1 mile SE of M1 Junction 39

Phoenix Park   (1922)

Dick Lane, Thornbury, Bradford,
BD3 7AT
☎   (01274) 667573
⊞   180
♨   C Lally (01274) 668218
✓   None
⊬   9 L 4982 yds SSS 64
⋔   WD/BH–U WE–NA
££   On application
⊕   Thornbury Roundabout (A647)

Pontefract & District   (1904)

Park Lane, Pontefract, WF8 4QS
☎   (01977) 792241
⊟   (01977) 792241
✉   manager@pdgc.co.uk
⊞   841
♨   RE Guiver (Mgr)
✓   NJ Newman (01977) 706806
⊬   18 L 6227 yds SSS 70
⋔   WD–I WE–after 3pm SOC–WD
exc Wed
££   £22 (£32)
⊕   Pontefract 1 mile on B6134. M62
Junction 32
↟   Alistair Mackenzie
■   www.pdgc.co.uk

Pontefract Park   (1973)

Public
Park Road, Pontefract, WF8
☎   (01977) 702799
⊬   18 L 4068 yds SSS 62
⋔   U
££   On application
⊕   Between Pontefract and M62
roundabout, nr racecourse

Queensbury   (1923)

Brighouse Road, Queensbury, Bradford,
BD13 1QF
☎   (01274) 882155
⊞   400 48(L) 47(J)
♨   B Cox
✓   D Delaney (01274) 816864
⊬   9 L 5008 yds SSS 65
⋔   U
££   £15 (£30)
⊕   4 miles SW of Bradford (A647)

Rawdon   (1896)

Buckstone Drive, Micklefield Lane,
Rawdon, LS19 6BD
☎   (0113) 250 6040
⊞   220 55(L) 50(J)
♨   RA Adams (0113) 250 6064
✓   (0113) 250 5017
⊬   9 L 5982 yds SSS 69
⋔   WD–H WE/BH–M SOC
££   £16
⊕   6 miles NW of Leeds nr A65/A658
junction

Riddlesden   (1927)

Howden Rough, Riddlesden, Keighley,
BD20 5QN
☎   (01535) 602148
⊞   400
♨   Mrs KM Brooksbank
(01535) 607646
⊬   18 L 4295 yds Par 63 SSS 61
⋔   U exc Sun–NA before 2pm
££   £15 (£20)
⊕   1 mile from Riddlesden, off Scott
Lane West. 3 miles N of Keighley,
off A650

Roundhay   (1923)

Public
Park Lane, Leeds, LS8 2EJ
☎   (0113) 266 2695
⊞   290
♨   RH McLauchlan
✓   JA Pape (0113) 266 1686
⊬   9 L 5322 yds SSS 65
⋔   U
££   On application
⊕   N of Leeds, off Moortown Ring
Road

Ryburn   (1910)

Norland, Sowerby Bridge, Halifax,
HX6 3QP
☎   (01422) 831355
⊞   300
♨   J Hoyle (01422) 843070
⊬   9 L 5127 yds SSS 65
⋔   U
££   £15 (£20)
⊕   3 miles S of Halifax

Sand Moor   (1926)

Alwoodley Lane, Leeds, LS17 7DJ
☎   (0113) 268 1685
⊟   (0113) 268 5180
⊞   540
♨   K Spencer
✓   P Tupling (0113) 268 3925

⊬   18 L 6429 yds SSS 71
⋔   WD–H by arrangement WE–NA
££   £36 (£45)
⊕   5 miles N of Leeds, off A61
↟   Dr A Mackenzie

Scarcroft   (1937)

Syke Lane, Leeds, LS14 3BQ
☎   (0113) 289 2311
⊟   (0113) 289 3835
✉   secretary@scarcroftgc.co.uk
⊞   580
♨   D Tear (Gen Mgr) (0113) 289 2311
✓   D Tear (0113) 289 2780
⊬   18 L 6426 yds SSS 71
⋔   WD–U WE/BH–M or by
arrangement SOC–WD
££   £30 D–£38 (£40)
⊕   7 miles N of Leeds, off A58
■   www.sgccwc.net

Shipley   (1896)

Beckfoot Lane, Cottingley Bridge,
Bingley, BD16 1LX
☎   (01274) 563212
⊟   (01274) 567739
⊞   600
♨   Mrs MJ Bryan (01274) 568652
✓   JR Parry (01274) 563674
⊬   18 L 6235 yds SSS 70
⋔   WD–U exc Tues–NA before 2pm
Sat–NA before 4pm
££   D–£35 (D–£40)
⊕   6 miles N of Bradford on A650
↟   Colt/Alison/Mackenzie/Braid
■   www.shipleygc.co.uk

Silsden   (1913)

Brunthwaite Lane, Brunthwaite, Silsden,
BD20 0ND
☎   (01535) 652998
⊟   (01535) 654273
⊞   300
♨   J Bellerby
⊬   18 L 5259 yds Par 67 SSS 66
⋔   Sat–restricted Sun–U after 1pm
££   £15 (£20)
⊕   5 miles N of Keighley, off A6034

South Bradford   (1906)

Pearson Road, Odsal, Bradford,
BD6 1BH
☎   (01274) 679195
⊞   200
♨   B Broadbent (01274) 670538
✓   P Cooke (01274) 673346
⊬   9 L 6076 yds SSS 69
⋔   WD–U WE–M
££   On application
⊕   Bradford 2 miles, nr Odsal Stadium

South Leeds   (1914)

Gipsy Lane, Ring Road, Beeston, Leeds
LS11 5TU
☎   (0113) 270 0479
✉   sec@slgc.freeserve.co.uk
⊞   450
♨   J Neal (0113) 277 1676
✓   M Lewis (0113) 270 2598
⊬   18 L 5865 yds SSS 68
⋔   WD–U WE–M SOC

££ £18 (£25)
🕸 4 miles S of Leeds. 2 miles from
M62 and M1

Temple Newsam (1923)
Public
Temple Newsam Road, Halton, Leeds,
LS15 0LN
☎ **(0113) 264 5624**
📖 500
🖎 G Hollins
✏ J Pape (0113) 264 7362
⮞ Lord Irwin 18 L 6448 yds SSS 71;
Lady Dorothy Wood 18 L 6229 yds
SSS 70
👥 U SOC
££ £7.50 (£9) Summer £7 (£8.50)
Winter
🕸 5 miles E of Leeds, off A63

Todmorden (1894)
Rive Rocks, Cross Stone, Todmorden,
0L14 8RD
☎ **(01706) 812986**
📖 179 44(L) 26(J)
🖎 G Holt (01706) 813653
⮞ 9 L 5902 yds SSS 68
👥 WD/BH–U WE–M SOC–WD
££ £15 (£20)
🕸 1 mile N of Todmorden, off A646

Wakefield (1891)
28 Woodthorpe Lane, Sandal, Wakefield,
WF2 6JH
☎ **(01924) 255104**
📠 (01924) 242752
📖 500
🖎 AJ McVicar (01924) 258778
✏ IM Wright (01924) 255380
⮞ 18 L 6653 yds SSS 72
👥 U H SOC–Wed–Fri
££ On application
🕸 3 miles S of Wakefield on A61. M1
Junction 39
🏠 Alex Herd

Waterton Park (1995)
The Balk, Walton, Wakefield, WF2 6QL
☎ **(01924) 259525**
📠 (01924) 256969
📖 650
🖎 L Lammas
✏ N Wood (01924) 255557
⮞ 18 L 6843 yds Par 72 SSS 73
👥 WD–H SOC
££ D–£30
🕸 4 miles SE of Wakefield centre
⊕ Driving range
🏠 Simon Gidman

West Bowling (1898)
Newall Hall, Rooley Lane, Bradford,
BD5 8LB
☎ **(01274) 724449**
📠 (01274) 393207
📖 500
🖎 IW Brogden (01274) 393207
✏ IA Marshall (01274) 728036
⮞ 18 L 5769 yds SSS 68
👥 WD–U H SOC
££ £24 (£30)
🕸 Junction of M606 and Bradford
Ring Road East

West Bradford (1900)
Chellow Grange, Haworth Road,
Bradford, BD9 6NP
☎ **(01274) 542767**
📠 (01274) 482079
📖 450
🖎 IP Milnes (Hon)
✏ NM Barber (01274) 542102
⮞ 18 L 5738 yds SSS 68
👥 U
££ £21 (£21)
🕸 3 miles W of Bradford (B6144)

Wetherby (1910)
Linton Lane, Linton, Wetherby,
LS22 4JF
☎ **(01937) 580089**
📠 (01937) 581915
📧 info@wetherbygolfclub.fsnet.co.uk
📖 630
🖎 L McGrae (Mgr) (01937) 580089
✏ M Daubney (01937) 580089
⮞ 18 L 6235 yds SSS 70
👥 WE–U after 10am SOC–WD H
££ £28 (£40)
🕸 ³/₄ mile W of Wetherby. A1
Wetherby roundabout
⊕ Driving range

Whitwood (1987)
Public
Altofts Lane, Whitwood, Castleford,
WF10 5PZ
☎ **(01977) 512835**
🖎 S Hicks (Hon)
✏ R Holland
⮞ 9 L 6176 yds SSS 69
👥 WD–U WE–booking necessary
££ On application
🕸 2 miles SW of Castleford (A655).
M62 Junction 31

Willow Valley (1993)
Pay and play
Clifton, Brighouse, HD6 4JB
☎ **(01274) 878624**

📠 (01274) 852805
📖 280
🖎 H Butterfield
✏ J Haworth
⮞ 18 & 9 hole courses
Academy course
👥 U
££ 18 hole:£23 (£28). 9 hole:£7 (£8)
🕸 SW of Leeds, M62 Junction 25
⊕ Driving range
🏠 Jonathan Gaunt

Woodhall Hills (1905)
Woodhall Road, Calverley, Pudsey,
LS28 5UN
☎ **(0113) 256 4771 (Clubhouse)**
📠 (0113) 295 4594
📖 550
🖎 J Armitage (0113) 255 4594
✏ W Lockett (0113) 256 2857
⮞ 18 L 6184 yds SSS 70
👥 WD–U Sat–U after 4.30pm Sun–U
after 9.30am
££ £20.50 (£25.50)
🕸 4 miles E of Bradford, off A647,
past Calverley GC

Woodsome Hall (1922)
Woodsome Hall, Fenay Bridge,
Huddersfield, HD8 0LQ
☎ **(01484) 602971**
📠 (01484) 608260
📖 279 130(L) 85(J)
🖎 TJ Mee (01484) 602739
RB Shaw (Hon)
✏ M Higginbottom (01484) 602034
⮞ 18 L 6080 yds SSS 69
👥 U H exc Tues–NA before 4pm SOC
££ £30 D–£40 (£50 D–£60)
🕸 6 miles SE of Huddersfield on
A629 Penistone road
🖥 www.woodsomehall.co.uk

Woolley Park (1995)
Woolley, Wakefield, WF4 2JS
☎ **(01226) 380144 (Bookings)**
📠 (01226) 390295
📖 500
🖎 D Rowbottom (Prop)
(01226) 382209
✏ J Baldwin
⮞ 18 L 6636 yds Par 71 SSS 72
👥 WD–U WE–restricted SOC
££ £15 (£22)
🕸 5 miles S of Wakefield on A61. M1
Junction 38, 2 miles
🏠 M Shattock
🖥 www.woolleypark.co.uk

Ireland

Co Antrim

Antrim   (1997)
Allen Park Golf Centre, 45 Castle Road, Antrim, BT41 4NA
- ☎ **(028) 9442 9001**
- 📠 (028) 9442 9001
- ✉ antrimgolfclub@aol.com
- 🏠 500
- 🏌 Marie Agnew (Mgr)
- 🏌 P Russell
- ⛳ 18 L 6110 m Par 72 SSS 72
- 👥 U
- £€ £14 (£16)
- 🚗 Antrim
- ⊕ Driving range

Ballycastle   (1890)
Cushendall Road, Ballycastle, BT64 6QP
- ☎ **(028) 2076 2536**
- 📠 (028) 2076 9909
- 🏠 920
- 🏌 BJ Dillon (Hon)
- 🏌 I McLaughlin (028) 2076 2506
- ⛳ 18 L 5927 yds SSS 70
- 👥 U H SOC
- £€ £20 (£30)
- 🚗 Between Portrush and Cushendall (A2)

Ballyclare   (1923)
25 Springvale Road, Ballyclare, BT39 9JW
- ☎ **(028) 9334 2352 (Clubhouse)**
- 📠 (028) 9332 2696
- ✉ ballyclaregolfclub@supanet.com
- 🏠 440
- 🏌 H McConnell (028) 9332 2696
- ⛳ 18 L 5840 yds SSS 71
- 👥 WD–U WE–NA before 4pm
- £€ £20 (£25)
- 🚗 1½ miles N of Ballyclare. 14 miles N of Belfast
- 🏠 T McAuley

Ballymena   (1903)
128 Raceview Road, Ballymena, BT42 4HY
- ☎ **(028) 2586 1207/1487**
- 📠 (028) 2586 1487
- 🏠 940
- 🏌 S Crummey (Hon)
- 🏌 K Revie
- ⛳ 18 L 5299 m Par 68 SSS 67
- 👥 WD/Sun–U SOC
- £€ £17 (£22)
- 🚗 2 miles E of Ballymena on A42

Bentra
Public
Slaughterford Road, Whitehead, BT38 9TG
- ☎ **(028) 9337 8996**
- 🏌 N Houston (028) 9335 1711
- ⛳ 9 L 3155 yds Par 36 SSS 34
- 👥 U

- £€ £8 (£11)
- 🚗 4 miles N of Carrickfergus on A2 Larne road
- 🏠 James Braid

Burnfield House
10 Cullyburn Road, Newtownabbey, BT36 8BN
- ☎ **(028) 9083 8737**
- ✉ michaelhj@ntlworld.com
- 🏌 MH Jackson (028) 9038 6652
- ⛳ 9 L 2751 yds Par 35 SSS 39
- 👥 U
- £€ £12 (£14)
- 🚗 10 miles N of Belfast (A2)

Bushfoot   (1890)
50 Bushfoot Road, Portballintrae, BT57 8RR
- ☎ **(028) 2073 1317**
- 📠 (028) 2073 1852
- ✉ bushfootgolfclub@btinternet.com
- 🏠 860
- 🏌 J Knox Thompson (Sec/Mgr)
- ⛳ 9 L 6001 yds SSS 68
- 👥 U Sat–NA after noon SOC
- £€ £15 (£19)
- 🚗 1 mile N of Bushmills. 4 miles E of Portrush

Cairndhu   (1928)
192 Coast Road, Ballygally, Larne, BT40 2QC
- ☎ **(028) 2858 3324**
- 📠 (028) 2858 3324
- 🏠 875
- 🏌 N Moore (028) 2858 3324
- 🏌 R Walker (028) 2858 3417
- ⛳ 18 L 6112 yds SSS 69
- 👥 U exc Sat–NA
- £€ £20 (£25)
- 🚗 4 miles N of Larne
- 🏠 JSF Morrison

Carrickfergus   (1926)
35 North Road, Carrickfergus, BT38 8LP
- ☎ **(028) 9336 3713**
- 📠 (028) 9336 3023
- ✉ carrickfergusgc@talk21
- 🏠 385
- 🏌 JW Thomson (Sec/Mgr)
- 🏌 M Stanford (028) 9335 1803
- ⛳ 18 L 5752 yds SSS 68
- 👥 U SOC
- £€ £18 (£25)
- 🚗 7 miles E of Belfast, off M5

Cushendall   (1937)
21 Shore Road, Cushendall, BT44 0NG
- ☎ **(028) 2177 1318**
- 🏠 834
- 🏌 S McLaughlin (028) 2175 8366
- ⛳ 9 L 4834 m SSS 63
- 👥 WE–restricted SOC
- £€ £13 (£18)
- 🚗 Cushendall, 25 miles N of Larne

Down Royal   (1990)
Dungarton Road, Maze, Lisburn, BT27 5RT
- ☎ **(028) 9262 1339**
- 📠 (028) 9262 1339
- 🏠 52
- 🏌 J Tinnion (Mgr)
- 🏌 C Calder
- ⛳ 18 L 6058 m Par 72 SSS 69
- 👥 U
- £€ £12 D–£17 (£24)
- 🚗 Lisburn, W of Belfast City (M1)
- 🏠 Stewart Assoc

Galgorm Castle   (1997)
200 Galgorm Road, Ballymena, BT42 1HL
- ☎ **(028) 2565 0210**
- 📠 (028) 2565 1151
- 🏠 500
- 🏌 B McGrown (Mgr)
- 🏌 P Collins
- ⛳ 18 L 6724 yds Par 72 SSS 72
- 👥 U SOC
- £€ £20 (£25)
- 🚗 Ballymena
- ⊕ Driving range
- 🖥 www.galgormcastle.co.uk

Gracehill   (1995)
Proprietary
141 Ballinlea Road, Stranocum, Ballymoney, BT53 8PX
- ☎ **(028) 2075 1209**
- 📠 (028) 2075 1074
- ✉ info@gracehillgolfclub.co.uk
- 🏠 360
- 🏌 M McClure (Mgr)
- 🏌 None
- ⛳ 18 L 6600 yds Par 72
- 👥 U
- £€ £15–£20 (£25)
- 🚗 6 miles N of Ballymoney (B66)
- 🏠 Frank Ainsworth
- 🖥 www.gracehillgolfclub.co.uk

Greenacres   (1996)
153 Ballyrobert Road, Ballyclare, BT39 9RT
- ☎ **(028) 9335 4111**
- 📠 (028) 9335 4166
- 🏠 340
- 🏌 P Watson
- ⛳ 18 L 5893 yds Par 70 SSS 68
- 👥 U
- £€ £12 (£18)
- 🚗 3 miles from Corrs Corner on B56
- ⊕ Floodlit driving range
- 🖥 www.greenacresgolfclub.co.uk

Greenisland   (1894)
156 Upper Road, Greenisland, Carrickfergus, BT38 8RW
- ☎ **(028) 9086 2236**
- ✉ greenisland.golf@virgin.net
- 🏠 740

   WJ McLaughlin (Hon) (028) 9086 3232
▷ 9 L 5536 metres Par 71 SSS 69
🏌 WD–U Sat–NA before 5pm SOC–exc Sat
£€ £12 (£18)
⛳ 9 miles NE of Belfast
🏠 H Middleton

Hilton Templepatrick

Castle Upton Estate, Paradise Walk, Templepatrick, BT39 0DD
☎ **(028) 9443 5542**
📠 (028) 9443 5511
✉ bill.donald@hilton.com
📖 350
   W Donald (Mgr)
✓ E Logue
▷ 18 L 7300 yds Par 71 SSS 71
🏌 U H
£€ £40 (£45)
⛳ 12 miles N of Belfast. M2 Junction 5. Belfast Airport 6 miles
⊕ Driving range
🏠 Jones/Feherty

Lambeg   (1986)

Bells Lane, Lambeg, Lisburn, BT27 4QH
☎ **(028) 9266 2738**
📠 (028) 9260 3432
📖 200
   B Jackson (Hon)
✓ I Murdock
▷ 18 L 4139 m Par 66 SSS 62
🏌 U SOC
£€ £7.40 (£9.40)
⛳ SW of Belfast, off Lisburn road

Larne   (1894)

54 Ferris Bay Road, Islandmagee, Larne, BT40 3RJ
☎ **(028) 9338 2228**
✉ info@larnegolfclub.co.uk
📖 420
   RI Johnston
▷ 9 L 6288 yds SSS 70
🏌 WD–U WE–M after 5pm SOC–WD/Sun
£€ £10 (£18)
⛳ 6 miles N of Whitehead on Browns Bay road
🏠 George Baillie

Lisburn   (1891)

68 Eglantine Road, Lisburn, BT27 5RQ
☎ **(028) 9267 7216**
📠 (028) 9260 3608
📖 1421
   GE McVeigh (Sec/Mgr)
✓ BR Campbell (028) 9267 7217
▷ 18 L 6647 yds Par 72 SSS 72
🏌 WD–U WE–M SOC–Mon & Thurs
£€ £25 (£30)
⛳ 3 miles S of Lisburn on A1
🏠 Hawtree

Mallusk   (1992)

Antrim Road, Glengormley, Newtownabbey, BT36 4RF
☎ **(028) 9084 3799**
📖 75

   J Patterson
▷ 9 L 4444 m SSS 62
🏌 U
£€ £6.50 (£8.75)
⛳ 4 miles NW of Newtownabbey (B95)

Massereene   (1895)

51 Lough Road, Antrim, BT41 4DQ
☎ **(028) 9442 9293**
📠 (028) 9448 7661
✉ massereenegc@utvinternet.com
📖 850
   K Stevens (028) 9442 8096
✓ J Smyth (028) 9446 4074
▷ 18 L 6602 yds SSS 72
🏌 U SOC
£€ £25 (£30)
⛳ 1 mile S of Antrim
🏠 Harold Swann
■ www.massereenegolfclub1895.com

Rathmore

Bushmills Road, Portrush, BT56 8JG
☎ **(028) 7082 2996**
   DR Williamson (Mgr)
▷ 18 L 6304 yds Par 70
🏌 U
£€ £30 (£35)
⛳ Portrush

Royal Portrush   (1888)

Dunluce Road, Portrush, BT56 8JQ
☎ **(028) 7082 2311**
📠 (028) 7082 3139
✉ info@royalportrushgolfclub.com
📖 997 297(L)
   Miss W Erskine
✓ G McNeill (028) 7082 3335
▷ Dunluce 18 L 6772 yds SSS 73; Valley 18 L 6273 yds SSS 70; Skerries-9 hole course
🏌 WD–I H exc Wed & Fri pm–NA Sat–NA before 3pm Sun–NA before 10.30am SOC
£€ Dunluce £85 (£95) Valley £30 (£37.50)
⛳ Portrush Coastal Rd ½ mile
⊕ Driving range
🏠 HS Colt
■ www.royalportrushgolfclub.com

Whitehead   (1904)

McCrae's Brae, Whitehead, Carrickfergus, BT38 9NZ
☎ **(028) 9337 0820**
📠 (028) 9337 0825
✉ robin@whiteheadgc.fsnet.co.uk
📖 1076
   RA Patrick (Hon)
✓ C Farr (028) 9337 0821
▷ 18 L 6050 yds SSS 69
🏌 WD–U WE–M SOC–exc Sat
£€ £15 (£20)
⛳ ½ mile from Whitehead, off road to Island Magee
🏠 AB Armstrong

Co Armagh

Ashfield   (1990)

Freeduff, Cullyhanna, Newry, BT35 0JJ
☎ **(028) 3086 8180**
📖 100
   J Quinn (Sec/Mgr)
✓ E Maney
▷ 18 L 5110 m Par 69 SSS 67
🏌 U
£€ £10 (£12)
⛳ 6 miles S of Newtownhamilton (B135)
⊕ Driving range
🏠 Frank Ainsworth

County Armagh   (1893)

Newry Road, Armagh, BT60 1EN
☎ **(028) 3752 2501**
📠 (028) 3752 5861
✉ june@golfarmagh.co.uk
📖 1350
   P McNaney (028) 3752 5861
✓ A Rankin (028) 3752 5864
▷ 18 L 6184 yds SSS 69
🏌 SOC
£€ £15 (£20)
⛳ 40 miles SW of Belfast by M1

Edenmore   (1992)

Drumnabreeze Road, Magheralin, Craigavon, BT67 0RH
☎ **(028) 9261 1310**
📠 (028) 9261 3310
✉ edenmoregc@aol.com
📖 620
   K Logan (Sec/Mgr)
▷ 18 L 6244 yds Par 71 SSS 70
🏌 U SOC
£€ £14 (£18)
⛳ 4 miles E of Lurgan (A3)
🏠 F Ainsworth

Loughgall

11-14 Main Street, Loughgall
☎ **(028) 3889 2900**
📠 (028) 3889 2902
   G Ferson (Mgr)
▷ 18 L 6229 yds Par 72
🏌 U SOC
£€ £14 (£16)
⛳ 8 miles W of Portadown (B77)
🏠 Don Patterson
■ www.armagh.gov.uk

Lurgan   (1893)

The Demesne, Lurgan, BT67 9BN
☎ **(028) 3832 2087 (Clubhouse)**
📠 (028) 3831 6166
📖 918
   Mrs M Sharpe
✓ D Paul (028) 3832 1068
▷ 18 L 6257 yds SSS 70
🏌 U SOC–Mon/Thurs/Fri am/Sun am
£€ £15 (£20)
⛳ Nr Brownlow Castle, Lurgan
🏠 Frank Pennink

Portadown (1902)
192 Gilford Road, Portadown, BT63 5LF
☎ **(028) 3835 5356**
🖵 (028) 3839 1394
📖 959
🏌 Mrs ME Holloway
✓ P Stevenson (028) 3833 4655
🏴 18 L 5794 yds SSS 70
👥 WD–U exc Tues
£€ £18 (£23)
🚗 3 miles S of Portadown, towards Gilford

Silverwood (1983)
Turmoyra Lane, Silverwood, Lurgan, BT66 6NG
☎ **(028) 3832 6606**
🖵 (028) 3834 7272
📖 280
🏌 K Devlin
✓ D Paul (028) 3832 6606
🏴 18 L 6459 yds Par 72 SSS 71
👥 U
£€ £12 (£15)
🚗 Lurgan 1 mile. M1 Junction 10
⊕ Floodlit driving range

Tandragee (1922)
Markethill Road, Tandragee, BT62 2ER
☎ **(028) 3884 0727 (Clubhouse)**
🖵 (028) 3884 0664
📧 office@tandragee.co.uk
📖 1205
🏌 D Clayton (028) 3884 1272
✓ D Keenan (028) 3884 1761
🏴 18 L 5754 m Par 71 SSS 70
👥 U SOC
£€ £15 (£20)
🚗 5 miles S of Portadown on A27
🏠 F Hawtree
■ www.tandragee.co.uk

Belfast

Ballyearl Golf Centre
Public
585 Doagh Road, Newtownabbey, BT36 5RZ
☎ **(028) 9084 8287**
🖵 (028) 9084 4896
✓ J Robinson (028) 9084 0899
🏴 9 L 2362 yds Par 3 course
👥 U
£€ £4.90 (£5.70)
🚗 N of Mossley on B59, via A8
⊕ Floodlit driving range

Balmoral (1914)
518 Lisburn Road, Belfast, BT9 6GX
☎ **(028) 9038 1514**
🖵 (028) 9066 6759
📖 925
🏌 RC McConkey (Mgr)
✓ G Bleakley (028) 9066 7747
🏴 18 L 5909 m SSS 70
👥 U exc Sat SOC–Mon & Thurs
£€ £20 (£30)
🚗 2 miles S of Belfast by Kings Hall

Belvoir Park (1927)
73 Church Road, Newtownbreda, Belfast, BT8 4AN
☎ **(028) 9049 1693**
🖵 (028) 9064 6113
📖 1100
🏌 Ann Vaughan (028) 9049 1693
✓ GM Kelly
🏴 18 L 6501 yds SSS 71
👥 U–booking necessary
£€ £33 (£38)
🚗 3 miles S of Belfast centre, off Newcastle road
🏠 HS Colt

Cliftonville (1911)
Westland Road, Belfast, BT14 6NH
☎ **(028) 9074 4158**
🖵 429
🏌 JM Henderson (Hon) (028) 9074 6595
🏴 9 L 6242 yds SSS 70
👥 U exc Sat
£€ £13 (£16)
🚗 Belfast

Dunmurry (1905)
91 Dunmurry Lane, Dunmurry, Belfast, BT17 9JS
☎ **(028) 9061 0834**
🖵 (028) 9060 2540
📧 dunmurrygc@hotmail.com
📖 493 127(L) 117(J)
🏌 T Cassidy (Golf Mgr)
✓ J Dolan (028) 9062 1314
🏴 18 L 6080 yds SSS 69
👥 Tues & Thurs–NA after 5pm Sat–NA before 5pm SOC
£€ £25 (£35) SOC–£23
🚗 Belfast 5 miles
🏠 T McAuley

Fortwilliam (1891)
Downview Avenue, Belfast, B15 4EZ
☎ **(028) 9037 0770**
🖵 (028) 9078 1891
📖 1100
🏌 M Purdy
✓ P Hanna (028) 9077 0980
🏴 18 L 5973 yds SSS 69
👥 U SOC
£€ £22 (£29)
🚗 2 miles N of Belfast on M2

Gilnahirk (1983)
Manns Corner, Upper Braniel Road, Belfast, BT5 7TX
☎ **(028) 9044 8477**
📖 200
🏌 A Carson
✓ K Gray
🏴 9 L 2699 m SSS 68
👥 U
£€ £9
🚗 3 miles SE of Belfast, off A23

The Knock Club (1895)
Summerfield, Dundonald, Belfast, BT16 2QX
☎ **(028) 9048 2249**

🖵 (028) 9048 7277
📖 900
🏌 Anne Armstrong (028) 9048 3251
✓ G Fairweather (028) 9048 3825
🏴 18 L 6407 yds SSS 71
👥 U SOC–Mon & Thurs
£€ D–£20 (£25)
🚗 4 miles E of Belfast on the Upper Newtownards Road
🏠 Colt/Mackenzie/Alison

Malone (1895)
240 Upper Malone Road, Dunmurry, Belfast, BT17 9LB
☎ **(028) 9061 2758**
🖵 (028) 9043 1394
📧 manager@malonegolfclub.co.uk
📖 759 379(L) 211(J)
🏌 JNS Agate (028) 9061 2758
✓ M McGee (028) 9061 4917
🏴 18 L 6599 yds SSS 71
9 L 3160 yds SSS 36
👥 Tues/Wed pm–NA Sat–NA before 3.30pm SOC–Mon & Thurs
£€ £40 (£45)
🚗 6 miles S of Belfast
🏠 J Harris/CK Cotton
■ www.malonegolfclub.co.uk

Ormeau (1893)
50 Park Road, Belfast, BT7 2FX
☎ **(028) 9064 1069 (Members)**
🖵 (028) 9064 6250
📖 280 70(L) 45(J)
🏌 R Barnes (028) 9064 0700
✓ (028) 9064 0999
🏴 9 L 5308 yds SSS 65
👥 U SOC
£€ £14 (£16.50)
🚗 2 miles S of Belfast

Shandon Park (1926)
73 Shandon Park, Belfast, BT5 6NY
☎ **(028) 9079 3730**
🖵 (028) 9040 2773
📖 1100
🏌 DG Jenkins (Mgr) (028) 9040 1856
✓ B Wilson (028) 9079 7859
🏴 18 L 6261 yds SSS 70
👥 WD–U Sat–NA before 5pm SOC
£€ £22 (£27)
🚗 3 miles E of Belfast on the Knock road

Co Carlow

Borris (1907)
Deerpark, Borris
☎ **(0503) 73310**
🖵 (0503) 73750
📖 475
🏌 N Lucas (0503) 73310
🏴 9 L 5680 m Par 70 SSS 69
👥 WD–U Sun–M SOC–WD/Sat
£€ €20
🚗 Borris

Carlow (1899)

Deer Park, Dublin Road, Carlow
- ☎ **(0503) 31695**
- ⌨ (0503) 40065
- 🕮 1300
- ✍ Mrs M Meaney
- ✎ A Gilbert (0503) 41745
- ⊳ 18 L 5844 m Par 70 SSS 71
- ♟ U SOC–WD
- ££ €42 (€54)
- 🚗 2 miles N of Carlow (N9) 50 miles S of Dublin (N7)
- ⛫ Tom Simpson
- ■ www.carlowgolfclub.com

Mount Wolseley (1996)

Tullow
- ☎ **(0503) 52055**
- ⌨ (0503) 52123
- 🕮 250
- ✍ D Morrissey (Mgr)
- ✎ J Bolger
- ⊳ 18 L 6497 m Par 72 SSS 74
- ♟ U
- ££ €44
- 🚗 15 miles E of Carlow (R275)

Co Cavan

Belturbet (1950)

Erne Hill, Belturbet
- ☎ **(049) 952 2287**
- 🕮 110
- ✍ PF Coffey (049) 22498
- ✎ None
- ⊳ 9 L 6118 m Par 72
- ♟ U SOC
- ££ €13
- 🚗 1 mile E of Belturbet

Blacklion (1962)

Toam, Blacklion, via Sligo
- ☎ **(072) 53024**
- 🕮 250
- ✍ P Maguire (Hon)
- ⊳ 9 L 5716 m SSS 69
- ♟ U SOC
- ££ D–€10 (D–€12)
- 🚗 12 miles SW of Enniskillen on A4 to N16
- ⛫ Eddie Hackett

Cabra Castle (1978)

Kingscourt
- ☎ **(042) 966 7030**
- ⌨ (042) 966 7039
- 🕮 130
- ✍ L McCaul
- ⊳ 9 L 5308 m Par 70
- ♟ U exc Sun–NA SOC
- ££ €11
- 🚗 2 miles E of Kingscourt

County Cavan (1894)

Arnmore House, Drumelis, Cavan
- ☎ **(049) 433 1541**
- ⌨ (049) 433 1541
- 🕮 800
- ✍ B Fitzsimmons
- ✎ B Noble
- ⊳ 18 L 5519 m SSS 69
- ♟ U
- ££ On application
- 🚗 2 miles W of Cavan on Killeshandra road
- ⊕ Driving range
- ⛫ Eddie Hackett

Slieve Russell G&CC (1994)

Ballyconnell
- ☎ **(049) 952 6458**
- ✉ slieve-russell@quinn-hotels.com
- 🕮 500
- ✍ I Hewson (049) 952 5090
- ✎ L McCool (049) 952 5090
- ⊳ 18 L 7053 yds Par 72 SSS 74
- 9 hole Par 3 course
- ♟ U SOC
- ££ €50 Sat–€65
- 🚗 15 miles N of Cavan Town
- ⊕ Driving range
- ⛫ Paddy Merrigan

Virginia (1945)

Park Hotel, Virginia
- ☎ **(049) 854 8066**
- 🕮 570
- ✍ S MacGabhann
- ⊳ 9 L 4139 m Par 64 SSS 62
- ♟ U
- ££ €12
- 🚗 35 miles SE of Cavan, nr Lough Ramor (N3)

Co Clare

Clonlara (1993)

Clonlara
- ☎ **(061) 354141**
- 🕮 85
- ✍ M Morris
- ⊳ 12 L 5289 m Par 70 SSS 69
- ♟ U
- ££ €9
- 🚗 8 miles NE of Limerick

Dromoland Castle (1964)

Newmarket-on-Fergus
- ☎ **(061) 368444**
- ⌨ (061) 368498
- 🕮 400
- ✍ J O'Halloran
- ✎ P Murphy
- ⊳ 18 L 6098 yds SSS 71
- ♟ U SOC
- ££ D–€36 (€42)
- 🚗 18 miles NW of Limerick. Shannon Airport 4 miles
- ■ www.dromoland.ie

East Clare (1992)

Bodyke
- ☎ **(061) 921322**
- 🕮 450
- ✍ N O'Donnell (Hon)
- ⊳ 18 L 5922 m Par 71 SSS 69
- ♟ U

- ££ €17
- 🚗 20 miles E of Ennis (R352)

Ennis (1907)

Drumbiggle, Ennis
- ☎ **(065) 682 4074**
- ⌨ (065) 684 1848
- 🕮 907
- ✍ N O'Donnell (Gen Mgr)
- ✎ M Ward (065) 682 0690
- ⊳ 18 L 5592 m Par 71 SSS 69
- ♟ U SOC
- ££ €30
- 🚗 1/2 mile NW of Ennis, off N18
- ■ www.golfclub.ennis.ie

Kilkee (1896)

East End, Kilkee
- ☎ **(065) 905 6048**
- ⌨ (065) 905 6977
- ✉ kilkeegolfclub@eircom.net
- 🕮 704
- ✍ M Culligan (Sec/Mgr)
- ⊳ 18 L 5928 m Par 71 SSS 71
- ♟ U SOC
- ££ €24
- 🚗 End of Kilkee Promenade. 10 miles NW of Kilrush
- ⛫ Eddie Hackett

Kilrush (1934)

Parknamoney, Kilrush
- ☎ **(065) 905 1138**
- ⌨ (065) 905 2633
- 🕮 338
- ✍ DF Nagle (Sec/Mgr) M Cody (Hon)
- ✎ J McDermott
- ⊳ 18 L 5986 yds Par 70 SSS 69
- ♟ U SOC
- ££ €21 (€25)
- 🚗 25 miles SW of Ennis on Lahinch-Ballybunion road
- ⛫ Arthur Spring
- ■ www.kilrushgolfclub.com

Lahinch (1892)

Lahinch
- ☎ **(065) 708 1003**
- ⌨ (065) 708 1592
- ✉ info@lahinchgolf.com
- 🕮 1250
- ✍ A Reardon (Sec/Mgr)
- ✎ R McCavery (065) 708 1408
- ⊳ Old 18 L 6699 yds SSS 74
  Castle 18 L 5620 yds SSS 69
- ♟ WD–U WE–NA 9–10.30am and 1–2pm SOC
- ££ Old–€110. Castle–€50
- 🚗 20 miles NW of Ennis on T69
- ⛫ Morris/Gibson/Mackenzie/Harris

Shannon (1966)

Shannon
- ☎ **(061) 471020**
- ⌨ (061) 471507
- 🕮 1050
- ✍ M Corry (061) 471849
- ✎ A Pike (061) 471551
- ⊳ 18 L 6515 yds Par 72 SSS 72
- ♟ WD–U SOC
- ££ €35
- 🚗 Shannon Airport

Spanish Point   (1915)
Spanish Point, Miltown Malbay
☎ **(065) 708 4219**
🕮 200
🖉 D Fitzgerald
🏳 9 L 4624 m Par 64 SSS 63
👤 U
£€ €35
⛳ 2 mile S of Miltown Malbay (N67). 20 miles W of Ennis
■ www.spanish-point.com

Woodstock   (1993)
Shanaway Road, Ennis
☎ **(065) 682 9463**
🖳 (065) 682 0304
🕮 400
🖉 Avril Guerin (Sec/Mgr)
🏳 18 L 5879 m SSS 71
👤 U
£€ €40
⛳ Ennis, 18 miles from Shannon Airport
🏠 Arthur Spring

Co Cork

Bandon   (1909)
Castlebernard, Bandon
☎ **(023) 41111**
🖳 (023) 44690
🕮 800
🖉 N O'Sullivan (Hon)
✓ P O'Boyle (023) 42224
🏳 18 L 5663 m Par 70 SSS 69
👤 U
£€ On application
⛳ Bandon 1¹/₂ miles. 18 miles SW of Cork

Bantry Bay   (1975)
Donemark, Bantry, West Cork
☎ **(027) 50579/53773**
🖳 (027) 53790
🖂 info@bantrygolf.com
🕮 650
🖉 J O'Sullivan (Mgr)
🏳 18 L 5914 m Par 71 SSS 72
👤 WD–U before 4.30 pm WE/BH–booking necessary SOC
£€ €40 (€40)
⛳ 1 mile N of Bantry on Glengarriff road (N71)
🏠 E Hackett/C O'Connor, Jnr
■ www.bantrygolf.com

Berehaven   (1902)
Millcove, Castletownbere
☎ **(027) 70700**
🖳 (027) 70700
🕮 134
🖉 B Twomey (Hon)
🏳 9 L 2841 yds SSS 67
👤 U SOC
£€ €20
⛳ 2 miles E of Castletownbere on Glengarriff road
🏠 James Healy

Charleville   (1909)
Charleville
☎ **(063) 81257**
🖳 (063) 81274
🖂 charlevillegolf@eircom.net
🕮 1250
🖉 P Nagle (Sec/Mgr)
✓ D Keating
🏳 18 L 6430 yds SSS 69 9 L 6750 yds SSS 72
👤 WD–U WE–book in advance SOC
£€ €28 (€35) SOC–€25 (€28)
⛳ 35 miles N of Cork on Limerick road
⊕ Driving range
■ www.charlevillegolf.com

Cobh   (1987)
Ballywilliam, Cobh
☎ **(021) 812399**
🖳 (021) 812615
🕮 120
🖉 H Cunningham
🏳 9 L 4576 m SSS 64
👤 WD–U WE–NA
£€ €11
⛳ 1 mile N of Cobh. 16 miles SE of Cork
🏠 Eddie Hackett

Coosheen   (1989)
Coosheen, Schull
☎ **(028) 28182**
🕮 200
🖉 L Morgan
🏳 9 L 4001 m Par 60 SSS 61
👤 U
£€ €14 (€14)
⛳ 15 miles S of Bantry

Cork   (1888)
Little Island, Cork
☎ **(021) 435 3451/3037**
🖳 (021) 435 3410
🖂 corkgolfclub@eircom.net
🕮 366 176 (L)
🖉 M Sands (021) 435 3451
✓ P Hickey (021) 435 3421
🏳 18 L 6065 m SSS 72
👤 WD–U H exc 12–2pm –M after 4pm Thurs–(Ladies Day)–phone in advance WE–NA before 2.30pm H
£€ €70 (€80)
⛳ 5 miles E of Cork, off N25
🏠 Dr A Mackenzie

Doneraile   (1927)
Doneraile
☎ **(022) 24137**
🕮 750
🖉 J O'Leary (022) 24379
🏳 9 L 5528 yds SSS 67
👤 WD/Sat–U
£€ €20
⛳ 8 miles NW of Mallow

Douglas   (1909)
Douglas, Cork
☎ **(021) 489 1086**
🖳 (021) 489 5297

🖂 admin@douglasgolfclub.ie
🕮 839
🖉 B Barrett (Mgr) (021) 489 5297
✓ GS Nicholson (021) 436 2055
🏳 18 L 5972 m SSS 71
👤 WD–U exc Tues WE–NA before 2pm SOC–WD
£€ €50
⛳ Cork 3 miles
🏠 P McEvoy
■ www.douglasgolfclub.ie

Dunmore   (1967)
Muckross, Clonakilty
☎ **(023) 34644**
🕮 430
🖉 L O'Donovan
🏳 9 L 4464 yds SSS 61
👤 WD–U exc Wed WE–M SOC–Sat
£€ €20
⛳ 3 miles S of Clonakilty
🏠 Eddie Hackett

East Cork   (1971)
Gortacrue, Midleton
☎ **(021) 463 1687**
🖳 (021) 461 3695
🖂 eastcorkgolfclub@eircom.net
🕮 600
🖉 M Moloney (Sec/Mgr)
✓ D MacFarlane
🏳 18 L 5207 m SSS 67
👤 WD–U WE–NA before noon BH–U
£€ €25
⛳ 2 miles N of Midleton on L35
⊕ Driving range
🏠 Eddie Hackett

Fermoy   (1892)
Corrin, Fermoy
☎ **(025) 32694**
🖳 (025) 33072
🕮 1000
🖉 K Murphy
✓ B Moriarty (025) 31472
🏳 18 L 5847 m SSS 70
👤 U SOC
£€ €23 (€30)
⛳ 2 miles S of Fermoy, off N8
🏠 Cdr John Harris

Fernhill   (1994)
Carrigaline
☎ **(021) 437 2226**
🖳 (021) 437 1011
🖂 fernhill@iol.ie
🕮 120
🖉 A Bowes (Mgr)
✓ W Callaghan (087) 284 1365
🏳 18 L 5766 m Par 70 SSS 67
👤 U
£€ €18 (€25)
⛳ 7 miles SE of Cork (R609), nr Ringskiddy
🏠 ML Bowes
■ www.fernhillgolfhotel.com

Fota Island   (1993)
Carrigtwohill, Cork
☎ **(021) 488 3710**

☎ (021) 453 2047
✉ reservations@fotaisland.ie
📖 650
🏌 Valerie Curran
✓ K Morris
🏳 18 L 6927 yds Par 71 SSS 73
👥 U
💶 €65 – €77 (€90)
🚗 8 miles E of Cork on N25
⊕ Driving range
🏠 O'Connor Jr/McEvoy/Howes

Frankfield (1984)

Frankfield, Douglas
☎ (021) 363124
📖 320
🏌 A MacFarlane
✓ D Whyte, M Ryan
🏳 9 L 4621 m SSS 65
👥 U SOC
💶 €6
🚗 S of Cork
⊕ Driving range

Glengarriff (1935)

Glengarriff
☎ (027) 63150
🖥 (027) 63575
📖 250
🏌 N Deasy (Hon)
🏳 9 L 4094 m SSS 66
👥 U
💶 D–€14 (€18)
🚗 1 mile E of Glengarriff (N71)

Harbour Point (1991)

Clash, Little Island
☎ (021) 353094
🖥 (021) 354408
📖 300
🏌 Mrs N Dwyer (Sec/Mgr)
✓ M O'Donovan (021) 353719
🏳 18 L 6063 yds SSS 72
👥 U SOC
💶 €20–€32
🚗 5 miles E of Cork
⊕ Floodlit driving range
🏠 Paddy Merrigan

Kanturk (1971)

Fairyhill, Kanturk
☎ (029) 50534
📖 410
🏌 T McAuliffe
✓ None
🏳 18 L 6262 yds Par 72 SSS 70
👥 U
💶 €15
🚗 2 miles SW of Kanturk (R579)
🏠 R Barry

Kinsale
Farrangalway (1993)

Farrangalway, Kinsale
☎ (021) 477 4722
🖥 (021) 477 3114
✉ kinsaleg@indigo.ie
📖 740
✓ G Broderick (021) 477 3258
🏳 18 L 6609 yds SSS 72

👥 WD–U WE–NA SOC
💶 €30
🚗 3 miles NW of Kinsale. 18 miles S of Cork
🏠 Jack Kenneally

Kinsale Ringenane (1912)

Ringenane, Belgooly, Kinsale
☎ (021) 477 2197
📖 740
✓ None
🏳 9 L 5332 yds SSS 68
👥 U SOC
💶 €17
🚗 2 miles E of Kinsale (R600). 16 miles S of Cork

Lee Valley G&CC (1993)

Clashanure, Ovens, Cork
☎ (021) 733 1721
🖥 (021) 733 1695
📖 450
🏌 C Nylan
✓ J Savage (021) 733 1758
🏳 18 L 6800 yds SSS 72
👥 U SOC
💶 €41
🚗 8 miles W of Cork (N22)
⊕ Floodlit driving range
🏠 C O'Connor Jr

Macroom (1924)

Lackaduve, Macroom
☎ (026) 41072
🖥 (026) 41391
✉ mcroomgc@iol.com
📖 650
🏌 C O'Sullivan (Mgr)
✓ None
🏳 18 L 5574 m Par 72 SSS 70
👥 U SOC
💶 €25 (€30)
🚗 Macroom Town, through Castle Arch. 25 miles W of Cork
🏠 Jack Kenneally

Mahon (1980)

Clover Hill, Blackrock, Cork
☎ (021) 294280
📖 450
🏌 T O'Connor
✓ T O'Connor
🏳 18 L 4818 m SSS 66
👥 U
💶 €15
🚗 SE of Cork City

Mallow (1948)

Ballyellis, Mallow
☎ (022) 21145
🖥 (022) 42501
📖 1500
🏌 D Curtin (Sec/Mgr)
✓ S Conway
🏳 18 L 6559 yds SSS 72
👥 WD–U before 5pm SOC
💶 €32 (€38)
🚗 1 mile SE of Mallow Bridge on Killavullen road
🏠 J Harris

Mitchelstown (1908)

Gurrane, Mitchelstown
☎ (025) 24072
📖 500
🏌 T Lewis
🏳 18 L 5157 m Par 67
👥 U SOC
💶 €25
🚗 30 miles NE of Cork
🏠 David Jones

Monkstown (1908)

Parkgarriffe, Monkstown
☎ (021) 484 1376
🖥 (021) 484 1722
✉ office@monkstowngolfclub.com
📖 900
🏌 H Madden (Sec/Mgr)
✓ B Murphy (021) 841686
🏳 18 L 5669 m SSS 69
👥 U SOC
💶 €37 (€44)
🚗 7 miles SE of Cork

Muskerry (1907)

Carrigrohane
☎ (021) 438 5297
🖥 (021) 451 6860
📖 803
🏌 H Gallagher
✓ WM Lehane (021) 438 1445
🏳 18 L 5786 m SSS 71
👥 Restricted at certain times–phone first SOC
💶 €35
🚗 7 miles NW of Cork. 2 miles W of Blarney

Old Head Golf Links (1997)

Kinsale
☎ (021) 477 8444
🖥 (021) 477 8022
✉ info@oldheadgolf.ie
🏌 J O'Brien (Gen Mgr)
🏳 18 L 7300 yds SSS 72
👥 U H
💶 €250
🚗 7 miles S of Kinsale
⊕ Driving range
🏠 Carr/Merrigan/Kirby/Hackett
■ www.oldheadgolflinks.com

Raffeen Creek (1989)

Ringaskiddy
☎ (021) 437 8430
📖 530
🏌 J Kiely
🏳 9 L 5098 m Par 70 SSS 67
👥 WD–U WE–U after noon
💶 €18
🚗 1 mile from Ringaskiddy Ferryport
🏠 Eddie Hackett

Skibbereen (1931)

Licknavar, Skibbereen
☎ (028) 21227
🖥 (028) 22994
✉ bookings@skibbgolf.com
📖 580
🏌 S Brett (Mgr)

For list of abbreviations and key to symbols see page 649

✓ None
⊵ 18 L 5474 m Par 71 SSS 69
👥 U SOC–Sat
££ €30
⊕ 1 mile W of Skibbereen. 52 miles SW of Cork
🏠 Eddie Hackett
■ www.skibbgolf.com

Youghal (1898)

Knockaverry, Youghal
☎ (024) 92787/92861
🖥 (024) 92641
✉ youghalgolfclub@eircom.net
📖 827
🗐 Margaret O'Sullivan
✓ L Burns (024) 92590
⊵ 18 L 5646 m SSS 70
👥 U
££ €25 (€32)
⊕ 30 miles E of Cork on N25 from Rosslare
🏠 Cdr Harris
■ www.youghalgolfclub.net

Co Donegal

Ballybofey & Stranorlar (1957)

The Glebe, Stranorlar
☎ (074) 31093
🖥 (074) 31058
📖 525
🗐 A Harkin (074) 31228
⊵ 18 L 5922 yds Par 68 SSS 68
👥 U SOC
££ €18 (€21)
⊕ Stranorlar ¹/₄ mile
🏠 PC Carr

Ballyliffin (1947)

Ballyliffin, Inishowen
☎ (077) 76119
🖥 (077) 76672
📖 828
🗐 C Doherty (Sec/Mgr)
✓ None
⊵ Old 18 L 6611 yds SSS 72
   Glashedy 18 L 6837 yds Par 72
👥 U SOC–WD
££ Old €30 Glashedy €44
⊕ 8 miles N of Buncrana. 15 miles N of Londonderry
🏠 Glashedy-Craddock/Ruddy
■ www.ballyliffingolfclub.com

Buncrana (1951)

Buncrana
☎ (077) 62279/20749
✉ buncranagc@eircom.net
📖 300
🗐 F McGrory (Hon) (077) 20749
✓ J Doherty
⊵ 9 L 4250 m SSS 62
👥 U
££ €8 – €13
⊕ S of Buncrana, nr Gateway Hotel

Bundoran (1894)

Bundoran
☎ (072) 41302
🖥 (072) 42014
📖 620
🗐 J McGagh (Sec/Mgr)
✓ D Robinson
⊵ 18 L 5688 m Par 70 SSS 70
👥 WD–U WE–restricted SOC
££ €30 (€40)
⊕ E boundary of Bundoran. 20 miles S of Donegal
🏠 H Vardon

Cruit Island (1985)

Kincasslagh, Dunglow
☎ (075) 43296
🖥 (075) 48028
📖 350
🗐 T Gallagher
✓ None
⊵ 9 L 5297 yds Par 68 SSS 64
👥 U SOC
££ €12 (€18)
⊕ 5 miles N of Dunglow, off R259
■ www.homepage.eircom.net /~cruitisland

Donegal (1960)

Murvagh, Laghey
☎ (073) 34054
🖥 (073) 34377
📖 650
🗐 J Nixon (073) 22166
   P Nugent (Gen Mgr)
⊵ 18 L 7271 yds SSS 73
👥 H SOC–exc Sun
££ €40 (€55)
⊕ 7 miles S of Donegal, off N15
🏠 Eddie Hackett
■ www.donegalgolfclub.ie

Dunfanaghy (1906)

Kill, Dunfanaghy, Letterkenny
☎ (074) 36335
🖥 (074) 36335
📖 390
🗐 J Moffitt
⊵ 18 L 5350 m Par 68 SSS 66
👥 U SOC
££ €22 (€27)
⊕ 25 miles NW of Letterkenny on N56
⊕ Driving range
🏠 Harry Vardon
■ www.golfdunfanaghy.com

Greencastle (1892)

Greencastle
☎ (077) 81013
🖥 (077) 81015
📖 750
🗐 B McCaul
✓ None
⊵ 18 L 5211 m SSS 67
👥 WD–U WE–restricted SOC
££ €18 (€24)
⊕ 21 miles NE of Londonderry, nr Moville
🏠 Eddie Hackett

Gweedore (1926)

Magheragallon, Derrybeg, Letterkenny
☎ (075) 31140
📖 200
⊕ O Ferry
⊵ 9 L 6201 yds SSS 69
👥 U
££ €10 (€12)
⊕ 3 miles N of Gweedore, off R257

Letterkenny (1913)

Barnhill, Letterkenny
☎ (074) 21150
🖥 (074) 21175
📖 790
🗐 S Gildea (074) 22453
⊵ 18 L 6239 yds SSS 71
👥 U–booking necessary SOC
££ €25 (€35)
⊕ 1 mile E of Letterkenny
🏠 Eddie Hackett

Narin & Portnoo (1931)

Narin, Portnoo
☎ (075) 45107
🖥 (074) 45107
✉ narinportnoo@eircom.net
📖 650
🗐 E Bonner (Hon)
✓ None
⊵ 18 L 5950 yds Par 69 SSS 68
👥 WD/Sat–U H Sun–NA before 2pm SOC
££ €25 (€30) SOC–€20 (€25)
⊕ 6 miles N of Ardara. West Donegal

North West (1891)

Lisfannon, Fahan
☎ (077) 61027
🖥 (077) 63284
📖 520
🗐 D Coyle (Hon)
✓ S McBriarty (077) 61715
⊵ 18 L 6239 yds SSS 70
👥 U
££ €21 (€28)
⊕ 2 miles S of Buncrana. 12 miles N of Londonderry

Otway (1893)

Saltpans, Rathmullan, Letterkenny
☎ (074) 58319
✉ gmcgivern@ntlworld.com
📖 97
🗐 G McGivern (Hon)
⊵ 9 L 4234 yds SSS 60
👥 U
££ €13
⊕ 15 miles NE of Letterkenny, by Lough Swilly

Portsalon (1891)

Portsalon, Fanad
☎ (074) 59459
🖥 (074) 59919
📖 500
🗐 P Doherty
⊵ 18 L 5878 yds Par 68 SSS 66
👥 U–phone in advance
££ €21 (€26)
⊕ 20 miles N of Letterkenny (R246)

Redcastle   (1983)

Redcastle, Moville
- ☎ **(077) 82073**
- ▥ 120
- ✍ D McCartney (Hon)
- ⊩ 9 L 6046 yds Par 72
- ⚇ U
- ££ €13
- ⇆ 15 miles N of Londonderry, by Lough Foyle (R238)

Rosapenna   (1894)

Downings, Rosapenna
- ☎ **(074) 55301**
- ▱ (074) 55128
- ✉ rosapenna@eircom.net
- ▥ 250
- ✍ N McManus
- ⊩ 18 L 6254 yds Par 70 SSS 71
- ⚇ U
- ££ €40 (€45)
- ⇆ 20 miles N of Letterkenny
- ⊕ Golf academy. Driving range
- ⌂ Morris/Vardon/Braid/Ruddy
- ■ www.rosapenna.ie

St Patricks Courses

(1994)

Carrigart
- ☎ **(074) 55114**
- ▱ (074) 55250
- ✍ D Walsh (Mgr)
- ⊩ 18 L 7108 yds Par 72 SSS 73
  18 L 5822 yds Par 71 SSS 71
- ⚇ U
- ££ €42 (€54)
- ⇆ 2 miles from Carrigart on Creeslough road
- ⌂ Hackett/O'Haire

Co Down

Ardglass   (1896)

Castle Place, Ardglass, BT30 7PP
- ☎ **(028) 4484 1219**
- ▱ (028) 4484 1841
- ▥ 901
- ✍ Miss D Polly
- ✓ P Farrell (028) 4484 1022
- ⊩ 18 L 5776 yds Par 70 SSS 69
- ⚇ U SOC
- ££ £20 (£26)
- ⇆ 7 miles SE of Downpatrick on B1

Ardminnan   (1995)

15 Ardminnan Road, Portaferry, BT22 1QJ
- ☎ **(028) 4277 1321**
- ▱ (028) 4277 1321
- ▥ 170
- ✍ E McGrattan
- ✓ T McCartney
- ⊩ 9 L 2766 m Par 70
- ⚇ U
- ££ £10 (£15)

- ⇆ 10 miles E of Downpatrick via ferry. 18 miles SE of Newtownards (A20)
- ⌂ Frank Ainsworth

Banbridge   (1913)

Huntly Road, Banbridge, BT32 3UR
- ☎ **(028) 4066 2342**
- ▱ (028) 4066 9400
- ▥ 850
- ✍ Mrs J Anketell (028) 4066 2211
- ⊩ 18 L 5590 m SSS 69
- ⚇ U SOC
- ££ £10 (£20)
- ⇆ 1 mile W of Banbridge
- ⌂ F Ainsworth
- ■ www.banbridgegolf.co.uk

Bangor   (1903)

Broadway, Bangor, BT20 4RH
- ☎ **(028) 9127 0922**
- ▱ (028) 9145 3394
- ✉ bgcsecretary@aol.com
- ▥ 1100
- ✍ DJ Ryan (Sec/Mgr)
- ✓ M Bannon
- ⊩ 18 L 6424 yds SSS 71
- ⚇ WD–U exc –M 1–2pm Wed–U before 4.45pm Sat–NA SOC
- ££ £25 Sun–£30
- ⇆ 1 mile S of Bangor, off Donaghadee road
- ⌂ James Braid

Blackwood   (1995)

150 Crawfordsburn Road, Bangor, BT19 1GB
- ☎ **(028) 9185 2706**
- ▱ (028) 9185 3785
- ▥ 240
- ✍ P Edgar, Debbie Hanna
- ✓ Debbie Hanna
- ⊩ 18 L 6392 yds SSS 70
- ⚇ U
- ££ On application
- ⇆ W of Bangor
- ⊕ Driving range

Bright Castle   (1970)

14 Coniamstown Road, Bright, Downpatrick, BT30 8LU
- ☎ **(028) 4484 1319**
- ▥ 100
- ✍ J McCawl (Hon)
- ⊩ 18 L 6700 yds Par 73 SSS 72
- ⚇ U SOC
- ££ £12 (£14)
- ⇆ 5 miles S of Downpatrick, off Killough road (B176)

Carnalea   (1927)

Station Road, Bangor, BT19 1EZ
- ☎ **(028) 9146 5004**
- ▱ (028) 9127 3989
- ▥ 800
- ✍ GY Steele (028) 9127 0368
- ✓ T Loughran (028) 9127 0122
- ⊩ 18 L 5647 yds SSS 67
- ⚇ U SOC–WD

- ££ £16.50 (£21)
- ⇆ By Carnalea Station, Bangor

Clandeboye   (1933)

Conlig, Newtownards, BT23 7PN
- ☎ **(028) 9127 1767/9147 3706**
- ▱ (028) 9147 3711
- ✉ contact@cgc-ni.com
- ▥ 1291
- ✍ R Eddis (Admin Mgr) (028) 9127 1767
- ✓ P Gregory (028) 9127 1750
- ⊩ Dufferin 18 L 6559 yds SSS 71
  Ava 18 L 5755 yds SSS 68
- ⚇ WD–U WE–M SOC
- ££ Dufferin–£27.50 (£33) Ava–£22
- ⇆ Conlig, off A21 Bangor-Newtownards road
- ⌂ Von Limburger/Alliss/Thomas
- ■ www.cgc-ni.com

Crossgar   (1993)

231 Derryboye Road, Crossgar, BT30 9DL
- ☎ **(028) 4483 1523**
- ▥ 105
- ✍ D Myles (Sec/Mgr)
- ⊩ 9 L 4170 m Par 64 SSS 63
- ⚇ U
- ££ £10 (£10)
- ⇆ 6 miles N of Downpatrick (A7)

Donaghadee   (1899)

84 Warren Road, Donaghadee, BT21 0PQ
- ☎ **(028) 9188 3624**
- ▱ (028) 9188 8891
- ✉ deegolf@freenet.co.uk
- ▥ 1135
- ✍ JRW Thomas
- ✓ G Drew (028) 9188 2392
- ⊩ 18 L 5614 m Par 71
- ⚇ U exc Sat–NA SOC–exc Sat
- ££ £22 (£25)
- ⇆ 6 miles S of Bangor on coast road. 18 miles E of Belfast

Downpatrick   (1930)

Saul Road, Downpatrick, BT30 6PA
- ☎ **(028) 4461 5947/2152**
- ▱ (028) 4461 7502
- ▥ 960
- ✍ BA Hitchins (028) 4461 5947
- ✓ (028) 4461 5167
- ⊩ 18 L 5702 m SSS 69
- ⚇ U SOC
- ££ £20 (£25)
- ⇆ 25 miles SE of Belfast (A1). Downpatrick 1½ miles
- ⌂ Hawtree
- ■ www.downpatrickgolfclub.com

Helen's Bay   (1896)

Golf Road, Helen's Bay, Bangor, BT19 1TL
- ☎ **(028) 9185 2601 (Clubhouse)**
- ▱ (028) 9185 2815
- ▥ 700
- ✍ PB Clarke (028) 9185 2815
- ⊩ 9 L 5261 m Par 68 SSS 67

♈ WD/Sun–U
Tues/Thurs/Sat–restricted
SOC–WD
££ On application
⛳ 9 miles E of Belfast, off A2

Holywood (1904)

Nuns Walk, Demesne Road, Holywood, BT18 9LE
☎ (028) 9042 2138
🖳 (028) 9042 5040
🕮 1000
✍ GA Fyfe (Gen Mgr)
(028) 9042 3135
⌁ P Gray (028) 9042 5503
🏴 18 L 5885 yds SSS 68
♈ WD–U exc 1.30–2.15pm Sat–after 5pm
££ £16 (£25)
⛳ 5 miles E of Belfast on Bangor road
■ www.holywoodgolfclub.co.uk

Kilkeel (1948)

Mourne Park, Kilkeel, BT34 4LB
☎ (028) 4176 2296/5095
🖳 (028) 4176 5579
🕮 720
✍ SC McBride (Hon)
(028) 4176 5095
⌁ None
🏴 18 L 6579 yds SSS 72
♈ U SOC–exc Sat
££ £18 (£22)
⛳ 3 miles W of Kilkeel on Newry road
⊕ Driving range
🏚 Badington/Hackett

Kirkistown Castle (1902)

142 Main Road, Cloughey, Newtownards, BT22 1JA
☎ (028) 4277 1233
🖳 (028) 4277 1699
🕮 948
✍ R Coulter (028) 4277 1233
⌁ J Peden (028) 4277 1004
🏴 18 L 5616 m Par 69 SSS 70
♈ WD/Sun–U Sat–NA before 2.30pm
££ £18.75 (£25.75)
⛳ 25 miles SE of Belfast
🏚 James Braid
■ www.kcgc.org

Mahee Island (1930)

Comber, Belfast, BT23 6ET
☎ (028) 9754 1234
🕮 500
✍ M Marshall (Hon)
⌁ A McCracken
🏴 9 L 2790 yds SSS 68
♈ U exc Sat–NA before 5pm
SOC–WD exc Mon
££ £10 (£15)
⛳ Strangford Lough, 14 miles SE of Belfast

Mount Ober G&CC (1985)

Ballymaconaghy Road, Knockbracken, Belfast, BT8 4SB
☎ (028) 9079 2108 (Bookings)
🖳 (028) 9070 5862

🕮 500
✍ D McNamara (Sec/Mgr)
⌁ G Loughrey (028) 9040 1811
🏴 18 L 5436 yds SSS 68
♈ WD–U Sat–NA before 3pm
Sun–NA before 10.30am SOC
££ £14 (£16)
⛳ 2 miles SW of Belfast, nr Four Winds
⊕ Floodlit driving range

Mourne (1946)

Club
36 Golf Links Road, Newcastle, BT33 0AN
☎ (028) 4372 3218
🖳 (028) 4372 2575
✉ secretary@mourne.freeserve.co.uk
🕮 385
✍ S Rooney (Hon)
🏴 Play over Royal Co Down
■ www.mournegc.freeserve.co.uk

Ringdufferin (1993)

Ringdufferin Road, Toye, Downpatrick, BT30 9PH
☎ (028) 4482 8812
🕮 260
✍ M Dallas (Hon)
🏴 18 L 4652 m Par 68 SSS 66
♈ U
££ £9 (£10)
⛳ 2 miles N of Killyleagh, off A22

Rockmount (1995)

28 Drumalig Road, Carryduff, Belfast, BT8 8EQ
☎ (028) 9081 2279
🖳 (028) 9081 5851
✉ d.patterson@btconnect.com
🕮 700
✍ D Patterson (Mgr)
🏴 18 L 6373 yds Par 72 SSS 71
♈ U
££ £20 (£24)
⛳ 8 miles S of Belfast (A24)
■ www.rockmountgolfclub.co.uk

Royal Belfast (1881)

Holywood, Craigavad, BT18 0BP
☎ (028) 9042 8165
🖳 (028) 9042 1404
🕮 1200
✍ Mrs SH Morrison
⌁ C Spence (028) 9042 8586
🏴 18 L 6184 yds SSS 70
♈ I Sat–NA before 4.30pm
££ £40 (£50)
⛳ E of Belfast on A2

Royal County Down (1889)

Newcastle, BT33 0AN
☎ (028) 4372 3314
🖳 (028) 4372 6281
✉ golf@royalcountydown.org
🕮 450
✍ JH Laidler
⌁ KJ Whitson (028) 4372 2419
🏴 Ch'ship 18 L 7065 yds SSS 74
Annesley 18 L 4708 yds SSS 63
♈ Contact Sec

££ Ch'ship–£95 (£105) Annesley–£18 (£28)
⛳ 30 miles S of Belfast
🏚 Tom Morris

Scrabo (1907)

233 Scrabo Road, Newtownards, BT23 4SL
☎ (028) 9181 2355
🖳 (028) 9182 2919
🕮 958
✍ Christine Hamill (Gen Mgr)
⌁ P McCrystal (028) 9181 7848
🏴 18 L 5699 m SSS 71
♈ WD–U WE–after 5pm SOC
££ £18 (£23)
⛳ 2 miles W of Newtownards, by Scrabo Tower

The Spa (1907)

Grove Road, Ballynahinch, BT24 8BR
☎ (028) 9756 2365
🖳 (028) 9756 4158
🕮 920
✍ TG Magee
🏴 18 L 6003 m SSS 72
♈ U exc Wed–NA after 3pm Sat–NA
££ £15 (£20)
⛳ 1 mile S of Ballynahinch. 15 miles S of Belfast

Temple (1994)

60 Church Road, Boardmills, Lisburn, BT27 6UP
☎ (028) 9263 9213
🖳 (028) 9263 8637
🕮 300
✍ D Kinnear (Sec/Mgr)
🏴 9 L 5451 yds Par 68 SSS 66
♈ U
££ £10 (£14)
⛳ 5 miles S of Belfast on Ballynahinch road

Warrenpoint (1893)

Lower Dromore Rd, Warrenpoint, BT34 3LN
☎ (028) 4175 2219 (Clubhouse)
🖳 (028) 4175 2918
✉ warrenpointgolfclub@talk21.com
🕮 1370
✍ M Trainor (028) 4175 3695
⌁ N Shaw (028) 4175 2371
🏴 18 L 5628 m SSS 70
♈ U SOC
££ £20 (£27)
⛳ 5 miles S of Newry
🏚 Tom Craddock

Co Dublin

Balbriggan (1945)

Blackhall, Balbriggan
☎ (01) 841 2229
🖳 (01) 841 3927
🕮 600
✍ M O'Halloran (Sec/Mgr) (01) 841 2229
⌁ None

☞ 18 L 5881 m SSS 71
⚏ WD–U WE–M SOC
£€ €32 (€35)
⚐ 1 mile S of Balbriggan on N1. 18 miles N of Dublin
⌂ Paramour/Stillwell/Ruddy
www.balbriggangolfclub.com

Balcarrick (1972)

Corballis, Donabate
☎ (01) 843 6228
⚏ (01) 843 6957
▥ 800
✍ Joan Byrne
⁄ S Rayfus
☞ 18 L 5940 m Par 73 SSS 71
⚏ WD–U Sat–NA before 10am Sun–NA SOC
£€ €24 (€30)
⚐ 2 miles E of Donabate. 18 miles N of Dublin

Ballinascorney (1971)

Ballinascorney, Tallaght, Dublin
☎ (01) 451 6430
▥ 500
☞ 18 L 5464 m Par 71 SSS 67
⚏ WD–U
£€ On application
⚐ 8 miles SW of Dublin

Beaverstown (1985)

Beaverstown, Donabate
☎ (01) 843 6439/6721
⚏ (01) 843 5059
✉ manager@beaverstown.com
▥ 835
✍ D Monaghan (Sec/Mgr) (01) 843 6439
☞ 18 L 5972 m Par 72 SSS 72
⚏ WD–U WE–phone first SOC
£€ €50 (€65)
⚐ 4 miles N of Dublin Airport
⌂ Hackett/McEvoy
■ www.beaverstown.com

Beech Park (1983)

Johnstown, Rathcoole
☎ (01) 458 0522
⚏ (01) 458 8365
▥ 550
✍ E Burke (Hon), P Muldowney (Mgr)
⁄ None
☞ 18 L 5730 m SSS 70
⚏ WD–U exc Tues/Wed–M WE–M BH–NA
£€ €30
⚐ Rathcoole 2 miles on Kilteel road. SW of Dublin
⌂ Eddie Hackett

Coldwinters (1994)

Newtown House, St Margaret's
☎ (01) 864 0324
⚏ (01) 834 1400
▥ 375
✍ Mrs K Yates
⁄ W Noble
☞ 18 L 5973 m SSS 71
9 L 3133 m SSS 31
⚏ U

£€ €13 (€20)
⚐ NW of Dublin. Airport 2 miles
⊕ Driving range. Golf Academy
⌂ Martin Hawtree

Corrstown (1993)

Corrstown, Killsallaghan
☎ (01) 864 0533
⚏ (01) 864 0537
▥ 1050
✍ J Kelly
⁄ P Gittens (01) 864 3322
☞ River 18 L 6077 m Par 72 SSS 71
Orchard 9 L 2792 m Par 35 SSS 69
⚏ Booking necessary
£€ €13
⚐ Dublin Airport 6 miles
⌂ E Connaughton
■ www.corrstown.com

Donabate (1925)

Balcarrick, Donabate
☎ (01) 843 6001
⚏ (01) 843 5012
▥ 913
✍ B Judd (01) 843 6346
⁄ H Jackson
☞ 18 L 6670 yds SSS 72
9 L 3200 yds Par 36
⚏ WE/BH–NA
£€ €30
⚐ 8 miles N of Dublin Airport on N1

Dublin Mountain (1993)

Gortlum, Brittas
☎ (01) 458 2570
⚏ (01) 458 2503
▥ 430
✍ F Carolan
☞ 18 L 5433 m Par 71
⚏ U
£€ €9
⚐ SW of Dublin

Dun Laoghaire (1910)

Eglinton Park, Tivoli Road, Dun Laoghaire
☎ (01) 280 3916
⚏ (01) 280 4868
▥ 880
✍ DA Peacock (Gen Mgr) (01) 280 3916
⁄ V Carey (01) 280 1694
☞ 18 L 5478 m SSS 69
⚏ WD–U exc 12–1.30pm SOC
£€ €42
⚐ 7 miles S of Dublin. Ferry Port 1 mile
⌂ HS Colt
■ www.dunlaoghairegolfclub.ie

Finnstown

Finnstown House Hotel, Lucan
☎ (01) 628 0644
⚏ (01) 628 1088
▥ 300
✍ M Doyle (01) 836 3423
☞ 9 L 5172 yds SSS 64
⚏ H SOC
£€ €14 (€19)

⚐ 7 miles W of Dublin
⌂ B Browne

Forrest Little (1972)

Forrest Little, Cloghran
☎ (01) 840 1763
⚏ (01) 840 1000
▥ 900
✍ T Greany (Sec/Mgr)
⁄ T Judd
☞ 18 L 5865 m SSS 70
⚏ WD–U WE–NA
£€ €36
⚐ Nr Dublin Airport
⌂ F Hawtree

Glencullen

Glencullen, Co Dublin
☎ (01) 295 2895
✍ G Davy
⁄ R Lucy
☞ 9 L 4705 m Par 69
⚏ U
£€ €15
⚐ 12 miles S of Dublin
■ www.glencullengc.ie

Hermitage (1905)

Lucan
☎ (01) 626 5396
✉ hermitagegolf@eircom.net
▥ 1153
✍ P Maguire (01) 626 8491
⁄ S Byrne (01) 626 8072
☞ 18 L 6032 m SSS 71
⚏ U SOC–WD
£€ €70 (€86)
⚐ Lucan 2 miles. 8 miles W of Dublin

Hibernian (1994)

City West Hotel, Saggert
☎ (01) 851 0565
⚏ (01) 831 5779
▥ 270
✍ B Cooling (Mgr)
☞ 18 L 6441 yds Par 70
⚏ U
£€ €32
⚐ 10 miles SW of Dublin, off N7
■ www.hiberniangolf.com

Hollywood Lakes (1992)

Ballyboughal
☎ (01) 843 3406/7
⚏ (01) 843 3002
✉ hollywoodlakes.gc@eircom.net
▥ 750
✍ AC Brogan (Sec/Mgr)
⁄ None
☞ 18 L 6834 yds Par 72 SSS 72
⚏ WD–U WE/BH–U after noon
£€ €30 (€35)
⚐ 10 miles N of Dublin Airport
⌂ Mel Flanagan

The Island (1890)

Corballis, Donabate
☎ (01) 843 6104
⚏ (01) 843 6860
▥ 800

P McDunphy (01) 843 6205
K Kelliher (01) 843 5005
18 L 6195 m SSS 73
WD–U WE–NA
€€ €100
14 miles N of Dublin
Hawtree
www.theislandgolfclub.com

Killiney (1903)
Ballinclea Road, Killiney
☎ (01) 285 2823
(01) 285 2823
520
MF Walsh
P O'Boyle (01) 285 6294
9 L 6220 yds SSS 70
U
€€ €38
8 miles S of Dublin
E Connaughton

Kilternan (1987)
Kilternan
☎ (01) 295 5559
(01) 295 5670
906
J Kinsella
Shop (01) 295 2986
18 L 5413 yds SSS 67
U SOC
€€ €21 (€26)
12 miles S of Dublin
Eddie Connaughton

Lucan (1897)
Celbridge Road, Lucan
☎ (01) 628 2106
(01) 628 2929
740
T O'Donnell (Sec/Mgr)
(01) 628 2106
18 L 5958 m Par 71 SSS 70
WD–U WE/BH–M SOC–WD exc Thurs
€€ €40
14 miles W of Dublin, nr Lucan on N4
Eddie Hackett

Luttrellstown Castle G&CC (1993)
Castleknock, Dublin 15
☎ (01) 808 9988
(01) 808 9989
golf@luttrellstown.ie
400
E Doyle (01) 808 9980
18 L 6384 m Par 72 SSS 73
U–soft spikes only SOC
€€ €85 (€95)
7 miles W of Dublin
Driving range
Bielenberg/Connaughton
www.luttrellstown.ie

Malahide (1892)
Beechwood, The Grange, Malahide
☎ (01) 846 1611
(01) 846 1270

malgc@clubi.ie
850
J McCormack (Sec/Mgr)
J Murray
27 L 6257-6633 yds SSS 70-72
WD–U WE–by arrangement SOC
€€ €50 (€85)
1½ miles S of Malahide. 10 miles N of Dublin, nr Airport
Eddie Hackett
www.malahidegolfclub.ie

Milltown (1907)
Lower Churchtown Road, Milltown, Dublin 14
☎ (01) 497 6090
(01) 497 6008
reception@milltowngolfclub.ie
1432
E Lawless (Gen Mgr)
J Harnett (01) 497 7072
18 L 5638 m Par 71 SSS 69
WD–U exc Tues & Wed pm Fri/WE–M BH–NA SOC–Mon & Thurs before 3.45pm
€€ €80
4 miles S of Dublin centre
Freddie Davis

Portmarnock (1894)
Portmarnock
☎ (01) 846 2794 (Clubhouse)
(01) 846 2601
971
JJ Quigley (01) 846 2968
J Purcell (01) 846 2634
27 holes:
6361-6497 m SSS 74-75
I WE–XL
€€ €90 (€115)
8 miles NE of Dublin

Portmarnock Hotel (1995)
Strand Road, Portmarnock
☎ (01) 846 1800
(01) 846 1077
golf@portmarnock.com
Moira Cassidy (Golf Dir)
(01) 846 1800
18 L 6260 m Par 71 SSS 73
U H
€€ €110 Residents–€80
8 miles NE of Dublin. Airport 15 mins
Bernhard Langer
www.portmarnock.com

Rush (1943)
Rush
☎ (01) 843 8177
(01) 843 8177
info@rushgolfclub.com
450
Noeline Quirile (Sec/Mgr)
9 L 5639 m Par 69 SSS 68
WD–U WE–M
€€ €29
16 miles N of Dublin, off N1
www.rushgolfclub.com

Silloge Park
Ballymun Road, Swords, Co Dublin, IRELAND
☎ (01) 862 0464
D D'Arcy
P O'Connor
18 L 5905 m Par 70
U
€€ €13
Swords, N of Dublin

Skerries (1905)
Hacketstown, Skerries
☎ (01) 849 1204 (Clubhouse)
(01) 849 1591
skerriesgolfclub@eircom.net
1060
A Burns (01) 849 1567
J Kinsella (01) 849 0925
18 L 6107 m Par 73 SSS 72
U SOC
€€ €40 (€45)
20 miles N of Dublin
www.skerriesgolfclub.ie

Slade Valley (1970)
Lynch Park, Brittas
☎ (01) 458 2739
(01) 458 2784
800
(01) 458 2183
J Dignam
18 L 5337 m SSS 68
WD–U am WE–M
€€ €20
8 miles W of Dublin, off N4
Sullivan/O'Brien

St Margaret's G&CC (1993)
St Margaret's, Dublin
☎ (01) 864 0400
(01) 864 0289
260
B Begley (Chief Exec)
18 L 6900 yds SSS 73
U SOC
€€ €60 (€80)
3 miles NW of Dublin Airport, between N1/N2
Driving range
Craddock/Ruddy
www.st-margarets.net

Swords (1996)
Balheary Avenue, Swords
☎ (01) 840 9819
(01) 840 9819
400
O McGuinness (Mgr)
18 L 5677 m Par 71 SSS 70
U
€€ €13
10 miles N of Dublin, nr Airport
T Halpin

Turvey (1994)
Turvey Avenue, Donabate
☎ (01) 843 5169
335

🔊 R Martin (Mgr)
🏳 18 hole course
🏌 U
££ €24 (€29)
�'t Donabate
🏠 Paddy McGuirk

Westmanstown (1988)
Clonsilla, Dublin 15
☎ **(01) 820 5817**
🖷 (01) 820 5858
📖 1000
🔊 JA Joyce (Hon)
🏳 18 L 5819 m SSS 70
🏌 U SOC
££ €30 (€36)
🚗 5 miles W of Dublin, nr Lucan
🏠 Eddie Hackett

Woodbrook (1926)
Dublin Road, Bray
☎ **(01) 282 4799**
🖳 (01) 282 1950
🖂 woodbrook@internet-ireland.ie
📖 1100
🔊 PF Byrne (Gen Mgr) (01) 282 4799
🏌 W Kinsella (01) 282 0205
🏳 18 L 6221 m SSS 72
🏌 WD–U WE–phone Sec SOC
££ €80 (€90)
🚗 11 miles SE of Dublin on N11
🏠 P McEvoy
⬛ www.woodbrook.ie

Dublin City

Carrickmines (1900)
Golf Lane, Carrickmines, Dublin 18
☎ **(01) 295 5972**
📖 600
🔊 TJB Webb (Hon)
🏳 9 L 6303 yds Par 71 SSS 69
🏌 U exc Wed/Sat–NA
££ €28 Sun–€31
🚗 6 miles S of Dublin

Castle (1913)
Woodside Drive, Rathfarnham,
Dublin 14
☎ **(01) 490 4207**
🖳 (01) 492 0264
📖 1400
🔊 LF Blackburne (Sec/Mgr)
🏌 D Kinsella (01) 492 0272
🏳 18 L 6270 yds SSS 70
🏌 Mon/Thurs/Fri–U Wed–U before
    12.30pm WE/BH–M SOC
££ €56
🚗 5 miles S of Dublin

Clontarf (1912)
Donnycarney House, Malahide Road,
Dublin 3
☎ **(01) 833 1892**
🖳 (01) 833 1933
🖂 info.cgc@indigo.ie
📖 1137
🔊 A Cahill (Mgr)
🏌 M Callan (01) 833 1877

🏳 18 L 5317 m SSS 68
🏌 U SOC
££ €38 (€50)
🚗 2 miles NE of Dublin city centre
🏠 HS Colt
⬛ www.clontarfgolfclub.ie

Deer Park (1974)
Deer Park Hotel, Howth
☎ **(01) 832 6039**
📖 340
🔊 BM Dunne (Hon)
🏌 None
🏳 18 L 6781 yds Par 72 SSS 71
    18 L 6475 yds Par 72 SSS 70
    12 hole Par 3 course
🏌 U SOC
££ €13
🚗 8 miles NE of Dublin
🏠 F Hawtree

Edmondstown (1944)
Rathfarnham, Dublin 16
☎ **(01) 493 2461**
🖳 (01) 493 3152
🖂 info@edmondstowngolfclub.ie
📖 600
🔊 SS Davies (01) 493 1082
🏌 A Crofton (01) 494 1049
🏳 18 L 6011 m Par 71 SSS 73
🏌 WD/BH–U SOC
££ €55 (€65)
🚗 5 miles S of Dublin. M50 Junction
    12
🏠 McEvoy/Cooke
⬛ www.edmondstowngolfclub.ie

Elm Green (1996)
Castleknock, Dublin 15
☎ **(01) 820 0797**
🖳 (01) 822 6668
📖 500
🔊 G Carr (Sec/Mgr)
🏌 A O'Connor
🏳 18 L 5300 m Par 71 SSS 66
🏌 U
££ €14 (€21)
🚗 NW Dublin
⊕ Floodlit driving range
🏠 Eddie Hackett

Elm Park (1927)
Nutley House, Donnybrook, Dublin 4
☎ **(01) 269 3438/269 3014**
🖳 (01) 269 4505
🖂 office@elmparkgolfclub.ie
📖 1750
🔊 A McCormack (01) 269 3438
🏌 S Green (01) 269 2650
🏳 18 L 5374 m SSS 69
🏌 U–phone Pro
££ €65 (€75)
🚗 3 miles S of Dublin

Foxrock (1893)
Torquay Road, Foxrock, Dublin 18
☎ **(01) 289 5668**
🖳 (01) 289 4943
📖 660
🔊 WM Daly (01) 289 3992

🏌 D Walker (01) 289 3414
🏳 9 L 5667 m Par 70 SSS 68
🏌 WD/BH/Sun–M Tues & Sat–NA
££ €36
🚗 5 miles S of Dublin

Grange (1911)
Whitechurch Road, Rathfarnham,
Dublin 14
☎ **(01) 493 2889**
🖳 (01) 493 9490
📖 1050 235(L) 210(J)
🔊 JA O'Donoghue (01) 493 2889
🏌 B Hamill (01) 493 2299
🏳 18 L 5517 m SSS 69
🏌 WD–U exc Tues/Wed pm–NA
    WE–M
££ €51
🚗 Rathfarnham, 5 miles from centre
    of Dublin

Hazel Grove (1988)
Mount Seskin Road, Jobstown, Dublin 24
☎ **(01) 452 0911**
📖 400 175(L)
🔊 J Matthews
🏌 None
🏳 9 L 5300 m SSS 67
🏌 Mon/Wed/Fri–U Sun–NA
    Tues/Thurs/Sat–restricted
££ €15
🚗 3 miles from Tallaght, off
    Blessington road
🏠 Eddie Hackett

Howth (1916)
Carrickbrack Road, Sutton, Dublin 13
☎ **(01) 832 3055**
🖳 (01) 832 1793
🖂 secretary@howthgolfclub.ie
📖 1200
🔊 Ms A MacNeice (01) 832 3055
🏌 JF McGuirk (01) 839 3895
🏳 18 L 5672 m SSS 69
🏌 WD–U exc Wed WE–M
££ €50
🚗 9 miles NE of Dublin, nr Sutton
    Cross
🏠 James Braid
⬛ www.howthgolfclub.ie

Kilmashogue (1994)
St Columba's College, Whitechurch,
Dublin 16
☎ **(087) 274 9844**
📖 260 200(L)
🔊 H Farrell
🏳 9 L 5320 m Par 70
🏌 M
🚗 Dublin

Newlands (1926)
Clondalkin, Dublin 22
☎ **(01) 459 2903**
🖳 (01) 459 3498
📖 1086
🔊 AT O'Neill (01) 459 3157
🏌 K O'Donnell (01) 459 3538
🏳 18 L 6184 yds SSS 70
🏌 WD–U am WE/BH–NA SOC
££ €42

🛵 6 miles SW of Dublin at Newlands
   Cross (N7)
🏠 James Braid

Rathfarnham (1899)

Newtown, Dublin 16
☎ **(01) 493 1201/493 1561**
🖥 (01) 493 1561
📖 561
🖊 DO Tipping (01) 493 1201
✓ B O'Hara
🏴 9 L 5787 m SSS 70
👥 U exc Tues & Sat–NA
££ €27
🛵 6 miles S of Dublin
🏠 John Jacobs

Royal Dublin (1885)

North Bull Island Nature Reserve,
Dollymount, Dublin 3
☎ **(01) 833 6346/1262**
🖥 (01) 833 6504
🖂 jlambe@theroyaldublingolfclub
   .com
📖 1050
🖊 JA Lambe (01) 833 1262
✓ L Owens (01) 833 6477 (Senior Pro
   C O'Connor Sr)
🏴 18 L 6925 yds SSS 73
👥 U H exc Wed Sat–NA before 4pm
   Sun–NA exc 10.30–12 noon
   SOC–WD
££ €100 (€115)
🛵 3 miles NE of Dublin, on coast road
   to Howth
⊕ Practice range
🏠 HS Colt
■ www.theroyaldublingolfclub.com

St Anne's (1921)

North Bull Island, Dollymount, Dublin 5
☎ **(01) 833 6471**
🖥 (01) 833 4618
📖 636
🖊 Shirley Sleator
✓ P Skerritt
🏴 18 L 5669 m Par 70 SSS 70
👥 WE/BH–NA SOC
££ €36 (€48)
🛵 Dublin 5 miles. M50, 5 miles
🏠 Eddie Hackett
■ www.stanneslinksgolf.com

Stackstown (1975)

Kellystown Road, Rathfarnham,
Dublin 16
☎ **(01) 494 2338**
🖥 (01) 493 3934
🖂 stackstowngolfclub@eircom.net
📖 1300
🖊 P Kennedy (Sec/Mgr)
   (01) 494 1993
✓ M Kavanagh (01) 494 4561
🏴 18 L 6494 m SSS 70
👥 WD–U before 12 noon WE–U after
   4.30pm
££ €30 (€38)
🛵 7 miles SE of Dublin. M50 junction
   13, 2 miles

Sutton (1890)

Cush Point, Sutton, Dublin 13
☎ **(01) 832 3013**
🖥 (01) 832 1603
🖂 info@suttongolfclub.org
📖 625
🖊 S Carroll (Hon)
✓ N Lynch (01) 832 1703
🏴 9 L 5624 m Par 70 SSS 67
👥 Tues–NA Sat–NA before 5.30pm
££ €25 (€35)
🛵 7 miles E of Dublin
■ www.suttongolfclub.org

Co Fermanagh

Castle Hume

Belleek Road, Enniskillen, BT93 7ED
☎ **(028) 6632 7077**
🖥 (028) 6632 7076
📖 270
🖊 Wilma Connor (Admin)
✓ S Donnelly (028) 6632 7077
🏴 18 L 5932 m Par 72 SSS 71
👥 U
££ £20/€35 (£25/€40)
🛵 Enniskillen (A46)
🏠 Tony Carroll

Enniskillen (1896)

Castlecoole, Enniskillen, BT74 6HZ
☎ **(028) 6632 5250**
🖥 (028) 6632 5250
🖂 enquiries@enniskillengolfclub.com
📖 480
🖊 R Ferguson
✓ None
🏴 18 L 5574 m Par 71 SSS 69
👥 U SOC
££ D–£15 (£18)
🛵 1 mile SE of Enniskillen, on
   Castlecoole Estate
🏠 TJ McAuley
■ www.enniskillengolfclub.com

Co Galway

Ardacong

Milltown Road, Tuam, Co Galway
☎ **(093) 25525**
🖊 Catherine Hahessy
🏴 18 L 6002 yds Par 70
££ €10
🛵 25 miles N of Galway

Athenry (1902)

Palmerstown, Oranmore
☎ **(091) 794466**
🖥 (091) 794971
🖂 athenrygc@eircom.net
📖 800
🖊 P Flattery (Sec/Mgr)
   (086) 825 4454
✓ R Ryan (091) 790599
🏴 18 L 6300 yds Par 70 SSS 70
👥 WD/Sat–U Sun–NA SOC

££ €26 (€32)
🛵 10 miles E of Galway on Athenry
   road (R348), off N6
🏠 Eddie Hackett

Ballinasloe (1894)

Rosgloss, Ballinasloe
☎ **(0905) 42126**
🖥 (0905) 42538
📖 925
🖊 M Kelly
✓ None
🏴 18 L 5865 m Par 72 SSS 70
👥 U SOC
££ €18 (€21)
🛵 Ballinasloe 2 miles
🏠 Hackett/Connaughton

Bearna (1996)

Corboley, Bearna
☎ **(091) 592677**
🖥 (091) 592674
🖂 info@bearnagolfclub.com
📖 500
🏴 18 L 5746 m Par 72 SSS 72
👥 U
££ €30 (€36)
🏠 RJ Browne
■ www.bearnagolfclub.com

Connemara (1973)

Ballyconneely, Clifden
☎ **(095) 23502/23602**
🖥 (095) 23662
🖂 links@iol.ie
📖 900
🖊 R Flaherty (Sec/Mgr)
✓ H O'Neill (095) 23502
🏴 18 L 6560 m SSS 72
👥 U H SOC
££ €45 – €50
🛵 8 miles SW of Clifden
🏠 Eddie Hackett

Connemara Isles

Annaghvane, Lettermore, Connemara
☎ **(091) 572498**
🖥 (091) 572214
📖 114
🖊 P O'Conghaile (Sec/Mgr)
🏴 9 L 5168 yds Par 70 SSS 67
👥 U SOC
££ €12–(€14)
🛵 3 miles W of Costello
🏠 Craddock/Ruddy

Curra West (1996)

Curra, Kylebrack, Loughrea
☎ **(091) 45121**
📖 60
🏴 18 L 4546 m Par 67
👥 U
££ €13
🛵 8 miles SE of Loughrea

Galway (1895)

Blackrock, Salthill, Galway
☎ **(091) 522033**
🖥 (091) 529783
📖 1020

🖉 P Fahy
✒ D Wallace (091) 523038
▷ 18 L 5828 m SSS 70
👥 Restricted Tues & Sun
££ €30 (€36)
🚗 3 miles W of Galway City

Galway Bay G&CC (1993)
Renville, Oranmore
☎ (091) 790500
🖳 (091) 792510
📖 425
🖉 Ann Hanley (Golf Dir)
✒ E O'Connor (091) 790503
▷ 18 L 6350 m SSS 73
👥 U H SOC
££ €42–€48
🚗 10 miles E of Galway City (N18)
⊕ Driving range. Golf Academy
🏠 C O'Connor Jr
■ www.gbaygolf.com

Glenlo Abbey
Glenlo Abbey Hotel, Bushy Park, Galway
☎ (091) 519698
🖳 (091) 519699
🖉 P Murphy (Sec/Mgr)
✒ P Murphy
▷ 9 L 5943 m Par 71
👥 U
££ €15
🚗 Galway Town
■ www.glenlo.com

Gort (1924)
Castlequarter, Gort
☎ (091) 632244
🖳 (091) 632387
🖂 info@gortgolf.com
📖 840
🖉 J Hannigan (Hon) (091) 631486
✒ None
▷ 18 L 5974 m Par 71
👥 U exc Sun am SOC
££ €22 (€26)
🚗 20 miles S of Galway
🏠 C O'Connor Jr
■ www.gortgolf.com

Loughrea (1924)
Graigue, Loughrea
☎ (091) 841049
🖳 (091) 847472
📖 400
🖉 M Hawkins (Mgr)
▷ 18 L 5261 m Par 69
👥 U SOC
££ €15
🚗 1 mile N of Loughrea, off Dublin-Galway road. 20 miles E of Galway
🏠 Eddie Hackett

Mountbellew (1929)
Shankill, Mountbellew, Ballinasloe
☎ (0905) 79259
🖳 (0905) 79274
📖 380
🖉 M Meehan (Mgr)
▷ 9 L 5214 m Par 69

👥 U SOC
££ €13
🚗 50km NE of Galway on N63

Oughterard (1973)
Gortreevagh, Oughterard
☎ (091) 552131
🖳 (091) 552733
📖 1000
🖉 J Waters
✒ M Ryan (Ext 201)
▷ 18 L 6752 yds SSS 69
👥 U SOC
££ €24
🚗 15 miles NW of Galway on N59
🏠 Harris/Merrigan

Portumna (1913)
Ennis Road, Portumna
☎ (0509) 41059
📖 600
🖉 D Frawley (Hon)
✒ R Clarke
▷ 18 L 5474 m Par 72 SSS 71
👥 U H SOC
££ €25
🚗 40 miles SE of Galway on Lough Derg
🏠 E Connaughton

Tuam (1904)
Barnacurragh, Tuam
☎ (093) 28993
🖳 (093) 26003
📖 700
🖉 V Gaffney (Sec/Mgr)
✒ L Smyth (093) 24091
▷ 18 L 5944 m Par 72 SSS 71
👥 Sun–NA SOC–WD
££ €23
🚗 20 miles N of Galway
🏠 Eddie Hackett

Co Kerry

Ardfert (1993)
Sackville, Ardfert, Tralee
☎ (066) 713 4744
🖳 (066) 713 4744
📖 171
🖉 T Lawlor
✒ N Cassidy
▷ 9 L 4754 m Par 66
👥 U
££ €22
🚗 60 miles NW of Tralee (R551)
⊕ Driving range
🏠 James Healy

Ballybeggan Park
Ballybeggan, Tralee, Co Kerry
☎ (066) 712 6188
🖉 P Colleran
▷ 9 L 6278 m Par 70
👥 U
££ €19
🚗 Tralee

Ballybunion (1893)
Sandhill Road, Ballybunion
☎ (068) 27146
🖳 (068) 27387
📖 648
🖉 J McKenna (Sec/Mgr)
✒ B O'Callaghan
▷ Old 18 L 6542 yds SSS 72
  Cashen 18 L 6477 yds SSS 70
👥 U SOC
££ Old–€110. New–€75
  Old+New D–€135
🚗 2 miles S of Ballybunion. 50 miles W of Limerick, via Tarbert
⊕ Driving range

Ballyheigue Castle (1995)
Ballyheigue, Tralee
☎ (066) 713 3555
🖳 (066) 713 3934
📖 350
🖉 J Casey (Sec/Mgr) (01) 713 3546
▷ 9 L 6292 m Par 72 SSS 74
👥 U
££ €15 (€15)
🚗 11 miles NW of Tralee (R551)
🏠 Roger Jones

Beaufort (1994)
Churchtown, Beaufort, Killarney
☎ (064) 44440
🖳 (064) 44752
🖂 beaufortgc@eircom.net
📖 300
🖉 C Kelly
✒ H Duggan
▷ 18 L 6605 yds Par 71 SSS 72
👥 WD–H SOC
££ €45 (€55)
🚗 7 miles W of Killarney, off N72
🏠 Dr Arthur Spring
■ www.beaufortgolfclub.com

Castlegregory
Stradbally, Castlegregory
☎ (066) 39444
📖 296
🖉 G O'Connor (Sec/Mgr)
▷ 9 L 5340 m SSS 68
👥 U SOC
££ €21
🚗 18 miles W of Tralee
🏠 Arthur Spring

Ceann Sibeal (1924)
Ballyferriter
☎ (066) 915 6255/6408
🖳 (066) 915 6409
📖 460
🖉 S Fahy (Mgr)
▷ 18 L 6690 yds SSS 71
👥 U SOC
££ €30 – €50
🚗 Dingle Peninsula, W of Tralee
🏠 Hackett/O'Connor Jr

Dooks (1889)
Glenbeigh
☎ (066) 976 8205
🖳 (066) 976 8476

office@dooks.com
900
D Mangan
18 L 5346 m Par 70 SSS 68
WD–U H before 5pm
WE/BH–phone first SOC
€40
3 miles N of Glenbeigh, on Ring of Kerry (N70)

Dunloe
Dunloe, Beaufort, Co Kerry
(064) 44578
K Crehan
K Crehan
9 L 4706 m Par 68
U
€20
8 miles W of killarney

Kenmare (1903)
Kenmare
(064) 41291
(064) 42061
info@kenmaregolfclub.com
600
S Duffield
None
18 L 5441 m SSS 69
U SOC
€40
20 miles S of Killarney on Cork road
Eddie Hackett

Kerries (1995)
Tralee
(066) 712 2112
280
H Barrett
9 L 2718 m Par 70
U
€19
Tralee

Killarney (1893)
Mahoney's Point, Killarney
(064) 31034
(064) 33065
reservations@killarney-golf.com
1500
T Prendergast
T Coveney (064) 31615
Mahoney's Point 18 L 6164 m SSS 72
Killeen 18 L 6475 m SSS 73
Lackabane 18 L 6410 m SSS 73
H SOC
On application
3 miles W of Killarney (N72)
Mahoney's Point-Longhurst/ Campbell; Killeen-Hackett/ O'Sullivan;, Lackabane-Steel
www.killarney-golf.com

Killorglin (1992)
Stealroe, Killorglin
(066) 976 1979
230

B Dodd
None
18 L 6464 yds SSS 72
U SOC
€23
1 mile from Killorglin on Tralee road (N70). 12 miles W of Killarney
Eddie Hackett

Listowel (1993)
Pay and play
Feale View, Listowel
(068) 21592
(068) 23387
Caroline Barrett
9 L 5728 yds Par 70 SSS 68
U SOC
9 holes–€12 18 holes–€18
Nr Listowel on N69
Eddie Hackett

Parknasilla (1974)
Parknasilla, Sneem
(064) 45122
(064) 45323
180
M Walsh (Mgr) (064) 45233
12 L 5284 m Par 69 SSS 67
U SOC
€25
Great Southern Hotel, 2 miles E of Sneem on Ring of Kerry
Arthur Spring

Ring of Kerry G&CC (1999)
Templenoe, Kenmare
(064) 42000
(064) 42533
reservations@ringofkerrygolf.com
212
E Edwards (Gen Mgr)
D O'Sullivan
18 L 6923 yds Par 72 SSS 73
U H
€70
4 miles W of Kenmare on N70
Eddie Hackett
www.ringofkerrygolf.com

Ross (1995)
Ross Road, Killarney
(064) 31125
(064) 31860
280
A O'Meara
A O'Meara
9 L 5674 m Par 72 SSS 72
U
18 holes–€21 9 holes–€14
In Killarney
Rodger Jones

Tralee (1896)
West Barrow, Ardfert
(066) 713 6379
(066) 713 6008
info@traleegolfclub.com
1241
A Byrne (Gen Mgr)
D Power

18 L 6252 m SSS 71
WD–U H before 4.30pm exc Wed–restricted Sat/BH–NA exc 11–1pm–H Sun–NA SOC–WD
€110
8 miles NW of Tralee, off Spa/Fenit road in Barrow
Arnold Palmer
www.traleegolfclub.com

Waterville (1889)
Waterville Golf Links, Ring of Kerry, Waterville
(066) 947 4102
(066) 947 4482
320
N Cronin
L Higgins
18 L 7225 yds SSS 74
U H SOC
€50–€120
1/4 mile N of Waterville on Ring of Kerry
Driving range
Hackett/Mulcahy

Co Kildare

Athy (1906)
Geraldine, Athy
(0507) 31729
(0507) 34710
info@athygolfclub.com
525
P Fleming (Hon)
None
18 L 6308 yds Par 71 SSS 69
WD–U Sat–M SOC
€20 (€30)
1 mile N of Athy on Kildare road
www.athygolfclub.com

Bodenstown (1983)
Bodenstown, Sallins
(045) 897096
650
J Hughes
Old 18 L 6132 m SSS 71; Ladyhill 18 L 5278 m SSS 68
U exc WE–NA (Old course)
€15
4 miles N of Naas on Clane road. 18 miles W of Dublin, off N7

Castlewarden G&CC (1989)
Straffan
(01) 458 9254
(01) 458 8972
565 225(L)
P Sheehan (Hon)
G Egan (01) 458 8219
18 L 6624 yds Par 72 SSS 71
WD–U WE–M SOC
€20–€27 (€27)
13 miles W of Dublin, off N7
Halpin/Browne
www.castlewardengolfclub.com

Celbridge Elm Hall

Elmhall, Celbridge, Co Kildare
- ☎ **(01) 628 8208**
- ♙ S Lawless
- ⌖ 9 L 5415 m Par 70
- ⚇ U
- ££ €19
- ⛳ 15 miles W of Dublin

Cill Dara (1920)

Little Curragh, Kildare Town
- ☎ **(045) 521433**
- ▭ 400
- ♙ F Curran (Hon)
- ⌁ M O'Boyle
- ⌖ 9 L 5842 m SSS 70
- ⚇ WD–U before 2pm exc Wed–NA Sat–NA after noon Sun/BH–NA SOC
- ££ €13
- ⛳ 1 mile W of Kildare town

Craddockstown (1991)

Blessington Road, Naas
- ☎ **(045) 897610**
- ▭ (045) 896968
- ▭ 580
- ♙ L Watson
- ⌖ 18 L 6134 m Par 71 SSS 70
- ⚇ U
- ££ €23
- ⛳ Naas
- ⛳ Arthur Spring

The Curragh (1883)

Curragh
- ☎ **(045) 441238/441714**
- ▭ (045) 442476
- ✉ curraghgolf@eircom.net
- ▭ 500 176(L)
- ♙ Ann Culleton (045) 441714
- ⌁ G Burke (045) 441896
- ⌖ 18 L 6035 m SSS 71
- ⚇ WD–U exc Tues–phone Sec
- ££ €30 (€35)
- ⛳ 3 miles S of Newbridge via M7 from Dublin
- ▪ www.curraghgolf-club.com

Highfield (1992)

Highfield House, Carbury
- ☎ **(0405) 31021**
- ▭ (0405) 31021
- ▭ 550
- ♙ P Duggan (Sec/Mgr)
- ⌁ P O'Hagan
- ⌖ 18 L 5707 m SSS 69
- ⚇ WD–U WE–U after 12 noon
- ££ €17 (€21)
- ⛳ 32 miles W of Dublin on N4
- ⛳ Alan Duggan
- ▪ www.highfield-golf.ie

The K Club (1991)

Straffan
- ☎ **(01) 601 7300**
- ▭ (01) 601 7399
- ✉ golf@kclub.ie
- ▭ 527

- ♙ P Crowe (Golf Dir)
- ⌁ E Jones, J McHenry
- ⌖ 18 L 7227 yds SSS 72
- ⚇ U H SOC–WD
- ££ €275
- ⛳ 18 miles SW of Dublin (N7)
- ⊕ Driving range
- ⛳ Arnold Palmer

Kilkea Castle (1995)

Castledermot
- ☎ **(0503) 45555**
- ▭ (0503) 45505
- ⌖ 18 L 6200 m Par 71 SSS 71
- ⚇ U
- ££ €36 (€42)
- ⛳ 7 miles N of Castledermot (R418)
- ⛳ David Cassidy

Killeen (1986)

Killeenbeg, Kill
- ☎ **(045) 866003**
- ▭ (045) 875881
- ▭ 170
- ♙ M Kelly
- ⌁ None
- ⌖ 18 L 5815 m Par 71 SSS 71
- ⚇ WD–U WE–NA before 10am
- ££ €25
- ⛳ 2 miles off N7 on Sallins road
- ⛳ Ruddy/Craddock

Knockanally (1985)

Donadea, North Kildare
- ☎ **(045) 869322**
- ▭ (045) 869322
- ✉ golf@knockanally.com
- ▭ 500
- ♙ N Lyons
- ⌁ M Darcy
- ⌖ 18 L 6424 yds SSS 71
- ⚇ U
- ££ €28 (€40)
- ⛳ 20 miles W of Dublin on Galway road (M4)
- ⛳ N Lyons

Leixlip (1994)

Leixlip
- ☎ **(01) 624 4978**
- ▭ (01) 624 6185
- ▭ 200
- ♙ J McKone
- ⌖ 9 L 6030 yds Par 72 SSS 70
- ⚇ U
- ££ €15 (€18)
- ⛳ 10 miles W of Dublin on N4
- ⛳ Eddie Hackett

Naas (1896)

Kerdiffstown, Naas
- ☎ **(045) 874644**
- ▭ (045) 896109
- ▭ 1000
- ♙ M Conway
- ⌖ 18 L 6232 m SSS 69
- ⚇ U SOC
- ££ €21 (€29)
- ⛳ 2 miles N of Naas
- ⛳ Arthur Spring

Newbridge (1997)

Tankardsgarden, Newbridge
- ☎ **(045) 486110**
- ▭ (045) 431289
- ▭ 220
- ♙ D Neylon (Hon)
- ⌖ 18 L 5960 m Par 72 SSS 72
- ⚇ U
- ££ €16 (€19)
- ⛳ 30 mins from Dublin on M7
- ⛳ Pat Suttle

Woodlands (1985)

Coolereagh, Coill Dubh
- ☎ **(045) 860777**
- ▭ (045) 860988
- ▭ 615
- ♙ J Russell
- ⌖ 18 L 6020 m Par 72 SSS 71
- ⚇ U
- ££ €14 (€18)
- ⛳ Naas
- ⛳ Tommy Halpin

Co Kilkenny

Callan (1929)

Geraldine, Callan
- ☎ **(056) 25136/25949**
- ▭ (056) 55155
- ▭ 750
- ♙ M Duggan (Hon)
- ⌁ J O'Dwyer (086) 817 2464
- ⌖ 18 L 6422 yds Par 72 SSS 70
- ⚇ U SOC
- ££ €25
- ⛳ 1 mile SE of Callan. 10 miles SW of Kilkenny
- ⛳ Bryan Moor

Castlecomer (1935)

Dromgoole, Castlecomer
- ☎ **(056) 41139**
- ▭ (056) 41139
- ✉ castlecomergolf@eircom.net
- ▭ 700
- ♙ M Dooley (Hon)
- ⌖ 9 L 5923 m Par 71 SSS 71
- ⚇ U SOC–WD
- ££ €20
- ⛳ 11 miles N of Kilkenny on N7
- ⛳ Pat Ruddy
- ▪ www.castlecomergolfclub.com

Kilkenny (1896)

Glendine, Kilkenny
- ☎ **(056) 65400**
- ▭ (056) 23593
- ▭ 950
- ♙ S O'Neill (056) 65400
- ⌁ J Bolger (056) 61730
- ⌖ 18 L 6500 yds SSS 70
- ⚇ U
- ££ €30 (36)
- ⛳ 1 mile N of Kilkenny, off N77

Mount Juliet (1991)

Thomastown

- ☎ **(056) 73000**
- 📠 (056) 73019
- ✍ Kim Thomas
- ✒ K Morris
- ⛳ 18 L 7299 yds Par 72 SSS 74
- 👥 U
- ££ €104 (€120)
- ⛴ 10 miles S of Kilkenny, off Dublin-Waterford road.
- ⊕ Driving range-residents and green fees. Golf Academy
- ⛩ Jack Nicklaus
- ■ www.mountjuliet.com

Mountain View (1997)

Kiltorcan, Ballyhale

- ☎ **(056) 68122**
- 📠 (056) 24655
- 📖 300
- ✍ M Kelly
- ⛳ 9 L 5025 m Par 70
- 👥 U
- ££ €13 (€13)
- ⛴ 12 miles S of Kilkenny
- ⛩ John O'Sullivan

Co Laois

Abbeyleix (1895)

Rathmoyle, Abbeyleix

- ☎ **(0502) 31450**
- 📖 500
- ✍ M Martin (Hon)
- ⛳ 18 L 6031 yds Par 72 SSS 70
- 👥 WD–U WE–NA SOC–WD/Sat
- ££ €15 (€25)
- ⛴ 10 miles S of Portlaoise. 60 miles SW of Dublin on Cork road
- ⛩ Mel Flanaghan

The Heath (1930)

The Heath, Portlaoise

- ☎ **(0502) 46533**
- 📠 (0502) 46566
- ✉ info@theheathgc.ie
- 📖 830
- ✍ J McNamara (Hon)
- ✒ (0502) 46622
- ⛳ 18 L 5873 m Par 71 SSS 70
- 👥 U
- ££ €16 (€30)
- ⛴ 4 miles E of Portlaoise
- ⊕ Floodlit driving range

Mountrath (1929)

Knockanina, Mountrath

- ☎ **(0502) 32558/32643**
- 📠 (0502) 32643
- 📖 800
- ✍ T O'Grady (0502) 32214
- ⛳ 18 L 6020 yds Par 71 SSS 69
- 👥 U
- ££ €20
- ⛴ 10 miles W of Portlaoise. Mountrath 2 miles

Portarlington (1908)

Garryhinch, Portarlington

- ☎ **(0502) 23115**
- 📠 (0502) 23044
- 📖 600
- ✍ D Cunningham (Hon)
- ⛳ 18 L 6004 m Par 71 SSS 71
- 👥 WD–U WE–restricted
- ££ €17 (€20)
- ⛴ Between Portarlington and Mountmellick on L116

Rathdowney (1930)

Coulnaboul West, Rathdowney

- ☎ **(0505) 46170**
- 📠 (0505) 46065
- 📖 600
- ✍ S Bolger (Hon)
- ⛳ 18 L 5864 m Par 71 SSS 70
- 👥 U exc Sun–NA SOC
- ££ €20 (€25)
- ⛴ 1 mile S of Rathdowney. 20 miles SW of Portlaoise
- ⛩ Hackett/Suttle

Co Leitrim

Ballinamore (1941)

Creevy, Ballinamore

- ☎ **(078) 44346**
- 📖 120
- ✍ J Cryan
- ⛳ 9 L 5514 m Par 70 SSS 68
- 👥 U SOC
- ⛴ 2 miles N of Ballinamore. 20 miles NE of Carrick-on-Shannon
- ⛩ Arthur Spring

Carrick-on-Shannon (1910)

Woodbrook, Carrick-on-Shannon

- ☎ **(079) 67015**
- 📖 210
- ✍ HP Gralton (Sec/Mgr)
- ⛳ 9 L 5584 yds SSS 68
- 👥 U
- ££ €14
- ⛴ 4 miles W of Carrick-on- Shannon on N4

Co Limerick

Abbeyfeale (1993)

Dromtrasna, Collins Abbeyfeale

- ☎ **(068) 32033**
- 📖 85
- ✍ M O'Riordan (Mgr)
- ✒ C Ahern
- ⛳ 9 L 4004 yds Par 61
- 👥 U
- ££ €10
- ⛴ 12 miles SW of Newcastle West

Adare Manor (1900)

Adare

- ☎ **(061) 396204**
- 📠 (061) 396800
- 📖 400
- ✍ M O'Donnell
- ✒ J Coyle
- ⛳ 18 L 5706 yds SSS 69
- 👥 WD–U WE–M
- ££ €25
- ⛴ 10 miles SW of Limerick
- ⛩ Sayers/Hackett

Castletroy (1937)

Castletroy, Limerick

- ☎ **(061) 335261**
- 📠 (061) 335373
- 📖 940
- ✍ L Hayes (061) 335753
- ✒ Shop (061) 330450
- ⛳ 18 L 5802 m SSS 71
- 👥 WD–U Sat am–U Sat pm/Sun–M SOC–Mon/Wed/Fri
- ££ €27 (€36)
- ⛴ 2 miles N of Limerick on Dublin road

Killeline (1993)

Newcastle West

- ☎ **(069) 61600**
- 📖 278
- ✍ A McCoy
- ⛳ 18 L 6700 yds Par 72
- 👥 U
- ££ €20
- ⛴ Newcastle West

Limerick (1891)

Ballyclough, Limerick

- ☎ **(061) 414083**
- 📠 (061) 415146
- 📖 1325
- ✍ P Murray (061) 415146
- ✒ L Harrington (061) 412492
- ⛳ 18 L 6479 yds SSS 71
- 👥 WD–U before 5pm exc Tues WE–M SOC–WD
- ££ €50
- ⛴ 3 miles S of Limerick

Limerick County G&CC

Ballyneety

- ☎ **(061) 351881**
- 📠 (061) 351384
- 📖 450
- ✍ J Heaton (Mgr)
- ✒ P Murphy
- ⛳ 18 L 6137 m Par 72 SSS 74
- 👥 U SOC
- ££ €24 (€30)
- ⛴ 5 miles S of Limerick (R512)
- ⊕ Driving range
- ⛩ Des Smyth
- ■ www.limerickcounty.com

Newcastle West (1938)

Ardagh

- ☎ **(069) 76500**
- 📠 (069) 76511
- 📖 510 120(L)
- ✍ P Lyons (Sec/Mgr)
- ⛳ 18 L 5905 m SSS 72
- 👥 U exc Sun–U after 4pm SOC
- ££ €21
- ⛴ 6 miles N of Newcastle West, off N21

⊕ Floodlit driving range
↑ Arthur Spring

Rathbane

Rathbane, Crossagalla, Limerick
☎ (061) 313655
✍ J Cassidy
✓ N Cassidy
⊳ 18 L 5671 m Par 70
👤 U
£€ €14
⛳ Limerick

Co Londonderry

Benone Par Three

53 Benone Avenue, Benone, Limavady, BT49 0LQ
☎ (028) 7775 0555
✍ MI Clark
⊳ 9 L 1427 yds Par 3 course
👤 U
£€ On application
⛳ 12 miles N of Limavady on A2 coast road

Brown Trout   (1984)

209 Agivey Road, Aghadowey, Coleraine, BT51 4AD
☎ (028) 7086 8209
📠 (028) 7086 8878
📧 bill@browntroutinn.com
📖 150
✍ B O'Hara (Sec/Mgr)
✓ K Revie
⊳ 9 L 2800 yds SSS 68
👤 U SOC
£€ £10 (£15)
⛳ 8 miles S of Coleraine at junction of A54/B66
↑ W O'Hara Sr
■ www.browntroutinn.com

Castlerock   (1901)

Circular Road, Castlerock, BT51 4TJ
☎ (028) 7084 8314
📠 (028) 7084 9440
📖 1100
✍ M Steen (Sec/Mgr)
✓ R Kelly
⊳ 18 L 6121 m SSS 72
   9 L 2457 m SSS 34
👤 WD–U exc Fri SOC
£€ 18 hole:£30 (£55) 9 hole:£12 (£15)
⛳ 5 miles W of Coleraine on A2
↑ Ben Sayers

City of Derry   (1912)

49 Victoria Road, Londonderry, BT47 2PU
☎ (028) 7134 6369
📠 (028) 7131 0008
📧 info@cityofderrygolfclub.com
📖 775
✍ M Doherty (028) 7131 1610
⊳ Prehen 18 L 6487 yds SSS 71
   Dunhugh 9 L 4708 yds SSS 63

👤 WD–U before 4pm –M after 4pm
   WE–UH SOC
£€ £15 (£20)
⛳ 3 miles from E end of Craigavon Bridge, towards Strabane
↑ Harry S Colt
■ www.cityofderrygolfclub.com

Foyle   (1994)

Alder Road, Londonderry, BT48 8DB
☎ (028) 7135 2222
📠 (028) 7135 3967
📧 mail@foylegolf.club24.co.uk
📖 265
✍ M Lapsley
✓ K McLaughlin
⊳ 18 L 6678 m SSS 72
   9 hole course
👤 U
£€ £12 (£15)
⛳ Londonderry
⊕ Driving range
↑ Frank Ainsworth
■ www.foylegolfcentre.co.uk

Kilrea   (1920)

Drumagarner Road, Kilrea
☎ (028) 2582 1048
📖 310
✍ DP Clarke
⊳ 9 L 4514 yds SSS 62
👤 Tues & Wed–NA after 5pm
   Sat–NA before 4pm
£€ £10 (£12.50)
⛳ Nr Kilrea on Maghera road. 15 miles S of Coleraine

Moyola Park   (1976)

15 Curran Road, Castledawson, Magherafelt, BT45 8DG
☎ (028) 7946 8468
📠 (028) 7946 8468
📖 940
✍ LWP Hastings (Hon)
✓ V Teague (028) 7946 8830
⊳ 18 L 6062 yds Par 71
👤 U SOC exc Sat
£€ £17 (£25)
⛳ 40 miles NW of Belfast by M2. 35 miles S of Coleraine
↑ Don Patterson

Portstewart   (1894)

117 Strand Road, Portstewart, BT55 7PG
☎ (028) 7083 2015
📠 (028) 7083 4097
📧 info@portstewartgc.co.uk
📖 1588
✍ M Moss BA (028) 7083 3839
✓ A Hunter (028) 7083 2601
⊳ Strand 18 L 6784 yds SSS 73
   Riverside 9 L 2662 yds Par 32
   Old 18 L 4733 yds SSS 62
👤 SOC–by arrangement
£€ Strand–£60 (£80). Riverside–£12 (£17). Old £10 (£14)
⛳ W boundary of Portstewart
■ www.portstewartgc.co.uk

Roe Park   (1993)

Roe Park Hotel, Limavady, BT49 9LB
☎ (028) 7776 0105
📖 300
✍ D Brockerton
✓ S Duffy
⊳ 18 L 6318 yds Par 70 SSS 71
👤 U
£€ £20 (£20)
⛳ Limavady
⊕ Driving range

Co Longford

County Longford   (1900)

Glack, Dublin Road, Longford
☎ (043) 46310
📠 (043) 47082
📖 800
✍ D Rooney
✓ D Keenaghan
⊳ 18 L 6008 yds SSS 69
👤 U SOC
£€ On application
⛳ Longford 1/2 mile on Dublin road
↑ Eddie Hackett

Co Louth

Ardee   (1911)

Town Parks, Ardee
☎ (041) 685 3227
📠 (041) 685 6137
📧 ardeegolf@oceanfree.net
📖 700
✍ MP Conoulty (Sec/Mgr)
✓ S Kirkpatrick
⊳ 18 L 6348 yds SSS 71
👤 U SOC
£€ €35 (€50)
⛳ 1/2 mile N of Ardee
⊕ Driving range
↑ Eddie Hackett

Carnbeg

Carnbeg, Dundalk, Co Louth
☎ (042) 933 2518
✍ P Kirk
✓ J Frawley
⊳ 18 L 6000 m Par 72
👤 U
£€ €18
⛳ Dundalk

County Louth   (1892)

Baltray, Drogheda
☎ (041) 982 2329
📠 (041) 982 2969
📖 1055
✍ M Delany
✓ P McGuirk (041) 982 2444
⊳ 18 L 6783 yds SSS 72
👤 By prior arrangement
£€ €75 (€95)
⛳ 3 miles NE of Drogheda
↑ Tom Simpson

Dundalk   (1904)

Blackrock, Dundalk
- ☎ **(042) 932 1731**
- ⌨ (042) 932 2022
- ✉ dkgc@iol.ie
- 📖 850
- ✎ T Sloane (Sec/Mgr)
- ⛳ J Cassidy (042) 932 2102
- ⛳ 18 L 6028 m Par 72
- 👥 U SOC
- ££ €26
- 🚗 3 miles S of Dundalk
- ■ www.eiresoft.com/dundalkgc

Greenore   (1896)

Greenore
- ☎ **(042) 937 3212/3678**
- ⌨ (042) 937 3678
- 📖 700
- ✎ R Daly
- ⛳ 18 L 6514 yds Par 71 SSS 71
- 👥 WD–U before 5pm WE/BH–by arrangement SOC
- ££ €24 (€30)
- 🚗 15 miles E of Dundalk on Carlingford Lough
- 🏠 Eddie Hackett

Killinbeg   (1991)

Killin Park, Dundalk
- ☎ **(042) 933 9303**
- ⌨ (042) 933 4320
- 📖 175
- ✎ T Bell (Sec/Mgr)
- ⛳ None
- ⛳ 18 L 4717 m Par 69 SSS 64
- 👥 U SOC
- ££ €15
- 🚗 2 miles NW of Dundalk on Castletown road

Seapoint   (1993)

Termonfeckin, Drogheda
- ☎ **(041) 982 2333**
- ⌨ (041) 982 2331
- ✉ golflinks@seapoint.ie
- 📖 530
- ✎ K Carrie
- ⛳ D Carroll (041) 988 1066
- ⛳ 18 L 6420 m Par 72 SSS 74
- 👥 U SOC
- ££ €40 – €50 (€60)
- 🚗 5 miles NE of Drogheda (R166)
- 🏠 Des Smyth
- ■ www.seapointgolfclub.com

Towneley Hall   (1994)

Tullyallen, Drogheda
- ☎ **(041) 942229**
- 📖 125
- ✎ O Quigley (Hon)
- ⛳ 9 L 5221 m Par 71 SSS 69
- 👥 U
- ££ €9
- 🚗 5 miles NW of Drogheda, off R168

Co Mayo

Achill   (1951)

Keel, Achill
- ☎ **(098) 43456**
- 📖 100
- ✎ DT Vesey
- ⛳ 9 L 2689 m Par 70 SSS 67
- 👥 U H SOC
- ££ €13
- 🚗 50 miles NW of Westport, on Achill Island
- 🏠 P Skerritt

Ashford Castle

Cong
- ☎ **(092) 46003**
- ⛳ 9 L 4500 yds SSS 68
- 👥 U SOC
- ££ €18
- 🚗 25 miles N of Galway on Lough Corrib
- 🏠 Eddie Hackett

Ballina   (1910)

Mossgrove, Shanaghy, Ballina
- ☎ **(096) 21050**
- ⌨ (096) 21050
- 📖 460
- ✎ P Connolly
- ⛳ 18 L 6103 yds Par 71
- 👥 WD–U Sun–NA before noon SOC–WD
- ££ €20
- 🚗 1 mile E of Ballina
- ■ www.ballinagolfclub.com

Ballinrobe   (1895)

Clooncastle, Ballinrobe
- ☎ **(092) 41118**
- ⌨ (092) 41889
- ✉ bgcgolf@iol.ie
- 📖 590
- ✎ T Moran (Sec/Mgr)
- ⛳ 18 L 6043 m Par 73 SSS 72
- 👥 U exc Sun–NA SOC
- ££ €30
- 🚗 2 miles NW of Ballinrobe on R331
- ⊕ Driving range
- 🏠 Eddie Hackett

Ballyhaunis   (1929)

Coolnaha, Ballyhaunis
- ☎ **(0907) 30014**
- 📖 300
- ✎ J Mooney (Hon)
- ⛳ 9 L 5413 m Par 70 SSS 68
- 👥 U exc Thurs (Ladies Day)–M Sun–NA SOC–WD
- ££ €13
- 🚗 2 miles N of Ballyhaunis

Carne Golf Links   (1995)

Carne, Belmullet
- ☎ **(097) 82292**
- ⌨ (097) 81477
- ✉ carnegolf@iol.ie
- 📖 350
- ✎ J O'Hara (Sec/Mgr)

- ⛳ 18 L 6119 m SSS 72
- 👥 U SOC
- ££ €40 W–€200
- 🚗 2 miles W of Belmullet. 40 miles W of Ballina
- 🏠 Eddie Hackett
- ■ www.carnegolflinks.com

Castlebar   (1910)

Hawthorn Avenue, Rocklands, Castlebar
- ☎ **(094) 21649**
- ⌨ (094) 26088
- 📖 950
- ✎ EJ Lonergan (086) 837 3944
- ⛳ 18 L 6500 yds Par 71 SSS 72
- 👥 WD/Sat–U Sun–NA
- ££ €24 (€30)
- 🚗 1 mile S of Castlebar, on Galway road
- 🏠 P McEvoy (1999)
- ■ www.castlebar.ie/golf

Claremorris   (1917)

Castlemacgarrett, Claremorris
- ☎ **(094) 71527**
- 📖 500
- ✎ A Finn (Hon)
- ⛳ 18 L 5827 yds Par 73 SSS 71
- 👥 WD–U before noon Sat–U before noon SOC
- ££ €23 (€25)
- 🚗 2 miles S of Claremorris (N17)
- 🏠 Tom Craddock

Mulranny   (1968)

Mulranny, Westport
- ☎ **(098) 36262**
- 📖 100
- ✎ C Moran (Hon)
- ⛳ 9 L 6255 yds Par 71 SSS 69
- 👥 U
- ££ €13
- 🚗 20 miles NW of Castlebar

Swinford   (1922)

Brabazon Park, Swinford
- ☎ **(094) 51378**
- 📖 300
- ✎ T Regan (094) 51502
- ⛳ 9 L 5901 yds SSS 68
- 👥 U SOC–exc Sun
- ££ €13
- 🚗 S of Swinford, off Kiltimagh road

Westport   (1908)

Carrowholly, Westport
- ☎ **(098) 28262/27070**
- ⌨ (098) 27217
- 📖 850
- ✎ M Walsh
- ⛳ A Mealia
- ⛳ 18 L 6653 yds SSS 72
- 👥 U SOC
- ££ €38 (€47)
- 🚗 2 miles W of Westport
- 🏠 F Hawtree
- ■ www.golfwestport.com

Co Meath

Ashbourne (1991)
Archerstown, Ashbourne
- ☎ (01) 835 2005
- 📠 (01) 835 2561
- 📖 645
- ✎ D O'Hare
- ⚲ J Dwyer
- ↦ 18 L 5778 m Par 71 SSS 70
- ♟ WD–U WE–NA before 1pm SOC
- ££ €32
- ⚬ 12 miles N of Dublin, off N2
- ⌂ Des Smyth

Black Bush (1987)
Thomastown, Dunshaughlin
- ☎ (01) 825 0021
- 📠 (01) 825 0400
- ✉ golf@blackbush.iol.ie
- 📖 950
- ✎ Kate O'Rourke (Admin)
- ⚲ S O'Grady
- ↦ 18 L 6930 yds SSS 73
  9 L 2800 yds SSS 35
- ♟ WD–U WE–NA before 4pm SOC
- ££ €26 (€32)
- ⚬ 1 mile E of Dunshaughlin, off N3.
  20 miles NW of Dublin
- ⊕ Driving range for members and
  green fees
- ⌂ Robert J Browne

County Meath (1898)
Newtownmoynagh, Trim
- ☎ (046) 31463
- 📠 (046) 37554
- 📖 800
- ✎ J McInerney (086) 274 9859
- ⚲ R Machin
- ↦ 18 L 6720 yds SSS 72
- ♟ WD–U exc Thurs WE–restricted
  SOC–exc Sun
- ££ €24 (€30)
- ⚬ 2 miles SW of Trim. 25 miles NW
  of Dublin
- ⌂ Hackett/Craddock
- ■ www.trimgolf.net

Gormanston College (1961)
Franciscan College, Gormanston
- ☎ (01) 841 2203
- 📖 160
- ✎ Br Laurence Brady
- ⚲ B Browne
- ↦ 9 L 1973 m Par 32
- ♟ NA
- ⚬ 22 miles N of Dublin

Headfort (1928)
Kells
- ☎ (046) 924 0146
- 📠 (046) 924 9282
- 📖 1100
- ✎ Nora Murphy (Admin)
  (046) 924 0146
- ⚲ B McGovern (046) 924 0639
- ↦ New 18 L 6164 m SSS 73
  Old 18 L 5973 m SSS 71
- ♟ U before 4pm exc NA 12.30–2pm
  SOC

- ££ New–€50. Old–€35 (€40)
- ⚬ 65km NW of Dublin on N3
- ⌂ Christy O'Connor Jr

Kilcock (1985)
Gallow, Kilcock
- ☎ (01) 628 7592
- 📠 (01) 628 7283
- 📖 650
- ✎ S Kelly (Sec/Mgr)
- ↦ 18 L 5794 m SSS 71
- ♟ U SOC
- ££ €25 Fri/WE–€32
- ⚬ 20 miles W of Dublin (N4)
- ⌂ E Hackett

Laytown & Bettystown (1909)
Bettystown
- ☎ (041) 982 7170/7534
- 📠 (041) 982 8506
- ✉ bettystowngolfclub@utvinternet
  .com
- 📖 850
- ✎ Helen Finnegan (041) 982 7170
- ⚲ RJ Browne (041) 982 8793
- ↦ 18 L 6454 yds SSS 72
- ♟ U SOC–WD
- ££ €45 (€55)
- ⚬ 25 miles N of Dublin

Moor Park (1993)
Moortown, Navan
- ☎ (046) 27661
- 📖 180
- ✎ M Fagan (Mgr)
- ↦ 18 L 5600 m Par 72 SSS 69
- ♟ U
- ££ €10
- ⚬ Navan

Royal Tara (1906)
Bellinter, Navan
- ☎ (046) 25244/25508/25584
- 📠 (046) 25508
- ✉ info@royaltaragolfclub.com
- 📖 1000
- ✎ P O'Brien (Hon),
  L Clarke (Gen Mgr)
- ⚲ A Whiston (046) 26009
- ↦ 18 L 5757 yds Par 71
  9 L 3184 yds Par 35
- ♟ U
- ££ €35 (€40)
- ⚬ 25 miles N of Dublin, off N3
- ■ www.royaltaragolfclub.com

South Meath
Longwood Road, Trim, Co Meath
- ☎ (046) 31471
- ✎ D Durney (Hon)
- ↦ 9 L 5612 m Par 70
- ♟ U
- ££ €10
- ⚬ S of Trim (R160)

Co Monaghan

Castleblayney (1985)
Onomy, Castleblayney
- ☎ (042) 974 9485
- 📖 275
- ✎ R Kernan (042) 974 0451
- ↦ 9 L 2678 yds SSS 66
- ♟ U SOC
- ££ €10 (€12)
- ⚬ Castleblayney town centre. 18
  miles SE of Monaghan
- ⌂ R Browne

Clones (1913)
Hilton Demesne, Clones
- ☎ (047) 56017/56913
- 📖 305
- ✎ M Taylor (049) 555 2354
- ↦ 18 L 6100 yds SSS 69
- ♟ WD–U WE–book in advance
- ££ €25
- ⚬ Hilton Park, 3km from Clones on
  Scotshouse Road

Mannan Castle (1993)
Donaghmoyne, Carrickmacross
- ☎ (042) 966 3308
- 📠 (042) 966 3195
- 📖 600
- ✎ R Howell (042) 966 2531
- ↦ 18 L 6020 yds Par 70 SSS 69
- ♟ U
- ££ €18
- ⚬ 4 miles N of Carrickmacross

Nuremore (1964)
Nuremore, Carrickmacross
- ☎ (042) 966 4016
- ✉ nuremore@eircom.net
- 📖 260
- ✎ A Capaldi
- ⚲ M Cassidy
- ↦ 18 L 5870 m Par 71 SSS 69
- ♟ U
- ££ €30 (€40)
- ⚬ 1 mile S of Carrickmacross on
  Dublin road
- ⌂ Eddie Hackett
- ■ www.nuremore-hotel.ie

Rossmore (1916)
Rossmore Park, Monaghan
- ☎ (047) 81316
- 📖 750
- ✎ J McKenna (Hon)
- ⚲ M Nicholson (047) 71222
- ↦ 18 L 6082 yds Par 70 SSS 69
- ♟ WD–U WE/BH–U SOC
- ££ €24
- ⚬ 2 miles S of Monaghan on
  Cootehill road
- ⌂ Des Smyth

Co Offaly

Birr (1893)
The Glenns, Birr
☎ **(0509) 20082**
🖥 (0509) 22155
📖 750
🖊 Mary O'Gorman (Hon)
✇ S O'Grady (0509) 21606
🏳 18 L 6216 yds SSS 70
👥 U SOC–exc Sun–NA 11.30–12
£€ €14 (€17)
🚗 2 miles W of Birr
⊕ Driving range
🏠 Eddie Connaughton

Castle Barna (1992)
Castlebarnagh, Daingean
☎ **(0506) 53384**
🖥 (0506) 53077
📖 400
🖊 E Mangan
🏳 18 L 5595 m Par 72 SSS 69
👥 U
£€ €12 (€17)
🚗 10 miles E of Tullamore (R402)
🏠 Alan Duggan

Edenderry (1910)
Kishawanny, Edenderry
☎ **(046) 973 1072**
🖥 (046) 973 3911
📧 enquiries@edenderrygolfclub.com
📖 1000
🖊 P O'Connell (044) 22211
🏳 18 L 6121 m Par 72 SSS 72
👥 WD–U exc Thurs (Ladies Day)
   WE–restricted SOC
£€ On application
🚗 1 mile E of Edenderry town
🏠 Havers/Hackett
■ www.edenderrygolfclub.com

Esker Hills G&CC
Tullamore, Co Offaly
☎ **(0506) 55999**
🖥 (0506) 55021
🖊 C Guinan
🏳 18 L 6669 yds Par 71
👥 U
£€ €25
🚗 Tullamore
■ www.eskerhillsgolf.com

Tullamore (1896)
Brookfield, Tullamore
☎ **(0506) 21439**
🖥 (0506) 41806
📧 tullamoregolfclub@eircom.net
📖 1000
🖊 J Barber-Loughnane
✇ D McArdle (0506) 51757
🏳 18 L 6428 yds Par 70 SSS 71
👥 WD exc Tues–U Sat–restricted
   Sun–NA SOC
£€ €32 (€40)
🚗 2½ miles S of Tullamore, off N52
🏠 Braid/Merrigan
■ www.tullamoregolfclub.com

Co Roscommon

Athlone (1892)
Hodson Bay, Athlone
☎ **(0902) 92073/92235**
🖥 (0902) 94080
📖 1000
🖊 I Dockery
✇ M Quinn
🏳 18 L 5854 m SSS 71
👥 U SOC
£€ D–€21 (€24)
🚗 3 miles N of Athlone on
   Roscommon road
🏠 F Hawtree

Ballaghaderreen (1937)
Aughalustia, Ballaghaderreen
☎ **(0907) 60295**
📖 350
🖊 J Corcoran (Hon)
🏳 9 L 5663 yds Par 70 SSS 66
👥 U SOC
£€ €15
🚗 Ballaghaderreen 3 miles
🏠 P Skerritt

Boyle (1911)
Knockadoo, Brusna, Boyle
☎ **(079) 62192/62594**
📖 145
🖊 D Conlon (Hon)
🏳 9 L 4914 m Par 67 SSS 64
👥 U SOC
£€ €12
🚗 1½ miles S of Boyle
🏠 Eddie Hackett

Castlerea (1905)
Clonallis, Castlerea
☎ **(0907) 21214**
📖 200
🖊 V Rabitte
🏳 9 L 5466 yds Par 68
👥 WD/Sat–U Sun–by arrangement
£€ €13
🚗 Knock Road, Castlerea

Roscommon (1904)
Moate Park, Roscommon
☎ **(0903) 26382**
🖥 (0903) 26043
📧 rosgolf@eircom.net
📖 720
🖊 C McConn
🏳 18 L 6059 m Par 72 SSS 71
👥 WD–U WE/BH–restricted SOC
£€ €25 (€25)
🚗 1 mile S of Roscommon
🏠 Eddie Connaughton

Strokestown (1995)
Strokestown
📖 200
🖊 L Glover (Hon) (078) 33528
🏳 9 L 5230 m Par 68 SSS 67
👥 U
£€ €12
🚗 15 miles N of Roscommon (R368).
   N5 to Longford/Westport

Co Sligo

Ballymote (1943)
Ballinascarrow, Ballymote
☎ **(071) 83504**
📖 250
🖊 J O'Connor
🏳 9 L 5302 m Par 68
👥 U
£€ €13
🚗 15 miles S of Sligo

County Sligo (1894)
Rosses Point
☎ **(071) 77134/77186**
🖥 (071) 77460
📧 cosligo@iol.ie
📖 1169
🖊 J Ironside (Mgr) (071) 77134
✇ J Robinson (071) 77171
🏳 18 L 6037 m SSS 72
   9 L 2795 m SSS 35
👥 U H–booking required SOC
£€ €60 Fri/WE–€75
🚗 5 miles NW of Sligo
🏠 Colt/Allison
■ www.countysligogolfclub.ie

Enniscrone (1931)
Ballina Road, Enniscrone
☎ **(096) 36297**
🖥 (096) 36657
📖 740
🖊 M Staunton (Sec/Mgr)
✇ C McGoldrick (096) 36666
🏳 18 L 6671 yds SSS 72
   9 L 3364 yds Par 72
👥 WD–U WE/BH–phone first SOC
£€ €45 (€60)
🚗 S of Enniscrone. Ballina 13 km
⊕ Driving range
🏠 Hackett/Steel
■ www.homepage.eircom.net
   /~enniscronegolf

Strandhill (1932)
Strandhill
☎ **(071) 68188**
🖥 (071) 68811
📖 450
🖊 Sandra Corcoran
✇ Golf Shop
🏳 18 L 6032 yds Par 69 SSS 68
👥 WD–U WE/BH–restricted SOC
£€ €30 (€36)
🚗 6 miles W of Sligo

Tubbercurry (1990)
Ballymote Road, Tubbercurry
☎ **(071) 85849**
📖 250
🖊 J Brennan
🏳 9 L 5478 m SSS 69
👥 U
£€ €13
🚗 20 miles S of Sligo
🏠 Eddie Hackett

For list of abbreviations and key to symbols see page 649

Co Tipperary

Ballykisteen   (1994)
Ballykisteen, Limerick Junction
- ☎ **(062) 33333**
- 🖳 260
- ✍ J Ryan
- ✒ D Reddan
- ⛳ 18 L 5765 yds Par 72
- 👥 U SOC–book in advance
- £€ €25
- ⛳ 3 miles NW of Tipperary town
- ⊕ Driving range
- 🏠 Des Smyth

Cahir Park   (1968)
Kilcommon, Cahir
- ☎ **(052) 41474**
- 🖳 (052) 42717
- 🖳 575
- ✍ J Costigan (052) 41146
- ✒ M Joseph (052) 43944
- ⛳ 18 L 6351 yds Par 71 SSS 71
- 👥 U SOC–WD/Sat
- £€ €21 (€24)
- ⛳ 1 mile S of Cahir
- ⊕ Driving range
- 🏠 Eddie Hackett

Carrick-on-Suir   (1939)
Garravoone, Carrick-on-Suir
- ☎ **(051) 640047**
- 🖳 (051) 640558
- 🖳 500
- ✍ A Murphy (Sec/Mgr)
- ⛳ 18 L 6061 m Par 72 SSS 70
- 👥 U exc Sun–NA before 11am SOC–WD/Sat
- £€ €22
- ⛳ 2 miles S of Carrick on Dungarvan road
- 🏠 Eddie Hackett

Clonmel   (1911)
Lyreanearla, Mountain Road, Clonmel
- ☎ **(052) 21138/24050**
- 🖳 (052) 24050
- 🖂 cgc@indigo.ie
- 🖳 820
- ✍ A Myles-Keating (052) 24050
- ✒ R Hayes (052) 24050
- ⛳ 18 L 6347 yds SSS 71
- 👥 WD–U WE–SOC
- £€ €30 Fri/WE–€35
- ⛳ 2 miles SW of Clonmel
- 🏠 Eddie Hackett

County Tipperary   (1993)
Dundrum, Cashel
- ☎ **(062) 71717**
- 🖳 (062) 71718
- 🖳 380
- ✍ W Crowe (Mgr)
- ⛳ 18 L 6955 yds SSS 73
- 👥 U SOC
- £€ €36 (€42)
- ⛳ 6 miles W of Cashel
- 🏠 Philip Walton
- ■ www.dundrumhousehotel.com

Nenagh   (1929)
Beechwood, Nenagh
- ☎ **(067) 34808**
- 🖳 (067) 34808
- 🖳 1200
- ✍ T Murphy (Hon)
- ✒ R Kelly (067) 33242
- ⛳ 18 L 6009 m Par 72 SSS 72
- 👥 U SOC
- £€ €30
- ⛳ 3 miles NE of Nenagh on old Birr road
- 🏠 Patrick Merrigan

Roscrea   (1892)
Derryvale, Roscrea
- ☎ **(0505) 21130**
- 🖳 (0505) 23410
- 🖳 500
- ✍ GP Maher (Hon)
- ⛳ 18 L 5782 m SSS 71
- 👥 U
- £€ €17 (€20)
- ⛳ 2 miles E of Roscrea on Dublin road (N7)
- 🏠 Arthur Spring

Slievenamon
Clonacody, Lisronagh, Co Tipperary
- ☎ **(052) 32213**
- ✍ K Lalor
- ⛳ 18 L 4135 m par 62
- 👥 U
- £€ €10
- ⛳ 8 miles N of Clonmel
- ■ www.slievnamongolfclub.com

Templemore   (1970)
Manna South, Templemore
- ☎ **(0504) 31502**
- 🖳 220
- ✍ M McGrath
- ⛳ 9 L 5442 yds SSS 67
- 👥 U exc Sun SOC
- £€ €13
- ⛳ ¹/₂ mile S of Templemore

Thurles   (1909)
Turtulla, Thurles
- ☎ **(0504) 21983/24599**
- 🖳 (0504) 24647
- 🖳 850
- ✍ C Murphy (Admin)
- ✒ S Hunt
- ⛳ 18 L 5904 m Par 72 SSS 71
- 👥 U
- £€ €25
- ⛳ 1 mile S of Thurles
- ⊕ Driving range
- 🏠 Lionel Hewson

Tipperary   (1896)
Rathanny, Tipperary
- ☎ **(062) 51119**
- 🖳 550
- ✍ J Considine (Sec/Mgr)
- ⛳ 18 L 5445 m Par 71 SSS 70
- 👥 U SOC
- £€ €17 (€20)
- ⛳ Tipperary 1 mile

Co Tyrone

Auchnacloy   (1995)
99 Tullyvar Road, Auchnacloy
- ☎ **(028) 8255 7050**
- 🖳 180
- ✍ S Houston
- ⛳ 9 L 5017 m Par 70 SSS 68
- 👥 U
- £€ £10 (£12)
- ⛳ 12 miles SW of Dungannon (B35)
- ⊕ Driving range

Dungannon   (1890)
34 Springfield Lane, Mullaghmore, Dungannon, BT70 1QX
- ☎ **(028) 8772 7338/2098**
- 🖳 (028) 8772 7338
- 🖂 dungannon.golfclub @btopenworld.com
- 🖳 840
- ✍ ST Hughes, Brenda McKenna (Sec/Mgr)
- ✒ Vivian Teague
- ⛳ 18 L 6046 yds SSS 69
- 👥 U
- £€ £18 (£22)
- ⛳ ¹/₂ mile NW of Dungannon on Donaghmore road

Fintona   (1904)
Eccleville Desmesne, 1 Kiln Street, Fintona, BT78 2BJ
- ☎ **(028) 8284 1480**
- 🖳 (028) 8284 1480
- 🖳 400
- ✍ V McCarney (028) 8284 0777
- ✒ P Leonard (028) 8284 1480
- ⛳ 9 L 5765 m Par 72 SSS 70
- 👥 U exc comp days SOC
- £€ £10 (£15)
- ⛳ 8 miles S of Omagh

Killymoon   (1889)
200 Killymoon Road, Cookstown, BT80 8SD
- ☎ **(028) 8676 3762**
- 🖳 (028) 8676 3762
- 🖂 kgcl@btopenworld.com
- 🖳 950
- ✍ V Wilson
- ✒ G Chambers
- ⛳ 18 L 5488 m SSS 69
- 👥 U H SOC
- £€ £14 (£18)
- ⛳ 1 mile S of Cookstown, off A29

Newtownstewart   (1914)
38 Golf Course Road, Newtownstewart, BT78 4HU
- ☎ **(028) 8166 1466**
- 🖳 (028) 8166 2506
- 🖂 newtown.stewart@lineone.net
- 🖳 700
- ✍ JE Mackin (028) 8167 1487
- ✒ None
- ⛳ 18 L 5341 m Par 70 SSS 69
- 👥 WD–U WE–NA after noon SOC
- £€ £12 (£17)

🚵 2 miles SW of Newtownstewart on B84
🏠 Frank Pennink
■ www.globalgolf.com/newtownstewart

Omagh (1910)
83A Dublin Road, Omagh, BT78 1HQ
☎ **(028) 8224 3160/1442**
🖳 (028) 8224 3160
🏢 817
🏌 Mrs F Caldwell
✓ None
🏳 18 L 5364 m SSS 68
👥 U SOC
££ £12 (£18)
🚵 1 mile from Omagh on Belfast-Dublin road

Strabane (1908)
Ballycolman, Strabane, BT82 9PH
☎ **(028) 7138 2271/2007**
🖳 (028) 7188 6514
🏢 800
🏌 G Glover (028) 7138 2007
✓ None
🏳 18 L 5552 m SSS 69
👥 WD–U WE–by arrangement SOC
££ £12 (£15)
🚵 ½ mile from Strabane, nr Fir Trees Hotel

Co Waterford

Dungarvan (1924)
Knocknagranagh, Dungarvan
☎ **(058) 43310/41605**
🖳 (058) 44113
📧 dungarvangc@eircom.net
🏢 900
🏌 Irene Howell (Mgr) (058) 43310
✓ D Hayes (058) 44707
🏳 18 L 6134 m Par 72 SSS 73
👥 U SOC
££ €28 (€35)
🚵 2 miles E of Dungarvan on N25. 25 miles W of Waterford
🏠 Maurice Fives
■ www.dungarvangolfclub.com

Dunmore East (1993)
Dunmore East
☎ **(051) 383151**
🖳 (051) 383151
🏢 300
🏌 M Skehan
🏳 18 L 6655 yds Par 72 SSS 70
👥 U
££ €14 (€21)
🚵 10 miles S of Waterford (R684)
🏠 J O'Riordan
■ www.dunmore-golf.com

Faithlegg (1993)
Faithlegg House, Faithlegg
☎ **(051) 382241**
🖳 (051) 382664
🏢 260
🏌 J Santry (Hon)

✓ T Higgins
🏳 18 L 6690 yds SSS 72
👥 U SOC
££ €36 (€50)
🚵 6 miles E of Waterford City on Dunmore East road
🏠 Patrick Merrigan

Gold Coast (1993)
Ballinacourty, Dungarvan
☎ **(058) 42249/44055**
🖳 (058) 43378
🏢 600
🏌 T Considine (058) 44055
✓ None
🏳 18 L 6171 m Par 72 SSS 72
👥 U SOC
££ €30 (€40)
🚵 E of Dungarvan, off R675
🏠 M Fives
■ www.goldcoastgolfclub.com

Lismore (1965)
Ballyin, Lismore
☎ **(058) 54026**
🖳 (058) 53338
🏢 450
🏌 S Hales
🏳 9 L 5291 m Par 69 SSS 67
👥 WD–U before 5pm –M after 5pm WE–phone first SOC–exc Sun
££ €14 (€18)
🚵 1 mile N of Lismore, off N72

Tramore (1894)
Newtown Hill, Tramore
☎ **(051) 386170/381247**
🖳 (051) 390961
🏢 1396
🏌 J Cox (Sec/Mgr)
✓ D Kiely
🏳 18 L 6055 m SSS 73
👥 U
££ €40 (€45)
🚵 7 miles S of Waterford
🏠 Capt Tippett
■ www.tramoregolfclub.com

Waterford (1912)
Newrath, Waterford
☎ **(051) 874182**
🖳 (051) 853405
🏢 961
🏌 J Condon (Sec/Mgr) (051) 876748
✓ J Condon
🏳 18 L 5722 m Par 71 SSS 70
👥 U
££ €26 (€30)
🚵 1 mile N of Waterford (N25)
🏠 Willie Park/James Braid

Waterford Castle (1991)
The Island, Ballinakill, Waterford
☎ **(051) 871633**
🖳 (051) 871634
🏢 450
🏌 M Garland
✓ None
🏳 18 L 6231 m Par 72 SSS 71
👥 U H SOC
££ €38

🚵 2 miles E of Waterford, off R683. Island in River Suir
⊕ Driving range
🏠 Des Smyth
■ www.waterfordcastle.com

West Waterford G&CC (1993)
Dungarvan
☎ **(058) 43216/41475**
🖳 (058) 44343
📧 info@westwaterfordgolf.com
🏢 350
🏌 T Whelan (Sec/Mgr)
🏳 18 L 6712 yds Par 72
👥 U SOC
££ €28 (€36)
🚵 4km W of Dungarvan, off N25
⊕ Practice range
🏠 Eddie Hackett
■ www.westwaterfordgolf.com

Co Westmeath

Ballinlough Castle
Clonmellon, Co Westmeath
☎ **(044) 64544**
🏌 T Brady
🏳 9 L 6114 m Par 70
👥 U
££ €13
🚵 25 miles NE of Mullingar

Delvin Castle (1992)
Clonyn, Delvin
☎ **(044) 64315**
🏢 330
🏌 F Dillon
✓ D Keenaghan
🏳 18 L 5818 m Par 70 SSS 68
👥 U
££ €20
🚵 15 miles NE of Mullingar (N52)

Glasson Hotel (1993)
Glasson, Athlone
☎ **(0902) 85120**
🖳 (0902) 85444
📧 info@glassongolf.ie
🏢 170
🏌 F Reid
✓ None
🏳 18 L 7120 yds Par 72 SSS 72
👥 U
££ €40
🚵 6 miles NE of Athlone (N55)
⊕ Golf Academy
🏠 C O'Connor Jr
■ www.glassongolf.ie

Moate (1900)
Aghanargit, Moate
☎ **(0902) 81271**
🖳 (0902) 81267
🏢 600
🏌 A O'Brien
🏳 18 L 6294 yds SSS 70
👥 U SOC–WD

£€ €15
🚗 Moate town centre
🏠 Bobby Browne

Mount Temple (1991)
Proprietary
Mount Temple, Moate
☎ (0902) 81841
🖥 (0902) 81957
📖 150
🏌 M Dolan
✔ None
⛳ 18 L 6500 yds SSS 71
👭 U H SOC
£€ €23
🚗 3 miles N of N6, between Athlone and Moate
🏠 Michael Dolan

Mullingar (1894)
Belvedere, Mullingar
☎ (044) 48366
🖥 (044) 41499
📖 560
🏌 Ann Scully
✔ J Burns
⛳ 18 L 6370 yds SSS 71
👭 U SOC
£€ €32
🚗 3 miles S of Mullingar (M52)
🏠 James Braid

Co Wexford

Courtown (1936)
Kiltennel, Gorey
☎ (055) 25166
🖥 (055) 25553
📧 courtown@aol.ie
📖 1600
🏌 D Cleere (Mgr)
✔ J Coone (055) 25860
⛳ 18 L 6398 yds SSS 71
👭 U SOC
£€ €30 (€42)
🚗 2 miles SE of Gorey
🏠 Harris
🖥 www.courtowngolfclub.com

Enniscorthy (1908)
Knockmarshall, Enniscorthy
☎ (054) 33191
📖 830
🏌 J Maguire
✔ M Sludds (054) 37600
⛳ 18 L 6115 m Par 72 SSS 72
👭 U exc Tues & Sun–phone first SOC
£€ €25 (€34)
🚗 1½ miles SW of Enniscorthy on New Ross road
⊕ Driving range
🏠 Eddie Hackett

New Ross (1905)
Tinneranny, New Ross
☎ (051) 421433
🖥 (051) 420098
📖 700
🏌 Kathleen Daly (Sec/Mgr)

⛳ 18 L 5751 m SSS 70
👭 U exc Sun SOC
£€ €18 (€24)
🚗 1 mile W of New Ross

Rosslare (1905)
Rosslare Strand, Rosslare
☎ (053) 32113 (Clubhouse)
    (053) 32203 (Bookings)
🖥 (053) 32263
📧 office@rosslaregolf.com
📖 1000
🏌 JF Hall (Mgr)
✔ J Young (053) 32032
⛳ 18 L 6782 yds Par 72 SSS 72
    12 L 3887 yds Par 46
👭 U SOC
£€ 18 hole:€35 (€50) 12 hole:€20
🚗 10 miles S of Wexford. Rosslare Ferry 6 miles
🏠 Hawtree/Taylor/O'Connor Jr
🖥 www.iol.ie~rgolfclb

St Helen's Bay (1993)
St Helen's, Kilrane, Rosslare Harbour
☎ (053) 33234
🖥 (053) 33803
📧 sthelens@iol.ie
📖 604
🏌 S Hession
✔ L Bowler
⛳ 18 L 6091 m SSS 72
👭 U SOC
£€ €25 (€32)
🚗 Nr Rosslare Ferry terminal
🏠 Philip Walton
🖥 www.sthelensbay.com

Tara Glen (1993)
Ballymoney, Gorey
☎ (055) 25413
🖥 (055) 25612
🏌 D Popplewell
⛳ 9 L 5826 m Par 72 SSS 70
👭 U
£€ €18
🚗 4 miles E of Gorey. 12 miles S of Arklow

Wexford (1960)
Mulgannon, Wexford
☎ (053) 42238
🖥 (053) 42243
📧 info@wexfordgolfclub.ie
📖 805
🏌 P Daly (Hon)
✔ D McGrane (053) 46300
⛳ 18 L 6338 yds Par 72 SSS 70
👭 U SOC
£€ €28 (€32)
🚗 Wexford ½ mile
🖥 www.wexfordgolfclub.ie

Co Wicklow

Arklow (1927)
Abbeylands, Arklow
☎ (0402) 32492
🖥 (0402) 91604
📧 arklowgolflinks@eircom.net

📖 500
🏌 B Timmons (Hon)
✔ None
⛳ 18 L 6475 yds Par 69 SSS 67
👭 WD–U Sat–U after 5pm Sun–NA SOC
£€ €40
🚗 1 mile from Arklow
🏠 Hawtree/Taylor/Hackett /Connaughton
🖥 www.arklowgolfclublinks.ie

Baltinglass (1928)
Baltinglass
☎ (0508) 81350
🖥 (0508) 81350
📖 399
🏌 O Cooney (Hon)
✔ M Murphy
⛳ 9 L 5554 m Par 68
👭 U SOC
£€ €13
🚗 38 miles S of Dublin (N81)

Blainroe (1978)
Blainroe
☎ (0404) 68168
🖥 (0404) 69369
📖 1100
🏌 W O'Sullivan (Sec/Mgr)
✔ J McDonald
⛳ 18 L 6175 m SSS 72
👭 U
£€ €45 (€56)
🚗 3 miles S of Wicklow on coast
🏠 FW Hawtree

Boystown
Baltyboys, Blessington, Co Wicklow
☎ (045) 867146
🏌 D McEvoy
⛳ 9 L 6950 yds Par 72
👭 U
£€ €16
🚗 Blessington, 15 miles SW of Dublin

Bray (1897)
Ravenswell Road, Bray
☎ (01) 286 2484
🖥 (01) 286 2484
📖 530
🏌 G Montgomery (Sec/Mgr)
✔ M Walby
⛳ 9 L 5642 m Par 70 SSS 69
👭 U before 6pm SOC–WD
£€ €24
🚗 12 miles S of Dublin

Charlesland G&CC (1993)
Greystones
☎ (01) 287 4350
🖥 (01) 287 4360
📧 teetimes@charlesland.com
📖 830
🏌 P Bradshaw (Gen Mgr)
✔ P Duignan
⛳ 18 L 6739 yds Par 72 SSS 71
👭 U SOC
£€ €45 (€60)
🚗 18 miles SE of Dublin
🏠 Eddie Hackett

Coollattin (1960)

Coollattin, Shillelagh
- ☎ **(055) 29125**
- 🖥 (055) 29125
- 📖 950
- ✍ D Byrne (Hon)
- 🏌 P Jones
- �︎ 18 L 6148 yds Par 70 SSS 69
- 👥 U
- ££ €35 (€45)
- 🚗 50 miles S of Dublin on Wicklow/Carlow border
- ⛳ Peter McEvoy

Delgany (1908)

Delgany
- ☎ **(01) 287 4536**
- 🖥 (01) 287 3977
- 📖 985
- ✍ RJ Kelly (Sec/Mgr)
- 🏌 G Kavanagh (01) 287 4697
- �︎ 18 L 6025 yds SSS 69
- 👥 U exc comp days SOC–Mon/Thurs/Fri am
- ££ €32 (€37)
- 🚗 18 miles S of Dublin, nr Greystones, off N11
- ⛳ H Vardon

Djouce (1995)

Roundwood
- ☎ **(01) 281 8585**
- 🖥 (01) 281 8522
- 📖 250
- ✍ D McGillycuddy (Mgr)
- ⏫ 9 L 6296 yds Par 71 SSS 70
- 👥 U SOC
- ££ €15 (€20)
- 🚗 15 miles NW of Wicklow (R764), off N11 at Kilmacanogue
- ⛳ Eddie Hackett

Druid's Glen (1995)

Newtownmountkennedy
- ☎ **(01) 287 3600**
- 🖥 (01) 287 3699
- 📖 200
- ✍ D Flinn (Gen Mgr)
- 🏌 E Darcy
- ⏫ 18 L 7026 yds Par 71 SSS 74
- 👥 U SOC
- ££ €104
- 🚗 20 miles S of Dublin (N11)
- ⊕ Golf Academy
- ⛳ Craddock/Ruddy

The European Club (1989)

Brittas Bay, Wicklow
- ☎ **(0404) 47415**
- 🖥 (0404) 47449
- ✉ info@theeuropeanclub.com
- 📖 120
- ✍ P Ruddy
- 🏌 None
- ⏫ 18 L 7089 yds SSS 71
- 👥 H SOC
- ££ €75 – €100
- 🚗 30 miles S of Dublin, off N11
- ⛳ Pat Ruddy

Glen of the Downs

Coolnaskeagh, Delgany, Co Wicklow
- ☎ **(01) 287 6240**
- ✍ R O'Hanrahan
- ⏫ 18 L 5891 m Par 71
- 👥 U
- ££ €51
- 🚗 Off N11, nr Delgany

Glenmalure (1993)

Greenane, Rathdrum
- ☎ **(0404) 46679**
- 🖥 (0404) 46783
- 📖 300
- ⏫ 18 L 5237 m Par 71 SSS 66
- 👥 U SOC
- ££ €18 (€21)
- 🚗 2 miles SW of Rathdrum on Glenmalure road

Greystones (1895)

Greystones
- ☎ **(01) 287 6624/4136**
- 🖥 (01) 287 3749
- ✉ secretary@greystonesgc.com
- 📖 850
- ✍ J Melody (01) 287 4136
- 🏌 K Holmes (01) 287 5308
- ⏫ 18 L 5322 m SSS 69
- 👥 WD–U
- ££ €45
- 🚗 Greystones, 18 miles S of Dublin
- ■ www.greystonesgc.com

Kilcoole (1992)

Kilcoole
- ☎ **(01) 287 2066**
- 🖥 (01) 201 0497
- ✉ adminkg@eircom.net
- 📖 375
- ✍ E Lonergan
- ⏫ 9 L 5506 m Par 70 SSS 69
- 👥 WD–U WE–NA before noon SOC–WD
- ££ €26 (€32)
- 🚗 S of Kilcoole on Newcastle road, off N11
- ⛳ Brian Williams

Old Conna (1987)

Ferndale Road, Bray
- ☎ **(01) 282 6055**
- 🖥 (01) 282 5611
- 📖 900
- ✍ D Diviney (Sec/Mgr)
- 🏌 P McDaid (01) 272 0022
- ⏫ 18 L 6551 yds SSS 72
- 👥 WD–U before 4pm WE/BH–NA SOC
- ££ €42 (€54)
- 🚗 2 miles N of Bray. 12 miles S of Dublin
- ⛳ Eddie Hackett
- ■ www.oldconna.com

Powerscourt (1996)

Powerscourt Estate, Enniskerry
- ☎ **(01) 204 6033**
- 🖥 (01) 276 1303
- ✉ golfclub@powerscourt.ie

- 📖 627
- ✍ B Gibbons (Mgr)
- 🏌 P Thompson
- ⏫ 18 L 5858 m Par 72 SSS 72
- 👥 U
- ££ €100
- 🚗 Enniskerry, 5 miles W of Bray
- ⊕ Driving range
- ⛳ Peter McEvoy
- ■ www.powerscourt.ie

Rathsallagh (1993)

Dunlavin
- ☎ **(045) 403316**
- 🖥 (045) 403295
- ✉ info@rathsallagh.com
- 📖 290
- ✍ J O'Flynn (045) 403316
- 🏌 B McDaid (045) 403316
- ⏫ 18 L 5943 m Par 72 SSS 72
- 👥 U
- ££ €75
- 🚗 14 miles S of Naas (R412)
- ⊕ Driving range
- ⛳ McEvoy/O'Connor Jr
- ■ www.rathsallagh.com

Roundwood (1995)

Ballinahinch, Newtownmountkennedy
- ☎ **(01) 281 8488**
- 🖥 (01) 284 3642
- ✍ M McGuirk
- ⏫ 18 L 6685 yds Par 72 SSS 72
- 👥 U
- ££ €41
- 🚗 15 miles NW of Wicklow (R764)

Tulfarris (1987)

Blessington Lakes
- ☎ **(045) 867644**
- 🖥 (045) 867000
- 📖 200
- ✍ A Williams (Mgr)
- 🏌 AV Williams
- ⏫ 18 L 7172 m SSS 74
- 👥 U SOC
- ££ €65 (€80)
- 🚗 30 miles S of Dublin, off N81
- ⊕ Driving range
- ⛳ Patrick Merrigan

Vartry Lakes (1997)

Proprietary
Roundwood
- ☎ **(01) 281 7006**
- 🖥 (01) 281 7006
- 📖 242
- ✍ J & A McDonald
- 🏌 None
- ⏫ 9 L 5276 m Par 70 SSS 70
- 👥 U SOC–WD/Sat
- ££ €12 (€18)
- 🚗 Roundwood village. SW of Bray, off N11
- ■ www.wicklow.ie

Wicklow (1904)

Dunbur Road, Wicklow
- ☎ **(0404) 67379**
- 📖 450
- ✍ J Kelly (Hon)

✓ D McLoughlin
⛳ 18 L 5695 m SSS 70
👫 SOC–WD/Sat
££ €28
🚗 32 miles S of Dublin, in Wicklow town
🏠 Craddock/Ruddy

Woodenbridge (1884)
Vale of Avoca, Arklow
☎ (0402) 35202
📠 (0402) 35754
📧 wgc@eircom.net
🗂 750
✎ H Crummy

⛳ 18 L 6400 yds Par 71 SSS 70
👫 U exc Sat & Thurs
££ €51 (€63)
🚗 4 miles W of Arklow. 45 miles S of Dublin
🏠 Patrick Merrigan
🖥 www.globalgolf.com

Scotland

Aberdeenshire

Aboyne (1883)
Formaston Park, Aboyne, AB34 5HP
☎ (013398) 86328
📠 (013398) 87078
📧 aboynegolf@btinternet.com
🗂 725 180(J)
✎ Mrs M MacLean (013398) 87078
✓ S Moir (013398) 86328
⛳ 18 L 5910 yds SSS 68
👫 U
££ On application
🚗 E end of Aboyne. 30 miles W of Aberdeen (A93)

Alford
Montgarrie Road, Alford, AB33 8AE
☎ (019755) 62178
📠 (019755) 62178
🗂 560
✓ None
⛳ 18 L 5483 yds Par 69 SSS 66
👫 WD–U WE–restricted on comp days SOC
££ £13 (£20)
🚗 25 miles W of Aberdeen on A944
🖥 www.golfalford.co.uk

Auchenblae (1894)
Public
Auchenblae, Laurencekirk, AB30 1TX
☎ (01561) 320002 (Bookings)
🗂 450
✎ J Thomson (01561) 320245
⛳ 9 L 2217 yds SSS 61
👫 U exc Wed & Fri 5.30–9pm
££ £9 (£12)
🚗 11 miles SW of Stonehaven. 3 miles W of A90 at Fordoun
🏠 Robin Hiseman

Ballater (1892)
Victoria Road, Ballater, AB35 5QX
☎ (013397) 55567
📠 (013397) 55057
🗂 670
✎ AE Barclay
✓ W Yule (013397) 55658
⛳ 18 L 6094 yds SSS 69
👫 U
££ On application
🚗 42 miles W of Aberdeen on A93
🖥 www.ballatergolfclub.co.uk

Banchory (1905)
Kinneskie Road, Banchory, AB31 5TA
☎ (01330) 822365
📠 (01330) 822491
📧 info@banchorygolfclub.co.uk
🗂 1000
✎ W Crighton
✓ D Naylor (01330) 822447
⛳ 18 L 5781 yds SSS 68
👫 WD–U WE–restricted
££ £20 (£23)
🚗 W of Banchory, off A93

Braemar (1902)
Cluniebank Road, Braemar, AB35 5XX
☎ (013397) 41618
🗂 300
✎ J Pennet (01224) 704471
⛳ 18 L 4916 yds SSS 64
👫 U SOC
££ £13 D–£17 (£17 D–£23) W–£60
🚗 Braemar ½ mile. 17 miles W of Ballater
🏠 J Anderson

Cruden Bay (1899)
Cruden Bay, Peterhead, AB42 0NN
☎ (01779) 812285
📠 (01779) 812945
📧 cbaygc@aol.com
🗂 1070
✎ Mrs R Pittendrigh (Sec/Mgr)
✓ RG Stewart (01779) 812414
⛳ 18 L 6395 yds SSS 72
   9 L 5106 yds SSS 65
👫 WD–U WE–H exc comp days
££ £50 D–£70 (£60)
🚗 22 miles NE of Aberdeen (A90)
⊕ Driving range
🏠 Thomas Simpson

Cullen (1879)
The Links, Cullen, Buckie, AB56 4WB
☎ (01542) 840685
📠 (01548) 841977
🗂 625
✎ LIG Findlay (01542) 840174
✓ None
⛳ 18 L 4610 yds Par 63 SSS 62
👫 U SOC
££ £12 D–£18 (£16 D–£22)
🚗 5 miles E of Buckie, off A98 between Aberdeen and Inverness
🏠 Tom Morris

Duff House Royal (1910)
The Barnyards, Banff, AB45 3SX
☎ (01261) 812062
📠 (01261) 812224
🗂 547 167(L) 132(J)
✎ Mrs J Corbett
✓ RS Strachan (01261) 812075
⛳ 18 L 6161 yds SSS 70
👫 WD–U H WE–H 8.30–11am and 12.30–3pm
££ £18–£24 (£24–£30)
🚗 Moray Firth coast, between Buckie and Fraserburgh
🏠 Dr A & Maj CA Mackenzie

Dunecht House (1925)
Dunecht, Skene, AB3 7AX
🗂 300
✎ B McIntosh (01330) 860223
⛳ 9 L 3135 yds SSS 70
👫 M
££ £8
🚗 12 miles W of Aberdeen on A944

Fraserburgh (1881)
Philorth, Fraserburgh, AB43 8TL
☎ (01346) 516616
📠 (01346) 516616
🗂 642 56(L) 119(J)
✎ J Mollison
⛳ 18 L 6308 yds SSS 70
   9 L 2400 yds Par 64
👫 U SOC
££ £17 D–£22 (£22 D–£27)
🚗 1 mile SE of Fraserburgh
🏠 James Braid
🖥 www.fraserburghgolfclub.net

Huntly (1892)
Cooper Park, Huntly, AB54 4SH
☎ (01466) 792643
📠 (01466) 792643
🗂 800
✎ EA Stott (01466) 792360
✓ (01466) 794181 (Shop)
⛳ 18 L 5399 yds SSS 66
👫 U SOC
££ £12 D–£18 (£18 D–£24) W–£65
🚗 N side of Huntly. 38 miles NW of Aberdeen, off A96
🖥 www.huntlygc.com

Inchmarlo (1995)
Glassel Road, Banchory, AB31 4BQ
- ☎ **(01330) 822557**
- ✎ HG Emsie (Gen Mgr)
  (01330) 822557 Ext 11
- ✓ P Lowe (01330) 822557 Ext 20
- ⊳ 18 L 6218 yds Par 71 SSS 70
  9 L 4300 yds Par 64 SSS 62
- 👥 U H SOC–WD
- ££ 18 hole:£30 (£35) 9 hole:£10 (£11)
- ⊛ ¹/₂ mile W of Banchory on A93
- ⊕ Floodlit driving range
- 🏠 Graeme Webster
- ▪ www.inchmarlo.com

Insch
Golf Terrace, Insch, AB52 6JY
- ☎ **(01464) 820363**
- 📠 (01464) 820363
- ✎ C McLachlan
- ⊳ 18 L 5350 yds SSS 67
- 👥 U
- ££ On application
- ⊛ 28 miles NW of Aberdeen, off A96

Inverallochy
Public
Whitelink, Inverallochy, Fraserburgh, AB43 8XY
- ☎ **(01346) 582000**
- 📖 400
- ✎ GM Young
- ✓ None
- ⊳ 18 L 5300 yds SSS 66
- 👥 U
- ££ D–£12 (£15)
- ⊛ 4 miles E of Fraserburgh, off A92

Inverurie (1923)
Blackhall Road, Inverurie, AB51 5JB
- ☎ **(01467) 620207**
- 📠 (01467) 621051
- ✉ administrator@inveruriegc.co.uk
- 📖 511 130(L)
- ✎ B Rogerson (01467) 624080
- ✓ M Lees (01467) 620193
- ⊳ 18 L 5711 yds SSS 68
- 👥 U SOC
- ££ £16 D–£20 (£20 D–£26)
- ⊛ 1 mile W of Inverurie. 16 miles NW of Aberdeen
- ▪ www.inveruriegc.co.uk

Keith (1963)
Mar Court, Fife Keith, Keith, AB55 5GF
- ☎ **(01542) 882469**
- 📠 (01542) 888176
- 📖 250
- ⊳ 18 L 5802 yds SSS 68
- 👥 U
- ££ £15 (£20)
- ⊛ Fife Park, W side of Keith

Kemnay (1908)
Monymusk Road, Kemnay, AB51 5RA
- ☎ **(01467) 642060 (Clubhouse),
  (01467) 643746 (Office)**
- 📠 (01467) 643746
- 📖 820
- ✎ B Robertson
- ✓ R McDonald (01647) 642225
- ⊳ 18 L 6342 yds Par 71 SSS 71
- 👥 U
- ££ £18 D–£24 (£22 D–£28)
- ⊛ 15 miles W of Aberdeen (B994, off A96)
- ▪ www.kemnaygolfclub.co.uk

Kintore (1911)
Balbithan Road, Kintore, AB51 0UR
- ☎ **(01467) 632631**
- 📠 (01467) 632995
- ✉ kintoregolfclub@lineone.net
- 📖 700
- ✎ J Black
- ⊳ 18 L 6019 yds SSS 69
- 👥 U
- ££ £13 (£19)
- ⊛ 12 miles NW of Aberdeen on A96

Longside
West End, Longside, Peterhead, AB42 7XJ
- ☎ **(01779) 821558**
- 📠 (01779) 821564
- 📖 569
- ✎ K Allan (01771) 622424
- ✓ None
- ⊳ 18 L 5225 yds Par 66 SSS 66
- 👥 U exc Sun–NA before 10.30am SOC
- ££ £10 D–£14 Sun–£15 D–£20
- ⊛ 5 miles W of Peterhead on A590

Lumphanan (1924)
10 Main Road, Lumphanan, Banchory, AB31 4PY
- ☎ **(013398) 83480**
- ✉ lumphanan.golf.club@lineone.net
- ✎ Mrs PA Thorn (013398) 83589
- ⊳ 9 L 3718 yds Par 62 SSS 62
- 👥 U
- ££ £6 D–£10 (£8 D–£14)
- ⊛ 25 miles W of Aberdeen on A980
- ▪ www.lineone.net~lumphanan.golf.club

McDonald (1927)
Hospital Road, Ellon, AB41 9AW
- ☎ **(01358) 720576**
- 📠 (01358) 720001
- ✉ mcdonald.golf@virgin.net
- 📖 750
- ✎ IA Shaw
- ✓ R Urquhart (01358) 722891
- ⊳ 18 L 5991 yds Par 70 SSS 70
- 👥 U
- ££ On application
- ⊛ 15 miles N of Aberdeen, off A90
- ▪ www.freespace.virgin.net/mcdonald.golf

Meldrum House (1998)
Meldrum House Estate, Oldmeldrum, AB51 0AE
- ☎ **(01651) 873553**
- 📠 (01651) 873635
- 📖 400
- ✎ J Caven (Golf Dir)
- ✓ N Marr
- ⊳ 18 L 6379 yds Par 70 SSS 72
- 👥 M
- ££ N/A
- ⊛ 11 miles N of Aberdeen on A947
- 🏠 Graeme Webster
- ▪ www.meldrumhouse.co.uk

Newburgh-on-Ythan (1888)
Newburgh, AB41 6BE
- ☎ **(01358) 789058**
- ✉ secretary@newburgh-on-ythan.co.uk
- 📖 540 60(L) 80(J)
- ✎ RV Bruce (01358) 789084
- ✓ None
- ⊳ 18 L 6162 yds SSS 71
- 👥 U exc Tues after 3pm & Sat before 1pm–NA
- ££ £16 (£21)
- ⊛ 12 miles N of Aberdeen (A975)
- ⊕ Driving range
- ▪ www.newburgh-on-ythan.co.uk

Newmachar (1989)
Swailend, Newmachar, Aberdeen, AB21 7UU
- ☎ **(01651) 863002**
- 📠 (01651) 863055
- ✉ newmachargolfclub@aol.com
- 📖 999
- ✎ DS Wade
- ✓ G Simpson (01651) 862127
- ⊳ 18 L 6659 yds Par 72 SSS 74
  18 L 6388 yds Par 72 SSS 71
- 👥 H SOC
- ££ Hawkshill £30 (£40) Swailend £15 (£20)
- ⊛ 12 miles N of Aberdeen on A947
- ⊕ Driving range
- 🏠 Dave Thomas
- ▪ www.newmachargolfclub.co.uk

Oldmeldrum (1885)
Kirk Brae, Oldmeldrum, AB51 0DJ
- ☎ **(01651) 872648/873555**
- 📠 (01651) 873555
- 📖 800
- ✎ J Page (01651) 872315
- ✓ H Love (01651) 873555
- ⊳ 18 L 5988 yds Par 70 SSS 69
- 👥 WD–U before 5pm WE–phone first
- ££ £14 (D–£24)
- ⊛ 17 miles N of Aberdeen on A947

Peterhead (1841)
Craigewan Links, Peterhead, AB42 1LT
- ☎ **(01779) 472149/480725**
- 📠 (01779) 480725
- ✉ phdgc@freenetname.co.uk
- 📖 500 45(L)
- ⊳ 18 L 6173 yds SSS 71
  9 L 2237 yds SSS 62
- 👥 U exc Sat–restricted
- ££ On application
- ⊛ 1 mile N of Peterhead
- 🏠 Willie Park Jr/James Braid

Rosehearty
c/o Mason's Arms Hotel, Rosehearty, Fraserburgh, AB43 7JJ
- ☎ **(01346) 571250 (Capt)**
- 📠 (01346) 571306
- 📖 220
- ✎ S Hornal
- ⊳ 9 L 2197 yds SSS 62

🐎 U
£€ D–£10 (D–£12)
🚗 4 miles W of Fraserburgh (B9031)

Rothes (1990)
Blackhall, Rothes, Aberlour, AB38 7AN
☎ (01340) 831443
🖥 (01340) 831443
📖 340
🏌 None
🏁 9 L 4972 yds Par 68 SSS 64
🐎 U
£€ £12 (£15)
🚗 ¹/₂ mile SW of Rothes. 10 miles S of Elgin on A941
🏠 John Souter

Royal Tarlair (1926)
Buchan Street, Macduff, AB44 1TA
☎ (01261) 832897
🖥 (01261) 833455
📧 info@royaltarlair.co.uk
📖 520
🏁 Mrs C Davidson
🏁 18 L 5866 yds SSS 68
🐎 U
£€ £15 D–£20
🚗 Macduff, 4 miles E of Banff. 45 miles E of Aberdeen
■ www.royaltarlair.co.uk

Stonehaven (1888)
Cowie, Stonehaven, AB39 3RH
☎ (01569) 762124
🖥 (01569) 765973
📧 stonehaven.golfclub@virgin.net
📖 500
🏁 WA Donald
🏌 None
🏁 18 L 5128 yds Par 66 SSS 65
🐎 Sat–NA before 3.45pm Sun–NA before 10.45am
£€ £16 (£22)
🚗 1 mile N of Stonehaven
🏠 A Simpson

Strathlene (1877)
Portessie, Buckie, AB56 2DJ
☎ (01542) 831798
🖥 (01542) 831798
📖 400
🏁 G Jappy
🏁 18 L 5977 yds SSS 69
🐎 U SOC
£€ D–£15 (D–£15)
🚗 ¹/₂ mile E of Buckie
🏠 G Smith
■ www.scottishholidays.net/strathlene

Tarland (1908)
Aberdeen Road, Tarland, AB34 4TB
☎ (013398) 81000
🖥 (013398) 81000
📖 400
🏁 Mrs L Ward (013398) 81967
🏁 9 L 5875 yds SSS 68
🐎 WD–U WE–enquiry advisable SOC–WD only
£€ £15 (£20)
🚗 5 miles NW of Aboyne. 30 miles W of Aberdeen
🏠 Tom Morris

Torphins (1896)
Bog Road, Torphins, AB31 4JU
☎ (013398) 82115
🖥 (013398) 82402
📧 stuart@macgregor5.fsnet.co.uk
📖 370
🏁 S MacGregor (013398) 82402
🏁 9 L 4738 yds SSS 64
🐎 U SOC
£€ £13 (£14)
🚗 1¹/₂ miles W of Torphins towards Lumphanan

Turriff (1896)
Rosehall, Turriff, AB53 4HD
☎ (01888) 562982
🖥 (01888) 568050
📧 grace@turriffgolf.scl.co.uk
📖 794
🏁 B Cook
🏌 JR Black (01888) 563025
🏁 18 L 6145 yds SSS 69
🐎 H WE–NA before 10am SOC
£€ £18 D–£22 (£22 D–£28)
🚗 35 miles N of Aberdeen (A947)
🏠 GM Fraser
■ www.turriffgolfclub.free-online.co.uk

Aberdeen Clubs

Bon Accord (1872)
Club
19 Golf Road, Aberdeen, AB2 1QB
☎ (01224) 633464
📖 450
🏁 FN Shand
🏁 Play over King's Links

Caledonian (1899)
Club
20 Golf Road, Aberdeen, AB2 1QB
☎ (01224) 632443
📖 620
🏁 JA Bridgeford
🏁 Play over King's Links

Northern (1897)
Club
King's Links, Aberdeen, AB24 5BQ
☎ (01224) 636440
🖥 (01224) 622679
📖 561
🏁 AW Garner
🏁 Play over King's Links

Aberdeen Courses

Auchmill (1975)
Bonnyview Road, West Heatheryfold, Aberdeen, AB2 7FQ
☎ (01224) 715214
📖 300
🏁 G Adams (01224) 715214
🏌 None
🏁 18 L 5883 yds Par 70 SSS 68
🐎 U

£€ On application
🚗 3 miles NW of Aberdeen city centre
🏠 Coles/Huggett

Balnagask (1955)
Public
St Fitticks Road, Aberdeen
☎ (01224) 871286
🖥 (01224) 873418
🏁 A Fraser
🏌 None
🏁 18 L 5472 metres SSS 69
🐎 U SOC
£€ £9 (£11.25)
🚗 1¹/₂ miles SE of Aberdeen

Deeside (1903)
Golf Road, Bieldside, Aberdeen, AB15 9DL
☎ (01224) 869457
🖥 (01224) 869457
📧 dgc@bieldside28.freeserve.co.uk
📖 1100
🏁 JW Keepe (Sec/Mgr) (01224) 869457
🏌 FJ Coutts (01224) 861041
🏁 18 L 6264 yds SSS 70
   9 L 3316 yds SSS 36
🐎 H
£€ £45 (£60)
🚗 3 miles SW of Aberdeen on A93

Hazlehead (1927)
Public
Hazlehead Park, Aberdeen, AB15 8BD
☎ (01224) 321830
🏌 I Smith
🏁 18 L 5673 metres SSS 70
   18 L 5303 metres SSS 68
   9 L 2531 metres SSS 34
🐎 U
£€ £9 (£11.25)
🚗 4 miles W of Aberdeen

King's Links
Public
Golf Road, King's Links, Aberdeen, AB24 5QB
☎ (01224) 632269
🏌 B Davidson (01224) 641577
🏁 18 L 5838 metres SSS 71
🐎 U
£€ £9.50 (£11.50)
🚗 1 mile E of Aberdeen
⊕ Driving range. Bon Accord, Caledonian and Northern Clubs play here

Murcar (1909)
Bridge of Don, Aberdeen, AB23 8BD
☎ (01224) 704354
🖥 (01224) 704354
📧 murcar-golf-club@lineone.net
📖 850
🏁 Barbara Rogerson (01224) 704354
🏌 G Forbes (01224) 704370
🏁 18 L 6287 yds SSS 71
   9 L 5369 yds SSS 67
🐎 H
£€ £45 (£55)
🚗 5 miles N of Aberdeen, off A90

A Simpson
www.murcar.co.uk

Peterculter (1989)

Oldtown, Burnside Road, Peterculter, AB14 0LN
- ☎ **(01224) 735245**
- 🖬 (01224) 735580
- ✉ info@peterculturgolfclub.co.uk
- 📖 925
- ✍ D Vannet (Mgr)
- ✓ D Vannet (01224) 734994
- ⊳ 18 L 6207 yds SSS 70
- 🕴 WD–U before 4pm WE–U SOC
- ££ £18–£24 (£20–£26)
- ⚬ 8 miles W of Aberdeen on A93
- ■ www.petercultergolfclub.co.uk

Portlethen (1983)

Badentoy Road, Portlethen, Aberdeen, AB12 4YA
- ☎ **(01224) 781090**
- 🖬 (01224) 781090
- 📖 1100
- ✓ Muriel Thomson (01224) 782571
- ⊳ 18 L 6670 yds SSS 72
- 🕴 WD–U exc Wed after 2pm Sat–NA before 4pm Sun–NA before 1pm
- ££ £15 D–£22 (£22)
- ⚬ 6 miles S of Aberdeen on A90
- 🕴 Donald Steel

Royal Aberdeen (1780)

Links Road, Bridge of Don, Aberdeen, AB23 8AT
- ☎ **(01224) 702571**
- 🖬 (01224) 826591
- ✉ admin@royalaberdeengolf.com
- 📖 350 100(J)
- ✍ GF Webster
- ✓ R MacAskill (Golf Dir) (01224) 702221
- ⊳ 18 L 6415 yds SSS 73 18 L 4066 yds SSS 60
- 🕴 I H SOC
- ££ £65 D–£90 (£75)
- ⚬ 2 miles N of Aberdeen on A90
- 🕴 Simpson/Braid
- ■ www.royalaberdeengolf.com

Westhill (1977)

Westhill Heights, Westhill, AB32 6RY
- ☎ **(01224) 742567**
- 🖬 (01224) 749124
- 📖 900
- ✍ Amelia Burt (Admin)
- ✓ G Bruce (01224) 740159
- ⊳ 18 L 5849 yds SSS 69
- 🕴 WD–U before 4.30pm Sat–M Sun–U
- ££ £14 D–£20 (£20 D–£25)
- ⚬ 8 miles W of Aberdeen, off A944
- 🕴 Charles Lawrie

Angus

Arbroath Artisan (1903)

Public
Elliot, Arbroath, DD11 2PE
- ☎ **(01241) 872069, (01241) 875837 (Bookings)**

🖬 (01241) 875837
📖 650
✍ J Knox
✓ L Ewart (01241) 875837
⊳ 18 L 6185 yds Par 70 SSS 69
🕴 WD–U SOC WE–NA before 10am
££ £18 D–£24 (£24 D–£32)
⚬ 1 mile SW of Arbroath on A92
🕴 James Braid

Brechin (1893)

Trinity, Brechin, DD9 7PD
- ☎ **(01356) 622383**
- 🖬 (01356) 626925
- 📖 650
- ✍ IA Jardine
- ✓ S Rennie (01356) 625270
- ⊳ 18 L 6200 yds SSS 70
- 🕴 U exc Wed SOC
- ££ £20 D–£28 (£25 D–£33)
- ⚬ 1 mile N of Brechin on B90

Caird Park (1926)

Public
Mains Loan, Caird Park, Dundee, DD4 9BX
- ☎ **(01382) 453606, (01382) 438871 (Starter)**
- 📖 350
- ✍ G Martin (01382) 461460
- ✓ J Black (01382) 459438
- ⊳ 18 L 6303 yds SSS 70 Yellow 9 L 1692 yds SSS 29 Red 9 L 1983 yds SSS 29
- 🕴 U SOC
- ££ Contact Starter
- ⚬ Off Kingsway by-pass, N of Dundee

Camperdown (1960)

Public
Camperdown Park, Dundee, DD4 9BX
- ☎ **(01382) 623398**
- 📖 250
- ✍ L Smith (01382) 815691
- ✓ R Brown (01382) 623398
- ⊳ 18 L 6561 yds SSS 72
- 🕴 U
- ££ £18 (£18)
- ⚬ 2 miles NW of Dundee (A923)

Downfield (1932)

Turnberry Ave, Dundee, DD2 3QP
- ☎ **(01382) 825595**
- 🖬 (01382) 813111
- ✉ downfieldgc@aol.com
- 📖 750
- ✍ Mrs M Stewart
- ✓ KS Hutton (01382) 889246
- ⊳ 18 L 6822 yds SSS 73
- 🕴 WD–U 9.30–noon and 2.18–3.42pm WE–limited access after 2pm
- ££ £16–£31 D–£26–£46 (£21–£36)
- ⚬ N of Dundee, off A923
- ■ www.downfieldgolf.co.uk

Edzell (1895)

High St, Edzell, DD9 7TF
- ☎ **(01356) 647283**
- 🖬 (01356) 648094

✉ secretary@edzellgolfclub.demon .co.uk
📖 700
✍ IG Farquhar (01356) 647283
✓ AJ Webster (01356) 648462
⊳ 18 L 6367 yds SSS 71 9 L 2057 yds Par 32
🕴 WD–NA 4.45–6.15pm WE–NA 7.30–10am & 12–2pm SOC
££ £24 D–£34 (£30 D–£44)
⚬ 6 miles N of Brechin on B966
⊕ Driving range
🕴 Bob Simpson

Forfar (1871)

Cunninghill, Arbroath Road, Forfar, DD8 2RL
- ☎ **(01307) 462120**
- 🖬 (01307) 468495
- 📖 520 150(L) 100(J)
- ✍ W Baird (01307) 463773
- ✓ P McNiven (01307) 465683
- ⊳ 18 L 6066 yds Par 69 SSS 70
- 🕴 U exc Sat SOC
- ££ £22 (£28)
- ⚬ 1½ miles E of Forfar on A932
- 🕴 Tom Morris/James Braid

Kirriemuir (1884)

Northmuir, Kirriemuir, DD8 4PN
- ☎ **(01575) 572144 (Clubhouse), (01575) 573317 (Starter)**
- 🖬 (01575) 574608
- 📖 850
- ✍ C Gowrie
- ✓ Mrs K Dallas (01575) 573317
- ⊳ 18 L 5510 yds SSS 67
- 🕴 WD–U WE–by arrangement SOC
- ££ £20 D–£26 (£25 D–£32)
- ⚬ NE outskirts of Kirriemuir. 17 miles N of Dundee
- 🕴 James Braid

Letham Grange (1987)

Letham Grange, Colliston, Arbroath, DD11 4RL
- ☎ **(01241) 890377**
- 🖬 (01241) 890725
- 📖 780
- ✍ D Speed
- ✓ Shop (01241) 890377
- ⊳ Old 18 L 6968 yds SSS 73 Glens 18 L 5528 yds SSS 68
- 🕴 WD–U WE–U after 10.30am SOC
- ££ Old £35 D–£40 (£35 D–£55) Glens £18 D–£20 (£20 D–£30)
- ⚬ 4 miles NW of Arbroath on A993
- 🕴 Old-Steel/Smith. New-T MacAuley

Monifieth Golf Links

Medal Starter's Box, Princes Street, Monifieth, DD5 4AW
- ☎ **(01382) 532767 (Medal), (01382) 532967 (Ashludie)**
- 🖬 (01382) 535553
- 📖 1700
- ✍ S Fyffe (01382) 535553
- ✓ I McLeod (01382) 532945
- ⊳ Medal 18 L 6650 yds SSS 72 Ashludie 18 L 5123 SSS 66
- 🕴 WD–U Sat–NA before 2pm Sun–NA before 10am SOC

For list of abbreviations and key to symbols see page 649

££   Medal £35 (£45). Ashludie £17
(£20). Medal+Ashludie £55 inc
catering
👟   6 miles E of Dundee
⊕   Abertay, Broughty, Grange/Dundee
and Monifieth clubs play here
■   www.monifiethgolf.co.uk

Montrose   (1562)
Public
Traill Drive, Montrose, DD10 8SW
☎   **(01674) 672932**
🖥   (01674) 671800
📧   secretary@montroselinks.co.uk
📖   1300
🏌   Mrs M Stewart
✓   J Boyd (01674) 672634
ⱶ   Medal 18 L 6544 yds SSS 72
Broomfield 18 L 4830 yds SSS 63
👤   Medal–WD–U Sat–NA before
2.30pm Sun–NA before 10am
Broomfield–U
££   Medal £32 (£36) Broomfield £16
(£18)
👟   1 mile from Montrose centre, off
A92
⊕   Royal Montrose, Caledonia and
Mercantile clubs play here
⌂   Willie Park (1903)
■   www.montroselinks.co.uk

Montrose Caledonia
(1896)
Club
Dorward Road, Montrose, DD10 8SW
☎   **(01674) 672313**
🏌   M Watson (01674) 672891
ⱶ   Play over Montrose courses

Montrose Mercantile
Club
East Links, Montrose, DD10 8SW
☎   **(01674) 672408**
📖   980
🏌   R Alexander (01674) 675716
ⱶ   Play over Montrose courses

Panmure   (1845)
Barry, Carnoustie, DD7 7RT
☎   **(01241) 853120**
🖥   (01241) 859737
📖   500
🏌   Maj (Retd) GW Paton
(01241) 855120
✓   N Mackintosh (01241) 852460
ⱶ   18 L 6317 yds Par 70 SSS 71
👤   WD/Sun–U Sat–NA
££   On application
👟   2 miles W of Carnoustie, off
A930

Royal Montrose   (1810)
Club
*Dorward Road, Montrose,
DD10 8SW*
☎   **(01674) 672376**
📖   650
🏌   JD Sykes (01674) 672785
ⱶ   Play over Montrose courses

Carnoustie Clubs

Carnoustie   (1842)
Club
3 Links Parade, Carnoustie, DD7 7JE
☎   **(01241) 852480**
🖥   (01241) 856459
📧   admin@carnoustiegolfclub.com
📖   900
🏌   WH Law
ⱶ   Play over Carnoustie courses

Carnoustie Caledonia   (1887)
Club
Links Parade, Carnoustie, DD7 7JF
☎   **(01241) 852115**
📖   640
🏌   JSB Robinson
ⱶ   Play over Carnoustie courses

Carnoustie Ladies   (1873)
Club
12 Links Parade, Carnoustie, DD7 7JF
☎   **(01241) 855252**
📖   96
🏌   Mrs JM Mitchell (01241) 855035
ⱶ   Play over Carnoustie courses

Carnoustie Mercantile
(1896)
Club
Links Parade, Carnoustie, DD7 7JE
📖   30
🏌   DG Ogilvie
ⱶ   Play over Carnoustie courses

Dalhousie   (1868)
Club
*c/o Glencoe Hotel, Links Parade,
Carnoustie, DD7 7JF*
☎   **(01241) 853273**
📖   150
🏌   WM Osler
ⱶ   Play over Carnoustie courses

Carnoustie Courses

Buddon Links   (1981)
Public
Links Parade, Carnoustie, DD7 7JE
☎   **(01241) 853249 (Starter),
(01241) 853789 (Bookings)**
🖥   (01241) 853720
🏌   G Duncan
ⱶ   18 L 5420 yds SSS 66
👤   WD–U WE–U after 11am
££   £20
👟   12 miles E of Dundee, by A92 or
A930

Burnside   (1914)
Public
Links Parade, Carnoustie, DD7 7JE
☎   **(01241) 855344 (Starter),
(01241) 853789 (Bookings)**
🖥   (01241) 853720
🏌   G Duncan
ⱶ   18 L 6020 yds SSS 69
👤   WD–U Sat–U after 2pm Sun–U
after 11.30am

££   £25
👟   12 miles E of Dundee, by A92 or
A930

Carnoustie Championship
(16th)
Public
Links Parade, Carnoustie, DD7 7JE
☎   **(01241) 853249 (Starter),
(01241) 853789 (Bookings)**
🖥   (01241) 853720
🏌   G Duncan
ⱶ   18 L 6941 yds SSS 75
👤   WD–H Sat–H after 2pm Sun–H
after 11.30am
££   £80
👟   12 miles E of Dundee, by A92 or
A930

Argyll & Bute

Blairmore & Strone   (1896)
High Road, Strone, Dunoon, PA23 8JJ
☎   **(01369) 840676**
📖   120
🏌   JC Fleming (01369) 860307
ⱶ   9 L 2122 yds SSS 62
👤   Mon–NA after 6pm Sat–NA
12–4pm
££   D–£10
👟   Strone, 8 miles N of Dunoon
⌂   James Braid

Bute   (1888)
*32 Marine Parade, Ardbeg, Rothesay,
Isle of Bute PA20 0LF*
📖   234
🏌   F Robinson (01700) 502158
ⱶ   9 L 2497 yds SSS 64
👤   U Sat–U after 11.30am
££   D–£8
👟   Stravanan Bay, 6 miles S of
Rothesay, off A845

Carradale   (1906)
Carradale, Campbeltown, PA28 6SA
☎   **(01583) 431321**
📖   324
🏌   Dr RJ Abernethy
✓   None
ⱶ   9 L 2370 yds SSS 64
👤   U
££   D–£10
👟   Carradale, 15 miles N of
Campbeltown (B842)

Colonsay
Owned privately
Isle of Colonsay, PA61 7YP
☎   **(019512) 316**
📖   100
🏌   K Byrne
ⱶ   18 L 4775 yds Par 72
👤   U
££   On application
👟   W coast of Colonsay, at Machrins

Cowal (1891)
Ardenslate Road, Dunoon, PA23 8LT
☎ **(01369) 705673**
🖥 (01369) 705673
✉ info@cowalgolfclub.co.uk
📖 900
✍ Mrs W Fraser (01369) 705673
⚐ RD Weir (01369) 702395
↦ 18 L 6063 yds SSS 70
👥 U
£€ £15 (£25)
⛳ NE boundary of Dunoon
🏠 James Braid (1928)

Craignure (1895)
Scallastle, Craignure, Isle of Mull, PA64 5AP
☎ **(01680) 300402**
✉ Mullair@btinternet.com
📖 102
✍ DS Howitt
↦ 9 L 5357 yds SSS 66
👥 U
£€ D–£15
⛳ 1 mile N of Craignure Ferry Terminal (Oban 40mins)

Dalmally (1986)
Old Saw Mill, Dalmally, PA33 1AS
☎ **(01838) 200370**
📖 120
✍ AJ Burke (01838) 200370
⚐ None
↦ 9 L 2277 yds Par 64 SSS 63
👥 U SOC
£€ R/D–£10
⛳ 1 mile W of Dalmally on A85
■ www.loch-awe.com/golfclub

Dunaverty (1889)
Southend, Campbeltown, PA28 6RF
☎ **(01586) 830677**
🖥 (01586) 830677
📖 430
✍ B Brannigan (Hon)
↦ 18 L 4799 yds SSS 63
👥 U
£€ £15 (£18)
⛳ 10 miles S of Campbeltown
■ www.redrival.com/dunaverty

Gigha (1992)
Isle of Gigha, Kintyre, PA41 7AA
☎ **(01583) 505242**
📖 30
✍ J Bannatyne
↦ 9 L 5042 yds SSS 65
👥 U
£€ D–£10
⛳ Off W coast of Kintyre

Glencruitten (1908)
Glencruitten Road, Oban, PA34 4PU
☎ **(01631) 562868**
📖 400
✍ AG Brown (01631) 564604
⚐ Shop (01631) 564115
↦ 18 L 4452 yds SSS 63
👥 U
£€ £17 (£20)

⛳ Oban 1 mile
🏠 James Braid

Helensburgh (1893)
25 East Abercromby Street, Helensburgh, G84 9HZ
☎ **(01436) 674173**
🖥 (01436) 671170
✉ thesecretary@helensburghgolfclub .org.uk
📖 863
✍ K Print (01436) 674173
⚐ D Fotheringham (01436) 675505
↦ 18 L 6104 yds Par 69 SSS 70
👥 WD–U WE–NA
£€ £25 D–£35
⛳ N of Helensburgh and A814. 8 miles W of Dumbarton
🏠 Tom Morris

Innellan (1891)
Knockamillie Road, Innellan, Dunoon
☎ **(01369) 830242**
📖 200
✍ A Wilson (01369) 702573
↦ 9 L 4878 yds SSS 64
👥 U SOC
£€ 18 holes–£12. 9 holes–£8
⛳ 4 miles S of Dunoon (A815)

Inveraray (1893)
North Cromalt, Inveraray, Argyll
☎ **(01499) 302508**
📖 175
✍ R Finnan
↦ 9 L 5600 yds SSS 68
👥 U SOC
£€ £10
⛳ 1 mile S of Inveraray on A83

Islay (1891)
Western Cottage, Port Ellen, Isle of Islay, PA42 7AT
☎ **(01496) 302409**
📖 400
✍ T Dunn
↦ 18 L 6226 yds SSS 70
👥 U SOC
£€ £30
⛳ Machrie, 5 miles N of Port Ellen
⊕ Driving range
🏠 Willie Campbell
■ www.islay.golf.btinternet.co.uk

Isle of Seil (1996)
Pay and play
Balvicar, Isle of Seil, PA34 4TL
☎ **(01852) 300348**
🖥 (01852) 300392
✉ b.r.m@tesco.net
📖 80
✍ B Mitchell
⚐ None
↦ 9 L 2335 yds Par 32
👥 U
£€ D–£6
⛳ 13 miles S of Oban on B844
🏠 Donald Campbell

Kyles of Bute (1906)
Tighnabruaich, PA21 2EE
☎ **(01700) 811603**
📖 160
✍ Dr J Thomson
↦ 9 L 2389 yds SSS 32
👥 U
£€ D–£10
⛳ 26 miles W of Dunoon

Lochgilphead (1963)
Blarbuie Road, Lochgilphead, PA31 8LE
☎ **(01546) 602340**
📖 250
✍ D MacVicar (01546) 602659
↦ 9 L 4484 yds SSS 63
👥 U SOC
£€ D–£10 (D–£10)
⛳ 1/2 mile N of Lochgilphead by Hospital

Lochgoilhead (1994)
Drymsynie Estates, Lochgoilhead, PA24 8AD
☎ **(01301) 703247**
🖥 (01301) 703538
⚐ None
↦ 9 L 1900 yds Par 60
👥 N of Lochgoilhead, off Rest & Be Thankful Road
£€ On application

Machrihanish (1876)
Machrihanish, Campbeltown, PA28 6PT
☎ **(01586) 810213**
🖥 (01586) 810221
📖 742 152(L) 178(J)
✍ Mrs A Anderson
⚐ K Campbell (01586) 810277
↦ 18 L 6225 yds SSS 71
9 hole course
👥 U
£€ £30 D–£50 exc Sat £40 D–£60
⛳ 5 miles W of Campbeltown

Millport (1888)
Millport, Isle of Cumbrae, KA28 0HB
☎ **(01475) 530311**
🖥 (01475) 530306
📖 288 120(L) 78(J)
✍ D Donnelly (01475) 530306
⚐ H Lee (01475) 530305
↦ 18 L 5828 yds SSS 69
👥 U SOC
£€ £20 D–£25 (£25 D–£31) W–£60
⛳ W of Millport (Largs car ferry)
🏠 James Braid

Port Bannatyne (1912)
Bannatyne Mains Road, Port Bannatyne, Isle of Bute, PA20 0PH
☎ **(01700) 504544**
📖 150
✍ Mrs BK Burnett (01700) 505142
↦ 13 L 5085 yds Par 68 SSS 65
👥 U
£€ £11 (£16)
⛳ 2 miles N of Rothesay
🏠 Peter Morrison

Rothesay (1892)

Canada Hill, Rothesay, Isle of Bute, PA20 9HN
☎ (01700) 503554
🖷 (01700) 503554
✉ pro@rothesaygolfclub.com
🕮 500
✓ J Dougal (01700) 503554
🏳 18 L 5395 yds SSS 66
🕅 WD–U WE–book with Pro SOC
££ On application
⛳ 1 mile E of Rothesay
⊕ Practice range
🏠 Braid/Sayers
■ www.rothesaygolfclub.com

Tarbert (1910)

Kilberry Road, Tarbert, PA29 6XX
☎ (01880) 820565
🕮 101
🏌 P Cupples
🏳 9 L 4460 yds SSS 63
🕅 U SOC
££ D–£10 W–£30
⛳ 1 mile W of Tarbert on B8024, off A83

Taynuilt (1987)

Taynuilt, PA35 1JE
☎ (01866) 822429
🖷 (01866) 822255 (phone first)
✉ michael.urwin@which.net
🏌 MJP Urwin (Hon) (01866) 833341
🏳 9 L 4510 yds Par 64 SSS 63
🕅 U
££ D–£10
⛳ 12 miles E of Oban on A85

Tobermory (1896)

Erray Road, Tobermory, Isle of Mull, PA75 6PS
🖷 (01688) 302140
🕮 180
🏌 J Weir (01688) 302338
🏳 9 L 2492 yds SSS 64
🕅 U
££ D–£13 W–£55
⛳ Tobermory, Isle of Mull
⊕ Tickets from Western Isles Hotel, Brown's shop and Fairways Lodge.
🏠 David Adams

Vaul (1920)

Scarinish, Isle of Tiree, PA77 6TP
🕮 100
🏌 P Campbell (01879) 220334
🏳 9 L 2837 yds Par 72 SSS 68
🕅 U
££ On application
⛳ 3 miles N of Scarinish, E end of Tiree. 40 min flight from Glasgow

Ayrshire

Annanhill (1957)

Public
Irvine Road, Kilmarnock, KA3 2RT
☎ (01563) 521512 (Starter)

🕮 350
🏌 T Denham (01563) 521644/525557
🏳 18 L 6270 yds SSS 70
🕅 WD/Sun–U Sat–NA SOC–exc Sat
££ On application
⛳ 1 mile N of Kilmarnock
🏠 J McLean

Ardeer (1880)

Greenhead Avenue, Stevenston, KA20 4JX
☎ (01294) 464542/465316
🖷 (01294) 465316
🕮 700
🏌 P Watson (01294) 465316
✓ R Summerfield (Starter) (01294) 601327
🏳 18 L 6409 yds SSS 72
🕅 U exc Sat–NA SOC–WD
££ £18 D–£30 Sun–£25 D–£40
⛳ 1/2 mile N of Stevenston, off A78
🏠 H Stutt

Auchenharvie (1981)

Public
Moor Park Road, West Brewery Park, Saltcoats, KA20 3HU
☎ (01294) 603103
🕮 50
🏌 W White (01294) 603775
✓ R Rodgers
🏳 9 L 5300 yds Par 66 SSS 65
🕅 WD–U WE–U after 9.30am
££ £5.50 (£7.30)
⛳ Low road between Saltcoats and Stevenston
⊕ Driving range

Ballochmyle (1937)

Ballochmyle, Mauchline, KA5 6LE
☎ (01290) 550469
🖷 (01290) 553657
🕮 750
🏌 RL Crawford
✓ None
🏳 18 L 5952 yds SSS 69
🕅 WD/WE–U BH–M SOC exc Sat
££ On application
⛳ 1 mile S of Mauchline on B705, off A76

Beith (1896)

Threepwood Road, Beith, KA15 2JR
☎ (01505) 503166 (Clubhouse)
🖷 (01505) 506814
🕮 400
🏌 M Murphy (01505) 506814 (am only)
🏳 18 L 4625 yds SSS 68
🕅 WD–U exc Tues–NA after 5pm Sat–NA before 2pm Sun–NA 1.30–2.30pm
££ £18 (£25)
⛳ Off Beith By-pass on A737

Belleisle (1927)

Public
Bellisle Park, Doonfoot Road, Ayr, KA7 4DU
☎ (01292) 441258
🖷 (01292) 442632

✓ D Gemmell (01292) 441314
🏳 18 L 6477 yds SSS 72
🕅 U SOC
££ £18 (£25)
⛳ S of Ayr in Belleisle Park
🏠 James Braid
■ www.golfsouthayrshire.com

Brodick (1897)

Brodick, Isle of Arran, KA27 8DL
☎ (01770) 302349
🖷 (01770) 302349
🕮 600
🏌 HM Macrae
✓ PS McCalla (01770) 302349
🏳 18 L 4736 yds SSS 64
🕅 U SOC
££ £18 D–£25 (£22 D–£30)
⛳ Brodick Pier 1 mile

Brunston Castle (1992)

Golf Course Road, Dailly, Girvan, KA26 9GD
☎ (01465) 811471
🖷 (01465) 811545
🕮 350
🏌 P Muirhead
✓ A Reid
🏳 18 L 6792 yds SSS 72
🕅 U–booking necessary SOC
££ £26 D–£45
⛳ 4 miles E of Girvan
⊕ Driving range
🏠 Donald Steel
■ www.brunstoncastle.co.uk

Caprington

Public
Ayr Road, Caprington, Kilmarnock, KA1 4UW
☎ (01563) 521915 (Starter)
🕮 400
🏌 DR Bray (01292) 474878
🏳 18 L 5810 yds SSS 68
   9 hole course
🕅 U
££ On application
⛳ 1 mile S of Kilmarnock (B7038)

Corrie (1892)

Corrie, Sannox, Isle of Arran, KA27 8JD
☎ (01770) 810223/810606
🕮 270
🏌 C Bell (01770) 600613
🏳 9 L 1948 yds SSS 61
🕅 U exc Thurs 12–2.30pm & Sat–NA
££ D–£12 W–£54
⛳ 6 miles N of Brodick

Dalmilling (1961)

Public
Westwood Avenue, Ayr, KA8 0QY
☎ (01292) 263893
🖷 (01292) 610543
✓ P Cheyney (Golf Mgr)
🏳 18 L 5724 yds SSS 68
🕅 U
££ £13 D–£21 (£16.50 D–£29)
⛳ NE boundary of Ayr, nr Ayr racecourse

Doon Valley (1927)

1 Hillside, Patna, Ayr, KA6 7JT
☎ **(01292) 531607**
🖳 (01292) 532489
📖 90
🎣 H Johnstone
✒ None
🏳 9 L 5858 yds SSS 70
👥 U
££ £10 (£15)
🏌 8 miles SE of Ayr (A713)

Girvan (1860)

Public
Golf Course Road, Girvan, KA26 9HW
☎ **(01465) 714272/714346 (Starter)**
🖳 (01465) 714346
📖 170
🎣 WB Tait
🏳 18 L 5095 yds SSS 64
👥 U
££ £13–£25
🏌 N side of Girvan (A77). 22 miles S of Ayr
🏠 James Braid

Glasgow GC Gailes (1892)

Gailes, Irvine, KA11 5AE
☎ **(01294) 311258**
🖳 (01294) 279366
✉ secretary@glasgow-golf.com
📖 1200
🎣 DW Deas (0141) 942 2011
Fax (0141) 942 0770
✒ J Steven (01294) 311561
🏳 18 L 6535 yds Par 71 SSS 72
👥 WD WE/BH–NA before 2.30pm SOC
££ £45 D–£60 (£58)
🏌 1 mile S of Irvine, off A78
🏠 Willie Park Jr
■ www.glasgowgailes-golf.com

Irvine (1887)

Bogside, Irvine, KA8 8SN
☎ **(01294) 275979**
📖 450
🎣 W McMahon
✒ K Erskine (01294) 275626
🏳 18 L 6408 yds SSS 71
👥 U SOC–WD
££ On application
🏌 1 mile N of Irvine towards Kilwinning

Irvine Ravenspark (1907)

Public
Kidsneuk Lane, Irvine, KA12 8SR
☎ **(01294) 271293**
✉ secretary@irgc.co.uk
📖 400
🎣 S Howie (01294) 553904
✒ P Bond (01294) 276467
🏳 18 L 6429 yds SSS 71
👥 U exc Sat U after 2.30 pm
££ £14 D–£25
🏌 N side of Irvine, off A737. 7 miles N of Troon
■ www.irgc.co.uk

Kilbirnie Place (1922)

Largs Road, Kilbirnie, KA25 7AT
☎ **(01505) 683398**
📖 450
🎣 Mrs C McGurk
✒ None
🏳 18 L 5411 yds SSS 67
👥 WD/Sun–U
f€ On application
🏌 ½ mile W of Kilbirnie, S of A760. 15 miles SW of Paisley

Kilmarnock (Barassie) (1887)

29 Hillhouse Road, Barassie, Troon, KA10 6SY
☎ **(01292) 313920/311077**
🖳 (01292) 318300
✉ barassiegc@lineone.net
📖 600
🎣 D Wilson (01292) 313920
✒ G Howie (01292) 311322
🏳 18 L 6484 yds SSS 74
9 L 2888 yds SSS 34
👥 WD–U WE–NA before 3pm SOC–Mon/Tues & Thurs
££ £50 (£60)
🏌 Opp Barassie Railway Station
🏠 Theodore Moone
■ www.kbgc.co.uk

Lamlash (1889)

Lamlash, Isle of Arran, KA27 8JU
☎ **(01770) 600296 (Clubhouse),**
(01770) 600196 (Starter)
🖳 (01770) 600296
📖 450
🎣 J Henderson
✒ None
🏳 18 L 4640 yds SSS 64
👥 U SOC
££ On application
🏌 3 miles S of Brodick on A841
🏠 Auchterlonie/Fernie
■ www.arrangolf.co.uk

Largs (1891)

Irvine Road, Largs, KA30 8EU
☎ **(01475) 674681 (Clubhouse)**
🖳 (01475) 673594
📖 800
🎣 DH Macgillivray (01475) 673594
✒ K Docherty (01475) 686192
🏳 18 L 6115 yds Par 70 SSS 71
👥 U SOC–WD
££ £30 D–£40 (£40)
🏌 1 mile S of Largs on A78
🏠 JH Stutt
■ www.largsgolfclub.co.uk

Lochranza (1991)

Pay and play
Lochranza, Isle of Arran, KA27 8HL
☎ **(0177083) 0273**
🖳 (0177083) 0600
✉ golf@lochgolf.co.uk
🎣 IM Robertson
🏳 18 L 5470 yds SSS 70
👥 U SOC–Apr–Oct
££ £15

🏌 14 miles N of Brodick
🏠 IM Robertson
■ www.lochgolf.co.uk

Loudoun Gowf (1909)

Galston, KA4 8PA
☎ **(01563) 821993/820551**
🖳 (01563) 820011
✉ secretary@loudoungowf.sol.uk
📖 850
🎣 L Gilliland (01563) 821993
🏳 18 L 6016 yds SSS 69
👥 WD–U WE–M
££ £21 D–£31
🏌 5 miles E of Kilmarnock on A71
■ www.loudoungowfclub.biz

Machrie Bay (1900)

Machrie Bay, Brodick, Isle of Arran, KA27 8DZ
☎ **(01770) 850232**
🖳 (01770) 850247
📖 160
🎣 J Milesi
✒ None
🏳 9 L 2200 yds Par 66 SSS 62
👥 U
££ D–£10 W–£35
🏌 10 miles W of Brodick
🏠 William Fernie

Maybole (1970)

Public
Memorial Park, Maybole, KA19
☎ **(01655) 889770**
🏳 9 L 2635 yds SSS 65
👥 U
££ £8 (£9)
🏌 S of Maybole, off A77. 8 miles S of Ayr

Muirkirk (1991)

Pay and play
c/o 65 Main Street, Muirkirk, KA18 3QR
☎ **(01290) 660184**
📖 100
🎣 R Bradford
🏳 9 L 5366 yds SSS 67
👥 U SOC
££ £9
🏌 12 miles W of M74 Junction 12 on A70

New Cumnock (1902)

Lochill, Cumnock Road, New Cumnock, KA18 4BQ
☎ **(01290) 423659**
📖 250
🎣 D Scott
🏳 9 L 2588 yds SSS 65
👥 U exc Sun am–NA
££ £5 D–£8
🏌 1 mile W of New Cumnock
🏠 William Fernie

Prestwick (1851)

2 Links Road, Prestwick, KA9 1QG
☎ **(01292) 477404**
🖳 (01292) 477255
✉ bookings@prestwickgc.co.uk

☐ 580
✎ IT Bunch
✓ FC Rennie (01292) 479483
⊳ 18 L 6668 yds SSS 73
👥 WD/Sun–I on application only
££ £85 D–£125
🚗 Prestwick Airport 1 mile, nr
   Railway Station
🏠 Tom Morris
■ www.prestwickgc.co.uk

Prestwick St Cuthbert
(1899)
East Road, Prestwick, KA9 2SX
☎ **(01292) 477101**
🖳 (01292) 671730
☐ 865
✎ JC Rutherford
⊳ 18 L 6470 yds SSS 71
👥 WD–U WE/BH–M SOC–WD
££ £24 D–£32
🚗 ¹/₂ mile E of Prestwick
■ www.stcuthbert.co.uk

Prestwick St Nicholas
(1851)
Grangemuir Road, Prestwick, KA9 1SN
☎ **(01292) 477608**
🖳 (01292) 473900
☐ 600 155(L) 68(J)
✎ PJ Carmichael
✓ Starter (01292) 473904
⊳ 18 L 5952 yds SSS 69
👥 WD–U WE–NA exc Sun pm
££ £36 D–£56 Sun pm–£41
🚗 Prestwick
🏠 C Hunter

Routenburn (1914)
Greenock Road, Largs, KA30 9AH
☎ **(01475) 673230**
☐ 350
✎ RB Connal (Mgr) (01475) 672757
✓ G McQueen (01475) 687240
⊳ 18 L 5650 yds SSS 68
👥 U–phone Pro SOC–WD
££ £14.50
🚗 N of Largs, off A78
🏠 James Braid

Royal Troon (1878)
Craigend Road, Troon, KA10 6EP
☎ **(01292) 311555**
🖳 (01292) 318204
✉ admin@royaltroon.com
☐ 800
✎ JW Chandler
✓ RB Anderson (01292) 313281
⊳ Old 18 L 7109 yds SSS 74
   Portland 18 L 6289 yds SSS 71
👥 Booking required – max 20.
   Mon/Tues/Thurs only–H
££ Old + Portland D–£170 (incl
   Lunch). Portland D–£100 (incl
   Lunch)
🚗 SE of Troon (B749). Prestwick
   Airport 3 miles
⊕ Practice range
🏠 W Fernie
■ www.royaltroon.com

Seafield (1930)
Public
*Belleisle Park, Doonfoot Road, Ayr,
KA7 4DU*
☎ **(01292) 441258**
🖳 (01292) 442632
✓ D Gemmell (Golf Mgr)
   (01292) 441314
⊳ 18 L 5498 yds SSS 66
👥 U
££ £13–£25
🚗 S of Ayr in Belleisle Park

Shiskine (1896)
*Shiskine, Blackwaterfoot, Isle of Arran,
KA27 8HA*
☎ **(01770) 860226**
🖳 (01770) 860205
☐ 550 154(L) 42(J)
✎ Mrs F Crawford (Mgr)
   (01770) 860548
⊳ 12 L 2990 yds SSS 42
👥 U SOC
££ £13 (£18)
🚗 11 miles SW of Brodick
🏠 Willie Fernie
■ www.shiskinegolf.com

Skelmorlie (1891)
Skelmorlie, Largs, PA17 5ES
☎ **(01475) 520152**
☐ 439
✎ Mrs A Fahey (Hon)
⊳ 18 L 5030 yds SSS 65
👥 U exc Sat (Apr–Oct)
££ D–£18 Sun–£20
🚗 Wemyss Bay Station 1¹/₂ miles
🏠 James Braid

Troon Municipal
Public
Harling Drive, Troon, KA10 6NF
☎ **(01292) 312464**
🖳 (01292) 312578
✓ G McKinlay
⊳ Lochgreen 18 L 6785 yds SSS 73
   Darley 18 L 6501 yds SSS 72
   Fullarton 18 L 4822 yds SSS 63
👥 U SOC
££ Lochgreen £19–£31 Darley
   £15–£29 Fullarton £13–£25
🚗 4 miles N of Prestwick at Station
   Brae

Troon Portland (1894)
Club
1 Crosbie Road, Troon KA10
☎ **(01292) 313488**
☐ 120
✎ G Clark (01292) 317367
⊳ Play over Portland at Royal Troon

Troon St Meddans (1907)
Club
Harling Drive, Troon, KA10 6NF
✉ troonstmeddans@btinternet.com
☐ 250
✎ J Trotter (01292) 220124
⊳ Play over Troon Municipal courses
   Lochgreen and Darley

Turnberry Hotel (1906)
Turnberry, KA26 9LT
☎ **(01655) 331000**
🖳 (01655) 331069
☐ 380
✎ P Burley (Golf Dir)
   (01655) 334000
✓ P Burley (01655) 334000
⊳ Ailsa 18 L 6976 yds SSS 72
   Kintyre 18 L 6719 yds SSS 71
   Arran 9 L 1996 yds Par 31
👥 On application
££ On application
🚗 18 miles S of Ayr on A77
⊕ Golf Academy. Driving range
🏠 Ailsa-Mackenzie Ross. Kintyre-
   Donald Steel
■ www.westin.com/turnberry

West Kilbride (1893)
*Fullerton Drive, Seamill, West Kilbride,
KA23 9HT*
☎ **(01294) 823911**
🖳 (01294) 829573
☐ 900
✎ H Armour
✓ G Ross (01294) 823042
⊳ 18 L 6452 yds SSS 71
👥 WD–U WE–M BH–NA SOC
££ On application
🚗 West Kilbride
🏠 Old Tom Morris/James Braid

Western Gailes (1897)
Gailes, Irvine, KA11 5AE
☎ **(01294) 311649**
🖳 (01294) 312312
✉ secretary@westerngailes.com
☐ 450
✎ AM McBean, DJ Lithgow (Mgr)
⊳ 18 L 6639 yds SSS 73
👥 WD–H Mon/Wed/Fri only
   (booking necessary)
££ £85 D–£115 Sun pm–£90
🚗 3 miles N of Troon (A78)
■ www.westerngailes.com

Whiting Bay (1895)
*Golf Course Road, Whiting Bay, Isle of
Arran, KA27 8PR*
☎ **(01770) 700775**
☐ 290
✎ Mrs M Auld (01770) 820208
⊳ 18 L 4405 yds SSS 63
👥 U
££ On application
🚗 8 miles S of Brodick

Borders

Duns (1894)
Hardens Road, Duns, TD11 3NR
☎ **(01361) 882194**
☐ 390
✎ A Preston (01361) 882194
✓ None
⊳ 18 L 6209 yds SSS 70
👥 U SOC
££ £18 (£21)
🚗 1 mile W of Duns, off A6105

Eyemouth (1894)

Gunsgreen House, Eyemouth,
TD14 5DX
☎ (018907) 50551 (Clubhouse)
📖 400
🏌 M Gibson (018907) 50004
↗ P Terras (018907) 50004
  C Maltman (Touring)
🏁 18 L 6520 yds SSS 72
🙋 U SOC
££ £20 (£25)
🚗 6 miles N of border, off A1
🏠 JR Bain

Galashiels (1884)

Ladhope Recreation Ground, Galashiels,
TD1 2NJ
☎ (01896) 753724
📖 366
🏌 R Gass (01896) 755307
🏁 18 L 5309 yds SSS 67
🙋 U SOC
££ £15 D–£20 (£20 D–£25)
🚗 ¼ mile NE of Galashiels, off A7
🏠 James Braid

Hawick (1877)

Vertish Hill, Hawick, TD9 0NY
☎ (01450) 372293
✉ thesecretary@hawickgolfclub.fsnet
  .co.uk
📖 600
🏌 J Reilly
🏁 18 L 5929 yds SSS 69
🙋 U
££ £21 D–£26
🚗 ½ mile S of Hawick
🌐 www.ukgolfer.com/hawick

The Hirsel (1948)

Kelso Road, Coldstream, TD12 4NJ
☎ (01890) 882678
🖨 (01890) 882233
📖 800
🏌 SA Galbraith (01890) 882233
🏁 18 L 6111 yds SSS 70
🙋 U SOC
££ £22 (£28)
🚗 ½ mile W of Coldstream (A697)

Innerleithen (1886)

Leithen Water, Leithen Road,
Innerleithen, EH44 6NL
☎ (01896) 830951
📖 175
🏌 S Wyse (01896) 830071
🏁 9 L 6066 yds SSS 69
🙋 U
££ £11 (£13)
🚗 1 mile N of Innerleithen on Heriot
  road
🏠 Willie Park

Jedburgh (1892)

Dunion Road, Jedburgh, TD8 6LA
☎ (01835) 863587
🖨 (01835) 862360
📖 300
🏌 G McEwen (01835) 862360
🏁 9 L 5600 yds Par 68 SSS 67

🙋 U
££ £16 (£16)
🚗 Jedburgh 1 mile (signposted from
  centre)
🏠 Willie Park
🌐 www.tweeddalepress.co.uk

Kelso (1887)

Golf Course Road, Kelso, TD5 7SL
☎ (01573) 223009
🖨 (01573) 228490
✉ golf@kelsogc.fsnet.co.uk
📖 400
🏌 DR Jack
🏁 18 L 6066 yds SSS 69
🙋 U SOC
££ £18 (£22)
🚗 1 mile N of Kelso, inside
  racecourse
🏠 James Braid

Langholm (1892)

Langholm, DG13 0JR
☎ (013873) 81408/81247
📖 150
🏌 WT Goodfellow
🏁 9 L 3090 yds SSS 70
🙋 U
££ £10 (£10)
🚗 21 miles N of Carlisle on A7
🌐 www.langholmgolfclub.co.uk

Lauder (1896)

Pay and play
Galashiels Road, Lauder, TD2 6QD
☎ (01578) 722526
✉ djdfamily@aol.com
📖 250
🏌 D Dickson (01578) 722526
🏁 9 L 6050 yds Par 72 SSS 69
🙋 U SOC
££ £10 (£10)
🚗 ½ mile W of Lauder
🏠 W Park Jr

Melrose (1880)

Dingleton Road, Melrose, TD6 9HS
☎ (01896) 822855
🖨 (01896) 822855
📖 309
🏌 J Orrett (01896) 822788
🏁 9 L 5579 yds Par 70 SSS 68
🙋 U exc during competitions
££ £18 D–£20
🚗 S boundary of Melrose, off A68

Minto (1928)

Denholm, Hawick, TD9 8SH
☎ (01450) 870220
🖨 (01450) 870126
✉ pat@mintogolfclub.freeserve.co.uk
📖 600
🏌 P Brown
↗ None
🏁 18 L 5542 yds SSS 67
🙋 H SOC
££ £25 (£30)
🚗 Denholm, 6 miles E of Hawick

Newcastleton (1894)

Holm Hill, Newcastleton, TD9 0QD
☎ (013873) 75257
🏌 FJ Ewart
↗ None
🏁 9 L 5426 yds Par 70 SSS 68
🙋 U SOC
££ £10
🚗 W of Newcastleton, off B6357 (via
  A7). M6 Junction 44
🏠 John Shade

Peebles (1892)

Kirkland Street, Peebles, EH45 8EU
☎ (01721) 720197
📖 650
🏌 H Gilmore
↗ C Imlah
🏁 18 L 6160 yds SSS 70
🙋 H SOC
££ £30 D–£45
🚗 23 miles S of Edinburgh, via A703
🏠 James Braid/HS Colt
🌐 www.peeblesgolfclub.co.uk

The Roxburghe Hotel (1997)

Heiton, Kelso, TD5 8JZ
☎ (01573) 450331
🖨 (01573) 450611
✉ golf@roxburghe.net
📖 300
🏌 Jeannette Thomson (Bookings)
↗ C Montgomerie (01573) 450333
🏁 18 L 6925 yds Par 72 SSS 73
🙋 By arrangement SOC
££ £50 (£70)
🚗 On A698 between Jedburgh and
  Kelso
⊕ Driving range
🏠 Dave Thomas
🌐 www.roxburghe.net

St Boswells (1899)

St Boswells, Melrose, TD6 0DE
☎ (01835) 823527
📖 320
🏌 JG Phillips
🏁 9 L 5274 yds SSS 66
🙋 U SOC
££ D–£15 (D–£15)
🚗 Off A68 at St Boswells Green, by
  River Tweed
🏠 Willie Park/Shade

Selkirk (1883)

The Hill, Selkirk, TD7 4NW
☎ (01750) 20621
📖 363
🏌 A Wilson
🏁 9 L 5560 yds SSS 68
🙋 WD–U exc Mon pm WE–phone
  first SOC
££ D–£18 (£18)
🚗 1 mile S of Selkirk on A7
🏠 Willie Park

Torwoodlee (1895)

Edinburgh Road, Galashiels,
Torwoodlee, TD1 2NE
☎ (01896) 752260

☎ (01896) 752260
🕮 550
✍ G Donnelly
➤ 18 L 6021 yds Par 69 SSS 70
👯 WD–U from 9.30am–1pm and after 2pm exc Thurs–NA from 4–6pm WE–by arrangement SOC
££ £25 D–£35 (£30 D–£40)
🚗 1 mile N of Galashiels on A7
🏠 Willie Park

Woll (1993)
Proprietary
Ashkirk, Selkirkshire, TD7 4NY
☎ **(01750) 32711**
✉ wollgolf@btinternet.com
🕮 360
➤ 9 L 6408 yds Par 72 SSS 71
👯 U SOC
££ D–£16
🚗 Ashkirk, 1 mile off A7

Clackmannanshire

Alloa (1891)
Schawpark, Sauchie, Alloa, FK10 3AX
☎ **(01259) 722745**
🖥 (01259) 218796
🕮 550 80(L) 130(J)
✍ T Crampton (Admin)
✓ W Bennett (01259) 724476
➤ 18 L 6240 yds Par 70 SSS 71
👯 WD–U WE–parties restricted
££ £24 D–£30 (£28 D–£35)
🚗 Sauchie, N of Alloa on A908
🏠 James Braid

Alva
Beauclerc Street, Alva, FK12 5LH
☎ **(01259) 760431**
🕮 320
➤ 9 L 2423 yds SSS 64
👯 U
££ On application
🚗 Back Road, Alva, on A91 Stirling-St Andrews road. Signs to Alva Glen

Braehead (1891)
Cambus, Alloa, FK10 2NT
☎ **(01259) 725766**
🖥 (01259) 214070
🕮 800
✍ Anne Nash
✓ TBA (01259) 722078
➤ 18 L 6086 yds SSS 69
👯 U–booking necessary SOC
££ £18.50 D–£24.50 (£24.50 D–£32.
🚗 2 miles W of Alloa (A907)
🏠 Robert Tait

Dollar (1890)
Brewlands House, Dollar, FK14 7EA
☎ **(01259) 742400**
🖥 (01259) 743497
✉ dollar.g.c @brewlandshousefreeserve.co.uk
🕮 375
✍ T Young

➤ 18 L 5242 yds SSS 66
👯 U SOC
££ £13.50 D–£17.50 (£22)
🚗 Dollar, off A91
🏠 Ben Sayers
⬛ www.mysite.freeserve.com /dollargolfclub

Tillicoultry (1899)
Alva Road, Tillicoultry, FK13 6BL
☎ **(01259) 750124**
🖥 (01259) 750124
🕮 400
✍ P Brown
➤ 9 L 2528 yds SSS 66
👯 WD/WE–U SOC
££ £12 (£16)
🚗 9 miles E of Stirling

Tulliallan (1902)
Kincardine, Alloa, FK10 4BB
☎ **(01259) 730396**
🖥 (01259) 733950
🕮 550 71(L) 100(J)
✍ NC Raleigh (Sec/Mgr)
✓ S Kelly (01259) 730798
➤ 18 L 5982 yds SSS 69
👯 U exc comp days
££ £16.50 (£21)
🚗 5 miles SE of Alloa
⬛ www.tulliallan-golf-club.co.uk

Dumfries & Galloway

Brighouse Bay (1999)
Pay and play
Borgue, Kirkcudbright, DG6 4TS
☎ **(01557) 870357**
🖥 (01557) 870357
✍ A Prewett-Stansfield, K Mercer
✓ J Davison (01557) 870409
➤ 18 L 6366 yds Par 73 SSS 72
👯 WD–U WE–booking advisable
££ £18 (£18)
🚗 6 miles SW of Kirkcudbright, off B727
⊕ Driving range
🏠 Duncan Gray

Castle Douglas (1905)
Abercromby Road, Castle Douglas, DG7 1BA
☎ **(01556) 502801**
🕮 510
✍ AD Millar (01556) 502099
➤ 9 L 5400 yds SSS 66
👯 U
££ £12
🚗 Off A75/A713, NE of Castle Douglas

Colvend (1905)
Sandyhills, Dalbeattie, DG5 4PY
☎ **(01556) 630398**
🖥 (01556) 630495
✉ sec.@colvendgolfclub.co.uk
🕮 500

✍ JB Henderson
➤ 18 L 5200 yds SSS 67
👯 U
££ D–£22
🚗 6 miles S of Dalbeattie on A710
🏠 Fernie/Soutar

Crichton (1884)
Bankend Road, Dumfries, DG1 4TH
☎ **(01387) 247894/702221**
🖥 (01387) 702223
🕮 600
➤ 9 L 3084 yds SSS 69
👯 WD–U before 3pm SOC
££ £12 D–£16
🚗 1 mile from Dumfries, nr Hospital

Dalbeattie (1894)
60 Maxwell Park, Dalbeattie, DG5 4LS
☎ **(01556) 611421/610311**
✉ arthurhowatson@aol.com
🕮 400
✍ A Howatson (01556) 610311
✓ None
➤ 9 L 5710 yds SSS 68
👯 U SOC
££ £15 (£15)
🚗 14 miles SW of Dumfries on A711/B794
⬛ www.dalbeattiegc.co.uk

Dumfries & County (1912)
Nunfield, Edinburgh Road, Dumfries, DG1 1JX
☎ **(01387) 253585**
🖥 (01387) 253585
✉ dumfriesc@aol.com
🕮 600 100(J)
✍ BRM Duguid (01387) 253585
✓ S Syme (01387) 268918
➤ 18 L 5928 yds SSS 69
👯 WD–U exc 11.30–2pm–NA Sat–NA Sun–NA before 10am
££ On application
🚗 1 mile NE of Dumfries, on A701
🏠 W Fernie
⬛ www.dumfriesandcounty-gc.fsnet .co.uk

Dumfries & Galloway (1880)
2 Laurieston Avenue, Maxwelltown, Dumfries, DG2 7NY
☎ **(01387) 253582**
🖥 (01387) 263848
✉ info@dggc.co.uk
🕮 750
✍ TM Ross (01387) 263848
✓ J Fergusson (01387) 256902
➤ 18 L 6325 yds SSS 70
👯 U
££ £27 (£33)
🚗 Dumfries
🏠 Willie Fernie

Gatehouse (1921)
'Innisfree', Laurieston, Castle Douglas, DG7 2PW
☎ **(01557) 814766 (Clubhouse), (01644) 450260 (Bookings)**
🖥 (01644) 450260
🕮 300

🏌 KA Cooper (01644) 450260
▷ 9 L 2521 yds SSS 66
🏃 U
£€ D–£10 (D–£10)
🚗 ¾ mile N of Gatehouse, off A75. 9
miles NW of Kirkcudbright

Gretna   (1991)

Kirtle View, Gretna, DG16 5HD
☎ (01461) 338464
🏌 G & E Birnie (Props)
▷ 9 L 6430 yds SSS 71
🏃 U SOC
£€ 9 holes–£5. 18 holes–£10
🚗 1 mile W of Gretna, off A75
⊕ Driving range
🏠 Nigel Williams

Hoddom Castle   (1973)

Pay and play
Hoddom Bridge, Ecclefechan, DG11 1AS
☎ (01576) 300251
🖳 (01576) 300757
🏌 D Laycock
▷ 9 L 2274 yds SSS 33
🏃 U
£€ £7 (£9)
🚗 2 miles SW of Ecclefechan on
B725. M74 Junction 6

Kirkcudbright   (1893)

*Stirling Crescent, Kirkcudbright,
DG6 4EZ*
☎ (01557) 330314
🖂 david@kirkcudbrightgolf.co.uk
📖 500
🏌 DA MacKenzie
▷ 18 L 5739 yds SSS 69
🏃 U H–phone first SOC
£€ £18 D–£23
🚗 ½ mile from Kirkcudbright town
centre

Lochmaben   (1926)

Castlehill Gate, Lochmaben, DG11 1NT
☎ (01387) 810552
🖂 lochmabengc@aol.com
📖 650
🏌 JM Dickie
▷ 18 L 5357 yds SSS 67
🏃 WD–U before 5pm WE–U exc
comp days SOC
£€ £18 D–£22 (£25 D–£30)
🚗 4 miles W of Lockerbie on A709. 8
miles NE of Dumfries
🏠 James Braid

Lockerbie   (1889)

Corrie Road, Lockerbie, DG11 2ND
☎ (01576) 203363
🖳 (01576) 203363
🖂 enquiries@lockerbiegolf
📖 530
🏌 J Thomson
▷ 18 L 5418 yds SSS 67
🏃 U exc Sun–NA before 11.30am
£€ £16 (£18)
🚗 ½ mile NE of Lockerbie, on Corrie
road
🏠 James Braid

Moffat   (1884)

Coatshill, Moffat, DG10 9SB
☎ (01683) 220020
🖳 (01683) 221802
🖂 moffatgolfclub@onetel.net.uk
📖 380
🏌 JW Mein (01683) 220020
✓ None
▷ 18 L 5259 yds Par 69 SSS 67
🏃 U exc Wed–NA after 3pm SOC
£€ £19 D–£23 (£26 D–£32)
🚗 A74(M) Junction 15. Follow signs
to Moffat
🏠 Ben Sayers
■ www.moffatgolfclub.co.uk

New Galloway   (1902)

New Galloway, Dumfries, DG7 3RN
☎ (01644) 450685
📖 280
🏌 NE White
▷ 9 L 5006 yds Par 68 SSS 67
🏃 U
£€ D–£13
🚗 S of New Galloway on A762.
20 miles N of Kirkcudbright
🏠 Baillie

Newton Stewart   (1981)

*Kirroughtree Avenue, Minnigaff, Newton
Stewart, DG8 6PF*
☎ (01671) 402172
📖 380
🏌 M Large
▷ 18 L 5903 yds Par 69 SSS 70
🏃 U H
£€ £22 D–£25 (£23 D–£27)
🚗 N of Newton Stewart, off A75

Pines Golf Centre

Pay and play
Lockerbie Road, Dumfries, DG1 3PF
☎ (01387) 247444
🖳 (01387) 249600
🖂 admin@pinesgolf.com
📖 160
🏌 B Gray (Mgr)
✓ B Gemmell (01387) 247444
▷ 18 L 5870 yds Par 68 SSS 69
🏃 U SOC
£€ £14 D–£18
🚗 By A75 Dumfries by-pass. M74
Junctions 15 or 17
⊕ Driving range
🏠 Duncan Gray
■ www.pinesgolf.com

Portpatrick   (1903)

Golf Course Road, Portpatrick, DG9 8TB
☎ (01776) 810273
🖳 (01776) 810811
🖂 enquiries@portpatrickgolfclub.com
📖 550
🏌 J McPhail
▷ Dunskey 18 L 5908 yds SSS 69
Dinvin 9 L 1504 yds Par 27
🏃 U H SOC
£€ £25 D–£35 (£30 D–£40) W–£120
Dinvin £10 D–£15
🚗 8 miles SW of Stranraer
🏠 CW Hunter

Powfoot   (1903)

Cummertrees, Annan, DG12 5QE
☎ (01461) 700276 (Bookings)
🖳 (01461) 700276
📖 920
🏌 BW Sutherland MBE (Mgr)
✓ G Dick (01461) 700327
▷ 18 L 6266 yds SSS 71
🏃 WD–U Sat–NA Sun–NA before
1pm
£€ Winter £15 5D–£60 Summer £25
D–£32 5D–£130
🚗 4 miles W of Annan. 15 miles SE
of Dumfries, off B724
🏠 James Braid

St Medan   (1905)

Monreith, Newton Stewart, DG8 8NJ
☎ (01988) 700358
📖 150
🏌 DR Graham (01988) 840214
▷ 9 L 2277 yds SSS 63
🏃 U SOC
£€ £15 (£15)
🚗 3 miles S of Port William, off A747
🏠 James Braid

Sanquhar   (1894)

*Blackaddie Road, Sanquhar, Dumfries,
DG4 6JZ*
☎ (01659) 50577
📖 180
🏌 D Hamilton (01659) 66095
▷ 9 L 5630 yds SSS 68
🏃 U–parties welcome
£€ D–£12 (D–£15)
🚗 ½ mile W of Sanquhar (A76). 30
miles N of Dumfries
🏠 W Fernie
■ www.scottishgolf.com

Southerness   (1947)

Southerness, Dumfries, DG2 8AZ
☎ (01387) 880677
🖳 (01387) 880644
📖 800
🏌 IA Robin
✓ None
▷ 18 L 6566 yds SSS 73
🏃 H–phone first SOC
£€ D–£40 (D–£50)
🚗 16 miles S of Dumfries, off A710
🏠 Mackenzie Ross
■ www.southernessgolfclub.com

Stranraer   (1905)

*Creachmore, Leswalt, Stranraer,
DG9 0LF*
☎ (01776) 870245
🖳 (01776) 870445
🖂 stranraergolf@btclick.com
📖 700
🏌 BC Kelly
▷ 18 L 6308 yds SSS 72
🏃 WE–NA before 9.30am and
11.45am–1.45pm
£€ £24 (£30)
🚗 2 miles NW of Stranraer on A718
🏠 James Braid
■ www.stranraergolfclub.net

For list of abbreviations and key to symbols see page 649

Thornhill (1893)

Blacknest, Thornhill, DG3 5DW
☎ **(01848) 330546**
📖 625
♟ J Tait
🏴 18 L 6085 yds SSS 70
👥 U
££ On application
⛳ 14 miles N of Dumfries (A76)

Wigtown & Bladnoch (1960)

Lightlands Terrace, Wigtown, DG8 9EF
☎ **(01988) 403354**
📖 170
♟ B Kaye
🏴 9 L 2731 yds SSS 67
👥 U SOC
££ £15 (£15)
⛳ Between Wigtown and Bladnoch, off A714
🏠 J Muir

Wigtownshire County (1894)

Mains of Park, Glenluce, Newton Stewart, DG8 0NN
☎ **(01581) 300420**
✉ enquiries @wigtownshirecountygolfclub.com
📖 420
♟ R McKnight
✏ None
🏴 18 L 5843 yds SSS 68
👥 U exc Wed–NA after 6pm
££ £21 D–£27 (£23 D–£29)
⛳ 8 miles E of Stranraer on A75
🏠 W Gordon Cunningham
■ www.wigtownshirecountygolfclub .com

Dunbartonshire

Balmore (1894)

Balmore, Torrance, G64 4AW
☎ **(01360) 620284**
📠 (01360) 622742
📖 750
♟ SB Keir (01360) 620284
✏ K Craggs (01360) 620123
🏴 18 L 5542 yds SSS 67
👥 WD–U SOC
££ On application
⛳ 4 miles N of Glasgow, off A807
🏠 Harry Vardon

Bearsden (1891)

Thorn Road, Bearsden, Glasgow, G61 4BP
☎ **(0141) 942 2351**
📖 600
♟ JL McComish
🏴 9 L 6014 yds SSS 69
👥 By arrangement
⛳ 6 miles NW of Glasgow

Cardross (1895)

Main Road, Cardross, Dumbarton, G82 5LB
☎ **(01389) 841213 (Clubhouse)**
📠 (01389) 842162
✉ golf@cardross.com
📖 850
♟ IT Waugh (01389) 841754
✏ R Farrell (01389) 841350
🏴 18 L 6469 yds SSS 72
👥 WD–U WE–M SOC
££ £28 D–£40
⛳ 4 miles W of Dumbarton on A814
🏠 Fernie (1904)/Braid(1921)
■ www.cardross.com

Clober (1951)

Craigton Road, Milngavie, Glasgow, G62 7HP
☎ **(0141) 956 1685**
📠 (0141) 955 1416
📖 700
♟ B Davidson
✏ (0141) 956 6963 (Golf Shop)
🏴 18 L 4963 yds SSS 65
👥 WD–U before 4pm WE–M BH–NA SOC–WD
££ £16
⛳ 7 miles NW of Glasgow
■ www.clober.com

Clydebank & District (1905)

Hardgate, Clydebank, G81 5QY
☎ **(01389) 383833**
📠 (01389) 383831
📖 780
♟ Mrs K Stoddart (01389) 383831
✏ PR Jamieson (01389) 383835
🏴 18 L 5823 yds SSS 68
👥 WD–H
££ On application
⛳ 2 miles N of Clydebank

Clydebank Municipal (1927)

Public
Overtoun Road, Dalmuir, Clydebank, G81 3RE
☎ **(0141) 952 8698 (Starter)**
📠 (0141) 952 6372
✏ R Bowman (0141) 952 6372
🏴 18 L 5349 yds SSS 66
👥 U exc Sat–NA 11am–2.30pm
££ On application
⛳ 8 miles W of Glasgow

Dougalston (1977)

Strathblane Road, Milngavie, Glasgow, G62 8HJ
☎ **(0141) 955 2434**
📠 (0141) 955 2406
📖 770
♟ Mrs H Everett
✏ C Everett
🏴 18 L 6225 yds SSS 71
👥 WD–U SOC
££ £22 (£28)
⛳ 7 miles N of Glasgow on A81
🏠 J Harris

Douglas Park (1897)

Hillfoot, Bearsden, Glasgow, G61 2TJ
☎ **(0141) 942 2220 (Clubhouse)**
📠 (0141) 942 0985
✉ secretary@douglasparkgolfclub.net
📖 470 270(L) 120(J)

JG Fergusson (0141) 942 0985

♟ JG Fergusson (0141) 942 0985
✏ D Scott (0141) 942 1482
🏴 18 L 5962 yds SSS 69
👥 M SOC
££ WD–£23
⛳ 6 miles NW of Glasgow, nr Hillfoot Station
🏠 Willie Fernie

Dullatur (1896)

1a Glendouglas Drive, Craigmarloch, Cumbernauld, G68 0DW
☎ **(01236) 723230**
📠 (01236) 727271
📖 580 64(L)
♟ Carol Millar (01236) 723230
✏ D Sinclair (01236) 794721
🏴 18 L 6312 yds SSS 70
   18 L 5875 yds SSS 68
👥 WD–U WE–M SOC
££ £20 (£30)
⛳ 3 miles N of Cumbernauld

Dumbarton (1888)

Broadmeadow, Dumbarton, G82 2BQ
☎ **(01389) 732830**
📠 (01389) 765995
📖 500
♟ DM Mitchell
🏴 18 L 6018 yds SSS 69
👥 WD–U WE–NA
££ D–£25
⛳ 1 mile N of Dumbarton

Hayston (1926)

Campsie Road, Kirkintilloch, Glasgow, G66 1RN
☎ **(0141) 776 1244**
📠 (0141) 776 9030
📖 440 70(L) 60(J)
♟ JV Carmichael (0141) 775 0723
✏ S Barnett (0141) 775 0882
🏴 18 L 6042 yds SSS 70
👥 WD–I before 4.30pm –M after 4.30pm WE–M
££ £25
⛳ 1 mile N of Kirkintilloch
🏠 James Braid

Hilton Park (1927)

Auldmarroch Estate, Stockiemuir Road, Milngavie, G62 7HB
☎ **(0141) 956 5124/1215**
📠 (0141) 956 4657
✉ info@hiltonparkgolfclub.fsnet .co.uk
📖 1200
♟ Mrs JA Dawson (0141) 956 4657
✏ W McCondichie (0141) 956 5125
🏴 Hilton 18 L 6054 yds SSS 70
   Allander 18 L 5374 yds SSS 69
👥 WD–U before 4pm
££ On application
⛳ 8 miles NW of Glasgow on A809
🏠 James Braid

Kirkintilloch (1895)

Todhill, Campsie Road, Kirkintilloch, G66 1RN
☎ **(0141) 776 1256**
📖 450 100(L) 100(J)

🖉 IM Gray (0141) 775 2387
🏳 18 L 5860 yds SSS 69
👫 M SOC
££ SOC–On application
🚗 7 miles N of Glasgow

Lenzie (1889)
19 Crosshill Road, Lenzie, G66 5DA
☎ **(0141) 776 1535**
💻 (0141) 777 7748
📖 501 125(L) 125(J)
🖉 SM Davidson (0141) 812 3018
✓ J McCallum (0141) 777 7748
🏳 18 L 5984 yds SSS 69
👫 M SOC
££ £24 D–£30
🚗 6 miles NE of Glasgow
■ www.lenziegolfclub.com

Loch Lomond
Rossdhu House, Luss, G83 8NT
☎ **(01436) 655555**
💻 (01436) 655500
🖉 K Williams
✓ C Campbell
🏳 18 L 7060 yds Par 71
👫 NA
🚗 20 miles NW of Glasgow on A82
🏠 Weiskopf/Morrish
■ www.lochlomond.com

Milngavie (1895)
Laighpark, Milngavie, Glasgow, G62 8EP
☎ **(0141) 956 1619**
💻 (0141) 956 4252
📧 secretary@milngaviegc.fsnet.co.uk
📖 390
🖉 S McInnes
✓ None
🏳 18 L 5818 yds SSS 68
👫 M SOC
££ On application
🚗 7 miles NW of Glasgow

Palacerigg (1975)
Public
Palacerigg Country Park, Cumbernauld, G67 3HU
☎ **(01236) 734969**
💻 (01236) 721461
📧 palacerigg-golfclub@lineone.net
📖 360
🖉 DSA Cooper
🏳 18 L 6444 yds Par 72 SSS 71
👫 U SOC
££ £8 (£10)
🚗 3 miles SE of Cumbernauld, off A80
🏠 Henry Cotton
■ www.palacerigggolfclub.co.uk

Ross Priory
Ross Loan, Gartocharn, Alexandria, G83 8NL
☎ **(01389) 830398**
💻 (01389) 830357
📖 800
🖉 R Cook
✓ None
🏳 9 L 5758 yds Par 70 SSS 68
👫 M

££ N/A
🚗 Off A881 at Gartocharn
🏠 George Campbell

Vale of Leven (1907)
Northfield Road, Bonhill, Alexandria, G83 9ET
☎ **(01389) 752351**
💻 (08707) 498950
📧 clubadministrator
@valeoflevengolfclub.org.uk
📖 600
🖉 R Barclay
✓ B Campbell (08707) 498914
🏳 18 L 5167 yds Par 67 SSS 66
👫 U H exc Sat (Apr–Sept) SOC (max 36 members)
££ £16 D–£24 (£20 D–£30)
🚗 Bonhill, 3 miles N of Dumbarton, off A82
■ www.valeoflevengolfclub.org.uk

Westerwood Hotel G&CC (1989)
St Andrews Drive, Cumbernauld, G68 0EW
☎ **(01236) 725281**
💻 (01236) 860730
📧 alantait@morton-hotels.com
📖 250
🖉 A Tait
✓ A Tait
🏳 18 L 6616 yds SSS 72
👫 U SOC
££ £27.50 (£30)
🚗 13 miles NE of Glasgow, off A80
🏠 Thomas/Ballesteros

Windyhill (1908)
Windyhill, Bearsden, G61 4QQ
☎ **(0141) 942 2349**
💻 (0141) 942 5874
📧 secretary@windyhill.co.uk
📖 650
🖉 W Proven
✓ C Duffy (0141) 942 7157
🏳 18 L 6254 yds SSS 70
👫 WD–U Sun–M SOC–WD
££ £20
🚗 8 miles NW of Glasgow
🏠 James Braid
■ www.windyhill.co.uk

Fife

Aberdour (1896)
Seaside Place, Aberdour, KY3 0TX
☎ **(01383) 860080**
💻 (01383) 860050
📧 aberdourgc@aol.com
📖 670
🖉 (01383) 860080
✓ D Gemmell (01383) 860256
🏳 18 L 5460 yds Par 67 SSS 66
👫 WD–book with Pro Sat–NA SOC
££ £20 (£30)
🚗 8 miles SE of Dunfermline, on coast
🏠 Robertson/Anderson

Anstruther (1890)
Marsfield Shore Road, Anstruther, KY10 3DZ
☎ **(01333) 310956**
💻 (01333) 312283
📖 500
🖉 J Boal
🏳 9 L 4504 yds SSS 63
👫 U SOC
££ £12 (£15)
🚗 9 miles S of St Andrews

Auchterderran (1904)
Public
Woodend Road, Cardenden, KY5 0NH
☎ **(01592) 721579**
📖 100
🖉 G McCrae
🏳 9 L 5400 yds SSS 66
👫 U SOC
££ £9 (£12)
🚗 1 mile N of Cardenden. 6 miles W of Kirkcaldy, off A910

Balbirnie Park (1983)
Balbirnie Park, Markinch, Glenrothes, KY7 6NR
☎ **(01592) 612095**
💻 (01592) 612383
📖 800
🖉 S Oliver (Admin)
✓ C Donnelly (01592) 752006
🏳 18 L 6210 yds SSS 70
👫 WE–booking essential
££ £27 D–£35 (£33 D–£45)
🚗 2 miles E of Glenrothes
🏠 Fraser Middleton

Ballingry
Pay and play
Lochore Meadows Country Park, Crosshill, Lochgelly, KY5 8BA
☎ **(01592) 860086**
📖 150
🏳 9 L 6482 yds SSS 71
👫 U
££ On application
🚗 2 miles N of Lochgelly (B920)

Burntisland (1797)
Club
51 Craigkennochie Terrace, Burntisland, KY3 9EN
☎ **(01592) 872728**
📖 100
🖉 AD McPherson
🏳 Play over Dodhead Course, Burntisland
■ www.burntislandgolfclub.co.uk

Burntisland Golf House Club (1898)
Dodhead, Burntisland, KY3 9LQ
☎ **(01592) 874093**
💻 (01592) 874093
📖 800
🖉 WK Taylor (Mgr) (01592) 874093
✓ P Wytrazek (01592) 872116
🏳 18 L 5965 yds SSS 70
👫 U H SOC
££ £17 D–£25 (£25 D–£37)

🖘 1 mile E of Burntisland on B923
🏛 Willie Park Jr/James Braid

Canmore (1897)
Venturefair Avenue, Dunfermline, KY12 0PE
- ☎ **(01383) 724969**
- 🖥 (01383) 731649
- 🕮 547 70(L) 85(J)
- ✍ C Stuart (01383) 513604
- 🏌 G Cook (01383) 728416
- ⛳ 18 L 5437 yds SSS 66
- 👥 WD–U WE–restricted
- ££ £16 D–£22 (£21 D–£32)
- 🖘 1 mile N of Dunfermline on A823
- 🏛 Ben Sayers

Charleton (1994)
Pay and play
Charleton, Colinsburgh, KY9 1HG
- ☎ **(01333) 340505**
- 🖥 (01333) 340583
- ✍ J Pattison
- ✏ A Hutton (01333) 330009
- ⛳ 18 L 6149 yds SSS 70
- 👥 U SOC
- ££ £18 (£22)
- 🖘 1 mile W of Colinsburgh, off B492
- ⊕ Driving range. 9 holes pitch & putt course
- 🏛 John Salvesen

Cowdenbeath (1991)
Public
Seco Place, Cowdenbeath, KY4 8PD
- ☎ **(01383) 511918**
- 🕮 400
- ✍ D Ferguson
- ⛳ 18 L 6100 yds SSS 69
- 👥 U
- ££ On application
- 🖘 In Cowdenbeath, signposted from A909/A92

Crail Golfing Society
(1786)
Balcomie Clubhouse, Fifeness, Crail, KY10 3XN
- ☎ **(01333) 450686**
- 🖥 (01333) 450416
- 🕮 1800
- ✍ A Busby (01333) 450686
- ✏ G Lennie (01333) 450960/450967
- ⛳ Balcomie 18 L 5922 yds SSS 69; Craighead 18 L 6728 yds Par 71 SSS 73
- 👥 U
- ££ £32 (£40)
- 🖘 11 miles SE of St Andrews
- 🏛 Balcomie-Tom Morris. Craighead-Gil Hanse
- 🖳 www.crailgolfingsociety.co.uk

Cupar (1855)
Hilltarvit, Cupar, KY15 5JT
- ☎ **(01334) 653549**
- 🖂 secretary@cupargolfclub.freeserve .co.uk
- 🕮 400
- ✍ JM Houston (01334) 654101

⛳ 9 L 5074 yds SSS 65
👥 WD–U Sat–NA SOC–WD/Sun
££ D–£15
🖘 10 miles W of St Andrews
🖳 www.cupargolfclub.co.uk

Drumoig
Leuchars, St Andrews, KY16 0DW
- ☎ **(01382) 541144**
- 🖥 (01382) 541133
- ✍ N Simpson (Gen Mgr)
- ✏ JM Farmer (Golf Mgr) (01382) 541144
- ⛳ 18 hole course
- 👥 U
- ££ On application
- 🖘 7 miles NW of St Andrews on A919
- ⊕ Driving range
- 🏛 Dave Thomas

Dunfermline (1887)
Pitfirrane, Crossford, Dunfermline, KY12 8QW
- ☎ **(01383) 723534**
- 🖂 pitfarrane@aol.com
- 🕮 690
- ✍ R De Rose
- ✏ C Nugent (01383) 729061
- ⛳ 18 L 6121 yds SSS 70
- 👥 WD–U 10–12 & 2–4pm WE–M SOC–WD
- ££ £25 D–£35
- 🖘 2 miles W of Dunfermline on A994
- 🏛 JR Stutt

Dunnikier Park (1963)
Public
Dunnikier Way, Kirkcaldy, KY1 3LP
- ☎ **(01592) 261599**
- 🖥 (01592) 642541
- 🖂 secretary@dpgc.fslife.co.uk
- 🕮 600 35(L) 75(J)
- ✍ N Crooks
- ✏ G Whyte (01592) 642121
- ⛳ 18 L 6601 yds SSS 72
- 👥 U SOC
- ££ £11.50 (£15.50)
- 🖘 N boundary of Kirkcaldy
- 🏛 R Stutt
- 🖳 www.dunnikierparkgolfclub.com

Earlsferry Thistle (1875)
Club
Melon Park, Elie, KY9 1AS
- 🕮 60
- ✍ AJ Stewart (01333) 330639
- ⛳ Play over Golf House Club Course

Falkland (1976)
Public
The Myre, Falkland, KY15 7AA
- ☎ **(01337) 857404**
- 🕮 350
- ✍ Mrs H Horsburgh
- ⛳ 9 L 2384 metres SSS 66
- 👥 U SOC
- ££ On application
- 🖘 5 miles N of Glenrothes on A912

Glenrothes (1958)
Public
Golf Course Road, Glenrothes, KY6 2LA
- ☎ **(01592) 754561/758686**
- 🖂 secretary@glenrothesgolf.org.uk
- 🕮 600 35(L) 50(J)
- ✍ Miss C Dawson
- ⛳ 18 L 6444 yds SSS 71
- 👥 U
- ££ £12 (£16)
- 🖘 Glenrothes West, off A92. M90 Junction 29
- 🏛 JR Stutt

Golf House Club (1875)
Elie, Leven, KY9 1AS
- ☎ **(01333) 330327**
- 🖥 (01333) 330895
- ✍ A Sneddon (01333) 330301
- ✏ R Wilson (01333) 330955
- ⛳ 18 L 6261 yds SSS 70 9 L 2277 yds SSS 32
- 👥 July–Sept ballot. WE–no party bookings. WE–NA before 3pm (May–Sept)
- ££ £38 D–£50 (£48 D–£60)
- 🖘 12 miles S of St Andrews

Kinghorn Ladies (1894)
Club
Golf Clubhouse, McDuff Crescent, Kinghorn, KY3 9RE
- ☎ **(01592) 890345**
- 🕮 38
- ⛳ Play over Kinghorn Municipal

Kinghorn Municipal (1887)
Public
McDuff Crescent, Kinghorn, KY3 9RE
- ☎ **(01592) 890345**
- 🕮 200
- ✍ I Gow (01592) 265445
- ✏ None
- ⛳ 18 L 5629 yds SSS 67
- 👥 U SOC
- ££ £11 (£16)
- 🖘 3 miles S of Kirkcaldy (A921)
- ⊕ Kinghorn and Kinghorn Thistle Clubs play here
- 🏛 Tom Morris

Kingsbarns Links
Kingsbarns, Fife, KY16 8QD
- ☎ **(01334) 460860**
- 🖥 (01334) 460877
- 🖂 info@kingsbarns.com
- ✍ D Scott (Golf Dir)
- ✏ D Scott
- ⛳ 18 hole course
- 👥 U
- ££ £125 D–£185
- 🖘 Between St Andrews and Crail on coast road (A917)
- ⊕ Driving range
- 🏛 Phillips/Parsinen
- 🖳 www.kingsbarns.com

Kirkcaldy (1904)
Balwearie Road, Kirkcaldy, KY2 5LT
- ☎ **(01592) 260370**
- 🖥 (01592) 205240

enquiries@kirkcaldygolfclub.sol
.co.uk
600
AC Thomson (01592) 205240
A Caira (01592) 203258
18 L 6040 yds SSS 70
U exc Sat–NA
££ £24–£30 Sun–£30–£38
S end of Kirkcaldy

Ladybank (1879)
Annsmuir, Ladybank, KY15 7RA
☎ **(01337) 830814,
(01337) 830725 (Starter)**
(01337) 831505
1000
D Allan
MJ Gray (01337) 830725
18 L 6601 yds SSS 72
WD–U 9.30am–4pm M–after 4pm
WE–NA
££ £35 (£45)
6 miles SW of Cupar, off A92 from
Melville Lodges roundabout

Leslie (1898)
*Balsillie Laws, Leslie, Glenrothes,
KY6 3EZ*
☎ **(01592) 620040**
300
G Lewis
9 L 4940 yds SSS 64
U
££ £5 (£8)
3 miles W of Glenrothes. M90
Junction 5/7, 11 miles

Leven Golfing Society (1820)
Club
Links Road, Leven, KY8 4HS
☎ **(01333) 426096/424229**
(01333) 424229
LGS@bosinternet.com
500
AJ McDonald (01333) 424229
Play over Leven Links

Leven Links (1846)
The Promenade, Leven, KY8 4HS
☎ **(01333) 421390 (Starter)**
(01333) 428859
secretary@leven-links.com
1200
(01333) 428859 (Links
Committee)
18 L 6434 yds SSS 71
WD–U before 5pm Sat–no parties
Sun–NA before 10.30am SOC
££ £30 (£35)
E of Leven, on promenade.
12 miles SW of St Andrews

Leven Thistle (1867)
Club
Balfour Street, Leven, KY8 4JF
☎ **(01333) 426397**
(01333) 439910
500
J Scott (01333) 426333
Play over Leven Links

Lochgelly (1895)
*Cartmore Road, Lochgelly, Kirkcaldy,
KY5 9PB*
☎ **(01592) 780174**
450
RF Stuart (01383) 512238
None
18 L 5454 yds SSS 66
U
££ £12 (£17)
NW edge of Lochgelly. 5 miles W
of Kirkcaldy

Lundin (1868)
Golf Road, Lundin Links, KY8 6BA
☎ **(01333) 320202**
(01333) 329743
secretary@lundingolfclub.co.uk
850
DR Thomson
DK Webster (01333) 320051
18 L 6394 yds SSS 71
WD–U Sat–NA before 2.30pm
Sun–restricted
££ £35 D–£45 (£45)
3 miles E of Leven
James Braid
www.lundingolfclub.co.uk

Lundin Ladies (1891)
Woodielea Road, Lundin Links, KY8 6AR
☎ **(01333) 320022 (Starter),
(01333) 320832 (Sec)**
lundinladies@madasafish.com
375
Marion Mitchell
9 L 4730 yds SSS 67
U
££ On application
3 miles E of Leven

Methil (1892)
Club
*Links House, Links Road, Leven,
KY8 4HS*
☎ **(01333) 425535**
(01333) 425187
50
ATJ Traill
Play over Leven Links

Pitreavie (1922)
*Queensferry Road, Dunfermline,
KY11 8PR*
☎ **(01383) 722591**
(01383) 722591
800
E Comerford
P Brookes (01383) 723151
18 L 6031 yds SSS 69
U–phone Pro SOC (Parties–max
36–must be booked in advance)
££ £19 D–£26 (£38)
2 miles off M90 Junction 2,
between Rosyth and Dunfermline
Dr A Mackenzie

St Michaels (1903)
Leuchars, St Andrews, KY16 0DX
☎ **(01334) 839365 (Clubhouse)**
(01334) 838789

stmichaelsgc@btclick.com
550
WA Spong (01334) 838666
18 L 5802 yds SSS 68
Sun am–NA (Mar–Oct) SOC
££ D–£22 (£30)
5 miles N of St Andrews on
Dundee road (A919)
www.stmichaelsgc.co.uk

Saline (1912)
Kinneddar Hill, Saline, KY12 9LT
☎ **(01383) 852591**
400
R Hutchison (01383) 852344
9 L 5302 yds SSS 66
U exc medal Sat
££ £9 (£11)
5 miles NW of Dunfermline

Scoonie (1951)
Public
North Links, Leven, KY8 4SP
☎ **(01333) 307007**
(01333) 307008
S Kuczerepa
None
18 L 4979 metres SSS 65
U SOC
££ On application
Adjoins Leven Links

Scotscraig (1817)
Golf Road, Tayport, DD6 9DZ
☎ **(01382) 552515**
(01382) 553130
900
BD Liddle
SJ Campbell
18 L 6550 yds SSS 72
WD–U WE–by prior arrangement
SOC
££ On application
10 miles N of St Andrews

Thornton (1921)
Station Road, Thornton, KY1 4DW
☎ **(01592) 771173 (Starter)**
(01592) 774955
700
BSL Main (01592) 771111
18 L 6155 yds Par 70 SSS 69
U
££ £15 D–£25 (£22 D–£32)
5 miles N of Kirkcaldy, off A92
www.thorntongolfclubfife.co.uk

St Andrews Clubs

The Royal & Ancient (1754)
Club
St Andrews, KY16 9JD
☎ **(01334) 460000**
(01334) 460001
thesecretary@randagc.org
1800
P Dawson
Play over St Andrews Links
www.randa.org www.opengolf.com

New   (1902)
Club
3-5 Gibson Place, St Andrews, KY16 9JE
☎ **(01334) 473426**
🖳 (01334) 477570
📧 golf@standrewsnewgolfclub.sol
.co.uk
🏠 1700
🏌 H Campbell Graham (Sec/Mgr)
🏴 Play over St Andrews Links courses
🌐 www.standrewsnewgolfclub.com

St Andrews   (1843)
Club
*Links House, 13 The Links, St Andrews,
KY16 9JB*
☎ **(01334) 473017**
🖳 (01334) 479577
📧 sec@thestandrewsgolfclub.co.uk
🏠 1600
🏌 T Gallacher (01334) 473017
🏴 Play over St Andrews Links
🌐 www.thestandrewsgolfclub.co.uk

St Andrews Thistle   (1817)
Club
*18 Morton Crescent, St Andrews,
KY16 8RA*
🏠 180
🏌 JD Gray (01334) 474668
🏴 Play over St Andrews Links

St Regulus Ladies'   (1913)
Club
9 Pilmour Links, St Andrews, KY16 9JG
📧 admin@st-regulus-lgc.fsnet.co.uk
🏠 245
🏌 Mrs J Lumsden (01334) 472249
🏴 Play over St Andrews Links

The St Rule Club   (1898)
Club
12 The Links, St Andrews, KY16 9JB
☎ **(01334) 472988**
🖳 (01334) 472988
📧 strule.club@virgin.net
🏠 284
🏌 Mrs J Allan
🏴 Play over St Andrews Links

St Andrews Courses

Balgove   (1993)
Public
*St Andrews Links Trust, Pilmour House,
St Andrews, KY16 9SF*
☎ **(01334) 466666**
🖳 (01334) 479555
🏌 AJR McGregor (Gen Mgr)
🏴 9 L 1520 yds Par 30
👥 U
££ £7 – £10
🚗 St Andrews Links, on A91
⊕ Driving range
🏛 Donald Steel
🌐 www.standrews.org.uk

Duke's   (1995)
Craigtoun, St Andrews, KY16 8NS
☎ **(01334) 474371**

🖂 (01334) 477668
📧 reservations@oldcoursehotel
.co.uk
🏠 350
🏌 S Toon (01334) 470214
🏌 R Walker (01334) 470214
🏴 18 L 7271 yds Par 72 SSS 75
👥 U H SOC
££ £65 (£75)
🚗 3 miles S of St Andrews on
Pitscottie road
⊕ Golf academy
🏛 Peter Thomson CBE
🌐 www.oldcoursehotel.co.uk

Eden   (1914)
Public
*St Andrews Links Trust, Pilmour House,
St Andrews, KY16 9SF*
☎ **(01334) 466666**
🖳 (01334) 479555
🏌 AJR McGregor (Gen Mgr)
🏴 18 L 6195 yds Par 70 SSS 70
👥 U SOC
££ £22 – £30
🚗 St Andrews Links, on A91
⊕ 3D-£65-£110 W-£130-£220
(unlimited play over Jubilee, New,
Eden and Strathtyrum courses).
Driving range
🏛 HS Colt
🌐 www.standrews.org.uk

Jubilee   (1897)
Public
*St Andrews Links Trust, Pilmour House,
St Andrews, KY16 9SF*
☎ **(01334) 466666**
🖳 (01334) 479555
🏌 AJR McGregor (Gen Mgr)
🏴 18 L 6742 yds Par 72 SSS 73
👥 U SOC
££ £30 –£45
🚗 St Andrews Links, on A91. Signs to
West Sands
⊕ 3D-£65-£110 W-£130-£220
(unlimited play over Jubilee,
Strathtyrum, Eden & New courses).
Driving range
🏛 Angus/Steel
🌐 www.standrews.org.uk

New   (1895)
Public
*St Andrews Links Trust, Pilmour House,
St Andrews, KY16 9SF*
☎ **(01334) 466666**
🖳 (01334) 479555
🏌 AJR McGregor (Gen Mgr)
🏴 18 L 6604 yds Par 71 SSS 73
👥 U SOC
££ £35 – £50
🚗 St Andrews Links, on A91. Signs to
West Sands
⊕ 3D-£65-£110 W-£130-£220
(unlimited play over Jubilee, New,
Eden and Strathtyrum courses).
Driving range
🏛 Old Tom Morris
🌐 www.standrews.org.uk

Old Course (15th Century)
Public
*St Andrews Links Trust, Pilmour House,
St Andrews, KY16 9SF*
☎ **(01334) 466666**
🖳 (01334) 479555
📧 linkstrust@standrews.org.uk
🏌 AJR McGregor (Gen Mgr)
🏴 18 L 6566 yds Par 72 SSS 72
👥 H I No Sun play
££ £72 – £105
🚗 St Andrews Links, on A91. Signs to
West Sands
⊕ Driving range
🌐 www.standrews.org.uk

Strathtyrum   (1993)
Public
*St Andrews Links Trust, Pilmour House,
St Andrews, KY16 9SF*
☎ **(01334) 466666**
🖳 (01334) 479555
🏌 AJR McGregor (Gen Mgr)
🏴 18 L 5094 yds Par 69 SSS 65
👥 U SOC
££ £16 – £20
🚗 St Andrews Links, on A91
⊕ 3D-£65-£110 W-£130-£220
(unlimited play over Jubilee, New,
Eden, Strathtyrum and Balgove
courses). Driving range
🏛 Donald Steel
🌐 www.standrews.org.uk

Glasgow

Alexandra Park   (1880)
Public
*Alexandra Park, Dennistoun, Glasgow,
G31 8SE*
☎ **(0141) 556 1294**
🏠 250
🏌 G Campbell
🏴 9 L 4562 yds Par 62
👥 U
££ On application
🚗 ¹/₂ mile E of Glasgow, nr M8
🏛 Graham McArthur

Bishopbriggs   (1907)
*Brackenbrae Road, Bishopbriggs,
Glasgow, G64 2DX*
☎ **(0141) 772 1810**
🖳 (0141) 762 2532
📧 bgcsecretary@dial.pipex.com
🏠 400 150(L) 110(J)
🏌 A Smith (0141) 772 8938
🏴 18 L 6041 yds SSS 69
👥 H SOC–WD
££ £20 D–£30
🚗 6 miles N of Glasgow on A803
🏛 James Braid
🌐 www.thebishopbriggsgolfclub.com

Cathcart Castle   (1895)
Mearns Road, Clarkston, G76 7YL
☎ **(0141) 638 0082**
🖳 (0141) 638 1201
🏠 950

🐿 IG Sutherland (0141) 638 9449
✒ S Duncan (0141) 638 3436
🏳 18 L 5832 yds SSS 68
👤 M SOC
££ £28 D–£40
⛳ 1 mile from Clarkston on B767

Cawder (1933)
Cadder Road, Bishopbriggs, Glasgow, G64 3QD
☎ **(0141) 761 1281**
📠 (0141) 761 1285
📧 secretary@cawdergolfclub.org.uk
📖 1400
🐿 (0141) 761 1282
✒ K Stevely (0141) 772 7102
🏳 Cawder 18 L 6279 yds SSS 71; Keir 18 L 5880 yds SSS 68
👤 WD–U SOC–WD
££ £30
⛳ N of Glasgow, off A803 Kirkintilloch Road
🏠 Braid/Steel
■ www.cawdergolfclub.org.uk

Cowglen (1906)
301 Barrhead Road, Glasgow, G43 1EU
☎ **(0141) 632 0556**
📖 485
🐿 RJG Jamieson (01505) 503000
✒ S Payne (0141) 649 9401
🏳 18 L 6079 yds SSS 69
👤 WD–by arrangement with Sec WE–M
££ £25.50 D–£35
⛳ 3 miles SW of Glasgow (B762)
🏠 James Braid

Glasgow (1787)
Killermont, Bearsden, Glasgow, G61 2TW
☎ **(0141) 942 1713**
📠 (0141) 942 0770
📧 secretary@glasgow-golf.com
📖 800
🐿 DW Deas (0141) 942 2011
✒ J Steven (0141) 942 8507
🏳 18 L 5977 yds Par 70 SSS 69
👤 M
⛳ 4 miles NW of Glasgow
🏠 Tom Morris Sr

Haggs Castle (1910)
70 Dumbreck Road, Dumbreck, Glasgow, G41 4SN
☎ **(0141) 427 0480**
📠 (0141) 427 1157
📖 900
🐿 A Williams (0141) 427 1157
✒ J McAlister (0141) 427 3355
🏳 18 L 6426 yds SSS 71
👤 WD–H SOC–Weds only
££ SOC–£40
⛳ SW Glasgow (B768). M77 Junct. 1
🏠 Dave Thomas (1998)

King's Park (1934)
Public
150A Croftpark Avenue, Croftfoot, Glasgow, G54
☎ **(0141) 630 1597**
🐿 PJ King

🏳 9 L 4236 yds Par 64 SSS 60
👤 U
££ On application
⛳ Croftfoot, 3¹/₂ miles S of Glasgow

Knightswood (1929)
Public
Knightswood Park, Lincoln Avenue, Glasgow, G13 3DN
☎ **(0141) 959 6358**
📖 40
🐿 J Dean (0141) 954 6495
✒ None
🏳 9 L 2793 yds Par 68 SSS 67
👤 U exc Wed & Fri before 9am and 10–11am–NA
££ £7.60
⛳ 4 miles NW of Glasgow, S of A82

Lethamhill (1933)
Public
Cumbernauld Road, Glasgow, G33 1AH
☎ **(0141) 770 6220**
📠 (0141) 770 0520
🏳 18 L 5946 yds SSS 68
👤 U
££ £7.20
⛳ 3 miles NE of Glasgow (A80)

Linn Park (1924)
Public
Simshill Road, Glasgow, G44 5TA
☎ **(0141) 633 0377**
🏳 18 L 4592 yds SSS 65
👤 U–phone 1 day in advance
££ £7.30 (£7.30)
⛳ 4 miles S of Glasgow, W of B766

Littlehill (1926)
Public
Auchinairn Road, Glasgow, G64 1UT
☎ **(0141) 772 1916**
🏳 18 L 6228 yds SSS 70
👤 U
££ On application
⛳ 3 miles NE of Glasgow, E of A803

Pollok (1892)
90 Barrhead Road, Glasgow, G43 1BG
☎ **(0141) 632 1080**
📠 (0141) 649 1398
📧 pollok.gc@lineone.net
📖 500
🐿 I Cumming (0141) 632 4351
✒ None
🏳 18 L 6358 yds SSS 70
👤 WD–I XL WE–NA SOC–WD
££ £32 D–£42 (£40)
⛳ 3 miles SW of Glasgow (B762). M77 Junction 2

Ralston (1903)
Strathmore Avenue, Ralston, Paisley, PA1 3DT
☎ **(0141) 882 1349**
📠 (0141) 883 9837
📖 440 165(L) 100(J)
🐿 J Pearson
✒ C Munro (0141) 810 4925
🏳 18 L 6100 yds SSS 69

👤 M SOC
⛳ 2 miles E of Paisley (A761)

Rouken Glen (1922)
Public
Stewarton Road, Thornliebank, Glasgow, G46 7UZ
☎ **(0141) 638 7044**
🏳 18 L 4800 yds SSS 63
👤 U SOC
££ On application
⛳ 5 miles S of Glasgow, W of A77
⊕ Driving range

Ruchill (1928)
Public
Ruchil Park, Brassey Street, Maryhill, Glasgow G20
📖 60
🏳 9 L 2240 yds SSS 31
👤 U
££ On application
⛳ 2 miles N of Glasgow, W of A879

Sandyhills (1905)
223 Sandyhills Road, Glasgow, G32 9NA
☎ **(0141) 778 1179**
📖 700
🐿 CJ Wilson
🏳 18 L 6253 yds SSS 71
👤 M SOC
££ £17.50
⛳ 4 miles SE of Glasgow, N of A74

Williamwood (1906)
Clarkston Road, Netherlee, Glasgow, G44 3YR
☎ **(0141) 637 1783**
📠 (0141) 571 0166
📖 911
🐿 TDM Hepburn
✒ S Marshall (0141) 637 2715
🏳 18 L 5878 yds SSS 69
👤 WD–H
££ £27
⛳ 5 miles S of Glasgow
🏠 James Braid

Highland

Caithness & Sutherland

Bonar Bridge/Ardgay (1904)
Bonar-Bridge, Ardgay, IV24 3EJ
☎ **(01863) 766199 (Clubhouse)**
📧 bonarardgaygolf@aol.com
📖 250
🐿 J Reid (01863) 766750
🏳 9 L 5162 yds SSS 66
👤 U
££ D–£12 (£12)
⛳ ¹/₂ mile N of Bonar-Bridge on A836. 12 miles W of Dornoch

Brora (1891)
Golf Road, Brora, KW9 6QS
- ☎ **(01408) 621417/621911**
- 🖵 (01408) 622157
- ✍ J Fraser
- ⊩ 18 L 6110 yds SSS 69
- 👥 U exc comp days –H for open comps SOC
- ££ £27 D–£32 (£30 D–£40)
- ⛳ 18 miles N of Dornoch (A9)
- 🏠 James Braid
- ■ www.broragolf.co.uk

The Carnegie Club (1995)
Skibo Castle, Clashmore, Dornoch, IV25 3RQ
- ☎ **(01862) 894600**
- 🖵 (01862) 894601
- ✍ A Grant
- ✓ D Thomson
- ⊩ 18 L 6671 yds Par 71 SSS 72
- 👥 H–booking required
- ££ £130 inc lunch
- ⛳ 3 miles SW of Dornoch
- 🏠 Donald Steel

Durness (1988)
Pay and play
Balnakeil, Durness, IV27 4PN
- ☎ **(01971) 511364**
- 🖵 (01971) 511321
- ✉ mackenziedurness@aol.com
- 📖 150
- ✍ Mrs L Mackay (01971) 511364
- ⊩ 9 L 5555 yds SSS 69
- 👥 U
- ££ D–£15 W–£50
- ⛳ 57 miles NW of Lairg on A838

Golspie (1889)
Ferry Road, Golspie, KW10 6ST
- ☎ **(01408) 633266**
- 🖵 (01408) 633393
- ✉ info@golspie-golf-club.co.uk
- 📖 315
- ✓ None
- ⊩ 18 L 5890 yds SSS 68
- 👥 U SOC
- ££ £25 D–£35
- ⛳ 11 miles N of Dornoch
- 🏠 James Braid
- ■ www.golspie-golf-club.co.uk

Helmsdale (1895)
Golf Road, Helmsdale, KW8 6JA
- 📖 50
- ✍ R Sutherland
- ⊩ 9 L 3720 yds SSS 61
- 👥 U
- ££ £5 D–£10 W–£25
- ⛳ 30 miles N of Dornoch (A9)

Lybster (1926)
Main Street, Lybster, KW1 6BL
- 📖 100
- ✍ AG Calder (01595) 721316
- ⊩ 9 L 1896 yds SSS 61
- 👥 U
- ££ D–£10
- ⛳ 13 miles S of Wick on A99

Reay (1893)
Reay, Thurso, Caithness, KW14 7RE
- ☎ **(01847) 811288**
- 🖵 (01847) 894189
- ✉ info@reaygolfclub.co.uk
- 📖 300
- ✍ W McIntosh
- ✓ None
- ⊩ 18 L 5831 yds Par 69 SSS 69
- 👥 U SOC
- ££ D–£20 W–£60
- ⛳ 11 miles W of Thurso
- 🏠 James Braid
- ■ www.reaygolfclub.co.uk

Royal Dornoch (1877)
Golf Road, Dornoch, IV25 3LW
- ☎ **(01862) 810219**
- 🖵 (01862) 810792
- ✉ rdgc@royaldornoch.com
- 📖 1127 220(L) 72(J)
- ✍ JS Duncan (Sec/Mgr) (01862) 811220
- ✓ A Skinner (01862) 810902
- ⊩ C'ship 18 L 6514 yds SSS 73
  Struie 18 L 5438 yds SSS 66
- 👥 C'ship–H Struie–U
- ££ On application
- ⛳ 45 miles N of Inverness, off A9, N of Dornoch
- ⊕ Helipad by clubhouse. Airstrip nearby
- ■ www.royaldornoch.com

Thurso (1893)
Newlands of Geise, Thurso, KW14 7XD
- ☎ **(01847) 893807**
- 📖 300
- ✍ Capt D Phillips (01847) 895433
- ⊩ 18 L 5828 yds SSS 69
- 👥 U
- ££ £11
- ⛳ 2 miles SW of Thurso

Ullapool
North Road, Ullapool, IV26 2TH
- ☎ **(01854) 613323**
- 🖵 (01854) 613133
- ✉ info@ullapool-golf.co.uk
- 📖 150
- ✓ None
- ⊩ 9 L 5338 yds Par 70 SSS 66
- 👥 U
- ££ £15 (£15) W–£50
- ⛳ Ullapool
- ■ www.ullapool-golf.co.uk

Wick (1870)
Reiss, Wick, KW1 5LJ
- ☎ **(01955) 602726**
- ✉ wickgolfclub@hotmail.com
- 📖 311
- ✍ D Shearer (01955) 602935
- ⊩ 18 L 6123 yds SSS 70
- 👥 U
- ££ On application
- ⛳ 3 miles N of Wick on A99
- ■ www.wickgolfclub.fsnet.co.uk

Inverness

Abernethy (1893)
Nethy Bridge, PH25 3EB
- ☎ **(01479) 821305**
- 🖵 (01479) 821305
- ✉ info@abernethygolfclub.com
- 📖 450
- ✍ RH Robbie
- ⊩ 9 L 2520 yds SSS 66
- 👥 U SOC
- ££ £13 (£16)
- ⛳ 5 miles S of Grantown (B970)
- ■ www.abernethygolfclub.com

Alness (1904)
Ardross Rd, Alness, Ross-shire, IV17 0QA
- ☎ **(01349) 883877**
- ✉ info@alnessgolfclub.co.uk
- 📖 300
- ✍ Mrs M Rogers
- ⊩ 18 L 4886 yds Par 67 SSS 64
- 👥 U SOC
- ££ £13 (£15)
- ⛳ ¼ mile N of Alness. 20 miles N of Inverness
- 🏠 I Scott Taylor
- ■ www.alness.com

Boat-of-Garten (1898)
Boat-of-Garten, PH24 3BQ
- ☎ **(01479) 831282**
- 🖵 (01479) 831523
- ✉ boatgolf@enterprise.net
- 📖 650
- ✍ P Smyth
- ⊩ 18 L 5866 yds SSS 69
- 👥 U–booking advisable
- ££ £28 D–£33 (£33 D–£38)
- ⛳ 27 miles SE of Inverness (A95)
- 🏠 James Braid
- ■ www.boatgolf.com

Carrbridge (1980)
Carrbridge, PH23 3AU
- ☎ **(01479) 841623 (Clubhouse)**
- ✉ enquiries@carrbridgegolf
- 📖 500
- ✍ Mrs AT Baird
- ⊩ 9 L 2623 yds Par 71 SSS 68
- 👥 U exc comp days–NA
- ££ D–£13 (D–£16)
- ⛳ 23 miles SE of Inverness, off A9
- ■ www.carrbridgegolf.com

Fort Augustus (1926)
Pay and play
Markethill, Fort Augustus, PH32 4AU
- ✉ info@fagc.co.uk
- 📖 110
- ✍ J Morgan (01320) 366758
- ⊩ 9 L 5454 yds SSS 67
- 👥 U
- ££ £12 D–£15
- ⛳ W end of Fort Augustus on A82
- 🏠 Harry S Colt
- ■ www.fagc.co.uk

Fort William (1974)
North Road, Fort William, PH33 6SN
- ☎ **(01397) 704464**
- ▥ 430
- ⋌ R Macintyre
- ⮞ 18 L 5686 metres SSS 71
- ♙ U
- ££ £20
- ⛳ 3 miles N of Fort William (A82)
- ⌂ JR Stutt

Fortrose & Rosemarkie
(1888)
Ness Road East, Fortrose, IV10 8SE
- ☎ **(01381) 620529**
- ▭ (01381) 621328
- ✉ secretary@fortrosegolfclub.co.uk
- ▥ 750
- ⋌ WT Baird
- ⮞ 18 L 5885 yds Par 72 SSS 69
- ♙ U SOC
- ££ £22 (£27)
- ⛳ Black Isle, 12 miles N of Inverness
- ⌂ James Braid
- ▬ www.fortrosegolfclub.co.uk

Grantown-on-Spey (1890)
Golf Course Road, Grantown-on-Spey, PH26 3HY
- ☎ **(01479) 872079**
- ▭ (01479) 873725
- ✉ secretary
  @grantownonspeygolfclub.co.uk
- ▥ 800
- ⋌ JS Macpherson
- ⮞ 18 L 5710 yds Par 70 SSS 68
- ♙ WD–U WE–U after 10am SOC
- ££ D–£20 (D–£25)
- ⛳ E side of Grantown (A95)
- ⌂ Park/Braid/Brown
- ▬ www.grantownonspeygolfclub
  .co.uk

Invergordon (1893)
King George Street, Invergordon, IV18 0BD
- ☎ **(01349) 852715**
- ▥ 170 30(L) 50(J)
- ⮞ 18 L 6030 yds Par 69 SSS 69
- ♙ U SOC
- ££ £15 (£15)
- ⛳ 15 miles NE of Dingwall
  (A9/B817)
- ⌂ A Rae (1994)

Inverness (1883)
Culcabock Road, Inverness, IV2 3XQ
- ☎ **(01463) 239882**
- ▭ (01463) 239882
- ▥ 1100
- ⋌ JS Thomson
- ✍ AP Thomson (01463) 231989
- ⮞ 18 L 6226 yds SSS 70
- ♙ WE/BH–restricted SOC
- ££ £29 D–£39 (£29 D–£39)
- ⛳ 1 mile S of Inverness
- ⌂ James Braid
- ▬ www.invernessgolfclub.co.uk

Kingussie (1891)
Gynack Road, Kingussie, PH21 1LR
- ☎ **(01540) 661374 (Clubhouse)**
- ▭ (01540) 662066
- ▥ 800
- ⋌ ND MacWilliam (01540) 661600
- ✍ None
- ⮞ 18 L 5555 yds SSS 68
- ♙ U
- ££ £19 D–£22 (£21 D–£27)
- ⛳ Kingussie (A9)
- ⌂ H Vardon
- ▬ www.kingussie-golf.co.uk

Loch Ness (1996)
Castle Heather, Inverness, IV2 6AA
- ☎ **(01463) 713334/5**
- ▭ (01463) 712695
- ✉ info@golflochness.com
- ▥ 600
- ⋌ ND Hampton (01463) 713335
- ✍ M Piggot (01463) 713334
- ⮞ 18 L 6772 yds Par 73 SSS 72
- ♙ U SOC
- ££ D–£25 (D–£30)
- ⛳ Culduthel, SW Inverness (A9)
- ⊕ Floodlit driving range
- ▬ www.golflochness.com

Muir of Ord (1875)
Great North Road, Muir of Ord, IV6 7SX
- ☎ **(01463) 870825**
- ▭ (01463) 871867
- ✉ muirgolf@supanet.com
- ▥ 700
- ⋌ Mrs J Gibson
- ✍ Shop (01463) 871311
- ⮞ 18 L 5557 yds SSS 68
- ♙ U SOC
- ££ D–£16 (£20) W–£50
- ⛳ 15 miles N of Inverness (A862)
- ⌂ James Braid

Nairn (1887)
Seabank Road, Nairn, IV12 4HB
- ☎ **(01667) 453208**
- ▭ (01667) 456328
- ✉ bookings@nairngolfclub.co.uk
- ▥ 1100
- ⋌ D Corstorphine (01667) 453208
- ✍ R Fyfe (01667) 452787
- ⮞ 18 L 6705 yds Par 72 SSS 74
  9 hole course
- ♙ U SOC
- ££ On application
- ⛳ Nairn West Shore (A96). 15 miles
  E of Inverness
- ⌂ Old Tom Morris/Braid/Simpson
- ▬ www.nairngolfclub.co.uk

Nairn Dunbar (1899)
Lochloy Road, Nairn, IV12 5AE
- ☎ **(01667) 452741**
- ▭ (01667) 456897
- ✉ secretary@nairndunbar.com
- ▥ 900
- ⋌ JS Falconer
- ✍ DH Torrance (01667) 453964
- ⮞ 18 L 6720 yds SSS 73
- ££ £35 D–£45 (£42 D–£56)

- ⛳ In Nairn
- ▬ www.nairndunbar.com

Newtonmore (1893)
Golf Course Road, Newtonmore, PH20 1AT
- ☎ **(01540) 673878**
- ▭ (01540) 670147
- ✉ secretary@newtonmoregolf.com
- ▥ 450
- ⋌ C Bisset
- ✍ R Henderson (01540) 673611
- ⮞ 18 L 6029 yds SSS 69
- ♙ U SOC
- ££ £18 D–£22 (£20 D–£27)
- ⛳ 4 miles W of Kingussie. 46 miles S
  of Inverness
- ▬ www.newtonmoregolf.com

Spean Bridge
Spean Bridge, Fort William, PH33
- ▥ 65
- ⋌ K Dalziel (01397) 703907
- ⮞ 9 hole course SSS 63
- ♙ U
- ££ D–£12
- ⛳ 9 miles N of Fort William on A82

Strathpeffer Spa (1888)
Golf Course Road, Strathpeffer, IV14 9AS
- ☎ **(01997) 421011/421219**
- ▭ (01997) 421011
- ▥ 360 50(L) 85(J)
- ⋌ N Roxburgh (01997) 421396
- ✍ G Lister (01997) 421011
- ⮞ 18 L 4792 yds SSS 64
- ♙ U SOC
- ££ £15 D–£21
- ⛳ ¼ mile N of Strathpeffer. 5 miles
  W of Dingwall
- ⌂ Willie Park/Tom Morris
- ▬ www.strathpeffergolf.co.uk

Tain (1890)
Chapel Road, Tain, IV19 1JE
- ☎ **(01862) 892314**
- ▭ (01862) 892099
- ✉ info@tain-golfclub.co.uk
- ▥ 500
- ⋌ Mrs KD Ross
- ✍ None
- ⮞ 18 L 6404 yds SSS 71
- ♙ U
- ££ £30 D–£36 (£36 D–£46)
- ⛳ 35 miles N of Inverness (A9). 8
  miles S of Dornoch
- ⌂ Tom Morris
- ▬ www.tain-golfclub.co.uk

Tarbat (1909)
Portmahomack, Tain, IV20 1YB
- ☎ **(01862) 871598**
- ▭ (01862) 871598
- ▥ 200
- ⋌ M Lane
- ⮞ 9 L 2568 yds SSS 65
- ♙ U SOC
- ££ D–£12
- ⛳ 10 miles E of Tain

Torvean (1962)
Public
Glenurquhart Road, Inverness, IV3 6JN
☎ **(01463) 711434 (Starter)**
⌨ (01463) 225651 (Sec)
📖 400
🏌 Mrs KM Gray (01463) 225651
✍ None
🏴 18 L 5784 yds SSS 68
👥 U
£€ £12.90 (£14.80)
⛳ SW of Inverness on A82

Orkney & Shetland

Orkney (1889)
Grainbank, Kirkwall, Orkney,
KW15 1RD
☎ **(01856) 872457**
⌨ (01856) 872457
📖 415
🏌 GR Donaldson (01856) 877533
🏴 18 L 5411 yds SSS 67
👥 U
£€ D–£15 W–£50
⛳ 1 mile W of Kirkwall
■ www.orkneygc.co.uk

Sanday (1977)
Sanday, Orkney, KW17 2BW
☎ **(01857) 600341**
⌨ (01857) 600341
📖 20
🏌 R Thorne
🏴 9 L 2776 yds Par 35
👥 U
£€ £10
⛳ 2 miles N of Lady on B9069

Shetland (1891)
Dale, Gott, Shetland, ZE2 9SB
☎ **(01595) 840369**
⌨ (01595) 840369
📖 400
🏌 E Groat
🏴 18 L 5776 yds SSS 68
👥 U
£€ D–£15
⛳ 3 miles N of Lerwick (A907)
🏛 Fraser Middleton
■ www.shetlandgolfclub.co.uk

Stromness (1890)
Stromness, Orkney, KW16 3DU
☎ **(01856) 850772**
📖 250
🏌 GA Bevan (01856) 850885
🏴 18 L 4762 yds SSS 63
👥 U
£€ D–£15
⛳ Stromness, 16 miles W of Kirkwall on Hoy Sound
■ www.stromnessgc.co.uk

Whalsay (1976)
Skaw Taing, Whalsay, Shetland,
ZE2 9AL
☎ **(01806) 566450/566481**

📖 100
🏌 C Hutchison
✍ None
🏴 18 L 6009 yds Par 70 SSS 68
👥 U SOC
£€ £10
⛳ 5 miles N of Symbister Ferry

West Coast

Askernish (1891)
Lochboisdale, Askernish, South Uist,
HS81 5ST
☎ **(01878) 700298**
📖 50
🏌 N Elliott
🏴 18 L 5114 yds SSS 67
👥 U
£€ £10
⛳ 5 miles NW of Lochboisdale
🏛 Tom Morris Sr

Barra
Cleat, Castlebay, Isle of Barra, HS9 5XX
☎ **(01871) 810591**
⌨ (01871) 810418
🏴 9 L 2396 yds
👥 U
£€ D–£5
⛳ 6 miles N of Castlebay

Gairloch (1898)
Gairloch, IV21 2BQ
☎ **(01445) 712407**
✉ secretary@gairlochgc.freeserve.co.uk
📖 285
🏌 A Shinkins
🏴 9 L 2281 yds SSS 64
👥 U–phone first
£€ D–£15 W–£49
⛳ 60 miles W of Dingwall in Wester Ross

Isle of Harris
Scarista, Isle of Harris, HS5 3HX
☎ **(01859) 502331**
✉ harrisgolf@ic24.net
📖 72
🏌 A Macsween
✍ None
🏴 9 L 2442 yds Par 68 SSS 64
👥 U
£€ £10 (£10)
⛳ 13 miles S of Tarbert on W coast
■ www.harrisgolf.com

Isle of Skye (1964)
Sconser, Isle of Skye, IV48 8TD
☎ **(01478) 650414**
📖 250
🏌 I Macmillan
🏴 9 L 4798 yds Par 66 SSS 64
👥 U
£€ D–£15
⛳ Between Broadford and Sligachan

Lochcarron (1908)
Lochcarron, Strathcarron, IV54 8YU
📖 124
🏌 AG Beattie ((01520) 766211
🏴 9 L 3575 yds Par 60 SSS 60
👥 U exc Sat 2–5pm–NA
£€ D–£10 W–£40
⛳ 1/2 mile E of Lochcarron in Wester Ross

Skeabost (1982)
Skeabost Bridge, Isle of Skye, IV51 9NP
☎ **(01470) 532202**
⌨ (01470) 532454
📖 80
🏌 DJ Matheson (01470) 532319 (Skeabost House Hotel)
🏴 9 L 3224 yds SSS 59
👥 U
£€ D–£13
⛳ 6 miles NW of Portree on Dunvegan road

Stornoway (1890)
Lady Lever Park, Stornoway, Isle of Lewis, HS2 0XP
☎ **(01851) 702240**
📖 400
🏌 JDF Watson (01851) 705486
🏴 18 L 5252 yds Par 68 SSS 67
👥 U exc Sun–NA SOC
£€ D–£15 W–£45
⛳ Off A857 in Lews Castle, Isle of Lewis
■ www.stornowaygolfclub.co.uk

Traigh
Camusdarach, Arisaig, PH39 4NT
☎ **(01687) 450337**
📖 160
🏌 H MacDougall (01687) 450628
✍ None
🏴 9 L 2405 yds Par 68 SSS 65
👥 U
£€ D–£14
⛳ 2 miles N of Arisaig on A830 Fort William-Mallaig road
🏛 John Salvesen

Lanarkshire

Airdrie (1877)
Rochsoles, Airdrie, ML6 0PQ
☎ **(01236) 762195**
⌨ (01236) 760584
✉ airdrie.golfclub@virgin.net
📖 450
🏌 DM Hardie
✍ J Carver (01236) 754360
🏴 18 L 6004 yds SSS 69
👥 M I WE/BH–NA SOC
£€ £15 D–£25
⛳ Airdrie 1 mile
🏛 James Braid

Bellshill (1905)
Community Road, Orbiston, Bellshill,
ML4 2RZ
☎ **(01698) 745124**

☐ 680
✍ J Sloan
ᐅ 18 L 5900 yds Par 69 SSS 69
👥 WD–U Sun–NA before 1.30pm
SOC
££ D–£20 (£30)
⬧ 30 miles W (A725) M74 Junction 5

Biggar (1895)
Public
The Park, Broughton Road, Biggar, ML12 6AH
☎ (01899) 220618 (Clubhouse), (01899) 220319 (Bookings)
☐ 140
✍ T Rodger (01698) 382311
✓ None
ᐅ 18 L 5537 yds SSS 67
👥 U–booking recommended
££ £10 (£12)
⬧ 12 miles SE of Lanark (A702)
🏠 Willie Park

Blairbeth (1910)
Burnside, Rutherglen, Glasgow, G73 4SF
☎ (0141) 634 3355 (Clubhouse)
☐ 450
✍ TI Whyte (0141) 634 3325
ᐅ 18 L 5518 yds SSS 68
👥 SOC–WD
££ On application
⬧ 1 mile S of Rutherglen

Bothwell Castle (1922)
Blantyre Road, Bothwell, Glasgow, G71 8PJ
☎ (01698) 853177
🖥 (01698) 854052
☐ 1000
✍ DA McNaught (01698) 854052
✓ A McCloskey (01698) 852052
ᐅ 18 L 6225 yds SSS 70
👥 WD–U 9.30–10.30am & 2.30–3.30pm
££ £24 D–£32
⬧ 2 miles N of Hamilton. M74 Junction 5

Calderbraes (1891)
57 Roundknowe Road, Uddingston, G71 7TS
☎ (01698) 813425
☐ 300
✍ S McGuigan (0141) 773 2287
ᐅ 9 L 5046 yds Par 66 SSS 67
👥 WD–U WE–M
££ D–£12
⬧ Start of M74

Cambuslang (1892)
30 Westburn Drive, Cambuslang, G72 7NA
☎ (0141) 641 3130
☐ 200 100(L) 75(J)
✍ RM Dunlop
ᐅ 9 L 5942 yds SSS 69
👥 M
££ On application
⬧ Cambuslang Station ³/₄ mile

Carluke (1894)
Hallcraig, Mauldslie Road, Carluke, ML8 5HG
☎ (01555) 770574/771070
🖥 (01555) 770574
☐ 460 100(L)
✍ T Pheely (01555) 770574
✓ C Ronald (01555) 751053
ᐅ 18 L 5805 yds SSS 68
👥 WD U before 4pm WE/BH–NA SOC
££ £23 D–£28
⬧ 20 miles SE of Glasgow

Carnwath (1907)
1 Main Street, Carnwath, ML11 8JX
☎ (01555) 840251
🖥 (01555) 841070
☐ 400
✍ Mrs L McPate
✓ None
ᐅ 18 L 5955 yds SSS 69
👥 WD–U before 4pm Sat–NA Sun–restricted
££ £16 D–£26 Sun–£22 D–£32
⬧ 7 miles E of Lanark

Cathkin Braes (1888)
Cathkin Road, Rutherglen, Glasgow, G73 4SE
☎ (0141) 634 6605
🖥 (0141) 630 9186
☐ 930
✍ H Millar
✓ S Bree (0141) 634 0650
ᐅ 18 L 6208 yds SSS 71
👥 WD–I
££ £25
⬧ 5 miles S of Glasgow (B759)
🏠 James Braid

Coatbridge Municipal (1971)
Public
Townhead Road, Coatbridge, ML52 2HX
☎ (01236) 28975
ᐅ 18 L 6020 yds SSS 69
👥 U
££ On application
⬧ Townhead, E of Glasgow. ¹/₂ mile E of M73
⊕ Driving range

Colville Park (1923)
Jerviston Estate, Motherwell, ML1 4UG
☎ (01698) 263017
🖥 (01698) 230418
☐ 900 64(L) 140(J)
✍ L Innes (01698) 262808
✓ J Currie (01698) 265779
ᐅ 18 L 6301 yds Par 71 SSS 70
👥 WD–U 11am–3pm exc Fri–NA WE–NA SOC–WD
££ £15 D–£25
⬧ 1 mile NE of Motherwell on A723
🏠 James Braid

Crow Wood (1925)
Cumbernauld Road, Muirhead, Glasgow, G69 9JF
☎ (0141) 799 2011

☐ (0141) 779 9148
☐ 700
✍ FM Davidson (0141) 779 4954
✓ B Moffat (0141) 779 1943
ᐅ 18 L 6168 yds Par 71 SSS 70
👥 WD–H (prior notice required) SOC
££ £23 D–£34
⬧ 5 miles NE of Glasgow, off A80
🏠 James Braid

Dalziel Park (1997)
100 Hagen Drive, Motherwell, ML1 5RZ
☎ (01698) 862862
🖥 (01698) 862863
☐ 400
✍ I Donnachie
✓ None
ᐅ 18 L 6137 yds Par 70
👥 WD–U SOC
££ £20
⬧ 5 miles E of Motherwell via A723 and B7029
⊕ Driving range
🏠 Nigel Williams

Douglas Water (1922)
Rigside, Lanark, ML11 9NB
☎ (01555) 880361
☐ 190
✍ D Hogg
ᐅ 9 L 2916 yds SSS 69
👥 U exc Sat–restricted
££ £8 (£10)
⬧ 7 miles S of Lanark. M74 Junctions 11 & 12

Drumpellier (1894)
Drumpellier Ave, Coatbridge, ML5 1RX
☎ (01236) 424139/428723
🖥 (01236) 428723
✉ administrator@drumpelliergc.freeserve.co.uk
☐ 500
✍ JM Craig
✓ D Ross (01236) 432971
ᐅ 18 L 6227 yds SSS 70
👥 I
££ £30 D–£40
⬧ 8 miles E of Glasgow
🏠 James Braid
◼ www.drumpellier.com

East Kilbride (1900)
Chapelside Road, Nerston, East Kilbride, G74 4PH
☎ (01355) 220913 (Clubhouse)
☐ 850
✍ WG Gray (01355) 247728
✓ P McKay (01355) 222192
ᐅ 18 L 6402 yds SSS 71
👥 M SOC–WD
££ £25 D–£35
⬧ 8 miles S of Glasgow

Easter Moffat (1922)
Mansion House, Plains, Airdrie, ML6 8NP
☎ (01236) 842878
🖥 (01236) 842904
✉ gordonmiller@emgc.freeserve.co.uk

📖 500
🏌 G Miller (01236) 620972
✏ G King (01236) 843015
🏴 18 L 6221 yds SSS 70
👤 WD only
£€ £20 D–£30
🚗 3 miles E of Airdrie

Hamilton (1892)
Riccarton, Ferniegair, Hamilton,
ML3 7UE
☎ (01698) 282872
📖 500
🏌 GM Chapman (01698) 459537
✏ R Forrest (01698) 282324
🏴 18 L 6255 yds SSS 71
👤 M or by arrangement with Sec
£€ On application
🚗 1¹/₂ miles S of Hamilton
🏺 James Braid

Hollandbush (1954)
Public
Acre Tophead, Lesmahagow, Coalburn,
ML11 0JS
☎ (01555) 893484
📖 420
🏌 R Lynch
✏ I Rae (01555) 893646
🏴 18 L 6246 yds SSS 70
👤 U
£€ £8.20 (9.50)
🚗 10 miles SW of Lanark, off A74,
between Lesmahagow and
Coalburn

Kirkhill (1910)
Greenlees Road, Cambuslang, Glasgow,
G72 8YN
☎ (0141) 641 3083 (Clubhouse)
📠 (0141) 641 8499
📖 570
🏌 J Young (0141) 641 8499
✏ D Williamson (0141) 641 7972
🏴 18 L 6030 yds SSS 70
👤 WD–by prior arrangement
WE/BH–NA SOC
£€ On application
🚗 Cambuslang, SE Glasgow
🏺 James Braid

Lanark (1851)
The Moor, Lanark, ML11 7RX
☎ (01555) 663219
📠 (01555) 663219
📧 lanarkgolfclub@talk21.com
📖 520 130(L) 150(J)
🏌 GH Cuthill
✏ A White (01555) 661456
🏴 18 L 6306 yds SSS 71
9 hole course
👤 WD–U until 4pm WE–M
£€ 18 hole: £26 D–£40 9 hole: £6
🚗 30 miles S of Glasgow, off A74
🏺 Tom Morris

Langlands (1985)
Public
Langlands Road, East Kilbride,
G75 0QQ
☎ (01355) 248173,
(01355) 224685 (Starter)

📠 (01355) 248121
📖 350
🏌 A Craik (01355) 248401
🏴 18 L 6201 yds Par 70 SSS 70
👤 U
£€ £8.70 (£10.10)
🚗 2 miles SE of East Kilbride, off
Strathaven Road
🏺 F Hawtree

Larkhall
Public
Burnhead Road, Larkhall, Glasgow
☎ (01698) 881113
📖 150
🏌 M Mallinson
🏴 9 L 6234 yds SSS 70
👤 U exc Tues 5–8pm & Sat 7am–5pm
£€ On application
🚗 SW of Larkhall on B7109. 10 miles
SE of Glasgow

Leadhills (1935)
2 Gowan Bank, Leadhills, ML16 6YB
☎ (01654) 74356
📠 (01654) 74356
📖 40
🏌 N Davies
🏴 9 L 2177 yds SSS 64
👤 U
£€ D–£5 (£5)
🚗 6 miles S of Abington, off A74

Mount Ellen (1905)
Lochend Road, Gartcosh, Glasgow,
G69 9EY
☎ (01236) 872277
📠 (01236) 872249
📖 480
🏌 WJ Dickson
✏ G Reilly
🏴 18 L 5525 yds SSS 68
👤 WD–U from 9am–4pm WE–NA
£€ On application
🚗 8 miles NE of Glasgow, W of M73

Mouse Valley (1993)
East End, Cleghorn, Lanark, ML11 8NR
☎ (01555) 870015
📠 (01555) 870022
📖 300
🏴 18 L 6300 yds SSS 72
9 L 2200 yds SSS 65
👤 U
£€ 18 hole: £12.50 (£15) 9 hole: £7 (£8)
🚗 2 miles W of Carnwath on A721
🏺 Graham Taylor

Shotts (1895)
Blairhead, Benhar Road, Shotts,
ML7 5BJ
☎ (01501) 820431
📖 700
🏌 GT Stoddart (01501) 825868
✏ J Strachan (01501) 822658
🏴 18 L 6205 yds SSS 70
👤 WD–U Sat–NA before 4.30pm
£€ £16 (£25)
🚗 18 miles E of Glasgow on B7057.
M8 Junction 5, 1¹/₂ miles
🏺 James Braid

Strathaven (1908)
Glasgow Road, Strathaven, ML10 6NL
☎ (01357) 520421
📠 (01357) 520539
📧 manager@strathavengolfclub
.fsbusiness.co.uk
📖 1000
🏌 AW Wallace
✏ S Kerr (01357) 521812
🏴 18 L 6226 yds SSS 71
👤 WD–I before 4pm WE–NA
£€ £25 D–£35
🚗 N of Strathaven, off Glasgow road
(A726)

Strathclyde Park
Public
Mote Hill, Hamilton, ML3 6BY
☎ (01698) 429350
📖 200
🏌 K Will
✏ W Walker (01698) 285511
🏴 9 L 6350 yds SSS 70
👤 U exc medal days (phone booking)
£€ 18 holes–£6.80 (£8)
🚗 Hamilton. M74 Junction 5
⊕ Driving range

Torrance House (1969)
Public
Strathaven Road, East Kilbride,
Glasgow, G75 0QZ
☎ (01355) 248638
📖 650
🏌 JB Asher (01355) 249720
✏ J Dunlop (013552) 33451
🏴 18 L 6415 yds SSS 71
👤 U
£€ £16
🚗 S of East Kilbride, off Strathaven
road (A726)

Wishaw (1897)
55 Cleland Road, Wishaw, ML2 7PH
☎ (01698) 372869 (Clubhouse)
📠 (01698) 357480
📖 475 100(L)
🏌 CR Innes (01698) 357480
✏ S Adair (01698) 358247
🏴 18 L 5999 yds SSS 69
👤 WD after 4pm WE–NA Sat–NA
£€ £15 D–£25 Sun–£20 D–£30 SOC
🚗 N of Wishaw town centre

Lothians

East Lothian

Aberlady (1912)
Club
Aberlady, EH32 0RB
📧 ithomps3@aol.com
📖 43
🏌 I Thompson (01875) 870029
🏴 Play over Kilspindie course

Bass Rock (1873)
Club
22 Smileyknowes Court, North Berwick, EH39 4RG
- 🖂 andelsthor@lineone.net
- ☎ 110
- ✍ A Thorburn (01620) 893391
- ⊳ Play over North Berwick

Castle Park (1994)
Pay and play
Gifford, Haddington, EH41 4PL
- ☎ **(01620) 810723**
- 🖶 (01620) 810723
- 🖂 stuartfortune@aol.com
- ☎ 360
- ✍ S Fortune (01620) 810733
- ✓ D Small (01368) 862872
- ⊳ 18 L 6121 yds Par 72 SSS 70
- 👥 U SOC
- ££ £14 D–£19 (£19 D–£25)
- 🚗 2 miles S of Gifford on Longyester road
- ⊕ Driving range
- ■ www.castleparkgolfclub.co.uk

Dirleton Castle (1854)
Club
15 The Pines, Gullane, EH31 2DT
- ☎ **(01620) 843591**
- ☎ 100
- ✍ J Taylor
- ⊳ Play over Gullane courses

Dunbar (1856)
East Links, Dunbar, EH42 1LL
- ☎ **(01368) 862317**
- 🖶 (01368) 865202
- ☎ 998
- ✍ Liz Thom
- ✓ J Montgomery (01368) 862086
- ⊳ 18 L 6404 yds SSS 71
- 👥 U SOC–exc Thurs
- ££ £37 D–£50 (£45 D–£60)
- 🚗 ½ mile E of Dunbar. 30 miles E of Edinburgh, off A1
- 🛈 Tom Morris

Gifford (1904)
Edinburgh Road, Gifford, EH41 4JE
- ☎ **(01620) 810591 (Starter)**
- 🖂 thesecretary@giffordgolfclub.fsnet.co.uk
- ☎ 570
- ✍ G MacColl (01620) 810267
- ⊳ 9 L 6050 yds SSS 69
- 👥 U–booking required
- ££ 18 holes–£15 D–£25
- 🚗 4 miles S of Haddington. 20 miles SE of Edinburgh (B6355)
- 🛈 Willie Watt

Glen (North Berwick) (1906)
East Links, Tantallon Terrace, North Berwick, EH39 4LE
- ☎ **(01620) 892726**
- 🖶 (01620) 895447
- 🖂 secretary@glengolfclub.co.uk
- ☎ 650
- ✍ K Fish
- ✓ Shop (01620) 894596
- ⊳ 18 L 6243 yds SSS 70
- 👥 U–booking recommended
- ££ £22 D–£32 (£30 D–£40)
- 🚗 20 miles E of Edinburgh, off A198
- 🛈 Braid/Sayers/Mackenzie Ross
- ■ www.glengolfclub.co.uk

Gullane (1882)
Gullane, EH31 2BB
- ☎ **(01620) 843115 (Starter)**
- 🖶 (01620) 842327
- 🖂 manager@gullanegolfclub.com
- ☎ 870 300(L) 60(J)
- ✍ SC Owram (01620) 842255
- ✓ J Hume (01620) 843111
- ⊳ No 1 18 L 6466 yds SSS 72
  No 2 18 L 6244 yds SSS 70
  No 3 18 L 5252 yds SSS 66
  6 hole children's course
- 👥 No 1–H Nos 2/3–U
- ££ No 1 £70 D–£95 (£85) No 2 £29 D–£41 (£35) No 3 £17 D–£25 (£24) Children's course free
- 🚗 18 miles E of Edinburgh on A198
- ⊕ Advance booking advisable
- ■ www.gullanegolfclub.com

Haddington (1865)
Amisfield Park, Haddington, EH41 4PT
- ☎ **(01620) 823627**
- 🖶 (01620) 826580
- 🖂 hadd.golf1@tesco.net
- ☎ 650
- ✍ DM Swarbrick (Mgr)
- ✓ J Sandilands (01620) 822727
- ⊳ 18 L 6317 yds SSS 70
- 👥 WD–U WE–U 10am–12 & 2–4pm
- ££ £20 (£30)
- 🚗 17 miles E of Edinburgh on A1. ¾ mile E of Haddington

The Honourable Company of Edinburgh Golfers (1744)
Muirfield, Gullane, EH31 2EG
- ☎ **(01620) 842123**
- 🖶 (01620) 842977
- ☎ 625
- ✍ Gp Capt JA Prideaux
- ⊳ 18 L 6601 yds SSS 73 (Championship L 7034 yds)
- 👥 WD–Tues & Thurs I H WE/BH–NA SOC
- ££ £90 D–£120
- 🚗 NE outskirts of Gullane, opposite sign for Greywalls Hotel on A198

Kilspindie (1867)
Aberlady, EH32 0QD
- ☎ **(01875) 870358**
- 🖶 (01875) 870358
- 🖂 kilspindie@btconnect.com
- ☎ 400 150(L) 60(J)
- ✍ PB Casely
- ✓ GJ Sked (01875) 870695
- ⊳ 18 L 5012 metres SSS 66
- 👥 Phone Sec in advance WD–U after 9.45am WE–U after 11am SOC
- ££ £27.50 D–£44 (£33 D–£55)
- 🚗 Aberlady, 17 miles E of Edinburgh
- 🛈 Ross/Sayers

Longniddry (1921)
Links Road, Longniddry, EH32 0NL
- ☎ **(01875) 852141**
- 🖶 (01875) 853371
- 🖂 secretary@longniddrygolfclub.co.uk
- ☎ 1100
- ✍ N Robertson
- ✓ WJ Gray (01875) 852228
- ⊳ 18 L 6260 yds SSS 70
- 👥 WD–U H SOC–WD after 9.18am
- ££ £35 D–£50 (£45)
- 🚗 13 miles E of Edinburgh, off A1
- 🛈 HS Colt
- ■ www.longniddrygolfclub.co.uk

Luffness New (1894)
Aberlady, EH32 0QA
- ☎ **(01620) 843114**
- 🖶 (01620) 842933
- 🖂 lngc@talk21.com
- ☎ 700
- ✍ Gp Capt AG Yeates (01620) 843336
- ✓ None
- ⊳ 18 L 6122 yds SSS 70
- 👥 H or I XL before 10am WE/BH–NA SOC
- ££ £37.50 D–£55
- 🚗 1 mile W of Gullane (A198)
- 🛈 Morris/Braid

Musselburgh (1938)
Monktonhall, Musselburgh, EH21 6SA
- ☎ **(0131) 665 2005**
- ☎ 1000
- ✍ G Finlay
- ✓ F Mann (0131) 665 7055
- ⊳ 18 L 6725 yds SSS 73
- 👥 WD–U before 4.30pm WE–NA before 10am
- ££ £25 (£35)
- 🚗 1 mile S of Musselburgh on B6415
- 🛈 James Braid

Musselburgh Old Course
Public
10 Balcarres Road, Musselburgh, EH21 7SD
- ☎ **(0131) 665 6981, (0131) 665 5438 (Starter)**
- 🖂 mocgc@breathemail.net
- ☎ 200
- ✍ L Freedman (0131) 665 4861
- ✓ None
- ⊳ 9 L 5748 yds SSS 69
- 👥 WD/BH–U WE–U after 1pm
- ££ 9 holes–£8
- 🚗 7 miles E of Edinburgh on A1
- ■ www.musselburgholdlinks.co.uk

North Berwick (1832)
West Links, Beach Road, North Berwick, EH39 4BB
- ☎ **(01620) 895040**
- 🖶 (01620) 893274
- 🖂 northberwickgc@aol.com
- ☎ 324
- ✍ NA Wilson (01620) 895040
- ✓ D Huish (01620) 893233
- ⊳ 18 L 6420 yds SSS 71

⚀ U H
£€ £42 D–£65 (£65) Winter–£22
D–£25 (£30)
⚆ Centre of North Berwick. 24 miles
E of Edinburgh (A198)

Royal Musselburgh   (1774)
*Prestongrange House, Prestonpans,
EH32 9RP*
☎ (01875) 810276
⌨ (01875) 810276
✉ royalmusselburgh@btinternet.com
♭ 800
⛓ TH Hardie (Sec/Mgr) J Hanratty
(Golf Sec) (01875) 819000
✓ J Henderson (01875) 810139
☟ 18 L 6237 yds SSS 70
⚀ U SOC
£€ £25 D–£35 (£35)
⚆ 8 miles E of Edinburgh on B1361
North Berwick road
⛰ James Braid
■ www.royalmusselburgh.co.uk

Tantallon   (1853)
Club
32 Westgate, North Berwick, EH39 4AH
☎ (01620) 892114
⌨ (01620) 894399
♭ 300
⛓ DA Leckie
☟ Play over North Berwick West
Links

Thorntree   (1856)
Club
*Prestongrange House, Prestonpans,
EH32 9RP*
☎ (01875) 810139
♭ 100
⛓ C Mackie
☟ Play over Royal
Musselburgh course

Whitekirk   (1995)
Whitekirk, North Berwick, EH39 5PR
☎ (01620) 870300
⌨ (01620) 870330
✉ countryclub@whitekirk.com
♭ 400
⛓ D Brodie
✓ P Wardell
☟ 18 L 6526 yds Par 72 SSS 72
⚀ U SOC
£€ £20 (£30)
⚆ 3 miles SE of North Berwick
(A198)
⊕ Practice range
⛰ Cameron Sinclair
■ www.whitekirk.com

Winterfield   (1935)
Public
*St Margarets, North Road, Dunbar,
EH42 1AU*
☎ (01368) 862280
♭ 350
✓ K Phillips (01368) 863562
☟ 18 L 5053 yds SSS 65
⚀ U
£€ On application–phone Pro
⚆ W side of Dunbar. 28 miles E of
Edinburgh (A1)

Midlothian

Baberton   (1893)
*50 Baberton Avenue, Juniper Green,
Edinburgh, EH14 5DU*
☎ (0131) 453 4911
⌨ (0131) 453 4678
✉ babertongolfclub@btinternet.com
♭ 900
⛓ BM Flockhart (0131) 453 4911
✓ K Kelly (0131) 453 3555
☟ 18 L 6129 yds SSS 70
⛓ WD–U Sun–2–4pm
£€ £25 D–£35 (£28 D–£38)
⚆ 5 miles SW of Edinburgh (A70)
⛰ Willie Park Jr
■ www.baberton.co.uk

Braid Hills   (1893)
Public
Braid Hills Road, Edinburgh, EH10 6JY
☎ (0131) 447 6666 (Starter)
☟ No 1 18 L 5731 yds Par 71 SSS 68
No 2 18 L 4832 yds Par 66 SSS 64
⛓ U–phone Starter. No 2 course
closed Sun
£€ £11 (£14)
⚆ 3 miles S of Edinburgh (A702)
⊕ No 2 course open Apr–Oct
⛰ Ferguson/McEwan

Braids United   (1897)
Club
*22 Braid Hills Approach, Edinburgh,
EH10 6JY*
☎ (0131) 452 9408
♭ 100
⛓ JS Forson
☟ Play over Braids 1 and 2

Broomieknowe   (1905)
*36 Golf Course Road, Bonnyrigg,
EH19 2HZ*
☎ (0131) 663 9317
⌨ (0131) 663 2152
♭ 500
⛓ JD Fisher
✓ M Patchett (0131) 660 2035
☟ 18 L 6200 yds Par 70
⛓ WD–U WE/BH–NA
£€ £19 D–£25 (£25)
⚆ 7 miles SE of Edinburgh
⛰ Braid/Hawtree
■ www.broomieknowe.com

Bruntsfield Links Golfing Society   (1761)
*The Clubhouse, 32 Barnton Avenue,
Edinburgh, EH4 6JH*
☎ (0131) 336 2006
⌨ (0131) 336 5538
✉ secretary@bruntsfield.sol.co.uk
♭ 1130
⛓ Cdr DM Sandford (0131) 336 1479
✓ B Mackenzie (0131) 336 4050
☟ 18 L 6407 yds SSS 71
⛓ WD–U WE–apply to Sec SOC–H
£€ £42 D–£60 (£47 D–£65)
⚆ 3 miles NW of Edinburgh, off A90
at Davidson Mains
⛰ Willie Park/Mackenzie/Hawtree

Carrick Knowe   (1930)
Public
Glendevon Park, Edinburgh, EH12 5VZ
☎ (0131) 337 1096 (Starter)
☟ 18 L 6184 yds SSS 68
⛓ U–phone Starter
£€ £12.50
⚆ 3 miles W of Edinburgh centre

Craigentinny   (1891)
Public
Fillyside Road, Edinburgh EH7
☎ (0131) 554 7501 (Starter)
☟ 18 L 5418 yds SSS 66
⛓ U–phone Starter
£€ £8.80–£9.65
⚆ 2¹/₂ miles NE of Edinburgh

Craigmillar Park   (1895)
*1 Observatory Road, Edinburgh,
EH9 3HG*
☎ (0131) 667 2837
✉ craigmillarparkgc@lineone.net
♭ 440 120(L) 70(J)
⛓ T Lawson (0131) 667 0047
✓ B McGhee (0131) 667 2850
☟ 18 L 5859 yds SSS 69
⛓ WD–I or H before 3.30pm
WE/BH–NA
£€ On application
⚆ Blackford, S of Edinburgh
⛰ James Braid

Duddingston   (1895)
*Duddingston Road West, Edinburgh,
EH15 3QD*
☎ (0131) 661 7688
⌨ (0131) 652 6057
♭ 600
⛓ IF Sproule (0131) 661 7688
✓ A McLean (0131) 661 4301
☟ 18 L 6473 yds SSS 72
⛓ WD–U WE–phone Pro SOC–Tues
& Thurs
£€ £35 D–£45 SOC–£25 D–£35
⚆ SE Edinburgh
■ www.duddingston-golf-club.com

Glencorse   (1890)
Milton Bridge, Penicuik, EH26 0RD
☎ (01968) 677177
⌨ (01968) 674399
♭ 700
⛓ W Oliver (01968) 677189
✓ C Jones (01968) 676481
☟ 18 L 5217 yds Par 64 SSS 66
⛓ WD–U SOC–WD/Sun pm
£€ £20 (£26)
⚆ 8 miles S of Edinburgh (A701)
⛰ Willie Park

Kings Acre   (1997)
Pay and play
Lasswade, EH18 1AU
☎ (0131) 663 3456
⌨ (0131) 663 7076
✉ info@kings-acregolf.com
⛓ Lizzie King
✓ A Murdoch (0131) 663 3456
☟ 18 L 6005 yds Par 70
Junior Par 3 course

☺ U SOC
££ £18 (£25)
∞ 3 miles S of Edinburgh, off A720
⊕ Floodlit driving range
⌂ Graeme Webster
■ www.kings-acregolf.com

Kingsknowe (1907)

326 Lanark Road, Edinburgh,
EH14 2JD
☎ (0131) 441 1144
⌨ (0131) 441 2079
▣ 819
∿ LI Fairlie (0131) 441 1145
√ C Morris (0131) 441 4030
⇀ 18 L 5981 yds SSS 69
☺ WD–U before 4pm WE–phone Pro
SOC–WD before 4pm
££ £20 (£30)
∞ SW Edinburgh
⌂ Herd/Braid

Liberton (1920)

297 Gilmerton Road, Edinburgh,
EH16 5UJ
☎ (0131) 664 3009
⌨ (0131) 666 0853
▣ 797
∿ TJ Watson
√ I Seath (0131) 664 1056
⇀ 18 L 5299 yds SSS 66
☺ WD–U before 5pm WE–NA before
2pm
££ £20
∞ 3 miles S of Edinburgh

Lothianburn (1893)

106a Biggar Road, Edinburgh,
EH10 7DU
☎ (0131) 445 2206
▣ 600 75(L) 100(J)
∿ WFA Jardine (0131) 445 5067
√ K Mungall (0131) 445 2288
⇀ 18 L 5662 yds SSS 68
☺ WD–U before 4.30pm –M after
4.30pm WE–NA SOC–H
££ £16.50 D–£22.50 (£22.50
D–£27.50)
∞ S of Edinburgh, on A702.
Lothianburn exit from Edinburgh
by-pass
⌂ James Braid (1928)
■ www.golfers.net

Marriott Dalmahoy
Hotel & CC

Dalmahoy, Kirknewton, EH27 8EB
☎ (0131) 335 8010
⌨ (0131) 335 3577
∿ I Burns (Golf Dir),
Mrs JM Bryans (Sec)
√ N Graham
⇀ East 18 L 6677 yds SSS 72
West 18 L 5185 yds SSS 66
☺ WD–U H SOC–WD
££ East–£65 (£80) West–£45 (£55)
∞ 7 miles W of Edinburgh on A71
⊕ Floodlit driving range
⌂ James Braid

Melville Golf Centre (1995)

Proprietary
Lasswade, Edinburgh, EH18 1AN
☎ (0131) 663 8038,
(0131) 654 0224 (24-hr Bookings)
⌨ (0131) 654 0814
✉ golf@melvillegolf.co.uk
▣ 50
∿ Mr & Mrs MacFarlane (Props)
√ G Carter (0131) 663 8038
⇀ 9 L 4604 yds Par 66 SSS 62
☺ U SOC
££ £8–£14 (£10–£16)
∞ 7 miles S of Edinburgh, signposted
off city by-pass on A7
⊕ Floodlit driving range
⌂ G Webster
■ www.melvillegolf.co.uk

Merchants of Edinburgh
(1907)

10 Craighill Gardens, Morningside,
Edinburgh, EH10 5PY
☎ (0131) 447 1219
⌨ (0131) 446 9833
✉ admin@merchantsgolf.com
▣ 1003
∿ J Elvin
NEM Colquhoun (0131) 447 8709
⇀ 18 L 4889 yds SSS 64
☺ WD–U before 4pm –M after 4pm
WE–M SOC–WD
££ £16
∞ SW of Edinburgh, off A701
⌂ Braid/Letters
■ www.merchantsgolf.com

Mortonhall (1892)

231 Braid Road, Edinburgh, EH10 6PB
☎ (0131) 447 2411
⌨ (0131) 447 8712
✉ clubhouse@mortonhallgc.co.uk
▣ 1000
∿ Ms BM Giefer (0131) 447 6974
√ DB Horn (0131) 447 5185
⇀ 18 L 6502 yds SSS 72
☺ H SOC
££ £30 (£30)
∞ 2 miles S of Edinburgh on A702
⌂ James Braid/FW Hawtree
■ www.mortonhallgc.co.uk

Murrayfield (1896)

43 Murrayfield Road, Edinburgh,
EH12 6EU
☎ (0131) 337 1009
⌨ (0131) 313 0721
▣ 815
∿ Mrs MK Thomson (0131) 337 3478
√ J Fisher (0131) 337 3479
⇀ 18 L 5764 yds Par 70 SSS 69
☺ WD–I WE–M
££ £30 (£35)
∞ 2 miles W of Edinburgh centre

Newbattle (1896)

Abbey Road, Eskbank, Dalkeith,
EH22 3AD
☎ (0131) 663 2123
⌨ (0131) 654 1810
✉ newbattlegolf@freeuk.com

▣ 600
∿ HG Stanners (0131) 663 1819
√ S McDonald (0131) 660 1631
⇀ 18 L 6012 yds SSS 70
☺ WD–U before 4pm WE–M
££ £20 D–£30
∞ 6 miles S of Edinburgh on A7 and
A68
⌂ HS Colt

Portobello (1853)

Public
Stanley Street, Portobello, Edinburgh,
EH15 1JJ
☎ (0131) 669 4361 (Starter)
⇀ 9 L 2405 yds SSS 64
☺ U–phone Starter
££ £8.80–£9.65
∞ 4 miles E of Edinburgh

Prestonfield (1920)

6 Priestfield Road North, Edinburgh,
EH16 5HS
☎ (0131) 667 9665
⌨ (0131) 667 9665
✉ prestonfield@btclick.com
▣ 900
∿ AS Robertson
√ J Macfarlane (0131) 667 8597
⇀ 18 L 6214 yds SSS 70
☺ WD–U WE–NA SOC–WD
££ £22 D–£33
∞ 2 miles SE of Edinburgh, off A7
Dalkeith Road
⌂ Peter Robertson
■ www.prestonfieldgolfclub.co.uk

Ratho Park (1928)

Ratho, Edinburgh, EH28 8NX
☎ (0131) 335 0069
⌨ (0131) 333 1752
✉ secretary.rpgc@btinternet.com
▣ 550 106(L) 72(J)
∿ JS Yates (0131) 335 0068
√ A Pate (0131) 333 1406
⇀ 18 L 5932 yds SSS 68
☺ U SOC–Tues/Wed/Thurs
££ £25 D–£35 (£35)
∞ 8 miles W of Edinburgh centre
(A71)
⌂ James Braid
■ www.rathoparkgolfclub.com

Ravelston (1912)

24 Ravelston Dykes Road, Edinburgh,
EH4 3NZ
☎ (0131) 315 2486
▣ 610
∿ J Lowrie
⇀ 9 L 5218 yds SSS 65
☺ WD–H
££ WD–£15
∞ Off Queensferry Road (A90). Turn
S at Blackhall
⌂ James Braid

Royal Burgess Golfing
Society of Edinburgh (1735)

181 Whitehouse Road, Barnton,
Edinburgh, EH4 6BY
☎ (0131) 339 2075

For list of abbreviations and key to symbols see page 649

☎ (0131) 339 3712
✉ secretary@royalburgess.co.uk
📖 620 60(J)
🏌 G Seeley (0131) 339 2075
✓ S Brian (0131) 339 6474
🏴 18 L 6494 yds SSS 71
👥 I SOC
££ On application
🚗 Queensferry Road (A90)
🏠 Tom Morris
▄ www.royalburgess.co.uk

Silverknowes　(1947)
Public
Silverknowes Parkway, Edinburgh, EH4 5ET
☎ **(0131) 336 3843 (Starter)**
🏴 18 L 6214 yds SSS 70
👥 U–phone Starter
££ £11 (£13.50)
🚗 4 miles N of Edinburgh

Swanston　(1927)
111 Swanston Road, Fairmilehead, Edinburgh, EH10 7DS
☎ **(0131) 445 2239**
🖥 (0131) 445 2239
📖 500
🏌 J Allan
✓ S Pardoe (0131) 445 4002
🏴 18 L 5004 yds SSS 65
👥 U exc comp days–NA WE–NA after 1pm
££ £15 D–£20 (£20 D–£25)
🚗 S of Edinburgh, off Biggar road (A702) Edinburgh By-pass
▄ www.swanstongolfclub.com

Torphin Hill　(1895)
Torphin Road, Edinburgh, EH13 0PG
☎ **(0131) 441 1100**
🖥 (0131) 441 7166
📖 450
🏌 AJ Hepburn
✓ J Browne
🏴 18 L 5230 yds SSS 66
👥 WD–U WE–U exc comp days SOC
££ D–£14 (D–£20)
🚗 SW boundary of Edinburgh

Turnhouse　(1897)
154 Turnhouse Road, Corstorphine, Edinburgh, EH12 0AD
☎ **(0131) 339 1014**
🖥 (0131) 339 1844
📖 640
🏌 AB Hay (0131) 539 5937
✓ J Murray (0131) 339 7701
🏴 18 L 6153 yds SSS 70
👥 M or by arrangement SOC
££ On application
🚗 W of Edinburgh (A9080)
▄ www.turnhousegc.com

Vogrie　(1990)
Pay and play
Vogrie Estate Country Park, Gorebridge, EH23 4NU
☎ **(01875) 821716**
🏴 9 hole course Par 66
👥 U

££ £5.70
🚗 SE of Edinburgh, off A68 (B6372)

West Lothian

Bathgate　(1892)
Edinburgh Road, Bathgate, EH48 1BA
☎ **(01506) 652232**
🖥 (01506) 636775
📖 580
🏌 WA Osborne (01506) 630505
✓ S Strachan (01506) 630553
🏴 18 L 6328 yds SSS 70
👥 U
££ £20 (£35)
🚗 15 miles W of Edinburgh. M8 Junction 4
🏠 Wm Park Sr

Bridgend & District　(1994)
Willowdean, Bridgend, Linlithgow, EH49 6NW
☎ **(01506) 834140**
🖥 (01506) 834706
🏌 R Irving
🏴 9 L 5192 yds Par 68 SSS 67
👥 U
££ £10 (£12)
🚗 Nr Linlithgow
▄ www.bridgendgolfclub.co.uk

Deer Park CC　(1978)
Golf Course Road, Knightsridge, Livingston, EH54 8AB
☎ **(01506) 446699**
🖥 (01506) 435608
✉ deerpark@muir-group.co.uk
📖 850
✓ B Dunbar
🏴 18 L 6688 yds SSS 72
👥 U SOC
££ £24 (£36)
🚗 N of Livingston. M8 Junction 3

Dundas Parks　(1957)
South Queensferry, EH30 9SS
📖 550
🏌 Mrs C Wood (0131) 319 1347
🏴 9 L 6056 yds SSS 70
👥 M I SOC
££ D–£10
🚗 Dundas Estate (Private). 1 mile S of Queensferry (A8000)

Greenburn　(1953)
6 Greenburn Road, Fauldhouse, EH47 9HJ
☎ **(01501) 770292**
✉ secretary@greenburngolfclub .fsnet.co.uk
📖 500
🏌 D Watson (01501) 744334
✓ M Leighton (01501) 771187
🏴 18 L 6210 yds SSS 71
👥 U
££ On application
🚗 4 miles S of M8 Junction 4 (East)/Junction 5 (West)

Harburn　(1921)
West Calder, EH55 8RS
☎ **(01506) 871256**
🖥 (01506) 870286
📖 500 80(L) 100(J)
🏌 J McLinden (01506) 871131
✓ S Mills (01506) 871582
🏴 18 L 5921 yds SSS 69
👥 U
££ £18 (£25)
🚗 2 miles S of W Calder on B7008, via A70 or A71

Linlithgow　(1913)
Braehead, Linlithgow, EH49 6QF
☎ **(01506) 842585**
🖥 (01506) 842764
📖 430
🏌 WS Christie
✓ S Rosie (01506) 844356
🏴 18 L 5729 yds SSS 68
👥 U exc Sat–NA SOC
££ £20 D–£25 Sun–£25 D–£30
🚗 SW of Linlithgow, off M9
🏠 Robert Simpson

Niddry Castle　(1983)
Castle Road, Winchburgh, EH52 2RQ
☎ **(01506) 891097**
📖 500
🏌 J Thomson
🏴 9 L 5476 yds SSS 67
👥 U
££ £13 (£19)
🚗 10 miles W of Edinburgh (B9080)

Polkemmet　(1981)
Public
Whitburn, Bathgate, EH47 0AD
☎ **(01501) 743905**
🏴 9 L 2967 metres SSS 37
👥 U
££ £4.95 (£5.75)
🚗 Between Whitburn and Harthill on B7066. M8 Junctions 4/5
⊕ Driving range

Pumpherston　(1895)
Drumshoreland Road, Pumpherston, EH53 0LQ
☎ **(01506) 432869**
🖥 (01506) 438250
📖 443 24(L) 100(J)
🏌 I McArthur (01506) 854584
✓ R Fyvie (01506) 433337
🏴 18 L 6006 yds Par 70 SSS 69
👥 WD–U SOC–WD
££ On application
🚗 14 miles W of Edinburgh. M8 Junction 3
🏠 Glen Andrews
▄ www.pumpherstongolfclub.com

Rutherford Castle　(1998)
West Linton, EH46 7AS
☎ **(01968) 661233**
🖥 (01968) 661233
✉ info@ruth-castlegc.co.uk
📖 150
✓ None

⌖ 18 L 6558 yds Par 72 SSS 71
👤 U SOC
£€ £15 (£25)
🚗 10 miles S of Edinburgh on A702
🏠 Bryan Moor
■ www.ruth-castlegc.co.uk

Uphall (1895)
Houston Mains, Uphall, EH52 6JT
☎ **(01506) 856404**
📠 (01506) 855358
📧 uphallgolfclub
@business-unmetered.com
📖 650
🏌 WA Crighton
⛳ G Law (01506) 855553
⌖ 18 L 5588 yds Par 69 SSS 67
👤 U
£€ £15 D–£20 (£20 D–£30)
🚗 7 miles W of Edinburgh Airport
(A8). M8 Junction 3

West Linton (1890)
West Linton, EH46 7HN
☎ **(01968) 660970**
📠 (01968) 660970
📖 750
🏌 AJ Mitchell (01968) 660970
⛳ I Wright (01968) 660256
⌖ 18 L 6132 yds SSS 70
👤 WD–U WE–phone Pro
£€ £20 D–£30 (£30)
🚗 18 miles S of Edinburgh on A702.

West Lothian (1892)
Airngath Hill, Linlithgow, EH49 7RH
☎ **(01506) 826030**
📠 (01506) 826030
📖 850
🏌 MJ Todd
⛳ C Gillies (01506) 825060
⌖ 18 L 6406 yds SSS 71
👤 WD–NA after 4pm WE–by
arrangement
£€ On application
🚗 1 mile N of Linlithgow, towards
Bo'ness
🏠 W Park Jr/Adams/Middleton

Moray

Buckpool (1933)
Barhill Road, Buckie, AB56 1DU
☎ **(01542) 832236**
📠 (01542) 832236
📖 500
🏌 Miss M Coull
⌖ 18 L 6257 yds SSS 70
👤 U
£€ £13 D–£15 (£20 D–£25)
🚗 W end of Buckpool, ¹/₂ mile off
A98

Dufftown (1896)
Tomintoul Road, Dufftown, AB55 4BS
☎ **(01340) 820325**
📠 (01340) 820325
📖 310
🏌 Mrs M Swann (Admin)

⛳ None
⌖ 18 L 5308 yds SSS 67
👤 U
£€ £12 D–£15
🚗 1 mile SW of Dufftown on B9009
■ www.speyside.moray.org
/dufftowngolfclub

Elgin (1906)
*Hardhillock, Birnie Road, Elgin,
IV30 8SX*
☎ **(01343) 542338**
📠 (01343) 542341
📖 854 113(L) 150(J)
🏌 DF Black
⛳ K Stables (01343) 542884
⌖ 18 L 6411 yds SSS 71
👤 WD–U after 9.30am WE–U after
10am SOC–WD SOC–WE by
arrangement
£€ £27 D–£37
🚗 1 mile S of Elgin on A941
⊕ Driving range
🏠 John MacPherson
■ www.elgingolfclub.com

Forres (1889)
Muiryshade, Forres, IV36 0RD
☎ **(01309) 672949**
📖 716 130(J)
🏌 Margaret Greenaway
⛳ S Aird (01309) 672250
⌖ 18 L 6141 yds SSS 70
👤 U SOC
£€ £14 (£20)
🚗 1 mile SE of Forres, off B9010

Garmouth & Kingston
(1932)
Garmouth, Fochabers, IV32 7NJ
☎ **(01343) 870388**
📠 (01343) 870388
📖 600
🏌 A Robertson (01343) 870231
⌖ 18 L 5935 yds SSS 69
👤 U SOC
£€ £18 D–£18 (£22 D–£25)
🚗 8 miles NE of Elgin

Hopeman (1909)
Hopeman, Moray, IV30 5YA
☎ **(01343) 830578**
📠 (01343) 830152
📧 hopemangc@aol.com
📖 700
🏌 J Fraser
⌖ 18 L 5590 yds SSS 67
👤 WD–U Sat–NA before 10am and
12.30–2pm Sun–NA before 9am
SOC
£€ £15 (£20)
🚗 7 miles NW of Elgin on B9012
🏠 J McKenzie
■ www.hopeman-golf-club.co.uk

Moray (1889)
Stotfield Road, Lossiemouth, IV31 6QS
☎ **(01343) 812018**
📠 (01343) 815102
📧 secretary@moraygolf.co.uk

📖 1500
🏌 SM Crane
⛳ A Thomson (01343) 813330
⌖ Old 18 L 6643 yds SSS 73
New 18 L 6005 yds SSS 69
👤 U H SOC
£€ On application
🚗 6 miles N of Elgin
⊕ Practice range
🏠 Old Tom Morris
■ www.moraygolf.co.uk

Spey Bay (1904)
*Spey Bay Hotel, Spey Bay, Fochabers,
IV32 7PJ*
☎ **(01343) 820424**
📠 (01343) 829282
📧 info@speybay.com
📖 200
🏌 I Ednie (Gen Mgr)
⌖ 18 L 6092 yds Par 70 SSS 69
👤 U
£€ £20 (£22)
🚗 7 miles W of Buckie, off A96
(B9104)
⊕ Driving range
🏠 Ben Sayers
■ www.speybay.com

Perth & Kinross

Aberfeldy (1895)
Taybridge Road, Aberfeldy, PH15 2BH
☎ **(01887) 820535**
📠 (01887) 820535
📖 200
🏌 P Woolley (01887) 829422
⌖ 18 L 5600 yds Par 68 SSS 66
👤 U
£€ £16 (£21)
🚗 10 miles W of Ballinluig, off A9
🏠 Souters

Alyth (1894)
Pitcrocknie, Alyth, PH11 8HF
☎ **(01828) 632268**
📠 (01828) 633491
📖 850
🏌 J Docherty
⛳ T Melville (01828) 632411
⌖ 18 L 6205 yds SSS 70
👤 U SOC
£€ On application
🚗 16 miles NW of Dundee (A91)
🏠 Tom Morris/James Braid
■ www.alythgolfclub.co.uk

Auchterarder (1892)
Ochil Road, Auchterarder, PH3 1LS
☎ **(01764) 662804**
📠 (01764) 662804
📖 820
🏌 WM Campbell
⛳ G Baxter (01764) 663711
⌖ 18 L 5757 yds SSS 68
👤 U SOC
£€ £22 D–£33 Sat–£27 D–£43
Sun–£43
🚗 1 mile SW of Auchterarder

Bishopshire (1903)
Pay and play
Kinnesswood, Kinross, KY13
- 150
- ✍ J Proudfoot (01592) 780203
- ▷ 10 L 4700 metres SSS 64
- ♚ U
- £€ £5 (£10)
- ⚑ 3 miles E of Kinross (A911). M90 Junction 7
- ♟ W Park

Blair Atholl (1896)
Invertilt Road, Blair Atholl, PH18 5TG
- ☎ (01796) 481407
- 🖷 (01796) 481751
- ▥ 445
- ✍ T Boon
- ▷ 9 L 5816 yds SSS 68
- ♚ U
- £€ £14.50 (£16.50)
- ⚑ 35 miles N of Perth, off A9

Blairgowrie (1889)
Rosemount, Blairgowrie, PH10 6LG
- ☎ (01250) 872594
- 🖷 (01250) 875451
- ▧ admin@blairgowrie-golf.co.uk
- ▥ 1200
- ✍ JN Simpson (Managing Sec) (01250) 872622
- ✓ C Dernie (01250) 873116
- ▷ Rosemount 18 L 6588 yds SSS 72; Landsdowne 18 L 6895 yds SSS 73; Wee 9 L 4614 yds SSS 63
- ♚ Mon/Tues/Thurs–U H 8am–12 & 2–3.30pm Wed/Fri/WE–restricted
- £€ On application
- ⚑ 1 mile S of Blairgowrie, off A93. 15 miles N of Perth
- ♟ Rosemount-Braid; Lansdowne-Alliss/Thomas; Wee-Old Tom Morris
- ■ www.blairgowrie.golf.co.uk

Callander (1890)
Aveland Road, Callander, FK17 8EN
- ☎ (01877) 330090
- 🖷 (01877) 330062
- ▧ callandergc@nextcall.net
- ▥ 500
- ✍ Mrs S Smart
- ✓ A Martin (01877) 330975
- ▷ 18 L 5185 yds SSS 65
- ♚ U SOC
- £€ £18 (£26)
- ⚑ Off A84, E end of Callander
- ♟ Tom Morris
- ■ www.callander.co.uk

Comrie (1891)
Laggan Braes, Comrie, PH6 2LR
- ☎ (01764) 670055
- ▥ 380
- ✍ S van der Walt (01786) 880727
- ▷ 9 L 3020 yds Par 70 SSS 70
- ♚ U exc Mon & Tues
- £€ £16 (£20)
- ⚑ 7 miles W of Crieff (A85)

Craigie Hill (1911)
Cherrybank, Perth, PH2 0NE
- ☎ (01738) 620829
- 🖷 (01738) 620829
- ▥ 625
- ✍ A Tunnicliffe (01738) 620829
- ✓ I Muir (01738) 622644
- ▷ 18 L 5386 yds SSS 67
- ♚ U exc Sat
- £€ £18 (£25)
- ⚑ W boundary of Perth
- ♟ Fernie/Anderson

Crieff (1891)
Perth Road, Crieff, PH7 3LR
- ☎ (01764) 652909 (Bookings)
- 🖷 (01764) 655096
- ▧ secretary@crieffgolf.co.uk
- ▥ 735
- ✍ JS Miller (01764) 652397
- ✓ DJW Murchie
- ▷ Ferntower 18 L 6402 yds SSS 72; Dornock 9 L 4772 yds SSS 63
- ♚ U H NA–12–2pm or after 5pm SOC
- £€ Ferntower £27 (£36) Dornock £12
- ⚑ 1 mile NE of Crieff (A85). 17 miles W of Perth
- ♟ James Braid
- ■ www.crieffgolf.co.uk

Dalmunzie (1948)
Glenshee, Blairgowrie, PH10 7QG
- ☎ (01250) 885226
- 🖷 (01250) 885225
- ▥ 52
- ✍ S Winton (Mgr)
- ▷ 9 L 2099 yds SSS 60
- ♚ U
- £€ D–£11.50
- ⚑ 22 miles N of Blairgowrie on A93. (Dalmunzie Hotel sign)

Dunkeld & Birnam (1892)
Fungarth, Dunkeld, PH8 0HU
- ☎ (01350) 727524
- 🖷 (01350) 728660
- ▥ 535
- ✍ RD Barrance
- ✓ None
- ▷ 18 L 5511 yds SSS 70
- ♚ WD–U WE–phone first
- £€ On application
- ⚑ Dunkeld 1 mile, off A923. 15 miles N of Perth
- ■ www.dunkeldandbirnamgolfclub.co.uk

Dunning (1953)
Rollo Park, Dunning, PH2 0QX
- ☎ (01764) 684747
- ▥ 580
- ✍ JR Stockley (01764) 684212
- ▷ 9 L 4885 yds Par 66 SSS 63
- ♚ WD–U Sat–NA before 4pm
- £€ £14 (£16)
- ⚑ 9 miles SW of Perth, off A9

Foulford Inn (1995)
Pay and play
Crieff, PH7 3LN
- ☎ (01764) 652407
- 🖷 (01764) 652407
- ▧ foulford@btclick.com
- ✍ M Beaumont
- ▷ 9 hole Par 3 course
- ♚ U
- £€ £4 D–£6
- ■ www.foulfordinn.co.uk

The Gleneagles Hotel
Auchterarder, PH3 1NF
- ☎ (01764) 694360 (Golf), (01764) 662231 (Hotel)
- ▧ golf.gleneagles@gleneagles.com
- ✍ G Marchbank (Golf Dir)
- ✓ S Smith (01764) 694343
- ▷ King's 18 L 6471 yds SSS 71 Queen's 18 L 5965 yds SSS 69 PGA Centenary 18 L 7081 SSS 74 9 hole Par 3 course
- ♚ U
- £€ May–Sept £110
- ⚑ 16 miles SW of Perth on A9
- ⊕ Driving range. Golf academy
- ♟ Braid/Nicklaus
- ■ www.gleneagles.com

Glenisla (1998)
Proprietary
Pitcrocknie Farm, Alyth, PH11 8JJ
- ☎ (01828) 632445
- 🖷 (01828) 633749
- ▥ 300
- ✍ E Wilson (Admin)
- ▷ 18 L 6402 yds Par 71 SSS 72
- ♚ U H
- £€ £22 (£26)
- ⚑ Nr Alyth (B954
- ■ www.golf-glenisla.co.uk

Green Hotel (1900)
2 The Muirs, Kinross, KY13 8AS
- ☎ (01577) 863407
- 🖷 (01577) 863180
- ▥ 450
- ✍ C Browne
- ▷ Red 18 L 6257 yds SSS 70 Blue 18 L 6456 yds SSS 71
- ♚ U
- £€ £15 D–£25 (£25 D–£35)
- ⚑ 17 miles S of Perth. M90 Junction 6/7

Kenmore (1992)
Pay and play
Mains of Taymouth, Kenmore, Aberfeldy, PH15 2HN
- ☎ (01887) 830226
- 🖷 (01887) 829059
- ▧ golf@taymouth.co.uk
- ▥ 120
- ✍ R Menzies (Mgr)
- ✓ None
- ▷ 9 L 6052 yds SSS 69
- ♚ U SOC
- £€ 9 holes–£9 (£10) 18 holes–£14 (£15)
- ⚑ Kenmore, 6 miles W of Aberfeldy on A827

🏠 D Menzies & Partners
⬛ www.taymouth.co.uk

Killin (1913)

Killin, FK21 8TX
☎ (01567) 820312
🖳 (01567) 820312
📧 info@killingolfclub.co.uk
📖 253
🏌 TL Taylor (01764) 656291
ጮ 9 L 5016 yds Par 66 SSS 65
👥 U SOC–Apr–Oct
££ £15 (£15)
⛳ Killin, W end of Loch Tay
🏠 John Duncan
⬛ www.killingolfclub.co.uk

King James VI (1858)

Moncreiffe Island, Perth, PH2 8NR
☎ (01738) 625170,
   (01738) 632460 (Starter)
🖳 (01738) 445132
📧 info@kjvigc.fsnet.co.uk
📖 675
🏌 Mrs H Blair (01738) 445132
✓ A Crerar (01738) 632460
ጮ 18 L 5664 yds SSS 69
👥 U exc Sat Sun–by reservation
££ £18 D–£25 Sun D–£30
⛳ Island in River Tay, Perth
🏠 Tom Morris
⬛ www.kingjamesvi.co.uk

Milnathort (1910)

*South Street, Milnathort, Kinross,
KY13 9XA*
☎ (01577) 864069
📧 milnathortgolf@ukgateway.net
📖 575
ጮ 9 L 5985 yds SSS 69
👥 U SOC
££ £13 D–£19 (£15 D–£21)
⛳ 1 mile N of Kinross. M90 Junction 6/7

Muckhart (1908)

*Drumburn Road, Muckhart, Dollar,
FK14 7JH*
☎ (01259) 781423
🖳 (01259) 781544
📧 enquiries@muckhartgolf.com
📖 550 125(L) 100(J)
🏌 CA Page
✓ K Salmoni (01259) 781493
ጮ 27 L 5895-6174 yds SSS 70-72
👥 U SOC
££ £20 D–£30 (£25 D–£35)
⛳ A91, 3 miles E of Dollar, towards Rumbling Bridge
⬛ www.muckhartgolf.com

Murrayshall (1981)

*Murrayshall, New Scone, Perth,
PH2 7PH*
☎ (01738) 554804
🖳 (01738) 552595
📧 info@murrayshall.com
📖 300
🏌 A Bryan (Mgr)
✓ AT Reid (01738) 552784
ጮ Murrayshall 18 L 6441 yds SSS 72
   Lynedoch 18 L 5362 yds SSS 69

👥 U SOC
££ Murrayshall £27 D–£45 Lynedoch £18 D–£32
⛳ 3 miles NE of Perth, off A94
⊕ Driving range. Indoor Golf Centre
🏠 Hamilton Stutt

Muthill (1911)

Peat Road, Muthill, PH5 2DA
☎ (01764) 681523
🖳 (01764) 681557
📧 muthillgolfclub@lineone.com
📖 400
🏌 J Elder (01764) 681523
ጮ 9 L 2371 yds SSS 63
👥 U SOC
££ £15 (£18)
⛳ 3 miles S of Crieff on A822
⬛ www.muthillgolfclub.co.uk

North Inch

Public
*c/o Perth & Kinross Council, 5 High
Street, Perth, PH1 5JS*
☎ (01738) 636481 (Starter)
🏌 G Harbut (01738) 475215
ጮ 18 L 4340 metres SSS 65
👥 U SOC
££ On application
⛳ Nr Perth and A9, by River Tay. Signs to Bell's Sports Centre

Pitlochry (1909)

*Pitlochry Estate Office, Pitlochry,
PH16 5NE*
☎ (01796) 472792 (Bookings)
🖳 (01796) 473599
📖 498
🏌 DCM McKenzie JP (01796) 472114
✓ G Hampton (01796) 472792
ጮ 18 L 5811 yds SSS 69
👥 U SOC
££ On application
⛳ N side of Pitlochry (A9). 28 miles NW of Perth
🏠 Fernie/Hutchison

Royal Perth Golfing Society

(1824)
Club
1/2 Atholl Crescent, Perth, PH1 5NG
☎ (01738) 622265
🖳 (01764) 664049
📖 250
🏌 DP McDonald (Gen Sec) (01738) 622265,
   L Rutherford (Golf Sec) (01764) 664049
ጮ Play over North Inch, Perth & Strathmore courses

St Fillans (1903)

*South Lochearn Rd, St Fillans,
PH26 2NJ*
☎ (01764) 685312
📧 stfillansgolf@aol.com
📖 400
🏌 J Stanyon (01764) 685300
ጮ 9 L 6054 yds SSS 69
👥 U SOC

££ £15 (£20)
⛳ 12 miles W of Crieff, on A85
🏠 W Auchterlonie
⬛ www.st-fillans-golf.com

Strathmore Golf Centre

(1995)
Pay and play
Leroch, Alyth, Blairgowrie, PH11 8NZ
☎ (01828) 633322
🖳 (01828) 633533
📖 350
🏌 C Spencer
✓ C Smith
ጮ 18 L 6454 yds Par 72 SSS 72
   9 L 1666 yds Par 29 SSS 58
👥 U SOC
££ 18 hole:£20 (£25) 9 hole:£8 (£10)
⛳ 5 miles E of Blairgowrie, off A926
⊕ Floodlit driving range
🏠 John Salvesen

Strathtay (1909)

*Lyon Cottage, Strathtay, Pitlochry,
PH9 0PG*
☎ (01887) 840211
📖 237
🏌 IA Ramsay
ጮ 9 L 4082 yds SSS 63
👥 U exc Thurs–NA after 5pm Sat–NA 10–10.30am Sun–NA 1–4pm SOC
££ D–£10
⛳ 4 miles W of Ballinluig (A827), towards Aberfeldy

Taymouth Castle (1923)

Kenmore, Aberfeldy, PH15 2NT
☎ (01887) 830228
🖳 (01887) 830228
📖 200
🏌 AA MacTaggart (Golf Dir)
✓ G Dott
ጮ 18 L 6066 yds SSS 69
👥 U WE–booking essential SOC
££ £20 D–£30 (£24 D–£38)
⛳ 6 miles W of Aberfeldy (A827)
🏠 James Braid

Whitemoss (1994)

*Whitemoss Road, Dunning, Perth,
PH2 0QX*
☎ (01738) 730300
📖 500
🏌 S Gaden
✓ None
ጮ 18 L 6200 yds Par 69 SSS 69
👥 U SOC
££ £15 (£15)
⛳ Aberuthven, 10 miles SW of Perth, off A9

Renfrewshire

Barshaw (1920)

Public
*Barshaw Park, Glasgow Road,
Paisley PA2*
☎ (0141) 889 2908
🖳 (0141) 840 2148

For list of abbreviations and key to symbols see page 649

103
W Collins (0141) 884 2533
18 L 5703 yds SSS 67
U
£8.50
1 mile E of Paisley Cross, off A737

Bonnyton　(1957)

Eaglesham, Glasgow, G76 0QA
(01355) 302781
(01355) 303151
950
A Hughes
K McWade (01355) 302256
18 L 6255 yds SSS 71
I SOC–WD
£40
2 miles W of Eaglesham. 6 miles S of Glasgow

Caldwell　(1903)

Caldwell, Uplawmoor, G78 4AU
(01505) 850329
(01505) 850604
CaldwellGolfClub@aol.com
450
HIF Harper (01505) 850366
S Forbes (01505) 850616
18 L 6195 yds SSS 70
WD–booking before 4pm–M after 4pm WE–M
On application
5 miles SW of Barrhead on A736 Glasgow-Irvine road

Cochrane Castle　(1895)

Scott Avenue, Craigston, Johnstone, PA5 0HF
(01505) 320146
(01505) 325338
secretary@cochranecastle.sol.co.uk
425
Mrs PIJ Quin
A Logan (01505) 328465
18 L 6194 yds Par 71 SSS 71
WD–U WE–M
£22 (£30)
1/2 mile S of Beith Road, Johnstone
Charles Hunter

East Renfrewshire　(1922)

Pilmuir, Newton Mearns, G77 6RT
(01355) 500256
(01355) 500323
450
DS McKenzie (Mgr)
S Russell (01355) 500206
18 L 6097 yds SSS 70
On application
£30 D–£40
2 miles SW of Newton Mearns
James Braid

Eastwood　(1893)

Muirshield, Loganswell, Newton Mearns, Glasgow G77 6RX
(01355) 500261
900
VE Jones (01355) 500280
I Darroch (01355) 500285

18 L 5666 yds SSS 68
WD SOC
£24 D–£30
9 miles SW of Glasgow
Theodore Moone

Elderslie　(1908)

63 Main Road, Elderslie, PA5 9AZ
(01505) 323956
(01505) 340346
432
Mrs A Anderson
R Bowman (01505) 320032
18 L 6165 yds SSS 70
M SOC–WD
£24 D–£32
2 miles SW of Paisley

Erskine　(1904)

Bishopton, PA7 5PH
(01505) 862302
400 140(L)
TA McKillop
P Thomson (01505) 862108
18 L 6287 yds SSS 70
WD–I WE–M
£27
5 miles NW of Paisley

Fereneze　(1904)

Fereneze Avenue, Barrhead, G78 1HJ
(0141) 881 1519
700
G McCreadie (0141) 881 7149
H Lee (0141) 880 7058
18 L 5962 yds SSS 70
M SOC–WD
D–£22
9 miles SW of Glasgow

Gleddoch　(1974)

Langbank, PA14 6YE
(01475) 540304
(01475) 540459
600
DW Tierney
K Campbell (01475) 540704
18 L 6375 yds SSS 71
WD–U WE–restricted SOC
£30
16 miles W of Glasgow (M8/A8)
J Hamilton Stutt

Gourock　(1896)

Cowal View, Gourock, PA19 1HD
(01475) 631001
(01475) 638307
ADT@gourockgolfclub.freeserve.co.uk
538 98(L) 86(J)
AD Taylor
J Mooney (01475) 636834
18 L 6408 yds SSS 72
WD–I before 4.30pm SOC
£20 (£27)
3 miles SW of Greenock, off A770. 7 miles W of Port Glasgow

Greenock　(1890)

Forsyth Street, Greenock, PA16 8RE
(01475) 720793
(01475) 791912
500 111(L) 110(J)
EJ Black (01475) 791912
P Morrison (01475) 787236
18 L 5888 yds SSS 69
9 L 2149 yds SSS 32
WD–U WE/BH–M
D–£25 (£30)
1 mile SW of Greenock on A8
James Braid
www.greenockgolfclub.co.uk

Kilmacolm　(1891)

Porterfield Road, Kilmacolm, PA13 4PD
(01505) 872139
(01505) 874007
888
R Weldin
I Nicholson (01505) 872695
18 L 5960 yds SSS 69
WD–U WE–M
£25 (£30)
10 miles W of Paisley (A761)

Lochwinnoch　(1897)

Burnfoot Road, Lochwinnoch, PA12 4AN
(01505) 842153
(01505) 843668
500
RJG Jamieson
G Reilly (01505) 843029
18 L 6243 yds SSS 71
WD–U before 4.30pm SOC–WD
£20 D–£20
9 miles SW of Paisley
www.lochwinnochgolf.co.uk

Old Ranfurly　(1905)

Ranfurly Place, Bridge of Weir, PA11 3DE
(01505) 613612 (Clubhouse)
(01505) 613214
375
QJ McClymont (01505) 613214
D McIntosh
18 L 6089 yds SSS 70
WD–I WE–M SOC
On application
7 miles W of Paisley, off A761

Paisley　(1895)

Braehead, Paisley, PA2 8TZ
(0141) 884 2292 (Clubhouse)
(0141) 884 3903
paisleygc@onetel.net.uk
805
J Hillis (0141) 884 3903
G Stewart (0141) 884 4114
18 L 6466 yds Par 71 SSS 72
WD–H SOC
£24 D–£32
Glenburn, S of Paisley
Stutt
www.paisleygc.com

Port Glasgow (1895)

Devol Farm, Port Glasgow, PA14 5XE
☎ **(01475) 704181**
📖 265
🖊 A Hughes (01475) 791214
🏴 18 L 5712 yds SSS 68
🏌 WD–U before 5pm –M after 5pm WE–NA SOC
💶 £15 D–£20 (£20 D–£30)
⛳ 1 mile S of Port Glasgow

Ranfurly Castle (1889)

Golf Road, Bridge of Weir, PA11 3HN
☎ **(01505) 612609**
📠 (01505) 610406
📧 secranfur@aol.com
📖 360 160(L) 100(J)
🖊 J King
✎ T Eckford (01505) 614795
🏴 18 L 6284 yds SSS 71
🏌 WD–H WE–M SOC–WD
💶 £25 D–£35
⛳ 7 miles W of Paisley (A761)
🏠 Kirkcaldy/Auchterlonie
■ www.ranfurlycastle.com

Renfrew (1894)

Blythswood Estate, Inchinnan Road, Renfrew, PA4 9EG
☎ **(0141) 886 6692**
📠 (0141) 886 1808
📧 secretary@renfrew.scottishgolf.com
📖 465 110(L) 80(J)
🖊 I Murchison
✎ D Grant (0141) 885 1754
🏴 18 L 6818 yds SSS 73
🏌 M SOC
💶 On application
⛳ 3 miles N of Paisley, nr Airport. M8 Junctions 26 or 27
🏠 Cdr JD Harris
■ www.renfrew.scottishgolf.com

Whinhill (1911)

Beith Road, Greenock, PA16
☎ **(01475) 24694**
📖 250
🖊 R Kirkpatrick (01475) 719260
✎ None
🏴 18 L 5504 yds SSS 68
🏌 U
💶 On application
⛳ Upper Greenock-Largs road
🏠 W Fernie

Whitecraigs (1905)

72 Ayr Road, Giffnock, Glasgow, G46 6SW
☎ **(0141) 639 4530**
📠 (0141) 616 3648
📧 wcraigsgc@aol.com
📖 1150
🖊 AG Keith CA
✎ A Forrow (0141) 639 2140
🏴 18 L 6013 yds SSS 70
🏌 WD–U before 5pm WE–M SOC–WD
💶 £40
⛳ 6 miles S of Glasgow (A77), nr Whitecraigs Station
■ www.thewhitecraigsgolfclub.co.uk

Stirlingshire

Aberfoyle (1890)

Braeval, Aberfoyle, FK8 3UY
☎ **(01877) 382493**
📖 600
🖊 RD Steele (01877) 382638
🏴 18 L 5218 yds SSS 66
🏌 WD–U WF–NA before 11.30am
💶 £15 D–£20 (£20 D–£28)
⛳ Braeval, 18 miles NW of Stirling (A81)

Balfron (1992)

Kepculloch Road, Balfron, G63 0QP
📧 golfbalfron@aol.com
📖 475
🖊 I Rubython (01360) 440915
✎ None
🏴 18 L 5903 yds Par 72 SSS 70
🏌 WD–U before 4pm WE–restricted SOC
💶 £15 (£15)
⛳ 18 miles NW of Glasgow, off A81
■ www.balfrongolfsociety.homepage.com

Bonnybridge (1925)

Larbert Road, Bonnybridge, Falkirk, FK4 1NY
☎ **(01324) 812822**
📧 bonnybridgegolfclub@hotmail.com
📖 425
🖊 J Mullen (01324) 812323
🏴 9 L 6058 yds SSS 70
🏌 WD–I SOC
💶 £16 D–£20
⛳ 3 miles W of Falkirk. M876 Junction 1

Bridge of Allan (1895)

Sunnylaw, Bridge of Allan, Stirling
☎ **(01786) 832332**
📖 513
🖊 TM Green
🏴 9 L 4932 yds SSS 66
🏌 U exc Sat
💶 £14 (£18)
⛳ 4 miles N of Stirling, off A9
🏠 Tom Morris Sr

Buchanan Castle (1936)

Proprietary
Drymen, G63 0HY
☎ **(01360) 660307**
📠 (01360) 660993
📖 830
🖊 R Kinsella
✎ K Baxter (01360) 660330
🏴 18 L 6015 yds SSS 69
🏌 By arrangement with Sec SOC
💶 £30 D–£40 (£30 D–£40)
⛳ 18 miles NW of Glasgow. 25 miles W of Stirling, off A811
🏠 James Braid

Campsie (1897)

Crow Road, Lennoxtown, Glasgow, G66 7HX
☎ **(01360) 310244**
📧 campsiegolfclub@aol.com
📖 650
🖊 NP Darroch (01360) 312249
✎ M Brennan (01360) 310920
🏴 18 L 5517 yds SSS 68
🏌 WD–U before 4.30pm SOC
💶 £20 D–£25 (£25)
⛳ N of Lennoxtown on B822 Fintry road
🏠 Auchterlonie/Stark

Dunblane New (1923)

Perth Road, Dunblane, FK15 0LJ
☎ **(01786) 821521**
📠 (01786) 821522
📖 700
🖊 JH Dunsmore
✎ RM Jamieson
🏴 18 L 5930 yds SSS 69
🏌 WD–U WE–M SOC
💶 £22 (£35)
⛳ E side of Dunblane. 6 miles N of Stirling

Falkirk (1922)

Stirling Road, Camelon, Falkirk, FK2 7YP
☎ **(01324) 611061/612219**
📠 (01324) 639573
📧 carmuirs.fgc@virgin.net
📖 700
🖊 J Elliott
🏴 18 L 6282 yds SSS 70
🏌 WD–U until 4pm Sat–NA SOC–exc Sat
💶 £20 D–£30 Sun–£40
⛳ 1½ miles W of Falkirk on A9
🏠 James Braid
■ www.falkirkcarmuirsgolfclub.co.uk

Falkirk Tryst (1885)

86 Burnhead Road, Larbert, FK5 4BD
☎ **(01324) 562415**
📠 (01324) 562054
📧 falkirktrystgc@tiscali.co.uk
📖 800
🖊 RC Chalmers (01324) 562054
✎ S Dunsmore (01324) 562091
🏴 18 L 6053 yds SSS 69
🏌 WD–U WE–M SOC–WD
💶 £22 D–£30
⛳ 3 miles NW of Falkirk on A88

Glenbervie (1932)

Stirling Road, Larbert, FK5 4SJ
☎ **(01324) 562605**
📠 (01324) 551054
📖 600
🖊 Dr Sheila Hartley
✎ J Chillas (01324) 562725
🏴 18 L 6423 yds Par 71 SSS 71
🏌 WD–U before 4pm WE–M SOC–Tues & Thurs
💶 £30 D–£40
⛳ 1 mile N of Larbert on A9. M876 Junction 2
🏠 James Braid

Grangemouth   (1973)
Public
Polmonthill, Polmont, FK2 0YA
☎ **(01324) 711500**
⌨ (01324) 717907
📖 700
🏌 I Hutton (Hon)
✒ SJ Campbell (01324) 503840
🏴 18 L 6527 yds SSS 70
👤 U–book with Pro SOC
£€ £12.50 D–£18 (£16 D–£21.50)
⛳ 3 miles NE of Falkirk. M9 Junct. 4

Kilsyth Lennox   (1900)
Tak-Ma-Doon Road, Kilsyth, G65 0RS
☎ **(01236) 823525 (Bookings)**
📖 250
🏌 AG Stevenson (01236) 823213
🏴 18 L 5930 yds Par 70
👤 WD–U until 5pm –M after 5pm
Sat–NA before 4pm Sun–NA
before 2pm SOC

£€ On application
⛳ N of Kilsyth and A803. 12 miles
NE of Glasgow

Polmont   (1901)
*Manuel Rigg, Maddiston, Falkirk,
FK2 0LS*
☎ **(01324) 711277 (Clubhouse)**
⌨ (01324) 712504
📖 300
🏌 P Lees (01324) 713811
🏴 9 L 3044 yds SSS 70
👤 U exc Sat–NA
£€ £8 Sun–£15
⛳ 4 miles SE of Falkirk on B805

Stirling   (1869)
Queen's Road, Stirling, FK8 3AA
☎ **(01786) 464098**
⌨ (01786) 450748
📧 enquiries@stirlinggolfclub.tv
📖 1000

🏌 AMS Rankin (01786) 464098
✒ I Collins (01786) 471490
🏴 18 L 6409 yds SSS 71
👤 WD–U SOC WE–NA
£€ £28 D–£40
⛳ ¹/₂ mile from Stirling centre. M9
Junction 10
🏠 Braid/Cotton
■ www.stirlinggolfclub.tv

Strathendrick   (1901)
Glasgow Road, Drymen, G63 0AA
☎ **(01360) 660695**
📖 480
🏌 M Quyn (01360) 660733
🏴 9 L 5116 yds SSS 64
👤 WD–U SOC–WD before 5pm
£€ £12
⛳ 25 miles W of Stirling, off A811
🏠 W Fernie

Wales

Cardiganshire

Aberystwyth   (1911)
Bryn-y-Mor, Aberystwyth, SY23 2HY
☎ **(01970) 615104**
⌨ (01970) 626622
📧 aberystwythgolf@talk21.com
📖 390
🏌 (01970) 625301
🏴 18 L 6119 yds SSS 71
👤 U SOC
£€ £18.50 (£22.50)
⛳ Aberystwyth ¹/₂ mile
🏠 H Varden

Borth & Ynyslas   (1885)
Borth, Ceredigion, SY24 5JS
☎ **(01970) 871202**
⌨ (01970) 871202
📖 550
🏌 GJ Pritchard
✒ JG Lewis (01970) 871557
🏴 18 L 6100 yds SSS 70
👤 WD–U WE/BH–by prior
arrangement SOC
£€ £22 (£30)
⛳ 8 miles N of Aberystwyth (B4353),
off A487

Cardigan   (1895)
Gwbert-on-Sea, Cardigan, SA43 1PR
☎ **(01239) 612035/621775**
⌨ (01239) 621775
📧 golf@cardigan.fsnet.co.uk
📖 600
🏌 JJ Jones (01239) 621775
✒ C Parsons (01239) 615359
🏴 18 L 6687 yds SSS 73
👤 H SOC
£€ D–£20 (£25) W–£80

⛳ 3 miles N of Cardigan
🏠 Grant/Hawtree
■ www.cardigangolf.co.uk

Cilgwyn   (1977)
Llangybi, Lampeter, SA48 8NN
☎ **(01570) 493286**
📖 290
🏌 JD Morgan
🏴 9 L 5327 yds SSS 67
👤 U SOC
£€ £10 (£15) W–£60
⛳ 5 miles NE of Lampeter, off A485
at Llangybi

Penrhos G&CC   (1991)
Llanrhystud, Aberystwyth, SY23 5AY
☎ **(01974) 202999**
⌨ (01974) 202100
📧 info@Penrhosgolf.co.uk
📖 300
🏌 R Rees-Evans
✒ P Diamond
🏴 18 L 6641 yds SSS 73
9 hole Par 3 course
👤 U SOC
£€ £20 (£25)
⛳ 9 miles S of Aberystwyth,
signposted off A487
⊕ Driving range
🏠 Jim Walters
■ www.Penrhosgolf.co.uk

Carmarthenshire

Ashburnham   (1894)
Cliffe Terrace, Burry Port, SA16 0HN
☎ **(01554) 832466**
⌨ (01554) 832466

📖 725
🏌 DK Williams (01554) 832269
✒ RA Ryder (01554) 833846
🏴 18 L 6916 yds SSS 72
👤 H
£€ £27 D–£32 (£32 D–£42)
⛳ 5 miles W of Llanelli (A484)

Carmarthen   (1907)
*Blaenycoed Road, Carmarthen,
SA33 6EH*
☎ **(01267) 281214**
📖 700
🏌 J Coe (01267) 281588
✒ P Gillis (01267) 281493
🏴 18 L 6245 yds SSS 71
👤 H SOC
£€ £20 (£25)
⛳ 4 miles NW of Carmarthen
🏠 JH Taylor

Derllys   (1993)
*Derllys Court, Llysonnen Road,
Carmarthen, SA33 5DT*
☎ **(01267) 211575/211309**
⌨ (01267) 211575
📖 48
🏌 R Walters
🏴 9 L 2859 yds Par 70 SSS 66
👤 U
£€ £10 D–£13 (£11 D–£14)
⛳ 4 miles W of Carmarthen, off A40
🏠 P Johnson

Garnant Park
Garnant, Ammanford, SA18 1NP
☎ **(01269) 826472**
⌨ (01269) 823365
📖 320
🏌 Mrs R Liles (01639) 844357

✓ None
▷ 18 L 6163 yds Par 72 SSS 72
👥 U SOC
£€ £11.50 (£15.50)
🚗 Ammanford and Pontardawe. M4
    Junction 45
🏠 Roger Jones

Glyn Abbey (1992)
Proprietary
Trimsaran, SA17 4LB
☎ **(01554) 810278**
🖥 (01554) 810889
📖 240
🏌 M Lane (Mgr) (01554) 810304
✓ M Stimson (01554) 810278
▷ 18 L 6173 yds Par 70 SSS 70
👥 U SOC
£€ £12 (£15)
🚗 4 miles NW of Llanelli, between
    Trimsaran and Carway
⊕ Driving range
🏠 Hawtree
■ www.glynabbey.co.uk

Glynhir (1909)
Glynhir Road, Llandybie, Ammanford,
SA18 2TF
☎ **(01269) 850472**
🖥 (01269) 851365
📖 700
🏌 D Kenchington, K Williams
    (01269) 851365
✓ D Prior (01269) 851010
▷ 18 L 6006 yds SSS 70
👥 WD/Sat–H Sun–NA SOC–WD
£€ Winter £10 (£12) 5D–£45 Summer
    £16 (£22) 5D–£70
🚗 3¹/₂miles N of Ammanford
🏠 Hawtree

Saron Golf Course
Pay and play
Penwern, Saron, Llandysul, SA44 4EL
☎ **(01559) 370705**
▷ 9 L 2091 yds Par 32
👥 U
£€ 9 holes–£7. 18 holes–£10
🚗 On A484 Newcastle Emlyn to
    Carmarthen road

Conwy

Abergele (1910)
Tan-y-Gopa Road, Abergele,
LL22 8DS
☎ **(01745) 824034**
🖥 (01745) 824772
📖 1250
🏌 CP Langdon
✓ I Runcie (01745) 823813
▷ 18 L 6520 yds SSS 71
👥 U SOC
£€ On application
🚗 Abergele Castle Grounds
🏠 David Williams

Betws-y-Coed (1977)
Clubhouse, Betws-y-Coed, LL24 0AL
☎ **(01690) 710556**
📧 betwsycoed.golfclub@tesco.net
📖 350
🏌 Mrs P Rowley
▷ 9 L 4996 yds SSS 64
👥 U SOC
£€ £16 (£21)
🚗 ¹/₄ mile off A5, in Betws-y-Coed

Conwy (Caernarvonshire)
(1890)
Morfa, Conwy, LL32 8ER
☎ **(01492) 593400**
🖥 (01492) 593363
📧 secretary@conwygolfclub.co.uk
📖 1000
🏌 DL Brown (01492) 592423
✓ JP Lees (01492) 593225
▷ 18 L 6936 yds SSS 74
👥 H WE–restricted SOC
£€ £28 (£35)
🚗 ¹/₂ mile W of Conway, off A55
■ www.conwygolfclub.co.uk

Llandudno (Maesdu)
(1915)
Hospital Road, Llandudno, LL30 1HU
☎ **(01492) 876450**
🖥 (01492) 871570
📧 george@maesdugolfclub.freeserve
    .co.uk
📖 1109
🏌 G Dean
✓ S Boulden (01492) 875195
▷ 18 L 6513 yds SSS 72
👥 U H–recognised GC members SOC
£€ £25 (£30)
🚗 1 mile S of Llandudno Station, nr
    Hospital

Llandudno (North Wales)
(1894)
72 Bryniau Road, West Shore,
Llandudno, LL30 2DZ
☎ **(01492) 875325**
🖥 (01492) 873355
📖 691
🏌 WR Williams (01492) 875325
✓ RA Bradbury (01492) 876878
▷ 18 L 6247 yds Par 71 SSS 71
👥 U SOC–phone Sec
£€ £25 (£35)
🚗 ¹/₄ mile from Llandudno on West
    Shore
■ www.northwales.uk.com/nwgc

Llanfairfechan (1971)
Llannerch Road, Llanfairfechan,
LL33 0EB
☎ **(01248) 680144**
📖 352
🏌 MJ Charlesworth (01248) 680524
▷ 9 L 3119 yds SSS 57
👥 U
£€ £10 (£10)
🚗 7 miles E of Bangor on A55

Old Colwyn (1907)
Woodland Avenue, Old Colwyn,
LL29 9NL
☎ **(01492) 515581**
📖 250
🏌 DA Jones
▷ 9 L 5243 yds SSS 66
👥 WD–U WE–by arrangement SOC
£€ £10 (£15)
🚗 2 miles E of Colwyn Bay, off A55
    Chester-Holyhead road

Penmaenmawr (1910)
Conway Old Road, Penmaenmawr,
LL34 6RD
☎ **(01492) 623330**
🖥 (01492) 622105
📖 600
🏌 Mrs JE Jones
▷ 9 L 5143 yds SSS 66
👥 U SOC
£€ £12 (£18)
🚗 4 miles W of Conway

Rhos-on-Sea (1899)
Penrhyn Bay, Llandudno, LL30 3PU
☎ **(01492) 549641**
🖥 (01492) 549100
📖 600
🏌 JM Bray
✓ M Macara
▷ 18 L 6064 yds SSS 69
👥 U
£€ £22 (£30)
🚗 On coast at Rhos-on-Sea. 4 miles E
    of Llandudno
🏠 Simpson

Denbighshire

Bryn Morfydd Hotel (1982)
Llanrhaeadr, Denbigh, LL16 4NP
☎ **(01745) 890280**
🖥 (01745) 890488
📖 250
✓ IP Jones
▷ 18 L 5800 yds Par 70 SSS 67
    9 hole Par 3 course
👥 U SOC
£€ £15 (£20)
🚗 2¹/₂ miles SE of Denbigh on A525
🏠 Duchess-Alliss/Thomas. Dukes-
    Muirhead/Henderson
■ www.bryn-morfydd.co.uk

Denbigh (1922)
Henllan Road, Denbigh, LL16 5AA
☎ **(01745) 814159**
🖥 (01745) 814888
📖 550
🏌 G Downs (01745) 816669
✓ M Jones (01745) 814159
▷ 18 L 5712 yds SSS 69
👥 U SOC
£€ On application
🚗 1 mile NW of Denbigh (B5382)

Kinmel Park   (1989)
Pay and play
Bodelwyddan, LL18 5SR
- ☎ **(01745) 833548**
- 📠 (01745) 824861
- 🏌 P Stebbings
- ✓ P Stebbings
- ⛳ 9 L 1550 yds Par 29
- 👥 U
- £€ £3.50 (£4)
- ⊕ Off A55, between Abergele and St Asaph
- ⊕ Driving range
- 🏠 Peter Stebbings

Prestatyn   (1905)
Marine Road East, Prestatyn, LL19 7HS
- ☎ **(01745) 854320**
- 📠 (01745) 888327
- ✉ prestatyngcmanager@freenet.co.uk
- 📖 680
- 🏌 R Woodruff (Mgr) (01745) 888353
- ✓ M Staton (01745) 852083
- ⛳ 18 L 6808 yds SSS 73
- 👥 H SOC
- £€ £25 (£30)
- ⊕ 1 mile E of Prestatyn
- 🏠 S Collins
- ■ www.prestatyngc.co.uk

Rhuddlan   (1930)
Meliden Road, Rhuddlan, LL18 6LB
- ☎ **(01745) 590217**
- 📠 (01745) 590472
- 📖 515 155(L) 80(J)
- 🏌 BP Jones
- ✓ A Carr (01745) 590898
- ⛳ 18 L 6471 yds SSS 71
- 👥 H Sun–M SOC–WD
- £€ £20 (£30)
- ⊕ 2 miles N of St Asaph, off A55
- 🏠 F Hawtree
- ■ www.rhuddlangolfclub.co.uk

Rhyl   (1890)
Coast Road, Rhyl, LL18 3RE
- ☎ **(01745) 353171**
- 📠 (01745) 353171
- 📖 600
- 🏌 I StC Doig
- ✓ T Leah
- ⛳ 9 L 6220 yds SSS 70
- 👥 U SOC
- £€ £20 (£25)
- ⊕ On A548 between Rhyl and Prestatyn
- 🏠 James Braid
- ■ www.rhylgolfclub.com

Ruthin-Pwllglas   (1920)
Pwllglas, Ruthin, LL15 2PE
- ☎ **(01824) 702296**
- 📠 (01978) 790692
- 📖 360
- 🏌 Mrs BK Tremayne (Hon) (01978) 790692
- ⛳ 10 L 5362 yds SSS 66
- 👥 U SOC
- £€ £12.50 (£18)
- ⊕ 2½ miles S of Ruthin

St Melyd   (1922)
The Paddock, Meliden Road, Prestatyn, LL19 8NB
- ☎ **(01745) 854405**
- 📠 (01745) 856908
- 📖 400
- 🏌 KJ Woodward, Mrs A Thompson
- ⛳ 9 L 5857 yds SSS 68
- 👥 U SOC
- £€ £18 (£22)
- ⊕ S of Prestatyn on A547
- ■ www.stmelydgolf.co.uk

Vale of Llangollen   (1908)
Holyhead Road, Llangollen, LL20 7PR
- ☎ **(01978) 860613**
- 📠 (01978) 860906
- 📖 850
- 🏌 AD Bluck (01978) 860906
- ✓ DI Vaughan (01978) 860040
- ⛳ 18 L 6656 yds Par 72 SSS 73
- 👥 U H SOC
- £€ £20 (£25)
- ⊕ 1½ miles E of Llangollen on A5

Flintshire

Caerwys   (1989)
Pay and play
Caerwys, Mold, CH7 5AQ
- ☎ **(01352) 720692**
- 📖 200
- 🏌 E Barlow
- ✓ N Lloyd
- ⛳ 9 L 3080 yds SSS 60
- 👥 U SOC
- £€ £4.50 (£5.50)
- ⊕ SW of Caerwys. 1½ miles S of A55 Express Way, between Holywell and St Asaph
- 🏠 Eleanor Barlow

DeVere Northop Country Park   (1994)
Northop, Chester, CH7 6WA
- ☎ **(01352) 840440**
- 📠 (01352) 840445
- 🏌 M Pritchard
- ✓ M Pritchard
- ⛳ 18 L 6802 yds Par 72
- 👥 U–phone first SOC
- £€ £40
- ⊕ 3 miles S of Flint, off A55
- ⊕ Driving range
- 🏠 John Jacobs

Flint   (1966)
Cornist Park, Flint, CH6 5HJ
- ☎ **(01352) 732327, (01244) 812974**
- 📠 (01244) 811885
- 📖 390
- 🏌 TE Owens
- ⛳ 9 L 5953 yds SSS 69
- 👥 WD–U before 5pm SOC–WD
- £€ D–£10 (£10)
- ⊕ 1 mile SW of Flint. End of M56, 8 miles

Hawarden   (1911)
Groomsdale Lane, Hawarden, Deeside, CH5 3EH
- ☎ **(01244) 531447**
- 📠 (01244) 536901
- 📖 480
- 🏌 MB Coppack
- ✓ A Rowlands (01244) 520809
- ⛳ 18 L 5809 yds SSS 69
- 👥 H SOC–WD
- £€ £18 (£24)
- ⊕ 6 miles W of Chester, off A55

Holywell   (1906)
Brynford, Holywell, CH8 8LQ
- ☎ **(01352) 710040/713937**
- 📠 (01352) 713937
- 📖 375 60(L)
- 🏌 JF Snead (01352) 713937
- ✓ M Parsley (01352) 710040
- ⛳ 18 L 6100 yds Par 70 SSS 70
- 👥 WD–U WE–SOC
- £€ £18 (£23)
- ⊕ 2 miles S of Holywell, off A5026

Kinsale
Pay and play
Llanerchymor, Holywell, CH8 9DX
- ☎ **(01745) 561080**
- 📠 (01745) 561079
- 📖 85
- 🏌 A Backhurst (Golf Dir)
- ✓ A Backhurst
- ⛳ 9 holes Par 71 SSS 70
- 👥 U
- £€ 9 holes–£6.60. 18 holes–£9.90
- ⊕ 4 miles N of Holywell on A548
- ⊕ Floodlit driving range
- 🏠 K Smith

Mold   (1909)
Cilcain Road, Pantymwyn, Mold, CH7 5EH
- ☎ **(01352) 740318/741513**
- 📠 (01352) 741517
- 📖 450 90(L) 95(J)
- 🏌 P Mather (01352) 741513
- ✓ M Jordan (01352) 740318
- ⛳ 18 L 5512 yds Par 67 SSS 67
- 👥 U SOC
- £€ £18 (£25)
- ⊕ 3 miles W of Mold
- 🏠 Hawtree

Old Padeswood   (1978)
Station Road, Padeswood, Mold, CH7 4JL
- ☎ **(01244) 547701 (Clubhouse)**
- 📖 500
- 🏌 B Slater (Hon)
- ✓ A Davies (01244) 547401
- ⛳ 18 L 6728 yds SSS 72
  9 hole Par 3 course
- 👥 U exc comp days SOC–WD
- £€ £18 D–£25 (£20)
- ⊕ 2 miles from Mold on A5118
- ■ www.oldpadeswoodgolfclub.co.uk

Padeswood & Buckley
(1933)
The Caia, Station Lane, Padeswood,
Mold CH7 4JD
- ☎ **(01244) 550537**
- 🖴 (01244) 541600
- 📖 592
- 🖊 JM Conway
- ✓ D Ashton (01244) 543636
- ⮑ 18 L 5982 yds Par 70 SSS 69
- 🙀 WD–U 9am–4pm –M after 4pm
  Sat–U Sun–NA SOC–WD Ladies
  Day–Wed
- ££ £20 (£25)
- 🚗 8 miles W of Chester, off A5118.
  2nd golf club on right
- 🏠 D Williams

Pennant Park
Proprietary
Whitford, Holywell, CH8 9EP
- ☎ **(01745) 560000**
- 🖊 P Roberts, R Jones
- ⮑ 18 holes Par 72
- 🙀 U SOC
- ££ £14 (£18)
- 🚗 Nr North Wales Expressway (A55)
- ⊕ Driving range. Academy course
- 🏠 Roger Jones
- ■ www.pennant-park.co.uk

Gwynedd

Aberdovey (1892)
Aberdovey, LL35 0RT
- ☎ **(01654) 767210**
- 🖴 (01654) 767027
- 📖 800
- 🖊 JM Griffiths (01654) 767493
- ✓ J Davies (01654) 767602
- ⮑ 18 L 6445 yds SSS 71
- 🙀 NA–8–9.30am & 1–2pm
- ££ On application
- 🚗 ¹/₂ mile W of Aberdovey (A493)
- 🏠 Braid/Fowler/Swan
- ■ www.aberdoveygolf.co.uk

Abersoch (1907)
Golf Road, Abersoch, LL53 7EY
- ☎ **(01758) 712636**
- 🖴 (01758) 712777
- 📖 700
- 🖊 A Drosinos Jones (01758) 712622
- ✓ A Drosinos Jones
- ⮑ 18 L 5819 yds SSS 69
- 🙀 U H SOC
- ££ £18 (£20)
- 🚗 ¹/₂ mile S of Abersoch (A55). 7
  miles S of Pwllheli
- 🏠 Harry Vardon
- ■ www.abersochgolf.co.uk

Bala (1973)
Penlan, Bala, LL23 7BC
- ☎ **(01678) 520359**
- 🖴 (01678) 521361
- 📖 340
- 🖊 G Rhys Jones

- ✓ T Davies
- ⮑ 10 L 4962 yds SSS 64
- 🙀 WD–U WE–NA pm SOC
- ££ £12 (£15) W–£40
- 🚗 ¹/₂ mile SW of Bala, off A494 to
  Dolgellau

Bala Lake Hotel
Bala, LL23 7YF
- ☎ **(01678) 520344/520111**
- 🖴 (01678) 521193
- 📖 50
- 🖊 D Pickering
- ⮑ 9 L 4280 yds SSS 61
- 🙀 U
- ££ On application
- 🚗 1¹/₂ miles S of Bala on B4403

Criccieth (1905)
Ednyfed Hill, Criccieth, LL52
- ☎ **(01766) 522154**
- 📖 200
- 🖊 MG Hamilton (01766) 522697
- ⮑ 18 L 5755 yds SSS 68
- 🙀 U
- ££ £12 Sun–£15
- 🚗 4 miles W of Portmadoc

Dolgellau (1911)
Hengwrt Estate, Pencefn Road,
Dolgellau, LL4 0SE
- ☎ **(01341) 422603**
- 📖 300
- 🖊 Ms JM May
- ✓ H Jones Davies
- ⮑ 9 L 4671 yds Par 66 SSS 63
- 🙀 U
- ££ £15 (£20)
- 🚗 ¹/₂ miles N of Dolgellau
- 🏠 J Medway

Ffestiniog (1893)
Y Cefn, Ffestiniog
- ☎ **(01766) 762637 (Clubhouse)**
- 📖 138
- 🖊 A Roberts (01766) 831829
- ⮑ 9 L 5032 metres Par 68 SSS 65
- 🙀 U
- ££ On application
- 🚗 1 mile E of Ffestiniog on Bala road
  (B4391)

Nefyn & District (1907)
Morfa Nefyn, Pwllheli, LL53 6DA
- ☎ **(01758) 720218 (Clubhouse)**
- 🖴 (01758) 720476
- 📧 nefyngolf@tesco.net
- 📖 880
- 🖊 JB Owens (01758) 720966
- ✓ J Froom (01758) 720102
- ⮑ 18 L 6548 yds SSS 71
  9 L 2618 yds SSS 34
- 🙀 U SOC
- ££ £26 D–£33 (£31 D–£36)
- 🚗 1¹/₂ miles W of Nefyn. 20 miles W
  of Caernarfon

Porthmadog (1905)
Morfa Bychan, Porthmadog, LL49 9UU
- ☎ **(01766) 512037 (Clubhouse)**

- 🖴 (01766) 514638
- 📖 920
- 🖊 Mrs A Richardson (Office Mgr)
  (01766) 514124
- ✓ P Bright (01766) 513828
- ⮑ 18 L 6363 yds Par 71 SSS 71
- 🙀 U H SOC
- ££ D–£25 (D–£30)
- 🚗 2 miles S of Porthmadog, towards
  Black Rock Sands
- 🏠 James Braid
- ■ www.porthmadog-golf-club.co.uk

Pwllheli (1900)
Golf Road, Pwllheli, LL53 5PS
- ☎ **(01758) 701644**
- 🖴 (01758) 701644
- 📖 820
- 🖊 D Roberts (Gen Mgr)
- ✓ J Pilkington (01758) 612520
- ⮑ 18 L 6091 yds SSS 69
- 🙀 U
- ££ £25 (£30)
- 🚗 ¹/₂ mile SW of Pwllheli
- 🏠 James Braid
- ■ www.pwllheligolfclub.co.uk

Royal St David's (1894)
Harlech, LL46 2UB
- ☎ **(01766) 780203**
- 🖴 (01766) 781110
- 📧 secretary@royalstdavids.co.uk
- 📖 880
- 🖊 DL Morkill (01766) 780361
- ✓ J Barnett (01766) 780857
- ⮑ 18 L 6571 yds SSS 73
- 🙀 U H–booking necessary SOC
- ££ £40 (£50)
- 🚗 W of Harlech on A496
- 🏠 H Finch-Hatton
- ■ www.royalstdavids.co.uk

Royal Town of Caernarfon
(1909)
Aberforeshore, LLanfaglan, Caernarfon,
LL54 5RP
- ☎ **(01286) 673967**
- 🖴 (01286) 672535
- 📧 caerngc@talk21.com
- 📖 735
- 🖊 G Jones (01286) 673783
- ✓ A Owen (01286) 678359
- ⮑ 18 L 5891 yds SSS 68
- 🙀 U SOC
- ££ £20 Sat–£28 Sun–£25
- 🚗 2¹/₂ miles SW of Caernarfon
- ■ www.caernarfongolfclub.co.uk

St Deiniol (1906)
Penybryn, Bangor, LL57 1PX
- ☎ **(01248) 353098**
- 📧 secretary@stdeiniol.fsbusiness
  .co.uk
- 📖 350
- 🖊 RD Thomas (01248) 370792
- ⮑ 18 L 5654 yds SSS 67
- 🙀 U SOC
- ££ £14 (£18)
- 🚗 Off A5/A55 Junction 11, 1 mile E
  of Bangor on A5122
- 🏠 James Braid

For list of abbreviations and key to symbols see page 649

Isle of Anglesey

Anglesey   (1914)
Station Road, Rhosneigr, LL64 5QX
☎ **(01407) 810219 (Clubhouse)**
🖬 (01407) 811127
✉ info@theangleseygolfclub.com
📖 450
🏌 VB Musgrave (Mgr)
   (01407) 811127
✓ M Parry (01407)811202
🏴 18 L 6330 yds SSS 70
👥 U H SOC
£€ £20
🚗 8 miles SE of Holyhead, off A4080
🏛 H Hilton
■ www.theangleseygolfclub.com

Baron Hill   (1895)
Beaumaris, LL58 8YW
☎ **(01248) 810231**
✉ golf@baronhill.co.uk
📖 360
🏌 A Pleming
🏴 9 L 5062 metres SSS 68
👥 U exc comp days SOC–WD & Sat
   (apply Sec)
£€ £15 W–£45
🚗 1 mile SW of Beaumaris

Bull Bay   (1913)
Bull Bay Road, Amlwch, LL68 9RY
☎ **(01407) 830213**
🖬 (01407) 832612
📖 700
🏌 I Furlong (Sec/Mgr)
   (01407) 830960
✓ J Burns (01407) 831188
🏴 18 L 6276 yds SSS 70
👥 H SOC
£€ £20 (£25)
🚗 ¹/₂ mile W of Amlwch on A5025
🏛 WH Fowler
■ www.bullbaygc.co.uk

Henllys Hall
Llanfaes, Beaumaris, LL58 8HU
☎ **(01248) 811717**
🖬 (01248) 811511
✓ P Maton
🏴 18 L 6062 yds Par 72
👥 U SOC
£€ £20 (£25)
🚗 2 miles N of Beaumaris (B5109)
🏛 Roger Jones

Holyhead   (1912)
Trearddur Bay, Holyhead, LL65 2YL
☎ **(01407) 763279/762119**
🖬 (01407) 763279
✉ mgrsec@aol.com
📖 790 396(L)
🏌 JA Williams
✓ S Elliott (01407) 762022
🏴 18 L 5540 metres SSS 70
👥 H SOC
£€ £19 D–£25 (£25 D–£29)
🚗 2 miles S of Holyhead
🏛 James Braid
■ www.holyheadgolfclub.co.uk

Llangefni   (1983)
Public
Llangefni, LL77 8YQ
☎ **(01248) 722193**
✓ P Lovell
🏴 9 L 1467 yds Par 28
👥 U
£€ £3.30 (£3.50)
🚗 ¹/₂mile S of Llangefni, off A5111
🏛 Hawtree

RAF Valley
Anglesey, LL65 3NY
☎ **(01407) 762241**
📖 150
🏌 MJ Constable (Mgr)
🏴 9 L 5604 yards SSS 68
👥 U – booking necessary
£€ D–£6 (£6)
🚗 RAF Valley base, off A55

Storws Wen   (1996)
Brynteg, Benllech, LL78 8JY
☎ **(01248) 852673**
🖬 (01248) 853843
📖 260
🏌 R Perry
✓ J Kelly
🏴 9 L 5002 yds Par 68 SSS 64
👥 U SOC
£€ £15 (£18)
🚗 2 miles from Benllech on B5108
🏛 K Jones

Mid Glamorgan

Aberdare   (1921)
Abernant, Aberdare, CF44 0RY
☎ **(01685) 871188 (Clubhouse)**
🖬 (01685) 872797
📖 500
🏌 T Mears (01685) 872797
✓ AW Palmer (01685) 878735
🏴 18 L 5875 yds SSS 69
👥 H SOC
£€ £17 (£21)
🚗 ¹/₂ mile E of Aberdare. 12 miles
   NW of Pontypridd

Bargoed   (1913)
Heolddu, Bargoed, CF81 9GF
☎ **(01443) 830143**
📖 548
🏌 G Williams (01443) 830608
🏴 18 L 6233 yds SSS 70
👥 WD–U WE–M SOC–WD
£€ £15
🚗 NW boundary of Bargoed. 8 miles
   N of Caerphilly (A469)

Bryn Meadows Golf Hotel   (1973)
The Bryn, Hengoed, CF8 7SM
☎ **(01495) 225590/224103**
🖬 (01495) 228272
📖 550
🏌 B Mayo
✓ B Hunter (01495) 221905

🏴 18 L 6156 yds SSS 69
👥 U
£€ £17.50 (£22.50)
🚗 6 miles N of Caerphilly (A469)
🏛 Mayo/Jefferies

Caerphilly   (1905)
Pencapel, Mountain Road, Caerphilly, CF83 1HJ
☎ **(029) 2088 3481**
🖬 (029) 2086 3441
📖 650
🏌 (029) 2086 3441
✓ J Hill (029) 2086 9104
🏴 13 L 5944 yds SSS 70
👥 WD–U H WE–M
£€ £24 W–£50
🚗 7 miles N of Cardiff, off A469

Castell Heights   (1982)
Pay and play
Blaengwynlais, Caerphilly, CF8 1NG
☎ **(029) 2088 6666 (Bookings)**
🖬 (029) 2086 9030
📖 600
🏌 S Bebb
🏴 9 L 2688 yds SSS 66
👥 U
£€ 9 holes–£4.50 (£5.50)
🚗 4 miles from M4 Junction 32
⊕ Driving range
🏛 J Page

Coed-y-Mwstwr   (1994)
Coychurch, Bridgend, CF35 6TN
☎ **(01656) 862121**
🖬 (01656) 864934
📖 260
🏌 HD James (Sec/Mgr)
🏴 12 L 6144 yds Par 70 SSS 70
👥 U H Sat–M SOC–WD
£€ £16 (£18)
🚗 2 miles W of M4 Junction 35

Creigiau   (1921)
Creigiau, Cardiff, CF15 9NN
☎ **(029) 2089 0263**
🖬 (029) 2089 0706
📖 700
🏌 AJ Greedy
✓ I Luntz (029) 2089 1909
🏴 18 L 6063 yds SSS 70
👥 WD–U WE/BH–M SOC–WD
£€ £30
🚗 5 miles NW of Cardiff. M4
   Junction 34

Llantrisant & Pontyclun   (1927)
Ely Valley Road, Talbot Green, Llantrisant, CF72 8AL
☎ **(01443) 222148**
✉ lpgc@barbox.net
📖 600
🏌 RW Rowsell (01443) 224601
✓ M Phillips (01443) 228169
🏴 18 L 5328 yds SSS 66
👥 WD–H WE/BH–M SOC–WD
£€ On application
🚗 10 miles NW of Cardiff. 2 miles N
   of M4 Junction 34

Maesteg (1912)

Mount Pleasant, Neath Road, Maesteg, CF34 9PR
- ☎ **(01656) 732037**
- 🖳 (01656) 734106
- 📖 720
- 🏌 RK Lewis (01656) 734106
- ⛳ 18 L 5929 yds SSS 69
- 👥 WD–H SOC
- £€ £17 (£20)
- ⛿ 1 mile W of Maesteg on B4282. M4 Junctions 36 or 40

Merthyr Tydfil (1909)

Cilsanws Mountain, Cefn Coed, Merthyr Tydfil, CF48 2NU
- ☎ **(01685) 723308**
- 📖 200
- 🏌 V Price
- ⚲ None
- ⛳ 18 L 5622 yds SSS 68
- 👥 U SOC–WD
- £€ £10 (£15)
- ⛿ 2 miles N of Merthyr Tydfil, off A470 at Cefn Coed
- 🏠 Price/Richard/Mathias

Morlais Castle (1900)

Pant, Dowlais, Merthyr Tydfil, CF48 2UY
- ☎ **(01685) 722822**
- 🖳 (01685) 722822
- 📧 meurig.price@lineone.net
- 📖 600
- 🏌 M Price
- ⚲ H Jarrett (01685) 388700
- ⛳ 18 L 6320 yds SSS 71
- 👥 WD–U Sat–NA 12–4pm Sun–NA 8am–12noon SOC
- £€ £16 (£20)
- ⛿ 3 miles N of Merthyr Tydfil, nr Mountain Railway

Mountain Ash (1907)

Cefnpennar, Mountain Ash, CF45 4DT
- ☎ **(01443) 472265 (Clubhouse)**
- 🖳 (01443) 479628
- 📖 530
- 🏌 G Matthews (01443) 479459
- ⚲ D Clark (01443) 478770
- ⛳ 18 L 5535 yds SSS 67
- 👥 WD–U H WE–M
- £€ £20
- ⛿ 9 miles NW of Pontypridd

Mountain Lakes (1988)

Heol Penbryn, Blaengwynlais, Caerphilly, CF83 1NG
- ☎ **(029) 2086 1128**
- 🖳 (029) 2086 3243
- 📖 480
- 🏌 DC Rooney (Hon)
- ⛳ 18 L 6300 yds SSS 72
- 👥 U SOC
- £€ £18 (£18)
- ⛿ 4 miles from M4 Junction 32
- 🏠 R Sandow

Pontypridd (1905)

Ty Gwyn Road, Pontypridd, CF37 4DJ
- ☎ **(01443) 402359**
- 🖳 (01443) 491622
- 📖 850
- 🏌 Vikki Hooley (01443) 409904
- ⚲ W Walters (01443) 491210
- ⛳ 18 L 5725 yds SSS 68
- 👥 WD–U H WE/BH–M H SOC–WD II
- £€ On application
- ⛿ E of Pontypridd, off A470. 12 miles NW of Cardiff

Pyle & Kenfig (1922)

Waun-y-Mer, Kenfig, Bridgend, CF33 4PU
- ☎ **(01656) 783093**
- 🖳 (01656) 772822
- 📧 secretary@pyleandkenfiggolfclub.co.uk
- 📖 860
- 🏌 (01656) 771613
- ⚲ R Evans (01656) 772446
- ⛳ 18 L 6741 yds Par 71 SSS 73
- 👥 WD–U H WE–M SOC
- £€ D–£35
- ⛿ 2 miles NW of Porthcawl. M4 Junction 37
- 🏠 HS Colt
- 🌐 www.pyleandkenfiggolfclub.co.uk

Rhondda (1910)

Penrhys, Ferndale, Rhondda, CF43 3PW
- ☎ **(01443) 433204**
- 🖳 (01443) 441384
- 📖 500
- 🏌 M Evans JP (01443) 441384
- ⚲ G Bebb (01443) 441385
- ⛳ 18 L 6428 yds SSS 71
- 👥 U H SOC
- £€ £15 (£20)
- ⛿ 6 miles W of Pontypridd

Royal Porthcawl (1891)

Rest Bay, Porthcawl, CF36 3UW
- ☎ **(01656) 782251**
- 🖳 (01656) 771687
- 📖 800
- 🏌 FW Prescott
- ⚲ P Evans (01656) 773702
- ⛳ 18 L 6685 yds SSS 74
- 👥 WD–I or H WE/BH–M SOC–H
- £€ On application
- ⛿ 22 miles W of Cardiff. M4 Junction 37
- ⊕ Driving range. Dormy House
- 🏠 Charles Gibson
- 🌐 www.royalporthcawl.com

Southerndown (1905)

Ewenny, Ogmore-by-Sea, Bridgend, CF32 0QP
- ☎ **(01656) 880326**
- 🖳 (01656) 880317
- 📧 southerndowngolf@btconnect.com
- 📖 700
- 🏌 AJ Hughes (01656) 880476
- ⚲ DG McMonagle
- ⛳ 18 L 6449 yds SSS 72
- 👥 U H

- £€ £30 (£40)
- ⛿ 3 miles S of Bridgend, nr Ogmore Castle ruins
- 🏠 W Fernie

Virginia Park (1993)

Pay and play
Virginia Park, Caerphilly, CF83 3SW
- ☎ **(029) 2086 3919**
- 📖 200
- 🏌 Mrs C Lewis
- ⚲ P Clark (029) 2085 0650
- ⛳ 9 L 4661 yds Par 66 SSS 63
- 👥 U SOC
- £€ On application
- ⛿ Caerphilly, 7 miles N of Cardiff
- ⊕ Driving range

Whitehall (1922)

The Pavilion, Nelson, Treharris, CF46 6ST
- ☎ **(01443) 740245**
- 📧 mark@wilde6755.freeserve.co.uk
- 📖 300
- 🏌 PM Wilde
- ⛳ 9 L 5666 yds SSS 68
- 👥 WD–U WE–M SOC
- £€ £18
- ⛿ 15 miles NW of Cardiff

Monmouthshire

Alice Springs (1989)

Bettws Newydd, Usk, NP5 1JY
- ☎ **(01873) 880708**
- 🖳 (01873) 880838
- 📖 350
- 🏌 KR Morgan
- ⚲ M Davies (01873) 880914
- ⛳ Red 18 L 5870 yds SSS 69
  Green 18 L 6438 yds SSS 72
- 👥 U SOC
- £€ £16 (£20)
- ⛿ 3 miles N of Usk on B4598
- ⊕ Driving range
- 🏠 Keith Morgan

Blackwood (1914)

Cwmgelli, Blackwood, NP12 1BR
- ☎ **(01495) 223152**
- 📖 300
- 🏌 AD Watkins
- ⚲ None
- ⛳ 9 L 5304 yds SSS 66
- 👥 WD–I SOC WE/BH–M
- £€ £14
- ⛿ 1/4 mile N of Blackwood

Caerleon (1974)

Pay and play
Broadway, Caerleon, NP6 1AY
- ☎ **(01633) 420342**
- 📖 150
- 🏌 P John
- ⚲ A Campbell
- ⛳ 9 L 3092 yds SSS
- 👥 U
- £€ 18 holes–£5 9 holes–£3.30
- ⛿ M4 Junction 25, 3 miles

⊕ Driving range
🏠 Donald Steel

The Celtic Manor Resort
(1995)
Coldra Woods, Newport, NP6 1JQ
☎ **(01633) 413000**
🖳 (01633) 410309
📖 450
🖊 S Wesson (01633) 413000
⌁ S Patience (01633) 413000
🏴 18 L 7001 yds Par 70 SSS 74
18 L 4094 yds Par 61 SSS 60
18 L 7403 yds Par 72 SSS 77
👥 H SOC
€€ On application
🏌 E of Newport on A48. M4 Junction 24
⊕ Golf Academy. Driving range
🏠 Robert Trent Jones Sr

Dewstow (1988)
Proprietary
Caerwent, NP26 5AH
☎ **(01291) 430444**
🖳 (01291) 425816
✉ info@dewstow.com
📖 850
🖊 D Bradbury (01291) 430444
⌁ J Skuse (01291) 430444
🏴 Valley 18 L 6091 yds Par 72 SSS 70;
Park 18 L 6226 yds Par 69 SSS 69
👥 U SOC
€€ £16 (£20)
🏌 Caerwent, 5 miles W of old Severn Bridge, off A48
⊕ Driving range
■ www.dewstow.com

Greenmeadow G&CC
(1979)
Treherbert Road, Croesyceiliog, Cwmbran, NP44 2BZ
☎ **(01633) 869321**
🖳 (01633) 868430
✉ info@greenmeadowgolf.com
📖 430
🖊 PJ Richardson (01633) 869321
⌁ D Woodman (01633) 862626
🏴 18 L 6078 yds Par 70 SSS 70
👥 WD–U WE–NA before 11am SOC
€€ On application
🏌 4 miles N of Newport on A4042. M4 Junction 26
⊕ Floodlit driving range
■ www.greenmeadowgolf.com

Llanwern (1928)
Tennyson Avenue, Llanwern, Newport, NP18 2DW
☎ **(01633) 412380**
🖳 (01633) 412029
📖 776
🖊 MW Penny (01633) 412029
⌁ S Price (01633) 413233
🏴 18 L 6115 yds SSS 69
👥 WD–U WE–restricted I H SOC
€€ WD–£20
🏌 1 mile S of M4 Junction 24

Marriott St Pierre Hotel & CC (1962)
St Pierre Park, Chepstow, NP16 6YA
☎ **(01291) 625261**
🖳 (01291) 629975
📖 840
🖊 TJ Cleary
⌁ Shop (01291) 635205
🏴 Old 18 L 6818 yds SSS 74;
Mathern 18 L 5732 yds SSS 68
👥 H SOC–WD
€€ On application
🏌 2 miles W of Chepstow (A48)
⊕ Driving range
🏠 CK Cotton

Monmouth (1896)
Leasbrook Lane, Monmouth, NP25 3SN
☎ **(01600) 712212**
🖳 (01600) 772399
✉ sec.mongc@barbox.net
📖 500
🖊 P Tully (01600) 772399
⌁ None
🏴 18 L 5698 yds SSS 69
👥 U SOC
€€ £15 (£20)
🏌 Signposted ¼ mile along A40 Monmouth-Ross road
🏠 George Walden
■ www.monmouthgolfclub.co.uk

Monmouthshire (1892)
Llanfoist, Abergavenny, NP7 9HE
☎ **(01873) 852606**
🖳 (01873) 852606
✉ secretary@mgcabergavenny.fsnet.co.uk
📖 520 103(L) 49(J)
🖊 R Bradley
⌁ (01873) 852532
🏴 18 L 5978 yds SSS 70
👥 WD–H SOC
€€ D–£30 (D–£35)
🏌 2 miles SW of Abergavenny
🏠 James Braid
■ www.monmouthshiregolfclub.co.uk

Newport (1903)
Great Oak, Rogerstone, Newport, NP10 9FX
☎ **(01633) 892643/894496**
🖳 (01633) 896676
✉ newportgolfclub.gwent @euphony.net
📖 800
🖊 JV Dinsdale (01633) 892643
⌁ PM Mayo (01633) 893271
🏴 18 L 6460 yds SSS 71
👥 WD–H
€€ £30 (£35)
🏌 3 miles W of Newport on B4591. M4 Junction 27, 1 mile
🏠 Ross/Fernie

Oakdale (1990)
Pay and play
Llwynon Lane, Oakdale, NP2 0NF
☎ **(01495) 220044**
🖊 M Lewis (Dir)

⌁ P Glynn (01495) 220440
🏴 9 L 1344 yds Par 28
👥 U SOC
€€ On application
🏌 15 miles NW of Newport via A467/B4251. M4 Junction 28
⊕ Driving range
🏠 Ian Goodenough

Parc (1990)
Pay and play
Church Lane, Coedkernew, Newport, NP1 9TU
☎ **(01633) 680933**
🖳 (01633) 681011
📖 450
🖊 C Hicks (Mgr), M Cleary (Sec)
⌁ J Skuse (01633) 680955
🏴 18 L 5512 yds SSS 67
👥 U SOC
€€ £11 (£13)
🏌 2 miles W of Newport on A48. M4 Junction 28
⊕ Floodlit driving range
🏠 B Thomas

Pontnewydd (1875)
Maesgwyn Farm, Upper Cwmbran, NP44 1AB
☎ **(01633) 482170**
🖳 (01633) 838598
✉ ctphillips@virgin.net
📖 250
🖊 CT Phillips (01633) 484447
🏴 11 L 5278 yds SSS 67
👥 WD–U WE–M SOC
€€ £15 (£15)
🏌 W outskirts of Cwmbran

Pontypool (1903)
Lasgarn Lane, Trevethin, Pontypool, NP4 8TR
☎ **(01495) 763655**
✉ pontypoolgolf@btconnect.com
📖 581 41(L) 80(J)
🖊 L Dodd
⌁ J Howard (01495) 755544
🏴 18 L 5712 yds SSS 69
👥 U H SOC
€€ £20 (£24)
🏌 1 mile N of Pontypool (A4042). M4 Junction 26
■ www.pontypoolgolf.co.uk

Raglan Parc
Parc Lodge, Raglan, NP5 2ER
☎ **(01291) 690077**
📖 380
🖊 T Lillistone
⌁ C Evans
🏴 18 L 6604 yds Par 73
👥 U
€€ £15 (£15)
🏌 Nr A40/A449 junction

The Rolls of Monmouth (1982)
The Hendre, Monmouth, NP25 5HG
☎ **(01600) 715353**
🖳 (01600) 713115

200
Mrs SJ Orton
None
18 L 6733 yds SSS 73
U SOC
£36 (£40)
3¹/₂ miles W of Monmouth on B4233

Shirenewton (1995)
Shirenewton, Chepstow, NP16 6RL
(01291) 641642
(01291) 641472
L Pagett (Mgr)
L Pagett (01291) 641471
18 L 6607 yds Par 72 SSS 72
U SOC
£16 (£18)
5 miles W of Chepstow, off A48. M4 Junction 22

Tredegar & Rhymney (1921)
Tredegar, Rhymney, NP2 3BQ
(01685) 840743
180
P Kenealy (07944) 843400
18 L 5564 yds SSS 68
U
£10
1¹/₂ miles W of Tredegar (B4256)

Tredegar Park (1923)
Parc-y-Brain Road, Rogerstone, Newport, NP10 9TG
(01633) 895219
(01633) 897152
800
AJ Trickett (01633) 894433
ML Morgan (01633) 894517
18 L 6564 yds SSS 72
H SOC–WD
D–£15 (£20)
W of Newport, off M4 Junction 27
R Sandow

Wernddu Golf Centre
Old Ross Road, Abergavenny, NP7 8NG
(01873) 856223
(01873) 852177
520
L Turvey
AA Ashmead
18 L 5500 yds Par 68 SSS 67
U
9 holes–£10. 18 holes–£15
1¹/₂ miles NE of Abergavenny on B4521
Floodlit driving range
www.wernddugolfclub.co.uk

West Monmouthshire (1906)
Golf Road, Pond Road, Nantyglo, Ebbw Vale, NP23 4QT
(01495) 310233/311361
(01495) 311361
300
SE Williams (01495) 310233
18 L 6118 yds SSS 69

WD/Sat–U Sun–M SOC–WD
£15
Nr Dunlop Semtex, off Brynmawr Bypass, towards Winchestown
Ben Sayers

Woodlake Park (1993)
Glascoed, Usk, NP4 0TE
(01291) 673933
(01291) 673811
golf@woodlake.co.uk
500
D Hawker
A Pritchard (01291) 671043
18 L 6300 yds Par 71 SSS 72
H SOC
Summer–£22.50 (£30) Winter–£15 (£20)
3 miles W of Usk, nr Llandegfedd reservoir
www.woodlake.co.uk

Pembrokeshire

Haverfordwest (1904)
Arnolds Down, Haverfordwest, SA61 2XQ
(01437) 763565
(01437) 764143
800
P Lewis (01437) 764523
A Pile (01437) 768409
18 L 5966 yds SSS 69
U SOC
£20 (£25)
1 mile E of Haverfordwest on A40
www.hwestgolf.homestead.com

Milford Haven (1913)
Hubberston, Milford Haven, SA72 3RX
(01646) 697762
(01646) 697870
380 65(L) 90(J)
WS Brown
D Williams (01646) 697762
18 L 6071 yds SSS 71
U SOC
£17.50 (£22.50)
W boundary of Milford Haven
www.mhgc.co.uk

Newport (Pembs) (1925)
Newport, SA42 0NR
(01239) 820244
(01239) 820244
400
A Payne (Mgr)
J Noott (01239) 615359
9 L 3089 yds SSS 68
U SOC
£18 (£22)
2¹/₂ miles NW of Newport, towards Newport Beach
James Braid

Priskilly Forest (1992)
Castle Morris, Haverfordwest, SA62 5EH
(01348) 840276

(01348) 840276
jevans@priskilly-forest.co.uk
P Evans
9 L 5874 yds Par 70 SSS 69
U SOC
9 holes–£10. 18 holes–£14 D–£16
2 miles off A40 at Letterston
J Walters
www.priskilly-forest.co.uk

St Davids City (1903)
Whitesands Bay, St Davids, SA62 6PT
(01437) 721751 (Clubhouse)
wjwilcox@hotmail.com
200
J Wilcox (01437) 720058
9 L 6117 yds SSS 70
U SOC
D–£15
2 miles W of St Davids. 15 miles NW of Haverfordwest

South Pembrokeshire (1970)
Military Road, Pembroke Dock, SA72 6SE
(01646) 621453
350
WD Owen (01646) 621453/621804
None
18 L 5638 yds SSS 69
U before 4.30pm SOC
On application
Pembroke Dock

Tenby (1888)
The Burrows, Tenby, SA70 7NP
(01834) 842978
(01834) 842978
800
BSR Warren (01834) 842978
M Hawkey (01834) 844447
18 L 6450 yds SSS 71
H SOC
£26 D–£35 (£32)
Tenby, South Beach
James Braid
www.tenbygolf.co.uk

Trefloyne (1996)
Trefloyne Park, Penally, Tenby, SA70 7RG
(01834) 842165
250
S Laidler (01834) 842165
18 L 6635 yds Par 71
U SOC
£21 (£26)
1¹/₂miles W of Tenby, off A4139 Pembroke road
FH Gilman
www.trefloynegolfcourse.co.uk

Powys

Brecon (1902)
Newton Park, Llanfaes, Brecon, LD3 8PA
(01874) 622004
210

For list of abbreviations and key to symbols see page 649

9 L 5256 yds Par 68 SSS 66
U SOC
£12
1/2 mile W of Brecon on A40
James Braid

Builth Wells   (1923)
Golf Club Road, Builth Wells, LD2 3NF
(01982) 553296
(01982) 551064
builthwellsgolfclub@btinternet.com
400
JN Jones
S Edwards
18 L 5376 yds SSS 67
U H SOC
£17 D–£22 (£23 D–£28)
W of Builth Wells on Llandovery road (A483)
www.builthwellsgolfclub.co.uk

Cradoc   (1967)
Penoyre Park, Cradoc, Brecon, LD3 9LP
(01874) 623658
(01874) 611711
secretary@cradoc.co.uk
750
Mrs EG Price (01874) 623658
R Davies (01874) 625524
18 L 6331 yds SSS 72
U SOC
£20 (£25)
2 miles NW of Brecon, off B4520
Driving range
CK Cotton
www.cradoc.co.uk

Knighton   (1905)
Ffrydd Wood, Knighton, LD7 1EF
(01547) 528646
(01547) 529284
150
AW Aspley (Hon)
9 L 5362 yds Par 68 SSS 66
U SOC
£10 (£12)
SW of Knighton. 20 miles NE of Llandrindod Wells
H Vardon

Llandrindod Wells   (1905)
Llandrindod Wells, LD1 5NY
(01597) 823873
(01597) 823873
secretary@lwgc.co.uk
490
(01597) 823873
Golf Shop (01597) 822247
18 L 5759 yds Par 69 SSS 69
U SOC
£17 (£22)
1/2 mile E of Llandrindod Wells centre
Harry Vardon
www.lwgc.co.uk

Machynlleth   (1904)
Ffordd Drenewydd, Machynlleth, SY20 8UH
(01654) 702000
231

9 L 5726 yds SSS 67
U Sun–NA before 11.30am SOC
£12 (£15)
1 mile E of Machynlleth, off A489

Rhosgoch   (1991)
Rhosgoch, Builth Wells, LD2 3JY
(01497) 851251
150
C Dance
9 L 5078 yds SSS 65
U SOC
£7 (£10)
5 miles N of Hay-on-Wye

St Giles Newtown   (1895)
Pool Road, Newtown, SY16 3AJ
(01686) 625844
350
DP Owen
9 L 6012 yds SSS 70
U SOC
£12.50 (£15)
1 mile E of Newtown (A483). 14 miles SW of Welshpool

St Idloes   (1920)
Owned privately
Penrhallt, Llanidloes, SY18 6LG
(01686) 412559
(01926) 889536
292
JC Green
P Parkin
9 L 5510 yds SSS 66
U H Sun–restricted SOC
£10 (£12) W–£45
1/2 mile from Llanidloes on Trefeglwys road (B4569)

Welsh Border Golf Complex   (1991)
Bulthy Farm, Bulthy, Middletown, SY21 8ER
(01743) 884247
200
J Watt
A Griffiths
9 L 3050 yds SSS 69
9 hole course
U SOC
£14
Between Shrewsbury and Welshpool on A458
Driving range
A Griffiths

Welshpool   (1929)
Golfa Hill, Welshpool, SY21 9AQ
(01938) 850249
welshpool.golfclub@virgin.net
400
D Lewis (01938) 810757
None
18 L 5708 yds Par 70 SSS 68
U
£12.50 D–£20.50 Winter–£15.50
4 1/2 miles W of Welshpool, on Dolgellau road (A458)
James Braid
www.welshpoolgolfclub.co.uk

South Glamorgan

Brynhill   (1921)
Port Road, Barry, CF62 8PN
(01446) 720277
700
P Gershenson (01446) 720277
P Fountain (01446) 740004
18 L 6352 yds SSS 71
WD/Sat–H Sun–NA SOC–WD
£20 Sat–£25 SOC–£17
A4050, 8 miles SW of Cardiff

Cardiff   (1921)
Sherborne Avenue, Cyncoed, Cardiff, CF23 6SJ
(029) 2075 3067
(029) 2068 0011
930
Mrs K Newling (029) 2075 3320
T Hanson (029) 2075 4772
18 L 6015 yds SSS 70
WD–H WE–M SOC–Thurs
£35 (£40)
3 miles N of Cardiff. 2 miles W of Pentwyn exit of A48(M). M4 Junction 29

Cottrell Park   (1996)
St Nicholas, Cardiff, CF5 6JY
(01446) 781781
(01446) 781187
1050
DW Marchant
S Birch
18 L 6606 yds Par 72 SSS 72
9 L 2807 yds Par 70 SSS 67
U H SOC–WD
18 hole:£25–£35 9 hole:£10–£15
4 miles W of Cardiff on A48. M4 Junction 33
Driving range
Bob Sandow

Dinas Powis   (1914)
Old Highwalls, Dinas Powis, CF64 4AJ
(029) 2051 2727
(029) 2051 2727
490
Ginny Golding
G Bennett (029) 2051 3682
18 L 5486 yds SSS 68
H SOC
D–£25 (£30)
3 miles SW of Cardiff (A4055)

Glamorganshire   (1890)
Lavernock Road, Penarth, CF64 5UP
(029) 2070 1185
(029) 2070 1185
glamgolf@btconnect.com
1100
BM Williams (029) 2070 1185
A Kerr-Smith (029) 2070 7401
18 L 6181 yds SSS 70
WD/WE–H SOC
£35 (£40)
5 miles SW of Cardiff

For list of abbreviations and key to symbols see page 649

Llanishen (1905)
Heol Hir, Cardiff, CF14 9UD
- ☎ **(029) 2075 5078**
- 🖃 (029) 2075 5078
- 📖 850
- ✍ (029) 2075 5078
- ✓ RA Jones (029) 2075 5076
- ⏃ 18 L 5327 yds SSS 67
- ⚇ WD–U WE–M H SOC–Thurs & Fri
- ££ £30
- ⛳ 5 miles N of Cardiff

Peterstone Lakes
Peterstone, Wentloog, Cardiff, CF3 2TN
- ☎ **(01633) 680009**
- 🖃 (01633) 680563
- ✉ peterstone_lakes@yahoo.com
- 📖 600
- ✍ P Millar
- ✓ P Glynn (01633) 680075
- ⏃ 18 L 6555 yds Par 72 SSS 72
- ⚇ U SOC
- ££ £18 (£25)
- ⛳ 3 miles S of Castleton, off A48. M4 Junction 28
- ⏚ Robert Sandow

Radyr (1902)
Drysgol Road, Radyr, Cardiff, CF15 8BS
- ☎ **(029) 2084 2408**
- 🖃 (029) 2084 3914
- ✉ manager@radyrgolf.co.uk
- 📖 880
- ✍ AM Edwards (Mgr) (029) 2084 2408
- ✓ R Butterworth (029) 2084 2476
- ⏃ 18 L 6053 yds SSS 70
- ⚇ SOC–Wed/Thurs/Fri
- ££ D–£38
- ⛳ 5 miles NW of Cardiff, off A470. M4 Junction 32
- ⏚ Braid/Holt
- ■ www.radyrgolf.co.uk

RAF St Athan (1977)
St Athan, Barry, CF62 4WA
- ☎ **(01446) 751043**
- 🖃 (01446) 751862
- 📖 450
- ✍ PF Woodhouse (01446) 797186
- ⏃ 9 L 6452 yds SSS 72
- ⚇ U exc Sun am–NA
- ££ £12 (£17)
- ⛳ 2 miles E of Llantwit Major. 10 miles S of Bridgend

St Andrews Major (1993)
Coldbrook Road, Cadoxton, Barry, CF6 3BB
- ☎ **(01446) 722227**
- 📖 350
- ✍ N Edmunds
- ⏃ 9 L 2931 yds
- ⚇ U SOC
- ££ 9 holes–£8. 18 holes–£13
- ⛳ Barry Docks Link road. M4 Junction 33
- ⏚ MRM Leisure

St Mary's Hotel G&CC (1990)
Pay and play
St Mary's Hill, Pencoed, CF35 5EA
- ☎ **(01656) 861100**
- 🖃 (01656) 863400
- 📖 800
- ✍ Kay Brazell
- ✓ J Peters (01656) 861599
- ⏃ 18 L 5291 yds Par 69 SSS 66
9 L 2426 yds Par 35
- ⚇ H SOC–WD
- ££ 18 hole:£15 (£17) 9 hole:£5 (£6)
- ⛳ Off M4 Junction 35
- ⊕ Floodlit driving range

St Mellons (1937)
St Mellons, Cardiff, CF3 2XS
- ☎ **(01633) 680401**
- 🖃 (01633) 681219
- 📖 550 89(L) 67(J)
- ✍ RH Boyce (01633) 680408
- ✓ B Thomas (01633) 680101
- ⏃ 18 L 6225 yds SSS 70
- ⚇ U exc Sat–NA SOC
- ££ £32
- ⛳ 4 miles E of Cardiff on A48. M4 Junction 28

Vale of Glamorgan Hotel G&CC
Hensol Park, Hensol, CF7 8JY
- ☎ **(01443) 665899**
- 🖃 (01443) 222220
- 📖 900
- ✍ Mrs L Edwards
- ✓ P Johnson
- ⏃ Lake 18 L 6507 yds Par 72
Hensol 9 L 3115 yds Par 36
- ⚇ H SOC
- ££ £25 (£30)
- ⛳ 1 mile from M 4 Junction 34
- ⊕ Driving range. Golf Academy
- ⏚ Peter Johnson

Wenvoe Castle (1936)
Wenvoe, Cardiff, CF5 6BE
- ☎ **(029) 2059 4371**
- 🖃 (029) 2059 4371
- 📖 540 100(L) 66(J)
- ✍ N Sims (029) 2059 4371
- ✓ J Harris (029) 2059 3649
- ⏃ 18 L 6422 yds SSS 71
- ⚇ WD–H WE/BH–M SOC–WD
- ££ £32
- ⛳ 4 miles W of Cardiff, off A4050

Whitchurch (1915)
Pantmawr Road, Whitchurch, Cardiff, CF4 6XD
- ☎ **(029) 2062 0125**
- 🖃 (029) 2052 9860
- 📖 780
- ✍ CR Innes (Mgr) (029) 2062 0985
- ✓ E Clark (029) 2061 4660
- ⏃ 18 L 6212 yds Par 71 SSS 71
- ⚇ U H SOC–Thurs
- ££ £35 (£40)
- ⛳ 3 miles NW of Cardiff on A470. M4 Junction 32

West Glamorgan

Allt-y-Graban (1993)
Allt-y-Graban Road, Pontlliw, Swansea, SA4 1DT
- ☎ **(01792) 885757**
- 📖 154
- ✍ Mrs M Lewis (Mgr)
- ✓ S Rees
- ⏃ 9 L 2210 yds Par 66 SSS 63
- ⚇ U SOC
- ££ 18 holes–£9 (£9) 9 holes–£6 (£6)
- ⛳ 3 miles of M4 Junction 47, on A48
- ⏚ FG Thomas

Clyne (1920)
120 Owls Lodge Lane, Mayals, Swansea, SA3 5DP
- ☎ **(01792) 401989**
- 🖃 (01792) 401078
- 📖 900
- ✍ RH Thompson FCA (Mgr)
- ✓ J Clewett (01792) 402094
- ⏃ 18 L 6334 yds SSS 71
- ⚇ U H SOC
- ££ £25 (£30)
- ⛳ 3 miles SW of Swansea
- ⊕ Driving range
- ⏚ Colt/Harris

Earlswood (1993)
Pay and play
Jersey Marine, Neath, SA10 6JP
- ☎ **(01792) 321578**
- ✍ Mrs D Goatcher (01792) 812198
- ✓ M Day
- ⏃ 18 L 5174 yds SSS 68
- ⚇ U SOC
- ££ £8
- ⛳ 5 miles E of Swansea, off A483 (B4290)

Fairwood Park (1969)
Blackhills Lane, Upper Killay, Swansea, SA2 7JN
- ☎ **(01792) 203648**
- 🖃 (01792) 297849
- 📖 650
- ✍ D Giltrap, J Pettifer (Mgr)
- ✓ G Hughes (01792) 299194
- ⏃ 18 L 6650 yds SSS 73
- ⚇ U SOC
- ££ £25 (£30)
- ⛳ 4 miles W of Swansea (A4118)
- ⏚ Hawtree

Glynneath (1931)
Penygraig, Pontneathvaughan, Glynneath, SA11 5UH
- ☎ **(01639) 720452**
- 🖃 (01639) 720452
- ✉ glynneathgolf@tiscali.co.uk
- 📖 644
- ✍ DA Fellowes
- ✓ N Evans
- ⏃ 18 L 5656 yds SSS 68
- ⚇ U H SOC
- ££ £17 (£22)
- ⛳ 2 miles NW of Glynneath on B4242. 15 miles NE of Swansea
- ⏚ Cotton/Pennink/Lawrie

Gower

Cefn Goleu, Three Crosses, Gowerton,
Swansea SA4 3HS
- ☎ (01792) 872480
- 🖳 (01792) 872480
- ✉ adrian.richards@gower-golf-club
  .demon.co.uk
- 🛏 600
- 🏌 JD Morgan (01792) 872480
- ✏ A Williamson (01792) 879905
- ⛳ 18 L 6450 yds Par 71 SSS 72
- 👥 H
- €€ £20
- ⛳ 5 miles W of Swansea, off B4295
- 🏠 Donald Steele

Inco   (1965)

Clydach, Swansea, SA6 5QR
- ☎ (01792) 841257
- 🛏 600
- 🏌 DE Jones (01792) 842929
- ⛳ 18 L 6064 yds Par 70 SSS 69
- 👥 U
- €€ £15 (£20)
- ⛳ N of Swansea (A4067)

Lakeside   (1992)

Pay and play
Water Street, Margam, Port Talbot,
SA13 2PA
- ☎ (01639) 899959
- 🛏 250
- 🏌 DM Jones
- ✏ M Wootton
- ⛳ 18 L 4550 yds Par 63 SSS 63
- 👥 U SOC
- €€ £9.50
- ⛳ Nr M4 Junction 38
- ⊕ Driving range
- 🏠 M Wootton

Langland Bay   (1904)

Langland Bay Road, Langland, Swansea,
SA3 4QR
- ☎ (01792) 366023
- 🖳 (01792) 361082
- 🛏 800
- 🏌 Mrs L Coleman (01792) 361721
- ✏ M Evans (01792) 366186
- ⛳ 18 L 5857 yds SSS 69
- 👥 U H SOC
- €€ £28 (£30)
- ⛳ 6 miles S of Swansea (A4067). M4
  Junction 45
- ■ www.langlandbaygolfclub.com

Morriston   (1919)

160 Clasemont Road, Morriston,
Swansea, SA6 6AJ
- ☎ (01792) 771079
- 🖳 (01792) 796528
- 🛏 585
- 🏌 WV Thomas (01792) 796528
- ✏ DA Rees (01792) 772335
- ⛳ 18 L 5785 yds SSS 68
- 👥 U H SOC–WD
- €€ £18 (£30)
- ⛳ 4 miles N of Swansea on A48. M4
  Junction 46, 1 mile

Neath   (1934)

Cadoxton, Neath, SA10 8AH
- ☎ (01639) 643615
- 🖳 (01639) 632759
- 🛏 750
- 🏌 DM Hughes (01639) 632759
- ✏ EM Bennett (01639) 633693
- ⛳ 18 L 6500 yds SSS 72
- 👥 WD–U WE–M SOC
- €€ Summer–£20 (£20) Winter £12
  (£12)
- ⛳ 2 miles NE of Neath (B4434)
- 🏠 James Braid

Palleg   (1930)

Palleg Road, Lower Cwmtwrch, Swansea
Valley, SA9 2QQ
- ☎ (01639) 842193
- 🛏 250
- 🏌 B Evans
- ✏ Sharon Roberts (01639) 845728
- ⛳ 9 L 3209 yds SSS 72
- 👥 WD–U Sat–NA Sun/BH–phone
  first SOC
- €€ On application
- ⛳ 15 miles NE of Swansea (A4067).
  M4 Junction 45

Pennard   (1896)

2 Southgate Road, Southgate, Swansea,
SA3 2BT
- ☎ (01792) 233131
- 🖳 (01792) 234797
- ✉ pigeon01@globalnet.co.uk
- 🛏 775
- 🏌 EM Howell (01792) 233131
- ✏ MV Bennett (01792) 233451
- ⛳ 18 L 6265 yds SSS 72
- 👥 U H SOC–WD only
- €€ £27 (£35) W–£90
- ⛳ 8 miles W of Swansea, by A4067
  and B4436
- ■ www.golfagent.com/clubsites
  /pennard

Pontardawe   (1924)

Cefn Llan, Pontardawe, Swansea,
SA8 4SH
- ☎ (01792) 863118
- 🖳 (01792) 830041
- ✉ pontardawe@btopenworld.com
- 🛏 574
- 🏌 K Davey (Hon), Mrs M Griffiths
  (Admin)
- ✏ G Hopkins (01792) 830977
- ⛳ 18 L 6101 yds SSS 70
- 👥 H SOC–WD
- €€ £22
- ⛳ 5 miles N of M4 Junction 45, off
  A4067

Swansea Bay   (1892)

Jersey Marine, Neath, SA10 6JP
- ☎ (01792) 812198
- 🛏 400
- 🏌 Mrs D Goatcher (01792) 814153
- ✏ M Day (01792) 816159
- ⛳ 18 L 6256 yds SSS 71
- 👥 U SOC
- €€ £17 (£24)
- ⛳ 5 miles E of Swansea, off A483
  (B4290). M4 Junction 42

Wrexham

Chirk   (1990)

Chirk, Wrexham, LL14 5AD
- ☎ (01691) 774407
- 🖳 (01691) 773878
- ✉ chirk-jackbarker@btinternet.com
- 🛏 500
- 🏌 MCA Moss
- ✏ M Maddison
- ⛳ 18 L 7045 yds Par 72 SSS 73
  9 hole Par 3 course
- 👥 U after 10am SOC
- €€ £18 D–£25 (£19 D–£25)
- ⛳ 8 miles S of Wrexham on A483
- ⊕ Driving range
- ■ www.jackbarker.com

Clays   (1992)

Bryn Estyn Road, Wrexham,
LL13 9UB
- ☎ (01978) 661406
- 🖳 (01978) 661417
- ✉ clays@wrexhamgolf.fsnet.co.uk
- 🛏 500
- ✏ D Larvin
- ⛳ 18 L 6000 yds Par 69
  Par 3 short course
- 👥 U SOC
- €€ £14 (£19)
- ⛳ Wrexham, off A534

Moss Valley   (1990)

Pay and play
Moss Road, Wrexham, LL11 6HA
- ☎ (01978) 720518
- 🖳 (01978) 720518
- 🛏 100
- 🏌 J Parry, J Lloyd (Mgr)
- ⛳ 9 L 2641 yds Par 68 SSS 67
- 👥 U
- €€ 9 holes–£6 (£8) 18 holes–£9
  (£12)
- ⛳ N of Wrexham, off A541
- ■ www.mossvalleygolf.com

Pen-y-Cae   (1993)

Ruabon Road, Pen-y-Cae, Wrexham,
LL14 1TW
- ☎ (01978) 810108
- 🛏 100
- 🏌 G Williams (Mgr)
- ⛳ 9 L 4280 yds Par 64 SSS 62
- 👥 U SOC–WD
- €€ 9 holes–£5 (£6) 18 holes–£7.50
  (£9.50)
- ⛳ 6 miles S of Wrexham, via
  A483/A539
- 🏠 John Day

Plassey   (1992)

Eyton, Wrexham, LL13 0SP
- ☎ (01978) 780020
- 🖳 (01978) 781397
- 🛏 165
- 🏌 J Taylor (01978) 780020
- ✏ S Ward (01978) 780020
- ⛳ 9 L 4962 yds Par 66 SSS 64

U SOC
£€ £12 (£14.50)
2 miles SW of Wrexham, off A483
⊕ 9 hole pitch & putt course
K Williams
www.plasseygolf.co.uk

Wrexham   (1904)

Holt Road, Wrexham, LL13 9SB

☎ **(01978) 261033**
📠 (01978) 364268
✉ info@wrexhamgolfclub.co.uk
📖 650

🏌 J Johnson (01978) 364268
✓ P Williams (01978) 351476
📐 18 L 6233 yds Par 70 SSS 70
H SOC–WD
£€ £22 (£27)
2 miles NE of Wrexham on A534
James Braid

Continent of Europe – Country and Region Index

For list of abbreviations and key to symbols see page 649

Austria

Innsbruck & Tirol

Achensee (1934)
6213 Pertisau/Tirol
☎ **(05243) 5377**
🖴 (05243) 6202
⯈ 9 L 5501 m SSS 70
👥 U H
£€ €35 (€40)
⛳ Pertisau, 50km NE of Innsbruck

Innsbruck-Igls (1935)
Oberdorf 11, 6074 Rinn
☎ **(05223) 78177**
🖴 (05223) 78177-77
⯈ Rinn 18 L 6055 m Par 71
Lans 9 L 4597 m Par 66
👥 H–booking necessary
£€ €43 (€52)
⛳ Rinn, 10km E of Innsbruck. Lans, 8km from Innsbruck
■ www.golfclub-innsbruck-igls.at

Kaiserwinkl GC Kössen
(1988)
6345 Kössen, Mühlau 1
☎ **(05375) 2122**
🖴 (05375) 2122-13
⯈ 18 L 5927 m CR 70.7 SR 127
👥 H
£€ €48 (€53)
⛳ 30km N of Kitzbühel, nr German border
🏠 Donald Harradine
■ www.golf-koessen.at

Kitzbühel (1955)
Schloss Kaps, 6370 Kitzbühel
☎ **(05356) 63007**
🖴 (05356) 63007-7
⯈ 9 L 6044 m Par 72
👥 H
£€ €58
⛳ Kitzbühel
🏠 J Morrison
■ www.golf.at.gckitzbuehel

Kitzbühel-Schwarzsee
(1988)
6370 Kitzbühel, Golfweg Schwarzsee 35
☎ **(05356) 71645**
🖴 (05356) 72785
⯈ 18 L 6247 m SSS 72
👥 H–booking necessary
£€ €47 – €55
⛳ 4km from Kitzbühel
🏠 G Hauser

Seefeld-Wildmoos (1968)
6100 Seefeld, Postfach 22
☎ **(05212) 3003-0**
🖴 (05212) 3722-22
⯈ 18 L 5894 m CR 72 SR 130
👥 H–booking necessary
£€ €38.50 – € 50
⛳ 7 km W of Seefeld. 24 km W of Innsbruck

🏠 Donald Harradine
■ www.seefeldgolf.com

Klagenfurt & South

Austria-Wörther See
9062 Moosburg, Golfstr 2
☎ **(04272) 83486**
🖴 (04272) 82055
⯈ 18 L 6011 m SSS 72
£€ €50
⛳ 3km N of Wörther See/Pörtschach
🏠 G Hauser

Bad Kleinkirchheim-Reichenau (1977)
9546 Bad Kleinkirchheim, Postfach 9
☎ **(04275) 594**
🖴 (04275) 594-4
⯈ 18 L 6074 m Par 72 SSS 72
👥 H
£€ €44 (€44)
⛳ Kleinkirchheim, 50 km NW of Klagenfurt, via Route 95
🏠 Donald Harradine

Kärntner (1927)
9082 Maria Wörth, Golfstr 3
☎ **(04273) 2515**
🖴 (04273) 2606
⯈ 18 L 5778 m Par 71
👥 H
£€ €44 (€51)
⛳ Dellach, S side of Wörther See. 15km W of Klagenfurt
■ www.golf.at

Klopeiner See-Turnersee
(1988)
9122 St Kanzian, Grabelsdorf 94
☎ **(04239) 3800-0**
🖴 (04239) 3800-18
⯈ 18 L 6114 m Par 72
👥 U
£€ €44
⛳ 25km E of Klagenfurt
🏠 Donald Harradine

Wörther See/Velden (1988)
9231 Köstenberg, Oberdorf 70
☎ **(04274) 7045/7087**
🖴 (04274) 708715
⯈ 18 L 6081 m SSS 72
👥 H
£€ €51
⛳ 30km W of Klagenfurt. 12km from Velden
🏠 Erhardt/Rossknecht
■ www.golf.at

Linz & North

Amstetten-Ferschnitz (1972)
3325 Ferschnitz, Gut Edla 18
☎ **(07473) 8293**

🖴 (07473) 82934
⯈ 18 holes Par 71
👥 U H
£€ €45 (€50)
⛳ 70km E of Linz
🏠 F Bouchard
■ www.golfclub-amstetten.at

Böhmerwald GC Ulrichsberg (1990)
4161 Ulrichsberg, Seitelschlag 50
☎ **(07288) 8200**
🖴 (07288) 8422
⯈ 18 L 6240 m SSS 73
9 hole Par 3 course
👥 U H
£€ €35 (€41)
⛳ 65km NW of Linz
🏠 Rossknecht/Erhardt

Haugschlag
3874 Haugschlag 160
☎ **(02865) 8441**
🖴 (02865) 8441-22
⯈ 18 L 6140 m SSS 72
18 L 6448 m SSS 74
18 hole Par 3 course
👥 H
£€ €46 (€62)
⛳ 25km N of Gmund. 140km NW of Vienna
■ www.golfresort.at

Herzog Tassilo (1991)
Blankenbergerstr 30, 4540 Bad Hall
☎ **(07258) 5480**
🖴 (07258) 5480-11
⯈ 18 L 5710 m SSS 70
👥 U
£€ €35 (€50)
⛳ 30km SW of Linz
🏠 Peter Mayerhofer
■ www.golf.at

Kremstal (1989)
Schachen 20, 4531 Kematen/Krems
☎ **(07228) 7644-0**
🖴 (07228) 7644-7
⯈ 18 L 5763 m Par 70
👥 H
£€ €36 (€50)
⛳ 20km W of Linz
🏠 Peter Mayerhofer
■ www.pgckremstal.at

Linz-St Florian (1960)
4490 St Florian, Tillysburg 28
☎ **(07223) 828730**
🖴 (07223) 828737
⯈ 18 L 5864 m Par 72 SSS 72
👥 H
£€ €51 (€62)
⛳ St Florian, 15km SE of Linz
🏠 Hanz Georg Erhardt

Linzer Luftenberg (1990)
4222 St Georgen, Am Luftenberg 1a
☎ **(07237) 3893**
🖴 (07237) 3893-40
⯈ 18 L 5862 m CR 69.9 SR 119

U H
££ €45 (€50)
🚗 15km NE of Linz
🏠 Keith Preston

Maria Theresia (1989)
Letten 5, 4680 Haag am Hausruck
☎ (07732) 3944
🖥 (07732) 3944-9
ᐱ 18 L 6055 m Par 72 SSS 72
👥 H
££ €36 (€44)
🚗 Between Passau and Wels. A8 exit Haag
🏠 Angst/Stärk
■ www.members.eunet.at /gcmariatheresia

Ottenstein (1988)
3532 Niedergrünbach 60
☎ (02826) 7476
🖥 (02826) 7476-4
ᐱ 18 L 6129 m CR 70.2 SR 123
👥 U
££ €37 (€45)
🚗 90km NE of Linz. 100km NW of Vienna
🏠 Preston/Zinterl/Erhardt
■ www.golfclub-ottenstein.at

St Oswald-Freistadt (1988)
Promenade 22, 4271 St Oswald
☎ (07945) 7938
🖥 (07945) 79384
ᐱ 9 L 5888 m Par 72
👥 WD–UH WE–U H restricted
££ €26 (€33)
🚗 40km N of Linz
🏠 Mel Flanegan

St Pölten Schloss Goldegg (1989)
3100 St Pölten Schloss Goldegg
☎ (02741) 7360/7060
🖥 (02741) 73608
ᐱ 18 L 6249 m SSS 73
👥 H or I
££ €29 (€36)
🚗 8km NW of St Pölten. 60km W of Vienna

Schärding-Pramtal (1994)
Maad 2, 4775 Taufkirchen/Pram
☎ (07719) 8110
🖥 (07719) 8110 15
ᐱ 18 L 6386 m CR 72.2 SR 119
👥 H
££ €38 (€43)
🚗 10km S of Schärding on B137
■ www.gcschaerding.at

Schloss Ernegg (1973)
3261 Steinakirchen, Schloss Ernegg
☎ (07488) 76770
🖥 (07488) 76771/71171
ᐱ 18 L 5803 m SSS 71
    9 L 2076 m SSS 62
👥 U
££ €33 (€40)
🚗 Steinakirchen, 80km SE of Linz. 125km W of Vienna

🏠 Tucker/Day
■ www.ernegg.at

Traunsee Kircham
4656 Kircham, Kampesberg 38
☎ (07619) 2576
🖥 (07619) 2576-11
ᐱ 18 L 5725 m Par 70 SSS 70
👥 U
££ €36 (€44)
🚗 10km E of Gmunden. 50km SW of Linz

Weitra (1989)
3970 Weitra, Hausschachen
☎ (02856) 2058
🖥 (02856) 2058-4
ᐱ 18 L 5916 m Par 72
👥 WD–U WE–H
££ €33 (€40)
🚗 75km NE of Linz, nr Czech border
🏠 M Gansdorfer

Wels (1981)
4616 Weisskirchen, Weyerbach 37
☎ (07243) 56038
🖥 (07243) 56685
ᐱ 18 L 6098 m Par 72
👥 H
££ €36 (€44)
🚗 5 km from Salzburg-Vienna highway. 8km SE of Wels
🏠 Hauser/Hunt Hastings

Salzburg Region

Bad Gastein (1960)
5640 Bad Gastein, Golfstrasse 6
☎ (06434) 2775
🖥 (06434) 2775-4
ᐱ 9 L 5986 m SSS 72
👥 H
££ €29 (€36)
🚗 Bad Gastein 2 km. Salzburg 100km
🏠 B von Limburger

Goldegg
5622 Goldegg, Postfach 6
☎ (06415) 8585
🖥 (06415) 8585-4
ᐱ 18 L 4693 m Par 70
👥 U
££ €40 (€45)
🚗 60km SW of Salzburg

Gut Altentann (1989)
Hof 54, 5302 Henndorf am Wallersee
☎ (06214) 6026-0
🖥 (06214) 6105-81
ᐱ 18 L 6103 m CR 70 SR 125
👥 H (max 34) – booking necessary
££ €56 – €67
🚗 Henndorf, 16km NE of Salzburg
🏠 Jack Nicklaus
■ www.gutaltentann.com

Gut Brandlhof G&CC
(1983)
5760 Saalfelden am Steinernen Meer, Hohlwegen 4
☎ (06582) 7800-555
🖥 (06582) 7800-529
ᐱ 18 L 6218 m SSS 72
👥 I H
££ €40 (€47)
🚗 Saalfelden, 70km SW of Salzburg towards Zell am See
🏠 Kofler

Kobernausserwald
5242 St Johann a.Walde, Strass 1
☎ (07743) 2719
🖥 (07743) 2719
ᐱ 18 L 5963 m Par 71 SSS 71
👥 U
££ €15 (€26)
🚗 30km E of Salzburg
🏠 Heinz Schmidbauer

Lungau (1991)
5582 St Michael, Feldnergasse 165
☎ (06477) 7448
🖥 (06477) 7448-4
ᐱ 18 L 6438 m CR 72.4 SR 121
    9 L 2502 m Par 56
👥 U – soft spikes only
££ €46 (€54)
🚗 St Michael, 120km S of Salzburg
🏠 Keith Preston
■ www.golfclub-lungau.at

Am Mondsee (1986)
St Lorenz 400, 5310 Mondsee
☎ (06232) 3835-0
🖥 (06232) 3835-83
ᐱ 18 L 6036 m SSS 72
👥 H
££ €40 (€47)
🚗 Mondsee, 25km E of Salzburg
🏠 Marc Miller

Radstadt Tauerngolf (1991)
Römerstrasse 18, 5550 Radstadt
☎ (06452) 5111
🖥 (06452) 7336
ᐱ 18 L 6023 m Par 71
    9 hole Par 3 course
👥 U
££ €42 (€48)
🚗 70km NW of Salzburg

Salzburg Fuschl (1995)
5322 Hof/Salzburg
☎ (06229) 2390
🖥 (06229) 2390
ᐱ 9 L 3650 m Par 62
    9 hole Par 3 course
👥 U
££ €22 – € 29
🚗 Hof, 12km E of Salzburg

Salzburg Klesheim (1955)
5071 Wals bei Salzburg, Schloss Klesheim
☎ (0662) 850851

☎ (0662) 857925
ℙ 9 L 5700 m SSS 70
※ U H–max 28 (men) 32 (women)
££ €47 (€47)
↝ 5km N of Salzburg
⌂ Robert Trent Jones Jr

Salzkammergut   (1933)
4820 Bad Ischl, Postfach 506
☎ (06132) 26340
▭ (06132) 26708
ℙ 18 L 5673 m Par 71
※ U
££ €40 (€50)
↝ 6 km W of Bad Ischl, nr Strobl. 50 km E of Salzburg
■ www.salzkammergut-golf.at

Urslautal   (1991)
Schinking 1, 5760 Saalfelden
☎ (06584) 2000
▭ (06584) 7475-10
ℙ 18 L 6030 m SSS 71
※ U H
££ €50 (€55)
↝ 80km SW of Salzburg
⌂ Keith Preston
■ www.golf-urslautal.at

Zell am See-Kaprun
(1983)
5700 Zell am See-Kaprun, Golfstr 25
☎ (06542) 56161
▭ (06542) 56161-16
ℙ 18 L 5980 m CR 71.2 SR 122
   18 L 6003 m CR 70.5 SR 125
※ H
££ €52 (€60)
↝ Zell am See, 80km SW of Salzburg
⌂ Harradine/Schauer
■ www.europasportregion.at/golfclub

Steiermark

Bad Gleichenberg   (1984)
Am Hoffeld 3, 8344 Bad Gleichenberg
☎ (03159) 3717
▭ (03159) 3065
ℙ 9 L 5422 m CR 69.5 SR 129
※ U
££ €29 (€35)
↝ 60km SE of Graz
⌂ Hauser

Dachstein Tauern   (1990)
8967 Haus/Ennstal, Oberhaus 59
☎ (03686) 2630
▭ (03686) 2630-15
ℙ 18 L 5910 m SSS 71
※ U
££ €60
↝ 2km from Schladming. 100km SE of Salzburg
⌂ Bernhard Langer
■ www.schladming-golf.at

Ennstal-Weissenbach G&LC   (1978)
8940 Liezen, Postfach 193
☎ (03612) 24821
▭ (03612) 24821-4
ℙ 18 L 5655 m SSS 70
※ U H I
££ €33 (€36)
↝ 100km SE of Salzburg. 100km NW of Graz
⌂ Gert Aigner

Furstenfeld   (1984)
8282 Loipersdorf, Gillersdorf 50
☎ (03382) 8533
▭ (03382) 8533-33
ℙ 18 L 6192 m SSS 72
※ U
££ €36 (€44)
↝ 70km E of Graz

Graz   (1989)
8051 Graz-Thal, Windhof 137
☎ (0316) 572867
▭ (0316) 572867-4
ℙ 9 L 5102 m CR 67 SR 112
※ U
££ €33 – €40 (€45)
↝ 10km W of Graz
⌂ Herwig Zisser

Gut Murstätten   (1989)
8403 Lebring, Oedt 14
☎ (03182) 3555
▭ (03182) 3688
ℙ 18 L 6398 m CR 70.5 SR 122
   9 hole course
※ H
££ €46 (€55)
↝ 25km S of Graz
⌂ J Dudok van Heel
■ www.gcmurstaetten.at

Maria Lankowitz   (1992)
Puchbacher Str 109, 8591 Maria Lankowitz
☎ (03144) 6970
▭ (03144) 6970-4
ℙ 18 L 6121 m SSS 72
※ U
££ €33 (€40)
↝ 40km W of Graz
⌂ Herwig Zisser

Murhof   (1963)
8130 Frohnleiten, Adriach 53
☎ (03126) 3010
▭ (03126) 3000-29
ℙ 18 L 6198 m Par 72
※ U H
££ €48 (€63)
↝ Frohnleiten, 25km N of Graz. 150km S of Vienna
⌂ B von Limburger

Murtal   (1995)
Frauenbachstr 51, 8724 Spielberg
☎ (03512) 75213
▭ (03512) 75213

ℙ 18 L 5951 m Par 72
※ H I
££ €40 (€44)
↝ Knittelfeld, 80km NW of Graz, via Route S36
⌂ Jeff Howes
■ www.gcmurtal.at

Reiting G&CC   (1990)
8772 Traboch, Schulweg 7
☎ (0663) 833308/(03847) 5008
▭ (03847) 5682
ℙ 9 L 6300 m Par 73 SSS 72
※ U
££ €26 (€30)
↝ 60km N of Graz

St Lorenzen   (1990)
8642 St Lorenzen, Gassing 22
☎ (03864) 3961
▭ (03864) 3961-2
ℙ 9 L 5374 m Par 70 SSS 70
※ U
££ €26 (€30)
↝ 60km N of Graz, nr Kapfenberg
⌂ Manfred Flasch

Schloss Frauenthal   (1988)
8530 Deutschlandsberg, Ulrichsberg 7
☎ (03462) 5717
▭ (03462) 5717-5
ℙ 18 L 5447 m SSS 70
※ U H
££ €45 (€55)
↝ 30km SW of Graz
⌂ Stephan Breisach
■ www.gcfrauenthal.at

Schloss Pichlarn   (1972)
8952 Irdning/Ennstal, Gatschen 28
☎ (03682) 22841-540
▭ (03682) 22841-580
ℙ 18 L 5863 m CR 70.7 SR 125
※ U
££ €43 (€51)
↝ 2km E of Irdning, off Salzburg-Graz road. 120km SE of Salzburg
⌂ Donald Harradine
■ www.pichlarn.at

Vienna & East

Adamstal   (1994)
Gaupmannsgraben 21, 3172 Ramsal
☎ (02764) 3500
▭ (02764) 3500-15
ℙ 18 L 5514 m CR 70 SR 128
※ U
££ €45 (€60)
↝ 65km SW of Vienna
⌂ Jeff Howes
■ www.adamstal.at

Bad Tatzmannsdorf G&CC   (1991)
Am Golfplatz 2, 7431 Bad Tatzmannsdorf
☎ (03353) 8282-0

🖳 (03353) 8282-1735
▷ 18 L 6304 m Par 73
   9 L 3660 m Par 60
👥 U H
€€ 18 hole:€43 (€55) 9 hole:€30 (€35)
⊕ 120km SE of Vienna
🏠 Rossknecht/Erhardt

Brunn G&CC   (1988)

2345 Brunn/Gebirge, Rennweg 50
☎ (02236) 31572/33711
🖳 (02236) 33863
▷ 18 L 6138 m Par 70 SSS 70
👥 H – soft spikes only
€€ €44 (€51)
⊕ 10km S of Vienna
🏠 G Hauser
■ www.golf.at

Colony Club Gutenhof   (1988)

2325 Himberg, Gutenhof
☎ (02235) 87055-0
🖳 (02235) 87055-14
▷ East 18 L 6335 m SSS 73
   West 18 L 6397 m SSS 73
👥 H
€€ €36 (€55)
⊕ 7km SE of Vienna
🏠 Rossknecht/Erhardt

Danube Golf-Wien   (1995)

Weingartenallee 22, 1220 Wien
☎ (0222) 25072
🖳 (0222) 25072-44
▷ 18 L 6130 m SSS 72
👥 H
€€ €40 (€40)
⊕ 15km NE of Vienna
🏠 Rossknecht/Erhardt

Eldorado Bucklige Welt   (1990)

Golfplatz 1, 2871 Zöbern
☎ (02642) 8451
🖳 (02642) 8451-52
▷ 18 L 4029m CR 64.5 SR 118
👥 H–max 45
€€ €35 (€50)
⊕ 90km S of Vienna via A2 Exit 80
🏠 Anton Reithofer
■ WWW.golf1.at

Enzesfeld   (1970)

2551 Enzesfeld
☎ (02256) 81272
🖳 (02256) 81272-4
▷ 18 L 6176 m SSS 72
👥 H
€€ €36 – € 44 (€58)
⊕ 32km S of Vienna. A2 Junction 29 (Leobersdorf)
🏠 Cdr John D Harris

Föhrenwald   (1968)

2700 Wiener Neustadt, Postfach 105
☎ (02622) 29171
🖳 (02622) 29171-4
▷ 18 L 6317 m SSS 72

👥 H
€€ €45 (€60)
⊕ 5 km S of Wiener Neustadt on Route B54
🏠 Jeff Howes

Fontana   (1996)

Fontana Allee 1, 2522 Oberwaltersdorf
☎ (02253) 606401
🖳 (02253) 606403
▷ 18 L 6088 m Par 72
👥 U–booking necessary. Soft spikes only
€€ €73 (€99)
⊕ 20km S of Vienna
🏠 Carrick/Erhardt

Hainburg/Donau   (1977)

2410 Hainburg, Auf der Heide 762
☎ (02165) 62628
🖳 (02165) 626283
▷ 18 L 6064 m SSS 72
👥 H
€€ €30 (€50)
⊕ 50km E of Vienna
🏠 G Hauser

Lengenfeld   (1995)

Am Golfplatz 1, 3552 Lengenfeld
☎ (02719) 8710
🖳 (02719) 8738
▷ 18 L 6130 m Par 72
👥 U
€€ €29 (€36)
⊕ 80km W of Vienna. Krems 8km

Neusiedlersee-Donnerskirchen   (1988)

7082 Donnerskirchen
☎ (02683) 8171
🖳 (02683) 817231
▷ 18 L 5937 m SSS 72
👥 H
€€ €36 (€36)
⊕ 45km SE of Vienna
🏠 Rossknecht-Erhardt

Schloss Ebreichsdorf   (1988)

2483 Ebreichsdorf, Schlossallee 1
☎ (02254)73888
🖳 (02254) 73888-13
▷ 18 L 6246 m Par 72 SSS 73
👥 WD–H WE–on request
€€ €36 (€51)
⊕ 28km S of Vienna
🏠 Keith Preston

Schloss Schönborn   (1987)

2013 Schönborn 4
☎ (02267) 2863/2879
🖳 (02267) 2879-19
▷ 27 L 6265-6474 m Par 72-73
👥 U H
€€ €44 (€58)
⊕ 40km N of Vienna

Schönfeld   (1989)

A-2291 Schönfeld, Am Golfplatz 1
☎ (02213) 2063

🖳 (02213) 20631
▷ 18 L 6185 m SSS 73
   9 hole Par 3 course
👥 H
€€ 18 hole:€36 (€50) 9 hole:€22 (€30)
⊕ 35km E of Vienna
🏠 G Hauser
■ www.golf.at

Semmering   (1926)

2680 Semmering
☎ (02664) 8154
🖳 (02664) 2114
▷ 9 L 3786 m SSS 60
👥 H
€€ €26 (€33)
⊕ 30km SW of Vienna Neustadt

Thayatal Drosendorf   (1994)

Autendorf 18, 2095 Drosendorf
☎ (02915) 62625
🖳 (02915) 62625
▷ 18 L 4289 m CR 64.4 SR 110
👥 U
€€ €18 (€29)
⊕ 100km NW of Vienna, nr Czech border (B4)
🏠 Rudolf Schedl

Wien   (1901)

1020 Wien, Freudenau 65a
☎ (0222) 728 9564 (Clubhouse), (0222) 728 9667 (Caddymaster)
🖳 (0222) 728 9564-20
▷ 18 L 5861 m SSS 71
👥 WE–NA
€€ €58
⊕ 10 mins SE of Vienna

Wienerberg   (1989)

1100 Wien, Gutheil Schoder 9
☎ (0222) 66123-7000
🖳 (0222) 66123-7789
▷ 9 L 5710 m SSS 70
👥 H
€€ €36
⊕ Vienna District 10
🏠 G Hauser

Wienerwald   (1981)

1130 Wien, Altgasse 27
☎ (0222) 877 3111 (Sec)
▷ 9 L 4652 m SSS 65
👥 H
€€ €22 (€36)
⊕ Laaben, 35km W of Vienna
🏠 Herbert Illo Holy

Vorarlberg

Bludenz-Braz   (1996)

Oberradin 60, 6751 Braz bei Bludenz
☎ (05552) 33503
🖳 (05552) 33503-3
▷ 12 L 5259 m Par 69 SSS 69
👥 M H
€€ D – € 32 (D – € 35)
⊕ 5km E of Bludenz
🏠 Maurice O'Fives

Bregenzerwald (1997)

Unterlitten 3a, 6943 Riefensberg
- ☎ **(05513) 8400**
- ⌨ (05513) 8400-4
- ▷ 18 L 5702 m Par 71
- ⚇ U I
- £€ €34 (€43)
- ⇄ 32km E of Bregenz. 150km E of Zürich
- ⌂ Kurt Rossknecht

Montafon-Zelfen (1992)

6774 Tschagguns, Zelfenstrasse 110
- ☎ **(05556) 77011**
- ⌨ (05556) 77045
- ▷ 9 L 3708 m Par 62 SSS 60
- ⚇ U H
- £€ €26
- ⇄ 60km S of Lake Constance
- ⌂ Stefan Breisach

Belgium

Antwerp Region

Bossenstein (1989)

Moor 16, Bossenstein Kasteel, 2520 Broechem
- ☎ **(03) 485 64 46**
- ⌨ (03) 485 78 41
- ▷ 18 L 6203 m SSS 72
  9 hole course
- ⚇ H
- £€ €25 (€37)
- ⇄ 15km E of Antwerp. 5km N of Lier
- ⌂ Paul Rolin

Cleydael (1988)

Kasteel Cleydael, 2630 Aartselaar
- ☎ **(03) 887 00 79/887 18 74**
- ⌨ (03) 887 00 15
- ▷ 18 L 6059 m SSS 72
- ⚇ H WE–NA before 2pm
- £€ €37 (€60)
- ⇄ 8km S of Antwerp. 40km N of Brussels
- ⌂ Paul Rolin

Inter-Mol (1984)

Goorstraat, 2400 Mol
- ☎ **(011) 39 17 80/60 02 46**
- ▷ 9 L 1557 m Par 29
- ⚇ H
- £€ €12 (€17)
- ⇄ Mol, 60km E of Antwerp

Kempense (1986)

Kiezelweg 78, 2400 Mol
- ☎ **(014) 81 46 41 (Clubhouse)**
- ⌨ (014) 81 62 78
- ▷ 18 L 5904 m Par 72
- ⚇ H
- £€ €30 (€42)
- ⇄ 60km E of Antwerp
- ⌂ Marc de Keyser

Lilse (1988)

Haarlebeek 3, 2275 Lille
- ☎ **(014) 55 19 30**
- ⌨ (014) 55 19 31
- ▷ 9 L 2007 m Par 64
- ⚇ U
- £€ €15 (€20)
- ⇄ Lille, 10km SW of Turnhout, nr E7. 25km E of Antwerp

Rinkven G&CC (1980)

Sint Jobsteenweg 120, 2970 Schilde
- ☎ **(03) 380 12 85**
- ⌨ (03) 384 29 33
- ▷ 27 hole course
- ⚇ H–phone before visit
- £€ €37 (€60)
- ⇄ 17 km NE of Antwerp, off E19

Royal Antwerp (1888)

Georges Capiaulei 2, 2950 Kapellen
- ☎ **(03) 666 84 56**
- ⌨ (03) 666 44 37
- ▷ 18 L 6140 m SSS 73
  9 L 2655 m SSS 34
- ⚇ WD–H (phone first)
- £€ €60 – € 75
- ⇄ Kapellen, 20km N of Antwerp
- ⌂ Willie Park/T Simpson
- ■ www.ragc.be

Steenhoven (1985)

Steenhoven 89, 2400 Postel-Mol
- ☎ **(014) 37 36 61**
- ⌨ (014) 37 36 62
- ▷ 18 L 5950 m SSS 71
- ⚇ H–booking necessary
- £€ €37 (€60)
- ⇄ 30 mins W of Antwerp
- ⌂ Pierre de Broqueville

Ternesse G&CC (1976)

Uilenbaan 15, 2160 Wommelgem
- ☎ **(03) 355 14 30**
- ⌨ (03) 355 14 35
- ▷ 18 L 5829 m Par 71
  9 L 1981 m Par 33
- ⚇ H–30
- £€ €50 (€62.50)
- ⇄ 5km E of Antwerp on E313
- ⌂ HJ Baker

Ardennes & South

Andenne (1988)

Ferme du Moulin 52, Stud, 5300 Andenne
- ☎ **(085) 84 34 04**
- ⌨ (085) 84 34 04
- ▷ 9 L 2447 m SSS 66
- ⚇ U
- £€ €12 (€17)
- ⇄ Andenne, 20km E of Namur
- ⌂ C Bertier

Château Royal d'Ardenne

Tour Léopold, Ardenne 6, 5560 Houyet
- ☎ **(082) 66 62 28**

- ⌨ (082) 66 74 53
- ▷ 18 L 5363 m SSS 71
- ⚇ H
- £€ €30 (€45)
- ⇄ 9km SE of Dinant on Rochefort road

Falnuée (1987)

Rue E Pirson 55, 5032 Mazy
- ☎ **(081) 63 30 90**
- ⌨ (081) 63 37 64
- ▷ 18 L 5700 m SSS 70
- ⚇ H
- £€ €30 (€45)
- ⇄ 18km NW of Namur. Mons-Liège highway Junction 13
- ⌂ J Jottrand
- ■ www.falnuee.be

Five Nations C C (1990)

Ferme du Grand Scley, 5372 Méan (Havelange)
- ☎ **(086) 32 32 32**
- ⌨ (086) 32 30 11
- ▷ 18 L 6066 m Par 72
- ⚇ WD–U WE–H
- £€ €35 (€45)
- ⇄ 30km S of Liège
- ⌂ Gary Player

Mont Garni (1989)

Rue du Mont Garni 3, 7331 Saint Ghislain
- ☎ **(065) 62 27 19**
- ⌨ (065) 62 34 10
- ▷ 18 L 6353 m Par 74
- ⚇ H
- £€ €30 (€45)
- ⇄ St Ghislain, 15km W of Mons. 65km SW of Brussels
- ⌂ T Macauley
- ■ www.golfmontgarni.be

Rougemont

Chemin du Beau Vallon 45, 5170 Profondeville
- ☎ **(081) 41 14 18**
- ⌨ (081) 41 21 42
- ▷ 18 L 5645 m Par 72
- ⚇ U
- £€ €25 (€37)
- ⇄ Profondeville, 10km S of Namur
- ■ www.users.skynet.be/rougemont

Royal GC du Hainaut (1933)

Rue de la Verrerie 2, 7050 Erbisoeul
- ☎ **(065) 22 96 10 (Clubhouse), (065) 22 02 00 (Sec)**
- ⌨ (065) 22 02 09
- ▷ 9 L 3117 m Par 36
  9 L 2925 m Par 36
  9 L 3218 m Par 36
- ⚇ U H (max 36)
- £€ €37 (€50)
- ⇄ 6km NW of Mons towards Ath on N56. Paris-Brussels motorway Junction 23
- ⌂ Martin Hawtree
- ■ www.viewgolf.net/RGCH

Brussels & Brabant

Bercuit   (1965)
Les Gottes 3, 1390 Grez-Doiceau
- ☎ **(010) 84 15 01**
- 🖥 (010) 84 55 95
- ⛳ 18 L 5931 m Par 72 SSS 72
- 👥 U H
- 💶 €50 (€100)
- 🚗 Grez-Doiceau, 27km SE of Brussels. Brussels-Namur highway exit 8
- 🏠 Robert Trent Jones Sr
- ■ www.golfdubercuit.be

Brabantse   (1982)
Steenwagenstraat 11, 1820 Melsbroek
- ☎ **(02) 751 82 05**
- 🖥 (02) 751 84 25
- ⛳ 18 L 5266 m Par 70
- 👥 H
- 💶 €35 (€45)
- 🚗 10km NE of Brussels, nr airport
- 🏠 Paul Rolin

La Bruyère   (1988)
Rue Jumerée 1, 1495 Sart-Dames-Avelines
- ☎ **(071) 87 72 67**
- 🖥 (071) 87 43 38
- ⛳ 18 L 5937 m SSS 71
- 👥 U
- 💶 €27.5 (€50)
- 🚗 40km S of Brussels towards Charleroi
- 🏠 Theys

Château de la Bawette   (1988)
Chaussée du Chateau Bawette 5, 1300 Wavre
- ☎ **(010) 22 33 32**
- 🖥 (010) 22 90 04
- ⛳ Parc 18 L 6076 m SSS 72
  Champs 9 L 2146 m SSS 63
- 👥 H–booking required
- 💶 €30 – €44 (€40 – €66)
- 🚗 1km N of Wavre. 15km S of Brussels. E411 Exit 5
- 🏠 Tom Macauley
- ■ www.golfduchateaudelabawette.be

Château de la Tournette
Chemin de Baudemont 23, 1400 Nivelles
- ☎ **(067) 89 42 66/89 42 68**
- 🖥 (067) 21 95 17
- ⛳ 18 L 6031 m Par 72
  18 L 6024 m Par 71
- 👥 H
- 💶 €30 (€50)
- 🚗 29km S of Brussels (E19)
- 🏠 Alliss/Clark

L'Empereur   (1989)
Rue Emile François 9, 1474 Ways (Genappe)
- ☎ **(067) 77 15 71**
- 🖥 (067) 77 18 33
- ⛳ 18 L 6157 m Par 72
  9 L 1660 m Par 31

- 👥 U H
- 💶 18 hole:€30 (€55) 9 hole:€20 (€30)
- 🚗 25km S of Brussels
- 🏠 Marcel Vercruyce
- ■ www.golfempereur.com

Hulencourt   (1989)
Bruyère d'Hulencourt 15, 1472 Vieux Genappe
- ☎ **(067) 79 40 40**
- 🖥 (067) 79 40 48
- ⛳ 18 L 6215 m Par 72
  9 hole Par 3 course
- 👥 H–max 36
- 💶 €55 (€80)
- 🚗 30km SE of Brussels
- 🏠 JM Rossi

Kampenhout   (1989)
Wildersedreef 56, 1910 Kampenhout
- ☎ **(016) 65 12 16**
- 🖥 (016) 65 16 80
- ⛳ 18 L 6142 m SSS 72
- 👥 H
- 💶 €25 (€37)
- 🚗 15km NE of Brussels (E19)
- 🏠 R de Vooght

Keerbergen   (1968)
Vlieghavelaan 50, 3140 Keerbergen
- ☎ **(015) 23 49 61**
- 🖥 (015) 23 57 37
- ⛳ 18 L 5503 m SSS 70
- 👥 H
- 💶 €35 (€50)
- 🚗 30km NE of Brussels
- 🏠 Frank Pennink
- ■ www.golf.be/keerbergen

Louvain-la-Neuve
Rue A Hardy 68, 1348 Louvain-la-Neuve
- ☎ **(010) 45 05 15**
- 🖥 (010) 45 44 17
- ⛳ 18 L 6226 m Par 72
- 👥 U
- 💶 €30 (€50)
- 🚗 20km SE of Brussels, off E411
- 🏠 J Dudok van Heel

Overijse   (1986)
Gemslaan 55, 3090 Overijse
- ☎ **(02) 687 50 30**
- 🖥 (02) 687 37 68
- ⛳ 9 L 5723 m Par 71
- 👥 H
- 💶 €20 (€37)
- 🚗 10km S of Brussels
- 🏠 Rossi

Pierpont   (1992)
1 Grand Pierpont, 6210 Frasnes-lez-Gosselies
- ☎ **(071) 85 17 75/85 14 19**
- 🖥 (071) 85 15 43
- ⛳ 18 L 6257 m Par 72
  5 hole Par 3 course
- 👥 U
- 💶 €30 (€60)
- 🚗 30km S of Brussels via N5
- 🏠 J Dudok van Heel
- ■ www.pierpont.be

Rigenée   (1981)
Rue de Châtelet 62, 1495 Villers-la-Ville
- ☎ **(071) 87 77 65**
- 🖥 (071) 87 77 83
- ⛳ 18 L 6031 m SSS 73
- 👥 H
- 💶 €27 (€45)
- 🚗 35km S of Brussels towards Charleroi
- 🏠 Rolin/Descampe

Royal Amicale Anderlecht   (1987)
Rue Scholle 1, 1070 Bruxelles
- ☎ **(02) 521 16 87**
- 🖥 (02) 521 51 56
- ⛳ 18 L 5037 m Par 70 CR 68.7 SR 123
- 👥 WD–U H WE–booking required
- 💶 €30 (€45)
- 🚗 SW Brussels

Royal Golf Club de Belgique   (1906)
Château de Ravenstein, 3080 Tervuren
- ☎ **(02) 767 58 01**
- 🖥 (02) 767 28 41
- ⛳ 18 L 6033 m SSS 72
  9 L 1960 m Par 32
- 👥 WD–H–max 20(men) 24(ladies)–phone first. Course closed Mon
- 💶 €90
- 🚗 Tervuren, 10km E of Brussels
- 🏠 Simpson

Royal Waterloo   (1923)
Vieux Chemin de Wavre 50, 1380 Ohain
- ☎ **(02) 633 18 50**
- 🖥 (02) 633 28 66
- ⛳ 18 L 6211 m SSS 72
  18 L 6224 m SSS 73
  9 L 2143 m SSS 33
- 👥 WD–H
- 💶 €80
- 🚗 22km SE of Brussels
- 🏠 Hawtree/Rolin

Sept Fontaines   (1987)
1021, Chaussée d'Alsemberg, 1420 Braine L'Alleud
- ☎ **(02) 353 02 46/353 03 46**
- 🖥 (02) 354 68 75
- ⛳ 18 L 6047 m Par 72 SSS 72
  18 L 4870 m Par 69 SSS 67
  9 hole short course
- 👥 U H
- 💶 €37 (€60)
- 🚗 Braine L'Alleud, 15km S of Brussels. Motorway exit 15
- 🏠 Rossi
- ■ www.golf-7fontaines.be

Winge G&CC   (1988)
Leuvensesteenweg 252, 3390 Sint Joris Winge
- ☎ **(016) 63 40 53**
- 🖥 (016) 63 21 40
- ⛳ 18 L 6049 m Par 72 CR 72.4

🕷 H
££ €35 (€50)
🏌 35km E of Brussels via Leuven
🏠 P Townsend
▬ www.golf.be/winge

East

Avernas

Route de Grand Hallet 19A,
4280 Hannut
☎ (019) 51 30 66
🖥 (019) 51 53 43
🏌 9 L 2674 m SSS 68
🕷 H
££ €17 (€22)
🏌 40km W of Liège. Brussels 50km
🏠 Hawtree/Cappart

Durbuy (1991)

Route d'Oppagne 34, 6940 Barvaux-su-
Ourthe
☎ (086) 21 44 54
🏌 18 L 5963 m SSS 72
9 hole Par 3 course
🕷 U
££ €32 (€45)
🏌 45km S of Liège
🏠 Martin Hawtree

Flanders Nippon Hasselt

(1988)
Vissenbroekstraat 15, 3500 Hasselt
☎ (011) 26 34 82
🖥 (011) 26 34 83
🏌 18 L 5966 m SSS 72
9 L 1750 m SSS 32
🕷 U H
££ €35 (€45)
🏌 5km E of Hasselt. 85km E of
Brussels
🏠 Rolin/Wirtz
▬ www.golf.be/flandersnippon

Henri-Chapelle (1988)

Rue du Vivier 3, 4841 Henri-Chapelle
☎ (087) 88 19 91
🖥 (087) 88 36 55
🏌 18 L 6040 m SSS 72
9 L 2168 m SSS 34
6 hole Par 3 course
🕷 18 hole:WE–H
££ 18 hole:€39 – € 49 9 hole:€19 – €29
🏌 15km NE of Liège. Aachen 10km
🏠 Steensels/Dudok van Heel

International Gomze (1986)

Sur Counachamps 8, 4140
Gomze Andoumont
☎ (041) 360 92 07
🖥 (041) 360 92 06
🏌 18 L 5918 m SSS 72
🕷 U H
££ On application
🏌 15km S of Liège. Spa 20km
🏠 Paul Rolin

Limburg G&CC (1966)

Golfstraat 1, 3530 Houthalen
☎ (089) 38 35 43
🖥 (089) 84 12 08
🏌 18 L 6049 m SSS 72
🕷 H
££ €45 (€55)
🏌 Houthalen, 15km N of Hasselt
🏠 Hawtree

Royal GC du Sart Tilman

(1939)
Route du Condroz 541, 4031 Liège
☎ (041) 336 20 21
🖥 (041) 337 20 26
🏌 18 L 6002 m SSS 72
🕷 H–booking required
££ D – € 38 (€50)
🏌 10km S of Liège on Route 620
(N35), towards Marche
🏠 T Simpson

Royal Golf des Fagnes

(1930)
1 Ave de l'Hippodrome, 4900 Spa
☎ (087) 79 30 30
🖥 (087) 79 30 39
🏌 18 L 6010 m Par 72
🕷 H–booking required
££ €37–50 (€45–55)
🏌 5km N of Spa. 35km SE of Liège
🏠 T Simpson

Spiegelven GC Genk

(1988)
Wiemesmeerstraat 109, 3600 Genk
☎ (089) 35 96 16
🖥 (089) 36 41 84
🏌 18 L 6198 m SSS 72
9 hole Par 3 course
🕷 H
££ €32 (€45)
🏌 Genk, 18km E of Hasselt. 20km N
of Maastricht
🏠 Ron Kirby

West & Oost
Vlaanderen

Damme G&CC (1987)

Doornstraat 16, 8340 Damme-Sijsele
☎ (050) 35 35 72
🖥 (050) 35 89 25
🏌 18 L 6046 m SSS 72
9 hole short course
🕷 H
££ €45 (€60)
🏌 7km E of Bruges. Knokke 15km
🏠 J Dudok van Heel
▬ www.golf.be/damme

Oudenaarde G&CC (1975)

Kasteel Petegem, Kortrykstraat 52,
9790 Wortegem-Petegem
☎ (055) 33 41 61
🖥 (055) 31 98 49

🏌 18 L 6172 m Par 72
9 L 2536 m Par 34
🕷 H
££ €40 (€50)
🏌 3 km SW of Oudenaarde
🏠 HJ Baker
▬ www.golf.be/oudenaarde

De Palingbeek (1991)

Eekhofstraat 14, 8902 Hollebeke I
eper
☎ (057) 20 04 36
🖥 (057) 21 89 58
🏌 18 L 6165 m Par 72
🕷 H
££ €35 (€47)
🏌 5km SE of Ieper, nr Hollebeke
🏠 HJ Baker
▬ www.golfpalingbeek.com

Royal Latem (1909)

9830 St Martens-Latem
☎ (092) 82 54 11
🖥 (092) 82 90 19
🏌 18 L 5767 m Par 72 SR 123
🕷 H
££ €50 (€65)
🏌 10 km SW of Ghent on route N43
Ghent-Deinze
▬ www.golf.be/latem

Royal Ostend (1903)

Koninklijke Baan 2, 8420 De Haan
☎ (059) 23 32 83
🖥 (059) 23 37 49
🏌 18 L 5618 m CR 70.1 SR 123
🕷 H–max 34
££ €40 – €50 (€50 – €60)
🏌 8km N of Ostend towards De
Haan
🏠 M Hawtree (1993/4)
▬ www.golfoostende.be

Royal Zoute (1899)

Caddiespad 14, 8300 Knokke-le-
Zoute
☎ (050) 60 16 17 (Clubhouse),
(050) 60 37 81 (Starter)
🖥 (050) 62 30 29
🏌 No 1 18 L 6172 m Par 72
No 2 18 L 3607 m Par 64
🕷 H No 1 course–max 20
WE–restricted
££ €85
🏌 Knokke-Heist
🏠 HS Colt

Waregem (1988)

Bergstraat 41, 8790 Waregem
☎ (056) 60 88 08
🖥 (056) 62 18 23
🏌 18 L 6038 m SSS 72
🕷 H Sun–NA before 1pm
££ €38 (€50)
🏌 30km SW of Ghent (E17)
🏠 Paul Rolin
▬ www.golf.be/waregem

Czech Republic

Karlovy Vary   (1904)
Prazska 125, PO Box 67, 360 01 Karlovy Vary
☎ **(017) 333 1001-2**
🖳 (017) 333 1101
▷ 18 L 6226 m SSS 72
👥 H
£€ 1100czk (1300czk)
⛳ 8km from Karlovy Vary (Road 6)
🏠 Noskowski

Lísnice   (1928)
252 10 Mnísek pod Brdy
☎ **(0318) 599 151**
🖳 (0318) 599 151
▷ 9 L 4948 m CR 66 SR 135
👥 H
£€ 800czk (1000czk)
⛳ 30km from Prague towards Dobrís
■ www.gkl.cz

Lokomotiva-Brno   (1967)
c/o Chlupova 7, 602 00 Brno
☎ **(05) 744615**
🖳 (05) 759309
▷ 9 L 4632 m SSS 68
👥 H
£€ 100czk (180czk)
⛳ Svratka, 80km NW of Brno. 100km SE of Prague
🏠 Chocholac

Mariánské Lázne   (1905)
PO Box 267, 353 01 Mariánské Lázne
☎ **(0165) 4300**
🖳 (0165) 625195
▷ 18 L 6195 m SSS 72
👥 H
£€ D–1000czk
⛳ 2km NE of Mariánské Lázne, opposite Golf Hotel

Park GC Ostrava   (1968)
Dolni 412, 747 15 Silherovice
☎ **(0595) 054144**
🖳 (0595) 054144
▷ 18 L 5593 m CR 70.3 SR 125
👥 H
£€ 1000czk (1200czk)
⛳ 15km N of Ostrava
🏠 Jan Cieslar
■ www.golf-ostrava.cz

Podebrady   (1964)
Na Zalesi 530, 29080 Podebrady
☎ **(0324) 610928**
🖳 (0324) 610981
▷ 18 L 5790 m CR 70.3 SR 114
👥 U H
£€ 600czk (800czk)
⛳ E side of Podebrady
🏠 Wagner/Havelka/Kodes
■ www.golfpodebrady.cz

Praha   (1926)
Na Morani 4, 128 00 Praha 2
☎ **(02) 292828/644 3828**
🖳 (02) 292828
▷ 9 L 5960 m SSS 72
👥 U
⛳ Prague-Motol, towards Plzen

Semily   (1970)
Bavlnarska 521, 513 01 Semily
☎ **(0431) 622443/624428**
🖳 (0431) 623000
▷ 9 L 4176 m Par 64
👥 WD–U WE–NA
£€ 400czk (600czk)
⛳ 2km from Semily. 100km NE of Prague
🏠 Schovánek/Janata
■ www.semily.cz

Denmark

Bornholm Island

Bornholm   (1972)
Plantagevej 3B, 3700 Rønne
☎ **56 95 68 54**
🖳 56 95 68 53
▷ 18 L 4819 m Par 68
  9 hole Par 3 course
👥 H
£€ 180kr
⛳ 4km E of Rønne, off Route 38 towards Aakirkeby
🏠 Frederik Dreyer
■ www.hjem.get2net.dk/bgk

Nexø
Dueodde Golfbane, Strandmarksvejen 14, 3730 Nexø
☎ **56 48 89 87**
🖳 56 48 89 69
▷ 18 L 5470 m CR 69.4 SR 124
👥 H
£€ 200kr (200kr)
⛳ 12km S of Nexø, nr Dueodde beach
🏠 Frederik Dreyer
■ www.dueodde-golf.dk

Nordbornholm-Rø   (1987)
Spellingevej 3, Rø, 3760 Gudhjem
☎ **56 48 40 50**
🖳 56 48 40 52
▷ 18 L 5369 m SSS 71
👥 WD–U WE–H
£€ D–200kr
⛳ Rø, 8km W of Gudhjem. 22km NE of Rønne
🏠 Anders Amilon
■ www.roegolfbane.dk

Funen

Faaborg   (1989)
Dalkildegards Allee 1, 5600 Faaborg
☎ **62 61 77 43**
🖳 62 61 79 34
▷ 18 L 5715 m Par 72
👥 U H
£€ D–200kr
⛳ 35km S of Odense
🏠 Frederik Dreyer

Lillebaelt   (1990)
O.Hougvej 130, 5500 Middelfart
☎ **64 41 80 11**
🖳 64 41 14 11
▷ 18 L 5586 m Par 71 CR 69.1
👥 H
£€ D–200kr
⛳ 2km from Middelfart. 45km W of Odense
🏠 Malling Petersen
■ www.gkl.dk

Odense   (1927)
Hestehaven 200, 5220 Odense SØ
☎ **65 95 90 00**
🖳 65 95 90 88
▷ 18 L 6098 m CR 71
  9 L 4044 m CR 61
👥 U H
£€ 250kr (300kr)
⛳ SE outskirts of Odense
🏠 Jan Sederholm
■ www.odensegolfklub.dk

Odense Eventyr   (1993)
Falen 227, 5250 Odense SV
☎ **66 17 11 44**
🖳 66 17 11 37
▷ 18 hole course Par 72
  9 hole course
👥 H
£€ 250kr (280kr)
⛳ 5km SW of Odense
🏠 Michael Møller
■ www.golfin.dk

SCT Knuds   (1954)
Slipshavnsvej 16, 5800 Nyborg
☎ **65 31 12 12**
🖳 65 30 28 04
▷ 18 L 5810 m CR 72
👥 H
£€ 250kr D–300kr (500kr)
⛳ 3km SE of Nyborg
🏠 Cotton/Dreyer
■ www.sct-knuds.dk

Svendborg   (1970)
Tordensgaardevej 5, Sørup, 5700 Svendborg
☎ **62 22 40 77**
🖳 62 20 29 77
▷ 18 L 5490 m CR 70.2 SR 127
👥 H–max 36
£€ 225kr (275kr)
⛳ 4km NW of Svendborg
🏠 Frederik Dreyer
■ www.svendborg-golf.dk

Vestfyns (1974)
Rønnemosegård, Krengerupvej 27,
5620 Glamsbjerg
- ☎ 63 72 19 20
- 📠 63 72 19 27
- ⛳ 18 L 5629 m Par 71 CR 71
- 🚹 H–max 48 (WE–max 36)
- ££ 200kr (300kr)
- ⛳ Glamsbjerg, 25km SW of Odense
- ■ www.golfonline.dk/klub/vestfyn

Greenland

Sondie Arctic Desert (1990)
Box 58, 3910 Kangerlussuaq, Greenland
- ☎ 29 91 14 13
- 📠 29 91 11 74
- ⛳ 18 L 5521 m SSS 72
- 🚹 U
- ⛳ 2km E of Kangerlussuaq Airport, Greenland
- 🏠 Ulf Larson

Jutland

Aalborg (1908)
Jaegersprisvej 35, Restrup Enge,
9000 Aalborg
- ☎ 98 34 14 76
- 📠 98 34 15 84
- ⛳ 18 L 6081 m CR 73.4
- 🚹 H (max 36)
- ££ 300kr (300kr)
- ⛳ 7 km SW of Aalborg
- 🏠 R Harris
- ■ www.aalborggk.dk

Aarhus (1931)
Ny Moesgaardvej 50, 8270 Hojbjerg
- ☎ 86 27 63 22
- 📠 86 27 63 21
- ⛳ 18 L 5725 m Par 72 CR 71
- 🚹 H
- ££ D–220kr (D–250kr)
- ⛳ 6km S of Aarhus, Route 451
- 🏠 Brian Huggett
- ■ www.aarhusgolf.dk

Blokhus Klit (1993)
Hunetorpvej 115, Box 230,
9490 Pandrup
- ☎ 98 20 95 00
- 📠 98 20 95 01
- ⛳ 18 L 5765 m CR 71
- 🚹 U H
- ££ 220kr (300kr)
- ⛳ 35km NW of Aalborg
- 🏠 Frederik Dreyer

Breinholtgård (1992)
Koksspangvej 17-19, 6710 Esbjerg V
- ☎ 75 11 57 00
- 📠 75 11 55 12
- ⛳ 27 holes Par 71
- 🚹 U H
- ££ 250kr

- ⛳ 11km N of Esbjerg
- 🏠 Gaunt/Trådsdahl

Brønderslev (1971)
PO Box 94, 9700 Brønderslev
- ☎ 98 82 32 81
- 📠 98 82 45 25
- ⛳ 18 L 5683 m CR 71
9 hole short course
- 🚹 H WE–booking necessary
- ££ 180kr (200kr)
- ⛳ 3km W of Brønderslev
- 🏠 Erik Schnack

Brundtlandbanen (2000)
Ostergade 63, 6520
Toftlund, DENMARK
- ☎ 73 83 16 00
- 📠 73 83 16 19
- ⛳ 18 L 5890 m Par 73
9 L 1255 m Par 29
- 🚹 H
- ££ 200kr (250kr)
- ⛳ Toftlund, central Jutland
- 🏠 Henrik Jacobsen
- ■ www.brundtlandbanen.dk

Dejbjerg (1966)
Letagervej 1, Dejbjerg, 6900 Skjern
- ☎ 97 35 00 09
- ⛳ 18 L 5275 m SSS 69
- 🚹 U H–max 36
- ££ D–170kr (D–200kr)
- ⛳ 6km N of Skjern. 25km from W coast on Skjern-Ringkøbing road (Route 28)
- 🏠 Schnack/Dreyer

Ebeltoft (1966)
Strandgårdshøj 8a, 8400 Ebeltoft
- ☎ 86 34 47 87/86 34 01 40
- ⛳ 18 L 5027 m Par 68 CR 67.6
- 🚹
- ££ D–200kr
- ⛳ 1km N of Ebeltoft
- 🏠 Frederik Dreyer

Esbjerg (1921)
Sønderhedevej 11, Marbaek,
6710 Esbjerg
- ☎ 75 26 92 19
- 📠 75 26 94 19
- ⛳ 18 L 6434 m CR 71
9 L 5520 m CR 70
- 🚹 U H
- ££ 250kr
- ⛳ 15km N of Esbjerg
- 🏠 Frederik Dreyer

Fanø Golf Links (1901)
Golfvejen 5, 6720 Fanø
- ☎ 76 66 00 77
- 📠 76 66 00 44
- ⛳ 18 L 5080 m CR 68.7
- 🚹 U
- ££ D–250kr
- ⛳ W side of Fanø Island. Ferry from Esbjerg 15 mins
- ■ www.fanoe-golf-links.dk

Grenaa (1981)
Vestermarken 1, 8500 Grenaa
- ☎ (86) 32 79 29
- ⛳ 18 L 5782 m Par 70
- 🚹 U
- ££ 150kr
- ⛳ 1km W of Grenaa. 60km NE of Aarhus
- 🏠 Dreyer/Sommer

Gyttegård (1974)
Billundvej 43, 7250 Hejnsvig
- ☎ 75 33 63 82
- 📠 75 33 68 20
- ⛳ 18 L 5548 m SSS 70
- 🚹 H
- ££ 200kr (250kr)
- ⛳ 2km NE of Hejnsvig. 5km SW of Billund
- 🏠 Amilon/Bossen

Haderslev (1971)
Viggo Carstensvej 7, 6100 Haderslev
- ☎ 74 52 83 01
- 📠 74 53 36 01
- ⛳ 18 L 5233 m CR 69
- 🚹 H
- ££ 220kr
- ⛳ 2km NW of Haderslev

Han Herreds
Starkaervej 20, 9690 Fjerritslev
- ☎ 98 21 26 66
- 📠 98 21 24 44
- ⛳ 18 L 5359 m CR 70.5
- 🚹 H
- ££ 150kr
- ⛳ 1km N of Fjerritslev. 40km W of Aalborg

Henne (1989)
Hennebysvej 30, 6854 Henne
- ☎ 75 25 56 10
- 📠 75 25 56 30
- ⛳ 18 L 5998 m Par 71 CR 72.5
9 hole Par 3 course
- 🚹 U H
- ££ 200kr
- ⛳ 19km NW of Varde. 35km N of Esbjerg
- 🏠 Frederik Dreyer
- ■ www.hennegolf.dk

Herning (1964)
Golfvej 2, 7400 Herning
- ☎ 97 21 00 33
- 📠 97 21 00 34
- ⛳ 18 L 5571 m CR 71.8
- 🚹 H
- ££ 150kr (200kr)
- ⛳ 2km E of Herning on Route 15
- 🏠 Dreyer/Baekgaard

Himmerland G&CC (1979)
Centervej 1, Gatten, 9640 Farsö
- ☎ 96 49 61 00
- 📠 98 66 14 56
- ⛳ Old 18 L 5422 m SSS 69 Par 70;
New 18 L 6102 m SSS 74 Par 73;
18 hole Par 3 course

☠ H
£€ 180kr D–230kr (270kr D–320kr)
♨ Gatten, 35km NW of Hobro
towards Løgstør (Route 29)
🏠 Jan Sederström

Hirtshals (1990)

Kjulvej 10, PO Box 51, 9850 Hirtshals
☏ **98 94 94 08**
🖥 98 94 19 35
› 18 L 5620 m Par 72
☠ U H max 48 WE–NA 10–12 noon
£€ 200kr
♨ 12km N of Hjørring
🏠 Erik Nielsen

Hjarbaek Fjord (1992)

Lynderup, 8832 Skals
☏ **86 69 62 88**
🖥 86 69 62 68
› 27 L 8595 m SSS 72
☠ H
£€ 230kr (270kr)
♨ 17km NW of Viborg
🏠 Henrik Jacobsen

Hjorring (1985)

Vinstrupvej, PO Box 215, 9800 Hjorring
☏ **98 91 18 28**
🖥 98 90 31 00
› 18 L 5945 m SSS 72
☠ H WE–NA 9–11am & 1.30–2.30pm
£€ 200kr (220kr)
♨ N of Hjorring. 50km N of Aalborg
🏠 Erik Schnack
■ www.hjoerringgolf.dk

Holmsland Klit

Klevevej 19, Søndervig, 6950 Ringkøbing
☏ **97 33 88 00**
🖥 97 33 86 80
› 18 L 5611 m SSS 69
☠ H
£€ 175kr
♨ 10km W of Ringkøbing
🏠 Leif Baekgaard

Holstebro (1970)

Råsted, 7570 Vemb
☏ **97 48 51 55**
› 18 L 5853 m CR 70.6
9 L 2510 m
☠ H
£€ 200kr (250kr)
♨ 13km W of Holstebro (Route 16)
🏠 Erik Schnack

Horsens (1972)

Silkeborgvej 44, 8700 Horsens
☏ **75 61 51 51**
🖥 75 61 40 51
› 18 L 6020 m CR 72.4
9 hole Par 3 course
£€ 220kr (250kr)
♨ 1 km W of Horsens towards
Silkeborg
🏠 Jan Sederholm
■ www.horsensgolf.dk

Hvide Klit (1972)

Hvideklitvej 28, 9982 Aalbaek
☏ **98 48 90 21/48 84 26**
🖥 98 48 91 12
› 18 L 5875 m SSS 72
☠ H
£€ 200kr (250kr)
♨ 3km N of Aalbaek. 24km N of
Frederikshavn
🏠 Anders Amilon

Juelsminde (1973)

Bobroholtvej 11a, 7130 Juelsminde
☏ **75 69 34 92**
🖥 75 69 46 11
› 18 L 5680 m SSS 72
☠ U H
£€ 200kr
♨ 20 km S of Horsens on coast. 2km
N of Juelsminde
🏠 Mehlsen/Jacobsen/Møller

Kaj Lykke (1988)

Kirkebrovej 5, 6740 Bramming
☏ **75 10 22 46**
🖥 75 10 26 68
› 18 L 5975 m CR 72.3 SR 131
Par 3 course
☠ H
£€ 200kr
♨ 18km E of Esbjerg
🏠 Bent Nielsen
■ www.kaj-lykke-golfklub.dk

Kalo (1992)

Aarhusvej 32, 8410 Rønde
☏ **86 37 36 00**
🖥 86 37 36 46
› 18 L 5936 m CR 72.2
☠ U
£€ 220kr (250kr)
♨ 20km E of Aarhus
🏠 Frederik Dreyer

Kolding (1933)

Egtved Alle 10, 6000 Kolding
☏ **75 52 37 93**
🖥 75 52 42 42
› 18 L 5376 m SSS 69
9 L 2065 m
☠ U
£€ 200kr (250kr)
♨ 3km N of Kolding
🏠 Jan Sederholm

Lemvig (1986)

Søgårdevejen 6, 7620 Lemvig
☏ **97 81 09 20**
🖥 97 81 09 20
› 18 L 5890 m CR 72
☠ H
£€ 200kr (200kr)
♨ 2km N of Lemvig. 35km NE of
Holstebro
🏠 Frederik Dreyer
■ www.home11.inet.tele.dk/lemviggk

Løkken (1990)

*Vrenstedvej 226, PO Box 43,
9480 Løkken*
☏ **98 99 26 57**

🖥 98 99 26 58
› 18 L 5902 m CR 72.3 SR 127
9 L 2964 m Par 29
☠ U H
£€ 200kr (200kr)
♨ 45km NW of Aalborg
🏠 Kaj Andersen
■ www.loekken-golfklub.dk

Nordvestjysk (1971)

Nystrupvej 19, 7700 Thisted
☏ **97 97 41 41**
› 18 L 5675 m CR 72
☠ H
£€ 150kr (150kr)
♨ 17km NW of Thisted
🏠 Schnack/Jacobsen

Odder (1990)

Akjaervej 200, Postbox 46, 8300 Odder
☏ **86 54 54 51**
› 18 L 5428 m Par 70 CR 70
☠ U
£€ 200kr (250kr)
♨ 4km SW of Odder, off Route 451
🏠 Frederik Dreyer

Randers (1958)

Himmelbovej, Fladbro, 8900 Randers
☏ **86 42 88 69**
🖥 86 40 88 69
› 18 L 5453 m SSS 70
9 hole Par 3 course
£€ 200kr (250kr)
♨ 5km W of Randers towards Langå
🏠 Mogens Harbo
■ www.randersgolf.dk

Ribe (1979)

Rønnehave, Snepsgårdevej 14, 6760 Ribe
☏ **30 73 65 18**
› 18 L 5430 m CR 69
☠ U
£€ 150kr
♨ 8 km SE of Ribe on Haderslev road
🏠 Frederik Dreyer

Rold Skov

Golfvej 1, 9520 Skørping
☏ **98 39 26 99**
🖥 98 39 26 52
› 18 L 5850 m SSS 72
☠ U H
£€ 220kr (250kr)
♨ 30km S of Aalborg
🏠 Henrik Jacobsen

Royal Oak (1992)

Golfvej, Jels, 6630 Rødding
☏ **74 55 32 94**
🖥 74 55 32 95
› 18 L 5967 m Par 72
☠ H–booking necessary. Soft spikes
only
£€ 300kr
♨ 25km SW of Kolding
■ www.royal-oak.dk

Saeby
Vandløsvej 50, 9300 Saeby
- ☎ 98 46 76 77
- ☐ 98 46 11 24
- ↦ 18 L 5944 m SSS 72
- ⚇ U
- ££ 200kr (200kr)
- ⛳ Saeby, 12km S of Fredrikshavn
- ⌂ Anders Amilon

Silkeborg (1966)
Sensommervej 15C, 8600 Silkeborg
- ☎ 86 85 33 99
- ☐ 86 85 35 22
- ↦ 18 L 5975 m SSS 72
- ⚇ WD–U exc Tues WE–NA pm
- ££ 225kr (275kr)
- ⛳ 5km E of Silkeborg
- ⌂ Frederik Dreyer
- ■ www.silkeborggc.dk

Sønderjyllands (1968)
Uge Hedegård, 6360 Tinglev
- ☎ 74 68 75 25
- ☐ 74 68 75 05
- ↦ 18 L 5856 m Par 71
- ⚇ H
- ££ 200kr (260kr)
- ⛳ 9km NE of Tinglev. 9km S of Abenraa
- ⌂ Erik Schnack
- ■ www.sdj-golfklub.dk

Varde (1991)
Gellerupvej 111b, 6800 Varde
- ☎ 75 22 49 44
- ☐ 75 22 48 35
- ↦ 18 L 6104 m Par 71
- ⚇ H
- ££ 200kr (250kr)
- ⛳ 20km N of Esbjerg
- ⌂ Erik Fauerholt

Vejle (1970)
Faellessletgard, Ibaekvej, 7100 Vejle
- ☎ 75 85 81 85
- ☐ 75 85 83 01
- ↦ 27 holes:
  5677-6148 m Par 71-73
  9 hole Par 3 course
- ⚇ H
- ££ 250kr (300kr)
- ⛳ 5 km SE of Vejle
- ⌂ J Malling Pedersen

Viborg (1973)
Spangsbjerg Alle 50, Overlund, 8800 Viborg
- ☎ 86 67 30 10
- ☐ 86 67 34 15
- ↦ 18 L 5767 m CR 72
- ⚇ WD–H 48 WE–H 36
- ££ 200kr (225kr)
- ⛳ 2 km E of Viborg
- ⌂ Frederik Dreyer
- ■ www.viborggolfklub.dk

Zealand

Asserbo (1946)
Bødkergaardsvej, 3300 Frederiksvaerk
- ☎ 47 72 14 90
- ☐ 47 72 14 26
- ↦ 18 L 5851 m Par 72
- ⚇ H
- ££ 300kr (350kr)
- ⛳ 3km from Frederiksvaerk towards Liseleje
- ⌂ Ross/Samuelsen
- ■ www.agc.dk

Copenhagen (1898)
Dyrehaven 2, 2800 Kgs. Lyngby
- ☎ 39 63 04 83
- ☐ 39 63 46 83
- ↦ 18 L 5761 m SSS 71
- ⚇ WD–U WE–NA before noon
- ££ 300kr (400kr)
- ⛳ 13 km N of Copenhagen, in deer park

Dragør
Kalvebodvej 100, 2791 Dragør
- ☎ 32 53 89 75
- ☐ 32 53 88 09
- ↦ 18 L 5864 m SSS 71
  6 hole Par 3 course
- ⚇ WD–U WE–U H
- ££ 250kr (300kr)
- ⛳ 15km SE of Copenhagen centre, nr Airport
- ⌂ Henning Jensen/Kierkegaard
- ■ www.dragor-golf.dk

Falster (1994)
Virketvej 44, 4863 Eskilstrup, Falster Island
- ☎ 54 43 81 43
- ☐ 54 43 81 23
- ↦ 18 L 5912 m Par 72
- ⚇ H
- ££ 225kr (275kr)
- ⛳ 20km NE of Nykøbing (Route 271)
- ⌂ Anders Amilon

Frederikssund (1974)
Egelundsgården, Skovnaesvej 9, 3630 Jaegerspris
- ☎ 47 31 08 77
- ☐ 47 31 21 88
- ↦ 18 L 5868 m SSS 71
- ⚇ WD–U H WE–H 30
- ££ 200kr (300kr)
- ⛳ 3km S of Frederikssund towards Skibby (Route 53)
- ⌂ Dreyer/Samuelsen

Furesø (1974)
Hestkøbgård, Hestkøb Vaenge 4, 3460 Birkerød
- ☎ 45 81 74 44
- ☐ 45 82 02 24
- ↦ 27 holes:
  5328-5641 m CR 70-71
- ⚇ H WD–NA before 9am WE–NA before noon

- ££ 250kr (350kr)
- ⛳ 25 km N of Copenhagen
- ⌂ Jan Sederholm
- ■ www.furesoegolfklub.dk

Gilleleje (1970)
Ferlevej 52, 3250 Gilleleje
- ☎ 49 71 80 56
- ☐ 49 71 80 86
- ↦ 18 L 6641 yds Par 72 CR 71
- ⚇ H–max 32
- ££ 280kr (350kr)
- ⛳ 62km N of Copenhagen
- ⌂ Jan Sederholm
- ■ www.gillelejegolfklub.dk

Hedeland (1980)
Staerkendevej 232A, 2640 Hedehusene
- ☎ 46 13 61 88/46 13 61 69
- ☐ 46 13 62 78
- ↦ 18 L 6070 m Par 72
  9 hole Par 3 course
- ⚇ H WE–NA before noon
- ££ 200kr (250kr)
- ⛳ 7km SE of Roskilde. 20km SW of Copenhagen
- ⌂ Jan Sederholm

Helsingør
GL Hellebaekvej, 3000 Helsingør
- ☎ 49 21 29 70
- ☐ 49 21 09 70
- ↦ 18 L 5612 m Par 71 CR 71
- ⚇ U H
- ££ 275–400kr (350–500kr)
- ⛳ 2km N of Helsingør

Hillerød (1966)
Nysøgårdsvej 9, Ny Hammersholt, 3400 Hillerød
- ☎ 48 26 50 46/48 25 40 30 (Pro)
- ☐ 48 25 29 87
- ↦ 18 L 5255 m CR 71
- ⚇ H WE–NA before noon
- ££ 300kr (350kr)
- ⛳ 3 km S of Hillerød
- ⌂ Sederholm/Knudsen

Holbaek (1964)
Dragerupvej 50, 4300 Holbaek
- ☎ 59 43 45 79
- ☐ 59 44 51 61
- ↦ 18 L 5290 m Par 70
- ⚇ U H
- ££ 240kr (280kr)
- ⛳ Kirsebaerholmen, 2km E of Holbaek
- ⌂ Dreyer/Sederholm
- ■ www.holbakgolfklub.dk

Køge (1970)
Gl.Hastrupvej12, 4600 Køge
- ☎ 56 65 10 00
- ☐ 56 65 13 45
- ↦ 18 L 6042 m Par 72
  9 L 3659 m Par 62
- ⚇ WE–H max 27
- ££ 270kr (320kr)
- ⛳ 3km S of Køge. Copenhagen 38 km

Kokkedal (1971)

Kokkedal Alle 9, 2970 Horsholm
- ☎ 45 76 99 59
- 📠 45 76 99 03
- ⛳ 18 L 5936 m Par 72
- 👥 H–WE pm only
- ££ 300kr (350kr)
- 🚗 Hørsholm, 30 km N of Copenhagen
- 🏠 Frank Pennink
- ■ www.kokkedalgolf.dk

Korsør (1996)

Ornumvej 8, Postbox 53, 4220 Korsør
- ☎ 58 37 18 36
- 📠 58 37 18 39
- ⛳ 18 L 5752 m CR 71.1 SR 130
- 👥 H–NA before 10am
- ££ 220 (275kr)
- 🚗 1km E of Korsør, on Korsør Bay
- ■ www.korsoergolf.dk

Mølleåens (1970)

Stenbaekgård, Rosenlundvej 3, 3540 Lynge
- ☎ 48 18 86 31/48 18 86 36 (Pro)
- 📠 48 18 86 43
- ⛳ 18 L 5494 m SSS 69
- 👥 H
- ££ 200kr (250kr)
- 🚗 32 km NW of Copenhagen
- 🏠 Jan Sederholm

Odsherred (1967)

4573 Højby
- ☎ 59 30 20 76
- 📠 59 30 36 76
- ⛳ 18 L 5536 m Par 71
- 👥 H
- ££ 200kr (240kr)
- 🚗 5km SW of Nykøbing
- 🏠 Amilon/Dreyer

Roskilde (1973)

Gedevad, Kongemarken 34, 4000 Roskilde
- ☎ 46 37 01 81
- 📠 46 32 85 79
- ⛳ 18 L 5700 m CR 71
- 👥 U H WE–NA before 10am
- ££ 250kr (300kr)
- 🚗 5km W of Roskilde
- 🏠 Jan Sederholm

Rungsted (1937)

Vestre Stationsvej 16, 2960 Rungsted Kyst
- ☎ 45 86 34 44
- 📠 45 86 57 70
- ⛳ 18 L 5918 m Par 71 CR 71.2 SR 129
- 👥 H–max 26 (WE–21) WE–NA before noon
- ££ 400kr (450kr)
- 🚗 Rungsted, 24km N of Copenhagen
- 🏠 Maj CA Mackenzie
- ■ www.rungstedgolfklub.dk

Simon's (1993)

Nybovej 5, 3490 Kvistgaard
- ☎ 49 19 14 78
- 📠 49 19 14 70
- ⛳ 18 L 6200 m SSS 74
- 👥 H–max 36
- ££ 300kr (450kr)
- 🚗 10km S of Helsingør. 35km N of Copenhagen
- 🏠 Martin Hawtree

Skjoldenaesholm (1992)

4174 Jystrup
- ☎ 57 53 87 00
- 📠 57 53 87 15
- ⛳ 18 L 5958 m SSS 71
- 👥 H–max 36
- ££ 260kr (310kr)
- 🚗 10km N of Ringsted. 60km SW of Copenhagen
- 🏠 Otto Bojesen
- ■ www.golfin.dk/sgc

Skovlunde Herlev (1980)

Syvendehusvej 111, 2730 Herlev
- ☎ 44 68 90 09
- 📠 44 68 90 04
- ⛳ 18 L 5125 m CR 67.8 SR 122 9 hole Par 3 course
- 👥 H
- ££ 250kr (300kr)
- 🚗 Herlev/Ballerup, 15km NW of Copenhagen
- 🏠 Torben Starup
- ■ www.shgk.dk

Søllerød

Brillerne 9, 2840 Holte
- ☎ 45 80 17 84, 45 80 18 77
- 📠 45 80 70 08
- ⛳ 18 L 5952 m SSS 72
- 👥 U
- ££ 280kr (350kr)
- 🚗 19km N of Copenhagen
- ■ www.sollerodgolf.dk

Sorø (1979)

Suserupvej 7a, 4180 Sorø
- ☎ 57 84 93 95
- 📠 57 84 85 58
- ⛳ 18 L 5693 m Par 71 CR 71
- 👥 H–max 42
- ££ 250kr (300kr)
- 🚗 6km S of Sorø. 15km W of Ringsted
- 🏠 Jan Sederholm
- ■ www.soroegolf.dk

Sydsjaellands (1974)

Borupgården, Mogenstrup, 4700 Naestved
- ☎ 55 76 15 55
- 📠 55 76 15 88
- ⛳ 18 L 5663 m CR 70.5
- 👥 H
- ££ 240kr (300kr)
- 🚗 10km SE of Naestved towards Praestø
- 🏠 Dreyer/Amillon

Vallensbaek (1985)

Golfsvinget 12, 2625 Vallensbaek
- ☎ 43 62 18 99
- 📠 43 62 18 33
- ⛳ 18 L 5965 m Par 71 CR 72 SR 123
- 👥 H
- ££ 220kr (260kr)
- 🚗 15km W of Copenhagen
- 🏠 Frederik Dreyer

Finland

Central

Etelä-Pohjanmaan (1986)

P O Box 136, 60101 Seinäjoki
- ☎ (06) 423 4545
- 📠 (06) 423 4547
- ⛳ 18 L 5806 m CR 71.9
- 👥 U
- ££ €34
- 🚗 5km E of Seinäjoki. 300km NW of Helsinki
- 🏠 Robert Trent Jones Jr
- ■ www.ruuhikoskigolf.fi

Karelia Golf (1987)

Vaskiportintie, 80780 Kontioniemi
- ☎ (013) 732411
- 📠 (013) 732472
- ⛳ 18 L 5619 m CR 71
- 👥 U H
- ££ €31
- 🚗 18km N of Joensuu. 460km NE of Helsinki
- 🏠 Kosti Kuronen

Kokkolan (1957)

P O Box 164, 67101 Kokkola
- ☎ (06) 822 1636
- 📠 (06) 822 1630
- ⛳ 18 L 5572 m SSS 71
- 👥 U H
- ££ €30
- 🚗 3km S of Kokkola. 500km N of Helsinki
- 🏠 KJ Indola

Laukaan Peurunkagolf (1989)

Valkolantie 68, 41530 Laukaa
- ☎ (014) 3377 300
- 📠 (014) 3377 305
- ⛳ 18 L 5547 m CR 71
- 👥 H
- ££ €40
- 🚗 28km NE of Jyväskylä. 300km N of Helsinki
- 🏠 Ronald Fream
- ■ www.golfpiste.com/lpg

Tarina Golf (1988)

Golftie 135, 71800 Siilinjärvi
- ☎ (017) 462 5299

☐ (017) 462 5269
⊳ Old 18 L 5593 m CR 70.2 SR 130
New 18 L 5866 m CR 71.5 SR 128
👥 U H
£€ €34 (€43)
⛳ 21km N of Kuopio (Route 5)
🏠 Kuronen/Sederholm

Vaasan (1969)
Golfkenttätie 61, 65380 Vaasa
☎ (06) 356 9989
☐ (06) 356 9091
⊳ 18 L 5602 m Par 72
👥 H or Green card
£€ €24
⛳ Kraklund, 6km SE of Vaasa on Route 724. 417km NW of Helsinki
🏠 Björn Eriksson

Helsinki & South

Aura Golf (1958)
Ruissalon Puistotie 536, 20100 Turku
☎ (02) 258 9201/9221
☐ (02) 258 9121
⊳ 18 L 5843 m SSS 71
👥 H–max 30 (men) 36 (women)
£€ €42 (€51)
⛳ Ruissalo Island, 9km W of Turku
🏠 Pekka Sivula
■ www.auragolf.fi

Espoo Ringside Golf (1990)
Niipperintie 20, 02920 Espoo
☎ (09) 849 4940
☐ (09) 853 7132
⊳ 18 L 5855 m SSS 72
👥 H
£€ €34 (€40)
⛳ 20km NW of Helsinki
🏠 Kosti Kuronen

Espoon Golfseura (1982)
Mynttiläntie 1, 02780 Espoo
☎ (09) 8190 3444
☐ (09) 8190 3434
⊳ 18 L 5920 m CR 72.3
👥 H
£€ €40
⛳ Espoo, 24km W of Helsinki
🏠 Jan Sederholm
■ www.espoongolfseura.fi

Harjattula G&CC (1989)
Harjattulantie 84, 20960 Turku
☎ (02) 276 2180
☐ (02) 258 7218
⊳ 18 L 6348 m Par 72 SSS 75
👥 H–max 36
£€ €35 (€43)
⛳ 22km S of Turku
🏠 Kosti Kuronen
■ www.harjattula.fi

Helsingin Golfklubi (1932)
Talin Kartano, 00350 Helsinki
☎ (09) 2252 3710
☐ (09) 2252 3732

⊳ 18 L 5486 m CR 68.7 SR 120
👥 H–max 24
£€ €45 (€50)
⛳ 7km W of Helsinki
🏠 Kosti Kuronen
■ www.helsingingolfklubi.fi

Hyvinkään (1989)
Golftie 63, 05880 Hyvinkää
☎ (019) 489390
☐ (019) 489392
⊳ 18 L 5457 m CR 72.1
👥 U H
£€ €29
⛳ 3km N of Hyvinkää. 50km N of Helsinki
🏠 Kosti Kuronen

Keimola Golf (1988)
Kirkantie 32, 01750 Vantaa
☎ (09) 276 6650
☐ (09) 896790
⊳ 27 L 5870-5924 m SSS 71-74
👥 WD–U before 3pm –M after 3pm WE–M H
£€ €27
⛳ 15km N of Helsinki
🏠 Pekka Wesamaa

Kurk Golf (1985)
02550 Evitskog
☎ (09) 819 0480
☐ (09) 819 04810
⊳ 18 L 5848 m Par 72
👥 H
£€ €38 (€47)
⛳ 40km W of Helsinki
🏠 Reijo Hillberg
■ www.kurkgolf.fi

Master Golf (1988)
Bodomintie 4, 029400 Espoo
☎ (09) 849 2300
☐ (09) 849 23011
⊳ 18 L 5708 m CR 71.2 SR 128
18 L 5375 m CR 70.1 SR 124
👥 WD before 2pm H–max 30 (M) 36 (L)
£€ €50 (€60)
⛳ 24km NW of Helsinki
🏠 Kuronen/Persson
■ www.mastergolf.fi

Meri-Teijo (1990)
Mathildedalin Kartano, 25860 Mathildedal
☎ (02) 736 3955
☐ (02) 736 3945
⊳ 18 L 5842 m CR 70.7
👥 U
£€ €19 (€24)
⛳ 20km S of Salo. 70km E of Turku

Messilä (1988)
Messiläntie 240, 15980 Messilä
☎ (03) 753 8171
☐ (03) 753 8174
⊳ 18 L 6013 m Par 73
👥 WD–U before 3pm
£€ D – € 30

⛳ 8km W of Lahti. 100km N of Helsinki
🏠 Kosti Kuronen

Nevas Golf (1988)
01190 Box
☎ (09) 272 6313
☐ (09) 272 6345
⊳ 18 L 5267 m CR 68.5
👥 U
£€ €35
⛳ 30km E of Helsinki
🏠 Kosti Kuronen

Nordcenter G&CC (1988)
10410 Aminnefors
☎ (019) 238850
☐ (019) 238871
⊳ 18 L 6375 m SSS 77
18 L 6069 m SSS 72
👥 H
£€ €59 (€71)
⛳ 80km W of Helsinki
🏠 Fream/Benz
■ www.nordcenter.com

Nurmijärven (1990)
Ratasillantie, 05100 Röykkä
☎ (09) 276 6230
☐ (09) 276 62330
⊳ 27 L 6002-6214 m SSS 73-75
👥 U
£€ €20–30
⛳ 23km W of Klaukkala. 50km NW of Helsinki

Peuramaa
02400 Kirkkonummi
☎ (09) 295 588
☐ (09) 2955 8210
⊳ 36 holes
👥 H
£€ €30 (€40)
⛳ 27km W of Helsinki
🏠 Kuronen/Persson
■ www.peuramaagolf.com

Pickala Golf (1986)
Golfkuja 5, 02580 Siuntio
☎ (09) 221 9080
☐ (09) 221 90899
⊳ Seaside 18 L 5820 m SSS 72
Park 18 L 5897 m SSS 72
👥 H
£€ €40 (€60)
⛳ 42km W of Helsinki, on South coast
🏠 Reijo Hillberg
■ www.pickalagolf.fi

Ruukkigolf (1986)
Brödtorp, 10420 Skuru
☎ (019) 245 4485
☐ (019) 245 4285
⊳ 18 L 6165 m Par 72
👥 U
£€ €20 (€29)
⛳ 85km W of Helsinki
🏠 Lasse Heikkinen

For list of abbreviations and key to symbols see page 649

Sarfvik (1984)

P O Box 27, 02321 Espoo
- ☎ **(09) 221 9000**
- 🖥 (09) 297 7134
- ⮂ 18 L 5690 m CR 70.5
  18 L 5399 m CR 69.8
- 👥 WD–U H
- £€ €67
- ⛳ 20km W of Helsinki
- 🏠 Jan Sederholm

St Laurence (1989)

Kaivurinkatu, 08200 Lohja
- ☎ **(019) 386603**
- 🖥 (019) 386666
- ⮂ 18 L 6240 m CR 71.5 SR 128
  18 L 6340 m CR 70.7 SR 120
- 👥 WD–H WE–M H
- £€ €50
- ⛳ 50km W of Helsinki
- 🏠 Kosti Kuronen

Sea Golf Rönnäs (1989)

Rönnäs, 07750 Isnäs
- ☎ **(019) 634434**
- 🖥 (019) 634458
- ⮂ 18 L 5541 m CR 70.5
- 👥 U
- £€ €5 (€9)
- ⛳ 27km SE of Porvoo. 80km E of Helsinki

Suur-Helsingin (1965)

Rinnekodintie 29, 02980 Espoo
- ☎ **(09) 855 8687**
- 🖥 (09) 855 0648
- ⮂ Lakisto 18 L 5551 m SSS 71
  Luukki 18 L 5085 m SSS 70
- 👥 U
- £€ €25
- ⛳ 25km N of Helsinki

Golf Talma (1989)

Nygårdintie 115-6, 04240 Talma
- ☎ **(09) 274 6540**
- 🖥 (09) 274 65432
- ⮂ 18 L 5809 m SSS 72
  18 L 5758 m SSS 72
  9 hole Par 3 course
- 👥 WD–H WE–M H
- £€ €50 (€60)
- ⛳ 35km N of Helsinki
- 🏠 Henrik Wartiainen

Tuusula (1983)

Kirkkotie 51, 04301 Tuusula
- ☎ **(042) 410241**
- 🖥 (09) 274 60860
- ⮂ 18 L 5626 m CR 71
- 👥 H
- £€ €37
- ⛳ 30km N of Helsinki, nr airport
- 🏠 Henrik Wartiainen
- 🖧 www.golfpiste.com/tgk

Virvik Golf (1981)

Virvik, 06100 Porvoo
- ☎ **(915) 579292**
- 🖥 (915) 579292
- ⮂ 18 L 5855 m SSS 72
- 👥 H
- £€ €20 (€24)
- ⛳ 18km SE of Porvoo. 66km E of Helsinki
- 🏠 Reijo Louhimo

North

Green Zone Golf (1987)

Näräntie, 95400 Tornio
- ☎ **(016) 431711**
- 🖥 (016) 431710
- ⮂ 18 L 5870 m SSS 73
- 👥 U
- £€ €20
- ⛳ 2km N of Tornio. 140km N of Oulu, on Finnish/Swedish border
- 🏠 Ake Persson

Katinkulta (1990)

88610 Vuokatti
- ☎ **(08) 669 7488**
- 🖥 (08) 669 7480
- ⮂ 18 L 6000 m Par 72
- 👥 H
- £€ €27 (€30)
- ⛳ 36km E of Kajaani. 600km N of Helsinki
- 🏠 Jan Sederholm

Oulu (1964)

Isokatu 99, 90120 Oulu
- ☎ **(08) 371666/531 5222**
- 🖥 (08) 379728/531 5129
- ⮂ 18 L 6160 m SSS 73
  9 L 2990 m SSS 73
- 👥 H
- £€ €34–37
- ⛳ Sanginsuu, 18km E of Oulu
- 🏠 Ronald Fream
- 🖧 www.golfpiste.com/ogk

South East

Imatran Golf (1986)

Golftie 11, 55800 Imatra
- ☎ **(05) 473 4954**
- 🖥 (05) 473 4953
- ⮂ 18 L 5738 m CR 71.4
- 👥 U
- £€ €29 (€29)
- ⛳ 6km N of Imatra. 270km E of Helsinki
- 🏠 Kosti Kuronen

Kartano Golf (1988)

P O Box 60, 79601 Joroinen
- ☎ **(017) 572257**
- 🖥 (017) 572263
- ⮂ 18 L 5597 m CR 71
- 👥 U
- £€ €22 (€29)
- ⛳ 20km S of Varkaus. 330km NE of Helsinki
- 🏠 Ake Persson

Kerigolf (1990)

Kerimantie 65, 58200 Kerimäki
- ☎ **(015) 252600**
- 🖥 (015) 252606
- ⮂ 18 L 6218 m Par 72 SSS 75
- 👥 H
- £€ €35
- ⛳ 15km E of Savonlinna. 350km NE of Helsinki
- 🏠 Ronald Fream
- 🖧 www.kerigolf.fi

Koski Golf (1987)

Eerolan Golfkeskus, 45700 Kuusankoski
- ☎ **(05) 864 4600**
- 🖥 (05) 864 4644
- ⮂ 18 L 6375 m Par 73
- 👥 H I
- £€ €35 (€40)
- ⛳ 3km E of Kuusankoski. 70km E of Lahti
- 🏠 Kosti Kuronen
- 🖧 www.koskigolf.com

Kymen Golf (1964)

Mussalo Golfcourse, 48310 Kotka
- ☎ **(05) 210 3700**
- 🖥 (05) 210 3730
- ⮂ 18 L 5672 m CR 70.6 SR 129
- 👥 H
- £€ €35
- ⛳ 5km W of Kotka, Mussalo Island. 130km E of Helsinki
- 🏠 Kosti Kuronen
- 🖧 www.kymengolf.fi

Lahden Golf (1959)

Takkulantie, 15230 Lahti
- ☎ **(03) 784 1311**
- 🖥 (03) 784 1311
- ⮂ 18 L 5547 m CR 71.7
- 👥 U H
- £€ €32 (€40)
- ⛳ 6km NE of Lahti. 110km NE of Helsinki

Porrassalmi (1989)

Annila, 50100 Mikkeli
- ☎ **(015) 335518/335446**
- 🖥 (015) 335446
- ⮂ 18 L 5430 m CR 69.8
- 👥 H
- £€ €30 – €35
- ⛳ 5km S of Mikkeli

Vierumäen Golfseura (1988)

Suomen Urheiluopisto, 19120 Vierumäki
- ☎ **(03) 842 4501**
- 🖥 (03) 842 4630
- ⮂ 18 L 5580 m CR 71.1
- 👥 U
- £€ €29
- ⛳ 25km NE of Lahti

South West

Porin Golfkerho (1939)
P O Box 25, 28601 Pori
☎ **(02) 630 3888**
🖳 (02) 630 38813
🗺 18 L 6160 m SSS 74
👥 H
€€ €34
⛳ 5km NW of Pori, at Kalafornia
🏠 Reijo Louhimo

River Golf (1988)
Taivalkunta, 37120 Nokia
☎ **(03) 340 0234**
🖳 (03) 340 0235
🗺 18 L 5616 m CR 70.8
👥 U
€€ €25
⛳ Nokia, 20km W of Tampere
🏠 Kosti Kuronen

Salo Golf (1988)
Liikuntapuisto 8, 24100 Salo
☎ **(02) 731 7321**
🖳 (02) 731 5600
🗺 18 L 5447 m CR 69
👥 U
€€ €20 (€25)
⛳ 110km W of Helsinki

Tammer Golf (1965)
Toimelankatu 4, 33560 Tampere
☎ **(03) 261 3316**
🖳 (03) 261 3130
🗺 18 L 5717 m CR 70
👥 U
€€ €25
⛳ Ruotula, 5km NE of Tampere

Tawast Golf (1987)
Tawastintie 48, 13270 Hämeenlinna
☎ **(03) 619 7502**
🖳 (03) 619 7503
🗺 18 L 6063 m Par 72
👥 WD–H–max 36 WE–M
€€ €34
⛳ 5km E of Hämeenlinna
🏠 Reijo Hillberg
🖥 www.htk.fi/tawg

Vammala (1991)
38100 Karkku
☎ **(03) 513 4070**
🖳 (03) 513 90711
🗺 18 L 5522 m CR 69.2
👥 H
€€ €20 (€27)
⛳ 11km N of Vammala. 210km NW of Helsinki
🏠 Kosti Kuronen

Wiurila G&CC (1990)
Viurilantie 126, 24910 Halikko
☎ **(02) 737 1400**
🖳 (02) 737 1404
🗺 18 L 5584 m CR 71.7
👥 U
€€ €22 (€27)

⛳ 5km W of Salo. 115km W of Helsinki

Yyteri Golf (1988)
Karhuluodontie 85, 28840 Pori
☎ **(02) 638 0380**
🖳 (02) 638 0385
🗺 18 L 5738 m Par 72
👥 II
€€ €34–42
⛳ 20km W of Pori
🏠 Reijo Louhimo
🖥 www.yyterilinks.com

France

Bordeaux & South West

Albret (1986)
Le Pusocq, 47230 Barbaste
☎ **05 53 65 53 69**
🖳 05 53 65 61 19
🗺 18 L 5911 m SSS 71
👥 U
€€ €21 (€26)
⛳ Barbaste, 30km W of Agen
🏠 JL Pega

Arcachon (1955)
35 Bd d'Arcachon, 33260 La Teste De Buch
☎ **05 56 54 44 00**
🖳 05 56 66 86 32
🗺 18 L 5930 m SSS 71
👥 U H
€€ €28.30 – €41.20
⛳ 60km SW of Bordeaux
🏠 CR Blandford

Arcangues (1991)
64200 Arcangues
☎ **05 59 43 10 56**
🖳 05 59 43 12 60
🗺 18 L 6142 m Par 72
👥 U
€€ On application
⛳ 3km SE of Biarritz
🏠 Ronald Fream

Ardilouse (1980)
Domaine de l'Ardilouse, 33680 Lacanau-Océan
☎ **05 56 03 25 60**
🖳 05 56 26 30 57
🗺 18 L 5932 m SSS 72
👥 H
⛳ 45km W of Bordeaux
🏠 John Harris

Biarritz (1888)
Ave Edith Cavell, 64200 Biarritz
☎ **05 59 03 71 80**

🖳 05 59 03 26 74
🗺 18 L 5402 m SSS 69
👥 U
€€ €35 (€55)
⛳ Biarritz
🏠 Willie Dunn

Biscarrosse (1989)
Route d'Ispe, 40600 Biscarrosse
☎ **05 58 09 84 93**
🖳 05 58 09 84 50
🗺 Lake 9 L 2172 m SSS 32
   Forest 9 L 3030 m SSS 36
👥 U
€€ €16 – €42
⛳ 80km SW of Bordeaux
🏠 Brizon/Veyssieres

Blue Green-Artiguelouve (1986)
Domaine St Michel, Pau-Artiguelouve, 64230 Artiguelouve
☎ **05 59 83 09 29**
🖳 05 59 83 14 05
🗺 18 L 6063 m Par 71
👥 U
€€ €29 (€36)
⛳ 8km NW of Pau, off Bayonne road
🏠 J Garaialde

Blue Green-Seignosse (1989)
Avenue du Belvédère, 40510 Seignosse
☎ **05 58 41 68 30**
🖳 05 58 41 68 31
🗺 18 L 6124 m Par 72
👥 U
€€ €40 – €60
⛳ 30km N of Biarritz, nr Airport
🏠 Robert von Hagge
🖥 www.golfseignosse.com

Bordeaux-Cameyrac (1972)
Cameyrac, 33450 St Sulpice
☎ **05 56 72 96 79**
🖳 05 56 72 86 56
🗺 18 L 5927 m SSS 72
   9 L 1188 m Par 28
⛳ 15km E of Bordeaux
🏠 Jacques Quenot

Bordeaux-Lac (1977)
Avenue de Pernon, 33300 Bordeaux
☎ **05 56 50 92 72**
🖳 05 56 29 01 84
🗺 18 L 6156 m SSS 72
   18 L 6159 m SSS 72
👥 U
€€ €23 (€33)
⛳ 2km N of Bordeaux
🏠 Jean Bourret
🖥 www.golfbordeauxlac.com

Bordelais (1900)
Domaine de Kater, Allee F Arago, 33200 Bordeaux-Caudéran
☎ **05 56 28 56 04**
🖳 05 56 28 59 71
🗺 18 L 4727 m SSS 67
👥 H–restricted Tues
€€ €35 (€45)
⛳ 3km NW of Bordeaux

For list of abbreviations and key to symbols see page 649

Casteljaloux   (1989)
Avenue du Lac, 47700 Casteljaloux
☎   05 53 93 51 60
🖳   05 53 93 04 10
🏴   18 L 5916 m SSS 72
👥   U
🏌   60km NW of Agen
🏠   Michel Gayon

Castelnaud   (1987)
'La Menuisière', 47290 Castelnaud de Gratecambe
☎   05 53 01 74 64
🖳   05 53 01 78 99
🏴   18 L 6322 m SSS 73
      9 L 2184 m SSS 27
🏌   10km N of Villeneuve on N21.
      40km N of Agen

Chantaco   (1928)
Route d'Ascain, 64500 St Jean-de-Luz
☎   05 59 26 14 22/05 59 26 19 22
🖳   05 59 26 48 37
🏴   18 L 5833 m SSS 70
👥   U H
£€   €45 – €56
🏌   2km S of St Jean-de-Luz, on Route d'Ascain
🏠   HS Colt
◼   www.golfdechantaco.com

Château des Vigiers   (1990)
24240 Monestier
☎   05 53 61 50 33
🖳   05 53 61 50 31
🏴   18 L 6003 m Par 72
      6 hole Academy course
👥   H
£€   €35 – €55
🏌   15km SW of Bergerac. 75km E of Bordeaux
🏠   Donald Steel
◼   www.vigiers.com

Chiberta   (1926)
Boulevard des Plages, 64600 Anglet
☎   05 59 63 83 20
🖳   05 59 63 30 56
🏴   18 L 5650 m SSS 70
👥   H–booking required
🏌   3km N of Biarritz. Airport 5km
🏠   T Simpson

Domaine de la Marterie
(1987)
St Felix de Reillac, 24260 Le Bugue
☎   05 53 05 61 00
🖳   05 53 05 61 01
🏴   18 L 6130 m Par 73
👥   U
£€   €26 (€36)
🏌   30km S of Perigueux, between La Douze and Le Bugue (D710)
🏠   Martine Lacroix
◼   www.marterie.fr

Graves et Sauternais   (1989)
St Pardon de Conques, 33210 Langon
☎   05 56 62 25 43

🏴   18 L 5810 m SSS 71
👥   U
🏌   5km from Langon. 45km SW of Bordeaux via A62

Gujan   (1990)
Route de Souguinet, 33470 Gujan Mestras
☎   05 57 52 73 73
🖳   05 56 66 10 93
🏴   18 L 6225 m SSS 72
      9 L 2635 m SSS 35
👥   U
£€   18 holes: €27 – 43
      9 holes: €21 – €26
🏌   12km E of Arcachon on RN 250.
      40km W of Bordeaux
🏠   Alain Prat

Hossegor   (1930)
333 Ave du Golf, 40150 Hossegor
☎   05 58 43 56 99
🖳   05 58 43 98 52
🏴   18 L 6001 m SSS 71
👥   H–max 35
£€   €40 – € 55
🏌   15km N of Bayonne, on coast
🏠   J Morrison
◼   www.golfhossegor.asso.fr

Makila
Route de Cambo, 64200 Bassussarry
☎   05 59 58 42 42
🖳   05 59 58 42 48
🏴   18 L 6176 m SSS 72
👥   H
£€   €34 – 46
🏌   5km SE of Biarritz. Airport 2km
🏠   R Roquemore

Médoc
Chemin de Courmateau, Louens, 33290 Le Pian Médoc
☎   05 56 70 11 90
🖳   05 56 70 11 99
🏴   Chateaux 18 L 6316 m SSS 73
      Vignes 18 L 6220 m SSS 73
👥   H
£€   €35 (€46)
🏌   20km NW of Bordeaux
🏠   Coore/Whitman

Moliets   (1989)
Rue Mathieu Desbieys, 40660 Moliets
☎   05 58 48 54 65
🖳   05 58 48 54 88
🏴   18 L 6172 m SSS 73
      9 hole course
👥   U H–max 30
£€   €34–53
🏌   Moliets, 40km N of Bayonne. 40km W of Dax
🏠   Robert Trent Jones Sr
◼   www.golfmoliets.com

La Nivelle   (1907)
Place William Sharp, 64500 Ciboure
☎   05 59 47 18 99/05 59 47 19 72
🏴   18 L 5570 m SSS 69
👥   U
🏌   2km S of St Jean-de-Luz

Pau   (1856)
Rue de Golf, 64140 Pau-Billère
☎   05 59 13 18 56
🖳   05 59 13 18 57
🏴   18 L 5312 m SSS 69
👥   H
£€   €35 – € 43
🏌   2km S of Pau. Bordeaux 200km
🏠   Willie Dunn

Périgueux   (1980)
Domaine de Saltgourde, 24430 Marsac
☎   05 53 53 02 35
🖳   05 53 09 46 29
🏴   18 L 6120 m SSS 72
👥   U
🏌   3km W of Périgueux, via Angoulême-Riberac road
🏠   Robert Berthet

Pessac   (1989)
Rue de la Princesse, 33600 Pessac
☎   05 57 26 03 33
🖳   05 56 36 52 89
🏴   18 L 5567-5935 m SSS 72
      9 L 2911 m SSS 36
      9 hole Par 3 course
👥   U
£€   €30 (€40)
🏌   4km W of Bordeaux
🏠   Olivier Brizon

Scottish Golf Aubertin
(1987)
64290 Aubertin
☎   05 59 82 70 69
🏴   18 L 4806 m Par 66
👥   U
🏌   20km S of Pau

Stade Montois   (1993)
Pessourdat, 40090 Saint Avit
☎   05 58 75 63 05
🖳   05 58 06 80 72
🏴   18 L 5944 m Par 71
👥   U
£€   €27 (€27)
🏌   Pau 80km. Biarritz 100km
🏠   J Garaialde

Brittany

Ajoncs d'Or   (1976)
Kergrain Lantic, 22410 Saint-Quay Portrieux
☎   02 96 71 90 74
🖳   02 96 71 40 83
🏴   18 L 6125 m SSS 72
👥   U
£€   €23–34 (€30–34)
🏌   17km N of Saint-Brieuc. 6km W of Étables-sur-Mer
🏠   Carlian-Des Heulles

Baden
Kernic, 56870 Baden
☎   02 97 57 18 96

☎ 02 97 57 22 05
⌇ 18 L 6145 m SSS 73
👥 U
🚗 12km SW of Vannes
🏠 Yves Bureau

Brest Les Abers   (1990)
Kerhoaden, 29810 Plouarzel
☎ **02 98 89 68 33**
⌇ 18 L 5060 m Par 71
👥 U
££ €31
🚗 15km W 0f Brest (D5)
🏠 Ch Dunoyer

Brest-Iroise   (1976)
Parc de Lann-Rohou, Saint-Urbain, 29800 Landerneau
☎ **02 98 85 16 17**
⌇ 02 98 85 19 39
⌇ 18 L 5672 m Par 71
   9 L 3329 m Par 37
👥 U
££ €32 (€35)
🚗 25km E of Brest
🏠 M Fenn

Cicé-Blossac   (1992)
Domaine de Cicé-Blossac, 35170 Bruz
☎ **02 99 52 79 79**
⌇ 02 99 57 93 60
⌇ 18 L 6343 m SSS 72
👥 U
🚗 Bruz, SW of Rennes (N177)
🏠 Macauley/Quenouille

Coatguelen   (1987)
Château de Coatguelen, 22290 Pléhédel
☎ **02 96 55 33 40**
⌇ 18 hole course
👥 U
££ €15 (€23)
🚗 10km S of Paimpol on D7. 35km from Saint-Brieuc

Dinard   (1890)
35800 St-Briac-sur-Mer
☎ **02 99 88 32 07**
⌇ 02 99 88 04 53
⌇ 18 L 5137 m Par 68
🚗 8km W of Dinard. 15km W of Saint-Malo

La Freslonnière   (1989)
Le Bois Briand, 35650 Le Rheu
☎ **02 99 14 84 01**
⌇ 02 99 14 94 98
⌇ 18 L 5756 m SSS 72 SR 125
👥 U
££ €31 – € 42
🚗 4km SW of Rennes, off N24
🏠 A du Bouexic

L'Odet   (1987)
Clohars-Fouesnant, 29950 Benodet
☎ **02 98 54 87 88**
⌇ 02 98 54 61 40
⌇ 18 L 5843 m SSS 72
   9 hole Par 3 course

👥 U H
££ €27–44
🚗 6km S of Benodet. 15km SE of Quimper
🏠 Robert Berthet

Les Ormes   (1988)
Château des Ormes, Epiniac, 35120 Dol-de-Bretagne
☎ **02 99 73 54 44**
⌇ 02 99 73 53 65
⌇ 18 L 5801 m SSS 72
👥 H
££ €31–41
🚗 8km S of Dol, off D795
🏠 A d'Ormesson

Pen Guen   (1926)
22380 Saint-Cast-le-Guildo
☎ **02 96 41 91 20**
⌇ 02 96 41 77 62
⌇ 18 L 4967m SSS 68
👥 U
££ €30–36
🚗 25km W of Dinard. 30km W of Saint-Malo

Pléneuf-Val André
Rue de la Plage des Vallées, 22370 Pléneuf-Val André
☎ **02 96 63 01 12**
⌇ 02 96 63 01 06
⌇ 18 L 6052 m Par 72
👥 U
££ €24–41
🚗 30km E of St Brieuc on coast. 60km W of St Malo
🏠 Alain Prat

Ploemeur Océan   (1990)
Kerham Saint-Jude, 56270 Ploemeur
☎ **02 97 32 81 82**
⌇ 02 97 32 80 90
⌇ 18 L 5957 m SSS 72 SR 126
👥 U H
££ €25 (€39)
🚗 10km from Lorient-Brest road, exit. Ploemeur
🏠 Macauley/Quenouille
🖥 www.formule-golf.com

Quimper-Cornouaille   (1959)
Manoir du Mesmeur, 29940 La Forêt-Fouesnant
☎ **02 98 56 97 09**
⌇ 02 98 56 86 81
⌇ 18 L 5451 m CR 69.6 SR 124
👥 U
££ €44 (€44)
🚗 15km SE of Quimper
🏠 F Hawtree
🖥 www.golfdecornouaille.com

Rennes Saint Jacques
B P 1117, 37136 St-Jacques-de-la-Lande
☎ **02 99 30 18 18**
⌇ 02 99 31 51 04
⌇ 18 L 6135 m Par 72
   9 L 2100 m Par 32
   9 hole short course

👥 U
££ €37
🚗 5km SW of Rennes
🏠 Robert Berthet

Rhuys-Kerver   (1988)
Formule Golf, Domaine de Kerver, 56730 St-Gildas-de-Rhuys
☎ **02 97 45 30 09**
⌇ 02 97 45 36 58
⌇ 18 L 6197 m SSS 73
👥 U
££ €35
🚗 30km S of Vannes
🏠 Olivier Brizon

Les Rochers   (1989)
Route d'Argentré du Plessis 3, 35500 Vitré
☎ **02 99 96 52 52**
⌇ 02 99 96 79 34
⌇ 18 L 5721 m Par 72
👥 U
££ €24 (€24)
🚗 Vitré, 30km E of Rennes
🏠 JC Varro

Sables-d'Or-les-Pins   (1925)
22240 Fréhel
☎ **02 96 41 42 57**
⌇ 02 96 41 51 44
⌇ 18 L 5586 m SSS 71
👥 U
££ €27–34
🚗 6km SW of Fréhel. 30km W of Dinard

St Laurent   (1975)
Ploemel, 56400 Auray
☎ **02 97 56 85 18**
⌇ 02 97 56 89 99
⌇ 18 L 6212 m SSS 72
   9 L 2705 m SSS 35
👥 U
££ €39
🚗 Ploemel, 16km SW of Auray
🏠 Fenn/Bureau

St Malo-Le Tronchet   (1986)
Le Tronchet, 35540 Miniac-Morvan
☎ **02 99 58 96 69**
⌇ 02 99 58 10 39
⌇ 18 L 5936 m SSS 72
   9 L 2684 m SSS 36
👥 U
££ D – € 40
🚗 23km S of St Malo, off RN 137
🏠 Hubert Chesneau

St Samson   (1965)
Route de Kérénoc, 22560 Pleumeur-Bodou
☎ **02 96 23 87 34**
⌇ 02 96 23 84 59
⌇ 18 L 5807 m Par 71
👥 U
££ €32 (€58)
🚗 7km N of Lannion on Tregastel road
🏠 Hawtree

For list of abbreviations and key to symbols see page 649

Sauzon   (1987)

Les Poulins, 56360 Belle-Ile-en-Mer
- ☎ 02 97 31 64 65
- ⤷ 18 L 5820 m Par 72
- 👤 U
- ⛳ Island off S coast of Brittany, near Quiberon
- 🏠 Yves Bureau

Val Queven   (1990)

Kerruisseau, 56530 Queven
- ☎ 02 97 05 17 96
- 02 97 05 19 18
- ⤷ 18 L 6127 m SSS 72 SR 118
- 👤 U Sun–restricted
- ££ €30 – € 44
- ⛳ 10km W of Lorient
- 🏠 Yves Bureau
- ■ www.formule-golf.com

Burgundy & Auvergne

Beaune-Levernois   (1990)

21200 Levernois
- ☎ 03 80 24 10 29
- 🖳 03 80 24 03 78
- ⤷ 18 L 6129 m Par 72
   9 L 1316 m Par 29
- 👤 U
- ££ €31 (€40)
- ⛳ 5km SE of Beaune (D470/D111)
- 🏠 Christian Piot

Chalon-sur-Saône   (1976)

Parc de Saint Nicolas, 71380 Chatenoy-en-Bresse
- ☎ 03 85 93 49 65
- 🖳 03 85 93 56 95
- ⤷ 18 L 5859 m SSS 71
- 👤 U
- ££ €25
- ⛳ 3km SE of Chalon. 125km N of Lyon
- 🏠 Michel Rio
- ■ www.golf_chalon_sur_saone.com

Chambon-sur-Lignon   (1986)

Riondet, La Pierre de la Lune, 43400 Le Chambon-sur-Lignon
- ☎ 04 71 59 28 10
- 🖳 04 71 65 87 14
- ⤷ 18 L 6110 m Par 72
- 👤 U
- ££ On application
- ⛳ 60km NW of Saint Etienne. 120km NW of Lyon
- 🏠 Michel Gayon
- ■ www.golf-chambon.com

Château d'Avoise   (1992)

9 Rue de Mâcon, 71210 Montchanin
- ☎ 03 85 78 19 19
- 🖳 03 85 78 15 16
- ⤷ 18 L 6350 m Par 72
- 👤 WD–U WE–H
- ⛳ 25km W of Chalon
- 🏠 Martin Hawtree

Château de Chailly

Chailly-sur-Armançon, 21320 Pouilly-en-Auxois
- ☎ 03 80 90 30 40
- 🖳 03 80 90 30 05
- ⤷ 18 L 6146 m SSS 72
- 👤 U
- ⛳ 45km SW of Dijon
- 🏠 Sprecher/Watine

Château de la Salle   (1989)

71260 La Salle-Mâcon Nord
- ☎ 03 85 36 09 71
- 🖳 03 85 36 06 70
- ⤷ 18 L 6024 m SSS 72
- 👤 U
- ££ €29 (€36)
- ⛳ 12km NW of Mâcon. Lyon 70km
- 🏠 Robert Berthet

Le Coiroux   (1977)

19190 Aubazine
- ☎ 03 55 27 25 66
- 🖳 03 55 27 29 33
- ⤷ 18 L 5400 m Par 70
- 👤 U
- ⛳ 15km E of Brive
- 🏠 Hubert Chesneau

Dijon-Bourgogne   (1972)

Bois des Norges, 21490 Norges-la-Ville
- ☎ 03 80 35 71 10
- 🖳 03 80 35 79 27
- ⤷ 18 L 6179 m SSS 72
- 👤 U
- ££ €29 (€38)
- ⛳ 7km N of Dijon towards Langres
- 🏠 Fenn/Radcliffe

Domaine de Roncemay   (1989)

89110 Chassy
- ☎ 03 86 73 50 50
- 🖳 03 86 73 69 46
- ⤷ 18 L 6401 m Par 72 SSS 73
- 👤 H WE–restricted
- ££ €31 (€43)
- ⛳ 15km W of Auxerre
- 🏠 Jeremy Pern

La Fredière   (1988)

La Fredière, Céron, 71110 Marcigny
- ☎ 03 85 25 27 40
- 🖳 03 85 25 06 12
- ⤷ 18 L 4529 m SSS 68
- 👤 U
- ££ €23–27
- ⛳ 35km NW of Roanne
- 🏠 Gilles Charmat

La Jonchère

Montgrenier, 23230 Gouzon
- ☎ 05 55 62 23 05
- ⤷ 18 L 5858 m SSS 71
- 👤 U
- ⛳ 30km SW of Montluçon. 100km NE of Limoges
- 🏠 J-L Pega

Limoges-St Lazare   (1976)

Avenue du Golf, 87000 Limoges
- ☎ 05 55 28 30 02
- ⤷ 18 L 6238 m SSS 73
- 👤 U
- ⛳ 2km S of Limoges on RN20
- 🏠 Hubert Chesneau

Mâcon La Salle   (1989)

La Salle-Mâcon Nord, 71260 La Salle
- ☎ 03 85 36 09 71
- 🖳 03 85 36 06 70
- ⤷ 18 L 6024 m Par 71
- 👤 H or green card
- ££ €29 (€36)
- ⛳ 5km N of Mâcon (A6)
- 🏠 Robert Berthet
- ■ www.golfmacon.com

Le Nivernais

Le Bardonnay, 58470 Magny Cours
- ☎ 03 58 18 30
- 🖳 03 58 04 04
- ⤷ 18 L 5670 m Par 71
- 👤 U
- ⛳ 12km S of Nevers on N7. 50km N of Moulins
- 🏠 Alain Prat

La Porcelaine

Célicroux, 87350 Panazol
- ☎ 05 55 31 10 69
- 🖳 05 55 31 10 69
- ⤷ 18 L 6035 m SSS 72
- 👤 U
- ££ €35 – € 40
- ⛳ 6km NE of Limoges
- 🏠 Jean Garaialde

St Junien   (1997)

Les Jouberties, 87200 Saint Junien
- ☎ 05 55 02 96 96
- 🖳 05 55 02 32 52
- ⤷ 18 L 5677 m Par 72 SSS 69.9
   9 hole course
- 👤 U
- ££ €22 (€25)
- ⛳ 30km W of Limoges (N141)
- ■ www.golfdesaintjunien.com

Sporting Club de Vichy   (1907)

Allée Baugnies, 03700 Bellerive/Allier
- ☎ 04 70 32 39 11
- 🖳 04 70 32 00 54
- ⤷ 18 L 5463 m SSS 70
- 👤 H
- ⛳ In Vichy
- 🏠 Arnaud Massy

Val de Cher   (1975)

03190 Nassigny
- ☎ 04 70 06 71 15
- ⤷ 18 L 5450 m Par 70
- 👤 U
- ££ €31
- ⛳ 20km N of Montluçon on N144
- 🏠 Bourret/Vigand

Les Volcans (1984)

La Bruyère des Moines, 63870 Orcines
- ☎ 04 73 62 15 51
- 📠 04 73 62 26 52
- ⏶ 18 L 6286 m SSS 73
   9 L 1377 m SSS 29
- 👥 U H
- ££ €37 (€43)
- ⚅ 12km W of Clermont-Ferrand on RN41
- ⛳ Lucien Roux
- ■ www.golfdesvolcans.com

Centre

Les Aisses (1992)

RN20 Sud, 45240 La Ferté St Aubin
- ☎ 02 38 64 80 87
- 📠 02 38 64 80 85
- ⏶ 27 L 6200 m Par 72
- 👥 U
- ££ €48
- ⚅ 30km S of Orléans. 140km S of Paris
- ⛳ Olivier Brizon

Ardrée (1988)

37360 St Antoine-du-Rocher
- ☎ 02 47 56 77 38
- 📠 02 47 56 79 96
- ⏶ 18 L 5758 m Par 70
- 👥 U
- ⚅ 10km N of Tours
- ⛳ Olivier Brizon

Les Bordes (1987)

41220 Saint Laurent-Nouan
- ☎ 02 54 87 72 13
- 📠 02 54 87 78 61
- ⏶ 18 L 6412 m Par 72
- 👥 U
- ££ €80 (€105)
- ⚅ 30km SW of Orléans
- ⛳ Robert van Hagge
- ■ www.lesbordes.com

Château de Cheverny

La Rousselière, 41700 Cheverny
- ☎ 02 54 79 24 70
- 📠 02 54 79 25 52
- ⏶ 18 L 6276 m Par 71
- 👥 U
- ££ €40
- ⚅ 15km S of Blois. 200km SW of Paris, via A10
- ⛳ O Van der Vynckt
- ■ www.golf-cheverny.com

Château de Maintenon

(1988)
Route de Gallardon, 28130 Maintenon
- ☎ 02 37 27 18 09
- 📠 02 37 27 10 12
- ⏶ 18 L 6393 m SSS 74
   9 L 1541 m SSS 30
- 👥 WD–U WE–restricted
- ⚅ 20km W of Rambouillet (D906). 70km SW of Paris
- ⛳ Michel Gayon

Château des Forges (1991)

Domaine des Forges, 79340 Menigoute
- ☎ 05 49 69 91 77
- ⏶ 18 L 6400 m Par 74
   9 L 3200 m Par 37
- 👥 U
- ££ €29 (€35)
- ⚅ 30km W of Poitiers
- ⛳ Bjorn Eriksson

Château des Sept Tours

(1989)
Le Vivier des Landes, 37330 Courcelles de Touraine
- ☎ 02 47 24 69 75
- 📠 02 47 24 23 74
- ⏶ 18 L 6194 m Par 72
- 👥 U
- ££ €31 (€38)
- ⚅ 35km NW of Tours
- ⛳ Donald Harradine

Cognac (1987)

Saint-Brice, 16100 Cognac
- ☎ 05 45 32 18 17
- 📠 05 45 35 10 76
- ⏶ 18 L 6142 m SSS 72
- 👥 H
- ⚅ 5km E of Cognac
- ⛳ Jean Garaialde

Le Connétable (1987)

Parc Thermal, 86270 La Roche Posay
- ☎ 05 49 86 25 10
- 📠 05 49 19 48 40
- ⏶ 18 L 6014 m SSS 72
- ££ €23 (€27)
- ⚅ La Roche-Posay, 20km E of Châtellerault. 40km NE of Poitiers
- ⛳ J Garaialde

Domaine de Vaugouard

(1987)
Chemin des Bois, Fontenay-sur-Loing, 45210 Ferrières
- ☎ 02 38 95 81 52
- 📠 02 38 95 79 78
- ⏶ 18 L 5914 m SSS 72
- ££ €29 (€53)
- ⚅ 10km N of Montargis. 100km S of Paris
- ⛳ Fromanger/Adam

Les Dryades (1987)

36160 Pouligny-Notre-Dame
- ☎ 02 54 30 28 00
- 📠 02 54 30 10 24
- ⏶ 18 L 6120 m SSS 72
- 👥 U
- ££ €31 (€38)
- ⚅ 10km S of La Châtre (D940). 60km SW of Bourges
- ⛳ Michel Gayon

Ganay (1991)

Prieuré de Ganay, 41220 St Laurent-Nouan
- ☎ 02 54 87 26 24

- ☎ 02 54 87 72 50
- ⏶ 27 hole course
- 👥 U
- ££ €15 (€21)
- ⚅ 130km S of Paris
- ⛳ Jim Shirley

Haut-Poitou (1987)

86130 Saint-Cyr
- ☎ 05 49 62 53 62
- 📠 05 49 88 71 14
- ⏶ 18 L 6590 m SSS 75
   9 L 1800 m Par 31
- 👥 U
- ££ €29 (€33)
- ⚅ 20km N of Poitiers. 70km S of Tours
- ⛳ HG Baker

Loudun-Roiffe (1985)

Domaine St Hilaire, 86120 Roiffe
- ☎ 05 49 98 78 06
- 📠 05 49 98 72 57
- ⏶ 18 L 6343 m Par 72
- 👥 U
- ££ €23 – € 35
- ⚅ 18km N of Loudun. 15km S of Saumur
- ⛳ Hubert Chesneau
- ■ www.golf-loudun.com

Marcilly (1986)

Domaine de la Plaine, 45240 Marcilly-en-Villette
- ☎ 02 38 76 11 73
- 📠 02 38 76 18 73
- ⏶ 18 L 6324 m SSS 73
   9 hole course
- 👥 U
- ££ €24 (€32)
- ⚅ 20km SE of Orléans
- ⛳ Olivier Brizon

Mazières (1987)

Le Petit Chêne, 79310 Mazières-en-Gâtine
- ☎ 05 49 63 20 95
- 📠 05 49 63 33 75
- ⏶ 18 L 6060 m SSS 72
- 👥 U
- ££ €25 (€33)
- ⚅ 15km SW of Parthenay. 25km NE of Niort
- ⛳ Robert Berthet

Mignaloux Beauvoir

Domaine de Beauvoir, 86550 Mignaloux Beauvoir
- ☎ 05 49 46 70 27
- 📠 05 49 55 31 95
- ⏶ 18 L 6032 m SSS 71
- 👥 WD–U WE–H
- ££ €26 – €31
- ⚅ 6km SE of Poitiers (RN147)
- ⛳ Olivier Brizon

Niort

Chemin du Grand Ormeau, 79000 Niort Romagne
- ☎ 05 49 09 01 41

☐ 05 49 73 41 53
🏳 18 L 5865 m Par 71
⚫ U
£€ €27 (€35)
🚗 80km W of Poitiers

Orléans Val de Loire
Château de la Touche, 45450 Donnery
☎ 02 38 59 25 15
☐ 02 38 57 01 98
🏳 18 L 5771 m SSS 71
⚫ U
🚗 16km E of Orléans
🏠 Trent Jones/Van der Vinckt

Golf du Perche (1987)
La Vallée des Aulnes, 28400 Souancé au Perche
☎ 02 37 29 17 33
☐ 02 37 29 12 88
🏳 18 L 6073 m Par 72
⚫ U
£€ €27 (€38)
🚗 60km SW of Chartres (D9). 130km SW of Paris
🏠 Laurent Heckly

La Picardière
Chemin de la Picardière, 18100 Vierzon
☎ 02 48 75 21 43
☐ 02 48 71 87 61
🏳 18 L 6077 m Par 72
⚫ U
£€ €29 (€34)
🚗 75km S of Orléans, off A71
🏠 JL Pega

La Prée-La Rochelle (1990)
Marsilly, 17137 Nieul-sur-Mer
☎ 05 46 01 24 42
☐ 05 46 01 25 84
🏳 18 L 6012 m SSS 72
⚫ U
£€ €24–38
🚗 6km N of La Rochelle
🏠 Olivier Brizon
🖥 www.golflarochelle.com

Royan (1977)
Maine-Gaudin, 17420 Saint-Palais
☎ 05 46 23 16 24
☐ 05 46 23 23 38
🏳 18 L 5970 m SSS 71
6 hole short course
⚫ U
£€ €25 – € 45
🚗 Saint-Palais, 7km W of Royan
🏠 Robert Berthet

Saintonge (1953)
Fontcouverte, 17100 Saintes
☎ 05 46 74 27 61
☐ 05 46 92 17 92
🏳 18 L 4971 m Par 68 SR 130
⚫ H
£€ €23 – € 32.50
🚗 2km NE of Saintes
🏠 Hervé Bertrand

Sancerrois (1989)
St Thibault, 18300 Sancerre
☎ 02 48 54 11 22
☐ 02 48 54 28 03
🏳 18 L 5820 m SSS 71
⚫ U
£€ €20 – € 30 (€28 – € 36)
🚗 45km NE of Bourges
🏠 Didier Fruchet
🖥 www.sancerre.net/golf

Sologne (1955)
Route de Jouy-le-Potier, 45240 La Ferté St Aubin
☎ 02 38 76 57 33
☐ 02 38 76 68 79
🏳 18 L 6400 yds SSS 72
⚫ U
£€ €17–18 (€20–26)
🚗 25km S of Orléans on RN20/D18. La Ferté St Aubin 4km

Sully-sur-Loire (1965)
L'Ousseau, 45600 Viglain
☎ 02 38 36 52 08
🏳 18 L 6154 m Par 72
9 L 3155 m Par 36
🚗 3km SW of Sully-sur-Loire

Touraine (1971)
Château de la Touche, 37510 Ballan-Miré
☎ 02 47 53 20 28
☐ 02 47 53 31 54
🏳 18 L 5671 m SSS 71
⚫ WE–H
£€ D – € 35 (D – € 46)
🚗 Ballan-Miré, 10km SW of Tours
🏠 Michael Fenn

Val de l'Indre (1989)
Villedieu-sur-Indre, 36320 Tregonce
☎ 02 54 26 59 44
☐ 02 54 26 06 37
🏳 18 L 6250 m SSS 72
⚫ U
£€ €27 (€35)
🚗 12km NW of Chateauroux. 80km SE of Tours on RN 143
🏠 Yves Bureau

Channel Coast & North

Abbeville (1989)
Route du Val, 80132 Grand-Laviers
☎ 03 22 24 98 58
☐ 03 22 24 49 61
🏳 18 L 6080 m Par 73
⚫ U
£€ €23 (€27)
🚗 3km NW of Abbeville
🏠 Didier Fruchet

L'Ailette
02000 Laon
☎ 23 24 83 99

☐ 23 24 84 66
🏳 18 L 6127 m Par 72
9 hole short course
⚫ WD–H WE–H restricted
£€ €28 (€37)
🚗 13km S of Laon. 45km NW of Reims
🏠 Michel Gayon

Amiens (1925)
80115 Querrieu
☎ 03 22 93 04 26
☐ 03 22 93 04 61
🏳 18 L 6114 m SSS 72
⚫ U
£€ €22–30 (€32–40)
🚗 7km NE of Amiens (D929)
🏠 Ross/Pennink

Apremont (1992)
60300 Apremont
☎ 03 44 25 61 11
☐ 03 44 25 11 72
🏳 18 L 6395 m SSS 73 SR 134
⚫ H
£€ €40 (€75)
🚗 45km N of Paris
🏠 John Jacobs
🖥 www.apremont-golf.com

Arras (1989)
Rue Briquet Taillandier, 62223 Anzin-St-Aubin
☎ 03 21 50 24 24
☐ 03 21 50 29 71
🏳 18 L 6150 m SSS 72
9 L 1550 m SSS 30
⚫ U
£€ €33 (€45)
🚗 50km S of Lille. 110km SE of Calais
🏠 JC Cornillot
🖥 www.arras-golfclub.com

Belle Dune
Promenade de Marquenterre, 80790 Fort-Mahon-Plage
☎ 03 22 23 45 50
☐ 03 22 23 93 41
🏳 18 L 5909 m Par 72 SSS 71
⚫ H or Green card
🚗 25km S of Le Touquet on coast
🏠 JM Rossi

Blue Green-Chantilly (1991)
Route d'Apremont, 60500 Vineuil St-Firmin
☎ 03 44 58 47 74
☐ 03 44 58 50 28
🏳 18 L 6209 m SSS 72
⚫ U
£€ €23–44
🚗 40km N of Paris (A1)
🏠 Huau/Nelson

Bois de Ruminghem (1991)
1613 Rue St Antoine, 62370 Ruminghem
☎ 03 21 85 30 33
☐ 03 21 36 38 38
🏳 18 L 6115 m Par 73

ⓦ U
£€ €38 (€38)
⊶ 20km NE of Calais
⌖ Bill Baker

Bondues (1968)
Château de la Vigne, BP 54, 59587 Bondues Cedex
☎ 03 20 23 20 62
▭ 03 20 23 24 11
▷ 18 L 6163 m SSS 73 SR 130
    18 L 6009 m SSS 72 SR 127
ⓦ H–max 30. Closed Tues
£€ €48 (€72)
⊶ 10km NE of Lille
⌖ Hawtree/Trent Jones

Brigode (1970)
36 Avenue de Golf, 59650 Villeneuve D'Ascq
☎ 03 20 91 17 86
▭ 03 20 05 96 36
▷ 18 L 6182 m SSS 72
ⓦ WD–H
⊶ 8km NE of Lille
⌖ HJ Baker

Champagne (1986)
02130 Villers-Agron
☎ 03 23 71 62 08
▭ 03 23 71 50 40
▷ 18 L 5760 m SSS 72
ⓦ U
£€ €30 (€40)
⊶ 25km SW of Reims, via E50
⌖ JC Cornillot
■ www.golf-de-champagne.com

Chantilly (1909)
Allée de la Ménagerie, 60500 Chantilly
☎ 03 44 57 04 43
▭ 03 44 57 26 54
▷ Vineuil 18 L 6597 m SSS 71
    Longeres 18 L 6378 m SSS 72
ⓦ WE–NA
£€ WD – € 61
⊶ 45km N of Paris
⌖ Tom Simpson

Château d'Humières (1990)
Château d'Humières, 60113 Monchy-Humières
☎ 03 44 42 39 51
▭ 03 44 42 48 92
▷ 18 L 6176 m SSS 73
ⓦ U
£€ €27 (€41)
⊶ 80km N of Paris. A1 Junction 11

Château de Raray
4 Rue Nicolas de Lancy, 60810 Raray
☎ 03 44 54 70 61
▭ 03 44 54 74 97
▷ 18 L 6455 m Par 72
    9 L 2921 m Par 35
ⓦ H
£€ €23–34 (€38–53)
⊶ 60km N of Paris (A1)
⌖ Patrick Leglise

Chaumont-en-Vexin (1963)
Château de Bertichère, 60240 Chaumont-en-Vexin
☎ 03 44 49 00 81
▭ 03 44 49 32 71
▷ 18 L 6195 m SSS 72
ⓦ H
£€ €23 (€46)
⊶ 65km NW of Paris
⌖ Donald Harradine

Compiègne (1896)
Ave Royale, 60200 Compiègne
☎ 03 44 38 48 00
▭ 03 44 40 23 59
▷ 18 L 6015 m Par 71
ⓦ U
£€ €23 (€38)
⊶ 80km NE of Paris
⌖ W Freemantel

Deauville l'Amiraute (1992)
CD 278, Tourgéville, 14800 Deauville
☎ 02 31 14 42 00
▭ 02 31 88 32 00
▷ 18 L 6055 m Par 73
ⓦ U
£€ €43–61 (€53–64)
⊶ 4km S of Deauville
⌖ Bill Baker
■ www.amiraute-resort.com

Domaine du Tilleul (1984)
Landouzy-la-Ville, 02140 Vervins
☎ 03 23 98 48 00
▭ 03 23 98 46 46
▷ 18 L 5203 m SSS 71
ⓦ Groups 10+ welcome
£€ €15–23 (€23–27)
⊶ 7km S of Hirson. 65km N of Reims

Dunkerque (1991)
Fort Vallières, Coudekerque-Village, 59380 Bergues
☎ 03 28 61 07 43
▭ 03 28 60 05 93
▷ 18 L 5710 m Par 71
£€ €21 (€27)
⊶ 5km E of Dunkerque
⌖ Robert Berthet

Hardelot Dunes Course (1991)
Ave du Golf, 62152 Hardelot
☎ 03 21 83 73 10
▭ 03 21 83 24 33
▷ 18 L 5713 m SSS 72
ⓦ U H
£€ €37 – € 61 (€49 – € 89)
⊶ 15km S of Boulogne
⌖ JP Cornillot

Hardelot Pins Course
Ave du Golf, 62152 Hardelot
☎ 03 21 83 73 10
▭ 03 21 83 24 33
▷ 18 L 5926 m SSS 73
ⓦ U
£€ €37–46 (€55 D – € 84)

⊶ 15km S of Boulogne
⌖ Tom Simpson (1931)

International Club du Lys (1929)
Rond-Point du Grand Cerf, 60260 Lamorlaye
☎ 03 44 21 26 00
▭ 03 44 21 35 52
▷ 18 L 6022 m Par 71
    18 L 4770 m Par 66
ⓦ WD–H WE–H (booking necessary)
£€ WD – € 46
⊶ 5km S of Chantilly. 40km N of Paris
⌖ Tom Simpson
■ www.golf-lys-chantilly.com

Morfontaine (1907)
60128 Mortefontaine
☎ 03 44 54 68 27
▭ 03 44 54 60 57
▷ 18 L 5803 m SSS 70.9
    9 L 2526 m Par 36
ⓦ Members' guests only
£€ NA
⊶ 10km S of Senlis. N of Paris
⌖ Tom Simpson

Mormal (1991)
Bois St Pierre, 59144 Preux-au-Sart
☎ 03 27 63 07 00
▭ 03 27 39 93 62
▷ 18 L 6022 m Par 72
ⓦ H
£€ €28 (€38)
⊶ 15km E of Valenciennes, off RN49
⌖ JC Cornillot
■ www.golf-mormal.com

Nampont-St-Martin (1978)
Maison Forte, 80120 Nampont-St-Martin
☎ 03 22 29 92 90/03 22 29 89 87
▭ 03 22 29 97 54
▷ Cygnes 18 L 6051 m SSS 72
    Belvédère 18 L 5145 m SSS 72
ⓦ U
£€ €20–23 (€31–37)
⊶ 50km S of Boulogne. Motorway A16 Junction 25
⌖ Thomas Chatterton

Pelves (1991)
Chemin de l'Enfer, 62118 Pelves
☎ 03 21 58 95 42
▭ 03 21 24 00 04
▷ 18 L 5958 m SSS 72
ⓦ U
⊶ 40km S of Lille. 180km N of Paris
⌖ Ogama

Rebetz (1988)
Route de Noailles, 60240 Chaumont-en-Vexin
☎ 03 44 49 15 54
▭ 03 44 49 14 26
▷ 18 L 6409 m SSS 73
ⓦ H
£€ €23 (€53)
⊶ Chaumont-en-Vexin, 65km NW of Paris, via D43

🏠 J-P Fourès
■ www.rebetz.com

Saint-Omer
Chemin des Bois, Acquin-Westbécourt,
62380 Lumbres
☎ 03 21 38 59 90
📠 03 21 93 02 47
▷ 18 L 6294 m Par 73
    9 L 2038 m Par 31
👥 U
💶 €26–40 (€34–49)
🚗 10km W of Saint-Omer. 40km S of
    Calais
🏠 J Dudok van Heel

Le Sart   (1910)
5 Rue Jean-Jaurès, 59650
Villeneuve D'Ascq
☎ 03 20 72 02 51
📠 03 20 98 73 28
▷ 18 L 5721 m SSS 71
👥 H
💶 €38 (€46 D – € 76)
🚗 5km E of Lille. Motorway Lille-
    Gand Junction 9 (Breucq-Le Sart)
🏠 Allan Macbeth

Thumeries   (1935)
Bois Lenglart, 59239 Thumeries
☎ 03 20 86 58 98
📠 03 20 86 52 66
▷ 18 L 5933 m SSS 72
👥 U
💶 €27 (€38)
🚗 10km N of Douai. 15km S of Lille
🏠 Boomer/Rossi

Le Touquet 'La Forêt'   (1904)
Ave du Golf, BP 41, 62520 Le Touquet
☎ 03 21 06 28 00
📠 03 21 06 28 01
▷ 18 L 5659 m SSS 70 SR 123
👥 U H
💶 €46 (€56)
🚗 2km S of Le Touquet. 30km S of
    Boulogne
🏠 H Hutchinson
■ www.opengolfclub.com

Le Touquet 'La Mer'   (1930)
Ave du Golf, BP 41, 62520 Le Touquet
☎ 03 21 06 28 00
📠 03 21 06 28 01
▷ 18 L 6275 m CR 74.9 SR 131
👥 U H
💶 €52 (€62)
🚗 As 'La Forêt'
🏠 HS Colt

Le Touquet 'Le Manoir'
(1994)
Ave du Golf, BP 41, 62520 Le Touquet
☎ 03 21 06 28 00
📠 03 21 06 28 01
▷ 9 L 2817 m Par 35 SR 118
👥 U
💶 €31 (€37)
🚗 As 'La Forêt'
🏠 HJ Baker

Val Secret   (1984)
Brasles, 02400 Château Thierry
☎ 03 23 83 07 25
📠 03 23 83 92 73
▷ 18 L 5540 m Par 70 SR 129
👥 U
💶 €25 (€40)
🚗 58km W of Reims via A4. Paris
    89km
■ www.valsecret.com

Vert Parc   (1991)
3 Route d'Ecuelles, 59480 Illies
☎ 03 20 29 37 87
📠 03 20 49 76 39
▷ 18 L 6328 m SSS 73
👥 U
🚗 18km SW of Lille
🏠 Patrice Simon

Wimereux   (1901)
Route d'Ambleteuse, 62930 Wimereux
☎ 03 21 32 43 20
📠 03 21 33 62 21
▷ 18 L 6150 m Par 72
👥 U
💶 €25 – € 40 (€35 – € 50)
🚗 6km N of Boulogne on D940. 30km
    S of Calais
🏠 Campbell/Hutchinson

Corsica

Spérone   (1990)
Domaine de Spérone, 20169 Bonifacio
☎ 04 95 73 17 13
📠 04 95 73 17 85
▷ 18 L 6106 m SSS 73
👥 H–max 28
💶 €50–75 W – € 230–435
🚗 S point of Corsica, SE of Bonifacio.
    25km S of Airport
🏠 Robert Trent Jones Sr

Ile de France

Ableiges   (1989)
95450 Ableiges
☎ 01 30 27 97 00
📠 01 30 27 97 10
▷ 18 L 6261 m Par 72
    9 L 2137 m Par 33
👥 18 holes:U H (max 30)
💶 18 holes: €23 (€38) 9 holes: €18
    (€23)
🚗 40km NW of Paris, nr Cergy
    Pontoise
🏠 Pern/Garaialde

Bellefontaine   (1987)
95270 Bellefontaine
☎ 01 34 71 05 02
📠 01 34 71 90 90
▷ 27 holes:
    6098-6306 m Par 72
👥 U

💶 €31 (€53)
🚗 27km N of Paris
🏠 Michel Gayon

Bondoufle   (1990)
Departmentale 31, 91070 Bondoufle
☎ 01 60 86 41 71
📠 01 60 86 41 56
▷ 18 L 6161 m SSS 73
👥 U H
🚗 30km S of Paris
🏠 Michel Gayon

Bussy-St-Georges   (1988)
Promenade des Golfeurs, 77600 Bussy-
St-Georges
☎ 01 64 66 00 00
📠 01 64 66 22 92
▷ 18 L 5890 m SSS 72
👥 U
💶 On application
🚗 20km E of Paris. Motorway A4
    Junction 12
🏠 Rolin/Cornillot

Cély   (1990)
Le Château, Route de Saint-Germain,
77930 Cély-en-Bière
☎ 01 64 38 03 07
📠 01 64 38 08 78
▷ 18 L 5874 m SSS 72
👥 U
💶 €34 (€53)
🚗 Fontainebleau 15km
🏠 Adam/Fromanger
■ www.celygolf.com

Cergy Pontoise   (1988)
2 Allee de l'Obstacle d'Eau,
95490 Vaureal
☎ 01 34 21 03 48
📠 01 34 21 03 34
▷ 18 L 6100 m SSS 72
👥 WD–U WE–U H
🚗 30km NW of Paris. A15 Junction
    12
🏠 Michel Gayon

Chevannes-Mennecy   (1994)
91750 Chevannes
☎ 01 64 99 88 74
📠 01 64 99 88 67
▷ 18 L 6307 m Par 72
👥 U
💶 €18 (€31)
🚗 45km S of Paris
🏠 A d'Ormesson

Clement Ader   (1990)
Domaine Château Pereire, 77220 Gretz
☎ 01 64 07 34 10
📠 01 64 07 82 10
▷ 18 L 6350 m CR 73.9 SR 145
👥 U
💶 On application
🚗 30km SE of Paris
🏠 Saito/Gayon
■ www.golfclementader.com

Coudray (1960)

Ave du Coudray, 91830 Le Coudray-Montceaux
- ☎ **01 64 93 81 76**
- 🖥 01 64 93 99 95
- ⤳ 18 L 5761 m Par 71
  9 L 1350 m Par 29
- 👥 II
- £€ €30 (€50)
- 🚗 35km S of Paris on A6 (Junction 11)
- ⌂ CK Cotton

Courson Monteloup (1991)

91680 Bruyères-le-Chatel
- ☎ **01 64 58 80 80**
- 🖥 01 64 58 83 06
- ⤳ 36 hole course:
  6171-6520 m SSS 72-75
- 👥 WD–U WE–M exc Jul/Aug
- £€ €38 (€61)
- 🚗 35km SW of Paris, off Route D3
- ⌂ Robert von Hagge
- ■ www.golf-stadefrancais.com

Crécy-la-Chapelle (1987)

Ferme de Monpichet, 77580 Crécy-la-Chapelle
- ☎ **01 64 04 70 75**
- ⤳ 18 L 6211 m SSS 72
- 👥 U
- 🚗 20km E of Paris by A4

Domaine de Belesbat (1989)

Courdimanche-sur-Essonne, 91820 Boutigny-sur-Essonne
- ☎ **01 69 23 19 10**
- 🖥 01 69 23 19 01
- ⤳ 18 L 6033 m SSS 72 SR 132
- 👥 H–Booking required
- £€ €50 (€100)
- 🚗 50km S of Paris, between Etampes and Fontainebleau
- ⌂ Fromanger/Adam
- ■ www.belesbat.com

Domont-Montmorency

Route de Montmorency, 95330 Domont
- ☎ **01 39 91 07 50**
- 🖥 01 39 91 25 70
- ⤳ 18 L 5775 m SSS 71
- 👥 H
- £€ €38 (€73)
- 🚗 18km N of Paris
- ⌂ Hawtree

Étiolles (1990)

Vieux Chemin de Paris, 91450 Étiolles
- ☎ **01 69 89 59 59**
- 🖥 01 69 89 59 60
- ⤳ 18 L 6239 m Par 74
  9 L 2665 m SSS 36
- 👥 U
- £€ €42 (€62.50)
- 🚗 30km S of Paris
- ⌂ Michel Gayon

Fontainebleau (1909)

Route d'Orleans, 77300 Fontainebleau
- ☎ **01 64 22 22 95**
- 🖥 01 64 22 63 76
- ⤳ 18 L 6074 m SSS 72
- 👥 WD–U WE–Jul/Aug only
- £€ WD – € 53
- 🚗 1km SW of Fontainebleau. 60km SE of Paris
- ⌂ Simpson/M Hawtree

Fontenailles (1991)

Domaine de Bois Boudran, 77370 Fontenailles
- ☎ **01 64 60 51 00**
- 🖥 01 60 67 52 12
- ⤳ 18 L 6256 m SSS 74
  9 L 2870 m
- 👥 WD–U WE–H
- £€ €27–31 (€49–69)
- 🚗 60km SE of Paris
- ⌂ Michel Gayon

Forges-les-Bains (1989)

Rue du Général Leclerc, 91470 Forges-les-Bains
- ☎ **01 64 91 48 18**
- 🖥 01 64 91 40 52
- ⤳ 18 L 6167 m SSS 72
- 👥 H or Green card
- £€ €30 (€50)
- 🚗 35km S of Paris, off A10
- ⌂ JM Rossi
- ■ www.golf-forgelesbains.com

La Forteresse (1989)

Domaine de la Forteresse, 77940 Thoury-Ferrottes
- ☎ **01 60 96 95 10**
- 🖥 01 60 96 01 41
- ⤳ 18 L 5888 m Par 72
- 👥 H or Green card
- £€ €29 (€53)
- 🚗 25km SE of Fontainebleau
- ⌂ Fromanger/Adam
- ■ www.golf-forteresse.com

Greenparc (1993)

Route de Villepech, 91280 St Pierre-du-Perray
- ☎ **01 60 75 40 60**
- 🖥 01 60 75 40 04
- ⤳ 18 L 5839 m SSS 71
- 👥 U
- £€ €18 (€38)
- 🚗 30km SW of Paris
- ⌂ Robin Nelson

L'Isle Adam (1995)

1 Chemin des Vanneaux, 95290 L'Isle Adam
- ☎ **01 34 08 11 11**
- 🖥 01 34 08 11 19
- ⤳ 18 L 6230 m Par 72
- 👥 U
- £€ €23—38 (€42–57)
- 🚗 30km N of Paris
- ⌂ Ronald Fream

Marivaux (1992)

Bois de Marivaux, 91640 Janvry
- ☎ **01 64 90 85 85**
- 🖥 01 64 90 82 22
- ⤳ 18 L 6116 m Par 72
- 👥 U H–max 36
- £€ €23–27 (€38–53)
- 🚗 25km SW of Paris
- ⌂ Macauley/Quenouille

Meaux-Boutigny (1985)

Rue de Barrois, 77470 Boutigny
- ☎ **01 60 25 63 98**
- 🖥 01 60 25 60 58
- ⤳ 18 L 5981 m SSS 72
  9 L 1499 m SSS 30
- 👥 U
- £€ €27 (€46)
- 🚗 45km E of Paris-Highway 4
- ⌂ Michel Gayon

Mont Griffon

RD 909, 95270 Luzarches
- ☎ **01 34 68 10 10**
- 🖥 01 34 68 04 10
- ⤳ 18 L 5897 m CR 70.8
- 👥 U
- £€ €34 (€54)
- 🚗 27km N of Paris, nr Chantilly
- ⌂ Nelson/Huau/Dongradi
- ■ www.golfhotelparis.com

Ormesson (1969)

Chemin du Belvedère, 94490 Ormesson-sur-Marne
- ☎ **01 45 76 20 71**
- 🖥 01 45 94 86 85
- ⤳ 18 L 6130 m SSS 72
- 👥 H
- £€ €31 (€53)
- 🚗 21km SE of Paris
- ⌂ Harris/CK Cotton

Ozoir-la-Ferrière (1926)

Château des Agneaux, 77330 Ozoir-la-Ferrière
- ☎ **01 60 02 60 79**
- 🖥 01 64 40 28 20
- ⤳ 18 L 5859 m Par 71
  9 L 2700 m Par 35
- 👥 U H
- £€ 18 holes: €32 (€61) 9 holes: €21 (€31)
- 🚗 25km SE of Paris via A4 (Porte de Bercy)
- ⌂ Sir Henry Cotton

Paris International (1991)

18 Route du Golf, 95560 Baillet-en-France
- ☎ **01 34 69 90 00**
- 🖥 01 34 69 97 15
- ⤳ 18 L 6319 m SSS 74
- 👥 Members and guests only
- £€ NA
- 🚗 24km NW of Paris
- ⌂ Jack Nicklaus

St Aubin   (1976)
Route du Golf, 91190 St Aubin
- ☎ **01 69 41 25 19**
- 🖥 01 69 41 02 25
- ⮃ 18 L 5971 m SSS 71
    9 L 1918 m SSS 31
- 👥 U
- ⛳ 30km SW of Paris
- 🏠 Berthet/Rio

St Germain-les-Corbeil
6 Ave du Golf, 91250 St Germain-les-Corbeil
- ☎ **01 60 75 81 54**
- 🖥 01 60 75 52 89
- ⮃ 18 L 5800 m SSS 71
- ⛳ 30km S of Paris

St Pierre du Perray   (1974)
Melun-Sénart, St Pierre du Perray, 91100 Corbeil
- ☎ **01 60 75 17 47**
- 🖥 01 69 89 00 73
- ⮃ 18 L 6169 m SSS 72
- 👥 U
- £€ £15 (£28)
- ⛳ 30km SE of Paris, off N6
- 🏠 Hubert Chesneau

Seraincourt   (1964)
Gaillonnet-Seraincourt, 95450 Vigny
- ☎ **01 34 75 47 28**
- 🖥 01 34 75 75 47
- ⮃ 18 L 5760 m SSS 70
- 👥 WD–U WE–H
- ⛳ 35km NW of Paris

Villarceaux   (1971)
Château du Couvent, 95710 Chaussy
- ☎ **01 34 67 73 83**
- 🖥 01 34 67 72 66
- ⮃ 18 L 6059 m Par 72
- 👥 H
- £€ €34 (€53)
- ⛳ 60km NW of Paris
- 🏠 M Backer

Languedoc-Roussillon

Cap d'Agde   (1989)
4 Ave des Alizés, 34300 Cap d'Agde
- ☎ **04 67 26 54 40**
- 🖥 04 67 26 97 00
- ⮃ 18 L 6160 m SSS 72
- 👥 U
- ⛳ 25km E of Béziers
- 🏠 Ronald Fream

Carcassonne   (1988)
Route de Ste-Hilaire, 11000 Carcassonne
- ☎ **06 13 20 85 43**
- 🖥 04 68 72 57 30
- ⮃ 18 L 5758 m Par 71
- 👥 U
- £€ €27 (€34)

- ⛳ 2km SW of Carcassonne
- 🏠 J-P Basurco

Coulondres   (1984)
72 Rue des Erables, 34980 Saint-Gely-du-Fesc
- ☎ **04 67 84 13 75**
- 🖥 04 67 84 06 33
- ⮃ 18 L 6175 m SSS 73
- 👥 U
- £€ €23 (€31)
- ⛳ 10km N of Montpellier towards Ganges
- 🏠 Donald Harradine
- 🖥 www.coulondres.com

Domaine de Falgos   (1992)
BP 9, 66260 St Laurent-de-Cerdans
- ☎ **04 68 39 51 42**
- 🖥 04 68 39 52 30
- ⮃ 18 L 5044 m SSS 68
- 👥 U
- £€ €32
- ⛳ 60km S of Perpignan, nr Spanish border (D115)

Fontcaude   (1991)
Route de Lodève, Domaine de Fontcaude, 34990 Juvignac
- ☎ **04 67 45 90 10**
- 🖥 04 67 45 90 20
- ⮃ 18 L 6992 m SSS 72
    9 hole short course
- 👥 U
- £€ €38–46
- ⛳ 6km W of Montpellier
- 🏠 C Pitman

La Grande-Motte   (1987)
Clubhouse du Golf, 34280 La Grande-Motte
- ☎ **04 67 56 05 00**
- 🖥 04 67 29 18 84
- ⮃ 18 L 6161 m CR 73.3 SR 133
    18 L 3076 m Par 58
    6 hole short course
- 👥 U
- £€ €38 (€46)
- ⛳ 18km E of Montpellier
- 🏠 Robert Trent Jones Sr

Montpellier Massane   (1988)
Domaine de Massane, 34670 Baillargues
- ☎ **04 67 87 87 87**
- 🖥 04 67 87 87 90
- ⮃ 18 L 6231 m Par 72
    9 hole Par 3 course
- 👥 U
- £€ €40 (€48)
- ⛳ 9km E of Montpellier. A9 Junction 28
- 🏠 Ronald Fream

Nîmes Campagne   (1968)
Route de Saint Gilles, 30900 Nîmes
- ☎ **04 66 70 17 37**
- 🖥 04 66 70 03 14
- ⮃ 18 L 6135 m SSS 72
- 👥 H
- £€ €38 (€46)

- ⛳ 7km S of Nîmes, by Airport
- 🏠 Morandi/Harradine

Nîmes-Vacquerolles   (1990)
Route de Sauve, 30900 Nîmes
- ☎ **04 66 23 33 33**
- 🖥 04 66 23 94 94
- ⮃ 18 L 6300 m SSS 72
- 👥 U
- £€ €28–40 (€37–40)
- ⛳ W of Nîmes centre (D999)
- 🏠 W Baker

St Cyprien   (1974)
Le Mas D'Huston, 66750 St Cyprien Plage
- ☎ **04 68 37 63 63**
- 🖥 04 68 37 64 64
- ⮃ 18 L 6480 m SSS 73
    9 L 2724 m SSS 35
- 👥 U H
- £€ €32 (€41)
- ⛳ 15km SE of Perpignan
- 🏠 Wright/Tomlinson

St Thomas   (1992)
Route de Bessan, 34500 Béziers
- ☎ **04 67 39 03 09**
- 🖥 04 67 39 10 65
- ⮃ 18 L 6130 m Par 72
- 👥 U
- £€ On application
- ⛳ 7km NE of Béziers (RN 113)
- 🏠 Patrice Lambert

Loire Valley

Angers   (1963)
Moulin de Pistrait, 49320 St Jean des Mauvrets
- ☎ **02 41 91 96 56**
- ⮃ 18 L 5460 m Par 70
- £€ €26 (€34)
- ⛳ 14km SE of Angers. Right bank of Loire.

Anjou G&CC   (1990)
Route de Cheffes, 49330 Champigné
- ☎ **02 41 42 01 01**
- 🖥 02 41 42 04 37
- ⮃ 18 L 6227 m SSS 72
    6 hole short course
- 👥 U H
- £€ €29 (€34)
- ⛳ 23km N of Angers
- 🏠 F Hawtree
- 🖥 www.anjougolf.com

Avrillé   (1988)
Château de la Perrière, 49240 Avrillé
- ☎ **02 41 69 22 50**
- 🖥 02 41 34 44 60
- ⮃ 18 L 6116 m SSS 71
    9 hole Par 3 course
- 👥 U
- £€ €21 (€31)
- ⛳ 5km N of Angers
- 🏠 Robert Berthet

Baugé-Pontigné   (1994)
Route de Tours, 49150 Baugé
☎   **02 41 89 01 27**
▱   02 41 89 05 50
⊵   18 L 5558 m Par 72
⚲   U
££   €20 (€29)
⚘   45km E of Angers. 70km SW of Tours
⌂   M Prat

La Bretesche   (1967)
Domaine de la Bretesche, 44780 Missillac
☎   **02 51 76 86 86**
▱   02 40 88 36 28
⊵   18 L 6080 m SSS 72
⚲   U
££   €40 (€60)
⚘   8km NW of Pontchâteau, between Nantes and Vannes
⌂   Cotton/Baker

Cholet   (1989)
Allée du Chêne Landry, 49300 Cholet
☎   **02 41 71 05 01**
▱   02 41 56 06 94
⊵   18 L 5792 m Par 71
⚲   WD–U WE–H
⚘   2km N of Cholet. 52km SE of Nantes
⌂   Olivier Brizon

La Domangère
La Roche-sur-Yon, Route de la Rochelle, 85310 Nesmy
☎   **02 51 07 65 90**
▱   02 51 07 65 95
⊵   18 L 6480 m SSS 72 SR 143
⚲   U
££   €27.50 – € 41
⚘   6km S of La Roche-sur-Yon. 70km S of Nantes
⌂   Michel Gayon
▮   www.golfdomangere.free.fr

Epinay   (1991)
Boulevard de l'Epinay, 44470 Carquefou
☎   **02 40 52 73 74**
▱   02 40 52 73 20
⊵   18 L 5790 m SSS 71
⚲   U
££   €26 (€35)
⚘   NE of Nantes
⌂   M Hawtree

Fontenelles
Saint-Gilles-Croix-de-Vie, 85220 Aiguillon-sur-Vie
☎   **02 51 54 13 94**
▱   02 51 55 45 77
⊵   18 L 6185 m Par 72
⚲   U
££   €21–39
⚘   6km E of St-Gilles-Croix-de-Vie. 75km SW of Nantes
⌂   Yves Bureau

Ile d'Or   (1988)
BP 10, 49270 La Varenne
☎   **02 40 98 58 00**
▱   02 40 98 51 62
⊵   18 L 6292 m Par 72
    9 L 1217 m Par 27
⚲   U H
⚘   30km NE of Nantes
⌂   Michel Gayon

International Barriere-La Baule   (1976)
44117 Saint-André-des Eaux
☎   **02 40 60 46 18**
▱   02 40 60 41 41
⊵   18 L 6055 m Par 72 SSS 73
    18 L 6301 m Par 72 SSS 74
    9 L 2969 m Par 36
⚲   H
££   €38–56. 9 hole:€21–32
⚘   Avrillac, 3km NE of La Baule
⌂   Alliss/Thomas/Gayon
▮   www.lucienbarriere.com

Laval-Changé   (1972)
Le Jariel, 53000 Changé-les-Laval
☎   **02 43 53 16 03**
▱   02 43 49 35 15
⊵   18 L 6068 m Par 72 SSS 72
    9 L 3388 m
⚲   U
££   €27
⚘   5km N of Laval. 60km E of Rennes
⌂   JP Foures

Le Mans Mulsanne   (1961)
Route de Tours, 72230 Mulsanne
☎   **02 43 42 00 36**
▱   02 43 42 21 31
⊵   18 L 5821 m SSS 71
⚲   H
££   €31–55 (€37–61)
⚘   Mulsanne, 12km S of Le Mans

Nantes
44360 Vigneux de Bretagne
☎   **02 40 63 25 82**
▱   02 40 63 64 86
⊵   18 L 5940 m SSS 72
⚲   H
££   €26 (€38)
⚘   12km NW of Nantes
⌂   Frank Pennink

Nantes Erdre   (1990)
Chemin du Bout des Landes, 44300 Nantes
☎   **02 40 59 21 21**
▱   02 51 84 94 50
⊵   18 L 5876 m SSS 71
⚲   U
££   €26 (€34)
⚘   Nantes
⌂   Yves Bureau
▮   www.ngc-nantes.fr

Les Olonnes
Gazé, 85340 Olonne-sur-Mer
☎   **02 51 33 16 16**

▱   02 51 33 10 45
⊵   18 L 6109 m Par 72
⚲   U
££   €24 – € 37
⚘   3km N of Les Sables d'Olonne
⌂   Bruno Parpoil

Pornic   (1912)
49 Boulevard de l'Océan, Sainte-Marie/Mer, 44210 Pornic
☎   **02 40 82 06 69**
▱   02 40 82 80 65
⊵   18 L 6119 m Par 72
⚲   U
££   €23–38
⚘   1km E of Pornic. 30km S of La Baule
⌂   Michel Gayon

Port Bourgenay   (1990)
Avenue de la Mine, Port Bourgenay, 85440 Talmont-St-Hilaire
☎   **02 51 23 35 45**
▱   02 51 23 35 48
⊵   18 L 5800 m SSS 72
⚲   U
££   €17–41
⚘   10km SE of Sables d'Olonne. 100km S of Nantes
⌂   Pierre Thevenin

Sablé-Solesmes
Domaine de l'Outinière, Route de Pincé, 72300 Sablé-sur-Sarthe
☎   **02 43 95 28 78**
▱   02 43 92 39 05
⊵   27 holes SSS 72:
    Forêt 9 L 3197 m
    Rivière 9 L 2992 m
    Cascade 9 L 3069 m
⚲   U
££   €40–49
⚘   40km SW of Le Mans
⌂   Michel Gayon

St Jean-de-Monts   (1988)
Ave des Pays de la Loire, 85160 Saint Jean-de-Monts
☎   **02 51 58 82 73**
▱   02 51 59 18 32
⊵   18 L 5962 m SSS 72
⚲   U
⚘   60km SW of Nantes on coast

Sargé-Le-Mans   (1990)
Rue de Bonnétable, 72190 Sargé-les Le Mans
☎   **02 43 76 25 07**
▱   02 43 76 45 25
⊵   18 L 6054 m SSS 72
⚲   U
££   €21 (€31)
⚘   6km NE of Le Mans
⌂   Antoine d'Ormesson

Savenay   (1990)
44260 Savenay
☎   **02 40 56 88 05**
▱   02 40 56 89 04
⊵   18 L 6335 m Par 73
    9 L 1122 m Par 30

🖁 U
£€ €24 – € 36
⊶ 36km W of Nantes. 30km E of La
Baule
🏠 Michel Gayon

Normandy

Bellême-St-Martin (1988)
Les Sablons, 61130 Bellême
☎ 02 33 73 00 07
🖁 02 33 73 00 17
⌲ 18 L 6011 m SSS 72
🖑 U
£€ €26 (€38)
⊶ 40km NE of Le Mans
🏠 Eric Vialatel

Beuzeval-Houlgate (†1981)
Route de Gonneville, 14510 Houlgate
☎ 02 31 24 80 49
🖁 02 31 28 04 48
⌲ 18 L 5558 m SSS 72
🖑 U
£€ €20–37
⊶ 2km S of Houlgate. 15km SW of
Deauville
🏠 Alliss/Thomas

Cabourg-Le Home (1907)
*38 Av Président Réné Coty, Le Home
Varaville, 14390 Cabourg*
☎ 02 31 91 25 56
🖁 02 31 91 18 30
⌲ 18 L 5234 m SSS 68
🖑 H
£€ €20–40
⊶ 4km W of Cabourg
🏠 Jackson/Brizon

Caen (1990)
Le Vallon, 14112 Bieville-Beuville
☎ 02 31 94 72 09
🖁 02 31 47 45 30
⌲ 18 holes SSS 72 Par 72
9 hole course
🖑 U
⊶ 5km N of Caen (D60)
🏠 F Hawtree

Champ de Bataille
*Château du Champ de Bataille, 27110
Le Neubourg*
☎ 02 32 35 03 72
🖁 02 32 35 83 10
⌲ 18 L 6575 m SSS 72
🖑 U
⊶ 28km NW of Evreux. 45km SW of
Rouen
🏠 Nelson/Huau

Clécy (1988)
Manoir de Cantelou, 14570 Clécy
☎ 02 31 69 72 72
🖁 02 31 69 70 22
⌲ 18 L 5965 m Par 72
🖑 U
£€ €20–38

⊶ 30km S of Caen, via D562
🏠 W Baker

Coutainville (1925)
Ave du Golf, 50230 Agon-Coutainville
☎ 02 33 47 03 31
🖁 02 33 47 38 42
⌲ 18 L 5045 m SSS 68
🖑 H
£€ €31
⊶ 12km W of Coutances. 75km S of
Cherbourg

Dieppe-Pourville (1897)
51 Route de Pourville, 76200 Dieppe
☎ 02 35 84 25 05
🖁 02 35 84 97 11
⌲ 18 L 5780 m Par 70
🖑 U
£€ €25 – € 42 (€42 – € 45)
⊶ 2km W of Dieppe towards
Pourville
🏠 Willie Park Jr
🖳 www.golf-dieppe.com

Étretat (1908)
BP No 7, Route du Havre, 76790 Étretat
☎ 02 35 27 04 89
⌲ 18 L 5994 m SSS 72
🖑 H
⊶ 25km N of Le Havre. Étretat 1km
🏠 Chantepie/Fruchet

Forêt Verte
Bosc Guerard, 76710 Montville
☎ 02 35 33 62 94
⌲ 18 L 7000 yds SSS 72
🖑 U
⊶ 10km N of Rouen
🏠 Thierry Huau

Granville (1912)
Bréville, 50290 Bréhal
☎ 02 33 50 23 06
🖁 02 33 61 91 87
⌲ 18 L 5854 m Par 71
9 L 2323 m Par 33
🖑 U
£€ 18 holes: €24 (€35) 9 holes: €15
(€20)
⊶ 5km N of Granville
🏠 Colt/Allison/Hawtree

Le Havre (1933)
*Hameau Saint-Supplix, 76930 Octeville-
sur-Mer*
☎ 02 35 46 36 50
🖁 02 35 46 32 66
⌲ 18 L 5830 m SSS 70
🖑 H
⊶ 10km N of Le Havre

Léry Poses (1989)
BP 7, 27740 Poses
☎ 02 32 59 47 42
⌲ 18 L 6242 m SSS 73
9 hole Par 3 course
🖑 U
⊶ 25km SE of Rouen
🏠 J Baker

New Golf Deauville (1929)
14 Saint Arnoult, 14800 Deauville
☎ 02 31 14 24 24
🖁 02 31 14 24 25
⌲ 18 L 5933 m SSS 71
9 L 3033 m SSS 72
🖑 U–booking required
£€ €46–76
⊶ 3km S of Deauville
🏠 Simpson/Cotton

Omaha Beach (1986)
Ferme St Sauveur, 14520 Port-en-Bessin
☎ 02 31 22 12 12
🖁 02 31 22 12 13
⌲ 18 L 6216 m SSS 72
9 L 2693 m SSS 35
🖑 U H
£€ €24–43
⊶ 8km N of Bayeux
🏠 Yves Bureau
🖳 www.best-channel-golfs.com

Parc de Brotonne (1991)
Jumièges, 76480 Duclair
☎ 02 35 05 32 97
🖁 02 35 37 99 97
⌲ 18 L 6040 m SSS 72
🖑 U
£€ €19 (€28.50)
⊶ 20km W of Rouen
🏠 JP Fourès

Rouen-Mont St Aignan
(1911)
*Rue Francis Poulenc, 76130 Mont
St Aignan*
☎ 02 35 76 38 65
🖁 02 35 75 13 86
⌲ 18 L 5522 m SSS 70
🖑 H WE–H after 4pm
£€ €23 – € 30 (€30 – € 46)
⊶ 4km N of Rouen

St Gatien Deauville (1987)
14130 St Gatien-des-Bois
☎ 02 31 65 19 99
🖁 02 31 65 11 24
⌲ 18 L 6272 m Par 72
9 L 3035 m Par 36
🖑 U
£€ €31 (€46)
⊶ 8km E of Deauville
🏠 Olivier Brizon

St Saëns (1987)
Domaine du Vaudichon, 76680 St Saëns
☎ 02 35 34 25 24
🖁 02 35 34 43 33
⌲ 18 L 5791 m SSS 70
🖑 U
£€ €34 (€46)
⊶ 30km NE of Rouen
🏠 D Robinson
🖳 www.golfstsaens.com

St Julien
*St Julien-sur-Calonne, 14130 Pont-
l'Évêque*
☎ 02 31 64 30 30

☎ 02 31 64 12 43
╠ 18 L 6035 m SSS 72
9 L 2275 m SSS 64
👥 U
££ €21–29 (€31–38)
🚗 3km SE of Pont l'Évêque
🏠 Prat/Baker

Le Vaudreuil (1962)

27100 Le Vaudreuil
☎ 02 32 59 02 60
🖥 02 32 59 43 88
╠ 18 L 6320 m SSS 74
👥 H
££ €27 (€42)
🚗 6km NE of Louviers. 25km SE of Rouen
🏠 F Hawtree

North East

Ammerschwihr

BP 19, Route des Trois Épis,
68770 Ammerschwihr
☎ 03 89 47 17 30
🖥 03 89 47 17 77
╠ 18 L 5795 m Par 70
9 hole short course
👥 U
££ €31 (€38)
🚗 8km W of Colmar. 70km S of Strasbourg
🏠 Robert Berthet

Bâle G&CC (1926)

Rue de Wentzwiller, 68220 Hagenthal-le-Bas
☎ 03 89 68 50 91
🖥 03 89 68 55 66
╠ 18 L 6255 m Par 72 SSS 73
👥 WD–H (max 28) WE–M
££ €70
🚗 15km SW of Bâle
🏠 B von Limburger
🖳 www.swissgolfnetwork.ch

Besançon (1968)

La Chevillotte, 25620 Mamirolle
☎ 03 81 55 73 54
🖥 03 81 55 88 64
╠ 18 L 6070 m SSS 73
👥 H
££ €35 (€41)
🚗 12km E of Besançon
🏠 Michael Fenn
🖳 www.golfbesancon.com

Bitche (1988)

Rue des Prés, 57230 Bitche
☎ 03 87 96 15 30
🖥 03 87 96 08 04
╠ 18 L 6082 m SSS 72
9 L 2293 m SSS 34
👥 U
🚗 75km NW of Strasbourg. 55km SE of Saarbrücken
🏠 Fromanger

Châlons-en-Champagne (1988)

La Grande Romanie, 51460 Courtisols
☎ 06 61 50 01 00
🖥 03 26 66 65 97
╠ 18 L 6578 m SSS 76
👥 U
££ €31 – € 38
🚗 St Etienne-au-Temple, 6km from A4 Junction 28
🏠 Alain Tribout

Château de Bournel (1990)

25680 Cubry
☎ 03 81 86 00 10
🖥 03 81 86 01 06
╠ 18 L 5767 m Par 71 CR 71.6 SR 133
👥 H
££ €33 (€50)
🚗 50km NE of Besançon
🏠 Robert Berthet
🖳 www.bournel.com

Combles-en-Barrois (1948)

14 Rue Basse, 55000 Combles-en-Barrois
☎ 03 29 45 16 03
🖥 03 29 45 16 06
╠ 18 L 6100 m Par 72
👥 H
££ €27 (€31)
🚗 80km W of Nancy, nr Bar-le-Duc
🏠 Michel Gayon

Coteaux de Champagne (1986)

Chemin de Bourdonnerie, BP 41, 51700 Dormans
☎ 03 26 58 25 09
🖥 03 26 59 33 88
╠ 18 L 5969 m Par 72
👥 U
🚗 Dormans, 20km SW of Reims
🏠 Olivier Brizon

Épinal (1985)

Rue du Merle-Blanc, 88001 Épinal
☎ 03 29 34 65 97
╠ 18 L 5700 m SSS 70
👥 H
🚗 Épinal, 70km S of Nancy
🏠 Michel Gayon

Faulquemont-Pontpierre (1993)

Rue du Golf, 57380 Faulquemont
☎ 03 87 29 21 21
🖥 03 87 90 76 25
╠ 18 L 6000 m SSS 72
9 hole par 3 course
👥 U
🚗 30km E of Metz
🏠 Flipo/Fourès

Forêt d'Orient

BP13 Rouilly-Sacey, 10220 Piney
☎ 03 25 46 37 78

╠ 18 L 6120 m Par 72
👥 U
🚗 20km E of Troyes
🏠 E Rossi

La Grange aux Ormes

La Grange aux Ormes, 57155 Marly
☎ 03 87 63 10 62
🖥 03 87 55 01 77
╠ 18 L 6200 m Par 72
9 L 2001 m Par 31
👥 U
££ €26 – € 34 (€29 – € 44)
🚗 3km S of Metz
🏠 Philippe Gourdon
🖳 www.grange-aux-ormes.com

Kempferhof (1988)

351 Rue du Moulin, 67115 Plobsheim
☎ 03 88 98 72 72
🖥 03 88 98 74 76
╠ 18 L 6024 m SSS 73 SR 145
👥 H
££ €30 (€90)
🚗 10km S of Strasbourg
🏠 Robert von Hagge
🖳 www.golf-kempferhof.com

La Largue G&CC (1988)

Rue du Golf, 68580 Mooslargue
☎ 03 89 07 67 67
🖥 03 89 25 62 83
╠ 18 L 6162 m SSS 72
👥 WD–H WE–NA before noon H
££ €38 (€53)
🚗 25km W of Basle
🏠 Jean Garaialde

Metz Technopole

Rue Félix Savart, 57070 Metz Technopole 2000
☎ 03 87 39 95 95
╠ 18 L 5774 m SSS 71
6 hole Par 3 course
👥 H or Green card
🚗 SE of Metz centre
🏠 Robert Berthet

Metz-Cherisey (1963)

Château de Cherisey, 57420 Cherisey
☎ 03 87 52 70 18
🖥 03 87 52 42 44
╠ 18 L 6172 m SSS 72
👥 H
££ €31 (€38)
🚗 15km SE of Metz
🏠 Donald Harradine

Nancy-Aingeray (1962)

Aingeray, 54460 Liverdun
☎ 03 83 24 53 87
╠ 18 L 5577 m SSS 69
👥 H
££ €31 (€38)
🚗 17km NW of Nancy
🏠 Michael Fenn

Nancy-Pulnoy (1993)
10 Rue du Golf, 54425 Pulnoy
- ☎ **03 83 18 10 18**
- 🖥 03 83 18 10 19
- ⊳ 18 L 6000 m SSS 72
- 9 hole Par 3 course
- 👥 WD–U WE–H
- ££ €26 (€38)
- ⊕ 10km E of Nancy
- ⌂ Hawtree/Flipo

Prunevelle (1930)
Ferme des Petits-Bans,
25420 Dampierre-sur-le-Doubs
- ☎ **03 81 98 11 77**
- 🖥 03 81 90 28 65
- ⊳ 18 L 6281 m SSS 73
- ⊕ 10km S of Montbéliard, on D126

Reims-Champagne (1928)
Château des Dames de France,
51390 Gueux
- ☎ **03 26 05 46 10**
- 🖥 03 26 05 46 19
- ⊳ 18 L 6026 m SSS 72
- 👥 U
- ££ €31 (€43)
- ⊕ 10km W of Reims
- ⌂ Michael Fenn

Rhin Mulhouse (1969)
Ile du Rhin, 68490 Chalampe
- ☎ **03 89 83 28 32**
- 🖥 03 89 83 28 42
- ⊳ 18 L 5991 m SSS 72
- 👥 WE–M
- ££ €44 (€56)
- ⊕ 20km E of Mulhouse
- ⌂ Donald Harradine

Rochat (1986)
1305 Route du Noirmont, 39220
Les Rousses
- ☎ **03 84 60 06 25**
- 🖥 03 84 60 01 73
- ⊳ 18 L 5388 m Par 71
- 👥 U
- ££ €27 (€38)
- ⊕ 30km N of Geneva (N5)

Rougemont-le-Château
(1990)
Route de Masevaux, 90110 Rougemont-
le-Château
- ☎ **03 84 23 74 74**
- 🖥 03 84 23 03 15
- ⊳ 18 L 6002 m SSS 72
- 👥 U H
- ££ €37 (€49)
- ⊕ 18km NE of Belfort. 25km NW of Mulhouse
- ⌂ Robert Berthet

Strasbourg (1934)
Route du Rhin, 67400 Illkirch
- ☎ **03 88 66 17 22**
- 🖥 03 88 65 05 67
- ⊳ 27 holes:
  6105-6138 m SSS 72-73

- 👥 WD–H (max 35)
- ££ WD only – € 35
- ⊕ 10km S of Strasbourg
- ⌂ Donald Harradine

Troyes-Cordelière (1957)
Château de la Cordelière,
10210 Chaource
- ☎ **03 25 40 18 76**
- 🖥 03 25 40 13 66
- ⊳ 18 L 6154 m SSS 72
- 👥 H
- ££ €27 (€38)
- ⊕ NE of Chaource on N443. 30km SE of Troyes
- ⌂ P Hirigoyen

Val de Sorne
Domaine de Val de Sorne,
39570 Vernantois
- ☎ **03 84 43 04 80**
- 🖥 03 84 47 31 21
- ⊳ 18 L 6000 m SSS 72
- 👥 U
- ££ €31–43
- ⊕ 5km SE of Lons-le-Saunier, between Geneva and Lyon
- ⌂ Hugues Lambert
- 🖳 www.valdesorne.com

Vittel
BP 122, 88804 Vittel-Cedex
- ☎ **03 29 08 18 80**
- ⊳ St Jean 18 L 6326 m SSS 72
  Peulin 18 L 6100 m SSS 72
  9 hole course
- ⊕ Vittel, 70km S of Nancy
- ⌂ Allison/Morrison/Begin

La Wantzenau (1991)
C D 302, 67610 La Wantzenau
- ☎ **03 88 96 37 73**
- 🖥 03 88 96 34 71
- ⊳ 18 L 6400 m SSS 72
- 👥 H
- ££ €43 (€61)
- ⊕ 12km N of Strasbourg
- ⌂ Pern/Garaialde

Paris Region

Béthemont-Chisan CC
(1989)
12 Rue du Parc de Béthemont,
78300 Poissy
- ☎ **01 39 75 51 13**
- 🖥 01 39 75 49 90
- ⊳ 18 L 6035 m SSS 72
- 👥 U
- ££ €38 (€76)
- ⊕ 30km W of Paris
- ⌂ Bernhard Langer

La Boulie
La Boulie, 78000 Versailles
- ☎ **01 39 50 59 41**
- ⊳ 18 L 6055 m SSS 71
  18 L 6206 m SSS 72
  9 hole course

- 👥 H WE–M
- ⊕ 15km SW of Paris

Disneyland Paris (1992)
1 Allee de la Mare Houleuse,
77400 Magny-le-Hongre
- ☎ **01 60 45 68 90**
- 🖥 01 60 45 68 33
- ⊳ 18 L 6221 m Par 72
  9 L 2905 m Par 36
- 👥 U
- ££ On application
- ⊕ 32km E of Paris via A4
- ⌂ Ronald Fream

Feucherolles (1992)
78810 Feucherolles
- ☎ **01 30 54 94 94**
- 🖥 01 30 54 92 37
- ⊳ 18 L 6358 m Par 72
- 👥 U
- ££ €46–53 (€58–75)
- ⊕ 23km W of Paris
- ⌂ JM Poellot

Fourqueux (1963)
Rue Saint Nom 36, 78112 Fourqueux
- ☎ **01 34 51 41 47**
- 🖥 01 39 21 00 70
- ⊳ 18 L 5578 m CR 70.5 SR 132
  9 L 2564 m CR 67.2 SR 126
- 👥 WD–U WE–M
- ⊕ 4km SW of St Germain-en-Laye, W of Paris

Isabella (1969)
RN12, Sainte-Appoline, 78370 Plaisir
- ☎ **01 30 54 10 62**
- 🖥 01 30 54 67 58
- ⊳ 18 L 5629 m SSS 71
- 👥 WD–H WE–NA
- ⊕ 28km W of Paris (RN12)
- ⌂ Paul Rolin

Joyenval (1992)
Chemin de la Tuilerie,
78240 Chambourcy
- ☎ **01 39 22 27 50**
- 🖥 01 39 79 12 90
- ⊳ Retz 18 L 6211 m Par 72
  Marly 18 L 6249 m Par 72
- 👥 M
- ⊕ 25km N of Paris, nr St Germain-en-Laye
- ⌂ Robert Trent Jones Sr

National (1990)
2 Avenue du Golf, 78280 Guyancourt
- ☎ **01 30 43 36 00**
- 🖥 01 30 43 85 58
- ⊳ Albatros 18 L 6495 m Par 72
  Aigle 18 L 5936 m Par 71
  Oiselet 9 L 2010 m Par 32
- 👥 H or Green card
- ££ €18–47 (€18–75)
- ⊕ St Quentin-en-Yvelines, SW of Paris (D36)
- ⌂ Chesneau/Von Hagge
- 🖳 www.golf-national.com

For list of abbreviations and key to symbols see page 649

Rochefort   (1964)
78730 Rochefort-en-Yvelines
☎ 01 30 41 31 81
⌨ 01 30 41 94 01
↦ 18 L 5735 m SSS 71
⚇ U
£€ €38–69
⛳ 45km SW of Paris
🏠 Hawtree

St Cloud   (1911)
60 Rue du 19 Janvier, Garches 92380
☎ 01 47 01 01 85
⌨ 01 47 01 19 57
↦ 18 L 5939 m SSS 72
   18 L 4823 m SSS 67
⚇ H
£€ €76 (€92)
⛳ Porte Dauphine, 9km W of Paris
🏠 HS Colt

St Germain   (1922)
Route de Poissy, 78100 St Germain-en-Laye
☎ 01 39 10 30 30
⌨ 01 39 10 30 31
↦ 18 L 6117 m SSS 72
   9 L 2030 m SSS 33
⚇ WD–H WE–M
£€ €61
⛳ 20km W of Paris
🏠 HS Colt
🖥 www.golfstgermain.org

St Quentin-en-Yvelines
RD 912, 78190 Trappes
☎ 01 30 50 86 40
↦ 18 L 5900 m SSS 71
   18 L 5753 m SSS 70
⚇ H
⛳ 20km SW of Paris
🏠 Hubert Chesneau

St Nom-La-Bretêche   (1959)
Hameau Tuilerie-Bignon, 78860 St Nom-La-Bretèche
☎ 01 30 80 04 40
⌨ 01 34 62 60 44
↦ 18 L 6685 yds SSS 72
   18 L 6712 yds SSS 72
⚇ H
£€ WD only – € 80
⛳ 24km W of Paris on A-13
🏠 F Hawtree

La Vaucouleurs   (1987)
Rue de l'Eglise, 78910 Civry-la-Forêt
☎ 01 34 87 62 29
⌨ 01 34 87 70 09
↦ Rivière 18 L 6138 m Par 73
   Vallons 18 L 5553 m SSS 70
⚇ H or Green card
£€ €34 (€57)
⛳ 50km W of Paris, between Mantes and Houdan
🏠 Michel Gayon

Les Yvelines
Château de la Couharde, 78940 La-Queue-les-Yvelines
☎ 01 34 86 48 89

☎ 01 34 86 50 31
↦ 18 L 6344 m Par 72
   9 L 2065 m Par 31
⚇ U
£€ €26 (€44)
⛳ Montfort-l'Amaury, 45km W of Paris
🏠 HJ Baker

Provence & Côte d'Azur

Aix Marseille   (1935)
13290 Les Milles
☎ 04 42 24 40 41/04 42 24 23 01
⌨ 04 42 39 97 48
↦ 18 L 6291 m SSS 73
⚇ H
£€ D – € 37 (D – € 43)
⛳ 7km SW of Aix-en-Provence. 30km N of Marseille
🏠 Peter Cannon

Barbaroux   (1989)
Route de Cabasse, 83170 Brignoles
☎ 04 94 69 63 63
⌨ 04 94 59 00 93
↦ 18 L 6367 m SSS 72
⚇ H
£€ €55
⛳ Brignoles, 50km E of Aix. 40km N of Toulon
🏠 Pete Dye/PB Dye
🖥 www.barbaroux.com

Les Baux de Provence   (1989)
Domaine de Manville, 13520 Les Baux-de-Provence
☎ 04 90 54 40 20
⌨ 04 90 54 40 93
↦ 9 L 2812 m SSS 36
⚇ U H
£€ €23 (€29)
⛳ 15km NE of Arles. 15km S of Avignon. 80km W of Marseilles
🏠 Martin Hawtree
🖥 www.golfsprovence.com

Beauvallon-Grimaud
Boulevard des Collines, 83120 Sainte-Maxime
☎ 04 94 96 16 98
↦ 9 L 2503 m SSS 34
⚇ H
⛳ 3km SW of Sainte Maxime

Biot   (1930)
La Bastide du Roy, 06410 Biot
☎ 04 93 65 08 48
⌨ 04 93 65 05 63
↦ 18 L 4511 m CR 62.7 SR 94
⚇ H
£€ €40 (€44)
⛳ Antibes 5km. Nice 15km

Cannes Mandelieu   (1891)
Route de Golf, 06210 Mandelieu
☎ 04 92 97 32 00

☎ 04 93 49 92 90
↦ 18 L 5871 m SSS 71
   9 L 2852 m SSS 33
⚇ U H
£€ €50 (€50)
⛳ Mandelieu, 7km W of Cannes

Cannes Mandelieu Riviera   (1990)
Avenue des Amazones, 06210 Mandelieu
☎ 04 92 97 49 49
⌨ 04 92 97 49 42
↦ 18 L 5736 m SSS 71
⚇ U H–max 36
£€ €40 (€44)
⛳ 10km SW of Cannes, off A8
🏠 Robert Trent Jones

Cannes Mougins   (1925)
175 Route d'Antibes, 06250 Mougins
☎ 04 93 75 79 13
⌨ 04 93 75 27 60
↦ 18 L 6263 m SSS 72
⚇ H–max 28
£€ €90
⛳ 8km NE of Cannes (D35)
🏠 Colt/Simpson (1925). Alliss/Thomas (1977)

Château L'Arc   (1985)
Domaine de Château L'Arc, 13710 Fuveau
☎ 04 42 53 89 09
⌨ 04 42 53 89 08
↦ 18 L 6300 m SSS 71
⚇ U
£€ €38
⛳ 15km SE of Aix-en-Provence
🏠 Michel Gayon
🖥 www.golfchateaularc.com

Châteaublanc
Les Plans, 84310 Morières-les-Avignon
☎ 04 90 33 39 08
⌨ 04 90 33 43 24
↦ 18 L 6141 m SSS 72
   9 L 1267 m Par 28
⚇ H
£€ €31 (€38)
⛳ 5km SE of Avignon, nr Airport
🏠 Thierry Sprecher
🖥 www.golfchateaublanc.com

Digne-les-Bains   (1990)
4 Route du Chaffaut, 0400 Digne-les-Bains
☎ 04 92 30 58 00
⌨ 04 92 30 58 13
↦ 18 L 5210 m SSS 68
⚇ U
⛳ 100km NE of Aix-en-Provence
🏠 Robert Berthet
🖥 www.golfdigne.com

Estérel Latitudes   (1989)
Ave du Golf, 83700 St Raphaël
☎ 04 94 52 68 30
⌨ 04 94 52 68 31
↦ 18 L 5921 m SSS 71
   9 L 1392 m Par 29

   U H
£€ €41–46
&⊷ 3km N of St-Raphaël
⌂ Robert Trent Jones

Frégate (1992)
Domaine de Frégate, RD 559, 83270
St Cyr-sur-Mer
☎ 04 94 29 38 00
⌨ 04 94 29 96 94
⊩ 18 L 6210 m SSS 72
   9 hole short course
   U
£€ €45 (€51)
&⊷ 25km W of Toulon on coast
⌂ Ronald Fream

Gap-Bayard (1988)
Centre d'Oxygénation, 05000 Gap
☎ 04 92 50 16 83
⌨ 04 92 50 17 05
⊩ 18 L 6023 m SSS 72
   U
£€ €33 (€38)
&⊷ 7km N of Gap. 80km S of Grenoble
⌂ Hugues Lambert

Grand Avignon (1989)
BP 121, Les Chênes Verts, 84270 Vedene
☎ 04 90 31 49 94
⌨ 04 90 31 01 21
⊩ 18 L 6046 m Par 72
   9 hole short course
   U
£€ €32 (€38)
&⊷ Vedene, 10km NE of Avignon
⌂ Georges Roumeas

La Grande Bastide (1990)
Chemin des Picholines, 06740
Châteauneuf de Grasse
☎ 04 93 77 70 08
⌨ 04 93 77 72 36
⊩ 18 L 6105 m SSS 72
   U H
£€ €44 (€49)
&⊷ Grasse, 17km N of Cannes
⌂ Cabell Robinson

Grasse CC (1992)
1 Route des Trois Ponts, 06130 Grasse
☎ 04 93 60 55 44
⌨ 04 93 60 55 19
⊩ 18 L 6021 m SSS 72
   U
£€ €46 (€49)
&⊷ 18km N of Cannes
⌂ JP Fourès

Le Lavandou
2 Ave du Cap Nègre, Cavalière, 83980
Le Lavandou
☎ 04 94 05 75 80
⊩ 18 L 5649 m Par 72
   U
&⊷ 50km E of Toulon, between Hyères
   and St Tropez
⌂ Yves Bureau

Luberon (1986)
La Grande Gardette, 04860 Pierrevert
☎ 04 92 72 17 19
⌨ 04 92 72 59 12
⊩ 18 L 6040 m SSS 72
   U
£€ €38
&⊷ 5km SW of Manosque. 45km NE of
   Aix
⌂ Artea
■ www.golf-du-luberon.com

Marseille La Salette (1988)
Impasse des Vaudrans, 13011
La Valentine Marseille
☎ 04 91 27 12 16
⌨ 04 91 27 21 33
⊩ 18 L 5436 m CR 71.7 SR 145
   H
£€ €33 (€42)
&⊷ Nr centre of Marseilles
⌂ Michel Gayon
■ www.opengolfclub.com

Miramas (1993)
Mas de Combe, 13140 Miramas
☎ 04 90 58 56 55
⌨ 04 90 17 38 73
⊩ 18 L 5670m Par 72
   H or Green card
£€ €17–23 (€23–31)
&⊷ 50km S of Avignon. 50km NW of
   Marseilles
⌂ Serge Giraud

Monte Carlo (1910)
Route du Mont-Agel, 06320 La Turbie
☎ 04 92 41 50 70
⌨ 04 93 41 09 55
⊩ 18 L 5679 m SSS 71
   H
£€ €61 (€76)
&⊷ Mont Agel, La Turbie, 10km N of
   Monte Carlo

Opio-Valbonne (1966)
Route de Roquefort-les-Pins, 06650 Opio
☎ 04 93 12 00 08
⌨ 04 93 12 26 00
⊩ 18 L 5892 m SSS 72 SR 123
   H
£€ €65
&⊷ 15km N of Cannes
⌂ Donald Harradine
■ www.opengolfclub.com

Pont Royal (1992)
Pont Royal, 13370 Mallemort
☎ 04 90 57 40 79
⌨ 04 90 59 45 83
⊩ 18 L 6303 m SSS 72
   H
£€ €31–46
&⊷ 35km SE of Avignon on N7,
   between Avignon and Aix
⌂ Severiano Ballesteros

Provence G&CC (1991)
Route de Fontaine de Vaucluse, L'Isle
sur la Sorgue, 84800 Saumane
☎ 04 90 20 20 65

   04 90 20 32 01
⊩ 18 L 6045 m SSS 72
   9 hole short course
   U
&⊷ 20km E of Avignon
⌂ Jean Garaialde

Roquebrune (1989)
CD 7, 83520 Roquebrune-sur-Argens
☎ 04 94 82 92 91
⌨ 04 94 82 94 74
⊩ 18 L 6031 m SSS 71
   H
£€ €40
&⊷ 35km N of Saint-Tropez. 40km SW
   of Cannes
⌂ Udo Barth

Royal Mougins (1993)
424 Avenue du Roi, 06250 Mougins
☎ 04 92 92 49 69, 04 92 92 49 79
⌨ 04 92 92 49 70
⊩ 18 L 6004 m SSS 72
   H
£€ €150 (inc lunch)
&⊷ 5km N of Cannes
⌂ Robert von Hagge
■ www.royalmougins.fr

St Endreol (1992)
Route de Bagnols-en-Fôret, 83920
La Motte
☎ 04 94 51 89 89
⌨ 04 94 51 89 90
⊩ 18 L 6219 m Par 72 CR 72.4
   U H
£€ €65
&⊷ 30km N of St Tropez. 30km W of
   Cannes
⌂ Michel Gayon

La Sainte-Baume (1988)
Golf Hotel, Domaine de Châteauneuf,
83860 Nans-les-Pins
☎ 04 94 78 60 12
⌨ 04 94 78 63 52
⊩ 18 L 6167 m SSS 72
   U
£€ €34–41 (€41)
&⊷ 30km SE of Aix-en-Provence, via
   A8 (exit Saint-Maximin)
⌂ Robert Berthet

Sainte-Maxime
Route de Débarquement, 83120 Sainte-
Maxime
☎ 04 94 55 02 02
⌨ 04 94 55 02 03
⊩ 18 L 6155 m SSS 71
   H
&⊷ 15km N of Saint Tropez. 80km W
   of Nice (RN98)
⌂ Donald Harradine

Servanes (1989)
Domaine de Servanes, 13890 Mouriès
☎ 04 90 47 59 95
⌨ 04 90 47 52 58
⊩ 18 L 6100m SSS 72
   H

££ €31 (€38)
⊗ 35km S of Avignon
↷ Sprecher/Watine

Taulane
Domaine du Château de Taulane, RN 85, 83840 La Martre
☎ 04 93 60 31 30
▢ 04 93 60 33 23
▷ 18 L 6250 m Par 72
♙ H
££ €31–46 (€53)
⊗ 55km N of Cannes on N85 (Route Napoleon)
↷ Gary Player

Valcros   (1964)
Domaine de Valcros, 83250 La Londe-les-Maures
☎ 04 94 66 81 02
▢ 04 94 66 90 48
▷ 18 L 5274 m SSS 69
♙ H
££ €45
⊗ 10km W of Le Lavandou
↷ F Hawtree

Valescure   (1895)
BP 451, 83704 St-Raphaël Cedex
☎ 04 94 82 40 46
▢ 04 94 82 41 42
▷ 18 L 5067 m Par 68
♙ U H
££ €46
⊗ 5km E of St-Raphaël
↷ Lord Ashcombe

Rhône-Alps

Aix-les-Bains   (1913)
Avenue du Golf, 73100 Aix-les-Bains
☎ 04 79 61 23 35
▢ 04 79 34 06 01
▷ 18 L 5519 m Par 70 SR 124
♙ H
££ €35 (€43)
⊗ 3km S of Aix
■ www.golf-aixlesbains.com

Albon   (1989)
Domaine de Senaud, Albon, 26140 St Rambert d'Albon
☎ 04 75 03 03 90
▢ 04 75 03 11 01
▷ 18 L 6108 m CR 70.4 SR 125
   9 L 1260 m Par 29
♙ U
££ €35 – € 44
⊗ 60km S of Lyon, motorway exit Chanas
↷ Antoine d'Ormesson
■ www.golf-albon.com

Annecy   (1953)
Echarvines, 74290 Talloires
☎ 04 50 60 12 89
▢ 04 50 60 08 80
▷ 18 L 5017 m SSS 68

♙ H
⊗ 13km E of Annecy
↷ Cecil Blandford

Annonay-Gourdan   (1988)
Domaine de Gourdan, 07430 Saint Clair
☎ 04 75 67 03 84
▢ 04 75 67 79 50
▷ 18 L 5900 m SSS 71
♙ U
⊗ 35km SE of St Etienne. 50km SW of Lyon
↷ Sprecher/Watine

Les Arcs
B P 18, 73706 Les Arcs Cedex
☎ 04 79 07 43 95
▢ 04 79 07 47 65
▷ 18 L 5547 m SSS 70
♙ H
⊗ 90 km E of Chambery on N90

Le Beaujolais   (1991)
69480 Lucenay-Anse
☎ 04 74 67 04 44
▢ 04 74 67 09 60
▷ 18 L 6137 m SSS 72
♙ U H
⊗ 25km N of Lyon

Bossey G&CC   (1985)
Château de Crevin, 74160 Bossey
☎ 04 50 43 95 50
▢ 04 50 95 32 57
▷ 18 L 5954 m Par 71
♙ WD–U WE–NA
££ €46
⊗ 6km S of Geneva
↷ Robert Trent Jones Jr

La Bresse
Domaine de Mary, 01400 Condessiat
☎ 04 74 51 42 09
▢ 04 74 51 40 09
▷ 18 L 6217 m Par 72
♙ WD–U WE–H
££ €34 (€45)
⊗ 15km SW of Bourg-en-Bresse, via RN73
↷ Jeremy Pern

Chamonix   (1934)
35 Route du Golf, 74400 Chamonix
☎ 04 50 53 06 28
▢ 04 50 53 38 69
▷ 18 L 6087 m SSS 72
♙ H
££ €31 – € 60 (€38 – € 60)
⊗ 3km N of Chamonix (RN 506). Geneva 80km
↷ Robert Trent Jones Sr
■ www.golfdechamonix.com

Le Clou   (1985)
01330 Villars-les-Dombes
☎ 04 74 98 19 65
▢ 04 74 98 15 15
▷ 18 L 5000 m SSS 67
♙ WD–U WE–H

⊗ 30km NE of Lyon
■ www.golfduclou.com

La Commanderie   (1964)
L'Aumusse-Crottet, 01290 Pont-de-Veyle
☎ 04 85 30 44 12
▢ 04 85 30 55 02
▷ 18 L 5560 m SSS 69
♙ H
⊗ 7km E of Mâcon on RN 79

Corrençon-en-Vercors   (1987)
Les Ritons, 38250 Corrençon-en-Vercors
☎ 04 76 95 80 42
▢ 04 76 95 84 63
▷ 18 L 5550 m Par 71
♙ U
⊗ 35km S of Grenoble, off D531
↷ Hugues Lambert

Divonne   (1931)
Ave des Thermes, 01220 Divonne-les-Bains
☎ 04 50 40 34 11
▢ 04 50 40 34 25
▷ 18 L 5858 m SSS 72
♙ H–max 30
££ €46 (€77)
⊗ Divonne ¹/₂ km. 18km N of Geneva
↷ Nakowski

Esery   (1990)
Esery, 74930 Reignier
☎ 04 50 36 58 70
▢ 04 50 36 57 62
▷ 18 L 6350 m SSS 73
   9 L 2024 m SSS 31
♙ WD–H WE–NA
££ €46
⊗ 10km S of Geneva
↷ Michel Gayon

Evian Masters   (1904)
Rive Sud du lac de Genève, 74500 Évian
☎ 04 50 26 85 00
▢ 04 50 75 65 54
▷ 18 L 6006 m SSS 72
♙ H
££ €32 – € 53 (€45 – € 64)
⊗ 2km W of Évian. 40km NE of Geneva Airport
↷ Cabell Robinson
■ www.royalparcevian.com

Flaine-Les-Carroz   (1984)
74300 Flaine
☎ 04 50 90 85 44
▢ 04 50 90 88 21
▷ 18 L 3693 m Par 63
♙ U
⊗ 4km N of Flaine. 60km SE of Geneva Airport
↷ Robert Berthet

Giez   (1991)
Lac d'Annecy, 74210 Giez
☎ 04 50 44 48 41
▢ 04 50 32 55 93

♐ 18 L 5820 m Par 72
9 L 2250 m Par 33
♔ H or Green card
££ €38 – € 46
⮌ 20km SE of Annecy
🛖 Didier Fruchet

Le Gouverneur

Château du Breuil, 01390 Monthieux
☎ 04 72 26 40 34
🖳 04 72 26 41 61
♐ 18 L 6477 m Par 72
18 L 5959 m Par 72
9 L 2365 m Par 34
♔ H or green card
££ €45
⮌ NE of Lyon, off A46
🛖 Fruchet/Sprecher

Grenoble-Bresson   (1990)

Route de Montavie, 38320 Eybens
☎ 04 76 73 65 00
🖳 04 76 73 65 51
♐ 18 L 6343 m SSS 72
♔ U
££ €35 (€41)
⮌ 10km SE of Grenoble
🛖 Robert Trent Jones Jr

Grenoble-Charmeil   (1988)

38210 St Quentin-sur-Isère
☎ 04 76 93 67 28
🖳 04 76 93 62 04
♐ 18 L 5733 m Par 73
♔ U
££ €31 (€40)
⮌ 15km NW of Grenoble, off A49
🛖 Perl/Garaialde
▪ www.bluegreen.com

Grenoble-Uriage   (1921)

Les Alberges, 38410 Uriage
☎ 04 76 89 03 47
🖳 04 76 73 15 80
♐ 9 L 2004 m Par 64
♔ U
££ €23 (€27)
⮌ 15km E of Grenoble
🛖 Watine/Sprecher

Lyon   (1921)

38280 Villette-d'Anthon
☎ 04 78 31 11 33
🖳 04 72 02 48 27
♐ 18 L 6229 m SSS 72
18 L 6727 m SSS 74
♔ U H
££ €34 (€50)
⮌ 20km E of Lyon
🛖 Fenn/Lambert

Lyon-Chassieu

Route de Lyon, 69680 Chassieu
☎ 04 78 90 84 77
🖳 04 78 90 88 85
♐ 18 L 5941 m Par 70
♔ H
⮌ 10km E of Lyon
🛖 Chris Pittman

Lyon-Verger   (1977)

69360 Saint-Symphorien D'Ozon
☎ 04 78 02 84 20
🖳 04 78 02 08 12
♐ 18 L 5800 m SSS 69
♔ U
££ €27 (€38)
⮌ 14km S of Lyon on A7, or RN7
2km S of Feyzin

Maison Blanche G&CC
(1991)

01170 Echenevex
☎ 04 50 42 44 42
🖳 04 50 42 44 43
♐ 18 L 6246 m SSS 72
9 L 1757 m Par 31
♔ WD–U H–max 30
⮌ 15km from Geneva
🛖 Harradine/Dongradi

Méribel   (1973)

BP 54, 73553 Méribel Cedex
☎ 04 79 00 52 67
🖳 04 79 00 38 85
♐ 18 L 5319 m SSS 70
♔ H
££ €41
⮌ 15km S of Moutiers. 35km S of
Albertville
🛖 Sprecher/Watine

Mionnay La Dombes   (1986)

Chemin de Beau-Logis, 01390 Mionnay
☎ 04 78 91 84 84
🖳 04 78 91 02 73
♐ 18 L 5763 m SSS 71
♔ U
££ €36 (€47.10)
⮌ 20km N of Lyon towards Bourg
🛖 Jacques Vouilloux

Mont-d'Arbois   (1964)

74120 Megève
☎ 04 50 21 29 79
🖳 04 50 93 02 63
♐ 18 L 6100 m SSS 72
♔ WE–restricted. Booking required
Jul/Aug
££ €31–46
⮌ 3km SE of Megève
🛖 Henry Cotton

St Etienne   (1989)

62 Rue St Simon, 42000 St Etienne
☎ 04 77 32 14 63
🖳 04 77 33 61 23
♐ 18 L 5700 m Par 72
6 hole Par 3 course
♔ U
££ €27 (€35)
⮌ Nr centre of St Etienne. Lyon 60km
🛖 Thierry Sprecher

Salvagny

*100 Rue des Granges, 69890 La Tour
de Salvagny*
☎ 04 78 48 83 60
🖳 04 78 48 00 16

♐ 18 L 6300 m SSS 73 Par 72
♔ U
⮌ Lyon 20km
🛖 Drancourt

La Sorelle   (1991)

*Domaine de Gravagnieux,
01320 Villette-sur-Ain*
☎ 04 74 35 47 27
🖳 04 74 35 44 51
♐ 18 L 6100 m SSS 72
♔ U
££ €28 (€37)
⮌ 50km NE of Lyon
🛖 Patrick Jacquier

Tignes   (1968)

Val Claret, 73320 Tignes
☎ 04 79 06 37 42 (Summer)
🖳 04 79 06 35 64
♐ 18 L 4810 m SSS 68
♔ H–max 35
££ €32
⮌ 50km E of Moutiers, off D902, nr
Italian border. 90km S of Chamonix

Valdaine   (1989)

*Domaine de la Valdaine,
Montboucher/Jabron,
26740 Montelimar-Montboucher*
☎ 04 75 00 71 33
🖳 04 75 01 24 49
♐ 18 L 5631 m SSS 71
♔ U
££ €31 (€43)
⮌ 4km E of Montelimar. 50km S of
Valence
🛖 TJ Macauley
▪ www.domainedelavaldaine.com

Valence St Didier   (1983)

26300 St Didier de Charpey
☎ 04 75 59 67 01
🖳 04 75 59 68 19
♐ 18 L 5807 m SSS 71
♔ U
££ €24 (€31)
⮌ 12km E of Valence
🛖 Thierry Sprecher

Toulouse & Pyrenees

Albi Lasbordes   (1989)

Château de Lasbordes, 81000 Albi
☎ 05 63 54 98 07
🖳 05 63 47 21 55
♐ 18 L 6200 m SSS 72
♔ U
££ €26 (€35)
⮌ 70km NE of Toulouse
🛖 Garaialde/Pern

Ariège   (1986)

Unjat, 09240 La Bastide-de-Serou
☎ 05 61 64 56 78
🖳 05 61 64 57 99
♐ 18 L 6000 m SSS 71
♔ H
££ €22 (€30)

⚪ Unjat, 20km NW of Foix
🏠 Michel Gayon

La Bigorre (1992)
Pouzac, 65200 Bagnères de Bigorre
☎ **05 62 91 06 20**
💻 05 62 91 06 20
⇝ 18 L 5909 m SSS 72
〽 U
⚪ 18km S of Tarbes. 150km W of Toulouse
🏠 Olivier Brizon

Château de Terrides (1986)
Domaine de Terrides, 82100 Labourgade
☎ **05 63 95 61 07**
💻 05 63 95 64 97
⇝ 18 L 6420 m SSS 71
〽 U
⚪ 45km NW of Toulouse
🏠 J-P Foures

Embats
Route de Montesquiou, 32000 Auch
☎ **05 62 05 20 80/05 62 61 10 11**
💻 05 62 05 92 55
⇝ 18 L 4751 m SSS 65
〽 U
£€ €23 (€26)
⚪ 4km W of Auch. 80km W of Toulouse
🏠 André Migret

Étangs de Fiac (1987)
Brazis, 81500 Fiac
☎ **05 63 70 64 70**
💻 05 63 75 32 91
⇝ 18 L 5800 m SSS 71
〽 U
£€ €26–34
⚪ 45km NE of Toulouse
🏠 M Hawtree

Florentin-Gaillac (1990)
Le Bosc, Florentin, 81150 Marssac-sur-Tarn
☎ **05 63 55 20 50**
💻 05 63 53 26 41
⇝ 18 L 6150 m SSS 71
〽 U
⚪ 10km W of Albi. 70km NE of Toulouse
🏠 Robert Berthet

Guinlet (1986)
32800 Eauze
☎ **05 62 09 80 84**
💻 05 62 09 84 50
⇝ 18 L 5565 m Par 71
〽 U
£€ €27 (€30)
⚪ 60km SW of Agen. 150km SE of Bordeaux
🏠 M Larrouy
■ www.guinlet.fr

Lannemezan
La Demi-Lune, 65300 Lannemezan
☎ **05 62 98 01 01**

⇝ 18 L 5872 m Par 70
〽 H
⚪ 38km SE of Tarbes
🏠 Hirigoyen/Laserre

Lourdes (1988)
Chemin du Lac, 65100 Lourdes
☎ **05 62 42 02 06**
💻 05 62 42 02 06
⇝ 18 L 5372 m Par 71 CR 70.6
〽 U
£€ €23–27 (€26–31)
⚪ 4km W of Lourdes, off D940
🏠 Olivier Brizon

Luchon (1908)
BP 40, 31110 Bagnères de Luchon
☎ **05 61 79 03 27**
⇝ 9 L 2375 m SSS 66
〽 H
⚪ Luchon, 90km SE of Tarbes. 145km S of Toulouse
🏠 Fenn/Hawtree

Mazamet-La Barouge (1956)
81660 Pont de l'Arn
☎ **05 63 61 08 00/05 63 67 06 72**
💻 05 63 61 13 03
⇝ 18 L 5623 m SSS 70
〽 U
£€ €27 (€36)
⚪ 2km N of Mazamet. 80km E of Toulouse. 80km W of Béziers
🏠 Mackenzie Ross/Hawtree

Toulouse (1951)
31320 Vieille-Toulouse
☎ **05 61 73 45 48**
💻 05 62 19 04 67
⇝ 18 L 5602 m Par 69
〽 U
£€ €38
⚪ 8km S of Toulouse
🏠 Hawtree

Toulouse-La Ramée
Ferme Cousturier, 31170 Tournefeuille
☎ **05 61 07 09 09**
💻 05 61 07 15 93
⇝ 18 L 5605 m SSS 69
9 hole short course
〽 H
⚪ SW of Toulouse
🏠 Hawtree

Toulouse-Palmola (1974)
Route d'Albi, 31660 Buzet-sur-Tarn
☎ **05 61 84 20 50**
💻 05 61 84 48 92
⇝ 18 L 6156 m SSS 73
〽 H
£€ €38 (€53)
⚪ 18km NE of Toulouse. A68 Junction 4
🏠 Michael Fenn

Toulouse-Seilh
Route de Grenade, 31840 Seilh
☎ **05 61 42 59 30**

💻 05 61 42 34 17
⇝ Red 18 L 6122 m SSS 72
Yellow 18 L 4202 m SSS 64
〽 H
£€ €31–36
⚪ 15km N of Toulouse. Blagnac Airport 5km
🏠 Jean Garaialde

Toulouse-Teoula
71 Avenue des Landes, 31830 Plaisance du Touch
☎ **05 61 91 98 80**
💻 05 61 91 49 66
⇝ 18 L 5500 m Par 69
〽 H or green card
£€ €31
⚪ 15km W of Toulouse
🏠 Martin Hawtree

Les Tumulus (1987)
1 Rue du Bois, 65310 Laloubère
☎ **05 62 45 14 50**
💻 05 62 45 11 82
⇝ 18 L 5050 m Par 70 CR 69.2 SR 127
〽 U
£€ €23 (€27)
⚪ 2km S of Tarbes, towards Bagnères
🏠 Charles de Ginestet
■ www.perso.fr/tumulus

Germany

Berlin & East

Balmer See (1995)
Drewinscher Weg 1, 17429 Neppermin
☎ **(038379) 28199**
💻 (038379) 28222
⇝ 27 L 5662-6090 m Par 71-73
〽 U H
£€ €36 (€46)
⚪ Usedom, 50km E of Greifswald
🏠 M Skeide

Berlin Motzener See (1991)
Am Golfplatz 5, 15741 Motzen
☎ **(033769) 50130**
💻 (033769) 50134
⇝ 18 L 6330 m Par 73
9 L 2756 m Par 54
〽 H–max 45. Booking necessary
£€ €35–45 (€70)
⚪ 30km S of Berlin
🏠 Kurt Rossknecht
■ www.golfclubmotzen.de

Berlin Wannsee (1895)
Golfweg 22, 14109 Berlin
☎ **(030) 806 7060**
💻 (030) 806 706-10
⇝ 18 L 6088 m SR 127
9 L 4442 m SR 102
〽 WD–U H WE–M

££ €55
⚷ Berlin (SW)
🏠 Harris Brothers (1925)
🖥 www.glcbw.de

Elbflorenz GC Dresden   (1992)

Ferdinand von Schillstr 4a, 01728 Possendorf
☎ **(035206) 2430**
🖳 (035206) 24317
🏁 18 L 5902 m Par 72
🕴 H
££ €35 (€40)
⚷ Dresden 12km
🏠 Dieter Sziedat
🖥 www.dresdnergolfclub.de

Palmerston Golf Resort (1991)

Parkallee 1, 15526 Bad Sarrow
☎ **(033631) 63300**
🖳 (033631) 63310
🏁 18 L 6118 m Par 72
　 18 L 6084 m Par 72
　 18 L 5593 m Par 71
　 9 hole course
🕴 U
££ €18 (€35)
⚷ 70km SE of Berlin
🏠 Palmer/Faldo/Eby/McEwan
🖥 www.palmerston.de

Potsdamer Tremmen   (1990)

Tremmener Landstrasse, 14641 Tremmen
☎ **(033233) 80244**
🖳 (033233) 80957
🏁 18 L 5921 m Par 72
🕴 H
££ €30 (€40)
⚷ SW of Berlin

Schloss Meisdorf   (1996)

Petersberger Trift 33, 06463 Meisdorf
☎ **(034743) 98450**
🖳 (034743) 98499
🏁 18 L 6236 m Par 72
🕴 U H
££ €20 (€30)
⚷ 70km S of Magdeburg
🏠 Gerd Osterkamp

Seddiner See   (1993)

Zum Weiher 44, 14552 Wildenbruch
☎ **(033205) 7320**
🖳 (033205) 73229
🏁 North 18 L 6259 m Par 72
　 South 18 L 6486 m Par 72
🕴 North–U H South–M H
££ North €35 (€45) South €50 (€60)
⚷ 40km SW of Berlin
🏠 North-Preissman. South-Trent Jones Jr

Semlin am See   (1992)

Ferchesarerstrasse 8b, 14712 Semlin
☎ **(03385) 5540**
🖳 (03385) 554400

🏁 18 L 6348 m SSS 73
🕴 H
££ €30 (€50)
⚷ 75km W of Berlin (B5/B188)
🏠 Christoph Städler
🖥 www.golfhotelsemlin.de

Bremen & North West

Bremer Schweiz   (1991)

Wölpscherstr 4, 28779 Bremen
☎ **(0421) 609 5331**
🖳 (0421) 609 5333
🏁 18 L 5858 m Par 72
🕴 H
££ €20
⚷ N of Bremen
🏠 Wolfgang Siegmann
🖥 www.golfclub-bremerschweiz.de

Club Zur Vahr   (1905)

Bgm-Spitta-Allee 34, 28329 Bremen
☎ **Bremen (0421) 204480, Garlstedt (04795) 417**
🖳 (0421) 244 9248
🏁 Garlstedt 18 L 6408 m CR 73.6 SR 136
　 Bremen 9 L 5777 m CR 68.5 SR 111
🕴 WD–H WE–M
££ Garlstedt – € 45 Bremen – € 30
⚷ Garlstedt-30km N of Bremen. Vahr-Bremen
🏠 B von Limburger

Herzogstadt Celle   (1985)

Beukenbusch 1, 29229 Celle
☎ **(05086) 395**
🖳 (05086) 8288
🏁 18 L 5915 m SSS 71
🕴 H
⚷ 6km NE of Celle, towards Lüneburg. 40km NE of Hanover
🏠 Wolfgang Siegmann

Küsten GC Hohe Klint   (1978)

Hohe Klint, 27478 Cuxhaven
☎ **(04723) 2737**
🖳 (04723) 5022
🏁 18 L 6047 m SSS 72
🕴 U H
££ €25 (€35)
⚷ 12km SW of Cuxhaven on Route 6, nr Oxstedt
🖥 www.golf-cuxhaven.de

Münster-Wilkinghege (1963)

Steinfurterstr 448, 48159 Münster
☎ **(0251) 214090**
🖳 (0251) 261518
🏁 18 L 5990 m SSS 71
🕴 WD–H WE–I
££ €30 (€40)
⚷ 2km N of Münster
🏠 W Siegmann

Oldenburgischer   (1964)

Am Golfplatz 1, 26180 Rastede
☎ **(04402) 7240**
🖳 (04402) 70417
🏁 18 L 6109 m SSS 72
🕴 WD–U WE–U H
££ €35 (€40)
⚷ 10km N of Oldenburg, nr Rastede
🏠 Von Limburger/Schnatmeyer

Ostfriesland   (1980)

Postbox 1220, 26634 Wiesmoor
☎ **(04944) 6440**
🖳 (04944) 6441
🏁 18 L 6183 m CR 72.7 SR 124
🕴 U
££ €30 (€35)
⚷ 25km SW of Wilhelmshaven
🏠 Frank Pennink
🖥 www.golfclub-ostfriesland.de

Soltau   (1982)

Hof Loh, 29614 Soltau
☎ **(05191) 967 63 33**
🖳 (05191) 967 63 34
🏁 18 L 6011 m SSS 73
　 9 L 2340 m SSS 54
🕴 H
££ €25 (€30)
⚷ Tetendorf, S of Soltau

Syke   (1989)

Schultenweg 1, 28857 Syke-Okel
☎ **(04242) 8230**
🖳 (04242) 8255
🏁 18 L 6266 m Par 73
🕴 U H
££ €25 (€30)
⚷ 20km S of Bremen

Tietlingen   (1979)

29683 Fallingbostel
☎ **(05162) 3889**
🖳 (05162) 7564
🏁 18 L 6193 m Par 72 SSS 73
🕴 H
££ €25 (€30)
⚷ 65km N of Hanover, between Walsrode and Fallingbostel
🏠 Bruns/Chadwick

Verden   (1988)

Holtumer Str 24, 27283 Verden
☎ **(04230) 1470**
🖳 (04230) 1550
🏁 18 hole course Par 72 SSS 72
🕴 U
££ €25 (€30)
⚷ 30km E of Bremen, nr Walle

Worpswede   (1974)

Giehlermühlen, 27729 Vollersode
☎ **(04763) 7313**
🖳 (04763) 6193
🏁 18 L 6200 m SSS 72
🕴 WD–U H WE–M H
££ €25 (€30)
⚷ Giehlermuhlen, 20km N of Bremen, off B74

Central North

Dillenburg
Auf dem Altscheid, 35687 Dillenburg
- ☎ (02771) 5001
- 📠 (02771) 5002
- ⮕ 18 L 6115 m Par 72
- ⛳ U H
- €€ €32 (€40)
- 🚗 30km S of Siegen. 100km N of Frankfurt

Hofgut Praforst (1992)
Postfach 1137, 36081 Hünfeld
- ☎ (06652) 9970
- 📠 (06652) 99755
- ⮕ 18 hole course
- 9 hole course
- ⛳ H–54 max
- €€ €36 (€46)
- 🚗 Hünfeld, 10km N of Fulda, off Route 27
- 🏠 Deutsche Golf Consult
- ■ www.praforst.de

Kassel-Wilhelmshöhe
(1958)
Ehlenerstr 21, 34131 Kassel
- ☎ (0561) 33509
- 📠 (0561) 37729
- ⮕ 18 L 5586 m SSS 70
- ⛳ U H
- €€ €30 (€40)
- 🚗 Wilhelmshöhe, 5km W of Kassel
- 🏠 Donald Harradine

Kurhessischer GC
Oberaula (1987)
Postfach 31, 36278 Oberaula
- ☎ (06628) 1573
- 📠 (06628) 919456
- ⮕ 18 L 6050 m SSS 72
- ⛳ U H
- €€ €25 (€35)
- 🚗 50km S of Kassel, nr Kircheim
- 🏠 Deutsche Golf Consult

Licher Golf (1992)
35423 Lich
- ☎ (06404) 91071
- 📠 (06404) 91072
- ⮕ 18 L 6065m SSS 72
- ⛳ H–booking necessary Sun–M
- €€ €35 (€55)
- 🚗 45km N of Frankfurt
- 🏠 Heinz Fehring

Rhoen (1971)
Am Golfplatz, 36145 Hofbieber
- ☎ (06657) 1334
- 📠 (06657) 914809
- ⮕ 18 L 5686 m CR 68.5 SR 127
- ⛳ H
- €€ €26 (€36)
- 🚗 Hofbieber, 11km E of Fulda
- 🏠 Kurt Peters
- ■ www.golfclub-fulda.de

Schloss Braunfels (1970)
Homburger Hof, 35619 Braunfels
- ☎ (06442) 4530
- 📠 (06442) 6683
- ⮕ 18 L 6085 m Par 73
- ⛳ WD–H (max 36) WE–H NA 10am–2pm
- €€ D – € 35 (€45)
- 🚗 70km N of Frankfurt
- 🏠 Bernhard von Limburger

Schloss Sickendorf (1990)
Schloss Sickendorf, 36341 Lauterbach
- ☎ (06641) 96130
- 📠 (06641) 961335
- ⮕ 18 L 6045 m Par 72 SSS 72
- ⛳ H
- €€ €25 (€35)
- 🚗 30km W of Fulda. 120km E of Frankfurt
- 🏠 Spangemacher

Winnerod
Parkstr 22, 35447 Reiskirchen
- ☎ (06408) 9513-0
- 📠 (06408) 9513-13
- ⮕ 18 L 6069 m Par 72
- 9 hole Par 3 course
- ⛳ U H
- €€ €25 (€45)
- 🚗 Hessen, 30km N of Frankfurt/Main
- 🏠 Michael Pinner

Zierenberg Gut Escheberg
(1995)
Gut Escheberg, 34289 Zierenberg
- ☎ (05606) 2608
- 📠 (05606) 2609
- ⮕ 18 L 6122 m Par 72
- ⛳ U H WE–booking necessary
- €€ €40 (€50)
- 🚗 20km NW of Kassel
- 🏠 Volker Püschel
- ■ www.golfclub-escheberg.de

Central South

Bad Kissingen (1910)
Euerdorferstr 11, 97688 Bad Kissingen
- ☎ (0971) 3608
- 📠 (0971) 60140
- ⮕ 18 L 5699 m SSS 70
- ⛳ U H
- €€ €35 (€40)
- 🚗 Bad Kissingen 2km. 65km N of Würzburg

Frankfurter (1913)
Golfstrasse 41, 60528 Frankfurt/Main
- ☎ (069) 666 2318
- 📠 (069) 666 7018
- ⮕ 18 L 6769 yds CR 72.5 SR 129
- ⛳ H–28 max
- €€ €52 (€60)
- 🚗 6km SW of Frankfurt, nr Airport
- 🏠 HS Colt
- ■ www.fgc.de

Hanau-Wilhelmsbad (1958)
Wilhelmsbader Allee 32, 63454 Hanau
- ☎ (06181) 82071
- 📠 (06181) 86967
- ⮕ 18 L 6110 m Par 73
- ⛳ WD–H WE–M H
- €€ €46 (€56)
- 🚗 4km NW of Hanau on B8-40/AB66. Frankfurt 15km

Hof Trages
Hofgut Trages, 63579 Freigericht, GERMANY
- ☎ (06055) 91380
- 📠 (06055) 913838
- ⮕ 18 L 5940 m CR 71.3 SR 127
- ⛳ WD–H WE–M
- €€ €50 (€60)
- 🚗 60km E of Frankfurt/Main
- 🏠 Kurt Rossknecht
- ■ www.hoftrages.de

Homburger (1899)
Saalburgchaussee 2, 61350 Bad Homburg
- ☎ (06172) 306808
- 📠 (06172) 32648
- ⮕ 10 holes Par 70 SSS 69
- ⛳ H
- €€ €25 (€35)
- 🚗 On B456 to Usingen

Idstein (2001)
Am Nassen Berg, 65510 Idstein
- ☎ (06126) 9322-13
- 📠 (06126) 9322-33
- ⮕ 18 L 6255 m Par 72
- ⛳ U
- €€ €15
- 🚗 25km N of Wiesbaden
- 🏠 Siegfried Heinz
- ■ www.golfpark-idstein.de

Idstein-Wörsdorf (1989)
Gut Henriettenthal, 65510 Idstein
- ☎ (06126) 9322-0
- 📠 (06126) 9322-22
- ⮕ 18 L 6140 m Par 72
- ⛳ WD–H WE–M
- €€ €25 (€35)
- 🚗 25km N of Wiesbaden
- 🏠 Siegfried Heinz
- ■ www.golfpark-idstein.de

Kitzingen (1980)
Larson Barracks, 97318 Kitzingen
- ☎ (09321) 4956
- 📠 (09321) 21936
- ⮕ 18 L 5956 m Par 71 SR 118
- ⛳ H + ID
- €€ €25 (€30)
- 🚗 20km E of Würzburg
- ■ www.golf.de

Kronberg G&LC (1954)
Schloss Friedrichshof, Hainstr 25, 61476 Kronberg/Taunus
- ☎ (06173) 1426
- 📠 (06173) 5953

⚑ 18 L 4941 m SSS 68
👥 WD–U H WE–M H
££ €45 (€55)
🚗 16km NW of Frankfurt
🏠 Harder/Harris

Main-Spessart (1990)
Postfach 1204, 97821 Marktheidenfeld-Eichenfürst
☎ (09391) 8435
🖥 (09391) 8816
⚑ 18 holes Par 72
    6 hole short course
👥 H–max 36
££ €26 (€36)
🚗 80km E of Frankfurt/Main
🏠 Harradine
■ www.main-spessart-golf.de

Main-Taunus (1979)
Lange Seegewann 2, 65205 Wiesbaden
☎ (06122) 52550/52208(Sec)
⚑ 18 L 6045 m SSS 72
👥 H
🚗 15km NW of Frankfurt Airport

Mannheim-Viernheim (1930)
Alte Mannheimer Str 3, 68519 Viernheim
☎ (06204) 607020
🖥 (06204) 607044
⚑ 18 L 6060 m SSS 72
👥 WD–H WE–M H (Summer)
🚗 10km NE of Mannheim

Maria Bildhausen
Rindhof 1, 97702 Münnerstadt
☎ (09766) 1601
🖥 (09766) 1602
⚑ 18 L 6047 m Par 72
    6 hole short course
👥 U
££ €30 (€35)
🚗 80km NE of Wurzburg
🏠 Christian Habeck

Neuhof
Hofgut Neuhof, 63303 Dreieich
☎ (06102) 327927/327010
🖥 (06102) 327012
⚑ 18 L 6151 m SSS 72
👥 WD–H WE–M
££ €50
🚗 Hofgut Neuhof, S of Frankfurt, off A3
🏠 Patrick Merrigan

Rhein Main (1977)
Steubenstrasse 9, 65189 Wiesbaden
☎ (0611) 373014
⚑ 18 L 6116 m SSS 71
👥 M
🚗 Wiesbaden 6km

Rheinblick
Weisser Weg, 65201 Wiesbaden-Frauenstein
☎ (0611) 420675
🖥 (0611) 941 0434

⚑ 18 L 6604 yds SSS 70
👥 Monday play only
🚗 2km from Wiesbaden at Hessen

Rheintal (1971)
An der Bundesstrr 291, 68723 Oftersheim
☎ (06202) 56390
⚑ 18 L 5840 m SSS 71
££ On application
🚗 Oftersheim, SE of Mannheim

St Leon-Rot (1996)
Opelstrasse 30, 68789 St Leon-Rot
☎ (06227) 86080
🖥 (06227) 860888
⚑ 18 L 6047 m Par 72
👥 WD–U before 2pm WE–M
££ €60 (€75)
🚗 20km S of Heidelberg
🏠 Hannes Schreiner

Spessart (1972)
Golfplatz Alsberg, 63628 Bad Soden-Salmünster
☎ (06056) 91580
🖥 (06056) 915820
⚑ 18 L 5956 m Par 72 SR 135
👥 H
££ €32 (€48) W – € 135
🚗 70km NE of Frankfurt, via A66 towards Fulda
🏠 Elliot Rowan
■ www.gc-spessart.de

Taunus Weilrod (1979)
Merzhauser Strasse, 61276 Weilrod-Altweilnau
☎ (06083) 95050
🖥 (06083) 950515
⚑ 18 L 5981 m CR 70.3
👥 H
££ €33 (€46)
🚗 25km NW of Bad Homburg
🏠 Donald Harradine
■ www.golfclub-taunus-weilrod.de

Wiesbadener (1893)
Chausseehaus 17, 65199 Wiesbaden
☎ (0611) 460238
🖥 (0611) 463251
⚑ 9 L 5320 m SSS 68
👥 WD–H (max 36) WE–H (max 28)
££ €30 (€60)
🚗 8km NW of Wiesbaden, towards Schlangenbad
🏠 Hirsch

Wiesloch-Hohenhardter Hof (1983)
Hohenhardter Hof, 69168 Wiesloch-Baiertal
☎ (06222) 78811-0
🖥 (06222) 78811-11
⚑ 18 L 5885 m SSS 72
👥 WD–H WE–M
££ €32 (€45)
🚗 17km S of Heidelberg
🏠 Harradine/Weishaupt
■ www.golfclub-wiesloch.de

Hamburg & North

Altenhof (1971)
Eckernförde, 24340 Altenhof
☎ (04351) 41227,
    (04351) 45800 (Pro)
🖥 (04351) 41227
⚑ 18 L 6066 m SSS 72
👥 H
££ €25 (€35)
🚗 3km S of Eckernförde. 25km NW of Kiel
🏠 Donald Harradine

Berhinderten (1994)
Gustav-Delle Str 18a, 22926 Ahrensburg
☎ (04102) 41544
🖥 (04102) 44516
⚑ 18 hole course
👥 U
££ On application
🚗 20km NE of Hamburg

Brodauer Mühle (1986)
Baumallee 14, 23730 Gut Beusloe
☎ (04561) 8140
🖥 (04561) 407397
⚑ 18 L 6113 m Par 72 SSS 72
👥 U H–36
££ €25 (€40)
🚗 30km N of Lübeck
🏠 Siegmann/Osterkamp

Buchholz-Nordheide
An der Rehm 25, 21244 Bucholz
☎ (04181) 36200
🖥 (04181) 97294
⚑ 18 L 6130 m SSS 72
👥 WD–U H WE–H I before 10am
££ €35 (€40)
🚗 30km S of Hamburg

Buxtehude (1982)
Zum Lehmfeld 1, 21614 Buxtehude
☎ (04161) 81333
🖥 (04161) 87268
⚑ 18 L 6480 m CR 73.6 SR 132
👥 H
££ €30 (€40)
🚗 30km SW of Hamburg on Route 73 from Harburg
🏠 Wolfgang Siegmann
■ www.golfclubbuxtehude.de

Deinster Mühle (1994)
Im Mühlenfeld 30, 21717 Deinste
☎ (04149) 925112
🖥 (04149) 925111
⚑ 18 L 5918 m CR 70.9 SR 123
👥 U H
££ €31 (€41)
🚗 50km SW of Hamburg
🏠 David Krause

Föhr (1966)
25938 Nieblum
☎ (04681) 580455
🖥 (04681) 580456
⚑ 18 L 5894 m CR 71.3 SR 120

Germany 883

H
£€ €35 (€40)
⚲ 1km SW of Wyk (Island of Föhr)

Gut Apeldör (1996)
Gut Apeldör, 25779 Hennstedt
☎ (04836) 8408
🖳 (04836) 8409
🏴 18 L 6048 m Par 72
6 hole short course
👤 U H
£€ €30 (€40)
⚲ 11km W of Heide. 110km N of Hamburg
🏠 DJ Krause
■ www.apeldoer.de

Gut Grambek (1981)
Schlosstr 21, 23883 Grambek
☎ (04542) 841474
🖳 (04542) 841476
🏴 18 L 5877 m SSS 71
👤 H
£€ €25 (€40)
⚲ 30km S of Lübeck. 50km E of Hamburg
■ www.gcgrambek.de

Gut Kaden (1984)
Kadenerstrasse 9, 25486 Alveslohe
☎ (04193) 9929-0
🖳 (04193) 992919
🏴 18 L 6076 m Par 72
9 hole course
👤 U H
£€ €40 (€55)
⚲ Alveslohe, 30km N of Hamburg

Gut Uhlenhorst (1989)
24229 Uhlenhorst
☎ (04349) 91700
🖳 (04349) 919400
🏴 18 L 6195 m SSS 72
👤 U
£€ €25 (€30)
⚲ 8km N of Kiel
🏠 Donald Harradine

Gut Waldhof (1969)
Am Waldhof, 24629 Kisdorferwohld
☎ (04194) 99740
🖳 (04194) 1251
🏴 18 L 5939 m CR 71.3 SR 128
👤 WD–H WE–M
£€ €35 (€45)
⚲ 34km N of Hamburg via A7 to Kaltenkirchen or B432
■ www.gut-waldhof.de

Gut Waldshagen (1996)
24306 Gut Waldshagen
☎ (04522) 766766
🖳 (04522) 766767
🏴 18 L 6372 m CR 73.1 SR 129
6 hole short course
👤 U
£€ €30 (€40)
⚲ 35km S of Kiel. 91km NE of Hamburg
■ www.gut-golf.de

Hamburg (1906)
In de Bargen 59, 22587 Hamburg
☎ (040) 812177
🖳 (040) 817315
🏴 18 L 5749 m CR 70.1 SR 126
👤 H WE–M
£€ €40 (€45)
⚲ Blankenese, 14km W of Hamburg
🏠 Colt/Allison/Morrison

Hamburg Ahrensburg (1964)
Am Haidschlag 39-45, 22926 Ahrensburg
☎ (04102) 51309
🖳 (04102) 81410
🏴 18 L 5782 m SSS 71
👤 WD–U WE–M only
⚲ 20km NE of Hamburg. Motorway exit Ahrensburg

Hamburg Hittfeld (1957)
Am Golfplatz 24, 21218 Seevetal
☎ (04105) 2331
🖳 (04105) 52571
🏴 18 L 5903 m SSS 71
👤 WD–U WE–M
£€ €30 (€40)
⚲ 25km S of Hamburg
🏠 Morrison/Gärtner

Hamburg Holm (1993)
Haverkamp 1, 25488 Holm
☎ (04103) 91330
🖳 (04103) 913313
🏴 27 holes CR 72.3 SR 124
👤 WD–U WE–M
£€ €40 (€45)
⚲ 20km W of Hamburg
🏠 Harradine/Rossknecht
■ www.gchh.de

Hamburg Walddörfer (1960)
Schevenbarg, 22949 Ammersbek
☎ (040) 605 1337
🖳 (040) 605 4879
🏴 18 L 6154 m SSS 73
18 hole pitch & putt course
👤 WD–U H WE–M H
£€ €40 (€50)
⚲ 20km N of Hamburg
🏠 B von Limburger

Hoisdorf (1977)
Hof Bornbek/Hoisdorf, 22952 Lütjensee
☎ (04107) 7831
🖳 (04107) 9934
🏴 18 L 5958 m Par 71
👤 WD–U WE–M only
£€ €35 (€40)
⚲ 25km NE of Hamburg

Jersbek
Oberteicher Weg, 22941 Jersbek
☎ (04532) 20950
🖳 (04532) 24779
🏴 18 L 5921 m SSS 71
👤 WD–H or I WE–M
£€ €30 (€35)
⚲ 20km N of Hamburg
🏠 Von Schinkel

Kieler GC Havighorst (1988)
Havighorster Weg 20, 24211 Havighorst
☎ (04302) 965980
🖳 (04302) 965981
🏴 18 L 6242 m Par 73 SSS 73
👤 WD–U H WE–H
£€ €25 (€30)
⚲ 10km S of Kiel. 85km N of Hamburg
🏠 Udo Barth

Lübeck-Travemünder (1921)
Kowitzberg 41, 23570 Lübeck-Travemünde
☎ (04502) 74018
🖳 (04502) 72182
🏴 27 L 6063 - 6152 m CR 72.8 SR 131
👤 H
£€ €30 (€40)
⚲ 18km NE of Lübeck. 70km NE of Hamburg
■ www.ltgk.de

Maritim Timmendorfer Strand (1973)
Am Golfplatz 3, 23669 Timmendorfer Strand
☎ (04503) 5152
🖳 (04503) 86344
🏴 North 18 L 6065 m SSS 72
South 18 L 3755 m SSS 60
👤 WE–booking required
£€ North D – € 30 (D – € 45) South D – € 25 (D – € 35)
⚲ 15km N of Lübeck
🏠 B von Limburger

Mittelholsteinischer Aukrug (1969)
Zum Glasberg 9, 24613 Aukrug-Bargfeld
☎ (04873) 595
🖳 (04873) 1698
🏴 18 L 6140 m SSS 72
👤 WD–H WE–H booking necessary
⚲ 10km W of Neumunster. Mitte exit on Route 430

Peiner Hof
Peiner Hag, 25497 Prisdorf
☎ (04101) 73790
🖳 (04101) 76640
🏴 18 holes CR 69.9 SR 126
👤 U
£€ €35 (€45)
⚲ 20km NW of Hamburg
■ www.peinerhof.de

An der Pinnau (1982)
Pinnebergerstr 81a, 25451 Quickborn-Rensel
☎ (04106) 81800
🖳 (04106) 82003
🏴 18 L 6023 m Par 72 SR 127
18 L 5231 m Par 72 SR 127
👤 H or I
£€ €35 (€45)
⚲ 25km NW of Hamburg, nr Quickborn

David Krause
www.pinnau.de

Am Sachsenwald (1985)
Am Riesenbett, 21521 Dassendorf
☎ (04104) 6120
🖳 (04104) 6551
🏌 18 L 6118 m SSS 72
👤 H
£€ €25 (€30)
🚗 20km SE of Hamburg
🏠 Deutsche Golf Consult

St Dionys (1972)
Widukindweg, 21357 St Dionys
☎ (04133) 213311
🖳 (04133) 213313
🏌 18 L 6125 m SSS 72
👤 By appointment only
£€ €40 (€50)
🚗 10km N of Lüneburg

Schloss Breitenberg
25524 Breitenberg
☎ (04828) 8188
🖳 (04828) 8100
🏌 27 hole course
👤 H
£€ €30 (€35)
🚗 50km N of Hamburg
🏠 Osterkamp/Krause
■ www.golfclubschlossbreitenberg.de

Schloss Lüdersburg (1985)
Lüdersburger Strasse 21, 21379 Lüdersburg
☎ (04139) 6970-0
🖳 (04139) 6970 70
🏌 18 L 6091 m SSS 73
   18 L 6107 m SSS 72
   4 hole par 3 course
👤 U H
£€ €30 (€47)
🚗 12km E of Lüneburg. 55km SE of Hamburg
🏠 Wolfgang Siegmann
■ www.luedersburg.de

Sylt
Am Golfplatz, 25996 Wenningstedt
☎ (04651) 99598-0
🖳 (04651) 45692
🏌 18 L 6200 m Par 72
👤 H-max 36
£€ €55
🚗 Sylt Island, 75km W of Flensburg
🏠 D Harradine

Treudelberg G&CC (1990)
Lemsahler Landstr 45, 22397 Hamburg
☎ (040) 608 22500
🖳 (040) 608 22444
🏌 18 L 6182 m SSS 72
   9 hole pitch & putt
👤 U H
£€ €35 (€45)
🚗 N of Hamburg centre
🏠 Donald Steel
■ www.treudelberg.com

Auf der Wendlohe
Oldesloerstr 251, 22457 Hamburg
☎ (040) 550 5014/5
🖳 (040) 550 3668
🏌 27 holes:
   5675-6050 m SSS 72
👤 WD-U WE-M
🚗 15km N of Hamburg
🏠 Ernst-Dietmar Hess

Wentorf-Reinbeker (1901)
Golfstrasse 2, 21465 Wentorf
☎ (040) 729 78066
🖳 (040) 729 78067
🏌 18 L 5698 m SSS 70
👤 WD-U H WE-M
£€ €30 (€35)
🚗 20km SE of Hamburg
🏠 Ernst Hess

Hanover & Weserbergland

Bad Salzuflen G&LC (1956)
Schwaghof 4, 32108 Bad Salzuflen
☎ (05222) 10773
🖳 (05222) 13954
🏌 18 L 6138 m Par 72
👤 H
£€ €30 (€35)
🚗 3km NE of Bad Salzuflen
🏠 B von Limburger

Braunschweig (1926)
Schwartzkopffstr 10, 38126 Braunschweig
☎ (0531) 691369
🏌 18 L 5893 m SSS 71
🚗 Braunschweig 5km

Burgdorf (1970)
Waldstr 15, 31303 Burgdorf-Ehlershausen
☎ (05085) 7628
🖳 (05085) 6617
🏌 18 L 6426 m SSS 74
👤 H
🚗 Burgdorf-Ehlershausen, 20km NE of Hanover

Gifhorn (1982)
Wilscher Weg 69, 38518 Gifhorn
☎ (05371) 16737
🖳 (05371) 51092
🏌 18 L 5972 m SSS 72
👤 H
£€ €25 (€35)
🚗 30km N of Braunschweig

Gütersloh Garrison
Princess Royal Barracks, BFPO 47
☎ (05241) 842606
🏌 9 L 5761 yds SSS 68
£€ £11
🚗 5km W of Gütersloh

Hameln (1985)
Schloss Schwöbber, 31855 Aerzen
☎ (05154) 9870
🖳 (05154) 9871-11
🏌 18 L 6222 m Par 73
   18 hole short course
🚗 10km SW of Hameln. 60km SW of Hanover

Hannover (1923)
Am Blauen See, 30823 Garbsen
☎ (05137) 73235
🏌 18 L 5855 m SSS 71
🚗 15km NW of Hanover

Hardenberg (1969)
Gut Levershausen, 37154 Northeim
☎ (05551) 61915
🖳 (05551) 61863
🏌 18 L 5970 m SSS 72
👤 H
£€ €32 (€42)
🚗 20km N of Göttingen, towards Northeim
🏠 Dr Siegmann
■ www.gchardenberg.de

Isernhagen (1983)
Auf Gut Lohne 22, 30916 Isernhagen
☎ (05139) 893185
🖳 (05139) 27033
🏌 18 L 6118 m SSS 72
👤 H-(max 34)
🚗 Gut Lohne, 12km NE of Hanover
■ www.golfclub-isernhagen.de

Langenhagen (1989)
Hainhaus 22, 30688 Langenhagen
☎ (0511) 736832
🖳 (0511) 726 1990
🏌 27 L 6161 m Par 72
👤 H
£€ €25 (€35)
🚗 25km N of Hannover
🏠 Siegmann

Lipperland zu Lage
Ottenhauserstr 100, 32791 Lage/Lippe
☎ (05232) 66829
🖳 (05232) 18165
🏌 18 L 6260 m SSS 73
👤 H
🚗 22km E of Bielefeld
🏠 Heinz Wolters

Lippischer (1980)
Huxoll 14, 32825 Blomberg-Cappel
☎ (05231) 459
🖳 (05236) 8102
🏌 18 L 5990 m CR 71.5 SR 126
👤 H
£€ €30 (€40)
🚗 12km E of Detmold
■ www.lippischergc.de

Marienfeld (1986)
Remse 27, 33428 Marienfeld
☎ (05247) 8880
🖳 (05247) 80386

🏌 18 L 5830 m CR 71.3 SR 132
👥 U H
💷 €30 (€40)
🚗 Gütersloh 10km
🏨 Spangemacher
▪ www.gc-marienfeld.de

Paderborner Land (1983)

Wilseder Weg 25, 33102 Paderborn
☎ (05251) 4377
🏌 18 L 5670 m SSS 68
👥 U
🚗 Salzkotten/Thule, between B-1 and B-64

Pyrmonter (1961)

Postfach 100 828, 31758 Hameln
☎ (05281) 8196
📠 (05281) 8196
🏌 18 L 5775 m SSS 70
👥 H
💷 €25 (€30)
🚗 4km S of Bad Pyrmont. 20km SW of Hameln
🏨 Donald Harradine

Ravensberger Land

Sudstrasse 96, 32130 Enger-Pödinghausen
☎ (09224) 79751
📠 (09224) 699446
🏌 18 hole course SSS 72
6 hole pitch & putt
👥 WD–H WE–M
💷 €20 (€25)
🚗 25km NE of Bielefeld towards Herford
🏨 Heinz Wolters

Senne GC Gut Welschof (1992)

Augustdorferstr 72, 33758 Schloss Holte-Stukenbrock
☎ (05207) 920936
📠 (05207) 88788
🏌 18 L 6246 m SSS 72
👥 U H
💷 €30 (€40)
🚗 20km S of Bielefeld
🏨 Christoph Städler

Sennelager (British Army) (1963)

Bad Lippspringe, BFPO 16
☎ (05252) 53794
📠 (05252) 53811
🏌 18 L 5658 m SSS 72
9 L 5214 m SSS 68
👥 H
💷 Forces–€20 (€25)
Civilians–€30 (€40)
🚗 9km E of Paderborn, off Route 1

Sieben-Berge Rheden (1965)

Postfach 1152, 31021 Gronau
☎ (05182) 52336
📠 (05182) 52336
🏌 18 L 5856 m SSS 71

👥 U H
💷 €25 (€30)
🚗 35km S of Hanover
🏨 B von Limburger

Weserbergland (1982)

Weissenfelder Mühle, 37647 Polle
☎ (05535) 8842
📠 (05535) 1225
🏌 18 holes SSS 72
👥 H
🚗 35km S of Hameln

Westfälischer Gütersloh

Gütersloher Str 127, 33397 Rietberg
☎ (05244) 2340/10528
📠 (05244) 1388
🏌 18 L 6135 m CR 71.6 SR 124
👥 U H
💷 €30 (€40)
🚗 8km SE of Gütersloh, nr Neuenkirchen
🏨 B von Limburger
▪ www.golf-gt.de

Widukind-Land (1985)

Auf dem Stickdorn 63, 32584 Löhne
☎ (05228) 7050
📠 (05228) 1039
🏌 18 hole course
👥 U H
💷 €30 (€35)
🚗 30km NE of Bielefeld
🏨 Dahlmeier/Brinkmeier

Munich & South Bavaria

Allgäuer G&LC (1984)

Hofgut Boschach, 87724 Ottobeuren
☎ (08332) 1310
📠 (08332) 5161
🏌 18 L 6096 m CR 71.1 SR 123
6 hole short course
👥 H
💷 €40 (€50)
🚗 2km S of Ottobeuren. 20km N of Kempten

Altötting-Burghausen (1986)

Piesing 4, 84533 Haiming
☎ (08678) 986903
📠 (08678) 986905
🏌 18 L 6281 m SSS 72/73
9 L 6002 m Par 70
👥 U
💷 €35 (€45)
🚗 Schloss Piesing, 4km N of Burghausen
🏨 G von Mecklenberg
▪ www.gc-altoetting-burghausen.de

Augsburg (1959)

Engelshofer Str 2, 86399 Bobingen-Burgwalden
☎ (08234) 5621

📠 (08234) 7855
🏌 18 L 6077 m CR 72.1 SR 133
👥 H–max 34
💷 €35 (€50)
🚗 18km SW of Augsburg
🏨 Kurt Rossknecht
▪ www.golfclub-augsburg.de

Bad Tölz (1973)

83646 Wackersberg
☎ (08041) 9994
📠 (08041) 2116
🏌 9 L 2886 m SSS 71
👥 WD–H WE–M
💷 €25 (€30)
🚗 5km W of Bad Tölz. 55km S of Munich

Bad Wörishofen

Schlingenerstr 27, 87668 Rieden
☎ (08346) 777
🏌 18 L 6318 m SSS 71
🚗 10km S of Bad Wörishofen

Beuerberg (1982)

Gut Sterz, 82547 Beuerberg
☎ (08179) 671/728
📠 (08179) 5234
🏌 18 L 6518 m SSS 74
👥 WD–H WE–M H
💷 €45 (€50)
🚗 Beuerberg, 45km SW of Munich
🏨 Donald Harradine

Im Chiemgau (1982)

Kötzing 1, 83339 Chieming
☎ (08669) 87330
📠 (08669) 87333
🏌 18 L 6221 m SSS 72
9 hole Par 3 course
👥 WD–H
💷 €40 (€55)
🚗 40km W of Salzburg. Munich 100km
🏨 J Dudok van Heel
▪ www.Golfchieming.de

Donauwörth (1995)

Lederstatt 1, 86609 Donauwörth
☎ (0906) 4044
📠 (0906) 999 8164
🏌 18 L 5939 m Par 72
👥 U H
💷 €30 (€40)
🚗 45km N of Augsburg
🏨 Peter Harradine

Ebersberg (1988)

Postfach 1351, 85554 Ebersberg
☎ (08094) 8106
📠 (08094) 8386
🏌 18 L 5907 m Par 72
6 hole Par 3 course
👥 U H
💷 €35 (€45)
🚗 Zaissing, 35km E of Munich
🏨 Thomas Himmel

Erding-Grünbach (1973)

Am Kellerberg, 85461 Grünbach
☎ **(08122) 49650**
🖳 (08122) 49684
🏳 18 L 6109 m SSS 72
👥 WD–H (max 35) WE–H (max 28)
£€ €35 (€45)
🛦 40km NE of Munich

Eschenried (1983)

Kurfürstenweg 10, 85232 Eschenried
☎ **(08131) 567410/567456**
🖳 (08131) 567418/567410
🏳 Eschenried 18 L 5935 m Par 72 SR 124
    Eschenhof 18 L 5550 m Par 70 SR 124
    Gröbenbach 9 L 1810 m Par 32
👥 U H
£€ Eschenried €45 (€55) Eschenhof €40 (€50) Gröbenbach €25 (€32)
🛦 8km NW of Munich
🏠 G von Mecklenburg
■ www.gc-eschenried.de

Feldafing (1926)

Tutzinger Str 15, 82340 Feldafing
☎ **(08157) 9334-0**
🖳 (08157) 9334-99
🏳 18 L 5724 m SSS 71
👥 WD–H WE–M
£€ €50 (€60)
🛦 32km S of Munich
🏠 B von Limburger

Garmisch-Partenkirchen (1928)

Gut Buchwies, 82496 Oberau
☎ **(08824) 8344**
🖳 (08824) 8344
🏳 18 L 6210 m Par 72
👥 U H
£€ €35 (€45)
🛦 10km N of Garmisch-Partenkirchen

Gut Ludwigsberg (1989)

Augsburgerstr 51, 86842 Turkheim
☎ **(08245) 3322**
🖳 (08245) 3789
🏳 18 L 6078 m Par 72
    9 hole Par 3 course
👥 U
£€ €35 (€45)
🛦 50km SW of Munich
🏠 Kurt Rossknecht

Gut Rieden

Gut Rieden, 82319 Starnberg
☎ **(08151) 90770**
🖳 (08151) 907711
🏳 18 L 6046 yds SSS 72
👥 H WE–M
£€ €40 (€50)
🛦 25km S of Munich

Hohenpähl (1988)

82396 Pähl
☎ **(08808) 9202-0**
🖳 (08808) 9202-22

🏳 18 L 5692 m Par 71 SR 126
👥 H
£€ €45 (€60)
🛦 40km S of Munich on B2
🏠 Kurt Rossknecht

Holledau

Weihern 3, 84104 Rudelzhausen
☎ **(08756) 96010**
🖳 (08756) 815
🏳 18 L 6085 m SSS 72
    9 hole course
👥 U H
£€ €25 (€40)
🛦 55km N of Munich

Höslwang im Chiemgau (1975)

Kronberg 3, 83129 Höslwang
☎ **(08075) 714**
🖳 (08075) 8134
🏳 18 L 6049 m Par 72 SSS 72
👥 H
£€ €40 (€50)
🛦 80km S of Munich
🏠 Thomas Himmel
■ www.golfclub-hoeslwang.de

Iffeldorf

Gut Rettenberg, 82393 Iffeldorf
☎ **(08856) 925555**
🖳 (08856) 925559
🏳 18 L 5904 m CR 70.6 SR 122
👥 U
£€ €40 – € 50 (€60)
🛦 45km S of Munich
🏠 Hery Beer

Landshut (1989)

Oberlippach 2, 84095 Furth-Landshut
☎ **(08704) 8378**
🖳 (08704) 8379
🏳 18 L 6251 m SSS 73
👥 H
£€ €35 (€45)
🛦 65 km E of Munich
🏠 Kurt Rossknecht

Mangfalltal G&LC

Oed 1, 83620 Feldkirchen-Westerham
☎ **(08063) 6300**
🖳 (08063) 6958
🏳 18 L 5742 m CR 70.4 SR 125
👥 WD–U WE–M
🛦 40km SE of Munich
■ www.glcm.de

Margarethenhof (1982)

Gut Steinberg, 83666 Waakirchen/Marienstein
☎ **(08022) 7506-0**
🖳 (08022) 74818
🏳 18 L 6056 m Par 71
👥 WD–H WE–before 10am
£€ €55 (€65)
🛦 Tegernsee, 45km S of Munich
🏠 Frank Pennink
■ www.margarethenhof.com

Memmingen Gut Westerhart (1994)

Westerhart 1b, 87740 Buxheim
☎ **(08331) 71016**
🖳 (08331) 71018
🏳 18 hole course
👥 U H
£€ €35 (€45)
🛦 120km W of Munich. Memmingen 5km

München Nord-Eichenried (1989)

Münchnerstr 57, 85452 Eichenried
☎ **(08123) 93080**
🖳 (08123) 930893
🏳 18 L 6318 m Par 73
👥 WD–U WE–M
£€ €50 (€80)
🛦 19km NE of Munich
🏠 Kurt Rossknecht
■ www.gc-eichenried.de

München West-Odelzhausen (1988)

Gut Todtenried, 85235 Odelzhausen
☎ **(08134) 1618**
🖳 (08134) 7623
🏳 18 L 6169 m Par 72 SSS 72
👥 I
£€ €30 (€45)
🛦 35km NW of Munich

München-Riedhof

82544 Egling-Riedhof
☎ **(08171) 7065**
🖳 (08171) 72452
🏳 18 L 6216 m SSS 72
👥 WD–U H
🛦 25km S of München
🏠 Heinz Fehring

Münchener (1910)

Tölzerstrasse 95, 82064 Strasslach
☎ **(08170) 450**
🖳 (08170) 611
🏳 Strasslach 27 L 6177 m SSS 72;
    Thalkirchen 9 L 2528 m SSS 69
👥 WD–H WE–M
£€ WD – € 60
🛦 Strasslach: 10km from Munich. Thalkirchen: Munich

Olching (1979)

Feursstrasse 89, 82140 Olching
☎ **(08142) 48290**
🖳 (08142) 482914
🏳 18 L 6028 m Par 72
👥 H WE–NA
£€ €40 (€50)
🛦 15km W of Munich
🏠 J Dudok van Heel

Pfaffing Wasserburger

München Ost, Köckmühle, 83539 Pfaffing
☎ **(08076) 1718**
🖳 (08076) 8594

P 18 L 6212 m SSS 73
9 hole course
U H
50km E of Münich
Kurt Rossknecht

Reit im Winkl-Kössen (1986)

Postfach 1101, 83237 Reit im Winkl
☎ **(05375) 628535**
📠 (05375) 628537
P 18 L 5221 m Par 70
U
££ €30 (€40)
🚗 100km SE of Munich
🏠 Georg Böhm

Rottaler G&CC (1972)

Am Fischgartl 2, 84332 Herbertsfelden
☎ **(08561) 5969**
📠 (08561) 2646
P 18 L 6105 m Par 72 SSS 72
U
££ €45
🚗 5km W of Pfarrkirchen on B388.
120km E of Munich
🏠 Donald Harradine

Rottbach (1995)

Weiherhaus 5, 82216 Rottbach
☎ **(08135) 93290**
📠 (08135) 932911
P 18 L 6409 m Par 72
U
££ €35 (€45)
🚗 20km NW of Munich
🏠 Thomas Himmel

St Eurach G&LC (1973)

Eurach 8, 82393 Iffeldorf
☎ **(08801) 1332**
📠 (08801) 2523
P 18 L 6509 m SSS 74
H exc Wed & Fri pm–NA WE–
NA
££ €50
🚗 40km S of Munich
🏠 Donald Harradine

Schloss Maxlrain

*Freiung 14, 83104 Maxlrain-
Tuntenhausen*
☎ **(08061) 1403**
📠 (08061) 30146
P 18 L 6083 m CR 73 SR 129
9 hole Par 3 course
U H
££ €46 (€60)
🚗 40km S of Munich
🏠 Paul Krings

Sonnenalp (1976)

Hotel Sonnenalp, 87527 Ofterschwang
☎ **(08321) 272181 (Sec)**
📠 (08321) 272242
P 18 L 5938 m SSS 71
🚗 4km W of Sonthofen
🏠 Donald Harradine

Starnberg (1986)

Uneringerstr, 82319 Starnberg
☎ **(08151) 12157**
📠 (08151) 29115
P 18 L 6057 m Par 72
WD–H WE–M
££ €40 (€50)
🚗 30km S of Munich
🏠 Kurt Rossknecht
🌐 www.gcstarnberg.de

Tegernseer GC Bad Wiessee (1958)

Robognerhof, 83707 Bad Wiessee
☎ **(08022) 8769**
📠 (08022) 82747
P 18 L 5459 m CR 68.6 SR 130
WD–H WE–H before 9.30am
££ €55 (€65)
🚗 Tegernsee, 50km S of Munich
🏠 D Harradine

Tutzing (1983)

82327 Tutzing-Deixlfurt
☎ **(08158) 3600**
📠 (08158) 7234
P 18 L 6159 m SSS 72
U H
££ €50
🚗 Starnberger See, 30km SW of
Munich

Waldegg-Wiggensbach (1988)

Hof Waldegg, 87487 Wiggensbach
☎ **(08370) 93073**
📠 (08370) 93074
P 18 L 5372 m CR 67.3 SR 117
H–max 36
££ €35 (€45)
🚗 10km W of Kempten, nr
Swiss/Austrian border

Wittelsbacher GC Rohrenfeld-Neuburg (1988)

Rohrenfeld, 86633 Neuburg/Donau
☎ **(08431) 44118**
📠 (08431) 41301
P 18 L 6350 m SSS 73
U H
££ €40 (€50)
🚗 7km E of Neuburg. 70km NW of
Munich
🏠 J Dudok van Heel
🌐 www.wittelbacher-golf.de

Wörthsee (1982)

Gut Schluifeld, 82237 Wörthsee
☎ **(08153) 93477-0**
📠 (08153) 4280
P 18 L 5913 m CR 70.2 SR 118
WD–H WE–M
££ €60 (€75)
🚗 Wörthsee, 20km W of Munich
🏠 Kurt Rossknecht
🌐 www.golfclub-woerthsee.de

Nuremberg & North Bavaria

Abenberg (1988)

Am Golfplatz 19, 91183 Abenberg
☎ **(09178) 98960**
📠 (09178) 989696
P 18 holes CR 72.3 SR 131
WD–H
££ €35 (€45)
🚗 10km S of Schwabach. 30km S of
Nuremberg

Bad Griesbach

Holzhäuser 8, 94086 Bad Griesbach
☎ **(08532) 790-0**
📠 (08532) 790-45
P Uttlau 18 L 6115 m SSS 72
Lederbach 18 L 5998 m SSS 71
Brunnwies 18 L 6029 m SSS 71
Beckenbauer 18 L 6500 m SSS 72
I H
££ €36 (€72)
🚗 28km SW of Passau
🏠 Kurt Rossknecht
🌐 www.hartl.de

Bad Windsheim (1992)

Am Weinturm 2, 91438 Bad Windsheim
☎ **(09841) 5027**
📠 (09841) 3448
P 18 L 6265 m Par 73 SSS 73
U
££ €30 (€40)
🚗 40km W of Nuremberg (B470)

Bamberg (1973)

Postfach 1525, 96006 Bamberg
☎ **(09547) 7212/7109**
📠 (09547) 7817
P 18 L 6175 m SSS 72
H
££ €30 (€40)
🚗 Gut Leimershof, 16km N of
Bamberg
🏠 Dieter Sziedat

Donau GC Passau-Rassbach (1986)

Rassbach 8, 94136 Thyrnau-Passau
☎ **(08501) 91313**
📠 (08501) 91314
P 18 L 5877 m Par 72
U
££ €36 (€41)
🚗 10km E of Passau
🏠 Götz Mecklenburg
🌐 www.golf-passau.de

Fränkische Schweiz (1974)

Kanndorf 8, 91316 Ebermannstadt
☎ **(09194) 4827**
📠 (09194) 5410
P 18 L 6050 m SSS 72
H
££ €30 (€40)
🚗 5km E of Ebermannstadt. 40km N
of Nuremberg

Fürth (1951)
Vacherstrasse 261, 90768 Fürth
☎ **(0911) 757522**
🖳 (0911) 973 2989
⮂ 18 L 6478 yds SSS 71
👥 H
£€ €25 (€40)
⛳ 20km W of Nuremburg
🏠 C Wagner (1992)

Gäuboden (1992)
Gut Fruhstorf, 94330 Aiterhofen
☎ **(09421) 72804**
🖳 (09421) 72804
⮂ 18 L 6233 m Par 72
👥 U H
£€ €30 (€35)
⛳ 40km SE of Regensburg, nr Straubing
🏠 Prof Schmidt

Hof (1985)
Postfach 1324, 95012 Hof
☎ **(09281) 43749**
🖳 (09821) 60318/709999
⮂ 18 L 6040 m SSS 72
👥 H
£€ €25 (€35)
⛳ 2km NE of Hof (B173)
🏠 Dieter Sziedat

Lauterhofen (1987)
Ruppertslohe 18, 92283 Lauterhofen
☎ **(09186) 1574**
🖳 (09186) 1527
⮂ 18 L 6054 m SSS 72
👥 H
£€ €35 (€45)
⛳ 25km SE of Nuremberg
🏠 Dillschnitter

Lichtenau-Weickershof
(1980)
Weickershof 1, 91586 Lichtenau
☎ **(09827) 92040**
🖳 (09827) 9204-44
⮂ 18 L 6218 m SSS 72
👥 WD–H (max 35) WE–M
£€ €30 (€40)
⛳ 10km E of Ansbach
🏠 Dieter Sziedat

Oberfranken Thurnau (1965)
Postfach 1349, 95304 Kulmbach
☎ **(09228) 319**
🖳 (09228) 7219
⮂ 18 L 6152 m SSS 72
👥 I H
⛳ Thurnau, 18km NW of Bayreuth. 14km SW of Kulmbach
🏠 Donald Harradine

Oberpfälzer Wald G&LC
(1977)
Ödengrub, 92431 Kemnath bei Fuhrn
☎ **(09439) 466**
🖳 (09439) 1247

⮂ 18 L 5799 m SSS 71
👥 I
£€ €25 (€30)
⛳ 10km E of Schwarzenfeld, towards Neunburg
🏠 Max Haseneder

Oberzwieselau (1990)
94227 Lindberg
☎ **(01049) 9922/2367**
🖳 (01049) 9922/2924
⮂ 18 L 5949 m SSS 72
👥 U H
£€ €40 (€50)
⛳ 170km NE of Munich
■ www.golfpark-oberzwieselau.de

Regensburg (1966)
93093 Jagdschloss Thiergarten
☎ **(09403) 505**
🖳 (09403) 4391
⮂ 18 L 5734 m CR 70.2 SR 131
👥 U
£€ €35 (€50)
⛳ 14km E of Regensburg, nr Walhalla
🏠 Harradine/Himmel

Regensburg-Sinzing
Minoritenhof 1, 93161 Sinzing
☎ **(0941) 32504**
🖳 (0941) 36299
⮂ 18 L 5984 m SSS 72
6 hole short course
👥 U H
£€ €30 (€35)
⛳ 7km SW of Regensburg

Am Reichswald (1960)
Schiestlstr 100, 90427 Nürnberg
☎ **(0911) 305730**
🖳 (0911) 301200
⮂ 18 L 6041 m CR 71.8 SR 129
👥 U H
£€ €45 (€65)
⛳ 10km N of Nuremberg

Sagmühle (1984)
Golfplatz Sagmühle 1, 94086 Bad Griesbach
☎ **(08532) 2038**
🖳 (08532) 3165
⮂ 18 L 6168 m SSS 72
👥 U
£€ €35 (€40)
⛳ 25km SW of Passau
🏠 Kurt Rossknecht

Schloss Fahrenbach (1993)
95709 Tröstau
☎ **(09232) 882-256**
🖳 (09232) 882-345
⮂ 18 L 5858 m Par 72 SSS 72
👥 U
£€ €30 (€35)
⛳ 15km W of Marktredwitz. 40km E of Bayreuth
🏠 Deutsche Golf Consult
■ www.golfhotel-fahrenbach.de

Schloss Reichmannsdorf
(1991)
Schlosshof 4, 96132 Schlüsselfeld
☎ **()9546) 9215-10**
🖳 (09546) 9224-0
⮂ 18 L 5800 m CR 70.8 SR 128
👥 H
£€ €30 (€35)
⛳ 7km from Schlüsselfeld
■ www.golfanlage-reichmannsdorf.de

Schlossberg (1985)
Grünbach 8, 94419 Reisbach
☎ **(08734) 7035**
🖳 (08734) 7795
⮂ 18 L 6070 m SSS 72
👥 U
£€ €35
⛳ Sommershausen, 15km from Dingolfing. 100km NE of Munich, off Route 11

Schmidmühlen G&CC
(1968)
Am Theilberg, 92287 Schmidmühlen
☎ **(09474) 701**
🖳 (09474) 8236
⮂ 18 L 5946 m Par 72
⛳ 35km NW of Regensburg

Schwanhof (1994)
Klaus Conrad Allee 1, 92706 Luhe-Wildenau
☎ **(09607) 92020**
🖳 (09607) 920248
⮂ 18 hole course SSS 72
👥 U H
£€ €35 (€45)
⛳ 80km N of Regensburg
🏠 Pate/Weisshaupt

Die Wutzschleife (1997)
Hillstedt 40, 92444 Rötz
☎ **(09976) 18460**
🖳 (09976) 18180
⮂ 18 L 4728 m Par 65
👥 U
£€ €25–30 (€30–35)
⛳ 70km N of Regensburg. 180km NE of Munich
🏠 Deutsche Golf Consult

Rhineland North

Aachen (1927)
Schurzelter Str 300, 52074 Aachen
☎ **(0241) 12501**
🖳 (0241) 171075
⮂ 18 L 6063 m Par 72
👥 H
£€ €40 (€50)
⛳ Seffent, 5km NW of Aachen
🏠 Murray/Morrison/Pennink

Ahaus
Schmäinghook 36, 48683 Ahaus-Alstätte
☎ **(02567) 405**

☐ (02567) 3524
☞ 18 hole course SSS 72
9 hole course
♙ U H
£€ €31 (€45)
⊶ 60km W of Münster
⌂ Deutsche Golf Consult
■ www.glc-ahaus.de

Alten Fliess (1995)

Am Alten Fliess 66, 50129 Bergheim
☎ (02238) 94410
☐ (02238) 944119
☞ 27 holes :
6050-6075 m Par 72
♙ U H–36 max
£€ €22–50 (€30–60)
⊶ 12km W of Cologne
⌂ Kurt Rossknecht

Artland (1988)

Westerholte 23, 49577 Ankum
☎ (05466) 301
☐ (05466) 91081
☞ 18 holes Par 72
♙ U H – booking required
£€ €32 (€42)
⊶ Ankum, 30km N of Osnabrück
⌂ Udo Schmidt
■ www.artlandgolf.de

Bergisch-Land

Siebeneickerst 386, 42111 Wuppertal
☎ (02053) 7177
☐ (02053) 7303
☞ 18 L 6037 m SSS 72
♙ WD–H WE–M
£€ €40
⊶ Elberfeld, 8km W of Wuppertal

Bochum (1982)

Im Mailand 127, 44797 Bochum
☎ (0234) 799832
☐ (0234) 795775
☞ 18 L 5300 m SSS 68
♙ WD–H
⊶ Bochum-Stiepel, 7km S of Bochum

Castrop-Rauxel

Dortmunder Str 383, 44577 Castrop-Rauxel
☎ (02305) 62027
☐ (02305) 61410
☞ 18 L 6181 m SSS 72
♙ U
⊶ 10km W of Dortmund

Dortmund (1956)

Reichmarkstr 12, 44265 Dortmund
☎ (0231) 774133/774609
☐ (0231) 774403
☞ 18 L 6174 m SSS 72
♙ WE–M
£€ €30 (€40)
⊶ 8km S of Dortmund
⌂ B von Limburger

Düsseldorf (1961)

Rommerljansweg 12, 40882 Ratingen
☎ (02102) 81092
☐ (02102) 81782
☞ 18 L 5905 m SSS 71
♙ WD–U WE–M
⊶ 11km N of Düsseldorf

Düsseldorf Hösel

In den Höfen 32, 40883 Ratingen
☎ (02102) 68629
☞ 18 L 6160 m SSS 72
♙ U
⊶ Hösel, 15km NE of Düsseldorf

Elfrather Mühle (1991)

An der Elfrather Mühle 145, 47802 Krefeld
☎ (02151) 4969-0
☐ (02151) 477459
☞ 18 L 6125 m Par 72 SSS 72
♙ H–max 36
£€ €35 (€45)
⊶ Krefeld 7km. Düsseldorf 25km
⌂ Ron Kirby

Erftaue (1991)

Zur Mühlenerft 1, 41517 Grevenbroich
☎ (02181) 280637
☐ (02181) 280639
☞ 18 L 6039 m Par 72
♙ WD–H WE–H after 1pm
£€ €30 (€40)
⊶ 25km SW of Düsseldorf
⌂ Karl Grohs

Essen Haus Oefte (1959)

Laupendahler Landstr, 45219 Essen-Kettwig
☎ (02054) 83911
☐ (02054) 83850
☞ 18 L 6011 m CR 71.7 SR 126
♙ U H
⊶ 14km SW of Essen

Essen-Heidhausen (1970)

Preutenborbeckstr 36, 45239 Essen
☎ (0201) 404111
☞ 18 L 5937 m SSS 71
♙ U H
⊶ 10km S of Essen on B224, nr Werden

Euregio Bad Bentheim (1987)

Postbox 1205, 48443 Bad Bentheim
☎ (05922) 6700
☐ (05922) 6701
☞ 18 L 5780 m CR 70.4 SR 130
♙ U exc Wed & Thurs–NA
£€ €35 (€45)
⊶ 55km N of Münster
⌂ Prof Schmidt
■ www.golfclub-euregio.de

Grevenmühle Ratingen (1988)

Grevenmühle, 40882 Ratingen-Homberg
☎ (02102) 9595-0
☐ (02102) 959515
☞ 18 L 6023 m Par 72

♙ WD–H WE–M
£€ €40 (€50)
⊶ 10km N of Düsseldorf
⌂ Peter Drecker

Haus Bey (1992)

An Haus bey 16, 41334 Nettetal
☎ (02153) 9197-0
☐ (02153) 919750
☞ 18 L 5948 m CR 71.8 SR 122
♙ U H
£€ €35 (€50)
⊶ 40km NW of Düsseldorf
⌂ Paul Krings
■ www.hausbey.de

Haus Kambach (1989)

Kambachstrasse 9-13, 52249 Eschweiler-Kinzweiler
☎ (02403) 37615
☐ (02403) 21270
☞ 18 L 6178 m SSS 72
♙ U
£€ €35 (€45)
⊶ 20km E of Aachen
⌂ Dieter Sziedat

Hubbelrath (1961)

Bergische Landstr 700, 40629 Düsseldorf
☎ (02104) 72178/71848
☐ (02104) 75685
☞ East 18 L 6208 m SSS 72
West 18 L 4325 m SSS 62
♙ WD–U WE–M H–max 28 East, 36 West
£€ East €50 (€60) West €40 (€50)
⊶ Hubbelrath, 13km E of Düsseldorf, on Route B7
⌂ B von Limburger

Hummelbachaue Neuss (1987)

Norfer Kirchstrasse, 41469 Neuss
☎ (02137) 91910
☐ (02137) 4016
☞ 18 L 6091 m Par 73
♙ WD–H WE–M
£€ €20–40 (€40)
⊶ 5km W of Düsseldorf
⌂ Udo Barth

Issum-Niederrhein (1973)

Pauenweg 68, 47661 Issum 1
☎ (02835) 92310
☐ (02835) 9231-20
☞ 18 L 5769 m CR 70.6 SR 125
♙ H
£€ €40 (€50)
⊶ 10km E of Geldern

Juliana (1979)

Frielinghausen 1, 45549 Sprockhövel
☎ (0202) 647070/648220
☐ (0202) 649891
☞ 18 L 6100 m SSS 71
♙ H
⊶ 30km E of Düsseldorf
⌂ De Buer

Köln G&LC

Golfplatz 2, 51429 Bergisch Gladbach
☎ **(02204) 92760**
📠 (02204) 927615
🏳 18 L 6090 m Par 72
👥 WD–H WE–NA
£€ WD – € 50
🏌 15km E of Cologne

Kosaido International

Am Schmidtberg 11, 40629 Düsseldorf
☎ **(02104) 77060**
📠 (02104) 770611
🏳 18 L 5562 m CR 70 SR 132
👥 WD–U WE–NA before 2.30pm
£€ €45 (€60)
🏌 10km NE of Düsseldorf
🏠 Tomizawa/Preissmann
■ www.kosaido.de

Krefeld (1930)

Eltweg 2, 47809 Krefeld
☎ **(02151) 570071/72**
🏳 18 L 6082 m SSS 72
👥 WD–U H–max 28
£€ €45 (€55)
🏌 7km SE of Krefeld. Düsseldorf 16km
🏠 B von Limburger

Mühlenhof (1990)

Mühlenhof, 47546 Kalkar
☎ **(02824) 924040**
📠 (02824) 924093
🏳 18 L 6103 m Par 72
👥 U
£€ €30 (€40)
🏌 80km N of Düsseldorf (B57)
🏠 Hans Herkberger
■ www.muehlenhof.net

Nordkirchen (1974)

Am Golfplatz 6, 59394 Nordkirchen
☎ **(02596) 9191**
📠 (02596) 9195
🏳 18 L 5828 m SSS 71
👥 WD–I WE–H
£€ €35 (€40)
🏌 30km S of Münster
🏠 Christoph Städtler
■ www.glc-nordkirchen.de

Op de Niep (1995)

Bergschenweg 71, 47506 Neukirchen-Vluyn
☎ **(02845) 28051**
📠 (02845) 28052
🏳 18 L 6374 m CR 72.8 SR 130
　 9 L 3926 m Par 66 CR 61.8
👥 WD–U H WE–M
£€ 18 holes: €25 (€40) 9 holes: €17 (€22)
🏌 20km W of Duisburg. 30km NW of Düsseldorf
🏠 Heinz Wolters

Osnabrück (1955)

Karmannstr 1, 49084 Osnabrück
☎ **(05402) 5636**

📠 (05402) 5257
🏳 18 L 5731 m Par 71
👥 U
£€ €35 (€50)
🏌 13km SE of Osnabrück
■ www.ogc.de

Rheine/Mesum (1998)

Wörstr 201, 48419 Rheine
☎ **(05975) 9490**
📠 (05975) 9491
🏳 18 L 6036 m Par 72 SSS 72
　 9 L 4442 m Par 68 SSS 64
👥 U H–max 36
£€ €22–32 (€35–45)
🏌 Gut Winterbrock, 40km W of Münster
🏠 Christoph Städler
■ www.golfsportclub.de

Rittergut Birkhof (1996)

Rittergut Birkhof, 41352 Korschenbroich
☎ **(02131) 510660**
📠 (02131) 510616
🏳 18 L 6037 m Par 73
　 9 hole Par 3 course
👥 I H
£€ €35 (€45)
🏌 20km W of Düsseldorf
🏠 Kurt Rossknecht

St Barbara's Royal Dortmund (1969)

Hesslingweg, 44309 Dortmund
☎ **(0231) 202551**
📠 (0231) 259183
🏳 18 L 5967 m SSS 73
👥 H–by prior arrangement
£€ €30 (€40)
🏌 Dortmund Brackel
🏠 Brig Jones/Maj Coleman

Schloss Georghausen (1962)

Georghausen 8, 51789 Lindlar-Hommerich
☎ **(02207) 4938**
📠 (02207) 81230
🏳 18 L 6045 m SSS 72
👥 H
£€ €35 (€45)
🏌 30km E of Cologne

Schloss Haag (1996)

Bartelter Weg 8, 47608 Geldern
☎ **(02831) 94777**
📠 (02831) 94778
🏳 18 L 6193 m Par 73
👥 H or I
£€ €25 (€30)
🏌 60km NW of Düsseldorf (Route 9)
🏠 W Hardes

Schloss Myllendonk (1965)

Myllendonkerstr 113, 41352 Korschenbroich 1
☎ **(02161) 641049**
📠 (02161) 648806
🏳 18 L 6120 m CR 71.3 SR 128
👥 H
£€ €48 (€55)

🏌 Korschenbroich, 5km E of Mönchengladbach
■ www.gc-schloss-myllendonk.de

Schmitzhof (1975)

Arsbeckerstr 160, 41844 Wegberg
☎ **(02436) 39090**
📠 (02436) 390915
🏳 18 L 6115 m CR 71.6 SR 132
👥 H
£€ €35 (€45)
🏌 Wegberg-Merbeck, 20km SW of Mönchengladbach
■ www.golfclubschmitzhof.de

Schwarze Heide

Gahlenerstrasse 44, 46244 Bottrop-Kirchellen
☎ **(02045) 82488**
📠 (02045) 83077
🏳 18 L 6051 m SSS 72
👥 I H
£€ €25 (€35)
🏌 55km N of Düsseldorf
🏠 Peter Drecker

Siegen-Olpe (1966)

Am Golfplatz, 57482 Wenden
☎ **(02762) 9762-0**
📠 (02762) 9762-12
🏳 18 L 5359 m CR 71.1 SR 127
👥 U H–max 36
£€ €40 (€45)
🏌 20km NW of Siegen

Siegerland (1993)

Berghäuser Weg, 57223 Kreuztal-Mittelhees
☎ **(02732) 59470**
📠 (02732) 594724
🏳 18 L 5865 m Par 72
👥 H
£€ €30 (€40)
🏌 15km N of Siegen
🏠 Spangemacher

Unna-Fröndenberg (1985)

Schwarzer Weg 1, 58730 Fröndenberg
☎ **(02373) 70068**
📠 (02373) 70069
🏳 18 L 6061 m CR 71.2 SR 123
　 9 hole Par 3 course
👥 M H (max 34)
£€ €35 (€45)
🏌 25km W of Dortmund
🏠 Karl Grohs
■ www.gcuf.de

Vechta-Welpe (1989)

Welpe 2, 49377 Vechta
☎ **(04441) 5539/82168**
📠 (04441) 852480
🏳 18 L 5957 m Par 72
👥 H
£€ €25 (€35)
🏌 50km SW of Bremen
🏠 Rainer Preissmann
■ www.golfclub-vechta.de

Velbert - Gut Kuhlendahl
Kuhlendahler Str 283, 42553 Velbert
- ☎ **(02053) 923290**
- 📠 (02053) 923291
- ⛳ 18 L 5608 m CR 70.4 SR 130
- 👥 H
- €€ €35 (€45)
- 🚗 Between Düsseldorf and Wuppertal
- 🏠 Grohs/Preissmann
- 🖥 www.gcvelbert.de

Vestischer GC Recklinghausen   (1974)
Bockholterstr 475, 45659 Recklinghausen
- ☎ **(02361) 93420**
- 📠 (02361) 934240
- ⛳ 18 L 6111 m SSS 72
- 👥 WD–H exc Mon–NA WE–M
- €€ €40 (€50)
- 🚗 Nr Loemühle Airport, N of Recklinghausen
- 🏠 Donald Harradine

Wasserburg Anholt
(1972)
Am Schloss 3, 46419 Isselburg Anholt
- ☎ **(02874) 3444**
- 📠 (02874) 29164
- ⛳ 18 L 6115 m SSS 72
- 👥 WD–U WE–H
- 🚗 Parkhotel, Wasserburg Anholt. 15 km W of Bocholt

West Rhine   (1956)
Javelin Barracks, BFPO 35
- ☎ **(02163) 974463**
- 📠 (02163) 80049
- ⛳ 18 L 6522 yds SSS 71
- 👥 WD–U WE–M
- €€ €30
- 🚗 On B230, 1km from Dutch/German border. 25km W of Mönchengladbach

Westerwald   (1979)
Steinebacherstr, 57629 Dreifelden
- ☎ **(02666) 8220**
- 📠 (02666) 8493
- ⛳ 18 holes SSS 72
- 👥 H
- €€ €30 (€40)
- 🚗 Hachenburg, 60km E of Bonn

Rhineland South

Bad Neuenahr G&LC
(1979)
Remagener Weg, 53474 Bad Neuenahr-Ahrweiler
- ☎ **(02641) 950950**
- 📠 (02641) 950 9595
- ⛳ 18 L 6060 m SSS 72
- 👥 WD–H WE–H before 10am & after 4pm
- €€ €40 (€50)

- 🚗 Bad Neuenahr, 40km S of Bonn
- 🏠 Grohs/Preismann

Bitburger Land   (1994)
Zur Weilersheck 1, 54636 Wissmannsdorf
- ☎ **(06527) 9272-0**
- 📠 (06527) 9272-30
- ⛳ 18 L 6168 m Par 72 SR 128
- 👥 H
- €€ €36 (€46)
- 🚗 25km NE of Trier
- 🏠 Karl Grohs
- 🖥 www.bitgolf.de

Bonn-Godesberg in Wachtberg   (1960)
Landgrabenweg, 53343 Wachtberg-Niederbachen
- ☎ **(0228) 344003**
- 📠 (0228) 340820
- ⛳ 18 L 5700 m Par 71
- 👥 WD–H WE–M
- €€ €35 (€45)
- 🚗 Niederbachem, 4km from Bad Godesberg
- 🏠 M Harris

Burg Overbach   (1984)
Postfach 1213, 53799 Much
- ☎ **(02245) 5550**
- 📠 (02245) 8247
- ⛳ 18 L 6056 m SSS 72
- 👥 H
- €€ €30 (€40)
- 🚗 Much, 45km E of Cologne, off A4
- 🏠 Deutsch Golf Consult
- 🖥 www.golfclub-burg-overbach.de

Burg Zievel   (1994)
Burg Zievel, 53894 Mechernich
- ☎ **(02256) 1651**
- 📠 (02256) 3479
- ⛳ 18 L 6143 m Par 72
- 👥 H
- €€ €15–35
- 🚗 30km S of Cologne
- 🏠 G Knappertz

Eifel   (1977)
Kölner Str, 54576 Hillesheim
- ☎ **(06593) 1241**
- 📠 (06593) 9421
- ⛳ 18 L 6017 m Par 72
- 👥 H–phone before play
- €€ €30 (€40)
- 🚗 70km S of Cologne
- 🏠 Grohs/Preismann

Gut Heckenhof   (1993)
53783 Eitorf
- ☎ **(02243) 83137**
- 📠 (02243) 83426
- ⛳ 18 L 6214 m SSS 72
- 👥 H
- €€ On request
- 🚗 40km SE of Cologne
- 🏠 William Amick

Internationaler GC Bonn
(1992)
Gut Grossenbusch, 53757 St Augustin
- ☎ **(02241) 39880**
- 📠 (02241) 398888
- ⛳ 18 L 5927 m Par 72
- 👥 U H
- €€ €35 (€50)
- 🚗 6km E of Bonn
- 🖥 www.golf-course-bonn.de

Jakobsberg   (1990)
Im Tal der Loreley, 56154 Boppard
- ☎ **(06742) 808491**
- 📠 (06742) 808493
- ⛳ 18 L 5950 m Par 72 SSS 72
- 👥 U
- €€ €35 (€45)
- 🚗 80km N of Mainz
- 🏠 Wolfgang Jersombek
- 🖥 www.jakobsberg.de

Kyllburger Waldeifel
Lietzenhof, 54597 Burbach
- ☎ **(06553) 961039**
- 📠 (06553) 3282
- ⛳ 18 hole course
- €€ On application
- 🚗 15km S of Siegen
- 🖥 www.golf-lietzenhof.de

Mittelrheinischer Bad Ems
(1938)
Denzerheide, 56130 Bad Ems
- ☎ **(02603) 6541**
- 📠 (02603) 13995
- ⛳ 18 L 6050 m SSS 72
- 👥 H
- €€ €40 (€55)
- 🚗 13km E of Koblenz, nr Bad Ems (6km)
- 🏠 Karl Hoffmann

Nahetal   (1971)
Drei Buchen, 55583 Bad Münster am Stein
- ☎ **(06708) 2145**
- 📠 (06708) 1731
- ⛳ 18 L 6065 m Par 72 SSS 72
- 👥 H
- €€ €35 (€45)
- 🚗 6 km S of Bad Kreuznach. 70km SW of Frankfurt
- 🏠 Armin Keller
- 🖥 www.golfclub-nahetal.de

Rhein Sieg   (1971)
Postfach 1216, 53759 Hennef
- ☎ **(02242) 6501**
- ⛳ 18 L 6081 m Par 72
- 🚗 Hennef, 30km SE of Cologne

Stromberg-Schindeldorf
(1987)
Park Village Golfanlagen, Buchenring 6, 55442 Stromberg
- ☎ **(06724) 93080**
- 📠 (06724) 930818
- ⛳ 18 L 5161 Par 68 SSS 68

U H–booking necessary
££ €30 (€42)
👟 5km from A61 exit Stromberg

Trier (1977)
54340 Ensch-Birkenheck
☎ **(06507) 993255**
🖳 (06507) 993257
🏴 18 L 6069 m Par 72
👥 H–max 36
££ €30 (€40)
👟 Trier 20km. Koblenz 80km

Waldbrunnen (1983)
Brunnenstr 11, 53578 Windhagen
☎ **(02645) 8041**
🖳 (02645) 8042
🏴 18 L 5787 m Par 71
👥 U
££ €30 (€40)
👟 30km S of Bonn
🏠 Donald Harradine

Wiesensee (1992)
Am Wiesensee, 56459 Westerburg-
Stahlhofen
☎ **(02663) 991192**
🖳 (02663) 991193
🏴 18 L 5917 m Par 72
9 hole Par 3 course
👥 H
££ €40 (€45)
👟 100km NW of Frankfurt. Cologne
80KM
🏠 E Bensing

Saar-Pfalz

Pfalz Neustadt (1971)
Im Lochbusch, 67435 Neustadt-
Geinsheim
☎ **(06327) 97420**
🖳 (06327) 974218
🏴 18 L 6180 m CR 72.1 SR 130
👥 U H WE–NA before 3pm
££ €40 (€55)
👟 Geinsheim, 15km SE of Neustadt
towards Speyer
🏠 B von Limburger

Saarbrücken (1961)
Oberlimbergerweg, 66798 Wallerfangen-
Gisingen
☎ **(06837) 91800/1584**
🖳 (06837) 91801
🏴 18 L 5971 m CR 71.9 SR 130
👥 H
££ €40 (€50)
👟 B406 towards Wallerfangen. 8km
N of Saarlouis
🏠 Donald Harradine
■ www.golfclub-saarbruecken.de

Websweiler Hof (1991)
Websweiler Hof, 66424 Homburg/Saar
☎ **(06841) 7777-60**
🖳 (06841) 7777-666

🏴 18 L 6188 m Par 72 SSS 74
👥 U H
££ €30 (€40)
👟 35km E of Saarbrücken
■ www.golf-saar.de

Westpfalz Schwarzbachtal
(1988)
66509 Rieschweiler
☎ **(06336) 6442**
🖳 (06336) 6408
🏴 18 L 5740 m Par 70
👥 H
👟 40km E of Saarbrücken

Woodlawn
6792 Ramstein Flugplatz
☎ **(06371) 476240**
🖳 (06371) 42158
🏴 18 L 6225 yds Par 70
👥 Military GC–visitors restricted
££ $16
👟 Ramstein 3km. Kaiserlautern 10km
■ www.ramsteingolf.com

Stuttgart &
South West

Bad Liebenzell
Golfplatz 1-9, 75378 Bad Liebenzell
☎ **(07052) 9325-0**
🖳 (07052) 9325-25
🏴 18 L 6113 m Par 72 SSS 72
18 L 5853 m Par 72 SSS 71
👥 H–max 33 WE–M 10.30am–2pm
££ €40 (€50)
👟 35km W of Stuttgart
🏠 Elger/Mühl

Bad Rappenau (1989)
Ehrenbergstrasse 25a, 74906
Bad Rappenau
☎ **(07264) 3666**
🖳 (07264) 3838
🏴 18 L 6103 m SSS 72
👥 U H
££ €30 (€40)
👟 10km NW of Heilbronn
🏠 Karl Gross

Bad Salgau (1995)
Koppelweg 103, 88348 Bad Salgau
☎ **(07581) 527459**
🖳 (07581) 527487
🏴 18 L 6190 m CR 71.8 SR 126
👥 U
££ €35 (€45)
👟 5km SW of Bad Salgau

Baden Hills GC Rastat
(1982)
Cabot Trail G208, 77836 Rheinmünster
☎ **(07229) 661501**
🖳 (07229) 661509
🏴 18 L 5906 m Par 72
👥 H–booking necessary

££ D – € 30 (D – € 40)
👟 10km W of Baden-Baden. 50km N
of Strasbourg

Baden-Baden (1901)
Fremersbergstr 127, 76530 Baden-
Baden
☎ **(07221) 23579**
🖳 (07221) 3025659
🏴 18 L 4282 m Par 64
👥 U
££ €35 (€50)
👟 Baden-Baden
🏠 Harry Vardon

Bodensee (1986)
Lampertsweiler 51, 88138 Weissensberg
☎ **(08389) 89190**
🖳 (08389) 923907
🏴 18 L 6112 m CR 72.1 SR 141
👥 H
££ €45 (€55)
👟 5km NE of Lindau/Bodensee
🏠 Robert Trent Jones Sr
■ www.gcbw.de

Freiburg (1970)
Krüttweg 1, 79199 Kirchzarten
☎ **(07661) 9847-0**
🖳 (07661) 984747
🏴 18 L 5945 m CR 71.8 SR 127
👥 H
££ €35 (€40)
👟 Freiburg-Kappel/Kirchzarten
🏠 B von Limburger

Fürstlicher Waldsee (1998)
Hopfenweiler, 88339 Bad Waldsee
☎ **(07524) 4017 200**
🖳 (07524) 4017 100
🏴 18 L 6474 m Par 72
9 hole Par 3 course
👥 U
££ 18 holes: €30 (€40) 9 holes: €13
(€20)
👟 60km SW of Ulm (Route 30)
🏠 Knauss/Himmel

Hechingen Hohenzollern
(1955)
Postfach 1124, 72379 Hechingen
☎ **(07471) 6478**
🏴 18 holes SSS 72
👥 WE–M
££ On application
👟 Hechingen, 50km S of Stuttgart

Heidelberg-Lobenfeld (1968)
Biddersbacherhof, 74931 Lobbach-
Lobenfeld
☎ **(06226) 952110**
🖳 (06226) 952111
🏴 18 L 5989 m SSS 72
👥 WD–H WE–M H
££ €40 (€50)
👟 20km E of Heidelberg
🏠 Donald Harradine

For list of abbreviations and key to symbols see page 649

Heilbronn-Hohenlohe (1964)
Hofgasse, 74639 Zweiflingen-
Friedrichsruhe
☎ **(07941) 920810**
🖩 (07941) 920819
🏌 18 L 5852 m CR 70.7 SR 121
👥 H
£€ €30 (€50)
🏌 25km W of Heilbronn, nr Öhringen
■ www.friedrichsruhe.de

Hetzenhof
Hetzenhof 7, 73547 Larch
☎ **(07172) 9180-0**
🖩 (07172) 9180-30
🏌 18 Holes Par 72 SR 131
6 hole short course
👥 WD–H WE–M
£€ €40
🏌 35km E of Stuttgart Airport, via
B29 and B297
■ www.golfclub-hetzenhof.de

Hohenstaufen (1959)
Unter den Ramsberg, 73072 Donzdorf-
Reichenbach
☎ **(07162) 27171/20050**
🏌 18 L 6540 yds SSS 72
🏌 15km E of Goppingen. 45km E of
Stuttgart

Kaiserhöhe (1995)
Im Laber 4, 74747 Ravenstein
☎ **(06297) 399**
🖩 (06297) 599
🏌 18 L 6049 m CR 71.3 SR 122
9 hole Par 3 course
👥 U H
£€ €30 (€45)
🏌 60km S of Würzburg
🏠 Kurt Rossknecht
■ www.gck.geoid.de

Konstanz (1965)
Langenrain, Kargegg, 78476 Allensbach
☎ **(07533) 5124**
🖩 (07533) 4897
🏌 18 L 6058 m SSS 72
👥 WD–I WE–H max 28
🏌 15km NW of Konstanz, nr
Langenrain

Lindau-Bad Schachen (1954)
Am Schönbühl 5, 88131 Lindau
☎ **(08382) 96170**
🖩 (08382) 961750
🏌 18 L 5871 m Par 71 SSS 71
£€ €45 (€55)
🏌 Nr Lindau, Bodensee

Markgräflerland Kandern (1984)
Feuerbacher Str 35, 79400 Kandern
☎ **(07626) 97799-0**
🖩 (07626) 97799-22
🏌 18 L 5931 m CR 71.5 SR 131
👥 WD–U WE–M
£€ €50 (€60)

🏌 Kandern, 10km N of Lörrach. 14km
NW of Basle
🏠 Grohs/Benz

Neckartal (1974)
Aldingerstr, Gebäude 975,
70806 Kornwestheim
☎ **(07141) 871319**
🖩 (07141) 81716
🏌 18 L 6310 m SSS 73
👥 WD–U WE–M
£€ €30 (€35)
🏌 5km NE of Stuttgart, nr
Kornwestheim
🏠 B von Limburger
■ www.golf.de/gcneckartal

Nippenburg (1993)
Nippenburg 21, 71701 Schwieberdingen
☎ **(07150) 39530**
🖩 (07150) 353518
🏌 18 L 5866 m Par 71
👥 H
£€ €35 (€50)
🏌 16km NW of Stuttgart
🏠 Bernhard Langer

Obere Alp (1989)
Am Golfplatz 1-3, 79780 Stühlingen
☎ **(07703) 9203-0**
🖩 (07703) 9203-18
🏌 18 L 6147 m SSS 71 SR 128
9 L 3522 m SSS 60
👥 H
£€ 18 hole:€40 (€50) 9 hole:€25 (€35)
🏌 40km N of Zürich, nr Swiss border
🏠 Karl Grohs
■ www.golf-oberealp.de

Oberschwaben-Bad Waldsee (1968)
Hopfenweiler 2d, 88339 Bad Waldsee
☎ **(07524) 5900**
🖩 (07524) 6106
🏌 18 L 5986 m CR 72.1 SR 133
👥 H–(max 34)
£€ €50 (€60)
🏌 Bad Waldsee, 60km SW of Ulm
🏠 Donald Harradine

Oeschberghof L & GC (1976)
Golfplatz 1, 78166 Donaueschingen
☎ **(0771) 84525**
🖩 (0771) 84540
🏌 18 L 6580 m SSS 74
9 L 4120 m SSS 62
👥 H
🏌 18 hole:€52 (€67) 9 hole:€31 (€47)
🏌 Donaueschingen, 60km E of
Freiburg
🏠 Deutsche Golf Consult

Owingen-Überlingen
Alte Owinger Str, 88696 Owingen
☎ **(07551) 83040**
🖩 (07551) 830422
🏌 18 L 6148 m SSS 72
👥 H

£€ €30 (€45)
🏌 5km N of Überlingen, nr Lake
Konstanz

Pforzheim Karlshäuser Hof (1987)
Karlshäuser Weg, 75248 Ölbronn-Dürrn
☎ **(07237) 9100**
🖩 (0723⁷/) 5161
🏌 18 hole course SSS 72
👥 H–max 36
£€ €35 (€45)
🏌 6km N of Pforzheim. 30km E of
Karlsruhe
🏠 Reinhold Weishaupt
■ www.gc-pf.de

Reischenhof (1987)
Industriestrasse 12, 88489 Wain
☎ **(07353) 1732**
🖩 (07373) 3824
🏌 27 L 5998 m CR 71.9 SR 129
👥 M H
£€ €40 (€50)
🏌 30km S of Ulm
🏠 Wolfgang Jersombeck
■ www.golf.de/gc-reischenhof

Reutlingen-Sonnenbühl (1987)
Im Zerg, 72820 Sonnenbühl
☎ **(07128) 92660**
🖩 (07128) 926692
🏌 18 L 6085 m SSS 72
👥 H
£€ €30 (€40)
🏌 40km S of Stuttgart

Rhein Badenweiler (1971)
79401 Badenweiler
☎ **(07632) 7970**
🖩 (07632) 797150
🏌 18 L 6134 m SSS 72
👥 WD–H WE–M
🏌 16km W of Badenweiler. 30km SW
of Freiburg
🏠 Donald Harradine

Rickenbach (1979)
Hennematt 20, 79736 Rickenbach
☎ **(07765) 777**
🖩 (07765) 544
🏌 18 L 5544 m CR 71 SR 134
👥 WD/Sat–U H exc Tues/Thurs am
Sun–NA before 3pm
£€ €50 (€60)
🏌 20km N of Bad Säckingen
🏠 Dudok van Heel/Himmel
■ www.golfclub-rickenbach.de

Schloss Klingenburg-Günzburg (1978)
Schloss Klingenburg, 89343 Jettingen-
Scheppach
☎ **(08225) 3030**
🖩 (08225) 30350
🏌 18 L 6237 m SSS 72
👥 H
£€ €35 (€50)

⛳ 40km W of Augsburg. 5km from
Stuttgart-Munich motorway, exit
Burgau
🏠 Harradine/Sziedat

Schloss Langenstein (1991)
Schloss Langenstein, 78359 Orsingen-
Nenzingen
☎ **(07774) 50651**
🖥 (07774) 50699
⮂ 18 L 6341 m CR 73.3 SR 124
9 hole course
👫 WD–H WE–H (restricted)
💷 €42 (€62)
⛳ 120km S of Stuttgart. 75km NE of
Zürich
🏠 Rod Whitman
◼ www.schloss-langenstein.com

Schloss Liebenstein (1982)
Postfach 27, 74380 Neckarwestheim
☎ **(07133) 9878-0**
🖥 (07133) 9878-18
⮂ 27 L 5890-6361 m SSS 71-73
👫 U
💷 €30 (€40)
⛳ 35km N of Stuttgart
🏠 Donald Harradine

Schloss Weitenburg (1984)
Sommerhalde 11, 72181 Starzach-Sulzau
☎ **(07472) 8061**
🖥 (07472) 8062
⮂ 18 L 5978 m CR 71.3 SR 123
9 hole course
👫 I or U
💷 18 holes: €35 (€45) 9 holes: €15
(€20)
⛳ 50km SW of Stuttgart in Neckar
Valley
🏠 Heinz Fehring

Sinsheim
Buchenauerhof 4, 74889 Sinsheim
☎ **(07265) 7258**
🖥 (07265) 7379
⮂ 18 hole course
👫 H
💷 €35 (€45)
⛳ 35km S of Heidelberg
🏠 Georg Boehm
◼ www.golfclubsinsheim.de

Steisslingen (1991)
Brunnenstr 4b, 78256 Steisslingen-
Wiechs
☎ **(07738) 7196**
🖥 (07738) 923297
⮂ 18 L 6145 m Par 72
6 hole course
👫 U
💷 €38 (€ 55)
⛳ 30km N of Konstanz
🏠 Dave Thomas
◼ www.golfclub-steisslingen.de

Stuttgarter Solitude (1927)
71297 Mönsheim
☎ **(07044) 911 0410**
🖥 (07044) 911 0420

⮂ 18 L 6045 m Par 72
👫 WD–H max 28 WE–M (phone
first)
💷 €45 (€55)
⛳ 30km W of Stuttgart
🏠 B von Limburger
◼ www.golfclub-stuttgart.com

Ulm/Neu-Ulm (1963)
Wochenauer Hof 2, 89186 Illerrieden
☎ **(07306) 929500**
🖥 (07306) 9295025
⮂ 18 L 6076 m SSS 72
👫 H–max 36
💷 €45 (€60)
⛳ 15km S of Ulm
🏠 Deutsche Golf Consult

Greece

Afandou (1973)
Afandou, Rhodes
☎ **(0241) 51255**
⮂ 18 L 6060 m Par 72
👫 U
⛳ Afandou, 20km S of Rhodes town

Corfu (1972)
PO Box 71, Ropa Valley, 49100 Corfu
☎ **(0661) 94220**
🖥 (0661) 94220
⮂ 18 L 6183 m SSS 72
👫 U
💷 €25 – € 50
⛳ Ermones Bay, 16km W of Corfu
town
🏠 Donald Harradine
◼ www.corfugolfclub.com

Glyfada (1962)
PO Box 70116, 166-10 Glyfada,
Athens
☎ **(01) 894 6459**
🖥 (01) 894 6834
⮂ 18 L 6189 m Par 72
👫 H
💷 €70 (€82)
⛳ 12km S of Athens
🏠 Donald Harradine
◼ www.athensgolfclub.com

Porto Carras G&CC
(1979)
Porto Carras, Halkidiki
☎ **(0375) 71381/71221**
⮂ 18 L 6086 m SSS 72
👫 U
⛳ Sithonia Peninsula, 100km SE of
Thessaloniki

Hungary

Birdland G&CC (1991)
Thermal krt.10, 9740 Bükfürdö
☎ **(94) 358060**
🖥 (94) 359000
⮂ 18 L 6459 m Par 72 SSS 71-75
9 hole Par 3 course
👫 U H
💷 £33
⛳ 120km SE of Vienna
🏠 G Hauser
◼ www.birdland.hu

Budapest G&CC
Becsi u.5, 2024 Kisoroszi
☎ **(1) 317 6025**
🖥 (1) 317 2749
⮂ 18 L 6089 m SSS 72
👫 U
💷 €25 (€30)
⛳ 35km N of Budapest via Highway
11
🏠 D Hajnal

Hencse National
Kossuth u.3, 7232 Hencse
☎ **(82) 481245**
🖥 (82) 481248
⮂ 18 L 6231 m Par 72
👫 U
💷 €27 (€32)
⛳ 20km from Kaposvar (SW
Hungary)
🏠 J Dudok van Heel
◼ www.hencsegc.com

Old Lake
PO Box 127, 2890 Tata-Remeteségpuszta
☎ **(34) 587620**
🖥 (34) 587623
⮂ 18 L 5915 m Par 72
👫 U H
💷 £17 (£27)
⛳ 5km from Tata. 60km W of
Budapest (M1)
🏠 Lázló Soproni
◼ www.oldlakegolf.com

Pannonia G&CC
Alcsútdoboz, 8087 Mariavölgy
☎ **(22) 594200**
🖥 (22) 594205
⮂ 18 L 5659 m CR 71.3 SR 123
👫 U
💷 €45 (€62)
⛳ Budapest 30km
🏠 H-G Erhardt
◼ www.pannonia-golf.hu

St Lorence G&CC
Pellérdi ut 55, 7634 Pécs
☎ **(72) 252844/252142**
🖥 (72) 252844/252173
⮂ 18 holes Par 72
👫 U
⛳ Szentlörinc, 11km W of Pécs

For list of abbreviations and key to symbols see page 649

Iceland

Akureyri (1935)
PO Box 317, 602 Akureyri
☎ **(462) 2974**
🖳 (461) 1755
🏌 18 L 5783 m Par 71
🏌 U H
££ 2500 Ikr
⛳ 1km from Akureyri (N coast)
🏠 Solnes/Gudmundsson
■ www.nett.is/ga

Borgarness (1973)
Hamar, 310 Borgarnes
☎ **(437) 1663**
🖳 (437) 2063
🏌 9 L 5548 m Par 72
🏌 U
££ 1200 Ikr
⛳ 5km W of Borgarnes. 100km N of Reykjavik (W coast)

Eskifjardar (1976)
735 Eskifjördur
🏌 9 L 4418 m Par 66
££ 1000 Ikr
⛳ 3km W of Eskifjördur (E coast)

Húsavík (1967)
PO Box 23, Kötlum, 640 Húsavík
☎ **(464) 1000**
🖳 (464) 1678
🏌 9 L 2460m Par 70
🏌 U
££ 1000 Ikr
⛳ 2km from Húsavík (N coast)
🏠 Nils Skjöld

Isafjardar (1978)
PO Box 367, 400 Isafjördur
☎ **(456) 5081**
🖳 (456) 4547
🏌 9 L 4980 m Par 70
🏌 U
££ 1000Ikr
⛳ 3km W of Isafjördur (NW coast)

Jökull (1973)
Postholf 67, 355 Olafsvík
☎ **(436) 1666**
🏌 9 L 4598 m Par 68
🏌 U
££ 1000 Ikr
⛳ 5km SE of Olafsvík (W coast)

Keilir (1967)
Box 148, 222 Hafnarfjördur
☎ **(565) 3360**
🖳 (565) 2560
🏌 18 L 5449 m Par 71
🏌 9 L 2748 m Par 36
🏌 U
££ 18 holes: 2000 Ikr 9 holes: 1000 Ikr
⛳ Hafnarfjördur, 10km S of Reykjavik
🏠 Hannes Thorsteinsson

Kopavogs og Gardabaejar (1994)
Postholf 214, 212 Gardabaer
☎ **(565) 7373**
🖳 (565) 9190
🏌 18 L 5437 m Par 70
🏌 U
££ 1700 Ikr
⛳ Gardabaer, S of Reykjavik

Leynir (1965)
PO Box 9, 300 Akranes
☎ **(431) 2711**
🖳 (431) 3711
🏌 18 L 5959 m Par 72
🏌 U
££ 2000Ikr
⛳ 2km from Akranes (SW coast)
🏠 H Thorsteinsson
■ www.leynir@aknet.is

Ness-Nesklúbburinn (1964)
PO Box 66, 172 Seltjarnarnes
☎ **(561) 1930**
🖳 (561) 1966
🏌 9 L 5374 m Par 72
🏌 U
££ 1500 Ikr
⛳ 3km W of Reykjavik

Oddafellowa (1990)
Urridavatnsdölum, 210 Gardabaer
☎ **(565) 9094**
🖳 (565) 9074
🏌 18 L 5830 m Par 71
🏌 U
££ 2500 Ikr
⛳ Gardabaer, S of Reykjavik
■ www.oddur.is

Olafsfjardar (1968)
Skeggjabrekku, 625 Olafsfjördur
☎ **(466) 2611**
🖳 (466) 2611
🏌 9 L 4570 m Par 66
🏌 U
££ 1000 Ikr
⛳ 60 km NW of Akureyri (N coast)

Reykjavíkur (1934)
Grafarholt, 112 Reykjavík
☎ **(585) 0200/0210**
🖳 (585) 0201
🏌 18 L 6075 m Par 71
🏌 18 L 6188 m Par 72
🏌 9 L 1761 m Par 32
🏌 U H
££ 4000–4800 Ikr
⛳ 10km E of Reykjavík
🏠 Skjold/Thorsteinsson
■ www.grgolf.is

Saudárkróks (1970)
Hlidarendi, Postholf 56, 550 Saudárkrókur
☎ **(453) 5075**
🏌 9 L 5902 m Par 72
🏌 U
££ 1000 Ikr
⛳ 2km W of Saudárkrókur (N coast)

Sudurnesja (1964)
PO Box 112, 232 Keflavik
☎ **(421) 4100**
🖳 (421) 5981
🏌 18 L 5861 m Par 72
🏌 U
££ 4000 Ikr
⛳ N of Keflavik (SW coast). Airport 5 km

Vestmannaeyja (1938)
Postholf 168, 902 Vestmannaeyar
☎ **(481) 2363**
🖳 (481) 2362
🏌 18 L 5322 m Par 70
🏌 U
££ 1500 Ikr
⛳ 2km W of Vestmannaeyar. Island off S coast - 20 min flight from Reykjavík

Italy

Como/Milan/Bergamo

Ambrosiano (1994)
Cascina Bertacca, 20080 Bubbiano-Milan
☎ **(0290) 840820**
🖳 (0290) 849365
🏌 18 L 6047 m Par 72
🏌 U
££ €37 (€57)
⛳ 25km SW of Milan
🏠 Cornish/Silva
■ www.k-grm.com

Barlassina CC (1956)
Via Privata Golf 42, 20030 Birago di Camnago (MI)
☎ **(0362) 560621/2**
🖳 (0362) 560934
🏌 18 L 6197 m SSS 72
🏌 WD–U
££ €56.80 (€80)
⛳ 22km N of Milan
🏠 J Morrison

Bergamo L'Albenza (1961)
Via Longoni 12, 24030 Almenno S. Bartolomeo (BG)
☎ **(035) 640028**
🖳 (035) 643066
🏌 27 L 6129-6253 m SSS 72
🏌 U–book by fax
££ €40 (€60)
⛳ 13km NW of Bergamo. Milan 45 km
🏠 Cotton/Sutton

Bogogno (1996)
Via Sant'Isidoro 1, 28010 Bogogno
☎ **(0322) 863339**

☎ (0322) 863798
🏌 18 L 6171 m Par 72
👥 U
£€ €50 (€65)
⛳ Bogogno, 25km N of Novara
🏠 Robert von Hagge

Brianza   (1996)

Cascina Cazzo, 20040 Usmate Velate
☎ **(039) 682 9089**
🖥 (039) 682 9059
🏌 18 L 5729 m Par 71 SSS 70
👥 U
£€ €25 (€40)
⛳ 24km NE of Milan. Monza 6km
🏠 Marco Croze

Carimate   (1962)

Via Airoldi, 22060 Carimate
☎ **(031) 790226**
🖥 (031) 790226
🏌 18 L 5982 m SSS 71
👥 U H
£€ €40 (€60)
⛳ 15km S of Como. 27km N of Milan
🏠 Pier Mancinelli

Castelconturbia   (1984)

Via Suno, 28010 Agrate Conturbia
☎ **(0322) 832093**
🖥 (0322) 832428
🏌 Red 9 L 3330 m Par 36
    Yellow 9 L 3070 m Par 36
    Blue 9 L 3210 m Par 36
👥 WD–H WE–M H
£€ €47 (€75)
⛳ 23km N of Novara. Milan 60 km
🏠 Robert Trent Jones Sr

Castello di Tolcinasco

(1993)
20090 Pieve Emanuele (MI)
☎ **(02) 9046 7201**
🏌 27 L 6253-6322 m Par 72
    9 hole Par 3 course
👥 U
£€ €40 (€50)
⛳ 12km S of Milan
🏠 Arnold Palmer

Franciacorta   (1986)

Via Provinciale 34b, 25040 Nigoline di Corte Franca, (Brescia)
☎ **(030) 984167**
🖥 (030) 984393
🏌 18 L 5924 m Par 72 SSS 72
    9 hole Par 3 course
👥 WD–U WE–NA before 2pm
£€ €35 (€50)
⛳ Nigoline, 25km E of Bergamo.
    Autostrada A4 exit Rovato
🏠 Dye/Croze

Lanzo Intelvi   (1962)

22024 Lanzo Intelvi (CO)
☎ **(031) 840169**
🏌 9 L 2438 m SSS 66
👥 U
⛳ 32km NW of Como

Menaggio & Cadenabbia

(1907)
Via Golf 12, 22010 Grandola E Uniti
☎ **(0344) 32103**
🖥 (0344) 30780
🏌 18 L 5455 m Par 70 SSS 69
👥 WD–H WE–H restricted
£€ €50 (€65)
⛳ 5km W of Menaggio. 40km N of
    Como
🏠 John Harris
📧 www.menaggio.it

Milano   (1928)

20052 Parco di Monza (MI)
☎ **(039) 303081/2/3**
🖥 (039) 304427
🏌 18 L 6414 m SSS 73
    9 L 2976 m SSS 36
👥 WD–H WE–by appointment
£€ €48 (€72)
⛳ 6km N of Monza. 18km NE of
    Milan
🏠 Gannon/Blandford

Molinetto CC   (1982)

SS Padana Superiore 11, 20063 Cernusco S/N (MI)
☎ **(02) 9210 5128/9210 5983**
🖥 (02) 9210 6635
🏌 18 L 6010 m Par 71
👥 WD–H WE–restricted
⛳ Cernusco, 10km E of Milan

Monticello   (1975)

Via Volta 4, 22070 Cassina Rizzardi
☎ **(031) 928055**
🖥 (031) 880207
🏌 18 L 6413 m SSS 72
    18 L 6056 m SSS 72
👥 WD–H WE–NA
£€ €40 (€50)
⛳ 10km SE of Como
🏠 Jim Fazio

La Pinetina   (1971)

Via al Golf 4, 22070 Carbonate (CO)
☎ **(031) 933202**
🖥 (031) 890342
🏌 18 L 5754 m Par 70 SSS 70
👥 WD–U WE–booking necessary
£€ €50 (€74)
⛳ 12km SW of Como. Milan 25km
🏠 Harris/ Albertini

Le Robinie   (1992)

Via per Busto Arsizio 9, 21058 Solbiate Olona (VA)
☎ **(039) 331 329260**
🖥 (039) 331 329266
🏌 18 L 6250 m Par 72 SSS 74
👥 WD–U WE–H
£€ €45 (€65)
⛳ 25km NW of Milan. Malpensa
    Airport 6km
🏠 Jack Nicklaus
📧 www.lerobinie.com

La Rossera   (1970)

Via Montebello 4, 24060 Chiuduno
☎ **(035) 838600**
🖥 (035) 442 7047
🏌 9 L 2510 m SSS 68
👥 U
£€ €27 (€32)
⛳ 2km from Chiuduno. 18km SE of
    Bergamo

Le Rovedine   (1978)

Via Carlo Marx, 20090 Noverasco di Opera (MI)
☎ **(02) 5760 6420/5760 2730**
🖥 (02) 5760 6405
🏌 18 L 6307 m SSS 72
👥 U
⛳ 4km S of Milan

Varese   (1934)

Via Vittorio Veneto 32, 21020 Luvinate (VA)
☎ **(0332) 227394/229302**
🖥 (0332) 222107
🏌 18 L 5936 m SSS 72
👥 WD–U H
£€ €40 (€60)
⛳ 5km NW of Varese
🏠 Gannon/Blandford

Vigevano   (1974)

Via Chitola 49, 27029 Vigevano (PV)
☎ **(0381) 346628/346077**
🖥 (0381) 346091
🏌 18 L 5678 m SSS 72
⛳ 25km SE of Novara. 35km SW of
    Milan

Villa D'Este   (1926)

Via Cantù 13, 22030 Montorfano (CO)
☎ **(031) 200200**
🖥 (031) 200786
🏌 18 L 5787 m SSS 71
👥 I H
⛳ Montorfano, 7km SE of Como
🏠 Peter Gannon

Zoate

20067 Zoate di Tribiano (MI)
☎ **(02) 9063 2183/9063 1861**
🖥 (02) 9063 1861
🏌 18 L 6122 m Par 72
👥 WD–U H
£€ €35 (€50)
⛳ Zoate, 17km SE of Milan
🏠 Marmori

Elba

Acquabona   (1971)

57037 Portoferraio, Isola di Elba (LI)
☎ **(0565) 940066**
🖥 (0565) 933410
🏌 9 L 5144 m SSS 67
👥 U
£€ €27–32

æ 5km NW of Porto Azzurro. 6km
NW of Porto Ferraio
⌂ Gianni Albertini

Emilia Romagna

Adriatic GC Cervia   (1985)
*Via Jelenia Gora No 6, 48016 Cervia-
Milano Marittima*
☎ (0544) 992786
⌨ (0544) 993410
⮀ 18 L 6246 m SSS 72
⋔ U H
££ €42 (50)
æ 20km SE of Ravenna
⌂ Marco Croze

Bologna   (1959)
*Via Sabattini 69, 40050 Monte San
Pietro (BO)*
☎ (051) 969100
⌨ (051) 672 0017
⮀ 18 L 6171 m SSS 72
⋔ U
££ €40 (€50)
æ 20km W of Bologna
⌂ Harris/Cotton

Croara   (1976)
29010 Croara di Gazzola
☎ (0523) 977105/977148
⌨ (0523) 977100
⮀ 18 L 6065 m SSS 72
⋔ H
££ €30 (€42)
æ 16km SW of Piacenza. 84km SE of
Milan
⌂ Buratti/Croze

Matilde di Canossa   (1987)
Via Casinazzo 1, 42100 San Bartolomeo
☎ (0522) 371295
⌨ (0522) 371204
⮀ 18 L 6231 m SSS 72
⋔ U
££ €30 (€40)
æ 50km NW of Bologna
⌂ Marco Croze

Modena G&CC   (1987)
*Via Castelnuovo Rangone 4, 41050
Colombaro di Formigine (MO)*
☎ (059) 553482
⌨ (059) 553696
⮀ 18 L 6423 m Par 72 SSS 74
9 hole Par 3 course
⋔ H
££ €40 (€60)
æ Formigine, 10km SW of Modena
⌂ Bernhard Langer

La Rocca   (1985)
Via Campi 8, 43038 Sala Baganza (PR)
☎ (0521) 834037
⌨ (0521) 834575
⮀ 18 L 6076 m SSS 71
⋔ U
££ €30 (€40)

æ 8km S of Parma
⌂ Marco Croze
▪ www.officeitalia.it/golflarocca

La Torre   (1992)
Via Limisano 10, Riolo Terme (RA)
☎ (0546) 74035
⌨ (0546) 74076
⮀ 18 L 6350 m Par 72
⋔ H
££ €20 (€25)
æ 30km SW of Bologna
⌂ Alberto Croze

Gulf of Genoa

Degli Ulivi   (1932)
Via Campo Golf 59, 18038 Sanremo
☎ (0184) 557093
⌨ (0184) 557388
⮀ 18 L 5203 m SSS 67
⋔ U
££ €37 (€55)
æ 5km N of Sanremo
⌂ Peter Gannon
▪ www.sanremogolf.it

Garlenda   (1965)
Via Golf 7, 17033 Garlenda
☎ (0182) 580012
⌨ (0182) 580561
⮀ 18 L 6085 m Par 72 SSS 72
⋔ H
££ €50 (€70)
æ 15km N of Alassio. Genoa 90km
⌂ John Harris
▪ www.garlendagolf.it

Marigola   (1975)
Via Vallata 5, 19032 Lerici (SP)
☎ (0187) 970193
⌨ (0187) 970193
⮀ 9 L 2116 m Par 49
⋔ U
æ 6km SE of La Spezia
⌂ Franco Marmori

Pineta di Arenzano   (1959)
Piazza del Golf 3, 16011 Arenzano (GE)
☎ (010) 911 1817
⌨ (010) 911 1270
⮀ 9 L 5527 m SSS 70
⋔ H
££ €30 (€42)
æ Arenzano Pineta, 20km W of
Genoa
⌂ Donald Harradine

Rapallo   (1930)
Via Mameli 377, 16035 Rapallo (GE)
☎ (0185) 261777
⌨ (0185) 261779
⮀ 18 L 5638 m Par 70
⋔ H WE–NA before noon
££ €40 (€60)
æ 25km SE of Genoa. A12 motorway
exit Rapallo
⌂ Cabell Robinson

Versilia   (1990)
Via Sipe 100, 55045 Pietrasanta (LU)
☎ (0584) 88 15 74
⌨ (0584) 75 22 72
⮀ 18 L 5873 m Par 71
⋔ U H
££ €52 – € 80
æ 30km N of Pisa on coast, nr Forte
dei Marmi
⌂ Marco Croze

Lake Garda & Dolomites

Asiago   (1967)
Via Meltar 2, 36012 Asiago (VI)
☎ (0424) 462721
⌨ (0424) 465133
⮀ 18 L 6005 m Par 70 SSS 71
⋔ U H
££ €40 (€55)
æ 3km N of Asiago. 50km N of
Vicenza
⌂ Peter Harradine
▪ www.golfasiago.it

Bogliaco   (1912)
Via Golf 21, 25088 Toscolano-Maderno
☎ (0365) 643006
⌨ (0365) 643006
⮀ 9 L 2650 m Par 70 SSS 69
⋔ H
££ €35 (€40)
æ Lake Garda, 40km NE of Brescia
▪ www.bogliaco.com

Ca' degli Ulivi   (1988)
*Via Ghiandare 2, 37010 Marciaga di
Costermano (VR)*
☎ (045) 725 6463/725 6485
⌨ (045) 725 6876
⮀ 18 L 6000 m SSS 72
9 hole course
æ Above village of Garda. Verona
Airport 35km

Campo Carlo Magno   (1922)
*Golf Hotel, 38084 Madonna di
Campiglio (TN)*
☎ (0465) 440622
⌨ (0465) 440298
⮀ 9 L 5148 m SSS 67
⋔ H
££ €37–50
æ Madonna di Campiglio 1 km. 74km
NW of Trento
⌂ Henry Cotton

Folgaria   (1987)
*Loc Costa di Folgaria, 38064
Folgaria (TN)*
☎ (0464) 720480
⌨ (0464) 720480
⮀ 9 L 2582 m SSS 70
⋔ H
££ €30 (€35)
æ 30km S of Trento, off A22
⌂ Marco Croze

Gardagolf CC (1985)
Via Angelo Omodeo 2, 25080 Soiano Del Lago (BS)
☎ **(0365) 674707 (Sec)**
🖷 (0365) 674788
🏳 18 L 6505 m SSS 74
    9 L 2635 m Par 35
👥 H
£€ €57 (€67)
⛳ Lake Garda, 30 km NE of Brescia.
🏠 Cotton/Pennink/Steel

Karersee-Carezza
Loc Carezza 171, 39056 Welschofen-Nova Levante
☎ **(0471) 612200**
🖷 (0471) 612200
🏳 9 L 5340 m SSS 68
👥 H
£€ €30 (€35)
⛳ 30km S of Bolzano
🏠 Marco Croze

Petersberg (1987)
Unterwinkel 5, 39040 Petersberg (BZ)
☎ **(0471) 615122**
🖷 (0471) 615229
🏳 18 L 5100 m Par 67 SSS 66
👥 U
£€ €42 (€52)
⛳ 35km SE of Bolzano, nr Nova Ponente
🏠 Marco Croze
🖥 www.golfclubpetersberg.it

Ponte di Legno (1980)
Corso Milano 36, 25056 Ponte di Legno (BS)
☎ **(0364) 900306**
🖷 (0364) 900555
🏳 9 L 4803 m SSS 68
👥 U
£€ €25 (€35)
⛳ 90km W of Trento, nr San Michele
🏠 Caremoli

Verona (1963)
Ca' del Sale 15, 37066 Sommacampagna
☎ **(045) 510060**
🖷 (045) 510242
🏳 18 L 6054 m SSS 72
👥 H
£€ €50 (€60)
⛳ 7km W of Verona
🏠 John Harris

Naples & South

Napoli (1983)
Via Campiglione 11, 80072 Arco Felice (NA)
☎ **(081) 526 4296**
🏳 9 L 4776 m SSS 68
👥 M
⛳ Pozzuoli, 10 km W of Naples

Porto d'Orra (1977)
PB 102, 88063 Catanzaro Lido
☎ **(0961) 791045**
🖷 (0961) 791444
🏳 9 L 5686 m SSS 70
👥 U
⛳ 9km N of Catanzaro Lido on coast

Riva Dei Tessali (1971)
74011 Castellaneta
☎ **(099) 843 9251**
🖷 (099) 843 9255
🏳 18 L 5960 m SSS 71
👥 U
£€ €30
⛳ 34km SW of Taranto
🏠 Marco Croze

San Michele
Loc Bosco 8/9, 87022 Cetraro (CS)
☎ **(0982) 91012**
🖷 (0982) 91430
🏳 9 L 2760 m SSS 70
👥 U H
£€ €15 (€17)
⛳ Cetraro, 50km N of Cosenza. 250km SE of Naples
🏠 Piero Mancinelli

Rome & Centre

Castelgandolfo (1987)
Via Santo Spirito 13, 00040 Castelgandolfo
☎ **(06) 931 2301/931 3084**
🖷 (06) 931 2244
🏳 18 L 6025 m SSS 72
👥 U H Sun–restricted
£€ €30 (€50)
⛳ 22km SE of Rome
🏠 Robert Trent Jones

Eucalyptus (1988)
Via Cogna 5, 04011 Aprilia (Roma)
☎ **(06) 927 46252**
🖷 (06) 926 8502
🏳 18 L 6310 m Par 72 SSS 73
👥 WD–U WE–U H
£€ €28 (€32)
⛳ 20km S of Rome on Aprilia-Anzio road
🏠 D'Onofrio
🖥 www.eucalyptusgolfclub.it

Fioranello
CP 96, 00134 Roma (RM)
☎ **(06) 713 8080**
🖷 (06) 713 8212
🏳 18 L 5360 m Par 70
👥 U
£€ €36 (€42)
⛳ Santa Maria, 17km SE of Rome
🏠 David Mezzacane

Fiuggi (1928)
Superstrada Anticolana 1, 03015 Fiuggi (FR)
☎ **(0775) 55250**

🖷 (0775) 506742
🏳 9 L 5697 m SSS 70
👥 U
⛳ 60km SE of Rome

Marco Simone (1989)
Via di Marco Simone, 00012 Guidonia (RM)
☎ **(0774) 366469**
🖷 (0774) 366476
🏳 18 L 6317 m SSS 73
    18 hole course Par 64
👥 U
⛳ 17km NE of Rome
🏠 Fazio/Mezzacane

Nettuno
Via della Campana 18, 00048 Nettuno (RM)
☎ **(06) 981 9419**
🖷 (06) 981 9419
🏳 18 L 6260 m SSS 72
👥 U H
£€ €25 (€35)
⛳ 60km S of Rome on coast
🏠 Marco Croze

Olgiata (1961)
Largo Olgiata 15, 00123 Roma
☎ **(06) 308 89141**
🖷 (06) 308 89968
🏳 18 L 6347 m SSS 73
    9 L 2947 m SSS 71
👥 U
£€ €50 (€65)
⛳ 19km NW of Rome, nr La Storta
🏠 CK Cotton

Parco de' Medici (1989)
Viale Parco de' Medici 165, 00148 Roma
☎ **(06) 655 3477**
🖷 (06) 655 3344
🏳 18 L 6303 m Par 71 SSS 73
    9 L 2620 m Par 34 SSS 68
👥 U
£€ €50 (€60)
⛳ 15km SW of Rome, nr Airport
🏠 Fabio/Mezzacane/Rebecchini
🖥 www.sheraton.com

Pescara (1992)
Contrado Cerreto 58, 66010 Miglianico (CH)
☎ **(0871) 959566**
🖷 (0871) 950363
🏳 18 L 6184 m Par 72 SSS 72
👥 U
£€ €25 (€35)
⛳ S of Pescara (Adriatic coast)

Le Querce
San Martino, 01015 Sutri (VT)
☎ **(0761) 68789**
🖷 (0761) 68142
🏳 18 L 6433 m SSS 72
👥 U
£€ €35
⛳ 42km N of Rome
🏠 Fazio/Mezzacane

Roma   (1903)
Via Appia Nuova 716A, 00178 Roma
- ☎ **(06) 780 3407**
- ⌨ (06) 783 46219
- ⚐ 18 L 5854 m Par 71 SSS 70
- 🏌 WD–H WE–M H
- £€ €35 (€50)
- ⛳ 7km SE of Rome towards Ciampino

Tarquinia
Loc Pian di Spille, Via degli Alina 271, 01016 Marina Velca/Tarquinia (VT)
- ☎ **(0766) 812109**
- ⚐ 9 L 5442 m SSS 69
- ⛳ 80km N of Rome on coast

Torvaianica
Via Enna 30, 00040 Marina di Ardea
- ☎ **(06) 913 3250**
- ⌨ (06) 913 3592
- ⚐ 9 L 4416 m SSS 64
- 🏌 H
- ⛳ 30km S of Rome
- 🏠 Leonardo Basili

Sardinia

Is Molas   (1975)
CP 49, 09010 Pula
- ☎ **(070) 924 1013/4**
- ⌨ (070) 924 2121
- ⚐ 18 L 6383 m SSS 72
  9 L 2966 m SSS 36
- £€ €60 (€70)
- ⛳ Pula, 32km S of Cagliari
- 🏠 Cotton/Pennink/Lurie

Pevero GC Costa Smeralda (1972)
07020 Porto Cervo
- ☎ **(0789) 96072/96210/96211**
- ⌨ (0789) 96572
- ⚐ 18 L 6186 m SSS 72
- 🏌 U H
- £€ €40–100
- ⛳ Porto Cervo, 30km N of Olbia, on Costa Smeralda
- 🏠 Robert Trent Jones

Sicily

Il Pìcciolo   (1988)
Via Picciolo, 195012 Castiglione di Sicilia
- ☎ **(0942) 986252**
- ⌨ (0942) 986252
- ⚐ 18 L 5810 m Par 72 SSS 71
- 🏌 H
- £€ €40 (€50)
- ⛳ 18km E of Taormina
- 🏠 Rota Carcamoli

Turin & Piemonte

Alpino Di Stresa   (1924)
Viale Golf Panorama 49, 28839 Vezzo (VB)
- ☎ **(0323) 20642/20101**
- ⌨ (0323) 20642
- ⚐ 9 L 5397 m Par 69 SSS 68
- 🏌 WE–U WE–restricted
- £€ 18 holes: €25 (€35) 9 holes: €17 (€25)
- ⛳ 7km W of Stresa. Milan 80km
- 🏠 Peter Gannon

Biella Le Betulle   (1958)
Valcarozza, 13887 Magnano (BI)
- ☎ **(015) 679151**
- ⌨ (015) 679276
- ⚐ 18 L 6427 m SSS 74
- 🏌 H
- £€ €65 (€72)
- ⛳ 17km SW of Biella
- 🏠 John Morrison
- ◼ www.lebetulle.com

Cervino   (1955)
11021 Cervinia-Breuil (AO)
- ☎ **(0166) 949131**
- ⌨ (0116) 949131
- ⚐ 9 L 4796 m SSS 66
- 🏌 U
- £€ €25–35
- ⛳ 53km NE of Aosta
- 🏠 Donald Harradine

Cherasco CC   (1982)
Via Fraschetta 8, 12062 Cherasco (CN)
- ☎ **(0172) 489772/488489**
- ⌨ (0172) 488304
- ⚐ 18 L 6041 m Par 72 SSS 72
- 🏌 H
- £€ €32 (€45)
- ⛳ Cherasco, 45km S of Turin
- 🏠 Gianmarco Croze
- ◼ www.golfcherasco.com

Claviere   (1923)
Strada Nazionale 45, 10050 Claviere (TO)
- ☎ **(0122) 878917**
- ⚐ 9 L 4650 m SSS 65
- 🏌 U
- ⛳ 96km W of Turin
- 🏠 Luzi

Courmayeur
11013 Courmayeur (AO)
- ☎ **(0165) 89103**
- ⚐ 9 L 2650 m SSS 67
- ⛳ 5km NE of Courmayeur

Cuneo   (1990)
Via degli Angeli 3, 12012 Mellana-Bóves (CN)
- ☎ **(0171) 387041**
- ⌨ (0171) 390763
- ⚐ 18 L 5851 m Par 71 SSS 70
- 🏌 U H
- £€ €35 (€45)

- ⛳ 80km S of Turin, nr Cúneo
- 🏠 Graham Cooke

Le Fronde   (1973)
Via Sant-Agostino 68, 10051 Avigliana (TO)
- ☎ **(011) 932 8053/0540**
- ⌨ (011) 932 0928
- ⚐ 18 L 5976 m SSS 71
- 🏌 WD–U WE–H max 34
- £€ €30 (€40)
- ⛳ Avigliana, 20km W of Turin
- 🏠 John Harris

I Girasoli   (1991)
Via Pralormo 315, 10022 Carmagnola (TO)
- ☎ **(011) 979 5088**
- ⌨ (011) 979 5228
- ⚐ 18 L 4585 m Par 65
- 🏌 H
- £€ €20 (€30)
- ⛳ 25km S of Turin
- ◼ www.girasoligolf.it

Iles Borromees
Loc Motta Rossa, 28833 Brovello Carpugnino (VB)
- ☎ **(0323) 929285**
- ⌨ (0323) 929190
- ⚐ 18 L 6445 m SSS 72
- 🏌 U
- £€ €40 (€60)
- ⛳ 5km S of Stresa. 80km NW of Milan
- 🏠 Marco Croze
- ◼ www.golfdesilesborromees.it

Golf dei Laghi   (1993)
Via Trevisani 6, 21028 Travedona Monate (VA)
- ☎ **(0332) 978101**
- ⌨ (0332) 977532
- ⚐ 18 L 6400 m Par 72 SSS 73
- 🏌 H
- £€ €30 (€50)
- ⛳ 30km SW of Varese. 50km NW of Milan
- 🏠 Piero Mancinelli

Margara   (1975)
Via Tenuta Margara 5, 15043 Fubine (AL)
- ☎ **(0131) 778555**
- ⌨ (0131) 778772
- ⚐ 18 L 6045 m SSS 72
- 🏌 U
- ⛳ 15km NW of Alessandria

La Margherita
Strada Pralormo 29, Carmagnola (TO)
- ☎ **(011) 979 5113**
- ⌨ (011) 979 5204
- ⚐ 18 L 6339 m SSS 73
- 🏌 U
- £€ €25 (€40)
- ⛳ 20km S of Turin
- 🏠 Croze/Ferraris

Piandisole   (1964)
Via Pineta 1, 28057 Premeno (NO)
☎ **(0323) 587100**
▷ 9 L 2830 m SSS 67
👥 U
⊸ Premeno, 30km N of Stresa

I Roveri   (1971)
Rotta Cerbiatta 24, 10070 Fiano (TO)
☎ **(011) 923 5719/923 5667**
🖳 (011) 923 5668
▷ 18 L 6218 m SSS 72
  9 L 3107 m SSS 36
👥 WE–NA
⊸ 16km NW of Turin. Caselle Airport 10km
🏠 Robert Trent Jones

La Serra   (1970)
Via Astigliano 42, 15048 Valenza (AL)
☎ **(0131) 954778**
🖳 (0131) 928294
▷ 9 L 2820 m SSS 70
👥 H
£€ €20 (€35)
⊸ 4km W of Valenza. 7km N of Alessandria
🏠 Migliorini

Sestrieres   (1932)
Piazza Agnelli 4, 10058 Sestrieres (TO)
☎ **(0122) 755170/76243**
🖳 (0122) 76294
▷ 18 L 4598 m Par 67 SSS 65
👥 U H
£€ €27 (€40)
⊸ Sestrieres, 96km W of Turin

Stupinigi   (1972)
Corso Unione Sovietica 506, 10135 Torino
☎ **(011) 347 2640**
🖳 (011) 397 8038
▷ 9 L 2175 m SSS 63
⊸ Mirafiore, Turin

Torino   (1924)
Via Agnelli 40, 10070 Fiano Torinese
☎ **(011) 923 5440/923 5670**
🖳 (011) 923 5886
▷ 18 L 6216 m SSS 72
  18 L 6214 m SSS 72
👥 U H
£€ €60 (€90)
⊸ 23km NW of Turin
🏠 Morrison/Croze/Cooke

Vinovo   (1986)
Via Stupinigi 182, 10048 Vinovo (TO)
☎ **(011) 965 3880**
🖳 (011) 962 3748
▷ 9 L 5732 m Par 72 SSS 71
👥 U
£€ €25 (€30)
⊸ Vinovo, 3km SW of Turin
🏠 Croce/Chiaravigcio

Tuscany & Umbria

Casentino   (1985)
Via Fronzola 6, Loc Il Palazzo, 52014 Poppi (Arezzo)
☎ **(0575) 529810**
🖳 (0575) 520167
▷ 9 L 5550 m Par 72 SSS 69
👥 WD–U WE–H
£€ €22 (€27)
⊸ Poppi, 50km SE of Florence
🏠 Brami/Baracchi
■ www.casentino.net/golf

Castelfalfi G&CC
50050 Montaione (FI)
☎ **(0571) 698093/4**
🖳 (0571) 698098
▷ 18 L 6095 m SSS 73
👥 H
⊸ 45km SW of Florence
🏠 Pier Mancinelli

Conero GC Sirolo   (1987)
Via Betellico 6, 60020 Sirolo (AN)
☎ **(071) 736 0613**
🖳 (071) 736 0380
▷ 18 L 6185 m Par 72
  9 hole course Par 29
👥 U
⊸ Sirolo, 20km SE of Ancona. Falconara Airport 25km
🏠 Marco Croze

Cosmopolitan G&CC   (1992)
Viale Pisorno 60, 56018 Tirrenia
☎ **(050) 33633**
🖳 (050) 384707
▷ 18 L 6291 m Par 73
👥 U
£€ €30
⊸ 15km SW of Pisa
🏠 David Mezzacane

Firenze Ugolino
Strada Chiantigiana 3, 50015 Grassina
☎ **(055) 230 1009/1085**
🖳 (055) 230 1141
▷ 18 L 5785 m SSS 70
👥 WD–H
£€ €57
⊸ Grassina, 10km S of Florence
🏠 Blandford/Gannon

Lamborghini-Panicale   (1992)
Loc Soderi 1, 06064 Panicale (PG)
☎ **(075) 837582**
🖳 (075) 837582
▷ 9 L 5872 m Par 72 SSS 70
👥 U H
£€ €24 (€29)
⊸ 30km W of Perugia, nr Lake Trasimeno
🏠 Ferruccio Lamborghini
■ www.lamborghinionline.it

Montecatini   (1985)
Via Dei Brogi 5, Loc Pievaccia, 51015 Monsummano Terme
☎ **(0572) 62218**
🖳 (0572) 617435
▷ 18 L 5932 m SSS 71
👥 WD–U H
⊸ 8km SE of Montecatini Terme. 50 km SW of Florence (A11)
🏠 Marco Croze

Le Pavoniere   (1986)
Via della Fattoria 6, 50047 Prato
☎ **(0574) 620855**
🖳 (0574) 624558
▷ 18 L 6464 m Par 72 SSS 73
👥 U
£€ €25 (€35)
⊸ Prato 10km. 25km W of Florence
🏠 Arnold Palmer

Perugia   (1959)
06074 Santa Sabina-Ellera
☎ **(075) 517 2204**
🖳 (075) 517 2370
▷ 18 L 5735 m Par 70 SSS 70
👥 U
£€ €37 (€45)
⊸ 6km NW of Perugia
🏠 David Mezzacane
■ www.golfclubperugia.it

Poggio dei Medici   (1995)
Via S Gavino 27, 50038 Scarperia Firenze
☎ **(055) 843 0436**
🖳 (055) 843 0439
▷ 18 L 6368 m Par 73 SSS 73
👥 U
£€ €65 (€75)
⊸ 27km from Florence
🏠 Fioravanti/Dassù
■ www.poggiodeimedici.com

Punta Ala   (1964)
Via del Golf 1, 58040 Punta Ala (GR)
☎ **(0564) 922121/922719**
🖳 (0564) 920182
▷ 18 L 6168 m SSS 72
👥 U
£€ €50 – € 80
⊸ 40km NW of Grosseto. Siena 90km. Florence 180km
■ www.puntaAla.net/golf

Tirrenia   (1968)
Viale San Guido, 56018 Tirrenia (PI)
☎ **(050) 37518**
🖳 (050) 33286
▷ 9 L 3065 m SSS 72
⊸ 15km SW of Pisa on coast

Venice & North East

Albarella
Isola di Albarella, 45010 Rosolina (RO)
☎ **(0426) 330124**

☎ (0426) 330628
🅿 18 L 6100 m SSS 72
👤 H
££ €40 (€50)
🏌 80km S of Venice
🏠 Harris/Croze

Ca' della Nave (1986)
Piazza Vittoria 14, 30030 Martellago
☎ (041) 540 1555
🖳 (041) 540 1926
🅿 18 L 6380 m SSS 73
9 L 1240 m Par 28
👤 H
🏌 Martellago, 12km NW of Venice
🏠 Arnold Palmer

Cansiglio (1956)
CP 152, 31029 Vittorio Veneto
☎ (0438) 585398
🖳 (0438) 585398
🅿 18 L 6007 m SSS 71
👤 WD–U WE–H
££ €40 (€50)
🏌 21km NE of Vittorio Veneto. 80km NE of Venice
🏠 Trent Jones/Croze

Colli Berici (1986)
Strada Monti Comunali, 36040 Brendola (VI)
☎ (0444) 601780
🖳 (0444) 400777
🅿 18 L 5798 m SSS 71
👤 U
££ €40 (€50)
🏌 Vicenza 10km. Venice 70km
🏠 Marco Croze

Frassanelle (1990)
35030 Frassanelle di Rovolon (PD)
☎ (049) 991 0722
🖳 (049) 991 0722
🅿 18 L 6180 m SSS 72
👤 H
££ €40 (€50)
🏌 20km S of Padova, nr Via dei Colli
🏠 Marco Croze

Lignano
Via Bonifica 3, 33054 Lignano Sabbiadoro (UD)
☎ (0431) 428025
🖳 (0431) 423230
🅿 18 L 6069 m Par 72
👤 H
££ €54 (€64)
🏌 90km E of Venice on coast
🏠 Marco Croze
■ www.golflignano.it

La Montecchia (1989)
Via Montecchia 12, 35030 Selvazzano (PD)
☎ (049) 805 5550
🖳 (049) 805 5737
🅿 18 L 6318 m SSS 73
9 L 3012 m Par 36
👤 U H

££ €50 (€55)
🏌 8km W of Padova. 40km W of Venice
🏠 T Macauley

Padova (1966)
35050 Valsanzibio di Galzigano
☎ (049) 913 0078
🖳 (049) 913 1193
🅿 18 L 6053 m SSS 72
👤 U
🏌 Valsanzibio, 20km S of Padua

San Floriano-Gorizia (1987)
Castello di San Floriano, 34070 San Floriano del Collio (GO)
☎ (0481) 884252/884234
🖳 (0481) 884252/884052
🅿 9 L 3810 m Par 62
👤 U
££ €25
🏌 6km NW of Gorizia. 50km SE of Udine, nr Slovenian border
🏠 Pellicciari

Trieste (1954)
Via Padriciano 80, 34012 Trieste
☎ (040) 226159/226270
🖳 (040) 226159
🅿 18 L 5883 m SSS 72
👤 U–closed Tues
££ €35 (€50)
🏌 Padriciano, 7km E of Trieste

Udine (1971)
Via dei Faggi 1, Località Villaverde, 33034 Fagagna (UD)
☎ (0432) 800418
🖳 (0432) 801312
🅿 18 L 5935 m Par 72
👤 H
££ €50 (€60)
🏌 15km NW of Udine
🏠 Marco Croze

Venezia (1928)
Via del Forte, 30011 Alberoni (Venezia)
☎ (041) 731015/731333
🖳 (041) 731339
🅿 18 L 6199 m SSS 72
👤 U H
££ €50 (€60)
🏌 Venice Lido
🏠 Cruickshank/Cotton

Villa Condulmer (1960)
Via della Croce 3, 31021 Zerman di Mogliano Veneto
☎ (041) 457062
🖳 (041) 457202
🅿 18 L 5995 m SSS 71
9 hole short course
👤 H
££ €40 (Sun – € 50)
🏌 Mogliano Veneto, 17km N of Venice
🏠 Harris/Croze

Luxembourg

Christnach (1993)
Am Lahr, 7641 Christnach
☎ 87 83 83
🖳 87 95 64
🅿 18 L 6210 m CR 71 SR 124
9 hole short course
👤 Greencard
££ €30 (€35)
🏌 25km N of Luxembourg city
■ www.golfclubchristnach.lu

Clervaux (1992)
Mecherwee, 9748 Eselborn
☎ 92 93 95
🖳 92 94 51
🅿 18 L 6144 m Par 72
👤 H
££ €26 (€28)
🏌 3km from Clervaux, North Luxembourg

Gaichel
Rue de Eischen, 8469 Gaichel
☎ 39 71 08
🖳 39 00 75
🅿 9 L 5155 m Par 70
👤 U H
££ €17 (€23)
🏌 10km W of Mersch on Belgian border

Grand-Ducal de Luxembourg (1936)
1 Route de Trèves, 2633 Senningerberg
☎ 34 00 90-1
🖳 34 83 91
🅿 18 L 5765 m SSS 71
👤 H
££ €45 (€55)
🏌 7km N of Luxembourg
🏠 Maj Simpson

Kikuoka CC Chant Val (1991)
Scheierhaff, 5412 Canach
☎ 35 61 35
🖳 35 74 50
🅿 18 L 6404 m SSS 74
👤 H
££ €35–52 (€67)
🏌 Canach, 15km E of Luxembourg City
🏠 Iwao Uematsu

Luxembourg Belenhaff (1993)
Domaine de Belenhaff, 6141 Junglinster
☎ 78 00 68-1
🖳 78 71 28
🅿 18 L 6120 m Par 72
👤 H or Green card
££ €43 (€52)
🏌 17km NE of Luxembourg, nr La Rochette

Malta

Royal Malta (1888)
Marsa LQA 06, Malta
☎ **(356) 21 23 93 02**
⌨ (356) 21 22 70 20
⊮ 18 L 5020 m SSS 67
👥 U exc Thurs–NA before 11am
    Sat–NA before noon
££ £M12–£M15
🚗 Marsa, 3 miles from Valetta

Netherlands

Amsterdam & Noord Holland

Amsterdam Old Course
(1990)
Zwarte Laantje 4, 1099 CE Amsterdam
☎ **(020) 694 3650**
⌨ (020) 663 4621
⊮ 9 L 5264 m SSS 68
👥 WE–H
££ €41
🚗 5km SE of Amsterdam

Amsterdamse (1934)
Bauduinlaan 35, 1047 HK Amsterdam
☎ **(020) 497 7866**
⌨ (020) 497 5966
⊮ 18 L 6124 m CR 73.1
👥 WD–H WE–M
££ €50 – € 65
🚗 10km W of Amsterdam
🏠 Rolin/Jol

Burg Purmerend (1989)
Westerweg 60, 1445 AD Purmerend
☎ **(0299) 689160**
⌨ (0299) 647081
⊮ 18 L 5994 m SSS 73
    9 hole course
👥 H
££ €41–50
🚗 16km N of Amsterdam
🏠 Tom McAuley

Haarlemmermeersche
Spieringweg 745, 2141 ED Cruquius
☎ **(023) 558 9000**
⌨ (023) 558 9009
⊮ 18 L 5747 m Par 73 CR 70
    9 hole short course
👥 H
££ €32 (€39)
🚗 Haarlemmermeer, W of Amsterdam
🏠 O'Connor Jr/Rijks

Heemskerkse (1998)
*Communicatieweg 18, 1967
PR Heemskerk*
☎ **(0251) 250088**
⌨ (0251) 241627
⊮ 18 L 6167 m CR 72.3 SR 130
👥 WD–U WE–M
££ €46
🚗 25km NW of Amsterdam

Kennemer G&CC (1910)
Kennemerweg 78, 2042 XT Zandvoort
☎ **(023) 571 2836/8456**
⌨ (023) 571 9520
⊮ 27 holes CR 71.5-73.2
    Van Hengel 9 L 2951 m
    Pennink 9 L 2916 m
    Colt 9 L 2942 m
👥 H WE–NA before 3pm
££ €75
🚗 Zandvoort, 6km W of Haarlem
🏠 Colt/Pennink/Van Henge

De Noordhollandse
(1982)
Sluispolderweg 6, 1817 BM Alkmaar
☎ **(072) 515 6807**
⌨ (072) 520 9918
⊮ 18 L 5865 m CR 70.6
👥 H
££ €39 (€50)
🚗 2km N of Alkmaar
🏠 Ryks/Dudok van Heel
🖥 www.dnhgc.nl

Olympus (1973)
*Abcouderstraatweg 46, 1105 AA
Amsterdam Zuid-Oost*
☎ **(0294) 285373**
⌨ (0294) 286347
⊮ 18 L 5926 m SSS 71
👥 U–phone first
££ €27
🚗 SE of Amsterdam, nr A2 and AMC
    Hospital
🏠 Dudok van Heel/Jol

Spaarnwoude (1977)
Het Hoge Land 2, 1981 LT Velsen-Zuid
☎ **(023) 538 2708**
⌨ (023) 538 7274
⊮ 18 L 5668 m Par 71
    9 L 2981 m Par 36
👥 H
££ €20
🚗 14km W of Amsterdam. 10km NE
    of Haarlem
🏠 Pennink/Jol

Waterlandse (1990)
*Buikslotermeerdijk 141, 1027
AC Amsterdam*
☎ **(020) 632 5650**
⌨ (0200 634 3506
⊮ 18 L 5156 m Par 71
££ €23
🚗 10km N of Amsterdam

Zaanse (1988)
Zuiderweg 68, 1456 NH Wijdewormer
☎ **(0299) 438199**
⌨ (0299) 438199
⊮ 9 L 5282 m Par 70
👥 WD–H WE–M
££ €40 (€45)
🚗 15km NE of Amsterdam
🏠 Gerard Jol
🖥 www.zaansegolfclub.com

Breda & South West

Brugse Vaart (1993)
Brugse Vaart 10, 4501 NE Oostburg
☎ **(0117) 453410**
⌨ (0117) 455511
⊮ 18 L 6305 m SSS 72
👥 U
££ €25 (€30)
🚗 15km N of Bruges, nr Knokke
🏠 Devos/Bauwens

Domburgsche (1914)
Schelpweg 26, 4357 BP Domburg
☎ **(0118) 586106**
⌨ (0118) 586109
⊮ 9 L 5415 m CR 69 SR 126
👥 H
££ €40 (€45)
🚗 15km NW of Middelburg

Efteling (1994)
Veldstraat 6, 5176 NB Kaatsheuvel
☎ **(0416) 288399**
⌨ (0416) 288439
⊮ 18 L 5896 m Par 72
👥 H
££ €41 (€50)
🚗 20km NE of Breda
🖥 www.efteling.com

Grevelingenhout (1988)
Oudendijk 3, 4311 NA Bruinisse
☎ **(0111) 482650**
⌨ (0111) 481566
⊮ 18 L 5951 m CR 70.7
    9 hole Par 3 course
👥 H
££ €40 – € 50
🚗 55km SW of Rotterdam
🏠 Donald Harradine

Oosterhoutse (1985)
Dukaatstraat 21, 4903 RN Oosterhout
☎ **(0162) 458759**
⌨ (0162) 433285
⊮ 18 L 5907 m CR 71 SR 126
👥 WD–H WE–M
££ €50
🚗 10km NE of Breda
🏠 J Dudok van Heel
🖥 www.ogcgolf.nl

Princenbosch (1991)
Bavelseweg 153, 5126 NM Gilze
☎ **(0161) 431811**

  18 L 5542 m Par 70
H–max 28
€27
10km SW of Breda

Reymerswael (1986)
Grensweg 21, 4411 ST Rilland Bath
(0113) 551265
(0113) 551264
9 L 5866 m CR 71.4 SR 126
6 hole course
H
€30 (€35)
20km W of Bergen op Zoom. 50km W of Breda, off A58
Dudok van Heel/Rijks
www.reymerswael.nl

Toxandria (1928)
Veenstraat 89, 5124 NC Molenschot
(0161) 411200
(0161) 411715
18 L 5834 m Par 72
WD–I Phone first
€50 (€70)
8km E of Breda
Morrison/Dudok van Heel
www.Toxandria.nl

De Woeste Kop (1986)
Justaasweg 4, 4571 NB Axel
(0115) 564467/564831 (Pro)
(0115) 564851
9 L 5424 m SSS 69
U
€20 (€30)
45km W of Antwerp
Paneels/Bosch

Wouwse Plantage (1981)
Zoomvlietweg 66, 4624 RP Bergen op Zoom
(0165) 377100
(0165) 377101
18 L 6162 m CR 72.1 SR 131
H WE–M
€50
10km E of Bergen-op-Zoom, nr Roosendaal
Pennink/Rolin
www.golfwouwseplantage.nl

East Central

Breuninkhof
Bussloselaan 6, 7383 RP Bussloo
(0571) 261955
(0571) 262089
9 L 6178 m SSS 72
U
€25 (€30)
100km E of Amsterdam
Eschauzier

Edese (1978)
Papendallaan 22, 6816 VD Arnhem
(026) 482 1985
(026) 482 1348

  18 L 5740 m SSS 70
H
€27 (€36)
National Sportcentrum Papendal. NW of Arnhem, towards Ede
Pennink/Dudok van Heel

De Graafschap (1987)
Sluitdijk 4, 7241 RR Lochem
(0573) 254323
(0573) 258450
18 L 6059 m CR 71.6
H–booking necessary
€41 (€45)
Lochem, 35km NW of Arnhem
www.lochemsegolfclub.nl

Hattemse G&CC (1930)
Veenwal 11, 8051 AS Hattem
(038) 444 1909
9 L 5808 yds SSS 68
WD–H WE–M+H
€18 (€23)
Hattem, 5km S of Zwolle
Del Court van Krimpen

Keppelse (1926)
Burg Kehrerstraat 52, 7002 LD Doetinchem
(0314) 343662
(0314) 366523
9 L 5360 m Par 70
H
€35 (€40)
Laag-Keppel, 25km E of Arnhem
JP Eschauzier

De Koepel (1983)
Postbox 88, 7640 AB Wierden
(0546) 576150/574070
(0546) 578109
9 L 2863 m SSS 70
WE–H
€23 (€27)
7km W of Almelo
F Pennink

Nunspeetse G&CC (1987)
Plesmanlaan 30, 8072 PT Nunspeet
(0341) 255255
(0341) 255285
27 L 6100 m Par 72
U
€45 (€50)
Nunspeet, 80km E of Amsterdam
Paul Rolin
www.nunspeetsegolf.nl

Rosendaelsche (1895)
Apeldoornseweg 450, 6816 SN Arnhem
(026) 442 1438
(026) 351 1196
18 L 6057 m CR 72.3 SR 132
WD–H WE–NA
€55
5km N of Arnhem on Route N50
Frank Pennink

Sallandsche De Hoek (1934)
PO Box 24, 7430 AA Diepenveen
(0570) 593269
(0570) 590102
18 L 5889 m SSS 71
WD–H WE–M H
€45
6km N of Deventer
Pennink/Steel

Sybrook (1992)
Veendijk 100, 7525 PZ Enschede
(0541) 530331
(0541) 531690
18 L 5878 m Par 71
WD–H WE–M
€36
10km N of Enschede
Rolin/Rijks

Twentsche (1926)
Almelosestraat 17, 7495 TG Ambt Delden
(074) 384 1167
(074) 384 1067
18 L 6178 m SSS 72
H
€45 (€50)
4km N of Delden
TJ McAuley
www.twentschegolfclub.nl

Veluwse (1957)
Nr 57, 7346 AC Hoog Soeren
(055) 519 1275
(055) 519 1275
9 L 6264 yds SSS 70
WD–U WD–H
€27 (€32)
5km W of Apeldoorn

Welderen (1994)
Grote Molenstraat 173, 6661 NH Elst
(0481) 376591
(0481) 377055
18 L 6015 m Par 72
WD–H WE–M
€36
Elst, S of Arnhem via A325 or A15
JE Eschauzier
www.welderen.nl

Eindhoven & South East

De Berendonck (1985)
Weg Door de Berendonck 40, 6603 LP Wijchen
(024) 642 0039
(024) 641 1254
18 L 5671 m Par 71 SSS 70
WE–restricted
€25 (€30)
5km SW of Nijmegen
J Dudok van Heel

Best G&CC
Golflaan 1, 5683 RZ Best
- ☎ (0499) 391443
- 🖶 (0499) 393221
- ⏳ 18 L 6079 m CR 71.7 SR 131
- 👥 H
- £€ €41 (€50)
- 🚗 Best, 5km NW of Eindhoven
- ⛳ J Dudok van Heel

Crossmoor G&CC   (1986)
Laurabosweg 8, 6006 VR Weert
- ☎ (0495) 518438
- 🖶 (0495) 518709
- ⏳ 18 L 6043 m Par 72
  9 hole Par 3 course
- 👥 H
- £€ €36 (€45)
- 🚗 Weert/Altweertheide, 30km SE of
  Eindhoven
- ⛳ J Dudok van Heel

De Dommel   (1928)
*Zegenwerp 12, 5271 NC
St Michielsgestel*
- ☎ (07355) 19168
- 🖶 (07355) 19441
- ⏳ 18 L 5607 m SSS 69
- 👥 WD–H WE–NA
- £€ €40 (€55)
- 🚗 10km S of Hertogenbosch
- ⛳ Colt/Steel

Eindhovensche Golf   (1930)
*Eindhovenseweg 300, 5553
VB Valkenswaard*
- ☎ (040) 201 4816
- 🖶 (040) 207 6177
- ⏳ 18 L 5918 m SSS 71
- 👥 H
- £€ €60
- 🚗 8km S of Eindhoven
- ⛳ HS Colt

Geijsteren G&CC   (1974)
Het Spekt 2, 5862 AZ Geijsteren
- ☎ (0478) 531809/532592
- 🖶 (0478) 532963
- ⏳ 18 L 6090 m Par 72
- 👥 WD–H WE–M
- £€ €45 (€50)
- 🚗 Off A73 Junction 9, N270 to
  Wanssum. 25km N of Venlo
- ⛳ Pennink/Steel

Gendersteyn   (1994)
Locht 140, 5504 RP Veldhoven
- ☎ (040) 253 4444
- 🖶 (040) 254 9747
- ⏳ 18 L 5770 m Par 72
- £€ €30 (€36)
- 🚗 10km SW of Eindhoven

Havelte   (1977)
*Postbus 29, Kolonieweg 2, 7970
AA Havelte*
- ☎ (0521) 342200
- 🖶 (0521) 343134
- ⏳ 18 L 6243 m CR 72.7 SR 135

H
- £€ €35 (€45)
- 🚗 30km SW of Assen (N371)
- ⛳ Donald Steel

Haviksoord   (1976)
*Maarheezerweg Nrd 11, 5595 XG
Leende (NB)*
- ☎ (040) 206 1818
- 🖶 (040) 206 2761
- ⏳ 9 L 5948 m CR 71.1 SR 136
- 👥 H
- £€ €35 (€40)
- 🚗 10km S of Eindhoven

Herkenbosch   (1991)
Stationsweg 100, 6075 CD Herkenbosch
- ☎ (0475) 529529
- 🖶 (0475) 533580
- ⏳ 18 L 5758 m Par 72
- 👥 U
- £€ €45 (€55)
- 🚗 20km S of Venlo, nr German
  border

Het Rijk van Nijmegen   (1985)
Postweg 17, 6561 KJ Groesbeek
- ☎ (024) 397 6644
- 🖶 (024) 397 6942
- ⏳ 18 L 6010 m CR 70.7
  18 L 5717 m CR 69.1
- 👥 H
- £€ €32 (€39)
- 🚗 5km E of Nijmegen
- ⛳ Paul Rolin
- 🖥 www.golfbaanhetrijkvannijmegen
  .nl

De Peelse Golf   (1991)
*Maasduinenweg 1, 5977 NP Eversoord-
Sevenum*
- ☎ (077) 467 8030
- 🖶 (077) 467 8031
- ⏳ 18 L 6047 m Par 72
- 👥 U H
- £€ €40 (€50)
- 🚗 20km W of Venlo
- ⛳ Alan Rijks

De Schoot   (1973)
*Schootsedijk 18, 5491 TD
Sint Oedenrode*
- ☎ (04134) 73011
- 🖶 (04134) 71358
- ⏳ 9 L 2886 m Par 72
- 👥 U
- £€ €27 (€32)
- 🚗 20km N of Eindhoven
- ⛳ A Rijks

Tongelreep G&CC   (1984)
*Charles Roelslaan 15, 5644
HX Eindhoven*
- ☎ (040) 252 0962
- 🖶 (040) 293 2238
- ⏳ 9 L 5345 m CR 69.2 SR 122
- 👥 WD–H WE–H by introduction only
- £€ €17.50 – € 30
- 🚗 Eindhoven
- ⛳ J van Rooy

Welschap   (1993)
Welschapsedijk 164, 5657 BB Eindhoven
- ☎ (040) 251 5797
- 🖶 (040) 252 9297
- ⏳ 18 L 5282 m Par 70
- £€ €27 (€32)
- 🚗 Eindhoven

Limburg Province

Brunssummerheide   (1985)
Rimburgerweg 50, Brunssum
- ☎ (045) 527 0968
- 🖶 (045) 527 3939
- ⏳ 27 L 5933 m Par 72
  9 hole Par 3 course
- 👥 U H
- £€ €36 (€45)
- 🚗 25km NE of Maastricht

Hoenshuis G&CC   (1987)
Hoensweg 17, 6367 GN Voerendaal
- ☎ (045) 575 3300
- 🖶 (045) 575 0900
- ⏳ 18 L 6074 m CR 71.2
- 👥 WE–NA 10am–2pm
- £€ €30 (€43)
- 🚗 Limburg, 10km NE of Maastricht
- ⛳ Paul Rolin

De Zuid Limburgse G&CC   (1956)
Dalbissenweg 22, 6281 NC Mechelen
- ☎ (043) 455 1397/1254
- 🖶 (043) 455 1576/3958
- ⏳ 18 L 5904 m Par 71
- 👥 WD–U WE–H
- £€ €34 (€43)
- 🚗 Mechelen, 25km SE of Maastricht
- ⛳ Hawtree/Snelder/Rolin

North

Gelpenberg   (1970)
Gebbeveenweg 1, 7854 TD Aalden
- ☎ (0591) 371929
- 🖶 (0591) 372422
- ⏳ 18 L 6031 m Par 71
- 👥 H
- £€ €40 (€50)
- 🚗 16km W of Emmen
- ⛳ Pennink/Steel

Holthuizen   (1985)
Oosteinde 7a, 9301 ZP Roden
- ☎ (050) 501 5103
- 🖶 (050) 501 3685
- ⏳ 9 L 6079 m SSS 72
- 👥 H
- £€ €32 (€36)
- 🚗 10km S of Groningen
- ⛳ Rijks/Eschauzier

Lauswolt G&CC   (1964)
*Van Harinxmaweg 8A, PO Box 36, 9244
ZN Beetsterzwaag*
- ☎ (0512) 383590/382594

☎ (0512) 383739
🖥 18 L 6087 m CR 71.5
🚹 H
££ €50 (€70)
⛳ Beetsterzwaag, 5km S of Drachten
🏠 Pennink/Steel

Noord Nederlandse G&CC
(1950)
Pollselaan 5, 9756 CJ Glimmen
☎ **(050) 406 2004**
🖥 (050) 406 1922
▷ 18 L 5660 m CR 69.9
🚹 H
££ €50
⛳ 12km S of Groningen, off A28
■ www.nngcc.nl

De Semslanden (1986)
*Nieuwe Dijk 1, 9514
BX Gasselternijveen*
☎ **(0599) 564661/565531**
🖥 (0599) 565594
▷ 18 L 5973 m CR 127
🚹 H
££ €27 (€32)
⛳ 25km E of Assen
🏠 Eschauzier/Thate/Jol

Vegilinbosschen
*Legemeersterweg 18, 8527 DS
Legemeer*
☎ **(0513) 499466**
🖥 (0513) 499777
▷ 18 L 5765 m SSS 71
🚹 H
££ €36 (€41)
⛳ 120km NE of Amsterdam
🏠 Allen Rijks

Rotterdam & The Hague

Broekpolder (1981)
*Watersportweg 100, 3138
HD Vlaardingen*
☎ **(010) 249 5566,
(010) 249 5555/249 5577**
🖥 (010) 249 5579
▷ 18 L 6048 m SSS 72
🚹 H
££ €34–45 (€45–57)
⛳ 15km W of Rotterdam, off A20
🏠 Frank Pennink

Capelle a/d IJssel (1977)
*Gravenweg 311, 2905 LB Capelle
a/d IJssel*
☎ **(010) 442 2485**
🖥 (010) 284 0606
▷ 18 L 5214 m SSS 68
🚹 WD–U WE–M
££ €39
⛳ 5km S of Rotterdam
🏠 Donald Harradine

Cromstrijen (1989)
Veerweg 26, 3281 LX Numansdorp
☎ **(0186) 654455**
🖥 (0186) 654681
▷ 18 L 6099 m Par 72
9 L 3800 m Par 62
🚹 H–max 28 (men) 34 (ladies)
££ €60 (€70)
⛳ 30km S of Rotterdam (A29)
🏠 Tom McAuley

De Hooge Bergsche (1989)
*Rottebandreef 40, 2661
JK Bergschenhoek*
☎ **(010) 522 0052/522 0703**
🖥 (010) 521 9350
▷ 18 L 5370 m Par 71 SR 116
🚹 U
££ €40 (€50)
⛳ Bergschenhoek, 2km NE of Rotterdam
🏠 Gerard Jol
■ www.hoogebergsche.nl

Koninklijke Haagsche G&CC (1893)
*Groot Haesebroekeseweg 22, 2243
EC Wassenaar*
☎ **(070) 517 9607**
🖥 (070) 514 0171
▷ 18 L 5674 m Par 72 SR 129
🚹 WD–H (max 24) WE–M
££ €100
⛳ 6km N of The Hague
🏠 Allison/Colt

Kralingen
Kralingseweg 200, 3062 CG Rotterdam
☎ **(010) 452 2283**
▷ 9 L 5220 yds CR 66.6
🚹 H
££ €35 (€40)
⛳ 5km from centre of Rotterdam
🏠 Copijn/Cotton

Leidschendamse Leeuwenbergh (1988)
Elzenlaan 31, 2495 AZ Den Haag
☎ **(070) 395 4556**
🖥 (070) 399 8615
▷ 18 L 5461 m Par 70
££ €55
⛳ E side of The Hague

De Merwelanden (1985)
*Golfbaan Crayestein, Baanhoekweg 50,
3313 LP Dordrecht*
☎ **(078) 621 1221**
🖥 (078) 616 1036
▷ 18 L 5722 m Par 71
🚹 U
££ €35 (€42.50)
⛳ 20km SE of Rotterdam
🏠 H & C Kuijsters

Noordwijkse (1915)
*Randweg 25, PO Box 70, 2200
AB Noordwijk*
☎ **(0252) 373761**

☎ (0252) 370044
▷ 18 L 5879 m CR 71.9
🚹 WD–H before noon and after 3pm
££ €57
⛳ 5km N of Noordwyk. 15 km NW of Leiden
🏠 Frank Pennink

Oude Maas (1975)
Veerweg 2a, 3161 EX Rhoon
☎ **(010) 501 5135**
🖥 (010) 501 5604
▷ 18 L 5471 m Par 71
🚹 H
££ €40 (€45)
⛳ Rhoon, 10km S of Rotterdam via A15
🏠 Pennink/Jol/Rijks
■ www.golfcluboudemaas.nl

Rijswijkse (1987)
Delftweg 58, 2289 AL Rijswijk
☎ **(070) 395 4864**
🖥 (070) 399 5040
▷ 18 L 5722 m Par 71 CR 69.5
🚹 H
££ €42 (€54)
⛳ 5km SE of The Hague
🏠 Steel/Rijks

Wassenaarse Rozenstein (1984)
*Dr Mansveltkade 15, 2242
TZ Wassenaar*
☎ **(070) 511 7846**
🖥 (070) 511 9302
▷ 18 L 5820 m SSS 70
🚹 H
££ €50 (€60)
⛳ 14km NE of The Hague
🏠 Dudok van Heel/Jol
■ www.rozenstein.nl

Westerpark Zoetermeer (1985)
Heuvelweg 3, 2716 DZ Zoetermeer
☎ **(079) 351 7283**
🖥 (079) 352 1335
▷ 18 L 5891 m Par 71
££ €32 (€36)
⛳ 10km E of The Hague (A12)

Zeegersloot (1984)
*Kromme Aarweg 5, PO Box 190, 2400
AD Alphen a/d Rijn*
☎ **(0172) 474567**
🖥 (0172) 494660
▷ 18 L 5793 m SSS 70
9 hole Par 3 course
🚹 U H
££ 18 hole:€38 (€52) 9 hole:€16.50 (€21)
⛳ Alphen, 15km N of Gouda. 20km S of Amsterdam
🏠 Gerard Jol

Utrecht & Hilversum

Almeerderhout   (1986)
Watersnipweg 19-21, 1341 AA Almere
- ☎ (036) 521 9130
- 🖥 (036) 521 9131
- ⮞ 27 L 6004-6046 m CR 71.9-72.2
  9 hole Par 3 course
- 👥 WD–U WE–M (Max h'cap 28)
- ££ €40 (€57.50)
- ⚲ 30km N of Hilversum
- ⌂ Dudok van Heel/Ryks

Anderstein
Woudenbergseweg 13a, 3953 ME Maarsbergen
- ☎ (0343) 431330
- 🖥 (0343) 432062
- ⮞ 18 L 6048 m CR 72
- 👥 WD–U WE–M only
- ££ €36–50
- ⚲ 20km E of Utrecht
- ⌂ Jol/Dudok van Heel

De Batouwe   (1990)
Oost Kanaalweg 1, 4011 LA Zoelen
- ☎ (0344) 624370
- 🖥 (0344) 613096
- ⮞ 18 L 5717 m Par 72 SSS 70
  9 hole Par 3 course
- 👥 U H–booking necessary
- ££ €43 (€57)
- ⚲ Tiel, 25km SE of Utrecht
- ⌂ Alan Rijks

Flevoland   (1979)
Bosweg 98, 8231 DZ Lelystad
- ☎ (0320) 230077
- 🖥 (0320) 230932
- ⮞ 18 L 5836 m Par 71
- 👥 WD–U H WE–M+H
- ££ €27 (€34)
- ⚲ Island of Flevoland. 1km NW of Lelystad. 45km N of Hilversum
- ⌂ JS Eschauzier

De Haar   (1974)
PO Box 104, Parkweg 5, 3450 AC Vleuten
- ☎ (030) 677 2860
- 🖥 (030) 677 3903
- ⮞ 9 L 6650 yds SSS 71
- 👥 WD–H WE–NA
- ££ €60
- ⚲ 10km NW of Utrecht
- ⌂ F Pennink

Hilversumsche   (1910)
Soestdijkerstraatweg 172, 1213 XJ Hilversum
- ☎ (035) 685 7060
- 🖥 (035) 685 3813
- ⮞ 18 L 6408 m Par 72
- 👥 Phone booking necessary
- ££ €45 (€57)
- ⚲ 3km E of Hilversum, nr Baarn
- ⌂ Burrows/Colt

De Hoge Kleij   (1985)
Appelweg 4, 3832 RK Leusden
- ☎ (033) 461 6944
- 🖥 (033) 465 2921
- ⮞ 18 L 6046 m SSS 72
- 👥 WD–H
- ££ €61
- ⚲ 1km SE of Amersfoort 20km NE of Utrecht via A28
- ⌂ Donald Steel

Nieuwegeinse   (1985)
Postbus 486, 3437 AL Nieuwegein
- ☎ (030) 604 2192/0769
- 🖥 (030) 604 2192
- ⮞ 9 L 4630 m Par 68 SSS 65
- 👥 WD–U WE–NA before 4pm
- ££ €20
- ⚲ 7km S of Utrecht
- ⌂ Paul Rolin

Utrechtse 'De Pan'   (1894)
Amersfoortseweg 1, 3735 LJ Bosch en Duin
- ☎ (030) 695 6427
- 🖥 (030) 696 3769
- ⮞ 18 L 5694 m Par 72 CR 70.1
- 👥 WD–M WE–NA
- ££ €60
- ⚲ 10km E of Utrecht, off A28
- ⌂ HS Colt

Zeewolde
Golflaan 1, 3896 LL Zeewolde
- ☎ (036) 522 2103
- 🖥 (036) 522 4100
- ⮞ 27 L 6259 m Par 72
  9 hole course Par 58
- 👥 H
- ££ €50
- ⚲ 20km N of Hilversum. 60km NE of Amsterdam
- ⌂ A Rijks
- ■ www.golfclub-zeewolde.nl

Norway

Arendal og Omegn   (1986)
Nes Verk, 4900 Tvedestrand
- ☎ 37 19 90 30
- 🖥 37 16 02 11
- ⮞ 18 L 5528 m Par 72
  9 hole course
- 👥 U
- ££ 250kr (300kr)
- ⚲ Nes Verk, 20km E of Arendal (E18). 95km NE of Kristiansand
- ■ www.arendalgk.no

Baerum   (1972)
Hellerudveien 26, 1350 Lommedalen
- ☎ 67 87 67 00
- 🖥 67 87 67 20
- ⮞ 18 L 5300 m Par 71
  9 hole short course

H–restricted. Max 28 (men) 32 (ladies). Booking advisable
- ££ 350kr
- ⚲ 10km W of Oslo. 10km N of Sandvika
- ⌂ Jeremy Turner

Bergen   (1937)
Erikveien 120, 5080 Eidsvåg
- ☎ 05 18 20 77
- ⮞ 9 L 4461 m Par 67
- 👥 U
- ££ 150kr
- ⚲ 8km N of Bergen

Borre   (1991)
Semb Hovedgaard, 3186 Horten
- ☎ 33 07 32 40
- 🖥 33 07 32 41
- ⮞ 18 L 6120 m Par 73
- 👥 H
- ££ 200kr (300kr)
- ⚲ Horten, 50km S of Drammen. 100km SW of Oslo
- ⌂ T Nordström

Borregaard   (1927)
PO Box 348, 1701 Sarpsborg
- ☎ 69 12 15 00
- 🖥 69 15 74 11
- ⮞ 9 L 4500 m SSS 65
- 👥 H
- ££ 150kr
- ⚲ Opsund, 1km N of Sarpsborg

Drøbak   (1988)
Belsjøveien 50, 1440 Drøbak
- ☎ 64 93 16 80
- 🖥 64 93 39 80
- ⮞ 18 L 5089 m Par 70
- 👥 H
- ££ 325kr (375kr)
- ⚲ 40km SE of Oslo
- ⌂ Hauser

Elverum   (1980)
PO Box 71, 2401 Elverum
- ☎ 62 41 35 88
- 🖥 62 41 55 13
- ⮞ 18 L 5845 m Par 72
- 👥 H
- ££ 200kr (220kr)
- ⚲ Starmoen Fritidspark, 10km E of Elverum. 35km E of Hamar. 150km N of Oslo

Grenland   (1976)
Luksefjellvn 578, 3721 Skien
- ☎ 35 59 07 03
- 🖥 35 59 06 10
- ⮞ 18 L 5777 m Par 72
- 👥 U
- ££ 250kr
- ⚲ 6km from Skien
- ⌂ Jan Sederholm

Groruddalen   (1988)
Postboks 37, Stovner, 0913 Oslo
- ☎ 22 79 05 60

☐ 22 79 05 79
☞ 9 L 2844 m CR 58.2 SR 102
⚇ U–before 3pm
££ 150kr
⊶ 15km N of Oslo
⌂ Leif Nilsson
▪ www.grorudgk.no

Hemsedal (1994)
3560 Hemsedal
☎ **32 06 23 77**
☐ 32 06 00 84
☞ 9 L 4816 m Par 68
⚇ U H
££ 180kr (240kr)
⊶ 40km N of Gol. 380km NW of Oslo
⌂ Leif Nilsson

Kjekstad (1976)
PO Box 201, 3440 Royken
☎ **31 29 79 90**
☐ 31 29 79 99
☞ 18 L 5100 m SSS 67
⚇ H
££ 250kr (300kr)
⊶ 12km SE of Drammen on Route 282. 40km SW of Oslo
⌂ Jan Sederholm

Kristiansand (1973)
PO Box 6090, Søm, 4602 Kristiansand
☎ **38 04 35 85**
☐ 38 04 34 15
☞ 9 L 2485 m SSS 70
⚇ U
££ D–150kr
⊶ 8 km E of Kristiansand (E18)

Larvik (1989)
Fritzøe Gård, 3267 Larvik
☎ **33 14 01 45**
☐ 33 14 01 49
☞ 18 L 6147 m Par 72
⚇ H
££ 300kr (400kr)
⊶ 3km S of Larvik on R301 to Stavern
⌂ Jan Sederholm
▪ www.larvikgolf.no

Narvik (1992)
8523 Elvegard
☎ **76 95 12 01**
☐ 76 95 12 06
☞ 18 L 5890 m Par 72
⚇ U H
££ 250kr
⊶ 30km S of Narvik
⌂ Jan Sederholm
▪ www.narvikgolf.no

Nes (1988)
Rommen Golfpark, 2160 Vormsund
☎ **63 91 20 30**
☐ 63 91 20 31
☞ 18 L 6001 m Par 72
⚇ H or Green card
££ 250kr (300kr)
⊶ 50km NE of Oslo, via E6/RV2
⌂ Hauser

Onsøy (1987)
Golfveien, 1626 Manstad
☎ **69 33 91 50**
☐ 69 33 35 24
☞ 18 L 5600 m Par 72
⚇ WD–U WE–H
££ 300kr
⊶ 10km W of Fredrikstad. Oslo 80km
⌂ Andersen/Mejstedt

Oppdal (1987)
PO Box 19, 7340 Oppdal
☎ **72 42 25 10**
☞ 9 L 2621 m Par 72
⚇ U
££ 150kr
⊶ 120km S of Trondheim
⌂ Jan Sederholm

Oppegård (1985)
Kongeveien 198, PO Box 50, 1416 Oppegård
☎ **66 81 59 90**
☐ 66 81 59 91
☞ 18 L 5280 m Par 71
⚇ U H
££ 250kr (350kr)
⊶ 22km S of Oslo
▪ www.oppegardgk.no

Oslo (1924)
Bogstad, 0757 Oslo
☎ **22 51 05 60**
☐ 22 51 05 61
☞ 18 L 6719 yds SSS 72
⚇ H–Max 20 (men) 28 (ladies) WD–restricted before 2pm WE–restricted after 2pm
££ 400kr (400kr)
⊶ 8km NW of Oslo. Signs to 'Bogstad Camping'.

Ostmarka (1989)
Postboks 63, 1914 Ytre Enebakk
☎ **64 92 38 40**
☐ 64 92 47 55
☞ 18 L 5640 m
⚇
££ 200kr (300kr)
⊶ 35km E of Oslo

Oustoen CC (1965)
PO Box 100, 1330 Fornebu
☎ **67 83 23 80/22 56 33 54**
☐ 67 53 95 44/22 59 91 83
☞ 18 L 5590m SSS 72
⚇ M
££ 500kr
⊶ Small island in Oslofjord, 10km W of Oslo

Skjeberg (1986)
PO Box 528, 1701 Sarpsborg
☎ **69 16 63 10**
☞ 18 L 5500 m Par 72
⚇ U
££ 150kr (200kr)
⊶ Hevingen, 2km N of Sarpsborg
⌂ Jan Sederholm

Sorknes (1990)
Sorknes Gaard, 2450 Rena
☎ **62 44 18 70**
☐ 62 44 00 27
☞ 18 L 6150 m SSS 72
⚇ U
££ 270kr (380kr)
⊶ 170km N of Oslo
⌂ Juul Soegaard
▪ www.sorknes.no

Stavanger (1956)
Longebakke 45, 4042 Hafrsfjord
☎ **51 55 54 31**
☐ 51 55 73 11
☞ 18 L 5751 m Par 71
⚇
££ 250kr
⊶ 6km SW of Stavanger
⌂ F Smith

Trondheim (1950)
PO Box 169, 7401 Trondheim
☎ **73 53 18 85**
☐ 73 52 75 05
☞ 9 L 5632 m SSS 72
⚇
££ 200kr
⊶ Trondheim 3 km
▪ www.trondheimgolfclubb.no

Tyrifjord (1982)
Postboks 91, 3529 Røyse
☎ **32 16 13 30**
☐ 32 16 13 40
☞ 18 L 5747 m Par 72 SR 140
⚇ U
££ 300kr (350kr)
⊶ 40km NW of Oslo (E16)
⌂ Sederholm/Eia
▪ www.tyrifjord-golfklubb.no

Vestfold (1958)
PO Box 64, 3108 Vear
☎ **33 36 25 00**
☐ 33 36 25 01
☞ 18 L 5979 m SSS 72
  9 hole course
⚇ H
££ 200kr (300kr)
⊶ Tønsberg 8km
⌂ Smith/Turner
▪ www.vestfoldgolfklubb.no

Poland

Amber Baltic (1993)
Baltycka Street 13, 72-514 Kolczewo
☎ **(091) 32 65 110/120**
☐ (091) 32 65 333
☞ 18 L 5802 m Par 72
  9 L 1307 m Par 28
⚇ U
££ €27 (€40)
⊶ 80km N of Szczecin
⌂ H-G Erhardt

For list of abbreviations and key to symbols see page 649

Portugal

Algarve

Alto G&CC   (1991)
Quinta do Alto do Poço, P O Box 1, 8501 906 Alvor
- ☎ **(0282) 460870**
- 🖳 (0282) 460879
- ☞ 18 L 6125 m SSS 73 SR 120
- 👥 U H
- ££ €56 – € 70
- ⛳ 2km W of Portimão
- ♿ Sir Henry Cotton
- ■ www.altoclub.com

Floresta Parque   (1987)
Vale do Poço, Budens, 8650 Vila do Bispo
- ☎ **(0282) 695333**
- 🖳 (0282) 695157
- ☞ 18 L 5787 m SSS 72
- 👥 U
- ££ €40
- ⛳ 16km W of Lagos, nr Salema
- ♿ Pepe Gancedo

Palmares   (1975)
Apartado 74, Meia Praia, 8600 901 Lagos
- ☎ **(0282) 790500**
- 🖳 (0282) 790509
- ☞ 18 L 5961 m Par 71 SSS 72
- 👥 U H
- ££ €45 – € 70
- ⛳ Meia Praia, 5km E of Lagos
- ♿ Frank Pennink
- ■ www.palmaresgolf.com

Penina   (1966)
PO Box 146, Penina, 8502 Portimao
- ☎ **(0282) 420200**
- 🖳 (0282) 420300
- ☞ Ch'ship 18 L 6343 m SSS 73; Resort 9 L 3987 m SSS 71; Academy 9 L 1851 m Par 30
- 👥 H–max 28 (M) or 36 (L) – soft spikes only
- ££ Ch'ship €65–90 Resort €37 Academy €33
- ⛳ 5km W of Portimao. 12km E of Lagos
- ♿ Sir Henry Cotton

Pestana   (1991)
Apartado 1011, 8400-908 Carvoeiro Lga
- ☎ **(0282) 340900**
- 🖳 (0282) 340901
- ☞ Gramacho 18 L 5919 m Par 72 SSS 71; Pinta 18 L 6727 m Par 71 SSS 72
- 👥 U
- ££ Garmacho €37–50 Pinta €50–70
- ⛳ 10km E of Portimão. 54km W of Faro Airport
- ♿ Ronald Fream
- ■ www.pestana.com

Pine Cliffs G&CC   (1991)
Pinhal do Concelho, 8200 Albufeira
- ☎ **(0289) 500100/501999**
- 🖳 (0289) 501950
- ☞ 9 L 2324 m Par 66 SSS 67
- 👥 U H
- ££ 9 hole: €27
- ⛳ 7km W of Vilamoura
- ♿ Martin Hawtree

Pinheiros Altos   (1992)
Quinta do Lago, 8135 Almancil
- ☎ **(0289) 359910**
- 🖳 (0289) 394392
- ☞ 18 L 6236 m Par 72
- 👥 H–phone first. Soft spikes only
- ££ €100
- ⛳ Quinta do Lago, 15km W of Faro
- ♿ Ronald Fream

Quinta do Lago   (1974)
Quinta Do Lago, 8135 Almancil
- ☎ **(0289) 390700/9**
- 🖳 (0289) 394013
- ☞ Quinta do Lago 18 L 6488 m SSS 72; Ria Formosa 18 L 6205 m SSS 72
- 👥 H–by prior arrangement
- ££ €65
- ⛳ 15km W of Faro. Airport 20km
- ♿ Mitchell/Lee

Salgados
Apartado 2362, Vale do Rabelho, 8200 917 Albufeira
- ☎ **(0289) 583030**
- 🖳 (0289) 591112
- ☞ 18 L 6080 m Par 72
- 👥 U
- ££ On application
- ⛳ W of Albufeira
- ♿ P de Vasconcelos

San Lorenzo   (1988)
Quinta do Lago, 8135 Almancil
- ☎ **(0289) 396522**
- 🖳 (0289) 396908
- ☞ 18 L 6238 m SSS 73
- 👥 H–restricted
- ££ €140
- ⛳ 16km W of Faro
- ♿ Joseph Lee

Vale de Milho   (1990)
Apartado 1273, Praia do Carvoeiro, 8401-911 Carvoeiro Lga
- ☎ **(0282) 358502**
- 🖳 (0282) 358497
- ☞ 9 hole Par 3 course
- 👥 U
- ££ 18 holes: €27 9 holes: €17
- ⛳ 2¹/₂ km E of Carvoeiro
- ♿ Dave Thomas

Vale do Lobo   (1968)
Vale Do Lobo, 8135-864 Vale do Lobo-Almançil
- ☎ **(0289) 353535**
- 🖳 (0289) 353003

- ☞ Ocean 18 L 5424 m Par 71 Royal 18 L 6050 m Par 72
- 👥 H
- ££ Ocean €90 Royal €110
- ⛳ 19km W of Faro. Airport 19km
- ♿ Cotton/Roquemore

Vila Sol   (1991)
Alto do Semino, Vilamoura, 8125 Quarteira
- ☎ **(0289) 300505**
- 🖳 (0289) 316499
- ☞ 27 L 6335 m Par SSS 72
- 👥 U H
- ££ €90
- ⛳ 5km E of Vilamoura. Faro Airport 10km
- ♿ Donald Steel

Vilamoura Laguna   (1990)
8125-507 Vilamoura, Algarve
- ☎ **(0289) 310180**
- 🖳 (0289) 310183
- ☞ 18 L 6133 m CR 71.1 SR 126
- 👥 H–max 28(M) 36(L)
- ££ €60
- ⛳ As Vilamoura Old
- ♿ Joseph Lee
- ■ www.vilamoura.net

Vilamoura Millennium   (2000)
8125-507 Vilamoura, Algarve
- ☎ **(0289) 310188**
- 🖳 (0289) 310183
- ☞ 18 L 6143 m CR 69.2 SR 113
- 👥 H–max 28(M) 36(L). Soft spikes only
- ££ €60
- ⛳ As Vilamoura Old
- ♿ Martin Hawtree
- ■ www.vilamoura.net

Vilamoura Old   (1969)
8125-507 Vilamoura, Algarve
- ☎ **(0289) 310341**
- 🖳 (0289) 310321
- ☞ 18 L 6254 m CR 70.9 SR 124
- 👥 H–max 24(M) 28(L) Soft spikes only
- ££ €110
- ⛳ Quarteira, 25km W of Faro
- ♿ Frank Pennink
- ■ www.vilamoura.net

Vilamoura Pinhal   (1976)
8125-507 Vilamoura, Algarve
- ☎ **(0289) 310390**
- 🖳 (0289) 310393
- ☞ 18 L 6206 m CR 70.4 SR 122
- 👥 H–max 28(M) 36(L)
- ££ €75
- ⛳ As Vilamoura Old
- ♿ Pennink/Trent Jones
- ■ www.vilamoura.net

Azores

Batalha (1995)
Rua do Bom Jesus, Aflitos, 9545-234
Fenais da Luz (Açores)
☎ **(0296) 298559/498560**
✆ (0296) 498284
🏳 18 L 6435 m CR 72.8 SR 131
🏌 H
£€ €40
🚗 Sao Miguel Island. Ponta Delgada 10km
🎯 Cameron/Powell
■ www.virtualazores.com/verdegolf

Furnas (1939)
Rua do Bom Jesus, Aflitos Furnas, 9545
Fenais da Luz (Açores)
☎ **(0296) 498559/584341**
✆ (0296) 498284/584651
🏳 18 L 6232 m SSS 72
🏌 H
£€ €40
🚗 São Miguel Island. Furnas Villa 5km
🎯 Mackenzie Ross/Cameron/Powell
■ www.virtualazores.com/verdegolf

Terceira Island (1954)
Caixa Postal 15, 9760 909 Praia da
Victória (Açores)
☎ **(0295) 902444**
✆ (0295) 902445
🏳 18 L 5790 m Par 72 SSS 70
🏌 U H
£€ €30
🚗 10km NW of Praia da Victoria

Lisbon & Central Portugal

Aroeira (1972)
Herdade da Aroeira, 2815-207 Charneca
da Caparica
☎ **(021) 297 9190**
✆ (021) 297 1238
🏳 18 L 6170 m CR 71 SR 123
  18 L 6195 m CR 72.3 SR 130
🏌 U H
£€ €45 (€62)
🚗 20km S of Lisbon, off Setúbal/Costa da Caparica road
🎯 Pennink/Steel
■ www.sil.pt

Belas
Alameda do Aqueducto, 2605-199 Belas
☎ **(021) 962 6600**
✆ (021) 962 6601
🏳 18 L 6200 m Par 72
🏌 U
🚗 W of Lisbon (N117)

Estoril (1945)
Avenida da República, 2765-273 Estoril
☎ **(021) 466 0367**
✆ (021) 468 2796

🏳 18 L 5313 m CR 67.9 SR 125
  9 L 2350 m SSS 65
🏌 WD–U WE–M
£€ €51 (€65)
🚗 N of Estoril on Sintra road. 30km W of Lisbon
🎯 Mackenzie Ross

Estoril-Sol Golf Academy (1976)
Quinta do Outeira, Linhó, 2710 Sintra
☎ **(01) 923 2461**
✆ (01) 923 2461
🏳 9 L 4118 m Par 66 SSS 66
🏌 U
🚗 7km N of Estoril. Lisbon 35km
🎯 Harris/Fream

Lisbon Sports Club (1922)
Casal da Carregueira, 2745 Belas
☎ **(01) 431 0077**
✆ (01) 431 2482
🏳 18 L 5216 m Par 69 SSS 69
🏌 U
£€ D – € 37 (D–47)
🚗 Belas, 20km NW of Lisbon
🎯 Hawtree

Marvao
Estrada do Monte Pobre, Sao Salvador
do d'Aramanha, 7330 Marvao
☎ **(045) 93755**
✆ (045) 93805
🏳 18 holes Par 72
🏌 U
🚗 25km N of Portalegre, nr Spanish border (N118/N246)

Montado
Apartado 40, Algeruz, 2950 Palmela
☎ **(065) 706648**
✆ (065) 706775
🏳 18 L 6060 m SSS 72
🏌 U
£€ €42
🚗 5km E of Setúbal. 40km S of Lisbon
🎯 Duarte Sottomayor

Penha Longa (1992)
Estrada da Lagoa Azul, Linhó, 2714-
511 Sintra
☎ **(021) 924 9011**
✆ (021) 924 9024
🏳 18 L 6290 m CR 70.2 SR 120
  9 L 2588 m Par 35
🏌 U H
£€ 18 hole:€81.70 (€104.30)
  9 hole:€31.20 (€40.80)
🚗 8km N of Estoril. 17km W of Lisbon
🎯 Robert Trent Jones Jr
■ www.caesarparkpenhalonga.com

Quinta da Beloura (1994)
Estrada de Albarraque, 2710 444 Sintra
☎ **(021) 910 6350**
✆ (021) 910 6359
🏳 18 L 5774 m Par 73 CR 71.2 SR 128

🏌 U
£€ D – € 35 (D – € 52)
🚗 Between Estoril and Sintra, off N9. Lisbon 34km
🎯 Rocky Roquemore
■ www.pestana.com

Quinta da Marinha (1984)
Quinta da Marinha, 2750 Cascais
☎ **(021) 486 0180**
✆ (021) 486 9032
🏳 18 L 6014 m CR 68.5 SR 114
🏌 U
£€ €61 (€76)
🚗 2km W of Cascais. 32km W of Lisbon
🎯 Robert Trent Jones
■ www.quintadamarinha.com

Quinta do Perú
Alameda da Serra 2, 2975-666 Quinta
do Conde
☎ **(021) 213 4320**
✆ (021) 213 4321
🏳 18 L 6036 m CR 72 SR 137
🏌 H
£€ €57 (€86)
🚗 E of Lisbon, off EN10
🎯 Rocky Roquemore
■ www.golfquintadoperu.com

Tróia Golf
Torralta, Tróia, 7570 Grandola
☎ **(065) 494112**
✆ (065) 494315
🏳 18 L 6338 m Par 72 SSS 74
🏌 U
£€ €27
🚗 S of Setúbal on Tróia peninsula. 50km S of Lisbon
🎯 Robert Trent Jones

Vimeiro
Praia do Porto Novo, Vimeiro, 2560
Torres Vedras
☎ **(061) 984157**
✆ (061) 984621
🏳 9 L 4781 m Par 68 SSS 67
🏌 U
£€ €25
🚗 Vimeiro, 20km N of Torres Vedras. 65km N of Lisbon
🎯 Frank Pennink

Madeira

Madeira (1991)
Sto Antonio da Serra, 9200
Machico, Madeira
☎ **(091) 552345/552356**
✆ (091) 552367
🏳 18 L 6040 m Par 72
🏌 U
£€ €40
🚗 25km E of Funchal. Airport 3km
🎯 Robert Trent Jones

Palheiro   (1993)

Sitio do Balancal, Sao Gonçalo, 9050-296 Funchal, Madeira
- ☎ **(0291) 792116,**
  (0291) 790120 (Bookings)
- 🖳 (0291) 792456
- ⮀ 18 L 6022 m SSS 71
- 👥 May–Sept–U Oct–April–H
- ££ €65
- ⚐ 5km from Funchal, off Airport road to Camacha
- 🛈 Cabell Robinson
- ■ www.madeira-golf.com

North

Amarante   (1997)

Quinta da Deveza, Fregim, 4600-670 Amarante
- ☎ **(0255) 446060**
- 🖳 (0255) 446202
- ⮀ 18 L 5085 m CR 65.4 SR 114
- 👥 H
- ££ €31 (€43.50)
- ⚐ 50km E of Oporto, off A4
- 🛈 J Santana da Silva

Golden Eagle G&CC

Quinta do Brincal, 2040 Rio Maior
- ☎ **(0243) 908148**
- 🖳 (0243) 908149
- ⮀ 18 L 6021 m Par 72
- 👥 H
- ££ €50 (€60)
- ⚐ 55km N of Lisbon, off N1 towards Leiria
- 🛈 R Roquemore

Miramar   (1932)

Av Sacadura Cabral, Miramar, 4405-0013 Arcozelo
- ☎ **(022) 762 2067**
- 🖳 (022) 762 7859
- ⮀ 9 L 2655 m Par 70 SSS 69
- 👥 H
- ££ €40 (€50)
- ⚐ 8km S of Oporto
- 🛈 Swan/Gordon

Montebelo

Farminhão, 3510 Viseu
- ☎ **(032) 856464**
- 🖳 (032) 856401
- ⮀ 18 L 6300 m Par 72 SSS 72
- 👥 U
- ⚐ 75km NE of Coimbra

Oporto   (1890)

Sisto-Paramos, 4500 Espinho
- ☎ **(022) 734 2008**
- 🖳 (022) 734 6895
- ⮀ 18 L 5780 m Par 71 SSS 70
- 👥 H WE–restricted
- ££ €50
- ⚐ Espinho, 15km S of Oporto

Ponte de Lima

Quinta de Pias, Fornelos, 4490 Ponte de Lima
- ☎ **(058) 43414**
- 🖳 (058) 743424
- ⮀ 18 L 6005 m Par 71 SSS 70
- 👥 U
- ⚐ 75km N of Oporto (N201)

Praia d'el Rey G&CC   (1997)

Vale de Janelas, Apartado 2, 2510 Obidos
- ☎ **(0262) 905005**
- 🖳 (0262) 905009
- ⮀ 18 L 6467 m Par 72 SSS 72
- 👥 U H
- ££ €65 (€85)
- ⚐ 65km N of Lisbon, nr Obidos (Motorway A 8)
- 🛈 Cabell Robinson
- ■ www.praia-del-rey.com

Quinta da Barca   (1997)

Barca do Lago, Gemezes, 4740 Esposende
- ☎ **(053) 966723**
- 🖳 (053) 969068
- ⮀ 9 L 2015 m Par 62
- 👥 U
- ££ €30 (€37)
- ⚐ 25km N of Oporto (IC1)
- 🛈 J Santana da Silva

Vidago

Pavilhão do Golfe, 5425 Vidago
- ☎ **(076) 907356**
- 🖳 (076) 996622
- ⮀ 9 L 2256m Par 66 SSS 64
- ⚐ 50km N of Vila Real. 130km NE of Oporto
- 🛈 Mackenzie Ross

Slovenia

G&CC Bled   (1937)

Ljublanska 5, 4260 Bled
- ☎ **(064) 700 777**
- 🖳 (064) 718 225
- ⮀ 18 L 6325 m SSS 73
  9 L 3092 m SSS 72
- 👥 H–36 max
- ££ €51 (€64)
- ⚐ 3km W of Bled. 50km NW of Ljubljana, nr Austro-Italian border
- 🛈 Donald Harradine
- ■ www.golf.bled.si

Castle Mokrice   (1992)

Terme Catez, Topliska Cesta 35, 8250 Brezice
- ☎ **(0608) 240751**
- 🖳 (0608) 57007
- ⮀ 18 holes SSS 70
- 👥 H
- ££ €29 (€32)
- ⚐ 30km N of Zagreb
- 🛈 Donald Harradine

Lipica   (1989)

Lipica 5, 66210 Sezana
- ☎ **(067) 31580**
- 🖳 (067) 72818
- ⮀ 9 L 6240 m SSS 71
- 👥 U
- ££ On application
- ⚐ 11km NE of Trieste. 85km SW of Ljubljana
- 🛈 Donald Harradine

Spain

Alicante & Murcia

Alicante   (1997)

C Vicente Hipolito 37, Playa San Juan, 03540 Alicante
- ☎ **(96) 515 37 94/515 20 43**
- 🖳 (96) 516 37 07
- ⮀ 18 L 6236 m Par 72
- 👥 U H
- ££ €54
- ⚐ Playa San Juan, N of Alicante
- 🛈 Severiano Ballesteros
- ■ www.alicantgolf.com

Altorreal   (1994)

Urb Altorreal, 30500 Molina de Segura (Murcia)
- ☎ **(968) 64 81 44**
- 🖳 (986) 64 82 48
- ⮀ 18 L 6239 m Par 72 SSS 73
- 👥 H
- ££ €30 (€36)
- ⚐ 10km from Murcia on Madrid road
- 🛈 Dave Thomas

Bonalba   (1993)

Partida de Bonalba, 03110 Mutxamiel (Alicante)
- ☎ **(96) 595 5955**
- ⮀ 18 L 6190m Par 72 SSS 73
- 👥 U
- ££ €48
- ⚐ 10km N of Alicante. A7 Junction 67
- 🛈 Ramón Espinosa
- ■ www.golfbonalba.com

Don Cayo   (1974)

Apartado 341, 0359 Altea La Vieja (Alicante)
- ☎ **(96) 584 80 46**
- 🖳 (96) 584 11 88
- ⮀ 9 L 6156 m SSS 72
- 👥 U H
- ⚐ 4km N of Altea, nr Callosa
- 🛈 Barber/Sanz

Ifach   (1974)

Crta Moraira-Calpe Km 3, Apdo 28, 03720 Benisa (Alicante)
- ☎ **(96) 649 71 14**

☎ (96) 649 71 14
▷ 9 L 3408 m SSS 59
👤 U
££ D – € 19
🚗 9km N of Calpe, towards Moraira
🏠 Javier Arana

Jávea (1981)

Apartado 148, 03730 Jávea, (Alicante)
☎ (96) 579 25 84
📠 (96) 646 05 54
▷ 9 L 6070 m SSS 71
👤 H
££ D – € 33
🚗 Lluca, Jávea. 90km NE of Alicante
🏠 Francisco Moreno

La Manga (1971)

Los Belones, 30385 Cartagena (Murcia)
☎ (968) 13 72 34
📠 (968) 15 72 72
▷ North 18 L 5780 m SSS 70
   South 18 L 6259 m SSS 73
   Princesa 18 L 5971 m SSS 72
👤 U
🚗 30km NE of Cartagena, nr Murcia
   airport
🏠 RD Putman

La Marquesa (1989)

Ciudad Quesada II, 03170
Rojales, (Alicante)
☎ (96) 671 42 58
📠 (96) 671 42 67
▷ 18 L 5840 m Par 72 SSS 70
👤 U
££ D – € 25
🚗 Rojales, 40km S of Alicante
🏠 Justo Quesada

Las Ramblas (1991)

Crta Alicante-Cartagena Km48, 03189
Urb Villamartin, Orihuela (Alicante)
☎ (96) 532 20 11
📠 (96) 532 21 59
▷ 18 L 5770 m SSS 71
👤 U H
££ €42
🚗 9km S of Torrevieja
🏠 José Gancedo

Real Campoamor (1989)

Crta Cartagena-Alicante Km48, Apdo
17, 03189 Orihuela-Costa (Alicante)
☎ (96) 532 13 66
📠 (96) 532 24 54
▷ 18 L 6203 m Par 72 SSS 73
👤 U H
££ €30
🚗 Torrevieja 9km (N332)
🏠 C Gracia Caselles

La Sella (1991)

Ctra La Xara-Jesús Pobre, 03749 Jesús
Pobre (Alicante)
☎ (96) 645 42 52/645 41 10
📠 (96) 645 42 01
▷ 18 L 6289 m CR 73.3 SR 136
👤 U H
££ €56

🚗 Denia 5km
🏠 Juan de la Cuadra

Villamartin (1972)

Crta Alicante-Cartagena Km50, 03189
Urb Villamartin, Orihuela (Alicante)
☎ (96) 676 51 27/676 51 60
📠 (96) 676 51 70
▷ 18 L 6132 m SSS 72
👤 U H
££ €48
🚗 8km S of Torrevieja
🏠 Paul Putman

Almería

Almerimar (1976)

Urb Almerimar, 04700 El
Ejido (Almería)
☎ (950) 48 02 34
📠 (950) 49 72 33
▷ 18 L 6111 m SSS 72
👤 U
🚗 35km W of Almería
🏠 Gary Player

Cortijo Grande (1976)

Apdo 2, Cortijo Grande, 04639
Turre (Almería)
☎ (951) 47 91 76
▷ 18 L 6024 m Par 72 SSS 71
👤 U
🚗 20km W of Turre. 85km N of
   Almería, nr Mojácar
🏠 PJ Polansky

La Envia (1993)

Apdo 51, 04720 Aguadulce (Almería)
☎ (950) 55 96 41
▷ 18 L 5810 m Par 72 SSS 70
👤 U
🚗 10km from Almería
🏠 F Mendoza

Playa Serena (1979)

Urb Playa Serena, 04740 Roquetas de
Mar (Almería)
☎ (950) 33 30 55
📠 (950) 33 30 55
▷ 18 L 6301 m Par 72
👤 H
££ €30–39
🚗 20km S of Almería
🏠 Gallardo/Alliss

Badajoz & West

Guadiana (1992)

Crta Madrid-Lisboa Km 393, Apdo 171,
06080 Badajoz
☎ (924) 44 81 88
▷ 18 L 6381 m Par 72 SSS 73
👤 U
🚗 Badajoz
🏠 Daniel Calero

Norba (1988)

Apdo 880, 10080 Cáceres
☎ (927) 23 14 41
📠 (927) 23 14 80
▷ 18 L 6422 m Par 72 SSS 74
👤 U
££ €24 (€36)
🚗 4km S of Cáceres
🏠 Carlos Corsini

Salamanca (1988)

Monte de Zarapicos, 37170
Zarapicos (Salamanca)
☎ (923) 32 91 02
▷ 18 L 6267 m Par 72 SSS 72
👤 U
🚗 W of Salamanca,nr Parada de
   Arriba (C-517)
🏠 Manuel Piñero

Balearic Islands

Canyamel

Urb Canyamel, Crta de Cuevas, 07580
Capdepera, (Mallorca)
☎ (971) 56 44 57
📠 (971) 56 53 80
▷ 18 L 6115 m SSS 72
👤 H
🚗 70km NE of Palma, nr Cala Ratjada
🏠 José Gancedo

Capdepera (1989)

Apdo 6, 07580 Capdepera, Mallorca
☎ (971) 56 58 75/56 58 57
📠 (971) 56 58 74
▷ 18 L 6284 m SSS 72
👤 U H
🚗 71km E of Palma, between Artá
   and Capdepera
🏠 Maples/Pape

Club Son Parc (1977)

Urb Son Parc, Mercadel (Menorca)
☎ (971) 18 88 75
📠 (971) 35 95 91
▷ 9 L 2791 m SSS 69
👤 U
££ 18 holes: €42–54 9 holes: €24–33
🚗 Mercadal, 18km N of Mahón
🏠 JF Martínez
🌐 www.clubsonparc.com

Ibiza (1990)

Apdo 1270, 07840 Santa Eulalia, (Ibiza)
☎ (971) 19 61 18
📠 (971) 19 60 51
▷ 18 L 6083 m SSS 72
   9 L 5867 m SSS 70
👤 H
££ €36–72
🚗 7km N of Ibiza town
🏠 Thomas/Rivero

Pollensa (1986)

Ctra Palma-Pollensa Km 49, 07460
Pollensa, (Mallorca)
☎ (971) 53 32 16
📠 (971) 53 32 65

For list of abbreviations and key to symbols see page 649

9 L 5304 m Par 70 SSS 70
U H
££ €52
Pollensa, 45km N of Palma
José Gancedo

Poniente (1978)
Costa de Calvia, 07181
Calvia (Mallorca)
☎ (971) 13 01 48
▢ (971) 13 01 76
18 L 6430 m SSS 72
U H
££ €65
12km SW of Palma towards Cala
Figuera
John Harris
www.ponientegolf.com

Pula Golf (1995)
Predio de Pula, 07550 Son
Servera (Mallorca)
☎ (971) 81 70 34
▢ (971) 81 70 35
18 L 6018 m Par 70
U H
££ €48 – € 72
70km NE of Palma

Royal Bendinat (1986)
C. Campoamor, 07015
Calviá, (Mallorca)
☎ (971) 40 52 00
▢ (971) 70 07 86
18 L 5768 m SSS 71
U H
7km W of Palma
Martin Hawtree

Santa Ponsa (1976)
Santa Ponsa, 07180 Calvia (Mallorca)
☎ (971) 69 02 11/69 08 00
▢ (971) 69 33 64
18 L 6520 m SSS 74
18 L 6053 m SSS 73
No 1–U H No 2–NA
££ €65
18km W of Palma
Folco Nardi

Son Antem (1993)
Apartado 102, 07620
Llucmajor, Mallorca
☎ (971) 12 92 00
▢ (971) 12 92 01
East 18 L 6327 m CR 73.9 SR 134
West 18 L 6293 m CR 74 SR 137
U
££ East – € 59.50 West – € 62.50
20km E of Palma (Route 717)
F López Segales

Son Servera (1967)
Costa de Los Pinos, 07759 Son
Servera, (Mallorca)
☎ (971) 84 00 96
▢ (971) 84 01 60
9 L 5956 m SSS 72
H
££ D – € 42

Son Servera, 64km E of Palma
John Harris

Son Vida (1964)
Urb Son Vida, 07013 Palma (Mallorca)
☎ (971) 79 12 10
▢ (971) 79 11 27
18 L 5740 m SSS 71
U H
££ €48
3km NW of Palma
FW Hawtree

Vall d'Or (1985)
Apdo 23, 07660 Cala D'Or, (Mallorca)
☎ (971) 83 70 68/83 70 01
▢ (971) 83 72 99
18 L 5799 m SSS 71
H
££ €63
60km E of Palma, between Cala
d'Or and Porto Colóm
Benz/Bendly

Barcelona & Cataluña

Aro-Mas Nou (1990)
Apdo 429, 17250 Playa de Aro
☎ (972) 82 69 00,
(972) 81 67 27 (Bookings)
▢ (972) 82 69 06
18 L 6218 m Par 72
9 holes Par 3 course
U H
££ €53 (€57)
35km SE of Gerona on coast. A7
Junction 9 Barcelona Airport
100km
Ramón Espinosa

Bonmont Terres Noves (1990)
Urb Terres Noves, 43300
Montroig (Tarragona)
☎ (977) 81 81 40
▢ (977) 81 81 46
18 L 6371 m SSS 72
U H
££ €33 (€48)
S of Tarragona. 130km S of
Barcelona
Robert Trent Jones Jr
www.bonmont.com

Caldes Internacional (1992)
Apdo 200, 08140 Caldes de
Montbui (Barcelona)
☎ (93) 865 38 28
18 L 6258 m Par 72 SSS 73
U
28km from Barcelona
Ramón Espinosa

Can Bosch (1984)
Trav de les Corts 322, 08029 Barcelona
☎ (93) 405 04 22/866 25 71
▢ (93) 419 9659
9 L 3027 m SSS 71
U H
35km NE of Barcelona
Ramon Espinosa

Costa Brava (1962)
La Masia, 17246 Sta Cristina
d'Aro (Gerona)
☎ (972) 83 71 50
▢ (972) 83 72 72
18 L 5573 m SSS 70
H
££ €36–57
Playa de Aro 5km. 30km SE of
Gerona
J Hamilton Stutt
www.golfcostabrava.com

Costa Dorada (1983)
Apartado 600, 43080 Tarragona
☎ (977) 65 33 61
18 L 6223 m SSS 73
Tarragona
José Gancedo

Empordà (1990)
Crta Torroella de Montgri, 17257
Gualta (Gerona)
☎ (972) 76 04 50/76 01 36
▢ (972) 75 71 00
27 L 5855-6112 m SSS 70-71
U H
££ €33 (€51)
35km E of Gerona, nr Pals. 130km
N of Barcelona
Robert von Hagge

Fontanals de Cerdanya (1994)
Fontanals de Cerdanya, 17538
Soriguerola (Girona)
☎ (972) 14 43 74
18 L 6454 m Par 72 SSS 74
U
2km from Alp de Puigcerdá

Girona (1992)
Urb Golf Girona, 17481 Sant Juliá de
Ramis, (Girona)
☎ (972) 17 16 41
▢ (972) 17 16 82
18 L 6100 m CR 72 SR 133
H–booking required
££ €33 (€52)
Sant Juliá de Ramis, 4km from
Girona. Barcelona 98km
Hawtree
www.golfgirona.com

Llavaneras (1945)
Camino del Golf, 08392 San Andres de
Llavaneras, (Barcelona)
☎ (93) 792 60 50
▢ (93) 795 25 58
18 L 4644 m SSS 66

U H
££   €36 (€72)
⊷   4km N of Mataró. 34km N of
     Barcelona (A19)
⌂   Hawtree/Espinosa

Masia Bach   (1990)

Ctra Martorell-Capellades, 08781 Sant Esteve Sesrovires

☎   (93) 772 8800
▢   (93) 772 8810
⟱   18 L 6039 m SSS 72
     9 L 3578 m SSS 62
⋔   H
££   €54 (€120)
⊷   30km NW of Barcelona
⌂   JM Olazábal

Osona Montanya   (1988)

Masia L'Estanyol, 08553 El Brull (Barcelona)

☎   (93) 884 01 70
▢   (93) 884 04 07
⟱   18 L 6036 m Par 72
     U H
⊷   60km NE of Barcelona
⌂   Dave Thomas

Pals   (1966)

Playa de Pals, 17526 Gerona

☎   (972) 63 60 06
▢   (972) 63 70 09
⟱   18 L 6222 m Par 73
⋔   U
⊷   40km E of Gerona. 135km NE of
     Barcelona
⌂   FW Hawtree

Peralada   (1993)

La Garriga, 17491 Peralada, Girona

☎   (972) 53 82 87
▢   (972) 53 82 36
⟱   18 L 5990 m SSS 71
⋔   H
££   €43 – € 63
⊷   Costa Brava, on French border.
     40km S of Perpignan Airport, nr
     Figueres
⌂   Jorge Soler
■   www.golfperalada.com

Real Cerdaña   (1929)

Apdo 63, Puigcerdá, (Gerona)

☎   (972) 88 13 38
⟱   18 L 5735 m SSS 70
⊷   Cerdaña, 1km from Puigcerdá
⌂   Javier Arana

Real Golf El Prat   (1956)

Apdo 10, 08820 El Prat de Llobregat, (Barcelona)

☎   (93) 379 02 78
▢   (93) 370 51 02
⟱   4 x 9 holes:
     6070-6266 m SSS 73-74
⋔   H
££   €72 (€144)
⊷   El Prat, Airport 3km. 15km S of
     Barcelona
⌂   Arana/Thomas

Reus Aiguesverds   (1989)

Crta Cambrils, Mas Guardiá, 43206 Reus

☎   (977) 75 27 25
▢   (977) 75 19 38
⟱   18 L 6905 yds SSS 72
⋔   U
££   €42
⊷   10km W of Tarragona. 100km S of
     Barcelona

Sant Cugat   (1914)

08190 Sant Cugat del Valles

☎   (93) 674 39 08/674 39 58
⟱   18 L 5209 m SSS 68
⊷   20km NW of Barcelona

Sant Jordi

Urb Sant Jordi d'Alfama, 43860 Ametlla de Mar, (Tarragona)

☎   (977) 49 34 57
▢   (977) 49 32 77
⟱   9 L 5696 m SSS 70
⋔   U H
⊷   50km S of Tarragona
⌂   Lauresno Nomen

Terramar   (1922)

Apdo 6, 08870 Sitges

☎   (93) 894 05 80/894 20 43
▢   (93) 894 70 51
⟱   18 L 5878 m Par 72
⋔   H
££   €42 (€66)
⊷   Sitges, 37km S of Barcelona
⌂   Hawtree/Piñero/Fazio

Torremirona   (1994)

Ctra N260 Km46, 17744 Navata (Girona)

☎   (972) 55 37 37
▢   (972) 55 37 16
⟱   18 L 6184 m Par 72
⋔   U
££   €47 (€63)
⊷   30km from Girona. A7 Junction 4
⌂   Joan Anglada

Vallromanes   (1972)

C/Afveras, 08188 Vallromanes, (Barcelona)

☎   (93) 572 90 64
▢   (93) 572 93 30
⟱   18 L 6038 m Par 72
⋔   H
⊷   23km N of Barcelona between
     Alella and Granollers. A7 Junction
     13
⌂   FW Hawtree

Burgos & North

Barganiza   (1982)

Apartado 277, 33080 Oviedo, Asturias

☎   (985) 74 24 68
⟱   18 L 5549 m SSS 70
⊷   12km N of Oviedo on Gijon old
     road
⌂   Victor García

Castillo de Gorraiz   (1993)

Urb Castillo de Gorraiz, 31620 Valle de Egues (Navarra)

☎   (948) 33 70 73
▢   (948) 33 73 15
⟱   18 L 6321 m CR 73.1 SR 130
⋔   U
££   €45 (€50)
⊷   4km from Pamplona
⌂   Cabell B Robinson
■   www.golfgorraiz.com

La Cuesta

Apdo 40, 33500 Llanes

☎   (98) 541 7084
▢   (98) 540 1973
⟱   9 L 5456 m SSS 69
⋔   U
⊷   3km from Llanes (N-634)

Izki Golf   (1992)

01119 Urturi (Alava)

☎   (945) 37 82 62
▢   (945) 37 82 66
⟱   18 L 6576 m Par 73
⋔   U
££   €24 (€40)
⊷   Urturi, 39km from Vitoria
⌂   Severiano Ballesteros

Larrabea   (1989)

Crta de Landa, 01170 Legutiano, (Alava)

☎   (945) 46 58 44/46 58 41
▢   (945) 46 57 25
⟱   18 L 5991 m Par 72
⋔   U
££   €30 (€36)
⊷   14km N of Vitoria, nr Villareal de
     Alava
⌂   José Gancedo

Laukariz   (1976)

Laukariz-Munguía, (Viscaya)

☎   (94) 674 08 58/674 04 62
⟱   18 L 6112 m SSS 72
⋔   U
⊷   15km N of Bilbao towards Mungía
⌂   RD Putman

Lerma   (1991)

Ctra Madrid-Burgos Km195, 09340 Lerma (Burgos)

☎   (947) 17 12 14/17 12 16
▢   (947) 17 12 16
⟱   18 L 6235 m SSS 72
⋔   H
⊷   30km S of Burgos, nr Villa Ducal
     de Lerma
⌂   Pepe Gancedo

La Llorea   (1994)

Crta Nacional 632, Km 62, 33394 Lloreda (Gijón)

☎   (985) 33 31 91
▢   (985) 36 47 26
⟱   18 L 5971 m Par 72
⋔   H
££   €33.66 (€39.76)
⊷   10km E of Gijón

🏠 Roland Fabret
■ www.golflallorea.com

Real Golf Castiello (1958)

Apdo Correos 161, 33200 Gijón
☎ (985) 36 63 13
🖅 (985) 13 18 00
☞ 18 L 4817 m Par 70
👥 WE–restricted
£€ €48
🚗 5km S of Gijón

Real Golf Neguri (1911)

Apdo Correos 9, 48990 Algorta
☎ (94) 469 02 00/04/08
☞ 18 L 6319 m SSS 72
6 hole Par 3 course
🚗 La Galea, 20km N of Bilbao
🏠 Javier Arana

Real Golf Pedreña (1928)

Apartado 233, Santander
☎ (942) 50 00 01/50 02 66
🖅 (942) 50 04 21
☞ 18 L 5745 m SSS 70
9 L 2740 m SSS 36
👥 H
£€ €34 (€54)
🚗 20km from Santander, on Bay of Santander
🏠 Colt/Ballesteros

Real San Sebastián (1910)

PO Box 6, Fuenterrabia, (Guipúzcoa)
☎ (943) 61 68 45/61 68 46
🖅 (943) 61 14 91
☞ 18 L 6020 m SSS 71
👥 WD–U H from 9–12 noon WE–NA
£€ €60 – €90
🚗 Jaizubia Valley, 14km NE of San Sebastián
🏠 P Hirigoyen

Real Zarauz (1916)

Apartado 82, Zarauz, (Guipúzcoa)
☎ (943) 83 01 45
☞ 9 L 5184 m SSS 68
🚗 Zarauz, 25km W of San Sebastián

Ulzama (1965)

31779 Guerendiain (Navarra)
☎ (948) 30 51 62
🖅 (948) 30 54 71
☞ 18 L 6246 m Par 72
👥 U
£€ On application
🚗 20km N of Pamplona
🏠 Javier Arana

Canary Islands

Amarilla (1988)

Urb Amarilla Golf, San Miguel de Abona, 38630 Santa Cruz de Tenerife
☎ (922) 73 03 19
🖅 (922) 73 00 85
☞ 18 L 6077 m Par 72

👥 H
£€ €60
🚗 6km SW of South Airport. 12km from Playa de las Americas
🏠 Donald Steel

Costa Teguise (1978)

Apdo 170, 35080 Arrecife de Lanzarote
☎ (928) 59 05 12
🖅 (928) 59 04 90
☞ 18 L 5853 m SSS 72
👥 U
£€ Summer €33 Winter €42
🚗 4km N of Arrecife
🏠 John Harris

Maspalomas (1968)

Av de Neckerman, Maspalomas, 35100 Gran Canaria
☎ (928) 76 25 81/76 73 43
🖅 (928) 76 82 45
☞ 18 L 6216 m SSS 72
👥 H
£€ Summer €36. Winter € 72
🚗 Maspalomas, S coast of Gran Canaria
🏠 Mackenzie Ross
■ www.maspalomasgolf.net

Real Golf Las Palmas (1891)

PO Box 93, 35380 Santa Brigida, Gran Canaria
☎ (928) 35 10 50/35 01 04
🖅 (928) 35 01 10
☞ 18 L 5690 m SSS 71
👥 WD–U WE–NA
£€ Summer €48. Winter € 73
🚗 Bandama, Las Palmas 14km
🏠 Mackenzie Ross

Real Tenerife (1932)

El Peñón, Tacoronte, Tenerife
☎ (922) 63 66 07
🖅 (922) 63 64 80
☞ 18 L 5750 m Par 71
👥 WD–H 8am–1pm
£€ €34
🚗 20km N of Santa Cruz. Puerto Cruz 15km
🏠 J Laynez

Golf del Sur (1987)

San Miguel de Abona, 38620 Tenerife (Canarias)
☎ (922) 73 81 70
🖅 (922) 78 82 72
☞ North 9 L 2913 m SSS 36
Links 9 L 2469 m SSS 34
South 9 L 2957 m SSS 36
👥 H
£€ €67
🚗 Airport 3km. Playa de las Américas 12km
🏠 Pepe Gancedo
■ www.golfdelsur.net

Cordoba

Córdoba (1976)

Apartado 436, 14080 Córdoba
☎ (957) 35 02 08
☞ 18 L 5964 m Par 72 SSS 73
👥 U
🚗 9km N of Córdoba, towards Obejo

Pozoblanco (1984)

Apdo 118, 14400 Pozoblanco, (Córdoba)
☎ (957) 33 91 71
🖅 (957) 33 91 71
☞ 9 L 3020 m Par 72
👥 U
🚗 Pozoblanco 3km
🏠 Carlos Luca

Galicia

Aero Club de Santiago (1976)

General Pardiñas 34, Santiago de Compostela (La Coruña)
☎ (981) 59 24 00
☞ 9 L 5816 m SSS 70
🚗 Santiago Airport

Aero Club de Vigo (1951)

Reconquista 7, 36201 Vigo
☎ (986) 48 66 45/48 75 09
☞ 9 L 5622 m SSS 60
🚗 Peinador Airport, 8km from Vigo

Domaio (1993)

San Lorenzo-Domaio, 36950 Moaña (Pontevedra)
☎ (986) 32 70 50
☞ 18 L 6110 m Par 72 SSS 73
👥 U
🏠 Ramón Espinosa

La Toja (1970)

Isla de La Toja, El Grove, Pontevedra
☎ (986) 73 01 58/73 08 18
🖅 (986) 73 31 22
☞ 9 L 5178 m SSS 72
👥 H
£€ €36–57
🚗 La Toja island. 30km W of Pontevedra
🏠 Ramón Espinosa

Granada

Granada

Avda de los Corsarios, 18110 Las Gabias (Granada)
☎ (958) 58 44 36
☞ 18 L 6037 m Par 71 SSS 73
👥 U
🚗 Las Gabias, 8km from Granada
🏠 Ramón Espinosa

Madrid Region

Barberán (1967)
Apartado 150.239, Cuatro Vientos,
28080 Madrid
☎ **(91) 509 00 59/509 11 40**
🖬 (91) 706 2174
🏳 9 L 6042 m SSS 72
🏌 M H
⛳ 10km SW of Madrid

La Dehesa (1991)
Calle Real 19, 28691 Villanueva
La Canada
☎ **(91) 815 70 22/815 70 37**
🖬 (91) 815 54 68
🏳 18 L 6456 m SSS 72
⛳ 35km NW of Madrid
🏛 Manuel Piñero

Herreria (1966)
PO Box 28200, San Lorenzo del
Escorial (Madrid)
☎ **(91) 890 51 11**
🏳 18 L 6050 m SSS 72
🏛 Escorial, 50km W of Madrid
🏛 Antonio Lucena

Jarama R.A.C.E. (1967)
Urb Ciudalcampo, 28707 San Sebastian
de los Reyes (Madrid)
☎ **(91) 657 00 01**
🖬 (91) 657 04 62
🏳 18 L 6505 m Par 72
9 hole Par 3 course
⛳ 28km N of Madrid on Burgos road
🏛 Javier Arana

Lomas-Bosque (1973)
Urb El Bosque, 28670 Villaviciosa de
Odón (Madrid)
☎ **(91) 616 75 00**
🖬 (91) 616 73 93
🏳 18 L 6075 m SSS 72
9 hole Par 3 course
🏌 WD–U H WE–M H
££ €25–78
⛳ 20km SW of Madrid
🏛 RD Putman

La Moraleja (1976)
La Moraleja, Alcobendas (Madrid)
☎ **(91) 650 07 00**
🏳 18 L 6016 m SSS 72
🏌 M
⛳ 9km N of Madrid on Burgos road
🏛 Jack Nicklaus

Nuevo De Madrid (1972)
Las Matas (Madrid)
☎ **(91) 630 08 20**
🏳 18 L 5647 m SSS 70
🏌 U H
⛳ 25km NW of Madrid on La Coruña
road

Olivar de la Hinojosa (1995)
Avda de Dublin, Campo de las Naciones,
28042 Madrid
☎ **(91) 721 18 89**

🏳 18 L 6163 m Par 72 SSS 72
🏌 U
⛳ Nr Madrid Airport M40

Puerta de Hierro (1896)
Avda de Miraflores, Ciudad Puerta de
Hierro, 28035 Madrid
☎ **(91) 316 1745**
🖬 (91) 373 8111
🏳 High 18 L 6375 m CR 72.5 SR 124
Low 18 L 6504 m CR 73.9 SR 130
🏌 M only
££ €78 (€162)
⛳ 4km N of Madrid (Route VI)
🏛 Harris/Simpson/Trent Jones

Los Retamares (1991)
Crta Algete-Alalpardo Km 2300, 28130
Valdeolmos (Madrid)
☎ **(91) 620 25 40**
🏳 18 L 6238 m Par 72 SSS 73
9 hole Par 3 course
🏌 U
⛳ 25km N of Madrid via N-1

Somosaguas (1971)
Avda de la Cabaña, 28223 Pozuelo de
Alarcón (Madrid)
☎ **(91) 352 16 47**
🖬 (91) 352 00 30
🏳 9 L 6054 m Par 72
⛳ Somosaguas
🏛 John Harris

Valdeláguila (1975)
Apdo 9, Alcalá de Henares (Madrid)
☎ **(91) 885 96 59**
🖬 (91) 885 96 59
🏳 9 L 5724 m Par 72
🏌 WD–U WE–NA
⛳ Villalbilla, 10km S of Alcalá

Villa de Madrid CC (1932)
Crta Castilla, 28040 Madrid
☎ **(91) 357 21 32**
🖬 (91) 549 07 97
🏳 27 L 5900-6321 m SSS 73-74
🏌 U H
££ €40 (€77)
⛳ 4km NW of Madrid, in the Casa del
Campo
🏛 Javier Arana

Malaga Region

Alhaurín (1994)
Crta 426 Km15, Alhaurín el Grande
☎ **(952) 59 59 70**
🖬 (952) 59 45 86
🏳 18 L 6221 m Par 72
18 hole Par 3 course
9 hole Par 3 course
🏌 U
££ €36
⛳ 6km from Mijas
🏛 Severiano Ballesteros

Añoreta (1989)
Avenida del Golf, 29730 Rincón de la
Victoria (Málaga)
☎ **(952) 40 40 00**
🖬 (952) 40 40 50
🏳 18 L 5976 m SSS 71
🏌 U
⛳ 12km E of Málaga
🏛 JM Canizares

La Cala (1991)
La Cala de Mijas, 29649 Mijas-
Costa (Málaga)
☎ **(952) 66 90 00, (952) 66 90 33**
🖬 (952) 66 90 34
🏳 North 18 L 6187 m Par 73
South 18 L 5966 m Par 72
6 hole Par 3 course
🏌 U H
££ €36 – € 63
⛳ 6km from Cala de Mijas, between
Fuengirola and Marbella
🏛 Cabell B Robinson
■ www.lacala.com

El Candado (1965)
Urb El Candado, El Palo, 29018
Málaga
☎ **(952) 29 93 40/1**
🏳 9 L 4676 m SSS 66
⛳ El Palo, 5km E of Málaga on Route
N340
🏛 Carlos Fernández

El Chaparral
Urb El Chaparral, Mijas-Costa
☎ **(952) 49 38 00**
🖬 (952) 49 40 51
🏳 18 L 5700 m SSS 71
🏌 U H
⛳ 5km W of Fuengirola on N340
🏛 Pepe Gancedo

Guadalhorce (1988)
Crtra de Cártama Km7, Apartado 48,
29590 Campanillas (Málaga)
☎ **(952) 17 93 78**
🖬 (952) 17 93 72
🏳 18 L 6194 m SSS 72
9 hole Par 3 course
🏌 WD–H before 1pm (booking
necessary) WE–M
££ €24–30
⛳ 8km W of Málaga
🏛 Kosti Kuronen

Lauro (1992)
Los Caracolillos, 29130 Alhaurín de la
Torre (Málaga)
☎ **(95) 241 27 67**
🖬 (95) 241 47 57
🏳 18 L 5971 m SSS 71
🏌 U
££ €46
⛳ 15km SW of Málaga airport on
Route A-366 towards Coín
🏛 Folco Nardi
■ www.laurogolf.com

Málaga Club de Campo
(1925)
Parador de Golf, Apdo 324,
29080 Málaga
☎ **(952) 38 12 55**
🖥 (952) 38 21 41
🏌 18 L 6249 m SSS 72
👤👤 U
⛳ Torremolinos 4km. 12km S of
Málaga, nr Airport
🏠 Tom Simpson

Mijas   (1976)
Apartado 145, Fuengirola, Málaga
☎ **(952) 47 68 43**
🖥 (952) 46 79 43
🏌 Lagos 18 L 6548 m Par 71 SSS 74;
Olivos 18 L 6009 m Par 72 SSS 72
👤👤 H–booking required Oct–Apr
££ €37
⛳ 4km NW of Fuengirola (Mijas
Valley)
🏠 Robert Trent Jones

Miraflores   (1989)
Urb Riviera del Sol, 29647 Mijas-Costa
☎ **(952) 93 19 60**
🖥 (952) 93 19 42
🏌 18 L 5113 m SSS 71
👤👤 U H
££ €55
⛳ 15km E of Marbella
🏠 Folco Nardi

Los Moriscos   (1974)
Costa Granada, Motril (Granada)
☎ **(958) 82 55 27**
🖥 (958) 25 52 51
🏌 9 L 5689 m SSS 72 Par 70
👤👤 U
⛳ 8km W of Motril, nr Salobrena.
80km E of Málaga
🏠 Ibergolf

Torrequebrada   (1976)
Apdo 120, Crta de Cadiz Km 220,
29630 Benalmadena
☎ **(95) 244 27 42**
🖥 (95) 256 11 29
🏌 18 L 5806 m Par 72 SSS 71
👤👤 H
££ €57
⛳ Benalmadena, 25km S of Málaga
🏠 Pepe Gancedo

Marbella & Estepona

Alcaidesa Links   (1992)
CN-340 Km124.6, 11315 La Linea (Cádiz)
☎ **(956) 79 10 40**
🖥 (956) 79 10 41
🏌 18 L 5766 m Par 72 SSS 71
👤👤 U–booking advised
££ €54
⛳ 15km E of Gibraltar. San Roque
3km
🏠 Alliss/Clark

Aloha   (1975)
Nueva Andalucia, 29660 Marbella
☎ **(952) 81 37 50/90 70 85/86,**
(952) 81 23 88 (Caddymaster)
🖥 (952) 81 23 89
🏌 18 L 6261 m SSS 72
9 hole short course
👤👤 H–booking necessary
££ €108
⛳ 8km W of Marbella, nr Puerto
Banus
🏠 Javier Arana

Los Arqueros   (1991)
Crta de Ronda Km43, 29679
Benahavis (Málaga)
☎ **(952) 78 46 00**
🖥 (952) 78 67 07
🏌 18 L 6130 m SSS 72
👤👤 H
££ €27
⛳ 5km N of San Pedro de Alcántara
🏠 Severiano Ballesteros

Atalaya G&CC   (1968)
Crta Benahavis 7, 29688 Málaga
☎ **(952) 88 28 12**
🖥 (952) 88 78 97
🏌 18 L 5856 m Par 72
18 L 5217 m Par 72
👤👤 U H
££ On application
⛳ 12km S of Marbella. 60km SW of
Málaga
🏠 Von Limburger/Krings

Las Brisas   (1968)
Apdo 147, 29660 Nueva
Andalucia (Málaga)
☎ **(952) 81 08 75/81 30 21**
🖥 (952) 81 55 18
🏌 18 L 6094 m SSS 72
👤👤 H–restricted
££ €120
⛳ 8km S of Marbella, nr Puerto Banus
🏠 Robert Trent Jones

La Cañada   (1982)
Ctra Guadiaro Km 1, 11311
Guadiaro (Cádiz)
☎ **(956) 79 41 00/79 44 11**
🖥 (956) 79 42 41
🏌 9 L 2873 m SSS 72
👤👤 U
⛳ Guadiaro, 2km from Sotogrande
🏠 Robert Trent Jones

La Duquesa G&CC   (1987)
Urb El Hacho, 29691 Manilva (Málaga)
☎ **(952) 89 04 25/89 04 26**
🖥 (952) 89 00 57
🏌 18 L 6142 m SSS 72
👤👤 U
⛳ 10km S of Estepona
🏠 Robert Trent Jones

Estepona   (1989)
Arroyo Vaquero, Apartado 532, 29680
Estepona (Málaga)
☎ **(952) 11 30 81**

🖥 (952) 11 30 80
🏌 18 L 5910 m Par 72 SSS 70
👤👤 U
££ €55
⛳ 5km W of Estepona (CN340)
🏠 Luis López
🖥 www.esteponagolf.com

Guadalmina   (1959)
Guadalmina Alta, San Pedro de
Alcántara, 29678 Marbella (Málaga)
☎ **(952) 88 65 22**
🖥 (952) 88 34 83
🏌 North 18 L 5825 m SSS 70
South 18 L 6075 m SSS 72
9 hole Par 3 course
👤👤 H (max 27M/35L)
££ €45
⛳ San Pedro, 12km W of Marbella
🏠 Arana/Nardi

Marbella   (1994)
CN 340 Km 188, 29600
Marbella (Málaga)
☎ **(952) 83 05 00**
🏌 18 L 5864 m Par 71 SSS 72
👤👤 U
⛳ Marbella
🏠 Robert Trent Jones

Monte Mayor   (1992)
Apdo 962, 29679 Benahavis (Málaga)
☎ **(95) 211 30 88**
🖥 (95) 211 30 87
🏌 18 L 5652 m Par 71 SSS 71
👤👤 U
££ €84 (inc buggy)
⛳ Between San Pedro and Estepona,
at Cancelada
🏠 Pepe Gancedo

Los Naranjos   (1977)
Apdo 64, 29660 Nueva
Andalucia, Marbella
☎ **(952) 81 52 06/81 24 28**
🖥 (952) 81 14 28
🏌 18 L 6484 m SSS 72
👤👤 U H
⛳ 8km S of Marbella, nr Puerto Banus
🏠 Robert Trent Jones Sr

El Paraiso   (1974)
Ctra Cádiz-Málaga Km 167, 29680
Estepona (Málaga)
☎ **(95) 288 38 35/288 38 46**
🖥 (95) 288 58 27
🏌 18 L 6116 m SSS 72
👤👤 U
££ €65
⛳ 14km S of Marbella
🏠 Player/Kirby

La Quinta G&CC   (1989)
Urb La Quinta, 29660 Nueva Andalucia
☎ **(952) 76 23 90**
🖥 (952) 76 23 99
🏌 27 L 5797-5945 m SSS 71-72
👤👤 U H
££ €72
⛳ 3km N of San Pedro de Alcántara
🏠 Piñero/García-Garrido

Rio Real   (1965)

Urb Rio Real, PO Box 82, 29600
Marbella (Málaga)

- ☎ **(95) 277 95 09**
- 📠 (95) 277 21 40
- ⛳ 18 L 6130 m SSS 72
- 👤 U
- 🚗 5km E of Marbella. Málaga Airport 50km
- �️ Javier Arana

San Roque   (1990)

CN 340 Km 126, San Roque,
11360 Cádiz

- ☎ **(956) 61 30 30/60/90**
- 📠 (956) 61 30 12/61 30 13
- ⛳ 18 L 6440 m SSS 74
- 👤 U H
- ££ €42
- 🚗 3km W of Sotogrande. 15km E of Gibraltar
- �️ Dave Thomas
- ■ www.sanroque.com

Santa María G&CC

Coto de los Dolores, Urb Elviria, Crta
N340 Km 192, 29600 Marbella
(Málaga)

- ☎ **(952) 83 03 86/83 03 88/83 10 36**
- 📠 (952) 83 08 70
- ⛳ 9 L 5792 m Par 71
- 👤 U
- 🚗 10km E of Marbella, opp Hotel Don Carlos
- �️ A García Garrido

Sotogrande   (1964)

Paseo del Parque, Apartado 14,
Sotogrande (Cádiz)

- ☎ **(956) 79 50 50/79 50 51**
- 📠 (956) 79 50 29
- ⛳ 18 L 6224 m SSS 74
  9 L 1299 m Par 29
- 👤 U
- 🚗 30km N of Gibraltar, nr Guadiaro
- �️ Robert Trent Jones

Valderrama   (1985)

11310 Sotogrande (Cadiz)

- ☎ **(956) 79 12 00**
- 📠 (956) 79 60 28
- ⛳ 18 L 7050 yds SSS 72
  9 hole Par 3 course
- 👤 H–12–2pm
- ££ €220
- 🚗 18km N of Gibraltar
- �️ Robert Trent Jones Sr
- ■ www.valderrama.com

La Zagaleta   (1994)

Crta San Pedro-Ronda Km 9,
29679 Benahavis

- ☎ **(95) 285 54 53**
- ⛳ 18 L 6039 m Par 72 SSS 72
- 👤 U
- 🚗 S of Marbella on Ronda road
- �️ Bradford Benz

Seville & Gulf of Cádiz

Bellavista   (1976)

Crta Huelva-Punta Umbría, Apdo
335, Huelva

- ☎ **(955) 31 90 17**
- 📠 (955) 31 90 25
- ⛳ 9 L 6270 m SSS 73
- 👤 U
- 🚗 Aljaraque, 6km SW of Huelva, towards Punta Umbria

Costa Ballena   (1997)

Crta Sta Maria-Chipiona, 11520 Rota

- ☎ **(956) 84 70 70**
- ⛳ 18 L 6187 m Par 72 SSS 72
- 👤 U
- �️ J-M Olazábal

Isla Canela   (1993)

Crta de la Playa, 21400
Ayamonte (Huelva)

- ☎ **(959) 47 72 63**
- 📠 (959) 47 72 71
- ⛳ 18 L 5937 m Par 72
- 👤 U H
- ££ €42
- 🚗 Ayamonte, 4km from Portuguese border
- �️ Juan Caterineu

Islantilla   (1993)

Urb Islantilla, Apdo 52, 21410 Isla
Cristina (Huelva)

- ☎ **(959) 48 60 39/48 60 49**
- 📠 (959) 48 61 04
- ⛳ 27 L 5926-6142 m SSS 72-73
- 👤 U H
- ££ €51
- 🚗 30km W of Huelva, nr Portuguese border
- �️ Canales/Recasens

Montecastillo   (1992)

Carretera de Arcos, 11406 Jérez

- ☎ **(956) 15 12 00**
- 📠 (956) 15 12 09
- ⛳ 18 L 6494 m SSS 72
- 👤 H
- ££ €90
- 🚗 10km NE of Jérez. 75km S of Seville
- �️ Jack Nicklaus

Montenmedio G&CC   (1996)

CN 340 Km42.5, 11150 Vejer-
Barbate (Cádiz)

- ☎ **(956) 45 12 16**
- 📠 (956) 45 12 95
- ⛳ 18 L 5897 m Par 72 SSS 72
- 👤 H
- ££ €75
- 🚗 Cádiz-Algeciras road (CN 340)
- �️ A Maldonado
- ■ www.monteenmedio.com

Novo Sancti Petri   (1990)

Urb Novo Sancti Petri, Playa de la
Barrosa, 11139 Chiclana de la Frontera

- ☎ **(956) 49 40 05**
- 📠 (956) 49 43 50
- ⛳ 18 L 6071 m Par 72
  18 L 6476 m Par 72
- 👤 U H
- ££ €54
- 🚗 La Barrosa, 24km SE of Cádiz. Jérez Airport 50km
- �️ Severiano Ballesteros
- ■ www.golf-novosancti.es

Pineda De Sevilla   (1939)

Apartado 1049, 41080 Sevilla

- ☎ **(954) 61 14 00**
- ⛳ 18 L 6120 m SSS 72
- 👤 U
- 🚗 3km S of Seville on Cádiz road
- �️ R & F Medina

Real Sevilla   (1992)

Autovía Sevilla-Utrera, 41089
Montequinto (Sevilla)

- ☎ **(954) 12 43 01**
- 📠 (954) 12 42 29
- ⛳ 18 L 6321 m SSS 73
- 👤 U H WE–booking necessary
- ££ €39
- 🚗 3km S of Seville
- �️ José María Olazabal
- ■ www.sevillagolf.com

Sevilla Golf   (1989)

Hacienda Las Minas, Ctra de Isla
Mayor, Aznalcazar (Sevilla)

- ☎ **(955) 75 04 14**
- ⛳ 9 L 5910 m Par 71
- 👤 U
- 🚗 15km W of Seville
- �️ A García Garrido

Vista Hermosa   (1975)

Apartado 77, Urb Vista Hermosa, 11500
Puerto de Santa María, Cádiz

- ☎ **(956) 87 56 05**
- ⛳ 9 L 5614 m Par 70
- 🚗 25km W of Cádiz

Zaudin

Crta Tomares-Mairena, 41940
Tomares (Sevilla)

- ☎ **(954) 15 41 59**
- 📠 (954) 15 33 44
- ⛳ 18 L 6192 m Par 71 SSS 72
- 👤 U
- ££ €43 (€60)
- 🚗 Cornisa del Aljarafe, 3km from Seville
- �️ Gary Player

Valencia & Castellón

El Bosque   (1989)

Crta Godelleta, 46370 Chiva-Valencia

- ☎ **(96) 180 41 42**

(96) 180 40 09
☞ 18 L 6384 m SSS 74
👤 U
⛳ Nr Chiva, 24km W of Valencia, off
Madrid road
🏠 Robert Trent Jones Sr

Costa de Azahar (1960)
*Ctra Grao-Benicasim, Castellón de
la Plana*
☎ (964) 22 70 64
☞ 9 L 2724 m SSS 70
⛳ 5km NE of Castellón, on coast
🏠 Angel Pérez

Escorpión (1975)
Apartado Correos 1, Betera (Valencia)
☎ (96) 160 12 11
🖂 (96) 169 01 87
☞ 27 L 6081-6383 m Par 71-73
👤 WD–H
£€ €60
⛳ Betera, 20km N of Valencia
🏠 Kirby/Vidaor

Manises (1964)
Apartado 22.029, Manises (Valencia)
☎ (96) 152 18 71
☞ 9 L 6094 m Par 73
⛳ 8km W of Valencia
🏠 Javier Arana

Mediterraneo CC (1978)
*Urb La Coma, 12190
Borriol, (Castellón)*
☎ (964) 32 16 53
🖂 (964) 32 16 53
☞ 18 L 6227 m Par 72
👤 H
£€ €36 (€42)
⛳ Borriol, 4km NW of Castellón
🏠 Ramón Espinosa
■ www.ccmediterraneo.com

Oliva Nova (1995)
46780 Oliva (Valencia)
☎ (096) 285 76 66
🖂 (096) 285 76 67
☞ 18 L 6270m Par 72
5 hole Par 3 course
👤 H
£€ €56
⛳ 15km N of Denia on N332. A7
Junction 61
🏠 Severiano Ballesteros
■ www.olivanovagolf.com

Panorámica (1995)
*Urb Panorámica, 12320 San
Jorge (Castellón)*
☎ (964) 49 30 72
☞ 18 L 6429 m Par 72 SSS 74
👤 U
⛳ A7 Junction 42 towards Vinaroz
🏠 Bernhardt Langer

El Saler (1968)
*Parador Luis Vives, 46012 El
Saler (Valencia)*
☎ (96) 161 11 86

(96) 162 70 16
☞ 18 L 6485 m SSS 75
👤 U
⛳ Oliva, 18km S of Valencia, towards
Cullera
🏠 Javier Arana

Valladolid

Entrepinos (1990)
*Avda del Golf 2, Urb Entrepinos, 47130
Simancas (Valladolid)*
☎ (983) 59 05 11/59 05 61
🖂 (983) 59 07 65
☞ 18 L 5215 m Par 69 SSS 69
👤 U H
£€ €32 (€45)
⛳ 15km SW of Valladolid
🏠 Manuel Piñero

Zaragoza

**Aero Club de
Zaragoza** (1966)
Coso 34, 50004 Zaragoza
☎ (976) 21 43 78
☞ 9 L 5042 m SSS 67
⛳ 12km SW of Zaragoza, by airbase

La Penaza (1973)
Apartado 3039, Zaragoza
☎ (976) 34 28 00/34 22 48
🖂 (976) 34 28 00
☞ 18 L 6122 m SSS 72
👤 H
⛳ 15km SW of Zaragoza on Madrid
road, nr airbase
🏠 FW Hawtree

Sweden

East Central

Ängsö (1979)
Bjönövägen 2, 721 30 Västerås
☎ (0171) 441012
🖂 (0171) 441049
☞ 18 hole course Par 72 SR 130
👤 H
£€ 220kr (300kr)
⛳ 15km E of Västerås
🏠 Åke Hultström

Arboga
PO Box 263, 732 25 Arboga
☎ (0589) 70100
☞ 18 L 5890 m Par 72
👤 U

£€ 180kr (240kr)
⛳ 5km S of Arboga
🏠 Sune Linde

Ärila (1951)
Nicolai, 611 92 Nyköping
☎ (0155) 216617
🖂 (0155) 267657
☞ 18 L 5826 m Par 72
👤 H
£€ 200kr (270kr)
⛳ 5km SE of Nyköping
🏠 Sköld/Linde

Askersund (1980)
Box 3002, 696 03 Ammeberg
☎ (0583) 34943
🖂 (0583) 34945
☞ 18 L 5835 m CR 71.2 SR 133
👤 H
£€ 220kr (280kr)
⛳ 10km SE of Askersund towards
Ammeberg. 1km on road to Kärra
🏠 Ronald Fream
■ www.golf.se/askersundsgk

Burvik
Burvik, 740 12 Knutby
☎ (0174) 43060
🖂 (0174) 43062
☞ 18 L 5785 m SSS 72
👤 U
£€ On application
⛳ 45km E of Uppsala. 70km N of
Stockholm
🏠 Bengt Lorichs

Edenhof (1991)
740 22 Bälinge
☎ (018) 334185
🖂 (018) 334186
☞ 18 L 5898 m SSS 72
👤 H
£€ 180kr (240kr)
⛳ 17km NW of Uppsala
🏠 Sune Linde

Enköping (1970)
Box 2006, 745 02 Enköping
☎ (0171) 20830
🖂 (0171) 20823
☞ 18 L 5660 m Par 71
👤 H
£€ 220kr (300kr)
⛳ 1km E of Enköping, off E18
■ www.enkopinggolf.se

Eskilstuna (1951)
Strängnäsvägen, 633 49 Eskilstuna
☎ (016) 142629
🖂 (016) 148729
☞ 18 L 5610 m SSS 70
👤 H
£€ 160kr (200kr)
⛳ 2km E of Eskilstuna. 20km E of
Örebro
🏠 Douglas Brasier

Fagersta   (1970)
Box 2051, 737 02 Fagersta
☎ **(0223) 54060**
🖳 (0223) 54000
🏳 18 L 5775 m Par 71
U
££ 140kr (180kr)
⛳ 7km W of Fagersta (Route 65).
70km N of Västerås

Frösåker   (1989)
Frösåker Gård, Box 17015, 720 17 Västerås
☎ **(021) 25401**
🖳 (021) 25485
🏳 18 L 5820 m Par 72
U H
££ 200kr (250kr)
⛳ 15km SE of Västerås
🏠 Sune Linde

Fullerö   (1988)
Jotsberga, 725 91 Västerås
☎ **(021) 50132**
🖳 (021) 50431
🏳 18 L 5633 m SSS 71
H
££ 200kr (280kr)
⛳ 6km SW of Västerås
🏠 Hultström/Sjöberg
🖥 www.golf.se/fullerogk

Gripsholm   (1991)
Box 133, 647 32 Mariefred
☎ **(0159) 350050**
🖳 (0159) 350059
🏳 18 L 6203 m Par 73 SR 128
H
££ 300kr (400kr)
⛳ Mariefred, 70km SW of Stockholm
🏠 Bengt Lorichs
🖥 www.golf.se/gripsholmsgk

Grönlund   (1989)
PO Box 38, 740 10 Almunge
☎ **(0174) 20670**
🖳 (0174) 20455
🏳 18 L 5865 m SSS 71
H
££ 200kr (260kr)
⛳ 20km E of Uppsala. 25km NE of Arlanda Airport
🏠 Åke Persson

Gustavsvik
Box 22033, 702 02 Örebro
☎ **(019) 244486**
🖳 (019) 246490
🏳 18 holes SSS 72
H
££ 200kr
⛳ 1km S of Örebro
🏠 Turner/Wirhed

Katrineholm   (1959)
Jättorp, 641 93 Katrineholm
☎ **(0150) 39270**
🖳 (0150) 39011
🏳 18 L 5850 m SSS 72
9 L 2850 m

U
££ 250kr (300kr)
⛳ 7km E of Katrineholm
🏠 Skjöld/Lorichs

Köping   (1963)
Box 278, 731 26 Köping
☎ **(0221) 81090**
🖳 (0221) 81277
🏳 18 L 5636 m Par 71
U
££ 200kr (250kr)
⛳ 3km N of Köping (E18)
🏠 Brasier/Sederholm

Kumla   (1987)
Box 46, 692 21 Kumla
☎ **(019) 577370**
🖳 (019) 577373
🏳 18 L 5845 m SSS 72
U
££ 200kr
⛳ 8km E of Kumla. 20km SE of Örebro
🏠 Jan Sederholm

Linde   (1984)
Dalkarlshyttan, 711 31 Lindesberg
☎ **(0581) 13960**
🖳 (0581) 12936
🏳 18 L 5539 m Par 71
H
££ 180kr (180kr)
⛳ 42km N of Örebro on R60. Lindesberg 2km
🏠 Jan Sederholm

Mosjö   (1989)
Mosjö Gård, 705 94 Örebrö
☎ **(019) 225780**
🖳 (019) 225045
🏳 18 L 6160 m Par 72
WD–U WE–H
££ 200kr (200kr)
⛳ 10km S of Örebrö
🏠 Åke Persson

Nora   (1988)
Box 108, 713 23 Nora
☎ **(0587) 311660**
🖳 (0587) 15050
🏳 18 L 5865 m Par 72
U
££ 200kr (240kr)
⛳ 33km N of Örebro
🏠 Jeremy Turner

Örebro   (1939)
Lanna, 719 93 Vintrosa
☎ **(019) 291065**
🖳 (019) 291055
🏳 18 L 5870 m Par 71
H–max 36
££ 260kr (320kr)
⛳ 18km W of Örebro on Route E18
🏠 Sköld/Sundblom/Berglund
🖥 www.golf.se/golfklubbar/orebrogk

Roslagen
Box 110, 761 22 Norrtälje
☎ **(0176) 237194**
🖳 (0176) 237103
🏳 18 L 5614 m SSS 72
9 L 2888 m SSS 36
H
££ 18 holes:250kr (300kr) 9 holes:150kr
⛳ 7km N of Norrtälje
🏠 TG Oxenstierna

Sala   (1970)
Norby Fallet 100, 733 92 Sala
☎ **(0224) 53077/53055/53064**
🖳 (0224) 53143
🏳 27 L 5895 m SSS 72
U
££ 220kr (270kr)
⛳ 8km E of Sala towards Uppsala, Route 67/72
🏠 Tedrup/Linde/Turner

Sigtunabygden   (1961)
Box 89, 193 22 Sigtuna
☎ **(08) 592 54012**
🖳 (08) 592 54167
🏳 18 L 5710 m SSS 72
H
££ 280kr (360kr)
⛳ Sigtuna, 50km N of Stockholm
🏠 Nils Sköld

Skepptuna
Skepptuna, 195 93 Märsta
☎ **(08) 512 93069**
🖳 (08) 512 93163
🏳 18 L 5745 m CR 71.4 SR 131
U H
££ 250kr (340kr)
⛳ 50km N of Stockholm, via Route 273
🏠 Jan Sederholm
🖥 www.skepptunagk.nu

Södertälje   (1952)
Box 9074, 151 09 Södertälje
☎ **(08) 550 91995**
🖳 (08) 550 62549
🏳 18 L 5875 m SSS 72
H WE–NA before 1pm
££ 300kr (350kr)
⛳ 4km W of Södertälje
🏠 Nils Sköld

Strängnäs   (1968)
Kilenlundavägen, 645 91 Strängnäs
☎ **(0152) 14731**
🖳 (0152) 14716
🏳 18 L 5625 m SSS 72
H
££ 240kr (300kr)
⛳ 3km S of Strängnäs
🏠 Anders Amilon

Torshälla   (1960)
Box 128, 64422 Torshälla
☎ **(016) 358722**
🖳 (016) 357491

☞ 18 L 5934 m Par 72
Ⓜ H
££ 200kr (250kr)
⌘ 5km N of Eskilstuna
⌂ Brasier/Linde

Tortuna
Nicktuna, Tortuna, 725 96 Västerås
☎ (021) 65300
⌨ (021) 65302
☞ 18 L 5750 m SSS 72
Ⓜ U
££ 150kr (180kr)
⌘ 10km N of Västerås
⌂ Husell/Hultström

Trosa (1972)
Box 80, 619 22 Trosa
☎ (0156) 22458
⌨ (0156) 22454
☞ 18 L 5727 m Par 72
Ⓜ H
££ 200kr
⌘ 5km W of Trosa, towards Uttervik
⌂ P Chamberlain

Upsala (1937)
Håmö Gård, Läby, 755 92 Uppsala
☎ (018) 460120
⌨ (018) 461205
☞ 18 L 5818 m SSS 72
  9 L 2674 m SSS 70
Ⓜ H
££ 300kr (350kr)
⌘ 10km W of Uppsala
⌂ Greger Paulsson

Vassunda (1989)
Smedby Gård, 741 91 Knivsta
☎ (018) 381230/381235
⌨ (018) 381416
☞ 18 L 6141 m Par 72
Ⓜ H
££ 240kr (340kr)
⌘ 45km N of Stockholm
⌂ Sune Linde

Västerås (1931)
Bjärby, 724 81 Västerås
☎ (021) 357543
⌨ (021) 357573
☞ 18 L 5250 m SSS 69
Ⓜ U
££ 200kr (250kr)
⌘ 2km N of Västerås
⌂ Nils Sköld

Far North

Boden (1946)
Tallkronsvägen 2, 961 51 Boden
☎ (0921) 72051
⌨ (0921) 72047
☞ 18 L 5495 m SSS 72
Ⓜ H
££ 250kr
⌘ 7km S of Boden
⌂ Björn Eriksson

Funäsdalsfjällen (1972)
Box 66, 840 95 Funäsdalen
☎ (0684) 21100
⌨ (0684) 21142
☞ 18 L 5300 m SSS 72
Ⓜ U
££ 180kr
⌘ Funäsdalen, nr Norwegian border
⌂ Sköld/Linde

Gällivare-Malmberget (1973)
Box 35, 983 21 Malmberget
☎ (0970) 20770
⌨ (0970) 20776
☞ 18 L 5528 m Par 71
Ⓜ H
££ 200kr
⌘ 4km NW of Gällivare, towards Malmberget
⌂ Jan Sederholm
🖳 www.gellivare/forening/golf

Haparanda (1989)
Mattiu 140, 953 35 Haparanda
☎ (0922) 10660
⌨ (0922) 15040
☞ 18 L 6230 m SSS 73
Ⓜ H
££ 160kr
⌘ 125km E of Luleå
⌂ Peter Chamberlain

Härnösand (1957)
Box 52, 871 22 Härnösand
☎ (0611) 67000
⌨ (0611) 66165
☞ 18 L 5819 m SSS 72
Ⓜ H
££ D–200kr (250kr)
⌘ Vägnön, 16km N of Härnösand on E4, towards Hemsö Island
⌂ Sköld/Turner
🖳 www.harnosand.gk.just.nu

Kalix (1990)
Box 32, 952 21 Kalix
☎ (0923) 15945/15935
⌨ (0923) 77735
☞ 18 L 5700m SSS 71
Ⓜ U
££ 160kr
⌘ 80km N of Luleå
⌂ Jan Sederholm

Luleå (1955)
Golfbaneväg 80, 975 96 Luleå
☎ (0920) 256300
⌨ (0920) 256362
☞ 18 L 5675 m Par 72
Ⓜ H
££ 250kr (250kr)
⌘ Rutvik, 12km E of Luleå
⌂ Skjöld/Tideman

Norrmjöle (1992)
905 82 Umeå
☎ (090) 81581
⌨ (090) 81565

☞ 18 L 5619 m Par 72
Ⓜ U
££ 200kr (220kr)
⌘ 19km S of Umeå
⌂ Acke Lundgren

Östersund-Frösö (1947)
Kungsgården 205, 832 96 Frösön
☎ (063) 576030
⌨ (063) 43765
☞ 18 L 6005 m Par 73
  9 hole Par 3 course
Ⓜ H
££ 200kr (220kr)
⌘ Island of Frösön, 8km from Ostersund
⌂ Nils Sköld
🖳 www.ofg.nu

Öviks GC Puttom (1967)
Ovansjö 1970, 891 95 Arnäsvall
☎ (0660) 254001
⌨ (0660) 254040
☞ 18 L 5795 m SSS 72
Ⓜ H
££ 180kr
⌘ 15km N of Örnsköldsvik on E4
⌂ Nils Sköld

Piteå (1960)
Nötöv 119, 941 41 Piteå
☎ (0911) 14990
⌨ (0911) 14960
☞ 18 L 5325 m Par 69
Ⓜ H
££ 160kr
⌘ 2km SE of Piteå
⌂ Jan Sederholm

Skellefteå (1967)
Rönnbäcken, 931 92 Skellefteå
☎ (0910) 779333
⌨ (0910) 779777
☞ 27 L 6135 m SSS 72
  Par 3 course
Ⓜ U H
££ 250kr (300kr)
⌘ Skellefteå 5km
⌂ Sköld/Carlsson/Larsson

Sollefteå (1970)
Box 213, 881 25 Sollefteå
☎ (0620) 21477/12670
⌨ (0620) 21477/12670
☞ 18 L 5770 m SSS 72
Ⓜ H
££ 180kr
⌘ Österforse, 15km SW of Sollefteå (Route 89)
⌂ Nils Sköld

Sundsvall (1952)
Golfvägen 5, 862 00 Kvissleby
☎ (060) 561056
⌨ (060) 561909
☞ 18 L 5885 m SSS 72
Ⓜ WD–H before noon WE–H after 10am
££ 180kr (200r)
⌘ Skottsund, 15km S of Sundsvall

Timrå

Golfbanevägen 2, 860 32 Fagervik
- ☎ **(060) 570153**
- ☐ (060) 578136
- ⋗ 18 L 5715 m Par 72
- ⋈ H
- ££ 180kr (200kr)
- ⚮ 1km S of Sundsvall airport
- ⌂ Sune Linde

Umeå (1954)

Lövön, 913 35 Holmsund
- ☎ **(090) 41071/41066**
- ☐ (090) 149120
- ⋗ 18 L 5751 m SSS 72
  9 L 2688 m SSS 70
- ⋈ U
- ££ 200kr
- ⚮ 16km SE of Umeå
- ⌂ Bo Engdahl

Gothenburg

Albatross (1973)

Lillhagsvägen, 422 50 Hisings-Backa
- ☎ **(031) 551901/550500**
- ☐ (031) 555900
- ⋗ 18 L 6020 m SSS 72
- ££ 220kr (250kr)
- ⚮ 10km N of Gothenburg on Hising Island

Chalmers

PO Box 40, 438 21 Landvetter
- ☎ **(031) 918430**
- ☐ (031) 916338
- ⋗ 18 L 5560 m SSS 71
- ⋈ WD–U H before 4pm –M H after 4pm WE–M H before 2pm –U H after 2pm
- ££ 200kr (200kr)
- ⚮ 20km E of Gothenburg. 2km from Landvetter airport
- ⌂ Gyllenhammar/Henrikson

Delsjö (1962)

Kallebäck, 412 76 Göteborg
- ☎ **(031) 406959**
- ☐ (031) 703 0431
- ⋗ 18 L 5703 m Par 71
- ⋈ H WE–NA before 1pm
- ££ 300kr
- ⚮ 5km E of Gothenburg (Route 40)
- ⌂ Douglas Brasier
- ▪ www.degk.se

Forsgårdens (1982)

Gamla Forsv 1, 434 47 Kungsbacka
- ☎ **(0300) 566350**
- ☐ (0300) 566351
- ⋗ 18 L 6110 m SSS 72
  9 L 2915 m
- ⋈ WD–U WE–NA before 2pm
- ££ 350kr (400kr)
- ⚮ 1km SE of Kungsbacka. 20km S of Gothenburg
- ⌂ Sune Linde
- ▪ www.forsgardensgk.org

Göteborg (1902)

Box 2056, 436 02 Hovås
- ☎ **(031) 282444**
- ☐ (031) 685333
- ⋗ 18 L 5935 yds SSS 70
- ⋈ WD–U H–max 28(M) 32 (L) WE–M before 2pm
- ££ 350kr (400kr)
- ⚮ 11km S of Gothenburg (Route 158)

Gullbringa (1968)

442 95 Kungälv
- ☎ **(0303) 227161**
- ☐ (0303) 227778
- ⋗ 18 L 5775 m Par 70
- ⋈ U
- ££ 220kr
- ⚮ 14km W of Kungälv, towards Marstrand
- ⌂ Douglas Brasier

Kungälv-Kode

Ö Knaverstad 140, 442 97 Kode
- ☎ **(0303) 51300**
- ☐ (0303) 50205
- ⋗ 18 L 5984 m Par 72
- ⋈ U
- ££ 200kr
- ⚮ 30km N of Gothenburg
- ⌂ Lars Andreasson

Kungsbacka (1971)

Hamra Gård 515, 429 44 Särö
- ☎ **(031) 936277**
- ☐ (031) 935085
- ⋗ 18 L 5855 m SSS 72
  9 L 2880 m SSS 36
- ⋈ WD–U WE–NA before 2pm
- ££ 250kr (300kr)
- ⚮ 7km N of Kungsbacka on Route 158
- ⌂ Pennink/Davidsson/Nordström

Lysegården (1966)

Box 532, 442 15 Kungälv
- ☎ **(0303) 223426**
- ☐ (0303) 223075
- ⋗ 18 L 5670 m SSS 71
  9 L 5444 m SSS 70
- ⋈ H
- ££ 200kr
- ⚮ 10km N of Kungälv
- ⌂ Röhss/Engström

Mölndals (1979)

Box 77, 437 21 Lindome
- ☎ **(031) 993030**
- ☐ (031) 994901
- ⋗ 18 L 5625 m SSS 73
- ⋈ H WE–NA before 11am
- ££ 250kr (300kr)
- ⚮ Lindome, 20km S of Gothenburg
- ⌂ Ronald Fream
- ▪ www.molndalsgk.o.se

Öijared (1958)

Pl 1082, 448 92 Floda
- ☎ **(0302) 30604**
- ☐ (0302) 35370

- ⋗ 18 L 5875 m Par 72
  18 L 5655 m Par 71
- ⋈ H WE–NA before 1pm
- ££ 250kr (250kr)
- ⚮ 35km NE of Gothenburg (E20), nr Nääs
- ⌂ Brasier/Amilon
- ▪ www.oijaredgk.o.se

Partille (1986)

Box 234, 433 24 Partille
- ☎ **(031) 987043**
- ☐ (031) 987757
- ⋗ 18 L 5475 m Par 70
- ⋈ WD–H WE–NA before 1pm
- ££ 220kr (220kr)
- ⚮ Öjersjö, 10km E of Gothenburg
- ⌂ Jan Sederholm
- ▪ www.golf.se/partillegk

Sjögärde

430 30 Frillesås
- ☎ **(0340) 657860**
- ☐ (0340) 657861
- ⋗ 18 L 5723 m SSS 72
  6 hole short course
- ⋈ H
- ££ 220kr (250kr)
- ⚮ 20km S of Kungsbacka
- ⌂ Lars Andreasson

Stenungsund (1993)

Lundby Pl 7480, 444 93 Spekeröd
- ☎ **(0303) 778470**
- ☐ (0303) 778350
- ⋗ 18 L 6245 m Par 72
- ⋈ WD–H WE–NA 10–12
- ££ 220kr (250kr)
- ⚮ 40km N of Gothenburg
- ⌂ Peter Nordwall
- ▪ www.golf.se/golfklubbar /stenungsundgk

Stora Lundby (1983)

Valters Väg 2, 443 71 Grabo
- ☎ **(0302) 44200**
- ☐ (0302) 44125
- ⋗ 18 L 6040 m Par 72
  9 hole Par 3 course
- ⋈ H
- ££ 180kr (220kr)
- ⚮ 25km NE of Gothenburg
- ⌂ Frank Pennink
- ▪ www.storalundbygk.o.se

Malmö & South Coast

Abbekas (1989)

Kroppsmarksvagen, 274 56 Abbekas
- ☎ **(0411) 533233**
- ☐ (0411) 533419
- ⋗ 18 L 5817 m Par 72
- ⋈ U H
- ££ 220kr (260kr)
- ⚮ 20km W of Ystad
- ⌂ Tommy Nordström

Barsebäck G&CC (1969)
246 55 Löddeköpinge
- ☎ **(046) 776230**
- ⌨ (046) 772630
- ▷ Old 18 L 5910 m Par 72
  New 18 L 6025 m Par 72
- ⋈ WD–H booking necessary
- ££ D–360kr
- ⊕ 35km N of Malmö
- ⌂ Bruce/Steel

Bokskogen (1963)
Torupsvägen 408-140, 230 40 Bara
- ☎ **(040) 406900**
- ⌨ (040) 406929
- ▷ Old 18 L 6006 m Par 72
  New 18 L 5542 m Par 71
- ⋈ H WE–after 1pm Old course
- ££ 400kr (400kr)
- ⊕ 15km SE of Malmö, off E65
- ⌂ Amilon/Sederholm/Lorichs

Falsterbo (1909)
Fyrvägen, 239 40 Falsterbo
- ☎ **(040) 470078/475078**
- ⌨ (040) 472722
- ▷ 18 L 6577 yds Par 71
- ⋈ H
- ££ D–300–450kr
- ⊕ 30km SW of Malmö
- ⌂ Gunnar Bauer
- ■ www.falsterbogk.com

Flommens (1935)
239 40 Falsterbo
- ☎ **(040) 475016**
- ⌨ (040) 473157
- ▷ 18 L 5735 m SSS 72
- ⋈ U H
- ££ 260–320kr (329kr)
- ⊕ 35km SW of Malmö
- ⌂ Bergendorff/Kristersson
- ■ www.flommensgk.com

Kävlinge (1991)
Box 138, 244 22 Kävlinge
- ☎ **(046) 736270**
- ⌨ (046) 728486
- ▷ 18 L 5800 m SSS 72
- ⋈ H
- ££ 200kr (280kr)
- ⊕ 12km N of Lund
- ⌂ Rolf Collijn

Ljunghusen (1932)
Kinellsvag, Ljunghusen, 236 42 Höllviken
- ☎ **(040) 450384**
- ⌨ (040) 454265
- ▷ 27 holes:
  L 5455-5895 m SSS 70-73
- ⋈ WD–U H WE–M before noon
- ££ 320kr (380kr)
- ⊕ Falsterbo Peninsula. 30km SW of Malmö
- ⌂ Douglas Brasier
- ■ www.ljgk.se

Lunds Akademiska (1936)
Kungsmarken, 225 92 Lund
- ☎ **(046) 99005**
- ⌨ (046) 99146
- ▷ 18 L 5780 m SSS 72
- ⋈ H
- ££ 160kr (200kr)
- ⊕ 5km E of Lund
- ⌂ Boström/Morrison

Malmö
Segesvängen, 212 27 Malmö
- ☎ **(040) 292535/292536**
- ⌨ (040) 292228
- ▷ 18 L 5750 m SSS 71
- ⋈ H
- ££ 280kr
- ⊕ NE of Malmö
- ⌂ Jan Sederholm
- ■ www.malmogolfklubb.com

Örestad (1986)
Golfvägen, Habo Ljung, 234 22 Lomma
- ☎ **(040) 410580**
- ⌨ (040) 416320
- ▷ 18 L 6036 m Par 73
  9 L 2923 m Par 35
  18 hole Par 3 course
- ⋈ H
- ££ 220kr (280kr)
- ⊕ 15km N of Malmö
- ⌂ Åke Persson
- ■ www.orestadsgk.com

Österlen (1945)
Lilla Vik, 272 95 Simrishamn
- ☎ **(0414) 412550**
- ⌨ (0414) 412551
- ▷ 18 L 5835 m CR 69.8
  18 L 5741 m CR 71.3
- ⋈ H
- ££ 300kr
- ⊕ Vik, 8km N of Simrishamn
- ⌂ Tommy Nordström
- ■ www.osterlensgk.com

Romeleåsen (1969)
Kvarnbrodda, 240 14 Veberöd
- ☎ **(046) 82012**
- ⌨ (046) 82113
- ▷ 18 L 5783 m Par 72
- ⋈ H
- ££ 220kr (280kr)
- ⊕ 6km S of Veberöd. 25km E of Malmö
- ⌂ Douglas Brasier
- ■ www.golf.romeleasensgk.com

Söderslätts
Ellaboda Grevier 260, 235 94 Vellinge
- ☎ **(040) 429680**
- ⌨ (040) 429684
- ▷ 18 L 5800 m SSS 72
  9 hole Par 3 course
- ⋈ WD–H WE–M H before noon
- ££ 250kr
- ⊕ 15km SE of Malmö
- ⌂ Sune Linde

Tegelberga (1988)
Alstad Pl 140, 231 96 Trelleborg
- ☎ **(040) 485690**
- ⌨ (040) 485691
- ▷ 27 L 6011 m CR 73.5
- ⋈ U H
- ££ 250kr (300kr)
- ⊕ 11km N of Trelleborg. 25km E of Malmö
- ⌂ Peter Chamberlain
- ■ www.golf.se/tegelbergagk

Tomelilla
Ullstorp, 273 94 Tomelilla
- ☎ **(0417) 13420**
- ⌨ (0417) 13657
- ▷ 18 L 6455 m Par 73 SSS 75
- ⋈ H
- ££ 240kr (240kr)
- ⊕ 15km N of Ystad. 60km E of Malmö
- ⌂ Tommy Nordström
- ■ www.tomelillagolfklubb.com

Trelleborg (1963)
Maglarp, Pl 431, 231 93 Trelleborg
- ☎ **(0410) 330460**
- ⌨ (0410) 330281
- ▷ 18 L 5278 m Par 70
- ⋈ U H
- ££ 200kr
- ⊕ 5km W of Trelleborg
- ⌂ Brasier/Chamberlain
- ■ www.trelleborgsgk.com

Vellinge (1991)
Toftadals Gård, 235 41 Vellinge
- ☎ **(040) 443255**
- ⌨ (040) 443179
- ▷ 18 L 5766 m SSS 72
  6 hole short course
- ⋈ WD–U WE–U H
- ££ 200kr (250kr)
- ⊕ 10km SE of Malmö
- ⌂ Tommy Nordström

Ystad (1930)
Längrevsvägen, 270 22 Köpingebro
- ☎ **(0411) 550350**
- ⌨ (0411) 550392
- ▷ 18 L 5800 m Par 72
- ⋈ U
- ££ 200–250kr
- ⊕ 7km E of Ystad, towards Simrishamn
- ⌂ Thure Bruce

North

Alvkarleby
Västanåvägen 5, 814 94 Alvkarleby
- ☎ **(026) 72757**
- ⌨ (026) 82307
- ▷ 18 L 5420 m Par 70
- ⋈ H
- ££ £13 (£19)
- ⊕ 25km from Gävle (Route 76)
- ⌂ Jan Sederholm
- ■ www.golf.alvkarleby.net

Avesta (1963)
Åsbo, 774 61 Avesta
☎ **(0226) 55913/10866/12766**
⌨ (0226) 12578
⏃ 18 L 5560 m SSS 71
👥 H
£€ 220kr (260kr)
🚣 3km NE of Avesta
🏠 Sune Linde
▣ www.golf.se/golfklubbar/avestagk

Bollnäs
Norrfly 4526, 823 91 Kilafors
☎ **(0278) 650540**
⌨ (0278) 651220
⏃ 18 L 5870 m Par 72
👥 H
£€ 180kr (200kr)
🚣 15km S of Bollnäs (Route 83)

Dalsjö (1989)
Dalsjö 3, 781 94 Borlänge
☎ **(0243) 220095**
⌨ (0243) 220140
⏃ 18 L 5715 m Par 72
👥 H
£€ 250kr (290kr)
🚣 5km NE of Borlänge
🏠 Jeremy Turner

Falun-Borlänge (1956)
Storgarden 10, 791 93 Falun
☎ **(023) 31015**
⌨ (023) 31072
⏃ 18 L 6085 m Par 72
👥 U
£€ 220kr (270kr)
🚣 Aspeboda, 8km N of Borlänge
🏠 Nils Sköld

Gävle (1949)
Bönavägen 23, 805 95 Gävle
☎ **(026) 120333/120338**
⌨ (026) 516468
⏃ 18 L 5735 m SSS 73
£€ 200kr (250kr)
🚣 3km N of Gävle

Hagge (1963)
Hagge, 771 90 Ludvika
☎ **(0240) 28087/28513**
⌨ (0240) 28515
⏃ 18 L 5519 m SSS 71
👥 H
£€ D–150kr
🚣 7km S of Ludvika
🏠 Sune Linde

Hofors (1965)
Box 117, 813 22 Hofors
☎ **(0290) 85125**
⌨ (0290) 85101
⏃ 18 L 5400 m Par 70
👥 U
£€ 180kr (200kr)
🚣 5km SE of Hofors
🏠 Sune Linde

Högbo (1962)
Daniel Tilas Väg 4, 811 92 Sandviken
☎ **(026) 215015**
⌨ (026) 215322
⏃ 18 L 5760 m Par 72
9 L 2590 m Par 35
👥 H
£€ 220kr (300kr)
🚣 6km N of Sandviken (Route 272)
🏠 Sköld/Linde

Hudiksvall (1964)
Tjuvskär, 824 01 Hudiksvall
☎ **(0650) 15930**
⌨ (0650) 18630
⏃ 18 L 5665 m SSS 72
👥 U
£€ 160kr
🚣 4km SE of Hudiksvall
🏠 Linde/Sköld

Leksand (1977)
Box 25, 793 21 Leksand
☎ **(0247) 14640**
⌨ (0247) 14157
⏃ 18 L 5263 m Par 70
👥 U
£€ 120kr (180kr)
🚣 2km N of Leksand
🏠 Nils Sköld

Ljusdal (1973)
Box 151, 827 23 Ljusdal
☎ **(0651) 16883**
⌨ (0651) 16883
⏃ 18 L 5920 m Par 72
👥 U
£€ 200kr
🚣 2km E of Ljusdal
🏠 Eriksson/Skjöld

Mora (1980)
Box 264, 792 24 Mora
☎ **(0250) 10182**
⌨ (0250) 10306
⏃ 18 L 5600 m Par 72
£€ 150kr
🚣 1km N of Mora. 40km NW of Rättvik
🏠 Sune Linde

Rättvik (1954)
Box 29, 795 21 Rättvik
☎ **(0248) 51030**
⌨ (0248) 12081
⏃ 18 L 5375 m SSS 70
👥 U
£€ 200–300kr
🚣 2km N of Rättvik

Sälenfjallens (1991)
Box 20, 780 67 Sälen
☎ **(0280) 20670**
⌨ (0280) 20670
⏃ 18 L 5710 m Par 72
👥 U H
£€ 220kr
🚣 230km NW of Borlänge. 400km NW of Stockholm

Sune Linde
▣ www.golf.se/salenfjallensgk

Säter (1984)
Box 89, 783 22 Säter
☎ **(0225) 50030**
⌨ (0225) 51424
⏃ 18 L 5781 m Par 72
👥 U
£€ 160kr
🚣 25km SE of Borlänge. 180km NW of Stockholm
🏠 Sune Linde

Snöå (1990)
Snöå Bruk, 780 51 Dala-Järna
☎ **(0281) 24072**
⌨ (0281) 24009
⏃ 18 L 5738 m SSS 73
👥 H
£€ 200kr
🚣 80km W of Borlänge, nr Dala-Järna (Route 71)
🏠 Åke Persson
▣ www.snoabruk.se/snoagk

Söderhamn (1961)
Box 117, 826 23 Söderhamn
☎ **(0270) 281300**
⌨ (0270) 281003
⏃ 18 L 5940 m Par 72
👥 H
£€ 200–220kr
🚣 8km N of Söderhamn
🏠 Nils Sköld
▣ www.soderhamnsgk.com

Sollerö (1991)
Levsnäs, 79290 Sollerön
☎ **(0250) 22236**
⌨ (0250) 22854
⏃ 18 L 7226 yds Par 72
👥 H
£€ 160kr
🚣 14km from Mora on Island of Sollerön in Siljan
🏠 JR Turner

Skane & South

Allerum (1992)
Pl 7592, 260 35 Ödåkra
☎ **(042) 93051**
⌨ (042) 93045
⏃ 18 L 6201 m SSS 73
👥 U
£€ 250–300kr
🚣 9km NE of Helsingborg
🏠 Hans Fock
▣ www.golf.se/golfklubbar/allerumgk

Ängelholm (1973)
Box 1117, 262 22 Ängelholm
☎ **(0431) 430260/431460**
⌨ (0431) 431568
⏃ 18 L 5760 m Par 72
👥 H (max 36)
£€ 200–250kr

🖙 10km E of Ängelholm on route 114
🕭 Jan Sederholm
▬ www.golf.se/golfklubbar
/angelholmsgk

Araslöv
Starvägen 1, 291 75 Färlöv
☎ **(044) 71600**
📠 (044) 71575
▷ 18 L 5817 m Par 72
👥 H or Green card
££ 160kr (220kr)
🖙 9km NW of Kristianstad (Route 19)
🕭 Sune Linde

Båstad (1929)
Box 1037, 269 21 Båstad
☎ **(0431) 73136**
📠 (0431) 73331
▷ 18 L 5632 m Par 71
18 L 6163 m Par 72
👥 H
££ 400kr
🖙 4km W of Båstad (Route 115)
🕭 Hawtree/Taylor/Nordström

Bedinge (1931)
Golfbanevägen, 231 76 Beddingestrand
☎ **(0410) 25514**
📠 (0410) 25411
▷ 18 L 5444 m Par 70
👥 H
££ 120 (160kr)
🖙 Beddingestrand, 20km E of
Trelleborg
🕭 Åke Persson

Bjäre
Salomonhög 3086, 269 93 Båstad
☎ **(0431) 361053**
📠 (0431) 361764
▷ 18 L 5550 m SSS 71
👥 H
££ 350kr
🖙 2km E of Båstad. 60km N of
Helsingborg
🕭 Svante Dahlgren

Bosjökloster (1974)
243 95 Höör
☎ **(0413) 25858**
📠 (0413) 25895
▷ 18 L 5890 m Par 72
👥 H
££ 180kr (220kr)
🖙 7km S of Höör. 40km NE of
Malmö
🕭 Douglas Brasier

Carlskrona (1949)
PO Almö, 370 24 Nättraby
☎ **(0457) 35123**
📠 (0457) 35090
▷ 18 L 5485 m Par 70
👥 U
££ D–220kr
🖙 18km SW of Karlskrona
🕭 Jan Sederholm
▬ www.carlskronagk.com

Degeberga-Widtsköfle
Box 71, 297 21 Degeberga
☎ **(044) 355035**
📠 (044) 355075
▷ 18 L 6129 m SSS 72
9 hole Par 3 course
👥 U
££ 100–170kr
🖙 20km S of Kristianstad

Eslöv (1966)
Box 150, 241 22 Eslöv
☎ **(0413) 18610**
📠 (0413) 18613
▷ 18 L 5610 m CR 70.7 SR 133
👥 H
££ 240kr (280kr)
🖙 4km S of Eslöv (Route 113)
🕭 Thure Bruce
▬ www.golf.se/golfklubbar/eslovsgk

Hässleholm (1978)
Skyrup, 282 95 Tyringe
☎ **(0451) 53111**
📠 (0451) 53138
▷ 18 L 5830 m SSS 72
👥 U
££ 200kr (240kr)
🖙 15km NW of Hässleholm
🕭 Persson/Bruce/Jensen

Helsingborg (1924)
260 40 Viken
☎ **(042) 236147**
▷ 9 L 4578 m Par 68
👥 U
££ 160kr (180kr)
🖙 15km NW of Helsingborg
🕭 W Hester

Karlshamn (1962)
Box 188, 374 23 Karlshamn
☎ **(0454) 50085**
📠 (0454) 50160
▷ 18 L 5861 m SSS 72
18 holes SSS 72
👥 H
££ 280kr
🖙 Morrum, 10 km W of Karlshamn
🕭 Brasier/Victorsson/Sederholm

Kristianstad (1924)
Box 41, 296 21 Åhus
☎ **(044) 247656**
📠 (044) 247635
▷ 18 L 5810 m SSS 72
9 L 2945 m SSS 36
👥 H
££ D–240kr (D–280kr)
🖙 18km SE of Kristianstad. Airport
20km
🕭 Brasier/Nordström

Landskrona (1960)
Erikstorp, 261 61 Landskrona
☎ **(0418) 446260**
📠 (0418) 446262
▷ Old 18 L 5700 m SSS 71
New 18 L 4300 m SSS 67

U
££ 240kr (280kr)
🖙 4km N of Landskrona, towards
Borstahusen

Mölle (1943)
260 42 Mölle
☎ **(042) 347520**
📠 (042) 347523
▷ 18 L 5292 m Par 70
👥 H–max 36
££ 320kr
🖙 Mölle, 35km NW of Helsingborg
🕭 Thure Bruce
▬ www.mollegk.m.se

Örkelljunga
Rya 472, 286 91 Örkelljunga
☎ **(0435) 53690/53640**
📠 (0435) 53670
▷ 18 L 5700 m SSS 72
👥 H
££ 200kr (240kr)
🖙 8km S of Örkelljunga. 40km NE of
Helsingborg (E4)
🕭 Hans Fock

Östra Göinge (1981)
Box 114, 289 21 Knislinge
☎ **(044) 60060**
📠 (044) 69060
▷ 18 L 5898 m Par 72
👥 H
££ 180kr (240kr)
🖙 20km N of Kristianstad
🕭 T Nordström
▬ www.golf.se/ostragoingegk

Perstorp (1964)
PO Box 87, 284 22 Perstorp
☎ **(0435) 35411**
📠 (0435) 35959
▷ 18 L 5675 m Par 71
6 hole short course
👥 H
££ 150kr (200kr)
🖙 1km S of Perstorp. 45km E of
Helsingborg
🕭 Amilon/Bruce/Persson

Ronneby (1963)
Box 26, 372 21 Ronneby
☎ **(0457) 10315**
📠 (0457) 10412
▷ 18 L 5323 m Par 72
👥 U
££ 250kr
🖙 3km S of Ronneby
▬ www.golf.se/ronnebygk

Rya (1934)
PL 5500, 255 92 Helsingborg
☎ **(042) 220182**
📠 (042) 220394
▷ 18 L 5599 m Par 72
👥 H
££ 260kr
🖙 10km S of Helsingborg
🕭 Petterson/Sundblom

St Arild (1987)
Golfvagen 48, 260 41 Nyhamnsläge
- ☎ **(042) 346860**
- 🖳 (042) 346042
- ╟ 18 L 5805 m Par 72
- ⋒ H
- ££ 260kr (260kr)
- ⤶ 50km N of Helsingborg
- ⌂ Jan Sederholm
- ▪ www.starild.se

Skepparslov (1984)
Udarpssäteri, 291 92 Kristianstad
- ☎ **(044) 229508**
- 🖳 (044) 229503
- ╟ 18 L 5996 m SSS 73
- ⋒ U
- ££ 180kr (250kr)
- ⤶ 7km W of Kristianstad
- ⌂ Rolf Collijn
- ▪ www.golf.se/golfklubbar
  /skepparslovsgk

Söderåsen (1966)
Box 41, 260 50 Billesholm
- ☎ **(042) 73337**
- 🖳 (042) 73963
- ╟ 18 L 5657 m Par 71
- ⋒ U
- ££ 300kr (330kr)
- ⤶ 20km E of Helsingborg
- ⌂ Thure Bruce
- ▪ www.golf.se/golfklubbar
  /soderasensgk

Sölvesborg
Box 63, 294 22 Sölvesborg
- ☎ **(0456) 70650**
- 🖳 (0456) 70650
- ╟ 18 L 5900 m Par 72
- ⋒ U
- ££ 240kr
- ⤶ 30km E of Kristianstad
- ⌂ Sune Linde

Svalöv (1989)
Månstorp Pl 1365, 268 90 Svalöv
- ☎ **(0418) 662462**
- 🖳 (0418) 663284
- ╟ 18 L 5874 m SSS 73
- ⋒ U
- ££ 230kr (280kr)
- ⤶ 20km E of Landskrona
- ⌂ Tommy Nordström
- ▪ www.golf.se/golfklubbar/svalovsgk

Torekov (1924)
Råledsu 31, 260 93 Torekov
- ☎ **(0431) 449841**
- 🖳 (0431) 364916
- ╟ 18 L 5701 m Par 72
- ⋒ Jun–Aug–H WE–M before noon
- ££ 220–280kr
- ⤶ 3km N of Torekov
- ⌂ Nils Sköld

Trummenas
373 02 Ramdala
- ☎ **(0455) 60505**

- 🖳 (0455) 60571
- ╟ 18 L 5600 m Par 72
  9 hole course
- ⋒ H
- ££ 200kr
- ⤶ 15km SE of Karlskrona, off Route 22
- ⌂ Ingmar Ericsson

Vasatorp (1973)
Box 13035, 250 13 Helsingborg
- ☎ **(042) 235058**
- 🖳 (042) 235135
- ╟ 18 L 5875 m SSS 72
  18 hole course
- ⋒ H–max 36
- ££ 300kr (400kr)
- ⤶ 9km E of Helsingborg
- ⌂ Bruce/Persson

Wittsjö (1962)
Ubbaltsgården, 280 22 Vittsjö
- ☎ **(0451) 22635**
- 🖳 (0451) 22567
- ╟ 18 L 5461 m Par 71
- ⋒ U
- ££ 160kr (200kr)
- ⤶ 2km SE of Vittsjö
- ⌂ Sköld/Amilon

South East

A 6 Golfklubb
Centralvägen, 553 05 Jönköping
- ☎ **(036) 308130**
- 🖳 (036) 308140
- ╟ 27 hole course:
  9 L 3185 m Par 38
  9 L 3115 m Par 37
  9 L 2935 m Par 36
- ⋒ U H
- ££ 250–300kr
- ⤶ 2km SE of Jönköping
- ⌂ Peter Nordwall

Älmhult (1975)
Pl 1215, 343 90 Älmhult
- ☎ **(0476) 14135**
- 🖳 (0476) 16565
- ╟ 18 L 5407 m SSS 71
- ⋒ U H
- ££ D–200kr
- ⤶ 2km E of Älmhult on Route 23
- ⌂ Persson/Söderberg

Åtvidaberg (1954)
Västantorp, 597 41 Åtvidaberg
- ☎ **(0120) 35425**
- 🖳 (0120) 13502
- ╟ 18 L 5565 m Par 71
- ⋒ U
- ££ 250kr (300kr)
- ⤶ 30km SE of Linköping
- ⌂ Brasier/Nordvall

Ekerum
387 92 Borgholm, Öland
- ☎ **(0485) 80000**

- 🖳 (0485) 80010
- ╟ 18 L 6045 m Par 72
  9 L 2875 m Par 36
- ⋒ U H
- ££ 200–370kr
- ⤶ 12km S of Borgholm. 25km N of Öland bridge
- ⌂ Peter Nordwall

Eksjö (1938)
Skedhult, 575 96 Eksjö
- ☎ **(0381) 13525**
- ╟ 18 L 5930 m SSS 72
- ⋒ WD–U WE–H
- ££ 200kr
- ⤶ 6km W of Eksjö on Nässjö road
- ⌂ Anders Amilon

Emmaboda (1976)
Kyrkogatan, 360 60 Vissefjärda
- ☎ **(0471) 20505/20540**
- 🖳 (0471) 20440
- ╟ 18 L 6165 m SSS 72
- ⋒ H
- ££ 200kr
- ⤶ 12km S of Emmaboda. 50km N of Karlskrona
- ▪ www.golf.se/golfklubbar
  /emmabodagk

Finspång (1965)
Viberga Gård, 612 92 Finspång
- ☎ **(0122) 13940**
- 🖳 (0122) 18888
- ╟ 27 L 5800 m SSS 72
- ⋒ U
- ££ 220kr (280kr)
- ⤶ 2km E of Finspång, Route 51. Norrköping 25km.
- ⌂ Sköld/Linde/Chamberlain

Gotska (1986)
Box 1119, 621 22 Visby, Gotland
- ☎ **(0498) 215545**
- 🖳 (0498) 256332
- ╟ 18 L 5202 m Par 69
  9 L 5414 m Par 72
- ⋒ U H
- ££ 18 holes:250kr. 9 holes:120kr
- ⤶ N outskirts of Visby
- ⌂ Jack Wenman

Grönhögen (1996)
PL 1270, 380 65 Öland
- ☎ **(0485) 665995**
- 🖳 (0485) 665999
- ╟ 18 L 5100 m Par 70
- ⋒ H
- ££ 120–180kr (140–280kr)
- ⤶ 45km S of Öland Bridge
- ⌂ Kenneth Nilsson
- ▪ www.gronhogen.se

Gumbalde
Box 35, 620 13 Ståga, Gotland
- ☎ **(0498) 482880**
- 🖳 (0498) 482884
- ╟ 18 L 5600 m SSS 71
- ⋒ U
- ££ 200–240kr

🏌 50km SE of Visby, Gotland island
⌂ Lars Lagergren

Hooks
560 13 Hok
☎ **(0393) 21420**
🖥 (0393) 21379
▷ 18 L 5758 m SSS 72
18 L 5750 m SSS 73
9 hole Par 3 course
👥 H
££ 300kr (350kr)
⛳ Hok, 30km SE of Jönköping, towards Växjö
⌂ Edberg/Bruce/Sederholm
◼ www.hooksgk.com

Isaberg (1968)
Nissafors Bruk, 330 27 Hestra
☎ **(0370) 336330**
🖥 (0370) 336325
▷ East 18 L 5823 m CR 71.8
West 18 L 5568 m CR 70.0
👥 H
££ 250kr (300kr)
⛳ Nissafors, 18km N of Gislaved. 60km S of Jönköping
⌂ Amilon/Bruce/Persson

Jönköping (1936)
Kettilstorp, 556 27 Jönköping
☎ **(036) 76567**
🖥 (036) 76511
▷ 18 L 5313 m Par 70
👥 Phone in advance H–max 30
££ 250kr (300kr)
⛳ Kettilstorp, 3km S of Jönköping
⌂ Frank Dyer
◼ www.golf.se/jonkopingsgk

Kalmar (1947)
Box 278, 391 23 Kalmar
☎ **(0480) 472111**
🖥 (0480) 472314
▷ Blue 18 L 5700 m SSS 72
Red 18 L 5634 m SSS 72
👥 H
££ 300kr (350kr)
⛳ 9km N of Kalmar via E22
⌂ Brasier/Sköld/Linde
◼ www.golf.se/golfklubbar/kalmargk

Lagan (1966)
Box 63, 340 14 Lagan
☎ **(0372) 30450/35460**
🖥 (0372) 35307
▷ 18 L 5539 m SSS 70
9 L 2419 m Par 34
👥 U
££ 160kr
⛳ Lagan, 10km N of Ljungby, on Route E4
⌂ Amilon/Persson/Magnusson

Landeryd (1987)
Bogestad Gård, 585 93 Linköping
☎ **(013) 362200**
🖥 (013) 362208
▷ North 18 L 5675 m SSS 72
South 18 L 5085 m SSS 68
9 hole short course

👥 U
££ 220kr (240kr)
⛳ 7km SE of Linköping
⌂ Nordström/Persson

Lidhems (1988)
360 14 Väckelsång
☎ **(0470) 33660**
🖥 (0470) 33761
▷ 18 L 5755 m Par 72
👥 H
££ 200kr
⛳ 30km S of Växjo (Road 30)
⌂ Ingmar Eriksson
◼ www.golf.se/lidhemsgk

Linköping (1945)
Box 15054, 580 15 Linköping
☎ **(013) 120646**
🖥 (013) 140769
▷ 18 L 5659 m SSS 71
👥 H
££ 250kr (300kr)
⛳ 3km SW of Linköping
⌂ Sundblom/Brasier

Mjölby (1986)
Blixberg, Miskarp, 595 92 Mjölby
☎ **(0142) 12570**
🖥 (0142) 16553
▷ 18 L 5485 m SSS 71
👥 H
££ 230kr (260kr)
⛳ 35km WSW of Linköping (E4)
⌂ Åke Persson
◼ www.mjolbygk.com

Motala (1956)
PO Box 264, 591 23 Motala
☎ **(0141) 50840**
🖥 (0141) 208990
▷ 18 L 5905 m Par 72
👥 U
££ 220kr (260kr)
⛳ 3km S of Motala via Route 50 or 32
⌂ Sköld/Sederholm

Nässjö (1988)
Box 5, 571 21 Nässjö
☎ **(0380) 10022**
🖥 (0380) 12082
▷ 18 L 5783 m Par 72
👥 U H
££ 170kr
⛳ 40km E of Jönköping
⌂ Bjorn Magnusson

Norrköping (1928)
Borg, 605 97 Norrköping
☎ **(011) 335235/183654**
🖥 (011) 335014
▷ 18 L 5860 m SSS 73
👥 U H
££ 250kr (300kr)
⛳ Klinga, 9km S of Norrköping on E4
⌂ Nils Sköld

Oskarshamn (1972)
Box 148, 572 23 Oskarshamn
☎ **(0491) 94033**
🖥 (0491) 94038
▷ 18 L 5545 m SSS 71
👥 H
££ 220kr (250kr)
⛳ 10km SW of Oskarshamn, nr Forshult
⌂ Nils Sköld

Skinnarebo
Skinnarebo, 555 93 Jönköping
☎ **(036) 69075**
🖥 (036) 362975
▷ 18 L 5686 m SSS 71
9 hole Par 3 course
👥 H
££ 180kr
⛳ 14km SW of Jönköping
⌂ Björn Magnusson

Söderköping (1983)
Hylinge, 605 96 Norrköping
☎ **(011) 70579**
▷ 18 L 5730 m SSS 72
👥 U
££ 180kr
⛳ Västra Husby, 9km W of Söderköping
⌂ Ronald Fream

Tobo (1971)
Fredensborg 133, 598 91 Vimmerby
☎ **(0492) 30346**
🖥 (0492) 30871
▷ 18 L 5720 m Par 72
👥 U
££ 200kr (240kr)
⛳ 10km S of Vimmerby, nr Storebro. 60km SW of Västervik
⌂ Brasier/Jensen
◼ www.tbgk.h.se

Tranås (1952)
Box 430, 573 25 Tranås
☎ **(0140) 311661**
🖥 (0140) 16161
▷ 18 L 5830 m SSS 72
👥 U
££ 240kr (280kr)
⛳ 2km N of Tranås

Vadstena (1957)
Hagalund, Box 122, 592 33 Vadstena
☎ **(0143) 12440**
🖥 (0143) 12709
▷ 18 L 5486 m Par 71
👥 U
££ 220kr (300kr)
⛳ 3km S of Vadstena, towards Vaderstad

Värnamo (1962)
Box 146, 331 21 Värnamo
☎ **(0370) 23123**
🖥 (0370) 23216
▷ 18 L 6253 m SSS 72
👥 U

£€ 200kr
⛳ 8km E of Värnamo on Route 127
🏠 Nils Sköld

Västervik (1959)

Box 62, Ekhagen, 593 22 Västervik
☎ (0490) 32420
📠 (0490) 32421
📝 18 L 5760 m Par 72
👥 U
£€ 200kr (250kr)
⛳ 1km E of Västervik
🏠 Sune linde

Växjö (1959)

Box 227, 351 05 Växjö
☎ (0470) 21515
📠 (0470) 21557
📝 18 L 5860 m Par 71
👥 H
£€ 250kr
⛳ 5km NW of Växjö
🏠 Douglas Brasier
💻 www.vaxjogk.com

Vetlanda (1983)

Box 249, 574 23 Vetlanda
☎ (0383) 18310
📠 (0383) 19278
📝 18 L 5552 m SSS 71
👥 U
£€ 160kr
⛳ Östanå, 3km W of Vetlanda. 80km
SE of Jönköping
🏠 Jan Sederholm

Visby

Kronholmen Västergarn, 620 20
Klintehamn, Gotland
☎ (0498) 245058
📠 (0498) 245240
📝 18 L 5765 m Par 72
9 hole course
👥 Jun–Aug–H
£€ 300kr
⛳ Kronholmen, 25km S of Visby,
Gotland island
🏠 Nordwall/Sköld
💻 www.golf.se/visbygk

Vreta Kloster

Box 144, 590 70 Ljungsbro
☎ (013) 169700
📠 (013) 169707
📝 18 L 5666 m Par 72
👥 H
£€ 160kr (200kr)
⛳ 15km N of Linköping
🏠 Sune Linde

South West

Alingsås (1985)

Hjälmared 4050, 441 95 Alingsås
☎ (0322) 52421
📝 18 L 5600 m SSS 72
👥 U
£€ 180kr (200kr)
⛳ 5km SE of Alingsås towards Borås

Bäckavattnet (1977)

Marbäck, 305 94 Halmstad
☎ (035) 44270
📠 (035) 44275
📝 18 L 5740 m Par 71
👥 H
£€ 220kr (280kr)
⛳ 13km E of Halmstad (RD25)
💻 www.backavattnetsgk.com

Billingen (1949)

St Kulhult, 540 17 Lerdala
☎ (0511) 80291
📠 (0511) 80244
📝 18 L 5470 m Par 71
👥 H
£€ 180kr
⛳ 20km NW of Skövde
🏠 Douglas Brasier

Borås (1933)

Östra Vik, Kråkered, 504 95 Borås
☎ (033) 250250
📠 (033) 250176
📝 North 18 L 6005 m Par 72
South 18 L 5085 m Par 69
👥 H–booking necessary
£€ 200kr (200kr)
⛳ 6km S of Borås, on Route 41
towards Varberg
🏠 Brasier/Persson

Ekarnas (1970)

Balders Väg 12, 467 31 Grästorp
☎ (0514) 12061
📠 (0514) 12062
📝 18 L 5501 m SSS 71
👥 H
£€ 200kr (220kr)
⛳ 25km E of Trollhätten. Lidköping
35km
🏠 Jan Andersson

Falkenberg (1949)

Golfvägen, 311 72 Falkenberg
☎ (0346) 50287
📠 (0346) 50997
📝 27 L 5575-5680 m SSS 72
👥 H
£€ 250–280kr
⛳ 5km S of Falkenberg

Falköping (1965)

Box 99, 521 02 Falköping
☎ (0515) 31270
📠 (0515) 31389
📝 18 L 5835 m Par 72
👥 H
£€ 220kr
⛳ 7km E of Falköping on Route 46
towards Skovde
🏠 Nils Sköld

Halmstad (1930)

302 73 Halmstad
☎ (035) 176800/176801
📠 (035) 176820
📝 18 L 5955 m CR 72.4
18 L 5542 m CR 69.9

👥 H WE–M before 1pm
£€ 480kr
⛳ Tylosand, 9km W of Halmstad
🏠 Sundblom/Sköld/Pennink

Haverdals (1988)

Slingervägen 35, 31042 Haverdal
☎ (035) 59530
📠 (035) 53890
📝 18 L 5840 m Par 72
👥 H
£€ 220kr
⛳ 11km NW of Halmstad
🏠 Anders Amilon

Hökensås (1962)

PO Box 116, 544 22 Hjo
☎ (0503) 16059
📠 (0503) 16156
📝 18 L 5540 m Par 72
9 hole course
👥 U
£€ 200kr (200kr)
⛳ 8km S of Hjo on Route 195
🏠 Sune Linde

Holms (1990)

Nannarp, 305 92 Halmstad
☎ (035) 38189
📠 (035) 38488
📝 18 L 5782 m Par 72
👥 H–max 36
£€ £24 (£30)
⛳ 15km from Halmstad
🏠 Peter Nordvall
💻 www.holmsgk.com

Hulta (1972)

Box 54, 517 22 Bollebygd
☎ (033) 204340
📠 (033) 204345
📝 18 L 6000 m SSS 72
👥 H
£€ 260kr
⛳ Bollebygd, 35km E of
Gothenburg
🏠 Jan Sederholm

Knistad G&CC

541 92 Skövde
☎ (0500) 463170
📠 (0500) 463075
📝 18 L 5790 m SSS 72
👥 H
£€ 200kr
⛳ 10km NE of Skövde
🏠 Jeremy Turner

Laholm (1964)

Box 101, 312 22 Laholm
☎ (0430) 30601
📠 (0430) 30891
📝 18 L 5430 m SSS 70
👥 U H
£€ 170kr (200kr)
⛳ 5 miles E of Laholm on Route 24
🏠 Jan Sederholm

Lidköping (1967)

Box 2029, 531 02 Lidköping
- ☎ **(0510) 546144**
- ☐ (0510) 546495
- �🏌 18 L 5382 m CR 68.6
- 👤 H
- ££ 180kr
- ⛳ 5km E of Lidköping
- 🏛 Douglas Brasier

Mariestad (1975)

Gummerstadsvägen 45, 542
94 Mariestad
- ☎ **(0501) 47147**
- ☐ (0501) 78117
- �🏌 18 L 5970 m SSS 73
- 👤 H
- ££ 200kr
- ⛳ 4km W of Mariestad, at Lake
  Vänern
- ◼ www.golf.se/mariestadsgk

Marks (1962)

Brättingstorpsvägen 28, 511 58 Kinna
- ☎ **(0320) 14220**
- ☐ (0320) 12516
- �🏌 18 L 5530 m Par 70
- 👤 H
- ££ 160kr (200kr)
- ⛳ Kinna, 30km S of Borås
- 🏛 Sköld/Sederholm

Onsjö (1974)

Box 6331 A, 462 42 Vänersborg
- ☎ **(0521) 68870**
- ☐ (0521) 17106
- �🏌 18 L 5730 m SSS 72
- 👤 U
- ££ 220kr (270kr)
- ⛳ 3km S of Vänersborg. 80km N of
  Gothenburg
- 🏛 Sköld/Linde
- ◼ www.golf.se/golfklubbar/onsjogk

Ringenäs (1987)

Strandlida, 305 91 Halmstad
- ☎ **(035) 161590**
- ☐ (035) 161599
- �🏌 27 L 5395-5615 m Par 71-72
- 👤 H
- ££ 200–320kr (320kr)
- ⛳ 10km NW of Halmstad
- 🏛 Sune Linde
- ◼ www.ringenasgolfbana.com

Skogaby (1988)

312 93 Laholm
- ☎ **(0430) 60190**
- ☐ (0430) 60225
- �🏌 18 L 5555 m Par 71
- 👤 U H
- ££ 140kr (180kr)
- ⛳ 10km E of Laholm. 30km SE of
  Halmstad
- 🏛 J Rosengren

Sotenas Golfklubb (1988)

Pl Onna, 450 46 Hunnebostrand
- ☎ **(0523) 52302**

- ☐ (0523) 52390
- �🏌 18 L 5695 m CR 71.1 SR 123
- 👤 H–max 33
- ££ 250kr (300kr)
- ⛳ 100km N of Gothenburg via E6
- 🏛 Jan Sederholm
- ◼ www.sotenasgolf.com

Töreboda (1965)

Box 18, 545 21 Töreboda
- ☎ **(0506) 12305**
- ☐ (0506) 12305
- �🏌 18 L 5355 m SSS 70
- 👤 U
- ££ 200kr
- ⛳ 7km E of Töreboda

Trollhättan (1963)

Stora Ekeskogen, 466 91 Sollebrunn
- ☎ **(0520) 441000**
- ☐ (0520) 441049
- �🏌 18 L 6200 m SSS 73
- 👤 U
- ££ 200kr
- ⛳ Koberg, 20km SE of Trollhättan
- 🏛 Nils Sköld

Ulricehamn (1947)

523 33 Ulricehamn
- ☎ **(0321) 10021**
- ☐ (0321) 16004
- �🏌 18 L 5509 m Par 71
- 👤 WD–H
- ££ 160kr (200kr)
- ⛳ Lassalyckan, 2km E of Ulricehamn

Vara-Bjertorp

Bjertorp, 535 91 Kvänum
- ☎ **(0512) 20261**
- ☐ (0512) 20261
- �🏌 18 L 6005 m Par 72
- 👤 H
- ££ 150kr (220kr)
- ⛳ 10km N of Vara. 110km NE of
  Gothenburg (E20)
- 🏛 Jan Sederholm
- ◼ www.golf.se/golfklubbar
  /varabjertorpgk

Varberg (1950)

430 10 Tvååker
- ☎ **(0340) 43446/37496**
- ☐ (0340) 43447
- �🏌 East 18 L 5440 m Par 71 CR 71
  West 18 L 6435 m Par 72 CR 76
- 👤 H
- ££ 260–320kr
- ⛳ East:15km E of Varberg. West:8km
  S of Varberg, nr E6
- 🏛 Sköld/Nordström
- ◼ www.varbergsgk.com

Vinberg (1992)

Sannagård, 311 95 Falkenberg
- ☎ **(0346) 19020**
- ☐ (0346) 19042
- �🏌 18 L 4050 m Par 65
- 👤 U
- ££ 160kr (180kr)
- ⛳ 5km E of Falkenberg on coast
- 🏛 Nilsson/Haglund

Stockholm

Ågesta (1958)

123 52 Farsta
- ☎ **(08) 447 3330**
- ☐ (08) 447 3337
- �🏌 18 L 5632 m SSS 72
  9 L 3404 m SSS 62
- 👤 WD–U
- ££ 400kr
- ⛳ Farsta, 15km S of Stockholm
- 🏛 Sköld/Sederholm

Botkyrka

Malmbro Gård, 147 91 Grödinge
- ☎ **(08) 530 29650**
- ☐ (08) 530 29409
- �🏌 18 holes Par 73
  9 hole Par 3 course
- 👤 WD–U H WE–H after 1pm
- ££ 250kr (300kr)
- ⛳ 30km S of Stockholm
- ◼ www.golf.se/botkyrkagk

Bro-Bålsta (1978)

Ginnlögs Väg, 197 91 Bro
- ☎ **(08) 582 41310**
- ☐ (08) 582 40006
- �🏌 18 L 6505 m Par 73
  9 L 1715 m Par 31
- 👤 WD–H (max 30) WE–NA
- ££ 350kr (400kr)
- ⛳ 40 km NW of Stockholm
- 🏛 Peter Nordwall

Djursholm (1931)

Hagbardsvägen 1, 182 63 Djursholm
- ☎ **(08) 5449 6451**
- ☐ (08) 5449 6456
- �🏌 18 L 5569 m SSS 71
  9 L 2135 m SSS 34
- 👤 WD–U H before 3pm –M after 3pm
  WE–M before 1pm –U H after 1pm
- ££ 400kr (400kr)
- ⛳ 12km N of Stockholm

Drottningholm (1958)

PO Box 183, 178 93 Drottningholm
- ☎ **(08) 759 0085**
- ☐ (08) 759 0851
- �🏌 18 L 5745 m SSS 71
- 👤 WD–U H before 3pm –M after 3pm
  WE–M before 3pm –U H after 3pm
- ££ 450kr
- ⛳ 16km W of Stockholm
- 🏛 Sundblom/Sköld

Fågelbro G&CC

Fågelbro Säteri, 139 60 Värmdö
- ☎ **(08) 571 41800**
- ☐ (08) 571 40671
- ⁤🏌 18 L 5522 m Par 71
- 👤 WD–H WE–M
- ££ 500kr (600kr)
- ⛳ 35km E of Stockholm
- 🏛 Eriksson/Oredsson

Haninge (1983)

Årsta Slott, 136 91 Haninge
- ☎ **(08) 500 32850**
- ☖ (08) 500 32851
- ⮞ 27 L 5930 m Par 73
- ⚇ WD–U before 1pm –M after 1pm
  WE–M before 1pm –U after 1pm
- ££ 400kr (450kr)
- ⚲ 30km S of Stockholm towards
  Nynäshamn
- ⌂ Jan Sederholm
- ■ www.haningegk.se

Ingarö (1962)

Fogelvik, 134 64 Ingarö
- ☎ **(08) 570 28244**
- ☖ (08) 570 28379
- ⮞ Old 18 L 5024 m SSS 71
  New 18 L 5203 m SSS 70
- ⚇ WD–U H WE–NA before 3pm
- ££ 350kr (400kr)
- ⚲ 30km E of Stockholm via Route
  222
- ⌂ Sköld/Eriksson
- ■ www.igk.se

Kungsängen (1992)

Box 133, 196 21 Kungsängen
- ☎ **(08) 584 50730**
- ☖ (08) 581 71002
- ⮞ Kings 18 L 6100 m Par 71
  Queens 18 L 5300 m Par 69
- ⚇ U H
- ££ Kings–600kr. Queens–400kr
- ⚲ 25km W of Stockholm via E18 to
  Brunna
- ⌂ Anders Forsbrand

Lidingö (1933)

Box 1035, 181 21 Lidingö
- ☎ **(08) 765 7911**
- ☖ (08) 765 5479
- ⮞ 18 L 5647 m SSS 72
- ⚇ WD–U H before 3pm –NA after
  3pm Sat–NA Sun–NA before 1pm
- ££ 400kr
- ⚲ 6km NE of Stockholm
- ⌂ MacDonald/Sundblom

Lindö (1978)

186 92 Vallentuna
- ☎ **(08) 511 72260**
- ☖ (08) 511 74122
- ⮞ 18 L 2850 m Par 71
- ⚇ U
- ££ 300kr (400kr)
- ⚲ Vallentuna, 20 km N of Stockholm
- ⌂ Åke Persson

Lindo Park

Lindö Park, 186 92 Vallentuna
- ☎ **(08) 511 70055 (Bookings)**
- ☖ (08) 511 70613
- ⮞ 18 L 5800 m SSS 72
  18 L 5795 m SSS 72
- ⚇ U H–book day before play
- ££ 300kr (400kr)
- ⚲ 30km N of Stockholm
- ⌂ Persson/Bruce/Eriksson
- ■ www.lindopark.se

Nya Johannesberg G&CC (1990)

762 95 Rimbo
- ☎ **(08) 514 50000**
- ☖ (08) 512 92390
- ⮞ 18 L 6328 m SSS 74
  9 hole course
- ⚇ H
- ££ 230kr (300kr)
- ⚲ 55km N of Stockholm
- ⌂ Donald Steel
- ■ www.golf.se/golfklubbar
  /johannesberggcc

Nynäshamn (1977)

Korunda 40, 148 91 Ösmo
- ☎ **(08) 524 30590/524 30599**
- ☖ (08) 524 30598
- ⮞ 27 L 5690 m SSS 72
- ⚇ H–phone first
- ££ 320kr (370kr)
- ⚲ Ösmo, 40km S of Stockholm
- ⌂ Sune Linde
- ■ www.nynashamnsgk.a.se

Österakers

Hagby 1, 184 92 Akersberga
- ☎ **(08) 540 85165**
- ☖ (08) 540 66832
- ⮞ 18 L 5792 m Par 72
  18 L 5780 m Par 72
- ⚇ H WE–NA after 2 pm
- ££ 320–380kr (380–450kr)
- ⚲ 30km NE of Stockholm
- ⌂ Sederholm/Tumba

Österhaninge (1992)

Husby, 136 91 Haninge
- ☎ **(08) 500 32077**
- ☖ (08) 500 32293
- ⮞ 18 L 5600 m Par 70
- ⚇ H
- ££ 240kr (300kr)
- ⚲ 35km S of Stockholm
- ⌂ Bengt Lorichs

Saltsjöbaden (1929)

Box 51, 133 21 Saltsjöbaden
- ☎ **(08) 717 0125**
- ☖ (08) 5561 6739
- ⮞ 18 L 5436 m SSS 71
  9 L 3756 m SSS 64
- ⚇ WD–U WE–M H before 2pm
- ££ 18 holes: D–420kr. 9 holes: 240kr
- ⚲ 15km E of Stockholm city, via
  Route 228

Sollentuna (1967)

Skillingegården, 192 77 Sollentuna
- ☎ **(08) 594 70995**
- ☖ (08) 594 70999
- ⮞ 18 L 5895 m SSS 72
- ⚇ WD–H before 3pm WE–H after
  3pm
- ££ 350kr
- ⚲ 19km N of Stockholm. 1km W of
  E4 (Rotebro)
- ⌂ Nils Sköld

Stockholm (1904)

Kevingestrand 20, 182 57 Danderyd
- ☎ **(08) 544 90710**
- ☖ (08) 544 90712
- ⮞ 18 L 5180 m SSS 69
- ⚇ WD–M after 3pm WE–M before
  3pm
- ££ 340kr (420kr)
- ⚲ 7km NE of Stockholm via Route
  E18

Täby (1968)

Skålhamra Gård, 187 70 Täby
- ☎ **(08) 510 23261**
- ☖ (08) 510 23441
- ⮞ 18 L 5776 m SSS 73
- ⚇ WD–H
- ££ 350–450kr
- ⚲ 15km N of Stockholm
- ⌂ Nils Sköld

Troxhammar

179 75 Skå
- ☎ **(08) 564 20610**
- ☖ (08) 560 24870
- ⮞ 27 holes Par 72
- ⚇ H–max 34
- ££ £30
- ⚲ 15km W of Stockholm, nr
  Drottningholm Castle
- ⌂ Jan Sederholm
- ■ www.golf.se/troxhammargk

Ullna (1981)

Rosenkälla, 184 94 Åkersberga
- ☎ **(08) 514 41230**
- ☖ (08) 510 26068
- ⮞ 18 L 5825 m Par 72
- ⚇ H
- ££ 600kr
- ⚲ 20km N of Stockholm via Route
  E18
- ⌂ Sven Tumba
- ■ www.ullnagolf.se

Ulriksdal

Box 8033, 171 08 Solna
- ☎ **(08) 857931**
- ⮞ 18 L 3900 m SSS 61
- ⚇ H
- ££ 130kr (160kr)
- ⚲ 8km N of Stockholm
- ⌂ Alec Backhurst

Vallentuna (1989)

Box 266, 186 24 Vallentuna
- ☎ **(08) 514 30560/1**
- ☖ (08) 514 30569
- ⮞ 18 L 5700 m SSS 72
- ⚇ WD–U WE–U after 1pm
- ££ 300kr (400kr)
- ⚲ 35km N of Stockholm
- ⌂ Sune Linde
- ■ www.vallentunagk.nu

Viksjö (1969)

Fjällens Gård, 175 45 Järfälla
- ☎ **(08) 580 31300/31310**
- ☖ (08) 580 31340

18 L 5930 m SSS 73
9 L 1830 m Par 30
U
£€ 9 holes:150kr (150kr) 18
   holes:300kr (300kr)
⚬ 18km NW of Stockholm
■ www.golf.se/viksjogk

Wäsby
Box 2017, 194 02 Upplands Väsby
☎ (08) 510 23345/23177
⊟ (08) 510 23364
▷ 18 L 6170 m SSS 72
   9 hole course
⚆ WD–U WE–H
£€ 250kr (350kr)
⚬ 20km N of Stockholm. 20km S of
   Airport
⚏ Björn Eriksson

Wermdö G&CC   (1966)
Torpa, 139 40 Värmdö
☎ (08) 574 60700
⊟ (08) 574 60729
▷ 18 L 5555 m Par 72
⚆ H WE–NA before 3pm
£€ 450kr (450kr)
⚬ 25km E of Stockholm via Route
   222
⚏ Nils Sköld

West Central

Arvika   (1974)
Box 197, 671 25 Arvika
☎ (0570) 54133
⊟ (0570) 54233
▷ 18 L 5815 m Par 72
⚆ H
£€ 200kr
⚬ 11km E of Arvika (Route 61)
⚏ Nils Sköld
■ www.arvikagk.nu

Billerud   (1961)
Valnäs, 660 40 Segmon
☎ (0555) 91313
⊟ (0555) 91306
▷ 18 L 5874 m SSS 72
⚆ H
£€ 180kr
⚬ Valnäs, 15km N of Säffle
⚏ Brasier/Sköld

Eda   (1992)
Noresund, 670 40 Åmotfors
☎ (0571) 34101
⊟ (0571) 34191
▷ 18 L 5575 m Par 72
⚆ U
£€ 230kr (260kr)
⚬ 30km W of Arvika
⚏ Leif Nilsson
■ www.edagk.com

Färgelanda
Box 23, 458 21 Färgelanda
☎ (0528) 20385

⊟ (0528) 20045
▷ 18 L 6000 m SSS 71
⚆ U
£€ 160kr
⚬ 23km N of Uddevalla. 100km N of
   Gothenburg
⚏ Åke Persson

Fjällbacka   (1965)
450 71 Fjällbacka
☎ (0525) 31150
⊟ (0525) 32122
▷ 18 L 5850 m SSS 72
⚆ H
£€ 250kr (350kr)
⚬ 2km N of Fjällbacka (Route 163)

Forsbacka   (1969)
Box 136, 662 23 Åmål
☎ (0532) 43073
⊟ (0532) 43116
▷ 18 L 5860 m SSS 72
⚆ H
£€ 220kr (300kr)
⚬ 6km W of Åmål (Route 164)
■ www.golf.se/golfklubbar
   /forsbackagk

Hammarö   (1991)
Sätter Tallbacken, 663 91 Hammarö
☎ (054) 521621
⊟ (054) 521863
▷ 18 L 6200 m Par 72
⚆ H
£€ 240kr (300kr)
⚬ 11km S of Karlstad
⚏ Sune Linde
■ www.golf.se/hammarogk

Karlskoga   (1975)
Bricketorp 647, 691 94 Karlskoga
☎ (0586) 728190
⊟ (0586) 728417
▷ 18 L 5705 m Par 72
£€ 180kr
⚬ Valåsen, 5km E of Karlskoga via
   Route E18
⚏ Sköld/Sederholm/Engdahl

Karlstad   (1957)
Höja 510, 655 92 Karlstad
☎ (054) 866353
⊟ (054) 866478
▷ 18 L 5970 m Par 72
   9 L 2875 m Par 36
⚆
£€ 250 kr (300kr)
⚬ 8km N of Karlstad (Route 63)
⚏ Sköld/Linde
■ www.golf.se/karlstadgk

Kristinehamn   (1974)
Box 337, 681 26 Kristinehamn
☎ (0550) 82310
⊟ (0550) 19535
▷ 18 L 5800 m SSS 72
⚆
£€ 250–300kr
⚬ 3km N of Kristinehamn

⚏ Sune Linde
■ www.golf.se/golfklubbar
   /kristinehamnsgk

Lyckorna   (1967)
Box 66, 459 22 Ljungskile
☎ (0522) 20176
⊟ (0522) 22304
▷ 18 L 5820 m SSS 72
⚆ H
£€ 200kr
⚬ 20km S of Uddevalla
⚏ Anders Amilon

Orust   (1981)
Morlanda 9404, 474 93 Ellös
☎ (0304) 53170
⊟ (0304) 53174
▷ 18 L 5770 m SSS 72
⚆ H
£€ 200–300kr
⚬ Ellös, 10km from Henån. 80km N
   of Gothenburg
⚏ Lars Andreasson
■ www.orustgk.org

Saxå   (1964)
Saxån, 682 92 Filipstad
☎ (0590) 24070
⊟ (0590) 24101
▷ 18 L 5680 m Par 72
⚆ U
£€ 160kr
⚬ 20km NE of Filipstad (Route 63)
⚏ Sköld/Bäckman

Skaftö   (1963)
Röd PL 4476, 450 34 Fiskebäckskil
☎ (0523) 23211
⊟ (0523) 23215
▷ 18 L 4831 m SSS 69
⚆ WD–H
£€ 150–300kr
⚬ 40km W of Uddevalla, through
   Fiskebäckskil
⚏ Sköld/Sederholm

Strömstad   (1967)
Golfbanevägen, 452 90 Strömstad 1
☎ (0526) 61788
⊟ (0526) 14766
▷ 18 L 5615 m SSS 71
⚆ H
£€ 250kr (300kr)
⚬ 6km N of Strömstad
⚏ Sköld/Sederholm
■ www.golf.se/stromstadgk

Sunne   (1970)
Box 108, 686 23 Sunne
☎ (0565) 14100/14210
⊟ (0565) 14855
▷ 18 hole course SSS 72
⚆ H
£€ 200kr
⚬ 2km S of Sunne. 60km N of
   Karlstad on Route 45
⚏ Jan Sederholm

Torreby (1961)

Torreby Slott, 455 93 Munkedal
- ☎ **(0524) 21365/21109**
- 🖥 (0524) 21351
- ⏸ 18 L 5885 m Par 72
- 👥 H
- ££ 200kr
- 🚗 Munkedal 8km. Uddevalla 30km.
- ⌂ Douglas Brasier

Uddeholm (1965)

Risäter 20, 683 93 Råda
- ☎ **(0563) 60564**
- 🖥 (0563) 60017
- ⏸ 18 L 5830 m SSS 72
- 👥 U H
- ££ D–160kr
- 🚗 Lake Råda, 80km N of Karlstad, via RD62

Switzerland

Bern

G&CC Blumisberg (1959)

3184 Wünnewil
- ☎ **(026) 496 34 38**
- 🖥 (026) 496 35 23
- ⏸ 18 L 6048 m Par 72
- 👥 WD–U H WE–M
- ££ 80fr (80fr)
- 🚗 Wünnewil, 16km SW of Bern
- ⌂ B von Limburger

Les Bois (1988)

Case Postale 26, 2336 Les Bois
- ☎ **(032) 961 10 03**
- 🖥 (032) 961 10 17
- ⏸ 9 L 3000 m Par 72
- 👥 WD–U WE–M
- ££ 75fr (90fr)
- 🚗 12km NE of La Chaux-de-Fonds, on Basel road
- ⌂ Jeremy Pern

Neuchâtel (1928)

Hameau de Voëns, 2072 Saint-Blaise
- ☎ **(032) 753 55 50**
- 🖥 (032) 753 29 40
- ⏸ 18 L 5913 m SSS 71
- 👥 H
- ££ 80fr (100fr)
- 🚗 Voëns/Saint-Blaise, 5km E of Neuchâtel. 30km W of Bern

Payerne (1996)

Domaine des Invuardes, 1530 Payerne
- ☎ **(026) 662 4220**
- 🖥 (026) 662 4221
- ⏸ 18 L 5450 m Par 70
- 👥 U H
- ££ 80fr (100fr)
- 🚗 50km W of Bern. 50km NE of Lausanne
- ⌂ Yves Bureau

Wallenried (1992)

1784 Wallenried
- ☎ **(026) 684 84 80**
- 🖥 (026) 684 84 90
- ⏸ 18 L 6000 m Par 72
- 👥 WD–U H
- ££ 70fr (90fr)
- 🚗 6km W of Fribourg
- ⌂ Ruzzo Reuss
- ■ www.swissgolfnetwork.ch

Wylihof (1994)

4542 Luterbach
- ☎ **(032) 682 28 28**
- 🖥 (032 682 65 17
- ⏸ 18 L 6580 yds Par 73
- 👥 WD–U H–max 36 WE–M H
- ££ 100fr (100fr)
- 🚗 40km N of Bern. 90km W of Zürich
- ⌂ Ruzzo Reuss von Plauen
- ■ www.golf.ch

Bernese Oberland

Interlaken-Unterseen (1964)

Postfach 110, 3800 Interlaken
- ☎ **(033) 823 60 16**
- 🖥 (033) 823 42 03
- ⏸ 18 L 5980 m Par 72
- 👥 H
- ££ 90fr (105fr)
- 🚗 Interlaken 3km
- ⌂ Donald Harradine
- ■ www.interlakengolf.ch

Riederalp (1986)

3987 Riederalp
- ☎ **(027) 927 29 32**
- 🖥 (027) 927 29 32
- ⏸ 9 L 3066 m SSS 55
- 👥 U
- ££ 45fr
- 🚗 10km NE of Brig
- ⌂ Donald Harradine

Lake Geneva & South West

Bonmont (1983)

Château de Bonmont, 1275 Chéserex
- ☎ **(022) 369 99 00**
- 🖥 (022) 369 99 09
- ⏸ 18 L 6165 m SSS 72
- 👥 WD–restricted WE–M
- ££ WD–90fr
- 🚗 3km from Nyon. 30km NE of Geneva
- ⌂ Donald Harradine

Les Coullaux (1989)

1846 Chessel
- ☎ **(024) 481 22 46**
- 🖥 (024) 481 22 46
- ⏸ 9 L 2940 m Par 58
- 👥 U

- ££ 25–40fr (30–50fr)
- 🚗 Chessel, between Evian and Montreux
- ⌂ Donald Harradine

Crans-sur-Sierre (1906)

C P 112, 3963 Crans-sur-Sierre
- ☎ **(027) 41 21 68**
- 🖥 (027) 41 95 68
- ⏸ 18 L 6170 m SSS 72
- 9 L 2729 m SSS 35
- 9 hole Par 3 course
- 👥 H
- ££ On application
- 🚗 20km E of Sion. Geneva 2 hrs

Domaine Impérial (1987)

Villa Prangins, 1196 Gland
- ☎ **(022) 999 06 00**
- 🖥 (022) 999 06 06
- ⏸ 18 L 6297 m SSS 74
- 👥 WD–H exc Mon am
- ££ WD–150fr
- 🚗 Nyon, 20km N of Geneva
- ⌂ Pete Dye

Geneva (1923)

70 Route de la Capite, 1223 Cologny
- ☎ **(022) 707 48 00**
- 🖥 (022) 707 48 20
- ⏸ 18 L 6150 m Par 72
- 👥 WD–am only Tues–Fri WE–M
- ££ 150fr
- 🚗 4km from centre of Geneva
- ⌂ Robert Trent Jones Sr

Lausanne (1921)

Route du Golf 3, 1000 Lausanne 25
- ☎ **(021) 784 84 84**
- 🖥 (021) 784 84 80
- ⏸ 18 L 6295 m SSS 74
- 👥 H
- ££ 90fr (110fr)
- 🚗 7km N of Lausanne towards Le Mont
- ⌂ Narbel/Harradine/Pern

Montreux (1898)

54 Route d'Evian, 1860 Aigle
- ☎ **(024) 466 46 16**
- 🖥 (024) 466 60 47
- ⏸ 18 L 6143 m Par 72 SSS 73
- 👥 H
- ££ 80fr (100fr)
- 🚗 Aigle, 15km S of Montreux
- ⌂ Donald Harradine

Sion (1995)

CP 639, Rte Vissigen 150, 1951 Sion
- ☎ **(027) 203 79 00**
- 🖥 (027) 203 79 01
- ⏸ 9 L 2315 m Par 33
- 👥 H–booking necessary
- ££ 18 holes: 61fr (79fr) 9 holes: 37fr (46fr)
- 🚗 Sion, 80km SE of Montreux
- ⌂ JL Tronchet

Verbier (1970)
1936 Verbier
☎ **(027) 771 53 14**
📠 (027) 771 60 93
👤 18 L 4880 m Par 69
👥 U
££ 50–70fr (80fr)
🚗 Centre of Verbier
🏠 Donald Harradine
■ www.verbiergolf.com

Villars (1922)
C P 152, 1884 Villars
☎ **(024) 495 42 14**
📠 (024) 495 42 18
👤 18 L 5250 m SSS 70
👥 U
££ 60fr (80fr)
🚗 5km E of Villars towards Les
Diablerets
🏠 Thierry Sprecher
■ www.golf-villars.ch

Lugano & Ticino

Lugano (1923)
6983 Magliaso
☎ **(091) 606 15 57**
📠 (091) 606 65 58
👤 18 L 5580 m Par 70
👥 H–max 36
££ 90fr (110fr)
🚗 8km W of Lugano towards Ponte
Tresa
🏠 Harradine/Robinson
■ www.golflugano.ch

Patriziale Ascona (1928)
Via al Lido 81, 6612 Ascona
☎ **(091) 791 21 32**
📠 (091) 791 07 06
👤 18 L 5933 m Par 71
👥 H–max 30
££ 90fr
🚗 5km W of Locarno
🏠 CK Cotton
■ www.golf.ascona.ch

St Moritz & Engadine

Arosa (1944)
Postfach 95, 7050 Arosa
☎ **(081) 377 42 42**
📠 (081) 377 46 77
👤 18 L 4340 m Par 66
👥 U
££ 70fr
🚗 30km S of Chur
🏠 D Harradine/P Harradine
■ www.arosa.ch/golf

Bad Ragaz (1957)
Hans Albrecht Strasse, 7310 Bad Ragaz
☎ **(081) 303 37 17**
📠 (081) 303 37 27
👤 18 L 5750 m Par 70
👥 H
££ D–120fr
🚗 20km N of Chur. 100km SE of
Zürich
🏠 Donald Harradine
■ www.resortragaz.ch

Davos (1929)
Postfach, 7260 Davos Dorf
☎ **(081) 46 56 34**
📠 (081) 46 25 55
👤 18 L 5208 yds Par 68
👥 WD–U
££ On application
🚗 1km outside Davos
🏠 Donald Harradine

Engadin (1893)
7503 Samedan
☎ **(081) 851 04 66**
📠 (081) 851 04 67
👤 18 L 6350 m SSS 73
👥 H
££ 90fr
🚗 Samedan, 6km NE of St Moritz
🏠 M Verdieri

Lenzerheide Valbella (1950)
7078 Lenzerheide
☎ **(081) 385 13 13**
📠 (081) 385 13 19
👤 18 L 5269 m SSS 69
👥 H
££ 60–80fr
🚗 20km S of Chur towards St Moritz
🏠 Donald Harradine

Vulpera (1923)
7552 Vulpera Spa
☎ **(081) 864 96 88**
📠 (081) 864 96 89
👤 9 L 1982 m SSS 62
👥 H
££ 60fr (70fr) W–290fr
🚗 Tarasp, nr Vulpera. 60km NE of St
Moritz
🏠 Dell/Spencer
■ www.swissgolfnetwork.ch-9holes-
vulpera

Zürich & North

Breitenloo (1964)
8309 Oberwil b. Bassersdorf
☎ **(01) 836 40 80**
📠 (01) 837 10 85
👤 18 L 6125 m Par 72 SSS 72
👥 WD–H by appointment WE–M H
££ 100fr
🚗 10km NE of Zürich Airport
🏠 Harradine/Pennink

Bürgenstock (1927)
6363 Bürgenstock
☎ **(041) 612 9010**
📠 (041) 612 9901
👤 9 L 2200 m Par 33
👥 I or H
££ 60fr (80fr)
🚗 15km S of Lucerne
🏠 Fritz Frey

Dolder (1907)
Kurhausstrasse 66, 8032 Zürich
☎ **(01) 261 50 45**
📠 (01) 261 53 02
👤 9 L 1735 m SSS 58
👥 WD–H WE–M
££ WD–70fr
🚗 Zürich

Entfelden (1988)
Postfach 230, Muhenstrasse 52,
5036 Oberentfelden
☎ **(062) 723 89 84**
📠 (062) 723 84 36
👤 9 L 3960 m SSS 60
👥 H
££ 50fr (70fr)
🚗 50km W of Zürich
🏠 Donald Harradine

Erlen (1988)
Schlossgut Eppishausen, Schlossstr 7,
8586 Erlen
☎ **(071) 648 29 30**
📠 (071) 648 29 40
👤 18 L 5913 m SSS 71
👥 H
££ 80fr (110fr)
🚗 30km NW of St Gallen. 60km W of
Zürich
🏠 Deutsche Golfconsult

Hittnau-Zürich G&CC (1964)
8335 Hittnau
☎ **(01) 950 24 42**
📠 (01) 951 01 66
👤 18 L 5519 m CR 69.4 SR 127
👥 WD–U WE–M
££ WD–110fr
🚗 Hittnau, 30km E of Zürich

Küssnacht (1994)
Sekretariat/Grossarni, 6403 Küssnacht
am Rigi
☎ **(041) 850 70 60**
📠 (041) 850 70 41
👤 18 L 5397 m Par 68
👥 WD–U H WE–M H
££ 100fr (120fr)
🚗 20km NE of Lucerne
🏠 Peter Harradine
■ www.kuessnacht.ch

Lucerne (1903)
Dietschiberg, 6006 Luzern
☎ **(041) 420 97 87**

☎ (041) 420 82 48
☞ 18 L 6082 m Par 72 SSS 71-73
✹ H
££ 80fr (100fr)
⛳ Lucerne 2km

Ostschweizerischer (1948)
9246 Niederbüren
☎ **(071) 422 18 56**
🖳 (071) 422 18 25
☞ 18 L 5920 m SSS 71
✹ WD–H
££ D–90fr
⛳ Niederbüren, 25km NW of St Gallen
🏠 Donald Harradine
■ www.osgc.ch

Schinznach-Bad (1929)
5116 Schinznach-Bad
☎ **(056) 443 12 26**
🖳 (056) 443 34 83
☞ 9 L 5670 m Par 71
✹ WD–U
££ 70fr
⛳ 6km S of Brugg. 35km W of Zürich

Schönenberg (1967)
8824 Schönenberg
☎ **(01) 788 90 40**
🖳 (01) 788 90 45
☞ 18 L 6205 m CR 73 SR 137
✹ WD–H–by appointment WE–M H
££ 90fr
⛳ 20km S of Zürich
🏠 Donald Harradine
■ www.swissgolfnetwork.ch

Sempachersee (1996)
6024 Hildisrieden, Lucerne
☎ **(041) 462 71 71**
🖳 (041) 462 71 72
☞ 18 L 6161 m Par 72 SR 127

9 L 3890 m Par 31
✹ WD–U H WE–M H
££ 90fr (90fr)
⛳ 13km NW of Lucerne
🏠 Kurt Rossknecht
■ www.golf-sempachersee.ch

Zürich-Zumikon (1929)
Weid 9, 8126 Zumikon
☎ **(01) 918 00 50**
🖳 (01) 918 00 37
☞ 18 L 6350 m Par 72 CR 73 SR 130
✹ WD–H by appointment WE–M
££ WD–150fr
⛳ 10km SE of Zürich
🏠 Donald Harradine
■ www.swissgolfnetwork.ch

Turkey

Gloria Golf
Acisu Mevkii PK27 Belek, Serik, Antalya
☎ **(242) 715 15 20**
🖳 (242) 715 15 25
☞ 18 holes Par 72
9 hole Academy course
✹ U
⛳ Antalya
🏠 Michel Gayon

Kemer G&CC
Goturk Koyu Mevkii Kemerburgaz, Eyup, Istanbul
☎ **(212) 239 70 10**
🖳 (212) 239 73 76
☞ 18 holes Par 73
✹ U–phone for booking
££ $50 ($90)
⛳ 30km from Istanbul
🏠 J Dudok van Heel

Klassis G&CC
Silivri, Istanbul
☎ **(212) 748 46 00**
🖳 (212) 748 46 43
☞ 18 L 6200 m Par 73
9 hole Par 3 course
✹ U
⛳ Istanbul
🏠 Tony Jacklin

National Antalya
Belek Turizm Merkesi, 07500 Serik, Antalya
☎ **(242) 725 46 20**
🖳 (242) 725 46 23
☞ 18 L 6232 m Par 72 SSS 72
9 L 1547 m Par 29
✹ H
££ £50
⛳ Belek, 30km from Antalya
🏠 Feherty/Jones
■ www.nationalturkey.com

Nobilis Golf (1998)
Acisu Mevkii, Belek, 07500 Serik, Antalya
☎ **(242) 1986/7**
🖳 (242) 1985
☞ 18 holes Par 72
✹ U
££ £35
⛳ 35km E of Antalya on Mediterranean coast
🏠 Dave Thomas

Tat Golf International
Belek International Golf, Kum Tepesi Belek, 07500 Serik, Antalya
☎ **(242) 725 53 03**
🖳 (242) 725 52 99
☞ 27 holes Par 72
✹ U
⛳ Antalya
🏠 Hawtree

General Index

A 6 Golfklubb, 925
Aachen, 888
Aalborg, 855
AAMI Australian Women's Open,
  223, 208
AAMI Women's Australian Tour,
  208
Aarhus, 855
Abbekas, 921
Abbeville, 866
Abbey Hill, 655
Abbey Hotel G & CC, 762
Abbeyleix, 793
Abbey Moor, 742
Abbeydale, 769
Abbeyfeale, 793
Abbotsley, 657
Abenberg, 887
Aberconwy Trophy, 264
Aberdare, 838
Aberdeenshire Ladies', 332
Aberdour, 815
Aberdovey, 837
Aberfeldy, 829
Aberfoyle, 833
Abergele, 835
Aberlady, 824
Abernethy, 820
Abersoch, 837
Aberystwyth, 834
Ableiges, 868
Aboyne, 802
Abridge G & CC, 679
Accrington & District, 704
Achensee, 847
Achill, 795
Acquabona, 896
Adamstal, 849
Adare Manor, 793
The Addington, 742
Addington Court, 742
Addington Palace, 742
Adriatic GC Cervia, 897
Advil Western Open, 154
Aero Club de Santiago, 914
Aero Club de Vigo, 914
Aero Club de Zaragoza, 918
Aerus Electrolux USA Championship,
  213
Afandou, 894
Ågesta, 928
Ahaus, 888
L'Ailette, 866
Air Canada Championship, 155
Airdrie, 822
Airlinks, 719
Les Aisses, 865
Aix Marseille, 875
Aix-les-Bains, 877
Ajoncs d'Or, 862

Akureyri, 895
Albarella, 900
Albatross, 921
Albi Lasbordes, 878
Albon, 877
Albret, 861
Alcaidesa Links, 916
Aldeburgh, 740
Aldenham G & CC, 692
Alder Root, 660
Alderley Edge, 660
Alderney, 659
Aldersey Green, 660
Aldwark Manor, 765
Aldwickbury Park, 692
Alexandra Park, 818
Alford, 802
Alfred Dunhill Championship, 126
Alfred Dunhill Cup, 194
Alfreton, 669
Algarve Open de Portugal, 128
Alhaurín, 915
Alicante, 910
Alice Springs, 839
Alingsås, 927
All-Ireland Inter-County
  Championship, 262
Allendale, 726
Allerthorpe Park, 764
Allerton Municipal, 716
Allerum, 923
Allestree Park, 669
Allgäuer G & LC, 885
Alloa, 812
Allt-y-Graban, 843
Almeerderhout, 906
Almerimar, 911
Älmhult, 925
Alness, 820
Alnmouth, 726
Alnmouth Village, 726
Alnwick, 726
Alston Moor, 667
Alten Fliess, 889
Altenhof, 882
Alto G & CC, 908
Alton, 687
Altorreal, 910
Altötting-Burghausen, 885
Altrincham Municipal, 660
Alva, 812
Alvaston Hall, 660
Alvkarleby, 922
Alwoodley, 771
Alyth, 829
Amarante, 910

Amarilla, 914
107th Amateur Championship, 227
Amber Baltic, 907
Ambrosiano, 895
American Express Challenge, 173
Amiens, 866
Ammerschwihr, 873
Ampfield Par Three, 687
Ampleforth College, 765
Amsterdam Old Course, 902
Amsterdamse, 902
Amstetten-Ferschnitz, 847
Andenne, 851
Anderstein, 906
Andover, 687
Ängelholm, 923
Angers, 870
Anglesey, 288, 838
Ängsö, 918
Angus, 288
Angus Ladies', 332
Anjou G & CC, 870
Annanhill, 808
Annecy, 877
Annonay-Gourdan, 877
Añoreta, 915
Anstruther, 815
Ansty, 756
The Antlers, 280
Antrim, 777
Antrobus, 660
The ANZ Championship, 127
ANZ Ladies Masters, 208
Appleby, 667
Apremont, 866
Aqualate, 732
Aquarius, 697
Araslöv, 924
Arboga, 918
Arbroath Artisan, 805
Arcachon, 861
Arcangues, 861
Arcot Hall, 726
Les Arcs, 877
Ardacong, 789
Ardee, 794
Ardeer, 808
Ardfert, 790
Ardglass, 784
Ardilouse, 861
Ardminnan, 784
Ardrée, 865
Arendal og Omegn, 906
Argyll and Bute, 288
Ariège, 878
Ärila, 918
Arkley, 692
Arklow, 800
Army, 687
Arnold Palmer Award, 367